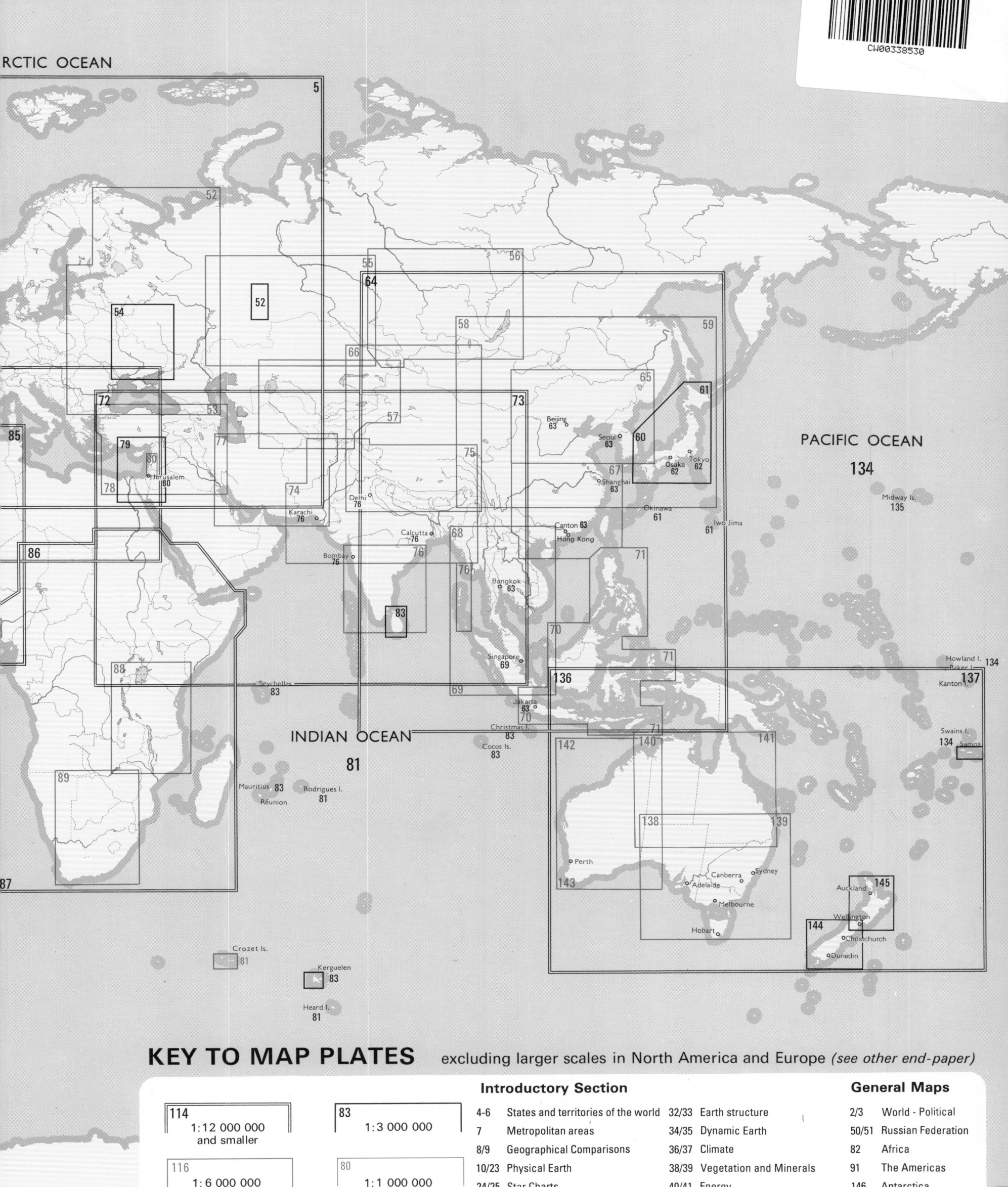

ARCTIC OCEAN

5

52

54

55

64

52

56

66

58

59

72

53

57

73

65

61

60

Beijing
63

Seoul
63

PACIFIC OCEAN

134

85

79

77

75

67

Osaka
62

Tokyo
62

Midway Is.
135

80

Jerusalem
80

Shanghai
63

78

74

Delhi
76

Okinawa
61

Iwo Jima
61

86

Karachi
76

Canton 63
Hong Kong

Calcutta
76

68

71

Bombay
76

76

70

Howland I.
Baker I. 134

88

76

Seychelles
83

83

Singapore
69

71

136

Kanton I. 137

INDIAN OCEAN

81

69

Jakarta
63

70

Swains I.
134 Samoa

Christmas I.
83

Cocos Is.
83

71

141

142

140

Mauritius 83
Réunion

Rodrigues I.
81

89

138

139

Auckland 145

Crozet Is.
81

Perth

Canberra Sydney
Adelaide

144 Wellington

87

Kerguelen
83

Melbourne

Christchurch

143

Dunedin

Heard I.
81

Hobart

KEY TO MAP PLATES excluding larger scales in North America and Europe *(see other end-paper)*

114		83	
1:12 000 000 and smaller		1:3 000 000	

116		80	
1:6 000 000 and smaller		1:1 000 000 and larger	

Inset maps of islands, cities, etc. are named

Introductory Section

4-6	States and territories of the world
7	Metropolitan areas
8/9	Geographical Comparisons
10/23	Physical Earth
24/25	Star Charts
26/27	Universe
28/29	Solar System
30/31	Space flight

32/33	Earth structure
34/35	Dynamic Earth
36/37	Climate
38/39	Vegetation and Minerals
40/41	Energy
42/43	Food and Population
44	Map projections

General Maps

2/3	World - Political
50/51	Russian Federation
82	Africa
91	The Americas
146	Antarctica
147	Arctic Ocean

THE TIMES ATLAS OF THE WORLD

CONCISE EDITION

TIMES BOOKS
A Division of HarperCollinsPublishers

Published in 1993 by
Times Books
A Division of **HarperCollins***Publishers*
77–85 Fulham Palace Road
Hammersmith
London W6 8JB

First Edition 1972
Reprinted with revisions 1973, 1974
Second Edition 1975
Reprinted 1976, 1978
Third Edition 1978
Reprinted with revisions 1979
Fourth Edition 1980
Reprinted with revisions 1982
Reprinted 1984
Fifth Edition 1986
Reprinted with revisions 1987, 1988,
1989, 1990, 1991
Sixth Edition 1992
Reprinted with revisions 1993

Copyright © Times Books and
Bartholomew 1993

Maps prepared by
Bartholomew, Edinburgh

Maps printed by
Bartholomew, The Edinburgh Press Limited

Index processed and typeset by
Stibo Datagrafik, Århus,
Denmark

Index printed by
Scotprint, Musselburgh,
Scotland

Books bound by
Sigloch, Künzelsau,
Germany

Geographical Consultants
Mr H.A.G. Lewis OBE
Mr P.J.M. Geelan

Physical Earth Maps by
Duncan Mackay

British Library Cataloguing in
Publication Data
The Times atlas of the world.
  Concise edition.–6th ed
  911

ISBN 0 7230 0493 5

FOREWORD

This new edition of *The Times Concise Atlas of the World* will, it is hoped, find as much favour with those who acquire a copy for the first time as it has with those familiar with the earlier editions.

Every effort has been made to ensure that the maps are as up-to-date as possible. The index of names has, in consequence, been augmented. It now contains some 100,000 entries but it still does not contain all the names which appear on the maps. The reader may, however, rest assured that the names of all important inhabited places and physical features are included together with the page number, country name and grid reference.

Great attention has been paid to the spelling of geographical names, a matter of great complexity due to the multiplicity of the World's languages, the diverse forms of writing or the absence of any writing system whatsoever. For want of a standard way of spelling names a variety of spellings has been used over the centuries establishing in each of the major languages of the world its own conventional way of spelling which differs greatly from the name found locally. In this atlas the name taken is always the name used by the official administering body. Where necessary that name has been converted into the Roman alphabet by systems which follow English language usage. Those systems accord with the transcription and transliteration systems accepted for official use in the United States and the United Kingdom. For added reference the English language conventional names have been added parenthetically e.g. Roma (Rome), Moskva (Moscow).

Names like maps often invoke political protestations. The status of areas, the international boundaries and the names associated with them as shown in this edition are those which reflect the situation pertaining on the ground at the time of publication: where boundaries are the subject of international dispute this portrayal will not win the approval of the contending parties but, in the view of the publishers, the function of an atlas is to show facts and not to adjudicate between the rights and wrongs of political issues.

In the introductory section is a list of countries of the World. It shows a world re-cast in a mould unforeseen and unforeseeable at the end of the Second World War. Yet the changes in the political scene are small in comparison with the way science has altered the pattern of life. No century in the world's history has witnessed changes so fundamental and widespread. Of more significance than the magnitude of the change is its rate, now such that any reliable prediction of the future beyond a decade or two cannot be made.

The trend is vividly demonstrated in the diagram showing the demand for energy but it is no less apparent under other subject headings.

Unabated growth of that kind cannot continue indefinitely. The maps which make up the body of the atlas show the physical and political world of to-day. How the same maps will look in the future depends on the size of the world's population; the pattern of settlement; the spread of industry; the availability of food, minerals and sources of energy; the world's vegetation, atmosphere and climate all of which are in risk of catastrophic change.

To sustain ever increasing numbers of people requires constant stock-taking of natural resources. Remote-sensing, a product of the space age, is now beginning to reveal its eventual capacity for the kind of global monitoring required.

The space age has barely dawned yet it has already stretched the confines of our world to include the solar system and embrace more and more of the universe.

Our atlas, therefore, includes the Earth we live on, the solar system and the universe beyond. May it bring pleasure and interest to all who use it.

CONTENTS

STATES AND TERRITORIES OF THE WORLD

State/Territory	Capital or main town	Sq. km	(Sq. miles)	Population	Date
A					
Afghanistan	Kābul	652,225	(251,773)	16,433,000	1991
Albania	Tiranë (Tirana)	28,750	(11,100)	3,250,000	1990
Algeria	El-Djezaïr (Algiers)	2,381,745	(919,355)	24,960,000	1990
American Samoa	Pago Pago	197	(76)	39,000	1990
Andorra	Andorra la Vella	465	(180)	52,000	1990
Angola	Luanda	1,246,700	(481,225)	10,020,000	1990
Anguilla	The Valley	91	(35)	7,019	1989
Antigua and Barbuda	St. John's	442	(171)	85,000	1990
Argentina	Buenos Aires	2,777,815	(1,072,240)	32,610,000*	1991
Armenia	Yerevan	30,000	(11,580)	3,300,000	1990
Aruba	Oranjestad	193	(75)	62,500	1988
Ascension	Georgetown	88	(34)	1,007	1988
Australia	Canberra	7,682,300	(2,965,370)	17,086,197	1990
Australian Capital Territory	Canberra	2,432	(939)	284,985	1990
New South Wales	Sydney	801,430	(309,350)	5,827,373	1990
Northern Territory	Darwin	1,346,200	(519,635)	157,304	1990
Queensland	Brisbane	1,727,000	(666,620)	2,906,838	1990
South Australia	Adelaide	984,380	(79,970)	1,439,157	1990
Tasmania	Hobart	68,330	(26,375)	456,663	1990
Victoria	Melbourne	227,600	(87,855)	4,379,981	1990
Western Australia	Perth	2,525,500	(974,845)	1,633,896	1990
Austria	Wien (Vienna)	83,855	(32,370)	7,761,700	1990
Azerbaijan	Baku	87,000	(33,580)	7,100,000	1990
Azores	Ponta Delgada	2,335	(901)	253,600	1988
B					
Bahamas	Nassau	13,865	(5,350)	254,685*	1990
Bahrain	Al Manāmah (Manama)	661	(255)	503,000	1990
Bangladesh	Dhaka	144,000	(55,585)	109,291,000	1990
Barbados	Bridgetown	430	(166)	257,082*	1990
Belgium	Bruxelles/(Brussels)	30,520	(11,780)	9,845,000	1990
Belize	Belmopan	22,965	(8,865)	188,000	1990
Belorussia	Minsk	208,000	(80,290)	10,200,000	1990
Benin	Porto Novo	112,620	(43,470)	4,736,000	1990
Bermuda	Hamilton	54	(21)	61,000	1990
Bhutan	Thimphu	46,620	(17,995)	1,517,000	1990
Bolivia	La Paz	1,098,575	(424,050)	7,400,000	1990
Bosnia-Herzegovina	Sarajevo	51,130	(19,735)	2,900,000	1993
Botswana	Gaborone	575,000	(221,950)	1,291,000	1990
Brazil	Brasília	8,511,965	(3,285,620)	153,322,000	1991
Brunei	Bandar Seri Begawan	5,765	(2,225)	266,000	1990
Bulgaria	Sofiya (Sofia)	110,910	(42,810)	9,011,000	1990
Burkina	Ouagadougou	274,122	(105,811)	9,001,000	1990
Burma	Rangoon	678,030	(261,720)	39,300,000	1990
Burundi	Bujumbura	27,835	(10,745)	5,458,000	1990
C					
Cambodia	Phnom Penh	181,000	(69,865)	8,700,000	1991
Cameroon	Yaoundé	475,500	(183,545)	11,834,000	1990
Canada	Ottawa	9,922,385	(3,830,840)	26,800,000	1991
Canary Islands	Las Palmas (on Gran Canaria) and Santa Cruz (on Tenerife)	7,275	(2,810)	1,589,403	1990
Cape Verde	Praia	4,035	(1,560)	370,000	1990
Cayman Islands	George Town	259	(100)	27,000	1990
Central African Republic	Bangui	624,975	(241,240)	3,039,000	1990
Chad	Ndjamena	1,284,000	(495,625)	5,679,000	1990
Channel Islands	St Helier (on Jersey) St Peter Port (on Guernsey)	194	(75)	140,711	1989
Chile	Santiago	751,625	(290,125)	13,386,000	1991
China	Beijing (Peking)	9,597,000	(3,704,440)	1,088,870,000	1989
Colombia	Bogotá	1,138,915	(439,620)	32,987,000	1990
Comoros	Moroni	1,860	(718)	551,000	1990
Congo	Brazzaville	342,000	(132,010)	2,271,000	1990
Croatia	Zagreb	56,540	(21,825)	4,726,000	1990
Cuba	Habana (Havana)	114,525	(44,205)	10,617,000	1990
Cyprus	Nicosia	9,250	(3,570)	707,000	1990
Czech Republic	Praha (Prague)	78,864	(30,433)	10,300,000	1992
D					
Denmark	København (Copenhagen)	43,075	(16,625)	5,140,000	1990
Djibouti	Djibouti	23,000	(8,800)	409,000	1990
Dominica	Roseau	751	(290)	81,200	1988
Dominican Republic	Santo Domingo	48,440	(18,700)	7,170,000	1990
E					
Ecuador	Quito	461,475	(178,130)	10,782,000	1990
Egypt	Cairo	1,000,250	(386,095)	57,000,000	1991
El Salvador	San Salvador	21,395	(8,260)	5,252,000	1990
Equatorial Guinea	Malabo	28,050	(10,825)	348,000	1990
Estonia	Tallinn	45,100	(17,413)	1,583,000	1991
Ethiopia	Ādīs Ābeba (Addis Ababa)	1,023,050	(394,895)	50,774,000	1990
F					
Faeroes	Tórshavn	1,399	(540)	47,663	1988
Falkland Islands	Port Stanley	12,175	(4,700)	2,000	1990
Fiji	Suva	18,330	(7,075)	765,000	1990
Finland	Helsinki	337,030	(130,095)	4,986,000	1990
France	Paris	543,965	(209,970)	56,556,000*	1990
French Guiana	Cayenne	91,000	(35,125)	93,540	1989
French Polynesia	Papeete	3,940	(1,520)	188,814*	1988
G					
Gabon	Libreville	267,665	(103,320)	1,172,000	1990
Gambia, The	Banjul	10,690	(4,125)	861,000	1990
Georgia	Tbilisi	69,700	(26,905)	5,400,000	1990
Germany	Berlin	356,840	(137,740)	78,500,000	1990
Baden-Württemberg	Stuttgart	35,730	(13,790)	9,400,000	1990
Bayern (Bavaria)	München (Munich)	70,545	(27,230)	11,000,000	1990
Berlin		883	(341)	3,400,000	1990
Brandenburg	Potsdam	29,059	(11,220)	2,700,000	1990
Bremen		404	(156)	700,000	1990
Hamburg		755	(291)	1,600,000	1990
Hessen	Wiesbaden	21,115	(8,150)	5,600,000	1990
Mecklenburg-Vorpommern	Schwerin	23,838	(9,204)	2,100,000	1990
Niedersachsen	Hannover	47,425	(18,305)	7,200,000	1990
Nordrhein-Westfalen	Dusseldorf	34,070	(13,150)	16,900,000	1990
Rheinland-Pfalz	Mainz	19,840	(7,660)	3,700,000	1990
Saarland	Saarbrücken	2,575	(994)	1,100,000	1990
Sachsen (Saxony)	Dresden	18,337	(7,080)	4,900,000	1990
Sachsen-Anhalt	Halle	20,445	(7,894)	3,000,000	1990
Schleswig-Holstein	Kiel	15,710	(6,065)	2,600,000	1990
Thüringen	Erfurt	16,251	(6,275)	2,500,000	1990
Ghana	Accra	238,305	(91,985)	15,028,000	1990
Gibraltar		6.5	(2.5)	30,689	1989
Greece	Athínai (Athens)	131,985	(50,954)	10,269,074*	1991
Greenland	Godthåb (Nuuk)	2,175,600	(839,780)	55,558	1990
Grenada	St George's	345	(133)	110,000	1989
Guadeloupe	Basse-Terre	1,780	(687)	344,000	1990
Guam	Agaña	450	(174)	132,726	1990
Guatemala	Guatemala	108,890	(42,030)	9,197,000	1990
Guinea	Conakry	245,855	(94,900)	5,756,000	1990
Guinea-Bissau	Bissau	36,125	(13,945)	965,000	1990
Guyana	Georgetown	214,970	(82,980)	990,000	1989

BOLD TYPE INDICATES INDEPENDENT STATE

ITALIC TYPE INDICATES DEPENDENT TERRITORIES AND STATES

* INDICATES THAT THE POPULATION FIGURE RELATES TO A CENSUS

State/Territory	Capital or main town	Sq. km	(Sq. miles)	Population	Date
H					
Haiti	Port-au-Prince	27,750	(10,710)	6,486,000	1990
Honduras	Tegucigalpa	112,085	(43,265)	5,105,000	1990
Hong Kong		1,062	(410)	5,448,000	1990
Hungary	Budapest	93,030	(35,910)	10,344,000	1991
I					
Iceland	Reykjavík	102,820	(39,690)	255,000	1990
India	New Delhi	3,166,830	(1,222,395)	843,930,861*	1991
Indonesia	Jakarta	1,919,445	(740,905)	179,321,641*	1990
Iran	Tehrān	1,648,000	(636,130)	58,031,000	1991
Iraq	Baghdad	438,445	(169,240)	18,920,000	1990
Ireland, Republic of (Eire)	Dublin (Baile Átha Cliath)	68,895	(26,595)	3,523,000	1991
Israel	Jerusalem	20,770	(8,015)	4,822,000	1990
Italy	Roma (Rome)	301,245	(116,280)	57,690,000	1990
Ivory Coast	Yamoussoukro	322,465	(124,470)	11,998,000	1990
J					
Jamaica	Kingston	11,425	(4,410)	2,420,000	1990
Japan	Tōkyō	396,700	(142,705)	123,612,000	1990
Jordan	Amman	90,650	(35,000)	3,170,000	1989
K					
Kazakhstan	Alma-Ata	2,717,300	(1,048,880)	16,700,000	1990
Kenya	Nairobi	582,645	(224,900)	24,032,000	1990
Kiribati	Bairiki	684	(264)	66,000	1990
Korea, North	Pyŏngyang	122,310	(47,210)	21,773,000	1990
Korea, South	Sŏul (Seoul)	98,445	(38,000)	43,302,000	1991
Kuwait	Al Kuwayt (Kuwait)	24,280	(9,370)	2,600,000	1991
Kyrgyzstan	Bishkek	198,500	(76,620)	4,400,000	1990
L					
Laos	Viangchan (Vientiane)	236,725	(91,375)	4,139,000	1990
Latvia	Rīga	63,700	(24,590)	2,686,000	1991
Lebanon	Beyrouth (Beirut)	10,400	(4,015)	3,200,000	1991
Lesotho	Maseru	30,345	(11,715)	1,774,000	1990
Liberia	Monrovia	111,370	(42,990)	2,607,000	1990
Libya	Ṭarābulus (Tripoli)	1,759,540	(679,180)	4,545,000	1990
Liechtenstein	Vaduz	160	(62)	29,000	1990
Lithuania	Vilnius	65,200	(25,165)	3,739,000	1991
Luxembourg	Luxembourg	2,585	(998)	384,000	1991
M					
Macao	Macao	17	(7)	479,000	1990
Macedonia	Skopje	25,715	(9,925)	2,033,964	1991
Madagascar	Antananarivo	594,180	(229,345)	11,197,000	1990
Madeira	Funchal	796	(307)	273,200	1988
Malawi	Lilongwe	94,080	(36,315)	8,556,000	1991
Malaysia	Kuala Lumpur	332,965	(128,525)	17,861,000	1990
Peninsular Malaysia	Kuala Lumpur	131,585	(50,790)	14,005,000	1988
Sabah	Kota Kinabalu	76,115	(29,380)	1,600,000	1988
Sarawak	Kuching	124,965	(48,235)	1,400,000	1988
Maldives	Malé	298	(115)	214,139	1990
Mali	Bamako	1,240,140	(478,695)	8,156,000	1990
Malta	Valletta	316	(122)	356,000	1990
Man, Isle of	Douglas	588	(227)	64,000	1990
Marshall Islands	Majuro	181	(69)	40,609	1988
Martinique	Fort-de-France	1,079	(417)	359,000	1990
Mauritania	Nouakchott	1,030,700	(397,850)	2,025,000	1990
Mauritius	Port Louis	1,865	(720)	1,075,000	1990
Mexico	Mexico City	1,972,545	(761,400)	81,140,952*	1990
Micronesia	Kolonia	702	(271)	109,000	1990
Moldavia	Kishinev	33,700	(13,010)	4,400,000	1990
Monaco	Monaco	1.6	(0.6)	29,876	1990
Mongolia	Ulaanbaatar (Ulan Bator)	1,565,000	(604,090)	2,095,000	1989
Montserrat	Plymouth	104	(40)	13,000	1990
Morocco (inc. W. Sahara)	Rabat	710,850	(274,460)	25,061,000	1990
Mozambique	Maputo	784,755	(302,915)	15,656,000	1990
N					
Namibia	Windhoek	824,295	(318,180)	1,781,000	1990
Nauru	Yaren	21	(8)	10,000	1990
Nepal	Kathmandu	141,415	(54,585)	18,916,000	1990
Netherlands	Amsterdam (seat of government: The Hague)	41,160	(15,891)	15,019,000	1991
Netherlands Antilles	Willemstad	800	(308)	192,866	1988
New Caledonia	Nouméa	19,105	(7,375)	144,051*	1989
New Zealand	Wellington	265,150	(102,350)	3,390,000	1990
Nicaragua	Managua	148,000	(57,130)	3,871,000	1990
Niger	Niamey	1,186,410	(457,955)	7,732,000	1989
Nigeria	Lagos (seat of government: Abuja)	923,850	(356,605)	108,542,000	1990
Northern Mariana Islands	Saipan	471	(182)	20,591	1988
Norway	Oslo	323,895	(125,025)	4,242,000	1990
O					
Oman	Masqaṭ (Muscat)	271,950	(104,970)	2,000,000	1990
P					
Pakistan	Islamabad	803,940	(310,320)	112,050,000	1990
Palau	Koror	365	(141)	14,106	1988
Panama	Panama	78,515	(30,305)	2,446,000	1991
Papua New Guinea	Port Moresby	462,840	(178,655)	3,699,000	1990
Paraguay	Asunción	406,750	(157,005)	4,277,000	1990
Peru	Lima	1,285,215	(496,095)	22,332,000	1990
Philippines	Manila	300,000	(115,800)	62,868,000	1991
Pitcairn Island	Adamstown	42	(16.2)	59	1990
Poland	Warszawa (Warsaw)	312,685	(120,695)	38,180,000	1990
Portugal	Lisboa (Lisbon)	91,630	(35,370)	10,525,000	1990
Puerto Rico	San Juan	8,960	(3,460)	3,599,000	1990
Q					
Qatar	Ad Dawḥah (Doha)	11,435	(4,415)	368,000	1990
R					
Réunion	Saint-Denis	2,510	(969)	596,000	1990
Romania	Bucureşti (Bucharest)	237,500	(91,675)	23,193,000	1991
Russian Federation	Moskva (Moscow)	17,078,005	(6,592,110)	148,100,000	1990
Rwanda	Kigali	26,330	(10,165)	7,181,000	1990
S					
St Kitts – Nevis	Basseterre	261	(101)	44,000	1990
St Helena	Jamestown	122	(47)	5,564	1988
St Lucia	Castries	616	(238)	146,600	1988
St Pierre and Miquelon	St Pierre	241	(93)	6,392*	1990
St Vincent	Kingstown	389	(150)	113,950	1987
San Marino	San Marino	61	(24)	24,000	1990
São Tomé and Príncipe	São Tomé	964	(372)	115,600	1988
Saudi Arabia	Ar Riyāḍ (Riyadh)	2,400,900	(926,745)	10,500,000	1991
Senegal	Dakar	196,720	(75,935)	7,327,000	1990
Seychelles	Victoria	404	(156)	67,000	1990
Sierra Leone	Freetown	72,325	(27,920)	4,151,000	1990

State/Territory	Capital or main town	Sq. km	(Sq. miles)	Population	Date
Singapore	Singapore	616	(238)	3,002,800*	1990
Slovakia	Bratislava	49,035	(18,927)	5,126,000	1992
Slovenia	Ljubljana	20,250	(7,815)	1,924,000	1990
Solomon Islands	Honiara	29,790	(11,500)	321,000	1990
Somalia	Muqdisho (Mogadishu)	630,000	(243,180)	7,497,000	1990
South Africa	Pretoria (administrative) Cape Town (legislative)	1,184,825	(457,345)	35,282,000	1990
Cape Province		656,640	(253,465)	4,901,261	1986
Natal		86,965	(33,570)	2,145,018	1985
Orange Free State		127,990	(49,405)	1,863,327	1987
Transvaal		268,915	(103,800)	7,532,179	1985
Spain	Madrid	504,880	(194,885)	38,991,000	1990
Sri Lanka	Colombo	65,610	(25,325)	16,993,000	1990
Sudan	Khartoum	2,505,815	(967,245)	25,204,000	1990
Surinam	Paramaribo	163,820	(63,235)	422,000	1990
Svalbard	Longyearbyen	62,000	(23,930)	3,942	1986
Swaziland	Mbabane	17,365	(6,705)	768,000	1990
Sweden	Stockholm	449,790	(173,620)	8,618,000	1991
Switzerland	Bern	41,285	(15,935)	6,712,000	1990
Syria	Dimashq (Damascus)	185,680	(71,675)	12,116,000	1990

T

State/Territory	Capital or main town	Sq. km	(Sq. miles)	Population	Date
Taiwan	T'ai-pei (Taipei)	35,990	(13,890)	19,700,000	1987
Tajikistan	Dushanbe	143,100	(55,235)	5,200,000	1990
Tanzania	Dodoma	939,760	(362,750)	25,635,000	1990
Thailand	Krung Thep (Bangkok)	514,000	(198,405)	54,532,000*	1990
Togo	Lomé	56,785	(21,920)	3,531,000	1990
Tonga	Nuku'alofa	699	(270)	95,000	1990
Trinidad and Tobago	Port of Spain	5,130	(1,980)	1,234,388*	1990
Tristan da Cunha		201	(78)	306	1988
Tunisia	Tunis	164,150	(63,360)	8,180,000	1990
Turkey	Ankara	779,450	(300,870)	58,687,000	1990
Turkmenistan	Ashkhabad	488,100	(188,405)	3,600,000	1990
Turks and Caicos Islands	Cockburn Town	430	(166)	11,696	1990
Tuvalu	Funafuti	24.6	(9.5)	10,000	1990

U

State/Territory	Capital or main town	Sq. km	(Sq. miles)	Population	Date
Uganda	Kampala	236,580	(91,320)	16,582,674*	1991
Ukraine	Kiev	603,700	(233,030)	51,800,000	1990
United Arab Emirates (U.A.E.)	Abu Dhabi	75,150	(29,010)	1,600,000	1988
United Kingdom of Great Britain and Northern Ireland (U.K.)	London	244,755	(94,475)	55,514,500*	1991
England	London	130,360	(50,320)	46,170,300*	1991
Northern Ireland	Belfast	14,150	(5,460)	1,589,000	1990
Scotland	Edinburgh	78,750	(30,400)	4,957,000*	1991
Wales	Cardiff	20,760	(8,015)	2,798,200*	1991
United States of America (U.S.A.)	Washington D.C.	9,363,130	(3,614,170)	248,709,873*	1990
Alabama	Montgomery	131,485	(50,755)	3,984,000*	1990
Alaska	Juneau	1,478,450	(570,680)	546,000*	1990
Arizona	Phoenix	293,985	(113,480)	3,619,000*	1990
Arkansas	Little Rock	134,880	(52,065)	2,337,000*	1990
California	Sacramento	404,815	(156,260)	29,279,000*	1990
Colorado	Denver	268,310	(103,570)	3,272,000*	1990
Connecticut	Hartford	12,620	(4,870)	3,227,000*	1990
Delaware	Dover	5,005	(1,930)	658,000*	1990
District of Columbia	Washington	163	(63)	575,000*	1990
Florida	Tallahassee	140,255	(54,140)	12,775,000*	1990
Georgia	Atlanta	150,365	(58,040)	6,387,000*	1990
Hawaii	Honolulu	16,640	(6,425)	1,095,000*	1990
Idaho	Boise	213,455	(82,390)	1,004,000*	1990
Illinois	Springfield	144,120	(55,630)	11,325,000*	1990
Indiana	Indianapolis	93,065	(35,925)	5,499,000*	1990
Iowa	Des Moines	144,950	(55,950)	2,767,000*	1990
Kansas	Topeka	211,805	(81,755)	2,467,000*	1990
Kentucky	Frankfort	102,740	(39,660)	3,665,000*	1990
Louisiana	Baton Rouge	115,310	(44,510)	4,181,000*	1990
Maine	Augusta	80,275	(30,985)	1,218,000*	1990
Maryland	Annapolis	25,480	(9,835)	4,733,000*	1990
Massachusetts	Boston	20,265	(7,820)	5,928,000*	1990
Michigan	Lansing	147,510	(56,940)	9,179,000*	1990
Minnesota	St Paul	206,030	(79,530)	4,359,000*	1990
Mississippi	Jackson	122,335	(47,220)	2,535,000*	1990
Missouri	Jefferson City	178,565	(68,925)	5,079,000*	1990
Montana	Helena	376,555	(145,350)	794,000*	1990
Nebraska	Lincoln	198,505	(76,625)	1,573,000*	1990
Nevada	Carson City	284,625	(109,865)	1,193,000*	1990
New Hampshire	Concord	23,290	(8,990)	1,103,000*	1990
New Jersey	Trenton	19,340	(7,465)	7,617,000*	1990
New Mexico	Sante Fe	314,255	(121,300)	1,490,000*	1990
New York	Albany	122,705	(47,365)	17,627,000*	1990
North Carolina	Raleigh	126,505	(48,830)	6,553,000*	1990
North Dakota	Bismarck	179,485	(69,280)	634,000*	1990
Ohio	Columbus	106,200	(40,995)	10,778,000*	1990
Oklahoma	Oklahoma City	177,815	(68,635)	3,124,000*	1990
Oregon	Salem	249,115	(96,160)	2,828,000*	1990
Pennsylvania	Harrisburg	116,260	(44,875)	11,764,000*	1990
Rhode Island	Providence	2,730	(1,055)	989,000*	1990
South Carolina	Columbia	78,225	(30,195)	3,272,000*	1990
South Dakota	Pierre	196,715	(75,930)	693,000*	1990
Tennessee	Nashville	106,590	(41,145)	4,822,000*	1990
Texas	Austin	678,620	(261,950)	16,825,000*	1990
Utah	Salt Lake City	212,570	(82,050)	1,711,000*	1990
Vermont	Montpelier	24,015	(9,270)	560,000*	1990
Virginia	Richmond	102,835	(39,695)	6,128,000*	1990
Washington	Olympia	172,265	(66,495)	4,827,000*	1990
West Virginia	Charleston	62,470	(24,115)	1,783,000*	1990
Wisconsin	Madison	140,965	(54,415)	4,870,000*	1990
Wyoming	Cheyenne	251,200	(96,965)	450,000*	1990
Uruguay	Montevideo	186,925	(72,155)	3,094,000	1990
Uzbekistan	Tashkent	447,400	(172,695)	20,300,000	1990

V

State/Territory	Capital or main town	Sq. km	(Sq. miles)	Population	Date
Vanuatu	Port Vila	14,765	(5,700)	147,000	1990
Vatican City	Vatican City	0.44	(0.17)	766	1988
Venezuela	Caracas	912,045	(352,050)	19,735,000	1990
Vietnam	Hanoi	329,566	(127,246)	66,200,000	1990
Virgin Islands (U.K.)	Road Town	153	(59)	13,000	1990
Virgin Islands (U.S.A.)	Charlotte Amalie	345	(133)	117,000	1990

W

State/Territory	Capital or main town	Sq. km	(Sq. miles)	Population	Date
Wallis and Futuna Islands	Mata-Utu	255	(98)	15,400	1988
Western Sahara		252,120	(97,345)	179,000	1990
Western Samoa	Apia	2,840	(1,095)	170,000	1990

Y

State/Territory	Capital or main town	Sq. km	(Sq. miles)	Population	Date
Yemen	San'ā	477,530	(184,325)	12,000,000	1990
Yugoslavia	Beograd (Belgrade)	102,170	(39,435)	10,406,742	1991
Montenegro	Podgorica	13,810	(5,330)	664,000	1990
Serbia	Beograd (Belgrade)	88,360	(34,105)	9,815,000	1990

Z

State/Territory	Capital or main town	Sq. km	(Sq. miles)	Population	Date
Zaire	Kinshasa	2,345,410	(905,330)	35,562,000	1990
Zambia	Lusaka	752,615	(290,510)	7,818,447*	1990
Zimbabwe	Harare	390,310	(150,660)	9,369,000	1990

METROPOLITAN AREAS

A metropolitan area is a continuous built-up area containing a number of cities and towns. The total combined population is given either as an estimate or from census returns.

Metropolitan areas with populations greater than 7 million.

Country	Metropolitan area	Population
Mexico	MEXICO CITY	18,748,000
Brazil	SÃO PAULO	17,112,712
USA	NEW YORK	16,198,000
Egypt	CAIRO	15,000,000
China	SHANGHAI	13,341,896
Argentina	BUENOS AIRES	12,604,018
India	BOMBAY	12,571,720
Japan	TOKYO	11,935,700
Brazil	RIO DE JANEIRO	11,205,567
South Korea	SEOUL	10,979,000
India	CALCUTTA	10,916,272
USA	LOS ANGELES	10,845,000
China	BEIJING	10,819,407
Indonesia	JAKARTA	9,253,000
France	PARIS	9,060,000
Russian Fed.	MOSCOW	9,000,000
China	TIANJIN	8,785,402
UK	LONDON	8,620,333
Japan	OSAKA-KOBE	8,520,000
India	DELHI	8,375,188
Philippines	MANILA–QUEZON CITY	7,832,000
Pakistan	KARACHI	7,702,000

Country	Metropolitan area	population
Afghanistan	Kābul	2,000,000
Algeria	Algiers	3,033,000
Angola	Luanda	1,717,000
Argentina	Buenos Aires	12,604,018
	Córdoba	1,136,000
	Rosario	1,084,000
Armenia	Yerevan	1,300,000
Australia	Adelaide	1,050,000
	Brisbane	1,302,000
	Canberra	310,000
	Melbourne	3,081,000
	Perth	1,193,000
	Sydney	3,657,000
Austria	Vienna	1,531,000
Azerbaijan	Baku	1,780,000
Bangladesh	Chittagong	2,289,000
	Dhākā	6,646,000
Belgium	Antwerp	473,082
	Brussels	970,501
Belorussia	Minsk	1,637,000
Brazil	Belem	1,418,061
	Belo Horizonte	3,615,234
	Brasília	1,803,478
	Curitiba	1,966,426
	Pôrto Alegre	2,906,472
	Recife	2,814,795
	Rio de Janeiro	11,205,567
	Salvador	2,424,878
	São Paulo	17,112,712
Bulgaria	Sofia	1,190,000
Burma	Rangoon	3,295,000
Canada	Montreal	3,034,100
	Ottawa	885,300
	Quebec	622,000
	Toronto	3,822,400
	Vancouver	1,586,600
	Winnipeg	648,500
Chile	Santiago	4,734,000
China	Anshan	2,517,080
	Baotou	1,257,000
	Beijing (Peking)	10,819,407
	Changchun	2,214,000
	Changsha	1,362,000
	Chengdu	3,004,000
	Chongqing	3,151,000
	Dalian	2,543,000
	Fushun	1,420,000
	Fuzhou	1,361,000
	Guangzhou (Canton)	3,671,000
	Guiyang	1,587,000
	Hangzhou	1,412,000
	Harbin	2,966,000
	Huainan	1,519,420
	Jilin	1,327,000
	Jinan	2,415,000
	Kunming	1,718,000
	Lanzhou	1,566,000
	Luoyang	1,227,000
	Nanchang	1,415,000
	Nanjing	2,265,000
	Qingdao	2,010,000
	Qiqihar	1,460,000
	Shanghai	13,341,896
	Shenyang	4,763,000
	Shijiazhuang	1,352,000
	Taiyuan	2,199,000
	Tangshan	1,590,000
	Tianjin	8,785,402
	Wuhan	3,921,000
	Xian	2,859,000
	Zhengzhou	1,759,000
	Zibo	2,400,000
Colombia	Barranquilla	1,019,000
	Bogotá	4,851,000
	Cali	1,555,000
	Medellín	1,585,000
Croatia	Zagreb	1,174,512
Cuba	Havana	2,099,000
Czech Republic	Prague	1,294,000
Denmark	Copenhagen	1,337,114
Dominican Republic	Santo Domingo	2,203,000
Ecuador	Guayaquil	1,764,170
	Quito	1,281,849
Egypt	Alexandria	3,684,000
	Cairo	15,000,000
	El Giza	1,670,800
Estonia	Tallinn	482,000
Ethiopia	Addis Ababa	1,891,000
France	Marseilles	1,087,000
	Paris	9,060,000
Georgia	Tbilisi	1,264,000
Germany	Berlin	3,400,000
	Bonn	280,000
	Bremen	700,000
	Cologne	934,000
	Dresden	501,000
	Duisburg	525,000
	Düsseldorf	567,000
	Essen–Dortmund	2,745,700
	Frankfurt	624,000
	Hamburg	1,600,000
	Hanover	497,000
	Leipzig	530,000
	Munich	1,631,000
	Nuremberg	477,000
	Stuttgart	560,000
Greece	Athens	3,097,000
Guatemala	Guatemala City	2,000,000
Haiti	Port-au-Prince	1,031,000
Hong Kong	Hong Kong	5,448,000
Hungary	Budapest	2,115,000
India	Ahmadabad	3,279,655
	Bangalore	4,086,548
	Bombay	12,571,720
	Calcutta	10,916,272
	Delhi	8,375,188
	Hyderabad	4,280,261
	Jaipur	1,514,425
	Kanpur	2,111,284
	Lucknow	1,642,134
	Madras	5,361,468
	Nagpur	1,661,409
	Pune	2,485,014
Indonesia	Bandung	2,535,000
	Jakarta	9,253,000
	Medan	1,850,000
	Semarang	1,224,000
	Surabaya	2,383,000
Iran	Isfahan	1,484,000
	Mashhad	1,882,000
	Tehran	6,773,000
Iraq	Baghdad	4,044,000
Ireland, (Rep. of)	Dublin	926,000
Israel	Jerusalem	508,000
	Tel Aviv	1,029,700
Italy	Milan	1,449,403
	Naples	1,204,149
	Rome	3,051,000
	Turin	1,002,863
Ivory Coast	Abidjan	2,168,000
Japan	Fukuoka	1,169,000
	Hiroshima	1,049,000
	Kawasaki	1,128,000
	Kitakyushu	1,030,000
	Kyoto	1,460,000
	Nagoya	2,160,000
	Osaka-Kobe	8,520,000
	Sapporo	1,670,000
	Tokyo	11,935,700
	Yokohama	3,220,000
Jordan	Amman	1,025,000
Kazakhstan	Alma-Ata	1,151,300
Kenya	Nairobi	1,503,000
Korea, North	Pyôngyang	2,230,000
Korea, South	Inchon	1,739,000
	Pusan	3,875,000
	Seoul	10,979,000
	Taegu	2,518,000
Kuwait	Kuwait	200,000
Latvia	Riga	915,000
Lebanon	Beirut	1,500,000
Libya	Tripoli	2,062,000
Lithuania	Vilnius	582,000
Malaysia	Kuala Lumpur	1,711,000
Mexico	Guadalajara	2,846,720
	Mexico City	18,748,000
	Monterrey	2,521,697
	Puebla de Zaragoza	1,267,000
Morocco	Casablanca	3,213,000
	Rabat	1,068,000
Netherlands	Amsterdam	1,062,000
	The Hague	683,631
	Rotterdam	1,037,000
New Zealand	Auckland	864,700
	Christchurch	303,400
	Wellington	325,700
Nicaragua	Managua	1,012,000
Nigeria	Abuja	523,900
	Lagos	4,100,000
Norway	Oslo	458,364
Pakistan	Faisalabad	1,507,000
	Islamabad	537,000
	Karachi	7,702,000
	Lahore	4,092,000
	Rawalpindi	1,099,000
Peru	Lima	6,404,500
Philippines	Manila–Quezon City	7,832,000
Poland	Warsaw	1,655,100
Portugal	Lisbon	1,603,000
	Oporto	1,314,794
Puerto Rico	San Juan	1,390,000
Romania	Bucharest	2,194,000
Russian Federation	Chelyabinsk	1,143,000
	Kazan	1,094,000
	Moscow	9,000,000
	Nizhniy Novgorod (formerly Gorkiy)	1,438,000
	Novosibirsk	1,436,000
	Omsk	1,148,000
	Perm	1,091,000
	Rostov-on-Don	1,020,000
	Samara (formerly Kuybyshev)	1,257,000
	St Petersburg (formerly Leningrad)	5,035,000
	Ufa	1,083,000
	Volgograd	999,000
	Yekaterinburg (formerly Sverdlovsk)	1,367,000
Saudi Arabia	Jeddah	1,800,000
	Riyadh	1,500,000
Senegal	Dakar	1,492,000
Singapore	Singapore	2,723,000
South Africa	Cape Town	2,310,000
	Durban	1,057,000
	Johannesburg	1,714,000
Spain	Barcelona	1,677,699
	Madrid	2,991,223
Sri Lanka	Colombo	616,000
Sudan	Khartoum	1,947,000
Sweden	Stockholm	1,662,000
Switzerland	Geneva	373,000
Syria	Aleppo	2,501,000
	Damascus	2,651,000
Taiwan	Kaohsiung	1,512,000
	Taipei	2,961,000
Tanzania	Dar-es-Salaam	1,657,000
Thailand	Bangkok	5,832,843
Tunisia	Tunis	1,636,000
Turkey	Ankara	3,022,236
	Istanbul	6,665,000
	Izmir	2,665,105
UK	Birmingham	2,207,800
	Glasgow	872,900
	Leeds	1,461,000
	Liverpool	1,227,700
	London	8,620,333
	Manchester	2,445,000
Ukraine	Dnepropetrovsk	1,179,000
	Donetsk	1,110,000
	Kharkov	1,611,000
	Kiev	2,624,000
	Odessa	1,115,000
Uruguay	Montevideo	1,197,000
USA	Atlanta	2,737,000
	Baltimore	2,342,000
	Boston	2,845,000
	Buffalo	959,000
	Chicago	6,216,000
	Cincinnati	1,449,000
	Cleveland	1,845,000
	Columbus	1,344,000
	Dallas – Fort Worth	3,766,000
	Denver	1,640,000
	Detroit	4,352,000
	Houston	3,247,000
	Indianapolis	1,237,000
	Kansas City	1,575,000
	Los Angeles	10,845,000
	Miami	1,814,000
	Milwaukee	1,398,000
	Minneapolis – St Paul	2,388,000
	New Orleans	1,307,000
	New York	16,198,000
	Oklahoma City	964,000
	Philadelphia	4,920,000
	Phoenix	2,030,000
	Pittsburg	2,094,000
	Portland	1,188,000
	Rochester	980,000
	Sacramento	1,385,000
	San Antonio	1,323,000
	San Diego	2,370,000
	San Francisco	5,028,000
	Seattle	1,862,000
	St Louis	2,467,000
	Tampa – St Petersburg	1,995,000
	Washington DC	3,734,000
Uzbekistan	Tashkent	2,100,000
Venezuela	Caracas	4,092,000
	Maracaibo	1,365,308
	Valencia	1,227,472
Vietnam	Haiphong	1,397,000
	Hanoi	1,088,862
	Ho Chi Minh (Saigon)	3,237,000
Yugoslavia	Belgrade	1,575,000
Zaire	Kinshasa	3,505,000

GEOGRAPHICAL COMPARISONS

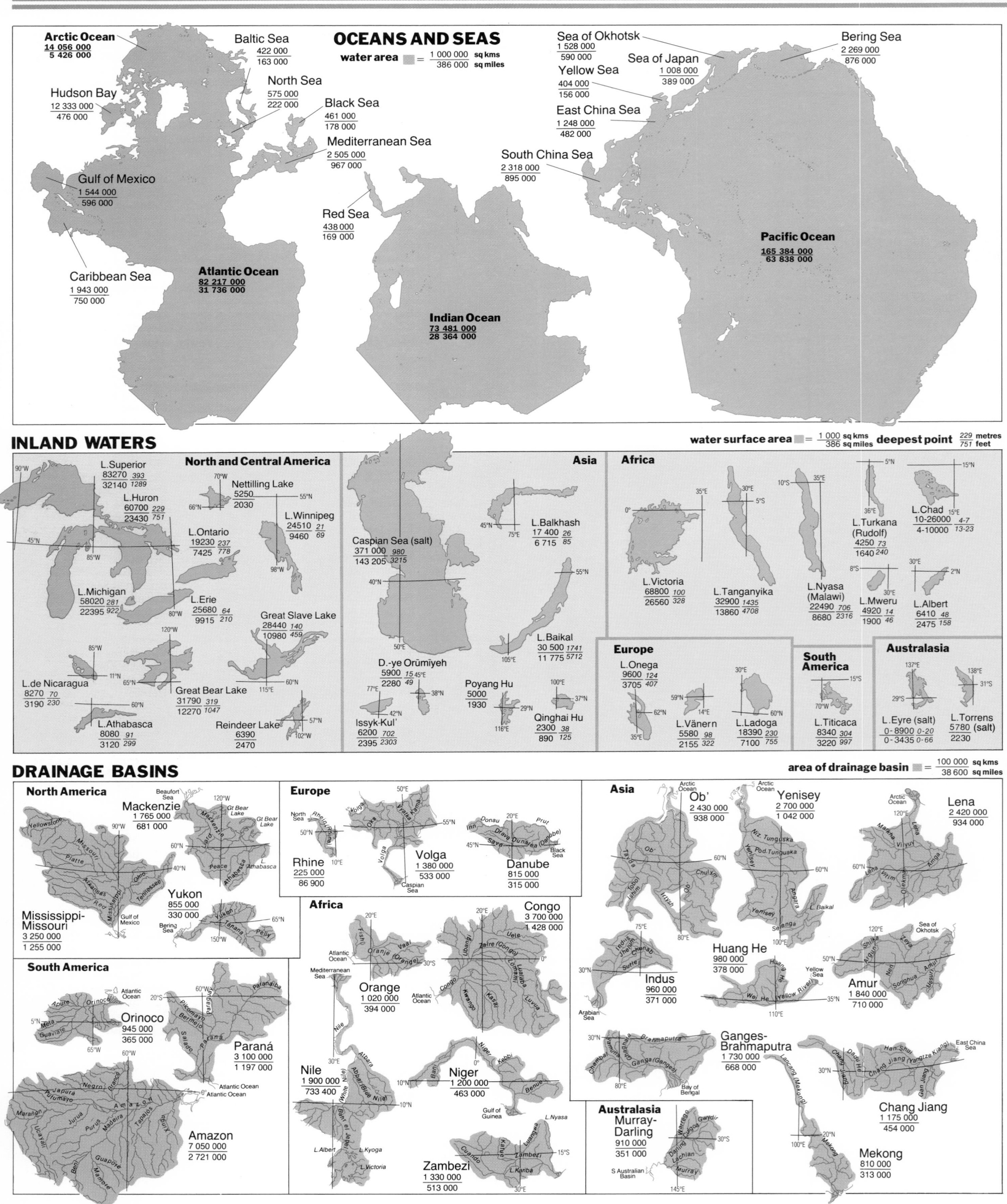

OCEANS AND SEAS

water area ■ = 1 000 000 sq kms / 386 000 sq miles

Arctic Ocean
14 056 000
5 426 000

Baltic Sea
422 000
163 000

Hudson Bay
12 333 000
476 000

North Sea
575 000
222 000

Black Sea
461 000
178 000

Mediterranean Sea
2 505 000
967 000

Gulf of Mexico
1 544 000
596 000

Red Sea
438 000
169 000

Caribbean Sea
1 943 000
750 000

Atlantic Ocean
82 217 000
31 736 000

Indian Ocean
73 481 000
28 364 000

South China Sea
2 318 000
895 000

Sea of Okhotsk
1 528 000
590 000

Sea of Japan
1 008 000
389 000

Yellow Sea
404 000
156 000

East China Sea
1 248 000
482 000

Bering Sea
2 269 000
876 000

Pacific Ocean
165 384 000
63 838 000

INLAND WATERS

water surface area ■ = 1 000 sq kms / 386 sq miles   deepest point 229 metres / 751 feet

North and Central America

L.Superior
83270 _393_
32140 _1289_

L.Huron
60700 _229_
23430 _751_

Nettilling Lake
5250
2030

L.Winnipeg
24510 _21_
9460 _69_

L.Ontario
19230 _237_
7425 _778_

L.Michigan
58020 _281_
22395 _922_

L.Erie
25680 _64_
9915 _210_

Great Slave Lake
28440 _140_
10980 _459_

L.de Nicaragua
8270 _70_
3190 _230_

Great Bear Lake
31790 _319_
12270 _1047_

L.Athabasca
8080 _91_
3120 _299_

Reindeer Lake
6390
2470

Asia

Caspian Sea (salt)
371 000 _980_
143 205 _3215_

L.Balkhash
17 400 _26_
6 715 _85_

L.Baikal
30 500 _1741_
11 775 _5712_

D.-ye Orūmīyeh
5900 _15_
2280 _49_

Poyang Hu
5000
1930

Issyk-Kul'
6200 _702_
2395 _2303_

Qinghai Hu
2300 _38_
890 _125_

Africa

L.Victoria
68800 _100_
26560 _328_

L.Tanganyika
32900 _1435_
13860 _4708_

L.Nyasa
(Malawi)
22490 _706_
8680 _2316_

L.Turkana
(Rudolf)
4250 _73_
1640 _240_

L.Chad
10-26000 _4-7_
4-10000 _13-23_

L.Mweru
4920 _14_
1900 _46_

L.Albert
6410 _48_
2475 _158_

Europe

L.Onega
9600 _124_
3705 _407_

L.Vänern
5580 _98_
2155 _322_

L.Ladoga
18390 _230_
7100 _755_

South America

L.Titicaca
8340 _304_
3220 _997_

Australasia

L.Eyre (salt)
0- 8900 _0-20_
0- 3435 _0-66_

L.Torrens
5780 (salt)
2230

DRAINAGE BASINS

area of drainage basin ■ = 100 000 sq kms / 38 600 sq miles

North America

Mackenzie
1 765 000
681 000

Yukon
855 000
330 000

Mississippi-Missouri
3 250 000
1 255 000

South America

Orinoco
945 000
365 000

Paraná
3 100 000
1 197 000

Amazon
7 050 000
2 721 000

Europe

Rhine
225 000
86 900

Volga
1 380 000
533 000

Danube
815 000
315 000

Africa

Orange
1 020 000
394 000

Nile
1 900 000
733 400

Niger
1 200 000
463 000

Zambezi
1 330 000
513 000

Congo
3 700 000
1 428 000

Asia

Ob'
2 430 000
938 000

Yenisey
2 700 000
1 042 000

Lena
2 420 000
934 000

Huang He
980 000
378 000

Indus
960 000
371 000

Amur
1 840 000
710 000

Ganges-Brahmaputra
1 730 000
668 000

Chang Jiang
1 175 000
454 000

Mekong
810 000
313 000

Australasia

Murray-Darling
910 000
351 000

MOUNTAIN HEIGHTS

Mountain	Metres	Feet	Location
Everest (Qomolangma Feng)	8,848	29,028	China-Nepal
K2 (Godwin Austen) (Qogir Feng)	8,611	28,250	Kashmir-China
Kangchenjunga	8,586	28,170	India-Nepal
Makalu	8,463	27,766	China-Nepal
Cho Oyu	8,201	26,906	China-Nepal
Dhaulagiri	8,167	26,795	Nepal
Manaslu	8,163	26,781	Nepal
Nanga Parbat	8,125	26,657	Kashmir
Annapurna	8,091	26,545	Nepal
Gasherbrum	8,068	26,470	Kashmir
Xixabangma Feng (Gosainthan)	8,012	26,286	Tibet, China
Distaghil Sar	7,885	25,869	Kashmir
Masherbrum	7,821	25,659	Kashmir
Nanda Devi	7,816	25,643	India
Kamet	7,756	25,446	India
Namjagbarwa Feng (Namcha Barwa)	7,756	25,446	Tibet, China
Gurla Mandhata	7,728	25,354	Tibet, China
Muztag	7,723	25,338	East Sinkiang, Tibet
Kongur Shan (Kungur)	7,719	25,325	China
Tirich Mir	7,690	25,230	Pakistan
Gongga Shan	7,556	24,790	Sichuan, China
Pik Kommunizma	7,495	24,590	Tajikistan
Pik Pobedy (Tomur Feng)	7,439	24,406	Kyrgyzstan-China
Aconcagua	6,960	22,834	Argentina
Ojos del Salado	6,880	22,572	Argentina-Chile
Bonete	6,872	22,546	Argentina
Huascarán	6,768	22,205	Peru
Sajama	6,542	21,463	Bolivia
Illampu	6,485	21,276	Bolivia
Chimborazo	6,310	20,702	Ecuador
McKinley	6,194	20,320	Alaska, U.S.A.
Logan	5,951	19,524	Yukon, Canada
Cotopaxi	5,896	19,344	Ecuador
Kilimanjaro	5,895	19,340	Tanzania
Citlaltépetl (Orizaba)	5,699	18,697	Mexico
Damávand	5,671	18,605	Iran
El'brus	5,642	18,510	Caucasus, Russian Federation
Kenya (Kirinyaga)	5,200	17,058	Kenya
Vinson Massif	5,140	16,860	Antarctica
Ararat (Büyük Ağri Daği)	5,123	16,808	Turkey
Jaya (Carstensz)	5,030	16,503	New Guinea, Indonesia
Mont Blanc	4,808	15,774	France-Italy
Ras Dashen	4,620	15,157	Ethiopia
Meru	4,565	14,979	Tanzania
Dom (Mischabel group)	4,545	14,910	Switzerland
Kirkpatrick	4,528	14,855	Antarctica
Karisimbi	4,507	14,786	Rwanda-Zaire
Matterhorn	4,478	14,690	Italy-Switzerland
Whitney	4,418	14,495	U.S.A.
Elbert	4,398	14,431	U.S.A.
Rainier	4,392	14,410	U.S.A.
Elgon	4,321	14,178	Kenya-Uganda
Mauna Kea	4,205	13,796	Hawaii, U.S.A.
Toubkal	4,165	13,664	Morocco
Cameroon (Caméroun)	4,095	13,435	Cameroon
Kinabalu	4,094	13,431	Sabah, Malaysia
Eiger	3,975	13,041	Switzerland
Erebus	3,794	12,447	Antarctica
Fuji	3,776	12,388	Japan
Cook	3,764	12,349	New Zealand
Teide	3,718	12,198	Canary Is.
Mulhacén	3,482	11,424	Spain
Etna	3,323	10,902	Sicily, Italy
Kosciusko	2,230	7,316	Australia

The mountains listed here are a selection from every continent rather than a strict numerical ordering.

RIVER LENGTHS

River	Kms	Miles	Location
Nile	6,695	4,160	Africa
Amazon	6,515	4,050	South America
Yangtze (Chang Jiang)	6,380	3,965	Asia
Mississippi-Missouri	6,019	3,740	U.S.A.
Ob'-Irtysh	5,570	3,460	Russian Federation-Kazakhstan
Yenisei	5,550	3,450	Russian Federation
Yellow River (Huang He)	5,464	3,395	China
Congo (Zaire)	4,667	2,900	Africa
Paraná	4,500	2,800	South America
Mekong	4,425	2,750	Asia
Amur	4,416	2,744	Russian Federation-China
Lena	4,400	2,730	Russian Federation
Mackenzie	4,250	2,640	Canada
Niger	4,030	2,505	Africa
Missouri	3,969	2,266	U.S.A.
Mississippi	3,779	2,348	U.S.A.
Murray-Darling	3,750	2,330	Australia
Volga	3,688	2,290	Russian Federation
Madeira	3,200	1,990	Brazil
Yukon	3,185	1,980	Canada-Alaska
Indus	3,180	1,975	Pakistan
Syrdar'ya	3,078	1,913	Kazakhstan
Salween	3,060	1,901	Asia
St Lawrence	3,058	1,900	Canada
São Francisco	2,900	1,800	Brazil
Rio Grande	2,870	1,785	U.S.A.-Mexico
Danube	2,850	1,770	Europe
Brahmaputra	2,840	1,765	India-Tibet
Euphrates	2,815	1,750	Iraq-Syria-Turkey
Pará-Tocantins	2,750	1,710	Brazil
Zambezi	2,650	1,650	Africa
Amudar'ya	2,620	1,630	Uzbekistan-Turkmenistan
Paraguay	2,600	1,615	South America
Nelson-Saskatchewan	2,570	1,600	Canada
Ural	2,534	1,575	Russian Federation-Kazakhstan
Ganges (Ganga)	2,510	1,560	India
Orinoco	2,500	1,555	Venezuela
Shabeelle	2,490	1,550	Somalia-Ethiopia
Arkansas	2,348	1,459	U.S.A.
Colorado	2,333	1,450	U.S.A.
Dnieper (Dnepr)	2,285	1,420	Ukraine-Belorussia
Irrawaddy	2,150	1,335	Burma
Don	1,870	1,162	Russian Federation
Orange	1,860	1,155	Africa
Rhine	1,320	820	Europe
Elbe	1,159	720	Germany-Czech Republic
Vistula (Wisła)	1,014	630	Poland
Loire	1,012	629	France
Tagus (Tejo)	1,006	625	Portugal-Spain

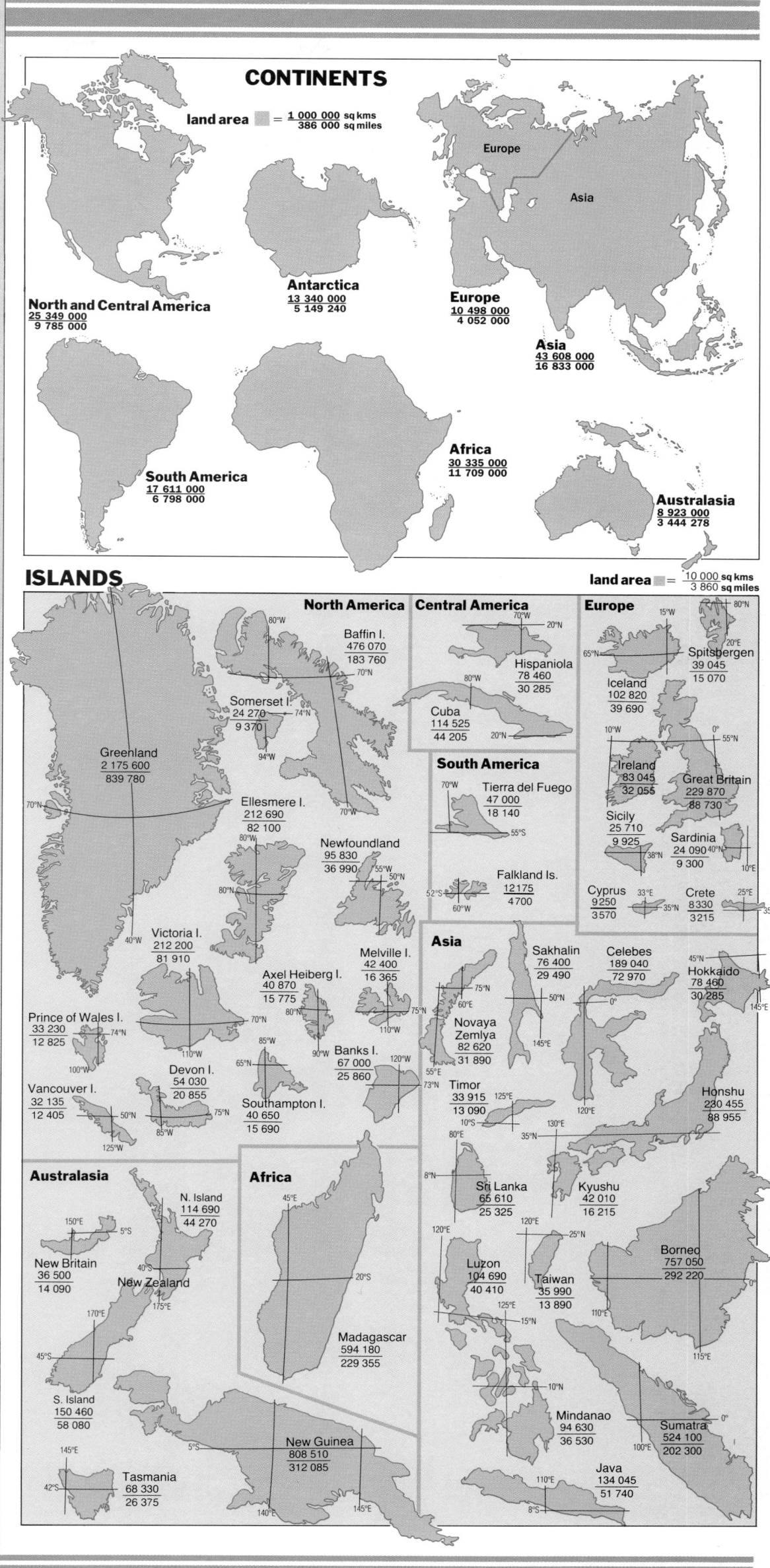

CONTINENTS

land area ▢ = 1 000 000 sq kms / 386 000 sq miles

North and Central America 25 349 000 / 9 785 000

South America 17 611 000 / 6 798 000

Antarctica 13 340 000 / 5 149 240

Africa 30 335 000 / 11 709 000

Europe 10 498 000 / 4 052 000

Asia 43 608 000 / 16 833 000

Australasia 8 923 000 / 3 444 278

ISLANDS

land area ▢ = 10 000 sq kms / 3 860 sq miles

North America — Baffin I. 476 070 / 183 760; Somerset I. 24 270 / 9 370; Greenland 2 175 600 / 839 780; Ellesmere I. 212 690 / 82 100; Victoria I. 212 200 / 81 910; Melville I. 42 400 / 16 365; Axel Heiberg I. 40 870 / 15 775; Prince of Wales I. 33 230 / 12 825; Banks I. 67 000 / 25 860; Devon I. 54 030 / 20 855; Vancouver I. 32 135 / 12 405; Southampton I. 40 650 / 15 690

Central America — Hispaniola 78 460 / 30 285; Cuba 114 525 / 44 205

South America — Tierra del Fuego 47 000 / 18 140; Falkland Is. 12 175 / 4 700; Newfoundland 95 830 / 36 990

Europe — Spitsbergen 39 045 / 15 070; Iceland 102 820 / 39 690; Ireland 83 045 / 32 055; Great Britain 229 870 / 88 730; Sicily 25 710 / 9 925; Sardinia 24 090 / 9 300; Cyprus 9250 / 3570; Crete 8330 / 3215

Asia — Sakhalin 76 400 / 29 490; Celebes 189 040 / 72 970; Hokkaido 78 460 / 30 285; Novaya Zemlya 82 620 / 31 890; Honshu 230 455 / 88 955; Timor 33 915 / 13 090; Sri Lanka 65 610 / 25 325; Kyushu 42 010 / 16 215; Luzon 104 690 / 40 410; Taiwan 35 990 / 13 890; Borneo 757 050 / 292 220; Mindanao 94 630 / 36 530; Sumatra 524 100 / 202 300; Java 134 045 / 51 740

Australasia — N. Island 114 690 / 44 270; New Britain 36 500 / 14 090; New Zealand; S. Island 150 460 / 58 080; Tasmania 68 330 / 26 375; New Guinea 808 510 / 312 085

Africa — Madagascar 594 180 / 229 355

SIBER
E
R
Kotuy
Lena
S
Honshu
Sakhalin
Kolyma
Hokkaido
Sea of Okhotsk
Novosibirskiye
Ostrova
ARCTIC
Kuril Islands
Kamchatka
OCEAN
Anadyr'
Ostrov
Vrangelya
Chukchi
Sea
Chukotskiy
Poluostrov
Bering
Sea
Bering Strait
Point Barrow
Beaufort
Sea
Bank
Island
Aleutian Islands
Yukon
Brooks Range
Alaska Range
Mount McKinley
Mackenzie Mountains
Mackenzie
Great
Bear
Lake
Aleutian Range
Kodiak Island
Gulf of Alaska
Coast Mountains
R O C K Y
Great
Slave L
NORTH
Midway Islands
Peace
Athabasca
Queen
Charlotte
Islands
PACIFIC
Vancouver
Island
Fraser
M o u n t a i n s
Mount Rainier
Mount St Helens
Columbia
Snake
Cascade Range
Hawaiian
Islands
Coast Ranges
Sierra Nevada
Great Salt
Lake
OCEAN
Mount
Whitney
Colorado
Gulf of California
Lower California
Sierra Madre Occiden

Yenisey
Ob'
Urals
Novaya Zemlya
Severnaya Zemlya
North Cape
SCANDINAVIA
Black Sea
Limit of permanent pack ice
Svalbard
Norwegian Sea
NORTH POLE
North Sea
Jan Mayen
Mediterranean Sea
BRITISH ISLES
Bay of Biscay
Denmark Strait
Iceland
Greenland
Ellesmere Island
Queen Elizabeth Islands
Parry Islands
Baffin Bay
NORTH AFRICA
Davis Strait
Victoria Island
Baffin Island
Cape Farewell
Madeira
NORTH
Canary Islands
Foxe Basin
Southampton Island
Hudson Strait
Cape Chidley
Labrador Sea
Azores
Hudson Bay
Labrador
Lake Athabasca
Churchill
Reindeer Lake
Southern Indian Lake
La Grande Rivière
Laurentian Highlands
Newfoundland
Cape Race
ATLANTIC
James Bay
Rupert
Saskatchewan
Lake Winnipeg
Nova Scotia
Lake Manitoba
Lake of the Woods
St Lawrence
Lake Superior
Cape Cod
Lake Huron
Lake Ontario
Lake Michigan
Missouri
Mississippi
Lake Erie
Great Plains
Platte
Ohio
Appalachian Mountains
Bermuda
OCEAN
Ozark Plateaus
Tennessee
Cape Hatteras
Arkansas
Savannah
Red River
Florida
Bahamas
Rio Grande
Gulf of Mexico
West Indies
Sierra Madre Oriental
Caribbean Sea
Orinoco
Yucatan

Colorado

Arkansas

Mississippi

Sierra Madre Occidental

Sierra Madre Oriental

Gulf of California

Lower California

Rio Grande

GULF

OF

MEXICO

Florida

Gulf of Campeche

Yucatan

W
C

G R

Popocatépetl ▲

Sierra Madre del Sur

*Gulf
of
Honduras*

Islas Revillagigedo

Lake
Nicaragua

Clipperton
Island

Isthmus

P A C I F I C

Isla del Coco

Isla de Malpelo

Galapagos Islands

O C E A N

BAHAMAS

WEST INDIES

GREATER ANTILLES

Cuba

Jamaica

Hispaniola

Puerto
Rico

CARIBBEAN

SEA

LESSER ANTILLES

NORTH

ATLANTIC

OCEAN

Bermuda

Trinidad

Gulf of
Darien

Panama

Gulf
of
Panama

Lake
Maracaibo

Cordillera

Occidental

Cauca

Magdalena

Cordillera Oriental

L L A N O S

Orinoco

Guiana

Roraima ▲

Highlands

Branco

Cotopaxi ▲

Chimborazo

Putumayo

Negro

Japurá

Amazon

Mouths
of the
Amazon

Marañón

Amazon

Juruá

Purus

Madeira

Tapajós

Xingu

Tocantins

Ucayali

A
N
D
E
S

Huascarán ▲

Madre de Dios

Parnaíba

Araguaia

São Francisco

MATO

GROSSO

Brazilian Highlands

Lake
Titicaca

Ancohuma ▲

Lake
Poopó

Salar
de
Uyuni

Atacama Desert

GRAN CHACO

Paraguay

Pilcomayo

Paraná

Lake Titicaca

Gran Chaco

Lake Poopó

Salar de Uyuni

Pilcomayo

Paraguay

Bermejo

Galapagos Islands

Salado

Paraná

Uruguay

Plate

San Félix   San Ambrosio

Aconcagua

Pampas

Juan Fernández

Colorado

Negro

S O U T H

Chubut

Chico

Patagonia

Deseado

Falkland Islands

Sala y Gomez

Tierra del Fuego

Easter Island

Cape Horn

Drake Passage

Elephant Island

P A C I F I C

South Shetland Islands

Ducie Island

Graham Land

ANTARCTIC PENINSULA

Palmer Land

Henderson Island

Pitcairn Island

Peter I Island

Bellingshausen Sea

O C E A N

Ellsworth Land

Rapa

S O U T H E R N

A N T

Marie Byrd Land

Ross Ice Shelf

Ross

Sea

Mount Erebus

Scott Island

Chatham Islands

Bounty Islands   Antipodes

Balleny Islands

New Zealand

Campbell Island

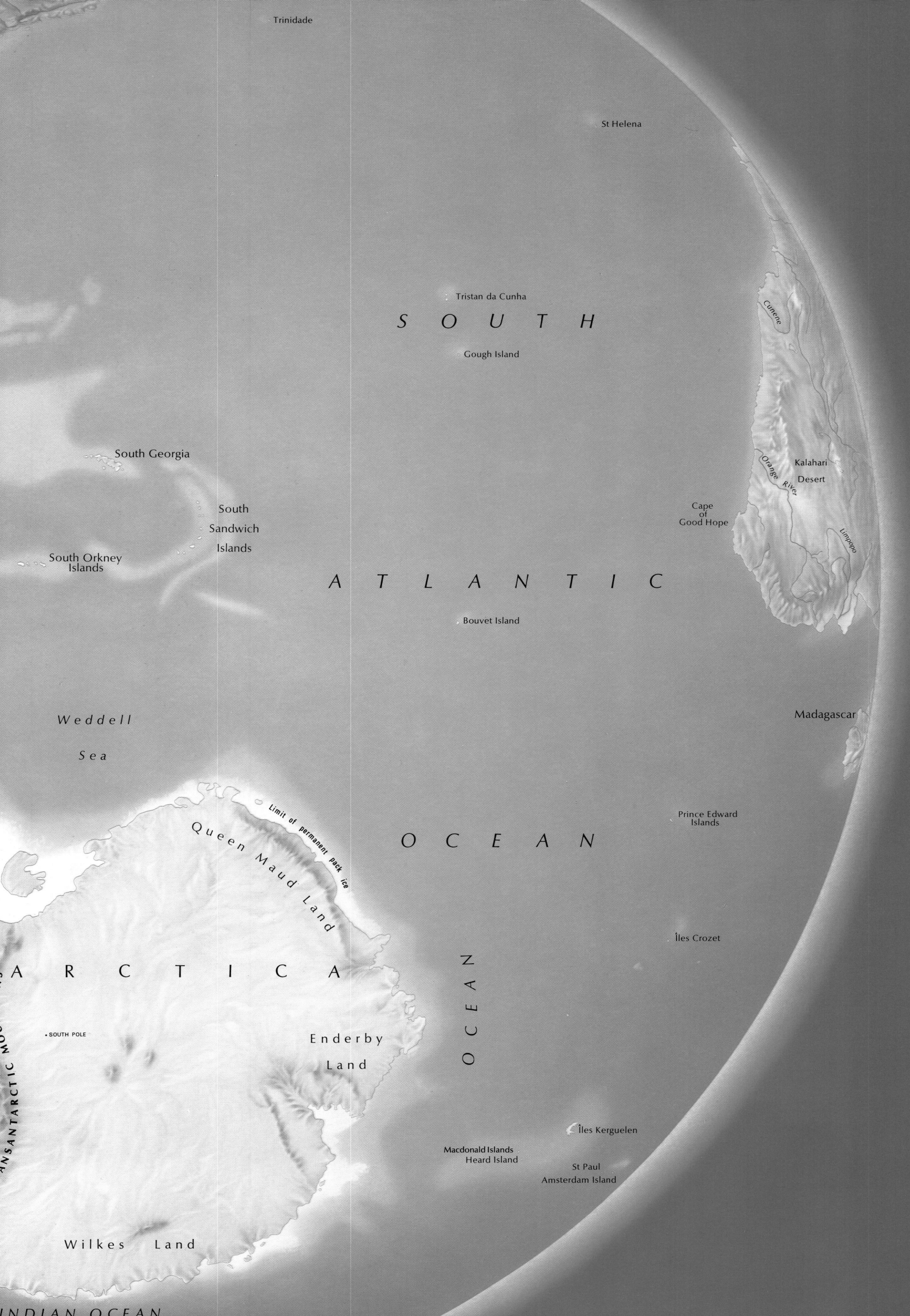

Trinidade

St Helena

Cunene

Tristan da Cunha

S O U T H

Gough Island

Kalahari
Desert

South Georgia

Orange River

Cape
of
Good Hope

South
Sandwich
Islands

South Orkney
Islands

A T L A N T I C

Bouvet Island

Madagascar

Weddell

Sea

Prince Edward
Islands

Limit of permanent pack ice

O C E A N

Queen Maud Land

Îles Crozet

A R C T I C A

O
C
E
A
N

TRANSANTARCTIC MOUNTAINS

• SOUTH POLE

Enderby
Land

Îles Kerguelen

Macdonald Islands
Heard Island

St Paul
Amsterdam Island

Wilkes   Land

INDIAN OCEAN

Iberian Peninsula
Sicily
Malta
Azores
Strait of Gibraltar
Chott Melrhir
El Jerid
Gulf of Sirte
Madeira
ATLAS MOUNTAINS
Canary Islands
NORTH ATLANTIC OCEAN
Hoggar
Tibesti
S A H A R A
Lac Faguibine
Cape Verde Islands
Sénégal
Cape Verde
Niger
S A H E L
Lake Chad
Gambia
Benue
Adamawa Highlands
Lake Volta
Grain Coast
Ivory Coast
Gold Coast
Slave Coast
Bight of Benin
Mouths of the Niger
Sanaga
Ubangi
Bioko
Gulf of Guinea
Príncipe
São Tomé
St Paul Rocks
Pagalu
Lac Mai-Ndombe
Congo
Kasai
Cuango
SOUTH AMERICA
Ascension
Bié Plateau
SOUTH ATLANTIC OCEAN
St Helena
Cunene
Okavango
Etosha Pan
Lake Ngami
Namib Desert
Orange River
Cape of Good Hope
Tristan da Cunha

Crete
Cyprus
rranean Sea

Lake Urmia
Caspian Sea

Pamirs
Tarim

Euphrates
Zagros Mountains
Hindu Kush
Karakoram
HIMALAYAS

Daryācheh-ye-Namak

Tigris

yan
Desert

Qattâra
Sinai
Gulf of Suez
Gulf of Aqaba

Dead Sea

Plateau of Iran

Plateau of Tibet

Helmand

Nile

The Great Oasis
Lake Nasser

ARABIAN

Persian Gulf

Thar Desert

Brahmaputr

PENINSULA

Gulf of Oman

Ganges (Ganga)

Nubian Desert

'Al Liwā'

Umm as Samim

Jebel Marra

Blue Nile

RED SEA

Maṣirah

Deccan

Godavari

White Nile

RUB AL KHĀLĪ

ARABIAN

SEA

Krishna

Lake Tana

Ethiopian Plateau

Danakil Desert

Bab el Mandeb

Gulf of Aden

Socotra

Laccadive Islands

Maldive Islands

Ceylon

Ogaden

Shabeelle

Uele

Lake Turkana

Rift Valley

Jubba

Lake Kyoga
Lake Albert
▲Mt Stanley
Lake Edward
Lake Victoria
Lake Kivu

INDIAN

Mount Kenya Tana

Lake Natron ▲ Kilimanjaro
Lake Eyasi

Seychelles

Chagos Archipelago

Luajaba

Rift Valley

Amirante Islands

Pemba Island
Zanzibar

Coëtivy Island

Lake Tanganyika

Mafia Island

Lake Upemba
Lake Mweru

Lake Rukwa

Aldabra Islands

Providence Islands

Lake Bangweulu

Rift Valley

Agalega Islands

Lake Nyasa

Comoro Islands

OCEAN

Lake Chilwa

Madagascar

Mozambique Channel

Zambezi

Lake Kariba

Tromelin

Makgadikgadi Pan

Limpopo

Rodrigues

Réunion
Mauritius

i

t

Vaal

Drakensberg

Desert

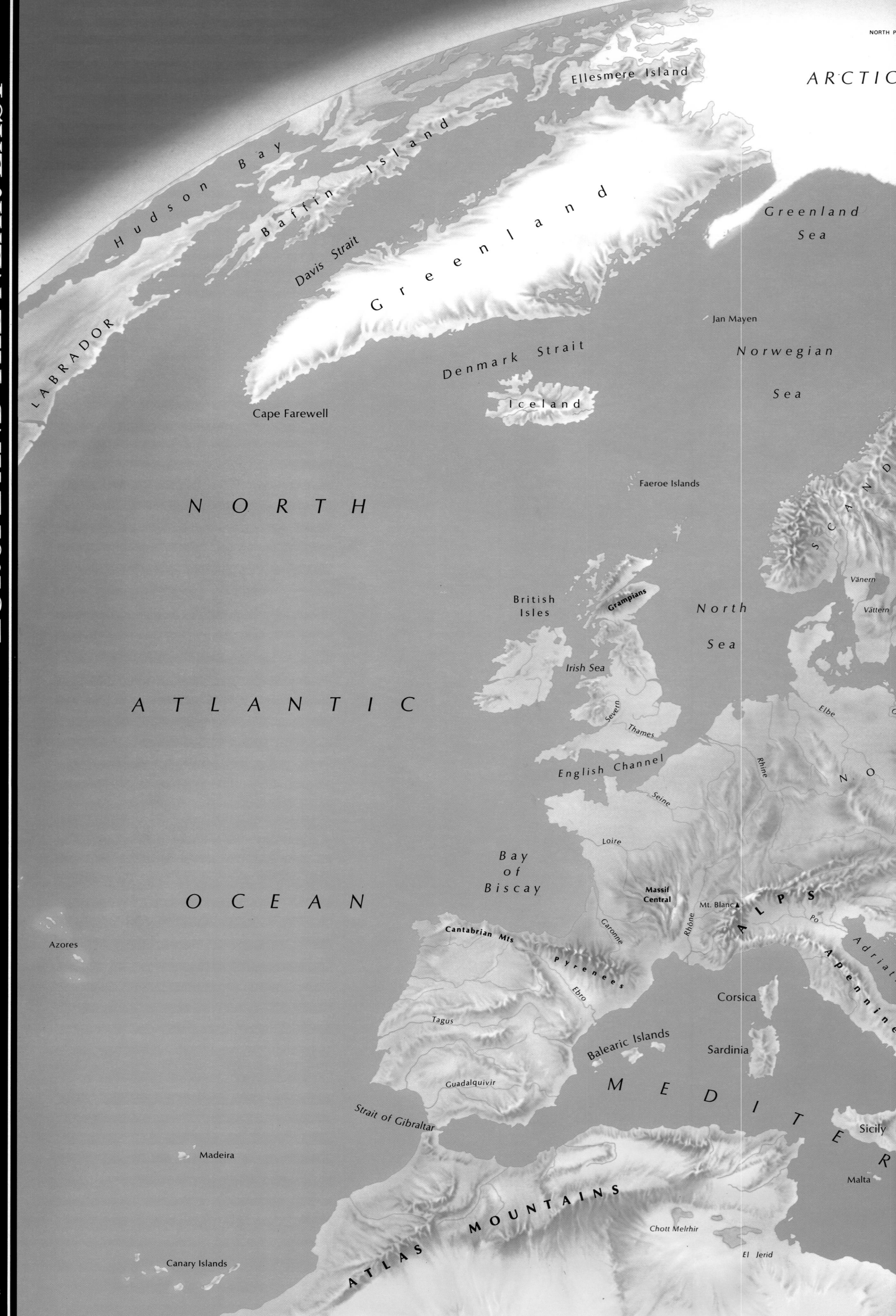

ARCTIC

NORTH PO

Ellesmere Island

Hudson Bay

Baffin Island

Greenland

Greenland
Sea

Davis Strait

Jan Mayen

LABRADOR

Denmark Strait

Norwegian

Cape Farewell

Iceland

Sea

Faeroe Islands

NORTH

Vänern

Vättern

British
Isles

Grampians

North

ATLANTIC

Irish Sea

Sea

Severn

Thames

Elbe

Rhine

N O

English Channel

Seine

OCEAN

Loire

Bay
of
Biscay

Massif
Central

Mt. Blanc

ALPS

Po

Rhône

Adriat

Cantabrian Mts

Garonne

Apennine

Pyrenees

Azores

Ebro

Corsica

Tagus

Balearic Islands

Sardinia

Guadalquivir

M E D I T E R

Strait of Gibraltar

Sicily

Madeira

Malta

ATLAS MOUNTAINS

Chott Melrhir

Canary Islands

El Jerid

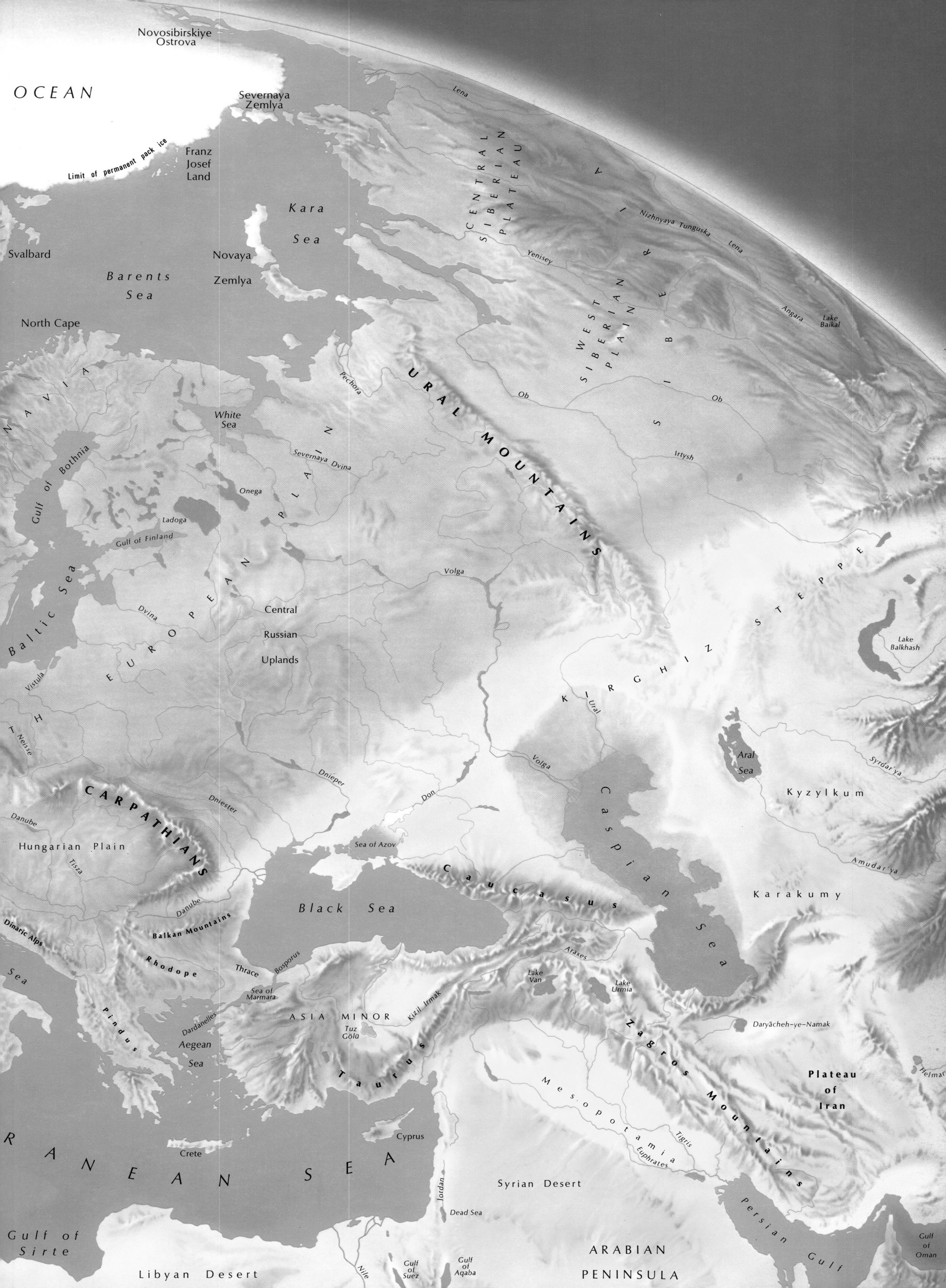

OCEAN

Novosibirskiye
Ostrova

Severnaya
Zemlya

Limit of permanent pack ice

Franz
Josef
Land

Svalbard

Kara
Sea

Barents
Sea

Novaya
Zemlya

North Cape

CENTRAL SIBERIAN PLATEAU

Lena

Nizhnyaya Tunguska   Lena

Yenisey

WESTERN SIBERIAN PLAIN

S I B E R I A

Angara

Lake
Baikal

White
Sea

Pechora

Severnaya Dvina

URAL MOUNTAINS

Ob

Ob

Irtysh

SCANDINAVIA

Gulf of Bothnia

Onega

Ladoga

Gulf of Finland

Baltic Sea

Dvina

EUROPEAN PLAIN

Central
Russian
Uplands

Volga

KIRGHIZ STEPPE

Lake
Balkhash

Vistula

Neisse

THE

Ural

Syrdar'ya

CARPATHIANS

Dniester

Dnieper

Don

Volga

Aral
Sea

Kyzylkum

Danube

Hungarian Plain

Tisza

Sea of Azov

Caspian Sea

Amudar'ya

Karakumy

Danube

Balkan Mountains

Dinaric Alps

Rhodope

Black   Sea

Caucasus

Sea

Pindus

Thrace

Bosporus

Sea of
Marmara

ASIA MINOR

Tuz
Gölü

Kizil Irmak

Araxes

Lake
Van

Lake
Urmia

Zagros Mountains

Daryācheh-ye-Namak

Plateau
of
Iran

Dardanelles

Aegean
Sea

Taurus

Mesopotamia

Helmar

RANEAN   SEA

Crete

Cyprus

Tigris

Euphrates

Persian Gulf

Gulf of
Sirte

Jordan

Dead Sea

Syrian Desert

ARABIAN

Gulf
of
Aqaba

Gulf
of
Suez

Nile

Libyan Desert

PENINSULA

Gulf
of
Oman

Barents Sea

Kheta

Scandinavia

White Sea

Pechora

CENTRAL

Baltic Sea

Lake Ladoga

Lake Onega

SIBERIAN

Ob

Nizhnyaya Tunguska

NORTH EUROPEAN PLAIN

WEST

PLATEAU

Dnieper

Ural Mountains

SIBERIAN

S
I
B

Yenisey

Angara

Volga

Tobol

Ishim

PLAIN

Don

Ural

Lake Baikal

Black Sea

Caucusus

Caspian Sea

KIRGHIZ

Ozero Tengiz

Ob

Hövsgöl Nuur

Selénga

Steppe

Aral Sea

Lake Balkhash

Ozero Zaysan

ALTAI

MONGO

Kyzylkum

Amudar'ya

Syrdar'ya

Ozero Alakol'

Karakumy

Ili

Ebinur Hu

Dzungaria

GOBI

Issyk Kul

Tien   Shan

Bosten Hu

Turfan Depression

Plateau of Iran

Pamirs

▲ Pik Kommunizma

Tarim

Lop Nur

Yellow River (Huang He)

Takla Makan

Hindu Kush

Karakoram

K2 ▲

Kunlun   Shan

Altun Shan

Qaidam Pendi

Qinghai Hu

Helmand

H
I
M
A
L
A
Y
A

Plateau of Tibet

Yangtze Kiang (Chang Jiang)

Yellow River (Huang He)

Qin Ling

Indus

Chenab

Sutlej

Salween

Red Basin

Indo-Gangetic

Brahmaputra

Yangtze Kiang (Chang Jiang)

Thar Desert

Plain

Everest ▲ ▲ Kangchenjunga

Nan Ling

Narmada

Ganges (Ganga)

Khasi Hills

Naga Hills

Mouths of the Ganges

Arabian

Mahanadi

Arakan

Red River (Song Hong)

Sea

Western Ghats

Deccan

Godavari

Eastern Ghats

Krishna

Irrawaddy

Gulf of Tongking

Bay of Bengal

Salween

Hainan

Laccadive Islands

Cauvery

Andaman Islands

Andaman Sea

INDOCHINA

Palk Strait

Chao Phraya

Maldive Islands

Ceylon

Kra Isthmus

Gulf of Thailand

Nicobar Islands

Malay Peninsula

Mekong

Strait of Malacca

INDIAN   OCEAN

Sumatra

Laptev Sea

Novosibirskiye
Ostrova

Alaska

Bering Strait

Nunivak
Island

Yana

Indigirka

Kolyma

Anadyr

B e r i n g

Verkhoyanskiy Khrebet

Lena

Vilyuy

S e a

Aleutian Islands

E

R

I

A

Aldan

Kht. Dzhungdzhur

Kamchatka

Komandorskiye
Ostrova

Yablonoyy Khrebet

S e a

o f

O k h o t s k

Kerulen

Shilka

Sakhalin

Kuril   Islands

Greater Khingan Range

Hulun
Nur

Amur

Sikhote Alin

Tatarskiy Proliv

I   A

M a n c h u r i a

Ussuri

Songhua

Oz
Khanka

Hokkaido

N O R T H

Midway
Islands

Changbai Shan

Korea

S e a

o f

J a p a n

Bo Hai

P A C I F I C

Honshu

Yellow River
(Huang He)

Y e l l o w

Korea Strait

Great Plain of China

S e a

Shikoku

O C E A N

Yangtze Kiang
(Chang Jiang)

Kyushu

Dongting Hu

Poyang Hu

Bonin Islands

E a s t

C h i n a

Volcano
Islands

Taiwan Strait

S e a

Ryukyu Islands

M
a
r
i
a
n
a
s

Marshall Islands

Taiwan

ang

P
H
I
L
I
P
P
I
N
E
S

S o u t h

Guam

Kiribati

C h i n a

Luzon

Paracel
Islands

S e a

Mindoro

Samar

C a r o l i n e   I s l a n d s

Panay

Palawan

Negros

Spratly
Islands

S u l u

Mindanao

S e a

C e l e b e s

S e a

Borneo

Admiralty
Islands

New Ireland

South

China

Sea

Celebes

Sea

Malay Peninsula

Strait of Malacca

S
u
m
a
t
r
a

*B
o
r
n
e
o*

B
o
r
n
e
o

*M
o
l
u
c
c
a
s*

Makassar Strait

Celebes

NOR

Ca

Banda

Sea

Arafur

Sea

J a v a

Sea

E
A
S
T

J a v a

Bali

Timor

I   N   D   I   E

S

Timor

Sea

Christmas Island

Cocos (Keeling) Islands

Arnhem Land

Victoria

Fitzroy

Kimberley
Plateau

Tanami
Desert

Barkly

I N D I A N

Great
Sandy
Desert

Ashburton

Macdonnell Ranges

Gibson
Desert

Lake
Amadeus

Sim
De

Finke

Gascoyne

Great Victoria Desert

Lake
Barlee

Lake
Moore

Nullarbor Plain

Lake
Gardner

Great Australian Bight

O C E A N

St Paul

S O U T H E R N

Kerguelen

Heard Island
Macdonald Islands

A N T A R C T I C A

roline Islands   Islands   Pohnpei   MICRONESIA   Marshall
Islands

TH PACIFIC OCEAN

SOUTH

M   E
L
A
N
E
S
I
A

Admiralty Islands

New Ireland

Bismarck
Sea

New Britain

Bougainville

Solomon Islands

New Guinea

Torres Strait

Great Barrier Reef

Cape
York
Peninsula

Gulf of
Carpentaria

Coral

Sea

Tableland

Flinders

Georgina

Great Dividing Range

Diamantina

Cooper Creek

Lake
Eyre

Barwon

Lake
Torrens

Darling

Murray

Lachlan

Murrumbidgee

Murray

Mount Kosciusko

Australian Alps

Bass Strait

Tasmania

Tasman

Sea

OCEAN

Nauru

Banaba

Kiribati

Santa
Cruz
Islands

Vanuatu

New
Caledonia

Norfolk Island

Lord Howe Island

New Zealand

Cook

Strait

Chatham Islands

Bounty Islands

Antipodes Islands

Auckland Islands

Campbell Island

Macquarie Island

P
O
L
Y
N
E
S
I
A

Line Islands

Tokelau
Islands

Tuvalu

PACIFIC

Samoan
Islands

Fiji

Tahiti
Society
Islands

Tonga

OCEAN

Kermadec Islands

STAR CHARTS

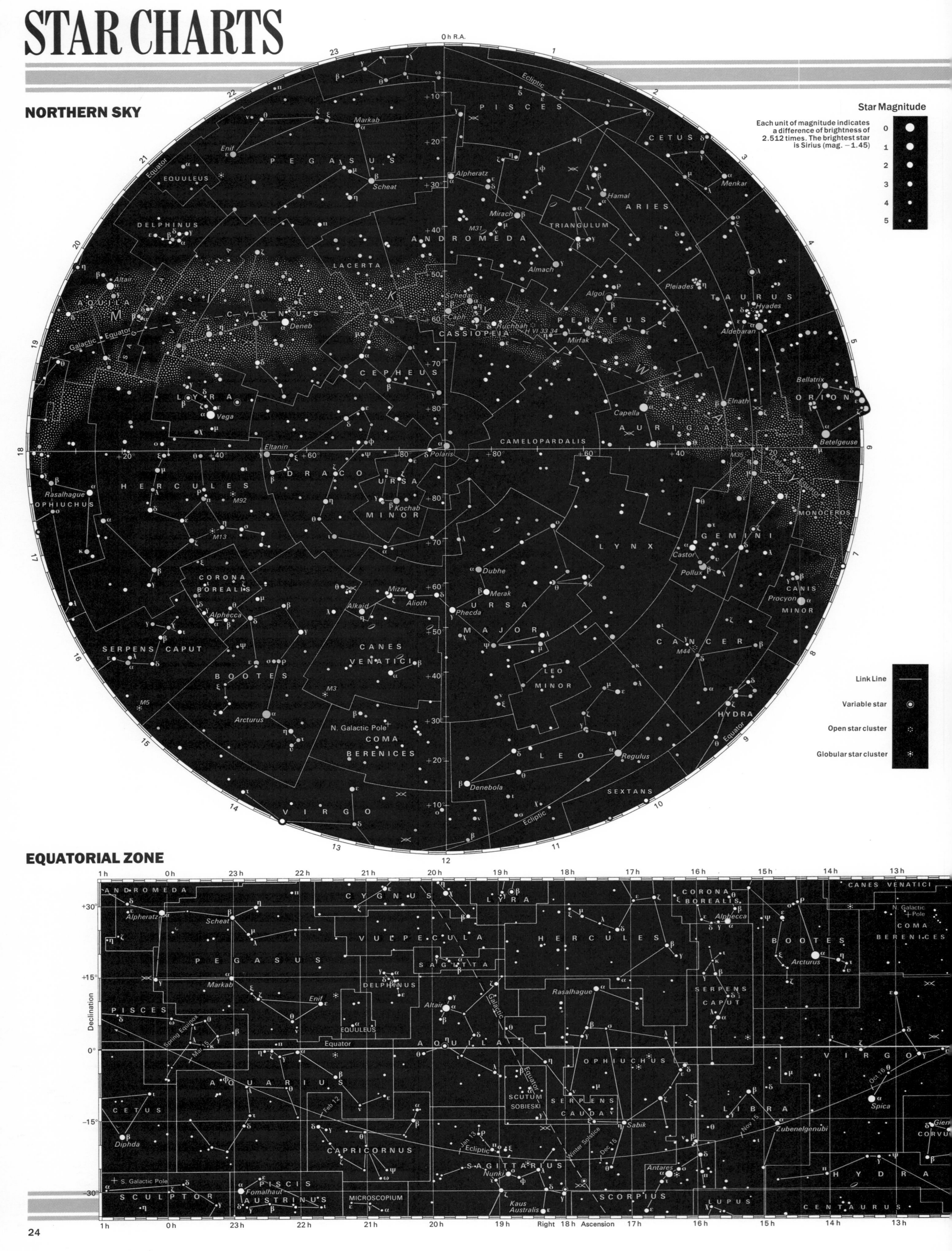

NORTHERN SKY

EQUATORIAL ZONE

Star Magnitude

Each unit of magnitude indicates a difference of brightness of 2.512 times. The brightest star is Sirius (mag. −1.45)

0	
1	
2	
3	
4	
5	

Link Line

Variable star

Open star cluster

Globular star cluster

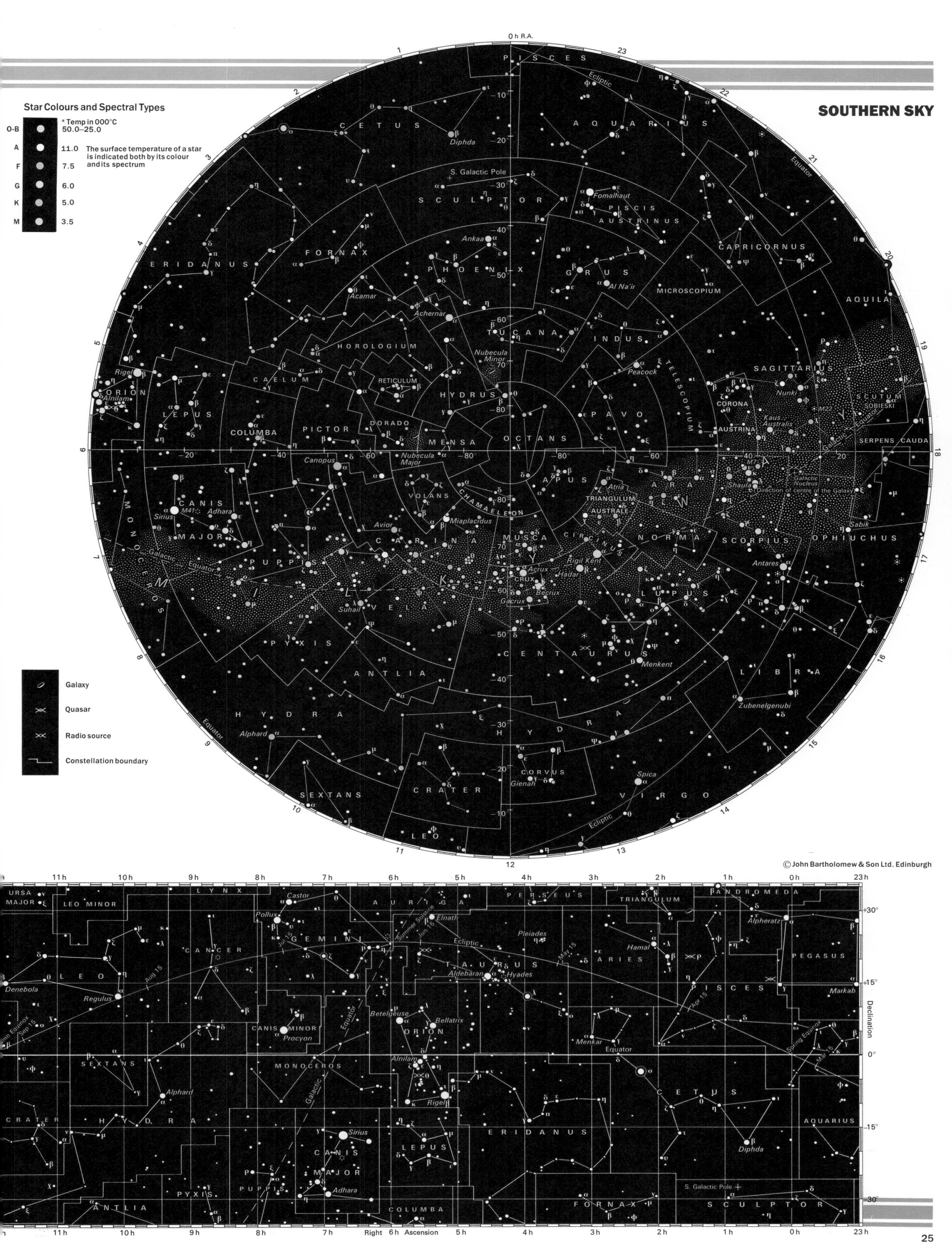

Star Colours and Spectral Types

		* Temp in 000°C
O-B	⬤	50.0–25.0
A	⬤	11.0
F	⬤	7.5
G	⬤	6.0
K	⬤	5.0
M	⬤	3.5

The surface temperature of a star is indicated both by its colour and its spectrum

Galaxy
Quasar
Radio source
Constellation boundary

© John Bartholomew & Son Ltd. Edinburgh

Right Ascension

Declination

25

UNIVERSE

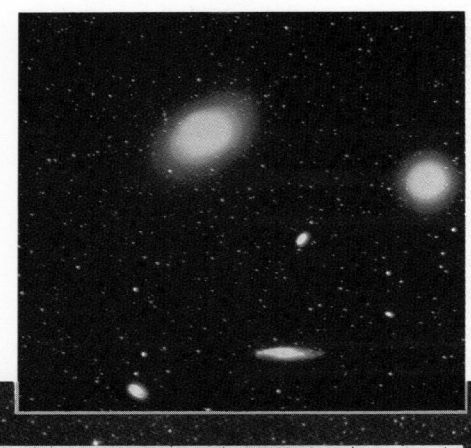

ORIGIN AND STRUCTURE OF THE UNIVERSE

Most astronomers believe that the Universe was created some ten to twenty thousand million years ago in an event often called the big bang or primordial fireball. The subsequent evolution of the universe can be described mathematically but the very early stages in particular are difficult to imagine.

The very high temperature mix of particles and radiation, the products of the big bang, expanded and cooled quickly allowing hydrogen and helium atoms to form and gravitate together to form huge clouds of gas. Turbulence within these contracting clouds caused them to fragment into rotating galaxy-sized clouds. Within these primitive galaxies smaller gas clouds condensed into clusters of stars, populating the galaxies much as we see them today. Most of these galaxies still belong to clusters, some containing thousands of members. There are probably several thousand million galaxies within the universe to the farthest distance so far observed.

Due to light travelling through space at a finite speed we see distant objects as they were when the light left them and in looking deep into space we also look far back in time. Over the past 40 years, larger optical telescopes, radio telescopes, space-borne instruments and computers have allowed astronomers to study the universe over a much wider range of the electromagnetic spectrum, much of it inaccessible from the Earth's surface.

Some galaxies are powerful emitters of radio waves and quasars, probably the nuclei of early galaxies, were first discovered by radio methods and later identified with optical objects: they appear so compact that they were mistaken for stars in our own galaxy. Many show very large 'red shifts' interpreted as velocities of recession which would make them amongst the most distant objects known. If all quasars are distant objects, it means that either our part of the universe is different from the rest or that they only occurred early on in the history of the universe. However, a few very experienced astronomers still believe they are nearer objects and that their red shifts have another origin. Perhaps the most difficult problem to be faced is that of finding reliable confirmation of estimates for the distances of the more distant galaxies and quasars.

In intergalactic space the more distant the object, the faster it seems to be receding from us. This is the expanding universe and the Hubble constant relates speed and distance. Already we believe we see objects receding at speeds approaching that of light or more then four-fifths of the way back to the big bang. However, the study of the universe even closer to its origin will be increasingly difficult and the moment of the big bang itself will be forever inaccessible to observation but the predicted isotropic background radiation from soon after this event has been observed.

Astronomy moves forward by theories to account for observations and further observations to test these theories. Two generally accepted simplifying principles were that our part of the universe is typical of the whole and that the same physical laws we apply to the present can also be applied to the past. The second principle is difficult to test back beyond the age of the Earth.

It is becoming more difficult to say what is a typical part of the universe now that surveys have confirmed a picture of the clustering of clusters of galaxies, which seem to be concentrated on a very large scale into 'walls' or surfaces with large intervening voids, likened to the surfaces of bubbles. Did these galaxies condense from this early distribution of gas or have these structures formed from existing galaxies? The formation of galaxies was probably largely completed within the first five billion years after the big bang when the universe was smaller, so the more distant galaxies or clusters of galaxies should be more closely packed as we look back into the past. This would be easier to test if galaxies were randomly distributed in space as was once thought and not concentrated in superclusters.

The average density of matter in the universe is thought to determine its future evolution, whether it will continue to grow larger, slow to a halt or eventually begin to contract. A current problem is that all the matter so far discovered in the universe in galaxies, interstellar dust and gas, stars and other forms appears to be insufficient to account for the behaviour of the universe as we find it. Some astronomers believe that as much as nine-tenths of the total matter in the universe remains to be discovered. It could be in the form of intergalactic matter, faint or dead stars or black holes, or hard to detect atomic particles such as neutrinos.

Black holes have been postulated to explain the origin of intense but small energy sources. If they exist they are so dense that not even light can escape from them so they can only be studied from the effects they have on nearby matter and radiation. Their strong gravitational fields draw in dust, gas, stars and perhaps even galaxies and the enormous amounts of energy released as this matter falls together and heats up produces light, heat and radio waves. As they become more massive their sphere of influence grows larger. Quasars may be the observable effects of the largest of black holes of the early universe, producing more light than a whole galaxy and very strong radiation at radio wavelengths. At the other end of the scale uncountable small or even microscopic black holes have been proposed to account for some extra mass. Knowledge of the nature, form and whereabouts of this 'missing mass' is of urgent importance.

Main picture The Large Magellanic Cloud (Nebecula Major), at 160,000 light years, is our nearest neighbour galaxy. The bright object (left centre) is the 30 Doradus or 'Tarantula' nebula near which SN1987A appeared.

Top Some of the thousands of elliptical and spiral galaxies in the Virgo cluster.

Top centre The Fornax cluster forms a small part of the Southern Supercluster of galaxies.

Bottom centre The spiral galaxy NGC 6744. Our galaxy is similar but being in a spiral arm ourselves, we see our stars concentrated into a bright band, the Milky Way.

Bottom The Pleiades (the 'seven sisters' of mythology) is a conspicuous star cluster in Taurus. Formed 80 million years ago, this cluster is 400 light years away.

Below In February 1987 a supernova (SN1987A) was discovered in the Large Magellanic Cloud being visible to the naked eye despite the LMC's great distance. The false-colour image by the Hubble Space Telescope in August 1990 shows expanding debris surrounding the exploding star as a red blob in the centre of the yellow ring of gas (1.3 light years across). This gas, expelled from the star thousands of years earlier, is being made to shine by radiation from the supernova explosion. The two blue stars to the left and right are not associated with the supernova.

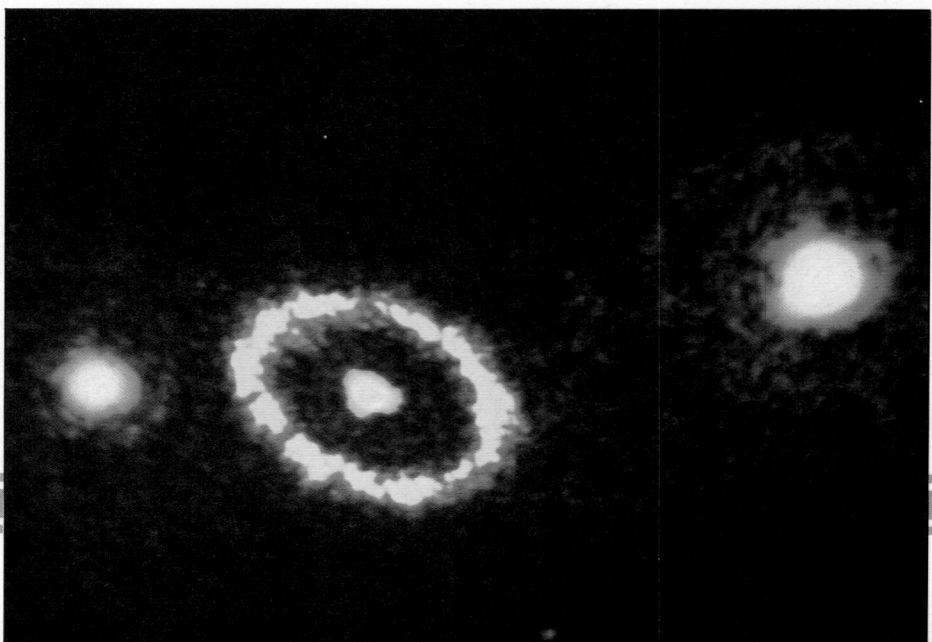

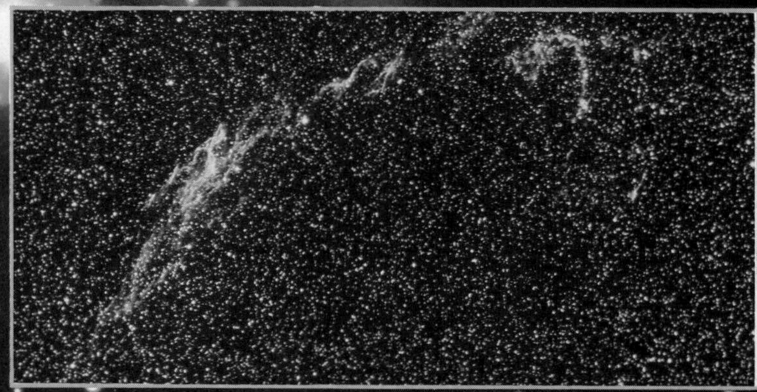

GALAXIES AND STARS

Galaxies take many forms from the giant globular galaxies, through ellipticals, spirals, barred spirals to irregular forms. This was once thought to be an evolutionary sequence but is now believed to reflect the speed with which star formation proceeded, the ellipticals turning their gas into stars before there was time for some of it to flatten into a disc where star formation could continue to form spiral arms.

The Virgo cluster is 75 million light years away and contains thousands of galaxies. On its fringes is the Local Group which contains our Milky Way system (the Galaxy), two other large spiral galaxies, the Magellanic Clouds and about twenty-five other smaller galaxies. These all lie within a distance of 5 million light years and form a gravitationally-bound group. In these galaxies astronomers can recognise many individual bright stars and nebulae while only exceptionally bright objects such as supernovae are visible in more distant galaxies.

Our Galaxy is a spiral, some hundred thousand light years across containing one or two hundred thousand million stars. At its centre in the direction of the great star clouds in Sagittarius is a massive core which may be like a supercluster of stars, almost a small galaxy in itself, and some astronomers believe, a black hole. The centre of the Galaxy is hidden by dust clouds from optical telescopes but these are largely transparent to some infrared and radio waves.

Like other similar galaxies it has two populations of stars. Population II stars form a more globular distribution and were formed first from hydrogen and helium. Population I stars lie mostly in the plane of the spiral arms and formed later from the flattened gas clouds and contain some heavier elements produced inside the first generation stars which were later expelled into space by exploding stars called supernovae. The Sun condensed from this contaminated gas and dust, and some of the matter left over from the birth of the Sun became the solar system. Without these heavier elements created inside stars there could be no Earth and no life as we know it. Elliptical galaxies contain mainly Population II stars.

Stars are still forming inside clouds of dust and gas such as the Horsehead Nebula in Orion. As the globules of gas contract they heat up until nuclear reactions start in their cores, turning hydrogen into helium. The outflow of radiation blows away remaining dust and gas to reveal a new star cluster. The stars are moving round the galactic centre, along with everything else in the Galaxy, and in time the stars in the cluster will disperse. The spiral arms are the areas of a galaxy where star formation is continuing and are mainly defined by a relatively small number of very bright hot stars. The bulk of the faint stars which greatly predominate are more uniformly spread throughout the galaxy.

The most massive stars use up their main source of energy quickly and fade within a few million years while a star such as the Sun, a yellow dwarf star, has been in much the same state for five thousand million years and will continue for as long again before major changes take place. When it can no longer convert hydrogen into helium it will start to convert helium to heavier elements swelling to become a red giant, enveloping the Earth and inner planets. However, these reactions can only proceed so far and as less heat is produced the Sun will shrink to become a very dense hot white dwarf about the size of the Earth, later cooling and fading to obscurity. Stars more than 1.4 times the mass of the Sun are unstable in the white-dwarf stage and collapse into even smaller bodies only a few kilometres across called neutron stars.

Above The Trifid Nebula is an example of a vast cloud of gas and dust. Globules of cold gas develop and condense and form new stars.
Below left The Hubble Space Telescope was released from the Shuttle Discovery in 1991. At 540 km above the Earth, objects can now be observed unhindered by the atmosphere.

Some collapse towards this stage so rapidly that the sudden generation of radiation blows off the outer layers of the star in a supernova explosion, for a few weeks giving off as much light as a whole galaxy of stars. Indeed supernovae are regularly observed in distant galaxies and can outshine the combined light of billions of more ordinary stars.

Early sky surveys revealed that many stars have companions; they appear double. Some were just chance alignments, but in many cases the stars are revolving around each other. The spectrograph reveals binary stars too close together to be seen directly. Stars show a wide variation in their colour, which is a measure of surface temperature, ranging from hot blue stars like Rigel through cooler yellow stars like Capella and the Sun to cool red stars like Betelgeuse. The spectrograph also tells astronomers about stars' composition.

Double stars give us stars' masses which range from about 50 times to one tenth that of the Sun while their diameters range from 2000 times the Sun to a hundredth or less. Stars differ in intrinsic brightness from 50,000 times (Deneb, Rigel) to only one-

Top left The Lagoon Nebula in the constellation of Sagittarius consists of a cloud of hydrogen and dust. The brightest region includes the new star Herschel 36, less than 10 000 years old.
Top right The Veil Nebula in Cygnus is the remnant of a supernova. The dust will eventually break up into small cold clouds.

thousandth that of the Sun. Many stars vary in brightness, the more violent changes occurring in novae and in supernovae where the collapse in seconds of a complete star can make it appear as bright as a whole galaxy.

Astronomers' means of studying the universe have widened dramatically over the past fifty years. Parts of the energy spectrum inaccessible from the ground can be studied from artificial satellites, from gamma rays, X-rays, ultra violet to some infrared wavelengths while infrared telescopes and radio telescopes are operated on the ground. New detectors, much more sensitive than photographic film, are now commonplace, and computer-controlled optics are making it possible to build eight- and ten-metre aperture optical telescopes. Radio telescopes on different continents can be linked together to give an equivalent aperture of thousands of kilometres, allowing very fine structure to be studied that even the best optical telescopes are unable to resolve. The Hubble Space Telescope, despite its problems, shows much finer detail than telescopes on the surface of the Earth. New facilities to detect neutrinos and gravity waves are planned.

SOLAR SYSTEM

Current theory suggests that the solar system condensed from a primitive solar nebula of gas and dust during an interval of a few tens of millions of years about 4600 million years ago. Gravity caused this nebula to contract, drawing most of its mass into the proto-sun at the centre. Turbulence gave the original cloud a tendency to rotate, and as it contracted conservation of angular momentum caused the proto-sun to spin faster and faster, forcing the remainder of the cloud into a disc shape.

The centre of the cloud heated up as it compressed, and so eventually became hot enough for the Sun to begin to shine, through nuclear energy released at its core. Meanwhile the surrounding disc cooled, allowing material to condense into solid form. Particles stuck together as they col-

lided and progressively larger bodies were built up. These swept up most of the debris to form the planets, which orbit the Sun close to the plane of the now vanished disc. The first materials to condense were the least volatile refractory compounds such as oxides of iron, nickel and aluminium. Decreasing temperature allowed rocky silicate material to appear followed by more volatile compounds such as water and methane. Thus composition of the planets progressed from less refractory cores to more volatile outer layers.

The planets nearest to the Sun are dense with metallic cores mantled by rocky silicate materials; planets further from the Sun accreted and retained large volumes of volatiles and are thus much more massive. They may have cores of rock and ice, surround-

ed by solid or liquid hydrogen enveloped in thick gassy atmospheres. These Gas Giants are accompanied by captured rocky and icy satellites which are mostly too small to have accreted and held atmospheres.

The subsequent evolution of the solar system was dominated by continuing chemical segregation within the planets and surface bombardment by waning numbers of smaller bodies. This bombardment was over by 3–4000 million years ago, although minor impacts still occur. Traces of these events remain on the surfaces of those bodies which have insufficient internal heat to drive any kind of resurfacing process.

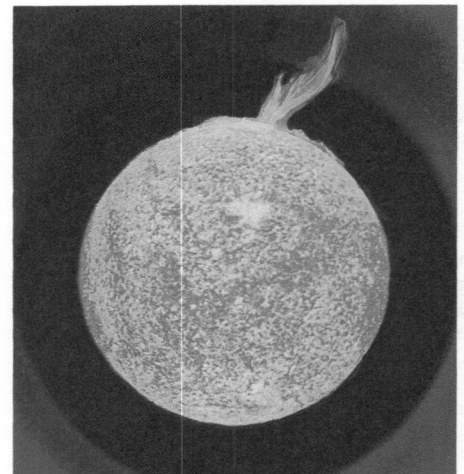

Right An ultra-violet image of the Sun from Skylab in 1973. A spectacular eruption of gas rises for half a million kilometres, channelled by the Sun's magnetic field.

	SUN	MERCURY	VENUS	EARTH	(MOON)	MARS	JUPITER	SATURN	URANUS	NEPTUNE	PLUTO
Mass (Earth=1)	333 400	0.055	0.815	1 (5.97 10²⁴kg)	0.012	0.107	317.8	95.2	14.5	17.2	0.003
Volume (Earth=1)	1 306 000	0.06	0.88	1	0.020	0.150	1 323	752	64	54	0.007
Density (water=1)	1.41	5.43	5.24	5.52	3.34	3.94	1.33	0.70	1.30	1.64	2.0
Equatorial diameter (km)	1 392 000	4878	12 104	12 756	3 476	6 794	142 800	120 000	52 000	48 400	2 302
Polar flattening	0	0	0	0.003	0	0.005	0.065	0.108	0.060	0.021	0
'Surface' gravity (Earth=1)	27.9	0.37	0.88	1	0.16	0.38	2.69	1.19	0.93	1.22	0.05
Number of satellites greater than 100 km diameter	—	0	0	1	—	0	7	13	7	6	1
Total number of satellites	—	0	0	1	—	2	16	17	15	8	1
Period of rotation (in Earth days)	25.38	58.65	−243 (retrograde)	23hr 56m 4 secs	27.32	1.03	0.414	0.426	−0.74 (retrograde)	0.67	−6.39 (retrograde)
Length of year (in Earth days and years)	—	88 days	224.7 days	365.26 days	—	687 days	11.86 years	29.46 years	84.01 years	164.8 years	247.7 years
Distance from Sun (max) Mkm	—	69.7	109	152.1	—	249.1	815.7	1 507	3 004	4 537	7 375
Distance from Sun (min) Mkm	—	45.9	107.4	147.1	—	206.7	740.9	1 347	2 735	4 456	4 425
Distance from Sun (mean) Mkm	—	57.9	108.9	149.6	—	227.9	778.3	1 427	2 870	4 497	5 900
Mean orbital velocity km/sec	—	47.9	35.0	29.8	—	24.1	13.1	9.6	6.8	5.4	4.7
Inclination of equator to orbit plane	7.25°	0.0°	177.3°	23.45°	6.68°	25.19°	3.12°	26.73°	97.86°	29.56°	122°
Inclination of orbit to ecliptic		7.01°	3.39°	0°	5.15°	1.85°	1.30°	2.48°	0.77°	1.77°	17.13°

	Mean Distance from Planet (1 000km)	Orbital Period (days) R=retrograde	Diameter (km)*
Mars			
Phobos	9.38	0.319	28x22x18
Deimos	23.46	1.262	16x12x12
Jupiter			
Metis	128.00	0.295	(40)
Adrastrea	129.00	0.297	(24x16)
Amalthea	181.30	0.498	(270x150)
Thebe	221.90	0.675	(100)
Io	421.60	1.769	3 630
Europa	670.90	3.551	3 138
Ganymede	1 070.00	7.155	5 262
Callisto	1 880.00	16.689	4 800
Leda	11 094.00	238.700	(15)
Himalia	11 480.00	250.600	(180)
Lysithea	11 720.00	259.200	(40)
Elara	11 737.00	259.700	(80)
Ananke	21 200.00	631R	(30)
Carme	22 600.00	692R	(45)
Pasiphae	23 500.00	735R	(70)
Sinope	23 700.00	758R	(40)
Saturn			
Atlas	137.70	0.602	40x30
Prometheus	139.50	0.613	140x80
Pandora	141.70	0.629	110x70
Epimetheus	151.40	0.694	140x100
Janus	151.50	0.695	220x160
Mimas	185.50	0.942	392
Enceladus	238.00	1.370	500
Tethys	294.70	1.888	1 060
Telesto	294.70	1.888	(24)
Calypso	294.70	1.888	30x20
Dione	377.40	2.737	1 120
Helene	377.40	2.737	36x30
Rhea	527.00	4.518	1 530
Titan	1 221.80	15.945	5 150
Hyperion	1 481.10	21.277	350x200
Iapetus	3 561.30	79.331	1 440
Phoebe	12 952.00	550.480R	220
Uranus			
Cordelia	49.75	0.335	(30)
Ophelia	53.76	0.376	(30)
Bianca	59.16	0.435	(50)
Cressida	61.77	0.464	(70)
Desdemona	62.66	0.475	(60)
Juliet	64.36	0.493	(80)
Portia	66.09	0.513	(110)
Rosalind	69.92	0.588	(60)
Belinda	75.26	0.624	(70)
Puck	85.89	0.762	150
Miranda	129.40	1.414	470
Ariel	191.20	2.520	1 160
Umbriel	266.00	4.144	1 170
Titania	435.90	8.706	1 580
Oberon	582.60	13.463	1 520
Neptune			
Naiad	48.20	0.296	(50)
Thalassa	50.00	0.312	(80)
Despina	52.50	0.333	(180)
Galatea	62.00	0.429	(150)
Larissa	73.60	0.554	(190)
Proteus	117.60	1.121	(400)
Triton	354.80	5.877	2 700
Nereid	5 513.40	360.160	(340)
Pluto			
Charon	19.64	6.387	1 190

*Many satellites are not spherical in shape, in which case two or three axes are quoted. Dimensions given in brackets are uncertain by at least ten per cent.

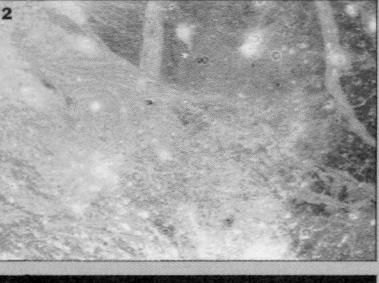

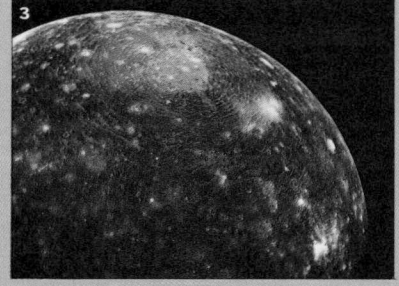

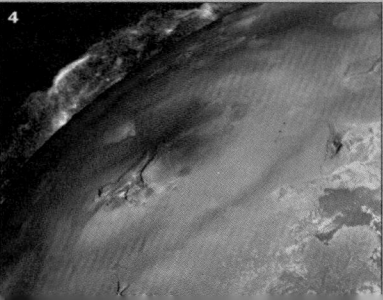

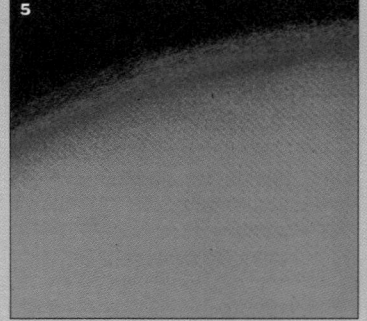

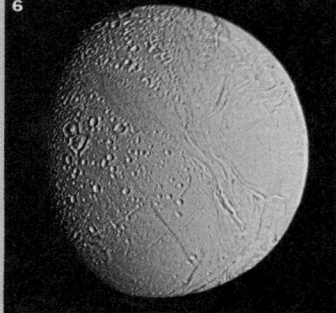

PLANETARY SATELLITES

All the planets except Mercury and Venus have bodies in orbit around them. The Earth-Moon system can be described as a double planet, whereas Mars' two satellites appear to be captured asteroids. The Gas Giants have a greater number of satellites ranging from bodies of less than 100 km across to larger moons of around 1000 km in diameter with rocky cores and usually icy crusts. Some of the more interesting bodies are illustrated here: the table on the left gives the full list.

1 Deimos is the smaller, outer irregular-shaped moon of Mars. The surface is covered by about 10 metres of loose rock.
2 The dark background material of **Ganymede** shows a high density of impact craters. The lighter network of grooves may have been formed by movements of the ice crust.
3 Callisto is among the most cratered in the Solar System with a surface at least 4 billion years old.
4 This Voyager 1 image of **Io** shows a plume of vaporized sulphur rising for 300 km above the first known active extraterrestrial volcano, Pele.
5 Titan is Saturn's largest moon and holds an extremely dense

atmosphere of nitrogen and methane above a surface of rock and ice.
6 Enceladus has experienced recent geological activity which has modified the cratered landscape.
7 The surface of **Mimas** is heavily cratered and shows no sign of geological activity.
8 This Voyager 2 mosaic of **Miranda** shows a variety of geological features.
9 Much of **Ariel**'s surface is pitted with craters 5 to 10 kms across and criss-crossed by valleys.
10 Titania displays many impact scars and also evidence of geological activity.

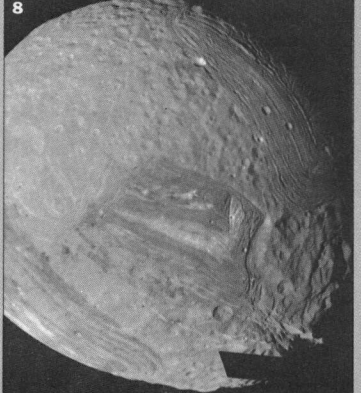

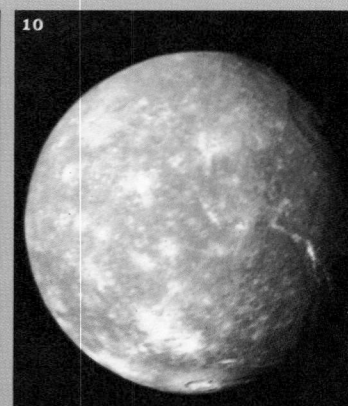

Left Io and Europa are clearly visible as they transit the face of Jupiter. The Great Red Spot of Jupiter has been observed for 300 years but the white ovals nearby did not appear until the 1930s. They are all centres of high pressure in this turbulent atmosphere.

Lower left The rings of Saturn lie in the equatorial plane and consist of countless small ice-covered particles. Tethys and Dione orbit Saturn at less than 400000km.

Below left The true-colour photograph of Uranus was taken from 9.1 million km by Voyager 2.

Below right Voyager 2 produced this composite false-colour image of Neptune in August 1989. The red edge around the planet is where the surrounding haze scatters sunlight.

GAS GIANTS

Jupiter has at least 16 satellites and a debris ring system about 50000km above the cloud tops. The outer atmosphere is all that can be directly observed of the planet itself. It is mostly hydrogen with lesser amounts of helium, ammonia, methane, water vapour and more exotic compounds. Jupiter's rapid rotation causes it to be flattened towards the poles. This rotation and heat flow convection from the interior cause complex weather patterns. Liquid droplets and solid particles of ammonia and other compounds, cause the clouds to be opaque. Where cloud systems interact vast storms can occur in the form of vortices. Some last only a few days, but the most persistent of these, the Great Red Spot, has been present since it was first detected in the 17th century.

The internal structure of Jupiter can be deduced. At about 1000km below the cloud tops hydrogen and helium may liquify to form a 10000km layer. Convection currents in this region generate the planet's intense magnetic field. The denser core, about 4% of the planet's mass, is mostly of rock and ice, with a little iron near the centre.

Saturn is the least dense of the planets. It has a stormy atmosphere situated above a 30000km layer of liquid molecular hydrogen and helium distorted by the planet's rotation. Below is a thin shell of liquid metallic hydrogen wrapped around a rock and ice core containing 25% of Saturn's mass.

The rings of Saturn are thought to be mostly made of icy debris, from 10m down to a few microns in size, derived from the break-up of a satellite. The rings are less than 1km thick but extend from above the cloud layer out to about 170000km from the centre. The rings are divided by gaps swept clear by complex gravitational interaction.

Uranus was little known until Voyager 2 flew by it in January 1986. It has a cloud cover even more featureless than either Jupiter or Saturn, and consists mostly of hydrogen. Unique among the planets, its axis is tilted almost into the plane of its orbit, with the south pole presently facing towards the Sun. Voyager 2 discovered ten more satellites and provided detailed images of the planet's eleven rings of icy debris.

Neptune provided a number of surprises when Voyager 2 flew by, on 24 August 1989, passing within 5,000km of the planet's north pole. The planet rotates in 16 hours 3 minutes, one hour faster than was believed to be the rate. Six new satellites were discovered, all irregular in shape and with impact craters, little changed since soon after their formation. Neptune has four rings. The magnetic axis is inclined 50° to the axis of rotation and displaced 10,000km from the centre. Neptune's atmosphere, a mixture of hydrogen, helium and methane, exhibits great turbulence. There is a great dark spot at 22°S latitude and a smaller dark spot nearer the south pole. Triton was found to be smaller than previous estimates.

Pluto, usually the most distant planet, is temporarily within the orbit of Neptune. The atmosphere is thought to be composed mostly of methane.

EARTHLIKE PLANETS

Mercury is the nearest planet to the Sun, spinning three times for every two orbits around the Sun. It has an exceptionally large metallic core which may be responsible for Mercury's weak magnetic field. Mercury is an airless world subject to vast extremes of temperature, from −180°C at night to 430°C near the middle of its long day.

The Mariner 10 spacecraft probe during the mid-1970s, revealed the surface to be dominated by heavily cratered areas dating from the early meteorite bombardment of the inner solar system. As the bombardment was tailing off Mercury's radius contracted by between 1 and 2km, forming compressional features (lobate scarps) which may have been caused by a change in the core from liquid to solid.

Venus has a dense atmosphere of 96% carbon dioxide mixed with nitrogen, oxygen, sulphur dioxide and water vapour which hides the surface under permanent cloud and maintains a mean surface temperature of about 480°C. The planet's slow rotation means that weather systems are driven mostly by solar heat, rather than by spin. As a result, beyond 10 kilometres above the surface, westerly winds of up to 100 m/sec cause a bulk rotation of the atmosphere in about four days.

Russian spacecraft have landed and sent back pictures of the surface. Imaging radar has been used to map most of the planet from orbiting spacecraft. The most recent survey by the Magellan probe began in 1990 and resolves features as small as 150m across. Mountains, valleys, impact craters and many other features have been mapped and 3-dimensional simulations generated by computer from the Magellan data.

Mars has a thin atmosphere of about 95% carbon dioxide mixed with other minor constituents. The polar caps consist of semi-permanent water ice and ephemeral solid carbon dioxide. Day and night surface temperatures vary between about −120°C and −20°C. Mars has two small satellites, each less than about 25km across, probably captured asteroids.

A variety of landscapes has been identified, including ancient heavily cratered terrains and plains which may consist of lava flows. There are several large volcanoes; the best preserved of these, Olympus Mons, rises 26km above the surface and is 550km across at its base.

Mars shows evidence of erosional processes. The effect of winds is seen in the degraded form of the older craters and the deposition of sand dunes. Dust storms frequently obscure the surface. The large channels, such as the 5000km long Valles Marineris, may have been cut by flowing water. Water is abundant in the polar caps and may be widespread held in as permafrost below the surface.

LUNAR DATA

Earth/Moon Mass Ratio	M_e/M_m 81.3015
Density (mean)	3.34g/cm³
Synodic Month (new Moon to new Moon)	29.530 588d
Sidereal Month (fixed star to fixed star)	27.321661 days
Inclination of Lunar orbit to ecliptic	5°8'43"
Inclination of equator to ecliptic	1°40'32"
Distance from Moon to Earth (mean)	384 400km (238 860 mi)
Optical libration	longitude ± 7.6° latitude ± 6.7°
Magnitude (mean of full Moon)	−12.7
Temperature	−153°C to + 134°C (−244°F to +273°F)
Escape velocity	2.38m/sec (1.48 mi/sec)
Diameter of Moon	3 476 km (2 160mi)
Surface gravity	162.2 cm/sec²

PHASES OF THE MOON

direction of light from Sun

New Moon

First quarter

Last quarter

Full Moon

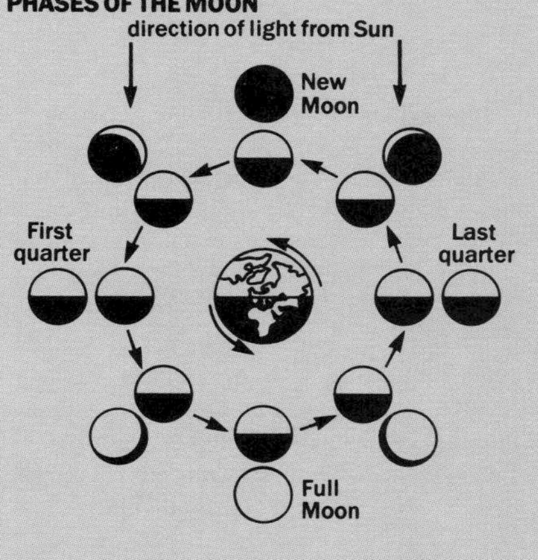

Above The Moon passes through a cycle of passes from New Moon to Full Moon.
Below An Apollo 16 photograph of the Moon.

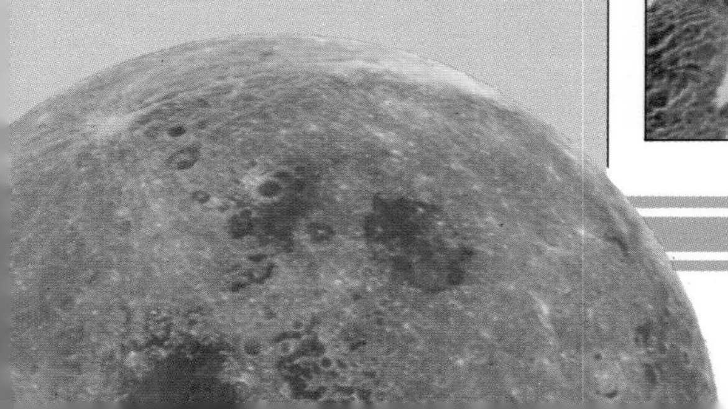

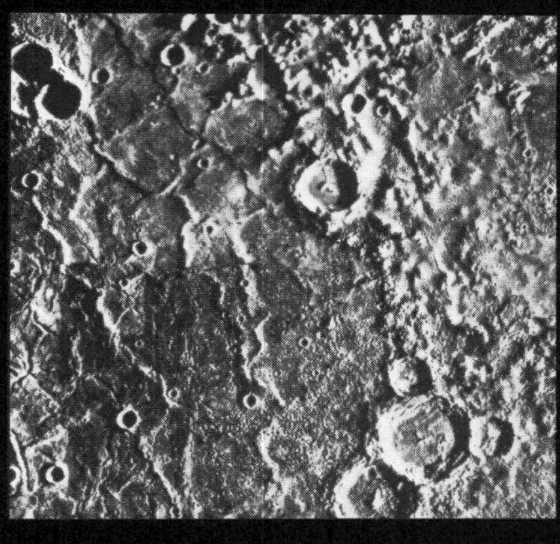

Above The Caloris basin of Mercury is the largest impact feature on the planet. The largest craters are some 200km wide.

Above right Mosaic of Mariner 9 images of Mars, showing the north polar ice cap and the enormous, extinct volcano, Olympus Mons, just below the centre of the image.

Right This Viking orbiter image of the surface of Mars shows the volcano, Olympus Mons, in more detail.

Below Radar mapping of Venus by the Magellan probe has provided this false-colour perspective view of Maat Mons, an 8km high volcano. The extensive lava flows give bright radar images suggesting that it may still be active.

29

SPACE FLIGHT

Possibly no other field of human endeavour has excited the imaginations of so many people over the past thirty-five years as the exploration of space. There are many difficulties involved in leaving the Earth. A large amount of energy is needed to lift a worthwhile payload 200km or more but it will fall back to the Earth's surface unless it is also given a velocity parallel to the ground of 29,000km per hour. To put a satellite into a higher orbit, or accelerate a spacecraft away from the Earth to the Moon or another planet, requires even greater energy and larger rockets for the same payload. Expendable rocket boosters are used which are jetisoned in stages as their fuel becomes exhausted.

On 4 October 1957 the USSR launched the first artificial satellite, Sputnik 1. The first American satellite, Explorer 1, followed within four months and discovered the Van Allen radiation belt about the Earth. The Russian lead in what developed into a space race was maintained by the first pictures of the far side of the Moon (Luna 3, 1959) and the first manned spaceflight (Yuri Gagarin, 1961), whereas the Americans at the same time were developing specialist satellites such as TIROS 1 (the first weather satellite), Transit 1B (the first navigation satellite) and Echo 1 (the first communications satellite), all launched in 1960.

During the 1960s and 1970s the nearby planets began to be investigated by flybys, orbiting probes and hard (crash) and soft landings, the Russians being more successful with Venus and the Americans with Mars. The surface of the Moon was studied by the US Ranger craft (1964/65) which resolved detail to a metre or so just before impact, the seven soft-landing Surveyors (1966/68) which surveyed potential manned landing sites and five Lunar Orbiters (1966/67) which provided what is still the only detailed survey of most of the lunar surface. Meanwhile the one-man Mercury and two-man Gemini flights of up to 14 days continued during which the techniques required for travel to the Moon were developed. On 20 July 1969 the first manned landing was made using the Saturn V rocket (US astronauts Armstrong, Aldrin and Collins, Apollo XI).

The Russian manned programme continued with longer flights in Earth orbit and the launch of their first Salyut space stations (from 1971) while their lunar program continued with robot exploration and the return of small samples to Earth.

The American probe Pioneer 10 (1972) was the first to cross the asteroid belt: both Pioneer 10 and 11 were, by 1992, well beyond the farthest planets and still being tracked. Skylab provided a useful working area in orbit (1973/74). A large part of Mercury was mapped by Mariner 10 (1973/

Top Right **The Hubble Space Telescope still attached to the Remote Manipulator Arm (lower right) of the Space Shuttle Discovery during deployment in 1990.**

Above **ESA's Ariane launch vehicle, developed and built in France, being prepared for flight at Kourou, French Guiana.**

Left **The first modules of the Mir space-station were launched into Earth orbit by the former USSR in 1986. It has been inhabited continuously by relays of cosmonauts.**

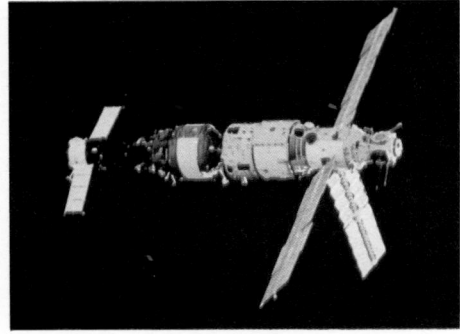

74), a survey that has not yet been repeated. The USSR started its long series of Venera spacecraft to Venus (from 1975) using orbiters and probes which descended to send back the first pictures of the surface and the US Viking 1 and 2 mapped Mars in great detail from orbit and their landers sampled the surface material, made tests for signs of life and recorded the weather (1976/77).

The US Voyagers 1 and 2 were launched in 1977 with Voyager 2 visiting Jupiter (1979), Saturn (1981), Uranus (1986) and Neptune (1989), sending back detailed images of all these planets and many of their satellites and discovering many new satellites and rings around Neptune. IRAS (1983) mapped the whole sky in the infra-red discovering many new objects: so much data was sent back in its few months operation that much is still not analysed. Other satellites observed gamma-rays, x-rays and the ultra-violet region of the spectrum while another large group of satellites looked towards the Earth to study the weather, the sea, land utilisation and many other aspects of the Earth's environment, many of which have commercial and military applications while both the USA and USSR have made much use of reconnaissance or spy satellites. The Soviet Mir space station which was launched in 1986 has been inhabited continuously by relays of cosmonauts, some of whom were in orbit for a year, some new modules having been added.

The UK launched only one small satellite before abandoning its own launch programme to join what is now the European Space Agency (ESA) which has used the Ariane rocket (developed and built in France from 1965) to launch both commercial satellites and space probes. China, Japan and India also now have their own launch capability and many nations use or participate in space projects of various kinds, especially in the fields of communications, weather and Earth resources.

The American ICE probe passed through the tail of comet Giacobini-Zinner in 1985 and two Japanese, two Soviet and the ESA Giotto made observations of Halley's comet in 1986, Giotto giving us the first close look at a comet's nucleus. Giotto is being re-activated to observe comet Grigg-Skjellerup in 1992. The Magellan orbiter commenced detailed radar mapping of Venus in 1989 and the Hubble Space Telescope was launched in 1990 by the Space Shuttle and despite problems with the optics is making observations of a quality impossible from the ground. Meanwhile, the spacecraft Galileo (1989) sent back the first-ever close-up picture of an asteroid, Gaspra (1991) on its way to Jupiter (1995). Ulysses (1990) which will pass over the Sun's poles (1994/95) will be swung out of the plane of the Earth's orbit by a close approach to Jupiter in 1992. Japan sent a small spacecraft carrying a tiny probe which was put into orbit around the Moon (1990). The Compton Gamma Ray Observatory was launched in 1991.

WEATHER SATELLITES
The impact of space flight on meteorology is becoming more obvious now that satellite pictures are routinely used as illustrations on TV weather forecasts. However, weather monitoring was among the major military and civil aims of the early space programme. Weather satellites can operate on a global basis, observing phenomena distant from meteorological observatories, such as over the ocean or unfriendly territory.

The most famous series of weather satellites, TIROS (Television and Infra-Red Observation Satellite), began with TIROS 1 in 1960 and continues, in advanced form, today. TIROS satellites are placed in non-synchronous orbits inclined to the equator to give close-up repeat coverage of middle and lower latitudes. Other satellites in higher,

Right **Weather satellites placed in geo-stationary orbits provide coverage over much of a hemisphere. However, to remain stationary relative to the ground they must be located over the equator, leading to severe foreshortening near the polar regions, as this Meteosat image shows.**

geosynchronous orbits provide effectively continuous low resolution coverage of almost complete hemispheres. A good example is the European Space Agency's Meteosats situated above 0°N, 0°W which have produced half-hourly images in the visible, water vapour infra-red and thermal infra-red bands since late 1977. The higher latitudes and polar regions, foreshortened by Meteosats, are best covered by weather satellites in lower, high inclination orbits.

Such satellites can detect and monitor hurricane formation and movement, allowing advance warning which has saved countless lives and minimised damage to property. More routinely, cloud patterns, water vapour content and vertical temperature profiles within the atmosphere and ground surface temperature are determined, which permit accurate forecasts a week in advance. Satellite observations are also essential for global investigation of the radiative properties of the Earth's surface and atmosphere so that we understand the dynamics of our climate much more fully than before the space age.

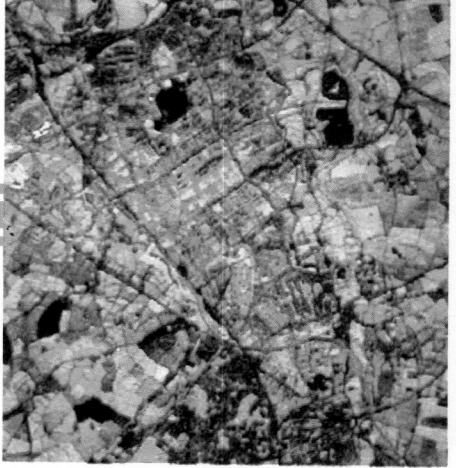

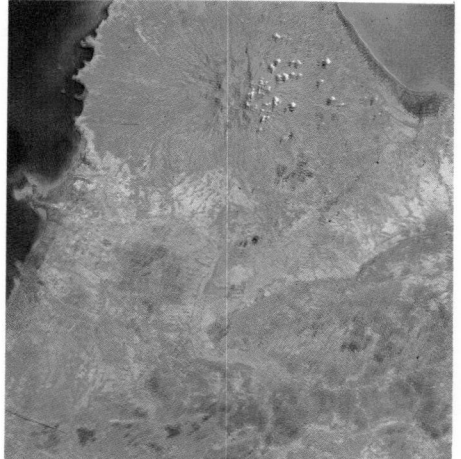

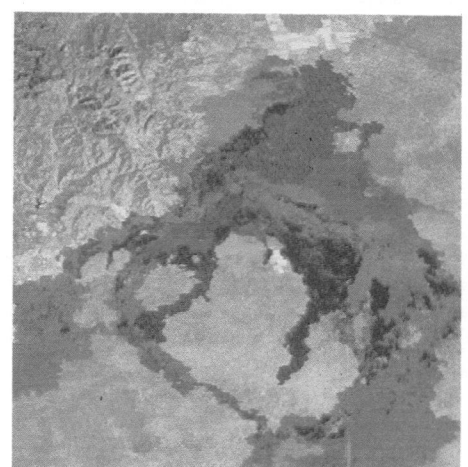

REMOTE SENSING

From orbit a camera or other imaging system is ideally placed to record and monitor large areas of the Earth on a regular basis. Photography is still useful in that it can provide a high resolution record, but it is restricted to visible and near infrared wavelengths and requires return of the film to Earth. Images recorded in digital form, not restricted to the photographic region of the spectrum, can be transmitted to a ground receiving station while the satellite continues in orbit. Computerised image processing techniques can reveal hidden structures within the data.

Digital images are recorded using electronic sensors. Usually the forward motion of the satellite is used to build up a picture line by line. The data within each line is broken into a string of numbers, each representing the brightness of one spot (or pixel) on the ground. This digital data may be transmitted in real time (direct to a ground receiving station or via a relay satellite), or recorded on board to be transmitted later as the satellite passes within range of a ground receiving station.

In order to cover most of the globe, remote sensing satellites are usually placed in polar orbits, highly inclined to the equator, which pass over a wide latitude range. Most are put in sun-synchronous orbit arranged so that the Earth rotates beneath them at a rate sufficient to keep the satellites over points at approximately the same local time throughout their north-south passage. The orbit then takes them from south to north on the nightside of the Earth before beginning another north-south passage further west at the same local time.

The most widely used satellite remote sensing data is that from multispectral scanners carried by the Landsat programme, begun in 1972. Initially known as ERTS (Earth Resources Technology Satellites),

Above left The false colour Landsat Thematic Mapper image of Milton Keynes, England, depicts built-up areas as blue, water black and vegetation red. The same image *above centre* has been computer enhanced to reveal recent landscape changes. Colour has been used to show areas of the same spectral characteristics. *Above right* Landsat Multispectral Scanner false colour image of the south coast of Portugal near Faro. The airport runway shows as a bright line by the lagoon in the lower left-hand corner.
Left Another multi-spectral Landsat image showing Gunung Muryo (1602m) and Tanjung (Cape) Bugel on the island of Java. This area is shown on page 70—N9.
Right Landsat Multispectral Scanner false colour image of Craters of the Moon in Idaho, U.S.A. There is little vegetation except in and near the mountainous area in the north-west.

the first three in the series were placed in near polar sun-synchronous orbits at an altitiude of about 920 km and overpassing the ground at about 09.30 local time. Complete global coverage, in four visible and near infrared bands with a pixel size of 80 m across, was achieved every 18 days. The succeeding generation of Landsats has a wider choice of spectral bands, a pixel size of 30 m and a global repeat every 16 days at an altitude of about 700 km. Landsat has enabled the observation of large-scale features in the Earth's crust, such as major folds and fault patterns, that from the surface (or an aircraft), cannot be seen in their entirety and often were not previously recognised, which has been used as an aid to hydrocar-

bon and mineral exploration. Some mineral occurrences are also highlighted by anomalous reflectance spectra which can be picked out especially well by the new sensors. The frequency repeat of Landsat coverage enables the monitoring of crops as they mature or are stricken by drought or disease, and the recording of major floods and forest fires. Changes in land use over the years since the programme began can be seen readily, without the expense of a large on-the-ground survey operation.

Nowadays we take live intercontinental television broadcasts for granted: these have been made possible only by the use of communication satellites. Civil communications satellites are the biggest group after

military satellites, and nearly half are in geosynchronous orbits. A single satellite can handle thousands of telephone and several television channels.

The large number of satellites interfere with some observations from the ground but the problem in space is potentially much more serious with thousands of items of space junk in orbit. These range from spent booster rockets to flecks of paint, which have damaged Space Shuttle windows. Even these very small items travelling at a high relative speed are potentially lethal to astronauts working outside. Although items more than a few centimetres across are regularly tracked by radar, the smaller pieces are effectively lost.

THE FUTURE

From a purely scientific point of view spaceflight could have a very bright future, extensions of known technology being sufficient for the manned exploration of the Moon and even Mars and further unmanned exploration of the universe. However, there has been a decline in public interest in space and with future projects requiring more resources, a difficulty in raising the necessary funds. In the USA projects such as the CRAF (Comet Rendezvous Asteroid Flyby) have been delayed repeatedly and the proposed Freedom space station was pronounced too ambitious but looks set to continue in redesigned form. With the present uncertainties concerning the states of the former USSR, the future scope of their space programme must be in doubt. Their space shuttle Buran has flown only twice, unmanned (to 1991), and the Mir space station is reported to need considerable repair and updating before 1994. Several designs for Mir 2 are under discussion. There is a Mars mission scheduled for 1994 and there has been open discussion of a manned expedition to Mars before 2010.

Other future missions include the US Mars Observer flight (1992) to map the surface for one Martian year, the ESA ISO (Infra-red Space Observatory) for launch in 1993 and the Cassini/Huygens Saturn NASA/ESA project for launch in 1995 with Saturn arrival in 2004 with touchdown on Titan the same year. Japan plans to launch Lunar-A to the Moon in 1996. ESA's space laboratory, Columbus, could be launched in 1998 and there are possible US Pluto Flyby and Neptune Orbiter missions in 2001-3.

Nearer to home is a trend to commercialisation of space ventures making it more expensive for developing countries and research institutes to afford to purchase data. Along with increasing emphasis on commercialisation comes a difficult period for space law. Despite United Nations treaties declaring outer space not subject to claims of sovereignty, many equatorial nations are claiming ownership of the geostationary orbit locations above. Problems loom also over the worldwide dissemination of increasingly high resolution imagery, because poor nations are disadvantaged compared with richer neighbours and foreign investors lacking the technology and expertise to process and interpret this information about their own resources. Similar unrest is developing over the direct broadcasting of television from satellites into territories whose governments wish to exercise political or moral censorship.

There are over a thousand satellites in Earth orbit, of which over a third are used for military purposes: these include surveillance, early warning and specialist communication satellites. Nuclear weapons are banned from space by treaty, but both superpowers have developed sophisticated anti-satellite weapons, such as hunter-killer satellites, which threaten the fragile secur-

Right The Jupiter probe Galileo is taking a gravity-assisted route to Jupiter with close approaches to Venus (1990) and Earth (1990 and 1992). In 1995 a probe will be released to descend through Jupiter's atmosphere while the main spacecraft orbits the planet. In October 1991 Galileo passed only 1600 km from asteroid Gaspra.

ity afforded by mutual surveillance by intelligence satellites.

Other satellite multispectral instruments are designed to monitor the oceans. For instance, the Nimbus 7 coastal-zone colour scanner (pixel size about 1 km) is sensitive in narrow spectral bands responsive to changes in chlorophyll concentration for mapping phytoplankton distribution and a thermal infrared channel which can show temperture variations and ocean surface currents.

Imaging by radar can be processed to give

a picture resembling a black and white photograph. This had been used over land to map tropical regions which are permanently cloud covered, to see through very dry sand deserts to the rocky structures beneath, and over the sea to determine roughness and wave patterns. Canada plans to launch such a satellite (Radarsat) to monitor sea-ice in Arctic waters. ERS-1, the ESA remote sensing satellite designed to study oceans, coastal regions and climates, was launched in 1991.

EARTH STRUCTURE

Internally the earth may be divided broadly into crust, mantle and core.

The crust is a thin shell constituting only 0.2% of the mass of the Earth. The continental crust varies in thickness from 20 to 90km and is less dense than ocean crust. Two-thirds of the continents are overlain by sedimentary rocks of average thickness less than 2km but attaining 20km. Ocean crust is on average 7km thick. It is composed of igneous rocks, basalts and gabbros.

Crust and mantle are separated by the Mohorovičić Discontinuity (Moho). The mantle differs from the crust. It is largely igneous. The upper mantle extends to 350km. There is a low velocity zone between 50km and 150km indicating a partial melting. The lower mantle has a more uniform composition. A sharp discontinuity defines the meeting of mantle and core. The inability of the outer core to transmit seismic waves suggests it is liquid. It is probably of metallic iron with other elements – sulphur, silicon, oxygen, potassium and hydrogen have all been suggested. The inner core is solid and probably of nickel-iron.

Temperature at the core-mantle boundary is about 3700°C and 4000°–4500°C in the inner core.

Evolution of the lithosphere, hydrosphere and atmosphere has been strongly influenced by the biosphere – the sphere of living things. The ancestral atmosphere lacked free oxygen. Plant life added oxygen to the atmosphere and transferred carbon dioxide to the crustal rocks and the hydrosphere. The composition of air at 79% nitrogen and 20% oxygen remains stable by the same mechanism.

Solar energy is distributed around the Earth by the atmosphere. Most of the weather and climate processes occur in the troposphere. The atmosphere also shields the Earth. Ozone which exists to the extent of 2 parts per million is at its maximum at 30km. It is the only gas which absorbs ultra-violet radiation. Water-vapour and CO_2 keep out infra-red radiation.

Above 80km nitrogen and oxygen cannot retain their molecular form. They tend to separate into atoms which become ionized (an ion is an atom lacking one or more of its electrons).

The ionosphere is a zone of ionized belts which reflect radio waves back to earth. These electrification belts change their position dependent on light and darkness and external factors.

Beyond the ionosphere, the magnetosphere extends to outer space. Ionized particles form a plasma (a fourth state of matter i.e. other than solid, liquid, gas) constrained by the Earth's magnetic field.

THE EARTH'S SHELLS

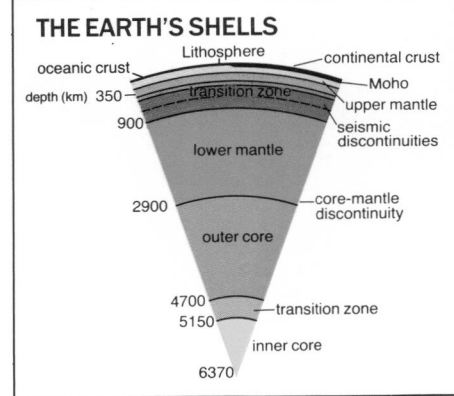

SEISMIC WAVES

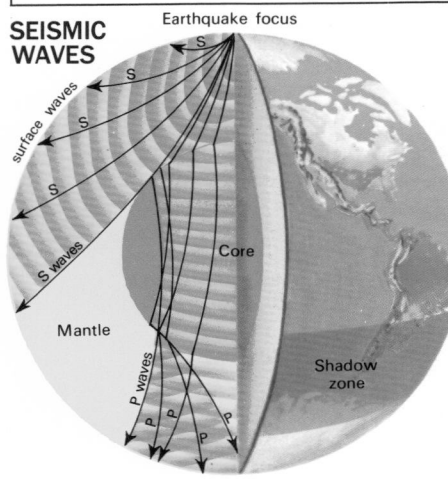

Above In an earthquake the shock generates vibrations, or seismic waves, which radiate in all directions from the focus. Surface waves travel close to the surface of the Earth. They cause most motion in the ground and, therefore, most damage to structures.

Other waves known as body waves pass through the body of the Earth. They are of two kinds. Primary (P) waves are compressional waves. They are able to travel through solids and fluids and cause the particles of the Earth to vibrate in the direction of travel of the wave. Secondary (S) waves are transverse, or shear, waves. They can only pass through solids. They travel at about half the velocity of 'P' waves and they vibrate at right angles to the path travelled by the wave.

Both types of wave obey normal rules of reflection and refraction. Their velocities depend on the nature of the medium through which they pass. Where the physical or chemical properties of the Earth change, the velocity and path of the waves are changed too. From the way the waves travel the nature of the internal layers of the Earth is revealed. By the same means the fluid nature of the outer core is confirmed. Because of the different paths followed by the two types of waves, there is a 'shadow zone' at 105° to 142° from the earthquake focus where both kinds of waves fail to reach the surface.

EARTH'S GRAVITY AND MAGNETIC FIELDS

The Earth is spheroidal in form because it is a rotating body. Were it not so it would take the form of a sphere. The shape is determined by the mass of the Earth and its rate of rotation. Centrifugal force acting outwards reduces the pull of gravity acting inwards so that gravity at the equator is less than at the poles. In theory gravity would be expected to vary progressively from the equator to the poles. In fact, it does not. Uneven distribution of matter within the Earth distorts the shape taken up by the mean sea-level surface (the geoid). In consequence a plumb-line or spirit-level may depart from the assumed vertical or horizontal. Moreover, the orbits of artificial satellites are perturbed by the irregularity of the Earth's gravity.

MAGNETISM

Like gravity, magnetism is strongest at the poles and weakest at the equator. The magnetic field of the Earth resembles that of a bar magnet displaced slightly from the geographical poles. It was long believed that the core being made of iron acted as a magnet but the temperatures prevailing there would destroy such magnetism. Today the belief is that electric currents generated in the semi-molten outer core are responsible for the magnetic field. The magnetic poles are not coincident with the geographical poles. Were a bar magnet substituted for the Earth's field it would not pass through the centre of the Earth but through a point in the plane of the equator about 1200km from the centre in the direction of Indonesia. The bar itself would be inclined at about 12° to the Earth's axis. The magnetic poles change their position from year to year so maps of magnetic declination used for navigation need to be updated annually.

Magnetism is expressed scientifically in three components, intensity, declination (departure from true north), and dip (the inclination in the vertical plane).

When molten rocks cool and solidify materials which are magnetic acquire the alignment of the Earth's local magnetic field at the time they solidified. The magnetism becomes frozen in the rocks. From this historic record the geographical position of the rocks at the time can be estimated from the magnetic alignments within the rocks. From such rock it was discovered that the Earth's magnetic poles had experienced a number of reversals the north pole becoming the south and vice-versa. A system of classification of the field allowed the ages of the various parts of the ocean floor to be deduced thus providing the evidence for sea-floor spreading and plate tectonics.

THE MAGNETOSPHERE

A stream of ionized gas, or plasma, the solar wind pours out from the Sun. Travelling at 1000km/sec its encounter with the Earth's magnetic field creates a bow shock wave. The magnetopause, the effective limit of the magnetic field, is pushed back to within 10 Earth radii measured in the direction of the Sun. It is stretched out in a long tail on the opposite side of the Earth. Between the bow-wave and magnetopause is the magnetosheath a region of charged particles producing fluctuations in the magnetic field. On the inner side of the magnetopause is a transition zone where charged particles react with the magnetic field and the magnetosheath. From this zone particles enter the internal magnetic field by the magnetic poles to produce aurorae. Particles trapped by the Earth's magnetism are deflected at the polar cusps and become trapped to form the Van Allen belts at about 5 Earth radii measured from the magnetic equator.

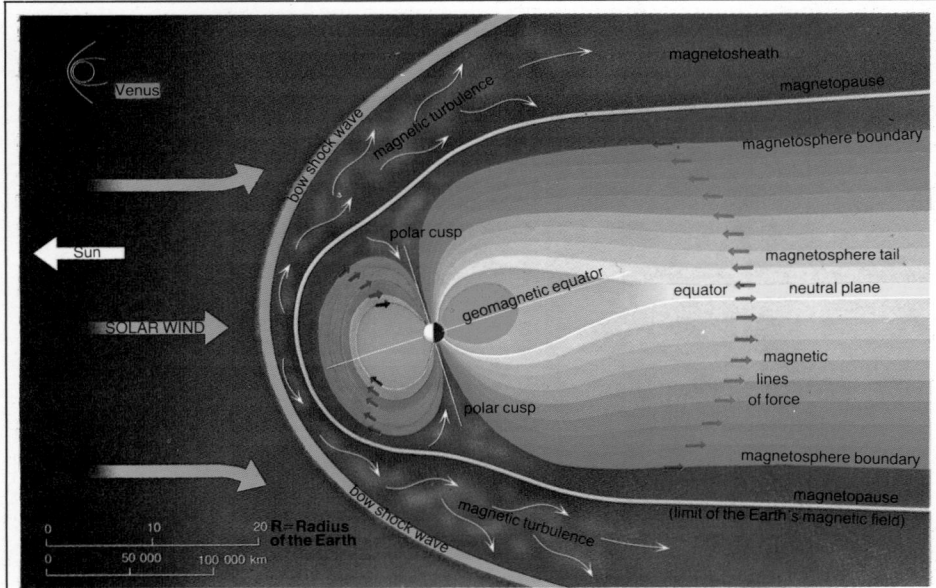

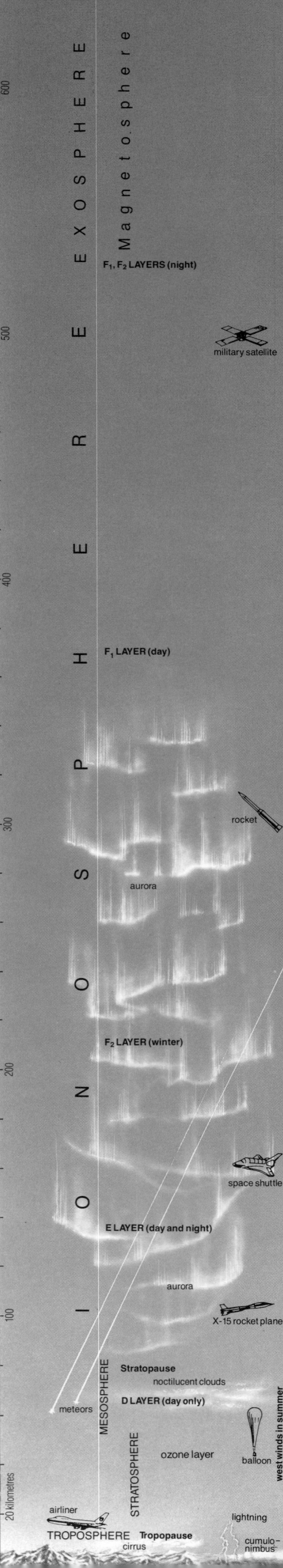

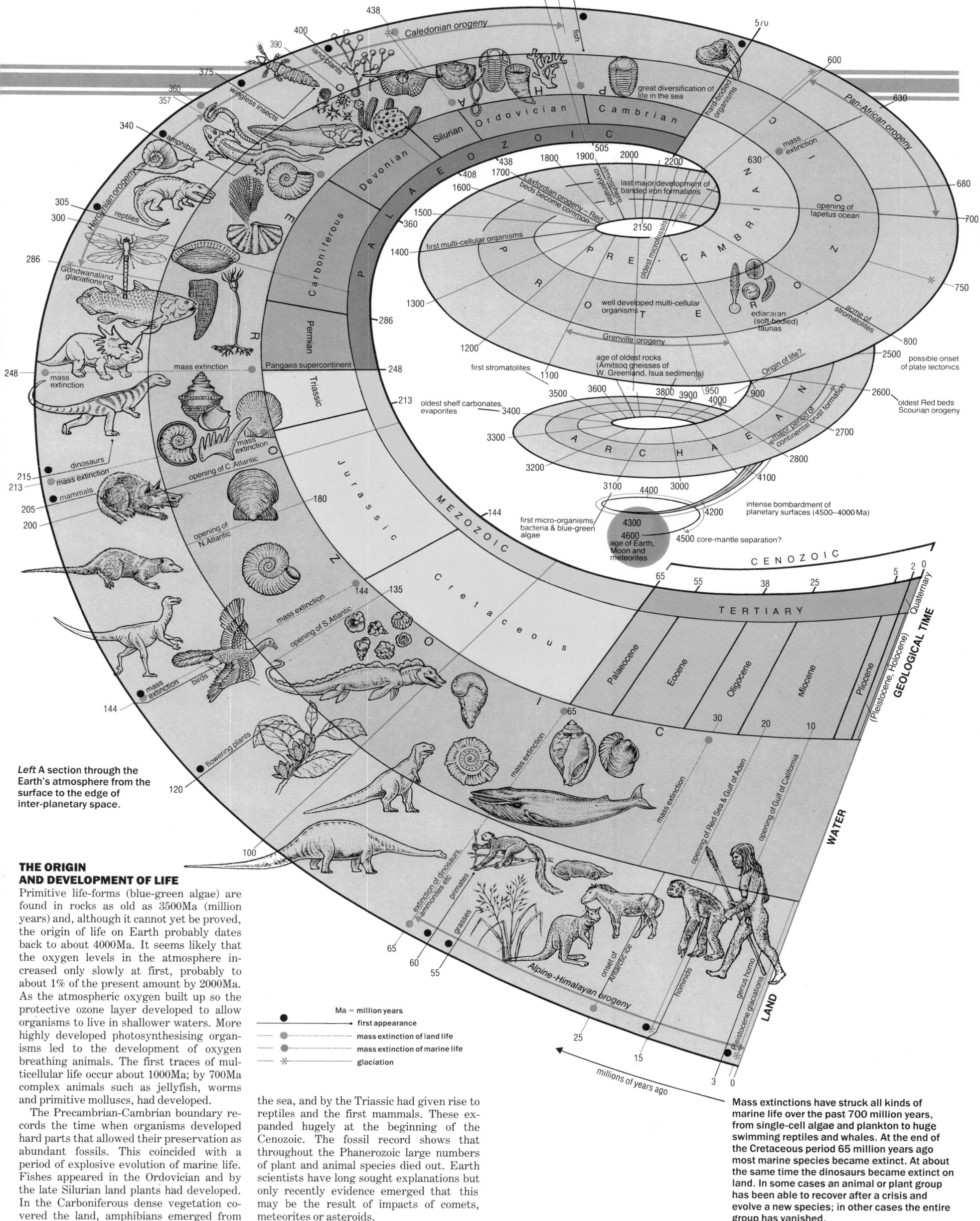

millions of years ago

Left A section through the Earth's atmosphere from the surface to the edge of inter-planetary space.

Ma = million years
● → first appearance
● --- mass extinction of land life
● --- mass extinction of marine life
✳ --- glaciation

THE ORIGIN AND DEVELOPMENT OF LIFE

Primitive life-forms (blue-green algae) are found in rocks as old as 3500Ma (million years) and, although it cannot yet be proved, the origin of life on Earth probably dates back to about 4000Ma. It seems likely that the oxygen levels in the atmosphere increased only slowly at first, probably to about 1% of the present amount by 2000Ma. As the atmospheric oxygen built up so the protective ozone layer developed to allow organisms to live in shallower waters. More highly developed photosynthesising organisms led to the development of oxygen breathing animals. The first traces of multicellular life occur about 1000Ma; by 700Ma complex animals such as jellyfish, worms and primitive molluscs, had developed.

The Precambrian-Cambrian boundary records the time when organisms developed hard parts that allowed their preservation as abundant fossils. This coincided with a period of explosive evolution of marine life. Fishes appeared in the Ordovician and by the late Silurian land plants had developed. In the Carboniferous dense vegetation covered the land, amphibians emerged from

the sea, and by the Triassic had given rise to reptiles and the first mammals. These expanded hugely at the beginning of the Cenozoic. The fossil record shows that throughout the Phanerozoic large numbers of plant and animal species died out. Earth scientists have long sought explanations but only recently evidence emerged that this may be the result of impacts of comets, meteorites or asteroids.

Mass extinctions have struck all kinds of marine life over the past 700 million years, from single-cell algae and plankton to huge swimming reptiles and whales. At the end of the Cretaceous period 65 million years ago most marine species became extinct. At about the same time the dinosaurs became extinct on land. In some cases an animal or plant group has been able to recover after a crisis and evolve a new species; in other cases the entire group has vanished.

DYNAMIC EARTH

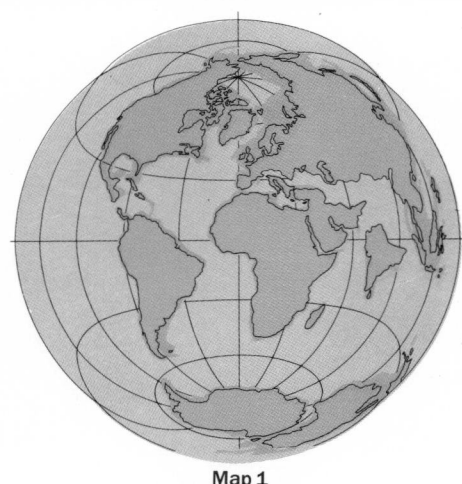

Map 1
50 million years ago

Map 2
100 million years ago

Map 3
150 million years ago

Map 4
200 million years ago

PLATE TECTONICS

Tectonics means the act of building. As applied to geology, the word, which comes from Greek, refers to study of the processes which produce faults, joints, folds and cleavage or cause magma to rise to the surface as the Earth's crust reacts to forces from below. Plate tectonics attribute such tectonic effects to the movement of the parts of the lithosphere. The lithosphere is defined as the rigid outer layer of the Earth consisting of the crust and the part of the upper mantle immediately below. Together they form a rigid layer which is split into a number of plates all in motion, like rafts, carrying the continents and the oceans with them to drift apart, to collide, to unite or sub-divide in a process of destruction and renewal. There are six major plates and a number of minor ones diverging, converging or sliding past each other at varying rates.

The plates are able to move because the rigid lithosphere rests on a less rigid asthenosphere a zone where the mantle is hotter and less resistant. Temperature increases at the rate of 20°C to 40°C with each km of depth in the outer parts of the Earth.

At mid-ocean ridges, a continuous chain some 40 000km in length running through all the oceans, new crust is created. Magma (hot molten rock) rises to flow out of the rift and solidify as pillow lavas or gabbros without reaching the crustal surface. The intrusion of new material forces the rift sides to move outwards and they are pushed further apart as still more magma injects itself into the rift. The rifts are regions of low seismic activity with a high heat flow.

Evidence of sea-floor spreading is provided by the magnetism locked into the rocks at the time they solidified. Evidence is also provided by the ocean sediments which become increasingly thicker outwards from the rift indicating a longer period of time for their deposition and consequently a greater age of the ocean floor on which they lie.

At mid-ocean ridges the plate margins are divergent (or extensional), new crust is formed and the boundary is said to be constructive. Where two plates meet the margins are convergent (or compressional) and are destructive. One plate slides under the other the plate margin descending at a steep angle, sometimes to a depth of 700km, into the asthenosphere, until melting occurs. Lighter material rises to attach itself to the underside of the continents. Continental plates containing much lighter material float over the ocean plates. Where the ocean plate is subducted, the subduction zone is marked by an ocean trench. Island areas are also formed in the oceans and young folded mountain ranges at the edge of a continent.

At some plate boundaries crust is neither created nor destroyed: the plates slide past each other at transform faults. The margins are translational and by type, conservative.

From study of all the oceans it can be said that the ocean floors are less than 200M years old. The Pacific plate contains only ocean crust. The other major plates consist of both continental and ocean crust. A fairly authoritative account can be given of the way the continents have drifted, divided and collided over the past 200M years. A very incomplete picture can be drawn of the course of events in the preceding 400M years and only a sketchy picture before that.

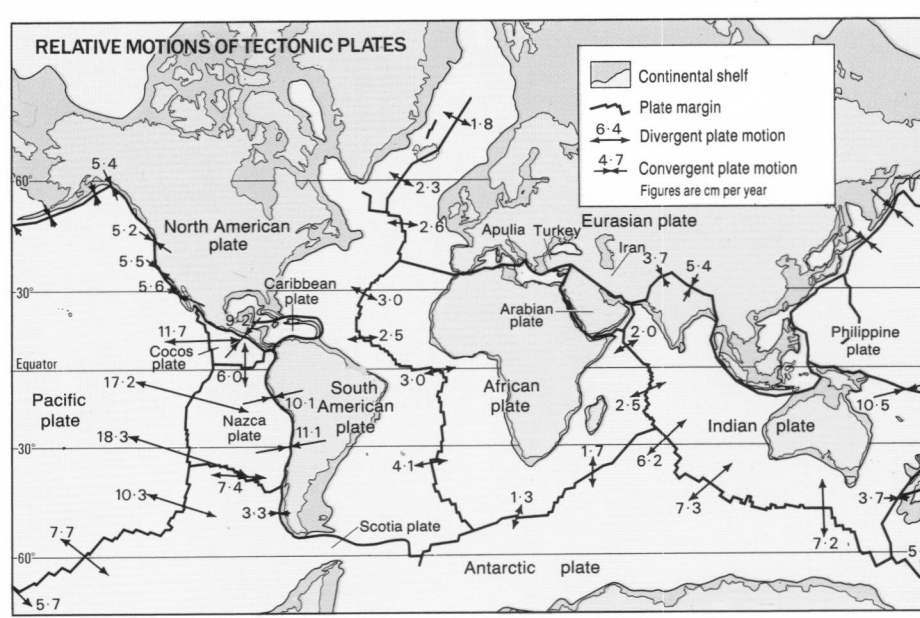

RELATIVE MOTIONS OF TECTONIC PLATES

	Continental shelf
	Plate margin
6·4	Divergent plate motion
4·7	Convergent plate motion
	Figures are cm per year

PLATE TECTONIC CYCLE

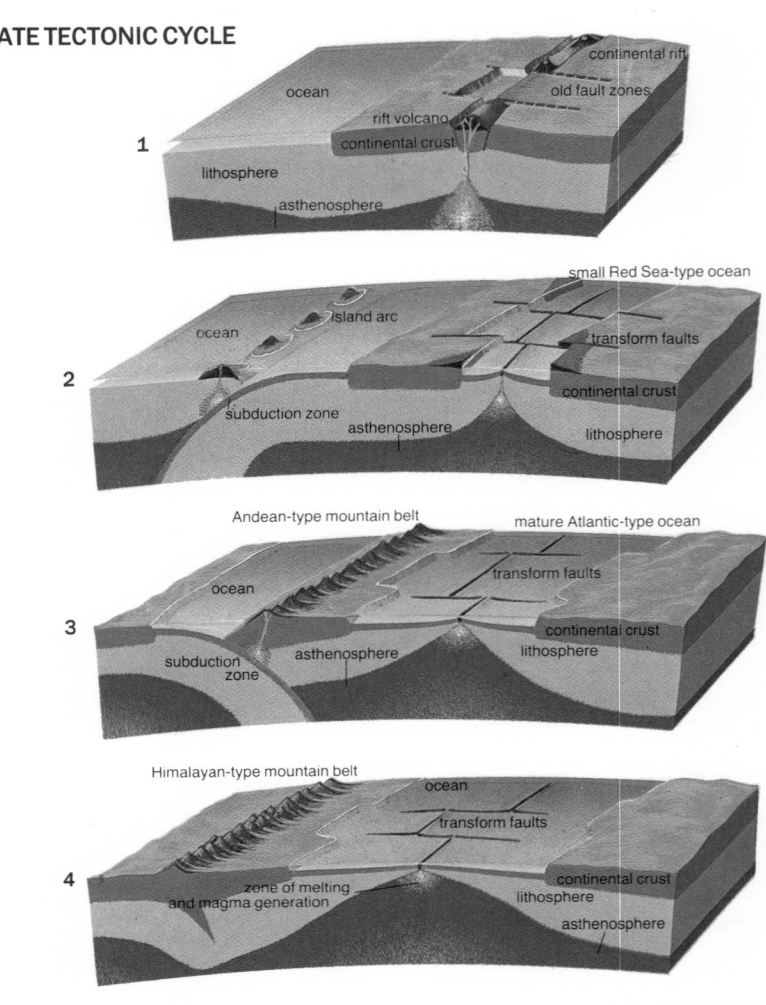

Above When continental lithosphere is subjected to tensional forces, it can become so attenuated that fault zones develop and crustal rocks subside. Hot magma rises from the asthenosphere to fill the space and that increases the heat flow through the lithosphere. Partial melting of mantle material ensues in the process of basaltic volcanism at a mid-ocean ridge. A rift develops in the continent and the two sides of the rift are forced further apart. Separation may be arrested after a while as in the case of the Rio Grande of south-west USA and the rift valley of East Africa. Should the process not be arrested, the rift will lengthen until the continent is split into two diverging plates.

1 Continental rifting in part following old faults in the continental basement.
2 Continental break-up with the formation of new oceanic crust in a small Red Sea-type ocean basin. Transform faults follow continental fractures.
3 A large mature Atlantic-type ocean basin has now formed on the site of the former continent. The subduction zone changes in direction (flips) to dip beneath the continent, forming a cordillera-type mountain belt.
4 Where continental collision occurs one continent partly underthrusts the other producing a Himalayan-type mountain belt underlain by thick continental crust (75-90km).

MAJOR TECTONIC FEATURES

Right Particular features are associated with different types of mineral deposits: continental rifts with tin and fluorine, mid-ocean ridges with marine metallic sulphides, island arcs and cordilleran-type mountains with a variety of metallic deposits.

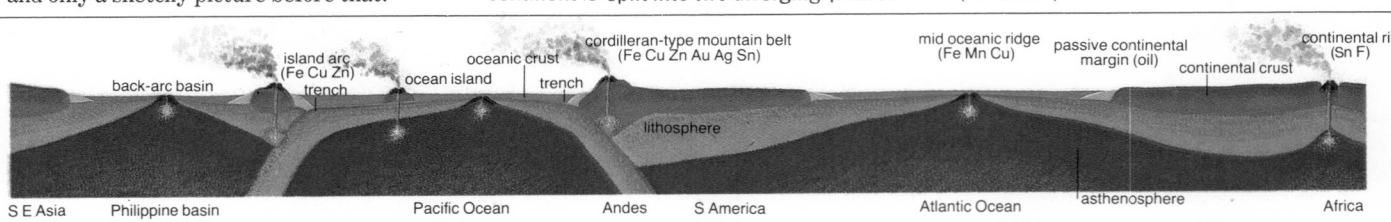

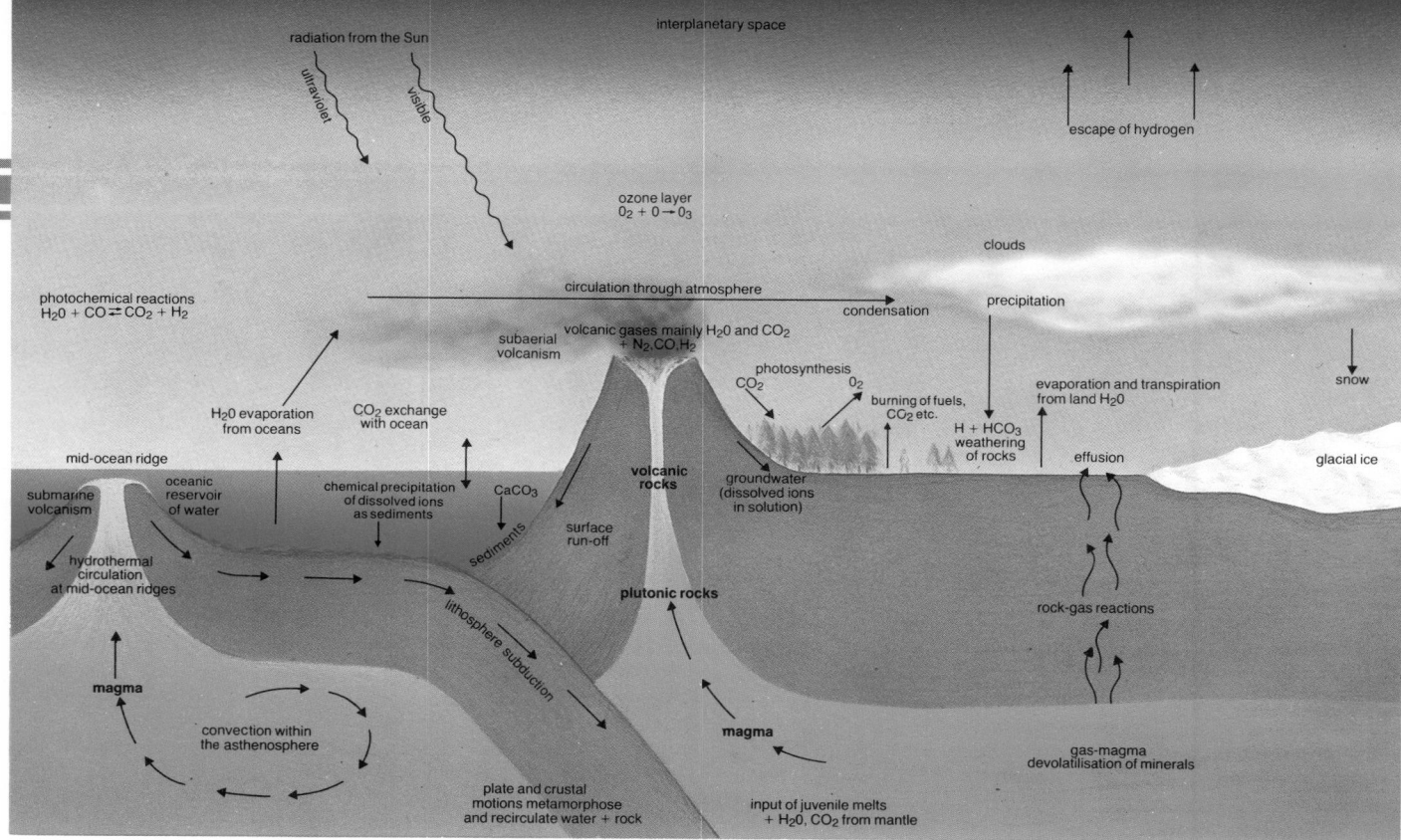

ROCK AND HYDROLOGICAL CYCLES

Left In the most familiar cycle rain falls onto the land, drains to the sea, evaporates, condenses into cloud and is precipitated onto the land again. Water is also released and recirculated as a result of plate movements and volcanic activity. In the rock cycle rocks are weathered and eroded, forming sediments which are in turn compacted into rocks that are eventually exposed and then weathered again. Man's industrial activity has modified the atmosphere by increasing the amount of CO_2 and adding other gases that may affect the vital ozone layer that shields the Earth from the Sun's ultra-violet rays. In the oceans, CO_2 and calcium are converted into calcium carbonate which forms sedimentary rocks which are re-cycled by the action of plate tectonics. In the atmosphere, CO_2, dust and water-vapour absorb infra-red energy and re-radiate it both to space and the atmosphere. If the level of CO_2 is increased, less of the Earth's own heat escapes to space, more is returned to the atmosphere and the Earth becomes warmer.

SURFACE PROCESSES

The lithosphere, the outermost layer of the Earth; the hydrosphere of salt and fresh water and the atmosphere composed of gases are all closely connected. There is a constant transfer of material from one to the other. The air in the atmosphere does not remain motionless. Convection and other influences impart complex patterns of motion in which matter is conveyed from one area to another. Atmospheric water vapour deposited on the lithosphere as water containing dissolved gases, reacts physically and chemically with surface rocks.

Variation in temperature, particularly frost, precipitation and winds cause a gradual fragmentation of surface rocks and physical decay in the process called weathering. Vegetation also plays its part in the alteration of surface rocks, by adding organic matter to weathered rocks to create soils and by resisting erosion. Water, however, is the major factor since it also acts as a transport medium.

Rivers transport enormous quantities of material varying from large boulders to particles of sand or clay carried in suspension. Where rivers overflow their banks, sand, gravel and clays are deposited in the flood plains to produce fertile valleys. On reaching the ocean or a lake the carrying capacity of the current is dissipated and material carried in suspension is deposited to form a delta.

Slumping of ocean floor material or earthquakes can put large quantities of fine sediments into suspension as a turbid layer which erodes the continental slope, thereby gathering more material all of which is deposited on the continental rise or the floor of the abyssal plain as "turbidites".

VOLCANOES

Almost all the world's active volcanoes, numbering 500–600 are located at convergent plate boundaries. Those are the volcanoes which give spectacular demonstrations of volcanic activity. Yet far greater volcanic activity continues unnoticed and without cessation at mid-ocean ridges where magma from the upper mantle is quietly being extruded on to the ocean floor to create new crustal material. The basalts erupted there are derived more or less directly from material of the mantle. Similar lavas are seen in the Columbia plateau, U.S.A. and the Deccan, India.

Chemical composition of magmas and the amount of gas they contain are important factors in determining the nature of a volcanic eruption. Gas-charged basalts produce cinder cones. Mount Etna in Italy has numerous such cinder cones. Violent eruptions usually occur when large clouds of lava come into contact with water to produce fine-grained ash. The name Surtseyan is given to this type after the volcanic island which appeared off Iceland in 1963. Andesites are more viscous. When charged with gas they erupt with explosive violence. Volcanoes like Fujiyama, Vesuvius and most of the other renowned volcanoes with steep sides are of this type.

Nuées ardentes (burning clouds) are extremely destructive. They are produced by rhyolitic magmas which erupt explosively sending molten lava fragments and gas at great speed down the mountain sides.

In spite of the destructiveness of many volcanoes people still live in their vicinity because of the fertile volcanic soils. Geothermal energy in regions of volcanic activity is another source of attraction.

EARTHQUAKES

Earthquakes are the manifestation of a slippage at a geological fault. The majority occur at tectonic plate boundaries. The interior of a plate tends to be stable and less subject to earthquakes. When plates slide past each other strain energy is suddenly released. Even though the amount of movement is very small the energy released is colossal. It is transferred in shock waves.

Most earthquakes originate at not very great depths – 5km or so. At the San Andreas fault earthquakes originate at about 20km depth. Over 70% of all foci are at depths of less than 70km. Some, however, may be as deep as 700km. The precise cause of those very deep earthquakes is not known. The point from which the earthquake is generated is the focus and the point on the surface immediately above the focus is the epicentre. Plotting the foci of deep earthquakes at convergent plate boundaries allows the path of the subducted plate to be traced.

Two types of scale are used to define the magnitude of earthquakes. In the logarithmic Richter Scale each unit is ten times the intensity of the next lower on the scale. The intensity is recorded by seismographs. There is no upper limit but the greatest magnitude yet recorded is 8·9.

The Modified Mercalli Earthquake Intensity Scale is in common use. It is based on the observed effects of an earthquake. At the lowest end the numeral I means the shock is felt by only a few people under special circumstances. A shock felt generally, with minor breakages indoors is classed as V. General alarm is equivalent to VIII and 'Panic' with varying categories of total destruction are graded IX to XII.

EXTERNAL INFLUENCES

Every day over a million tons of extra-terrestrial material falls on the Earth. Most of this material is ultra-fine cosmic dust. Only a small proportion of the incoming material actually reaches the surface of the Earth. Most is burned up by friction with the atmosphere where it vaporises after being heated to incandescence when it may be seen as so-called shooting stars.

Meteors come both sporadically and in showers. They are part of the solar system and rotate round the Sun. When the Earth comes in contact with them a meteor display occurs.

Occasionally a larger body survives passage through the atmosphere and strikes the ground. One very large meteorite fell in Arizona about 25,000 years ago. Meteor Crater is the result. Another devastating impact occurred in 1908 when an object struck the Tunguska area of Siberia, devastating an area of several kilometres radius in which all the trees were felled.

Tektites are curious objects. They are small and glassy and are found lying on the surface of several places - Australia, South-East Asia, Ivory Coast, Czech Republic and Slovakia. Terrestrial and extra-terrestrial origins have been ascribed to them. They have the appearance of melted rocks formed as the result of meteorite impact but no local evidence of such impact has been detected at any of the sites.

It seems inevitable that a comet or an asteroid will, in the course of time, collide with the Earth. Both comets and asteroids pass within the Earth's orbit. A collision will occur if the Earth happens to be located in that part of its orbit when one or the other crosses it.

Left When the Earth's crust bends under compression, folds develop. The simplest of these is a monocline, a one-sided fold, although downfolds (synclines) and upfolds (anticlines) are more usual. Increasing pressure steepens the side facing the pressure until one side is pushed under the other, to form a recumbent fold. Finally it may break along its axis, one limb being thrust over the other. Mountain chains often demonstrate intense folding between converging plates.

Faults occur when the Earth's crust breaks, often causing earthquakes. When tension stretches the crust normal faulting occurs and the rocks on one side of the fault-plane override those on the other.

A horst is a block of the crust thrust up between faults; the reverse is a graben or rift valley. Repeated horst and graben forms give basin and range topography as in Nevada, USA.

The upward movement of a plug of salt, some thousands of feet in depth, may force up strata and the surface layers to form a salt dome, often associated with oil and gas.

FOLDING AND FAULTING

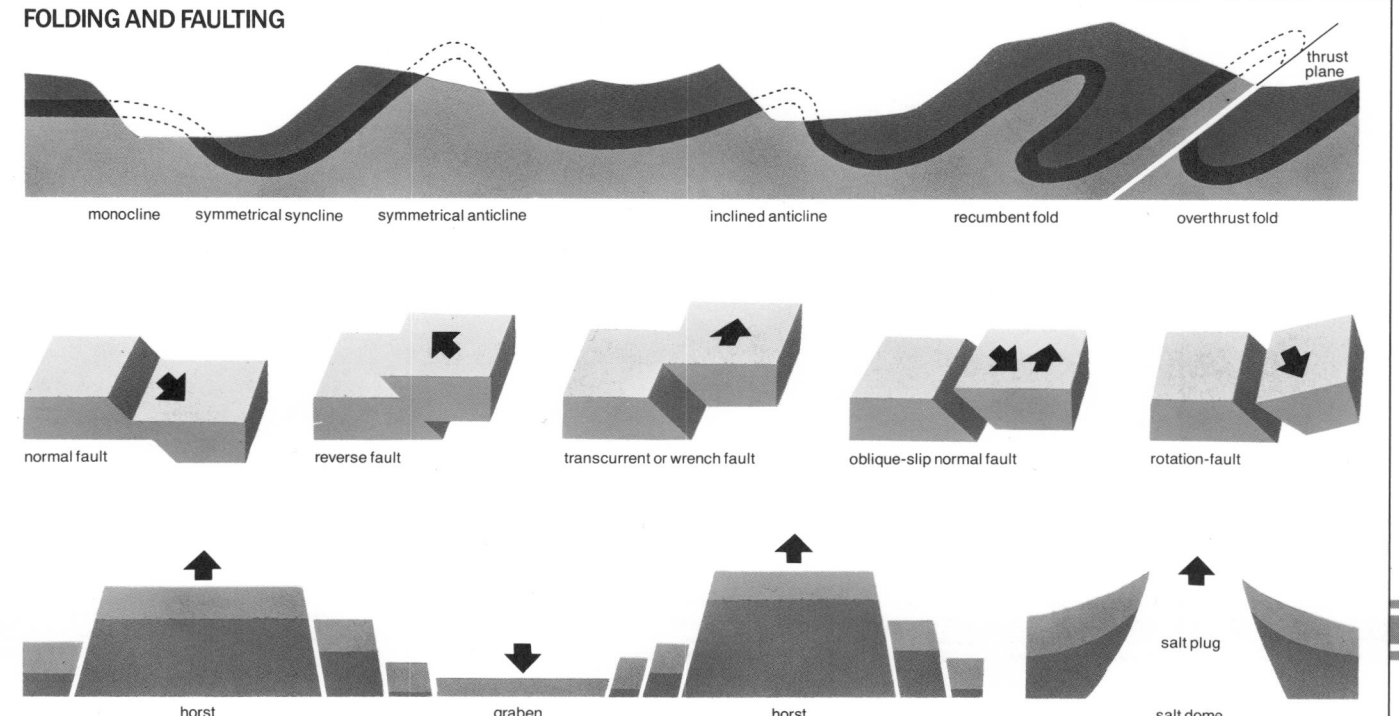

CLIMATE

Climate is generally said to be the average weather conditions observed over a long period. The factors which determine climate are temperature and rainfall.

Although heated slightly by the passage of the Sun's rays the atmosphere is warmed by the re-radiation of solar heat energy stored in the oceans and continents. Air which contains as much water vapour as possible (i.e. the air is saturated) is said to have a relative humidity of 100 and half-saturated air, 50. Air at a temperature of 32°C (90°F) can hold more than nine times as much water vapour as air at 0°C (32°F). For this reason polar regions have low precipitation.

Near the equator where the north-east and south-east trade winds meet is a zone known as the Inter-tropical Convergence Zone. Here warm, water-laden air rises to some 12-15km in altitude, its high content of water-vapour visible as cumulonimbus clouds. On cooling with altitude rain falls. This low-pressure doldrum zone of light winds has daily afternoon rains.

The two tropics are zones of descending air and, therefore, high atmospheric pressure and low rainfall. On the other hand, the arctic and antarctic circles are low pressure zones and between them and the tropics the winds are 'anti-trade' i.e. blowing from the SW and NW respectively in the northern and southern hemispheres. This is the zone of the 'westerlies' in which weather is determined by depressions (low-pressure centres) and anti-cyclones (high pressure centres), the first rain-bearing, the second dry. In the polar regions the winds tend to be easterly. The poles themselves are high-pressure areas.

But for the rotation of the Earth, winds would blow south or north from high-pressure zones at the poles and tropics towards the polar circles and equator. Rotation and centrifugal force impart a west or east motion. The system of pressure belts moves from 6° to 10° north or south following the seasonal movements of the Sun.

Continents and oceans also influence the global pattern especially in the northern hemisphere where most land lies. The interiors of N. America and Eurasia become very hot in summer and very cold in winter causing air to flow respectively from and to the oceans. Monsoons are an expression of this seasonal reversal of direction.

Tropical cyclones (typhoons and hurricanes and many local names) are highly destructive systems. They occur in a belt between 5° and 30° latitude, the majority in the northern hemisphere. They can be 800km in diameter, rotating clockwise in the southern hemisphere and counter-clockwise in the northern. Wind speeds above Force

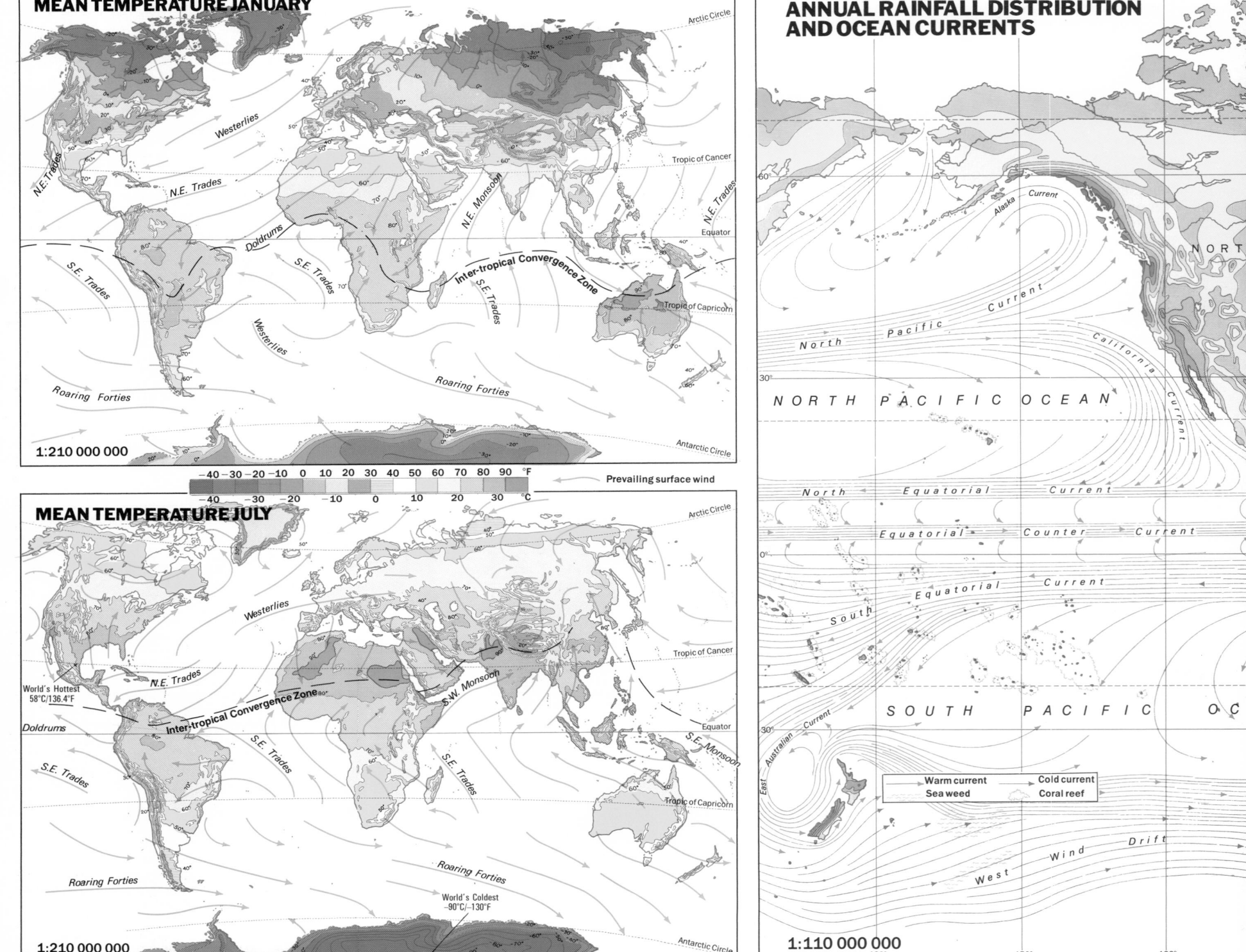

MEAN TEMPERATURE JANUARY   1:210 000 000

MEAN TEMPERATURE JULY   1:210 000 000

World's Hottest 58°C/136.4°F
Doldrums
World's Coldest −90°C/−130°F

Prevailing surface wind

°F −40 −30 −20 −10 0 10 20 30 40 50 60 70 80 90
°C −40 −30 −20 −10 0 10 20 30

ANNUAL RAINFALL DISTRIBUTION AND OCEAN CURRENTS   1:110 000 000

NORTH PACIFIC OCEAN
SOUTH PACIFIC OCEAN

Warm current   Cold current
Sea weed   Coral reef

84	97	104
12.0	over 16.0	over 16.0
10	**11**	**12**
Trees uprooted considerable damage.	Major destruction.	Disastrous destruction

Left In 1805, the British admiral, Francis Beaufort, devised a sequence of numbers to indicate the force of winds at sea. Associated effects at sea and on land were added later to show that 'white horses' occasional at Force 3 became widespread at Force 6, that waves became higher and longer, that spray and foam increased with turbulence until visibility was affected. Wind speeds were added later still. More scientific methods exist but the scale is easily assimilable and the Beaufort number with temperature; pressure; precipitation; visibility and outlook together provide a concise weather summary.

12, seas rising to 16–17m and torrential rain cause the destruction.

Far from destructive are the Chinook of N. America and the Föhn winds of the Alps. Air, depleted of moisture, is warmed in its descent of the rain-shadow side of high mountain ranges.

Tsunamis, destructive ocean waves, are not the result of weather but of submarine seismic activity. A wave of no more than 1m but travelling at 650km/hr can rise to 16m or more on impact with the shore.

Right Waterspouts are sea tornadoes, short-lived phenomena lasting from one minute to half-an-hour. A rapidly gyrating vortex descends from a cumulus or cumulonimbus cloud whipping the sea and sucking up a column of water from 1m to 300m diameter which travels with the cloud but with the base moving at a different speed. High velocity peripheral winds, the disturbed sea-surface and descent of water inflict the damage. It should be noted that the African tornado, also highly destructive, is actually a violent squall.

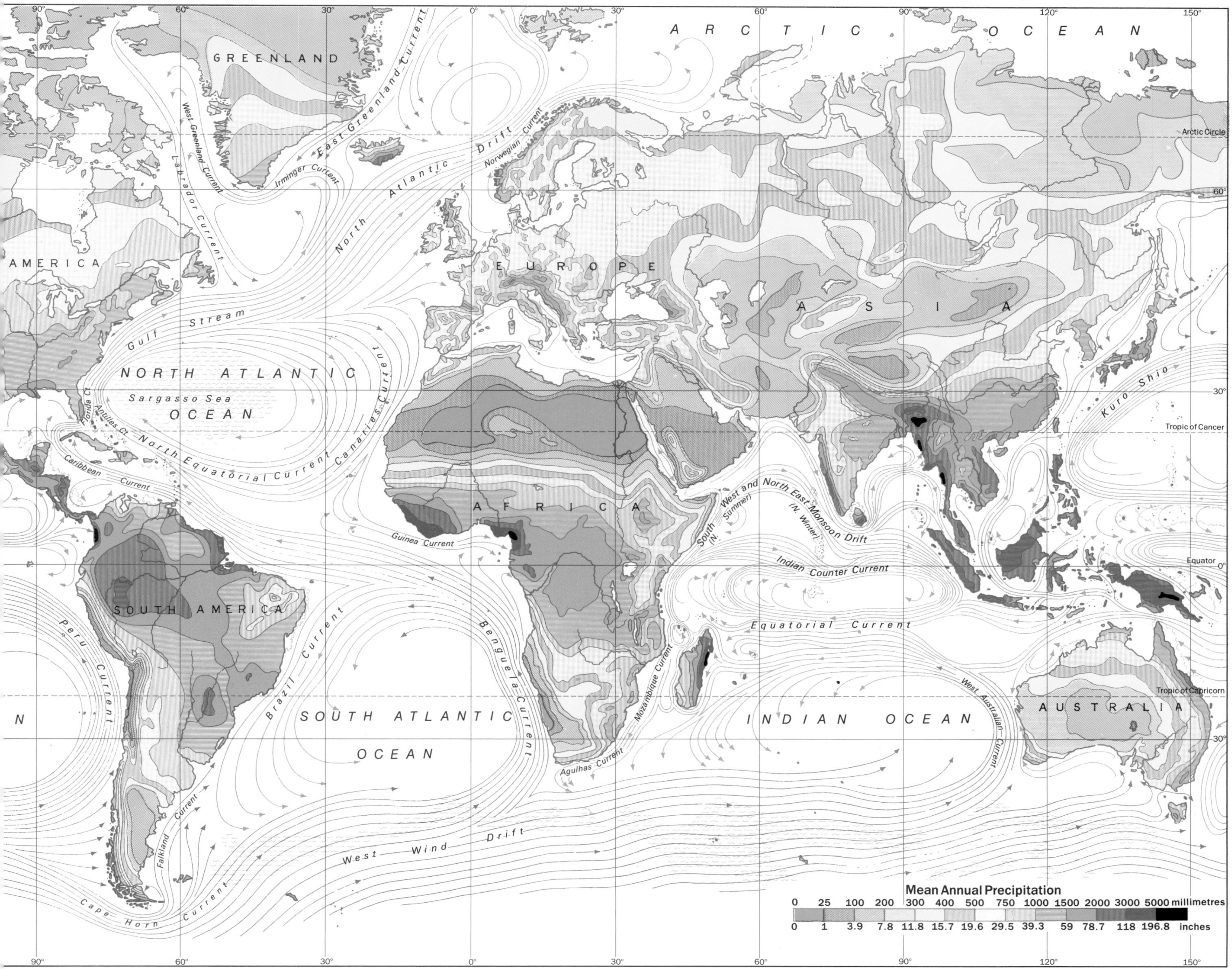

Mean Annual Precipitation

	0	25	100	200	300	400	500	750	1000	1500	2000	3000	5000 millimetres
	0	1	3.9	7.8	11.8	15.7	19.6	29.5	39.3	59	78.7	118	196.8 inches

VEGETATION

In a world so subordinated to human beings, it is salutary to be reminded that the atmosphere itself and fertile soils which support agriculture are the creations of plant life. Yet there is far less general concern for the preservation of plants threatened with extinction than there is over endangered animal species.

Perhaps the most remarkable feature of plant life is its almost complete ubiquity. Unless inhibited by ice, plants establish themselves wherever conditions allow and once established encourage the formation or collection of soil and the means to generate their species. The type of plant is determined primarily by climate and soil. Soil is composed of solid, liquid and gas, the solid part being the primary parent rock with secondary rock material changed through moisture and chemical reaction. Humus, decayed vegetable matter, is both solid and liquid. The gas is air.

Russian research first linked soil type to climate, so Russian terms are used for soils. Vegetation zones broadly match soil classes. Thus in the tundra, low temperature and a permanently frozen sub-soil retard organic decay. Thaw in the peaty surface produces swamps. Trees and shrubs are sparse and stunted. South of the tundra is the boreal forest (taiga) of coniferous trees, largely evergreen with some deciduous trees. Their resinous leaves protect against extreme cold and limit transpiration. Soils are podzols, a name applied to whitish-grey sandy soils in which leaching has taken place, a process by which water percolates downwards carrying organic and other matter in solution. These soils are acid. The coniferous vegetation does not produce a rich humus when it decays. Because Siberian rivers flow north the lower reaches are still frozen when the upper reaches thaw. Floods then ensue.

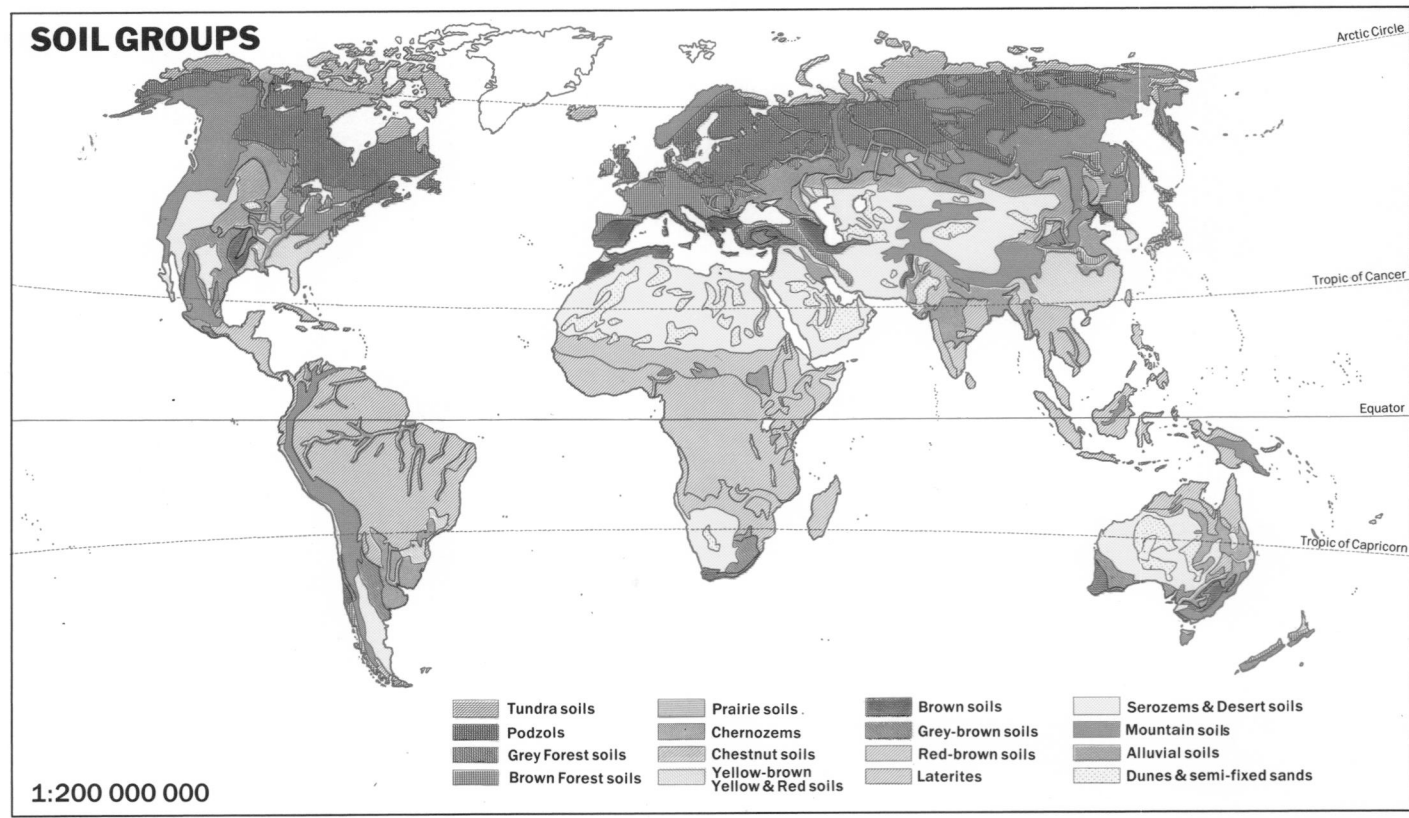

SOIL GROUPS

1:200 000 000

Tundra soils	Prairie soils	Brown soils	Serozems & Desert soils
Podzols	Chernozems	Grey-brown soils	Mountain soils
Grey Forest soils	Chestnut soils	Red-brown soils	Alluvial soils
Brown Forest soils	Yellow-brown Yellow & Red soils	Laterites	Dunes & semi-fixed sands

Trees of the taiga are, therefore, less healthy than those of N. America.

South of the taiga the mixed coniferous and deciduous temperate forests merge into a zone of deciduous forests where trees have a resting period in winter and summers are dry enough and warm enough to allow humus to form. Further south again are the chernozems, fine-grained loams rich in humus hence their name 'black-earth'. This is the zone of the naturally occurring wooded grassy steppes. The soils are of various kinds but they are very like the loess of northern China where the cohesive properties of the soil allow it to form vertical faces. These fertile soils which are found in Europe, Asia and N. & S. America have all been given over to agriculture.

South again are the rather less fertile chestnut soils of the true steppes. Next follow red and grey soils of the semi-desert and desert steppes.

Beyond the hot deserts are the tropical grasslands and finally at the equator the rain forests (selva) where very tall evergreen trees form a dense forest, denser in S. America than in Africa or Asia. The resting period in which the trees shed their leaves occurs at various times throughout the year.

More than two fifths of all living things on earth are found in the rain forests and there is a tremendous variety of trees and other forms of life in even a small area of forest.

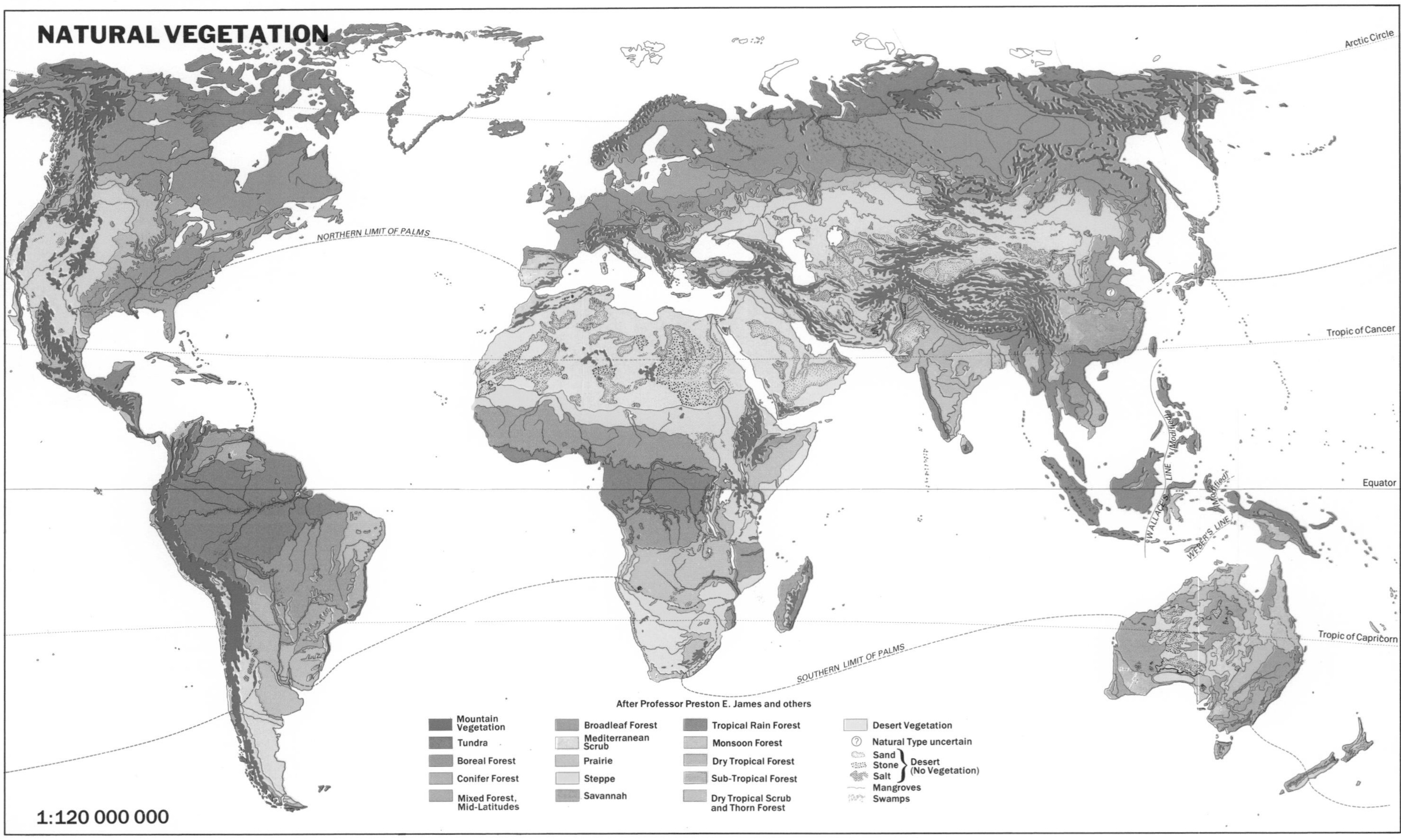

NATURAL VEGETATION

NORTHERN LIMIT OF PALMS

SOUTHERN LIMIT OF PALMS

After Professor Preston E. James and others

1:120 000 000

Mountain Vegetation	Broadleaf Forest	Tropical Rain Forest	Desert Vegetation
Tundra	Mediterranean Scrub	Monsoon Forest	Natural Type uncertain
Boreal Forest	Prairie	Dry Tropical Forest	Sand / Stone / Salt — Desert (No Vegetation)
Conifer Forest	Steppe	Sub-Tropical Forest	Mangroves
Mixed Forest, Mid-Latitudes	Savannah	Dry Tropical Scrub and Thorn Forest	Swamps

Rare metals

Uranium, the best known and most important of the rare metals owes the expansion of its production to the development of nuclear power and related industries. North America is the largest producer but there are significant deposits in Australia, South Africa, Niger and France. **Niobium**, a metal used in alloys and toolmaking is mined mainly in Brazil, Canada and Russian Federation, while **Tantalum**, a corrosion resistant metal valuable to the electronic and chemical industries is found in N. America and Nigeria.

Precious metals

Over and above their more glamorous associations, gold, platinum and silver have a wide range of applications within industry including electronics, chemicals and photography. South Africa dominates the western world's production of **gold** and **platinum**,

Above Manganese nodules form gradually over millions of years around a foreign body. Although they occur over 20% of the ocean floor, only in limited areas are they of economic importance.

accounting for over 30% of total output (the major platinum mines are located in Bophuthatswana). Russian Federation, also a substantial producer of platinum is the other major gold producing country while smaller amounts are found in North America and several other localities worldwide. **Silver** production is less dominated by any one country and is mined throughout the Americas, Central Asia and Australia.

Chemical and Fertilizer minerals

This grouping embraces a variety of minerals occurring in a range of forms and requiring very different recovery techniques. Their usage is widespread in chemical processes throughout industry, **apatite**, **potash** and **phosphate rock** being especially

important in the manufacture of fertilizers. Phosphate rock is exploited widely, though the main volume of production is from U.S.A., Russian Federation and Morocco. The former U.S.S.R., North America, Germany and France are the leading suppliers of potash. Sources of **borax, fluorite** and **sulphur** occur throughout N. America, Europe and western Asia, with U.S.A. a leading producer of all three.

Other Industrial minerals

Asbestos, well-known as a fibrous insulating material; it is produced in Central Asia, North America, Canada, Southern Africa, China and Italy. **China clay**, a fine white clay used in the paper, ceramic and cosmetic industries is found in China, Europe and U.S.A.

Magnesite, a magnesium ore comes particularly from Central Asia, Europe and China for use in the production of refractories and chemicals.

Mica, used as an electrical insulator, is principally produced in U.S.A. and in smaller quantities throughout Europe and Asia.

Talc, a soft greasy mineral is used as a lubricant and in paper manufacture, paint and cosmetics. Production is mainly from U.S.A., Russian Federation and Europe.

Light metals

Aluminium is extracted from bauxite, an ore occurring in feldspars and other silicates which readily breaks down in tropical conditions. It is therefore often found as a surface crust in tropical areas. Principal producers are Australia, Guinea and Jamaica with smaller but substantial amounts from S.E. Europe, Central Asia and the northern regions of South America. **Titanium** is a heat resistant metal used in high grade steel alloys largely in the aircraft and aerospace industries. The two main ores, rutile and ilmenite,

are widespread and plentiful; the main sources include Brazil, Canada and Norway.

Iron

Iron is the second most abundant metallic element in the Earth's crust after aluminium. Rarely found as a free metal it exists in ores of varying constitutions which are smelted to produce metallic iron. Further processing produces steel and combination with other metals makes special steels and alloys. Iron ore is mined in many locations but the principal producing areas are Ukraine, Russian Federation, Australia, Brazil and U.S.A. followed by Canada, China and India. Many other countries produce smaller but nonetheless substantial tonnages.

Ferro-alloy metals

These metals are variously mined in many locations throughout the world but, taken collectively, the most important producing areas are the former U.S.S.R., South Africa and Canada followed by U.S.A. and China. All of these metals offer specific qualities and properties for the manufacture of a variety of special steels and alloys. **Nickel** and **chromium**, for example, are necessary for the production of high quality stainless steel whilst **vanadium** and **tungsten** help produce very hard steels.

Base metals

Generally mined as ores and compounds the free metal is released after smelting. **Antimony, copper, tin** and **zinc** are important in the making of alloys but each has individual uses related to its specific properties. Copper, **lead**, tin and zinc for example, are corrosion resistant under certain conditions, and the liquidity of **mercury** has obvious uses. Often found together or in combination with other metals, they are distributed widely over the earth's surface and there are many significant producing countries.

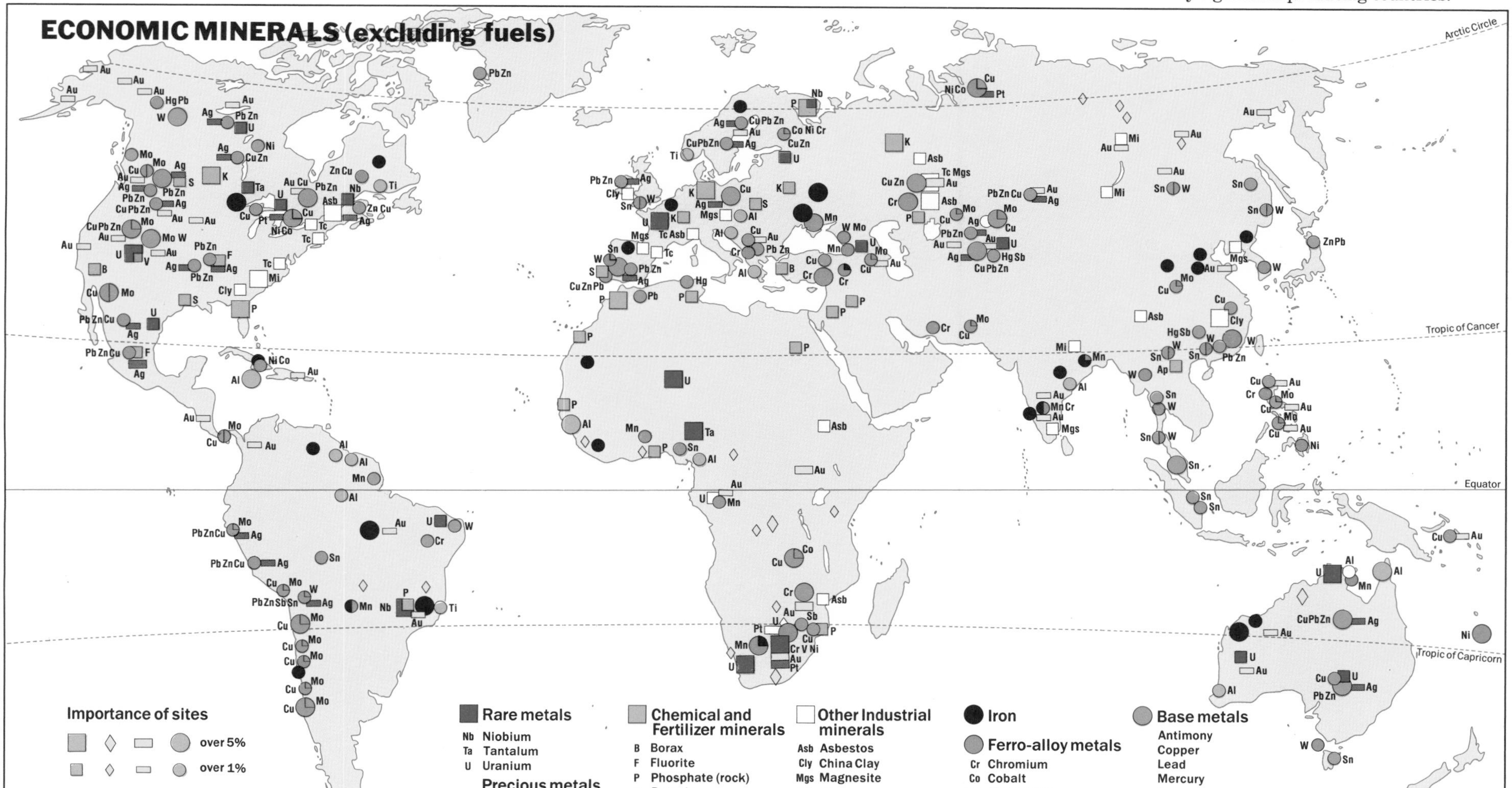

ECONOMIC MINERALS (excluding fuels)

Importance of sites

over 5%

over 1%

World yield and known reserves of each mineral

1:130 000 000

Rare metals
Nb Niobium
Ta Tantalum
U Uranium

Precious metals
Au Gold
Pt Platinum
Ag Silver
Diamonds

Chemical and Fertilizer minerals
B Borax
F Fluorite
P Phosphate (rock)
K Potash
S Sulphur
Ap Apatite

Other Industrial minerals
Asb Asbestos
Cly China Clay
Mgs Magnesite
Mi Mica
Tc Talc

Light metals
Al Aluminium
Ti Titanium

Iron

Ferro-alloy metals
Cr Chromium
Co Cobalt
Mn Manganese
Mo Molybdenum
Ni Nickel
W Tungsten
V Vanadium

Base metals
Antimony
Copper
Lead
Mercury
Tin
Zinc

ENERGY

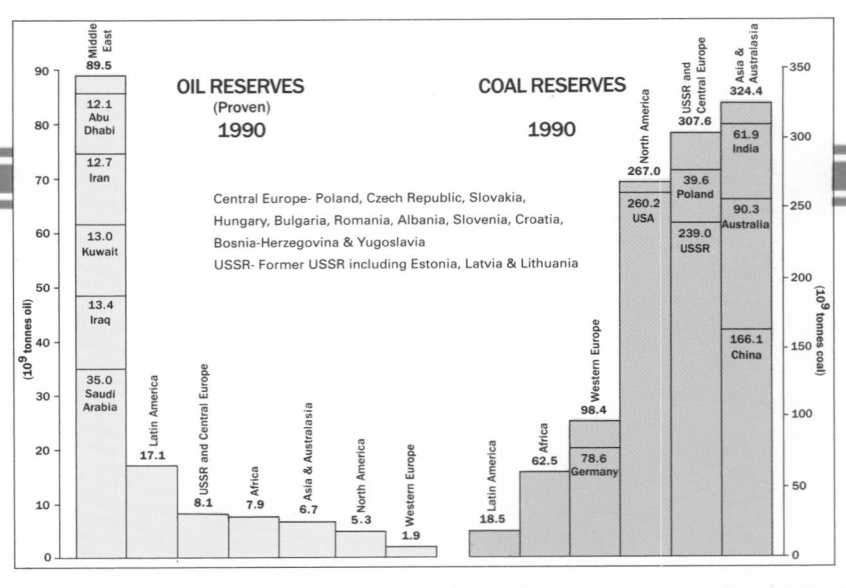

OIL RESERVES (Proven) 1990   **COAL RESERVES** 1990

Central Europe- Poland, Czech Republic, Slovakia, Hungary, Bulgaria, Romania, Albania, Slovenia, Croatia, Bosnia-Herzegovina & Yugoslavia
USSR- Former USSR including Estonia, Latvia & Lithuania

Taken together, the maps and diagrams though concerned with energy, give in graphic form, a summary of two centuries of economic growth.

Coal powered the industrial revolution and replaced wood as the primary source for industrial and domestic heat.

From the end of World War I another economic transformation began. Oil which had been used since remotest times to provide light and heat began to achieve major industrial importance. The last coal-fired ships vanished from the seas and with them the coal-bunkering stations disposed around the world. On land the internal-combustion engine replaced the horse; oil-fired electricity generation began to challenge coal-fired plants.

The end of World War II marked the start of unparalleled economic growth. Between 1950 and 1990 world energy demand increased four-fold, the steepest rise occurring between 1960 and 1970. In this period coal lost its pre-eminence as a source of energy. An oil industry developed to produce a variety of fuels and lubricants. It contained a large petro-chemical element.

Eighty per cent of this stupendous industrial expansion was based in North America (particularly the U.S.A.), Europe, the former U.S.S.R. and Japan. Oil and gas were the sources of the additional energy required for the expansion and the Middle East was the source of half the oil consumed.

The oil producing and exporting nations (OPEC) decided to raise the price of oil in 1973 thus bringing to an end the era of low-price energy. Revolution in Iran and the outbreak of war between Iraq and Iran caused a further escalation in price in 1979. Oil was then 17 times dearer than in 1972. Demand fell. The continued search for alternative sources was intensified. Rate of production fell below rate of discovery once more. Middle East share of world oil production fell from 50% to 27% by 1990. However, the Middle East still possesses over 50% of proved reserves.

Off-shore technology in exploration and exploitation have created a new oil technology. Operations in Alaska and Siberia have taxed the ingenuity of the oil-industry in combating severe climatic conditions.

Oil and gas reserves are constantly reviewed as new discoveries are made but the life of both is relatively short. Coal reserves are probably adequate for the next 250 years. In the coming decades the use of oil will increasingly be restricted to areas like transport where no alternative exists. Coal will once more be in the ascendancy. Coal gas which has been virtually replaced by natural gas may once more be used. Extraction of oil from coal may also be practised. Other sources of oil and gas are bituminous shales and tar sands.

Among the possible alternative energy sources are those in which the energy expended is renewed. Wind-generation and tidal power are two such examples. Although they may well be economically operated the installation costs are prodigious.

Nuclear energy alone promises to be capable of meeting future demands. Early promises of this form of generation providing abundant and cheap energy were not fulfilled. Fears that the supply of uranium would run out have been dispelled by enrichment techniques which yield 50 to 60 times the output. Strong opposition from those concerned for the environment has been the principle reason why the nuclear industry has been retarded. The accident at Three-Mile Island in the United States in 1979 had a profound effect on public opinion which was reinforced by the Chernobyl' disaster in the Ukraine in April 1986.

Still further options remain. All nuclear energy at the moment is based on nuclear fission. If nuclear fusion can be harnessed then an unlimited supply of energy could be provided by the oceans. The process would be the same as that by which the Sun creates its energy. Geothermal power is practical and feasible. Another source is the transformation of the Sun's light into electricity by photovoltaique techniques. Alternatively, solar energy can be converted into micro-waves by satellite. Such methods are for the next century, not this.

SOURCES OF ENERGY

Oil
Gas
Coal
Lignite
Uranium
Hydro-Electric
Oil pipeline
Gas pipeline

COMPARATIVE DEVELOPMENT
as shown by Energy Consumption

6.3%
21.3%
64.3%
7.8%

High 8.0
2.0
0.2
Low

Percentage of total world population

Energy consumption per head (metric tons coal equivalent)

1:59 000 000

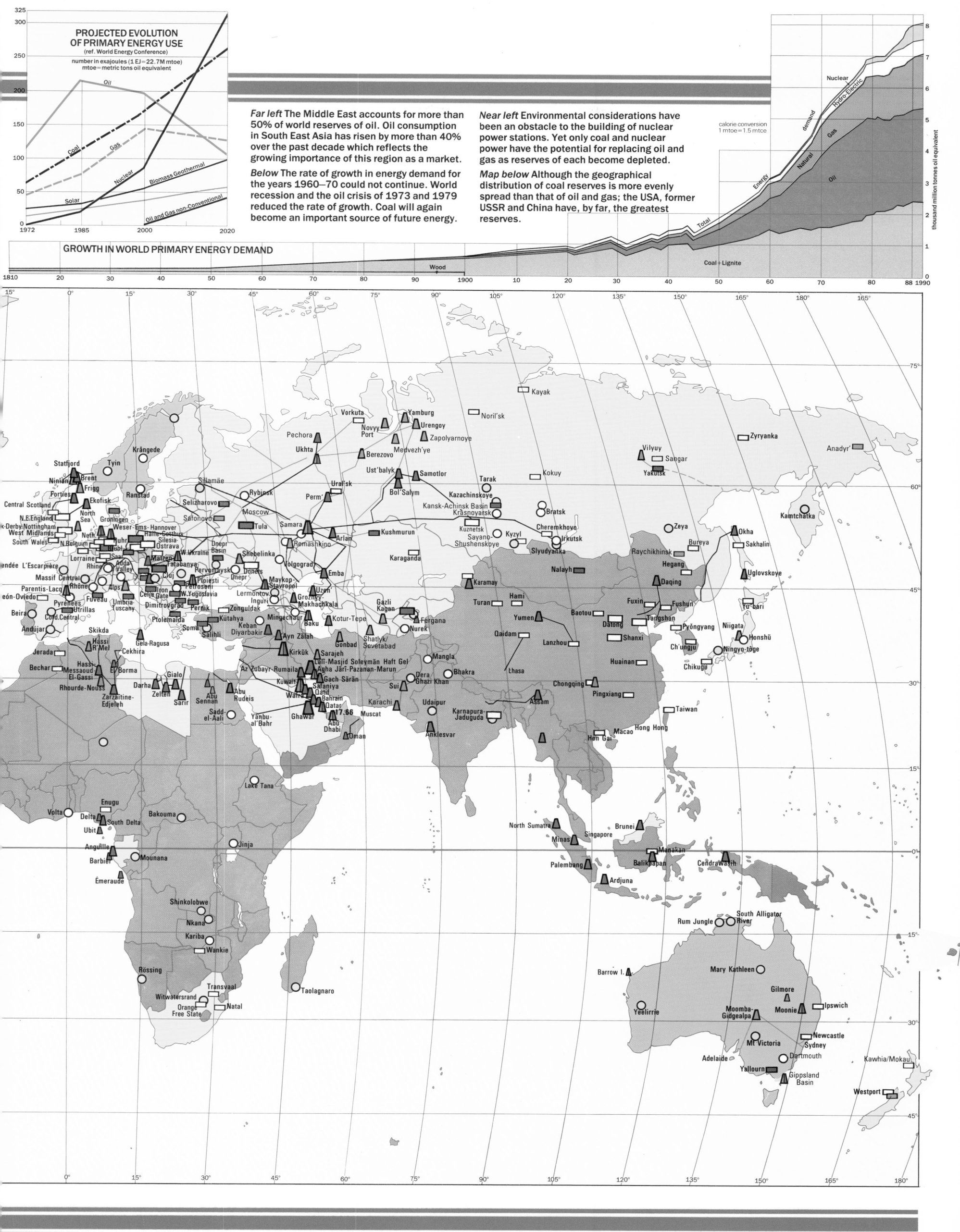

PROJECTED EVOLUTION OF PRIMARY ENERGY USE
(ref. World Energy Conference)

number in exajoules (1 EJ = 22.7M mtoe)
mtoe = metric tons oil equivalent

Oil

Coal

Gas

Nuclear

Biomass Geothermal

Solar

Oil and Gas non-Conventional

Far left The Middle East accounts for more than 50% of world reserves of oil. Oil consumption in South East Asia has risen by more than 40% over the past decade which reflects the growing importance of this region as a market.

Below The rate of growth in energy demand for the years 1960–70 could not continue. World recession and the oil crisis of 1973 and 1979 reduced the rate of growth. Coal will again become an important source of future energy.

Near left Environmental considerations have been an obstacle to the building of nuclear power stations. Yet only coal and nuclear power have the potential for replacing oil and gas as reserves of each become depleted.

Map below Although the geographical distribution of coal reserves is more evenly spread than that of oil and gas; the USA, former USSR and China have, by far, the greatest reserves.

calorie conversion
1 mtoe = 1.5 mtce

Nuclear

Hydro-Electric

Gas
Natural

Oil

Energy
demand

Total

thousand million tonnes oil equivalent

GROWTH IN WORLD PRIMARY ENERGY DEMAND

Wood

Coal + Lignite

FOOD

With a world population which has doubled in the half-century between 1925 and 1975, it is a source of wonderment that more people are not starving. Especially since a further increase of 25% in the number of mouths to feed occurred in the decade up to 1985. It is still more remarkable when it is remembered that only about 11% of the Earth's land surface is under cultivation and that includes areas of non-food products like rubber. The credit for this achievement must be given to the development of artificial fertilizers; the conditioning of plants to alien climates; the development of high-yield seeds and new strains and generally improved agricultural technology. There is no great reserve of land ready to be brought into crop production. The outlook for the future is of a world in which the poorest areas have the highest population growth and the greatest difficulty in producing sufficient food. Matters of immediate concern are the current rate of soil erosion through the felling of trees, over-cropping, and the loss of fertility of world soils through unwise use of artificial fertilizers. Animal manure and vegetable waste are frequently used as fuel. Cash crops are planted where food·crops are needed. Even if organic matter were returned to the soil and all the land were devoted to food crops, the required yields would not necessarily be achieved. In many of the poorest areas improved seeds and fertilizers would still be required. Food provision is not therefore, simply a matter of agricultural technology and distribution. Political and social factors are also involved.

From the land now under cultivation 98% of all food is produced. The other 2% comes from the sea. Unless, through some miracle of laboratory science, protein can be artificially created in sufficient quantities, the sea is the only major source available in the immediate future for supplementing the food potential of the land. Fish-farming, practised in East Asia for four thousand years, has been taken up in several parts of the world but it has been restricted to certain types of fish and shell-fish. The land, however, remains the main source of food and future yields depend on soil conservation and recovery; the development of new strains; conservation of food plants now under threat of extinction; elimination of pests and diseases; improved animal husbandry; investigating new sources of vegetable protein and synthetic food production.

Nutritional standards vary from nation to nation as do diets. North America, Western Europe, Australia and New Zealand are the great meat-eaters; East Asia consumes more fish and less meat but much of the world is dependent on cereal crops, beans and pulses. In overall calorie terms the best-fed nations take in on average, daily, almost three times the average of the worst-fed. Comparing the daily calorie intake of average low-calorie groups of countries with Canada, the United States, Argentina, Western Europe, Australia, and New Zealand there is a gap of more than 1300 calories. Reducing this disparity must depend on improved local food production provided at the same time the present high rate of population growth can be abated.

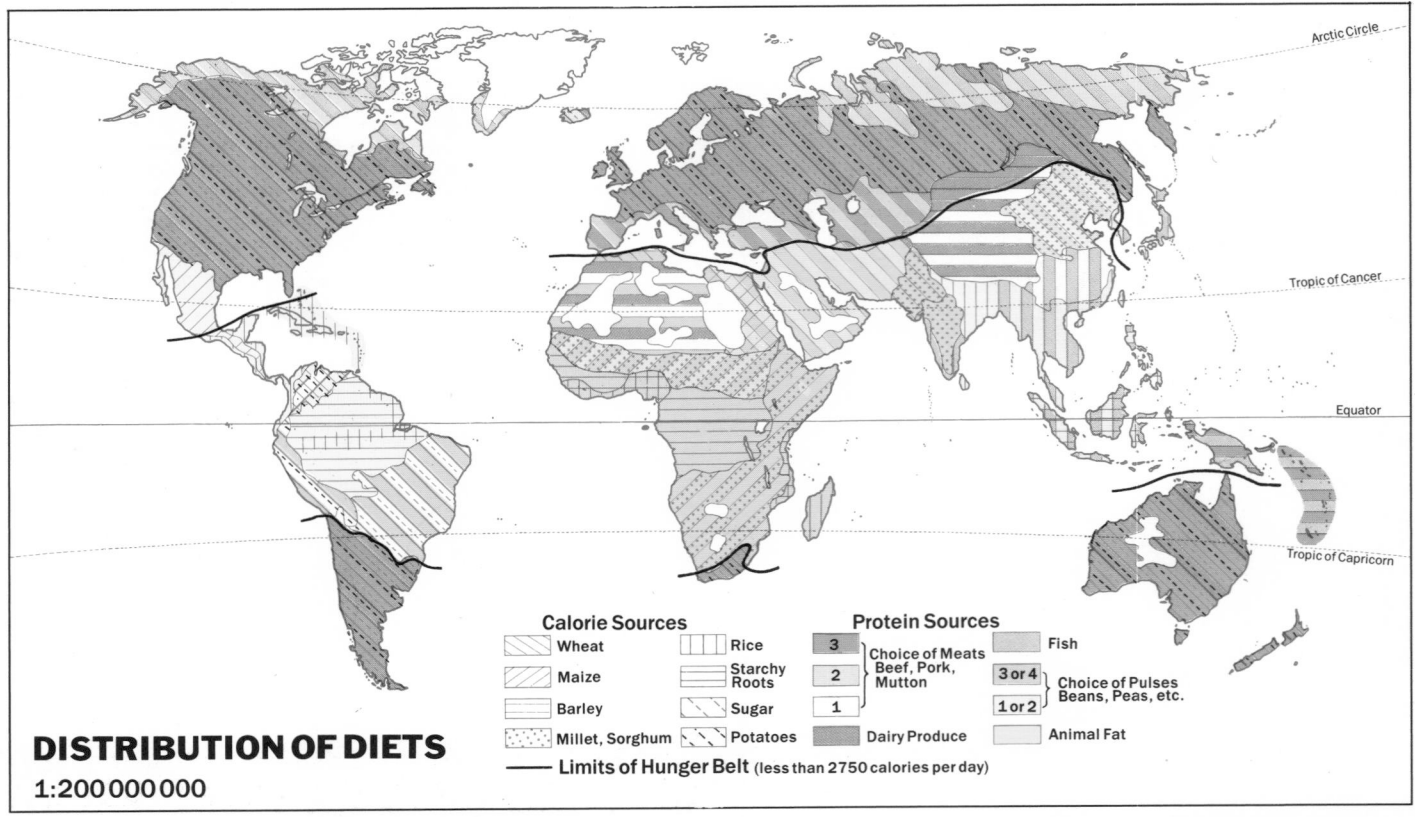

DISTRIBUTION OF DIETS
1:200 000 000

Calorie Sources
- Wheat
- Maize
- Barley
- Millet, Sorghum
- Rice
- Starchy Roots
- Sugar
- Potatoes

Protein Sources
- 3 Choice of Meats Beef, Pork, Mutton
- 2
- 1
- Dairy Produce
- Fish
- 3 or 4 Choice of Pulses Beans, Peas, etc.
- 1 or 2
- Animal Fat

— Limits of Hunger Belt (less than 2750 calories per day)

FOOD SOURCES

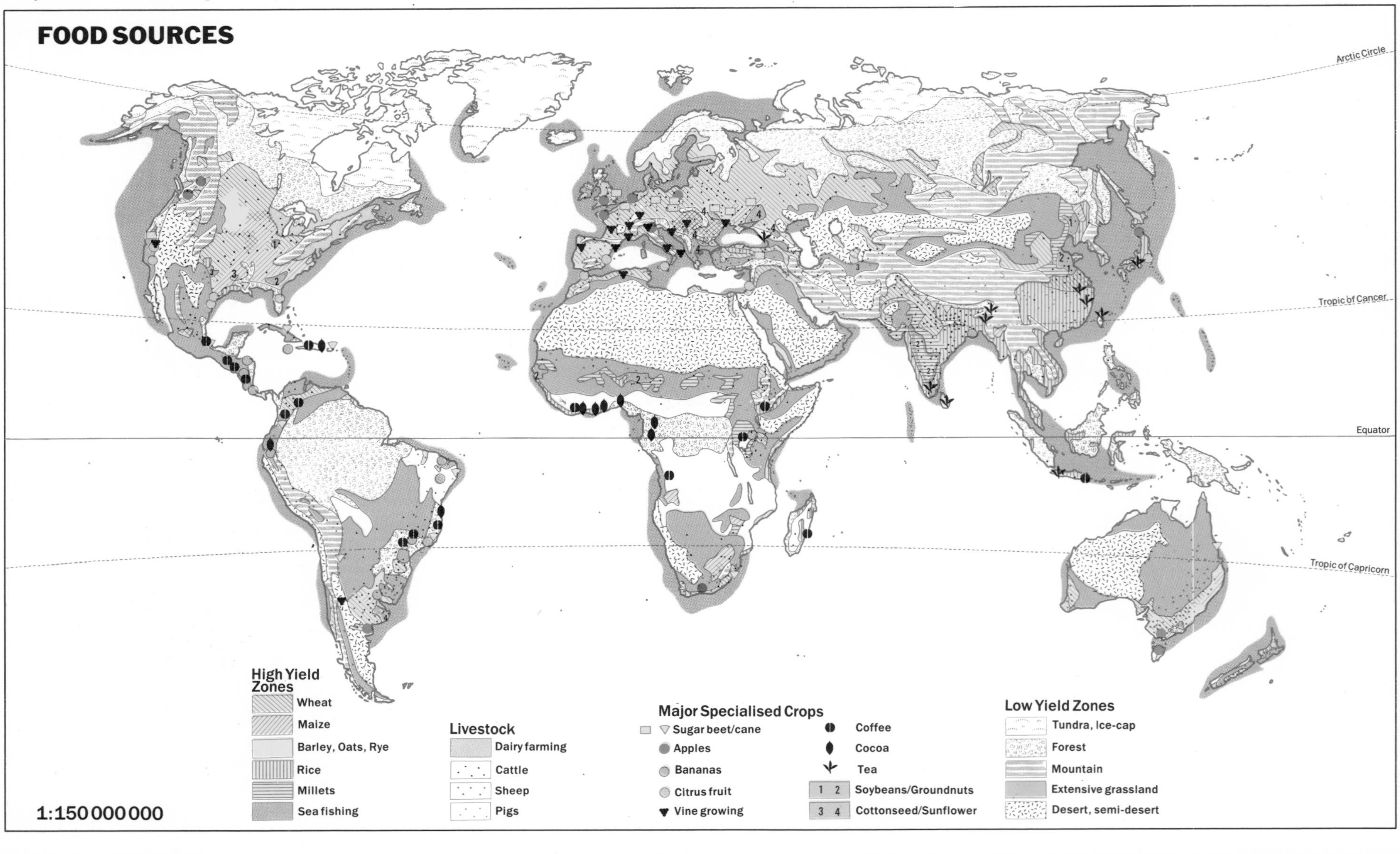

1:150 000 000

High Yield Zones
- Wheat
- Maize
- Barley, Oats, Rye
- Rice
- Millets
- Sea fishing

Livestock
- Dairy farming
- Cattle
- Sheep
- Pigs

Major Specialised Crops
- Sugar beet/cane
- Apples
- Bananas
- Citrus fruit
- Vine growing
- Coffee
- Cocoa
- Tea
- 1 2 Soybeans/Groundnuts
- 3 4 Cottonseed/Sunflower

Low Yield Zones
- Tundra, Ice-cap
- Forest
- Mountain
- Extensive grassland
- Desert, semi-desert

POPULATION

In the view of many people, proliferation of the human race is, in itself and its environmental consequences, a threat to the future of all life on this planet. The twentieth century promises to close with 3.6 times as many people as there were at the beginning. Fortunately, the high rate of annual increase (1.99%) of the period up to 1975 has been reduced, and consequently, there will be almost 1.5 billion fewer people at the end of the century than was at one time anticipated. Assuming that the present growth (1.67%) continues, there will be 6.1 billion people by AD2000.

For any country a growth rate in excess of 2% can spell disaster: 2% means a doubling of population in 35 years, 2.5% gives a doubling in 28 years and a growth of 3.5% doubles in only 20 years. Rate of growth is dependent on the number of live births, infant mortality and the death rate. The increase in numbers has been largely the result of reduction in infant mortality and the death rate in adults. People are living longer and a reduction in the number of live births may well be counterbalanced by prolonged life.

There is a kind of north-south divide, if one excludes Australia and New Zealand, with the technologically developed world approaching zero growth while the rest of the world continues to increase, in some areas at an alarming rate. In Africa, many countries have a growth rate of more than 3% in spite of shorter life expectancy and higher infant mortality (114 per 1000 compared with 16 for Europe and 12 for North America). The Middle Eastern countries although sparsely populated are now seeing increases of well over 4%

Today, Albania alone in Europe has a rate of growth in excess of 2%. The United Kingdom, Italy, Sweden, Denmark, Austria, Belgium and Bulgaria have achieved a growth rate of less than 0.2%, with Germany and Hungary now experiencing negative growth. Japan and the former U.S.S.R. have achieved a rate below 1%.

China's policy of population control has brought the growth rate down to 1.3% not far removed from U.S.A. and Canada (both 1.0%) the highest of the northern nations. India, likewise has, by its birth control policy, slowed its rate of growth yet at present rates the combined populations of China and India will exceed 2½ billion by the end of the century at which time the population of Asia will have equalled or surpassed the total world population of 1975.

In Central and South America a high average birth-rate by country is accompanied by a general lowering of the death-rate which for most of the area is about the same as that of Canada and U.S.A., Europe, the former U.S.S.R., Japan, China, Australia and New Zealand all of which are either 10 or less per 1000 compared with 10 to 20 for Africa and Southern Asia (except Malaysia, Thailand and Philippines). Life expectancy is lowest in parts of Africa and Asia – below 40 years compared with over 70 for almost all the developed world.

Increased longevity, reduced infant mortality and a high birth rate will inevitably change the numbers of young and old who live as dependents. Providing for them is a great challenge for the next few generations.

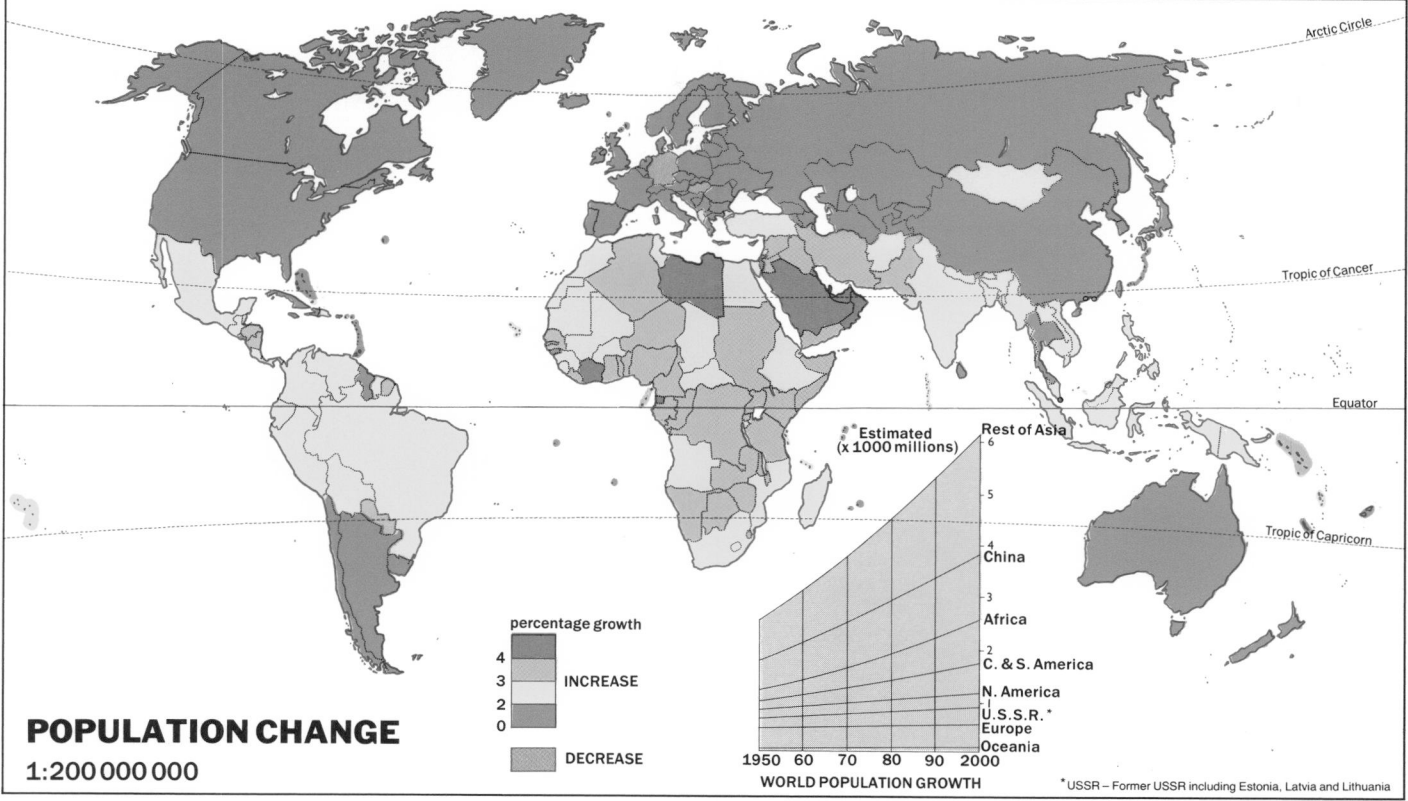

POPULATION CHANGE
1:200 000 000

percentage growth

4
3   INCREASE
2
0

DECREASE

*Estimated (x 1000 millions)

Rest of Asia
China
Africa
C. & S. America
N. America
U.S.S.R.*
Europe
Oceania

1950 60 70 80 90 2000
WORLD POPULATION GROWTH

*USSR – Former USSR including Estonia, Latvia and Lithuania

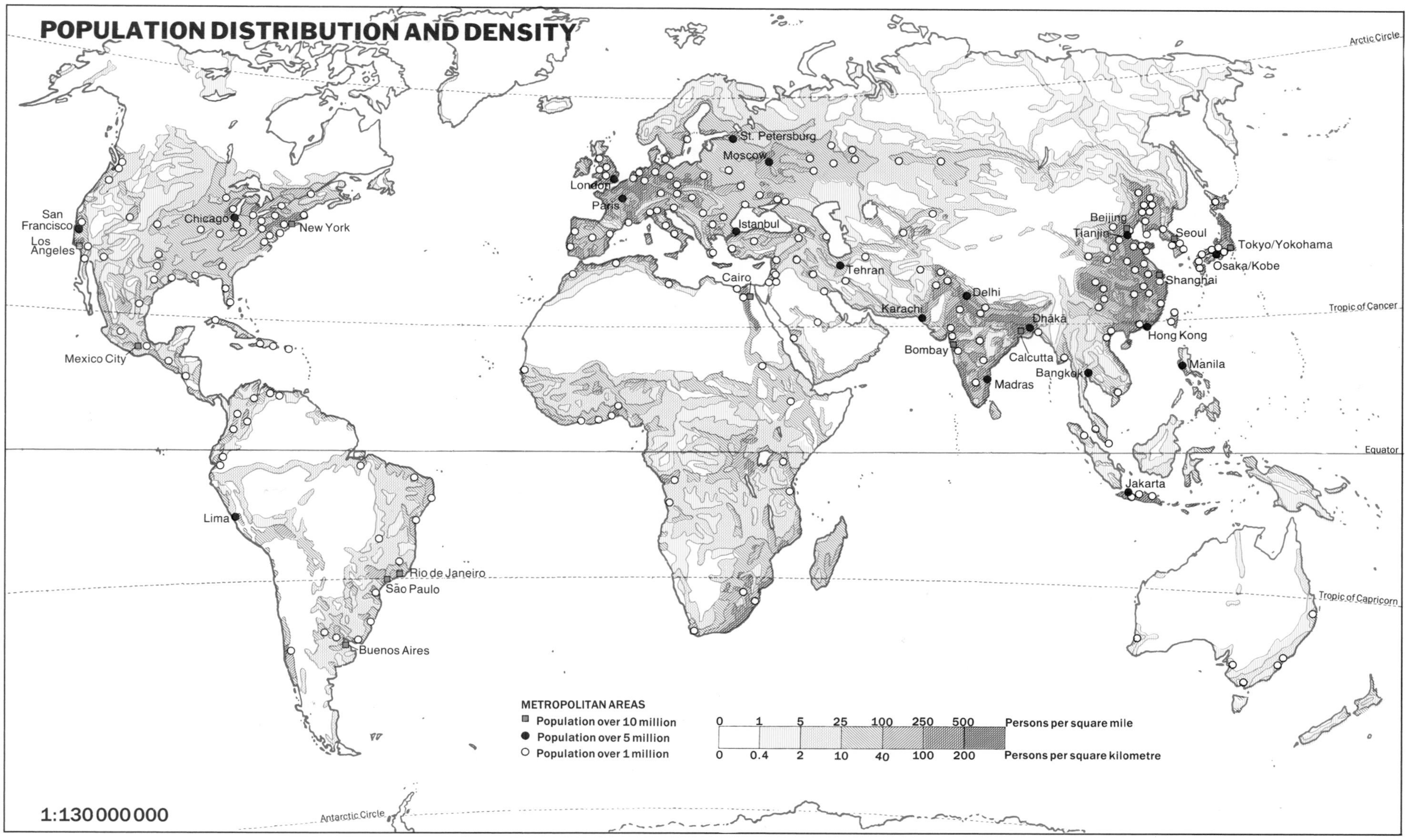

POPULATION DISTRIBUTION AND DENSITY

METROPOLITAN AREAS
- ◻ Population over 10 million
- ● Population over 5 million
- ○ Population over 1 million

0   1   5   25   100   250   500   Persons per square mile
0   0.4   2   10   40   100   200   Persons per square kilometre

1:130 000 000

MAP PROJECTIONS

Map projection is the means by which the imaginary lines of latitude and longitude (the graticule) on a three-dimensional globe are transferred to two-dimensional paper. This transfer cannot be made without error of some kind. Most map projections are no more than a mathematical arrangement of the lines of latitude and longitude to try to achieve a specified result but their underlying principles are firmly based on the concept of perspective projection from a view-point, or light-source onto a plane, a cone or a cylinder tangent to (touching) the globe or secant to (cutting) it.

MAPS OF THE HEMISPHERE

Orthographic projection gives the view as seen from an infinite distance. It is most used for the visible face of the Moon. Other azimuthal projections are best explained by their polar case. In the *stereographic* the projection is from one pole on to a plane tangent at the other. Meridians and parallels plot as circles, arcs of circles or straight lines. In the *equidistant*, the straight, radiating meridians are true to scale. The parallels are equally-spaced concentric circles. Distances are correct along a meridian (but not in other directions). In *Lambert's Equal-Area*, the parallels are so spaced that the area enclosed by two meridians and any two parallels is in true proportion to the corresponding area on the globe.

REGIONAL MAPS

In the *conic with one standard parallel*, the parallel of tangency is made true to scale. Others are concentric circles drawn from the apex of the cone, usually at their correct spacing. Scale errors are reduced with *two standard parallels* of true length and spacing. Neither projection is conformal or equal-area but they can be made so. The conformal version of both has been widely used in topographic maps and aeronautical charts. *Bonne*, a modified conic with one standard parallel is equal-area. The central meridian and all parallels are correctly subdivided. The standard parallel is true to scale. Other parallels are arcs of circles concentric with it. Meridians are curved lines where they are straight in the other two.

The cylinder and the cone can be opened to form a plane and, therefore, serve for projection of the graticule. Either may be tangent, with one standard parallel, or be secant, with two in order to reduce scale-errors overall. Projections may preserve shape (be *conformal*) or area (when they are called *equal-area*) or preserve distance from a central point (be *equidistant*). No two of those properties can exist in a single projection. A projection may dispense with all three in favour of another property e.g. minimum scale-error. It may just aim at good general shape for land, ocean or a region.

POLAR PROJECTIONS

The *gnomonic* is the projection (view) from the centre of the Earth. The limit plotted here is 45° from the tangent point (the pole). This gives a circle equal in radius to 90° (the equator) on the *orthographic* projection. The other two projections are plotted on this same equator. They are, therefore, not to scale but they show the way the parallels are equally spaced in the *equidistant*; are increasingly spaced in the *stereographic* and become very crowded near the equator in the *orthographic* projection.

WORLD MAPS

Mercator is conformal (scale at any point is the same in all directions). Lines of constant bearing (loxodromes or rhumb lines) plot as straight lines, hence its importance to navigators. *Gall's* projection, a kind of stereographic is neither conformal nor equal-area. A cylinder is secant at 45°N and S. Projection is from a point on the equator diametrically opposite. *"The Times"* projection has Gall's parallels but the meridians are modified from the sinusoidal and considerably less curved. In the *sinusoidal* projection, the central meridian is perpendicular to the equator and half its length. Parallels are straight, equally spaced and equally subdivided. Meridians drawn through the subdivisions are sine curves. In *Mollweide*, the central meridian cuts the equator and all parallels at right angles. All are subdivided equally. Meridians 90° east and west of centre form a circle equal in area to a hemisphere. From that equation the spacing of the parallels can be calculated. *Hammer's* projection, derived from Lambert's equal-area, has the equator doubled in length. All three projections are equal-area. *Winkel Tripel* is the mean of Hammer and Plate Carrée. It is not equal-area. *Plate Carrée*, the simplest projection (not shown here) is a system of squares based on the equator.

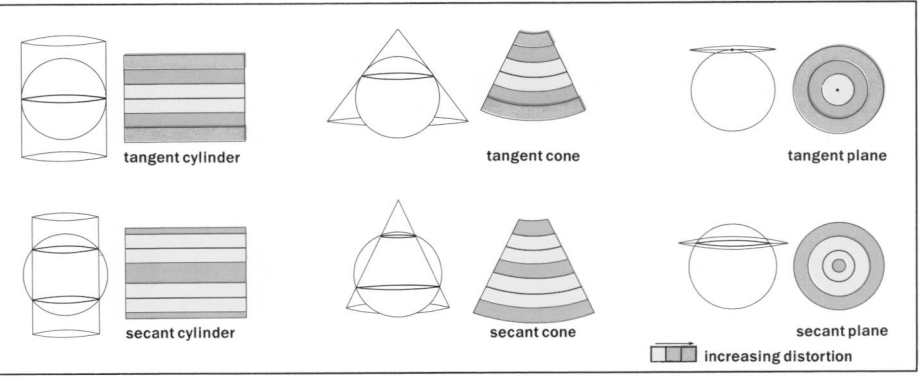

tangent cylinder • tangent cone • tangent plane

secant cylinder • secant cone • secant plane

increasing distortion

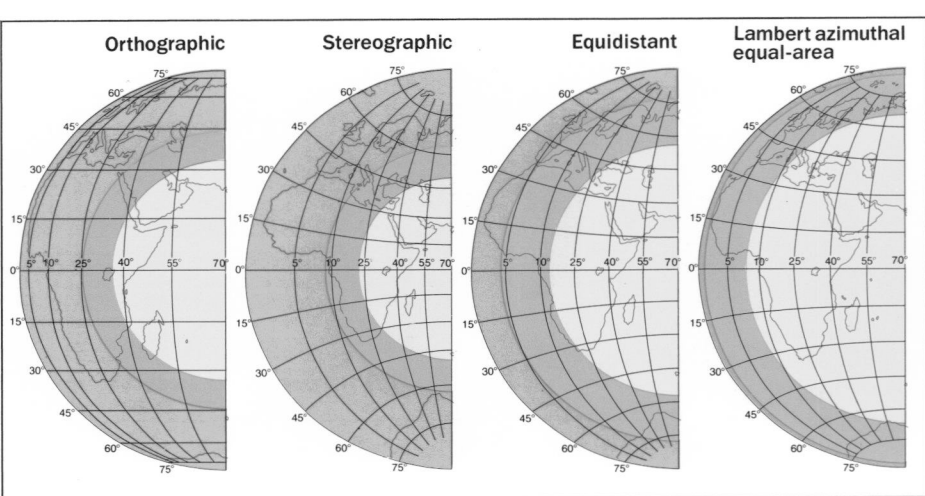

Orthographic • Stereographic • Equidistant • Lambert azimuthal equal-area

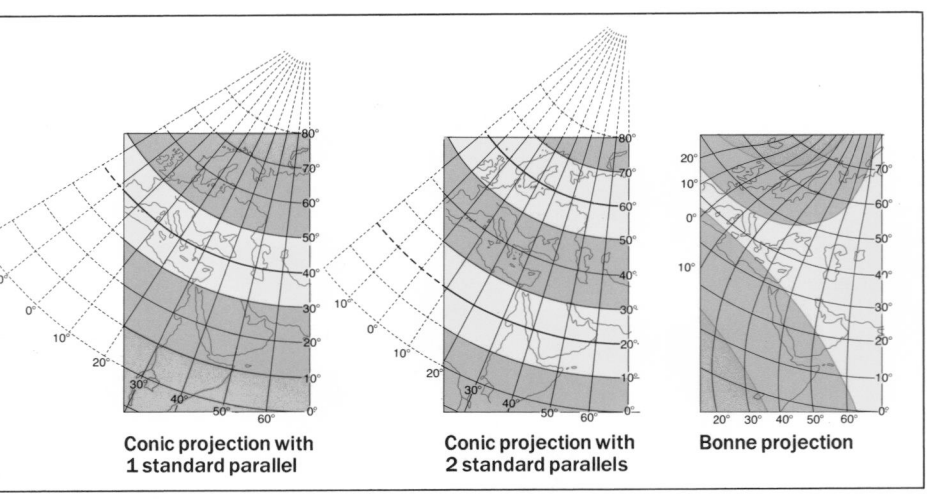

Conic projection with 1 standard parallel • Conic projection with 2 standard parallels • Bonne projection

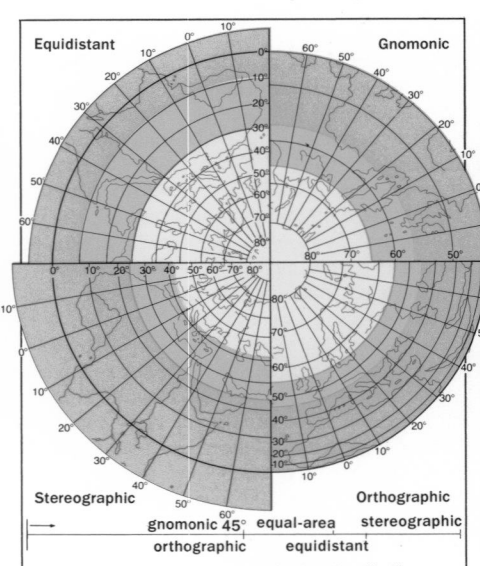

Equidistant • Gnomonic • Stereographic • Orthographic

gnomonic 45° equal-area orthographic
orthographic equidistant

The bar scale shows the comparative lengths of half-meridians (90°) in four projections. To these, Lambert's Equal-Area has been added.

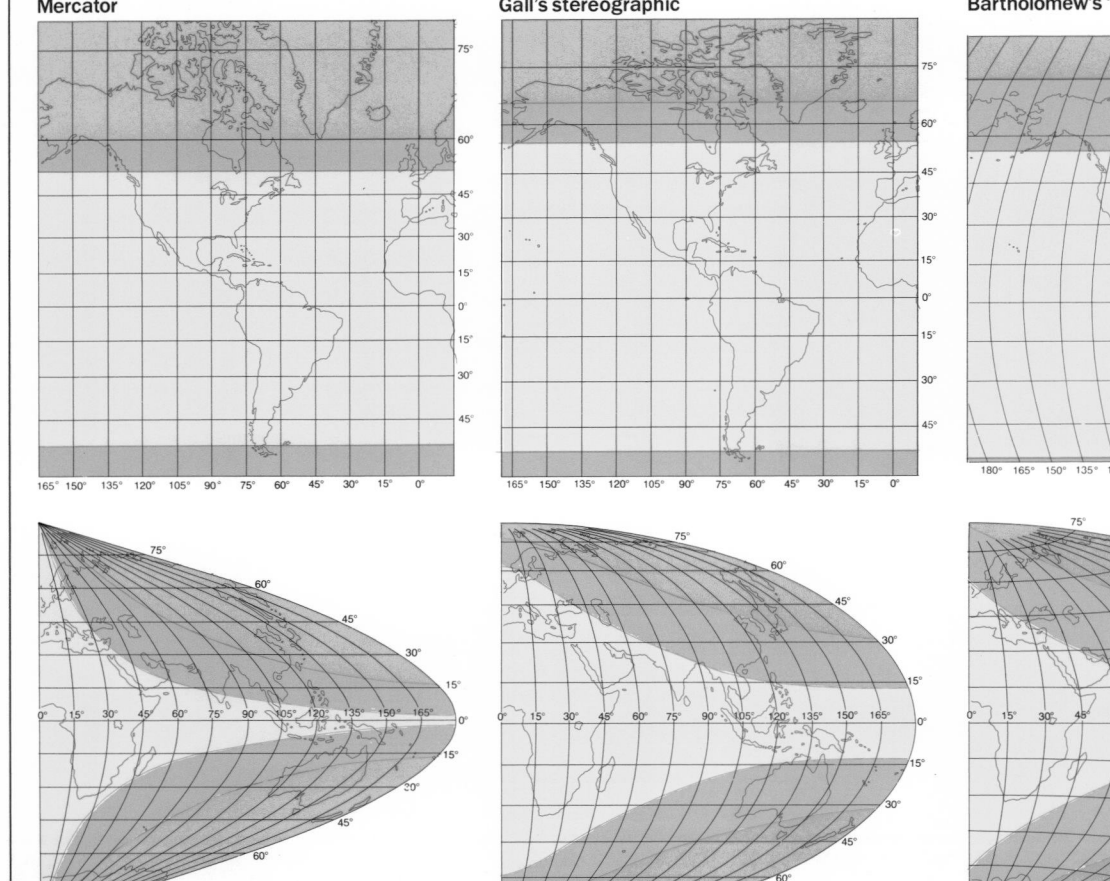

Mercator • Gall's stereographic • Bartholomew's 'The Times'

Sinusoidal (Sanson-Flamsteed) • Mollweide • Hammer (Hammer-Aitoff)

BOUNDARIES

- International
- International, Undefined or Alignment Uncertain
- Limits of Sovereignty across Water Areas
- Autonomous, Federal State
- Main Administrative
- Other Administrative
- Offshore Administrative
- Armistice, Cease-Fire Line
- Demilitarised Zone
- National Park
- Reserve, Reservation

COMMUNICATIONS

- Main Railways
- Other Railway
- Light Railway
- Projected Railways
- Railway Tunnels
- Road Tunnel
- Special Highway *Projected*
- Main Road *Projected*
- Other Road *Projected*
- Tracks
- Car Ferries
- Rail Ferries
- Navigable Canals *Locks*
- Projected or Disused Canal
- Drainage or Irrigation Canal
- Canal Tunnel
- Tunnel Aqueduct

LAKE TYPES

- Fresh-water
- Reservoir *Dam*
- Seasonal Fresh
- Seasonal Brackish
- Salt-lake, Lagoon
- Perennial Salt-lake
- Seasonal Salt-lake
- Saline Mud-flat
- Salt-flat

LANDSCAPE FEATURES

- Ice-field and Glaciers
- Ice-cap, Ice-sheet
- Lava-fields
- Lava-fields
- Sand Desert, Dunes
- Saline Marsh, Salt Desert
- Marsh, Swamp
- Swamp, Flood-area
- Mangrove Swamp
- Tidal Area
- Atoll

OTHER FEATURES

- River, Stream
- Seasonal Watercourses
- Seasonal Flood-plain
- Undefined Course of River
- Pass; Gorges
- Waterfalls, Rapids
- Dam, Barrage
- Escarpments
- Flood Dyke
- Limits of Ice-shelf
- Reefs
- Rocks
- Spot Depth · 9650
- Lighthouse
- Lightship; Beacon
- Waterhole, Well
- Active Volcano
- Summit, Peak
- Oil Wells
- Oil or Natural Gas Pipeline
- Mine
- Site of Battle
- Historic Site
- Historic Ruin
- Ancient Walls
- Mosque, Sheikh's Tomb
- Cathedral, Monastery, Church
- International or Main Airport
- Airport, Airfield

CITY MAPS

- State Boundary
- County, Department Boundary
- City Limits
- Borough, District Boundary
- Main Railways *Station*
- Other Railways *Bridge*
- Projected Railways
- Underground Railway *Station*
- Special Highway *Projected*
- Main Road
- Secondary Road
- Other Road, Street
- Track
- Road Tunnel
- Bridge; Flyover
- Seaway *Locks*
- Canals
- Drainage Canal
- Waterfalls, Rapids
- Historic Walls
- Airports
- Racecourses
- Stadium
- Cemetery; Churches
- Woodland, Park
- Built-up Area

STYLES OF LETTERING

- T O G O — Country Name
- ALBERTA — -Major Administrative Divisions
- KENT CHER — -Other
- PARIS Bern — National Capitals
- Omsk
- Denver — Administrative Centres
- Kraków
- GANDER Gatwick — Airports
- *M O A B* — Historic Region
- *D E C C A N*
- *S I N A I* — Physical Regions
- *Mato Grosso*
- *ATLAS Nile* — Physical Features
- *Mt Blanc Thames*
- *BASIN Ridge* — Ocean Bottom Features
- *M A S A I* — Tribal Name

PRINCIPAL MAP ABBREVIATIONS

A.	1. Alp, Alpen, Alpi. 2. Alt	Cᵐᵃ	Cima	Hⁿ	Horn	Mᵍⁿᵃ	Montagna	Por.	Porog
Abbᵉ	Abbaye	Cⁿᵒ	Corno	Hosp.	1. Hospice, Hospiz. 2. Hospital	Mᵍⁿᵉ	Montagne	Port.	Portugal, Portuguese
A.C.T.	Australian Capital Territory	Cᵒ	Cerro	Ht.	Haut	Mkt.	Markt	pᵒᵛ	Poluostrov
Aig.	Aiguille	Constⁿ	Construction	Hte.	Haute	Mon.	Monasterio, Monastery	P.P.	Pulau-pulau
Akr.	Akra, Akrotírion	Cord.	Cordillera	Hᵗᵉʳ	Hinter	Mont.	Monument	Pr.	1. Proliv.
Anch.	Anchorage	Cr.	Creek	Hᵞ	Highway	Mt.	Mont, Mount, Mountain		2. Przylądek. 3. Prince
A.O.	Avtonomnaya Oblast'	Cuch.	Cuchilla	I.	Ile, Ilha, Insel, Isla, Island, Isle, Isola, Isole	Mte.	Monte	Promᵞ	Promontory
Appⁿᵒ	Appennino	Cucᵘ	Cuccuru			Mᵗᵉˢ	Montes	Prop.	Proposed
Aqued.	Aqueduct	Cy.	City	IJ.	IJssel	Mti.	Monti, Munti	PROT.	Protectorate
Ar.	Arroyo	Czo.	Cozzo	im.	imeni	Mts.	Mounts, Mountains	PROV.	Provincial
Arch.	Archipel, Archipelago, Archipiélago	D.	1. Da, Dag, Dagh, Dağı, Dağları. 2. Danau. 3. Darreh. 4. Daryácheh	In.	1. Inder, Indre, Inner, Inre. 2. Inlet	N.	1. Nam. 2. Neu, Ny. 2. Nevado, Nudo. 4. Noord, Nord. Nórre, Nørre. North. 5. Nos	Psa	Presa
				IND.	India			pᵃᵒ	Passo
Arr.	Arrecife	-d-	-dake	Inf.	Inferior, -e, Inférieure			Pt.	1. Point. 2. Pont
Ay.	Ayia, Ayioi, Áyion, Áyios	D.C.	District of Columbia	Int.	International	Nᵃ	Nuestra	pᵗ	1. Petit. 2. Point.
B.	1. Baai, Bahia, Baia, Baie, Baja, Bay, Bucht, Bukhta, Bukt. 2. Bad. 3. Ban. 4. Barazh, Barrage, Barragem. 5. Bayou. 6. Bir. 7. Bonto. 8. Bulu	Den.	Denmark	Iᵃ	Iles, Ilhas, Islands, Islas, Isles	Nat.	National		3. Pont
		Dists.	Districts	ISR.	Israel	N.D.	Notre Dame	Pᵗᵃ	1. Ponta, Punta. 2. Puerta
		Div.	Division	Isth.	Isthmus	Nᵈʳ	Neder, Nieder	Pᵗᵉ	1. Pointe. 2. Ponte.
		Dj.	Djebel	J.	1. Jabal, Jebel, Jibál. 2. Järvi, Jaure, Jazira, Jezero, Jezioro. 3. Jökull	N.E.	North East		Puente
		Dns.	Downs			Neth.	Netherlands	Pᵗᵒ	1. Porto, Puerto. 2. Ponto, Punto
		Dz.	Dzong			Nizh.	Nizhne, -neye, -niy, -nyaya	Pᶻᵒ	Pizzo
Bᶜ	Banc	E.	East	Jap.	Japan, Japanese	Nizm.	Nizmennost	Q.	Qala, Qara, Qarn
Bᶜᵃ	Boca	Eil.	Eiland, Eilanden	Jct.	Junction	N.O.	Noord Oost, Nord Ost	R.	1. Reka, Rio, River, Rivière, Rud, Rzeka. 2. Ria
Bel.	Belgium, Belgian	Escarp.	Escarpment	K.	1. Kaap, Kap, Kapp. 2. Kaikyō. 3. Kato. 4. Kerang, Kering. 5. Kiang. 6. Kirke. 7. Ko. 8. Koh, Küh, Kúhha. 9. Kólpos. 10. Kopf. 11. Kuala. 12. Kyst	Nor.	Norway, Norwegian		
Bg.	Berg	Est.	Estación			Nᵒˢ	Nudos	Ra.	Range
Bge	Barrage	Eᵗᵍ	Etang			Nov.	Novyy, -aya, -iye, -oye	Rap.	Rapids
Bgt.	Bight, Bugt	F.	Firth			Nᵗʳ	Nether	Rᵈ	Rocca
Bⁱ	Bani, Beni	F.D.	Federal District			N.W.	North West	Rᵈ	Road
Bj	Burj	Fj.	1. Fjell. 2. Fjord, Fjördur			N.Z.	New Zealand	REC.	Recreation
Bᵏ	Bank	Fᵏ	Fork			O.	1. Old. 2. Oost, Ost. 3. Ostrov	Res.	Reservoir
Bk.	Buku	Fl.	Fleuve					Resp.	Respublika
Bⁿ	Basin	F.France	France, French	Kan.	Kanal, Kanaal	Ō.	1. Ōstre. 2. Öy	Rᶠ	Reef
Bol.	Bol'shoy, -oye, -aya, -iye	Ft.	Fort	Kap.	Kapelle	Ø.	1. Østre. 2. Øy	Rᵍᵉ	Ridge
		Fᵗᵉ	Fonte	Kep.	Kepulauan	Obl.	Oblast	Rⁱᵇ	Ribeira
Bos.	Bosanski	Fy.	Ferry	Kg.	Kampong, Kompong, Kong	Oᵇᵗ	Ouder	Rly.	Railway
Br.	1. Branch. 2. Bredning. 3. Bridge, Brücke. 4. Britain, British. 5. Burun	-g	-gawa			Oᵍᵗ	Oguilet	Rom.	Romania, Romanian
		G.	1. Gebel. 2. Ghedir. 3. Gól, Gölü, Gôl. 4. Golfe, Golfo, Gulf. 5. Gompa. 6. Gora, Gory. 7. Guba, 8. Gunung	Kh.	1. Khawr. 2. Khirbet, Khiábán, -e. 3. Khowr	Ogl.	Oglat	Rᵗᵉ	Route
						O.L.V.	Onze Lieve Vrouw	Rus. Fed.	Russian Federation
Bt.	Bukit			Khr.	Khrebet	Or.	Orr, Oros	S.	1. Salar, Salina. 2. San. 3. Saw. 4. See. 5. Seto. 6. Sjö. 7. Sör. South, Syd. 8. Sung. 9. sur. 10. Sebjet
Bü.	Büyük			Kl.	1. Kechil. 2. Klein, -e	Orm.	Ormos		
Bukh.	Bukhta	Geb.	Gebergte, Gebirge	Kör.	Körfez, -i	Os(t)	Ostrova		
C.	1. Čabo, Cap, Cape. 2. Česká, -é, -ý. 3. Col.	Geogˡ	Geographical	Kr.	Kangar	Ot.	Olet		
		Gez.	Gezira	Kü.	Küçük	Ov.	Over, Övre		
Çᵃ	Çay	Ghub.	Ghubba	L.	1. Lac, Lago, Lagôa, Lake, Liman, Limni, Liqen, Loch, Lough. 2. Lam	Oᵛᵃ	Ostrov, -a	Sᵃ	Serra, Sierra
Cabᵒ	Cabeço	Gl.	1. Gamle, Gammel. 2. Glacier			Oz.	Ozero	Sab.	Sabkhat
Cach.	Cachoeira, -o	Gp.	Group			P.	1. Pass. 2. Pic, Pico, Piz. 3. Pulau. 4. Pou	Sᶜ	Scoglio
Can.	1. Canal. 2. Canale. 3. Canavese.	Gr.	1. Graben. 2. Gross, -e, Grande	Lag.	Lagoon, Laguna, -e			Sᵈ	Sound, Sund
		Gᵛ	Gasr	Lᵈ	Land	Pal.	Palace, Palacio, Palais	S.E.	South East
Cas.	Castle	Grˡᵉˢ	Grottes	Ldg.	Landing	Pass.	Passage	Seb.	Sebjet, Sebkhat, Sebkra
Cat.	1. Cataract. 2. Catena	Gt.	Great, Groot, -e	Lit.	Little	Peg.	Pegunungan		
Cath.	Cathedral	H.	1. Hawr. 2. Hill. 3. Hoch. 4. Hora, Hory	Lⁱ	Lille	Pen.	Peninsula, Penisola	Sev.	Sever, -naya, -nyy
Cᵈ	Ciudad			M.	1. Mae, Me. 2. Meer. 3. Muang. 4. Muntii. 5. Muong. 6. Mys. 7. Monte	Per.	Pereval	Sᵍⁿᵒ	Stagno
Cerv.	Červená, -é	Halv.	Halvey			Ph.	Phum	Sh.	1. Sh'aib. 2. Sharif. 3. Shatt. 4. Shima. 5. Shankou
Ch.	1. Chapel, Chapelle. 2. Chott. 2. Chaung. 3. Chott.	Har.	Harbour			Phn.	Phnom		
		Hᵈ	Head			Pᵍᵍ	Poggio		
		H.E.P.	Hydro-Electric Power	m	metre/s	Plat.	Plateau	Sⁱ	Sidi
Chan.	Channel	Hᵍˢ	Hegység	Mal.	Malyy, -aya, -oye	Plosk.	Ploskogor'ye	Sᵏⁿᵒˡ	Sandknoll
Chᵘ	Château	Hᵗˢ	Heights	Mem.	Memorial	Pⁿᵗᵒ	Pantano	Sˡ	Sal
Chⁿᵉ	Chaine	Hⁱ	Hasi, Hasy	Mex.	Mexico, Mexican	Pⁿᵗᵉ	Pointe	Sˡⁱ	Sieve
Chˡᵉ	Chapelle	Hist.	Historic	Mᶠ	Massif	Pol.	Poluostrov	Sᵐᵗ	Seamount
								Snᵃ	Senhora
								Snᵒ	Senhoro
								Sp.	1. Spain, Spanish. 2. Spitze
								Spᵏ	Seapeak

Spr.	Spring
Sˡ	Sönder, Sønder
Sr.	Sredniy, -nyaya
Sᵗ	Saint, Sint, Staryy
St.	1. State. 2. Stor. Store. 3. Stung
Sᵗᵃ	Santa
Sta.	Station
Stby.	Staby, Statsjonsby
Sᵗᵉ	Sainte
Ste.	Store
Sten.	Stenón, Stenós
Sᵗᵒ	Santo
Str.	Strait
Sv.	Svaty, Sveti
S.W.	South West
T.	1. Tal. 2. Tal, Tall, Tell. 3. Tepe, Tepesi
Talsp.	Talsperre
Tel.	Teluk
Terr.	Terrace
Terrʸ	Territory
Tg.	Tanjung
Thwy.	Throughway, Thruway
Tk.	Teluk
Tᵐᵗ	Tablemount
Tᵒ	Tando
Tpk.	Turnpike
Terr.	Trench, Trough
Tᵗᵉ	Torre
Tun.	Tunnel
U	Uad
U.A.E.	United Arab Emirates
Ug.	Udjung
U.K.	United Kingdom
Unt.	Unter
Upᵗ	Upper
U.S.A.	United States of America
V.	1. Val, Valle. 2. Väster, Vest, Vester. 3. Vatn. 4. Ville. 5. Vorder. 6. Volcán
Vᵃ	Vila
Vdkhr.	Vodokhranilishche
Vel.	Velikiy, -aya, -iye
Ven.	Venezuela, Venezuelan
Verkh.	Verkhniy, -neye, -ne, -nyaya
Vn.	Volcán
Vol.	Volcán, Volcano, Vulkán
Vost.	Vostochnyy
Vozv.	Vozvyshennost'
W.	1. Wadi. 2. Wald. 3. Wan. 4. Water. 5. Well. 6. West
Wᵗ	Wester
Wᵃ	-yama
Yᵗ	Ytre, Ytter, Ytri
Yuzh.	Yuzhnaya, -no, -nyy
Z.	Zaliv
Zᵃ	Zaliv
Zap.	Zapadnyy, -aya, -o, -oye
Zem.	Zemlya

ARCTIC OCEAN
BEAUFORT SEA
GREENLAND
BAFFIN BAY
HUDSON BAY
RUSSIAN FEDERATION
Novo Sibirskiye Ostrova
Os. Vrangelya (Wrangel I.)
USA ALASKA
Bering Str.
BERING SEA
SEA OF OKHOTSK
Aleutian Islands
Sakhalin
Kuril Is.
SEA OF JAPAN
Hokkaidō
Honshū
JAPAN
Tokyō
Yokhama
CANADA
Victoria I.
Banks I.
Devon I.
Baffin I.
Davis Str.
Newfoundland
UNITED STATES OF AMERICA
San Francisco
Los Angeles
San Diego
Seattle
Portland
Vancouver
Chicago
Detroit
Toronto
Montreal
Ottawa
New York
Philadelphia
Baltimore
Washington
Houston
New Orleans
Atlanta
Miami
MEXICO
Monterrey
Guadalajara
Mexico City
GULF OF MEXICO
THE BAHAMAS
CUBA
Habana
JAMAICA
Hispaniola
Port au Prince
Santo Domingo
San Juan
CARIBBEAN SEA
Managua
San José
Barranquilla
Maracaibo
Caracas
VENEZUELA
Medellín
Bogotá
COLOMBIA
Quito
ECUAD.
Guayaquil
PERU
Lima
BRAZIL
Belém
Recife
Salvador
Brasília
Belo Horizonte
São Paulo
Rio de Janeiro
La Paz
BOLIVIA
PARAGUAY
Asunción
Córdoba
Rosario
Santiago
Buenos Aires
Montevideo
URUG.
ARGENTINA
Falkland Is. (UK)
C. Horn
NORTH PACIFIC OCEAN
SOUTH PACIFIC OCEAN
NORTH ATLANTIC OCEAN
Tropic of Cancer
Equator
Tropic of Capricorn
Hawaiian Is. (USA)
Honolulu
Midway I. (USA)
Wake I. (USA)
Marshall Is.
Caroline Is.
KIRIBATI
NAURU
Phoenix Is.
Marquesas (Fr.)
TUVALU
SOLOMON IS.
PAPUA NEW GUINEA
Samoa (USA)
W. SAMOA
FIJI
TONGA
Tuamotu (Fr.)
Tahiti
Cook Is.
New Caledonia (Fr.)
VANUATU
CORAL SEA
AUSTRALIA
Brisbane
Sydney
Canberra
Melbourne
TASMANIA
Hobart
TASMAN SEA
NEW ZEALAND
Auckland
Wellington
Christchurch
Dunedin
Chatham Is.
Kermadec Is. (NZ)
Norfolk I. (Aust.)
Clipperton (Fr.)
Islas Galápagos (Ecuador)
Sala y Gómez (Chile)
Easter I.
Islas Juan Fernández (Chile)
Population Key
Capitals | Cities & Towns
over 3 mill.
over 1 mill.
under 1 mill.
Communications
Roads
Railways
Main Shipping Routes
Other Shipping Routes
Limits of Pack-ice
Permanent Pack-ice
Average Winter Limit
West of 90° Greenwich

CHANGES OF SOVEREIGNTY
since World War II
1:125 000 000
Independence gained since 1939 from former sovereign powers:
UK
Belgium
Denmark
France
Italy
Japan
Neths.
Spain
USA
Portugal
S. Africa
Yug.
Year of Independence
60 = 1960:
Territory ceded or annexed since 1939
Territory annexed by the former USSR between 1939 and 1945
Boundary adjustments
Transfers of territory
Independent before 1939
Dependent territory
Area of the former USSR
F/B6813

ARCTIC OCEAN

BARENTS SEA

RUSSIAN FEDERATION

KAZAKHSTAN

MONGOLIA

CHINA

INDIA

SAUDI ARABIA

LIBYA

EGYPT

SUDAN

CHAD

NIGER

MALI

MAURITANIA

ALGERIA

ETHIOPIA

SOMALIA

KENYA

TANZANIA

ZAIRE

ANGOLA

ZAMBIA

NAMIBIA

BOTSWANA

SOUTH AFRICA

MADAGASCAR

ATLANTIC OCEAN

INDIAN OCEAN

PACIFIC OCEAN

AUSTRALIA

NEW ZEALAND

JAPAN

1:66 000 000
(45° N. & S.)

TIME ZONES
1:125 000 000

Zone Times are the Standard Times kept on land and sea compared with 12 hours (noon) Greenwich Mean Time. Daylight Saving Time (normally one hour in advance of local Standard Time), which is observed by certain countries for part of the year, is not shown on the map.

John Bartholomew & Son Ltd. Edinburgh

RUSSIAN FEDERATION
KAZAKHSTAN
UZBEKISTAN
TURKMENISTAN
FINLAND
ESTONIA
LATVIA
LITHUANIA
BELORUSSIA
UKRAINE
MOLDAVIA
ROMANIA
BULGARIA
GREECE
TURKEY
GEORGIA
ARMENIA
AZERBAIJAN
SYRIA
IRAQ
IRAN (PERSIA)
CYPRUS
LEBANON
ISRAEL
JORDAN
SAUDI ARABIA
KUWAIT
BARENTS SEA
KARA SEA
BLACK SEA
CASPIAN SEA
PERSIAN GULF
Novaya Zemlya
Kol'skiy Poluostrov
Lappland
Moskva
Sankt-Peterburg
Helsinki
Tallinn
Riga
Minsk
Kiyev
Khar'kov
Odessa
Dnepropetrovsk
Donetsk
Rostov-na-Donu
Volgograd
Astrakhan
Saratov
Samara
Kazan'
Nizhniy Novgorod
Yaroslavl'
Izhevsk
Ufa
Perm'
Yekaterinburg
Chelyabinsk
Magnitogorsk
Orenburg
Omsk
Novosibirsk
Pavlodar
Tbilisi
Baku
Yerevan
Tabriz
Tehran
Esfahan
Baghdad
Al Basrah
Halab
Dimashq
Beyrouth
Jerusalem
Tel Aviv-Yafo
Ankara
Istanbul
Izmir
Edirne
Sofiya
București
Athinai
Thessaloniki
Kriti
Alexandria
Cairo
Sevastopol'
Simferopol'
Krym
Aral'skoye More (Aral Sea)
Plato Ustyurt
Longitude East 45° of Greenwich
1:15M
km
miles

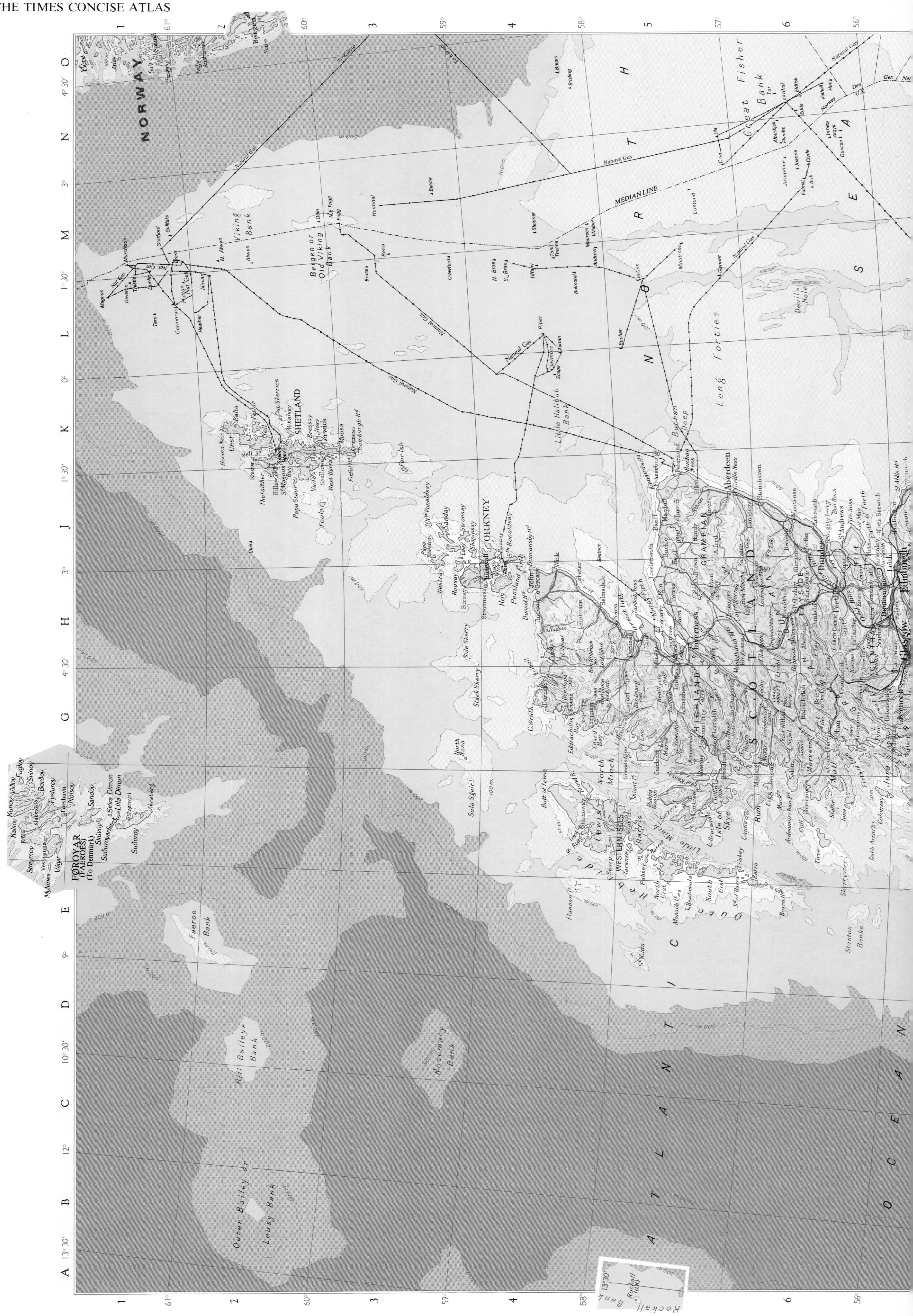

NORWAY

N O R T H   S E A

MEDIAN LINE

Viking Bank

Bergen or Old Viking Bank

Great Fisher Bank

Long Forties

Little Halibut Bank

Buchan Deep

Devil's Hole

SHETLAND

ORKNEY

SCOTLAND

GRAMPIAN

HIGHLAND

TAYSIDE

CENTRAL

STRATHCLYDE

Aberdeen

Inverness

Edinburgh

Glasgow

WESTERN ISLES

Outer Hebrides

Inner Hebrides

North Minch

Little Minch

The Minch

Isle of Skye

Isle of Lewis

Butt of Lewis

Pentland Firth

Wick

C. Wrath

North Rona

Sula Sgeir

Stack Skerry

Sule Skerry

Fair Isle

Foula

Fetlar

Unst

Yell

Magnus

FÖROYAR
(FAEROES)
(To Denmark)

Faeroe Bank

Rosemary Bank

Bill Baileys Bank

Outer Bailey or Lousy Bank

Rockall Bank

Rockall

ATLANTIC   OCEAN

Natural Gas

Piper

Beryl

Brent

Ninian

Forties

CONIC PROJECTION

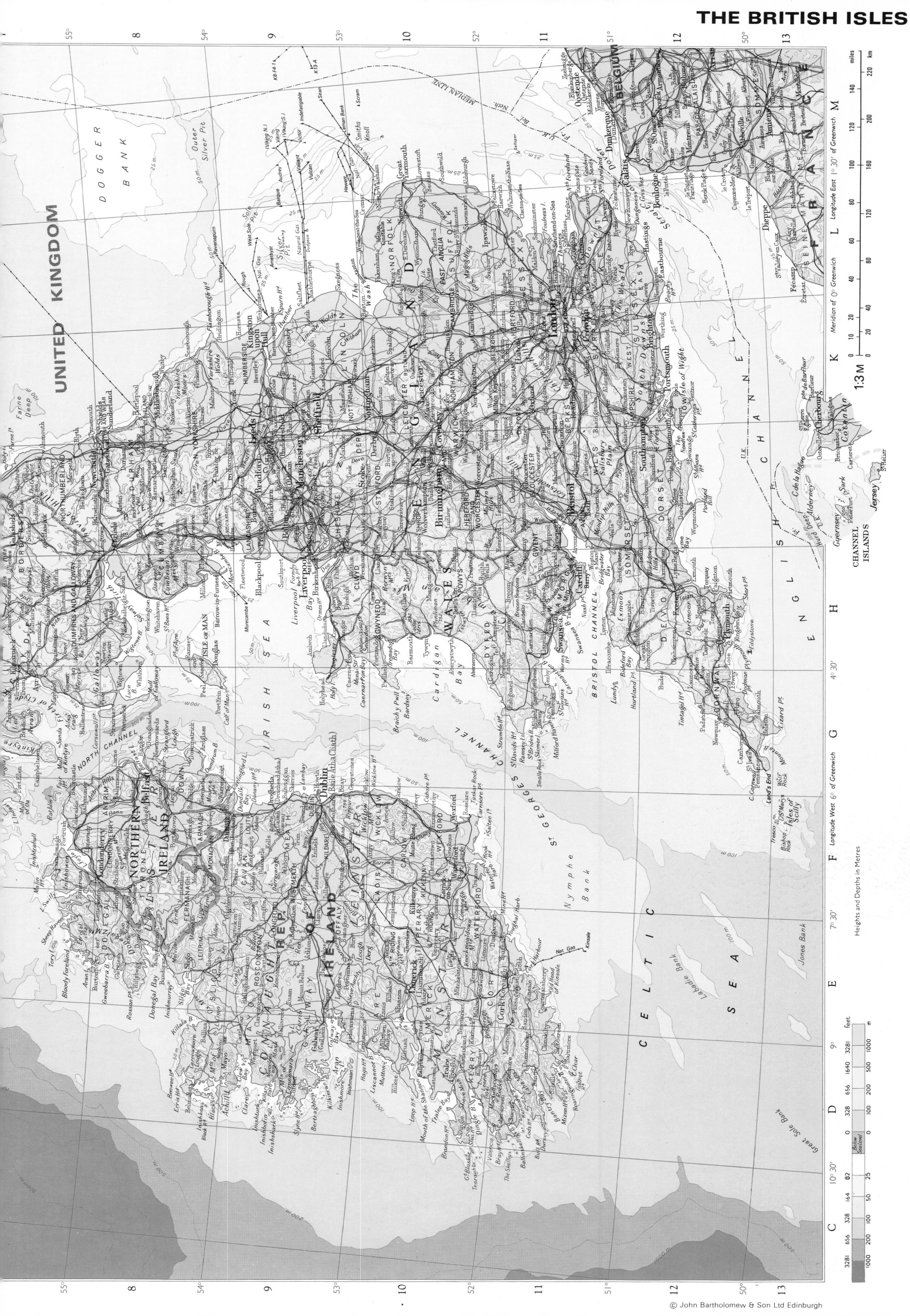
UNITED KINGDOM
REP. OF IRELAND
NORTHERN IRELAND
ENGLAND
WALES
IRISH SEA
CELTIC SEA
ENGLISH CHANNEL
BRISTOL CHANNEL
ST GEORGE'S CHANNEL
NORTH CHANNEL
DOGGER BANK
FRANCE
BELGIUM
CHANNEL ISLANDS
ISLE OF MAN
London
Dublin
Belfast
Cork
Cardiff
Birmingham
Manchester
Liverpool
Leeds
Sheffield
Bristol
Plymouth
Southampton
Newcastle
1:3M
Longitude East 1° 30' of Greenwich
Meridian of 0° Greenwich
Longitude West 6° of Greenwich
Heights and Depths in Metres

A
B
C
D
5°
4°
53°
52°
51°
1
2
3
4
5
6
7
To Dublin & Dun Laoghaire
To Rosslare
To Cork
ANGLESEY
GWYNEDD
CLWYD
MERSEYSIDE
CHESHIRE
SHROPSHIRE
WALES
POWYS
DYFED
HEREFORD AND WORCESTER
WEST GLAMORGAN
MID GLAMORGAN
SOUTH GLAMORGAN
GWENT
AVON
SOMERSET
DEVON
CORNWALL
DORSET
CARDIGAN BAY
Caernarfon Bay
Tremadoc Bay
St Brides Bay
Carmarthen Bay
BRISTOL CHANNEL
Bridgwater Bay
Bideford Bay
Bude Bay
Lyme Bay
Exmoor Forest
Dartmoor Forest
Bodmin Moor
Manchester
Salford
Liverpool
Birkenhead
Chester
Wrexham
Holyhead
Bangor
Caernarfon
Aberystwyth
Cardigan
Fishguard (Abergwaun)
Carmarthen (Caerfyrddin)
Swansea (Abertawe)
Newport (Casnewydd)
CARDIFF (Caerdydd)
Bristol
Shrewsbury
Telford
Wolverhampton
Hereford
Brecon (Aberhonddu)
Weston super-mare
Barnstaple
Taunton
Exeter
Plymouth
Torquay
Truro
Dorchester
Weymouth
Lundy
Bill of Portland
Longitude West 3° of Greenwich
CONIC PROJECTION
metres
feet
609
2000
304
1000
152
500
76
250
0
0
Below Sea Level

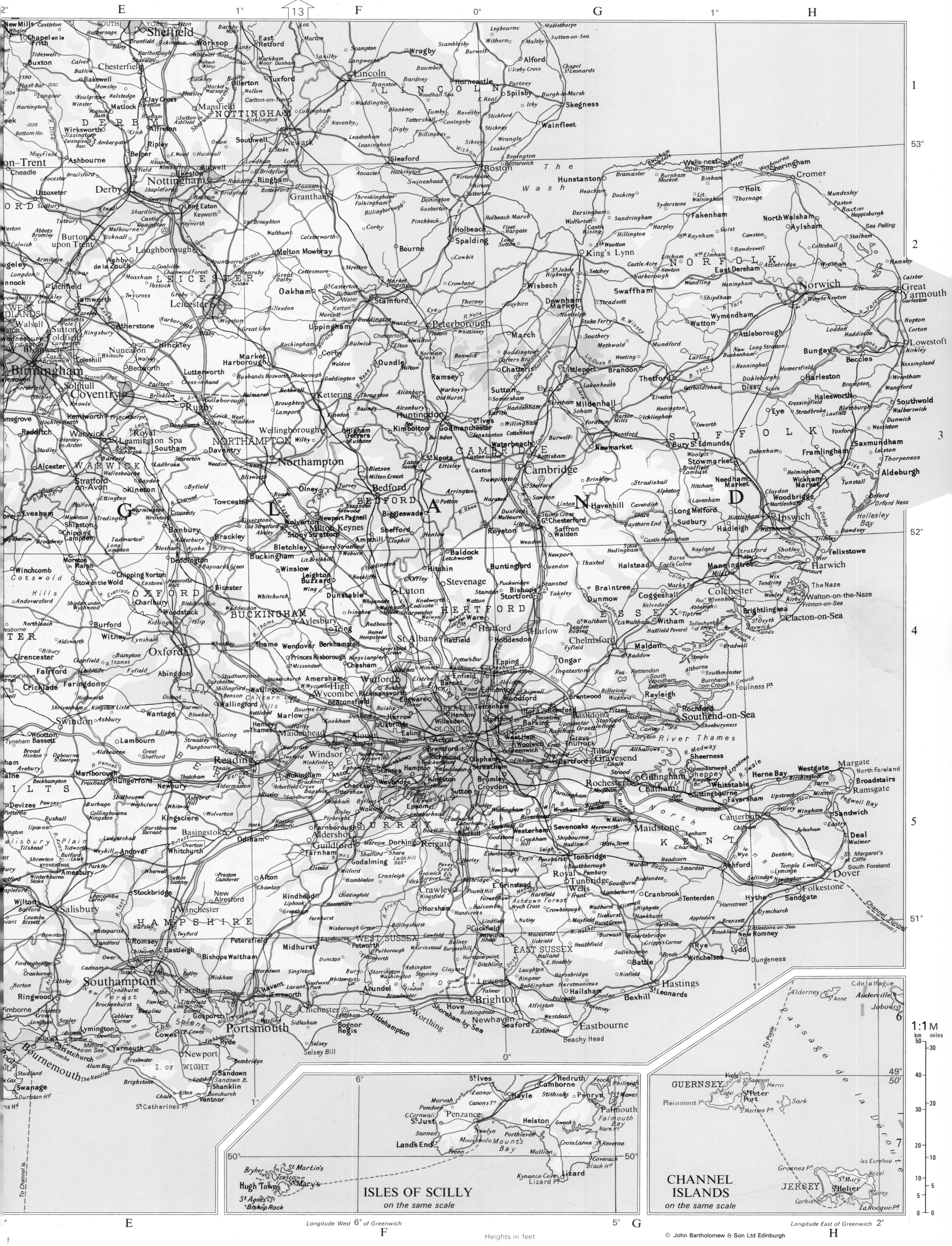

ISLES OF SCILLY
on the same scale

CHANNEL ISLANDS
on the same scale

GUERNSEY

JERSEY

1:1 M

Heights in feet

Longitude West 6° of Greenwich

Longitude East of Greenwich 2°

© John Bartholomew & Son Ltd Edinburgh

THAMES ESTUARY

GREATER LONDON

LONDON

THAMES

E S S E X

K E N T

S U R R E Y

B E R K S H I R E

BUCKINGHAM

H E R T F O R D

Southend-on-Sea · Chelmsford · Brentwood · Basildon · Billericay · Rayleigh · South Benfleet · Canvey Island · Tilbury · Gravesend · Northfleet · Dartford · Swanley · Bexley · Bromley · Greenwich · Newham · Barking · Redbridge · Havering · Romford · Dagenham · Ilford · Chigwell · Epping · Harlow · Cheshunt · Hoddesdon · Hertford · Ware · Welwyn Garden City · Hatfield · St. Albans · Potters Bar · Barnet · Borehamwood · Watford · Bushey · Harrow · Hemel Hempstead · Harpenden · Berkhamsted · Chesham · Amersham · High Wycombe · Beaconsfield · Rickmansworth · Chalfont St. Giles · Slough · Maidenhead · Windsor · Bracknell · Camberley · Farnborough · Aldershot · Woking · Guildford · Dorking · Leatherhead · Ashtead · Epsom · Ewell · Banstead · Reigate · Sevenoaks · Tonbridge · Maidstone · Sittingbourne · Gillingham · Chatham · Rochester

Westminster · Kensington and Chelsea · Camden · Islington · Hackney · Haringey · Enfield · Tower Hamlets · Southwark · Lambeth · Wandsworth · Hammersmith · Ealing · Hillingdon · Hounslow · Richmond upon Thames · Kingston upon Thames · Merton · Sutton · Croydon · Lewisham · Catford · Eltham · Woolwich

Staines · Egham · Chertsey · Sunbury · Walton on Thames · Weybridge · Esher · Feltham · Ashford · London Heathrow

© Times Books Ltd

1:300 000

0 5 10 15 km

0 5 10 miles

51° 45'   51° 30'   51° 15'

0° 45'   0° 30'   0° 15'   0° 00'   0° 15'   0° 30'

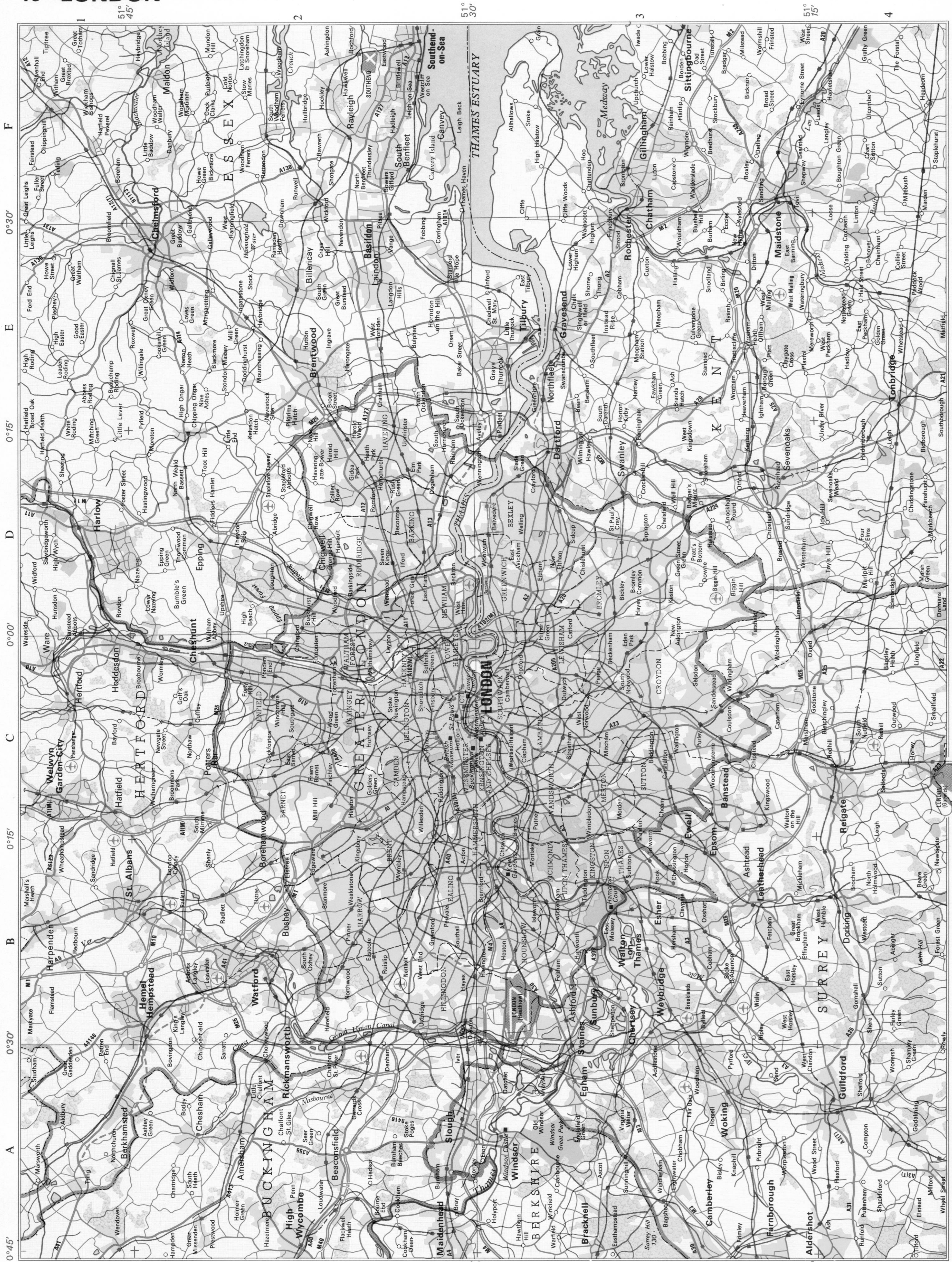

A 3°00' B 2°45' C 2°30' D 2°15' E

IRISH SEA

Southport
Marshside
Birkdale
Churchtown
Mere Brow
Sollom
Crosston
Eccleston
Euxton
White Coppice
Chorley
Anglezarke Moor
Tutton Moor
Edenfield
Whitworth
Summit
Wardle
M82

LANCASHIRE

Formby
Ormskirk
Skelmersdale
Wigan
Chorley
Limbrick
Belmont
Winter Hill
Rivington
Horwich
Red Rock
Bolton
Bury
Rochdale
Littleborough
Hollingworth Lake
GREATER MANCHESTER

Liverpool
LIVERPOOL BAY
Crosby
Bootle
Wallasey
Birkenhead
MERSEYSIDE
St. Helens
Kirkby
Huyton
Prescot
Newton-le-Willows
Haydock
Leigh
Worsley
Salford
MANCHESTER
Ashton-under-Lyne
Stalybridge
Droylsden
Denton
Hyde
Stockport

Widnes
Runcorn
Ellesmere Port
Warrington
CHESHIRE
Northwich
Macclesfield
PEAK DISTRICT NATIONAL PARK
Wilmslow
Altrincham
Sale
Cheadle
Knutsford

R. MERSEY

CLWYD
DEE

53°30'
53°15'
3°30'

A 3°00' B 2°45' C 2°30' D 2°15' E

A 2°15' B 2°00' C 1°45' D 1°30' E 1°15'

STAFFORD
Cannock
Lichfield
Brownhills
Walsall
Tamworth
Atherstone
LEICESTER
Hinckley
Nuneaton
Bedworth
Wolverhampton
Willenhall
Wednesbury
Sutton Coldfield
West Bromwich
Dudley
Smethwick
WEST MIDLANDS
BIRMINGHAM
Solihull
Coventry
Kenilworth
Royal Leamington Spa
WARWICK
Kidderminster
Stourbridge
Halesowen
Bromsgrove
Redditch
WORCESTER AND HEREFORD
SALOP
Rugby

52°30'
52°15'

A 2°15' B 2°00' C 1°45' D 1°30' E 1°15'

0 5 10 15 km
0 5 10 miles
1:300 000
© Times Books Ltd

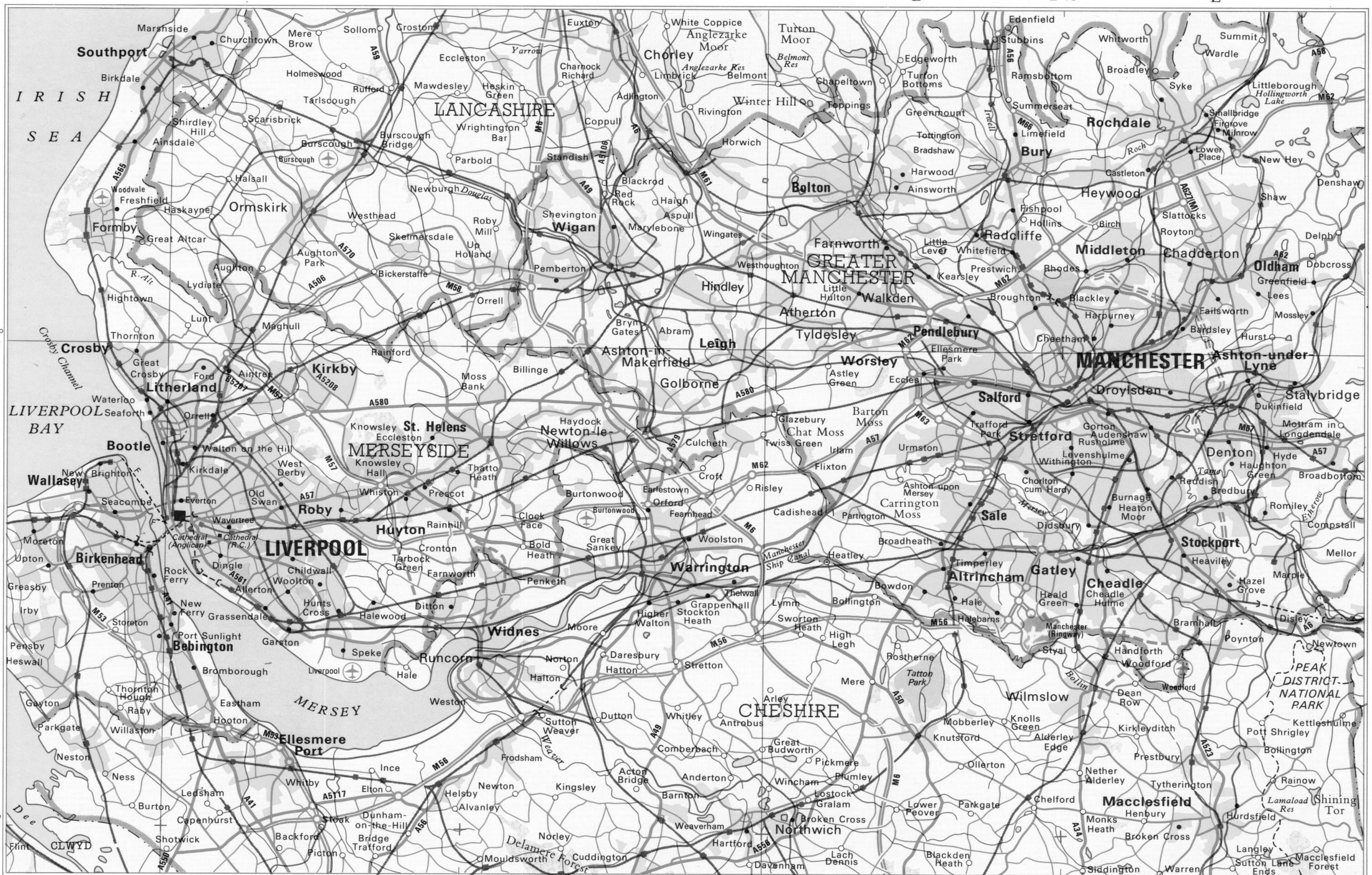

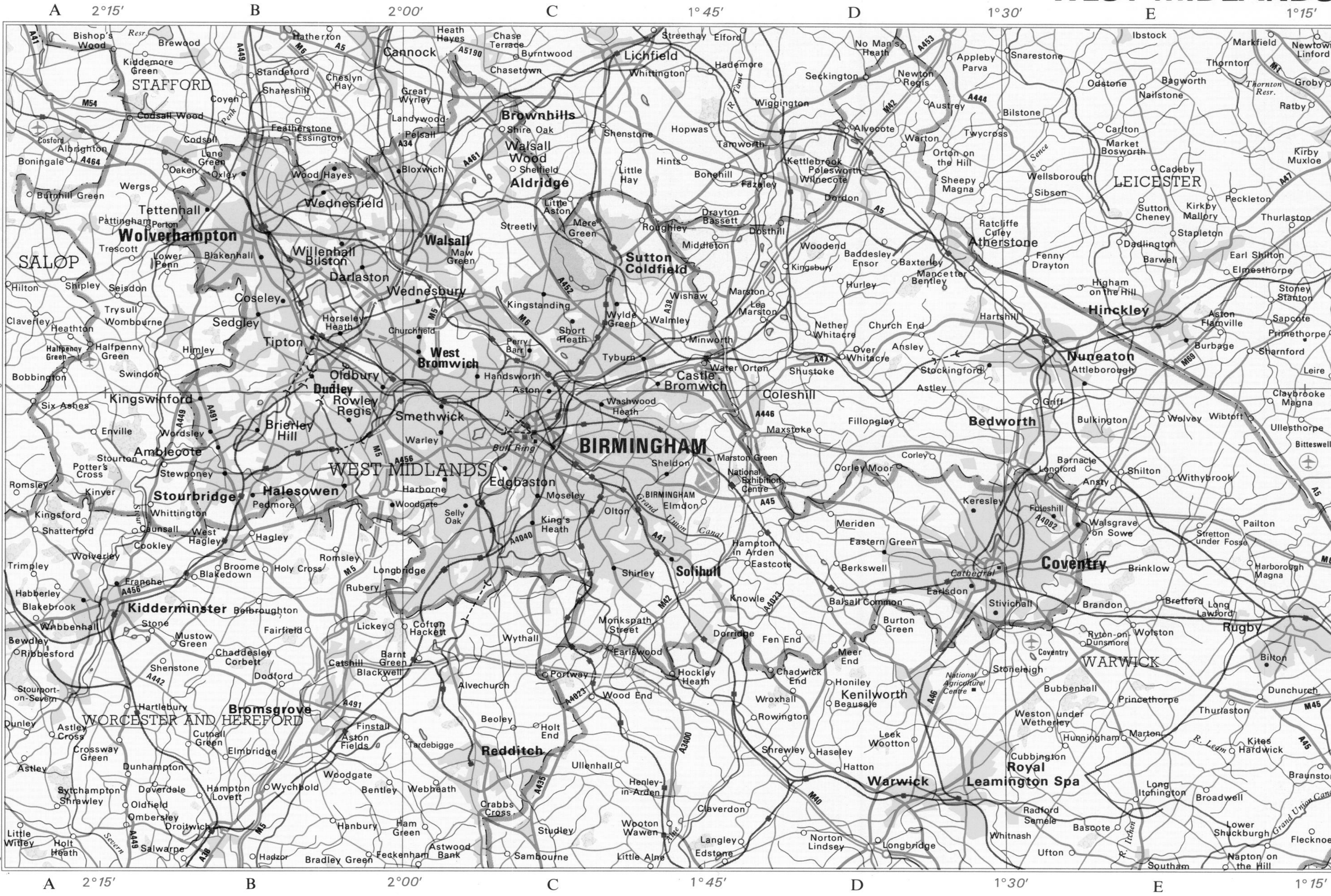

A   7°   B   6°   C   5°   D   4°   E

Major regions and features:

TAYSIDE

CENTRAL

STRATHCLYDE

SCOTLAND

DUMFRIES AN...

NORTHERN IRELAND

LONDONDERRY

ANTRIM

TYRONE

DOWN

ARMAGH

MONAGHAN

CAVAN

REP. OF IRELAND

LOUTH

MEATH

NORTH CHANNEL

IRISH SEA

ISLE OF MAN

JURA

ISLAY

ARRAN

KINTYRE

Firth of Clyde

Firth of Lorn

Sound of Jura

Belfast Lough

Lough Neagh

Strangford L.

Dundrum Bay

Dundalk Bay

Mourne Mountains

Lough Foyle

Lough Swilly

Selected towns/cities:

Glasgow, Paisley, Motherwell, Hamilton, Kilmarnock, Ayr, Stirling, Falkirk, Dumbarton, Greenock, Port Glasgow, Irvine, Troon, Prestwick, Cumnock, Maybole, Girvan, Stranraer, Newton Stewart, Wigtown, Whithorn, Kirkcudbright, Castle Douglas, Dalbeattie, Dumfries, Thornhill, Moniaive, Sanquhar, Biggar, Lanark

Londonderry, Coleraine, Limavady, Strabane, Omagh, Cookstown, Magherafelt, Ballymena, Larne, Antrim, Carrickfergus, Belfast, Lisburn, Bangor, Newtownards, Donaghadee, Downpatrick, Newcastle, Newry, Armagh, Portadown, Lurgan, Craigavon, Banbridge, Dungannon, Enniskillen, Monaghan, Cavan, Dundalk, Drogheda, Dublin (Baile Átha Cliath), Dún Laoghaire, Mullingar, Trim, Oban, Campbeltown

Douglas, Ramsey, Peel, Castletown (Isle of Man)

Snaefell 2034

CONIC PROJECTION

NORTH SEA
FIRTH OF FORTH
FIFE
LOTHIAN
BORDERS
GALLOWAY
NORTHUMBERLAND
TYNE AND WEAR
DURHAM
CUMBRIA
CLEVELAND
NORTH YORKSHIRE
ENGLAND
LANCASHIRE
WEST YORKS
GREATER MANCHESTER
MERSEYSIDE
SOUTH YORKSHIRE
HUMBERSIDE
LINCOLNSHIRE
DERBY
NOTTINGHAM
CHESHIRE
Dundee
Arbroath
Carnoustie
St. Andrews
Edinburgh
Leith
Dunbar
Haddington
Kirkcaldy
Berwick-upon-Tweed
Lindisfarne or Holy I.
Farne Is
Peebles
Galashiels
Melrose
Kelso
Coldstream
Jedburgh
Hawick
Langholm
Lockerbie
Carlisle
Newcastle upon Tyne
Tynemouth
S. Shields
Gateshead
Sunderland
Hexham
Durham
Hartlepool
Redcar
Middlesbrough
Stockton
Darlington
Whitby
Scarborough
Filey
Bridlington
Flamborough Hd
York
Leeds
Bradford
Halifax
Huddersfield
Wakefield
Kingston upon Hull
Grimsby
Cleethorpes
Spurn Head
Doncaster
Barnsley
Sheffield
Rotherham
Manchester
Salford
Stockport
Oldham
Rochdale
Bolton
Wigan
Blackburn
Preston
Blackpool
Lancaster
Morecambe
Barrow-in-Furness
Kendal
Windermere
Penrith
Keswick
Southport
Liverpool
Birkenhead
Warrington
St. Helens
Harrogate
Ripon
Richmond
Thirsk
Malton
Pickering
Beverley
Selby
Goole
Scunthorpe
Gainsborough
Lincoln
River Humber
Cleveland Hills
Holderness
1:1 M
km miles
56°
55°
54°
3°
2°
1°
0°
F
G
H
J
1
2
3
4
5
6
9
Meridian of 0° Greenwich
Heights in feet

14 IRELAND

ATLANTIC OCEAN

NORTHERN IRELAND

REP. OF IRELAND (ÉIRE)

ULSTER · CONNAUGHT · LEINSTER · MUNSTER

DONEGAL · LONDONDERRY · ANTRIM · TYRONE · FERMANAGH · DOWN · ARMAGH · MONAGHAN · CAVAN · LEITRIM · SLIGO · MAYO · ROSCOMMON · LONGFORD · WESTMEATH · MEATH · LOUTH · DUBLIN · KILDARE · OFFALY · GALWAY · CLARE · LAOIS · CARLOW · WICKLOW · WEXFORD · KILKENNY · TIPPERARY · LIMERICK · KERRY · CORK · WATERFORD

Belfast · Dublin (Baile Átha Cliath) · Londonderry (Derry) · Cork (Corcaigh) · Limerick (Luimneach) · Galway (Gaillimh) · Waterford (Port Láirge) · Sligo · Wexford · Kilkenny · Athlone

IRISH SEA · NORTH CHANNEL · ST GEORGE'S CHANNEL · Donegal Bay · Galway Bay · Dingle Bay · Bantry Bay · Clew Bay · Dundalk Bay

ISLAY · ARRAN · KINTYRE · Mull of Kintyre · Firth of Clyde · Rathlin I. · Achill Island · Aran Islands · Valencia I.

to Douglas · to Holyhead · to Fishguard · to Pembroke Dock · to Swansea

Heights and Depths in metres · CONIC PROJECTION · 1:1.5 M · Longitude West 8° of Greenwich

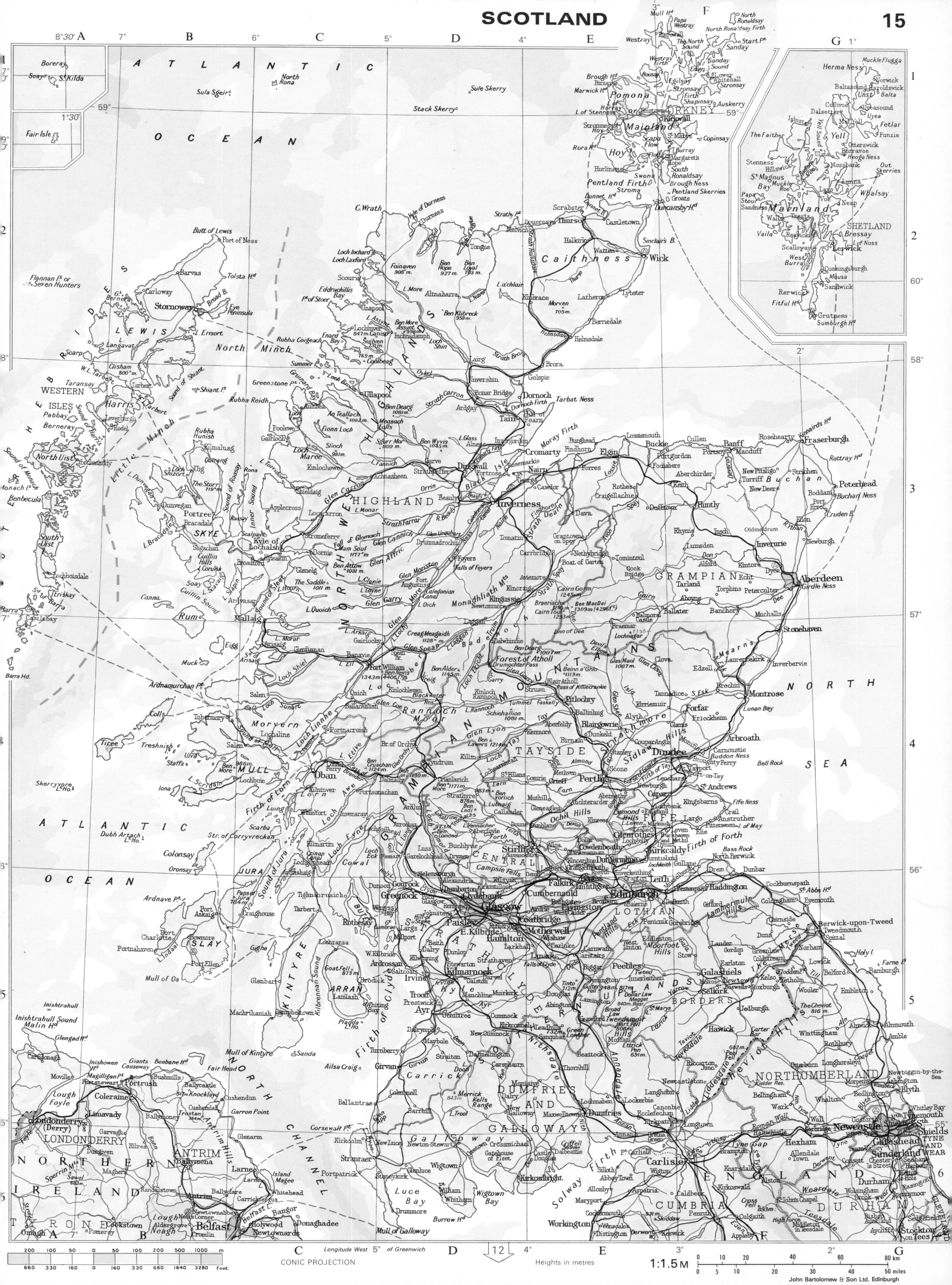
ATLANTIC OCEAN
NORTH SEA
St. Kilda
Fair Isle
North Rona
Sula Sgeir
Sule Skerry
Stack Skerry
ORKNEY
Mainland
Hoy
Pomona
Kirkwall
Westray
Sanday
Stronsay
Pentland Firth
SHETLAND
Lerwick
Yell
Unst
Fetlar
Whalsay
Fair Isle
Sumburgh Hd
Butt of Lewis
LEWIS
Stornoway
Harris
North Uist
Benbecula
South Uist
Barra
WESTERN ISLES
HEBRIDES
North Minch
Little Minch
SKYE
Portree
Rum
Canna
Eigg
Muck
Coll
Tiree
MULL
Iona
Colonsay
JURA
ISLAY
KINTYRE
ARRAN
Caithness
Thurso
Wick
C. Wrath
Durness
Tongue
Ben Hope 927m.
Ben Loyal 763m.
Foinaven 908m.
Ben Klibreck 959m.
Ullapool
HIGHLAND
NORTH WEST HIGHLANDS
Dornoch
Tain
Invergordon
Dingwall
Cromarty
Moray Firth
Inverness
Nairn
Forres
Elgin
Buckie
Banff
Fraserburgh
Peterhead
Huntly
Inverurie
Aberdeen
GRAMPIAN
Cairn Gorm 1245m.
Ben MacDui 1309m (4296 f.)
Braeriach
Stonehaven
Montrose
Arbroath
Forfar
Dundee
TAYSIDE
Perth
Pitlochry
Blairgowrie
Forest of Atholl
GRAMPIAN MOUNTAINS
Fort William
Ben Nevis 1343m. (4406 f.)
Mallaig
Kyle of Lochalsh
Glen More
Loch Ness
Caledonian Canal
Kingussie
Aviemore
Rannoch Moor
Oban
Firth of Lorn
Loch Linnhe
Loch Awe
Loch Fyne
Loch Lomond
Stirling
CENTRAL
FIFE
St. Andrews
Kirkcaldy
Glenrothes
Firth of Forth
Edinburgh
LOTHIAN
Leith
Dunbar
Haddington
Berwick-upon-Tweed
Falkirk
Cumbernauld
Glasgow
Clydebank
Paisley
Greenock
Coatbridge
Motherwell
Hamilton
E. Kilbride
STRATHCLYDE
Kilmarnock
Irvine
Ardrossan
Ayr
Firth of Clyde
Girvan
Carrick
SOUTHERN UPLANDS
BORDERS
Galashiels
Peebles
Selkirk
Hawick
Jedburgh
Kelso
Cheviot Hills
The Cheviot 816m.
DUMFRIES AND GALLOWAY
Dumfries
Stranraer
Wigtown
Kirkcudbright
Solway Firth
Mull of Galloway
Carlisle
CUMBRIA
Workington
NORTHUMBERLAND
Newcastle
Gateshead
Sunderland
TYNE AND WEAR
Durham
DURHAM
ENGLAND
Hexham
Blyth
NORTH CHANNEL
NORTHERN IRELAND
LONDONDERRY
ANTRIM
Londonderry (Derry)
Coleraine
Portrush
Ballymena
Larne
Antrim
Belfast
Bangor
Lough Neagh
Lough Foyle
Malin Hd.
Mull of Kintyre
Longitude West 5° of Greenwich
CONIC PROJECTION
Heights in metres
1:1.5M
John Bartholomew & Son Ltd. Edinburgh

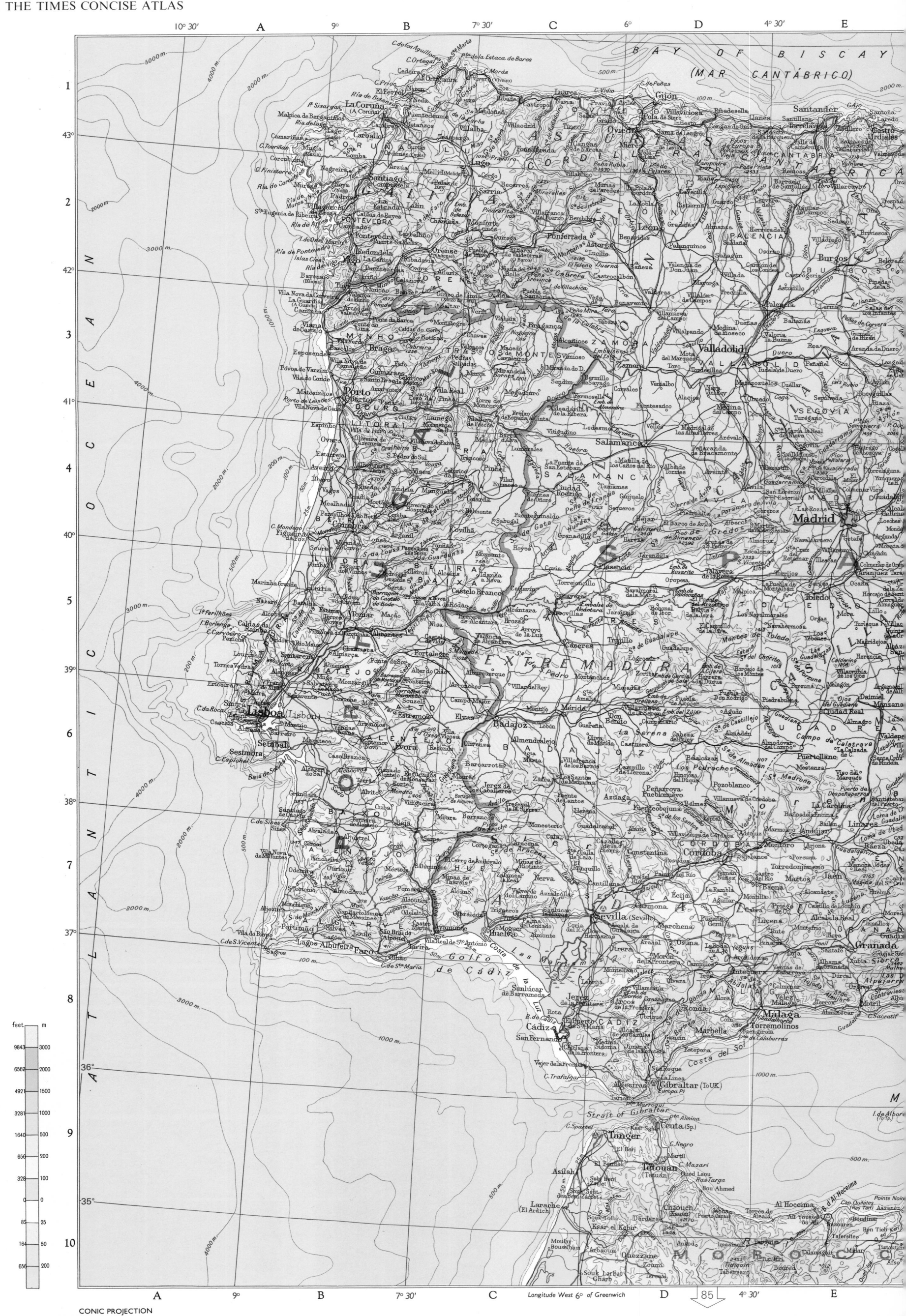
BAY OF BISCAY
(MAR CANTÁBRICO)
ATLANTIC OCEAN
CORDILLERA CANTÁBRICA
ASTURIAS
GALICIA
LEÓN
PORTUGAL
SPAIN
EXTREMADURA
ANDALUCÍA
CASTILLA LA NUEVA
MOROCCO
Golfo de Cádiz
Strait of Gibraltar
Costa del Sol
Costa de la Luz
Sierra Morena
Sierra de Gredos
Sierra de Guadarrama
Montes de Toledo
La Coruña
Santiago de Compostela
Lugo
Oviedo
Gijón
Santander
Burgos
Valladolid
Salamanca
Madrid
Toledo
Porto
Coimbra
Lisboa (Lisbon)
Setúbal
Évora
Badajoz
Mérida
Cáceres
Sevilla (Seville)
Córdoba
Granada
Málaga
Cádiz
Huelva
Faro
Gibraltar (To UK)
Tanger
Ceuta (Sp.)
Tetouan
Larache
Al Hoceima
C. Finisterre
C. de S. Vicente
C. Trafalgar
Longitude West 6° of Greenwich
85

GOLFE DE GASCOGNE (GOLFO DE GASCUÑA)
FRANCE
GOLFE DU LION
Toulouse
Montpellier
Marseille
Narbonne
Perpignan
ANDORRA
Bilbao
San Sebastián
Pamplona
Logroño
Zaragoza
Lérida
Gerona
Barcelona
Tarragona
Tortosa
Castellón de la Plana
Valencia
Golfo de Valencia
Alicante
Murcia
Cartagena
Albacete
Cuenca
Teruel
Almería
MALLORCA (MAJORCA)
Palma
MENORCA (MINORCA)
Mahón
Ciudadela
IBIZA (IVIZA)
Formentera
ISLAS BALEARES
(BALEARIC ISLANDS)
(To Spain)
MEDITERRANEAN SEA
Oran
Mostaganem
Tlemcen
Sidi Bel Abbès
ALGERIA
Longitude East 3° of Greenwich
Meridian of 0° Greenwich
MADRID
1:60 000
CIUDAD UNIVERSITARIA
CHAMARTIN
TETUAN
CHAMBERÍ
SALAMANCA
MONCLOA
Casa de Campo
Puerta del Sol
Parque del Retiro
RETIRO
Atocha
ARGANZUELA
CARABANCHEL
LATINA
VALLECAS
Delicias
1:3 M
km miles
© John Bartholomew & Son Ltd Edinburgh

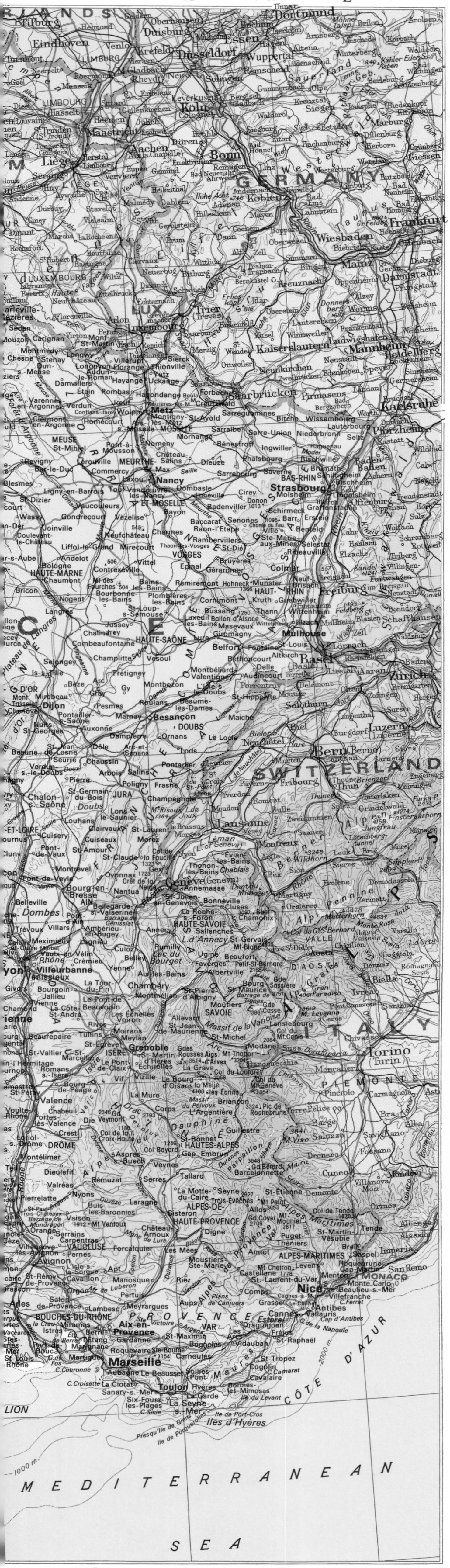

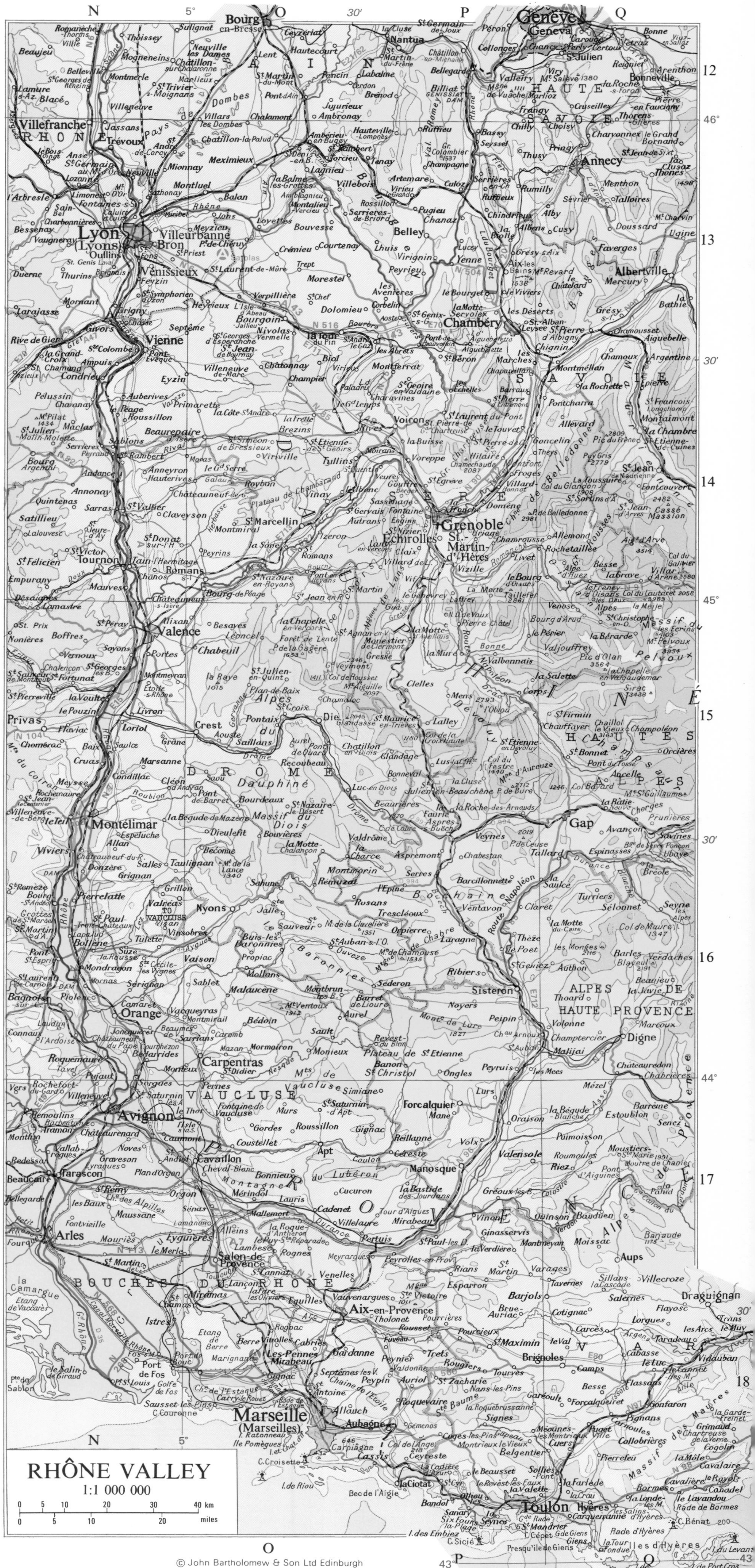

RHÔNE VALLEY

1:1 000 000

0 5 10 20 30 40 km

0 10 20 miles

43

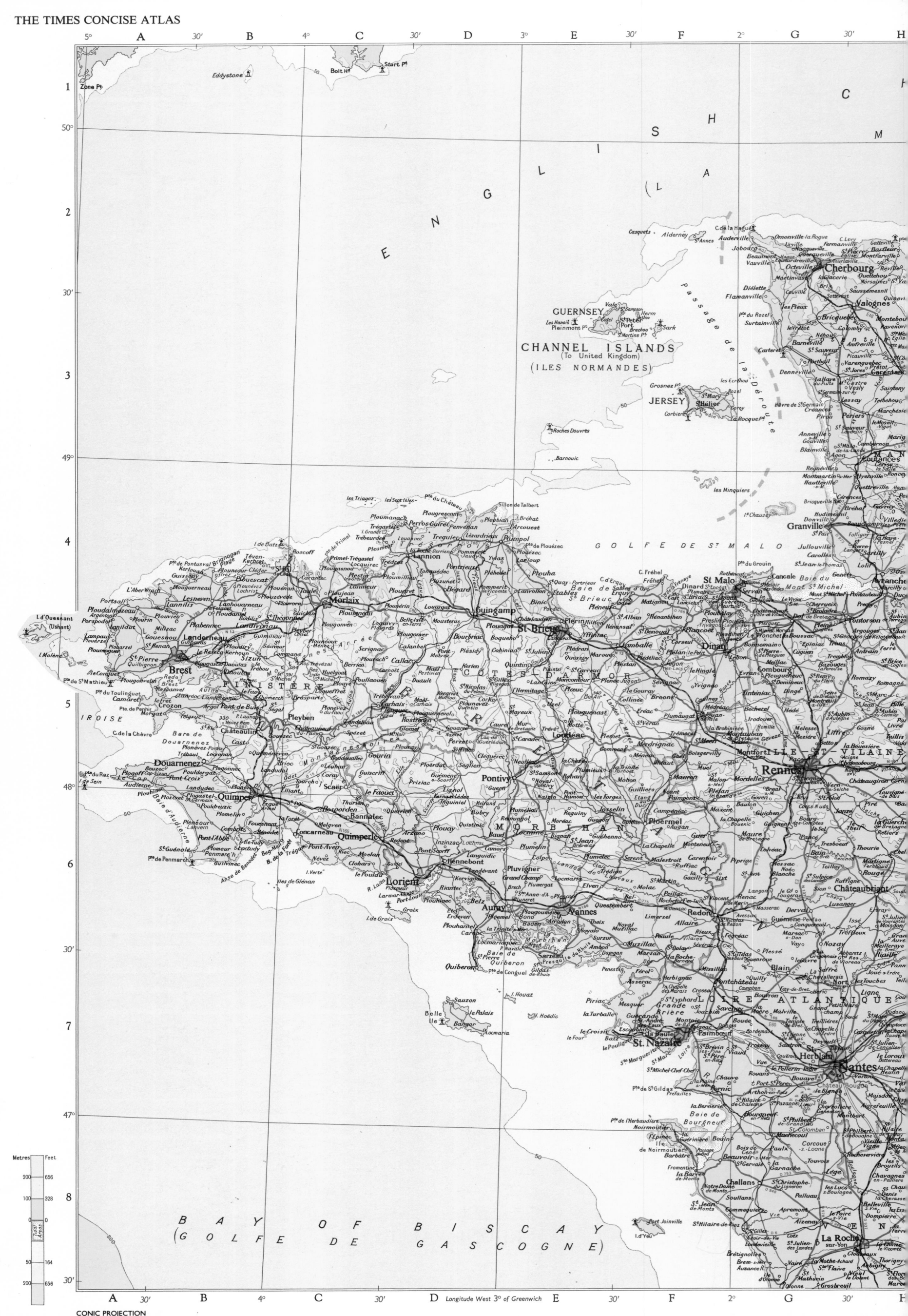

ENGLISH CHANNEL

(LA MANCHE)

CHANNEL ISLANDS
(To United Kingdom)
(ILES NORMANDES)

GUERNSEY

JERSEY

Cherbourg

Valognes

GOLFE DE St MALO

Granville

St Malo

Avranches

Mont St Michel

Dinan

CÔTES-D'OR

Morlaix

Guingamp

St Brieuc

I. d'Ouessant
(Ushant)

Brest

ILLE-ET-VILAINE

Rennes

FINISTÈRE

Châteaulin

Pleyben

Pontivy

BRETAGNE

Douarnenez

Ploërmel

Quimper

Châteaubriant

Quimperlé

MORBIHAN

Concarneau

Redon

Lorient

Vannes

Auray

Quiberon

LOIRE ATLANTIQUE

Belle Ile

St Nazaire

Herblain

Nantes

BAY   OF   BISCAY

(GOLFE   DE   GASCOGNE)

La Roche sur Yon

CONIC PROJECTION

Metres Feet
200 656
100 328
0 0
50 164
200 656

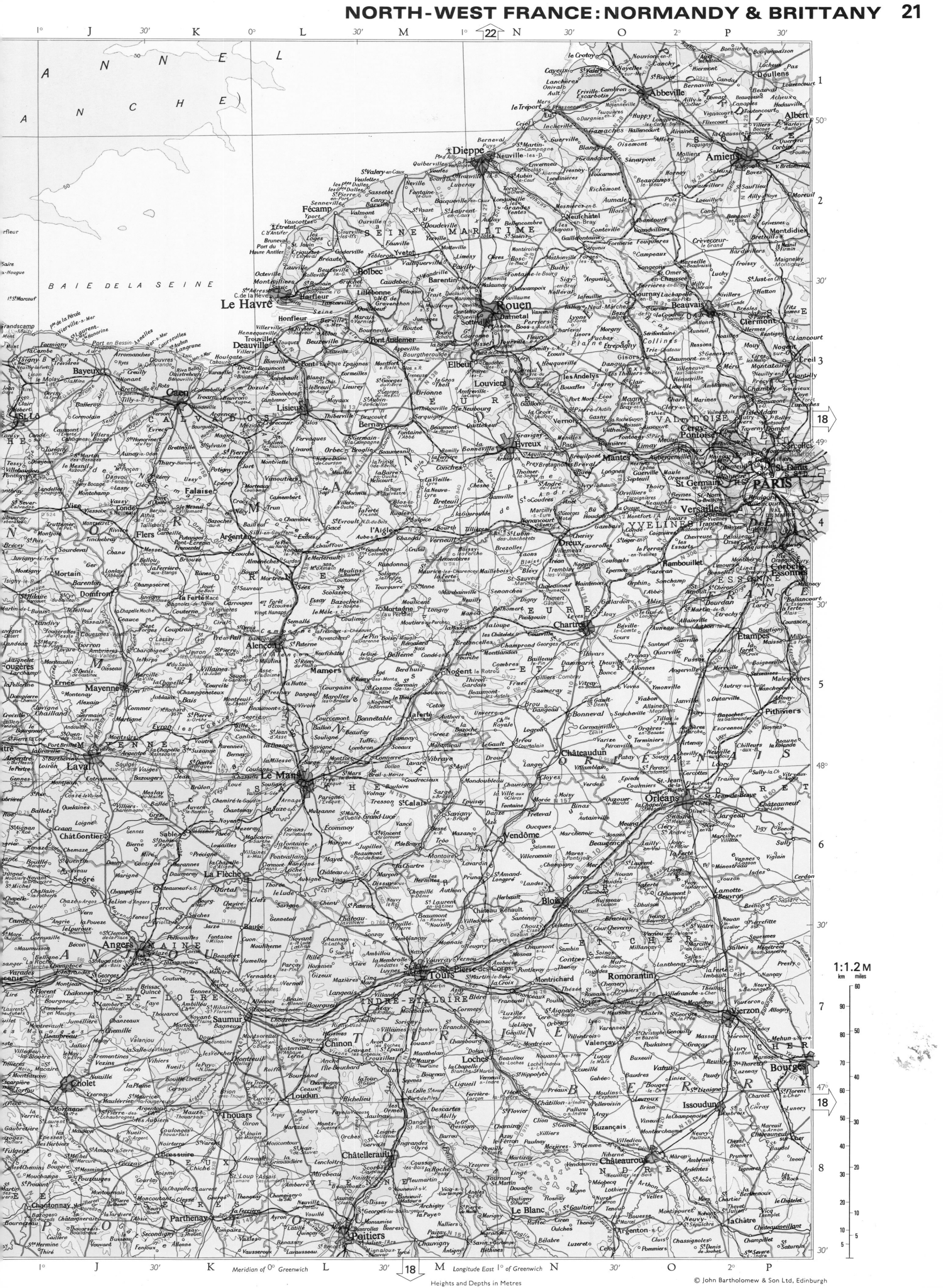

1:1.2 M

© John Bartholomew & Son Ltd, Edinburgh

LA MANCHE
BAIE DE LA SEINE
SEINE MARITIME
CALVADOS
EURE
ORNE
MANCHE
MAYENNE
SARTHE
EURE-ET-LOIR
LOIRET
LOIR-ET-CHER
INDRE-ET-LOIRE
MAINE-ET-LOIRE
DEUX-SÈVRES
VIENNE
INDRE
CHER
VAL D'OISE
YVELINES
ESSONNE
SOMME
OISE
Le Havre
Rouen
Dieppe
Fécamp
Amiens
Abbeville
Beauvais
Caen
Bayeux
Lisieux
Évreux
Chartres
Dreux
PARIS
Versailles
Alençon
Le Mans
Laval
Angers
Tours
Orléans
Blois
Vendôme
Saumur
Cholet
Poitiers
Châtellerault
Châteauroux
Bourges
Vierzon
Issoudun
Romorantin
Châteaudun
Étampes
Rambouillet
Meridian of 0° Greenwich
Longitude East 1° of Greenwich
km miles
Heights and Depths in Metres

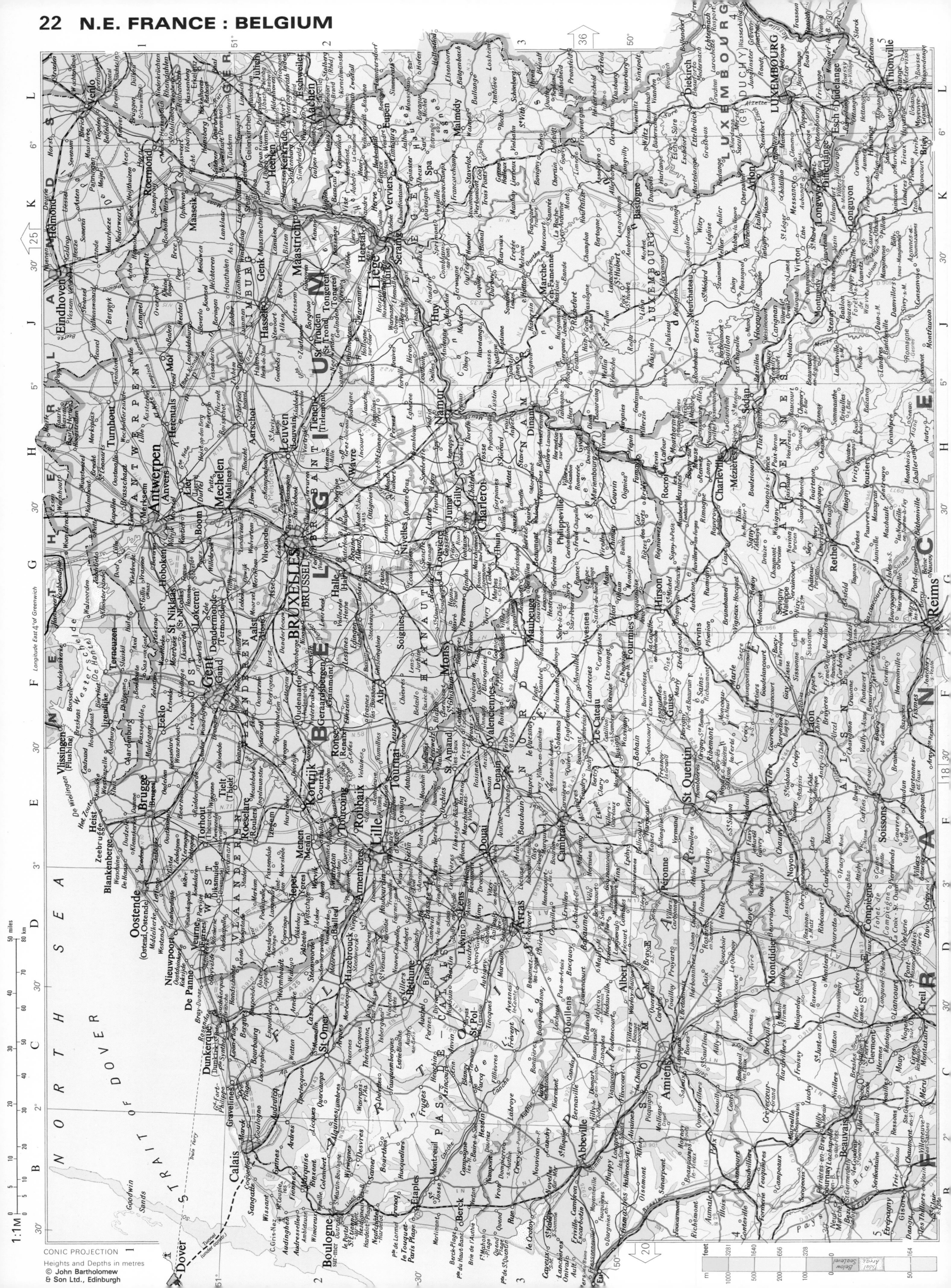

CONIC PROJECTION
Heights and Depths in metres

1:1M

PARIS

OISE
SEINE-ET-MARNE
MARNE
HAUTS-DE-SEINE
VAL-D'OISE
YVELINES
ESSONNE
EURE-ET-LOIR

Meaux
Melun
Mantes-la-Jolie
Versailles
Rambouillet
Corbeil-Essonnes
Villeneuve-St-Georges
St-Germain-en-Laye
Aéroport Charles de Gaulle
Orly

1:300 000

0   5   10   15 km
0   5   10 miles

© Times Books Ltd

BRUSSELS

Map 1: Amsterdam / The Hague

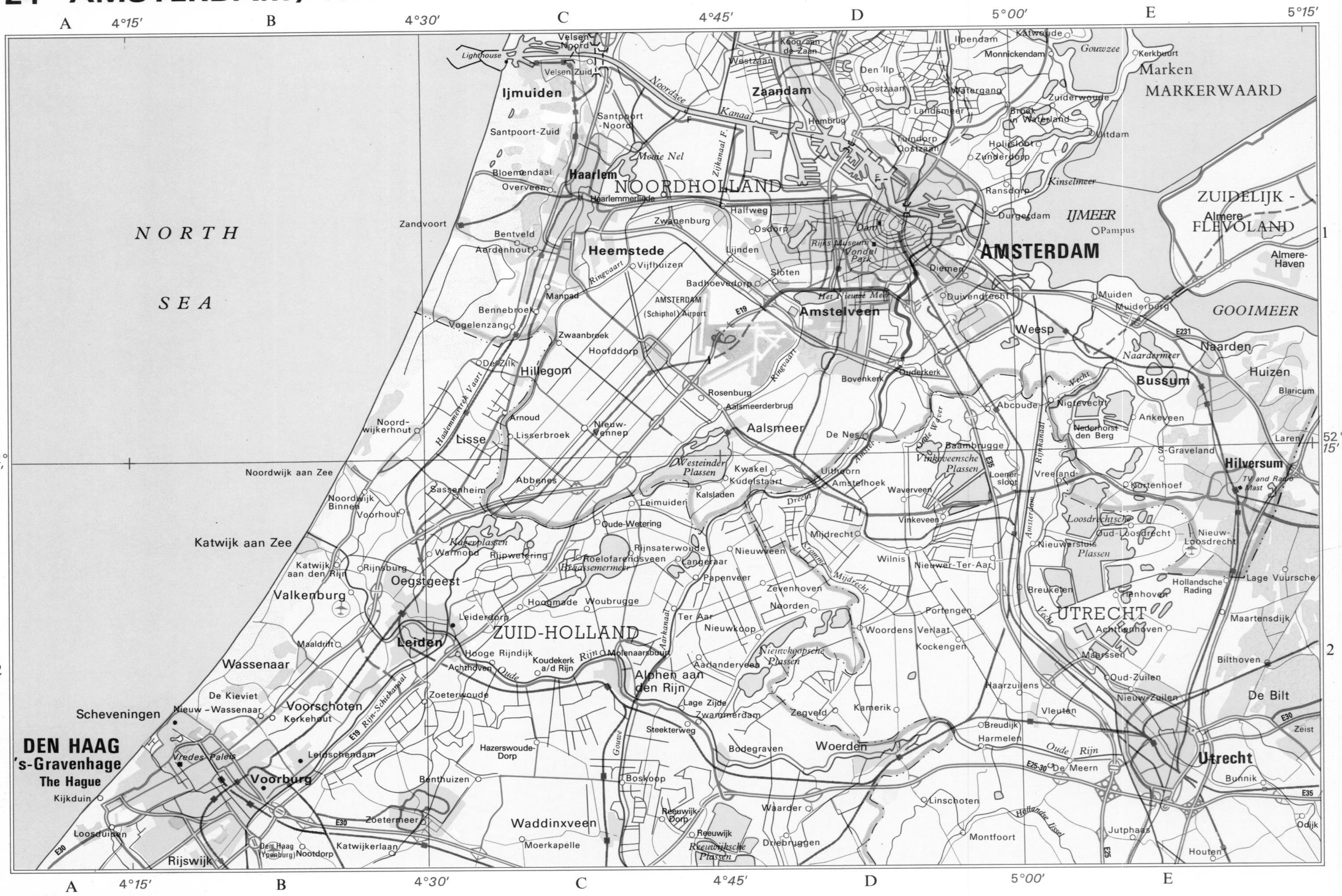

Grid references (top): A 4°15′ B 4°30′ C 4°45′ D 5°00′ E 5°15′

NORTH SEA

NOORDHOLLAND

Ijmuiden · Velsen-Noord · Velsen Zuid · Zaandam · Zandvoort · Haarlem · Heemstede · Bloemendaal · Overveen · Aardenhout · Bentveld · Halfweg · Zwanenburg · Oostzaan · Den Ilp · Watergang · Marken · MARKERWAARD · Monnickendam · Kwadijk · Hembrug · Oostzaan · Landsmeer · Ransdorp · Durgerdam · Kinselmeer

AMSTERDAM

Amstelveen · AMSTERDAM (Schiphol Airport) · Het Nieuwe Meer · Sloten · Osdorp · Badhoevedorp · Diemen · Duivendrecht · Muiden · Muiderberg · Weesp · Naarden · Bussum · Huizen · Blaricum · Ankeveen · Nederhorst den Berg · S-Graveland · Hilversum · TV and Radio Mast · Laren · ZUIDELIJK - Almere FLEVOLAND · Almere-Haven · IJMEER · GOOIMEER · Pampus

ZUID-HOLLAND

Hillegom · Bennebroek · Vogelenzang · De Zilk · Hoofddorp · Aalsmeer · Kudelstaart · Uithoorn · Amstelhoek · Wilnis · Mijdrecht · Vinkeveen · Abcoude · Nigtevecht · Vreeland · Loosdrecht · Nieuw-Loosdrecht · Lage Vuursche · Maartensdijk

Noordwijk aan Zee · Noordwijk Binnen · Voorhout · Lisse · Lisserbroek · Sassenheim · Warmond · Katwijk aan Zee · Katwijk aan den Rijn · Rijnsburg · Oegstgeest · Leiden · Leiderdorp · Hoogmade · Woubrugge · Ter Aar · Nieuwkoop · Noorden · Zevenhoven · Nieuwveen · Woerdens Verlaat · Kockengen · Portengen · Breukelen · UTRECHT · Maarssen · Oud-Zuilen · De Bilt · Nieuw Zuilen · Bilthoven · Zeist

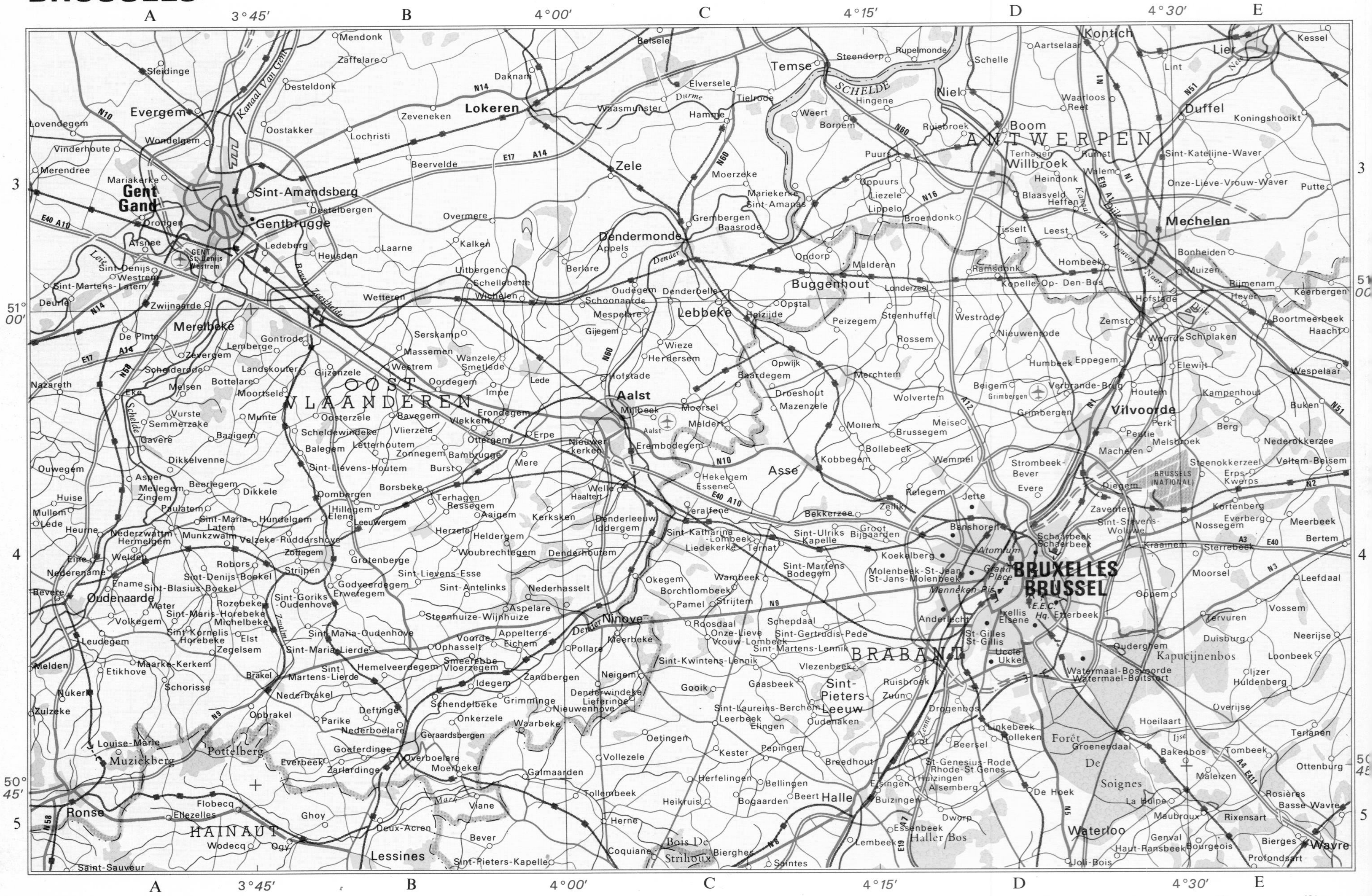

Valkenburg · Wassenaar · Scheveningen · Nieuw-Wassenaar · Voorschoten · Voorburg · **DEN HAAG** 's-Gravenhage The Hague · Kijkduin · Loosduinen · Rijswijk · Leidschendam · Zoetermeer · Benthuizen · Boskoop · Waddinxveen · Moerkapelle · Reeuwijk · Bodegraven · Woerden · Harmelen · De Meern · Montfoort · Linschoten · Jutphaas · Houten · Bunnik · Odijk

Katwijkerlaan · Nootdorp · Zoeterwoude · Hazerswoude Dorp · Steekterweg · Zwammerdam · Alphen aan den Rijn · Koudekerk a/d Rijn · Aarlanderveen · Zegveld · Kamerik · Zegveld

Scale 1:300 000

Map 2: Brussels

Grid references (top): A 3°45′ B 4°00′ C 4°15′ D 4°30′ E

OOST VLAANDEREN

Evergem · Lokeren · Gent/Gand · Sint-Amandsberg · Gentbrugge · Ledeberg · Merelbeke · Destelbergen · Zele · Dendermonde · Lebbeke · Aalst · Ninove · Geraardsbergen · Ronse · Oudenaarde · Zottegem · Brakel · Nazareth · Deinze

ANTWERPEN · Boom · Willebroek · Puurs · Bornem · Mechelen · Duffel · Lier · Kontich · Temse · Niel · Schelle · SCHELDE

BRABANT

BRUXELLES BRUSSEL · Vilvoorde · Zaventem (BRUSSELS NATIONAL) · Anderlecht · Halle · Asse · Wemmel · Jette · Schaerbeek · Grimbergen · Waterloo · Braine · Hoeilaart · Overijse · Tervuren · Wavre

HAINAUT · Lessines · Flobecq

Scale bar: 0 5 10 15 km / 0 5 10 miles

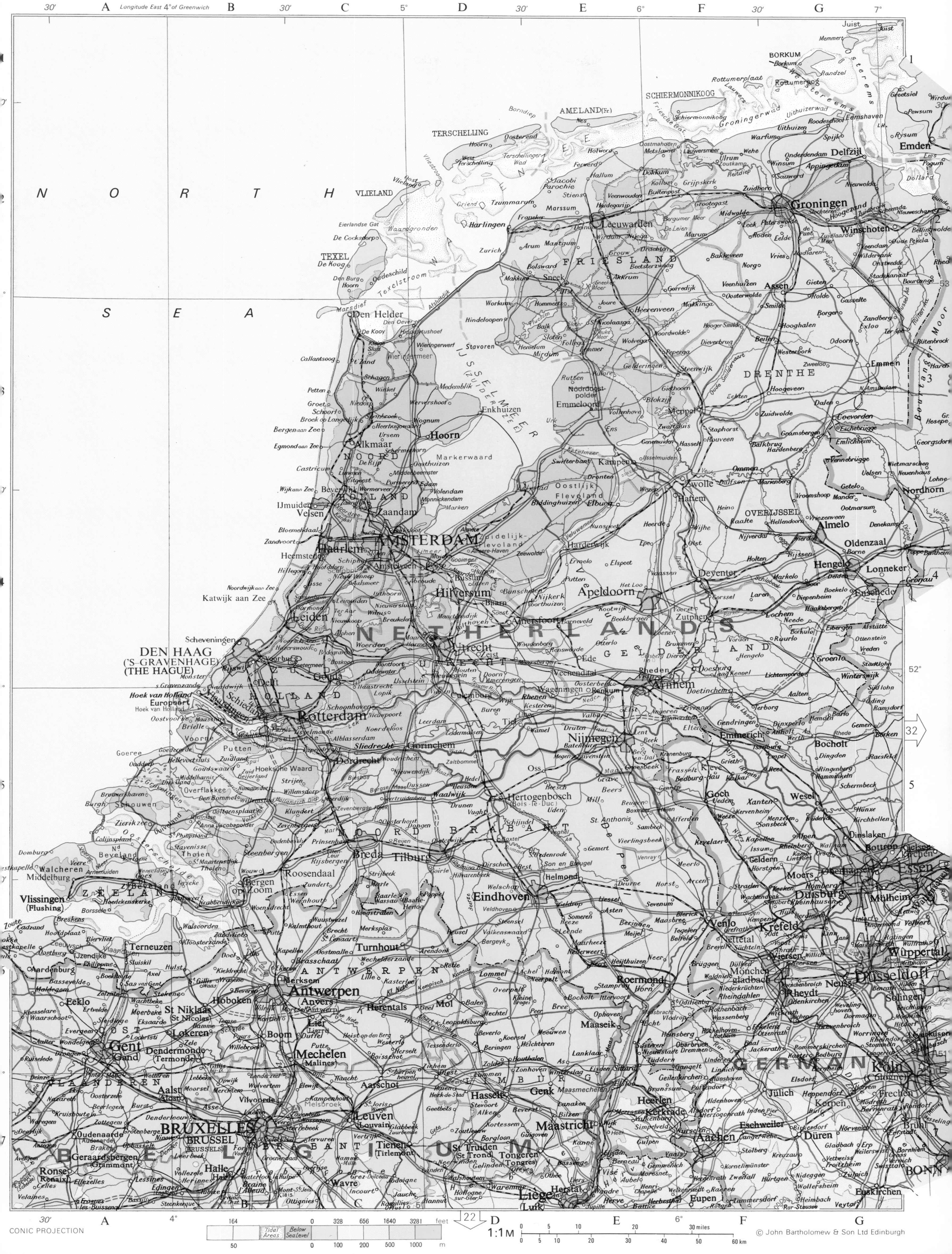

Longitude East 4° of Greenwich

NORTH SEA

NETHERLANDS

Provinces and regions
FRIESLAND · DRENTHE · OVERIJSSEL · GELDERLAND · NOORD HOLLAND · ZUID HOLLAND · UTRECHT · NOORD BRABANT · ZEELAND · LIMBURG

Major cities and towns
AMSTERDAM · Rotterdam · DEN HAAG ('S-GRAVENHAGE) (THE HAGUE) · Utrecht · Haarlem · Leiden · Groningen · Leeuwarden · Assen · Zwolle · Enschede · Hengelo · Almelo · Oldenzaal · Deventer · Apeldoorn · Zutphen · Arnhem · Nijmegen · Hertogenbosch (Bois-le-Duc) · Tilburg · Breda · Eindhoven · Helmond · Venlo · Roermond · Maastricht · Heerlen · Kerkrade · Sittard · Middelburg · Vlissingen (Flushing) · Terneuzen · Dordrecht · Gorinchem · Gouda · Delft · Schiedam · Hoek van Holland · Europoort · Den Helder · Alkmaar · Hoorn · Enkhuizen · Hilversum · Amersfoort · Ede · Hengelo · Winterswijk · Doetinchem · Emmen · Coevorden · Hoogeveen · Meppel · Steenwijk · Heerenveen · Sneek · Harlingen · Franeker · Dokkum · Delfzijl · Winschoten · Stadskanaal

Islands
TEXEL · VLIELAND · TERSCHELLING · AMELAND (Fr) · SCHIERMONNIKOOG · BORKUM · JUIST

Water features
IJSSEL MEER (ZUIDER ZEE) · Markerwaard · Markermeer · Sneeker Meer · Dollard · Waddenzee · Texelstroom · Marsdiep

GERMANY
Emden · Emmerich · Kleve · Goch · Xanten · Wesel · Bocholt · Borken · Essen · Duisburg · Mülheim · Krefeld · Viersen · Mönchengladbach · Neuss · Düsseldorf · Rheydt · Solingen · Wuppertal · Köln · Aachen · Düren · Jülich · Eschweiler · BONN

BELGIUM
Antwerpen (Anvers) · Gent (Gand) · Mechelen (Malines) · Leuven (Louvain) · BRUXELLES (BRUSSEL) · Hasselt · Genk · Turnhout · Herentals · Lier · Roosendaal · Bergen op Zoom · Maaseik · Tongeren (Tongres) · St Truiden (St Trond) · Liège (Luik) · Eupen · Eekloo · Lokeren · St Niklaas · Aalst · VLAANDEREN · OOST · WEST · BRABANT · LIMBURG

CONIC PROJECTION

1:1 M

© John Bartholomew & Son Ltd Edinburgh

Tidal Areas · Below Sea Level

feet 164 · 0 · 328 · 656 · 1640 · 3281
m 50 · 0 · 100 · 200 · 500 · 1000

miles 0 · 5 · 10 · 20 · 30
km 0 · 10 · 20 · 30 · 40 · 50 · 60

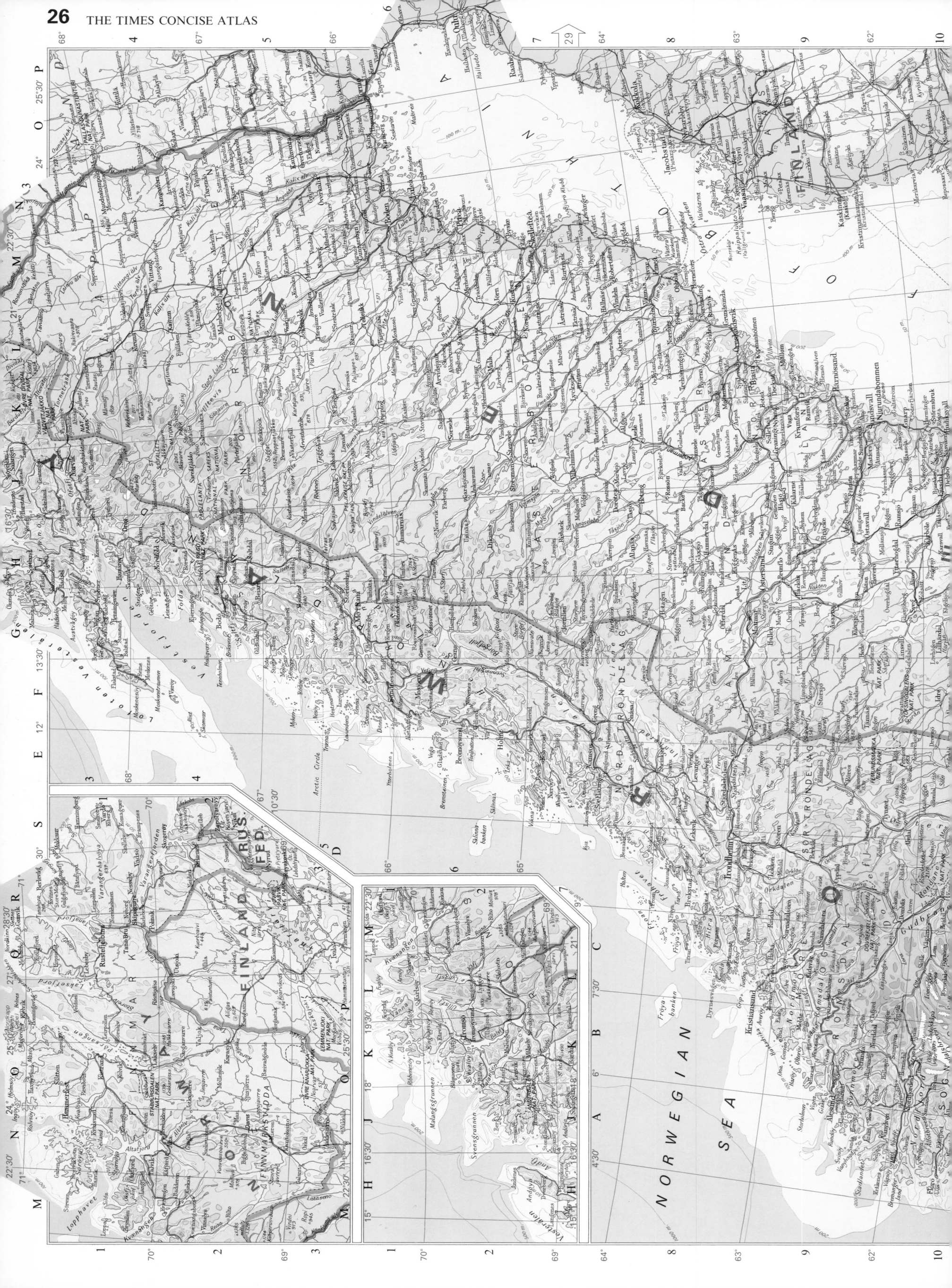
NORWEGIAN SEA
FINLAND
RUS. FED.
FINLAND
29

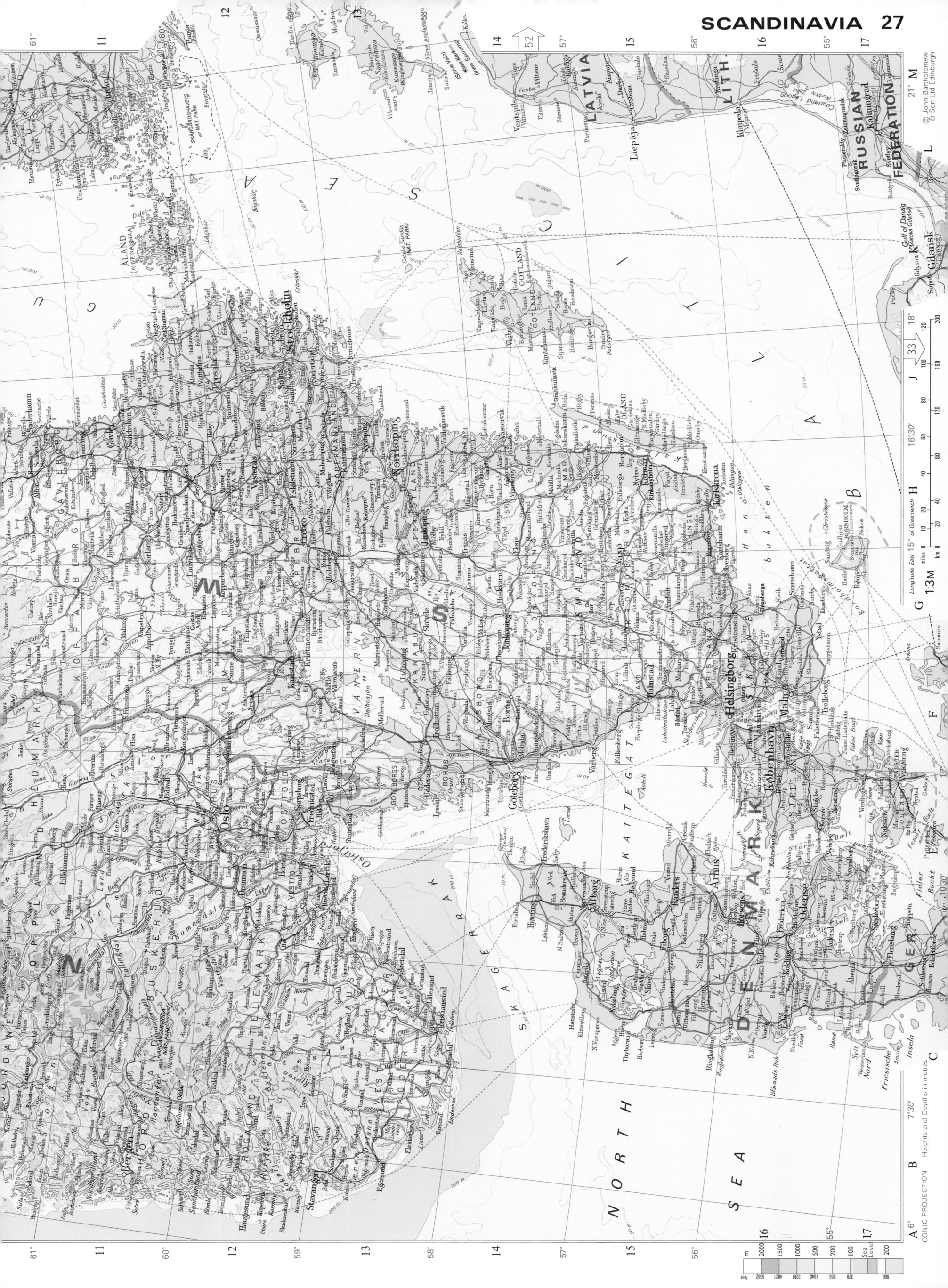

NORTH SEA
SKAGERRAK
KATTEGAT
BALTIC SEA
GULF OF BOTHNIA
DENMARK
SWEDEN
NORWAY
LATVIA
LITH.
RUSSIAN FEDERATION
GER.
Oslo
Stockholm
København
Göteborg
Bergen
Stavanger
Malmö
Helsingborg
Gdańsk
Kaliningrad
Liepāja
Ventspils
Klaipeda
GOTLAND
ÖLAND
BORNHOLM
Longitude East 15° of Greenwich
1:3M
CONIC PROJECTION
Heights and Depths in metres
© John Bartholomew & Son Ltd Edinburgh

SKAGERRAK
KATTEGAT
DENMARK
JYLLAND
JUTLAND
SJÆLLAND
FYN
FÜNEN
LOLLAND
FALSTER
GERMANY
ICELAND
Skagen
Hirtshals
Hjørring
Frederikshavn
Læsø
Jammerbugt
Ålborg
Limfjorden
Thisted
Nykøbing
MORS
Skive
Viborg
Randers
Hobro
Mariager
Anholt
Grenå
Århus
Silkeborg
Herning
Holstebro
Ringkøbing
Skjern
Horsens
Vejle
Fredericia
Kolding
Esbjerg
Ribe
Fanø
Rømø
Haderslev
Åbenrå
Sønderborg
Tønder
Flensburg
Sylt
Westerland
FRIESISCHE INSELN
Föhr
Amrum
Odense
Nyborg
Svendborg
Middelfart
Assens
Fåborg
Ærø
Langeland
Rudkøbing
Samsø
Kalundborg
Holbæk
Roskilde
Køge
Slagelse
Korsør
Ringsted
Næstved
Vordingborg
Nakskov
Maribo
Nykøbing
Fehmarn
Femer Bælt
Store Bælt
Lille Bælt
Smålandsfarvandet
Reykjavík
Akureyri
Faxaflói
Húnaflói
Breidhafjördhur
Kattegat
Scale 1:1M
km
miles
feet
m
Longitude East 10° of Greenwich

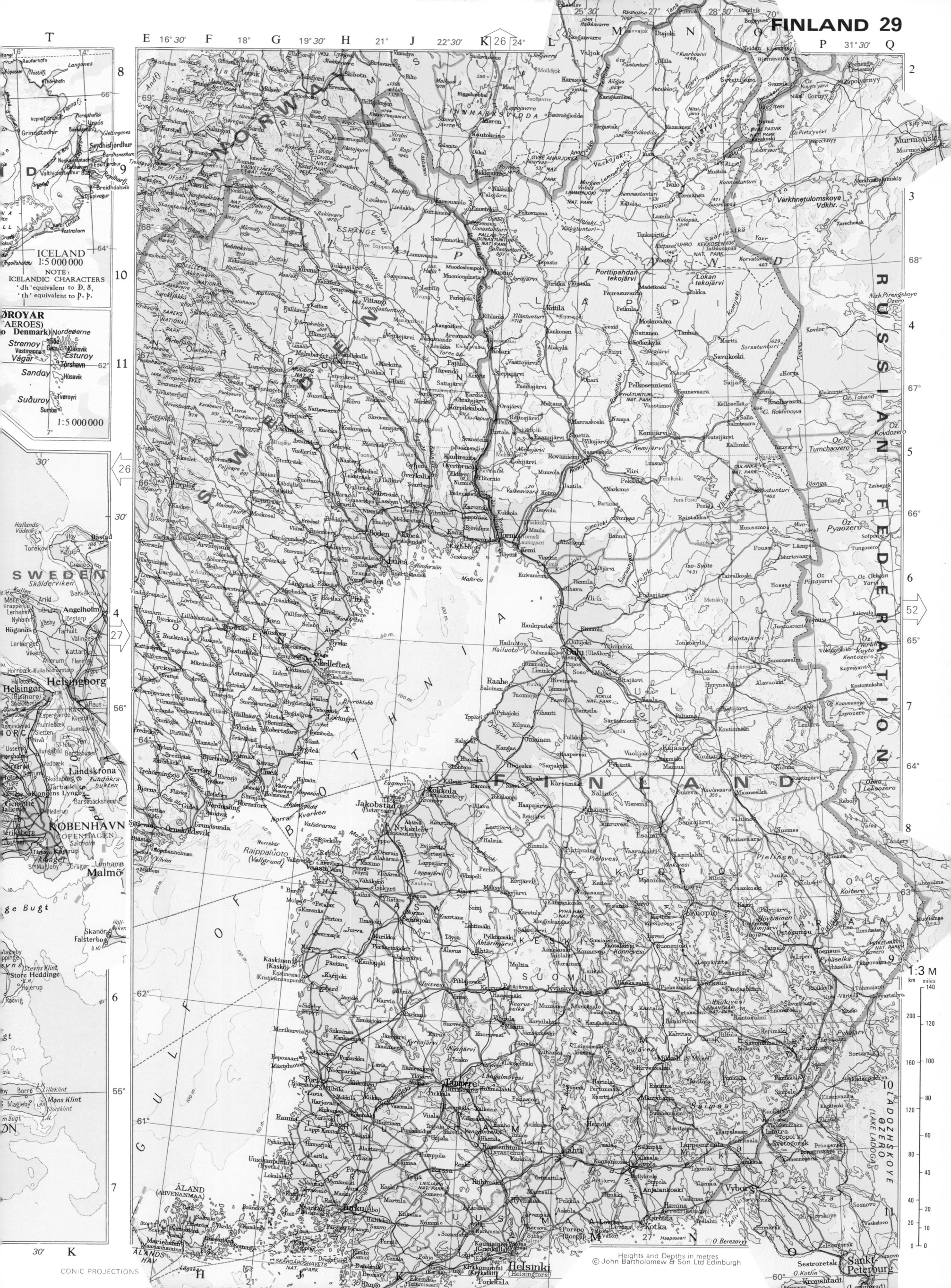
ICELAND
1:5 000 000
NOTE:
ICELANDIC CHARACTERS
'dh' equivalent to Ð, ð,
'th' equivalent to Þ, þ.
FØROYAR
(FAEROES)
Stremoy
Vágar
Tórshavn
Sanday
Suðuroy
1:5 000 000
SWEDEN
Helsingborg
Landskrona
KØBENHAVN
(COPENHAGEN)
Malmö
NORWAY
SWEDEN
Narvik
Kiruna
Gällivare
Boden
Luleå
Piteå
Skellefteå
Umeå
Örnsköldsvik
GULF OF BOTHNIA
Vaasa
Kokkola
Jakobstad
Oulu
Raahe
Kemi
Tornio
Rovaniemi
Ivalo
Kuopio
Jyväskylä
Tampere
Pori
Rauma
Turku (Åbo)
Helsinki (Helsingfors)
Lahti
Kotka
Hamina
Lappeenranta
Mikkeli
Joensuu
Vyborg
Sankt-Peterburg
Murmansk
ÅLAND (AHVENANMAA)
ÅLANDS HAV
FINLAND
SUOMI
LAPPI
OULU
KUOPIO
KESKI-SUOMI
RUSSIAN FEDERATION
LADOZHSKOYE OZERO (LAKE LADOGA)
1:3 M
Heights and Depths in metres
© John Bartholomew & Son Ltd Edinburgh
CONIC PROJECTIONS

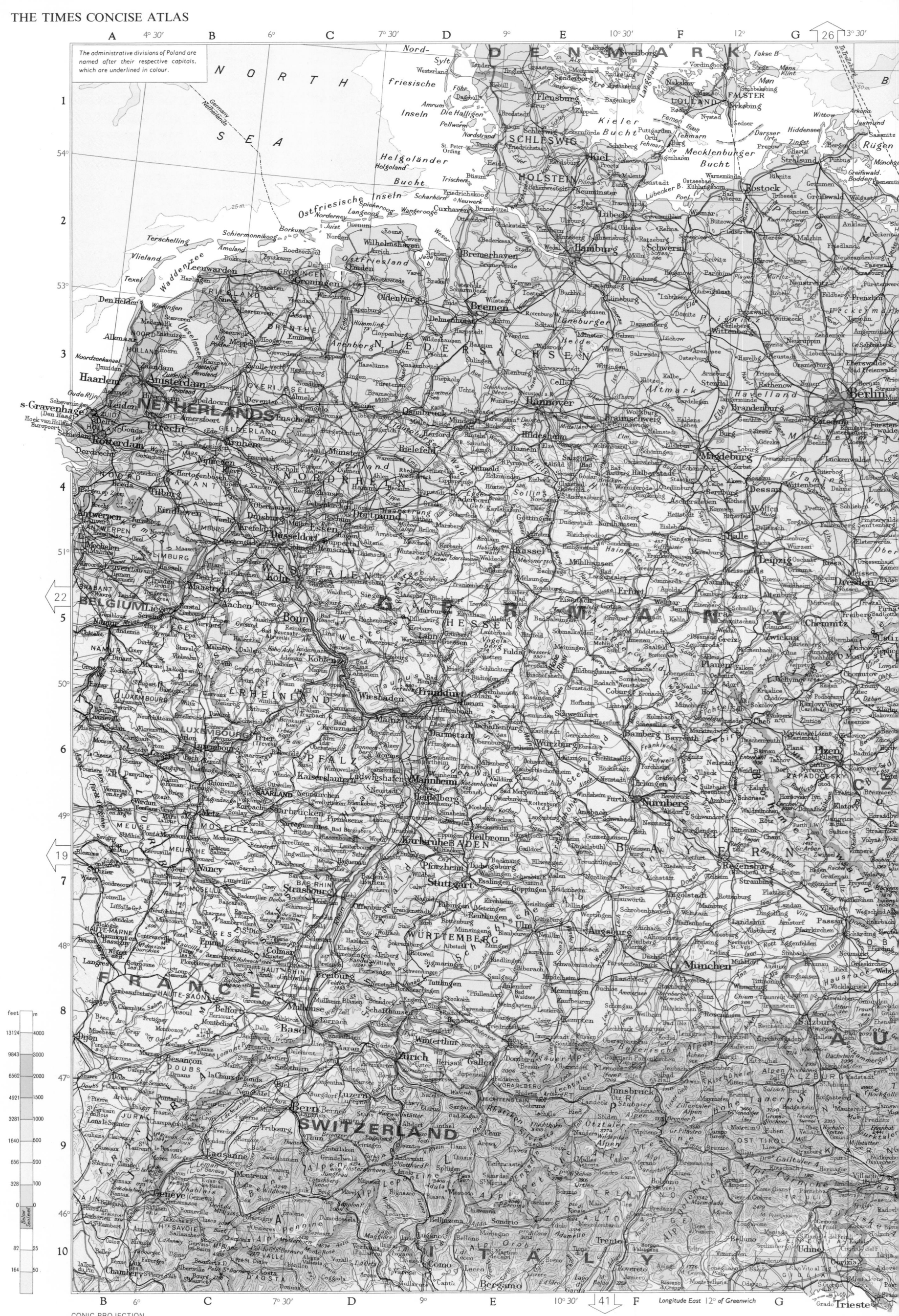

The administrative divisions of Poland are named after their respective capitals, which are underlined in colour.
NORTH SEA
DENMARK
NETHERLANDS
BELGIUM
LUXEMBOURG
GERMANY
FRANCE
SWITZERLAND
ITALY
Amsterdam
Rotterdam
Hamburg
Bremen
Hannover
Berlin
Köln
Frankfurt
Stuttgart
München
Nürnberg
Zürich
Bern
Genève
Strasbourg
Dresden
Leipzig
Brussels
Basel
Innsbruck
Trieste
Longitude East 12° of Greenwich

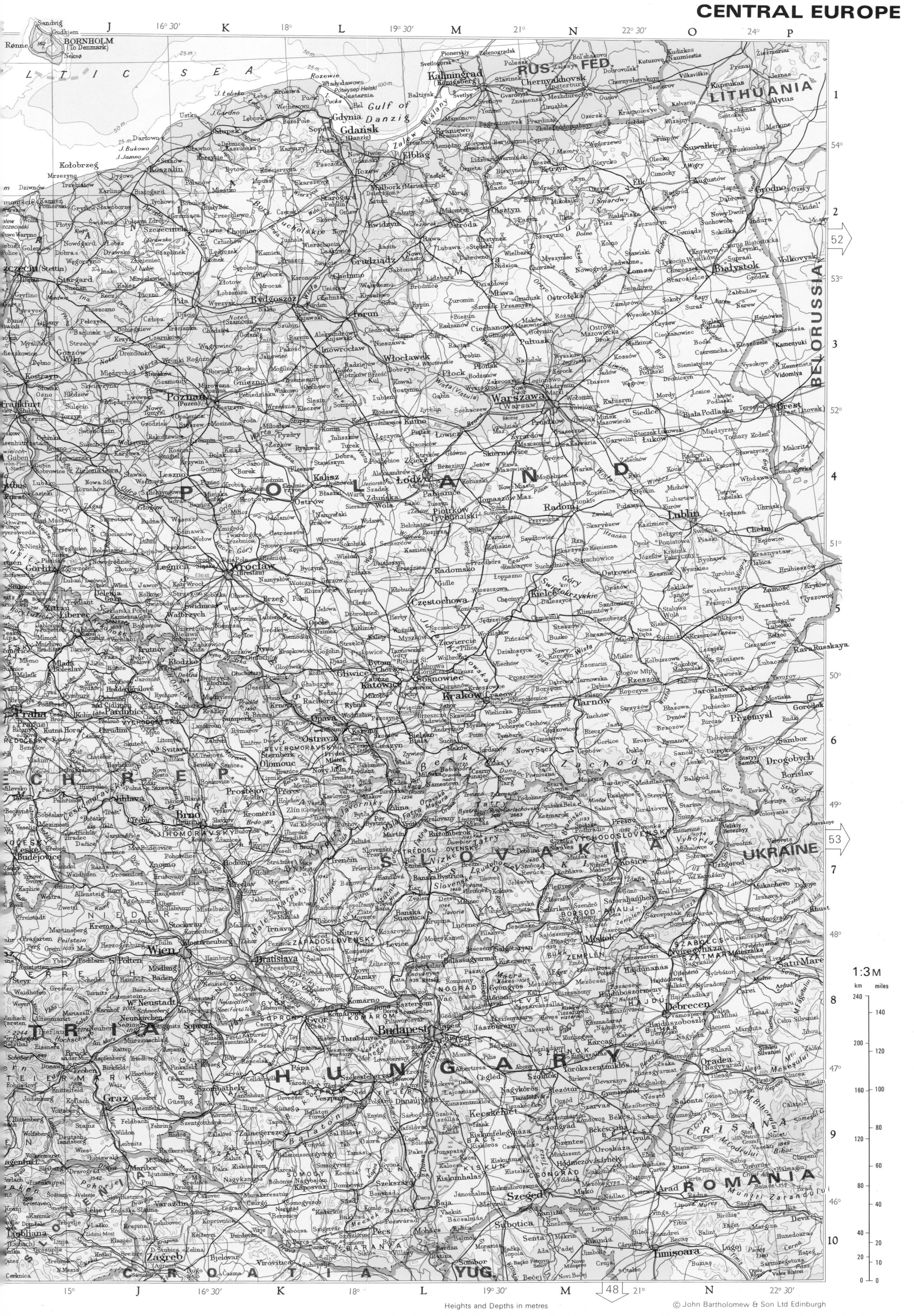

1:3 M

Heights and Depths in metres

© John Bartholomew & Son Ltd Edinburgh

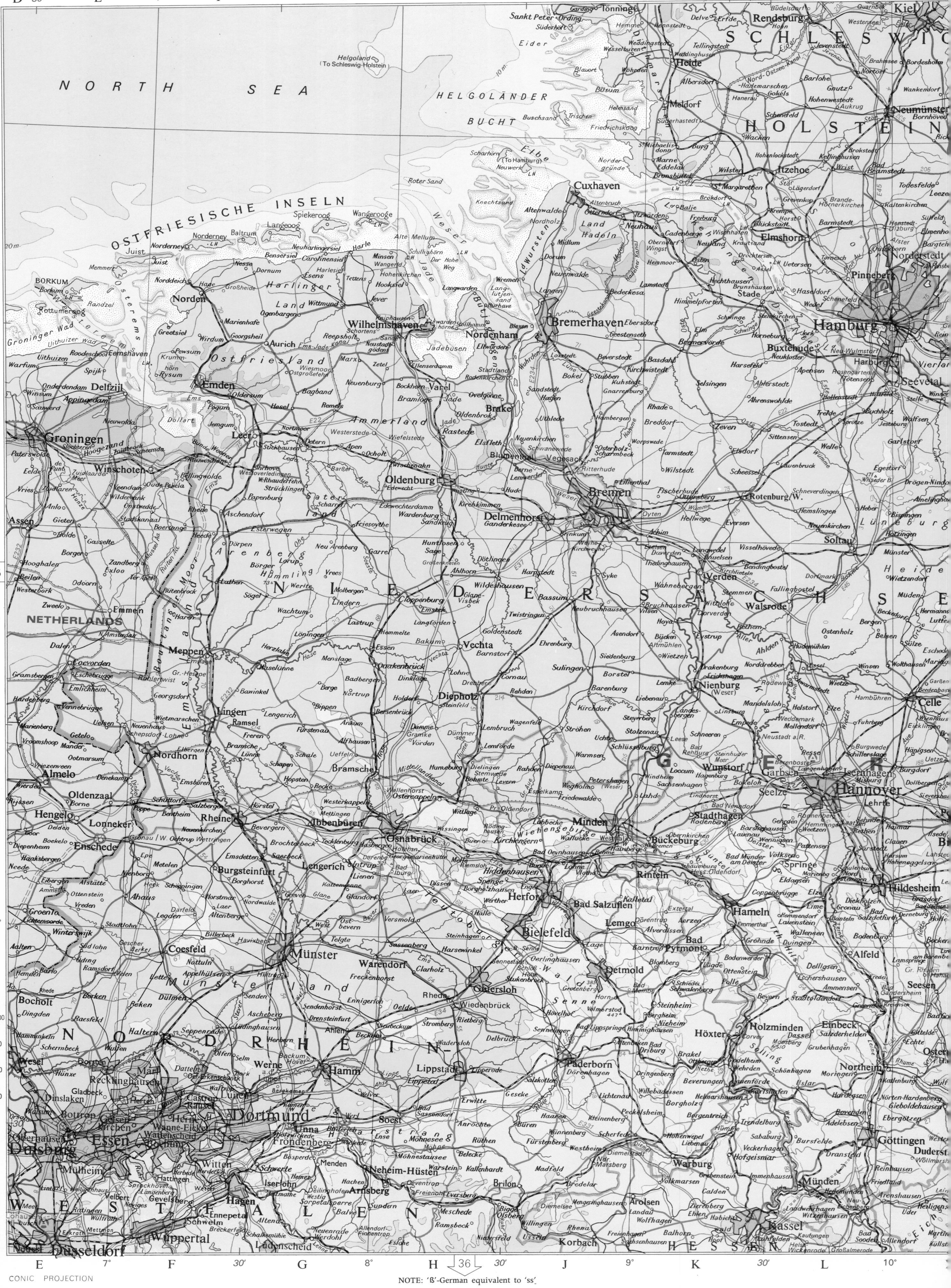

NORTH SEA

HELGOLÄNDER BUCHT

OSTFRIESISCHE INSELN

Helgoland
(To Schleswig-Holstein)

SCHLESWIG

HOLSTEIN

NORTH SEA

BORKUM

OSTFRIESLAND

NETHERLANDS

NIEDERSACHSEN

GERMANY

NORDRHEIN-WESTFALEN

HESSEN

Groningen
Emden
Wilhelmshaven
Nordenham
Bremerhaven
Cuxhaven
Hamburg
Neumünster
Meldorf
Heide
Itzehoe
Elmshorn
Norderstedt
Pinneberg
Buxtehude
Harburg
Seevetal
Stade
Oldenburg
Delmenhorst
Bremen
Rotenburg (W.)
Soltau
Verden
Walsrode
Nienburg (Weser)
Celle
Meppen
Lingen
Nordhorn
Almelo
Oldenzaal
Hengelo
Enschede
Rheine
Ibbenbüren
Osnabrück
Vechta
Cloppenburg
Diepholz
Minden
Bückeburg
Stadthagen
Wunstorf
Seelze
Hannover
Hildesheim
Burgsteinfurt
Lengerich
Herford
Bielefeld
Bad Salzuflen
Lemgo
Hameln
Bad Pyrmont
Münster
Warendorf
Gütersloh
Detmold
Paderborn
Holzminden
Einbeck
Coesfeld
Bocholt
Wesel
Hamm
Lippstadt
Soest
Höxter
Göttingen
Warburg
Dortmund
Essen
Duisburg
Mülheim
Hagen
Iserlohn
Arnsberg
Brilon
Korbach
Kassel
Düsseldorf
Wuppertal
Lüdenscheid

Leer
Aurich
Norden
Wittmund
Jever
Varel
Brake
Rastede
Wildeshausen
Syke
Sulingen
Twistringen
Bassum
Rendsburg

CONIC PROJECTION

MECKLENBURGER BUCHT

LÜBECKER BUCHT

Greifswalder Bodden

Lübeck
Eutin
Wismar
Grevesmühlen
Schwerin
Rostock
Warnemünde
Bad Doberan
Güstrow
Teterow
Demmin
Anklam
Greifswald
Wolgast
Stralsund
Ueckermünde
Stettiner Haff
USEDOM

MECKLENBURG-VORPOMMERN

Waren
Malchin
Neubrandenburg
Strasburg
Pasewalk
Neustrelitz
Prenzlau
Parchim
Ludwigslust
Pritzwalk
Wittstock
Templin
Angermünde
Lüneburg
Salzwedel
Perleberg
Wittenberge
Neuruppin
Eberswalde
Bad Freienwalde
Bernau
Gardelegen
Stendal
Rathenow
Tangermünde
Nauen
Oranienburg
BRANDENBURG
BERLIN
Gifhorn
Wolfsburg
Helmstedt
Haldensleben
Burg
Genthin
Brandenburg
Potsdam
Köpenick
Strausberg
Magdeburg
Oschersleben
Schönebeck
Belzig
Luckenwalde
Zossen
Jüterbog
Lübben
Halberstadt
Wernigerode
Blankenburg
Stassfurt
Bernburg
Köthen (Anhalt)
Aschersleben
Quedlinburg
Zerbst
Roßlau
Dessau
Coswig
Wittenberg
Bitterfeld
Torgau
Finsterwalde
Eisleben
Hettstedt
Sangerhausen
Nordhausen
Halle
Neustadt
Merseburg
Querfurt
Delitzsch
Eilenburg
Wurzen
Elsterwerda
Leipzig
Riesa
Oschatz
Grimma

SACHSEN-ANHALT
SACHSEN
THÜRINGEN

1:1M

km miles

Heights and Depths in metres

© John Bartholomew & Son Ltd Edinburgh

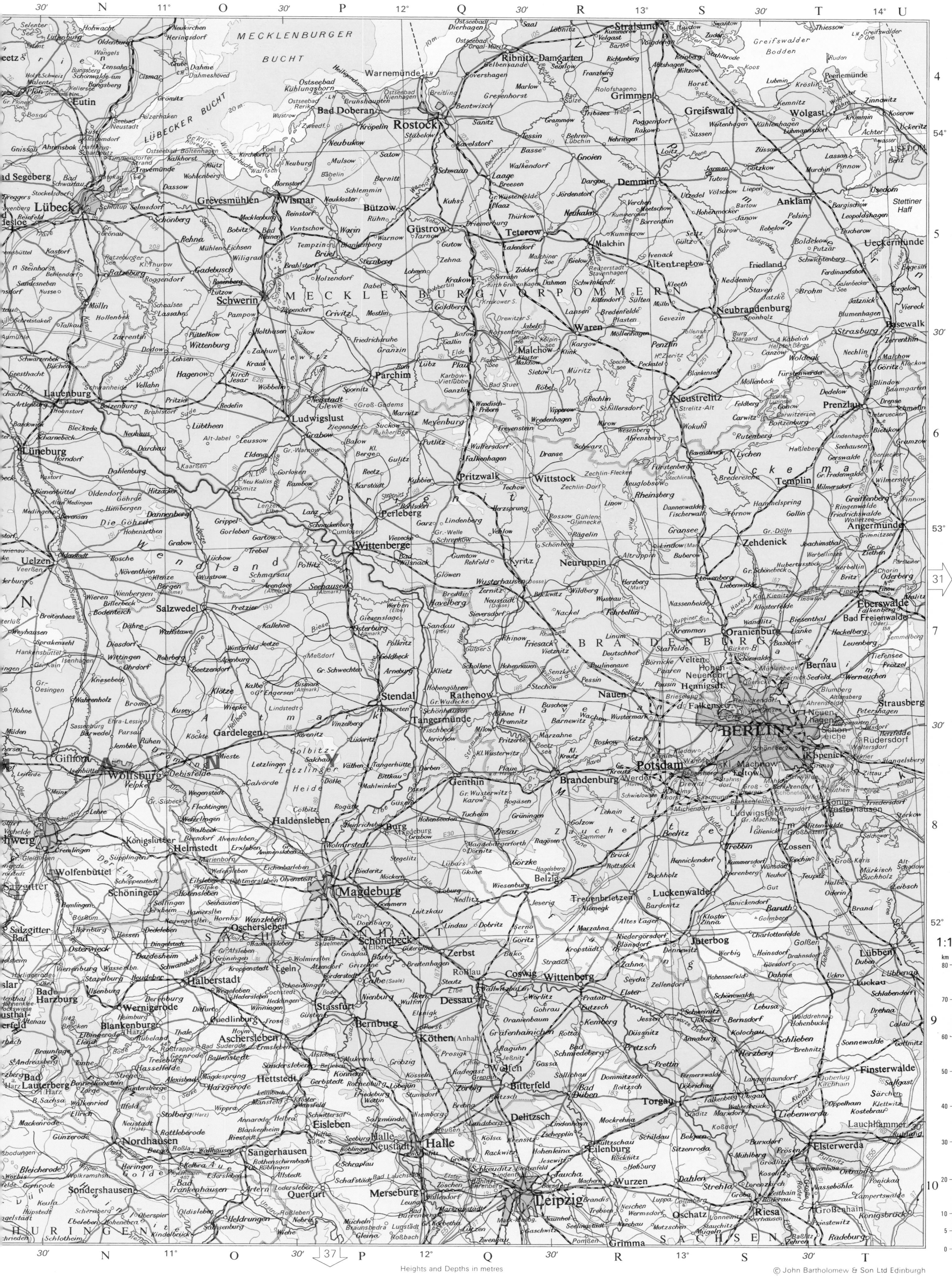

HAMBURG

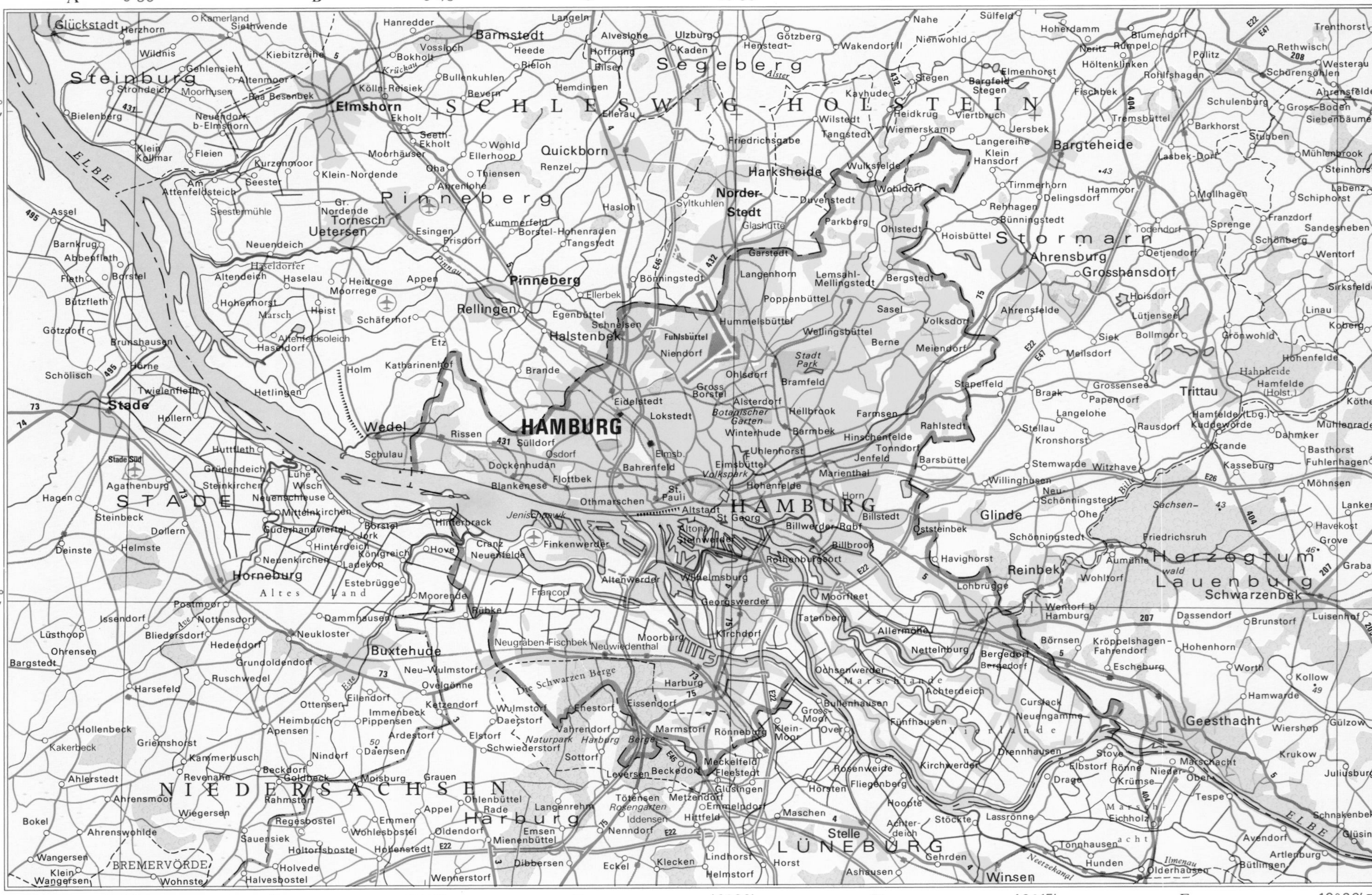

Grid: A 9°30′ · B 9°45′ · C 10°00′ · D 10°15′ · E 10°30′ F
53°45′ · 53°30′

SCHLESWIG-HOLSTEIN · Steinburg · Segeberg · Stormarn · Pinneberg · STADE · NIEDERSACHSEN · Harburg · LÜNEBURG · Herzogtum Lauenburg

Selected places: Glückstadt, Elmshorn, Quickborn, Norderstedt, Harksheide, Ahrensburg, Bargteheide, Pinneberg, Uetersen, Wedel, Stade, **HAMBURG**, Buxtehude, Horneburg, Reinbek, Glinde, Schwarzenbek, Geesthacht, Winsen

ELBE

BERLIN

Grid: A 13°00′ · B 13°15′ · C 13°30′ · D 13°45′ E
52°30′

BRANDENBURG · Nauen · Falkensee · Potsdam · Werder · **BERLIN** · Spandau · Charlottenburg · Schöneberg · Wilmersdorf · Steglitz · Zehlendorf · Lichterfelde · Teltow · Wittenau · Tegel · Reinickendorf · Pankow · Wedding · Mitte · Friedrichshain · Weissensee · Prenzlauer Berg · Tiergarten · Kreuzberg · Tempelhof · Neukölln · Mariendorf · Britz · Buckow · Marienfelde · Lichtenrade · Köpenick · Friedrichshagen · Oberschöneweide · Niederschöneweide · Johannisthal · Karlshorst · Biesdorf · Marzahn · Hohenschönhausen · Bernau · Werneuchen · Strausberg · Erkner · Zeuthen · Königs Wusterhausen · Ludwigsfelde

1:300 000

0 5 10 15 km
0 5 10 miles

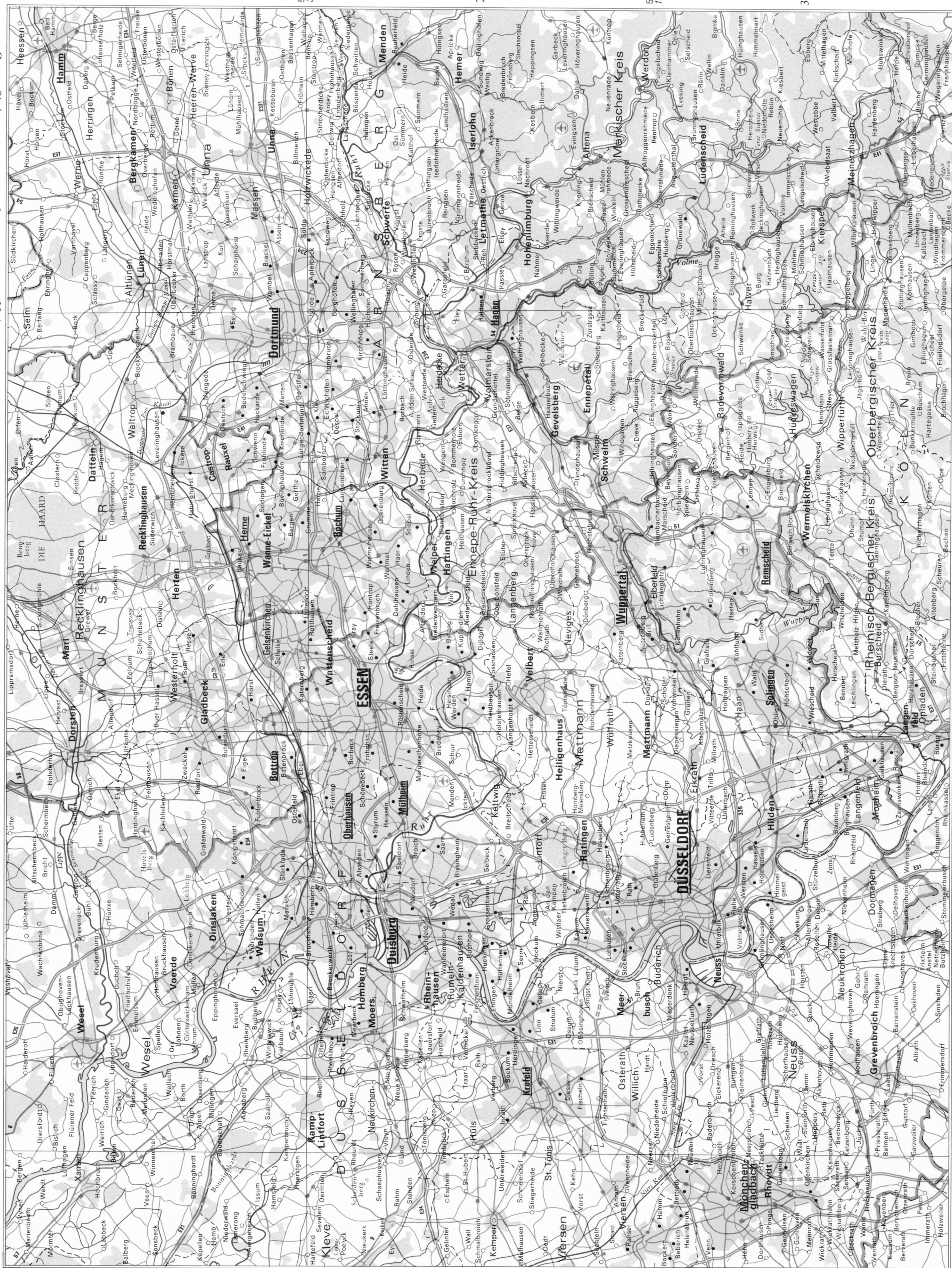

1:300 000

© Times Books Ltd

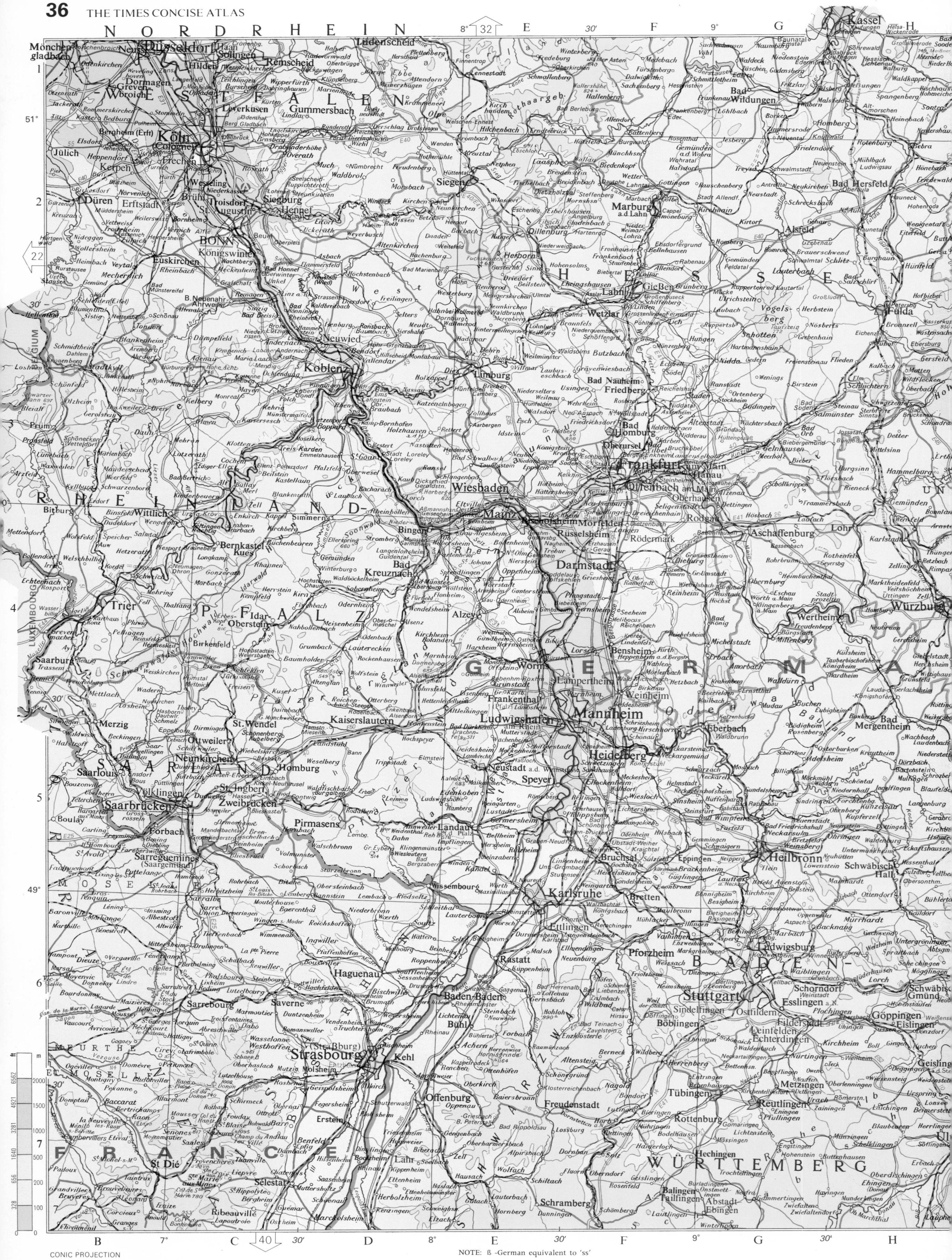

NORDRHEIN

GERMANY

RHEINLAND-PFALZ

HESSEN

SAARLAND

BADEN-WÜRTTEMBERG

FRANCE

LUXEMBOURG

BELGIUM

Major cities and towns: Mönchengladbach, Düsseldorf, Remscheid, Solingen, Leverkusen, Köln (Cologne), Bonn, Königswinter, Siegburg, Hennef, Siegen, Marburg a.d. Lahn, Alsfeld, Bad Hersfeld, Kassel, Fulda, Gießen, Wetzlar, Limburg, Neuwied, Koblenz, Frankfurt am Main, Offenbach am Main, Hanau, Wiesbaden, Mainz, Rüsselsheim, Darmstadt, Aschaffenburg, Würzburg, Bingen, Bad Kreuznach, Alzey, Worms, Mannheim, Ludwigshafen, Heidelberg, Heilbronn, Trier, Idar-Oberstein, Kaiserslautern, Neustadt a.d. Weinstrasse, Speyer, Eberbach, Bad Mergentheim, Saarbrücken, Völklingen, Zweibrücken, Neunkirchen, Homburg, Pirmasens, Landau, Karlsruhe, Bretten, Pforzheim, Ludwigsburg, Stuttgart, Esslingen a.N., Göppingen, Haguenau, Baden-Baden, Rastatt, Strasbourg, Kehl, Offenburg, Freudenstadt, Tübingen, Reutlingen, Saverne, Sarrebourg, St Dié, Sélestat

CONIC PROJECTION

NOTE: ß — German equivalent to 'ss'

ft m
6562 2000
4921 1500
3281 1000
1640 500
656 200
328 100
0

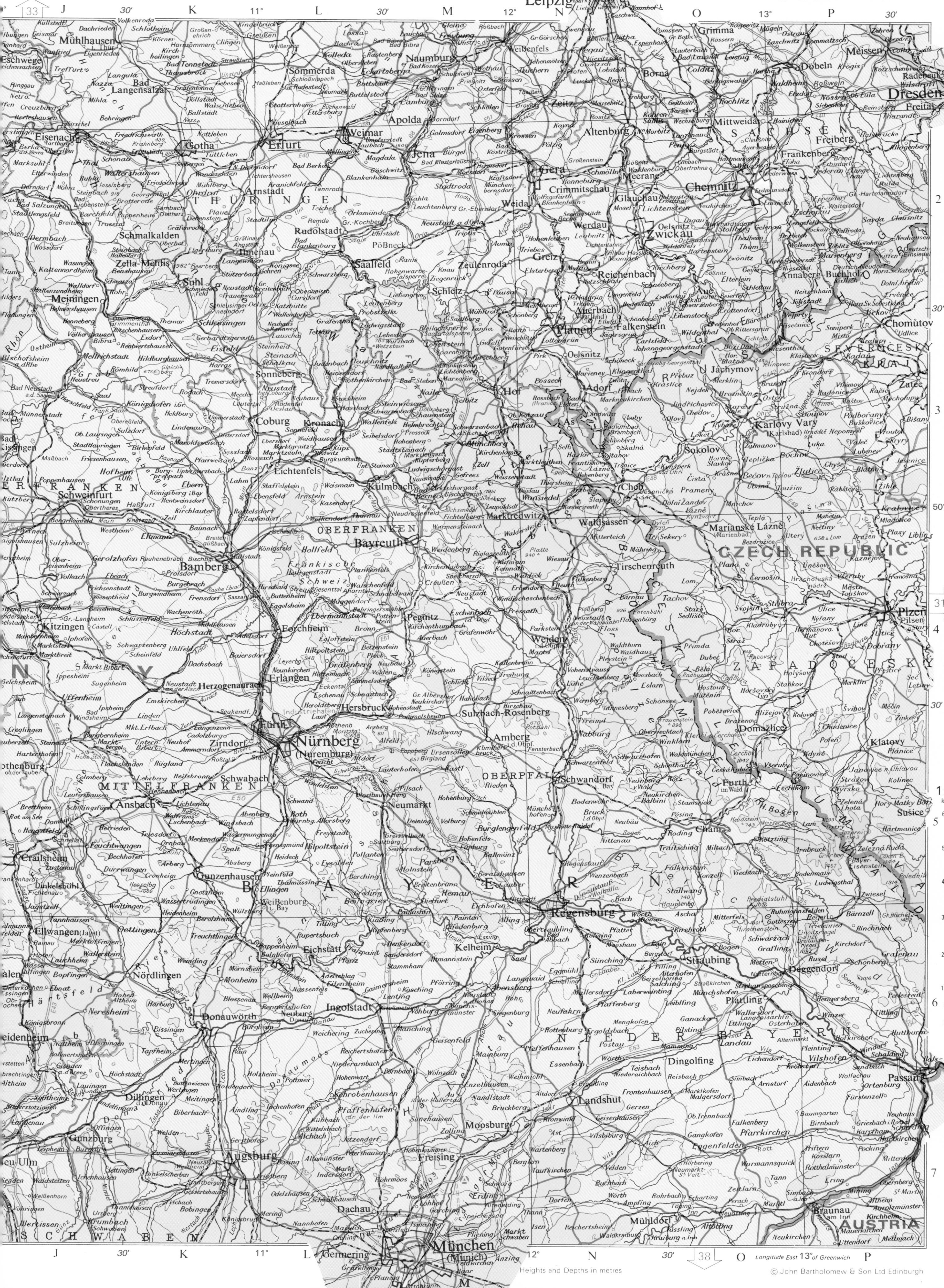
Leipzig
Dresden
Erfurt
Weimar
Jena
Gera
Chemnitz
Zwickau
Plauen
Hof
Bayreuth
Bamberg
Coburg
Schweinfurt
Nürnberg (Nuremberg)
Fürth
Erlangen
Regensburg
Ingolstadt
Augsburg
München (Munich)
Landshut
Passau
Straubing
Plzeň
Karlovy Vary
Cheb
THÜRINGEN
SACHSEN
OBERFRANKEN
MITTELFRANKEN
OBERPFALZ
NIEDERBAYERN
SCHWABEN
CZECH REPUBLIC
ZÁPADOČESKÝ
AUSTRIA
33
31
38
1:1M
Longitude East 13° of Greenwich
Heights and Depths in metres

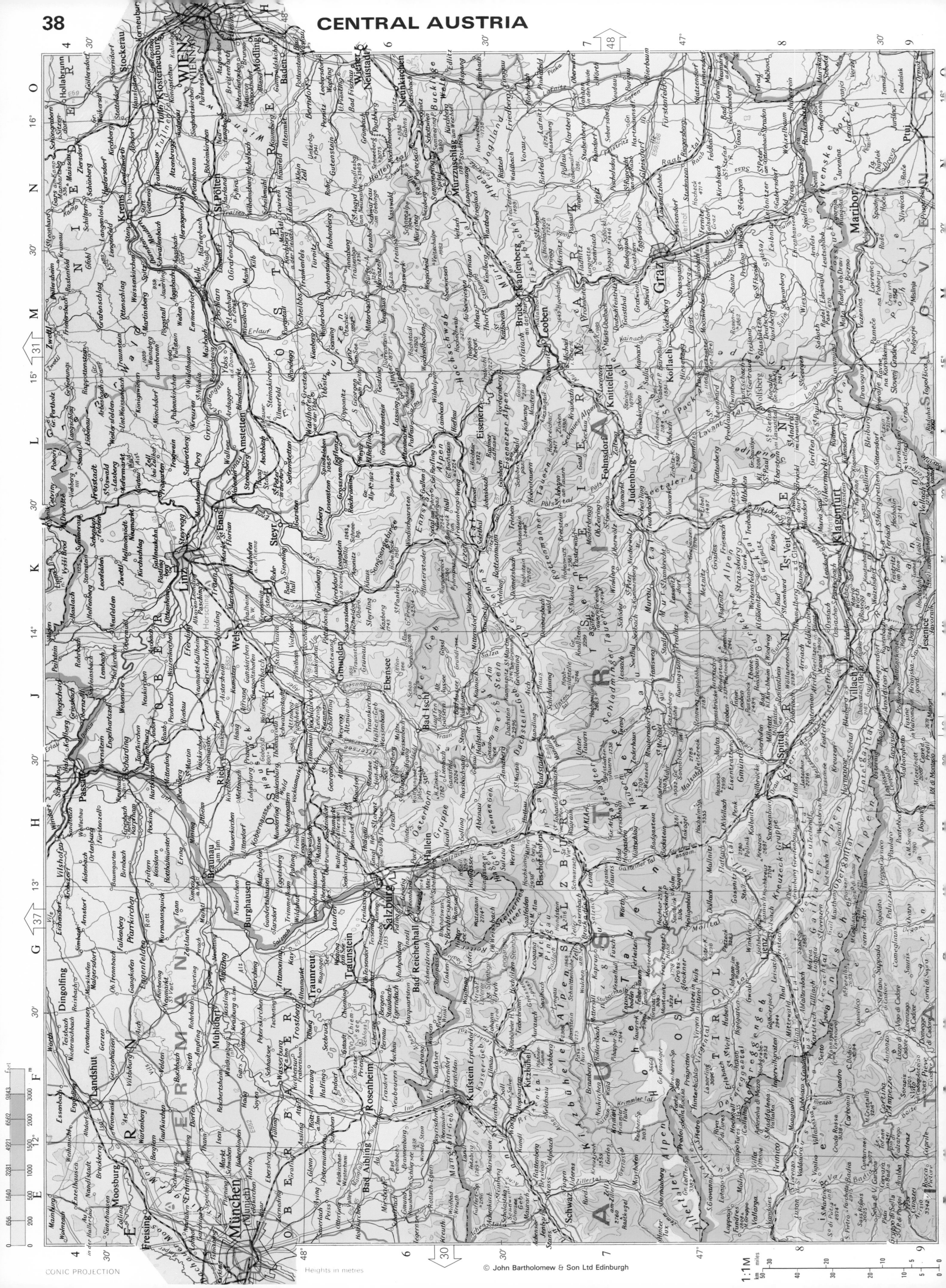

WIEN (VIENNA)
Linz
Salzburg
Graz
Klagenfurt
Villach
Maribor
München (Munich)
Passau
Landshut
Rosenheim
Innsbruck
St Pölten
Krems
Steyr
Wels
Leoben
Bruck
Judenburg
Spittal
Lienz
Kitzbühel
Kufstein
Bad Ischl
Hallein
Braunau
Freising
Moosburg
Wiener Neustadt
Baden
Mödling
Stockerau
Ptuj
Jesenice
AUSTRIA
GERMANY
ITALY
YUGOSLAVIA
CZECHOSLOVAKIA
HUNGARY
NIEDER ÖSTERREICH
OBER ÖSTERREICH
STEIERMARK
KÄRNTEN
SALZBURG
TIROL
OBERBAYERN
NIEDERBAYERN
Hohe Tauern
Niedere Tauern
Dachstein
Karawanken
Heights in metres
CONIC PROJECTION
1:1M

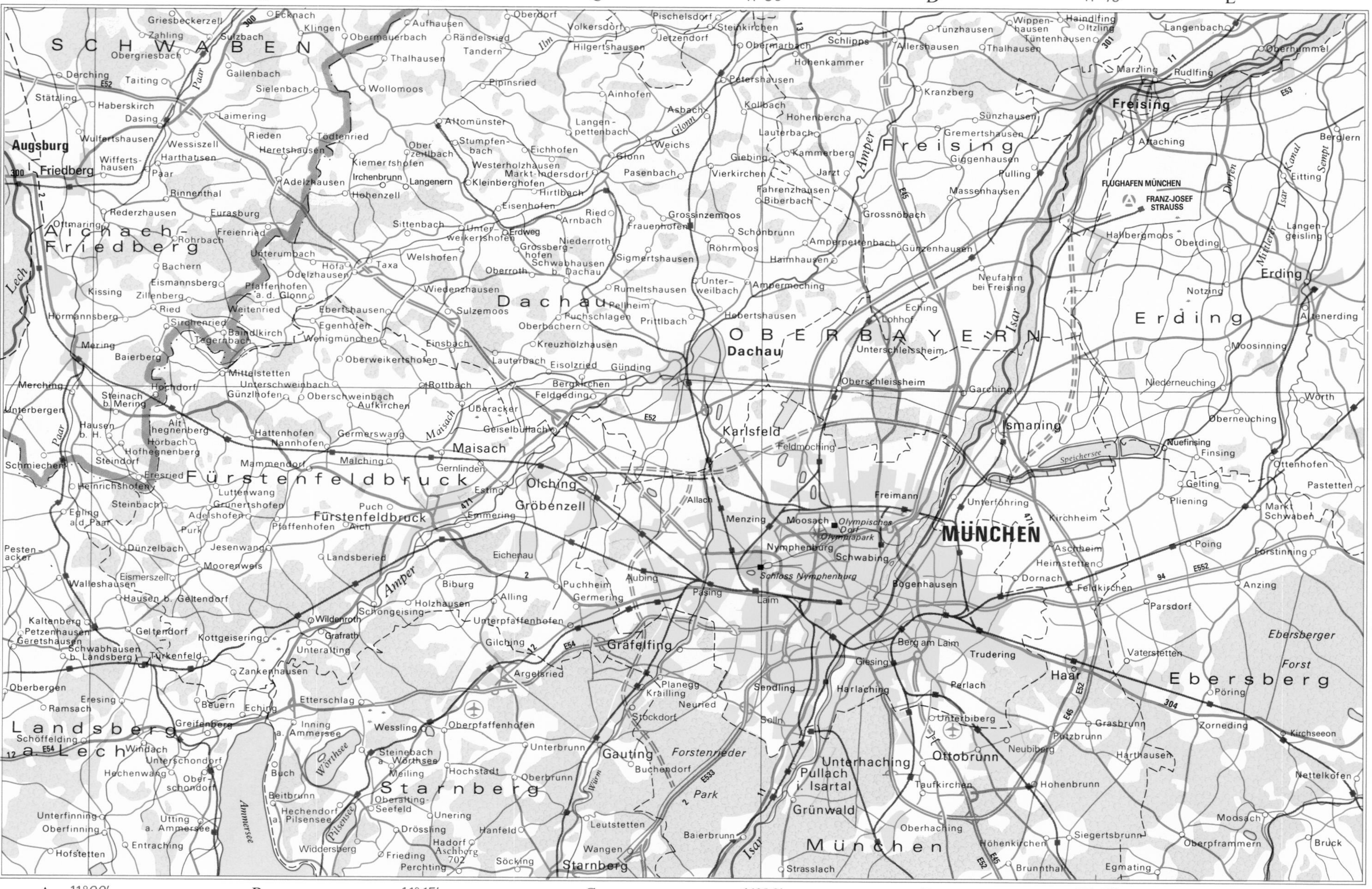

MILAN

1:300 000

© Times Books Ltd

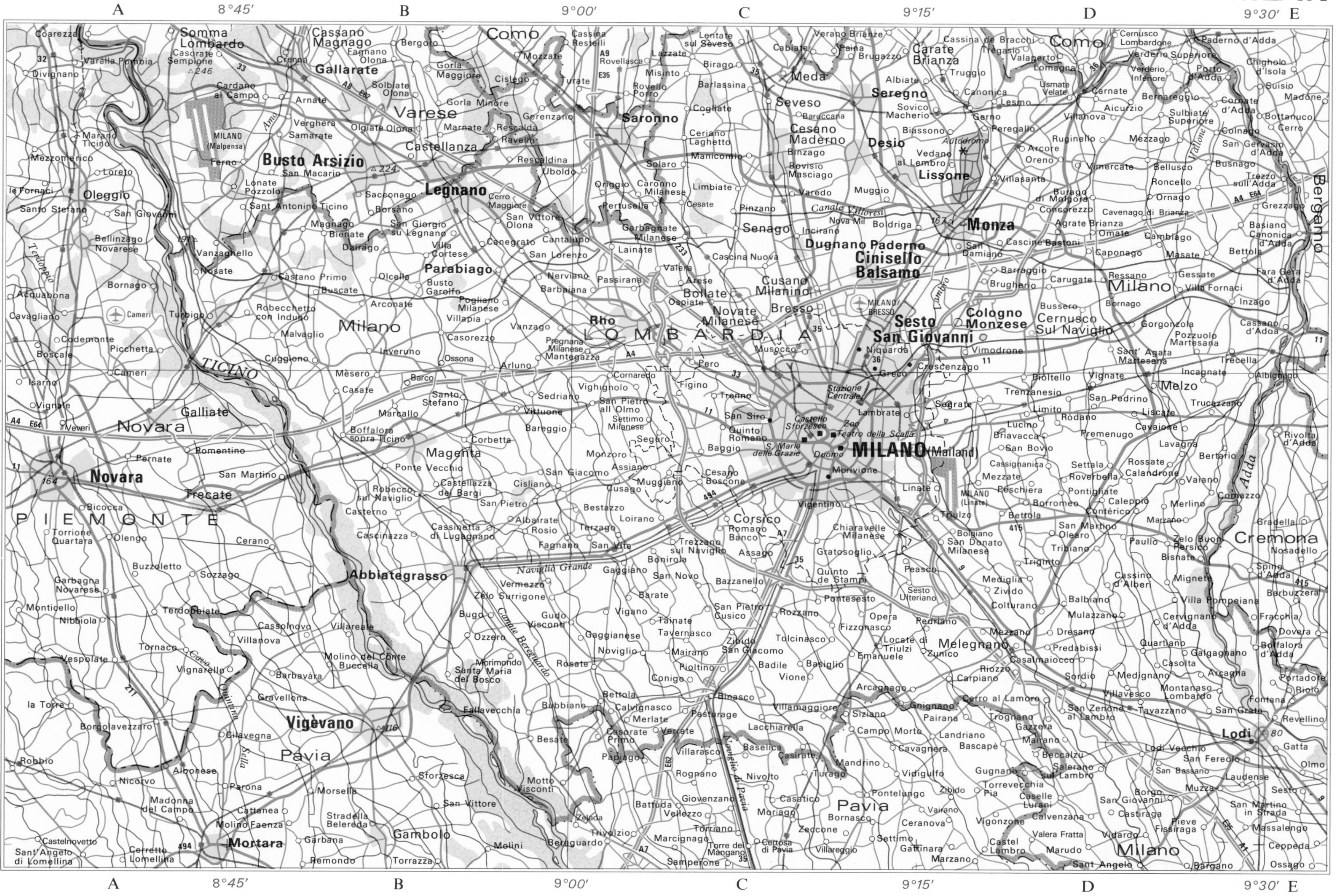

CONIC PROJECTION

Heights and Depths in metres

	328	656	1640	1381	4921	6562	9843	13124	feet
	100	200	500	1000	1500	2000	3000	4000	m

Longitude East 9° of Greenwich

1:1M

0 5 10   20   30   40   50 km

© John Bartholomew & Son Ltd Edinburgh

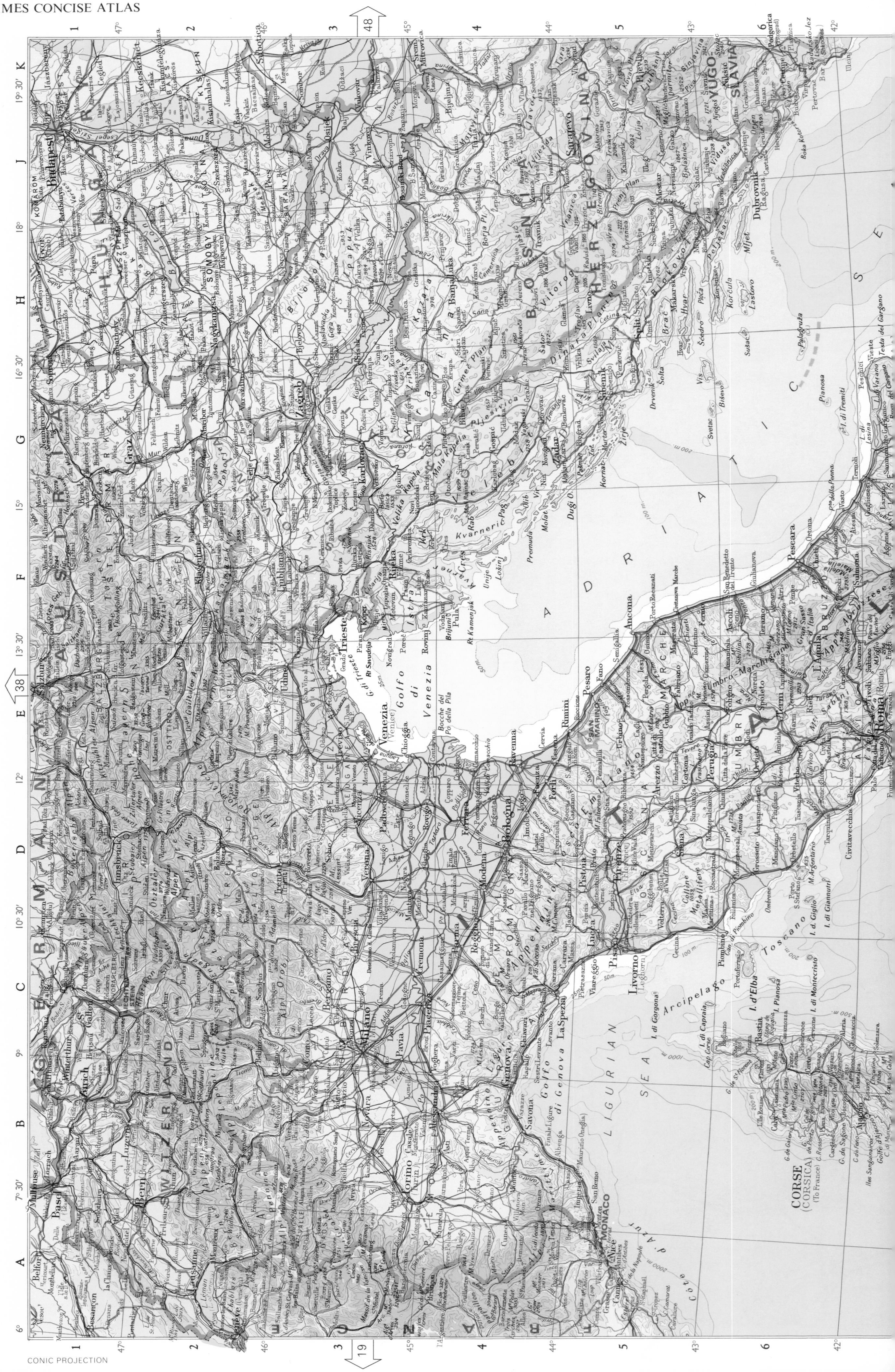
Budapest
Zagreb
Trieste
Venezia
Milano
Bologna
Firenze
Roma
Ancona
Pescara
Genova
Torino
Dubrovnik
Sarajevo
Ljubljana
CORSE (CORSICA)
CONIC PROJECTION

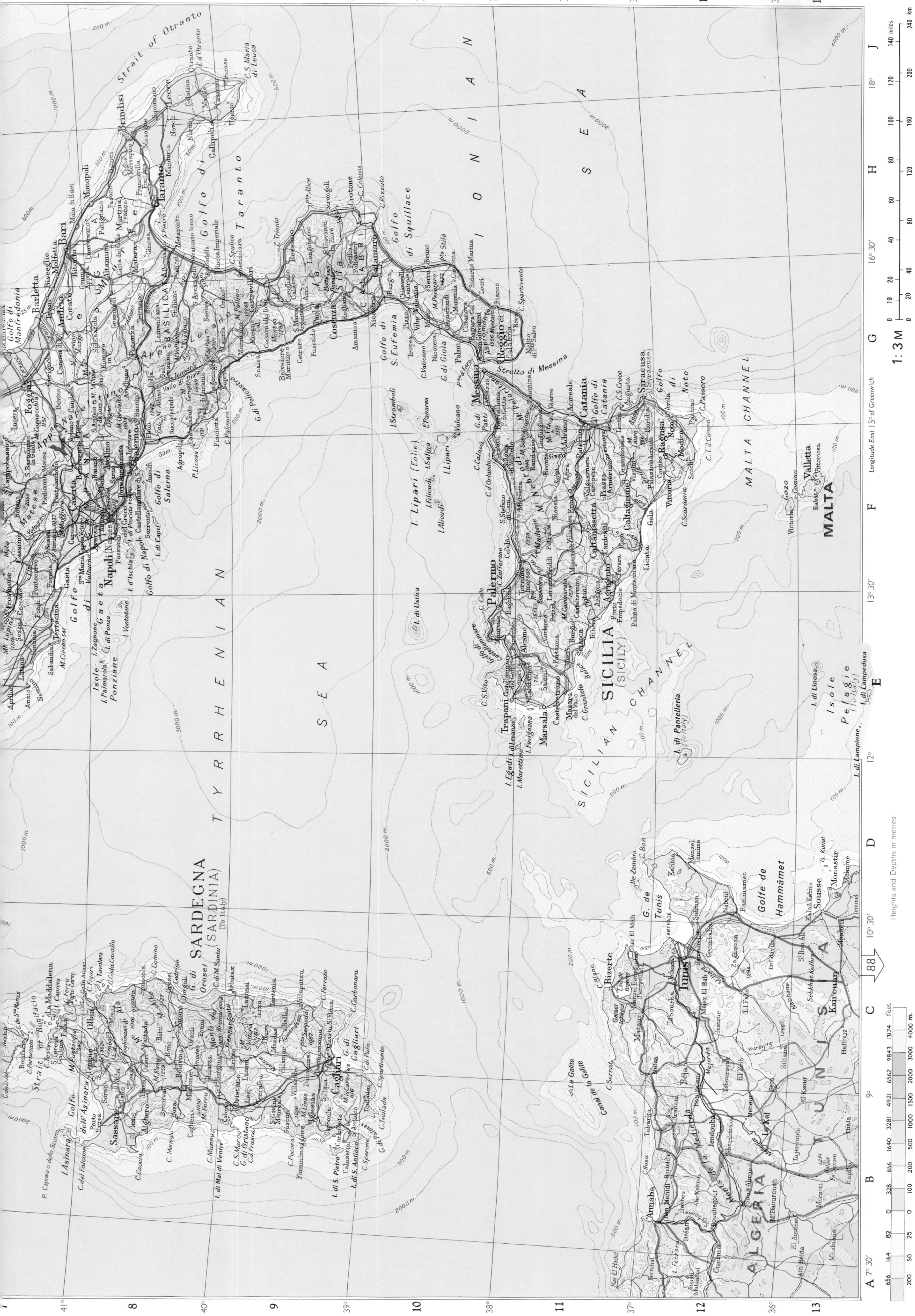

I O N I A N   S E A

T Y R R H E N I A N   S E A

SICILIAN CHANNEL

MALTA CHANNEL

Strait of Otranto

Golfo di Taranto

Golfo di Squillace

Golfo di S.Eufemia

Golfo di Gioia

Golfo di Catania

Golfo di Noto

Golfo di Manfredonia

Golfo di Napoli

Golfo di Gaeta

Golfo di Salerno

Stretto di Messina

G. di Patti

SARDEGNA (SARDINIA) (To Italy)

G. di Orosei

SICILIA (SICILY)

MALTA

Isole Pelagie (To Italy)

T U N I S I A

A L G E R I A

Golfe de Hammâmet

G. de Tunis

Brindisi

Lecce

Taranto

Bari

Barletta

Foggia

Napoli (Naples)

Salerno

Catanzaro

Reggio di Calabria

Messina

Catania

Siracusa

Ragusa

Palermo

Trapani

Marsala

Caltanissetta

Cagliari

Sassari

Tunis

Bizerte

Sousse

Kairouan

Valletta

Crotone

Cosenza

Rossano

1:3 M

Heights and Depths in metres

Longitude East 15° of Greenwich

Milano / Milan
Novara
Vercelli
Torino / Turin
Moncalieri
Chieri
Asti
Alessandria
Tortona
Voghera
Pavia
Piacenza
Cremona
Lodi
Crema
Casalpusterlengo
Stradella

Pinerolo
Carmagnola
Racconigi
Bra
Alba
Acqui Terme
Ovada
Nizza Monferrato
Novi Ligure
Bobbio

Cavour
Savigliano
Cherasco
Fossano
Mondovi
Cuneo
Dogliani
Ceva
Garessio

FRANCE

Savona
Albisola Marina
Varazze
Genova (Genoa)
S. Pier d'Arena
Sturla
Nervi
Rapallo
Sta Margherita Ligure
Portofino
Chiavari
Sestri Levante
La Spezia
Sarzane
Carrara
Massa
Marina di Carrara

Finale Lig.
Pietra Ligure
Albenga
Alassio
Laigueglia
Capo Mele
Diano Marina
Oneglia
Imperia
Porto Maurizio
San Remo
Ventimiglia
Bordighera
Menton
Monte-Carlo
MONACO
Nice
Antibes
Cannes
COTE D'AZUR

GOLFO DI GENOVA

LIGURIAN SEA

RIVIERA DI PONENTE
RIVIERA DI LEVANTE

Viareggio
Torre d. Lago Puccini
Livorno (Leghorn)

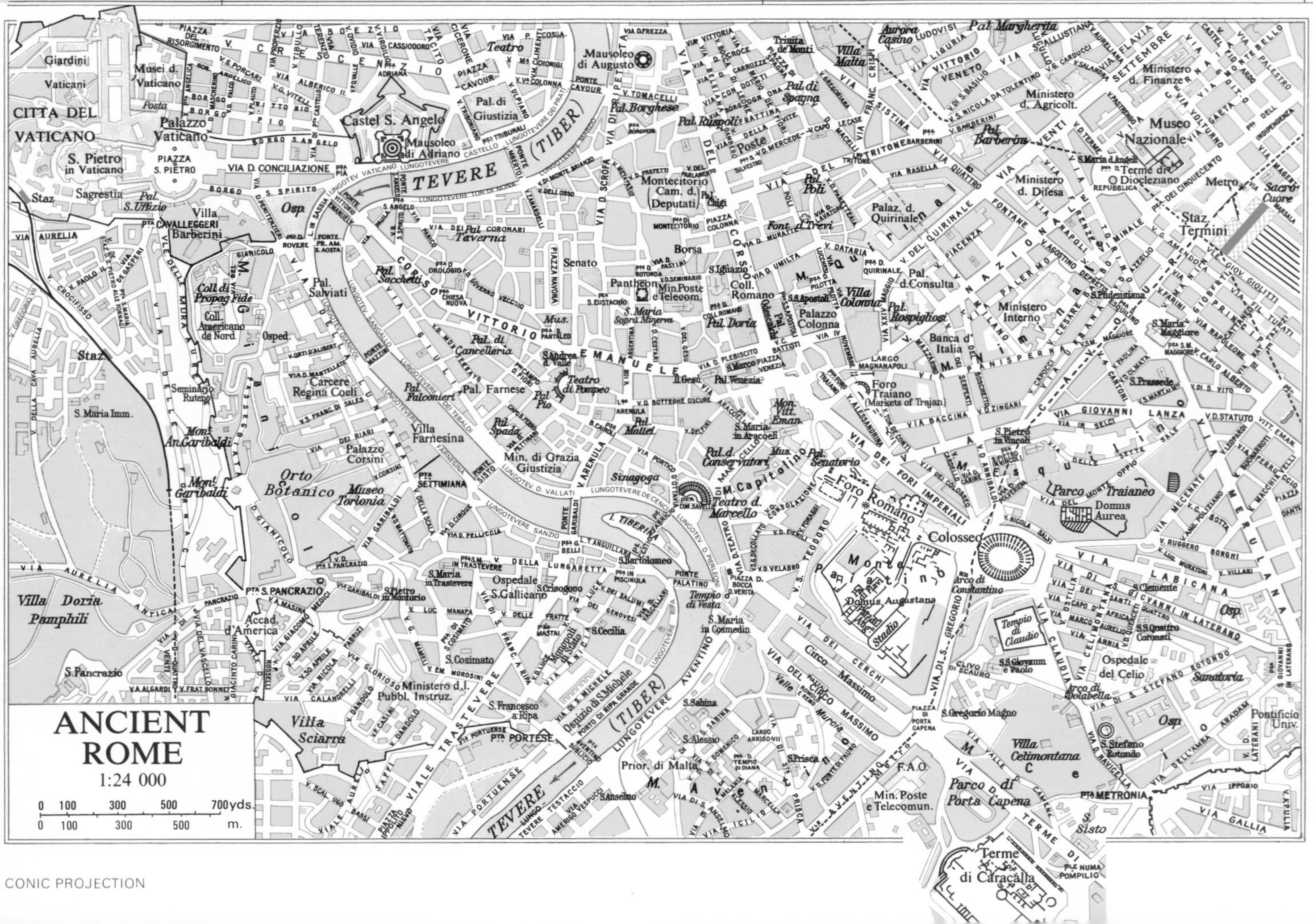

ANCIENT ROME
1:24 000

CITTA DEL VATICANO
S. Pietro in Vaticano
Castel S. Angelo
TEVERE (TIBER)
Villa Doria Pamphili
Orto Botanico
Museo Torlonia

0 100 300 500 700 yds.

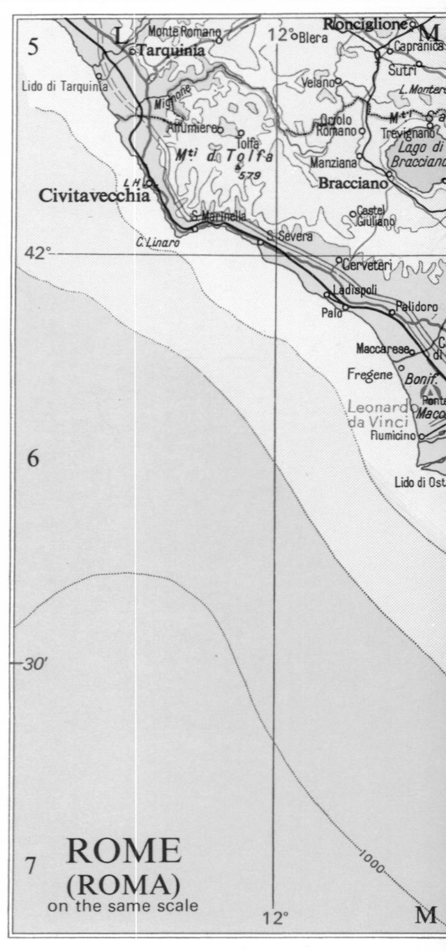

ROME (ROMA)
on the same scale

Tarquinia
Civitavecchia
Bracciano
Leonardo da Vinci Fiumicino

NAPLES
(NAPOLI)
on the same scale

1:1 M

Heights and Depths in metres

© John Bartholomew & Son Ltd Edinburgh

CROATIA

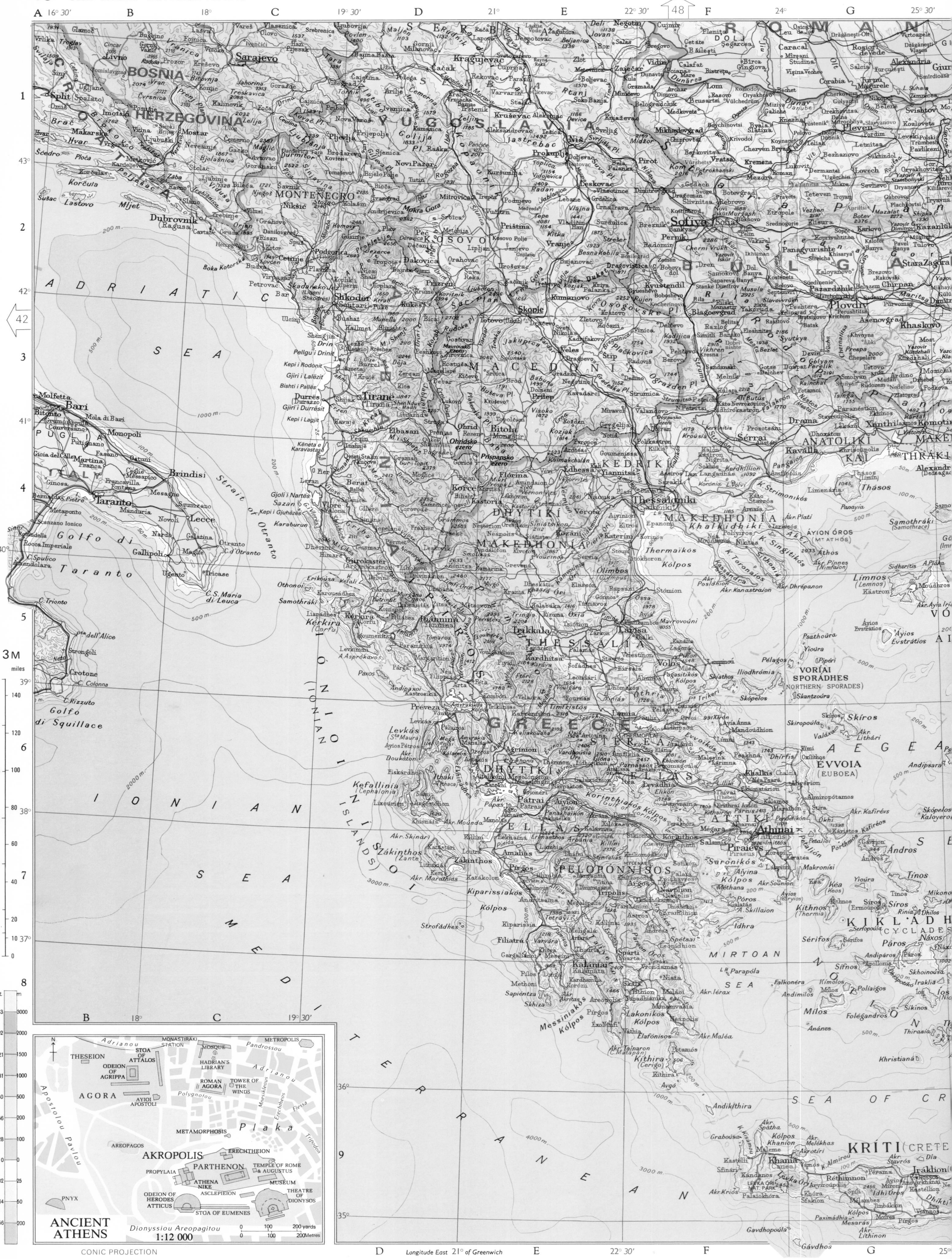

BOSNIA-HERZEGOVINA

Sarajevo

YUGOSLAVIA

MONTENEGRO

Dubrovnik (Ragusa)

ADRIATIC SEA

Skopje

KOSOVO

Priština

Niš

Sofiya (Sofia)

BULGARIA

ROMANIA

MACEDONIA

Tiranë (Tirana)

ALBANIA

Durrës (Durazzo)

Elbasan

Ohrid

Bitola (Monastir)

PUGLIA

Bari

Brindisi

Taranto

Lecce

Golfo di Taranto

Golfo di Squillace

Strait of Otranto

IONIAN SEA

IONIAN ISLANDS

Kérkira (Corfu)

DHYTIKÍ MAKEDHONÍA

Thessaloníki

MAKEDHONÍA

Khalkidhikí

ÁYION ÓROS (MT ÁTHOS)

ANATOLIKÍ MAKEDHONÍA

ANATOLIKÍ THRÁKI

Kaválla

Dráma

Sérrai

Thásos

Ioánnina

ÍPIROS

THESSALÍA

Tríkkala

Kardhítsa

Lárisa

Vólos

VORÍAI SPORÁDHES (NORTHERN SPORADES)

Skíros

GREECE

STEREÁ ELLÁS

DHYTIKÍ ELLÁS

Agrínion

Pátrai

Athínai

Piraiévs (Piraeus)

EVVOIA (EUBOEA)

AEGEAN SEA

PELOPÓNNISOS

Kórinthos

Spárti

Kalámai

Kithira (Cerigo)

KIKLÁDHES (CYCLADES)

Náxos

Páros

Mílos

Sifnos

MIRTOAN SEA

MEDITERRANEAN SEA

SEA OF CRETE

KRÍTI (CRETE)

Khaniá

Réthimnon

Iráklion

ANCIENT ATHENS
1:12 000

THESEION

STOA OF ATTALOS

ODEION OF AGRIPPA

AGORA

HADRIAN'S LIBRARY

ROMAN AGORA

TOWER OF THE WINDS

MONASTIRÁKI STATION

MOSQUE

METROPOLIS

AYIOI APOSTOLI

METAMORPHOSIS

Plaka

AREOPAGOS

AKROPOLIS

PARTHENON

PROPYLAIA

ATHENA NIKE

ERECHTHEION

TEMPLE OF ROME & AUGUSTUS

MUSEUM

ODEION OF HERODES ATTICUS

ASCLEPIEION

PNYX

THEATRE OF DIONYSOS

STOA OF EUMENES

Dionyssiou Areopagitou

CONIC PROJECTION

Longitude East 21° of Greenwich

1:3M

km   miles

240

140

200

120

160

100

120

80

80

40

40

20

0

ISTANBUL
(CONSTANTINOPLE)
1 : 110 000

BOSPORUS
1 : 1 100 000

CORFU
(KÉRKIRA)
(To Greece)
1 : 1 200 000

RHODES
(RÓDHOS)
(To Greece)
1 : 1 200 000

ATHENS – PIRÆUS
(ATHÍNAI – PIRAIÉVS)
1 : 150 000

The names of provinces in Bulgaria are named after their respective capitals, which are underlined in colour.

Heights and Depths in metres

© John Bartholomew & Son Ltd Edinburgh

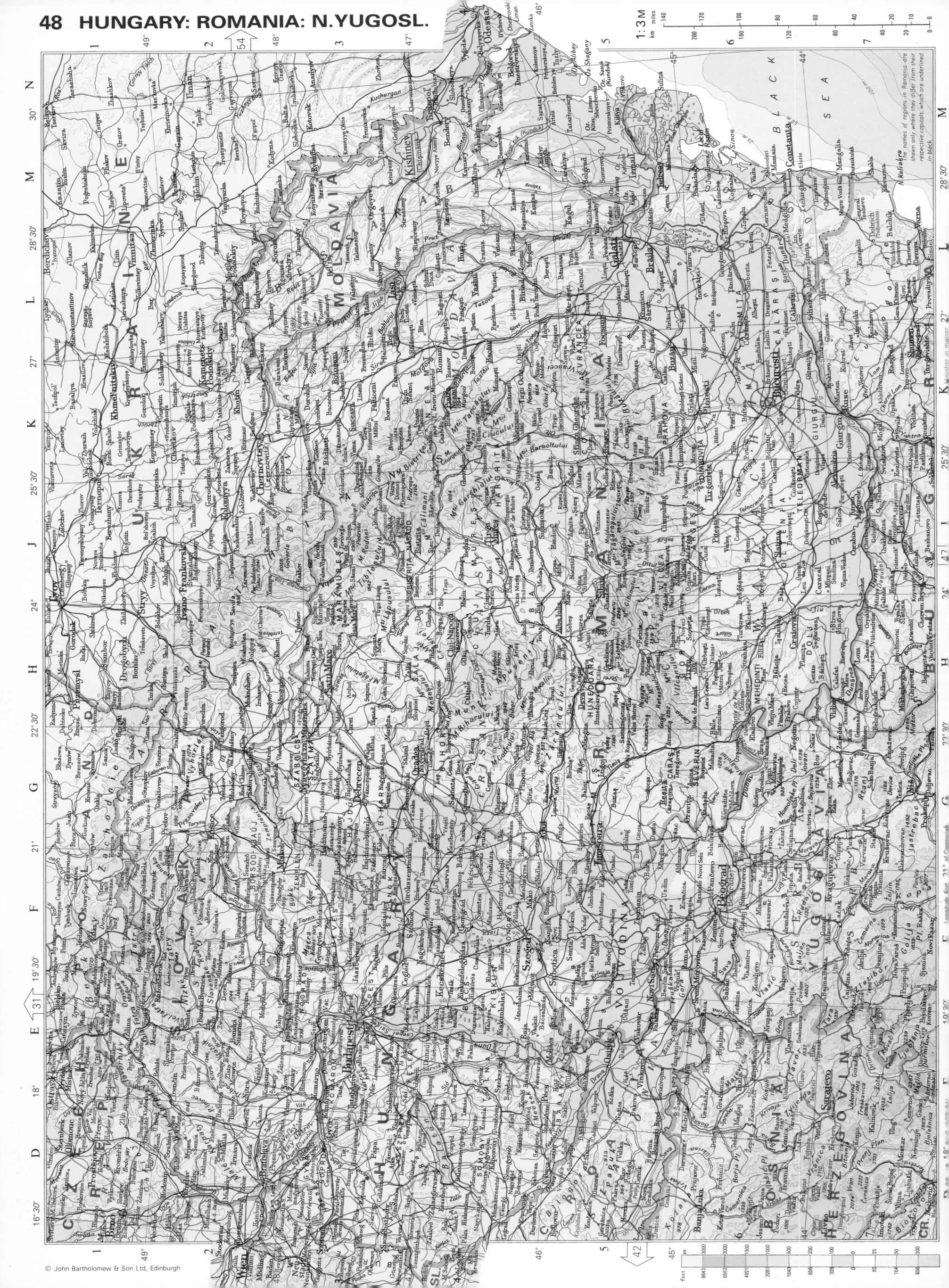
1:3M
BLACK SEA
The names of regions in Romania are shown only where they differ from their respective capitals, which are underlined in black
MOLDAVIA
Kishinev
Odessa
Iaşi
Galaţi
Brăila
Constanţa
Bucureşti
Ploieşti
Braşov
Sibiu
Cluj-Napoca
Oradea
Timişoara
Craiova
Ruse
Varna
Debrecen
Miskolc
Budapest
Szeged
Kecskemét
Bratislava
Wien
Beograd
Novi Sad
Sarajevo
Lvov
Chernovtsy
Ivano-Frankovsk
Ternopol
Vinnitsa
Kosice
Subotica
Osijek
Szombathely
Gyor
Pecs
Dunărea
Tisza

MOSCOW

GULF OF FINLAND

SANKT - PETERBURG

Kronshtadt
Ostrov Kotlin
Lomonosov
Petrodvorets
Strel'na
Krasnoye Selo
Pushkin
Pavlovsk
Sofiya
Kolpino
Pontonnyy
Otradnoye
Pavlovo
Dubrovka
Vsevolozhsk
Pargolovo
Levashovo
Sestroretsk
LENINGRAD AIRPORT

MOSKVA

MOSKVA
GOROD MOSKVA
Kremlin
Red Square
Bol'shoi Theatre

Kryukovo
Skhodnya
SHEREMET'YEVO AIRPORT
Dolgoprudnyy
Khimki
Mytishchi
Kaliningrad
Shchelkovo
Ivanteyevka
Fryazino
Tushino
Krasnogorsk
Dedovsk
Kuntsevo
Odintsovo
Balashikha
Reutov
Zheleznodorozhnyy
Lyubertsy
Elektrougli
Zhukovskiy
Lyublino
Biryulevo
Lytkarino
Ramenskoye
Oktyabr'skiy
VNUKOVO AIRPORT
Aprelevka
MOSKVA

1 : 300 000

0 5 10 15 km
0 5 10 miles

© Times Books Ltd

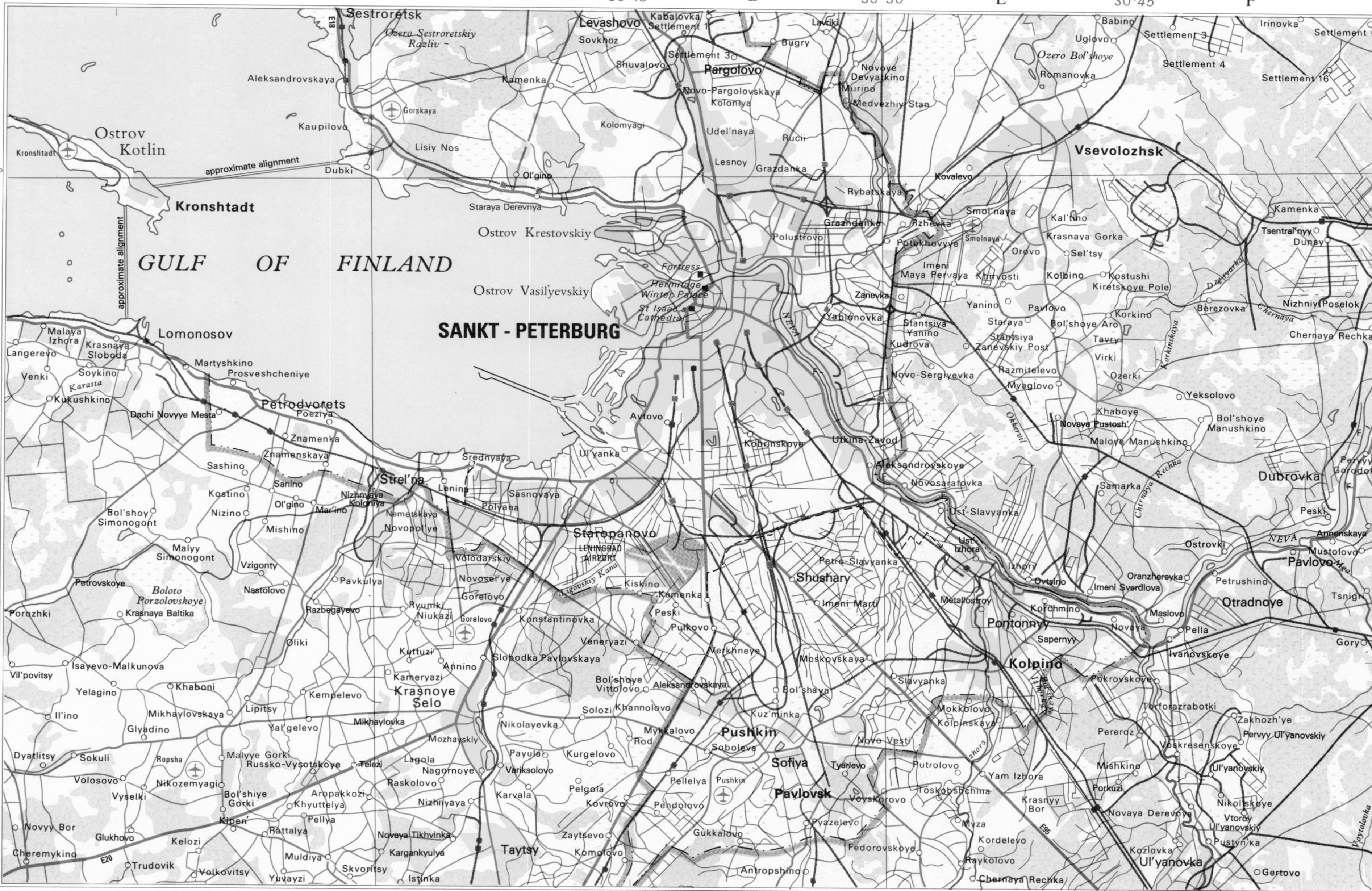

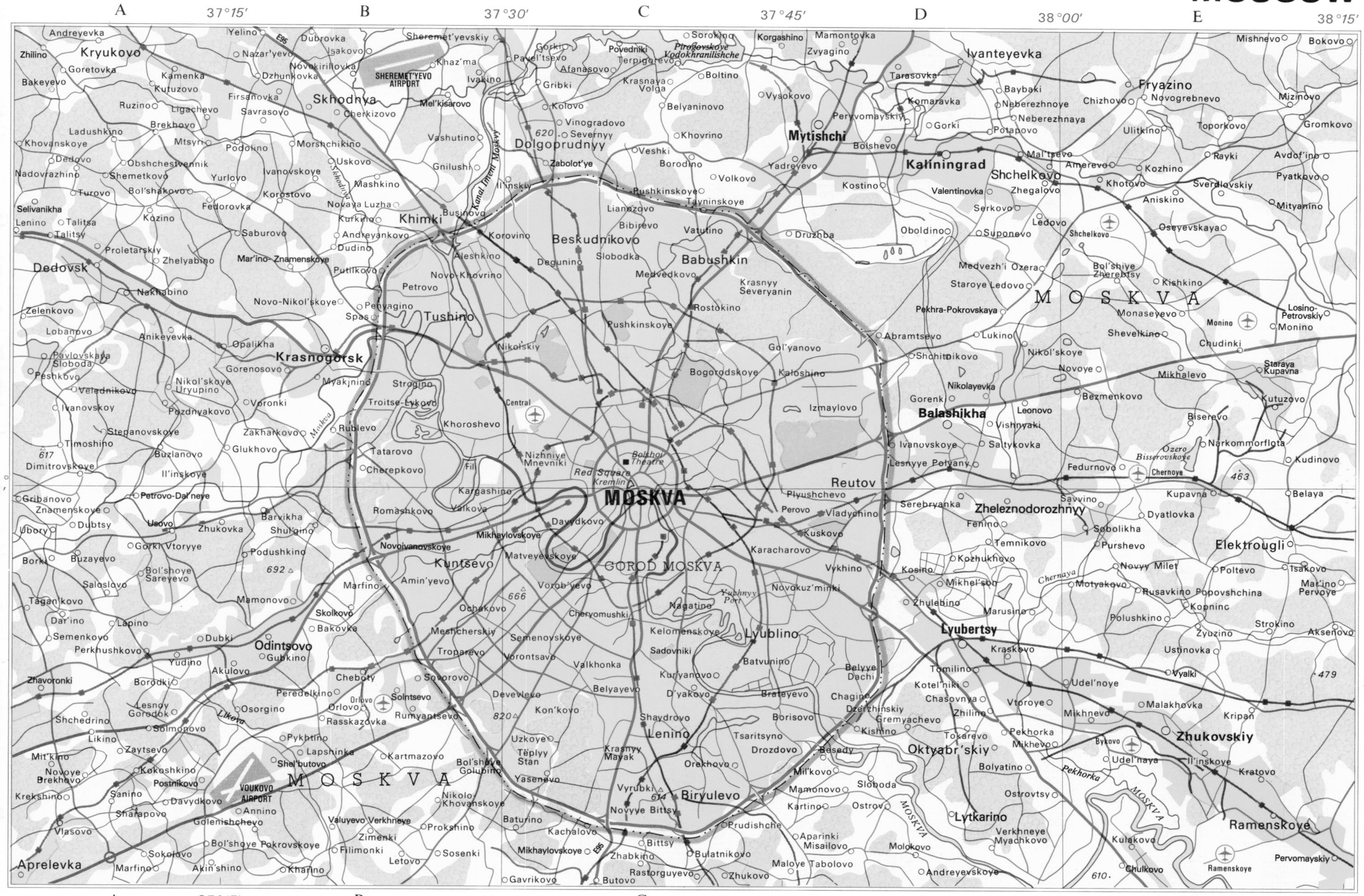

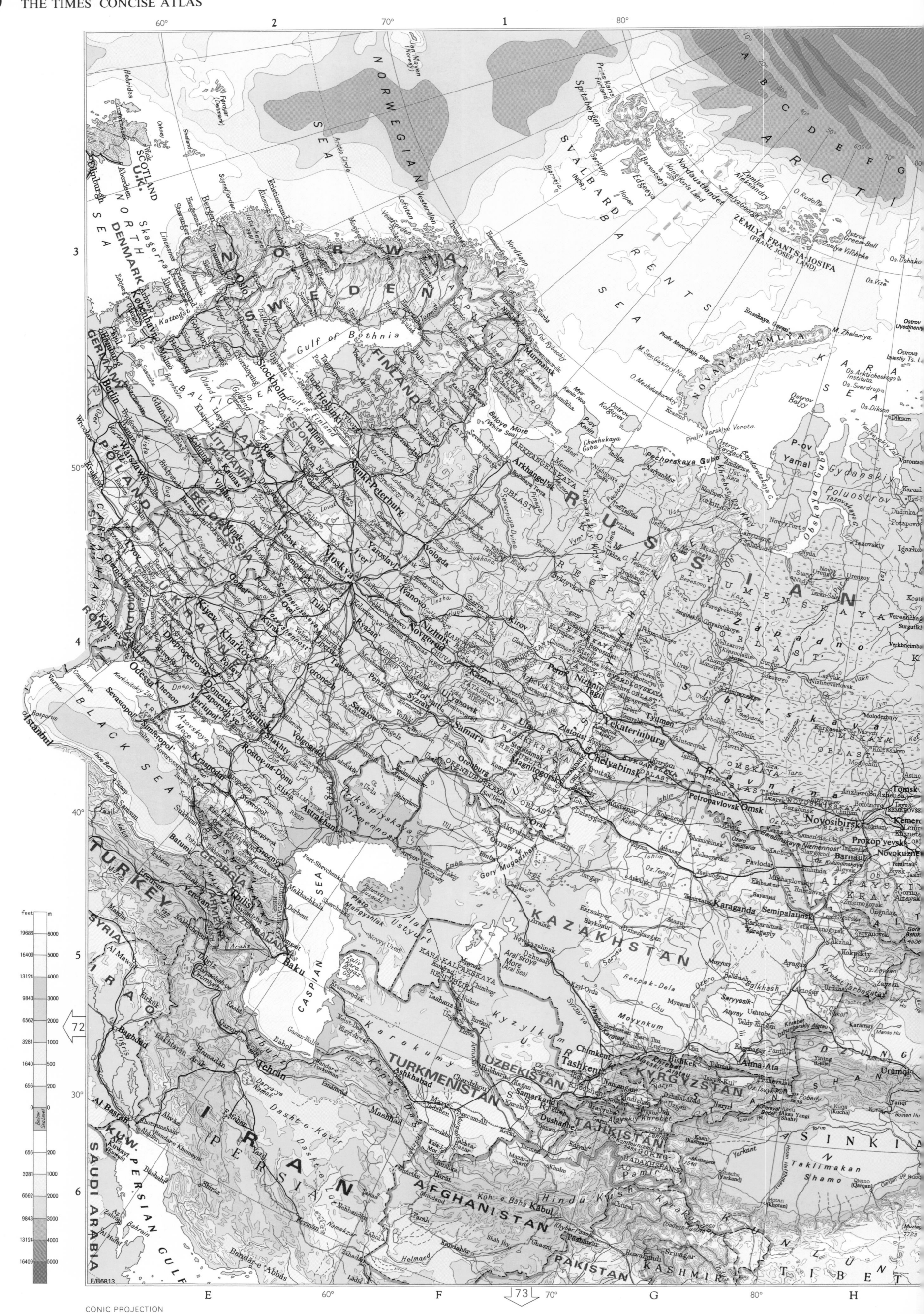

NORWEGIAN SEA
ARCTIC
SVALBARD (NOR.)
Spitsbergen
BARENTS SEA
ZEMLYA FRANTSA-IOSIFA (FRANZ JOSEF LAND)
NOVAYA ZEMLYA
KARA SEA
NORTH SEA
SCOTLAND
U.K.
NORWAY
SWEDEN
FINLAND
DENMARK
GERMANY
POLAND
LITHUANIA
LATVIA
ESTONIA
BELORUSSIA
UKRAINE
MOLDOVA
ROM.
BALTIC SEA
Gulf of Bothnia
Gulf of Finland
Beloye More (White Sea)
RUSSIAN FEDERATION
BLACK SEA
CASPIAN SEA
Aral'skoye More (Aral Sea)
TURKEY
SYRIA
IRAQ
IRAN
PERSIA
GEORGIA
ARMENIA
AZERBAIJAN
KAZAKHSTAN
UZBEKISTAN
TURKMENISTAN
KYRGYZSTAN
TAJIKISTAN
AFGHANISTAN
PAKISTAN
KASHMIR
TIBET
SAUDI ARABIA
KUW.
PERSIAN GULF
Oslo
Stockholm
Helsinki
Tallinn
Riga
Vilnius
Minsk
Warszawa
Berlin
København
Sankt-Peterburg
Moskva
Kiyev
Khar'kov
Odessa
Istanbul
Tbilisi
Yerevan
Baku
Tehran
Baghdad
Kabul
Tashkent
Bishkek
Alma-Ata
Dushanbe
Ashkhabad
Samarkand
Volgograd
Rostov-na-Donu
Astrakhan'
Samara
Kazan'
Nizhniy Novgorod
Perm'
Yekaterinburg
Chelyabinsk
Omsk
Novosibirsk
Tomsk
Barnaul
Karaganda
Semipalatinsk
Arkhangel'sk
Murmansk
Vologda
Yaroslavl'
Kirov
Ufa
Orenburg
Magnitogorsk
Saratov
Voronezh
Krasnodar
Sevastopol'
Simferopol'
Batumi
Kara Kum
Kyzylkum
Hindu Kush
Pamir
Taklimakan Shamo
Dasht-e-Kavir
Zapadno Sibirskaya Ravnina
Prikaspiyskaya Nizmennost'
feet
m
19686 6000
16409 5000
13124 4000
9843 3000
6562 2000
3281 1000
1640 500
656 200
0 0
Below Sea level
656 200
3281 1000
6562 2000
9843 3000
13124 4000
16409 5000
72
73
E
F
G
H
60°
70°
80°
50°
40°
30°
F/B6813

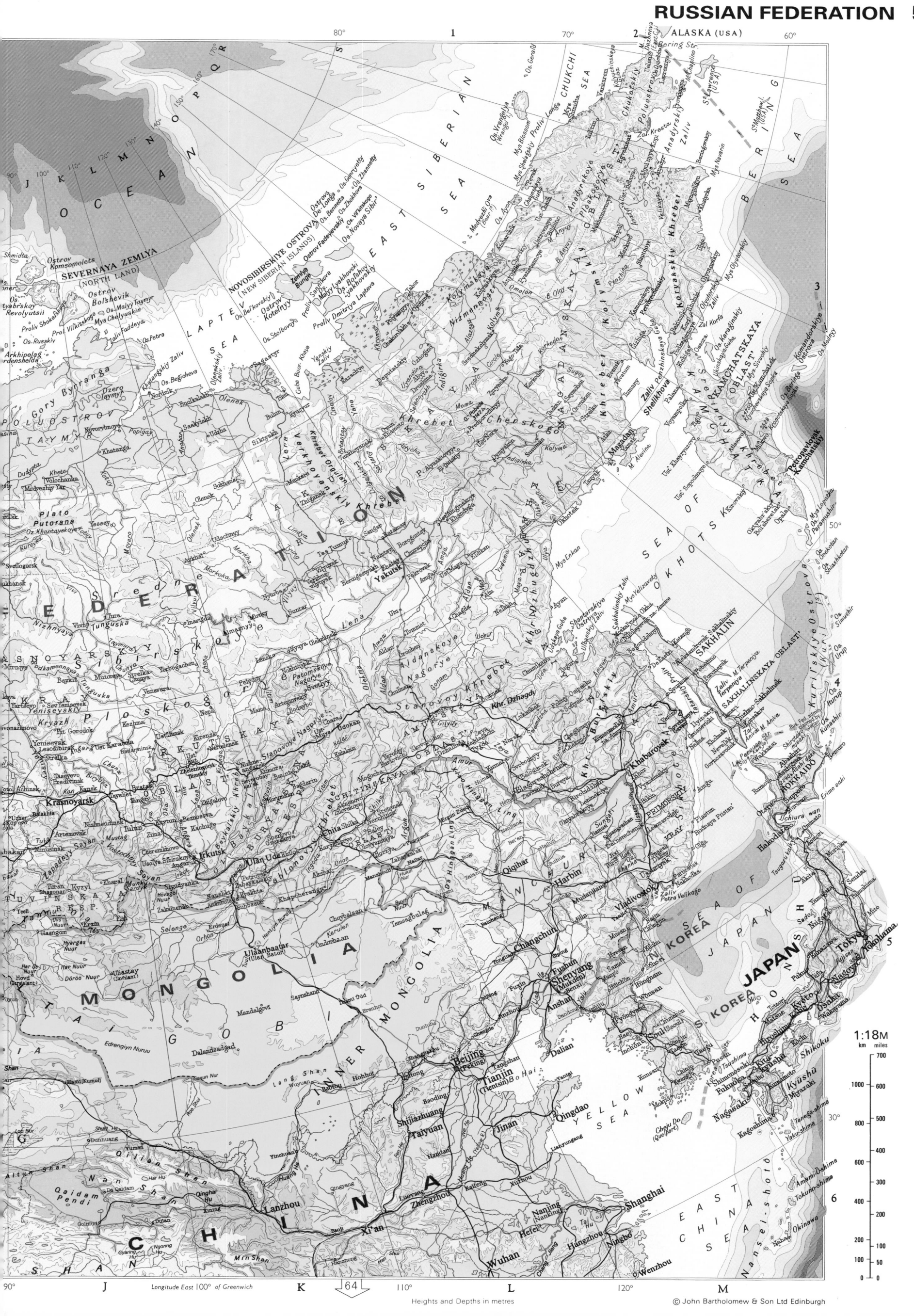

ALASKA (USA)

ARCTIC OCEAN

SEVERNAYA ZEMLYA
(NORTH LAND)

NOVOSIBIRSKIYE OSTROVA
(NEW SIBERIAN ISLANDS)

LAPTEV SEA

EAST SIBERIAN SEA

CHUKCHI SEA

BERING SEA

POLUOSTROV TAYMYR

KAMCHATSKAYA OBLAST'

Petropavlovsk-Kamchatskiy

FEDERATION

Yakutsk

SEA OF OKHOTSK

Magadan

SAKHALIN

SAKHALINSKAYA OBLAST'

HOKKAIDO

Khabarovsk

PRIMORSKIY KRAY

Krasnoyarsk

IRKUTSK OBLAST'

BURYAT

CHITINSKAYA OBLAST'

Irkutsk
Ulan-Ude

Chita

Vladivostok

SEA OF JAPAN

HONSHU

Tokyo

JAPAN

Nagoya
Kyoto
Osaka

MONGOLIA

Ulaanbaatar (Ulan Bator)

INNER MONGOLIA

MANCHURIA

Harbin
Qiqihar
Changchun
Shenyang (Mukden)
Anshan
Fushun

N. KOREA
P'yongyang

S. KOREA
Seoul

SHIKOKU

KYUSHU

GOBI

YELLOW SEA

Beijing (Peking)
Tianjin (Tientsin)
Dalian
Qingdao
Jinan
Taiyuan
Shijiazhuang

Bo Hai

Qilian Shan
Nan Shan
Altun Shan

Qaidam Pendi

Lanzhou

Xi'an

Zhengzhou
Luoyang

CHINA

Wuhan

Shanghai

Nanjing (Nanking)
Hefei
Hangzhou
Ningbo
Wenzhou

EAST CHINA SEA

Nansei-shoto

1:18M

km   miles

700
600
500
400
300
200
100
50
0

1000
800
600
400
200
100
0

Longitude East 100° of Greenwich

Heights and Depths in metres

© John Bartholomew & Son Ltd Edinburgh

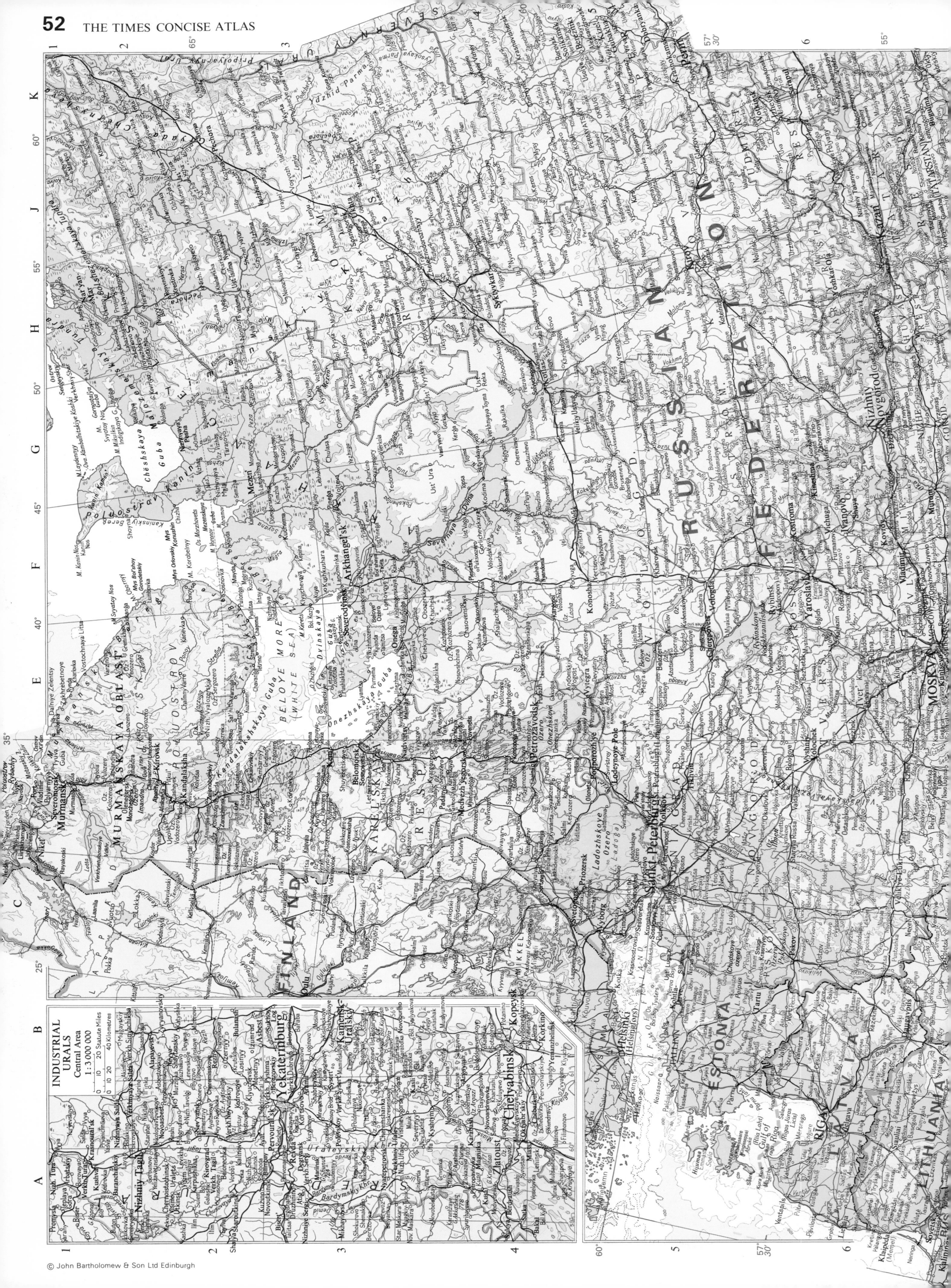

INDUSTRIAL URALS
Central Area
1:3 000 000

POLAND
BELORUSSIA
UKRAINE
RUSSIA
KAZAKHSTAN
ROMANIA
BULGARIA
TURKEY
GEORGIA
AZERBAIJAN

CASPIAN SEA

BLACK SEA (CHERNOYE MORE) (KARA DENİZ)

AZOVSKOYE MORE (SEA OF AZOV)

KALMYTSKAYA RESPUBLIKA

WARSZAWA
Lublin
VILNIUS
MINSK
Smolensk
Bryansk
KIEV (Kiyev)
Odessa
Kishinev
Bucureşti (Bucharest)
İstanbul (Constantinople)
Samara
Saratov
Volgograd
Voronezh
Kursk
Kharkov
Donetsk
Rostov-na-Donu
Astrakhan
Krasnodar
Novorossiysk
Sochi
Sukhumi
Batumi
TBILISI
Kutaisi
Makhachkala
Grozny
Stavropol
Armavir
Nikolayev
Kherson
Sevastopol
Simferopol
Yalta
Kerch
Zaporozhye
Dnepropetrovsk
Krivoy Rog
Cherkassy
Kremenchug
Poltava
Melitopol
Mariupol
Taganrog
Novoshakhtinsk
Shakhty
Kamensk-Shakhtinskiy
Ryazan
Tula
Kaluga
Orel
Tambov
Penza
Ulyanovsk
Samara
Bryansk
Zhitomir
Vinnitsa
Chernovtsy
Ternopol
Lvov
Sinop
Samsun
Trabzon
Zonguldak
Varna
Burgas
Constanţa
Galaţi
Ploieşti

1:6 M

CONIC PROJECTION

feet m 4000 3000 2000 1500 1000 500 200 100 0
400 km 320 240 160 80 40 0

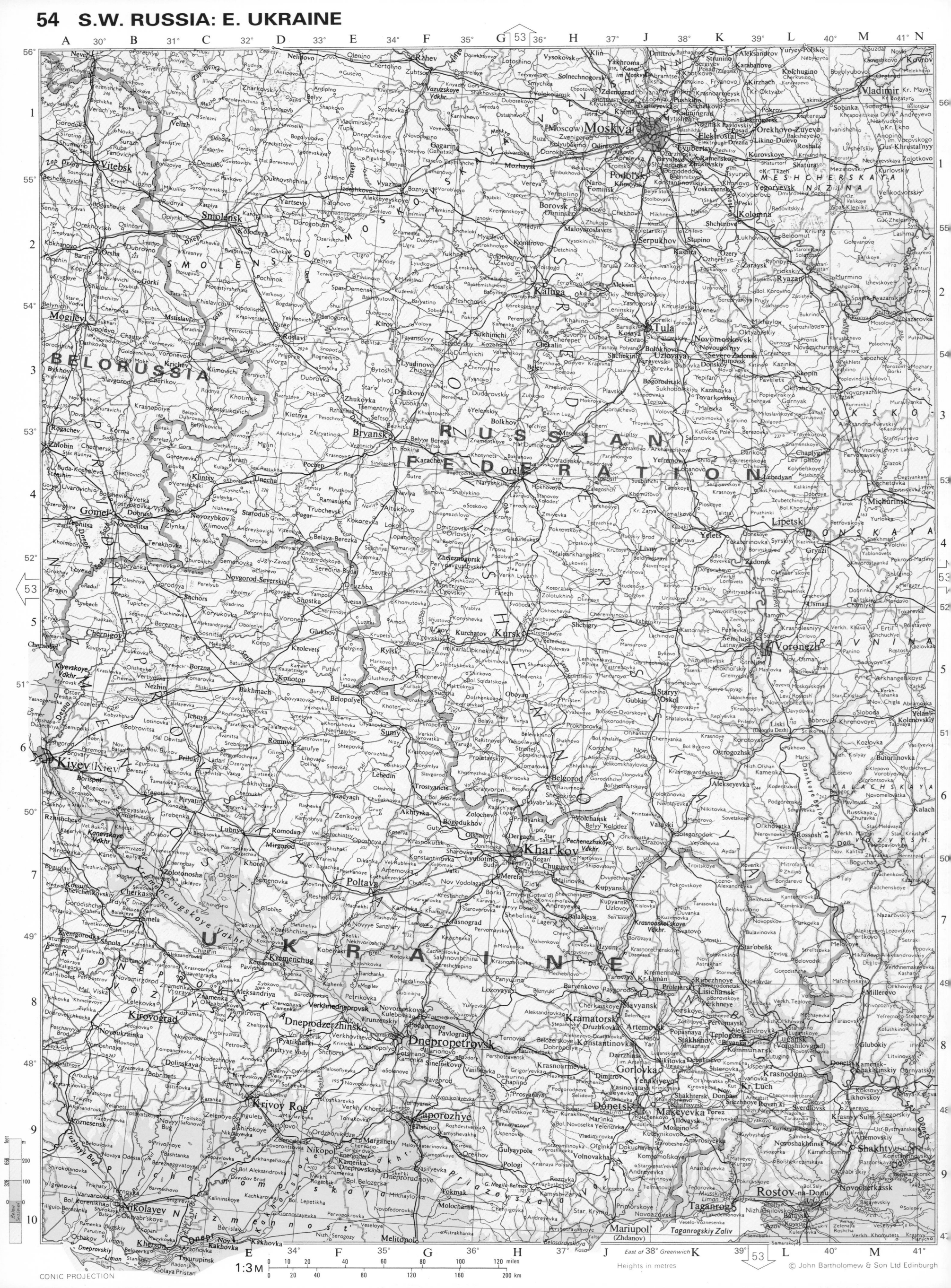

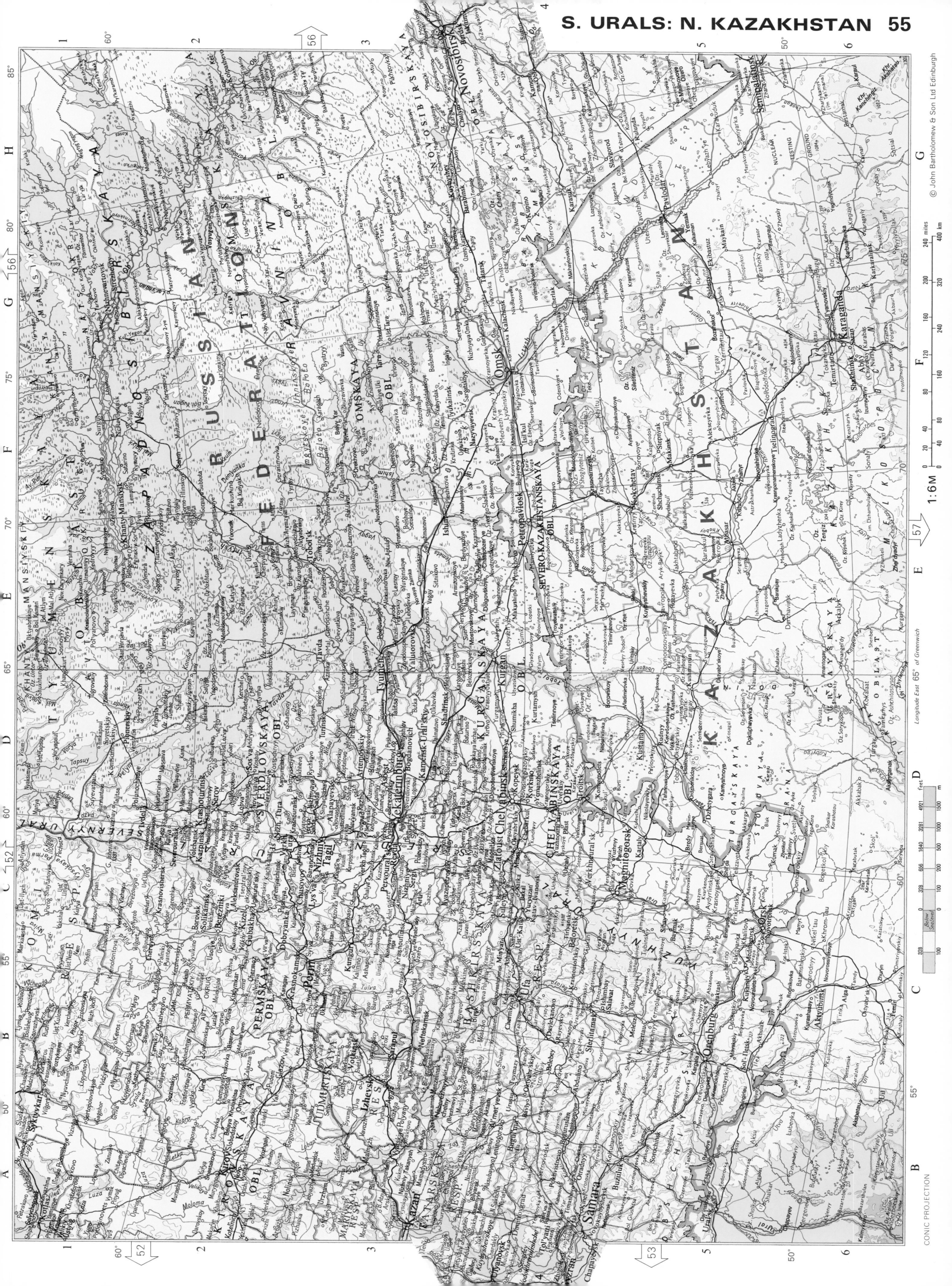
1:6M
CONIC PROJECTION
© John Bartholomew & Son Ltd Edinburgh
RUSSIAN FEDERATION
KAZAKHSTAN
Omsk
Novosibirsk
Karaganda
Samara
Perm
Ufa
Orenburg

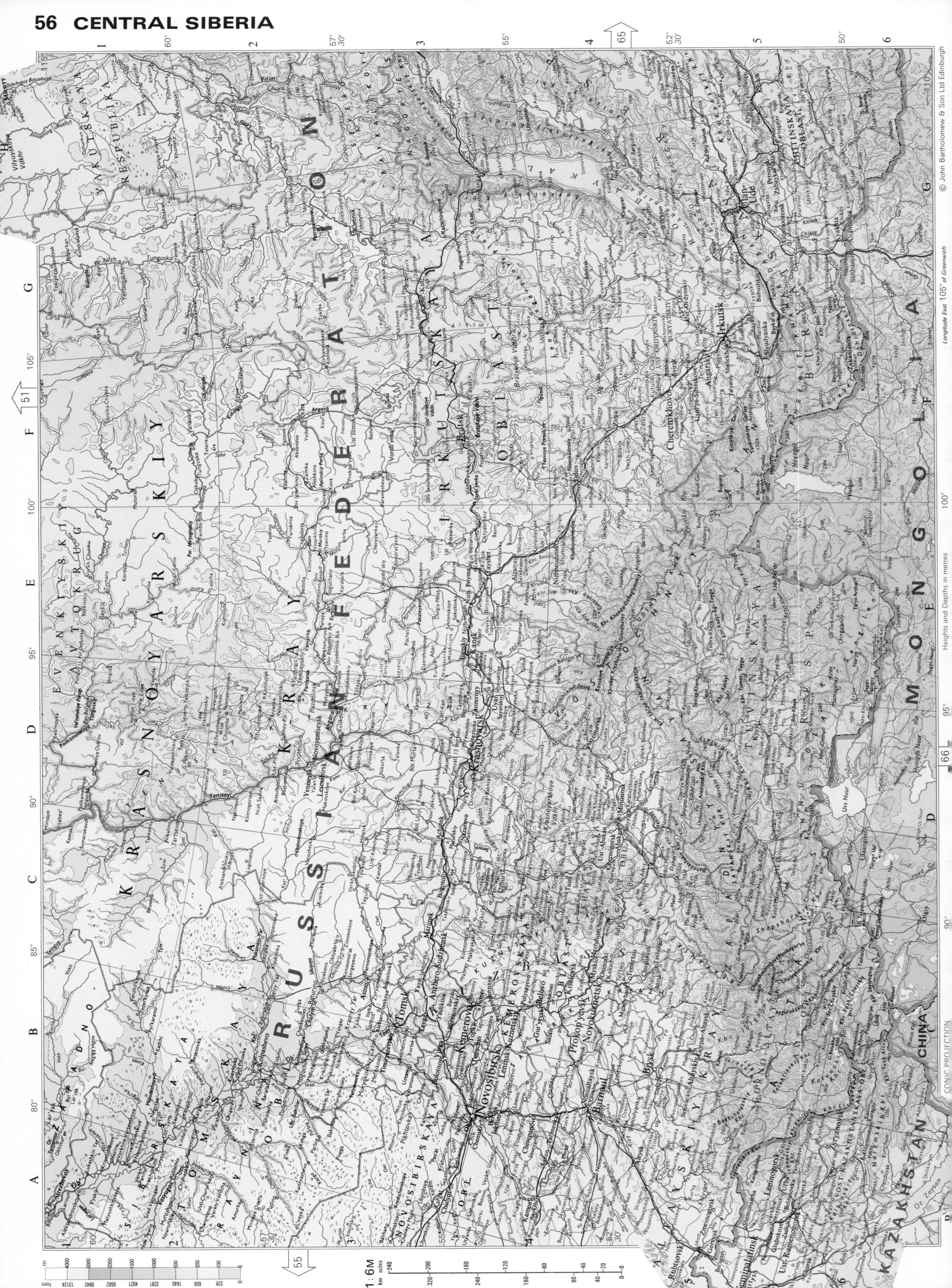

© John Bartholomew & Son Ltd Edinburgh

Longitude East 105° of Greenwich

Heights and Depths in metres

CONIC PROJECTION

1:6M

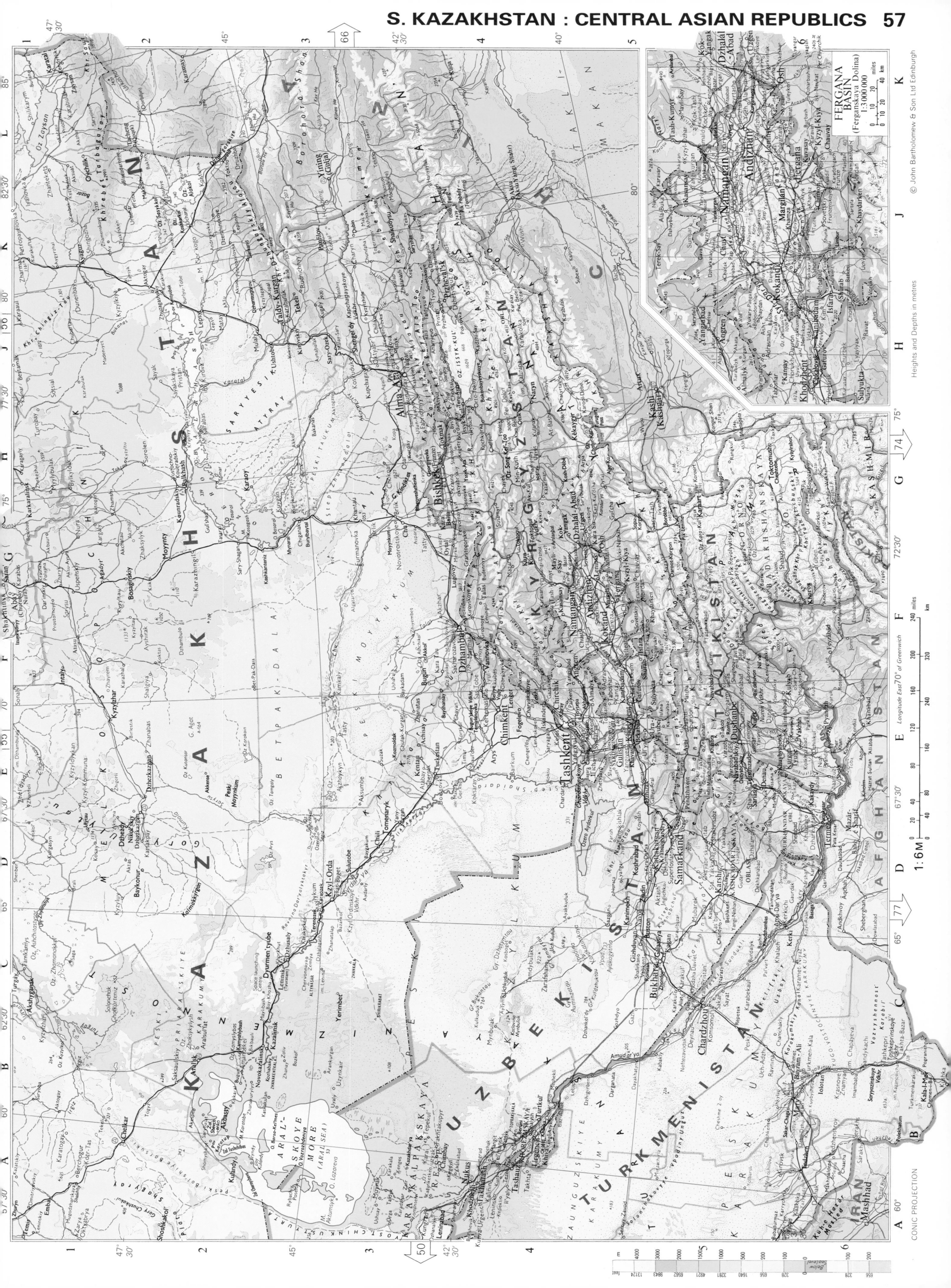

FERGANA BASIN
(Ferganskaya Dolina)
1:3000000

Heights and Depths in metres

CONIC PROJECTION

1:6M

56

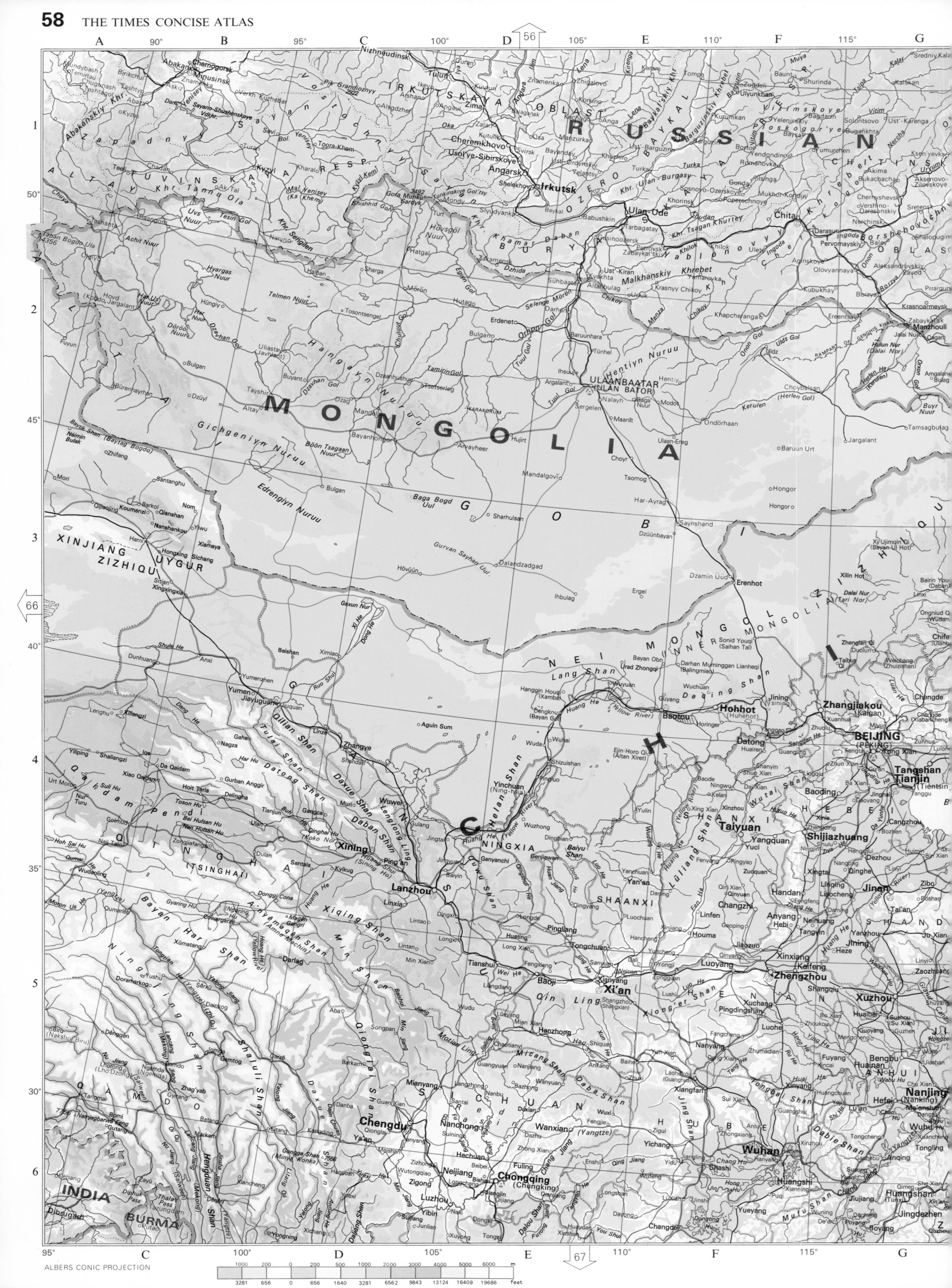

66

67

ALBERS CONIC PROJECTION

m	1000	200	0	200	500	1000	2000	3000	4000	5000	6000
feet	3281	656	0	656	1640	3281	6562	9843	13124	16409	19686

SEA OF OKHOTSK

Continuation on the same scale

SEA OF JAPAN

HOKKAIDO

Sapporo

Asahikawa

Otaru

Muroran

Hakodate

Aomori

SOUTH KOREA

Pusan

KOREA STRAIT (Tsushima-kaikyō)

Tsushima

Kita-Kyūshū

Fukuoka

Saga

Sasebo

Nagasaki

Kumamoto

Kagoshima

Miyazaki

Nobeoka

Ōita

Beppu

Matsue

Tottori

Hiroshima

Okayama

Kurashiki

Kōbe

Matsuyama

Kōchi

Tokushima

JAPAN

feet / m

9843 / 3000
6562 / 2000
4921 / 1500
3281 / 1000
1640 / 500
656 / 200
328 / 100
0 / 0
656 / 200
6562 / 2000
13124 / 4000
26248 / 8000

CONIC PROJECTION

Top coordinate labels: J 136° K 137° L 138° M 139° N ... 142° Q 143°

Latitude markings (right margin): 5, 40°, 6, 39°, 7, 38°, 8, 37°, 9, 36°, 10, 35°, 11, 34°, 12, 13, 14

Prefectures / regions:
AOMORI, AKITA, IWATE, YAMAGATA, MIYAGI, NIIGATA, FUKUSHIMA, TOYAMA, NAGANO, GUMMA, TOCHIGI, IBARAKI, SAITAMA, TOKYO, KANAGAWA, CHIBA, YAMANASHI, SHIZUOKA, GIFU, AICHI, FUKUI, ISHIKAWA, MIE, SHIGA, NAGANO

Major cities:
Aomori, Hirosaki, Hachinohe, Morioka, Akita, Sakata, Sendai, Yamagata, Fukushima, Kōriyama, Iwaki, Niigata, Nagaoka, Joetsu, Takada, Kanazawa, Komatsu, Toyama, Takaoka, Nagano, Matsumoto, Takasaki, Maebashi, Utsunomiya, Mito, Hitachi, Omiya, Urawa, Kawagoe, TOKYO, Kawasaki, Yokohama, Yokosuka, Chiba, Hachiōji, Odawara, Numazu, Shimizu, Shizuoka, Hamamatsu, Toyohashi, Okazaki, Nagoya, Yokkaichi, Gifu, Ōgaki, Tsu, Matsusaka, Fukui, Takefu

Seas and oceans:
SEA OF JAPAN, PACIFIC OCEAN

Bays:
Mutsu-wan, Toyama-wan, Sagami-wan, Suruga-wan, Tōkyō-wan, Ise-wan, Mikawa-wan

Islands:
Sado, Awa-shima, Tobi-shima, Izu, Ō-shima, To-shima, Nii-jima, Kōzu-shima, Miyake-jima, Mikura-jima, Hachijō-jima, Inamba-jima, Onohara-jima

Capes/points:
Shiriya-zaki, Shirakami-misaki, Oga-hantō, Nyūdō-zaki, Iro-zaki, Omae-zaki, Daiō-zaki, Shiono-misaki, Inubō-saki, Nojima-zaki

Heights and Depths in metres
East 136° of Greenwich

Inset maps:

IWO JIMA 1:300 000
Iō-Jima (Iwo Jima), Motoyama, Suribachi-yama, Kitano-hana, Kangoku-iwa, Kama-iwa, Higashi-iwa, Tobiishi-hana, Futatsu-ne
Statute Miles 0 1 2 3; Kilometres 0 1 2

OKINAWA 1:1 200 000
Hedo-misaki, Hedo, Ukae, Sosu, Ada, Aha, Arakawa, Nago, Naha, Naha Airport, Shuri, Itoman, Gushikami, Kin, Nakijin, Ie-jima
Miles 0 10; Kilometres 0 10

Scale: 1:3 M
km / miles scale bar: 200 / 140, 170, 160 / 100, 120 / 80, 60, 80 / 40, 40 / 20, 20, 0

© John Bartholomew & Son Ltd Edinburgh

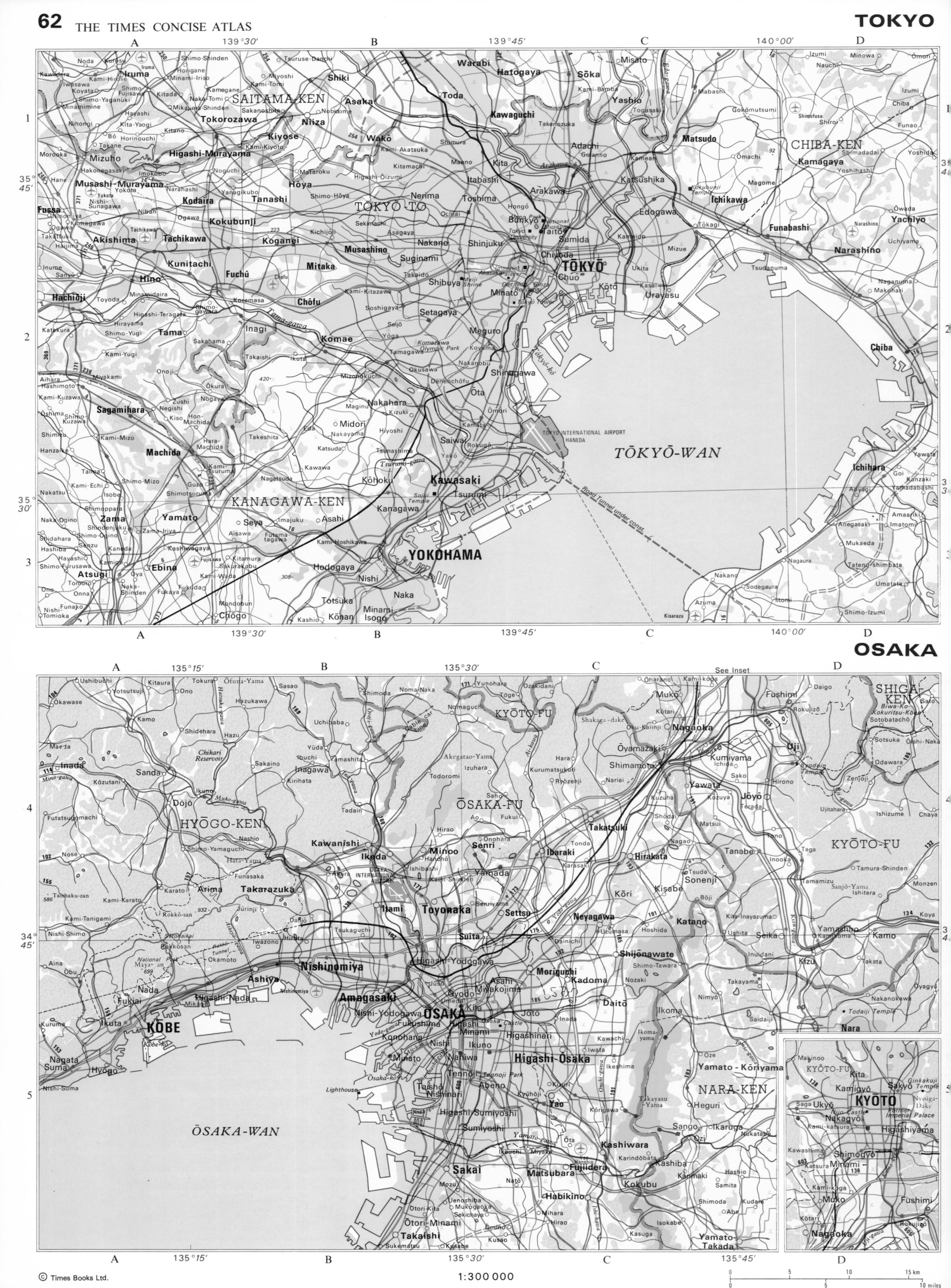

OSAKA

SAITAMA-KEN

Noda
Kurosu
Iruma
Tsuruse-Danchi
Warabi
Hatogaya
Misato
Izumi
Minowa
Ōmori

Tokorozawa
Shiki
Toda
Sōka
Yashio
Chiba
CHIBA-KEN

Niiza
Asaka
Kawaguchi
Matsudo
Kamagaya

Kiyose
Wako
Adachi
Ichikawa

Higashi-Murayama
Hōya
TOKYO-TO
Itabashi
Nerima
Katsushika

Musashi-Murayama
Toshima
Kokubunji
Temple

Kodaira
Tanashi
Arakawa
Edogawa

Fussa
Akishima
Tachikawa
Kōganei
Nakano
Shinjuku
Sumida
Funabashi
Narashino

Kunitachi
Fuchū
Mitaka
Musashino
Suginami
Chiyoda
TOKYO
Chuo
Kōto
Chiba

Hachiōji
Hino
Chōfu
Setagaya
Shibuya
Minato
Urayasu

Tama
Inagi
Komae
Meguro
Shinagawa
TOKYO-WAN

Machida
Nakahara
Ōta
Kamata
TOKYO INTERNATIONAL AIRPORT HANEDA
Ichihara

KANAGAWA-KEN
Kawasaki
Tsurumi
Yokohama

Sagamihara

Zama
Yamato
Seya
Asahi
Kanagawa

Atsugi
Ebina
Hodogaya
Nishi
Naka
Totsuka
Minami Isogo
Chōgo
Kōnan

KYOTO-FU
SHIGA-KEN

Fushimi
Nagaoka
Uji

HYOGO-KEN
OSAKA-FU

Kawanishi
Minoo
Senri
Ibaraki
Hirakata
KYOTO-FU

Ikeda
Yamada
Kōri

Takarazuka
Itami
Toyonaka
Settsu
Neyagawa
Katano

Nishinomiya
Suita
Shijonawate

Ashiya
Higashi-Yodogawa
Moriguchi
Kadoma

KOBE
Amagasaki
OSAKA
Daitō
Ikoma

Higashi-Ōsaka
NARA-KEN
Nara

OSAKA-WAN
Sakai
Yao
Kashiwara

Matsubara
Fujiidera
Kokubu

Habikino
Yamato-Kōriyama

Takaishi

KYOTO-FU
KYOTO
Higashiyama

1 : 300 000

SEOUL

1:300000

PEKING

1:300000

SHANGHAI

1:300000

CANTON

1:100 000

BANGKOK

1:300000

JAKARTA

1:300000

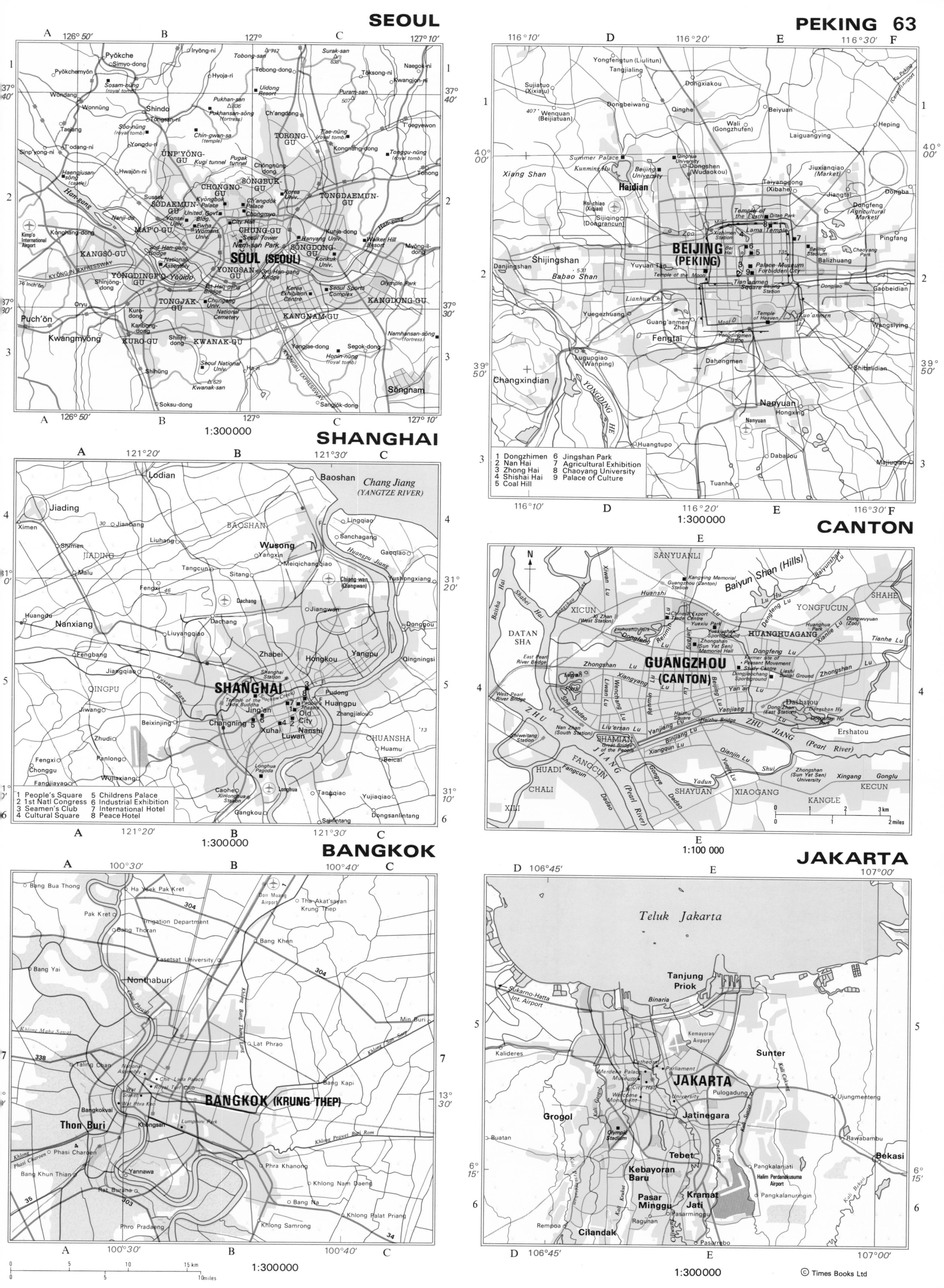

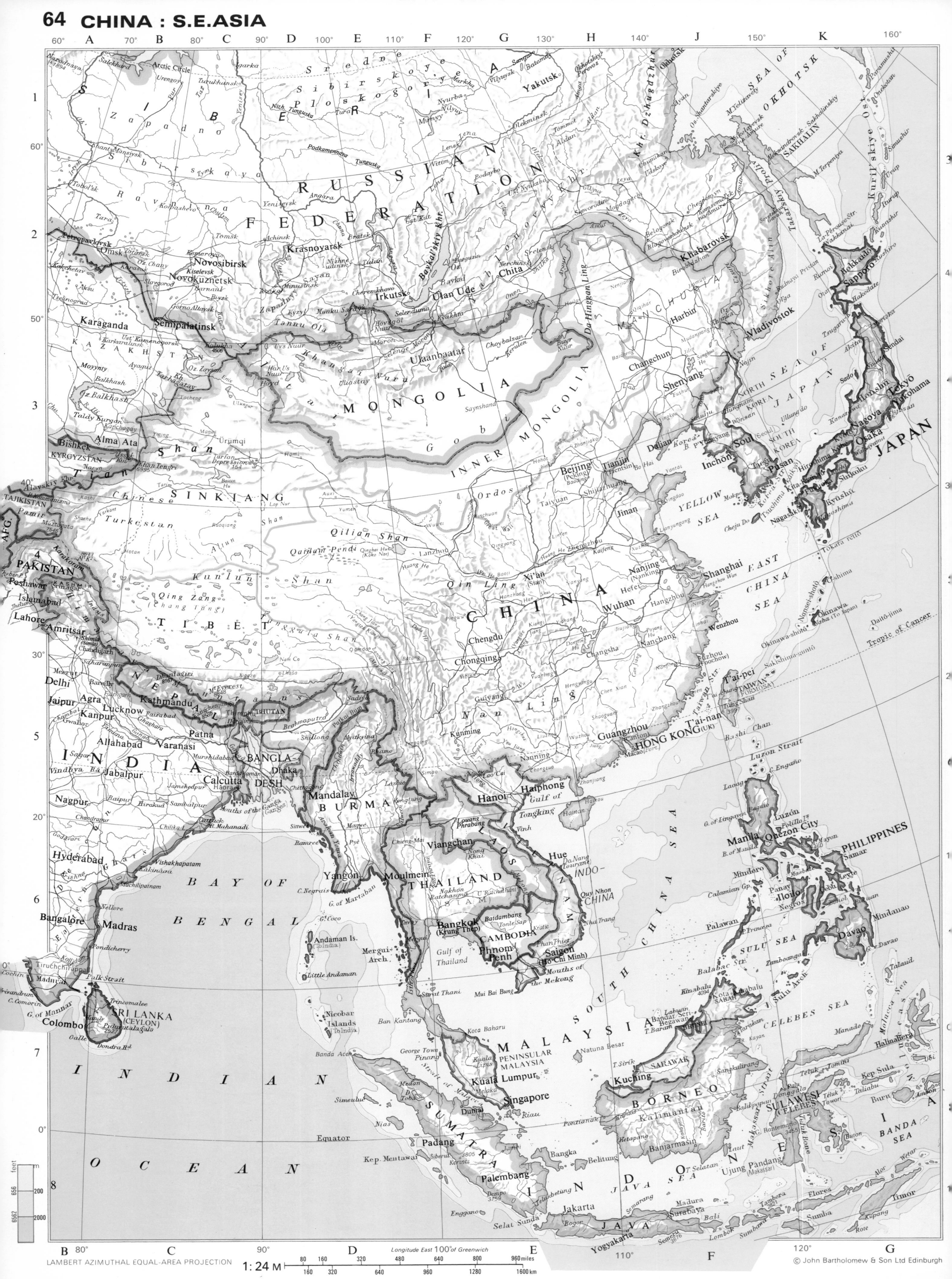

MONGOLIA
RUSSIAN FEDERATION
NORTH KOREA
SOUTH KOREA
JAPAN
SEA OF JAPAN
YELLOW SEA
(HUANG HAI)
KOREA BAY
BO HAI
(GULF OF CHIHLI)
HEILONGJIANG
JILIN
LIAONING
HEBEI
SHANXI
SHANDONG
HENAN
NEI MONGOL
(INNER MONGOLIAN AUT REGION)
BEIJING
Tianjin
Shenyang
Harbin
Changchun
Dalian
P'YŎNGYANG
SOUL (SEOUL)
Pusan
Vladivostok
Qingdao
1:6 M
CONIC PROJECTION
Heights and Depths in metres

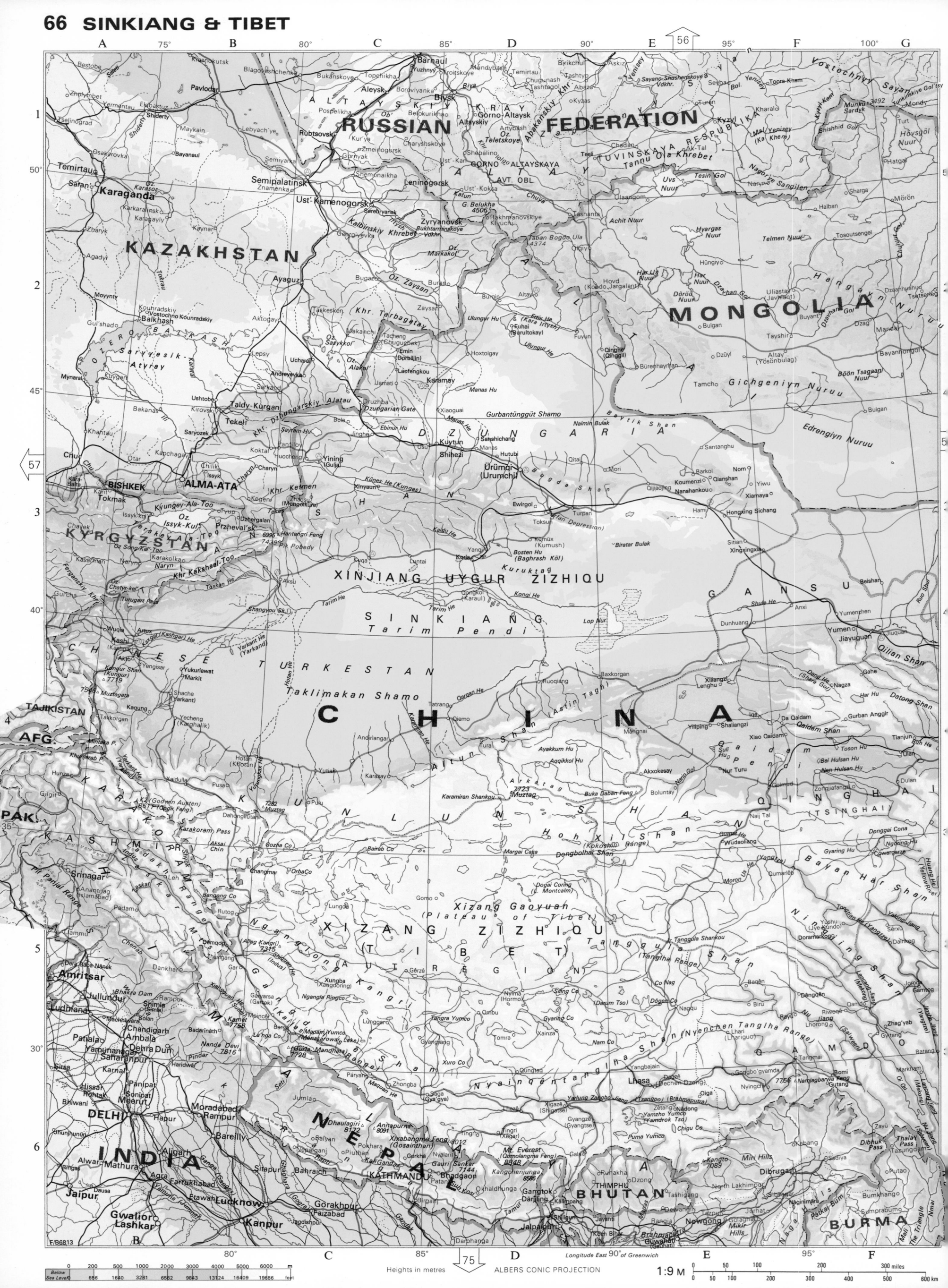

RUSSIAN FEDERATION
KAZAKHSTAN
MONGOLIA
KYRGYZSTAN
TAJIKISTAN
AFG.
PAK.
CHINA
INDIA
NEPAL
BHUTAN
BURMA
ALTAYSKIY KRAY
GORNO ALTAYSKAYA AVT. OBL.
TUVINSKAYA RESPUBLIKA
XINJIANG UYGUR ZIZHIQU
SINKIANG
Tarim Pendi
CHINESE TURKESTAN
Taklimakan Shamo
DZUNGARIA
TIEN SHAN
KUNLUN SHAN
KARAKORAM
KASHMIR
XIZANG ZIZHIQU (TIBET AUTONOMOUS REGION)
Xizang Gaoyuan (Plateau of Tibet)
QINGHAI (TSINGHAI)
GANSU
Qaidam Pendi
Gurbantünggüt Shamo
Nyainqentanglha Shan
Tanggula Shan
Gangdise Shan
Hoh Xil Shan
Altun Shan
Bayan Har Shan
Qilian Shan
Ozero Balkhash
Lop Nur
Barnaul
Semipalatinsk
Karaganda
Ust'-Kamenogorsk
Alma-Ata
Bishkek
Ürümqi (Urumchi)
Kashi (Kashgar)
Lhasa
Kathmandu
Thimphu
Delhi
Srinagar
Mt. Everest 8848
Heights in metres
ALBERS CONIC PROJECTION
Longitude East 90° of Greenwich
1:9 M
Below Sea Level 0 200 500 1000 2000 3000 4000 5000 6000 m
656 1640 3281 6562 9843 13124 16409 19686 feet
0 50 100 200 300 miles
0 50 100 200 300 400 500 600 km

CHINA
SICHUAN
GUIZHOU
YUNNAN
GUANGXI
GUANGDONG
HUNAN
HUBEI
JIANGXI
FUJIAN
ZHEJIANG
ANHUI
TAIWAN (FORMOSA)
TAIWAN STRAIT
SOUTH CHINA SEA
GULF OF TONGKING
HAINAN
VIETNAM
LAOS
HONG KONG
MACAO
HONG KONG 1:300,000
Kowloon
Victoria
Shanghai
Hangzhou
Nanjing
Wuhan
Changsha
Nanchang
Fuzhou
Xiamen
Guangzhou
Nanning
Guiyang
Kunming
Chongqing
Chengdu
Hanoi
Haiphong
Haikou
Zhanjiang
Shantou
Tropic of Cancer
CONIC PROJECTION
1:6M
Heights and Depths in metres
Longitude East 114° of Greenwich

CHINA
INDO-CHINA
BURMA (MYANMAR)
THAILAND
LAOS
VIETNAM
CAMBODIA (KAMPUCHEA)
BANGLADESH
INDIA
HANOI
HAIPHONG
BANGKOK (KRUNG THEP)
YANGON
MANDALAY
PHNOM PENH
SAIGON (HO CHI MINH)
VIANGCHAN (VIENTIANE)
Da Nang
Nanning
HAINAN
GULF OF TONKING
GULF OF THAILAND
BAY OF BENGAL
Gulf of Martaban
ANDAMAN SEA
ANDAMAN ISLANDS
MERGUI ARCHIPELAGO
Mouths of the Irrawaddy
Ten Degree Channel

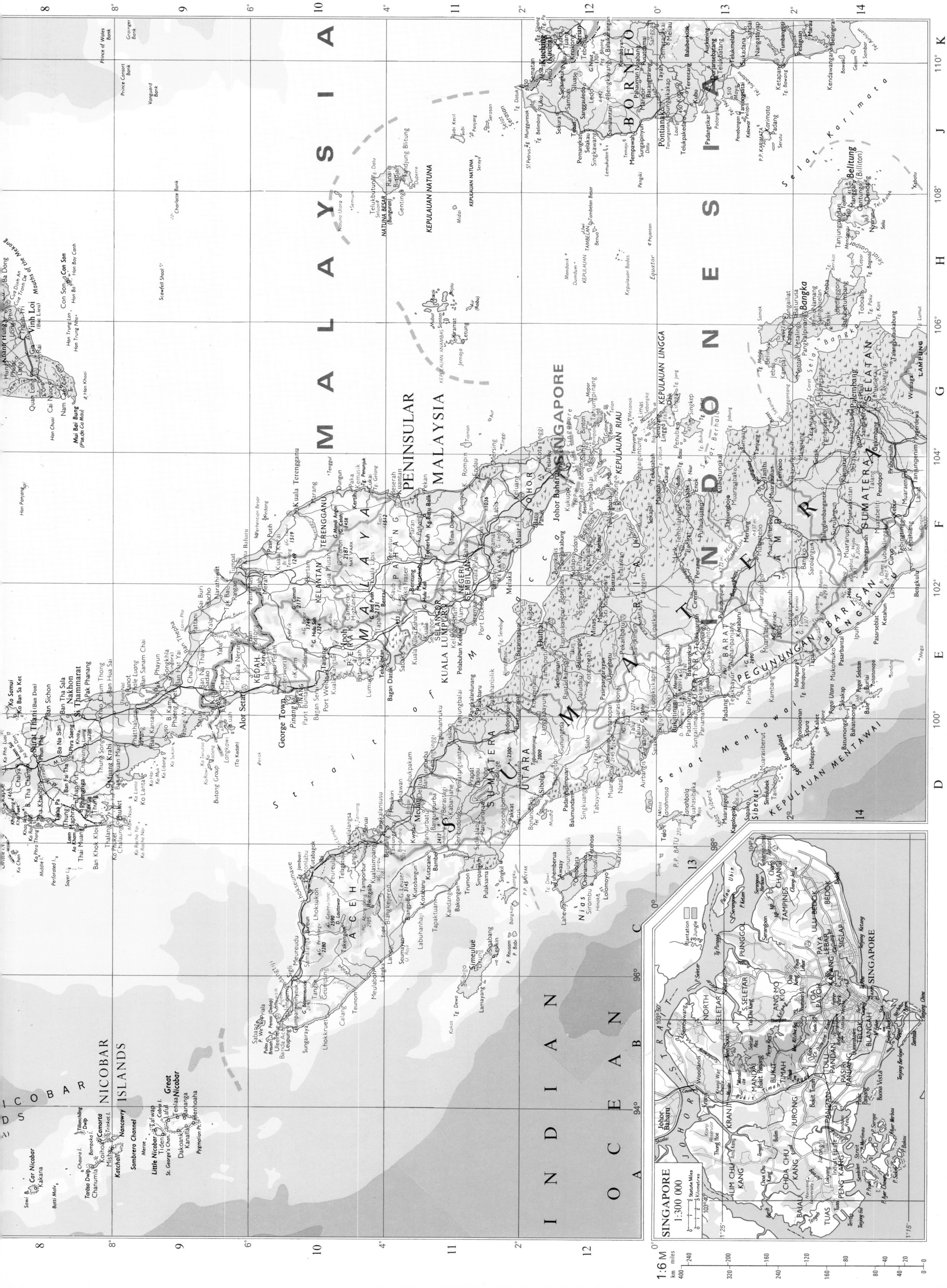

MALAYSIA

PENINSULAR MALAYSIA

BORNEO

INDONESIA

SUMATERA

SUMATERA UTARA

ACEH

NICOBAR ISLANDS

INDIAN OCEAN

KUALA LUMPUR

SINGAPORE

George Town

Pinang

Johor Baharu

KEDAH

PERAK

KELANTAN

TERENGGANU

PAHANG

JOHOR

NEGERI SEMBILAN

KEPULAUAN RIAU

KEPULAUAN LINGGA

KEPULAUAN NATUNA

NATUNA BESAR

PEGUNUNGAN BARISAN

JAMBI

BENGKULU

SUMATERA SELATAN

LAMPUNG

Bangka

Belitung (Billiton)

Kuching

Pontianak

Nias

Siberut

KEPULAUAN MENTAWAI

Strait of Malacca

Strait of Singapore

Equator

SINGAPORE

1:300 000

CHANGI
SELETAR
PAYA LEBAR
TAMPINES
BEDOK
JURONG
TUAS
WOODLANDS
Johor Bahru

Plantation
Jungle

MERCATOR PROJECTION

Heights and Depths in metres

1:6 M

© John Bartholomew & Son Ltd Edinburgh

BORNEO & CELEBES

PHILIPPINES

MALAYSIA

BRUNEI

SABAH

SARAWAK

BORNEO

KALIMANTAN

KALIMANTAN BARAT

KALIMANTAN TIMUR

KALIMANTAN TENGAH

KALIMANTAN SELATAN

SULAWESI (CELEBES)

SULAWESI TENGAH

SULAWESI SELATAN

Kuching (Kucing)

Pontianak

Balikpapan

Samarinda

Banjarmasin

Palangkaraya

Palu

Parigi

Poso

Palopo

Pare Pare

Majene

Watampone

Ujung Pandang (Makassar)

Sungguminasa

Bandar Seri Begawan

Kota Kinabalu (Jesselton)

Sandakan

Zamboanga

CELEBES SEA

SULU SEA

Balabac Strait

SULU ARCHIPELAGO

TURTLE ISLANDS

Selat Karimata

Makassar Strait

Teluk Tomini

KEPULAUAN NATUNA

Natuna Besar (Bunguran)

KEPULAUAN LAUT KECIL

JAVA SEA

JAVA (JAWA)
(To Indonesia)

JAKARTA (BATAVIA)

Serang

Bandung

Bogor

Cirebon

Semarang

Surakarta

Surabaya

Madura

JAWA TENGAH

JAWA TIMUR

SUMATERA SELATAN

LAMPUNG

Palembang

Tanjungkarang Telukbetung

BALI

Denpasar

Lombok

BALI SEA

INDONES

Longitude East 116° of Greenwich

Longitude East 110° of Greenwich

MERCATOR PROJECTION

Heights and Depths in metres

| feet | 22967 | 16404 | 9843 | 3281 | 656 | 0 | 328 | 656 | 1640 | 3281 | 6562 |
| m | 7000 | 5000 | 3000 | 1000 | 200 | 0 | 100 | 200 | 500 | 1000 | 2000 |

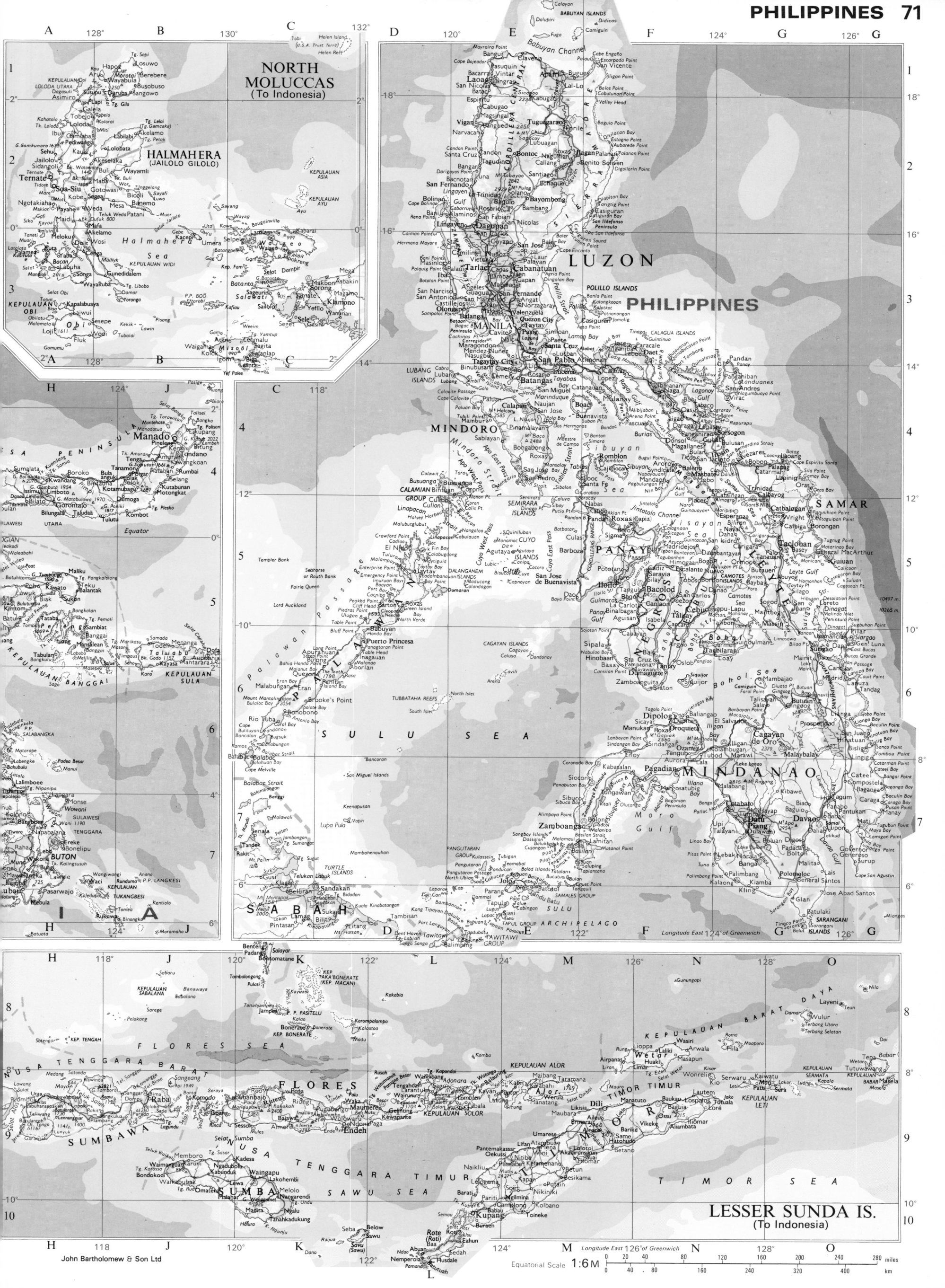
NORTH MOLUCCAS
(To Indonesia)
HALMAHERA
(JAILOLO GILOLO)
Halmahera Sea
LUZON
PHILIPPINES
MINDORO
PANAY
NEGROS
SAMAR
LEYTE
MINDANAO
PALAWAN
SULU SEA
SULU ARCHIPELAGO
SABAH
MANILA
Moro Gulf
Sibuyan Sea
Visayan Sea
Bohol Sea
Babuyan Channel
FLORES SEA
NUSA TENGGARA BARAT
NUSA TENGGARA TIMUR
SUMBAWA
FLORES
SUMBA
SAWU SEA
TIMOR
TIMOR SEA
KEPULAUAN BARAT DAYA
LESSER SUNDA IS.
(To Indonesia)
Longitude East 124° of Greenwich
Longitude East 126° of Greenwich
John Bartholomew & Son Ltd
Equatorial Scale 1:6M

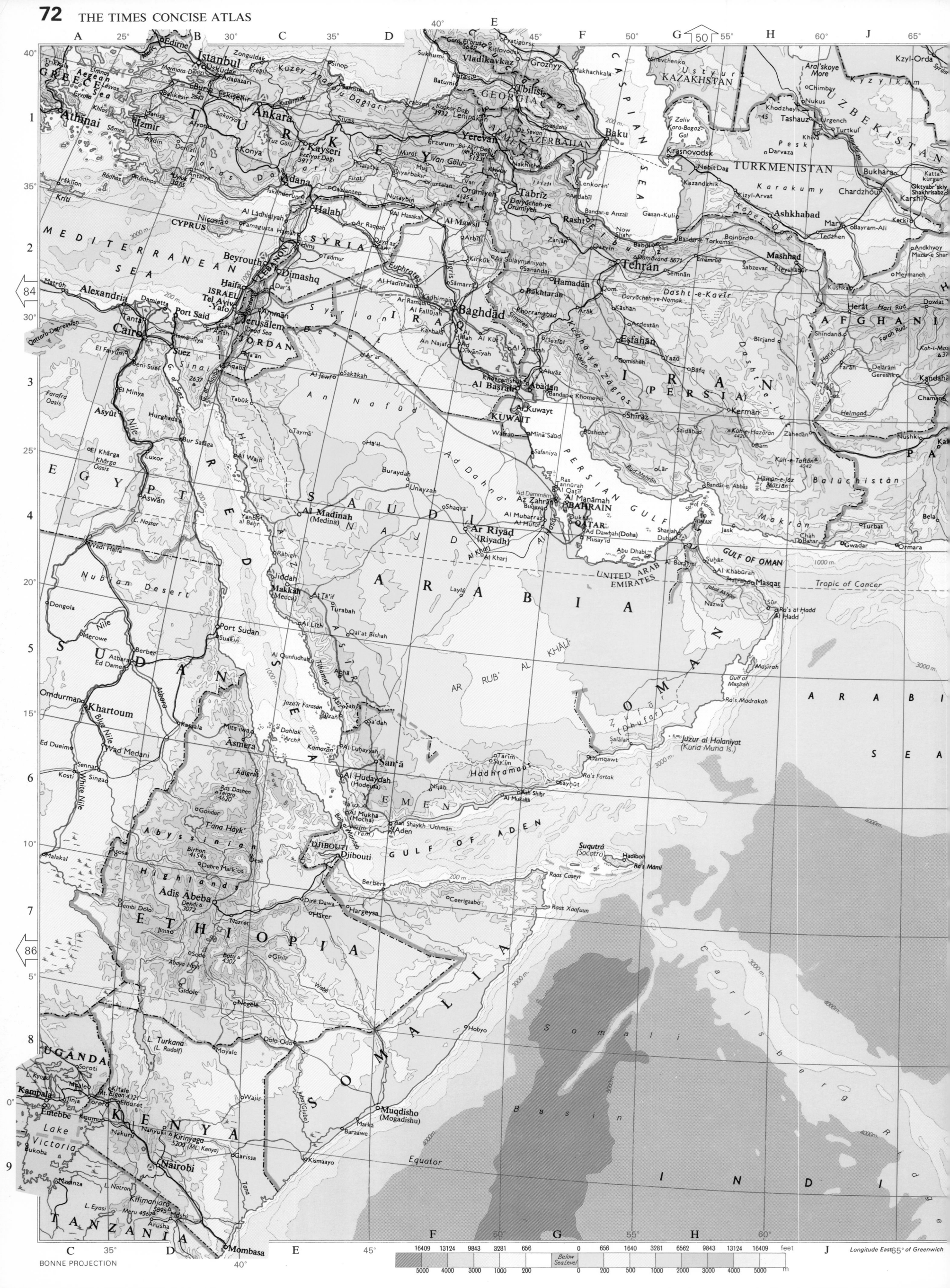

MOYYNKUM
KAZAKHSTAN
Dzhambul
Bishkek
KYRGYZSTAN
Alma-Ata
Tashkent
TIAN SHAN
Ürümqi
SINKIANG
(XINJIANG)
Taklimakan Shamo
CHINA
KUN LUN SHAN
Qing Zang
Chang Tang
(XIZANG)
TIBET
Lhasa
Chengdu
Chongqing
(Chungking)
Kunming
KASHMIR
Islamabad
Rawalpindi
Lahore
Amritsar
Delhi
KATHMANDU
NEPAL
BHUTAN
Mt. Everest
8848
Thimphu
BANGLA DESH
Dhaka
Calcutta
BURMA
Mandalay
VIETNAM
Hanoi
Jaipur
Kanpur
Lucknow
Allahabad
Varanasi
Patna
Ahmadabad
Vadodara
Surat
INDIA
Nagpur
Bombay
Pune
Hyderabad
BAY OF BENGAL
Yangon
Moulmein
Pegu
THAILAND
Bangkok
(Krung Thep)
CAMBODIA
GULF OF THAILAND
Bangalore
Madras
Pondicherry
Mysore
Coimbatore
ANDAMAN ISLANDS
(To India)
NICOBAR ISLANDS
(To India)
LACCADIVE ISLANDS
(To India)
Cochin
Madurai
Trivandrum
C. Comorin
SRI LANKA
(CEYLON)
Colombo
Kandy
George Town
PENINSULAR MALAYSIA
Kuala Lumpur
MALDIVES
Male
INDIAN OCEAN

1:15 M
0 100 200 400 600 800 1000 1200 1400 km
0 50 100 200 300 400 500 600 700 800 miles

Heights and Depths in metres

© John Bartholomew & Son Ltd Edinburgh

CHINA
XIZANG GAOYUAN (PLATEAU OF TIBET)
XIZANG ZIZHIQU
TIBET (AUT. REGION)
QINGHAI (TSINGHAI)
Tanggula Shan
Nyainqêntanglha Shan
Gangdisê Shan
Nyenchen Tanglha
Lhasa
Xigazê
Nagqu
Gyangzê (Gyangtse)
Yarlung Zangbo Jiang (Tsangpo) (Brahmaputra)
Nu Jiang (Salween)
NEPAL
KATHMANDU
Mt. Everest (Qomolangma Feng) 8848 (29028ft)
Cho Oyu 8201
Makalu 8463
Kangchenjunga 8598
Dhaulagiri 8167
Annapurna 8091
Manaslu 8163
SIKKIM
Gangtok
THIMPHU
BHUTAN
ARUNACHAL PRADESH
ASSAM
Guwahati
Dibrugarh
NAGALAND
MEGHALAYA
Shillong
MANIPUR
Imphal
TRIPURA
Agartala
MIZORAM
BANGLADESH
DHAKA (DACCA)
Narayanganj
Chittagong
Khulna
Rajshahi
Mymensingh
Sylhet
Comilla
WEST BENGAL
Calcutta
Haora
BIHAR
Patna
Gaya
Ranchi
Jamshedpur
Dhanbad
Bhagalpur
Muzaffarpur
Darbhanga
Varanasi (Benares)
Gorakhpur
Allahabad
ORISSA
Cuttack
Bhubaneshwar
Puri
Sambalpur
Raipur
Vishakhapatam
Vizianagaram
Chota Nagpur
Mouths of the Ganges (or Ganga)
Padma
BAY OF BENGAL
BURMA
CHIN STATE
KACHIN STATE
SHAN STATE
Mandalay
Sittwe
Mt. Victoria 3053
Henzada
Bassein
Cox's Bazar
Rahmapur
Brahmapur

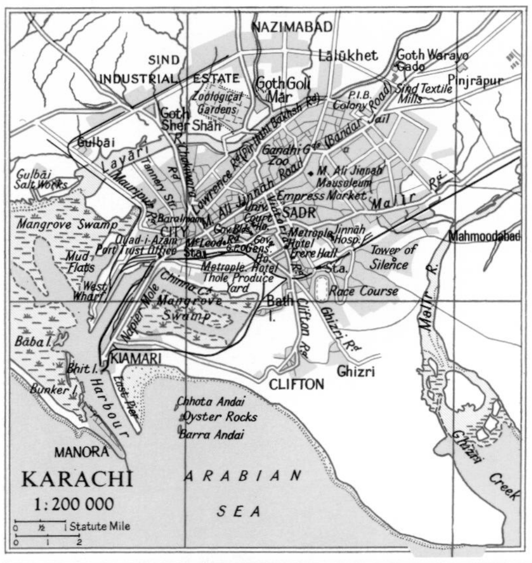

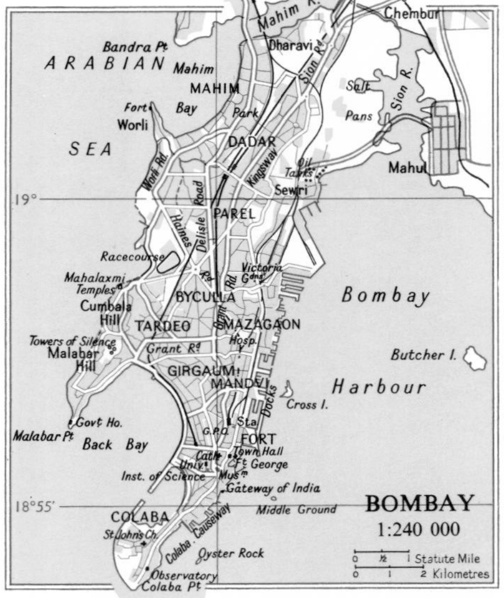

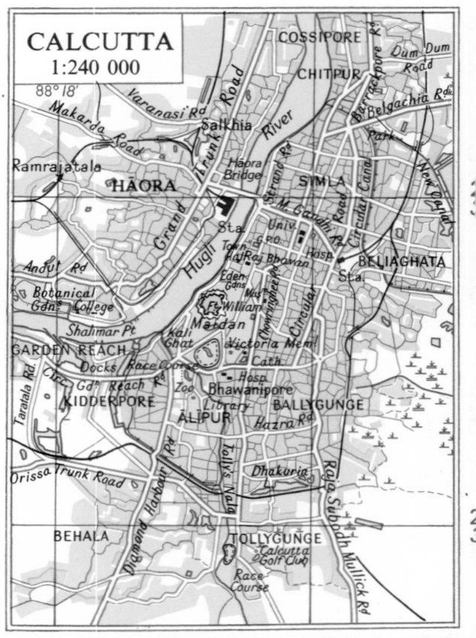

KARACHI
1:200 000

BOMBAY
1:240 000

DELHI
1:240 000

CALCUTTA
1:240 000

MAHARASHTRA

MADHYA PRADESH

ORISSA

ANDHRA PRADESH

KARNATAKA

TAMIL NADU

SRI LANKA
(CEYLON)

ANDAMAN ISLANDS

NICOBAR ISLANDS

LAKSHADWEEP
(Laccadive Islands)

Laccadive, Minicoy and Amindivi Islands
(India)

MALDIVES

Arabian Sea

Bay of Bengal

Bombay
Pune (Poona)
Nasik
Ahmadnagar
Solapur
Hyderabad
Secunderabad
Warangal
Vijayawada
Guntur
Vishakhapatnam
Kakinada
Rajahmundry
Eluru
Nellore
Madras
Bangalore
Mysore
Mangalore
Hubli
Dharwad
Belgaum
Kolhapur
Coimbatore
Madurai
Tiruchchirappalli
Salem
Vellore
Pondicherry
Cochin (Kochi)
Ernakulam
Trivandrum (Thiruvananthapuram)
Quilon (Kollam)
Calicut (Kozhikode)
Trichur (Thrissur)
Cape Comorin
Nagercoil
Tuticorin
Tirunelveli
Jaffna
Trincomalee
Colombo
Kandy
Galle
Port Blair
North Andaman
Middle Andaman
South Andaman
Little Andaman
Car Nicobar
Great Nicobar
Little Nicobar

Nine Degree Channel
Eight Degree Channel
Ten Degree Channel
Coco Channel

Gulf of Mannar
Palk Strait
Adam's Bridge

Mouths of the Godavari

1:6M

Heights and Depths in metres

ALBERS CONIC PROJECTION

© John Bartholomew & Son Ltd Edinburgh

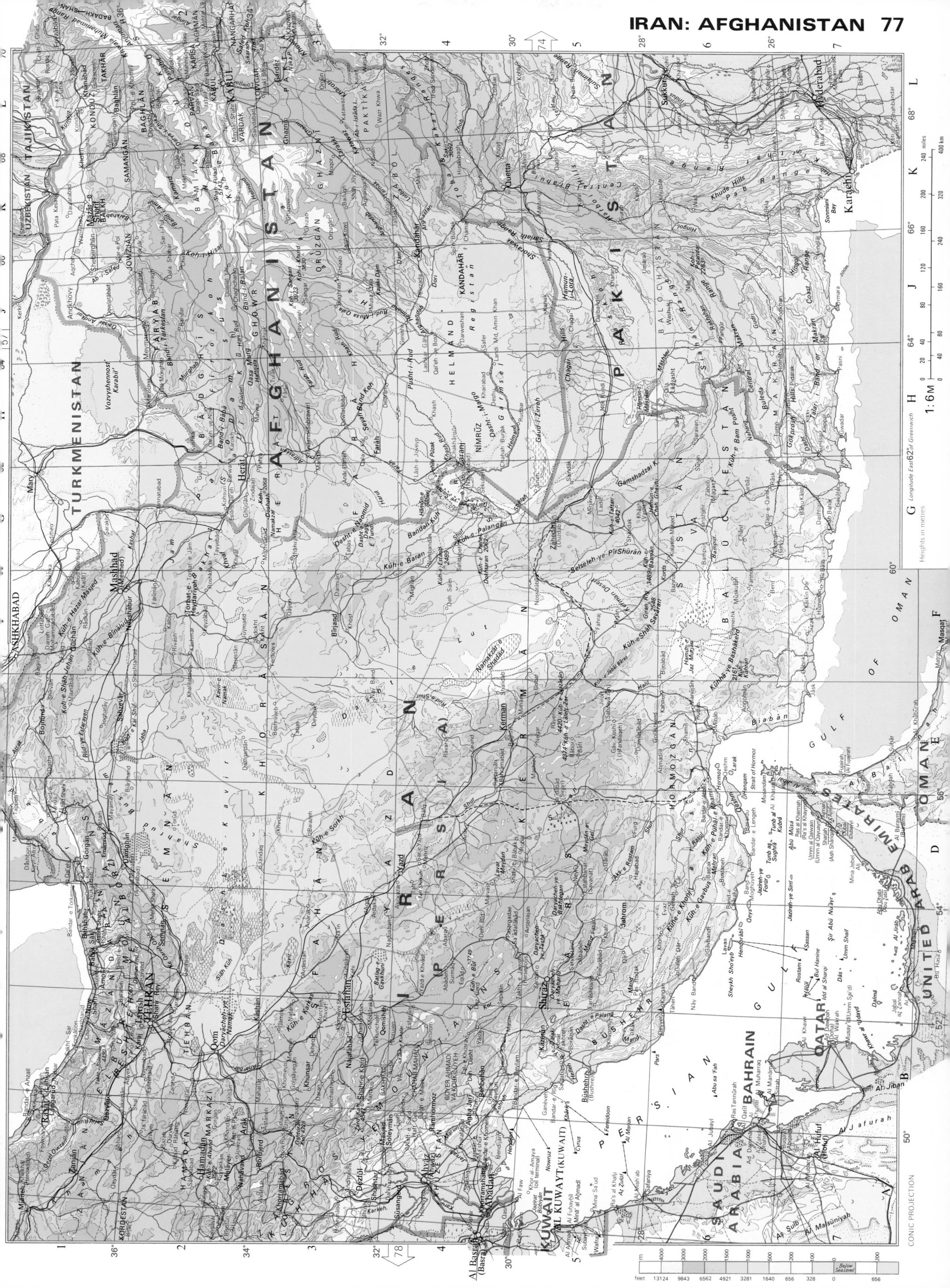

AFGHANISTAN
IRAN
PAKISTAN
TURKMENISTAN
UZBEKISTAN
TAJIKISTAN
KUWAIT
QATAR
BAHRAIN
SAUDI ARABIA
UNITED ARAB EMIRATES
OMAN
PERSIAN GULF
GULF OF OMAN
Strait of Hormoz
TEHRAN
KABUL
Mashhad
Herat
Kandahar
Quetta
Karachi
Hyderabad
Sukkur
Esfahan
Shiraz
Kerman
Yazd
Zahedan
Bandar-e Abbas
Ahvaz
Abadan
Hamadan
Qom
Kashan
Semnan
Gorgan
Mary
ASHKHABAD
Masqat
Al Basrah
Al Kuwayt (Kuwait)
Dasht-e Kavir
Dasht-e Lut
Registan
Makran Coast Range
Central Makran Range
Kirthar Range
Siahan Range
Chagai Hills
Toba Kakar Range
Sulaiman Range
Paropamisus
Band-i-Turkestan
Kuh-e Baba
Zagros Mountains
Elburz Mountains
Helmand
Hari Rud
Farah Rud
Indus
CONIC PROJECTION
1:6M
Longitude East 62° of Greenwich
Heights in metres
feet 13124 9843 6562 4921 3281 1640 656 328 0 656
m 4000 3000 2000 1500 1000 500 200 100 0 200
Below Sea Level
0 20 40 80 120 160 240 miles
0 40 80 160 240 320 400 km

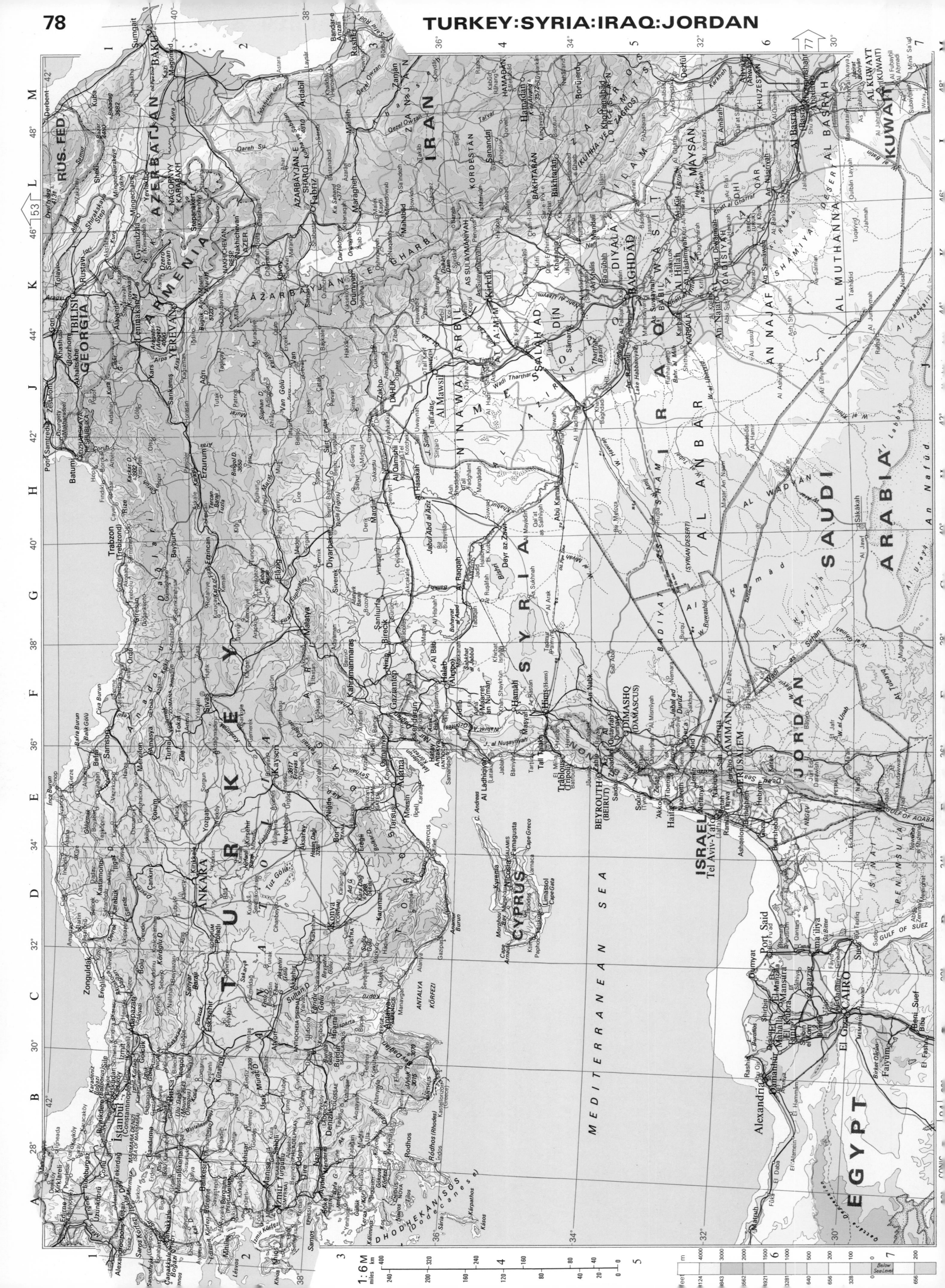

TURKEY
SYRIA
IRAQ
JORDAN
SAUDI ARABIA
IRAN
EGYPT
CYPRUS
ISRAEL
KUWAIT
GEORGIA
ARMENIA
AZERBAIJAN
MEDITERRANEAN SEA
ANKARA
İstanbul
DIMASHQ (DAMASCUS)
BAGHDĀD
AMMAN
BEYROUTH (BEIRUT)
CAIRO
1:6M

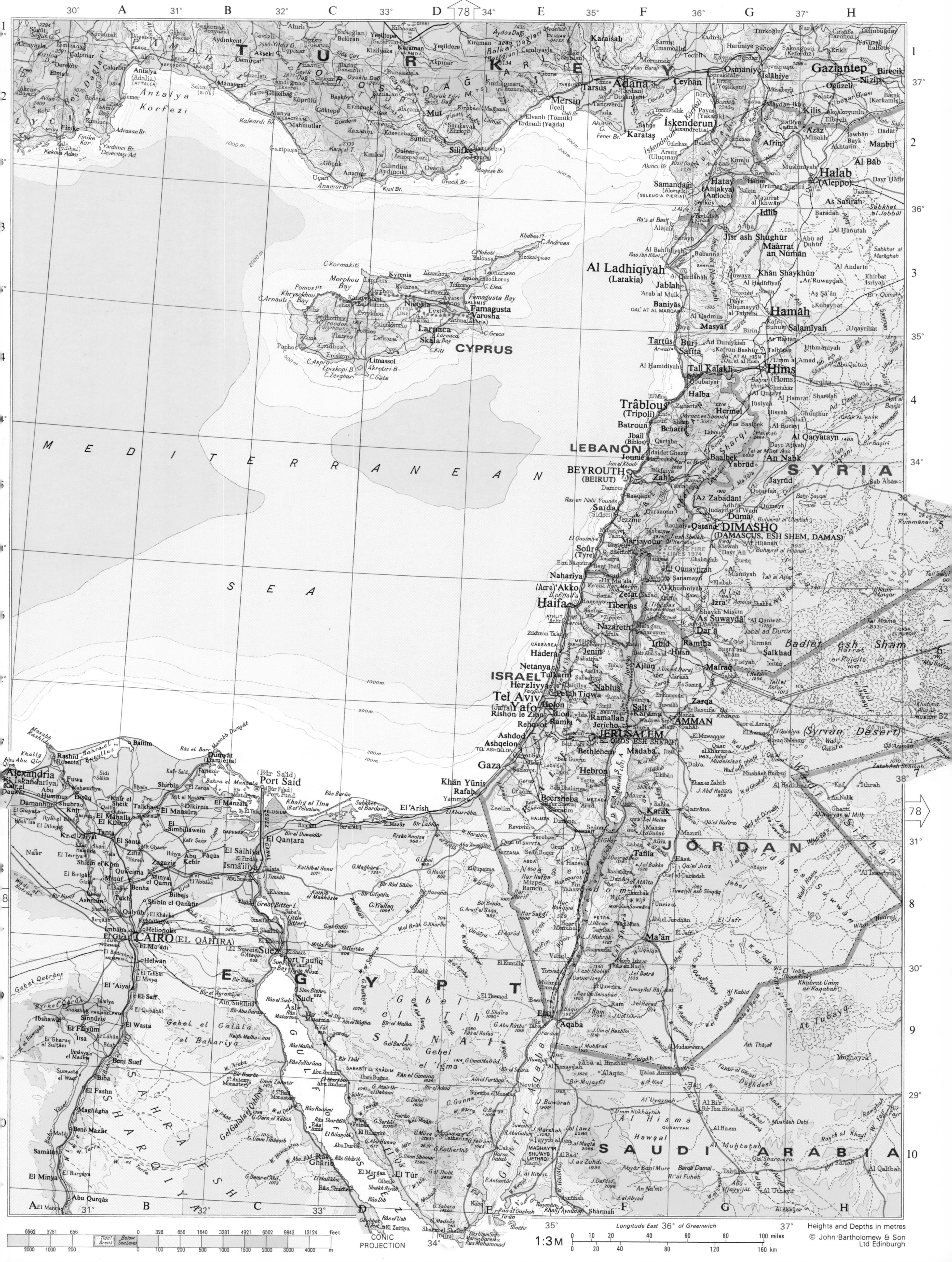

TURKEY

CYPRUS

MEDITERRANEAN SEA

SYRIA

LEBANON

BEYROUTH (BEIRUT)

DIMASHQ (DAMASCUS, ESH SHEM, DAMAS)

Al Ladhiqiyah (Latakia)

Hamah

Hims (Homs)

Trâblous (Tripoli)

ISRAEL

Tel Aviv

JERUSALEM (EL QUDS ESH SHERIF)

Haifa

Nazareth

AMMAN

JORDAN

Gaza

EGYPT

CAIRO (EL QÂHIRA)

Alexandria (El Iskandariya)

Port Said (Bûr Sa'îd)

Suez

SAUDI ARABIA

SINAI

Aqaba

Elat

Gaziantep

Halab (Aleppo)

CONIC PROJECTION

1:3 M

Heights and Depths in metres

© John Bartholomew & Son Ltd Edinburgh

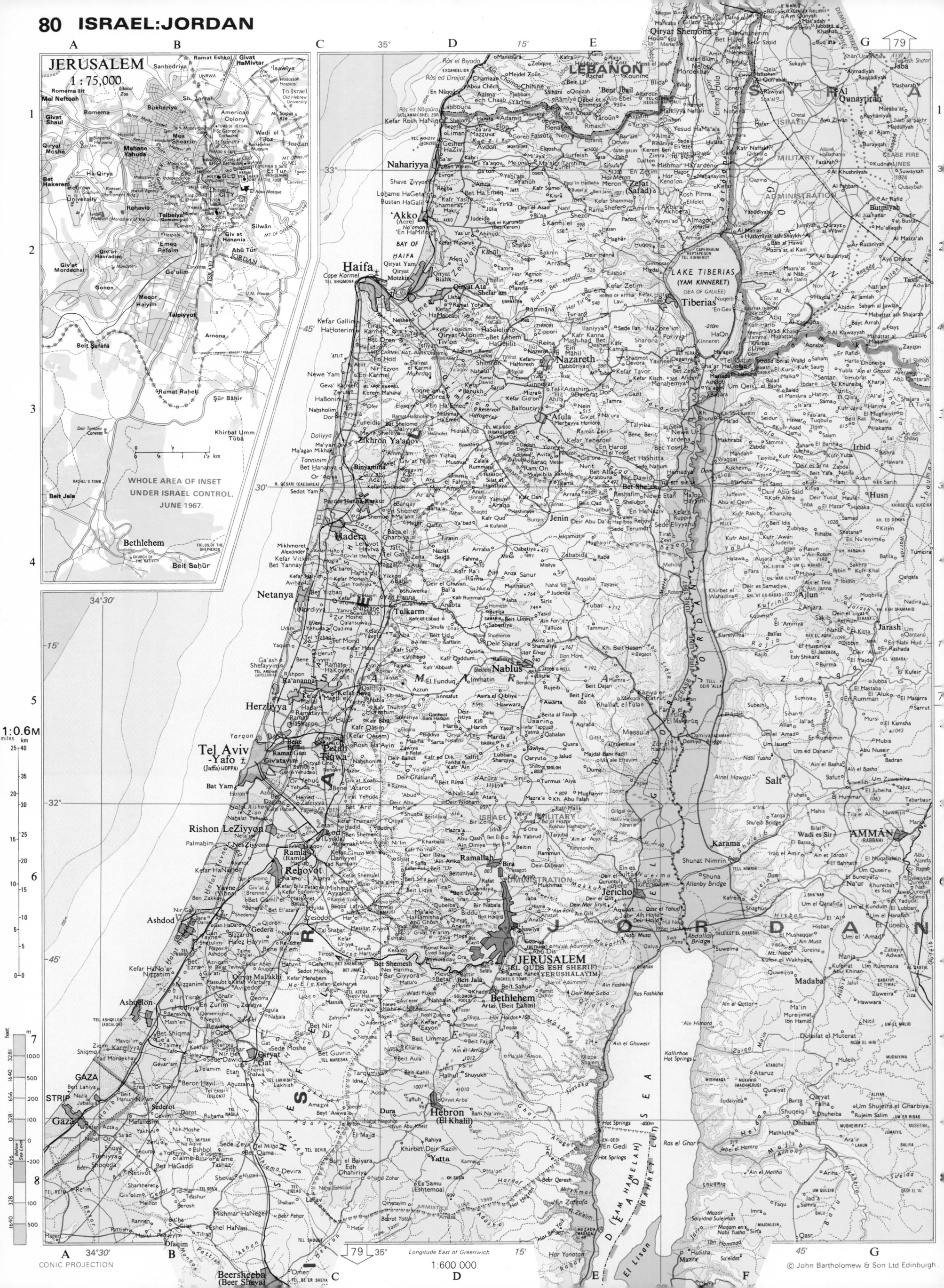
JERUSALEM
1 : 75,000
WHOLE AREA OF INSET UNDER ISRAEL CONTROL, JUNE 1967.
Bethlehem
LEBANON
SYRIA
JORDAN
LAKE TIBERIAS (YAM KINNERET) (SEA OF GALILEE)
Tiberias
Haifa
Nahariyya
'Akko (Acre)
BAY OF HAIFA
Nazareth
Afula
Jenin
Hadera
Netanya
Tulkarm
Nablus
Herzliyya
Tel Aviv -Yafo (Jaffa) (JOPPA)
Bat Yam
Rishon LeZiyyon
Ramla
Rehovot
Lod (Lydda)
Ashdod
Ashqelon
GAZA STRIP
Gaza
Qiryat Gat
Beersheba (Beer Sheva)
Hebron (El Khalil)
Ramallah
Jericho
JERUSALEM (EL QUDS ESH SHERIF) (YERUSHALAYIM)
Bethlehem (Beit Lahm)
Irbid
Jarash
Ajlun
Salt
AMMAN (RABBAH)
Madaba
Dhiban
Karama
Allenby Bridge
DEAD SEA (YAM HAMELAH) (BAHRET LUT)
El Lisan
Qiryat Shemona
Zefat (Safad)
Al Qunaytirah
ISRAEL MILITARY ADMINISTRATION
CEASE FIRE LINES 1974
1:0.6M
CONIC PROJECTION
Longitude East of Greenwich
1:600 000
© John Bartholomew & Son Ltd Edinburgh

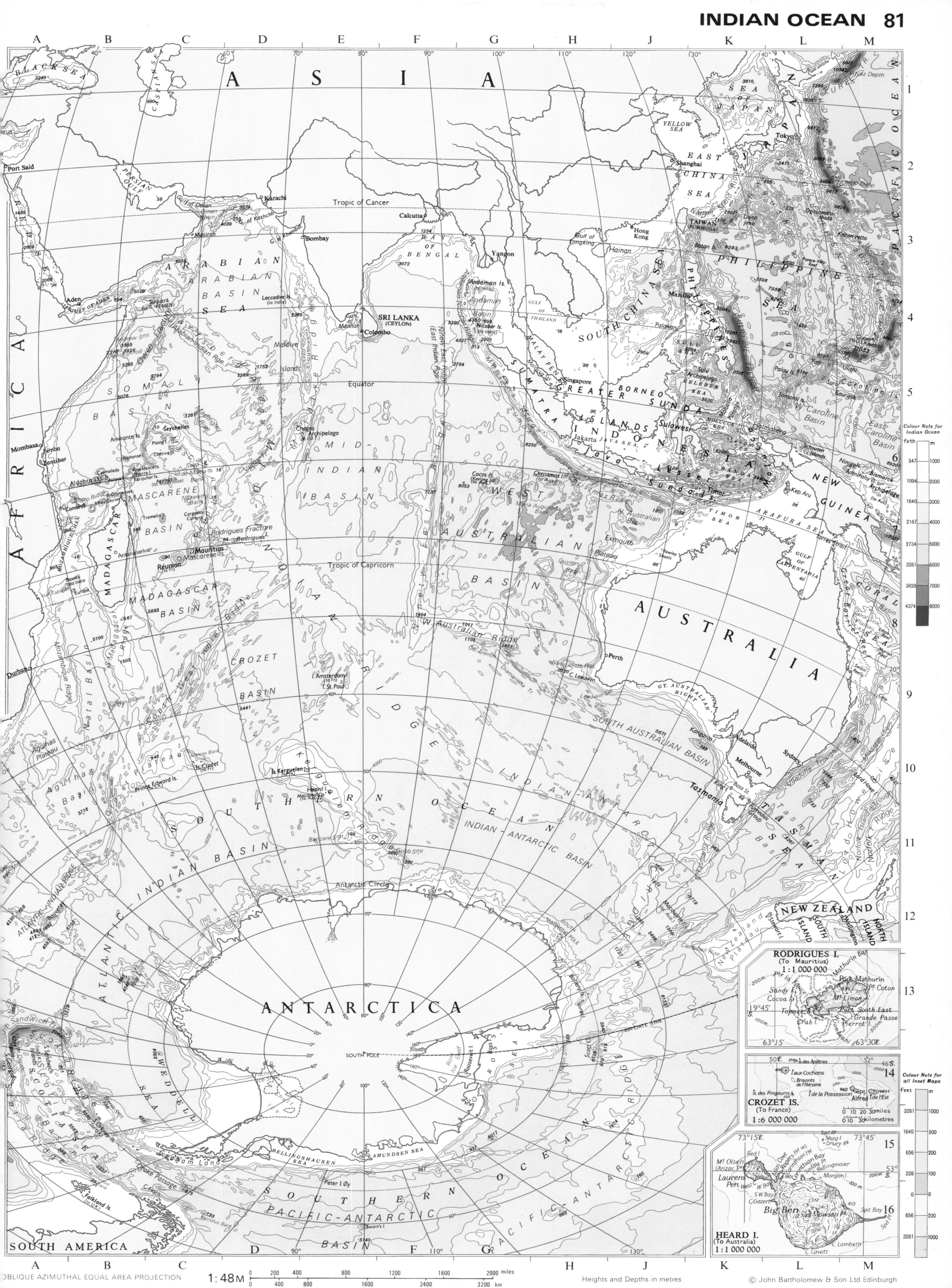

OBLIQUE AZIMUTHAL EQUAL AREA PROJECTION   1:48M   Heights and Depths in metres

1:24 M

MILLER'S PROLATED STEREOGRAPHIC PROJECTION

SRI LANKA
(CEYLON)
1 : 2 400 000

COCOS IS.
(KEELING IS.)
(To Australia)
1 : 1 000 000

CHRISTMAS I.
(To Australia)
1 : 1 000 000

SEYCHELLES
1 : 3 000 000

MAHÉ
1 : 1 000 000

MAURITIUS
1 : 1 000 000

RÉUNION
(To France) 1 : 1 000 000

KERGUELEN
(To France)
1 : 3 000 000

LAMBERT CONFORMAL
CONIC PROJECTION

Heights in metres

© John Bartholomew & Son Ltd Edinburgh

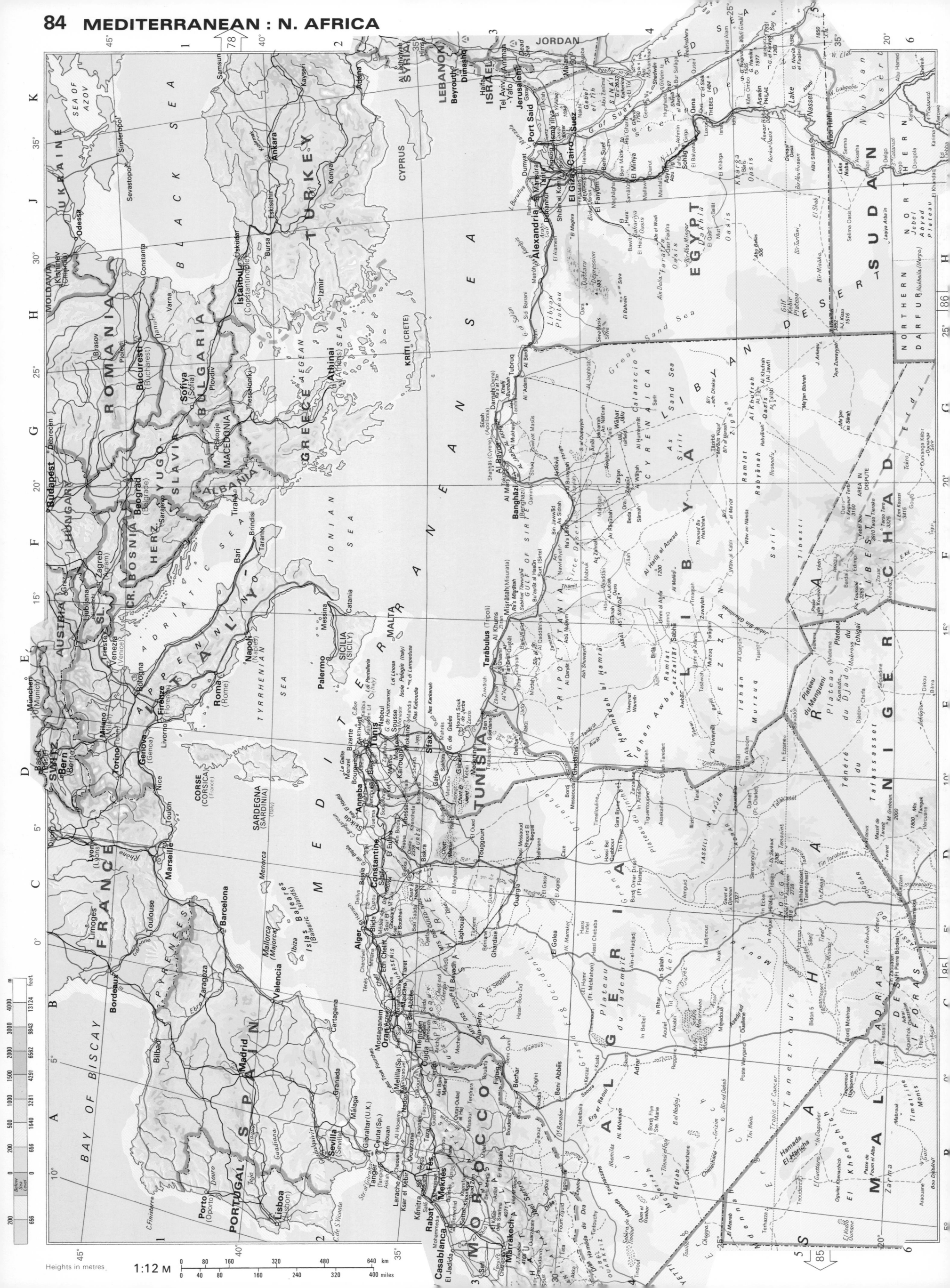
MEDITERRANEAN SEA
BLACK SEA
IONIAN SEA
TYRRHENIAN SEA
AEGEAN SEA
ADRIATIC SEA
BAY OF BISCAY
SAHARA
FRANCE
SPAIN
PORTUGAL
ITALY
SWITZ.
AUSTRIA
HUNGARY
ROMANIA
BULGARIA
YUGOSLAVIA
ALBANIA
GREECE
TURKEY
UKRAINE
MOLDAVIA
CYPRUS
SYRIA
LEBANON
ISRAEL
JORDAN
EGYPT
LIBYA
TUNISIA
ALGERIA
MOROCCO
MALI
NIGER
CHAD
SUDAN
MALTA
Heights in metres
1:12 M
km
miles

AÇORES (AZORES) (Portugal)
on the same scale

MADEIRA (Portugal)

ISLAS CANARIAS (CANARY ISLANDS) (Spain)

PORTUGAL
SPAIN
MEDITERRANEAN SEA

MOROCCO
ALGERIA
TUNISIA
LIBYA

WESTERN SAHARA

MAURITANIA

MALI

NIGER

SAHARA

Tropic of Cancer

SENEGAL
THE GAMBIA
GUINEA-BISSAU
GUINEA
SIERRA LEONE
LIBERIA
IVORY COAST
BURKINA (UPPER VOLTA)
GHANA
TOGO
BENIN
NIGERIA
CAMEROON

GULF OF GUINEA
BIGHT OF BENIN
BIGHT OF BIAFRA (BONNY)

SAO TOME AND PRINCIPE
EQUATORIAL GUINEA

CAPE VERDE (ILHAS DO CABO VERDE)
on the same scale

LAMBERT AZIMUTHAL EQUAL AREA PROJECTION
Meridian of 0° Greenwich
Heights in metres
1:12 M

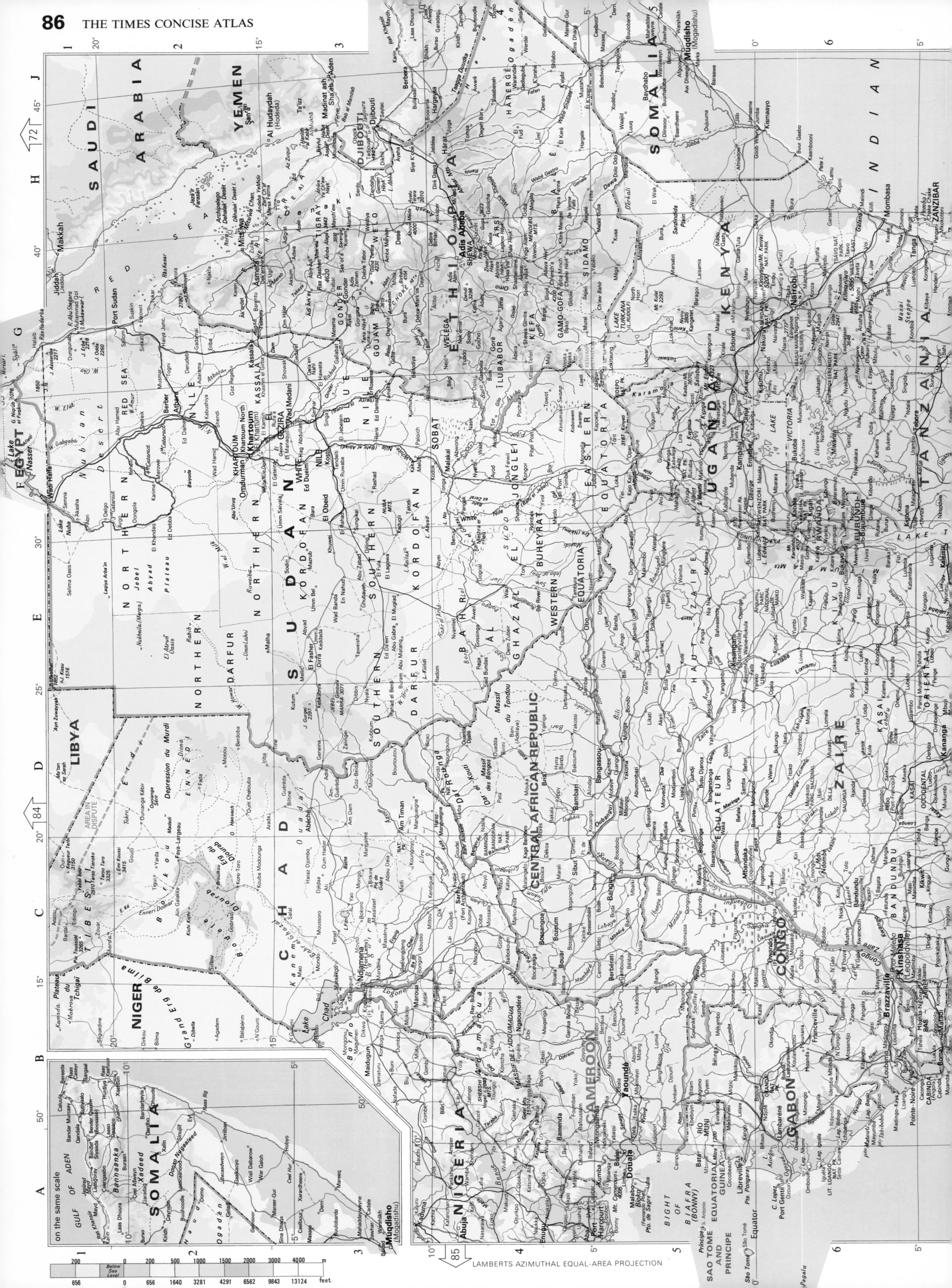

SAUDI ARABIA
YEMEN
EGYPT
LIBYA
SUDAN
CHAD
NIGER
NIGERIA
CAMEROON
CENTRAL AFRICAN REPUBLIC
ETHIOPIA
DJIBOUTI
SOMALIA
KENYA
UGANDA
RWANDA
BURUNDI
TANZANIA
ZAIRE
CONGO
GABON
EQUATORIAL GUINEA
SAO TOME AND PRINCIPE
RED SEA
LAKE VICTORIA
Khartoum
Addis Ababa
Nairobi
Kampala
Kinshasa (Léopoldville)
Brazzaville
Ndjamena
Bangui
Yaoundé
Libreville
Muqdisho (Mogadishu)
Djibouti
Şan'ā'
Mombasa
Abuja
on the same scale
GULF OF ADEN
72
84
85
LAMBERTS AZIMUTHAL EQUAL-AREA PROJECTION
200 0 200 500 1000 1500 2000 3000 4000 m
656 0 656 1640 3281 4291 6562 9843 13124 feet
Below Sea Level

Heights in metres

1:12M

© John Bartholomew & Son Ltd Edinburgh

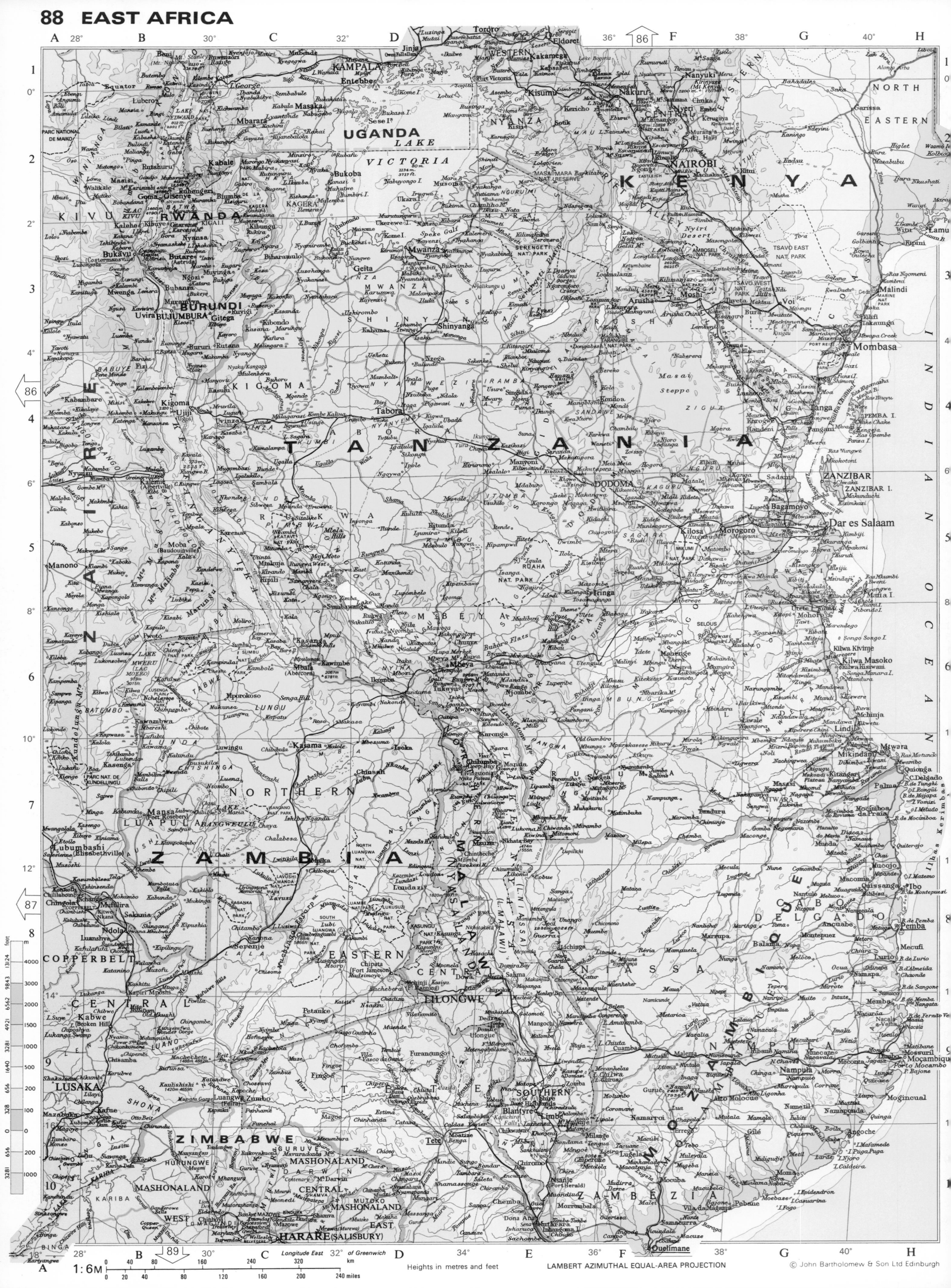

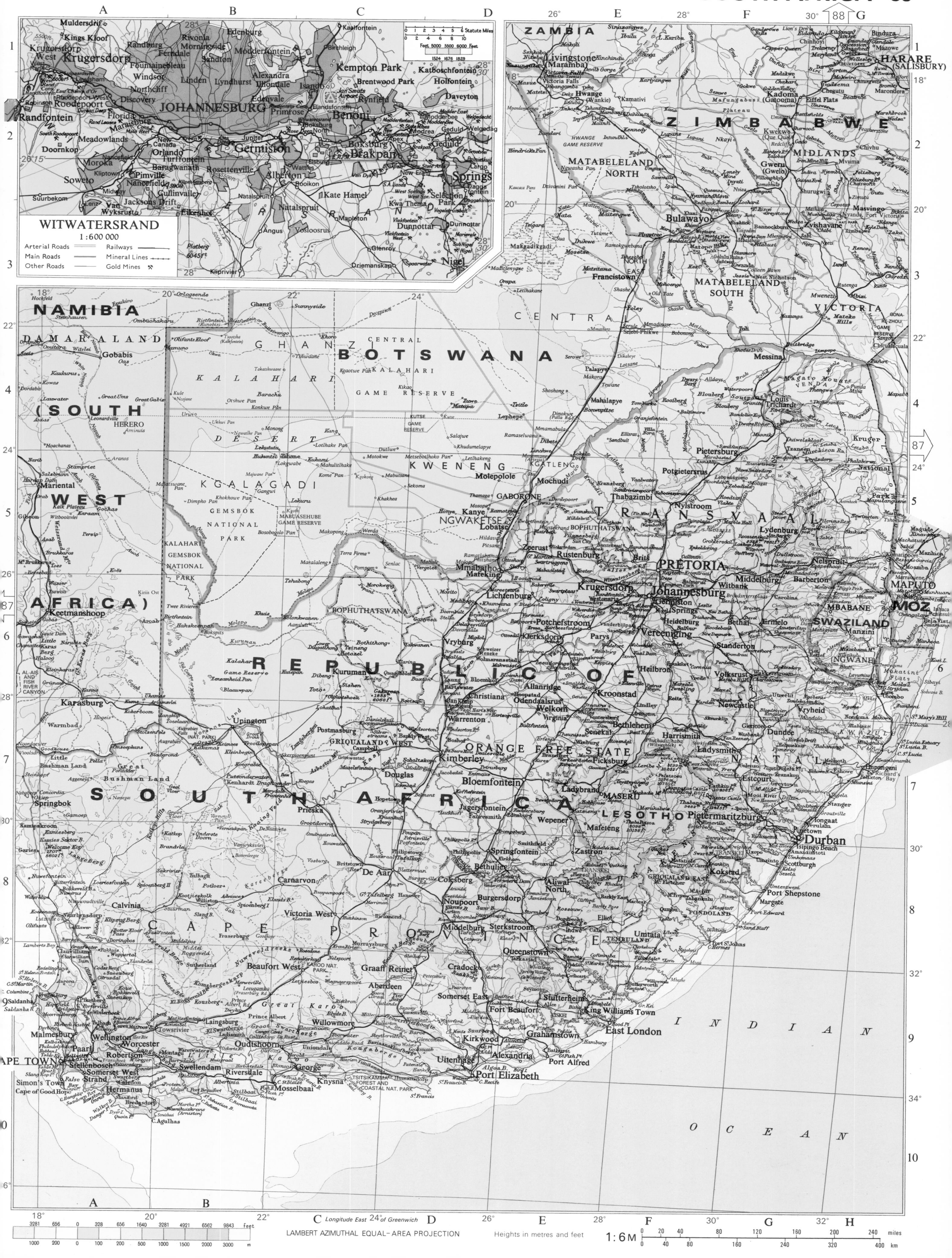

WITWATERSRAND
1:600 000

Arterial Roads — Railways
Main Roads — Mineral Lines
Other Roads — Gold Mines ✕

Inset (Witwatersrand): Muldersdrif, Kings Kloof, Krugersdorp, West Krugersdorp, Randburg, Rivonia, Morningside, Sandton, Edenburg, Modderfontein, Birchleigh, Kaalfontein, Kempton Park, Katboschfontein, Hollfontein, Ferndale, Fournainebleau, Windsor, Linden, Lyndhurst, Alexandra, Isando, Jan Smuts Airport, Brentwood Park, Daveyton, Northcliff, Discovery, JOHANNESBURG, Primrose, Edenvale, Elandsfontein, Benoni, Randfontein, Florida, Maraisburg, New Canada, Roodepoort West, Rand Leases, Orlando, Turffontein, Germiston, Boksburg, Brakpan, Springs, Soweto, Moroka, Nancefield, Pimville, Rosettenville, Alberton, Kwa Thema, Kliptown, Midway, Suurbekom, Lenz, Jackson's Park, Natalspruit, Booikon, Kate Hamel, New Era, Selection Park, Dunnottar, Vosloosrus, Mapleton, Glenroy, Nigel, Driemanskap, Kliprivier

ZAMBIA — Livingstone (Maramba), Victoria Falls, Hwange (Wankie), HWANGE GAME RESERVE, Kamativi

ZIMBABWE — Bulawayo, MATABELELAND NORTH, MATABELELAND SOUTH, MIDLANDS, Gweru (Gwelo), Kwekwe (Que Que), Zvishavane, HARARE (SALISBURY), Bindura, Marondera, Kadoma (Gatooma), VICTORIA, GONA RE ZHOU GAME RESERVE, Masvingo (Fort Victoria), Beitbridge, Messina

NAMIBIA (SOUTH WEST AFRICA) — DAMARALAND, HERERO, Gobabis, Windhoek, WEST, Mariental, Keetmanshoop, Karasburg, Warmbad, AI-AIS AND FISH RIVER CANYON, Springbok, BUSHMAN LAND

BOTSWANA — GHANZI, Ghanzi, KALAHARI, CENTRAL KALAHARI GAME RESERVE, KWENENG, NGWAKETSE, Molepolole, Mochudi, GABORONE, Kanye, Lobatse, Francistown, Orapa, KALAHARI GEMSBOK NATIONAL PARK, GEMSBOK NATIONAL PARK, MABUASEHUBE GAME RESERVE

REPUBLIC OF SOUTH AFRICA — TRANSVAAL, Pietersburg, Potgietersrus, Nylstroom, Thabazimbi, Rustenburg, Brits, PRETORIA, Lydenburg, Nelspruit, Barberton, Krugersdorp, JOHANNESBURG, Germiston, Witbank, Middelburg, Ermelo, Carolina, Standerton, Klerksdorp, Potchefstroom, Vereeniging, Heidelberg, BOPHUTHATSWANA, Mafeking, Lichtenburg, Zeerust, Vryburg, Kuruman, GRIQUALAND WEST, Kimberley, Douglas, ORANGE FREE STATE, Kroonstad, Welkom, Virginia, Bloemfontein, Bethlehem, Harrismith, Ladysmith, Newcastle, Vryheid, Dundee, NATAL, KWAZULU, Pietermaritzburg, Durban, Pinetown, LESOTHO, MASERU, Mafeteng, Wepener, Zastron, Aliwal North, Burgersdorp, TRANSKEI, Umtata, Kokstad, Port Shepstone, Margate, CAPE PROVINCE, De Aar, Carnarvon, Victoria West, Beaufort West, Graaff Reinet, Cradock, Queenstown, CISKEI, King Williams Town, East London, Grahamstown, Port Elizabeth, Uitenhage, Oudtshoorn, George, Mosselbaai, Knysna, Swellendam, Worcester, Paarl, CAPE TOWN, Stellenbosch, Cape of Good Hope, Simon's Town, Hermanus, Cape Agulhas, Malmesbury, Saldanha

SWAZILAND — MBABANE, Manzini, NGWANE

MOZAMBIQUE (MOZ) — MAPUTO

INDIAN OCEAN

LAMBERT AZIMUTHAL EQUAL-AREA PROJECTION
Heights in metres and feet
1:6M

LAMBERT AZIMUTHAL EQUAL-AREA PROJECTION   Heights and Depths in metres   1 : 48 000 000

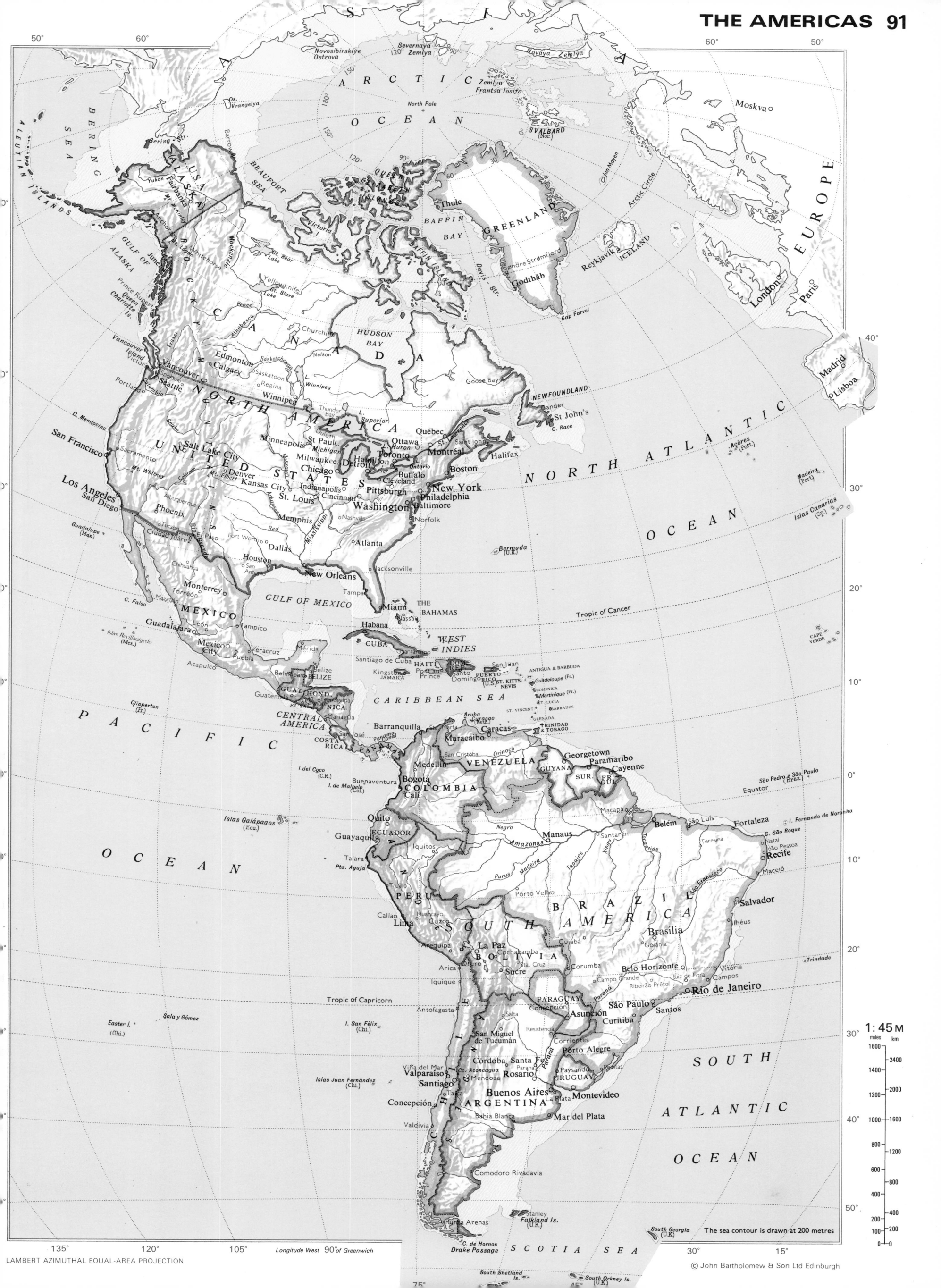

ASIA

ARCTIC OCEAN

North Pole

Novosibirskiye Ostrova

Severnaya Zemlya

Zemlya Frantsa Iosifa

Os. Vrangelya

Moskva

SVALBARD (Nor.)

Jan Mayen

Novaya Zemlya

BERING SEA

BEAUFORT SEA

Barrow

EUROPE

ALEUTIAN ISLANDS

Thule

BAFFIN BAY

GREENLAND

Kap Farvel

Reykjavik ICELAND

Godthåb

London

Paris

GULF OF ALASKA

ALASKA USA

Fairbanks

Mt. McKinley

Yukon

Whitehorse

Gt. Bear Lake

Yellowknife

Gt. Slave Lake

QUEEN ELIZABETH IS.

Victoria I.

Baffin Island

Davis Str.

Andre Strömfjord

Arctic Circle

Madrid Lisboa

Prince Rupert Queen Charlotte

Juneau

ROCKY

Peace

Athabasca

L. Athabasca

CANADA

HUDSON BAY

Churchill

Nelson

Goose Bay

Madeira (Port.)

Vancouver Island Victoria

Vancouver

Seattle

Portland

NORTH AMERICA

Edmonton

Calgary

Saskatoon

Regina

Saskatchewan

L. Winnipeg

Thunder Bay

NEWFOUNDLAND

Gander

St John's

C. Race

Açores (Port.)

C. Mendocino

San Francisco

Sacramento

UNITED STATES

Salt Lake City

Winnipeg

Duluth

Minneapolis

St Paul

L. Superior

L. Michigan

L. Huron

Ottawa

Toronto

Montréal

Québec

Saint John

Halifax

L. Ontario

Boston

NORTH ATLANTIC OCEAN

Mt. Whitney

Los Angeles

San Diego

Denver

Mt. Elbert

Colorado

Milwaukee

Chicago

Detroit

Cleveland

Buffalo

Pittsburgh

New York

Philadelphia

Baltimore

Washington

Indianapolis

Cincinnati

Kansas City

St. Louis

Nashville

OCEAN

Phoenix

Tucson

Albuquerque

Rio Grande

Ciudad Juárez

El Paso

Red

Fort Worth

Dallas

Memphis

Atlanta

Norfolk

Bermuda (U.K.)

Madeira (Port.)

Guadalupe (Mex.)

Chihuahua

Houston

San Antonio

Mississippi

Jacksonville

Islas Canarias (Sp.)

Monterrey

Torreón

MEXICO

GULF OF MEXICO

New Orleans

Tampa

Miami

Nassau

THE BAHAMAS

Tropic of Cancer

C. Falso

Mazatlán

Guadalajara

León

Tampico

Veracruz

Mérida

Habana

CUBA

WEST INDIES

CAPE VERDE

Islas Revillagigedo (Mex.)

Mexico City

Puebla

Acapulco

Belize

Belmopan BELIZE

Santiago de Cuba

HAITI

DOM. REP.

San Juan

PUERTO RICO (U.S.)

ANTIGUA & BARBUDA

Guadeloupe (Fr.)

Clipperton (Fr.)

GUAT. HOND.

Guatemala

EL SALV. NICA.

Kingston

JAMAICA

Port-au-Prince

Santo Domingo

ST. KITTS-NEVIS

DOMINICA

Martinique (Fr.)

CENTRAL AMERICA

Managua

San José

COSTA RICA

PANAMA

CARIBBEAN SEA

ST. LUCIA

ST. VINCENT

BARBADOS

GRENADA

TRINIDAD & TOBAGO

PACIFIC

I. del Coco (C.R.)

I. de Malpelo (Col.)

Buenaventura

Medellín

Bogotá

COLOMBIA

Cali

Barranquilla

Maracaibo

Aruba

Caracas

San Cristóbal

Orinoco

VENEZUELA

GUYANA

Georgetown

Paramaribo

SUR.

FR. GU.

Cayenne

São Pedro e São Paulo (Braz.)

OCEAN

Islas Galápagos (Ecu.)

Quito

ECUADOR

Guayaquil

Iquitos

Negro

Manaus

Santarém

Macapá

Belém

São Luís

Fortaleza

Equator

I. Fernando de Noronha

C. São Roque

Natal

João Pessoa

Recife

Talara

Pta. Aguja

Trujillo

Amazonas

Purus

Madeira

Tapajós

Xingu

Teresina

PERU

Huancayo

Cuzco

Pôrto Velho

BRAZIL

Maceió

Callao

Lima

SOUTH

Salvador

Ilhéus

AMERICA

Arequipa

La Paz

Cochabamba

BOLIVIA

Sta. Cruz

Cuiabá

Brasília

Goiânia

São Francisco

Belo Horizonte

Vitória

Arica

Sucre

Corumbá

Campo Grande

Ribeirão Prêto

Juiz de Fora

Campos

Iquique

Tropic of Capricorn

Antofagasta

PARAGUAY

Concepción

Asunción

Paraná

São Paulo

Santos

Rio de Janeiro

1:45 M

Easter I. (Chi.)

Sala y Gómez

I. San Félix (Chi.)

Salta

Resistencia

Corrientes

Curitiba

Pôrto Alegre

miles km

1600 2400

1400 2000

San Miguel de Tucumán

Córdoba

Santa Fe

Paraná

URUGUAY

SOUTH

1200

Islas Juan Fernández (Chi.)

Viña del Mar

Valparaíso

Santiago

Co. Aconcagua

Mendoza

Rosario

La Plata

Montevideo

ATLANTIC

1000 1600

800

Concepción

Buenos Aires

ARGENTINA

Mar del Plata

OCEAN

600 800

400

Valdivia

Bahía Blanca

Trindade

200

CHILE

Comodoro Rivadavia

200

0 0

Punta Arenas

Stanley

Falkland Is. (U.K.)

South Georgia (U.K.)

The sea contour is drawn at 200 metres

Drake Passage

C. de Hornos

SCOTIA SEA

South Shetland

South Orkney Is.

50° 60° 60° 50°

40°

30°

20°

10°

0°

10°

20°

30°

40°

50°

135° 120° 105° 30° 15°

Projection by courtesy of the
National Geographic Society, Washington, D.C.

© John Bartholomew & Son Ltd Edinburgh

Longitude West 100° of Greenwich

ATLANTIC

OCEAN

BERMUDA
(To U.K.)
Hamilton

Tropic of Cancer

THE
BAHAMAS

WEST

INDIES

HISPANIOLA

LEEWARD ISLANDS

1:12.5M

miles   km
500 ── 800
         700
400 ── 600
         500
300 ── 400
200 ──
         300
100 ──
         200
         100
          50
   0 ──   0

2

3

4

5

6

7

8

HABANA
(HAVANA)

CUBA

JAMAICA
Kingston

HAITI
Port au Prince

DOMINICAN
REPUBLIC
Santo
Domingo

PUERTO RICO
(To U.S.A.)

WINDWARD ISLANDS

BELIZE

HONDURAS

NIC.

CARIBBEAN   SEA

ANTILLES

LESSER

GRE ATER

ANTILLES

VEN.

NETHERLANDS
ANTILLES

126   128

Heights in feet   Depths in metres

Chicago   Detroit   New York   Philadelphia   Boston
Washington   Baltimore   Pittsburgh   Cleveland   Cincinnati   Columbus
Milwaukee   Atlanta   Birmingham   Montgomery   Charlotte   Charleston
Jacksonville   Orlando   Tampa   Miami   Miami Beach   Ft. Lauderdale   West Palm Beach
Nassau   New Providence
OTTAWA   Toronto   Montreal   Québec   Hull   Hamilton   Buffalo
INDIANA   OHIO   KENTUCKY   TENNESSEE   VIRGINIA   WEST VIRGINIA
NORTH CAROLINA   SOUTH CAROLINA   GEORGIA   ALABAMA   FLORIDA
PENNSYLVANIA   NEW YORK   MASS.   NEW BRUNSWICK   PRINCE EDWARD I.   MAINE
ST. LAWRENCE   Gulf of Saint Lawrence   Halifax   Cape Breton I.

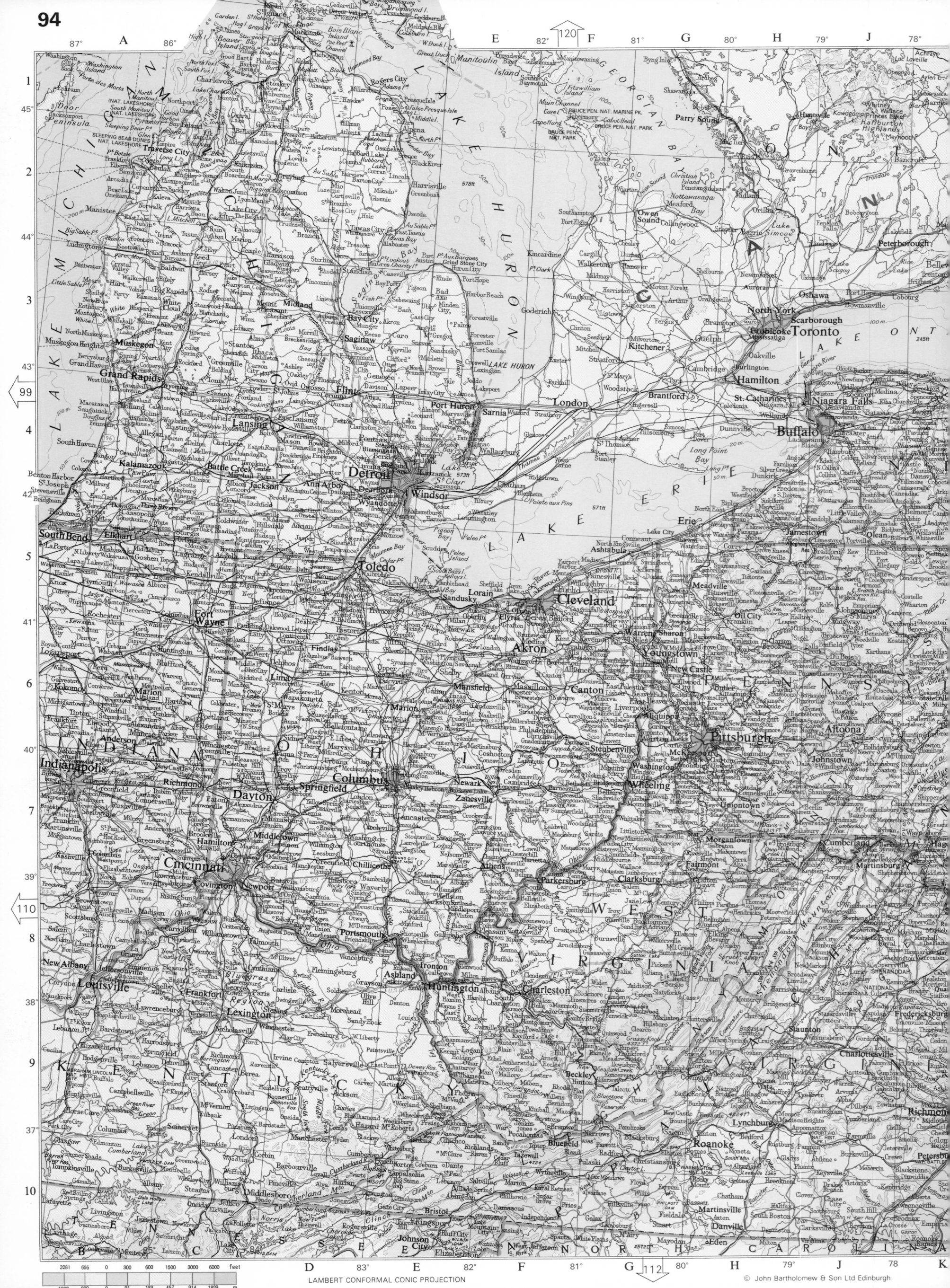

Longitude West 76° of Greenwich

1:3M

0 10 20 30 40 60 80 100 120 miles
0 20 40 80 120 160 km

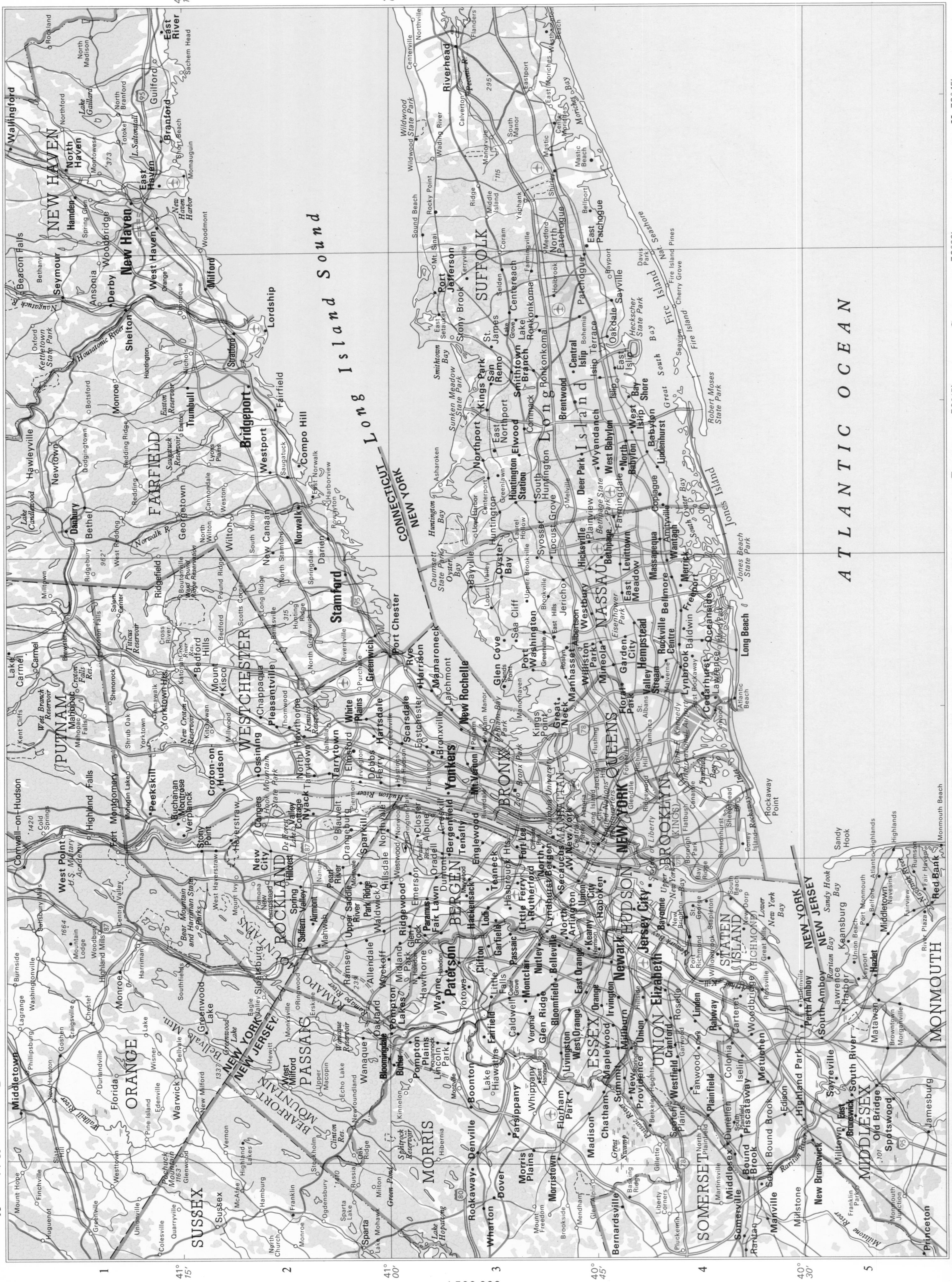

ATLANTIC OCEAN

Long Island Sound

CONNECTICUT
NEW YORK

NEW YORK
NEW JERSEY

NEW HAVEN
FAIRFIELD
PUTNAM
WESTCHESTER
ORANGE
ROCKLAND
SUSSEX
PASSAIC
MORRIS
BERGEN
ESSEX
UNION
HUDSON
RICHMOND
STATEN ISLAND
BRONX
MANHATTAN
QUEENS
BROOKLYN (KINGS)
NASSAU
SUFFOLK
NEW YORK
SOMERSET
MIDDLESEX
MONMOUTH

RAMAPO MOUNTAINS
BEARFORT MOUNTAIN

New Haven
Bridgeport
Stamford
Danbury
Norwalk
White Plains
Yonkers
Newark
Elizabeth
Paterson
Jersey City
NEW YORK
Riverhead
Patchogue
Port Jefferson
Hempstead
Middletown
Morristown

1:500 000

© Times Books Ltd

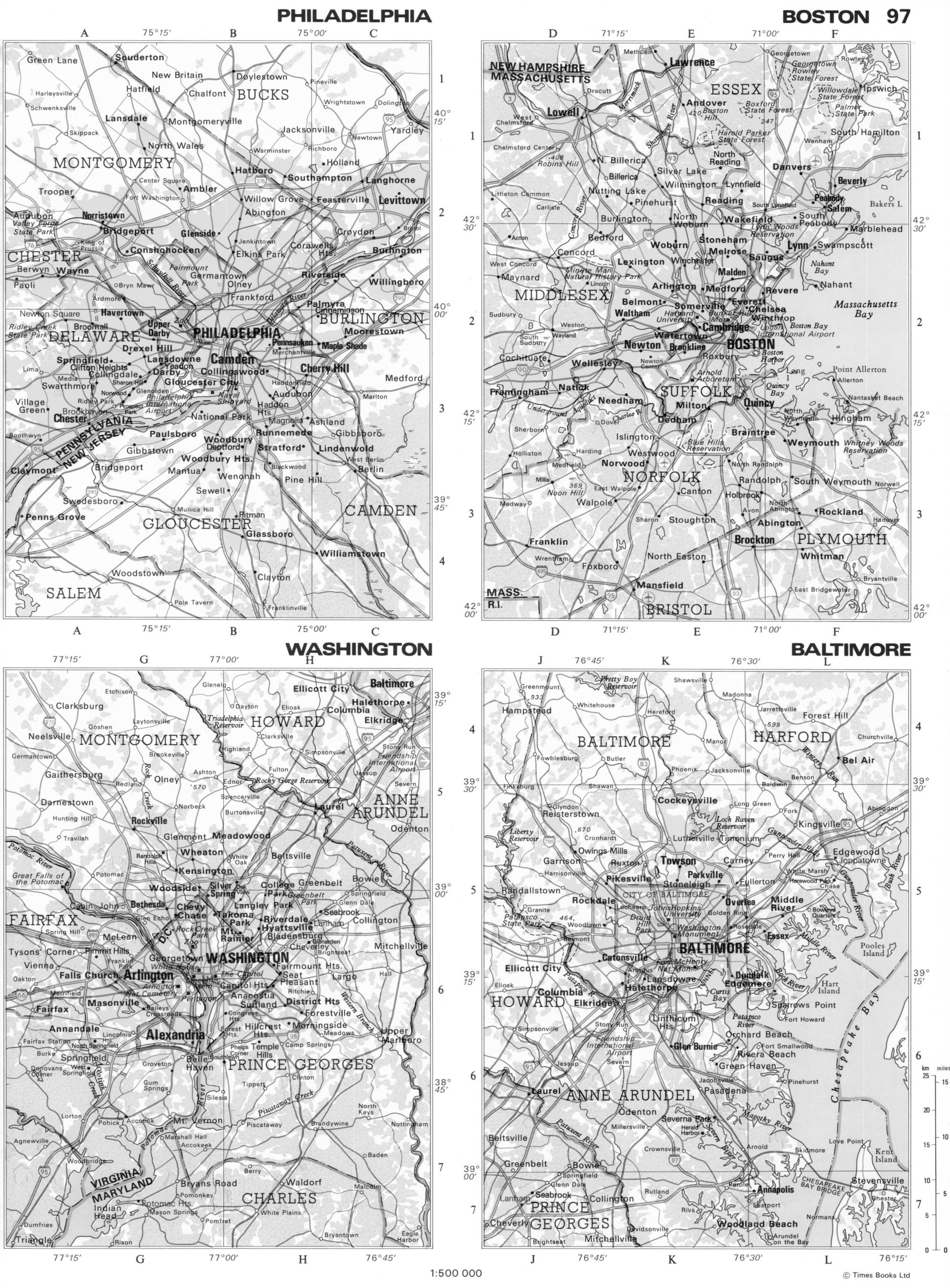

1:500 000

© Times Books Ltd

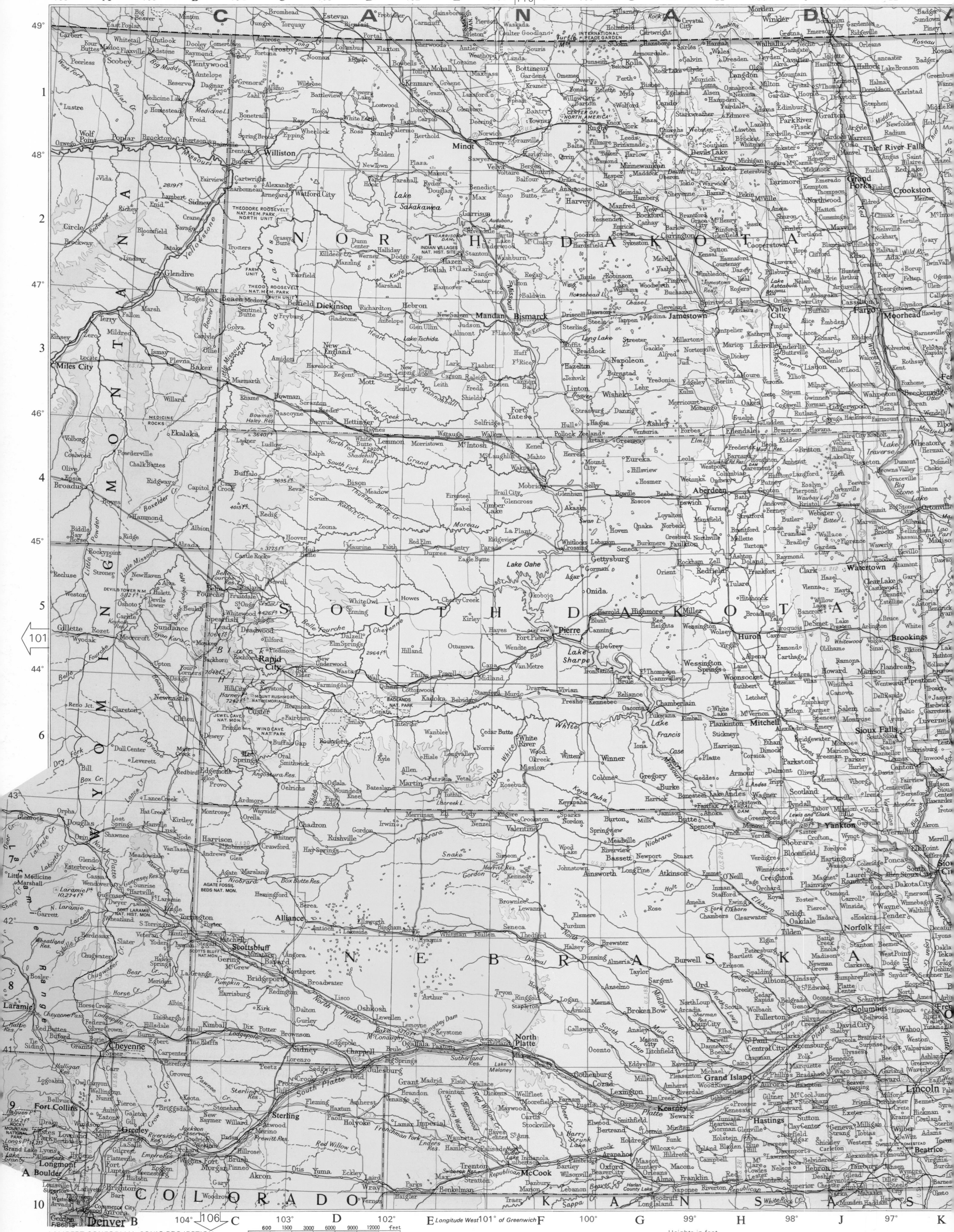

CANADA

MONTANA

NORTH DAKOTA

SOUTH DAKOTA

WYOMING

NEBRASKA

COLORADO

KANSAS

Minot

Bismarck · Mandan

Jamestown

Valley City

Fargo · Moorhead

Grand Forks · Crookston

Thief River Falls

Dickinson

Williston

Miles City

Glendive

Aberdeen

Watertown

Huron

Brookings

Pierre · Fort Pierre

Rapid City

Deadwood · Lead · Spearfish

Sioux Falls

Mitchell

Chamberlain

Yankton

Gillette

Newcastle

Cheyenne

Laramie

Fort Collins

Greeley · Longmont · Boulder

Denver

Scottsbluff · Gering

Alliance

Chadron

North Platte

Grand Island

Kearney · Hastings

Columbus

Lincoln

Norfolk

Lake Sakakawea

Lake Oahe

Lake Sharpe

Theodore Roosevelt Nat. Mem. Park

Mount Rushmore National Memorial

Wind Cave Nat. Park

Jewel Cave Nat. Mon.

Devils Tower N.M.

Badlands Nat. Park

Agate Fossil Beds Nat. Mon.

Scotts Bluff Nat. Mon.

Rocky Mountain National Park

LAMBERT CONFORMAL CONIC PROJECTION

Longitude West of Greenwich

Heights in feet

600 1500 3000 6000 9000 12000 feet
183 457   914   1829 2743 3658 m

ONTARIO
LAKE SUPERIOR
LAKE MICHIGAN
MICHIGAN
WISCONSIN
IOWA
ILLINOIS
MISSOURI
Lake of the Woods
Upper Red Lake
Lower Red Lake
Mille Lacs
Isle Royale
Apostle Islands (NAT. LAKESHORE)
Keweenaw Peninsula
Thunder Bay
Duluth
Superior
Minneapolis
St. Paul
St Cloud
Rochester
La Crosse
Eau Claire
Wausau
Green Bay
Appleton
Oshkosh
Sheboygan
Manitowoc
Madison
Milwaukee
Racine
Kenosha
Waukegan
Chicago
Gary
Rockford
Dubuque
Cedar Rapids
Waterloo
Davenport
Moline
Rock Island
Des Moines
Iowa City
Burlington
Peoria
Bloomington
Champaign
Decatur
Springfield
Quincy
Council Bluffs
Sault Ste Marie
Marquette
Escanaba
on the same scale
1:3M
0 10 20 40 60 80 100 miles
0 20 40 80 120 160 km
© John Bartholomew & Son Ltd Edinburgh

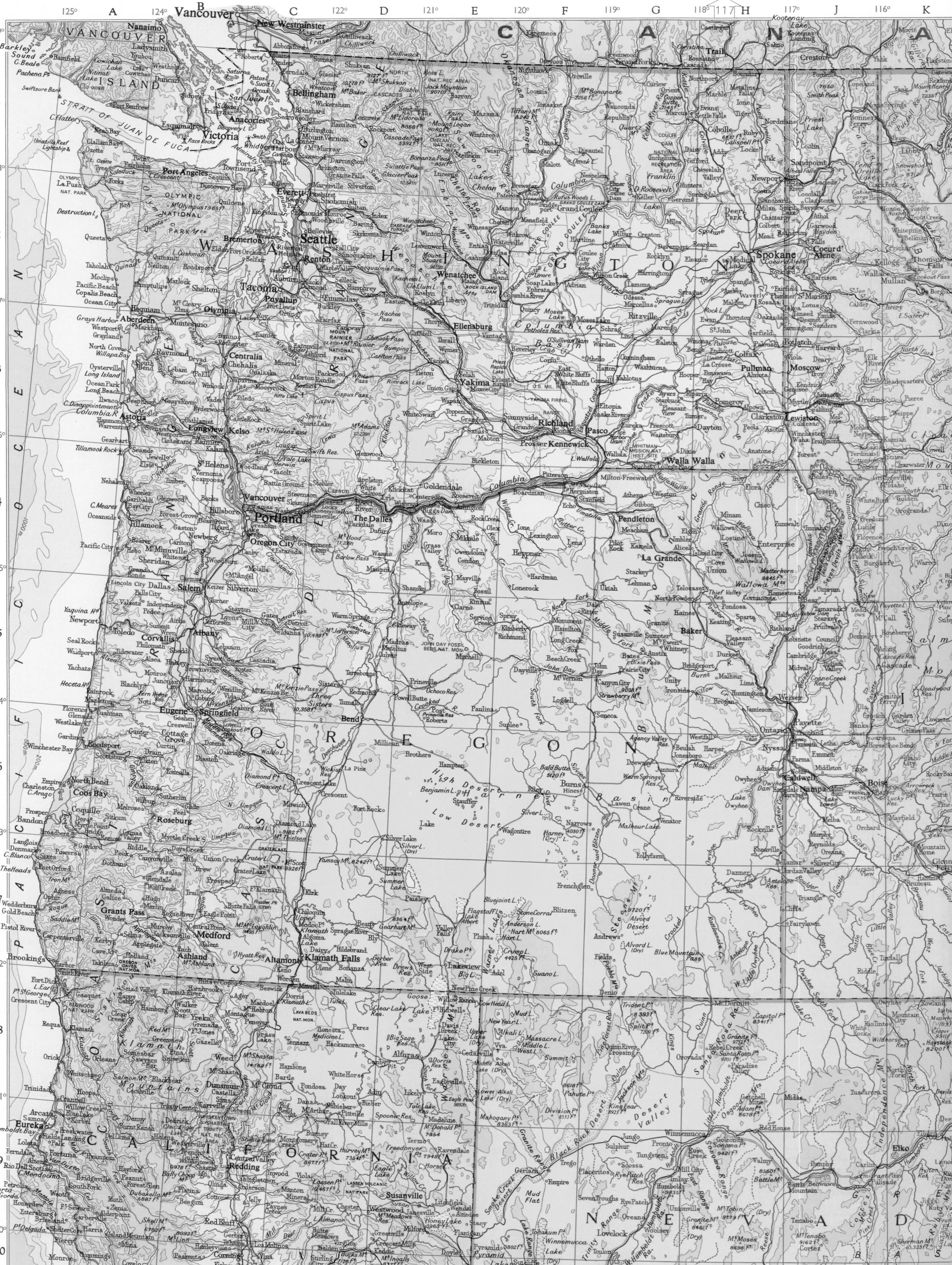

C A N A D A

VANCOUVER ISLAND

WASHINGTON

OREGON

CALIFORNIA

NEVADA

IDAHO

P A C I F I C   O C E A N

STRAIT OF JUAN DE FUCA

Vancouver
New Westminster
Nanaimo
Victoria
Bellingham
Anacortes
Port Angeles
Everett
Seattle
Bremerton
Tacoma
Olympia
Aberdeen
Centralia
Chehalis
Yakima
Ellensburg
Wenatchee
Spokane
Coeur d'Alene
Moscow
Pullman
Richland
Pasco
Kennewick
Walla Walla
Pendleton
La Grande
Baker
Astoria
Longview
Kelso
Vancouver
Portland
Oregon City
The Dalles
Salem
Albany
Corvallis
Newport
Eugene
Springfield
Bend
Coos Bay
Roseburg
Grants Pass
Medford
Ashland
Klamath Falls
Lakeview
Burns
Ontario
Nyssa
Caldwell
Nampa
Boise
Eureka
Redding
Susanville
Alturas
Winnemucca
Elko

Columbia River
Snake River
John Day R.
MOUNT RAINIER NATIONAL PARK
CRATER LAKE NATIONAL PARK
OLYMPIC NATIONAL PARK
MT ST HELENS
MT HOOD 11235 ft
MT SHASTA

LAMBERT CONFORMAL CONIC PROJECTION

Heights in feet
Depths in metres

PACIFIC OCEAN
San Francisco
Los Angeles
San Diego
Sacramento
Fresno
Oakland
San Jose
Stockton
Bakersfield
Santa Barbara
Reno
Carson City
NEVADA
YOSEMITE NATIONAL PARK
SEQUOIA NATIONAL PARK
KINGS CANYON NATIONAL PARK
DEATH VALLEY NATIONAL MONUMENT
MOJAVE DESERT
CHANNEL ISLANDS
Santa Catalina I.
San Clemente I.
GULF OF SANTA CATALINA
OAHU
(HONOLULU COUNTY)
Honolulu
Pearl City
Kaneohe
Kailua
1:1M
HAWAIIAN ISLANDS
(To U.S.A.)
1:9 000 000
also on page 135
KAUAI
NIIHAU
MOLOKAI
LANAI
MAUI
KAHOOLAWE
HAWAII
LAMBERT CONFORMAL CONIC PROJECTION
Longitude West of Greenwich

Heights in feet Depths in metres

© John Bartholomew & Son Ltd Edinburgh

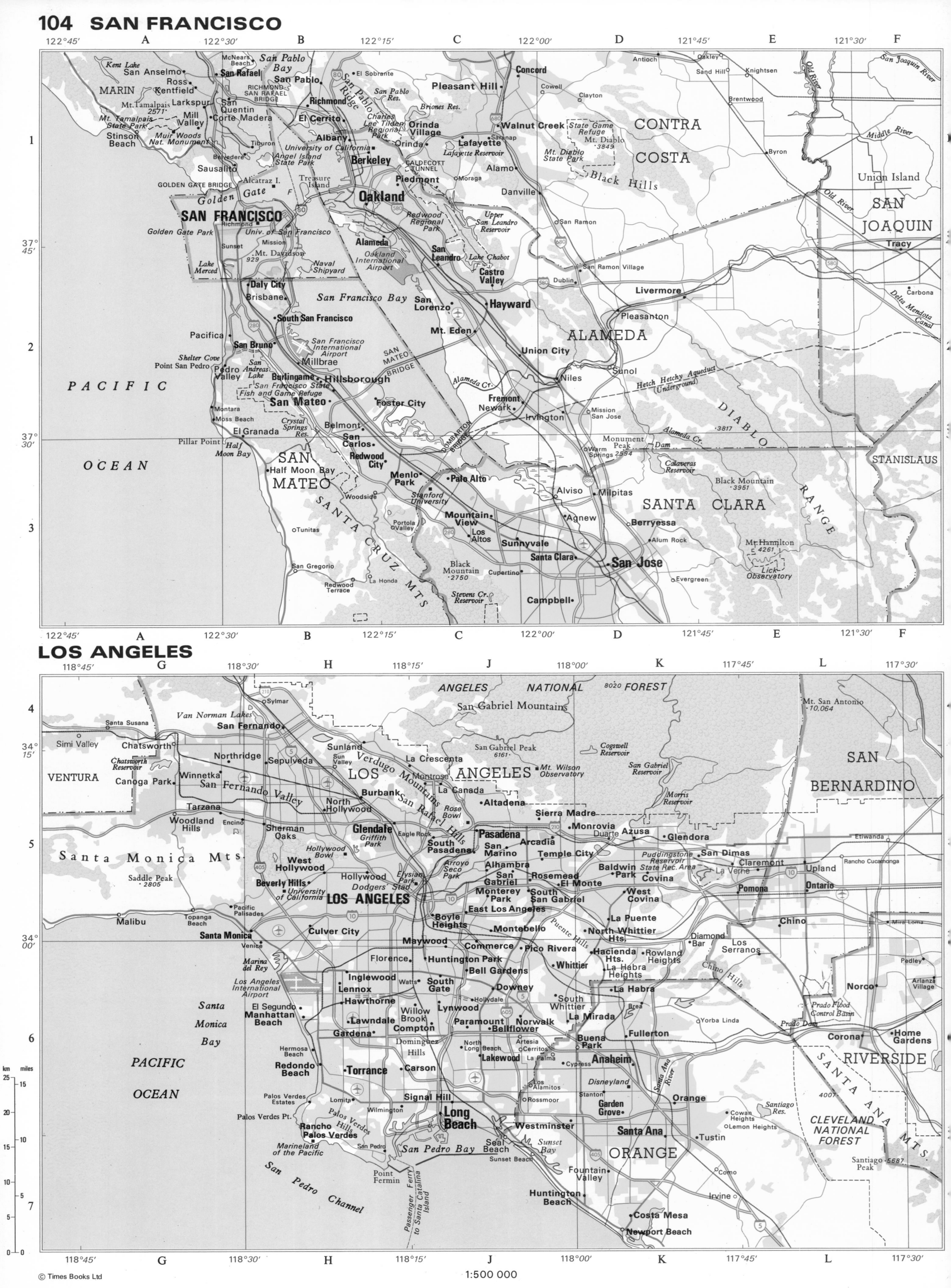

MARIN

Kent Lake
McNears Beach
San Anselmo
San Rafael
San Pablo Bay
San Pablo
El Sobrante
Concord
Antioch
Oakley
Sand Hill
Knightsen
San Joaquin River

Ross
Kentfield
Larkspur
RICHMOND-SAN RAFAEL BRIDGE
Richmond
Pleasant Hill
Cowell
Clayton
Brentwood
Mt. Tamalpais 2571
Mt. Tamalpais State Park
Mill Valley
Corte Madera
San Quentin
El Cerrito
San Pablo Ridge
San Pablo Res.
Briones Res.
Walnut Creek
State Game Refuge
Mt. Diablo 3849
CONTRA COSTA
Byron

Stinson Beach
Muir Woods Nat. Monument
Tiburon
Albany
Charles Lee Tilden Regional Park
Orinda Village
Orinda
Lafayette
Saranap
Lafayette Reservoir
Mt. Diablo State Park
Black Hills
Union Island

Belvedere
University of California
Angel Island State Park
Berkeley
CALDECOTT TUNNEL
Alamo
SAN JOAQUIN

Sausalito
Alcatraz I.
Treasure Island
Piedmont
oMoraga
Danville
Tracy

GOLDEN GATE BRIDGE
Golden Gate
Oakland
Redwood Regional Park
Upper San Leandro Reservoir
oSan Ramon

SAN FRANCISCO
Richmond
Univ. of San Francisco
Golden Gate Park
Sunset
Mission
Alameda
San Leandro
Castro Valley
Lake Chabot
San Ramon Village
Dublin

Lake Merced
Mt. Davidson 929
Naval Shipyard
Oakland International Airport
San Lorenzo
Hayward
Livermore

Daly City
Brisbane
San Francisco Bay
Mt. Eden
Pleasanton

Pacifica
South San Francisco
Union City
Sunol
Carbona

San Bruno
San Francisco International Airport
Millbrae
Niles
Hetch Hetchy Aqueduct (Underground)
Delta Mendota Canal

Shelter Cove
Point San Pedro
Pedro Valley
San Andreas Lake
Burlingame
Hillsborough
SAN MATEO BRIDGE
Alameda Cr.
Fremont
Newark
DIABLO RANGE

Montara
Moss Beach
San Francisco State Fish and Game Refuge
San Mateo
Foster City
Irvington
Mission San Jose
3817

PACIFIC OCEAN
El Granada
Crystal Springs Res.
Belmont
DUMBARTON BRIDGE
Monument Peak 2594
Dam
Alameda Cr.
STANISLAUS

Pillar Point
Half Moon Bay
San Carlos
Redwood City
Warm Springs
Calaveras Reservoir
Black Mountain 3951

SAN MATEO
Half Moon Bay
Menlo Park
Palo Alto
Alviso
Milpitas
SANTA CLARA
Mt. Hamilton 4261

Woodside
Stanford University
Mountain View
Los Altos
Agnew
Berryessa
Lick Observatory

Tunitas
Portola Valley
Sunnyvale
Alum Rock

San Gregorio
Black Mountain 2750
Santa Clara
San Jose
Evergreen

Redwood Terrace
La Honda
Cupertino
Stevens Cr. Reservoir
Campbell

ANGELES NATIONAL FOREST 8020
Mt. San Antonio 10,064

Simi Valley
Santa Susana
Sylmar
San Gabriel Mountains
San Gabriel Peak 6161
Cogswell Reservoir
SAN BERNARDINO

Chatsworth
Van Norman Lakes
San Fernando
Sunland
Verdugo Mountains
La Crescenta
Montrose
Mt. Wilson Observatory

VENTURA
Chatsworth Reservoir
Northridge
Sepulveda
Sun Valley
La Canada
Morris Reservoir

LOS ANGELES
Winnetka
Canoga Park
San Fernando Valley
Burbank
North Hollywood
San Rafael Hills
Rose Bowl
Altadena
Sierra Madre
Monrovia
Duarte
Azusa
Glendora
Etiwanda

Woodland Hills
Tarzana
Encino
Sherman Oaks
Glendale
Griffith Park
Eagle Rock
Pasadena
Arcadia
Temple City
Puddingstone Reservoir
San Dimas
Rancho Cucamonga

Santa Monica Mts.
Saddle Peak 2805
West Hollywood
Hollywood Bowl
South Pasadena
San Marino
Alhambra
Rosemead
State Rec. Area
La Verne
Claremont
Upland

Beverly Hills
University of California
Hollywood
Dodgers Stad.
Elysian Park
San Gabriel
Monterey Park
El Monte
Baldwin Park
Covina
Pomona
Ontario

Malibu
Pacific Palisades
Topanga Beach
Los Angeles
South San Gabriel
West Covina
Chino

Santa Monica
Culver City
Boyle Heights
East Los Angeles
Montebello
Puente Hills
North Whittier Hts.
La Puente
Diamond Bar
Los Serranos

Venice
Maywood
Commerce
Pico Rivera
Hacienda Hts.
Rowland Heights
Norco

Santa Monica Bay
Marina del Rey
Los Angeles International Airport
Florence
Huntington Park
Bell Gardens
Whittier
La Habra Heights
Chino Hills

El Segundo
Manhattan Beach
Lennox
Watts
South Gate
Downey
South Whittier
La Habra
La Mirada
Brea
Yorba Linda
Prado Flood Control Basin

Hawthorne
Lawndale
Willow Brook
Lynwood
Paramount
Norwalk
Buena Park
Fullerton
Pedley

Hermosa Beach
Gardena
Compton
Hollydale
Bellflower
Artesia
Cerritos
La Palma
Cypress
Home Gardens

Redondo Beach
Torrance
Dominguez Hills
Carson
North Long Beach
Lakewood
Anaheim
Corona
RIVERSIDE
Arlanza Village

Palos Verdes Estates
Lomita
Wilmington
Los Alamitos
Stanton
Garden Grove
Orange
Santiago Res.
Cowan Heights
Lemon Heights

Rancho Palos Verdes
Palos Verdes Pt.
Palos Verdes Hills
San Pedro
Signal Hill
Rossmoor
Disneyland
Santiago Peak 5687

PACIFIC OCEAN
Point Fermin
Marineland of the Pacific
Long Beach
Seal Beach
Sunset Bay
Fountain Valley
ORANGE
CLEVELAND NATIONAL FOREST

San Pedro Bay
Sunset Beach
Westminster
Santa Ana
Tustin
Como
Irvine

San Pedro Channel
Passenger Ferry to Santa Catalina Island
Huntington Beach
Newport Beach
Costa Mesa
SANTA ANA MTS

1:500 000

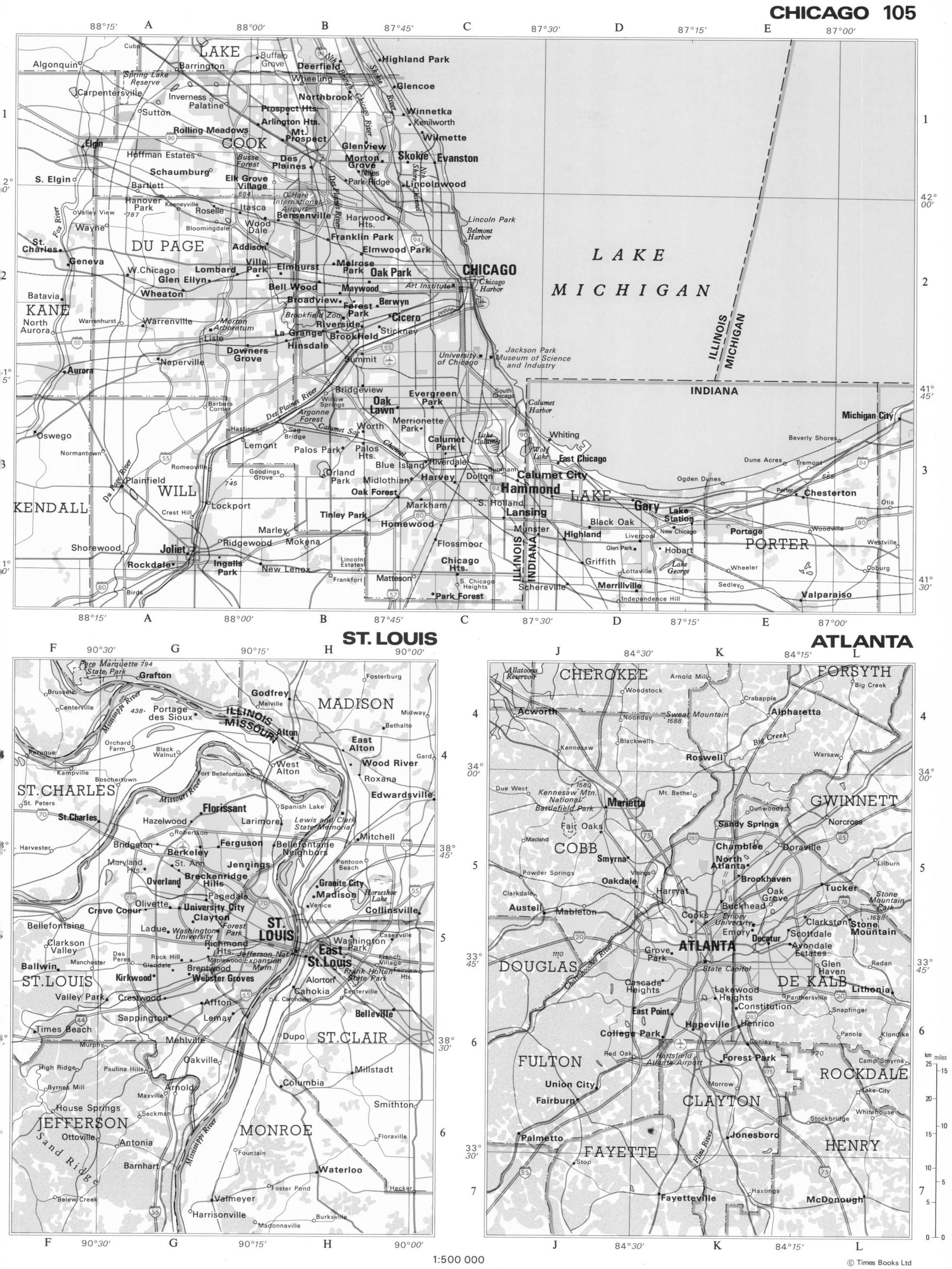

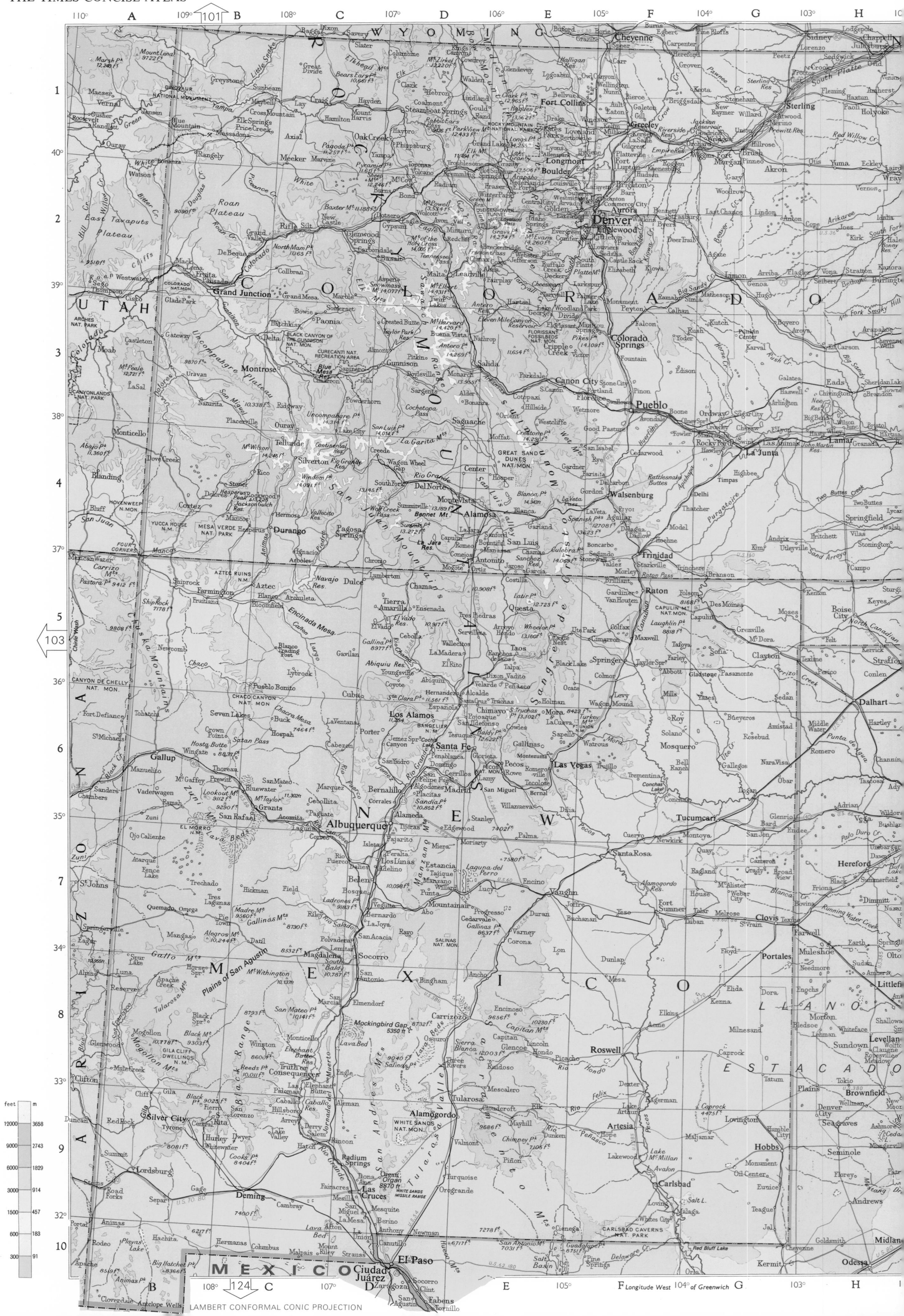
WYOMING
UTAH
COLORADO
NEW MEXICO
ARIZONA
MEXICO
ROCKY MOUNTAINS
SAN JUAN MOUNTAINS
SANGRE DE CRISTO MTS
LLANO ESTACADO
Denver
Cheyenne
Fort Collins
Greeley
Boulder
Colorado Springs
Pueblo
Grand Junction
Durango
Alamosa
Trinidad
Raton
Santa Fe
Los Alamos
Las Vegas
Albuquerque
Gallup
Farmington
Socorro
Roswell
Tucumcari
Clovis
Alamogordo
Las Cruces
Carlsbad
Hobbs
Deming
Silver City
El Paso
Ciudad Juárez
101
103
124
Longitude West of Greenwich
LAMBERT CONFORMAL CONIC PROJECTION
feet
m
12000
3658
9000
2743
6000
1829
3000
914
1500
457
600
183
300
91

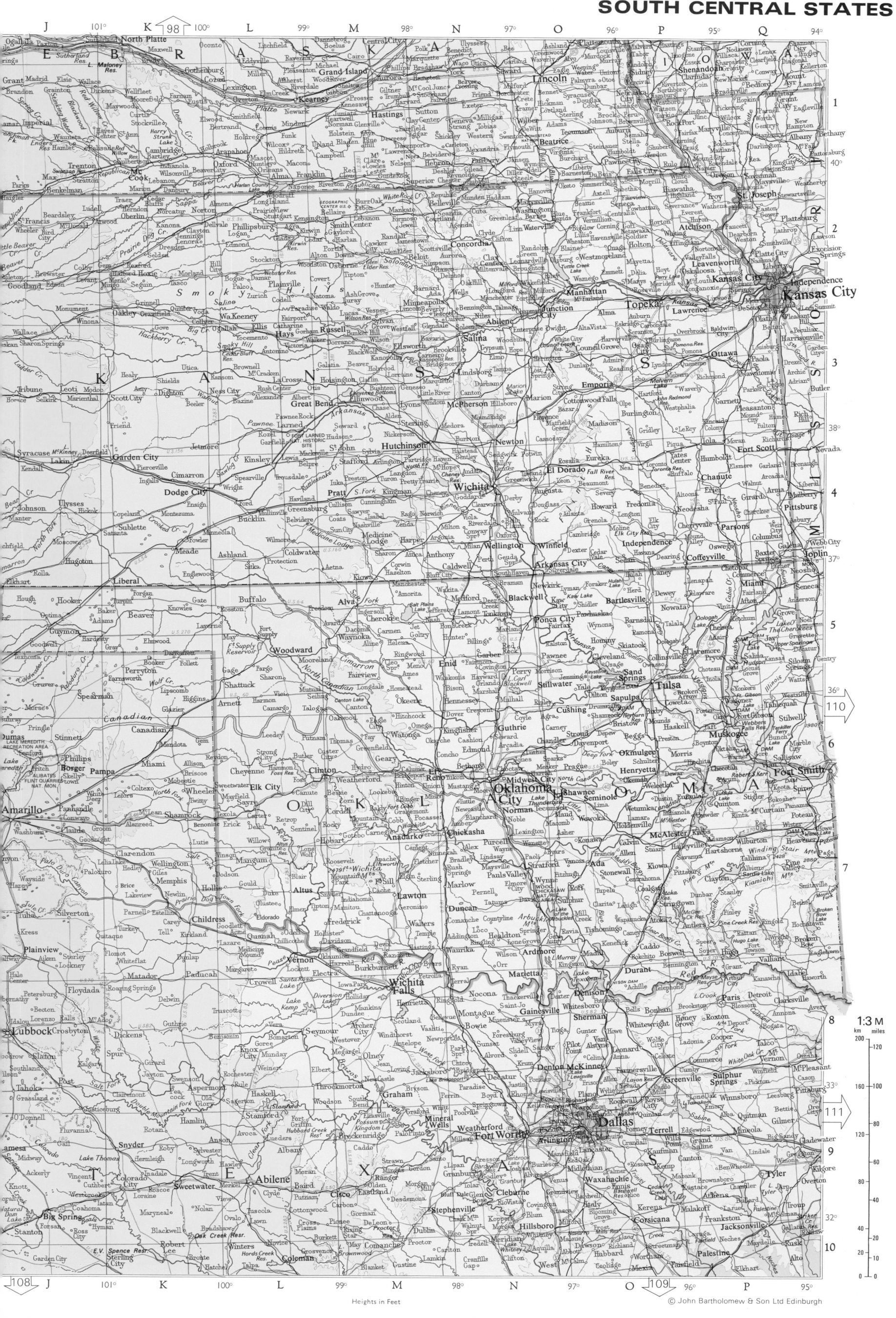
98
108
109
110
111
NEBRASKA
IOWA
KANSAS
MISSOURI
OKLAHOMA
TEXAS
North Platte
Grand Island
Lincoln
Kearney
Hastings
Beatrice
St. Joseph
Topeka
Kansas City
Independence
Lawrence
Salina
Hutchinson
Wichita
Dodge City
Garden City
Emporia
Joplin
Tulsa
Oklahoma City
Enid
Norman
Lawton
Muskogee
Fort Smith
Amarillo
Lubbock
Wichita Falls
Abilene
Fort Worth
Dallas
Arlington
Denton
Sherman
Tyler
1:3 M
km
miles
Heights in Feet

Northward continuation of TEXAS on same scale

NEW MEXICO

OKLAHOMA

HOUSTON
1: 600 000

LAMBERT CONFORMAL CONIC PROJECTION

OKLAHOMA
ARKANSAS
LOUISIANA
TEXAS
GULF OF MEXICO
Dallas
Fort Worth
Houston
San Antonio
Austin
Galveston
Corpus Christi
Shreveport
Beaumont
Port Arthur
Waco
Laredo
Brownsville
Wichita Falls
Texarkana
Little Rock
Hot Springs
Lake Charles
Tyler
Longview
Victoria
Matamoros
Reynosa
1:3M
km miles
FORT WORTH-DALLAS
1: 720 000
Heights in feet
Depths in metres
Longitude West 99° of Greenwich
110
111

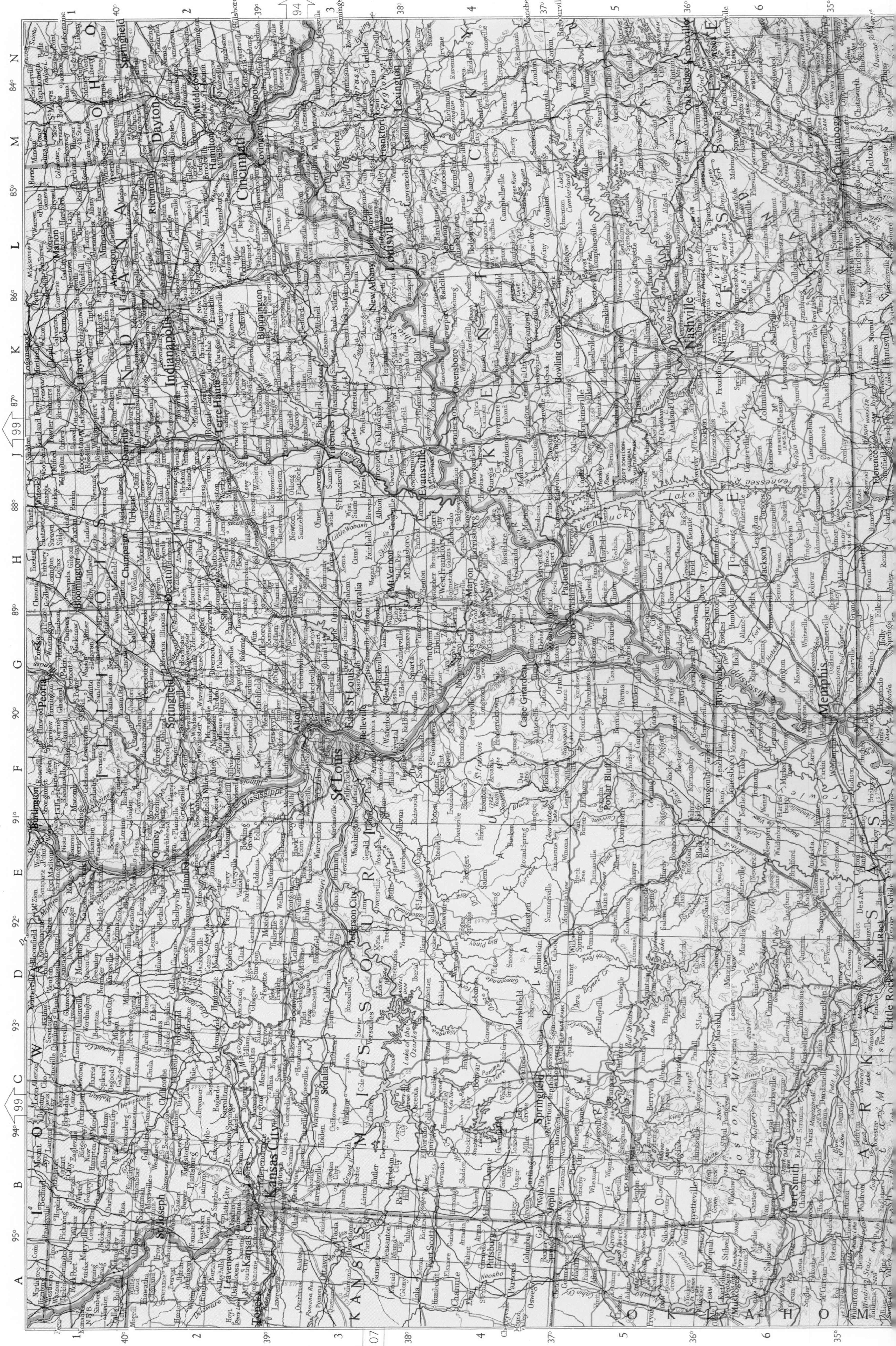

LAMBERT CONFORMAL CONIC PROJECTION

1:3 M

ST LOUIS
1:300 000

NEW ORLEANS
1:300 000

GEORGIA
ALABAMA
MISSISSIPPI
LOUISIANA
TEXAS
FLORIDA
ARKANSAS

Atlanta
Rome
Gadsden
Anniston
Decatur
Birmingham
Bessemer
Tuscaloosa
Columbus
Montgomery
Selma
Meridian
Columbus
Greenville
Greenwood
Jackson
Vicksburg
Natchez
Hattiesburg
Laurel
Biloxi
Gulfport
Mobile
Pensacola
Panama City
Tallahassee
New Orleans
Baton Rouge
Lafayette
Lake Charles
Alexandria
Monroe
Shreveport
Longview
Texarkana
El Dorado
Pine Bluff
Hot Springs
Beaumont
Port Arthur
Orange
Galveston
Baytown

GULF OF MEXICO

Mississippi Sound
Lake Pontchartrain
Mobile Bay

Longitude West 90° of Greenwich

Heights in feet Depths in metres

© John Bartholomew & Son Ltd Edinburgh

feet
3281
1000
656
200
0
m
1000
3000 914
1500 457
600 183
300 91
0

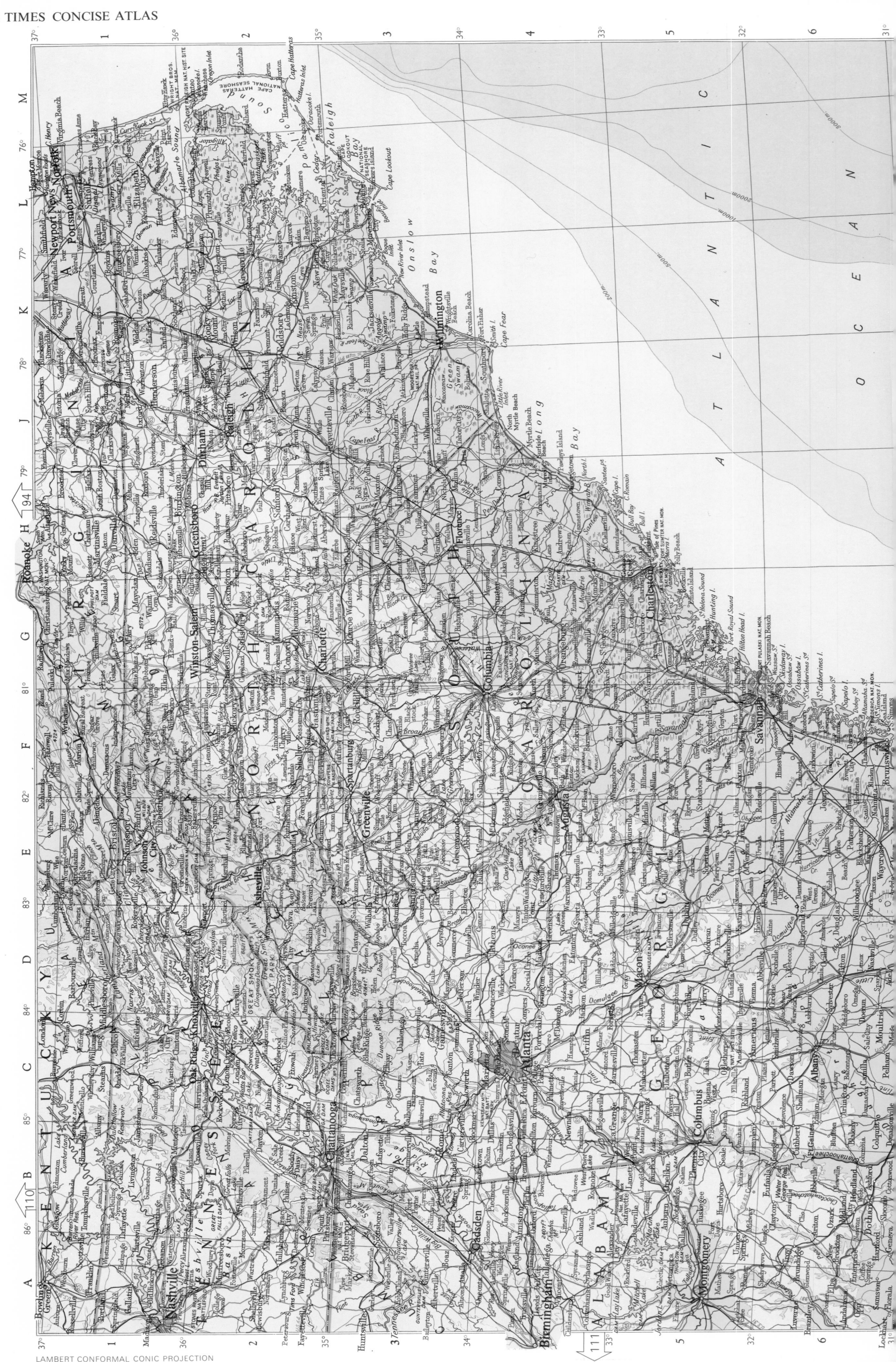

LAMBERT CONFORMAL CONIC PROJECTION

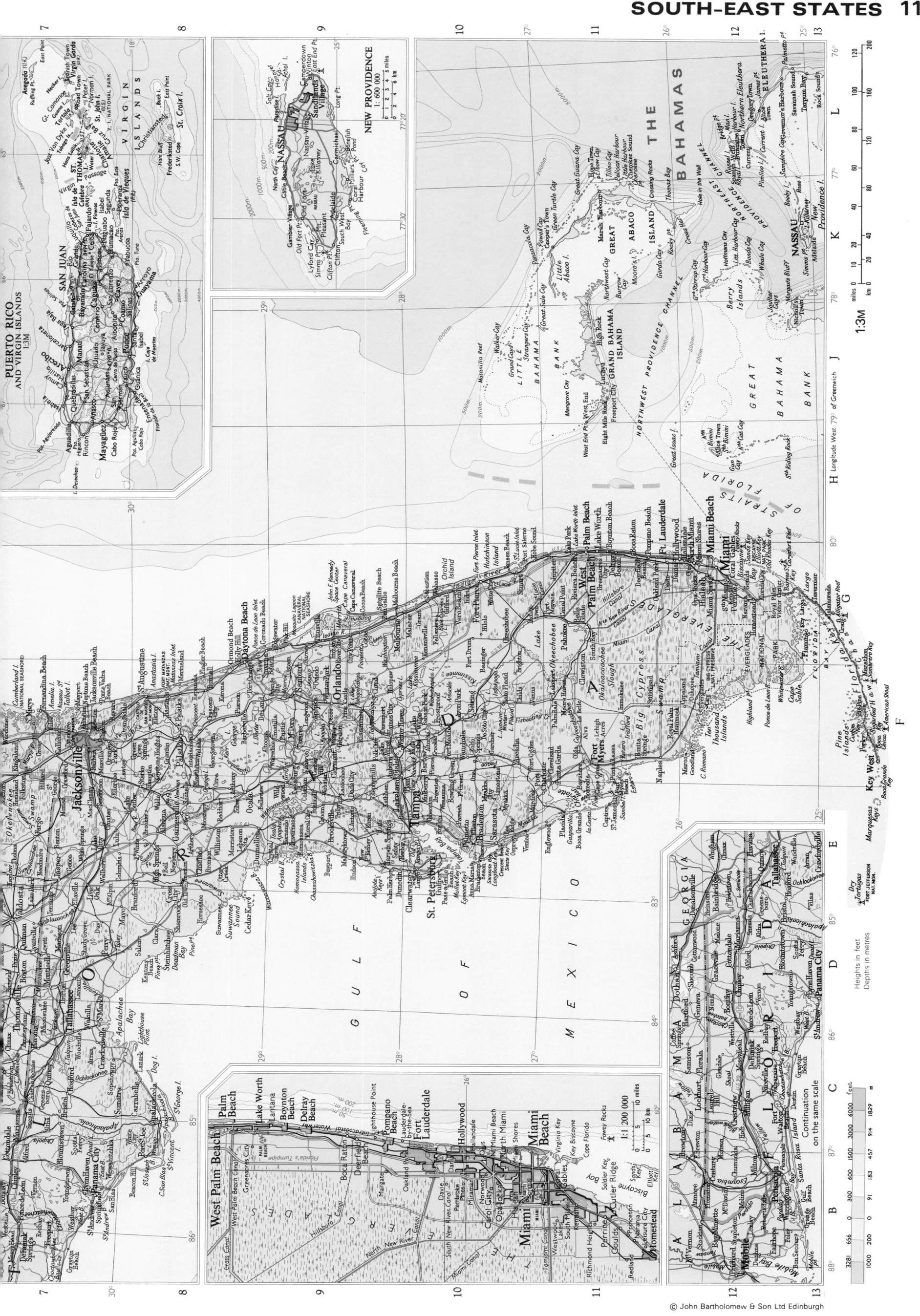
PUERTO RICO AND VIRGIN ISLANDS
1:3M
NEW PROVIDENCE
1: 600 000
THE BAHAMAS
GULF OF MEXICO
FLORIDA
STRAITS OF FLORIDA
1:1 200 000
Continuation on the same scale
1:3M
Longitude West of Greenwich
Heights in feet
Depths in metres

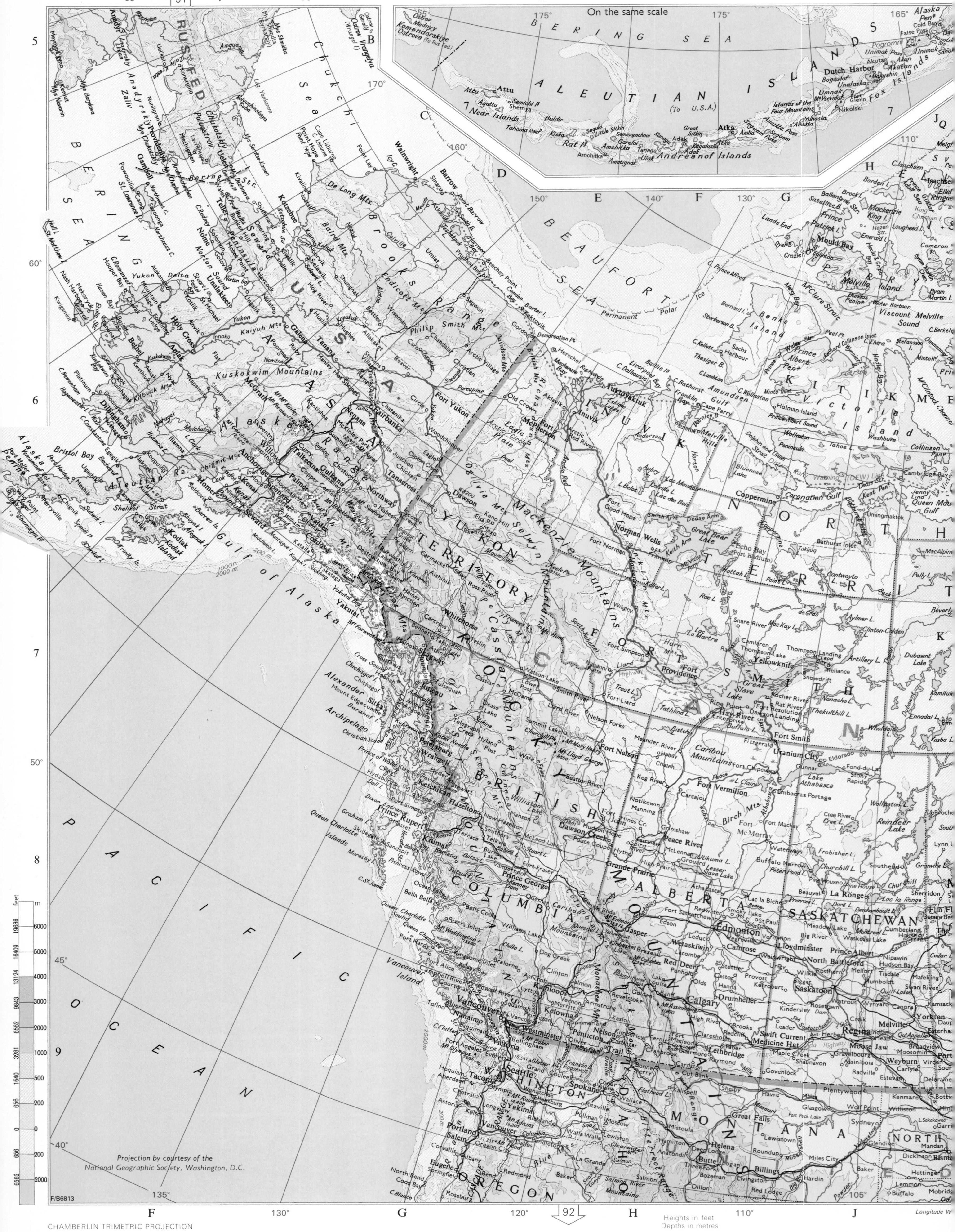

On the same scale

BERING SEA

ALEUTIAN ISLANDS
(To U.S.A.)

Near Islands
Rat Is.
Andreanof Islands
Fox Islands
Dutch Harbor

BEAUFORT SEA

R U S . F E D .

CHUKCHI SEA

U . S . A .
A L A S K A

Brooks Range
Alaska Range

Fairbanks
Anchorage
Juneau

Gulf of Alaska

YUKON TERRITORY

Whitehorse

Mackenzie Mountains

NORTH WEST TERRITORIES

Great Bear Lake

Yellowknife

Great Slave Lake

Lake Athabasca

BRITISH COLUMBIA

Prince George

Vancouver
Vancouver Island

ALBERTA

Edmonton
Calgary

SASKATCHEWAN

Saskatoon
Regina

P A C I F I C   O C E A N

WASHINGTON

Seattle
Spokane

OREGON
Portland
Salem

IDAHO

MONTANA

NORTH

Projection by courtesy of the
National Geographic Society, Washington, D.C.

Heights in feet
Depths in metres

GREENLAND
(KALAALLIT NUNAAT)
ICELAND
BAFFIN BAY
DAVIS STRAIT
DENMARK STRAIT
LABRADOR SEA
ATLANTIC OCEAN
NEWFOUNDLAND
HUDSON BAY
HUDSON STRAIT
FOXE BASIN
Baffin Island
Devon Island
Ungava Bay
LABRADOR
QUEBEC
ONTARIO
MANITOBA
NEW BRUNSWICK
NOVA SCOTIA
PRINCE EDWARD I.
Island of Newfoundland
Gulf of Saint Lawrence
Anticosti Island
Cape Breton I.
LAKE SUPERIOR
LAKE HURON
L. ERIE
ONTARIO
James Bay
Southampton Island
Coats I.
Mansel I.
Melville Peninsula
Boothia Peninsula
Somerset Island
Lancaster Sound
Jones Sound
Kane Basin
Thule
Godthåb (Nuuk)
Frederikshåb (Paamiut)
Holsteinsborg
Godhavn (Qeqertarsuaq)
Upernavik
Angmagssalik
Reykjavik
Akureyri
Scoresbysund
Arctic Circle
Frobisher Bay
Schefferville
Goose Bay
Churchill
Winnipeg
Thunder Bay
Sault Ste Marie
Sudbury
Toronto
Ottawa
Montréal
Québec
Halifax
Saint John
Fredericton
Charlottetown
St John's
Corner Brook
Gander
Boston
New York
Buffalo
Detroit
Minneapolis
St Paul
Duluth
Milwaukee
MINNESOTA
WISCONSIN
MICHIGAN
MAINE
NEW YORK
VERMONT
NEW HAMPSHIRE
MASS.
1:12.5M
km
miles
© John Bartholomew & Son Ltd Edinburgh

ARCTIC OCEAN

CHUKCHI SEA

BERING STRAIT

BEROOKS RANGE

CANADA

RUSSIA (CHUKOTSKIY POLUOSTROV)

U.S.A.

ALASKA RANGE

NORTON SOUND

BRISTOL BAY

KUSKOKWIM BAY

GULF OF ALASKA

Arctic Circle

Point Barrow

Barrow · Wainwright · Point Hope · Point Lay · Kotzebue · Noatak · Noorvik · Nome · Teller · Shishmaref · Wales · Gambell · St. Lawrence I. · Unalakleet · Mountain Village · Hooper Bay · Bethel · Kwethluk · Dillingham · Kodiak · Fairbanks · College · Nenana · Tanana · Anchorage · Palmer · Willow · Wasilla · Spenard · Whittier · Kenai · Seward · Homer · Seldovia · Cordova · Valdez · Fort Yukon · McGrath · Holy Cross · Chignik · Dutch Harbor · Unalaska I. · Unimak I. · Fort Randall · Nunivak I. · Pribilof Is. · St. Paul · St. George · Kwigillingok

DENALI (Mt McKinley)

WRANGELL MTS · st ELIAS MTS · CHUGACH MTS · KENAI MTS

ALEUTIAN ISLANDS

NEAR ISLANDS · RAT ISLANDS · ANDREANOF ISLANDS · FOX ISLANDS

ATTU I. · KISKA I. · AMCHITKA I. · TANAGA I. · ADAK I. · ATKA I. · KANAGA I.

ATKA · AMLIA I. · UMNAK I. · UNALASKA I. · ISLANDS OF THE FOUR MOUNTAINS

KODIAK ISLAND · SHUMAGIN ISLANDS

on the same scale

CONIC PROJECTION

Heights in feet
Depths in metres

1 : 6 M

| feet | 6562 | 656 | 0 | 600 | 1500 | 3000 | 6000 | 9000 | 12000 |
| m | 2000 | 200 | 0 | 183 | 457 | 914 | 1829 | 2743 | 3658 |

miles 0 20 40 80 120 160 200 240

km 0 40 80 160 240 320 400

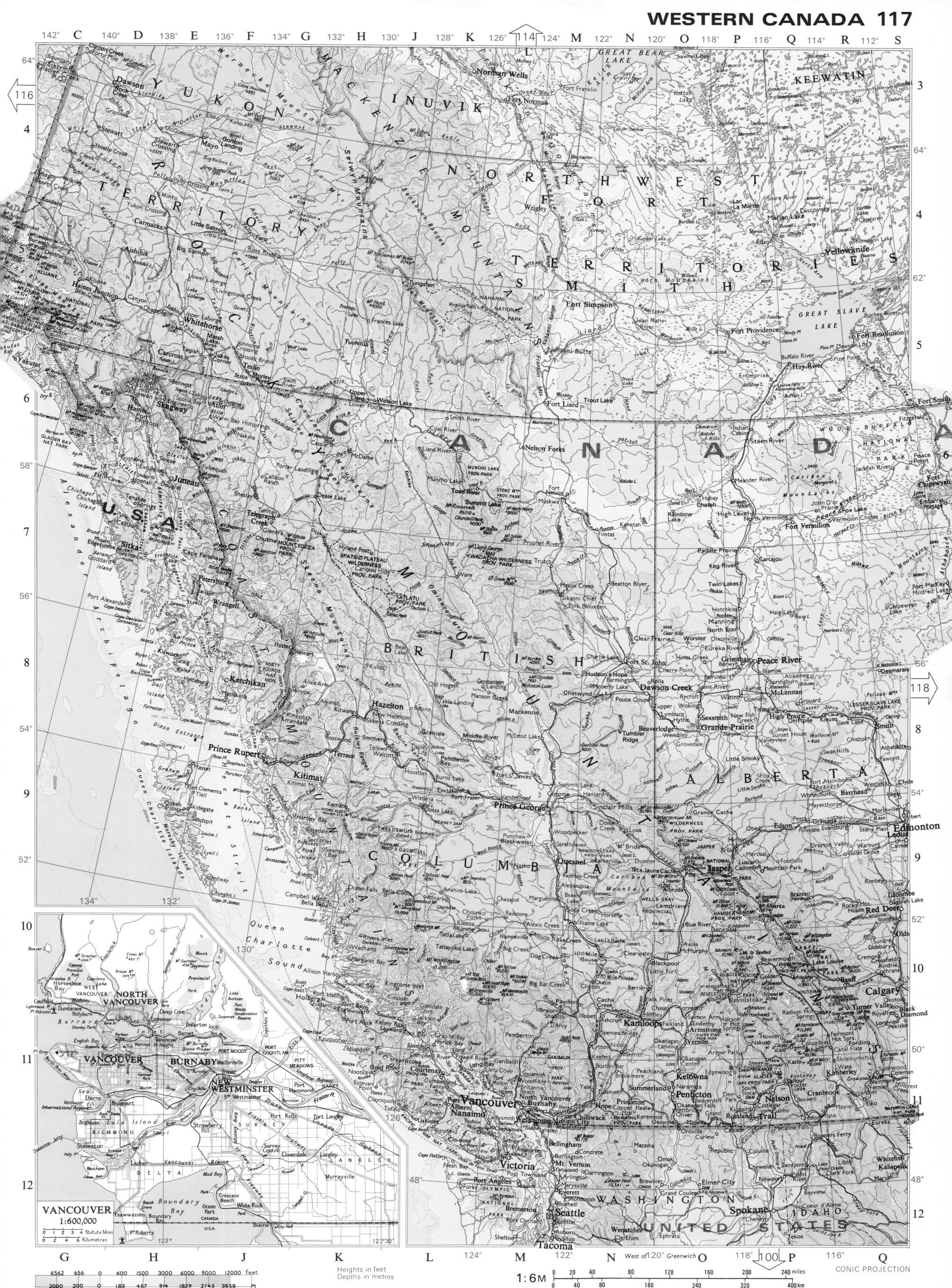

VANCOUVER
1:600,000

Heights in feet
Depths in metres

1 : 6M

CONIC PROJECTION

WINNIPEG
1:300 000
KILDONAN
Brooklands
ST. JAMES
TRANSCONA
ST. BONIFACE
Tuxedo
Charleswood
ST. CHARLES
Fort Whyte
ST. VITAL
Continuation
on the same scale
Winnipeg
Selkirk
Steinbach
Kenora
Dryden
Fort Frances
International Falls
Rainy River
ONTA
Peace River
High Prairie
Lesser Slave Lake
SWAN HILLS
Athabasca
Lac la Biche
Edmonton
Red Deer
Calgary
Banff
Lake Louise
Medicine Hat
Lethbridge
Fort Macleod
Cardston
Drumheller
Lloydminster
North Battleford
Saskatoon
Swift Current
Kindersley
Maple Creek
ALBERTA
SASKA
BRITISH COLUMBIA
ROCKY MOUNTAINS
CYPRESS HILLS
GREAT SAND HILLS
CANADA
U.S.A.
117
115
101
CONIC PROJECTION
Longitude West

MANITOBA

SASKATCHEWAN

LAKE NIPIGON 852ft.

ONTARIO

LAKE WINNIPEG

LAKE WINNIPEGOSIS

LAKE MANITOBA

Winnipeg

Regina

Prince Albert

Brandon

Thompson

Flin Flon

The Pas

Dauphin

Yorkton

Melville

Swan River

Norway House

Grand Rapids

RIDING MOUNTAIN NATIONAL PARK

DUCK MTN. PROV. PARK

PORCUPINE HILLS

PASQUIA HILLS

LAC LA RONGE PROVINCIAL PARK

Churchill River

Saskatchewan River

Qu'Appelle River

Nelson River

Trans Canada Highway

CANADA
U.S.A.

1:3M
km   miles
200 120
160 100
120   80
      60
 80   40
 40   20
      10
  0   0

© John Bartholomew & Son Ltd Edinburgh

115
99
94
LAKE NIPIGON
LAKE SUPERIOR
LAKE MICHIGAN
LAKE HURON
GEORGIAN BAY
LAKE ERIE
ONTARIO
MICHIGAN
JAMES
Thunder Bay
Sault Ste. Marie
Marquette
Sudbury
Timmins
Kapuskasing
Hearst
Cochrane
Detroit
Windsor
London
Flint
Lansing
Saginaw
Bay City
Sarnia
Port Huron
Hamilton
Kitchener
Guelph
Isle Royale NATIONAL PARK
Keweenaw Peninsula
Saginaw Bay
North Channel
Manitoulin Island
OTTAWA
1:240 000
HULL
VANIER
TORONTO
1:300 000
NORTH YORK
EAST YORK
SCARBOROUGH
ETOBICOKE
LAKE ONTARIO
Longitude West 81° of Greenwich
Feet
Metres
3000
914
1500
457
600
183
300
91
0
0

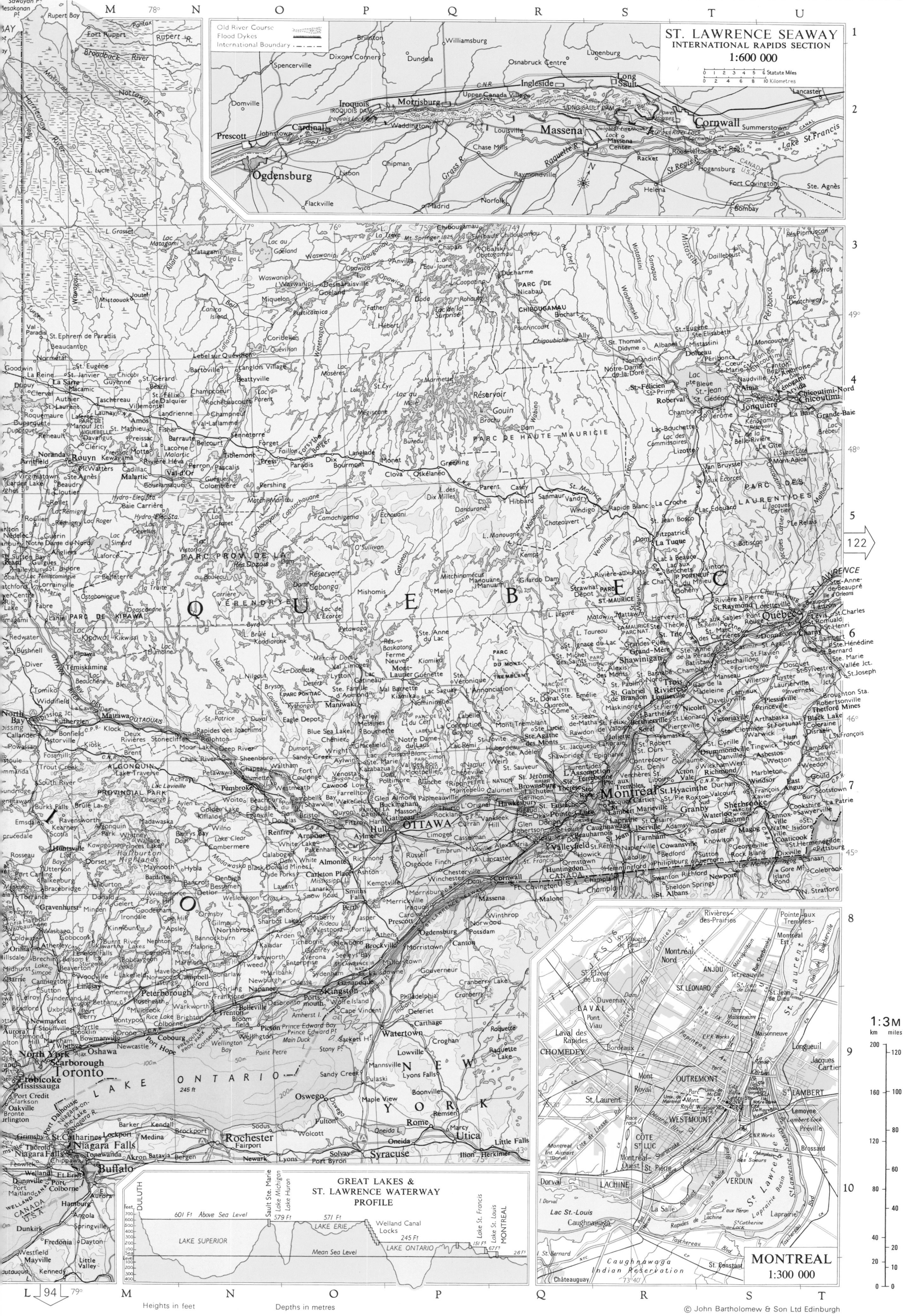

ST. LAWRENCE SEAWAY
INTERNATIONAL RAPIDS SECTION
1:600 000

Old River Course
Flood Dykes
International Boundary

Statute Miles
Kilometres

Inset (St. Lawrence Seaway): Brinston · Williamsburg · Dundela · Osnabruck Centre · Lunenburg · Spencerville · Dixons Corners · Morrisburg · Upper Canada Village · Ingleside · Long Sault · Lancaster · Domville · Iroquois · IROQUOIS DAM · Iroquois Lock · Waddington · LONG SAULT DAM · Cornwall · Summerstown · Prescott · Johnstown · Cardinal · Louisville · Massena · Chase Mills · Moses Saunders Power Dam · St. Regis · Ste. Agnès · Ogdensburg · Lisbon · Chipman · Grass R. · Raquette R. · Raymondville · Hogansburg · Fort Covington · Flackville · Madrid · Norfolk · Helena · Bombay · CANADA U.S.A. · Lake St. Francis

MONTREAL
1:300 000

Montreal inset: Rivières-des-Prairies · Pointe-aux-Trembles · Montréal Est · St. Vincent de Paul · St. Elzéar de Laval · Montréal Nord · ANJOU · ST. LÉONARD · St. Jean de Dieu · LAVAL · Duvernay · Tetreaultville · Chomedey · Laval des Rapides · Bordeaux · Maisonneuve · Longueuil · Jacques Cartier · Outremont · Mont Royal · St. Laurent · St. Lambert · Dorval · Montreal Int. Airport (Dorval) · Montréal Ouest · WESTMOUNT · Lemoyne · Lachine · CÔTE ST. LUC · VERDUN · Preville · LaSalle · Caughnawaga Indian Reservation · St. Constant · Châteauguay · Brossard

GREAT LAKES & ST. LAWRENCE WATERWAY PROFILE

DULUTH · Sault Ste. Marie · Lake Michigan · Lake Huron · Welland Canal Locks · Lake St. Francis · MONTREAL

601 Ft Above Sea Level · 579 Ft · 571 Ft · LAKE ERIE · 245 Ft · LAKE ONTARIO · LAKE SUPERIOR · Mean Sea Level · 151 Ft · 67 Ft · 26 Ft

1:3M
km · miles

Province / major labels: QUEBEC · ONTARIO · NEW YORK · CANADA · U.S.A. · LAKE ONTARIO · LAKE ERIE

Parks: PARC DE LA VÉRENDRYE · PARC DE KIPAWA · PARC DE HAUTE-MAURICIE · PARC DES LAURENTIDES · PARC DU MONT TREMBLANT · PARC PONTIAC · ALGONQUIN PROVINCIAL PARK · LA VÉRENDRYE

Major cities/towns: Montréal · Québec · Ottawa · Hull · Toronto · Mississauga · Scarborough · North York · Etobicoke · Oshawa · Buffalo · Rochester · Syracuse · Utica · Watertown · Kingston · Peterborough · Barrie · Orillia · Niagara Falls · St. Catharines · Chicoutimi · Chicoutimi-Nord · Jonquière · Alma · Shawinigan · Trois-Rivières · Rivière-du-Loup · Drummondville · Sherbrooke · Granby · Rouyn · Val-d'Or · Malartic · Noranda · North Bay · Pembroke · Renfrew · Cornwall · Massena · Ogdensburg · Brockville · Prescott · Thetford Mines · Victoriaville · Asbestos · Arthabaska

Heights in feet · Depths in metres

122 →

72° A 71° B 70° C 69° D 68° E 67° F 66° G 65° H 64° 115 J 63°
1
2
3
4
5
6
7
8
9
10
52°
51°
50°
49°
48°
47°
46°
45°
44°
115
121
Q U É B E C
NEW BRUNSWICK
PRINCE EDW
ISLAND
M A I N E
U. S. A.
N O V A S C O
ST. LAWRENCE (ST-LAURENT)
G U
S T L
GASPÉ PENINSULA
HONGUEDO PASSAGE
JACQUES-CARTIER PASSAGE
ANTICOSTI
BAY OF FUNDY
Shickshock Mountains
Réservoir Manicouagan
Lac Bréhat
Otish Mountains
Gagnon
Sept-Îles
Port-Cartier-Ouest
Port Cartier
Baie Comeau
Forestville
Chicoutimi
Jonquière
Alma
Kénogami
La Baie
Tadoussac
Rivière-du-Loup
Trois Pistoles
Rimouski
Mont Joli
Matane
Ste. Anne des Monts
Cap Chat
Amqui
Gaspé
Chandler
Campbellton
Dalhousie
Bathurst
Edmundston
Madawaska
Fort Kent
Grand Falls
Presque Isle
Caribou
Houlton
Woodstock
Fredericton
Chatham
Newcastle
Moncton
Saint John
Charlottetown
Summerside
Truro
Amherst
New Glasgow
Halifax
Dartmouth
Windsor
Kentville
Yarmouth
Digby
Liverpool
Lunenburg
Shelburne
Bangor
Augusta
Waterville
Lewiston
Auburn
Portland
South Portland
Old Orchard Beach
Biddeford
Sanford
Kennebunk
Kittery
Bar Harbor
Québec
Lévis
Montmagny
La Malbaie
Baie St. Paul
Thetford Mines
Mégantic
Mingan
Port Menier
Moisie
Sherbrooke
feet
m
3000
914
1500
457
600
183
300
91
0
0
656
200
3281
1000
B 70° C 69° D 68° E 67° F 66° G 65° H 64° J 63°

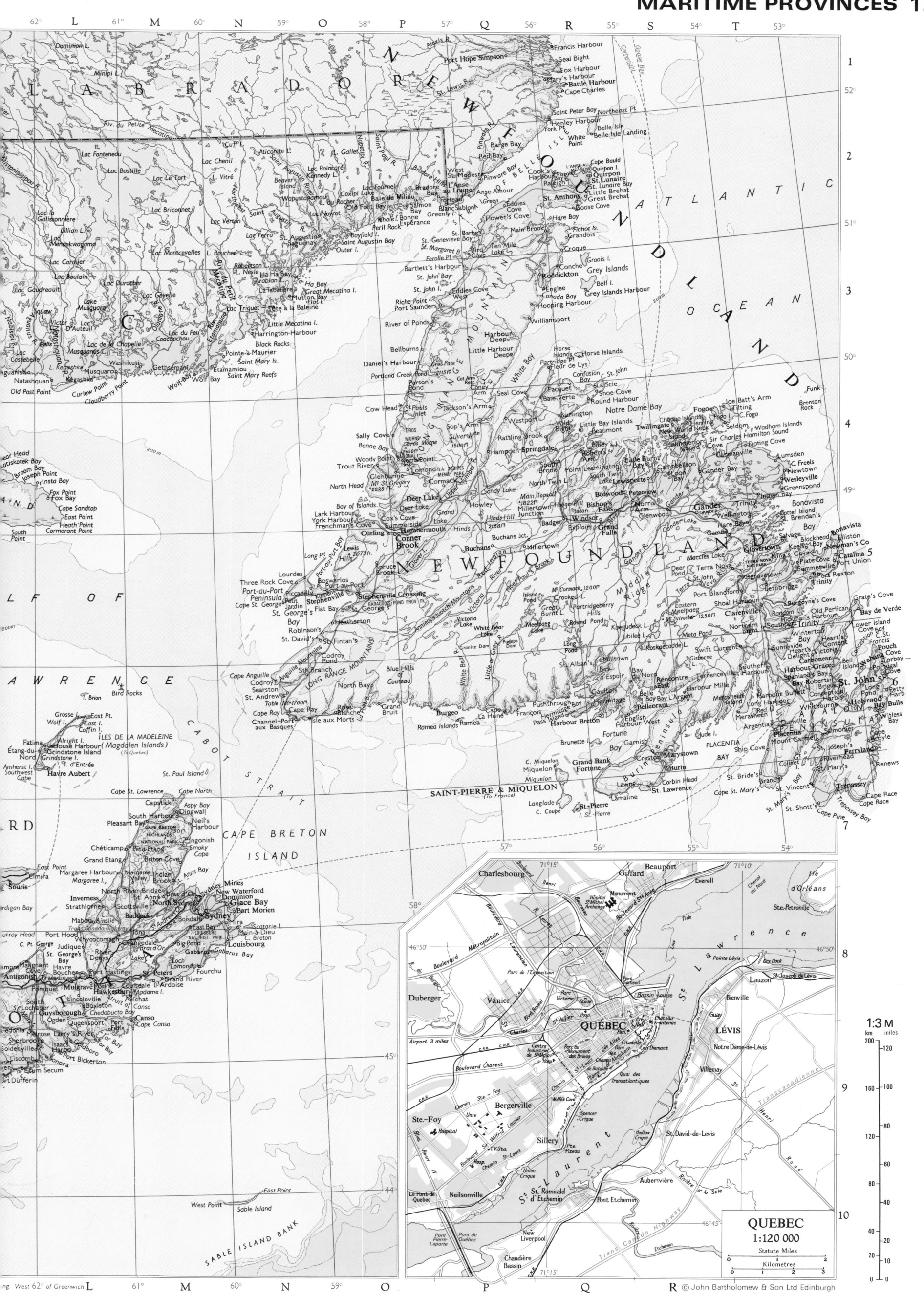
LABRADOR
NEWFOUNDLAND
ATLANTIC OCEAN
STRAIT OF BELLE ISLE
LONG RANGE MOUNTAINS
CABOT STRAIT
GULF OF ST. LAWRENCE
CAPE BRETON ISLAND
AVALON PENINSULA
ÎLES DE LA MADELEINE (Magdalen Islands)
SAINT-PIERRE & MIQUELON (To France)
SABLE ISLAND BANK
Sable Island
Port Hope Simpson
Battle Harbour
Cape Charles
Belle Isle
St. Anthony
Roddickton
Harbour Deep
Daniel's Harbour
Baie Verte
Twillingate
Fogo
Springdale
Deer Lake
Humbermouth
Corner Brook
Stephenville
Stephenville Crossing
St. George's
Port-au-Port
Channel-Port aux Basques
Cape Ray
Burgeo
Ramea
Harbour Breton
Grand Falls
Windsor
Bishop's Falls
Botwood
Lewisporte
Gander
Gambo
Glovertown
Bonavista
Catalina
Trinity
Clarenville
Grand Bank
Fortune
Marystown
Burin
St. Lawrence
Placentia
Harbour Grace
Carbonear
Bay Roberts
St. John's
Ferryland
Trepassey
Cape Race
St.-Pierre
Miquelon
Havre Aubert
Cape North
Cheticamp
Inverness
Baddeck
North Sydney
Sydney
Glace Bay
Louisbourg
St. Peters
Port Hawkesbury
Mulgrave
Antigonish
Guysborough
Canso
Souris
Pictou
QUEBEC
1:120 000
Statute Miles
Kilometres
Charlesbourg
Beauport
Giffard
Vanier
Duberger
Ste.-Foy
Sillery
Lévis
Lauzon
Bienville
St. Laurent
Île d'Orléans
St. Romuald d'Etchemin
New Liverpool
Chaudière Bassin
Trans Canada Highway
1:3 M
km
miles

ARIZONA
UNITED STATES
NEW MEXICO
TEXAS
SONORA
CHIHUAHUA
COAHUILA
BAJA CALIFORNIA
BAJA CALIFORNIA SUR
DURANGO
ZACATECAS
SINALOA
NAYARIT
JALISCO
MICHOACAN
MEXICO

Golfo de California

PACIFIC OCEAN

Tropic of Cancer

San Diego
Tijuana
Ensenada
Mexicali
Yuma
El Centro
Tucson
Nogales
Cananea
Agua Prieta
Douglas
El Paso
Ciudad Juárez
Las Cruces
Carlsbad
Hobbs
Midland
Odessa
Hermosillo
Guaymas
Empalme
Ciudad Obregón
Navojoa
Los Mochis
Chihuahua
Delicias
Ciudad Camargo
Hidalgo del Parral
Santa Bárbara
Nueva Rosita
Monclova
Gómez Palacio
Ciudad Lerdo
Torreón
Matamoros
Parras
San Pedro de las Colonias
Culiacán
Durango
La Paz
Mazatlán
Tepic
Aguascalientes
Zacatecas
León
Guadalajara
Irapuato
Salamanca
Manzanillo
Colima
Morelia
Uruapan

MEXICO CITY
1:250 000
Naucalpan de Juárez
Azcapotzalco
Villa Gustavo A. Madero
Tacuba
Lomas Chapultepec
Bosque de Chapultepec
Mixcoac
Iztacalco
Iztapalapa
Coyoacán
Ciudad Universitaria
Villa Obregón
Tlalpan
Aeropuerto Internacional

PANAMA CANAL
1: 900 000
CARIBBEAN SEA
Colón
Cristóbal
Gatún
Balboa
PANAMÁ
PACIFIC OCEAN

Statute Miles
Kilometres

feet
13124 4000
9843 3000
6562 2000
3281 1000
1640 500
656 200
m

Continuation on the same scale

CARIBBEAN SEA

GULF OF MEXICO

Bahía de Campeche

HONDURAS

NICARAGUA

COSTA RICA

PANAMA

Golfo de Panamá

Pen. de Azuero

Golfo de Chiriquí

TEGUCIGALPA

MANAGUA

S. JOSE

PANAMA

Golfo L de Honduras

Mosquitia

MÉXICO

GUATEMALA

BELIZE

BELMOPAN

EL SALVADOR

SAN SALVADOR

YUCATAN

QUINTANA ROO

CAMPECHE

CHIAPAS

OAXACA

GUERRERO

Mérida

Campeche

Chetumal

Veracruz

Tampico

Ciudad Madero

Puebla

Toluca

Cuernavaca

Acapulco

Chilpancingo

Oaxaca

Tuxtla Gutiérrez

Tapachula

Quezaltenango

San Antonio

Monterrey

Ciudad Victoria

Laredo

Nuevo Laredo

Matamoros

Brownsville

Reynosa

McAllen

Golfo de Tehuantepec

Sierra Madre del Sur

Golfo de Honduras

San Pedro Sula

Tela

La Ceiba

1 : 6 M

Heights and Depths in metres

Longitude West 100° of Greenwich

© John Bartholomew & Son Ltd Edinburgh

Continued on inset

CURAÇAO
1:1 500 000
ARUBA
1:1 500 000
BONAIRE
1:1.5m
Willemstad
Oranjestad
Kralendijk
FLORIDA
U.S.A.
Palm Beach
West Palm Beach
Ft. Lauderdale
Miami
Miami Beach
Key West
Straits of Florida
GRAND BAHAMA
GREAT ABACO
ELEUTHERA
NEW PROVIDENCE
Nassau
ANDROS
CAT I.
SAN SALVADOR (WATLING)
GREAT EXUMA
LONG I.
ACKLINS I.
GREAT INAGUA
THE BAHAMAS
Great Bahama Bank
Tropic of Cancer
Yucatan Channel
HABANA
(HAVANA)
Matanzas
Pinar del Rio
Cienfuegos
Santa Clara
Sancti Spíritus
Trinidad
Ciego de Avila
Camagüey
Nuevitas
Las Tunas
Holguín
Bayamo
Manzanillo
Santiago de Cuba
Guantánamo
Baracoa
CUBA
Isla de la Juventud
(Isla de Pinos)
Golfo de Batabanó
Windward Passage
MEXICO
Cancún
I. de Cozumel
Grand Cayman
Little Cayman
Cayman Brac
CAYMAN TRENCH
Montego Bay
Kingston
JAMAICA
Jamaica Channel
Jérémie
Les Cayes
Pedro Bank
Rosalind Bank
Serranilla Bank
Alice Shoal
Swan Is
(To Hond)
Islas de la Bahía
Roatán
Utila
La Ceiba
HONDURAS
Cabo Gracias á Dios
Mosquitia
Cayos Miskito
NICARAGUA
Managua
León
Granada
Matagalpa
Bluefields
Lago de Nicaragua
I. de Providencia (Col.)
I. de San Andrés (Col.)
Roncador Bank
Serrana Bank
Quita Sueño Bank
COSTA RICA
SAN JOSÉ
Limón
Puntarenas
PANAMA
Colón
Golfo de Panamá
Golfo de los Mosquitos
Archipiélago de las Perlas
Golfo del Darién
Península de Azuero
COLOMBIA
Barranquilla
Cartagena
Santa Marta
Sierra Nevada de Santa Marta
CARIBBEAN SEA
PACIFIC OCEAN
CONIC PROJECTION
Longitude West 74° of Greenwich
113
125
128
feet
m
13124 4000
9843 3000
6562 2000
3281 1000
1640 500
656 200
0 0
Below Sea Level
656 200
6562 2000
13124 4000
22966 7000

TOBAGO
1:1 500 000

JAMAICA
1:1 500 000

TRINIDAD
1:1 500 000

PART OF MAINLAND VENEZUELA

Port of Spain
San Fernando
Point Fortin

MARTINIQUE
1:1 500 000

Fort-de-France

GUADELOUPE
1:1 500 000

Basse Terre
Pointe-à-Pitre
MARIE GALANTE
Grand Bourg

1:1.5m.
ST. KITTS
(ST. CHRISTOPHER)
BASSETERRE
ST. KITTS - NEVIS
NEVIS

1:1.5m.
ANTIGUA
ST. JOHN'S

1:1.5m.
GRENADA
St. George's

1:1.5m.
BARBADOS
BRIDGETOWN

TURKS & CAICOS ISLANDS (U.K.)

HISPANIOLA

DOMINICAN REPUBLIC
SANTO DOMINGO
Santiago
Cap-Haïtien
Puerto Plata

PORT-AU-PRINCE
Jacmel

PUERTO RICO (U.S.)
SAN JUAN
Ponce
Mayagüez

VIRGIN IS.
Charlotte Amalie
ST. CROIX (U.S.)

PUERTO RICO TRENCH
Milwaukee Depth 9200m

LEEWARD ISLANDS

ANGUILLA (U.K.)
SAINT MARTIN
ST. KITTS & NEVIS
ANTIGUA & BARBUDA
ST. JOHN'S
MONTSERRAT (U.K.)
GUADELOUPE (To France)
Basse Terre
Pointe-à-Pitre
Marie Galante (Fr.)

DOMINICA
Roseau

MARTINIQUE (To France)
Fort-de-France

ST LUCIA
CASTRIES

ST VINCENT
KINGSTOWN
The Grenadines

BARBADOS
Bridgetown

GRENADA
St. George's

CARIBBEAN SEA

LESSER ANTILLES

WINDWARD ISLANDS

ARUBA (Neth.)
Oranjestad
CURAÇAO (Neth.)
Willemstad
BONAIRE (Neth.)

Los Roques Trench
Bonaire Trench

Isla de Margarita
La Asunción
Porlamar
Los Testigos

TRINIDAD AND TOBAGO
TOBAGO
Scarborough
TRINIDAD
Port of Spain
San Fernando

VENEZUELA
CARACAS
Maracaibo
Lago de Maracaibo
Barquisimeto
Valencia
Maracay
Barcelona
Cumaná
Carúpano
Maturín
Ciudad Bolívar
El Tigre
Golfo de Venezuela
Pen. de Guajira

GUY.

1:6 M

Heights and Depths in metres

© John Bartholomew & Son Ltd Edinburgh

NICARAGUA

COSTA RICA

PANAMA

COLOMBIA

VENEZUELA

ECUADOR

PERU

BOLIVIA

CHILE

ARG.

BRASIL

GUYANA

TRINIDAD & TOBAGO

GRENADA

ST LUCIA

ST VINCENT

BARBADOS

S O U T H   P A C I F I C   O C E A N

GALAPAGOS ISLANDS
(ARCHIPIÉLAGO DE COLÓN)
(To Ecuador)

On the same scale

Culpepper
Wenman
Pinta (Abingdon)
Marchena (Bindloe)
Genovesa (Tower)
San Salvador (James I.)
Santa Cruz (Indefatigable I.)
San Cristóbal (Chatham I.)
Fernandina (Narborough I.)
Isla Isabela (Albemarle I.)
Santa María (Charles I.)
Española (Hood I.)

LAMBERT AZIMUTHAL EQUAL AREA PROJECTION

Heights in metres

Tropic of Capricorn

Caracas
Bogotá
Medellín
Cali
Quito
Guayaquil
Lima
Callao
La Paz
Manaus
Maracaibo
Barranquilla
Cartagena
Arequipa
Antofagasta
Iquique

m   feet
6000   19685
5000   16404
4000   13123
3000   8843
2000   6562
1000   3281
500   1640
200   656
0   0
Below Sea Level
200   656

Longitude West 50° of Greenwich
NORTH ATLANTIC OCEAN
SURINAME
FRENCH GUIANA
BRAZIL
PARAGUAY
Paramaribo
Cayenne
New Amsterdam
Georgetown
Macapá
Belém
São Luís
Fortaleza (Ceará)
Natal
João Pessoa
Recife (Pernambuco)
Maceió
Aracaju
Salvador (Bahia)
Teresina
Brasília
Goiânia
Belo Horizonte
Vitória
Campos
Rio de Janeiro
São Paulo
Santos
Campinas
Ribeirão Prêto
Uberaba
Uberlândia
Campo Grande
Corumbá
Cuiabá
Santarém
Marabá
Montes Claros
Ilhéus
Campina Grande
Juazeiro do Norte
Feira de Santana
Londrina
Presidente Prudente
Anápolis
Equator
Rocas
Fernando de Noronha (To Brazil)
I. Martin Vaz
I. Trindade (To Brazil)
Mouths of the Amazon
Ilha de Marajó
Ilha de Maracá
Serra dos Carajás
Serra do Roncador
Chapada Diamantina
Serra do Espinhaço
Planalto de Mato Grosso
Pantanal do Taquari
Serra Tumucumaque
Arquipélago dos Abrolhos
1:12 M
km miles
0 80 160 240 320 400 480
0 160 320 480 640 800
G H J K L M
55° 50° 45° 40° 35° 30°
10° 5° 0° 5° 10° 15° 20°
1 2 3 4 5 6 7 8

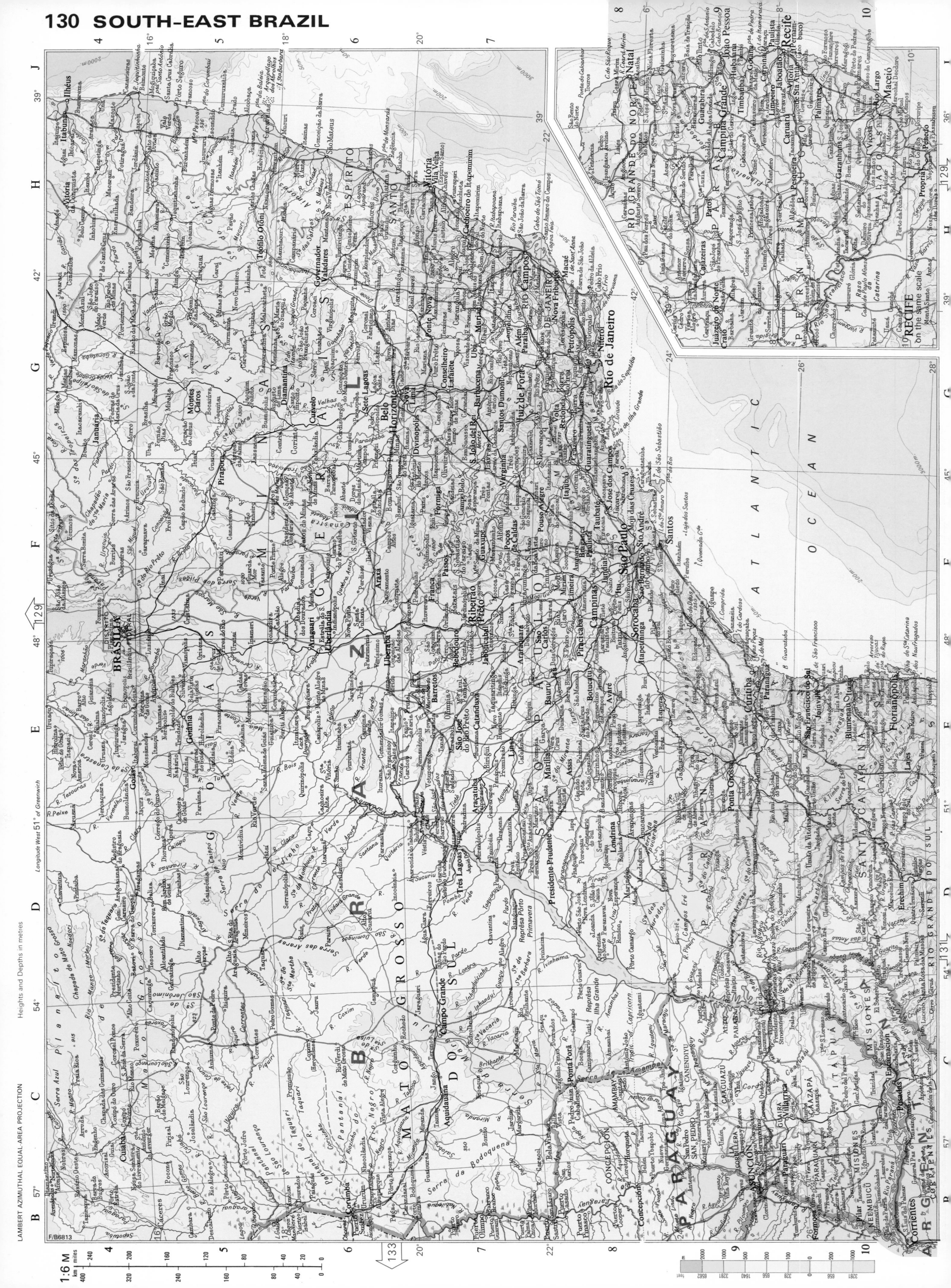

LAMBERT AZIMUTHAL EQUAL AREA PROJECTION

Longitude West 51° of Greenwich

Heights and Depths in metres

F/B6813

RECIFE
on the same scale

1:6 M

km miles

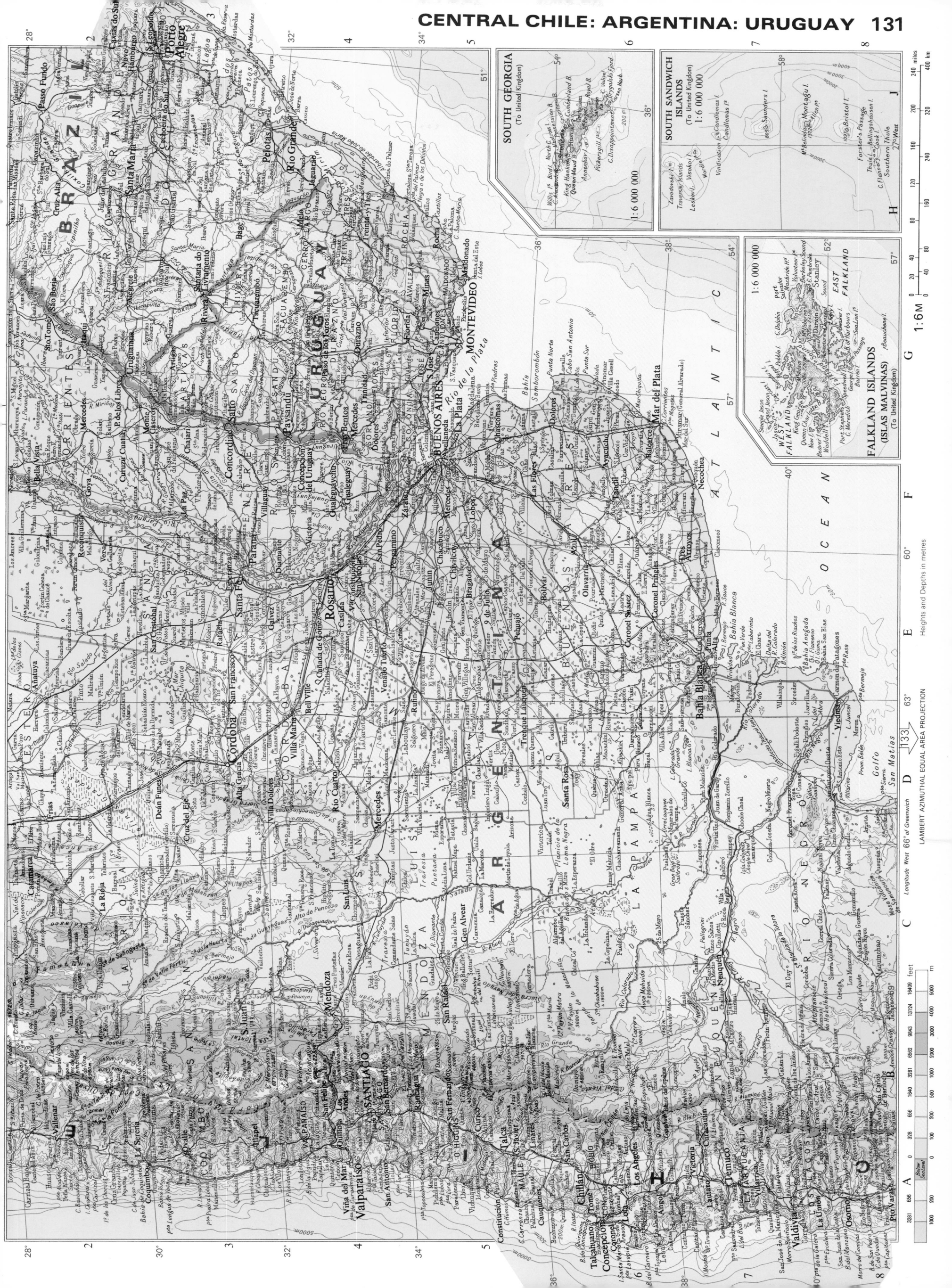

SOUTH GEORGIA
(To United Kingdom)
1:6 000 000

SOUTH SANDWICH
ISLANDS
(To United Kingdom)
1:6 000 000

FALKLAND ISLANDS
(ISLAS MALVINAS)
(To United Kingdom)
1:6 000 000

1:6M

Heights and Depths in metres

LAMBERT AZIMUTHAL EQUAL-AREA PROJECTION

BUENOS AIRES

1:300 000

© Times Books Ltd

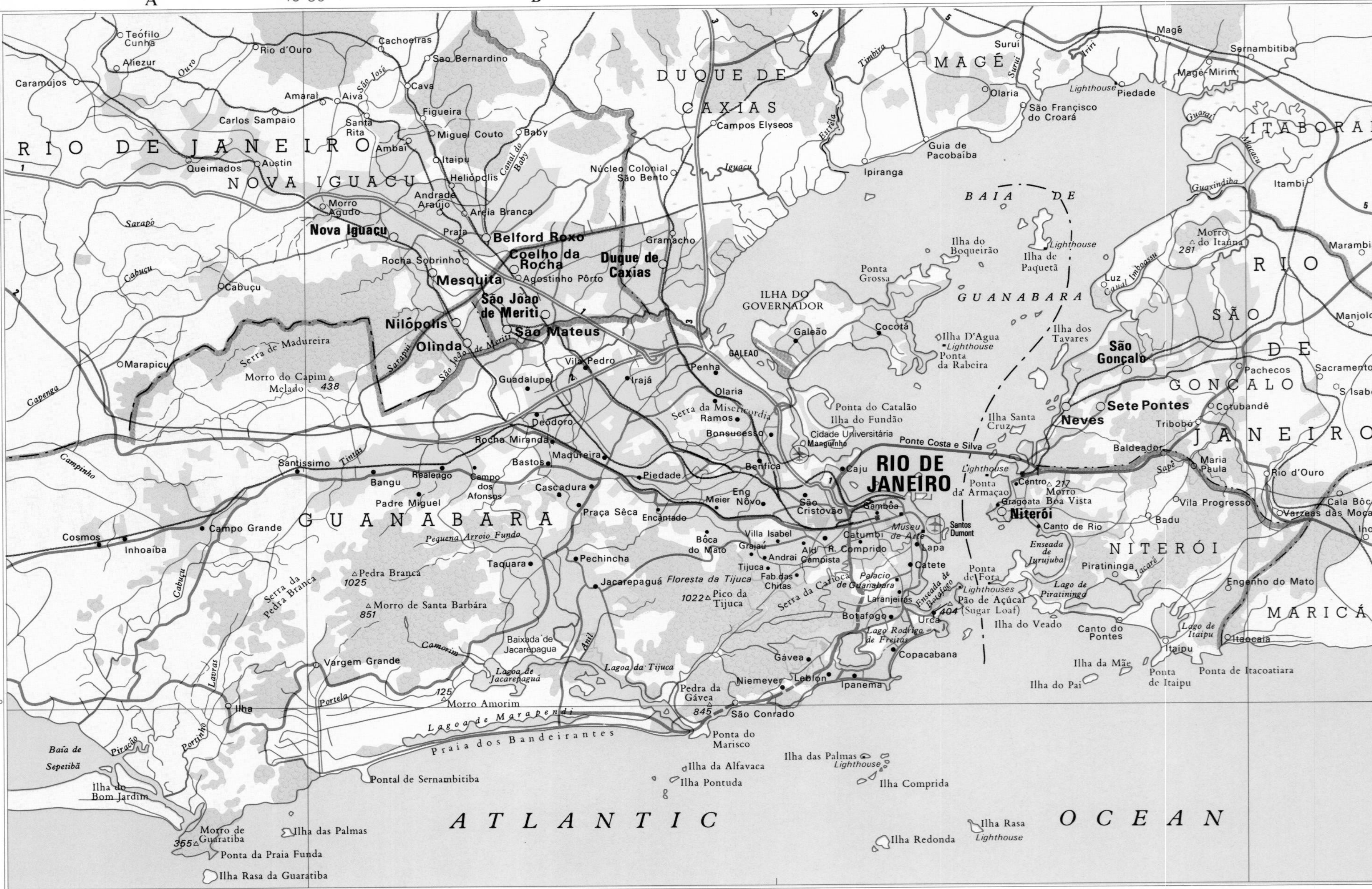

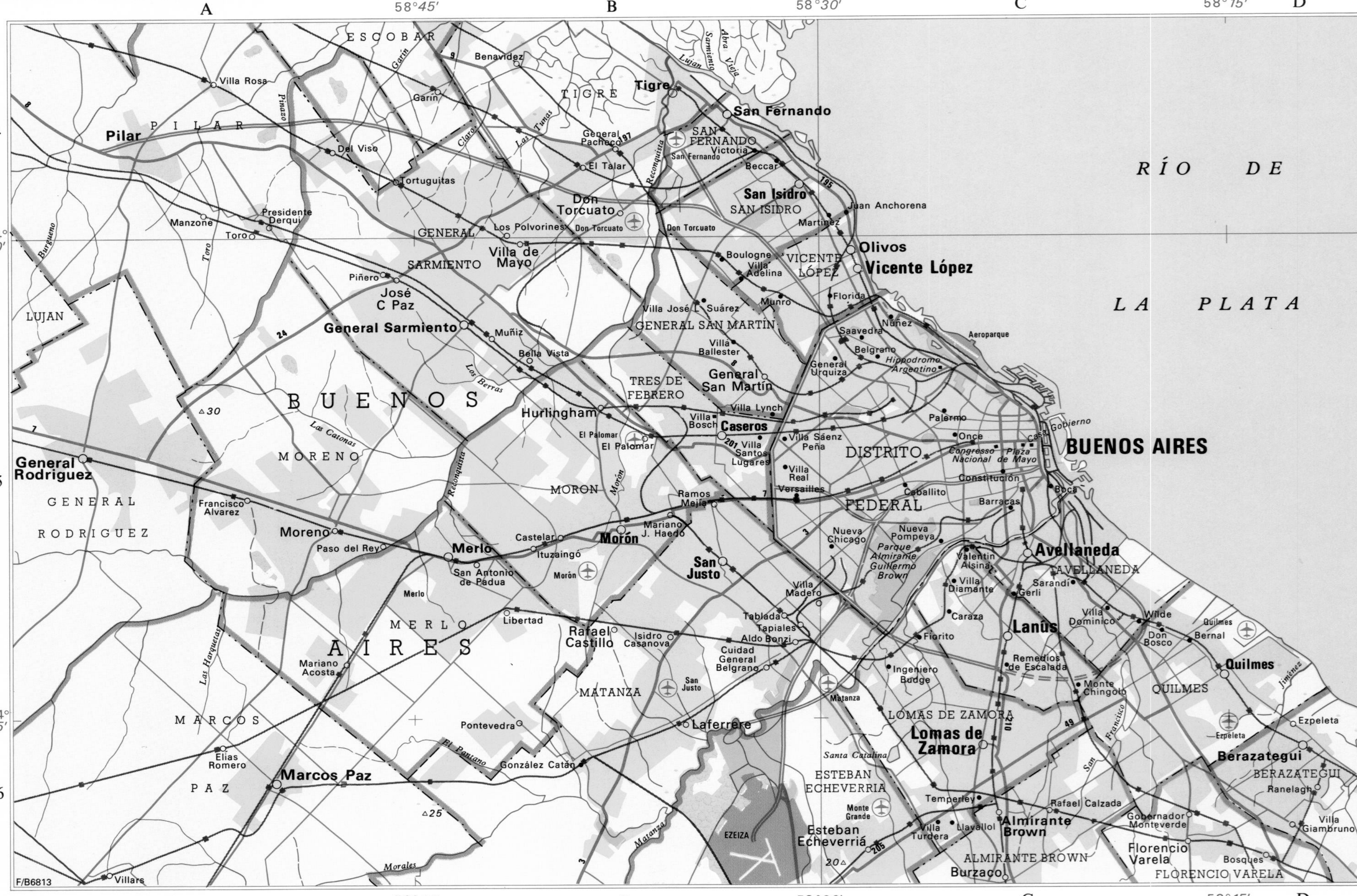

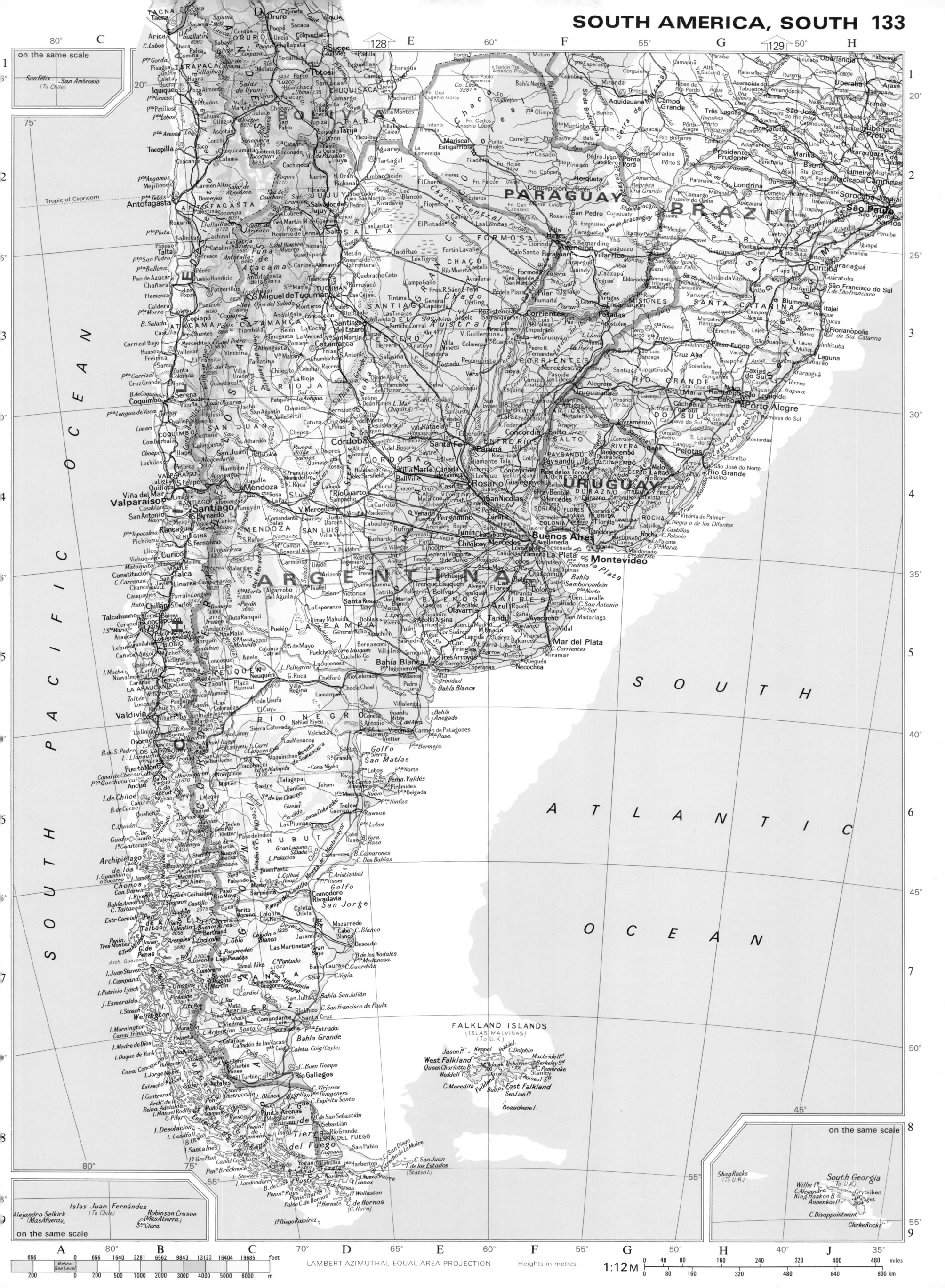
on the same scale
San Félix
San Ambrosio
(To Chile)
Tropic of Capricorn
BOLIVIA
PARAGUAY
BRAZIL
URUGUAY
ARGENTINA
CHILE
SOUTH PACIFIC OCEAN
SOUTH ATLANTIC OCEAN
FALKLAND ISLANDS
(ISLAS MALVINAS)
(To U.K.)
West Falkland
East Falkland
Tierra del Fuego
South Georgia
(To U.K.)
Shag Rocks
Islas Juan Fernández
Alejandro Selkirk
(MasAfuera)
Robinson Crusoe
(MasAtierra)
(To Chile)
Sta Clara
Santiago
Buenos Aires
Montevideo
Asunción
Valparaíso
Córdoba
Rosario
Mendoza
Porto Alegre
São Paulo
Curitiba
Bahía Blanca
Mar del Plata
Comodoro Rivadavia
Punta Arenas
Río Gallegos
Antofagasta
Concepción
LAMBERT AZIMUTHAL EQUAL AREA PROJECTION
Heights in metres
1:12M
Below Sea Level
656 0 656 1640 3281 6562 9843 13123 16404 19685 feet
200 0 200 500 1000 2000 3000 4000 5000 6000 m
0 40 80 160 240 320 400 480 miles
0 80 160 320 480 640 800 km

19 WESTERN SAMOA 1:3 000 000
SAVAII
Falealupo · C. Puava Safotu · Fagamalo
Asau · Matautu Pt. · Samalaeulu
Falelima · Maugaafi Sataua
Salailua · Vaiafai · Mulifanua Strait · Mailelegai Pt.
C. Asuisui · Iaga · Apolima Apia
Samatau · Faleolo · Aflamalu · Lefaga
C. Mulitapuili · Matautu · Salani Bay Upolu · Saluafata
Sataii B. · Nuusafe'e · Falealili Bay · Aleipata Is.
UPOLU

20 AMERICAN SAMOA 1:3 000 000
TUTUILA
Pago Pago
Tu USAF Matatula
Leone · Steps Pt.
MANUA IS.
Ofu Olosega
Ta'u (To U.S.A.) · Luma · group
Tau

16 HOWLAND I. (To U.S.A.) 1:300 000
Landing · Settlement (Uninhabited)

17 JARVIS I. (To U.S.A.) 1:300 000
Landing · Settlement (Uninhabited)

15 BAKER I. (To U.S.A.) 1:300 000
Landing · Settlement (Uninhabited)

18 SWAINS I. (To U.S.A.) 1:300 000
Fala Ane Pt. · Taulaga Pt. · Lagoon · Etena · Landing

14 KANTON I. (To Kiribati) 1:600 000
CANTON AIRPORT
Northside · DOCK
Boat Channel · SEAPLANE ANCHORAGE
Southside
Pyramid Pt.

13 RAROTONGA (To New Zealand) 1:600 000
Avatiu · Avarua · Matavera
Arorangi · Ikurangi · Te Rua Manga
Tupapa · Ngatangiia
Raemaru · Matatonga · Oneroa
Titikaveka

12 TAHITI AND MOOREA (To France) 1:1 200 000
MOOREA
Papetoai · Opunohu B. · Pt. Aroa · Pt. Faupo
Pt. Haurii · Tiamae · Cook B. · Mahina
Paopao · Maatea · Arevareva · Pt. Venus · Mahaena
Haapiti · Afareaitu · Papeete · Uporohu
Afareaitu · Faaa · Tiarei
Pt. Nuupere · Taapuna · Hitiaa
Pt. Tataa · Punaauia · Faone
MOOREA · Aorai 2066m · L. Vaihiria
Punaauia · Opohona
Paea · 1696 m · TAHITI
Maraa · Uutofai Faone
Papara · Nairiri · C. Tahara'a
Atimaono · Mataiea · Port Phaeton · Taravao B. · Pt. Tatatua · Tautira
Vairao · Matiti · Presqu'île de Taiarapu · Rooniu 1332 m
Teahupoo · Tomono · Tapati
Pt. Vaiau

11 TUAMOTU AND SOCIETY ISLANDS (To France) 1:12 000 000

Feet 13,124 6562 · 0 · 1640 3281 6562 feet
Metres 4000 2000 · 0 · 500 1000 2000 Metres

KING GEORGE ISLANDS
Ahe · Manihi · Tepoto · Napuka
ARCHIPEL · Takapoto · Takaroa · Tikei · DISAPPOINTMENT IS.
Mataiva · Arutua · Apataki · Takume · Fangatau
Tikehau · Rangiroa · ÎLES PALLISER · Kaukura · Rotava · Toau · Takaroa · Aratika · DES · Raroia · Fakahina
Makatea · Kauehi · Katiu · Makemo · Taenga · Tekokoto · Fakaina
ARCHIPEL DE TAHITI · Fakarava · Faaite · Tuanake · Hiti · TUAMOTU · Rekareka
Maupiti · Motu Iti · ÎLES · Tahanea · Motutunga · Marutea · Tatakoto
Mopelia · SOUS LE · Anaa · Haraiki · Hikueru · Yauere · Amanu
Scilly · VENT · Tetiaroa · Reitoru · Marokau · Hao
ÎLES DU VENT · Moorea · Faaite · Hereheretue · Ravahere · Nengonengo · Akiaki · Pukarua · Reao
Maiao · TAHITI · Presqu'île de Taiarapu · Manuhangi · Vanavana · Nukutavake · Pinaki
Tubuai Manu · Mehetia · Anuanu Raro · DUKE OF GLOUCESTER IS. · Tureia
Anuanu Runga · Nukutepipi · Vahanga · Tenararo

TUAMOTU AND SOCIETY ISLANDS (To France) 1:12 000 000
100 Statute Miles
100 200 Kilometres

ASIA · SEA OF OKHOTSK · BERING SEA · ARCTIC OCEAN · ALEUTIAN TRENCH
Beijing (Peking) · Vladivostok · Kamchatka Pen. · Sakhalin · Kurile Ridge · Kurile Trench
Shanghai · YELLOW SEA · Korean Pen. · JAPAN · Tokyo · Osaka
EAST CHINA SEA · Okinawa · Nansei Shoto · Iwo Jima · MID-PACIFIC MOUNTAINS · HAWAIIAN IS.
Hong Kong · TAIWAN · Nansei Shoto · Bonin Is. · Minami Tori Shima · Marcus I. · Wake I. (To U.S.A.) · Midway Is.
Hainan · PHILIPPINE SEA · NORTHERN MARIANAS · Saipan · Tinian · Rota · Guam
SOUTH CHINA SEA · Manila · PHILIPPINES · MICRONESIA · MARSHALL ISLANDS · Bikini · Eniwetok
Palawan · SULU SEA · Mindanao · CAROLINE ISLANDS · GILBERT ISLANDS
INDIAN OCEAN · Singapore · BORNEO · CELEBES SEA · W. Caroline Basin · East Caroline Basin · NAURU · KIRIBATI · PHOENIX IS.
SUMATRA · GREATER SUNDA ISLANDS · Sulawesi · Halmahera · MELANESIA · Bismarck Archipel · New Ireland · New Britain · SOLOMON IS. · TUVALU (ELLICE IS.) · TOKELAU (N.Z.)
Java · LESSER SUNDA ISLANDS · Flores · Timor · NEW GUINEA · Bougainville · Guadalcanal · Sta. Cruz Is. · WESTERN SAMOA
INDONESIA · Timor · ARAFURA SEA · GULF OF CARPENTARIA · CORAL SEA · New Hebrides · VANUATU · FIJI · Viti Levu · TONGA · COOK IS.
JAVA TRENCH · TIMOR SEA · AUSTRALIA · New Caledonia · Norfolk I. · South Fiji Basin
Brisbane · Sydney · Lord Howe Rise · Norfolk Ridge · Kermadec Ridge
Melbourne · TASMAN SEA · NEW ZEALAND · NORTH ISLAND · Auckland · Wellington · Chatham Rise · Chatham Is.
Tasmania · SOUTH ISLAND · Stewart I. · Kermadec Trench
Macquarie Ridge · Campbell I. · Auckland Is. · Antipodes Is. (To N.Z.)
ROSS SEA · ANTARCTICA

fathoms	Metres
547	1000
1094	2000
1640	3000
2187	4000
2734	5000
3281	6000
3828	7000
4374	8000

Note:– All the Island Groups shown as insets on this plate are situated East of the International Date Line.

LAMBERT AZIMUTHAL PROJECTION

NORTH AMERICA
CENTRAL AMERICA
SOUTH AMERICA
Arctic Circle
Tropic of Cancer
Equator
Tropic of Capricorn
Antarctic Circle
San Francisco
Los Angeles
Mexico
Panama
Lima
Santiago
Islas Galápagos
Is. Revillagigedo
Clipperton
MARQUESAS
TUAMOTU
SOCIETY IS.
TUBUAI IS.
Pitcairn I.
Easter I.
Mendocino Seascarp
Murray Seascarp
Molokai Fracture Zone
Clarion Fracture Zone
Clipperton Fracture Zone
Easter Island Fracture Zone
Challenger Fracture Zone
Eltanin Fracture Zone
EAST PACIFIC RISE
EAST PACIFIC RIDGE
PACIFIC-ANTARCTIC RIDGE
SOUTH EAST PACIFIC BASIN
Peru Basin
Chile Basin
Middle America Trench
PERU-CHILE TRENCH
Cocos Ridge
Carnegie Ridge
Tuamotu Ridge
Austral Ridge
Sala y Gómez Ridge
Graham Land
AMUNDSEN SEA
feet 3281 656 0 328 656 1640 3281 4921 6562 9843 13124 feet
metres 1000 200 0 100 200 500 1000 1500 2000 3000 4000 metres
This Colour Note covers all insets except Tuamotu and Marquesas Is.
KAUAI
NIIHAU
OAHU
HONOLULU
MOLOKAI
LANAI
MAUI
KAHOOLAWE
HAWAII
Hilo
Mauna Kea
Mauna Loa
Kaiwi Channel
Alenuihaha Channel
Kauai Channel
HAWAIIAN IS.
(To U.S.A.)
1:3 000 000
MIDWAY IS.
(To U.S.A.)
1:300 000
Sand Island
Eastern I.
PALMYRA I.
(To U.S.A.)
1:300 000
TABUAERAN (FANNING I.)
(to Kiribati)
1:900 000
KIRITIMATI (CHRISTMAS I.)
(to Kiribati)
1:2 400 000
PITCAIRN I.
(To U.K.)
1:210 000
Adamstown
ROBINSON CRUSOE (JUAN FERNANDEZ)
(To Chile)
1:1 200 000
San Juan Bautista
MARQUESAS IS.
(ÎS. MARQUISES)
(To France)
1:6 000 000
Nuku Hiva
Ua Huka
Ua Pu
Hiva Oa
Fatu Hiva
Tahuata
See Tuamotu Inset for Colour Note
GAMBIER IS.
(ÎLES GAMBIER)
(To France)
1:600 000
Mangareva
Rikitea
EASTER I.
(I. DE PASCUA)
(RAPA NUI)
(To Chile)
1:600 000
Hanga Roa
1:48M
miles
km

MOLUCCAS

INDONESIA

SULAWESI (Celebes)

SERAM SEA

BANDA SEA

IRIAN JAYA

NEW GUINEA

BISMARCK ARCHIPELAGO

BISMARCK SEA

PAPUA NEW GUINEA

Port Moresby

Gulf of Papua

FLORES SEA

TIMOR SEA

ARAFURA SEA

Torres Strait

Thursday I.

C. York

INDIAN OCEAN

Java Trench

Darwin

Arnhem Land

Gove Pen.

Gulf of Carpentaria

Cape York Peninsula

CORAL SEA ISLANDS

Coral Sea Plateau

Cairns

Townsville

NORTHERN TERRITORY

Tennant Creek

Barkly Tableland

Mount Isa

QUEENSLAND

Mackay

Great Sandy Desert

WESTERN AUSTRALIA

AUSTRALIA

Gibson Desert

Alice Springs

Macdonnell Ranges

Ayers Rock (Uluru)

Simpson Desert

Rockhampton

Great Victoria Desert

SOUTH AUSTRALIA

L. Eyre North

L. Eyre South

L. Torrens

L. Gairdner

NEW SOUTH WALES

Broken Hill

Perth

Fremantle

Kalgoorlie

Nullarbor Plain

Great Australian Bight

Eucla

Port Augusta

Whyalla

Port Lincoln

Adelaide

Sydney

Newcastle

Wollongong

CANBERRA

VICTORIA

Ballarat

Geelong

Melbourne

Mount Gambier

Bass Strait

King I.

Flinders I.

Furneaux Group

TASMANIA

Launceston

Hobart

SOUTH AUSTRALIAN BASIN

BONNE PROJECTION

East of 140° Greenwich

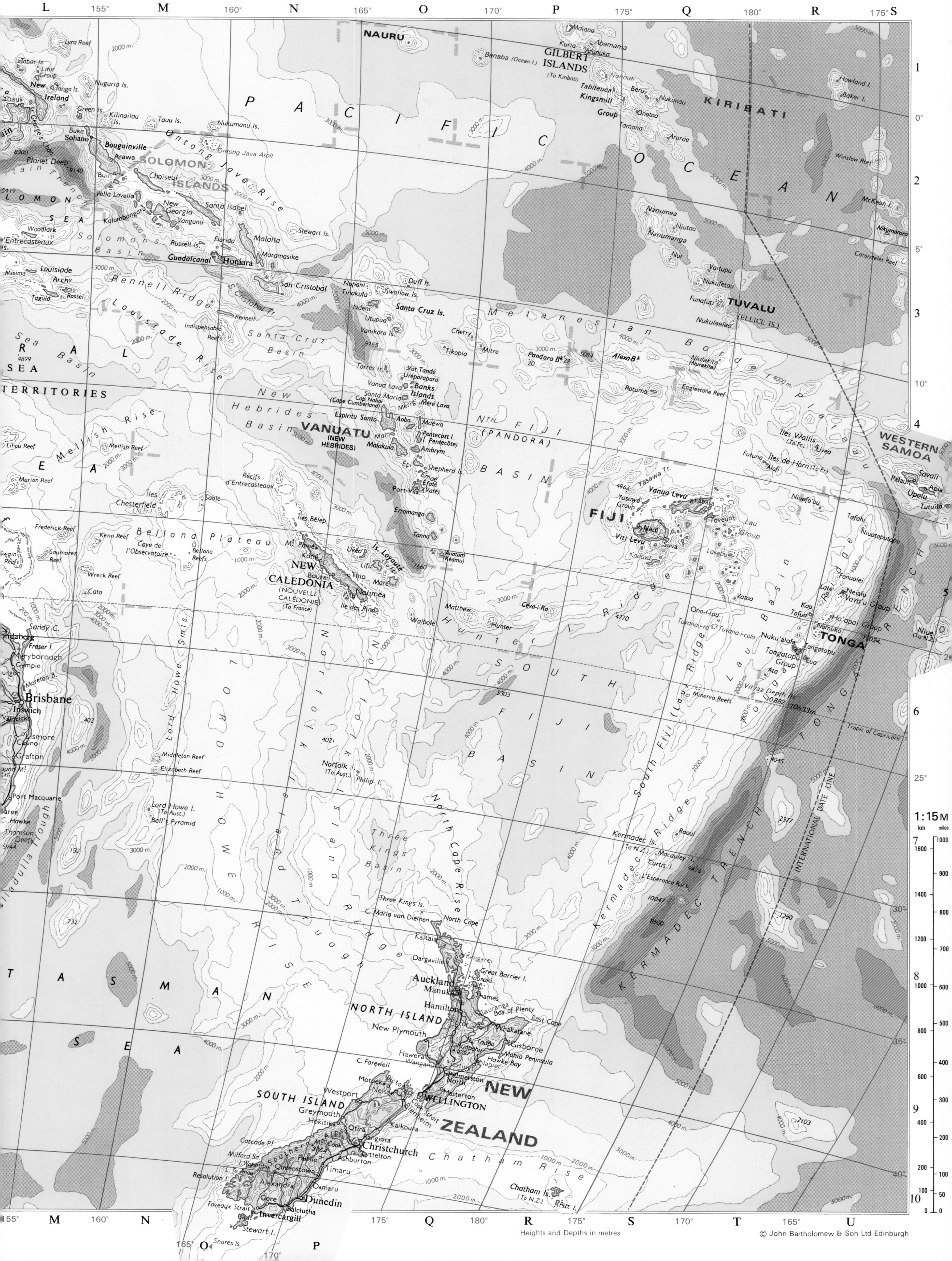

PACIFIC OCEAN

NAURU

GILBERT ISLANDS (To Kiribati)

KIRIBATI

Maiana
Abemama
Aranuka
Banaba (Ocean I.)
Kuria
Tabiteuea
Kingsmill Group
Nonouti
Beru
Nukunau
Onotoa
Tamana
Arorae

Howland I.
Baker I.

Winslow Reef

McKean I.

Nikumaroro

Nanumea
Niutao
Nanumanga
Nui
Vaitupu
Nukufetau
Funafuti
TUVALU (ELLICE IS.)
Nukulaelae
Carondelet Reef

Lyra Reef
Tabar Is.
Lihir Group
Nuguria Is.
New Ireland
Tanga Is.
Green Is.
Kilinailau Is.
Tau Is.
Nukumanu Is.
Ontong Java Rise
Ontong Java Atoll

Buka
Sohano
Bougainville
Arawa
Buin
SOLOMON ISLANDS
Planet Deep
Choiseul
Vella Lavella
New Georgia
Yangunu
Santa Isabel
Kolombangara
Russell Is.
Florida
Malaita
Stewart Is.
Maramasike

Woodlark
D'Entrecasteaux
Misima
Louisiade Arch.
Tagula
Rossel

SOLOMON SEA

Guadalcanal
Honiara
San Cristobal
Rennell
Indispensable Reefs

SOLOMON BASIN
Rennell Ridge
Louisiade Rise

Nupani
Tinakula
Swallow Is.
Duff Is.
Ndeni
Santa Cruz Is.
Utupua
Vanikoro Is.
Cherry
Mitre
Tikopia
Santa Cruz Basin

Melanesian Border Plateau

Pandora Bk
Alexa Bk
Rotuma
Niulakita (Nurakita)
Eggleston Reef

CORAL SEA

AUSTRALIAN TERRITORIES

Mellish Rise
Lihou Reef
Mellish Reef
Marion Reef

Chesterfield (To Fr.)
Îles Chesterfield

Torres Is.
Vot Tandé
Ureparapara
Vanua Lava
Banks Islands
Santa Maria
Cap Nahoi (Cape Cumberland)
Méré Lava
Mera
Espiritu Santo
Aoba
Maéwo
Malo
Pentecost I. (I. Pentecôte)
Malakula
Ambrym
Épi
Shepherd Is.
Emae
Éfaté (Vaté)
Port-Vila
Erromanga
Tanna
Anatom (Keamu)

VANUATU (NEW HEBRIDES)

New Hebrides Basin

NTH FIJI (PANDORA) BASIN

Îles Wallis (To Fr.)
Uvea
Futuna
Îles de Horn (To Fr.)
Alofi

WESTERN SAMOA
Savaii
Palauli
Apia
Upolu
Tutuila

Tafahi
Niuatoputapu
Niuafo'ou

Yasawa Tr.
Vanua Levu
Yasawa Group
Taveuni
Lau Group
Nadi
Viti Levu
Suva
Kadavu
Lakemba
FIJI

Frederick Reef
Saumarez Reef
Wreck Reef
Cato
Kenn Reef
Bellona Reefs
Caye de l'Observatoire
Bellona Plateau

Mt Panié
Ouégoa
Koné
Bourail
NEW CALEDONIA (NOUVELLE CALÉDONIE) (To France)
Thio
Nouméa
Île des Pins
Récifs d'Entrecasteaux
Îles Bélep
Is. Loyauté
Ouvéa
Lifou
Maré

Matthew
Hunter
Walpole
Ceva-i-Ra

Vatoa
Ono-i-Lau
Tuvana-i-ra
Tuvana-i-colo

NORTH FIJI BASIN

Hunter Ridge

Lau Ridge

SOUTH FIJI BASIN

Lau Basin

Vityaz Depth
Minerva Reefs

Kao
Tofua
Nomuka
Ha'apai Group
Nuku'alofa
TONGA
Tongatapu Group
'Eua
Ata

Neiafu
Vava'u Group
Fonualei
Late

Niue (To N.Z.)

Bundaberg
Sandy C.
Fraser I.
Maryborough
Gympie
Brisbane
Ipswich
Warwick
Lismore
Casino
Grafton

TASMAN SEA

Lord Howe Smts.

Middleton Reef
Elizabeth Reef

Norfolk Ridge

Lord Howe Rise

Norfolk I. (To Aust.)
Philip I.

NORFOLK ISLAND RIDGE

SOUTH FIJI BASIN

Kermadec Is. (To N.Z.)
Raoul
Macauley I.
Curtis I.
L'Esperance Rock

KERMADEC TRENCH

KERMADEC RIDGE

Three Kings Basin

Three King's Is.
C. Maria van Diemen
North Cape

North Cape Rise

Kaitaia
Dargaville
Whangarei
Great Barrier I.
Auckland
Manukau
Hamilton
Thames
Tauranga
Bay of Plenty
East Cape
NORTH ISLAND
New Plymouth
Whakatane
Gisborne
Taupo
Ruapehu
Mahia Peninsula
Hawera
Hawke Bay
Wanganui
Napier
Masterton
C. Farewell
Motueka
Picton
Nelson
Palmerston North
Blenheim
WELLINGTON
Cook Strait

NEW ZEALAND

Westport
Greymouth
Hokitika
Otira
Kaikoura
SOUTH ISLAND
Cascade Pt.
Haast
Wanaka
Arthur's Pass
Rangiora
Christchurch
Lyttelton
Ashburton
Timaru
Alexandra
Oamaru
Milford Sd.
Queenstown
Cromwell
COOK
Resolution I.
Gore
Dunedin
Foveaux Strait
Balclutha
Bluff
Invercargill
Stewart I.
Snares Is.

Chatham Rise

Chatham Is. (To N.Z.)
Pitt I.

Heights and Depths in metres

1:15M
km miles

© John Bartholomew & Son Ltd Edinburgh

LAMBERT AZIMUTHAL EQUAL-AREA PROJECTION

Heights and Depths in metres

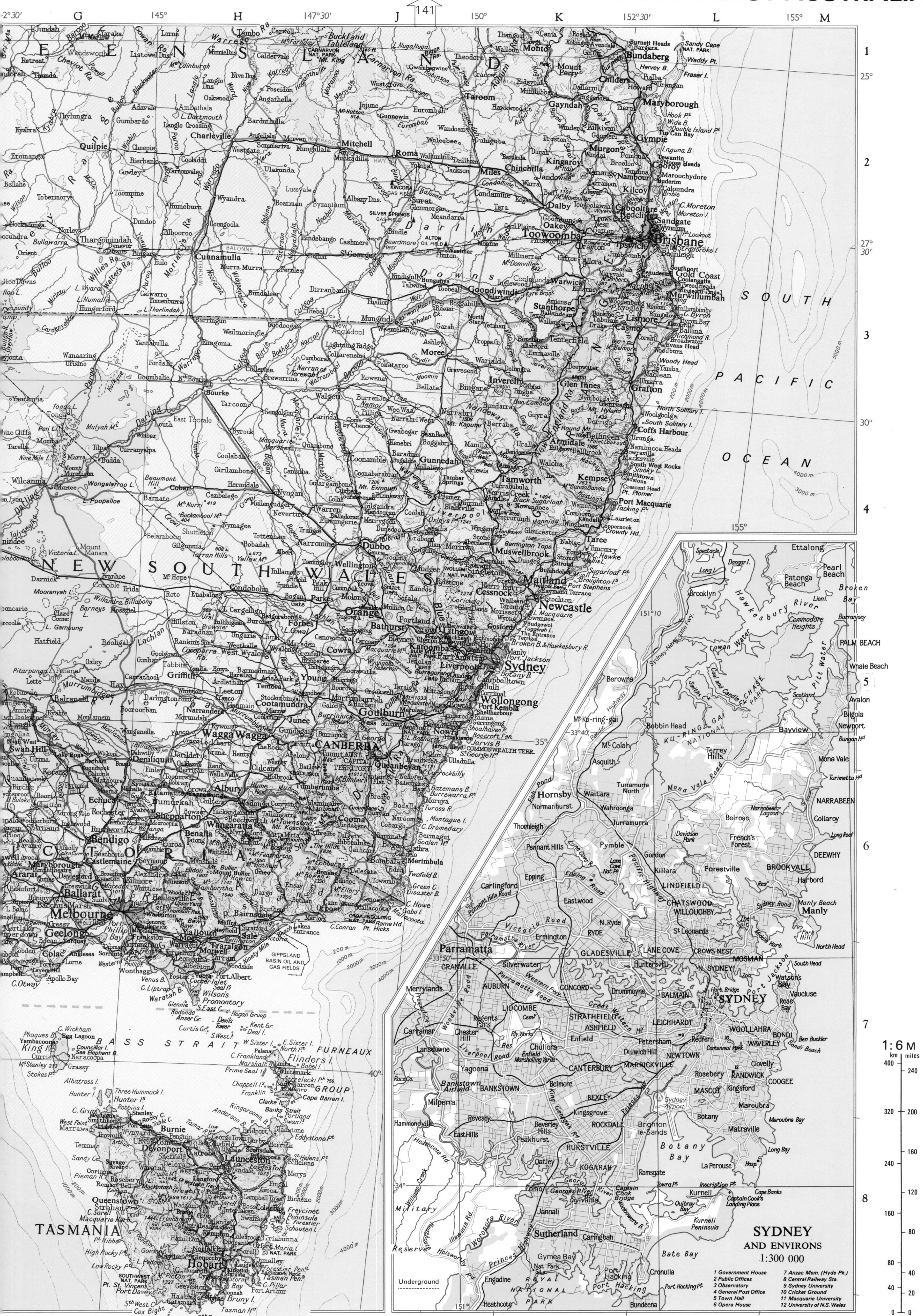

QUEENSLAND

NEW SOUTH WALES

VICTORIA

TASMANIA

SOUTH PACIFIC OCEAN

BASS STRAIT

FURNEAUX GROUP

Brisbane
Sydney
Melbourne
Canberra
Hobart
Newcastle
Wollongong
Bundaberg
Maryborough
Gympie
Toowoomba
Ipswich
Gold Coast
Lismore
Grafton
Coffs Harbour
Armidale
Tamworth
Port Macquarie
Taree
Dubbo
Orange
Bathurst
Cowra
Goulburn
Wagga Wagga
Albury
Griffith
Deniliquin
Bendigo
Ballarat
Geelong
Swan Hill
Shepparton
Wangaratta
Launceston
Devonport
Burnie

SYDNEY AND ENVIRONS
1:300 000

Parramatta
Liverpool
Manly
Mosman
Hornsby
Chatswood
Bankstown
Sutherland
Botany Bay
Port Jackson
KU-RING-GAI CHASE NATIONAL PARK
ROYAL NATIONAL PARK
PALM BEACH
Broken Bay
Hawkesbury River

1 Government House
2 Public Offices
3 Observatory
4 General Post Office
5 Town Hall
6 Opera House
7 Anzac Mem. (Hyde Pk.)
8 Central Railway Sta.
9 Cricket Ground
10 Sydney University
11 Macquarie University
12 University of N.S.W.

Underground

1:6 M

km   miles

© John Bartholomew & Son Ltd, Edinburgh

Longitude East 145° of Greenwich

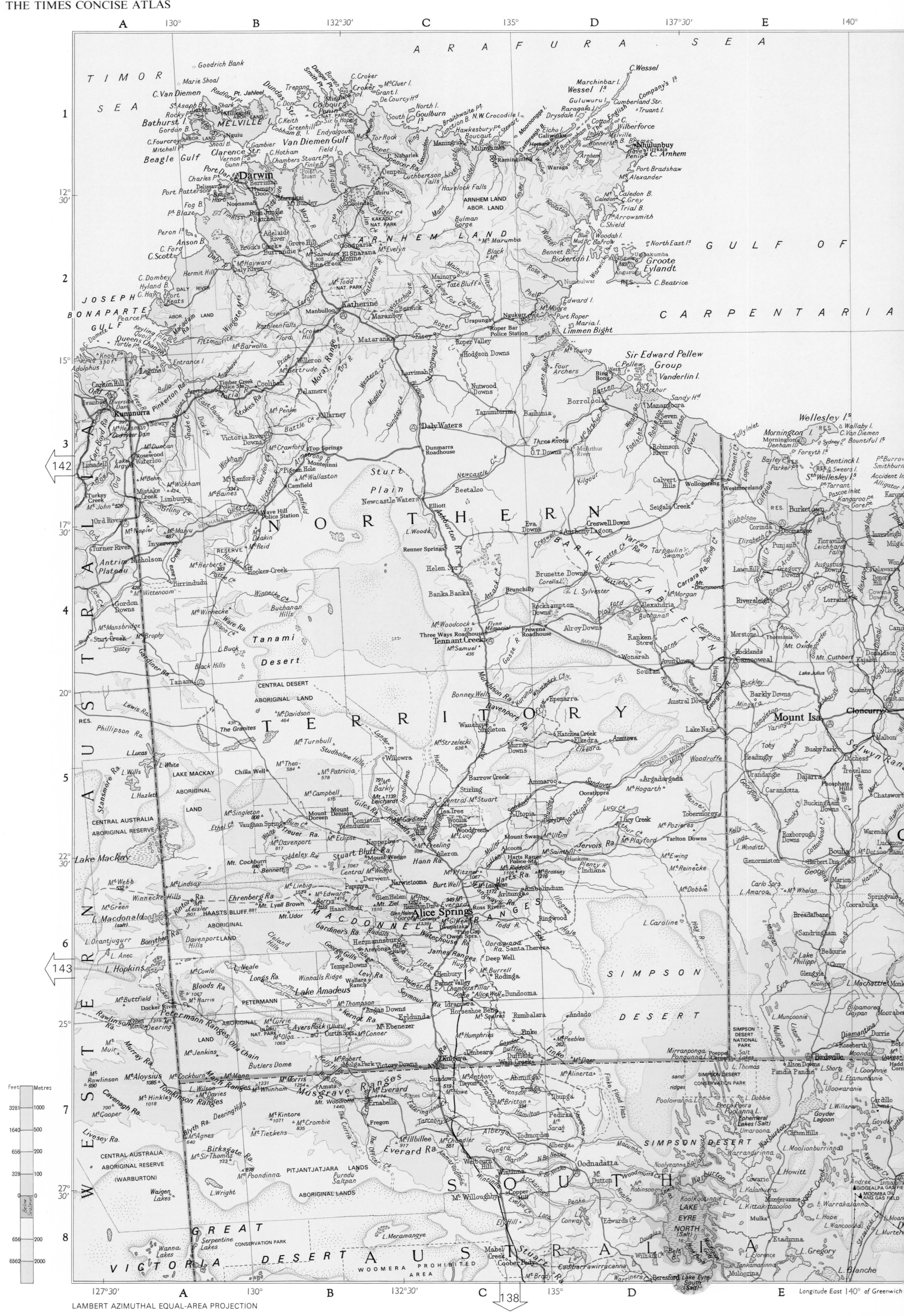

LAMBERT AZIMUTHAL EQUAL-AREA PROJECTION

Longitude East 140° of Greenwich

BRISBANE
1:300 000

Statute Miles
0 1 2 3
Kilometres

1:6 M
km miles
400 — 240
— 200
320 — 160
240 — 120
160 — 80
— 40
— 20
0 — 0

Heights and Depths in metres

© John Bartholomew & Son Ltd. Edinburgh

LAMBERT AZIMUTHAL EQUAL-AREA PROJECTION

PERTH
AND ENVIRONS
1:300 000

1. Government House
2. G.P.O.
3. Art Gallery
4. Parliament House
5. University
6. Zoo & Botanical Gardens

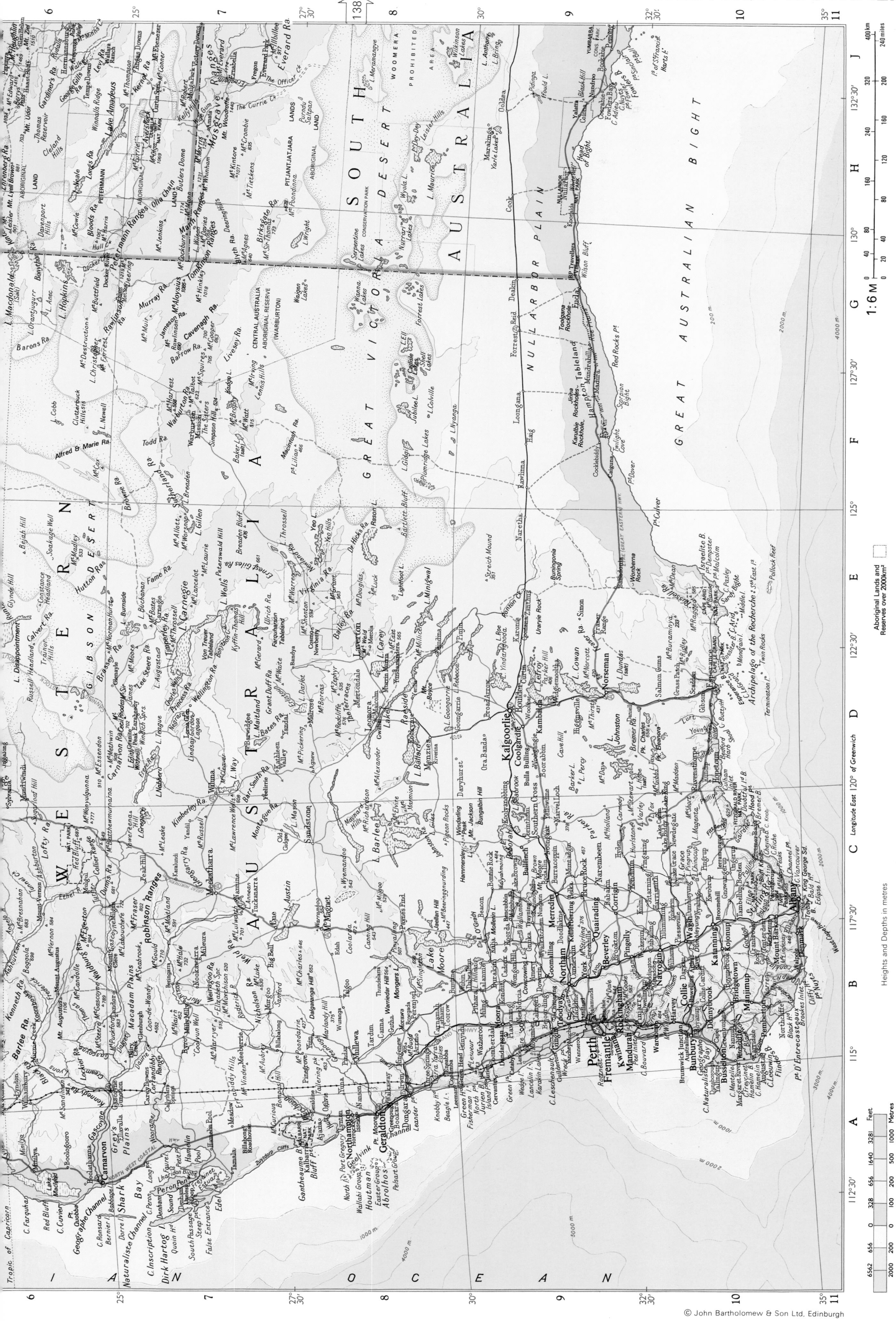

WESTERN AUSTRALIA

SOUTH AUSTRALIA

GIBSON DESERT

GREAT VICTORIA DESERT

NULLARBOR PLAIN

GREAT AUSTRALIAN BIGHT

INDIAN OCEAN

Tropic of Capricorn

Shark Bay

Carnarvon

Geraldton

Northampton

Perth
Fremantle
Mandurah
Bunbury
Busselton
Albany

Kalgoorlie
Coolgardie
Boulder

Norseman

Esperance

Meekatharra

Wiluna

Laverton

Leonora

Menzies

Southern Cross

Merredin

Northam

York

Katanning

Narrogin

Collie

Cook

Forrest

Reid

Eucla

Madura

Mundrabilla

Balladonia

Robinson Ranges

Barlee Ra.

Kennedy Ra.

Barrow Ra.

Warburton Ranges

Petermann Ranges

Musgrave Ranges

Everard Ra.

Rawlinson Ra.

WOOMERA PROHIBITED AREA

CENTRAL AUSTRALIA ABORIGINAL RESERVE (WARBURTON)

ABORIGINAL LAND

L. Macdonald

L. Hopkins

L. Amadeus

L. Carnegie

L. Wells

L. Disappointment

L. Moore

Lake Barlee

Lake Carey

Lake Rason

L. Cowan

L. Dundas

Forrest Lakes

Serpentine Lakes

GREAT EASTERN HWY

Longitude East 120° of Greenwich

1:6 M

Heights and Depths in metres

Aboriginal Lands and Reserves over 2000km²

Feet
6562
3281
1640
656
328
0

Metres
2000
1000
500
200
100
0
200
656
2000
4000
6562

0 40 80 120 160 200 240 280 320 360 400 km
0   40   80   120   160   200   240 miles

© John Bartholomew & Son Ltd. Edinburgh

CHRISTCHURCH
AND ENVIRONS
1:300 000

Statute Miles
0   1   2   3   4   5

0   1   2   3   4   5
Kilometres

DUNEDIN
AND ENVIRONS
1:300 000

Longitude East 170° of Greenwich

CONIC PROJECTION

© John Bartholomew & Son Ltd Edinburgh

3281 656   0   656 1640 3281 6562 9843   Feet
1000 200   0   200 500 1000 2000 3000   Metres

AUCKLAND AND ENVIRONS
1:300 000

(Auckland inset labels: Greenhithe, Glenfield, Pupuke, Takapuna, Hobsonville, Beach Haven, Hillcrest, Birkdale, BIRKENHEAD, NORTHCOTE, Devonport, North Head, Browns I., Motukorea Channel, WAITEMATA HARBOUR, Henderson, Te Atatu, Pt Chevalier, Ponsonby, Grey Lynn, AUCKLAND, NEWMARKET, Kohimarama, Glendowie, St Heliers, Mission Bay, Orakei, Bucklands Beach, Howick, Pakuranga, MT ALBERT, EDEN, Kemuera, Remuera, Three Kings, One Tree Hill, MT ROSKILL, ONEHUNGA, MT WELLINGTON, New Lynn, Green Bay, Blockhouse Bay, Lynfield, Waikowhai, Hillsborough, Mangere Br., Mangere, Mangere East, Favona, OTAHUHU, PAPATOETOE, MANUKAU CITY, Papakura, Waiuku, MANUKAU HARBOUR, Auckland International Airport, Cornwallis)

NORTHLAND
Three Kings Is., Surville Cliffs, North Cape, C. Reinga, C. Maria van Diemen, Kaitaia, Kaikohe, Whangarei, Dargaville, Bay of Islands, Kerikeri, Hokianga Hr., Kaipara Harbour

AUCKLAND
Helensville, Warkworth, Takapuna, Auckland, Manukau, Papakura, Pukekohe, Waiuku, HAURAKI GULF, Great Barrier I., Little Barrier I., Coromandel Peninsula, Mercury Is.

THAMES VALLEY
Thames, Paeroa, Waihi, Te Aroha, Firth of Thames

WAIKATO
Huntly, Morrinsville, Hamilton, Cambridge, Matamata, Te Awamutu, Putaruru, Te Kuiti, Raglan Hr., Aotea Hr., Kawhia Hr.

BAY OF PLENTY
Mount Maunganui, Tauranga, Te Puke, Whakatane, Kawerau, Opotiki, Rotorua, White I., C. Runaway

EAST CAPE
Gisborne, East Cape, Tuahine Pt., Gable End Foreland, Table Cape, Mahia Peninsula

TONGARIRO
Taumarunui, Turangi, Taupo, Taihape, L. Taupo

TARANAKI
New Plymouth, Waitara, Inglewood, Stratford, Eltham, Hawera, Patea, Wanganui, C. Egmont, Mt Egmont

HAWKE'S BAY
Wairoa, Napier, Hastings, Havelock North, Waipawa, Waipukurau, Dannevirke, C. Kidnappers, Hawke Bay

MANAWATU
Wanganui, Marton, Feilding, Palmerston North, Foxton, Bulls

HOROWHENUA
Levin, Otaki, Shannon

WAIRARAPA
Masterton, Carterton, Greytown, Featherston, Martinborough, C. Palliser

WELLINGTON
Porirua, Upper Hutt, Lower Hutt, Petone, Eastbourne, Paraparaumu, Kapiti I., COOK STRAIT

NELSON
Motueka, Nelson, Richmond, Takaka, C. Farewell, Farewell Spit, Golden Bay, TASMAN BAY, ABEL TASMAN NAT. PARK, D'Urville I.

MARLBOROUGH
Picton, Blenheim, Havelock, Cloudy Bay, Cape Campbell

NORTH ISLAND
TASMAN SEA, PACIFIC OCEAN, North Taranaki Bight, South Taranaki Bight

Heights in feet
Depths in metres

Longitude East 174° of Greenwich

© John Bartholomew & Son Ltd, Edinburgh

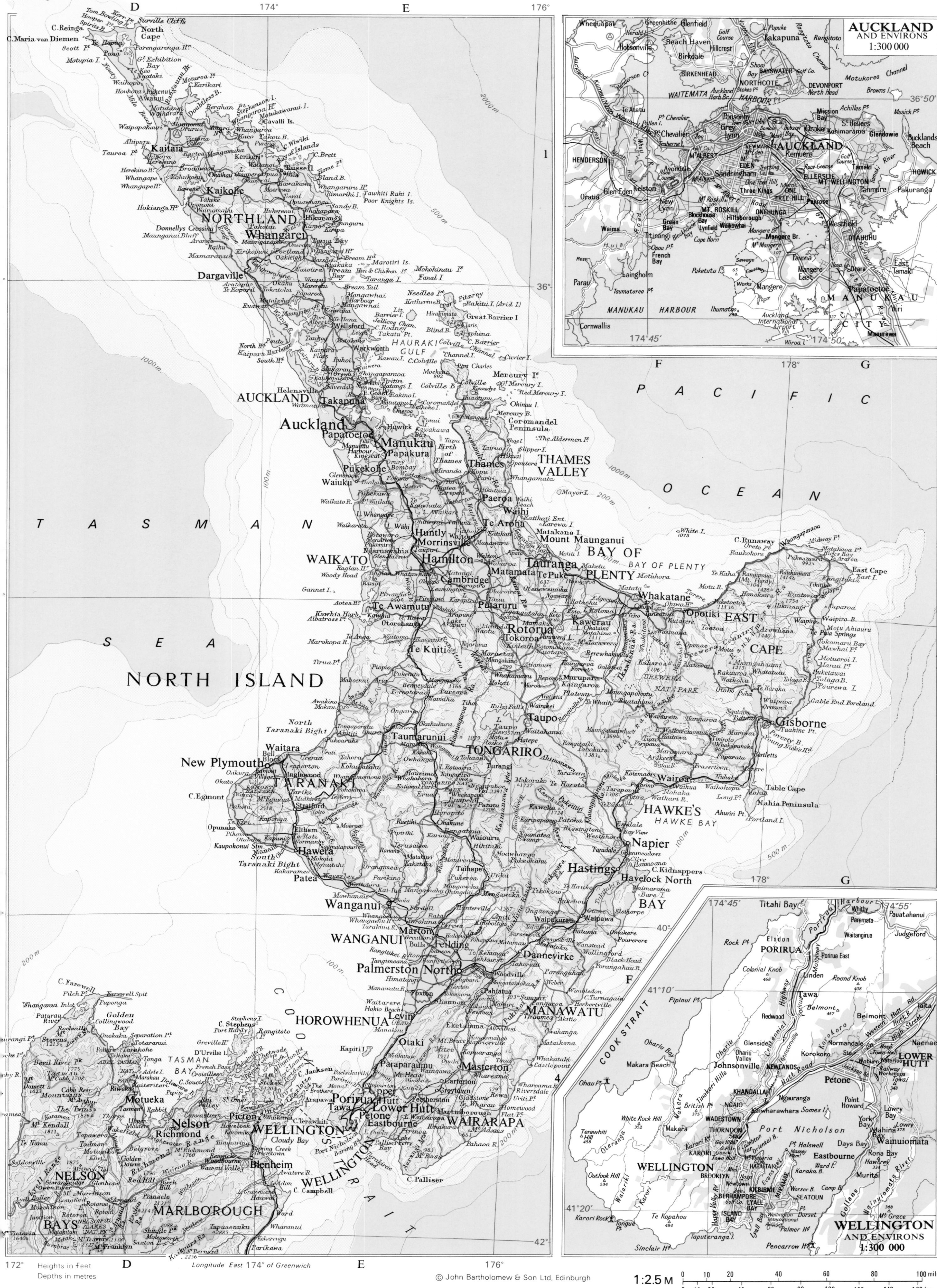

1:2.5 M

0 10 20 40 60 80 100 miles
0 20 40 60 80 100 120 140 160 km

WELLINGTON AND ENVIRONS
1:300 000

(Wellington inset labels: Titahi Bay, PORIRUA, Porirua East, Tawa, Belmont, Johnsonville, NEWLANDS, KHANDALLAH, NGAIO, WADESTOWN, THORNDON, KARORI, WELLINGTON, BROOKLYN, KILBIRNIE, SEATOUN, LYALL BAY, Island Bay, Port Nicholson, Eastbourne, Petone, LOWER HUTT, Days Bay, Wainuiomata, Pencarrow Hd., Baring Head, COOK STRAIT)

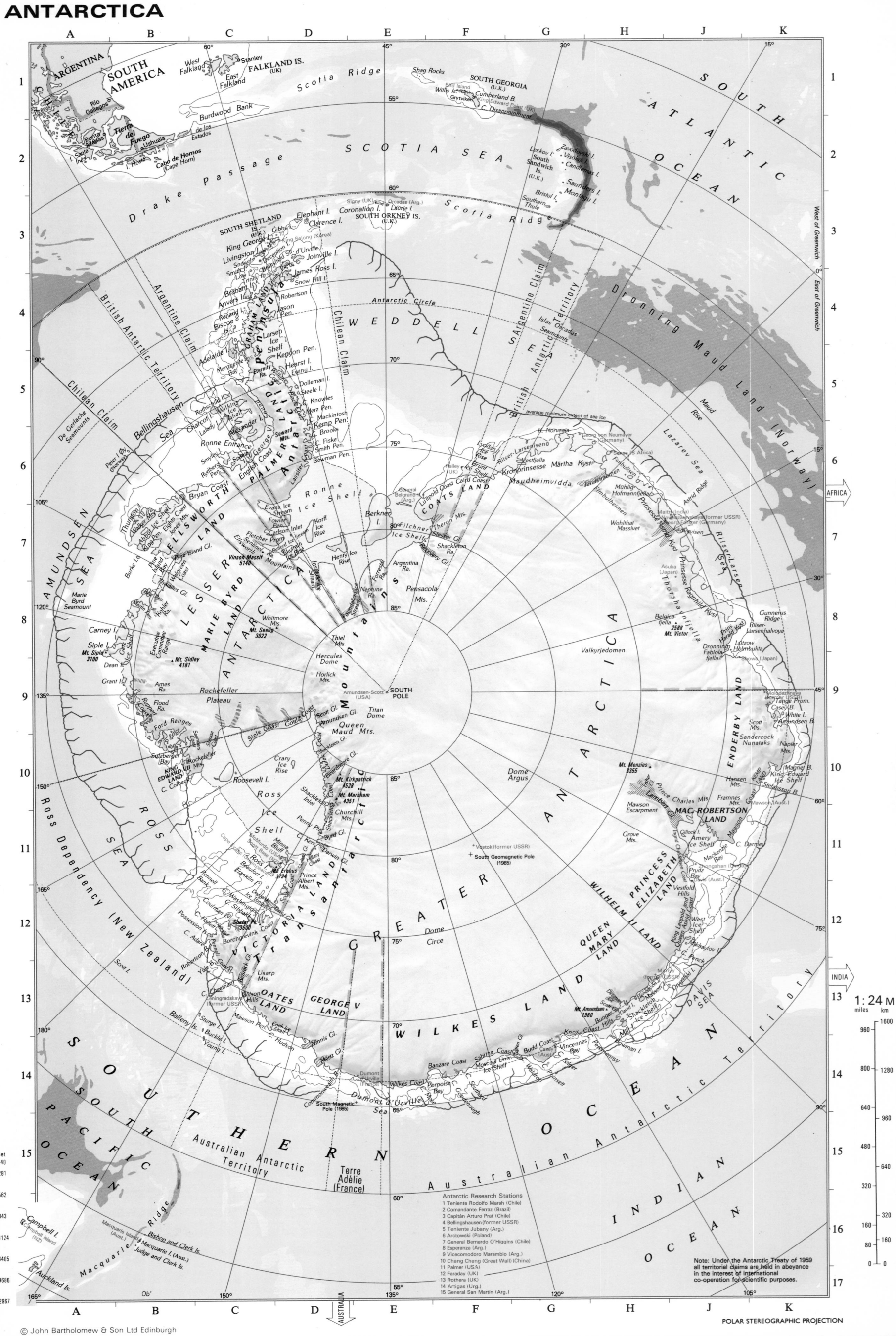

1 : 24 M

Antarctic Research Stations
1 Teniente Rodolfo Marsh (Chile)
2 Comandante Ferraz (Brazil)
3 Capitán Arturo Prat (Chile)
4 Bellingshausen (former USSR)
5 Teniente Jubany (Arg.)
6 Arctowski (Poland)
7 General Bernardo O'Higgins (Chile)
8 Esperanza (Arg.)
9 Vicecomodoro Marambio (Arg.)
10 Chang Cheng (Great Wall) (China)
11 Palmer (USA)
12 Faraday (UK)
13 Rothera (UK)
14 Artigas (Urg.)
15 General San Martín (Arg.)

Note: Under the Antarctic Treaty of 1959 all territorial claims are held in abeyance in the interest of international co-operation for scientific purposes.

© John Bartholomew & Son Ltd Edinburgh

POLAR STEREOGRAPHIC PROJECTION

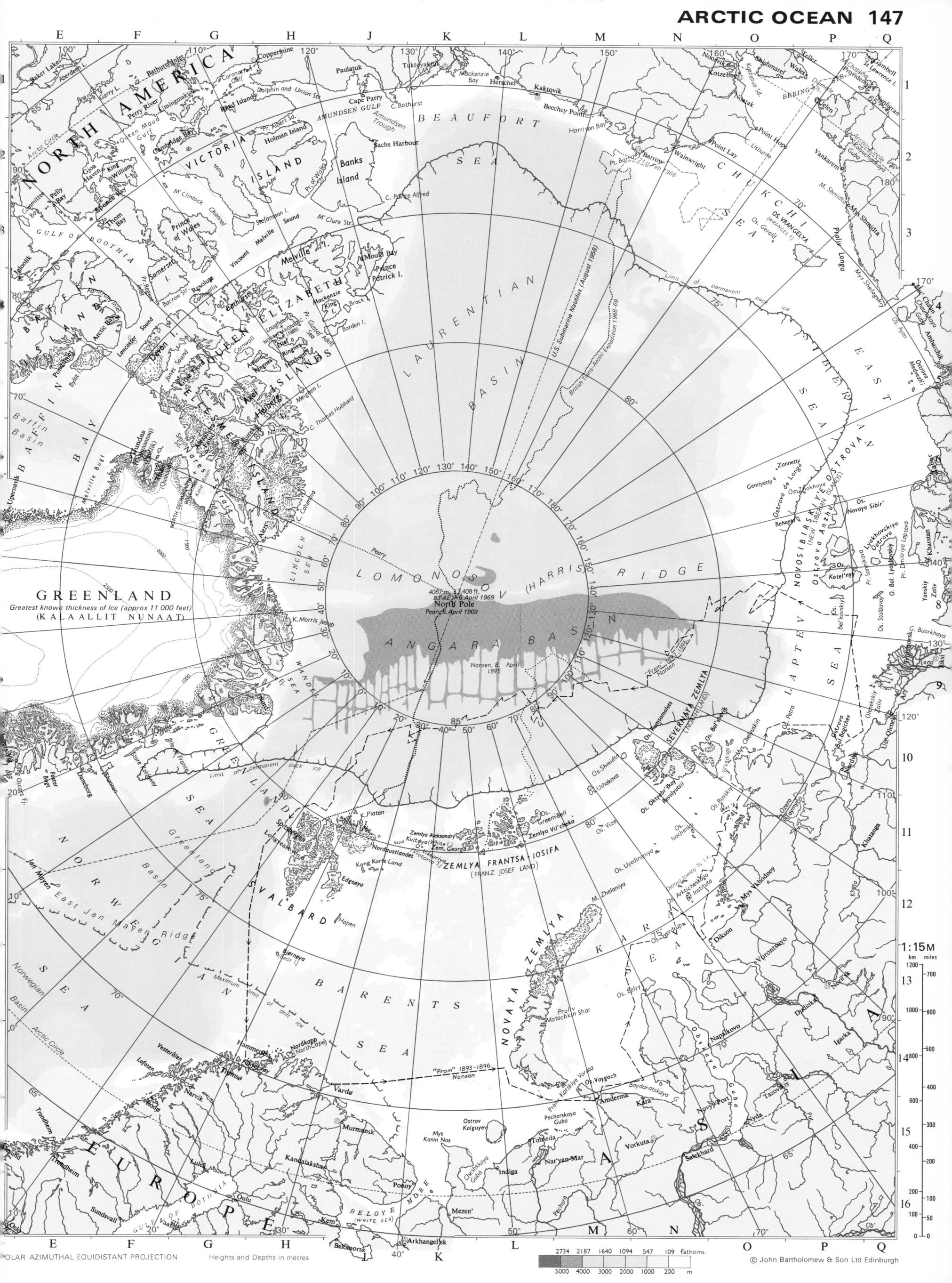

POLAR AZIMUTHAL EQUIDISTANT PROJECTION

Heights and Depths in metres

2734	2187	1640	1094	547	109	fathoms
5000	4000	3000	2000	1000	200	m

GLOSSARY

Language Abbreviations

The entries in this short glossary have been restricted to the less widely-known geographical terms. It also omits terms which are visually similar eg. banc, banco, bank.

Afr	Afrikaans	*Kor*	Korean
Alb	Albanian	*Lao*	Laotian
Ar	Arabic	*Lap*	Lappish
Ben	Bengali	*Lat*	Latvian
Ber	Berber	*Mal*	Malay
Bul	Bulgarian	*Mlg*	Malagasy
Bur	Burmese	*Mon*	Mongolian
Cam	Cambodian	*Nor*	Norwegian
Ch	Chinese	*Per*	Persian
Cz	Czech	*Pol*	Polish
Dan	Danish	*Por*	Portuguese
Dut	Dutch	*Rom*	Romanian
Est	Estonian	*Rus*	Russian
Fae	Faeroese	*Sca*	Scandinavian
Fin	Finnish	*S-C*	Serbo-Croat
Fr	French	*Sla*	Slavonic
Gae	Gaelic	*Som*	Somali
Ger	German	*Sp*	Spanish
Gr	Greek	*Swe*	Swedish
Heb	Hebrew	*Th*	Thai (Siamese)
Hin	Hindi	*Tib*	Tibetan
Hun	Hungarian	*Tu*	Turkish
Ice	Icelandic	*Ur*	Urdu
Ind	Indonesian	*Vt*	Vietnamese
It	Italian	*Wel*	Welsh
Jpn	Japanese		

Name	Language	Meaning
A, –å, –á	*Sca, Ice*	stream
Adasi	*Tu*	island
Adrar	*Ber*	mountains
Aiguille	*Fr*	peak, needle
Ain, 'Aīn, 'Ayn	*Ar*	spring, well
Akrotírion	*Gr*	cape, point
Ala–	*Fin*	lower
Alt–a, –o	*It, Por, Sp*	upper
Ao	*Ch, Th*	bay
Arro-io, yo	*Por, Sp*	watercourse
Au	*Cam*	river
Aust–	*Nor*	east(ern)
Ayía, Ayios	*Gr*	saint
Ba	*Vt*	mountain
Bāb	*Ar*	strait
Bādiyah, Badiet	*Ar*	desert
Baelt	*Dan*	strait
Bahía	*Sp*	bay
Baḩr, Baḩrah	*Ar*	sea, channel
Baixo	*Por*	lower
Baj–a, –o	*Sp*	lower
Ban	*Cam, Lao, Th*	village
–bana	*Jpn*	point, cape
Bandao	*Ch*	peninsula
Bandar	*Ar, Mal, Per,*	port, harbour
Bas, –se	*Fr*	lower
Batin, Batn	*Ar*	depression
Be'er(ot)	*Heb*	well(s)
Bei	*Ch*	north(ern)
Bereg	*Rus*	bank, shore
–berg, Berg(e)	*Sca, Ger*	mountain(s)
Bid	*Ar*	waterhole
Bir, Bîr, B'ir	*Ar*	well
Birk–at, –et	*Ar*	well, pool
–bjerg	*Dan*	hill
Boca	*Por, Sp*	mouth
Bocche	*It*	mouths, estuary
Boğazi	*Tu*	strait
Bol'sh–e, –aya, –oy	*Rus*	big
Bonom	*Vt*	mountain
–botn, –botten	*Nor, Swe*	valley floor
Bouche	*Fr*	mouth, estuary
–bre(en)	*Nor*	glacier
Bredning	*Dan*	bay
Bucht	*Ger*	bay
Bugt	*Dan*	bay
Bukhta	*Rus*	bay
Bukt(en)	*Nor, Swe*	bay
Bur–un, –nu	*Tu*	point, cape
Cabo	*Por, Sp*	cape, highland
Caka	*Tib*	salt lake
cañad–a, –ón	*Sp*	ravine, gorge
Canon	*Sp*	canyon
Cap, Capo	*Fr, It*	cape, headland
Cerro	*Sp*	hill, peak
Chaco	*Sp*	jungle region
Chaine, Chaîne	*Fr*	mountain chain
Chiang	*Th*	town
Chott	*Ar*	salt lake, marsh
Cima, Cime	*It, Sp, Fr*	summit
Citta	*It*	town, city
Ciudad	*Sp*	town, city
Co	*Tib*	lake
Col	*Fr*	high pass
Cordillera	*Sp*	mountain chain
Corn –e, –o	*Fr, It*	peak
Côte	*Fr*	coast, slope
Cu Lao	*Vt*	island
Cua	*Vt*	estuary inlet
Cun	*Ch*	village
Da	*Vt*	river
Da	*Ch*	big
Dag–i	*Tu*	mountain
Dagh	*Per*	mountain
Daglar–i	*Tu*	mountains
–dal, –ur	*Sca, Ice,Afr*	valley
–dalur	*Ice*	valley
Dao	*Ch*	island
Darreh	*Per*	valley
Daryachech	*Per*	lake
Dasht	*Per, Ur*	desert
Denizi	*Tu*	sea
–diep	*Dut*	channel
Djebel, Djibal	*Ar*	mountain
–djup	*Ice*	fjord
Do, –do	*Vt, Kor*	island
Dolina	*Rus*	valley
Dong	*Ch*	east(ern)
Dorf, –dorf	*Ger, Afr*	village
–dwip	*Hin*	island
Eiland(en)	*Afr, Dut*	island(s)
–elv(a)	*Nor*	river
Embalse	*Sp*	reservoir
Embouchure	*Fr*	estuary
'Emeq	*Heb*	plain
Erg	*Ar*	desert with dunes
Eski	*Tu*	old
Espigao	*Por*	upland
Estero	*Sp*	inlet, estuary; swamp
Estrecho	*Sp*	strait
Estreito	*Por*	strait
Etang	*Fr*	lake, lagoon
–ye(jar)	*Ice*	island(s)
Ezers	*Lat*	lake
Fels	*Ger*	rock
Feng	*Ch*	peak
Fiume	*It*	river
–fjall, fjell	*Swe, Nor*	mountain
–fjord(en)	*Dan, Nor*	fjord; lagoon
–fjordhur	*Ice*	fjord
–floi	*Ice*	bay
Foce, Foci	*It*	river-mouth
–fonn	*Nor*	glacier
Fuente	*Sp*	source, well
Gang	*Ch*	harbour
–gata	*Jpn*	inlet, lagoon
–gawa	*Jpn*	river
Gebel	*Ar*	mountain
Gebirge	*Ger*	mountains
Geziret	*Ar*	island
Gipfel	*Ger*	peak
Gji	*Alb*	inlet, bay
Gletscher	*Ger*	glacier
Gobi	*Mon*	desert
Gol	*Mon*	river
Göl(u)	*Tu*	lake
Gonglu	*Ch*	highway
Gor–a, –y	*Rus, (Sla)*	mountain(s)
–got	*Kor*	point, cape
Greben'	*Rus*	ridge
Gryada	*Rus*	ridge
Guan	*Ch*	pass
Guba	*Rus*	bay
–gunto	*Jpn*	island, group
Gunung	*Ind, Mal*	mountain
–haehyop	*Kor*	strait
Haff	*Ger*	bay
Hai	*Ch*	sea
Halbinsel	*Ger*	peninsula
halvoya	*Nor*	peninsula
Ham(m)ad–a	*Ar*	plateau
Hamakhtesh	*Heb*	depression
Hassi	*Ar*	well
–haug	*Nor*	hill
–havn	*Dan, Fae, Nor*	harbour
He	*Ch*	river
–hede, hei	*Dan, Nor*	heath
–hegyseg	*Hun*	mountains
Heide	*Ger*	heath, moor
Hka	*Bur*	river
–ho	*Nor*	peak
Hon	*Vt*	island
Hory	*Cz*	mountains
Hot	*Mon*	town
Hu	*Ch*	lake
Ia	*Vt*	stream, river
imeni	*Rus*	in the name of
Ipsoma	*Gr*	high ground
Irhzer	*Ber*	watercourse
Irmak	*Tu*	large river
'Irq	*Ar*	sand dunes
Iso–	*Fin*	big
Jabal	*Ar*	mountain
–jarv, –i	*Est, Fin*	lake
–jaure, javrre	*Lap*	lake
Jazīrah	*Ar*	island
Jezioro	*Pol*	lake
Jiang	*Ch*	river
–jima	*Jpn*	island
–jok–i, –ka	*Fin, Lap*	river
–jokull	*Ice*	glacier
–kai	*Jpn*	bay, inlet, sea
–kaikyo	*Jpn*	strait
Kamen'	*Rus*	stone
–kawa	*Jpn*	river
Kefar	*Heb*	village
Kenet	*Alb*	inlet
Kep	*Alb*	point, cape
Kepulauan	*Ind*	archipelago, islands
Khalig, Khalij	*Ar*	bay, gulf
Khawr	*Ar*	inlet
Khersonisos	*Gr*	peninsula
Khrebet	*Rus*	mountain range
Klit	*Dan*	dunes
Klong	*Th*	canal, creek
–ko	*Jpn*	lake, inlet
Ko	*Th*	island
Kofel, Koge(e)l	*Ger*	dome-shaped hill
Kolpos	*Gr*	gulf
Kopf	*Ger*	hill
Körfezi(i)	*Tu*	bay, gulf
Kosa	*Rus*	spit of land
Kray	*Rus*	region
Kryazh	*Rus*	ridge
Kuh(ha)	*Per*	mountains(s)
Kum	*Rus*	sandy desert
–kundo	*Kor*	island group
Laem	*Th*	point
Lago	*It, Por, Sp*	lake
laht	*Est*	bay
Lam	*Th*	stream
Lande	*Ger*	sandy moor, heath
Laut	*Ind*	sea
Lednik	*Rus*	glacier
Les	*Cz, Rus*	woods, forest
les, lez	*Fr*	near, beside
Lieh-tao	*Ch*	group of islands
Liman	*Rus*	bay, gulf
Liman–i	*Tu*	harbour, port
Limni	*Gr*	lake, lagoon
Ling	*Ch*	mountain range
Llano	*Sp*	plain, prairie
Llyn	*Wel*	lake
Lohatanjona	*Mlg*	point
Loma	*Sp*	hill
Lu	*Ch*	street, road
Madinat	*Ar*	town, city
Mae Nam	*Th*	river
Mal	*Alb*	mountain(s)
Mal–a, –o, –yy	*Sla*	small
Male	*Cz*	small
Marsa, Mersa	*Ar*	anchorage, inlet
Masabb	*Ar*	canal, estuary
Mega, Magal–a, –o	*Gr*	big
Mesto	*Sla*	place, town
Mikr–i, on	*Gr*	small
Mina'	*Ar*	port, harbour
Moni	*Gr*	monastery
More	*Rus*	sea
Muntii	*Rom*	mountains
Mynydd	*Wel*	mountain
–myr	*Nor, Swe*	moor, swamp
Mys	*Rus*	cape
na	*Sla*	on
nad	*Sla*	above, over
Nafud	*Ar*	desert, dune
Nagor'ye	*Rus*	highland, uplands
Nagy–	*Hun*	big, great
Nahr	*Ar*	river
Nakhon	*Th*	town
Nam	*Bur, Th, Vt*	river
Nan	*Ch*	south(ern)
Ne–a, –on, –os	*Gr*	new
Nei	*Ch*	inner
–nes	*Ice, Nor*	point, cape
Ngoc	*Vt*	mountain, peak
–ni	*Kor*	village
Nizhn–eye, –iy	*Rus*	lower
Nizina	*Cz, Rus*	lowland
Nizmennost'	*Rus*	lowlands
Nos	*Bul, Rus*	ness, point
Nosy	*Mlg*	island
Nov–a, –o	*Sla*	new
Nuur	*Mon*	lake
Ny–	*Sca*	new
ø, øy	*Sca*	island
Okrug	*Rus*	district
–oog	*Ger*	island
Ormos	*Gr*	bay
Oros (Ori)	*Ger*	mountain(s)
Ostrov(a)	*Rus*	island(s)
Otok(i)	*S–C*	island(s)
Oued	*Ar*	dry river-bed
Ozero (Ozera)	*Rus*	lake(s)
pää	*Fin*	hill
Pal–a, –ai, –o, –io	*Gr*	old
Parbat	*Ur*	mountain
Pegunungan	*Ind*	mountain range
Pelabohan	*Mal*	harbour
Pellg	*Alb*	bay
Pendi	*Ch*	basin
Pereval	*Rus*	pass
Pertuis	*Fr*	opening, strait
Perv–o, –yy	*Rus*	first
Peski	*Rus*	sands, desert
Pingyuan	*Ch*	plain
Ploskogor'ye	*Rus*	plateau
Pod	*Sla*	under, sub–
Poluostrov	*Rus*	peninsula
Polwysep	*Pol*	peninsula
Porogi	*Rus*	rapids
Poselok	*Rus*	settlement
Pradesh	*Hin*	state
presqu'île	*Fr*	peninsula
Pri	*Rus*	near, cis–
Proliv	*Rus*	strait
Protok–a	*Rus*	channel
pulau	*Ind, Mal*	island(s)
Puy	*Fr*	peak
Qi	*Ch*	admin. div.
Qiao	*Ch*	bridge
Qiryat	*Heb*	town
Qu	*Tib*	stream
Quan	*Ch*	spring
Qundao	*Ch*	archipelago
Rade	*Fr*	roadstead
rags	*Lat*	point, cape
Ramlat	*Ar*	sands
–rani	*Ice*	spur
Ra's	*Ar, Per*	point, cape
Ravnina	*Rus*	plain
Rayon	*Rus*	district
Represa	*Por*	dam
Reshteh	*Per*	mountain range
–retsugan	*Jpn*	chain of rocks
–retto	*Jpn*	chain of islands
–rev	*Nor*	reef, cliff
Ri	*Tib*	mountain
–ri	*Kor*	village
Rosh	*Heb*	point, cape
Rt	*S–C*	point, cape
Rubha	*Gae*	point, cape
Rud (khaneh)	*Per*	river
Rudohorie	*Cz*	mountains
–saar(i)	*Est, Fin*	island
Sabkhat	*Ar*	salt-flat
Saghir	*Ar*	small
sahra	*Ar*	plain
saḩrā', saḩārā	*Ar*	desert(s)
–saki, –misaki	*Jpn*	point, cape
San, –san	*Lao, Jpn, Kor*	mountain
Sebkra	*Ar*	salt-flat
Selat	*Ind*	strait, channel
Selatan	*Ind, Mal*	south(ern)
selka	*Fin*	ridge; open water
Selo	*Rus, S–C*	village
Selva	*Sp*	forest
–sen	*Jpn*	mountain
–seto	*Jpn*	strait, channel
Sever–o, –naya	*Rus*	north(ern)
Shamo	*Ch*	desert
Shan	*Ch*	mountain(s)
Shandi	*Ch*	mountainous area
Shang	*Ch*	upper
Shankou	*Ch*	pass
Shanmai	*Ch*	mountain range
Shatt	*Ar*	river (–mouth)
–shima	*Jpn*	island
–shoto	*Jpn*	group of islands
Shuiku	*Ch*	reservoir
–sjo	*Nor*	lake
So	*Dan, Nor*	lake
Song	*Vt*	river
Spitze	*Ger*	peak
Sredn–a, –e, –ayz	*Sla*	middle
Sredn–e, –eye, –iy, –yaya	*Rus*	middle
Star–a, –e	*Cz*	old
Star–a, –i	*S–C*	old
Star–aya, –oye, –yy, –yye	*Rus*	old
Step'	*Rus*	steppe
Stor–, Stora	*Swe*	big
–suido	*Jpn*	strait, channel
Sungai	*Ind, Mal*	river
–suo	*Fin*	swamp, marsh
Sveti	*S–C*	saint
Szenti–	*Hun*	saint
–take	*Jpn*	peak
Tanjong	*Ind, Mal*	cape, point
Tao	*Ch*	island
Tasek	*Mal*	lake
Tassili	*Ber*	plateau
Tau	*Rus*	mountain(s)
Tekojarvi	*Fin*	reservoir
Teluk	*Ind*	bay
Tengah	*Ind*	middle
Tepe–si	*Tu*	hill, peak
Thale	*Th*	lake
Timur	*Ind*	east(ern)
–tjakka	*Lap*	mountain
–to	*Jpn*	island
–tong	*Kor*	village
Tonle	*Cam*	lake
–udden	*Swe*	point, cape
Uj–	*Hun*	new
Ujung	*Ind*	point, cape
Urzyq	*Ar*	area of dunes
Ust'ye	*Rus*	estuary
Utara, Uttar	*Ind, Hin*	north(ern)
v	*Sla*	in
-vaara(t)	*Fin*	hill(s)
–vag	*Nor*	bay
–vann, Vatn	*Nor*	lake
–varos	*Hun*	town
–varre	*Nor*	mountain
Vast–er, –ra	*Swe*	western
Vaux	*Fr*	valleys
Velik–a, –o, –aya	*Sla*	big
Verkhn–e, –aya, –iy	*Rus*	upper
–vesi	*Fin*	water, lake
Vig–ik	*Dan, Nor*	bay
Vinh	*Vt*	bay
Vodokhranil-ishche	*Rus*	reservoir
Vorota	*Rus*	gate, strait
Vostochn–aya, –yy	*Rus*	eastern
Vozvyshennost'	*Rus*	uplands
Vpadina	*Rus*	depression
Vrch(y)	*Cz*	mountain(s)
Vung	*Vt*	bay, gulf
Vysok–aya, –o, –iy	*Rus*	high
Vyssh–aya, –e, –iy	*Rus*	higher
Wad	*Dut*	sand-flat
Wadi	*Ar*	watercourse
Wai	*Ch*	outer
Wan	*Ch*	bay
–wan	*Jpn*	bay
Wielk–a, –i, –o	*Pol*	big
Wysok–a, –i, –o	*Pol*	high
Xi	*Ch*	west; stream
Xia	*Ch*	lower; gorge
Xian	*Ch*	country
Xiao	*Ch*	small
Xu	*Ch*	islet
Yam	*Heb*	lake, sea
–yama	*Jpn*	mountain(s)
Ye	*Bur*	island
Yli–	*Fin*	upper
Yoma	*Bur*	mountain range
You	*Ch*	right
Yuzhn–o, –yy	*Rus*	southern
Za	*Rus*	behind, beyond
–zaki	*Jpn*	point, cape
Zalew, Zaliv	*Pol, Rus*	bay
–zan	*Jpn*	mountain
Zapadn–aya, –o	*Rus*	western
Zapovednik	*Rus*	reserve
Zemlya	*Rus*	land
–zhen	*Ch*	town
Zhong	*Ch*	middle
Zhou	*Ch*	islet
Zui	*Ch*	point, spit
Zuid	*Dut*	south
Zuidelijk	*Dut*	southern

Abbreviations used in the Index

Abbreviation	Meaning
Afghan	Afghanistan
Afr	Africa, African
Ala	Alabama
Amer	America, American
Anc mon	Ancient monument
Anc site	Ancient site
Arch	Archipel, archipelago, archipiélago
Arg	Argentina
Ariz	Arizona
Ark	Arkansas
Aust	Australia
Aut	Autonomous
B	Bay
Berks	Berkshire
Br	British
Br Col	British Columbia
Bucks	Buckinghamshire
C	Cape
Cal, Calif	California
Can	Canal
Cat(s)	Cataract(s)
Cent	Central
Chan	Channel
Co	County, Coast
Colo	Colorado
Conn	Connecticut
Czech	Czechoslovakia
Den	Denmark
Dept	Department, Département
Des	Desert
Dist	District
Div	Division
Dom Rep	Dominican Republic
E	East, Eastern
Eng	England, English
Eq, Equat	Equatorial
Est	Estuary
Fed	Federation
Fj	Fjord
Fr	French
G	Gulf
Ger	Germany
Gla	Glacier
Gloucs	Gloucestershire
Grp	Group
Gt	Great
Hants	Hampshire
Hbr	Harbour
Hd	Head
H.E.	Hydro Electric
Herts	Hertfordshire
Hist reg	Historic region
Hist site	Historic site
I, isld	Island
Ind	Indian
Is, islds	Islands
Isld king	Island kingdom
Isth	Isthmus
Jct, junc, junct	Junction
L	Lake
Lancs	Lancashire
Lincs	Lincolnshire
Lt Ho	Lighthouse
Madhya Prad	Madhya Pradesh
Man	Manitoba
Mass	Massachusetts
Med	Mediterranean
Mich	Michigan
Minn	Minnesota
Miss	Mississippi
Mon	Monument
Mont	Montana
Moz	Mozambique
Mt, Mte	Mountain
Mth(s)	Mouth(s)
Mt ra	Mountain range
Mts	Mountains
N	North, Northern, New
Nat Park	National Park
Neth, Nether, Neths	Netherlands
Nev	Nevada
New Bruns	New Brunswick
New Hamps	New Hampshire
New Mex	New Mexico
Nfld	Newfoundland
Notts	Nottinghamshire
N Scotia	Nova Scotia
N S W	New South Wales
N W Terr	Northwest Territories
N Y	New York
Oc	Ocean
Okla	Oklahoma
Old prov	Old province
Oxon	Oxford, Oxfordshire
Pac	Pacific
Pass	Passage
Pen	Peninsula
Penn	Pennsylvania
People's Rep	People's Republic
Physical reg	Physical region
Pk	Peak
Plat	Plateau
Port	Portugal, Portuguese
Pr	Prince
Prefect	Prefecture
Princ	Principality
Prom	Promontory
Prot	Protectorate
Prov	Province
Pt, Pta, Pto	Point
Qnsld	Queensland
R	Rio, river
Ra	Range
Rdg	Ridge
Reg	Region
Rep	Republic
Res	Reservoir
Rus. Fed.	Russian Federation
S	South, Southern
Sa	Serra, Sierra
Sask	Saskatchewan
Sd	Sound
Sk	Shuiku (reservoir)
Span	Spanish
Spr	Spring
St, Ste	Saint, Sainte
Sta	Station
Staffs	Staffordshire
Stat Area	Statistical Area
Str	Strait
Switz	Switzerland
Tenn	Tennessee
Terr	Territory
Tex	Texas
Tribal dist	Tribal district
U.A.E.	United Arab Emirates
U.K.	United Kingdom
Union Terr	Union Territory
U.S.A.	United States of America
V	Valley
Ven	Venezuela
Vict	Victoria
Virg	Virginia
Vol	Volcano
W	West, Western
Wash	Washington
W I	West Indies
Wilts	Wiltshire
Wyo	Wyoming
Yorks	Yorkshire

Czech Republic and Slovakia
Although the maps in this edition have been revised to take account of the independence of the Czech Republic and Slovakia, the index reflects the previous political situation.

Aa — Águilas

A

22 C2 **Aa** *R* France
32 E9 **Aa** *R* Germany
41 J2 **Aach** Germany
25 F7 **Aachen** Germany
37 J6 **Aalen** Germany
80 D1 **Aalma edh Chaab** Lebanon
25 C4 **Aalsmeer** Netherlands
22 G2 **Aalst** Belgium
25 G5 **Aalten** Netherlands
22 E1 **Aalter** Belgium
29 M9 **Äänekoski** Finland
29 M4 **Aapajärvi** Finland
115 O3 **Aappilattoq** Greenland
40 H3 **Aarau** Switzerland
36 E3 **Aarbergen** Germany
25 A6 **Aardenburg** Netherlands
40 H3 **Aargau** *canton* Switzerland
22 H2 **Aarschot** Belgium
Aasiaat *see* **Egedesminde**
16 E9 **Aazanèn** Morocco
58 D5 **Aba** China
85 F7 **Aba** Nigeria
86 F5 **Aba** Zaire
128 G5 **Abacaxis** *R* Brazil
113 K11 **Abaco, Great** *isld* Bahamas
113 K11 **Abaco, Little** *isld* Bahamas
77 A4 **Abadan** Iran
77 C5 **Ābādeh** Iran
130 F6 **Abadia dos Dourados** Brazil
85 D2 **Abadla** Algeria
130 F6 **Abaeté** Brazil
129 J4 **Abaetetuba** Brazil
65 C2 **Abag Qi** China
133 F3 **Abai** Paraguay
103 P4 **Abajo Pk** Utah U.S.A.
86 A4 **Abakaliki** Nigeria
56 D4 **Abakan** Russian Federation
56 C5 **Abakanskiy Khrebet** *mts* Russian Federation
85 E6 **Abala** Niger
85 F5 **Abalak** Niger
85 E4 **Abalessa** Algeria
137 P1 **Abamama** *isld* Kiribati
128 D6 **Abancay** Peru
21 O2 **Abancourt** France
45 L1 **Abano Terme** Italy
77 C4 **Abarqū** Iran
60 S1 **Abashiri** Hokkaido Japan
125 K5 **Abasolo** Mexico
55 F3 **Abatskoye** Russian Federation
136 K4 **Abau** Papua New Guinea
86 G3 **Ābay** *R* Ethiopia
57 G1 **Abay** Kazakhstan
86 G4 **Ābaya Hāyt'** *L* Ethiopia
20 G6 **Abbaretz** France
99 S3 **Abbaye, Pt** Michigan U.S.A.
86 H3 **Abbe, L** Ethiopia
21 O4 **Abbé,l'** France
9 G4 **Abberton** England
21 O1 **Abbeville** France
111 L10 **Abbeville** Alabama U.S.A.
112 D6 **Abbeville** Georgia U.S.A.
111 D12 **Abbeville** Louisiana U.S.A.
112 E3 **Abbeville** South Carolina U.S.A.
118 J8 **Abbey** Saskatchewan Canada
14 B4 **Abbeyfeale** Ireland
12 E4 **Abbey Head** Scotland
14 D4 **Abbeyleix** Ireland
141 G2 **Abbey Pk** Queensland Australia
13 F6 **Abbeystead** England
41 J7 **Abbiategrasso** Italy
26 K6 **Abborrträsk** Sweden
141 J4 **Abbot B** Queensland Australia
146 B7 **Abbot Ice Shelf** Antarctica
141 J5 **Abbot,Mt** Queensland Australia
8 D6 **Abbotsbury** England
117 M11 **Abbotsford** British Columbia Canada
13 F2 **Abbotsford** Scotland
99 Q5 **Abbotsford** Wisconsin U.S.A.
106 F5 **Abbott** New Mexico U.S.A.
109 K4 **Abbott** Texas U.S.A.
74 E1 **Abbottabad** Pakistan
25 C4 **Abcoude** Netherlands
16 D8 **Abdalagís, Sa. de** *mts* Spain
78 H3 **'Abd al Azīz** *mts* Turkey
80 F6 **Abdallah Br** Jordan
52 H6 **Abdi** Russian Federation
53 H7 **Abdulino** Russian Federation
86 D3 **Abéché** Chad
17 F3 **Abejar** Spain
22 D2 **Abele** Belgium
86 G4 **Ābeltī** Ethiopia
26 E7 **Abelvaer** Norway
26 G6 **Abelvattnet** *L* Sweden
37 K5 **Abenberg** Germany
16 E6 **Abenjar** *R* Spain
16 E6 **Abenojar** Spain
28 C6 **Åbenrå** Denmark
Åbenrå-Sønderborg *co see* **Sønderjylland** *co*
37 M6 **Abens** *R* Germany
37 M6 **Abensberg** Germany
85 E7 **Abeokuta** Nigeria
8 B1 **Aber** Wales
86 G4 **Ābera** Ethiopia
8 B3 **Aberaeron** Wales
13 E1 **Aberargie** Scotland
8 C4 **Aberavon** Wales
20 A4 **Aber-Benoit** *R* France
15 F3 **Aberchirder** Scotland
121 S7 **Abercorn** Quebec Canada
Abercorn Zambia *see* **Mbala**
139 J5 **Abercrombie** *R* New South Wales Australia
8 C4 **Aberdare** Wales
88 F2 **Aberdare Mts** *ra* Kenya
8 B2 **Aberdaron** Wales
Aberdeen *co see* **Grampian** *reg*
139 K4 **Aberdeen** New South Wales Australia
118 L6 **Aberdeen** Saskatchewan Canada
89 D9 **Aberdeen** S Africa
15 F3 **Aberdeen** Scotland
101 N7 **Aberdeen** Idaho U.S.A.
95 L7 **Aberdeen** Maryland U.S.A.
111 H8 **Aberdeen** Mississippi U.S.A.
112 H2 **Aberdeen** North Carolina U.S.A.
98 H4 **Aberdeen** South Dakota U.S.A.
100 B3 **Aberdeen** Washington U.S.A.
147 E1 **Aberdeen L** Northwest Territories Canada
13 E1 **Aberdour** Scotland
8 B2 **Aberdyfi** Wales
15 E4 **Aberfeldy** Scotland
8 B1 **Aberffraw** Wales
8 B1 **Aberffraw B** Wales
13 G6 **Aberford** England
141 H5 **Aberfoyle** Queensland Australia
12 D1 **Aberfoyle** Scotland
8 C4 **Abergavenny** Wales
8 C1 **Abergele** Wales
85 D7 **Abergourou** Ivory Coast
141 H4 **Abergowrie** Queensland Australia
8 C3 **Abergwesyn** Wales
8 B4 **Abergwili** Wales
13 F1 **Aberlady** Scotland
Abermo *see* **Barmouth**
119 O8 **Abernethy** Saskatchewan Canada
13 E1 **Abernethy** Scotland
8 B3 **Aberporth** Wales
8 B2 **Abersoch** Wales
Aberteifi *see* **Cardigan**
8 C4 **Abertillery** Wales
12 E1 **Aberuthven** Scotland
20 A4 **Aber Wrach,L'** France
8 B3 **Aberystwyth** Wales
45 J3 **Abetone** Italy
52 K2 **Abez'** Russian Federation
38 G8 **Abfaltersbach** Austria
53 F9 **Abganerovo** Russian Federation
72 E5 **Abhā** Saudi Arabia
85 D7 **Abidjan** Ivory Coast
28 B7 **Abild** Denmark
28 B4 **Abild Å** *R* Denmark
118 F4 **Abilene** Alberta Canada
107 N3 **Abilene** Kansas U.S.A.
108 H3 **Abilene** Texas U.S.A.
94 J9 **Abilene** Virginia U.S.A.
21 M8 **Abilly** France
9 E4 **Abingdon** England
99 Q9 **Abingdon** Illinois U.S.A.
94 E10 **Abingdon** Virginia U.S.A.
141 G4 **Abingdon Downs** Queensland Australia
141 J4 **Abingdon Reef** Gt Barrier Reef Australia
12 E3 **Abington** Scotland
53 E11 **Abinsk** Russian Federation
106 D5 **Abiquiu** New Mexico U.S.A.
26 K3 **Abisko** Sweden
120 J2 **Abitibi** *R* Ontario Canada
120 J3 **Abitibi Canyon** Ontario Canada
120 K4 **Abitibi,L** Ontario Canada
86 G3 **Abīy Ādī** Ethiopia
86 G4 **Abiyata Hāyk'** *L* Ethiopia
53 F11 **Abkhazskaya Respublika** Georgia
21 O4 **Ablis** France
21 L3 **Ablon** France
138 C2 **Abminga** South Australia Australia
Åbo *see* **Turku**
106 D7 **Abo** New Mexico U.S.A.
74 F3 **Abohar** India
85 D7 **Aboisso** Ivory Coast
85 E7 **Abomey** Benin
69 C10 **Abongabong, Gunung** *mt* Sumatra
86 B5 **Abong Mbang** Cameroon
48 F3 **Abony** Hungary
71 D6 **Aborlan** Philippines
26 J8 **Åbosjo** Sweden
86 C3 **Abou Deïa** Chad
15 F3 **Aboyne** Scotland
Abqaiq *see* **Buqayq**
110 L4 **Abraham Lincoln Nat. Hist. Site** Kentucky U.S.A.
133 E6 **Abra, L. del** Argentina
99 S5 **Abrams** Wisconsin U.S.A.
54 J1 **Abramtsevo** Russian Federation
16 B5 **Abrantes** Portugal
124 C4 **Abreojos, Pta** *C* Mexico
36 C6 **Abreschwiller** France
84 J5 **Abri** Sudan
9 G4 **Abridge** England
129 L7 **Abrolhos, Arquipélago dos** *islds* Brazil
48 H4 **Abrud** Romania
118 B8 **Abruzzi,Mt** British Columbia Canada
42 F6 **Abruzzo** *prov* Italy
98 J2 **Absaraka** North Dakota U.S.A.
101 P5 **Absaroka Ra** Mont/Wyoming U.S.A.
101 Q4 **Absarokee** Montana U.S.A.
37 K5 **Absberg** Germany
21 J8 **Absie,l'** France
38 H6 **Abtenau** Austria
36 H1 **Abterode** Germany
36 H6 **Abtsgmünd** Germany
33 S4 **Abtshagen** Germany
79 H3 **Abū aḍ Ḍuhūr** Syria
80 G6 **Abu 'Alanda** Jordan
71 L10 **Abuan** Indonesia
84 H5 **Abu Ballas** *mt* Egypt
80 D5 **'Abud** Jordan
77 D7 **Abu Dhabi** U.A.E.
79 D10 **Abu Durba** Egypt
79 F8 **Ābū el Jurdhān** Jordan
128 F5 **Abufari** Brazil
86 E3 **Abu Gabra** Sudan
84 J6 **Abu Hamed** Sudan
79 A7 **Abu Hummus** Egypt
85 F7 **Abuja** Nigeria
78 H4 **Abū Kamāl** Syria
79 B8 **Abu Kebîr** Egypt
61 O8 **Abukuma** *R* Japan
61 O9 **Abukuma-kōchi** *hills* Japan
86 E3 **Abu Matariq** Sudan
86 D5 **Abumonbazi** Zaire
77 D7 **Abū Mūsá** *isld* U.A.E.
128 E5 **Abuná** Brazil
84 E3 **Abū Nujaym** Libya
80 G3 **Abu Qanṭarah** Syria
79 A10 **Abu Qurqâs** Egypt
60 E14 **Aburatsu** Japan
74 E6 **Abu Road** India
79 D10 **Abu Rudeis** Egypt
77 B6 **Abu Sa'fah** *oil well* Persian Gulf
86 G1 **Abu Shagara, Ras** *C* Sudan
80 F5 **Abu Sidra** Israel
84 J5 **Abu Simbel** *hist site* Egypt
60 O3 **Abuta** Japan
84 J4 **Abu Tig** Egypt
86 F2 **Abu 'Uruq** Sudan
124 F5 **Abuya** Mexico
86 G3 **Ābuye Mēda** *mt* Ethiopia
71 G5 **Abuyog** Philippines
86 E3 **Abu Zabad** Sudan
Abū Ẓabi *see* **Abu Dhabi**
84 J4 **Abu Zenîma** Egypt
86 F4 **Abwong** Sudan
28 D2 **Åby** Denmark
27 H15 **Åby** Kalmar Sweden
27 H13 **Åby** Östergotland Sweden
86 E3 **Abyad** Sudan
26 L6 **Åby älv** *R* Sweden
28 D2 **Åbybro** Denmark
142 C5 **Abydos** W Australia Australia
86 E4 **Abyei** Sudan
77 B2 **Ābyek** Iran
127 N4 **Abymes** Guadeloupe W Indies
26 M6 **Åbyn** Sweden
72 D6 **Abyssinian Highlands** Ethiopia
55 C4 **Abzakovo** Russian Federation
55 C5 **Abzanovo** Russian Federation
141 K2 **Acacia Ridge** *dist* Brisbane, Qnsld Australia
118 G7 **Acadia Valley** Alberta Canada
130 E8 **Acaí** Brazil
108 B4 **Acala** Texas U.S.A.
125 J7 **Acámbaro** Mexico
126 F10 **Acandí** Colombia
124 G6 **Acaponeta** Mexico
125 K9 **Acapulco de Juárez** Mexico
129 J4 **Acará** *R* Brazil
129 K4 **Acarau** Brazil
130 C9 **Acaray, R** Paraguay
130 H9 **Acari** Brazil
128 D7 **Acari** *R* Peru
127 K10 **Acarigua** Venezuela
125 K8 **Acatlán** Mexico
125 M9 **Acayucan** Mexico
45 P5 **Acciano** Italy
140 F3 **Accident Inlet** Queensland Australia
97 G6 **Accotink** *R* Virginia U.S.A.
94 F9 **Accoville** West Virginia U.S.A.
85 D7 **Accra** Ghana
13 F6 **Accrington** England
69 C10 **Aceh** *prov* Sumatra
101 M7 **Acequia** Idaho U.S.A.
43 F8 **Acerra** Italy
41 K2 **Ach** *R* Germany
128 E2 **Achaguas** Venezuela
74 G8 **Achalpur** India
38 E7 **Ache** *R* Austria
84 E6 **Achegour** Niger
22 J1 **Achel** Belgium
38 F6 **Achen** *R* Germany
59 J2 **Acheng** China
119 P4 **Acheninni L** Saskatchewan Canada
38 E6 **Achenkirch** Austria
41 P2 **Achen Pass** Germany
38 E6 **Achen-Tal** *R* Austria
41 P2 **Achenwald** Austria
36 E6 **Achern** Germany
144 D5 **Acheron** *R* New Zealand
21 P1 **Acheux-en-Amienois** France
22 D3 **Achicourt** France
22 D3 **Achiet-le-Grand** France
53 F11 **Achikulak** Russian Federation
14 B3 **Achill** Ireland
109 L2 **Achille** Oklahoma U.S.A.
32 K6 **Achim** Germany
55 G1 **Achimovy 2-ye** Russian Federation
56 D3 **Achinsk** Russian Federation
55 E2 **Achiry** Russian Federation
57 E3 **Achisay** Kazakhstan
58 B2 **Achit Nuur** *L* Mongolia
15 C3 **Achnasheen** Scotland
33 T4 **Achter-Wasser** *L* Germany
53 E10 **Achuyevo** Russian Federation
86 F5 **Achwa** *R* Uganda
20 G5 **Acigne** France
78 D3 **Acı Gölü** *L* Turkey
47 K7 **Acıpayam** Turkey
43 G11 **Acireale** Sicily
108 F3 **Ackerly** Texas U.S.A.
111 G8 **Ackerman** Mississippi U.S.A.
99 N7 **Ackley** Iowa U.S.A.
126 G3 **Acklins I** Bahamas
111 M7 **Ackworth** Georgia U.S.A.
71 F5 **Aclan Pt** Philippines
14 C2 **Aclare** Ireland
9 H2 **Acle** England
118 D7 **Acme** Alberta Canada
106 F8 **Acme** New Mexico U.S.A.
112 J3 **Acme** North Carolina U.S.A.
108 H1 **Acme** Texas U.S.A.
106 C6 **Acomita** New Mexico U.S.A.
133 D4 **Aconcagua** *mt* Argentina
131 B4 **Aconcagua** *R* Chile
85 A1 **Açores** *islds* Atlantic Oc
87 F10 **Acornhoek** S Africa
A Coruña *see* **Lá Coruña**
45 N4 **Acqualagna** Italy
42 D6 **Acquapendente** Italy
21 N3 **Acquigny** France
44 D2 **Acqui Terme** Italy
138 D4 **Acraman, L** South Australia Australia
128 D5 **Acre** *state* Brazil
128 E5 **Acre** *R* Brazil
80 D2 **Acre** Israel
43 G9 **Acri** Italy
44 D3 **Acroscia** *R* Italy
48 D3 **Acs** Hungary
48 E3 **Acsa** Hungary
135 N10 **Actaeon Grp** *islds* Pacific Oc
9 F5 **Acton** England
102 F7 **Acton** California U.S.A.
101 R4 **Acton** Montana U.S.A.
8 D4 **Acton Turville** England
121 S7 **Acton Vale** Quebec Canada
130 H8 **Açu** Brazil
129 K4 **Açude Areras** *L* Brazil
130 E9 **Acunguí** Brazil
130 C4 **Açurizal** Brazil
45 O6 **Acuto** Italy
112 C3 **Acworth** Georgia U.S.A.
61 Q12 **Ada** Okinawa
107 N2 **Ada** Kansas U.S.A.
94 B4 **Ada** Michigan U.S.A.
98 K2 **Ada** Minnesota U.S.A.
94 D6 **Ada** Ohio U.S.A.
107 O7 **Ada** Oklahoma U.S.A.
48 F5 **Ada** Serbia Yugoslavia
85 C5 **Adafer** *reg* Mauritania
119 O8 **Adair** Saskatchewan Canada
99 M8 **Adair** Iowa U.S.A.
110 A5 **Adair** Oklahoma U.S.A.
103 L10 **Adair, B. de** Mexico
112 C3 **Adairsville** Georgia U.S.A.
16 D4 **Adaja** *R* Spain
144 A6 **Ada, L** New Zealand
47 J6 **Adala** Turkey
27 D11 **Adals-elv** *R* Norway
26 J8 **Ådalshøen** Sweden
Adama *see* **Nazrēt**
80 F5 **Adamah** Jordan
84 G3 **Adam, Al'** Libya
103 P7 **Adamana** Arizona U.S.A.
130 D7 **Adamantina** Brazil
117 O10 **Adamant Mt** British Columbia Canada
86 B4 **Adamaoua** *reg* Cameroon
42 D2 **Adamello** *mt* Italy
80 D1 **Adamit** Israel
133 F8 **Adam,Mt** Falkland Is
55 C5 **Adamovka** Russian Federation
100 H8 **Adam Peak** *mt* Nevada U.S.A.
102 B3 **Adams** California U.S.A.
95 O4 **Adams** Massachusetts U.S.A.
99 O6 **Adams** Minnesota U.S.A.
98 K9 **Adams** Nebraska U.S.A.
98 H1 **Adams** North Dakota U.S.A.
107 J5 **Adams** Oklahoma U.S.A.
110 J5 **Adams** Tennessee U.S.A.
99 R6 **Adams** Wisconsin U.S.A.
83 J8 **Adam's Bridge** Sri Lanka/India
117 O10 **Adams L** British Columbia Canada
145 E4 **Adams, Mt** New Zealand
100 D3 **Adams,Mt** Washington U.S.A.
107 P7 **Adamson** Oklahoma U.S.A.
83 K11 **Adam's Peak** Sri Lanka
102 D2 **Adams Pk** California U.S.A.
95 L6 **Adamstown** Pennsylvania U.S.A.
121 S7 **Adamsville** Quebec Canada
111 K8 **Adamsville** Alabama U.S.A.
94 F6 **Adamsville** Ohio U.S.A.
110 H6 **Adamsville** Tennessee U.S.A.
109 J4 **Adamsville** Texas U.S.A.
103 M3 **Adamsville** Utah U.S.A.
16 D6 **Adamuz** Spain
78 E3 **Adana** Turkey
118 H6 **Adanac** Saskatchewan Canada
70 E5 **Adang,Teluk** *B* Kalimantan
78 C1 **Adapazari** Turkey
86 G2 **Adarama** Sudan
146 C12 **Adare, C** Antarctica
70 D5 **Adas** Kalimantan
80 D8 **Adasha** *R* Israel
141 G7 **Adavale** Queensland Australia
103 J3 **Adaven** Nevada U.S.A.
99 M7 **Adaza** Iowa U.S.A.
41 M5 **Adda** *R* Italy
9 E3 **Adderbury** England
109 M6 **Addicks** Texas U.S.A.
13 G6 **Addingham** England
107 N7 **Addington** Oklahoma U.S.A.
80 E3 **Addirim** Israel
111 E11 **Addis** Louisiana U.S.A.
Addis Ababa *see* **Ādīs Abeba**
111 J7 **Addison** Alabama U.S.A.
95 U2 **Addison** Maine U.S.A.
95 K4 **Addison** New York U.S.A.
109 O8 **Addison** Texas U.S.A.
95 O2 **Addison** Vermont U.S.A.
94 G8 **Addison** West Virginia U.S.A.
73 L9 **Addu Atoll** Maldives
79 G4 **Ad Duraykish** Syria
100 H1 **Addy** Washington U.S.A.
112 D6 **Adel** Georgia U.S.A.
99 M8 **Adel** Iowa U.S.A.
100 F7 **Adel** Oregon U.S.A.
138 B8 **Adelaide** South Australia Australia
126 F2 **Adelaide** New Providence I Bahamas
146 C5 **Adelaide I** Antarctica
115 K4 **Adelaide Pen** Northwest Territories Canada
140 B2 **Adelaide River** N Terr Australia
102 G7 **Adelanto** California U.S.A.
Adelaye *see* **Bani**
40 G5 **Adelboden** Switzerland
32 L9 **Adelebsen** Germany
142 E3 **Adele I** W Australia Australia
145 D4 **Adele I** New Zealand
106 D7 **Adelino** New Mexico U.S.A.
37 J6 **Adelmannsfelden** Germany
127 J2 **Adelphi** Jamaica
37 L6 **Adelschlag** Germany
37 K4 **Adelsdorf** Germany
36 G5 **Adelsheim** Germany
17 G4 **Ademuz** Spain
72 F6 **Aden** Yemen
36 B3 **Adenau** Germany
85 F5 **Aderbissinat** Niger
71 G6 **Adgaoan** *R* Mindanao Philippines
79 G5 **'Adhrā'** Syria
80 D2 **'Adi** Israel
136 G2 **Adi** *isld* W Irian
86 G3 **Ādī Ārk'ey** Ethiopia
138 B4 **Adieu, Cape** South Australia Australia
45 K1 **Adige** *R* Italy
86 G3 **Ādīgrat** Ethiopia
74 H9 **Adilabad** India
86 F5 **Adilang** Uganda
78 J2 **Adilcevaz** Turkey
59 L2 **Adimi** Russian Federation
100 E8 **Adin** California U.S.A.
22 D1 **Adinkerke** Belgium
95 N2 **Adirondack Mts** New York U.S.A.
86 G4 **Ādīs Abeba** Ethiopia
86 G4 **Ādīs Alem** Ethiopia
86 G3 **Ādīs Zemen** Ethiopia
86 G3 **Ādī Ugrī** Ethiopia
78 G3 **Adiyaman** Turkey
48 L4 **Adjud** Romania
53 E11 **Adler** Russian Federation
8 D1 **Adlington** England
118 J9 **Admiral** Saskatchewan Canada
145 D4 **Admiralty B** New Zealand
116 K1 **Admiralty Bay** Alaska U.S.A.
142 F2 **Admiralty G** W Australia Australia
117 F7 **Admiralty I** Alaska U.S.A.
117 F7 **Admiralty I Nat Mon** Alaska U.S.A.
115 L3 **Admiralty Inlet** Northwest Territories Canada
100 C1 **Admiralty Inlet** Washington U.S.A.
136 K2 **Admiralty Is** Bismarck Arch
107 O3 **Admire** Kansas U.S.A.
38 K6 **Admont** Austria
133 E5 **Adolfo Alsina** Argentina
26 J5 **Adolfsström** Sweden
142 G3 **Adolphus I** W Australia Australia
71 L9 **Adonara** *isld* Indonesia
76 C3 **Adoni** India
48 E3 **Adony** Hungary
80 C7 **Adora** Jordan
80 C8 **Adorayim** *R* Israel
32 J10 **Adorf** Germany
37 N3 **Adorf** Germany
86 B4 **Adoumaoua, Massif de l'** *mts* Cameroon
18 E9 **Adour** *R* France
16 E8 **Adra** Spain
43 F11 **Adrano** Sicily
85 D3 **Adrar** Algeria
85 B4 **Adrar** *reg* Mauritania
85 E4 **Adrar des Iforas** *mt reg* Algeria/Mali
85 E5 **Adrar Quezzeine** *mts* Mali
85 A4 **Adrar Souttouf** *reg* Mauritania
77 H3 **Adraskand** *R* Afghanistan
57 F4 **Adrasman** Tajikistan
86 D3 **Adré** Chad
84 E4 **Adri** Libya
42 E3 **Adria** Italy
112 E5 **Adrian** Georgia U.S.A.
99 L6 **Adrian** Minnesota U.S.A.
110 B3 **Adrian** Missouri U.S.A.
100 H6 **Adrian** Oregon U.S.A.
100 F2 **Adrian** Washington U.S.A.
94 G8 **Adrian** West Virginia U.S.A.
Adrianople *see* **Edirne**
45 N2 **Adriatic Sea**
28 D7 **Adsbøl** Denmark
103 N10 **Aduana del Sasabe** Mexico
41 K4 **Adula Gruppe** *mt* Switzerland
80 C7 **'Adullam** *dist* Israel
110 G4 **Advance** Missouri U.S.A.
142 E5 **Adverse Well** W Australia Australia
122 H8 **Advocate Harbour** Nova Scotia Canada
86 G3 **Ādwa** Ethiopia
80 G2 **'Adwān** Syria
108 B8 **Ady** Texas U.S.A.
51 N2 **Adycha** *R* Russian Federation
53 E10 **Adygeyskaya Avtonomnyy Oblast'** Russian Federation
78 H1 **Adzharskaya Respublika** Georgia
85 D7 **Adzope** Ivory Coast
28 E5 **Æbelø** *isld* Denmark
46 G6 **Aegean Sea** Greece
28 E7 **Ærø** *isld* Denmark
8 B3 **Aeron,R** Wales
28 E7 **Ærøskøbing** Denmark
40 G3 **Aesch** Switzerland
118 D9 **Aetna** Alberta Canada
107 M4 **Aetna** Kansas U.S.A.
52 H5 **Afanas'yevo** Russian Federation
47 R14 **Afándou** Rhodes Greece
80 D2 **Afeq** Israel
20 F6 **Aff** *R* France
85 B5 **Affollé** *reg* Mauritania
77 H3 **Afghanistan** *rep* Asia
86 H5 **Afgooye** Somalia
86 A4 **Afikpo** Nigeria
53 E11 **Afips** *R* Russian Federation
80 F2 **Afiq** Syria
26 D8 **Åfjord** Norway
85 E2 **Aflou** Algeria
86 H5 **Afmadow** Somalia
129 L5 **Afogados da Ingázeira** Brazil
116 L7 **Afognak I** Alaska U.S.A.
85 B5 **Afollé** *reg* Mauritania
8 C2 **Afon Dyfi** *R* Wales
130 C4 **Afonso** Brazil
45 Q8 **Afragola** Italy
86 H3 **Āfrēra YeCh'ew Hāyk'** *L* Ethiopia
82 **Africa**
52 D1 **Afrikanda** Russian Federation
79 G2 **'Afrīn** Syria
40 A3 **Afrique,Mt** France
38 J8 **Afritz** Austria
16 E10 **Afso** Morocco
99 M8 **Afton** Iowa U.S.A.
99 O5 **Afton** Minnesota U.S.A.
106 D9 **Afton** New Mexico U.S.A.
95 M4 **Afton** New York U.S.A.
107 Q5 **Afton** Oklahoma U.S.A.
99 R7 **Afton** Wisconsin U.S.A.
101 P7 **Afton** Wyoming U.S.A.
129 H4 **Afua** Brazil
80 E3 **'Afula** Israel
80 E3 **'Afula 'Illit** Israel
78 C2 **Afyon** Turkey
86 B2 **Agadem** Niger
85 F5 **Agadès** Niger
85 C2 **Agadir** Morocco
57 G1 **Agadyr'** Kazakhstan
85 F7 **Agaie** Nigeria
121 L2 **Again** *R* Quebec Canada
85 F5 **Agalak, Mt** Niger
83 H6 **Agalega Is** Mauritius Indian Oc
125 M2 **Agalta,Sa.de** *ra* Honduras
55 F1 **Agan** *R* Russian Federation
61 N8 **Agano** Japan
55 C4 **Agapovka** Russian Federation
74 G7 **Agar** India
98 F5 **Agar** South Dakota U.S.A.
28 C5 **Ågård** Denmark
86 G4 **Āgaro** Ethiopia
117 N11 **Agassiz** British Columbia Canada
106 G2 **Agate** Colorado U.S.A.
98 C7 **Agate** Nebraska U.S.A.
98 C7 **Agate Fossil Beds Nat. Mon.** Nebraska U.S.A.
73 L6 **Agatti** *isld* Lakshadweep Indian Oc
120 F5 **Agawa** Ontario Canada
101 N2 **Agawam** Montana U.S.A.
85 D7 **Agboville** Ivory Coast
18 H9 **Agde** France
18 H9 **Agde,Cap d'** France
28 E6 **Ågedrup** Denmark
61 L10 **Agematsu** Japan
18 F8 **Agen** France
100 G6 **Agency Valley Res** Oregon U.S.A.
107 N2 **Agenda** Kansas U.S.A.
100 C8 **Ager** California U.S.A.
28 E5 **Agernæs** Denmark
28 B3 **Agerø** *isld* Denmark
28 C6 **Agerskov** Denmark
28 G6 **Agersø** Denmark
28 E2 **Agersted** Denmark
28 H5 **Agerup** Denmark
89 A7 **Aggeneys** S Africa
28 A3 **Agger** Denmark
36 C2 **Agger** *R* Germany
28 C3 **Aggersborg** Denmark
28 A3 **Agger Tange** *pen* Denmark
38 M5 **Aggsbach** Austria
77 K3 **Aghangai** Afghanistan
116 J8 **Aghiyuk I** Alaska U.S.A.
85 B4 **Aghwinit** Mauritania
85 B4 **Aghzoumal, Sabkhat** *salt lake* Western Sahara
124 E4 **Agiabampo** Mexico
58 F1 **Aginskoye** Russian Federation
43 F11 **Agira** Sicily
18 G10 **Agly** *R* France
85 B3 **Agmar** Mauritania
45 L1 **Agna** Italy
118 L2 **Agnes Lake** Ontario Canada
142 F3 **Agnes, Mt** W Australia Australia
143 G7 **Agnes, Mt** W Australia Australia
100 A7 **Agness** Oregon U.S.A.
143 D8 **Agnew** W Australia Australia
85 D7 **Agnibilekrou** Ivory Coast
48 J5 **Agnita** Romania
42 D3 **Agno** *R* Italy
42 F7 **Agnone** Italy
44 E1 **Agogna** *R* Italy
20 G3 **Agon** France
67 B3 **Agong** China
38 K6 **Agonitz** Austria
42 E2 **Agordo** Italy
45 O6 **Agosta** Italy
18 G9 **Agout** *R* France
74 H5 **Agra** India
107 L2 **Agra** Kansas U.S.A.
107 O6 **Agra** Oklahoma U.S.A.
53 G11 **Agrakhanskiy Poluostrov** *pen* Russian Federation
Agram *see* **Zagreb**
17 H3 **Agramunt** Spain
17 F3 **Agreda** Spain
43 G8 **Agri** *R* Italy
78 J2 **Ağrı** Turkey
71 E3 **Agria Pt** Luzon Philippines
111 H11 **Agricola** Mississippi U.S.A.
43 F11 **Agrigento** Sicily
131 B7 **Agrio,R** Argentina
43 F8 **Agropoli** Italy
45 N6 **Agro Pontino** *plain* Italy
47 O12 **Agrós** Greece
71 E3 **Agta Pt** Philippines
124 G6 **Agua Brava, L** Mexico
103 L9 **Agua Caliente** Arizona U.S.A.
129 H8 **Água Clara** Brazil
127 K9 **Aguada Grande** Venezuela
128 C2 **Aguadas** Colombia
127 L5 **Aguadilla** Puerto Rico
109 K8 **Agua Dulce** Texas U.S.A.
103 M7 **Agua Fria** *R* Arizona U.S.A.
109 H9 **Agualeguas** Mexico
102 H8 **Aguanga** California U.S.A.
123 K3 **Aguanish** Quebec Canada
124 F3 **Agua Nueva** Mexico
109 J9 **Agua Nueva** Texas U.S.A.
123 K3 **Aguanus R** Quebec Canada
130 E7 **Aguapeí** *R* Brazil
128 G7 **Aguape,Sa** *mts* Brazil
131 G2 **Aguapey** *R* Argentina
124 E2 **Agua Prieta** Mexico
128 F8 **Aguaray** Argentina
130 C8 **Aguaray Guazú,R** Paraguay
A Guardia *see* **La Guardia** Spain
128 C4 **Aguarico** *R* Ecuador
17 G3 **Aguas** *R* Spain
120 C4 **Aguasabon Dam** Ontario Canada
108 E6 **Agua Salada** Mexico
130 H10 **Águas Belas** Brazil
124 H7 **Aguascalientes** Mexico
130 H5 **Aguas Formosas** Brazil
128 C5 **Aguaytia** Peru
16 D6 **Agudo** Spain
130 E8 **Agudos** Brazil
16 B4 **Agueda** Portugal
16 C4 **Agueda** *R* Spain
85 E5 **Aguelhok** Mali
85 C4 **Aguelt el Melha** Mauritania
45 O4 **Agugliano** Italy
85 F6 **Aguié** Niger
103 L8 **Aguila** Arizona U.S.A.
106 F4 **Aguilar** Colorado U.S.A.
16 E2 **Aguilar de Campoo** Spain
109 H8 **Aguilares** Texas U.S.A.
17 F7 **Águilas** Spain

38 J6 **Alm** *R* Austria
38 G7 **Alm** Austria
122 H8 **Alma** New Brunswick Canada
121 T4 **Alma** Quebec Canada
110 B6 **Alma** Arkansas U.S.A.
106 D2 **Alma** Colorado U.S.A.
112 E6 **Alma** Georgia U.S.A.
107 O2 **Alma** Kansas U.S.A.
94 C3 **Alma** Michigan U.S.A.
110 C2 **Alma** Missouri U.S.A.
98 G9 **Alma** Nebraska U.S.A.
99 P5 **Alma** Wisconsin U.S.A.
57 H3 **Alma-Ata** Kazakhstan
16 A6 **Almada** Portugal
141 G3 **Almaden** Queensland Australia
16 D6 **Almadén** Spain
16 D6 **Almadén, Sa. de** *mts* Spain
80 F2 **Almagor** Israel
71 G5 **Almagro** *isld* Philippines
48 G6 **Almăjului Muntii** *mts* Romania
84 F4 **Al Malāqī** *well* Libya
57 E4 **Almalyk** Uzbekistan
102 C1 **Almanor, L** California U.S.A.
17 G6 **Almansa** Spain
16 D2 **Almanza** Spain
117 K7 **Alma Peak** British Columbia Canada
17 F3 **Almarza** Spain
48 H3 **Almaş** *R* Romania
130 E4 **Almas, R das** Brazil
17 F3 **Almazán** Spain
57 E4 **Almazar** Uzbekistan
54 K8 **Almaznaya** Ukraine
56 H1 **Almaznyy** Russian Federation
27 H12 **Almby** Sweden
32 J9 **Alme** *R* Germany
27 H15 **Älmeboda** Sweden
100 B7 **Almeda** Oregon U.S.A.
129 H4 **Almeirim** Brazil
16 B5 **Almeirim** Portugal
25 G4 **Almelo** Netherlands
107 L2 **Almena** Kansas U.S.A.
129 K7 **Almenara** Brazil
17 F7 **Almenara, Sa. de** *mt* Spain
17 F3 **Almenar de Soria** Spain
16 C3 **Almendra, Embalse de** *res* Spain
16 C6 **Almendralejo** Spain
21 L4 **Alménêches** France
55 D4 **Al'menevo** Russian Federation
8 D6 **Almer** England
25 D4 **Almere** Netherlands
25 D4 **Almere-Haven** Netherlands
17 F7 **Almería** *prov* Spain
17 F8 **Almería** Spain
98 G8 **Almeria** Nebraska U.S.A.
17 F8 **Almería,G.de** Spain
52 H7 **Al'met'yevsk** Russian Federation
27 G15 **Älmhult** Sweden
16 E8 **Almijara, Sierra de** *mts* Spain
28 C5 **Almind** Vejle Denmark
28 C4 **Almind** Viborg Denmark
100 G2 **Almira** Washington U.S.A.
130 E9 **Almirante Tamandaré** Brazil
46 G6 **Almiropótamos** Greece
46 F5 **Almirós** Greece
46 G9 **Almiroú Kólpos** *G* Crete Greece
101 M7 **Almo** Idaho U.S.A.
16 B7 **Almodôvar** Portugal
16 E6 **Almodóvar del Campo** Spain
17 F5 **Almodóvar del Pinar** Spain
133 D3 **Almogasta** Argentina
94 K4 **Almond** New York U.S.A.
99 R5 **Almond** Wisconsin U.S.A.
15 E4 **Almond,R** Scotland
8 D4 **Almondsbury** England
106 D3 **Almont** Colorado U.S.A.
94 D4 **Almont** Michigan U.S.A.
98 E3 **Almont** North Dakota U.S.A.
121 O7 **Almonte** Ontario Canada
16 C5 **Almonte** *R* Spain
74 H4 **Almora** India
16 E4 **Almorox** Spain
100 H3 **Almota** Washington U.S.A.
79 F9 **Al Mudawwara** Jordan
86 H3 **Al Mukhā** Yemen
27 G15 **Almundsryd** Sweden
16 E8 **Almuñécar** Spain
27 H14 **Almvik** Sweden
101 P8 **Almy** Wyoming U.S.A.
111 E7 **Almyra** Arkansas U.S.A.
13 G3 **Aln Br** England
15 D3 **Alness** Scotland
13 G3 **Alnmouth** England
26 J9 **Alnö** Sweden
13 G3 **Alnwick** England
137 R4 **Alofi** *isld* Îles de Horn Pacific Oc
94 C1 **Aloha** Michigan U.S.A.
68 B1 **Alon** Burma
139 H9 **Alonnah** Tasmania Australia
71 E5 **Alonon Pt** Philippines
119 T8 **Alonsa** Manitoba Canada
71 M9 **Alor** *isld* Indonesia
16 D8 **Alora** Spain
71 M8 **Alor,Kep** *isld* Indonesia
71 L9 **Alor,Selat** Indonesia
69 E9 **Alor Setar** Malaysia
16 C7 **Alosno** Spain
Alost *see* **Aalst**
143 G7 **Aloysius, Mt** W Australia Australia
52 D2 **Alozero** Russian Federation
133 E5 **Alpachiri** Argentina
38 E7 **Alpbach** Austria
19 Q14 **Alpe d'Huez** *mt* France
110 C5 **Alpena** Arkansas U.S.A.
94 D1 **Alpena** Michigan U.S.A.
98 H5 **Alpena** South Dakota U.S.A.
94 H8 **Alpena** West Virginia U.S.A.
17 G6 **Alpera** Spain
129 J5 **Alpercatas, Serra das** *mts* Brazil
19 K8 **Alpes-de-Haute-Provence** *dept* France
19 O15 **Alpes du Dauphiné** *mts* France
19 K9 **Alpes-Maritime** *dept* France
46 D2 **Alpet** *mt* Albania
44 C3 **Alpet** *mt* Italy
141 H6 **Alpha** Queensland Australia
99 Q8 **Alpha** Illinois U.S.A.
95 M6 **Alpha** New Jersey U.S.A.
94 J9 **Alpha** Virginia U.S.A.
25 C4 **Alphen** Netherlands
83 H5 **Alphonse I** Seychelles Indian Oc
16 B5 **Alpiarça** Portugal
44 B1 **Alpignano** Italy
103 P8 **Alpine** Arizona U.S.A.
108 D5 **Alpine** Texas U.S.A.
36 E7 **Alpirsbach** Germany
16 B7 **Alportel,S Braz de** Portugal
4 F7 **Alps, The** *mt ra* Europe
47 L5 **Alpu** Turkey
79 G3 **Al Qadmūs** Syria
22 B2 **Alquines** France
79 G4 **Al Quşayr** Syria
84 E3 **Al Quşbāt** Libya
79 G5 **Al Quţayfah** Syria
123 L6 **Alright I** Madeleine Is, Quebec Canada
28 E5 **Alrø** *isld* Denmark
140 D4 **Alroy Downs** N Terr Australia
28 E3 **Als** Denmark
28 D7 **Als** *isld* Denmark
19 K4 **Alsace** *prov* France
118 H7 **Alsask** Saskatchewan Canada
17 F2 **Alsasua** Spain
25 F7 **Alsdorf** Germany
100 B5 **Alsea** Oregon U.S.A.
117 E6 **Alsek** *R* British Columbia Canada
98 H1 **Alsen** North Dakota U.S.A.
36 D4 **Alsenz** Germany
110 F2 **Alsey** Illinois U.S.A.
36 G2 **Alsfeld** Germany
28 D6 **Als Fjord** *inlet* Denmark
36 E4 **Alsheim** Germany
26 J5 **Alsjaur** *L* Sweden
33 P9 **Alsleben** Germany
28 A5 **Alslev** Denmark
28 C6 **Alslev Kro** Denmark
28 F4 **Ålsø** Denmark
26 F6 **Alstahaug** Norway
32 E8 **Alstätte** Germany
95 P3 **Alstead** New Hampshire U.S.A.
26 F6 **Alsten** *isld* Norway
32 M5 **Alster** *R* Germany
13 F4 **Alston** England
27 M15 **Alsunga** Latvia
26 N2 **Alta** Norway
101 L4 **Alta** Montana U.S.A.
26 N2 **Altaelv** *R* Norway
26 N1 **Altafjord** *inlet* Norway
131 D3 **Alta Gracia** Argentina
127 J9 **Altagracia** Venezuela
128 E2 **Altagracia de Orituco** Venezuela
109 L6 **Altair** Texas U.S.A.
128 E7 **Altamachí** Bolivia
112 E6 **Altamaha** *R* Georgia U.S.A.
133 E4 **Alta Melincué** Argentina
129 H4 **Altamira** Brazil
125 N9 **Altamirano** Mexico
102 C4 **Altamont** California U.S.A.
110 H2 **Altamont** Illinois U.S.A.
100 D7 **Altamont** Oregon U.S.A.
98 K5 **Altamont** South Dakota U.S.A.
110 L6 **Altamont** Tennessee U.S.A.
101 P8 **Altamont** Wyoming U.S.A.
144 B6 **Alta, Mt** New Zealand
43 H8 **Altamura** Italy
65 B2 **Altan Bulag** China
56 E6 **Altanbulag** Mongolia
124 D2 **Altar** Mexico
118 G7 **Altario** Alberta Canada
124 F5 **Altata** Mexico
45 R7 **Altavilla Irpina** Italy
99 O6 **Alta Vista** Iowa U.S.A.
107 O3 **Alta Vista** Kansas U.S.A.
94 H9 **Altavista** Virginia U.S.A.
66 D2 **Altay** China
58 C2 **Altay** Mongolia
56 C5 **Altay** *mts* Russian Federation
56 C5 **Altayskiy** Russian Federation
56 B5 **Altayskiy Kray** *terr* Russian Federation
37 L5 **Altdorf** Germany
37 N6 **Altdorf** Niederbayern Germany
41 J4 **Altdorf** Switzerland
17 G6 **Altea** Spain
33 O6 **Alte Elde** *R* Germany
32 H5 **Alte Mellum** Germany
36 B3 **Altenahr** Germany
33 M9 **Altenau** Germany
32 J9 **Altenbeken** Germany
32 F8 **Altenberge** Germany
32 J5 **Altenbruch** Germany
37 N2 **Altenburg** Germany
37 M7 **Altenerding** Germany
36 C4 **Altenglan** Germany
36 E1 **Altenhundem** Germany
36 D2 **Altenkirchen** Germany
38 L6 **Altenmarkt** Ober Österreich Austria
38 H7 **Altenmarkt** Salzburg Austria
37 P6 **Altenmarkt** Germany
33 N6 **Alten Medingen** Germany
36 H6 **Altenstadt** Baden-Württemberg Germany
36 F3 **Altenstadt** Hessen Germany
36 F6 **Altensteig** Germany
33 S5 **Altentreptow** Germany
32 J5 **Altenwalde** Germany
16 B5 **Alter do Chão** Portugal
33 R8 **Altes Lager** Germany
26 K3 **Altevatn** *L* Norway
111 L11 **Altha** Florida U.S.A.
37 J6 **Altheim** Germany
111 E7 **Altheimer** Arkansas U.S.A.
38 K8 **Althofen** Austria
9 G4 **Althorne** England
13 H6 **Althorpe** England
138 D6 **Althorpe Is** South Australia Australia
139 G3 **Altiboullin, L** New South Wales Australia
45 M1 **Altino** Italy
47 H5 **Altınoluk** Turkey
47 L5 **Altıntaş** Turkey
47 K8 **Altınyala** Turkey
33 O6 **Alt-Jabel** Germany
19 K5 **Altkirch** France
33 T7 **Altlandsberg** Germany
36 E5 **Altleiningen** Germany
37 M6 **Altmannstein** Germany
95 L3 **Altmar** New York U.S.A.
33 O7 **Altmark** *reg* Germany
36 H1 **Altmorschen** Germany
37 K5 **Altmühl** *R* Germany
32 K7 **Altmühlen** Germany
15 D2 **Altnaharra** Scotland
111 A10 **Alto** Texas U.S.A.
16 B6 **Alto Alentejo** *prov* Portugal
130 D5 **Alto Araguaia** Brazil
126 G4 **Alto Cedro** Cuba
130 C4 **Alto Coité** Brazil
130 D5 **Alto Garças** Brazil
87 G9 **Alto Molocue** Mozambique
44 D3 **Alto,Monte** Italy
37 L7 **Altomünster** Germany
9 F5 **Alton** England
102 A1 **Alton** California U.S.A.
110 F3 **Alton** Illinois U.S.A.
95 L3 **Alton** New York U.S.A.
103 M4 **Alton** Utah U.S.A.
118 D1 **Altona** Manitoba Canada
99 Q8 **Altona** Illinois U.S.A.
101 P9 **Altonah** Utah U.S.A.
138 E2 **Alton Downs** South Australia Australia
141 J8 **Alton Oilfield** Queensland Australia
111 K7 **Altoona** Alabama U.S.A.
113 F9 **Altoona** Florida U.S.A.
107 P4 **Altoona** Kansas U.S.A.
94 J6 **Altoona** Pennsylvania U.S.A.
128 G8 **Alto Paraguay** *dept* Paraguay
130 C9 **Alto Paraná** *dept* Paraguay
129 J5 **Alto Parnaiba** Brazil
45 J4 **Altopascio** Italy
129 H7 **Alto Sucuriú** Brazil
38 G5 **Altötting** Germany
129 J4 **Alto Turi** Brazil
130 C10 **Alto Uruguai** Brazil
126 A1 **Alto Vista** *hill* Aruba W Indies
13 F6 **Altrincham** England
33 R7 **Altruppin** Germany
33 T8 **Alt-Schadow** Germany
54 F4 **Altukhovo** Russian Federation
78 K4 **Altun Köprü** Iraq
66 C4 **Altun Shan** *mts* China
99 O5 **Altura** Minnesota U.S.A.
100 E8 **Alturas** California U.S.A.
113 F10 **Alturas** Florida U.S.A.
107 L7 **Altus** Oklahoma U.S.A.
107 L6 **Altus Res** Oklahoma U.S.A.
41 M2 **Altusried** Germany
36 B6 **Altwiller** France
57 C2 **Altynasar** Kazakhstan
55 D3 **Altynay** Russian Federation
53 G10 **Altyn-Khutsan, Ozero** Russian Federation
52 C6 **Alūksne** Latvia
28 D4 **Alum** Denmark
9 E6 **Alum Bay** England
133 C5 **Aluminé** Argentina
26 M6 **Ålund** Sweden
27 K11 **Alunda** Sweden
103 K6 **Alunite** Nevada U.S.A.
76 C3 **Alur** India
53 D11 **Alushta** Ukraine
17 F4 **Alustante** Spain
83 J11 **Alutgama** Sri Lanka
83 K9 **Alut Oya** Sri Lanka
Aluva *see* **Alwaye**
84 E4 **Al 'Uwaynāt** Libya
16 B4 **Alva** *R* Portugal
12 E1 **Alva** Scotland
113 F11 **Alva** Florida U.S.A.
94 D10 **Alva** Kentucky U.S.A.
107 M5 **Alva** Oklahoma U.S.A.
98 B5 **Alva** Wyoming U.S.A.
16 B7 **Alvalade** Portugal
125 M8 **Alvarado** Mexico
109 K3 **Alvarado** Texas U.S.A.
128 F4 **Alvaraes** Brazil
26 E9 **Alvdal** Norway
118 L6 **Alvena** Saskatchewan Canada
33 O8 **Alvensleben** Germany
32 K8 **Alverdissen** Germany
117 D5 **Alverstone Mt** Alaska/Yukon Terr U.S.A./Canada
27 A11 **Alversund** Norway
27 G15 **Alvesta** Sweden
8 D4 **Alveston** England
27 G10 **Älvho** Sweden
110 J1 **Alvin** Illinois U.S.A.
109 M6 **Alvin** Texas U.S.A.
99 S4 **Alvin** Wisconsin U.S.A.
45 P6 **Alvito** Italy
16 B6 **Alvito** Portugal
27 J11 **Älvkarleby** Sweden
98 K9 **Alvo** Nebraska U.S.A.
109 K2 **Alvord** Texas U.S.A.
100 G7 **Alvord L** Oregon U.S.A.
26 F10 **Älvros** Sweden
27 F14 **Älvsborg** *reg* Sweden
26 M6 **Älvsbyn** Sweden
27 F14 **Älvsered** Sweden
99 M2 **Alvwood** Minnesota U.S.A.
78 H6 **Al Wadyān** *reg* Iraq/Saudi Arabia
84 G4 **Al Wāḩah** Libya
87 E12 **Alwal Nth** S Africa
74 G5 **Alwar** India
76 C5 **Alwaye** India
13 F3 **Alwinton** England
6 M2 **Alwyn** *oil rig* North Sea
110 C7 **Aly** Arkansas U.S.A.
140 D2 **Alyangula** N Terr Australia
51 N2 **Alyaskitovyy** Russian Federation
55 E2 **Alymka** *R* Russian Federation
15 E4 **Alyth** Scotland
31 P1 **Alytus** Lithuania
38 G5 **Alz** *R* Germany
98 B4 **Alzada** Montana U.S.A.
36 G3 **Alzenau** Germany
22 L4 **Alzette** *R* Luxembourg
36 E4 **Alzey** Germany
128 F2 **Amacuro Delta** Venezuela
140 B6 **Amadeus,L** N Terr Australia
86 F4 **Amadi** Sudan
115 M4 **Amadjuak L** Northwest Territories Canada
60 J11 **Amagasaki** Japan
29 K5 **Amager** *isld* Denmark
60 D12 **Amagi** Japan
61 N11 **Amagi-san** *mt* Japan
22 G5 **Amagne** France
21 L4 **Amain, Mt. d'** France
116 F9 **Amak I** Alaska U.S.A.
60 C13 **Amakusa-nada** *sea* Japan
60 D13 **Amakusa-Shimo-shima** *isld* Japan
60 D13 **Amakusa-shotō** *islds* Japan
84 G4 **Āmāl** Libya
27 F12 **Åmål** Sweden
76 F2 **Amalapuram** India
43 F8 **Amalfi** Italy
46 E7 **Amaliás** Greece
16 C5 **Amalia,Sta** Spain
74 F8 **Amalner** India
129 G8 **Amambai** Brazil
130 C8 **Amambaí, Serra de** *mts* Brazil/Paraguay
130 C8 **Amambay** *dept* Paraguay
133 F2 **Amambay, Sa. de** *mts* Brazil/Paraguay
128 F4 **Amaná,L** Brazil
40 D2 **Amance** France
40 D3 **Amancey** France
94 E7 **Amanda** Ohio U.S.A.
42 E6 **Amandola** Italy
55 E6 **Amangel'dy** Kazakhstan
55 D4 **Amankaragay** Kazakhstan
60 J10 **Amano-hashidate** *inlet* Japan
43 G9 **Amantea** Italy
55 E5 **Amantogay** Kazakhstan
87 F12 **Amanzimtoti** S Africa
129 H3 **Amapa** Brazil
78 L6 **Amārah, Al** Iraq
88 F9 **Amaramba,L** Mozambique
129 K5 **Amarante** Brazil
119 T8 **Amaranth** Manitoba Canada
68 C2 **Amarapura** Burma
102 H5 **Amargosa Ra** California U.S.A.
106 D5 **Amarilla** New Mexico U.S.A.
108 C8 **Amarillo** Texas U.S.A.
131 B4 **Amarillo,Cerro** *pk* Argentina
75 J7 **Amarkantak** India
129 J6 **Amaro Leite** Brazil
140 E6 **Amaroo,L** Queensland Australia
61 N7 **Amarume** Japan
80 D8 **'Amasa** Jordan
99 S3 **Amasa** Michigan U.S.A.
45 O7 **Amaseno** Italy
85 B3 **Amasine** Western Sahara
78 D1 **Amasra** Turkey
78 F1 **Amasya** Turkey
138 B2 **Amata** South Australia Australia
128 E4 **Amataura** Brazil
125 N9 **Amatenango** Mexico
87 F11 **Amatikulu** S Africa
124 H7 **Amatitán** Mexico
125 L8 **Amatlan** Mexico
124 G7 **Amatlán de Cañas** Mexico
61 O10 **Amatsu-Kominato** Japan
22 J2 **Amay** Belgium
Amazon *R see* **Amazonas** *R*
119 M7 **Amazon** Saskatchewan Canada
128 E4 **Amazonas** *state* Brazil
128 D4 **Amazonas** *div* Colombia
128 C5 **Amazonas** *dept* Peru
129 H4 **Amazonas** *R* S America
128 E3 **Amazonas** *state* Venezuela
110 B2 **Amazonia** Missouri U.S.A.
129 J3 **Amazon,Mouths of the** Brazil
80 C7 **Amazya** Israel
74 E1 **Amb** Pakistan
74 G9 **Ambajogai** India
74 G3 **Ambala** India
83 J11 **Ambalangodo** Sri Lanka
87 H12 **Ambalavao** Madagascar
140 C6 **Ambalindum** N Terr Australia
85 G8 **Ambam** Cameroon
86 G3 **Āmba Maryam** Ethiopia
83 K10 **Amban Ganga** *R* Sri Lanka
87 H10 **Ambanje** Madagascar
70 N9 **Ambarawa** Java
51 Q2 **Ambarchik** Russian Federation
18 E8 **Ambarès et Lagrave** France
52 D2 **Ambarnyy** Russian Federation
141 H7 **Ambathala** Queensland Australia
128 C4 **Ambato** Ecuador
87 H11 **Ambato-Boeny** Madagascar
87 H11 **Ambatolampy** Madagascar
131 C2 **Ambato,Sa** *ra* Argentina
18 F7 **Ambazac** France
107 N6 **Amber** Oklahoma U.S.A.
100 H2 **Amber** Washington U.S.A.
116 J8 **Amber B** Alaska U.S.A.
37 M5 **Amberg** Germany
99 T4 **Amberg** Wisconsin U.S.A.
9 E1 **Ambergate** England
127 H4 **Ambergris Cays** *islds* Turks & Caicos Is
19 O13 **Ambérieu-en-Bugey** France
120 J8 **Amberley** Ontario Canada
144 D5 **Amberley** New Zealand
22 K3 **Amberloup** Belgium
21 L8 **Amberre** France
18 H7 **Ambert** France
18 G9 **Ambialet** France
85 B6 **Ambidédi** Mali
75 K7 **Ambikapur** India
71 E4 **Ambil** *isld* Philippines
21 L7 **Ambillou** France
21 K7 **Ambillou-Château** France
87 H10 **Ambilobe** Madagascar
117 H7 **Ambition,Mt** British Columbia Canada
21 P3 **Amblainville** France
13 G3 **Amble** England
116 J3 **Ambler** *R* Alaska U.S.A.
13 F5 **Ambleside** England
22 B2 **Ambleteuse** France
22 L3 **Amblève** Belgium
87 H12 **Amboasary** Madagascar
87 H11 **Ambodifototra** Madagascar
87 H12 **Ambohimahasoa** Madagascar
21 N7 **Amboise** France
20 E6 **Ambon** France
136 F2 **Ambon** Moluccas Indonesia
87 H12 **Amborompotsy** Madagascar
86 G6 **Amboseli, L** Kenya
87 H12 **Ambositra** Madagascar
87 H13 **Ambovombe** Madagascar
103 J7 **Amboy** California U.S.A.
99 R8 **Amboy** Illinois U.S.A.
95 N6 **Amboy,S** New Jersey U.S.A.
21 O8 **Ambrault** France
94 G6 **Ambridge** Pennsylvania U.S.A.
21 J5 **Ambrières-les-Vallées** France
87 B7 **Ambriz** Angola
19 O12 **Ambronay** France
112 D6 **Ambrose** Georgia U.S.A.
98 C1 **Ambrose** North Dakota U.S.A.
137 O5 **Ambrym** *isld* Vanuatu
71 E2 **Ambuklao Dam** Luzon Philippines
71 K9 **Ambulombo Vol** Indonesia
70 O10 **Ambulu** Java
70 O9 **Ambunten** Java
76 D4 **Ambur** India
141 J7 **Amby** Queensland Australia
27 C12 **Åmdal** Norway
86 D3 **Am Dam** Chad
85 E4 **Amded** *watercourse* Algeria
50 F2 **Amderma** Russian Federation
75 O2 **Amdo** China
86 G3 **Amedamit** *mt* Ethiopia
102 D1 **Amedee** California U.S.A.
25 E2 **Ameland** *isld* Netherlands
42 E6 **Amelia** Italy
98 H7 **Amelia** Nebraska U.S.A.
94 K9 **Amelia** Virginia U.S.A.
113 F7 **Amelia I** Florida U.S.A.
32 M6 **Amelinghausen** Germany
43 H9 **Amendolara** Italy
67 A5 **Ameng** China
17 J2 **Amer** Spain
102 D2 **American** *R* California U.S.A.
130 F8 **Americana** Brazil
101 N7 **American Falls** Idaho U.S.A.
103 N1 **American Fork** Utah U.S.A.
138 E6 **American River** South Australia Australia
134 E1 **American Samoa** *islds* Pacific Oc
113 F13 **American Shoal** *lighthouse* Florida U.S.A.
112 C5 **Americus** Georgia U.S.A.
25 D4 **Amerongen** Netherlands
25 D4 **Amersfoort** Netherlands
9 F4 **Amersham** England
143 B9 **Amery** W Australia Australia
99 O4 **Amery** Wisconsin U.S.A.
146 J11 **Amery Ice Shelf** Antarctica
99 N7 **Ames** Iowa U.S.A.
98 K8 **Ames** Nebraska U.S.A.
107 M5 **Ames** Oklahoma U.S.A.
118 E3 **Amesbury** Alberta Canada
9 E5 **Amesbury** England
95 R4 **Amesbury** Massachusetts U.S.A.
118 J1 **Amesdale** Ontario Canada
120 F3 **Ameson** Ontario Canada
146 B9 **Ames Range** *mts* Antarctica
94 F7 **Amesville** Ohio U.S.A.
7 L9 **Amethyst** *oil rig* North Sea
122 J8 **Amet Sound** Nova Scotia Canada
46 F6 **Amfiklia** Greece
46 E6 **Amfilokhia** Greece
46 F4 **Amfipolis** Greece
46 E6 **Ámfissa** Greece
20 H3 **Amfreville** France
21 M3 **Amfreville-la-Campagne** France
51 N2 **Amga** Russian Federation
51 M3 **Amga** *R* Russian Federation
58 G2 **Amgalang Bulag** China
51 N4 **Amgu** Russian Federation
59 L2 **Amgu** Russian Federation
86 D3 **Am Guéréda** Chad
85 F3 **Amguid** Algeria
59 K1 **Amgun'** *R* Russian Federation
86 G3 **Amhara** *reg* Ethiopia
Amherst *see* **Kyaikkami**
122 H8 **Amherst** Nova Scotia Canada
106 H1 **Amherst** Colorado U.S.A.
95 T2 **Amherst** Maine U.S.A.
95 P4 **Amherst** Massachusetts U.S.A.
98 G9 **Amherst** Nebraska U.S.A.
95 Q4 **Amherst** New Hampshire U.S.A.
94 E5 **Amherst** Ohio U.S.A.
98 J4 **Amherst** South Dakota U.S.A.
94 H9 **Amherst** Virginia U.S.A.
120 G10 **Amherstburg** Ontario Canada
94 F9 **Amherstdale** West Virginia U.S.A.
123 K6 **Amherst I** Madeleine Is, Quebec Canada
121 O8 **Amherst I** Ontario Canada
99 R5 **Amherst Junction** Wisconsin U.S.A.
142 F4 **Amherst, Mt** W Australia Australia
42 D6 **Amiata,Monte** Italy
98 C3 **Amidon** North Dakota U.S.A.
141 K8 **Amiens** Queensland Australia
21 P2 **Amiens** France
78 H5 **Amij,Wadi** Iraq
46 E4 **Amindaion** Greece
73 L6 **Amindivi Is** Lakshadweep Indian Oc
60 H10 **Amino** Japan
87 C10 **Aminuis** Namibia
79 F4 **Amioun** Lebanon
80 F1 **'Amir** Israel
83 H5 **Amirante Is** Indian Oc
118 F6 **Amisk** Alberta Canada
119 P4 **Amisk L** Saskatchewan Canada
106 G6 **Amistad** New Mexico U.S.A.
108 G106 **Amistad Nat. Recreation Area** Texas U.S.A.
108 F6 **Amistad Res** Mexico
111 F11 **Amite** Louisiana U.S.A.
111 C7 **Amity** Arkansas U.S.A.
95 O6 **Amityville** Long I, New York U.S.A.
75 L5 **Amlekhganj** Nepal
27 C13 **Amli** Norway
8 B1 **Amlwch** Wales
80 G6 **'Ammān** Jordan
8 C4 **Ammanford** Wales
26 H5 **Ammarfjallet** *mt* Sweden
26 H6 **Ammarnäs** Sweden
140 D5 **Ammaroo** N Terr Australia
115 Q4 **Ammassalik** Greenland
28 E4 **Ammelhede** Denmark
33 P10 **Ammendorf** Germany
32 L9 **Ammensen** Germany
41 O2 **Ammer** *R* Germany
41 N2 **Ammer Gebirge** *mt* Germany
32 G6 **Ammerland** *reg* Germany
41 O2 **Ammerland** Germany
116 R2 **Ammerman Mt** Yukon Territory Canada
37 K5 **Ammerndorf** Germany
41 O1 **Ammer See** *L* Germany
80 F2 **'Ammi 'ad** Israel
101 O6 **Ammon** Idaho U.S.A.
68 G5 **Amnat Charoen** Thailand
Amne Machin *see* **A'nyêmaqên Shan**
80 F2 **Amnun** Israel
77 C1 **Āmol** Iran
130 B6 **Amolar** Brazil
36 F2 **Amöneburg** Germany
36 G4 **Amorbach** Germany
131 F2 **Amores** *R* Argentina
47 H8 **Amorgós** *isld* Greece
107 M5 **Amorita** Oklahoma U.S.A.
111 H8 **Amory** Mississippi U.S.A.
121 M4 **Amos** Quebec Canada
103 J8 **Amos** California U.S.A.
28 G5 **Åmose Å** *R* Denmark
27 H11 **Åmot** Sweden
27 D12 **Åmot Akershus** Norway
27 C12 **Åmotsdal** Norway
85 B3 **Amott** Morocco
Amoy *see* **Xiamen**
70 D5 **Ampah** Kalimantan
70 G5 **Ampana** Sulawesi Indonesia
87 G12 **Ampanihy** Madagascar
130 F8 **Amparo** Brazil
87 H11 **Ampasimanolotra** Madagascar
128 D7 **Ampato, Cord. de** *mts* Peru
70 Q10 **Ampenan** Indonesia
37 M7 **Amper** *R* Germany
37 N7 **Ampfing** Germany
103 O9 **Amphitheater** Arizona U.S.A.
70 G5 **Ampibaku** Sulawesi
85 F7 **Ampier** Nigeria
13 G5 **Ampleforth** England
70 G5 **Ampoa** Sulawesi Indonesia
17 H4 **Amposta** Spain
9 F3 **Ampthill** England
19 N14 **Ampuis** France
17 J2 **Ampurdán** *dist* Spain
80 D2 **'Amqa** Israel
122 E5 **Amqui** Quebec Canada
74 G8 **Amravati** India
74 D8 **Amreli** India
74 F3 **Amritsar** India
30 D1 **Amrum** *isld* Germany
26 K7 **Åmsele** Sweden
38 J7 **Am Stein** *mt* Austria
25 C4 **Amstelveen** Netherlands
24 **Amsterdam** *conurbation* Netherlands
25 C4 **Amsterdam** Netherlands
113 C7 **Amsterdam** Georgia U.S.A.
101 L7 **Amsterdam** Idaho U.S.A.
95 N4 **Amsterdam** New York U.S.A.
94 G6 **Amsterdam** Ohio U.S.A.
81 E9 **Amsterdam, I** Indian Oc
38 L5 **Amstetten** Austria
27 F12 **Ämtervik, V** Sweden
86 D3 **Am Timan** Chad
28 B2 **Amtoft** Denmark
41 L2 **Amtzell** Germany
127 J9 **Amuay** Venezuela
57 D5 **Amu-Dar'ya** Turkmenistan
57 B4 **Amudar'ya** *R* Turkmenistan/Uzbekistan
147 H5 **Amund Ringness I** Northwest Territories Canada
146 K9 **Amundsen B** Antarctica
146 D9 **Amundsen Glacier** Antarctica
147 J1 **Amundsen Gulf** Northwest Territories Canada
146 H13 **Amundsen, Mt** Antarctica
146 E9 **Amundsen-Scott** *U.S.A. Base* Antarctica
146 A8 **Amundsen Sea** Antarctica
147 J2 **Amundsen Trough** Arctic Oc
27 H10 **Amungen** *L* Sweden
70 D6 **Amuntai** Kalimantan
59 L1 **Amur** *R* Russian Federation
71 J4 **Amurang** Sulawesi Indonesia
71 J4 **Amurang Teluk** *B* Sulawesi Indonesia
144 D5 **Amuri Pass** New Zealand
17 F1 **Amurrio** Spain
59 L1 **Amursk** Russian Federation
59 J1 **Amurskaya Oblast'** *prov* Russian Federation
55 C4 **Amurskiy** Russian Federation
46 E6 **Amvrakía, L** Greece
46 D6 **Amvrakikós Kólpos** *G* Greece
54 K9 **Amvrosiyevka** Ukraine
107 K3 **Amy** Kansas U.S.A.
56 D4 **Amyl** *R* Russian Federation
120 F4 **Amyot** Ontario Canada
68 B3 **An** Burma
70 G6 **Anabanua** Sulawesi
138 F5 **Ana Branch** *R* New South Wales Australia
80 D4 **Anabta** Jordan
102 E7 **Anacapa Is** California U.S.A.
45 Q8 **Anacapri** Italy
127 M10 **Anaco** Venezuela
111 C10 **Anacoco** Louisiana U.S.A.
101 N3 **Anaconda** Montana U.S.A.
101 M4 **Anaconda Range** Montana U.S.A.
100 C1 **Anacortes** Washington U.S.A.
107 M6 **Anadarko** Oklahoma U.S.A.
130 H10 **Anadia** Brazil
16 B4 **Anadia** Portugal
78 F1 **Anadolu Dağlari** *mt* Turkey
47 N10 **Anadolufeneri** Turkey
47 N10 **Anadoluhlsarı** Turkey
51 R2 **Anadyr** Russian Federation
51 R2 **Anadyrskoye Ploskogor'ye** *tableland* Russian Federation
47 H8 **Anáfi** *isld* Greece
26 F9 **Anafjället** *mt* Sweden
47 H8 **Anafópoulo** *isld* Greece
130 H4 **Anagé** Brazil
45 O6 **Anagni** Italy
102 F8 **Anaheim** California U.S.A.
117 L9 **Anahim Lake** British Columbia Canada
135 O1 **Anahola** Hawaiian Is
125 J4 **Anáhuac** Mexico
111 B12 **Anahuac** Texas U.S.A.
102 R11 **Anahulu** *R* Hawaiian Is
76 C5 **Anaimalai Hills** India
75 K10 **Anakapalle** India
141 J6 **Anakie** Queensland Australia
116 M2 **Anaktuvuk Pass** Alaska U.S.A.
87 H10 **Analalava** Madagascar
128 F4 **Anama** Brazil
119 T7 **Anama Bay** Manitoba Canada
126 E4 **Ana Maria, Cayos de** *islds* Cuba
69 G11 **Anambas, Kepulauan** *isld* Indonesia
61 L8 **Anamizu** Japan
98 F2 **Anamoose** North Dakota U.S.A.
129 G3 **Anamu** *R* Brazil
78 D3 **Anamur** Turkey
60 H12 **Anan** Japan
46 G8 **Anánes** *isld* Greece
71 J7 **Anano** *isld* Indonesia
76 C3 **Anantapur** India
74 F2 **Anantnag** Kashmir
48 M3 **Anan'yev** Ukraine
53 E11 **Anapa** Russian Federation
43 G11 **Anapo** *R* Sicily
129 J7 **Anápolis** Brazil
129 H4 **Anapú** *R* Brazil
77 D4 **Anār** Iran
77 C3 **Anārak** Iran
77 G3 **Anār Darrah** Afghanistan
26 F8 **Anaris Fjällen** *mt* Sweden
26 O3 **Anarjokka** *R* Norway/Finland
127 L5 **Añasco** Puerto Rico
26 M7 **Ånåset** Sweden
113 F8 **Anastasia I** Florida U.S.A.
78 D2 **Anatolia** *reg* Turkey
46 E3 **Anatoliki Makedhonia Kai Thráki** *admin region* Greece
137 O6 **Anatom** *isld* Vanuatu
100 H3 **Anatone** Washington U.S.A.
80 E6 **'Anatot** Jordan
29 O7 **Änättijärvi** *L* Finland
131 E2 **Añatuya** Argentina
128 F3 **Anauá** *R* Brazil
78 H5 **Anbār, Al** *prov* Iraq
69 G8 **An Bien** Vietnam
128 C5 **Ancash** *dept* Peru
9 F2 **Ancaster** England
101 O4 **Anceney** Montana U.S.A.
21 H7 **Ancenis** France
21 L7 **Anché** France
130 H7 **Anchieta** Brazil
106 E8 **Ancho** New Mexico U.S.A.
116 N6 **Anchorage** Alaska U.S.A.
94 B8 **Anchorage** Kentucky U.S.A.
94 E4 **Anchor Bay** Michigan U.S.A.
144 A6 **Anchor I** New Zealand
116 M7 **Anchor Point** Alaska U.S.A.
127 J2 **Anchovy** Jamaica
65 C5 **Anci** China
121 T6 **Ancienne Lorette** *airport* Quebec Canada
113 E9 **Anclote Keys** *islds* Florida U.S.A.
128 E7 **Ancohuma** *mt* Bolivia
128 C6 **Ancón** Peru
45 O4 **Ancona** Italy
128 C3 **Ancon de Sardinas B.de** Ecuador
95 O4 **Ancram** New York U.S.A.
22 D4 **Ancre** *R* France
13 F2 **Ancroft** England
13 F3 **Ancrum** Scotland
88 G8 **Ancuabe** Mozambique
133 C6 **Ancud** Chile
133 C5 **Andacollo** Argentina
140 D7 **Andado** N Terr Australia
128 D6 **Andahuaylas** Peru
107 N4 **Andale** Kansas U.S.A.
133 D3 **Andalgala** Argentina
26 C9 **Åndalsnes** Norway
16 D7 **Andalucia** *reg* Spain
111 K10 **Andalusia** Alabama U.S.A.
68 A6 **Andaman Islands** Bay of Bengal
138 D4 **Andamooka** South Australia Australia
52 G5 **Andanga** Russian Federation
77 L2 **Andarāb** Afghanistan
129 K6 **Andaria** Brazil
79 H3 **Andarīn, Al** Syria
67 B5 **Ande** China
86 H2 **Andeba Ye Midir Zerf Ch'af** *C* Ethiopia
41 K4 **Andeer** Switzerland
52 H1 **Andeg** Russian Federation
21 N3 **Andelle** *R* France
19 J4 **Andelot** France
21 N3 **Andelys,les** France
22 J3 **Andenne** Belgium
85 E5 **Anderamboukane** Mali
26 J2 **Ånderdalen Nat. Park** Norway
41 J4 **Andermatt** Switzerland
36 C3 **Andernach** Germany
36 C3 **Andernach-Land** Germany
57 F6 **Anderov** Tajikistan
26 L7 **Andersfors** Sweden
114 G4 **Anderson** *R* Northwest Territories Canada
100 C9 **Anderson** California U.S.A.
94 B6 **Anderson** Indiana U.S.A.
110 B5 **Anderson** Missouri U.S.A.
112 E3 **Anderson** South Carolina U.S.A.
139 H8 **Anderson Bay** Tasmania Australia
68 A6 **Anderson I** Andaman Is
100 F7 **Anderson L** Oregon U.S.A.
101 K6 **Anderson Ranch Res** Idaho U.S.A.
112 C5 **Andersonville** Georgia U.S.A.
110 L2 **Andersonville** Indiana U.S.A.
27 G14 **Anderstorp** Sweden
95 N4 **Andes** New York U.S.A.
133 D3 **Andes, Cordillera de los** *mts* S America
98 H6 **Andes,L** South Dakota U.S.A.
87 H11 **Andevoranto** Madagascar
26 H2 **Andfjord** *inlet* Norway
76 D2 **Andhra Pradesh** *prov* India
17 F2 **Andía,Sierra de** *mt* Spain
83 J10 **Andigama** Sri Lanka
46 F9 **Andikithira** *isld* Greece
87 H11 **Andilamena** Madagascar
46 G8 **Andímilos** *isld* Greece
46 G7 **Andipáros** *isld* Greece
47 P13 **Andipaxoi** *isld* Greece
47 H6 **Andipsara** *isld* Greece
78 F3 **Andırın** Turkey
66 C4 **Andirlangar** China
47 H5 **Ándissa** Greece
53 G12 **Andiyskoye Koysu** *R* Russian Federation
57 F4 **Andizhan** Uzbekistan
77 J1 **Andkhvoy** Afghanistan
36 C7 **Andlau** France
87 H10 **Andoany** Madagascar
40 F1 **Andolsheim** France
52 E4 **Andomskiy Pogost** Russian Federation
65 G6 **Andong** S Korea
65 D7 **Andongwei** China
141 F1 **Andoom** Queensland Australia
44 D4 **Andora** Italy
26 J3 **Andörja** *isld* Norway
17 J2 **Andorra** *princ* Pyrenees
17 H2 **Andorra la Vella** Andorra
21 J5 **Andouille** France
9 E5 **Andover** England
95 R2 **Andover** Maine U.S.A.
95 Q3 **Andover** New Hampshire U.S.A.
95 N6 **Andover** New Jersey U.S.A.
94 K4 **Andover** New York U.S.A.
94 G5 **Andover** Ohio U.S.A.
98 J4 **Andover** South Dakota U.S.A.
9 E4 **Andoversford** England
26 H2 **Andöya** *isld* Norway
130 D7 **Andradina** Brazil
17 J5 **Andraix** Majorca
116 O10 **Andreanof Is** Aleutian Is
52 D6 **Andreapol'** Russian Federation
12 D5 **Andreas** I of Man U.K.
79 E3 **Andreas,C** Cyprus
87 H11 **Andreba** Madagascar
138 F2 **Andree,L** South Australia Australia
115 R3 **Andrée Land** Greenland
130 G7 **Andrel lándia** Brazil
31 M4 **Andrespol** Poland
118 E5 **Andrew** Alberta Canada
6 L4 **Andrew** *oil rig* North Sea
99 Q7 **Andrew** Iowa U.S.A.
68 B3 **Andrew B** Burma
143 E10 **Andrew, Mt** W Australia Australia
94 B6 **Andrews** Indiana U.S.A.
98 C7 **Andrews** Nebraska U.S.A.
112 D2 **Andrews** North Carolina U.S.A.
100 G7 **Andrews** Oregon U.S.A.
112 H4 **Andrews** South Carolina U.S.A.
108 E3 **Andrews** Texas U.S.A.
53 H8 **Andreyevka** Russian Federation
54 N1 **Andreyevo** Russian Federation
53 D9 **Andreyevo-Ivanovka** Ukraine
55 E2 **Andreyevskoye, Oz** *L* Russian Federation
53 D8 **Andreykovichi** Russian Federation
43 G7 **Andria** Italy
46 D2 **Andrijevica** Montenegro Yugoslavia
46 E7 **Andrítsaina** Greece
106 G4 **Andrix** Colorado U.S.A.
87 G12 **Androka** Madagascar
116 G9 **Andronica I** Alaska U.S.A.
Andropov *see* **Rybinsk**
126 E2 **Andros** *isld* Bahamas
46 G7 **Ándros** *isld* Greece
95 R2 **Androscogg** *R* New Hamps/Maine U.S.A.
53 G7 **Androsovka** Russian Federation
126 F2 **Andros Town** Andros Bahamas
73 L6 **Androth I** Lakshadweep Indian Oc
76 A5 **Āndrott** *isld* Indian Oc
53 C8 **Andrushevka** Ukraine
31 L6 **Andrychów** Poland
55 D2 **Andryushino** Russian Federation
26 K2 **Andselv** Norway
16 E6 **Andújar** Spain
87 C8 **Andulo** Angola
18 H8 **Anduze** France
27 G14 **Aneby** Sweden
143 G6 **Anec, L** W Australia Australia
131 B8 **Anecón Grande** *pk* Argentina
85 E5 **Anefis** Mali
113 L7 **Anegada** *isld* Virgin Is
133 E6 **Anegado, B** Argentina
85 E7 **Anécho** Togo
118 K7 **Anerley** Saskatchewan Canada
118 K9 **Aneroid** Saskatchewan Canada
21 N4 **Anet** France
98 J2 **Aneta** North Dakota U.S.A.
67 E3 **Anfu** China
140 B3 **Angalarri** *R* N Terr Australia
133 C2 **Angamos, Pta** *C* Chile
125 J8 **Angangue** Mexico
59 H2 **Ang'angxi** China
56 D2 **Angara** *R* Russian Federation
147 K8 **Angara Basin** Arctic Oc
56 F4 **Angarsk** Russian Federation
140 B7 **Angas Downs** N Terr Australia
142 G6 **Angas Ra** W Australia Australia
138 E5 **Angaston** South Australia Australia
71 E3 **Angat** Luzon Philippines
130 E8 **Angatuba** Brazil
26 H9 **Ånge** Sweden
26 H10 **Ängebo** Sweden
124 C3 **Angel de la Guarda** *isld* Mexico
71 E3 **Angeles** Luzon Philippines
128 F2 **Angel Falls** *waterfall* Venezuela
27 F15 **Ängelholm** Sweden
94 J4 **Angelica** New York U.S.A.
111 B10 **Angelina** *R* Texas U.S.A.
28 D7 **Angeln** *reg* Germany
43 G8 **Angelo de Lom,S** Italy
27 H12 **Ängelsberg** Sweden
102 D3 **Angels Camp** California U.S.A.
38 N7 **Anger** Austria
41 J6 **Angera** Italy
26 J8 **Ångermanälven** *R* Sweden
26 K9 **Ångermanälven** *isld* Sweden
32 E10 **Angermund** Germany
21 J7 **Angers** France
26 G10 **Ängersjö** Sweden
21 O5 **Angerville** France
26 M5 **Ängeså** Sweden
26 N5 **Ängesan** *R* Sweden
26 L8 **Ängesön** *isld* Sweden
70 E5 **Anggana** Kalimantan
70 G7 **Anggowala, Bk** *mt* Sulawesi Indonesia
45 M4 **Anghiari** Italy
112 J2 **Angier** North Carolina U.S.A.
115 K5 **Angikuni L** Northwest Territories Canada
8 A4 **Angle** Wales
144 A7 **Anglem, Mt** New Zealand
120 D4 **Angler** Ontario Canada
139 G7 **Anglesea** Victoria Australia
Anglesey *co see* **Gwynedd**
8 B1 **Anglesey** *isld* Wales
21 M8 **Angles sur-l'Anglin** France
18 D9 **Anglet** France
109 M6 **Angleton** Texas U.S.A.
118 J7 **Anglia** Saskatchewan Canada
21 L8 **Angliers** France
21 N8 **Anglin** *R* France
Angmagssalik *see* **Ammassalik**
88 G10 **Angoche** Mozambique
77 E6 **Angohrān** Iran
131 A6 **Angol** Chile
87 C8 **Angola** *rep* Africa
94 B5 **Angola** Indiana U.S.A.
94 H4 **Angola** New York U.S.A.
90 K11 **Angola Basin** Atlantic Oc
112 K3 **Angola Swamp** North Carolina U.S.A.
117 F7 **Angoon** Alaska U.S.A.
98 C8 **Angora** Nebraska U.S.A.
124 E5 **Angostura** Mexico
125 J6 **Angostura** Mexico
128 D3 **Angostura I, Salto** *cataract* Colombia
124 E2 **Angostura, Presa de la** *res* Mexico
125 N9 **Angostura, Psa. de la** *res* Mexico
98 C6 **Angostura Reserve** South Dakota U.S.A.
18 F7 **Angoulême** France
18 F7 **Angoumois** *prov* France
129 K8 **Angra dos Reis** Brazil
45 R8 **Angri** Italy
21 J6 **Angrie** France
37 L2 **Angstedt-Gräfinau** Germany
68 E5 **Ang Thong** Thailand
17 G2 **Angués** Spain
126 E3 **Anguila Isles** Bahamas
127 N5 **Anguilla** *isld* Lesser Antilles
45 L1 **Anguillara Ven** Italy
123 N6 **Anguille, C** Newfoundland Canada
86 E6 **Angumu** Zaire
65 C5 **Anguo** China
140 D2 **Angurugu** Northern Territory Australia
Angus *co see* **Tayside** *reg*
98 K1 **Angus** Minnesota U.S.A.
119 Q8 **Angusville** Manitoba Canada
88 C10 **Angwa** *R* Zimbabwe
129 H8 **Anhandui** *R* Brazil
28 H3 **Anholt** *isld* Denmark
28 H3 **Anholt** Denmark
67 D2 **Anhua** China
58 G5 **Anhui** *prov* China
130 C5 **Anhumas** Brazil
Anhwei *prov see* **Anhui** *prov*
61 O5 **Aniai** Japan
116 H6 **Aniak** Alaska U.S.A.
116 H8 **Aniakchak Nat Mon and Preserve** Alaska U.S.A.
116 H8 **Aniakchak Vol. Crater** Alaska U.S.A.
80 F2 **Ani'am** Syria
22 E3 **Aniche** France
130 E5 **Anicuns** Brazil
47 H8 **Ánidhros** *isld* Greece
85 E7 **Anié** Togo
45 N6 **Aniene** *R* Italy
18 E10 **Anie, Pic d'** *mt* Spain/France
55 D5 **Anikhovka** Russian Federation
52 F5 **Anikovo** Russian Federation
106 C4 **Animas** *R* Colorado U.S.A.
106 B10 **Animas** New Mexico U.S.A.
124 C3 **Animas,Pta Las** *C* Mexico
68 C5 **Anin** Burma
48 G5 **Anina** Romania
103 M6 **Anita** Arizona U.S.A.
99 M8 **Anita** Iowa U.S.A.
71 G5 **Anitaguipan Pt** Philippines
130 E10 **Anitápolis** Brazil

116 J2 **Aniuk** *R* Alaska U.S.A.
59 M2 **Aniva, Zaliv** *B* Russian Federation
99 R4 **Aniwa** Wisconsin U.S.A.
22 E4 **Anizy-le-Château** France
29 M11 **Anjalankoski** Finland
74 D7 **Anjar** India
80 G4 **'Anjara** Jordan
67 F1 **Anji** China
65 G2 **Anjia** China
Anjiang *see* **Qianyang**
Anjiangying *see* **Luanping**
61 L11 **Anjō** Japan
21 H7 **Anjou** *reg* France
87 G10 **Anjouan** *isld* Comoros
87 H11 **Anjozorobe** Madagascar
59 J4 **Anjŭ** N Korea
77 L2 **Anjuman** *reg* Afghanistan
87 G12 **Ankaboa, Tanjona** *C* Madagascar
58 E5 **Ankang** China
78 D2 **Ankara** Turkey
87 H11 **Ankaratra** *mt* Madagascar
27 H14 **Ankarsrum** Sweden
26 J6 **Ankarsund** Sweden
87 G12 **Ankazoabo** Madagascar
99 N8 **Ankeny** Iowa U.S.A.
68 J6 **An Khe** Vietnam
33 T5 **Anklam** Germany
74 E8 **Ankleshwar** India
86 G4 **Ānkober** Ethiopia
16 D10 **Ankod** Morocco
38 H7 **Ankogel** *mt* Austria
87 E7 **Ankoro** Zaire
52 E6 **An'kovo** Russian Federation
32 G7 **Ankum** Germany
13 H6 **Anlaby** England
67 E3 **Anle** China
22 K4 **Anlier** Belgium
68 H7 **An Loc** Vietnam
67 B4 **Anlong** China
68 G5 **Anlong Veng** Cambodia
58 F5 **Anlu** China
26 F8 **Ånn** Sweden
25 C3 **Anna** Netherlands
53 F8 **Anna** Russian Federation
110 G4 **Anna** Illinois U.S.A.
94 C6 **Anna** Ohio U.S.A.
109 L2 **Anna** Texas U.S.A.
85 F1 **Annaba** Algeria
38 H7 **Annaberg** Austria
37 P2 **Annaberg-Buchholz** Germany
79 G4 **An Nabk** Syria
33 S9 **Annaburg** Germany
84 G4 **An Nāfūrah** Libya
128 G3 **Annai** Guyana
25 B5 **Anna Jacobapolder** Netherlands
61 M9 **Annaka** Japan
94 K8 **Anna, L** Virginia U.S.A.
68 G3 **Annam** *reg* Vietnam
113 E10 **Anna Maria** Florida U.S.A.
13 E4 **Annan** Scotland
141 J5 **Annandale** Queensland Australia
15 E5 **Annandale** Scotland
99 M4 **Annandale** Minnesota U.S.A.
13 E3 **Annan Water** Scotland
133 C7 **Anna Pink, B** Chile
142 D4 **Anna Plains** W Australia Australia
95 L8 **Annapolis** Maryland U.S.A.
122 G9 **Annapolis R** Nova Scotia Canada
75 K4 **Annapurna** *mt* Nepal
94 D4 **Ann Arbor** Michigan U.S.A.
33 O9 **Annarode** Germany
78 L7 **An Nāsirīyah** Iraq
99 R8 **Annawan** Illinois U.S.A.
143 C7 **Annean, L** W Australia Australia
21 L3 **Annebault** France
19 Q13 **Annecy** France
40 D6 **Annecy,L.d'** France
131 H6 **Annenkov Is** S Georgia
141 K2 **Annerley** *dist* Brisbane, Qnsld Australia
117 H8 **Annette I** Alaska U.S.A.
20 G3 **Anneville-sur-Mer** France
19 N14 **Anneyron** France
68 J6 **An Nhon** Vietnam
141 G2 **Annie** *R* Queensland Australia
123 P5 **Annieopsquotch Mts** Newfoundland Canada
58 D6 **Anning He** *R* China
28 J5 **Annisse** Denmark
111 L8 **Anniston** Alabama U.S.A.
140 D5 **Annitowa** N Terr Australia
40 G5 **Anniviers Val d'** Switzerland
Annobón *isld see* **Pagalu** *isld*
90 L9 **Annobón** *isld* Equat Guinea
109 N2 **Annona** Texas U.S.A.
19 N14 **Annonay** France
127 L2 **Annotto Bay** Jamaica
22 D2 **Annœulin** France
36 D5 **Annweiler** Germany
46 G9 **Áno Arkhánai** Crete Greece
99 N4 **Anoka** Minnesota U.S.A.
98 H7 **Anoka** Nebraska U.S.A.
47 P13 **Ano Lefkimmi** Greece
54 M1 **Anopino** Russian Federation
22 G4 **Anor** France
87 H10 **Anorontany, Tanjona** *C* Madagascar
36 B7 **Anould** France
46 G9 **Áno Viánnos** Crete Greece
47 O12 **Ano Virón** Greece
68 J7 **An Phuoc** Vietnam
65 C5 **Anping** China
67 C6 **Anpu** China
67 C6 **Anpu Gang** *B* China
58 G5 **Anqing** China
65 D6 **Anqiu** China
25 F6 **Anrath** Germany
67 D3 **Anren** China
32 H9 **Anröchte** Germany
22 K2 **Ans** Belgium
28 B5 **Ansager** Denmark
65 A6 **Ansai** China
37 K5 **Ansbach** Germany
40 A6 **Anse** France
127 H5 **Anse-à-Galets** Haiti
127 J5 **Anse-à-Pitre** Haiti
122 H5 **Anse-au-Griffon** Quebec Canada
126 H5 **Anse-à-Veau** Haiti
127 N4 **Anse Bertrand** Guadeloupe W Indies
126 G5 **Anse d'Hainault** Haiti
98 G8 **Anselmo** Nebraska U.S.A.
22 H3 **Anseremme** Belgium
139 H7 **Anser Gr** *islds* Tasmania Australia
122 B5 **Anse St.Jean,L'** Quebec Canada
127 L4 **Anses d'Arlets, Les** Martinique W Indies
59 H3 **Anshan** China
67 B3 **Anshun** China
131 B3 **Ansilta** *pk* Argentina
131 B3 **Ansilta, Cord. de** *ra* Argentina
109 P3 **Ansley** Louisiana U.S.A.
98 G8 **Ansley** Nebraska U.S.A.
140 B2 **Anson B** N Terr Australia
85 E5 **Ansongo** Mali
94 C6 **Ansonia** Ohio U.S.A.
120 K4 **Ansonville** Ontario Canada
112 G2 **Ansonville** North Carolina U.S.A.
28 C6 **Anst** Denmark
94 F8 **Ansted** West Virginia U.S.A.
15 F4 **Anstruther** Scotland
128 D6 **Anta** Peru
Antakya *see* **Hatay**
78 C3 **Antalya** Turkey
87 H11 **Antananarivo** Madagascar
87 H11 **Antanifotsy** Madagascar
87 H12 **Antanimora** Madagascar
146 **Antarctica**
90 D16 **Antarctic Circle**
146 D6 **Antarctic Pen** Antarctica
81 C10 **Antares Bank** Indian Oc
130 H11 **Antas** Brazil
130 D10 **Antas,R das** Brazil
15 C3 **An Teallach** *mt* Scotland
118 J8 **Antelope** Saskatchewan Canada
98 B1 **Antelope** Montana U.S.A.
98 D3 **Antelope** North Dakota U.S.A.
109 J2 **Antelope** Texas U.S.A.
101 Q9 **Antelope** Utah U.S.A.
87 E10 **Antelope** Zimbabwe
100 H7 **Antelope Cr** Oregon U.S.A.
130 H9 **Antenor Navarro** Brazil
16 D7 **Antequera** Spain
130 B9 **Antequera,Pto** Paraguay
106 D3 **Antero Pk** Colorado U.S.A.
106 E3 **Antero Res** Colorado U.S.A.
38 F8 **Anterselva di Mezzo** Italy
107 N4 **Anthony** Kansas U.S.A.
106 D9 **Anthony** New Mexico U.S.A.
108 A3 **Anthony** New Mex/Tex U.S.A.
138 C4 **Anthony, L** South Australia Australia
140 D4 **Anthony Lagoon** N Terr Australia
138 C2 **Anthony,Mt** South Australia Australia
85 C3 **Anti Atlas** *mts* Morocco
44 B4 **Antibes** France
44 B4 **Antibes,C.d'** France
127 N9 **Antica, I** Venezuela
45 N5 **Anticoli Corrado** Italy
122 J4 **Anticosti I** Quebec Canada
21 L2 **Antifer,C.d'** France
21 M8 **Antigny** France
123 K8 **Antigonish** Nova Scotia Canada
125 O10 **Antigua** Guatemala
127 P4 **Antigua** *isld* Lesser Antilles
127 O6 **Antigua and Barbuda** *islds* West Indies
127 N4 **Antigues Pte. d'** Guadeloupe W Indies
118 B3 **Antikameg** Alberta Canada
133 C5 **Antilhue** Chile
126 G4 **Antilla** Cuba
103 N3 **Antimony** Utah U.S.A.
Antioch *see* **Hatay**
102 C3 **Antioch** California U.S.A.
99 S7 **Antioch** Illinois U.S.A.
98 D7 **Antioch** Nebraska U.S.A.
18 E6 **Antioche, Pertuis d'** *B* France
128 C2 **Antioquia** *div* Colombia
80 C5 **Antipatris** Israel
52 D6 **Antipovo** Russian Federation
128 C4 **Antisana** *mt* Ecuador
119 Q9 **Antler** Saskatchewan Canada
98 E1 **Antler** North Dakota U.S.A.
107 P7 **Antlers** Oklahoma U.S.A.
133 C2 **Antofagasta** Chile
133 D3 **Antofagasta de la Sierra** Argentina
133 D3 **Antofalla** *vol* Argentina
109 O1 **Antoine** Arkansas U.S.A.
22 E2 **Antoing** Belgium
44 F2 **Antola,Monte** Italy
106 G2 **Anton** Colorado U.S.A.
108 E2 **Anton** Texas U.S.A.
87 J11 **Antongila, Helodrano** *B* Madagascar
87 G12 **Antongo** Madagascar
130 E9 **Antonina** Brazil
107 L3 **Antonino** Kansas U.S.A.
48 K1 **Antoniny** Ukraine
129 K7 **Antônio** *R* Brazil
130 G7 **Antônio Carlos** Brazil
130 G6 **Antônio Dias** Brazil
Antonio Enes *see* **Angoche**
130 C8 **Antônio João** Brazil
106 D4 **Antonito** Colorado U.S.A.
54 D10 **Antonovka** Ukraine
47 H1 **Antonovo** Bulgaria
126 D3 **Antón Recio** Cuba
21 P4 **Antony** France
140 D4 **Antony Lagoon** N Terr Australia
20 H5 **Antrain** France
52 C4 **Antrea** Russian Federation
36 G5 **Antrefftal** Germany
14 E2 **Antrim** *co* N Ireland
14 E2 **Antrim** N Ireland
95 P3 **Antrim** New Hampshire U.S.A.
95 K5 **Antrim** Pennsylvania U.S.A.
14 E2 **Antrim Hills** N Ireland
142 G4 **Antrim Plat** W Australia Australia
87 G11 **Antsalova** Madagascar
52 D5 **Antsiferovo** Russian Federation
87 H11 **Antsirabe** Madagascar
87 J11 **Antsirakosy, Tanjona** *C* Madagascar
87 H10 **Antsirañana** Madagascar
52 C5 **Antsla** Estonia
87 H10 **Antsohihy** Madagascar
29 N10 **Anttola** Finland
65 G3 **Antu** China
Antwerp *see* **Antwerpen**
95 M2 **Antwerp** New York U.S.A.
94 C5 **Antwerp** Ohio U.S.A.
22 H1 **Antwerpen** Belgium
14 E3 **An Uaimh** Ireland
75 L8 **Anugul** India
116 F6 **Anukslak L** Alaska U.S.A.
26 K8 **Anundsjö** Sweden
74 E4 **Anupgarh** India
83 K9 **Anuradhapura** Sri Lanka
Anvers *see* **Antwerpen**
45 P6 **Anversa degli Abruzzi** Italy
146 C4 **Anvers Island** Antarctica
116 G5 **Anvik** Alaska U.S.A.
121 P3 **Anvilla** Quebec Canada
117 G4 **Anvil Range** Yukon Territory Canada
22 C3 **Anvin** France
58 C3 **Anxi** China
67 F4 **Anxi** China
67 A1 **An Xian** China
67 D2 **Anxiang** China
65 C5 **Anxin** China
138 C5 **Anxious B** South Australia Australia
58 F4 **Anyang** China
70 K9 **Anyar** Java
58 C5 **A'nyêmaqên Shan** *mts* China
65 B7 **Anyi** China
67 E2 **Anyi** China
67 D7 **Anyou** China
117 J8 **Anyox** British Columbia Canada
67 E4 **Anyuan** China
52 J3 **An'yudin** Russian Federation
67 B1 **Anyue** China
51 Q2 **Anyuy** *R* Russian Federation
42 B3 **Anza** *R* Italy
118 F2 **Anzac** Alberta Canada
17 G2 **Anzánigo** Spain
40 H6 **Anzasca, Valle** Italy
18 F10 **Anzat** France
65 B6 **Anze** China
22 E2 **Anzegem** Belgium
56 C3 **Anzhero-Sudzhensk** Russian Federation
147 P7 **Anzhu Os** *isld* Russian Federation
22 E3 **Anzin** France
38 E5 **Anzing** Germany
45 N7 **Anzio** Italy
128 F2 **Anzoátegui** *state* Venezuela
45 K2 **Anzola dell'Emilia** Italy
137 O5 **Aoba** *isld* Vanuatu
59 L5 **Aoga-shima** *isld* Japan
65 D3 **Aohan Qi** China
18 E10 **Aoiz** Spain
61 O5 **Aomori** Japan
60 N3 **Aonae** Japan
144 C6 **Aorangi** *admin region* New Zealand
145 E4 **Aorangi Mts** New Zealand
145 D4 **Aorere R** New Zealand
68 D7 **Ao Sawi** *B* Thailand
40 F6 **Aosta** Italy
145 E3 **Aotea Harbour** New Zealand
85 C5 **Aouker** *reg* Mauritania
85 E3 **Aoulef** Algeria
67 B3 **Aoxi** China
60 G10 **Aoya** Japan
86 C1 **Aozou** Chad
103 P10 **Apache** Arizona U.S.A.
109 J1 **Apache** Oklahoma U.S.A.
106 B8 **Apache Creek** New Mexico U.S.A.
103 N8 **Apache Junct** Arizona U.S.A.
103 O10 **Apache Pk** Arizona U.S.A.
113 C7 **Apalachee B** Florida U.S.A.
112 C2 **Apalachia Dam** North Carolina U.S.A.
113 C8 **Apalachicola** Florida U.S.A.
128 D3 **Apaporis** *R* Colombia
130 B8 **Apa.R** Brazil/Paraguay
130 D7 **Âparecida do Tabuado** Brazil
144 B7 **Aparima R** New Zealand
71 E1 **Aparri** Luzon Philippines
70 E6 **Apar, Teluk** *B* Kalimantan
145 D2 **Apata** New Zealand
48 E5 **Apatin** Serbia Yugoslavia
52 D1 **Apatity** Russian Federation
124 H8 **Apatzingán** Mexico
116 C5 **Apavawook C** St Lawrence I, Alaska U.S.A.
52 C5 **Ape** Latvia
45 M4 **Apecchio** Italy
119 S3 **Apeganau L** Manitoba Canada
25 E4 **Apeldoorn** Netherlands
32 G6 **Apen** Germany
33 O7 **Apenburg** Germany
32 L6 **Apensen** Germany
128 E6 **Apere** *R* Bolivia
112 J2 **Apex** North Carolina U.S.A.
41 L1 **Apfingen** Germany
101 L1 **Apgar** Montana U.S.A.
80 C5 **Aphek** Israel
116 E6 **Aphrewn** *R* Alaska U.S.A.
86 E5 **Api** Zaire
134 C1 **Apia** Western Samoa
129 G5 **Apiacás,Serra dos** *mts* Brazil
130 E9 **Apiaí** Brazil
45 R7 **Apice** Italy
71 J9 **Api,Gunung** *vol* Indonesia
70 E2 **Apin-Apin** Sabah
130 B10 **Apipe Grande** *isld* Argentina
106 F4 **Apishapa** *R* Colorado U.S.A.
70 G5 **Api,Tg** *C* Sulawesi Indonesia
145 E3 **Apiti** New Zealand
125 K8 **Apizaco** Mexico
124 H5 **Apizolaya** Mexico
56 F2 **Aplinskiy Porog** *falls* Russian Federation
129 L5 **Apodi** *R* Brazil
71 E4 **Apo East Pass** Philippines
47 Q14 **Apolakkiá** Rhodes Greece
37 M1 **Apolda** Germany
Apollonia *see* **Sūsah**
46 G8 **Apollonia** Greece
128 E6 **Apolo** Bolivia
113 F9 **Apopka** Florida U.S.A.
113 F9 **Apopka,L** Florida U.S.A.
133 G1 **Aporé** *R* Brazil
129 H3 **Aporema** Brazil
99 Q2 **Apostle Is** Michigan U.S.A.
133 F3 **Apostoles** Argentina
54 E9 **Apostolovo** Ukraine
128 G3 **Apoteri** Guyana
71 E4 **Apo West Pass** Philippines
94 E10 **Appalachia** Virginia U.S.A.
94 F10 **Appalachian Mts** U.S.A.
27 G11 **Äppelbo** Sweden
32 F9 **Appelhülsen** Germany
44 D3 **Appennino Ligure** *mt* Italy
42 C4 **Appennino Tosco-Emiliano** *mts* Italy
42 E5 **Appennino Umbro-Marchigiano** *mts* Italy
36 D6 **Appenweier** Germany
41 K3 **Appenzell** *canton* Switzerland
13 G6 **Apperley Br** England
21 M3 **Appeville** France
41 O5 **Appiano sulla Strada del Vino** Italy
25 G2 **Appingedam** Netherlands
109 N4 **Appleby** Texas U.S.A.
13 F4 **Appleby-in-Westmorland** England
142 A2 **Applecross** *dist* Perth, W Aust Australia
8 B5 **Appledore** Devon England
9 G5 **Appledore** Kent England
102 D3 **Applegate** California U.S.A.
100 B7 **Applegate** Oregon U.S.A.
122 H8 **Apple River** Nova Scotia Canada
109 N4 **Apple Springs** Texas U.S.A.
95 S2 **Appleton** Maine U.S.A.
100 D4 **Appleton** Washington U.S.A.
99 S5 **Appleton** Wisconsin U.S.A.
110 B3 **Appleton City** Missouri U.S.A.
94 J9 **Appomattox** Virginia U.S.A.
54 J1 **Aprelevka** Russian Federation
22 J5 **Apremont** France
20 G8 **Apremont** Vendée France
27 M15 **Apriki** Latvia
43 E7 **Aprilia** Italy
46 G2 **Apriltsi** Bulgaria
53 E11 **Apsheronsk** Russian Federation
138 F6 **Apsley** Victoria Australia
121 M8 **Apsley** Ontario Canada
140 B1 **Apsley Str** N Terr Australia
19 O17 **Apt** France
45 H3 **Apuane** Italy
135 V6 **Apua Pt** Hawaiian Is
130 D8 **Apucarana** Brazil
130 D8 **Apucarana, Serra Da** *mts* Brazil
71 D6 **Apurauan** Philippines
128 E2 **Apure** *state* Venezuela
128 D6 **Apurímac** *dept* Peru
48 H4 **Apuseni Muntii** *mt* Romania
88 D6 **Apwa** Tanzania
79 F9 **'Aqaba** Jordan
84 J4 **Aqaba,G.of** Red Sea
77 J1 **Aqchah** Afghanistan
78 K2 **Aq Chai** Iran
77 D1 **Āq Qal'eh** Iran
66 D4 **Aqqikkol Hu** *L* China
80 G3 **'Aqraba** Jordan
103 L7 **Aquarius Mts** Arizona U.S.A.
103 N4 **Aquarius Plat** Utah U.S.A.
130 B8 **Aquidabán,R** Paraguay
130 C7 **Aquidauana** Brazil
130 C6 **Aquidauana,R** Brazil
124 G3 **Aquiles Serdán** Mexico
109 K4 **Aquilla** Texas U.S.A.
126 H5 **Aquin** Haiti
45 P7 **Aquino** Italy
75 L6 **Ara** India
17 G2 **Ara** *R* Spain
80 F3 **Arab** *R* Jordan
79 F3 **'Arab al Mulk** Syria
38 E8 **Arabba** Italy
112 D6 **Arabi** Georgia U.S.A.
111 K12 **Arabi** New Orleans, Louisiana U.S.A.
Arabian Gulf *see* **Persian Gulf**
123 N3 **Arabian L** Quebec Canada
84 H3 **Arabs Gulf** Egypt
78 D1 **Araç** Turkey
128 F3 **Araçá** *R* Brazil
129 L6 **Aracaju** Brazil
130 C9 **Aracanguy, Mt de** Paraguay
126 G9 **Aracataca** Colombia
129 L4 **Aracati** Brazil
130 E7 **Araçatuba** Brazil
16 C7 **Aracena** Spain
16 C7 **Aracena, Sa. de** *mts* Spain
130 G5 **Araçuaí** Brazil
48 G4 **Arad** Romania
86 D2 **Arada** Chad
56 D5 **Aradanskiy Khrebet** *mts* Russian Federation
81 L7 **Arafura Sea** Aust/New Guinea
129 H7 **Aragarças** Brazil
78 J1 **Aragats** *mt* Armenia
61 M9 **Ara-gawa** *R* Japan
100 A6 **Arago,Cape** Oregon U.S.A.
17 G2 **Aragón** *R* Spain
17 G4 **Aragon** *reg* Spain
43 F11 **Aragona** Sicily
17 F4 **Aragoncillo** *mt* Spain
128 E2 **Aragua** *state* Venezuela
129 J6 **Araguaçu** Brazil
128 F2 **Aragua de Barcelona** Venezuela
129 H3 **Araguari** *R* Brazil
129 J7 **Araguari** Brazil
133 H1 **Araguari** *R* Brazil
129 J5 **Araguatins** Brazil
53 F12 **Aragvi** *R* Georgia
144 C5 **Arahura** New Zealand
61 M8 **Arai** Japan
79 E8 **Araif el Naqa** *mt* Egypt
80 G8 **Ara'ir** Jordan
85 E3 **Arak** Algeria
77 A2 **Arāk** Iran
61 N8 **Arakai-yama** *mt* Japan
128 G2 **Arakaka** Guyana
78 G4 **Arak, Al** Syria
116 A4 **Arakamchechen, Ostrov** *isld* Russian Federation
68 A2 **Arakan** *prov* Burma
68 B2 **Arakan Yoma** *ra* Burma
46 F6 **Arákhova** Greece
46 D5 **Árakhthos** *R* Greece
76 D4 **Arakkonam** India
120 C2 **Ara L** Ontario Canada
57 B2 **Aral'sk** Kazakhstan
57 A3 **Aral'skoye More** *sea* Kazakhstan/Uzbekistan
55 B6 **Aralsor, Oz** *L* Kazakhstan
26 A9 **Åram** Norway
141 G6 **Aramac** *R* Queensland Australia
141 H6 **Aramac** Queensland Australia
125 K5 **Aramberri** Mexico
19 N17 **Aramon** France
43 C7 **Aranci, G** Sardinia
16 E3 **Aranda de Duero** Spain
17 F3 **Aranda de Moncayo** Spain
87 B10 **Arandis** Namibia
145 D1 **Aranga** New Zealand
128 E7 **Arani** Bolivia
76 D4 **Arani** India
14 C1 **Aran I** Ireland
16 E4 **Aranjuez** Spain
8 C2 **Aran Mawddwy** *mt* Wales
89 A5 **Aranos** Namibia
109 L7 **Aransas B** Texas U.S.A.
109 K8 **Aransas Pass** Texas U.S.A.
130 E6 **Arantes,R** Brazil
137 P1 **Aranuka** *isld* Kiribati
85 D5 **Araouane** Mali
106 E1 **Arapaho** *mt* Colorado U.S.A.
106 H3 **Arapahoe** Colorado U.S.A.
98 G9 **Arapahoe** Nebraska U.S.A.
101 R7 **Arapahoe** Wyoming U.S.A.
128 E7 **Arapa,L** Peru
145 E4 **Arapawa I** New Zealand
133 F4 **Arapey** Uruguay
131 G3 **Arapey Grande** *R* Uruguay
130 H10 **Arapiraca** Brazil
78 G2 **Arapkir** Turkey
130 D8 **Arapongas** Brazil
145 E3 **Arapuni** New Zealand
130 E10 **Araquari** Brazil
78 H6 **'Ar'ar** Saudi Arabia
80 D4 **'Ar'Ara** Israel
133 H3 **Araranguá** Brazil
129 J8 **Araraquara** Brazil
130 F8 **Araras** São Paulo Brazil
130 D6 **Araras,Serra das** Mato Grosso Brazil
130 D9 **Araras, Serra das** *mts* Paraná Brazil
139 G6 **Ararat** Victoria Australia
Ararat,Mt *see* **Bügük Ağri**
129 K4 **Arari** Brazil
75 M5 **Araria** India
130 G8 **Araruama L.de** Brazil
78 H6 **Arar,Wadi** Saudi Arabia
80 D5 **A-ras** Jordan
78 J1 **Aras** *R* Turkey
17 G5 **Aras de Alpuente** Spain
126 A1 **Arasji** Aruba W Indies
145 D2 **Aratapu** New Zealand
145 F3 **Aratiatia** New Zealand
61 O7 **Arato** Japan
128 F5 **Araua** *R* Brazil
128 D2 **Arauca** Colombia
133 C5 **Arauco** Chile
127 K10 **Araure** Venezuela
80 E2 **'Arav** Israel
74 E6 **Aravalli Range** India
137 M3 **Arawa** Bougainville I Papua New Guinea
144 B6 **Arawata R** New Zealand
129 J7 **Araxá** Brazil
128 F1 **Araya,P.de** Venezuela
61 P14 **Ara-zaki** *C* Okinawa
17 G3 **Arba** *R* Spain
86 G4 **Ārba Minch'** Ethiopia
43 C9 **Arbatax** Sardinia
52 G5 **Arbazh** Russian Federation
40 C2 **Arbecey** France
37 K5 **Arberg** Germany
78 J4 **Arbīl** *prov* Iraq
27 H12 **Arboga** Sweden
27 H12 **Arbogaån** *R* Sweden
40 C4 **Arbois** France
41 K2 **Arbon** Switzerland
101 N7 **Arbon** Idaho U.S.A.
119 O5 **Arborfield** Saskatchewan Canada
9 F5 **Arborfield Cross** England
119 U8 **Arborg** Manitoba Canada
99 R4 **Arbor Vitae** Wisconsin U.S.A.
27 H10 **Arbrå** Sweden
13 F1 **Arbroath** Scotland
102 B2 **Arbuckle** California U.S.A.
113 F10 **Arbuckle,L** Florida U.S.A.
109 K1 **Arbuckle Mts** Oklahoma U.S.A.
107 O7 **Arbuckles, Lake of the** Oklahoma U.S.A.
110 F5 **Arbyrd** Missouri U.S.A.
19 J5 **Arc** France
19 O18 **Arc** *R* France
18 E8 **Arcachon** France
94 J4 **Arcade** New York U.S.A.
118 A3 **Arcadia** Alberta Canada
113 F10 **Arcadia** Florida U.S.A.
94 A6 **Arcadia** Indiana U.S.A.
107 Q4 **Arcadia** Kansas U.S.A.
111 D9 **Arcadia** Louisiana U.S.A.
99 U5 **Arcadia** Michigan U.S.A.
110 F4 **Arcadia** Missouri U.S.A.
98 G8 **Arcadia** Nebraska U.S.A.
94 D5 **Arcadia** Ohio U.S.A.
107 N6 **Arcadia** Oklahoma U.S.A.
99 P5 **Arcadia** Wisconsin U.S.A.
95 T2 **Arcadia Nat. Park** Maine U.S.A.
43 G8 **Arcangelo,S** Italy
94 C7 **Arcanum** Ohio U.S.A.
21 L8 **Arçay** France
102 G3 **Arc Dome** *mt* Nevada U.S.A.
45 P6 **Arce** Italy
125 J8 **Arcelia** Mexico
25 F6 **Arcen** Netherlands
45 N4 **Arcévia** Italy
46 F1 **Archar** Bulgaria
95 M5 **Archbald** Pennsylvania U.S.A.
94 C5 **Archbold** Ohio U.S.A.
112 H2 **Archdale** North Carolina U.S.A.
141 F2 **Archer** *R* Queensland Australia
113 E8 **Archer** Florida U.S.A.
141 F2 **Archer Bend Nat. Park** Queensland Australia
109 J2 **Archer City** Texas U.S.A.
141 K2 **Archerfield Airfield** Brisbane, Qnsld Australia
141 H3 **Archer Pt** Queensland Australia
119 O6 **Archerwill** Saskatchewan Canada
40 E1 **Arches** France
103 P3 **Arches Nat. Park** Utah U.S.A.
110 B3 **Archie** Missouri U.S.A.
21 M8 **Archigny** France
119 M8 **Archive** Saskatchewan Canada
106 C5 **Archuleta** New Mexico U.S.A.
18 H4 **Arcis sur Aube** France
138 C2 **Arckaringa** *R* South Australia Australia
101 M6 **Arco** Idaho U.S.A.
98 K5 **Arco** Minnesota U.S.A.
119 P9 **Arcola** Saskatchewan Canada
99 S10 **Arcola** Illinois U.S.A.
111 F8 **Arcola** Mississippi U.S.A.
45 K1 **Árcole** Italy
18 H6 **Arconce** *R* France
138 D4 **Arcoona** South Australia Australia
131 B7 **Arco, Paso de** Arg/Chile
130 F7 **Arcos** Brazil
16 D8 **Arcos de la Frontera** Spain
16 B3 **Arcos de Vale de Vez** Portugal
17 G3 **Arcos,Sierra de** *mt* Spain
76 D4 **Arcot** India
20 D4 **Arcouest,l'** France
130 H10 **Arcoverde** Brazil
19 J5 **Arc-Senans** France
147 F4 **Arctic Bay** Northwest Territories Canada
90 J2 **Arctic Circle**
116 D4 **Arctic Lagoon** Alaska U.S.A.
147 **Arctic Ocean**
114 F4 **Arctic Red River** Northwest Territories Canada
116 P2 **Arctic Village** Alaska U.S.A.
146 D3 **Arctowski, Henryk** *Poland Base* Antarctica
45 L1 **Arcugnano** Italy
22 E5 **Arcy-Ste. Restitue** France
44 G2 **Arda** *R* Italy
78 M2 **Ardabīl** Iran
38 L5 **Ardagger** Austria
78 J1 **Ardahan** Turkey
77 C3 **Ardakan** Esfahān Iran
77 B4 **Ardal** Iran
27 C10 **Årdal** Opland Norway
27 B12 **Årdal** Rogaland Norway
14 C2 **Ardara** Ireland
118 K7 **Ardath** Saskatchewan Canada
52 F6 **Ardatov** Russian Federation
120 K7 **Ardbeg** Ontario Canada
12 B2 **Ardbeg** Scotland
45 N6 **Ardea** Italy
18 H8 **Ardèche** *dept* France
14 E3 **Ardee** Ireland
119 S8 **Arden** Manitoba Canada
121 O8 **Arden** Ontario Canada
103 J5 **Arden** Nevada U.S.A.
138 E4 **Arden Mt** South Australia Australia
18 H3 **Ardennes** *dept* France
22 H4 **Ardennes** France
21 O8 **Ardentes** France
12 D1 **Ardentinny** Scotland
77 C3 **Ardestān** Iran
15 D3 **Ardgay** Scotland
14 F2 **Ardglass** N Ireland
46 E4 **Ardhéa** Greece
16 C6 **Ardila,R** Spain
119 M9 **Ardill** Saskatchewan Canada
124 H6 **Ardilla, Cerro La** *pk* Mexico
46 G3 **Ardino** Bulgaria
18 E10 **Ardisa** Spain
70 P9 **Ardjasa** Java
70 O9 **Ardjuna,G** *mt* Java
145 F3 **Ardkeen** New Zealand
118 D6 **Ardley** Alberta Canada
15 D4 **Ardlui** Scotland
12 C2 **Ardminish** Scotland
139 H6 **Ardmona** Victoria Australia
118 G4 **Ardmore** Alberta Canada
107 N7 **Ardmore** Oklahoma U.S.A.
98 C6 **Ardmore** South Dakota U.S.A.
110 K6 **Ardmore** Tennessee U.S.A.
14 D5 **Ardmore B** Ireland
15 B4 **Ardnamurchan Pt** Scotland
15 B5 **Ardnave Pt** Scotland
98 J1 **Ardoch** North Dakota U.S.A.
22 B2 **Ardres** France
12 C1 **Ardrishaig** Scotland
138 E5 **Ardrossan** South Australia Australia
118 D5 **Ardrossan** Alberta Canada
15 D5 **Ardrossan** Scotland
14 F2 **Ards Pen** N Ireland
12 B2 **Ardtalla** Scotland
48 H3 **Ardud** Romania
15 C3 **Ardvasar** Scotland
53 F7 **Ardym** Russian Federation
26 F8 **Åre** Sweden
26 N4 **Areavaara** Sweden
127 L5 **Arecibo** Puerto Rico
131 F5 **Areco** *R* Argentina
48 J5 **Areful** Romania
129 L4 **Areia Branca** Brazil
45 Q7 **Areinzo** Italy
118 K6 **Arelee** Saskatchewan Canada
27 E12 **Aremark** Norway
36 B3 **Aremberg** Germany
118 H9 **Arena** Saskatchewan Canada
71 E6 **Arena** Philippines
95 N4 **Arena** New York U.S.A.
133 C7 **Arenales** *mt* Chile
130 C4 **Arenápolis** Brazil
71 F4 **Arena Pt** Luzon Philippines
124 E6 **Arena, Pta** *C* Mexico
16 D4 **Arenas de S.Pedro** Spain
128 D8 **Arenas,Pta** *C* Chile
32 F7 **Arenberg** *reg* Germany
27 C13 **Arendal** Norway
22 J1 **Arendonk** Belgium
33 O7 **Arendsee** Germany
32 L10 **Arenshausen** Germany
19 Q12 **Arenthon** France
28 D2 **Arentsminde** Denmark
17 J3 **Arenys de Mar** Spain
46 E8 **Areópolis** Greece
128 D7 **Arequipa** Peru
129 H4 **Arere** Brazil
18 E8 **Arès** France
16 D3 **Arévalo** Spain
140 B6 **Areyonga** N Terr Australia
42 D5 **Arezzo** Italy
46 E7 **Arfará** Greece
17 F2 **Arga** *R* Spain
140 D5 **Argadargada** N Terr Australia
58 E2 **Argalant** Mongolia
16 E5 **Argamasilla de Alba** Spain
16 E4 **Arganda** Spain
16 B4 **Arganil** Portugal
71 F6 **Argao** Philippines
45 P6 **Argatone, M** *mt* Italy
55 D3 **Argayash** Russian Federation
55 D3 **Argazi, Oz** Russian Federation
18 H10 **Argelès sur Mer** France
41 L2 **Argen** *R* Germany
21 K3 **Argences** France
19 Q18 **Argens** *R* France
117 P10 **Argenta** British Columbia Canada
45 L2 **Argenta** Italy
101 N4 **Argenta** Montana U.S.A.
21 K4 **Argentan** France
42 D6 **Argentario,Monte** Italy
18 G7 **Argentat** France
44 B3 **Argentera Mt** Italy
21 P4 **Argenteuil** Seine-et-Oise France
123 S6 **Argentia** Newfoundland Canada
40 E6 **Argentières** France
44 C4 **Argentina** *R* Italy
131 D5 **Argentina** *rep* S America
146 E7 **Argentina Range** *mts* Antarctica
90 E13 **Argentine Basin** Atlantic Oc
133 C8 **Argentino,L** Argentina
20 A4 **Argenton** France
21 K7 **Argenton** *R* France
21 K8 **Argenton-Château** France
21 O8 **Argenton-sur-Creuse** France
122 C3 **Argent,R à l'** Quebec Canada
21 J5 **Argentre** France
21 H5 **Argentré-du-Plessis** France
18 G5 **Argent sur Sauldre** France
48 J5 **Argeş** *R* Romania
48 J5 **Argeş** *reg* Romania
48 J6 **Argeşel** *R* Romania
77 J4 **Arghandab** *R* Afghanistan
77 K4 **Arghastan** *R* Afghanistan
84 J6 **Argo** Sudan
20 B5 **Argol** France
46 F7 **Argolikós Kólpos** *B* Greece
107 N4 **Argonia** Kansas U.S.A.
22 J5 **Argonne** *reg* France
99 S4 **Argonne** Wisconsin U.S.A.
70 O9 **Argopura G** *mt* Java
101 N5 **Argora** Idaho U.S.A.
46 F7 **Argos** Greece
94 A5 **Argos** Indiana U.S.A.
46 E4 **Árgos Orestikón** Greece
20 H4 **Argouges** France
18 D10 **Arguedas** Spain
21 O2 **Argueil** France
20 F5 **Arguenon** *R* France
59 H1 **Argun** *R* China/Rus Fed
85 E6 **Argungu** Nigeria
146 G10 **Argus, Dome** *ice dome* Antarctica
102 G6 **Argus Ra** California U.S.A.
98 J2 **Argusville** North Dakota U.S.A.
21 N8 **Argy** France
122 G10 **Argyle** Nova Scotia Canada
112 E6 **Argyle** Georgia U.S.A.
94 E3 **Argyle** Michigan U.S.A.
98 K1 **Argyle** Minnesota U.S.A.
99 R7 **Argyle** Wisconsin U.S.A.
142 G3 **Argyle, L** W Australia Australia
Argyll *co see* **Strathclyde and Highland** *regions*
6 M6 **Argyll** *oil rig* North Sea
Argyrokastron *see* **Gjirokastër**
65 E3 **Ar Horquin Qi** China
28 E4 **Århus** Denmark
28 E4 **Århus** *co* Denmark
145 E3 **Aria** New Zealand
139 H5 **Ariah Pk** New South Wales Australia
60 D13 **Ariake-kai** *G* Japan
87 C11 **Ariamsvlei** Namibia
43 G7 **Ariano Irpino** Italy
45 M2 **Ariano Nel Polésine** Italy
128 D3 **Ariari** *R* Colombia
73 L8 **Ari Atoll** Maldives
85 D6 **Aribinda** Burkina
128 D7 **Arica** Chile
128 D4 **Arica** Colombia
45 N6 **Ariccia** Italy
123 M8 **Arichat** C Breton I, Nova Scotia
60 J11 **Arida** Japan
60 J11 **Arida-gawa** *R* Japan
85 B3 **Aridal, Sabkhat** *salt lake* Western Sahara
143 E10 **Arid, C** W Australia Australia
83 J12 **Aride I** Seychelles
Arid I *see* **Rakitu I**
18 G9 **Ariège** *dept* France
18 G10 **Ariège** *R* France
80 D5 **Ari'el** Jordan
100 C4 **Ariel** Washington U.S.A.
48 H4 **Arieş** *R* Romania
80 G8 **Ariha** Jordan
79 G3 **Arīḩā** Syria
106 H2 **Arikaree** *R* Colorado U.S.A.
60 C13 **Arikawa** Japan
29 K4 **Arild** Sweden
48 F7 **Arilje** Serbia Yugoslavia
128 F5 **Arima** Brazil
60 J11 **Arima** Japan
127 O2 **Arima** Trinidad
101 N7 **Arimo** Idaho U.S.A.
128 G3 **Arinda** Guyana
129 G6 **Arinos** *R* Brazil
129 J7 **Arinos** Brazil
101 M9 **Arinosa** Utah U.S.A.
99 L8 **Arion** Iowa U.S.A.
127 P1 **Aripo, Mt** Trinidad
128 D2 **Ariporo** *R* Colombia
128 F5 **Aripuana** *R* Brazil
128 F5 **Ariquemes** Brazil
130 D5 **Ariranha** *R* Brazil
15 C4 **Arisaig** Scotland
79 D7 **'Arîsh, El** Egypt
117 J9 **Aristazabal I** British Columbia Canada
133 D7 **Aristizábal, C** Argentina
111 L10 **Ariton** Alabama U.S.A.
43 C9 **Aritzo** Sardinia
103 N10 **Arivaca** Arizona U.S.A.
87 H11 **Arivonimamo** Madagascar
17 F3 **Ariza** Spain
18 F9 **Arize** *R* France
133 D5 **Arizona** Argentina
103 L7 **Arizona** *state* U.S.A.
124 D2 **Arizpe** Mexico
27 F12 **Årjäng** Sweden
26 J5 **Arjeplog** Sweden
128 D1 **Arjona** Colombia
16 E7 **Arjona** Spain
51 O2 **Arka** Russian Federation
110 F7 **Arkabutla Res** Mississippi U.S.A.
53 F8 **Arkadak** Russian Federation
109 O1 **Arkadelphia** Arkansas U.S.A.
55 E5 **Arkalyk** Kazakhstan
109 O1 **Arkansas** *state* U.S.A.
110 C6 **Arkansas** *R* Arkansas U.S.A.
111 E8 **Arkansas City** Arkansas U.S.A.
107 O4 **Arkansas City** Kansas U.S.A.
111 E7 **Arkansas Post Nat. Mem** Arkansas U.S.A.
84 G5 **Arkanu Jebel** *mt* Libya
138 E4 **Arkaroola** South Australia Australia
47 J9 **Arkása** Kárpathos I Greece
66 D4 **Arkatag** *mts* China
117 F5 **Arkell,Mt** Yukon Territory Canada
27 G15 **Arkelstorp** Sweden
47 V14 **Arkhángelos** Rhodes Greece
52 F3 **Arkhangel'sk** Russian Federation
53 F11 **Arkhangel'skoye** Russian Federation
59 K2 **Arkhara** Russian Federation
53 D7 **Arkhipovka** Russian Federation
53 D8 **Arkino** Russian Federation
14 E4 **Arklow** Ireland
47 H7 **Árkoi** *isld* Greece
120 J9 **Arkona** Ontario Canada
30 H1 **Arkona** Germany
27 J13 **Arkösund** Sweden
94 K4 **Arkport** New York U.S.A.
52 H6 **Arkul'** Russian Federation
95 N4 **Arkville** New York U.S.A.
27 J12 **Ärla** Sweden
18 H7 **Arlanc** France
16 E2 **Arlanza** *R* Spain
41 M3 **Arlberg** *pass* Austria
101 L2 **Arlee** Montana U.S.A.
19 N17 **Arles** Bouches du Rhône France
18 G10 **Arles** Pyrénées-Orientales France
22 E3 **Arleux** France
100 J5 **Arling** Idaho U.S.A.
8 D4 **Arlingham** England
103 M8 **Arlington** Arizona U.S.A.
102 G8 **Arlington** California U.S.A.
106 G3 **Arlington** Colorado U.S.A.
113 F7 **Arlington** Florida U.S.A.
112 C6 **Arlington** Georgia U.S.A.
99 P7 **Arlington** Iowa U.S.A.
107 M4 **Arlington** Kansas U.S.A.
110 G5 **Arlington** Kentucky U.S.A.
99 M5 **Arlington** Minnesota U.S.A.
98 K8 **Arlington** Nebraska U.S.A.
94 D6 **Arlington** Ohio U.S.A.
100 E4 **Arlington** Oregon U.S.A.
98 J5 **Arlington** South Dakota U.S.A.
110 G6 **Arlington** Tennessee U.S.A.
109 N9 **Arlington** Texas U.S.A.
95 O3 **Arlington** Vermont U.S.A.
95 K8 **Arlington** Virginia U.S.A.
117 M11 **Arlington** Washington U.S.A.
101 T8 **Arlington** Wyoming U.S.A.
99 S7 **Arlington Heights** Illinois U.S.A.
110 E4 **Arlington Res** Missouri U.S.A.
85 F5 **Arlit** Niger
22 K4 **Arlon** Belgium
140 C6 **Arltunga** N Terr Australia
107 Q4 **Arma** Kansas U.S.A.
118 E8 **Armada** Alberta Canada
143 B9 **Armadale** W Australia Australia
12 E2 **Armadale** Scotland
122 B7 **Armagh** Quebec Canada
14 E2 **Armagh** *co* N Ireland
14 E2 **Armagh** N Ireland
18 F9 **Armagnac** *reg* France
18 H5 **Armançon** *R* France
47 H9 **Armathia** *isld* Greece
13 F4 **Armathwaite** England
53 F10 **Armavir** Russian Federation
Armaynskaya S.S.R. *see* **Armenia**
128 C3 **Armenia** Colombia
78 K1 **Armenia** *rep* E Europe
48 G5 **Armeniş** Romania
22 D2 **Armentières** France
21 M4 **Armentières** Eure France
101 P2 **Armington** Montana U.S.A.
101 S6 **Arminto** Wyoming U.S.A.
119 Q6 **Armit** Saskatchewan Canada
9 E2 **Armitage** England
55 E3 **Armizonskoye** Russian Federation
119 N5 **Armley** Saskatchewan Canada
98 H6 **Armour** South Dakota U.S.A.
98 G1 **Armourdale** North Dakota U.S.A.
120 D3 **Arms** Ontario Canada
36 E4 **Armsheim** Germany
101 N5 **Armstead** Montana U.S.A.
140 B3 **Armstrong** *R* N Terr Australia
117 O10 **Armstrong** British Columbia Canada
99 T9 **Armstrong** Illinois U.S.A.
99 M6 **Armstrong** Iowa U.S.A.
110 D2 **Armstrong** Missouri U.S.A.
109 K9 **Armstrong** Texas U.S.A.
59 L2 **Armu** *R* Russian Federation
74 H9 **Armur** India
47 J4 **Armutcuk Dağ** *mt* Turkey
47 K4 **Armutlu** Turkey
53 D10 **Armyansk** Ukraine
28 B7 **Arnå** *R* Denmark
21 L6 **Arnage** France
46 F4 **Arnaia** Greece
28 R9 **Arnarstapi** Iceland
118 D1 **Arnaud** Manitoba Canada
115 M6 **Arnaud,R** Quebec Canada
79 C3 **Arnauti, C** Cyprus
18 J5 **Arnay le Duc** France
28 B4 **Arnborg** Denmark
37 P5 **Arnbruck** Germany
33 Q7 **Arneburg** Germany
18 D10 **Arnedo** Spain
98 C2 **Arnegard** North Dakota U.S.A.
22 C2 **Arneke** France
26 M6 **Arnemark** Sweden
25 A6 **Arnemuiden** Netherlands
27 E11 **Årnes** Norway
107 L5 **Arnett** Oklahoma U.S.A.
94 F9 **Arnett** West Virginia U.S.A.
28 R9 **Arngerdhareyri** Iceland
25 E5 **Arnhem** Netherlands
140 D1 **Arnhem,C** N Terr Australia
140 C2 **Arnhem Land** *reg* N Terr Australia
140 C2 **Arnhem Land Aboriginal Land** N Terr Australia
21 N4 **Arnières** France
45 H4 **Arno** *R* Italy
138 D5 **Arno Bay** South Australia Australia
102 D3 **Arnold** California U.S.A.
110 F3 **Arnold** Missouri U.S.A.
98 F8 **Arnold** Nebraska U.S.A.
94 H6 **Arnold** Pennsylvania U.S.A.
99 L6 **Arnolds Park** Iowa U.S.A.
38 J8 **Arnoldstein** Austria
21 P7 **Arnon** *R* France
119 V3 **Arnot** Manitoba Canada
26 L1 **Arnöy** Norway
16 B2 **Arnoya** *R* Spain
12 D1 **Arnprior** Scotland
32 G10 **Arnsberg** Germany
13 F5 **Arnside** England
37 K2 **Arnstadt** Germany
37 L3 **Arnstein** Germany
37 O6 **Arnstorf** Germany
121 L4 **Arntfield** Quebec Canada
28 B6 **Arnum** Denmark
128 F2 **Aro** *R* Venezuela
127 K9 **Aroa** Venezuela
87 C11 **Aroab** Namibia
46 E7 **Aroánia** *mt* Greece
124 H4 **Arocha** Mexico
130 C7 **Aroeira** Brazil
32 K10 **Arolsen** Germany
55 E3 **Aromashevo** Russian Federation
21 J5 **Aron** France
21 J5 **Aron** *R* Mayenne France
42 B3 **Arona** Italy
122 E7 **Aroostook** New Brunswick Canada
95 S7 **Aroostook** *R* Maine U.S.A.
116 E6 **Aropuk L** Alaska U.S.A.
137 Q2 **Arorae** *isld* Kiribati
71 F4 **Aroroy** Philippines
28 D6 **Arøsund** Denmark
127 O2 **Arouca** Trinidad
17 F9 **Aroui, Mt** Morocco
145 F3 **Arowhana** *mt* New Zealand
106 G3 **Aroya** Colorado U.S.A.
109 M3 **Arp** Texas U.S.A.
57 G4 **Arpa** Kyrgyzstan
18 G8 **Arpajon** France
21 P4 **Arpajon** France
48 J5 **Arpasu de Jos** Romania
55 D1 **Arpavla** Russian Federation
120 K4 **Arpin** Ontario Canada
45 P6 **Arpino** Italy
45 L1 **Arquà Petrarca** Italy
45 L1 **Arquà Polesine** Italy
21 N2 **Arques** *R* France
22 C2 **Arques** Pas-de-Calais France
21 N2 **Arques-la-Bataille** France
80 E2 **'Arraba** Israel
141 F7 **Arrabury** Queensland Australia
36 B6 **Arracourt** France
20 E6 **Arradon** France
131 D2 **Arraga** Argentina
16 C4 **Arrago** *R* Spain
129 J6 **Arraias** Brazil
16 B6 **Arraiolos** Portugal
14 C4 **Arra Mts** Ireland
119 Q7 **Arran** Saskatchewan Canada
15 C5 **Arran** *isld* Scotland
111 M11 **Arran** Florida U.S.A.
80 E4 **'Arrana** Jordan
117 H8 **Arrandale** British Columbia Canada
78 G4 **Ar Raqqah** Syria
84 F4 **Ar Rāqūbah** Libya
22 D3 **Arras** Pas-de-Calais France
79 G4 **Ar Rastan** Syria
18 F9 **Arrats** *R* France

28 B5 **Arre** Denmark
18 F10 **Arreau** France
128 E3 **Arrecifal** Colombia
85 B3 **Arrecife** Canary Is
20 C5 **Arrée,Mtgne.d'** France
28 J5 **Arresø** *L* Denmark
106 C9 **Arrey** New Mexico U.S.A.
45 L4 **Arrezzo** *reg* Italy
38 J8 **Arriach** Austria
125 N9 **Arriaga** Mexico
106 G2 **Arriba** Colorado U.S.A.
141 G6 **Arrilalah** Queensland Australia
28 B6 **Arrild** Denmark
9 F3 **Arrington** England
143 B8 **Arrino** W Australia Australia
12 D1 **Arrochar** Scotland
133 G4 **Arroio Grande** Brazil
21 J3 **Arromanches** France
16 C5 **Arronches** Portugal
44 M6 **Arrone** *R* Italy
18 F9 **Arros** *R* France
21 N5 **Arrou** France
18 H6 **Arroux** *R* France
101 Q2 **Arrow Cr** Montana U.S.A.
117 P10 **Arrowhead** British Columbia Canada
119 O2 **Arrow L** Ontario Canada
14 C2 **Arrow,L** Ireland
117 O10 **Arrow Park** British Columbia Canada
110 D2 **Arrow Rock** Missouri U.S.A.
100 K6 **Arrowrock Res** Idaho U.S.A.
138 F4 **Arrowsmith Mt** New South Wales Australia
144 C5 **Arrowsmith, Mt** New Zealand
140 D2 **Arrowsmith Pt** N Terr Australia
144 B6 **Arrowtown** New Zealand
118 D8 **Arrow Wood** Alberta Canada
16 C5 **Arroyo de la Luz** Spain
108 F6 **Arroyo de la Zorra** *R* Mexico
131 F6 **Arroyo Grande** *R* Argentina
102 D6 **Arroyo Grande** California U.S.A.
106 E5 **Arroyo Hondo** New Mexico U.S.A.
131 F4 **Arroyo Negro** *R* Uruguay
103 J8 **Arroyo Seco** *R* California U.S.A.
128 F6 **Arroyos,L de Los** Bolivia
130 B9 **Arroyos-y-Esteros** Paraguay
130 C4 **Arruda** Brazil
78 G4 **Ar Ruşāfah** Syria
79 H3 **Ar Ruwayḑah** Syria
28 D3 **Års** Denmark
77 C5 **Arsenajan** Iran
118 J3 **Arsenault L** Saskatchewan Canada
117 Q3 **Arseno L** Northwest Territories Canada
59 K3 **Arsen'yev** Russian Federation
55 C3 **Arshinka** Russian Federation
86 G4 **Ārsī** *prov* Ethiopia
41 O6 **Arsiero** Italy
76 C4 **Arsikere** India
52 G6 **Arsk** Russian Federation
26 J9 **Årskogen** Sweden
57 G4 **Arslanbal** Kyrgyzstan
45 O5 **Arsoli** Italy
19 K3 **Ars-sur-Moselle** France
27 J11 **Årsunda** Sweden
79 F2 **Arsuz** Turkey
22 D5 **Arsy** France
46 D5 **Árta** Greece
17 K5 **Artá** Majorca
80 D7 **Artas** Jordan
98 G4 **Artas** South Dakota U.S.A.
17 K5 **Artá,Sierra de,Mt** Majorca
124 H8 **Arteaga** Mexico
59 K3 **Artem** Russian Federation
19 P13 **Artemare** France
126 C3 **Artemisa** Cuba
51 J3 **Artemovak** Russian Federation
54 G7 **Artemovka** Ukraine
56 D4 **Artemovsk** Russian Federation
53 F9 **Artemovskiy** Russian Federation
45 N6 **Artena** Italy
21 O5 **Artenay** France
33 O10 **Artern** Germany
17 H3 **Artesa de Segre** Spain
Artesia *see* **Mosomane**
111 H8 **Artesia** Mississippi U.S.A.
98 J5 **Artesian** South Dakota U.S.A.
109 H7 **Artesia Wells** Texas U.S.A.
26 G6 **Artfjallet** *mt* Sweden
121 T6 **Arthabaska** Quebec Canada
18 E9 **Arthez** France
21 O3 **Arthies** France
21 O8 **Arthon** France
20 G7 **Arthon-en-Retz** France
139 H8 **Arthur** *R* Tasmania Australia
110 H2 **Arthur** Illinois U.S.A.
98 E8 **Arthur** Nebraska U.S.A.
98 J2 **Arthur** North Dakota U.S.A.
109 M2 **Arthur City** Texas U.S.A.
138 E4 **Arthur,L** South Australia Australia
139 H8 **Arthur,L** Tasmania Australia
142 E4 **Arthur, Mt** W Australia Australia
145 D4 **Arthur, Mt** New Zealand
141 K5 **Arthur Pt** Queensland Australia
143 B10 **Arthur River** W Australia Australia
144 C5 **Arthur's Pass** New Zealand
126 G2 **Arthur's Town** Cat I Bahamas
55 C3 **Arti** Russian Federation
146 C3 **Artigas** *Uruguay Base* Antarctica
133 F4 **Artigas** Uruguay
114 J5 **Artillery L** Northwest Territories Canada
29 M11 **Artjärvi** Finland
118 H6 **Artland** Saskatchewan Canada
33 M6 **Artlenburg** Germany
22 C3 **Artois** *prov* France
102 B2 **Artois** California U.S.A.
22 D3 **Artois Collines d'** France
46 E6 **Artotína** Greece
78 F1 **Artova** Turkey
Artsakan Nor *see* **Qagan Nur** *L*
48 M5 **Artsiz** Ukraine
66 B4 **Artux** China
71 B1 **Aru** Halmahera Indonesia
86 F5 **Aru** Zaire
129 H6 **Aruanã** Brazil
126 A2 **Aruba** *isld* W Indies
18 E9 **Arudy** France
80 E8 **Arugot** *R* Jordan
136 G3 **Aru,Kep** *islds* Moluccas Indonesia
25 D2 **Arum** Netherlands
128 F4 **Arumá** Brazil
61 Q12 **Arume** *B* Okinawa
75 Q4 **Arunachal Pradesh** *prov* India
9 F6 **Arundel** England
144 C5 **Arundel** New Zealand
9 F5 **Arun,R** England
28 E6 **Årup** Denmark
76 D6 **Aruppukkottai** India
80 D5 **'Arūra** Jordan
88 F3 **Arusha** Tanzania
70 G4 **Arus,Tg** *C* Sulawesi Indonesia
70 B5 **Arut** *R* Kalimantan
70 E6 **Aru,Tg** *C* Kalimantan
83 K9 **Aruvi Aru** *R* Sri Lanka
86 D5 **Aruwimi** *R* Zaire
106 E2 **Arvada** Colorado U.S.A.
101 T5 **Arvada** Wyoming U.S.A.
26 K7 **Arvån** Sweden
58 D2 **Arvayheer** Mongolia
40 D5 **Arve** *R* France
26 K5 **Arvestuottar** *mt* Sweden
74 H8 **Arvi** India
121 T4 **Arvida** Quebec Canada
26 K6 **Arvidsjaur** Sweden
27 F12 **Arvika** Sweden
102 F6 **Arvin** California U.S.A.
94 J9 **Arvonia** Virginia U.S.A.
65 E1 **Arxan** China
147 Q9 **Ary** Russian Federation
55 C3 **Aryazh** Russian Federation
47 O13 **Aryirádhes** Greece
46 G9 **Aryiroúpolis** Crete Greece
55 E4 **Aryk-Balyk** Kazakhstan
57 E4 **Arys'** *R* Kazakhstan
57 E4 **Arys'** Kazakhstan
57 D2 **Arys,Ozero** *L* Kazakhstan
20 E6 **Arz** *R* France
20 F6 **Arzal, Barrage d'** *dam* France
52 F6 **Arzamas** Russian Federation
20 D6 **Arzano** France
37 N3 **Arzberg** Germany
37 L5 **Arzberg** *mt* Germany
32 K8 **Ärzen** Germany
85 D1 **Arzew** Algeria
36 B3 **Arzfeld** Germany
53 F10 **Arzgir** Russian Federation
41 O6 **Arzignano** Italy
41 N3 **Arzl** Austria
20 E6 **Arzon** France
16 B2 **Arzúa** Spain
22 K1 **As** Belgium
37 N3 **Aš** Czechoslovakia
26 E8 **Ås** Norway
28 E2 **Aså** Denmark
27 F14 **Åsa** Sweden
87 C11 **Asab** Namibia
74 D1 **Asadābād** Afghanistan
69 D11 **Asahan** *R* Sumatra
60 G10 **Asahi** *R* Japan
61 O10 **Asahi** Chiba Japan
60 Q2 **Asahi-dake** *mt* Japan
61 N7 **Asahi-dake** *mt* Japan
60 Q2 **Asahikawa** Japan
86 H3 **Āsalē** *L* Ethiopia
61 M9 **Asama yama** *vol* Japan
65 G6 **Asan Man** *B* S Korea
75 M7 **Asansol** India
26 G9 **Åsarna** Sweden
84 F5 **Asawanwah** Libya
36 C2 **Asbach** Germany
71 C3 **Asbakin** W Irian
55 D3 **Asbest** Russian Federation
121 T7 **Asbestos** Quebec Canada
89 C7 **Asbestos Mts** S Africa
107 Q4 **Asbury** Kansas U.S.A.
110 B4 **Asbury** Missouri U.S.A.
Ascalon *see* **Tel Ashqelon**
90 B12 **Ascension** *isld* Atlantic Oc
128 F7 **Ascensión** Bolivia
124 E2 **Ascensión** Chihuahua Mexico
126 A1 **Ascension** Curaçao W Indies
37 O6 **Ascha** Germany
38 L5 **Aschbach** Austria
33 M4 **Ascheberg** Germany
32 G9 **Ascheberg** Nordrhein-Westfalen Germany
32 F6 **Aschendorf** Germany
21 O5 **Aschères-le-Marché** France
33 O9 **Aschersleben** Germany
17 H3 **Asco** Spain
12 C2 **Ascog** Scotland
42 F6 **Ascoli Piceno** Italy
141 K1 **Ascot** *dist* Brisbane, Qnsld Australia
9 F5 **Ascot** England
133 D2 **Ascotán** Chile
86 H3 **Āseb** Ethiopia
27 H14 **Åseda** Sweden
85 E4 **Asedjrad** *hills* Algeria
53 H7 **Asekeyevoye** Russian Federation
86 G4 **Āsela** Ethiopia
26 J7 **Åsele** Sweden
26 E8 **Åsen** Norway
27 G10 **Åsen** Sweden
32 K7 **Asendorf** Germany
46 G3 **Asenovgrad** Bulgaria
27 B13 **Åseral** Norway
79 G5 **Aşfar, Tall al** *mt* Syria
22 G5 **Asfeld-la-ville** France
27 D12 **Asgårdstr** Norway
55 C3 **Asha** Russian Federation
80 C8 **Ashan** *R* Israel
52 J5 **Ashan** Russian Federation
55 C3 **Ashap** Russian Federation
9 E1 **Ashbourne** England
112 D6 **Ashburn** Georgia U.S.A.
142 B6 **Ashburton** *R* W Australia Australia
8 C6 **Ashburton** England
144 C5 **Ashburton** New Zealand
140 C4 **Ashburton Ra** N Terr Australia
9 E4 **Ashbury** England
95 N6 **Ashbury Park** New Jersey U.S.A.
99 L3 **Ashby** Minnesota U.S.A.
9 E2 **Ashby de la Zouch** England
57 D2 **Ashchikol', Ozero** *L* Kazakhstan
57 C1 **Ashchitastysor, Ozero** *L* Kazakhstan
117 N10 **Ashcroft** British Columbia Canada
80 B6 **Ashdod** Israel
109 N2 **Ash Down** Arkansas U.S.A.
9 G5 **Ashdown Forest** England
112 H2 **Asheboro** North Carolina U.S.A.
107 O7 **Asher** Oklahoma U.S.A.
119 T7 **Ashern** Manitoba Canada
108 H7 **Asherton** Texas U.S.A.
112 E2 **Asheville** North Carolina U.S.A.
110 E5 **Ash Flat** Arkansas U.S.A.
9 G5 **Ashford** England
113 D11 **Ashford** Alabama U.S.A.
100 C3 **Ashford** Washington U.S.A.
9 E5 **Ashford Hill** England
103 M6 **Ashfork** Arizona U.S.A.
141 K1 **Ashgrove** *dist* Brisbane, Qnsld Australia
107 M2 **Ash Grove** Kansas U.S.A.
110 C4 **Ash Grove** Missouri U.S.A.
145 E4 **Ashhurst** New Zealand
60 Q2 **Ashibetsu** Japan
61 N9 **Ashikaga** Japan
9 F6 **Ashington** England
61 N9 **Ashio** Japan
52 G6 **Ashit** *R* Russian Federation
60 J11 **Ashiya** Japan
60 G13 **Ashizuri-misaki** *C* Japan
77 D4 **Ashkazar** Iran
77 F1 **Ashkhabad** Iran
77 F1 **Ashkhabad** Turkmenistan
13 F3 **Ashkirk** Scotland
99 T9 **Ashkum** Illinois U.S.A.
111 L8 **Ashland** Alabama U.S.A.
110 F2 **Ashland** Illinois U.S.A.
107 L4 **Ashland** Kansas U.S.A.
94 E8 **Ashland** Kentucky U.S.A.
95 S7 **Ashland** Maine U.S.A.
101 T4 **Ashland** Montana U.S.A.
98 K8 **Ashland** Nebraska U.S.A.
95 Q3 **Ashland** New Hampshire U.S.A.
94 E6 **Ashland** Ohio U.S.A.
100 C7 **Ashland** Oregon U.S.A.
95 L6 **Ashland** Pennsylvania U.S.A.
94 K9 **Ashland** Virginia U.S.A.
99 Q3 **Ashland** Wisconsin U.S.A.
110 J5 **Ashland City** Tennessee U.S.A.
144 D5 **Ashley** New Zealand
110 G3 **Ashley** Illinois U.S.A.
94 C3 **Ashley** Michigan U.S.A.
98 G3 **Ashley** North Dakota U.S.A.
120 K4 **Ashley Mine** Ontario Canada
55 E3 **Ashlyk** *R* Russian Federation
118 F4 **Ashmont** Alberta Canada
108 E3 **Ashmore** Texas U.S.A.
142 E1 **Ashmore Reef** Timor Sea
79 A8 **Ashmûn** Egypt
80 F1 **Ashmura** Syria
95 N5 **Ashokan Res** New York U.S.A.
60 R2 **Ashoro** Japan
80 B7 **Ashqelon** Israel
78 J4 **Ash Sharqat** Iraq
72 F6 **Ash Shaykh' Uthmān** Yemen
72 F6 **Ash Shihr** Yemen
84 E4 **Ash Shuwayrif** Libya
94 G5 **Ashtabula** Ohio U.S.A.
98 J2 **Ashtabula,L** North Dakota U.S.A.
74 F9 **Ashti** India
77 A2 **Ashtiān** Iran
121 O7 **Ashton** Ontario Canada
101 O5 **Ashton** Idaho U.S.A.
99 R8 **Ashton** Illinois U.S.A.
94 B3 **Ashton** Michigan U.S.A.
98 H5 **Ashton** South Dakota U.S.A.
13 F6 **Ashton-in-Makerfield** England
142 F3 **Ashton Ra** W Australia Australia
13 F6 **Ashton-under-Lyne** England
115 N7 **Ashuanipi,L** Labrador, Nfld Canada
121 R3 **Ashuapmuchuan** *R* Quebec Canada
78 J4 **Ashur** Iraq
78 J6 **Ashuriyah, Al** Iraq
111 K8 **Ashville** Alabama U.S.A.
79 G3 **'Āsi** *R* Syria/Lebanon
42 D3 **Asiago** Italy
71 C2 **Asia Pulau Pulau** *islds* Indonesia
71 F4 **Asid Gulf** Philippines
124 H6 **Asientos** Mexico
45 K1 **Asigliano Ven** Italy
75 L9 **Āsika** India
85 C1 **Asilah** Morocco
71 A1 **Asimiro** Halmahera Indonesia
43 B7 **Asinara, Golfo dell'** Sardinia
43 B7 **Asinara, I** Sardinia
56 C3 **Asino** Russian Federation
78 H2 **Aşkale** Turkey
53 D10 **Askaniya Nova** Ukraine
55 C4 **Askarovo** Russian Federation
14 C4 **Askeaton Adare** Ireland
27 D12 **Asker** Norway
13 G6 **Askern** England
27 G13 **Askersund** Sweden
72 H1 **Askhabad** Turkmenistan
26 J7 **Åskilje** Sweden
27 E12 **Askim** Norway
112 K2 **Askin** North Carolina U.S.A.
55 C3 **Askino** Russian Federation
28 G7 **Askø** Denmark
29 M11 **Askola** Finland
65 J3 **Askol'd, O** *isld* Russian Federation
28 C6 **Askov** Denmark
99 O3 **Askov** Minnesota U.S.A.
13 F5 **Askrigg** England
27 A10 **Askvoll** Norway
79 C9 **Asl** Egypt
47 K5 **Aslanapa** Turkey
79 E2 **Aslanköy Dere** *str* Turkey
74 D1 **Asmar** Afghanistan
Asmara *see* **Āsmera**
86 G2 **Āsmera** Ethiopia
29 K5 **Asminderød** Denmark
28 F5 **Asnæs** *pen* Denmark
28 G5 **Asnæs** Denmark
21 J3 **Asnelles** France
27 G15 **Åsnen** Sweden
27 E11 **Åsnes** Norway
129 G3 **Asoenangka** Brazil
45 J1 **Asola** Italy
28 S9 **Asólfsstadhir** Iceland
60 E13 **Aso Nat. Park** Japan
86 F3 **Āsosa** Ethiopia
86 G1 **Asoteriba, Jebel** *mt* Sudan
100 H3 **Asotin** Washington U.S.A.
85 E3 **Asouf** *watercourse* Algeria
60 C11 **Asō-wan** *B* Japan
60 E13 **Aso zan** *vol* Japan
36 G6 **Aspach** Germany
48 C3 **Aspang** Austria
26 G8 **Aspås** Sweden
13 E4 **Aspatria** England
17 G6 **Aspe** Spain
26 J8 **Aspeå** Sweden
106 D2 **Aspen** Colorado U.S.A.
101 P8 **Aspen** Wyoming U.S.A.
118 D6 **Aspen Beach Prov. Park** Alberta Canada
36 G6 **Asperg** Germany
28 D6 **Asperup** Denmark
19 P16 **Aspremont** France
46 D5 **Asprókavos, Akr** *C* Greece
47 P13 **Asprókavos, Akra** *C* Greece
43 G10 **Aspromonte** *mts* Italy
123 M7 **Aspy B** C Breton I, Nova Scotia
118 K6 **Asquith** Saskatchewan Canada
79 H3 **Aş Şā'ān** Syria
74 D1 **Assad-Abad** Afghanistan
79 H2 **As Safirah** Syria
21 K8 **Assais-les-Jumeaux** France
75 O5 **Assam** *prov* India
85 F5 **Assamakka** Niger
95 M8 **Assateague I** Maryland U.S.A.
22 G2 **Asse** Belgium
19 Q17 **Asse** *R* France
119 V2 **Assean L** Manitoba Canada
89 G6 **Assegai** *R* Swaziland
85 F3 **Assekaifaf** Algeria
85 F4 **Assekreme** *mt* Algeria
32 K5 **Assel** Germany
21 K5 **Asse la Boisne** France
22 K3 **Asselborn** Luxembourg
25 G3 **Assen** Netherlands
36 F3 **Assenheim** Germany
28 E3 **Assens** Århus Denmark
28 D6 **Assens** Fyn Denmark
20 F7 **Asserac** France
22 J3 **Assesse** Belgium
122 G2 **Assigny,L** Quebec Canada
118 L9 **Assinboia** Saskatchewan Canada
28 B4 **Assing** Denmark
118 L9 **Assiniboia** Saskatchewan Canada
117 Q10 **Assiniboine,Mt** Br Col/Alberta Canada
119 Q8 **Assiniboine R** Manitoba/Sask Canada
84 G4 **As Sirīr** *sands* Libya
46 F4 **Ássiros** Greece
129 H8 **Assis** Brazil
42 E5 **Assisi** Italy
36 D3 **Assmannshausen** Germany
41 K6 **Asso** Italy
78 G4 **As Sukhnah** Syria
87 H9 **Assumption** *isld* Seychelles
110 G2 **Assumption** Illinois U.S.A.
78 K5 **Aş Suwayrah** Iraq
36 C5 **Assweiler** Germany
37 N7 **Ast** Germany
27 E10 **Asta** *R* Norway
18 F8 **Astaffort** France
47 H9 **Astakidha** *isld* Greece
46 E6 **Astakós** Greece
77 A1 **Astaneh** Iran
28 E2 **Åsted** Nordjylland Denmark
28 B3 **Åsted** Viborg Denmark
25 E6 **Asten** Netherlands
77 C1 **Asterabad** Iran
44 D2 **Asti** Italy
16 E1 **Astillero** Spain
Astin Tagh *mt ra see* **Altun Shan**
47 H8 **Astipálaia** *isld* Greece
9 E1 **Aston** England
8 D3 **Aston Cross** England
74 F1 **Astor** Kashmir
16 C2 **Astorga** Spain
99 Q9 **Astoria** Illinois U.S.A.
100 B3 **Astoria** Oregon U.S.A.
98 K5 **Astoria** South Dakota U.S.A.
27 F15 **Åstorp** Sweden
121 L6 **Astorville** Ontario Canada
87 H10 **Astove** *isld* Br Indian Oc Terr
53 G10 **Astrakhan'** Russian Federation
55 E5 **Astrakhanka** Kazakhstan
26 L7 **Åsträsk** Sweden
146 J6 **Astrid Ridge** *ridge* Antarctica
46 F7 **Astros** Greece
28 E6 **Astrup** Fyn Denmark
28 B5 **Åstrup** Ribe Denmark
28 D6 **Åstrup** Sønderjylland Denmark
28 J7 **Åstrup** *isld* Storstrøm Denmark
28 D5 **Åstrup** Vejle Denmark
16 E2 **Astudillo** Spain
45 N7 **Astura** *R* Italy
16 C1 **Asturias** *reg* Spain
9 F3 **Astwood** England
146 J8 **Asuka** *Japan Base* Antarctica
28 E6 **Åsum** Denmark
133 F3 **Asunción** Paraguay
27 H14 **Asunden** *L* Sweden
28 E5 **As Vig** *B* Denmark
84 J5 **Aswân** Egypt
84 J5 **Aswan High Dam** Egypt
84 J4 **Asyût** Egypt
48 E3 **Aszód** Hungary
137 R6 **Ata** *isld* Pacific Oc
57 E3 **Atabay** Kazakhstan
47 L7 **Atabey** Turkey
133 C3 **Atacama** *reg* Chile
128 E8 **Atacama, Des de** Chile
133 D3 **Atacama, Puna de** *plateau* Argentina
48 L2 **Ataki** Moldavia
85 E7 **Atakpamé** Togo
130 J10 **Atalaia** Brazil
46 F6 **Atalándi** Greece
128 D6 **Atalaya** Peru
130 H6 **Ataléia** Brazil
71 M9 **Atambua** Timor Indonesia
61 N10 **Atami** Japan
115 O5 **Atammik** Greenland
55 F4 **Atansor, Oz** *L* Kazakhstan
79 C9 **'Ataqa, G** *mt* Egypt
85 B4 **Atar** Mauritania
80 D5 **'Atara** Jordan
80 F7 **Ataroth** Jordan
106 B7 **Atarque** New Mexico U.S.A.
80 F7 **Ataruz** Jordan
Atas *isld see* **South I** Cocos Is
102 D6 **Atascadero** California U.S.A.
109 J6 **Atascosa** *R* Texas U.S.A.
57 F1 **Atasu** Kazakhstan
68 C4 **Atatano** *R* Burma
78 G3 **Ataturk Baraji** *res* Turkey
17 F2 **Atauri** Spain
71 M9 **Atauro** *isld* Indonesia
86 F2 **Atbara** Sudan
86 G2 **Atbara** *R* Sudan
55 E5 **Atbasar** Kazakhstan
57 H4 **At-Bash** Kyrgyzstan
111 E12 **Atchafalaya Bay** Louisiana U.S.A.
107 P2 **Atchison** Kansas U.S.A.
116 G5 **Atchueelinguk** *R* Alaska U.S.A.
112 C3 **Atco** Georgia U.S.A.
95 N7 **Atco** New Jersey U.S.A.
17 F3 **Ateca** Spain
58 E4 **A-t'eng-hsi-lien** China
124 G7 **Atenguillo** Mexico
61 O7 **Aterazawa** Japan
42 F6 **Aterno** *R* Italy
42 D2 **Atesine,Alpi** Italy
42 F6 **Atessa** Italy
22 F2 **Ath** Belgium
117 D4 **Athabasca** Alberta Canada
114 J6 **Athabasca, L** Alberta/Sask Canada
119 Q4 **Athapap** Manitoba Canada
119 Q4 **Athapapuskow L** Manitoba Canada
28 C4 **Atheden** *reg* Denmark
110 B1 **Athelstan** Iowa U.S.A.
100 G4 **Athena** Oregon U.S.A.
14 C3 **Athenry** Ireland
121 P8 **Athens** Ontario Canada
Athens Greece *see* **Athínai**
110 K7 **Athens** Alabama U.S.A.
112 D4 **Athens** Georgia U.S.A.
99 R10 **Athens** Illinois U.S.A.
109 O3 **Athens** Louisiana U.S.A.
95 S2 **Athens** Maine U.S.A.
94 B4 **Athens** Michigan U.S.A.
94 E7 **Athens** Ohio U.S.A.
95 L5 **Athens** Pennsylvania U.S.A.
112 C2 **Athens** Tennessee U.S.A.
109 M3 **Athens** Texas U.S.A.
99 Q4 **Athens** Wisconsin U.S.A.
121 L8 **Atherley** Ontario Canada
9 E2 **Atherstone** England
141 H3 **Atherton** Queensland Australia
13 F6 **Atherton** England
85 E7 **Athiémé** Benin
22 F4 **Athies** Aisne France
22 D4 **Athies** Somme France
46 F7 **Athínai** Greece
21 K4 **Athis-de-l'Orne** France
14 C3 **Athleague** Ireland
14 D3 **Athlone** Ireland
79 D3 **Athna** Cyprus
76 B2 **Athni** India
144 B6 **Athol** New Zealand
100 J2 **Athol** Idaho U.S.A.
95 P4 **Athol** Massachusetts U.S.A.
113 L9 **Athol I** New Providence I Bahamas
122 F6 **Atholville** New Brunswick Canada
46 G4 **Áthos** *mt* Greece
Athos, Mt *reg see* **Áyion Óros**
79 G9 **Ath Thāyat** *mt* Saudi Arabia
22 K4 **Athus** Belgium
14 E4 **Athy** Ireland
86 C3 **Ati** Chad
145 F3 **Atiamuri** New Zealand
130 F8 **Atibaia** Brazil
128 D7 **Atico** Peru
123 N2 **Aticonipi L** Quebec Canada
17 F3 **Atienza** Spain
119 Q4 **Atik** Manitoba Canada
117 Q8 **Atikameg** Alberta Canada
119 R4 **Atikameg Lake** Manitoba Canada
99 P1 **Atikokan** Ontario Canada
115 N7 **Atikonak, L** Labrador, Nfld Canada
122 H1 **Atikonal L** Labrador, Nfld Canada
118 J1 **Atikwa L** Ontario Canada
71 E3 **Atimonan** Philippines
45 P6 **Atina** Italy
76 D5 **Atirampattinam** India
116 P9 **Atka** Aleutian Is
51 P2 **Atka** Russian Federation
53 F8 **Atkarsk** Russian Federation
116 J1 **Atkasuk** Alaska U.S.A.
110 D6 **Atkins** Arkansas U.S.A.
99 Q8 **Atkinson** Illinois U.S.A.
98 G7 **Atkinson** Nebraska U.S.A.
112 J3 **Atkinson** North Carolina U.S.A.
71 B3 **Atkri** W Irian
105 **Atlanta** *conurbation* Georgia U.S.A.
111 M8 **Atlanta** Georgia U.S.A.
101 K6 **Atlanta** Idaho U.S.A.
110 G1 **Atlanta** Illinois U.S.A.
94 A6 **Atlanta** Indiana U.S.A.
107 O4 **Atlanta** Kansas U.S.A.
110 D2 **Atlanta** Missouri U.S.A.
95 K4 **Atlanta** New York U.S.A.
109 N2 **Atlanta** Texas U.S.A.
99 L8 **Atlantic** Iowa U.S.A.
112 L3 **Atlantic** North Carolina U.S.A.
95 N7 **Atlantic City** New Jersey U.S.A.
101 R7 **Atlantic City** Wyoming U.S.A.
95 N6 **Atlantic Highlands** New Jersey U.S.A.
90 J15 **Atlantic-Indian Basin** Southern Oc
90 J14 **Atlantic-Indian Ridge** S Atlantic Oc
128 D1 **Atlántico** *div* Colombia
90 **Atlantic Oc**
90 E5 **Atlantis Fracture** Atlantic Oc
94 D4 **Atlas** Michigan U.S.A.
85 C2 **Atlas, Haut** *mts* Morocco
85 C2 **Atlas, Moyen** *mts* Morocco
85 E2 **Atlas Saharien** *mts* Algeria
118 G8 **Atlee** Alberta Canada
117 G6 **Atlin** British Columbia Canada
80 C3 **'Atlit** Israel
125 K8 **Atlixco** Mexico
26 A10 **Atlöy** *isld* Norway
76 D3 **Atmakur** India
113 B11 **Atmore** Alabama U.S.A.
117 L9 **Atnarko** British Columbia Canada
26 D10 **Atnasjö** *L* Norway
55 E2 **Atnis** Russian Federation
60 E11 **Atō** Japan
87 H12 **Atofinandrahana** Madagascar
107 O7 **Atoka** Oklahoma U.S.A.
102 G6 **Atolia** California U.S.A.
101 N6 **Atomic City** Idaho U.S.A.
124 H7 **Atotonilco el Alto** Mexico
77 E1 **Atrak** *R* Iran
27 F14 **Atran** Sweden
26 L7 **Åträsk** Sweden
128 C2 **Atrato** *R* Colombia
42 F6 **Atri** Italy
45 R8 **Atripaida** Italy
56 G4 **Atsikyak** Russian Federation
61 N10 **Atsugi** Japan
61 N7 **Atsumi** Japan
61 L11 **Atsumi-hantō** *pen* Japan
140 C4 **Attack Cr** N Terr Australia
111 K7 **Attalla** Alabama U.S.A.
68 H5 **Attapu** Laos
47 U14 **Attaviros** *mt* Rhodes Greece
115 L7 **Attawapiskat** Ontario Canada
80 G1 **Aţ Ţayḩah** Syria
36 D1 **Attendorn** Germany
38 J6 **Attersee** Austria
110 J1 **Attica** Indiana U.S.A.
107 M4 **Attica** Kansas U.S.A.
94 D3 **Attica** Michigan U.S.A.
94 J4 **Attica** New York U.S.A.
94 E5 **Attica** Ohio U.S.A.
22 E5 **Attichy** France
40 B5 **Attignat** France
22 H5 **Attigny** France
46 F6 **Attikí** *admin region* Greece
95 Q5 **Attleboro** Massachusetts U.S.A.
9 H2 **Attleborough** England
9 H2 **Attlebridge** England
26 J9 **Attmar** Sweden
109 N4 **Attoyac Bayou** *R* Texas U.S.A.
116 J9 **Attu** Aleutian Is
115 O4 **Attu** Greenland
76 D5 **Attur** India
133 D5 **Atuel** *R* Argentina
131 C6 **Atuel, Banados del** *swamps* Argentina
27 H13 **Åtvid** Sweden
27 H13 **Åtvidaberg** Sweden
119 P8 **Atwater** Saskatchewan Canada
102 D4 **Atwater** California U.S.A.
99 M4 **Atwater** Minnesota U.S.A.
13 H6 **Atwick** England
106 G1 **Atwood** Colorado U.S.A.
110 H2 **Atwood** Illinois U.S.A.
107 J2 **Atwood** Kansas U.S.A.
94 F6 **Atwood Res** Ohio U.S.A.
53 G7 **Atyashevo** Russian Federation
38 N5 **Atzenbrugg** Austria
33 P9 **Atzendorf** Germany
36 D2 **Au** Rheinland-Pfalz Germany
128 E4 **Auati-Paraná** *R* Brazil
135 S3 **Auau Chan** Hawaiian Is
37 J4 **Aub** Germany
19 P18 **Aubagne** France
22 K4 **Aubange** Belgium
71 F2 **Aubarede Pt** Luzon Philippines
18 H4 **Aube** *R* France
18 H4 **Aube** *dept* France
22 K2 **Aubel** Belgium
22 E3 **Aubencheul-Au-Bac** France
22 G4 **Aubenton** France
21 O4 **Aubergenville** France
83 L13 **Aubert,C** Kerguelen Indian Oc
21 M4 **Aube-sur-Rille** France
18 F7 **Aubeterre** France
21 J8 **Aubiers, les** France
21 L6 **Aubigné** Sarthe France
22 D3 **Aubigny** Pas-de-Calais France
20 H8 **Aubigny** Vendée France
18 G5 **Aubigny sur Nère** France
18 G8 **Aubin** France
18 H8 **Aubrac, Mts d'** France
103 M6 **Aubrey Cliffs** Arizona U.S.A.
143 B7 **Aubrey, Mt** W Australia Australia
114 G4 **Aubry L** Northwest Territories Canada
141 K7 **Auburn** *R* Queensland Australia
111 L9 **Auburn** Alabama U.S.A.
102 C3 **Auburn** California U.S.A.
110 G2 **Auburn** Illinois U.S.A.
94 B5 **Auburn** Indiana U.S.A.
107 P3 **Auburn** Kansas U.S.A.
110 K5 **Auburn** Kentucky U.S.A.
95 R2 **Auburn** Maine U.S.A.
94 C3 **Auburn** Michigan U.S.A.
99 L9 **Auburn** Nebraska U.S.A.
95 L4 **Auburn** New York U.S.A.
117 M12 **Auburn** Washington U.S.A.
113 F9 **Auburndale** Florida U.S.A.
99 R5 **Auburndale** Wisconsin U.S.A.
141 K7 **Auburn Ra** Queensland Australia
18 G7 **Aubusson** France
133 D5 **Auca Mahuida,Sa** *mt* Argentina
52 B6 **Auce** Latvia
18 F9 **Auch** France
22 C3 **Auchel** France
12 E4 **Auchencairn** Scotland
12 D4 **Auchenmalg** Scotland
85 F7 **Auchi** Nigeria
12 D3 **Auchinleck** Scotland
12 E1 **Auchterarder** Scotland
13 E1 **Auchterderran** Scotland
13 E1 **Auchtermuchty** Scotland
22 C2 **Auchy-au-Bois** France
113 D7 **Aucilla** *R* Florida U.S.A.
145 F1 **Auckland** New Zealand
145 E2 **Auckland** *admin region* New Zealand
68 D6 **Auckland B** Burma
18 G9 **Aude** *R* France
18 G9 **Aude** *dept* France
120 C2 **Auden** Ontario Canada
Audenarde *see* **Oudenaarde**
18 E8 **Audenge** France
20 G2 **Auderville** France
20 A5 **Audierne** France
20 B6 **Audierne, B. d'** France
83 L14 **Audierne, Bd'** Kerguelen Indian Oc
40 E3 **Audincourt** France
22 B2 **Audinghen** France
45 N4 **Auditore** Italy
8 D2 **Audlem** England
22 B2 **Audresselles** France
7 M9 **Audrey** *oil rig* North Sea
22 C2 **Audruicq** France
99 M8 **Audubon** Iowa U.S.A.
98 E2 **Audubon Lake** *res* North Dakota U.S.A.
19 J3 **Audun le Roman** France
32 G6 **Aue** *R* Germany
37 O2 **Aue** Germany
84 E4 **Auenat Uennin** Libya
36 G5 **Auenstein** Germany
37 N2 **Auerbach** Germany
36 F4 **Auerbach** Hessen Germany
41 N2 **Auer Berg** *mt* Germany
37 O2 **Auerswalde** Germany
111 E12 **Au Far, Point** Louisiana U.S.A.
21 N2 **Auffay** France
20 F6 **Augan** France
141 H7 **Augathella** Queensland Australia
14 E2 **Aughnacloy** N Ireland
14 E4 **Aughrim** Ireland
89 B7 **Augrabies** S Africa
89 B7 **Augrabies Falls** Orange R S Africa
94 D2 **Au Gres** Michigan U.S.A.
37 K7 **Augsburg** Germany
143 B10 **Augusta** W Australia Australia
43 G11 **Augusta** Sicily
110 E6 **Augusta** Arkansas U.S.A.
112 E4 **Augusta** Georgia U.S.A.
110 F1 **Augusta** Illinois U.S.A.
107 O4 **Augusta** Kansas U.S.A.
94 C8 **Augusta** Kentucky U.S.A.
95 S2 **Augusta** Maine U.S.A.
94 B4 **Augusta** Michigan U.S.A.
101 N2 **Augusta** Montana U.S.A.
99 P5 **Augusta** Wisconsin U.S.A.
143 E7 **Augusta, L** W Australia Australia
116 R6 **Augusta,Mt** Yukon Territory Canada
94 H8 **Augusta Springs** Virginia U.S.A.
116 L7 **Augustine I** Alaska U.S.A.
130 G6 **Augusto de Lima** Brazil
130 H8 **Augusto Severo** Brazil
31 O2 **Augustów** Poland
140 E4 **Augustus Downs** Queensland Australia
142 E3 **Augustus Island** W Australia Australia
143 B6 **Augustus, Mt** W Australia Australia
37 M6 **Au in der Hallertau** Germany
40 B2 **Aujon** *R* France
6 M6 **Auk** *oil rig* North Sea
32 L4 **Aukrug** Germany
26 K6 **Auktsjaur** Sweden
112 K1 **Aulander** North Carolina U.S.A.
142 E5 **Auld, L** W Australia Australia
18 E6 **Aulnay de Saintonge** France
21 P5 **Aulnay-la-Rivière** France
20 B5 **Aulne** *R* France
118 H1 **Aulneau Pen** Ontario Canada
22 F3 **Aulnoye** France
106 F1 **Ault** Colorado U.S.A.
15 C3 **Aultbea** Scotland
54 F8 **Auly** Ukraine
37 M2 **Auma** *R* Germany
37 M2 **Auma** Germany
21 O2 **Aumale** France
18 G6 **Aumance** *R* France
22 K5 **Aumetz** France
57 C4 **Auminzatau,Gory** *mt* Uzbekistan
40 C4 **Aumont** France
18 H8 **Aumont** Lozère France
33 M5 **Aumühle** Germany
21 J3 **Aunay-sur-Odon** France
74 F10 **Aundh** India
21 L6 **Aune** *R* France
21 O5 **Auneau** France
21 P3 **Auneuil** France
68 B3 **Aunglan** Burma
28 E4 **Auning** Denmark
18 E6 **Aunis** *prov* France
87 C11 **Auob** *R* Namibia
71 J5 **Auponhia** Moluccas Indonesia
19 Q17 **Aups** France
69 G11 **Aur** *isld* Malaysia
29 K11 **Aura** Finland
26 C9 **Aura** *R* Norway
37 K4 **Aurach** *R* Germany
74 H5 **Auraiya** India
29 K11 **Aurajoki** *R* Finland
74 F9 **Aurangabad** India
20 E6 **Auray** France
21 J3 **Aure** *R* France
26 C8 **Aure** Norway
19 O16 **Aurel** France
99 L7 **Aurelia** Iowa U.S.A.
85 F1 **Aurès** *mts* Algeria
32 F6 **Aurich** Germany
130 E5 **Aurilândia** Brazil
18 G8 **Aurillac** France
19 P18 **Auriol** France
70 B5 **Aurkuning** Kalimantan
27 B11 **Aurland** Norway
130 H9 **Aurora** Brazil
121 L9 **Aurora** Ontario Canada
106 F2 **Aurora** Colorado U.S.A.
99 S8 **Aurora** Illinois U.S.A.
94 C7 **Aurora** Indiana U.S.A.
107 N2 **Aurora** Kansas U.S.A.
110 C5 **Aurora** Missouri U.S.A.
98 H9 **Aurora** Nebraska U.S.A.
112 L2 **Aurora** North Carolina U.S.A.
103 N3 **Aurora** Utah U.S.A.
19 P15 **Aurouze, Mt d'** France
76 D4 **Auroville** India
26 C9 **Aursjöen** *L* Norway
27 E12 **Aurskog** Norway
26 E9 **Aursunden** *L* Norway
141 F2 **Aurukun** Queensland Australia
45 P7 **Aurunci Monti** Italy
87 C11 **Aus** Namibia
94 C2 **Au Sable** *R* Michigan U.S.A.
95 O2 **Ausable Forks** New York U.S.A.
94 D2 **Au Sable Pt** Michigan U.S.A.
128 D6 **Ausangate** *mt* Peru
80 F4 **Ausara** Jordan
88 B7 **Aushi** Zambia
15 F1 **Auskerry** Scotland
45 O7 **Ausoni, Monti** *mt* Italy
41 K3 **Ausser-Rhoden** *dist* Switzerland
8 D4 **Aust** England
27 C13 **Austad** Norway
27 C13 **Aust Agder Fylker** Norway
112 C4 **Austell** Georgia U.S.A.
Austerlitz *see* **Slavkov**
119 T9 **Austin** Manitoba Canada
99 O6 **Austin** Minnesota U.S.A.
101 N3 **Austin** Montana U.S.A.
100 G5 **Austin** Oregon U.S.A.
94 J5 **Austin** Pennsylvania U.S.A.
109 K5 **Austin** Texas U.S.A.
143 C8 **Austin, L** W Australia Australia
109 M4 **Austonio** Texas U.S.A.
140 E5 **Austral Downs** N Terr Australia
136 **Australia** *dominion* Australia
146 F15 **Australian Antarctic Territory** Antarctica
143 B10 **Australind** W Australia Australia
135 M11 **Austral Ridge** Pacific Oc
26 D8 **Austråt** Norway
27 A11 **Austrheim** Norway
38 E7 **Austria** *rep* Cent Europe
26 G3 **Austvågöy** *isld* Norway
109 L7 **Austwell** Texas U.S.A.
21 N6 **Autainville** France
128 G4 **Autazes** Brazil
22 K4 **Autelbas** Belgium
18 G9 **Auterive** France
123 L3 **Auteuil, L. d'** Quebec Canada
22 C3 **Authie** *R* France
121 M4 **Authier** Quebec Canada
21 K7 **Authion** *R* France
21 M6 **Authon** Loir-et-Cher France
21 M5 **Authon-du-Perche** France
21 O5 **Authon-la-Plaine** France
124 G8 **Autlán de Navarro** Mexico
45 O6 **Autore, M** *mt* Italy
99 U3 **Au Train** Michigan U.S.A.
19 P14 **Autrans** France
21 P5 **Autruy-sur-Juine** France
22 H5 **Autry** France
18 H6 **Autun** France
140 B3 **Auvergne** N Terr Australia
18 H7 **Auvergne** *prov* France
21 K6 **Auvers-le-Hamon** France
21 P3 **Auvers-sur-Oise** France
18 F7 **Auvezère** *R* France
22 G4 **Auvillers-les-Forges** France
21 L8 **Auxances** *R* France
94 E2 **Aux Barques, Pt** Michigan U.S.A.
18 H5 **Auxerre** France
21 P1 **Auxi-le-Château** France
40 B3 **Auxonne** France
110 E2 **Auxvasse** Missouri U.S.A.
128 F2 **Auyán Tepui** *mt* Venezuela
115 M4 **Auyuittuq Nat Park** NW Terr
20 G8 **Auzance** *R* France
18 G6 **Auzances** France
68 B2 **Ava** Burma
110 G4 **Ava** Illinois U.S.A.
110 D5 **Ava** Missouri U.S.A.
26 M5 **Avafors** Sweden
18 F6 **Availles-Limouzine** France
116 H1 **Avalik** *R* Alaska U.S.A.
18 H5 **Avallon** France
102 F8 **Avalon** California U.S.A.
111 F8 **Avalon** Mississippi U.S.A.
95 N7 **Avalon** New Jersey U.S.A.
108 C3 **Avalon, L** New Mexico U.S.A.
123 T6 **Avalon Pen** Newfoundland Canada
131 F2 **Avalos** *R* Argentina
124 J5 **Avalos** Mexico
19 Q15 **Avançon** France
107 M5 **Avard** Oklahoma U.S.A.
129 J8 **Avaré** Brazil
53 G12 **Avarskoye Koysu** *R* Russian Federation
47 H4 **Ávas** Greece
116 E9 **Avatanak I** Aleutian Is
26 H7 **Avaträsk** Sweden
26 L5 **Avaudden** Sweden
26 K6 **Avaviken** Sweden
102 H6 **Avawatz Mts** California U.S.A.
47 N10 **Avci Koru** *forest* Turkey
54 J8 **Avdeyevka** Ukraine
9 E5 **Avebury** England
16 D4 **Aveinte** Spain
129 G4 **Aveiro** Brazil
16 B4 **Aveiro** Portugal
77 A2 **Avej** Iran
22 E2 **Avelgem** Belgium
94 G6 **Avella** Pennsylvania U.S.A.
133 F4 **Avellaneda** Argentina
45 R8 **Avellino** Italy
102 D6 **Avenal** California U.S.A.
40 F4 **Avenches** Switzerland
95 Q4 **Aver** Massachusetts U.S.A.
28 E6 **Avernak By** *B* Denmark
26 B8 **Averöy** *isld* Norway
45 Q8 **Aversa** Italy
100 K2 **Avery** Idaho U.S.A.
99 O8 **Avery** Iowa U.S.A.
109 N2 **Avery** Texas U.S.A.
111 E12 **Avery Island** Louisiana U.S.A.
22 F3 **Avesnes** France
22 D3 **Avesnes le Comte** France
22 E3 **Avesnes-les-Aubert** France
90 C7 **Aves Ridge** Atlantic Oc
20 G6 **Avessac** France
27 H11 **Avesta** Sweden
18 F8 **Aveyron** *R* France
18 G8 **Aveyron** *dept* France
45 O5 **Avezzano** Italy
46 E5 **Avgó** *mt* Greece
46 F8 **Avgó** *isld* Greece
47 H9 **Avgó** *isld* Greece
133 E3 **Aviá Terai** Argentina
15 E3 **Aviemore** Scotland
144 C6 **Aviemore, L** New Zealand
115 P5 **Avigaat** Greenland
80 B7 **Avigedor** Israel
43 G8 **Avigliano** Italy
19 N17 **Avignon** France
16 D4 **Avila** *prov* Spain
16 D4 **Ávila, Sa. de** *mts* Spain
16 D1 **Avilés** Spain
40 D3 **Avilley** France
109 N3 **Avinger** Texas U.S.A.
22 D3 **Avion** France
47 O12 **Aviótes** Greece
95 K5 **Avis** Pennsylvania U.S.A.
41 O5 **Avisio** *R* Italy
80 E1 **Avivim** Israel
16 B5 **Aviz** Portugal
46 F6 **Avlón** Greece
28 B4 **Avlum** Denmark
80 G2 **Avne Etan** Syria
80 G2 **Avné Etan** Syria
28 H6 **Avnø Fjord** *inlet* Denmark
28 F6 **Avnslev** Denmark
139 G6 **Avoca** Victoria Australia
14 E4 **Avoca** Ireland
144 C5 **Avoca** New Zealand
94 E3 **Avoca** Michigan U.S.A.
95 K4 **Avoca** New York U.S.A.
108 H3 **Avoca** Texas U.S.A.
14 E4 **Avoca,Vale of** Ireland
138 D5 **Avoid B** South Australia Australia
117 O10 **Avola** British Columbia Canada
43 G12 **Avola** Sicily
8 D5 **Avon** *co* England
15 E3 **Avon** *R* Scotland
106 D2 **Avon** Colorado U.S.A.
95 P5 **Avon** Connecticut U.S.A.
110 F1 **Avon** Illinois U.S.A.
99 M4 **Avon** Minnesota U.S.A.
101 N3 **Avon** Montana U.S.A.
94 K4 **Avon** New York U.S.A.
112 M2 **Avon** North Carolina U.S.A.
94 E5 **Avon** Ohio U.S.A.
98 H6 **Avon** South Dakota U.S.A.
141 K6 **Avondale** Queensland Australia
103 M8 **Avondale** Arizona U.S.A.
106 F3 **Avondale** Colorado U.S.A.
110 B2 **Avondale** Missouri U.S.A.
109 L8 **Avondale** Texas U.S.A.
140 D4 **Avon Downs** N Terr Australia
141 H5 **Avon Downs** Queensland Australia
94 E5 **Avon Lake** Ohio U.S.A.
119 M8 **Avonlea** Saskatchewan Canada
21 L7 **Avon-les-Roches** France
94 H6 **Avonmore** Pennsylvania U.S.A.
8 D4 **Avonmouth** England
113 F10 **Avon Park** Florida U.S.A.
143 B9 **Avon, R** W Australia Australia
9 E3 **Avon, R** England
9 E5 **Avon, R** England
130 E10 **Avoredo** *lighthouse* Brazil
40 D3 **Avoudrey** France
65 A1 **Avraga** Mongolia
20 H4 **Avranches** France
22 D4 **Avre** *R* France
21 N4 **Avre** *R* Eure France
36 B6 **Avricourt** France
48 J5 **Avrig** Romania
22 K5 **Avril** France
48 E7 **Avtovac** Bosnia-Herzegovina
61 P12 **Awa** Okinawa
69 C12 **Awaay** Indonesia
60 H11 **Awaji-shima** *isld* Japan
145 E3 **Awakino** New Zealand
84 E4 **Awāl** *watercourse* Libya
70 Q10 **Awang** Indonesia
145 D1 **Awanui** New Zealand
86 H4 **Āwarē** Ethiopia
144 B7 **Awarua** New Zealand
86 G4 **Āwasa Hāyk'** *L* Ethiopia
86 H4 **Āwash** Ethiopia
61 N7 **Awa-shima** *isld* Japan
85 D7 **Awaso** Ghana
57 K4 **Awat** China
86 G4 **Āwat'a** *R* Ethiopia
145 E4 **Awatere R** New Zealand

84 E4 **Awbārī** Libya
86 H5 **Aw Dheegle** Somalia
12 C1 **Awe,L** Scotland
112 H4 **Awendaw** South Carolina U.S.A.
84 G4 **Awjilah** Libya
70 G6 **Awo** *R* Sulawesi Indonesia
117 Q4 **Awry L** Northwest Territories Canada
85 B4 **Awserd** Mauritania
116 J2 **Awuna** *R* Alaska U.S.A.
8 D5 **Axbridge** England
25 A6 **Axel** Netherlands
27 F14 **Axelfors** Sweden
147 H5 **Axel Heiberg I** Northwest Territories Canada
106 C1 **Axial** Colorado U.S.A.
128 G4 **Axinim** Brazil
18 G10 **Ax-les-Thermes** France
8 D6 **Axminster** England
112 E6 **Axson** Georgia U.S.A.
107 O2 **Axtell** Kansas U.S.A.
27 G13 **Axvall** Sweden
18 H3 **Ay** France
20 H3 **Ay** *R* France
128 C4 **Ayabaca** Peru
60 J10 **Ayabe** Japan
78 D1 **Ayaç** Turkey
133 F5 **Ayacucho** Argentina
128 D6 **Ayacucho** Peru
68 B1 **Ayadaw** Burma
57 K1 **Ayaguz** Kazakhstan
57 D4 **Ayakkuduk** Uzbekistan
66 D4 **Ayakkum Hu** *L* China
16 C7 **Ayamonte** Spain
78 E1 **Ayancık** Turkey
80 C6 **Ayanot** Israel
126 G10 **Ayapel** Colombia
128 D6 **Ayaviri** Peru
77 L1 **Āybak** Afghanistan
13 G4 **Aycliffe** England
55 E4 **Aydabul'** Kazakhstan
54 L8 **Aydar** *R* Ukraine
57 D4 **Aydarkul', Ozero** *L* Uzbekistan
112 K2 **Ayden** North Carolina U.S.A.
47 J7 **Aydın** Turkey
78 A3 **Aydın** Turkey
Aydıncık *see* **Gılındire**
47 J7 **Aydin Dağlar** *mts* Turkey
79 B1 **Aydınkent** Turkey
47 N11 **Aydınlı** Turkey
55 C5 **Aydrlinskiy** Russian Federation
86 H3 **Ayelu Terara** *mt* Ethiopia
40 G5 **Ayer** Switzerland
17 G2 **Ayerbe** Spain
100 G3 **Ayers** Washington U.S.A.
140 C7 **Ayers Ra** N Terr Australia
140 B7 **Ayers Rock** *mt* N Terr Australia
55 F3 **Ayev** *R* Russian Federation
19 O16 **Aygues** *R* France
56 C5 **Aygulaskiy Khrebet** *mts* Russian Federation
46 F5 **Ayiá** Greece
46 F6 **Ayía Ánna** Greece
46 G5 **Ayía Iríni Akra** *C* Greece
47 H5 **Ayiássos** Greece
46 G4 **Áyion Óros** *reg* Greece
46 F7 **Áyios** *isld* Greece
46 G5 **Áyios Evstrátios** *isld* Greece
47 O12 **Ayios Matthaíos** Greece
46 G9 **Áyios Míron** Crete Greece
47 H9 **Ayios Nikólaos** Crete Greece
46 D6 **Ayios Pétros** Greece
79 D3 **Ayios Seryios** Cyprus
79 E3 **Ayios Theodhoros** Cyprus
116 L2 **Ayiyak** *R* Alaska U.S.A.
47 H7 **Aykathonisi** *isld* Greece
86 G3 **Āykel** Ethiopia
47 H7 **Ay Kírikos** Greece
36 B4 **Ayl** Germany
121 N7 **Aylen,L** Ontario Canada
119 M8 **Aylesbury** Saskatchewan Canada
9 F4 **Aylesbury** England
144 D5 **Aylesbury** New Zealand
122 H8 **Aylesford** Nova Scotia Canada
9 H5 **Aylesham** England
117 D6 **Aylesworth, Mt** Br Col/Alaska Canada/U.S.A.
16 E3 **Ayllón** Spain
16 E3 **Ayllón, Sa. de** *mts* Spain
121 P7 **Aylmer** Quebec Canada
114 J5 **Aylmer L** Northwest Territories Canada
118 B7 **Aylmer,Mt** Alberta Canada
119 O5 **Aylsham** Saskatchewan Canada
9 H2 **Aylsham** England
121 O7 **Aylwin** Quebec Canada
17 F6 **Ayna** Spain
79 H4 **'Ayn al Bayḑā'** Syria
78 J3 **Ayn Diwār** Syria
9 E3 **Aynho** England
112 H4 **Aynor** South Carolina U.S.A.
80 G1 **Ayn Ziwān** Syria
84 G5 **'Ayn Zuwayyah** *well* Libya
147 Q4 **Ayon,Ostrov** *isld* Russian Federation
17 G5 **Ayora** Spain
85 E6 **Ayorou** Niger
55 G2 **Aypolovo** Russian Federation
Ayr *co see* **Strathclyde** *reg*
141 H4 **Ayr** Queensland Australia
12 D3 **Ayr** Scotland
98 H9 **Ayr** Nebraska U.S.A.
98 J2 **Ayr** North Dakota U.S.A.
21 L8 **Ayron** France
99 M6 **Ayrshire** Iowa U.S.A.
141 G5 **Ayrshire Downs** Queensland Australia
55 F4 **Aysarinskoye** Kazakhstan
13 G5 **Aysgarth** England
86 H3 **Āysha** Ethiopia
57 F1 **Ayshirak** Kazakhstan
57 G3 **Aytau** *mts* Kazakhstan
13 H5 **Ayton** N Yorks England
13 F2 **Ayton** Scotland
47 J2 **Aytos** Bulgaria
57 C4 **Aytym** Uzbekistan
61 P7 **Ayukawahama** Japan
65 C2 **Ayulhai** China
124 G7 **Ayutla** Mexico
68 E5 **Ayutthaya** Thailand
78 A2 **Ayvacik** Turkey
47 H5 **Ayvalık** Turkey
22 K3 **Aywaille** Belgium
80 E1 **Ayyelet Ha Shahar** Israel
77 D1 **Āzād Shahr** Iran
100 B7 **Azalea** Oregon U.S.A.
61 P13 **Azama** Okinawa
79 G7 **Azamān, Qā'** *depression* Saudi Arabia
75 K5 **Azamgarh** India
55 C3 **Azangulovo** Russian Federation
55 D2 **Azanka** Russian Federation
22 J5 **Azannes-et-Soumazannes** France
77 A1 **Āzarān** Iran
78 K2 **Āzārbāyjān-e Gharbī** Iran
78 L2 **Āzārbāyjān-e Sharqī** Iran
85 G6 **Azare** Nigeria
52 E5 **Azatskoye, Oz** *L* Russian Federation
21 N8 **Azay-le-Ferron** France
21 L7 **Azay-le-Rideau** France
21 M7 **Azay-sur-Cher** France
21 K8 **Azay-sur-Thouet** France
79 H2 **A'zāz** Syria
Azbine *reg* Niger *see* **Aïr ou Azbine**
21 N6 **Azé** Loire France
40 G7 **Azeglio** Italy
78 L1 **Azerbaijan** *rep* E Europe
Azerbaydzhanskaya S.S.R. *see* **Azerbaijan**
19 N13 **Azergues** *R* France
53 F7 **Azeyevo** Russian Federation
55 G4 **Azhbulat, Oz** *L* Kazakhstan
56 C5 **Azho-Tayga, Gora** *mt* Russian Federation
85 C2 **Azilal** Morocco
22 C3 **Azincourt** France
86 A6 **Azingo, L** Gabon
95 R1 **Aziscoos L** Maine U.S.A.
84 E3 **'Azīzīyah, Al** Libya
16 C7 **Aznalcóllar** Spain
128 C4 **Azogues** Ecuador
52 G2 **Azopol'ye** Russian Federation
Azores *islds see* **Açores**
90 G5 **Azores-Cape St Vincent Ridge** Atlantic Oc
86 D3 **Azoum** *R* Chad
54 L9 **Azov** Russian Federation
Azov,Sea of *see* **Azovskoye More**
54 L9 **Azovskiy Kanal** Russian Federation
53 E10 **Azovskoye More** Rus Fed/Ukraine
17 F1 **Azpeitia** Spain
85 C2 **Azrou** Morocco
103 L9 **Aztec** Arizona U.S.A.
106 C5 **Aztec** New Mexico U.S.A.
106 B5 **Aztec Ruins Nat.Mon** New Mexico U.S.A.
127 J5 **Azua** Dominican Rep
16 D6 **Azuaga** Spain
17 G3 **Azuara** Spain
128 C4 **Azuay** *prov* Ecuador
60 C12 **Azuch-Ō-shima** *isld* Japan
17 F6 **Azuer** *R* Spain
125 O6 **Azuero,Pen.de** Panama
131 B3 **Azufre, P. del** Chile
48 K5 **Azuga** Romania
133 F5 **Azul** Argentina
131 B5 **Azul** *pk* Chile
125 P9 **Azul** *R* Mexico
131 B8 **Azul, Cerro** *pk* Neuquén Argentina
130 E7 **Azul Paulista, Mte** Brazil
130 C4 **Azul,Serra** *mts* Mato Grosso Brazil
61 O8 **Azuma-yama** *mt* Japan
80 B8 **Azza** Israel
79 G5 **Az Zabadānī** Syria
84 F4 **Az Zahrah** Libya

B

71 L10 **Baa** Indonesia
41 M3 **Baad** Austria
70 E4 **Baai** *R* Kalimantan
25 F6 **Baal** Germany
79 G4 **Baalbek** Lebanon
86 H5 **Baardheere** Somalia
25 C6 **Baarle-Hertog** Belgium
25 C6 **Baarle Nassau** Netherlands
25 D4 **Baarn** Netherlands
60 D14 **Baba** Japan
46 E4 **Baba** *mt* Macedonia Yugoslavia
47 H5 **Baba Burun** *C* Turkey
78 M1 **Babadag** *mt* Azerbaijan
48 M6 **Babadag** Romania
47 J3 **Babaeski** Turkey
128 C4 **Babahoyo** Ecuador
71 G7 **Babak** Philippines
143 C9 **Babakin** W Australia Australia
77 K2 **Bābā, Koh-i-** *mts* Afghanistan
79 H2 **Bāb, Al** Syria
72 E6 **Bab al Mandab** *str* Arabia/Djibouti
79 G3 **Bābannā** Syria
67 B5 **Babao** China
71 O8 **Babar** *isld* Indonesia
71 O9 **Babar,Kep** *islds* Indonesia
70 O9 **Babat** Java
57 E5 **Babatag, Khr** *mts* Tajikistan/Uzbekistan
88 E4 **Babati** Tanzania
71 L10 **Babau** Timor Indonesia
80 G7 **Babayir et Tiwal** Jordan
101 M1 **Babb** Montana U.S.A.
116 S2 **Babbage** *R* Yukon Territory Canada
143 A6 **Babbage I** W Australia Australia
99 P2 **Babbitt** Minnesota U.S.A.
99 Q5 **Babcock** Wisconsin U.S.A.
33 P5 **Bäbelin** Germany
88 C5 **Babemba** *tribe* Zaire
88 C7 **Babemba** *tribe* Zambia
36 F4 **Babenhausen** Hessen Germany
31 M6 **Babia Góra** *mts* Czech/Poland
124 E3 **Babicora** Mexico
124 F3 **Babicora, L. de** Mexico
78 K5 **Bābil** *prov* Iraq
141 H3 **Babinda** Queensland Australia
117 L8 **Babine L** British Columbia Canada
117 K8 **Babine Ra** British Columbia Canada
69 C11 **Babi, Pulau** *isld* Indonesia
136 G2 **Babo** W Irian
48 D4 **Babócsa** Hungary
77 C1 **Bābol** Iran
103 N10 **Baboquivari Pk** Arizona U.S.A.
142 E4 **Babrongan Tower** *mt* W Australia Australia
113 F10 **Babson Park** Florida U.S.A.
36 G5 **Babstadt** Germany
16 D9 **Bab Taza** Morocco
67 B3 **Babu** China
46 E3 **Babuna** *mt* Macedonia Yugoslavia
56 G5 **Babushkin** Russian Federation
71 E1 **Babuyan** *islds* Philippines
71 D6 **Babuyan** Philippines
71 E1 **Babuyan Ch** Philippines
124 E4 **Baca** Mexico
86 A2 **Bacaadweyn** Somalia
124 E4 **Bacabáche** Mexico
129 G5 **Bacabal** Brazil
129 H4 **Bacaja** *R* Brazil
71 A3 **Bacan** *isld* Indonesia
124 E3 **Bacanora** Mexico
71 E1 **Bacarra** Philippines
48 K4 **Bacău** Romania
68 G1 **Bac Can** Vietnam
19 K4 **Baccarat** France
122 G10 **Baccaro Pt** Nova Scotia Canada
45 L1 **Bacchiglione** *R* Italy
41 H5 **Baceno** Italy
48 L4 **Băceşti** Romania
68 H2 **Bac Giang** Vietnam
37 N5 **Bach** Germany
94 D3 **Bach** Michigan U.S.A.
127 J10 **Bachaquero** Venezuela
36 D3 **Bacharach** Germany
115 M2 **Bache Pen** Northwest Territories Canada
124 F3 **Bachiniva** Mexico
68 J2 **Bach Long Vi** *isld* Vietnam
69 E9 **Bacho** Thailand
37 L1 **Bachra** Germany
57 J5 **Bachu** China
115 K4 **Back** *R* Northwest Territories Canada
48 E5 **Backa** *reg* Serbia Yugoslavia
27 G14 **Bäckaby** Sweden
48 E5 **Bačka Palanka** Serbia Yugoslavia
48 F5 **Bačka Topola** Serbia Yugoslavia
95 L10 **Back Bay** Virginia U.S.A.
117 J4 **Backbone Ranges** Northwest Territories Canada
26 H8 **Backe** Sweden
27 F13 **Bäckefors** Sweden
27 G12 **Bäckhammar** Sweden
36 G6 **Backnang** Germany
119 U10 **Backoo** North Dakota U.S.A.
48 F5 **Bačko Petrovo Selo** Serbia Yugoslavia
138 E6 **Backstaiys Pass** South Australia Australia
26 H6 **Bäckstrand** Sweden
99 M3 **Backus** Minnesota U.S.A.
8 D5 **Backwell** England
Bac Lieu *see* **Vinh Loi**
71 E2 **Bacnotan** Luzon Philippines
127 P5 **Bacolet** Grenada
45 Q8 **Bacoli** Italy
71 F5 **Bacolod** Philippines
71 E4 **Baco, Mt** Philippines
112 C6 **Baconton** Georgia U.S.A.
21 N2 **Bacqueville-en-Caux** France
48 E4 **Bácsalmás** Hungary
48 E4 **Bács-Kiskun** *co* Hungary
9 H2 **Bacton** England
124 F5 **Bacubirito** Mexico
71 G7 **Baculin Bay** Mindanao Philippines
13 F6 **Bacup** England
129 J4 **Bacuri,I de** Brazil
98 F5 **Bad** *R* South Dakota U.S.A.
Bada *see* **Xilin**
75 L7 **Bada Barabil** India
37 N6 **Bad Abbach** Germany
76 B5 **Badagara** India
38 E6 **Bad Aibling** Germany
129 J4 **Badajós** Brazil
16 C6 **Badajoz** *prov* Spain
16 C6 **Badajoz** Spain
128 F4 **Badajoz, L** Brazil
77 L1 **Badakhshān** *prov* Afghanistan
17 J3 **Badalona** Spain
76 B3 **Badami** India
75 M7 **Bādāmpāhārh** India
56 E3 **Badan, Khrebet** *mts* Russian Federation
65 H3 **Badaohe** China
Badaojiang *see* **Hunjiang**
124 F5 **Badariguato** Mexico
74 H3 **Badarīnaāth** India
70 D2 **Badas** Brunei
69 H12 **Badas,Kep** *isld* Indonesia
38 J6 **Bad Aussee** Austria
94 E3 **Bad Axe** Michigan U.S.A.
32 G7 **Badbergen** Germany
36 D5 **Bad Bergzabern** Germany
37 L2 **Bad Berka** Germany
36 E1 **Bad Berleburg** Germany
37 M3 **Bad Berneck** Germany
36 B3 **Bad Bertrich** Germany
37 M1 **Bad Bibra** Sachsen-Anhalt Germany
37 L2 **Bad Blankenburg** Germany
37 J3 **Bad Bocklet** Germany
32 L5 **Bad Bramstedt** Germany
123 M7 **Baddeck** C Breton I, Nova Scotia
32 M8 **Baddeckenstedt** Germany
26 M2 **Badderen** Norway
33 P4 **Bad Doberan** Germany
32 K9 **Bad Driburg** Germany
33 R9 **Bad Düben** Germany
36 E5 **Bad Dürkheim** Germany
33 Q10 **Bad Dürrenberg** Germany
37 N3 **Bad Elster** Germany
36 D3 **Bad Ems** Germany
48 C2 **Baden** Austria
119 Q6 **Baden** Manitoba Canada
20 E6 **Baden** France
41 H3 **Baden** Switzerland
94 G6 **Baden** Pennsylvania U.S.A.
36 E6 **Baden-Baden** Germany
15 D4 **Badenoch** Scotland
19 K4 **Badenviller** France
36 G6 **Baden-Württemberg** Germany
45 P1 **Baderna** Croatia
33 U7 **Bad Freienwalde** Germany
36 G5 **Bad Friedrichshall** Germany
32 M9 **Bad Gandersheim** Germany
118 F1 **Badger** Manitoba Canada
123 Q5 **Badger** Newfoundland Canada
102 E5 **Badger** California U.S.A.
98 K1 **Badger** Minnesota U.S.A.
101 Q5 **Badger Basin** Wyoming U.S.A.
77 H2 **Bādghīs** Afghanistan
38 N8 **Bad Gleichenberg** Austria
36 C2 **Bad Godesberg** Germany
30 H5 **Bad Gottleuba** Germany
32 M9 **Bad Grund** Germany
38 K5 **Bad Hall** Austria
33 N9 **Bad Harzburg** Germany
36 E6 **Bad Herrenalb** Germany
36 H2 **Bad Hersfeld** Germany
38 H7 **Bad Hofgastein** Austria
36 F3 **Bad Homburg** Germany
36 C2 **Bad Honnef** Germany
45 K1 **Badia Polesine** Italy
45 M4 **Badia Tedalda** Italy
32 H8 **Bad Iburg** Germany
79 H6 **Badiet esh Sham** *desert* Jordan/Syria
74 C6 **Badin** Pakistan
112 G2 **Badin** North Carolina U.S.A.
112 G2 **Badin L** North Carolina U.S.A.
38 J6 **Bad Ischl** Austria
37 J3 **Bad Kissingen** Germany
33 O5 **Bad Kleinen** Germany
37 M2 **Bad Klosterlausnitz** Germany
37 M1 **Bad Kösen** Germany
36 D4 **Bad Kreuznach** Germany
98 C2 **Bad Lands** *reg* North Dakota U.S.A.
98 E6 **Badlands Nat.Park** South Dakota U.S.A.
37 K1 **Bad Langensalza** Germany
33 P10 **Bad Lauchstädt** Germany
37 O1 **Bad Lausik** Germany
33 M9 **Bad Lauterberg** Germany
38 K8 **Bad Leonhard** Austria
37 K2 **Bad Liebenstein** Germany
36 F6 **Bad Liebenzell** Germany
32 J9 **Bad Lippspringe** Germany
32 J9 **Bad Meinberg** Germany
36 H5 **Bad Mergentheim** Germany
32 K8 **Bad Münder am Deister** Germany
36 D4 **Bad Münster** Germany
36 B2 **Bad Münstereifel** Germany
31 H4 **Bad Muskau** Germany
36 F3 **Bad Nauheim** Germany
32 K8 **Bad Nenndorf** Germany
36 C2 **Bad Neuenahr** Germany
36 C2 **Bad Neuenahr-Ahrweiler** Germany
37 J3 **Bad Neustadt** Germany
32 J8 **Bad Oeynhausen** Germany
33 M5 **Bad Oldersloe** Germany
68 H4 **Ba Don** Vietnam
67 C1 **Badong** China
69 H8 **Ba Dong** Vietnam
36 B6 **Badonviller** France
36 G3 **Bad Orb** Germany
65 D6 **Badou** China
36 E7 **Bad Peterstal** Germany
32 K9 **Bad Pyrmont** Germany
36 G5 **Bad Rappenau** Germany
38 G6 **Bad Reichenhall** Germany
36 E7 **Bad Rippoldsau** Germany
32 M8 **Bad Salzdetfurth** Germany
33 P8 **Bad Salzelmen** Germany
36 H2 **Bad Salzschlirf** Germany
32 J8 **Bad Salzuflen** Germany
37 J2 **Bad Salzungen** Germany
32 H9 **Bad Sassendorf** Germany
33 R9 **Bad Schmiedeberg** Germany
36 F5 **Bad Schönborn** Germany
36 E3 **Bad Schwalbach** Germany
33 N5 **Bad Schwartau** Germany
33 M5 **Bad Segeberg** Germany
36 E3 **Bad Soden** Germany
32 L10 **Bad Sooden** Germany
37 M3 **Bad Steben** Germany
33 Q6 **Bad Stuer** Germany
33 O9 **Bad Suderode** Germany
37 M1 **Bad Sulza** Germany
33 R4 **Bad Sülze** Germany
36 F6 **Bad Teinach-Zavelstein** Germany
37 K1 **Bad Tennstedt** Germany
41 P2 **Bad Tölz** Germany
141 F1 **Badu I** Queensland Australia
83 L10 **Badulla** Sri Lanka
36 F3 **Bad Vilbel** Germany
38 O6 **Bad Voslau** Austria
102 H5 **Badwater** *L* California U.S.A.
36 G1 **Bad Wildungen** Germany
33 P7 **Bad Wilsnack** Germany
36 G5 **Bad Wimpfen** Germany
37 J5 **Bad Windsheim** Germany
59 K1 **Badzhal'skiy Khrebet** *mt* Russian Federation
26 O2 **Baeivašgiedde** Norway
28 C5 **Bække** Denmark
28 A4 **Bækmarksbro** Denmark
28 E3 **Bælum** Denmark
16 E7 **Baena** Spain
36 D6 **Baerenthal** France
128 C4 **Baeza** Ecuador
16 E7 **Baeza** Spain
47 J7 **Bafa Gölü** *L* Turkey
86 B4 **Bafang** Cameroon
85 B6 **Bafata** Guinea-Bissau
115 K3 **Baffin** *dist* Northwest Territories Canada
109 K8 **Baffin B** Texas U.S.A.
147 E6 **Baffin Basin** Arctic Oc
115 N3 **Baffin Bay** Greenland/Canada
90 E2 **Baffin-Greenland Rise** Atlantic Oc
115 M3 **Baffin I** Northwest Territories Canada
141 K6 **Baffle Creek** Queensland Australia
86 B5 **Bafia** Cameroon
85 B6 **Bafing** *R* Guinea/Mali
79 H2 **Bafliyun** Syria
85 B6 **Bafoulabé** Mali
86 B4 **Bafoussam** Cameroon
77 D4 **Bāfq** Iran
78 E1 **Bafra** Turkey
86 E5 **Bafwasende** Zaire
58 D3 **Baga Bogd Uul** *mt* Mongolia
71 E3 **Bagac Bay** Luzon Philippines
76 B2 **Bagalkot** India
88 G5 **Bagamoyo** Tanzania
69 E11 **Bagan Datuk** Malaysia
71 G7 **Baganga** Mindanao Philippines
71 F7 **Baganian Peninsula** Mindanao Philippines
69 E10 **Bagan Serai** Malaysia
69 E11 **Bagansiapiapi** Sumatra
142 A3 **Baganup L** W Australia Australia
58 E2 **Baga Nuur** Mongolia
44 H2 **Baganza** *R* Italy
55 D3 **Bagaryak** Russian Federation
32 G6 **Bagband** Germany
109 K10 **Bagdad** Mexico
103 L7 **Bagdad** Arizona U.S.A.
103 J7 **Bagdad** California U.S.A.
110 L3 **Bagdad** Kentucky U.S.A.
58 F1 **Bagdarin** Russian Federation
131 G3 **Bagé** Brazil
28 F7 **Bagenkop** Denmark
101 S8 **Baggs** Wyoming U.S.A.
78 K5 **Baghdād** Iraq
78 K5 **Baghdād** *prov* Iraq
77 A4 **Bāgh-e Malek** Iran
75 N7 **Bagherhat** Bangladesh
43 F10 **Bagheria** Sicily
77 E4 **Baghīn** Iran
77 L1 **Baghlān** Afghanistan
77 J3 **Baghran** Afghanistan
Baghrash Köl *L see* **Bosten Hu** *L*
14 E4 **Baginbun Hd** Ireland
69 H14 **Baginda, Tanjong** *C* Indonesia
99 L2 **Bagley** Minnesota U.S.A.
99 P7 **Bagley** Wisconsin U.S.A.
116 Q6 **Bagley Icefield** Alaska U.S.A.
45 L3 **Bagnacavallo** Italy
43 G10 **Bagnara Cálabra** Italy
110 D3 **Bagnell Dam** Missouri U.S.A.
18 F9 **Bagnères de Bigorre** France
18 F10 **Bagnères de Luchon** France
40 F6 **Bagnes,Val De** Switzerland
21 K7 **Bagneux** Maine-et-Loire France
45 J3 **Bagni di Lucca** Italy
41 L5 **Bagni di Masino** Italy
44 B3 **Bagni di Vinádio** Italy
45 K4 **Bagno A Ripoli** Italy
45 L4 **Bagno di Romagna** Italy
21 K4 **Bagnoles-de-l'Orne** France
45 L1 **Bagnoli di Sopra** Italy
45 L1 **Bagnolo di Po** Italy
45 J2 **Bagnolo in Piano** Italy
44 H1 **Bagnolo Mella** Italy
45 J1 **Bagnolo San Vito** Italy
19 N16 **Bagnols-sur-Cèze** France
Bago *see* **Pegu**
28 D6 **Bågø** *isld* Denmark
85 C6 **Bagoe** *R* Ivory Co/Mali
Bagong *see* **Sansui**
77 L2 **Bagrāmī** Afghanistan
31 M1 **Bagrationovsk** Russian Federation
9 F5 **Bagshot** England
65 E3 **Bag Tal** China
128 C5 **Bagua** Peru
85 F5 **Baguezane, Mt** Niger
71 N9 **Baguia** Timor Indonesia
71 E2 **Baguio** Luzon Philippines
71 G7 **Baguio** Mindanao Philippines
71 F2 **Baguio Pt** Luzon Philippines
86 C3 **Baguirmi** *dist* Chad
126 E2 **Bahama Bank,Great** Bahamas
126 F1 **Bahama Bank, Little** Bahamas
126 F2 **Bahamas, The** W Indies
127 M4 **Baham, Pte** Martinique W Indies
75 N6 **Baharampur** India
84 H4 **Baharīya Oasis** Egypt
69 E14 **Bahatmonga** Indonesia
70 D3 **Bahau** *R* Sarawak
70 D6 **Bahaur** Kalimantan
74 E4 **Bahawalnagar** Pakistan
74 D4 **Bahawalpur** Pakistan
79 G1 **Bahçe** Turkey
88 E4 **Bahi** Tanzania
129 K6 **Bahia** *state* Brazil
131 E7 **Bahía Blanca** Argentina
125 L1 **Bahía, Islas de la** Honduras
124 C3 **Bahía Kino** Mexico
133 D7 **Bahía Laura** Argentina
133 C6 **Bahía Pargua** Chile
124 B4 **Bahía Tortugas** Mexico
86 G3 **Bahir Dar** Ethiopia
48 L3 **Bahluiul** *R* Romania
48 J4 **Bahnea** Romania
88 B5 **Baholoholo** *tribe* Zaire
70 G6 **Bahombelu** Sulawesi Indonesia
70 G6 **Bahomonte** Sulawesi
69 H8 **Ba,Hon** *isld* Vietnam
79 A7 **Bahra el Burullus** *lagoon* Egypt
79 B7 **Bahra el Manzala** *lagoon* Egypt
75 J5 **Bahraich** India
77 B6 **Bahrain** *sheikhdom* Persian Gulf
86 D3 **Bahr Aouk** *R* Chad
86 C4 **Bahr Aoukale** *R* Cent Afr Republic
86 F3 **Bahr el Abiad** *R* Sudan
86 E4 **Bahr el Arab** *watercourse* Sudan
86 F3 **Bahr el Azraq** *R* Sudan
86 E4 **Bahr el Ghazal** *R* Sudan
86 E4 **Bahr el Ghazal** *prov* Sudan
86 F4 **Bahr ez Zeraf** *R* Sudan
79 H5 **Bahr Şaygal Sab 'Ābār** *L* Syria
71 H6 **Bahubulu** *isld* Sulawesi Indonesia
77 G7 **Bāhu Kālat** Iran
129 J4 **Baiã** Brazil
48 H6 **Baia de Aramă** Romania
48 H4 **Baia de Cris** Romania
16 B6 **Baia de Setúbal** Portugal
87 B9 **Baia doz Tigres** Angola
128 F7 **Baia Grande,L** Brazil
48 H3 **Baia Mare** Romania
45 R8 **Baiano** Italy
48 H3 **Baia Sprie** Romania
77 D3 **Baiazeh** Iran
86 C4 **Baïbokoum** Chad
65 H3 **Baicaogou** China
57 K4 **Baicheng** China
65 F2 **Baicheng** China
48 K5 **Băicoi** Romania
121 N5 **Baie Carrière** Quebec Canada
122 D4 **Baie-Comeau** Quebec Canada
126 H5 **Baie de Henne** Haiti
122 E5 **Baie de Sables** Quebec Canada
123 P2 **Baie-du-Milieu** Quebec Canada
115 M7 **Baie-du-Poste** Quebec Canada
122 G6 **Baie du Vin** New Brunswick Canada
68 F7 **Baie,I.de la** Cambodia
122 K3 **Baie Johan Beetz** Quebec Canada
127 N4 **Baie Mahault** Guadeloupe W Indies
36 E7 **Baiersbronn** Germany
122 C5 **Baie Ste.Catherine** Quebec Canada
122 H4 **Baie Ste.Clair** Quebec Canada
122 B6 **Baie St.Paul** Quebec Canada
122 E4 **Baie Trinité** Quebec Canada
122 J7 **Baie Verte** New Brunswick Canada
123 Q4 **Baie Verte** Newfoundland Canada
67 D3 **Baifang** China
Baiguan *see* **Shangyu**
74 J7 **Baihar** India
58 F5 **Baihe** China
65 B6 **Baijiazhuang** China
Baikal *L see* **Baykal,Ozero** *L*
75 K7 **Baikunthpur** India
Bailādila *see* **Kirandul**
Bailādila *see* **Kirandul**
65 E1 **Bailang** China
Baile Átha *see* **Dublin**
48 J6 **Băile Govora** Romania
48 G6 **Băile Herculane** Romania
16 E6 **Bailén** Spain
48 J5 **Baile Olăneşti** Romania
48 H6 **Băileşti** Romania
48 K4 **Băile Tuşnad** Romania
22 G3 **Baileux** Belgium
106 E2 **Bailey** Colorado U.S.A.
112 J2 **Bailey** North Carolina U.S.A.
143 D8 **Bailey Ra** W Australia Australia
111 K7 **Baileyton** Alabama U.S.A.
95 U1 **Baileyville** Maine U.S.A.
14 D3 **Bailieborough** Ireland
67 D3 **Bailin** China
129 H3 **Bailique, I** Brazil
21 N5 **Bailleau-le-Pin** France
22 D2 **Bailleul** France
21 K4 **Bailleul** Orne France
22 D3 **Bailleul-Sire-Berthoult** France
115 K2 **Baillie Hamilton I** Northwest Territories Canada
114 G3 **Baillie Is** Northwest Territories Canada
127 M4 **Baillif** Guadeloupe W Indies
77 K3 **Bailugh** Afghanistan
87 C8 **Bailundo** Angola
111 M11 **Bainbridge** Georgia U.S.A.
95 M4 **Bainbridge** New York U.S.A.
94 D7 **Bainbridge** Ohio U.S.A.
20 G6 **Bain-de-Bretagne** France
140 B3 **Baines, Mt** N Terr Australia
127 H5 **Bainet** Haiti
Baini *see* **Yuqing**
19 K4 **Bains-les-Bains** France
13 H6 **Bainton** England
98 B1 **Bainville** Montana U.S.A.
Baiona *see* **Bayona** Spain
59 J2 **Baiquan** China
66 C4 **Bairab Co** *L* China
109 H3 **Baird** Texas U.S.A.
116 E6 **Baird Inlet** Alaska U.S.A.
116 G3 **Baird Mts** Alaska U.S.A.
65 D3 **Bairin Youqi** China
58 G3 **Bairin Zuoqi** China
139 J7 **Bairnsdale** Victoria Australia
101 S7 **Bairoil** Wyoming U.S.A.
79 H7 **Bā'ir, Wādī** *watercourse* Jordan
20 H6 **Bais** Ille-et-Vilaine France
21 K5 **Bais** Mayenne France
18 F8 **Baïse** *R* France
Baisha *see* **Jiande**
65 B7 **Baisha** China
67 B2 **Baisha** China
67 C7 **Baisha** China
65 B7 **Baisha Shuiku** *res* China
67 E3 **Baishi Feng** *mt* China
65 A7 **Baishui** China
58 D5 **Baishui Jiang** *R* China
22 E2 **Baisieux** France
45 J3 **Baiso** Italy
52 B6 **Baisogala** Lithuania
74 J4 **Baitadi** Nepal
68 G3 **Bai Thoung** Vietnam
19 N15 **Baix** France
65 C6 **Baixiang** China
65 A3 **Baixingt** China
65 E3 **Baixingt** China
16 B6 **Baixo Alentejo** *prov* Portugal
130 H6 **Baixo Guandu** Brazil
87 C9 **Baixo Longa** Angola
65 C5 **Baiyang Dian** *L* China
67 C1 **Baiyangping** China
Baiyashi *see* **Dong'an**
58 D4 **Baiyin** China
86 F2 **Baiyuda** Sudan
67 E3 **Baiyun Shan** *mt* China
58 E4 **Baiyu Shan** *mts* China
67 B1 **Baizi** China
48 E4 **Baja** Hungary
124 B3 **Baja California** *state* Mexico
70 Q10 **Bajan** Indonesia
124 J4 **Baján** Mexico
124 B3 **Baja, Pta** *C* Mexico
69 H11 **Bajau** *isld* Indonesia
71 K9 **Bajawa** Flores Indonesia
48 F7 **Bajina Bašta** Serbia Yugoslavia
48 E5 **Bajmok** Serbia Yugoslavia
128 C2 **Bajo Baudo** Colombia
70 N9 **Bajonegoro** Java
126 E7 **Bajo Nuevo** Caribbean
141 K6 **Bajool** Queensland Australia
28 C7 **Bajstrup** Denmark
48 D4 **Bak** Hungary
70 E3 **Bakajan, G** *mt* Kalimantan
55 C4 **Bakal** Russian Federation
86 D4 **Bakala** Cent Afr Republic
57 J2 **Bakanas** *R* Kazakhstan
57 H3 **Bakanas** Kazakhstan
70 E6 **Bakaucengal** Kalimantan
56 B3 **Bakchar** *R* Russian Federation
85 B6 **Bakel** Senegal
133 C7 **Baker** *R* Chile
103 H6 **Baker** California U.S.A.
101 M4 **Baker** Idaho U.S.A.
98 B3 **Baker** Montana U.S.A.
103 K2 **Baker** Nevada U.S.A.
98 G1 **Baker** North Dakota U.S.A.
100 H5 **Baker** Oregon U.S.A.
94 J7 **Baker** West Virginia U.S.A.
103 N7 **Baker Butte** *mt* Arizona U.S.A.
137 R1 **Baker I** Pacific Oc
117 G8 **Baker I** Alaska U.S.A.
95 R7 **Baker L** Maine U.S.A.
143 F7 **Baker Lake** W Australia Australia
115 K5 **Baker Lake** Northwest Territories Canada
100 D1 **Baker,Mt** Washington U.S.A.
125 P9 **Bakers** Belize
102 F6 **Bakersfield** California U.S.A.
112 E1 **Bakersfield** North Carolina U.S.A.
108 E5 **Bakersfield** Texas U.S.A.
95 P2 **Bakersfield** Vermont U.S.A.
9 E1 **Bakewell** England
77 G2 **Bakharz** *reg* Iran
53 D11 **Bakhchisaray** Ukraine
54 D5 **Bakhmach** Ukraine
78 L4 **Bākhtarān** Iran
77 B3 **Bakhtiarī va Chahār Mahāll** *prov* Iran
77 B4 **Bakhtiyāri** Iran
47 J5 **Bakır** *R* Turkey
47 M11 **Bakırköy** Turkey
29 T9 **Bakkagerdhi** Iceland
25 F2 **Bakkeveen** Netherlands
47 K7 **Baklan** Turkey
86 G4 **Bako** Ethiopia
85 C7 **Bako** Ivory Coast
69 C11 **Bakongan** Sumatra
48 D4 **Bakony** *mts* Hungary
86 D4 **Bakouma** Cent Afr Republic
85 C6 **Bakoye** *R* Guinea/Mali
54 L1 **Baksheyevo** Russian Federation
26 K6 **Baktsjaure** Sweden
78 M1 **Baku** Azerbaijan
71 G6 **Bakulin Pt** Mindanao Philippines
32 H7 **Bakum** Germany
69 G12 **Bakung** *isld* Indonesia
121 L7 **Bala** Ontario Canada
80 D4 **Bal'a** Jordan
78 D2 **Bâlâ** Turkey
8 C2 **Bala** Wales
71 C7 **Balabac Str** Borneo/Philippines
70 E6 **Balabalangan, Kep** *islds* Indonesia
71 H8 **Balabalangan Pulau Pulau** *islds* Indonesia
54 H1 **Balabanovo** Russian Federation
71 C7 **Balabec** *isld* Palawan Philippines
54 G9 **Balabino** Ukraine
128 E6 **Bala,Cerros de** *mts* Bolivia
48 H6 **Bălăciţa** Romania
127 J2 **Balaclava** Jamaica
77 B1 **Baladeh** Iran
80 F3 **Balad el Basha** Jordan
80 F3 **Balad el Mansura** Jordan
56 F4 **Balagansk** Russian Federation
74 J8 **Balaghat** India
17 H3 **Balaguer** Spain
70 B5 **Balaiberkuak** Kalimantan
70 B4 **Balaikarangan** Kalimantan
68 A2 **Balaing** Burma
69 D12 **Balaipungut** Sumatra
70 B6 **Balairiam** Kalimantan
70 B4 **Balaisepuac** Kalimantan
70 K8 **Balak, Gunung** Sumatra
138 E5 **Balaklava** South Australia Australia
54 H7 **Balakleya** Ukraine
8 C2 **Bala L** Wales
87 G8 **Balama** Mozambique
70 E1 **Balambangan** *isld* Indonesia
77 H2 **Balā Morghāb** Afghanistan
40 B6 **Balan** France
48 K4 **Bălan** Romania
125 O9 **Balancán** Mexico
71 E3 **Balanga** Luzon Philippines
75 K8 **Balāngīr** India
71 H5 **Balantak** Sulawesi
70 M9 **Balapulang** Java
71 F5 **Balaring** Negros Philippines
70 G6 **Balase** *R* Sulawesi
48 E2 **Balassagyarmat** Hungary
84 H4 **Balât** Egypt
48 D4 **Balaton** *L* Hungary
99 L5 **Balaton** Minnesota U.S.A.
48 D4 **Balatonfüred** Hungary
48 D4 **Balatonszentgyörgy** Hungary
71 L9 **Balauring** Flores Indonesia
124 F10 **Balboa** Panama
14 E3 **Balbriggan** Ireland
141 H8 **Balbuna** Queensland Australia
13 G6 **Balby** England
86 J5 **Balcad** Somalia
144 D5 **Balcairn** New Zealand
138 E4 **Balcanoona** South Australia Australia
131 F6 **Balcarce** Argentina
119 O8 **Balcarres** Saskatchewan Canada
48 H6 **Bălceşti** Romania
47 J1 **Balchik** Bulgaria
109 O9 **Balch Springs** Texas U.S.A.
144 B7 **Balclutha** New Zealand
9 F5 **Balcombe** England
100 F6 **Bald Butte** *mt* Oregon U.S.A.
94 K6 **Bald Eagle Mt** Pennsylvania U.S.A.
41 H3 **Baldegg See** *L* Switzerland
6 M3 **Balder** *oil rig* North Sea
143 C11 **Bald Hd** W Australia Australia
44 D2 **Baldichieri d'Asti** Italy
110 E6 **Bald Knob** Arkansas U.S.A.
94 F9 **Bald Knob** West Virginia U.S.A.
101 L5 **Bald Mt** Idaho U.S.A.
103 J4 **Bald Mt** Nevada U.S.A.
9 F4 **Baldock** England
119 T2 **Baldock L** Manitoba Canada
42 D3 **Baldo,Monte** Italy
113 F7 **Baldwin** Florida U.S.A.
110 A3 **Baldwin** Kansas U.S.A.
94 B3 **Baldwin** Michigan U.S.A.
98 F2 **Baldwin** North Dakota U.S.A.
99 O5 **Baldwin** Wisconsin U.S.A.
102 H7 **Baldwin L** California U.S.A.
116 F3 **Baldwin Pen** Alaska U.S.A.
118 H6 **Baldwinton** Saskatchewan Canada
95 P4 **Baldwinville** Massachusetts U.S.A.
95 R3 **Baldwin, W** Maine U.S.A.
111 H7 **Baldwyn** Mississippi U.S.A.
119 R7 **Baldy Mt** Manitoba Canada
103 P8 **Baldy Pk** Arizona U.S.A.
106 E6 **Baldy Pk** New Mexico U.S.A.
57 E5 **Bal'dzhuvon** Tajikistan
86 H4 **Balē** *prov* Ethiopia
69 E14 **Bale** Indonesia
17 J5 **Baleares, Islas** *arch* Spain
Balearic Is *see* **Baleares, Islas** *arch*
70 C4 **Baleh** *R* Sarawak
130 H5 **Baleia, Pta da** *C* Brazil
115 N6 **Baleine,à la** *R* Quebec Canada
83 L14 **Baleiniers, Golfe des** Kerguelen Indian Oc
71 C7 **Balembangan** *isld* Sabah
22 J1 **Balen** Belgium
48 K6 **Băleni** Romania
71 E3 **Baler** Luzon Philippines
71 E3 **Baler Bay** Luzon Philippines
15 E5 **Balerno** Scotland
75 M8 **Bāleshwar** India
58 G1 **Baley** Russian Federation
141 H5 **Balfe's Creek** Queensland Australia
48 D4 **Bal Földvár** Hungary
26 K7 **Bålforsen** Sweden
117 P11 **Balfour** British Columbia Canada
144 B6 **Balfour** New Zealand
98 F2 **Balfour** North Dakota U.S.A.
142 D6 **Balfour Downs** W Australia Australia
12 D1 **Balfron** Scotland
77 F1 **Bālgirān** Iran
142 G5 **Balgo Hill** W Australia Australia
119 N8 **Balgonie** Saskatchewan Canada
32 K10 **Balhorn** Germany
86 B4 **Bali** Cameroon
70 P10 **Bali** *isld* Indonesia
71 F6 **Baliangao** Mindanao Philippines
69 D11 **Balige** Sumatra
31 N6 **Baligród** Poland
65 D4 **Balihan** China
47 J5 **Balıkesir** Turkey
78 G4 **Balīkh** *R* Syria
86 C3 **Bal Illi** *R* Chad
70 G2 **Balimbing Tawitaw** *isld* Philippines
69 E10 **Baling** Malaysia
70 C3 **Balingian** *R* Sarawak
70 C3 **Balingian** Sarawak
65 D3 **Balinqiao** China
48 G5 **Balint** Romania
70 P9 **Bali Sea** Indonesia
70 P10 **Bali,Selat** Bali/Java
70 G2 **Baliungan** Tawitawi Philippines
130 D5 **Baliza** Brazil
32 K5 **Balje** Germany
118 K6 **Baljennie** Saskatchewan Canada
25 E3 **Balk** Netherlands
48 G3 **Balkány** Hungary
55 C4 **Balkany** Russian Federation
55 E4 **Balkashino** Kazakhstan
25 F3 **Balkbrug** Netherlands
77 K1 **Balkh** *prov* Afghanistan
77 K1 **Balkhab** *R* Afghanistan
57 G2 **Balkhash** Kazakhstan
57 G2 **Balkhash, Ozero** *L* Kazakhstan
74 H9 **Balkonda** India
15 C4 **Ballachulish** Scotland
143 E9 **Balladonia** W Australia Australia
14 C3 **Ballaghaderreen** Ireland
21 P4 **Ballancourt-sur-Essonne** France
141 K8 **Ballandean** Queensland Australia
26 J3 **Ballangen** Norway
101 R4 **Ballantine** Montana U.S.A.
15 C5 **Ballantrae** Scotland
119 O4 **Ballantyne Bay** Saskatchewan Canada
114 H2 **Ballantyne Str** Northwest Territories Canada
43 C9 **Ballao** Sardinia
139 G6 **Ballarat** Victoria Australia
102 G5 **Ballarat** California U.S.A.
143 D8 **Ballard, L** W Australia Australia
80 F4 **Ballas** Jordan
15 E3 **Ballater** Scotland
12 D5 **Ballaugh** I of Man U.K.
28 F4 **Balle** Denmark
21 K6 **Ballée** France
28 F5 **Ballen** Denmark
133 C3 **Ballena,Pta** *C* Chile
33 O9 **Ballenstedt** Germany
146 C13 **Balleny Islands** Antarctica
21 J3 **Balleroy** France
29 K5 **Ballerup** Denmark
112 C3 **Ball Ground** Georgia U.S.A.
75 L6 **Ballia** India
14 B2 **Ballina** Ireland
14 C3 **Ballinasloe** Ireland
14 C3 **Ballindine** Ireland
28 B3 **Balling** Denmark
14 C4 **Ballingarry** Ireland
108 H4 **Ballinger** Texas U.S.A.
15 E4 **Ballinluig** Scotland
14 B3 **Ballinrobe** Ireland
14 A5 **Ballinskelligs B** Ireland
37 J6 **Ballmertshofen** Germany
118 B7 **Ball,Mt** Alberta Canada
12 D1 **Balloch** Scotland
21 L5 **Ballon** France
19 K5 **Ballon d'Alsace** *mt* France
21 H6 **Ballots** France
46 D4 **Ballsh** Albania
137 M8 **Ball's Pyramid** *isld* Pacific Oc
37 K1 **Ballstädt** Germany
95 O4 **Ballston Spa** New York U.S.A.
28 B6 **Ballum** Denmark
14 E2 **Ballybay** Ireland
14 D2 **Ballybofey** Ireland
14 B4 **Ballybunnion** Ireland
14 B2 **Ballycastle** Ireland
14 E1 **Ballycastle** N Ireland
14 E2 **Ballyclare** N Ireland
14 D2 **Ballyconnell** Ireland
14 D5 **Ballycotton B** Ireland
14 C4 **Ballyduff** Ireland
14 C3 **Ballygar** Ireland
14 D2 **Ballygawley** N Ireland
12 B2 **Ballygrant** Scotland
14 D2 **Ballyhaise** Ireland
14 C3 **Ballyhaunis** Ireland
14 C4 **Ballyhoura Hills** Ireland
14 D3 **Ballyjamesduff** Ireland
14 D3 **Ballymahon** Ireland
14 E2 **Ballymena** N Ireland
14 E1 **Ballymoney** N Ireland
14 C2 **Ballymote** Ireland
14 F2 **Ballynahinch** N Ireland
14 F2 **Ballyquintin Pt** N Ireland
14 D4 **Ballyragget** Ireland
14 C2 **Ballyshannon** Ireland
14 E3 **Ballytore** Ireland
14 B3 **Ballyvaughan** Ireland
12 D3 **Balmaclellan** Scotland
12 D1 **Balmaha** Scotland
95 M2 **Balmat** New York U.S.A.
48 G3 **Balmazújváros** Hungary
40 F7 **Balme** Italy
40 G5 **Balmhorn** *mt* Switzerland
141 K1 **Balmoral** *dist* Brisbane, Qnsld Australia
138 F6 **Balmoral** Victoria Australia
119 U8 **Balmoral** Manitoba Canada
144 D5 **Balmoral** New Zealand
6 L4 **Balmoral** *oil rig* North Sea
15 E3 **Balmoral Castle** Scotland
108 D5 **Balmorhea** Texas U.S.A.
13 F1 **Balmullo** Scotland
74 A4 **Balochistān** *prov* Pakistan
87 B8 **Balombo** Angola
141 J7 **Balonne** *R* Queensland Australia
141 J8 **Balonne R** Queensland Australia
55 D2 **Balotovskoye** Russian Federation
74 E6 **Balotra** India
33 P6 **Balow** Germany
12 D1 **Balquhidder** Scotland
75 K5 **Balrampur** India
48 J6 **Balş** Romania
99 O4 **Balsam L** Wisconsin U.S.A.
121 M8 **Balsam Lake** Ontario Canada
129 J5 **Balsas** Brazil
124 H8 **Balsas** *R* Mexico
26 K2 **Balsfjord** *inlet* Norway
26 K2 **Balsfjord** Norway
45 P6 **Balsorano** Italy
27 J12 **Bålsta** Sweden
26 G3 **Balstad** Norway
48 M3 **Balta** Ukraine
98 F1 **Balta** North Dakota U.S.A.
16 E3 **Baltanás** Spain
16 B3 **Baltar** Spain
133 F4 **Baltasar Brum** Uruguay
98 K6 **Baltic** South Dakota U.S.A.
27 H16 **Baltic Sea** N Europe
79 B7 **Baltīm** Egypt
14 B5 **Baltimore** Ireland
87 E10 **Baltimore** S Africa
95 L7 **Baltimore** Maryland U.S.A.
97 **Baltimore** *conurbation* Maryland U.S.A.
14 E4 **Baltinglass** Ireland
Baltit *see* **Hunza**
31 M1 **Baltiysk** Russian Federation
32 F5 **Baltrum** Germany
80 G8 **Balu** *R* Jordan
80 G8 **Balu** Jordan

77 G6	Balūchestān va Sīstān	Iran
	Balūchistān prov see	
	Balochistān	
72 J3	Balūchistān reg	Pakistan/Iran
70 C3	Balui R	Sarawak
71 E7	Balukbaluk isld	Philippines
69 D12	Balumundan	Sumatra
70 C5	Baluran, Gunung mt	Kalimantan
75 N6	Balurghat	India
71 G8	Balut isld	Philippines
32 G10	Balve	Germany
52 C6	Balvi	Latvia
47 J5	Balya	Turkey
84 J4	Balyana, El	Egypt
56 H4	Bal Yeravnoye, Oz L	Russian Federation
56 C4	Balyksa	Russian Federation
56 E5	Balyktyg Khem R	Russian Federation
118 C7	Balzac	Alberta Canada
77 F5	Bam	Iran
67 B4	Bama	China
86 B3	Bama	Nigeria
141 F1	Bamaga	Queensland Australia
85 C6	Bamako	Mali
128 C5	Bambamarca	Peru
71 E3	Bamban	Luzon Philippines
71 E2	Bambang	Luzon Philippines
71 E8	Bambannan isld	Philippines
86 D4	Bambari	Cent Afr Republic
141 H4	Bambaroo	Queensland Australia
13 F6	Bamber Br	England
37 K4	Bamberg	Germany
112 F4	Bamberg	South Carolina
86 E5	Bambesa	Zaire
86 E5	Bambili	Zaire
86 C5	Bambio	Cent Afr Republic
27 D13	Bamble	Norway
142 D5	Bamboo Creek	W Australia Australia
142 C5	Bamboo Springs	W Australia Australia
83 M13	Bambou Mts	Mauritius
130 F7	Bambui	Brazil
70 D5	Bambulung	Kalimantan
13 G2	Bamburgh	England
86 B4	Bamenda	Cameroon
117 L11	Bamfield	British Columbia Canada
77 K2	Bāmīān	Afghanistan
67 C4	Bamian	China
65 F3	Bamiancheng	China
	Bamiantong see Muling	
86 C4	Bamingui R	Cent Afr Republic
86 C4	Bamingui-Bangoran Nat. Park	Cent Afr Republic
68 G6	Bam Nak	Cambodia
68 E5	Bamnet Narong	Thailand
124 E5	Bamoa	Mexico
69 A8	Bam Posht, Kūh-e mts	Iran
77 H6	Bam Posht, Kūh-e mts	Iran
8 C8	Bampton	England
9 E4	Bampton	England
77 G6	Bampūr	Iran
77 G6	Bampūr R	Iran
74 J9	Bāmrāgad	India
	Ba Na	Vietnam
137 O1	Banaba isld	Pacific Oc
129 L5	Banabulú Açude res	Brazil
14 D3	Banagher	Ireland
71 E4	Banahao, Mt	Luzon Philippines
86 E5	Banalia	Zaire
68 G7	Banam	Cambodia
85 C6	Banamba	Mali
124 D2	Banámichi	Mexico
141 K6	Banana	Queensland Australia
129 H6	Bananal, Ilha do	Brazil
113 G9	Banana R	Florida U.S.A.
130 J9	Bananeiras	Brazil
76 G7	Bananga	Nicobar Is
68 F6	Ban Aranyaprathet	Thailand
47 J3	Banarli	Turkey
69 D8	Ba Na San	Thailand
48 F6	Banatska Novo Selo	Serbia Yugoslavia
15 C4	Banavie	Scotland
71 J8	Banawaja isld	Indonesia
78 B2	Banaz	Turkey
68 E4	Ban Bang Mun Nak	Thailand
68 E4	Ban Bang Rakam	Thailand
71 G6	Banbayan Pt	Mindanao Philippines
69 E10	Ban Betong	Thailand
68 J6	Ban Bik	Vietnam
14 E2	Banbridge	N Ireland
68 E5	Ban Bua Chum	Thailand
68 D7	Ban Bua Yai	Thailand
68 E5	Ban Bu Khanum	Thailand
68 G5	Ban Bungxai	Laos
68 H5	Ban Bungxai	Laos
9 E3	Banbury	England
71 D3	Bancalan	Palawan Philippines
138 F4	Bancannia, L	New South Wales Australia
85 A4	Banc d'Arguin Nat. Park	Mauritania
68 D3	Ban Chang Khoeng	Thailand
68 C5	Ban Channabot	Thailand
68 D3	Ban Chiang Dao	Thailand
15 F3	Banchory	Scotland
68 D4	Ban Chum Phae	Thailand
125 Q8	Banco Chinchorro isld	Mexico
71 D7	Bancoron isld	Philippines
121 N7	Bancroft	Ontario Canada
100 O7	Bancroft	Idaho U.S.A.
99 M6	Bancroft	Iowa U.S.A.
98 J5	Bancroft	South Dakota U.S.A.
48 J4	Band	Romania
74 J6	Banda	India
69 C11	Bandahara, Gunung mt	Sumatra
61 N7	Bandai-Asahi Nat.Pk	Japan
61 O8	Bandai-san mt	Japan
85 B7	Banda Jumaa	Sierra Leone
27 C12	Bandaksli L	Norway
85 C7	Bandama R	Ivory Coast
68 G5	Ban Dan	Thailand
77 G4	Bandan Kuh mt	Iran
	Bandar see Machilipatnam	
77 J2	Bandar	Afghanistan
87 F9	Bandar	Mozambique
75 J4	Bandar	Nepal
70 K8	Bandaragung	Sumatra
86 B2	Bandarbeyla	Somalia
77 E7	Bandar-e' Abbas	Iran
77 A1	Bandar-e Anzalī	Iran
77 B4	Bandar-e Deylam	Iran
77 D6	Bandar-e Khoemir	Iran
77 A4	Bandar-e Khomeynī	Iran
77 A4	Bandar-e Lengeh	Iran
77 B5	Bandar-e Rīg	Iran
77 D1	Bandar-e Torkeman	Iran
86 B1	Bandar Murcaay	Somalia
70 D2	Bandar Seri Begawan	Brunei
136 F3	Banda Sea	Indonesia
88 E7	Bandawe	Malawi
22 J3	Bande	Belgium
16 B2	Bande	Spain
129 K8	Bandeira mt	Brazil
130 F7	Bandeira mt	Brazil
130 E8	Bandeirantes	Brazil
130 D8	Bandeirantes, I. dos	Brazil
106 D6	Bandelier Nat.Mon	New Mexico U.S.A.
77 D6	Band-e Moghūyeh	Iran
71 D3	Bandera	Luzon Philippines
106 G4	Bandera	Mexico
69 B10	Banderas, B de	Mexico
28 G7	Bandholm	Denmark
85 D6	Bandiagara	Mali
77 K2	Band-i-Amur R	Afghanistan
77 J2	Band-i-Balān mts	Afghanistan
78 B1	Bandırma	Turkey
47 J4	Bandırma Körfezi G	Turkey
77 J2	Band-i-Turkestan mts	Afghanistan
70 M9	Bandjar	Java
70 D6	Bandjarmasin	Kalimantan
70 M9	Bandjarnegara	Java
19 P18	Bandol	France
	Ban Don see Surat Thani	
14 C5	Bandon R	Ireland
14 C5	Bandon	Ireland
100 A5	Bandon	Oregon U.S.A.
68 G4	Ban Dong	Laos
68 F4	Ban Don Khi	Thailand
14 E4	Bandra	India
14 E2	Bandundu	Zaire
71 E1	Bandung	Java
69 D8	Bandung	Sumatra
69 F12	Bandung	Sumatra
68 H4	Ban Dupre	Laos
101 N4	Bandy	Virginia U.S.A.
101 N4	Bandya	W Australia Australia
48 L5	Băneasa	Romania
78 K4	Baneh	Iran
71 B2	Banema	Halmahera Indonesia
68 F1	Ban Nam Sau	Vietnam
68 F3	Ban Na Noi	Thailand
68 F3	Ban Naphong	Laos
68 F3	Ban Na Sabaeng	Thailand
68 F3	Ban Na Thawi	Thailand
126 F2	Bannerman Town	Eleuthera Bahamas
40 H6	Bannio	Italy
41 H6	Bannio-Anzino	Italy
121 N8	Bannockburn	Ontario Canada
144 B6	Bannockburn	New Zealand
12 E1	Bannockburn	Scotland
101 M5	Bannock Pass	Idaho/Montana U.S.A.
101 N7	Bannock Ra	Idaho U.S.A.
68 E3	Ban Noi	Thailand
68 E2	Ban Nong Kha	Laos
68 E5	Ban Nong Makha	Thailand
68 F5	Ban Nong Met	Laos
68 F5	Ban Nong Waeng	Thailand
74 D2	Banni	Pakistan
17 J2	Bañolas	Spain
19 P16	Banon	France
124 H6	Bánok	Mexico
31 L7	Bánovce	Czechoslovakia
74 G6	Banow	Andarāb
68 F3	Ban Pak Bong	Thailand
68 D3	Ban Pak Chan	Thailand
68 D6	Ban Pak Khlong	Thailand
68 D6	Ban Pak Nam	Thailand
68 E3	Ban Pak Neun	Laos
68 F5	Ban Pak Thong Chai	Thailand
68 D5	Ban Phachi	Thailand
68 G4	Ban Phaeng	Thailand
68 F5	Ban Phai	Thailand
68 E6	Ban Phanat Nikhom	Thailand
68 H5	Ban Phattaya	Thailand
68 H5	Ban Phon	Laos
68 G5	Ban Phon Ngam	Thailand
68 D4	Ban Phran Katai	Thailand
68 H5	Ban Phrom Phirom	Thailand
68 F5	Ban Phutthaisong	Thailand
	Ban Pla Soi see Chon Buri	
71 N8	Ban Pong	Thailand
138 E4	Ban Saen To	Thailand
68 E2	Ban Sai	Laos
70 E5	Ban Sai Yok	Thailand
75 M6	Ban Sanam Chai	Thailand
130 G7	Ban Sangae	Thailand
	Ban Saraphi Chae Hom	Thailand
128 C3	Ban Sattahip	Thailand
127 P6	Ban Sawi	Thailand
130 G9	Bansalpaha	Thailand
68 G4	Ban Sichon	Thailand
85 A4	Ban Sop Huai Hai	Thailand
68 D4	Ban Sop Prap	Thailand
68 D4	Ban Sot	Laos
102 R12	Ban Suwai	Thailand
94 F5	Banswara	India
113 F8	Ban Ta Khli	Thailand
71 J9	Bantal	Sumbawa Indonesia
70 F7	Bantaeng	Sulawesi
128 D2	Bantal	Sumatra
83 M8	Bantam	Cocos Is Indian Oc
33 P9	Ban Tan	Thailand
126 H4	Ban Ta Ruang	Thailand
71 E3	Bantayan isld	Philippines
32 L8	Bantein	Germany
70 L9	Banten	Java
68 E5	Ban Tha Chang	Thailand
68 G5	Ban Tham Khae	Thailand
127 M9	Ban Thap Phung	Thailand
68 E8	Ban Tha Song Yang	Thailand
68 F5	Ban Tha Tako	Thailand
68 H4	Ban Thateng	Laos
68 D4	Ban Tha Uthen	Thailand
68 E3	Ban Thepha	Thailand
22 J5	Bantheville	France
68 F5	Ban Thung Luang	Thailand
71 F4	Banton isld	Philippines
14 H6	Bantry	Ireland
98 F11	Bantry	North Dakota U.S.A.
14 B6	Bantry B	Ireland
70 N9	Bantul	Java
74 N8	Bantval	India
68 E6	Ban Waeng Noi	Thailand
68 G4	Ban Wang Saphong	Thailand
68 E6	Ban Keo Lom	Vietnam
68 G4	Ban Wang Ta Mua	Thailand
8 D5	Banwell	England
68 F4	Ban Wiang Khuk	Thailand
48 G3	Banya	Bulgaria
69 C11	Banyak, Kep. isld	Indonesia
68 H5	Ban Yang Talat	Thailand
68 D8	Ban Yok Khlo	Thailand
68 F4	Ban Khuan Mao	Thailand
141 K1	Banyo dist	Brisbane, Qnsld Australia
86 B4	Banyo	Cameroon
26 K3	Banyoles	France
70 N9	Banyumas	Java
70 P10	Banyuwangi R	Java
37 L3	Banz	Germany
145 Q13	Banzare Coast	Antarctica Southern Oc
32 J7	Bao'an	China
37 O3	Bärenbrush	Germany
21 M2	Baode	China
65 G4	Baode	China
65 D7	Baoding	China
67 K3	Baoji	China
67 C2	Baojing	China
	Bakang see Horqin Zouyi Zhongqi	
68 G1	Baokang	China
68 D2	Bao Lac	Vietnam
68 H5	Bao Loc	Vietnam
65 J1	Baoqing	China

67 G1	Baoshan	China
68 J3	Baoting	China
58 E3	Baotou	China
85 C6	Baoulé R	Mali
59 G5	Baoying	China
	Baoyou see Ledong	
76 E3	Bapatla	India
22 D3	Bapaume	France
103 N8	Bapchule	Arizona U.S.A.
121 M7	Baptiste	Ontario Canada
80 D4	Bāqa el Gharbiya	Israel
66 E5	Baqen	China
79 F9	Bāqir, J mt	Jordan
78 K5	Ba'Qūbah	Iraq
80 F3	Baqura	Jordan
22 H4	Bar R	France
48 L1	Bar	Ukraine
42 J6	Bar Montenegro Yugoslavia
86 F3	Bara	Sudan
74 G5	Bara	India
43 H7	Bari	Italy
85 F1	Baria	Algeria
71 M6	Barie	Indonesia
128 F2	Barima, Pta C	Venezuela
127 J10	Barinas	Venezuela
128 D2	Barinas	Venezuela
79 J9	Barisan R	Sumatra
100 D2	Baring	Missouri U.S.A.
121 N4	Baring, Washington U.S.A.
143 E10	Baring, Mt W Australia Australia
28 D5	Bāring Vig B	Denmark
127 J10	Barinitas	Venezuela
20 F8	Baripada	India
130 E8	Bariri	Brazil
21 M4	Barre-en-Ouche, la	France
129 K6	Barreiras	Brazil
129 G4	Barreiras	Brazil
118 F6	Barreirinha	Brazil
129 J5	Barreirinhas	Brazil
130 D4	Barreiro	Brazil
16 A6	Barreiro	Portugal
130 D8	Barreiros	Brazil
130 K5	Barren R	Kentucky U.S.A.
58 D5	Barren Is	Alaska U.S.A.
27 H11	Barken, N L	Sweden
94 J3	Barker, New York U.S.A.
143 D9	Barker L W Australia Australia
19 P16	Barret de Lioure	France
102 H9	Barrettos	Brazil
99 P4	Barrett L California U.S.A.
142 F4	Barrett, Mt W Australia Australia
118 C4	Barrhead	Alberta Canada
12 D2	Barrhead	Scotland
15 D5	Barrhill	Scotland
121 L8	Barrie	Ontario Canada
120 H7	Barrie I	Ontario Canada
101 N3	Barrier Range	New South Wales Australia
117 N10	Barrière	British Columbia Canada
138 F4	Barrington Tops	New South Wales Australia
141 H8	Barrington	New South Wales Australia
9 E1	Barrow R	England
26 G5	Barrow	Alaska U.S.A.
69 F13	Barrow	Alaska U.S.A.
141 H8	Barrow-in-Furness	England
127 L4	Barrow Pt	Queensland Australia
147 M2	Barrow, Pt	Alaska U.S.A.
143 F7	Barrow Ra W Australia Australia
127 P4	Barrows	Manitoba Canada
98 G2	Barrow Str	Northwest Territories Canada
115 Q6	Barry	Wales
103 O9	Barry	Illinois U.S.A.
121 P6	Barrys Bay	Ontario Canada
14 B3	Barryton	Michigan U.S.A.
144 C5	Barrytown	New Zealand
95 M3	Barryville	New York U.S.A.
29 H6	Barsakelmes	Kazakhstan
78 L6	Barsé	Denmark
78 L6	Barsebäckshamn	Sweden
92 K8	Barsi	India
32 K6	Barsinghausen	Germany
77 D1	Barstow California U.S.A.
108 Q4	Barstow Texas U.S.A.
84 G3	Bardī, Al Libya
139 J4	Barumini	Sardinia
37 F6	Bārnstorf	Germany
84 F7	Baro R	Ethiopia
85 F7	Baro	Nigeria
94 J6	Baroda see Vadodara	
122 K5	Baronissi	Italy
45 P8	Barony, Les reg	France
32 P3	Barons	Alberta Canada
143 E8	Baron's R W Australia Australia
14 B5	Bardstown	Kentucky U.S.A.
36 F6	Baronville	France
84 K9	Barotseland	reg Zambia
80 G8	Barqā Israel
95 R5	Barqay	Israel
128 E2	Barquisimeto Venezuela
94 B2	Barr France
21 J4	Barr Scotland
13 H6	Barr Colorado U.S.A.
129 K6	Barra isld Scotland
130 E4	Barra Brazil
130 E4	Barra Bonita Brazil
127 J12	Barra Head Scotland
21 L4	Barra Mansa Brazil
128 C4	Barranca Peru
128 D2	Barrancabermeja Colombia
127 J10	Barrancas R Corrientes Argentina
127 H9	Barrancas Colombia
127 N10	Barrancas Venezuela
131 B6	Barrancas, R Mendoza Argentina
16 B7	Barrancos Portugal
133 F3	Barranqueras Argentina
126 G9	Barranquilla Colombia
19 P14	Barraux France
17 F5	Barrax Spain
43 G8	Barré Italy
71 G5	Basey Samar Philippines

(Remaining columns continue with index entries in the same format — coordinate reference, place name and qualifier, country/region — through to the column ending "...Bates Idaho U.S.A." at the page's lower right.)

100 G5 **Bates** Oregon U.S.A.
112 F4 **Batesburg** South Carolina U.S.A.
98 D6 **Batesland** South Dakota U.S.A.
143 E7 **Bates,Mt** W Australia Australia
143 D7 **Bates Ra** W Australia Australia
110 E6 **Batesville** Arkansas U.S.A.
110 L2 **Batesville** Indiana U.S.A.
111 G7 **Batesville** Mississippi U.S.A.
109 H7 **Batesville** Texas U.S.A.
52 D5 **Batetskiy** Russian Federation
122 E7 **Bath** New Brunswick Canada
8 D5 **Bath** England
127 M3 **Bath** Jamaica
110 F1 **Bath** Illinois U.S.A.
95 S3 **Bath** Maine U.S.A.
95 K4 **Bath** New York U.S.A.
112 L2 **Bath** North Carolina U.S.A.
112 F4 **Bath** South Carolina U.S.A.
98 H4 **Bath** South Dakota U.S.A.
127 P4 **Bath** Nevis W Indies
86 C3 **Batha** *R* Chad
68 G6 **Batheay** Cambodia
12 E2 **Bathgate** Scotland
98 J1 **Bathgate** North Dakota U.S.A.
139 J5 **Bathurst** New South Wales Australia
122 G6 **Bathurst** New Brunswick Canada
Bathurst The Gambia *see* **Banjul**
141 G2 **Bathurst Bay** Queensland Australia
114 G3 **Bathurst,C** Northwest Territories Canada
140 B1 **Bathurst I** N Terr Australia
115 K2 **Bathurst I** Northwest Territories Canada
114 J4 **Bathurst Inlet** Northwest Territories Canada
142 E3 **Bathurst Is** W Australia Australia
85 D7 **Batié** Burkina
70 G6 **Batikala,Tg** *B* Sulawesi Indonesia
48 E5 **Batina** Croatia
78 L7 **Batin, Wadi al** Iraq
69 E10 **Bati Putih, Gunung** *mt* Malaysia
121 S6 **Batiscan** Quebec Canada
121 T5 **Batiscan,L** Quebec Canada
77 C3 **Batlag-e-Gavkhuni** Iran
13 G6 **Batley** England
78 H3 **Batman** Turkey
85 F1 **Batna** Algeria
71 F4 **Bato,L** Luzon Philippines
111 E11 **Baton Rouge** Louisiana U.S.A.
86 B5 **Batouri** Cameroon
130 D4 **Batovi** Brazil
68 H7 **Ba Tri** Vietnam
42 H3 **Batrina** Croatia
79 F4 **Batroûn** Lebanon
26 R1 **Båtsfjord** Norway
80 D3 **Bat Shelomo** Israel
45 L1 **Battáglia Terme** Italy
140 D3 **Batten** *R* N Terr Australia
36 F1 **Battenberg** Germany
143 C6 **Batthewmurnarna** *mt* W Australia Australia
83 L10 **Batticaloa** Sri Lanka
22 K2 **Battice** Belgium
69 A8 **Batti Malv** *isld* Nicobar Is
45 R8 **Battipaglia** Italy
9 G6 **Battle** England
140 B3 **Battle Cr** N Terr Australia
100 J7 **Battle Cr** Idaho U.S.A.
101 Q1 **Battle Cr** Montana U.S.A.
98 J8 **Battle Cr** Nebraska U.S.A.
118 H9 **Battle Creek** Saskatchewan Canada
94 B4 **Battle Creek** Michigan U.S.A.
8 D2 **Battlefield** England
118 J6 **Battleford** Saskatchewan Canada
118 J5 **Battlefords Prov.Park,The** Saskatchewan Canada
100 C4 **Battle Ground** Washington U.S.A.
123 R1 **Battle Harbour** Labrador, Nfld Canada
102 G1 **Battle Mt** Nevada U.S.A.
118 F6 **Battle R** Alberta Canada
118 H6 **Battle R** Saskatchewan Canada
98 D1 **Battleview** North Dakota U.S.A.
48 G4 **Battonya** Hungary
118 J8 **Battrum** Saskatchewan Canada
70 D4 **Batuajau, Bt** *mt* Kalimantan
71 H8 **Batuata** *isld* Indonesia
69 F11 **Batu Balik, Kampung** Malaysia
69 H14 **Batubetumbang** Indonesia
70 D3 **Batu Bora** *mt* Sarawak
70 D4 **Batubrok, Bt** *mt* Kalimantan
70 G5 **Batudaka** Indonesia
70 C4 **Batuesambang, Bukit** *mt* Kalimantan
69 E10 **Batu Gajah** Malaysia
71 H5 **Batuhitam,Tg** *C* Sulawesi Indonesia
70 D4 **Batuilangmebang, G** *mt* Kalimantan
70 P10 **Batukau, Bt** *mt* Bali Indonesia
71 H9 **Batulanteh** Indonesia
71 H9 **Batulanteh** *mt* Indonesia
70 D6 **Batulein** Kalimantan
70 D3 **Batu Mabun** *mt* Sarawak
78 H1 **Batumi** Georgia
69 D14 **Batumonga** Indonesia
69 F12 **Batu Pahat** Malaysia
69 C13 **Batu,Pulaupulau** *isld* Indonesia
70 F4 **Batuputih** Kalimantan
70 K8 **Baturaja** Sumatra Indonesia
70 N9 **Baturetno** Java
70 P10 **Batur, Gunung** *mt* Java
52 D6 **Baturino** Russian Federation
129 L4 **Baturité** Brazil
69 H14 **Baturusa** Indonesia
69 E13 **Batusangkar** Sumatra
70 G6 **Batusitanduk** Sulawesi
70 F3 **Batu Tg** *B* Kalimantan
71 L10 **Batutuah** Indonesia
80 B5 **Bat Yam** Israel
20 F7 **Batz** France
20 B4 **Batz,I. de** France
71 H7 **Baubau** Sulawesi Indonesia
86 A3 **Bauchi** Nigeria
20 D6 **Baud** France
75 L8 **Bauda** India
128 C2 **Baudo, Sa. de** *mts* Colombia
21 O7 **Baudres** France
19 Q17 **Bauduen** France
21 K6 **Baugé** France
19 Q13 **Bauges** *dist* France
140 D3 **Bauhinia** N Terr Australia
141 J6 **Bauhinia Downs** Queensland Australia
71 N9 **Baukau** Timor
70 G7 **Baula** Sulawesi Indonesia
123 R2 **Bauld,C** Newfoundland Canada
20 F7 **Baule,la** France
20 G6 **Baulon** France
41 J3 **Bauma** Switzerland
9 F1 **Baumber** England
19 K5 **Baume-les-Dames** France
33 T6 **Baumgarten** Germany
37 O7 **Baumgarten** Germany
36 C4 **Baumholder** Germany
70 G6 **Bauna** Sulawesi
37 K3 **Baunach** *R* Germany
37 K4 **Baunach** Germany
70 C6 **Baung** Kalimantan
58 F1 **Baunt** Russian Federation
128 F6 **Baures** Bolivia
130 E8 **Bauru** Brazil
130 D6 **Baús** Brazil
52 B6 **Bauska** Latvia
31 H4 **Bautzen** Germany
109 P1 **Bauxite** Arkansas U.S.A.
Bavaria *see* **Bayern**
107 N3 **Bavaria** Kansas U.S.A.
22 F3 **Bavay** France
89 C9 **Baviaanskloofberge** *mts* S Africa
124 E2 **Bavispe** Mexico
70 C5 **Bawan** Kalimantan
139 H7 **Baw Baw, Mt** Victoria Australia
9 H2 **Bawdeswell** England
9 H3 **Bawdsey** England
70 O8 **Bawean** *isld* Java
32 F7 **Bawinkel** Germany
84 H4 **Bawîti** Egypt
120 D3 **Bawk** Ontario Canada
85 D6 **Bawku** Ghana
68 C3 **Bawlake** Burma
118 E6 **Bawlf** Alberta Canada
68 A2 **Bawli Bazar** Burma
68 B4 **Bawmi** Burma
13 G6 **Bawtry** England
68 F1 **Ba Xat** Vietnam
58 G4 **Ba Xian** China
67 B2 **Ba Xian** China
66 D4 **Baxkorgan** China
112 E6 **Baxley** Georgia U.S.A.
99 N8 **Baxter** Iowa U.S.A.
99 M3 **Baxter** Minnesota U.S.A.
101 S10 **Baxter Mt** Colorado U.S.A.
110 B4 **Baxter Springs** Kansas U.S.A.
122 C7 **Baxter State Park** Maine U.S.A.
80 D3 **Bayada** Israel
126 F4 **Bayamo** Cuba
127 L5 **Bayamón** Puerto Rico
59 J2 **Bayan** China
55 G5 **Bayanaul** Kazakhstan
56 G4 **Bayanday** Russian Federation
Bayan Gol *see* **Dengkou**
58 C5 **Bayan Har Shan** China
58 D2 **Bayanhongor** Mongolia
65 E1 **Bayan Hot** China
65 A3 **Bayan Hure** China
Bayan Huxu *see* **Horqin Youyi Zhongqi**
65 C3 **Bayan Nur Sum** China
58 E3 **Bayan Obo** China
126 E10 **Bayano L.** Panama
Bayan Qagan *see* **Qahar Youyi Houqi**
65 F1 **Bayan Qagan** China
65 E2 **Bayan Qagan** China
113 F7 **Bayard** Florida U.S.A.
99 M8 **Bayard** Iowa U.S.A.
98 C8 **Bayard** Nebraska U.S.A.
94 H7 **Bayard** West Virginia U.S.A.
19 Q15 **Bayard, Col** *pass* France
65 B1 **Bayasgalant** Mongolia
47 L6 **Bayat** Turkey
71 F6 **Bayawan** Negros Philippines
71 G5 **Baybay** Leyte Philippines
112 L2 **Bayboro** North Carolina U.S.A.
123 U6 **Bay Bulls** Newfoundland Canada
78 H1 **Bayburt** Turkey
69 H8 **Bay Canh, Hon** *isld* Vietnam
94 D3 **Bay City** Michigan U.S.A.
100 B4 **Bay City** Oregon U.S.A.
109 M7 **Bay City** Texas U.S.A.
99 O5 **Bay City** Wisconsin U.S.A.
84 G3 **Baydā,Al** Libya
50 F2 **Baydaratskaya Guba** *G* Russian Federation
123 U5 **Bay de Verde** Newfoundland Canada
86 H5 **Baydhabo** Somalia
123 R6 **Bay du Nord** Newfoundland Canada
37 P5 **Bayer-Eisenstein** Germany
41 O2 **Bayerische Alpen** *mt* Germany
37 N5 **Bayerischer Wald** *mts* Germany
37 K5 **Bayern** *land* Germany
21 J3 **Bayeux** France
120 J9 **Bayfield** Ontario Canada
99 Q3 **Bayfield** Wisconsin U.S.A.
123 O2 **Bayfield I** Quebec Canada
122 E5 **Bayfield Mtn** Quebec Canada
57 D3 **Baygakum** Kazakhstan
55 D4 **Baygara** Kazakhstan
98 A4 **Bay Horse** Montana U.S.A.
47 J6 **Bayındır** Turkey
55 D3 **Baykalovo** Russian Federation
56 G4 **Baykal,Ozero** *L* Russian Federation
56 F5 **Baykal'sk** Russian Federation
56 G4 **Baykal'skiy Khrebet** *mts* Russian Federation
56 D5 **Bay-Khaak** Russian Federation
57 C2 **Bay-Khozha** Kazakhstan
55 C3 **Baykibashevo** Russian Federation
56 E1 **Baykit** Russian Federation
57 D1 **Baykonur** Kazakhstan
71 E3 **Bay, Laguna de** Luzon Philippines
123 R6 **Bay l'Argent** Newfoundland Canada
140 E3 **Bayley Pt** Queensland Australia
55 C4 **Baymak** Russian Federation
48 L4 **Baymakliya** Moldavia
111 J11 **Bay Minette** Alabama U.S.A.
9 E4 **Baynard's Green** England
71 E2 **Bayombong** Luzon Philippines
19 K4 **Bayon** France
16 B2 **Bayona** Spain
18 E9 **Bayonne** France
71 E5 **Bayo Pt** Panay Philippines
111 E7 **Bayou Bartholomew** *R* Arkansas U.S.A.
111 D9 **Bayou D'Arbonne** Louisiana U.S.A.
111 D9 **Bayou D'Arbonne L** Louisiana U.S.A.
110 E6 **Bayou de View** *R* Arkansas U.S.A.
111 H11 **Bayou La Batre** Alabama U.S.A.
111 F12 **Bayou Lafourche** *R* Louisiana U.S.A.
111 E9 **Bayou Macon** *R* Louisiana U.S.A.
111 E7 **Bayou Meto** *R* Arkansas U.S.A.
111 F9 **Bayou Pierre** *R* Mississippi U.S.A.
111 E12 **Bayou Vista** Louisiana U.S.A.
128 B5 **Bayovar** Peru
113 E9 **Bayport** Florida U.S.A.
94 D3 **Bay Port** Michigan U.S.A.
99 O5 **Bayport** Minnesota U.S.A.
117 K10 **Bay Pt** British Columbia Canada
71 D5 **Bay Pt** Philippines
47 H5 **Bayramiç** Turkey
37 M4 **Bayreuth** Germany
123 T6 **Bay Roberts** Newfoundland Canada
58 F1 **Baysa** Russian Federation
111 G11 **Bay St.Louis** Mississippi U.S.A.
113 F11 **Bayshore** Florida U.S.A.
95 O6 **Bay Shore** Long I, New York U.S.A.
112 E1 **Bays Mt** Tennessee U.S.A.
56 E5 **Bay-Soot** Russian Federation
111 G10 **Bay Springs** Mississippi U.S.A.
Baytag Bogdo *see* **Baytik Shan**
9 G3 **Baythorn End** England
66 E2 **Baytik Shan** *mt ra* China/Mongolia
109 N6 **Baytown** Texas U.S.A.
145 F3 **Bay View** New Zealand
117 P12 **Bayview** Idaho U.S.A.
57 E3 **Bayzhansay** Kazakhstan
17 F7 **Baza** Spain
48 K1 **Bazaliya** Ukraine
22 G5 **Bazancourt** France
57 K1 **Bazar** *R* Kazakhstan
107 O3 **Bazar** Kansas U.S.A.
53 G12 **Bazardyuzyu, Gora** *mt* Azerbaijan/Rus Fed
52 G6 **Bazarnyye Mataki** Russian Federation
87 G10 **Bazaruto, I** Mozambique
18 E8 **Bazas** France
17 F7 **Baza,Sierra de** Spain
22 J4 **Bazeilles** France
67 B1 **Bazhong** China
48 G6 **Baziaş** Romania
18 G9 **Baziége** France
121 Q5 **Bazin** *R* Quebec Canada
107 L3 **Bazine** Kansas U.S.A.
77 G5 **Bazmām, Kūh-e** *mt* Iran
77 F6 **Bazman** Iran
21 M5 **Bazoche-Gouet,la** France
22 F5 **Bazoches** France
21 K4 **Bazoches-au-Houlme** France
21 P5 **Bazoches-les Gallerandes** France
21 L4 **Bazoches-sur-Hoëne** France
21 L5 **Bazoge,la** France
21 H8 **Bazoges-en Paillers** France
21 J8 **Bazoges-en-Pareds** France
21 J5 **Bazougers** France
20 G5 **Bazouges-la-Perouse** France
45 K3 **Bazzano** Italy
79 F4 **Bcharre** Lebanon
112 E6 **Beach** Georgia U.S.A.
98 C3 **Beach** North Dakota U.S.A.
95 N7 **Beach Haven** New Jersey U.S.A.
138 E6 **Beachport** South Australia Australia
95 N7 **Beachwood** New Jersey U.S.A.
9 G6 **Beachy Head** England
143 C9 **Beacon** W Australia Australia
95 O5 **Beacon** New York U.S.A.
118 H4 **Beacon Hill** Saskatchewan Canada
113 B8 **Beacon Hill** Florida U.S.A.
139 H8 **Beaconsfield** Tasmania Australia
9 F4 **Beaconsfield** England
13 G2 **Beadnell** England
142 E3 **Beagle Bay** W Australia Australia
133 D8 **Beagle, Canal** *str* Chile/Arg
140 A1 **Beagle G** N Terr Australia
143 A8 **Beagle I** W Australia Australia
142 E3 **Beagle Reef** W Australia Australia
87 H10 **Bealanana** Madagascar
117 L11 **Beale,C** British Columbia Canada
94 K8 **Bealeton** Virginia U.S.A.
108 F3 **Beals Cr** Texas U.S.A.
118 C1 **Beaman** Manitoba Canada
8 D6 **Beaminster** England
100 J4 **Bear** Idaho U.S.A.
101 O7 **Bear** *R* Idaho U.S.A.
111 J7 **Bear Cr** Alabama U.S.A.
107 J4 **Bear Cr** Kansas U.S.A.
99 S5 **Bear Cr** Wisconsin U.S.A.
98 B8 **Bear Cr** Wyoming U.S.A.
101 Q4 **Bearcreek** Montana U.S.A.
95 M5 **Bear Cr.Res** Pennsylvania U.S.A.
111 D8 **Bearden** Arkansas U.S.A.
120 C3 **Beardmore** Ontario Canada
146 D10 **Beardmore Glacier** Antarctica
141 J8 **Beardmore Res** Queensland Australia
103 M8 **Beardsley** Arizona U.S.A.
107 J2 **Beardsley** Kansas U.S.A.
110 F1 **Beardstown** Illinois U.S.A.
123 K4 **Bear Head** Anticosti I, Quebec
118 J7 **Bear Hills,The** Saskatchewan Canada
Bear I *see* **Bjørnøya**
115 L7 **Bear I** Northwest Territories Canada
14 B5 **Bear I** Ireland
120 K6 **Bear Island** Ontario Canada
119 V3 **Bear L** Manitoba Canada
101 O7 **Bear L** Idaho/Utah U.S.A.
117 K7 **Bear Lake** British Columbia Canada
94 A2 **Bear Lake** Michigan U.S.A.
98 B5 **Bear Lodge Mts** Wyoming U.S.A.
101 M3 **Bearmouth** Montana U.S.A.
121 M4 **Béarn** Quebec Canada
18 E9 **Béarn** *prov* France
101 Q1 **Bearpaw Mt** Montana U.S.A.
146 B8 **Bear Pen** Antarctica
119 N4 **Bear R** Saskatchewan Canada
101 N8 **Bear R.City** Utah U.S.A.
12 D2 **Bearsden** Scotland
101 S9 **Bears Ears Pk** Colorado U.S.A.
115 K7 **Bearskin L** Ontario Canada
74 F3 **Beas** *R* India
18 D9 **Beasain** Spain
17 F6 **Beas de Segura** Spain
127 J6 **Beata, I** Dominican Rep
40 G4 **Beatenberg** Switzerland
117 P10 **Beaton** British Columbia Canada
6 J4 **Beatrice** *oil rig* North Sea
111 J10 **Beatrice** Alabama U.S.A.
98 K9 **Beatrice** Nebraska U.S.A.
140 D2 **Beatrice,C** Aust
142 F3 **Beatrice,Mt** W Australia Australia
107 O2 **Beattie** Kansas U.S.A.
15 E5 **Beattock** Scotland
117 N7 **Beatton River** British Columbia Canada
119 N6 **Beatty** Saskatchewan Canada
102 H5 **Beatty** Nevada U.S.A.
100 D7 **Beatty** Oregon U.S.A.
121 N4 **Beattyville** Quebec Canada
94 D9 **Beattyville** Kentucky U.S.A.
19 N17 **Beaucaire** France
21 O2 **Beaucamps-le-Vieux** France
121 L3 **Beaucanton** Quebec Canada
21 M6 **Beauce** *plain* France
122 B7 **Beauceville** Quebec Canada
20 H4 **Beauchamps** France
131 G8 **Beauchene I** Falkland Is
121 M6 **Beauchêne, Lac** Quebec Canada
40 E2 **Beaucourt** France
141 L8 **Beaudesert** Queensland Australia
121 L4 **Beaudry** Quebec Canada
21 L5 **Beaufay** France
40 E6 **Beaufort** France
22 L4 **Beaufort** Luxembourg
70 D2 **Beaufort** Sabah
112 L3 **Beaufort** North Carolina U.S.A.
112 G5 **Beaufort** South Carolina U.S.A.
79 F5 **Beaufort Castle** *hist site* Lebanon
21 K7 **Beaufort-en-Vallée** France
146 C11 **Beaufort I** Antarctica
112 L3 **Beaufort Inlet** North Carolina U.S.A.
116 R2 **Beaufort Lag** Alaska U.S.A.
147 K2 **Beaufort Sea** Arctic Oc
89 B9 **Beaufort West** S Africa
21 O6 **Beaugency** France
121 R7 **Beauharnois** Quebec Canada
121 Q7 **Beauharnois Power Canal** Quebec Canada
19 N12 **Beaujeu** France
19 Q16 **Beaujeu** France
18 H6 **Beaujolais, Mts du** France
95 S6 **Beau L** Maine/New Brunswick U.S.A./Canada
9 E6 **Beaulieu** England
21 N7 **Beaulieu-lès-Loches** France
15 D3 **Beauly** Scotland
15 D3 **Beauly, R** Scotland
8 B1 **Beaumaris** Wales
21 M3 **Beaumesnil** France
22 D3 **Beaumetz-les-Loges** France
22 G3 **Beaumont** Belgium
123 R4 **Beaumont** Newfoundland Canada
21 L8 **Beaumont** Vienne France
144 B6 **Beaumont** New Zealand
102 H8 **Beaumont** California U.S.A.
107 O4 **Beaumont** Kansas U.S.A.
111 H10 **Beaumont** Mississippi U.S.A.
111 B11 **Beaumont** Texas U.S.A.
18 F9 **Beaumont de Lomogne** France
18 F8 **Beaumont de Périgord** France
22 J4 **Beaumont-en-Argonne** France
21 L3 **Beaumont-en-Auge** France
22 E3 **Beaumont-en-Cambrésis** France
20 G2 **Beaumont-Hague** France
21 M6 **Beaumont-la-Ronce** France
21 M3 **Beaumont-le-Roger** France
21 M5 **Beaumont-les-Autels** France
21 L6 **Beaumont-Pied-de-Bœuf** France
21 P3 **Beaumont-sur-Oise** France
21 L5 **Beaumont-sur-Sarthe** France
19 J5 **Beaune** France
21 P5 **Beaune-la Rolande** France
121 T6 **Beauport** Quebec Canada
21 J7 **Beaupréau** France
21 P1 **Beauquesne** France
22 H3 **Beauraing** Belgium
40 B7 **Beaurepaire d'Isère** France
19 P15 **Beaurières** France
22 F5 **Beaurieux** France
118 E1 **Beausejour** Manitoba Canada
139 H6 **Beauty,Mt** Victoria Australia
21 P3 **Beauvais** France
118 C9 **Beauvais Lake Prov. Park** Alberta Canada
118 K3 **Beauval** Saskatchewan Canada
21 P1 **Beauval** France
118 F5 **Beauvallon** Alberta Canada
20 F8 **Beauvoir-sur-Mer** France
118 F4 **Beaver** *R* Alberta Canada
117 L5 **Beaver** *R* Yukon Terr/Br Col Canada
116 O3 **Beaver** Alaska U.S.A.
107 M3 **Beaver** Kansas U.S.A.
98 F3 **Beaver** *R* North Dakota U.S.A.
108 D7 **Beaver** Oklahoma U.S.A.
100 B4 **Beaver** Oregon U.S.A.
94 G6 **Beaver** Pennsylvania U.S.A.
103 L3 **Beaver** *R* Utah U.S.A.
103 M3 **Beaver** Utah U.S.A.
122 J9 **Beaverbank** Nova Scotia Canada
122 G6 **Beaver Brook** New Brunswick Canada
98 G9 **Beaver City** Nebraska U.S.A.
116 O4 **Beaver Cr** Alaska U.S.A.
106 G2 **Beaver Cr** Colorado U.S.A.
101 N5 **Beaver Cr** Idaho U.S.A.
107 J2 **Beaver Cr** Kansas U.S.A.
110 D5 **Beaver Cr** Missouri U.S.A.
98 B3 **Beaver Cr** Montana U.S.A.
98 F9 **Beaver Cr** Nebraska U.S.A.
98 B6 **Beaver Cr** Wyoming U.S.A.
117 C4 **Beaver Creek** Yukon Territory Canada
98 J9 **Beaver Crossing** Nebraska U.S.A.
110 K4 **Beaver Dam** Kentucky U.S.A.
99 S6 **Beaver Dam** Wisconsin U.S.A.
117 O11 **Beaverdell Falls** British Columbia Canada
94 G6 **Beaver Falls** Pennsylvania U.S.A.
101 N4 **Beaverhead** *R* Montana U.S.A.
101 M4 **Beaverhead Mts** Idaho/Montana U.S.A.
118 E5 **Beaverhill L** Alberta Canada
99 V4 **Beaver I** Michigan U.S.A.
123 N2 **Beaver Island L** Quebec Canada
99 U3 **Beaver L** Michigan U.S.A.
117 N9 **Beaver Lake** British Columbia Canada
117 O8 **Beaverlodge** Alberta Canada
117 P10 **Beavermouth** British Columbia Canada
116 J5 **Beaver Mts** Alaska U.S.A.
118 F4 **Beaver R** Alberta Canada
118 H4 **Beaver R** Saskatchewan Canada
118 K4 **Beaver R** Saskatchewan Canada
110 C5 **Beaver Res** Arkansas U.S.A.
95 M3 **Beaver R.Flow** New York U.S.A.
121 L8 **Beaverton** Ontario Canada
94 C3 **Beaverton** Michigan U.S.A.
100 C4 **Beaverton** Oregon U.S.A.
95 K6 **Beavertown** Pennsylvania U.S.A.
99 T9 **Beaverville** Illinois U.S.A.
74 F5 **Beawar** India
133 D4 **Beazley** Argentina
131 C4 **Bebedero, Salina** Argentina
129 J8 **Bebedouro** Brazil
36 G6 **Bebenhausen** Germany
129 L4 **Beberibe** Brazil
36 H2 **Bebra** Germany
47 H2 **Bebrovo** Bulgaria
9 H3 **Beccles** England
48 F5 **Bečej** Serbia Yugoslavia
48 K5 **Beceni** Romania
16 C2 **Becerreá** Spain
126 C7 **Becerro,Cayos** *reefs* Caribbean
85 D2 **Béchar** Algeria
116 J7 **Becharaf National Monument** Alaska U.S.A.
116 J8 **Becharof L** Alaska U.S.A.
85 D7 **Bechem** Ghana
144 C5 **Beche, Mt de la** New Zealand
20 G5 **Bécherel** France
46 G1 **Bechet** Romania
116 F9 **Bechevin B** Alaska U.S.A.
37 K5 **Bechhofen** Germany
Bechuanaland Prot *see* **Botswana**
31 H6 **Bechyně** Czechoslovakia
32 M7 **Beckedorf** Germany
13 E4 **Beckfoot** England
9 E5 **Beckhampton** England
36 B5 **Beckingen** Germany
8 D5 **Beckington** England
94 F9 **Beckley** West Virginia U.S.A.
144 B6 **Becks** New Zealand
32 H9 **Beckum** Germany
109 N3 **Beckville** Texas U.S.A.
102 D2 **Beckwourth** California U.S.A.
48 J3 **Beclean** Romania
21 J6 **Bécon** France
19 O16 **Béconne** France
9 G4 **Becontree** England
37 O3 **Bečov nad Teplou** Czechoslovakia
108 F2 **Becton** Texas U.S.A.
31 K6 **Bečva** *R* Czechoslovakia
84 F4 **Beda** Libya
70 O10 **Bedadung** *R* Java
13 G5 **Bedale** England
18 H9 **Bédarieux** France
19 N16 **Bedarrides** France
36 B1 **Bedburg** Germany
8 B1 **Beddgelert** Wales
9 G6 **Beddingham** England
119 R9 **Bede** Manitoba Canada
20 G5 **Bédée** France
28 E4 **Beder** Denmark
32 J5 **Bederkesa** Germany
55 C3 **Bedeyeva Polyana** Russian Federation
122 J9 **Bedford** Nova Scotia Canada
121 S7 **Bedford** Quebec Canada
9 F3 **Bedford** England
110 K3 **Bedford** Indiana U.S.A.
99 M9 **Bedford** Iowa U.S.A.
94 B8 **Bedford** Kentucky U.S.A.
95 Q4 **Bedford** New Hampshire U.S.A.
94 J6 **Bedford** Pennsylvania U.S.A.
94 H9 **Bedford** Virginia U.S.A.
101 P7 **Bedford** Wyoming U.S.A.
141 H3 **Bedford C** Queensland Australia
142 F3 **Bedford Downs** W Australia Australia
143 D10 **Bedford Harb** W Australia Australia
127 P5 **Bedford Pt** Grenada
9 F3 **Bedfordshire** *co* England
74 D7 **Bedi** India
69 H14 **Bedinggong** Indonesia
13 G3 **Bedlington** England
19 O16 **Bédoin** France
41 O5 **Bedollo** Italy
69 E11 **Bedongkong** Sumatra
140 E6 **Bedourie** Queensland Australia
142 A4 **Bedout I** W Australia Australia
8 A7 **Bedruthan Steps** England
28 C6 **Bedsted** Denmark
9 E3 **Bedworth** England
98 J8 **Bee** Nebraska U.S.A.
110 E6 **Beebe** Arkansas U.S.A.
98 G4 **Beebe** South Dakota U.S.A.
141 H7 **Beechal** *R* Queensland Australia
94 K5 **Beech Cr** Pennsylvania U.S.A.
110 J4 **Beech Creek** Kentucky U.S.A.
100 F5 **Beech Creek** Oregon U.S.A.
99 T8 **Beecher** Illinois U.S.A.
110 H2 **Beecher City** Illinois U.S.A.
116 N1 **Beechey Point** Alaska U.S.A.
110 L4 **Beech Fork** *R* Kentucky U.S.A.
110 K2 **Beech Grove** Indiana U.S.A.
99 S3 **Beechwood** Michigan U.S.A.
139 H6 **Beechworth** Victoria Australia
118 K8 **Beechy** Saskatchewan Canada
32 M7 **Beedenbostel** Germany
100 C9 **Beegum** California U.S.A.
25 E5 **Beek** Gelderland Netherlands
25 E4 **Beekbergen** Netherlands
111 E9 **Beekman** Louisiana U.S.A.
107 K3 **Beeler** Kansas U.S.A.
33 R8 **Beelitz** Germany
98 K8 **Beemer** Nebraska U.S.A.
33 O8 **Beendorf** Germany
141 L8 **Beenleigh** Queensland Australia
37 K2 **Beerberg** *mt* Germany
33 S8 **Beeren** Germany
36 F4 **Beerfelden** Germany
113 E10 **Bee Ridge** Florida U.S.A.
143 C8 **Beeringgnurding, Mt** W Australia Australia
22 F2 **Beerlegem** Belgium
79 F8 **Beer Menuha** Israel
22 E1 **Beernem** Belgium
79 E9 **Beer Ora** Israel
80 C8 **Be'er Pehar** Israel
25 E5 **Beers** Netherlands
80 C8 **Beersheba** Israel
Be'er Sheva *see* **Beersheba**
25 D6 **Beerze** *R* Netherlands
31 H3 **Beeskow** Germany
87 E11 **Beestekraal** S Africa
9 E2 **Beeston** England
140 C3 **Beetaloo** N Terr Australia
25 F2 **Beetsterzwaag** Netherlands
33 O7 **Beetzendorf** Germany
33 R8 **Beetz-see** *L* Germany
109 K7 **Beeville** Texas U.S.A.
86 D5 **Befale** Zaire
87 H11 **Befandriana** Madagascar
86 D5 **Befori** Zaire
20 D4 **Bégard** France
8 B4 **Begelly** Wales
127 P4 **Beggars Pt** Antigua W Indies
107 O6 **Beggs** Oklahoma U.S.A.
86 F4 **Bēgī** Ethiopia
51 L1 **Begicheva, Ostrov** *isld* Russian Federation
20 C6 **Beg-Meil** France
27 D11 **Begna** *R* Norway
28 E4 **Begtrup Vig** *B* Denmark
19 N15 **Begude-de-Mazenc, la** France
77 B4 **Behbehān** Iran
33 N5 **Behlendorf** Germany
117 H8 **Behm Can** Alaska U.S.A.
140 A3 **Behn, Mt** N Terr Australia
22 L3 **Beho** Belgium
33 R4 **Behren-Lübchin** Germany
37 L4 **Behringersmühle** Germany
77 C1 **Behshahr** Iran
59 J2 **Bei'an** China
26 G4 **Beiarn** Norway
67 B2 **Beibei** China
67 A1 **Beichuan** China
65 A6 **Beichuan He** *R* China
65 D5 **Beidaihehaibin** China
32 M10 **Beienrode** Germany
37 O2 **Beierfeld** Germany
68 J2 **Beihai** China
36 G6 **Beihingen** Germany
66 F4 **Bei Hulsan Hu** *L* China
67 D4 **Bei Jiang** *R* China
63 **Beijing** *conurbation* China
85 A5 **Beila** Mauritania
25 G3 **Beilen** Netherlands
68 J3 **Beili** China
68 K1 **Beiliu** China
37 L5 **Beilngries** Germany
36 G5 **Beilstein** Baden-Württemberg Germany
36 E2 **Beilstein** Hessen Germany
36 C3 **Beilstein** Rheinland-Pfalz Germany
67 B6 **Beilun Ai** *pass* China
36 H7 **Beimerstetten** Germany
44 C1 **Beinasco** Italy
22 G5 **Beine** France
36 E6 **Beinheim** France
15 E4 **Beinn a' Ghlo** *mt* Scotland
40 H3 **Beinwil** Switzerland
67 B4 **Beipan Jiang** *R* China
65 E4 **Beipiao** China
87 F9 **Beira** Mozambique
16 B4 **Beira Alta** *prov* Portugal
16 B5 **Beira Baixa** *prov* Portugal
16 B4 **Beira Litoral** *prov* Portugal
Beirut *see* **Beyrouth**
118 D7 **Beiseker** Alberta Canada
58 C3 **Beishan** China
65 F2 **Beitaolaizhao** China
87 E10 **Beitbridge** Zimbabwe
15 D5 **Beith** Scotland
80 D6 **Beit Hanīnā** Jordan
80 F4 **Beit Idis** Jordan
80 D7 **Beit Jala** Jordan
80 D7 **Beit Kahil** Jordan
80 A7 **Beit Lahiya** Israel
80 D7 **Beit Lahm** Jordan
80 E1 **Beit Lif** Lebanon
80 G3 **Beit Ras** Jordan
80 D7 **Beit Sahur** Jordan
26 E7 **Beitstad** Norway
26 E8 **Beitstadfjord** *inlet* Norway
48 G4 **Beius** Romania
67 G2 **Beiyandang Shan** *mt* China
65 E4 **Beizhen** China
65 D6 **Beizhen** China
16 B6 **Beja** Portugal
43 C12 **Béja** Tunisia
143 E6 **Bejah Hill** W Australia Australia
85 E1 **Bejaïa** Algeria
85 F1 **Bejaïa, Golfe de** *G* Algeria
16 D4 **Béjar** Spain
77 F2 **Bejestān** Iran
143 B9 **Bejoording** W Australia Australia
57 E4 **Bekabad** Tajikistan
70 L9 **Bekasi** Java
48 F4 **Békés** *co* Hungary
48 G4 **Békés** Hungary
48 G4 **Békéscsaba** Hungary
85 D7 **Bekwai** Ghana
Bela *see* **Villach**
74 B5 **Bela** Pakistan
86 B2 **Bélabérim** Niger
86 B4 **Bélabo** Cameroon
21 N8 **Bélâbre** France
48 G6 **Bela Crkva** Serbia Yugoslavia
56 B5 **Bel'agash** Kazakhstan
20 E5 **Bel Air** *mt* France
20 F6 **Bel-Air** France
95 L7 **Bel Air** Maryland U.S.A.
70 D4 **Belajan** *R* Kalimantan
70 D4 **Belajan, G** *mt* Kalimantan
16 D6 **Belalcázar** Spain
74 H9 **Belampalli** India
37 O4 **Bělá nad Radbuzou** Czechoslovakia
71 J4 **Belang** Sulawesi Indonesia
119 U5 **Bélanger Pt** Manitoba Canada
119 U5 **Bélanger R** Manitoba Canada
70 B6 **Belangiran** Kalimantan
46 E1 **Bela Palanka** Serbia Yugoslavia
139 H4 **Belaraboon** New South Wales Australia
Belarus *see* **Belorussia**
129 G8 **Bela Vista** Brazil
87 F11 **Bela Vista** Mozambique
130 C8 **Bela Vista** Paraguay
130 E5 **Bela Vista de Goiás** Brazil
69 D11 **Belawan** Sumatra
54 G5 **Belaya** Russian Federation
54 E4 **Belaya-Berezka** Russian Federation
54 M8 **Belaya-Kalitva** Russian Federation
55 B2 **Belaya Kholunitsa** Russian Federation
48 N1 **Belaya Tserkov'** Ukraine
44 D2 **Belbo** *R* Italy
48 L3 **Belceşti** Romania
115 K2 **Belcher Chan** Northwest Territories Canada
115 M6 **Belcher, Les Iles** Northwest Territories Canada
17 G3 **Belchite** Spain
14 D2 **Belcoo** N Ireland
121 N4 **Belcourt** Quebec Canada
98 G1 **Belcourt** North Dakota U.S.A.
102 C1 **Belden** California U.S.A.
98 D1 **Belden** North Dakota U.S.A.
94 B3 **Belding** Michigan U.S.A.
52 D5 **Belebelka** Russian Federation
55 B4 **Belebey** Russian Federation
86 J5 **Beledweyne** Somalia
129 J4 **Belém** Brazil
129 L5 **Belém de São Francisco** Brazil
128 C3 **Belén** Colombia
129 G8 **Belén** Paraguay
108 A1 **Belen** New Mexico U.S.A.
131 G3 **Belén,Cuchilla de** *mt* Uruguay
124 H7 **Belén del Refugio** Mexico
46 G1 **Belene** Bulgaria
137 N5 **Belep,Îles** New Caledonia
86 G3 **Beles** *R* Ethiopia
16 B2 **Belesar, Embalse de** *res* Spain
54 H3 **Belev** Russian Federation
86 C5 **Bélézé** Cent Afr Republic
100 C2 **Belfair** Washington U.S.A.
122 K7 **Belfast** Prince Edward I Canada
144 B4 **Belfast** New Zealand
14 F2 **Belfast** N Ireland
95 S2 **Belfast** Maine U.S.A.
25 F6 **Belfeld** Netherlands
98 C3 **Belfield** North Dakota U.S.A.
86 F3 **Bēlfodiya** Ethiopia
13 G2 **Belford** England
19 K5 **Belfort** France
40 E2 **Belfort, Terr De** France
101 Q4 **Belfry** Montana U.S.A.
76 B3 **Belgaum** India
19 P18 **Belgentier** France
33 S10 **Belgern** Germany
146 H8 **Belgicafjella** *ra* Antarctica
99 T6 **Belgium** Wisconsin U.S.A.
22 E2 **Belgium** *kingdom* W Europe
54 H6 **Belgorod** Russian Federation
48 N4 **Belgorod Dnestrovskiy** Ukraine
53 E8 **Belgorodkaya Oblast'** *prov* Russian Federation
Belgrade *see* **Beograd**
101 O4 **Belgrade** Montana U.S.A.
98 H8 **Belgrade** Nebraska U.S.A.
133 F5 **Belgrano** Argentina
131 E7 **Belgrano,Pto** Argentina
47 M10 **Belgrat Ormani** *forest* Turkey
145 D4 **Belgrove** New Zealand
85 F3 **Bel Guebbour, Hassi** Algeria
112 L2 **Belhaven** North Carolina U.S.A.
85 F2 **Belhirane** Algeria
21 N4 **Belhomert** France
43 E11 **Belice** *R* Sicily
53 G12 **Belidzhi** Russian Federation
47 H1 **Beli Lom** *R* Bulgaria
48 E5 **Beli Manastir** Croatia
70 K8 **Belimbing** Indonesia
69 J12 **Belimbing, Tanjong** *C* Indonesia
18 E8 **Belin** France
86 B5 **Bélinga** Gabon
94 H7 **Belington** West Virginia U.S.A.
69 G13 **Belinyu** Indonesia
46 F3 **Belitsa** Bulgaria
69 J14 **Belitung** *isld* Indonesia
125 P9 **Belize** Belize
125 P9 **Belize** Central America
48 G6 **Beljanića** *mt* Serbia Yugoslavia
143 C9 **Belka** W Australia Australia
99 O9 **Belknap** Iowa U.S.A.
100 K2 **Belknap** Montana U.S.A.
147 P8 **Bel'kovskiy Os** *isld* Russian Federation
141 K7 **Bell** Queensland Australia
121 N3 **Bell** *R* Quebec Canada
113 E8 **Bell** Florida U.S.A.
117 J9 **Bella Bella** British Columbia Canada
18 F6 **Bellac** France
133 F4 **Bellaco** Uruguay
117 K9 **Bella Coola** British Columbia Canada
107 M2 **Bellaire** Kansas U.S.A.
94 B2 **Bellaire** Michigan U.S.A.
94 G6 **Bellaire** Ohio U.S.A.
109 M6 **Bellaire** Texas U.S.A.
141 G7 **Bellalie** Queensland Australia
42 C2 **Bellano** Italy
76 C3 **Bellary** India
40 G5 **Bella Tola** *mt* Switzerland
131 F2 **Bella Vista** Argentina
128 C4 **Bellavista** Loreto Peru
128 C5 **Bellavista** San Martin Peru
139 J8 **Bell B** Tasmania Australia
145 E3 **Bell Block** New Zealand
141 K5 **Bell Cay** *isld* Gt Barrier Reef Aust
110 E3 **Belle** Missouri U.S.A.
123 R6 **Belle B** Newfoundland Canada
33 P9 **Belleben** Germany
94 D6 **Belle Center** Ohio U.S.A.
40 E7 **Bellecôte** *mt* France
19 P14 **Belledonne, Pic de** *mt* France
94 D6 **Bellefontaine** Ohio U.S.A.
94 K6 **Bellefonte** Pennsylvania U.S.A.
98 C5 **Belle Fourche** South Dakota U.S.A.
98 A5 **Belle Fourche** *R* Wyoming U.S.A.
18 G5 **Bellegarde** France
19 P12 **Bellegarde** France
18 G7 **Bellegarde-en-Marche** France
113 G11 **Belle Glade** Florida U.S.A.
40 E3 **Belleherbe** France
20 D7 **Belle Ile** France
123 R2 **Belle Isle** Newfoundland Canada
20 D4 **Belle-Isle-en-Terre** France
123 R2 **Belle Isle Landing** Belle Isle, Nfld
123 Q2 **Belle Isle,Strait of** Newfoundland Canada
21 M5 **Bellême** France
110 K5 **Belle Meade** Tennessee U.S.A.
103 N6 **Bellemont** Arizona U.S.A.
21 N2 **Bellencombre** France
141 H3 **Bellenden Ker** *ra* Queensland Australia
22 E4 **Bellenglise** France
123 R6 **Belleoram** Newfoundland Canada
119 M8 **Belle Plaine** Saskatchewan Canada
99 O8 **Belle Plaine** Iowa U.S.A.
107 N4 **Belle Plaine** Kansas U.S.A.
99 N5 **Belle Plaine** Minnesota U.S.A.
110 H3 **Belle Rive** Illinois U.S.A.
121 T4 **Belle-Rivière,Lac de la** Quebec Canada
121 M5 **Belleterre** Quebec Canada
94 F7 **Belle Valley** Ohio U.S.A.
40 E5 **Bellevaux** France
40 B4 **Bellevesvre** France
113 E8 **Belleview** Florida U.S.A.
121 N8 **Belleville** Ontario Canada
19 N12 **Belleville** France
110 G3 **Belleville** Illinois U.S.A.
107 N2 **Belleville** Kansas U.S.A.
95 L3 **Belleville** New York U.S.A.
94 K6 **Belleville** Pennsylvania U.S.A.
94 F7 **Belleville** West Virginia U.S.A.
99 R7 **Belleville** Wisconsin U.S.A.
20 H8 **Belleville sur Vie** France
141 G3 **Bellevue** Queensland Australia
118 C9 **Bellevue** Alberta Canada
101 L6 **Bellevue** Idaho U.S.A.
99 Q7 **Bellevue** Iowa U.S.A.
94 B4 **Bellevue** Michigan U.S.A.
94 E5 **Bellevue** Ohio U.S.A.
109 J2 **Bellevue** Texas U.S.A.
100 C2 **Bellevue** Washington U.S.A.
19 P13 **Belley** France
110 H1 **Bellflower** Illinois U.S.A.
110 E2 **Bellflower** Missouri U.S.A.
36 E5 **Bellheim** Germany
123 R3 **Bell I.** Newfoundland Canada
123 T6 **Bell I** Newfoundland Canada
22 E4 **Bellicourt** France
21 H7 **Belligne** France
13 F3 **Bellingham** England
98 K4 **Bellingham** Minnesota U.S.A.
100 C1 **Bellingham** Washington U.S.A.
146 D3 **Bellingshausen** *former U.S.S.R. Base* Antarctica
146 B6 **Bellingshausen Sea** Antarctica
25 H2 **Bellingwolde** Netherlands
41 K5 **Bellinzona** Switzerland
118 E4 **Bellis** Alberta Canada
36 F2 **Bellnhausen** Germany
12 C2 **Bellochantuy** Scotland
137 M6 **Bellona Plateau** Coral Sea
102 C3 **Bellota** California U.S.A.
21 K4 **Bellou-en-Houlme** France
95 P3 **Bellows Falls** Vermont U.S.A.
21 P3 **Belloy-en-France** France
115 L5 **Bell Pen** Northwest Territories Canada
138 C4 **Bell,Pt** South Australia Australia
106 F6 **Bell Ranch** New Mexico U.S.A.
13 F1 **Bell Rock** Scotland
110 G6 **Bells** Tennessee U.S.A.
109 L2 **Bells** Texas U.S.A.
119 Q6 **Bellsite** Manitoba Canada
42 E2 **Belluno** Italy
131 D4 **Bell Ville** Argentina
94 E6 **Bellville** Ohio U.S.A.
109 L6 **Bellville** Texas U.S.A.
106 E1 **Bellvue** Colorado U.S.A.
111 C10 **Bellwood** Louisiana U.S.A.
98 J8 **Bellwood** Nebraska U.S.A.
94 J6 **Bellwood** Pennsylvania U.S.A.
118 D9 **Belly R** Alberta Canada
95 N6 **Belmar** New Jersey U.S.A.
16 D6 **Bélmez** Spain
99 N7 **Belmond** Iowa U.S.A.
142 B1 **Belmont** *dist* Perth, W Aust Australia
119 S9 **Belmont** Manitoba Canada
122 J8 **Belmont** Nova Scotia Canada
120 J10 **Belmont** Ontario Canada
102 H3 **Belmont** Nevada U.S.A.
95 Q3 **Belmont** New Hampshire U.S.A.
94 K4 **Belmont** New York U.S.A.
112 F2 **Belmont** North Carolina U.S.A.
109 K6 **Belmont** Texas U.S.A.
94 K8 **Belmont** Virginia U.S.A.
99 Q7 **Belmont** Wisconsin U.S.A.
129 L7 **Belmonte** Brazil
16 C4 **Belmonte** Portugal
17 F5 **Belmonte** Spain
125 P9 **Belmopan** Belize
141 F4 **Belmore** *R* Queensland Australia
14 A2 **Belmullet** Ireland
130 H4 **Belo Campo** Brazil
56 C3 **Belogorsk** Russian Federation
59 J1 **Belogorsk** Russian Federation
55 E1 **Belogorye** Russian Federation
54 M6 **Belogor'ye** Voronezhskaya obl Russian Federation
46 F1 **Belogradchik** Bulgaria
87 G13 **Beloha** Madagascar
129 K7 **Belo Horizonte** Brazil
107 M2 **Beloit** Kansas U.S.A.
99 R7 **Beloit** Wisconsin U.S.A.
130 H10 **Belo Jardim** Brazil
48 M5 **Beloles'ye** Ukraine
129 H4 **Belo Monte** Brazil
52 D3 **Belomorsk** Russian Federation
147 J16 **Belomorsk** Russian Federation
52 D3 **Belomorsko-Baltiyskiy** Russian Federation
54 L2 **Beloomut** Russian Federation
70 G6 **Belopa** Sulawesi
54 F5 **Belopol'ye** Ukraine
16 E2 **Belorado** Spain
79 C1 **Belōran** Turkey
55 C4 **Beloretsk** Russian Federation
54 B3 **Belorussia** *rep* E Europe

111 F10 Bogue Chitto Mississippi U.S.A.
112 K3 Bogue Inlet North Carolina U.S.A.
54 B2 Bogushevsk Belorussia
54 B7 Boguslav Ukraine
31 J5 Boguszów Poland
127 L2 Bog Walk Jamaica
70 D4 Boh R Kalimantan
65 D5 Bo Hai G China
22 E4 Bohain France
65 D5 Bohai Wan B China
119 M8 Boharm Saskatchewan Canada
38 N5 Böheimkirchen Austria
30 H6 Bohemia old region Czechoslovakia
142 F4 Bohemia Downs W Australia Australia
85 E7 Bohicon Benin
42 F2 Bohiniska Bistrica Slovenia
37 N1 Böhlen Germany
32 K7 Böhme Germany
37 N4 Böhmer Wald mts Germany
32 H8 Bohmte Germany
33 Q7 Böhne Germany
71 G6 Bohol isld Philippines
71 F6 Bohol Str Philippines
16 D5 Bohonal de Ibor Spain
48 D4 Böhönye Hungary
65 A2 Böhöt Mongolia
80 B8 Bohu Israel
128 F4 Boiaçu Brazil
43 F7 Boiano Italy
122 F7 Boiestown New Brunswick Canada
21 P5 Boigneville France
122 B5 Boileau Quebec Canada
130 C9 Boi Preto,Serra de mts Brazil
130 F8 Boi, Pta. do C Brazil
129 J7 Bois R Brazil
94 C1 Bois Blanc I Michigan U.S.A.
123 M7 Boisdale C Breton I, Nova Scotia
40 D4 Bois d' Amont France
20 G8 Bois-de-Cené France
18 H5 Bois du Roi mt France
100 J6 Boise Idaho U.S.A.
106 H5 Boise City Oklahoma U.S.A.
20 F5 Boisgervilly France
21 N3 Bois Guillaume France
114 G4 Bois, Lac Des L Northwest Territories Canada
Bois-le-Duc see 's-Hertogenbosch
21 K8 Boismé France
18 H7 Bois Noirs hills France
22 H1 Boisschot Belgium
119 R9 Boissevain Manitoba Canada
21 M4 Boissy-les-Perche France
21 M5 Boissy-Maugis France
38 F9 Boite R Italy
130 F8 Boituva Brazil
33 T6 Boitzenburg Germany
33 N6 Boize R Germany
33 N6 Boizenburg Germany
46 C3 Bojana R Albania
28 E6 Bøjden Denmark
71 E1 Bojeador,C Luzon Philippines
77 E1 Bojnūrd Iran
69 D13 Bojo isld Indonesia
70 K9 Bojong Java
48 F5 Boka Serbia Yugoslavia
42 J6 Boka Kotorska B Montenegro Yugoslavia
85 F7 Bokani Nigeria
70 G4 Bokat Sulawesi
85 B6 Boké Guinea
113 E11 Bokeelia Florida U.S.A.
32 J6 Bokel Germany
32 K8 Bokeloh Germany
56 F4 Bokhan Russian Federation
68 H6 Bo Kheo Cambodia
89 A8 Bokkeveld Berg mt S Africa
27 A12 Boknfjorden inlet Norway
56 B6 Boko Kazakhstan
57 H4 Bokonbayevskoye Kyrgyzstan
86 C3 Bokoro Chad
107 Q6 Bokoshe Oklahoma U.S.A.
86 D6 Bokote Zaire
59 H2 Bo-ko-tu China
68 D7 Bokpyin Burma
86 D6 Bokungu Zaire
68 C5 Bok Ye-gan isld Burma
70 G5 Bolaäng Sulawesi Indonesia
86 D6 Bolaiti Zaire
85 A6 Bolama Guinea-Bissau
124 H7 Bolaños Mexico
67 C5 Bolao China
21 L2 Bolbec France
55 E2 Bolchary Russian Federation
99 M9 Bolckow Missouri U.S.A.
48 E4 Bölcske Hungary
33 T5 Boldekow Germany
28 C6 Bolderslev Denmark
48 K5 Boldeşti-Scăeni Romania
66 C3 Bole China
85 D7 Bole Ghana
101 N2 Bole Montana U.S.A.
48 H1 Bolekhov Ukraine
86 D6 Boleko Zaire
100 J4 Boles Idaho U.S.A.
31 J4 Bolesławiec Poland
107 O6 Boley Oklahoma U.S.A.
85 D6 Bolgatanga Ghana
121 O4 Bolger Quebec Canada
48 M5 Bolgrad Ukraine
59 K2 Boli China
86 C6 Bolia Zaire
26 L7 Boliden Sweden
111 H9 Boligee Alabama U.S.A.
71 D2 Bolinao,C Luzon Philippines
48 K6 Bolintin Vale Romania
71 H4 Boliohutu,Gunung mt Sulawesi Indonesia
131 E6 Bolívár Argentina
128 D2 Bolívar div Colombia
128 C3 Bolivar Colombia
128 C4 Bolivar prov Ecuador
110 C4 Bolivar Missouri U.S.A.
94 J4 Bolivar New York U.S.A.
110 H6 Bolivar Tennessee U.S.A.
128 E2 Bolivar state Venezuela
128 F2 Bolivar,Cerro mt Venezuela
109 N6 Bolivar Pen Texas U.S.A.
127 J10 Bolivar, Pico mt Venezuela
128 E7 Bolivia rep S America
112 J3 Bolivia North Carolina U.S.A.
46 E1 Boljevac Serbia Yugoslavia
78 E3 Bolkar Dağları mts Turkey
27 D12 Bolkesjö Norway
120 G4 Bolkow Ontario Canada
31 J5 Bolków Poland
36 H6 Boll Germany
41 H2 Boll Germany
27 F14 Bollebygd Sweden
45 K4 Bolle,Le Italy
36 B4 Bollendorf Germany
19 N16 Bollène France
40 G4 Bolligen Switzerland
28 B5 Bølling Denmark
8 D1 Bollington England
27 H10 Bollnäs Sweden
141 H8 Bollon Queensland Australia
27 G15 Bolmen L Sweden
9 F6 Bolney England
71 F5 Bolo Panay Philippines
86 C6 Bolobo Zaire
71 E7 Bolod Islands Philippines
42 D4 Bologna Italy
19 J4 Bologne France
52 D6 Bologovo Russian Federation
54 J2 Bolokhovo Russian Federation
86 C5 Bolomba Zaire
86 D6 Bolombo Zaire
59 L2 Bolon' Russian Federation
125 P7 Bolonchén de Rejón Mexico
71 F7 Bolong Mindanao Philippines
59 L2 Bolon,Oz L Russian Federation
71 F1 Bolos Pt Luzon Philippines
43 B8 Bolotana Sardinia
56 B3 Bolotnoye Russian Federation
68 H5 Bolovens, Plateau des Laos
131 C2 Bolsa,Cerro pk Argentina
42 D6 Bolsena,L.di Italy
31 N1 Bol'shakovo Russian Federation
54 F9 Bolshaya Belozerka Ukraine
55 F3 Bol'shaya Tava R Russian Federation
52 F3 Bol'shaya Tavra Russian Federation
56 G1 Bol'shaya Yerema R Russian Federation
55 F3 Bol'sherech'ye Russian Federation
51 P3 Bol'sheretsk Russian Federation
55 C3 Bolshe-ustikinskoye Russian Federation
54 B4 Bol'shevik Belorussia
51 K1 Bol'shevik, Ostrov isld Russian Federation
55 F3 Bolshiye Uki Russian Federation
56 B1 Bolshoi Megtyg'yegan R Russian Federation
48 J1 Bol'shovtsy Ukraine
55 E1 Bol'shoy Atlym Russian Federation
55 F1 Bol'shoy Balyk R Russian Federation
147 P10 Bol'shoy Begichev,Os isld Russian Federation
56 H2 Bol'shoy Chuya R Russian Federation
55 E3 Bol'shoye Sorokino Russian Federation
55 G4 Bol'shoye Topol'noye, Oz L Russian Federation
55 G4 Bol'shoye Yaravoye, Oz L Russian Federation
55 E1 Bol'shoy Kamen' Russian Federation
55 F2 Bol'shoy Kun'yak Russian Federation
55 D3 Bol'shoy Kuyash Russian Federation
51 O1 Bolshoy Lyakhovskiy,Ostrov isld Russian Federation
56 D2 Bol'shoy Pit R Russian Federation
55 F1 Bolshoy Salym R Russian Federation
59 L1 Bol'shoy Shantar,Oz isld Russian Federation
55 E1 Bol'shoy Tap R Russian Federation
52 C5 Bol'shoy Tyuters, Os. isld Estonia
55 F3 Bol'shoy Uvat, Oz L Russian Federation
56 D5 Bolshoy Yenisey R Russian Federation
55 F2 Bol'shoy Yugan R Russian Federation
124 G4 Bolsón de Mapimí desert Mexico
25 E2 Bolsward Netherlands
17 H2 Boltaña Spain
8 C7 Bolt Head England
121 L9 Bolton Ontario Canada
13 F6 Bolton England
112 J3 Bolton North Carolina U.S.A.
13 G6 Bolton Br England
119 W4 Bolton L Manitoba Canada
13 F5 Bolton le-Sands England
78 C1 Bolu Turkey
66 E4 Boluntay China
14 A5 Bolus Hd Ireland
54 F3 Bolva R Russian Federation
47 L6 Bolvadin Turkey
78 C2 Bolvadin Turkey
8 B6 Bolventor England
48 E5 Bóly Hungary
47 H2 Bolyarovo Bulgaria
42 D2 Bolzano Italy
86 B7 Boma Zaire
22 K3 Bomal Luxembourg/Belgium
86 B5 Bomandjokou Congo
109 H2 Bomarton Texas U.S.A.
86 C5 Bomassa Congo
74 E9 Bombay India
145 E2 Bombay New Zealand
87 H11 Bombetoka,B.de Madagascar
86 F5 Bombo Uganda
86 C5 Bomboma Zaire
130 H10 Bom Conselho Brazil
129 J7 Bom Despacho Brazil
66 E6 Bomi China
85 B7 Bomi Hills Liberia
130 J9 Bom Jardim Brazil
130 D5 Bom Jardim de Goiás Brazil
128 E5 Bom Jardin Brazil
129 K5 Bom Jesus Brazil
129 K5 Bom Jesus da Gurgueia, Serra mts Brazil
129 K6 Bom Jesus da Lapa Brazil
130 H7 Bom Jesus do Itabapoana Brazil
130 H7 Bom Jesus do Norte Brazil
27 A12 Bömlafjorden inlet Norway
27 A12 Bömlo Norway
86 E5 Bomokandi R Zaire
86 C5 Bomongo Zaire
143 B7 Bompas Hill W Australia Australia
130 E10 Bom Retiro Brazil
130 G7 Bom Sucesso Brazil
118 D5 Bon Accord Alberta Canada
94 K9 Bon Air Virginia U.S.A.
127 K8 Bonaire isld Lesser Antilles
127 K9 Bonaire Trench Caribbean
116 R6 Bona,Mt Alaska U.S.A.
69 D12 Bonandolok Sumatra
139 J6 Bonang Victoria Australia
125 M3 Bonanza Nicaragua
106 D3 Bonanza Colorado U.S.A.
100 D7 Bonanza Oregon U.S.A.
106 A1 Bonanza Utah U.S.A.
127 J5 Bonao Dominican Rep
99 P9 Bonaparte Iowa U.S.A.
142 E2 Bonaparte Arch W Australia Australia
100 F1 Bonaparte,Mt Washington U.S.A.
15 D3 Bonar Bridge Scotland
121 N8 Bonarlaw Ontario Canada
116 G5 Bonasila Dome mt Alaska U.S.A.
127 N3 Bonasse Trinidad
44 G3 Bonassola Italy
122 G5 Bonaventure Quebec Canada
122 H5 Bonaventure I Quebec Canada
123 T5 Bonavista Newfoundland Canada
40 C3 Bonboillon France
138 D4 Bon Bon South Australia Australia
85 G1 Bon,C Tunisia
106 F4 Boncarbo Colorado U.S.A.
21 O5 Bonce France
13 F3 Bonchester Br Scotland
9 E6 Bonchurch England
101 T10 Bond Colorado U.S.A.
86 B6 Bonda Gabon
28 C7 Bonden Au R Germany
45 K2 Bondeno Italy
86 D5 Bondo Zaire
71 F4 Bondoc Penin Luzon Philippines
71 F4 Bondoc Pt Luzon Philippines
71 H9 Bondokodi Sumbawa Indonesia
36 F6 Bondorf Germany
85 D7 Bondoukou Ivory Coast
70 O9 Bondowoso Java
126 F2 Bonds Cay isld Bahamas
144 C5 Bonds Peak mt New Zealand
99 S5 Bonduel Wisconsin U.S.A.
101 P6 Bondurant Wyoming U.S.A.
101 O6 Bone Idaho U.S.A.
70 G6 Bonebone Sulawesi
113 L9 Bonefish Pond New Providence I Bahamas
71 H7 Bonelipu Indonesia
70 G7 Bonelowe Indonesia
68 G4 Boneng Laos
71 K8 Boneogeh Indonesia
71 K8 Bonerate isld Indonesia
71 K8 Bonerate Indonesia
26 K3 Bones Norway
15 E5 Boness Scotland
98 H6 Bonesteel South Dakota U.S.A.
131 C2 Bonete,Cerro pk Argentina
70 G7 Bone, Teluk B Sulawesi Indonesia
98 C1 Bonetraill North Dakota U.S.A.
121 L6 Bonfield Ontario Canada
71 E4 Bongabong Philippines
86 D5 Bongandanga Zaire
70 F2 Bongao Philippines
70 M9 Bongkok mt Java
71 G7 Bongo isld Mindanao Philippines
86 C3 Bongor Chad
68 J5 Bong Son Vietnam
109 L2 Bonham Texas U.S.A.
118 L1 Bonheur Ontario Canada
12 D2 Bonhill Scotland
36 C7 Bonhomme, Col du pass France
43 B7 Bonifacio,Str.of Corsica/Sardinia
111 L11 Bonifay Florida U.S.A.
Bonin Is see Ogasawara-shoto
103 P9 Bonita Arizona U.S.A.
111 E9 Bonita Louisiana U.S.A.
113 F11 Bonita Springs Florida U.S.A.
130 C7 Bonito Brazil
69 E13 Bonjol Sumatra
36 C2 Bonn Germany
18 G6 Bonnat France
19 Q12 Bonne France
19 P15 Bonne R France
123 P4 Bonne Bay Newfoundland Canada
21 L3 Bonnebosq France
22 G3 Bonne Esperance Belgium
123 P2 Bonne Espérance Quebec Canada
21 P4 Bonnelles France
20 G5 Bonnemain France
101 M3 Bonner Montana U.S.A.
140 D1 Bonner Mt N Terr Australia
100 J1 Bonners Ferry Idaho U.S.A.
110 B2 Bonner Springs Kansas U.S.A.
28 A3 Bonnet Denmark
21 L5 Bonnétable France
110 F4 Bonne Terre Missouri U.S.A.
21 P2 Bonneuil-les-Eaux France
21 M8 Bonneuil-Matours France
21 N5 Bonneval Eure-et-Loir France
40 F7 Bonneval-sur-Arc France
40 D4 Bonnevaux France
19 Q12 Bonneville France
100 D4 Bonneville Oregon U.S.A.
101 R6 Bonneville Wyoming U.S.A.
21 N3 Bonneville,la France
101 N7 Bonneville Pk Idaho U.S.A.
101 L9 Bonneville Salt Flats Utah/Nev U.S.A.
138 F6 Bonney,L South Australia Australia
140 C5 Bonney Well N Terr Australia
21 P1 Bonnières Pas-de-Calais France
21 O3 Bonnières Seine-et-Oise France
143 C9 Bonnie Rock W Australia Australia
19 O17 Bonnieux France
36 G5 Bönnigheim Germany
36 H3 Bonnland Germany
18 G5 Bonny France
85 F8 Bonny Nigeria
Bonny, Bight Of see Biafra, Bight Of
106 H2 Bonny Res Colorado U.S.A.
122 F8 Bonny River New Brunswick Canada
118 G4 Bonnyville Alberta Canada
20 E6 Bono France
43 C8 Bono Sardinia
110 F6 Bono Arkansas U.S.A.
71 C6 Bonobond Palawan Philippines
60 D14 Bōno-misaki C Japan
68 H7 Bonom Mhai mt Vietnam
43 B8 Bonorva Sardinia
21 M8 Bonres France
111 J11 Bon Secour Alabama U.S.A.
70 E4 Bontang Kalimantan
89 A9 Bonteberg mts S Africa
85 B7 Bonthe Sierra Leone
71 E2 Bontoc Luzon Philippines
71 K8 Bontomatane Indonesia
70 G7 Bontosunggu Sulawesi
109 O5 Bon Wier Texas U.S.A.
48 E4 Bonyhád Hungary
143 G6 Bonython Ra N Terr/W Aust Australia
141 F1 Booby I Queensland Australia
113 K12 Booby I Bahamas
127 M3 Booby South Pt Jamaica
36 D7 Boofzheim France
138 C4 Bookabie South Australia Australia
143 A8 Bookara W Australia Australia
103 P2 Book Cliffs Utah U.S.A.
108 D7 Booker Texas U.S.A.
94 H9 Booker T. Washington Nat Mon Virginia U.S.A.
85 C7 Boola Guinea
142 B6 Boolaloo W Australia Australia
143 A6 Boolathanna W Australia Australia
138 E5 Booleroo Centre South Australia Australia
143 A6 Boologooro W Australia Australia
22 G1 Boom Belgium
94 B2 Boon Michigan U.S.A.
141 L8 Boonah Queensland Australia
106 F3 Boone Colorado U.S.A.
99 N7 Boone Iowa U.S.A.
112 F1 Boone North Carolina U.S.A.
94 H9 Boones Mill Virginia U.S.A.
110 C6 Booneville Arkansas U.S.A.
110 N4 Booneville Kentucky U.S.A.
110 H7 Booneville Mississippi U.S.A.
94 D9 Booneville Res Kentucky U.S.A.
141 H6 Boongoondoo Queensland Australia
127 P4 Boon Pt Antigua W Indies
94 K7 Boonsboro Maryland U.S.A.
58 C2 Bööntsagaan Nuur L Mongolia
102 A2 Boonville California U.S.A.
110 J3 Boonville Indiana U.S.A.
110 D3 Boonville Missouri U.S.A.
95 M3 Boonville New York U.S.A.
71 B3 Boo,Pulau Pulau islds W Irian
143 D9 Boorabbin W Australia Australia
86 H4 Boorama Somalia
21 N3 Boos France
Boosaaso see Bender Qaasim
13 E5 Boot England
147 E3 Boothia, Gulf of Northwest Territories Canada
115 K3 Boothia Pen Northwest Territories Canada
111 J8 Boothton Alabama U.S.A.
13 E5 Bootle England
13 F6 Bootle England
37 J6 Bopfingen Germany
89 C6 Bophuthatswana homeland S Africa
65 C6 Boping China
36 D3 Boppard Germany
20 E5 Boqueho France
129 K6 Boqueirão, Serra do mts Brazil
128 F8 Boquerón dept Paraguay
108 E6 Boquillas Texas U.S.A.
108 E6 Boquillas del Carmen Mexico
37 O4 Bor Czechoslovakia
86 E4 Bo R Sudan
27 G14 Bor Sweden
78 E3 Bor Turkey
48 G6 Bor Serbia Yugoslavia
135 M10 Bora-Bora isld Society Is Pacific Oc
101 M5 Borah Pk Idaho U.S.A.
27 F14 Borås Sweden
77 B5 Borāzjān Iran
128 G4 Borba Brazil
28 B4 Borbjerg Denmark
71 G5 Borbon Cebu Philippines
130 H9 Borborema, Planalto da plateau Brazil
48 K3 Borca Romania
48 L6 Borcea R Romania
146 C12 Borchgrevink Coast coast Antarctica
78 H1 Borçka Turkey
138 D6 Borda,C South Australia Australia
47 K7 Bor Dağı mt Turkey
18 E8 Bordeaux France
98 B8 Bordeaux Wyoming U.S.A.
57 G5 Bordëbë Kyrgyzstan
143 C10 Borden W Australia Australia
122 J7 Borden Prince Edward I Canada
118 K6 Borden Saskatchewan Canada
114 H2 Borden I Northwest Territories Canada
115 L3 Borden Pen Northwest Territories Canada
95 N6 Bordentown New Jersey U.S.A.
15 F5 Borders reg Scotland
138 F6 Bordertown South Australia Australia
32 M4 Bordesholm Germany
28 S9 Bordheyri Iceland
44 C4 Bordighera Italy
85 D3 Bordj Flye Ste Marie Algeria
85 F2 Bordj Messaouda Algeria
85 E4 Bordj Mokhtar Algeria
85 F3 Bordj Omar Driss Algeria
6 F1 Borðoy isld Faeroes
57 H4 Bordunskiy Kyrgyzstan
85 D5 Boré Mali
143 D8 Boreas,Mt W Australia Australia
31 K4 Borek Poland
Borgå see Porvoo
28 S9 Borgarnes Iceland
44 C1 Bórgaro Torinese Italy
26 G3 Borge Norway
26 G6 Börgefjell mt Norway
32 K9 Borgentreich Germany
32 G7 Börger Germany
25 G3 Borger Netherlands
108 C8 Borger Texas U.S.A.
32 K9 Borgholz Germany
32 H8 Borgholzhausen Germany
32 F8 Borghorst Germany
43 H10 Borgia Italy
22 J2 Borgloon Belgium
28 D2 Børglum Denmark
40 G5 Borgne R Switzerland
41 O5 Borgo Italy
45 J4 Borgo a Mozzano Italy
45 J1 Borgoforte Italy
44 E1 Borgolavezzaro Italy
45 N6 Borgo Montello Italy
44 F1 Borgonovo Val Tidone Italy
45 M4 Borgo Pace Italy
45 K2 Borgo Panigale Italy
45 O5 Borgorose Italy
42 D5 Borgo S. Lorenzo Italy
41 J6 Borgoticino Italy
44 G3 Borgo Val di Taro Italy
42 D2 Borgo Valsugana Italy
41 H7 Borgo Vercelli Italy
26 H9 Borgsjö Sweden
27 F14 Borgstena Sweden
12 D4 Borgue Scotland
26 B9 Borgund Norway
27 C10 Borgund Norway
26 H8 Borgvattnet Sweden
98 B8 Borie Wyoming U.S.A.
68 F3 Borikhane Laos
31 O6 Borinya Ukraine
26 S2 Boris Gleb Russian Federation
31 O6 Borislav Ukraine
57 E3 Borisovka Kazakhstan
55 F4 Borisovskoye Russian Federation
54 B6 Borispol Ukraine
87 H11 Boriziny Madagascar
130 C9 Borja Paraguay
17 F3 Borja Spain
42 H4 Borja Planina Bosnia-Herzegovina
17 H3 Borjas Blancas Spain
26 M6 Börjelslandet Sweden
32 F9 Bork Germany
32 E9 Borken Germany
36 G1 Borken Germany
54 H7 Borki Ukraine
28 D5 Børkop Denmark
86 C2 Borkou dist Chad
52 C6 Borkovichi Belorussia
25 G4 Borkulo Netherlands
32 E5 Borkum Germany
27 H11 Borlänge Sweden
47 J6 Borlu Turkey
44 D3 Bormida di Millésimo R Italy
44 D3 Bormida di Spigno R Italy
42 C2 Bormio Italy
37 O1 Borna Germany
25 E2 Borndiep Netherlands
25 G4 Borne Netherlands
70 B4 Borneo isld E Indies
16 C3 Bornes mt Portugal
36 B2 Bornheim Germany
27 H16 Bornholm isld Denmark
27 G16 Bornholmsgattet str Sweden/Denmark
32 M4 Bornhöved Germany
33 R7 Börnicke Germany
33 R8 Bornim Germany
86 B3 Borno prov Nigeria
16 D8 Bornos, Embalse de res Spain
86 E4 Boro R Sudan
48 K3 Boroaia Romania
70 M9 Borobudur ruins Java
71 E5 Borocay isld Panay Philippines
51 N2 Borogontsy Russian Federation
57 L3 Borohoro Shan mt ra China
71 H4 Boroko Sulawesi Indonesia
85 D6 Boromo Burkina
102 G6 Boron California U.S.A.
141 K6 Bororen Queensland Australia
13 G5 Boroughbridge England
56 B5 Borovlyanka Russian Federation
55 F4 Borovoye Kazakhstan
54 H1 Borovsk Russian Federation
55 E3 Borovskiy Russian Federation
55 D4 Borovskoy Kazakhstan
27 G16 Borrby Sweden
29 K6 Borre Denmark
33 R5 Borrenthin Germany
138 E5 Borrika South Australia Australia
28 B5 Borris Denmark
14 E4 Borris Ireland
14 D4 Borrisoleigh Ireland
140 D3 Borroloola N Terr Australia
27 J13 Börrum Sweden
48 J3 Borşa Romania
58 G1 Borsch Chovochnyy Khrebet mt Russian Federation
33 R10 Borsdorf Germany
48 K4 Borsec Romania
26 P1 Börselv Norway
48 H2 Borshava R Ukraine
48 K2 Borshchev Ukraine
48 F2 Borsod-Abaúj Zemplén Hungary
25 A6 Borssele Netherlands
33 N8 Börssum Germany
29 K5 Borstahusen Sweden
32 J7 Borstel Germany
57 K3 Bortala He R China
8 B3 Borth Wales
18 G7 Bort-les-Orgues France
26 G9 Börtnan Sweden
58 F1 Borto Russian Federation
77 B4 Borūjen Iran
77 A3 Borūjerd Iran
28 E4 Borum Denmark
28 H5 Borup Denmark
98 K2 Borup Minnesota U.S.A.
56 D4 Borus,Khrebet mts Russian Federation
31 K2 Bory Tucholskie forest Poland
31 M5 Borzęcin Poland
78 J1 Borzhomi Georgia
54 D5 Borzna Ukraine
58 G1 Borzya R Russian Federation
58 G1 Borzya Russian Federation
57 G1 Bosaginskiy Kazakhstan
48 E5 Bosanski Brod Croatia
42 G4 Bosanski Petrovac Bosnia-Herzegovina
33 M4 Bosau Germany
8 B6 Boscastle England
95 Q3 Boscawen New Hampshire U.S.A.
45 K1 Boschi Santa Anna Italy
21 N2 Bosc-le-Hard France
99 Q6 Boscobel Wisconsin U.S.A.
9 E6 Boscombe England
45 Q8 Boscotrecase Italy
67 B5 Bose China
38 K7 Bosenstein,Gross mt Austria
65 D6 Boshan China
89 D7 Boshof S Africa
77 E3 Boshruyeh Iran
46 E2 Bosilegrad Serbia Yugoslavia
27 G12 Bosjön Sweden
25 C4 Boskoop Netherlands
98 A8 Bosler Wyoming U.S.A.
8 D1 Bosley England
42 H4 Bosna R Bosnia-Herzegovina
Bosna i Hercegovina see Bosnia-Herzegovina
42 H4 Bosnia-Herzegovina rep S Europe
86 C5 Bosobolo Zaire
61 O10 Bōsō-hantō pen Japan
32 G10 Bösperde Germany
Bosporus str see Karadeniz Boğazı str
106 D7 Bosque New Mexico U.S.A.
124 G2 Bosque Bonito Mexico
86 C4 Bossambélé Cent Afr Republic
86 C4 Bossangoa Cent Afr Republic
86 C4 Bossemtele Cent Afr Republic
111 C9 Bossier City Louisiana U.S.A.
87 C9 Bossiesvlei Namibia
86 B3 Bosso Niger
66 D3 Bosten Hu L China
9 F2 Boston England
113 D7 Boston Georgia U.S.A.
95 Q4 Boston Massachusetts U.S.A.
97 Boston conurbation Massachusetts U.S.A.
117 N11 Boston Bar British Columbia Canada
127 M2 Boston Bay Jamaica
138 D5 Boston I South Australia Australia
110 C6 Boston Mts Arkansas U.S.A.
13 G6 Boston Spa England
28 F6 Bøstrup Fyn Denmark
28 D4 Bøstrup Viborg Denmark
48 E5 Bosut R Croatia
123 O5 Boswarlos Newfoundland Canada
117 P11 Boswell British Columbia Canada
99 T9 Boswell Indiana U.S.A.
107 P7 Boswell Oklahoma U.S.A.
94 H6 Boswell Pennsylvania U.S.A.
110 C2 Bosworth Missouri U.S.A.
74 D7 Botad India
139 K5 Botany B New South Wales Australia
26 J8 Boteå Sweden
46 G2 Botev mt Bulgaria
46 F2 Botevgrad Bulgaria
118 E6 Botha Alberta Canada
9 F1 Bothamsall England
87 E11 Bothaville S Africa
13 E4 Bothel England
117 M12 Bothell Washington U.S.A.
26 L8 Bothnia,Gulf of Sweden/Finland
139 H8 Bothwell Tasmania Australia
120 J10 Bothwell Ontario Canada
12 D2 Bothwell Scotland
16 B3 Boticas Portugal
87 D10 Botletle R Botswana
9 E6 Botley England
48 M4 Botna R Moldavia
28 H7 Bøtø Denmark
71 D3 Botolan Pt Luzon Philippines
48 K3 Botoşani Romania
65 C5 Botou China
68 H4 Bo Trach Vietnam
22 L3 Botrange mt Belgium
26 L7 Botsmark Sweden
89 C4 Botswana rep Africa
43 G9 Botte Donato mt Italy
89 A8 Botter Kloof Pass S Africa
89 B8 Bottersleegte S Africa
9 F2 Bottesford England
98 F1 Bottineau North Dakota U.S.A.
9 G3 Bottisham England
127 N6 Bottom Saba W Indies
9 E1 Bottom House England
45 M1 Bottrighe Italy
32 E9 Bottrop Germany
46 F1 Botunya R Bulgaria
123 R4 Botwood Newfoundland Canada
85 C7 Bouaflé Ivory Coast
21 N3 Bouafles France
16 D9 Bou Ahmed Morocco
85 D7 Bouaké Ivory Coast
86 C4 Bouala Cent Afr Republic
86 C4 Bouar Cent Afr Republic
85 D2 Bouârfa Morocco
43 A12 Bouati Mahmoud Algeria
20 G7 Bouaye France
30 H6 Boubín mt Czechoslovakia
86 C4 Bouca Cent Afr Republic
18 D9 Boucau France
140 C1 Boucaut B N Terr Australia
21 K4 Boucé Orne France
22 E3 Bouchain France
21 L7 Bouchard, l'Île France
22 D4 Bouchavesnes France
43 B12 Bouchegouf Algeria
123 N2 Boucher,L Quebec Canada
19 N17 Bouches-du-Rhône dept France
121 P6 Bouchette Quebec Canada
22 D4 Bouchoir France
85 D2 Boudenib Morocco
16 E9 Boudinar Morocco
85 D5 Bou Djébéha Mali
40 A2 Boudreville France
40 E4 Boudry Switzerland
20 G7 Bouée France
21 O8 Bouesse France
20 H5 Bouexière, la France
122 E3 Bouffard,L Quebec Canada
83 K14 Bœuf, Nez de pk Réunion
137 M3 Bougainville isld Papua New Guinea
142 F2 Bougainville, C W Australia Australia
141 H3 Bougainville Reef Gt Barrier Reef Aust
71 C2 Bougainville,Selat W Irian
85 F1 Bougaroun,C Algeria
21 O7 Bouges le-Château France
Bougie see Bejaïa
85 C6 Bougouni Mali
43 C11 Bouhairet Benzart G Tunisia
17 G9 Bou Hanifa Algeria
17 G9 Bou Hanifa, Barrage de Algeria
127 M4 Bouillante Guadeloupe W Indies
21 M3 Bouille,la France
21 K7 Bouillé Loretz France
21 J6 Bouillé-Ménard France
22 J4 Bouillon Belgium
20 G8 Bouin France
85 C3 Bou Izakam Morocco
85 B3 Boujdour Western Sahara
85 B3 Boukra Western Sahara
123 L3 Boulain,L Quebec Canada
19 K3 Boulay France
143 D9 Boulder W Australia Australia
98 A9 Boulder Colorado U.S.A.
101 N3 Boulder Montana U.S.A.
103 N4 Boulder Utah U.S.A.
101 Q7 Boulder Wyoming U.S.A.
103 K5 Boulder Can Nevada U.S.A.
103 K6 Boulder City Nevada U.S.A.
102 B4 Boulder Cr California U.S.A.
100 J7 Boulder Cr Idaho U.S.A.
121 N5 Bouleau, L. au Quebec Canada
102 H9 Boulevard California U.S.A.
140 E6 Boulia Queensland Australia
20 H8 Boulogne R France
22 B2 Boulogne France
21 P4 Boulogne-Billancourt France
21 M6 Bouloire France
85 C5 Boulouli Mali
85 D6 Boulsa Burkina
22 H5 Boult-aux-Bois France
85 G6 Boultoum Niger
22 H4 Boulzicourt France
86 C5 Boumba R Cameroon
85 D7 Bouna Ivory Coast
117 C3 Boundary Alaska U.S.A.
102 F4 Boundary Pk Nevada U.S.A.
118 J9 Boundary Plateau Mont/Sask U.S.A./Canada
85 C7 Boundiali Ivory Coast
68 H6 Boung Long Cambodia
68 E2 Boun Neua Laos
106 E4 Bountiful Colorado U.S.A.
140 E3 Bountiful Is Queensland Australia
118 K7 Bounty Saskatchewan Canada
21 J8 Boupère, le France
21 P1 Bouquemaison France
110 E3 Bourbeuse R Missouri U.S.A.
94 A5 Bourbon Indiana U.S.A.
110 E3 Bourbon Missouri U.S.A.
83 L14 Bourbon,C Kerguelen Indian Oc
18 H6 Bourbon-Lancy France
18 H6 Bourbon l'Archambault France
18 H6 Bourbonnais prov France
40 C2 Bourbonne les Bains France
18 G7 Bourboule,la France
19 J5 Bourboune les Bassigny France
22 C2 Bourbourg France
19 O13 Bourbre R France
20 D5 Bourbriac France
19 O15 Bourdeaux France
36 B6 Bourdonnay France
16 E10 Boured Morocco
85 D5 Bourem Mali
18 E7 Bourg Gironde France
18 G7 Bourganeuf France
21 M3 Bourg-Archard France
18 H7 Bourg Argental France
19 Q15 Bourg d'Arud France
19 O14 Bourg-de-Péage France
20 G6 Bourg-des-Comptes France
21 M2 Bourg Dun France
19 O12 Bourg-en-Bresse France
21 P7 Bourges France
22 F5 Bourg et Comin France
40 C6 Bourget,L.du France
21 P4 Bourget,le Paris France
18 G10 Bourg-Madame France
21 K6 Bourg-Neuf France
20 F7 Bourgneuf,B.de France
21 J7 Bourgneuf-en-Mauges France
20 G7 Bourgneuf-en-Retz France
21 J5 Bourgneuf,le France
22 G5 Bourgogne France
19 O13 Bourgoin France
40 E6 Bourg-St-Maurice France
21 M3 Bourgtheroulde-Infreville France
21 K3 Bourguébus France
21 L7 Bourgueil France
120 K4 Bourkes Ontario Canada
121 N4 Bourlamaque Quebec Canada
22 E3 Bourlon France
121 P4 Bourmont Quebec Canada
40 C1 Bourmont France
21 M7 Bournan France
21 L7 Bournand France
9 F2 Bourne England
115 K1 Bourne,C Northwest Territories Canada
9 F4 Bourne End England
9 E6 Bournemouth England
21 M3 Bourneville France
21 H8 Bournezeau France
18 E8 Bourriot Bergonce France
32 F7 Bourtanger Moor Germany
21 M4 Bourth France
22 B2 Bourthes France
86 D3 Bourtoutou Chad
22 L4 Bous Luxembourg
85 E1 Bou Saâda Algeria
43 B12 Bou Salem Tunisia
103 K8 Bouse Arizona U.S.A.
103 K8 Bouse Wash R Arizona U.S.A.
36 B5 Bous/Saar Germany
18 G6 Boussac France
20 G4 Boussac,la France
21 H7 Boussay France
22 L5 Bousse France
86 C3 Bousso Chad
43 B12 Bouteldja Algeria
21 P5 Boutigny France
85 B5 Boutilimit Mauritania
18 E6 Boutonne R France
143 B10 Bouvard,C W Australia Australia
19 O13 Bouvesse France
90 J14 Bouvet I S Atlantic Oc
81 A12 Bouvetøy isld S Atlantic Oc
20 G7 Bouvron France
36 C6 Bouxwiller France
85 F6 Bouza Niger
21 O8 Bouzanne R France
36 B5 Bouzonville France
28 C7 Bov Denmark
43 G11 Bova Italy
32 L9 Bovenden Germany
70 C4 Boven Kapuas mts Sarawak
28 F6 Bovense Denmark
26 C10 Böverdal Norway
21 P2 Boves France
44 C3 Boves Italy
8 C6 Bovey Tracey England
22 K3 Bovigny Belgium
100 J3 Bovill Idaho U.S.A.
43 G7 Bovino Italy
28 A4 Bøvlingbjerg Denmark
45 L1 Bovolenta Italy
45 K1 Bovolone Italy
8 C6 Bow England
98 D1 Bowbells North Dakota U.S.A.
127 M3 Bowden Jamaica
113 F7 Bowden Florida U.S.A.
98 G4 Bowdle South Dakota U.S.A.
101 S1 Bowdoin,L Montana U.S.A.
112 B4 Bowdon Georgia U.S.A.
98 G2 Bowdon North Dakota U.S.A.
143 B10 Bowelling W Australia Australia
141 J5 Bowen R Queensland Australia
141 J5 Bowen Queensland Australia
110 E1 Bowen Illinois U.S.A.
141 H5 Bowen Downs Queensland Australia
117 M11 Bowen I British Columbia Canada
140 B1 Bowen Str N Terr Australia
95 M7 Bowers Delaware U.S.A.
94 D7 Bowersville Ohio U.S.A.
101 L5 Bowery Pk Idaho U.S.A.
13 F5 Bowes England
143 B8 Bowgada W Australia Australia
141 H5 Bowie Queensland Australia
103 P9 Bowie Arizona U.S.A.
106 C3 Bowie Colorado U.S.A.
109 K2 Bowie Texas U.S.A.
118 F9 Bow Island Alberta Canada
78 L3 Bowkan Iran
12 D2 Bowling Scotland
113 F10 Bowling Green Florida U.S.A.
110 J2 Bowling Green Indiana U.S.A.
110 K4 Bowling Green Kentucky U.S.A.
110 E2 Bowling Green Missouri U.S.A.
94 D5 Bowling Green Ohio U.S.A.
95 K8 Bowling Green Virginia U.S.A.
141 H4 Bowling Green,C Queensland Australia
112 D3 Bowman Georgia U.S.A.
98 C3 Bowman North Dakota U.S.A.
146 H14 Bowman I Antarctica
146 D6 Bowman Peninsula pen Antarctica
121 M9 Bowmanville Ontario Canada
15 B5 Bowmore Scotland
118 C7 Bowness Alberta Canada
13 F5 Bowness England
118 C7 Bow R Alberta Canada
142 G3 Bow River W Australia Australia
117 N9 Bowron Lake Prov. Park British Columbia Canada
117 J7 Bowser L British Columbia Canada
119 Q6 Bowsman Manitoba Canada
118 B7 Bow Valley Prov. Park Alberta Canada
36 H5 Boxberg Germany
98 C7 Box Butte Res Nebraska U.S.A.
98 A6 Box Cr Wyoming U.S.A.
101 P1 Box Elder Montana U.S.A.
98 C5 Box Elder South Dakota U.S.A.
106 F2 Box Elder Cr Colorado U.S.A.
98 B4 Boxelder Cr Montana U.S.A.
101 R2 Boxelder Cr Montana U.S.A.
9 F5 Box Hill England
27 H13 Boxholm Sweden
58 G5 Bo Xian China
65 D6 Boxing China
25 E5 Boxmeer Netherlands
25 D5 Boxtel Netherlands
78 E1 Boyabat Turkey
128 D2 Boyacá div Colombia
47 K3 Boyalık Turkey
58 G6 Boyang China
143 B10 Boyanup W Australia Australia
111 D10 Boyce Louisiana U.S.A.
94 J7 Boyce Virginia U.S.A.
143 D8 Boyce,Mt W Australia Australia
46 F1 Boychinovtsi Bulgaria
119 V3 Boyd Manitoba Canada
101 Q4 Boyd Montana U.S.A.
109 K2 Boyd Texas U.S.A.
123 S4 Boyd's Cove Newfoundland Canada
94 J10 Boydton Virginia U.S.A.
65 C5 Boye China
99 L7 Boyer R Iowa U.S.A.
99 L7 Boyer Iowa U.S.A.
77 B4 Boyer Ahmadī va Kohkīlūyeh prov Iran
106 G3 Boyero Colorado U.S.A.
95 M6 Boyertown Pennsylvania U.S.A.
98 A4 Boyes Montana U.S.A.
95 K10 Boykins Virginia U.S.A.
118 E4 Boyle Alberta Canada
14 C3 Boyle Ireland
111 F8 Boyle Mississippi U.S.A.
123 L8 Boylston Nova Scotia Canada
141 K6 Boyne R Queensland Australia
14 E3 Boyne R Ireland
94 C1 Boyne City Michigan U.S.A.
94 C1 Boyne Falls Michigan U.S.A.
21 P5 Boynes France
110 C1 Boynton Missouri U.S.A.
107 P6 Boynton Oklahoma U.S.A.
113 G11 Boynton Beach Florida U.S.A.
86 E5 Boyoma Falls Zaire
101 R6 Boysen Res Wyoming U.S.A.
143 B10 Boyup Brook W Australia Australia
47 J8 Bozburun Turkey
47 H5 Bozcaada isld Turkey
47 L5 Boz Dağ mt Turkey
79 G2 Bozdağ mt Turkey
47 J6 Boz Dağları mts Turkey
47 J7 Bozdoğan Turkey
101 P4 Bozeman Montana U.S.A.
Bozen see Bolzano
86 C5 Bozene Zaire
31 K1 Boże Pole Poland
65 C5 Bozhen China
37 O3 Boží Dar Czechoslovakia
78 D3 Bozkır Turkey
54 F1 Boznya Russian Federation
78 G3 Bozova Turkey
48 G6 Bozovici Romania
55 F5 Bozshakol' Kazakhstan
45 J1 Bozzolo Italy
138 A4 BP Travellers Village South Australia Australia
44 C2 Bra Italy
22 G2 Brabançonne prov Belgium
22 G2 Brabant prov Belgium
146 C4 Brabant I Antarctica
119 O2 Brabant L Saskatchewan Canada
28 E4 Brabrand Denmark
28 H6 Bråby Denmark
42 H5 Brač isld Croatia
15 B3 Bracadale Scotland
129 H6 Braça Menor R Brazil
44 M5 Bracciano Italy
42 E6 Bracciano,Lago di Italy
44 M5 Bracciano, Lago di Italy
121 L7 Bracebridge Ontario Canada
21 O6 Bracieux France
26 H9 Bräcke Sweden
118 J9 Bracken Saskatchewan Canada
109 J6 Bracken Texas U.S.A.
36 G5 Brackenheim Germany
13 G6 Brackenhill England
119 S5 Bracken L Manitoba Canada
108 G6 Brackettville Texas U.S.A.
9 E3 Brackley England
9 F5 Bracknell England
32 J9 Brackwede Germany

12 E1 Braco Scotland
43 G8 Bradano R Italy
98 F3 Braddock North Dakota U.S.A.
94 H6 Braddock Pennsylvania U.S.A.
99 L9 Braddyville Iowa U.S.A.
113 E10 Bradenton Florida U.S.A.
113 E10 Bradenton Beach Florida U.S.A.
28 B7 Braderup Germany
121 L8 Bradford Ontario Canada
8 D5 Bradford England
13 G6 Bradford England
110 E6 Bradford Arkansas U.S.A.
99 R8 Bradford Illinois U.S.A.
99 N7 Bradford Iowa U.S.A.
95 T1 Bradford Maine U.S.A.
95 P3 Bradford New Hampshire U.S.A.
94 C6 Bradford Ohio U.S.A.
94 J5 Bradford Pennsylvania U.S.A.
95 Q5 Bradford Rhode I U.S.A.
94 B9 Bradfordsville Kentucky U.S.A.
111 C8 Bradley Arkansas U.S.A.
102 D6 Bradley California U.S.A.
99 T8 Bradley Illinois U.S.A.
107 N7 Bradley Oklahoma U.S.A.
110 D5 Bradleyville Missouri U.S.A.
94 D5 Bradner Ohio U.S.A.
123 P2 Bradore Bay Quebec Canada
123 P2 Bradore Hills Quebec Canada
140 B3 Bradshaw N Terr Australia
98 J9 Bradshaw Nebraska U.S.A.
142 F3 Bradshaw,Mt W Australia Australia
119 R9 Bradwardine Manitoba Canada
118 L7 Bradwell Saskatchewan Canada
9 G4 Bradwell England
98 F8 Brady Nebraska U.S.A.
109 H4 Brady Texas U.S.A.
117 E6 Brady Glacier Alaska U.S.A.
138 C3 Brady,Mt South Australia Australia
28 D5 Brædstrup Denmark
138 E5 Braemar South Australia Australia
15 E3 Braemar Scotland
15 E3 Braeriach mt Scotland
16 B3 Braga Portugal
131 E5 Bragado Argentina
129 J4 Bragança Brazil
16 C3 Bragança Portugal
130 F8 Bragança Paulista Brazil
112 E6 Braganza Georgia U.S.A.
110 G5 Bragg City Missouri U.S.A.
118 C7 Bragg Creek Prov. Park Alberta Canada
54 B5 Bragin Belorussia
99 N4 Braham Minnesota U.S.A.
33 N6 Brahlstorf Mecklenburg-Vorpommern Germany
75 O7 Brahmanbaria Bangladesh
75 L9 Brahmapur India
75 P5 Brahmaputra R S Asia
32 L4 Brahmsee L Germany
77 K5 Brahui,Cen reg Pakistan
99 S8 Braidwood Illinois U.S.A.
48 L5 Brăila Romania
9 E2 Brailsford England
98 J8 Brainard Nebraska U.S.A.
22 F5 Braine France
22 G2 Braine L'Alleud Belgium
22 G2 Braine-le Château Belgium
22 G2 Braine-le Comte Belgium
99 M3 Brainerd Minnesota U.S.A.
21 L7 Brain-sur-Allonnes France
9 G4 Braintree England
13 E4 Braithwaite England
111 G12 Braithwaite Louisiana U.S.A.
140 C1 Braithwaite Pt N Terr Australia
22 J2 Braives Belgium
89 F4 Brak R S Africa
32 H6 Brake Germany
22 F2 Brakel Belgium
32 K9 Brakel Germany
85 B5 Brakna reg Mauritania
57 D1 Brali Kazakhstan
117 M10 Bralorne British Columbia Canada
107 N5 Braman Oklahoma U.S.A.
Brambach see Radiumbad-Brambach
38 F7 Bramberg Austria
13 G6 Bramham England
32 H6 Bramloge Germany
28 B6 Bramming Denmark
44 B3 Bram,Monte Italy
26 J9 Bramö isld Sweden
9 H3 Brampton England
98 J3 Brampton North Dakota U.S.A.
141 J5 Brampton I Queensland Australia
32 G8 Bramsche Germany
141 G1 Bramwell Queensland Australia
94 F9 Bramwell West Virginia U.S.A.
9 G2 Brancaster England
13 G4 Brancepeth England
123 T7 Branch Newfoundland Canada
99 U6 Branch Michigan U.S.A.
95 K4 Branchport New York U.S.A.
112 G4 Branchville South Carolina U.S.A.
130 B7 Branco R Mato Grosso Brazil
128 F3 Branco R Roraima Brazil
130 J9 Branco,Cabo Brazil
131 B2 Branco,R Argentina
41 L3 Brand Austria
37 O3 Brand Czechoslovakia
87 B10 Brandberg mt Namibia
26 H9 Brändbo Sweden
28 C5 Brande Denmark
32 L5 Brande-Hörnerkirchen Germany
101 T4 Brandenberg Montana U.S.A.
33 R8 Brandenburg Germany
33 R7 Brandenburg land Germany
110 K4 Brandenburg Kentucky U.S.A.
37 P2 Brand-Erbisdorf Germany
28 C6 Branderup Denmark
13 H6 Brandesburton England
89 E7 Brandfort S Africa
33 R10 Brandis Germany
29 J11 Brändö Finland
119 S9 Brandon Manitoba Canada
9 G3 Brandon England
106 H3 Brandon Colorado U.S.A.
98 E9 Brandon Nebraska U.S.A.
95 O3 Brandon Vermont U.S.A.
99 S6 Brandon Wisconsin U.S.A.
14 A4 Brandon B Ireland
14 A4 Brandon Hd Ireland
14 E4 Brandon Hill mt Ireland
14 A4 Brandon Mt Ireland
95 N3 Brandreth New York U.S.A.
13 G5 Brandsby England
133 F5 Brandsen Argentina
28 D6 Brandsø isld Denmark
110 E5 Brandsville Missouri U.S.A.
98 K5 Brandt South Dakota U.S.A.
27 F11 Brandval Norway
87 D12 Brandvlei S Africa
94 K8 Brandy Virginia U.S.A.
95 L8 Brandywine Maryland U.S.A.
48 K6 Brănești Romania
95 P5 Branford Connecticut U.S.A.
113 E8 Branford Florida U.S.A.
27 L17 Braniewo Poland
31 M1 Braniewo Poland
31 M6 Branisko mts Czechoslovakia
18 E8 Branne France
102 A2 Branscomb California U.S.A.
146 C3 Bransfield Str Antarctica
106 G4 Branson Colorado U.S.A.
110 C5 Branson Missouri U.S.A.
9 F1 Branston England
118 D8 Brant Alberta Canada
70 O9 Brantas Java
70 O10 Brantas R Java
120 K9 Brantford Ontario Canada
98 H2 Brantford North Dakota U.S.A.
111 K10 Brantley Alabama U.S.A.
18 F7 Brantôme France
138 F7 Branxholme Victoria Australia
123 M8 Bras d'or L Nova Scotia Canada
99 O9 Brashear Missouri U.S.A.
128 E6 Brasiléia Brazil
129 J7 Brasília Brazil
129 G4 Brasília Legal Brazil
52 C6 Braslav Belorussia
48 K5 Brasov Romania
20 C5 Brasparts France
85 F8 Brass Nigeria
22 G1 Brasschaat Belgium
140 C6 Brassey Mt N Terr Australia
143 D6 Brassey Ra W Australia Australia
70 E2 Brassey Ra mts Sabah
139 G5 Brassi New South Wales Australia
28 D4 Brassø L Denmark
95 R1 Brassua L Maine U.S.A.
48 H4 Bratca Romania
48 L5 Brates, L Romania
46 G1 Brateş, Lacul L Romania
31 K7 Bratislava Czechoslovakia
46 G3 Bratsigovo Bulgaria
56 F3 Bratsk Russian Federation
56 F3 Bratskoye Vodokhranilishche res Russian Federation
48 M2 Bratslav Ukraine
26 K7 Bratten Sweden
95 P4 Brattleboro Vermont U.S.A.
32 M8 Brau Germany
36 D3 Braubach Germany
36 G2 Brauerschwend Germany
38 H5 Braunau Austria
36 E3 Braunfels Germany
33 N9 Braunlage Germany
33 P10 Braunsbedra Germany
Braunsberg see Braniewo Poland
33 N8 Braunschweig Germany
8 B5 Braunton England
36 B2 Brauweiler Germany
131 D4 Brava, L. la Argentina
94 G7 Brave Pennsylvania U.S.A.
27 H13 Bråviken L Sweden
131 D2 Bravo,Sa mt Argentina
14 E3 Bray Ireland
22 D4 Bray-Dunes France
22 E5 Braye France
21 M6 Braye,R France
21 O3 Bray-et-Lû France
8 C5 Brayford England
14 A5 Bray Hd Ireland
115 M4 Bray I Northwest Territories Canada
110 C2 Braymer Missouri U.S.A.
18 H4 Bray sur Seine France
22 D4 Bray-sur-Somme France
118 A6 Brazeau Alberta Canada
118 B6 Brazeau Dam Alberta Canada
128 F6 Brazil rep S America
110 J2 Brazil Indiana U.S.A.
90 G11 Brazil Basin Atlantic Oc
109 M6 Brazoria Texas U.S.A.
109 L4 Brazos R Texas U.S.A.
86 C6 Brazzaville Congo
42 H6 Brčko Bosnia-Herzegovina
31 K2 Brda R Poland
48 D1 Brdo mt Czechoslovakia
140 E6 Breadalbane Queensland Australia
143 E7 Breaden Bluff hill W Australia Australia
143 F7 Breaden,L W Australia Australia
141 K1 Breakfast Creek dist Brisbane, Qnsld Australia
144 A6 Breaksea I New Zealand
144 B7 Breaksea Is New Zealand
141 L6 Breaksea Spit Queensland Australia
20 G5 Bréal-sous-Montfort France
8 D4 Bream England
6 N4 Bream oil rig North Sea
145 E1 Bream Bay New Zealand
27 F15 Breared Sweden
21 L2 Bréaute France
111 E11 Breaux Bridge Louisiana U.S.A.
48 K5 Breaza Romania
70 K9 Brebes Java
70 M9 Brebes,Tg C Java
121 U4 Brébeuf, L Quebec Canada
122 B5 Brébeuf,L Quebec Canada
18 H4 Brécey France
20 E6 Brech France
36 E3 Brechen Germany
120 B8 Brechin Ontario Canada
15 F4 Brechin Scotland
20 F3 Brechou isld Channel Is English Chan
22 H1 Brecht Belgium
106 D2 Breckenridge Colorado U.S.A.
98 K3 Breckenridge Minnesota U.S.A.
110 C2 Breckenridge Missouri U.S.A.
109 J3 Breckenridge Texas U.S.A.
133 C8 Brecknock, Pen Chile
31 K7 Břeclav Czechoslovakia
8 C4 Brecon Wales
8 C4 Brecon Beacons mts Wales
Breconshire co see Powys, Gwent, Mid Glamorgan counties
25 C5 Breda Netherlands
99 M7 Breda Iowa U.S.A.
26 M7 Bredåker Sweden
27 H15 Bredåkra Sweden
27 G14 Bredaryd Sweden
87 D12 Bredasdorp S Africa
33 Q7 Breddin Germany
32 K6 Breddorf Germany
28 D6 Brede Denmark
9 G6 Brede England
28 B6 Brede Å R Denmark
28 B6 Bredebro Denmark
32 J10 Bredelar Germany
22 E1 Bredene Belgium
33 R5 Bredenfelde Germany
119 P8 Bredenbury Saskatchewan Canada
33 S6 Bredereiche Germany
28 C7 Bredevad Denmark
26 L6 Bredsel Sweden
27 G12 Bredsjö Sweden
30 E1 Bredstedt Germany
28 C5 Bredsten Denmark
26 K8 Bredträsk Sweden
55 D4 Bredy Russian Federation
22 K1 Bree Belgium
89 A9 Breede R S Africa
110 G3 Breese Illinois U.S.A.
33 S5 Breesen Germany
46 E3 Bregalnica R Macedonia Yugoslavia
41 H2 Brege R Germany
41 L2 Bregenz Austria
41 L3 Bregenzer Ache R Austria
41 L3 Bregenzer Wald mt Austria
28 G5 Bregninge Denmark
48 H6 Bregovo Bulgaria
20 G4 Bréhal France
20 E4 Bréhat isld France
122 B1 Bréhat, L Quebec Canada
33 Q9 Brehna Germany
33 T9 Brehnitz Germany
36 E2 Breidenbach Germany
28 R9 Breidhafjördhur B Iceland
28 T9 Breidhdalsvik Iceland
98 E3 Breien North Dakota U.S.A.
21 L5 Breil-sur-Mérize,le France
26 B10 Breim Norway
40 G1 Breisach Germany
37 M5 Breitenbrunn Germany
33 Q10 Breitenfeld Germany
37 K4 Breitengüssbach Germany
33 P9 Breitenhagen Germany
33 M7 Breitenhees Germany
37 O3 Breitenhof Germany
33 S6 Breiter Luzinsee L Germany
40 G5 Breithorn mt Switzerland
33 Q9 Breitling Germany
37 J2 Breitungen Germany
26 M1 Breivikbotn Norway
28 A6 Brejning Denmark
129 K4 Brejo Brazil
94 C3 Brekenridge Michigan U.S.A.
26 E9 Brekken Norway
28 B9 Brekstad Norway
26 A10 Bremangerland isld Norway
41 L6 Brembana, Val Italy
41 L6 Brembo R Italy
32 J6 Bremen Germany
112 B4 Bremen Georgia U.S.A.
94 A5 Bremen Indiana U.S.A.
94 E7 Bremen Ohio U.S.A.
140 D1 Bremer isld N Terr Australia
143 C10 Bremer Bay W Australia Australia
32 J5 Bremerhaven Germany
143 D10 Bremer Ra W Australia Australia
117 M12 Bremerton Washington U.S.A.
32 K6 Bremervörde Germany
41 H3 Bremgarten Switzerland
116 Q6 Bremner R Alaska U.S.A.
109 L4 Bremond Texas U.S.A.
26 E6 Bremsteinen lighthouse Norway
139 H3 Brenda New South Wales Australia
28 D6 Brenderup Denmark
45 K1 Brendola Italy
8 C5 Brendon Hills England
109 L5 Brenham Texas U.S.A.
21 N8 Brenne reg France
21 M6 Brenne R Indre-et-Loire France
41 O3 Brenner Austria
101 M5 Brenner Montana U.S.A.
41 O4 Brennero Italy
41 O3 Brenner Pass Austria/Italy
41 M6 Breno Italy
42 C3 Breno Italy
19 P12 Brénod France
36 B5 Brenschelbach Germany
121 M6 Brent Ontario Canada
6 M1 Brent oil rig North Sea
111 J9 Brent Alabama U.S.A.
41 N5 Brenta R Italy
41 N5 Brenta, Gruppa di mt Italy
9 F5 Brentford England
98 H4 Brentford South Dakota U.S.A.
123 T4 Brenton Rock Newfoundland Canada
9 G4 Brentwood England
102 C4 Brentwood California U.S.A.
37 J6 Brenz R Germany
9 G5 Brenzett England
89 G6 Brereton Park S Africa
45 J2 Brescello Italy
41 M6 Brescia Italy
25 A6 Breskens Netherlands
Breslau see Wrocław
21 O2 Bresle R France
21 P3 Bresles France
143 C6 Bresnahan,Mt W Australia Australia
41 P4 Bressanone Italy
40 B5 Bresse reg France
21 K8 Bressuire France
31 O3 Brest Belorussia
20 B5 Brest France
20 F5 Brest à Nantes, Canal de France
46 E1 Brestovac Serbia Yugoslavia
20 A5 Brest,Rade de B France
83 J14 Bretagne, Pnte de Réunion Indian Oc
21 N4 Bretagnolles France
48 K4 Brețcu Romania
18 G8 Bretenoux France
21 M4 Breteuil-sur-Iton France
21 P2 Breteuil-sur-Noye France
20 G8 Brétignolles-sur-Mer France
21 P4 Brétigny France
118 C5 Breton Alberta Canada
21 M5 Bretoncelles France
111 G12 Breton I Louisiana U.S.A.
18 E6 Breton, Pertuis d' B France
95 N6 Breton Woods New Jersey U.S.A.
38 K7 Bretstein Austria
145 E1 Brett, C New Zealand
36 F5 Bretten Germany
21 K3 Bretteville France
21 K3 Bretteville-l'Orgueilleuse France
37 J5 Brettheim Germany
36 G5 Bretzfeld Germany
36 G4 Breuberg Germany
69 B10 Breueh, Pulau isld Sumatra
21 L3 Breuil-en-Auge,le France
21 N4 Breuilpont France
25 D4 Breukelen Netherlands
40 C1 Breuvannes France
21 O4 Bréval France
112 E2 Brevard North Carolina U.S.A.
129 H4 Breves Brazil
27 D12 Brevik Norway
95 T2 Brewer Maine U.S.A.
95 L3 Brewerton New York U.S.A.
113 E10 Brewster Florida U.S.A.
107 J2 Brewster Kansas U.S.A.
98 G8 Brewster Nebraska U.S.A.
95 O5 Brewster New York U.S.A.
94 F6 Brewster Ohio U.S.A.
117 O11 Brewster Washington U.S.A.
115 R3 Brewster, Kap C Greenland
144 B6 Brewster, Mt New Zealand
111 J10 Brewton Alabama U.S.A.
25 F6 Breyell Germany
Brezhnev see Naberezhnyye Chelny
19 O14 Brezins France
46 F2 Breznik Bulgaria
48 F2 Brezno Czechoslovakia
38 M8 Brezno Slovenia
48 J5 Brezoi Romania
21 N4 Brézolles France
16 D2 Brezo, Sa. del mts Spain
46 G2 Brezovo Bulgaria
42 H3 Brezovo Polje mt Croatia
86 D4 Bria Cent Afr Republic
103 M4 Brian Head Utah U.S.A.
18 G5 Briare France
141 L7 Bribie I Queensland Australia
108 G1 Brice Texas U.S.A.
99 N6 Bricelyn Minnesota U.S.A.
48 M1 Brichany Moldavia
110 E7 Brickeys Arkansas U.S.A.
19 J4 Bricon France
123 M2 Briconnet,L Quebec Canada
20 G3 Bricquebec France
20 G4 Bricqueville-sur-Mer France
14 C4 Bride R Ireland
12 D5 Bride I of Man U.K.
8 C6 Bridell Wales
8 B6 Bridestowe England
119 U3 Bridgar Manitoba Canada
117 M10 Bridge R British Columbia Canada
101 M7 Bridge Idaho U.S.A.
112 D6 Bridgeboro Georgia U.S.A.
12 B2 Bridgend Islay Scotland
13 E1 Bridgend Tayside Scotland
8 C4 Bridgend Wales
12 E1 Bridge of Allan Scotland
12 D3 Bridge of Doon Scotland
12 D2 Bridge of Weir Scotland
110 L7 Bridgeport Alabama U.S.A.
102 E3 Bridgeport California U.S.A.
95 O5 Bridgeport Connecticut U.S.A.
107 N3 Bridgeport Kansas U.S.A.
98 C8 Bridgeport Nebraska U.S.A.
100 H5 Bridgeport Oregon U.S.A.
100 F2 Bridgeport Washington U.S.A.
109 K2 Bridgeport, L Texas U.S.A.
102 E3 Bridgeport Res California U.S.A.
113 L12 Bridge Pt Bahamas
101 R4 Bridger Montana U.S.A.
101 P4 Bridger Pk Montana U.S.A.
101 S8 Bridger Pk Wyoming U.S.A.
95 M7 Bridgeton New Jersey U.S.A.
112 K2 Bridgeton North Carolina U.S.A.
143 B10 Bridgetown W Australia Australia
127 P6 Bridgetown Barbados
122 G9 Bridgetown Nova Scotia Canada
122 K8 Bridgeville Nova Scotia Canada
100 B9 Bridgeville California U.S.A.
122 H9 Bridgewater Nova Scotia Canada
95 S7 Bridgewater Maine U.S.A.
95 R5 Bridgewater Massachusetts U.S.A.
98 J6 Bridgewater South Dakota U.S.A.
94 J8 Bridgewater Virginia U.S.A.
138 F7 Bridgewater,C Victoria Australia
94 A5 Bridgman Michigan U.S.A.
8 D2 Bridgnorth England
95 R2 Bridgton Maine U.S.A.
8 C5 Bridgwater England
13 H5 Bridlington England
139 H8 Bridport Tasmania Australia
8 D6 Bridport England
18 G4 Brie reg France
20 B5 Brie France
25 B5 Brielle Netherlands
112 F4 Brier Creek Georgia U.S.A.
119 M8 Briercrest Saskatchewan Canada
118 F4 Brierville Alberta Canada
122 F9 Brier I Nova Scotia Canada
22 H5 Brieulles-sur-Bar France
21 O4 Brieval France
22 K5 Briey France
40 G5 Brig Switzerland
41 H1 Brigach R Germany
120 H10 Brigden Ontario Canada
13 H6 Brigg England
109 K5 Briggs Texas U.S.A.
98 B9 Briggsdale Colorado U.S.A.
101 N8 Brigham City Utah U.S.A.
13 G6 Brighouse England
8 B6 Brightley England
103 M5 Bright Angel Pt Arizona U.S.A.
9 H4 Brightlingsea England
138 E6 Brighton South Australia Australia
121 N8 Brighton Ontario Canada
9 F6 Brighton England
98 B10 Brighton Colorado U.S.A.
113 F10 Brighton Florida U.S.A.
110 F2 Brighton Illinois U.S.A.
99 P8 Brighton Iowa U.S.A.
94 D4 Brighton Michigan U.S.A.
141 F6 Brighton Downs Queensland Australia
145 D4 Brightwater New Zealand
20 B4 Brignogan-Plage France
123 T6 Brigus Newfoundland Canada
17 F4 Brihuega Spain
42 F4 Brijuni isld Croatia
26 G4 Briksvoer isld Norway
130 C7 Brilhante,R Brazil
106 F5 Brilliant New Mexico U.S.A.
99 S5 Brillion Wisconsin U.S.A.
32 J10 Brilon Germany
99 R9 Brimfield Illinois U.S.A.
43 H8 Brindisi Italy
138 C4 Bring,L South Australia Australia
94 E6 Brinkhaven Ohio U.S.A.
9 G3 Brinkley England
110 E7 Brinkley Arkansas U.S.A.
9 E3 Brinklow England
53 E10 Brinkovskaya Russian Federation
32 J6 Brinkum Germany
138 E5 Brinkworth South Australia Australia
21 P6 Brinon-sur-Sauldre France
98 G1 Brinsmade North Dakota U.S.A.
113 C7 Brinson Georgia U.S.A.
21 J6 Briollay France
21 O8 Brion Indre France
123 L6 Brion, I Madeleine Is, Quebec Canada
21 M3 Brionne France
21 H7 Brion-près-Thouet France
18 H7 Brioude France
21 K4 Briouze France
141 L8 Brisbane Queensland Australia
141 L7 Brisbane R Queensland Australia
108 D8 Briscoe Texas U.S.A.
45 L3 Brisighella Italy
6 N4 Brisk oil rig North Sea
21 K7 Brissac-Quincé France
41 J4 Bristenstock mt Switzerland
122 E7 Bristol New Brunswick Canada
121 O7 Bristol Quebec Canada
8 D5 Bristol England
106 H3 Bristol Colorado U.S.A.
95 P5 Bristol Connecticut U.S.A.
113 C7 Bristol Florida U.S.A.
112 E6 Bristol Georgia U.S.A.
94 B5 Bristol Indiana U.S.A.
95 Q3 Bristol New Hampshire U.S.A.
95 M6 Bristol Pennsylvania U.S.A.
95 Q5 Bristol Rhode I U.S.A.
98 J4 Bristol South Dakota U.S.A.
95 O2 Bristol Vermont U.S.A.
94 E10 Bristol Virginia/Tenn U.S.A.
116 G8 Bristol B Alaska U.S.A.
8 C5 Bristol Chan England/Wales
146 G3 Bristol I S Sandwich Is Atlantic Oc
103 J7 Bristol L California U.S.A.
103 J7 Bristol Mts California U.S.A.
103 K3 Bristol Silver Nevada U.S.A.
107 O6 Bristow Oklahoma U.S.A.
117 M11 Britannia Beach British Columbia Canada
146 A3 British Antarctic Terr Antarctica
117 K7 British Columbia prov Canada
115 L1 British Empire Ra Northwest Territories Canada
British Guiana see Guyana
British Honduras see Belize
81 E6 British Ind.Oc.Terr colony Indian Oc
116 Q2 British Mts Alaska/Yukon Terr U.S.A./Canada
British N. Borneo see Sabah
British Solomon Is see Solomon Is.
123 M7 Briton Cove C Breton I, Nova Scotia
8 C4 Briton Ferry Wales
87 E11 Brits S Africa
87 D12 Britstown S Africa
120 K7 Britt Ontario Canada
99 N6 Britt Iowa U.S.A.
27 G14 Brittatorp Sweden
107 N6 Britton Oklahoma U.S.A.
98 J4 Britton South Dakota U.S.A.
138 C2 Britton,Mt South Australia Australia
33 T7 Britz Germany
18 G7 Brive-la-Gaillarde France
16 E2 Briviesca Spain
20 G2 Brix France
38 F7 Brixental V Austria
8 C7 Brixham England
48 D1 Brno Czechoslovakia
27 F12 Bro Sweden
112 D3 Broad R Georgia U.S.A.
112 F3 Broad R South Carolina U.S.A.
118 J6 Broadacres Saskatchewan Canada
95 N3 Broadalbin New York U.S.A.
143 D9 Broad Arrow W Australia Australia
121 M1 Broadback R Quebec Canada
15 B2 Broad Bay Scotland
100 A6 Broadbent Oregon U.S.A.
109 N4 Broaddus Texas U.S.A.
15 C3 Broadford Scotland
14 B2 Broad Haven Ireland
8 A4 Broad Haven Wales
9 E5 Broad Hinton England
142 D5 Broadhurst Ra W Australia Australia
98 H5 Broadland South Dakota U.S.A.
15 E2 Broad Law Scotland
116 N5 Broad Pass Alaska U.S.A.
141 J5 Broad Sound Queensland Australia
141 K5 Broad Sound Chan Queensland Australia
141 J6 Broadsound Ra Queensland Australia
9 H5 Broadstairs England
98 A4 Broadus Montana U.S.A.
119 P8 Broadview Saskatchewan Canada
101 R3 Broadview Montana U.S.A.
108 A9 Broadview New Mexico U.S.A.
9 F6 Broadwater England
98 D8 Broadwater Nebraska U.S.A.
8 E3 Broadway England
8 D6 Broadwey England
8 D6 Broadwindsor England
145 D1 Broadwood New Zealand
126 C3 Broa, Ensenada de la B Cuba
28 D7 Broager Denmark
28 E6 Broby Denmark
27 G15 Broby Sweden
119 Q1 Brochet Manitoba Canada
122 C4 Brochet,L.au Quebec Canada
32 G5 Brochterbeck Germany
121 Q4 Brochu,L Quebec Canada
119 J7 Brock Saskatchewan Canada
99 L9 Brock Nebraska U.S.A.
32 L6 Brockel Germany
33 N9 Brocken mt Germany
9 E6 Brockenhurst England
118 D9 Brocket Alberta Canada
98 H1 Brocket North Dakota U.S.A.
114 H2 Brock I Northwest Territories Canada
13 H6 Brocklesby England
142 B5 Brockman,Mt W Australia Australia
94 K3 Brockport New York U.S.A.
98 G7 Brocksburg Nebraska U.S.A.
140 B2 Brock's Creek N Terr Australia
95 Q4 Brockton Massachusetts U.S.A.
98 B1 Brockton Montana U.S.A.
121 P8 Brockville Ontario Canada
98 B4 Brockway Montana U.S.A.
94 J5 Brockway Pennsylvania U.S.A.
110 J2 Brocton Illinois U.S.A.
94 H4 Brocton New York U.S.A.
48 F7 Brodarevo Serbia Yugoslavia
118 L7 Broderick Saskatchewan Canada
115 L3 Brodeur Pen Northwest Territories Canada
99 R7 Brodhead Wisconsin U.S.A.
48 G6 Brodica Serbia Yugoslavia
12 C2 Brodick Scotland
94 K10 Brodnax Virginia U.S.A.
31 L2 Brodnica Poland
55 D3 Brodokalmak Russian Federation
25 C3 Broek op Langedijk Netherlands
100 H5 Brogan Oregon U.S.A.
21 M3 Broglie France
20 F5 Brohinière,la France
36 C3 Brohl-Lützing Germany
33 T5 Brohm-Cosa Germany
33 M8 Broistedt Germany
31 N3 Brok Poland
99 R4 Brokaw Wisconsin U.S.A.
32 K5 Brokdorf Germany
107 P5 Broken Arrow Oklahoma U.S.A.
139 K5 Broken Bay New South Wales Australia
98 G8 Broken Bow Nebraska U.S.A.
107 Q7 Broken Bow Oklahoma U.S.A.
107 Q7 Broken Bow L Oklahoma U.S.A.
138 F4 Broken Hill New South Wales Australia
Broken Hill Zambia see Kabwe
129 G3 Brokopondomeer L Suriname
29 K12 Bromarv Finland
33 N7 Brome Germany
8 D3 Bromfield England
98 C1 Bromhead Saskatchewan Canada
9 G5 Bromley England
27 D11 Bromma Norway
28 E7 Bromme Denmark
70 O9 Bromo mt Java
13 H5 Brompton England
99 O9 Bromsgrove England
8 D3 Bromyard England
19 N13 Bron France
40 A6 Bron France
110 B4 Bronaugh Missouri U.S.A.
28 D2 Brønderslev Denmark
28 E5 Brøndum Denmark
8 B3 Bronllys Wales
37 L4 Bronn Germany
27 G15 Brönnestad Sweden
55 E2 Bronnikovo Russian Federation
26 F6 Brønnøysund Norway
36 H2 Bronnzell Germany
28 B6 Brøns Denmark
113 E8 Bronson Florida U.S.A.
94 B5 Bronson Michigan U.S.A.
109 N4 Bronson Texas U.S.A.
120 J9 Bronte Ontario Canada
43 F11 Bronte Sicily
108 G4 Bronte Texas U.S.A.
139 H8 Bronte Park Tasmania Australia
95 O6 Bronx New York U.S.A.
41 O5 Bronzolo Italy
122 E3 Brooch L Quebec Canada
99 T9 Brook Indiana U.S.A.
94 K8 Brooke Virginia U.S.A.
109 O4 Brookeland Texas U.S.A.
113 E8 Brooker Florida U.S.A.
71 C6 Brooke's Pt Palawan Philippines
122 J8 Brookfield Nova Scotia Canada
110 C2 Brookfield Missouri U.S.A.
111 F10 Brookhaven Mississippi U.S.A.
119 N9 Brooking Saskatchewan Canada
100 A7 Brookings Oregon U.S.A.
98 K5 Brookings South Dakota U.S.A.
141 H4 Brook Is.Lt.Ho Queensland Australia
9 G6 Brookland England
94 K5 Brookland Pennsylvania U.S.A.
112 F5 Brooklet Georgia U.S.A.
121 M9 Brooklin Ontario Canada
95 Q4 Brookline Massachusetts U.S.A.
110 K2 Brooklyn Indiana U.S.A.
99 O8 Brooklyn Iowa U.S.A.
94 C4 Brooklyn Michigan U.S.A.
111 G10 Brooklyn Mississippi U.S.A.
95 O6 Brooklyn New York U.S.A.
95 M5 Brooklyn Pennsylvania U.S.A.
117 N11 Brookmere British Columbia Canada
94 H10 Brookneal Virginia U.S.A.
99 N4 Brook Park Minnesota U.S.A.
110 H4 Brookport Illinois U.S.A.
118 F8 Brooks Alberta Canada
95 S2 Brooks Maine U.S.A.
101 Q2 Brooks Montana U.S.A.
117 G5 Brooks Brook Yukon Territory Canada
119 N5 Brooksby Saskatchewan Canada
146 D6 Brooks, Cape C Antarctica
109 M6 Brookshire Texas U.S.A.
116 D4 Brooks Mt Alaska U.S.A.
116 M5 Brooks,Mt Alaska U.S.A.
116 K2 Brooks Range Alaska U.S.A.
99 O3 Brookston Minnesota U.S.A.
109 M2 Brookston Texas U.S.A.
113 E9 Brooksville Florida U.S.A.
111 H8 Brooksville Mississippi U.S.A.
143 B9 Brookton W Australia Australia
95 U1 Brookton Maine U.S.A.
95 L4 Brooktondale New York U.S.A.
110 M2 Brookville Indiana U.S.A.
107 N3 Brookville Kansas U.S.A.
94 H5 Brookville Pennsylvania U.S.A.
111 J8 Brookwood Alabama U.S.A.
141 L7 Brooloo Queensland Australia
123 K4 Broom B Anticosti I, Quebec
142 D4 Broome W Australia Australia
143 C10 Broomehill W Australia Australia
142 F3 Broome, Mt W Australia Australia
20 F5 Broons France
99 L4 Brooten Minnesota U.S.A.
142 G4 Brophy,Mt W Australia Australia
143 F7 Brophy,Mt W Australia Australia
15 E2 Brora Scotland
28 B5 Brørup Denmark
27 G16 Brösarp Sweden
14 D3 Brosna R Ireland
48 K3 Brosteni Romania
68 A7 Brothers islds Andaman Is
100 E6 Brothers Oregon U.S.A.
145 E4 Brothers, The New Zealand
84 K4 Brothers,The islds Red Sea
37 J2 Brotterode Germany
21 N5 Brou France
13 F4 Brough England
15 E1 Brough Hd Orkney Scotland
15 F2 Brough Ness Scotland
9 F3 Broughton England
13 E5 Broughton Cumbria England
12 E2 Broughton Scotland
110 H4 Broughton Illinois U.S.A.
107 N2 Broughton Kansas U.S.A.
121 T6 Broughton Station Quebec Canada
15 F4 Broughty Ferry Scotland
86 C2 Broulkou Chad
36 B7 Brouvelieures France
25 A5 Brouwershaven Netherlands
20 H8 Brouzils,les France
40 E4 Brove R Switzerland
85 C7 Brovio Liberia
28 D2 Brovst Denmark
99 L3 Browerville Minnesota U.S.A.
71 C5 Brown Bank Palawan Philippines
94 E3 Brown City Michigan U.S.A.
107 L3 Brownell Kansas U.S.A.
143 E7 Browne Ra W Australia Australia
108 E2 Brownfield Texas U.S.A.
119 P9 Browning Saskatchewan Canada
110 C1 Browning Missouri U.S.A.
101 M1 Browning Montana U.S.A.
144 C5 Browning Pass New Zealand
143 C9 Brown,L W Australia Australia
119 M8 Brownlee Saskatchewan Canada
98 F7 Brownlee Nebraska U.S.A.
138 F3 Brown,Mt South Australia Australia
138 E4 Brown,Mt South Australia Australia
142 A3 Brown,Mt W Australia Australia
138 C4 Brown Pt South Australia Australia
141 G3 Brown R Queensland Australia
120 J3 Brownrigg Ontario Canada
144 B7 Browns New Zealand
110 J3 Browns Illinois U.S.A.
109 M3 Brownsboro Texas U.S.A.
121 Q7 Brownsburg Quebec Canada
110 K2 Brownsburg Indiana U.S.A.
126 E2 Browns Cay isld Bahamas
145 E2 Browns I New Zealand
98 C8 Brownson Nebraska U.S.A.
127 K2 Brown's Town Jamaica
94 A8 Brownstown Indiana U.S.A.
99 N4 Browns Valley Minnesota U.S.A.
110 L2 Brownsville Indiana U.S.A.
110 K4 Brownsville Kentucky U.S.A.
100 C5 Brownsville Oregon U.S.A.
94 H6 Brownsville Pennsylvania U.S.A.
110 G6 Brownsville Tennessee U.S.A.
109 K10 Brownsville Texas U.S.A.
99 M5 Brownton Minnesota U.S.A.
99 R7 Browntown Wisconsin U.S.A.
111 J8 Brownville Alabama U.S.A.
99 L9 Brownville Nebraska U.S.A.
95 M3 Brownville New York U.S.A.
95 S1 Brownville Junc Maine U.S.A.
109 J4 Brownwood, L Texas U.S.A.
142 E2 Browse I Australia
142 E2 Browse I Indian Oc
15 E5 Broxburn Scotland
112 E6 Broxton Georgia U.S.A.
16 C5 Brozas Spain
45 K4 Brozzi Italy
45 P1 Brtonigla Croatia
18 F4 Bruay France
22 F3 Bruay-sur-l'Escaut France
127 P6 Bruce Barbados
118 E5 Bruce Alberta Canada
144 B6 Bruce New Zealand
6 L3 Bruce oil rig North Sea
111 G7 Bruce Mississippi U.S.A.
99 P4 Bruce Wisconsin U.S.A.
144 B5 Bruce Bay New Zealand
99 R3 Bruce Crossing Michigan U.S.A.
120 J9 Brucefield Ontario Canada
142 C5 Bruce,Mt W Australia Australia
120 J7 Bruce Pen Ontario Canada
120 J7 Bruce Peninsula National Marine Park nat park Ontario Canada
120 J7 Bruce Peninsula National Park nat park Ontario Canada
143 C9 Bruce Rock W Australia Australia
110 H5 Bruceton Tennessee U.S.A.
109 K4 Bruceville Texas U.S.A.
19 K4 Bruche R France
32 K7 Bruchhausen-Vilsen Germany
36 F3 Bruchköbel Germany
36 F5 Bruchsal Germany
31 K7 Bruck Austria
33 R8 Brück Germany
37 L4 Bruck Bayern Germany
38 M7 Bruck-an-der-Mur Austria
37 M6 Bruckberg Germany
38 L8 Brückl Austria
21 K3 Brucourt France
19 P18 Brue-Auriac France
118 E5 Bruederheim Alberta Canada
33 P5 Brüel Germany
14 C4 Bruff Ireland
20 H7 Bruffière,la France
Bruges see Brugge
40 H3 Brugg Switzerland
22 E1 Brugge Belgium
36 D1 Brügge Germany
25 F6 Brüggen Germany
45 L1 Brugine Italy
44 F2 Brugnato, L. di Italy
36 B2 Brühl Germany
94 H5 Bruin Pennsylvania U.S.A.
103 O2 Bruin Pt Utah U.S.A.
117 P9 Brûlé Alberta Canada
98 E8 Brule Nebraska U.S.A.
99 P3 Brule Wisconsin U.S.A.
121 N6 Brûlé, L Quebec Canada
121 M7 Brûlé Lake Ontario Canada
21 K6 Brûlon France
22 J4 Brûly Belgium
129 K6 Brumado Brazil
25 F4 Brummen Netherlands
140 C4 Brunchilly N Terr Australia
43 C8 Bruncu Spina mt Sardinia
108 H7 Brundage Texas U.S.A.
111 L10 Brundidge Alabama U.S.A.
100 K7 Bruneau Idaho U.S.A.
22 G4 Brunehamel France
70 D2 Brunei state Borneo
70 D2 Brunei B Brunei
Brunei Town see Bandar Seri Begawan
140 D4 Brunette Downs N Terr Australia
123 Q6 Brunette I Newfoundland Canada
21 L2 Bruneval France
26 G8 Brunflo Sweden
109 J8 Bruni Texas U.S.A.
42 D2 Brunico Italy
118 D1 Brunkild Manitoba Canada
Brünn see Brno
37 N2 Brunn Germany
29 K4 Brunnby Sweden
41 J3 Brunnen Switzerland
119 M6 Bruno Saskatchewan Canada
99 O3 Bruno Minnesota U.S.A.
32 K5 Brunsbüttelkoog Germany
32 L5 Brunshausen Germany
25 E7 Brunssum Netherlands
Brunswick see Braunschweig
112 F6 Brunswick Georgia U.S.A.
95 S3 Brunswick Maine U.S.A.
94 K7 Brunswick Maryland U.S.A.
94 F5 Brunswick Ohio U.S.A.
143 E3 Brunswick B W Australia Australia
143 B10 Brunswick Junction W Australia Australia
120 G3 Brunswick L Ontario Canada
133 C8 Brunswick, Pen. de Chile
31 K6 Bruntál Czechoslovakia
146 F6 Brunt Ice Shelf ice shelf Antarctica
139 H9 Bruny I Tasmania Australia
47 H3 Brusartsi Bulgaria
106 G1 Brush Colorado U.S.A.
95 N2 Brushton New York U.S.A.
112 F1 Brushy Mts North Carolina U.S.A.
130 E10 Brusque Brazil
Brussels see Bruxelles
120 J9 Brussels Ontario Canada
99 T5 Brussels Wisconsin U.S.A.
22 G2 Bruxelles Belgium
24 Bruxelles conurbation Belgium
19 K4 Bruyères France
20 G5 Bruz France
128 E2 Bruzual Venezuela
22 F5 Bry France
94 C5 Bryan Ohio U.S.A.
109 L5 Bryan Texas U.S.A.
146 C6 Bryan Coast Antarctica
54 K8 Bryanka Ukraine
138 F5 Bryan,Mt South Australia Australia
53 G11 Bryansk Russian Federation
54 F3 Bryansk Russian Federation
53 D8 Bryanskaya Oblast' prov Russian Federation
109 P1 Bryant Arkansas U.S.A.
110 M1 Bryant Indiana U.S.A.
110 D5 Bryant Cr Missouri U.S.A.
95 R2 Bryant Pond Maine U.S.A.
22 C3 Bryas France
103 M4 Bryce Canyon Nat. Park Utah U.S.A.
144 B7 Bryndwr New Zealand
8 F7 Bryher isld Isles of Scilly England
8 C4 Bryn-amman Wales
8 C3 Bryn-crug Wales
8 C1 Bryneglwys Wales
26 M1 Brynilen Norway
8 C4 Bryn Mawr Wales
48 L2 Brynzeny Moldavia
28 D4 Bryrup Denmark
112 D2 Bryson City North Carolina U.S.A.
121 N6 Bryson,L Quebec Canada
48 G6 Brza Palanka Serbia Yugoslavia
31 K5 Brzeg Poland
31 L3 Brzešć Kuj Poland
31 M6 Brzesko Poland
31 L5 Brzeszcze Poland
31 M4 Brzeziny Poland
31 L4 Brzeźnica Poland
31 N6 Brzozów Poland
21 O4 Bû France
88 E8 Bua R Malawi
71 H5 Buabuang Sulawesi
71 H5 Buagi Indonesia
21 J4 Buais France
69 D12 Buatan Sumatra
84 F3 Bu'ayrāt al Hasūn Libya
33 S7 Buberow Germany
89 F2 Bubi R Zimbabwe
77 A5 Būbīyān, Jazīrat isld Kuwait
20 D6 Bubry France
71 F6 Bubuan isld Mindanao Philippines
13 H6 Bubwith England
87 F10 Bubye R Zimbabwe
47 L7 Bucak Turkey
128 D2 Bucaramanga Colombia
71 G6 Bucas Grande Philippines
141 J5 Bucasia Queensland Australia
111 H10 Bucatunna Mississippi U.S.A.
142 E3 Buccaneer Arch W Australia Australia
43 G8 Buccino Italy
48 K3 Bucecea Romania
47 K3 Bü Çekmece Turkey
48 J1 Buchach Ukraine
6 L5 Buchan oil rig North Sea
15 F3 Buchan dist Scotland
140 D4 Buchanan R N Terr Australia

119	P7	**Buchanan** Saskatchewan Canada
85	B7	**Buchanan** Liberia
112	B4	**Buchanan** Georgia U.S.A.
99	U8	**Buchanan** Michigan U.S.A.
106	F7	**Buchanan** New Mexico U.S.A.
98	G2	**Buchanan** North Dakota U.S.A.
94	H9	**Buchanan** Virginia U.S.A.
109	J5	**Buchanan Dam** Texas U.S.A.
140	B4	**Buchanan Hills** N Terr Australia
141	H5	**Buchanan,L** Queensland Australia
143	E7	**Buchanan,L** W Australia Australia
109	J5	**Buchanan, L** Texas U.S.A.
115	M3	**Buchan Gulf** Northwest Territories Canada
15	G3	**Buchan Ness** Scotland
123	Q5	**Buchans** Newfoundland Canada
123	Q5	**Buchans Jnct** Newfoundland Canada
133	E4	**Buchardo** Argentina
		Bucharest *see* **Bucureşti**
37	N7	**Buchbach** Germany
36	G4	**Buchen** Germany
36	C4	**Büchenbeuren** Germany
37	L1	**Buchenwald** Germany
32	L6	**Buchholz** Germany
33	R8	**Buchholz** Germany
41	N2	**Buching** Germany
41	N1	**Buchloe** Germany
15	D4	**Buchlyvie** Scotland
41	K3	**Buchs** Switzerland
21	N2	**Buchy** France
106	C6	**Buck** New Mexico U.S.A.
9	F3	**Buckden** England
32	K8	**Bückeburg** Germany
32	K7	**Bücken** Germany
103	M8	**Buckeye** Arizona U.S.A.
94	E7	**Buckeye Lake** Ohio U.S.A.
95	K7	**Buckeystown** Maryland U.S.A.
8	C7	**Buckfastleigh** England
94	G8	**Buckhannon** West Virginia U.S.A.
15	E4	**Buckhaven & Methil** Scotland
98	C5	**Buckhorn** Wyoming U.S.A.
15	E3	**Buckie** Scotland
121	P7	**Buckingham** Quebec Canada
9	E3	**Buckingham** England
94	J9	**Buckingham** Virginia U.S.A.
140	D1	**Buckingham B** N Terr Australia
140	E5	**Buckingham Downs** Queensland Australia
140	B4	**Buck,L** N Terr Australia
118	C5	**Buck L** Alberta Canada
116	G4	**Buckland** Alaska U.S.A.
119	V1	**Buckland L** Manitoba Canada
145	G1	**Bucklands Beach** New Zealand
141	J6	**Buckland Tableland** Queensland Australia
146	C13	**Buckle I** Antarctica
140	E5	**Buckley** *R* Queensland Australia
110	H1	**Buckley** Illinois U.S.A.
94	B2	**Buckley** Michigan U.S.A.
100	C2	**Buckley** Washington U.S.A.
38	O6	**Bucklige Welt** *reg* Austria
107	L4	**Bucklin** Kansas U.S.A.
110	D2	**Bucklin** Missouri U.S.A.
		Buckner Bay *see* **Nakagusuku-wan**
102	C2	**Bucks** California U.S.A.
103	L7	**Buckskin Mts** Arizona U.S.A.
102	C2	**Bucks Mt** California U.S.A.
95	T2	**Bucksport** Maine U.S.A.
33	Q7	**Bückwitz** Germany
31	K6	**Bučovice** Czechoslovakia
86	B6	**Buco Zau** Angola
22	D3	**Bucquoy** France
122	H7	**Buctouche** New Brunswick Canada
48	K6	**Bucureşti** Romania
71	E7	**Bucutua** *isld* Philippines
22	F4	**Bucy-les-Pierrepont** France
98	D3	**Bucyrus** North Dakota U.S.A.
26	B9	**Bud** Norway
68	D7	**Buda** *isld* Burma
109	K5	**Buda** Texas U.S.A.
48	E3	**Budafok** Hungary
54	B4	**Buda-Koshelevo** Belorussia
68	B1	**Budalin** Burma
48	E3	**Budapest** Hungary
74	H4	**Budaun** India
9	E1	**Budby** England
146	G14	**Budd Coast** Antarctica
53	F10	**Buddenovsk** Russian Federation
143	B8	**Budd,Mt** W Australia Australia
15	F4	**Buddon Ness** Scotland
8	B6	**Bude** England
32	L4	**Büdelsdorf** Germany
32	G9	**Büderich** Germany
141	L7	**Buderim** Queensland Australia
22	K4	**Buderscheid** Luxembourg
48	K6	**Budeşti** Romania
139	K5	**Budgewoi** New South Wales Australia
28	S9	**Budhardalur** Iceland
29	T9	**Budhareyri** Iceland
28	R9	**Budhir** Iceland
29	T9	**Búdhir** Iceland
131	A7	**Budi,L.del** Chile
36	G3	**Büdingen** Germany
86	C5	**Budjala** Zaire
8	C6	**Budleigh Salterton** England
45	L2	**Budrio** Italy
70	F6	**Budungbudung** Sulawesi
42	J6	**Budva** Montenegro Yugoslavia
54	H7	**Budy** Ukraine
86	A5	**Buéa** Cameroon
19	P16	**Buech** *R* France
21	N4	**Buéil** France
102	D7	**Buellton** California U.S.A.
128	C3	**Buenaventura** Colombia
71	E4	**Buenavista** Philippines
71	G6	**Buenavista** Mindanao Philippines
106	D3	**Buena Vista** Colorado U.S.A.
112	C5	**Buena Vista** Georgia U.S.A.
94	H9	**Buena Vista** Virginia U.S.A.
126	E3	**Buenavista, B. de** Cuba
17	F4	**Buendia, Embalse de** Spain
		Buene *R* *see* **Bojana**
131	A8	**Bueno** *R* Chile
130	E4	**Buenolândia** Brazil
129	K7	**Buenópolis** Brazil
131	E6	**Buenos Aires** *prov* Argentina
132		**Buenos Aires** *conurbation* Argentina
128	D4	**Buenos Aires** Colombia
133	C7	**Buenos Aires,L** Chile/Arg
127	N3	**Buenos Ayres** Trinidad
133	D7	**Buen Pasto** Argentina
133	D8	**Buen Tiempo,C** Argentina
130	H4	**Buerarema** Brazil
40	E5	**Buet,Mt** France
117	Q6	**Buffalo** *R* Alberta/N W Terr Canada
89	G6	**Buffalo** *R* S Africa
110	C5	**Buffalo** *R* Arkansas U.S.A.
107	P4	**Buffalo** Kansas U.S.A.
110	L4	**Buffalo** Kentucky U.S.A.
98	K3	**Buffalo** *R* Minnesota U.S.A.
99	N4	**Buffalo** Minnesota U.S.A.
110	C4	**Buffalo** Missouri U.S.A.
101	Q3	**Buffalo** Montana U.S.A.
94	J4	**Buffalo** New York U.S.A.
107	L5	**Buffalo** Oklahoma U.S.A.
112	F3	**Buffalo** South Carolina U.S.A.
98	C4	**Buffalo** South Dakota U.S.A.
110	J6	**Buffalo** *R* Tennessee U.S.A.
99	P5	**Buffalo** *R* Wisconsin U.S.A.
101	T5	**Buffalo** Wyoming U.S.A.
101	Q5	**Buffalo Bill Dam** Wyoming U.S.A.
101	Q5	**Buffalo Bill Res** Wyoming U.S.A.
99	N6	**Buffalo Center** Iowa U.S.A.
106	E2	**Buffalo Creek** Colorado U.S.A.
119	M9	**Buffalo Gap** Saskatchewan Canada
98	C6	**Buffalo Gap** South Dakota U.S.A.
118	E6	**Buffalo, L** Alberta Canada
117	Q5	**Buffalo L** Northwest Territories Canada
108	E1	**Buffalo L** Texas U.S.A.
139	H6	**Buffalo,Mt** Victoria Australia
118	J3	**Buffalo Narrows** Saskatchewan Canada
119	M8	**Buffalo Pound Prov Park** Saskatchewan Canada
127	L2	**Buff Bay** Jamaica
112	C3	**Buford** Georgia U.S.A.
98	C1	**Buford** North Dakota U.S.A.
98	A8	**Buford** Wyoming U.S.A.
48	K6	**Buftea** Romania
31	O4	**Bug** *R* Belorussia/Poland etc
128	C3	**Buga** Colombia
18	G10	**Bugarach, Pic de** *mt* France
58	G1	**Bugarikhta** Russian Federation
47	J4	**Buğdaylı** Turkey
70	N9	**Bugel,Tg** Java
40	B6	**Bugey** *dist* France
		Buggs Island Lake *see* **John H. Kerr Res.** N Carolina/Virginia
88	D1	**Bugiri** Uganda
26	R2	**Bugøynes** Norway
54	C10	**Bugskiy Liman** *lagoon* Ukraine
71	C6	**Bugsuk** *isld* Palawan Philippines
59	H2	**Bugt** China
18	F8	**Bugue,Le** France
71	E1	**Buguey** Luzon Philippines
78	K2	**Bügük Ağri** *mt* Turkey
57	F3	**Bugun'** Kazakhstan
57	E3	**Bugun'skoye Vodokhranilishche** *res* Kazakhstan
78	G4	**Buhayrat al Asad** *L* Syria
87	F9	**Buhera** Zimbabwe
58	C4	**Buh He** *R* China
71	F4	**Buhi** Luzon Philippines
36	E6	**Bühl** Germany
101	L7	**Buhl** Idaho U.S.A.
99	O2	**Buhl** Minnesota U.S.A.
36	E6	**Bühlerhöhe** Germany
36	E6	**Bühlertal** Germany
36	H5	**Bühlertann** Germany
88	E6	**Buhoro Flats** Tanzania
48	K4	**Buhuşi** Romania
117	N7	**Buick** British Columbia Canada
25	C4	**Buiksloot** Netherlands
8	C3	**Builth Wells** Wales
137	M3	**Buin** Bougainville I Papua New Guinea
41	M4	**Buin,Piz** *mt* Switz/Austria
130	H10	**Buique** Brazil
36	B2	**Buir** Germany
22	B3	**Buire-le-Sec** France
22	F4	**Buironfosse** France
19	O16	**Buis-les-Baronnies** France
25	F2	**Buitenpost** Netherlands
67	B7	**Bui Thon** Vietnam
122	J2	**Buit,L** Quebec Canada
16	E7	**Bujalance** Spain
46	E2	**Bujanovac** Serbia Yugoslavia
17	G3	**Bujaraloz** Spain
42	F3	**Buje** Croatia
88	B3	**Bujumbura** Burundi
48	D3	**Bük** Hungary
137	L3	**Buka** *isld* Papua New Guinea
66	E4	**Buka Daban Feng** *mt* China
88	D2	**Bukakata** Uganda
87	E7	**Bukama** Zaire
88	D2	**Bukasa I** Uganda
88	B3	**Bukavu** Zaire
88	C2	**Bukene** Tanzania
88	B3	**Bukeye** Burundi
57	C5	**Bukhara** Uzbekistan
46	F2	**Bukhovo** Bulgaria
56	B6	**Bukhtarminskoye Vodokhranilishche** *res* Kazakhstan
70	C6	**Bukitlidi** Kalimantan
69	E13	**Bukittinggi** Sumatra
48	F2	**Bükk** *mt* Hungary
79	F8	**Bukka, J. el** *mt* Jordan
48	D4	**Bükösd** Hungary
33	Q9	**Buko** Germany
88	C2	**Bukoba** Tanzania
48	J2	**Bukovina** *old prov* Romania/Ukraine
31	J1	**Bukowo,Jezioro** *L* Poland
136	G2	**Bula** Moluccas Indonesia
71	H4	**Bula anguki** Sulawesi
41	J2	**Bülach** Switzerland
56	H5	**Bulagansk** Russian Federation
65	D2	**Bulag Sum** China
139	K4	**Bulahdelah** New South Wales Australia
71	E4	**Bulalacao** Philippines
71	E5	**Bulalacao** Calamian Group Philippines
71	F4	**Bulan** Philippines
71	E7	**Bulan** *isld* Philippines
55	D3	**Bulanash** Russian Federation
55	C4	**Bulanavo** Russian Federation
89	F3	**Bulawayo** Zimbabwe
55	F3	**Bulayevo** Kazakhstan
28	C2	**Bulbjerg** *hill* Denmark
47	K6	**Buldan** Turkey
74	G8	**Buldana** India
77	H6	**Buleda** *reg* Pakistan
70	P10	**Buleleng** Bali Indonesia
89	G5	**Bulembu** Swaziland
9	E5	**Bulford** England
58	B2	**Bulgan** Mongolia
58	D2	**Bulgan** Mongolia
58	C3	**Bulgan** Mongolia
56	F5	**Bulgan** Mongolia
46	F2	**Bulgaria** *rep* E Europe
47	J2	**Bŭlgarovo** Bulgaria
47	K6	**Bulgaz Dağ** *mt* Turkey
40	C1	**Bulgnéville** France
77	C7	**Bul Hanine** *oil well* Persian Gulf
71	B2	**Buli** Halmahera Indonesia
71	C6	**Buliluyan,C** Palawan Philippines
141	K1	**Bulimba** *dist* Brisbane, Qnsld Australia
141	L2	**Bulimba Cr** Brisbane, Qnsld Australia
67	B4	**Buliu He** *R* China
117	K8	**Bulkley** *R* British Columbia Canada
143	D9	**Bulla Bulling** W Australia Australia
22	L3	**Bullange** Belgium
16	E5	**Bullaque** *R* Spain
109	M3	**Bullard** Texas U.S.A.
27	E13	**Bullaren S** *L* Sweden
17	F6	**Bullas** Spain
141	G8	**Bullawarra,L** Queensland Australia
86	H3	**Bullaxaar** Somalia
36	C3	**Bullay** Germany
127	L3	**Bull Bay** Jamaica
112	H5	**Bull Bay** South Carolina U.S.A.
40	F4	**Bulle** Switzerland
138	F4	**Bullea,L** New South Wales Australia
116	O1	**Bullen** Alaska U.S.A.
126	A1	**Bullen Baai** *B* Curaçao
139	H6	**Buller, Mt** Victoria Australia
145	D4	**Buller R** New Zealand
143	C9	**Bullfinch** W Australia Australia
103	K6	**Bullhead City** Nevada U.S.A.
112	H5	**Bull I** South Carolina U.S.A.
102	H7	**Bullion Mts** California U.S.A.
101	R3	**Bull Mts** Montana U.S.A.
141	G5	**Bullock** *R* Queensland Australia
141	G8	**Bulloo** *R* Queensland Australia
141	G8	**Bulloo Downs** Queensland Australia
141	F8	**Bulloo, L** Queensland Australia
133	F8	**Bull Pt** Falkland Is
118	B9	**Bull R** British Columbia Canada
145	E4	**Bulls** New Zealand
127	J3	**Bull Savannah** Jamaica
110	D5	**Bull Shoals Lake** Missouri U.S.A.
22	D3	**Bully** France
100	C9	**Bully Choop Mt** California U.S.A.
140	C2	**Bulman Gorge** N Terr Australia
139	G6	**Buloke,L** Victoria Australia
77	L2	**Bulola** Afghanistan
136	K3	**Bulolo** Papua New Guinea
138	F5	**Bulpunga** New South Wales Australia
87	E11	**Bultfontein** S Africa
71	G7	**Buluan** Mindanao Philippines
70	G7	**Bulubulu** Sulawesi
70	E3	**Bulu, G** *mt* Kalimantan
70	G7	**Bulukumba** Sulawesi
51	M1	**Bulun** Russian Federation
86	D7	**Bulungu** Zaire
71	G4	**Bulusan** Luzon Philippines
118	F6	**Bulwark** Alberta Canada
9	E2	**Bulwell** England
141	L1	**Bulwer I** Brisbane, Qnsld Australia
9	F2	**Bulwick** England
119	N8	**Bulyea** Saskatchewan Canada
86	D5	**Bumba** Zaire
84	G3	**Bumbah, Khalīj** Libya
48	H5	**Bumbeşti-Jiu** Romania
103	M7	**Bumble Bee** Arizona U.S.A.
70	G4	**Bumbulan** Sulawesi Indonesia
70	F2	**Bum-Bum** Sabah
70	M9	**Bumiaju** Java
66	F6	**Bumkhang** Burma
100	D3	**Bumping L** Washington U.S.A.
40	F4	**Bümpliz** Switzerland
75	O5	**Bumthang** Bhutan
109	O5	**Buna** Texas U.S.A.
71	G7	**Bunawan** Mindanao Philippines
143	B10	**Bunbury** W Australia Australia
110	B6	**Bunch** Oklahoma U.S.A.
14	E4	**Bunclody** Ireland
14	D1	**Buncrana** Ireland
141	K6	**Bundaberg** Queensland Australia
141	H8	**Bundaleer** Queensland Australia
32	F6	**Bunde** Germany
32	J8	**Bünde** Germany
140	D5	**Bundey** *R* N Terr Australia
74	F6	**Bundi** India
111	C11	**Bundick L** Louisiana U.S.A.
111	C11	**Bundicks Cr** Louisiana U.S.A.
140	C6	**Bundooma** N Terr Australia
14	C2	**Bundoran** Ireland
68	J6	**Bun Duc** Vietnam
12	B1	**Bunessan** Scotland
71	G7	**Bunga** *R* Mindanao Philippines
143	C9	**Bungalbin Hill** W Australia Australia
9	H3	**Bungay** England
68	E5	**Bung Boraphet** *L* Thailand
146	H13	**Bunger Hills** Antarctica
141	J7	**Bungil** *R* Queensland Australia
71	H6	**Bunginkela** *isld* Sulawesi Indonesia
68	F3	**Bung Kan** Thailand
70	G6	**Bungku** Sulawesi Indonesia
87	C7	**Bungo** Angola
60	G2	**Bungo-suidō** *str* Japan
141	J8	**Bungunya** Queensland Australia
		Bunguran *see* **Natuna Besar**
		Bunguran Utara, Kepulauan *see* **Natuna Besar**
86	B3	**Buni** Nigeria
86	F5	**Bunia** Zaire
143	E9	**Buningonia Spring** *spring* W Australia Australia
70	E3	**Bunju** *isld* Kalimantan
110	E4	**Bunker** Missouri U.S.A.
141	K6	**Bunker Grp** *islds* Gt Barrier Reef Aust
116	E4	**Bunker Hill** Alaska U.S.A.
110	G2	**Bunker Hill** Illinois U.S.A.
110	K1	**Bunker Hill** Indiana U.S.A.
107	M3	**Bunker Hill** Kansas U.S.A.
103	K5	**Bunkerville** Nevada U.S.A.
87	E8	**Bunkeya** Zaire
111	D11	**Bunkie** Louisiana U.S.A.
113	F8	**Bunnell** Florida U.S.A.
145	E4	**Bunnythorpe** New Zealand
70	G4	**Bunobagu** Sulawesi
68	H7	**Bu Noi** Vietnam
17	G5	**Buñol** Spain
25	D4	**Bunschoten** Netherlands
143	B8	**Buntine** W Australia Australia
9	F4	**Buntingford** England
70	D5	**Buntok** Kalimantan
70	D5	**Buntokecil** Kalimantan
141	K1	**Bunyaville** *dist* Brisbane, Qnsld Australia
68	E3	**Bun Yun** Thailand
51	L1	**Buolkalakh** Russian Federation
68	J6	**Buon Me Thuot** Vietnam
51	N1	**Buor-khaya, Guba** *G* Russian Federation
80	G1	**Buq'ātā** Syria
77	A7	**Buqayq** Saudi Arabia
28	A4	**Bur** Denmark
88	G3	**Bura** Kenya
86	A1	**Buraan** Somalia
71	L10	**Buraen** Timor Indonesia
		Buraimi *see* **Buraymī, Al**
143	B9	**Burakin** W Australia Australia
86	E3	**Buram** Sudan
143	E10	**Buraminya,Mt** W Australia Australia
141	K2	**Buranda** *dist* Brisbane, Qnsld Australia
75	J3	**Burang** China
130	H5	**Buranhaém** Brazil
45	M1	**Burano** Italy
86	J4	**Burao** Somalia
111	G12	**Buras** Louisiana U.S.A.
71	G5	**Burauen** Leyte Philippines
72	E3	**Buraydah** Saudi Arabia
55	C3	**Burayevo** Russian Federation
79	G4	**Burayj, Al** Syria
77	D7	**Buraymī, Al** U.A.E.
80	G1	**Burayqah** Syria
36	E2	**Burbach** Germany
9	E5	**Burbage** England
102	F7	**Burbank** California U.S.A.
98	K9	**Burchard** Nebraska U.S.A.
139	H5	**Burcher** New South Wales Australia
99	N6	**Burchinal** Iowa U.S.A.
57	C5	**Burdalyk** Turkmenistan
141	H5	**Burdekin** *R* Queensland Australia
141	H5	**Burdekin Falls** Queensland Australia
117	M7	**Burden,Mt** British Columbia Canada
118	F9	**Burdett** Alberta Canada
95	L4	**Burdett** New York U.S.A.
48	K3	**Burdujeni** Romania
78	C3	**Burdur** Turkey
47	L7	**Burdur Gölü** *L* Turkey
90	E14	**Burdwood Bank** Atlantic Oc
86	G3	**Burē** Ethiopia
86	G4	**Burē** Ethiopia
26	M7	**Bureå** Sweden
121	P4	**Bureau, L** Quebec Canada
59	K1	**Bureinskiy, Khrebet** *mts* Russian Federation
32	J9	**Büren** Germany
25	D5	**Buren** Netherlands
58	B2	**Bürenhayrhan** Mongolia
65	B1	**Bürentsogt** Mongolia
59	K1	**Bureya** *R* Russian Federation
59	J2	**Bureya** Russian Federation
9	E4	**Burford** England
32	K5	**Burg** Germany
33	P8	**Burg** Germany
36	D5	**Burgalben** Germany
47	J2	**Burgas** Bulgaria
38	O7	**Burgau** Austria
37	J7	**Burgau** Germany
112	J3	**Burgaw** North Carolina U.S.A.
47	N11	**Burgaz** Turkey
47	N11	**Burgaz** *isld* Turkey
37	J5	**Burgbernheim** Germany
32	M8	**Burgdorf** Germany
40	G3	**Burgdorf** Switzerland
100	K4	**Burgdorf** Idaho U.S.A.
37	K4	**Burgebrach** Germany
37	M2	**Bürgel** Germany
48	C3	**Burgenland** *prov* Austria
123	P6	**Burgeo** Newfoundland Canada
87	E12	**Burgersdorp** S Africa
9	F6	**Burgess Hill** England
95	L9	**Burgess Store** Virginia U.S.A.
13	E4	**Burgh** England
25	A5	**Burgh** Netherlands
36	H2	**Burghaun** Germany
38	G5	**Burghausen** Germany
37	L6	**Burgheim** Germany
9	G1	**Burgh-le-Marsh** England
43	E11	**Burgio** Sicily
36	H3	**Burgjoss** Germany
37	L3	**Burgkunstadt** Germany
37	N5	**Burglengenfeld** Germany
16	E2	**Burgos** *prov* Spain
16	E2	**Burgos** Spain
37	K3	**Burgpreppach** Germany
36	H3	**Burgsinn** Germany
36	G4	**Bürgstadt** Germany
37	O2	**Burgstädt** Germany
33	S6	**Burg Stargard** Germany
32	F8	**Burgsteinfurt** Germany
27	K14	**Burgsvik** Sweden
17	G2	**Burguete** Spain
36	F2	**Burgwald** Germany
32	L7	**Burgwedel** Germany
37	K4	**Burgwindheim** Germany
47	H5	**Burhaniye** Turkey
32	H5	**Burhave** Germany
130	E8	**Buri** Brazil
69	E14	**Buriai** Indonesia
71	F4	**Burias** *isld* Philippines
71	F4	**Burias Pass** Luzon Philippines
123	R6	**Burin** Newfoundland Canada
68	F5	**Buriram** Thailand
130	E7	**Buritama** Brazil
128	G6	**Buriti** *R* Brazil
130	E6	**Buriti Alegre** Brazil
129	K5	**Buriti Bravo** Brazil
130	F4	**Buritis** Brazil
80	C8	**Burj el Baiyara** Jordan
79	G4	**Burj Sāfīta** Syria
28	C7	**Burkal** Denmark
109	J1	**Burkburnett** Texas U.S.A.
140	F5	**Burke** *R* Queensland Australia
140	E6	**Burke** *R* Queensland Australia
100	K2	**Burke** Idaho U.S.A.
98	G6	**Burke** South Dakota U.S.A.
109	N4	**Burke** Texas U.S.A.
117	K9	**Burke Chan** British Columbia Canada
146	B7	**Burke I** Antarctica
144	C6	**Burke Pass** New Zealand
110	L5	**Burkesville** Kentucky U.S.A.
140	E4	**Burketown** Queensland Australia
109	H4	**Burkett** Texas U.S.A.
94	J9	**Burkeville** Virginia U.S.A.
37	O2	**Burkhardtsdorf** Germany
85	D6	**Burkina** *rep* W Africa
98	G4	**Burkmere** South Dakota U.S.A.
121	L7	**Burk's Falls** Ontario Canada
55	G4	**Burla** Russian Federation
36	G7	**Burladingen** Germany
141	G5	**Burleigh** Queensland Australia
109	K3	**Burleson** Texas U.S.A.
13	G6	**Burley** England
101	M7	**Burley** Idaho U.S.A.
8	D3	**Burley Gate** England
55	D4	**Burli** Kazakhstan
55	B5	**Burlin** Kazakhstan
107	P3	**Burlingame** Kansas U.S.A.
123	Q4	**Burlington** Newfoundland Canada
121	L9	**Burlington** Ontario Canada
106	H2	**Burlington** Colorado U.S.A.
99	P9	**Burlington** Iowa U.S.A.
107	P3	**Burlington** Kansas U.S.A.
95	N6	**Burlington** New Jersey U.S.A.
112	H1	**Burlington** North Carolina U.S.A.
95	O2	**Burlington** Vermont U.S.A.
117	M11	**Burlington** Washington U.S.A.
101	R5	**Burlington** Wyoming U.S.A.
110	A1	**Burlington Junction** Missouri U.S.A.
8	D2	**Burlton** England
57	J2	**Burlyu-Tobe** Kazakhstan
80	G5	**Burma** Jordan
68	B2	**Burma** *rep* S E Asia
139	H6	**Burmah Forest** Victoria Australia
55	D1	**Burmantovo** Russian Federation
101	N9	**Burmester** Utah U.S.A.
118	C9	**Burmis** Alberta Canada
144	D5	**Burnbrae** New Zealand
109	J5	**Burnet** Texas U.S.A.
141	K7	**Burnett** *R* Queensland Australia
141	K6	**Burnett Heads** Queensland Australia
100	D9	**Burney** California U.S.A.
8	C5	**Burnham** England
144	D5	**Burnham** New Zealand
95	S2	**Burnham** Maine U.S.A.
94	K6	**Burnham** Pennsylvania U.S.A.
9	G2	**Burnham Deepdale** England
9	G2	**Burnham Market** England
9	G4	**Burnham-on-Crouch** Essex England
40	F2	**Burnhaupt** France
139	H8	**Burnie** Tasmania Australia
13	H5	**Burniston** England
13	F6	**Burnley** England
13	G4	**Burnopfield** England
57	F3	**Burnoye** Kazakhstan
101	T10	**Burns** Colorado U.S.A.
100	F6	**Burns** Oregon U.S.A.
98	B8	**Burns** Wyoming U.S.A.
13	G5	**Burnsall** England
110	M5	**Burnside** Kentucky U.S.A.
94	J6	**Burnside** Pennsylvania U.S.A.
143	E7	**Burnside,L** W Australia Australia
117	L8	**Burns Lake** British Columbia Canada
98	G3	**Burnstad** North Dakota U.S.A.
122	G6	**Burnsville** New Brunswick Canada
110	H7	**Burnsville** Mississippi U.S.A.
112	E2	**Burnsville** North Carolina U.S.A.
94	G8	**Burnsville** West Virginia U.S.A.
101	P8	**Burntfork** Wyoming U.S.A.
126	G3	**Burnt Ground** Long I Bahamas
13	E1	**Burntisland** Scotland
122	J1	**Burnt L** Labrador, Nfld Canada
116	Q3	**Burnt Paw** Alaska U.S.A.
100	H5	**Burnt R** Oregon U.S.A.
100	B9	**Burnt Ranch** California U.S.A.
121	M8	**Burnt River** Ontario Canada
119	R3	**Burntwood L** Manitoba Canada
33	S5	**Burow** Germany
66	D2	**Burqin** China
119	M6	**Burr** Saskatchewan Canada
138	E5	**Burra** South Australia Australia
143	C9	**Burracoppin** W Australia Australia
139	K5	**Burragorang L** New South Wales Australia
15	F2	**Burray** Scotland
46	D3	**Burrel** Albania
140	C6	**Burrell,Mt** N Terr Australia
13	E1	**Burrelton** Scotland
139	J5	**Burrendong Res.** New South Wales Australia
17	G5	**Burriana** Spain
13	H6	**Burringham** England
124	J3	**Burro** Mexico
108	F6	**Burro** Mexico
99	P6	**Burr Oak** Iowa U.S.A.
107	M2	**Burr Oak** Kansas U.S.A.
94	B5	**Burr Oak** Michigan U.S.A.
94	E7	**Burr Oak Res** Ohio U.S.A.
103	L7	**Burro Cr** Arizona U.S.A.
108	E6	**Burro, Serranias del** *mts* Mexico
113	K11	**Burrow Cay** Bahamas
140	F3	**Burrowes, Pt** Queensland Australia
15	D6	**Burrow Head** Scotland
107	N3	**Burrton** Kansas U.S.A.
140	B2	**Burrundie** N Terr Australia
133	E3	**Burruyacú** Argentina
111	G13	**Burrwood** Louisiana U.S.A.
8	B4	**Burry Port** Wales
78	B1	**Bursa** Turkey
84	J4	**Bur Safâga** Egypt
36	C1	**Burscheid** Germany
13	F6	**Burscough** England
32	L9	**Bursfelde** Germany
8	D1	**Burslem** England
28	G7	**Bursø** Denmark
22	F2	**Burst** Belgium
118	H8	**Burstall** Saskatchewan Canada
99	M6	**Burt** Iowa U.S.A.
98	D3	**Burt** North Dakota U.S.A.
138	F4	**Burta** New South Wales Australia
94	C1	**Burt L** Michigan U.S.A.
9	E6	**Burton** England
98	G7	**Burton** Nebraska U.S.A.
109	L5	**Burton** Texas U.S.A.
8	B4	**Burton** Wales
13	H5	**Burton Agnes** England
13	F5	**Burton-in-Kendal** England
112	D3	**Burton L** Georgia U.S.A.
14	C2	**Burtonport** Ireland
9	E2	**Burton upon Trent** England
26	L7	**Burträsk** Sweden
122	F7	**Burtts Corner** New Brunswick Canada
138	F5	**Burtundy** New South Wales Australia
140	C6	**Burt Well** N Terr Australia
136	F2	**Buru** *isld* Moluccas Indonesia
84	J3	**Burullus** *L* Egypt
		Burultokay *see* **Fuhai**
88	B3	**Burundi** *rep* Cent Africa
88	B3	**Bururi** Burundi
85	F7	**Burutu** Nigeria
8	D3	**Burwarton** England
9	G6	**Burwash** England
9	G1	**Burwell** England
98	G8	**Burwell** Nebraska U.S.A.
33	S10	**Burxdorf** Germany
121	T7	**Bury** Quebec Canada
9	F6	**Bury** England
13	F6	**Bury** Greater Manchester England
56	F5	**Buryatskaya Respublika** Russian Federation
9	G3	**Bury St.Edmunds** England
43	E11	**Busambra, Rca** *mt* Sicily
71	F7	**Busan B** Mindanao Philippines
87	D7	**Busango** Zaire
118	D5	**Busby** Alberta Canada
101	T4	**Busby** Montana U.S.A.
44	B2	**Busca** Italy
33	R7	**Buschow** Germany
32	J4	**Buschsand** *isld* Germany
46	E3	**Buševa Planina** *mt* Macedonia Yugoslavia
46	D3	**Bushat** Albania
77	B5	**Būshehr** Iran
88	C2	**Bushenyi** Uganda
95	M5	**Bushkill** Pennsylvania U.S.A.
87	C9	**Bushland** *homeland* Namibia
108	B8	**Bushland** Texas U.S.A.
121	L6	**Bushnell** Ontario Canada
113	E9	**Bushnell** Florida U.S.A.
110	F1	**Bushnell** Illinois U.S.A.
98	C8	**Bushnell** Nebraska U.S.A.
107	M3	**Bushton** Kansas U.S.A.
140	E5	**Bushy Park** Queensland Australia
89	F1	**Busi** *R* Zimbabwe
88	E1	**Busia** Uganda
22	E3	**Busigny** France
86	D5	**Businga** Zaire
86	C6	**Busira** *R* Zaire
48	J1	**Busk** Ukraine
27	C11	**Buskerud** *reg* Norway
31	M5	**Busko** Poland
37	P3	**Buškovice** Czechoslovakia
55	D4	**Buskul'** Kazakhstan
71	B1	**Busobuso** Halmahera Indonesia
79	G6	**Buşrá ash Shām** Syria
19	K5	**Bussang** France
40	E2	**Bussang,Col.de** *pass* France
21	J8	**Busseau,le** France
143	B10	**Busselton** W Australia Australia
44	H2	**Busseto** Italy
99	O8	**Bussey** Iowa U.S.A.
41	N7	**Bussolengo** Italy
25	D4	**Bussum** Netherlands
77	D6	**Bustaneh** Iran
80	D2	**Bustan Ha Galil** Israel
141	K6	**Bustard Hd** Queensland Australia
48	K5	**Buşteni** Romania
42	B3	**Busto Arsizio** Italy
57	C4	**Buston** Uzbekistan
71	D4	**Busuanga** Philippines
86	D5	**Busu Djanoa** Zaire
32	J4	**Büsum** Germany
86	D5	**Buta** Zaire
131	G2	**Butai** *R* Brazil
70	O9	**Butak, G** *mt* Java
69	D9	**Butang Group** *isld* Thailand
133	D5	**Buta Ranquil** Argentina
88	B3	**Butare** Rwanda
71	F3	**Butaunan** *isld* Philippines
		Bute *co see* **Strathclyde** *reg*
138	E5	**Bute** South Australia Australia
15	C5	**Bute** *isld* Scotland
117	J9	**Butedale** British Columbia Canada
117	L10	**Bute Inlet** British Columbia Canada
88	B1	**Butembo** Zaire
22	L3	**Bütgenbach** Belgium
		Butha Qi *see* **Zalantun**
68	A2	**Buthidaung** Burma
47	P12	**Buthrotum** *hist site* Albania
86	F5	**Butiaba** Uganda
86	B1	**Butiyaalo** Somalia
32	H5	**Butjadingen** *reg* Germany
55	D3	**Butka** Russian Federation
68	B3	**Butle** *R* Burma
111	H9	**Butler** Alabama U.S.A.
112	C5	**Butler** Georgia U.S.A.
94	C5	**Butler** Indiana U.S.A.
110	M3	**Butler** Kentucky U.S.A.
110	B3	**Butler** Missouri U.S.A.
95	N6	**Butler** New Jersey U.S.A.
94	E6	**Butler** Ohio U.S.A.
107	L6	**Butler** Oklahoma U.S.A.
94	H6	**Butler** Pennsylvania U.S.A.
98	J4	**Butler** South Dakota U.S.A.
138	B2	**Butlers Dome** *mt* N Terr Australia
80	G2	**Butmiye** Syria
71	H7	**Buton** *isld* Sulawesi Indonesia
71	H7	**Buton, Selat** *str* Indonesia
46	D5	**Butrintit, Liqen i** *L* Albania
41	K3	**Bütschwil** Switzerland
45	K1	**Buttapietra** Italy
101	N4	**Butte** Montana U.S.A.
98	H7	**Butte** Nebraska U.S.A.
98	F2	**Butte** North Dakota U.S.A.
100	C7	**Butte Falls** Oregon U.S.A.
37	L1	**Buttelstedt** Germany
102	C1	**Butte Meadows** California U.S.A.
36	G7	**Buttenhausen** Germany
37	L4	**Buttenheim** Germany
37	K6	**Buttenwiesen** Germany
100	F4	**Butter Cr** Oregon U.S.A.
99	M6	**Butterfield** Minnesota U.S.A.
13	E5	**Buttermere** England
9	G2	**Butterwick** England
87	E12	**Butterworth** S Africa
14	C4	**Buttevant** Ireland
143	G6	**Buttfield, Mt** W Australia Australia
27	K14	**Buttle** Sweden
117	L11	**Buttle L** British Columbia Canada
15	B2	**Butt of Lewis** Scotland
115	K6	**Button B** Manitoba Canada
115	N5	**Button Is** Northwest Territories Canada
102	E6	**Buttonwillow** California U.S.A.
37	L1	**Buttstädt** Germany
98	J3	**Buttzville** North Dakota U.S.A.
71	G6	**Butuan** Mindanao Philippines
71	G6	**Butuan B** Mindanao Philippines
		Butung *isld see* **Buton**
54	M6	**Buturlinovka** Russian Federation
68	H6	**Bu Tu Suay** Vietnam
36	F3	**Butzbach** Germany
33	P5	**Bützow** Germany
86	J4	**Buuhoodle** Somalia
86	J5	**Buulobarde** Somalia
86	H6	**Buur Gaabo** Somalia
84	H5	**Buurhakaba** Somalia
26	E9	**Buvika** Norway
79	E10	**Buwārah, J** *mt* Saudi Arabia
21	L8	**Buxerolles** France
21	O7	**Buxeuil** France
32	L6	**Buxtehude** Germany
9	E1	**Buxton** England
112	M2	**Buxton** North Carolina U.S.A.
19	J6	**Buxy** France
55	C3	**Buy** *R* Russian Federation
58	C2	**Buyant** Mongolia
65	A1	**Buyant** Mongolia
58	G2	**Buyr Nuur** *L* Mongolia
47	N11	**Büyük** *isld* Turkey
47	N11	**Büyükada** Turkey
47	N10	**Büyükdere** Turkey
47	H4	**Büyük Kemikli Br** *C* Turkey
47	J7	**Büyük Menderes** *R* Turkey
21	N8	**Buzançais** France
22	H5	**Buzancy** France
48	K5	**Buzău** *R* Romania
48	K5	**Buzău** Romania
48	K5	**Buzăului Muntii** *mt* Romania
55	B4	**Buzdyak** Russian Federation
60	E12	**Buzen** Japan
87	F9	**Buzi** Mozambique
48	G5	**Buziaş** Romania
55	C4	**Buzov'yazy** Russian Federation
95	R5	**Buzzards B** Massachusetts U.S.A.
8	C4	**Bwlch** Wales
27	H11	**By** Sweden
47	H1	**Byala** Bulgaria
46	F1	**Byala Slatina** Bulgaria
114	J2	**Byam Martin I** Northwest Territories Canada
109	K1	**Byars** Oklahoma U.S.A.
31	O4	**Bychawa** Poland
31	L4	**Byczyna** Poland
31	K2	**Bydgoszcz** Poland
		Byelorussia *see* **Belorussia**
106	F2	**Byers** Colorado U.S.A.
109	J1	**Byers** Texas U.S.A.
94	F7	**Byesville** Ohio U.S.A.
9	E3	**Byfield** England
9	F5	**Byfleet** England
26	L7	**Bygdeå** Sweden
26	L7	**Bygdeträsk** Sweden
27	C10	**Bygdin** *L* Norway
26	L7	**Bygdsiljum** Sweden
28	D5	**Bygholm Å** *R* Denmark
27	C13	**Bygland** Norway
27	C13	**Byglandsfj** Norway
110	G7	**Byhalia** Mississippi U.S.A.
54	B3	**Bykhov** Belorussia
27	B12	**Bykle** Norway
27	B12	**Bykleheiane** Norway
59	M2	**Bykov** Russian Federation
28	C7	**Bylderup** Denmark
57	H1	**Bylkyldak** Kazakhstan
115	M3	**Bylot I** Northwest Territories Canada
140	F4	**Bynoe** *R* Queensland Australia
140	B2	**Bynoe Harbour** N Terr Australia
101	N2	**Bynum Res** Montana U.S.A.
111	F9	**Byram** Mississippi U.S.A.
146	D11	**Byrd Glacier** Antarctica
121	O5	**Byrd,L** Quebec Canada
13	F3	**Byrness** England
143	B7	**Byro** W Australia Australia
112	D5	**Byromville** Georgia U.S.A.
102	C4	**Byron** California U.S.A.
99	R7	**Byron** Illinois U.S.A.
95	R2	**Byron** Maine U.S.A.
101	R5	**Byron** Wyoming U.S.A.
139	L3	**Byron Bay** New South Wales Australia
51	J1	**Byrranga,Gory** *mt* Russian Federation
109	J2	**Byrson** Texas U.S.A.
28	F2	**Byrum** Denmark
26	M7	**Byske** Sweden
26	L6	**Byske älv** *R* Sweden
48	F1	**Bystra** *mt* Czechoslovakia
55	F2	**Bystryy** Russian Federation
31	K5	**Bystrzyca Kłodzka** Poland
51	N2	**Bytantay** *R* Russian Federation
31	L6	**Bytča** Czechoslovakia
31	L5	**Bytom** Poland
54	F3	**Bytosh** Russian Federation
31	K1	**Bytów** Poland
		Byzantium *see* **İstanbul**
141	J7	**Byzantium** Queensland Australia
31	M3	**Bzura** *R* Poland

C

130	B9	**Caacupé** Paraguay
130	C9	**Caaguazú** *dept* Paraguay
133	F3	**Caaguazu** Paraguay
130	C9	**Caaguazú, Cord de** *mts* Paraguay
87	C8	**Caála** Angola
130	B10	**Caapucú** Paraguay
130	C8	**Caarapó** Brazil
130	F5	**Caatinga** Brazil
130	C10	**Caazapá** Paraguay
129	G7	**Cabacal** *R* Brazil
130	H9	**Cabaceiras** Brazil
126	E3	**Cabaiguán** Cuba
71	E3	**Cabalantian** Luzon Philippines
71	G5	**Cabalian** Leyte Philippines
106	C9	**Caballo** New Mexico U.S.A.
128	D4	**Caballococha** Peru
106	C9	**Caballo Res** New Mexico U.S.A.
124	G3	**Caballos Mesteños, Llano de los** Mexico
71	E3	**Cabanatuan** Luzon Philippines
122	D6	**Cabano** Quebec Canada
71	E2	**Cabarruyan** *isld* Luzon Philippines
19	Q18	**Cabasse** France
141	K1	**Cabbage Tree Cr** Brisbane, Qnsld Australia
16	B2	**Cabe** *R* Spain
130	F4	**Cabeceiras** Brazil
130	J9	**Cabedelo** Brazil
99	S8	**Cabery** Illinois U.S.A.
16	D6	**Cabeza del Buey** Spain
128	F7	**Cabezas** Bolivia
106	C6	**Cabezon** New Mexico U.S.A.
71	F6	**Cabilao** *isld* Philippines
127	J9	**Cabimas** Venezuela
107	P5	**Cabin Creek** Oklahoma U.S.A.
86	B7	**Cabinda** Angola
100	J1	**Cabinet Gorge Dam** Idaho U.S.A.
100	J1	**Cabinet Mts** Idaho U.S.A.
71	E8	**Cabingan** *isld* Philippines
99	P3	**Cable** Wisconsin U.S.A.
113	L9	**Cable Beach** New Providence I Bahamas
133	D7	**Cabo Blanco** Argentina
17	F8	**Cabo de Gata,Sierra del** Spain
88	G8	**Cabo Delgado** *dist* Mozambique
130	G8	**Cabo Frio** Brazil
121	O5	**Cabonga, Rés** Quebec Canada
110	D4	**Cabool** Missouri U.S.A.
141	L7	**Caboolture** Queensland Australia
88	D9	**Cabora Bassa Dam** Mozambique
133	D6	**Cabo Raso** Argentina
113	H7	**Cabo Rojo** Puerto Rico
110	E6	**Cabot** Arkansas U.S.A.
120	J7	**Cabot Head** *C* Ontario Canada
123	M6	**Cabot Str** Nfld/Nova Scotia Canada
21	K3	**Cabourg** France
85	A8	**Cabo Verde, Ilhas do** *islds* Atlantic Oc
71	E4	**Cabra** *isld* Philippines
16	E7	**Cabra del Santo Cristo** Spain
69	A9	**Cabra I** Nicobar Is
127	J5	**Cabral** Dominican Rep
130	G5	**Cabral,Serra do** *mts* Brazil
43	B9	**Cabras** Sardinia
19	P15	**Cabre, Col de** *pass* France
16	B3	**Cabreira** *mt* Portugal
17	J5	**Cabrera** *isld* Balearic Is
127	K5	**Cabrera** Dominican Rep
16	C2	**Cabrera** *R* Spain
126	F4	**Cabreras** *R* Cuba
16	C2	**Cabrera,Sierra** *mt* Spain
118	J8	**Cabri** Saskatchewan Canada
17	F5	**Cabriel** *R* Spain
19	O18	**Cabriès** France
102	G9	**Cabrillo Nat Mon** California U.S.A.
127	M4	**Cabrits, I** Martinique W Indies
130	G10	**Cabrobó** Brazil
128	E2	**Cabruta** Venezuela
71	E7	**Cabucan** *isld* Philippines
71	E2	**Cabugao** Luzon Philippines
71	E5	**Cabulauan** *isld* Philippines
124	E2	**Cabullona** Mexico
71	G8	**Caburan** Mindanao Philippines
128	E1	**Cabure** Venezuela
71	F1	**Cabutunan Pt** Luzon Philippines
133	G3	**Caçador** Brazil
46	D1	**Čačak** Serbia Yugoslavia
122	F3	**Cacaoui L** Quebec Canada
130	F8	**Cacapava** Brazil
133	G4	**Caçapava do Sul** Brazil
94	J7	**Cacapon** *R* West Virginia U.S.A.
68	H2	**Cac Ba** *isld* Vietnam
43	B8	**Caccia,C** Sardinia
133	G3	**Cacequi** Brazil
129	G7	**Cáceraes** Brazil
130	B5	**Cáceres** Brazil
16	C5	**Cáceres** *prov* Spain
16	C5	**Cáceres** Spain
110	E6	**Cache** *R* Arkansas U.S.A.
110	G4	**Cache** *R* Illinois U.S.A.
107	M7	**Cache** Oklahoma U.S.A.
120	K6	**Cache Bay** Ontario Canada
102	B3	**Cache Cr** California U.S.A.
85	A6	**Cacheu** Guinea-Bissau
129	G5	**Cachimbo, Serra do** *mts* Brazil
133	D2	**Cachinal** Chile
87	C8	**Cachingues** Angola
129	L6	**Cachoeira** Brazil
130	E6	**Cachoeira Alta** Brazil
130	E5	**Cachoeira de Goiás** Brazil
131	H3	**Cachoeira do Sul** Brazil
130	F8	**Cachoeira Paulista** Brazil
130	H7	**Cachoeiro de Itapemirim** Brazil
102	E7	**Cachuma, L** California U.S.A.
16	E7	**Cacín** *R* Spain
42	H3	**Cačinci** Croatia
71	D5	**Cacnipa** *isld* Philippines
87	C8	**Cacolo** Angola
87	C8	**Caconda** Angola
86	B7	**Cacongo** Angola
122	C6	**Cacouna** Quebec Canada
103	M8	**Cactus** Arizona U.S.A.
109	H8	**Cactus** Texas U.S.A.
118	H6	**Cactus Lake** Saskatchewan Canada
102	H4	**Cactus Ra** Nevada U.S.A.
130	D6	**Caçu** Brazil
87	B9	**Caculavar** *R* Angola
129	K6	**Caculé** Brazil
130	D5	**Caçununga** Brazil
86	J5	**Cadale** Somalia
31	L6	**Čadca** Czechoslovakia
111	C7	**Caddo** *R* Arkansas U.S.A.
107	O7	**Caddo** Oklahoma U.S.A.
109	J3	**Caddo** Texas U.S.A.
111	B9	**Caddo L** Texas U.S.A.
109	L2	**Caddo Mills** Texas U.S.A.
45	J2	**Cadelbosco di Sopra** Italy
111	F12	**Cade,L.de** Louisiana U.S.A.
140	C1	**Cadell** *R* N Terr Australia
141	F5	**Cadell** *R* Queensland Australia
128	D6	**Cadena del Pantiacolla** Peru
32	K5	**Cadenberge** Germany
19	O17	**Cadenet** France
125	K5	**Cadereyta** Mexico
8	C2	**Cader Idris** *mt* Wales
112	H4	**Cades** South Carolina U.S.A.
138	D3	**Cadibarrawirracanna,L** South Australia Australia
19	P18	**Cadière-d'Azur** France
71	F3	**Cadig Mts** Philippines
121	M4	**Cadillac** Quebec Canada
118	K9	**Cadillac** Saskatchewan Canada
18	E8	**Cadillac** France
94	B2	**Cadillac** Michigan U.S.A.
18	G10	**Cadi, Sierra del** *mts* Spain
71	F5	**Cadiz** Negros Philippines
16	C8	**Cádiz** Spain
16	D8	**Cádiz** *prov* Spain
103	J7	**Cadiz** California U.S.A.

162
Cadiz — Capoeiras, Cachoeira das

110 J5 Cadiz Kentucky U.S.A.
94 G6 Cadiz Ohio U.S.A.
16 C8 Cádiz, B. de Spain
103 J7 Cadiz L California U.S.A.
118 G6 Cadogan Alberta Canada
117 P9 Cadomin Alberta Canada
38 F9 Cadore reg Italy
99 P5 Cadott Wisconsin U.S.A.
117 P7 Cadotte R Alberta Canada
143 B9 Cadoux W Australia Australia
8 C5 Cadoxton Wales
41 N6 Cadria,Monte Italy
45 L1 Ca Emo Italy
21 K3 Caen France
13 H6 Caenby Corner England
8 C1 Caergwrle Wales
Caergybi see Holyhead
8 D4 Caerleon Wales
8 B1 Caernarfon Wales
8 B1 Caernarfon B Wales
Caernarvon co see Gwynedd
8 C4 Caerphilly Wales
8 C3 Caersws Wales
8 D4 Caerwent Wales
80 C3 Caesarea Israel
80 F1 Caesarea Philippi Syria
112 E2 Caesars Head South Carolina U.S.A.
130 G6 Caete Brazil
129 K6 Caetite Brazil
130 E7 Cafelândia Brazil
83 K14 Cafres,Pl.des Réunion Indian Oc
129 G3 Cafuini R Brazil
71 E1 Cagayan R Luzon Philippines
71 G6 Cagayan de Oro Mindanao Philippines
71 E6 Cagayan Is Philippines
47 J5 Çağiş Turkey
42 E5 Cagli Italy
43 C9 Cagliari Sardinia
43 C9 Cagliari,G.di Sardinia
44 B4 Cagnes France
71 F4 Cagraray isld Philippines
127 L5 Caguas Puerto Rico
111 J9 Cahaba R Alabama U.S.A.
21 J3 Cahagnes France
14 B5 Caha Mts Ireland
14 D4 Caher Ireland
14 A5 Cahirsiveen Ireland
14 E4 Cahore Pt Ireland
18 G8 Cahors France
87 G9 Caia Mozambique
129 G6 Caiabis, Serra dos Brazil
87 D8 Caianda Angola
45 Q7 Caianello Italy
129 H7 Caiapó R Brazil
130 D5 Caiapônia Brazil
130 D5 Caiapo, Serra do mts Brazil
45 Q7 Caiazzo Italy
126 E3 Caibarién Cuba
68 H7 Cai Be Vietnam
130 J9 Caicará Brazil
128 E2 Caicara Bolívar Venezuela
128 F2 Caicara Monagas Venezuela
129 L5 Caico Brazil
127 H4 Caicos Is W Indies
Caidian see Hanyang
143 F9 Caiguna W Australia Australia
21 J8 Caillère, la France
122 E1 Cailleteau,L Quebec Canada
128 D7 Cailloma Peru
111 E12 Caillou B Louisiana U.S.A.
126 G5 Caimanera Cuba
71 D3 Caiman Pt Luzon Philippines
109 J5 Cain City Texas U.S.A.
87 B9 Cainde Angola
133 D1 Caine R Bolivia
122 G7 Cains R New Brunswick Canada
99 N9 Cainsville Missouri U.S.A.
69 G8 Cai Nuoc Vietnam
45 P6 Caira, M mt Italy
146 F6 Caird Coast Antarctica
12 C1 Cairnbaan Scotland
94 J6 Cairnbrook Pennsylvania U.S.A.
139 G6 Cairn Curran Dam Victoria Australia
15 E3 Cairn Gorm mt Scotland
116 K6 Cairn Mt Alaska U.S.A.
12 C4 Cairnryan Scotland
141 H3 Cairns Queensland Australia
15 E3 Cairn Toul mt Scotland
79 B8 Cairo Egypt
44 D3 Cairo Italy
113 C7 Cairo Georgia U.S.A.
110 G4 Cairo Illinois U.S.A.
110 D2 Cairo Missouri U.S.A.
98 H8 Cairo Nebraska U.S.A.
95 N4 Cairo New York U.S.A.
94 C6 Cairo Ohio U.S.A.
94 F7 Cairo West Virginia U.S.A.
67 A3 Caishentang China
67 F1 Caishi China
9 H2 Caister England
13 H6 Caistor England
15 E2 Caithness dist Scotland
87 B8 Caitou Angola
87 C9 Caiundo Angola
48 K4 Căiuţi Romania
45 Q8 Caivano Italy
141 G8 Caiwarro Queensland Australia
22 D4 Caix France
Caiyuanzhen see Shengsi
67 F1 Caizi Hu China
128 C5 Cajamarca dept Peru
128 C5 Cajamarca Peru
18 G8 Cajarc France
130 H9 Cajàzeiras Brazil
48 F7 Čajetina Serbia Yugoslavia
71 F4 Cajidiocan Philippines
48 E7 Čajniče Bosnia-Herzegovina
130 F7 Cajuru Brazil
47 L8 Çakırlar Turkey
47 N11 Çakmakmlar Turkey
47 K6 Çal Turkey
16 C7 Cala Spain
85 F7 Calabar Nigeria
121 O7 Calabogie Ontario Canada
127 L10 Calabozo Venezuela
43 G9 Calabria prov Italy
71 D5 Calabugdong Philippines
16 D8 Calaburras, Pta. de Spain
128 E7 Calacoto Bolivia
46 F1 Calafat Romania
133 C8 Calafate Argentina
71 F5 Calagnaan isld Philippines
71 F3 Calagua islds Philippines
17 F2 Calahorra Spain
122 E8 Calais New Brunswick Canada
22 B2 Calais France
95 T8 Calais Maine U.S.A.
Calais,Pas de see Dover,Str.of
128 F5 Calama Brazil
133 D2 Calama Chile
126 G9 Calamar Colombia
71 D4 Calamian Group islds Philippines
99 Q7 Calamine Wisconsin U.S.A.
22 L2 Calamine,la Belgium
48 H5 Călan Romania
128 F4 Calanaque Brazil
17 G4 Calanda Spain
41 K4 Calanda mt Switzerland
71 E5 Calandagan isld Philippines
87 C7 Calandula Angola
69 B10 Calang Sumatra
20 D5 Calanhel France
84 G4 Calanscio Sand Sea Libya
71 E4 Calapan Philippines
100 C5 Calapooia R Oregon U.S.A.
48 K6 Călăraşi reg Romania
48 L6 Călăraşi Romania
20 D5 Calarhel France
43 B9 Calasetta Sardinia
17 F6 Calasparra Spain
43 E11 Calatafimi Sicily
17 F3 Calatayud Spain
48 H4 Călăţele Romania
33 T9 Calau Germany
71 F4 Calauag Philippines
43 F10 Calavà, C Sicily
102 C4 Calaveras Res California U.S.A.
71 E4 Calavite,Cape Philippines
71 E1 Calayan isld Luzon Philippines
71 G4 Calbayog Philippines
33 P9 Calbe Germany
71 G5 Calbiga Samar Philippines
131 A8 Calbuco pk Chile
129 L5 Calcanhar, Pta. do C Brazil
111 C12 Calcasieu L Louisiana U.S.A.
128 B4 Calceta Ecuador
133 E3 Calchaqui Argentina
45 J4 Calci Italy
45 J1 Calcinato Italy
129 H3 Calcoene Brazil
75 N7 Calcutta India
48 J6 Căldăraru Romania
128 C2 Caldas div Colombia
16 A5 Caldas da Rainha Portugal
17 J3 Caldas de Montbuy Spain
16 B2 Caldas de Reyes Spain
16 B3 Caldas do Gerês Portugal
130 E5 Caldas Novas Brazil
13 E4 Caldbeck England
88 G10 Caldeira isld Mozambique
32 K10 Calden Germany
117 G7 Calder Alaska U.S.A.
100 J2 Calder Idaho U.S.A.
133 C3 Caldera Chile
125 M5 Caldera Costa Rica
45 K2 Calderara di Reno Italy
12 E2 Caldercruix Scotland
16 E5 Calderina mt Spain
141 H7 Caldervale Queensland Australia
8 D4 Caldicot Wales
100 J6 Caldwell Idaho U.S.A.
107 N4 Caldwell Kansas U.S.A.
94 F7 Caldwell Ohio U.S.A.
109 L5 Caldwell Texas U.S.A.
8 B4 Caldy I Wales
89 E8 Caledon R S Africa
89 A10 Caledon S Africa
122 G9 Caledonia Nova Scotia Canada
94 B4 Caledonia Michigan U.S.A.
99 P6 Caledonia Minnesota U.S.A.
94 K4 Caledonia New York U.S.A.
94 E6 Caledonia Ohio U.S.A.
15 D3 Caledonian Canal Scotland
140 D2 Caledon,Mt N Terr Australia
17 J3 Calella Spain
141 J5 Calen Queensland Australia
124 G3 Calera Mexico
111 K8 Calera Alabama U.S.A.
124 H6 Calera Victor Rosales Mexico
128 D7 Caleta Buena Chile
133 D8 Caleta Coig est Argentina
133 D7 Caleta Olivia Argentina
131 B8 Caleufu R Argentina
103 J9 Calexico California U.S.A.
12 D5 Calf of Man isld I of Man U.K.
118 C7 Calgary Alberta Canada
106 F2 Calhan Colorado U.S.A.
111 M7 Calhoun Georgia U.S.A.
110 J4 Calhoun Kentucky U.S.A.
111 G8 Calhoun City Mississippi U.S.A.
112 E3 Calhoun Falls South Carolina U.S.A.
128 C3 Cali Colombia
47 K4 Çalı Turkey
71 G5 Calicoan isld Samar Philippines
110 D5 Calico Rock Arkansas U.S.A.
68 A7 Calicut Andaman Is
76 B5 Calicut India
102 F6 Caliente California U.S.A.
103 K4 Caliente Nevada U.S.A.
127 O2 California Trinidad
102 C1 California state U.S.A.
110 D3 California Missouri U.S.A.
94 H6 California Pennsylvania U.S.A.
124 D4 California,G.de Mexico
102 F6 California Hot Springs California U.S.A.
48 J5 Călimăneşti Romania
48 J3 Călimani, Muntii mts Romania
76 D5 Calimere,Pt India
133 D4 Calingasta Argentina
143 B9 Calingiri W Australia Australia
Calino isld see Kálimnos isld
111 D8 Calion Arkansas U.S.A.
103 J8 Calipatria California U.S.A.
100 H1 Calispell Peak Washington U.S.A.
71 E5 Calis Pt Philippines
102 B3 Calistoga California U.S.A.
87 D12 Calitzdorp S Africa
71 E4 Calivite Passage Philippines
109 O5 Call Texas U.S.A.
138 F3 Callabonna R South Australia Australia
113 F7 Callahan Florida U.S.A.
14 D4 Callan Ireland
121 L6 Callander Ontario Canada
12 D1 Callander Scotland
71 E2 Callang Luzon Philippines
25 C3 Callantsoog Netherlands
128 C6 Callao Peru
99 O10 Callao Missouri U.S.A.
103 L2 Callao Utah U.S.A.
95 L9 Callao Virginia U.S.A.
142 D5 Callawa W Australia Australia
98 G8 Callaway Nebraska U.S.A.
43 B12 Calle, la Algeria
125 K6 Calles Mexico
141 K6 Callide Queensland Australia
109 J7 Calliham Texas U.S.A.
118 D3 Calling L Alberta Canada
118 E3 Calling River Alberta Canada
8 B7 Callington England
141 K6 Calliope Queensland Australia
117 H6 Callison Ranch British Columbia Canada
17 G6 Callosa de Ensarriá Spain
143 B7 Callytharra Springs W Australia Australia
118 D5 Calmar Alberta Canada
99 P6 Calmar Iowa U.S.A.
36 F6 Calmbach Germany
118 L2 Calm L Ontario Canada
9 E5 Calne England
71 G4 Calolbon Philippines
71 F6 Calolot Mindanao Philippines
113 F11 Caloosahatchee R Florida U.S.A.
43 G8 Calore R Italy
141 L7 Caloundra Queensland Australia
17 H6 Calpe Spain
101 P7 Calpet Wyoming U.S.A.
79 A2 Çalpınar Turkey
102 D2 Calpine California U.S.A.
125 K8 Calpulálpam Mexico
120 F3 Calstock Ontario Canada
43 F11 Caltagirone Sicily
43 F11 Caltanissetta Sicily
47 K7 Çaltepe mt Turkey
87 C7 Caluango Angola
87 C8 Calucinga Angola
87 B8 Calulo Angola
121 Q7 Calumet Quebec Canada
99 S2 Calumet Michigan U.S.A.
107 M6 Calumet Oklahoma U.S.A.
87 B8 Caluquembe Angola
71 E6 Calusa isld Philippines
40 G7 Caluso Italy
86 B1 Caluula Somalia
71 E5 Caluya isld Philippines
103 O8 Calva Arizona U.S.A.
18 E3 Calvados dept France
45 K4 Calvana,Monte Della Italy
9 E1 Calver England
140 D3 Calvert R N Terr Australia
111 H10 Calvert Alabama U.S.A.
109 L5 Calvert Texas U.S.A.
110 H4 Calvert City Kentucky U.S.A.
140 D3 Calvert Hills N Terr Australia
117 J10 Calvert I British Columbia Canada
94 K8 Calverton Virginia U.S.A.
143 E6 Calvert Ra W Australia Australia
124 H7 Calvillo Mexico
119 T10 Calvin North Dakota U.S.A.
107 O7 Calvin Oklahoma U.S.A.
89 A8 Calvinia S Africa
45 Q7 Calvi Risorta Italy
45 J1 Calvisano Italy
16 D4 Calvitero mt Spain
33 O8 Calvörde Germany
36 F6 Calw-Hirsau Germany
112 J2 Calypso North Carolina U.S.A.
87 C7 Camabatela Angola
129 L7 Camacá Brazil
87 B8 Camacaio Angola
124 H5 Camache Mexico
121 O5 Camachigama,L Quebec Canada
87 C8 Camacupa Angola
127 L10 Camaguán Venezuela
126 F4 Camagüey Cuba
126 E3 Camagüey, Arch. de islds Cuba
69 E10 Camah, Gunung Malaysia
128 G5 Camaitu R Brazil
126 E3 Camajuani Cuba
128 D7 Camaña Peru
71 G5 Camandag Samar Philippines
100 C1 Camano I Washington U.S.A.
87 D8 Camanongue Angola
130 C6 Camapuã Mato Grosso Brazil
133 G4 Camaquã Rio Grande do Sul Brazil
131 H3 Camaquã,R Brazil
128 F4 Camara Brazil
128 G6 Camarare R Brazil
17 H3 Camarasa,Embalse de Spain
18 G9 Camarès France
19 N16 Camaret France
20 A5 Camaret Finistère France
107 L5 Camargo Oklahoma U.S.A.
19 N17 Camargue, La reg France
102 E7 Camarillo California U.S.A.
16 A1 Camariñas Spain
124 F6 Camaronero, L. del Mexico
133 D6 Camarones Argentina
101 N5 Camas Idaho U.S.A.
100 C4 Camas Washington U.S.A.
101 L6 Camas Cr Idaho U.S.A.
100 B6 Camas Valley Oregon U.S.A.
Ca Mau, Pte De see Mui Bai Bung
87 C7 Camaxilo Angola
16 B2 Cambados Spain
142 E4 Camballin W Australia Australia
130 B5 Cambara Brazil
Cambay, G. of see Khambhat, G. of
8 B6 Cambeak England
21 H3 Cambe, la France
36 E3 Camberg Germany
20 H3 Cambernon France
68 F6 Cambodia rep S E Asia
13 G3 Cambois England
18 E9 Cambo les B France
130 E10 Camboriú Brazil
8 A7 Camborne England
22 E3 Cambrai France
16 B1 Cambre Spain
21 L3 Cambremer France
102 C6 Cambria California U.S.A.
99 R6 Cambria Wisconsin U.S.A.
7 H10 Cambrian Mts Wales
144 B6 Cambrians New Zealand
120 K9 Cambridge Ontario Canada
9 G3 Cambridge England
127 J2 Cambridge Jamaica
145 E2 Cambridge New Zealand
100 J5 Cambridge Idaho U.S.A.
99 Q8 Cambridge Illinois U.S.A.
99 N8 Cambridge Iowa U.S.A.
107 O4 Cambridge Kansas U.S.A.
95 L8 Cambridge Maryland U.S.A.
95 Q4 Cambridge Massachusetts U.S.A.
99 N4 Cambridge Minnesota U.S.A.
98 F9 Cambridge Nebraska U.S.A.
95 O3 Cambridge New York U.S.A.
94 F6 Cambridge Ohio U.S.A.
Cambridge and I of Ely co see Cambridgeshire
114 J4 Cambridge Bay Northwest Territories Canada
142 G2 Cambridge G W Australia Australia
9 F3 Cambridgeshire co England
94 G5 Cambridge Springs Pennsylvania U.S.A.
17 H3 Cambrils Spain
22 D3 Cambrin France
21 O1 Cambron France
87 C8 Cambundi-Catembo Angola
130 F7 Cambuquira Brazil
37 M1 Camburg Germany
12 D2 Cambuslang Scotland
139 K5 Camden New South Wales Australia
111 J10 Camden Alabama U.S.A.
111 D8 Camden Arkansas U.S.A.
95 M7 Camden Delaware U.S.A.
95 S2 Camden Maine U.S.A.
94 C5 Camden Michigan U.S.A.
95 N7 Camden New Jersey U.S.A.
95 M3 Camden New York U.S.A.
112 G3 Camden South Carolina U.S.A.
110 H5 Camden Tennessee U.S.A.
111 B11 Camden Texas U.S.A.
116 P1 Camden B Alaska U.S.A.
94 G8 Camden on Gauley West Virginia U.S.A.
142 E3 Camden Sd W Australia Australia
110 D3 Camdenton Missouri U.S.A.
87 D8 Cameia,Parque Nacional da Angola
8 B6 Camelford England
8 B7 Camel,R England
87 B7 Camembe Angola
21 L4 Camembert France
45 O4 Camerano Italy
45 O4 Camerata Picena Italy
42 E5 Camerino Italy
103 N6 Cameron Arizona U.S.A.
99 Q9 Cameron Illinois U.S.A.
111 C12 Cameron Louisiana U.S.A.
110 B2 Cameron Missouri U.S.A.
101 O4 Cameron Montana U.S.A.
106 G7 Cameron New Mexico U.S.A.
95 K4 Cameron New York U.S.A.
112 H2 Cameron North Carolina U.S.A.
94 J5 Cameron Pennsylvania U.S.A.
109 L5 Cameron Texas U.S.A.
94 G7 Cameron West Virginia U.S.A.
99 P4 Cameron Wisconsin U.S.A.
88 C6 Cameron B Zambia
141 F8 Cameron Corner Queensland Australia
141 G5 Cameron Downs Queensland Australia
120 B3 Cameron Falls Ontario Canada
69 E10 Cameron Highlands Malaysia
117 O6 Cameron Hills Alberta Canada
114 J2 Cameron I Northwest Territories Canada
144 A7 Cameron Mts New Zealand
86 B4 Cameroon rep Africa
85 F8 Cameroun, Mt Cameroon
129 J4 Cameta Brazil
140 B3 Camfield N Terr Australia
140 B3 Camfield R N Terr Australia
71 G6 Camiguin isld Philippines
71 E1 Camiguin isld Luzon Philippines
71 E3 Camiling Luzon Philippines
111 M10 Camilla Georgia U.S.A.
133 D1 Camiña Chile
16 B3 Caminha Portugal
102 D3 Camino California U.S.A.
129 J4 Camiranga Brazil
133 E2 Camiri Bolivia
128 D6 Camisea R Peru
87 D7 Camissombo Angola
117 R4 Camlaren Northwest Territories Canada
79 E1 Camlıyayla Turkey
95 K5 Cammal Pennsylvania U.S.A.
43 F11 Cammarata, Monte mt Sicily
33 R8 Cammer Germany
124 E4 Camoa Mexico
125 M3 Camoapa Nicaragua
129 K4 Camocim Brazil
41 K5 Camoghe mt Switzerland
44 F3 Camogli Italy
41 M6 Camonica,Val Italy
140 E4 Camooweal Queensland Australia
129 H3 Camopi Fr Guiana
20 E6 Camors France
69 A8 Camorta Nicobar Is
71 G5 Camotes Islands Philippines
71 G5 Camotes Sea Philippines
124 G8 Camotlán de Miraflores Mexico
41 M6 Camowiche,Alpi mt Italy
42 E7 Campagna reg Italy
45 M1 Campagna Lupia Italy
45 M5 Campagnano di Roma Italy
22 B3 Campagne-lès-Hesdin France
125 L2 Campamento Honduras
133 F4 Campana Argentina
124 H4 Campana Mexico
133 B7 Campana, I Chile
130 C8 Campanario Mato Grosso Brazil
130 H6 Campanário Minas Gerais Brazil
133 C5 Campanario mt Chile/Arg
16 D6 Campanario Spain
45 Q8 Campanella, Pta C Italy
130 F7 Campanha Brazil
45 R7 Campania reg Italy
117 J9 Campania I British Columbia Canada
141 H5 Campaspe R Queensland Australia
102 C2 Camp Beale California U.S.A.
141 J6 Campbell R Queensland Australia
102 C4 Campbell California U.S.A.
110 F5 Campbell Missouri U.S.A.
98 H9 Campbell Nebraska U.S.A.
95 K4 Campbell New York U.S.A.
94 G5 Campbell Ohio U.S.A.
145 E4 Campbell, C New Zealand
121 N8 Campbellford Ontario Canada
68 D7 Campbell I Burma
102 R12 Campbell Industrial Pk Hawaiian Is
146 A16 Campbell Island N Z Base Antarctica
117 J9 Campbell Island British Columbia Canada
140 B5 Campbell, Mt N Terr Australia
117 D3 Campbell, Mt Yukon Territory Canada
74 E2 Campbellpore Pakistan
142 G2 Campbell Ra W Australia Australia
117 L10 Campbell River British Columbia Canada
121 O7 Campbell's Bay Quebec Canada
99 S6 Campbellsport Wisconsin U.S.A.
110 L4 Campbellsville Kentucky U.S.A.
122 F6 Campbellton New Brunswick Canada
123 S4 Campbellton Newfoundland Canada
109 J7 Campbellton Texas U.S.A.
139 K5 Campbelltown New South Wales Australia
139 J8 Campbell Town Tasmania Australia
12 C3 Campbeltown Scotland
20 G7 Campbon France
98 C4 Camp Crook South Dakota U.S.A.
99 Q6 Camp Douglas Wisconsin U.S.A.
21 O2 Campeaux France
125 O8 Campeche Mexico
90 A6 Campeche Bank Atlantic Oc
125 N8 Campeche, B.de Mexico
126 F4 Campechuela Cuba
20 F6 Campénéac France
139 G7 Camperdown Victoria Australia
113 L9 Camperdown New Providence I Bahamas
119 R7 Camperville Manitoba Canada
141 K2 Camphill dist Brisbane, Qnsld Australia
111 L9 Camp Hill Alabama U.S.A.
45 K4 Campi Bisenzio Italy
45 Q8 Campi Flegrei Italy
16 D6 Campillo de Llerena Spain
16 D7 Campillos Spain
130 H9 Campina Grande Brazil
130 F8 Campinas Brazil
130 E6 Campina Verde Brazil
102 F5 Camp Nelson California U.S.A.
86 A5 Campo Cameroon
18 F10 Campo Spain
106 H4 Campo Colorado U.S.A.
43 F7 Campobasso Italy
122 F9 Campobello I New Brunswick Canada
130 F7 Campo Belo Brazil
130 E10 Campo Belo do Sul Brazil
45 L1 Campodarsego Italy
16 E6 Campo de Calatrava physical reg Spain
16 E5 Campo de Criptana Spain
129 H6 Campo de Diauarum Brazil
126 G9 Campo de la Cruz Colombia
130 D10 Campo Erê Brazil
130 E6 Campo Florido Brazil
129 K6 Campo Formoso Brazil
45 J2 Campogalliano Italy
133 E3 Campo Gallo Argentina
133 G2 Campo Grande Brazil
130 C7 Campo Grande Mato Grosso Brazil
130 B9 Campo Grande airport Paraguay
130 E9 Campo Largo Brazil
45 L1 Campolongo Maggiore Italy
129 K4 Campo Maior Brazil
130 D9 Campo Mourão Brazil
130 D10 Campo Novo Brazil
45 H3 Camporgiano Italy
130 H7 Campos Brazil
130 F6 Campos Altos Brazil
45 K2 Camposanto Italy
45 R7 Camposauro mt Italy
130 D10 Campos de Palmas plains Brazil
130 F8 Campos do Jordão Brazil
130 D9 Campos Eré Brazil
133 G3 Campos Novos Brazil
41 J5 Campo Tencia mt Switzerland
128 E3 Campo Troco Colombia
42 D2 Campo Tures Italy
99 P9 Camp Point Illinois U.S.A.
102 D6 Camp Roberts California U.S.A.
109 H5 Camp San Saba Texas U.S.A.
12 D1 Campsie Fells Scotland
111 C10 Campti Louisiana U.S.A.
94 D9 Campton Kentucky U.S.A.
95 Q3 Campton New Hampshire U.S.A.
102 C2 Camptonville California U.S.A.
103 N7 Camp Verde Arizona U.S.A.
68 J7 Cam Ranh Vietnam
118 E5 Camrose Alberta Canada
45 L1 Camsano Vicentino Italy
117 M4 Camsell Range Northwest Territories Canada
45 K3 Camugnano Italy
47 J4 Çan Turkey
122 G7 Canaan New Brunswick Canada
127 M2 Canaan Tobago
95 O4 Canaan Connecticut U.S.A.
121 T8 Canaan Vermont U.S.A.
103 N4 Canaan Pk Utah U.S.A.
122 G8 Canaan R New Brunswick Canada
129 J6 Cana Brava R Brazil
130 F5 Canabrava Brazil
71 C6 Canabungan isld Philippines
114 Canada dominion N America
123 Q3 Canada B Newfoundland Canada
131 E4 Canãda de Gómez Argentina
95 R8 Canada Falls Maine U.S.A.
95 M5 Canadensis Pennsylvania U.S.A.
106 F5 Canadian R New Mexico U.S.A.
108 D8 Canadian R Texas U.S.A.
108 D8 Canadian Texas U.S.A.
133 D8 Cañadón de las Vacas Argentina
133 D6 Cañadón Grande, Sa ra Argentina
112 G4 Canadys South Carolina U.S.A.
42 G4 Čanak Croatia
47 N10 Çanak R Turkey
47 H4 Canakkale Turkey
47 H4 Çanakkale Boğazi str Turkey
43 B11 Canal de la Galite str Tunisia
127 H5 Canal de St. Marc Haiti
129 H3 Canal do Norte Brazil
129 J4 Canal do Sul Brazil
117 Q10 Canal Flats British Columbia Canada
110 G5 Canalou Missouri U.S.A.
113 G11 Canal Point Florida U.S.A.
94 E7 Canal Winchester Ohio U.S.A.
128 D5 Canama Brazil
95 K4 Canandaigua L New York U.S.A.
124 D2 Cananea Mexico
130 F9 Cananéia Brazil
128 E3 Canapiari,Co mt Colombia
21 P1 Canaples France
130 E6 Canápolis Brazil
128 C4 Cañar prov Ecuador
126 C4 Canarreos,Arch.de los Cuba
90 F6 Canary Basin Atlantic Oc
85 A3 Canary Is Atlantic Oc
94 K4 Canaseraga New York U.S.A.
130 E4 Canastra, Serra da mts Goiás Brazil
130 F7 Canastra, Serra da mts Minas Gerais Brazil
124 G5 Canatlán Mexico
44 B1 Canave Italy
16 C5 Cañaveral Spain
113 G9 Canaveral, C Florida U.S.A.
113 G9 Canaveral National Seashore Florida U.S.A.
17 F4 Cañaveras Spain
129 L7 Canavieiras Brazil
38 E9 Canazei Italy
139 H4 Canbelego New South Wales Australia
139 J6 Canberra Aust Capital Terr Australia
138 A6 Canberra & Environs Australia
100 E8 Canby California U.S.A.
98 K5 Canby Minnesota U.S.A.
100 C4 Canby Oregon U.S.A.
20 G4 Cancale France
41 M4 Cancano, Lago di Italy
45 Q8 Cancello Italy
45 Q7 Cancello ed Arnone Italy
22 B3 Canche R France
21 O1 Canchy France
18 F8 Cancon France
125 Q7 Cancún Mexico
45 K3 Canda, M mt Italy
47 H6 Çandarlı Turkey
47 H6 Çandarlı Körfezi G Turkey
21 P1 Candas France
21 H6 Candé France
16 B5 Candeeiros,Sa.de Portugal
128 F5 Candeias R Brazil
130 F7 Candeias Brazil
43 G7 Candela Italy
45 N4 Candelara Italy
130 C10 Candelaria Argentina
124 F2 Candelaria Mexico
108 C5 Candelaria Texas U.S.A.
139 J6 Candelo New South Wales Australia
Candia see Iráklion
119 O8 Candiac Saskatchewan Canada
45 L1 Candiana Italy
130 D9 Cândido de Abreu Brazil
130 E8 Cândido Mota Brazil
116 F4 Candle Alaska U.S.A.
119 M5 Candle L Saskatchewan Canada
146 G2 Candlemas I S Sandwich Is S Atlantic Oc
95 O5 Candlewood,L Connecticut U.S.A.
118 J6 Cando Saskatchewan Canada
98 G1 Cando North Dakota U.S.A.
133 G3 Candói Brazil
143 B6 Candolle, Mt W Australia Australia
71 E2 Candon Luzon Philippines
95 L4 Candor New York U.S.A.
112 H2 Candor North Carolina U.S.A.
120 K5 Cane Ontario Canada
Canea see Khaniá
94 J4 Caneadea New York U.S.A.
129 J6 Canéia Brazil
133 G3 Canela Brazil
133 F4 Canelones Uruguay
130 C9 Canendiyu dept Paraguay
133 C5 Cañete Chile
128 C6 Cañete R Peru
17 F4 Cañete Spain
107 P4 Caney Kansas U.S.A.
107 O7 Caney Oklahoma U.S.A.
110 L6 Caney Fork R Tennessee U.S.A.
110 K4 Caneyville Kentucky U.S.A.
111 C8 Canfield Arkansas U.S.A.
94 G5 Canfield Ohio U.S.A.
18 E10 Canfranc Spain
87 C8 Cangamba Angola
87 C7 Cangandala Angola
16 C1 Cangas de Narcea Spain
16 D1 Cangas de Onís Spain
21 N7 Cangey France
69 E9 Canglun Malaysia
87 C8 Cangoa Angola
89 B9 Cango Caves S Africa
87 D8 Cangombe Angola
59 H1 Cangshan China
65 D7 Cangshan China
130 J9 Canguaretama Brazil
133 G4 Canguçu Brazil
131 H3 Canguçu,Sa.do mt Brazil
87 C8 Cangumbe Angola
67 D5 Cangwu China
67 B1 Cangxi China
65 C5 Cang Xian China
68 D1 Cangyuan China
65 C5 Cangzhou China
130 H10 Canhotinho Brazil
115 N6 Caniapiscau R Quebec Canada
115 N7 Caniapiscau,Lac Quebec Canada
121 N3 Canica I Quebec Canada
43 F11 Canicatti Sicily
71 G5 Canigao Ch Philippines
18 G10 Canigou mt France
17 F7 Caniles Spain
117 N10 Canim L British Columbia Canada
129 K5 Caninde R Brazil
71 E5 Canipo isld Philippines
15 C2 Canisp Mt Scotland
94 K4 Canisteo New York U.S.A.
95 K4 Canisteo R New York U.S.A.
21 H3 Canisy France
124 H6 Cañitas Mexico
17 F7 Canjáyar Spain
78 D1 Çankırı Turkey
71 E3 Canlubang Luzon Philippines
118 B7 Canmore Alberta Canada
143 B8 Canna W Australia Australia
15 B3 Canna isld Scotland
76 B5 Cannanore India
110 K4 Cannelton Indiana U.S.A.
41 J5 Cannero Riviera Italy
44 B4 Cannes France
45 J1 Canneto s. Oglio Italy
122 H8 Canning Nova Scotia Canada
116 O2 Canning R Alaska U.S.A.
98 G5 Canning South Dakota U.S.A.
143 C8 Canning Hill W Australia Australia
142 B2 Canning River W Australia Australia
142 B2 Cannington dist Perth, W Aust Australia
121 L8 Cannington Ontario Canada
142 B2 Canning Vale W Australia Australia
41 J5 Cannobio Italy
99 O5 Cannon R Minnesota U.S.A.
98 E3 Cannonball R North Dakota U.S.A.
98 F3 Cannon Ball North Dakota U.S.A.
99 O5 Cannon Falls Minnesota U.S.A.
139 J7 Cann R Victoria Australia
133 G3 Canoas Brazil
130 D10 Canõas, R. das Brazil
140 F4 Canobie Queensland Australia
130 F6 Canoeiros Brazil
118 J3 Canoe L Saskatchewan Canada
117 O9 Canoe R British Columbia Canada
130 E10 Canoinhas Brazil
15 F5 Canonbie Scotland
106 E3 Canon City Colorado U.S.A.
106 C5 Cañon Largo R New Mexico U.S.A.
94 G6 Canonsburg Pennsylvania U.S.A.
112 F6 Canoochia R Georgia U.S.A.
138 F5 Canopus South Australia Australia
119 P7 Canora Saskatchewan Canada
43 G7 Canosa di Puglia Italy
127 O8 Canouan isld Lesser Antilles
98 J6 Canova South Dakota U.S.A.
139 J5 Canowindra New South Wales Australia
47 K6 Çanşa Turkey
71 F6 Cansilan Pt Negros Philippines
123 M8 Canso Nova Scotia Canada
123 L8 Canso,Str.of Nova Scotia Canada
16 E1 Cantabria prov Spain
18 D10 Cantabria,Sierra de mts Spain
Cantábrica, Mar see Biscay, Bay of
45 K3 Cantagallo Italy
18 G7 Cantal dept France
45 Q6 Cantalupo nel Sánnio Italy
127 O2 Cantaro Trinidad
127 M10 Cantaura Venezuela
21 N3 Canteleu France
122 E8 Canterbury New Brunswick Canada
9 H5 Canterbury England
144 D5 Canterbury admin region New Zealand
144 D6 Canterbury Bight New Zealand
144 C6 Canterbury Plains New Zealand
45 O6 Canterna, L. di Italy
68 G7 Can Tho Vietnam
102 G6 Cantil California U.S.A.
71 G6 Cantilan Mindanao Philippines
16 D7 Cantillana Spain
129 K5 Canto do Buriti Brazil
63 Canton conurbation China
Canton China see Guangzhou
112 C3 Canton Georgia U.S.A.
110 F1 Canton Illinois U.S.A.
107 N3 Canton Kansas U.S.A.
95 R2 Canton Maine U.S.A.
111 F9 Canton Mississippi U.S.A.
110 E1 Canton Missouri U.S.A.
101 O3 Canton Montana U.S.A.
121 P8 Canton New York U.S.A.
112 E2 Canton North Carolina U.S.A.
94 F6 Canton Ohio U.S.A.
107 M5 Canton Oklahoma U.S.A.
95 L5 Canton Pennsylvania U.S.A.
98 K6 Canton South Dakota U.S.A.
109 M3 Canton Texas U.S.A.
121 T4 Canton-Bégin Quebec Canada
134 A5 Canton I Pacific Oc
107 M5 Canton L Oklahoma U.S.A.
110 D1 Cantril Iowa U.S.A.
41 K6 Cantù Italy
118 J8 Cantuar Saskatchewan Canada
130 D9 Cantú,R Brazil
130 D9 Cantú, Serra do mt Brazil
130 G10 Canudos Brazil
133 F5 Cañuelas Argentina
128 G4 Canuma Brazil
128 F5 Canutama Brazil
107 L6 Canute Oklahoma U.S.A.
124 G4 Canutillo Mexico
108 A4 Canutillo Texas U.S.A.
145 D4 Canvastown New Zealand
9 G5 Canvey I England
118 L5 Canwood Saskatchewan Canada
21 M2 Cany-Barville France
120 F5 Canyon Ontario Canada
117 E5 Canyon Yukon Territory Canada
108 F1 Canyon Texas U.S.A.
101 P5 Canyon Wyoming U.S.A.
100 G5 Canyon City Oregon U.S.A.
100 K6 Canyon Cr Idaho U.S.A.
118 C3 Canyon Creek Alberta Canada
101 N3 Canyon Creek Montana U.S.A.
103 P5 Canyon de Chelly Nat.Mon Arizona U.S.A.
101 O3 Canyon Ferry Dam Montana U.S.A.
103 N8 Canyon L Arizona U.S.A.
109 J6 Canyon L Texas U.S.A.
103 P3 Canyonlands Nat. Park Utah U.S.A.
117 K4 Canyon Ranges Northwest Territories Canada
100 B7 Canyonville Oregon U.S.A.
87 D7 Canzar Angola
33 T6 Canzow Germany
67 B5 Cao Bang Vietnam
65 C5 Caogoubu China
67 A3 Cao Hai L China
65 F4 Cao He R China
65 F4 Caohekou China
Caojiahe see Qichun
12 C2 Caolisport, L Scotland
87 C7 Caombo Angola
68 J6 Cao Nguen Dar Lac plateau Vietnam
122 F1 Caopacho L Quebec Canada
122 F2 Caopacho R Quebec Canada
121 Q3 Caopatina, L Quebec Canada
65 F3 Caoshi China
67 D3 Caoshi China
65 C7 Cao Xian China
98 F5 Capa South Dakota U.S.A.
87 D7 Capaia Angola
128 E2 Capanaparo R Venezuela
129 J4 Capanema Brazil
130 D9 Capanema, R Brazil
45 J4 Capannoli Italy
45 J4 Capannori Italy
130 F5 Capão Redondo Brazil
130 H7 Caparaó,Sa do mts Brazil
128 E3 Caparro, Co mt Colombia
71 E3 Capas Luzon Philippines
127 J9 Capatárida Venezuela
48 H5 Căpăţînei, Muntii mt Romania
71 D7 Capayan Sulu isld Philippines
18 D9 Capbreton France
122 F4 Cap Chat Quebec Canada
121 S6 Cap de la Madeleine Quebec Canada
18 G8 Capdenac France
122 H4 Cap de Rabast Quebec Canada
122 H5 Cap-d'Espoir Quebec Canada
95 R4 Cape Ann Massachusetts U.S.A.
143 E10 Cape Arid Nat Park W Australia Australia
139 J8 Cape Barren I Tasmania Australia
90 K12 Cape Basin Atlantic Oc
Cape Bastion see Jinmu Jido
123 M7 Cape Breton Highlands Nat Pk C Breton I, Nova Scotia
123 N7 Cape Breton I Nova Scotia Canada
123 U6 Cape Broyle Newfoundland Canada
113 G9 Cape Canaveral Florida U.S.A.
123 R1 Cape Charles Labrador, Nfld Canada
95 L9 Cape Charles Virginia U.S.A.
85 D7 Cape Coast Ghana
95 S5 Cape Cod Massachusetts U.S.A.
95 R5 Cape Cod B Massachusetts U.S.A.
95 R5 Cape Cod Canal Massachusetts U.S.A.
95 R5 Cape Cod Nat.Seashore Massachusetts U.S.A.
113 F11 Cape Coral Florida U.S.A.
115 M5 Cape Dorset Northwest Territories Canada
115 N4 Cape Dyer Northwest Territories Canada
146 C11 Cape Evans Antarctic Base Antarctica
112 K4 Cape Fear North Carolina U.S.A.
110 G4 Cape Girardeau Missouri U.S.A.
112 M2 Cape Hatteras North Carolina U.S.A.
115 N5 Cape Hopes Advance Quebec Canada
Cape Horn see Hornos, C. de
112 H4 Cape I South Carolina U.S.A.
116 F3 Cape Krusenstern Nat Mon Alaska U.S.A.
143 B10 Capel W Australia Australia
129 L6 Capela Brazil
123 P6 Cape la Hune Newfoundland Canada
8 C1 Capel Curig Wales
143 D10 Cape Le Grand Nat Park W Australia Australia
130 G5 Capelinha Brazil
116 E2 Cape Lisburne Alaska U.S.A.
141 J6 Capella Queensland Australia
22 F4 Capelle-en-Thierache, la France
22 K4 Capellen Luxembourg
87 C9 Capelongo Angola
95 N8 Cape May New Jersey U.S.A.
87 C7 Capenda-Camulemba Angola
89 A10 Cape of Good Hope S Africa
114 G3 Cape Parry Northwest Territories Canada
89 B8 Cape Province S Africa
89 A10 Cape Pt S Africa
141 H5 Cape R Queensland Australia
123 T7 Cape Race Newfoundland Canada
142 A5 Cape Range Nat Park W Australia Australia
123 N6 Cape Ray Newfoundland Canada
80 F2 Capernaum Israel
112 H5 Cape Romain South Carolina U.S.A.
103 N5 Cape Royal Arizona U.S.A.
113 F12 Cape Sable pen Florida U.S.A.
122 G10 Cape Sable I Nova Scotia Canada
122 F9 Cape St.Mary Nova Scotia Canada
123 S7 Cape St. Mary's lighthouse Newfoundland Canada
127 O5 Capesterre Marie Galante W Indies
127 N4 Capesterre-Belle-Eau Guadeloupe W Indies
45 P5 Capestrallo Italy
89 A9 Cape Town S Africa
90 E7 Cape Verde Fracture Atlantic Oc
90 G7 Cape Verde Is rep Atlantic Oc
90 G7 Cape Verde Plateau Atlantic Oc
95 M9 Capeville Virginia U.S.A.
95 L2 Cape Vincent New York U.S.A.
15 C2 Cape Wrath Scotland
141 F1 Cape York Pen Queensland Australia
127 H5 Cap-Haïtien Haiti
130 B9 Capiatá Paraguay
128 E3 Capibara Venezuela
130 J9 Capiberibe R Brazil
133 F4 Capilla Argentina
133 E4 Capilla del Monte Argentina
129 J4 Capim R Brazil
128 E7 Capinota Bolivia
41 H6 Capio, Monte Italy
45 O6 Capistrello Italy
121 O5 Capitachouane R Quebec Canada
106 E8 Capitan New Mexico U.S.A.
146 C3 Capitan Arturo Prat Chile Base Antarctica
130 C8 Capitán Bado Paraguay
131 A8 Capitanes, Pta C Chile
106 E8 Capitan Mts New Mexico U.S.A.
42 E6 Capitignano Italy
98 B4 Capitol Montana U.S.A.
100 H8 Capitol Peak mt Nevada U.S.A.
103 N3 Capitol Reef Nat. Park Utah U.S.A.
122 G5 Caplan Quebec Canada
20 A5 Cap, Le pen France
71 E5 Capnoyan isld Philippines
88 D9 Capoche R Mozambique
129 G5 Capoeiras, Cachoeira das waterfall Brazil

44 D4 Capo Mele Italy
139 K3 Capoompeta mt New South Wales Australia
45 O5 Cappadocia Italy
36 F2 Cappel Germany
14 D4 Cappoquin Ireland
127 O7 Cap Pt St Lucia
42 C5 Capraia, I.di Italy
43 B7 Caprara o dello Scorno, Pta pt Sardinia
120 K6 Capreol Ontario Canada
43 C7 Caprera, I Sardinia
44 E4 Caprese Michelangelo Italy
45 Q8 Capri Italy
45 Q7 Capriati a Volturno Italy
141 K5 Capricorn Chan Gt Barrier Reef Aust
141 K6 Capricorn Grp islds Gt Barrier Reef Aust
143 B6 Capricorn Ra W Australia Australia
42 D3 Caprino Veronese Italy
87 D9 Caprivi Strip Namibia
108 D2 Caprock New Mexico U.S.A.
123 M7 Capstick C Breton I, Nova Scotia
135 U5 Captain Cook Hawaiian Is
139 J6 Captain's Flat New South Wales Australia
18 E8 Captieux France
113 E11 Captiva Florida U.S.A.
45 Q7 Capua Italy
71 E7 Capual isld Philippines
83 K12 Capucin Pt Mahé I Indian Oc
71 G4 Capul Philippines
106 D4 Capulin Colorado U.S.A.
106 G5 Capulin New Mexico U.S.A.
128 D3 Caqueta div Colombia
128 D4 Caquetá R Colombia
71 E4 Carabao isld Philippines
128 D6 Carabaya, Cord.de mts Peru
128 F4 Carabinani R Brazil
128 E1 Carabobo state Venezuela
48 J6 Caracal Romania
127 L9 Caracas Venezuela
129 K5 Caracol Brazil
130 C7 Caracol Brazil
125 J8 Caracuaro Mexico
71 G7 Caraga Mindanao Philippines
14 B4 Caragh,L Ireland
131 G4 Caraguatá R Uruguay
130 F8 Caraguata-tuba Brazil
130 C9 Caraguatay Paraguay
133 C5 Carahue Chile
130 H5 Caraí Brazil
12 C2 Cara I Scotland
129 H5 Carajás, Serra dos mts Brazil
18 G9 Caraman France
20 D3 Caramat Ontario Canada
71 F4 Caramoan Pen Philippines
128 F5 Caranapatuba Brazil
130 G7 Carandaí Brazil
130 B6 Carandazal Brazil
140 E5 Carandotta Queensland Australia
129 K8 Carangola Brazil
128 F3 Caransaca,Co mt Venezuela
48 G5 Caransebeş Romania
20 C4 Carantec France
130 B9 Carapeguá Paraguay
138 D5 Carappee Hill South Australia Australia
122 H6 Caraquet New Brunswick Canada
122 H6 Caraquet Bay New Brunswick Canada
128 B4 Caráquez,B.de Ecuador
48 G5 Caraşova Romania
48 G5 Caraş-Severin reg Romania
125 N2 Caratasca Honduras
130 G6 Caratinga Brazil
69 G14 Carat, Tanjung C Indonesia
128 E4 Carauari Brazil
130 H8 Caraúbas Brazil
106 D6 Caravaca de la Cruz Spain
41 L7 Caravaggio Italy
130 H5 Caravelas Brazil
128 D7 Caraveli Peru
43 B9 Caravius, M. is mt Sardinia
128 C5 Caraz Peru
130 H5 Carazinho Brazil
16 B2 Carballiño Spain
16 B1 Carballo Spain
16 B1 Carba, Sa. de la mts Spain
119 S9 Carberry Manitoba Canada
101 U1 Carbert Montana U.S.A.
118 D7 Carbon Alberta Canada
43 C9 Carbonara,C Sardinia
45 K1 Carbonara di Po Italy
118 D5 Carbondale Alberta Canada
106 C2 Carbondale Colorado U.S.A.
107 P3 Carbondale Kansas U.S.A.
95 M5 Carbondale Pennsylvania U.S.A.
123 T6 Carbonear Newfoundland Canada
17 F8 Carboneras Spain
111 J8 Carbon Hill Alabama U.S.A.
43 B9 Carbonia Sardinia
38 F8 Carbonin Italy
130 G5 Carbonita Brazil
18 F9 Carbonne France
17 G5 Carcagente Spain
117 P7 Carcajou Alberta Canada
18 E7 Carcans, Etang de L France
71 F5 Carcar Cebu Philippines
131 E4 Carcaraña R Argentina
18 G9 Carcassonne France
128 C3 Carchi prov Ecuador
139 J5 Carcoar New South Wales Australia
117 F5 Carcross Yukon Territory Canada
142 A6 Cardabia W Australia Australia
47 K7 Cardak Turkey
119 R8 Cardale Manitoba Canada
68 F7 Cardamomes,Chaine des mts Cambodia
125 K6 Cárdenas Mexico
139 G3 Cardenyabba R New South Wales Australia
133 C7 Cardiel,L Argentina
8 C5 Cardiff Wales
Cardigan co see Dyfed
8 B3 Cardigan Wales
123 K7 Cardigan B Prince Edward I Canada
8 B2 Cardigan B Wales
121 P8 Cardinal Ontario Canada
94 E6 Cardington Ohio U.S.A.
17 J3 Cardona Spain
17 J3 Cardoner,R Spain
127 J9 Cardón,Pta Venezuela
130 E7 Cardoso Brazil
130 F9 Cardoso,I.do Brazil
144 B6 Cardrona New Zealand
144 B6 Cardrona, Mt New Zealand
119 M9 Cardross Saskatchewan Canada
12 D2 Cardross Scotland
118 D9 Cardston Alberta Canada
141 H4 Cardwell Queensland Australia
41 O6 Carega, Cima mt Italy
48 G3 Carei Romania
127 O2 Carenage Trinidad
22 D3 Carency France
20 H3 Carentan France
20 F6 Carentoir France
8 B4 Carew Wales
101 M6 Carey Idaho U.S.A.
94 D6 Carey Ohio U.S.A.
108 G1 Carey Texas U.S.A.
143 B7 Carey Downs W Australia Australia
143 D8 Carey, L W Australia Australia
81 C7 Cargados Carajos islds Indian Oc
18 L10 Cargèse Corsica
120 J8 Cargill Ontario Canada
13 E1 Cargill Scotland
141 G5 Cargoon Queensland Australia
20 C5 Carhaix-Plouguer France
122 E1 Carheil,L Quebec Canada
47 J7 Caria hist reg Turkey
130 H7 Cariacica Brazil
127 N9 Cariaco Venezuela
126 F10 Caribana,Pta Colombia
126 C5 Caribbean Sea Central America
117 N9 Cariboo Mts British Columbia Canada
117 K5 Caribou R Northwest Territories Canada
122 K8 Caribou Nova Scotia Canada
116 G9 Caribou R Alaska U.S.A.
95 S7 Caribou Maine U.S.A.
117 K7 Caribou Hide British Columbia Canada
122 K8 Caribou I Nova Scotia Canada
120 E5 Caribou I Ontario Canada
117 R5 Caribou Is Northwest Territories Canada
101 O6 Caribou Mt Idaho U.S.A.
117 Q6 Caribou Mts Alberta Canada
124 F4 Carichic Mexico
119 Q9 Carievale Saskatchewan Canada
71 G5 Carigara Leyte Philippines
22 J4 Carignan France
44 C2 Carignano Italy
121 Q7 Carillon Quebec Canada
139 J4 Carinda New South Wales Australia
17 G3 Cariñena Spain
129 K6 Carinhanha Brazil
45 P7 Carinola Italy
129 J6 Caripare Brazil
127 N9 Caripe Venezuela
127 N9 Caripito Venezuela
130 D9 Caririaçu Brazil
128 F5 Caritianas Brazil
130 G9 Cariús Brazil
107 N5 Carl Blackwell, L Oklahoma U.S.A.
22 E4 Carlepont France
17 G5 Carlet Spain
122 F8 Carleton Quebec Canada
94 D4 Carleton Michigan U.S.A.
98 J9 Carleton Nebraska U.S.A.
122 F6 Carleton,Mt New Brunswick Canada
121 O7 Carleton Place Ontario Canada
122 K4 Carleton Pt Quebec Canada
98 B5 Carlile Wyoming U.S.A.
103 H1 Carlin Nevada U.S.A.
36 B5 Carling France
14 E2 Carlingford Ireland
110 G2 Carlinville Illinois U.S.A.
142 B2 Carlisle dist Perth, W Aust Australia
13 F4 Carlisle England
110 E7 Carlisle Arkansas U.S.A.
110 J3 Carlisle Indiana U.S.A.
94 C8 Carlisle Kentucky U.S.A.
95 K6 Carlisle Pennsylvania U.S.A.
112 F3 Carlisle South Carolina U.S.A.
127 P6 Carlisle B Barbados
143 F8 Carlisle Lakes W Australia Australia
18 G10 Carlitte mt France
43 B9 Carloforte Sardinia
13 E2 Carlops Scotland
133 E6 Carlos Ameghino, Istmo Argentina
133 E5 Carlos Casares Argentina
130 H5 Carlos Chagas Brazil
131 G4 Carlos Reyles Uruguay
14 E4 Carlow co Ireland
14 E4 Carlow Ireland
15 B2 Carloway Scotland
Carlsbad Czechoslovakia see Karlovy Vary
102 G8 Carlsbad California U.S.A.
108 C3 Carlsbad New Mexico U.S.A.
108 C3 Carlsbad Caverns Nat. Park New Mexico U.S.A.
72 H7 Carlsberg Ridge Indian Oc
37 O3 Carlsfeld Germany
99 T3 Carlshend Michigan U.S.A.
118 L6 Carlton Saskatchewan Canada
99 O3 Carlton Minnesota U.S.A.
100 B4 Carlton Oregon U.S.A.
109 J4 Carlton Texas U.S.A.
142 G3 Carlton Hill W Australia Australia
9 F1 Carlton-on-Trent England
100 D3 Carlton Pass Washington U.S.A.
12 E2 Carluke Scotland
119 P9 Carlyle Saskatchewan Canada
110 G3 Carlyle Illinois U.S.A.
98 B3 Carlyle Montana U.S.A.
118 D1 Carman Manitoba Canada
118 D8 Carmangay Alberta Canada
123 S4 Carmanville Newfoundland Canada
Carmarthen co see Dyfed
8 B4 Carmarthen Wales
8 C4 Carmarthen Van mt Wales
18 G8 Carmaux France
119 M6 Carmel Saskatchewan Canada
102 C5 Carmel California U.S.A.
94 A7 Carmel Indiana U.S.A.
110 K2 Carmel Indiana U.S.A.
95 O5 Carmel New York U.S.A.
95 S2 Carmel Maine U.S.A.
80 D3 Carmel,Mt Israel
112 E3 Carmel, Mt South Carolina U.S.A.
80 D3 Carmel National Park, Mt Israel
133 F4 Carmelo Uruguay
127 J9 Carmelo Venezuela
102 C5 Carmel Valley California U.S.A.
126 G10 Carmen Colombia
124 F2 Carmen R Mexico
125 L8 Carmen isld Mexico
71 G6 Carmen Philippines
101 M4 Carmen Idaho U.S.A.
107 M5 Carmen Oklahoma U.S.A.
133 D2 Carmen Alto Chile
130 C10 Carmen del Paraná Paraguay
133 E6 Carmen de Patagones Argentina
131 B2 Carmen,R.del Chile
133 D5 Carmensa Argentina
108 E7 Carmen, Sa. del mts Mexico
110 H3 Carmi Illinois U.S.A.
113 L9 Carmichael New Providence I Bahamas
118 J8 Carmichael Saskatchewan Canada
141 J5 Carmila Queensland Australia
109 L5 Carmine Texas U.S.A.
130 G7 Carmo Brazil
44 D3 Carmo mt Italy
130 F7 Carmo da Cachoeira Brazil
130 F6 Carmo do Paranaiba Brazil
143 C9 Carmody, L W Australia Australia
16 D7 Carmona Spain
13 H5 Carnaby England
20 D6 Carnac France
143 B8 Carnamah W Australia Australia
138 F4 Carnanto,L South Australia Australia
143 A6 Carnarvon W Australia Australia
89 C8 Carnarvon S Africa
141 H7 Carnarvon Nat. Park Queensland Australia
141 J7 Carnarvon Ra Queensland Australia
143 D7 Carnarvon Ra W Australia Australia
71 C5 Carnatic Shoal S China Sea
14 D2 Carndonagh Ireland
119 Q9 Carnduff Saskatchewan Canada
8 C1 Carnedd Llewelyn mt Wales
143 E7 Carnegie W Australia Australia
107 M6 Carnegie Oklahoma U.S.A.
94 G6 Carnegie Pennsylvania U.S.A.
143 E7 Carnegie, L W Australia Australia
90 A9 Carnegie Ridge Pacific Oc
21 K4 Carneille, la France
107 N3 Carneiro Kansas U.S.A.
131 A6 Carnero,B.del Chile
112 D3 Carnesville Georgia U.S.A.
146 B8 Carney isld Antarctica
99 T4 Carney Michigan U.S.A.
107 O6 Carney Oklahoma U.S.A.
13 F5 Carnforth England
42 E2 Carniche, Alpi mts Italy
69 A8 Car Nicobar isld Nicobar Is
22 E3 Carnières France
20 C5 Carnoët France
86 C5 Carnot Cent Afr Republic
138 D5 Carnot,C South Australia Australia
19 Q18 Carnoules France
13 F1 Carnoustie Scotland
14 E4 Carnsore Pt Ireland
12 E2 Carnwath Scotland
116 N3 Caro Alaska U.S.A.
94 D3 Caro Michigan U.S.A.
141 K4 Carola Cay isld Gt Barrier Reef Australia
112 F2 Caroleen North Carolina U.S.A.
129 J5 Carolina Brazil
128 C3 Carolina Colombia
87 F11 Carolina S Africa
112 K3 Carolina Beach North Carolina U.S.A.
118 C6 Caroline Alberta Canada
144 B6 Caroline New Zealand
135 M9 Caroline I Pacific Oc
134 E7 Caroline Is Pacific Oc
140 D6 Caroline, L N Terr Australia
32 G5 Carolinensiel Germany
144 A6 Caroline Pk New Zealand
142 F3 Caroline Ra W Australia Australia
20 G4 Carolles France
119 M8 Caron Saskatchewan Canada
137 S3 Carondelet Reef Phoenix Is Pacific Oc
127 O2 Caroni Trinidad
128 F2 Caroni R Venezuela
127 O2 Caroni Swamp Trinidad
127 J9 Carora Venezuela
121 O7 Carp Ontario Canada
103 K4 Carp Nevada U.S.A.
53 B9 Carpathian Mts E Europe
48 H5 Carpaţii Meridionali mts Romania
41 M7 Carpenédolo Italy
141 G4 Carpentaria Downs Queensland Australia
140 E2 Carpentaria,Gulf of Australia
98 B8 Carpenter Wyoming U.S.A.
99 S7 Carpentersville Illinois U.S.A.
100 A7 Carpenterville Oregon U.S.A.
19 O16 Carpentras France
45 J2 Carpi Italy
19 P18 Carpiagne mt France
130 J8 Carpina Brazil
45 J3 Carpineti Italy
46 E3 Carpineto Romano Italy
45 R8 Cârpiniş Romania
102 E7 Carpinteria California U.S.A.
98 E1 Carpio North Dakota U.S.A.
117 M8 Carp L British Columbia Canada
103 M2 Carp L Utah U.S.A.
94 C1 Carp Lake Michigan U.S.A.
138 F6 Carpolac Victoria Australia
20 H7 Carquefou France
19 Q18 Carqueiranne France
106 F1 Carr Colorado U.S.A.
113 C8 Carrabelle Florida U.S.A.
119 O6 Carragana Saskatchewan Canada
14 B3 Carra,L Ireland
16 B4 Carramulo, Sa. do mts Portugal
131 A5 Carranza,C Chile
125 J4 Carranza, Presa V. res Mexico
128 F2 Carrao R Venezuela
44 H3 Carrara Italy
102 H5 Carrara Nevada U.S.A.
140 D4 Carrara Range N Terr Australia
17 F4 Carrascosa del Campo Spain
17 G7 Carrascoy,Sierra de mts Spain
139 H5 Carrathool New South Wales Australia
14 B5 Carrauntoohil mt Ireland
142 G3 Carr Boyd Ra W Australia Australia
15 E3 Carrbridge Scotland
133 F2 Carreria Paraguay
131 B6 Carrero,Cerro pk Argentina
127 O8 Carriacou isld Lesser Antilles
15 D5 Carrick Scotland
14 F2 Carrickfergus N Ireland
14 E3 Carrickmacross Ireland
14 C3 Carrick on Shannon Ireland
14 D4 Carrick-on-Suir Ireland
111 G11 Carriere Mississippi U.S.A.
121 N5 Carrière,L Quebec Canada
110 H4 Carriers Mills Illinois U.S.A.
138 E4 Carrieton South Australia Australia
131 B8 Carri Lafquén, L Argentina
98 G2 Carrington North Dakota U.S.A.
16 D2 Carrion R Spain
16 D2 Carrión de los Condes Spain
127 H8 Carrizal Colombia
124 F2 Carrizal Mexico
133 C3 Carrizal Bajo Chile
131 B2 Carrizal, Pta C Chile
102 E6 Carrizo Cr California U.S.A.
106 G5 Carrizo Cr New Mex/Tex U.S.A.
103 P5 Carrizo Mts Arizona U.S.A.
108 H7 Carrizo Springs Texas U.S.A.
106 E8 Carrizozo New Mexico U.S.A.
119 R9 Carroll Manitoba Canada
99 M7 Carroll Iowa U.S.A.
98 J7 Carroll Nebraska U.S.A.
111 H8 Carrollton Alabama U.S.A.
112 B4 Carrollton Georgia U.S.A.
110 F2 Carrollton Illinois U.S.A.
94 B8 Carrollton Kentucky U.S.A.
111 G8 Carrollton Mississippi U.S.A.
110 D2 Carrollton Missouri U.S.A.
94 F6 Carrollton Ohio U.S.A.
109 O8 Carrollton Texas U.S.A.
94 J6 Carrolltown Pennsylvania U.S.A.
99 T7 Carrollville Wisconsin U.S.A.
141 F4 Carron R Queensland Australia
12 E1 Carronbridge Scotland
119 V4 Carrot R Manitoba Canada
119 N5 Carrot River Saskatchewan Canada
21 K4 Carrouges France
14 E4 Carrowmore L Ireland
118 H6 Carruthers Saskatchewan Canada
100 C8 Carrville California U.S.A.
95 N2 Carry Falls Res New York U.S.A.
19 O18 Carry-le-Rouet France
78 F1 Çarşamba Turkey
118 D8 Carseland Alberta Canada
13 E1 Carse of Gowrie dist Scotland
45 O5 Carseolani, Mti Italy
9 E1 Carsington Resr. England
45 O5 Carsoli Italy
99 L8 Carson Iowa U.S.A.
102 E2 Carson R Nevada U.S.A.
98 E3 Carson North Dakota U.S.A.
100 D4 Carson Washington U.S.A.
94 C3 Carson City Michigan U.S.A.
102 E2 Carson City Nevada U.S.A.
146 D7 Carson Inlet inlet Antarctica
102 F2 Carson L Nevada U.S.A.
142 F3 Carson, R W Australia Australia
102 F2 Carson Sink dry lake Nevada U.S.A.
94 E3 Carsonville Michigan U.S.A.
12 D3 Carsphairn Scotland
118 C7 Carstairs Alberta Canada
12 E2 Carstairs Scotland
Carstensz, G see Jaya Pk
128 C1 Cartagena Colombia
17 G7 Cartagena Spain
128 C3 Cartago Colombia
125 N5 Cartago Costa Rica
102 F5 Cartago California U.S.A.
108 G6 Carta Valley Texas U.S.A.
101 P2 Carter Montana U.S.A.
107 L6 Carter Oklahoma U.S.A.
101 P8 Carter Wyoming U.S.A.
13 F3 Carter Bar England
20 G3 Carteret France
141 G2 Carter, Mt Queensland Australia
9 G3 Carters Bridge England
111 M7 Cartersville Georgia U.S.A.
101 T3 Cartersville Montana U.S.A.
145 E4 Carterton New Zealand
43 C12 Carthage Tunisia
85 G1 Carthage ruins Tunisia
109 P1 Carthage Arkansas U.S.A.
99 P9 Carthage Illinois U.S.A.
94 B7 Carthage Indiana U.S.A.
111 G9 Carthage Mississippi U.S.A.
110 B4 Carthage Missouri U.S.A.
95 M3 Carthage New York U.S.A.
112 H2 Carthage North Carolina U.S.A.
98 J5 Carthage South Dakota U.S.A.
94 B10 Carthage Tennessee U.S.A.
109 N3 Carthage Texas U.S.A.
120 J6 Cartier Ontario Canada
142 E1 Cartier I Timor Sea
22 F3 Cartignies France
13 F5 Cartmel England
45 N4 Cartoceto Italy
48 J6 Cartojani Romania
115 O7 Cartwright Labrador, Nfld Canada
119 S9 Cartwright Manitoba Canada
98 C2 Cartwright North Dakota U.S.A.
129 L5 Caruaru Brazil
130 H10 Caruarú Brazil
128 F1 Carúpano Venezuela
129 K4 Carutapera Brazil
110 G5 Caruthersville Missouri U.S.A.
94 D9 Carver Kentucky U.S.A.
22 D3 Carvin France
16 A5 Carvoeira,C Portugal
128 F4 Carvoeiro Brazil
101 M1 Carway Alberta Canada
141 H6 Carwell Queensland Australia
33 S6 Carwitz Germany
111 F9 Cary Mississippi U.S.A.
112 J2 Cary North Carolina U.S.A.
139 G3 Caryapundy Swamp New S Wales/Queensland
113 G12 Carysfort Reef Florida U.S.A.
45 K3 Carzolano,Mt Italy
133 C4 Casablanca Chile
85 C2 Casablanca Morocco
130 F7 Casa Branca Brazil
16 B6 Casa Branca Portugal
42 F7 Casacalenda Italy
41 L5 Casaccia Switzerland
127 P3 Casa Cruz, C Trinidad
124 E2 Casa de János Mexico
129 G8 Casado Paraguay
103 N9 Casa Grande Arizona U.S.A.
103 N9 Casa Grande Nat. Mon Arizona U.S.A.
17 G5 Casa Ibáñez Spain
41 L7 Casalbuttano Italy
45 Q7 Casal di Principe Italy
44 D1 Casale Italy
45 M6 Casalecchio di Reno Italy
45 J2 Casalgrande Italy
45 H2 Casalmaggiore Italy
45 J1 Casaloldo Italy
44 G1 Casalpusterlengo Italy
45 P6 Casalvieri Italy
45 P8 Casamicciola Terme Italy
116 E4 Casapedaga Alaska U.S.A.
108 C6 Casa Piedra Texas U.S.A.
43 J8 Casarano Italy
124 F2 Casas Grandes Mexico
109 O9 Casa View Texas U.S.A.
100 J5 Cascade Idaho U.S.A.
101 O2 Cascade Montana U.S.A.
95 Q2 Cascade New Hampshire U.S.A.
100 D4 Cascade Locks Oregon U.S.A.
117 N11 Cascade Mts Br Col/Wash Canada
100 D1 Cascade Pass Washington U.S.A.
100 C7 Cascade Ra U.S.A.
100 K5 Cascade Res Idaho U.S.A.
100 D2 Cascade Tunnel Washington U.S.A.
100 C5 Cascadia Oregon U.S.A.
16 A6 Cascais Portugal
122 G5 Cascapedia Quebec Canada
122 F5 Cascapedia R Quebec Canada
130 D9 Cascavel Brazil
45 J4 Cascina Italy
95 R2 Casco Maine U.S.A.
99 T5 Casco Wisconsin U.S.A.
95 R3 Casco B Maine U.S.A.
45 M3 Casemurate Italy
45 L4 Casentina Italy
133 D3 Caseros Argentina
45 L3 Caserta Italy
94 D3 Caseville Michigan U.S.A.
146 G14 Casey Australia Base Antarctica
121 Q5 Casey Quebec Canada
99 T10 Casey Illinois U.S.A.
146 K9 Casey B Antarctica
86 B1 Casey, Raas C Somalia
14 D4 Cashel Ireland
87 F9 Cashel Zimbabwe
107 N6 Cashion Oklahoma U.S.A.
141 J7 Cashmere Queensland Australia
100 E2 Cashmere Washington U.S.A.
99 Q6 Cashton Wisconsin U.S.A.
71 E2 Casiguran Luzon Philippines
71 F2 Casiguran B Luzon Philippines
71 F2 Casiguran Sound Luzon Philippines
133 E4 Casilda Argentina
48 L6 Casimcea Romania
130 G8 Casimiro de Abreu Brazil
45 L4 Casina Italy
139 L3 Casino New South Wales Australia
128 E3 Casiquiare R Venezuela
124 D2 Casita Mexico
31 J6 Čáslav Czechoslovakia
128 C5 Casma Peru
71 G5 Casogoran B Philippines
45 L3 Casola Valsenio Italy
109 N2 Cason Texas U.S.A.
45 Q8 Casória Italy
102 A2 Caspar California U.S.A.
17 G3 Caspe Spain
101 T7 Casper Wyoming U.S.A.
111 C9 Caspiana Louisiana U.S.A.
53 G10 Caspian Sea
20 F2 Casquets Lt.Ho English Chan
144 C5 Cass R New Zealand
144 C5 Cass New Zealand
110 C6 Cass Arkansas U.S.A.
94 D3 Cass R Michigan U.S.A.
94 H8 Cass West Virginia U.S.A.
98 B7 Cassa Wyoming U.S.A.
18 G8 Cassagnes-Bégonhès France
87 D8 Cassai Angola
130 F7 Cássai Brazil
Cassaigne see Sidi Ali
87 D8 Cassamba Angola
43 G9 Cassano allo Ionio Italy
94 D3 Cass City Michigan U.S.A.
121 P7 Casselman Ontario Canada
98 J3 Casselton North Dakota U.S.A.
19 Q14 Casse Massion mt France
117 J6 Cassiar British Columbia Canada
117 H6 Cassiar Mts British Columbia Canada
130 D6 Cassilândia Brazil
139 J4 Cassilis New South Wales Australia
141 G5 Cassilis Queensland Australia
87 C9 Cassinga Angola
142 F2 Cassini I W Australia Australia
133 G4 Cassino Brazil
45 P6 Cassino Italy
129 H3 Cassiporé R Brazil
19 P18 Cassis France
99 M2 Cass L Minnesota U.S.A.
107 O3 Cassoday Kansas U.S.A.
94 B5 Cassopolis Michigan U.S.A.
110 C5 Cassville Missouri U.S.A.
99 Q7 Cassville Wisconsin U.S.A.
20 B5 Cast France
45 K1 Castagnaro Italy
102 F7 Castaic California U.S.A.
129 J4 Castanhal Brazil
131 B3 Castaño R Argentina
133 D4 Castaño Argentina
124 J4 Castaños Mexico
127 M1 Castara Tobago
17 G3 Castejón,Mt.de Spain
45 J1 Castelbelforte Italy
45 L3 Castel Bolognese Italy
45 J1 Castel d'Ario Italy
42 D4 Castel del Rio Italy
42 F7 Castel di Sangro Italy
45 L4 Castel Focognano Italy
45 P7 Castelforte Italy
45 L4 Castelfranco di Sopra Italy
45 J4 Castelfranco Emilia Italy
42 D3 Castelfranco Veneto Veneto Italy
45 J1 Castel Goffredo Italy
18 F8 Casteljaloux France
37 J4 Castell Germany
109 J5 Castell Texas U.S.A.
100 C8 Castella California U.S.A.
43 F8 Castellabate Italy
43 E10 Castellammare del Golfo Sicily
45 Q8 Castellammare di Stabia Italy
40 G7 Castellamonte Italy
45 J2 Castellarano Italy
133 F5 Castelli Argentina
45 K3 Castello di Serravalle Italy
17 G4 Castellón prov Spain
17 G5 Castellón de la Plana Spain
17 G4 Castellote Spain
45 J1 Castellucchio Italy
45 N6 Castel Madama Italy
45 N4 Castel Maggiore Italy
45 K1 Castelmassa Italy
18 G9 Castelnaudary France
18 E7 Castelnau de Médoc France
18 F8 Castelnau de Montratier France
18 F9 Castelnau-Magnoac France
45 J2 Castel novo di Sotto Italy
45 H3 Castel novo ne'Monti Italy
45 H3 Castelnuovo di Garfagnana Italy
45 N5 Castelnuovo di Porto Italy
45 J3 Castelnuovo di Verona Italy
130 H7 Castelo Brazil
16 B5 Castelo de Vide Portugal
45 O4 Castelplanio Italy
45 M6 Castel Porziano Italy
45 R8 Castel San Giorgio Italy
45 L4 Castel San Niccolo Italy
45 L3 Castel San Pietro Terme Italy
18 F8 Castelsarrasin France
44 F1 Castel S.Giov Italy
43 F11 Castelterminі Sicily
45 P5 Castelvecchio Subequo Italy
43 E11 Castelvetrano Sicily
45 P7 Castel Volturno Italy
45 J3 Castenaso Italy
41 M7 Castenedolo Italy
138 F6 Casterton Victoria Australia
18 E9 Castets France
122 F7 Castigan Mts New Brunswick Canada
45 K3 Castiglione dei Pepoli Italy
45 J1 Castiglione delle Stiviere Italy
45 H3 Castiglione di Garfagnana Italy
45 L4 Castiglion Fibocchi Italy
42 D5 Castiglion Fiorentino Italy
94 K4 Castile New York U.S.A.
133 C3 Castilla Chile
16 D4 Castilla La Vieja reg Spain
71 E4 Castillejos Luzon Philippines
16 D5 Castillejo, Sa. de mts Spain
127 J3 Castilletes Venezuela
133 C7 Castillo mt Chile
131 B4 Castillo,Cerro del pk Argentina
113 F8 Castillo de San Marcos Nat. Mon Florida U.S.A.
124 H3 Castillón Mexico
18 F8 Castillon et Capitourlan France
18 F8 Castillonnès France
133 D7 Castillo,Pampa del plain Argentina
133 G4 Castillos Uruguay
95 T2 Castine Maine U.S.A.
9 G2 Castle Acre England
14 B3 Castlebar Ireland
12 E4 Castlebay Scotland
14 D3 Castlebellingham Ireland
111 J10 Castleberry Alabama U.S.A.
14 E2 Castleblayney Ireland
9 E3 Castle Bromwich England
13 F4 Castle Carrock England
8 D5 Castle Cary England
14 D4 Castlecomer Ireland
100 J7 Castle Cr Idaho U.S.A.
103 N2 Castle Dale Utah U.S.A.
14 D3 Castlederg N Ireland
14 E4 Castledermot Ireland
103 K8 Castle Dome Mts Arizona U.S.A.
9 E2 Castle Donington England
12 E4 Castle Douglas Scotland
12 E3 Castlefern Scotland
13 G6 Castleford England
101 L7 Castleford Idaho U.S.A.
100 H1 Castlegar British Columbia Canada
103 O2 Castle Gate Utah U.S.A.
90 C1 Castle Harbour Bermuda
112 K3 Castle Hayne North Carolina U.S.A.
103 M8 Castle Hot Sp Arizona U.S.A.
126 G3 Castle I Bahamas
14 B4 Castleisland Ireland
139 G6 Castlemaine Victoria Australia
14 B4 Castlemaine Ireland
14 C4 Castlemartyr Ireland
118 B7 Castle, Mt Alberta Canada
117 F3 Castle Mt Yukon Territory Canada
102 D6 Castle Mt California U.S.A.
101 L5 Castle Peak Idaho U.S.A.
145 F4 Castlepoint New Zealand
14 D3 Castlepollard Ireland
14 C3 Castlerea Ireland
139 J4 Castlereagh R New South Wales Australia
140 D1 Castlereagh B N Terr Australia
9 G2 Castle Rising England
106 F2 Castle Rock Colorado U.S.A.
98 C5 Castle Rock South Dakota U.S.A.
101 O8 Castle Rock Utah U.S.A.
100 C3 Castle Rock Washington U.S.A.
99 R6 Castle Rock Res Wisconsin U.S.A.
13 G4 Castleside England
9 E1 Castleton England
127 L2 Castleton Jamaica
103 P3 Castleton Utah U.S.A.
95 O3 Castleton Vermont U.S.A.
95 O4 Castleton on Hudson New York U.S.A.
12 D5 Castletown I of Man U.K.
14 B5 Castletown Bere Ireland
14 F2 Castlewellan N Ireland
98 J5 Castlewood South Dakota U.S.A.
108 D6 Castolon Texas U.S.A.
118 F6 Castor Alberta Canada
111 C9 Castor Louisiana U.S.A.
111 D9 Castor R Louisiana U.S.A.
95 M3 Castorland New York U.S.A.
20 H3 Castre, Mt France
18 G9 Castres France
25 C3 Castricum Netherlands
127 O7 Castries St Lucia
133 C6 Castro Chile
16 D2 Castrocalbón Spain
45 L3 Castrocaro Italy
45 O6 Castro dei Volsci Italy
16 E2 Castrogeriz Spain
16 C1 Castropol Spain
32 F9 Castrop-Rauxel Germany
16 E1 Castro Urdiales Spain
16 B7 Castro Verde Portugal
43 G9 Castrovillari Italy
102 C5 Castroville California U.S.A.
109 J6 Castroville Texas U.S.A.
16 D6 Castuera Spain
88 G10 Casuarina isld Mozambique
142 G2 Casuarina, Mt W Australia Australia
116 N6 Caswell Alaska U.S.A.
144 A6 Caswell Sd New Zealand
48 E3 Čata Czechoslovakia
87 C8 Catabola Angola
143 B9 Cataby W Australia Australia
127 J2 Catadupa Jamaica
130 G7 Cataguases Brazil
111 D10 Catahoula L Louisiana U.S.A.
71 F4 Cataiñgan Philippines
78 J2 Çatak Turkey
78 J3 Çatak R Turkey
130 F6 Catalão Brazil
47 J3 Çatalca Turkey
47 J5 Çatal Dağı mt Turkey
127 K5 Catalina, I Dominican Rep
139 H9 Catamaran Tasmania Australia
131 D2 Catamarca Argentina
133 D3 Catamarca prov Argentina
71 F4 Catanauan Philippines
87 F9 Catandica Mozambique
71 G4 Catanduanes isld Philippines
130 E7 Catanduva Brazil
130 D8 Catanduvas Brazil
43 G11 Catania Sicily
43 G11 Catania,Golfo di Sicily
43 H10 Catanzaro Italy
113 K7 Cataó Puerto Rico
111 F12 Cataouatche,L Louisiana U.S.A.
110 K2 Cataract L Indiana U.S.A.
130 C9 Cataratas del Iguazú waterfalls Arg/Brazil
71 G4 Catarman Philippines
71 G7 Catarman Pt Mindanao Philippines
123 Q3 Cat Arm Reservoir res Newfoundland Canada
17 G5 Catarroja Spain
95 M6 Catasauqua Pennsylvania U.S.A.
128 D2 Catatumbo R Venezuela/Colombia
111 M9 Cataula Georgia U.S.A.
129 G4 Catavara Brazil
99 Q4 Catawba Wisconsin U.S.A.
112 F2 Catawba L South Carolina U.S.A.
95 L6 Catawissa Pennsylvania U.S.A.
87 F9 Cataxa Mozambique
71 G5 Catbalogan Samar Philippines
126 E2 Cat Cays islds Bahamas
101 R2 Cat Creek Montana U.S.A.
22 F3 Cateau,Le France
71 G7 Catel Mindanao Philippines
20 E3 Catel Channel Is
22 E3 Catelet, le France
125 M8 Catemaco Mexico
45 P5 Catena di Monte Sirente Italy
130 J10 Catende Brazil
118 J5 Cater Saskatchewan Canada
9 F5 Caterham England
87 B7 Catete Angola
107 L3 Catharine Kansas U.S.A.
98 G2 Cathay North Dakota U.S.A.
139 J6 Cathcart New South Wales Australia
87 E12 Cathcart S Africa
108 D5 Cathedral Mt Texas U.S.A.
109 P1 Catherine,L Arkansas U.S.A.
103 M2 Catherine, Mt Utah U.S.A.
127 L2 Catherine's Peak Jamaica
89 F8 Cathkin Pk mt Lesotho
100 B3 Cathlamet Washington U.S.A.
94 D1 Cathro Michigan U.S.A.
126 G2 Cat I Bahamas
111 G11 Cat I Mississippi U.S.A.
22 F3 Catillon-sur-Sambre France
85 A6 Catio Guinea-Bissau
128 F3 Catisimiña Venezuela
79 F1 Çatkit Suyu R Turkey
115 K7 Cat Lake Ontario Canada
94 E8 Catlettsburg Kentucky U.S.A.
99 T9 Catlin Illinois U.S.A.
144 B7 Catlins R New Zealand
137 M6 Cato isld Coral Sea
95 L3 Cato New York U.S.A.
94 K7 Catoctin Mt Maryland/Virg U.S.A.
130 H9 Catolé do Rocha Brazil
42 E5 Catria,Monte Italy
133 E5 Catriló Argentina
128 F3 Catrimani Brazil
95 O4 Catskill New York U.S.A.
95 N4 Catskill Mts New York U.S.A.
94 J4 Cattaraugus New York U.S.A.
22 L5 Cattenom France
13 F6 Catterall England
13 G5 Catterick England
45 N4 Cattolica Italy
87 F11 Catuane Mozambique
133 D4 Catuna Argentina
128 E3 Cauaburi R Brazil
45 M1 Cavàrzere Italy
129 J4 Cauaxi R Brazil
71 F6 Cauayan Negros Philippines
128 C3 Cauca div Colombia
128 C3 Cauca,R Colombia
72 E1 Caucasus mt ra Georgia/Rus Fed etc
119 V3 Cauchon L Manitoba Canada
95 R7 Caucomgomoc L Maine U.S.A.
21 M2 Caudebec France
21 N3 Caudebec-les-Elbeuf France
17 G6 Caudete Spain
22 E3 Caudry France
88 C9 Cauese Mts Mozambique
121 R7 Caughnawaga Quebec Canada
71 G6 Cauit Pt Philippines
20 F5 Caulnes France
43 G10 Caulonia Italy
19 N17 Caumont France
21 J3 Caumont-l'Eventé France
126 E4 Caunao R Cuba
18 G9 Caunes France
87 C7 Caungulu Angola
131 A5 Cauquenes Chile
133 C5 Cauquenes Chile
128 F2 Caura R Venezuela
20 D5 Caurel France
122 E5 Causapscal Quebec Canada
18 G8 Caussade France
128 F6 Cautário R Brazil
18 E10 Cauterets France
131 A7 Cautin prov Chile
126 F4 Cauto Cuba
21 L2 Cauville France
21 L2 Caux reg France
45 R8 Cava Italy
16 B3 Cavado R Portugal
40 H7 Cavaglia Italy
19 O17 Cavaillon France
19 Q18 Cavalaire France
129 J6 Cavalcante Brazil
41 O5 Cavalese Italy
98 J1 Cavalier North Dakota U.S.A.
119 U10 Cavalier North Dakota U.S.A.
145 D1 Cavalli Is New Zealand
109 L7 Cavallo, Pass Texas U.S.A.
85 C7 Cavally R Ivory Co/Liberia
14 D3 Cavan co Ireland
14 D3 Cavan Ireland
47 K7 Çavdır Turkey
45 N6 Cave Italy
144 C6 Cave New Zealand
110 E6 Cave City Arkansas U.S.A.
94 B9 Cave City Kentucky U.S.A.
103 N8 Cavecreek Arizona U.S.A.
143 D9 Cave Hill W Australia Australia
110 H4 Cave in Rock Illinois U.S.A.
130 E10 Caveiras,R Brazil
100 B7 Cave Junction Oregon U.S.A.
120 C2 Cavell Ontario Canada
118 J6 Cavell Saskatchewan Canada
143 G7 Cavenagh Ra W Australia Australia
138 F6 Cavendish Victoria Australia
118 G8 Cavendish Alberta Canada
9 G3 Cavendish England
45 M2 Ca Venier Italy
131 G3 Cavera R Brazil
131 G3 Cavera, Serra do mts Brazil
68 C7 Cavern I Burma
130 D9 Cavernoso, Serra do mts Brazil
120 C4 Cavers Ontario Canada
9 F5 Caversham England
111 L7 Cave Spring Georgia U.S.A.
103 K3 Cave Valley Nevada U.S.A.
129 H3 Caviana isld Brazil
18 E7 Cavignac France
71 G6 Cavili Philippines
71 E3 Cavite Luzon Philippines
48 H3 Cavnic Romania
45 N6 Cavo, M mt Italy
44 B2 Cavour Italy
98 H5 Cavour South Dakota U.S.A.
45 J2 Cavriago Italy
42 J6 Cavtat Croatia
15 E3 Cawdor Scotland
107 M2 Cawker City Kansas U.S.A.
138 F4 Cawndilla L New South Wales Australia
Cawnpore see Kanpur
13 G6 Cawood England
121 P7 Cawood Low Quebec Canada
9 H2 Cawston England
130 G7 Caxambu Brazil
129 K4 Caxias Brazil
128 D4 Caxias Amazonas Brazil
131 H2 Caxias do Sul Brazil
87 B7 Caxito Angola
9 F3 Caxton England
12 D2 Caxton Gibbet England
47 L6 Çay Turkey
47 K3 Çayağzı Turkey
128 C3 Cayambe vol Ecuador
112 F4 Cayce South Carolina U.S.A.
68 F8 Cay Dua B Vietnam
78 H1 Çayeli Turkey
129 H3 Cayenne Fr Guiana
21 O1 Cayeux-sur-Mer France
127 L5 Cayey Puerto Rico
18 H9 Caylar, le France
118 D8 Cayley Alberta Canada
18 G8 Caylus France
126 E5 Cayman Brac isld W Indies
126 D5 Cayman, Grand isld W Indies
126 D5 Cayman, Little isld W Indies
90 A6 Cayman Trench Caribbean
68 G7 Cay Mit Vietnam
86 A2 Caynabo Somalia
125 P9 Cayo Belize
127 P4 Cayon St Kitts W Indies
126 F2 Cay Sal Bank Bahamas
126 D3 Cayucos California U.S.A.
99 T10 Cayuga Indiana U.S.A.
98 J3 Cayuga North Dakota U.S.A.
109 M4 Cayuga Texas U.S.A.
95 L4 Cayuga L New York U.S.A.
16 D7 Cazalla de la Sierra Spain
48 L6 Căzăneşti Romania
18 E9 Cazaubon France
18 E8 Cazaux, Etang de L France
85 F2 Caze Algeria
95 M4 Cazenovia New York U.S.A.
18 F9 Cazères France
42 G4 Cazin Bosnia-Herzegovina
42 H3 Čazma Croatia
87 D8 Cazombo Angola
16 E7 Cazorla Spain
87 F9 Cazula Mozambique
16 D2 Cea R Spain
48 K3 Ceahlău Romania
48 K4 Ceahlău mt Romania
Ceanannus Mór see Kells
130 J8 Ceará Mirim Brazil
20 J5 Ceaucé France
48 H6 Ceauru, Lacu L Romania
21 L7 Ceaux-en-Loudun France
119 P5 Ceba Saskatchewan Canada
125 O6 Cebaco,I Panama
124 G4 Ceballos Mexico
106 C6 Cebolla New Mexico U.S.A.
130 D10 Cebollar Argentina
133 G4 Cebollati R Uruguay
17 F3 Cebollera mt Spain
106 C6 Cebolleta New Mexico U.S.A.
16 E4 Cebreros Spain
71 F5 Cebu Philippines
71 F7 Cebuano Barracks Mindanao Philippines
43 E7 Ceccano Italy
48 E4 Cece Hungary
36 C4 Cecil Ohio U.S.A.
99 S5 Cecil Wisconsin U.S.A.
141 K8 Cecil Plains Queensland Australia
143 D7 Cecil Rhodes, Mt mt W Australia Australia
95 M7 Cecilton Maryland U.S.A.
100 B8 Cecilville California U.S.A.
42 D5 Cecina Italy
16 C5 Ceclavín Spain
99 O7 Cedar R Iowa U.S.A.
107 M2 Cedar Kansas U.S.A.
99 U5 Cedar Michigan U.S.A.
98 H8 Cedar R Nebraska U.S.A.
111 H8 Cedarbluff Mississippi U.S.A.
94 F9 Cedar Bluff Virginia U.S.A.

107 L3 **Cedar Bluff Res** Kansas U.S.A.
107 K2 **Cedar Bluffs** Kansas U.S.A.
98 K8 **Cedar Bluffs** Nebraska U.S.A.
103 M4 **Cedar Breaks Nat.Mon** Utah U.S.A.
99 T6 **Cedarburg** Wisconsin U.S.A.
98 E6 **Cedar Butte** South Dakota U.S.A.
110 D3 **Cedar City** Missouri U.S.A.
103 L4 **Cedar City** Utah U.S.A.
98 D3 **Cedar Cr** North Dakota U.S.A.
109 K5 **Cedar Creek** Texas U.S.A.
109 O9 **Cedar Crest** Texas U.S.A.
109 L3 **Cedar Cr. L** Texas U.S.A.
101 L7 **Cedar Cr.Res** Idaho U.S.A.
99 O7 **Cedar Falls** Iowa U.S.A.
94 F8 **Cedar Grove** West Virginia U.S.A.
99 T6 **Cedar Grove** Wisconsin U.S.A.
127 P4 **Cedar Grove** Antigua W Indies
112 L2 **Cedar I** North Carolina U.S.A.
95 M9 **Cedar I** Virginia U.S.A.
113 D8 **Cedar Key** Florida U.S.A.
119 R5 **Cedar L** Manitoba Canada
108 E3 **Cedar L** Texas U.S.A.
99 T8 **Cedar Lake** Indiana U.S.A.
109 M7 **Cedar Lane** Texas U.S.A.
102 G3 **Cedar Mts** Nevada U.S.A.
94 D5 **Cedar Pt** Ohio U.S.A.
99 P8 **Cedar Rapids** Iowa U.S.A.
98 H8 **Cedar Rapids** Nebraska U.S.A.
95 K5 **Cedar Run** Pennsylvania U.S.A.
120 H10 **Cedar Springs** Ontario Canada
94 B3 **Cedar Springs** Michigan U.S.A.
111 L7 **Cedartown** Georgia U.S.A.
107 O4 **Cedar Vale** Kansas U.S.A.
106 E7 **Cedarvale** New Mexico U.S.A.
127 L2 **Cedar Valley** Jamaica
100 E8 **Cedarville** California U.S.A.
95 M7 **Cedarville** New Jersey U.S.A.
110 N2 **Cedarville** Ohio U.S.A.
106 F4 **Cedarwood** Colorado U.S.A.
94 K8 **Cedon** Virginia U.S.A.
119 O9 **Cedoux** Saskatchewan Canada
43 C8 **Cedrino** *R* Sardinia
130 G9 **Cedro** Brazil
124 B3 **Cedros** *isld* Mexico
124 E4 **Cedros** Mexico
127 N3 **Cedros Pt** Trinidad
138 C4 **Ceduna** South Australia Australia
86 J4 **Ceel Afweyn** Somalia
86 A3 **Ceelbuur** Somalia
86 A2 **Ceel Hur** Somalia
86 A1 **Ceerigaabo** Somalia
43 F10 **Cefalù** Sicily
16 E3 **Cega** *R* Spain
48 F3 **Cegléd** Hungary
43 H8 **Ceglie Messapico** Italy
17 F6 **Cehegin** Spain
67 B4 **Ceheng** China
48 H3 **Cehu Silvaniei** Romania
48 G4 **Ceica** Romania
128 E3 **Cejal** Colombia
87 C8 **Cela** Angola
Celah, Gunung *see* **Mandi Angin, Gunung**
45 P5 **Celano** Italy
16 B2 **Celanova** Spain
125 J7 **Celaya** Mexico
Celebes *isld see* **Sulawesi**
70 G3 **Celebes Sea** Indonesia
109 L2 **Celeste** Texas U.S.A.
94 C6 **Celina** Ohio U.S.A.
94 B10 **Celina** Tennessee U.S.A.
109 L2 **Celina** Texas U.S.A.
17 G4 **Cella** Spain
48 D3 **Celldömölk** Hungary
32 M7 **Celle** Germany
22 E2 **Celles** Belgium
21 M7 **Celle-St.Avant,la** France
21 N6 **Cellettes** France
21 N8 **Celon** France
16 B3 **Celorico de Basto** Portugal
7 E12 **Celtic Sea** British Isles/ France
47 L7 **Çeltikçi** Turkey
47 H4 **Çeltik Gölü** *L* Turkey
41 O5 **Cembra** Italy
107 M7 **Cement** Oklahoma U.S.A.
94 C4 **Cement City** Michigan U.S.A.
46 D1 **Čemerna Planina** *mt* Serbia Yugoslavia
42 H4 **Čemernica** *mt* Bosnia-Herzegovina
48 E7 **Čemerno** Bosnia-Herzegovina
8 B1 **Cemlyn B** Wales
8 B1 **Cemmaes** Wales
17 F6 **Cenajo, Embalse del** *res* Spain
8 B3 **Cenarth** Wales
136 H2 **Cenderawasih, Teluk** *B* W Irian
71 A3 **Cenga** Indonesia
44 G2 **Ceno** *R* Italy
133 C6 **Cenoa** *R* Argentina
86 C4 **Cent.Afr.Rep** Equat Africa
130 D8 **Centenario do Sul** Brazil
112 H3 **Centenary** South Carolina U.S.A.
101 T8 **Centennial** Wyoming U.S.A.
103 L8 **Centennial Wash** *R* Arizona U.S.A.
106 D4 **Center** Colorado U.S.A.
110 E2 **Center** Missouri U.S.A.
98 E2 **Center** North Dakota U.S.A.
111 B10 **Center** Texas U.S.A.
94 E6 **Centerburg** Ohio U.S.A.
99 O4 **Center City** Minnesota U.S.A.
95 L9 **Center Cross** Virginia U.S.A.
113 F9 **Center Hill** Florida U.S.A.
110 L5 **Center Hill L** Tennessee U.S.A.
95 P6 **Center Moriches** Long I, New York U.S.A.
95 Q3 **Center Ossipee** New Hampshire U.S.A.
109 H6 **Center Point** Texas U.S.A.
110 D1 **Centerville** Iowa U.S.A.
111 E12 **Centerville** Louisiana U.S.A.
94 H6 **Centerville** Pennsylvania U.S.A.
98 K6 **Centerville** South Dakota U.S.A.
110 J6 **Centerville** Tennessee U.S.A.
109 M4 **Centerville** Texas U.S.A.
101 O9 **Centerville** Utah U.S.A.
100 E4 **Centerville** Washington U.S.A.
108 E6 **Centinela, Picacho del** *pk* Mexico
124 H3 **Centinela, Pico del** *mt* Mexico
42 D4 **Cento** Italy
44 G3 **Cento Croci, Passo di** Italy
107 O7 **Centrahoma** Oklahoma U.S.A.
89 D3 **Central** *dist* Botswana
130 B9 **Central** *dept* Paraguay
15 D4 **Central** *reg* Scotland
116 P4 **Central** Alaska U.S.A.
106 B9 **Central** New Mexico U.S.A.
112 E3 **Central** South Carolina U.S.A.
103 L4 **Central** Utah U.S.A.
86 C4 **Central African Republic** Africa
118 L8 **Central Butt** Saskatchewan Canada
106 E2 **Central City** Colorado U.S.A.
99 P7 **Central City** Iowa U.S.A.
110 J4 **Central City** Kentucky U.S.A.
98 H8 **Central City** Nebraska U.S.A.
94 J6 **Central City** Pennsylvania U.S.A.
140 B5 **Central Desert Aboriginal Land** N Terr Australia
95 Q5 **Central Falls** Rhode I U.S.A.
110 G3 **Centralia** Illinois U.S.A.
107 O2 **Centralia** Kansas U.S.A.
110 D2 **Centralia** Missouri U.S.A.
100 C3 **Centralia** Washington U.S.A.
94 G8 **Centralia** West Virginia U.S.A.
94 B1 **Central Lake** Michigan U.S.A.
140 C5 **Central Mt. Stewart** N Terr Australia
100 C7 **Central Point** Oregon U.S.A.
136 J2 **Central Ra** Papua New Guinea
56 **Central Siberia**
95 L3 **Central Square** New York U.S.A.
102 B1 **Central Valley** California U.S.A.
111 L7 **Centre** Alabama U.S.A.
144 A7 **Centre I** New Zealand
122 E7 **Centreville** New Brunswick Canada
122 F9 **Centreville** Nova Scotia Canada
111 J9 **Centreville** Alabama U.S.A.
95 L7 **Centreville** Maryland U.S.A.
94 B5 **Centreville** Michigan U.S.A.
111 E10 **Centreville** Mississippi U.S.A.
111 J11 **Century** Florida U.S.A.
94 G7 **Century** West Virginia U.S.A.
67 B4 **Cenwanglao Shan** *mt* China
67 C5 **Cenxi** China
48 E7 **Čeotina** *R* Bosnia-Herzegovina/Yugoslavia
19 P18 **Cépet,C** France
Cephalonia *isld* Greece *see* **Kefallinia** *isld*
41 M5 **Cepina** Italy
44 C4 **Ceppo Monte** *mt* Italy
45 O6 **Ceprano** Italy
21 L6 **Cérans-Foulletourte** France
128 E2 **Cerbatana, Sa. de la** *mts* Venezuela
103 K6 **Cerbat Mts** Arizona U.S.A.
18 H10 **Cerbère, C** France
16 B7 **Cercal** Portugal
16 E4 **Cercedilla** Spain
37 O5 **Čerchov** *mt* Czechoslovakia
21 O6 **Cercottes** France
18 H6 **Cercy la Tour** France
18 G10 **Cerdaña** *dist* Spain
21 P6 **Cerdon** France
18 G8 **Cère** *R* France
45 K1 **Cerea** Italy
118 G7 **Cereal** Alberta Canada
45 L1 **Ceregnano** Italy
21 N7 **Ceré-la-Ronde** France
20 H4 **Cérences** France
130 E4 **Ceres** Brazil
40 F7 **Ceres** Italy
87 C12 **Ceres** S Africa
13 F1 **Ceres** Scotland
102 C4 **Ceres** California U.S.A.
45 J1 **Ceresara** Italy
40 F7 **Ceresole Reale** Italy
18 G10 **Céret** France
126 G10 **Cereté** Colombia
87 J9 **Cerf** *isld* Br Indian Oc Terr
83 J12 **Cerf I** Mahé I Indian Oc
121 P6 **Cerf. L du** Quebec Canada
22 G3 **Cerfontaine** Belgium
21 P3 **Cergy-Pontoise** France
44 D3 **Ceriale** Italy
43 G7 **Cerignola** Italy
Cerigo *isld* Greece *see* **Kíthira** *isld*
18 G6 **Cerilly** France
21 J3 **Cerisy-la-Forêt** France
20 H3 **Cerisy-la-Salle** France
21 J8 **Cérizay** France
47 J3 **Çerkesköy** Turkey
42 F3 **Cerknica** Slovenia
48 G4 **Cermei** Romania
48 H5 **Cerna** *R* Romania
48 L5 **Cerna** Romania
48 L6 **Cernavodă** Romania
19 K5 **Cernay** France
8 D6 **Cerne Abbas** England
42 H3 **Cernik** Croatia
37 O4 **Černošin** Czechoslovakia
109 H9 **Cerralvo** Mexico
124 E5 **Cerralvo** *isld* Mexico
45 J4 **Cerreto Guidi** Italy
44 H3 **Cerreto, Passo di** Italy
45 R7 **Cerreto Sannita** Italy
8 C1 **Cerrigydrudion** Wales
46 D3 **Cerrik** Albania
106 D6 **Cerrillos** New Mexico U.S.A.
125 J6 **Cerritos** Mexico
130 E9 **Cêrro Azul** Brazil
128 C6 **Cerro de Pasco** Peru
127 L5 **Cerro de Punta** *pk* Puerto Rico
110 H2 **Cerro Gordo** Illinois U.S.A.
131 G4 **Cerro Largo** *dept* Uruguay
127 J9 **Cerrón** *mt* Venezuela
124 F4 **Cerro Prieto** Mexico
21 K7 **Cersay** France
45 K4 **Certaldo** Italy
143 B9 **Cervantes** W Australia Australia
43 G7 **Cervaro** *R* Italy
45 P7 **Cervaro** Italy
43 G8 **Cervati, M** *mt* Italy
44 H2 **Cervellino** *mt* Italy
17 H3 **Cervera** Spain
17 F2 **Cervera del Rio Alhama** Spain
16 D2 **Cervera de P** Spain
42 E4 **Cervia** Italy
43 G8 **Cervialto, M** *mt* Italy
45 R7 **Cervinara** Italy
41 H7 **Cervo** *R* Italy
44 D4 **Cervo** Italy
128 D2 **César** *div* Colombia
126 H10 **César,R** Colombia
42 E4 **Cesena** Italy
45 M3 **Cesenatico** Italy
52 C6 **Cēsis** Latvia
37 O5 **Česká Kubice** Czechoslovakia
31 H5 **Česká Lípa** Czechoslovakia
31 H7 **Ceské Budějovice** Czechoslovakia
31 H6 **Českézemé** *reg* Czechoslovakia
31 J6 **Českomoravská Vysočina** *mts* Czechoslovakia
31 H5 **Český Brod** Czechoslovakia
31 H7 **Český Krumlov** Czechoslovakia
37 O4 **Český les Sumava** *mts* Czechoslovakia
48 E1 **Český Těšín** Czechoslovakia
78 A2 **Çesme** Turkey
47 H6 **Çeşnie** Turkey
139 K5 **Cessnock** New South Wales Australia
48 H6 **Cetate** Romania
42 H5 **Cetina** *R* Croatia
42 J6 **Cetinje** Montenegro Yugoslavia
21 M5 **Ceton** France
43 G9 **Cetraro** Italy
19 P15 **Ceuse, Pic de** *mt* France
85 C1 **Ceuta** *Spanish exclave* Morocco
16 D9 **Ceuta** Spain
137 P6 **Ceva-i-Ra** *reef* Pacific Oc
41 N5 **Cevedale** *mt* Italy
18 H8 **Cevennes** *mts* France
78 G3 **Ceylânpınar** Turkey
Ceylon *rep see* **Sri Lanka** *rep*
119 N9 **Ceylon** Saskatchewan Canada
99 M6 **Ceylon** Minnesota U.S.A.
19 P18 **Ceyreste** France
57 B6 **Chaacha** Turkmenistan
19 P16 **Chabestan** France
19 O15 **Chabeuil** France
142 A6 **Chabjuwardoo B** W Australia Australia
18 H5 **Chablis** France
19 P16 **Chabre, Mt de** France
19 Q16 **Chabrières** France
21 O7 **Chabris** France
133 C1 **Chaca** Chile
131 E5 **Chacabuco** Argentina
127 N1 **Chacachacare I** Trinidad
133 D2 **Chacance** Chile
133 C6 **Chacao, Canal de** Chile
133 D6 **Chacays, Sa. de los** *mts* Argentina
131 C6 **Chachahuen,Sa** *mt* Argentina
128 D7 **Chachani** *mt* Peru
128 C5 **Chachapoyas** Peru
68 E6 **Chachoengsao** Thailand
74 D6 **Chachro** Pakistan
133 E3 **Chaco** *prov* Argentina
128 F8 **Chaco** *dept* Paraguay
133 E3 **Chaco Austral** *reg* Argentina
133 E2 **Chaco Boreal** *reg* Paraguay
106 B5 **Chaco Canyon Nat. Mon** New Mexico U.S.A.
133 E2 **Chaco Central** *reg* Argentina
117 H8 **Chacon,C** Prince of Wales I, Alaska
129 G5 **Chacorãco, Cachoeira do** *waterfall* Brazil
106 C6 **Chacra Mesa** *mt* New Mexico U.S.A.
86 C3 **Chad** *rep* Equat Africa
56 D5 **Chadan** Russian Federation
112 J3 **Chadbourn** North Carolina U.S.A.
131 C6 **Chadileo,R** Argentina
133 D5 **Chadileuvú** *R* Argentina
86 B3 **Chad,L** Equat Africa
56 F2 **Chadobets** *R* Russian Federation
98 D7 **Chadron** Nebraska U.S.A.
99 R7 **Chadwick** Illinois U.S.A.
48 M4 **Chadyr Lunga** Moldavia
110 G4 **Chaffee** Missouri U.S.A.
94 J4 **Chaffee** New York U.S.A.
74 A4 **Chagai** Pakistan
77 H5 **Chagai Hills** Pakistan
53 H8 **Chagan** *R* Kazakhstan/Rus Fed
51 N3 **Chagda** Russian Federation
8 C6 **Chagford** England
77 J2 **Chaghcharān** Afghanistan
55 E4 **Chaglinka** *R* Kazakhstan
40 A4 **Chagny** France
52 E5 **Chagoda** Russian Federation
52 E5 **Chagodoshcha** *R* Russian Federation
81 E6 **Chagos Arch** Indian Oc
94 F5 **Chagrin Falls** Ohio U.S.A.
127 O2 **Chaguanas** Trinidad
127 N1 **Chaguaramas** Trinidad
127 L10 **Chaguaramas** Venezuela
77 H4 **Chahah Burjak** Afghanistan
77 G7 **Chāh Bahār** Iran
77 G5 **Chah Ghevhī, Hamūn-e** *L* Iran
77 L1 **Chāh-i-Ghab** Afghanistan
78 K4 **Chah-I-Surkh** Iraq
68 E5 **Chai Badan** Thailand
75 L7 **Chāībāssa** India
Chaigoubu *see* **Huai'an**
21 J5 **Chailland** France
19 P14 **Chaine de Belledonne** *mts* France
85 E6 **Chaîne de l'Atakora** *mts* Benin
19 N17 **Chaine des Alpilles** *mts* France
18 H7 **Chaise Dieu, la** France
69 D8 **Chaiya** Thailand
68 E5 **Chaiyaphum** Thailand
20 H8 **Chaize-le-Vicomte,la** France
131 F3 **Chajari** Argentina
116 L6 **Chakachamna L** Alaska U.S.A.
74 F2 **Chak Amru** Pakistan
88 G4 **Chake Chake** Tanzania
77 H4 **Chakhānsūr** Afghanistan
74 E2 **Chakwal** Pakistan
128 D7 **Chala** Peru
87 F8 **Chalabesa** Zambia
40 C4 **Chalain,L.de** France
18 F7 **Chalais** France
59 H2 **Cha-lan-t'un** China
128 D7 **Chala,Pta** Peru
125 P10 **Chalatenango** Honduras
69 D9 **Chalaung** Thailand
124 H6 **Chalchihuites** Mexico
125 P11 **Chalchuapa** El Salvador
Chalcis *see* **Khalkís**
9 E6 **Chale** England
122 G6 **Chaleurs, Baie des** Quebec/New Bruns Canada
128 D6 **Chalhuanca** Peru
133 C7 **Chalia** *R* Argentina
88 B7 **Chali,L** Zambia
19 J5 **Chalindrey** France
67 D3 **Chaling** China
74 F8 **Chalisgaon** India
9 G5 **Chalk** England
98 B4 **Chalk Buttes** Montana U.S.A.
109 K3 **Chalk Mountain** Texas U.S.A.
121 N6 **Chalk River** Ontario Canada
144 A7 **Chalky Inlet** New Zealand
116 Q3 **Chalkyitsik** Alaska U.S.A.
21 H6 **Challain-la-Potherie** France
20 G8 **Challans** France
133 D1 **Challapata** Bolivia
115 M1 **Challenger Mts** Northwest Territories Canada
22 H5 **Challerange** France
101 L5 **Challis** Idaho U.S.A.
52 E2 **Chal'mny Varre** Russian Federation
75 N7 **Chalna** Bangladesh
52 D4 **Chalna** Russian Federation
21 J7 **Chalonnes** France
18 H4 **Chalons-sur-Marne** France
19 J6 **Chalon-sur-Saône** France
65 J3 **Chaluhe** China
18 F7 **Châlus** France
57 B4 **Chalysh** Uzbekistan
37 O5 **Cham** *R* Germany
37 O5 **Cham** Germany
106 E4 **Chama** Colorado U.S.A.
106 D5 **Chama** New Mexico U.S.A.
74 B3 **Chaman** Pakistan
68 E6 **Chamao,Khao** *mt* Thailand
106 D5 **Chama, R** New Mexico U.S.A.
128 C5 **Chamaya** *R* Peru
74 G2 **Chamba** India
73 M3 **Chambal** *R* Madhya Prad/Rajasthan India
40 B7 **Chambaran, Plat. de** France
126 E3 **Chambas** Cuba
119 M8 **Chamberlain** Saskatchewan Canada
98 G6 **Chamberlain** South Dakota U.S.A.
95 R7 **Chamberlain L** Maine U.S.A.
142 G3 **Chamberlain R** W Australia Australia
116 P2 **Chamberlin,Mt** Alaska U.S.A.
103 P6 **Chambers** Arizona U.S.A.
98 H7 **Chambers** Nebraska U.S.A.
140 B1 **Chambers B** N Terr Australia
94 K7 **Chambersburg** Pennsylvania U.S.A.
99 T4 **Chambers I** Wisconsin U.S.A.
138 C1 **Chambers Pillar** *pk* N Terr Australia
19 P13 **Chambéry** France
88 C7 **Chambeshi** *R* Zambia
128 C4 **Chambira** *R* Peru
21 P3 **Chambly** France
21 L4 **Chambois** France
18 H7 **Chambon, le** Loire France
121 S4 **Chambord** Quebec Canada
21 O6 **Chambord** France
21 M7 **Chambourg-sur-Indre** France
66 E5 **Chamdo** *prov* China
124 G8 **Chamela** Mexico
77 B4 **Cham-e Zeydun** Iran
77 B3 **Chamgordan** Iran
133 D4 **Chamical** Argentina
106 D5 **Chamita** New Mexico U.S.A.
86 G4 **Chamo Hāyk'** *L* Ethiopia
110 E3 **Chamois** Missouri U.S.A.
74 H3 **Chamoli** India
40 E6 **Chamonix** France
19 P16 **Chamouse,Mt.de** France
75 K7 **Champa** India
89 F7 **Champagne Castle** *mt* Lesotho
40 C4 **Champagnole** France
142 E3 **Champagny Is** W Australia Australia
99 S9 **Champaign** Illinois U.S.A.
131 D3 **Champaqui** *pk* Argentina
68 G5 **Cham Pasak** Laos
121 N4 **Champcoeur** Quebec Canada
36 C7 **Champ du Feu** *mt* France
21 O8 **Champenoise,la** France
21 K5 **Champgeneteux** France
19 O14 **Champier** France
21 J6 **Champigné** France
21 N6 **Champigny** France
21 L8 **Champigny le Sec** France
21 L7 **Champigny-sur-Veude** France
21 P8 **Champillet** France
22 J3 **Champion** Belgium
118 D8 **Champion** Alberta Canada
99 T3 **Champion** Michigan U.S.A.
94 G5 **Champion Heights** Ohio U.S.A.
121 S6 **Champlain** Quebec Canada
95 O2 **Champlain** New York U.S.A.
121 R8 **Champlain** New York U.S.A.
95 O3 **Champlain Canal** New York U.S.A.
19 J5 **Champlitte** France
40 B2 **Champlitte** France
121 N4 **Champneuf** Quebec Canada
19 Q15 **Champoléon** France
40 G6 **Champorcher** Italy
21 N5 **Champrond** France
21 J4 **Champsecret** France
21 J7 **Champtocé** France
20 H7 **Champtoceaux** France
76 C5 **Chamrajnagar** India
19 P14 **Chamrousse** France
16 B5 **Chamusca** Portugal
69 E9 **Chana** Thailand
18 H8 **Chanac** France
131 B2 **Chañaral** *R* Chile
133 C3 **Chañaral** Chile
131 B2 **Chañaral, I** Chile
98 K6 **Chancellor** South Dakota U.S.A.
133 C5 **Chanco** Chile
21 M4 **Chandai** France
116 P2 **Chandalar** *R* Alaska U.S.A.
116 N3 **Chandalar** Alaska U.S.A.
111 G11 **Chandeleur Sound** Louisiana U.S.A.
122 H5 **Chandler** Quebec Canada
116 M2 **Chandler** *R* Alaska U.S.A.
103 N8 **Chandler** Arizona U.S.A.
107 O6 **Chandler** Oklahoma U.S.A.
109 M3 **Chandler** Texas U.S.A.
116 L2 **Chandler L** Alaska U.S.A.
138 C2 **Chandler,Mt** South Australia Australia
99 Q9 **Chandlerville** Illinois U.S.A.
128 D6 **Chandless** *R* Peru/Brazil
75 O7 **Chandpur** Bangladesh
74 H9 **Chandrapur** India
77 G6 **Chānf** Iran
Chang'an *see* **Rong'an**
65 A7 **Chang'an** China
87 F9 **Changara** Mozambique
65 G4 **Changbai** China
65 G4 **Changbai Shan** *mt ra* China
146 D3 **Chang Cheng** *China Base* Antarctica
68 J3 **Changcheng** China
67 B1 **Changchi** China
65 F3 **Changchun** China
65 F2 **Changchunling** China
67 F1 **Changdang Hu** *L* China
67 D2 **Changde** China
123 S4 **Change I** Newfoundland Canada
65 B7 **Changge** China
65 E5 **Changhai** China
58 F5 **Chang Hu** *L* China
67 F1 **Changhua** China
67 G4 **Chang-hua** Taiwan
67 C7 **Changhua Jiang** *R* China
67 C1 **Chang Jiang** *R* China
67 C7 **Changjiang** China
67 E2 **Chang Jiang** *R* Jiangxi China
65 G4 **Changjin Res** N Korea
68 F6 **Chang,Ko** *isld* Thailand
65 D6 **Changle** China
67 G2 **Changle** China
67 F4 **Changle** China
65 D5 **Changli** China
59 H3 **Changling** China
66 B5 **Changmar** China
67 A2 **Changning** China
67 D3 **Changning** China
65 C4 **Changping** China
Changpuzhen *see* **Suining**
65 C6 **Changqing** China
65 F5 **Changsan-got** *C* N Korea
67 D2 **Changsha** China
67 F2 **Changshan** China
65 E5 **Changshan Qundao** *islds* China
65 D4 **Changshanyu** China
67 B2 **Changshou** China
67 G1 **Changshu** China
67 B3 **Changshun** China
67 F4 **Changtai** China
65 G2 **Changting** China
67 E4 **Changting** China
65 F3 **Changtu** China
65 G2 **Changwu** China
67 F1 **Changxing** China
65 E5 **Changxing Dao** *isld* China
67 D1 **Changyang** China
65 D6 **Changyi** China
59 H4 **Changyon** N Korea
65 C7 **Changyuan** China
Changzhai *see* **Changshun**
65 B6 **Changzhi** China
67 G1 **Changzhou** Jiangsu China
67 E1 **Changzhuyuan** China
83 J8 **Chankanai** Sri Lanka
116 H8 **Chankluit I** Alaska U.S.A.
69 C8 **Chan,Ko** *isld* Thailand
21 L7 **Channay-sur-Lathan** France
145 E2 **Channel I** New Zealand
102 E8 **Channel Is** California U.S.A.
20 E3 **Channel Islands** English Chan
123 N6 **Channel-Port aux Basques** Newfoundland Canada
143 C10 **Channel Pt** W Australia Australia
126 F3 **Channel Rock** Bahamas
76 C4 **Channiapatna** India
119 P4 **Channing** *airfield* Manitoba Canada
99 S3 **Channing** Michigan U.S.A.
108 B8 **Channing** Texas U.S.A.
16 B2 **Chantada** Spain
21 K6 **Chantenay** Sarthe France
68 F6 **Chanthaburi** Thailand
21 P3 **Chantilly** France
21 H8 **Chantonnay** France
115 K4 **Chantrey Inlet** Northwest Territories Canada
21 J4 **Chanu** France
69 A8 **Chanumla** Nicobar Is
107 P4 **Chanute** Kansas U.S.A.
110 A4 **Chanute** Kansas U.S.A.
55 G3 **Chany** Russian Federation
21 J7 **Chanzeaux** France
17 G10 **Chanzy** Algeria
Chao'an *see* **Chaozhou**
65 C6 **Chaocheng** China
16 D9 **Chaoen** Morocco
58 G5 **Chao Hu** *L* China
128 C5 **Chao, I** Peru
68 E5 **Chao Phraya Ra** Thailand
65 E1 **Chaor He** *R* China
58 E5 **Chaotianyi** China
67 F1 **Chao Xian** China
Chaoyang *see* **Huinan**
59 K2 **Ch'ao-Yang** China
67 E5 **Chaoyang** Guangdong China
65 E4 **Chaoyang** Liaoning China
65 A7 **Chaoyi** China
67 E5 **Chaozhou** China
129 J5 **Chapada das Mangabeiras** *mts* Brazil
129 K6 **Chapada Diamantina** *mts* Brazil
129 K5 **Chapada do Araripe** *mts* Brazil
130 C4 **Chapada dos Guimarães** Brazil
129 K4 **Chapadinha** Brazil
121 Q3 **Chapais** Quebec Canada
124 H7 **Chapala,L.de** Mexico
129 K8 **Chaparao,Serra do** *mts* Brazil
53 H8 **Chapayev** Kazakhstan
57 C6 **Chapayeva, Imeni** Turkmenistan
53 G7 **Chapayevsk** Russian Federation
121 N7 **Chapeau** Quebec Canada
130 D10 **Chapecó** Brazil
130 D10 **Chapecózinho** *R* Brazil
9 E1 **Chapel en le Frith** England
112 H2 **Chapel Hill** North Carolina U.S.A.
110 K6 **Chapel Hill** Tennessee U.S.A.
21 K5 **Chapelle-au-Riboul,la** France
40 D1 **Chapelle-aux-Bois, La** France
20 H7 **Chapelle Basse Mer, la** France
21 M7 **Chapelle, Blanche-St. Martin, la** France
20 G6 **Chapelle-Bouexic,la** France
21 K6 **Chapelle d'Aligné, la** France
18 G5 **Chapelle d' Angillon,la** France
20 F7 **Chapelle-des-Marais,la** France
21 H6 **Chapelle-Glain,la** France
20 H7 **Chapelle-Heulin,la** France
22 J4 **Chapelle, la** France
20 F6 **Chapelle,La** Morbihan France
123 L3 **Chapelle,L. de la** Quebec Canada
21 K4 **Chapelle-Moche,la** France
21 J5 **Chapelle-Rainsouin,la** France
21 N5 **Chapelle Royale** France
21 K8 **Chapelle St. Laurent, la** France
21 O6 **Chapelle-st.Mesmin,la** France
20 G7 **Chapelle-sur-Erdre, La** France
9 G1 **Chapel St Leonards** England
127 K2 **Chapelton** Jamaica
13 G6 **Chapeltown** England
99 Q10 **Chapin** Illinois U.S.A.
110 F2 **Chapin** Illinois U.S.A.
120 G4 **Chapleau** *R* Ontario Canada
120 G5 **Chapleau** Ontario Canada
120 H4 **Chapleau-Nemecosenda Wild R. Prov. Pk** Ontario Canada
118 L8 **Chaplin** Saskatchewan Canada
147 P1 **Chaplina,Mys** *C* Russian Federation
54 H8 **Chaplino** Ukraine
54 L3 **Chaplygin** Russian Federation
111 K10 **Chapman** Alabama U.S.A.
107 N3 **Chapman** Kansas U.S.A.
101 R1 **Chapman** Montana U.S.A.
98 H8 **Chapman** Nebraska U.S.A.
117 O10 **Chapman,Mt** British Columbia Canada
142 F3 **Chapman R** W Australia Australia
109 K8 **Chapman Ranch** Texas U.S.A.
94 E9 **Chapmanville** West Virginia U.S.A.
52 E2 **Chapoma** Russian Federation
98 D8 **Chappell** Nebraska U.S.A.
109 L5 **Chappell Hill** Texas U.S.A.
139 J8 **Chappell Is** Tasmania Australia
95 L8 **Chaptico** Maryland U.S.A.
18 E7 **Chapus, le** France
120 K4 **Chaput** Ontario Canada
128 E7 **Chaqui** Bolivia
133 D1 **Chaqui** Bolivia
74 G2 **Char** Kashmir
85 B4 **Char** Mauritania
51 L3 **Chara** Russian Federation
133 E1 **Charagua** Bolivia
124 E4 **Charay** Mexico
98 C2 **Charbonneau** North Dakota U.S.A.
40 C3 **Charcenne** France
21 K5 **Charchigné** France
109 K7 **Charco** Texas U.S.A.
146 C5 **Charcot I** Antarctica
118 G3 **Chard** Alberta Canada
8 D6 **Chard** England
57 E4 **Chardara** Kazakhstan
57 E4 **Chardarinskoye Vdkhr** *res* Kazakhstan/Uzbekistan
94 F5 **Chardon** Ohio U.S.A.
126 G5 **Chardonnière** Haiti
57 C5 **Chardzhou** Turkmenistan
18 E7 **Charente** *R* France
18 E7 **Charente** *dept* France
18 E7 **Charente-Maritime** *dept* France
21 M3 **Charentonne** *R* France
18 G6 **Charenton-sur-Cher** France
86 C3 **Chari** *R* Chad
77 L2 **Chārīkār** Afghanistan
9 G5 **Charing** England
116 D2 **Chariot** Alaska U.S.A.
18 H5 **Charité, la** France
99 N8 **Chariton** Iowa U.S.A.
99 N9 **Chariton** *R* Iowa U.S.A.
110 D2 **Chariton** *R* Missouri U.S.A.
128 G2 **Charity** Guyana
52 H2 **Charkayuvom** Russian Federation
74 H6 **Charkhari** India
9 E4 **Charlbury** England
22 H3 **Charleroi** Belgium
94 H6 **Charleroi** Pennsylvania U.S.A.
119 Q3 **Charles** Manitoba Canada
121 T6 **Charlesbourg** Quebec Canada
95 M9 **Charles,C** Virginia U.S.A.
99 O6 **Charles City** Iowa U.S.A.
115 M5 **Charles I** Northwest Territories Canada
143 B8 **Charles,Mt** W Australia Australia
143 D10 **Charles Pk** W Australia Australia
140 B1 **Charles Pt** N Terr Australia
144 A6 **Charles Sd** New Zealand
144 C4 **Charleston** New Zealand
110 B6 **Charleston** Arkansas U.S.A.
99 S10 **Charleston** Illinois U.S.A.
111 F7 **Charleston** Mississippi U.S.A.
110 G5 **Charleston** Missouri U.S.A.
100 A6 **Charleston** Oregon U.S.A.
112 H5 **Charleston** South Carolina U.S.A.
112 C2 **Charleston** Tennessee U.S.A.
94 F8 **Charleston** West Virginia U.S.A.
103 J5 **Charleston Pk** Nevada U.S.A.
14 C3 **Charlestown** Ireland
94 B8 **Charlestown** Indiana U.S.A.
95 P3 **Charlestown** New Hampshire U.S.A.
94 K7 **Charles Town** West Virginia U.S.A.
127 P4 **Charlestown** Nevis W Indies
118 A1 **Charles Wood** Manitoba Canada
Charlet,Ft *see* **Djanet**
21 N3 **Charleval** France
141 H7 **Charleville** Queensland Australia
22 H4 **Charleville-Mézières** France
94 B1 **Charlevoix** Michigan U.S.A.
94 B1 **Charlevoix,L** Michigan U.S.A.
116 Q4 **Charley** *R* Alaska U.S.A.
117 N7 **Charlie Lake** British Columbia Canada
18 H6 **Charlieu** France
94 C4 **Charlotte** Michigan U.S.A.
112 G2 **Charlotte** North Carolina U.S.A.
109 J7 **Charlotte** Texas U.S.A.
127 M5 **Charlotte Amalie** Virgin Is
117 L9 **Charlotte L** British Columbia Canada
27 F12 **Charlottenberg** Sweden
33 S7 **Charlottenburg** Berlin
33 S9 **Charlottenfelde** Germany
94 J8 **Charlottesville** Virginia U.S.A.
122 J7 **Charlottetown** Prince Edward I Canada
Charlotte Town Grenada *see* **Gouyave**
127 N1 **Charlotteville** Tobago
139 G6 **Charlton** Victoria Australia
120 K5 **Charlton** Ontario Canada
115 M7 **Charlton I** Northwest Territories Canada
19 K4 **Charmes** France
40 F4 **Charmey** Switzerland
40 F3 **Chärmoille** Switzerland
8 D6 **Charmouth** England
21 M8 **Charnizay** France
142 F3 **Charnley,R** W Australia Australia
121 T6 **Charny** Quebec Canada
60 R2 **Charo-gawa** *R* Japan
18 H6 **Charolles** France
21 P8 **Charost** France
52 E4 **Charozero** Russian Federation
122 J2 **Charpeney,L** Quebec Canada
21 O3 **Chars** France
74 D1 **Charsadda** Pakistan
57 D5 **Charshanga** Turkmenistan
56 B6 **Charsk** Kazakhstan
99 L7 **Charter Oak** Iowa U.S.A.
141 H5 **Charters Towers** Queensland Australia
122 A8 **Chartierville** Quebec Canada
21 M6 **Chartre,la** France
21 N5 **Chartres** France
57 F4 **Charvakskoye Vdkhr.** Uzbekistan
19 Q13 **Charvin, Mt** France
19 Q13 **Charvonnex** France
56 B5 **Charysh** *R* Russian Federation
131 F5 **Chascomas** Argentina
117 O10 **Chase** British Columbia Canada
107 M3 **Chase** Kansas U.S.A.
99 P6 **Chaseburg** Wisconsin U.S.A.
94 J10 **Chase City** Virginia U.S.A.
98 G3 **Chase L** North Dakota U.S.A.
55 D3 **Chashi** Russian Federation
57 B5 **Chashkent** Turkmenistan
99 N5 **Chaska** Minnesota U.S.A.
144 B7 **Chaslands Mistake** New Zealand
117 N10 **Chasm** British Columbia Canada
52 D1 **Chasnachorr, Gora** *mt* Russian Federation
52 E3 **Chasovenskaya** Russian Federation
52 H4 **Chasovo** Russian Federation
54 J8 **Chasov Yar** Ukraine
113 E9 **Chassahowitzka B** Florida U.S.A.
99 S2 **Chassell** Michigan U.S.A.
18 F7 **Chasseneuil** France
18 H8 **Chassezac** *R* France
21 O8 **Chassignoles** France
21 K5 **Chassille** France
55 E3 **Chastoozer'ye** Russian Federation
52 H6 **Chastyye** Russian Federation
21 J8 **Châtaigneraie,la** France
116 O4 **Chatanika** Alaska U.S.A.
121 L10 **Chatauqua L** New York U.S.A.
127 O8 **Chateaubelair** St Vincent
20 G7 **Chateau Bougon** *airport* France
20 H5 **Châteaubourg** France
20 H6 **Châteaubriant** France
18 H5 **Château Chinon** France
19 O18 **Château d'If** *isld* France
18 E7 **Château d'Oléron, le** France
21 L6 **Château-du-Loir** France
21 N5 **Châteaudun** France
21 P4 **Châteaufort** France
95 N2 **Chateaugay** New York U.S.A.
20 H5 **Châteaugiron** France
21 J6 **Château-Gontier** France
21 L6 **Château-la-Vallière** France
20 B5 **Châteaulin** France
21 P8 **Châteaumeillant** France
19 N14 **Châteauneuf-de-Galaure** France
20 G4 **Châteauneuf-d'Ille-et-Vilaine** France
20 C5 **Châteauneuf-du-Faou** France
21 N4 **Châteauneuf-en-Thymerais** France
18 E7 **Châteauneuf-sur-Charente** France
21 P8 **Châteauneuf-sur-Cher** France
21 P6 **Châteauneuf-sur-Loire** France
21 J6 **Châteauneuf-sur-Sarthe** France
22 G4 **Château-Porcien** France
20 D4 **Château,Pte.du** France
19 Q16 **Châteauredon** France
19 N17 **Châteaurenard** France
21 M6 **Château-Renault** France
122 A7 **Chateau Richer** Quebec Canada
21 O8 **Châteauroux** Indre France
19 K4 **Château Salins** France
18 H3 **Château-Thierry** France
121 R5 **Chateauvert, L** Quebec Canada
127 O4 **Châteaux, Pte. des** Guadeloupe W Indies
117 O6 **Chateh** Alberta Canada
20 E4 **Châtelaudren** France
22 H3 **Châtelet** Belgium
21 P8 **Châtelet,le** France
21 N5 **Châtelets,les** France
18 H7 **Chatelguyon** France
40 A2 **Chatellenot** France
21 M8 **Châtellerault** France
36 C7 **Chatenois** France
99 O6 **Chatfield** Minnesota U.S.A.
122 G6 **Chatham** New Brunswick Canada
120 H10 **Chatham** Ontario Canada
9 G5 **Chatham** England
117 F7 **Chatham** Alaska U.S.A.
99 R10 **Chatham** Illinois U.S.A.
110 G2 **Chatham** Illinois U.S.A.
111 D9 **Chatham** Louisiana U.S.A.
95 S5 **Chatham** Massachusetts U.S.A.
95 O4 **Chatham** New York U.S.A.
94 H10 **Chatham** Virginia U.S.A.
137 R10 **Chatham Is** Pacific Oc
117 H8 **Chatham Sd** British Columbia Canada
133 C8 **Chatham Stokes** *mt* Chile
22 K4 **Châtillon** Belgium
40 G6 **Châtillon** Italy
18 G5 **Châtillon-Coligny** France
19 P12 **Châtillon de Michaille** France
21 H5 **Châtillon-en-Vendelais** France
19 O13 **Chatillon-la-Palud** France
21 N8 **Châtillon-sur-Indre** France
18 G5 **Châtillon-sur-Loire** France
57 F4 **Chatkal** *R* Kyrgyzstan
57 F4 **Chatkal'skiy Khr** *mts* Kyrgyzstan/Uzbekistan
111 H10 **Chatom** Alabama U.S.A.
75 L6 **Chatra** India
21 O8 **Châtre, la** France
140 F5 **Chatsworth** Queensland Australia
120 K8 **Chatsworth** Ontario Canada
112 C3 **Chatsworth** Georgia U.S.A.
110 H1 **Chatsworth** Illinois U.S.A.
95 N7 **Chatsworth** New Jersey U.S.A.
89 G2 **Chatsworth** Zimbabwe
111 L8 **Chattahoochee** *R* Alabama/ Georgia
111 M11 **Chattahoochee** Florida U.S.A.
112 B2 **Chattanooga** Tennessee U.S.A.
100 H2 **Chattaroy** Washington U.S.A.
94 E9 **Chattaroy** West Virginia U.S.A.
9 G3 **Chatteris** England
144 B6 **Chatto Cr** New Zealand
13 G2 **Chatton** England
111 L7 **Chattooga** *R* Georgia/ Alabama U.S.A.
112 D3 **Chattooga** *R* S Carolina/ Georgia U.S.A.
112 D2 **Chatuge L** North Carolina U.S.A.
68 E5 **Chaturat** Thailand
57 H4 **Chatyr-Kël' Ozero** *L* Kyrgyzstan
20 H8 **Chauché** France
18 H8 **Chaudes-Aigues** France
22 K2 **Chaudfontaine** Belgium
Chau Doc *see* **Chau Phu**
21 J7 **Chaudron-en-Mauges** France
22 E5 **Chaudun** France
116 H6 **Chauekuktuli L** Alaska U.S.A.
19 Q15 **Chauffayer** France
68 B2 **Chauk** Burma
75 R5 **Chaukan Pass** Burma/India
22 D4 **Chaulnes** France
40 B4 **Chaumergy** France
40 D3 **Chaumont** *mt* France
19 J4 **Chaumont** Haute-Marne France
21 O3 **Chaumont-en-Vexin** France
22 G4 **Chaumont-Porcien** France
21 N7 **Chaumont-sur-Loire** France
21 O6 **Chaumont-sur-Tharonne** France
94 E7 **Chauncey** Ohio U.S.A.
68 D6 **Chaungwabyin** Burma
68 C4 **Chaungzon** Burma
51 Q2 **Chaunskaya Guba** *G* Russian Federation
22 E4 **Chauny** France
68 G7 **Chau Phu** Vietnam
69 A8 **Chaura I** Nicobar Is
20 G4 **Chausey Is** France
21 P2 **Chaussée-Tirancourt,la** France
19 J6 **Chaussin** France
54 B3 **Chausy** Belorussia
94 H4 **Chautauqua** New York U.S.A.
94 H4 **Chautauqua L** New York U.S.A.
57 F4 **Chauvay** Kyrgyzstan
20 G7 **Chauvé** France
21 N6 **Chauvigny** Loir-et-Cher France
21 M8 **Chauvigny** Vienne France
118 G6 **Chauvin** Alberta Canada
19 K5 **Chaux de Fonds, la** France
40 E3 **Chaux de Fonds, La** Switzerland
20 H8 **Chavagnes-en-Paillers** France
19 N14 **Chavanay** France
52 E2 **Chavan'ga** Russian Federation
130 D4 **Chavantina** Brazil
130 D7 **Chavantina** Brazil
16 C3 **Chaves** Portugal
94 D9 **Chavies** Kentucky U.S.A.
22 F5 **Chavignon** France
87 D8 **Chavuma** Zambia
69 D8 **Chawang** Thailand
9 F5 **Chawton** England
56 G2 **Chaya** *R* Russian Federation
88 C7 **Chaya, L** Zambia
57 E3 **Chayan** Kazakhstan
57 G4 **Chayek** Kyrgyzstan
52 H6 **Chaykovskiy** Russian Federation
78 K2 **Chāypareh** Iran
66 F6 **Ch'a-yü** China
21 J6 **Chazé-sur-Argos** France
52 H4 **Chazhegovo** Russian Federation
133 E4 **Chazon** Argentina
95 O2 **Chazy** New York U.S.A.
118 D7 **Cheadle** Alberta Canada
9 E2 **Cheadle** England
111 L8 **Cheaha Mt** Alabama U.S.A.
94 H7 **Cheat** *R* West Virginia U.S.A.
110 J5 **Cheatham L** Tennessee U.S.A.
37 N3 **Cheb** Czechoslovakia
55 D4 **Chebarkul'** Russian Federation
52 G6 **Cheboksary** Russian Federation
94 C1 **Cheboygan** Michigan U.S.A.
52 E5 **Chebsara** Russian Federation
53 G11 **Checheno-Ingushskaya Respublika** Russian Federation
54 B4 **Chechersk** Belorussia
31 M5 **Chęciny** Poland
107 P6 **Checotah** Oklahoma U.S.A.
21 P6 **Chécy** France
123 L8 **Chedabucto B** Nova Scotia Canada
8 D5 **Cheddar** England
83 K9 **Cheddikulam** Sri Lanka
68 A3 **Cheduba** *isld* Burma
68 A3 **Cheduba** Burma
68 A3 **Cheduba Str** Burma
118 G2 **Cheecham** Alberta Canada
120 J2 **Cheepash** *R* Ontario Canada
120 G1 **Cheepay** *R* Ontario Canada
141 G7 **Cheepie** Queensland Australia
119 O1 **Cheeseman L** Ontario Canada
106 E2 **Cheesman,L** Colorado U.S.A.
146 C13 **Cheetham,C** Antarctica
18 E6 **Chef-Boutonne** France
111 G11 **Chef Menteur** Louisiana U.S.A.
Chefoo *see* **Yantai**
116 E6 **Chefornak** Alaska U.S.A.
121 R3 **Chef,R.du** Quebec Canada
59 K1 **Chegdomyn** Russian Federation
85 C3 **Chegga** Mauritania
116 A3 **Chegitun** *R* Russian Federation
89 G2 **Chegutu** Zimbabwe
100 B3 **Chehalis** *R* Washington U.S.A.
100 C3 **Chehalis** Washington U.S.A.
67 B4 **Chehe** China

87 F8 **Cheif Serenje** Zambia
21 L7 **Cheillé** France
59 J5 **Cheju** S Korea
65 G8 **Cheju do** *isld* S Korea
65 G8 **Cheju haehyŏp** *str* S Korea
54 H2 **Chekalin** Russian Federation
52 H7 **Chekan** Russian Federation
54 J1 **Chekhov** Russian Federation
Chekiang *prov see* **Zhejiang**
55 G2 **Chekino** Russian Federation
51 N3 **Chekunda** Russian Federation
52 E3 **Chekuyevo** Russian Federation
119 O6 **Chelan** Saskatchewan Canada
100 F2 **Chelan** Washington U.S.A.
100 E1 **Chelan,L** Washington U.S.A.
100 E1 **Chelan Range** Washington U.S.A.
116 M5 **Chelatna L** Alaska U.S.A.
133 D5 **Chelforó** Argentina
85 F1 **Chelia** *mt* Algeria
85 E1 **Chélif** *R* Algeria
55 C3 **Chelkakovo** Russian Federation
57 A1 **Chelkar** Kazakhstan
31 O4 **Chełm** Poland
31 L2 **Chełmno** Poland
120 J6 **Chelmsford** Ontario Canada
9 G4 **Chelmsford** England
52 E3 **Chelmuzhi** Russian Federation
31 L2 **Chełmża** Poland
99 O8 **Chelsea** Iowa U.S.A.
94 C4 **Chelsea** Michigan U.S.A.
107 P5 **Chelsea** Oklahoma U.S.A.
95 P3 **Chelsea** Vermont U.S.A.
8 D4 **Cheltenham** England
20 H6 **Chelun** France
17 G5 **Chelva** Spain
55 D3 **Chelyabinsk** Russian Federation
55 D4 **Chelyabinskaya Oblast'** *prov* Russian Federation
94 F8 **Chelyan** West Virginia U.S.A.
56 C5 **Chelyush** Russian Federation
51 K1 **Chelyuskin,Mys** *C* Russian Federation
117 M11 **Chemainus** British Columbia Canada
100 C4 **Chemawa** Oregon U.S.A.
21 J6 **Chemaze** France
87 F9 **Chemba** Mozambique
57 B6 **Chemen-i-Bit** Turkmenistan
21 N7 **Chemery** France
22 H4 **Chémery-sur-Bar** France
21 J7 **Chemillé** France
21 M6 **Chemillé-sur-Dême** France
40 B4 **Chemin** France
21 K6 **Chemiré-le-Gaudin** France
37 O2 **Chemnitz** Germany
95 R7 **Chemquasabamticook L** Maine U.S.A.
56 B4 **Chemskiy** Russian Federation
95 K4 **Chemung** *R* New York U.S.A.
116 O4 **Chena** *R* Alaska U.S.A.
74 D3 **Chenab** *R* Pakistan
85 D3 **Chenachane** *watercourse* Algeria
85 D3 **Chenachane** Algeria
116 O4 **Chena Hot Springs** Alaska U.S.A.
95 M4 **Chenango** *R* New York U.S.A.
86 G4 **Ch'ench'a** Ethiopia
22 K2 **Chênée** Belgium
18 G6 **Chénérailles** France
121 P7 **Chénéville** Quebec Canada
107 N4 **Cheney** Kansas U.S.A.
100 H2 **Cheney** Washington U.S.A.
111 D10 **Cheneyville** Louisiana U.S.A.
76 E4 **Chengalpattu** India
65 C6 **Cheng'an** China
67 B4 **Chengbihe Shuiku** *res* China
67 C3 **Chengbu** China
65 A7 **Chengcheng** China
Chengchow *see* **Zhengzhou**
65 D4 **Chengde** China
67 E1 **Chengdong Hu** *L* China
67 A1 **Chengdu** China
67 A4 **Chenggong** China
67 E5 **Chenghai** China
67 A4 **Chengjiang** China
65 D5 **Chengkou** China
67 C1 **Chengkou** China
67 C7 **Chengmai** China
65 E6 **Chengshan Jiao** *pen* China
Chengtu *see* **Chengdu**
65 C7 **Chengwu** China
65 E6 **Chengyang** China
67 F2 **Chengyang** China
65 E5 **Chengzitan** China
121 O6 **Chenier** Quebec Canada
123 N2 **Chenil,L** Quebec Canada
36 B7 **Cheniménil** France
65 D7 **Cheniu Shan** *isld* China
65 D7 **Chenjiagang** China
65 C7 **Chenliu** China
110 H1 **Chenoa** Illinois U.S.A.
21 N7 **Chenonceaux** France
40 B3 **Chenôve** France
67 G1 **Chenqian Shan** *isld* China
21 L6 **Chenu** France
67 C2 **Chenxi** China
67 D4 **Chen Xian** China
Chenying *see* **Wannian**
68 J6 **Cheo Reo** Vietnam
67 F3 **Chepan** China
46 G3 **Chepelare** Bulgaria
128 C5 **Chepén** Peru
133 D4 **Chepes** Argentina
8 D4 **Chepstow** Wales
99 Q3 **Chequamegon B** Wisconsin U.S.A.
21 M7 **Cher** *R* France
22 K3 **Cherain** Belgium
44 C2 **Cherasco** Italy
106 G3 **Cheraw** Colorado U.S.A.
111 G10 **Cheraw** Mississippi U.S.A.
112 H3 **Cheraw** South Carolina U.S.A.
20 G2 **Cherbourg** France
85 E1 **Cherchell** Algeria
52 J4 **Cherdyn'** Russian Federation
20 G6 **Chère** *R* France
52 B2 **Cheremisskoye** Russian Federation
56 F4 **Cheremkhovo** Russian Federation
55 D3 **Cheremshanka** Russian Federation
55 D1 **Cheremukhovo** Russian Federation
56 D4 **Cheremushki** Russian Federation
56 B4 **Cherepanovo** Russian Federation
54 H2 **Cherepet'** Russian Federation
52 E5 **Cherepovets** Russian Federation
52 D5 **Chereptsovo** Russian Federation
118 C5 **Cherhill** Alberta Canada
54 C3 **Cherikov** Belorussia
21 N4 **Cherisy** France
54 J8 **Cherkasskoye** Ukraine
53 F11 **Cherkessk** Russian Federation
46 G1 **Cherkovitsa** Bulgaria
55 F4 **Cherlak** Russian Federation
52 J5 **Chermoz** Russian Federation
141 K1 **Chermside** *dist* Brisbane, Qnsld Australia
116 H9 **Chernabura I** Alaska U.S.A.
46 G3 **Chernatitsa** *hills* Bulgaria
55 D2 **Chernaya** *R* Russian Federation
52 H5 **Chernaya Kholunitsa** Russian Federation
48 J2 **Chernaya Tisa** *R* Ukraine
Chernenko *see* **Sharypovo**
47 J1 **Chernevo** Bulgaria
54 C5 **Chernigov** Ukraine
59 K3 **Chernigovka** Russian Federation
116 F9 **Cherni I** Alaska U.S.A.
55 C4 **Chernikovsk** Russian Federation
47 H1 **Cherni Lom** *R* Bulgaria
46 F2 **Cherni Vrŭkh** *mt* Bulgaria
53 D8 **Chernobyl'** Ukraine
56 D4 **Chernogorsk** Russian Federation
55 C2 **Chernoistochinsk** Russian Federation
55 G4 **Chernoretskoye** Kazakhstan
55 F4 **Chernousovka** Russian Federation
52 G6 **Chernovskoye** Russian Federation
48 K2 **Chernovtsy** Ukraine
55 E2 **Chernoye** Russian Federation
55 E3 **Chernoye, Oz** *L* Russian Federation
55 C3 **Chernushka** Russian Federation
52 G3 **Chernut'yevo** Russian Federation
31 N1 **Chernyakhovsk** Russian Federation
52 J2 **Chernysheva, Gryada** *ridge* Russian Federation
58 G1 **Chernyshevsk** Russian Federation
31 O1 **Chernyshevskoye** Russian Federation
53 G10 **Chernyye Zemli** Russian Federation
55 C5 **Chernyy Otrog** Russian Federation
53 G9 **Chernyy Yar** Russian Federation
110 J7 **Cherokee** Alabama U.S.A.
99 L7 **Cherokee** Iowa U.S.A.
107 Q4 **Cherokee** Kansas U.S.A.
107 M5 **Cherokee** Oklahoma U.S.A.
109 J5 **Cherokee** Texas U.S.A.
112 D1 **Cherokee Dam** Tennessee U.S.A.
94 D10 **Cherokee L** Tennessee U.S.A.
111 B9 **Cherokee,L** Texas U.S.A.
113 K11 **Cherokee Pt** Bahamas
110 B5 **Cherokees, L O'The** Oklahoma U.S.A.
126 F1 **Cherokee Sound** Great Abaco I Bahamas
55 E2 **Cherpiya** Russian Federation
75 O6 **Cherrapunji** India
20 G4 **Cherrueix** France
137 O4 **Cherry** *isld* Santa Cruz Is
103 K2 **Cherry Cr** Nevada U.S.A.
98 E5 **Cherry Cr** South Dakota U.S.A.
94 H4 **Cherry Creek** New York U.S.A.
103 K1 **Cherry Cr.Mt** Nevada U.S.A.
95 U2 **Cherryfield** Maine U.S.A.
117 O7 **Cherry Point** Alberta Canada
107 P4 **Cherryvale** Kansas U.S.A.
95 N4 **Cherry Valley** New York U.S.A.
112 F2 **Cherryville** North Carolina U.S.A.
56 G3 **Cherskogo,Gora** *mt* Russian Federation
51 O2 **Cherskogo,Khrebet** *mts* Russian Federation
17 H4 **Cherta** Spain
54 M7 **Chertkovo** Russian Federation
54 E1 **Chertolino** Russian Federation
9 F5 **Chertsey** England
144 C5 **Chertsey** New Zealand
52 F6 **Cherusti** Russian Federation
19 O13 **Cheruy,Pt.de** France
52 G4 **Cherva** Russian Federation
48 N3 **Chervonoz-namenka** Ukraine
9 E3 **Cherwell,R** England
94 C3 **Chesaning** Michigan U.S.A.
94 E8 **Chesapeake** Ohio U.S.A.
95 L10 **Chesapeake** Virginia U.S.A.
95 L8 **Chesapeake B** U.S.A.
95 L8 **Chesapeake Beach** Maryland U.S.A.
95 M7 **Chesapeake City** Maryland U.S.A.
9 F4 **Chesham** England
8 D1 **Cheshire** *co* England
95 O4 **Cheshire** Massachusetts U.S.A.
52 G2 **Chëshskaya Guba** *B* Russian Federation
57 G5 **Cheshtebe** Tajikistan
88 B6 **Chesi,L** Zambia
8 D6 **Chesil Bank** England
120 J8 **Chesley** Ontario Canada
55 D4 **Chesma** Russian Federation
112 F2 **Chesnee** South Carolina U.S.A.
22 H5 **Chesne, le** Ardennes France
21 M4 **Chesne,le** Eure France
122 H9 **Chester** Nova Scotia Canada
8 D1 **Chester** England
110 B6 **Chester** Arkansas U.S.A.
100 D9 **Chester** California U.S.A.
95 P5 **Chester** Connecticut U.S.A.
101 O5 **Chester** Idaho U.S.A.
110 G4 **Chester** Illinois U.S.A.
95 L7 **Chester** *R* Maryland U.S.A.
95 P4 **Chester** Massachusetts U.S.A.
101 P1 **Chester** Montana U.S.A.
98 J9 **Chester** Nebraska U.S.A.
95 M6 **Chester** Pennsylvania U.S.A.
112 F3 **Chester** South Carolina U.S.A.
109 N5 **Chester** Texas U.S.A.
95 P3 **Chester** Vermont U.S.A.
94 K9 **Chester** Virginia U.S.A.
122 H9 **Chester Basin** Nova Scotia Canada
9 E1 **Chesterfield** England
101 O7 **Chesterfield** Idaho U.S.A.
110 F2 **Chesterfield** Illinois U.S.A.
112 G3 **Chesterfield** South Carolina U.S.A.
94 K9 **Chesterfield** Virginia U.S.A.
137 M5 **Chesterfield, Îles** Coral Sea
115 K5 **Chesterfield Inlet** Northwest Territories Canada
94 F7 **Chesterhill** Ohio U.S.A.
9 F2 **Chesterton** England
99 T8 **Chesterton** Indiana U.S.A.
95 L7 **Chestertown** Maryland U.S.A.
95 O3 **Chestertown** New York U.S.A.
121 P7 **Chesterville** Ontario Canada
109 O3 **Chestnut** Louisiana U.S.A.
94 H6 **Chestnut Ridge** Pennsylvania U.S.A.
144 D5 **Chest Pk** New Zealand
95 R7 **Chesuncook L** Maine U.S.A.
95 M7 **Cheswold** Delaware U.S.A.
56 C3 **Chet'** *R* Russian Federation
68 A7 **Chetamale** Andaman Is
99 P4 **Chetek** Wisconsin U.S.A.
123 L7 **Cheticamp** C Breton I, Nova Scotia
73 L6 **Chetlat** *isld* Lakshadweep Indian Oc
107 P4 **Chetopa** Kansas U.S.A.
76 A5 **Chettlatt** *isld* Indian Oc
125 P8 **Chetumal** Mexico
145 E4 **Chetwode Is** New Zealand
117 N8 **Chetwynd** British Columbia Canada
116 E6 **Chevak** Alaska U.S.A.
19 O17 **Cheval-Blanc** France
20 G7 **Chevallerais, La** Loire-Atlantique France
21 O5 **Chevilly** France
118 L6 **Cheviot** Saskatchewan Canada
144 D5 **Cheviot** New Zealand
13 F3 **Cheviot Hills** England/Scotland
141 G7 **Cheviot Ra** Queensland Australia
21 K6 **Cheviré-le-Rouge** France
20 A5 **Chèvre, C. de la** France
111 E12 **Chevreuil, Point** Louisiana U.S.A.
21 P4 **Chevreuse** France
40 E7 **Chevril,L** France
20 G7 **Chevrolière, la** France
88 D9 **Chewa** Mozambique
86 G5 **Ch'ew Bahir** *L* Ethiopia
100 H1 **Chewelah** Washington U.S.A.
8 D5 **Chew valley L** England
107 L6 **Cheyenne** Oklahoma U.S.A.
98 D5 **Cheyenne** *R* South Dakota U.S.A.
108 D4 **Cheyenne** Texas U.S.A.
98 B8 **Cheyenne** Wyoming U.S.A.
107 M3 **Cheyenne Bottoms** Kansas U.S.A.
98 A8 **Cheyenne Pass** Wyoming U.S.A.
106 H3 **Cheyenne Wells** Colorado U.S.A.
18 H8 **Cheylard, le** France
143 C10 **Cheyne B** W Australia Australia
117 M9 **Chezacut** British Columbia Canada
21 P8 **Chezal-Benoît** France
20 E5 **Chèze,la** France
75 L6 **Chhapra** India
74 H6 **Chhatarpur** India
75 L9 **Chhatrapur** India
68 G6 **Chhlong** Cambodia
68 H6 **Chhlong** *R* Cambodia
74 F7 **Chhota Udepur** India
68 G7 **Chhuk** Cambodia
116 H9 **Chiachi I** Alaska U.S.A.
67 G5 **Chia-i** Taiwan
66 D5 **Chia-jen Ts'o** *L* China
40 F7 **Chialamberto** Italy
66 D5 **Chia-man-t'e-k'a-mu Hu** *L* China
87 B9 **Chiange** Angola
68 E2 **Chiang Saen** Thailand
42 E6 **Chiani** *R* Italy
125 N9 **Chiapa del Corzo** Mexico
45 O4 **Chiaravalle** Italy
43 G10 **Chiaravalle Centrale** Italy
41 L5 **Chiareggio** Italy
41 L6 **Chiari** Italy
125 K8 **Chiautla** Mexico
44 F3 **Chiavari** Italy
41 K5 **Chiavenna** Italy
61 O10 **Chiba** *prefect* Japan
61 O10 **Chiba** Japan
61 P13 **Chibana** Okinawa
87 B9 **Chibia** Angola
68 E5 **Chi Bon Dam** Thailand
121 P3 **Chibougamau** *R* Quebec Canada
121 Q3 **Chibougamau** Quebec Canada
121 R3 **Chibougamau,Parc de** Quebec Canada
88 B8 **Chibuluma** Zambia
60 G9 **Chiburi-shima** *isld* Japan
87 F10 **Chibuto** Mozambique
87 E8 **Chibwe** Zambia
99 T8 **Chicago** Illinois U.S.A.
105 **Chicago** *conurbation* Illinois U.S.A.
99 T8 **Chicago Heights** Illinois U.S.A.
122 F5 **Chic-Chocs,Parc des** Quebec Canada
117 E7 **Chichagof I** Alaska U.S.A.
85 C2 **Chichaoua** Morocco
21 K8 **Chiché** France
65 C4 **Chicheng** China
125 P7 **Chichén Itza** *ruins* Mexico
9 F6 **Chichester** England
142 C5 **Chichester Ra** W Australia Australia
142 B5 **Chichester Ra Nat Park** W Australia Australia
61 N10 **Chichibu** Japan
61 M9 **Chichibu Tama Nat. Park** Japan
56 C3 **Chichka-Yul** *R* Russian Federation
95 K9 **Chickahominy** *R* Virginia U.S.A.
112 B3 **Chickamauga** Georgia U.S.A.
112 B2 **Chickamauga Dam** Tennessee U.S.A.
111 H10 **Chickasawhay** *R* Mississippi U.S.A.
107 O7 **Chickasaw Nat. Recreation Area** Oklahoma U.S.A.
107 N6 **Chickasha** Oklahoma U.S.A.
116 R4 **Chicken** Alaska U.S.A.
8 D5 **Chicklade** England
16 C8 **Chiclana de la Frontera** Spain
128 C5 **Chiclayo** Peru
133 D6 **Chico** *R* Argentina
71 E2 **Chico** *R* Luzon Philippines
102 C2 **Chico** California U.S.A.
100 H4 **Chico** Oregon U.S.A.
109 K2 **Chico** Texas U.S.A.
133 D3 **Chicoana** Argentina
121 M4 **Chicobi,L** Quebec Canada
87 F10 **Chicomo** Mozambique
125 K7 **Chicontepec** Mexico
87 D7 **Chicopa** *R* Angola
95 P4 **Chicopee** Massachusetts U.S.A.
121 T4 **Chicoutimi** Quebec Canada
121 T5 **Chicoutimi** *R* Quebec Canada
122 B5 **Chicoutimi, Parc des** Quebec Canada
89 G4 **Chicualacuala** Mozambique
76 D5 **Chidambaram** India
9 F5 **Chiddingford** England
109 O2 **Chidester** Arkansas U.S.A.
115 N5 **Chidley,C** Quebec Canada
100 F1 **Chief Joseph Dam** Washington U.S.A.
113 E8 **Chiefland** Florida U.S.A.
120 J8 **Chiefs Pt** Ontario Canada
67 B5 **Chiem Hoa** Vietnam
87 E7 **Chiengi** Zambia
68 D3 **Chieng-Mai** Thailand
42 F5 **Chienti** *R* Italy
44 C1 **Chieri** Italy
22 K5 **Chiers** *R* France
41 L5 **Chiesa** Italy
41 M5 **Chiese** *R* Italy
42 F6 **Chieti** Italy
22 F2 **Chièvres** Belgium
130 H5 **Chifre,Serra do** *mts* Brazil
57 G2 **Chiganak** Kazakhstan
61 N10 **Chigasaki** Japan
116 J8 **Chiginigak Vol., Mt** Alaska U.S.A.
54 D7 **Chigirin** Ukraine
116 L6 **Chigmit Mts** Alaska U.S.A.
122 H8 **Chignecto B** Nova Scotia/New Bruns Canada
116 H8 **Chignik** Alaska U.S.A.
19 Q13 **Chignin** France
121 R3 **Chigoubiche, L** Quebec Canada
87 F10 **Chigubo** Mozambique
66 E6 **Chigu Co** *L* China
9 G4 **Chigwell** England
Chihli,G. of *see* **Bo Hai**
124 F3 **Chihuahua** Mexico
131 B7 **Chihuido Medio** *pk* Argentina
57 D3 **Chiili** Kazakhstan
67 C6 **Chikan** China
107 N5 **Chikaskia** *R* Okla/Kansas U.S.A.
76 C4 **Chik Ballapur** India
52 C6 **Chikhachevo** Russian Federation
60 O3 **Chikiu-misaki** *C* Japan
76 B4 **Chikmagalur** India
56 G5 **Chikoy** *R* Russian Federation
68 G6 **Chikreng** *R* Cambodia
60 D12 **Chikugo** *R* Japan
60 D12 **Chikugo** Japan
61 M9 **Chikuma** *R* Japan
116 H6 **Chikuminuk L** Alaska U.S.A.
61 N11 **Chikura** Japan
88 E10 **Chikwawa** Malawi
68 A2 **Chi-kyaw** Burma
117 L9 **Chilanko Forks** British Columbia Canada
74 F1 **Chilas** Kashmir
83 J10 **Chilaw** Sri Lanka
128 C6 **Chilca, Pta. de** *pt* Peru
102 D2 **Chilcoot** California U.S.A.
117 M10 **Chilcotin** *R* British Columbia Canada
141 K3 **Chilcott I** Gt Barrier Reef Aust
141 K7 **Childers** Queensland Australia
111 K8 **Childersburg** Alabama U.S.A.
108 G1 **Childress** Texas U.S.A.
103 M9 **Childs** Arizona U.S.A.
113 F10 **Childs** Florida U.S.A.
133 C6 **Chile** *rep* S America
128 C5 **Chilete** Peru
76 C3 **Chilgājūr** India
9 G5 **Chilham** England
110 C3 **Chilhowee** Missouri U.S.A.
94 F10 **Chilhowie** Virginia U.S.A.
116 K6 **Chilikadrotna** *R* Alaska U.S.A.
75 L9 **Chilika Lake** India
87 E8 **Chililabombwe** Zambia
89 G2 **Chilimanzi** Zimbabwe
59 H1 **Chi-liu Ho** *R* China
117 F6 **Chilkat** *R* Alaska U.S.A.
117 M10 **Chilko** *R* British Columbia Canada
141 G3 **Chillagoe** Queensland Australia
131 A6 **Chillán** Chile
140 B5 **Chilla Well** N Terr Australia
21 P5 **Chilleurs-aux-Bois** France
99 R9 **Chillicothe** Illinois U.S.A.
110 C2 **Chillicothe** Missouri U.S.A.
94 D7 **Chillicothe** Ohio U.S.A.
109 H1 **Chillicothe** Texas U.S.A.
139 G6 **Chillingollah** Victoria Australia
100 D1 **Chilliwack** British Columbia Canada
19 P13 **Chilly** France
101 M5 **Chilly** Idaho U.S.A.
116 J6 **Chilnuk Mts** Alaska U.S.A.
133 C6 **Chiloé** *prov* Chile
135 R14 **Chiloe, I. de** Chile
88 C8 **Chilonga** Zambia
87 F8 **Chilongazi** Zambia
100 D7 **Chiloquin** Oregon U.S.A.
125 K9 **Chilpancingo** Mexico
139 H6 **Chiltern** Victoria Australia
9 F4 **Chiltern Hills** England
99 S5 **Chilton** Wisconsin U.S.A.
88 E7 **Chilumba** Malawi
67 G4 **Chi-lung** Taiwan
88 F9 **Chilwa,L** Malawi
9 E6 **Chilworth** England
125 M9 **Chimalapa** Mexico
87 F9 **Chimanimani** Zimbabwe
87 F10 **Chimanimani Nat. Park** Zimbabwe
22 G3 **Chimay** Belgium
106 E6 **Chimayo** New Mexico U.S.A.
57 A3 **Chimbay** Uzbekistan
128 C4 **Chimborazo** *mt* Ecuador
128 C5 **Chimbote** Peru
88 C8 **Chimbwin-gombi** *mt* Zambia
55 E3 **Chimeyevo** Russian Federation
57 F4 **Chimion** Kyrgyzstan
48 M4 **Chimishliya** Moldavia
57 E4 **Chimkent** Kazakhstan
123 P4 **Chimney Cove** Newfoundland Canada
108 B3 **Chimney Peak** New Mexico U.S.A.
106 E9 **Chimney Pk** New Mexico U.S.A.
83 J12 **Chimney Rocks** Seychelles
87 F9 **Chimoio** Mozambique
118 E9 **Chin** Alberta Canada
65 F7 **Chin** *isld* S Korea
58 D4 **China** *rep* E Asia
95 S2 **China** Maine U.S.A.
68 C4 **China Bakir** *R* Burma
124 G5 **Chinacates** Mexico
112 G2 **China Grove** North Carolina U.S.A.
125 L3 **Chinandega** Nicaragua
102 F9 **China Pt** California U.S.A.
109 K4 **China Spring** Texas U.S.A.
108 C6 **Chinati Mts** Texas U.S.A.
57 E4 **Chinaz** Uzbekistan
120 J7 **Chin, Cape** Ontario Canada
128 C6 **Chincha Alta** Peru
117 O6 **Chinchaga** *R* Alberta Canada
128 C6 **Chincha, Is** Peru
141 K7 **Chinchilla** Queensland Australia
17 F6 **Chinchilla de Monte Aragón** Spain
128 C4 **Chinchipe** *R* Ecuador/Peru
16 E4 **Chinchón** Spain
95 M9 **Chincoteague** Virginia U.S.A.
95 M8 **Chincoteague B** Maryland U.S.A.
87 G9 **Chinde** Mozambique
73 P4 **Chindwin** *R* Burma
61 P14 **Chinen** Okinawa
88 E8 **Chinengue** Mozambique
66 B4 **Chinese Turkestan** *reg* Xinjiang Uygur Zizhiqu China
67 D1 **Ching-Chiang Res** China
Chinghai *prov see* **Qinghai** *prov*
55 B5 **Chingirlau** Kazakhstan
88 A8 **Chingola** Zambia
87 B8 **Chingoroi** Angola
87 C8 **Chinguai** Angola
73 P4 **Chin Hills** Burma
88 C10 **Chinhoyi** Zimbabwe
116 L8 **Chiniak,C** Alaska U.S.A.
Chining *see* **Jining**
74 E3 **Chiniot** Pakistan
124 E4 **Chinipas** Mexico
116 L7 **Chinitna B** Alaska U.S.A.
65 G7 **Chinju** S Korea
86 D4 **Chinko** *R* Cent Afr Republic
103 P5 **Chinle** Arizona U.S.A.
103 P5 **Chinle V** Arizona U.S.A.
103 P5 **Chinle Wash** Arizona U.S.A.
67 F4 **Chin-men** Taiwan
143 C10 **Chinocup, L** W Australia Australia
21 L7 **Chinon** France
118 G7 **Chinook** Alberta Canada
101 Q1 **Chinook** Montana U.S.A.
100 D3 **Chinook Pass** Washington U.S.A.
103 M7 **Chino Valley** Arizona U.S.A.
87 F8 **Chinsali** Zambia
88 D7 **Chinsali** Zambia
68 A1 **Chin State** Burma
75 P8 **Chin State** *prov* Burma
76 E1 **Chintalnar** India
88 E7 **Chintheche** Malawi
126 G10 **Chinú** Colombia
22 J4 **Chiny** Belgium
55 G3 **Chinyavino** Russian Federation
42 E3 **Chioggia** Italy
Chios *isld see* **Khíos** *isld*
88 D8 **Chipata** Zambia
87 E9 **Chipepo** Zambia
88 D9 **Chipera** Mozambique
88 E10 **Chiperone** *mt* Mozambique
119 T1 **Chipewyan,L** Manitoba Canada
117 R7 **Chipewyan Lake** Alberta Canada
87 E8 **Chipili** Zambia
65 C6 **Chiping** China
87 F10 **Chipinge** Zimbabwe
117 Q9 **Chip Lake** Alberta Canada
111 L11 **Chipley** Florida U.S.A.
111 M9 **Chipley** Georgia U.S.A.
74 E10 **Chiplun** India
122 G7 **Chipman** New Brunswick Canada
120 D3 **Chipman L** Ontario Canada
88 E8 **Chipoka** Malawi
111 L11 **Chipola** *R* Florida U.S.A.
88 A9 **Chiposhya, L** Zambia
68 G7 **Chi Pou** Cambodia
121 L9 **Chippawa** Ontario Canada
8 D5 **Chippenham** England
99 L4 **Chippewa** *R* Minnesota U.S.A.
99 P5 **Chippewa Falls** Wisconsin U.S.A.
99 P4 **Chippewa Lake** Wisconsin U.S.A.
13 F6 **Chipping** England
9 E3 **Chipping Campden** England
9 E4 **Chipping Norton** England
8 D4 **Chipping Sodbury** England
46 F1 **Chiprovtsi** Bulgaria
128 C6 **Chiquian** Peru
128 D2 **Chiquinquirá** Colombia
131 F6 **Chiquita, L. Mar** Buenos Aires Argentina
128 F7 **Chiquitos, Llanos de** Bolivia
128 B4 **Chira** *R* Peru
76 E3 **Chirala** India
87 F9 **Chiramba** Mozambique
128 C3 **Chirambirá, Pta** *pt* Colombia
77 J2 **Chiras** Afghanistan
57 E4 **Chirchik** Uzbekistan
87 F10 **Chiredzi** Zimbabwe
89 G3 **Chiredzi** *R* Zimbabwe
109 N4 **Chireno** Texas U.S.A.
111 B10 **Chireno** Texas U.S.A.
84 E5 **Chirfa** Niger
103 P9 **Chirica Hua Nat.Mon** Arizona U.S.A.
103 P10 **Chiricahua Pk** Arizona U.S.A.
126 H10 **Chiriguaná** Colombia
116 K9 **Chirikof I** Alaska U.S.A.
75 P8 **Chiringa** Bangladesh
125 N5 **Chiriqui,G.de** Panama
75 K7 **Chirmiri** India
47 J1 **Chirnogeni** Romania
13 F2 **Chirnside** Scotland
15 F5 **Chirnside** Borders Scotland
88 E10 **Chiromo** Malawi
46 G2 **Chirpan** Bulgaria
Chirua, L *see* **Chilwa, L**
87 E9 **Chirundu** Zimbabwe
22 D4 **Chiry-Ourscamps** France
88 B9 **Chisamba** Zambia
116 R5 **Chisana** Alaska U.S.A.
116 Q6 **Chisana Glacier** Alaska U.S.A.
44 B2 **Chisane** *R* Italy
119 R4 **Chisel Lake** Manitoba Canada
88 D6 **Chisenga** Malawi
55 C4 **Chishmy** Russian Federation
118 C4 **Chisholm** Alberta Canada
95 R2 **Chisholm** Maine U.S.A.
99 O2 **Chisholm** Minnesota U.S.A.
74 E4 **Chishtian Mandi** Pakistan
67 B2 **Chishui** China
67 F4 **Chishui** China
67 B3 **Chishui He** *R* China
88 B7 **Chisi** *isld* Zambia
Chisimaio *see* **Kismaayo**
87 F8 **Chisimba Falls** Zambia
Chişinău *see* **Kishinev**
48 G4 **Chişineu-Criş** Romania
108 D6 **Chisos Mts** Texas U.S.A.
108 C5 **Chispa Cr** Texas U.S.A.
116 P5 **Chistochina** Alaska U.S.A.
55 G4 **Chisto-ozernoye** Russian Federation
52 H6 **Chistopol** Russian Federation
55 E4 **Chistopol'ye** Kazakhstan
55 G4 **Chistovo** Russian Federation
55 F4 **Chistyakovskoye** Kazakhstan
88 E8 **Chisumulu** *isld* Mozambique
58 F1 **Chita** Russian Federation
87 B9 **Chitado** Angola
116 L4 **Chitanana** *R* Alaska U.S.A.
58 C5 **Chi-t'ang** China
61 K11 **Chita wan** *G* Japan
52 G4 **Chitayevo** Russian Federation
118 K5 **Chitek** Saskatchewan Canada
119 S6 **Chitek L** Manitoba Canada
87 C8 **Chitembo** Angola
45 L4 **Chitignano** Italy
116 P6 **Chitina** Alaska U.S.A.
116 Q6 **Chitina** *R* Alaska U.S.A.
56 G5 **Chitinskaya Oblast'** *prov* Russian Federation
60 P3 **Chitose** Japan
76 C3 **Chitradurga** India
74 J6 **Chitrakut** India
74 D1 **Chitral** Pakistan
125 O6 **Chitré** Panama
75 O7 **Chittagong** Bangladesh
75 M7 **Chittaranjan** India
74 F6 **Chittaurgarh** India
143 B9 **Chittering** W Australia Australia
76 D4 **Chittoor** India
76 C5 **Chittur** India
89 G1 **Chitungwiza** Zimbabwe
88 F8 **Chiulézi** *R* Mozambique
87 D9 **Chiume** Angola
42 D2 **Chiusa** Italy
42 D5 **Chiusi** Italy
45 L4 **Chiusi di Verna** Italy
87 G8 **Chiuta, L** Malawi
88 E9 **Chiuta,L** Mozambique
17 G5 **Chiva** Spain
40 G7 **Chivasso** Italy
124 C4 **Chivato,Pta** *C* Mexico
128 D7 **Chivay** Peru
87 B9 **Chivemba** Angola
89 G2 **Chivhu** Zimbabwe
131 E5 **Chivilcoy** Argentina
106 H3 **Chivington** Colorado U.S.A.
22 F4 **Chivy** France
67 D6 **Chixi** China
125 O10 **Chixoy** *R* Guatemala
89 E1 **Chizarira Hills** Zimbabwe
52 F2 **Chizha** Russian Federation
Chizhou *see* **Guichi**
60 H10 **Chizu** Japan
55 F4 **Chkalovo** Kazakhstan
57 H6 **Chkalovsk** Tajikistan
52 D2 **Chkalovskiy** Russian Federation
31 J5 **Chlumec nad Cidlinou** Czechoslovakia
31 M5 **Chmielnik** Poland
65 F5 **Cho** *isld* N Korea
65 G7 **Ch'o** *isld* S Korea
68 G5 **Choam Ksan** Cambodia
131 B3 **Choapo,R** Chile
87 D9 **Chobe Nat. Park** Botswana
9 F5 **Chobham** England
68 G2 **Cho Bo** Vietnam
31 J5 **Choceň** Czechoslovakia
121 O5 **Chochocouane** *R* Quebec Canada
67 B6 **Cho Chu** Vietnam
31 J4 **Chocianów** Poland
128 C2 **Chocó** *div* Colombia
103 K8 **Chocolate Mts** Arizona U.S.A.
103 J8 **Chocolate Mts** California U.S.A.
95 Q3 **Chocorua** New Hampshire U.S.A.
112 K2 **Chocowinity** North Carolina U.S.A.
107 N6 **Choctaw** Oklahoma U.S.A.
111 K11 **Choctawhatchee B** Florida U.S.A.
37 O3 **Chodov** Czechoslovakia
31 K3 **Chodzież** Poland
133 D5 **Choele Choel** Argentina
88 C9 **Chofombo** Mozambique
68 H7 **Cho Giua** Vietnam
119 N5 **Choiceland** Saskatchewan Canada
137 M3 **Choiseul** *isld* Solomon Is
133 F8 **Choiseul Sd** Falkland Is
19 Q12 **Choisy** France
22 D5 **Choisy-au-Bac** France
124 E4 **Choix** Mexico
31 H3 **Chojna** Poland
31 K2 **Chojnice** Poland
31 J4 **Chojnów** Poland
61 O6 **Chōkai-san** *mt* Japan
86 G3 **Ch'ok'ē Mts** Ethiopia
98 K4 **Chokio** Minnesota U.S.A.
57 G3 **Choknar** Kazakhstan
57 H4 **Choktal** Kyrgyzstan
51 O1 **Chokurdakh** Russian Federation
87 F10 **Chókwé** Mozambique
102 D6 **Cholame** California U.S.A.
102 D6 **Cholame Cr** California U.S.A.
133 C4 **Cholchagua** *prov* Chile
21 J7 **Cholet** France
13 F3 **Chollerford** England
68 H7 **Cho Lon** Vietnam
57 H4 **Cholpon** Kyrgyzstan
57 H4 **Cholpon-Ata** Kyrgyzstan
125 K8 **Cholula** Mexico
125 L3 **Choluleca** Honduras
87 E9 **Choma** Zambia
68 F7 **Chomna** Cambodia
68 G2 **Cho Moi** Vietnam
75 N5 **Chomo Lhari** *mt* Bhutan/China
68 D3 **Chom Thong** Thailand
37 P3 **Chomutov** Czechoslovakia
56 H1 **Chona** *R* Russian Federation
68 E6 **Chon Buri** Thailand
68 E4 **Chon Daen** Thailand
128 B4 **Chone** Ecuador
67 F3 **Chong'an** China
67 G1 **Chongde** China
65 H4 **Ch'ŏngjin** N Korea
65 F5 **Chŏngju** N Korea
65 G6 **Ch'ŏngju** S Korea
68 F6 **Chong Kal** Cambodia
65 C4 **Chongli** China
67 G1 **Chongming** China
67 G1 **Chongming Dao** *isld* China
67 A1 **Chongqing** China
67 B2 **Chongqing** China
67 E3 **Chongren** China
67 E4 **Chongshi** China
88 B9 **Chongwe** *R* Zambia
67 E2 **Chongyang** China
67 F3 **Chongyang Xi** *R* China
67 E4 **Chongyi** China
56 D5 **Chongyz-Tayga, Gora** *mt* Russian Federation
68 H1 **Chongzuo** China
65 G7 **Chŏnju** S Korea
133 C6 **Chonos,Arch.de los** *islds* Chile
125 N9 **Chontalpa** Mexico
68 H7 **Chon Thanh** Vietnam
75 M4 **Cho Oyu** *pk* China/Nepal
48 G2 **Chop** Ukraine
13 G5 **Chop Gate** England
68 H7 **Cho Phuoc Hai** Vietnam
130 D9 **Chopim, R** Brazil
130 D9 **Chopimzinho** Brazil
95 M8 **Choptank** *R* Maryland U.S.A.
56 F3 **Chora** *R* Russian Federation
68 G1 **Cho Ra** Vietnam
33 T7 **Chorin** Germany
16 E5 **Chorito, Sa. del** *mts* Spain
57 F5 **Chorku** Kyrgyzstan
13 F6 **Chorley** England
131 B2 **Choros** *R* Chile
131 B2 **Choros,I.de los** Chile
31 O2 **Choroszcz** Poland
141 G6 **Chorregon** Queensland Australia
128 C6 **Chorrillos** Peru
130 G10 **Chorrochó** Brazil
48 K1 **Chortkov** Ukraine
31 M2 **Chorzele** Poland
31 L5 **Chorzów** Poland
Chōsen-kaikyō *see* **Nishi-suido**
61 O10 **Chōshi** Japan
133 C5 **Chos Malal** Argentina
65 G5 **Choson-Man** *B* N Korea
31 J2 **Choszczno** Poland
128 C5 **Chota** Peru
75 K7 **Chota Nagpur** *reg* India
101 N2 **Choteau** Montana U.S.A.
107 P5 **Choteau** Oklahoma U.S.A.
31 J6 **Chotěbor** Czechoslovakia
37 P4 **Chotěšov** Czechoslovakia
85 E2 **Chott ech Chergui** *salt lake* Algeria
85 E1 **Chott El Hodna** *marsh* Algeria
85 F2 **Chott El Jerid** *salt flats* Tunisia
85 F2 **Chott Melrhir** *salt flats* Algeria
21 L7 **Chouzé-sur-Loire** France
21 N6 **Chouzy-sur-Cisse** France
112 L1 **Chowan** *R* North Carolina U.S.A.
102 D4 **Chowchilla** California U.S.A.
138 F5 **Chowilla Dam** South Australia Australia
117 O9 **Chown,Mt** Alberta Canada
58 F2 **Choybalsan** Mongolia
40 C3 **Choye** France
65 A1 **Choyr** Mongolia
31 K6 **Chřiby** *dist* Czechoslovakia
48 D1 **Chřiby** Czechoslovakia
109 L5 **Chriesman** Texas U.S.A.
99 T10 **Chrisman** Illinois U.S.A.
89 G6 **Chrissiesmeer** S Africa
144 D5 **Christabel, L** New Zealand
127 P6 **Christchurch** *parish* Barbados
9 E6 **Christchurch** England
144 B4 **Christchurch** New Zealand
116 P3 **Christian** Alaska U.S.A.
127 K2 **Christiana** Jamaica
89 D6 **Christiana** S Africa
95 L7 **Christiana** Pennsylvania U.S.A.
115 N3 **Christian,C** Northwest Territories Canada
120 K8 **Christian I** Ontario Canada
94 C6 **Christiansburg** Ohio U.S.A.
110 M1 **Christiansburg** Ohio U.S.A.
94 G9 **Christiansburg** Virginia U.S.A.
28 C6 **Christiansfeld** Denmark
115 O4 **Christianshåb** Greenland
28 C4 **Christianshede** Denmark
27 H16 **Christiansø** *isld* Denmark
127 M6 **Christiansted** Virgin Is
69 C8 **Christie I** Burma
119 V2 **Christie L** Manitoba Canada
101 Q2 **Christina** Montana U.S.A.
118 G3 **Christina,L** Alberta Canada
100 G1 **Christina L** British Columbia Canada
144 B6 **Christina, Mt** New Zealand
118 G2 **Christina R** Alberta Canada
109 J7 **Christine** Texas U.S.A.
142 F4 **Christmas Creek** W Australia Australia
Christmas I *see* **Kiritimati**
83 M9 **Christmas I** Indian Oc
120 H2 **Christopher Falls** Ontario Canada
143 G6 **Christopher, L** W Australia
108 G4 **Christoval** Texas U.S.A.
131 H3 **Christovão Pereira,Pte** Brazil
106 D4 **Chromo** Colorado U.S.A.
31 J6 **Chrudim** Czechoslovakia
31 L5 **Chrzanow** Poland
57 G3 **Chu** Kazakhstan
57 F3 **Chu** *R* Kazakhstan/Kyrgyzstan
125 O10 **Chuacús,Sa.de** *ra* Guatemala
67 F2 **Chuankeng** China
67 G1 **Chuansha** China
57 J1 **Chubartau** Kazakhstan
103 J7 **Chubbuck** California U.S.A.
61 L9 **Chubu-Sangaku Nat. Park** Japan
133 D6 **Chubut** *R* Argentina
133 D6 **Chubut** *prov* Argentina
Chuchow *see* **Zhuzhou**
103 J8 **Chuckwalla Mts** California U.S.A.
133 E4 **Chucul** Argentina
37 P5 **Chudenice** Czechoslovakia
55 D4 **Chudinovo** Russian Federation
8 C6 **Chudleigh** England
141 G4 **Chudleigh Park** Queensland Australia
120 K6 **Chudleigh River Valley** Ontario Canada
52 D5 **Chudovo** Russian Federation
Chudskoye, Ozero *see* **Peipus, L**
116 M7 **Chugach Is** Alaska U.S.A.
116 O6 **Chugach Mts** Alaska U.S.A.
60 F11 **Chūgoku sanchi** *mts* Japan
Chuguchak *see* **Tacheng**
56 C4 **Chugunash** Russian Federation
55 F3 **Chugunly** Russian Federation
54 H7 **Chuguyev** Ukraine
98 B8 **Chugwater** Wyoming U.S.A.
98 B8 **Chugwater Cr** Wyoming U.S.A.
103 N9 **Chuichu** Arizona U.S.A.
59 L1 **Chukchagirskoye, Oz** *L* Russian Federation
147 O3 **Chukchi Sea** Arctic Oc
52 F5 **Chukhloma** Russian Federation
52 F5 **Chukhlomskoye, Oz** *L* Russian Federation
116 A3 **Chukotskiy Poluostrov** Russian Federation
56 G2 **Chula** *R* Russian Federation
112 D6 **Chula** Georgia U.S.A.
99 N10 **Chula** Missouri U.S.A.
94 K9 **Chula** Virginia U.S.A.
57 E3 **Chulak-Kurgan** Kazakhstan
52 G3 **Chulasa** Russian Federation
102 G9 **Chula Vista** California U.S.A.
116 N5 **Chulitna** *R* Alaska U.S.A.
51 M3 **Chul'man** Russian Federation
8 C6 **Chulmleigh** England
128 B5 **Chulucanas** Peru
58 D2 **Chuluut Gol** *R* Mongolia
56 B3 **Chulym** Russian Federation
56 D3 **Chulym** *R* Russian Federation
56 C5 **Chulyshman** *R* Russian Federation
56 C5 **Chulyshmunskiy Khrebet** *mts* Russian Federation
74 H2 **Chumar** Kashmir
133 D3 **Chumbicha** Argentina
56 C6 **Chumek** Kazakhstan
47 H2 **Chumerna** *mt* Bulgaria
59 L1 **Chumikan** Russian Federation
68 D7 **Chumphon** Thailand
68 E5 **Chum Saeng** Thailand
111 J11 **Chumuckla** Florida U.S.A.
56 B4 **Chumysh** *R* Russian Federation
56 E2 **Chuna** *R* Russian Federation
67 F2 **Chun'an** China
65 G6 **Ch'unch'ŏn** S Korea
111 H11 **Chunchula** Alabama U.S.A.
75 N7 **Chunchura** India
Chungking *see* **Chongqing**
66 C6 **Chung-pa** China
68 K3 **Chung-yüan** China
65 H3 **Chunhua** China
56 E1 **Chunku** *R* Russian Federation
58 D6 **Chün-lien** China
67 C1 **Chunmuying** China
83 K8 **Chunnakam** Sri Lanka
56 E2 **Chunoyar** Russian Federation
56 E1 **Chunya** *R* Russian Federation
88 D6 **Chunya** Tanzania
59 J3 **Chunyang** China
69 G8 **Chuoi,Hon** *isld* Vietnam
52 D2 **Chupa** Russian Federation
127 O1 **Chupara Pt** Trinidad
128 D6 **Chuquibambilla** Peru
133 D2 **Chuquicamata** Chile
133 E2 **Chuquisaca** *dept* Bolivia
52 H6 **Chur** Russian Federation
41 L4 **Chur** Switzerland
52 J5 **Churaki** Russian Federation
51 N2 **Churapcha** Russian Federation
55 C3 **Churayevo** Russian Federation
119 Q8 **Churchbridge** Saskatchewan Canada
95 L8 **Church Creek** Maryland U.S.A.
94 E10 **Church Hill** Tennessee U.S.A.
115 N7 **Churchill** *R* Labrador, Nfld Canada
115 K6 **Churchill** Manitoba Canada
118 L3 **Churchill** *R* Saskatchewan Canada
8 D5 **Churchill** England
101 M7 **Churchill** Idaho U.S.A.
118 J2 **Churchill L** Saskatchewan Canada
95 R7 **Churchill L** Maine U.S.A.
146 D11 **Churchill Mts** Antarctica
117 L6 **Churchill Pk** British Columbia Canada
119 W1 **Churchill R** Manitoba Canada
8 C6 **Churchingford** England
111 D11 **Church Point** Louisiana U.S.A.
122 F9 **Church Pt** Nova Scotia Canada
98 G1 **Churchs Ferry** North Dakota U.S.A.
8 D2 **Church Stretton** England
94 K3 **Churchville** New York U.S.A.
94 H8 **Churchville** Virginia U.S.A.
99 M7 **Churdan** Iowa U.S.A.
56 D5 **Chureg-Tag,Gora** *mt* Russian Federation
41 K3 **Churfirsten** *mt* Switzerland
75 K6 **Churk** India
52 F3 **Churkino** Russian Federation
74 F4 **Churu** India
94 B5 **Churubusco** Indiana U.S.A.
128 E1 **Churuguara** Venezuela
52 F4 **Chushevitsy** Russian Federation
106 B5 **Chuska Mts** Ariz/New Mex U.S.A.
55 C2 **Chusovaya** *R* Russian Federation
55 C2 **Chusovoy** Russian Federation
52 J4 **Chusovskoy** Russian Federation
57 F4 **Chust** Uzbekistan
122 D4 **Chute-aux-Outardes** Quebec Canada
122 A4 **Chute-des-Passes** Quebec Canada
134 F7 **Chuuk Is** Caroline Is Pacific Oc
52 J4 **Chuval** Russian Federation
52 G6 **Chuvashskaya Respublika** Russian Federation
67 F1 **Chu Xian** China
61 N9 **Chūzenji-ko** *L* Japan
37 P3 **Chyše** Czechoslovakia
88 F3 **Chyulu Ra** Kenya
70 M9 **Ciamis** Java
45 N6 **Ciampino** Italy
70 L9 **Cianjur** Java
42 C4 **Ciano d'Enza** Italy
103 O7 **Cibecue** Arizona U.S.A.
70 L9 **Cibinong** Java
48 H5 **Cibinului,Munţii** *mts* Romania
103 K8 **Cibola** Arizona U.S.A.
70 L9 **Ci Buni** *R* Java
124 D2 **Cibuta** Mexico
42 F3 **Čičarija** *mt* Croatia

166

Cicciano — Colonial Beach

45 R8 **Cicciano** Italy
94 A6 **Cicero** Indiana U.S.A.
95 L3 **Cicero** New York U.S.A.
129 L6 **Cicero Dantas** Brazil
46 E1 **Čicevac** Serbia Yugoslavia
67 G1 **Cicheng** China
17 F2 **Cidacos** *R* Spain
70 L9 **Cidaun** Java
78 D1 **Cide** Turkey
31 J5 **Cidlina** *R* Czechoslovakia
31 M3 **Ciéchanow** Poland
31 N3 **Ciechanowiec** Poland
31 L3 **Ciechocinek** Poland
126 E4 **Ciego de Avila** Cuba
70 L9 **Ciemas** Java
128 D1 **Ciénaga** Colombia
126 G10 **Ciénaga de Oro** Colombia
126 G10 **Ciénaga Grande** *marshy lake* Colombia
106 E9 **Cienega** New Mexico U.S.A.
124 H5 **Ciénega del Carmen** Mexico
124 H5 **Cieneguilla** Mexico
124 D3 **Cieneguita** Mexico
126 D3 **Cienfuegos** Cuba
22 J3 **Ciergnon** Belgium
31 O5 **Cieszanow** Poland
31 L6 **Cieszyn** Poland
17 G6 **Cieza** Spain
31 M6 **Ciężkowice** Poland
47 M10 **Çiftalan** Turkey
47 L5 **Çifteler** Turkey
17 F4 **Cifuentes** Spain
70 K9 **Cigeulis** Java
40 H7 **Cigliano** Italy
17 F5 **Cigüela** *R* Spain
78 D2 **Cihanbeyli** Turkey
124 G8 **Cihuatlán** Mexico
16 D5 **Cijara, Embalse de** *res* Spain
70 M9 **Cikalong** Java
46 D4 **Çikës, Mal i** *mt* Albania
70 M9 **Cilacap** Java
70 L9 **Cilangkahan** Java
78 J1 **Cildir G** *L* Turkey
67 D2 **Cili** China
8 C3 **Cilycwm** Wales
103 J6 **Cima** California U.S.A.
70 L9 **Cimahi** Java
70 M9 **Ci Manuk** *R* Java
106 C3 **Cimarron** Colorado U.S.A.
107 K4 **Cimarron** Kansas U.S.A.
106 F5 **Cimarron** New Mexico U.S.A.
107 M5 **Cimarron** *R* Okla/Kansas U.S.A.
31 O2 **Cimochy** Poland
42 D4 **Cimone, M** *mt* Italy
48 H4 **Cîmpeni** Romania
48 H4 **Cîmpia Turzii** Romania
48 K5 **Cîmpina** Romania
48 J5 **Cîmpulung** Romania
48 K3 **Cîmpulung Moldovenesc** Romania
48 K4 **Cîmpuri** Romania
128 E2 **Cinaruco** *R* Venezuela
18 F10 **Cinca** *R* Spain
42 H5 **Cincar** *mt* Bosnia-Herzegovina
99 O9 **Cincinnati** Iowa U.S.A.
94 C7 **Cincinnati** Ohio U.S.A.
95 M4 **Cincinnatus** New York U.S.A.
126 E4 **Cinco-Balas, Cayo** *islds* Cuba
116 H8 **Cinder** *R* Alaska U.S.A.
8 D4 **Cinderford** England
48 K5 **Cîndeşti** Romania
48 H5 **Cîndrelu** *mt* Romania
47 J7 **Çine** *R* Turkey
47 J7 **Çine** Turkey
22 J3 **Ciney** Belgium
16 B3 **Cinfães** Portugal
70 F5 **Cinoko, Tanjong** *C* Sulawesi
21 L7 **Cinq Mars** France
68 A7 **Cinque I** Andaman Is
129 J5 **Cinta,Serra da** *mts* Brazil
85 A4 **Cintra, G.de** Western Sahara
45 O6 **Ciociaria** Italy
48 J6 **Ciolăneşti** Romania
70 M9 **Cipatuja** Java
67 E3 **Ciping** China
21 K5 **Ciral** France
17 G4 **Cirat** Spain
146 E12 **Circe, Dome** *ice dome* Antarctica
43 E7 **Circeo, M** *mt* Italy
43 E7 **Circeo, M** *lighthouse* Italy
116 P4 **Circle** Alaska U.S.A.
98 A2 **Circle** Montana U.S.A.
94 E7 **Circleville** Ohio U.S.A.
103 M3 **Circleville** Utah U.S.A.
70 M9 **Cirebon** Java
9 E4 **Cirencester** England
69 E13 **Cirenti** Sumatra
21 P3 **Cires-les-Mello** France
19 K4 **Cirey** France
36 B6 **Cirey-sur-Vezouse** France
44 C1 **Ciriè** Italy
18 E8 **Ciron** *R* France
21 N8 **Ciron** France
44 G3 **Cisa, Passo di** Italy
99 S9 **Cisco** Illinois U.S.A.
109 J3 **Cisco** Texas U.S.A.
103 P3 **Cisco** Utah U.S.A.
89 E9 **Ciskei** *homeland* S Africa
48 K5 **Cislău** Romania
33 N4 **Cismar** Germany
31 N6 **Cisna** Poland
48 J5 **Cisnadie** Romania
110 H3 **Cisne** Illinois U.S.A.
128 C2 **Cisneros** Colombia
133 C6 **Cisnes** *R* Chile
70 L9 **Cisompet** Java
100 D3 **Cispus** *R* Washington U.S.A.
100 D3 **Cispus Pass** Washington U.S.A.
21 N6 **Cisse** *R* France
37 O3 **Čistá** Czechoslovakia
109 K6 **Cistern** Texas U.S.A.
45 N6 **Cisterna di Latina** Italy
16 D2 **Cistierna** Spain
129 G3 **Citare** *R* Brazil
125 L8 **Citlaltépetl** Mexico
113 E8 **Citra** Florida U.S.A.
111 H10 **Citronelle** Alabama U.S.A.
87 C12 **Citrusdal** S Africa
42 D3 **Cittadella** Italy
42 E6 **Citta della Pieve** Italy
42 E5 **Città di Castello** Italy
43 G10 **Cittanova** Italy
142 A1 **City Beach** *dist* Perth, W Aust Australia
113 G9 **City Point** Florida U.S.A.
48 K5 **Ciucaşu** *mt* Romania
48 H4 **Ciucea** Romania
48 K4 **Ciucului Muntii** *mt* Romania
108 G6 **Ciudad Acuña** Mexico
125 J8 **Ciudad Altamirano** Mexico
128 F2 **Ciudad Bolívar** Venezuela
109 J9 **Ciudad Camargo** Mexico
124 G4 **Ciudad Camargo** Mexico
125 O8 **Ciudad del Carmen** Mexico
124 G3 **Ciudad Delicias** Mexico
17 K4 **Ciudadela** Spain
127 N10 **Ciudad Guayana** Venezuela
124 F3 **Ciudad Guerrero** Mexico
124 H8 **Ciudad Guzmán** Mexico
125 N10 **Ciudad Hidalgo** Mexico
106 D10 **Ciudad Juárez** Mexico
124 H5 **Ciudad Lerdo** Mexico
125 L6 **Ciudad Madero** Mexico
125 K6 **Ciudad Mante** Mexico
124 E4 **Ciudad Obregón** Mexico
128 F2 **Ciudad Piar** Venezuela
16 E6 **Ciudad Real** *prov* Spain
16 E6 **Ciudad Real** Spain
16 C4 **Ciudad Rodrigo** Spain
125 N10 **Ciudad Tecún Umán** Mexico
Ciudad Trujillo *see* **Santo Domingo** Dominican Rep
125 K6 **Ciudad Victoria** Mexico
48 G4 **Ciumeghiu** Romania
48 L5 **Ciuşlea** Romania
47 K5 **Civan Daği** *mt* Turkey
42 E2 **Cividale del F** Italy
42 E6 **Civita Castellana** Italy
42 F5 **Civitanova Marche** Italy
44 L5 **Civitavecchia** *lighthouse* Italy
45 L3 **Civitella di Romagna** Italy
45 O6 **Civitella Roveto** Italy
44 B1 **Civrari Monte** Italy
18 F6 **Civray** France
21 P8 **Civray** Cher France
47 K6 **Çivril** Turkey
67 G1 **Cixi** China
65 C6 **Ci Xian** China
78 J3 **Cizre** Turkey
12 C2 **Clachan** Scotland
100 C4 **Clackamas** *R* Oregon U.S.A.
143 B9 **Clackline** W Australia Australia
Clackmannon *co see* **Central** *reg*
9 H4 **Clacton-on-Sea** England
12 C1 **Cladich** Scotland
107 M3 **Claflin** Kansas U.S.A.
100 J1 **Clagstone** Idaho U.S.A.
20 E6 **Claie,R** France
21 L8 **Clain** *R* France
119 N6 **Clair** Saskatchewan Canada
6 J2 **Clair** *oil rig* North Sea
68 G1 **Claire** *R* Vietnam
98 J4 **Claire City** South Dakota U.S.A.
117 R6 **Claire, L** Alberta Canada
108 G2 **Clairemont** Texas U.S.A.
94 H6 **Clairton** Pennsylvania U.S.A.
19 J6 **Clairvaux** France
21 N8 **Claise** *R* France
100 A1 **Clallam Bay** Washington U.S.A.
18 H5 **Clamecy** France
102 G2 **Clan Alpine Mts** Nevada U.S.A.
101 N3 **Clancy** Montana U.S.A.
144 C6 **Clandeboye** New Zealand
118 F5 **Clandonald** Alberta Canada
9 E4 **Clanfield** England
111 K9 **Clanton** Alabama U.S.A.
119 S8 **Clanwilliam** Manitoba Canada
87 C12 **Clanwilliam** S Africa
12 C2 **Claonaig** Scotland
9 F5 **Clapham** England
13 F5 **Clapham** N Yorks England
44 B3 **Clapier, Mt** France
141 F4 **Clara** *R* Queensland Australia
14 D3 **Clara** Ireland
113 D8 **Clara** Florida U.S.A.
99 L5 **Clara City** Minnesota U.S.A.
68 C7 **Clara I** Burma
141 F4 **Claraville** Queensland Australia
138 E5 **Clare** South Australia Australia
9 G3 **Clare** England
14 C3 **Clare** *R* Ireland
14 C4 **Clare** *co* Ireland
99 M7 **Clare** Iowa U.S.A.
94 C3 **Clare** Michigan U.S.A.
14 C4 **Clarecastle** Ireland
139 G5 **Clare Corner** New South Wales Australia
14 A3 **Clare I** Ireland
142 A2 **Claremont** *dist* Perth, W Aust Australia
127 K2 **Claremont** Jamaica
95 P3 **Claremont** New Hampshire U.S.A.
98 H4 **Claremont** South Dakota U.S.A.
141 G2 **Claremont Is** Gt Barrier Reef Australia
14 C3 **Claremorris** Ireland
139 L3 **Clarence** *R* New South Wales Australia
144 D5 **Clarence** New Zealand
99 P8 **Clarence** Iowa U.S.A.
99 O10 **Clarence** Missouri U.S.A.
110 D2 **Clarence Cannon Res** Missouri U.S.A.
146 D3 **Clarence I** South Shetland Is Antarctica
133 C8 **Clarence,I** Chile
140 B1 **Clarence Str** N Terr Australia
117 G8 **Clarence Str** Alaska U.S.A.
126 G3 **Clarence Town** Long I Bahamas
121 O8 **Clarendon** Ontario Canada
127 K3 **Clarendon** *parish* Jamaica
110 E7 **Clarendon** Arkansas U.S.A.
94 H5 **Clarendon** Pennsylvania U.S.A.
108 G1 **Clarendon** Texas U.S.A.
123 S5 **Clarenville** Newfoundland Canada
118 D8 **Claresholm** Alberta Canada
19 P16 **Claret** France
98 B6 **Clareton** Wyoming U.S.A.
32 H9 **Clarholz** Germany
141 F4 **Clarina** *R* Queensland Australia
99 L9 **Clarinda** Iowa U.S.A.
127 M10 **Clarines** Venezuela
94 H5 **Clarington** Pennsylvania U.S.A.
99 N7 **Clarion** Iowa U.S.A.
94 H5 **Clarion** *R* Pennsylvania U.S.A.
94 H5 **Clarion** Pennsylvania U.S.A.
126 H4 **Clarion Bank** Bahamas
145 E2 **Claris** New Zealand
107 O7 **Clarita** Oklahoma U.S.A.
102 H8 **Clark** *L* California U.S.A.
101 T9 **Clark** Colorado U.S.A.
110 D2 **Clark** Missouri U.S.A.
98 J5 **Clark** South Dakota U.S.A.
101 N4 **Clark Canyon Res** Montana U.S.A.
103 M7 **Clarkdale** Arizona U.S.A.
141 G4 **Clarke** *R* Queensland Australia
122 F3 **Clarke City** Quebec Canada
139 J8 **Clarke I** Tasmania Australia
118 K4 **Clarke L** Saskatchewan Canada
141 J5 **Clarke Ra** Queensland Australia
141 H4 **Clarke River** Queensland Australia
112 D3 **Clarkesville** Georgia U.S.A.
98 L5 **Clarkfield** Minnesota U.S.A.
100 J1 **Clark Fork** Idaho U.S.A.
117 Q12 **Clark Fork** *R* Idaho U.S.A.
112 E4 **Clark Hill Dam** Georgia U.S.A.
112 E4 **Clark Hill L** *res* Georgia U.S.A.
100 J2 **Clarkia** Idaho U.S.A.
116 K6 **Clark,L** Alaska U.S.A.
117 M3 **Clark,Mt** Northwest Territories Canada
103 J6 **Clark Mt** California U.S.A.
106 E1 **Clark Pk** Colorado U.S.A.
120 J8 **Clark Pt** Ontario Canada
111 D9 **Clarks** Louisiana U.S.A.
98 J8 **Clarks** Nebraska U.S.A.
101 Q5 **Clarks** *R* Wyoming U.S.A.
110 H6 **Clarksburg** Tennessee U.S.A.
94 G7 **Clarksburg** West Virginia U.S.A.
111 F7 **Clarksdale** Mississippi U.S.A.
99 N6 **Clarks Grove** Minnesota U.S.A.
122 G10 **Clark's Harbour** Nova Scotia Canada
110 K1 **Clarks Hill** Indiana U.S.A.
144 C6 **Clarks Junction** New Zealand
121 L9 **Clarkson** Ontario Canada
98 J8 **Clarkson** Nebraska U.S.A.
142 E4 **Clarkson, Mt** W Australia Australia
116 H7 **Clarks Point** Alaska U.S.A.
94 D4 **Clarkston** Michigan U.S.A.
101 O3 **Clarkston** Montana U.S.A.
100 H3 **Clarkston** Washington U.S.A.
127 K2 **Clark's Town** Jamaica
144 B7 **Clarksville** New Zealand
110 C6 **Clarksville** Arkansas U.S.A.
110 F2 **Clarksville** Illinois U.S.A.
99 O7 **Clarksville** Iowa U.S.A.
94 B4 **Clarksville** Michigan U.S.A.
110 J5 **Clarksville** Tennessee U.S.A.
109 M2 **Clarksville** Texas U.S.A.
94 J10 **Clarksville** Virginia U.S.A.
112 J3 **Clarkton** North Carolina U.S.A.
109 K8 **Clarkwood** Texas U.S.A.
100 E5 **Clarno** Oregon U.S.A.
129 H7 **Claro** *R* Brazil
22 E3 **Clary** France
141 H6 **Claude** *R* Queensland Australia
108 C8 **Claude** Texas U.S.A.
130 G7 **Cláudio** Brazil
32 M8 **Clauen** Germany
37 O2 **Claussnitz** Germany
33 M9 **Clausthal-Zellerfeld** Germany
71 E1 **Claveria** Luzon Philippines
118 L8 **Clavet** Saskatchewan Canada
19 N14 **Claveyson** France
112 F5 **Claxton** Georgia U.S.A.
102 C3 **Clay** California U.S.A.
110 J4 **Clay** Kentucky U.S.A.
109 L5 **Clay** Texas U.S.A.
94 F8 **Clay** West Virginia U.S.A.
107 N2 **Clay Center** Kansas U.S.A.
98 H9 **Clay Center** Nebraska U.S.A.
110 H3 **Clay City** Illinois U.S.A.
110 J2 **Clay City** Indiana U.S.A.
110 N4 **Clay City** Kentucky U.S.A.
9 E1 **Clay Cross** England
118 J9 **Claydon** Saskatchewan Canada
9 H3 **Claydon** England
18 H6 **Clayette, la** France
103 L5 **Clayhole Wash** *creek* Arizona U.S.A.
118 J1 **Clay L** Ontario Canada
6 K4 **Claymore** *oil rig* North Sea
107 P5 **Claymore** Oklahoma U.S.A.
117 L11 **Clayoquot** British Columbia Canada
103 O8 **Claypool** Arizona U.S.A.
103 O7 **Clay Springs** Arizona U.S.A.
94 G6 **Claysville** Pennsylvania U.S.A.
138 E3 **Clayton** *R* South Australia Australia
9 F6 **Clayton** England
111 L10 **Clayton** Alabama U.S.A.
112 D3 **Clayton** Georgia U.S.A.
101 L5 **Clayton** Idaho U.S.A.
99 Q9 **Clayton** Illinois U.S.A.
110 K2 **Clayton** Indiana U.S.A.
107 K2 **Clayton** Kansas U.S.A.
106 G5 **Clayton** New Mexico U.S.A.
95 L2 **Clayton** New York U.S.A.
112 J2 **Clayton** North Carolina U.S.A.
107 P7 **Clayton** Oklahoma U.S.A.
95 R7 **Clayton Lake** Maine U.S.A.
13 F6 **Clayton-le-Moors** England
94 G9 **Claytor Lake** Virginia U.S.A.
95 M4 **Clayville** New York U.S.A.
131 F4 **Clé** *R* Argentina
107 O7 **Clear Boggy Cr** Oklahoma U.S.A.
99 L2 **Clearbrook** Minnesota U.S.A.
144 C6 **Clearburn** New Zealand
14 B5 **Clear,C** Ireland
94 G8 **Clearco** West Virginia U.S.A.
103 O7 **Clear Cr** *R* Arizona U.S.A.
101 T5 **Clear Cr** Wyoming U.S.A.
100 B8 **Clear Creek** California U.S.A.
116 O7 **Cleare,C** Alaska U.S.A.
99 M9 **Clearfield** Iowa U.S.A.
94 J5 **Clearfield** Pennsylvania U.S.A.
101 N8 **Clearfield** Utah U.S.A.
108 G3 **Clear Fork** *R* Texas U.S.A.
117 O7 **Clear Hills** Alberta Canada
14 B5 **Clear I** Ireland
119 S8 **Clear L** Manitoba Canada
121 N7 **Clear, L** Ontario Canada
102 B2 **Clear L** California U.S.A.
99 N6 **Clear L** Iowa U.S.A.
109 P4 **Clear L** Louisiana U.S.A.
99 N4 **Clear L** Minnesota U.S.A.
98 K5 **Clear L** South Dakota U.S.A.
103 M2 **Clear L** Utah U.S.A.
99 O4 **Clear L** Wisconsin U.S.A.
100 D8 **Clear L. Res** California U.S.A.
101 T5 **Clearmont** Wyoming U.S.A.
117 O7 **Clear Prairie** Alberta Canada
117 N10 **Clearwater** British Columbia Canada
113 E10 **Clearwater** Florida U.S.A.
100 J3 **Clearwater** *R* Idaho U.S.A.
100 K3 **Clearwater** Idaho U.S.A.
107 N4 **Clearwater** Kansas U.S.A.
98 H7 **Clearwater** Nebraska U.S.A.
119 Q4 **Clearwater L. Prov. Park** Manitoba Canada
100 K3 **Clearwater Mts** Idaho U.S.A.
118 B6 **Clearwater R** Alberta Canada
110 F4 **Clearwater Res** Missouri U.S.A.
99 L2 **Clearwter** *R* Minnesota U.S.A.
143 D7 **Cleaver, Mt** W Australia Australia
107 O2 **Cleburne** Kansas U.S.A.
109 K3 **Cleburne** Texas U.S.A.
21 K4 **Clécy** France
8 B4 **Cleddau, R** Wales
20 B4 **Cléder** France
8 D3 **Clee Hill** England
100 D2 **Cle Elum L** Washington U.S.A.
13 H6 **Cleethorpes** England
7 L8 **Cleeton** *gas field* North Sea
118 H5 **Cleeves** Saskatchewan Canada
40 B1 **Clefmont** France
21 K6 **Clefs** France
109 J7 **Clegg** Texas U.S.A.
20 D5 **Cléguérec** France
140 B6 **Cleland Hills** N Terr Australia
22 K4 **Clemency** Luxembourg
102 C3 **Clements** California U.S.A.
115 N1 **Clements Markham Inlet** Northwest Territories Canada
122 G9 **Clementsport** Nova Scotia Canada
122 G9 **Clementsvale** Nova Scotia Canada
94 F8 **Clendenin** West Virginia U.S.A.
94 F6 **Clendening Res** Ohio U.S.A.
8 D3 **Cleobury Mortimer** England
71 D5 **Cleopatra Needle** *mt* Philippines
107 M5 **Cleo Springs** Oklahoma U.S.A.
21 L7 **Cléré** France
21 N2 **Clères** France
121 M4 **Cléricy** Quebec Canada
40 D2 **Clerjus, Le** France
142 C3 **Clerke Reef** Indian Oc
133 J9 **Clerke Rocks** S Georgia
141 J6 **Clermont** Queensland Australia
122 B6 **Clermont** Quebec Canada
21 P3 **Clermont** Oise France
113 F9 **Clermont** Florida U.S.A.
99 P6 **Clermont** Iowa U.S.A.
94 J5 **Clermont** Pennsylvania U.S.A.
21 K6 **Clermont-Créans** France
19 J3 **Clermont en Argonne** France
18 H7 **Clermont Ferrand** France
18 H9 **Clermont l'Herault** France
121 L4 **Clerval** Quebec Canada
40 D3 **Clerval** France
22 L3 **Clervaux** Luxembourg
21 O3 **Cléry-en-Vexin** France
21 O6 **Cléry-St. André** France
22 D4 **Clery-sur-Somme** France
42 D2 **Cles** Italy
21 K8 **Clessé** France
138 D5 **Cleve** South Australia Australia
8 D5 **Clevedon** England
13 G4 **Cleveland** *co* England
110 D6 **Cleveland** Arkansas U.S.A.
113 F11 **Cleveland** Florida U.S.A.
112 D3 **Cleveland** Georgia U.S.A.
101 O7 **Cleveland** Idaho U.S.A.
99 N5 **Cleveland** Minnesota U.S.A.
111 F8 **Cleveland** Mississippi U.S.A.
101 Q1 **Cleveland** Montana U.S.A.
95 M3 **Cleveland** New York U.S.A.
112 G2 **Cleveland** North Carolina U.S.A.
98 G3 **Cleveland** North Dakota U.S.A.
94 F5 **Cleveland** Ohio U.S.A.
107 O5 **Cleveland** Oklahoma U.S.A.
112 E2 **Cleveland** South Carolina U.S.A.
112 C2 **Cleveland** Tennessee U.S.A.
109 M5 **Cleveland** Texas U.S.A.
103 O2 **Cleveland** Utah U.S.A.
99 T6 **Cleveland** Wisconsin U.S.A.
141 H4 **Cleveland, C** Queensland Australia
13 G4 **Cleveland Hills** England
130 D10 **Clevelândia** Brazil
101 M1 **Cleveland,Mt** Montana U.S.A.
113 G11 **Clewiston** Florida U.S.A.
9 H2 **Cley** England
14 A3 **Clifden** Ireland
144 A7 **Clifden** New Zealand
106 B9 **Cliff** New Mexico U.S.A.
100 D3 **Cliffdell** Washington U.S.A.
71 D5 **Cliff Head** Philippines
101 O5 **Cliff Lake** Montana U.S.A.
94 D3 **Clifford** Michigan U.S.A.
98 J2 **Clifford** North Dakota U.S.A.
94 H9 **Clifford** Virginia U.S.A.
99 Q4 **Clifford** Wisconsin U.S.A.
100 H7 **Cliffs** Idaho U.S.A.
112 F2 **Cliffside** North Carolina U.S.A.
141 K8 **Clifton** Queensland Australia
113 K9 **Clifton** New Providence I Bahamas
8 D5 **Clifton** England
103 P8 **Clifton** Arizona U.S.A.
99 T9 **Clifton** Illinois U.S.A.
107 N2 **Clifton** Kansas U.S.A.
95 N6 **Clifton** New Jersey U.S.A.
98 B6 **Clifton** Wyoming U.S.A.
94 H9 **Clifton Forge** Virginia U.S.A.
138 E2 **Clifton Hills** South Australia Australia
113 K9 **Clifton Pt** New Providence I Bahamas
118 J9 **Climax** Saskatchewan Canada
106 D2 **Climax** Colorado U.S.A.
111 M11 **Climax** Georgia U.S.A.
94 B4 **Climax** Michigan U.S.A.
98 K2 **Climax** Minnesota U.S.A.
112 C2 **Clinch** *R* Tennessee U.S.A.
94 E9 **Clinchco** Virginia U.S.A.
94 E10 **Clinch Mt** Tenn/Virg U.S.A.
94 E10 **Clinchport** Virginia U.S.A.
117 P9 **Cline, Mt** Alberta Canada
37 K1 **Clingen** Germany
112 D2 **Clingmans Dome** Tennessee U.S.A.
108 A4 **Clint** Texas U.S.A.
117 N10 **Clinton** British Columbia Canada
120 J9 **Clinton** Ontario Canada
144 B7 **Clinton** New Zealand
110 D6 **Clinton** Arkansas U.S.A.
95 P5 **Clinton** Connecticut U.S.A.
99 S9 **Clinton** Illinois U.S.A.
99 T10 **Clinton** Indiana U.S.A.
99 Q8 **Clinton** Iowa U.S.A.
110 H5 **Clinton** Kentucky U.S.A.
111 E11 **Clinton** Louisiana U.S.A.
95 S2 **Clinton** Maine U.S.A.
95 Q4 **Clinton** Massachusetts U.S.A.
94 D4 **Clinton** Michigan U.S.A.
98 K4 **Clinton** Minnesota U.S.A.
111 F9 **Clinton** Mississippi U.S.A.
110 C3 **Clinton** Missouri U.S.A.
101 M3 **Clinton** Montana U.S.A.
95 M3 **Clinton** New York U.S.A.
107 M6 **Clinton** Oklahoma U.S.A.
112 F3 **Clinton** South Carolina U.S.A.
112 C1 **Clinton** Tennessee U.S.A.
99 S7 **Clinton** Wisconsin U.S.A.
114 J5 **Clinton-Colden L** Northwest Territories Canada
114 E5 **Clinton Creek** Yukon Territory Canada
99 S5 **Clintonville** Wisconsin U.S.A.
103 N7 **Clints Well** Arizona U.S.A.
110 C1 **Clio** Iowa U.S.A.
94 D3 **Clio** Michigan U.S.A.
112 H3 **Clio** South Carolina U.S.A.
21 N8 **Clion** France
135 Q7 **Clipperton** *atoll* Pacific Oc
15 B3 **Clisham Mt** Lewis Scotland
20 H7 **Clisson** France
13 F6 **Clitheroe** England
118 D6 **Clive** Alberta Canada
145 F3 **Clive** New Zealand
101 M9 **Clive** Utah U.S.A.
117 O4 **Clive L** Northwest Territories Canada
118 J6 **Cloan** Saskatchewan Canada
14 D3 **Cloghan** Ireland
14 D2 **Clogher** N Ireland
14 E3 **Clogher Hd** Ireland
20 C6 **Clohars** France
140 F5 **Clonagh** Queensland Australia
14 C5 **Clonakilty** Ireland
14 C5 **Clonakilty B** Ireland
140 F4 **Cloncurry** *R* Queensland Australia
140 F5 **Cloncurry** Queensland Australia
14 E3 **Clondalkin** Ireland
14 E4 **Clonegal** Ireland
14 D2 **Clones** Ireland
59 J3 **Clŏngjin** N Korea
14 D4 **Clonmel** Ireland
99 L4 **Clontarf** Minnesota U.S.A.
117 L11 **Clo-oose** British Columbia Canada
9 F3 **Clophill** England
32 H7 **Cloppenburg** Germany
99 O3 **Cloquet** Minnesota U.S.A.
130 B9 **Clorinda** Argentina
12 E3 **Closeburn** Scotland
123 L3 **Cloudberry Pt** Quebec Canada
106 E9 **Cloudcroft** New Mexico U.S.A.
101 S5 **Cloud Pk** Wyoming U.S.A.
145 E4 **Cloudy Bay** New Zealand
116 J5 **Cloudy Mt** Alaska U.S.A.
121 L4 **Cloutier** Quebec Canada
20 H8 **Clouzeaux, les** France
121 P4 **Clova** Quebec Canada
15 E4 **Clova** Scotland
8 B5 **Clovelly** England
13 F2 **Clovenfords** Scotland
112 F2 **Clover** South Carolina U.S.A.
94 J10 **Clover** Virginia U.S.A.
102 A3 **Cloverdale** California U.S.A.
110 K2 **Cloverdale** Indiana U.S.A.
106 B10 **Cloverdale** New Mexico U.S.A.
110 K4 **Cloverport** Kentucky U.S.A.
106 G7 **Clovis** New Mexico U.S.A.
8 D3 **Clows Top** England
21 N6 **Cloyes** France
14 C5 **Cloyne** Ireland
21 O8 **Cluis** France
48 H4 **Cluj** *reg* Romania
48 H4 **Cluj-Napoca** Romania
8 C3 **Clun** England
139 G7 **Clunes** Victoria Australia
140 E6 **Cluny** Queensland Australia
118 E8 **Cluny** Alberta Canada
102 H1 **Cluro** Nevada U.S.A.
40 E5 **Cluses** France
41 L6 **Clusone** Italy
120 J3 **Clute** Ontario Canada
144 B6 **Clutha** *R* New Zealand
144 A6 **Clutha/Central Otago** *admin region* New Zealand
144 B7 **Clutha R** New Zealand
99 O7 **Clutier** Iowa U.S.A.
117 P3 **Clut L** Northwest Territories Canada
143 F6 **Clutterbuck Hills** W Australia Australia
8 C1 **Clwyd** *R* Wales
8 C1 **Clwyd** *co* Wales
113 D7 **Clyattville** Georgia U.S.A.
8 C4 **Clydach** Wales
118 D4 **Clyde** Alberta Canada
115 N3 **Clyde** Northwest Territories Canada
144 B6 **Clyde** New Zealand
6 M6 **Clyde** *oil rig* North Sea
107 N2 **Clyde** Kansas U.S.A.
95 L3 **Clyde** New York U.S.A.
98 H1 **Clyde** North Dakota U.S.A.
94 E5 **Clyde** Ohio U.S.A.
109 H3 **Clyde** Texas U.S.A.
12 D2 **Clydebank** Scotland
12 D3 **Clyde,Firth of** Scotland
121 O7 **Clyde Forks** Ontario Canada
101 P4 **Clyde Park** Montana U.S.A.
122 G10 **Clyde R** Nova Scotia Canada
12 D2 **Clyde,R** Scotland
144 B7 **Clydevale** New Zealand
99 S6 **Clyman** Wisconsin U.S.A.
94 H6 **Clymer** Pennsylvania U.S.A.
8 B1 **Clynnog-fawr** Wales
8 C3 **Clyro** Wales
8 C6 **Clyst Honiton** England
16 C4 **Coa** *R* Portugal
103 H8 **Coachella** California U.S.A.
123 M3 **Coacoachou L** Quebec Canada
108 F3 **Coahoma** Texas U.S.A.
124 H4 **Coahuila** *state* Mexico
117 K5 **Coal** *R* Br Col/Yukon Terr Canada
94 F8 **Coal** *R* West Virginia U.S.A.
99 S8 **Coal City** Illinois U.S.A.
124 H8 **Coalcomán de Matamoros** Mexico
116 Q4 **Coal Creek** Alaska U.S.A.
118 E9 **Coaldale** Alberta Canada
102 G3 **Coaldale** Nevada U.S.A.
144 C5 **Coalgate** New Zealand
107 O7 **Coalgate** Oklahoma U.S.A.
94 E8 **Coal Grove** Ohio U.S.A.
110 C6 **Coal Hill** Arkansas U.S.A.
144 A7 **Coal I** New Zealand
102 D5 **Coalinga** California U.S.A.
101 T9 **Coalmont** Colorado U.S.A.
94 J6 **Coalport** Pennsylvania U.S.A.
117 K6 **Coal River** British Columbia Canada
94 E7 **Coalton** Ohio U.S.A.
9 E2 **Coalville** England
101 O9 **Coalville** Utah U.S.A.
98 A4 **Coalwood** Montana U.S.A.
127 L5 **Coamo** Puerto Rico
128 F4 **Coari** Brazil
144 C6 **Coastal North Otago** *admin region* New Zealand
117 G7 **Coast Mts** British Columbia Canada
141 K7 **Coast Ra** Queensland Australia
141 K7 **Coast Ra** *mts* Queensland Australia
100 B9 **Coast Range** *mts* U.S.A.
102 A1 **Coast Rge** California U.S.A.
12 E2 **Coatbridge** Scotland
125 L8 **Coatepec** Mexico
95 M6 **Coatesville** Pennsylvania U.S.A.
121 T7 **Coaticook** Quebec Canada
107 M4 **Coats** Kansas U.S.A.
112 J2 **Coats** North Carolina U.S.A.
115 L5 **Coats I** Northwest Territories Canada
146 E7 **Coats Land** Antarctica
110 D1 **Coatsville** Iowa U.S.A.
125 M8 **Coatzacoalcos** Mexico
121 L5 **Cobalt** Ontario Canada
101 L4 **Cobalt** Idaho U.S.A.
125 O10 **Cobán** Guatemala
139 H4 **Cobar** New South Wales Australia
139 J6 **Cobargo** New South Wales Australia
99 Q7 **Cobb** Wisconsin U.S.A.
139 J6 **Cobberas,Mt** Victoria Australia
143 F6 **Cobb, L** W Australia Australia
9 E6 **Cobblers Corner** England
145 D4 **Cobb Res** New Zealand
139 G7 **Cobden** Victoria Australia
121 O7 **Cobden** Ontario Canada
110 G4 **Cobden** Illinois U.S.A.
122 J8 **Cobequid B** Nova Scotia Canada
122 J8 **Cobequid Mts** Nova Scotia Canada
14 C5 **Cóbh** Ireland
140 B1 **Cobham B** N Terr Australia
128 E6 **Cobija** Bolivia
95 N4 **Cobleskill** New York U.S.A.
121 M8 **Coboconk** Ontario Canada
121 M9 **Cobourg** Ontario Canada
140 B1 **Cobourg Pen** N Terr Australia
143 B6 **Cobra** W Australia Australia
139 H6 **Cobram** New South Wales Australia
101 L8 **Cobre** Nevada U.S.A.
127 L2 **Cobre, R** Jamaica
87 F8 **Cobue** Mozambique
37 K3 **Coburg** Germany
100 B5 **Coburg** Oregon U.S.A.
115 M2 **Coburg I** Northwest Territories Canada
16 D3 **Coca** Spain
128 D7 **Cocachacra** Peru
128 D6 **Cocamá** Peru
42 C2 **Coca, Pzo. di** Italy
45 M3 **Coccolia** Italy
17 G6 **Cocentaina** Spain
128 E7 **Cochabamba** Bolivia
128 C3 **Cocha, L** Colombia
127 N9 **Coche, I** Venezuela
106 D3 **Cochetopa Pass** Colorado U.S.A.
76 C6 **Cochin** India
68 G7 **Cochin** *reg* Vietnam
128 E8 **Cochinoca** Argentina
126 D3 **Cochinos, B. de** Cuba
103 P9 **Cochise** Arizona U.S.A.
103 P9 **Cochise Head** *mt* Arizona U.S.A.
106 D6 **Cochiti L** New Mexico U.S.A.
112 D5 **Cochran** Georgia U.S.A.
118 C7 **Cochrane** Alberta Canada
120 J3 **Cochrane** Ontario Canada
133 C7 **Cochrane, L** Chile/Arg
94 G5 **Cochranton** Pennsylvania U.S.A.
33 O9 **Cochstedt** Germany
142 E3 **Cockatoo I** W Australia Australia
15 E3 **Cock Bridge** Scotland
141 G3 **Cockburn** *R* Queensland Australia
138 F4 **Cockburn** South Australia Australia
133 C8 **Cockburn, Canal** *str* Chile
127 J4 **Cockburn Harbour** Turks & Caicos Is
120 G7 **Cockburn I** Ontario Canada
140 B6 **Cockburn, Mt** N Terr Australia
140 A7 **Cockburn, Mt** N Terr Australia
142 G3 **Cockburn Ra** W Australia Australia
142 A3 **Cockburn Sd** W Australia Australia
13 F2 **Cockburnspath** Scotland
126 G2 **Cockburn Town** San Salvador Bahamas
13 F2 **Cockenzie** Scotland
13 F6 **Cockerham** England
13 E4 **Cockermouth** England
95 L7 **Cockeysville** Maryland U.S.A.
143 F9 **Cocklebiddy** W Australia Australia
127 J2 **Cockpit** *pk* Jamaica
127 J2 **Cockpit Country, The** *reg* Jamaica
109 N9 **Cockrell Hill** Texas U.S.A.
15 F5 **Cocksburnpath** Scotland
89 D9 **Cockscomb** *mt* S Africa
129 J5 **Côco** *R* Brazil
125 M2 **Coco** *R* Honduras/Nicaragua
113 G9 **Cocoa** Florida U.S.A.
113 G9 **Cocoa Beach** Florida U.S.A.
126 E3 **Coco, Cayo** *isld* Cuba
111 F12 **Cocodrie** Louisiana U.S.A.
100 J1 **Cocolalla** Idaho U.S.A.
103 M6 **Coconino Plat** Arizona U.S.A.
139 H5 **Cocoparra Rge** New South Wales Australia
71 E5 **Cocoro** *isld* Philippines
127 P2 **Cocos B** Trinidad
81 G6 **Cocos I** Indian Oc
90 A8 **Cocos I** Pacific Oc
90 A8 **Cocos Ridge** Pacific Oc
83 L13 **Cocotte, Mt** Mauritius
124 H7 **Cocula** Mexico
6 M5 **Cod** *oil rig* North Sea
43 C8 **Coda Cavallo, C** Sardinia
48 L4 **Codăeşti** Romania
128 F4 **Codajas** Brazil
107 L2 **Codell** Kansas U.S.A.
118 L8 **Coderre** Saskatchewan Canada
119 N5 **Codette** Saskatchewan Canada
144 A7 **Codfish I** New Zealand
115 N6 **Cod I** Labrador, Nfld Canada
9 F4 **Codicote** England
42 E4 **Codigoro** Italy
48 J5 **Codlea** Romania
129 K4 **Codó** Brazil
44 G1 **Codogno** Italy
127 N6 **Codrington** Barbuda W Indies
123 N6 **Codroy** Newfoundland Canada
123 O5 **Codroy Pond** Newfoundland Canada
48 G4 **Codrului Muntii** *mts* Romania
122 G8 **Cody** New Brunswick Canada
98 E7 **Cody** Nebraska U.S.A.
101 Q5 **Cody** Wyoming U.S.A.
94 E10 **Coeburn** Virginia U.S.A.
121 N8 **Coe Hill** Ontario Canada
141 F2 **Coen** *R* Queensland Australia
141 G2 **Coen** Queensland Australia
32 F9 **Coesfeld** Germany
83 H5 **Coëtivy Is** Seychelles Indian Oc
100 J2 **Coeur d'Alene** Idaho U.S.A.
22 E5 **Coeuvres et Valsery** France
25 G3 **Coevorden** Netherlands
21 K5 **Coevrons, les** *mts* France
20 G8 **Coëx** France
112 E6 **Coffee** Georgia U.S.A.
117 D4 **Coffee Creek** Yukon Territory Canada
101 P2 **Coffee Creek** Montana U.S.A.
110 G2 **Coffeen** Illinois U.S.A.
111 L10 **Coffee Springs** Alabama U.S.A.
111 G8 **Coffeeville** Mississippi U.S.A.
107 P4 **Coffeyville** Kansas U.S.A.
138 D5 **Coffin B** South Australia Australia
123 L6 **Coffin I** Madeleine Is, Quebec Canada
139 L4 **Coffs Harbour** New South Wales Australia
17 G5 **Cofrentes** Spain
48 M6 **Cogealac** Romania
9 G4 **Coggeshall** England
42 B3 **Coggiola** Italy
99 P7 **Coggon** Iowa U.S.A.
43 B8 **Coghinas** *R* Sardinia
43 C8 **Coghinas, L.d** Sardinia
142 G4 **Coghlan, Mt** W Australia Australia
18 E7 **Cognac** France
40 F6 **Cogne, V.de** Italy
44 E3 **Cogoleto** Italy
16 E4 **Cogolludo** Spain
41 N5 **Cógolo** Italy
98 J3 **Cogswell** North Dakota U.S.A.
101 T2 **Cohagen** Montana U.S.A.
20 E5 **Cohiniac** France
94 K4 **Cohocton** New York U.S.A.
95 K4 **Cohocton** *R* New York U.S.A.
95 O4 **Cohoes** New York U.S.A.
139 G6 **Cohuna** Victoria Australia
112 C3 **Cohutta** Georgia U.S.A.
125 O6 **Coiba, I** Panama
133 C8 **Coig** *R* Argentina
21 O4 **Coignières** France
133 C7 **Coihaique** Chile
76 C5 **Coimbatore** India
129 G7 **Coimbra** Brazil
16 B4 **Coimbra** Portugal
16 D8 **Coin** Spain
110 A1 **Coin** Iowa U.S.A.
128 E7 **Coipasa, L** Bolivia
Coire *see* **Chur** Switzerland
19 N15 **Coiron, Mts du** France
128 E2 **Cojedes** *state* Venezuela
128 B3 **Cojimies** Ecuador
48 H4 **Cojocna** Romania
127 J9 **Cojoro** Venezuela
133 D7 **Cojudo Blanco** *mt* Argentina
47 N10 **Cok** *R* Turkey
99 M4 **Cokato** Minnesota U.S.A.
94 G6 **Cokeburg** Pennsylvania U.S.A.
101 P7 **Cokeville** Wyoming U.S.A.
26 O2 **Cokkarassa** *mt* Norway
139 G7 **Colac** Victoria Australia
144 A7 **Colac** New Zealand
131 B2 **Colanguil, Cerro de** *mt* Argentina
130 H6 **Colatina** Brazil
36 F2 **Cölbe** Germany
146 B10 **Colbeck, C** Antarctica
100 H2 **Colbert** Washington U.S.A.
33 P8 **Colbitz** Germany
33 P8 **Colbitz-Letzlinger Heide** Germany
121 N8 **Colborne** Ontario Canada
107 J2 **Colby** Kansas U.S.A.
99 Q5 **Colby** Wisconsin U.S.A.
128 D7 **Colca** *R* Peru
9 G4 **Colchester** England
95 P5 **Colchester** Connecticut U.S.A.
99 Q9 **Colchester** Illinois U.S.A.
8 D5 **Cold Ashton** England
116 F9 **Cold B** Alaska U.S.A.
44 B2 **Col de Longet** France
94 J4 **Colden** New York U.S.A.
13 F4 **Cold Fell** *mt* England
13 F2 **Coldingham** Scotland
37 O1 **Colditz** Germany
118 G4 **Cold L** Alberta Canada
119 Q3 **Cold L** Manitoba Canada
99 M4 **Cold Spring** Minnesota U.S.A.
109 M5 **Coldspring** Texas U.S.A.
13 F2 **Coldstream** Scotland
121 L8 **Coldwater** Ontario Canada
107 L4 **Coldwater** Kansas U.S.A.
94 C5 **Coldwater** Michigan U.S.A.
111 F7 **Coldwater** *R* Mississippi U.S.A.
110 M1 **Coldwater** Ohio U.S.A.
108 C7 **Coldwater Cr** Texas/Okla U.S.A.
120 D4 **Coldwell** Ontario Canada
139 H8 **Colebrook** Tasmania Australia
121 T8 **Colebrook** New Hampshire U.S.A.
110 C3 **Cole Camp** Missouri U.S.A.
116 Q2 **Coleen** *R* Alaska U.S.A.
8 D4 **Coleford** England
94 J5 **Colegrove** Pennsylvania U.S.A.
141 F2 **Coleman** *R* Queensland Australia
118 C9 **Coleman** Alberta Canada
113 E9 **Coleman** Florida U.S.A.
94 C3 **Coleman** Michigan U.S.A.
109 H4 **Coleman** Texas U.S.A.
22 B2 **Colembert** France
138 F6 **Coleraine** Victoria Australia
121 T7 **Coleraine** Quebec Canada
14 E1 **Coleraine** N Ireland
99 N2 **Coleraine** Minnesota U.S.A.
118 G9 **Coleridge** Alberta Canada
98 J7 **Coleridge** Nebraska U.S.A.
139 J8 **Coles B** Tasmania Australia
89 D8 **Colesberg** S Africa
8 E4 **Colesborne** England
9 E2 **Coleshill** England
128 D7 **Coles, Pta** *C* Peru
118 H7 **Coleville** Saskatchewan Canada
102 E3 **Coleville** California U.S.A.
119 O9 **Colfax** Saskatchewan Canada
102 D2 **Colfax** California U.S.A.
110 H1 **Colfax** Illinois U.S.A.
110 K1 **Colfax** Indiana U.S.A.
99 N8 **Colfax** Iowa U.S.A.
111 D10 **Colfax** Louisiana U.S.A.
106 F5 **Colfax** New Mexico U.S.A.
100 H3 **Colfax** Washington U.S.A.
99 P4 **Colfax** Wisconsin U.S.A.
119 O9 **Colgate** Saskatchewan Canada
133 D7 **Colhué Huapí, L** Argentina
131 B5 **Coliauco** Argentina
131 B7 **Colico, L** Chile
25 A5 **Colijnsplaat** Netherlands
124 H8 **Colima** Mexico
129 K5 **Colinas** Brazil
13 F1 **Colinsburgh** Scotland
118 D4 **Colinton** Alberta Canada
13 E2 **Colinton** Scotland
12 C2 **Colintraive** Scotland
15 B4 **Coll** *isld* Scotland
139 H4 **Collabah** New South Wales Australia
139 J3 **Collarenebri** New South Wales Australia
106 C2 **Collbran** Colorado U.S.A.
42 D5 **Colle di Val d'Elsa** Italy
89 F3 **Colleen Bawn** Zimbabwe
116 O4 **College** Alaska U.S.A.
110 M2 **College Corner** Indiana U.S.A.
110 K6 **College Grove** Tennessee U.S.A.
111 M8 **College Park** Georgia U.S.A.
95 L7 **College Park** Maryland U.S.A.
100 G3 **College Place** Washington U.S.A.
109 L5 **College Station** Texas U.S.A.
45 P6 **Collelongo** Italy
139 H3 **Collerina** New South Wales Australia
42 C5 **Collesalvetti** Italy
45 J4 **Collesalvetti** Italy
45 R7 **Colle Sannita** Italy
109 N9 **Colleyville** Texas U.S.A.
45 N6 **Colli Albani** Italy
139 J4 **Collie** New South Wales Australia
143 B10 **Collie** W Australia Australia
143 B10 **Collie Cardiff** W Australia Australia
142 E3 **Collier B** W Australia Australia
113 F12 **Collier City** Florida U.S.A.
143 C6 **Collier Ra** *mts* W Australia Australia
110 G6 **Collierville** Tennessee U.S.A.
8 B6 **Colliford L** England
12 E3 **Collin** Scotland
45 J3 **Collina, Passo di** Italy
20 E5 **Collinée** France
21 O3 **Collines-du-Vexin, Plaine et** France
9 E5 **Collingbourne Kingston** England
9 F1 **Collingham** England
13 G6 **Collingham** England
95 N7 **Collingswood** New Jersey U.S.A.
141 F5 **Collingwood** Queensland Australia
120 K8 **Collingwood** Ontario Canada
145 D4 **Collingwood** New Zealand
112 E5 **Collins** Georgia U.S.A.
111 G10 **Collins** Mississippi U.S.A.
110 C4 **Collins** Missouri U.S.A.
101 O2 **Collins** Montana U.S.A.
94 J4 **Collins** New York U.S.A.
114 J3 **Collinson Pen** Northwest Territories Canada
111 E9 **Collinston** Louisiana U.S.A.
14 E3 **Collinstown** Ireland
141 J5 **Collinsville** Queensland Australia
111 L7 **Collinsville** Alabama U.S.A.
110 G3 **Collinsville** Illinois U.S.A.
107 P5 **Collinsville** Oklahoma U.S.A.
110 J6 **Collinwood** Tennessee U.S.A.
41 M6 **Collio** Italy
120 J1 **Collis** Ontario Canada
37 Q1 **Cölln** Germany
19 Q18 **Collobrières** France
131 B8 **Collon Cura** *R* Argentina
14 C2 **Collooney** Ireland
107 K2 **Collyer** Kansas U.S.A.
40 F1 **Colmar** France
37 J5 **Colmberg** Germany
133 E3 **Colmena** Argentina
16 E8 **Colmenar** Spain
16 E4 **Colmenar de Oreja** Spain
16 E4 **Colmenar Vieja** Spain
109 N5 **Colmesneil** Texas U.S.A.
12 D3 **Colmonell** Scotland
21 J5 **Colmont** *R* France
106 F5 **Colmor** New Mexico U.S.A.
13 F6 **Colne** England
9 G4 **Colne, R** England
124 A2 **Colnett, C** Mexico
139 K5 **Colo** *R* New South Wales Australia
99 N7 **Colo** Iowa U.S.A.
41 O7 **Cologna** Italy
45 K1 **Cologna Veneta** Italy
Cologne *see* **Köln**
99 N5 **Cologne** Minnesota U.S.A.
94 A4 **Coloma** Michigan U.S.A.
99 R5 **Coloma** Wisconsin U.S.A.
21 K3 **Colombelles** France
40 A1 **Colombey les Deux Églises** France
129 J8 **Colombia** Brazil
108 H8 **Colombia** Mexico
128 C3 **Colombia** *rep* S America
90 B7 **Colombian Basin** Atlantic Oc
121 N4 **Colombiere** Quebec Canada
83 J11 **Colombo** Sri Lanka
20 G3 **Colomby** France
98 G6 **Colome** South Dakota U.S.A.
133 E4 **Colón** Argentina
126 D3 **Colón** Cuba
125 P5 **Colón** Panama
94 B5 **Colon** Michigan U.S.A.
138 B4 **Colona** South Australia Australia
126 G3 **Colonel Hill** Crooked I Bahamas
131 F5 **Colonia** Uruguay
133 D5 **Colonia Catriel** Argentina
131 D7 **Colonia Choele Choel** *isld* Argentina
133 F4 **Colonia del Sac** Uruguay
124 E2 **Colonia Díaz** Mexico
133 D7 **Colonia las Heras** Argentina
95 K8 **Colonial Beach** Virginia U.S.A.

Colonial Heights — Cotulla

167

94 K9 **Colonial Heights** Virginia U.S.A.
95 L9 **Colonial Nat. Hist. Park** Virginia U.S.A.
130 H4 **Colônia, R** Brazil
125 M2 **Colón, Montañas de** *ra* Honduras
43 H9 **Colonna, C** Italy
119 M7 **Colonsay** Saskatchewan Canada
15 B4 **Colonsay** *isld* Scotland
107 P3 **Colony** Kansas U.S.A.
131 D7 **Colorada Grande, L** Argentina
127 N10 **Coloradito** Venezuela
131 B5 **Colorado** *R* Chile
106 B2 **Colorado** *state* U.S.A.
103 L5 **Colorado** *R* Arizona U.S.A.
106 B2 **Colorado** *R* Colorado U.S.A.
109 J4 **Colorado** *R* Texas U.S.A.
103 J10 **Colorado, Cerro** *pk* Mexico
108 G3 **Colorado City** Texas U.S.A.
131 E7 **Colorado, Delta del R** Argentina
106 B2 **Colorado Nat.Mon** Colorado U.S.A.
103 N5 **Colorado Plat** Arizona U.S.A.
103 K7 **Colorado R.Aqueduct** California U.S.A.
106 F3 **Colorado Springs** Colorado U.S.A.
16 C4 **Colorico da Beira** Portugal
45 H2 **Colorno** Italy
19 Q17 **Colostre** *R* France
125 L10 **Colotepec** Mexico
124 H6 **Colotlán** Mexico
20 E6 **Colpo** France
120 K8 **Colpoys B** Ontario Canada
133 D1 **Colquechaca** Bolivia
111 M10 **Colquitt** Georgia U.S.A.
9 F2 **Colsterworth** England
101 T4 **Colstrip** Montana U.S.A.
108 D8 **Coltexo** Texas U.S.A.
9 H2 **Coltishall** England
102 G7 **Colton** California U.S.A.
95 L8 **Colton** Maryland U.S.A.
95 N2 **Colton** New York U.S.A.
98 K6 **Colton** South Dakota U.S.A.
103 O2 **Colton** Utah U.S.A.
100 H3 **Colton** Washington U.S.A.
117 O10 **Columbia** *R* British Columbia Canada
111 L10 **Columbia** Alabama U.S.A.
113 E7 **Columbia** Florida U.S.A.
110 F3 **Columbia** Illinois U.S.A.
94 B9 **Columbia** Kentucky U.S.A.
111 D9 **Columbia** Louisiana U.S.A.
95 L7 **Columbia** Maryland U.S.A.
111 G10 **Columbia** Mississippi U.S.A.
110 D3 **Columbia** Missouri U.S.A.
112 L2 **Columbia** North Carolina U.S.A.
95 L6 **Columbia** Pennsylvania U.S.A.
112 F3 **Columbia** South Carolina U.S.A.
98 H4 **Columbia** South Dakota U.S.A.
110 J6 **Columbia** Tennessee U.S.A.
94 J9 **Columbia** Virginia U.S.A.
100 E4 **Columbia** *R* Wash/Oregon U.S.A.
117 O11 **Columbia** *R* Wash/Br Col U.S.A./Canada
100 F2 **Columbia Basin** *reg* Washington U.S.A.
115 N1 **Columbia, C** Northwest Territories Canada
94 B5 **Columbia City** Indiana U.S.A.
95 L8 **Columbia, Dist. of (D.C.)** U.S.A.
101 L1 **Columbia Falls** Montana U.S.A.
116 O6 **Columbia Glacier** Alaska U.S.A.
117 Q10 **Columbia Lake** British Columbia Canada
117 P9 **Columbia, Mt** Br Col/Alberta Canada
114 G7 **Columbia Mts** British Columbia Canada
111 K8 **Columbiana** Alabama U.S.A.
94 G6 **Columbiana** Ohio U.S.A.
100 E2 **Columbia River** Washington U.S.A.
98 H4 **Columbia Road Res** South Dakota U.S.A.
95 O4 **Columbiaville** New York U.S.A.
106 D1 **Columbine** Colorado U.S.A.
101 T6 **Columbine** Wyoming U.S.A.
89 A9 **Columbine, C** S Africa
17 H5 **Columbretes, I** Spain
111 M9 **Columbus** Georgia U.S.A.
110 L2 **Columbus** Indiana U.S.A.
107 Q4 **Columbus** Kansas U.S.A.
111 H8 **Columbus** Mississippi U.S.A.
101 Q4 **Columbus** Montana U.S.A.
98 J8 **Columbus** Nebraska U.S.A.
106 C10 **Columbus** New Mexico U.S.A.
98 D1 **Columbus** North Dakota U.S.A.
94 D7 **Columbus** Ohio U.S.A.
109 L6 **Columbus** Texas U.S.A.
99 R6 **Columbus** Wisconsin U.S.A.
126 G3 **Columbus Bank** Bahamas
99 P8 **Columbus City** Iowa U.S.A.
126 G2 **Columbus Mon** San Salvador Bahamas
126 G2 **Columbus Pt** Cat I Bahamas
127 M2 **Columbus Pt** Tobago
102 B2 **Colusa** California U.S.A.
12 E4 **Colvend** Scotland
94 J6 **Colver** Pennsylvania U.S.A.
145 E2 **Colville** New Zealand
116 L2 **Colville** *R* Alaska U.S.A.
100 H1 **Colville** Washington U.S.A.
114 G4 **Colville L** Northwest Territories Canada
143 F8 **Colville, Lake** W Australia Australia
137 Q8 **Colville Ridge** *sea feature* Pacific Oc
13 F3 **Colwell** England
99 O6 **Colwell** Iowa U.S.A.
8 C1 **Colwyn Bay** Wales
8 C6 **Colyford** England
45 M2 **Comacchio** Italy
125 O10 **Comalapa** Guatemala
125 N8 **Comalcalco** Mexico
131 B8 **Comallo** *R* Argentina
48 K6 **Comana** Romania
107 N7 **Comanche** Oklahoma U.S.A.
109 J4 **Comanche** Texas U.S.A.
146 D3 **Comandante Ferraz** *Brazil Base* Antarctica
133 D7 **Comandante Luis Piedrabuena** Argentina
133 D4 **Comandante Salas** Argentina
48 K4 **Comănești** Romania
48 K5 **Comarnic** Romania
125 L2 **Comayagua** Honduras
16 B4 **Comba Dão** Portugal
112 G5 **Combahee** *R* South Carolina U.S.A.
133 C4 **Combarbala** Chile
40 C2 **Combeaufontaine** France
8 B5 **Combe Martin** England
120 H10 **Comber** Ontario Canada
14 F2 **Comber** N Ireland
121 N7 **Combermere** Ontario Canada
68 A3 **Combermere B** Burma
109 K9 **Combes** Texas U.S.A.
22 D3 **Combles** France
69 F12 **Combol** *isld* Indonesia
20 G5 **Combourg** France
139 L4 **Comboyne** New South Wales Australia
21 N5 **Combres** France
20 B6 **Combrit** France
94 D9 **Combs** Kentucky U.S.A.
131 D4 **Comechingones, Sa. de** *ra* Argentina
38 G8 **Comeglians** Italy
38 G8 **Comelico** Italy
130 E6 **Comendador Gomes** Brazil
111 L9 **Comer** Alabama U.S.A.
112 D3 **Comer** Georgia U.S.A.
14 D4 **Comeragh Mts** Ireland
130 H5 **Comercinho** Brazil
98 B1 **Comertown** Montana U.S.A.
141 J6 **Comet** *R* Queensland Australia
141 J6 **Comet** Queensland Australia
109 J6 **Comfort** Texas U.S.A.
99 M5 **Comfrey** Minnesota U.S.A.
75 O7 **Comilla** Bangladesh
22 E2 **Comines** France
43 F12 **Comino** *isld* Malta
43 C8 **Comino, C** Sardinia
94 C2 **Comins** Michigan U.S.A.
43 F12 **Comiso** Sicily
125 N9 **Comitán de Dominguez** Mexico
20 C5 **Commana** France
121 L7 **Commanda** Ontario Canada
18 G6 **Commentry** France
20 G8 **Commequiers** France
21 J5 **Commer** France
112 D3 **Commerce** Georgia U.S.A.
107 Q5 **Commerce** Oklahoma U.S.A.
109 M2 **Commerce** Texas U.S.A.
106 F2 **Commerce City** Colorado U.S.A.
19 J4 **Commercy** France
45 J1 **Commessaggio** Italy
121 S4 **Commissaires, Lac des** Quebec Canada
115 L4 **Committee B** Northwest Territories Canada
146 D14 **Commonwealth B** Antarctica
138 C3 **Commonwealth Hill** South Australia Australia
139 K6 **Commonwealth Terr** New South Wales Australia
41 K6 **Como** Italy
106 E2 **Como** Colorado U.S.A.
111 G7 **Como** Mississippi U.S.A.
133 D7 **Comodoro Rivadavia** Argentina
41 K5 **Como, Lago di** Italy
124 D4 **Comondú** Mexico
125 J7 **Comonfort** Mexico
76 C6 **Comorin, C** India
81 B7 **Comoro Ridge** Indian Oc
87 G10 **Comoros** *islds, rep* Indian Oc
118 G7 **Compeer** Alberta Canada
22 D5 **Compiègne** France
22 D5 **Compiègne, Forêt de** France
124 G7 **Compostela** Mexico
71 G7 **Compostela** Mindanao Philippines
130 F9 **Comprida, I** São Paulo Brazil
102 A2 **Comptche** California U.S.A.
102 F8 **Compton** California U.S.A.
99 R8 **Compton** Illinois U.S.A.
12 E1 **Comrie** Scotland
95 O3 **Comstock** New York U.S.A.
108 F6 **Comstock** Texas U.S.A.
45 O4 **Cona** Italy
66 E5 **Co Nag** *L* China
85 B7 **Conakry** Guinea
133 D6 **Cona Niyeo** Argentina
112 C3 **Conasauga** *R* Georgia U.S.A.
98 D6 **Conata** South Dakota U.S.A.
45 N4 **Conca** *R* Italy
108 H6 **Concan** Texas U.S.A.
20 C6 **Concarneau** France
130 H9 **Conceição** Paraíba Brazil
130 H6 **Conceição da Barra** Brazil
130 E6 **Conceiçao das Alagoas** Brazil
129 J5 **Conceiçao do Araguaia** Brazil
130 G6 **Conceição do Mato Dentro** Brazil
133 D3 **Concepción** Argentina
128 E6 **Concepcion** Beni Bolivia
128 F7 **Concepción** Santa Cruz Bolivia
131 A6 **Concepción** Chile
124 C2 **Concepcion** *R* Mexico
130 B8 **Concepción** *dept* Paraguay
130 B8 **Concepción** Paraguay
131 A6 **Concepción, B. del** Chile
133 B8 **Concepción, Can** *str* Chile
130 C10 **Concepción de la Sierra** Argentina
124 J5 **Concepción del Oro** Mexico
131 F4 **Concepción del Uruguay** Argentina
128 F7 **Concepción, L** Bolivia
124 D4 **Concepción, Pta** *C* Mexico
99 M9 **Conception** Missouri U.S.A.
123 U6 **Conception B** Newfoundland Canada
87 B10 **Conception B** Namibia
123 T6 **Conception Harb** Newfoundland Canada
126 G3 **Conception I** Bahamas
83 K12 **Conception I** Mahé I Indian Oc
124 G6 **Concha** Mexico
130 E8 **Conchas** Brazil
106 F6 **Conchas** New Mexico U.S.A.
106 F6 **Conchas Lake** New Mexico U.S.A.
21 M4 **Conches** France
133 D2 **Conchi** Chile
124 G4 **Concho** Mexico
103 P7 **Concho** Arizona U.S.A.
107 N6 **Concho** Oklahoma U.S.A.
108 G4 **Concho** *R* Texas U.S.A.
108 B7 **Conchos, Rio** Mexico
102 B4 **Concord** California U.S.A.
111 M8 **Concord** Georgia U.S.A.
94 C4 **Concord** Michigan U.S.A.
98 K7 **Concord** Nebraska U.S.A.
95 Q3 **Concord** New Hampshire U.S.A.
112 G2 **Concord** North Carolina U.S.A.
95 Q2 **Concord** Vermont U.S.A.
131 F3 **Concordia** Argentina
130 D10 **Concórdia** Brazil
124 F6 **Concordia** Mexico
107 N2 **Concordia** Kansas U.S.A.
110 C3 **Concordia** Missouri U.S.A.
45 J2 **Concórdia sulla Secchia** Italy
100 D1 **Concrete** Washington U.S.A.
68 G3 **Con Cuong** Vietnam
101 O7 **Conda** Idaho U.S.A.
141 K7 **Condamine** *R* Queensland Australia
141 K7 **Condamine** Queensland Australia
18 G7 **Condat** France
129 L6 **Cónde** Brazil
98 H4 **Conde** South Dakota U.S.A.
88 E9 **Condédzi** *R* Mozambique
125 L3 **Condega** Nicaragua
21 M5 **Condé-sur-Huîsne** France
22 F3 **Condé-sur-l'Escaut** France
21 J4 **Condé-sur-Noireau** France
21 O4 **Condé-sur-Vesgres** France
21 H3 **Condé-sur-Vire** France
130 H4 **Condeúba** Brazil
139 H5 **Condobolin** New South Wales Australia
18 F9 **Condom** France
100 E4 **Condon** Oregon U.S.A.
142 C5 **Condon Creek** *B* W Australia Australia
128 C4 **Condor, Cord. del** *mts* Ecuador/Peru
12 D2 **Condorrat** Scotland
19 N14 **Condrieu** France
22 J3 **Condroz** Belgium
142 E3 **Cone B** W Australia Australia
111 K10 **Conecuh** *R* Alabama U.S.A.
42 E3 **Conegliano** Italy
17 J5 **Conejera** *isld* Balearic Is
106 D4 **Conejos** Colorado U.S.A.
94 H6 **Conemaugh** *R* Pennsylvania U.S.A.
45 O4 **Cónero, M** *mt* Italy
133 E6 **Conesa** Argentina
94 K4 **Conesus L** New York U.S.A.
99 P8 **Conesville** Iowa U.S.A.
94 F6 **Conesville** Ohio U.S.A.
123 Q4 **Coney Arm** Newfoundland Canada
90 C1 **Coney I** Bermuda
95 O6 **Coney Island** New York U.S.A.
40 D2 **Conflans** France
19 J3 **Conflans-Jarny** France
21 P4 **Conflans-Ste. Honorine** France
21 P2 **Conflans-Ste. Honorine Villers-Bretonneux** France
94 H7 **Confluence** Pennsylvania U.S.A.
18 F6 **Confolens** France
103 L2 **Confusion Range** Utah U.S.A.
130 B9 **Confuso, R** Paraguay
14 B3 **Cong** Ireland
112 G4 **Congaree** *R* South Carolina U.S.A.
112 G4 **Congaree Swamp Nat. Mon** South Carolina U.S.A.
67 D5 **Conghua** China
67 C4 **Congjiang** China
8 D1 **Congleton** England
86 C6 **Congo** *rep* W Africa
85 C6 **Congo** *R* West Africa
Congo (Brazzaville) *rep see* **Congo** *rep*
Congo (Kinshasa) *rep see* **Zaïre** *rep*
130 G7 **Congonhas** Brazil
8 D5 **Congresbury** England
118 L9 **Congress** Saskatchewan Canada
21 H6 **Congrier** France
68 J5 **Cong Tum** Vietnam
20 D7 **Conguel, Pte. de** France
133 C6 **Cónico** *mt* Chile/Arg
21 N5 **Conie** *R* France
106 E2 **Conifer** Colorado U.S.A.
9 F1 **Coningsby** England
13 G6 **Conisbrough** England
140 B5 **Coniston** N Terr Australia
120 K6 **Coniston** Ontario Canada
13 E5 **Coniston** England
141 G4 **Conjuboy** Queensland Australia
118 F3 **Conklin** Alberta Canada
108 B7 **Conlen** Texas U.S.A.
21 K5 **Conlie** France
40 C4 **Conliège** France
120 K4 **Connaught** Ontario Canada
14 B3 **Connaught** *prov* Ireland
142 E6 **Connaughton, Mt** W Australia Australia
19 N16 **Connaux** France
94 G5 **Conneaut** Ohio U.S.A.
94 G5 **Conneautville** Pennsylvania U.S.A.
95 P3 **Connecticut** *R* U.S.A.
95 O5 **Connecticut** *state* U.S.A.
15 C4 **Connel Ferry** Scotland
100 G3 **Connell** Washington U.S.A.
94 H6 **Connellsville** Pennsylvania U.S.A.
141 F6 **Connemara** Queensland Australia
14 B3 **Connemara** *dist* Ireland
101 L4 **Conner** Montana U.S.A.
138 B2 **Conner, Mt** N Terr Australia
140 B7 **Conner, Mt** N Terr Australia
21 M5 **Connerre** France
94 B7 **Connersville** Indiana U.S.A.
14 B2 **Conn, L** Ireland
142 F2 **Connor, Mt** W Australia Australia
122 D6 **Connors** New Brunswick Canada
141 J5 **Connors Ra** *mts* Queensland Australia
128 C4 **Cononaco** *R* Ecuador
112 F2 **Conover** North Carolina U.S.A.
99 R3 **Conover** Wisconsin U.S.A.
33 S6 **Conow** Germany
20 G6 **Conquereuil** France
118 K7 **Conquest** Saskatchewan Canada
20 A5 **Conquet, le** France
130 F6 **Conquista** Brazil
101 O1 **Conrad** Montana U.S.A.
139 J7 **Conran, C** Victoria Australia
99 Q4 **Conrath** Wisconsin U.S.A.
109 M5 **Conroe** Texas U.S.A.
109 M5 **Conroe, L** Texas U.S.A.
45 L2 **Consandolo** Italy
121 N9 **Consecon** Ontario Canada
130 G7 **Conselheiro Lafaiete** Brazil
45 L3 **Conselice** Italy
45 L1 **Conselve** Italy
22 J5 **Consenvoye** France
13 G4 **Consett** England
95 M6 **Conshohocken** Pennsylvania U.S.A.
22 H4 **Cons-la-Grandville** France
126 C3 **Consolación del Sur** Cuba
69 H8 **Con Son** *isld* Vietnam
69 H8 **Con Son** Vietnam
118 G6 **Consort** Alberta Canada
95 M3 **Constableville** New York U.S.A.
Constance *see* **Konstanz**
143 E6 **Constance Headland** *hill* W Australia Australia
Constance, L *see* **Bodensee**
128 F5 **Constância dos Baetas** Brazil
48 M6 **Constanța** Romania
16 D7 **Constantina** Spain
85 F1 **Constantine** Algeria
94 B5 **Constantine** Michigan U.S.A.
116 H7 **Constantine, C** Alaska U.S.A.
117 C5 **Constantine, Mt** Yukon Territory Canada
Constantinople *see* **İstanbul**
127 N4 **Constant, Morne** *hill* Guadeloupe W Indies
127 L2 **Constant Spring** Jamaica
131 A5 **Constitución** Chile
141 J6 **Consuelo** Queensland Australia
118 H9 **Consul** Saskatchewan Canada
101 L8 **Contact** Nevada U.S.A.
130 G7 **Contagalo** Brazil
128 D5 **Contamana** Peru
128 F3 **Contão** Brazil
131 D4 **Contara** *R* Argentina
45 M1 **Contarina** Italy
129 K6 **Cóntas** *R* Brazil
21 O2 **Conteville** France
40 F5 **Conthey** Switzerland
21 J6 **Contigné** France
103 O10 **Continental** Arizona U.S.A.
94 C5 **Continental** Ohio U.S.A.
106 C4 **Continental Res** Colorado U.S.A.
95 Q3 **Contoocook** New Hampshire U.S.A.
125 Q7 **Contoy, I** Mexico
16 E8 **Contraviesa, Sa** *mts* Spain
121 R7 **Contrecoeur** Quebec Canada
133 C8 **Contreras, I** Chile
21 N7 **Contres** Loir-et-Cher France
22 H5 **Contreuve** France
40 C1 **Contrexéville** France
130 G6 **Contria** Brazil
118 F7 **Control** Alberta Canada
36 C5 **Contwig** Germany
114 J4 **Contwoyto L** Northwest Territories Canada
21 P2 **Conty** France
126 H10 **Convención** Colombia
43 H8 **Conversano** Italy
94 B6 **Converse** Indiana U.S.A.
111 C10 **Converse** Louisiana U.S.A.
94 C6 **Convoy** Ohio U.S.A.
110 D6 **Conway** Arkansas U.S.A.
99 M9 **Conway** Iowa U.S.A.
110 D4 **Conway** Missouri U.S.A.
95 Q3 **Conway** New Hampshire U.S.A.
112 K1 **Conway** North Carolina U.S.A.
98 J1 **Conway** North Dakota U.S.A.
112 H4 **Conway** South Carolina U.S.A.
8 C1 **Conway B** Wales
141 J5 **Conway, C** Queensland Australia
138 D3 **Conway, L** South Australia Australia
110 D6 **Conway, L** Arkansas U.S.A.
140 C6 **Conway, Mt** N Terr Australia
95 Q2 **Conway, N** New Hampshire U.S.A.
144 D5 **Conway R** New Zealand
107 N4 **Conway Springs** Kansas U.S.A.
8 B4 **Conwil Elvet** Wales
8 C1 **Conwy** Wales
8 C1 **Conwy R** Wales
112 C4 **Conyers** Georgia U.S.A.
22 K3 **Coo** Belgium
138 C3 **Coober Pedy** South Australia Australia
9 G6 **Cooden** England
142 A3 **Coogee** *dist* Perth, W Aust Australia
142 A3 **Coogee L** W Australia Australia
142 C5 **Cooglegong** W Australia Australia
141 J7 **Coogoon** *R* Queensland Australia
140 C2 **Cooinda** N Terr Australia
138 B4 **Cook** South Australia Australia
99 O2 **Cook** Minnesota U.S.A.
99 K9 **Cook** Nebraska U.S.A.
133 C9 **Cook, B.de** Chile
117 K10 **Cook, C** British Columbia Canada
101 Q4 **Cooke City** Montana U.S.A.
143 B9 **Cooke, Mt** W Australia Australia
94 B10 **Cookeville** Tennessee U.S.A.
9 F4 **Cookham** England
146 D13 **Cook Ice Shelf** Antarctica
118 D5 **Cooking L** Alberta Canada
116 L7 **Cook Inlet** Alaska U.S.A.
134 L10 **Cook Is** Pacific Oc
144 C5 **Cook, Mt** New Zealand
117 D5 **Cook, Mt** Alaska/Yukon Terr U.S.A./Canada
99 U4 **Cooks** Michigan U.S.A.
123 Q2 **Cook's Hbr** Newfoundland Canada
121 T7 **Cookshire** Quebec Canada
141 H2 **Cook's Passage** Queensland Australia
106 C9 **Cooks Pk** New Mexico U.S.A.
121 L8 **Cookstown** Ontario Canada
14 E2 **Cookstown** N Ireland
145 E4 **Cook Strait** New Zealand
141 H3 **Cooktown** Queensland Australia
141 H7 **Cooladdi** Queensland Australia
139 J4 **Coolah** New South Wales Australia
139 H5 **Coolamon** New South Wales Australia
139 L3 **Coolangatta** New South Wales Australia
141 L8 **Coolangatta** Queensland Australia
143 C8 **Coolarda** *hill* W Australia Australia
142 A2 **Coolbellup, L** W Australia Australia
112 G2 **Cooleemee** North Carolina U.S.A.
143 D9 **Coolgardie** W Australia Australia
140 B3 **Coolibah** N Terr Australia
103 N9 **Coolidge** Arizona U.S.A.
112 D6 **Coolidge** Georgia U.S.A.
109 L4 **Coolidge** Texas U.S.A.
127 P4 **Coolidge** *airport* Antigua W Indies
103 O8 **Coolidge Dam** Arizona U.S.A.
143 B8 **Coolimba** W Australia Australia
100 J1 **Coolin** Idaho U.S.A.
141 K8 **Coolmunda Dam** Queensland Australia
142 A4 **Cooloongup, L** W Australia Australia
94 F7 **Coolville** Ohio U.S.A.
143 B7 **Coolyun Well** W Australia Australia
139 J6 **Cooma** New South Wales Australia
14 A5 **Coomacarrea** *mt* Ireland
9 E5 **Coombe Bissett** England
8 D4 **Coombe Hill** England
143 B9 **Coomberdale** W Australia Australia
139 J4 **Coonabarabran** New South Wales Australia
138 F6 **Coonalpyn** South Australia Australia
139 J4 **Coonamble** New South Wales Australia
143 E9 **Coonana** W Australia Australia
138 F6 **Coonawarra** South Australia Australia
138 F5 **Coonbah Roadhouse** New South Wales Australia
138 D4 **Coondambo** South Australia Australia
Coondapoor *see* **Kundāpura**
142 C5 **Coongan, R** W Australia Australia
141 H8 **Coongoola** Queensland Australia
138 C2 **Coongra** *R* South Australia Australia
138 F2 **Cooninnie, L** South Australia Australia
76 C5 **Coonoor** India
99 M8 **Coon Rapids** Iowa U.S.A.
99 N4 **Coon Rapids** Minnesota U.S.A.
140 C1 **Cooper** *R* N Terr Australia
129 G8 **Cooper** Paraguay
109 M2 **Cooper** Texas U.S.A.
141 F7 **Cooper Cr** Qnsld/S Aust Australia
141 F7 **Cooper Creek** *R* Queensland Australia
144 A6 **Cooper I** New Zealand
143 G7 **Cooper, Mt** W Australia Australia
139 L4 **Coopernook** New South Wales Australia
141 K2 **Coopers Plains** *dist* Brisbane, Qnsld Australia
113 K11 **Cooper's Town** Bahamas
126 F1 **Coopers Town** Great Abaco I Bahamas
95 M4 **Cooperstown** New York U.S.A.
98 H2 **Cooperstown** North Dakota U.S.A.
94 B3 **Coopersville** Michigan U.S.A.
127 O3 **Coora** Trinidad
138 B4 **Coorabie** South Australia Australia
140 F6 **Coorabulka** Queensland Australia
143 B7 **Coor-de-Wandy** *mt* W Australia Australia
138 E6 **Coorong, The** *L* South Australia Australia
143 B8 **Coorow** W Australia Australia
141 L7 **Cooroy** Queensland Australia
111 L7 **Coosa** *R* Alabama U.S.A.
112 C3 **Coosawattee** *R* Georgia U.S.A.
112 F5 **Coosawhatchie** *R* South Carolina U.S.A.
100 A6 **Coos Bay** Oregon U.S.A.
139 J5 **Cootamundra** New South Wales Australia
14 E2 **Cootehill** Ireland
141 K7 **Cooyar** Queensland Australia
131 B6 **Copahué** *pk* Chile
133 C5 **Copahue** *mt* Chile/Arg
100 A2 **Copalis Beach** Washington U.S.A.
109 K7 **Copano B** Texas U.S.A.
100 C8 **Copco** California U.S.A.
106 H2 **Cope** Colorado U.S.A.
128 F4 **Copea, Paraná** *R* Brazil
113 F12 **Copeland** Florida U.S.A.
100 J1 **Copeland** Idaho U.S.A.
107 K4 **Copeland** Kansas U.S.A.
94 B2 **Copemish** Michigan U.S.A.
Copenhagen *see* **København**
95 M3 **Copenhagen** New York U.S.A.
133 E5 **Copetonas** Argentina
139 K3 **Copeton Res.** New South Wales Australia
133 C3 **Copiapó** Chile
133 D3 **Copiapo** *vol* Chile
15 F2 **Copinsay** Scotland
138 E4 **Copley** South Australia Australia
128 D6 **Coporaque** Peru
45 L2 **Copparo** Italy
120 G3 **Coppell** Ontario Canada
109 N8 **Coppell** Texas U.S.A.
129 G2 **Coppename** *R* Suriname
32 L8 **Coppenbrügge** Germany
116 P5 **Copper** *R* Alaska U.S.A.
109 K4 **Copperas Cove** Texas U.S.A.
100 G1 **Copper Butte** *mt* Washington U.S.A.
116 P6 **Copper Center** Alaska U.S.A.
120 J6 **Copper Cliff** Ontario Canada
99 T2 **Copper Hbr** Michigan U.S.A.
138 C3 **Copper Hill** South Australia Australia
114 H4 **Coppermine** Northwest Territories Canada
120 F6 **Coppermine Pt** *C* Ontario Canada
117 N11 **Copper Mt** British Columbia Canada
100 K8 **Copper Mt** Nevada U.S.A.
117 Q5 **Copp L** Northwest Territories Canada
48 J4 **Copșa Mică** Romania
131 B6 **Copulhue, Paso del** Arg/Chile
75 L3 **Coqên** China
22 B2 **Coquelles** France
13 G3 **Coquet I** England
13 G3 **Coquet, R** England
Coquilhatville *see* **Mbandaka**
100 A6 **Coquille** Oregon U.S.A.
131 B2 **Coquimbo** Chile
101 P7 **Cora** Wyoming U.S.A.
46 G1 **Corabia** Romania
130 G5 **Coração de Jesus** Brazil
139 L3 **Coraki** New South Wales Australia
120 J2 **Coral** Ontario Canada
71 C6 **Coral B** Palawan Philippines
113 L9 **Coral Harbour** New Providence I Bahamas
115 L5 **Coral Harbour** Northwest Territories Canada
137 K4 **Coral Sea Islands Terr** Australasia
99 P8 **Coralville Lake** *res* Iowa U.S.A.
101 L1 **Coram** Montana U.S.A.
139 G7 **Corangamite, L** Victoria Australia
129 G3 **Corantijn** *R* Suriname
94 G6 **Coraopolis** Pennsylvania U.S.A.
43 G7 **Corato** Italy
20 C5 **Coray** France
21 P4 **Corbeil-Essonnes** France
19 P13 **Corbelin** France
22 F5 **Corbény** France
120 K8 **Corbetton** Ontario Canada
21 P2 **Corbie** France
20 F3 **Corbiere** Channel Is
18 G10 **Corbières** *reg* France
18 H5 **Corbigny** France
94 C10 **Corbin** Kentucky U.S.A.
123 R7 **Corbin Hd** Newfoundland Canada
45 M1 **Córbola** Italy
16 D7 **Corbones** *R* Spain
13 F4 **Corbridge** England
9 F2 **Corby** Lincs England
9 F2 **Corby** Northants England
Corcaigh *see* **Cork**
36 B7 **Corcieux** France
102 E5 **Corcoran** California U.S.A.
20 G8 **Corcoué-sur-Logne** France
133 C6 **Corcovado** *mt* Chile
133 C6 **Corcovado, Golfo** Chile
16 A2 **Corcubion** Spain
112 D6 **Cordele** Georgia U.S.A.
107 M6 **Cordell** Oklahoma U.S.A.
20 G7 **Cordemais** France
18 G8 **Cordes** France
129 J5 **Cordilheiras, Serra das** *mts* Brazil
16 D1 **Cordillera Cantábrica** *mts* Spain
128 C3 **Cordillera Central** *mts* Colombia
127 J5 **Cordillera Central** *mts* Dominican Rep
125 O5 **Cordillera Central** *mts* Panama
128 C5 **Cordillera Central** *mts* Peru
71 E2 **Cordillera Central** *mts* Luzon Philippines
127 J10 **Cordillera de Mérida** *mts* Venezuela
128 C3 **Cordillera Occidental** *mts* Colombia
128 D2 **Cordillera Oriental** *mts* Colombia
71 F5 **Cordilleras Ra** Panay Philippines
138 F2 **Cordillo Downs** South Australia Australia
130 G6 **Cordisburgo** Brazil
131 D3 **Córdoba** Argentina
131 D4 **Cordoba** *prov* Argentina
128 C2 **Córdoba** *div* Colombia
125 L8 **Cordoba** Mexico
16 D7 **Córdoba** *prov* Spain
16 D7 **Córdoba** Spain
131 D3 **Cordoba, Sierra de** *ra* Argentina
128 C6 **Córdova** Peru
111 J8 **Cordova** Alabama U.S.A.
116 P6 **Cordova** Alaska U.S.A.
99 Q8 **Cordova** Illinois U.S.A.
121 N8 **Cordova Mines** Ontario Canada
116 P6 **Cordova Pk** Alaska U.S.A.
45 J3 **Coreglia Antelminelli** Italy
140 F4 **Corella** *R* Queensland Australia
140 D4 **Corella L** N Terr Australia
141 G5 **Corfield** Queensland Australia
45 P5 **Corfinio** Italy
Corfu *isld* Greece *see* **Kérkira** *isld*
94 J4 **Corfu** New York U.S.A.
100 F3 **Corfu** Washington U.S.A.
16 C2 **Corgo** Spain
130 C6 **Corguinho** Brazil
45 N6 **Cori** Italy
16 C5 **Coria** Spain
16 C7 **Coria del R** Spain
45 N4 **Coriano** Italy
121 O3 **Coribelle** Quebec Canada
139 K5 **Coricudgy** *mt* New South Wales Australia
43 H9 **Corigliano Calabro** Italy
45 O4 **Corinaldo** Italy
141 K2 **Corinda** *dist* Brisbane, Qnsld Australia
140 E4 **Corinda** Queensland Australia
141 K3 **Coringa Is** Gt Barrier Reef Aust
141 K3 **Coringa Is** Coral Sea
139 H8 **Corinna** Tasmania Australia
101 N8 **Corinne** Utah U.S.A.
Corinth *see* **Kórinthos**
101 S4 **Corinth** Montana U.S.A.
95 O3 **Corinth** New York U.S.A.
Corinth, Gulf of *see* **Korinthiakós Kólpos**
143 C9 **Corinthian** W Australia Australia
130 G6 **Corinto** Brazil
130 C6 **Corixinha, R** Brazil
14 C5 **Cork** *co* Ireland
14 C5 **Cork** Ireland
20 D5 **Corlay** France
43 E11 **Corleone** Sicily
47 J3 **Çorlu** Turkey
123 P4 **Cormack** Newfoundland Canada
123 Q5 **Cormack** *mt* Newfoundland Canada
21 O5 **Cormainville** France
21 L3 **Cormeilles** France
21 M7 **Cormery** France
22 F5 **Cormicy** France
123 L2 **Cormier, L** Quebec Canada
21 J3 **Cormolain** France
119 R4 **Cormorant** Manitoba Canada
6 L1 **Cormorant** *oil rig* North Sea
123 L4 **Cormorant Pt** Anticosti I, Quebec
107 M6 **Corn** Oklahoma U.S.A.
41 M6 **Corna** Italy
45 P6 **Cornacchia, Monte** Italy
32 H7 **Cornau** Germany
21 K7 **Corne** France
112 D3 **Cornelia** Georgia U.S.A.
133 G2 **Cornélio Procópio** Brazil
99 S9 **Cornell** Illinois U.S.A.
99 P4 **Cornell** Wisconsin U.S.A.
123 P5 **Corner Brook** Newfoundland Canada
139 H7 **Corner Inlet** Victoria Australia
110 K6 **Cornersville** Tennessee U.S.A.
111 D9 **Corney L** Louisiana U.S.A.
103 P6 **Cornfields** Arizona U.S.A.
13 F2 **Cornhill-on-Tweed** England
20 H5 **Cornille** France
40 E2 **Cornimont** France
119 P9 **Corning** Saskatchewan Canada
110 F5 **Corning** Arkansas U.S.A.
99 M9 **Corning** Iowa U.S.A.
107 O2 **Corning** Kansas U.S.A.
99 L9 **Corning** Missouri U.S.A.
95 K4 **Corning** New York U.S.A.
94 E7 **Corning** Ohio U.S.A.
Corn Is *see* **Maiz, Is. del**
141 G5 **Cornish** *R* Queensland Australia
95 P3 **Cornish Flat** New Hampshire U.S.A.
142 F5 **Cornish, Mt** W Australia Australia
45 J3 **Corno alle Scale** *mt* Italy
42 F6 **Corno, M** *mt* Italy
20 B5 **Cornouaille** *reg* France
21 J6 **Cornuaille, la** France
100 H4 **Cornucopia** Oregon U.S.A.
99 P3 **Cornucopia** Wisconsin U.S.A.
18 H9 **Cornus** France
121 Q7 **Cornwall** Ontario Canada
8 B7 **Cornwall** *co* England
115 K2 **Cornwallis I** Northwest Territories Canada
138 D5 **Corny Pt** South Australia Australia
127 K9 **Coro** Venezuela
130 G6 **Coroaci** Brazil
129 K4 **Coroatá** Brazil
87 B9 **Coroca** *R* Angola
128 E7 **Corocoro** Bolivia
128 E7 **Coroico** Bolivia
130 F6 **Coromandel** Brazil
145 E2 **Coromandel** New Zealand
76 E5 **Coromandel Coast** India
145 E2 **Coromandel Peninsula** New Zealand
21 J7 **Coron** France
71 E4 **Coron** Philippines
138 F4 **Corona** New South Wales Australia
102 G8 **Corona** California U.S.A.
106 E7 **Corona** New Mexico U.S.A.
119 M9 **Coronach** Saskatchewan Canada
102 G9 **Coronado** California U.S.A.
71 F7 **Coronado B** Mindanao Philippines
125 N5 **Coronado, B.de** Costa Rica
113 G8 **Coronado Beach** Florida U.S.A.
103 O10 **Coronado Nat. Mem** Arizona U.S.A.
118 F6 **Coronation** Alberta Canada
114 H4 **Coronation G** Northwest Territories Canada
146 E3 **Coronation I** S Orkney Is Antarctica
142 E2 **Coronation Is** W Australia Australia
71 E5 **Coron B** Philippines
71 E5 **Coron Delian** *isld* Philippines
131 A6 **Coronel** Chile
133 E5 **Coronel Dorrego** Argentina
130 G6 **Coronel Fabriciano** Brazil
130 C9 **Coronel Oviedo** Paraguay
130 C4 **Coronel Ponce** Brazil
131 E6 **Coronel Pringles** Argentina
131 E6 **Coronel Suárez** Argentina
133 F5 **Coronel Vidal** Argentina
144 B6 **Coronet Pk** New Zealand
128 D7 **Coropuna** *mt* Peru
46 D4 **Çorovodë** Albania
139 H6 **Corowa** New South Wales Australia
126 G10 **Corozal** Colombia
127 O1 **Corozal Pt** Trinidad
20 G6 **Corps-Nuds** France
130 C10 **Corpus** Argentina
109 K8 **Corpus Christi** Texas U.S.A.
133 D1 **Corque** Bolivia
101 L6 **Corral** Idaho U.S.A.
16 E5 **Corralde Almaguer** Spain
124 G5 **Corrales** Mexico
16 D3 **Corrales** Spain
133 F4 **Corrales** Uruguay
126 D3 **Corralillo** Cuba
124 F2 **Corralitos** Mexico
143 B7 **Corrandibby Ra** *mts* W Australia Australia
14 B3 **Corraun** Ireland
14 B3 **Corraun Pen** Ireland
99 L7 **Correctionville** Iowa U.S.A.
71 E3 **Corregidor** Luzon Philippines
130 E5 **Córrego do Ouro** Brazil
129 J6 **Corrente** Brazil
130 D6 **Corrente, R** Goiás Brazil
43 F12 **Correnti, C.I. de** Sicily
129 K6 **Correntina** Brazil
106 C7 **Correo** New Mexico U.S.A.
18 G7 **Corrèze** *dept* France
18 G7 **Corrèze** *R* France
45 K1 **Corrèzzo** Italy
45 M1 **Corrézzola** Italy
14 B3 **Corrib, L** Ireland
12 C2 **Corrie** Scotland
130 B10 **Corrientes** Argentina
131 F2 **Corrientes** *prov* Argentina
133 F3 **Corrientes** *R* Argentina
128 C4 **Corrientes** *R* Peru
133 F5 **Corrientes, C** Argentina
126 B4 **Corrientes, C** Cuba
124 G7 **Corrientes, C** Mexico
109 N5 **Corrigan** Texas U.S.A.
143 C9 **Corrigin** W Australia Australia
139 K5 **Corrimal** New South Wales Australia
13 H6 **Corringham** England
14 B4 **Corrofin** Ireland
94 H5 **Corry** Pennsylvania U.S.A.
139 J6 **Corryong** Victoria Australia
12 C1 **Corryvreckan, Str.of** Scotland
18 L11 **Corse-du-Sud** *dept* Corsica
20 F5 **Corseul** France
12 C3 **Corsewall Pt** Scotland
8 D5 **Corsham** England
18 L10 **Corsica** *isld* France
98 H6 **Corsica** South Dakota U.S.A.
109 L3 **Corsicana** Texas U.S.A.
12 E3 **Corsock Br** Scotland
8 D5 **Corston** England
13 E2 **Corstorphine** Scotland
115 P5 **Cort Adelaer, Kap** *C* Greenland
103 N9 **Cortaro** Arizona U.S.A.
16 C7 **Cortegana** Spain
130 J10 **Cortès** Brazil
106 B4 **Cortez** Colorado U.S.A.
102 H1 **Cortez** Nevada U.S.A.
38 F8 **Cortina d'Ampezzo** Italy
98 K9 **Cortland** Nebraska U.S.A.
95 L4 **Cortland** New York U.S.A.
94 G5 **Cortland** Ohio U.S.A.
9 H2 **Corton** England
42 D5 **Cortona** Italy
85 B6 **Corubal** *R* Guinea/Guinea-Bissau
16 B6 **Coruche** Portugal
78 H1 **Çoruh** *R* Turkey
15 B3 **Coruisk, L** Scotland
78 E1 **Çorum** Turkey
130 B6 **Corumbá** Brazil
130 E4 **Corumbá de Goiás** Brazil
130 E6 **Corumbaíba** Brazil
130 E5 **Corumbá, R** Brazil
130 H5 **Corumbaú, Pta. do** *C* Brazil
128 F6 **Corumbiara** *R* Brazil
128 F2 **Corumo** *R* Venezuela
16 B1 **Coruña** *prov* Spain
94 C4 **Corunna** Michigan U.S.A.
130 H11 **Coruripe** Brazil
101 L3 **Corvallis** Montana U.S.A.
100 B5 **Corvallis** Oregon U.S.A.
38 E8 **Corvara in Badia** Italy
32 K9 **Corvey** Germany
8 C2 **Corwen** Wales
107 M4 **Corwin** Kansas U.S.A.
116 E7 **Corwin, C** Alaska U.S.A.
101 P4 **Corwin Springs** Montana U.S.A.
94 A8 **Corydon** Indiana U.S.A.
110 K3 **Corydon** Indiana U.S.A.
99 N9 **Corydon** Iowa U.S.A.
110 J4 **Corydon** Kentucky U.S.A.
94 J5 **Corydon** Pennsylvania U.S.A.
9 G5 **Coryton** England
21 K6 **Corzé** France
Cos *isld see* **Kos** *isld*
124 F5 **Cosalá** Mexico
125 M8 **Cosamaloapan** Mexico
43 G9 **Cosenza** Italy
9 E6 **Cosham** England
94 F6 **Coshocton** Ohio U.S.A.
81 B6 **Cosmoledo Is** Indian Oc
143 E8 **Cosmo Newberry** W Australia Australia
99 M5 **Cosmos** Minnesota U.S.A.
18 G5 **Cosne** France
18 G6 **Cosne-d'Allier** France
102 G5 **Coso Junction** California U.S.A.
133 E4 **Cosquin** Argentina
21 J6 **Cossé-le-Vivien** France
21 O6 **Cosson** *R* France
109 K6 **Cost** Texas U.S.A.
17 G7 **Costa Blanca** *reg* Spain
17 K3 **Costa Brava** *reg* Spain
16 C7 **Costa de la Luz** *reg* Spain
17 F8 **Costa del Sol** Spain
45 L1 **Costa di Rovigo** Italy
113 E11 **Costa I, La** Florida U.S.A.
102 G8 **Costa Mesa** California U.S.A.
125 M4 **Costa Rica** *rep* Central America
124 C2 **Costa Rica** Mexico
123 K3 **Costebelle, L** Quebec Canada
94 J5 **Costello** Pennsylvania U.S.A.
Costermansville *see* **Bukavu**
48 J6 **Costeşhi** Romania
95 T1 **Costigan** Maine U.S.A.
106 E5 **Costilla** New Mexico U.S.A.
33 Q9 **Coswig** Germany
71 G7 **Cotabato** Mindanao Philippines
128 E8 **Cotagaita** Bolivia
128 D7 **Cotahuasi** Peru
102 B3 **Cotati** California U.S.A.
130 H6 **Cotaxé, R** Brazil
121 Q7 **Côteau Station** Quebec Canada
118 K7 **Coteau, The** Saskatchewan Canada
126 G5 **Coteaux** Haiti
111 E12 **Cote Blanche B** Louisiana U.S.A.
44 B4 **Côte d'Azur** France
19 J5 **Côte d'Or** *dept* France
19 J5 **Côte d'Or** France
20 G3 **Cotentin** *pen* France
18 C4 **Côtes d'Armor** *dept* France
141 J6 **Cotherstone** Queensland Australia
13 F4 **Cotherstone** England
19 Q18 **Cotignac** France
45 L3 **Cotignola** Italy
128 F3 **Cotinga** *R* Brazil
85 E7 **Cotonou** Benin
128 C4 **Cotopaxi** *vol* Ecuador
106 E3 **Cotopaxi** Colorado U.S.A.
9 E4 **Cotswold Hills** England
100 B6 **Cottage Grove** Oregon U.S.A.
112 G5 **Cottageville** South Carolina U.S.A.
94 F8 **Cottageville** West Virginia U.S.A.
31 H4 **Cottbus** Germany
123 T5 **Cottel I** Newfoundland Canada
9 G3 **Cottenham** England
110 D5 **Cotter** Arkansas U.S.A.
83 M14 **Cotter, C** Mauritius
142 A2 **Cottesloe Beach** *dist* Perth, W Aust Australia
9 F2 **Cottesmore** England
129 H3 **Cottica** Suriname
13 H6 **Cottingham** England
99 O2 **Cotton** Minnesota U.S.A.
140 E6 **Cottonbush Cr** Queensland Australia
111 J8 **Cottondale** Alabama U.S.A.
111 L11 **Cottondale** Florida U.S.A.
140 D1 **Cotton I** N Terr Australia
119 V3 **Cotton L** Manitoba Canada
110 E6 **Cotton Plant** Arkansas U.S.A.
111 D11 **Cottonport** Louisiana U.S.A.
109 O3 **Cotton Valley** Louisiana U.S.A.
111 L10 **Cottonwood** Alabama U.S.A.
103 N7 **Cottonwood** Arizona U.S.A.
100 C9 **Cottonwood** California U.S.A.
100 J3 **Cottonwood** Idaho U.S.A.
99 M5 **Cottonwood** *R* Minnesota U.S.A.
98 E6 **Cottonwood** South Dakota U.S.A.
109 H3 **Cottonwood** Texas U.S.A.
103 L6 **Cottonwood Cliffs** Arizona U.S.A.
107 O3 **Cottonwood Falls** Kansas U.S.A.
103 O6 **Cottonwood Wash** *R* Arizona U.S.A.
127 J5 **Cotuí** Dominican Rep
109 H7 **Cotulla** Texas U.S.A.

18 E7 **Coubre, Pointe de la** *pt* France
142 F3 **Couchman Ra** W Australia Australia
22 E4 **Coucy-le-Château Auffrique** France
21 N7 **Couddes** France
22 C1 **Coudekerque-Branche** France
99 P4 **Couderay** Wisconsin U.S.A.
94 J5 **Coudersport** Pennsylvania U.S.A.
21 O3 **Coudray-St. Germer, le** France
21 M6 **Coudrecieux** France
21 N4 **Coudres** France
122 B6 **Coudres, I.aux** Quebec Canada
138 D6 **Coüedic, C.de** South Australia Australia
20 G7 **Couëron** France
21 J5 **Couesmes-Vaucé** France
20 H5 **Couesnon** *R* France
20 H7 **Couffé** France
100 C3 **Cougar** Washington U.S.A.
18 F6 **Couhé** France
14 A5 **Coulagh B** Ireland
21 L5 **Coulans** France
15 C2 **Coulbeag Mt** Scotland
100 F2 **Coulee City** Washington U.S.A.
100 G1 **Coulee Dam** Washington U.S.A.
100 G1 **Coulee Dam Nat. Recreation Area** Washington U.S.A.
21 L5 **Coulimer** France
146 C12 **Coulman I** Antarctica
21 O6 **Coulmiers** France
22 B2 **Coulogne** France
21 O4 **Coulombs** Eure France
121 O6 **Coulonge** *R* Quebec Canada
18 E6 **Coulonges-Sur-l'Autize** France
21 K8 **Coulonges Thouarsais** France
21 H4 **Coulouvray-Boisbenâtre** France
119 R9 **Coulter** Manitoba Canada
102 D4 **Coulterville** California U.S.A.
110 G3 **Coulterville** Illinois U.S.A.
116 F4 **Council** Alaska U.S.A.
100 J5 **Council** Idaho U.S.A.
99 L8 **Council Bluffs** Iowa U.S.A.
107 O3 **Council Grove** Kansas U.S.A.
8 D2 **Cound** England
107 N7 **Countyline** Oklahoma U.S.A.
15 E4 **Coupar Angus** Scotland
123 Q7 **Coupe, C** Langlade I Atlantic Oc
100 C1 **Coupeville** Washington U.S.A.
109 K5 **Coupland** Texas U.S.A.
22 B2 **Couple, Mt** France
21 K5 **Couptrain** France
117 S3 **Courageous L** Northwest Territories Canada
21 P5 **Courances** France
122 B8 **Courcelles** Quebec Canada
21 L5 **Courcemont** France
21 N6 **Cour Cheverny** France
21 K5 **Courcité** France
21 L5 **Courgains** France
27 M16 **Courland Lagoon** Lithuania/Rus Fed
21 J8 **Courlay** France
18 H7 **Courpière** France
22 D3 **Courrières** France
18 H9 **Coursan** France
21 K3 **Courseulles** France
18 H5 **Courson les Carrières** France
21 N5 **Courtalain** France
40 F3 **Courtelary** Switzerland
117 L11 **Courtenay** British Columbia Canada
98 H2 **Courtenay** North Dakota U.S.A.
18 G7 **Courtine, la** France
110 J7 **Courtland** Alabama U.S.A.
107 N2 **Courtland** Kansas U.S.A.
99 M5 **Courtland** Minnesota U.S.A.
95 K10 **Courtland** Virginia U.S.A.
14 C5 **Courtmacsherry** Ireland
109 L5 **Courtney** Texas U.S.A.
21 L4 **Courtomer** France
Courtrai *see* **Kortrijk**
22 H2 **Court Saint-Etienne** Belgium
118 L8 **Courval** Saskatchewan Canada
21 N5 **Courville** France
109 O3 **Coushatta** Louisiana U.S.A.
83 J12 **Cousin I** Seychelles
22 G3 **Cousolre** France
21 M8 **Coussay-les-Bois** France
19 O17 **Coustellet** France
87 D9 **Coutada do Mucusso** Angola
20 H3 **Coutances** France
21 K4 **Couterne** France
22 J2 **Couthuin** Belgium
18 E7 **Coutras** France
101 N1 **Coutts** Alberta Canada
21 K7 **Coutures** France
127 O2 **Couva** Trinidad
20 G2 **Couville** France
22 H3 **Couvin** Belgium
22 F4 **Couvron-et-Aumencourt** France
48 K5 **Covasna** Romania
48 K5 **Covasna** *reg* Romania
109 N1 **Cove** Arkansas U.S.A.
100 H4 **Cove** Oregon U.S.A.
112 K2 **Cove City** North Carolina U.S.A.
103 M3 **Cove Fort** Utah U.S.A.
100 B10 **Covelo** California U.S.A.
94 K7 **Cove Mt** Pennsylvania U.S.A.
126 G10 **Coveñas** Colombia
9 E3 **Coventry** England
95 L8 **Cove Point** Maryland U.S.A.
107 M2 **Covert** Kansas U.S.A.
94 A4 **Covert** Michigan U.S.A.
94 J9 **Covesville** Virginia U.S.A.
16 B4 **Covilhã** Portugal
116 K7 **Coville, L** Alaska U.S.A.
112 D4 **Covington** Georgia U.S.A.
99 T9 **Covington** Indiana U.S.A.
94 C7 **Covington** Kentucky U.S.A.
111 F11 **Covington** Louisiana U.S.A.
99 S3 **Covington** Michigan U.S.A.
94 C6 **Covington** Ohio U.S.A.
107 N5 **Covington** Oklahoma U.S.A.
110 G6 **Covington** Tennessee U.S.A.
109 K3 **Covington** Texas U.S.A.
94 G9 **Covington** Virginia U.S.A.
120 G5 **Cow** *R* Ontario Canada
15 C4 **Cowal** Scotland
139 J5 **Cowal, L** New South Wales Australia
119 R6 **Cowan** Manitoba Canada
110 K6 **Cowan** Tennessee U.S.A.
140 E4 **Cowan Downs** Queensland Australia
138 F6 **Cowangie** Victoria Australia
118 K4 **Cowan L** Saskatchewan Canada
143 D9 **Cowan, Lake** W Australia Australia
101 P4 **Cowan, Mt** Montana U.S.A.
121 S7 **Cowansville** Quebec Canada
138 D3 **Coward Springs** South Australia Australia
58 C5 **Cowargarzê** China
138 E2 **Cowarie** South Australia Australia
9 F2 **Cowbit** England
103 L2 **Cowboy Pass** Utah U.S.A.
8 C5 **Cowbridge** Wales
143 B9 **Cowcowing L** W Australia Australia
100 G2 **Cow Cr** Washington U.S.A.
110 H2 **Cowden** Illinois U.S.A.
13 E1 **Cowdenbeath** Scotland
101 T9 **Cowdrey** Colorado U.S.A.
138 D5 **Cowell** South Australia Australia
94 G8 **Cowen** West Virginia U.S.A.
139 H7 **Cowes** Victoria Australia
9 E6 **Cowes** England
107 P6 **Coweta** Oklahoma U.S.A.
9 F6 **Cowfold** England
123 P4 **Cow Head** Newfoundland Canada
100 E8 **Cow Head L** California U.S.A.
100 A1 **Cowichan, L** British Columbia Canada
140 A6 **Cowle, Mt** N Terr Australia
98 H9 **Cowles** Nebraska U.S.A.
106 E6 **Cowles** New Mexico U.S.A.
141 G7 **Cowley** Queensland Australia
118 D9 **Cowley** Alberta Canada
101 R5 **Cowley** Wyoming U.S.A.
100 C3 **Cowlitz** *R* Washington U.S.A.
100 D3 **Cowlitz Pass** Washington U.S.A.
94 H8 **Cowpasture** *R* Virginia U.S.A.
112 F2 **Cowpens** South Carolina U.S.A.
112 F2 **Cowpens Nat.Bat.Site** South Carolina U.S.A.
139 J5 **Cowra** New South Wales Australia
130 G4 **Coxa, R** Brazil
139 H9 **Cox Bight** Tasmania Australia
13 G4 **Coxhoe** England
130 C4 **Coxibó do Ouro** Brazil
130 C6 **Coxim** Brazil
123 O2 **Coxipi L** Quebec Canada
130 C4 **Coxipó da Ponté** Brazil
143 F6 **Cox,Mt** W Australia Australia
140 D3 **Cox R** N Terr Australia
95 O4 **Coxsackie** New York U.S.A.
75 O8 **Cox's Bazar** Bangladesh
123 P4 **Cox's Cove** Newfoundland Canada
108 B6 **Coyame** Mexico
108 D5 **Coyanosa Cr** Texas U.S.A.
21 P3 **Coye-la-Forêt** France
107 N6 **Coyle** Oklahoma U.S.A.
102 C4 **Coyote** California U.S.A.
102 H6 **Coyote L** California U.S.A.
102 F5 **Coyote Peak** California U.S.A.
103 L9 **Coyote Pk** Arizona U.S.A.
124 D5 **Coyote, Pta** *C* Mexico
124 F6 **Coyotitán** Mexico
98 G9 **Cozad** Nebraska U.S.A.
44 B2 **Cozie Alpi** *mt* Italy
124 C2 **Cozón, Cerro** *mt* Mexico
125 Q7 **Cozumel, I.de** Mexico
100 F3 **Crab Cr** Washington U.S.A.
141 F1 **Crab I** Queensland Australia
139 J4 **Craboon** New South Wales Australia
94 C9 **Crab Orchard** Kentucky U.S.A.
112 C2 **Crab Orchard** Tennessee U.S.A.
110 G4 **Crab Orchard L** Illinois U.S.A.
127 H2 **Crab Pond Pt** Jamaica
139 H7 **Crab Pt** Victoria Australia
8 B6 **Crackington Haven** England
8 D2 **Crackleybank** England
Cracow *see* **Kraków**
141 K7 **Cracow** Queensland Australia
139 H8 **Cradle, Mt** Tasmania Australia
138 E4 **Cradock** South Australia Australia
89 D9 **Cradock** S Africa
117 G8 **Craig** Alaska U.S.A.
101 S9 **Craig** Colorado U.S.A.
113 G13 **Craig** Florida U.S.A.
99 L9 **Craig** Missouri U.S.A.
101 O2 **Craig** Montana U.S.A.
98 K8 **Craig** Nebraska U.S.A.
15 E3 **Craigellachie** Scotland
13 E1 **Craigend** Scotland
15 C5 **Craighouse** Scotland
12 D2 **Craigie** Scotland
144 C5 **Craigieburn** New Zealand
100 J3 **Craigmont** Idaho U.S.A.
116 R6 **Craig, Mt** Alaska U.S.A.
118 E7 **Craigmyle** Alberta Canada
13 E1 **Craigrothie** Scotland
94 H8 **Craigsville** Virginia U.S.A.
14 D4 **Craiguenamanagh** Ireland
119 M7 **Craik** Saskatchewan Canada
13 F1 **Crail** Scotland
37 J5 **Crailsheim** Germany
48 H6 **Craiova** Romania
13 E2 **Cramond** Scotland
121 Q8 **Cranberry, L** New York U.S.A.
119 Q4 **Cranberry Portage** Manitoba Canada
9 E6 **Cranborne** England
143 C10 **Cranbrook** W Australia Australia
117 Q11 **Cranbrook** British Columbia Canada
9 G5 **Cranbrook** England
119 R8 **Crandall** Manitoba Canada
98 J4 **Crandall** South Dakota U.S.A.
109 L3 **Crandall** Texas U.S.A.
99 S4 **Crandon** Wisconsin U.S.A.
127 P6 **Crane** Barbados
110 C5 **Crane** Missouri U.S.A.
98 B2 **Crane** Montana U.S.A.
100 G6 **Crane** Oregon U.S.A.
108 E4 **Crane** Texas U.S.A.
100 J5 **Crane Cr.Res** Idaho U.S.A.
118 H8 **Crane L** Saskatchewan Canada
119 M9 **Crane Valley** Saskatchewan Canada
109 K4 **Cranfills Gap** Texas U.S.A.
9 F5 **Cranleigh** England
100 A8 **Crannell** California U.S.A.
13 F2 **Cranshaws** Scotland
95 Q5 **Cranston** Rhode I U.S.A.
13 H6 **Cranswick** England
21 J6 **Craon** France
22 F5 **Craonne** France
18 H7 **Craponne-sur-Arzon** France
98 H1 **Crary** North Dakota U.S.A.
146 D10 **Crary Ice Rise** *ice rise* Antarctica
48 H3 **Crasna** *R* Romania
48 L4 **Crasna** Romania
48 H3 **Crasnei, Muntii** *mt* Romania
100 C7 **Crater L** Oregon U.S.A.
100 C7 **Crater Lake Nat. Park** Oregon U.S.A.
100 D9 **Crater Peak** *mt* California U.S.A.
101 M6 **Craters of the Moon Nat.Mon** Idaho U.S.A.
43 G9 **Crati** *R* Italy
130 G9 **Crato** Brazil
21 L7 **Cravant-les Coteaux** Indre-et-Loire France
119 N8 **Craven** Saskatchewan Canada
130 F7 **Cravinhos** Brazil
128 D2 **Cravo Norte** *R* Colombia
6 L3 **Crawford** *oil rig* North Sea
12 E3 **Crawford** Scotland
112 D4 **Crawford** Georgia U.S.A.
111 H8 **Crawford** Mississippi U.S.A.
98 C7 **Crawford** Nebraska U.S.A.
109 K4 **Crawford** Texas U.S.A.
12 E3 **Crawfordjohn** Scotland
140 B3 **Crawford,Mt** N Terr Australia
95 Q2 **Crawford Notch** New Hampshire U.S.A.
71 D5 **Crawford Pt** Philippines
110 K1 **Crawfordsville** Indiana U.S.A.
111 M11 **Crawfordville** Florida U.S.A.
112 E4 **Crawfordville** Georgia U.S.A.
9 F5 **Crawley** England
8 C4 **Cray** Wales
9 G5 **Crayford** England
116 P4 **Crazy Mts** Alaska U.S.A.
101 P3 **Crazy Mts** Montana U.S.A.
101 P4 **Crazy Pk** Montana U.S.A.
101 T5 **Crazy Woman Cr** Wyoming U.S.A.
15 D4 **Creag Meagaidh** *mt* Scotland
143 B6 **Cream, R** W Australia Australia
20 G3 **Créances** France
118 L4 **Crean L** Saskatchewan Canada
40 A5 **Crêches** France
22 B3 **Crécy-en-Pontieu** France
22 F4 **Crécy-sur-Serre** France
8 C6 **Crediton** England
12 D4 **Cree Bridge** Scotland
106 D4 **Creede** Colorado U.S.A.
112 J1 **Creedmoor** North Carolina U.S.A.
101 R9 **Creek** Colorado U.S.A.
94 H6 **Creekside** Pennsylvania U.S.A.
113 L9 **Creek Village** New Providence I Bahamas
114 J6 **Cree L** Saskatchewan Canada
124 F4 **Creel** Mexico
119 O9 **Creelman** Saskatchewan Canada
120 K8 **Creemore** Ontario Canada
12 D3 **Cree, R** Scotland
114 J6 **Cree River** Saskatchewan Canada
12 D4 **Creetown** Scotland
37 J5 **Creglingen** Germany
119 P4 **Creighton** Saskatchewan Canada
98 H7 **Creighton** Nebraska U.S.A.
120 J6 **Creighton Mine** Ontario Canada
21 P3 **Creil** France
44 G1 **Crema** Italy
47 R14 **Cremasti** Rhodes Greece
19 O13 **Crémieu** France
118 C7 **Cremona** Alberta Canada
44 G1 **Crémona** Italy
111 F7 **Crenshaw** Mississippi U.S.A.
18 E8 **Créon** France
48 F5 **Crepaja** Serbia Yugoslavia
129 G5 **Crepori** *R* Brazil
22 D5 **Crépy-en-Valois** France
120 K6 **Crerar** Ontario Canada
42 F4 **Cres** Croatia
98 G4 **Cresbard** South Dakota U.S.A.
107 N6 **Crescent** Oklahoma U.S.A.
113 G10 **Crescent Beach** Florida U.S.A.
112 J4 **Crescent Beach** South Carolina U.S.A.
100 A8 **Crescent City** California U.S.A.
139 K4 **Crescent Head** New South Wales Australia
113 F8 **Crescent L** Florida U.S.A.
100 D6 **Crescent L** Oregon U.S.A.
100 B1 **Crescent, L** Washington U.S.A.
100 E9 **Crescent Mills** California U.S.A.
103 J6 **Crescent Pk** Nevada U.S.A.
99 O6 **Cresco** Iowa U.S.A.
45 L2 **Crespino** Italy
8 B4 **Cresselly** Wales
109 K3 **Cresson** Texas U.S.A.
139 H8 **Cressy** Tasmania Australia
139 G7 **Cressy** Victoria Australia
19 O15 **Crest** France
94 E6 **Crestline** Ohio U.S.A.
100 J1 **Creston** British Columbia Canada
123 R6 **Creston** Newfoundland Canada
99 M8 **Creston** Iowa U.S.A.
101 L1 **Creston** Montana U.S.A.
100 G2 **Creston** Washington U.S.A.
101 S8 **Creston** Wyoming U.S.A.
106 E3 **Crestone Pk** Colorado U.S.A.
111 K11 **Crestview** Florida U.S.A.
110 J6 **Crestview** Tennessee U.S.A.
119 M8 **Crestwynd** Saskatchewan Canada
112 L2 **Creswell** North Carolina U.S.A.
100 B6 **Creswell** Oregon U.S.A.
115 K3 **Creswell B** Northwest Territories Canada
140 D4 **Creswell Downs** N Terr Australia
139 G7 **Creswick** Victoria Australia
19 J6 **Crêt de la Neige** *mt* France
Crete *isld see* **Kriti** *isld*
99 T8 **Crete** Illinois U.S.A.
98 K9 **Crete** Nebraska U.S.A.
98 H3 **Crete** North Dakota U.S.A.
46 G9 **Crete, Sea of** Greece
21 J3 **Creully** France
17 K2 **Creus, C** Spain
18 G6 **Creuse** *dept* France
21 N8 **Creuse** *R* France
37 M4 **Creussen** Germany
37 J1 **Creuzburg** Germany
45 K2 **Crevalcore** Italy
21 P2 **Crèvecoeur-le-Grand** France
21 L3 **Crèvecœur** France
17 G6 **Crevillente** Spain
41 H5 **Crevola** Italy
8 D1 **Crewe** England
94 J9 **Crewe** Virginia U.S.A.
8 D6 **Crewkerne** England
12 D1 **Crianlarich** Scotland
8 B2 **Criccieth** Wales
9 E1 **Crich** England
118 K9 **Crichton** Saskatchewan Canada
133 H3 **Criciuma** Brazil
9 E3 **Crick** England
8 C4 **Crickhowell** Wales
9 E4 **Cricklade** England
94 C6 **Cridersville** Ohio U.S.A.
12 E1 **Crieff** Scotland
21 N1 **Criel-sur-Mer** France
15 E6 **Criffell** *mt* Scotland
42 F3 **Crikvenica** Croatia
117 E6 **Crillon, Mt** Alaska U.S.A.
99 O1 **Crilly** Ontario Canada
Crimea *see* **Krymskaya Oblast'**
37 N2 **Crimmitschau** Germany
12 C1 **Crinan** Scotland
15 C4 **Crinan Canal** Scotland
106 E3 **Cripple Creek** Colorado U.S.A.
116 J5 **Cripple Landing** Alaska U.S.A.
9 G6 **Cripps's Corner** England
21 L2 **Criquetot-l'Esneval** France
48 G4 **Crişana** Romania
130 F5 **Cristalina** Brazil
129 H6 **Cristalino** *R* Brazil
38 F8 **Cristallo** *mt* Italy
126 H10 **Cristóbal Colón, Pico** *mt* Colombia
48 J4 **Cristuru Secuiesc** Romania
48 G4 **Crişul Alb** *R* Romania
48 G4 **Crişul Negru** *R* Romania
48 H4 **Crişul Repede** *R* Romania
94 C8 **Crittenden** Kentucky U.S.A.
33 P5 **Crivitz** Germany
99 S4 **Crivitz** Wisconsin U.S.A.
38 L9 **Črna** Slovenia
46 E3 **Crna** *R* Macedonia Yugoslavia
Crna Gora *see* **Montenegro**
46 E2 **Crna Gora** *mt* Macedonia/Serbia Yugoslavia
46 E2 **Crna Trava** Serbia Yugoslavia
46 D3 **Crni Drim** *R* Macedonia Yugoslavia
38 M9 **Črni-vrh** *mt* Slovenia
14 B3 **Croagh Patrick Mt** Ireland
139 J7 **Croajingolong Nat. Park** Victoria Australia
42 G4 **Croatia** *rep* S Europe
41 O5 **Croce, C** *mt* Italy
43 G11 **Croce, S., C** Sicily
110 D4 **Crocker** Missouri U.S.A.
70 D2 **Crocker Ra** Borneo
12 E3 **Crocketford** Scotland
109 M4 **Crockett** Texas U.S.A.
9 G5 **Crockham Hill** England
21 K4 **Crocy** France
38 F8 **Croda Rossa** *mt* Italy
110 J4 **Crofton** Kentucky U.S.A.
98 J7 **Crofton** Nebraska U.S.A.
142 D5 **Crofton,Mt** W Australia Australia
95 M3 **Croghan** New York U.S.A.
19 O18 **Croisette, C** France
20 E7 **Croisic,le** France
22 D3 **Croisilles** France
145 D4 **Croisilles Harbour** New Zealand
127 H5 **Croix des Bouquets** Haiti
19 P15 **Croix Haute, Col de la** *pass* France
21 H5 **Croixille,la** France
21 M7 **Croix,la** France
122 B2 **Croix, L.à la** Quebec Canada
122 E8 **Croix R** New Brunswick Canada
22 D5 **Croix-St.Ouen, la** France
21 N3 **Croix-st.Leufroy,la** France
120 K8 **Croker, Cape** Ontario Canada
140 B2 **Croker Hill** N Terr Australia
140 C1 **Croker I** N Terr Australia
15 D3 **Cromarty** Scotland
15 D3 **Cromarty Firth** Scotland
138 B2 **Crombie, Mt** South Australia Australia
119 Q9 **Cromer** Manitoba Canada
9 H2 **Cromer** England
144 B6 **Cromwell** New Zealand
99 O3 **Cromwell** Minnesota U.S.A.
144 C5 **Cronadun** New Zealand
37 K5 **Cronheim** Germany
13 F5 **Crook** Cumbria England
13 G4 **Crook** Durham England
98 D9 **Crook** Colorado U.S.A.
107 K4 **Crooked Cr** Kansas U.S.A.
100 G7 **Crooked Cr** Oregon U.S.A.
126 G3 **Crooked I** Bahamas
126 G3 **Crooked I.Passage** Bahamas
123 Q5 **Crooked L** Newfoundland Canada
113 F10 **Crooked L** Florida U.S.A.
117 M8 **Crooked R** British Columbia Canada
100 E5 **Crooked R** Oregon U.S.A.
119 O6 **Crooked River** Saskatchewan Canada
13 F2 **Crookham** England
14 B5 **Crookhaven** Ireland
109 M2 **Crook, L** Texas U.S.A.
13 F5 **Crooklands** England
12 E1 **Crook of Devon** Scotland
98 K2 **Crookston** Minnesota U.S.A.
98 F7 **Crookston** Nebraska U.S.A.
94 E7 **Crooksville** Ohio U.S.A.
139 J5 **Crookwell** New South Wales Australia
14 C4 **Croom** Ireland
113 E9 **Croom** Florida U.S.A.
139 K3 **Croppa Cr** New South Wales Australia
9 E3 **Cropredy** England
123 R2 **Croque** Newfoundland Canada
141 G3 **Crosbie** *R* Queensland Australia
99 N3 **Crosby** Minnesota U.S.A.
111 E10 **Crosby** Mississippi U.S.A.
98 C1 **Crosby** North Dakota U.S.A.
109 M6 **Crosby** Texas U.S.A.
108 F2 **Crosbyton** Texas U.S.A.
8 D5 **Cross** England
85 F7 **Cross** *R* Nigeria
20 F7 **Crossac** France
12 C2 **Crossaig** Scotland
87 B10 **Cross, C** Namibia
113 D8 **Cross City** Florida U.S.A.
111 E8 **Crossett** Arkansas U.S.A.
13 F4 **Cross Fell** England
118 C7 **Crossfield** Alberta Canada
13 E1 **Crossgates** Scotland
8 C3 **Cross Gates** Wales
8 B4 **Cross Hands** Wales
113 K12 **Cross Harbour** Bahamas
14 C5 **Crosshaven** Ireland
12 D3 **Crosshill** Scotland
112 F3 **Cross Hill** South Carolina U.S.A.
113 K11 **Crossing Rocks** Bahamas
121 O8 **Cross, L** Ontario Canada
111 C9 **Cross L** Louisiana U.S.A.
119 U4 **Cross Lake** Manitoba Canada
144 D5 **Crossley, Mt** New Zealand
118 D4 **Cross L. Prov. Park** Alberta Canada
12 B5 **Crossmaglen** N Ireland
103 K7 **Crossman Pk** Arizona U.S.A.
12 E4 **Crossmichael** Scotland
14 B2 **Crossmolina** Ireland
106 B1 **Cross Mountain** Colorado U.S.A.
109 H3 **Cross Plains** Texas U.S.A.
94 B1 **Cross Village** Michigan U.S.A.
110 L6 **Crossville** Tennessee U.S.A.
116 P5 **Crosswind L** Alaska U.S.A.
45 J2 **Crostolo** *R* Italy
94 E3 **Croswell** Michigan U.S.A.
110 L3 **Crothersville** Indiana U.S.A.
43 H9 **Crotone** Italy
21 O1 **Crotoy,le** France
37 O3 **Crottendorf** Germany
100 K5 **Crouch** Idaho U.S.A.
9 G4 **Crouch, R** England
22 E5 **Crouy** France
21 L7 **Crouzilles** France
101 S4 **Crow Agency** Montana U.S.A.
139 H4 **Crowal** *R* New South Wales Australia
9 G5 **Crowborough** England
8 C5 **Crowcombe** England
106 F1 **Crow Cr** Colorado U.S.A.
111 F7 **Crowder** Mississippi U.S.A.
107 P6 **Crowder** Oklahoma U.S.A.
118 F1 **Crowduck L.** Manitoba Canada
139 L4 **Crowdy Hd** New South Wales Australia
108 H2 **Crowell** Texas U.S.A.
139 G7 **Crowes** Victoria Australia
101 Q6 **Crowheart** Wyoming U.S.A.
139 H4 **Crowl** *R* New South Wales Australia
9 F2 **Crowland** England
13 H6 **Crowle** England
106 G3 **Crowley** Colorado U.S.A.
111 D11 **Crowley** Louisiana U.S.A.
102 F4 **Crowley, L** California U.S.A.
94 E8 **Crown City** Ohio U.S.A.
103 M7 **Crown King** Arizona U.S.A.
106 B6 **Crown Point** New Mexico U.S.A.
95 O3 **Crown Point** New York U.S.A.
115 L4 **Crown Prince Frederick I** Northwest Territories Canada
127 M2 **Crown Pt** Tobago
99 T8 **Crown Pt** Indiana U.S.A.
101 O3 **Crow Peak** Montana U.S.A.
141 K7 **Crow's Nest** Queensland Australia
118 C9 **Crowsnest Pass** Alberta/Br Col Canada
99 M3 **Crow Wing** *R* Minnesota U.S.A.
13 G4 **Croxdale** England
8 B5 **Croyde** England
141 F4 **Croydon** Queensland Australia
142 C5 **Croydon** W Australia Australia
9 F5 **Croydon** England
144 B7 **Croydon** New Zealand
83 L13 **Croy, Î de** Kerguelen Indian Oc
94 J8 **Crozet** Virginia U.S.A.
81 D9 **Crozet Basin** Indian Oc
81 C10 **Crozet, Îs** Indian Oc
81 B10 **Crozet Plateau** Indian Oc
114 G2 **Crozier Chan** Northwest Territories Canada
20 B5 **Crozon** France
19 N15 **Cruas** France
126 D3 **Cruces** Cuba
128 C2 **Cruces, Pta** *pt* Colombia
22 L4 **Cruchten** Luxembourg
94 H7 **Crucible** Pennsylvania U.S.A.
15 G3 **Cruden B** Scotland
8 D2 **Crudgington** England
8 D4 **Crudwell** England
111 F8 **Cruger** Mississippi U.S.A.
21 M4 **Crûlai** France
14 E2 **Crumlin** N Ireland
100 F7 **Crump L** Oregon U.S.A.
19 Q12 **Cruseilles** France
22 K5 **Crusnes** France
133 E4 **Cruz** Argentina
133 G3 **Cruz Alta** Brazil
131 D3 **Cruz del Eje** Argentina
130 G8 **Cruzeiro** Brazil
133 G2 **Cruzeiro do Oeste** Brazil
128 D5 **Cruzeiro do Sul** Brazil
133 C3 **Cruz Grande** Chile
128 C3 **Cruz, La** Colombia
18 G9 **Cruzy** France
117 M8 **Crysdale, Mt** British Columbia Canada
106 C2 **Crystal** *R* Colorado U.S.A.
103 K5 **Crystal** Nevada U.S.A.
98 J1 **Crystal** North Dakota U.S.A.
113 E9 **Crystal B** Florida U.S.A.
138 E5 **Crystal Brook** South Australia Australia
119 T9 **Crystal City** Manitoba Canada
108 H7 **Crystal City** Texas U.S.A.
99 S3 **Crystal Falls** Michigan U.S.A.
99 S7 **Crystal L** Illinois U.S.A.
99 U5 **Crystal L** Michigan U.S.A.
99 N6 **Crystal Lake** Iowa U.S.A.
113 E9 **Crystal River** Florida U.S.A.
119 M6 **Crystal Springs** Saskatchewan Canada
111 F9 **Crystal Springs** Mississippi U.S.A.
99 U6 **Crystal Valley** Michigan U.S.A.
48 F4 **Csanytelek** Hungary
48 E3 **Csepel Sziget** *R* Hungary
48 F4 **Csongrád** *co* Hungary
48 F4 **Csongrád** Hungary
48 D3 **Csorna** Hungary
48 F4 **Csorvas** Hungary
48 E3 **Csóványos** *mt* Hungary
48 D4 **Csurgó** Hungary
127 L9 **Cúa** Venezuela
88 F9 **Cuambo** Mozambique
87 D9 **Cuando** *R* Angola
87 C9 **Cuangar** Angola
87 C7 **Cuango** Angola
86 C7 **Cuango** Zaire
87 B7 **Cuanza** *R* Angola
67 A7 **Cua Rao** Vietnam
133 F4 **Cuareim** Brazil
131 F3 **Cuaro** *R* Uruguay
133 E4 **Cuarto** *R* Argentina
124 H4 **Cuatro Ciénegas de Carranza** Mexico
68 H4 **Cua Tung** Vietnam
124 F3 **Cuauhtémoc** Mexico
124 G8 **Cuautitlán** Mexico
125 K8 **Cuautla** Mexico
16 B6 **Cuba** Portugal
110 F1 **Cuba** Illinois U.S.A.
107 N2 **Cuba** Kansas U.S.A.
110 E3 **Cuba** Missouri U.S.A.
106 D5 **Cuba** New Mexico U.S.A.
94 J4 **Cuba** New York U.S.A.
126 D4 **Cuba** *rep* W Indies
103 M10 **Cubabi, Cerro** *pk* Mexico
99 Q7 **Cuba City** Wisconsin U.S.A.
127 M9 **Cubagua, I** Venezuela
143 B10 **Cuballing** W Australia Australia
87 C9 **Cubango** *R* Angola
130 F8 **Cubatão** Brazil
119 N4 **Cub Hills** Saskatchewan Canada
127 K10 **Cubiro** Venezuela
48 J6 **Cuca** Romania
133 C6 **Cucao, B.de** Chile
133 F4 **Cuchilla de Haedo** *hills* Uruguay
9 F5 **Cuckfield** England
9 E1 **Cuckney** England
94 K9 **Cuckoo** Virginia U.S.A.
87 C8 **Cucumbi** Angola
124 D2 **Cucurpe** Mexico
128 D2 **Cúcuta** Colombia
99 T7 **Cudahy** Wisconsin U.S.A.
76 D5 **Cuddalore** India
76 D3 **Cuddapah** India
141 F7 **Cuddapan,L** Queensland Australia
102 G6 **Cuddeback L** California U.S.A.
113 F13 **Cudjoe Key** *isld* Florida U.S.A.
119 M6 **Cudworth** Saskatchewan Canada
143 C7 **Cue** W Australia Australia
16 E3 **Cuéllar** Spain
128 C4 **Cuenca** Ecuador
71 E4 **Cuenca** Philippines
17 F4 **Cuenca** Spain
17 F5 **Cuenca** *prov* Spain
124 H5 **Cuencamé de Ceniceros** Mexico
17 F4 **Cuenca, Serrania de** *mts* Spain
125 K8 **Cuernavaca** Mexico
109 K6 **Cuero** Texas U.S.A.
19 Q18 **Cuers** France
106 F6 **Cuervo** New Mexico U.S.A.
102 D6 **Cuesta Pass** California U.S.A.
126 G4 **Cueto** Cuba
17 F7 **Cuevas del Almanzora** Spain
133 E2 **Cuevo** Bolivia
22 E5 **Cuffies** France
123 N2 **Cuff L** Quebec Canada
19 P18 **Cuges-les-Pins** France
48 H5 **Cugir** Romania
43 B8 **Cuglieri** Sardinia
20 G5 **Cuguen** France
130 C4 **Cuiabá** Brazil
14 D2 **Cuilcagh** *mt* N Ireland
15 B3 **Cuillin Hills** Scotland
87 C7 **Cuilo** *R* Angola
59 J2 **Cuiluan** China
87 C8 **Cuima** Angola
22 D2 **Cuinchy** France
36 B4 **Cuint** Germany
22 E5 **Cuise-la-Motte** France
130 H9 **Cuité** Brazil
130 H6 **Cuité, R** Brazil
87 C9 **Cuito** *R* Angola
87 C9 **Cuito Cuanavale** Angola
128 F4 **Cuiuni** *R* Brazil
110 E2 **Cuivre** *R* Missouri U.S.A.
71 E7 **Cujangan** *isld* Philippines
48 H6 **Cujmir** Romania
69 F10 **Cukai** Malaysia
78 J3 **Çukurca** Turkey
68 H4 **Cu Lai** Vietnam
18 G6 **Culan** France
68 J5 **Cu Lao Bo Bai** *isld* Vietnam
68 J5 **Cu Lao Cham** *isld* Vietnam
68 J7 **Cu Lao Hon** *isld* Vietnam
68 J5 **Cu Lao Re** *isld* Vietnam
71 F5 **Culasi** Panay Philippines
98 B1 **Culbertson** Montana U.S.A.
98 F9 **Culbertson** Nebraska U.S.A.
139 H6 **Culcairn** New South Wales Australia
22 G4 **Cul-des-Sarts** Belgium
106 E4 **Culebra Pk** Colorado U.S.A.
16 C3 **Culebra, Sa de la** *mts* Spain
25 D5 **Culemborg** Netherlands
87 C9 **Culevai** Angola
141 H8 **Culgoa** *R* N S W/Qnsld Australia
139 H3 **Culgoa, R** New S Wales/Queensland
124 F5 **Culiacán** Mexico
124 F5 **Culiacancito** Mexico
71 D5 **Culion** Philippines
129 H6 **Culiseu** *R* Brazil
17 F7 **Cúllar de Baza** Spain
139 J5 **Cullarin Rge** New South Wales Australia
15 F3 **Cullen** Scotland
17 G5 **Cullera** Spain
107 M4 **Cullison** Kansas U.S.A.
111 K7 **Cullman** Alabama U.S.A.
141 G5 **Culloden** *R* Queensland Australia
8 C6 **Cullompton** England
125 M2 **Culmi** Honduras
8 D3 **Culmington** England
19 P13 **Culoz** France
94 J8 **Culpeper** Virginia U.S.A.
128 A7 **Culpepper** *isld* Galapagos Is
15 E5 **Culter Fell** Scotland
129 H6 **Culuene** *R* Brazil
99 U8 **Culver** Indiana U.S.A.
107 N3 **Culver** Kansas U.S.A.
100 D5 **Culver** Oregon U.S.A.
144 D5 **Culverden** New Zealand
143 E10 **Culver,Pt** W Australia Australia
129 K4 **Cuma, B.de** Brazil
47 H4 **Cumalı** Turkey
128 F1 **Cumana** Venezuela
127 N9 **Cumanacoa** Venezuela
47 J6 **Cumaovası** Turkey
130 E6 **Cumari** Brazil
Cumberland *co see* **Cumbria**
117 L11 **Cumberland** British Columbia Canada
99 M8 **Cumberland** Iowa U.S.A.
94 D9 **Cumberland** Kentucky U.S.A.
94 J7 **Cumberland** Maryland U.S.A.
94 F7 **Cumberland** Ohio U.S.A.
110 J5 **Cumberland** *R* Tennessee U.S.A.
94 J9 **Cumberland** Virginia U.S.A.
99 O4 **Cumberland** Wisconsin U.S.A.
Cumberland, C *see* **Nahoï, C**
110 J5 **Cumberland City** Tennessee U.S.A.
94 D10 **Cumberland Gap** Tenn/Virg U.S.A.
119 P5 **Cumberland House** Saskatchewan Canada
113 F7 **Cumberland I** Georgia U.S.A.
141 J5 **Cumberland Is** Queensland Australia
119 P4 **Cumberland L** Saskatchewan Canada
94 B10 **Cumberland, L** Kentucky U.S.A.
110 L5 **Cumberland, L** Kentucky U.S.A.
94 D10 **Cumberland Mt** Tennessee U.S.A.
115 N4 **Cumberland Pen** Northwest Territories Canada
111 K7 **Cumberland Plateau** Alabama U.S.A.
99 R2 **Cumberland Pt** Michigan U.S.A.
94 D10 **Cumberland R** Kentucky U.S.A.
94 J7 **Cumberland Res** Pennsylvania U.S.A.
115 N4 **Cumberland Sound** Northwest Territories Canada
140 D1 **Cumberland Str** N Terr Australia
12 E2 **Cumbernauld** Scotland
139 J3 **Cumborah** New South Wales Australia
133 C7 **Cumbrera** *mt* Chile
13 E4 **Cumbria** *co* England
76 D3 **Cumbum** India
109 M2 **Cumby** Texas U.S.A.
44 B2 **Cumiana** Italy
129 G4 **Cumina** *R* Brazil
129 G3 **Cuminapanema** *R* Brazil
13 E4 **Cummertrees** Scotland
112 C3 **Cumming** Georgia U.S.A.
102 A2 **Cummings** California U.S.A.
98 J2 **Cummings** North Dakota U.S.A.
138 D5 **Cummins** South Australia Australia
142 F4 **Cummins Ra** W Australia Australia
139 J5 **Cumnock** New South Wales Australia
12 D3 **Cumnock** Scotland
124 E2 **Cumpas** Mexico
78 D3 **Çumra** Turkey
124 E3 **Cumuripa** Mexico
130 H5 **Cumuruxatiba** Brazil
127 O2 **Cumuto** Trinidad
126 E3 **Cunagua** Cuba
129 H3 **Cunani** Brazil
124 D6 **Cuñaño** Mexico
131 G3 **Cuñapiru** *R* Uruguay
133 C5 **Cunco** Chile
142 D5 **Cuncudgerie Hill** W Australia Australia
143 B9 **Cunderdin** W Australia Australia
128 D3 **Cundinamarca** *div* Colombia
87 B9 **Cunene** *R* Angola
44 C3 **Cúneo** Italy
138 C4 **Cungena** South Australia Australia
17 H6 **Cunillera** *isld* Balearic Is
18 H7 **Cunlhat** France
141 H8 **Cunnamulla** Queensland Australia
107 M4 **Cunningham** Kansas U.S.A.
100 G3 **Cunningham** Washington U.S.A.
127 O2 **Cunupia** Trinidad
21 K7 **Cuon** France
119 N8 **Cupar** Saskatchewan Canada
13 E1 **Cupar** Scotland
128 C2 **Cupica, G.de** Colombia
46 E1 **Ćuprija** Serbia Yugoslavia
100 J4 **Cuprum** Idaho U.S.A.
124 D5 **Cupula, P** Mexico
71 B1 **Cur** Halmahera Indonesia
129 G7 **Curabá** *R* Brazil
129 L5 **Curaçá** Brazil
126 B1 **Curaçao** *isld* W Indies
131 B7 **Curacáutin** Chile
131 D7 **Curaco, R** Argentina
131 E6 **Cura Malal, Cerro** *pk* Argentina
133 C5 **Curanilahue** Chile
128 C4 **Curaray** *R* Peru/Ecuador
131 B4 **Curaumilla, Pta de** *C* Chile
48 K6 **Curcani** Romania
21 K7 **Curçay-sur-Dive** France
138 D4 **Curdlawidny Lagoon** South Australia Australia
9 E2 **Curdworth** England
18 H5 **Cure** *R* France
106 C3 **Curecanti Nat. Recreation Area** Colorado U.S.A.
83 M13 **Curepipe** Mauritius
133 C5 **Curepto** Chile
127 O10 **Curiapo** Venezuela
131 B5 **Curico** Chile
131 D8 **Curico, L** Argentina
128 E4 **Curicuriari** *R* Brazil
83 J12 **Curieuse I** Seychelles
130 J9 **Curimataú** *R* Brazil
143 A7 **Curious,Mt** W Australia Australia
128 D3 **Curiplaya** Colombia
133 H3 **Curitiba** Brazil
130 E10 **Curitibanos** Brazil
100 G1 **Curlew** Washington U.S.A.
141 J5 **Curlew I** Queensland Australia
139 K4 **Curlewis** New South Wales Australia
111 H12 **Curlew Is** Louisiana U.S.A.
116 F5 **Curlew L** Alaska U.S.A.
123 L3 **Curlew Pt** Quebec Canada
123 O5 **Curling** Newfoundland Canada
138 E4 **Curnamona** South Australia Australia
44 F2 **Curone** *R* Italy
139 K4 **Currabubula** New South Wales Australia
130 H9 **Currais Novas** Brazil
138 C2 **Curralulla** *R* South Australia Australia
121 Q7 **Curran** Ontario Canada
94 D2 **Curran** Michigan U.S.A.
103 J3 **Currant** Nevada U.S.A.
139 G4 **Curranyalpa** New South Wales Australia
141 F7 **Currawilla** Queensland Australia
126 F2 **Current** Eleuthera Bahamas
110 E4 **Current** *R* Missouri U.S.A.
113 L12 **Current I** Bahamas
139 G7 **Currie** Tasmania Australia
13 E2 **Currie** Scotland
99 L5 **Currie** Minnesota U.S.A.
103 K1 **Currie** Nevada U.S.A.
112 J3 **Currie** North Carolina U.S.A.
138 B2 **Currie Cr., The** South Australia Australia
119 U1 **Currie L** Manitoba Canada
140 B7 **Currie,Mt** N Terr Australia
112 L1 **Currituck** North Carolina U.S.A.
112 M1 **Currituck Sound** North Carolina U.S.A.
139 K6 **Currockbilly, Mt** New South Wales Australia
110 E2 **Curryville** Missouri U.S.A.
37 L2 **Cursdorf** Germany
45 L1 **Curtarolo** Italy
48 J5 **Curtea de Argeş** Romania
48 G4 **Curtici** Romania
143 D9 **Curtin** W Australia Australia
100 B6 **Curtin** Oregon U.S.A.
140 B7 **Curtin Springs** N Terr Australia
16 B1 **Curtis** Spain
111 C9 **Curtis** Louisiana U.S.A.
99 V3 **Curtis** Michigan U.S.A.
98 F9 **Curtis** Nebraska U.S.A.
141 L6 **Curtis Chan** Gt Barrier Reef Australia
139 H7 **Curtis Group** *islds* Tasmania Australia
141 K6 **Curtis I** Queensland Australia
137 R8 **Curtis I** Kermadec Is Pacific Oc
94 D2 **Curtisville** Michigan U.S.A.
129 G4 **Curuá** Brazil
129 H5 **Curuaés** *R* Brazil
129 H3 **Curuá, I** Brazil
129 G3 **Curuapanema** *R* Brazil
128 D5 **Curuçá** *R* Brazil
129 J4 **Curuca** Brazil
133 F2 **Curuguaty** Paraguay
69 F14 **Curup** Sumatra
129 J4 **Cururupu** Brazil
131 F2 **Curuzú Cuatiá** Argentina
129 K7 **Curvelo** Brazil
94 J6 **Curwensville** Pennsylvania U.S.A.
14 E1 **Cushendall** N Ireland
14 E1 **Cushendun** N Ireland
99 M3 **Cushing** Minnesota U.S.A.
107 O6 **Cushing** Oklahoma U.S.A.
111 B10 **Cushing** Texas U.S.A.
110 E6 **Cushman** Arkansas U.S.A.
101 Q3 **Cushman** Montana U.S.A.
100 A6 **Cushman** Oregon U.S.A.
100 B2 **Cushman, L** Washington U.S.A.
124 F3 **Cusihuiráchic** Mexico
45 H3 **Cusna, Mt** Italy
18 H6 **Cusset** France
112 C5 **Cusseta** Georgia U.S.A.
99 O1 **Cusson** Minnesota U.S.A.
144 D5 **Cust** New Zealand
101 S3 **Custer** Montana U.S.A.
98 C6 **Custer** South Dakota U.S.A.
101 S4 **Custer Battlefield Nat.Mon** Montana U.S.A.
107 M6 **Custer City** Oklahoma U.S.A.
45 J1 **Custoza** Italy
117 O8 **Cutbank** *R* Alberta Canada
101 N1 **Cut Bank** Montana U.S.A.
119 P5 **Cut Beaver L** Saskatchewan Canada
111 A8 **Cuthand Cr** Texas U.S.A.
112 C6 **Cuthbert** Georgia U.S.A.
98 H6 **Cuthbert** South Dakota U.S.A.
108 F3 **Cuthbert** Texas U.S.A.
140 E4 **Cuthbert, Mt** Queensland Australia
45 J3 **Cutigliano** Italy
118 H6 **Cut Knife** Saskatchewan Canada
120 H6 **Cutler** Ontario Canada
116 H3 **Cutler** *R* Alaska U.S.A.
102 E5 **Cutler** California U.S.A.
95 T9 **Cutler** Maine U.S.A.
14 C3 **Cutra, L** Ireland
22 E4 **Cuts** France
139 H3 **Cuttaburra** *R* New South Wales Australia
75 L8 **Cuttack** India
103 O8 **Cutter** Arizona U.S.A.
81 H7 **Cuvier Basin** Indian Oc
143 A6 **Cuvier,C** W Australia Australia
145 E2 **Cuvier I** New Zealand
87 C8 **Cuvo** *R* Angola
32 J5 **Cuxhaven** Germany
Cu Xu, I *see* **Quan Dao Co To**
94 F5 **Cuyahoga** *R* Ohio U.S.A.
94 F5 **Cuyahoga Falls** Ohio U.S.A.
102 E6 **Cuyama** *R* California U.S.A.
71 E3 **Cuyapo** Luzon Philippines
71 E5 **Cuyo** *isld* Philippines
71 E5 **Cuyo East Passage** Philippines
71 E5 **Cuyo West Passage** Philippines
99 N3 **Cuyuna** Minnesota U.S.A.
128 G2 **Cuyuni** *R* Guyana
125 N2 **Cuyu Tigni** Nicaragua
128 E8 **Cuzco** *mt* Bolivia
128 D6 **Cuzco** Peru
42 H5 **Čvrsnica** *mt* Bosnia-Herzegovina
8 C4 **Cwmbran** Wales
88 B3 **Cyangugu** Rwanda
31 H3 **Cybinka** Poland
Cyclades *islds see* **Kikládhes** *islds*
139 H9 **Cygnet** Tasmania Australia
119 W2 **Cygnet L** Manitoba Canada
138 D6 **Cygnet River** South Australia Australia
118 B5 **Cynthia** Alberta Canada
110 M3 **Cynthiana** Kentucky U.S.A.
110 G4 **Cypress** Illinois U.S.A.
111 C10 **Cypress** Louisiana U.S.A.
109 M6 **Cypress** Texas U.S.A.
111 A8 **Cypress Cr** Texas U.S.A.
109 N3 **Cypress Cr., Lit** Texas U.S.A.
118 H9 **Cypress Hills** Saskatchewan Canada
118 G9 **Cypress Hills Prov. Park** Alberta Canada
113 F9 **Cypress L** Florida U.S.A.
119 S9 **Cypress River** Manitoba Canada
79 D4 **Cyprus** *rep* Mediterranean Sea
84 G4 **Cyrenaica** *reg* Libya
Cyrene *see* **Shaḩḩāt**
77 A5 **Cyrus** *oil well* Persian Gulf
115 N5 **Cyrus Field B** Northwest Territories Canada
22 E2 **Cysoing** France
31 J2 **Czaplinek** Poland

118 G6 **Czar** Alberta Canada
31 M4 **Czarna** *R* Poland
31 O2 **Czarna Białestocka** Poland
31 K2 **Czarne** Poland
31 K3 **Czarnków** Poland
31 M6 **Czarny Dunajec** Poland
31 M6 **Czchów** Poland
31 J6 **Czechoslovakia** *rep* Europe
31 K3 **Czempin** Poland
31 O3 **Czeremcha** Poland
Czernowitz *see* **Chernovtsy**
31 K2 **Czersk** Poland
31 J3 **Czerwieńsk** Poland
31 L5 **Częstochowa** Poland
31 J2 **Człopa** Poland
31 K2 **Człuchów** Poland
31 N3 **Czyżew** Poland

D

36 D2 **Daaden** Germany
65 F2 **Da'an** China
71 F5 **Daanbantayan** Cebu Philippines
122 B7 **Daaquam** Quebec Canada
67 B2 **Daba** China
79 F7 **Dabāb, J. Ed** *mt* Jordan
127 J9 **Dabajuro** Venezuela
85 D7 **Dabakala** Ivory Coast
58 D4 **Daban Shan** *mt* China
48 E3 **Dabas** Hungary
67 C1 **Daba Shan** *mts* China
86 G3 **Dabat** Ethiopia
128 C2 **Dabeiba** Colombia
68 C4 **Dabein** Burma
33 P5 **Dabel** Germany
70 C4 **Dabhoi** India
31 H2 **Dabie** Poland
67 E1 **Dabie Shan** *mts* China
79 G10 **Dabl Mushāsh** *well* Saudi Arabia
36 C6 **Dabo** France
85 B6 **Dabola** Guinea
85 D7 **Dabou** Ivory Coast
85 D7 **Daboya** Ghana
36 C1 **Dabringhausen** Germany
31 O2 **Dąbrowa** Poland
31 L5 **Dąbrowa Górnicza** Poland
31 M2 **Dąbrówno** Poland
65 D7 **Dabu** China
67 E4 **Dabu** China
65 F2 **Dabusu Pao** *L* China
Dacca *see* **Dhaka**
65 C5 **Dachang** China
37 L7 **Dachau** Germany
37 L7 **Dachauer Moos** *marshes* Germany
37 K4 **Dachsbach** Germany
38 J7 **Dachstein** *mt* Austria
38 J7 **Dachstein-Gebirge** *mts* Austria
31 J6 **Dačice** Czechoslovakia
107 M5 **Dacoma** Oklahoma U.S.A.
128 G3 **Dadanawa** Guyana
79 H2 **Dādāt** Syria
70 D2 **Daday** Turkey
113 E9 **Dade City** Florida U.S.A.
111 L9 **Dadeville** Alabama U.S.A.
74 B4 **Dadhar** Pakistan
65 D7 **Dadian** China
65 G3 **Dadianzi** China
71 C3 **Dadi, Tg** *C* W Irian
68 J1 **Dadong** China
18 G9 **Dadou** *R* France
27 H11 **Dådran** Sweden
74 E8 **Dadra & Nagar Haveli** *Union Terr* India
74 G4 **Dadri** India
74 B5 **Dadu** Pakistan
68 H7 **Da Dung** *R* Vietnam
48 L6 **Dăeni** Romania
65 C4 **Da'erhao** China
140 D7 **Daer,Mt** N Terr Australia
71 F3 **Daet** Philippines
67 B3 **Dafang** China
80 F1 **Dafna** Israel
119 N7 **Dafoe** Saskatchewan Canada
68 B4 **Daga** *R* Burma
27 C11 **Dagali** Norway
85 A5 **Dagana** Senegal
47 K5 **Dagardı** Turkey
71 A1 **Dagasuli** Indonesia
30 D1 **Dagebüll** Germany
9 G4 **Dagenham** England
53 G11 **Dagestanskaya Respublika** Russian Federation
102 H7 **Daggett** California U.S.A.
99 T4 **Daggett** Michigan U.S.A.
78 K5 **Daghgharah, Al** Iraq
27 G12 **Daglösen** Sweden
98 B1 **Dagmar** Montana U.S.A.
65 D5 **Dagu** China
67 A3 **Daguan** China
21 K7 **Daguenière,la** France
71 E2 **Dagupan** Luzon Philippines
94 J5 **Dagus Mines** Pennsylvania U.S.A.
68 C4 **Dagwin** Burma
141 G4 **Dagworth** Queensland Australia
66 E6 **Dagzê** China
79 E10 **Dahab** Egypt
117 L4 **Dahadinni** *R* Northwest Territories Canada
67 D5 **Dahao Dao** *isld* China
65 J1 **Dahezhen** China
59 H2 **Da Hinggan Ling** *mt ra* China
32 G10 **Dahle** Germany
36 B3 **Dahleim** Germany
33 R10 **Dahlen** Germany
33 N6 **Dahlenburg** Germany
33 S8 **Dahlewitz** Germany
95 K8 **Dahlgren** Virginia U.S.A.
112 C3 **Dahlonega** Georgia U.S.A.
33 O4 **Dahme** Germany
33 T8 **Dahme** *R* Germany
33 S9 **Dahme** Germany
33 P5 **Dahmen** Germany
33 O4 **Dahmeshöved** Germany
36 D5 **Dahn** Germany
72 F3 **Dahnā, Ad** *reg* Saudi Arabia
74 F7 **Dāhod** India
78 J3 **Dahok** Iraq
Dahomey *rep see* **Benin, Rep. of**
66 B4 **Dahongliutan** China
65 E4 **Dahongqi** China
67 D1 **Dahong Shan** *mts* China
33 N7 **Dähre** Germany
78 J3 **Dahuk** Iraq
78 J3 **Dahūk** *prov* Iraq
65 E4 **Dahushan** China
139 G5 **Dahwilly** New South Wales Australia
71 O8 **Dai** *isld* Indonesia
48 K7 **Daia** Romania
65 C5 **Daicheng** China
65 B4 **Dai Hai** *L* China
69 G13 **Daik** Indonesia
68 C4 **Daik-U** Burma
75 J4 **Dailekh** Nepal
121 T3 **Daillebout, L** Quebec Canada
60 G9 **Daimanji-san** *mt* Japan
16 E5 **Daimiel** Spain
109 N2 **Daingerfield** Texas U.S.A.
61 K10 **Dainichiga-take** *pk* Japan
66 F5 **Dainkog** China
141 H3 **Daintree** *R* Queensland Australia
141 H3 **Daintree** Queensland Australia
61 K11 **Daiō** Japan
65 E2 **Daiqin Tal** China
Dairen *see* **Dalian**
84 J4 **Dairût** Egypt
100 D7 **Dairy** Oregon U.S.A.
143 B7 **Dairy Creek** W Australia Australia
60 G10 **Dai-sen** *mt* Japan
60 G10 **Dai sen-Oki Nat. Park** Japan
109 N5 **Daisetta** Texas U.S.A.
67 G1 **Dai Shan** *isld* China
67 F4 **Daishan** China
129 K5 **Dais Irmaos, Serra** *mts* Brazil
100 G1 **Daisy** Washington U.S.A.
58 F4 **Dai Xian** China
Daiyue *see* **Shanyin**
67 F4 **Daiyun Shan** *mts* China
127 J5 **Dajabón** Dominican Rep
140 E5 **Dajarra** Queensland Australia
58 D5 **Dajin Chuan** *R* China
67 G2 **Dajing** China
45 P1 **Dajla** Croatia
70 D5 **Daju** Kalimantan
85 A6 **Dakar** Senegal
67 D4 **Dakengkou** China
67 D5 **Dakengkou** China
68 H5 **Dak Gle** Vietnam
85 A4 **Dakhla, Ad** Western Sahara
84 H4 **Dakhla Oasis** Egypt
68 H5 **Dak Kon** Vietnam
69 A9 **Dakoank** Nicobar Is
85 F6 **Dakoro** Niger
99 F7 **Dakota** Illinois U.S.A.
99 P6 **Dakota** Minnesota U.S.A.
99 M7 **Dakota City** Iowa U.S.A.
98 K7 **Dakota City** Nebraska U.S.A.
46 D2 **Dakovica** Serbia Yugoslavia
48 E5 **Dakovo** Croatia
28 D3 **Dal** Denmark
27 E11 **Dal** Norway
87 D8 **Dala** Angola
27 J11 **Dalä** *L* Sweden
41 L3 **Dalaas Tal** Austria
85 B6 **Dalaba** Guinea
65 A4 **Dalad Qi** China
Dalai *see* **Da'an**
Dalai Nor *L see* **Hulun Nur** *L*
58 G3 **Dalai Nur** *L* China
27 G11 **Dala-Järna** Sweden
78 B3 **Dalaman** *R* Turkey
58 D3 **Dalandzadgad** Mongolia
71 E5 **Dalanganem** *islds* Philippines
27 K12 **Dalarö** Sweden
70 B3 **Dalat** Sarawak
68 J7 **Da Lat** Vietnam
71 C6 **Dalawan B** Philippines
77 J5 **Dalbandin** Pakistan
15 E6 **Dalbeattie** Scotland
141 H5 **Dalbeg** Queensland Australia
27 F13 **Dalbosjön** *L* Sweden
141 K7 **Dalby** Queensland Australia
28 F5 **Dalby** Denmark
27 F11 **Dalby** Sweden
12 D5 **Dalby** I of Man U.K.
28 E3 **Dalbyneder** Denmark
28 E3 **Dalbyover** Denmark
27 A10 **Dale** Norway
27 A11 **Dale** Norway
110 K3 **Dale** Indiana U.S.A.
100 G5 **Dale** Oregon U.S.A.
94 J6 **Dale** Pennsylvania U.S.A.
109 K6 **Dale** Texas U.S.A.
8 A4 **Dale** Wales
110 L5 **Dale Hollow L** Kentucky/Tennessee
118 D8 **Dalemead** Alberta Canada
143 B9 **Dale,Mt** W Australia Australia
25 G3 **Dalen** Netherlands
28 B7 **Daler** Denmark
31 M5 **Daleszyce** Poland
68 A2 **Dalet** *R* Burma
68 A3 **Dalet** Burma
68 A2 **Daletme** Burma
110 L1 **Daleville** Indiana U.S.A.
27 H10 **Dalfors** Sweden
25 F4 **Dalfsen** Netherlands
143 B8 **Dalgaranger Hill** W Australia Australia
139 J6 **Dalgety** New South Wales Australia
12 E1 **Dalginross** Scotland
141 F5 **Dalgonally** Queensland Australia
108 B7 **Dalhart** Texas U.S.A.
114 G3 **Dalhousie, C** Northwest Territories Canada
65 A7 **Dali** China
59 H4 **Dalian** China
58 D6 **Daliang Shan** China
65 E5 **Dalian Wan** *B* China
71 G7 **Daliao** Philippines
106 D7 **Dalies** New Mexico U.S.A.
65 A6 **Dali He** *R* China
Dalinghe *see* **Jin Xian**
80 D3 **Daliyat el Karmil** Israel
65 G4 **Dalizi** China
48 E5 **Dalj** Croatia
15 E5 **Dalkeith** Scotland
14 E3 **Dalkey** Ireland
141 K7 **Dallarnil** Queensland Australia
119 U7 **Dallas** Manitoba Canada
111 M8 **Dallas** Georgia U.S.A.
100 B5 **Dallas** Oregon U.S.A.
109 N10 **Dallas** Texas U.S.A.
99 P4 **Dallas** Wisconsin U.S.A.
99 N8 **Dallas Center** Iowa U.S.A.
99 P9 **Dallas City** Illinois U.S.A.
95 L7 **Dallastown** Pennsylvania U.S.A.
102 D4 **Dallas Warner Res** California U.S.A.
100 D4 **Dalles, The** Oregon U.S.A.
117 G8 **Dall I** Alaska U.S.A.
116 F6 **Dall L** Alaska U.S.A.
116 N3 **Dall Mt** Alaska U.S.A.
85 E6 **Dallol Bosso** *watercourse* Niger
77 C7 **Dalmā** *isld* U.A.E.
133 E4 **Dalmacio Velez Sarsfield** Argentina
12 D1 **Dalmally** Scotland
42 G4 **Dalmatia** *reg* Croatia
55 D3 **Dalmatovo** Russian Federation
12 D3 **Dalmellington** Scotland
118 L6 **Dalmeny** Saskatchewan Canada
28 G6 **Dalmose** Denmark
12 D2 **Dalmuir** Scotland
59 L3 **Dal'negorsk** Russian Federation
59 K2 **Dal'nerechensk** Russian Federation
52 F6 **Dal'neye-Konstantinovo** Russian Federation
52 E1 **Dal'niye Zelentsy** Russian Federation
85 C7 **Daloa** Ivory Coast
67 C5 **Dalongdong Shuiku** *res* China
67 B3 **Dalou Shan** *mt ra* China
121 M4 **Dalquier** Quebec Canada
118 D7 **Dalroy** Alberta Canada
15 D5 **Dalry** Dumfries & Galloway Scotland
15 D5 **Dalry** Strathclyde Scotland
141 H4 **Dalrymple** Queensland Australia
15 D5 **Dalrymple** Scotland
141 J5 **Dalrymple,Mt** Queensland Australia
29 K11 **Dalsbruk** Finland
28 S9 **Dalsmynni** Iceland
13 F4 **Dalston** England
75 L6 **Dāltenganj** India
120 F4 **Dalton** Ontario Canada
13 E3 **Dalton** Scotland
112 C3 **Dalton** Georgia U.S.A.
95 O4 **Dalton** Massachusetts U.S.A.
98 D8 **Dalton** Nebraska U.S.A.
95 M5 **Dalton** Pennsylvania U.S.A.
115 R4 **Dalton, Kap** *C* Greenland
69 E12 **Daludalu** Sumatra
65 F5 **Dalu Dao** *isld* China
28 E6 **Dalum** Denmark
68 E2 **Daluo** China
65 H2 **Daluolemi** China
65 G1 **Daluozhen** China
71 E1 **Dalupiri** *isld* Philippines
71 G4 **Dalupiri** Philippines
12 E3 **Dalveen P** Scotland
28 S9 **Dalvík** Iceland
143 B9 **Dalwallinu** W Australia Australia
15 D4 **Dalwhinnie** Scotland
36 F1 **Dalwigksthal** Germany
109 N9 **Dalworthington Gardens** Texas U.S.A.
140 B2 **Daly** *R* N Terr Australia
102 B4 **Daly City** California U.S.A.
140 B2 **Daly R** N Terr Australia
140 B2 **Daly River** N Terr Australia
140 D1 **Daly River Aboriginal Land** N Terr Australia
140 C3 **Daly Waters** N Terr Australia
98 D5 **Dalzell** South Dakota U.S.A.
79 G10 **'Damaj, Bargā** *hill* Saudi Arabia
74 E8 **Daman** India
79 A7 **Damanhûr** Egypt
65 C4 **Damaqun Shan** *mt ra* China
71 B3 **Damar** *isld* Indonesia
71 O8 **Damar** *isld* Indonesia
107 L2 **Damar** Kansas U.S.A.
86 C5 **Damara** Cent Afr Republic
87 B10 **Damara** *homeland* Namibia
89 A4 **Damaraland** *tribal area* Namibia
95 S2 **Damariscotta L** Maine U.S.A.
Damas *see* **Dimashq**
Damascus *see* **Dimashq**
110 D6 **Damascus** Arkansas U.S.A.
95 K7 **Damascus** Maryland U.S.A.
94 F10 **Damascus** Virginia U.S.A.
131 B5 **Damas, Paso de las** Chile/Arg
86 B3 **Damaturu** Nigeria
77 C2 **Damavand** Iran
87 C7 **Damba** Angola
36 C7 **Dambach** France
83 K10 **Dambulla** Sri Lanka
68 J4 **Dam Cau Hai** Vietnam
126 G5 **Dame Marie** Haiti
20 E6 **Damgan** France
77 D1 **Dāmghān** Iran
28 A4 **Damhus Å** *R* Denmark
65 D3 **Damiao** China
48 L4 **Dămieneşti** Romania
21 L5 **Damigni** France
65 C6 **Daming** China
67 C5 **Daming Shan** *mts* China
80 F5 **Damiya** Jordan
80 F5 **Damiya Br** Jordan
71 E8 **Dammai** *isld* Philippines
77 B6 **Dammām, Ad** Saudi Arabia
21 O5 **Dammarie** France
18 G3 **Dammartin-en-Goële** France
22 E1 **Damme** Belgium
32 H7 **Damme** Germany
74 H7 **Damoh** India
109 M6 **Damon** Texas U.S.A.
85 D7 **Damongo** Ghana
79 F5 **Damour** Lebanon
70 F4 **Dampelas, Tg** *C* Celebes
22 K4 **Dampicourt** Belgium
142 B5 **Dampier** W Australia Australia
142 B5 **Dampier Arch** W Australia Australia
142 E4 **Dampier Downs** W Australia Australia
40 C2 **Dampierre-sur-Saône** France
71 C3 **Dampir, Selat** *str* W Irian
70 O10 **Dampit** Java
28 J7 **Damsholte** Denmark
19 J3 **Damvillars** France
21 N4 **Damville** France
22 J5 **Dâmvillers** France
80 F1 **Dan** Israel
112 H1 **Dan** *R* North Carolina U.S.A.
94 J10 **Dan** *R* Virginia U.S.A.
119 M6 **Dana** Saskatchewan Canada
71 K10 **Dana** *isld* Indonesia
79 F8 **Danā** Jordan
99 S9 **Dana** Illinois U.S.A.
110 J2 **Dana** Indiana U.S.A.
85 C7 **Danané** Ivory Coast
68 J4 **Da Nang** Vietnam
75 L6 **Danapur** India
116 G9 **Dana Vol** Alaska U.S.A.
58 D5 **Danba** China
85 F6 **Danbatta** Nigeria
95 O5 **Danbury** Connecticut U.S.A.
98 F9 **Danbury** Nebraska U.S.A.
95 Q3 **Danbury** New Hampshire U.S.A.
109 M6 **Danbury** Texas U.S.A.
99 O4 **Danbury** Wisconsin U.S.A.
103 J7 **Danby L** California U.S.A.
119 T6 **Dancing Point** Manitoba Canada
143 B9 **Dandaragan** W Australia Australia
74 J4 **Dandel Dhura** Nepal
76 B3 **Dandeli** India
139 H7 **Dandenong** Victoria Australia
59 H3 **Dandong** China
74 E2 **Dandot** Pakistan
121 Q5 **Dandurand, L** Quebec Canada
99 R6 **Dane** Wisconsin U.S.A.
147 E10 **Daneborg** Greenland
109 L6 **Danevang** Texas U.S.A.
65 A8 **Danfeng** China
67 E6 **Dangan Liedao** *isld* China
57 E5 **Dangara** Tajikistan
65 J2 **Dangbizhen** China
Dangcheng *see* **Xiangshan**
87 B7 **Dange** Angola
21 N5 **Dangeau** France
140 B1 **Danger Pt** *inlet* N Terr Australia
89 A10 **Danger Pt** S Africa
21 M8 **Dangé-St-Romain** France
21 L5 **Dangeul** France
66 F4 **Dang He** *R* China
86 G3 **Dangila** Ethiopia
68 G5 **Dangrek, Chaine des** *mts* Cambodia
125 P9 **Dangriga** Belize
65 C7 **Dangshan** China
67 F1 **Dangtu** China
21 O3 **Dangu** France
67 D1 **Dangyang** China
68 J7 **Da Nhim** *R* Vietnam
113 G11 **Dania** Florida U.S.A.
101 P7 **Daniel** Wyoming U.S.A.
42 E2 **Daniele del Friuli, S** Italy
122 D3 **Daniel-Johnston Dam** Quebec Canada
143 D10 **Daniell** W Australia Australia
144 D5 **Daniells, L** New Zealand
123 P3 **Daniels Harbour** Newfoundland Canada
118 J1 **Daniels L** Ontario Canada
95 Q5 **Danielson** Connecticut U.S.A.
112 D3 **Danielsville** Georgia U.S.A.
52 F5 **Danilov** Russian Federation
42 J6 **Danilovgrad** Montenegro Yugoslavia
55 F4 **Danilovka** Kazakhstan
52 J3 **Danilovka** Russian Federation
52 E3 **Danilovo** Russian Federation
58 F4 **Daning** China
67 C1 **Daningchang** China
Danjiang *see* **Leishan**
68 J6 **Dan Kia** Vietnam
67 A1 **Danleng** China
98 H8 **Dannebrog** Nebraska U.S.A.
115 Q4 **Dannebrog Ø** *isld* Greenland
28 G7 **Dannemare** Denmark
27 J11 **Dannemora** Sweden
95 O2 **Dannemora** New York U.S.A.
33 O6 **Dannenberg** Germany
33 S6 **Dannenwalde** Germany
100 H7 **Danner** Oregon U.S.A.
145 F4 **Dannevirke** New Zealand
68 E4 **Dan Sai** Thailand
144 C6 **Danseys Pass** New Zealand
67 E5 **Danshui** China
68 B4 **Danson B** Burma
94 C4 **Dansville** Michigan U.S.A.
94 K4 **Dansville** New York U.S.A.
94 E10 **Dante** Virginia U.S.A.
76 E1 **Dantewara** India
Dantu *see* **Zhenjiang**
Danube *R* Austria/Germany *see* **Donau** *R*
Danube *R* Bulgaria/Yugoslavia *see* **Dunav** *R*
Danube *R* Czechoslovakia *see* **Dunaj** *R*
Danube *R* Hungary *see* **Duna** *R*
Danube *R* Romania *see* **Dunărea** *R*
68 B4 **Danubyu** Burma
70 D4 **Danumparai** Kalimantan
110 G1 **Danvers** Illinois U.S.A.
99 L4 **Danvers** Minnesota U.S.A.
101 Q2 **Danvers** Montana U.S.A.
121 S7 **Danville** Quebec Canada
110 C6 **Danville** Arkansas U.S.A.
112 D5 **Danville** Georgia U.S.A.
99 T9 **Danville** Illinois U.S.A.
110 K2 **Danville** Indiana U.S.A.
95 R2 **Danville** Maine U.S.A.
94 E6 **Danville** Ohio U.S.A.
95 L6 **Danville** Pennsylvania U.S.A.
95 P2 **Danville** Vermont U.S.A.
94 H10 **Danville** Virginia U.S.A.
94 F8 **Danville** West Virginia U.S.A.
21 J4 **Danvou-la-Ferrière** France
67 C7 **Dan Xian** China
67 F1 **Danyang** China
21 N6 **Danzé** France
67 B3 **Danzhai** China
67 C5 **Danzhu** China
Danzig *see* **Gdańsk**
98 G3 **Danzig** North Dakota U.S.A.
31 L1 **Danzig, G. of** Poland
71 E5 **Dao** Panay Philippines
16 B4 **Dão** *R* Portugal
Daokou *see* **Hua Xian**
21 J6 **Daon** France
20 B5 **Daoulas** France
85 D3 **Daoura** *watercourse* Algeria/Morocco
68 J2 **Dao Vinh Thuc** *isld* Vietnam
67 D4 **Dao Xian** China
67 B2 **Daozhen** China
71 G6 **Dapa** Philippines
85 E6 **Dapaog** Togo
111 J11 **Daphne** Alabama U.S.A.
71 F6 **Dapiak, Mt** Philippines
65 E4 **Dapingfang** China
71 F6 **Dapitan** Philippines
74 E10 **Dapoli** India
118 D4 **Dapp** Alberta Canada
Dapu *see* **Liucheng**
66 F4 **Da Qaidam** China
65 E5 **Daqin Dao** *isld* China
59 J2 **Daqing** China
65 F1 **Daqing** China
65 A4 **Daqing Shan** *mt ra* China
65 B4 **Daqing Shan** *mts* China
Daqin Tal *see* **Naiman Qi**
67 G1 **Daqu Shan** *isld* China
85 A5 **Dara** Senegal
79 G6 **Dar'ā** Syria
77 D5 **Dārāb** Iran
48 K2 **Darabani** Romania
71 F5 **Daraga** Philippines
85 G2 **Daraj** Libya
48 J1 **Darakhov** Ukraine
71 G5 **Daram** *isld* Philippines
77 B3 **Daran** Iran
48 D5 **Darány** Hungary
58 F1 **Darasun** Russian Federation
85 G6 **Darazo** Nigeria
52 B6 **Darbėnai** Lithuania
101 L3 **Darby** Montana U.S.A.
116 F4 **Darby C** Alaska U.S.A.
116 F4 **Darby Mts** Alaska U.S.A.
33 N6 **Darchau** Germany
142 E3 **D'Arcole Is** W Australia Australia
117 M10 **D'Arcy** British Columbia Canada
118 J7 **D'Arcy** Saskatchewan Canada
110 C6 **Dardanelle** Arkansas U.S.A.
102 E3 **Dardanelle** California U.S.A.
Dardanelles *str see* **Çanakkale Boğazi** *str*
33 N9 **Dardesheim** Germany
46 C1 **Đarđevica Tara** Montenegro Yugoslavia
Dar el Beida *see* **Casablanca**
86 D4 **Dar-el-Kouti** *dist* Cent Afr Republic
88 G5 **Dar es Salaam** Tanzania
144 D5 **Darfield** New Zealand
Darfur *prov* Sudan *see* **Northern and Southern Darfur** *provs*
74 D1 **Dargai** Pakistan
57 B4 **Darganata** Turkmenistan
145 D1 **Dargaville** New Zealand
21 O1 **Dargnies** France
139 H6 **Dargo** Victoria Australia
33 R5 **Dargun** Germany
58 E2 **Darhan** Mongolia
59 F3 **Darhan Muminggan Lianheqi** China
47 N11 **Darıca** Turkey
112 F6 **Darien** Georgia U.S.A.
126 F10 **Darién, G.del** Colombia/Panama
125 Q5 **Darién, Serrania del** *ra* Panama
71 E2 **Darigayos Pt** Luzon Philippines
55 B5 **Dar'inskoye** Kazakhstan
125 L3 **Darío** Nicaragua
66 D6 **Dārjiling** India
143 B10 **Darkan** W Australia Australia
138 D5 **Darke Peak** South Australia Australia
77 A4 **Darkhazineh** Iran
58 C5 **Darlag** China
138 F5 **Darling** *R* South Australia Australia
141 J8 **Darling Downs** *reg* Queensland Australia
119 T9 **Darlingford** Manitoba Canada
115 M1 **Darling Pen** Northwest Territories Canada
13 G5 **Darlington** England
101 M6 **Darlington** Idaho U.S.A.
99 M9 **Darlington** Missouri U.S.A.
112 H3 **Darlington** South Carolina U.S.A.
99 Q7 **Darlington** Wisconsin U.S.A.
139 H5 **Darlington Pt** New South Wales Australia
143 D8 **Darlot, L** W Australia Australia
31 J1 **Darłowo** Poland
48 K3 **Dărmăneşti** Romania
77 F3 **Darmiān** Iran
118 L8 **Darmody** Saskatchewan Canada
36 F4 **Darmstadt** Germany
84 G3 **Darnah** Libya
111 E9 **Darnell** Louisiana U.S.A.
21 N3 **Darnetal** France
139 G5 **Darnick** New South Wales Australia
114 G4 **Darnley B** Northwest Territories Canada
146 J11 **Darnley, C** Antarctica
17 G3 **Daroda** Spain
57 F5 **Daroot-Korgon** Kyrgyzstan
52 G5 **Darovskoy** Russian Federation
141 G6 **Darr** *R* Queensland Australia
141 K2 **Darra** Brisbane, Qnsld Australia
77 F1 **Darreh Gaz** Iran
100 D1 **Darrington** Washington U.S.A.
86 D4 **Dar Rounga** *reg* Cent Afr Republic
108 D7 **Darrouzett** Texas U.S.A.
76 D3 **Darsi** India
30 G1 **Darsser Ort** *C* Germany
9 G5 **Dartford** England
138 F7 **Dartmoor** Victoria Australia
8 C6 **Dartmoor Forest** England
141 H7 **Dartmouth** *L* Queensland Australia
122 J9 **Dartmouth** Nova Scotia Canada
8 C7 **Dartmouth** England
122 H4 **Dartmouth R** Quebec Canada
139 J6 **Dartmouth Res** Victoria Australia
31 J1 **Dartowo** Poland
8 C6 **Dart, R** England
14 C2 **Dartry Mts** Ireland
136 J3 **Daru** Papua New Guinea
71 B1 **Daruba** Halmahera Indonesia
66 E5 **Darum Tso** *L* China
42 H3 **Daruvar** Croatia
15 D5 **Darvel** Scotland
13 F6 **Darwen** England
77 J4 **Darweshan** Afghanistan
140 B1 **Darwin** N Terr Australia
133 F8 **Darwin** Falkland Is
102 G5 **Darwin** California U.S.A.
88 C10 **Darwin** *dist* Zimbabwe
133 C7 **Darwin, Can** *str* Chile
146 D11 **Darwin Glacier** *glacier* Antarctica
78 K3 **Daryācheh-ye Orūmīyeh** *L* Iran
77 C7 **Dās** *isld* U.A.E.
22 L3 **Dasburg** Germany
75 L8 **Dashapalla** India
67 C1 **Dashennongjia** *mt* China
65 A4 **Dashetai** China
Dashiqiao *see* **Yingkou**
65 E1 **Dashizhai** China
77 E1 **Dasht** Iran
77 H7 **Dasht** *R* Pakistan
77 C2 **Dasht-e-Kavir** Iran
77 G7 **Dashtiari** Iran
65 C3 **Dashui Nur** China
120 J9 **Dashwood** Ontario Canada
37 L7 **Dasing** Germany
71 E7 **Dassalan** *isld* Philippines
32 L9 **Dassel** Germany
99 M4 **Dassel** Minnesota U.S.A.
33 N5 **Dassow** Germany
77 E2 **Dastgardān** Iran
70 D4 **Datadian** Kalimantan
70 D4 **Datagenojang** Kalimantan
65 C4 **Datan** China
68 J1 **Datang** China
47 J8 **Datça** Turkey
9 F5 **Datchet** England
60 O3 **Date** Japan
103 L7 **Date Cr** Arizona U.S.A.
103 L9 **Dateland** Arizona U.S.A.
74 H6 **Datia** India
67 F4 **Datian** China
106 C7 **Datil** New Mexico U.S.A.
67 F1 **Datong** China
65 F1 **Datong** Heilongjiang China
65 B4 **Datong** Shanxi China
58 C4 **Datong Shan** *mt ra* China
140 F6 **Datson,Mt** Queensland Australia
59 M2 **Datta** Russian Federation
32 F9 **Datteln** Germany
69 J12 **Datu** *isld* Indonesia
69 J11 **Datuk, Tanjong** *C* Indonesia/Malaysia
65 J2 **Daubikhe** *R* Russian Federation
74 D2 **Daud Khel** India
32 K7 **Dauelsen** Germany
115 N1 **Daugaard Jensen Land** Greenland
28 D5 **Daugård** Denmark
52 C6 **Daugava** *R* Latvia
52 C6 **Daugav'pils** Latvia
77 K1 **Daulatabad** Afghanistan
74 F9 **Daulatabad** India
128 C4 **Daule** Ecuador
41 M3 **Daumen** *mt* Germany
21 K6 **Daumeray** France
36 B3 **Daun** Germany
74 F9 **Daund** India
68 C6 **Daung Kyun** *isld* Burma
119 R7 **Dauphin** Manitoba Canada
95 L6 **Dauphin** Pennsylvania U.S.A.
19 O14 **Dauphiné** *prov* France
111 H11 **Dauphin I** Alabama U.S.A.
119 S7 **Dauphin L** Manitoba Canada
85 F6 **Daura** Nigeria
74 G5 **Dausa** India
15 E3 **Dava** Scotland
76 B3 **Davangere** India
71 G7 **Davao** Mindanao Philippines
71 G7 **Davao Gulf** Mindanao Philippines
12 C3 **Davarr I** Scotland
121 S6 **Daveluyville** Quebec Canada
22 D4 **Davenescourt** France
121 M4 **Davengus** Quebec Canada
116 J5 **Davenport** Alaska U.S.A.
102 B4 **Davenport** California U.S.A.
113 F9 **Davenport** Florida U.S.A.
99 Q8 **Davenport** Iowa U.S.A.
98 J9 **Davenport** Nebraska U.S.A.
95 N4 **Davenport** New York U.S.A.
107 O6 **Davenport** Oklahoma U.S.A.
100 G2 **Davenport** Washington U.S.A.
141 F6 **Davenport Downs** Queensland Australia
140 A6 **Davenport Hills** N Terr Australia
140 B5 **Davenport,Mt** N Terr Australia
140 C5 **Davenport Ra** N Terr Australia
9 E3 **Daventry** England
80 E3 **Daverat** Israel
32 K7 **Daverden** Germany
125 N5 **David** Panama
98 J8 **David City** Nebraska U.S.A.
146 D12 **David Glacier** *glacier* Antarctica
146 H13 **David I** Antarctica
119 M7 **Davidson** Saskatchewan Canada
112 G2 **Davidson** North Carolina U.S.A.
107 L7 **Davidson** Oklahoma U.S.A.
140 B5 **Davidson,Mt** N Terr Australia
116 Q2 **Davidson Mts** Alaska U.S.A.
8 B6 **Davidstow** England
113 G11 **Davie** Florida U.S.A.
138 A2 **Davies, Mt** South Australia Australia
26 A10 **Davik** Norway
109 K5 **Davilla** Texas U.S.A.
119 N8 **Davin** Saskatchewan Canada
146 J11 **Davis** *Australia Base* Antarctica
119 M5 **Davis** Saskatchewan Canada
102 C3 **Davis** California U.S.A.
99 R7 **Davis** Illinois U.S.A.
107 N7 **Davis** Oklahoma U.S.A.
98 K6 **Davis** South Dakota U.S.A.
94 H7 **Davis** West Virginia U.S.A.
112 E5 **Davisboro** Georgia U.S.A.
99 N9 **Davis City** Iowa U.S.A.
100 E8 **Davis Creek** California U.S.A.
103 K6 **Davis Dam** Arizona U.S.A.
115 N6 **Davis Inlet** Labrador, Nfld Canada
94 H7 **Davis, Mt** Pennsylvania U.S.A.
108 C5 **Davis Mts** Texas U.S.A.
94 D3 **Davison** Michigan U.S.A.
146 J13 **Davis Sea** Antarctica
115 O4 **Davis Str** Greenland/Canada
110 E4 **Davisville** Missouri U.S.A.
55 C4 **Davlekanovo** Russian Federation
41 L4 **Davos** Switzerland
79 F2 **Davudi Dağı** *mts* Turkey
94 F9 **Davy** West Virginia U.S.A.
56 G5 **Davydov, Gora** *mt* Russian Federation
143 D9 **Davyhurst** W Australia Australia
65 F3 **Dawa** China
65 E4 **Dawa** China
86 H5 **Dawa** *R* Ethiopia
Dawei *see* **Tavoy**
141 K6 **Dawes Ra** Queensland Australia
77 B7 **Dawḩah, Ad** Qatar
68 D4 **Dawlan** Burma
8 C6 **Dawlish** England
110 C2 **Dawn** Missouri U.S.A.
108 E1 **Dawn** Texas U.S.A.
68 C4 **Dawna Ra** Burma
141 J6 **Dawson** *R* Queensland Australia
117 D3 **Dawson** Yukon Territory Canada
111 M10 **Dawson** Georgia U.S.A.
98 K5 **Dawson** Minnesota U.S.A.
98 G3 **Dawson** North Dakota U.S.A.
107 P5 **Dawson** Oklahoma U.S.A.
109 L4 **Dawson** Texas U.S.A.
119 R6 **Dawson Bay** Manitoba Canada
117 N8 **Dawson Creek** British Columbia Canada
117 Q5 **Dawson Landing** Northwest Territories Canada
117 Q5 **Dawson Lodge** Northwest Territories Canada
117 P10 **Dawson, Mt** British Columbia Canada
117 D4 **Dawson Range** Yukon Territory Canada
110 J4 **Dawson Springs** Kentucky U.S.A.
141 K7 **Dawson Vale** Queensland Australia
111 M7 **Dawsonville** Georgia U.S.A.
67 E1 **Dawu** China
79 H4 **Daww, Ad** *depression* Syria
18 E9 **Dax** France
67 B1 **Da Xian** China
68 H1 **Daxin** China
65 E6 **Daxindian** China
65 C5 **Daxing** China
59 J3 **Daxinggou** China
36 E5 **Daxlanden** Germany
67 C4 **Daxu** China
67 C5 **Daxuan** China
Daxue *see* **Wencheng**
58 D4 **Daxue Shan** *mt ra* China
58 D5 **Daxue Shan** *mt ra* China
67 F3 **Daxu Shan** *pass* China
100 D8 **Day** California U.S.A.
113 D7 **Day** Florida U.S.A.
57 B4 **Dayakhatyn** Turkmenistan
65 F4 **Dayang He** *R* China
67 C5 **Dayao Shan** *mts* China
67 E5 **Daya Wan** *B* China
67 E1 **Daye** China
67 A1 **Dayi** China
67 B4 **Dayi** China
Dayishan *see* **Guanyun**
139 G6 **Daylesford** Victoria Australia
102 G5 **Daylight Pass** California U.S.A.
133 F4 **Dayman** *R* Uruguay
131 F3 **Dayman, Cuchilla del** *mts* Uruguay
143 D9 **Day, Mt** W Australia Australia
67 C2 **Dayong** China
79 G5 **Dayr 'Alī** Syria
79 G4 **Dayr 'Aţiyah** Syria
78 H4 **Dayr az Zawr** Syria
79 H2 **Dayr Ḩāfir** Syria
79 G3 **Dayr Shumayyil al Taḩtāni** Syria
100 B7 **Days Creek** Oregon U.S.A.
118 E6 **Daysland** Alberta Canada
99 M7 **Dayton** Iowa U.S.A.
94 J4 **Dayton** New York U.S.A.
94 C7 **Dayton** Ohio U.S.A.
94 H6 **Dayton** Pennsylvania U.S.A.
112 B2 **Dayton** Tennessee U.S.A.
109 N5 **Dayton** Texas U.S.A.
100 H3 **Dayton** Washington U.S.A.
101 S5 **Dayton** Wyoming U.S.A.
113 F8 **Daytona Beach** Florida U.S.A.
67 E4 **Dayu** China
67 E4 **Dayu Ling** *mt* China
58 G4 **Da Yunhe** *R* China
100 F5 **Dayville** Oregon U.S.A.
98 H2 **Dazey** North Dakota U.S.A.
67 F4 **Dazhang Xi** *R* China
67 B1 **Dazhu** China
47 K7 **Dazkırı** Turkey
67 B2 **Dazu** China
89 D8 **De Aar** S Africa
99 T3 **Dead** *R* Michigan U.S.A.
116 N1 **Deadhorse** Alaska U.S.A.
101 Q5 **Dead Indian Pk** Wyoming U.S.A.
111 L11 **Dead L** Florida U.S.A.
113 D8 **Deadman B** Florida U.S.A.
103 H7 **Deadman L** California U.S.A.
126 G3 **Deadman's Cay** Long I Bahamas
103 K6 **Dead Mts** Cal/Nev U.S.A.
95 R1 **Dead R** Maine U.S.A.
80 E8 **Dead Sea** Israel/Jordan
95 R8 **Deadwater L** Maine U.S.A.
98 C5 **Deadwood** South Dakota U.S.A.
100 K5 **Deadwood Res** Idaho U.S.A.
140 C2 **Deaf Adder Cr** N Terr Australia
143 G9 **Deakin** W Australia Australia
140 B4 **Deakin,Mt** N Terr Australia
9 H5 **Deal** England
95 L8 **Deale** Maryland U.S.A.
139 H7 **Deal I** Tasmania Australia
95 M8 **Deal Island** Maryland U.S.A.
58 G6 **De'an** China
110 D1 **Dean** Iowa U.S.A.
117 K9 **Dean Ch** British Columbia Canada
141 H5 **Deane,Mt** Queensland Australia
8 D4 **Dean, Forest of** England
131 D3 **Deán Funes** Argentina
146 B9 **Dean I** *isld* Antarctica
143 E10 **Dean,Mt** W Australia Australia
117 L9 **Dean R** British Columbia Canada
95 M4 **Deansboro** New York U.S.A.
94 D4 **Dearborn** Michigan U.S.A.
110 B2 **Dearborn** Missouri U.S.A.
107 P4 **Dearing** Kansas U.S.A.
100 J3 **Deary** Idaho U.S.A.
114 G4 **Dease Arm** *B* Northwest Territories Canada
116 K1 **Dease Inlet** Alaska U.S.A.
117 J6 **Dease Lake** British Columbia Canada
147 G2 **Dease Str** Northwest Territories Canada
102 G5 **Death Valley** California U.S.A.
21 L3 **Deauville** France
101 R5 **Deaver** Wyoming U.S.A.
70 B4 **Debak** Sarawak
54 K8 **Debal'tsevo** Ukraine
67 B5 **Debao** China
46 D3 **Debar** Macedonia Yugoslavia
116 H4 **Debauch Mt** Alaska U.S.A.
84 J6 **Debba, Ed** Sudan
80 F1 **Debbe** *R* Israel
118 L5 **Debden** Saskatchewan Canada
127 O3 **Débé** Trinidad
122 E7 **Debec** New Brunswick Canada
80 E1 **Debel et Emmeya** Lebanon
9 H3 **Debenham** England
9 H3 **Deben, R** England
106 B2 **De Beque** Colorado U.S.A.
109 N3 **De Berry** Texas U.S.A.
52 H5 **Debessy** Russian Federation
31 N5 **Dębica** Poland
31 N4 **Dęblin** Poland
31 K1 **Dębnica Kaszubska** Poland
31 H3 **Dębno** Poland
85 D5 **Débó, L** Mali
143 C9 **Deborah,L** W Australia Australia
142 F3 **Deborah,Mt** W Australia Australia
116 O5 **Deborah, Mt** Alaska U.S.A.
100 K2 **De Borgia** Montana U.S.A.
48 F6 **Debrc** Serbia Yugoslavia
86 G4 **Debre Birhan** Ethiopia
48 G3 **Debrecen** Hungary
86 G3 **Debre Mark'os** Ethiopia
86 G3 **Debre Tabor** Ethiopia
71 E2 **Debutunan Pt** Luzon Philippines
46 D2 **Dečani** Serbia Yugoslavia
111 K7 **Decatur** Alabama U.S.A.
110 B5 **Decatur** Arkansas U.S.A.
111 M8 **Decatur** Georgia U.S.A.
99 S10 **Decatur** Illinois U.S.A.
110 H2 **Decatur** Illinois U.S.A.
94 C6 **Decatur** Indiana U.S.A.
99 N9 **Decatur** Iowa U.S.A.
94 B4 **Decatur** Michigan U.S.A.
111 G9 **Decatur** Mississippi U.S.A.
98 K7 **Decatur** Nebraska U.S.A.
109 K2 **Decatur** Texas U.S.A.
110 H6 **Decaturville** Tennessee U.S.A.
18 G8 **Decazeville** France
76 C4 **Deccan** *plateau* India
121 M5 **Decelles, Lac** Quebec Canada
89 C3 **Deception** *watercourse* Botswana
115 M5 **Déception** Quebec Canada
146 C3 **Deception Island** S Shetland Is Antarctica
Dechen Dzong *see* **Dagzê**
122 E2 **Dechêne, L** Quebec Canada
110 K6 **Decherd** Tennessee U.S.A.
22 E3 **Dechy** France
118 F1 **Decimal** Manitoba Canada
43 B9 **Decimomannu** Sardinia
31 H5 **Děčin** Czechoslovakia
117 F7 **Decision, C** Alaska U.S.A.
18 H6 **Decize** France
119 R8 **Decker** Manitoba Canada
110 J3 **Decker** Indiana U.S.A.
101 T4 **Decker** Montana U.S.A.
106 E2 **Deckers** Colorado U.S.A.
25 C2 **De Cocksdorp** Netherlands
140 C1 **De Courcy Hd** N Terr Australia
48 E4 **Decs** Hungary
48 J4 **Deda** Romania
Dedap *see* **Penasi, Pulau**
9 E4 **Deddington** England
Dedéagach *see* **Alexandroúpolis**
33 N8 **Dedeleben** Germany
33 T6 **Dedelow** Germany
99 M8 **Dedham** Iowa U.S.A.
46 E3 **Dedino** Macedonia Yugoslavia
130 F9 **Dedo de Deus** *mt* Brazil
85 D6 **Dedougou** Burkina
52 C6 **Dedovichi** Russian Federation
100 B9 **Dedrick** California U.S.A.
55 B5 **Dedurovka** Kazakhstan
83 J10 **Deduru Oya** *R* Sri Lanka
56 E1 **Dedushka, Porog** *falls* Russian Federation
88 E9 **Dedza** Malawi
15 F3 **Dee** *R* Scotland
14 C4 **Deel** *R* Ireland
112 H2 **Deep** *R* North Carolina U.S.A.
Deep Bay Malawi *see* **Chilumba**
122 G9 **Deep Brook** Nova Scotia Canada
100 J7 **Deep Cr** Idaho U.S.A.
94 H7 **Deep Creek L** Maryland U.S.A.
103 L2 **Deep Creek Ra** Utah U.S.A.
107 O6 **Deep Fork** *R* Oklahoma U.S.A.
112 F1 **Deep Gap** North Carolina U.S.A.
121 N6 **Deep River** Ontario Canada
95 P5 **Deep River** Connecticut U.S.A.
99 O8 **Deep River** Iowa U.S.A.
100 B3 **Deep River** Washington U.S.A.
102 G4 **Deep Sp** California U.S.A.
139 K3 **Deepwater** New South Wales Australia
110 C3 **Deepwater** Missouri U.S.A.
140 C6 **Deep Well** N Terr Australia
8 C1 **Dee, R** England/Wales
12 E4 **Dee, R** Scotland
110 C6 **Deer** Arkansas U.S.A.
100 D9 **Deer Cr** California U.S.A.
99 L3 **Deer Cr** Minnesota U.S.A.
98 F9 **Deer Cr** Nebraska U.S.A.
101 T7 **Deer Cr** Wyoming U.S.A.
107 N5 **Deer Creek** Oklahoma U.S.A.
103 N1 **Deer Cr.Res** Utah U.S.A.
107 J3 **Deerfield** Kansas U.S.A.
113 G11 **Deerfield Beach** Florida U.S.A.
122 F9 **Deer I** New Brunswick Canada
116 F9 **Deer I** Alaska U.S.A.
95 T2 **Deer I** Maine U.S.A.
116 F3 **Deering** Alaska U.S.A.
98 E1 **Deering** North Dakota U.S.A.
138 A2 **Deering Hills** South Australia Australia
143 G7 **Deering,Mt** W Australia Australia
123 P4 **Deer Lake** Newfoundland Canada
22 E2 **Deerlijk** Belgium
101 N3 **Deer Lodge** Montana U.S.A.
111 H10 **Deer Park** Alabama U.S.A.
100 H2 **Deer Park** Washington U.S.A.
117 O11 **Deer Pk** British Columbia Canada
123 S5 **Deer Pond** Newfoundland Canada
99 N2 **Deer River** Minnesota U.S.A.
99 T3 **Deerton** Michigan U.S.A.
106 F2 **Deer Trail** Colorado U.S.A.
99 N3 **Deerwood** Minnesota U.S.A.
111 F7 **Deeson** Mississippi U.S.A.
100 K8 **Deeth** Nevada U.S.A.
Defeng *see* **Liping**
38 F8 **Defereggengeb** *mt* Austria
38 F8 **Defereggental** *V* Austria
95 M2 **Deferiet** New York U.S.A.
133 F5 **Defferrari** Argentina
99 L8 **Defiance** Iowa U.S.A.
94 C5 **Defiance** Ohio U.S.A.
111 K11 **De Funiak Springs** Florida U.S.A.
16 B6 **Degebe** *R* Portugal
27 G16 **Degeberga** Sweden
86 H4 **Degeh Bur** Ethiopia
85 F8 **Degema** Nigeria
27 G12 **Degerfors** Sweden
146 A6 **De Gerlache Seamounts** *seamounts* Antarctica
37 O6 **Deggendorf** Germany
36 H6 **Deggingen** Germany
47 J6 **Degirmendere** Turkey
99 L4 **De Graff** Minnesota U.S.A.
110 N1 **Degraff** Ohio U.S.A.
111 C7 **De Gray Res** Arkansas U.S.A.
142 C5 **De Grey** W Australia Australia
98 G5 **De Grey** South Dakota U.S.A.
142 D5 **De Grey R** W Australia Australia
55 D3 **Degtyarsk** Russian Federation
22 E1 **De Haan** Belgium
86 H2 **Dehalak' Desēt, Archipelago** Ethiopia
86 H2 **Dehalak' Desēt I** Ethiopia
77 C4 **Deh Bīd** Iran
77 B4 **Deh-Dasht** Iran
74 E8 **Dehej** India
85 G2 **Dehiba** Tunisia
74 H3 **Dehra Dun** India
75 L6 **Dehri** India
36 E3 **Dehrn** Germany
77 F4 **Deh Salm** Iran
67 F4 **Dehua** China
59 J3 **Dehui** China
36 E5 **Deidesheim** Germany
86 E4 **Deim Zubeir** Sudan
37 M5 **Deining** Germany
25 E2 **Deinum** Netherlands
22 F2 **Deinze** Belgium

170
Deir Abu Said — Djoum

80 F4 **Deir Abu Said** Jordan
80 F4 **Deir es Samadiya** Jordan
80 D5 **Deir Istiya** Jordan
80 E6 **Deir Mar Jiryis** Jordan
80 D4 **Deir Sharal** Jordan
32 K8 **Deister** *hills* Germany
48 H3 **Dej** Romania
46 D3 **Dêja** *mt* Albania
71 B2 **Dejailolo, Selat** *str* Indonesia
28 A5 **Dejbjerg** Denmark
27 F12 **Deje** Sweden
86 G3 **Dejen** Ethiopia
67 C2 **Dejiang** China
99 S8 **De Kalb** Illinois U.S.A.
111 H9 **De Kalb** Mississippi U.S.A.
109 N2 **De Kalb** Texas U.S.A.
95 M2 **De Kalb Junc** New York U.S.A.
59 M1 **De Kastri** Russian Federation
86 G2 **Dek'emhāre** Ethiopia
86 D6 **Dekese** Zaire
86 C4 **Dékoa** Cent Afr Republic
25 C2 **De Koog** Netherlands
111 G12 **Delacroix** Louisiana U.S.A.
106 F4 **Delagua** Colorado U.S.A.
100 J6 **Delamar** Idaho U.S.A.
103 K4 **Delamar Mts** Nevada U.S.A.
140 B3 **Delamere** N Terr Australia
113 F8 **De Land** Florida U.S.A.
102 E6 **Delano** California U.S.A.
103 M3 **Delano Peak** Utah U.S.A.
77 H3 **Delārām** Afghanistan
118 K4 **Delaronde L** Saskatchewan Canada
110 G1 **Delavan** Illinois U.S.A.
99 S7 **Delavan** Wisconsin U.S.A.
95 N5 **Delaware** *R* U.S.A.
95 M7 **Delaware** *state* U.S.A.
107 P2 **Delaware** *R* Kansas U.S.A.
94 D6 **Delaware** Ohio U.S.A.
107 P5 **Delaware** Oklahoma U.S.A.
145 D4 **Delaware B** New Zealand
95 M7 **Delaware B** U.S.A.
95 M7 **Delaware City** Delaware U.S.A.
108 C4 **Delaware Cr** Texas/New Mex U.S.A.
94 D6 **Delaware Res** Ohio U.S.A.
118 E9 **Del Bonita** Alberta Canada
32 J9 **Delbrück** Germany
118 D6 **Delburne** Alberta Canada
111 E12 **Delcambre** Louisiana U.S.A.
106 F4 **Delcarbon** Colorado U.S.A.
46 F3 **Delčevo** Macedonia Yugoslavia
87 E8 **Delcommune, L** Zaire
25 G4 **Delden** Netherlands
119 R9 **Deleau** Manitoba Canada
139 J6 **Delegate** New South Wales Australia
25 F2 **De Leien** Netherlands
40 F3 **Delémont** Switzerland
109 J3 **De Leon** Texas U.S.A.
29 H11 **Delet Teili** *chan* Finland
22 C2 **Delettes** France
102 B2 **Delevan** California U.S.A.
94 J4 **Delevan** New York U.S.A.
130 F7 **Delfinópolis** Brazil
25 B5 **Delfshaven** Netherlands
25 B4 **Delft** Netherlands
83 J8 **Delft** *isld* Sri Lanka
25 G2 **Delfzijl** Netherlands
100 A9 **Delgada, Pt** California U.S.A.
133 E6 **Delgada, Pta** Argentina
88 H7 **Delgado, C** Mozambique
86 F1 **Delgo** Sudan
120 K10 **Delhi** Ontario Canada
74 G4 **Delhi** India
99 P7 **Delhi** Iowa U.S.A.
111 E9 **Delhi** Louisiana U.S.A.
107 L6 **Delhi** Oklahoma U.S.A.
70 K9 **Deli** *isld* Java
118 E7 **Delia** Alberta Canada
107 P2 **Delia** Kansas U.S.A.
129 H3 **Delices** Fr Guiana
109 O1 **Delight** Arkansas U.S.A.
77 B3 **Delijan** Iran
46 E1 **Deli Jovan** *mt* Serbia Yugoslavia
58 C4 **Delingha** China
118 K7 **Delisle** Saskatchewan Canada
140 B2 **Delissaville** N Terr Australia
69 D11 **Delitua** Sumatra
33 Q9 **Delitzsch** Germany
110 F6 **Dell** Arkansas U.S.A.
101 N5 **Dell** Montana U.S.A.
36 C2 **Dellbrück** Germany
40 E2 **Delle** France
101 N9 **Delle** Utah U.S.A.
103 L5 **Dellenbaugh, Mt** Arizona U.S.A.
26 J10 **Dellen, N** *L* Sweden
32 L9 **Delligsen** Germany
100 B9 **Del Loma** California U.S.A.
98 K6 **Dell Rapids** South Dakota U.S.A.
107 L2 **Dellvale** Kansas U.S.A.
85 E1 **Dellys** Algeria
102 G9 **Del Mar** California U.S.A.
99 Q7 **Delmar** Iowa U.S.A.
95 M8 **Delmar** Maryland U.S.A.
118 J6 **Delmas** Saskatchewan Canada
32 J6 **Delmenhorst** Germany
130 H10 **Delmiro Gouveia** Brazil
98 H6 **Delmont** South Dakota U.S.A.
103 K4 **Delmues** Nevada U.S.A.
42 F3 **Delnice** Croatia
106 D4 **Del Norte** Colorado U.S.A.
116 F2 **De Long Mts** Alaska U.S.A.
139 H8 **Deloraine** Tasmania Australia
119 R9 **Deloraine** Manitoba Canada
13 F6 **Delph** England
46 E6 **Delphi** Greece
110 K1 **Delphi** Indiana U.S.A.
107 N2 **Delphos** Kansas U.S.A.
94 C6 **Delphos** Ohio U.S.A.
113 G11 **Delray Beach** Florida U.S.A.
124 D2 **Del Río** Mexico
108 G6 **Del Rio** Texas U.S.A.
26 J10 **Delsbo** Sweden
106 B3 **Delta** Colorado U.S.A.
110 G4 **Delta** Missouri U.S.A.
94 C5 **Delta** Ohio U.S.A.
95 L7 **Delta** Pennsylvania U.S.A.
103 M2 **Delta** Utah U.S.A.
119 T8 **Delta Beach** Manitoba Canada
141 F3 **Delta Downs** Queensland Australia
116 O4 **Delta Junction** Alaska U.S.A.
102 C4 **Delta Mendota Canal** California U.S.A.
95 M3 **Delta Res** New York U.S.A.
95 L9 **Deltaville** Virginia U.S.A.
94 B4 **Delton** Michigan U.S.A.
139 K3 **Delungra** New South Wales Australia
74 D8 **Delvada** India
109 K5 **Del Valle** Texas U.S.A.
32 K4 **Delve** Germany
46 D5 **Delvinákion** Greece
46 D5 **Delvinë** Albania
108 G2 **Delwin** Texas U.S.A.
48 J2 **Delyatin** Ukraine
55 B4 **Dema** *R* Russian Federation
118 K8 **Demaine** Saskatchewan Canada
70 N9 **Demak** Java
16 E2 **Demando, S. de la** *mts* Spain
116 R2 **Demarcation Pt** Alaska U.S.A.
86 D7 **Demba** Zaire
86 D4 **Dembia** Cent Afr Republic
86 F4 **Dembī Dolo** Ethiopia
48 G2 **Demecser** Hungary
22 J2 **Demer** *R* Belgium
Demerara *see* **Georgetown** Guyana
54 C1 **Demidov** Russian Federation
55 D3 **Demina** Russian Federation
106 C9 **Deming** New Mexico U.S.A.
100 C1 **Deming** Washington U.S.A.
128 F3 **Demini** *R* Brazil
79 B2 **Demirçat** Turkey
47 K5 **Demirci** Turkey
47 N11 **Demirciler** Turkey
47 J6 **Demirköprü Baraji** *L* Turkey
47 J3 **Demirköy** Turkey
33 S5 **Demmin** Germany
128 F5 **Democracia** Brazil
111 J9 **Demopolis** Alabama U.S.A.
68 C3 **Demoso** Burma
143 E10 **Dempster, Pt** W Australia Australia
74 H2 **Dêmqog** India
55 F2 **Dem'yanka** *R* Russian Federation
52 D5 **Demyansk** Russian Federation
55 E2 **Dem'yanskoye** Russian Federation
22 E3 **Denain** France
86 H3 **Denakil** *tribal dist* Ethiopia
116 O5 **Denali** Alaska U.S.A.
116 M5 **Denali Nat Park and Preserve** Alaska U.S.A.
86 H4 **Denan** Ethiopia
114 J7 **Denare Beach** Saskatchewan Canada
57 E5 **Denau** Uzbekistan
Denbigh *co see* **Clwyd and Gwynedd** *counties*
121 N7 **Denbigh** Ontario Canada
8 C1 **Denbigh** Wales
116 G4 **Denbigh, C** Alaska U.S.A.
25 B5 **Den Bommel** Netherlands
25 C2 **Den Burg** Netherlands
68 E4 **Den Chai** Thailand
69 J14 **Dendang** Indonesia
22 G2 **Dender** *R* Belgium
22 G2 **Denderleeuw** Belgium
22 G1 **Dendermonde** Belgium
25 D3 **Den Dever** Netherlands
86 G4 **Dendi** *mt* Ethiopia
118 K8 **Dendron** Saskatchewan Canada
25 H4 **Denekamp** Netherlands
55 C1 **Denezhkin Kamen', G** *mt* Russian Federation
65 B7 **Dengfeng** China
58 E3 **Dengkou** China
66 F5 **Dêngqên** China
58 F5 **Deng Xian** China
65 C4 **Dengyoufang** China
65 E6 **Dengzhou** China
24 A2 **Den Haag** *conurbation* Netherlands
143 A7 **Denham** W Australia Australia
9 F4 **Denham** England
140 E3 **Denham I** Queensland Australia
141 J5 **Denham Ra** Queensland Australia
143 A7 **Denham Sd** W Australia Australia
111 F11 **Denham Springs** Louisiana U.S.A.
25 C3 **Den Helder** Netherlands
118 K6 **Denholm** Saskatchewan Canada
13 F3 **Denholm** Scotland
17 G7 **Denia** Spain
138 C4 **Denial Bay** South Australia Australia
122 C6 **Deniau** Quebec Canada
139 G6 **Deniliquin** New South Wales Australia
100 G7 **Denio** Oregon U.S.A.
83 J12 **Denis I** Seychelles
99 L7 **Denison** Iowa U.S.A.
109 L2 **Denison** Texas U.S.A.
107 O8 **Denison Dam** Oklahoma U.S.A.
140 B5 **Denison, Mt** N Terr Australia
116 K7 **Denison, Mt** Alaska U.S.A.
142 G4 **Denison Plains** W Australia Australia
141 J4 **Denison Pt** Queensland Australia
52 J2 **Denisovka** Komi Respublika Russian Federation
83 K11 **Deniyaya** Sri Lanka
47 K7 **Denizli** Turkey
37 L6 **Denkendorf** Germany
139 K4 **Denman** New South Wales Australia
146 H13 **Denman Glacier** Antarctica
143 B10 **Denmark** W Australia Australia
122 J8 **Denmark** Nova Scotia Canada
28 **Denmark** *kingdom* N W Europe
100 A7 **Denmark** Oregon U.S.A.
112 F4 **Denmark** South Carolina U.S.A.
99 T5 **Denmark** Wisconsin U.S.A.
115 R4 **Denmark Str** Greenland/Iceland
20 G3 **Denneville** France
33 S9 **Dennewitz** Germany
94 F6 **Dennison** Ohio U.S.A.
95 R5 **Dennis Port** Massachusetts U.S.A.
144 C4 **Denniston** New Zealand
94 H10 **Denniston** Virginia U.S.A.
12 E1 **Denny** Scotland
100 B9 **Denny** California U.S.A.
12 E2 **Dennyloanhead** Scotland
95 U2 **Dennysville** Maine U.S.A.
70 P10 **Denpasar** Bali Indonesia
70 G6 **Densongi** Sulawesi
13 F5 **Dent** England
100 J3 **Dent** Idaho U.S.A.
48 G5 **Denta** Romania
40 G5 **Dent Blanche** *mt* Switzerland
40 E5 **Dent du Midi** *mt* Switzerland
9 H5 **Denton** England
112 E6 **Denton** Georgia U.S.A.
94 E8 **Denton** Kentucky U.S.A.
95 M8 **Denton** Maryland U.S.A.
109 K2 **Denton** Texas U.S.A.
137 L3 **D'Entrecasteaux Is** Papua New Guinea
106 E2 **Denver** Colorado U.S.A.
100 J4 **Denver** Idaho U.S.A.
94 A6 **Denver** Indiana U.S.A.
99 O7 **Denver** Iowa U.S.A.
95 L6 **Denver** Pennsylvania U.S.A.
108 E3 **Denver City** Texas U.S.A.
118 H6 **Denzil** Saskatchewan Canada
86 B4 **Déo** *R* Cameroon
74 G4 **Deoband** India
75 M6 **Deogarh** India
68 J4 **Deo Hai Van** Vietnam
74 E9 **Deolali** India
21 O8 **Déols** France
68 J6 **Deo Ma** Vietnam
22 D1 **De Panne** Belgium
25 E5 **De Peel** Netherlands
99 S5 **De Pere** Wisconsin U.S.A.
94 J4 **Depew** New York U.S.A.
107 O6 **Depew** Oklahoma U.S.A.
65 C6 **Deping** China
22 F2 **De Pinte** Belgium
70 L9 **Depok** Java
109 M2 **Deport** Texas U.S.A.
95 M4 **Deposit** New York U.S.A.
128 F3 **Depósito** Brazil
95 Q4 **Depot** New Hampshire U.S.A.
120 K7 **Depot Harbour** Ontario Canada
86 D2 **Depression du Murdi** Chad
9 E5 **Deptford** England
142 C5 **Depuch I** W Australia Australia
99 R8 **Depue** Illinois U.S.A.
25 G2 **De Punt** Netherlands
51 O2 **Deputatskiy** Russian Federation
58 C6 **Dêqên** China
67 G1 **Deqing** China
67 D5 **Deqing** China
111 B7 **De Queen** Arkansas U.S.A.
111 C11 **De Quincy** Louisiana U.S.A.
77 L5 **Dera Bugti** Pakistan
74 D3 **Dera Ghazi Khan** Pakistan
74 D3 **Dera Ismail Khan** Pakistan
46 D2 **Đeravica** *mt* Serbia Yugoslavia
48 L1 **Derazhnya** Ukraine
33 Q8 **Derben** Germany
78 M1 **Derbent** Russian Federation
86 D4 **Derbisaka** Cent Afr Republic
139 J8 **Derby** Tasmania Australia
142 E3 **Derby** W Australia Australia
9 E2 **Derby** England
95 O5 **Derby** Connecticut U.S.A.
99 N9 **Derby** Iowa U.S.A.
107 N4 **Derby** Kansas U.S.A.
109 H7 **Derby** Texas U.S.A.
95 P2 **Derby Center** Vermont U.S.A.
9 E1 **Derbyshire** *co* England
16 D9 **Derdara** Morocco
48 G3 **Derecske** Hungary
47 K8 **Dereköy** Turkey
47 M10 **Dereköy** *R* Turkey
78 A1 **Derekoy** Turkey
33 N8 **Der Elm** *hills* Germany
33 N9 **Derenburg** Germany
52 D4 **Derevyanka** Russian Federation
14 D2 **Derg** *R* N Ireland
54 H6 **Dergachi** Ukraine
14 D2 **Derg, L** Ireland
32 H5 **Der Hohe Weg** *sandbank* Germany
111 C11 **De Ridder** Louisiana U.S.A.
25 C3 **De Rijp** Netherlands
139 G7 **Derinallum** Victoria Australia
47 N11 **Derince** Turkey
86 H5 **Derkali** Kenya
54 L8 **Derkul** *R* Rus Fed/Ukraine
46 G1 **Dermantsi** Bulgaria
37 J2 **Dermbach** Germany
111 E8 **Dermott** Arkansas U.S.A.
Derna *see* **Darnah**
87 C11 **Dernberg, C** Namibia
32 M8 **Derneburg** Germany
111 F12 **Dernieres, Is** Louisiana U.S.A.
138 C2 **De Rose Hill** South Australia Australia
20 G3 **Déroute,Pass de la** France
14 D3 **Derravaragh, L** Ireland
86 J5 **Derri** Somalia
Derry *see* **Londonderry**
95 Q4 **Derry** New Hampshire U.S.A.
106 C9 **Derry** New Mexico U.S.A.
94 H6 **Derry** Pennsylvania U.S.A.
140 D5 **Derry Downs** N Terr Australia
14 C2 **Derryveagh Mts** Ireland
36 D1 **Derschlag** Germany
9 G2 **Dersingham** England
86 G2 **Derudeb** Sudan
95 M4 **De Ruyter** New York U.S.A.
20 G6 **Derval** France
46 E6 **Dervéni** Greece
42 H4 **Derventa** Bosnia-Herzegovina
140 B6 **Derwent** N Terr Australia
139 H8 **Derwent** *R* Tasmania Australia
118 F5 **Derwent** Alberta Canada
12 E4 **Derwent, R** England
13 E4 **Derwent Water** *L* England
55 E5 **Derzhavinsk** Kazakhstan
133 D4 **Desaguadero** *R* Argentina
131 B5 **Desague, Cerro** *pk* Argentina
110 E7 **Des Arc** Arkansas U.S.A.
110 F4 **Des Arc** Missouri U.S.A.
102 G2 **Desatoya Mts** Nevada U.S.A.
9 F3 **Desborough** England
130 B5 **Descalvado** Mato Grosso Brazil
130 F7 **Descalvado** São Paulo Brazil
124 A1 **Descanso** Mexico
102 H9 **Descanso** California U.S.A.
21 M8 **Descartes** France
121 S6 **Deschaillons** Quebec Canada
100 E4 **Deschutes** *R* Oregon U.S.A.
109 J3 **Desdemona** Texas U.S.A.
86 G3 **Desē** Ethiopia
45 M1 **Dese** *R* Italy
133 P7 **Deseado** Argentina
41 N7 **Desenzano del Garda** Italy
103 M2 **Deseret** Utah U.S.A.
101 N9 **Deseret Pk** Utah U.S.A.
121 N8 **Deseronto** Ontario Canada
103 J8 **Desert Center** California U.S.A.
102 H8 **Desert Hot Springs** California U.S.A.
121 O6 **Desért, L** Quebec Canada
101 M8 **Desert Pk** Utah U.S.A.
103 J5 **Desert Ra** Nevada U.S.A.
100 G8 **Desert Valley** Nevada U.S.A.
103 N5 **Desert View** Arizona U.S.A.
127 M4 **Deshaies** Guadeloupe W Indies
67 A3 **Deshengpo** China
98 J9 **Deshler** Nebraska U.S.A.
94 D5 **Deshler** Ohio U.S.A.
74 E5 **Deshnok** India
77 H4 **Deshu** Afghanistan
124 B1 **Desierto de Altar** *desert* Mexico
17 H4 **Desierto de las Palmas** Spain
98 E1 **Des Lacs** *R* North Dakota U.S.A.
118 D3 **Desmarais** Alberta Canada
121 O3 **Desmaraisville** Quebec Canada
100 J2 **Desmet** Idaho U.S.A.
101 L3 **De Smet** Montana U.S.A.
98 J5 **De Smet** South Dakota U.S.A.
130 B10 **Desmochados** Paraguay
99 M7 **Des Moines** *R* Iowa U.S.A.
99 N8 **Des Moines** Iowa U.S.A.
99 L6 **Des Moines** *R* Minnesota U.S.A.
106 G5 **Des Moines** New Mexico U.S.A.
54 B6 **Desna** *R* Ukraine
54 E2 **Desnogorsk** Russian Federation
133 C8 **Desolación, I** Chile
71 G5 **Desolation Pt** Philippines
110 G4 **De Soto** Illinois U.S.A.
107 Q3 **De Soto** Kansas U.S.A.
110 F3 **De Soto** Missouri U.S.A.
99 P6 **De Soto** Wisconsin U.S.A.
113 F10 **De Soto City** Florida U.S.A.
16 E6 **Despeñaperros, Pto. de** Spain
99 T7 **Des Plaines** Illinois U.S.A.
48 G6 **Despotovac** Serbia Yugoslavia
83 H5 **Desroches** *isld* Seychelles
33 Q9 **Dessau** Germany
40 E3 **Dessoubre** *R* France
111 K11 **Destin** Florida U.S.A.
31 K5 **Deštná** *mt* Poland
138 E6 **D'Estrees, B** South Australia Australia
117 D5 **Destruction Bay** Yukon Territory Canada
100 A2 **Destruction I** Washington U.S.A.
143 G6 **Destruction,Mt** W Australia Australia
22 B2 **Desvres** France
48 G5 **Deta** Romania
87 E9 **Dete** Zimbabwe
32 G6 **Detern** Germany
121 N7 **Detlor** Ontario Canada
32 J9 **Detmold** Germany
94 D1 **Detour Passage** Michigan U.S.A.
99 U4 **Detour, Pt** Michigan U.S.A.
94 D1 **Detour Village** Michigan U.S.A.
94 D4 **Detroit** Michigan U.S.A.
109 M2 **Detroit** Texas U.S.A.
122 H4 **Détroit d'Honguedo** Quebec Canada
99 L3 **Detroit Lakes** Minnesota U.S.A.
94 D4 **Detroit R** Michigan U.S.A.
100 C5 **Detroit Res** Oregon U.S.A.
37 J4 **Dettelbach** Germany
36 G6 **Dettenhausen** Germany
36 H3 **Detter** Germany
36 F7 **Dettingen** Baden-Württemberg Germany
36 G3 **Dettingen** Bayern Germany
36 C6 **Dettwiller** France
68 G5 **Det Udom** Thailand
48 E2 **Detva** Czechoslovakia
74 G8 **Deūlgaon Rāja** India
25 E6 **Deurne** Netherlands
37 Q2 **Deutsch-Einsiedel** Germany
33 R7 **Deutschhof** Germany
48 D3 **Deutschkreutz** Austria
37 P2 **Deutsch-Neudorf** Germany
122 B2 **Deux Décharges, L** Quebec Canada
121 M6 **Deux Rivieres** Ontario Canada
18 E6 **Deux-Sèvres** *dept* France
48 H5 **Deva** Romania
16 D1 **Deva** *R* Spain
110 E7 **De Valls Bluff** Arkansas U.S.A.
48 F3 **Dévaványa** Hungary
47 L8 **Devecitaşi Adası** *isld* Turkey
48 D3 **Devecser** Hungary
78 E2 **Develi** Turkey
25 F4 **Deventer** Netherlands
112 D4 **Devereux** Georgia U.S.A.
86 H4 **De Verme Falls** Ethiopia
6 L1 **Deveron** *oil rig* North Sea
15 F3 **Deveron** *R* Scotland
46 E1 **Devica** *mt* Serbia Yugoslavia
74 D5 **Devikot** India
21 N3 **Deville** France
116 E3 **Devil Mt** Alaska U.S.A.
145 D4 **Devil River Pk** New Zealand
108 F5 **Devils** *R* Texas U.S.A.
14 D4 **Devilsbit Mt** Ireland
8 C3 **Devils Bridge** Wales
102 E6 **Devils Den** California U.S.A.
15 E4 **Devil's Elbow** Scotland
116 K5 **Devils Elbow** *V* Alaska U.S.A.
102 E3 **Devils Gate** California U.S.A.
89 E1 **Devil's Gorge** Zambia
6 L6 **Devil's Hole** North Sea
99 Q2 **Devils I** Michigan U.S.A.
110 H4 **Devil's Kitchen L** Illinois U.S.A.
98 H1 **Devils Lake** North Dakota U.S.A.
100 K8 **Devils L. Res** Nevada U.S.A.
117 G6 **Devils Paw** *mt* Br Col/Alaska Canada/U.S.A.
102 E4 **Devils Pk** California U.S.A.
103 J7 **Devils Playground** *desert* California U.S.A.
126 G2 **Devil's Point** Cat I Bahamas
102 E4 **Devils Postpile Nat.Mon** California U.S.A.
101 O8 **Devils Slide** Utah U.S.A.
139 H7 **Devils Tower** *isld* Tasmania Australia
98 B5 **Devils Tower** Wyoming U.S.A.
46 G3 **Devin** Bulgaria
109 J6 **Devine** Texas U.S.A.
80 C8 **Devira** Israel
9 E5 **Devizes** England
74 F6 **Devli** India
107 M7 **Devol** Oklahoma U.S.A.
46 D4 **Devoll** *R* Albania
118 D5 **Devon** Alberta Canada
120 G5 **Devon** Ontario Canada
8 C6 **Devon** *co* England
101 O1 **Devon** Montana U.S.A.
115 L2 **Devon I** Northwest Territories Canada
139 H8 **Devonport** Tasmania Australia
8 B7 **Devonport** England
80 E3 **Devora** Israel
78 D1 **Devrek** *R* Turkey
78 D1 **Devrez** *R* Turkey
89 G2 **Devuli** *R* Zimbabwe
52 H6 **Devyaternya** Russian Federation
52 E4 **Devyatiny** Russian Federation
55 E2 **Devyatkova** Russian Federation
70 F7 **Dewakang Besar** *isld* Indonesia
70 F7 **Dewakang Ketjil** *isld* Indonesia
107 P6 **Dewar** Oklahoma U.S.A.
118 H7 **Dewar Lake** Saskatchewan Canada
74 G7 **Dewas** India
69 B11 **Dewa, Tanjong** *C* Indonesia
118 G5 **Dewberry** Alberta Canada
98 H9 **Deweese** Nebraska U.S.A.
103 M7 **Dewey** Arizona U.S.A.
107 P5 **Dewey** Oklahoma U.S.A.
98 C6 **Dewey** South Dakota U.S.A.
94 E9 **Dewey Res** Kentucky U.S.A.
22 E1 **De Wielingen** Belgium/Neths
118 C8 **De Winton** Alberta Canada
111 E7 **De Witt** Arkansas U.S.A.
94 C4 **De Witt** Michigan U.S.A.
110 C2 **De Witt** Missouri U.S.A.
98 K9 **De Witt** Nebraska U.S.A.
95 L3 **De Witt** New York U.S.A.
13 G6 **Dewsbury** England
67 F2 **Dexing** China
111 D7 **Dexter** Arkansas U.S.A.
99 M8 **Dexter** Iowa U.S.A.
107 O4 **Dexter** Kansas U.S.A.
95 S1 **Dexter** Maine U.S.A.
94 D4 **Dexter** Michigan U.S.A.
99 O6 **Dexter** Minnesota U.S.A.
110 G5 **Dexter** Missouri U.S.A.
108 C2 **Dexter** New Mexico U.S.A.
95 L2 **Dexter** New York U.S.A.
109 L2 **Dexter** Texas U.S.A.
113 F8 **Dexter, L** Florida U.S.A.
99 Q5 **Dexterville** Wisconsin U.S.A.
138 B3 **Dey-Dey, L** South Australia Australia
22 L3 **Deyfeldt** Belgium
77 E3 **Deyhuk** Iran
57 C5 **Deynau** Turkmenistan
136 H3 **Deyong, Tanjung** *C* W Irian
77 B6 **Deyyer** Iran
117 E5 **Dezadeash L** Yukon Territory Canada
77 A3 **Dezfūl** Iran
77 B4 **Dez Gerd** Iran
65 C6 **Dezhou** China
41 M6 **Dezzo** Italy
46 E7 **Dháfni** Greece
79 G6 **Dhahab, Wādī adh** *watercourse* Syria
Dhahran *see* **Z̧ahrān, Az**
75 O7 **Dhaka** Bangladesh
79 D3 **Dhali** Cyprus
75 J8 **Dhamtari** India
75 M7 **Dhanbad** India
74 J4 **Dhangarhi** Nepal
109 H6 **D'Hanis** Texas U.S.A.
75 M5 **Dhankuta** Nepal
76 D6 **Dhanushkodi** India
74 F7 **Dhar** India
76 C5 **Dharapuram** India
75 K7 **Dharmajaygarh** India
76 D4 **Dharmapuri** India
76 C3 **Dharmavaram** India
74 G2 **Dharmshāla** India
86 A1 **Dharoor** *R* Somalia
85 C5 **Dhar Oualata** *plateau* Mauritania
76 B3 **Dhārwād** India
66 C6 **Dhaulagiri** *mt* Nepal
74 G5 **Dhaulpur** India
75 L8 **Dhenkanal** India
47 H7 **Dhenoúsa** *isld* Greece
46 D4 **Dhërmi** Albania
46 E5 **Dheskáti** Greece
46 G8 **Dhespotikó** *isld* Greece
40 A4 **Dheune** *R* France
80 G7 **Dhiban** Jordan
46 F7 **Dhídhimoi** Greece
47 H3 **Dhidhimótikhon** Greece
46 G9 **Dhikti Ori** *mt* Crete Greece
46 G7 **Dhílos** *isld* Greece
46 E7 **Dhimitsána** Greece
78 L6 **Dhī Qar** *prov* Iraq
80 F8 **Dhira** Jordan
46 F6 **Dhírfis** *mt* Greece
47 H7 **Dhodhekánisos** *islds* Greece
74 G5 **Dholpur** India
46 E5 **Dhomokós** Greece
76 C3 **Dhone** India
74 D8 **Dhoraji** India
46 G3 **Dhoxáton** Greece
46 G7 **Dhragonisi** *isld* Greece
47 O12 **Dhráhstis, Akra** *C* Greece
74 D7 **Dhrangadhra** India
46 F5 **Dhrépanon, Ákr** *C* Greece
46 D5 **Dhrin** *R* Albania
75 N5 **Dhuburi** India
Dhufar *see* **Z̧ufār**
21 O6 **Dhuison** France
74 F8 **Dhule** India
74 E2 **Dhulian** Pakistan
86 B2 **Dhuudo** Somalia
46 E6 **Dhytikí Ellas** *admin region* Greece
46 E4 **Dhytikí Makedhonía** *admin region* Greece
46 G9 **Dia** *isld* Crete Greece
129 H2 **Diable, I.du** Fr Guiana
40 F5 **Diablerets** *mt* Switzerland
100 D1 **Diablo L** Washington U.S.A.
127 K2 **Diablo, Mt** Jamaica
108 C4 **Diablo, Sa** *mts* Texas U.S.A.
127 O7 **Diablotin, Morne** *hill* Dominica
99 M9 **Diagonal** Iowa U.S.A.
85 B6 **Dialakoto** Senegal
131 E4 **Diamante** Argentina
133 D4 **Diamante** *R* Argentina
141 F6 **Diamantina** *R* Queensland Australia
129 K7 **Diamantina** Brazil
130 G6 **Diamantina** Minas Gerais Brazil
141 F6 **Diamantina Lakes** Queensland Australia
129 G6 **Diamantino** Brazil
130 C4 **Diamantino** Mato Grosso Brazil
130 D5 **Diamantino** Mato Grosso Brazil
110 B5 **Diamond** Missouri U.S.A.
118 E9 **Diamond City** Alberta Canada
75 N7 **Diamond Harb** India
144 D5 **Diamond Harbour** New Zealand
102 S12 **Diamond Hd** Hawaiian Is
141 K3 **Diamond Islets** Gt Barrier Reef Australia
100 C6 **Diamond L** Oregon U.S.A.
103 J2 **Diamond Mts** Nevada U.S.A.
100 C6 **Diamond Peak** *mt* Oregon U.S.A.
103 J2 **Diamond Pk** Nevada U.S.A.
102 D3 **Diamond Springs** California U.S.A.
101 P8 **Diamondville** Wyoming U.S.A.
94 G8 **Diana** West Virginia U.S.A.
141 J3 **Diana Bank** Gt Barrier Reef Aust
28 G5 **Dianaland** Denmark
67 C6 **Dianbai** China
Dianbu *see* **Feidong**
67 A4 **Dian Chi** *L* China
67 B1 **Dianjiang** China
44 D4 **Diano Marina** Italy
129 J6 **Dianópolis** Brazil
65 H2 **Diaoling** China
85 E6 **Diapaga** Burkina
71 F2 **Diapitan B** Luzon Philippines
46 F4 **Diavata** Greece
68 A6 **Diavolo, Mt** Andaman Is
65 A5 **Dibabu** China
87 D7 **Dibaya** Zaire
86 D3 **Dibbis** Sudan
66 F6 **Dibhuk Pass** India/Burma
86 B4 **Dibi** Cameroon
109 N4 **Diboll** Texas U.S.A.
66 E6 **Dibrugarh** India
75 Q5 **Dibrugarh** India
71 E3 **Dicapanisan Pt** Luzon Philippines
Diciosănmărtin *see* **Tîrnăveni**
98 E9 **Dickens** Nebraska U.S.A.
108 G2 **Dickens** Texas U.S.A.
95 R6 **Dickey** Maine U.S.A.
98 H3 **Dickey** North Dakota U.S.A.
98 D3 **Dickinson** North Dakota U.S.A.
109 M6 **Dickinson** Texas U.S.A.
9 H3 **Dickleburgh** England
36 D3 **Dickscheid-Geroldstein** Germany
110 J5 **Dickson** Tennessee U.S.A.
95 M5 **Dickson City** Pennsylvania U.S.A.
78 H3 **Dicle** *R* Turkey
45 L4 **Dicomano** Italy
71 F1 **Didacas** *isld* Luzon Philippines
9 E4 **Didcot** England
85 C6 **Didiéni** Mali
109 L8 **Dido** Texas U.S.A.
118 C7 **Didsbury** Alberta Canada
74 F5 **Didwana** India
121 S4 **Didyme** Quebec Canada
19 O15 **Die** France
89 G5 **Die Berg** *mt* S Africa
36 B5 **Diebling** France
85 D6 **Diébougou** Burkina
36 F4 **Dieburg** Germany
118 K7 **Diefenbaker, L** Saskatchewan Canada
33 N6 **Die Göhrde** *reg* Germany
131 F3 **Diego Lamas** Uruguay
133 D9 **Diego Ramírez, Is** Chile
Diego Suarez *see* **Antsiranana**
30 D1 **Die Halligen** *inlet* Germany
32 L8 **Diekholzen** Germany
22 L4 **Diekirch** Luxembourg
20 G2 **Diélette** France
32 H8 **Dielingen** Germany
85 C6 **Diema** Mali
32 K9 **Diemel** *R* Germany
36 C6 **Diemeringen** France
68 F2 **Dien Bien Phu** Vietnam
68 G3 **Dien Chau** Vietnam
32 J8 **Diepenau** Germany
25 G4 **Diepenheim** Netherlands
32 H7 **Diepholz** Germany
21 N2 **Dieppe** France
127 P4 **Dieppe Bay Town** St Kitts W Indies
36 D2 **Dierdorf** Germany
25 F4 **Dieren** Netherlands
33 Q4 **Dierhagen** Germany
36 D2 **Dieringhausen** Germany
109 N1 **Dierks** Arkansas U.S.A.
65 F2 **Di'er Songhua Jiang** *R* China
33 N7 **Diesdorf** Germany
41 J2 **Diessenhofen** Switzerland
22 J2 **Diest** Belgium
110 H2 **Dieterich** Illinois U.S.A.
37 K3 **Dietersdorf** Germany
37 M5 **Dietfurt** Germany
41 H3 **Dietikon** Switzerland
101 L7 **Dietrich** Idaho U.S.A.
36 F3 **Dietzenbach** Germany
19 O15 **Dieulefit** France
19 K4 **Dieuze** France
25 F3 **Dieverbrug** Netherlands
36 B2 **Die Ville** *reg* Germany
36 E3 **Diez** Germany
65 D7 **Difang** China
22 K4 **Differdange** Luxembourg
67 F1 **Digang** China
75 Q5 **Digboi** India
122 G9 **Digby** Nova Scotia Canada
9 F1 **Digby** England
83 M14 **Digby, C** Kerguelen Indian Oc
122 F9 **Digby Neck** Nova Scotia Canada
107 K3 **Dighton** Kansas U.S.A.
95 Q5 **Dighton** Massachusetts U.S.A.
94 B2 **Dighton** Michigan U.S.A.
74 G9 **Diglur** India
19 Q16 **Digne** France
21 N4 **Digny** France
18 H6 **Digoin** France
71 F2 **Digollorin Pt** Luzon Philippines
71 G7 **Digos** Mindanao Philippines
74 G8 **Digras** India
136 H3 **Digul** *R* W Irian
86 H5 **Diinsoor** Somalia
71 E5 **Diit** *isld* Philippines
22 H2 **Dijle** *R* Belgium
19 J5 **Dijon** France
86 C4 **Dik** Chad
89 E4 **Dikabeye** Botswana
26 H6 **Dikanäs** Sweden
86 H3 **Dikhil** Djibouti
47 H5 **Dikili** Turkey
79 B7 **Dîkirnis** Egypt
22 D2 **Dikkebus** Belgium
67 F3 **Dikou** China
83 K11 **Dikoya** Sri Lanka
55 D2 **Dikoye, Oz** *L* Russian Federation
22 D1 **Diksmuide** Belgium
50 H1 **Dikson** Russian Federation
50 G1 **Dikson, Ostrov** *isld* Russian Federation
86 B3 **Dikwa** Nigeria
47 J7 **Dilek Dağ** *mt* Turkey
71 M9 **Dili** Timor Indonesia
106 E6 **Dilia** New Mexico U.S.A.
68 A6 **Diligent Str** Andaman Is
68 J7 **Di Linh** Vietnam
47 N11 **Diliskelesi Ist** *lighthouse* Turkey
119 M8 **Dilke** Saskatchewan Canada
103 O6 **Dilkon** Arizona U.S.A.
36 E2 **Dill** *R* Germany
118 G6 **Dillberry L. Prov Park** Alberta Canada
107 L6 **Dill City** Oklahoma U.S.A.
36 E2 **Dillenburg** Germany
98 K9 **Diller** Nebraska U.S.A.
109 H7 **Dilley** Texas U.S.A.
86 E3 **Dilling** Sudan
36 B5 **Dillingen** Germany
116 H7 **Dillingham** Alaska U.S.A.
118 H3 **Dillon** Saskatchewan Canada
106 D2 **Dillon** Colorado U.S.A.
101 N4 **Dillon** Montana U.S.A.
112 H3 **Dillon** South Carolina U.S.A.
144 D5 **Dillon Cone** *mt* New Zealand
94 E6 **Dillon Res** Ohio U.S.A.
95 K6 **Dillsburg** Pennsylvania U.S.A.
94 J9 **Dillwyn** Virginia U.S.A.
87 D8 **Dilolo** Zaire
75 P6 **Dimapur** India
124 F6 **Dimas** Mexico
79 G5 **Dimashq** Syria
86 D7 **Dimbelenge** Zaire
85 D7 **Dimbokro** Ivory Coast
138 F6 **Dimboola** Victoria Australia
48 J5 **Dîmbo Viţa** *R* Romania
48 J6 **Dîmboviţa** *reg* Romania
141 H3 **Dimbulah** Queensland Australia
54 J8 **Dimitrov** Ukraine
54 E8 **Dimitrova** Ukraine
47 H2 **Dimitrovgrad** Bulgaria
53 G7 **Dimitrovgrad** Russian Federation
46 F1 **Dimitrovgrad** Serbia Yugoslavia
46 G2 **Dimitrov, Yazovir G.** *res* Bulgaria
108 E1 **Dimmitt** Texas U.S.A.
98 H6 **Dimock** South Dakota U.S.A.
79 F7 **Dīmona** Israel
46 F1 **Dimovo** Bulgaria
71 G5 **Dinagat** *isld* Philippines
71 G5 **Dinagat Sound** Philippines
75 N6 **Dinajpur** Bangladesh
20 F5 **Dinan** France
22 H3 **Dinant** Belgium
47 L6 **Dinar** Turkey
42 G4 **Dinara Planina** *R* Bosnia-Herzegovina/Croatia
20 F4 **Dinard-St.Enogat** France
86 F3 **Dinder** *R* Sudan
76 C5 **Dindigul** India
109 K7 **Dinero** Texas U.S.A.
86 C7 **Dinga** Zaire
71 E3 **Dingalan B** Luzon Philippines
68 K3 **Ding'an** China
58 E4 **Dingbian** China
32 E9 **Dingden** Germany
20 G5 **Dingé** France
33 M10 **Dingelstädt** Germany
33 O9 **Dingelstedt** Germany
48 K3 **Dîngeni** Romania
75 M4 **Dinggyê** China
67 G1 **Dinghai** China
101 O7 **Dingle** Idaho U.S.A.
14 A4 **Dingle B** Ireland
67 E4 **Dingnan** China
141 J6 **Dingo** Queensland Australia
37 O6 **Dingolfing** Germany
71 E1 **Dingras** Luzon Philippines
65 C7 **Dingtao** China
85 B6 **Dinguiraye** Guinea
123 M7 **Dingwall** C Breton I, Nova Scotia
15 D3 **Dingwall** Scotland
58 D4 **Dingxi** China
65 C5 **Ding Xian** China
65 B5 **Dingxiang** China
65 C5 **Dingxing** China
65 E6 **Dingzi Gang** *B* China
69 H8 **Dinh An, Cua** *river mouth* Vietnam
67 B6 **Dinh Lap** Vietnam
25 H4 **Dinkel** *R* Netherlands
37 J5 **Dinkelsbühl** Germany
37 K7 **Dinkelscherben** Germany
32 H7 **Dinklage** Germany
103 O5 **Dinnebito Wash** *creek* Arizona U.S.A.
13 G3 **Dinnington** England
87 E10 **Dinokwe** Botswana
118 K1 **Dinorwic L** Ontario Canada
101 Q9 **Dinosaur Nat.Mon** Utah/Colo U.S.A.
78 J4 **Dīn, Şalāḩ ad** *prov* Iraq
32 E9 **Dinslaken** Germany
118 K7 **Dinsmore** Saskatchewan Canada
113 F7 **Dinsmore** Florida U.S.A.
70 K8 **Dintiteladas** *C* Sumatra
102 E5 **Dinuba** California U.S.A.
94 K9 **Dinwiddie** Virginia U.S.A.
25 F5 **Dinxperlo** Netherlands
27 G15 **Diö** Sweden
85 C6 **Dioila** Mali
116 C4 **Diomede Is** Bering Str
51 S2 **Diomida, Ostrova** *islds* Russian Federation
22 H3 **Dion** Belgium
86 D2 **Diona** Chad
130 D10 **Dionisio Cerqueira** Brazil
130 D5 **Diorama** Brazil
48 F2 **Diósgyör** Hungary
85 A6 **Diouloulou** Senegal
85 C6 **Dioura** Mali
85 A6 **Diourbel** Senegal
74 C6 **Diplo** Pakistan
71 F6 **Dipolog** Mindanao Philippines
22 L4 **Dippach** Luxembourg
12 C2 **Dippen** Scotland
12 C3 **Dippin** Scotland
144 B6 **Dipton** New Zealand
74 D1 **Dir** Pakistan
27 B13 **Dirdal** Norway
141 G2 **Direction,C** Queensland Australia
83 M8 **Direction I** Cocos Is Indian Oc
86 H4 **Dirē Dawa** Ethiopia
125 L4 **Diriamba** Nicaragua
87 D9 **Dirico** Angola
43 F11 **Dirillo** *R* Sicily
143 A7 **Dirk Hartog I** W Australia Australia
84 E6 **Dirkou** Niger
25 B5 **Dirksland** Netherlands
13 F1 **Dirleton** Scotland
36 C5 **Dirmingen** Germany
86 E3 **Dirra** Sudan
141 J8 **Dirranbandi** Queensland Australia
103 O3 **Dirty Devil** *R* Utah U.S.A.
102 T13 **Disappearing I** Hawaiian Is
131 H6 **Disappointment, C** S Georgia
100 A3 **Disappointment, C** Washington U.S.A.
135 N9 **Disappointment Is** Tuamotu Arch Pacific Oc
143 E6 **Disappointment,L** W Australia Australia
139 K6 **Disaster B** New South Wales Australia
100 F1 **Disautel** Washington U.S.A.
37 J6 **Dischingen** Germany
117 Q4 **Discovery** Northwest Territories Canada
138 F7 **Discovery B** S Aust/Vict Australia
127 K1 **Discovery Bay** Jamaica
100 C2 **Discovery Bay** Washington U.S.A.
100 C1 **Discovery I** Washington U.S.A.
90 J13 **Discovery Tablemount** S Atlantic Oc
142 E5 **Discovery Well** W Australia Australia
41 J4 **Disentis** Switzerland
13 G5 **Dishforth** England
116 J5 **Dishkakat** Alaska U.S.A.
116 J5 **Dishna** *R* Alaska U.S.A.
80 F1 **Dishon** *R* Israel
80 F1 **Dishon** Israel
115 O4 **Disko** *isld* Greenland
115 O4 **Diskofjord** Greenland
119 M8 **Disley** Saskatchewan Canada
140 F4 **Dismal** *R* Queensland Australia
98 F8 **Dismal** *R* Nebraska U.S.A.
95 L10 **Dismal Swamp** Virginia U.S.A.
52 C6 **Disna** Belorussia
22 K2 **Dison** Belgium
95 K9 **Disputanta** Virginia U.S.A.
121 T7 **Disraëli** Quebec Canada
9 H3 **Diss** England
21 L8 **Dissay** France
21 L6 **Dissay-sous-Courcillon** France
32 H8 **Dissen** Germany
122 C4 **Dissimieux, L** Quebec Canada
100 C6 **Disston** Oregon U.S.A.
79 A7 **Disûq** Egypt
9 F6 **Ditchling** England
33 O9 **Ditfurt** Germany
32 K4 **Dithmarschen** *reg* Germany
43 F11 **Dittaino** *R* Sicily
36 G6 **Ditzingen** Germany
74 D8 **Diu** India
71 G6 **Diuata Mts** Mindanao Philippines
21 K7 **Dive** *R* France
52 D5 **Divenskaya** Russian Federation
121 L6 **Diver** Ontario Canada
110 G2 **Divernon** Illinois U.S.A.
142 G3 **Diversion Dam** W Australia Australia
109 H2 **Diversion L** Texas U.S.A.
21 K3 **Dives** *R* France
21 K3 **Dives sur Mer** France
20 G2 **Divette** *R* France
26 L3 **Dividal** *R* Norway
106 E3 **Divide** Colorado U.S.A.
141 H6 **Dividing Range** Queensland Australia
71 F2 **Divilacan B** Luzon Philippines
87 F10 **Divinhe** Mozambique
130 G7 **Divinopólis** Brazil
22 C3 **Divion** France
100 F8 **Division Peak** *mt* Nevada U.S.A.
53 F10 **Divnoye** Russian Federation
85 C7 **Divo** Ivory Coast
78 G2 **Divriği** Turkey
74 B5 **Diwana** Pakistan
78 K6 **Dīwānīyah, Ad** Iraq
121 O4 **Dix** Quebec Canada
98 C8 **Dix** Nebraska U.S.A.
95 R2 **Dixfield** Maine U.S.A.
111 K8 **Dixiana** Alabama U.S.A.
111 K10 **Dixie** Alabama U.S.A.
113 D7 **Dixie** Georgia U.S.A.
100 K4 **Dixie** Idaho U.S.A.
100 G3 **Dixie** Washington U.S.A.
100 G5 **Dixie Pass** Oregon U.S.A.
102 F2 **Dixie Valley** Nevada U.S.A.
121 Q5 **Dix Milles, L.des** Quebec Canada
95 S2 **Dixmont** Maine U.S.A.
95 O2 **Dix Mt** New York U.S.A.
Dixmude *see* **Diksmuide**
102 C3 **Dixon** California U.S.A.
99 R8 **Dixon** Illinois U.S.A.
110 D4 **Dixon** Missouri U.S.A.
101 L2 **Dixon** Montana U.S.A.
98 K7 **Dixon** Nebraska U.S.A.
106 E5 **Dixon** New Mexico U.S.A.
101 S8 **Dixon** Wyoming U.S.A.
117 G8 **Dixon Entrance** *str* Br Col/Alaska Canada/U.S.A.
111 J9 **Dixons Mills** Alabama U.S.A.
117 P7 **Dixonville** Alberta Canada
94 H6 **Dixonville** Pennsylvania U.S.A.
67 A4 **Dixu** China
121 T7 **Dixville** Quebec Canada
78 K5 **Diyālá** *prov* Iraq
78 H3 **Diyarbakır** Turkey
65 H3 **Diyingou** China
74 B9 **Diz** Pakistan
77 H6 **Diz** Pakistan
67 C2 **Dizhuang** China
8 B6 **Dizzard Pt** England
86 B5 **Dja** *R* Cameroon
84 E5 **Djado** Niger
84 E5 **Djado, Pl.du** Niger
71 A2 **Djailolo** Halmahera Indonesia
Djailolo Gilolo *isld see* **Halmahera** *isld*
Djajapura *see* **Jayapura**
86 B6 **Djambala** Congo
69 F13 **Djambi** *prov* Sumatra
70 L9 **Djampang-Kulon** Java
85 F4 **Djanet** Algeria
70 E6 **Djangeru** Kalimantan
70 E3 **Djanlonong** Kalimantan
85 E3 **Djaret** *watercourse* Algeria
70 L9 **Djatinegara** Java
70 M9 **Djatiwangi** Java
86 B2 **Djbella** Niger
69 G13 **Djebus** Indonesia
86 C3 **Djédaa** Chad
85 E2 **Djedi** *watercourse* Algeria
85 E2 **Djelfa** Algeria
86 E4 **Djéma** Cent Afr Republic
70 F7 **Djeneponto** Sulawesi
Djerba, I de *see* **Jerba, I de**
86 B4 **Djérem** *R* Cameroon
Djezair, El *see* **Alger**
85 D6 **Djibasso** Burkina
85 D6 **Djibo** Burkina
86 H3 **Djibouti** Djibouti
86 H3 **Djibouti** *rep* N E Africa
86 D7 **Djokopunda** Zaire
86 D5 **Djolu** Zaire
70 D7 **Djorong** Kalimantan
86 B6 **Djoué** *R* Congo
85 C5 **Djouf, El** *reg* Mauritania/Mali
85 E7 **Djougou** Benin
86 B5 **Djoum** Cameroon

86 C2 **Djourab** *dist* Chad
86 F5 **Djugu** Zaire
29 T9 **Djupivogur** Iceland
27 H11 **Djura** Sweden
27 K12 **Djursholm** Sweden
28 E4 **Djursland** *reg* Denmark
111 G10 **D'Lo** Mississippi U.S.A.
51 O1 **Dmitriya Lapteva, Proliv** *str* Russian Federation
55 G3 **Dmitriyevka** Russian Federation
54 G4 **Dmitriyev-L'govskiy** Russian Federation
54 J1 **Dmitrov** Russian Federation
54 D6 **Dmitrovka** Ukraine
54 G4 **Dmitrovsk-Orlovskiy** Russian Federation
54 B4 **Dnepr** *R* Belorussia/Rus Fed etc
54 F8 **Dneprodzerzhinsk** Ukraine
54 G8 **Dnepropetrovsk** Ukraine
54 F9 **Dneprorudnoye** Ukraine
53 C7 **Dneprovskaya Nizmennost** *lowland* Belorussia/Ukraine
54 C10 **Dneprovskiy Liman** *lagoon* Ukraine
53 C9 **Dnestr** *R* Europe
48 M4 **Dnestrovsk** Moldavia
48 N4 **Dnestrovskiy Liman** *lagoon* Ukraine
Dnieper *R see* **Dnepr** *R*
Dniester *R see* **Dnestr** *R*
52 C5 **Dno** Russian Federation
77 K2 **Doāb Mekh-i-Zarīn** Afghanistan
122 F7 **Doaktown** New Brunswick Canada
70 E7 **Doangdoangan Besar** *isld* Indonesia
70 E7 **Doangdoangan Ketjil** *isld* Indonesia
67 B6 **Doan Hung** Vietnam
86 C4 **Doba** Chad
33 Q5 **Dobbertin** Germany
138 E2 **Dobbie, L** South Australia Australia
140 E6 **Dobbie,Mt** N Terr Australia
109 M5 **Dobbin** Texas U.S.A.
31 M6 **Dobczyce** Poland
52 B6 **Dobele** Latvia
37 P1 **Döbeln** Germany
33 T9 **Doberlug Kirchhain** Germany
31 J3 **Dobiegniew** Poland
133 E5 **Doblas** Argentina
136 G3 **Dobo** Moluccas Indonesia
48 E6 **Doboj** Bosnia-Herzegovina
112 F6 **Doboy Sd** Georgia U.S.A.
31 J2 **Dobra** Poland
37 M3 **Döbraberg** *mt* Germany
37 P4 **Dobřany** Czechoslovakia
38 J8 **Dobratsch** *mt* Austria
31 M2 **Dobre Miasto** Poland
48 G4 **Dobresti** Romania
48 H6 **Dobreta-Turnu-Severin** Romania
38 J8 **Döbriach** Austria
47 J1 **Dobrich** Bulgaria
33 S9 **Döbrichau** Germany
46 F3 **Dobrinishte** Bulgaria
31 H6 **Dobříš** Czechoslovakia
33 Q8 **Dobritz** Germany
31 L5 **Dobrodzień** Poland
31 O6 **Dobromil** Ukraine
54 J8 **Dobropol'ye** Ukraine
48 J6 **Dobroteşti** Romania
54 F2 **Dobroye** Russian Federation
54 C4 **Dobrush** Belorussia
54 C4 **Dobryanka** Ukraine
31 L3 **Dobrzyn** Poland
48 F2 **Dobšiná** Czechoslovakia
144 C5 **Dobson** New Zealand
144 B6 **Dobson** *R* New Zealand
112 G1 **Dobson** North Carolina U.S.A.
8 B7 **Dobwalls** England
127 N1 **Docas del Dragón** *chan* Trinidad/Ven
71 D7 **Doc Can** *isld* Sulu Arch Philippines
130 G6 **Doce, R** Brazil
143 G6 **Docker Cr** W Australia Australia
140 A6 **Docker River** N Terr Australia
9 G2 **Docking** England
26 H9 **Dockmyr** Sweden
142 F4 **Dockrell, Mt** W Australia Australia
26 K8 **Docksta** Sweden
36 B3 **Dockweiler** Germany
109 H10 **Doctor Cos** Mexico
143 E8 **Doctor Hicks Ra** W Australia Australia
Doctor Petru Groza *see* **Ştei**
121 P3 **Doda, L** Quebec Canada
76 C4 **Dod Ballapur** India
13 F2 **Doddington** England
109 O2 **Doddridge** Arkansas U.S.A.
118 E5 **Dodds** Alberta Canada
Dodecanese *islds see* **Dhodhekánisos** *islds*
98 K8 **Dodge** Nebraska U.S.A.
98 D2 **Dodge** North Dakota U.S.A.
99 O5 **Dodge Center** Minnesota U.S.A.
107 K4 **Dodge City** Kansas U.S.A.
99 Q7 **Dodgeville** Wisconsin U.S.A.
8 B7 **Dodman Pt** England
88 E5 **Dodoma** Tanzania
33 O6 **Dodow** Germany
118 J7 **Dodsland** Saskatchewan Canada
109 P3 **Dodson** Louisiana U.S.A.
101 R1 **Dodson** Montana U.S.A.
47 K5 **Dodurga** Turkey
22 G1 **Doel** Belgium
112 D6 **Doerun** Georgia U.S.A.
25 F4 **Doesburg** Netherlands
25 F5 **Doetinchem** Netherlands
71 J5 **Dofa** Indonesia
36 F6 **Doffingen** Germany
66 D5 **Dogai Coring** *L* China
47 H6 **Doğanbey Burun** *C* Turkey
78 G1 **Doğankent** Turkey
79 F2 **Doğankent** Turkey
117 M10 **Dog Creek** British Columbia Canada
66 E5 **Dogên Co** *L* China
47 L5 **Döğer** Turkey
7 M8 **Dogger Bank** North Sea
127 N5 **Dog I** Lesser Antilles
144 B7 **Dog I** New Zealand
113 C8 **Dog I** Florida U.S.A.
119 T7 **Dog L** Manitoba Canada
99 R1 **Dog L** Ontario Canada
44 C2 **Dogliani** Italy
38 H9 **Dogna** Italy
60 G9 **Dōgo** *isld* Japan
85 E6 **Dogondoutchi** Niger
60 G10 **Dōgo-yama** *mt* Japan
118 C7 **Dog Pound** Alberta Canada
126 E2 **Dog Rocks** Bahamas
78 K2 **Doğubayazit** Turkey
127 P4 **Dogwood Pt** Nevis W Indies
Doha *see* **Dawḥah, Ad**
Dohad *see* **Dāhod**
75 P7 **Dohazar** Bangladesh
121 S5 **Doheny** Quebec Canada
33 N4 **Döhnsdorf** Germany
71 A1 **Doi** Indonesia
68 D3 **Doi Saket** Thailand
22 H3 **Doische** Belgium
130 E8 **Dois Córregos** Brazil
46 F3 **Dojran** Macedonia Yugoslavia
46 F3 **Dojrawsko ezero** *L* Macedonia Yugoslavia
27 D11 **Dokka** Norway
26 M4 **Dokkas** Sweden
28 E3 **Dokkedal** Denmark
25 E2 **Dokkum** Netherlands
55 D5 **Dokuchayevka** Kazakhstan
54 J9 **Dokuchayevsk** Ukraine
136 H3 **Dolak** *isld* W Irian
98 H5 **Doland** South Dakota U.S.A.
121 S4 **Dolbeau** Quebec Canada
32 G9 **Dolberg** Germany
20 G4 **Dol-de Bretagne** France
19 J5 **Dôle** France
125 N5 **Dolega** Panama
42 G3 **Dolenjske Toplice** Slovenia
8 C3 **Dolfor** Wales
8 C2 **Dolgellau** Wales
95 N3 **Dolgeville** New York U.S.A.
116 G9 **Dolgoi I** Alaska U.S.A.
55 E3 **Dolgovskoye** Russian Federation
48 H2 **Dolgoye** Ukraine
43 C9 **Dolianova** Sardinia
48 H2 **Dolina** Ukraine
59 M2 **Dolinsk** Russian Federation
54 D8 **Dolinskaya** Ukraine
71 A3 **Dolit** Indonesia
46 F1 **Dolj** Romania
46 E1 **Doljevac** Serbia Yugoslavia
38 G8 **Döllach** Austria
12 E1 **Dollar** Scotland
118 J9 **Dollard** Saskatchewan Canada
122 F3 **Dollard, L** Quebec Canada
15 E5 **Dollar Law** *mt* Scotland
32 F6 **Dollart** *inlet* Germany/Neths
32 M8 **Dollbergen** Germany
33 P8 **Dolle** Germany
146 D5 **Dolleman I** Antarctica
28 C4 **Dollerup** Denmark
37 L6 **Dollnstein** Germany
21 M5 **Dollon** France
37 K1 **Döllstädt** Germany
46 G1 **Dolna Mitropbliya** Bulgaria
46 E3 **Dolneni** Macedonia Yugoslavia
46 G1 **Dolni Dŭbnik** Bulgaria
37 Q2 **Dolní Jiřetín** Czechoslovakia
31 J6 **Dolni Královice** Czechoslovakia
37 O3 **Dolní Žandov** Czechoslovakia
45 M1 **Dolo** Italy
70 F5 **Dolo** Sulawesi
19 P13 **Dolomieu** France
42 D2 **Dolomitiche, Alpi** Italy
Dolonnur *see* **Duolun**
86 H5 **Dolo Odo** Ethiopia
131 F6 **Dolores** Argentina
125 P9 **Dolores** Guatemala
17 G6 **Dolores** Spain
131 F4 **Dolores** Uruguay
106 B3 **Dolores** *R* Colorado U.S.A.
106 B4 **Dolores** Colorado U.S.A.
125 J7 **Dolores Hidalgo** Mexico
133 F8 **Dolphin, C** Falkland Is
127 H1 **Dolphin Hd** *hill* Jamaica
87 B11 **Dolphin Hd** Namibia
142 B5 **Dolphin I** W Australia Australia
13 E2 **Dolphinton** Scotland
114 H4 **Dolphin & Union Str** Northwest Territories Canada
38 G8 **Dölsach** Austria
31 K4 **Dolsk** Poland
68 G3 **Do Luong** Vietnam
21 M7 **Dolus-le-Sec** France
8 C1 **Dolwyddelan** Wales
136 H2 **Dom** *mt* W Irian
122 H2 **Domagaya L** Labrador, Nfld Canada
119 U9 **Domain** Manitoba Canada
47 K5 **Domaniç** Turkey
47 K5 **Domaniç Daği** *mt* Turkey
21 P1 **Domart-en-Ponthieu** France
37 O5 **Domažlice** Czechoslovakia
55 C5 **Dombarovskiy** Russian Federation
26 D9 **Dombås** Norway
19 K4 **Dombasle** France
87 B8 **Dombe Grande** Angola
140 A2 **Dombey,C** N Terr Australia
48 E4 **Dombóvár** Hungary
48 G2 **Dombrád** Hungary
37 J5 **Dombühl** Germany
25 A5 **Domburg** Netherlands
103 K9 **Dome** Arizona U.S.A.
117 N9 **Dome Creek** British Columbia Canada
40 E7 **Dôme-de-Chasseforêt** France
103 K8 **Dome Rock Mts** Arizona U.S.A.
144 D5 **Domett** New Zealand
145 D4 **Domett, Mt** New Zealand
36 B6 **Domèvre** France
21 J4 **Domfront** France
106 D6 **Domingo** New Mexico U.S.A.
127 O7 **Dominica** *isld* Lesser Antilles
127 J5 **Dominican Rep** W Indies
123 M7 **Dominion** C Breton I, Nova Scotia
115 M4 **Dominion, C** Northwest Territories Canada
119 U9 **Dominion City** Manitoba Canada
123 L1 **Dominion L** Labrador, Nfld Canada
115 O7 **Domino** Labrador, Nfld Canada
33 O6 **Dömitz** Germany
21 H4 **Domjean** France
130 G6 **Dom Joaquim** Brazil
41 K4 **Domleschg** *R* Switzerland
18 F8 **Domme** France
25 D6 **Dommel** *R* Netherlands
33 R9 **Dommitzsch** Germany
86 A2 **Domo** Ethiopia
54 J1 **Domodedovo** Russian Federation
41 H5 **Domodossola** Italy
21 P3 **Domont** France
146 E14 **Domont d'Urville Sea** Antarctica
40 D1 **Dompaire** France
21 H5 **Dompierre-du-Chemin** France
22 B3 **Dompierre-sur-Authie** France
20 H8 **Dompierre-sur-Yon** France
36 B7 **Domptail** France
71 J9 **Dompu** Sumbawa Indonesia
119 M6 **Domremy** Saskatchewan Canada
26 K8 **Domsjö** Sweden
88 E9 **Domue** *pk* Mozambique
131 B6 **Domuyo** *pk* Argentina
141 K8 **Domville** *mt* Queensland Australia
141 K8 **Domville,Mt** Queensland Australia
46 F6 **Domvraina** Greece
42 F2 **Domžale** Slovenia
141 J5 **Don** *R* Queensland Australia
20 G6 **Don** *R* France
22 D2 **Don** France
124 E4 **Don** Mexico
54 L5 **Don** *R* Russian Federation
15 F3 **Don** *R* Scotland
106 D9 **Dona Ana** New Mexico U.S.A.
45 M1 **Donada** Italy
14 F2 **Donaghadee** N Ireland
139 G6 **Donald** Victoria Australia
121 M8 **Donald** Ontario Canada
118 E6 **Donalda** Alberta Canada
144 A6 **Donald, Mt** New Zealand
140 F4 **Donaldson** Queensland Australia
109 P1 **Donaldson** Arkansas U.S.A.
98 K1 **Donaldson** Minnesota U.S.A.
111 E11 **Donaldsonville** Louisiana U.S.A.
112 C6 **Donalsonville** Georgia U.S.A.
14 E3 **Donard** Ireland
124 G5 **Donato Guerra** Mexico
38 L5 **Donau** *R* Austria
37 L6 **Donau** *R* Germany
41 J2 **Donaueschingen** Germany
37 L6 **Donaumoos** *reg* Germany
37 K6 **Donauried** *reg* Germany
37 N5 **Donaustauf** Germany
37 K6 **Donauwörth** Germany
118 K7 **Donavon** Saskatchewan Canada
38 M7 **Donawitz** Austria
54 J8 **Donbass (Donetskiy Ugol'nyy Basseyn)** Ukraine
16 D6 **Don Benito** Spain
140 B1 **Don,C** N Terr Australia
13 G6 **Doncaster** England
95 K8 **Doncaster** Maryland U.S.A.
22 H4 **Donchery** France
22 K4 **Doncols** Luxembourg
87 B7 **Dondo** Angola
87 F9 **Dondo** Mozambique
71 E6 **Dondonay** *isld* Philippines
70 G4 **Dondo, Teluk** *B* Sulawesi
70 G4 **Dondo, Tg** *C* Sulawesi
73 N7 **Dondra Head** *C* Sri Lanka
48 L2 **Dondyushany** Moldavia
14 C2 **Donegal** Ireland
14 D2 **Donegal** *co* Ireland
14 C2 **Donegal Bay** *B* Ireland
14 B4 **Donegal Pt** Ireland
110 K5 **Donelson** Tennessee U.S.A.
14 C4 **Doneraile** Ireland
54 J8 **Donetsk** Ukraine
53 E9 **Donetskiy Kryazh** *mts* Rus Fed/Ukraine
127 J2 **Don Figuerero Mts** Jamaica
86 B4 **Donga** *R* Nigeria
59 K2 **Dong'an** China
67 D3 **Dong'an** China
68 J5 **Dong An** Vietnam
143 A8 **Dongara** W Australia
74 J8 **Dongargarh** India
66 D4 **Dongbolhai Shan** *mts* China
Dongchangshou *see* **Xinle**
Dongcun *see* **Haiyang**
68 H2 **Dong Dang** Vietnam
65 C6 **Dong'e** China
25 C5 **Dongen** Netherlands
20 F7 **Donges** France
68 J3 **Dongfang** China
65 J1 **Dongfanghong** China
65 F3 **Dongfeng** China
70 F5 **Donggala** Sulawesi
58 C4 **Donggi Cona** *L* China
67 D1 **Donggong** China
65 F4 **Donggou** China
67 E3 **Donggu** China
67 E5 **Dongguan** China
65 C6 **Dongguang** China
68 H4 **Dong Ha** Vietnam
65 D7 **Donghai** China
67 C6 **Donghai Dao** *isld* China
58 D3 **Dong He** *R* China
58 E4 **Dong He** *R* China
68 H4 **Dong Hoi** Vietnam
Donghuang *see* **Xishui** Guizhou
67 C4 **Dongjiang** China
65 H2 **Dongjingcheng** China
70 F6 **Dongkait, Tanjong** *C* Sulawesi
70 G4 **Dongkalang** Sulawesi
68 H1 **Dong Khe** Vietnam
67 C3 **Dongkou** China
67 B4 **Donglan** China
Dongliao *see* **Liaoyuan**
65 F3 **Dongliao He** *R* China
67 B5 **Dongling** China
67 E1 **Dongliu** China
65 C7 **Dongming** China
68 H7 **Dong Nai** *R* Vietnam
59 K2 **Dongning** China
87 C8 **Dongo** Angola
41 K5 **Dongo** Italy
86 C5 **Dongo** Zaire
84 J6 **Dongola** Sudan
86 C5 **Dongou** Congo
68 E4 **Dong Phraya Fai** *ra* Thailand
68 E5 **Dong Phraya Yen** Thailand
Dongping *see* **Anhua**
65 C7 **Dongping** China
65 C6 **Dongping Hu** *L* China
68 H7 **Dong Sai** Vietnam
67 F5 **Dongshan** China
67 F5 **Dongshan Dao** *isld* China
67 E6 **Dongsha Qundao** *isld* China
65 A5 **Dongsheng** China
67 B2 **Dongsheng** China
67 D2 **Dongting Hu** *L* China
67 G3 **Dongtou** China
67 B6 **Dong Trieu** Vietnam
65 D2 **Dong Ujimqin Qi** China
68 G1 **Dong Van** Vietnam
87 D8 **Dongwe** *R* Zambia
67 B2 **Dongxi** China
67 E2 **Dongxiang** China
65 D7 **Dongxi Lian Dao** *isld* China
65 G1 **Dongxing** China
67 B6 **Dongxing** China
67 G2 **Dongyang** China
65 D6 **Dongying** China
67 F1 **Dongzhi** China
109 L4 **Donie** Texas U.S.A.
9 F2 **Donington** England
110 F5 **Doniphan** Missouri U.S.A.
117 D4 **Donjek** *R* Yukon Territory Canada
48 G6 **Donji Milanovac** Serbia Yugoslavia
42 H4 **Donji Vakuf** Bosnia-Herzegovina
18 H6 **Donjon, le** France
99 S3 **Donken** Michigan U.S.A.
26 F5 **Dönna** *isld* Norway
109 J9 **Donna** Texas U.S.A.
121 T6 **Donnacona** Quebec Canada
42 B3 **Donnas** Italy
36 B6 **Donnelay** France
110 G2 **Donnellson** Illinois U.S.A.
117 P8 **Donnelly** Alberta Canada
100 J5 **Donnelly** Idaho U.S.A.
98 K4 **Donnelly** Minnesota U.S.A.
145 D1 **Donnelly's Crossing** New Zealand
102 D2 **Donner Pass** California U.S.A.
38 K7 **Donnersbach** Austria
38 K7 **Donnersbach Wald** Austria
36 D4 **Donnersberg** *mt* Germany
100 G6 **Donner und Blitzen** *R* Oregon U.S.A.
26 F5 **Dönnes** Norway
143 B10 **Donnybrook** W Australia Australia
98 E1 **Donnybrook** North Dakota U.S.A.
19 K4 **Donon** *mt* France
36 C7 **Donon, Col du** *pass* France
94 H6 **Donora** Pennsylvania U.S.A.
140 F4 **Donor's Hill** Queensland Australia
Donostia *see* **San Sebastian**
99 T9 **Donovan** Illinois U.S.A.
102 D4 **Don Pedro Res** California U.S.A.
13 G6 **Don, R** England
54 K3 **Donskoy** Russian Federation
54 L6 **Donskoye Belogorye** Russian Federation
28 B5 **Donslund** Denmark
68 C4 **Donthami** *R* Burma
20 G4 **Donville** France
36 H6 **Donzdorf** Germany
18 G7 **Donzenac** France
19 N16 **Donzère** France
18 H5 **Donzy** France
143 C9 **Doodlakine** W Australia Australia
109 H4 **Doole** Texas U.S.A.
142 C5 **Dooleena** *mt* W Australia Australia
98 B1 **Dooley** Montana U.S.A.
121 O6 **Doolittle, L** Quebec Canada
140 E4 **Doomadgee** Queensland Australia
116 M3 **Doonerak, Mt** Alaska U.S.A.
12 D3 **Doon, L** Scotland
12 D3 **Doon, R** Scotland
25 D4 **Doorn** Netherlands
99 T5 **Door Pen** Wisconsin U.S.A.
86 A2 **Dooxo Nugaaleed** *V* Somalia
44 B1 **Dora** Italy
111 J8 **Dora** Alabama U.S.A.
106 G8 **Dora** New Mexico U.S.A.
42 B3 **Dora Baltea** *R* Italy
124 G4 **Dorado** Mexico
142 E5 **Dora,L** W Australia Australia
66 F5 **Doramarkog** China
113 F9 **Dora, Mt** Florida U.S.A.
98 K3 **Doran** Minnesota U.S.A.
27 G15 **Dörarp** Sweden
18 F6 **Dorat, le** France
Dorbiljin *see* **Emin**
Dorbiljin *see* **Emin**
Dorbod *see* **Siziwang Qi**
65 F1 **Dorbod** China
122 H8 **Dorchester** New Brunswick Canada
8 D6 **Dorchester** England
9 E4 **Dorchester** England
98 J9 **Dorchester** Nebraska U.S.A.
99 Q4 **Dorchester** Wisconsin U.S.A.
115 M4 **Dorchester, C** Northwest Territories Canada
89 A4 **Dordabis** Namibia
18 F7 **Dordogne** *dept* France
18 E8 **Dordogne** *R* France
25 C5 **Dordrecht** Netherlands
18 H7 **Dore** *R* France
140 B5 **Doreen, Mt** N Terr Australia
118 K4 **Doré L** Saskatchewan Canada
18 G7 **Dore, Mont** *mt* France
100 C6 **Dorena** Oregon U.S.A.
32 H8 **Dörenberg** *mt* Germany
32 J9 **Dörenhagen** Germany
118 E6 **Dorenlee** Alberta Canada
32 J8 **Dörentrup** Germany
130 F6 **Dores do Indaiá** Brazil
37 N7 **Dorfen** Germany
32 L7 **Dorfmark** Germany
33 R6 **Dorf Zechlin** Germany
43 C8 **Dorgali** Sardinia
77 J4 **Dori** *R* Afghanistan
85 D6 **Dori** Burkina
75 K5 **Dorīghāt** India
89 A8 **Doring** *R* S Africa
118 J4 **Dorintosh** Saskatchewan Canada
120 B4 **Dorion** Ontario Canada
121 Q7 **Dorion** Quebec Canada
140 B2 **Dorisvale** N Terr Australia
9 F5 **Dorking** England
36 B1 **Dormagen** Germany
18 H3 **Dormans** France
19 N13 **D'Or, Mt** France
41 L3 **Dornbirn** Austria
36 E2 **Dornburg** Germany
37 M1 **Dorndorf** Germany
37 J2 **Dorndorf** Germany
48 K3 **Dorneşti** Romania
36 F7 **Dornhan** Germany
15 C3 **Dornie** Scotland
48 J3 **Dornişoara** Romania
33 Q8 **Dörnitz** Germany
15 D3 **Dornoch** Scotland
15 D3 **Dornoch Firth** Scotland
13 E4 **Dornock** Scotland
65 A2 **Dornogovĭ** *prov* Mongolia
36 F7 **Dornstetten** Germany
32 F5 **Dornum** Germany
48 E3 **Dorog** Hungary
54 E2 **Dorogobuzh** Russian Federation
52 F2 **Dorogorskoye** Russian Federation
48 K3 **Dorohoi** Romania
54 H1 **Dorokhovo** Russian Federation
26 H7 **Dorotea** Sweden
118 E7 **Dorothy** Alberta Canada
52 G5 **Dorovitsa** Russian Federation
32 F7 **Dörpen** Germany
107 M3 **Dorrance** Kansas U.S.A.
143 A7 **Dorre I** W Australia Australia
139 L4 **Dorrigo** New South Wales Australia
8 D2 **Dorrington** England
100 D8 **Dorris** California U.S.A.
100 E8 **Dorris Res** California U.S.A.
121 M7 **Dorset** Ontario Canada
8 D6 **Dorset** *co* England
94 G5 **Dorset** Ohio U.S.A.
95 O3 **Dorset** Vermont U.S.A.
32 E9 **Dorsten** Germany
32 G9 **Dortmund** Germany
32 J5 **Dorum** Germany
86 E5 **Doruma** Zaire
121 R7 **Dorval** Quebec Canada
36 H5 **Dörzbach** Germany
133 D6 **Dos Bahías, C** Argentina
125 P9 **Dos Bocas** Belize
103 P9 **Dos Cabezas** Arizona U.S.A.
77 G2 **Doshakh, Koh-I** *mt* Afghanistan
71 E4 **Dos Hermanas** *isld* Philippines
16 D7 **Dos Hermanas** Spain
68 H2 **Do Son** Vietnam
102 D5 **Dos Palos** California U.S.A.
46 G3 **Dospat** Bulgaria
121 T6 **Dosquet** Quebec Canada
102 A2 **Dos Rios** California U.S.A.
109 H5 **Doss** Texas U.S.A.
33 R6 **Dosse** *R* Germany
85 E6 **Dosso** Niger
45 J1 **Dossobuono** Italy
50 E4 **Dossor** Kazakhstan
28 D3 **Døstrup** Denmark
94 K9 **Doswell** Virginia U.S.A.
111 L10 **Dothan** Alabama U.S.A.
100 B7 **Dothan** Oregon U.S.A.
123 T4 **Doting Cove** Newfoundland Canada
116 P5 **Dot Lake** Alaska U.S.A.
32 H7 **Dötlingen** Germany
101 S10 **Dotsero** Colorado U.S.A.
36 H5 **Döttingen** Germany
21 N8 **Douadic** France
22 E3 **Douai** France
86 A5 **Douala** Cameroon
20 B5 **Douarnenez** France
20 B5 **Douarnenez, Baie de** France
109 N6 **Double Bayou** Texas U.S.A.
126 D3 **Double Headed Shot Cays** *islds* Bahamas
68 C5 **Double I** Burma
141 L7 **Double Island Pt** Queensland Australia
108 G2 **Double Mountain Fork** *R* Texas U.S.A.
102 F6 **Double Mt** California U.S.A.
116 L6 **Double Peak** Alaska U.S.A.
141 H4 **Double Pt** *C* Queensland Australia
111 J7 **Double Springs** Alabama U.S.A.
31 J6 **Doubrava** *R* Czechoslovakia
19 J6 **Doubs** *R* France
40 D3 **Doubs** *dept* France
40 F3 **Doubs** *R* Switzerland
142 E3 **Doubtful B** W Australia Australia
143 C10 **Doubtful Island B** W Australia Australia
144 A6 **Doubtful Sd** New Zealand
145 D1 **Doubtless B** New Zealand
40 C4 **Doucier** France
21 M2 **Doudeville** France
99 O9 **Douds** Iowa U.S.A.
21 K7 **Doué-la-Fontaine** Maine-et-Loire France
85 D6 **Douentza** Mali
144 A7 **Doughboy Bay** New Zealand
138 D3 **Douglas** *R* South Australia Australia
119 S9 **Douglas** Manitoba Canada
121 O7 **Douglas** Ontario Canada
89 C7 **Douglas** S Africa
12 E3 **Douglas** Scotland
12 D5 **Douglas** I of Man U.K.
117 F6 **Douglas** Alaska U.S.A.
103 P10 **Douglas** Arizona U.S.A.
112 E6 **Douglas** Georgia U.S.A.
99 U7 **Douglas** Michigan U.S.A.
98 K9 **Douglas** Nebraska U.S.A.
98 E2 **Douglas** North Dakota U.S.A.
100 E2 **Douglas** Washington U.S.A.
98 A7 **Douglas** Wyoming U.S.A.
117 J9 **Douglas Chan** British Columbia Canada
106 B2 **Douglas Cr** Colorado U.S.A.
112 D1 **Douglas Dam** Tennessee U.S.A.
94 C1 **Douglas L** Michigan U.S.A.
112 D2 **Douglas L** Tennessee U.S.A.
12 E2 **Douglas Mill** Scotland
143 E8 **Douglas,Mount** W Australia Australia
116 L7 **Douglas, Mt** Alaska U.S.A.
120 J8 **Douglas Pt** Ontario Canada
107 O4 **Douglass** Kansas U.S.A.
122 G6 **Douglastown** New Brunswick Canada
122 H5 **Douglastown** Quebec Canada
111 M8 **Douglasville** Georgia U.S.A.
22 F3 **Doui** Belgium
46 D6 **Doukáton,Akr** *C* Greece
19 J4 **Doulevant le Château** France
21 P1 **Doullens** France
20 H7 **Doulon** France
14 A5 **Doulus Hd** Ireland
86 B5 **Doumé** Cameroon
67 D5 **Doumen** China
67 A5 **Doumuge** China
12 D1 **Doune** Scotland
15 E2 **Dounreay** Scotland
85 C7 **Douobé** *R* Liberia
37 P3 **Doupov** Czechoslovakia
22 F3 **Dour** France
130 E6 **Dourada, Cachoeira** *rapids* Brazil
129 J6 **Dourada,Serra** *mts* Brazil
130 E5 **Dourada,Serra** *mts* Brazil
130 B6 **Dourados** Brazil
130 C8 **Dourados** Brazil
133 F2 **Dourados** *R* Brazil
130 D8 **Dourados,Serra dos** *mts* Brazil
21 P4 **Dourdan** France
18 G9 **Dourdou** *R* France
22 B3 **Douriez** France
16 C3 **Douro** *R* Portugal
16 B3 **Douro Litoral** *prov* Portugal
Doushi *see* **Gong'an**
19 Q13 **Doussard** France
20 H3 **Douve** *R* France
21 K3 **Douvres-la-Délivrande** France
19 N14 **Doux** *R* France
18 E9 **Douze** *R* France
22 J4 **Douzy** France
45 L3 **Dovadola** Italy
106 B4 **Dove Creek** Colorado U.S.A.
142 C5 **Dove,Mt** W Australia Australia
139 H9 **Dover** Tasmania Australia
28 D4 **Dover** Denmark
9 E1 **Dove,R** England
9 H5 **Dover** England
110 C6 **Dover** Arkansas U.S.A.
95 M7 **Dover** Delaware U.S.A.
113 E9 **Dover** Florida U.S.A.
112 F5 **Dover** Georgia U.S.A.
110 N3 **Dover** Kentucky U.S.A.
95 Q3 **Dover** New Hampshire U.S.A.
95 N6 **Dover** New Jersey U.S.A.
112 K2 **Dover** North Carolina U.S.A.
94 F6 **Dover** Ohio U.S.A.
107 N6 **Dover** Oklahoma U.S.A.
110 J5 **Dover** Tennessee U.S.A.
95 S1 **Dover Foxcroft** Maine U.S.A.
143 F10 **Dover,Pt** W Australia Australia
22 C1 **Dover,Str.of** France/England
38 J9 **Dovje** Slovenia
28 F7 **Dovnsklint** Denmark
26 D9 **Dovre** Norway
26 D9 **Dovrefjell** Norway
26 D9 **Dovrefjell Nat. Park** Norway
88 D8 **Dowa** Malawi
94 A5 **Dowagiac** Michigan U.S.A.
143 B9 **Dowerin** W Australia Australia
Dow, L. *see* **Xau, L.**
8 C4 **Dowlais** Wales
77 J1 **Dowlatābād** Afghanistan
77 H3 **Dowlatābād** Afghanistan
77 E5 **Dowlatābād** Iran
77 J2 **Dowlat Yār** Afghanistan
118 F7 **Dowling** Alberta Canada
14 F2 **Down** *co* N Ireland
99 T8 **Downers Grove** Illinois U.S.A.
102 F8 **Downey** California U.S.A.
101 N7 **Downey** Idaho U.S.A.
141 K1 **Downfall Cr** Brisbane, Qnsld Australia
9 G2 **Downham Market** England
102 D2 **Downieville** California U.S.A.
99 O9 **Downing** Missouri U.S.A.
95 M6 **Downingtown** Pennsylvania U.S.A.
14 F2 **Downpatrick** N Ireland
14 B2 **Downpatrick Hd** Ireland
107 M2 **Downs** Kansas U.S.A.
101 Q6 **Downs Mt** Wyoming U.S.A.
95 M4 **Downsville** New York U.S.A.
9 E5 **Downton** England
117 L9 **Downton,Mt** British Columbia Canada
8 B6 **Downtown** England
99 N7 **Dows** Iowa U.S.A.
77 L2 **Dowshī** Afghanistan
7 L9 **Dowsing Lightship** North Sea
69 C12 **Dowu, Tanjung** *C* Indonesia
102 D1 **Doyle** California U.S.A.
110 L6 **Doyle** Tennessee U.S.A.
144 D5 **Doyleston** New Zealand
95 M6 **Doylestown** Pennsylvania U.S.A.
106 D3 **Doyleville** Colorado U.S.A.
60 F9 **Dōzen** *islds* Japan
59 K4 **Dōzen Nishi Jima** *isld* Japan
111 K10 **Dozier** Alabama U.S.A.
121 N5 **Dozois, Rés** Quebec Canada
21 K3 **Dozulé** France
45 L3 **Dozza** Italy
85 C2 **Drâa** *R* Morocco/Algeria
36 C2 **Drabenderhöhe** Germany
28 F4 **Dråby** Denmark
19 P15 **Drac** *R* France
130 D7 **Dracena** Brazil
46 E3 **Dračevo** Macedonia Yugoslavia
36 E5 **Drachenfels** *mt* Germany
25 F2 **Drachten** Netherlands
95 Q4 **Dracut** Massachusetts U.S.A.
28 F6 **Dræby** Denmark
48 L6 **Dragalina** Romania
26 H7 **Dragan** *L* Sweden
48 J6 **Drăgăneşti-Olt** Romania
48 K6 **Drăgăneşti-Vlaşca** Romania
48 J6 **Drăgăşani** Romania
103 O2 **Dragerton** Utah U.S.A.
46 E3 **Dragoevo** Macedonia Yugoslavia
46 F2 **Dragoman** Bulgaria
45 K2 **Dragoncello** Italy
Dragon's Mouths *chan see* **Bocas del Dragon**
103 O9 **Dragoon** Arizona U.S.A.
29 K5 **Dragør** Denmark
46 F2 **Dragovistica** Bulgaria
29 J11 **Dragsfjärd** Finland
28 B3 **Dragstrup** Denmark
19 Q17 **Draguignan** France
33 T9 **Drahnsdorf** Germany
100 B6 **Drain** Oregon U.S.A.
22 G4 **Draize** France
139 K3 **Drake** New South Wales Australia
119 M7 **Drake** Saskatchewan Canada
103 M7 **Drake** Arizona U.S.A.
98 A9 **Drake** Colorado U.S.A.
98 F2 **Drake** North Dakota U.S.A.
32 K7 **Drakenburg** Germany
89 F8 **Drakensberg** *mts* S Africa
89 G5 **Drakensberg Garden** S Africa
146 B3 **Drake Passage** Antarctica
100 E7 **Drake Peak** *mt* Oregon U.S.A.
102 B4 **Drakes Bay** California U.S.A.
110 J4 **Drakesboro** Kentucky U.S.A.
94 J10 **Drakes Branch** Virginia U.S.A.
46 G3 **Dráma** Greece
27 D12 **Drammen** Norway
27 D12 **Dramsfj** *inlet* Norway
40 F5 **Drance** *R* Switzerland
48 L4 **Drânceni** Romania
27 D12 **Drangedal** Norway
40 E5 **Dranse** *R* France
33 R6 **Dranse** Germany
32 L9 **Dransfeld** Germany
28 C5 **Drantum** Denmark
112 H1 **Draper** North Carolina U.S.A.
98 F6 **Draper** South Dakota U.S.A.
101 O9 **Draper** Utah U.S.A.
117 D6 **Draper, Mt** Alaska U.S.A.
74 F1 **Dras** Kashmir
38 G8 **Drau** *R* Austria
38 N9 **Drava** *R* Slovenia
42 G2 **Dravograd** Slovenia
31 J2 **Drawa** *R* Poland
31 J2 **Drawsko** Poland
141 K8 **Drayton** Queensland Australia
98 J1 **Drayton** North Dakota U.S.A.
118 B5 **Drayton Val** Alberta Canada
37 O5 **Draženov** Czechoslovakia
43 B12 **Dréan** Algeria
37 P2 **Drebach** Germany
32 H7 **Drebber** Germany
48 E2 **Drégelypalánk** Hungary
33 M5 **Dreggers** Germany
36 F3 **Dreieichenhain** Germany
Dreihausen *see* **Ebsdorfergrund**
38 F7 **Dreiherrn-Spitze** *mt* Italy/Austria
36 B3 **Dreis** Germany
40 G1 **Dreisam** *R* Germany
37 P6 **Dreitannenriegel** *mt* Germany
28 E7 **Drejø** Denmark
13 F1 **Drem** Scotland
46 F2 **Dren** Bulgaria
33 T6 **Drense** Germany
32 G9 **Drensteinfurt** Germany
25 G3 **Drenthe** *prov* Netherlands
120 H10 **Dresden** Ontario Canada
37 Q1 **Dresden** Germany
107 K2 **Dresden** Kansas U.S.A.
98 H1 **Dresden** North Dakota U.S.A.
94 E6 **Dresden** Ohio U.S.A.
110 H5 **Dresden** Tennessee U.S.A.
52 C6 **Dretun'** Belorussia
21 N4 **Dreux** France
26 F10 **Drevsjö** Norway
111 F8 **Drew** Mississippi U.S.A.
100 C7 **Drew** Oregon U.S.A.
33 Q5 **Drewitzer See** *L* Germany
100 G6 **Drewsey** Oregon U.S.A.
100 E7 **Drews Res** Oregon U.S.A.
110 B3 **Drexel** Missouri U.S.A.
31 J3 **Drezdenko** Poland
52 E6 **Drezna** Russian Federation
54 K1 **Drezna** Russian Federation
36 E2 **Driedorf** Germany
113 D7 **Drifton** Florida U.S.A.
118 B3 **Driftpile** Alberta Canada
120 J3 **Driftwood** Ontario Canada
94 J5 **Driftwood** Pennsylvania U.S.A.
101 O6 **Driggs** Idaho U.S.A.
141 J7 **Drillham** Queensland Australia
46 D2 **Drim** *R* Serbia Yugoslavia
14 B5 **Drimoleague** Ireland
46 D2 **Drin** *R* Albania
48 E7 **Drina** *R* Bosnia-Herzegovina/Yugoslavia
32 K9 **Dringenberg** Germany
46 D3 **Drinit, Pellgu i** *B* Albania
46 D3 **Drin i zi** *R* Albania
119 M8 **Drinkwater** Saskatchewan Canada
109 J5 **Dripping Springs** Texas U.S.A.
109 K8 **Driscoll** Texas U.S.A.
52 C6 **Drissa** *R* Belorussia
26 D9 **Driva** *R* Norway
26 D9 **Drivstua** Norway
42 G5 **Drniš** Croatia
41 N6 **Dro** Italy
27 E12 **Dröbak** Norway
31 M3 **Drobin** Poland
55 F4 **Drobyshevo** Russian Federation
48 G4 **Drocea** *mt* Romania
32 K5 **Drochtersen** Germany
22 D3 **Drocourt** France
26 H3 **Drog** Norway
32 M6 **Drögen Nindorf** Germany
14 E3 **Drogheda** Ireland
14 E3 **Drogheda B** Ireland
48 H1 **Drogobych** Ukraine
31 O3 **Drohiczyn** Poland
8 D3 **Droitwich** England
48 L2 **Drokiya** Moldavia
36 D1 **Drolshagen** Germany
139 H7 **Dromana** Victoria Australia
14 F2 **Dromara** N Ireland
19 O15 **Drôme** *dept* France
21 J3 **Drome** *R* Calvados France
139 K6 **Dromedary,C** New South Wales Australia
33 O8 **Dromling** Germany
14 D3 **Dromod** Ireland
14 D2 **Dromore** N Ireland
14 C2 **Dromore West** Ireland
44 B3 **Dronero** Italy
9 E1 **Dronfield** England
22 F1 **Drongen** Belgium
18 F7 **Dronne** *R* France
146 J8 **Dronning Fabiolafjella** *ra* Antarctica
28 E2 **Dronninglund** Denmark
146 H4 **Dronning Maud Land** Antarctica
119 Q7 **Dropmore** Manitoba Canada
18 F8 **Dropt** *R* France
31 J7 **Drosendorf** Austria
74 D1 **Drosh** Pakistan
28 G6 **Drøsselbjerg** Denmark
21 N5 **Droué** France
120 E2 **Drowning** *R* Ontario Canada
37 N1 **Droyssig** Germany
21 L3 **Drucourt** France
118 J7 **Druid** Saskatchewan Canada
8 C2 **Druid** Wales
126 A1 **Druif** Aruba W Indies
36 C6 **Drulingen** France
118 E7 **Drumheller** Alberta Canada
14 D4 **Drum Hills** Ireland
14 D3 **Drumlish** Ireland
144 B7 **Drummond** New Zealand
101 M3 **Drummond** Montana U.S.A.
99 P3 **Drummond** Wisconsin U.S.A.
94 D1 **Drummond I** Michigan U.S.A.
95 L10 **Drummond,L** Virginia U.S.A.
140 D4 **Drummond,Mt** N Terr Australia
141 H6 **Drummond Ra** Queensland Australia
121 S7 **Drummondville** Quebec Canada
12 D4 **Drummore** Scotland
15 D3 **Drumnadrochit** Scotland
15 D4 **Drumochter Pass** Scotland
107 O6 **Drumright** Oklahoma U.S.A.
14 C2 **Drumshanbo** Ireland
12 D1 **Drumvaich** Scotland
25 D5 **Drunen** Netherlands
119 V8 **Drunken Point** *C* Manitoba Canada
13 G3 **Druridge B** England
145 E2 **Drury** New Zealand
117 F4 **Drury L** Yukon Territory Canada
36 D6 **Drusenheim** France
31 O1 **Druskininkai** Lithuania
25 E5 **Druten** Netherlands
52 C6 **Druya** Belorussia
54 E4 **Druzhba** Ukraine
51 O2 **Druzhina** Russian Federation
55 C3 **Druzhinino** Russian Federation
54 J8 **Druzhkovka** Ukraine
42 G4 **Drvar** Bosnia-Herzegovina
42 G5 **Drvenik** *isld* Croatia
100 B3 **Dryad** Washington U.S.A.
46 G2 **Dryanovo** Bulgaria
117 D6 **Dry B** Alaska U.S.A.
118 J1 **Dryberry L** Ontario Canada
119 Q2 **Drybrough** Manitoba Canada
101 R5 **Dry Cr** Wyoming U.S.A.
118 K1 **Dryden** Ontario Canada
94 D4 **Dryden** Michigan U.S.A.
95 L4 **Dryden** New York U.S.A.
108 E5 **Dryden** Texas U.S.A.
110 E4 **Dry Fork** *R* Missouri U.S.A.
98 A6 **Dry Fork** *R* Wyoming U.S.A.
146 J13 **Drygalski I.** Antarctica
146 C12 **Drygalski Ice Tongue** *ice tongue* Antarctica
8 C3 **Drygarn Fawr** *mt* Wales
127 K2 **Dry Harbour Mts** Jamaica
102 G2 **Dry L** Nevada U.S.A.
122 F1 **Drylake** Labrador, Nfld Canada
103 K5 **Dry Lake** Nevada U.S.A.
103 K4 **Dry Lake Valley** Nevada U.S.A.
12 D1 **Drymen** Scotland
111 D10 **Dry Prong** Louisiana U.S.A.
141 G4 **Dry R** Queensland Australia
140 D1 **Drysdale I** N Terr Australia
142 F2 **Drysdale River Nat Park** W Australia Australia
113 E13 **Dry Tortugas** *islds* Florida U.S.A.
85 G7 **Dschang** Cameroon
99 V5 **Dtblin** Michigan U.S.A.
86 D5 **Dua** *R* Zaire
127 K9 **Duaca** Venezuela
67 C4 **Du'an** China
Duancun *see* **Wuxiang**
95 N2 **Duane** New York U.S.A.
141 J6 **Duaringa** Queensland Australia
127 J5 **Duarte, Pico** *mt* Dominican Rep
130 E8 **Duartina** Brazil
130 D8 **Duas Onças,Ilha das** Brazil
20 D5 **Duault** France
109 P3 **Dubach** Louisiana U.S.A.
77 D7 **Dubai** U.A.E.
100 B9 **Dubakella Mt** California U.S.A.
114 J5 **Dubawnt** *R* Northwest Territories Canada
Dubayy *see* **Dubai**
139 J4 **Dubbo** New South Wales Australia
56 C1 **Dubches** *R* Russian Federation
37 O4 **Dubec** Czechoslovakia
33 T9 **Duben** Germany
55 C5 **Dubenskiy** Russian Federation
12 B1 **Dubh Artach** *isld* Scotland
48 G1 **Dubiecko** Poland
57 K3 **Dubin** Kazakhstan
124 F2 **Dublán** Mexico
120 J9 **Dublin** Ontario Canada
14 E3 **Dublin** *co* Ireland
14 E3 **Dublin** Ireland
112 E5 **Dublin** Georgia U.S.A.
94 B7 **Dublin** Indiana U.S.A.
111 F7 **Dublin** Mississippi U.S.A.
94 D6 **Dublin** Ohio U.S.A.
109 J3 **Dublin** Texas U.S.A.
52 E6 **Dubna** *R* Russian Federation
54 H2 **Dubna** Russian Federation
101 N5 **Dubois** Idaho U.S.A.
99 K9 **Du Bois** Nebraska U.S.A.
94 J5 **Du Bois** Pennsylvania U.S.A.
101 Q6 **Dubois** Wyoming U.S.A.
48 M3 **Dubossary** Moldavia
54 K3 **Dubovka** Russian Federation
85 B7 **Dubréka** Guinea
54 E3 **Dubrovka** Russian Federation
42 J6 **Dubrovnik** Croatia
54 B2 **Dubrovno** Belorussia
55 E2 **Dubrovnoye** Russian Federation
119 P8 **Dubuc** Saskatchewan Canada
99 Q7 **Dubuque** Iowa U.S.A.
52 G6 **Dub'yazy** Russian Federation
20 F6 **Duc,Etang au** *L* France
20 H4 **Ducey** France
67 E2 **Duchang** China
121 Q3 **Ducharme** Quebec Canada
30 H5 **Duchcov** Czechoslovakia
33 T5 **Ducherow** Germany
101 P9 **Duchesne** Utah U.S.A.
140 E5 **Duchess** Queensland Australia
118 F8 **Duchess** Alberta Canada
141 F1 **Ducie** *R* Queensland Australia
135 O11 **Ducie I** Pacific Oc
110 J6 **Duck** *R* Tennessee U.S.A.
119 R6 **Duck Bay** Manitoba Canada
111 G8 **Duck Hill** Mississippi U.S.A.
118 L6 **Duck Lake** Saskatchewan Canada
119 Q7 **Duck Mt** *ra* Manitoba Canada
119 R7 **Duck Mt. Prov. Park** Manitoba Canada
112 C2 **Ducktown** Tennessee U.S.A.
103 J3 **Duckwater** Nevada U.S.A.
103 J3 **Duckwater Pk** Nevada U.S.A.
21 M3 **Duclair** France
102 E6 **Ducor** California U.S.A.
127 L4 **Ducos** Martinique W Indies
9 F2 **Duddington** England
22 L5 **Dudelange** Luxembourg
36 B4 **Dudeldorf** Germany
32 M9 **Duderstadt** Germany
109 P3 **Dudgemona** *R* Louisiana U.S.A.
7 L9 **Dudgeon Lightship** North Sea
50 H2 **Dudinka** Russian Federation
8 D2 **Dudley** England
112 D5 **Dudley** Georgia U.S.A.
110 F5 **Dudley** Missouri U.S.A.
54 G3 **Dudorovskiy** Russian Federation
47 N10 **Dudullu** Turkey
36 C5 **Dudweiler** Germany
51 J1 **Dudypta** *R* Russian Federation
22 E1 **Dudzele** Belgium
85 C7 **Duékoué** Ivory Coast
16 D3 **Dueñas** Spain
16 C2 **Duerna** *R* Spain
17 F3 **Duero** *R* Spain
112 E3 **Due West** South Carolina U.S.A.
146 D10 **Dufek Coast** Antarctica
119 O8 **Duff** Saskatchewan Canada
22 H1 **Duffel** Belgium
138 C2 **Duffield** *R* N Terr Australia
140 C7 **Duffield** N Terr Australia
118 C5 **Duffield** Alberta Canada
137 O3 **Duff Is** Santa Cruz Is
15 E3 **Dufftown** Scotland
122 F2 **Dufresne,L** Quebec Canada
122 G2 **Dufresne Lake** Quebec Canada
100 D4 **Dufur** Oregon U.S.A.
140 F5 **Dugald** *R* Queensland Australia
103 N7 **Dugas** Arizona U.S.A.
111 D9 **Dugdemona** *R* Louisiana U.S.A.
110 J2 **Dugger** Indiana U.S.A.
42 F4 **Dugi O** Croatia
54 H2 **Dugna** Russian Federation
141 G1 **Dugong I** Gt Barrier Reef Aust
118 E6 **Duhamel** Alberta Canada
131 D2 **Duice, R** Argentina
128 E3 **Duida, Co** *mt* Venezuela
141 F2 **Duifken Pt** Queensland Australia

32 L8 **Duingen** Germany
32 E10 **Duisburg** Germany
25 A5 **Duiveland** Netherlands
67 C4 **Dujiang** China
86 H5 **Dujuuma** Somalia
46 E2 **Dukat** Serbia/Macedonia Yugoslavia
107 L7 **Duke** Oklahoma U.S.A.
117 H8 **Duke I** Alaska U.S.A.
141 K5 **Duke Is** Queensland Australia
135 N10 **Duke of Gloucester Is** Pacific Oc
142 F4 **Dukes Dome** *mt* W Australia Australia
86 F4 **Duk Faiwil** Sudan
77 B7 **Dukhān** Qatar
53 G8 **Dukhovnitskoye** Russian Federation
54 D1 **Dukhovshchina** Russian Federation
59 L1 **Duki** Russian Federation
31 N6 **Dukla** Poland
52 C6 **Dukstas** Lithuania
111 F12 **Dulac** Louisiana U.S.A.
58 C4 **Dulan** China
8 B1 **Dulas B** Wales
71 G7 **Dulawan** Mindanao Philippines
116 K4 **Dulbi** *R* Alaska U.S.A.
106 D5 **Dulce** New Mexico U.S.A.
80 G7 **Duleilat el Muterat** Jordan
51 N2 **Dulgalakh** *R* Russian Federation
47 J1 **Dŭlgopol** Bulgaria
141 F1 **Dulhunty** *R* Queensland Australia
70 D3 **Dulit Ra** Sarawak
67 C4 **Duliu Jiang** *R* China
71 G5 **Duljugan Pt** Leyte Philippines
25 F6 **Dülken** Germany
75 P6 **Dullabchara** India
98 B6 **Dull Center** Wyoming U.S.A.
32 F9 **Dülmen** Germany
67 A5 **Dulong** China
47 J1 **Dulovo** Bulgaria
99 O3 **Duluth** Minnesota U.S.A.
8 C5 **Dulverton** England
71 F6 **Dumaguete** Negros Philippines
69 E12 **Dumai** Sumatra
47 J6 **Dumanlı Dağı** *mt* Turkey
71 F7 **Dumanquilas B** Mindanao Philippines
71 D5 **Dumaran** *isld* Philippines
139 K3 **Dumaresq** *R* New S Wales/Queensland
111 E8 **Dumas** Arkansas U.S.A.
108 C8 **Dumas** Texas U.S.A.
79 G5 **Dumayr** Syria
79 G5 **Dumayr,Jebel** *mts* Syria
83 K10 **Dumbanagala** *mt* Sri Lanka
12 D2 **Dumbarton** Scotland
48 F2 **Ďumbier** *mt* Czechoslovakia
143 C10 **Dumbleyung** W Australia Australia
143 C10 **Dumbleyung, L** W Australia Australia
86 B3 **Dumboa** Nigeria
48 J4 **Dumbrăveni** Romania
48 L5 **Dumbrăveni** Romania
69 H12 **Dumdum** *isld* Indonesia
Dumfries *co see* **Dumfries and Galloway** *reg*
12 E3 **Dumfries** Scotland
15 D5 **Dumfries and Galloway** *reg* Scotland
54 G3 **Duminichi** Russian Federation
48 K5 **Dumitreşti** Romania
75 M6 **Dumka** India
119 N9 **Dummer** Saskatchewan Canada
32 H7 **Dümmersee** *L* Germany
71 J4 **Dumoga** Sulawesi
71 H4 **Dumoga Ketjil** Sulawesi
121 N6 **Dumoine, L** Quebec Canada
98 K4 **Dumont** Minnesota U.S.A.
146 E14 **Dumont d'Urville** *France Base* Antarctica
121 O6 **Dumont,L** Quebec Canada
36 B3 **Dümpelfeld** Germany
65 J1 **Dumune** China
79 B7 **Dumyât** Egypt
48 E4 **Duna** *R* Hungary
48 D3 **Dunaj** *R* Czechoslovakia
31 M6 **Dunajec** *R* Poland
14 E3 **Dunany Pt** Ireland
48 E4 **Dunapataj** Hungary
48 L6 **Dunărea** *R* Romania
48 E4 **Dunaújváros** Hungary
48 F5 **Dunav** *R* S Europe
46 F1 **Dunavtsi** Bulgaria
48 K2 **Dunayevtsy** Ukraine
144 C6 **Dunback** New Zealand
141 F3 **Dunbar** Queensland Australia
13 F1 **Dunbar** Scotland
107 P7 **Dunbar** Oklahoma U.S.A.
101 N9 **Dunbar** Utah U.S.A.
94 F8 **Dunbar** West Virginia U.S.A.
99 S4 **Dunbar** Wisconsin U.S.A.
Dunbarton *co see* **Strathclyde** *reg*
118 L7 **Dunblane** Saskatchewan Canada
12 E1 **Dunblane** Scotland
14 E3 **Dunboyne** Ireland
100 B1 **Duncan** British Columbia Canada
6 M6 **Duncan** *oil rig* North Sea
103 P9 **Duncan** Arizona U.S.A.
98 J8 **Duncan** Nebraska U.S.A.
107 N7 **Duncan** Oklahoma U.S.A.
101 Q6 **Duncan** Wyoming U.S.A.
141 F1 **Duncan Is** Queensland Australia
117 R4 **Duncan L** Northwest Territories Canada
140 A3 **Duncan, Mt** N Terr Australia
14 E4 **Duncannon** Ireland
95 K6 **Duncannon** Pennsylvania U.S.A.
68 A7 **Duncan Passage** Andaman Is
112 C3 **Duncan Ridge** Georgia U.S.A.
127 K1 **Duncans** Jamaica
15 E2 **Duncansby Hd** Scotland
126 G3 **Duncan Town** Bahamas
109 N10 **Duncanville** Texas U.S.A.
9 E3 **Dunchurch** England
13 F6 **Duncombe** England
9 F6 **Duncton** England
52 B6 **Dundaga** Latvia
120 K8 **Dundalk** Ontario Canada
14 E2 **Dundalk** Ireland
14 E3 **Dundalk B** Ireland
147 F6 **Dundas** Northwest Territories Canada
115 N2 **Dundas** Greenland
94 E7 **Dundas** Ohio U.S.A.
117 H8 **Dundas I** British Columbia Canada
143 D9 **Dundas L** W Australia Australia
140 B1 **Dundas Str** N Terr Australia
89 G7 **Dundee** S Africa
13 F1 **Dundee** Scotland
94 D5 **Dundee** Michigan U.S.A.
95 L4 **Dundee** New York U.S.A.
109 J2 **Dundee** Texas U.S.A.
26 G5 **Dunderlands-dal** *V* Norway
Dund Hot *see* **Zhenglan Qi**
141 G8 **Dundoo** Queensland Australia
12 E4 **Dundrennan** Scotland
14 F2 **Dundrum** N Ireland
14 F2 **Dundrum B** N Ireland
118 L7 **Dundurn** Saskatchewan Canada
144 C7 **Dunedin** New Zealand
113 E9 **Dunedin** Florida U.S.A.
139 J4 **Dunedoo** New South Wales Australia
57 J1 **Dunenbay** Kazakhstan
14 D1 **Dunfanaghy** Ireland
15 E4 **Dunfermline** Scotland
120 J9 **Dungannon** Ontario Canada
14 E2 **Dungannon** N Ireland
74 E7 **Dungarpur** India
14 D4 **Dungarvan** Ireland
14 D4 **Dungarvan Harb** Ireland
9 G6 **Dungeness** England
133 D8 **Dungeness,Pta** Arg/Chile
14 E2 **Dungiven** N Ireland
14 C2 **Dungloe** Ireland
139 K4 **Dungog** New South Wales Australia
86 E5 **Dungu** Zaire
69 F10 **Dungun** Malaysia
86 G1 **Dungunab** Sudan
142 G3 **Dunham** *R* W Australia Australia
9 F1 **Dunham** England
59 J3 **Dunhua** China
58 B3 **Dunhuang** China
141 J7 **Dunkeld** Queensland Australia
138 F6 **Dunkeld** Victoria Australia
15 E4 **Dunkeld** Scotland
106 E9 **Dunken** New Mexico U.S.A.
22 C1 **Dunkerque** France
Dunkirk *see* **Dunkerque**
119 M8 **Dunkirk** Saskatchewan Canada
110 L1 **Dunkirk** Indiana U.S.A.
101 O1 **Dunkirk** Montana U.S.A.
121 L10 **Dunkirk** New York U.S.A.
86 G3 **Dunkur** Ethiopia
85 D7 **Dunkwa** Ghana
14 E3 **Dún Laoghaire** Ireland
99 L8 **Dunlap** Iowa U.S.A.
107 O3 **Dunlap** Kansas U.S.A.
106 F7 **Dunlap** New Mexico U.S.A.
108 G1 **Dunlap** Texas U.S.A.
14 E3 **Dunlavin** Ireland
109 J6 **Dunlay** Texas U.S.A.
14 E3 **Dunleer** Ireland
18 G6 **Dun-le-Palestel** France
6 L1 **Dunlin** *oil rig* North Sea
119 T4 **Dunlop** Manitoba Canada
120 J9 **Dunlop** Ontario Canada
12 D2 **Dunlop** Scotland
14 B5 **Dunmanus B** Ireland
14 B5 **Dunmanway** Ireland
140 C3 **Dunmarra Roadhouse** N Terr Australia
14 C3 **Dunmore** Ireland
95 M5 **Dunmore** Pennsylvania U.S.A.
113 L12 **Dunmore Town** Bahamas
126 F2 **Dunmore Town** Eleuthera Bahamas
9 G4 **Dunmow** England
112 J2 **Dunn** North Carolina U.S.A.
98 D2 **Dunn Center** North Dakota U.S.A.
99 M6 **Dunnell** Minnesota U.S.A.
113 E8 **Dunnellon** Florida U.S.A.
15 E2 **Dunnet B** Scotland
15 E2 **Dunnet Hd** Scotland
12 E1 **Dunning** Scotland
98 F8 **Dunning** Nebraska U.S.A.
36 E7 **Dunningen** Germany
143 C6 **Dunns Ra** W Australia Australia
120 G6 **Dunn Valley** Ontario Canada
121 L10 **Dunnville** Ontario Canada
139 G6 **Dunolly** Victoria Australia
12 D2 **Dunoon** Scotland
100 J9 **Dunphy** Nevada U.S.A.
14 A4 **Dunquin** Ireland
84 J5 **Dunqul Oasis** Egypt
120 G4 **Dunrankin** Ontario Canada
119 S9 **Dunrea** Manitoba Canada
13 F2 **Duns** Scotland
144 D5 **Dunsandel** New Zealand
143 B10 **Dunsborough** W Australia Australia
98 G1 **Dunseith** North Dakota U.S.A.
100 C8 **Dunsmuir** California U.S.A.
9 F4 **Dunstable** England
144 B6 **Dunstan Mts** New Zealand
117 O9 **Dunster** British Columbia Canada
8 C5 **Dunster** England
31 K7 **Dun Streda** Czechoslovakia
18 G6 **Dun sur Auron** France
22 J5 **Dun-sur-Meuse** France
120 K8 **Duntroon** Ontario Canada
144 C6 **Duntroon** New Zealand
36 D6 **Duntzenheim** France
15 B3 **Dunvegan** Scotland
15 B3 **Dunvegan,L** Scotland
123 T6 **Dunville** Newfoundland Canada
9 H3 **Dunwich** England
58 G3 **Duolun** China
76 D3 **Dūpādu** India
67 D4 **Dupang Ling** *mts* China
121 L4 **Duparquet** Quebec Canada
69 J11 **Duperre I** Indonesia
94 B8 **Dupont** Indiana U.S.A.
95 M5 **Dupont** Pennsylvania U.S.A.
98 E4 **Dupree** South Dakota U.S.A.
121 L4 **Dupuy** Quebec Canada
142 B5 **Dupuy,C** W Australia Australia
101 N1 **Dupuyer** Montana U.S.A.
130 G8 **Duque de Caxias** Brazil
133 B8 **Duque de York,I** Chile
103 O10 **Duquesne** Arizona U.S.A.
94 H6 **Duquesne** Pennsylvania U.S.A.
110 G3 **Du Quoin** Illinois U.S.A.
80 D7 **Dura** Jordan
41 M2 **Durach** Germany
142 F3 **Durack,R** W Australia Australia
142 F3 **Durack Ra** W Australia Australia
78 E1 **Durağan** Turkey
141 K7 **Durah** Queensland Australia
47 J5 **Durak** Turkey
106 E7 **Duran** New Mexico U.S.A.
19 Q16 **Durance** *R* France
99 R7 **Durand** Illinois U.S.A.
94 D4 **Durand** Michigan U.S.A.
99 P5 **Durand** Wisconsin U.S.A.
124 G5 **Durango** Mexico
18 D9 **Durango** Spain
106 C4 **Durango** Colorado U.S.A.
47 J1 **Durankulak** Bulgaria
111 G8 **Durant** Mississippi U.S.A.
107 O8 **Durant** Oklahoma U.S.A.
16 E3 **Duratón** *R* Spain
131 G4 **Durazno** *dept* Uruguay
131 G4 **Durazno** Uruguay
Durazzo *see* **Durrës**
89 G7 **Durban** S Africa
56 C6 **Durbat-Daba, Pereval** *pass* Mongolia/Rus Fed
27 M15 **Durbe** Latvia
94 H8 **Durbin** West Virginia U.S.A.
22 J3 **Durbuy** Belgium
16 E8 **Dúrcal** Spain
36 B2 **Düren** Germany
75 J8 **Durg** India
75 M7 **Durgapur** India
120 K8 **Durham** Ontario Canada
121 S7 **Durham** Quebec Canada
13 G4 **Durham** *co* England
13 G4 **Durham** England
102 C2 **Durham** California U.S.A.
107 N3 **Durham** Kansas U.S.A.
95 R3 **Durham** New Hampshire U.S.A.
112 J2 **Durham** North Carolina U.S.A.
122 F7 **Durham Br** New Brunswick Canada
141 F7 **Durham Downs** Queensland Australia
12 E3 **Durisdeer** Scotland
100 H5 **Durkee** Oregon U.S.A.
36 E6 **Durlach** Germany
9 E6 **Durlston Hd** England
36 E6 **Durmersheim** Germany
42 J5 **Durmitor** *mt* Montenegro Yugoslavia
15 D2 **Durness** Scotland
38 N5 **Durnstein** Austria
123 L3 **Durocher,L** Quebec Canada
38 M6 **Durrenstein** *mt* Austria
46 C3 **Durrës** Albania
46 C3 **Durrësit, Gjiri i** *B* Albania
140 F7 **Durrie** Queensland Australia
14 D4 **Durrow** Ireland
37 J5 **Dürrwangen** Germany
14 A5 **Dursey Hd** Ireland
14 A5 **Dursey I** Ireland
8 D4 **Dursley** England
8 C5 **Durston** England
47 K5 **Dursunbey** Turkey
21 K6 **Durtal** France
Duru *see* **Wuchuan**
28 B3 **Durup** Denmark
47 K3 **Durusu Gölü** *L* Turkey
79 G6 **Durūz, Jabal ad** *mts* Syria
145 D4 **D'Urville I** New Zealand
77 J2 **Durzab** Afghanistan
120 D1 **Dusey** *R* Ontario Canada
57 A6 **Dushak** Turkmenistan
67 B4 **Dushan** China
57 E5 **Dushanbe** Tajikistan
65 C4 **Dushikou** China
95 L5 **Dushore** Pennsylvania U.S.A.
47 J2 **Dŭskotna** Bulgaria
144 A6 **Dusky Sd** New Zealand
32 E10 **Düsseldorf** Germany
25 C5 **Dussen** Netherlands
41 J4 **Düssist** *mt* Switzerland
33 R9 **Düssnitz** Germany
107 O6 **Dustin** Oklahoma U.S.A.
83 J9 **Dutch B** Sri Lanka
Dutch Guiana *see* **Surīname**
116 D10 **Dutch Harbor** Aleutian Is
101 M9 **Dutch Mt** Utah U.S.A.
89 C4 **Dutlwe** Botswana
52 J3 **Dutovo** Russian Federation
85 F6 **Dutsan Wai** Nigeria
141 G5 **Dutton** *R* Queensland Australia
120 J10 **Dutton** Ontario Canada
101 O2 **Dutton** Montana U.S.A.
138 D4 **Dutton,L** South Australia Australia
103 M3 **Dutton,Mt** Utah U.S.A.
119 N7 **Duval** Saskatchewan Canada
127 H5 **Duvalierville** Haiti
121 N6 **Duval,L** Quebec Canada
55 C3 **Duvan** Russian Federation
144 D5 **Duvauchelle** New Zealand
26 F8 **Duved** Sweden
127 J5 **Duvergé** Dominican Rep
52 D3 **Duvogero** Russian Federation
22 D5 **Duvy** France
95 R4 **Duxbury** Massachusetts U.S.A.
9 G3 **Duxford** England
67 B4 **Duyang Shan** *mts* China
68 C4 **Duyinzeik** Burma
67 B3 **Duyun** China
78 C1 **Düzce** Turkey
47 H1 **Dve Mogili** Bulgaria
26 H2 **Dverberg** Norway
52 F3 **Dvina, Severnaya** *R* Russian Federation
52 E2 **Dvinskaya Guba** *B* Russian Federation
54 C1 **Dvin'ye,Oz** *L* Russian Federation
31 K6 **Dvorec** Czechoslovakia
31 J5 **Dvůr Králové** Czechoslovakia
88 D8 **Dwangwa** *R* Malawi
143 B10 **Dwarda** W Australia Australia
74 C7 **Dwarka** India
89 E5 **Dwars Berg** *mts* S Africa
143 B10 **Dwellingup** W Australia Australia
99 S8 **Dwight** Illinois U.S.A.
107 O3 **Dwight** Kansas U.S.A.
98 J8 **Dwight** Nebraska U.S.A.
94 F9 **Dwight** Virginia U.S.A.
100 K3 **Dworshak Res.** Idaho U.S.A.
106 C9 **Dwyer** New Mexico U.S.A.
98 B7 **Dwyer** Wyoming U.S.A.
54 F3 **Dyat'kovo** Russian Federation
28 D7 **Dybbøl** Denmark
28 A3 **Dybe Kirke** Denmark
28 H6 **Dybsø Fjord** *inlet* Denmark
119 R4 **Dyce** Manitoba Canada
15 F3 **Dyce** Scotland
99 T5 **Dyckesville** Wisconsin U.S.A.
110 H5 **Dyer** Tennessee U.S.A.
114 G2 **Dyer B** Northwest Territories Canada
120 J7 **Dyer Bay** Ontario Canada
110 G5 **Dyersburg** Tennessee U.S.A.
99 P7 **Dyersville** Iowa U.S.A.
8 B3 **Dyfed** *co* Wales
8 B2 **Dyfi** *R* Wales
31 J1 **Dygowo** Poland
31 J7 **Dyje** *R* Czechoslovakia
53 F11 **Dykhtau** *mt* Georgia/Rus Fed
22 H2 **Dyle** *R* Belgium
9 G5 **Dymchurch** England
118 K1 **Dyment** Ontario Canada
8 D4 **Dymock** England
141 G8 **Dynevor Downs** Queensland Australia
31 N6 **Dynów** Poland
102 F4 **Dyor** Nevada U.S.A.
28 E6 **Dyreborg** Denmark
26 C8 **Dyrnesvågen** Norway
26 J2 **Dyröy** Norway
119 N8 **Dysart** Saskatchewan Canada
13 E1 **Dysart** Scotland
99 O7 **Dysart** Iowa U.S.A.
47 J2 **Dyulevo** Bulgaria
47 J2 **Dyulino** Bulgaria
78 L1 **Dyul'tydag** *mt* Russian Federation
57 C2 **Dyurmen'tyube** Kazakhstan
58 D2 **Dzaanhushuu** Mongolia
58 C2 **Dzag** Mongolia
58 F3 **Dzamïn Üüde** Mongolia
87 H10 **Dzaoudzi** Comoros
56 E6 **Dzargal Hid** Mongolia
58 C2 **Dzavhan Gol** *R* Mongolia
30 H5 **Džban** *mt* Czechoslovakia
54 J8 **Dzerzhinsk** Ukraine
57 K2 **Dzerzhinskoye** Kazakhstan
59 K1 **Dzhagdy,Khrebet** *mts* Russian Federation
56 D5 **Dzhakul', Gora** *mt* Russian Federation
57 G4 **Dzhalal-Abad** Kyrgyzstan
59 H1 **Dzhalinda** Russian Federation
55 B5 **Dzhambeyty** Kazakhstan
57 C4 **Dzhankel'dy** Uzbekistan
57 J2 **Dzhansugurov** Kazakhstan
56 D5 **Dzhebashskiy Khrebet** *mts* Russian Federation
46 G3 **Dzhebel** Bulgaria
57 J3 **Dzhergalan** Kyrgyzstan
55 D5 **Dzhetygara** Kazakhstan
57 C4 **Dzhetymtau, Gory** *mt* Uzbekistan
57 D1 **Dzhezdy** Kazakhstan
57 E1 **Dzhezkazgan** Kazakhstan
56 G5 **Dzhida** *R* Russian Federation
56 F5 **Dzhidinskiy,Khrebet** *mts* Mongolia/Rus Fed
57 B4 **Dzhigirbent** Turkmenistan
57 E4 **Dzhizak** Uzbekistan
56 D4 **Dzhoyskiy Khrebet** *mts* Russian Federation
57 D5 **Dzhuma** Uzbekistan
57 K2 **Dzhungarskiy Alatau, Khrebet** *mts* Kazakhstan
48 L2 **Dzhurin** Ukraine
57 C2 **Dzhusaly** Kazakhstan
31 M2 **Działdowo** Poland
31 M5 **Działoszyce** Poland
31 L4 **Działoszyn** Poland
31 L2 **Dzierżgoń** Poland
31 K5 **Dzierżoniów** Poland
125 O7 **Dzitbalché** Mexico
31 H1 **Dziwnów** Poland
56 E5 **Dzöölon** Mongolia
52 B6 **Džūkste** Latvia
66 C3 **Dzungaria** *reg* China
66 C2 **Dzungarian Gate** *pass* China/Kazakhstan
58 E3 **Dzüünbayan** Mongolia
65 C1 **Dzüünbulag** Mongolia
58 B2 **Dzüyl** Mongolia

E

106 H3 **Eads** Colorado U.S.A.
103 P7 **Eagar** Arizona U.S.A.
101 T10 **Eagle** Colorado U.S.A.
100 J6 **Eagle** Idaho U.S.A.
110 M3 **Eagle** *R* Kentucky U.S.A.
98 K9 **Eagle** Nebraska U.S.A.
99 S7 **Eagle** Wisconsin U.S.A.
101 R5 **Eagle** Wyoming U.S.A.
98 E4 **Eagle Butte** South Dakota U.S.A.
107 M6 **Eagle City** Oklahoma U.S.A.
102 G6 **Eagle Crags** California U.S.A.
121 O6 **Eagle Depot** Quebec Canada
141 K1 **Eagle Farm** *dist* Brisbane, Qnsld Australia
99 N7 **Eagle Grove** Iowa U.S.A.
99 S2 **Eagle Harbor** Michigan U.S.A.
139 J9 **Eaglehawk Neck** Tasmania Australia
119 O1 **Eaglehead L** Ontario Canada
119 T5 **Eagle I** Manitoba Canada
118 J1 **Eagle L** Ontario Canada
100 E9 **Eagle L** California U.S.A.
95 S6 **Eagle L** Maine U.S.A.
95 R7 **Eagle L** Maine U.S.A.
113 F10 **Eagle Lake** Florida U.S.A.
109 L6 **Eagle Lake** Texas U.S.A.
103 J8 **Eagle Mts** California U.S.A.
106 E5 **Eagle Nest** New Mexico U.S.A.
108 G7 **Eagle Pass** Texas U.S.A.
100 E8 **Eagle Peak** *mt* California U.S.A.
114 F4 **Eagle Plain** Yukon Territory Canada
100 C7 **Eagle Point** Oregon U.S.A.
99 S2 **Eagle River** Michigan U.S.A.
99 R4 **Eagle River** Wisconsin U.S.A.
94 H9 **Eagle Rock** Virginia U.S.A.
12 D2 **Eaglesham** Scotland
137 Q4 **Eaglestone Reef** Pacific Oc
116 O4 **Eagle Summit** Alaska U.S.A.
103 L8 **Eagle Tail Mts** Arizona U.S.A.
109 N1 **Eagleton** Arkansas U.S.A.
107 Q7 **Eagletown** Oklahoma U.S.A.
100 E8 **Eagleville** California U.S.A.
71 L10 **Eahun** Roti Indonesia
61 O7 **Eai-gawa** *R* Japan
68 H6 **Ea Kan** *R* Vietnam
9 F4 **Ealing** England
144 C6 **Ealing** New Zealand
143 D7 **Earaheedy** W Australia Australia
8 D3 **Eardisland** England
117 L11 **Ear Lakes Cove** British Columbia Canada
110 F6 **Earle** Arkansas U.S.A.
99 M8 **Earlham** Iowa U.S.A.
102 E6 **Earlimart** California U.S.A.
99 L8 **Earling** Iowa U.S.A.
110 J4 **Earlington** Kentucky U.S.A.
100 A8 **Earl,L** California U.S.A.
144 A6 **Earl Mts** New Zealand
13 F2 **Earlston** Scotland
121 L5 **Earlton** Ontario Canada
99 S8 **Earlville** Illinois U.S.A.
99 P7 **Earlville** Iowa U.S.A.
13 E1 **Earn,Br.of** Scotland
117 F4 **Earn L** Yukon Territory Canada
12 D1 **Earn,L** Scotland
12 E1 **Earn,R** Scotland
144 B6 **Earnslaw, Mt** New Zealand
103 K7 **Earp** California U.S.A.
13 G3 **Earsdon** England
9 F6 **Easebourne** England
13 G4 **Easington** Durham England
13 J6 **Easington** Humberside England
13 G5 **Easingwold** England
112 E3 **Easley** South Carolina U.S.A.
110 F3 **East Alton** Illinois U.S.A.
121 T7 **East Angus** Quebec Canada
123 M7 **East B** C Breton I, Nova Scotia
113 B7 **East B** Florida U.S.A.
111 G12 **East B** Louisiana U.S.A.
111 B12 **East B** Texas U.S.A.
112 G1 **East Bend** North Carolina U.S.A.
95 L7 **East Berlin** Pennsylvania U.S.A.
109 L6 **East Bernard** Texas U.S.A.
9 G6 **Eastbourne** England
145 G4 **Eastbourne** New Zealand
94 H6 **East Brady** Pennsylvania U.S.A.
8 D5 **East Brent** England
111 J10 **East Brewton** Alabama U.S.A.
71 G6 **East Bucas** Philippines
101 O1 **East Butte** *mt* Montana U.S.A.
127 J4 **East Caicos** *isld* Turks & Caicos Is
145 G2 **East Cape** New Zealand
145 F3 **East Cape** *admin region* New Zealand
99 T8 **East Chicago** Indiana U.S.A.
64 G4 **East China Sea**
145 E2 **East Coast Bays** New Zealand
118 E7 **East Coulee** Alberta Canada
9 G6 **Eastdean** England
9 G2 **East Dereham** England
99 Q7 **East Dubuque** Illinois U.S.A.
103 K2 **East Ely** Nevada U.S.A.
118 J9 **Eastend** Saskatchewan Canada
143 A8 **Easter Grp** *islds* W Australia Australia
135 U16 **Easter I** Pacific Oc
141 F5 **Eastern Creek** Queensland Australia
84 J4 **Eastern Desert** Egypt
86 F4 **Eastern Equatoria** *prov* Sudan
76 C4 **Eastern Ghats** *mts* India
123 S5 **Eastern Meelpaeg** *L* Newfoundland Canada
119 S5 **Easterville** Manitoba Canada
122 E7 **East Florenceville** New Brunswick Canada
120 J3 **Eastford** Ontario Canada
99 Q9 **East Galesburg** Illinois U.S.A.
102 G2 **Eastgate** Nevada U.S.A.
East Germany *see* **Germany**
101 M1 **East Glacier Park** Montana U.S.A.
9 F5 **East Grinstead** England
8 D1 **Eastham** England
95 P6 **East Hampton** Long I, New York U.S.A.
95 P4 **Easthampton** Massachusetts U.S.A.
101 O3 **East Helena** Montana U.S.A.
9 G6 **East Hoathly** England
123 L6 **East I** Madeleine Is, Quebec Canada
9 E4 **East Ilsley** England
95 P4 **East Jaffrey** New Hampshire U.S.A.
147 E12 **East Jan Mayen Rdg** Norwegian Sea
122 J9 **East Jeddore** Nova Scotia Canada
122 G10 **East Jordan** Nova Scotia Canada
94 B1 **East Jordan** Michigan U.S.A.
9 G1 **East Keal** England
122 G9 **East Kemptville** Nova Scotia Canada
12 D2 **East Kilbride** Scotland
95 R6 **East L** Maine U.S.A.
99 U5 **East Lake** Michigan U.S.A.
109 J3 **Eastland** Texas U.S.A.
94 C4 **East Lansing** Michigan U.S.A.
9 E6 **Eastleigh** England
110 N1 **East Liberty** Ohio U.S.A.
13 F2 **East Linton** Scotland
94 G6 **East Liverpool** Ohio U.S.A.
89 E9 **East London** S Africa
East Lothian *co see* **Lothian** *reg*
94 E8 **East Lynn** West Virginia U.S.A.
115 M7 **Eastmain** Quebec Canada
112 D5 **Eastman** Georgia U.S.A.
141 H6 **Eastmere** Queensland Australia
143 E8 **East, Mt** W Australia Australia
8 D3 **Eastnor** England
99 R9 **Easton** Illinois U.S.A.
95 Q4 **Easton** Massachusetts U.S.A.
99 N6 **Easton** Minnesota U.S.A.
110 B2 **Easton** Missouri U.S.A.
95 M6 **Easton** Pennsylvania U.S.A.
100 D2 **Easton** Washington U.S.A.
112 G4 **Eastover** South Carolina U.S.A.
East Pakistan *see* **Bangladesh**
113 F8 **East Palatka** Florida U.S.A.
94 G6 **East Palestine** Ohio U.S.A.
102 B2 **East Park Res** California U.S.A.
99 N8 **East Peru** Iowa U.S.A.
117 N8 **East Pine** British Columbia Canada
123 L6 **East Point** Madeleine Is, Quebec Canada
121 L1 **East Point** Ontario Canada
123 L7 **East Point** Prince Edward I Canada
123 N10 **East Point** Sable I, Nova Scotia
111 M8 **East Point** Georgia U.S.A.
94 E9 **East Point** Kentucky U.S.A.
119 M9 **East Poplar** Saskatchewan Canada
106 E2 **East Portal** Colorado U.S.A.
110 G5 **East Prairie** Missouri U.S.A.
122 G10 **East Pubnico** Nova Scotia Canada
94 G9 **East Rainelle** West Virginia U.S.A.
100 H9 **East Range** Nevada U.S.A.
9 F1 **East Retford** England
9 H5 **Eastry** England
110 F3 **East St Louis** Illinois U.S.A.
147 P5 **East Siberian Sea** Arctic Oc
139 J7 **East Sister I** Tasmania Australia
100 K2 **East Sister Peak** *mt* Idaho U.S.A.
9 F1 **East Stoke** England
8 D5 **East Stour** England
9 G6 **East Sussex** *co* England
94 D2 **East Tawas** Michigan U.S.A.
139 H4 **East Toorale** New South Wales Australia
119 N4 **East Trout L** Saskatchewan Canada
99 S7 **East Troy** Wisconsin U.S.A.
103 N7 **East Verde** *R* Arizona U.S.A.
95 M9 **Eastville** Virginia U.S.A.
13 E1 **East Wemyss** Scotland
9 E1 **East Wood** England
138 C2 **Eateringinna Cr** South Australia Australia
98 B9 **Eaton** Colorado U.S.A.
110 L1 **Eaton** Indiana U.S.A.
110 M2 **Eaton** Ohio U.S.A.
118 H7 **Eatonia** Saskatchewan Canada
94 C4 **Eaton Rapids** Michigan U.S.A.
9 F3 **Eaton Socon** England
112 D4 **Eatonton** Georgia U.S.A.
100 C3 **Eatonville** Washington U.S.A.
17 F9 **Eau, C. de l'** Morocco
99 U7 **Eau Claire** Michigan U.S.A.
99 P5 **Eau Claire** *R* Wisconsin U.S.A.
99 P5 **Eau Claire** Wisconsin U.S.A.
122 G1 **Eau-Claire, L. à l'** Labrador, Nfld Canada
115 M6 **Eau Claire, L. à l'** Quebec Canada
113 G9 **Eau Gallie** Florida U.S.A.
121 Q3 **Eau-Jaune, L. a l'** Quebec Canada
21 N2 **Eaulne** *R* France
134 E7 **Eauripik - New Guinea Rise** Pacific Oc
18 F9 **Eauze** France
141 G2 **Ebagoola** Queensland Australia
125 K6 **Ebano** Mexico
36 D1 **Ebbe** *mts* Germany
13 H5 **Ebberston** England
28 D6 **Ebberup** Denmark
8 C4 **Ebbw Vale** Wales
86 B5 **Ebebiyin** Equat Guinea
33 N10 **Ebeleben** Germany
28 F4 **Ebeltoft** Denmark
28 F4 **Ebeltoft Vig** *B* Denmark
119 P7 **Ebenezer** Saskatchewan Canada
99 U3 **Eben Junction** Michigan U.S.A.
94 J6 **Ebensburg** Pennsylvania U.S.A.
38 J6 **Ebensee** Austria
37 K3 **Ebensfeld** Germany
36 G5 **Eberbach** Germany
78 C2 **Eber Gölü** Turkey
32 M9 **Ebergötzen** Germany
37 L4 **Ebermannstadt** Germany
37 K3 **Ebern** Germany
36 D4 **Ebernburg** Germany
110 M4 **E Bernstadt** Kentucky U.S.A.
36 H6 **Ebersbach** Germany
36 H3 **Ebersburg** Germany
37 L3 **Ebersdorf** Germany
36 F4 **Eberstadt** Germany
38 L8 **Eberstein** Austria
33 T7 **Eberswalde** Germany
60 P2 **Ebetsu** Japan
55 F4 **Ebeyty, Oz** *L* Russian Federation
67 A2 **Ebian** China
36 G7 **Ebingen** Germany
60 D13 **Ebino** Japan
66 C3 **Ebinur Hu** *L* China
79 G3 **Ebla** *anc site* Syria
37 J6 **Ebnat** Germany
41 K3 **Ebnat** Switzerland
86 D5 **Ebola** *R* Zaire
43 G8 **Eboli** Italy
86 B5 **Ebolowa** Cameroon
37 K4 **Ebrach** Germany
9 F2 **E Bridgford** England
44 F2 **Ebro** *mt* Italy
16 E2 **Ebro** *R* Spain
16 E2 **Ebro, Embalse del** *res* Spain
36 E2 **Ebschloh** *mt* Germany
36 F2 **Ebsdorfergrund** Germany
33 M6 **Ebstorf** Germany
22 G2 **Ecaussines** Belgium
13 E3 **Ecclefechan** Scotland
13 F2 **Eccles** Scotland
94 F9 **Eccles** West Virginia U.S.A.
13 G6 **Ecclesfield** England
8 D2 **Eccleshall** England
127 P2 **Ecclesville** Trinidad
47 H4 **Eceabat** Turkey
40 E4 **Echallens** Switzerland
21 L4 **Échauffour** France
85 E1 **Ech Cheliff** Algeria
67 E1 **Echeng** China
101 U5 **Echeta** Wyoming U.S.A.
19 P14 **Échirolles** France
61 J10 **Echizen-misaki** *C* Japan
99 L5 **Echo** Minnesota U.S.A.
100 F4 **Echo** Oregon U.S.A.
101 O9 **Echo** Utah U.S.A.
103 K5 **Echo B** Nevada U.S.A.
120 G6 **Echo Bay** Ontario Canada
103 N5 **Echo Cliffs** Arizona U.S.A.
139 H8 **Echo,L** Tasmania Australia
121 P5 **Échouani L** Quebec Canada
122 H4 **Echouerie, L'** Quebec Canada
119 O8 **Echo Valley Prov. Park** Saskatchewan Canada
25 E6 **Echt** Netherlands
15 F3 **Echt** Scotland
32 M9 **Echte** Germany
25 F3 **Echten** Netherlands
22 L4 **Echternach** Luxembourg
139 G6 **Echuca** Victoria Australia
36 F3 **Echzell** Germany
16 D7 **Écija** Spain
36 H5 **Eckartshausen** Germany
98 H3 **Eckelson** North Dakota U.S.A.
37 L4 **Eckental** Germany
30 E1 **Eckernförde** Germany
109 J5 **Eckert** Texas U.S.A.
13 F3 **Eckford** Scotland
8 D3 **Eckington** England
9 E1 **Eckington** England
12 C1 **Eck,L** Scotland
98 D9 **Eckley** Colorado U.S.A.
94 F9 **Eckman** West Virginia U.S.A.
118 C6 **Eckville** Alberta Canada
32 H5 **Eckwarderhörne** Germany
111 K9 **Eclectic** Alabama U.S.A.
143 C11 **Eclipse I** W Australia Australia
140 B5 **Eclipse, Mt** N Terr Australia
115 M3 **Eclipse Sound** Northwest Territories Canada
21 L6 **Écommoy** France
110 L2 **Economy** Indiana U.S.A.
121 O5 **Écorces,L.aux** Quebec Canada
21 O3 **Ecos** France
21 K4 **Écouché** France
21 N3 **Ecouis** France
21 L4 **Écouves, Forêt d'** France
22 J4 **Ecouviez** Belgium
22 C2 **Ecques** France
20 G3 **Ecréhou, les** English Chan
111 G7 **Ecru** Mississippi U.S.A.
128 C4 **Ecuador** *rep* S America
21 N7 **Écueillé** France
123 K9 **Ecum Secum** Nova Scotia Canada
86 H3 **Ēd** Ethiopia
143 B8 **Edah** W Australia Australia
118 J5 **Edam** Saskatchewan Canada
25 D3 **Edam** Netherlands
15 F1 **Eday** Scotland
118 E6 **Edberg** Alberta Canada
109 K9 **Edcouch** Texas U.S.A.
6 N6 **Edda** *oil rig* North Sea
86 E3 **Ed Da'ein** Sudan
86 F3 **Ed Damazin** Sudan
86 F2 **Ed Damer** Sudan
86 F2 **Ed Debba** Sudan
32 K5 **Eddelak** Germany
123 Q2 **Eddies Cove** Newfoundland Canada
13 E2 **Eddleston** Scotland
15 C2 **Eddrachillis B** Scotland
86 F3 **Ed Dueim** Sudan
100 K2 **Eddy** Montana U.S.A.
109 K4 **Eddy** Texas U.S.A.
8 B7 **Eddystone Lt. Ho** English Chan
139 J8 **Eddystone Pt** Tasmania Australia
99 O8 **Eddyville** Iowa U.S.A.
110 H4 **Eddyville** Kentucky U.S.A.
98 G8 **Eddyville** Nebraska U.S.A.
25 E4 **Ede** Netherlands
85 E7 **Ede** Nigeria
86 B5 **Edéa** Cameroon
27 G11 **Edebäck** Sweden
27 K11 **Edebo** Sweden
130 E5 **Edéia** Brazil
48 F2 **Edelény** Hungary
143 A7 **Edel Land** *pen* W Australia Australia
139 J6 **Eden** New South Wales Australia
119 S8 **Eden** Manitoba Canada
101 O2 **Eden** Montana U.S.A.
94 J4 **Eden** New York U.S.A.
94 H10 **Eden** North Carolina U.S.A.
112 H1 **Eden** North Carolina U.S.A.
98 J4 **Eden** South Dakota U.S.A.
108 H4 **Eden** Texas U.S.A.
101 O8 **Eden** Utah U.S.A.
99 S6 **Eden** Wisconsin U.S.A.
101 Q7 **Eden** Wyoming U.S.A.
9 G5 **Edenbridge** England
89 D7 **Edenburg** S Africa
144 B7 **Edendale** New Zealand
14 D3 **Edenderry** Ireland
13 F6 **Edenfield** England
138 F6 **Edenhope** Victoria Australia
120 J8 **Edenhurst** Ontario Canada
36 E5 **Edenkoben** Germany
119 R2 **Eden L** Manitoba Canada
9 G5 **Eden,R** England
71 N9 **Eden,Tg** *C* Indonesia
112 L1 **Edenton** North Carolina U.S.A.
94 C3 **Edenville** Michigan U.S.A.
119 N8 **Edenwold** Saskatchewan Canada
36 E1 **Eder** *R* Germany
36 G1 **Edermünde** Germany
33 O10 **Edersleben** Germany
36 F1 **Ederstausee** *res* Germany
36 G1 **Edertal** Germany
27 F13 **Edet, L** Sweden
32 G6 **Edewecht** Germany
32 G6 **Edewechterdamm** Germany
101 R4 **Edgar** Montana U.S.A.
98 J9 **Edgar** Nebraska U.S.A.
111 F11 **Edgard** Louisiana U.S.A.
142 D5 **Edgar, Mt** W Australia Australia
142 E4 **Edgar Ra** W Australia Australia
110 E4 **Edgar Springs** Missouri U.S.A.
95 R5 **Edgartown** Massachusetts U.S.A.
109 M9 **Edgecliff** Texas U.S.A.
145 F2 **Edgecumbe** New Zealand
112 F4 **Edgefield** South Carolina U.S.A.
119 O8 **Edgeley** Saskatchewan Canada
98 H3 **Edgeley** North Dakota U.S.A.
115 N5 **Edgell I** Northwest Territories Canada
110 D6 **Edgemont** Arkansas U.S.A.
98 C6 **Edgemont** South Dakota U.S.A.
50 B1 **Edgeöya** *isld* Spitzbergen
109 O5 **Edgerly** Louisiana U.S.A.
118 G6 **Edgerton** Alberta Canada
94 C5 **Edgerton** Ohio U.S.A.
99 R7 **Edgerton** Wisconsin U.S.A.
101 T6 **Edgerton** Wyoming U.S.A.
113 G9 **Edgewater** Florida U.S.A.
117 O11 **Edgewood** British Columbia Canada
110 H3 **Edgewood** Illinois U.S.A.
95 L7 **Edgewood** Maryland U.S.A.
106 D6 **Edgewood** New Mexico U.S.A.
109 M3 **Edgewood** Texas U.S.A.
9 F4 **Edgware** England
80 C8 **Edh Dhahiriya** Jordan
46 E4 **Édhessa** Greece
144 B6 **Edievale** New Zealand
36 C3 **Ediger-Eller** Germany
84 F5 **Edimpi** Chad
99 N5 **Edina** Minnesota U.S.A.
94 G5 **Edinboro** Pennsylvania U.S.A.
99 R10 **Edinburg** Illinois U.S.A.
111 G9 **Edinburg** Mississippi U.S.A.
98 J1 **Edinburg** North Dakota U.S.A.
109 J9 **Edinburg** Texas U.S.A.
94 J8 **Edinburg** Virginia U.S.A.
13 E2 **Edinburgh** Scotland
110 L2 **Edinburgh** Indiana U.S.A.
141 H7 **Edinburgh, Mt** Queensland Australia
22 F2 **Edingen** Belgium
47 H3 **Edirne** Turkey
102 F6 **Edison** California U.S.A.
106 F3 **Edison** Colorado U.S.A.
111 M10 **Edison** Georgia U.S.A.
112 G4 **Edisto** *R* South Carolina U.S.A.
112 G5 **Edisto Island** South Carolina U.S.A.
138 E6 **Edithburgh** South Australia Australia
117 P9 **Edith Cavell,Mt** Alberta Canada
101 O3 **Edith, Mt** Montana U.S.A.
143 D7 **Edith Withnell, L** W Australia Australia
85 F3 **Edjeleh** Algeria
143 D8 **Edjudina** W Australia Australia
13 G3 **Edlingham** England
38 O6 **Edlitz** Austria
95 M4 **Edmeston** New York U.S.A.
107 L2 **Edmond** Kansas U.S.A.
107 N6 **Edmond** Oklahoma U.S.A.
100 C2 **Edmonds** Washington U.S.A.
141 H3 **Edmonton** Queensland Australia
118 D5 **Edmonton** Alberta Canada
9 F4 **Edmonton** England
94 C3 **Edmore** Michigan U.S.A.
98 H1 **Edmore** North Dakota U.S.A.
122 D6 **Edmundston** New Brunswick Canada
109 L7 **Edna** Texas U.S.A.
13 F2 **Ednam** Scotland
27 J13 **Ed, O** Sweden
61 N10 **Edo-gawa** *R* Japan
27 M14 **Edole** Latvia
42 C2 **Edolo** Italy
26 C8 **Edoy** *isld* Norway
47 J5 **Edremit** Turkey
47 H5 **Edremit Körfezi** *B* Turkey
58 C3 **Edrengiyn Nuruu** *mt* Mongolia
109 K8 **Edroy** Texas U.S.A.
27 K12 **Edsbro** Sweden
27 H13 **Edsbruk** Sweden
27 H10 **Edsbyn** Sweden
26 J8 **Edsele** Sweden
58 D3 **Edsin Gol** China
117 P9 **Edson** Alberta Canada
107 J2 **Edson** Kansas U.S.A.
27 J14 **Ed, V** Sweden
118 E4 **Edwand** Alberta Canada
139 G6 **Edward** *R* New South Wales Australia
140 D2 **Edward I** N Terr Australia
120 B4 **Edward I** Ontario Canada
88 B2 **Edward, L** Zaire
140 B6 **Edward, Mt** N Terr Australia
141 F2 **Edward River** Queensland Australia
102 G7 **Edwards** California U.S.A.
99 Q8 **Edwards** *R* Illinois U.S.A.
111 F9 **Edwards** Mississippi U.S.A.
95 M2 **Edwards** New York U.S.A.
94 A5 **Edwardsburg** Michigan U.S.A.
138 D3 **Edwards Creek** South Australia Australia
144 B7 **Edwardson, C** New Zealand
144 A6 **Edwardson Sd** New Zealand
108 G5 **Edwards Plateau** Texas U.S.A.
110 G3 **Edwardsville** Illinois U.S.A.
15 F4 **Edzell** Scotland
117 H7 **Edziza, Mt** British Columbia Canada
22 F1 **Eeklo** Belgium
100 B9 **Eel** *R* California U.S.A.
94 B6 **Eel** *R* Indiana U.S.A.
25 G2 **Eelde** Netherlands
25 D4 **Eem** *R* Netherlands
25 D4 **Eem Meer** Netherlands
25 G2 **Eemshaven** Netherlands
89 B6 **Eenzamheid Pan** *salt lake* S Africa
22 E1 **Eernegem** Belgium
137 O5 **Éfaté** *isld* Vanuatu
38 K5 **Eferding** Austria
99 N2 **Effie** Minnesota U.S.A.
99 P6 **Effigy Mounds Nat. Mon.** Iowa U.S.A.
110 H2 **Effingham** Illinois U.S.A.
107 P2 **Effingham** Kansas U.S.A.
48 M6 **Eforie** Romania
80 D7 **Efrata** Jordan
71 B3 **Ef Torobi** *isld* W Irian
28 B5 **Eg** Denmark
28 E4 **Egå** Denmark
18 D10 **Ega** *R* Spain
43 E10 **Egadi, I** Sicily
133 F5 **Egaña** Argentina
103 K2 **Egan Range** Nevada U.S.A.
121 N7 **Eganville** Ontario Canada
85 F7 **Egbe** Nigeria
98 B8 **Egbert** Wyoming U.S.A.
28 H5 **Egebjerg** Denmark
115 O4 **Egedesminde** Greenland
116 J7 **Egegik B** Alaska U.S.A.
98 G1 **Egeland** North Dakota U.S.A.
33 O9 **Egeln** Germany
28 D7 **Egen** Denmark
28 F4 **Egens** Denmark
28 E3 **Egense** Denmark
37 J6 **Eger** *R* Germany
48 F3 **Eger** Hungary
28 D7 **Egernsund** Denmark
27 A13 **Egersund** Norway
143 C6 **Egerton, Mt** W Australia Australia
32 M6 **Egestorf** Germany
41 L3 **Egg** Austria
27 D11 **Eggedal** Norway
31 J7 **Eggenburg** Austria
37 O7 **Eggenfelden** Germany
33 U5 **Eggesin** Germany
28 G6 **Eggeslevmagle** Denmark
99 T4 **Egg Harbor** Wisconsin U.S.A.
95 N7 **Egg Harbor City** New Jersey U.S.A.
95 N7 **Egg Harbor, Gt** New Jersey U.S.A.
95 N7 **Egg Harbor, Little** New Jersey U.S.A.
116 G5 **Egg I** Alaska U.S.A.
139 G7 **Egg Lagoon** Tasmania Australia
13 G4 **Eggleston** England
37 N6 **Eggmühl** Germany
37 L4 **Eggolsheim** Germany
9 F5 **Egham** England
22 H2 **Eghezee** Belgium
28 G6 **Egholm** *isld* Denmark
28 D2 **Egholm** *isld* Nordjylland Denmark
15 F1 **Egilsay** Scotland
142 C5 **Eginbah** W Australia Australia
85 D3 **Eglab,El** *reg* Algeria
18 G7 **Egletons** France
36 G1 **Egling** Germany
13 G3 **Eglingham** England
144 B6 **Eglinton** *R* New Zealand
114 H2 **Eglinton I** Northwest Territories Canada
41 J2 **Eglisau** Switzerland
37 L4 **Egloffstein** Germany
25 C3 **Egmond aan Zee** Netherlands
122 H7 **Egmont B** Prince Edward I Canada
113 E10 **Egmont Key** *isld* Florida U.S.A.
145 E3 **Egmont, Mt** New Zealand
145 E3 **Egmont Village** New Zealand
28 J6 **Egøje** Denmark

118 D4 Egremont Alberta Canada
47 L6 Eğret Turkey
47 L7 Eğridir Turkey
78 C2 Egridir Gölü L Turkey
47 K5 Eğrigöz Dağı mt Turkey
13 H5 Egton England
28 C5 Egtved Denmark
71 E7 Eguet Pt Philippines
19 O17 Eguilles France
18 G6 Éguzon France
28 C6 Egvad Denmark
48 F3 Egyek Hungary
84 H4 Egypt rep Africa
112 F5 Egypt Georgia U.S.A.
111 H8 Egypt Mississippi U.S.A.
109 L6 Egypt Texas U.S.A.
79 F4 Ehden Lebanon
36 H7 Ehingen Germany
33 Q8 Ehle R Germany
32 K10 Ehlen Germany
36 F6 Ehningen Germany
33 N7 Ehra-Lessien Germany
113 E9 Ehren Florida U.S.A.
103 K8 Ehrenberg Arizona U.S.A.
140 B6 Ehrenberg Ra N Terr Australia
36 D3 Ehrenbreitstein Germany
32 J7 Ehrenburg Germany
37 O2 Ehrenfriedersdorf Germany
112 F4 Ehrhardt South Carolina U.S.A.
36 E2 Ehringshausen Germany
60 D14 Ei Japan
36 E2 Eibach Germany
36 E2 Eibelshausen Germany
37 J4 Eibelstadt Germany
37 O3 Eibenstock Germany
25 G4 Eibergen Netherlands
38 M8 Eibiswald Austria
33 O8 Eichenbarleben Germany
37 O6 Eichendorf Germany
37 M5 Eichhofen Germany
32 M10 Eichsfeld mts Germany
37 L6 Eichstätt Germany
40 G1 Eichstetten Germany
36 F5 Eichtersheim Germany
33 T8 Eichwalde Germany
36 H2 Eichzell Germany
32 M7 Eicklingen Germany
27 D12 Eidanger Norway
26 B9 Eide Norway
32 J4 Eider Germany
32 L4 Eider R Germany
6 F1 Eiði Faeroes
26 G3 Eidsfjord Norway
27 D12 Eidsfoss Norway
27 F11 Eidskog Norway
26 C9 Eidsvåg Norway
141 K7 Eidsvold Queensland Australia
27 E11 Eidsvoll Norway
25 C2 Eierlandse Gat Netherlands
36 B3 Eifel mts Germany
89 F2 Eiffel Flats Zimbabwe
37 J1 Eigenrieden Germany
40 G4 Eiger mt Switzerland
15 B4 Eigg isld Scotland
113 J11 Eight Mile Rock Bahamas
146 B7 Eights Coast Antarctica
142 D4 Eighty Mile Beach W Australia Australia
26 A10 Eikefjord Norway
27 D12 Eikeren R Norway
26 C9 Eikesdalsvatn L Norway
139 H6 Eildon Victoria Australia
33 R10 Eilenburg Germany
129 G3 Eilerts de Haan Geb mts Suriname
33 O8 Eilsleben Germany
32 L8 Eime Germany
33 M7 Eimke Germany
27 E11 Eina Norway
141 G4 Einasleigh Queensland Australia
32 L9 Einbeck Germany
25 D6 Eindhoven Netherlands
32 L4 Einfeld Germany
68 B4 Einme Burma
36 C5 Einöd Germany
37 P6 Einödsriegel mt Germany
Einsiedel see Deutsch-Einsiedel
79 F8 Ein Yahav Israel
Éire rep see Ireland, Rep of
120 G4 Eire River Ontario Canada
128 E5 Eirunepe Brazil
22 L4 Eisch R Luxembourg
22 K2 Eisden Belgium
25 E7 Eisden Netherlands
36 C4 Eisen Germany
37 J2 Eisenach Germany
36 E4 Eisenberg Germany
37 M2 Eisenberg Germany
38 L6 Eisenerz Austria
38 L7 Eisenerzer-Alpen mts Austria
106 E2 Eisenhower Tunnel Colorado U.S.A.
38 J8 Eisenhut mt Austria
31 H3 Eisenhüttenstadt Germany
38 L8 Eisenkappel Austria
48 D3 Eisenstadt Austria
38 J8 Eisentratten Austria
38 L5 Eisenwurzen reg Austria
36 D2 Eiserfeld Germany
37 K3 Eisfeld Germany
33 P9 Eisleben Germany
36 H6 Eislingen Germany
37 L6 Eitensheim Germany
36 H2 Eiterfeld Germany
36 C2 Eitorf Germany
17 G2 Ejea de los Caballeros Spain
87 G12 Ejeda Madagascar
28 D5 Ejer Bavnehoj hill Denmark
28 B3 Ejerslev Denmark
127 J10 Ejido Venezuela
65 A5 Ejin Horo Qi China
65 C2 Ej Nur China
28 B3 Ejsing Denmark
28 C5 Ejstrup Denmark
85 D7 Ejura Ghana
98 B4 Ekalaka Montana U.S.A.
27 J15 Ekby Sweden
22 F2 Eke Belgium
29 K12 Ekenäs Finland
22 G1 Ekeren Belgium
145 E4 Eketahuna New Zealand
26 N5 Ekfors Sweden
46 D6 Ekhinádhes isld Greece
46 G3 Ekhinos Greece
55 G5 Ekibastuz Kazakhstan
59 K1 Ekimchan Russian Federation
116 N6 Eklutna Alaska U.S.A.
6 N6 Ekofisk oil rig North Sea
27 J12 Ekoln L Sweden
22 F1 Eksaarde Belgium
27 G11 Ekshärad Sweden
27 G14 Eksjö Sweden
26 L7 Ekträsk Sweden
115 L7 Ekwan R Ontario Canada
116 J7 Ekwok Alaska U.S.A.
68 C3 Ela Burma
El Aaiún see Laâyoune
46 F8 Elafónisos isld Greece
111 F7 Elaine Arkansas U.S.A.
80 E5 El 'Ajājira Jordan
103 H10 El Alamo Mexico
75 K10 Elamanchili India
99 R5 Eland Wisconsin U.S.A.
89 E5 Elands R S Africa
89 C8 Elands Berg mt S Africa
8 C3 Elan Valley Reservoirs Wales
43 B13 El Aouinet Algeria
41 L4 Ela, Piz mt Switzerland
16 D7 El Arahal Spain
El Arâich see Larache Morocco
124 C4 El Arco Mexico
80 F5 El Ardah Jordan
141 H4 El Arish Queensland Australia
46 E5 Elassón Greece
79 E9 Elat Israel
46 F6 Elátia Greece
86 E2 El Atrun Oasis Sudan
80 D7 El 'Azar Jordan
78 G2 Elâziğ Turkey
111 K10 Elba Alabama U.S.A.
101 M7 Elba Idaho U.S.A.
98 H8 Elba Nebraska U.S.A.
94 J3 Elba New York U.S.A.
42 C6 Elba, I.d' Italy
126 H10 El Banco Colombia
16 D4 El Barco de Avila Spain
46 D3 Elbasan Albania
127 K10 El Baúl Venezuela
32 J5 Elbe est Germany
33 M6 Elbe R Germany
33 N5 Elbe-Lübeck Kanal Germany
79 G4 El Beqa'a R Lebanon
110 J3 Elberfield Indiana U.S.A.
32 F8 Elbergen Germany
99 O7 Elberon Iowa U.S.A.
109 J2 Elbert Texas U.S.A.
99 U5 Elberta Michigan U.S.A.
106 D2 Elbert,Mt Colorado U.S.A.
112 E3 Elberton Georgia U.S.A.
21 N3 Elbeuf France
33 N9 Elbingerode Germany
78 F2 Elbistan Turkey
31 L1 Elblag Poland
17 F6 El Bonillo Spain
124 H6 El Bordo Mexico
16 D9 El Borj Morocco
118 L7 Elbow Saskatchewan Canada
113 L11 Elbow Cay isld Bahamas
98 K4 Elbow L Minnesota U.S.A.
118 C8 Elbow R Alberta Canada
124 J6 El Bozal Mexico
53 F11 El'brus mt Russian Federation
86 E4 El Buheyrat prov Sudan
25 E4 Elburg Netherlands
16 E3 El Burgo de Osma Spain
100 K9 Elburz Nevada U.S.A.
77 B1 Elburz Mountains Iran
102 H9 El Cajon California U.S.A.
128 F2 El Callao Venezuela
16 D5 El Campillo de la Jara Spain
109 L6 El Campo Texas U.S.A.
102 H9 El Capitan Res California U.S.A.
128 C2 El Carmen Colombia
124 G5 El Casco Mexico
17 G3 El Castellar Spain
103 J9 El Centro California U.S.A.
128 F7 El Cerro Bolivia
16 C7 El Cerro de Andévalo Spain
124 F3 El Charco Mexico
17 G6 Elche Spain
17 F6 Elche de la Sierra Spain
125 N9 El Chichón vol Mexico
124 G3 El Chilicote Mexico
127 K9 El Chino Venezuela
99 R4 Elcho Wisconsin U.S.A.
140 D1 Elcho I N Terr Australia
133 E2 El Chorro Argentina
124 H5 El Cobre Mexico
128 D2 El Cocuy Colombia
126 C3 El Cotorro Cuba
126 G4 El Cristo Cuba
108 B5 El Cuervo Mexico
32 L8 Eldagsen Germany
124 C2 El Dátil Mexico
33 Q6 Elde R Germany
33 O6 Eldena Germany
138 F4 Elder,L South Australia Australia
99 R5 Elderon Wisconsin U.S.A.
6 N6 Eldfisk oil rig North Sea
126 A4 El Díaz Mexico
126 G10 El Difícil Colombia
33 M7 Eldingen Germany
124 G8 El Divisadero Mexico
128 C3 El Diviso Colombia
124 B2 El Doctor Mexico
99 O9 Eldon Iowa U.S.A.
110 D3 Eldon Missouri U.S.A.
100 B2 Eldon Washington U.S.A.
99 N7 Eldora Iowa U.S.A.
130 C10 Eldorado Argentina
130 E9 Eldorado Brazil
114 J6 Eldorado Saskatchewan Canada
124 F5 Eldorado Mexico
109 P2 El Dorado Arkansas U.S.A.
110 H4 Eldorado Illinois U.S.A.
107 O4 El Dorado Kansas U.S.A.
107 L7 Eldorado Oklahoma U.S.A.
108 G5 Eldorado Texas U.S.A.
128 F2 El Dorado Venezuela
89 G1 Eldorado Zimbabwe
100 D1 Eldorado,Mt Washington U.S.A.
103 K6 Eldorado Mts Nevada U.S.A.
110 B4 El Dorado Springs Missouri U.S.A.
88 E1 Eldoret Kenya
98 K2 Eldred Minnesota U.S.A.
95 N5 Eldred New York U.S.A.
94 J5 Eldred Pennsylvania U.S.A.
27 F15 Eldsberga Sweden
100 H2 Eleanor Washington U.S.A.
143 D10 Eleanora Pk W Australia Australia
102 E3 Eleanor, L California U.S.A.
89 E4 Elebe mt Botswana
109 J1 Electra Texas U.S.A.
101 P5 Electric Pk Mont/Wyoming U.S.A.
135 O1 Eleele Hawaiian Is
52 B6 Eleja Latvia
48 G4 Elek Hungary
54 K1 Elektrogorsk Russian Federation
54 K1 Elektrostal' Russian Federation
22 J2 Elemalle Belgium
47 H2 Elena Bulgaria
128 D4 El Encanto Colombia
33 N9 Elend Germany
106 C8 Elephant Butte New Mexico U.S.A.
106 C8 Elephant Butte Res New Mexico U.S.A.
68 G7 Elephant, Chaine de l' mts Cambodia
146 D3 Elephant I South Shetland Is Antarctica
83 K8 Elephant Pass Sri Lanka
116 G3 Elephant Point Alaska U.S.A.
46 F3 Eleshnitsa Bulgaria
128 E3 El Esmeralda Venezuela
128 C3 El Espinal Colombia
56 H4 Elesun Russian Federation
84 J5 Elet, Wadi watercourse Sudan
85 F1 El Eulma Algeria
113 L12 Eleuthera I Bahamas
99 P5 Eleva Wisconsin U.S.A.
106 E3 Eleven Mile Canyon Res Colorado U.S.A.
110 E5 Eleven Point R Missouri U.S.A.
46 F6 Elevsis Greece
22 H2 Elewijt Belgium
20 C5 Elez R France
80 G2 El Fahham Syria
43 C12 El Fahs Tunisia
86 E3 El Fasher Sudan
16 D9 El Fendek Morocco
16 B1 El Ferrol Spain
117 E6 Elfin Cove Alaska U.S.A.
119 O7 Elfros Saskatchewan Canada
86 H4 El Fud Ethiopia
124 E4 El Fuerte Mexico
86 E3 El Fula Sudan
80 D5 El Fundug Jordan
26 E9 Elgå Norway
26 E9 Elgepiggen mt Norway
37 K2 Elgersburg Germany
86 F3 El Geteina Sudan
86 F3 El Gezira prov Sudan
80 F5 El Ghor Jordan
119 R9 Elgin Manitoba Canada
122 G8 Elgin New Brunswick Canada
15 E3 Elgin Scotland
103 O10 Elgin Arizona U.S.A.
99 S7 Elgin Illinois U.S.A.
99 P7 Elgin Iowa U.S.A.
98 H8 Elgin Nebraska U.S.A.
103 K4 Elgin Nevada U.S.A.
98 E3 Elgin North Dakota U.S.A.
107 M7 Elgin Oklahoma U.S.A.
100 H4 Elgin Oregon U.S.A.
109 K5 Elgin Texas U.S.A.
103 O3 Elgin Utah U.S.A.
141 H5 Elgin Downs Queensland Australia
86 F5 Elgon, Mt Uganda
17 H2 El Grado Spain
124 G8 El Grullo Mexico
128 D3 El Guamo Colombia
84 H4 El Harra Egypt
86 F3 El Hawata Sudan
85 E3 El Homr Algeria
87 D7 Elias Garcia Angola
127 J5 Elías Piña Dominican Rep
109 J3 Eliasville Texas U.S.A.
108 D2 Elida New Mexico U.S.A.
119 U9 Elie Manitoba Canada
13 F1 Elie Scotland
46 F6 Elikón mt Greece
29 M11 Elimäki Finland
46 F2 Elin Pelin Bulgaria
95 R3 Eliot Maine U.S.A.
29 O10 Elisenvaara Russian Federation
129 K5 Eliseu Martins Brazil
80 E6 Elisha' Jordan
53 F10 Elista Russian Federation
106 F2 Elizabeth Colorado U.S.A.
99 Q7 Elizabeth Illinois U.S.A.
109 P5 Elizabeth Louisiana U.S.A.
95 N6 Elizabeth New Jersey U.S.A.
94 F7 Elizabeth West Virginia U.S.A.
112 L1 Elizabeth City North Carolina U.S.A.
95 R5 Elizabeth Is Massachusetts U.S.A.
142 F3 Elizabeth, Mt W Australia Australia
122 F6 Elizabeth,Mt New Brunswick Canada
101 P9 Elizabeth Mt Utah U.S.A.
137 M7 Elizabeth Reef Pacific Oc
143 B7 Elizabeth Spring W Australia Australia
94 E10 Elizabethton Tennessee U.S.A.
94 B7 Elizabethtown Indiana U.S.A.
94 B9 Elizabethtown Kentucky U.S.A.
95 O2 Elizabethtown New York U.S.A.
112 J3 Elizabethtown North Carolina U.S.A.
95 L6 Elizabethtown Pennsylvania U.S.A.
Elizabethville see Lubumbashi
95 L6 Elizabethville Pennsylvania U.S.A.
138 E6 Eliza,L South Australia Australia
18 D9 Elizondo Spain
124 G4 El Jaralito Mexico
86 F3 El Jebelein Sudan
126 E4 El Jibaro Cuba
31 N2 Ełk Poland
102 A2 Elk California U.S.A.
110 B5 Elk R Missouri U.S.A.
108 B3 Elk New Mexico U.S.A.
95 M7 Elk R Penn/Maryland U.S.A.
110 K6 Elk R Tennessee U.S.A.
94 F8 Elk R West Virginia U.S.A.
101 P6 Elk Wyoming U.S.A.
99 P7 Elkader Iowa U.S.A.
86 F2 El Kamlin Sudan
101 R5 Elk Basin Wyoming U.S.A.
100 K4 Elk City Idaho U.S.A.
107 P4 Elk City Kansas U.S.A.
107 L6 Elk City Oklahoma U.S.A.
102 B2 Elk Creek California U.S.A.
140 D5 Elkedra N Terr Australia
43 B12 El Kef Tunisia
85 C2 El Kelaâ des Srarhna Morocco
86 H4 Ēl Kerē Ethiopia
102 C3 Elk Grove California U.S.A.
86 F2 El Khandaq Sudan
79 E7 El Kharrûba Egypt
94 B5 Elkhart Indiana U.S.A.
107 J4 Elkhart Kansas U.S.A.
109 M4 Elkhart Texas U.S.A.
99 T6 Elkhart Lake Wisconsin U.S.A.
101 S9 Elkhead Mts Colorado U.S.A.
119 Q9 Elkhorn Manitoba Canada
99 L8 Elk Horn Iowa U.S.A.
98 H7 Elkhorn R Nebraska U.S.A.
99 S7 Elkhorn Wisconsin U.S.A.
47 H2 Elkhovo Bulgaria
112 G1 Elkin North Carolina U.S.A.
118 E5 Elk I. Nat. Park Alberta Canada
108 C2 Elkins New Mexico U.S.A.
94 H8 Elkins West Virginia U.S.A.
94 B2 Elk L Michigan U.S.A.
120 K5 Elk Lake Ontario Canada
95 K4 Elkland Pennsylvania U.S.A.
110 K7 Elkmont Alabama U.S.A.
106 D1 Elk Mt Colorado U.S.A.
101 T8 Elk Mt Wyoming U.S.A.
100 K1 Elko British Columbia Canada
100 K9 Elko Nevada U.S.A.
101 P8 Elkol Wyoming U.S.A.
86 H4 Ēl K'oran Ethiopia
101 N3 Elk Park Montana U.S.A.
112 F1 Elk Park North Carolina U.S.A.
118 G5 Elk Point Alberta Canada
98 K7 Elk Pt South Dakota U.S.A.
118 C9 Elk R British Columbia Canada
99 N4 Elk R Minnesota U.S.A.
94 B2 Elk Rapids Michigan U.S.A.
43 C12 El Krib Tunisia
100 J3 Elk River Idaho U.S.A.
43 B13 El Ksour Tunisia
106 B1 Elk Springs Colorado U.S.A.
113 F8 Elkton Florida U.S.A.
110 J5 Elkton Kentucky U.S.A.
95 M7 Elkton Maryland U.S.A.
99 O6 Elkton Minnesota U.S.A.
100 B6 Elkton Oregon U.S.A.
98 K5 Elkton South Dakota U.S.A.
110 K6 Elkton Tennessee U.S.A.
94 J8 Elkton Virginia U.S.A.
79 E9 El Kuntilla Egypt
94 C10 Elk Valley Tennessee U.S.A.
110 G4 Elkville Illinois U.S.A.
79 G4 El Laboue Lebanon
86 E3 El Lagowa Sudan
83 K10 Ellamulla Sri Lanka
12 C1 Ellanbeich Scotland
13 G6 Elland England
143 A7 Ellavalla W Australia Australia
113 D7 Ellaville Florida U.S.A.
111 M9 Ellaville Georgia U.S.A.
20 D5 Elle R France
37 N3 Ellefeld Germany
114 J2 Ellef Ringnes I Northwest Territories Canada
143 C10 Elleker W Australia Australia
95 O2 Ellenburg New York U.S.A.
95 M8 Ellendale Delaware U.S.A.
111 F12 Ellendale Louisiana U.S.A.
98 H3 Ellendale North Dakota U.S.A.
103 O3 Ellen,Mt Utah U.S.A.
95 P2 Ellen,Mt Vermont U.S.A.
143 C10 Ellen Pk W Australia Australia
13 E4 Ellen,R England
100 E2 Ellensburg Washington U.S.A.
32 H6 Ellenserdamm Germany
113 E10 Ellenton Florida U.S.A.
95 N5 Ellenville New York U.S.A.
36 C3 Ellenz-Poltersdorf Germany
112 G2 Eller North Carolina U.S.A.
112 H2 Ellerbe North Carolina U.S.A.
113 E7 Ellerbee Florida U.S.A.
36 D4 Ellerspring mt Germany
144 B6 Ellery, L New Zealand
139 J6 Ellery,Mt Victoria Australia
8 D2 Ellesmere England
115 L2 Ellesmere I Northwest Territories Canada
144 D5 Ellesmere, L New Zealand
8 D1 Ellesmere Port England
110 K2 Ellettsville Indiana U.S.A.
22 F2 Ellezelles Belgium
20 C5 Elliant France
Ellice Is. see Tuvalu islds state
95 L7 Ellicott City Maryland U.S.A.
94 J4 Ellicottville New York U.S.A.
28 D3 Ellidshøj Denmark
112 C3 Ellijay Georgia U.S.A.
28 E2 Elling Denmark
28 F6 Ellinge Denmark
37 K5 Ellingen Germany
13 G3 Ellington England
110 F4 Ellington Missouri U.S.A.
107 M3 Ellinwood Kansas U.S.A.
89 E8 Elliot S Africa
95 L8 Elliot Maryland U.S.A.
112 G3 Elliot South Carolina U.S.A.
142 E4 Elliot Lake W Australia Australia
120 H6 Elliot Lake Ontario Canada
141 H4 Elliot, Mt Queensland Australia
140 C3 Elliott N Terr Australia
99 L8 Elliott Iowa U.S.A.
98 J3 Elliott North Dakota U.S.A.
113 G12 Elliott Key isld Florida U.S.A.
122 H4 Ellis B Quebec Canada
89 E4 Ellisras S Africa
138 C5 Elliston South Australia Australia
123 T5 Elliston Newfoundland Canada
101 N3 Elliston Montana U.S.A.
94 G9 Elliston Virginia U.S.A.
111 G10 Ellisville Mississippi U.S.A.
143 G8 Ell, L W Australia Australia
38 F6 Ellmau Austria
36 F6 Ellmendingen Germany
15 F3 Ellon Scotland
74 F8 Ellora India
112 G4 Elloree South Carolina U.S.A.
33 N9 Ellrich Germany
118 E4 Ellscott Alberta Canada
110 F5 Ellsinore Missouri U.S.A.
107 M3 Ellsworth Kansas U.S.A.
95 T2 Ellsworth Maine U.S.A.
99 L6 Ellsworth Minnesota U.S.A.
98 D7 Ellsworth Nebraska U.S.A.
99 O5 Ellsworth Wisconsin U.S.A.
109 J1 Ellsworth,L Oklahoma U.S.A.
146 B7 Ellsworth Land Antarctica
146 C7 Ellsworth Mts Antarctica
37 J6 Ellwangen Germany
94 G6 Ellwood City Pennsylvania U.S.A.
32 H6 Ellwürden Germany
32 K5 Elm Germany
41 K4 Elm Switzerland
99 O6 Elma Iowa U.S.A.
100 B2 Elma Washington U.S.A.
133 C6 El Maitén Argentina
47 K8 Elmalı Turkey
86 F3 El Manaquil Sudan
124 A2 El Maneadero Mexico
124 G5 El Martinez Mexico
109 L7 Elmaton Texas U.S.A.
103 J9 El Mayor Mexico
79 D7 El Mazâr Egypt
112 K2 Elm City North Carolina U.S.A.
98 G9 Elm Cr Nebraska U.S.A.
118 D1 Elm Creek Manitoba Canada
107 N6 Elm Cr.Res.,E Oklahoma U.S.A.
108 A2 Elmendorf New Mexico U.S.A.
127 J9 El Mene de Mauroa Venezuela
32 M5 Elmenhorst Germany
99 O10 Elmer Missouri U.S.A.
95 M7 Elmer New Jersey U.S.A.
109 H1 Elmer Oklahoma U.S.A.
100 G1 Elmer City Washington U.S.A.
43 B13 El Meskiana Algeria
99 T8 Elmhurst Illinois U.S.A.
79 F4 El Mīna Lebanon
123 K7 Elmira Prince Edward I Canada
102 C3 Elmira California U.S.A.
94 C1 Elmira Michigan U.S.A.
95 L4 Elmira New York U.S.A.
103 M8 El Mirage Arizona U.S.A.
98 H4 Elm L South Dakota U.S.A.
109 K4 Elm Mott Texas U.S.A.
107 N3 Elmo Kansas U.S.A.
99 L9 Elmo Missouri U.S.A.
101 T8 Elmo Wyoming U.S.A.
16 E4 El Molar Spain
108 G7 El Moral Mexico
139 G6 Elmore Victoria Australia
111 K9 Elmore Alabama U.S.A.
99 M6 Elmore Minnesota U.S.A.
94 D5 Elmore Ohio U.S.A.
109 K1 Elmore City Oklahoma U.S.A.
106 B6 El Morro Nat.Mon New Mexico U.S.A.
122 J9 Elmsdale Nova Scotia Canada
32 L5 Elmshorn Germany
98 D5 Elm Springs South Dakota U.S.A.
36 D5 Elmstein Germany
122 J8 Elmsvale Nova Scotia Canada
86 E3 El Muglad Sudan
120 J8 Elmwood Ontario Canada
110 G1 Elmwood Illinois U.S.A.
107 K5 Elmwood Oklahoma U.S.A.
99 O5 Elmwood Wisconsin U.S.A.
18 G10 Elne France
71 D5 El Nido Philippines
118 D7 Elnora Alberta Canada
110 J3 Elnora Indiana U.S.A.
86 F3 El Obeid Sudan
111 G12 Eloi Bay Louisiana U.S.A.
80 D1 Elon Israel
80 E5 Elon Moré Jordan
110 K6 Elora Tennessee U.S.A.
20 B5 Elorn R France
128 C4 El Oro prov Ecuador
125 J8 El Oro Mexico
124 F6 Elota Mexico
103 N9 Eloy Arizona U.S.A.
124 G5 El Palmito Mexico
128 F2 El Pao Venezuela
16 E4 El Pardo Spain
99 R9 El Paso Illinois U.S.A.
108 A4 El Paso Texas U.S.A.
131 B4 El Peñón pk Chile
14 C3 Elphin Ireland
141 J5 Elphinstone Queensland Australia
119 R8 Elphinstone Manitoba Canada
127 N9 El Pilar Venezuela
133 E2 El Pintado Argentina
83 K11 Elpitiya Sri Lanka
102 E4 El Portal California U.S.A.
128 C5 El Portugues Peru
108 B4 El Porvenir Mexico
16 D5 El Puente del Arzobispo Spain
16 C8 El Puerto de Sta. Maria Spain
80 D5 Elqana Jordan
80 E1 El Qouzah Lebanon
131 B2 Elqui R Chile
79 E8 El Quşeima Egypt
79 F9 El Quweira Jordan
124 G6 El Regocijo Mexico
108 F7 El Remolino Mexico
125 J6 El Retorno Mexico
116 N5 Elridge Glacier Alaska U.S.A.
106 D5 El Rito New Mexico U.S.A.
16 C7 El Ronquillo Spain
99 M4 Elrosa Minnesota U.S.A.
118 J7 Elrose Saskatchewan Canada
99 Q6 Elroy Wisconsin U.S.A.
124 H6 El Rucio Mexico
117 F4 Elsa Yukon Territory Canada
42 D5 Elsa R Italy
109 K9 Elsa Texas U.S.A.
124 G6 El Salto Mexico
125 P11 El Salvador rep Central America
71 G6 El Salvador Mindanao Philippines
120 H4 Elsas Ontario Canada
108 A6 El Sauz Mexico
109 J9 El Sauz Texas U.S.A.
25 E4 Elsberg hill Netherlands
110 F2 Elsberry Missouri U.S.A.
32 K6 Elsdorf Germany
32 H8 Else R Germany
22 L3 Elsenborn Belgium
36 F5 Elsenz R Germany
140 C2 Elsey N Terr Australia
26 G5 Elsfjord Norway
32 H6 Elsfleth Germany
98 E9 Elsie Nebraska U.S.A.
100 B4 Elsie Oregon U.S.A.
103 M3 Elsinore Utah U.S.A.
102 G8 Elsinore L California U.S.A.
25 E7 Elsloo Netherlands
98 F7 Elsmere Nebraska U.S.A.
107 P4 Elsmore Kansas U.S.A.
33 Q9 Elsnigk Germany
130 C10 El Soberbio Argentina
127 M10 El Socorro Venezuela
127 L10 El Sombrero Venezuela
116 K1 Elson Lagoon Alaska U.S.A.
25 E4 Elspeet Netherlands
25 E5 Elst Netherlands
9 F5 Elstead England
33 R9 Elster Germany
33 Q10 Elster R Germany
37 N2 Elsterberg Germany
33 T10 Elsterwerda Germany
145 F3 Elsthorpe New Zealand
9 F4 Elstree England
108 A6 El Sueco Mexico
124 G8 El Tabaco Mexico
16 C2 El Teleno mt Spain
25 F5 Elten Germany
37 O2 Elterlein Germany
9 G5 Eltham England
145 E3 Eltham New Zealand
79 E9 El Thamad Egypt
128 F2 El Tigre Venezuela
9 F3 Eltisley England
37 K4 Eltmann Germany
128 E2 El Tocuyo Venezuela
109 P5 Elton Louisiana U.S.A.
100 G3 Eltopia Washington U.S.A.
133 C3 El toro Chile
102 G8 El Toro California U.S.A.
133 C3 El Tránsito Chile
124 C2 El Tren Mexico
124 D6 El Triunfo Mexico
118 K1 Eltrut L Ontario Canada
127 O2 El Tucuche mt Trinidad
133 C8 El Turbio Argentina
36 E3 Eltville Germany
76 E2 Eluru India
119 Q9 Elva Manitoba Canada
52 C5 Elva Estonia
106 D5 El Vado New Mexico U.S.A.
128 C2 El Valle Colombia
127 L9 El Valle Venezuela
12 E3 Elvanfoot Scotland
79 E2 Elvanlı Turkey
27 E10 Elvdal Norway
26 N2 Elvebakken Norway
20 E6 Elven France
27 E11 Elverum Norway
125 L3 El Viejo Nicaragua
128 D2 El Vigia Venezuela
128 D5 Elvira Brazil
114 J3 Elvira,C Northwest Territories Canada
142 B5 Elvire, Mt W Australia Australia
143 C8 Elvire, Mt W Australia Australia
142 G4 Elvire, R W Australia Australia
44 D1 Elvo R Italy
133 C4 El Volcán Chile
86 H5 El Wak Kenya
101 O1 Elwell, L res Montana U.S.A.
99 S8 Elwood Illinois U.S.A.
94 B6 Elwood Indiana U.S.A.
110 B2 Elwood Missouri U.S.A.
98 G9 Elwood Nebraska U.S.A.
9 G3 Ely England
99 P8 Ely Iowa U.S.A.
99 P2 Ely Minnesota U.S.A.
103 K2 Ely Nevada U.S.A.
80 D3 Elyaqim Israel
138 C3 Ely Hill South Australia Australia
99 N5 Elysian Minnesota U.S.A.
36 E3 Elz Germany
40 H1 Elz R Germany
36 E7 Elzach Germany
124 G5 El Zape Mexico
32 L7 Elze Germany
27 G10 Emådalen Sweden
137 O5 Émaé isld Vanuatu
77 D1 Emāmrūd Iran
27 H14 Emån R Sweden
50 E4 Emba R Kazakhstan
57 A1 Emba Kazakhstan
122 G1 Embar Labrador, Nfld Canada
133 E2 Embarcación Argentina
110 H2 Embarras R Illinois U.S.A.
117 R6 Embarras Portage Alberta Canada
99 O2 Embarrass Minnesota U.S.A.
98 J3 Embden North Dakota U.S.A.
60 P1 Embetsu Japan
128 D5 Embira R Brazil
101 R5 Emblem Wyoming U.S.A.
13 G3 Embleton England
47 U14 Embóna Rhodes Greece
121 P7 Embrun Ontario Canada
88 F2 Embu Kenya
32 F6 Emden Germany
99 R9 Emden Illinois U.S.A.
67 A2 Emei China
67 A2 Emei Shan mt China
80 F1 Emeq Ḥula Israel
80 D2 'Emeq Zevulun Israel
98 J2 Emerado North Dakota U.S.A.
141 J6 Emerald Queensland Australia
114 H2 Emerald I Northwest Territories Canada
71 D5 Emergency Pt Philippines
142 E3 Emeriau Pt W Australia Australia
115 N7 Emeril Labrador, Nfld Canada
119 U9 Emerson Manitoba Canada
99 L8 Emerson Iowa U.S.A.
98 K7 Emerson Nebraska U.S.A.
98 J6 Emery South Dakota U.S.A.
47 K5 Emet Turkey
101 P4 Emigrant Montana U.S.A.
102 D2 Emigrant Gap California U.S.A.
100 J9 Emigrant Pass Nevada U.S.A.
101 P4 Emigrant Pk Montana U.S.A.
103 J4 Emigrant Valley Nevada U.S.A.
86 C2 Emi Koussi mt Chad
42 D4 Emilia-Romagna prov Italy
40 F6 Emilius, M Italy
57 L2 Emin China
66 C2 Emin China
47 J2 Emine,N Bulgaria
94 B8 Eminence Kentucky U.S.A.
110 E4 Eminence Missouri U.S.A.
47 J2 Eminska Planina plateau Bulgaria
47 K7 Emir R Turkey
78 C2 Emirdag Turkey
139 J7 Emita Flinders I, Tasmania Australia
94 H5 Emlenton Pennsylvania U.S.A.
32 E7 Emlichheim Germany
27 H15 Emmaboda Sweden
126 B1 Emmastad Curaçao
27 N13 Emmaste Estonia
95 M6 Emmaus Pennsylvania U.S.A.
139 K3 Emmaville New South Wales Australia
40 G4 Emme R Switzerland
118 L3 Emmeline L Saskatchewan Canada
25 E3 Emmeloord Netherlands
25 G3 Emmen Netherlands
41 H3 Emmen Switzerland
40 G4 Emmen Tal Switzerland
25 F5 Emmerich Germany
28 B7 Emmerlev Denmark
32 K8 Emmern Germany
38 M5 Emmersdorf Austria
28 B7 Emmerske Denmark
32 K9 Emmerthal Germany
32 K8 Emmerthal Germany
141 G6 Emmet Queensland Australia
100 J6 Emmet Idaho U.S.A.
98 H7 Emmet Nebraska U.S.A.
99 M6 Emmetsburg Iowa U.S.A.
107 O2 Emmett Kansas U.S.A.
76 C3 Emmiganuru India
95 K7 Emmitsburg Maryland U.S.A.
103 O1 Emmons,Mt Utah U.S.A.
99 N1 Emo Ontario Canada
48 F3 Emőd Hungary
109 M3 Emory Texas U.S.A.
108 D6 Emory Pk Texas U.S.A.
124 D4 Empalme Mexico
89 G7 Empangeni S Africa
32 K7 Empede Germany
133 F3 Empedrado Argentina
25 F5 Empel Germany
112 D5 Empire Georgia U.S.A.
99 U5 Empire Michigan U.S.A.
100 F9 Empire Nevada U.S.A.
100 A6 Empire Oregon U.S.A.
106 F1 Empire Res Colorado U.S.A.
42 D5 Empoli Italy
107 O3 Emporia Kansas U.S.A.
94 K10 Emporia Virginia U.S.A.
94 J5 Emporium Pennsylvania U.S.A.
118 G8 Empress Alberta Canada
22 J3 Emptinne Belgium
19 N14 Empurany France
98 G2 Emrick North Dakota U.S.A.
32 F6 Ems R Germany
32 F8 Emsbüren Germany
32 F9 Emscher R Germany
121 L7 Emsdale Ontario Canada
32 G8 Emsdetten Germany
32 G6 Ems-Jade Kanal Germany
37 K4 Emskirchen Germany
32 F7 Emslage Germany
36 G1 Emstal Germany
32 H7 Emstek Germany
9 F6 Emsworth England
65 G3 Emu China
141 F3 Emu Ck Queensland Australia
61 L10 Ena Japan
27 J10 Enånger Sweden
80 D4 'Enav Jordan
80 C3 'En Ayyala Israel
101 T8 Encampment Wyoming U.S.A.
17 H4 Encanade mt Spain
108 B6 Encantada Mexico
124 B2 Encantada, Cerro de la Mexico
131 H3 Encantadas,Sa mts Brazil
124 C4 Encantado, Cerro mt Mexico
71 E3 Encanto,C Luzon Philippines
124 H7 Encarnación Mexico
130 C10 Encarnación Paraguay
118 E8 Enchant Alberta Canada
85 D7 Enchi Ghana
106 C5 Encinada Mesa tableland New Mexico U.S.A.
109 H7 Encinal Texas U.S.A.
108 A6 Encinillas Mexico
102 G8 Encinitas California U.S.A.
108 B1 Encino New Mexico U.S.A.
108 B2 Encinoso New Mexico U.S.A.
128 D2 Encontrados Venezuela
138 E6 Encounter B South Australia Australia
133 G4 Encruzilhada do Sul Brazil
48 G2 Encs Hungary
117 L8 Endako British Columbia Canada
69 F11 Endau R Malaysia
69 F11 Endau Malaysia
71 K9 Ende isld Flores Indonesia
99 R6 Endeavor Wisconsin U.S.A.
141 H3 Endeavour Queensland Australia
119 P6 Endeavour Saskatchewan Canada
141 F1 Endeavour Str Queensland Australia
108 A8 Endee New Mexico U.S.A.
71 K9 Endeh Indonesia
28 E5 Endelave Denmark
134 K8 Enderbury I Phoenix Is Pacific Oc
117 O10 Enderby British Columbia Canada
142 B5 Enderby I W Australia Australia
146 J10 Enderby Land Antarctica
98 J3 Enderlin North Dakota U.S.A.
98 E9 Enders Res Nebraska U.S.A.
118 E7 Endiang Alberta Canada
95 L4 Endicott New York U.S.A.
100 H3 Endicott Washington U.S.A.
117 G7 Endicott Arm pen Alaska U.S.A.
116 L3 Endicott Mts Alaska U.S.A.
117 G4 End,Mt Yukon Territory Canada
8 D1 Endon England
80 E3 'En Dor Israel
140 C1 Endyalgout I N Terr Australia
128 D6 Ene R Peru
143 B8 Eneabba W Australia Australia
55 C5 Energetik Russian Federation
54 F9 Energodar Ukraine
134 G7 Enewetak atoll Marshall Is Pacific Oc
47 H4 Enez Turkey
78 A1 Enez Turkey
79 F4 Enfe Lebanon
43 C12 Enfida Tunisia
122 J9 Enfield Nova Scotia Canada
9 F4 Enfield England
110 H3 Enfield Illinois U.S.A.
95 P3 Enfield New Hampshire U.S.A.
112 K1 Enfield North Carolina U.S.A.
127 K5 Engaño, C Dominican Rep
71 E1 Engaño,C Luzon Philippines
60 R1 Engaru Japan
28 B7 Enge Germany
80 E8 En Gedi Israel
41 H4 Engelberg Switzerland
112 M2 Engelhard North Carolina U.S.A.
38 J5 Engelhartszell Austria
53 G8 Engel's Russian Federation
36 C2 Engelskirchen Germany
41 J2 Engen Germany
130 C4 Engenho Brazil
138 D3 Engenina R South Australia Australia
32 J8 Enger Germany
26 E10 Engerdal Norway
27 F10 Engeren,L Norway
36 D3 Engers Germany
28 C4 Engesvang Denmark
80 F2 'En Gev Israel
Enghien see Edingen
21 P4 Enghien-les-Bains France
117 F6 Engineer British Columbia Canada
22 J2 Engis Belgium
70 B4 Engkilili Sarawak
8 D3 England U.K.
111 E7 England Arkansas U.S.A.
106 C8 Engle New Mexico U.S.A.
123 Q3 Englee Newfoundland Canada
119 N6 Englefield Saskatchewan Canada
117 K10 Englewood British Columbia Canada
106 F2 Englewood Colorado U.S.A.
113 E11 Englewood Florida U.S.A.
107 L4 Englewood Kansas U.S.A.
112 C2 Englewood Tennessee U.S.A.
110 K3 English Indiana U.S.A.
122 E4 English Bay Quebec Canada
116 L7 English Bay Alaska U.S.A.
7 H13 English Channel England/France
146 C6 English Coast Antarctica
140 D1 English Company's Is N Terr Australia
127 P4 English Harbour Town Antigua W Indies
123 R6 English Harbour W Newfoundland Canada
119 N1 English River Ontario Canada
52 D2 Engozero Russian Federation
36 G7 Engstingen Germany
17 G6 Énguera Spain
52 B6 Engure Latvia
80 D3 'En Ha'Emeq Israel
80 D2 'En HaMifraz Israel
80 E3 'En Ḥarod Israel
79 F8 'En Ḥazeva Israel
80 C3 'En Hod Israel
98 B2 Enid Montana U.S.A.
107 N5 Enid Oklahoma U.S.A.
111 G7 Enid L Mississippi U.S.A.
142 B5 Enid, Mt W Australia Australia
118 A3 Enilda Alberta Canada
36 G7 Eningen Germany
60 P3 Eniwa Japan
60 P3 Eniwa dake mt Japan
85 C5 Enji Mauritania
80 C3 'En Karmel Israel
36 D5 Enkenbach-Alsenborn Germany
25 D3 Enkhuizen Netherlands
36 C4 Enkirch Germany
27 J12 Enköping Sweden
128 G8 En Madrejón Paraguay
114 J5 Ennadai Northwest Territories Canada
86 E3 En Nahud Sudan
86 D2 Ennedi plateau Chad
14 D3 Ennell,L Ireland
32 F10 Ennepetal Germany
127 H5 Ennery Haiti
139 H3 Enngonia New South Wales Australia
32 H9 Ennigerloh Germany
98 D5 Enning South Dakota U.S.A.
27 E13 Enningdal Norway
14 C4 Ennis Ireland
101 O4 Ennis Montana U.S.A.
109 L3 Ennis Texas U.S.A.
14 E4 Enniscorthy Ireland
14 D2 Enniskillen N Ireland
14 B4 Ennistimon Ireland
80 D1 Enn Nâqoûra Lebanon
38 K6 Ennstaler Alpen mts Austria
80 G4 En Nu'eiyima Jordan
29 P9 Eno Finland
108 E2 Enochs Texas U.S.A.
141 K1 Enoggera dist Brisbane, Qnsld Australia
69 F13 Enok Sumatra
98 J8 Enola Nebraska U.S.A.
29 O9 Enonkoski Finland
29 K3 Enontekiö Finland
112 F3 Enoree R South Carolina U.S.A.
112 F3 Enoree South Carolina U.S.A.
95 P2 Enosburg Falls Vermont U.S.A.
67 D5 Enping China
70 F6 Enrekang Sulawesi
71 E2 Enrile Luzon Philippines
127 J5 Enriquillo, Lago de Dominican Rep
25 E3 Ens Netherlands
139 J6 Ensay Victoria Australia
25 G4 Enschede Netherlands
36 B5 Ensdorf Germany
32 H10 Ense Germany
133 F4 Ensenada Argentina
124 A2 Ensenada Mexico
106 D5 Ensenada New Mexico U.S.A.
126 B3 Ensenada de Guadiana B Cuba
36 C5 Ensheim Germany
80 D4 'En Shemer Israel
67 C1 Enshi China
118 D8 Ensign Alberta Canada
107 K4 Ensign Kansas U.S.A.
99 U4 Ensign Michigan U.S.A.
19 K5 Ensisheim France
28 F4 Enslev Denmark
9 E4 Enstone England
86 F5 Entebbe Uganda
37 N4 Entenbühl mt Germany
12 E3 Enterkinfoot Scotland
117 P5 Enterprise Northwest Territories Canada
121 O8 Enterprise Ontario Canada
111 L10 Enterprise Alabama U.S.A.
107 N3 Enterprise Kansas U.S.A.
111 H9 Enterprise Mississippi U.S.A.
100 H4 Enterprise Oregon U.S.A.
103 L4 Enterprise Utah U.S.A.
71 D5 Enterprise Pt Philippines
100 E2 Entiat Mts Washington U.S.A.
70 C4 Entimau, Bt mt Sarawak
17 F8 Entinas,Pta. De Las Spain
133 D8 Entrada,Pta Argentina
18 H5 Entrains France
21 J6 Entrammes France
140 A3 Entrance I N Terr Australia
18 G8 Entraygues France
143 B10 Entrecasteaux, Pt.d' W Australia Australia
137 N5 Entrecasteaux, Récifs D' reefs New Caledonia
83 J14 Entre-Deux Réunion Indian Oc
123 L6 Entré, I. d' Madeleine Is, Quebec Canada
129 H5 Entre Rios Brazil
130 G7 Entre Rios de Minas Brazil
36 F6 Entringen Germany
103 M7 Entro Arizona U.S.A.
89 E2 Entuba Zimbabwe
118 C5 Entwistle Alberta Canada
85 F7 Enugu Nigeria
100 D2 Enumclaw Washington U.S.A.
21 N2 Envermeu France
27 H11 Enviken Sweden
8 D3 Enville England
128 D5 Envira Brazil
67 B1 Enyang China
48 E4 Enying Hungary
144 C5 Enys, Mt New Zealand
36 F6 Enz R Germany
45 H2 Enza R Italy
80 E8 'En Ẕafẕafa Israel
61 M10 Enzan Japan
37 M6 Enzelhausen Germany
36 E6 Enzklösterle Germany
80 B7 En Ẕurim Israel
36 F6 Enzweihingen Germany
111 D11 Eola Louisiana U.S.A.
110 E2 Eolia Missouri U.S.A.
21 L3 Epaignes France
45 P8 Epameo, M mt Italy

174

Epaney — Fall River Mills

21 K4 Epaney France
46 F4 Epanomí Greece
32 F8 Epe Germany
25 E4 Epe Netherlands
133 E5 Epecuén,L Argentina
22 E3 Epéhy France
140 D5 Epenarra N Terr Australia
22 C2 Éperlecques France
18 H3 Épernay France
87 B9 Epernbe Namibia
21 O4 Épernon France
111 H9 Epes Alabama U.S.A.
21 J8 Epesses, les France
36 C7 Epfig France
138 E2 Ephemeral Lakes South Australia Australia
103 N2 Ephraim Utah U.S.A.
95 L6 Ephrata Pennsylvania U.S.A.
100 F2 Ephrata Washington U.S.A.
137 O5 Épi isld Vanuatu
88 G10 Epidendron isld Mozambique
46 F7 Epídhavros Greece
21 O6 Epieds France
17 G3 Épila Spain
19 K4 Epinal France
20 F8 Epine, l' Vendée France
20 G5 Epiniac France
98 J6 Epiphany South Dakota U.S.A.
79 C4 Episkopi Cyprus
21 O4 Epône France
36 B5 Eppelborn Germany
37 P2 Eppendorf Germany
22 F4 Eppes France
22 G3 Eppe-Sauvage France
9 G4 Epping England
95 Q3 Epping New Hampshire U.S.A.
98 C1 Epping North Dakota U.S.A.
36 F5 Eppingen Germany
36 E3 Eppstein Germany
98 A4 Epsie Montana U.S.A.
9 F5 Epsom England
21 M6 Epuisay France
87 C10 Epukiro Namibia
13 H6 Epworth England
99 Q7 Epworth Iowa U.S.A.
77 C4 Eqlīd Iran
110 H4 Equality Illinois U.S.A.
86 D5 Equateur prov Zaire
86 E4 Equatoria prov Sudan
73 L9 Equatorial Chan Maldives
85 F8 Equatorial Guinea rep W Africa
20 G2 Equeurdreville France
95 M5 Equmunk Pennsylvania U.S.A.
60 O4 Era Japan
86 E4 Era watercourse Sudan
141 H7 Erac R Queensland Australia
71 C6 Eran Palawan Philippines
71 C6 Eran Bay Palawan Philippines
111 D12 Erath Louisiana U.S.A.
78 F1 Erbaa Turkey
36 D5 Erbach R Germany
36 H7 Erbach Baden-Württemberg Germany
36 G4 Erbach Hessen Germany
86 G1 Erba, Jebel mt Sudan
37 N4 Erbendorf Germany
135 N4 Erben Tablemount Pacific Oc
36 C4 Erbes Kopf mt Germany
20 H6 Erbray France
22 D4 Ercheu France
78 J2 Erciş Turkey
78 E2 Erciyas Dag Turkey
45 Q8 Ercolana Italy
48 E3 Ercsi Hungary
48 E3 Erd Hungary
65 H2 Erdaohezi China
65 G3 Erdao Jiang R China
47 J4 Erdek Turkey
47 J4 Erdek Körfezi B Turkey
79 E2 Erdemli Turkey
56 F6 Erdenet Mongolia
20 D6 Erdeven France
86 D2 Erdi dist Chad
37 M7 Erding Germany
37 M7 Erdinger Moos marsh Germany
9 E2 Erdington England
37 P2 Erdmannsdorf Germany
36 B3 Erdorf Germany
20 H6 Erdre R France
20 F5 Éréac France
128 F2 Erebato R Venezuela
146 D11 Erebus, Mt vol Ross I Antarctica
78 K6 Erech Iraq
130 D10 Erechim Brazil
58 G2 Ereentsav Mongolia
Ereğli see Marmaraereğlisi
78 C1 Ereğli Turkey
71 H7 Ereke Indonesia
47 L7 Eren R Turkey
47 K8 Eren Dağ mt Turkey
65 D2 Eren Gobi China
65 B3 Erenhot China
Erenköy see İntepe
47 N11 Erenköy Turkey
129 G4 Erepecu, L Brazil
16 D3 Eresma R Spain
47 H5 Eressós Greece
80 B7 Erez Israel
22 K3 Erezée Belgium
32 K4 Erfde Germany
89 E7 Erfenis Dam res S Africa
65 A4 Erfenzi China
85 D2 Erfoud Morocco
36 B2 Erft R Germany
36 B2 Erftstadt Germany
37 L2 Erfurt Germany
56 D4 Ergak-Targak-Tayga, Khrebet mts Russian Federation
78 G2 Ergani Turkey
85 D4 Erg Chech desert region Mali/Algeria
86 C2 Erg du Djourab dist Chad
65 A3 Ergel Mongolia
47 H3 Ergene R Turkey
85 D3 Erg er Raoui desert region Algeria
85 C3 Erg Iguid sand desert Algeria/Mauritania
55 E1 Erginskiy Sor, Oz L Russian Federation
52 C6 Ērgli Latvia
37 N6 Ergolding Germany
37 N6 Ergoldsbach Germany
65 G1 Ergu China
20 B6 Ergué-Armel France
86 C3 Erguig R Chad
Ergun He R see Argun R
59 H1 Ergun Youqi China
59 H1 Ergun Zuoqi China
37 O7 Erharting Germany
16 D2 Eria R Spain
86 G2 Eriba Sudan
16 A6 Ericeira Portugal
32 K7 Erichshagen Germany
107 L6 Erick Oklahoma U.S.A.
119 S8 Erickson Manitoba Canada
122 G2 Eric L Quebec Canada
99 N1 Ericsburg Minnesota U.S.A.
98 H8 Ericson Nebraska U.S.A.
98 A9 Erie Colorado U.S.A.
99 Q8 Erie Illinois U.S.A.
107 P4 Erie Kansas U.S.A.
94 D5 Erie Michigan U.S.A.
103 J6 Erie Nevada U.S.A.
98 J2 Erie North Dakota U.S.A.
94 G4 Erie Pennsylvania U.S.A.
120 J10 Erieau Ontario Canada
94 G4 Erie,L U.S.A./Canada
79 H1 Erikli Turkey
47 O12 Erikoúsa isld Greece
119 T8 Eriksdale Manitoba Canada
46 E7 Erimanthos mt Greece
60 R4 Erimo-misaki C Japan
22 C3 Erin France
37 P7 Ering Germany
27 H15 Eringsboda Sweden
127 N3 Erin Pt Trinidad
15 A3 Eriskay isld Scotland
9 G5 Erith England
46 F6 Erithraí Greece
Eritrea see Ertra
25 F6 Erkelenz Germany
27 K12 Erken Sweden
33 T8 Erkner Germany
86 G2 Erkowit Sudan
32 E10 Erkrath Germany
38 F6 Erl Austria
Erlangdiang see Dawu
37 L4 Erlangen Germany
94 C7 Erlanger Kentucky U.S.A.
38 M5 Erlauf R Austria
37 N3 Erlbach Germany
140 C7 Erldunda N Terr Australia
36 F3 Erlensee Germany
111 C8 Erling,L Arkansas U.S.A.
65 G3 Erlong Shan mt China
38 F8 Erlsbach Austria
25 E4 Ermelo Netherlands
89 F6 Ermelo S Africa
78 D3 Ermenek Turkey
79 D2 Ermenek R Turkey
71 M9 Ermera Indonesia
Ermoúpolis see Síros
33 O9 Ermsleben Germany
138 B2 Ernabella South Australia Australia
138 B2 Ernabella R South Australia Australia
76 C6 Ernakulam India
36 E1 Erndtebrück Germany
14 C2 Erne R Ireland
21 J5 Ernée France
21 J5 Ernée R France
14 D2 Erne,L.Lower N Ireland
14 D2 Erne,L.Upper N Ireland
143 E7 Ernest Giles Ra W Australia Australia
144 A7 Ernest Is New Zealand
135 M12 Ernest Legouve Reef Pacific Oc
117 G8 Ernest Sd Alaska U.S.A.
118 L8 Ernfold Saskatchewan Canada
45 O6 Ernici, Monti mt Italy
36 G4 Ernstthal Germany
76 C5 Erode India
78 J2 Erois Turkey
141 G7 Eromanga Queensland Australia
111 D9 Eros Louisiana U.S.A.
36 B2 Erp Germany
22 G3 Erquelinnes Belgium
20 F4 Erquy France
20 F4 Erquy, C.d' France
143 B7 Errabiddy Hills W Australia Australia
85 D2 Er Rachidia Morocco
86 F3 Er Rahad Sudan
80 G6 Er Rajib Jordan
88 F10 Errego Mozambique
14 C1 Errigal mt Ireland
28 G7 Errindlev Denmark
14 A2 Erris Hd Ireland
28 D5 Erritsø Denmark
111 G12 Errol I Louisiana U.S.A.
137 O5 Erromango isld Vanuatu
86 F3 Er Roseires Sudan
46 D4 Ersekë Albania
118 E6 Erskine Alberta Canada
142 F4 Erskine, Mount W Australia Australia
26 M6 Ersnäs Sweden
36 D7 Erstein France
19 L4 Ersteir France
36 H3 Erthal Germany
54 M5 Ertil' Russian Federation
66 D2 Ertix He R China
86 G2 Ertra prov Ethiopia
47 J5 Ertugrul Turkey
22 F1 Ertvelde Belgium
145 E3 Erua New Zealand
138 E4 Erudina South Australia Australia
27 H12 Ervalla Sweden
21 K6 Erve R France
37 Q2 Ervěnice Czechoslovakia
22 D3 Ervillers France
112 J2 Erwin North Carolina U.S.A.
112 E1 Erwin Tennessee U.S.A.
32 H9 Erwitte Germany
119 P6 Erwood Saskatchewan Canada
8 C3 Erwood Wales
33 O8 Erxleben Germany
46 D3 Erzen R Albania
37 N3 Erzgebirge Germany
56 E5 Erzin Russian Federation
79 G2 Erzin Turkey
78 G2 Erzincan Turkey
78 H2 Erzurum Turkey
52 B6 Erzvilkas Lithuania
60 P4 Esan-misaki C Japan
21 J3 Esaue R France
28 A6 Esbjerg Denmark
107 M2 Esbon Kansas U.S.A.
17 G2 Esca R Spain
18 E10 Esca R Spain
130 J10 Escada Brazil
103 N4 Escalante R Utah U.S.A.
103 N4 Escalante Utah U.S.A.
103 L4 Escalante Des Utah U.S.A.
131 A8 Escalera,Pta Chile
124 G4 Escalón Mexico
16 E4 Escalona Spain
111 J11 Escambia R Florida U.S.A.
99 T3 Escanaba R Michigan U.S.A.
99 T4 Escanaba Michigan U.S.A.
125 O8 Escárcega Mexico
21 H7 Escarpière, l' France
22 E3 Escaut R France
36 E3 Esch Germany
22 L5 Esch Luxembourg
36 G4 Eschau Germany
36 F3 Eschborn Germany
22 K4 Eschdorf Luxembourg
32 E7 Eschebrügge Germany
32 M7 Eschede Germany
37 L4 Eschenau Germany
37 M4 Eschenbach Germany
36 E2 Eschenberg Germany
32 L9 Eschershausen Germany
40 G4 Escholzmatt Switzerland
116 G3 Eschscholtz B Alaska U.S.A.
22 K4 Esch-sur-la-Sûre Luxembourg
37 J1 Eschwege Germany
25 F7 Eschweiler Germany
127 K5 Escocesa, B Dominican Rep
130 H5 Escondido Brazil
102 G8 Escondido California U.S.A.
20 F7 Escoublac France
122 C5 Escoumins,R Quebec Canada
21 P5 Escrennes France
13 G6 Escrick England
124 G6 Escuinapa de Hidalgo Mexico
122 F5 Escuminac Quebec Canada
122 H6 Escuminac, Pt New Brunswick Canada
86 B5 Eséka Cameroon
Eşen see Kestep
47 N10 Esenceli Turkey
32 G5 Esens Germany
17 H2 Esera R Spain
77 B3 Eşfahān Iran
16 E3 Esgueva R Spain
80 B8 Eshbol Israel
80 B8 Eshel Ha Nasi Israel
9 F5 Esher England
77 L1 Eshkamesh Afghanistan
57 F6 Eshkāshem Afghanistan
87 F11 Eshowe S Africa
Esh Shem see Dimashq
77 B2 Eshtehard Iran
80 D8 Eshtemoa Jordan
87 E10 Esigodini Zimbabwe
42 E5 Esino R Italy
141 K7 Esk Queensland Australia
139 H8 Esk R Tasmania Australia
116 N6 Eska Alaska U.S.A.
118 L8 Eskbank Saskatchewan Canada
145 F3 Eskdale New Zealand
13 E5 Eskdale Green England
14 C2 Eske, L Ireland
47 K7 Eskere Turkey
29 T9 Eskifjordhur Iceland
28 H5 Eskildstrup Denmark
28 H7 Eskilstrup Denmark
27 H12 Eskilstuna Sweden
122 J3 Eskimo I Quebec Canada
114 F4 Eskimo Lakes Northwest Territories Canada
115 K5 Eskimo Point Northwest Territories Canada
78 D1 Eskipazar Turkey
47 L5 Eskişehir Turkey
13 H5 Esk,R England
15 E5 Esk,R Scotland
107 O3 Eskridge Kansas U.S.A.
16 D2 Esla R Spain
16 D3 Esla, Embalse del res Spain
78 L4 Eslamabad-e Gharb Iran
77 G2 Eslām Qal'eh Afghanistan
37 O4 Eslarn Germany
32 H10 Eslohe Germany
27 F16 Eslöv Sweden
47 K6 Eşme Turkey
141 G4 Esmeralda Queensland Australia
126 E4 Esmeralda Cuba
133 B7 Esmeralda, I Chile
128 C3 Esmeraldas Ecuador
98 G1 Esmond North Dakota U.S.A.
98 J5 Esmond South Dakota U.S.A.
120 D2 Esnagami L Ontario Canada
120 F4 Esnagi L Ontario Canada
22 J2 Esnaux Belgium
27 E11 Espa Norway
127 J8 Espada,Pta Colombia
18 G8 Espalion France
17 H6 Espalmador isld Balearic Is
120 J6 Espanola Ontario Canada
128 B8 Española isld Galapagos Is
113 F8 Espanola Florida U.S.A.
106 D6 Espanola New Mexico U.S.A.
19 P17 Esparron France
102 B3 Esparto California U.S.A.
125 M5 Esparza Costa Rica
28 E6 Espe Denmark
27 D10 Espedals-vatn L Norway
32 J8 Espelkamp Germany
116 E3 Espenberg,C Alaska U.S.A.
37 N1 Espenhain Germany
88 F8 Esperança Mozambique
143 D10 Esperance W Australia Australia
143 D10 Esperance B W Australia Australia
146 D3 Esperanza Argentina Base Graham Land Antarctica
131 E3 Esperanza Argentina
124 E4 Esperanza Mexico
113 K7 Esperanza Puerto Rico
108 B4 Esperanza Texas U.S.A.
125 M2 Esperanza, Sa. de la ra Honduras
29 K5 Espergærde Denmark
45 P7 Esperia Italy
16 A6 Espichel,C Portugal
16 D6 Espiel Spain
130 E10 Espigão,Serra do mts Brazil
16 D2 Espigüete mt Spain
128 D6 Espinar Peru
19 Q16 Espinasses France
124 J4 Espinazo Mexico
130 G6 Espinhaço,Serra,do mt Brazil
16 B4 Espinho Portugal
131 G2 Espinilho, Serra do ra Brazil
130 G4 Espinosa Brazil
130 H6 Espirito Santo state Brazil
124 D5 Espiritu Santo isld Mexico
137 O5 Espiritu Santo isld Vanuatu
125 Q8 Espiritu Santo, B. del Mexico
133 D8 Espiritu Santo,C Chile/Arg
71 G4 Espiritu Santo,C Philippines
125 P7 Espita Mexico
123 R6 Espoir, B. d' Newfoundland Canada
16 B3 Esposende Portugal
40 D2 Esprels France
87 F10 Espungabera Mozambique
100 F3 Esquatzel Coulee R Washington U.S.A.
124 E2 Esqueda Mexico
133 C6 Esquel Argentina
22 C2 Esquelbecq France
100 B1 Esquimalt British Columbia Canada
117 M11 Esquimalt British Columbia Canada
133 F3 Esquina Argentina
29 K4 Esrum Sø L Denmark
55 D1 Ess R Russian Federation
80 F3 Es Samt Jordan
80 D8 Es Samu Jordan
85 C2 Essaouira Morocco
80 G3 Es Sarih Jordan
21 O4 Essarts-le-Roi, les France
20 H8 Essarts, les Vendée France
21 L4 Essay France
85 E2 Es Seggeur watercourse Algeria
32 L7 Essel Germany
22 G1 Essen Belgium
32 G7 Essen Niedersachsen Germany
32 E10 Essen Nordrhein-Westfalen Germany
37 N6 Essenbach Germany
143 D6 Essendon, Mt W Australia Australia
120 H10 Essex Ontario Canada
9 G4 Essex co England
103 J7 Essex California U.S.A.
95 P5 Essex Connecticut U.S.A.
99 L9 Essex Iowa U.S.A.
101 M1 Essex Montana U.S.A.
95 O2 Essex New York U.S.A.
95 O2 Essex Junct Vermont U.S.A.
94 D3 Essexville Michigan U.S.A.
37 M6 Essing Germany
37 J6 Essingen Germany
36 G6 Esslingen Germany
21 P4 Essonne dept France
21 P5 Essonne R France
52 D4 Essoyla Russian Federation
100 C4 Estacada Oregon U.S.A.
16 B1 Estaca de Bares, Pta. de la Spain
106 G8 Estacado, Llano plain New Mex/Tex U.S.A.
103 K10 Estacion Doctor Mexico
103 K10 Estacion France Mexico
103 K9 Estación Mèdanos Mexico
133 E8 Estados, I. de los Argentina
18 G10 Estagel France
71 F2 Estagno Pt Luzon Philippines
77 D5 Eşţahbānāt Iran
120 K6 Estaire Ontario Canada
22 D2 Estaires France
129 L6 Estância Brazil
108 A1 Estancia New Mexico U.S.A.
17 F7 Estancias, Sierra de las mts Spain
77 G4 Estand, Kūh-e- mt Iran
125 O9 Estapilla Mexico
16 B4 Estarreja Portugal
18 F10 Estats, Pic d' mt Spain
40 E4 Estavayer le Lac Switzerland
89 F7 Estcourt S Africa
32 L6 Este R Germany
42 D3 Este Italy
125 L3 Esteli Nicaragua
17 F2 Estella Spain
98 K5 Estelline South Dakota U.S.A.
16 D5 Estena R Spain
16 D7 Estepa Spain
16 D8 Estepona Spain
133 G4 Este, Pta. del Uruguay
116 N4 Ester Alaska U.S.A.
98 A7 Esterbrook Wyoming U.S.A.
119 P8 Esterhazy Saskatchewan Canada
18 H4 Esternay France
113 F11 Estero Florida U.S.A.
102 C6 Estero B California U.S.A.
133 C8 Estero Obstrucción Chile
125 K6 Esteros Mexico
133 E2 Esteros Paraguay
133 F3 Esteros del Iberá swamp Argentina
18 F10 Esterri de Aneu Spain
32 G6 Esterwegen Germany
98 A9 Estes Pk Colorado U.S.A.
119 P9 Estevan Saskatchewan Canada
117 J9 Estevan Group islds British Columbia Canada
117 K11 Estevan Point British Columbia Canada
118 G7 Esther Alberta Canada
99 M6 Estherville Iowa U.S.A.
112 F5 Estill South Carolina U.S.A.
18 H4 Estissac France
119 N8 Estlin Saskatchewan Canada
118 J7 Eston Saskatchewan Canada
52 B5 Estonia rep E Europe
Estonskaya S.S.R. see Estonia
16 A6 Estoril Portugal
19 Q17 Estoublon France
22 C2 Estree Blanche France
22 D5 Estrées St. Denis France
133 G4 Estreito Brazil
130 F6 Estrêla do Indaiá Brazil
130 F6 Estrêla do Sul Brazil
16 B4 Estrela, Sa. da mts Portugal
103 M9 Estrella Arizona U.S.A.
102 D6 Estrella R California U.S.A.
103 M8 Estrella,Sierra mt Arizona U.S.A.
129 K6 Estrelto, Serra do mts Brazil
16 A6 Estremadura prov Portugal
16 B6 Estremoz Portugal
129 J5 Estrondo, Serra do mts Brazil
28 E3 Estruplund Denmark
118 H8 Estuary Saskatchewan Canada
28 B3 Estvad Denmark
48 E3 Esztergom Hungary
20 E4 Étables France
138 E3 Etadunna South Australia Australia
115 M2 Etah Greenland
19 J3 Etain France
22 K4 Étalle Belgium
123 N3 Etamamiou,R Quebec Canada
123 N3 Etamamu Quebec Canada
123 N3 Etamamu R Quebec Canada
21 P5 Etampes France
138 F2 Etamunbanie,L South Australia Australia
80 B7 Etan Israel
18 H6 Étang France
123 L6 Étang-du-Nord Madeleine Is, Quebec Canada
22 B2 Étaples France
74 H6 Etawa India
119 V1 Etawney L Manitoba Canada
124 E4 Etchojoa Mexico
20 D6 Etel France
27 K14 Etelhem Gotland Sweden
85 E5 Etelia Mali
32 K7 Etelsen Germany
122 B5 Eternité,L Quebec Canada
146 C5 Eternity Ra Antarctica
98 H6 Ethan South Dakota U.S.A.
22 K4 Ethe Belgium
111 E11 Ethel Louisiana U.S.A.
111 G8 Ethel Mississippi U.S.A.
110 D2 Ethel Missouri U.S.A.
94 F9 Ethel West Virginia U.S.A.
119 R7 Ethelbert Manitoba Canada
140 A5 Ethel Cr N Terr Australia
141 G3 Ethel Cr Queensland Australia
142 D6 Ethel Creek W Australia Australia
143 C6 Ethel R W Australia Australia
111 H8 Ethelsville Alabama U.S.A.
119 N6 Ethelton Saskatchewan Canada
141 G4 Etheridge R Queensland Australia
101 R6 Ethete Wyoming U.S.A.
86 G4 Ethiopia socialist state Africa
101 N1 Ethridge Montana U.S.A.
47 H5 Etili Turkey
40 F5 Etivaz, l' L Switzerland
116 J2 Etivluk R Alaska U.S.A.
27 D10 Etna R Norway
95 S2 Etna Maine U.S.A.
101 M8 Etna Utah U.S.A.
43 F11 Etna, Monte vol Sicily
27 A12 Etne Norway
27 D11 Etnedal Norway
121 L9 Etobicoke Ontario Canada
111 B10 Etoile Texas U.S.A.
116 D6 Etolin,C Alaska U.S.A.
117 G7 Etolin I Alaska U.S.A.
116 E6 Etolin Str Alaska U.S.A.
119 P6 Etomami Saskatchewan Canada
141 J5 Eton Queensland Australia
120 F5 Eton Ontario Canada
9 F5 Eton England
22 K5 Eton France
87 C9 Etosha Nat. Park Namibia
87 C9 Etosha Pan Namibia
112 B3 Etowah R Georgia U.S.A.
112 C2 Etowah Tennessee U.S.A.
22 F4 Etreaupont France
21 P5 Etrechy France
22 E4 Etreillers France
21 O3 Étrépagny France
21 L2 Étretat France
22 F4 Etreux France
22 D3 Étricourt-Manancourt France
40 A4 Etrigny France
46 F2 Etropole Bulgaria
22 F3 Etrœungt France
22 L4 Ettelbrück Luxembourg
36 D7 Ettenheim Germany
25 C5 Etten-Leur Netherlands
37 L1 Ettersburg Germany
100 A9 Ettersburg California U.S.A.
37 J2 Etterwinden Germany
9 E3 Ettington England
37 O6 Ettling Germany
36 E6 Ettlingen Germany
142 C5 Ettrick W Australia Australia
144 B6 Ettrick New Zealand
99 P5 Ettrick Wisconsin U.S.A.
15 E5 Ettrick Pen mt Scotland
13 E3 Ettrick Water Scotland
80 G6 Et Tuneib Jordan
80 G3 Et Turra Jordan
26 N5 Etu-Aapua mt Sweden
9 E2 Etwall England
124 G7 Etzatlán Mexico
37 P1 Etzdorf Germany
118 F9 Etzikom Alberta Canada
118 F9 Etzikom Coulee R Alberta Canada
21 N1 Eu France
137 S6 'Eua isld Tonga
139 H5 Euabalong New South Wales Australia
94 C9 Eubank Kentucky U.S.A.
36 H4 Eubigheim Germany
Euboea isld see Évvoia isld
143 G9 Eucla W Australia Australia
98 K2 Euclid Minnesota U.S.A.
94 F5 Euclid Ohio U.S.A.
139 J6 Eucumbene,L New South Wales Australia
122 G3 Eudites,L.des Quebec Canada
111 E8 Eudora Arkansas U.S.A.
138 E5 Eudunda South Australia Australia
37 J3 Euerdorf Germany
111 L10 Eufala Alabama U.S.A.
107 P6 Eufaula Oklahoma U.S.A.
107 P6 Eufaula L Oklahoma U.S.A.
43 G10 Eufemia,S.,Golfo di Italy
45 L1 Euganei, Colli hills Italy
100 B5 Eugene Oregon U.S.A.
124 B4 Eugenia, Pta C Mexico
130 C8 Eugênio Penzo Brazil
29 K8 Eugmo isld Finland
139 J5 Eugowra New South Wales Australia
37 O1 Eula R Germany
109 N9 Euless Texas U.S.A.
141 H8 Eulo Queensland Australia
112 F6 Eulonia Georgia U.S.A.
139 J4 Eumaungerie New South Wales Australia
16 B1 Eume R Spain
141 J5 Eungella Queensland Australia
111 D11 Eunice Louisiana U.S.A.
108 D3 Eunice New Mexico U.S.A.
22 L2 Eupen Belgium
78 J5 Euphrates R S W Asia
111 G8 Eupora Mississippi U.S.A.
27 M10 Eura Finland
29 J10 Eurajoki Finland
18 F3 Eure dept France
21 N3 Eure R France
18 F4 Eure-et-Loir dept France
115 L1 Eureka Northwest Territories Canada
100 A9 Eureka California U.S.A.
99 R9 Eureka Illinois U.S.A.
107 O4 Eureka Kansas U.S.A.
101 L1 Eureka Montana U.S.A.
103 J2 Eureka Nevada U.S.A.
98 G4 Eureka South Dakota U.S.A.
101 N10 Eureka Utah U.S.A.
100 G3 Eureka Washington U.S.A.
116 O6 Eureka Lodge Alaska U.S.A.
117 O7 Eureka River Alberta Canada
115 L2 Eureka Snd Northwest Territories Canada
110 C5 Eureka Springs Arkansas U.S.A.
102 G4 Eureka Valley California U.S.A.
138 F4 Eurinilla R South Australia Australia
138 F4 Euriowie New South Wales Australia
139 H6 Euroa Victoria Australia
141 J7 Eurombah R Queensland Australia
141 J7 Eurombah Queensland Australia
81 B8 Europa isld Mozambique Chan
16 D8 Europa Pt Gibraltar
25 B5 Europoort Netherlands
61 J11 Eushimi Japan
36 B2 Euskirchen Germany
109 L3 Eustace Texas U.S.A.
113 F9 Eustis Florida U.S.A.
98 F9 Eustis Nebraska U.S.A.
139 G5 Euston New South Wales Australia
111 J9 Eutaw Alabama U.S.A.
112 G4 Eutawville South Carolina U.S.A.
33 N4 Eutin Germany
36 F7 Eutingen Germany
117 K9 Eutsuk L British Columbia Canada
33 R9 Eutzsch Germany
13 F6 Euxton England
111 E10 Eva Louisiana U.S.A.
108 C7 Eva Oklahoma U.S.A.
140 C4 Eva Downs N Terr Australia
87 C9 Evale Angola
99 M5 Evan Minnesota U.S.A.
139 H8 Evandale Tasmania Australia
100 H1 Evans Washington U.S.A.
118 B5 Evansburg Alberta Canada
115 L1 Evans,C Northwest Territories Canada
94 G6 Evans City Pennsylvania U.S.A.
139 L3 Evans Head New South Wales Australia
146 C7 Evans Ice Stream ice stream Antarctica
115 M7 Evans,L Quebec Canada
117 O9 Evans,Mt Alberta Canada
106 E2 Evans,Mt Colorado U.S.A.
101 M3 Evans, Mt Montana U.S.A.
115 L5 Evans Str Northwest Territories Canada
99 T7 Evanston Illinois U.S.A.
101 P8 Evanston Wyoming U.S.A.
120 H7 Evansville Ontario Canada
116 M3 Evansville Alaska U.S.A.
110 G3 Evansville Illinois U.S.A.
110 J3 Evansville Indiana U.S.A.
99 L3 Evansville Minnesota U.S.A.
99 R7 Evansville Wisconsin U.S.A.
101 T7 Evansville Wyoming U.S.A.
109 J4 Evant Texas U.S.A.
94 B3 Evart Michigan U.S.A.
94 D10 Evarts Kentucky U.S.A.
18 G6 Evaux France
47 H5 Evciler Turkey
99 O2 Eveleth Minnesota U.S.A.
138 C3 Evelyn Ck South Australia Australia
140 C2 Evelyn, Mt N Terr Australia
26 J3 Evenes Norway
110 E5 Evening Shade Arkansas U.S.A.
56 D1 Evenkiyskiy Avtonomnyy Okrug dist Russian Federation
80 E1 Even Menaḥem Israel
51 P2 Evensk Russian Federation
80 C4 Even Yehuda Israel
141 G2 Eve Pk Queensland Australia
22 G3 Evêque Belgium
120 B4 Everard Ontario Canada
138 D4 Everard,L South Australia Australia
140 C6 Everard, Mt N Terr Australia
138 B2 Everard,Mt South Australia Australia
138 C2 Everard Ra South Australia Australia
28 H6 Everdrup Denmark
22 G2 Evere Belgium
107 P2 Everest Kansas U.S.A.
75 M5 Everest, Mt China/Nepal
94 J6 Everett Pennsylvania U.S.A.
100 C2 Everett Washington U.S.A.
112 F6 Everett City Georgia U.S.A.
95 O4 Everett, Mt Massachusetts U.S.A.
22 F1 Evergem Belgium
113 F12 Everglades Florida U.S.A.
113 G12 Everglades Nat. Park Florida U.S.A.
111 K10 Evergreen Alabama U.S.A.
106 E2 Evergreen Colorado U.S.A.
112 J3 Evergreen North Carolina U.S.A.
109 M10 Everman Texas U.S.A.
27 G16 Everöd Sweden
32 H10 Eversberg Germany
32 K6 Eversen Germany
141 G6 Evesham Queensland Australia
118 H6 Evesham Saskatchewan Canada
9 E3 Evesham England
40 D5 Evian-les-Bains France
29 K8 Evijärvi Finland
85 G8 Evinayong Mbini Equat Guinea
46 E6 Évinos R Greece
27 C13 Evje Norway
80 D2 Evlayim Israel
40 G5 Evolène Switzerland
16 B6 Évora Portugal
20 G5 Evran France
21 K3 Evrecy France
47 H4 Evreşe Turkey
21 N3 Évreux France
21 K5 Évron France
80 D2 Evron Israel
46 E3 Évropos Greece
47 H3 Évros R Greece
46 E7 Evrótas R Greece
21 P4 Evry France
79 C3 Evrykhou Cyprus
46 G6 Évvoia isld Greece
102 R12 Ewa Hawaiian Is
102 R12 Ewa Bch Hawaiian Is
100 H2 Ewan Washington U.S.A.
116 P5 Ewan L Alaska U.S.A.
127 K2 Ewarton Jamaica
86 B6 Ewc Congo
9 F5 Ewell England
36 E2 Ewersbach Germany
94 D8 Ewing Kentucky U.S.A.
99 P9 Ewing Missouri U.S.A.
98 H7 Ewing Nebraska U.S.A.
146 D5 Ewing I Antarctica
140 D6 Ewing, Mt N Terr Australia
66 D3 Ewirgol China
128 E6 Exaltación Bolivia
118 G7 Excel Alberta Canada
110 B2 Excelsior Missouri U.S.A.
102 E3 Excelsior Mt California U.S.A.
102 F3 Excelsior Mts Nevada U.S.A.
117 F6 Excursion Alaska U.S.A.
37 K3 Exdorf Germany
146 B8 Executive Committee Ra Antarctica
99 P4 Exeland Wisconsin U.S.A.
8 C5 Exe,R England
120 J9 Exeter Ontario Canada
8 C6 Exeter England
102 E5 Exeter California U.S.A.
110 C5 Exeter Missouri U.S.A.
98 J9 Exeter Nebraska U.S.A.
95 R4 Exeter New Hampshire U.S.A.
117 S3 Exeter L Northwest Territories Canada
8 C5 Exford England
99 M8 Exira Iowa U.S.A.
99 O9 Exline Iowa U.S.A.
25 G3 Exloo Netherlands
21 L4 Exmes France
8 C6 Exminster England
8 C5 Exmoor Forest England
95 M9 Exmore Virginia U.S.A.
142 A5 Exmouth W Australia Australia
8 C6 Exmouth England
142 A5 Exmouth Gulf W Australia Australia
117 Q3 Exmouth L Northwest Territories Canada
81 H7 Exmouth Plateau Indian Oc
46 E8 Éxo Nímfi Greece
141 J6 Expedition Ra Queensland Australia
123 R5 Exploits R Newfoundland Canada
118 B7 Exshaw Alberta Canada
32 K8 Extertal Germany
8 C5 Exton England
16 C5 Extremadura reg Spain
128 D6 Extremo Brazil
126 F2 Exuma Sd Bahamas
116 P6 Eyak Alaska U.S.A.
80 C5 Eyal Israel
88 E3 Eyasi,L Tanzania
27 C13 Eydehamn Norway
9 F2 Eye England
9 H3 Eye England
118 L8 Eyebrow Saskatchewan Canada
13 F2 Eyemouth Scotland
18 G7 Eygurande France
28 S10 Eyjafjalla ice cap Iceland
28 S8 Eyjafjördhur inlet Iceland
86 A2 Eyl Somalia
18 F8 Eymet France
18 G7 Eymoutiers France
9 E4 Eynsham England
99 O6 Eyota Minnesota U.S.A.
28 S10 Eyrarbakki Iceland
140 E6 Eyre R Queensland Australia
143 F9 Eyre W Australia Australia
118 H7 Eyre Saskatchewan Canada
14 C3 Eyrecourt Ireland
138 E4 Eyre,Mt South Australia Australia
144 B6 Eyre Mts New Zealand
138 D3 Eyre North, L South Australia Australia
138 D5 Eyre Pen South Australia Australia
138 D3 Eyre South, L South Australia Australia
119 R1 Eyrie L Manitoba Canada
37 L5 Eysölden Germany
32 K7 Eystrup Germany
6 F1 Eysturoy isld Faeroes
19 N14 Eyzin France
47 H5 Ezine Turkey
77 A3 Ezna Iran

F

134 C12 Faaone Tahiti Pacific Oc
45 J2 Fabbrico Italy
108 A4 Fabens Texas U.S.A.
27 D10 Fåberg Norway
117 P4 Faber L Northwest Territories Canada
121 L5 Fabre Quebec Canada
42 E5 Fabriano Italy
130 E9 Fábrica de Papel Brazil
48 L6 Făcăeni Romania
128 D3 Facatativa Colombia
141 K6 Facing I Queensland Australia
18 E8 Facture France
133 C7 Facundo Argentina
86 D2 Fada Chad
85 E6 Fada N'Gourma Burkina
51 K1 Faddeya,Zaliv G Russian Federation
51 O1 Fadeyevskiy, Ostrov isld Russian Federation
73 L7 Fadippolu Atoll Maldives
42 D4 Faenza Italy
115 O5 Færingehavn Greenland
6 E1 Faeroe Bank N Atlantic Oc
Færøerne see Faeroes
6 F1 Faeroes islds N Atlantic Oc
86 C4 Fafa R Cent Afr Republic
85 E5 Fafa Mali
71 C3 Fafanlap W Irian
16 B3 Fafe Portugal
86 H4 Fafen watercourse Ethiopia
48 J5 Făgăraş Romania
48 J5 Făgăraşului, Muntii mts Romania
26 G10 Fågelsjö Sweden
27 H14 Fagerhult Sweden
27 H12 Fagersta Sweden
48 G5 Făget Romania
48 H3 Făgetului, Muntii mts Romania
45 L3 Faggiola, M mt Italy
85 F6 Faggo Nigeria
71 C3 Fagita W Irian
45 P5 Fagnano Alto Italy
133 D8 Fagnano, L Chile/Arg
22 G3 Fagnes Belgium
85 D5 Faguibine,L Mali
77 F5 Fahraj Iran
41 O5 Fai Della Paganella Italy
41 J5 Faido Switzerland
Faifo see Hoi An
121 O4 Faillon,L Quebec Canada
106 D9 Fairacres New Mexico U.S.A.
141 J6 Fairbairn Res Queensland Australia
103 O10 Fairbank Arizona U.S.A.
99 O7 Fairbank Iowa U.S.A.
116 O4 Fairbanks Alaska U.S.A.
95 R2 Fairbanks Maine U.S.A.
109 M6 Fairbanks Texas U.S.A.
112 H3 Fair Bluff North Carolina U.S.A.
94 C7 Fairborn Ohio U.S.A.
111 M8 Fairburn Georgia U.S.A.
98 C6 Fairburn South Dakota U.S.A.
99 S9 Fairbury Illinois U.S.A.
98 J9 Fairbury Nebraska U.S.A.
94 H7 Fairchance Pennsylvania U.S.A.
99 Q5 Fairchild Wisconsin U.S.A.
98 H1 Fairdale North Dakota U.S.A.
144 C4 Fairdown New Zealand
144 B7 Fairfax New Zealand
111 L9 Fairfax Alabama U.S.A.
99 M5 Fairfax Minnesota U.S.A.
99 L9 Fairfax Missouri U.S.A.
107 O5 Fairfax Oklahoma U.S.A.
112 F5 Fairfax South Carolina U.S.A.
98 H6 Fairfax South Dakota U.S.A.
95 O2 Fairfax Vermont U.S.A.
100 C2 Fairfax Washington U.S.A.
127 P6 Fairfield Barbados
111 K8 Fairfield Alabama U.S.A.
102 B3 Fairfield California U.S.A.
95 O5 Fairfield Connecticut U.S.A.
101 L6 Fairfield Idaho U.S.A.
110 H3 Fairfield Illinois U.S.A.
99 P8 Fairfield Iowa U.S.A.
95 S2 Fairfield Maine U.S.A.
101 N2 Fairfield Montana U.S.A.
98 H9 Fairfield Nebraska U.S.A.
98 C2 Fairfield North Dakota U.S.A.
95 K7 Fairfield Pennsylvania U.S.A.
109 L4 Fairfield Texas U.S.A.
95 P2 Fairfield Vermont U.S.A.
100 H2 Fairfield Washington U.S.A.
119 T7 Fairford Manitoba Canada
9 E4 Fairford England
110 C4 Fair Grove Missouri U.S.A.
95 R5 Fairhaven Massachusetts U.S.A.
95 L3 Fair Haven New York U.S.A.
95 O3 Fair Haven Vermont U.S.A.
100 B1 Fairholm Washington U.S.A.
118 J5 Fairholme Saskatchewan Canada
113 B12 Fairhope Alabama U.S.A.
15 A2 Fair I Scotland
71 C5 Fairie Queen Philippines
107 Q5 Fairland Oklahoma U.S.A.
144 C6 Fairlie New Zealand
12 D2 Fairlie Scotland
141 G3 Fairlight Queensland Australia
141 G5 Fairlight Queensland Australia
119 Q9 Fairlight Saskatchewan Canada
144 B6 Fairlight New Zealand
99 M6 Fairmont Minnesota U.S.A.
98 J9 Fairmont Nebraska U.S.A.
112 H3 Fairmont North Carolina U.S.A.
107 N5 Fairmont Oklahoma U.S.A.
94 G7 Fairmont West Virginia U.S.A.
117 Q10 Fairmont Hot Springs British Columbia Canada
118 H7 Fairmount Saskatchewan Canada
111 M7 Fair Mount Georgia U.S.A.
94 B6 Fairmount Indiana U.S.A.
95 M8 Fairmount Maryland U.S.A.
98 K3 Fairmount North Dakota U.S.A.
115 M5 Fair Ness C Northwest Territories Canada
13 F2 Fairnilee Scotland
110 E6 Fairoaks Arkansas U.S.A.
102 C3 Fair Oaks California U.S.A.
99 T8 Fair Oaks Indiana U.S.A.
106 E2 Fairplay Colorado U.S.A.
110 C4 Fair Play Missouri U.S.A.
107 L2 Fairport Kansas U.S.A.
99 U4 Fairport Michigan U.S.A.
95 K3 Fairport New York U.S.A.
95 L9 Fair Port Virginia U.S.A.
94 F5 Fairport Harbor Ohio U.S.A.
141 G3 Fairview Queensland Australia
117 O7 Fairview Alberta Canada
99 Q9 Fairview Illinois U.S.A.
107 P2 Fairview Kansas U.S.A.
94 C2 Fairview Michigan U.S.A.
98 B2 Fairview Montana U.S.A.
107 M5 Fairview Oklahoma U.S.A.
94 G4 Fairview Pennsylvania U.S.A.
98 K6 Fairview South Dakota U.S.A.
103 N2 Fairview Utah U.S.A.
94 G7 Fairview West Virginia U.S.A.
117 D6 Fairweather,C Alaska U.S.A.
117 E6 Fairweather,Mt Br Col/Alaska Canada/U.S.A.
119 N5 Fairy Glen Saskatchewan Canada
74 E3 Faisalabad India
112 J2 Faison North Carolina U.S.A.
22 H4 Faissault France
98 D4 Faith South Dakota U.S.A.
79 A9 Faiyûm,El Egypt
66 C6 Faizabad India
127 M5 Fajardo Puerto Rico
135 N10 Fakarava atoll Tuamotu Arch Pacific Oc
9 G2 Fakenham England
136 G2 Fakfak W Irian
28 J6 Fakse Denmark
28 J6 Fakse Ladeplads Denmark
65 F3 Faku China
21 K4 Falaise France
117 P5 Falaise L Northwest Territories Canada
46 F3 Falakrón mt Greece
68 A1 Falam Burma
80 D5 Falama Jordan
48 L4 Fălciu Romania
106 F3 Falcon Colorado U.S.A.
128 D1 Falcón state Venezuela
45 O4 Falconara Marittima Italy
120 K6 Falconbridge Ontario Canada
17 G9 Falcon,C Algeria
43 B8 Falcone,C.del Sardinia
94 H4 Falconer New York U.S.A.
109 H9 Falcon L Texas/Mexico U.S.A./Mexico
28 E6 Faldsled Denmark
85 B6 Falémé R Senegal/Mali
52 H5 Falenki Russian Federation
27 H13 Falerum Sweden
48 L3 Faleshty Moldavia
109 J8 Falfurrias Texas U.S.A.
117 P8 Falher Alberta Canada
100 A9 Falk California U.S.A.
121 L7 Falkenberg Ontario Canada
37 N4 Falkenberg Germany
33 T7 Falkenberg Brandenburg Germany
33 S9 Falkenberg Brandenburg Germany
37 O7 Falkenberg Niederbayern Germany
27 F15 Falkenberg Sweden
33 Q6 Falkenhagen Germany
33 S7 Falkensee Germany
37 N3 Falkenstein Germany
37 O5 Falkenstein Germany
12 E2 Falkirk Scotland
117 O10 Falkland British Columbia Canada
13 E1 Falkland Scotland
131 G8 Falkland Is Atlantic Oc
133 E8 Falkland Sd Falkland Is
110 H7 Falkner Mississippi U.S.A.
46 F8 Falkonéra isld Greece
27 F13 Falköping Sweden
111 K7 Falkville Alabama U.S.A.
125 P9 Fallabón Guatemala
102 G8 Fall Brook California U.S.A.
100 D2 Fall City Washington U.S.A.
99 P5 Fall Creek Wisconsin U.S.A.
33 N8 Fallersleben Germany
26 L6 Fällfors Sweden
28 E5 Falling Denmark
32 L7 Fallingbostel Germany
15 C3 Fall of Glomach Scotland
98 A3 Fallon Montana U.S.A.
102 F2 Fallon Nevada U.S.A.
95 Q5 Fall River Massachusetts U.S.A.
100 D8 Fall River Mills California U.S.A.

107 O4 **Fall R.Res** Kansas U.S.A.
95 N5 **Fallsburg, S** New York U.S.A.
95 K8 **Falls Church** Virginia U.S.A.
99 L9 **Falls City** Nebraska U.S.A.
100 B5 **Falls City** Oregon U.S.A.
109 J7 **Falls City** Texas U.S.A.
94 J5 **Falls Cr** Pennsylvania U.S.A.
15 E5 **Falls of Clyde** Scotland
15 D3 **Falls of Foyers** Scotland
78 J5 **Fallūjah, Al** Iraq
22 H3 **Falmagne** Belgium
9 F6 **Falmer** England
8 A7 **Falmouth** England
127 J1 **Falmouth** Jamaica
94 C8 **Falmouth** Kentucky U.S.A.
95 R5 **Falmouth** Massachusetts U.S.A.
94 B2 **Falmouth** Michigan U.S.A.
94 K8 **Falmouth** Virginia U.S.A.
127 P4 **Falmouth** Antigua W Indies
95 R3 **Falmouth-Foreside** Maine U.S.A.
8 B7 **Fal,R** England
89 A10 **False B** S Africa
116 F9 **False Pass** Aleutian Is
141 F2 **False Pera Hd** Queensland Australia
94 D1 **False Presque I** Michigan U.S.A.
17 H3 **Falset** Spain
127 J5 **Falso, C** Dominican Rep
124 E6 **Falso,C** Mexico
133 D9 **Falso C. de Hornos** Chile
28 H7 **Falster** *isld* Denmark
29 K6 **Falsterbo** Sweden
13 F3 **Falstone** England
42 D5 **Falterona, M** *mt* Italy
48 K3 **Fălticeni** Romania
27 H11 **Falun** Sweden
79 D3 **Famagusta** Cyprus
86 F3 **Famaka** Sudan
133 D3 **Famatina** Argentina
133 D3 **Famatina, Sa. de** *mts* Argentina
22 J3 **Famenne** Belgium
143 E7 **Fame Ra** W Australia Australia
143 F6 **Family Well** W Australia Australia
71 C3 **Fam, Kepulauan** *isld* W Irian
102 E6 **Famoso** California U.S.A.
71 C2 **Fan** *isld* W Irian
14 D1 **Fanad Hd** Ireland
145 E1 **Fanal I** New Zealand
45 J3 **Fanano** Italy
67 F1 **Fanchang** China
110 H5 **Fancy Farm** Kentucky U.S.A.
87 H12 **Fandriana** Madagascar
47 R14 **Fánes** Rhodes Greece
86 F4 **Fangak** Sudan
58 F5 **Fangcheng** China
67 C6 **Fangcheng** China
67 C1 **Fangdou Shan** *mts* China
28 E6 **Fangel** Denmark
65 B5 **Fanglan** China
65 B6 **Fangshan** China
67 C1 **Fang Xian** China
65 G2 **Fangzheng** China
65 D6 **Fangzi** China
65 F3 **Fanjiatun** China
111 B12 **Fannett** Texas U.S.A.
111 G9 **Fannin** Mississippi U.S.A.
109 K7 **Fannin** Texas U.S.A.
Fanning I *see* **Tabuaeran**
77 F6 **Fannuj** Iran
117 L11 **Fanny Bay** British Columbia Canada
119 U9 **Fannystelle** Manitoba Canada
28 A6 **Fanø** *isld* Denmark
42 E5 **Fano** Italy
65 B5 **Fanshi** China
68 F1 **Fan Si Pan** *mt* Vietnam
65 C7 **Fan Xian** China
20 D5 **Faouët,le** France
20 B5 **Faou,le** France
80 F8 **Faqu** Jordan
79 B8 **Fâqûs** Egypt
80 F4 **Fara** Jordan
146 C4 **Faraday** *U.K. Base* Graham Land Antarctica
141 H6 **Faraday, Mt** Queensland Australia
86 E5 **Faradje** Zaire
87 H12 **Farafangana** Madagascar
45 Q8 **Faraglioni** Italy
77 H3 **Farāh** Afghanistan
77 H3 **Farah Rud** *R* Afghanistan
45 N5 **Fara in Sabina** Italy
102 A4 **Farallon Is** California U.S.A.
85 D6 **Faramana** Burkina
85 B6 **Faranah** Guinea
86 H2 **Farasān, Jazā'ir** *isld* Red Sea
84 J5 **Farâyid,G.El** *mt* Egypt
28 C4 **Fårbæk** Denmark
110 E2 **Farber** Missouri U.S.A.
26 J6 **Fårberg** Sweden
48 J3 **Farcău** *mt* Romania
85 C3 **Farciya, Al** Western Sahara
16 E7 **Fardes** *R* Spain
28 A4 **Fåre** Denmark
36 B5 **Farebersviller** France
9 E6 **Fareham** England
28 H6 **Farendløse** Denmark
28 G5 **Fårevejle** Denmark
116 L5 **Farewell** Alaska U.S.A.
145 D4 **Farewell, C** New Zealand
98 K3 **Fargo** North Dakota U.S.A.
107 L5 **Fargo** Oklahoma U.S.A.
29 K4 **Farhult** Sweden
28 C7 **Fårhus** Denmark
80 F5 **Fari'a el Jiftlick** Jordan
121 Q3 **Faribault** Quebec Canada
99 N5 **Faribault** Minnesota U.S.A.
75 N7 **Faridpur** Bangladesh
84 G3 **Farigh** *watercourse* Libya
16 A5 **Farilhões** *isld* Portugal
26 H10 **Färilla** Sweden
85 A6 **Farim** Guinea-Bissau
9 E4 **Faringdon** England
27 K12 **Faringe** Sweden
106 E4 **Farista** Colorado U.S.A.
27 H15 **Färjestaden** Sweden
80 D5 **Farkha** Jordan
118 H1 **Farlane** Ontario Canada
141 J5 **Farleigh** Queensland Australia
121 O6 **Farley** Quebec Canada
99 P7 **Farley** Iowa U.S.A.
106 F5 **Farley** New Mexico U.S.A.
98 J6 **Farmer** South Dakota U.S.A.
99 S9 **Farmer City** Illinois U.S.A.
109 O8 **Farmers Branch** Texas U.S.A.
99 T10 **Farmersburg** Indiana U.S.A.
99 P7 **Farmersburg** Iowa U.S.A.
109 L2 **Farmersville** Texas U.S.A.
111 D9 **Farmerville** Louisiana U.S.A.
95 N6 **Farmingdale** New Jersey U.S.A.
98 D6 **Farmingdale** South Dakota U.S.A.
117 N8 **Farmington** British Columbia Canada
102 D4 **Farmington** California U.S.A.
99 Q9 **Farmington** Illinois U.S.A.
99 P9 **Farmington** Iowa U.S.A.
95 R2 **Farmington** Maine U.S.A.
99 N5 **Farmington** Minnesota U.S.A.
110 F4 **Farmington** Missouri U.S.A.
95 Q3 **Farmington** New Hampshire U.S.A.
106 B5 **Farmington** New Mexico U.S.A.
101 O9 **Farmington** Utah U.S.A.
100 H2 **Farmington** Washington U.S.A.
94 G7 **Farmington** West Virginia U.S.A.
94 B6 **Farmland** Indiana U.S.A.
98 C2 **Farm Unit** North Dakota U.S.A.
112 K2 **Farmville** North Carolina U.S.A.
94 J9 **Farmville** Virginia U.S.A.
98 F9 **Farnam** Nebraska U.S.A.
9 F5 **Farnborough** England
8 D1 **Farndon** England
7 K7 **Farne Deep** North Sea
13 G2 **Farne Is** England
112 C2 **Farner** Tennessee U.S.A.
27 C10 **Farnes** Norway
121 S7 **Farnham** Quebec Canada
9 F5 **Farnham** England
94 H4 **Farnham** New York U.S.A.
117 P10 **Farnham,Mt** British Columbia Canada
9 G5 **Farningham** England
13 F6 **Farnworth** England
129 G4 **Faro** Brazil
117 G4 **Faro** Yukon Territory Canada
28 H7 **Farø** *isld* Denmark
16 B7 **Faro** Portugal
27 K14 **Fårö** *isld* Gotland Sweden
71 G6 **Farol Pt** Philippines
43 G10 **Faro,Pta d** Sicily
86 B4 **Faro R** Cameroon
16 B2 **Faro, Sa del** *mts* Spain
27 K14 **Fårösund** Gotland Sweden
87 J10 **Farquhar Is** Br Indian Oc Terr
83 H6 **Farquhar Is** Seychelles Indian Oc
143 E7 **Farquharson Tableland** W Australia Australia
141 F6 **Farrars Cr** Queensland Australia
26 H5 **Farras** *mt* Sweden
77 C5 **Farrāshband** Iran
94 G5 **Farrell** Pennsylvania U.S.A.
121 P7 **Farrellton** Quebec Canada
8 D5 **Farrington Gurney** England
28 C6 **Farris** Denmark
77 C5 **Fārs** Iran
46 E5 **Fársala** Greece
77 H3 **Fārsī** Afghanistan
28 C3 **Farsø** Denmark
99 O8 **Farson** Iowa U.S.A.
101 Q7 **Farson** Wyoming U.S.A.
27 B13 **Farsund** Norway
130 D10 **Fartura,Serra da** *mts* Brazil
28 D4 **Fårvang** Denmark
115 P6 **Farvel,Kap** *C* Greenland
94 C3 **Farwell** Michigan U.S.A.
98 H8 **Farwell** Nebraska U.S.A.
108 D1 **Farwell** Texas U.S.A.
77 J2 **Fāryab** *prov* Afghanistan
77 C5 **Fasā** Iran
43 H8 **Fasano** Italy
109 J7 **Fashing** Texas U.S.A.
79 A10 **Fashn,El** Egypt
28 B5 **Faster** Denmark
28 C4 **Fasterholt** Denmark
14 B5 **Fastnet Rock** Ireland
74 F7 **Fatehabad** India
74 H5 **Fatehgarh** India
45 O7 **Fate, Mt. delle** Italy
54 G4 **Fatezh** Russian Federation
78 J4 **Fathan,Al** Iraq
121 P3 **Father,L** Quebec Canada
123 L6 **Fatima** Madeleine Is, Quebec Canada
16 B5 **Fatima** Portugal
78 F1 **Fatsa** Turkey
135 N9 **Fatu Hiva** *isld* Marquesas Is Pacific Oc
86 C6 **Fatunda** Zaire
110 B2 **Faucett** Missouri U.S.A.
40 D6 **Faucigny** *dist* France
19 K4 **Faucilles, Mts** France
45 J4 **Fauglia** Italy
40 G4 **Faulhorn** *mt* Switzerland
98 G4 **Faulkton** South Dakota U.S.A.
111 J9 **Faunsdale** Alabama U.S.A.
22 C2 **Fauquembergues** France
117 O11 **Fauquier** British Columbia Canada
48 L5 **Făurei** Romania
89 D7 **Fauresmith** S Africa
26 H4 **Fauske** Norway
118 B3 **Faust** Alberta Canada
95 N2 **Faust** New York U.S.A.
101 N9 **Faust** Utah U.S.A.
21 M2 **Fauville** France
43 F11 **Favara** Sicily
19 Q13 **Faverges** France
21 O4 **Faverolles** Eure France
9 G5 **Faversham** England
43 E11 **Favignana, I** Sicily
28 C4 **Favrholt** Denmark
77 A5 **Faw, Al** Iraq
118 C4 **Fawcett** Alberta Canada
118 D3 **Fawcett L** Alberta Canada
9 E6 **Fawley** England
115 L7 **Fawn** *R* Ontario Canada
28 R9 **Faxa-flói** *B* Iceland
26 J8 **Faxälven** *R* Sweden
27 F10 **Faxfj** *mt* Norway
107 M6 **Fay** Oklahoma U.S.A.
86 C2 **Faya-Largeau** Chad
54 F2 **Fayansovyy** Russian Federation
85 B4 **Faydat as Sadra** Western Sahara
20 G7 **Fay-de-Bretagne** France
21 J7 **Faye-d'Anjou** France
119 Q3 **Faye Lake** Manitoba Canada
21 L8 **Faye-la-Vineuse** France
111 J8 **Fayette** Alabama U.S.A.
99 P7 **Fayette** Iowa U.S.A.
99 U4 **Fayette** Michigan U.S.A.
111 E10 **Fayette** Mississippi U.S.A.
110 D2 **Fayette** Missouri U.S.A.
94 C5 **Fayette** Ohio U.S.A.
103 N2 **Fayette** Utah U.S.A.
110 B5 **Fayetteville** Arkansas U.S.A.
111 M8 **Fayetteville** Georgia U.S.A.
112 J2 **Fayetteville** North Carolina U.S.A.
110 N2 **Fayetteville** Ohio U.S.A.
110 K6 **Fayetteville** Tennessee U.S.A.
109 L6 **Fayetteville** Texas U.S.A.
94 F8 **Fayetteville** West Virginia U.S.A.
22 F3 **Fay le Franc** Belgium
109 J9 **Faysville** Texas U.S.A.
80 G1 **Fazārah** Syria
74 F3 **Fazilka** India
85 B4 **Fdérik** Mauritania
14 B4 **Feale** *R* Ireland
102 C3 **Feather** *R* California U.S.A.
102 C2 **Feather Falls** California U.S.A.
145 E4 **Featherston** New Zealand
139 H6 **Feathertop,Mt** Victoria Australia
101 K6 **Featherville** Idaho U.S.A.
144 A6 **Febrero Pt** New Zealand
21 L2 **Fécamp** France
40 F1 **Fecht** *R* France
133 F4 **Federación** Argentina
98 A8 **Federal** Wyoming U.S.A.
99 M2 **Federal Dam** Minnesota U.S.A.
95 M8 **Federalsburg** Maryland U.S.A.
27 A11 **Fedje** *isld* Norway
98 J5 **Fedora** South Dakota U.S.A.
14 B3 **Feeagh,L** Ireland
36 D7 **Fegersheim** France
28 B3 **Feggesund** *chan* Denmark
20 F6 **Fégréac** France
48 H2 **Fehérhyarmat** Hungary
30 F1 **Fehmarn** *isld* Germany
33 R7 **Fehrbellin** Germany
38 O8 **Fehring** Austria
130 H8 **Feia, Lagoa** *L* Brazil
65 C6 **Feicheng** China
67 F1 **Feidong** China
65 C7 **Fei Huang** *R* China
128 D5 **Feijó** Brazil
67 D5 **Feilai Xia** *R* China
145 E4 **Feilding** New Zealand
Feira *see* **Luangwa** Zambia
129 L6 **Feira de Santana** Brazil
38 J8 **Feistritz** Austria
38 K8 **Feistritz-im-Ros** Austria
67 F1 **Feixi** China
65 D7 **Fei Xian** China
65 C6 **Feixiang** China
129 K8 **Feja, L** Brazil
48 E3 **Fejér** *co* Hungary
28 G7 **Fejø** *isld* Denmark
28 F4 **Fejrup** Denmark
48 D5 **Fekete Viz** *R* Hungary
17 K5 **Felanitx** Majorca
9 F5 **Felbridge** England
99 T3 **Felch** Michigan U.S.A.
36 G2 **Feldatal** Germany
38 N8 **Feldbach** Austria
28 F4 **Feldballe** Denmark
33 S6 **Feldberg** Germany
40 H2 **Feldberg** *mt* Germany
28 C3 **Feldingbjerg** Denmark
41 L3 **Feldkirch** Austria
131 F3 **Feliciano** *R* Argentina
83 J12 **Felicité I** Seychelles
94 C8 **Felicity** Ohio U.S.A.
73 L8 **Felidu Atoll** Maldives
130 G6 **Felixlândia** Brazil
106 F8 **Felix,R** New Mexico U.S.A.
108 C3 **Felix, Rio** New Mexico U.S.A.
9 H4 **Felixstowe** England
108 B5 **Félix U. Gómez** Mexico
36 B4 **Fell** Germany
36 G6 **Fellbach** Germany
18 G7 **Felletin** France
13 G4 **Felling** England
127 M2 **Fellowship** Jamaica
113 G10 **Fellsmere** Florida U.S.A.
45 K2 **Felonica** Italy
9 F6 **Felpham** England
36 G1 **Felsberg** Germany
28 C7 **Felsted** Denmark
108 B7 **Felt** Oklahoma U.S.A.
13 G3 **Felton** England
102 B4 **Felton** California U.S.A.
111 L8 **Felton** Georgia U.S.A.
98 K2 **Felton** Minnesota U.S.A.
42 D2 **Feltre** Italy
28 G7 **Femer Bælt** *str* Denmark/Germany
28 F4 **Femmøller** Denmark
28 H7 **Femø** *isld* Denmark
28 G7 **Femø Sund** *chan* Denmark
26 E9 **Femund** Norway
26 F9 **Femundsmarka Nat. Park** Norway
87 G13 **Fenambosy, Fenambosy** *pt* Madagascar
106 B7 **Fence Lake** New Mexico U.S.A.
65 B7 **Fencheng** China
121 M8 **Fenelon Falls** Ontario Canada
79 F2 **Fener Burun** *C* Turkey
36 B6 **Fénétrange** France
21 J6 **Feneu** France
59 H3 **Fengcheng** China
67 E2 **Fengcheng** China
67 D5 **Fengchuan** China
67 B2 **Fengdu** China
58 F4 **Fengfeng** China
67 B3 **Fenggang** China
67 G2 **Fenghua** China
67 C3 **Fenghuang** China
67 C1 **Fengjie** *R* China
67 D5 **Fengkai** China
65 F2 **Fengle** China
67 D1 **Fengle** China
67 E5 **Fengliang** China
65 A7 **Fenglingdu** China
65 D5 **Fengnan** China
65 C4 **Fengning** China
67 G2 **Fengqiao** China
65 C7 **Fengqiu** China
65 D5 **Fengrun** China
65 D4 **Fengshan** China
67 B4 **Fengshan** China
58 G4 **Fengtai** China
67 F4 **Fengting** China
67 B5 **Fengwu** China
65 C7 **Feng Xian** China
67 G1 **Fengxian** China
58 E5 **Fengxiang** China
67 E2 **Fengxin** China
Fengyi *see* **Zheng'an**
Fengyizhen *see* **Maowen**
67 G4 **Feng-Yuan** Taiwan
65 B4 **Fengzhen** China
65 B6 **Fen He** *R* China
116 H2 **Feniak L** Alaska U.S.A.
21 K8 **Fenioux** France
14 B4 **Fenit** Ireland
100 J4 **Fenn** Idaho U.S.A.
99 Q7 **Fennimore** Wisconsin U.S.A.
94 A4 **Fennville** Michigan U.S.A.
9 F3 **Fenny Stratford** England
87 H11 **Fenoarivo Atsinanana** Madagascar
28 H6 **Fensmark** Denmark
9 F3 **Fenstanton** England
119 M6 **Fenton** Saskatchewan Canada
109 P5 **Fenton** Louisiana U.S.A.
94 D4 **Fenton** Michigan U.S.A.
95 L10 **Fentress** Virginia U.S.A.
135 L10 **Fenua Ura** *isld* Society Is Pacific Oc
121 L9 **Fenwick** Ontario Canada
13 G2 **Fenwick** England
12 D2 **Fenwick** Strathclyde Scotland
94 G8 **Fenwick** West Virginia U.S.A.
119 O7 **Fenwood** Saskatchewan Canada
99 Q5 **Fenwood** Wisconsin U.S.A.
65 B6 **Fenxi** China
65 B6 **Fenyang** China
67 E3 **Fenyi** China
22 H3 **Fépin** France
26 E9 **Feragen** *L* Norway
100 J3 **Ferdinand** Idaho U.S.A.
110 K3 **Ferdinand** Indiana U.S.A.
33 T5 **Ferdinandshof** Germany
18 H4 **Fère-Champenoise** France
77 A5 **Fereidoon** *oil well* Persian Gulf
20 F7 **Férel** France
22 E4 **Fère,La** France
26 E8 **Feren** *L* Norway
45 O6 **Ferentino** Italy
57 F4 **Fergana** Uzbekistan
57 K6 **Fergana Basin** Tajikistan/Uzbekistan
57 G4 **Ferganskiy Khr** *mts* Kyrgyzstan
101 Q2 **Fergus** Montana U.S.A.
98 K3 **Fergus Falls** Minnesota U.S.A.
140 B2 **Fergusson** *R* N Terr Australia
118 E6 **Ferintosh** Alberta Canada
85 C7 **Ferkessédougou** Ivory Coast
120 B2 **Ferland** Ontario Canada
14 D2 **Fermanagh** *co* N Ireland
20 H2 **Fermanville** France
121 P6 **Ferme Neuve** Quebec Canada
33 S9 **Fermerswalde** Germany
45 N4 **Fermignano** Italy
42 F5 **Fermo** Italy
16 C3 **Fermoselle** Spain
14 C4 **Fermoy** Ireland
128 A8 **Fernandina** *isld* Galapagos Is
113 F7 **Fernandina Beach** Florida U.S.A.
90 G9 **Fernando de Noronha** *isld* Atlantic Oc
130 E7 **Fernandópolis** Brazil
Fernando Póo *isld* *see* **Bioko**
16 D7 **Fernán Núñez** Spain
130 G5 **Fernão Dias** Brazil
100 C1 **Ferndale** Washington U.S.A.
98 H4 **Ferney** South Dakota U.S.A.
9 F5 **Fernhurst** England
118 B9 **Fernie** British Columbia Canada
141 H8 **Fernlee** Queensland Australia
102 E2 **Fernley** Nevada U.S.A.
41 N3 **Fern Pass** Austria
100 B5 **Fern Ridge Res** Oregon U.S.A.
14 E4 **Ferns** Ireland
144 D5 **Fernside** New Zealand
36 F2 **Fernwald** Germany
100 J2 **Fernwood** Idaho U.S.A.
111 F10 **Fernwood** Mississippi U.S.A.
123 P2 **Ferolle Pt** Newfoundland Canada
47 H4 **Férrai** Greece
42 D4 **Ferrara** Italy
17 G9 **Ferrat,C** Algeria
44 B4 **Ferrat,Cape** France
43 C9 **Ferrato,C** Sardinia
16 B6 **Ferreira do Alentejo** Portugal
129 H3 **Ferreira Gomes** Brazil
130 D7 **Ferreiros** Brazil
20 H5 **Ferré, le** France
128 C5 **Ferreñafe** Peru
18 E8 **Ferret,C** France
40 F6 **Ferret,Col** *pass* Switz/Italy
19 K5 **Ferreue** France
111 E10 **Ferriday** Louisiana U.S.A.
118 C6 **Ferrier** Alberta Canada
21 K4 **Ferrière-aux-Étangs,la** France
21 K8 **Ferriere,la** Deux Sèvres France
20 H8 **Ferrière,la** Vendée France
21 M7 **Ferrière-Larçon** France
18 G4 **Ferrières** France
21 O2 **Ferrières-en-Bray** France
21 M4 **Ferrière-sur-Risle,la** France
28 A3 **Ferring** Denmark
28 A3 **Ferring Sø** Denmark
99 P9 **Ferris** Illinois U.S.A.
95 O2 **Ferrisburg** Vermont U.S.A.
101 S7 **Ferris Mts** Wyoming U.S.A.
28 F6 **Ferritslev** Denmark
43 C7 **Ferro,C** Sardinia
130 G6 **Ferros** Brazil
123 N2 **Ferru,L** Quebec Canada
43 B8 **Ferru, M** *mt* Sardinia
94 G10 **Ferrum** Virginia U.S.A.
116 N5 **Ferry** Alaska U.S.A.
99 U6 **Ferry** Michigan U.S.A.
13 G6 **Ferrybridge** England
123 U6 **Ferryland** Newfoundland Canada
107 P5 **Ferry Res** Oklahoma U.S.A.
99 U6 **Ferrysburg** Michigan U.S.A.
8 B4 **Ferryside** Wales
99 P6 **Ferryville** Wisconsin U.S.A.
55 C4 **Fershampenuaz** Russian Federation
28 H5 **Ferslev** Denmark
21 P5 **Ferté-Alais,la** France
21 M5 **Ferté-Bernard,la** France
21 M4 **Ferté-Fresnel, la** France
18 H4 **Ferté Gaucher,La** France
21 O7 **Ferté-Imbault,la** France
22 F4 **Ferté, la** France
21 K4 **Ferté-Macé,la** France
21 O6 **Ferté-St.Aubin,la** France
21 O6 **Ferté-St. Cyr,la** France
18 H4 **Ferté sur Jouarre, la** France
21 M4 **Ferté-Vidame,la** France
98 K2 **Fertile** Minnesota U.S.A.
48 D3 **Fertöszentmiklos** Hungary
Fertö Tór *see* **Neusiedler See**
21 L3 **Fervaques** France
41 M3 **Ferwall Gruppe** *mt* Austria
25 E2 **Ferwerd** Netherlands
85 C2 **Fès** Morocco
86 C7 **Feshi** Zaire
98 G2 **Fessenden** North Dakota U.S.A.
19 P15 **Festre, Col du** *pass* France
22 D2 **Festubert** France
110 F3 **Festus** Missouri U.S.A.
48 L6 **Feteşti** Romania
14 D4 **Fethard** Ireland
47 K8 **Fethiye** Turkey
47 K8 **Fethiye Körfezi** *B* Turkey
43 A12 **Fetzara, L** Algeria
37 L5 **Feucht** Germany
41 N3 **Feuchten** Austria
37 J5 **Feuchtwangen** Germany
118 K7 **Feudal** Saskatchewan Canada
21 O3 **Feuillie, la** France
123 M3 **Feu, L. du** Quebec Canada
21 O2 **Feuquières** France
21 O1 **Feuquières-en-Vimeu** France
18 H7 **Feurs** France
77 L1 **Feyzābād** Afghanistan
77 F2 **Feyzābād** Iran
84 E4 **Fezzan** *reg* Libya
8 C2 **Ffestiniog** Wales
8 C4 **Fforest Fawr** *mts* Wales
133 D3 **Fiambalá** Argentina
45 O5 **Fiamignano** Italy
87 H11 **Fianarantsoa** Madagascar
86 C4 **Fianga** Chad
40 F7 **Fiano** Italy
48 G5 **Fibiş** Romania
45 K2 **Ficarolo** Italy
86 G4 **Fichē** Ethiopia
123 R2 **Fichot I** Newfoundland Canada
37 M3 **Fichtelberg** Germany
37 O3 **Fichtelberg** *mt* Germany
37 M3 **Fichtelfebirge** *mts* Germany
37 J5 **Fichtenau** Germany
89 E7 **Ficksburg** S Africa
44 H2 **Fidenza** Italy
119 V1 **Fidler L** Manitoba Canada
135 O4 **Fieberling Table Mt** Pacific Oc
106 C7 **Field** New Mexico U.S.A.
94 G10 **Fieldale** Virginia U.S.A.
140 B1 **Field I** N Terr Australia
118 K6 **Fielding** Saskatchewan Canada
100 G7 **Fields** Oregon U.S.A.
100 A9 **Fields Landing** California U.S.A.
139 H8 **Field West Mt** Tasmania Australia
48 J5 **Fieni** Romania
22 B2 **Fiennes** France
46 D4 **Fier** Albania
19 P13 **Fier** *R* France
42 D2 **Fiera di Primiero** Italy
106 B9 **Fierro** New Mexico U.S.A.
13 E1 **Fife** *reg* Scotland
109 H4 **Fife** Texas U.S.A.
119 M9 **Fife L** Saskatchewan Canada
13 F1 **Fife Ness** Scotland
139 J5 **Fifield** New South Wales Australia
99 Q4 **Fifield** Wisconsin U.S.A.
101 R5 **Fifteen Mile Cr** Wyoming U.S.A.
17 G9 **Figalo,C** Algeria
43 C8 **Figari,C** Sardinia
18 G8 **Figeac** France
27 J14 **Figeholm** Sweden
45 K4 **Figline Valdarno** Italy
127 P4 **Fig Tree** Nevis W Indies
16 B4 **Figuera da Foz** Portugal
16 B5 **Figuera dos Vinhos** Portugal
17 J2 **Figueras** Spain
Figueres *see* **Figueras**
85 D2 **Figuig** Morocco
137 Q5 **Fiji** *islds* Pacific Oc
17 F7 **Filabres, Sierra de los** *mts* Spain
129 J5 **Filadélfia** Brazil
128 F8 **Filadelfia** Paraguay
48 F2 **Filakovo** Czechoslovakia
146 E7 **Filchner Ice Shelf** Antarctica
36 G6 **Filderstadt** Germany
27 C10 **Filefj** *mt* Norway
119 R4 **File L** Manitoba Canada
101 L7 **Filer** Idaho U.S.A.
45 O6 **Filettino** Italy
13 H5 **Filey** England
46 D5 **Filiátes** Greece
46 E7 **Filiatrá** Greece
43 F10 **Filicudi, I** Italy
85 E6 **Filingué** Niger
31 O1 **Filipów** Poland
27 G12 **Filipstad** Sweden
41 L4 **Filisur** Switzerland
48 H6 **Fillaşi** Romania
22 C3 **Fillièvres** France
119 O9 **Fillmore** Saskatchewan Canada
102 F7 **Fillmore** California U.S.A.
94 J4 **Fillmore** New York U.S.A.
98 G1 **Fillmore** North Dakota U.S.A.
103 M3 **Fillmore** Utah U.S.A.
36 H6 **Fils** *R* Germany
28 C5 **Filskov** Denmark
28 A5 **Filsø** Denmark
8 D4 **Filton** England
86 H4 **Filtu** Ethiopia
146 H6 **Fimbulheimen** *ra* Antarctica
146 H6 **Fimbulisen** *ice shelf* Antarctica
42 D4 **Finale Emilia** Italy
44 D3 **Finale Ligure** Italy
17 F7 **Fiñana** Spain
94 H9 **Fincastle** Virginia U.S.A.
121 P7 **Finch** Ontario Canada
9 F4 **Finchley** England
28 C4 **Finderup** Denmark
15 E3 **Findhorn** *R* Scotland
15 E3 **Findhorn** Scotland
78 H1 **Fındıklı** Turkey
79 E2 **Findıkpınarı** Turkey
119 M8 **Findlater** Saskatchewan Canada
99 S10 **Findlay** Illinois U.S.A.
94 D5 **Findlay** Ohio U.S.A.
117 P10 **Findlay,Mt** British Columbia Canada
9 F6 **Findon** England
9 F3 **Finedon** England
139 J8 **Fingal** Tasmania Australia
98 J3 **Fingal** North Dakota U.S.A.
110 H6 **Finger** Tennessee U.S.A.
115 K7 **Finger L** Ontario Canada
95 L4 **Finger Lakes** New York U.S.A.
14 E3 **Finglas** Ireland
88 C9 **Fingoe** *mt* Mozambique
88 C9 **Fingoe** Mozambique
47 L8 **Finike** Turkey
47 P12 **Finiq** Albania
16 A2 **Finisterre,C** Spain
138 D2 **Finke** *R* N Terr Australia
140 C7 **Finke** N Terr Australia
138 D2 **Finke Flood Flats** South Australia Australia
140 C6 **Finke Gorge** N Terr Australia
138 C4 **Finke,Mt** South Australia Australia
140 D7 **Finke, R** N Terr Australia
29 L8 **Finland** *rep* N Europe
99 P2 **Finland** Minnesota U.S.A.
52 C5 **Finland, Gulf of** Estonia/Finland/Rus Fed
114 G6 **Finlay** *R* British Columbia Canada
99 O3 **Finlayson** Minnesota U.S.A.
98 J2 **Finley** North Dakota U.S.A.
109 M1 **Finley** Oklahoma U.S.A.
119 O2 **Finmark** Ontario Canada
14 D2 **Finn** *R* Ireland
12 D1 **Finnart** Scotland
118 E7 **Finnegan** Alberta Canada
26 H4 **Finneid** Norway
36 D1 **Finnentrop** Germany
26 L7 **Finnforsfallet** Sweden
141 H3 **Finnigan, Mt** Queensland Australia
140 B2 **Finniss** *R* N Terr Australia
138 C5 **Finniss,C** South Australia Australia
26 O1 **Finnmark** *county* Norway
26 N2 **Finnmarksvidda** *reg* Norway
116 J6 **Finn Mt** Alaska U.S.A.
27 F11 **Finnskog** Norway
27 F11 **Finnskoga,S** Sweden
26 K2 **Finnsnes** Norway
26 M6 **Finnträsk** Sweden
33 T7 **Finow** Germany
33 T7 **Finowfurt** Germany
33 T7 **Finow Kanal** Germany
27 H13 **Finspång** Sweden
40 H4 **Finsteraarhorn** *mt* Switzerland
33 T9 **Finsterwalde** Germany
15 E1 **Finstown** Scotland
29 H11 **Finström** Finland
36 E4 **Finthen** Germany
14 D2 **Fintona** N Ireland
12 D1 **Fintry** Scotland
142 C5 **Finucane I** W Australia Australia
141 F5 **Finucane Ra** Queensland Australia
40 F5 **Fionnay** Switzerland
15 C3 **Fionn Loch** *L* Scotland
12 B1 **Fionphort** Scotland
45 J2 **Fiorano Modenese** Italy
144 A6 **Fiordland Nat. Park** New Zealand
44 G2 **Fiorenzuola d'Arda** Italy
45 N4 **Fiorenzuola di Focara** Italy
88 C5 **Fip** Tanzania
78 G2 **Firat** *R* Turkey
102 D5 **Firebaugh** California U.S.A.
116 M6 **Fire I** Alaska U.S.A.
42 D5 **Firenze** Italy
42 D4 **Firenzuola** Italy
98 E4 **Firesteel** South Dakota U.S.A.
48 H3 **Firiza** Romania
133 E4 **Firmat** Argentina
18 H7 **Firminy** France
118 L9 **Fir Mt** Saskatchewan Canada
74 H5 **Firozabad** India
77 H2 **Firozkoh** *reg* Afghanistan
74 F3 **Firozpur** India
112 F2 **First R** North Carolina U.S.A.
116 R2 **Firth** *R* Alaska/Yukon Terr U.S.A./Canada
77 C5 **Firūzābād** Iran
37 K7 **Fischach** Germany
36 C4 **Fischbach** Germany
38 M7 **Fischbacher Alpen** *mts* Austria
33 Q7 **Fischbeck** Germany
36 E2 **Fischelbach** Germany
41 M3 **Fischen** Germany
109 J6 **Fischer** Texas U.S.A.
32 K6 **Fischerhude** Germany
33 S6 **Fischerwall** Germany
89 A5 **Fish** *watercourse* Namibia
9 E6 **Fishbourne** England
102 E4 **Fish Camp** California U.S.A.
116 L1 **Fish Cr** Alaska U.S.A.
101 M6 **Fish Cr.Res** Idaho U.S.A.
113 F10 **Fisheating Cr** Florida U.S.A.
121 N4 **Fisher** Quebec Canada
111 C10 **Fisher** Louisiana U.S.A.
98 K2 **Fisher** Minnesota U.S.A.
119 U7 **Fisher Branch** Manitoba Canada
146 H10 **Fisher Glacier** Antarctica
143 A9 **Fisherman I** W Australia Australia
95 M9 **Fishermans I** Virginia U.S.A.
115 L5 **Fisher Str** Northwest Territories Canada
116 E9 **Fisher Vol** Aleutian Is
8 B4 **Fishguard** Wales
8 A3 **Fishguard B** England
95 L8 **Fishing Creek** Maryland U.S.A.
117 M4 **Fish L** Northwest Territories Canada
116 M4 **Fish L** Alaska U.S.A.
103 N3 **Fish L** Utah U.S.A.
94 D3 **Fish Pt** Michigan U.S.A.
102 A3 **Fish Rock** California U.S.A.
101 Q4 **Fishtail** Montana U.S.A.
101 M4 **Fishtrap** Montana U.S.A.
94 E9 **Fishtrap L** Kentucky U.S.A.
46 D6 **Fiskárdho** Greece
28 C3 **Fiskbæk** Denmark
95 P4 **Fiskdale** Massachusetts U.S.A.
118 J7 **Fiske** Saskatchewan Canada
146 D6 **Fiske, C** Antarctica
115 O5 **Fiskenæsset** Greenland
28 S9 **Fiskivötn** *lakes* Iceland
22 F5 **Fismes** France
95 Q4 **Fitchburg** Massachusetts U.S.A.
86 C3 **Fitri, L** Chad
28 C5 **Fitting** Denmark
9 F6 **Fittleworth** England
128 D6 **Fitzcarrald** Peru
143 C10 **Fitzgerald** *R* W Australia Australia
117 R6 **Fitzgerald** Alberta Canada
112 D6 **Fitzgerald** Georgia U.S.A.
143 C10 **Fitzgerald River Nat Park** W Australia Australia
109 L1 **Fitzhugh** Oklahoma U.S.A.
117 K10 **Fitzhugh Sd** British Columbia Canada
22 C5 **Fitz James** France
140 B2 **Fitzmaurice** *R* N Terr Australia
121 S5 **Fitzpatrick** Quebec Canada
133 D7 **Fitz Roy** Argentina
141 K6 **Fitzroy** *R* Queensland Australia
133 C7 **Fitz Roy** *mt* Chile/Arg
142 F4 **Fitzroy Crossing** W Australia Australia
121 O7 **Fitzroy Harbour** Ontario Canada
141 H3 **Fitzroy I** Queensland Australia
142 E4 **Fitzroy R** W Australia Australia
120 J7 **Fitzwilliam I** Ontario Canada
42 E7 **Fiuggi** Italy
45 J3 **Fiumalbo** Italy
Fiume *see* **Rijeka**
42 E7 **Fiumicino** Italy
45 M3 **Fiumi Uniti** *R* Italy
144 A6 **Five Fingers Pen** New Zealand
122 H8 **Five Islands** Nova Scotia Canada
101 R6 **Fivemile Cr** Wyoming U.S.A.
14 D2 **Fivemiletown** N Ireland
144 B6 **Five Rivers** New Zealand
88 B4 **Fizi** Zaire
26 L4 **Fjällåsen** Sweden
26 G6 **Fjällfjällen** *mt* Sweden
26 F9 **Fjällnäs** Sweden
28 H7 **Fjelde** Denmark
28 F3 **Fjellerup** Denmark
28 E6 **Fjelsted** Denmark
28 D6 **Fjelstrup** Denmark
28 C2 **Fjerritslev** Denmark
27 B10 **Fjordane** *reg* Norway
27 B13 **Fjotland** Norway
27 D11 **Flå** Norway
37 K5 **Flachslanden** Germany
28 A3 **Flade Sø** Denmark
28 B6 **Fladså** *R* Denmark
37 J2 **Fladungen** Germany
106 G2 **Flagler** Colorado U.S.A.
113 F8 **Flagler Beach** Florida U.S.A.
103 N6 **Flagstaff** Arizona U.S.A.
95 R1 **Flagstaff L** Maine U.S.A.
100 E7 **Flagstaff L** Oregon U.S.A.
100 K1 **Flagstone** British Columbia Canada
28 G6 **Flakkebjerg** Denmark
26 F3 **Flakstad** Norway
27 B11 **Flåm** Norway
20 G2 **Flamanville** France
99 Q4 **Flambeau** *R* Wisconsin U.S.A.
99 Q3 **Flambeau Res** Wisconsin U.S.A.
13 H5 **Flamborough Hd** England
133 C3 **Flamenco** Chile
131 E8 **Flamenco, I** Argentina
33 R9 **Fläming** *reg* Germany
101 Q8 **Flaming Gorge Res** Utah/Wyoming U.S.A.
113 G12 **Flamingo** Florida U.S.A.
18 F10 **Flamisell** *R* Spain
36 C2 **Flammersfeld** Germany
127 O2 **Flanagin Town** Trinidad
99 O1 **Flanders** Ontario Canada
22 D2 **Flandre** *prov* France
22 E3 **Flandre** France
98 K5 **Flandreau** South Dakota U.S.A.
102 E1 **Flanigan** Nevada U.S.A.
38 H6 **Flankenmarkt** Austria
26 K8 **Flärke** Sweden
98 E3 **Flasher** North Dakota U.S.A.
26 H7 **Flåsjön** *L* Sweden
117 K5 **Flat** *R* Northwest Territories Canada
94 B3 **Flat** *R* Michigan U.S.A.
109 K4 **Flat** Texas U.S.A.
123 O5 **Flat Bay** Newfoundland Canada
118 C4 **Flatbush** Alberta Canada
111 J8 **Flat Creek** Alabama U.S.A.
101 L2 **Flathead L** Montana U.S.A.
101 L1 **Flathead Mts** Montana U.S.A.
117 Q11 **Flathead R** Idaho U.S.A.
5 C5 **Flat Holm** *isld* Bristol Channel England
141 J5 **Flat I** Queensland Australia
118 E4 **Flat L** Alberta Canada
144 A6 **Flat Mt** New Zealand
109 K6 **Flatonia** Texas U.S.A.
110 F4 **Flat River** Missouri U.S.A.
110 J3 **Flat Rock** Illinois U.S.A.
94 B7 **Flat Rock** Indiana U.S.A.
141 H2 **Flattery, C** Queensland Australia
100 A1 **Flattery,C** Washington U.S.A.
38 K8 **Flattnitz** Austria
94 F9 **Flat Top** West Virginia U.S.A.
101 R3 **Flatwillow** Montana U.S.A.
94 G8 **Flatwoods** West Virginia U.S.A.
41 O3 **Flaurling** Austria
27 C12 **Flåv** *L* Norway
28 E2 **Flavenskjold** Denmark
22 F4 **Flavigny le Grd. et Beaurain** France
22 E4 **Flavy le Martel** France
8 D5 **Flax Bourton** England
118 H7 **Flaxcombe** Saskatchewan Canada
116 P1 **Flaxman I** Alaska U.S.A.
98 D1 **Flaxton** North Dakota U.S.A.
98 A1 **Flaxville** Montana U.S.A.
20 B4 **Flèche** *R* France
21 K6 **Flèche, La** France
33 O8 **Flechtingen** Germany
113 K9 **Fleeming Pt** New Providence I Bahamas
118 F6 **Fleet** Alberta Canada
9 G2 **Fleet Hargate** England
141 H5 **Fleetwood** Queensland Australia
13 E6 **Fleetwood** England
95 M6 **Fleetwood** Pennsylvania U.S.A.
36 G5 **Flein** Germany
95 N4 **Fleischmanns** New York U.S.A.
27 B13 **Flekkefjord** Norway
27 C13 **Flekkeröy** *isld* Norway
Flemhude *see* **Quarnbek**
119 Q8 **Fleming** Saskatchewan Canada
98 D9 **Fleming** Colorado U.S.A.
94 D8 **Flemingsburg** Kentucky U.S.A.
95 N6 **Flemington** New Jersey U.S.A.
90 F4 **Flemish Cap** Atlantic Oc
28 E6 **Flemløse** Denmark
27 J12 **Flen** Sweden
29 K4 **Fleninge** Sweden
28 C7 **Flensburg** Germany
28 D7 **Flensburger Förde** *inlet* Denmark/Germany
21 N7 **Fléré-la-Rivière** France
21 J4 **Flers** France
22 D3 **Flers** France
101 N2 **Flesher** Montana U.S.A.
120 K8 **Flesherton** Ontario Canada
112 E2 **Fletcher** North Carolina U.S.A.
107 M7 **Fletcher** Oklahoma U.S.A.
94 D2 **Fletcher Pond** Michigan U.S.A.
146 C7 **Fletcher Promontory** *pen* Antarctica
9 F2 **Fletton** England
18 F9 **Fleurance** France
123 Q3 **Fleur de Lys** Newfoundland Canada
122 H2 **Fleur-de-May,L** Labrador, Nfld Canada
40 E4 **Fleurier** Switzerland
22 H3 **Fleurus** Belgium
21 N3 **Fleury-sur-Andelle** France
68 G1 **Fleuve Rouge** *R* Vietnam
36 H3 **Flieden** Germany
41 K4 **Flims** Switzerland
9 G5 **Flimwell** England
140 F4 **Flinders** *R* Queensland Australia
143 B10 **Flinders B** W Australia Australia
141 G2 **Flinders Group** *islds* Gt Barrier Reef Aust
139 J7 **Flinders I** Tasmania Australia
141 J4 **Flinder's Passage** Australia
141 J4 **Flinders Reefs** Gt Barrier Reef Aust
138 E4 **Flinders Rge** South Australia Australia
22 E3 **Flines-le-Râches** France
119 Q4 **Flin Flon** Manitoba Canada
Flint *co* *see* **Clwyd**
110 K7 **Flint** *R* Alabama U.S.A.
111 M10 **Flint** *R* Georgia U.S.A.
94 D3 **Flint** Michigan U.S.A.
8 C1 **Flint** Wales
107 O4 **Flint Hills** Kansas U.S.A.
135 M9 **Flint I** Pacific Oc
120 E3 **Flint L** Ontario Canada
118 L9 **Flintoft** Saskatchewan Canada
141 J8 **Flinton** Queensland Australia
110 D5 **Flippin** Arkansas U.S.A.
112 C4 **Flirt** *R* Georgia U.S.A.
27 F11 **Flisa** Norway
27 H14 **Fliseryd** Sweden
17 H3 **Flix** Spain
13 H6 **Flixborough** England
21 P1 **Flixecourt** France
22 H4 **Flize** France
13 G6 **Flockton Moor** England
111 J11 **Flomaton** Florida U.S.A.
108 G1 **Flomot** Texas U.S.A.
36 E4 **Flonheim** Germany
67 D1 **Flood Basin** *L* Hubei China
146 B9 **Flood Ra** Antarctica
99 O3 **Floodwood** Minnesota U.S.A.
110 H3 **Flora** Illinois U.S.A.
94 A6 **Flora** Indiana U.S.A.
111 F9 **Flora** Mississippi U.S.A.
100 H4 **Flora** Oregon U.S.A.
18 H8 **Florac** France
111 K10 **Florala** Alabama U.S.A.
113 E9 **Floral City** Florida U.S.A.
142 B5 **Flora, Mt** W Australia Australia
141 H3 **Flora Pass** Gt Barrier Reef Aust
140 E4 **Floraville** Queensland Australia
142 A1 **Floreat Park** *dist* Perth, W Aust Australia
22 H3 **Floreffe** Belgium
Florence *see* **Firenze**
110 J7 **Florence** Alabama U.S.A.
103 N8 **Florence** Arizona U.S.A.
106 E3 **Florence** Colorado U.S.A.
100 J4 **Florence** Idaho U.S.A.
107 O3 **Florence** Kansas U.S.A.
94 C8 **Florence** Kentucky U.S.A.
111 F9 **Florence** Mississippi U.S.A.
101 L3 **Florence** Montana U.S.A.
95 N6 **Florence** New Jersey U.S.A.
100 A6 **Florence** Oregon U.S.A.
112 H3 **Florence** South Carolina U.S.A.
98 J4 **Florence** South Dakota U.S.A.
109 K5 **Florence** Texas U.S.A.
99 S4 **Florence** Wisconsin U.S.A.
103 N8 **Florence Junc** Arizona U.S.A.
102 F4 **Florence L** California U.S.A.
128 F8 **Florencia** Argentina
128 C3 **Florencia** Colombia
22 H3 **Florennes** Belgium
22 J4 **Florenville** Belgium
131 F5 **Flores** *R* Argentina
85 A1 **Flores** *isld* Azores Atlantic Oc
130 H9 **Flores** Brazil
125 P9 **Flores** Guatemala
71 K9 **Flores** *isld* Indonesia
131 F4 **Flores** *dept* Uruguay
48 L3 **Floreshty** Moldavia
117 K11 **Flores I** British Columbia Canada
71 J8 **Flores Sea** Indonesia
130 H10 **Floresta** Brazil
109 J6 **Floresville** Texas U.S.A.
108 E3 **Florey** Texas U.S.A.
129 K5 **Floriano** Brazil
128 E5 **Floriano Peixoto** Brazil
130 E10 **Florianopólis** Brazil
126 E4 **Florida** Cuba
137 N3 **Florida** *isld* Solomon Is
131 G5 **Florida** Uruguay
113 B12 **Florida** *state* U.S.A.
94 C5 **Florida** Ohio U.S.A.
113 G12 **Florida B** Florida U.S.A.
113 F13 **Florida Keys** *islds* Florida U.S.A.
113 H12 **Florida,Str.of** U.S.A./Bahamas
130 B10 **Florida,V** Paraguay
43 G11 **Floridia** Sicily
109 O4 **Florien** Louisiana U.S.A.
46 E4 **Flórina** Greece
99 O9 **Floris** Iowa U.S.A.
106 E3 **Florissant** Colorado U.S.A.
106 E3 **Florissant Fossilbeds Nat. Mon.** Colorado U.S.A.
26 A10 **Flörö** Norway
36 G3 **Flörsbach** Germany
47 M11 **Florya** Turkey
37 N4 **Floss** Germany
37 N4 **Flossenbürg** Germany
15 F2 **Flotta** Scotland
118 J4 **Flotten L** Saskatchewan Canada
103 M3 **Flowell** Utah U.S.A.
120 J7 **Flowerpot I. Nat. Park** Ontario Canada
123 Q2 **Flower's Cove** Newfoundland Canada
98 K7 **Floyd** *R* Iowa U.S.A.
108 D1 **Floyd** New Mexico U.S.A.
108 F2 **Floydada** Texas U.S.A.
103 M6 **Floyd,Mt** Arizona U.S.A.
27 D11 **Fluberg** Norway
41 L4 **Flüela Pass** Switzerland
21 O6 **Fluery les Aubrais** France
25 E3 **Fluessen** *R* Netherlands
71 A3 **Fluk** Indonesia
111 F11 **Fluker** Louisiana U.S.A.
20 G5 **Flume** *R* France
17 G3 **Flumen** *R* Spain
43 B9 **Fluminimaggiore** Sardinia
36 F7 **Fluorn** Germany
Flushing Netherlands *see* **Vlissingen**
94 D3 **Flushing** Michigan U.S.A.
94 F6 **Flushing** Ohio U.S.A.
108 F3 **Fluvanna** Texas U.S.A.
18 G10 **Fluvia** *R* Spain
28 C4 **Fly** Denmark
136 J3 **Fly** *R* Indonesia/Papua New Guinea
83 M9 **Flying Fish Cove** Christmas I Indian Oc
140 C2 **Flying Fox Cr** N Terr Australia
28 A4 **Flynder Kirke** Denmark
28 B3 **Flynder Sø** *L* Denmark
6 M6 **Flyndre** *oil rig* North Sea
109 L4 **Flynn** Texas U.S.A.
140 C4 **Flynn Mem** N Terr Australia
119 O7 **Foam Lake** Saskatchewan Canada
73 L9 **Foa Mulaku I** Maldives
47 H6 **Foça** Turkey

176

Focant — Freuchie

22 J3 **Focant** Belgium
45 H3 **Foce d. Radici** *mt* Italy
15 E3 **Fochabers** Scotland
42 E4 **Foci del Po** Italy
48 L5 **Focşani** Romania
28 H6 **Fodby** Denmark
21 P7 **Foëcy** France
140 D3 **Foelsche** *R* N Terr Australia
67 D5 **Fogang** China
140 B2 **Fog B** N Terr Australia
57 E4 **Fogelevo** Kazakhstan
43 G7 **Foggia** Italy
42 E5 **Foglia** *R* Italy
45 N7 **Fogliano** *L* Italy
29 H11 **Föglö** Finland
123 S4 **Fogo** Newfoundland Canada
88 G10 **Fogo** *isld* Mozambique
123 S4 **Fogo,C** Newfoundland Canada
28 C4 **Fogstrup** Denmark
38 L7 **Fohnsdorf** Austria
28 A7 **Föhr** *isld* Germany
45 R7 **Foiana in Val Fortore** Italy
14 A5 **Foilclogh** *mt* Ireland
15 D2 **Foinaven,Mt** Scotland
18 G10 **Foix** France
52 H6 **Foki** Russian Federation
54 F3 **Fokina, imeni** Russian Federation
54 F3 **Fokino** Russian Federation
26 D9 **Fokstua** Norway
26 G4 **Folda** *inlet* Norway
48 F4 **Földeák** Hungary
26 F7 **Foldereid** Norway
28 B6 **Foldingbro** Denmark
28 C6 **Folding Kirke** Denmark
28 B6 **Fole** Denmark
46 G8 **Folégandros** *isld* Greece
89 E3 **Foley** Botswana
111 J11 **Foley** Alabama U.S.A.
113 D7 **Foley** Florida U.S.A.
99 N4 **Foley** Minnesota U.S.A.
120 H4 **Foleyet** Ontario Canada
115 M4 **Foley I** Northwest Territories Canada
27 B11 **Folgefonna** *gla* Norway
116 J5 **Folger** Alaska U.S.A.
146 G14 **Folger, Cape** *C* Antarctica
20 B4 **Folgoët, le** France
42 E6 **Foligno** Italy
9 H5 **Folkestone** England
9 F2 **Folkingham** England
113 E7 **Folkston** Georgia U.S.A.
112 K3 **Folkstone** North Carolina U.S.A.
26 D9 **Folla** *R* Norway
26 D9 **Folldal** Norway
28 E4 **Følle** Denmark
25 E3 **Follega** Netherlands
28 G5 **Føllenslev** Denmark
20 H4 **Folligny** France
26 G8 **Föllinge** Sweden
27 E12 **Follo** Norway
42 D6 **Follonica** Italy
112 H5 **Folly Beach** South Carolina U.S.A.
100 G6 **Follyfarm** Oregon U.S.A.
102 C3 **Folsom** California U.S.A.
111 F11 **Folsom** Louisiana U.S.A.
106 G5 **Folsom** New Mexico U.S.A.
102 C3 **Folsom L** California U.S.A.
48 L5 **Folteşti** Romania
126 E3 **Fómento** Cuba
52 F6 **Fominki** Russian Federation
52 G2 **Fominskaya** Russian Federation
52 F5 **Fominskoye** Russian Federation
99 M7 **Fonda** Iowa U.S.A.
95 N4 **Fonda** New York U.S.A.
98 F1 **Fonda** North Dakota U.S.A.
114 J6 **Fond-du-Lac** Saskatchewan Canada
99 S6 **Fond du Lac** Wisconsin U.S.A.
94 D10 **Fonde** Kentucky U.S.A.
21 M7 **Fondettes** France
43 E7 **Fondi** Italy
45 O7 **Fondi, L. di** Italy
26 E8 **Fongen** *mt* Norway
43 C8 **Fonni** Sardinia
16 C1 **Fonsagrada** Spain
28 D6 **Fønsskov** Denmark
22 G3 **Fontaine** Belgium
21 N6 **Fontaine** Loir-et-Cher France
18 G4 **Fontainebleau** France
19 O17 **Fontaine-de-Vaucluse** France
40 B2 **Fontaine-Française** France
21 M3 **Fontaine-l'Abbé** France
21 N2 **Fontaine-le-Bourg** France
21 M2 **Fontaine-le-Dun** France
40 B3 **Fontaine-lès-Dijon** France
21 K6 **Fontaine-Milon** France
21 L6 **Fontaine-St. Martin,la** France
133 C6 **Fontana,L** Argentina
112 D2 **Fontana L** North Carolina U.S.A.
45 P6 **Fontana Liri** Italy
45 L3 **Fontanelice** Italy
117 N6 **Fontas** British Columbia Canada
40 D7 **Fontcouvert** France
38 F7 **Fonte** Italy
128 E4 **Fonte Boa** Brazil
128 G6 **Fonte do Pau d'Água** Brazil
18 E6 **Fontenay-le-Comte** France
21 O3 **Fontenay-St.Père** France
123 L2 **Fonteneau,L** Quebec Canada
122 H5 **Fontenelle** Quebec Canada
101 P7 **Fontenelle Fork** *R* Wyoming U.S.A.
101 P7 **Fontenelle Res** Wyoming U.S.A.
22 E2 **Fontenoy** Belgium
21 L7 **Fontevrault l'Abbaye** France
8 D6 **Fontmell Magna** England
22 L5 **Fontoy** France
137 S5 **Fonualei** *isld* Tonga
48 D4 **Fonyód** Hungary
Foochow *see* **Fuzhou** Fujian
103 M2 **Fool Cr.Res** Utah U.S.A.
117 P9 **Foothills** Alberta Canada
99 R7 **Footville** Wisconsin U.S.A.
41 H5 **Foppiano** Italy
27 J14 **Föra** Sweden
107 O5 **Foraker** Oklahoma U.S.A.
116 M5 **Foraker,Mt** Alaska U.S.A.
19 K3 **Forbach** France
36 E6 **Forbach** Germany
139 J5 **Forbes** New South Wales Australia
99 O2 **Forbes** Minnesota U.S.A.
98 H4 **Forbes** North Dakota U.S.A.
117 P10 **Forbes, Mt** Alberta Canada
85 F7 **Forcados** Nigeria
19 Q18 **Forcalqueiret** France
19 P17 **Forcalquier** France
38 E8 **Forchetta** *mt* Italy
37 L4 **Forchheim** Germany
36 H5 **Forchtenberg** Germany
13 F2 **Ford** England
107 L4 **Ford** Kansas U.S.A.
94 C9 **Ford** Kentucky U.S.A.
99 T3 **Ford** *R* Michigan U.S.A.
140 A2 **Ford, C** N Terr Australia
102 E6 **Ford City** California U.S.A.
94 H6 **Ford City** Pennsylvania U.S.A.
26 A10 **Förde** Norway
145 E3 **Fordell** New Zealand
33 P9 **Förderstedt** Germany
9 G3 **Fordham** England
9 E6 **Fordingbridge** England
103 J8 **Ford L** California U.S.A.
110 D4 **Fordland** Missouri U.S.A.
31 L2 **Fordon** Poland
146 B9 **Ford Ranges** Antarctica
139 H3 **Ford's Br** New South Wales Australia
110 K4 **Fordsville** Kentucky U.S.A.
109 K6 **Fordtran** Texas U.S.A.
98 J1 **Fordville** North Dakota U.S.A.
111 D8 **Fordyce** Arkansas U.S.A.
98 J7 **Fordyce** Nebraska U.S.A.
26 G5 **Fore** Norway
85 B7 **Forécariah** Guinea
8 C5 **Foreland,The** England
115 Q4 **Forel, Mont** *mt* Greenland
109 N2 **Foreman** Arkansas U.S.A.
118 F9 **Foremost** Alberta Canada
22 G2 **Forest** Belgium
120 H9 **Forest** Ontario Canada
100 J3 **Forest** Idaho U.S.A.
111 G9 **Forest** Mississippi U.S.A.
94 D6 **Forest** Ohio U.S.A.
118 E6 **Forestburg** Alberta Canada
109 K2 **Forestburg** Texas U.S.A.
110 F6 **Forest City** Arkansas U.S.A.
99 N6 **Forest City** Iowa U.S.A.
112 F2 **Forest City** North Carolina U.S.A.
95 M5 **Forest City** Pennsylvania U.S.A.
142 B3 **Forestdale** *dist* Perth, W Aust Australia
95 O3 **Forest Dale** Vermont U.S.A.
109 O1 **Forester** Arkansas U.S.A.
94 E3 **Forester** Michigan U.S.A.
100 B9 **Forest Glen** California U.S.A.
101 Q3 **Forestgrove** Montana U.S.A.
100 B4 **Forest Grove** Oregon U.S.A.
102 D2 **Foresthill** California U.S.A.
111 D10 **Forest Hill** Louisiana U.S.A.
109 M9 **Forest Hill** Texas U.S.A.
141 G4 **Forest Home** Queensland Australia
139 J8 **Forestier, C** Tasmania Australia
139 J9 **Forestier Pen** Tasmania Australia
99 O4 **Forest Lake** Minnesota U.S.A.
15 D4 **Forest of Atholl** Scotland
99 N4 **Foreston** Minnesota U.S.A.
95 M3 **Forestport** New York U.S.A.
98 J1 **Forest River** North Dakota U.S.A.
9 G5 **Forest Row** England
122 C5 **Forestville** Quebec Canada
102 B3 **Forestville** California U.S.A.
94 E3 **Forestville** Michigan U.S.A.
94 H4 **Forestville** New York U.S.A.
122 C5 **Forestville, Parc de** Quebec Canada
20 C6 **Forêt, B.de la** *B* France
19 J3 **Forêt d'Argonne** France
20 C6 **Forêt, la** France
21 P5 **Forêt-Ste Croix, la** France
18 H7 **Forez, Mts du** France
15 F4 **Forfar** Scotland
118 K7 **Forgan** Saskatchewan Canada
107 K5 **Forgan** Oklahoma U.S.A.
20 E5 **Forges, les** France
21 O2 **Forges-les-Eaux** France
121 O4 **Forget** Quebec Canada
119 P9 **Forget** Saskatchewan Canada
41 N2 **Forggen See** *L* Germany
45 P8 **Forio** Italy
110 G6 **Forked Deer** *R* Tennessee U.S.A.
119 R7 **Fork River** *R* Manitoba Canada
100 A2 **Forks** Washington U.S.A.
144 C5 **Forks, The** New Zealand
94 J9 **Fork Union** Virginia U.S.A.
42 E4 **Forli** Italy
45 M3 **Forlimpopoli** Italy
14 E4 **Forlorn Pt** Ireland
98 J3 **Forman** North Dakota U.S.A.
13 E6 **Formby** England
138 D6 **Formby B** South Australia Australia
13 E6 **Formby Pt** England
45 M5 **Formello** Italy
17 H6 **Formentera** *isld* Balearic Is
21 O2 **Formerie** France
43 F7 **Formia** Italy
130 F7 **Formiga** Brazil
126 G5 **Formigas Bank** Caribbean
45 J2 **Formigine** Italy
45 L2 **Formignana** Italy
21 J3 **Formigny** France
26 F7 **Formofoss** Norway
Formosa *see* **Taiwan**
133 F3 **Formosa** Argentina
129 J6 **Formosa** *R* Brazil
129 J7 **Formosa** Brazil
129 J6 **Formosa do Rio Prêto** Brazil
129 G6 **Formosa, Serra** *mts* Brazil
Formosa Strait *see* **Taiwan Str**
130 F4 **Formoso** Brazil
107 M2 **Formoso** Kansas U.S.A.
28 F4 **Fornæs** *C* Denmark
17 K4 **Fornells** Menorca
38 G8 **Forni Avoltri** Italy
6 F1 **Føroyar** *islds* N Atlantic Oc
15 E3 **Forres** Scotland
143 G9 **Forrest** W Australia Australia
119 S9 **Forrest** Manitoba Canada
99 S9 **Forrest** Illinois U.S.A.
146 E7 **Forrestal Ra** Antarctica
117 G8 **Forrester I** Alaska U.S.A.
142 C2 **Forrestfield** *dist* Perth, W Aust Australia
143 G8 **Forrest Lakes** W Australia Australia
143 G6 **Forrest, Mt** W Australia Australia
99 R7 **Forreston** Illinois U.S.A.
142 G3 **Forrest River Mission** W Australia Australia
26 J9 **Fors** Sweden
26 J3 **Forsa** Norway
26 J10 **Forsa** Sweden
108 F3 **Forsan** Texas U.S.A.
27 B13 **Forsand** Norway
141 G4 **Forsayth** Queensland Australia
27 J11 **Forsbacka** Sweden
27 F12 **Forshaga** Sweden
27 F13 **Forshem** Sweden
27 F15 **Förslöv** Sweden
27 K11 **Forsmark** Sweden
26 J8 **Forsmo** Sweden
26 K5 **Forsnäs** Sweden
26 C8 **Forsnes** Norway
29 K11 **Forssa** Finland
31 H4 **Forst** Germany
139 L4 **Forster** New South Wales Australia
112 D4 **Forsyth** Georgia U.S.A.
99 S10 **Forsyth** Illinois U.S.A.
101 T3 **Forsyth** Montana U.S.A.
121 O4 **Forsythe** Quebec Canada
145 E4 **Forsyth I** New Zealand
140 E3 **Forsyth Is** Queensland Australia
141 G6 **Forsyth Ra** Queensland Australia
74 E4 **Fort Abbas** Pakistan
111 E10 **Fort Adams** Mississippi U.S.A.
115 L7 **Fort Albany** Ontario Canada
129 L4 **Fortaleza** Brazil
128 E5 **Fortaleza de Ituxi** Brazil
122 G9 **Fort Anne Nat. Hist. Park** Nova Scotia Canada
Fort Archambault *see* **Sarh**
94 J7 **Fort Ashby** West Virginia U.S.A.
118 C4 **Fort Assiniboine** Alberta Canada
99 S7 **Fort Atkinson** Wisconsin U.S.A.
15 D3 **Fort Augustus** Scotland
87 E12 **Fort Beaufort** S Africa
122 H8 **Fort Beau Sejour Nat. Hist. Park** New Brunswick Canada
101 R1 **Fort Belknap Agency** Montana U.S.A.
111 M9 **Fort Benning** Georgia U.S.A.
101 P2 **Fort Benton** Montana U.S.A.
100 E8 **Fort Bidwell** California U.S.A.
118 K3 **Fort Black** Saskatchewan Canada
103 P9 **Fort Bowie Nat. Hist. Site** Arizona U.S.A.
102 A2 **Fort Bragg** California U.S.A.
110 J3 **Fort Branch** Indiana U.S.A.
101 P8 **Fort Bridger** Wyoming U.S.A.
99 K8 **Fort Calhoun** Nebraska U.S.A.
Fort Carnot *see* **Ikongo**
Fort Charlet *see* **Djanet**
Fort Chimo *see* **Kuujjuaq**
117 R6 **Fort Chipewyan** Alberta Canada
98 E2 **Fort Clark** North Dakota U.S.A.
107 M6 **Fort Cobb** Oklahoma U.S.A.
98 A9 **Fort Collins** Colorado U.S.A.
140 F5 **Fort Constantine** Queensland Australia
121 O7 **Fort Coulonge** Quebec Canada
95 N2 **Fort Covington** New York U.S.A.
Fort Dauphin *see* **Tôlañaro**
111 L9 **Fort Davis** Alabama U.S.A.
108 D5 **Fort Davis** Texas U.S.A.
108 D5 **Fort Davis Nat. Hist. Site** Texas U.S.A.
103 P6 **Fort Defiance** Arizona U.S.A.
127 L4 **Fort de France** Martinique W Indies
111 K10 **Fort Deposit** Alabama U.S.A.
100 A8 **Fort Dick** California U.S.A.
99 M7 **Fort Dodge** Iowa U.S.A.
110 J5 **Fort Donelson Nat Mil Park** Tennessee U.S.A.
113 G10 **Fort Drum** Florida U.S.A.
9 E3 **Fort Dunlop** England
123 P2 **Forteau** Labrador, Nfld Canada
130 B6 **Forte Coimbra** Brazil
44 H4 **Forte dei Marmi** Italy
121 L10 **Fort Erie** Ontario Canada
142 B5 **Fortescue R** W Australia Australia
142 C5 **Fortescue, R** W Australia Australia
95 L9 **Fort Eustis** Virginia U.S.A.
95 T7 **Fort Fairfield** Maine U.S.A.
112 K4 **Fort Fisher** North Carolina U.S.A.
Fort Flatters *see* **Bordj Omar Driss**
99 N1 **Fort Frances** Ontario Canada
117 M3 **Fort Franklin** Northwest Territories Canada
117 L8 **Fort Fraser** British Columbia Canada
112 F6 **Fort Frederica Nat. Mon** Georgia U.S.A.
111 L10 **Fort Gaines** Georgia U.S.A.
Fort Garaud *see* **Fdérik**
106 E4 **Fort Garland** Colorado U.S.A.
118 B1 **Fort Garry** Manitoba Canada
94 E8 **Fort Gay** West Virginia U.S.A.
115 M7 **Fort George** Quebec Canada
15 D3 **Fort George** Scotland
107 P6 **Fort Gibson** Oklahoma U.S.A.
107 P5 **Fort Gibson L** Oklahoma U.S.A.
114 G4 **Fort Good Hope** Northwest Territories Canada
113 F10 **Fort Green** Florida U.S.A.
138 F3 **Fort Grey** New South Wales Australia
109 H3 **Fort Griffin** Texas U.S.A.
12 E2 **Forth** Scotland
Fort Hall *see* **Murang'a** Kenya
101 N6 **Fort Hall** Idaho U.S.A.
13 F1 **Forth, Firth of** Scotland
115 L7 **Fort Hope** Ontario Canada
12 D1 **Forth, R** Scotland
103 O10 **Fort Huachuca** Arizona U.S.A.
121 S6 **Fortierville** Quebec Canada
6 L5 **Forties** *oil rig* North Sea
122 H9 **Forties Settlement** Nova Scotia Canada
103 K3 **Fortification Ra** Nevada U.S.A.
128 F8 **Fortin Carlos Antonio López** Paraguay
101 L1 **Fortine** Montana U.S.A.
128 G8 **Fortin Falcón** Paraguay
133 F2 **Fortin Gen. Caballero** Paraguay
128 F8 **Fortin General Eugenio Garay** Paraguay
128 F8 **Fortin Infante Rivarola** Paraguay
122 E3 **Fortin, L** Quebec Canada
133 E3 **Fortin Lavalle** Argentina
128 F8 **Fortin Linares** Paraguay
133 F2 **Fortin Madrejón** Paraguay
128 F7 **Fortin Ravelo** Bolivia
128 G8 **Fortin Rojas Silva** Paraguay
128 F7 **Fortin Suárez Arana** Bolivia
128 G7 **Fortin Teniente Américo Picco** Paraguay
Fort Jameson Zambia *see* **Chipata**
113 E13 **Fort Jefferson Nat.Mon** Florida U.S.A.
Fort Johnston *see* **Mangochi**
100 C8 **Fort Jones** California U.S.A.
118 G4 **Fort Kent** Alberta Canada
95 S6 **Fort Kent** Maine U.S.A.
100 C7 **Fort Klamath** Oregon U.S.A.
94 B9 **Fort Knox** Kentucky U.S.A.
Fort Lallemande *see* **Belhirane**
Fort Lamy *see* **N'djamena**
98 B7 **Fort Laramie** Wyoming U.S.A.
98 B7 **Fort Laramie Nat. Hist. Mon.** Wyoming U.S.A.
107 L3 **Fort Larned Nat. Hist. Site** Kansas U.S.A.
113 G11 **Fort Lauderdale** Florida U.S.A.
112 G3 **Fort Lawn** South Carolina U.S.A.
100 C2 **Fort Lewis** Washington U.S.A.
117 M5 **Fort Liard** Northwest Territories Canada
127 J5 **Fort Liberté** Haiti
98 F3 **Fort Lincoln** North Dakota U.S.A.
112 C2 **Fort Loudon Lake** Tennessee U.S.A.
98 B9 **Fort Lupton** Colorado U.S.A.
106 G3 **Fort Lyon** Colorado U.S.A.
108 G5 **Fort McKavett** Texas U.S.A.
117 S7 **Fort MacKay** Alberta Canada
101 S5 **Fort Mackenzie** Wyoming U.S.A.
118 D9 **Fort Macleod** Alberta Canada
Fort McMahon *see* **El Homr**
118 F2 **Fort McMurray** Alberta Canada
114 F4 **Fort McPherson** Northwest Territories Canada
99 P9 **Fort Madison** Iowa U.S.A.
22 B3 **Fort Mahon Plage** France
Fort Manning *see* **Mchinji**
113 F8 **Fort Matanzas Nat.Mon** Florida U.S.A.
113 F10 **Fort Meade** Florida U.S.A.
112 G2 **Fort Mill** South Carolina U.S.A.
98 C9 **Fort Morgan** Colorado U.S.A.
106 G1 **Fort Morgan** Colorado U.S.A.
113 F11 **Fort Myers** Florida U.S.A.
113 E11 **Fort Myers Beach** Florida U.S.A.
117 M6 **Fort Nelson** British Columbia Canada
117 L3 **Fort Norman** Northwest Territories Canada
113 F10 **Fort Ogden** Florida U.S.A.
43 G7 **Fortore** *R* Italy
111 L7 **Fort Payne** Alabama U.S.A.
101 T2 **Fort Peck L** *res* Montana U.S.A.
113 G10 **Fort Pierce** Florida U.S.A.
98 F5 **Fort Pierre** South Dakota U.S.A.
Fort Pierre Bordes *see* **Tin Zaouaten**
95 N4 **Fort Plain** New York U.S.A.
117 P5 **Fort Providence** Northwest Territories Canada
112 G5 **Fort Pulaski Nat. Mon** Georgia U.S.A.
119 O8 **Fort Qu' Appelle** Saskatchewan Canada
112 M2 **Fort Raleigh Nat.Hist.Site** North Carolina U.S.A.
116 F9 **Fort Randall** Alaska U.S.A.
98 H6 **Fort Randall Dam** South Dakota U.S.A.
94 C6 **Fort Recovery** Ohio U.S.A.
114 J5 **Fort Reliance** Northwest Territories Canada
117 R5 **Fort Resolution** Northwest Territories Canada
101 Q5 **Fortress Mt** Wyoming U.S.A.
123 M8 **Fortress of Louisburg Nat. Hist. Park** C Breton I, Nova Scotia
98 F3 **Fort Rice** North Dakota U.S.A.
107 O2 **Fort Riley** Kansas U.S.A.
99 M3 **Fort Ripley** Minnesota U.S.A.
87 E10 **Fort Rixon** Zimbabwe
98 C7 **Fort Robinson** Nebraska U.S.A.
100 D6 **Fort Rock** Oregon U.S.A.
144 B7 **Fortrose** New Zealand
Fort Rosebery Zambia *see* **Mansa**
102 A3 **Fort Ross** California U.S.A.
Fort Rousset *see* **Owando**
121 M1 **Fort Rupert** Quebec Canada
117 L8 **Fort St. James** British Columbia Canada
117 N7 **Fort St. John** British Columbia Canada
Fort Sandeman *see* **Zhob**
118 D5 **Fort Saskatchewan** Alberta Canada
107 Q4 **Fort Scott** Kansas U.S.A.
115 L6 **Fort Severn** Ontario Canada
100 B9 **Fort Seward** California U.S.A.
107 M7 **Fort Sill** Oklahoma U.S.A.
117 N5 **Fort Simpson** Northwest Territories Canada
114 G5 **Fort Smith** *dist* Northwest Territories Canada
117 R5 **Fort Smith** Northwest Territories Canada
107 Q6 **Fort Smith** Arkansas U.S.A.
101 T8 **Fort Steele** Wyoming U.S.A.
108 E5 **Fort Stockton** Texas U.S.A.
108 C1 **Fort Sumner** New Mexico U.S.A.
112 H5 **Fort Sumter Nat.Mon** South Carolina U.S.A.
107 L5 **Fort Supply** Oklahoma U.S.A.
108 E7 **Fort Supply Res** Oklahoma U.S.A.
103 P8 **Fort Thomas** Arizona U.S.A.
98 G5 **Fort Thompson** South Dakota U.S.A.
107 P7 **Fort Towson** Oklahoma U.S.A.
27 C10 **Fortun** Norway
17 G6 **Fortuna** Spain
100 A9 **Fortuna** California U.S.A.
98 C1 **Fortuna** North Dakota U.S.A.
116 F6 **Fortuna Lodge** Alaska U.S.A.
123 R6 **Fortune** Newfoundland Canada
106 E6 **Fort Union Nat.Mon** New Mexico U.S.A.
112 D5 **Fort Valley** Georgia U.S.A.
117 Q6 **Fort Vermilion** Alberta Canada
Fort Victoria *see* **Masvingo**
94 B7 **Fortville** Indiana U.S.A.
111 K11 **Fort Walton Beach** Florida U.S.A.
101 R6 **Fort Washakie** Wyoming U.S.A.
94 B5 **Fort Wayne** Indiana U.S.A.
113 E8 **Fort White** Florida U.S.A.
118 A2 **Fort Whyte** Manitoba Canada
15 C4 **Fort William** Scotland
109 M10 **Fort Worth** Texas U.S.A.
98 F3 **Fort Yates** North Dakota U.S.A.
116 R5 **Fortymile** *R* Alaska U.S.A.
116 P3 **Fort Yukon** Alaska U.S.A.
77 D6 **Forūr, Jazīreh-ye** *isld* Iran
22 J2 **Forville** Belgium
119 N9 **Forward** Saskatchewan Canada
52 H5 **Fosforitnaya** Russian Federation
67 D5 **Foshan** China
115 L2 **Fosheim Pen** Northwest Territories Canada
26 D8 **Fosna** Norway
26 E7 **Fosnes** Norway
107 L6 **Foss** Oklahoma U.S.A.
44 C2 **Fossano** Italy
22 H3 **Fosse** Belgium
100 E4 **Fossil** Oregon U.S.A.
101 P8 **Fossil** Wyoming U.S.A.
101 P8 **Fossil Butte Nat. Mon.** Wyoming U.S.A.
142 F4 **Fossil Downs** W Australia Australia
121 L6 **Fossmill** Ontario Canada
42 E5 **Fossombrone** Italy
119 O6 **Fosston** Saskatchewan Canada
99 L2 **Fosston** Minnesota U.S.A.
139 H7 **Foster** Victoria Australia
121 S7 **Foster** Quebec Canada
98 J7 **Foster** Nebraska U.S.A.
100 C5 **Foster** Oregon U.S.A.
147 E10 **Foster Bugt** Greenland
99 T4 **Foster City** Michigan U.S.A.
117 D6 **Foster, Mt.** Yukon Territory Canada
118 J8 **Fosterton** Saskatchewan Canada
110 K6 **Fosterville** Tennessee U.S.A.
94 D5 **Fostoria** Ohio U.S.A.
109 M5 **Fostoria** Texas U.S.A.
67 F4 **Fotan** China
142 F5 **Fotheringham, Mt** W Australia Australia
21 O2 **Foucarmont** France
36 C7 **Fouday** France
20 B6 **Fouesnant** France
86 B6 **Fougamou** Gabon
20 H5 **Fougères** France
83 K13 **Fougères,Pl.des** Réunion Indian Oc
40 D2 **Fougerolles** France
21 J5 **Fougerolles-du-Plessis** France
21 P2 **Fouilloy** France
109 O2 **Fouke** Arkansas U.S.A.
68 B3 **Foul** *isld* Burma
84 K5 **Foul Bay** Egypt
9 G4 **Foulness Pt** England
13 E5 **Foulney** *isld* England
144 C4 **Foulwind, C** New Zealand
86 B4 **Foumban** Cameroon
85 C3 **Foum el Hassan** Morocco
85 C2 **Foum Zguid** Morocco
146 D8 **Foundation Ice Stream** *ice stream* Antarctica
106 F3 **Fountain** Colorado U.S.A.
99 U5 **Fountain** Michigan U.S.A.
99 O6 **Fountain** Minnesota U.S.A.
112 K2 **Fountain** North Carolina U.S.A.
103 N2 **Fountain Grn** Utah U.S.A.
111 E8 **Fountain Hill** Arkansas U.S.A.
112 E3 **Fountain Inn** South Carolina U.S.A.
16 B7 **Foupana** *R* Portugal
140 D3 **Four Archers** *mt* N Terr Australia
18 E7 **Fouras** France
101 U1 **Four Buttes** Montana U.S.A.
21 M5 **Fourche, la** France
110 B7 **Fourche la Fave** *R* Arkansas U.S.A.
19 J4 **Fourchies, Mts des** France
123 M8 **Fourchu** C Breton I, Nova Scotia
103 P4 **Four Corners** Utah U.S.A.
98 B5 **Four Corners** Wyoming U.S.A.
140 A1 **Fourcroy, C** N Terr Australia
20 E7 **Four, le** *isld* France
22 G3 **Fourmies** France
83 K14 **Fournaise, Piton de la** *vol* Réunion Indian Oc
46 E5 **Fournás** Greece
83 L13 **Fourneau** *isld* Mauritius
123 P2 **Fournel, L** Quebec Canada
22 D2 **Fournes-en-Weppes** France
122 G2 **Fournier, L** Quebec Canada
47 H7 **Foúrnoi** *isld* Greece
127 K3 **Four Paths** Jamaica
19 N17 **Fourques** France
13 F3 **Fourstones** England
99 R3 **Fourteenmile Pt** Michigan U.S.A.
85 B6 **Fouta Djalon** *mt reg* Guinea
85 B5 **Fouta Ferlo** *reg* Senegal
8 D5 **Fovant** England
144 A7 **Foveaux Strait** New Zealand
28 C3 **Fovlum** Denmark
8 B7 **Fowey** England
113 G12 **Fowey Rocks** Florida U.S.A.
126 F2 **Fowl Cay** *isld* Bahamas
106 F3 **Fowler** Colorado U.S.A.
99 T9 **Fowler** Indiana U.S.A.
107 K4 **Fowler** Kansas U.S.A.
94 C3 **Fowler** Michigan U.S.A.
101 O1 **Fowler** Montana U.S.A.
146 C7 **Fowler Peninsula** *pen* Antarctica
138 B4 **Fowler Pt** South Australia Australia
138 B4 **Fowlers B** South Australia Australia
138 F4 **Fowlers Gap** New South Wales Australia
109 J7 **Fowlerton** Texas U.S.A.
94 C4 **Fowlerville** Michigan U.S.A.
110 G6 **Fowlkes** Tennessee U.S.A.
111 M11 **Fowlstown** Georgia U.S.A.
77 A1 **Fowman** Iran
115 K6 **Fox** *R* Manitoba Canada
99 S8 **Fox** *R* Illinois U.S.A.
99 U3 **Fox** *R* Michigan U.S.A.
99 T4 **Fox** Michigan U.S.A.
99 P9 **Fox** *R* Missouri U.S.A.
100 F5 **Fox** Oregon U.S.A.
99 S5 **Fox** *R* Wisconsin U.S.A.
123 L4 **Fox B** Anticosti I, Quebec
94 H5 **Foxburg** Pennsylvania U.S.A.
117 P8 **Fox Creek** Alberta Canada
115 M4 **Foxe Basin** Northwest Territories Canada
115 L4 **Foxe Chan** Northwest Territories Canada
115 M5 **Foxe Pen** Northwest Territories Canada
119 M5 **Foxford** Saskatchewan Canada
14 B3 **Foxford** Ireland
123 R1 **Fox Harbour** Labrador, Nfld Canada
13 H5 **Foxholes** England
98 K3 **Foxhome** Minnesota U.S.A.
116 P8 **Fox Islands** *isld* Aleutian Is
143 C10 **Fox, L** W Australia Australia
99 S7 **Fox Lake** Illinois U.S.A.
99 S6 **Fox Lake** Wisconsin U.S.A.
101 T8 **Foxpark** Wyoming U.S.A.
144 C5 **Fox Peak** *mt* New Zealand
123 L4 **Fox Pt** Anticosti I, Quebec
117 L7 **Fox R** British Columbia Canada
145 E4 **Foxton** New Zealand
118 H8 **Fox Valley** Saskatchewan Canada
119 Q8 **Foxwarren** Manitoba Canada
111 G10 **Foxworth** Mississippi U.S.A.
15 D3 **Foyers** Scotland
14 D2 **Foyle** *R* N Ireland
14 D1 **Foyle, L** Ireland
14 B4 **Foynes** Ireland
16 C1 **Foz** Spain
87 B9 **Foz do Cunene** Angola
128 D5 **Foz do Gregório** Brazil
130 C9 **Foz do Iguaçú** Brazil
128 F5 **Foz do Jamari** Brazil
128 D5 **Foz do Jordao** Brazil
128 E4 **Foz do Jutai** Brazil
128 E4 **Foz do Mamoriá** Brazil
128 D5 **Foz do Riozinho** Brazil
67 E1 **Foziling Shuiku** *res* China
128 E5 **Foz Tarauacá** Brazil
95 L6 **Frackville** Pennsylvania U.S.A.
8 B7 **Fraddon** England
17 H3 **Fraga** Spain
36 B7 **Fraize** France
22 F3 **Frameries** Belgium
95 Q4 **Framingham** Massachusetts U.S.A.
9 H3 **Framlingham** England
36 G3 **Frammersbach** Germany
146 J10 **Framnes Mts** Antarctica
31 O5 **Frampol** Poland
130 F7 **Franca** Brazil
83 M14 **Francais, Port-aux-** *France Base* Kerguelen Indian Oc
43 H8 **Francavilla Fontana** Italy
18 **France** *rep* W Europe
147 F10 **France, Ile de** Greenland
138 F6 **Frances** South Australia Australia
117 J5 **Frances** *R* Yukon Territory Canada
100 B3 **Frances** Washington U.S.A.
140 B2 **Frances Creek** N Terr Australia
117 J5 **Frances L** Yukon Territory Canada
101 N1 **Frances, L** Montana U.S.A.
127 K5 **Francés Viejo, C** Dominican Rep
99 U9 **Francesville** Indiana U.S.A.
86 B6 **Franceville** Gabon
19 J6 **Franche Comté** *prov* France
119 O8 **Francis** Saskatchewan Canada
107 O7 **Francis** Oklahoma U.S.A.
98 G6 **Francis Case, L** South Dakota U.S.A.
128 D4 **Francisco de Orellana** Peru
124 H5 **Francisco I. Madero** Coahuila Mexico
124 G5 **Francisco I. Madero** Durango Mexico
130 C9 **Francisco, S** *R* Brazil
130 G5 **Francisco Sá** Brazil
123 R1 **Francis Harbour** Labrador, Nfld Canada
95 Q1 **Francis, L** New Hampshire U.S.A.
89 E3 **Francistown** Botswana
123 Q6 **François** Newfoundland Canada
117 K8 **François L** British Columbia Canada
127 M4 **François, Le** Martinique W Indies
45 L2 **Francolino** Italy
22 K2 **Francorchamps** Belgium
101 Q6 **Francs Pk** Wyoming U.S.A.
21 N7 **Francueil** France
25 E2 **Franeker** Netherlands
118 C9 **Frank** Alberta Canada
36 F1 **Frankenau** Germany
36 F2 **Frankenbach** Germany
37 P2 **Frankenberg** Germany
36 F1 **Frankenberg/Eder** Germany
37 J5 **Frankenhardt** Germany
37 J5 **Frankenhöhe** *mts* Germany
94 D3 **Frankenmuth** Michigan U.S.A.
36 D5 **Frankenstein** Germany
36 E4 **Frankenthal** Germany
37 M3 **Frankenwald** *mts* Germany
127 K2 **Frankfield** Jamaica
121 N8 **Frankford** Ontario Canada
110 E2 **Frankford** Missouri U.S.A.
94 G9 **Frankford** West Virginia U.S.A.
94 A6 **Frankfort** Indiana U.S.A.
107 O2 **Frankfort** Kansas U.S.A.
94 C8 **Frankfort** Kentucky U.S.A.
99 U5 **Frankfort** Michigan U.S.A.
95 M3 **Frankfort** New York U.S.A.
94 D7 **Frankfort** Ohio U.S.A.
98 H5 **Frankfort** South Dakota U.S.A.
36 F3 **Frankfurt am Main** Germany
31 H3 **Frankfurt an der Oder** Germany
37 K6 **Fränkische Alb** *mts* Germany
37 L4 **Fränkische Schweiz** *reg* Germany
139 J7 **Frankland, C** Tasmania Australia
111 L8 **Franklin** Georgia U.S.A.
101 O7 **Franklin** Idaho U.S.A.
94 A7 **Franklin** Indiana U.S.A.
110 K5 **Franklin** Kentucky U.S.A.
111 E12 **Franklin** Louisiana U.S.A.
95 T2 **Franklin** Maine U.S.A.
95 Q4 **Franklin** Massachusetts U.S.A.
101 Q3 **Franklin** Montana U.S.A.
98 H9 **Franklin** Nebraska U.S.A.
95 Q3 **Franklin** New Hampshire U.S.A.
95 N5 **Franklin** New Jersey U.S.A.
95 M4 **Franklin** New York U.S.A.
112 D2 **Franklin** North Carolina U.S.A.
94 C7 **Franklin** Ohio U.S.A.
94 H5 **Franklin** Pennsylvania U.S.A.
110 K6 **Franklin** Tennessee U.S.A.
109 L4 **Franklin** Texas U.S.A.
95 L10 **Franklin** Virginia U.S.A.
94 H8 **Franklin** West Virginia U.S.A.
114 G3 **Franklin B** Northwest Territories Canada
100 G1 **Franklin D. Roosevelt L** Washington U.S.A.
99 R8 **Franklin Grove** Illinois U.S.A.
138 D5 **Franklin Harb** South Australia Australia
146 C11 **Franklin I** Antarctica
120 K7 **Franklin I** Ontario Canada
103 J1 **Franklin L** Nevada U.S.A.
117 L3 **Franklin Mts** Northwest Territories Canada
144 A6 **Franklin Mts** New Zealand
116 P2 **Franklin Mts** Alaska U.S.A.
116 H1 **Franklin, Pt** Alaska U.S.A.
139 J8 **Franklin Snd** Tasmania Australia
115 K3 **Franklin Str** Northwest Territories Canada
111 F11 **Franklinton** Louisiana U.S.A.
112 J1 **Franklinton** North Carolina U.S.A.
94 J4 **Franklinville** New York U.S.A.
112 H2 **Franklinville** North Carolina U.S.A.
100 J6 **Franklin Whitney** *airport* Idaho U.S.A.
144 D5 **Franklyn, Mt** New Zealand
37 J3 **Fränk Saale** *R* Germany
139 H7 **Frankston** Victoria Australia
109 M3 **Frankston** Texas U.S.A.
99 T7 **Franksville** Wisconsin U.S.A.
144 B6 **Frankton** New Zealand
101 R5 **Frannie** Wyoming U.S.A.
87 B10 **Fransfontein** Namibia
26 H9 **Fränsta** Sweden
9 G5 **Frant** England
37 N3 **Františkovy Lázně** Czechoslovakia
147 L11 **Frantsa-Iosifa, Zemlya** Arctic Oc
120 F4 **Franz** Ontario Canada
33 R4 **Franzburg** Germany
144 C5 **Franz Josef Gla** New Zealand
Franz Josef Land *see* **Frantsa-Iosifa, Zemlya**
38 G7 **Franz-Josefs Höhe** *mt* Austria
43 B9 **Frasca, C. d** Sardinia
42 E7 **Frascati** Italy
100 C1 **Fraser** *R* British Columbia Canada
106 E2 **Fraser** Colorado U.S.A.
87 D12 **Fraserburg** S Africa
15 F3 **Fraserburgh** Scotland
120 J3 **Fraserdale** Ontario Canada
141 L7 **Fraser I** Queensland Australia
143 C7 **Fraser, Mt** W Australia Australia
143 E9 **Fraser Range** W Australia Australia
69 E11 **Fraser's Hill** Malaysia
145 F3 **Frasertown** New Zealand
119 U8 **Fraserwood** Manitoba Canada
46 D4 **Frashër** Albania
48 K6 **Frăsinet** Romania
19 K6 **Frasne** France
22 F2 **Frasnes-les-Buissenal** Belgium
25 F5 **Frasselt** Germany
45 J3 **Frassinoro** Italy
120 F5 **Frater** Ontario Canada
45 L1 **Fratta Polesine** Italy
41 J2 **Frauenfeld** Switzerland
33 S10 **Frauenhain** Germany
37 O5 **Frauenstein** *mt* Germany
37 K2 **Frauenwald** Germany
28 E6 **Fraugde** Denmark
131 F4 **Fray Bentos** Uruguay
21 N5 **Frazé** France
99 L3 **Frazee** Minnesota U.S.A.
101 T1 **Frazer** Montana U.S.A.
142 A6 **Frazer I** W Australia Australia
120 B3 **Frazer L** Ontario Canada
36 B2 **Frechen** Germany
16 D2 **Frechilla** Spain
32 G9 **Freckenhorst** Germany
99 S2 **Freda** Michigan U.S.A.
98 E3 **Freda** North Dakota U.S.A.
36 E1 **Fredeburg** Germany
32 L9 **Freden** Germany
29 K5 **Fredensborg** Denmark
94 C2 **Frederic** Michigan U.S.A.
99 O4 **Frederic** Wisconsin U.S.A.
95 M7 **Frederica** Delaware U.S.A.
28 D5 **Fredericia** Denmark
99 Q9 **Frederick** Illinois U.S.A.
95 K7 **Frederick** Maryland U.S.A.
107 L7 **Frederick** Oklahoma U.S.A.
98 H4 **Frederick** South Dakota U.S.A.
120 J3 **Frederick House** *R* Ontario Canada
137 L6 **Frederick Reef** Coral Sea
99 O7 **Fredericksburg** Iowa U.S.A.
95 L6 **Fredericksburg** Pennsylvania U.S.A.
94 K8 **Fredericksburg** Virginia U.S.A.
117 F7 **Frederick Sd** Alaska U.S.A.
110 F4 **Fredericktown** Missouri U.S.A.
94 E6 **Fredericktown** Ohio U.S.A.
122 F8 **Fredericton** New Brunswick Canada
122 F8 **Fredericton Junct** New Brunswick Canada
28 C4 **Frederiks** Denmark
29 K5 **Frederiksberg** Denmark
28 C5 **Frederikshåb** Denmark
115 P5 **Frederikshåb** Greenland
115 O5 **Frederikshåb Isblink** Greenland
28 F2 **Frederikshavn** Denmark
28 H5 **Frederikssund** Denmark
113 L8 **Frederiksted** Virgin Is
28 J5 **Frederiksværk** Denmark
128 C2 **Fredonia** Colombia
103 M5 **Fredonia** Arizona U.S.A.
107 P4 **Fredonia** Kansas U.S.A.
110 H4 **Fredonia** Kentucky U.S.A.
94 H4 **Fredonia** New York U.S.A.
98 G3 **Fredonia** North Dakota U.S.A.
109 J5 **Fredricksburg** Texas U.S.A.
26 K7 **Fredrika** Sweden
27 E12 **Fredrikstad** Norway
110 E3 **Freeburg** Missouri U.S.A.
95 K6 **Freeburg** Pennsylvania U.S.A.
100 J4 **Freedom** Idaho U.S.A.
110 K2 **Freedom** Indiana U.S.A.
107 L5 **Freedom** Oklahoma U.S.A.
100 E9 **Freedonyer Peak** *mt* California U.S.A.
95 N6 **Freehold** New Jersey U.S.A.
94 C3 **Freeland** Michigan U.S.A.
95 M5 **Freeland** Pennsylvania U.S.A.
138 E4 **Freeling Heights** *mt* South Australia Australia
140 C6 **Freeling Mt** N Terr Australia
102 E3 **Freel Peak** California U.S.A.
123 T4 **Freels, C** Newfoundland Canada
118 B4 **Freeman** *R* Alberta Canada
98 J6 **Freeman** South Dakota U.S.A.
110 K1 **Freeman, L** Indiana U.S.A.
111 G12 **Freemason I** Louisiana U.S.A.
122 F9 **Freeport** Nova Scotia Canada
111 K11 **Freeport** Florida U.S.A.
99 R7 **Freeport** Illinois U.S.A.
95 R3 **Freeport** Maine U.S.A.
94 F6 **Freeport** Ohio U.S.A.
94 H6 **Freeport** Pennsylvania U.S.A.
109 M7 **Freeport** Texas U.S.A.
113 J11 **Freeport City** Grand Bahama I
109 J8 **Freer** Texas U.S.A.
99 U5 **Freesoil** Michigan U.S.A.
126 F2 **Freetown** Eleuthera Bahamas
122 J7 **Freetown** Prince Edward I Canada
85 B7 **Freetown** Sierra Leone
94 A8 **Freetown** Indiana U.S.A.
127 P4 **Freetown** Antigua W Indies
95 L4 **Freeville** New York U.S.A.
16 C6 **Fregenal de la Sierra** Spain
138 B2 **Fregon** South Australia Australia
20 F4 **Fréhel** France
20 F4 **Fréhel, C** France
26 C8 **Frei** Norway
36 G6 **Freiberg** Germany
37 P2 **Freiberg** Germany
37 O1 **Freiberger Mulde** *R* Germany
40 G1 **Freiburg** Germany
32 K10 **Freienhagen** Germany
32 H10 **Freienohl** Germany
36 G3 **Freiensteinau** Germany
37 M4 **Freihung** Germany
36 D2 **Freilingen** Germany
133 C3 **Freirina** Chile
36 C4 **Freisen** Germany
37 M7 **Freising** Germany
38 L4 **Freistadt** Austria
16 C3 **Freixo de Espada à Cinta** Portugal
28 D2 **Frejlev** Denmark
143 B9 **Fremantle** W Australia Australia
94 C5 **Fremont** Indiana U.S.A.
99 V6 **Fremont** Michigan U.S.A.
98 K8 **Fremont** Nebraska U.S.A.
112 K2 **Fremont** North Carolina U.S.A.
94 D5 **Fremont** Ohio U.S.A.
103 O3 **Fremont** *R* Utah U.S.A.
101 N8 **Fremont I** Utah U.S.A.
101 Q7 **Fremont L** Wyoming U.S.A.
106 D2 **Fremont Pass** Colorado U.S.A.
101 Q6 **Fremont Pk** Wyoming U.S.A.
20 F4 **Frênaye, B.de la** France
112 D2 **French Broad** *R* Tennessee U.S.A.
94 D9 **Frenchburg** Kentucky U.S.A.
94 G5 **French Cr** Pennsylvania U.S.A.
100 J4 **French Creek** Idaho U.S.A.
102 T13 **French Frigate Shoals** Hawaiian Is
100 G7 **Frenchglen** Oregon U.S.A.
129 H3 **French Guiana** *French dept* S America
100 C9 **French Gulch** California U.S.A.
139 H7 **French I** Victoria Australia
110 K3 **French Lick** Indiana U.S.A.
102 F2 **Frenchman** Nevada U.S.A.
95 T2 **Frenchman Bay** Maine U.S.A.
118 H5 **Frenchman Butte** Saskatchewan Canada
139 H8 **Frenchman Cap** Tasmania Australia
101 S1 **Frenchman Cr** Mont/Sask U.S.A./Canada
103 J5 **Frenchman Flat** *dry lake* Nevada U.S.A.
98 E9 **Frenchman Fork** *R* Nebraska U.S.A.
118 J9 **Frenchman R** Saskatchewan Canada
123 O4 **Frenchman's Cove** Newfoundland Canada
14 C3 **Frenchpark** Ireland
145 D4 **French Pass** New Zealand
French Terr. of the Afars and the Issas (FTAI) *see* **Djibouti** *rep*
95 M6 **Frenchtown** New Jersey U.S.A.
22 B2 **Frencq** France
19 Q14 **Frêne, Pic du** *mt* France
21 M3 **Freneuse-sur-Risle** France
37 K4 **Frensdorf** Germany
31 L6 **Frenštát** Czechoslovakia
32 G8 **Freren** Germany
143 D7 **Frere Ra** W Australia Australia
129 H5 **Fresco** *R* Brazil
14 D4 **Freshford** Ireland
144 B6 **Freshford Plain** New Zealand
9 E6 **Freshwater** England
100 A9 **Freshwater** California U.S.A.
21 L5 **Fresnay** France
21 L5 **Fresnaye-sur-Chédouet, la** France
40 C2 **Fresnes** France
22 F3 **Fresnes-sur-L'Escaut** France
124 H6 **Fresnillo de González Echeverría** Mexico
102 E4 **Fresno** *R* California U.S.A.
102 E5 **Fresno** California U.S.A.
101 P1 **Fresno Res** Montana U.S.A.
21 N2 **Fresnoy-Folny** France
22 E4 **Fresnoy-le-Grand** France
40 C4 **Fresse, Mt.de** France
21 O1 **Fressenneville** France
27 B10 **Fresvik** Norway
21 N6 **Fréteval** France
27 B11 **Fretheim** Norway
19 J5 **Fretigney** France
20 A5 **Fret,le** France
13 E1 **Freuchie** Scotland

36 G4 **Freudenberg** Baden-Württemberg Germany
36 D2 **Freudenberg** Nordrhein-Westfalen Germany
36 E7 **Freudenstadt** Germany
22 C3 **Frévent** France
140 D4 **Frewena Roadhouse** N Terr Australia
94 H4 **Frewsburg** New York U.S.A.
37 M1 **Freyburg** Germany
143 A10 **Freycinet, C** W Australia Australia
143 A7 **Freycinet Estuary** *inlet* W Australia Australia
139 J8 **Freycinet Pen** Tasmania Australia
33 Q6 **Freyenstein** Germany
36 B5 **Freyming** France
37 L5 **Freystadt** Germany
30 H7 **Freyung** Germany
85 B6 **Fria** Guinea
87 B9 **Fria, C** Namibia
102 E5 **Friant** California U.S.A.
102 E5 **Friant Dam** California U.S.A.
102 E6 **Friant-Kern Canal** California U.S.A.
127 P4 **Friar's B., North** St Kitts W Indies
83 L10 **Friar's Hood** *mt* Sri Lanka
111 F7 **Friars Port** Mississippi U.S.A.
131 D2 **Frias** Argentina
40 F4 **Fribourg** Switzerland
36 E3 **Frickhofen** Germany
22 D3 **Fricourt** France
100 B1 **Friday Harbour** Washington U.S.A.
141 F1 **Friday I** Queensland Australia
13 H5 **Fridaythorpe** England
38 O7 **Friedberg** Austria
37 K7 **Friedberg** Bayern Germany
36 F3 **Friedberg** Hessen Germany
33 P9 **Friedeburg** Germany
38 M4 **Friedersbach** Austria
33 T8 **Friedersdorf** Germany
32 L10 **Friedland** Germany
33 T5 **Friedland** Germany
37 K2 **Friedrichroda** Germany
36 F3 **Friedrichsdorf** Germany
33 T7 **Friedrichsfelde** Germany
41 K2 **Friedrichshafen** Germany
33 T8 **Friedrichshagen** Germany
32 J4 **Friedrichskoog** Germany
33 P5 **Friedrichsruhe** Germany
30 E1 **Friedrichstadt** Germany
33 T6 **Friedrichswalde** Germany
37 K2 **Friedrichswerth** Germany
36 G2 **Frielendorf** Germany
107 K3 **Friend** Kansas U.S.A.
98 J9 **Friend** Nebraska U.S.A.
Friendly Is *see* **Tonga**
127 K2 **Friendship** *pk* Jamaica
95 S3 **Friendship** Maine U.S.A.
94 J4 **Friendship** New York U.S.A.
94 D8 **Friendship** Ohio U.S.A.
99 R6 **Friendship** Wisconsin U.S.A.
70 C2 **Friendship Shoal** S China Sea
94 H7 **Friendsville** Maryland U.S.A.
27 D12 **Frierfjord** *inlet* Norway
94 F10 **Fries** Virginia U.S.A.
38 K8 **Friesach** Austria
33 R7 **Friesack** Germany
25 F2 **Friesche Gat** Netherlands
36 D7 **Friesenheim** Germany
28 A7 **Friesische Inseln** *islds* Germany
25 E2 **Friesland** Netherlands
32 G6 **Friesoythe** Germany
83 J12 **Frigate** *isld* Seychelles
6 M3 **Frigg** *oil rig* North Sea
45 J3 **Frignano** Italy
9 H4 **Frinton-on-Sea** England
124 H6 **Frío** Mexico
109 J7 **Frio** *R* Texas U.S.A.
130 H8 **Frio, C** Brazil
15 F4 **Friockheim** Scotland
108 E1 **Frio Draw** *R* New Mex/Tex U.S.A.
36 F6 **Friolzheim** Germany
22 L4 **Frisange** Luxembourg
109 L2 **Frisco** Texas U.S.A.
111 J10 **Frisco City** Alabama U.S.A.
103 L3 **Frisco Mt** Utah U.S.A.
108 C8 **Fritch** Texas U.S.A.
8 B6 **Frithelstock Stone** England
36 G1 **Fritzlar** Germany
42 E2 **Friuli-Venezia-Giulia** *prov* Italy
21 O1 **Friville-Escarbotin** France
12 E5 **Frizington** England
26 D8 **Froan** *isld* Norway
119 P9 **Frobisher** Saskatchewan Canada
115 N5 **Frobisher Bay** Northwest Territories Canada
114 J6 **Frobisher L** Saskatchewan Canada
8 D1 **Frodsham** England
19 P14 **Froges** France
118 G5 **Frog L** *L* Alberta Canada
26 D8 **Frohavet** *inlet* Norway
37 O1 **Frohburg** Germany
33 S7 **Frohnau** Germany
33 P8 **Frohse** Germany
98 B1 **Froid** Montana U.S.A.
22 G3 **Froid-Chapelle** Belgium
130 F5 **Fróis** Brazil
21 P2 **Froissy** France
36 B2 **Froitzheim** Germany
52 H4 **Frolovskaya** Russian Federation
55 E1 **Froly** Russian Federation
101 R4 **Fromberg** Montana U.S.A.
31 M1 **Frombork** Poland
138 E3 **Frome** *R* South Australia Australia
8 D5 **Frome** England
127 H1 **Frome** Jamaica
138 E4 **Frome Downs** South Australia Australia
138 E4 **Frome, L** South Australia Australia
22 D2 **Fromelles** France
21 K4 **Fromentel** France
20 F8 **Fromentine** France
32 G10 **Fröndenberg** Germany
36 F2 **Fronhausen** Germany
16 B5 **Fronteira** Portugal
18 E6 **Frontenay Rohan-Rohan** France
37 O6 **Frontenhausen** Germany
125 N8 **Frontera** Mexico
124 E2 **Fronteras** Mexico
118 J9 **Frontier** Saskatchewan Canada
101 P8 **Frontier** Wyoming U.S.A.
18 H9 **Frontignan** France
106 E1 **Front Range** Colorado U.S.A.
94 J8 **Front Royal** Virginia U.S.A.
28 F6 **Frørup** Denmark
33 O9 **Frose** Germany
43 E7 **Frosinone** Italy
28 B3 **Frøslev** Denmark
20 G7 **Frossay** France
109 L3 **Frost** Texas U.S.A.
26 E8 **Frosta** Norway
94 J7 **Frostburg** Maryland U.S.A.
113 F10 **Frostproof** Florida U.S.A.
28 B2 **Frøstrup** Denmark
26 G7 **Frostviken** Sweden
37 K2 **Fröttstädt** Germany
19 K4 **Frouard** France
119 O9 **Froude** Saskatchewan Canada
27 H12 **Frövi** Sweden
9 E5 **Froxfield** England
26 C8 **Fröya** *isld* Norway
26 B8 **Fröyabanken** Norway
22 C3 **Fruges** France
106 B2 **Fruita** Colorado U.S.A.
111 H10 **Fruitdale** Alabama U.S.A.
98 C5 **Fruitdale** South Dakota U.S.A.
100 J5 **Fruitland** Idaho U.S.A.
106 B5 **Fruitland** New Mexico U.S.A.
101 P9 **Fruitland** Utah U.S.A.
144 B6 **Fruitlands** New Zealand
100 J5 **Fruitvale** Idaho U.S.A.
48 K3 **Frumuşica** Romania
Frunze *see* **Bishkek**
54 F8 **Frunzenskiy** Ukraine
48 M3 **Frunzovka** Ukraine
48 F5 **Fruška Gora** *mt* Serbia Yugoslavia
130 E7 **Frutal** Brazil
40 G4 **Frutigen** Switzerland
102 B2 **Fruto** California U.S.A.
54 K1 **Fryanovo** Russian Federation
98 C3 **Fryburg** North Dakota U.S.A.
48 E1 **Frýdek Místek** Czechoslovakia
95 R2 **Fryeburg** Maine U.S.A.
27 F11 **Fryksände** Sweden
46 E5 **Ftéri** *mt* Greece
67 F3 **Fu'an** China
45 J4 **Fucecchio** Italy
Fucheng *see* **Qiongshan**
65 C6 **Fucheng** China
65 B7 **Fucheng** China
36 E2 **Fuchskauten** *mt* Germany
60 G11 **Fuchū** Japan
67 D4 **Fuchuan** China
59 G6 **Fuchun Jiang** *R* China
42 F7 **Fucino, Piana del** Italy
61 P5 **Fudai** Japan
67 G3 **Fuding** China
16 D8 **Fuengirola** Spain
108 G7 **Fuente** Mexico
17 G7 **Fuente Alamo de Murcia** Spain
16 C6 **Fuente de Cantos** Spain
16 C4 **Fuenteguinaldo** Spain
16 D6 **Fuenteobejuna** Spain
16 D3 **Fuentesaúco** Spain
17 G3 **Fuentes de Ebro** Spain
16 C4 **Fuentes de Oñoro** Spain
130 B7 **Fuerte Olimpo** Paraguay
85 B3 **Fuerteventura** *isld* Canary Is
71 E1 **Fuga** *isld* Luzon Philippines
38 E7 **Fügen** Austria
28 H6 **Fuglebjerg** Denmark
6 F1 **Fugloy** *isld* Faeroes
26 L1 **Fugløy** *isld* Norway
28 F7 **Fuglsbølle** Denmark
65 C7 **Fugou** China
65 B5 **Fugu** China
Fuguo *see* **Zhanhua**
66 D2 **Fuhai** China
77 A5 **Fuḩayḩīl, Al** Kuwait
33 Q9 **Fuhne** *R* Germany
32 L7 **Fuhrberg** Germany
21 H7 **Fuilet, le** France
77 E7 **Fujairah** U.A.E.
Fujayrah, Al *see* **Fujairah**
67 F3 **Fujian** *prov* China
67 B1 **Fu Jiang** *R* China
61 M11 **Fujieda** Japan
61 M10 **Fuji Hakone Izu Nat. Park** Japan
61 M10 **Fuji-kawa** *R* Japan
59 K2 **Fujin** China
61 M10 **Fujinomiya** Japan
61 N9 **Fujioka** Japan
61 O5 **Fujisaki** Japan
61 M10 **Fuji-san** *vol* Japan
61 N10 **Fujisawa** Japan
61 M10 **Fujiyoshida** Japan
61 N5 **Fukaura** Japan
61 N9 **Fukaya** Japan
Fukien *prov see* **Fujian**
60 J10 **Fukuchiyama** Japan
60 B13 **Fukue** Japan
60 B13 **Fukue-jima** *isld* Japan
61 K9 **Fukui** Japan
60 D12 **Fukuma** Japan
61 K9 **Fukuno** Japan
60 D12 **Fukuoka** Japan
61 N6 **Fukura** Japan
61 L11 **Fukuroi** Japan
61 O8 **Fukushima** *prefect* Japan
60 O4 **Fukushima** Hokkaido Japan
61 O8 **Fukushima** Honshu Japan
60 G11 **Fukuyama** Honshu Japan
60 D14 **Fukuyama** Kyūshū Japan
60 H10 **Fukuzaki** Japan
85 B6 **Fulacunda** Guinea-Bissau
77 C1 **Fulād Mahalleh** Iran
36 H2 **Fulda** *R* Germany
36 H2 **Fulda** Germany
99 L6 **Fulda** Minnesota U.S.A.
36 G1 **Fuldabrück** Germany
13 G6 **Fulford** England
58 D6 **Fulin** China
67 B2 **Fuling** China
67 F3 **Fuling** China
141 F5 **Fullarton** *R* Queensland Australia
127 N3 **Fullarton** Trinidad
102 G8 **Fullerton** California U.S.A.
94 E8 **Fullerton** Kentucky U.S.A.
109 P4 **Fullerton** Louisiana U.S.A.
98 H8 **Fullerton** Nebraska U.S.A.
6 M6 **Fulmar** *oil rig* North Sea
65 F2 **Fulongquan** China
48 E4 **Fülöpszállás** Hungary
41 O3 **Fulpmes** Austria
111 J10 **Fulton** Alabama U.S.A.
111 C8 **Fulton** Arkansas U.S.A.
99 Q8 **Fulton** Illinois U.S.A.
94 A6 **Fulton** Indiana U.S.A.
107 Q3 **Fulton** Kansas U.S.A.
110 H5 **Fulton** Kentucky U.S.A.
111 C11 **Fulton** Louisiana U.S.A.
111 H7 **Fulton** Mississippi U.S.A.
110 E3 **Fulton** Missouri U.S.A.
95 L3 **Fulton** New York U.S.A.
94 E6 **Fulton** Ohio U.S.A.
98 J6 **Fulton** South Dakota U.S.A.
95 N4 **Fultonham** New York U.S.A.
95 N4 **Fultonville** New York U.S.A.
27 F10 **Fuluälven** *R* Sweden
27 F10 **Fulufj** *mt* Sweden
27 F10 **Fulunäs** Sweden
22 H4 **Fumay** France
18 F8 **Fumel** France
41 N5 **Fumo, Mt** Italy
61 N10 **Funabashi** Japan
137 Q3 **Funafuti** *atoll* Tuvalu
60 E14 **Funahiki** Japan
Funan *see* **Fusui**
65 F4 **Funan** China
26 F9 **Funäsdalen** Sweden
85 A2 **Funchal** Madeira
16 B7 **Funcheira** Portugal
126 G9 **Fundación** Colombia
130 H6 **Fundão** Brazil
124 E4 **Fundición** Mexico
38 E8 **Fundres** Italy
48 K6 **Fundulea** Romania
41 N3 **Fundus Feiler** *mt* Austria
122 G8 **Fundy, B. of** Nova Scotia/New Bruns Canada
122 G8 **Fundy Nat. Park** New Brunswick Canada
Funen *isld see* **Fyn** *isld*
102 H5 **Funeral Peak** California U.S.A.
87 F10 **Funhalouro** Mozambique
65 D5 **Funing** China
67 B5 **Funing** China
98 G9 **Funk** Nebraska U.S.A.
123 T4 **Funk I** Newfoundland Canada
141 J5 **Funnel** *R* Queensland Australia
117 F6 **Funter** Alaska U.S.A.
85 F6 **Funtua** Nigeria
65 C5 **Fuping** China
65 A7 **Fuping** China
67 F4 **Fuqing** China
112 J2 **Fuquay Springs** North Carolina U.S.A.
88 D9 **Furancungo** Mozambique
60 Q2 **Furano** Japan
59 J2 **Furao** China
46 G1 **Furculeşti** Romania
80 C3 **Furēidis** Israel
60 Q3 **Furenai** Japan
60 T2 **Füren ko** *L* Japan
29 K5 **Furesø** *L* Denmark
36 G5 **Fürfeld** Baden-Württemberg Germany
36 D4 **Fürfeld** Rheinland-Pfalz Germany
77 D5 **Furg** Iran
112 F5 **Furman** South Carolina U.S.A.
52 F6 **Furmanov** Russian Federation
57 G3 **Furmanovka** Kazakhstan
12 C1 **Furnace** Scotland
130 F7 **Furnas Dam** Brazil
139 J8 **Furneaux Group** *islds* Tasmania Australia
138 F6 **Furner** South Australia Australia
Furnes *see* **Veurne**
27 E11 **Furnes** Norway
118 H5 **Furness** Saskatchewan Canada
67 B2 **Furong Jiang** *R* China
67 E3 **Furong Shan** *mt* China
32 G7 **Fürstenau** Germany
33 S6 **Fürstenberg** Germany
36 F1 **Fürstenberg** Germany
38 O7 **Fürstenfeld** Austria
37 L7 **Fürstenfeldbrück** Germany
30 H3 **Fürstenwalde** Germany
33 T6 **Fürstenwerder** Germany
37 P6 **Fürstenzell** Germany
36 F4 **Fürth** Germany
37 O5 **Furth im Wald** Germany
41 H1 **Furtwangen** Germany
60 O2 **Furuhira** Japan
61 O7 **Furukawa** Japan
61 L9 **Furukawa** Japan
115 L4 **Fury & Hecla Str** Northwest Territories Canada
27 A11 **Fusa** Norway
128 D3 **Fusagasuga** Colombia
45 Q8 **Fusaro** *L* Italy
43 G9 **Fuscaldo** Italy
38 G7 **Fusch** Austria
32 M8 **Fuse** *R* Germany
65 B6 **Fushan** China
65 E6 **Fushan** China
68 J3 **Fushan** China
13 E2 **Fushiebridge** Scotland
61 K9 **Fushiki** Japan
59 H3 **Fushun** China
67 A2 **Fushun** China
45 L3 **Fusignano** Italy
118 H7 **Fusilier** Saskatchewan Canada
Fusin *see* **Fuxin**
45 M1 **Fusina** Italy
41 J5 **Fusio** Switzerland
59 J3 **Fusong** China
41 N2 **Füssen** Germany
28 D4 **Fussing Sø** *L* Denmark
67 B5 **Fusui** China
61 L11 **Futagawa** Japan
60 E12 **Futago-san** *mt* Japan
60 D11 **Futaoi-jima** *isld* Japan
45 K3 **Futa, Passo di** Italy
61 O5 **Futatsui** Japan
61 N13 **Futatsu-ne** *rocks* Japan
61 P13 **Futemma** Okinawa
61 N10 **Futtsu** Japan
137 R4 **Futuna** *isld* Îles de Horn Pacific Oc
67 F3 **Futun Xi** *R* China
79 A7 **Fuwa** Egypt
65 E5 **Fu Xian** China
67 A4 **Fuxian Hu** *L* China
65 E3 **Fuxin** China
Fuxing *see* **Wangmo**
58 G5 **Fuyang** China
67 F1 **Fuyang** China
67 F5 **Fuyang** China
67 G3 **Fuying Dao** *isld* China
59 H2 **Fuyu** China
59 K2 **Fuyuan** China
67 A4 **Fuyuan** China
66 D2 **Fuyun** China
48 F3 **Füzesabony** Hungary
48 G3 **Füzesgyarmat** Hungary
67 E3 **Fuzhou** Fujian China
67 F2 **Fuzhou** Jiangxi China
65 F5 **Fuzhoucheng** China
9 E4 **Fyfield** England
9 G4 **Fyfield** Essex England
28 E6 **Fyn** *isld* Denmark
28 F6 **Fyn** *co* Denmark
12 C1 **Fyne, L** Scotland
28 D7 **Fynshav** Denmark
28 F5 **Fynshoved** *C* Denmark
27 C12 **Fyresv** *L* Norway
127 O3 **Fyzabad** Trinidad

G

86 A2 **Gaalkacyo** Somalia
70 C4 **Gaat** *R* Sarawak
52 D4 **Gabanova** Russian Federation
123 M8 **Gabarouse** C Breton I, Nova Scotia
17 J3 **Gabarras, Mts** Spain
18 F9 **Gabarret** France
102 G3 **Gabbs** Nevada U.S.A.
102 F3 **Gabbs Valley Ra** Nevada U.S.A.
87 B8 **Gabela** Angola
Gaberones *see* **Gaborone**
85 F2 **Gabès** Tunisia
85 G2 **Gabès, Golfe de** Tunisia
84 J5 **Gabgaba, Wadi** *watercourse* Sudan
102 C5 **Gabilan Ra** California U.S.A.
31 M3 **Gąbin** Poland
145 G3 **Gable End Foreland** New Zealand
117 K9 **Gable Mt** British Columbia Canada
139 J7 **Gabo** *isld* Victoria Australia
28 C6 **Gabøl** Denmark
86 B6 **Gabon** *rep* Equat Africa
89 D5 **Gaborone** Botswana
95 N2 **Gabriels** New York U.S.A.
16 C4 **Gabriel y Galán, Embalse** *res* Spain
77 F7 **Gābrik** Iran
46 G2 **Gabrovo** Bulgaria
85 B6 **Gabú** Guinea-Bissau
83 L14 **Gaby** *isld* Kerguelen Indian Oc
21 L4 **Gacé** France
77 B4 **Gach Sārān** Iran
20 F6 **Gacilly, la** France
98 G3 **Gackle** North Dakota U.S.A.
48 E7 **Gacko** Bosnia-Herzegovina
85 B3 **Ga'da, Al** Western Sahara
76 B3 **Gadag** India
86 G2 **Gadamai** Sudan
28 C5 **Gadbjerg** Denmark
26 G7 **Gäddede** Sweden
32 J8 **Gadderbaum** Germany
33 O5 **Gadebusch** Germany
80 D3 **Gadish** Israel
17 F8 **Gador, Sierra de** Spain
80 F1 **Gadot** Israel
118 E6 **Gadsby** Alberta Canada
111 L8 **Gadsden** Alabama U.S.A.
103 K9 **Gadsden** Arizona U.S.A.
28 J5 **Gadstrup** Denmark
76 C2 **Gadwal** India
54 F6 **Gadyach** Ukraine
89 G2 **Gadzema** Zimbabwe
86 C5 **Gadzi** Cent Afr Republic
20 F5 **Gaël** France
48 J6 **Găeşti** Romania
43 F7 **Gaeta** Italy
45 P8 **Gaeta, Gulf of** Italy
112 F2 **Gaffney** South Carolina U.S.A.
71 A2 **Gafi** *isld* Indonesia
38 L6 **Gaflenz** Austria
85 F2 **Gafsa** Tunisia
57 E4 **Gafurov** Tajikistan
57 H6 **Gafurov** Tajikistan
71 B3 **Gag** *isld* Indonesia
54 F1 **Gagarin** Russian Federation
106 B9 **Gage** New Mexico U.S.A.
107 L5 **Gage** Oklahoma U.S.A.
122 H7 **Gage, C** Prince Edward I Canada
99 R4 **Gagen** Wisconsin U.S.A.
19 O15 **Gagère, P. de la** *mt* France
122 F8 **Gagetown** New Brunswick Canada
36 E6 **Gaggenau** Germany
52 F6 **Gagino** Russian Federation
27 H11 **Gagnef** Sweden
85 C7 **Gagnoa** Ivory Coast
122 D2 **Gagnon** Quebec Canada
121 P6 **Gagnon, L** Quebec Canada
52 H4 **Gagshor** Russian Federation
66 F4 **Gahe** China
38 N6 **Gahns** *mt* Austria
89 A6 **Gaiab** *watercourse* Namibia
130 B5 **Gaiba** *L* Bolivia/Brazil
75 N6 **Gaibanda** Bangladesh
48 L4 **Găiceana** Romania
47 H10 **Gaïdhouronisi** *isld* Crete Greece
38 J8 **Gail** *R* Austria
36 H6 **Gaildorf** Germany
18 G9 **Gaillac** France
122 E1 **Gaillarbois, L** Quebec Canada
21 O2 **Gaillefontaine** France
21 N3 **Gaillon** France
38 G8 **Gailtaler Alpen** *mts* Austria
133 D6 **Gaiman** Argentina
37 L6 **Gaimersheim** Germany
94 B10 **Gainesboro** Tennessee U.S.A.
111 H9 **Gainesville** Alabama U.S.A.
113 E8 **Gainesville** Florida U.S.A.
109 K2 **Gainesville** Texas U.S.A.
13 G4 **Gainford** England
119 Q9 **Gainsborough** Saskatchewan Canada
13 H6 **Gainsborough** England
47 P13 **Gäïos** Greece
138 D4 **Gairdner Lake** South Australia Australia
15 C3 **Gairloch** Scotland
15 C4 **Gairlochy** Scotland
15 E3 **Gairn** *R* Scotland
38 L7 **Gaishorn** Austria
95 K7 **Gaithersburg** Maryland U.S.A.
65 E4 **Gai Xian** China
70 P9 **Gajam** Indonesia
76 B3 **Gajendragara** India
89 C6 **Gakarosa** *mt* S Africa
116 P5 **Gakona** Alaska U.S.A.
52 E4 **Gakugsa** Russian Federation
66 D6 **Gala** China
15 F5 **Gala** *R* Scotland
57 C5 **Galaasiya** Uzbekistan
77 H2 **GāLā, Band-i-** *mts* Afghanistan
83 K10 **Galagedera** Sri Lanka
118 F6 **Galahad** Alberta Canada
79 B9 **Galâla el Baharîya, G. el** *mts* Egypt
79 C10 **Galâla el Qiblîya, G. el** *mts* Egypt
17 G4 **Galamocha** Spain
88 G3 **Galana** *R* Kenya
69 G12 **Galang Besar** *isld* Indonesia
26 N3 **Galanito** Norway
48 D2 **Galanta** Czechoslovakia
128 A7 **Galapagos Is** Pacific Oc
13 F2 **Galashiels** Scotland
101 O1 **Galata** Montana U.S.A.
46 F7 **Galatás** Greece
145 F3 **Galatea** New Zealand
106 G3 **Galatea** Colorado U.S.A.
137 R8 **Galathea Depth** Pacific Oc
48 L5 **Galati** Romania
110 H4 **Galatia** Illinois U.S.A.
107 M3 **Galatia** Kansas U.S.A.
43 J8 **Galatina** Italy
Galatz *see* **Galati**
19 O14 **Galaure** *R* France
94 G10 **Galax** Virginia U.S.A.
46 E6 **Galaxidhion** Greece
47 N10 **Galaza Burun** *C* Turkey
141 F3 **Galbraith** Queensland Australia
124 J5 **Gal. Cepeda** Mexico
26 C10 **Galdhöpiggen** *mt* Norway
124 F2 **Galeana** Mexico
130 G8 **Galeão** Brazil
45 L4 **Galeata** Italy
77 C6 **Galeh Dār** Iran
71 A2 **Galela** Indonesia
116 J4 **Galena** Alaska U.S.A.
99 Q7 **Galena** Illinois U.S.A.
107 Q4 **Galena** Kansas U.S.A.
95 M7 **Galena** Maryland U.S.A.
110 C5 **Galena** Missouri U.S.A.
109 G9 **Galena Park** Texas U.S.A.
33 T5 **Galenbecker See** *L* Germany
127 P3 **Galeota Pt** Trinidad
17 F7 **Galera** Spain
128 B3 **Galera, Pta** *pt* Ecuador
131 A8 **Galera, Pta. de la** Chile
99 Q9 **Galesburg** Illinois U.S.A.
94 B4 **Galesburg** Michigan U.S.A.
99 P5 **Galesville** Wisconsin U.S.A.
120 K1 **Galeton** Ontario Canada
98 B9 **Galeton** Colorado U.S.A.
94 K5 **Galeton** Pennsylvania U.S.A.
83 J13 **Galets, Pte des** Réunion Indian Oc
13 F6 **Galgate** England
83 K10 **Galgiriya** *mt* Sri Lanka
117 M11 **Galiano I** British Columbia Canada
19 Q14 **Galibier, Col du** *pass* France
100 B7 **Galice** Oregon U.S.A.
48 J1 **Galich** Ukraine
46 F1 **Galiche** Bulgaria
52 F5 **Galichskoye, Oz** *L* Russian Federation
16 B2 **Galicia** Spain
99 U8 **Galien** Michigan U.S.A.
141 H5 **Galilee, L** Queensland Australia
80 F2 **Galilee, Sea of** Israel
127 L2 **Galina Pt** Jamaica
94 E6 **Galion** Ohio U.S.A.
127 M4 **Galion, Baie du** Martinique W Indies
123 O2 **Galissonnière, L.la** Quebec Canada
43 C11 **Galite, La** Tunisia
103 O9 **Galiurov Mts** Arizona U.S.A.
140 D1 **Galiwinku** N Terr Australia
55 D3 **Galkino** Russian Federation
86 G3 **Gallabat** Sudan
42 B3 **Gallarate** Italy
21 O4 **Gallardon** France
99 N10 **Gallatin** Missouri U.S.A.
101 O4 **Gallatin** *R* Montana U.S.A.
110 K5 **Gallatin** Tennessee U.S.A.
109 M4 **Gallatin** Texas U.S.A.
101 O4 **Gallatin Gateway** Montana U.S.A.
101 O4 **Gallatin Pk** Montana U.S.A.
101 P4 **Gallatin Ra** Mont/Wyoming U.S.A.
83 K11 **Galle** Sri Lanka
17 G3 **Gállego** *R* Spain
133 C8 **Gallegos** *R* Argentina
106 G6 **Gallegos** New Mexico U.S.A.
45 J4 **Galleno** Italy
123 O2 **Gallet** *L* Quebec Canada
14 C5 **Galley Hd** Ireland
45 J3 **Gallicano** Italy
45 N6 **Gallicano nel Lazio** Italy
46 F4 **Gallikós** *R* Greece
33 Q5 **Gallin** Germany
106 D5 **Gallina Pk** New Mexico U.S.A.
44 D3 **Gallinara** *isld* Italy
106 E6 **Gallinas** New Mexico U.S.A.
108 B1 **Gallinas Peak** New Mexico U.S.A.
128 D1 **Gallinas, Pta** *C* Colombia
43 H8 **Gallipoli** Italy
Gallipoli Turkey *see* **Gelibolu**
94 E8 **Gallipolis** Ohio U.S.A.
94 J6 **Gallitzin** Pennsylvania U.S.A.
26 L4 **Gällivare** Sweden
45 Q7 **Gallo** Italy
17 F4 **Gallo** *R* Spain
26 H9 **Gällö** Sweden
43 E10 **Gallo, C** Sicily
17 F4 **Gallocanta, L.de** Spain
41 M5 **Gallo, Lago di** Italy
106 B8 **Gallo Mts** New Mexico U.S.A.
95 L3 **Galloo I** New York U.S.A.
7 M11 **Galloper Lightship** North Sea
15 D6 **Galloway** Scotland
27 F14 **Gällstad** Sweden
106 B6 **Gallup** New Mexico U.S.A.
17 G3 **Gallur** Spain
45 K4 **Galluzzo** Italy
85 F6 **Galmi** Niger
139 J5 **Galong** New South Wales Australia
83 K9 **Galoya** Sri Lanka
83 L10 **Gal Oya** *R* Sri Lanka
83 L10 **Gal Oya Nat. Park** Sri Lanka
124 H5 **Gal. Simon Bolivar** Mexico
28 C6 **Galsted** Denmark
12 D2 **Galston** Scotland
26 J9 **Galström** Sweden
102 C3 **Galt** California U.S.A.
99 N9 **Galt** Missouri U.S.A.
85 B3 **Galtat Zemmour** Western Sahara
28 D4 **Galten** Denmark
26 N1 **Galten** Norway
124 F3 **Gal. Trías** Mexico
41 M4 **Galtür** Austria
14 C4 **Galtymore** *mt* Ireland
99 R8 **Galva** Illinois U.S.A.
94 A6 **Galveston** Indiana U.S.A.
111 B12 **Galveston** Texas U.S.A.
131 E4 **Galvez** Argentina
14 B3 **Galway** *co* Ireland
14 B3 **Galway** Ireland
14 B3 **Galway Bay** Ireland
71 B3 **Gam** *isld* Indonesia
71 C3 **Gam** *isld* W Irian
21 O2 **Gamaches** France
61 L11 **Gamagōri** Japan
131 E8 **Gama, I** Argentina
94 B10 **Gamaliel** Kentucky U.S.A.
71 G4 **Gamay Bay** Philippines
75 N4 **Gamba** China
85 D6 **Gambaga** Ghana
21 O4 **Gambais** France
45 J4 **Gambassi Terme** Italy
45 R6 **Gambatesa** Italy
86 F4 **Gambēla** Ethiopia
116 B5 **Gambell** St Lawrence I, Alaska U.S.A.
45 M3 **Gambettola** Italy
85 A6 **Gambia** *R* The Gambia/Senegal
85 A6 **Gambia, The** *rep* W Africa
94 E6 **Gambier** Ohio U.S.A.
140 B1 **Gambier, C** N Terr Australia
138 D6 **Gambier Is** South Australia Australia
135 R15 **Gambier Is** Pacific Oc
113 L9 **Gambier Village** New Providence I Bahamas
124 F9 **Gamboa** Panama
86 C6 **Gamboma** Congo
141 G3 **Gamboola** Queensland Australia
86 C5 **Gamboula** Cent Afr Republic
71 H4 **Gambuta** *mt* Sulawesi
Gamcaka *see* **Lelai**
130 J10 **Gameleira** Brazil
71 A2 **Gamkunoro Gunung** *mt* Indonesia
71 A2 **Gamlaba** Indonesia
27 H14 **Gamleby** Sweden
26 M6 **Gammelstad** Sweden
36 G7 **Gammertingen** Germany
16 D4 **Gamo** *R* Spain
86 G4 **Gamo-Gofa** *prov* Ethiopia
83 K10 **Gampola** Sri Lanka
77 G5 **Gamshadzai K** *mts* Iran
66 F5 **Gamtog** China
26 Q1 **Gamvik** Norway
18 E9 **Gan** France
73 L9 **Gan** Maldives
37 O6 **Ganacker** Germany
103 P6 **Ganado** Arizona U.S.A.
109 L6 **Ganado** Texas U.S.A.
121 O8 **Gananoque** Ontario Canada
67 C7 **Gancheng** China
Gand *see* **Gent**
87 B8 **Ganda** Angola
70 F6 **Gandadiwata G** *mt* Sulawesi
87 D7 **Gandajika** Zaire
74 B4 **Gandava** Pakistan
123 S5 **Gander** Newfoundland Canada
123 S4 **Gander Bay** Newfoundland Canada
32 J6 **Ganderkesee** Germany
123 R5 **Gander R** Newfoundland Canada
17 H3 **Gandesa** Spain
74 D7 **Gāndhīdhām** India
74 E7 **Gāndhīnagar** India
74 F6 **Gāndhi Sāgar** *L* India
17 G6 **Gandia** Spain
28 E2 **Gandrup** Denmark
103 L2 **Gandy** Utah U.S.A.
77 B5 **Ganēveh** Iran
83 K10 **Ganewatta** Sri Lanka
74 H5 **Gangā** *R* India
74 G9 **Gangakher** India
Gangā, Mouths of the *see* **Ganges, Mouths of the**
133 D6 **Gan Gan** Argentina
74 E4 **Ganganagar** India
68 B1 **Gangaw** Burma
76 C3 **Gangawati** India
75 R6 **Gangaw Range** Burma
66 C5 **Gangdisê Shan** *mt ra* China
25 F7 **Gangelt** Germany
Ganges *R see* **Gangā** *R*
18 H9 **Ganges** France
75 N8 **Ganges, Mouths of the** Bangladesh/India
27 F14 **Gånghester** Sweden
37 O7 **Gangkofen** Germany
65 F4 **Gangou** China
75 N5 **Gangtok** India
65 A6 **Ganguyi** China
67 E3 **Gan Jiang** *R* China
Ganjig *see* **Horqin Zuoyi Houqi**
139 H5 **Ganmam** New South Wales Australia
18 H6 **Gannat** France
6 L5 **Gannet** *oil rig* North Sea
145 E2 **Gannet I** New Zealand
101 L6 **Gannett** Idaho U.S.A.
101 Q6 **Gannett Pk** Wyoming U.S.A.
80 C5 **Ganne Yehuda** Israel
98 G5 **Gannvalley** South Dakota U.S.A.
80 C6 **Gan Shelomo** Israel
58 C3 **Gansu** *prov* China
85 C7 **Ganta** Liberia
Gantang *see* **Taiping**
143 A8 **Gantheaume B** W Australia Australia
138 E6 **Gantheaume, C** South Australia Australia
142 D4 **Gantheaume Pt** W Australia Australia
69 J14 **Gantung** Indonesia
67 E4 **Gan Xian** China
58 E4 **Ganyanchi** China
80 B6 **Gan Yavne** Israel
87 D11 **Ganyesa** S Africa
65 D7 **Ganyu** China
65 D4 **Ganzhao** China
Ganzhe *see* **Minhou**
67 E4 **Ganzhou** China
33 Q6 **Ganzlin** Germany
85 D5 **Gao** Mali
67 E2 **Gao'an** China
Gaobeidian *see* **Xincheng**
65 C5 **Gaocheng** China
67 F1 **Gaochun** China
Gaocun *see* **Mayang**
65 B5 **Gaocun** China
67 D5 **Gaohe** China
67 E1 **Gaohebu** China
65 A5 **Gaojiabu** China
65 A7 **Gaoling** China
67 B4 **Gaolou Ling** *mt* China
65 D6 **Gaomi** China
67 E4 **Gaopi** China
65 B7 **Gaoping** China
65 D6 **Gaoqing** China
67 C3 **Gaosha** China
65 B4 **Gaoshan** China
65 E3 **Gaotaishan** China
65 C6 **Gaotang** China
85 D6 **Gaoua** Burkina
85 B6 **Gaoual** Guinea
67 A2 **Gao Xian** China
65 C7 **Gaoxianji** China
58 G4 **Gaoyang** China
65 C6 **Gaoyi** China
59 G5 **Gaoyou** China
59 G5 **Gaoyou Hu** *L* China
67 C6 **Gaozhou** China
19 Q15 **Gap** France
71 E3 **Gapan** Luzon Philippines
19 P18 **Gapeau** *R* France
66 C5 **Gar** China
85 F3 **Gara Brune** Algeria
86 A2 **Garadag** Somalia
43 C11 **Garaet Ichkeul** *L* Tunisia
139 J3 **Garah** New South Wales Australia
47 H1 **Gara Khitrino** Bulgaria
14 C3 **Gara, L** Ireland
130 H10 **Garanhuns** Brazil
71 H9 **Garantah** Indonesia
130 F5 **Garapuava** Brazil
86 D4 **Garba** Cent Afr Republic
107 N5 **Garber** Oklahoma U.S.A.
100 B9 **Garberville** California U.S.A.
9 G3 **Garboldisham** England
130 E8 **Garça** Brazil
130 D4 **Garças** *R* Brazil
37 M7 **Garching** Germany
106 E4 **Garcia** Colorado U.S.A.
16 D5 **Garcia de Sola, Embalse de** *res* Spain
130 D7 **Garcias** Brazil
18 H8 **Gard** *dept* France
18 H9 **Gard** *R* France
41 N6 **Garda, Lago di** Italy
19 O18 **Gardanne** France
98 J1 **Gardar** North Dakota U.S.A.
27 J15 **Gårdby** Sweden
33 O7 **Gardelegen** Germany
99 U4 **Garden** Michigan U.S.A.
100 J6 **Gardena** Idaho U.S.A.
98 F1 **Gardena** North Dakota U.S.A.
111 K7 **Garden City** Alabama U.S.A.
107 K4 **Garden City** Kansas U.S.A.
110 B3 **Garden City** Missouri U.S.A.
112 F5 **Garden City** South Carolina U.S.A.
98 J5 **Garden City** South Dakota U.S.A.
108 F4 **Garden City** Texas U.S.A.
101 O8 **Garden City** Utah U.S.A.
109 H7 **Gardendale** Texas U.S.A.
102 G8 **Garden Grove** California U.S.A.
99 N9 **Garden Grove** Iowa U.S.A.
142 A3 **Garden I** W Australia Australia
143 B9 **Garden I** W Australia Australia
99 V4 **Garden I** Michigan U.S.A.
111 G12 **Garden I Bay** Louisiana U.S.A.
140 B1 **Garden Point** N Terr Australia
119 V9 **Gardenton** Manitoba Canada
100 K5 **Garden Valley** Idaho U.S.A.
77 L3 **Gardēz** Afghanistan
120 J3 **Gardiner** Ontario Canada
95 S2 **Gardiner** Maine U.S.A.
101 P4 **Gardiner** Montana U.S.A.
106 F5 **Gardiner** New Mexico U.S.A.
100 A6 **Gardiner** Oregon U.S.A.
118 L7 **Gardiner Dam** Saskatchewan Canada
140 C5 **Gardiner, Mt** N Terr Australia
142 G4 **Gardiner Ra** Australia
95 P5 **Gardiners I** New York U.S.A.
140 B6 **Gardiner's Range** N Terr Australia
32 J4 **Garding** Germany
106 E4 **Gardner** Colorado U.S.A.
113 F10 **Gardner** Florida U.S.A.
99 S8 **Gardner** Illinois U.S.A.
95 P4 **Gardner** Massachusetts U.S.A.
95 U2 **Gardner L** Maine U.S.A.
102 E3 **Gardnerville** Nevada U.S.A.
31 K1 **Gardno, Jezioro** *L* Poland
27 G13 **Gårdsjö** Sweden
26 H6 **Gardsjönas** Sweden
27 J15 **Gärdslösa** Sweden
Gardula *see* **Gīdolē**
12 D1 **Gare L** Scotland
12 D1 **Garelochhead** Scotland
42 H3 **Garešnica** Croatia
44 D3 **Garessio** Italy
85 F3 **Garet el Djenoun** *mt* Algeria
45 H3 **Garfagnane** *R* Italy
110 C5 **Garfield** Arkansas U.S.A.
112 E5 **Garfield** Georgia U.S.A.
107 L3 **Garfield** Kansas U.S.A.
101 N9 **Garfield** Utah U.S.A.
100 H2 **Garfield** Washington U.S.A.
101 N5 **Garfield Mt** Idaho/Montana U.S.A.
46 E7 **Gargaliánoi** Greece
16 D5 **Gargáligas** *R* Spain
42 G7 **Gargano, Promontorio del** *prom* Italy
120 E5 **Gargantua, C** Ontario Canada
26 N2 **Gargia** Norway
41 N6 **Gargnano** Italy
26 J6 **Gargnäs** Sweden
13 F6 **Gargrave** England
12 D1 **Gargunnock** Scotland
52 B6 **Gargždai** Lithuania
74 H7 **Garhakota** India
55 D2 **Gari** Russian Federation
100 B4 **Garibaldi** Oregon U.S.A.
117 M11 **Garibaldi Prov. Park** British Columbia Canada
43 F7 **Garigliano** *R* Italy
15 F3 **Garioch** Scotland
88 G2 **Garissa** Kenya
119 R7 **Garland** Manitoba Canada
107 Q4 **Garland** Kansas U.S.A.
98 K9 **Garland** Nebraska U.S.A.
112 J3 **Garland** North Carolina U.S.A.
94 H5 **Garland** Pennsylvania U.S.A.
109 O9 **Garland** Texas U.S.A.
101 N8 **Garland** Utah U.S.A.
101 R5 **Garland** Wyoming U.S.A.
44 E1 **Garlasco** Italy
12 D4 **Garlieston** Scotland
18 E9 **Garlin** France
111 K10 **Garlrand** Alabama U.S.A.
32 M6 **Garlstorf** Germany
57 F5 **Garm** Tajikistan
41 O3 **Garmisch-Partenkirchen** Germany
77 H4 **Garmsel** *reg* Afghanistan
20 G8 **Garnache, la** France
99 P7 **Garnavillo** Iowa U.S.A.
122 J2 **Garneau, R** Quebec Canada
101 Q3 **Garneill** Montana U.S.A.
99 N6 **Garner** Iowa U.S.A.
112 J2 **Garner** North Carolina U.S.A.
118 E4 **Garner Lake Prov. Park** *pk* Alberta Canada
101 M3 **Garnet** Montana U.S.A.
115 M4 **Garnet Bay** Northwest Territories Canada
107 P3 **Garnett** Kansas U.S.A.
18 F9 **Garonne** *R* France
130 E11 **Garopaba** Brazil
74 F6 **Garoth** India
86 B4 **Garoua** Cameroon
86 B4 **Garoua Boulai** Cameroon
119 V3 **Garraway** Manitoba Canada
32 H7 **Garrel** Germany
98 K6 **Garretson** South Dakota U.S.A.
94 B5 **Garrett** Indiana U.S.A.
94 H7 **Garrett** Pennsylvania U.S.A.
101 U7 **Garrett** Wyoming U.S.A.
94 F5 **Garrettsville** Ohio U.S.A.
119 N5 **Garrick** Saskatchewan Canada
99 O7 **Garrison** Iowa U.S.A.
94 D8 **Garrison** Kentucky U.S.A.
99 N3 **Garrison** Minnesota U.S.A.
101 N3 **Garrison** Montana U.S.A.
95 O5 **Garrison** New York U.S.A.
98 E2 **Garrison** North Dakota U.S.A.
109 N4 **Garrison** Texas U.S.A.
103 L3 **Garrison** Utah U.S.A.
98 E2 **Garrison Dam** North Dakota U.S.A.
16 C5 **Garrovillas** Spain
15 D4 **Garry** *L* Scotland
115 K4 **Garry L** Northwest Territories Canada
101 S4 **Garryowen** Montana U.S.A.
88 H3 **Garsen** Kenya
28 D5 **Gårslev** Denmark
27 G16 **Gärsnäs** Sweden
118 G2 **Garson L** Alberta Canada
32 M7 **Garssen** Germany
38 F7 **Garsstein** *mt* Austria
13 F6 **Garstang** England
13 F6 **Garston** England
144 B6 **Garston** New Zealand
18 F6 **Gartempe** *R* France
8 C3 **Garth** Wales
8 C2 **Garthmyl** Wales
Gartok *see* **Garyarsa**
33 O6 **Gartow** Germany
31 H2 **Gartz** Germany
70 M9 **Garut** Java
13 F2 **Garvald** Scotland
15 D3 **Garve** Scotland
144 B6 **Garvie Mts** New Zealand
31 N4 **Garwolin** Poland
100 J2 **Garwood** Idaho U.S.A.
109 L6 **Garwood** Texas U.S.A.
98 C9 **Gary** Colorado U.S.A.
99 T8 **Gary** Indiana U.S.A.
98 K2 **Gary** Minnesota U.S.A.
98 K5 **Gary** South Dakota U.S.A.
109 N3 **Gary** Texas U.S.A.
94 F9 **Gary** West Virginia U.S.A.
66 C5 **Garyarsa** China
60 F11 **Garyū zan** *mt* Japan
33 Q6 **Garz** Germany
58 C5 **Garzê** China
128 C3 **Garzón** Colombia
50 E5 **Gasan-Kuli** Turkmenistan
33 Q10 **Gaschwitz** Germany
45 J4 **Gasciana Terme** Italy
94 B6 **Gas City** Indiana U.S.A.
18 E9 **Gascogne** *prov* France
18 D8 **Gascogne, G. de** France/Spain
110 E3 **Gasconade** *R* Missouri U.S.A.
122 H5 **Gascons** Quebec Canada
98 C3 **Gascoyne** North Dakota U.S.A.
143 B7 **Gascoyne Junction** W Australia Australia
143 B6 **Gascoyne, Mt** W Australia Australia
143 A6 **Gascoyne, R** W Australia Australia
Gascuña, Golfo de *see* **Gascogne, G.de**
86 G2 **Gash** *R* Ethiopia
85 G7 **Gashaka** Nigeria
74 G1 **Gasherbrum** *mt* Kashmir
85 G6 **Gashua** Nigeria
Gashuun Nuur *L see* **Gaxun Nur**
26 H4 **Gaskacok** *mt* Norway
21 O3 **Gasny** France
126 E4 **Gaspar** Cuba
127 J5 **Gaspar Hernández** Dominican Rep
113 E11 **Gasparilla** *isld* Florida U.S.A.
69 H14 **Gaspar, Selat** *str* Indonesia
122 H5 **Gaspé** Quebec Canada
122 H5 **Gaspé, B. de** Quebec Canada
122 H5 **Gaspé, C** Quebec Canada
122 F5 **Gaspé Pen** Quebec Canada
122 H9 **Gaspereau** *L* Nova Scotia Canada
122 G7 **Gaspereau Forks** New Brunswick Canada
122 F5 **Gaspesie, Parc de la** Quebec Canada
100 B8 **Gasquet** California U.S.A.
61 O7 **Gassan** *mt* Japan
94 G8 **Gassaway** West Virginia U.S.A.
25 G3 **Gasselte** Netherlands
85 F2 **Gassi, El** Algeria
40 G7 **Gassino Tor** Italy
44 C1 **Gassino Torinese** Italy
85 G7 **Gassol** Nigeria
103 J5 **Gass Pk** Nevada U.S.A.
28 E3 **Gassum** Denmark
38 H7 **Gasteiner Tal** Austria
Gasteiz *see* **Vitoria**
100 B4 **Gaston** Oregon U.S.A.
112 F2 **Gastonia** North Carolina U.S.A.
94 J10 **Gaston, L** Virginia U.S.A.
47 O12 **Gastoúri** Greece
133 D6 **Gastre** Argentina
17 F8 **Gata, C.de** Spain
117 K6 **Gataga** *R* British Columbia Canada
48 G5 **Gătaia** Romania
16 C4 **Gata, Sa. de** *mts* Spain
52 D5 **Gatchina** Russian Federation
108 D7 **Gate** Oklahoma U.S.A.
94 E10 **Gate City** Virginia U.S.A.
12 D4 **Gatehouse of Fleet** Scotland
100 C5 **Gates** Oregon U.S.A.
13 G4 **Gateshead** England
116 L3 **Gates of the Arctic Nat Park and Preserve** Alaska U.S.A.
101 O3 **Gates of the Mts** *pass* Montana U.S.A.
112 L1 **Gatesville** North Carolina U.S.A.
109 K4 **Gatesville** Texas U.S.A.
106 B3 **Gateway** Colorado U.S.A.
100 K1 **Gateway** Montana U.S.A.
100 D5 **Gateway** Oregon U.S.A.
21 L7 **Gâtine** *reg* France
121 P5 **Gatineau** *R* Quebec Canada
121 P7 **Gatineau** Quebec Canada
21 J8 **Gâtine Hauteurs de** *hills* France
112 D2 **Gatlinburg** Tennessee U.S.A.
80 D1 **Ga'ton** Israel
Gatooma *see* **Kadoma**
33 S8 **Gatow** Germany
61 N7 **Gatsugi** Japan
20 H2 **Gatteville** France
41 H6 **Gattinara** Italy
141 K8 **Gatton** Queensland Australia
124 E9 **Gatun** Panama
125 O5 **Gatún L** Panama
9 F5 **Gatwick Airport** England
36 E4 **Gau-Algesheim** Germany
21 H8 **Gaubretière, la** France
16 D8 **Gaucin** Spain
16 D6 **Gaudalmellato** *R* Spain
77 H5 **Gaud-I-Zirreh** *salt desert* Afghanistan
123 K3 **Gaudreault, L** Quebec Canada
119 U1 **Gauer** *L* Manitoba Canada
Gauhati *see* **Guwahati**
26 E9 **Gauldalen** *R* Norway
94 F8 **Gauley Bridge** West Virginia U.S.A.
21 M5 **Gault, le** France
123 R6 **Gaultois** Newfoundland Canada

21 N5 **Gault-St.Denis, le** France
69 F13 **Gaung** Sumatra
36 E4 **Gau-Odernheim** Germany
66 D6 **Gauri Sankar** *mt* Nepal/China
27 D10 **Gausdal, Ö** Norway
27 D10 **Gausdal, V** Norway
27 C12 **Gausta** *mt* Norway
77 G7 **Gavāter** Iran
77 C6 **Gāvbandī** Iran
77 C6 **Gavbus Kūh-e** *mt* Iran
46 F10 **Gavdhopoúla** *isld* Greece
46 G10 **Gávdhos** *isld* Crete Greece
18 E9 **Gave de Pau** *R* France
130 H4 **Gavião, R** Brazil
106 C5 **Gavilan** New Mexico U.S.A.
102 D7 **Gaviota** California U.S.A.
77 E5 **Gāv Koshī** Iran
27 J11 **Gävle** Sweden
27 J11 **Gävlebukten** *B* Sweden
20 H4 **Gavray** France
20 G6 **Gavre, le** France
52 E6 **Gavrilov Yam** Russian Federation
52 F5 **Gavrino** Russian Federation
46 G7 **Gávrion** Greece
74 G8 **Gawilgarh** India
138 E5 **Gawler** South Australia Australia
138 D4 **Gawler Ranges** South Australia Australia
26 H8 **Gåxsjö** Sweden
58 D3 **Gaxun Nur** *L* China
99 S2 **Gay** Michigan U.S.A.
75 L6 **Gaya** India
85 E6 **Gaya** Niger
85 F6 **Gaya** Nigeria
17 H3 **Gaya** *R* Spain
65 H3 **Gaya He** *R* China
70 F2 **Gaya, Pulau** *isld* Sabah
9 E3 **Gaydon** England
107 M2 **Gaylord** Kansas U.S.A.
94 C1 **Gaylord** Michigan U.S.A.
99 M5 **Gaylord** Minnesota U.S.A.
100 A7 **Gaylord** Oregon U.S.A.
141 K7 **Gayndah** Queensland Australia
52 H4 **Gayny** Russian Federation
48 M2 **Gaysin** Ukraine
99 Q6 **Gays Mills** Wisconsin U.S.A.
52 E5 **Gayutino** Russian Federation
98 J7 **Gayville** South Dakota U.S.A.
48 M2 **Gayvoron** Ukraine
79 E7 **Gaza** Egypt
85 F6 **Gazaoua** Niger
80 A7 **Gaza Strip** Israel
100 C8 **Gazelle** California U.S.A.
21 O4 **Gazeran** France
57 D4 **Gazgan** Uzbekistan
78 F3 **Gaziantep** Turkey
78 D3 **Gazipaşa** Turkey
57 C4 **Gazli** Uzbekistan
45 J1 **Gazoldo degli Ippoliti** Italy
45 K1 **Gazzo Veronese** Italy
45 J1 **Gazzuolo** Italy
85 C7 **Gbanga** Liberia
85 F7 **Gboko** Nigeria
31 L1 **Gdańsk** Poland
52 C5 **Gdov** Russian Federation
31 L1 **Gdynia** Poland
80 B7 **Ge'a** Israel
100 B3 **Gearhart** Oregon U.S.A.
100 E7 **Gearhart Mt** Oregon U.S.A.
107 M6 **Geary** Oklahoma U.S.A.
71 B3 **Gebe** *isld* Indonesia
37 K1 **Gebesee** Germany
47 N11 **Gebze** Turkey
86 G3 **Gedaref** Sudan
141 F3 **Geddes** *R* Queensland Australia
98 H6 **Geddes** South Dakota U.S.A.
9 F3 **Geddington** England
36 G3 **Gedern** Germany
28 H7 **Gedesby** Denmark
70 L9 **Gede, Tg** *C* Java
28 C4 **Gedhus** Denmark
22 H4 **Gedinne** Belgium
47 K5 **Gediz** Turkey
47 J6 **Gediz** *R* Turkey
86 H4 **Gedlegubē** Ethiopia
Gedong *see* **Fangshan**
70 B4 **Gedong** Sarawak
28 H7 **Gedser** Denmark
28 C3 **Gedsted** Denmark
70 K8 **Gedungpakuan** Sumatra
142 E4 **Geegully Ck** W Australia Australia
22 H1 **Geel** Belgium
139 G7 **Geelong** Victoria Australia
143 A8 **Geelvink Chan** W Australia Australia
89 A7 **Geel Vloer** S Africa
110 D6 **Geers Ferry L** Arkansas U.S.A.
25 C5 **Geertruidenberg** Netherlands
32 J5 **Geestekanal** Germany
32 J5 **Geestenseth** Germany
33 M6 **Geesthacht** Germany
22 J2 **Geetbets** Belgium
139 H9 **Geeveston** Tasmania Australia
37 M3 **Gefell** Germany
80 C7 **Gefen** Israel
37 M3 **Gefrees** Germany
65 E2 **Gegenmiao** China
65 D5 **Gegu** China
65 G7 **Gehaku** *lighthouse* S Korea
36 G2 **Gehau** Germany
21 N7 **Gehée** France
32 L8 **Gehrden** Germany
67 F1 **Ge Hu** *L* China
85 G6 **Geidam** Nigeria
41 P3 **Geierspitze** *mt* Austria
120 B2 **Geikie I** Ontario Canada
141 G2 **Geikie Ra** Queensland Australia
25 F7 **Geilenkirchen** Germany
27 C11 **Geilo** Norway
33 R5 **Geilow** Germany
36 E5 **Geinsheim** Germany
26 B9 **Geiranger** Norway
37 N6 **Geiselhöring** Germany
37 J4 **Geiselwind** Germany
37 M6 **Geisenfeld** Germany
37 N7 **Geisenhausen** Germany
36 D3 **Geisenheim** Germany
41 J2 **Geisingen** Germany
36 F7 **Geislingen** Germany
36 H6 **Geislingen an der Steige** Germany
37 J1 **Geismar** Germany
36 D6 **Geispolsheim** France
88 D3 **Geita** Tanzania
37 O1 **Geithain** Germany
27 D12 **Geithus** Norway
26 G6 **Geittind** *mt* Norway
73 R5 **Gejiu** China
43 F11 **Gela** *R* Sicily
43 F11 **Gela** Sicily
86 J4 **Geladī** Ethiopia
88 F3 **Gelai** *mt* Tanzania
33 Q4 **Gelbensande** Germany
37 J4 **Gelchsheim** Germany
25 F3 **Gelderingen** Netherlands
25 F4 **Gelderland** Netherlands
25 D5 **Geldermalsen** Netherlands
25 F5 **Geldern** Germany
25 E6 **Geldrop** Netherlands
47 J5 **Gelembe** Turkey
37 O2 **Gelenau** Germany
121 M8 **Gelert** Ontario Canada
47 H4 **Gelibolu** Turkey
78 D1 **Gelicek** Turkey
79 H1 **Gelinbuğday** Turkey
22 J2 **Gelinden** Belgium
67 F4 **Geling** China
86 J4 **Gelinsoor** Somalia
71 L9 **Gelinting** Flores Indonesia
36 G3 **Gelnhausen** Germany
28 C6 **Gelså** *R* Denmark
Gelsdorf *see* **Grafschaft**
32 F9 **Gelsenkirchen** Germany
28 D6 **Gelsted** Denmark
28 D7 **Gelting** Germany
69 G14 **Gelumbang** Sumatra
118 E8 **Gem** Alberta Canada
107 K2 **Gem** Kansas U.S.A.
69 F11 **Gemas** Malaysia
22 H2 **Gembloux** Belgium
32 E9 **Gemen** Germany
86 C5 **Gemena** Zaire
19 P18 **Gémenos** France
78 F2 **Gemerek** Turkey
86 H3 **Gemerī Hāyk'** *L* Ethiopia
25 E5 **Gemert** Netherlands
47 K4 **Gemlik Körfezi** *B* Turkey
22 K2 **Gemmenich** Belgium
36 F5 **Gemmingen** Germany
42 E2 **Gemona del Friuli** Italy
18 E7 **Gémozac** France
84 J4 **Gemsa** Egypt
89 B5 **Gemsbok Nat. Park** Botswana
36 B2 **Gemünd** Germany
36 H3 **Gemünden** Bayern Germany
36 F2 **Gemünden** Hessen Germany
36 D4 **Gemünden** Rheinland-Pfalz Germany
70 E7 **Gemuru** Kalimantan
86 H4 **Genalē** *R* Ethiopia
22 G2 **Genappe** Belgium
27 F16 **Genarp** Sweden
45 N6 **Genazzano** Italy
78 H2 **Genç** Turkey
18 F6 **Gençay** France
25 F5 **Gendringen** Netherlands
107 N7 **Gene Autry** Oklahoma U.S.A.
86 D3 **Geneina** Sudan
25 F3 **Genemuiden** Netherlands
133 E5 **General Acha** Argentina
133 E5 **General Alvear** Argentina
131 C5 **General Alvear** Mendoza Argentina
130 C9 **General Aquvino** Paraguay
133 E4 **General Arenales** Argentina
130 C10 **General Artigas** Paraguay
146 E6 **General Belgrano II** *Argentina Base* Antarctica
146 D3 **General Bernardo O'Higgins** *Chile Base* Graham Land Antarctica
130 D4 **General Caneiro** Brazil
133 E3 **General Capdevila** Argentina
102 F5 **General Grant Grove Sctn** California U.S.A.
133 F5 **General Guido** Argentina
17 G5 **Generalisimo, Emb. de** Spain
133 F3 **General José de San Martín** Argentina
133 E5 **General La Madrid** Argentina
133 F5 **General Lavalle** Argentina
71 G6 **General Luna** Philippines
71 G5 **General MacArthur** Philippines
133 F5 **General Madariaga** Argentina
128 E8 **General Martin M. de Güemes** Argentina
130 B10 **General Paz** Argentina
133 C6 **General Paz, L** Argentina
146 C5 **General San Martín** *Argentina Base* Antarctica
71 G7 **General Santos** Philippines
47 J1 **General Toshevo** Bulgaria
109 H9 **General Treviño** Mexico
133 E5 **General Viamonte** Argentina
100 J3 **Genesee** Idaho U.S.A.
94 D3 **Genesee** Michigan U.S.A.
94 K4 **Genesee** *R* New York U.S.A.
99 Q8 **Geneseo** Illinois U.S.A.
107 M3 **Geneseo** Kansas U.S.A.
94 K4 **Geneseo** New York U.S.A.
20 G7 **Geneston** France
20 H4 **Genêts** France
Geneva *see* **Genève**
111 L10 **Geneva** Alabama U.S.A.
111 M9 **Geneva** Georgia U.S.A.
94 C6 **Geneva** Indiana U.S.A.
98 J9 **Geneva** Nebraska U.S.A.
94 G5 **Geneva** Ohio U.S.A.
109 O4 **Geneva** Texas U.S.A.
Geneva, L *see* **Léman, Lac**
99 S7 **Geneva, L** Wisconsin U.S.A.
120 J6 **Geneva Lake Mine** Ontario Canada
40 D5 **Genève** Switzerland
36 E7 **Gengenbach** Germany
68 D1 **Gengma** China
Genhe *see* **Ergun Zuoqi**
59 H1 **Gen He** *R* China
120 J3 **Genier** Ontario Canada
16 E7 **Genil** *R* Spain
21 N7 **Génillé** France
58 E4 **Genjiawan** China
22 K2 **Genk** Belgium
60 D12 **Genkai-nada** *sea* Japan
40 B3 **Genlis** France
25 E5 **Gennep** Netherlands
28 C6 **Genner** Denmark
21 K7 **Gennes** Maine-et-Loire France
21 J6 **Gennes** Mayenne France
21 H6 **Gennes-sur-Seiche** France
21 L6 **Genneteil** France
21 P4 **Gennevilliers** France
Genoa *see* **Genova**
139 J6 **Genoa** Victoria Australia
106 G2 **Genoa** Colorado U.S.A.
113 E7 **Genoa** Florida U.S.A.
99 S7 **Genoa** Illinois U.S.A.
98 J8 **Genoa** Nebraska U.S.A.
102 E2 **Genoa** Nevada U.S.A.
94 D5 **Genoa** Ohio U.S.A.
99 P6 **Genoa** Wisconsin U.S.A.
99 S7 **Genoa City** Wisconsin U.S.A.
101 O1 **Genou** Montana U.S.A.
21 O7 **Genouilly** Cher France
44 E3 **Genova** Italy
128 B7 **Genovesa** *isld* Galapagos Is
51 P1 **Genriyetty, Ostrov** *isld* Russian Federation
22 F1 **Gent** Belgium
70 P9 **Genteng** Indonesia
70 L9 **Genteng** Java
33 Q8 **Genthin** Germany
111 K12 **Gentilly** New Orleans, Louisiana U.S.A.
69 H11 **Genting** *isld* Indonesia
118 B1 **Gent Lon** Manitoba Canada
29 K5 **Gentofte** Denmark
110 B5 **Gentry** Arkansas U.S.A.
99 M9 **Gentry** Missouri U.S.A.
45 N6 **Genzano di Roma** Italy
48 H5 **Geoagiu** Romania
143 B10 **Geographe B** W Australia Australia
143 A6 **Geographe Chan** W Australia Australia
107 M2 **Geographic Center of US** Kansas U.S.A.
22 H3 **Geopinnes** Belgium
138 D3 **George** *R* South Australia Australia
115 N6 **George** *R* Quebec Canada
83 M14 **George** *C* Kerguelen Indian Oc
89 C9 **George** S Africa
116 J5 **George** *R* Alaska U.S.A.
99 L6 **George** Iowa U.S.A.
123 L8 **George B** Nova Scotia Canada
140 B6 **George Gills Ra** N Terr Australia
139 J6 **George, L** New South Wales Australia
138 F6 **George, L** South Australia Australia
142 E5 **George, L** W Australia Australia
99 W3 **George, L** Ontario Canada
88 C1 **George, L** Uganda
116 N6 **George, L** Alaska U.S.A.
113 F8 **George, L** Florida U.S.A.
37 L5 **Georgensgmünd** Germany
37 K2 **Georgenthal** Germany
90 C4 **Georges Bank** Atlantic Oc
144 A6 **George Sd** New Zealand
90 A11 **Georgetown** Ascension I
141 G4 **Georgetown** Queensland Australia
138 E5 **Georgetown** South Australia Australia
139 H8 **George Town** Tasmania Australia
122 K7 **Georgetown** Prince Edward I Canada
129 G2 **Georgetown** Guyana
69 E10 **Georgetown** Malaysia
144 C6 **Georgetown** New Zealand
127 O8 **Georgetown** St Vincent
85 B6 **Georgetown** The Gambia
110 E6 **Georgetown** Arkansas U.S.A.
102 D3 **Georgetown** California U.S.A.
95 M8 **Georgetown** Delaware U.S.A.
113 F8 **Georgetown** Florida U.S.A.
111 L10 **Georgetown** Georgia U.S.A.
101 O7 **Georgetown** Idaho U.S.A.
99 T10 **Georgetown** Illinois U.S.A.
94 C8 **Georgetown** Kentucky U.S.A.
111 F10 **Georgetown** Mississippi U.S.A.
94 D8 **Georgetown** Ohio U.S.A.
112 H4 **Georgetown** South Carolina U.S.A.
109 K5 **Georgetown** Texas U.S.A.
121 S7 **Georgeville** Quebec Canada
146 C6 **George VI Sound** Antarctica
146 D13 **George V Land** Antarctica
109 J7 **George West** Texas U.S.A.
146 H7 **Georg Forster** *Germany Base* Antarctica
53 F12 **Georgia** *rep* E Europe
112 C5 **Georgia** *state* U.S.A.
111 K10 **Georgiana** Alabama U.S.A.
120 J7 **Georgian B** Ontario Canada
117 L11 **Georgia, St. of** British Columbia Canada
140 E5 **Georgina** *R* N Terr Australia
140 E5 **Georgina** *R* N Terr/Queensland Australia
140 E5 **Georgina** *R* Queensland Australia
140 E4 **Georgina Cr** N Terr Australia
47 J2 **Georgi Traykov** Bulgaria
Georgiu-Dezh *see* **Liski**
53 F11 **Georgiyevsk** Russian Federation
32 F7 **Georgsdorf** Germany
32 F6 **Georgsheil** Germany
32 H8 **Georgsmarienhütte** Germany
146 G6 **Georg von Neumayer** *Germany Base* Antarctica
41 N4 **Gepatschhaus** Austria
21 J4 **Ger** France
28 E2 **Gerå** *R* Denmark
37 K2 **Gera** *R* Germany
37 N2 **Gera** Germany
22 F2 **Geraardsbergen** Belgium
36 H5 **Gerabronn** Germany
119 Q8 **Gerald** Saskatchewan Canada
110 E3 **Gerald** Missouri U.S.A.
143 A8 **Geraldine** W Australia Australia
144 C6 **Geraldine** New Zealand
101 P2 **Geraldine** Montana U.S.A.
51 S2 **Geral'd, Ostrov** *islds* Russian Federation
143 A8 **Geraldton** W Australia Australia
120 C3 **Geraldton** Ontario Canada
120 D3 **Geraldton** Ontario Canada
130 E10 **Geral, Serra** *mts* Brazil
80 B8 **Gerar** *R* Israel
19 K4 **Gérardmer** France
143 E7 **Gerard, Mt** W Australia Australia
80 G4 **Gerasa** Jordan
55 F2 **Gerasimovka** Russian Federation
100 C9 **Gerber** California U.S.A.
100 D7 **Gerber Res** Oregon U.S.A.
33 P9 **Gerbstedt** Germany
36 H4 **Gerchsheim** Germany
78 H3 **Gercuş** Turkey
116 L6 **Gerdine, Mt** Alaska U.S.A.
78 D1 **Gerede** Turkey
77 J4 **Gereshk** Afghanistan
17 F7 **Gérgal** Spain
40 A4 **Gergy** France
37 K3 **Gerhardtsgereuth** Germany
69 E10 **Gerik** Malaysia
98 C8 **Gering** Nebraska U.S.A.
37 O1 **Geringswalde** Germany
100 F9 **Gerlach** Nevada U.S.A.
48 F1 **Gerlachovsky** *mt* Czechoslovakia
36 H4 **Gerlachsheim** Germany
28 H5 **Gerlev** Denmark
28 G6 **Gerlev** Denmark
36 G6 **Gerlingen** Germany
38 E7 **Gerlostal** *R* Austria
133 E4 **Germania** Argentina
117 L8 **Germansen Landing** British Columbia Canada
110 G3 **Germantown** Illinois U.S.A.
95 K7 **Germantown** Maryland U.S.A.
95 O4 **Germantown** New York U.S.A.
94 C7 **Germantown** Ohio U.S.A.
110 G6 **Germantown** Tennessee U.S.A.
30 D5 **Germany** *rep* Europe
47 J7 **Germencik** Turkey
37 L7 **Germering** Germany
36 E5 **Germersheim** Germany
89 F6 **Germiston** S Africa
28 C5 **Gerndrup** Denmark
36 E6 **Gernsbach** Germany
36 F4 **Gernsheim** Germany
61 L10 **Gero** Japan
70 P10 **Gerokgak** Bali Indonesia
36 B3 **Gerolstein** Germany
37 J4 **Gerolzhofen** Germany
100 G1 **Gerome** Washington U.S.A.
17 J2 **Gerona** *prov* Spain
17 J3 **Gerona** Spain
17 J2 **Gerona** Spain
103 O8 **Geronimo** Arizona U.S.A.
107 M7 **Geronimo** Oklahoma U.S.A.
139 K5 **Gerringong** New South Wales Australia
18 F9 **Gers** *dept* France
18 F9 **Gers** *R* France
36 H3 **Gersfeld** Germany
36 F4 **Gersprenz** *R* Germany
37 J6 **Gerstetten Herbrechtingen** Germany
37 K7 **Gersthofen** Germany
37 J2 **Gerstingen** Germany
116 P5 **Gerstle** *R* Alaska U.S.A.
33 T6 **Gerswalde** Germany
140 B3 **Gertrude, Mt** N Terr Australia
48 K2 **Gertsa** Ukraine
80 C4 **Gerulim** Israel
19 O15 **Gervanne** *R* France
66 C5 **Gêrzê** China
78 E1 **Gerze** Turkey
37 N7 **Gerzen** Germany
32 E9 **Gescher** Germany
32 J9 **Geseke** Germany
80 D1 **Gesher HaZiv** Israel
22 H4 **Gespunsart** France
37 K7 **Gessertshausen** Germany
44 B3 **Gesso** *R* Italy
21 H7 **Gesté** France
28 C5 **Gesten** Denmark
86 H4 **Gestro, Wabē** *R* Ethiopia
26 H8 **Gesunden** *L* Sweden
29 H11 **Geta** Finland
16 E4 **Getafe** Spain
100 H8 **Getchell Mine** Nevada U.S.A.
22 J2 **Gete** *R* Belgium
123 M3 **Gethsémani** Quebec Canada
28 A3 **Gettrup** Denmark
95 K7 **Gettysburg** Pennsylvania U.S.A.
98 G5 **Gettysburg** South Dakota U.S.A.
67 B4 **Getu He** *R* China
130 D10 **Getúlio Vargas** Brazil
146 B8 **Getz Ice Shelf** Antarctica
107 N4 **Geuda Springs** Kansas U.S.A.
69 C11 **Geumapang** *R* Sumatra
69 C10 **Geumpang** Sumatra
69 C10 **Geureudong, Gunung** *mt* Sumatra
139 J4 **Geurie** New South Wales Australia
80 C3 **Geva' Karmel** Israel
32 F10 **Gevelsberg** Germany
80 B7 **Gever'am** Israel
20 G5 **Geveze** France
33 S5 **Gevezin** Germany
46 E3 **Gevgelija** Macedonia Yugoslavia
19 K6 **Gex** France
79 C2 **Geydik Dağ** *mt* Turkey
37 O2 **Geyer** Germany
36 G4 **Geyersberg** *mt* Germany
47 H5 **Geyikli** Turkey
101 P2 **Geyser** Montana U.S.A.
81 B7 **Geyser, Banc du** Madagascar
28 S9 **Geysir** Iceland
47 L4 **Geyve** Turkey
84 D3 **Ghadāmis** Libya
80 G2 **Ghadir al Bustan** Syria
73 N3 **Ghaghara** *R* India
85 D7 **Ghana** *rep* W Africa
84 E5 **Ghanīmah, Jabal Bin** *mts* Libya
89 B3 **Ghanzi** Botswana
89 C4 **Ghanzi** *dist* Botswana
80 E7 **Ghar** *R* Jordan
78 K6 **Gharab** Iraq
85 E2 **Ghardaia** Algeria
43 B12 **Ghardimaou** Tunisia
43 C11 **Ghar El Melh** Tunisia
84 J4 **Gharib, Gebel** Egypt
84 E3 **Gharyan** Libya
84 E5 **Ghāt** Libya
75 M7 **Ghatsila** India
86 E4 **Ghazāl, Al** *prov* Sudan
17 F9 **Ghazaouet** Algeria
74 G4 **Ghaziabad** India
77 L3 **Ghaznī** Afghanistan
77 K3 **Ghazoor** Afghanistan
99 O2 **Gheen** Minnesota U.S.A.
Ghent *see* **Gent**
94 B8 **Ghent** Kentucky U.S.A.
99 L5 **Ghent** Minnesota U.S.A.
Gheorghe Gheorghiu-Dei *see* **Oneşti**
48 K4 **Gheorgheni** Romania
48 H3 **Gherla** Romania
43 B8 **Ghilarza** Sardinia
48 K4 **Ghimeş Făget** Romania
133 C7 **Ghio, L** Argentina
22 F2 **Ghislenghien** Belgium
77 J3 **Ghizao** Afghanistan
118 L1 **Ghost** *R* Ontario Canada
117 Q4 **Ghost L** Northwest Territories Canada
117 P9 **Ghost Mt** British Columbia Canada
77 J2 **Ghowr** *prov* Afghanistan
86 E3 **Ghubaysh** Sudan
Ghudamis *see* **Ghadāmis**
79 H4 **Ghunthur** Syria
77 G2 **Ghūriān** Afghanistan
22 D1 **Ghyvelde** France
68 H7 **Gia Dinh** Vietnam
68 H6 **Gia Nghia** Vietnam
42 D6 **Giannutri, I.di** Italy
89 F7 **Giants Castle** *mt* S Africa
14 E1 **Giant's Causeway** N Ireland
83 K9 **Giants Tank** *L* Sri Lanka
70 P10 **Gianyar** Indonesia
69 G8 **Gia Rai** Vietnam
43 G11 **Giarre** Sicily
18 G7 **Giat** France
44 B1 **Giaveno** Italy
126 F4 **Gibara** Cuba
98 H9 **Gibbon** Nebraska U.S.A.
100 G4 **Gibbon** Oregon U.S.A.
101 M4 **Gibbons Pass** Montana U.S.A.
101 M4 **Gibbonsville** Idaho U.S.A.
142 F3 **Gibb River** W Australia Australia
99 S3 **Gibbs City** Michigan U.S.A.
146 D3 **Gibbs I** S Shetland Is Antarctica
143 C10 **Gibbs, Mt** W Australia Australia
87 C11 **Gibeon** Namibia
26 K2 **Gibostad** Norway
16 C7 **Gibraleón** Spain
16 D8 **Gibraltar** *colony* S W Europe
127 J10 **Gibraltar** Venezuela
16 D9 **Gibraltar, Str of** Spain/Africa
111 C9 **Gibsland** Louisiana U.S.A.
100 C8 **Gibson** California U.S.A.
112 E4 **Gibson** Georgia U.S.A.
101 Q3 **Gibson** Montana U.S.A.
94 D5 **Gibsonburg** Ohio U.S.A.
99 S9 **Gibson City** Illinois U.S.A.
143 D6 **Gibson Des** W Australia Australia
117 M11 **Gibsons** British Columbia Canada
143 D10 **Gibson Soak** W Australia Australia
113 E10 **Gibsonton** Florida U.S.A.
112 H1 **Gibsonville** North Carolina U.S.A.
58 B2 **Gichgeniyn Nuruu** *mt* Mongolia
52 H5 **Gidayevo** Russian Federation
79 D8 **Giddi, G el** Egypt
109 L5 **Giddings** Texas U.S.A.
26 K8 **Gideå** Sweden
26 K8 **Gideå** *R* Sweden
110 G5 **Gideon** Missouri U.S.A.
141 F6 **Gideon, Mt** Queensland Australia
138 F3 **Gidgealpa Gas Field** South Australia Australia
143 F8 **Gidgi, L** W Australia Australia
31 L5 **Gidle** Poland
86 G4 **Gīdolē** Ethiopia
36 H4 **Giebelstadt** Germany
32 M9 **Gieboldehausen** Germany
18 G5 **Gien** France
37 J6 **Giengen** Germany
19 Q18 **Giens** France
19 N13 **Gier** *R* France
33 P7 **Giesenslage** Germany
36 F2 **Giessen** Germany
25 G2 **Gieten** Netherlands
25 F3 **Giethoorn** Netherlands
84 J4 **Gifatin I** Egypt
13 F2 **Gifford** Scotland
113 G10 **Gifford** Florida U.S.A.
99 N7 **Gifford** Iowa U.S.A.
100 G1 **Gifford** Washington U.S.A.
33 N8 **Gifhorn** Germany
61 K10 **Gifu** Japan
124 D5 **Giganta, Sa de la** Mexico
124 E9 **Gigante** Panama
124 G3 **Gigantes, Llanos de los** Mexico
15 C5 **Gigha** *isld* Scotland
42 D6 **Giglio, I. del** Italy
18 H9 **Gignac** France
19 P17 **Gignac** France
19 O18 **Gignac** France
40 F6 **Gignod** Italy
16 D1 **Gijón** Spain
103 P9 **Gila** *R* Arizona U.S.A.
106 B9 **Gila** New Mexico U.S.A.
103 M9 **Gila Bend** Arizona U.S.A.
103 L8 **Gila Bend Mts** Arizona U.S.A.
106 B8 **Gila Cliff Dwellings Nat.Mon** New Mexico U.S.A.
103 K9 **Gila Mts** Arizona U.S.A.
78 K4 **Gilān-e Gharb** Iran
121 R5 **Gilardo Dam** Quebec Canada
71 B2 **Gila, Tanjong** *C* Indonesia
48 H4 **Gilău** Romania
141 F3 **Gilbert** *R* Queensland Australia
103 N8 **Gilbert** Arizona U.S.A.
99 O2 **Gilbert** Minnesota U.S.A.
102 G3 **Gilbert** Nevada U.S.A.
94 F9 **Gilbert** West Virginia U.S.A.
137 P2 **Gilbert Is** Pacific Oc
117 L10 **Gilbert, Mt** British Columbia Canada
116 O6 **Gilbert, Mt** Alaska U.S.A.
111 H10 **Gilbertown** Alabama U.S.A.
101 P9 **Gilbert Pk** Utah U.S.A.
119 R7 **Gilbert Plains** Manitoba Canada
141 G4 **Gilbert River** Queensland Australia
28 J4 **Gilbjerghoved** *C* Denmark
129 J5 **Gilbués** Brazil
98 J1 **Gilby** North Dakota U.S.A.
98 B9 **Gilcrest** Colorado U.S.A.
13 G6 **Gildersome** England
26 G4 **Gildeskal** Norway
101 P1 **Gildford** Montana U.S.A.
88 G10 **Gilé** Mozambique
95 R2 **Gilead** Maine U.S.A.
98 J9 **Gilead** Nebraska U.S.A.
143 G6 **Giles** W Australia Australia
143 G7 **Giles** W Australia Australia
108 G1 **Giles** Texas U.S.A.
143 C8 **Giles, L** W Australia Australia
140 B5 **Giles Ra** N Terr Australia
84 H5 **Gilf Kebir Plateau** Egypt
139 K3 **Gilgai** New South Wales Australia
139 J4 **Gilgandra** New South Wales Australia
80 E6 **Gilgat** Jordan
139 J3 **Gil Gil** *R* New South Wales Australia
88 F2 **Gilgil** Kenya
74 F1 **Gilgit** Kashmir
139 H4 **Gilgunnia** New South Wales Australia
117 J9 **Gil I** British Columbia Canada
70 P10 **Gilimanuk** Bali Indonesia
79 D2 **Gilındire** Turkey
46 D1 **Giljeva Planina** *mt* Serbia Yugoslavia
98 B9 **Gill** Colorado U.S.A.
115 K6 **Gillam** Manitoba Canada
28 J4 **Gilleleje** Denmark
143 E7 **Gillen, L** W Australia Australia
140 C6 **Gillen, Mt** N Terr Australia
138 D4 **Gilles, L** South Australia Australia
103 M8 **Gillespie** Arizona U.S.A.
110 G2 **Gillespie** Illinois U.S.A.
144 B5 **Gillespies Pt** New Zealand
111 E7 **Gillett** Arkansas U.S.A.
95 L5 **Gillett** Pennsylvania U.S.A.
109 K6 **Gillett** Texas U.S.A.
99 S5 **Gillett** Wisconsin U.S.A.
98 A5 **Gillette** Wyoming U.S.A.
109 N1 **Gillham** Arkansas U.S.A.
26 G9 **Gillhov** Sweden
110 C2 **Gilliam** Missouri U.S.A.
141 F5 **Gilliat** *R* Queensland Australia
141 F5 **Gilliat** Queensland Australia
13 G5 **Gilling** England
8 D5 **Gillingham** England
9 G5 **Gillingham** England
109 O5 **Gillis** Louisiana U.S.A.
14 C2 **Gill, L** Ireland
146 J11 **Gillock I** *isld* Antarctica
99 T4 **Gills Rock** Wisconsin U.S.A.
22 G3 **Gilly** Belgium
99 S9 **Gilman** Illinois U.S.A.
99 O8 **Gilman** Iowa U.S.A.
101 N2 **Gilman** Montana U.S.A.
99 Q4 **Gilman** Wisconsin U.S.A.
110 C1 **Gilman City** Missouri U.S.A.
109 N3 **Gilmer** Texas U.S.A.
101 M5 **Gilmore** Idaho U.S.A.
99 M7 **Gilmore City** Iowa U.S.A.
121 N8 **Gilmour** Ontario Canada
86 F4 **Gīlo** *R* Ethiopia
48 H6 **Gilort** *R* Romania
117 N9 **Gilpin** British Columbia Canada
118 L8 **Gilroy** Saskatchewan Canada
102 C4 **Gilroy** California U.S.A.
28 R9 **Gilsfjördhur** *inlet* Iceland
13 F3 **Gilsland** England
98 H9 **Giltner** Nebraska U.S.A.
8 C4 **Gilwern** Wales
51 M3 **Gilyuy** *R* Russian Federation
86 D3 **Gimbala** *mt* Sudan
127 O8 **Gimie** *mt* St Lucia
101 L6 **Gimlet** Idaho U.S.A.
119 V8 **Gimli** Manitoba Canada
27 K11 **Gimo** Sweden
52 D3 **Gimoly** Russian Federation
18 F9 **Gimone** *R* France
18 F9 **Gimont** France
26 G3 **Gimsöy** Norway
80 C6 **Gimzo** Israel
19 P17 **Ginasservis** France
141 J6 **Gindie** Queensland Australia
76 D4 **Gingee** India
36 H6 **Gingen** Germany
127 J2 **Ginger Hill** Jamaica
141 K6 **Gin Gin** Queensland Australia
143 B9 **Gingin** W Australia Australia
71 G6 **Gingoog B** Philippines
86 H4 **Gīnīr** Ethiopia
80 E3 **Ginnegar** Israel
28 F4 **Ginnerup** Denmark
80 F2 **Ginnosar** Israel
43 H8 **Ginosa** Italy
61 P13 **Ginowan** Okinawa
16 B2 **Ginzo de Limia** Spain
45 K3 **Giogo di Casaglia** Italy
45 K3 **Giogo di Scarperia** Italy
45 P6 **Gioia dei Marsi** Italy
43 G10 **Gioia,G.di** Italy
45 Q7 **Gioia Sannitica** Italy
46 E6 **Gióna** *mt* Greece
41 J5 **Giornico** Switzerland
43 H9 **Giovanni in Fiore, S** Italy
45 K4 **Giovi** *mt* Italy
139 H7 **Gippsland** Victoria Australia
139 J7 **Gippsland Basin Oil & Gas Fields** Victoria Australia
142 A6 **Giralia** W Australia Australia
31 N6 **Giraltovce** Czechoslovakia
40 D1 **Girancourt** France
77 F5 **Giran Rig** *mt* Iran
99 R10 **Girard** Illinois U.S.A.
107 Q4 **Girard** Kansas U.S.A.
94 G5 **Girard** Ohio U.S.A.
94 G4 **Girard** Pennsylvania U.S.A.
108 G2 **Girard** Texas U.S.A.
128 D3 **Girardot** Colombia
15 F3 **Girdle Ness** Scotland
78 G1 **Giresun** Turkey
84 J4 **Girga** Egypt
74 D8 **Gir Hills** India
86 C5 **Giri** *R* Zaire
75 M6 **Giridih** India
139 H4 **Girilambone** New South Wales Australia
83 K10 **Giriulla** Sri Lanka
19 K5 **Giromagny** France
Girona *see* **Gerona**
18 E7 **Gironde** *R* France
18 E8 **Gironde** *dept* France
17 J2 **Gironella** Spain
18 G9 **Girou** *R* France
119 V9 **Giroux** Manitoba Canada
130 C11 **Giruá** Brazil
15 D5 **Girvan** *R* Scotland
15 D5 **Girvan** Scotland
119 M7 **Girvin** Saskatchewan Canada
108 E4 **Girvin** Texas U.S.A.
116 H4 **Gisasa** *R* Alaska U.S.A.
145 G3 **Gisborne** New Zealand
13 F6 **Gisburn** England
123 S6 **Gisburn L** Newfoundland Canada
117 M8 **Giscome** British Columbia Canada
103 N7 **Gisela** Arizona U.S.A.
88 B2 **Gisenye** Rwanda
26 A9 **Giske** *isld* Norway
28 F6 **Gislev** Denmark
28 H5 **Gislinge** Denmark
21 O3 **Gisors** France
37 K1 **Gispersleben** Germany
57 E5 **Gissar** Tajikistan
57 E5 **Gissarskiy Khrebet** *mts* Tajikistan/Uzbekistan
22 D1 **Gistel** Belgium
88 B3 **Gitega** Burundi
32 M9 **Gittelde** Germany
Giuba *R* *see* **Jubba** *R*
41 N6 **Giudicarie Val** Italy
45 Q8 **Giugliano in Campo** Italy
45 O6 **Giuliano di Roma** Italy
42 F6 **Giulianova** Italy
48 J3 **Giumalău** *mt* Romania
48 L6 **Giurgeni** Romania
48 K4 **Giurgeului, Muntii** *mts* Romania
47 H1 **Giurgiu** Romania
48 K6 **Giurgiu** *reg* Romania
80 C3 **Giv'at 'Ada** Israel
80 C5 **Giv'atayim** Israel
28 C5 **Give** Denmark
22 D3 **Givenchy-en-Gohelle** France
22 H3 **Givet** Belgium
19 N13 **Givors** France
22 G3 **Givry** Belgium
19 J6 **Givry** France
40 A4 **Givry** France
28 C5 **Givskud** Denmark
89 F4 **Giyani** S Africa
79 B8 **Gîza, El** Egypt
21 L7 **Gizeux** France
57 C4 **Gizhduvan** Uzbekistan
51 Q2 **Gizhiga** Russian Federation
22 F4 **Gizy** France
31 N1 **Gizycko** Poland
27 C10 **Gjende** *L* Norway
27 C10 **Gjendesheim** Norway
28 E3 **Gjerlev** Denmark
28 D4 **Gjern** Denmark
28 F3 **Gjerrild** Denmark
27 C13 **Gjerstad** Norway
26 F7 **Gjersvik** Norway
26 D9 **Gjevil-vatn** *L* Norway
46 D4 **Gjirokastër** Albania
115 K4 **Gjoa Haven** Northwest Territories Canada
28 D2 **Gjøl** Denmark
28 C3 **Gjørup** Denmark
27 C13 **Gjovdal** Norway
27 E11 **Gjövik** Norway
46 C4 **Gjuhëzës, Kepi i** *C* Albania
78 E1 **Gķirmak** *R* Turkey
22 H2 **Glabbeek Zuurbemde** Belgium
123 N7 **Glace Bay** Nova Scotia Canada
20 G2 **Glacerie, la** France
117 P10 **Glacier** British Columbia Canada
117 E6 **Glacier B** Alaska U.S.A.
117 E6 **Glacier Bay Nat. Park** Alaska U.S.A.
117 E6 **Glacier Bay Nat Park and Preserve** Alaska U.S.A.
116 O6 **Glacier I** Alaska U.S.A.
116 Q4 **Glacier Mt** Alaska U.S.A.
117 O10 **Glacier Nat. Park** British Columbia Canada
101 M1 **Glacier Nat. Park** Montana U.S.A.
100 D1 **Glacier Peak** Washington U.S.A.
115 M2 **Glacier Str** Northwest Territories Canada
36 B2 **Gladbach** Germany
32 E9 **Gladbeck** Germany
99 O7 **Gladbrook** Iowa U.S.A.
107 L2 **Glade** Kansas U.S.A.
36 F2 **Gladenbach** Germany
106 B3 **Glade Park** Colorado U.S.A.
94 F10 **Glade Spring** Virginia U.S.A.
109 N3 **Gladewater** Texas U.S.A.
119 N9 **Gladmar** Saskatchewan Canada
26 E6 **Gladstad** Norway
141 K6 **Gladstone** Queensland Australia
138 E5 **Gladstone** South Australia Australia
139 J8 **Gladstone** Tasmania Australia
119 T8 **Gladstone** Manitoba Canada
145 E4 **Gladstone** New Zealand
99 T4 **Gladstone** Michigan U.S.A.
110 B2 **Gladstone** Missouri U.S.A.
98 D3 **Gladstone** North Dakota U.S.A.
94 C3 **Gladwin** Michigan U.S.A.
94 H8 **Glady** West Virginia U.S.A.
94 H9 **Gladys** Virginia U.S.A.
117 G6 **Gladys L** British Columbia Canada
28 G6 **Glænø** *isld* Denmark
27 F12 **Glafsfj** *L* Sweden
118 K7 **Glamis** Saskatchewan Canada
15 F4 **Glamis** Scotland
103 J8 **Glamis** California U.S.A.
42 H4 **Glamoc** Bosnia-Herzegovina
Glamorgan *co see* **W., Mid & S.Glam.** *counties*
28 E6 **Glamsbjerg** Denmark
38 K8 **Glan** *R* Austria
36 D4 **Glan** *R* Germany
71 G8 **Glan** Mindanao Philippines
27 H13 **Glan** *L* Sweden
14 B4 **Glanaruddery Mts** Ireland
19 P15 **Glandage** France
19 Q14 **Glandon, Col du** *pass* France
32 G8 **Glandorf** Germany
32 G8 **Glane** *R* Germany
38 K8 **Glanegg** Austria
41 J4 **Glärnisch** *mt* Switzerland
41 K3 **Glarus** Switzerland
107 N2 **Glasco** Kansas U.S.A.
95 O4 **Glasco** New York U.S.A.
99 R9 **Glasford** Illinois U.S.A.
127 H1 **Glasgow** Jamaica
12 D2 **Glasgow** Scotland
94 B10 **Glasgow** Kentucky U.S.A.
110 D2 **Glasgow** Missouri U.S.A.
101 T1 **Glasgow** Montana U.S.A.
94 H9 **Glasgow** Virginia U.S.A.
38 M8 **Glashutten** Austria
133 D6 **Glasier** Argentina
118 J5 **Glaslyn** Saskatchewan Canada
15 E4 **Glas Maol** *mt* Scotland
119 M9 **Glasnevin** Saskatchewan Canada
95 M7 **Glassboro** New Jersey U.S.A.
108 D5 **Glass Mts** Texas U.S.A.
8 D5 **Glastonbury** England
41 J3 **Glatt** *R* Switzerland
37 N2 **Glauchau** Germany
47 H1 **Glavinitsa** Bulgaria
108 D7 **Glazier** Texas U.S.A.
52 H5 **Glazov** Russian Federation
31 K2 **Głda** *R* Poland
110 H5 **Gleason** Tennessee U.S.A.
99 R4 **Gleason** Wisconsin U.S.A.
94 K5 **Gleasonton** Pennsylvania U.S.A.
103 P10 **Gleeson** Arizona U.S.A.
37 K3 **Gleichberg** *mt* Germany
118 D8 **Gleichen** Alberta Canada
33 P10 **Gleina** Germany
38 L7 **Glein Alpe** *mts* Austria
38 N7 **Gleisdorf** Austria
28 B5 **Glejbjerg** Denmark
98 C7 **Glen** Nebraska U.S.A.
95 Q2 **Glen** New Hampshire U.S.A.
100 A6 **Glenada** Oregon U.S.A.
15 D3 **Glen Affric** Scotland
145 E2 **Glen Afton** New Zealand
121 P7 **Glen Almond** Quebec Canada
112 F2 **Glen Alpine** North Carolina U.S.A.
20 C6 **Glénans, Iles de** France
15 D5 **Glen App** Scotland
144 B6 **Glenaray** New Zealand
14 F2 **Glenarm** N Ireland
12 D1 **Glen Artney** Scotland
119 O8 **Glenavon** Saskatchewan Canada
144 C6 **Glenavy** New Zealand
143 D7 **Glenayle** W Australia Australia
118 K9 **Glenbain** Saskatchewan Canada
12 C2 **Glenbarr** Scotland
139 K4 **Glenbawn Reservoir** New South Wales Australia
119 S9 **Glenboro** Manitoba Canada
145 E2 **Glenbrook** New Zealand
143 B7 **Glenburgh** W Australia Australia
98 E1 **Glenburn** North Dakota U.S.A.
138 F6 **Glenburnie** South Australia Australia
123 P4 **Glenburnie** Newfoundland Canada
95 L7 **Glen Burnie** Maryland U.S.A.
118 K5 **Glenbush** Saskatchewan Canada
15 D3 **Glen Cannich** Scotland
103 N5 **Glen Canyon** Arizona U.S.A.
103 N4 **Glen Canyon Nat. Recreation Area** Utah U.S.A.
15 C3 **Glen Carron** *R* Scotland
13 E1 **Glencarse** Scotland
15 E4 **Glen Clova** Scotland
138 F6 **Glencoe** South Australia Australia
120 J10 **Glencoe** Ontario Canada
89 G7 **Glencoe** S Africa
111 L8 **Glencoe** Alabama U.S.A.
99 M5 **Glencoe** Minnesota U.S.A.
106 E8 **Glencoe** New Mexico U.S.A.
98 F4 **Glencross** South Dakota U.S.A.
103 M8 **Glendale** Arizona U.S.A.
102 F7 **Glendale** California U.S.A.
111 K11 **Glendale** Florida U.S.A.
107 N3 **Glendale** Kansas U.S.A.
103 K5 **Glendale** Nevada U.S.A.
94 C7 **Glendale** Ohio U.S.A.
100 B7 **Glendale** Oregon U.S.A.
94 G7 **Glendale** West Virginia U.S.A.
117 L10 **Glendale Cove** British Columbia Canada
12 C1 **Glendaruel** Scotland
139 K5 **Glen Davis** New South Wales Australia
106 E1 **Glendevey** Colorado U.S.A.
12 E1 **Glendevon** Scotland
98 B2 **Glendive** Montana U.S.A.
98 A7 **Glendo** Wyoming U.S.A.
118 F4 **Glendon** Alberta Canada
111 F8 **Glendora** Mississippi U.S.A.
14 C2 **Glendowan Mts** Ireland
141 H4 **Gleneagle** Queensland Australia
15 E4 **Gleneagles** Scotland
107 M2 **Glen Elder** Kansas U.S.A.
138 E5 **Glenelg** South Australia Australia
138 F6 **Glenelg** *R* Victoria Australia
15 C3 **Glenelg** Scotland
119 S8 **Glenella** Manitoba Canada
119 P9 **Glen Ewen** Saskatchewan Canada
12 D1 **Glen Falloch** Scotland
13 E1 **Glenfarg** Scotland
95 M3 **Glenfield** New York U.S.A.
98 H2 **Glenfield** North Dakota U.S.A.
15 C4 **Glenfinnan** Scotland
109 L6 **Glen Flora** Texas U.S.A.
14 D1 **Glengad Hd** Ireland
14 B5 **Glengariff** Ireland
15 C3 **Glen Garry** *R* Scotland
15 D4 **Glen Garry** Scotland
143 C7 **Glengarry Ra** W Australia Australia
127 L2 **Glengoffe** Jamaica
140 E6 **Glengyle** Queensland Australia
144 B7 **Glenham** New Zealand
98 F4 **Glenham** South Dakota U.S.A.
140 C6 **Glen Helen** N Terr Australia
140 C6 **Glen Helen Gorge** N Terr Australia
145 D4 **Glenhope** New Zealand
139 K3 **Glen Innes** New South Wales Australia
118 K8 **Glen Kerr** Saskatchewan Canada
99 V5 **Glen L** Michigan U.S.A.
12 D4 **Glenluce** Scotland
139 G4 **Glen Lyon** New South Wales Australia
15 D4 **Glen Lyon** Scotland
95 L5 **Glen Lyon** Pennsylvania U.S.A.
145 E2 **Glen Massey** New Zealand
109 P5 **Glenmora** Louisiana U.S.A.
15 D3 **Glen More** Scotland
141 J7 **Glenmorgan** Queensland Australia
15 D3 **Glen Moriston** Scotland
102 B2 **Glenn** California U.S.A.
116 P5 **Glennallen** Alaska U.S.A.
14 C3 **Glennamaddy** Ireland
139 H7 **Glennie** *isld* Victoria Australia
94 D2 **Glennie** Michigan U.S.A.
103 P9 **Glenn, Mt** Arizona U.S.A.
100 K7 **Glenns Ferry** Idaho U.S.A.
102 F6 **Glennville** California U.S.A.
112 F6 **Glennville** Georgia U.S.A.
12 D1 **Glen Ogle** Scotland
144 B7 **Glenomaru** New Zealand
117 H7 **Glenora** British Columbia Canada
139 H8 **Glenorchy** Tasmania Australia
144 B6 **Glenorchy** New Zealand
15 D4 **Glen Orchy** Scotland
141 F4 **Glenore** Queensland Australia
144 B7 **Glenore** New Zealand
140 E6 **Glenormiston** Queensland Australia
139 L4 **Glenreagh** New South Wales Australia
108 A8 **Glenrio** New Mex/Tex U.S.A.
121 Q7 **Glen Robertson** Ontario Canada
98 A7 **Glenrock** Wyoming U.S.A.
109 K3 **Glen Rose** Texas U.S.A.
13 E1 **Glenrothes** Scotland
142 F3 **Glenroy** W Australia Australia
95 O3 **Glens Falls** New York U.S.A.
15 E4 **Glen Shee** Scotland
118 L7 **Glenside** Saskatchewan Canada
15 D4 **Glen Spean** Scotland
28 D3 **Glenstrup Sø** *L* Denmark
101 T1 **Glentana** Montana U.S.A.
14 C2 **Glenties** Ireland
144 C5 **Glentunnel** New Zealand
118 L9 **Glentworth** Saskatchewan Canada
98 E3 **Glen Ullin** North Dakota U.S.A.
15 D3 **Glen Urquhart** Scotland
120 K5 **Glenvale** Ontario Canada
99 T7 **Glenview** Illinois U.S.A.
99 N6 **Glenville** Minnesota U.S.A.
98 H9 **Glenville** Nebraska U.S.A.
94 G8 **Glenville** West Virginia U.S.A.
112 D2 **Glenville L** North Carolina U.S.A.
123 S5 **Glenwood** Newfoundland Canada
111 K10 **Glenwood** Alabama U.S.A.
111 C7 **Glenwood** Arkansas U.S.A.
112 E5 **Glenwood** Georgia U.S.A.
94 B7 **Glenwood** Indiana U.S.A.
99 L8 **Glenwood** Iowa U.S.A.
99 L4 **Glenwood** Minnesota U.S.A.
99 O9 **Glenwood** Missouri U.S.A.
106 B8 **Glenwood** New Mexico U.S.A.

Glenwood — Grandpré 179

112 F2 **Glenwood** North Carolina U.S.A.
100 B4 **Glenwood** Oregon U.S.A.
103 N3 **Glenwood** Utah U.S.A.
100 D3 **Glenwood** Washington U.S.A.
94 E8 **Glenwood** West Virginia U.S.A.
99 O4 **Glenwood** Wisconsin U.S.A.
106 C2 **Glenwood Springs** Colorado U.S.A.
118 D9 **Glenwoodville** Alberta Canada
28 F4 **Glesborg** Denmark
33 N4 **Gleschendorf** Germany
41 H4 **Gletsch** Switzerland
118 H7 **Glidden** Saskatchewan Canada
99 Q3 **Glidden** Wisconsin U.S.A.
100 B6 **Glide** Oregon U.S.A.
33 S8 **Glienick** Germany
33 S7 **Glienicke** Germany
14 B4 **Glin** Ireland
32 M5 **Glinde** Germany
31 M3 **Glinojeck** Poland
48 J1 **Glinyany** Ukraine
26 G9 **Glissjöberg** Sweden
26 C10 **Glittertind** *mt* Norway
31 L5 **Gliwice** Poland
46 D4 **Gllavë** Albania
103 O8 **Globe** Arizona U.S.A.
48 C3 **Gloggnitz** Austria
31 J4 **Głogów** Poland
31 K5 **Głogówek** Poland
31 N5 **Głogów Małopolski** Poland
33 Q8 **Gloine** Germany
20 D5 **Glomel** France
26 G5 **Glomfjord** Norway
26 E9 **Glomma** *R* Norway
26 L6 **Glommerstrask** Sweden
27 J15 **Glönminge** Sweden
130 H10 **Glória** Brazil
106 E6 **Glorieta** New Mexico U.S.A.
87 H10 **Glorieuses, Is** Indian Oc
116 C6 **Glory of Russia C** Alaska U.S.A.
21 L3 **Glos** France
21 M4 **Glos-la-Ferrière** France
13 G6 **Glossop** England
21 M3 **Glos-sur-Risle** France
111 E10 **Gloster** Mississippi U.S.A.
29 K5 **Glostrup** Denmark
52 G3 **Glotovo** Russian Federation
139 K4 **Gloucester** New South Wales Australia
8 D4 **Gloucester** England
95 R4 **Gloucester** Massachusetts U.S.A.
95 L9 **Gloucester** Virginia U.S.A.
95 M7 **Gloucester City** New Jersey U.S.A.
141 J4 **Gloucester I** Queensland Australia
94 E7 **Glouster** Ohio U.S.A.
123 P5 **Glover I** Newfoundland Canada
95 N3 **Gloversville** New York U.S.A.
33 Q7 **Glöwen** Germany
31 M4 **Głowno** Poland
54 M8 **Glubokiy** Russian Federation
56 B5 **Glubokoye** Kazakhstan
31 K5 **Głuchołazy** Poland
28 D7 **Glucksburg** Germany
32 K5 **Glückstadt** Germany
28 D5 **Glud** Denmark
28 C4 **Gludsted** Denmark
54 E5 **Glukhov** Ukraine
52 F6 **Glukhovo** Russian Federation
69 B10 **Glumpangminyeuk** Sumatra
29 K5 **Glumslöv** Sweden
28 H6 **Glumsø** Denmark
13 F6 **Glusburn** England
55 E4 **Glyadyanskoye** Russian Federation
48 K2 **Glyboka** Ukraine
8 B1 **Glyder Fawr** *mt* Wales
143 E6 **Glynde Hill** W Australia Australia
95 L7 **Glyndon** Maryland U.S.A.
98 K3 **Glyndon** Minnesota U.S.A.
28 B3 **Glyngøre** Denmark
8 C4 **Glynneath** Wales
8 C4 **Glyntawe** Wales
31 J7 **Gmünd** Austria
38 J6 **Gmunden** Austria
33 P9 **Gnadau** Germany
94 F6 **Gnadenhutten** Ohio U.S.A.
26 J9 **Gnarp** Sweden
32 K6 **Gnarrenburg** Germany
38 N8 **Gnas** Austria
27 J12 **Gnesta** Sweden
28 G4 **Gniben** *C* Denmark
31 L2 **Gniew** Poland
31 K3 **Gniezno** Poland
33 M4 **Gnissau** Germany
46 E2 **Gnjilane** Serbia Yugoslavia
33 R5 **Gnoien** Germany
8 D2 **Gnosall** England
37 K5 **Gnotzheim** Germany
143 C10 **Gnowangerup** W Australia
143 B9 **Gnuka** W Australia
32 L4 **Gnutz** Germany
76 A3 **Goa, Daman & Diu** *terr* India
139 K6 **Goalen Head** New South Wales Australia
75 O5 **Goalpara** India
71 H9 **Goang** Indonesia
12 C2 **Goat Fell** *mt* Scotland
13 H5 **Goathland** England
101 M1 **Goat Mt** Montana U.S.A.
87 F11 **Goba** Mozambique
89 A4 **Gobabis** Namibia
58 D3 **Gobi Desert** Mongolia
60 J12 **Gobō** Japan
8 C2 **Gobowen** England
25 F5 **Goch** Germany
87 C10 **Gochas** Namibia
86 G4 **Gocho** Ethiopia
36 F5 **Gochsheim** Germany
79 C2 **Göçuk** Turkey
9 F5 **Godalming** England
74 J9 **Godavari** *R* India
76 F2 **Godavari, Mouths of the** India
122 E4 **Godbout** Quebec Canada
122 E4 **Godbout, R** Quebec Canada
117 E7 **Goddard** Alaska U.S.A.
107 N4 **Goddard** Kansas U.S.A.
36 F4 **Goddelau-Wolfskehlen** Germany
46 F1 **Godech** Bulgaria
27 H13 **Godegård** Sweden
32 K9 **Godelheim** Germany
47 L8 **Gödene** Turkey
120 J9 **Goderich** Ontario Canada
21 L2 **Goderville** France
22 D2 **Godewaersvelde** France
121 O8 **Godfrey** Ontario Canada
110 F3 **Godfrey** Illinois U.S.A.
115 O4 **Godhavn** Greenland
74 E7 **Godhra** India
109 K3 **Godley** Texas U.S.A.
144 C5 **Godley Gl** New Zealand
144 C5 **Godley R** New Zealand
9 F3 **Godmanchester** England
71 J5 **Godo** *mt* Indonesia
48 E3 **Gödöllö** Hungary
9 E6 **Godshill** England
115 K7 **Gods L** Manitoba Canada
9 F5 **Godstone** England
115 O5 **Godthåb** Greenland
112 J2 **Godwin** North Carolina U.S.A.
Godwin Austen *mt see* **K2** *mt*
25 A5 **Goedereede** Netherlands
121 O3 **Goeland** Quebec Canada
25 A5 **Goeree** Netherlands
25 A6 **Goes** Netherlands
107 P2 **Goff** Kansas U.S.A.
103 J7 **Goffs** Carolina U.S.A.
95 Q3 **Goffstown** New Hampshire U.S.A.
120 J5 **Gogama** Ontario Canada
60 F10 **Gō-gawa** *R* Japan
99 R3 **Gogebic** Michigan U.S.A.
99 R3 **Gogebic Range** *mts* Michigan U.S.A.
37 K7 **Goggingen** Germany
41 H5 **Goglio** Italy
7 L10 **Gog Magog Hills** England
36 B6 **Gogney** France
22 F3 **Gognies-Chaussée** Belgium
142 F4 **Gogo** W Australia Australia
31 K5 **Gogolin** Poland
86 E4 **Gogrial** Sudan
33 Q9 **Gohrau** Germany
33 N6 **Göhrde** Germany
130 J9 **Goiana** Brazil
130 E6 **Goiandira** Brazil
130 E4 **Goianésia** Brazil
130 E5 **Goiânia** Brazil
130 J9 **Goianinha** *lighthouse* Brazil
130 E4 **Goiás** Brazil
130 D5 **Goiás** *state* Brazil
130 E6 **Goiatuba** Brazil
12 D1 **Goil, L** Scotland
130 D9 **Goio Erê** Brazil
25 D5 **Goirle** Netherlands
45 J1 **Goito** Italy
86 G3 **Gojam** *prov* Ethiopia
86 G4 **Gojeb** *R* Ethiopia
61 J11 **Gojō** Japan
61 O6 **Gojōme** Japan
47 K5 **Gök** *R* Turkey
76 B2 **Gokak** India
47 K7 **Gökbel** *mt* Turkey
47 H4 **Gökçeada** *isld* Turkey
47 K5 **Gökçedağ** Turkey
79 C2 **Gökdere** *str* Turkey
32 K4 **Gokels** Germany
78 A3 **Gökova Körfezi** Turkey
77 H7 **Gokprosh Hills** Pakistan
78 D3 **Göksu** *R* Turkey
78 F2 **Göksun** Turkey
68 C1 **Gokteik** Burma
47 K7 **Göktepe** Turkey
47 K8 **Gök Tepe** *mt* Turkey
79 C2 **Göktepe** Turkey
87 E9 **Gokwe** Zimbabwe
27 C11 **Gol** Norway
75 P5 **Golaghat** India
80 G2 **Golan** Syria
31 K3 **Gołańcz** Poland
77 E6 **Golāshkerd** Iran
54 D10 **Golaya Pristan'** Ukraine
77 E5 **Golbaf** Iran
77 L2 **Golbahār** Afghanistan
38 G8 **Gölbnerjoch** *mt* Austria
74 H10 **Golconda** India
110 H4 **Golconda** Illinois U.S.A.
100 H9 **Golconda** Nevada U.S.A.
Gölcük *see* **Etili**
47 N11 **Gölcük** Turkey
94 K5 **Gold** Pennsylvania U.S.A.
31 N1 **Gołdap** Poland
100 A7 **Gold Beach** Oregon U.S.A.
33 P7 **Goldbeck** Germany
33 Q5 **Goldberg** Germany
123 L8 **Goldboro** Nova Scotia Canada
101 O1 **Gold Butte** Montana U.S.A.
141 L8 **Gold Coast** Queensland Australia
28 C7 **Goldelund** Germany
117 P10 **Golden** British Columbia Canada
98 A10 **Golden** Colorado U.S.A.
100 K4 **Golden** Idaho U.S.A.
110 E1 **Golden** Illinois U.S.A.
145 D4 **Golden Bay** New Zealand
110 B4 **Golden City** Missouri U.S.A.
100 E4 **Goldendale** Washington U.S.A.
144 D4 **Golden Downs** New Zealand
33 N10 **Goldene Aue** Germany
102 B4 **Golden Gate** California U.S.A.
102 B4 **Golden Gate Nat. Recreation Area** California U.S.A.
103 J4 **Golden Gate Ra** Nevada U.S.A.
127 M3 **Golden Grove** Jamaica
121 N7 **Golden Lake** Ontario Canada
111 F12 **Golden Meadow** Louisiana U.S.A.
110 H5 **Golden Pond** Kentucky U.S.A.
118 H8 **Golden Prairie** Saskatchewan Canada
127 P4 **Golden Rock** *airport* St Kitts W Indies
101 N8 **Golden Spike Nat. Hist. Site** Utah U.S.A.
32 H7 **Goldenstedt** Germany
14 C4 **Golden Vale** Ireland
123 K8 **Goldenville** Nova Scotia Canada
99 N7 **Goldfield** Iowa U.S.A.
102 G4 **Goldfield** Nevada U.S.A.
109 J7 **Goldfinch** Texas U.S.A.
101 M9 **Gold Hill** Utah U.S.A.
102 G4 **Gold Point** Nevada U.S.A.
118 K1 **Gold Rock** Ontario Canada
119 R1 **Goldsand L** Manitoba Canada
95 M7 **Goldsboro** Maryland U.S.A.
112 K2 **Goldsboro** North Carolina U.S.A.
108 E4 **Goldsmith** Texas U.S.A.
102 H6 **Goldstone L** California U.S.A.
142 C5 **Goldsworthy** W Australia Australia
142 C5 **Goldsworthy, Mt** W Australia Australia
109 J4 **Goldthwaite** Texas U.S.A.
112 F3 **Goldville** South Carolina U.S.A.
78 J1 **Göle** Turkey
85 E2 **Golea, El** Algeria
89 G6 **Golela** S Africa
31 H2 **Goleniów** Poland
102 E7 **Goleta** California U.S.A.
16 C7 **Golfo de Cádiz** Spain
43 E10 **Golfo di Castellammare** Sicily
43 E7 **Golfo di Gaeta** Italy
44 E3 **Golfo di Genova** Italy
45 N1 **Golfo di Venezia** Adriatic Sea
47 K7 **Gölgel Dağ** *mts* Turkey
138 F5 **Gol Gol** New South Wales Australia
109 K7 **Goliad** Texas U.S.A.
46 D1 **Golija Planina** *mt* Serbia Yugoslavia
65 E2 **Golin Baixing** China
Gollel *see* **Lavumisa**
33 T6 **Gollin** Germany
38 H6 **Golling** Austria
33 S10 **Gollmberg** *pk* Germany
33 T9 **Gollmitz** Germany
47 J6 **Gölmarmara** Turkey
33 S8 **Golmberg** *pk* Germany
37 M2 **Golmsdorf** Germany
66 E4 **Golmud** China
71 E4 **Golo** *isld* Philippines
52 H1 **Golodnaya Guba, Oz** *L* Russian Federation
57 E4 **Golodnaya Step'** Kazakhstan/Uzbekistan
86 H4 **Gololcha** Ethiopia
88 E9 **Golomoti** Malawi
48 N2 **Golovanevsk** Ukraine
116 F4 **Golovin** Alaska U.S.A.
60 T2 **Golovnino** Kuril Is Russian Federation
77 B3 **Golpāyegān** Iran
47 L4 **Gölpazarı** Turkey
116 G5 **Golsovia** Alaska U.S.A.
15 E3 **Golspie** Scotland
33 T9 **Golssen** Germany
28 D2 **Gølstrup** Denmark
107 M5 **Goltry** Oklahoma U.S.A.
31 L2 **Gołub** Poland
55 F4 **Golubovka** Kazakhstan
89 F3 **Golulu Ruins** Zimbabwe
87 B7 **Golungo Alto** Angola
98 C3 **Golva** North Dakota U.S.A.
46 G3 **Golyam Perelik** *mt* Bulgaria
31 M3 **Gołymin** Poland
54 C2 **Golynki** Russian Federation
55 E3 **Golyshmanovo** Russian Federation
33 R8 **Golzow** Germany
88 B2 **Goma** Zaire
85 G6 **Gombe** Nigeria
44 H4 **Gombo** Italy
70 M9 **Gombong** Java
47 H5 **Gömeç** Turkey
54 B4 **Gomel'** Belorussia
85 A3 **Gomera** *isld* Canary Is
124 H5 **Gómez Palacio** Mexico
125 K4 **Gómez, Presa M.R.** *res* Mexico
20 F5 **Gommené** France
33 P8 **Gommern** Germany
66 C5 **Gomo** China
71 A3 **Gomumu** *isld* Indonesia
127 H5 **Gonaïves** Haiti
51 M3 **Gonam** *R* Russian Federation
89 G3 **Gona-re-zhou Game Res.** Zimbabwe
126 H5 **Gonâve, Île de la** Haiti
48 G2 **Gönc** Hungary
19 Q14 **Goncelin** France
74 D8 **Gondal** India
36 F5 **Gondelsheim** Germany
86 G3 **Gonder** Ethiopia
86 G3 **Gonder** *prov* Ethiopia
74 J8 **Gondia** India
19 J4 **Gondrecourt** France
80 F1 **Gonen** Israel
47 J4 **Gönen** *R* Turkey
47 J4 **Gönen** Turkey
19 Q18 **Gonfaron** France
21 L2 **Gonfreville l'Orcher** France
83 K11 **Gongala** *mt* Sri Lanka
67 D1 **Gong'an** China
66 E5 **Gongbo'gyamda** China
67 C4 **Gongcheng** China
75 O4 **Gonggar** China
58 D6 **Gongga Shan** *mt* China
57 K3 **Gongliu** China
Gonglüe *see* **Donggu**
85 G6 **Gongola** *R* Nigeria
139 H4 **Gongolgon** New South Wales Australia
67 D3 **Gongpingxu** China
67 D2 **Gongtian** China
65 B7 **Gong Xian** China
65 D4 **Gongyingzi** China
Gongzhuling *see* **Huaide**
31 O2 **Goniądz** Poland
88 G4 **Gonja** Tanzania
36 G7 **Gönningen** Germany
46 E5 **Gónnos** Greece
61 P5 **Gonohe** Japan
60 C12 **Gōnoura** Japan
40 D3 **Gonsans** France
99 L2 **Gonvick** Minnesota U.S.A.
45 J2 **Gonzaga** Italy
102 C5 **Gonzales** California U.S.A.
109 K6 **Gonzales** Texas U.S.A.
36 C4 **Gonzerath** Germany
86 H6 **Goob Weyn** Somalia
94 K9 **Goochland** Virginia U.S.A.
146 F14 **Goodenough, C** Antarctica
121 M8 **Gooderham** Ontario Canada
119 O7 **Goodeve** Saskatchewan Canada
94 B1 **Good Hart** Michigan U.S.A.
99 V4 **Good Hbr. B** Michigan U.S.A.
89 B8 **Goodhope** S Africa
116 E4 **Goodhope** *R* Alaska U.S.A.
116 F3 **Goodhope B** Alaska U.S.A.
87 C12 **Good Hope, C. of** S Africa
117 L10 **Good Hope, Mt** British Columbia Canada
87 C11 **Goodhouse** S Africa
99 O5 **Goodhue** Minnesota U.S.A.
101 L7 **Gooding** Idaho U.S.A.
107 J2 **Goodland** Kansas U.S.A.
119 R9 **Goodlands** Manitoba Canada
83 M12 **Goodlands** Mauritius
110 K5 **Goodlettsville** Tennessee U.S.A.
99 S4 **Goodman** Wisconsin U.S.A.
116 F7 **Goodnews B** Alaska U.S.A.
108 C8 **Goodnight** Texas U.S.A.
139 H3 **Goodooga** New South Wales Australia
140 B2 **Goodparla** N Terr Australia
116 P4 **Goodpaster** *R* Alaska U.S.A.
106 F3 **Good Pasture** Colorado U.S.A.
98 B9 **Goodrich** Colorado U.S.A.
100 J5 **Goodrich** Idaho U.S.A.
98 F2 **Goodrich** North Dakota U.S.A.
111 B11 **Goodrich** Texas U.S.A.
99 Q4 **Goodrich** Wisconsin U.S.A.
140 B1 **Goodrich Bank** N Terr Australia
117 P10 **Goodsir, Mt** British Columbia Canada
118 H4 **Goodsoil** Saskatchewan Canada
119 P7 **Good Spirit L** Saskatchewan Canada
103 J6 **Goodsprings** Nevada U.S.A.
119 O9 **Goodwater** Saskatchewan Canada
111 K8 **Good Water** Alabama U.S.A.
107 J5 **Goodwell** Oklahoma U.S.A.
8 A3 **Goodwick** Wales
121 L4 **Goodwin** Ontario Canada
103 M7 **Goodwin** Arizona U.S.A.
98 K5 **Goodwin** South Dakota U.S.A.
7 M11 **Goodwin Sands** English Chan
144 C6 **Goodwood** New Zealand
9 F6 **Goodwood Park** England
13 H6 **Goole** England
139 H5 **Goolgowi** New South Wales Australia
139 J4 **Goolma** New South Wales Australia
139 J5 **Gooloogong** New South Wales Australia
138 E6 **Goolwa** South Australia Australia
140 C1 **Goomadeer** *R* N Terr Australia
143 B9 **Goomalling** W Australia Australia
139 H3 **Goombalie** New South Wales Australia
141 K7 **Goombungee** Queensland Australia
141 K7 **Goomeri** Queensland Australia
141 K8 **Goondiwindi** Queensland Australia
143 D9 **Goongarrie** W Australia Australia
143 D8 **Goongarrie, L** W Australia Australia
141 J5 **Goonyella** Queensland Australia
25 G4 **Goor** Netherlands
117 P8 **Goose** *R* Alberta Canada
115 N7 **Goose Bay** Labrador, Nfld Canada
144 D5 **Goose Bay** New Zealand
101 R5 **Gooseberry Cr** Wyoming U.S.A.
118 G6 **Gooseberry L. Prov. Park** Alberta Canada
123 R2 **Goose Cove** Newfoundland Canada
101 M7 **Goose Cr** Idaho U.S.A.
112 G4 **Goose Creek** South Carolina U.S.A.
101 M8 **Goose Cr. Mts** Utah U.S.A.
101 T7 **Goose Egg** Wyoming U.S.A.
116 F9 **Goose I** Alaska U.S.A.
119 Q4 **Goose L** Manitoba Canada
100 E8 **Goose L** California U.S.A.
76 C3 **Gooty** India
75 L9 **Gopalpur** India
31 L3 **Gopło, Jezioro** *L* Poland
36 H6 **Göppingen** Germany
103 K10 **Gora** *isld* Mexico
31 K4 **Góra** Poland
31 N4 **Gora Kalwaria** Poland
75 K5 **Gorakhpur** India
42 J5 **Goransko** Montenegro Yugoslavia
48 E7 **Goražde** Bosnia-Herzegovina
113 K11 **Gorda Cay** *isld* Bahamas
128 D7 **Gorda, Pta** *C* Chile
19 O17 **Gordes** France
47 J6 **Gördes** Turkey
86 D4 **Gordil** Cent Afr Republic
28 B6 **Gørding** Denmark
111 J8 **Gordo** Alabama U.S.A.
139 H8 **Gordon** *R* Tasmania Australia
13 F2 **Gordon** Scotland
116 R2 **Gordon** Alaska U.S.A.
106 F4 **Gordon** Colorado U.S.A.
112 D5 **Gordon** Georgia U.S.A.
98 D7 **Gordon** Nebraska U.S.A.
109 J3 **Gordon** Texas U.S.A.
99 P3 **Gordon** Wisconsin U.S.A.
13 E3 **Gordon Arms** Scotland
140 B1 **Gordon B** N Terr Australia
140 B3 **Gordon Cr** N Terr Australia
98 E7 **Gordon Cr** Nebraska U.S.A.
142 G4 **Gordon Downs** W Australia Australia
139 H8 **Gordon L.** Tasmania Australia
118 G2 **Gordon, L** Alberta Canada
117 R4 **Gordon L** Northwest Territories Canada
117 F4 **Gordon Landing** Yukon Territory Canada
94 B10 **Gordonsville** Tennessee U.S.A.
94 J8 **Gordonsville** Virginia U.S.A.
141 H3 **Gordonvale** Queensland Australia
86 C4 **Goré** Chad
86 G4 **Gorē** Ethiopia
144 B7 **Gore** New Zealand
107 P6 **Gore** Oklahoma U.S.A.
120 H7 **Gore Bay** Ontario Canada
144 D5 **Gore Bay** New Zealand
13 E2 **Gorebridge** Scotland
109 H2 **Goree** Texas U.S.A.
54 J2 **Gorelki** Russian Federation
95 Q2 **Gore Mt** Vermont U.S.A.
140 E4 **Gore Pt** Queensland Australia
116 M7 **Gore Pt** Alaska U.S.A.
106 D2 **Gore Ra** Colorado U.S.A.
110 H4 **Goreville** Illinois U.S.A.
20 F3 **Gorey** Channel Is
14 E4 **Gorey** Ireland
77 D1 **Gorgān** Iran
147 K11 **Gorga, Zemlya** *isld* Russian Federation
83 K14 **Gorge** *R* Réunion Indian Oc
142 C5 **Gorge Ra** W Australia Australia
141 H4 **Gorge Ra., The** Queensland Australia
128 C3 **Gorgona** *isld* Colombia
42 C5 **Gorgona, I.di** Italy
41 K6 **Gorgonzola** Italy
86 G3 **Gorgora** Ethiopia
85 G6 **Gorgoram** Nigeria
101 O9 **Gorgorza** Utah U.S.A.
107 L3 **Gorham** Kansas U.S.A.
95 R3 **Gorham** Maine U.S.A.
95 Q2 **Gorham** New Hampshire U.S.A.
95 K4 **Gorham** New York U.S.A.
53 F12 **Gori** Georgia
46 D4 **Goricë** Albania
99 O9 **Gorin** Missouri U.S.A.
25 C5 **Gorinchem** Netherlands
9 E4 **Goring** England
27 H10 **Göringen** Sweden
78 L2 **Goris** Armenia
52 E6 **Goritsy** Russian Federation
42 F3 **Gorizia** Italy
42 G3 **Gorjanci** *mts* Yugoslavia
52 G3 **Gorka** Russian Federation
75 L4 **Gorkhā** Nepal
Gor'kiy *see* **Nizhniy Novgorod**
Gor'kovskaya Oblast' *see* **Nizhegorodskaya Oblast'**
52 F6 **Gor'kovskoye Vodokhranilishche** *res* Russian Federation
33 O6 **Gorleben** Germany
9 H2 **Gorleston** England
28 G5 **Gørlev** Denmark
31 N6 **Gorlice** Poland
52 F3 **Gorlichevskaya** Russian Federation
31 H4 **Görlitz** Germany
28 J5 **Gørløse** Denmark
33 O6 **Gorlosen** Germany
98 F5 **Gorman** South Dakota U.S.A.
109 J3 **Gorman** Texas U.S.A.
94 H7 **Gormania** Maryland U.S.A.
139 H8 **Gormanston** Tasmania Australia
43 F11 **Gornalunga** *R* Sicily
47 H1 **Gorna Oryakhovitsa** Bulgaria
55 E2 **Gornaya Subbota** Russian Federation
65 J2 **Gorniye Klyuchi** Russian Federation
46 D1 **Gornji Milanovac** Serbia Yugoslavia
42 H5 **Gornji Vakuf** Bosnia-Herzegovina
56 C5 **Gorno-Altaysk** Russian Federation
56 C5 **Gorno-Altayskaya Avtonomnyy Oblast'** Russian Federation
57 G5 **Gorno-Badakhshanskaya Avtonomnyy Oblast'** *prov* Tajikistan
56 H2 **Gorno-Chuyskiy** Russian Federation
55 E2 **Gorno Slinkina** Russian Federation
52 G1 **Gornostal'ya Guba** *B* Russian Federation
54 M8 **Gornyatskiy** Russian Federation
29 P2 **Gornyy** Russian Federation
48 N1 **Gornyy Tikich** *R* Ukraine
45 M2 **Goro** Italy
48 J2 **Gorodenka** Ukraine
52 F6 **Gorodets** Russian Federation
52 F1 **Gorodetskiy, Mys Bol'shoy** *C* Russian Federation
54 C7 **Gorodishche** Ukraine
52 D6 **Gorodnya** Russian Federation
54 A1 **Gorodok** Belorussia
136 K3 **Goroka** Papua New Guinea
138 F6 **Goroke** Victoria Australia
52 F6 **Gorokhovets** Russian Federation
87 F9 **Gorongosa** Mozambique
71 H4 **Gorontalo** Sulawesi
31 M1 **Górowo Iławeckie** Poland
25 F2 **Gorredijk** Netherlands
120 J9 **Gorrie** Ontario Canada
21 J5 **Gorron** France
33 S9 **Görsdorf** Germany
54 K8 **Gorskoye** Ukraine
25 F4 **Gorssel** Netherlands
14 C3 **Gort** Ireland
14 C1 **Gortahork** Ireland
14 B3 **Gorumna I** Ireland
130 G4 **Gorutuba, R** Brazil
57 A2 **Gory Chushkakul'** *mt* Kazakhstan
53 C8 **Goryn'** *R* Belorussia/Ukraine
31 M5 **Góry Świętokrzyskie** *mts* Poland
42 E6 **Gorzano, M** *mt* Italy
33 Q8 **Görzke** Germany
31 L4 **Gorzów** Poland
31 J3 **Gorzów Wielkopolski** Poland
Gosainthan *mt see* **Xixabangma Feng**
9 F2 **Gosberton** England
37 M2 **Göschwitz** Germany
61 N8 **Gosen** Japan
139 K5 **Gosford** New South Wales Australia
102 E5 **Goshen** California U.S.A.
94 B5 **Goshen** Indiana U.S.A.
95 N5 **Goshen** New York U.S.A.
100 B6 **Goshen** Oregon U.S.A.
101 O10 **Goshen** Utah U.S.A.
94 H9 **Goshen** Virginia U.S.A.
61 O5 **Goshogawara** Japan
127 N4 **Gosier** Guadeloupe W Indies
33 M9 **Goslar** Germany
20 H5 **Gosné** France
142 C2 **Gosnells** *dist* Perth, W Aust Australia
42 G4 **Gospić** Croatia
9 E6 **Gosport** England
110 K2 **Gosport** Indiana U.S.A.
111 G10 **Goss** Mississippi U.S.A.
33 Q9 **Gossa** Germany
41 K3 **Gossau** Switzerland
22 G3 **Gosselies** Belgium
26 B9 **Gossen** *isld* Norway
140 C4 **Gosse R** N Terr Australia
86 E4 **Gossinga** Sudan
38 J6 **Gossl** Austria
38 H8 **Gössnitz** Austria
37 N2 **Gössnitz** Germany
46 D3 **Gostivar** Macedonia Yugoslavia
38 L6 **Göstling** Austria
38 L6 **Göstlinger Alpen** *mts* Austria
31 K4 **Gostyn** Poland
31 L3 **Gostynin** Poland
27 H13 **Göta Kanal** Sweden
107 M6 **Gotebo** Oklahoma U.S.A.
27 E14 **Göteborg** Sweden
27 E13 **Göteborgs Och Bohus** *county* Sweden
85 G7 **Gotel Mts** Nigeria
61 M10 **Gotemba** Japan
37 K2 **Gotha** Germany
27 K14 **Gothem** Gotland Sweden
98 F9 **Gothenburg** Nebraska U.S.A.
85 E6 **Gothéye** Niger
27 K14 **Gotland** *isld* Sweden
27 K14 **Gotland** *county* Sweden
27 H12 **Götlunda** Sweden
60 B12 **Gotō-rettō** *islds* Japan
71 B2 **Gotowasi** Indonesia
46 F3 **Gotse Delchev** Bulgaria
27 K13 **Gotska Sandön** *isld* Sweden
60 F10 **Gōtsu** Japan
44 G3 **Gottero** *mt* Italy
37 O6 **Gotteszell** Germany
36 F2 **Göttingen** Hessen Germany
32 L9 **Göttingen** Niedersachsen Germany
26 K8 **Gottne** Sweden
117 M10 **Gott Pk** British Columbia Canada
28 C2 **Gøttrup** Denmark
Gottwaldov *see* **Zlín**
Gotval'd *see* **Zmiyev**
41 L3 **Götzis** Austria
20 D5 **Gouarec** France
65 E4 **Goubangzi** China
25 C4 **Gouda** Netherlands
86 C4 **Goudeï** Chad
22 F4 **Goudelancourt** France
9 G5 **Goudhurst** England
85 B6 **Goudiry** Senegal
85 G6 **Goudoumaria** Niger
120 F4 **Goudreau** Ontario Canada
25 B5 **Goudswaard** Netherlands
20 G4 **Gouesnière, la** France
20 B5 **Gouesnou** France
20 E5 **Gouet** *R* France
20 C5 **Gouézec** France
112 E4 **Gough** Georgia U.S.A.
90 J13 **Gough I** S Atlantic Oc
118 E6 **Gough L** Alberta Canada
40 D2 **Gouhenans** France
121 Q4 **Gouin, Rés** Quebec Canada
120 F6 **Goulais River** Ontario Canada
139 K4 **Goulburn** *R* New South Wales Australia
139 J5 **Goulburn** New South Wales Australia
140 C1 **Goulburn Is** N Terr Australia
121 T7 **Gould** Quebec Canada
111 E8 **Gould** Arkansas U.S.A.
106 D1 **Gould** Colorado U.S.A.
107 L7 **Gould** Oklahoma U.S.A.
99 V3 **Gould City** Michigan U.S.A.
146 D9 **Gould Coast** Antarctica
143 B7 **Gould, Mt** W Australia Australia
85 C6 **Goumbou** Mali
46 E4 **Gouménissa** Greece
40 E3 **Goumois** France
85 D5 **Goundam** Mali
86 C4 **Goundi** Chad
46 E7 **Goúra** Greece
86 C2 **Gouradi** Chad
20 F5 **Gouray, le** France
18 F8 **Gourdon** France
85 G6 **Gouré** Niger
21 K8 **Gourgé** France
20 C5 **Gourin** France
120 F4 **Gourlay L** Ontario Canada
85 D5 **Gourma Rharous** Mali
21 O3 **Gournay-en-Bray** France
86 C2 **Gouro** Chad
12 D2 **Gourock** Scotland
139 J6 **Gourock Rge** New South Wales Australia
118 K9 **Gouverneur** Saskatchewan Canada
95 M2 **Gouverneur** New York U.S.A.
47 O12 **Gouviá** Greece
21 P3 **Gouvieux** France
20 G3 **Gouville** France
22 K3 **Gouvy** Belgium
127 P5 **Gouyave** Grenada
22 E3 **Gouzeaucourt** France
18 G6 **Gouzon** France
119 N7 **Govan** Saskatchewan Canada
12 D2 **Govan** Scotland
140 D1 **Gove** N Terr Australia
107 K3 **Gove** Kansas U.S.A.
20 G5 **Goven** France
118 H9 **Govenlock** Saskatchewan Canada
140 D1 **Gove Pen** N Terr Australia
48 J2 **Goverla** *mt* Ukraine
130 H6 **Governador Valadares** Brazil
100 D4 **Government Camp** Oregon U.S.A.
71 G7 **Governor Generoso** Philippines
122 K8 **Governor, L** Nova Scotia Canada
113 L12 **Governor's Harbour** Bahamas
145 D4 **Gowanbridge** New Zealand
94 J4 **Gowanda** New York U.S.A.
141 G6 **Gowan Ra** Queensland Australia
110 B2 **Gower** Missouri U.S.A.
8 B4 **Gower Inn** Wales
120 K5 **Gowganda** Ontario Canada
14 D3 **Gowna, L** Ireland
99 M7 **Gowrie** Iowa U.S.A.
131 F2 **Goya** Argentina
127 N4 **Goyave** Guadeloupe W Indies
138 C2 **Goyder** *R* N Terr Australia
140 D2 **Goyder** *R* N Terr Australia
138 E2 **Goyder Lagoon** South Australia Australia
123 M3 **Goyelle, L** Quebec Canada
128 C6 **Goyllarisquizga** Peru
47 L4 **Göynük** Turkey
61 P6 **Goyō-zan** *mt* Japan
86 D3 **Goz-Beïda** Chad
66 C4 **Gozha Co** *L* China
43 F12 **Gozo** *isld* Malta
86 G2 **Goz Regeb** Sudan
89 D9 **Graaff Reinet** S Africa
36 E5 **Graben-Neudorf** Germany
85 C8 **Grabo** Ivory Coast
46 F9 **Graboúsa** *isld* Crete Greece
55 F4 **Grabovo** Kazakhstan
33 O6 **Grabow** Germany
33 P6 **Grabow** Mecklenburg-Vorpommern Germany
33 P8 **Grabow** Sachsen-Anhalt Germany
31 L4 **Grabów** Poland
42 G4 **Gračac** Croatia
48 E6 **Gračanica** Bosnia-Herzegovina
21 O7 **Graçay** France
101 O7 **Grace** Idaho U.S.A.
98 H2 **Grace City** North Dakota U.S.A.
121 O6 **Gracefield** Quebec Canada
143 C10 **Grace, L** W Australia Australia
122 G1 **Grace L** Labrador, Nfld Canada
107 M6 **Gracemont** Oklahoma U.S.A.
141 K2 **Graceville** *dist* Brisbane, Qnsld Australia
111 L11 **Graceville** Florida U.S.A.
98 K4 **Graceville** Minnesota U.S.A.
110 J5 **Gracey** Kentucky U.S.A.
38 O8 **Grad** Slovenia
48 E6 **Gradačac** Bosnia-Herzegovina
129 H5 **Gradaús, Serra dos** *mts* Brazil
26 H5 **Graddis** Norway
16 D2 **Gradefes** Spain
46 E3 **Gradeska Pl** *mt* Macedonia Yugoslavia
48 H5 **Grădistea Muncelului** Romania
33 S9 **Graditz** Germany
70 P10 **Gradjagan** Java
42 E3 **Grado** Italy
16 C1 **Grado** Spain
46 E3 **Gradsko** Macedonia Yugoslavia
111 E7 **Grady** Arkansas U.S.A.
108 D1 **Grady** New Mexico U.S.A.
28 A5 **Grådyb** *chan* Denmark
102 D2 **Graeagle** California U.S.A.
28 C5 **Grædstrup** Denmark
28 H7 **Grænge** Denmark
28 J4 **Græsted** Denmark
99 M6 **Graettinger** Iowa U.S.A.
37 P6 **Grafenau** Germany
37 L4 **Gräfenberg** Germany
33 Q9 **Gräfenhainichen** Germany
37 K2 **Gräfenroda** Germany
38 M5 **Grafenschlag** Austria
37 L2 **Gräfenthal** Germany
37 K1 **Gräfentonna** Germany
37 M4 **Grafenwöhr** Germany
38 N5 **Grafenwörth** Austria
36 D6 **Graffenstaden** Germany
Gräfinau *see* **Angstedt-Gräfinau**
37 O6 **Grafling** Germany
109 J3 **Graford** Texas U.S.A.
32 F10 **Grafrath** Germany
36 C2 **Grafschaft** Germany
139 L3 **Grafton** New South Wales Australia
110 F3 **Grafton** Illinois U.S.A.
95 O4 **Grafton** New York U.S.A.
98 J1 **Grafton** North Dakota U.S.A.
94 E5 **Grafton** Ohio U.S.A.
94 G7 **Grafton** West Virginia U.S.A.
99 T6 **Grafton** Wisconsin U.S.A.
141 H3 **Grafton, C** Queensland Australia
133 C8 **Grafton, Is** Chile
103 K3 **Grafton, Mt** Nevada U.S.A.
141 H3 **Grafton Pass** Gt Barrier Reef Australia
45 R8 **Gragnano** Italy
117 M7 **Graham** *R* British Columbia Canada
119 N1 **Graham** Ontario Canada
109 J2 **Graham** Texas U.S.A.
117 G9 **Graham I** British Columbia Canada
115 K2 **Graham I** Northwest Territories Canada
118 C2 **Graham L** Alberta Canada
95 T2 **Graham L** Maine U.S.A.
146 C4 **Graham Land** *pen* Antarctica
103 P9 **Graham, Mt** Arizona U.S.A.
89 E9 **Grahamstown** S Africa
95 N5 **Grahamsville** New York U.S.A.
42 J6 **Grahovo** Montenegro Yugoslavia
42 A3 **Graie, Alpi** Italy
14 E4 **Graigue** Ireland
107 K2 **Grainfield** Kansas U.S.A.
118 D7 **Grainger** Alberta Canada
98 E9 **Grainton** Nebraska U.S.A.
129 J5 **Grajau** Brazil
31 N2 **Grajewo** Poland
52 H6 **Grakhovo** Russian Federation
16 B4 **Gralheira, Sa** *mts* Portugal
28 C6 **Gram** Denmark
46 F1 **Gramada** Bulgaria
18 G8 **Gramat** France
47 J2 **Gramatikovo** Bulgaria
32 H7 **Gramke** Germany
43 F11 **Grammichele** Sicily
Grammont *see* **Geraardsbergen**
33 R4 **Grammow** Germany
15 F3 **Grampian** *reg* Scotland
15 D4 **Grampian Mt** Scotland
138 F6 **Grampians** *mts* Victoria Australia
25 G3 **Gramsbergen** Netherlands
46 D4 **Gramsh** Albania
33 U6 **Gramzow** Germany
44 B3 **Grana** *R* Italy
126 G10 **Granada** Colombia
125 M4 **Granada** Nicaragua
16 E7 **Granada** Spain
16 E7 **Granada** *prov* Spain
106 H3 **Granada** Colorado U.S.A.
16 C4 **Granadilla** Spain
133 D7 **Gran Altiplanicie Central** *plain* Argentina
14 D3 **Granard** Ireland
45 K2 **Granarolo dell'Emilia** Italy
38 G7 **Granat-Spitze** *mt* Austria
133 D7 **Gran Baja** *hills* Argentina
131 C7 **Gran Bajo Salitroso** *salt lake* Argentina
109 K3 **Granbury** Texas U.S.A.
121 S7 **Granby** Quebec Canada
106 E1 **Granby** Colorado U.S.A.
110 B5 **Granby** Missouri U.S.A.
98 A9 **Granby, L** Colorado U.S.A.
85 A3 **Gran Canaria** *isld* Canary Is
40 B2 **Grancey** France
133 E3 **Gran Chaco** *reg* Argentina
127 O2 **Gran Couva** Trinidad
111 E12 **Grand** *R* Louisiana U.S.A.
99 M9 **Grand** *R* Missouri U.S.A.
98 E4 **Grand** *R* South Dakota U.S.A.
20 H6 **Grand-Auverne** France
119 P1 **Grand B** Ontario Canada
113 J11 **Grand Bahama** *isld* Bahamas
123 R6 **Grand Bank** Newfoundland Canada
90 E4 **Grand Banks of Nfld** Atlantic Oc
85 D8 **Grand Bassam** Ivory Coast
122 F8 **Grand Bay** New Brunswick Canada
119 V8 **Grand Beach** Manitoba Canada
119 V8 **Grand Beach Prov. Park** Manitoba Canada
120 J9 **Grand Bend** Ontario Canada
94 D4 **Grand Blanc** Michigan U.S.A.
19 Q13 **Grand Bornand** France
127 N5 **Grand Bourg** Guadeloupe W Indies
123 O6 **Grand Bruit** Newfoundland Canada
127 J4 **Grand Caicos** *isld* Turks & Caicos Is
21 H3 **Grandcamp-Maisy** France
65 D7 **Grand Canal** China
14 D3 **Grand Canal** Ireland
111 C9 **Grand Cane** Louisiana U.S.A.
19 Q17 **Grand Cañon du Verdon** France
103 M5 **Grand Canyon** *gorge* Arizona U.S.A.
103 M5 **Grand Canyon Nat. Park** Arizona U.S.A.
103 M5 **Grand Canyon Village** Arizona U.S.A.
113 J10 **Grand Cays** *islds* Bahamas
118 G4 **Grand Centre** Alberta Canada
85 C8 **Grand Cess** Liberia
20 E6 **Grand Champ** France
20 G7 **Grand-champ** France
111 D12 **Grand Cheniere** Louisiana U.S.A.
19 P13 **Grand Colombier** *mt* France
100 F2 **Grand Coulee** Washington U.S.A.
21 N3 **Grand Couronne** France
21 O2 **Grandcourt** France
127 N4 **Grand Cul de Sac Marin** *B* Guadeloupe W Indies
128 C6 **Grande** *R* Peru
131 G3 **Grande** *R* Uruguay
122 G6 **Grande-Anse** New Brunswick Canada
127 O4 **Grande Anse** Guadeloupe W Indies
133 D8 **Grande, B** Argentina
121 U4 **Grande-Baie** Quebec Canada
45 M2 **Grande Bonificazione Ferrarese** Italy
20 F7 **Grande Brière** *reg* France
83 K14 **Grande Brûlé** Réunion Indian Oc
19 P14 **Grande Chartreuse** *mts* France
133 D5 **Grande Colorado** *R* Argentina
18 H8 **Grande Combe, la** France
87 G10 **Grande Comore** *isld* Comoros
131 H2 **Grande, Coxilha** *mt* Brazil
131 G4 **Grande, Cuchilla** *ra* Uruguay
129 G4 **Grande do Curuai, L** Brazil
122 H5 **Grande Grève** Quebec Canada
129 K8 **Grande, I** Brazil
20 C4 **Grande, I** France
45 M3 **Grande, M** *mt* Italy
128 F7 **Grande, Monte** *mts* Bolivia
128 F7 **Grande O'Guapay** *R* Bolivia
117 O8 **Grande Prairie** Alberta Canada
127 M2 **Grande, R** Jamaica
86 B2 **Grand Erg de Bilma** Niger
85 E2 **Grand Erg Occidental** *desert* Algeria
122 H5 **Grande Rivière** Quebec Canada
127 P1 **Grande Rivière** Trinidad
127 L4 **Grande Rivière** Martinique W Indies
127 H5 **Grande Rivière du Nord** Haiti
100 H4 **Grande Ronde** *R* Oregon U.S.A.
122 C5 **Grandes Bergeronnes** Quebec Canada
21 M2 **Grandes Dalles, les** France
129 K5 **Grande, Serra** *mts* Brazil
121 S6 **Grandes Piles** Quebec Canada
21 N2 **Grandes Ventes, les** France
123 L7 **Grand Etang** C Breton I, Nova Scotia
127 P5 **Grand Etang** *L* Grenada
127 N4 **Grande Terre** *isld* Guadeloupe W Indies
122 G4 **Grande Vallée** Quebec Canada
127 N3 **Grande Vigie,Pte.de la** Guadeloupe W Indies
122 E6 **Grand Falls** New Brunswick Canada
123 R5 **Grand Falls** Newfoundland Canada
103 N6 **Grand Falls** Arizona U.S.A.
108 E4 **Grandfalls** Texas U.S.A.
112 F1 **Grandfather Mt** North Carolina U.S.A.
107 M7 **Grandfield** Oklahoma U.S.A.
100 G1 **Grand Forks** British Columbia Canada
98 J2 **Grand Forks** North Dakota U.S.A.
22 C1 **Grand Fort Philippe** France
20 G6 **Grand Fougeray, le** France
95 N4 **Grand Gorge** New York U.S.A.
127 J5 **Grand Gosier** Haiti
22 K3 **Grand-Halleux** Belgium
122 F9 **Grand Harbour** New Brunswick Canada
99 U6 **Grand Haven** Michigan U.S.A.
111 G11 **Grand I** Louisiana U.S.A.
99 U3 **Grand I** Michigan U.S.A.
98 H9 **Grand I** Nebraska U.S.A.
121 M9 **Grand I** New York U.S.A.
113 F8 **Grandin** Florida U.S.A.
110 F5 **Grandin** Missouri U.S.A.
98 J2 **Grandin** North Dakota U.S.A.
117 O3 **Grandin, Lac** Northwest Territories Canada
111 G12 **Grand Isle** Louisiana U.S.A.
95 O2 **Grand Isle** Vermont U.S.A.
131 F7 **Grand Jason** *isld* Falkland Is
99 M7 **Grand Junct** Iowa U.S.A.
106 B2 **Grand Junction** Colorado U.S.A.
94 A4 **Grand Junction** Michigan U.S.A.
110 G6 **Grand Junction** Tennessee U.S.A.
101 N3 **Grand Kohrs Ranch Nat. Hist. Site** Montana U.S.A.
122 E8 **Grand L** New Brunswick Canada
123 P4 **Grand L** Newfoundland Canada
94 D1 **Grand L** Michigan U.S.A.
94 C6 **Grand L** Ohio U.S.A.
122 F2 **Grand Lac Germain** Quebec Canada
106 E1 **Grand Lake** Colorado U.S.A.
111 C11 **Grand Lake** Louisiana U.S.A.
95 S7 **Grand Lakes L** Maine U.S.A.
94 C4 **Grand Ledge** Michigan U.S.A.
20 G7 **Grand Lieu, Lac de** France
28 H5 **Grandløse** Denmark
95 S7 **Grand L Seboeis** Maine U.S.A.
21 L6 **Grand-Lucé, le** France
99 V3 **Grand Marais** Michigan U.S.A.
99 Q2 **Grand Marais** Minnesota U.S.A.
111 M13 **Grand Marais State Park** St Louis
121 S6 **Grand-Mère** Quebec Canada
106 C2 **Grand Mesa** Colorado U.S.A.
122 E2 **Grandmesnil, L** Quebec Canada
117 P10 **Grand Mt** British Columbia Canada
123 R2 **Grandois** Newfoundland Canada
16 B6 **Grândola** Portugal
16 B6 **Grândola, Sa. de** *mt* Portugal
117 E6 **Grand Pacific Glacier** British Colombia Canada
110 C2 **Grand Pass** Missouri U.S.A.
99 R2 **Grand Portage** Minnesota U.S.A.
109 L3 **Grand Prairie** Texas U.S.A.
109 N9 **Grand Prairie** Texas U.S.A.
22 H5 **Grandpré** France

180 **Grand Pressigny, le — Guanajay**

21 M8 **Grand Pressigny, le** France
21 N3 **Grand Quevilly** France
94 F5 **Grand R** Ohio U.S.A.
119 S5 **Grand Rapids** Manitoba Canada
94 B4 **Grand Rapids** Michigan U.S.A.
99 N2 **Grand Rapids** Minnesota U.S.A.
22 G3 **Grandrieu** Belgium
18 H8 **Grandrieu** France
123 M8 **Grand River** C Breton I, Nova Scotia
99 N9 **Grand River** Iowa U.S.A.
100 B4 **Grand Ronde** Oregon U.S.A.
127 P5 **Grand Roy** Grenada
42 A3 **Grand St. Bernard, Col du** *pass* Switz/Italy
109 M3 **Grand Saline** Texas U.S.A.
129 H3 **Grand Santi** Fr Guiana
40 E4 **Grandson** Switzerland
111 G12 **Grand Terre Is** Louisiana U.S.A.
101 P6 **Grand Teton** *mt* Wyoming U.S.A.
101 P6 **Grand Teton Nat. Park** Wyoming U.S.A.
127 J4 **Grand Turk I** Turks & Caicos Is
106 B2 **Grand Valley** Colorado U.S.A.
119 R7 **Grandview** Manitoba Canada
100 J7 **Grand View** Idaho U.S.A.
110 B3 **Grandview** Missouri U.S.A.
109 K3 **Grandview** Texas U.S.A.
100 F3 **Grandview** Washington U.S.A.
94 B4 **Grandville** Michigan U.S.A.
36 B7 **Grandvillers** France
21 O2 **Grandvilliers** France
103 L5 **Grand Wash** *creek* Arizona U.S.A.
103 L6 **Grand Wash Cliffs** Arizona U.S.A.
19 N15 **Grâne** France
26 F6 **Grane** Norway
17 G3 **Grañén** Spain
44 B2 **Granero** *mt* Italy
121 N5 **Granet, L** Quebec Canada
14 C4 **Graney, L** Ireland
27 G11 **Grangarde** Sweden
58 D4 **Grangca** China
27 H11 **Grängeberg** Sweden
127 H1 **Grange Hill** Jamaica
40 E5 **Grange, Mont de** *mt* France
12 E1 **Grangemouth** Scotland
99 P9 **Granger** Missouri U.S.A.
109 K5 **Granger** Texas U.S.A.
100 E3 **Granger** Washington U.S.A.
101 Q8 **Granger** Wyoming U.S.A.
36 B7 **Granges-sur-Vologne** France
100 J4 **Grangeville** Idaho U.S.A.
26 J8 **Graninge** Sweden
107 L7 **Granite** Oklahoma U.S.A.
100 G5 **Granite** Oregon U.S.A.
98 A8 **Granite** Wyoming U.S.A.
117 L10 **Granite Bay** British Columbia Canada
111 M12 **Granite City** St Louis
110 F3 **Granite City** Illinois U.S.A.
99 L5 **Granite Falls** Minnesota U.S.A.
112 F2 **Granite Falls** North Carolina U.S.A.
100 D1 **Granite Falls** Washington U.S.A.
116 N7 **Granite I** Alaska U.S.A.
99 T3 **Granite I** Michigan U.S.A.
100 H9 **Granite Mt** Nevada U.S.A.
103 J7 **Granite Mts** California U.S.A.
143 D7 **Granite Peak** W Australia Australia
102 H6 **Granite Peak** California U.S.A.
100 H8 **Granite Peak** *mt* Nevada U.S.A.
101 Q4 **Granite Pk** Montana U.S.A.
101 M9 **Granite Pk** Utah U.S.A.
101 R7 **Granite Pk** Wyoming U.S.A.
99 T3 **Granite Pt** Michigan U.S.A.
116 Q6 **Granite Range** Alaska U.S.A.
100 F9 **Granite Range** Nevada U.S.A.
140 B5 **Granites, The** *pk* N Terr Australia
112 F4 **Graniteville** South Carolina U.S.A.
130 G9 **Granito** Brazil
144 C4 **Granity** New Zealand
129 K4 **Granja** Brazil
127 J5 **Granja, Pta. de la** Dominican Rep
27 J14 **Grankullavik** Sweden
133 D6 **Gran Laguna Salada** *L* Argentina
118 F9 **Granlea** Alberta Canada
133 E6 **Gran Lorenzo** Argentina
26 G8 **Granlunda** Sweden
124 F3 **Gran Morelos** Mexico
27 G13 **Gränna** Sweden
111 B7 **Grannis** Arkansas U.S.A.
98 E1 **Grano** North Dakota U.S.A.
17 J3 **Granollers** Spain
42 A3 **Gran Paradiso** *mt* Italy
133 E5 **Gran Pico** Argentina
42 D2 **Gran Pilastro** *mt* Italy/Austria
133 E4 **Gran Pinto** Argentina
44 B2 **Gran Queyron** *mt* Italy/France
133 D5 **Gran Roca** Argentina
42 F6 **Gran Sasso d'Italia** Italy
33 S6 **Gransee** Germany
120 D2 **Grant** Ontario Canada
113 G10 **Grant** Florida U.S.A.
99 M8 **Grant** Iowa U.S.A.
94 B3 **Grant** Michigan U.S.A.
101 M4 **Grant** Montana U.S.A.
98 E9 **Grant** Nebraska U.S.A.
107 P8 **Grant** Oklahoma U.S.A.
99 M9 **Grant City** Missouri U.S.A.
143 D7 **Grant Duff Ra** W Australia Australia
9 F2 **Grantham** England
146 B9 **Grant I** *isld* Antarctica
140 C1 **Grant I** N Terr Australia
117 P3 **Grant L** Northwest Territories Canada
116 E4 **Grantley Hbr** Alaska U.S.A.
143 E8 **Grant, Mt** W Australia Australia
120 J9 **Granton** Ontario Canada
13 E2 **Granton** Scotland
99 Q5 **Granton** Wisconsin U.S.A.
15 E3 **Grantown on Spey** Scotland
142 E4 **Grant Ra** W Australia Australia
103 J3 **Grant Ra** Nevada U.S.A.
26 K7 **Granträsk** Sweden
116 M6 **Grants** Alaska U.S.A.
106 C6 **Grants** New Mexico U.S.A.
99 O4 **Grantsburg** Wisconsin U.S.A.
101 L3 **Grantsdale** Montana U.S.A.
13 F2 **Grantshouse** Scotland
100 B7 **Grants Pass** Oregon U.S.A.
101 N9 **Grantsville** Utah U.S.A.
94 F8 **Grantsville** West Virginia U.S.A.
111 M8 **Grantville** Georgia U.S.A.
20 G4 **Granville** France
99 R8 **Granville** Illinois U.S.A.
99 L7 **Granville** Iowa U.S.A.
95 O3 **Granville** New York U.S.A.
98 F1 **Granville** North Dakota U.S.A.
94 E6 **Granville** Ohio U.S.A.
94 K6 **Granville** Pennsylvania U.S.A.
122 G9 **Granville Ferry** Nova Scotia Canada
133 E5 **Gran Villegas** Argentina
119 R2 **Granville L** Manitoba Canada
33 P6 **Granzin** Germany
130 G5 **Grão Mogol** Brazil
109 M4 **Grapeland** Texas U.S.A.
102 F7 **Grapevine** California U.S.A.
109 N8 **Grapevine** Texas U.S.A.
109 K3 **Grapevine Res** Texas U.S.A.
42 D3 **Grappa, Monte** *mt* Italy
126 G5 **Grappler Bk** Caribbean
27 H11 **Gräsberg** Sweden
32 M8 **Grasdorf** Germany
87 F10 **Graskop** S Africa
114 H5 **Gras,L.de** Northwest Territories Canada
13 E5 **Grasmere** England
27 K11 **Gräsö** Sweden
95 M2 **Grass** *R* New York U.S.A.
101 R6 **Grass Creek** Wyoming U.S.A.
44 B4 **Grasse** France
121 M3 **Grasset, L** Quebec Canada
13 G5 **Grassington** England
100 C8 **Grass Lake** California U.S.A.
108 F2 **Grassland** Texas U.S.A.
118 K9 **Grasslands Nat Park** Saskatchewan Canada
145 E4 **Grassmere, L** New Zealand
143 D10 **Grass Patch** W Australia Australia
119 T3 **Grass R** Manitoba Canada
101 R2 **Grassrange** Montana U.S.A.
119 Q4 **Grass River Prov. Park** Manitoba Canada
102 C2 **Grass Valley** California U.S.A.
100 E4 **Grass Valley** Oregon U.S.A.
139 G8 **Grassy** Tasmania Australia
98 C2 **Grassy Butte** North Dakota U.S.A.
126 F3 **Grassy Cr** Andros Bahamas
118 G7 **Grassy Island L** Alberta Canada
94 G8 **Grassy Knob** *mt* West Virginia U.S.A.
118 F9 **Grassy Lake** Alberta Canada
28 D7 **Gråsten** Denmark
27 F13 **Grästorp** Sweden
26 J3 **Gratangen** Norway
123 U5 **Grate's Cove** Newfoundland Canada
99 R7 **Gratiot** Wisconsin U.S.A.
94 C7 **Gratis** Ohio U.S.A.
26 L6 **Gråträsk** Sweden
28 D4 **Grauballe** Denmark
41 K4 **Graubünden** *canton* Switzerland
18 H9 **Grau-du-Roi,le** France
17 H2 **Graus** Spain
131 H2 **Gravata** Brazil
25 E5 **Grave** Netherlands
118 L9 **Gravelbourg** Saskatchewan Canada
22 C2 **Gravelines** France
21 H5 **Gravelle, la** France
87 F10 **Gravelotte** S Africa
121 L8 **Gravenhurst** Ontario Canada
36 F3 **Grävenwiesbach** Germany
101 L3 **Grave Pk** Idaho U.S.A.
18 E7 **Grave, Pte de** *C* France
139 K3 **Gravesend** New South Wales Australia
9 G5 **Gravesend** England
19 N17 **Graveson** France
110 B5 **Gravette** Arkansas U.S.A.
21 N3 **Gravigny** France
21 L2 **Graville** France
43 G8 **Gravina di Puglia** Italy
99 M9 **Gravity** Iowa U.S.A.
28 D3 **Gravlev** Denmark
26 E7 **Gravvik** Norway
99 V5 **Grawn** Michigan U.S.A.
119 N8 **Gray** Saskatchewan Canada
19 J5 **Gray** France
112 D4 **Gray** Georgia U.S.A.
95 R3 **Gray** Maine U.S.A.
108 D7 **Gray** Oklahoma U.S.A.
100 A3 **Grayland** Washington U.S.A.
117 L6 **Grayling** *R* British Columbia Canada
94 C2 **Grayling** Michigan U.S.A.
116 R3 **Grayling Fk.** *R* Alaska U.S.A.
13 F5 **Grayrigg** England
100 A3 **Grays Harbor** Washington U.S.A.
101 O6 **Grays L** Idaho U.S.A.
119 P8 **Grayson** Saskatchewan Canada
94 E8 **Grayson** Kentucky U.S.A.
111 D9 **Grayson** Louisiana U.S.A.
120 A2 **Grayson L** Ontario Canada
106 E2 **Grays Pk** Colorado U.S.A.
94 B1 **Grays Reef** Michigan U.S.A.
100 B3 **Grays River** Washington U.S.A.
9 G5 **Grays Thurrock** England
111 K11 **Grayton Beach** Florida U.S.A.
110 H3 **Grayville** Illinois U.S.A.
54 G6 **Grayvoron** Russian Federation
38 M7 **Graz** Austria
16 D8 **Grazalema** Spain
46 E2 **Grdelica** Serbia Yugoslavia
13 G6 **Greasbrough** England
117 M4 **Greasy L** Northwest Territories Canada
138 B5 **Great Australian Bight** Australia
9 G4 **Great Baddow** England
113 J12 **Great Bahama Bank** Bahamas
145 E2 **Great Barrier I** New Zealand
136 **Great Barrier Reef** Australia
141 H3 **Great Barrier Reef Marine Park** Queensland Australia
95 O4 **Great Barrington** Massachusetts U.S.A.
141 H4 **Great Basalt Wall** Queensland Australia
103 H1 **Great Basin** Nevada U.S.A.
117 L3 **Great Bear** *R* Northwest Territories Canada
114 H4 **Great Bear L** Northwest Territories Canada
107 M3 **Great Bend** Kansas U.S.A.
98 K3 **Great Bend** North Dakota U.S.A.
89 A9 **Great Berg** *R* S Africa
15 B2 **Great Bernera** *isld* Scotland
14 A4 **Great Blasket I.** Ireland
122 F3 **Great Boule I** Quebec Canada
123 R2 **Great Brehat** Newfoundland Canada
8 D1 **Great Budworth** England
123 Q5 **Great Burnt L.** Newfoundland Canada
89 A7 **Great Bushman Land** *reg* S Africa
94 J7 **Great Cacapon** West Virginia U.S.A.
9 F2 **Great Casterton** England
9 G3 **Great Chesterford** England
123 T7 **Great Colinet I.** Newfoundland Canada
12 D2 **Great Cumbrae** *isld* Scotland
9 F2 **Great Dalby** England
118 K6 **Great Deer** Saskatchewan Canada
101 S9 **Great Divide** Colorado U.S.A.
139 **Great Dividing Ra** Australia
13 H5 **Great Driffield** England
120 H7 **Great Duck I.** Ontario Canada
146 E12 **Greater Antarctica** Antarctica
Greater Khingan Range *see* **Da Hinggan Ling**
13 F6 **Greater Manchester** *co* England
145 D1 **Great Exhibition Bay** New Zealand
126 F3 **Great Exuma** *isld* Bahamas
101 O2 **Great Falls** Montana U.S.A.
112 G3 **Great Falls** South Carolina U.S.A.
110 L6 **Great Falls Dam** Tennessee U.S.A.
110 L6 **Great Falls L** Tennessee U.S.A.
89 E9 **Great Fish** *R* S Africa
6 N6 **Great Fisher Bank** North Sea
89 E9 **Great Fish Pt.** *lighthouse* S Africa
145 E4 **Greatford** New Zealand
127 K3 **Great Goat I** Jamaica
9 F2 **Great Gonerby** England
113 K11 **Great Guana Cay** *isld* Bahamas
9 F5 **Greatham** England
126 F2 **Great Harbour Cay** *isld* Bahamas
144 A6 **Great I** New Zealand
145 D1 **Great I** New Zealand
126 H4 **Great Inagua** *isld* Bahamas
Great Indian Desert *see* **Thar**
113 H11 **Great Isaac I** Bahamas
89 A6 **Great Karas Berg** *mts* Namibia
89 C9 **Great Karoo** *reg* S Africa
89 E9 **Great Kei** *R* S Africa
141 K6 **Great Keppel I** Queensland Australia
139 H8 **Great L** Tasmania Australia
112 K3 **Great L** North Carolina U.S.A.
8 D3 **Great Malvern** England
145 E2 **Great Mercury I** New Zealand
9 F4 **Great Missenden** England
136 J3 **Great NE Channel** Australia/Papua New Guinea
69 A9 **Great Nicobar** *isld* Nicobar Is
9 F4 **Great Offley** England
8 C1 **Great Ormes Head** Wales
95 P6 **Great Peconic B** Long I, New York U.S.A.
127 J3 **Great Pedro Bluff** Jamaica
95 T2 **Great Pond** Maine U.S.A.
95 R5 **Great Pt** Massachusetts U.S.A.
122 G10 **Great Pubnico L** Nova Scotia Canada
127 J2 **Great R** Jamaica
88 E5 **Great Ruaha** *R* Tanzania
95 N3 **Great Sacandaga L** New York U.S.A.
113 J11 **Great Sale Cay** Bahamas
101 N8 **Great Salt L** Utah U.S.A.
101 M9 **Great Salt L.Des** Utah U.S.A.
106 E4 **Great Sand Dunes Nat.Mon** Colorado U.S.A.
118 H8 **Great Sand Hills** Saskatchewan Canada
142 D5 **Great Sandy Desert** W Australia Australia
141 L7 **Great Sandy I** Queensland Australia
9 E5 **Great Shefford** England
9 G3 **Great Shelford** England
89 G4 **Great Shingwidzi** *R* S Africa
114 H5 **Great Slave L** Northwest Territories Canada
112 D2 **Great Smoky Mts** Tenn/N Carolina U.S.A.
117 L7 **Great Snow Mt** British Columbia Canada
7 D13 **Great Sole Bank** Atlantic Oc
95 O6 **Great South Bay** Long I, New York U.S.A.
113 K12 **Great Stirrup Cay** *isld* Bahamas
8 B6 **Great Torrington** England
87 C10 **Great Ums** Namibia
138 B3 **Great Victoria Desert** South Australia Australia
122 J8 **Great Village** Nova Scotia Canada
Great Wall *China Base* Antarctica *see* **Chang Cheng**
9 G4 **Great Waltham** England
95 U2 **Great Wass I** Maine U.S.A.
139 H8 **Great Western Tiers** Tasmania Australia
68 C7 **Great West Torres I** Burma
13 G5 **Great Whernside** *mt* England
9 H2 **Great Yarmouth** England
27 E13 **Grebbestad** Sweden
36 G2 **Grebenau** Germany
36 G3 **Grebenhain** Germany
54 D6 **Grebenka** Ukraine
32 K10 **Grebenstein** Germany
38 K7 **Grebenzen** *mt* Austria
85 F4 **Greboun, Mt** Niger
43 F8 **Greco, Torre del** Italy
37 L5 **Greding** Germany
16 D4 **Gredos, Sa. de** *mts* Spain
28 B6 **Gredstedbro** Denmark
46 E6 **Greece** *rep* S Europe
98 B9 **Greeley** Colorado U.S.A.
98 H8 **Greeley** Nebraska U.S.A.
115 L1 **Greely Fiord** Northwest Territories Canada
50 F1 **Greem Bell, Ostrov** *isld* Russian Federation
107 O2 **Green** Kansas U.S.A.
112 E2 **Green** *R* North Carolina U.S.A.
113 G11 **Greenacres City** Florida U.S.A.
95 M8 **Greenbackville** Maryland U.S.A.
99 T5 **Green Bay** Wisconsin U.S.A.
94 G8 **Greenbrier** *R* West Virginia U.S.A.
94 D2 **Greenbush** Michigan U.S.A.
98 K1 **Greenbush** Minnesota U.S.A.
143 B10 **Greenbushes** W Australia Australia
139 K6 **Green Cape** New South Wales Australia
110 K2 **Greencastle** Indiana U.S.A.
94 K7 **Greencastle** Pennsylvania U.S.A.
126 F2 **Green Cay** *isld* Bahamas
99 O9 **Green City** Missouri U.S.A.
118 B4 **Green Court** Alberta Canada
113 F8 **Green Cove Springs** Florida U.S.A.
32 L9 **Greene** Germany
99 O7 **Greene** Iowa U.S.A.
95 M4 **Greene** New York U.S.A.
98 E1 **Greene** North Dakota U.S.A.
143 G6 **Greene, Mt** W Australia Australia
112 E1 **Greeneville** Tennessee U.S.A.
102 C5 **Greenfield** California U.S.A.
110 F2 **Greenfield** Illinois U.S.A.
94 B7 **Greenfield** Indiana U.S.A.
99 M8 **Greenfield** Iowa U.S.A.
95 P4 **Greenfield** Massachusetts U.S.A.
110 C4 **Greenfield** Missouri U.S.A.
94 D7 **Greenfield** Ohio U.S.A.
107 M6 **Greenfield** Oklahoma U.S.A.
110 H5 **Greenfield** Tennessee U.S.A.
110 C5 **Green Forest** Arkansas U.S.A.
143 B9 **Green Head** W Australia Australia
127 O2 **Green Hill** Trinidad
140 B1 **Greenhill I** N Terr Australia
143 B9 **Greenhills** W Australia Australia
144 B7 **Greenhills** New Zealand
102 F6 **Greenhorn Mts** California U.S.A.
141 H3 **Green I** Queensland Australia
143 B9 **Green I** W Australia Australia
123 Q2 **Green I** Newfoundland Canada
144 B7 **Green I** New Zealand
116 O6 **Green I** Alaska U.S.A.
121 Q4 **Greening** Quebec Canada
137 L2 **Green Is** Papua New Guinea
127 H1 **Green Island** Jamaica
144 C7 **Green Island** New Zealand
71 D5 **Green Island B** Philippines
144 A7 **Green Islets** New Zealand
117 N10 **Green L** British Columbia Canada
99 S6 **Green L** Wisconsin U.S.A.
118 K4 **Green Lake** Saskatchewan Canada
109 L7 **Green Lake** Texas U.S.A.
115 P2 **Greenland** *isld terr* Arctic
127 P6 **Greenland** Barbados
90 H1 **Greenland Basin** Arctic Oc
90 G2 **Greenland-Iceland Rise** N Atlantic Oc
144 B6 **Greenland Res** New Zealand
147 G10 **Greenland Sea** Arctic Oc
13 F2 **Greenlaw** Scotland
107 O2 **Greenleaf** Kansas U.S.A.
12 E1 **Greenloaning** Scotland
15 E5 **Green Lowther** *mt* Scotland
138 C5 **Greenly I** South Australia Australia
123 P2 **Greenly I** Quebec Canada
145 F3 **Greenmeadows** New Zealand
106 D2 **Green Mt Res** Colorado U.S.A.
95 O3 **Green Mts** Vermont U.S.A.
101 S7 **Green Mts** Wyoming U.S.A.
12 D2 **Greenock** Scotland
14 E2 **Greenore** Ireland
14 E4 **Greenore Pt** Ireland
143 A8 **Greenough** W Australia Australia
116 R2 **Greenough, Mt** Alaska U.S.A.
Greenpeace *Antarctic Base see* **Cape Evans**
112 G5 **Green Pond** South Carolina U.S.A.
95 P5 **Greenport** Long I, New York U.S.A.
122 D6 **Green R** New Brunswick Canada
101 Q8 **Green River** Wyoming U.S.A.
94 B9 **Green R. Res** Kentucky U.S.A.
111 J9 **Greensboro** Alabama U.S.A.
111 M11 **Greensboro** Florida U.S.A.
112 D4 **Greensboro** Georgia U.S.A.
112 H1 **Greensboro** North Carolina U.S.A.
95 P2 **Greensboro** Vermont U.S.A.
94 B7 **Greensburg** Indiana U.S.A.
107 L4 **Greensburg** Kansas U.S.A.
94 B9 **Greensburg** Kentucky U.S.A.
111 F11 **Greensburg** Louisiana U.S.A.
94 H6 **Greensburg** Pennsylvania U.S.A.
141 K2 **Greenslopes** *dist* Brisbane, Qnsld Australia
123 T4 **Greenspond** Newfoundland Canada
94 J7 **Green Spring** West Virginia U.S.A.
94 D5 **Green Springs** Ohio U.S.A.
99 O9 **Greentop** Missouri U.S.A.
94 B6 **Greentown** Indiana U.S.A.
113 K11 **Green Turtle Cay** *isld* Bahamas
110 H2 **Greenup** Illinois U.S.A.
141 H4 **Greenvale** Queensland Australia
85 C8 **Greenville** Liberia
111 K10 **Greenville** Alabama U.S.A.
100 E9 **Greenville** California U.S.A.
113 D7 **Greenville** Florida U.S.A.
110 G3 **Greenville** Illinois U.S.A.
110 J4 **Greenville** Kentucky U.S.A.
95 S1 **Greenville** Maine U.S.A.
94 B3 **Greenville** Michigan U.S.A.
111 E8 **Greenville** Mississippi U.S.A.
110 F4 **Greenville** Missouri U.S.A.
95 Q4 **Greenville** New Hampshire U.S.A.
95 N4 **Greenville** New York U.S.A.
112 K2 **Greenville** North Carolina U.S.A.
94 C6 **Greenville** Ohio U.S.A.
94 G5 **Greenville** Pennsylvania U.S.A.
112 E3 **Greenville** South Carolina U.S.A.
109 L2 **Greenville** Texas U.S.A.
94 H8 **Greenville** Virginia U.S.A.
119 N2 **Greenwater L** Ontario Canada
119 O6 **Greenwater L. Prov. Park** Saskatchewan Canada
119 S9 **Greenway** Manitoba Canada
98 G4 **Greenway** South Dakota U.S.A.
9 G5 **Greenwich** England
107 N4 **Greenwich** Kansas U.S.A.
95 O3 **Greenwich** New York U.S.A.
94 E5 **Greenwich** Ohio U.S.A.
103 N3 **Greenwich** Utah U.S.A.
100 G1 **Greenwood** British Columbia Canada
110 B6 **Greenwood** Arkansas U.S.A.
102 D3 **Greenwood** California U.S.A.
95 M8 **Greenwood** Delaware U.S.A.
94 A7 **Greenwood** Indiana U.S.A.
94 C10 **Greenwood** Kentucky U.S.A.
111 C9 **Greenwood** Louisiana U.S.A.
111 F8 **Greenwood** Mississippi U.S.A.
98 K9 **Greenwood** Nebraska U.S.A.
112 E3 **Greenwood** South Carolina U.S.A.
98 H7 **Greenwood** South Dakota U.S.A.
99 Q5 **Greenwood** Wisconsin U.S.A.
111 H8 **Greenwood Springs** Mississippi U.S.A.
100 J3 **Greer** Idaho U.S.A.
112 E3 **Greer** South Carolina U.S.A.
111 C7 **Greeson, L** Arkansas U.S.A.
32 F5 **Greetsiel** Germany
21 M5 **Greez** France
25 F6 **Grefrath** Germany
119 S9 **Gregg** Manitoba Canada
111 B9 **Greggton** Texas U.S.A.
118 F2 **Gregoire L** Alberta Canada
128 D5 **Gregório** *R* Brazil
98 G6 **Gregory** South Dakota U.S.A.
140 E4 **Gregory Downs** Queensland Australia
142 G5 **Gregory L** W Australia Australia
143 C7 **Gregory, L** W Australia Australia
141 G4 **Gregory Ra** Queensland Australia
142 D5 **Gregory Ra** W Australia Australia
113 L12 **Gregory Town** Bahamas
38 H8 **Greifenburg** Austria
41 J3 **Greifensee** *L* Switzerland
33 T6 **Greiffenberg** Germany
33 S4 **Greifswald** Germany
33 T4 **Greifswalder Bodden** Germany
33 T4 **Greifswalder Oie** *isld* Germany
38 K7 **Greimberg** *mt* Austria
38 L5 **Grein** Austria
41 J4 **Greina Pass** Switzerland
38 M5 **Greinerwald** *woods* Austria
37 L5 **Greisselbach** Germany
37 N2 **Greiz** Germany
52 E1 **Gremikha** Russian Federation
33 N4 **Gremsmühlen** Germany
28 F4 **Grenå** Denmark
127 P5 **Grenada** *isld* Lesser Antilles
100 C8 **Grenada** California U.S.A.
111 G8 **Grenada** Mississippi U.S.A.
18 E9 **Grenade** France
18 F9 **Grenade sur Garonne** France
127 O8 **Grenadines, The** *islds* Lesser Antilles
40 F3 **Grenchen** Switzerland
28 C5 **Grene** Denmark
28 F1 **Grenen** *C* Denmark
139 J5 **Grenfell** New South Wales Australia
119 P8 **Grenfell** Saskatchewan Canada
19 P14 **Grenoble** France
107 O4 **Grenola** Kansas U.S.A.
98 C1 **Grenora** North Dakota U.S.A.
26 S2 **Grense/Jakobselv** Norway
127 P5 **Grenville** Grenada
106 G5 **Grenville** New Mexico U.S.A.
98 J4 **Grenville** South Dakota U.S.A.
141 G1 **Grenville C** Queensland Australia
117 J9 **Grenville Chan** British Columbia Canada
117 L10 **Grenville, Mt** British Columbia Canada
19 P17 **Gréoux-les-Bains** France
33 Q9 **Greppin** Germany
33 Q4 **Gresenhorst** Germany
100 C4 **Gresham** Oregon U.S.A.
70 O9 **Gresik** Java
19 P15 **Gresse** France
19 Q13 **Grésy-sur-Isère** France
139 K5 **Greta** New South Wales Australia
.13 G5 **Greta Br** England
119 U9 **Gretna** Manitoba Canada
111 G12 **Gretna** Louisiana U.S.A.
111 J13 **Gretna** New Orleans, Louisiana U.S.A.
94 H10 **Gretna** Virginia U.S.A.
13 E3 **Gretna Green** Scotland
37 K1 **Greussen** Germany
45 K4 **Greve** Italy
25 A5 **Grevelingen** Netherlands
32 G8 **Greven** Germany
46 E4 **Grevená** Greece
36 B1 **Grevenbroich** Germany
32 L5 **Grevenkop** Germany
33 O5 **Grevesmühlen** Germany
27 F16 **Grevie** Sweden
29 K4 **Grevie** Sweden
28 H5 **Grevinge** Denmark
101 R5 **Greybull** Wyoming U.S.A.
140 D2 **Grey, C** N Terr Australia
101 Q4 **Greycliff** Montana U.S.A.
99 M4 **Grey Eagle** Minnesota U.S.A.
117 F4 **Grey Hunter Pk** Yukon Territory Canada
123 R3 **Grey I** Newfoundland Canada
123 R3 **Grey Is** Newfoundland Canada
144 C5 **Greymouth** New Zealand
123 Q5 **Grey R** Newfoundland Canada
141 G8 **Grey Ra** Qnsld/N S W
141 G8 **Grey Range** Queensland Australia
101 P6 **Greys** *R* Wyoming U.S.A.
143 A7 **Grey's Plains** W Australia Australia
13 F4 **Greystoke** England
101 R9 **Greystone** Colorado U.S.A.
14 E3 **Greystones** Ireland
145 E4 **Greytown** New Zealand
89 G7 **Greytown** S Africa
22 H2 **Grez-Doiceau** Belgium
21 J6 **Grez-en-Bouère** France
46 D4 **Griba** *mt* Albania
81 F11 **Gribb Seamount** Southern Oc
86 C4 **Gribingui** *R* Cent Afr Republic
52 D2 **Gridino** Russian Federation
102 C2 **Gridley** California U.S.A.
99 S9 **Gridley** Illinois U.S.A.
107 P3 **Gridley** Kansas U.S.A.
87 D11 **Griekwastad** S Africa
25 D2 **Griend** Netherlands
37 P7 **Griesbach** Germany
36 F4 **Griesheim** Germany
41 O3 **Gries im Sellrain** Austria
Griessen *see* **Klettgau**
25 F5 **Grieth** Germany
38 L8 **Griffen** Austria
111 M8 **Griffin** Georgia U.S.A.
113 F9 **Griffin, L** Florida U.S.A.
116 Q1 **Griffin Pt** Alaska U.S.A.
139 H5 **Griffith** New South Wales Australia
115 K3 **Griffith I** Northwest Territories Canada
110 E6 **Griffithville** Arkansas U.S.A.
112 K2 **Grifton** North Carolina U.S.A.
99 Q10 **Griggsville** Illinois U.S.A.
41 K6 **Grigna** *mt* Italy
19 N16 **Grignan** France
18 E8 **Grignols** France
48 M3 **Grigoriopol'** Moldavia
25 F2 **Grijpskerk** Netherlands
86 C4 **Grimari** Cent Afr Republic
19 Q18 **Grimaud** France
21 L8 **Grimaudière, la** France
48 K1 **Grimaylov** Ukraine
139 G8 **Grim, C** Tasmania Australia
102 C2 **Grimes** California U.S.A.
100 K5 **Grimes Pass** Idaho U.S.A.
33 R10 **Grimma** Germany
33 S4 **Grimmen** Germany
Grimmenthal *see* **Obermassfeld-Grimmenthal**
33 T7 **Grimnitzsee** Germany
121 L9 **Grimsby** Ontario Canada
13 H6 **Grimsby** England
41 H4 **Grimsel** *mt* Switzerland
28 S8 **Grimsey** *isld* Iceland
117 P7 **Grimshaw** Alberta Canada
27 C13 **Grimstad** Norway
28 B5 **Grimstrup** Denmark
28 R10 **Grindavik** Iceland
40 H4 **Grindelwald** Switzerland
28 C3 **Grinderslev** Denmark
28 B5 **Grindsted Å** Denmark
95 S8 **Grindstone** Maine U.S.A.
94 E2 **Grind Stone City** Michigan U.S.A.
123 L6 **Grindstone Island** Quebec Canada
119 U7 **Grindstone Prov. Park** Manitoba Canada
119 V7 **Grindstone Pt** Manitoba Canada
99 O8 **Grinnell** Iowa U.S.A.
107 K2 **Grinnell** Kansas U.S.A.
115 K2 **Grinnell Pen** Northwest Territories Canada
42 F2 **Grintavec** *mt* Slovenia
13 G5 **Grinton** England
26 C8 **Grip** *lighthouse* Norway
33 O6 **Grippel** Germany
89 F8 **Griqualand E** *reg* S Africa
89 C7 **Griqualand W** *reg* S Africa
40 F6 **Grisanche, Val** Italy
115 L2 **Grise Fiord** Northwest Territories Canada
45 L1 **Grisignano** Italy
69 F14 **Grisik** Sumatra
22 B2 **Gris Nez, C** France
18 F9 **Grisolles** France
27 K11 **Grisslehamn** Sweden
99 L8 **Griswold** Iowa U.S.A.
52 H4 **Griva** Russian Federation
21 P2 **Grivesnes** France
40 F6 **Grivola** *mt* Italy
33 P9 **Grizeline** Germany
85 D3 **Grizim** Algeria
117 N3 **Grizzly Bear Mt** Northwest Territories Canada
26 C9 **Grjotli** Norway
42 G4 **Grmeč Plan** Bosnia-Herzegovina
123 R3 **Groais I** Newfoundland Canada
33 S10 **Gröba** Germany
33 Q10 **Gröbers** Germany
27 M15 **Grobina** Latvia
9 E2 **Groby** England
33 P9 **Gröbzig** Germany
28 B7 **Gröde-Appelland** *isld* Germany
31 O2 **Gródek** Poland
31 K5 **Grodków** Poland
33 S10 **Grödlitz** Germany
31 O2 **Grodno** Belorussia
31 J3 **Grodzisk** Poland
31 M3 **Grodzisk Mazowiecki** Poland
89 C8 **Groen** *watercourse* S Africa
22 G2 **Groenendaal** Belgium
25 G4 **Groenlo** Netherlands
109 L4 **Groesbeck** Texas U.S.A.
25 E5 **Groesbeek** Netherlands
25 C3 **Groet** Netherlands
32 K8 **Grohnde** Germany
22 F3 **Groise, la** France
37 N1 **Groitzsch** Germany
20 D6 **Groix** France
20 D6 **Groix, I de** France
31 M4 **Grójec** Poland
43 C12 **Grombalia** Tunisia
28 C7 **Grønå** *R* Denmark
32 L8 **Gronau** Niedersachsen Germany
32 F8 **Gronau** Nordrhein-Westfalen Germany
28 B4 **Grønbjerg** Denmark
26 F7 **Grong** Norway
28 C4 **Grønhøj** Denmark
33 O9 **Gröningen** Germany
25 G2 **Groningen** Netherlands
25 F2 **Groningerwad** Netherlands
119 N5 **Gronlid** Saskatchewan Canada
115 P5 **Grønnedal** Greenland
26 F5 **Grönöy** Norway
27 K12 **Grönskär** *lighthouse* Sweden
27 H14 **Grönskåra** Sweden
28 J7 **Grønsund** *chan* Denmark
89 D9 **Groot** *R* S Africa
140 D2 **Groote Eylandt** *isld* N Terr Australia
25 F2 **Grootegast** Netherlands
89 B9 **Groot Swartberge** *mts* S Africa
89 C8 **Groot Tafelberg** *mt* S Africa
87 D11 **Grootvloer** *L* S Africa
89 B7 **Groot Vloer** S Africa
89 E9 **Groot Winterberg** *mt* S Africa
22 K4 **Grosbous** Luxembourg
20 G8 **Grosbreuil** France
127 O7 **Gros Islet** St Lucia
27 G14 **Grosjö** Sweden
123 P4 **Gros Morne** *pk* Newfoundland Canada
122 G4 **Gros Morne** Quebec Canada
127 H5 **Gros Morne** Haiti
127 L4 **Gros Morne** Martinique W Indies
123 P4 **Gros Morne Nat. Park** Newfoundland Canada
19 J6 **Grosne** *R* France
20 F3 **Grosnez Pt** Channel Is
41 M5 **Grosotto** Italy
123 P3 **Gros Pate** *pk* Newfoundland Canada
113 F7 **Gross** Florida U.S.A.
37 M4 **Gross Albershof** Germany
40 H4 **Gross Aletsch Gl** Switzerland
32 L10 **Grossalmerode** Germany
33 O9 **Gross Alsleben** Germany
33 P8 **Gross Ammensleben** Germany
37 P5 **Gross Arber** *mt* Germany
33 S8 **Grossbeeren** Germany
33 T8 **Grossbesten** Germany
33 M10 **Grossbodungen** Germany
37 O1 **Gross Bothen** Germany
36 G5 **Grossbottwar** Germany
37 L2 **Gross-Breitenbach** Germany
33 T7 **Gross-Dölln** Germany
37 M2 **Gross Ebersdorf** Germany
123 L6 **Grosse I** Madeleine Is, Quebec Canada
36 F2 **Grossenbuseck** Germany
37 K1 **Grossenehrich** Germany
33 O7 **Gross Engersen** Germany
33 T10 **Grossenhain** Germany
32 H7 **Grossenkneten** Germany
37 N2 **Grossenstein** Germany
127 N4 **Grosse Pointe** Guadeloupe W Indies
33 S10 **Grosse Röder** *R* Germany
42 D6 **Grosseto** Italy
51 N4 **Grossevichi** Russian Federation
36 D5 **Gross Eyberg** *mt* Germany
36 E3 **Gross Feldberg** *mt* Germany
33 T6 **Gross Fredenwalde** Germany
36 E4 **Gross-Gerau** Germany
33 M8 **Gross Gleidingen** Germany
38 G7 **Gross-Glockner** Austria
33 P6 **Gross-Godems** Germany
37 N1 **Gross Görschen** Germany
33 N5 **Gross Gronau** Germany
33 M5 **Gross Hansdorf** Germany
37 P2 **Gross Hartmannsdorf** Germany
32 F5 **Grossheide** Germany
37 M1 **Gross Heringen** Germany
33 M7 **Gross-Kain** Germany
36 E4 **Gross Karlbach** Germany
33 O4 **Gross Klützhöved** Germany
37 L2 **Gross Kochberg** Germany
33 Q10 **Gross Korbetha** Germany
33 T8 **Gross Köris** Germany
33 R8 **Gross Kreutz** Germany
37 N6 **Gross Laaber** *R* Germany
37 J4 **Gross-Langheim** Germany
36 H2 **Grosslüder** Germany
33 S8 **Gross-Machnow** Germany
37 M6 **Grossmehring** Germany
33 M7 **Gross-Oesingen** Germany
36 G4 **Grossostheim** Germany
33 M4 **Gross Plöner See** *L* Germany
37 P6 **Gross Rachel** *mt* Germany
38 L6 **Grossraming** Austria
32 M9 **Gross Rhüden** Germany
36 B5 **Grossrosseln** Germany
37 L1 **Gross Rudestedt** Germany
33 T7 **Gross Schönebeck** Germany
33 P7 **Gross Schwechten** Germany
33 T8 **Gross Selchower See** *L* Germany
33 N8 **Gross-Sisbeck** Germany
33 S6 **Gross Stechlinsee** *L* Germany
36 H6 **Gross Süssen** Germany
36 F4 **Gross-Umstadt** Germany
37 P2 **Gross Waltersdorf** Germany
33 P6 **Gross-Warnow** Germany
33 Q6 **Gross Welle** Germany
33 Q7 **Gross Wudicke** Germany
33 R5 **Gross Wüstenfelde** Germany
33 Q8 **Gross Wusterwitz** Germany
33 T7 **Gross Ziethen** Germany
36 F4 **Gross-Zimmern** Germany
36 B6 **Gros Tenquin** France
21 M3 **Gros Theil, le** France
42 F3 **Grosuplje** Slovenia
141 J5 **Grosvenor Downs** Queensland Australia
116 K7 **Grosvenor, L** Alaska U.S.A.
101 P6 **Gros Ventre Ra** Wyoming U.S.A.
32 J9 **Grotenberg** *mt* Germany
22 F2 **Grotenberge** Belgium
22 H1 **Grote Nete** *R* Belgium
95 Q5 **Groton** Connecticut U.S.A.
95 Q4 **Groton** Massachusetts U.S.A.
95 L4 **Groton** New York U.S.A.
98 H4 **Groton** South Dakota U.S.A.
95 P2 **Groton** Vermont U.S.A.
26 G4 **Grötöy** Norway
45 Q8 **Grotta Azzurra** Italy
45 O7 **Grotta delle Capre** Italy
22 J3 **Grotte-de-Han** Belgium
19 N16 **Grottes de St. Marcel** France
94 J8 **Grottoes** Virginia U.S.A.
36 F5 **Grotzingen** Germany
117 P8 **Grouard** Alberta Canada
20 G4 **Grouin, Pte.du** France
120 H4 **Groundhog** *R* Ontario Canada
101 M6 **Grouse** Idaho U.S.A.
101 M8 **Grouse Creek** Utah U.S.A.
25 E2 **Grouw** Netherlands
27 C13 **Grovane** Norway
107 Q5 **Grove** Oklahoma U.S.A.
94 E7 **Grove City** Ohio U.S.A.
94 G5 **Grove City** Pennsylvania U.S.A.
117 O8 **Grovedale** Alberta Canada
140 B2 **Grove Hill** N Terr Australia
111 J10 **Grove Hill** Alabama U.S.A.
28 C4 **Grove Kirke** Denmark
102 D4 **Groveland** California U.S.A.
26 F9 **Grövelsjön** Sweden
146 H11 **Grove Mts** Antarctica
98 B9 **Grover** Colorado U.S.A.
101 P7 **Grover** Wyoming U.S.A.
111 C12 **Groves** Texas U.S.A.
109 M4 **Groveton** Texas U.S.A.
95 Q2 **Groveton** Vermont U.S.A.
145 D4 **Grovetown** New Zealand
112 E4 **Grovetown** Georgia U.S.A.
101 P6 **Grovont** Wyoming U.S.A.
103 L9 **Growler** Arizona U.S.A.
103 L9 **Growler Mts** Arizona U.S.A.
47 J1 **Grozd'ovo** Bulgaria
45 P1 **Groznjan** Croatia
57 F3 **Groznoye** Kyrgyzstan
53 G11 **Groznyy** Russian Federation
41 J4 **Gr. Scheerh** *mt* Switzerland
33 O4 **Grube** Germany
32 L9 **Grubenhagen** Germany
42 H3 **Grubišno Polje** Croatia
37 P6 **Grubweg** Germany
21 M2 **Gruchet-le-Valasse** France
42 J6 **Gruda** Croatia
47 J2 **Grudovo** Bulgaria
31 M2 **Grudusk** Poland
31 L2 **Grudziadz** Poland
128 D8 **Gruesa, Pta** *C* Chile
122 B6 **Grues, I. aux** Quebec Canada
44 C1 **Grugliasco** Italy
12 B2 **Gruinart** Scotland
109 J9 **Grulla** Texas U.S.A.
36 D4 **Grumbach** Germany
43 H7 **Grumo Appula** Italy
27 F12 **Grums** Sweden
37 O2 **Gruna** Germany
15 C3 **Grunard Bay** Scotland
33 T8 **Grunau** Germany
87 C11 **Grünau** Namibia
36 G6 **Grunbach** Germany
36 F2 **Grünberg** Germany
36 G3 **Gründau** Germany
Gründelhardt *see* **Frankenhardt**
26 K8 **Grundsunda** Sweden
26 J8 **Grundtjärn** Sweden
99 O7 **Grundy Center** Iowa U.S.A.
120 K7 **Grundy Lake Prov. Park** Ontario Canada
28 D7 **Grünholz** Germany
124 J5 **Gruñidora** Mexico
33 Q8 **Grüningen** Germany
36 F2 **Grüningen** Germany
36 H4 **Grünsfeld** Germany
36 E4 **Grünstadt** Germany
38 E8 **Gruppo** *mt* Italy
41 L4 **Grüsch** Switzerland
108 C7 **Gruver** Texas U.S.A.
40 F4 **Gruyère, L. de la** Switzerland
52 B6 **Gruzdžiai** Lithuania
Gruzinskaya S.S.R. *see* **Georgia**
54 L4 **Gryazi** Russian Federation
52 F5 **Gryazovets** Russian Federation
31 M6 **Grybów** Poland
27 H11 **Grycksbo** Sweden
31 J2 **Gryfice** Poland
31 H2 **Gryfino** Poland
99 L1 **Grygla** Minnesota U.S.A.
27 G12 **Grythyttehed** Sweden
26 H3 **Grytöy** *L* Norway
26 C9 **Grytten** Norway
131 H6 **Grytviken** S Georgia
31 J2 **Grzmiąca** Poland
41 O3 **Gschnitz** Austria
36 H6 **Gschwend** Germany
40 F5 **Gstaad** Switzerland
40 F5 **Gsteig** Switzerland
19 P15 **Guâ** France
75 L7 **Gua** India
41 O7 **Gua** *R* Italy
128 D3 **Guacamayas** Colombia
126 F4 **Guacanayabo, G.de** Cuba
127 L9 **Guacara** Venezuela
103 M9 **Gu Achi** Arizona U.S.A.
128 D2 **Guachiria** *R* Colombia
130 C8 **Guaçu** Brazil
124 H7 **Guadalajara** Mexico
16 E4 **Guadalajara** Spain
17 F4 **Guadalajara** *prov* Spain
137 M3 **Guadalcanal** *isld* Solomon Is
16 D6 **Guadalcanal** Spain
16 E6 **Guadalén** *R* Spain
17 F7 **Guadalentin** *R* Spain
16 D8 **Guadalete** *R* Spain
16 E8 **Guadalfeo** *R* Spain
16 E8 **Guadalhorce** *R* Spain
16 E6 **Guadalimar** *R* Spain
17 F6 **Guadalmena** *R* Spain
16 D6 **Guadalmez** *R* Spain
17 G3 **Guadalope** *R* Spain
16 D7 **Guadalquivir** *R* Spain
131 C5 **Guadal, Sa. de** Argentina
108 A4 **Guadalupe** Mexico
124 H6 **Guadalupe** Mexico
71 F5 **Guadalupe** Cebu Philippines
102 D7 **Guadalupe** California U.S.A.
109 J6 **Guadalupe** *R* Texas U.S.A.
108 C4 **Guadalupe Pk** Texas U.S.A.
16 D5 **Guadalupe, Sa de** *mts* Spain
124 G5 **Guadalupe Victoria** Durango Mexico
124 F4 **Guadalupe y Calvo** Mexico
16 E4 **Guadarrama, Sa. de** *mts* Spain
17 F5 **Guadazaón** *R* Spain
127 N4 **Guadeloupe** *islds* Lesser Antilles
16 E6 **Guadiana** *R* Portugal/Spain
16 E7 **Guadiano Menor** *R* Spain
16 D6 **Guadiato** *R* Spain
17 F4 **Guadiela** *R* Spain
16 E7 **Guadix** Spain
133 C6 **Guafo** *isld* Chile
127 P2 **Guaico** Trinidad
130 C7 **Guaicuras** Brazil
128 F2 **Guaina** Venezuela
128 E3 **Guainia** *R* Colombia
130 C9 **Guaíra** Brazil
130 C9 **Guaira** Paraguay
133 C6 **Guaitecas, Is** Chile
126 F4 **Guajaba, Cayo** *isld* Cuba
128 E6 **Guajará Mirim** Brazil
128 E5 **Guajarraã** Brazil
128 F5 **Guajaturaba** Brazil
124 H4 **Guaje, Llano de** *reg* Mexico
125 L2 **Guajiniquil** Honduras
128 D1 **Guajira** *div* Colombia
128 D1 **Guajira, Pena de** *pen* Colombia
102 A3 **Gualala** California U.S.A.
42 E5 **Gualdo Tadino** Italy
131 F4 **Gualeguay** *R* Argentina
131 F4 **Gualeguay** Argentina
133 F4 **Gualeguaychu** Argentina
131 D8 **Gualicho Salina** *salt pan* Argentina
128 E7 **Guallatiri** *mt* Chile
45 J2 **Gualtieri** Italy
134 E6 **Guam** *isld* Mariana Is Pacific Oc
129 J4 **Guamá** *R* Brazil
129 J4 **Guamá** Brazil
127 K9 **Guama** Venezuela
133 B6 **Guamblin, I** Chile
133 E5 **Guamini** Argentina
124 E5 **Guamúchil** Mexico
69 E10 **Gua Musang** Malaysia
65 C5 **Gu'an** China
126 C3 **Guanabacoa** Cuba
130 G8 **Guanabara** Brazil
125 M4 **Guanacaste, Cord. de** *ra* Costa Rica
124 G5 **Guanacevi** Mexico
126 B3 **Guanahacabibes, Pen. de** Cuba
126 C3 **Guanajay** Cuba

124 J7 **Guanajuato** Mexico
129 K6 **Guanambi** Brazil
128 C5 **Guañape, I** Peru
127 O2 **Guanapo** Trinidad
128 E2 **Guanarito** Venezuela
65 B5 **Guancen Shan** *mt ra* China
67 C6 **Guanchang** China
133 D3 **Guandacol** Argentina
65 G3 **Guandi** China
67 C1 **Guandiankou** China
126 B3 **Guane** Cuba
67 B1 **Guang'an** China
67 E3 **Guangchang** China
67 F1 **Guangde** China
65 D3 **Guangdegong** China
67 D5 **Guangdong** *prov* China
67 F2 **Guangfeng** China
67 A1 **Guangfu** China
67 A1 **Guanghan** China
Guanghua *see* **Laohekou**
65 B6 **Guanghua** China
67 E2 **Guangji** China
58 F4 **Guangling** China
65 E5 **Guanglu Dao** *isld* China
67 F1 **Guangming Ding** *mt* China
67 B4 **Guangnan** China
67 D5 **Guangning** China
65 C6 **Guangping** China
65 D6 **Guangrao** China
67 E1 **Guangshan** China
58 F5 **Guangshui** China
67 B5 **Guangxi** *prov* China
67 F1 **Guangyang** China
58 E5 **Guangyuan** China
67 F3 **Guangze** China
67 D5 **Guangzhou** China
65 C6 **Guangzong** China
130 G6 **Guanhães** Brazil
65 D7 **Guanhu** China
127 L5 **Guánica** Puerto Rico
128 F2 **Guanipa** *R* Venezuela
67 D3 **Guanjiazui** China
67 B4 **Guanling** China
67 C1 **Guanmian Shan** *mts* China
65 D7 **Guannan** China
100 F7 **Guano L** Oregon U.S.A.
65 G1 **Guansongzhen** China
Guansuo *see* **Guanling**
128 F1 **Guanta** Venezuela
126 G4 **Guantánamo** Cuba
126 G5 **Guantánamo, B. de** Cuba
65 C6 **Guantao** China
65 C4 **Guanting Shuiku** *res* China
65 C6 **Guan Xian** China
67 A1 **Guan Xian** China
67 D4 **Guanyang** China
65 D7 **Guanyun** China
130 F7 **Guapé** Brazil
128 C3 **Guapi** Colombia
133 G3 **Guaporé** Brazil
130 J9 **Guarabira** Brazil
130 D10 **Guarama** Brazil
130 F8 **Guarantinguetá** Brazil
130 H7 **Guarapari** Brazil
130 D9 **Guarapuava** Brazil
130 E9 **Guaraqueçaba** Brazil
130 E7 **Guararapes** Brazil
130 J10 **Guararapes** Brazil
17 G2 **Guara, Sa. de** Spain
18 E10 **Guara, Sierra de** *mts* Spain
130 E9 **Guaratuba** Brazil
45 O6 **Guarcino** Italy
16 C4 **Guarda** Portugal
17 F7 **Guardal** *R* Spain
130 F5 **Guarda Mor** Brazil
127 L10 **Guardatinajas** Venezuela
13 F1 **Guardbridge** Scotland
133 E6 **Guardia Mitre** Argentina
133 D7 **Guardián, C** Argentina
45 R7 **Guardia Sanframondi** Italy
16 D2 **Guardo** Spain
16 B4 **Guardunha Sa.da** *mts* Portugal
128 F5 **Guariba** *R* Amazonas Brazil
127 L10 **Guárico** *R* Venezuela
128 E2 **Guárico** *state* Venezuela
130 D10 **Guarita** *R* Brazil
124 E5 **Guasave** Mexico
128 C3 **Guascama, Pta** *pt* Colombia
125 K7 **Guasima** Mexico
130 C9 **Guassú, R** Brazil
42 D4 **Guastalla** Italy
125 O10 **Guatemala** *rep* Central America
126 G4 **Guatemala** Cuba
125 O10 **Guatemala** Guatemala
127 L9 **Guatire** Venezuela
128 E3 **Guaviare** *R* Colombia
128 D3 **Guaviare** *div* Colombia
126 F4 **Guayabal** Cuba
128 E2 **Guayabal** Venezuela
128 D3 **Guayabero** *R* Colombia
131 C3 **Guayaguas, Sa. da** *ra* Argentina
127 P3 **Guayaguayare** Trinidad
127 L5 **Guayama** Puerto Rico
128 C4 **Guayaquil** Ecuador
128 B4 **Guayaquil, Golfo de** Ecuador
128 E6 **Guayaramerin** Bolivia
128 B4 **Guayas** *prov* Ecuador
133 B7 **Guayeco Arch** *islds* Chile
124 D4 **Guaymas** Mexico
131 F3 **Guayquiraró, R** Argentina
130 F7 **Guazupé** Brazil
86 G3 **Guba** Ethiopia
87 E8 **Guba** Zaire
67 A2 **Gubai** China
52 J5 **Gubakha** Russian Federation
71 G4 **Gubat** Philippines
42 E5 **Gubbio** Italy
52 J4 **Gubdor** Russian Federation
65 D4 **Gubeikou** China
31 H4 **Guben** Germany
31 H4 **Gubin** Germany
54 J5 **Gubkin** Russian Federation
47 H2 **Gŭbŭbovo** Bulgaria
65 C6 **Gucheng** China
67 D1 **Gucheng** China
17 G4 **Gudar, Sa. de** *mts* Spain
28 F6 **Gudbjerg** Denmark
26 C9 **Gudbrandsdalen** Norway
28 D5 **Gudenå** *R* Denmark
36 G1 **Gudensberg** Germany
36 F4 **Gudernheim** Germany
28 D6 **Guderup** Denmark
27 G16 **Gudhjem** Denmark
28 F6 **Gudme** Denmark
77 J6 **Gudri** *R* Pakistan
65 B7 **Gudui** China
28 G6 **Gudum** Denmark
28 E3 **Gudumholm** Denmark
28 A3 **Gudum Kirke** Denmark
76 D3 **Gudur** India
27 B11 **Gudvangen** Norway
19 K5 **Guebwiller** France
133 C6 **Guechucuicui, Pta** Chile
85 B7 **Guéckédou** Guinea
21 M5 **Gué-de-la-Chaîne** France
21 O4 **Gue-de-Longroi, le** France
20 E6 **Guegon** France
121 N4 **Guéguen** *L* Quebec Canada
20 E6 **Guéhenno** France
16 E7 **Güéjar Sierra** Spain
86 C3 **Guelengdeng** Chad
85 F1 **Guelma** Algeria
85 B3 **Guelmine** Western Sahara
98 H3 **Guelph** North Dakota U.S.A.
85 D5 **Guem** Mali
36 C7 **Guémar** France
20 G6 **Guémene-Penfao** France
20 D5 **Guéméné-sur-Scorff** France
121 P6 **Guenette** Quebec Canada
133 C7 **Guenguel** *R* Argentina
20 G6 **Guenroue** France
20 F6 **Guer** France
16 C6 **Gueraña** Spain
20 F7 **Guérande** France
86 C3 **Guéra, Pic de** *mt* Chad
85 E2 **Guerara** Algeria
20 H6 **Guerche-de-Bretagne, la** France
18 G6 **Guerche-sur-l'Aubois, la** France
86 D3 **Guéréda** Chad
18 G6 **Guéret** France
121 L5 **Guerin** Quebec Canada
20 F8 **Guérinière, la** France
20 D5 **Guerlédan, L.de** France
20 D5 **Guern** France
18 D9 **Guernica** Spain
119 M7 **Guernsey** Saskatchewan Canada
98 B7 **Guernsey** Wyoming U.S.A.
20 E3 **Guernsey I** Channel Is
98 B7 **Guernsey Res** Wyoming U.S.A.
21 M4 **Guerouldé, la** France
109 J9 **Guerra** Texas U.S.A.
21 O2 **Guerville** France
85 D4 **Guettara, El** Mali
18 H6 **Gueugnon** France
111 D12 **Gueydan** Louisiana U.S.A.
41 K4 **Güferhorn** *mt* Switzerland
38 E6 **Güffert-Spitze** *mt* Austria
86 G4 **Gugā** *mt* Ethiopia
86 G4 **Guga** *mt* Ethiopia
42 F7 **Guglionesi** Italy
48 H5 **Gugu** *mt* Romania
70 K9 **Guhakolak, Tanjong** *C* Java
33 R6 **Gühlen-Glienecke** Germany
130 C4 **Guia** Brazil
20 G6 **Guichen** France
67 F1 **Guichi** China
125 M9 **Guichicovi** Mexico
20 C4 **Guiclan** France
20 D6 **Guidel** France
86 B4 **Guider** Cameroon
98 H9 **Guide Rock** Nebraska U.S.A.
67 B3 **Guiding** China
45 J1 **Guidizzolo** Italy
67 D3 **Guidong** China
19 P13 **Guiers** *R* France
85 A5 **Guiers, L. de** Senegal
45 J3 **Guiglia** Italy
85 C7 **Guiglo** Ivory Coast
20 G6 **Guignen** France
22 J2 **Guigoven** Belgium
127 L9 **Güigüi** Venezuela
Guihua *see* **Mingxi**
87 F10 **Guija** Mozambique
67 C4 **Gui Jiang** *R* China
67 G2 **Guiji Shan** *mts* China
143 B9 **Guilderton** W Australia Australia
143 B9 **Guildford** W Australia Australia
9 F5 **Guildford** England
95 Q2 **Guildhall** Vermont U.S.A.
65 E1 **Guiler Gol** *R* China
95 P5 **Guilford** Connecticut U.S.A.
95 S1 **Guilford** Maine U.S.A.
112 H1 **Guilford Ct. Ho. Nat. Mil. Park** North Carolina U.S.A.
67 C4 **Guilin** China
20 F6 **Guillac** France
20 F5 **Guilliers** France
20 B6 **Guilvinec, le** France
16 B3 **Guimaraes** Portugal
71 F5 **Guimaras** *isld* Philippines
71 F5 **Guimaras Str** Philippines
20 B5 **Guimiliau** France
111 J8 **Guin** Alabama U.S.A.
125 M3 **Güina** Nicaragua
71 F5 **Guinauayan** *isld* Philippines
126 E3 **Guinchos Cay** *isld* Cuba
102 B3 **Guinda** California U.S.A.
71 G6 **Guindulman** Philippines
85 B6 **Guinea** *rep* W Africa
90 J8 **Guinea Basin** Atlantic Oc
85 A6 **Guinea-Bissau** *rep* W Africa
85 E8 **Guinea, Gulf of** W Africa
122 C3 **Guinecourt, L** Quebec Canada
126 D3 **Güines** Cuba
22 B2 **Guines** France
20 D4 **Guingamp** France
71 F5 **Guintacan** *isld* Philippines
71 F3 **Guintinua** *isld* Philippines
110 E6 **Guion** Arkansas U.S.A.
20 B5 **Guipavas** France
67 C5 **Guiping** China
17 F1 **Guipúzcoa** *prov* Spain
85 D5 **Guir** Mali
126 C3 **Güira de Melena** Cuba
130 D5 **Guiratinga** Brazil
129 H3 **Guisanbourg** Fr Guiana
13 G5 **Guisborough** England
22 E4 **Guiscard** France
20 C5 **Guiscriff** France
22 F4 **Guise** France
13 G6 **Guiseley** England
20 B4 **Guisseny** France
9 G2 **Guist** England
71 G5 **Guiuan** Philippines
22 E4 **Guivry** France
67 F2 **Guixi** China
67 C5 **Gui Xian** China
67 B3 **Guiyang** Guizhou China
67 B3 **Guizhou** *prov* China
74 D7 **Gujarat** *prov* India
74 F2 **Gujranwala** Pakistan
74 F2 **Gujrat** Pakistan
67 C1 **Gujunba** China
103 N9 **Gu Komelik** Arizona U.S.A.
54 L8 **Gukovo** Russian Federation
58 D4 **Gulang** China
139 J4 **Gulargambone** New South Wales Australia
74 G10 **Gulbarga** India
52 C6 **Gulbene** Latvia
57 G4 **Gul'cha** Kyrgyzstan
28 A5 **Guldager** Denmark
28 E5 **Guldbjerg** Denmark
28 H7 **Guldborg** Denmark
36 D4 **Guldental** Germany
27 H12 **Guldsmedshyttan** Sweden
76 B2 **Guledagudda** India
79 E1 **Gülek** Turkey
27 A10 **Gulen** Norway
112 H2 **Gulf** North Carolina U.S.A.
111 J11 **Gulf Beach** Florida U.S.A.
141 G4 **Gulf Highway** Queensland Australia
111 H11 **Gulf Islands Nat Seashore** Mississippi U.S.A.
113 E10 **Gulfport** Florida U.S.A.
111 G11 **Gulfport** Mississippi U.S.A.
Gulf, The *see* **Persian Gulf**
26 R1 **Gulgofjorden** Norway
139 J4 **Gulgong** New South Wales Australia
67 B2 **Gulin** China
57 E4 **Gulistan** Uzbekistan
33 P6 **Gülitz** Germany
Gulja *see* **Yining**
116 P5 **Gulkana** Alaska U.S.A.
118 D6 **Gull** *L* Alberta Canada
27 H15 **Gullabo** Sweden
13 F1 **Gullane** Scotland
119 O1 **Gull Bay** Ontario Canada
28 D4 **Gullev** Denmark
6 L1 **Gullfaks** *oil rig* North Sea
28 S9 **Gullfoss** *waterfall* Iceland
99 V4 **Gull I** Michigan U.S.A.
99 V3 **Gulliver** Michigan U.S.A.
99 M3 **Gull L** Minnesota U.S.A.
118 J8 **Gull Lake** Saskatchewan Canada
26 K6 **Gullön** Sweden
27 G13 **Gullspång** Sweden
26 M5 **Gullträsk** Sweden
47 J7 **Güllük** Turkey
47 J7 **Güllük Körfezi** *B* Turkey
65 F2 **Gulong** China
25 E7 **Gulpen** Netherlands
33 Q7 **Gülper See** *L* Germany
47 H5 **Gülpınar** Turkey
77 G2 **Gulran** Afghanistan
78 E2 **Gülşehir** Turkey
26 J8 **Gulsele** Sweden
57 G2 **Gul'shad** Kazakhstan
33 S5 **Gültz** Germany
86 F5 **Gulu** Uganda
141 J7 **Guluguba** Queensland Australia
140 D1 **Guluwuru I** N Terr Australia
59 H1 **Gulya** Russian Federation
46 G1 **Gulyantsi** Bulgaria
54 H9 **Gulyaypole** Ukraine
33 S4 **Gülzow** Germany
141 G7 **Gumbardo** Queensland Australia
26 M7 **Gumboda** Sweden
140 B5 **Gum Cr** N Terr Australia
85 F6 **Gumel** Nigeria
125 K6 **Gümez** Mexico
16 E3 **Gumiel de Hizán** Spain
75 L7 **Gumla** India
61 M9 **Gumma** *prefect* Japan
36 D1 **Gummersbach** Germany
85 F6 **Gummi** Nigeria
71 E2 **Gumotgong** Luzon Philippines
69 C10 **Gumpang** *R* Sumatra
94 K9 **Gum Spring** Virginia U.S.A.
33 Q7 **Gumtow** Germany
67 A5 **Gumu** China
47 L7 **Gümüşgün** Turkey
78 G1 **Gümüşhane** Turkey
74 G6 **Guna** India
86 G3 **Guna, Terara** *mt* Ethiopia
139 H5 **Gunbar** New South Wales Australia
113 H12 **Gun Cay** Bahamas
58 F1 **Gunda** Russian Federation
139 J6 **Gundagai** New South Wales Australia
37 J6 **Gundelfingen** Germany
36 G5 **Gundelsheim** Germany
28 C3 **Gundersted** Denmark
36 E4 **Gundheim** Germany
70 N9 **Gundik** Java
86 D5 **Gundji** Zaire
28 H7 **Gundslev** Denmark
71 B3 **Gunedidalem** Indonesia
47 K6 **Güney** Turkey
119 N2 **Gunflint** Ontario Canada
86 C7 **Gungu** Zaire
119 U5 **Gunisao** *R* Manitoba Canada
119 V5 **Gunisao** *L* Manitoba Canada
103 L4 **Gunlock** Utah U.S.A.
114 J6 **Gunnar** Saskatchewan Canada
26 J6 **Gunnarn** Sweden
26 M5 **Gunnarsbyn** Sweden
141 H4 **Gunnawarra** Queensland Australia
115 R4 **Gunnbjørn Fjeld** *mt* Greenland
27 J14 **Gunnebo** Sweden
139 K4 **Gunnedah** New South Wales Australia
146 K8 **Gunnerus Ridge** Antarctica
141 J7 **Gunnewin** Queensland Australia
139 J5 **Gunning** New South Wales Australia
8 B7 **Gunnislake** England
106 B3 **Gunnison** *R* Colorado U.S.A.
106 D3 **Gunnison** Colorado U.S.A.
101 N8 **Gunnison I** Utah U.S.A.
140 B1 **Gunn Pt** N Terr Australia
140 E4 **Gunpowder** *R* Queensland Australia
101 N1 **Gunsight** Montana U.S.A.
76 C3 **Guntakal** India
100 B6 **Gunter** Oregon U.S.A.
109 L2 **Gunter** Texas U.S.A.
33 N9 **Güntersberge** Germany
36 E4 **Guntersblum** Germany
111 K7 **Guntersville** Alabama U.S.A.
119 U8 **Gunton** Manitoba Canada
111 H7 **Guntown** Mississippi U.S.A.
76 E2 **Guntur** India
71 N8 **Gunungapi** *isld* Indonesia
70 B3 **Gunung Ayer** Sarawak
70 E6 **Gunungbatubesar** Kalimantan
69 C12 **Gunungsitoli** Indonesia
70 K8 **Gunungsugih** Sumatra
69 D12 **Gunungtua** Sumatra
75 K9 **Gunupur** India
118 J7 **Gunworth** Saskatchewan Canada
143 B9 **Gunyidi** W Australia Australia
37 J7 **Günz** *R* Germany
37 J7 **Günzburg** Germany
37 K5 **Gunzenhausen** Germany
33 N9 **Günzerode** Germany
67 B5 **Guohua** China
65 C4 **Guojiatun** China
Guoluezhen *see* **Lingbao**
58 G5 **Guoyang** China
65 B5 **Guoyangzhen** China
65 D7 **Gupei** China
48 K3 **Gura Humorului** Romania
66 F4 **Gurban Anggir** China
65 B3 **Gurban Obo** China
66 D2 **Gurbantünggüt Shamo** *desert* China
138 E6 **Gurchen B** South Australia Australia
74 F2 **Gurdaspur** India
111 C8 **Gurdon** Arkansas U.S.A.
47 K6 **Güre** Turkey
74 G4 **Gurgaon** India
86 D3 **Gurgei, Jebel** *mt* Sudan
129 K5 **Gurgueia** *R* Brazil
127 N11 **Guri** Venezuela
128 F2 **Guri, Embalse de** *res* Venezuela
130 E6 **Gurinhatã** Brazil
46 D4 **Gur-i-Topit** *mt* Albania
38 J8 **Gurk** *R* Austria
47 H2 **Gurkovo** Bulgaria
38 K8 **Gurktal** *V* Austria
38 J8 **Gurktaler Alpen** *mts* Austria
66 C5 **Gurla Mandhata** *mt* China
57 B4 **Gurlen** Uzbekistan
110 K7 **Gurley** Alabama U.S.A.
98 D8 **Gurley** Nebraska U.S.A.
88 D10 **Guro** Mozambique
59 L1 **Gurskoye** Russian Federation
88 F9 **Gurué** Mozambique
78 F2 **Gürün** Turkey
129 H4 **Gurupá** Brazil
129 J4 **Gurupi** *R* Brazil
129 J6 **Gurupi** Brazil
129 J4 **Gurupi, C** Brazil
87 F9 **Guruve** Zimbabwe
76 D2 **Guruzala** India
58 D3 **Gurvan Sayhan Uul** *mt* Mongolia
50 E4 **Gur'yev** Kazakhstan
56 C4 **Gur'yevsk** Russian Federation
85 F6 **Gusau** Nigeria
33 P8 **Güsen** Germany
31 N1 **Gusev** Russian Federation
59 H4 **Gushan** China
101 Q9 **Gusher** Utah U.S.A.
67 E1 **Gushi** China
61 P14 **Gushikami** Okinawa
61 P13 **Gushikawa** Okinawa
70 E1 **Gusi** Sabah
52 G7 **Gusikha** Russian Federation
46 D2 **Gusinje** Montenegro Yugoslavia
56 G5 **Gusinoozersk** Russian Federation
56 G5 **Gusinoye, Oz** *L* Russian Federation
52 F6 **Gus'Khrustal'nyy** Russian Federation
46 D4 **Gusmar** Albania
67 B2 **Gusong** China
43 B9 **Guspini** Sardinia
48 C3 **Güssing** Austria
45 J1 **Gussola** Italy
27 G11 **Gustav Adolf** Sweden
115 Q4 **Gustav Holm, Kap** *C* Greenland
127 N6 **Gustavia** Lesser Antilles
124 C2 **Gustavo Sotelo** Mexico
117 F6 **Gustavus** Alaska U.S.A.
33 P9 **Güsten** Germany
36 E2 **Gusternhain** Germany
102 C4 **Gustine** California U.S.A.
109 J4 **Gustine** Texas U.S.A.
33 S4 **Gustow** Germany
33 Q5 **Güstrow** Germany
27 H13 **Gusum** Sweden
48 K1 **Gusyatin** Ukraine
36 E7 **Gutach** Germany
66 E6 **Gutarg** China
56 E4 **Gutarskiy Khrebet** *mts* Russian Federation
38 L5 **Gutau** Austria
37 M3 **Gutenfürst** Germany
38 N6 **Gutenstein** Austria
33 P9 **Gütergltick** Germany
32 H9 **Gütersloh** Germany
143 B8 **Gutha** W Australia Australia
110 J5 **Guthrie** Kentucky U.S.A.
99 M2 **Guthrie** Minnesota U.S.A.
98 F1 **Guthrie** North Dakota U.S.A.
107 N6 **Guthrie** Oklahoma U.S.A.
108 G2 **Guthrie** Texas U.S.A.
99 M8 **Guthrie Center** Iowa U.S.A.
119 R3 **Guthrie L** Manitoba Canada
67 F3 **Gutian** China
125 L7 **Gutiérrez Zamora** Mexico
Guting *see* **Yutai**
33 S8 **Gut-Neuhof** Germany
33 Q5 **Gutow** Germany
38 L8 **Guttaring** Austria
99 P7 **Guttenberg** Iowa U.S.A.
87 F9 **Gutu** Zimbabwe
54 G6 **Guty** Ukraine
33 S5 **Gützkow** Germany
80 C7 **Guvrin** *R* Israel
75 O5 **Guwahati** India
36 G1 **Guxhagen** Germany
65 B6 **Gu Xian** China
65 C4 **Guyan** China
128 G3 **Guyana** *rep* S America
94 E8 **Guyandotte** *R* West Virginia U.S.A.
58 F3 **Guyang** China
65 A4 **Guyang** China
121 M4 **Guyenne** Quebec Canada
18 E8 **Guyenne** *prov* France
9 G2 **Guyhirn** England
Guyi *see* **Sanjiang** Guangxi
107 J5 **Guymon** Oklahoma U.S.A.
116 R6 **Guyot Glacier** Alaska U.S.A.
139 K4 **Guyra** New South Wales Australia
123 L8 **Guysborough** Nova Scotia Canada
112 F5 **Guyton** Georgia U.S.A.
79 B2 **Güzelbağ** Turkey
67 C2 **Guzhang** China
58 G5 **Guzhen** China
Guzhou *see* **Rongjiang**
124 F2 **Guzmán, L. de** Mexico
31 N1 **Gvardeysk** Russian Federation
48 K1 **Gvardeyskoye** Ukraine
53 D10 **Gvardeyskoye** Ukraine
48 J2 **Gvozdets** Ukraine
68 B4 **Gwa** Burma
89 E2 **Gwaai** Zimbabwe
139 J4 **Gwabegar** New South Wales Australia
38 G8 **Gwabl** Austria
74 B10 **Gwadar** Pakistan
89 E2 **Gwai** *R* Zimbabwe
8 B1 **Gwalchmai** Wales
143 D8 **Gwalia** W Australia Australia
74 H5 **Gwalior** India
141 J7 **Gwambegwine** Queensland Australia
89 F3 **Gwanda** Zimbabwe
86 E5 **Gwane** Zaire
8 B3 **Gwbert-on-Sea** Wales
68 B2 **Gwebin** Burma
14 C2 **Gweebarra B** Ireland
Gwelo *see* **Gweru**
100 E4 **Gwendolen** Oregon U.S.A.
8 D4 **Gwent** *co* Wales
89 F2 **Gweru** *R* Zimbabwe
89 F2 **Gweru** Zimbabwe
99 T3 **Gwinn** Michigan U.S.A.
98 J3 **Gwinner** North Dakota U.S.A.
139 J3 **Gwydir** *R* New South Wales Australia
8 B1 **Gwynedd** *co* Wales
118 D6 **Gwynne** Alberta Canada
19 J5 **Gy** France
Gya'gya *see* **Saga**
78 L1 **Gyandzha** Azerbaijan
66 C5 **Gyangrang** China
Gyangtse *see* **Gyangzê**
66 D6 **Gyangzê** China
66 D5 **Gyaring Co** *L* China
58 C5 **Gyaring Hu** *L* China
50 G1 **Gydanskiy Poluostrov** *pen* Russian Federation
75 L4 **Gyirong** China
66 F5 **Gyitang** China
8 C2 **Gylchedd** *mt* Wales
115 P5 **Gyldenløves Fjord** Greenland
28 H5 **Gyldenløves Høj** *hill* Denmark
26 N5 **Gyljen** Sweden
28 E5 **Gylling** Denmark
28 E5 **Gylling Næs** Denmark
141 L7 **Gympie** Queensland Australia
68 B3 **Gyobingauk** Burma
61 N9 **Gyōda** Japan
48 F4 **Gyomaendrőd** Hungary
48 F3 **Gyöngyös** *R* Hungary
48 F3 **Gyöngyös** Hungary
48 E4 **Gyönk** Hungary
48 D3 **Györ** Hungary
48 D3 **Györ-Sopron** Hungary
106 D2 **Gypsum** Colorado U.S.A.
107 N3 **Gypsum** Kansas U.S.A.
117 Q5 **Gypsum Pt** Northwest Territories Canada
119 T7 **Gypsumville** Manitoba Canada
28 H5 **Gyrstinge** Denmark
27 J11 **Gysinge** Sweden
46 F2 **Gyueshevo** Bulgaria
48 G4 **Gyula** Hungary
52 D6 **Gzhat'** *R* Russian Federation
Gzhatsk *see* **Gagarin**

H

22 H2 **Haacht** Belgium
37 M4 **Haag** Germany
25 G4 **Haaksbergen** Netherlands
36 C1 **Haan** Germany
137 S5 **Ha'apai Group** *islds* Tonga
29 L8 **Haapajärvi** Finland
29 L9 **Haapamäki** Finland
29 L7 **Haapavesi** Finland
52 B5 **Haapsalu** Estonia
25 C4 **Haarlem** Netherlands
32 G9 **Haarstrang** Germany
144 B5 **Haast** New Zealand
140 B6 **Haast Bluff** N Terr Australia
25 C5 **Haastrecht** Netherlands
140 A6 **Haasts Bluff Aboriginal Land** N Terr Australia
80 G4 **Habaka** Jordan
126 C3 **Habana** Cuba
83 K9 **Habarane** Sri Lanka
86 G5 **Habaswein** Kenya
117 O6 **Habay** Alberta Canada
22 K4 **Habay-la-Neuve** Belgium
78 J5 **Habbamyah** Iraq
32 K10 **Habichtswald** *wood* Germany
75 O6 **Habiganj** Bangladesh
65 C3 **Habirag** China
80 G7 **Habis** *R* Jordan
80 C5 **Habla** Israel
27 K14 **Hablingo** Sweden
27 G14 **Habo** Sweden
59 N3 **Habomai-Shoto** *islds* Kuril Is Pacific Oc
80 C3 **Ha Bonim** Israel
60 P1 **Haboro** Japan
22 L3 **Habscheid** Germany
61 N11 **Habuminato** Japan
131 B7 **Hachado, Paso de** Arg/Chile
32 G10 **Hachen** Germany
36 D2 **Hachenburg** Germany
59 L5 **Hachijō Jima** *isld* Japan
61 N5 **Hachimori** Japan
60 O2 **Hachinai dake** *mt* Japan
59 M3 **Hachinohe** Japan
59 L4 **Hachiōjio** Japan
106 B10 **Hachita** New Mexico U.S.A.
100 D8 **Hackamore** California U.S.A.
26 G9 **Hackås** Sweden
103 L6 **Hackberry** Arizona U.S.A.
111 C12 **Hackberry** Louisiana U.S.A.
107 K3 **Hackberry Cr** Kansas U.S.A.
118 E6 **Hackett** Alberta Canada
110 B6 **Hackett** Arkansas U.S.A.
95 N6 **Hackettstown** New Jersey U.S.A.
111 J7 **Hackleburg** Alabama U.S.A.
138 E4 **Hack, Mt** South Australia Australia
13 H5 **Hackness** England
87 C8 **Haco** Angola
68 H2 **Ha Coi** Vietnam
36 E3 **Hadamar** Germany
80 C5 **Hadar** Israel
98 J7 **Hadar** Nebraska U.S.A.
72 H4 **Ḩadd, Al** Oman
107 N2 **Haddam** Kansas U.S.A.
9 G3 **Haddenham** England
13 F2 **Haddington** Scotland
9 H2 **Haddiscoe** England
112 D4 **Haddock** Georgia U.S.A.
73 L8 **Haddunmahti Atoll** Maldives
85 F6 **Hadejia** *R* Nigeria
27 D11 **Hadeland** Norway
32 J5 **Hadelner Kanal** Germany
32 K4 **Hademarschen** Germany
80 C4 **Ḩadera** Israel
80 C4 **Hadera** *R* Israel
38 N5 **Hadersdorf** Austria
Haderslev *co see* **Sønderjylland** *co*
28 C6 **Haderslev** Denmark
28 B4 **Haderup** Denmark
72 F5 **Hadhramaut** *reg* Yemen
72 G6 **Ḩadībōh** Socotra
79 G3 **Ḩadīdīyah** Syria
43 A11 **Hadid, Ras El** *C* Algeria
85 F1 **Hadid, Ras El** *C* Algeria
78 D3 **Hadım** Turkey
78 J4 **Hadithah, Al** Iraq
9 G3 **Hadleigh** England
9 G4 **Hadleigh** England
114 J3 **Hadley B** Northwest Territories Canada
144 C6 **Hadlow** New Zealand
33 O9 **Hadmersleben** Germany
80 F2 **Ḩad Nes** Syria
26 G3 **Hadsel** Norway
26 G3 **Hädselöy** *isld* Norway
28 E4 **Hadsten** Denmark
28 E3 **Hadsund** Denmark
116 O3 **Hadweenzic** *R* Alaska U.S.A.
131 G3 **Haedo, Cuchilla de** *ra* Uruguay
65 F5 **Haeju** N Korea
80 C7 **Ha-Ela** Israel
28 E6 **Hæsinge** Denmark
41 O3 **Hafelekar Sp** *mt* Austria
80 C6 **Hafez Ḩayyim** Israel
28 R9 **Haffjördhur** *B* Iceland
33 N4 **Haffkrug-Scharbeutz** Germany
115 N2 **Haffner Bjerg** *mt* Greenland
118 K6 **Hafford** Saskatchewan Canada
43 C13 **Haffouz** Tunisia
78 F2 **Hafik** Turkey
74 E2 **Hafizabad** Pakistan
75 P6 **Haflong** India
28 S9 **Hafnarfjördhur** Iceland
38 H7 **Hafner** *mt* Austria
77 A4 **Haft Gel** Iran
77 H2 **Haftqala** *R* Afghanistan
Hafun *see* **Xaafuun** Somalia
86 F3 **Hag Abdullah** Sudan
112 F5 **Hagan** Georgia U.S.A.
27 J11 **Hagaström** Sweden
32 F5 **Hage** Germany
80 D3 **Ha Gelilit** Israel
33 R8 **Hagelsberg** *mt* Germany
116 G7 **Hagemeister I** Alaska U.S.A.
119 M6 **Hagen** Saskatchewan Canada
32 F10 **Hagen** Germany
32 K8 **Hagenburg** Germany
38 H6 **Hagen-Gebirge** *mts* Austria
33 O6 **Hagenow** Germany
101 L7 **Hagerman** Idaho U.S.A.
106 F8 **Hagerman** New Mexico U.S.A.
27 H13 **Hägerstad** Sweden
94 B7 **Hagerstown** Indiana U.S.A.
94 K7 **Hagerstown** Maryland U.S.A.
120 K10 **Hagersville** Ontario Canada
27 G11 **Hagfors** Sweden
26 G8 **Häggenås** Sweden
13 G2 **Haggerston** England
85 B3 **Haggounia, Al** Western Sahara
26 G8 **Häggsjön** Sweden
68 G1 **Ha Giang** Vietnam
48 K4 **Hăgimaş** *mt* Romania
61 L10 **Hagiwara** Japan
8 D3 **Hagley** England
19 K3 **Hagondage** France
112 G3 **Hagood** South Carolina U.S.A.
80 C5 **Ḩagor** Israel
80 F1 **Ha Gosherim** Israel
14 B4 **Hags Hd** Ireland
118 L6 **Hague** Saskatchewan Canada
95 O3 **Hague** New York U.S.A.
98 F3 **Hague** North Dakota U.S.A.
20 G2 **Hague, C. de la** France
19 L4 **Haguenau** France
98 A9 **Hagues Pk** Colorado U.S.A.
Hague, The *see* **Den Haag**
18 E9 **Haguetmau** France
123 O3 **Haha Bay** Quebec Canada
122 B5 **Ha Ha, L** Quebec Canada
80 D6 **Ha Hamisha** Jordan
113 D7 **Hahira** Georgia U.S.A.
37 M4 **Hahnbach** Germany
36 D2 **Hahnbei** Germany
33 M9 **Hahnenklee-Bockswiese** Germany
80 C3 **Ha Ḩoterim** Israel
67 G1 **Hai'an** China
67 C6 **Hai'an** China
65 E4 **Haicheng** China
67 F4 **Haicheng** China
37 N5 **Haidhof** Germany
43 B13 **Haïdra** Tunisia
37 O5 **Haidstein** *mt* Germany
68 H2 **Hai Duong** Vietnam
22 J2 **Haien** Belgium
80 C2 **Ḩaifa** Israel
80 D2 **Ḩaifa, Bay of** Israel
67 E5 **Haifeng** China
143 F9 **Haig** W Australia Australia
36 E2 **Haiger** Germany
36 F7 **Haigerloch** Germany
117 P7 **Haig Lake** Alberta Canada
98 E10 **Haigler** Nebraska U.S.A.
65 D5 **Hai He** *R* China
67 C6 **Haikang** China
60 C12 **Haiki** Japan
69 D9 **Hai,Ko** *isld* Thailand
68 K2 **Haikou** China
135 T3 **Haiku** Hawaiian Is
75 P6 **Hailakandi** India
59 G2 **Hailar** China
101 L6 **Hailey** Idaho U.S.A.
121 L5 **Haileybury** Ontario Canada
107 P7 **Haileyville** Oklahoma U.S.A.
59 J3 **Hailin** China
67 D6 **Hailing Dao** *isld* China
65 J3 **Hailong** China
68 J7 **Hai Long** Vietnam
9 G6 **Hailsham** England
59 J2 **Hailun** China
29 L6 **Hailuoto** *isld* Finland
29 L6 **Hailuoto** Finland
32 M8 **Haimar** Germany
67 G1 **Haimen** China
67 G2 **Haimen** China
67 C7 **Hainan** *prov* China
68 D2 **Hai-nang** Burma
Hainan Strait *see* **Qiongzhou Haixia**
22 F2 **Hainaut** Belgium
22 F3 **Hainaut** France
31 K7 **Hainburg** Austria
117 F6 **Haines** Alaska U.S.A.
100 H5 **Haines** Oregon U.S.A.
113 F9 **Haines City** Florida U.S.A.
117 E5 **Haines Junction** Yukon Territory Canada
22 G3 **Haine-St-Paul** Belgium
38 N5 **Hainfeld** Austria
68 B4 **Haing** *R* Burma
37 P2 **Hainichen** Germany
67 G1 **Haining** China
33 N10 **Hainleite** Germany
37 Q2 **Hainsberg** Germany
94 D4 **Haintramck** Michigan U.S.A.
68 H2 **Haiphong** Vietnam
118 F5 **Hairy Hill** Alberta Canada
65 E3 **Haisgai** China
127 H5 **Haiti** *rep* W Indies
68 J3 **Haitou** China
65 F2 **Haituo** China
103 N9 **Haivana Nakya** Arizona U.S.A.
102 G5 **Haiwee Res** California U.S.A.
65 D5 **Haixing** China
86 G2 **Haiya Junct** Sudan
67 G1 **Haiyan** China
65 E6 **Haiyang** China
65 F5 **Haiyang Dao** *isld* China
Haiyou *see* **Sanmen**
67 B5 **Haiyuan** China
68 H1 **Haiyuan** China
48 G3 **Hajdú-Bihar** *co* Hungary
48 G3 **Hajdúböszörmény** Hungary
48 G3 **Hajdúdorog** Hungary
48 G3 **Hajdúhadház** Hungary
48 G3 **Hajdúnánás** Hungary
48 G3 **Hajdúszoboszló** Hungary
61 M7 **Hajiki-saki** *C* Japan
79 G9 **Ḩājj** Saudi Arabia
31 O3 **Hajnówka** Poland
65 F7 **Hajo** *isld* S Korea
68 A1 **Haka** Burma
135 V5 **Hakalou** Hawaiian Is
80 G3 **Hakama** Jordan
87 E7 **Hakansson** *mts* Zaire
27 F13 **Håkantorp** Sweden
144 A7 **Hakapoua, L** New Zealand
61 N8 **Hakase-yama** *mt* Japan
144 C6 **Hakataramea** New Zealand
60 G11 **Hakata shima** *isld* Japan
131 B8 **Hakelhuincul, Altiplanicie de** *plateau* Argentina
Hakha *see* **Haka**
78 J3 **Hakkâri** Turkey
26 M5 **Hakkas** Sweden
61 J11 **Hakken-zan** *mt* Japan
61 O5 **Hakkōda san** Japan
60 Q1 **Hako dake** *mt* Japan
59 M3 **Hakodate** Japan
60 O4 **Hakodate wan** *B* Japan
61 K9 **Haku-san** *vol* Japan
61 K9 **Hakusan Nat. Park** Japan
Hal *see* **Halle** Belgium
79 H2 **Ḩalab** Syria
78 G4 **Halabiye** Syria
78 K4 **Halabja** Iraq
65 F2 **Halahai** China
86 G1 **Halaib** Sudan
79 D8 **Halâl, G** *mt* Egypt
72 H5 **Halaniyat, Juzur al** *islds* Arabian Sea
48 G3 **Halasto** *L* Hungary
79 G9 **Ḩālat 'Ammār** Saudi Arabia
48 K3 **Hălăuceşti** Romania
135 S2 **Halawa** Hawaiian Is
80 F4 **Halawa** Jordan
135 S2 **Halawa, C** Hawaiian Is
79 G4 **Halba** Lebanon
86 H3 **Halba Desêt** *isld* Red Sea
56 E6 **Halban** Mongolia
33 T8 **Halbe** Germany
33 O9 **Halberstadt** Germany
8 C6 **Halberton** England
119 O9 **Halbrite** Saskatchewan Canada
145 E4 **Halcombe** New Zealand
71 E4 **Halcon, Mt** Philippines
117 P10 **Halcyon Hot Springs** British Columbia Canada
28 E3 **Hald** Århus Denmark
28 C3 **Hald** Viborg Denmark
28 H6 **Haldagerlille** Denmark
27 E12 **Halden** Norway
33 O8 **Haldensleben** Germany
28 C4 **Hald Sø** *L* Denmark
28 E4 **Haldum** Denmark
74 H4 **Haldwani** India
140 D6 **Hale** *R* N Terr Australia
106 H2 **Hale** Colorado U.S.A.
94 D2 **Hale** Michigan U.S.A.
110 C2 **Hale** Missouri U.S.A.
135 T3 **Haleakala Crater** Hawaiian Is
108 F1 **Hale Center** Texas U.S.A.
135 Q2 **Haleiwa** Hawaiian Is
143 B7 **Hale, Mt** W Australia Australia
135 R2 **Halena** Hawaiian Is
112 B2 **Hales Bar Dam** Tennessee U.S.A.
9 D3 **Halesowen** England
9 G5 **Hale Street** England
9 H3 **Halesworth** England
111 J7 **Haleyville** Alabama U.S.A.
144 B7 **Halfmoon Bay** New Zealand
9 E3 **Halford** England
107 K2 **Halford** Kansas U.S.A.
117 M7 **Halfway** *R* British Columbia Canada
94 K7 **Halfway** Maryland U.S.A.
100 H5 **Halfway** Oregon U.S.A.
108 F1 **Halfway** Texas U.S.A.
116 K6 **Halfway Mt** Alaska U.S.A.
25 C4 **Halfweg** Netherlands
80 B7 **Halib** Israel
121 M7 **Haliburton** Ontario Canada
141 H4 **Halifax** Queensland Australia
123 J9 **Halifax** Nova Scotia Canada
13 G6 **Halifax** England
112 K1 **Halifax** North Carolina U.S.A.
95 L6 **Halifax** Pennsylvania U.S.A.
94 H10 **Halifax** Virginia U.S.A.
141 H4 **Halifax B** Queensland Australia
141 H4 **Halifax, Mt** Queensland Australia
29 K11 **Halikko** Finland
77 E5 **Halil** *R* Iran
79 G4 **Halīmah** *mt* Lebanon
70 L9 **Halimun, G** *mt* Java
Haliut *see* **Urad Zhongqi**
76 B3 **Haliyal** India
26 N4 **Halju** *mt* Sweden
28 D6 **Halk** Denmark
116 L1 **Halkett, C** Alaska U.S.A.
118 E6 **Halkirk** Alberta Canada
15 E2 **Halkirk** Scotland
26 O2 **Halkkavarre** *mt* Norway
101 M3 **Hall** Montana U.S.A.
26 J8 **Hälla** Sweden
9 G6 **Halland** England
26 F8 **Hålland** Sweden
27 F15 **Halland** *county* Sweden
113 G12 **Hallandale** Florida U.S.A.
27 F15 **Hallandsås** *hills* Sweden
29 K4 **Hallands Väderö** *isld* Sweden
138 D5 **Hall B** South Australia Australia
115 N1 **Hall Basin** Canada/Greenland
119 S8 **Hallboro** Manitoba Canada
22 G2 **Halle** Belgium
32 H8 **Halle** Germany
33 P10 **Halle** Germany
27 H15 **Hälleberga** Sweden
120 G3 **Hallebourg** Ontario Canada
28 G5 **Halleby Å** *R* Denmark
100 K9 **Halleck** Nevada U.S.A.
27 G12 **Hällefors** Sweden
38 H6 **Hallein** Austria
26 G8 **Hallen** Sweden
36 F1 **Hallenberg** Germany
21 O2 **Hallencourt** France
28 F4 **Hallendrup** Denmark
33 P10 **Halle-Neustadt** Germany
26 H9 **Hällesjö** Sweden
146 C12 **Hallett, Cape** *C* Antarctica
109 L6 **Hallettsville** Texas U.S.A.
146 F6 **Halley** *U.K. Base* Antarctica
111 E8 **Halley** Arkansas U.S.A.
116 B6 **Hall I** Bering Sea
98 D2 **Halliday** North Dakota U.S.A.
98 A9 **Halligan Res** Colorado U.S.A.
27 D11 **Hallingdalselv** *R* Norway
27 C11 **Hallingskarvet** *mt* Norway
27 B11 **Hallingskeid** Norway
115 L4 **Hall Lake** *L* Northwest Territories Canada
27 J11 **Hållnäs** Sweden
119 V10 **Hallock** Minnesota U.S.A.
118 K8 **Hallonquist** Saskatchewan Canada
115 N5 **Hall Pen** Northwest Territories Canada
110 G6 **Halls** Tennessee U.S.A.
8 C7 **Hallsands** England
27 H12 **Hallsberg** Sweden
142 G4 **Halls Creek** W Australia Australia
138 F6 **Halls Gap** Victoria Australia
37 K4 **Hallstadt** Germany
27 H12 **Hallstahammar** Sweden
106 G3 **Hall Station** Colorado U.S.A.
38 J6 **Hallstatt** Austria
27 K11 **Hallstavik** Sweden
95 M5 **Hallstead** Pennsylvania U.S.A.
111 C9 **Hall Summit** Louisiana U.S.A.
110 D2 **Hallsville** Missouri U.S.A.
109 N3 **Hallsville** Texas U.S.A.
81 A8 **Hall Table Mt** Indian Oc
41 O3 **Halltal** Austria
94 J5 **Hallton** Pennsylvania U.S.A.
22 E2 **Halluin** France
25 E2 **Hallum** Netherlands
28 E2 **Hallund** Denmark
28 C5 **Hallundbæk** Denmark
26 H8 **Hallviken** Sweden
98 K1 **Halma** Minnesota U.S.A.
71 B2 **Halmahera** *isld* Indonesia
71 B3 **Halmahera** *sea* Indonesia
48 H3 **Halmeu** Romania
27 F15 **Halmstad** Sweden
43 C12 **Halq el Oued** Tunisia
28 E2 **Hals** Denmark
26 C8 **Halsa** Norway
37 P2 **Halsbrucke** Germany
36 F2 **Halsdorf** Germany
98 F8 **Halsey** Nebraska U.S.A.
100 B5 **Halsey** Oregon U.S.A.
71 D5 **Halsey Harbour** Philippines
28 H5 **Halsnæs** *pen* Denmark
28 G6 **Halsskov** Denmark
98 K2 **Halstad** Minnesota U.S.A.
9 G4 **Halstead** England
107 N4 **Halstead** Kansas U.S.A.
36 B5 **Halstroff** France
29 L8 **Halsua** Finland
26 E9 **Haltdalen** Norway
26 D7 **Halten** Norway
32 F9 **Haltern** Germany
29 J2 **Halti** *mt* Finland
109 M9 **Haltom City** Texas U.S.A.
13 F4 **Haltwhistle** England
77 C7 **Ḩālūl** *isld* Qatar
71 K10 **Halura** *isld* Indonesia
36 C1 **Halver** Germany
118 L8 **Halvorgate** Saskatchewan Canada
28 D2 **Halvrimmen** Denmark
141 K7 **Haly, Mt** Queensland Australia
22 E4 **Ham** France
80 G3 **Ham** Jordan
60 F12 **Hama** Japan
60 F11 **Hamada** Japan
85 F3 **Hamada de Tinrhert** *stony desert* Algeria
85 D4 **Hamada El Haricha** *reg* Mali
77 A2 **Hamadān** Iran
85 C3 **Hamada Tounassine** *stony desert* Algeria
80 F3 **Ḩamadya** Israel
79 G3 **Ḩamāh** Syria
61 P13 **Hamahika-jima** *isld* Okinawa
61 L11 **Hamakita** Japan
60 P2 **Hamamasu** Japan
59 L5 **Hamamatsu** Japan
60 T2 **Hamanaka** Japan
61 L11 **Hamana ko** *L* Japan
80 C4 **Ha Ma 'Pil** Israel
27 E11 **Hamar** Norway
98 H2 **Hamar** North Dakota U.S.A.
26 H3 **Hamaröy** Norway
60 H10 **Hamasaka** Japan
84 J5 **Hamâta, Gebel** *mt* Egypt
80 F3 **Hamat Gader** Jordan
60 Q1 **Hama-Tombetsu** Japan
36 C5 **Hambach** France
83 L11 **Hambantota** Sri Lanka
98 G2 **Hamberg** North Dakota U.S.A.
32 J6 **Hambergen** Germany
117 O9 **Hamber Prov. Park** British Columbia Canada
9 F5 **Hambledon** England
13 G6 **Hambleton** England
13 G5 **Hambleton Hills** England
100 D8 **Hambone** California U.S.A.
32 L7 **Hambühren** Germany
34 **Hamburg** *conurbation* Germany
111 E8 **Hamburg** Arkansas U.S.A.
100 B8 **Hamburg** California U.S.A.
99 L9 **Hamburg** Iowa U.S.A.
95 N5 **Hamburg** New Jersey U.S.A.
94 J4 **Hamburg** New York U.S.A.
95 M6 **Hamburg** Pennsylvania U.S.A.
20 H4 **Hambye** France
95 M4 **Hamden** New York U.S.A.
94 E7 **Hamden** Ohio U.S.A.
29 L10 **Hame** *prov* Finland
29 K10 **Hämeenkyrö** Finland
29 L11 **Hämeenlinna** Finland
143 A10 **Hamelin B** W Australia Australia
143 A7 **Hamelin Pool** W Australia Australia
32 K8 **Hameln** Germany
101 N6 **Hamer** Idaho U.S.A.
33 O8 **Hamersleben** Germany
142 C5 **Hamersley** W Australia Australia
142 B5 **Hamersley Ra** W Australia Australia
142 B6 **Hamersley Ra. Nat Park** W Australia Australia
33 P7 **Hamerten** Germany
65 G5 **Hamhŭng** N Korea
66 E3 **Hami** China
140 F6 **Hamilton** *R* Queensland Australia
140 F6 **Hamilton** Queensland Australia
138 C2 **Hamilton** *R* South Australia Australia
139 H8 **Hamilton** Tasmania Australia
138 F6 **Hamilton** Victoria Australia
90 B2 **Hamilton** Bermuda
121 L9 **Hamilton** Ontario Canada
145 E2 **Hamilton** New Zealand
12 D2 **Hamilton** Scotland
111 J7 **Hamilton** Alabama U.S.A.
101 S9 **Hamilton** Colorado U.S.A.
111 M9 **Hamilton** Georgia U.S.A.
99 P9 **Hamilton** Illinois U.S.A.
94 C5 **Hamilton** Indiana U.S.A.
107 O4 **Hamilton** Kansas U.S.A.
94 A4 **Hamilton** Michigan U.S.A.
101 L3 **Hamilton** Montana U.S.A.
95 M4 **Hamilton** New York U.S.A.
119 U10 **Hamilton** North Dakota U.S.A.
94 C7 **Hamilton** Ohio U.S.A.
100 F5 **Hamilton** Oregon U.S.A.
109 J4 **Hamilton** Texas U.S.A.
100 D1 **Hamilton** Washington U.S.A.
102 C2 **Hamilton City** California U.S.A.
101 R6 **Hamilton Dome** Wyoming U.S.A.
140 C6 **Hamilton Downs** N Terr Australia
115 O7 **Hamilton Inlet** Labrador, Nfld Canada

182 **Hamilton,L — Hébert, L**

111 C7 **Hamilton,L** Arkansas U.S.A.
103 J2 **Hamilton, Mt** Nevada U.S.A.
29 N11 **Hamina** Finland
74 J6 **Hamirpur** India
Hamitabat *see* **İsparta**
94 C5 **Hamler** Ohio U.S.A.
94 A5 **Hamlet** Indiana U.S.A.
98 E9 **Hamlet** Nebraska U.S.A.
112 H3 **Hamlet** North Carolina U.S.A.
138 E5 **Hamley Bridge** South Australia Australia
94 K3 **Hamlin** New York U.S.A.
108 G3 **Hamlin** Texas U.S.A.
94 E8 **Hamlin** West Virginia U.S.A.
94 A2 **Hamlin L** Michigan U.S.A.
32 G9 **Hamm** Germany
17 G9 **Hammam Bou Hadjar** Algeria
43 D12 **Hammamet** Tunisia
85 G1 **Hammamet, G de** Tunisia
85 G1 **Hammam Lif** Tunisia
29 H11 **Hammarland** Finland
27 F11 **Hammarsbyn** Sweden
29 M3 **Hammastunturi** *mt* Finland
22 G1 **Hamme** Belgium
32 J6 **Hamme** *R* Germany
28 D4 **Hammel** Denmark
36 H3 **Hammelburg** Germany
28 F4 **Hammelev** Denmark
28 C6 **Hammelev** Denmark
33 S6 **Hammelspring** Germany
22 H2 **Hamme-Mille** Belgium
26 H8 **Hammerdal** Sweden
147 H14 **Hammerfest** Norway
28 D3 **Hammershøj** Denmark
143 C9 **Hammersley L** W Australia Australia
36 C3 **Hammerstein** Germany
13 G6 **Hammerton** England
28 C4 **Hammerum** Denmark
100 K7 **Hammett** Idaho U.S.A.
32 E9 **Hamminkeln** Germany
107 L6 **Hammon** Oklahoma U.S.A.
138 E4 **Hammond** South Australia Australia
99 T8 **Hammond** Illinois U.S.A.
110 H2 **Hammond** Illinois U.S.A.
111 F11 **Hammond** Louisiana U.S.A.
98 B4 **Hammond** Montana U.S.A.
95 M2 **Hammond** New York U.S.A.
100 B3 **Hammond** Oregon U.S.A.
99 O5 **Hammond** Wisconsin U.S.A.
94 D1 **Hammond B** Michigan U.S.A.
141 F1 **Hammond I** Queensland Australia
95 K4 **Hammondsport** New York U.S.A.
122 G8 **Hammond Vale** New Brunswick Canada
102 C2 **Hammonton** California U.S.A.
95 N7 **Hammonton** New Jersey U.S.A.
26 O1 **Hamnbukt** Norway
26 L2 **Hamneidet** Norway
26 S1 **Hamningberg** Norway
68 G7 **Ham Ninh** Vietnam
121 T7 **Ham Nord** Quebec Canada
26 L4 **Håmojokk** Sweden
22 K1 **Hamont** Belgium
86 G2 **Hamoyet, Jebel** *mt* Sudan
123 Q4 **Hampden** Newfoundland Canada
144 C6 **Hampden** New Zealand
98 H1 **Hampden** North Dakota U.S.A.
95 T2 **Hampden Highlands** Maine U.S.A.
28 C4 **Hampen** Denmark
36 B6 **Hampont** France
9 E5 **Hampshire** *co* England
122 F8 **Hampstead** New Brunswick Canada
95 K7 **Hampstead** Maryland U.S.A.
112 K3 **Hampstead** North Carolina U.S.A.
122 G8 **Hampton** New Brunswick Canada
9 F5 **Hampton** England
111 D8 **Hampton** Arkansas U.S.A.
113 E8 **Hampton** Florida U.S.A.
111 M8 **Hampton** Georgia U.S.A.
99 N7 **Hampton** Iowa U.S.A.
98 J9 **Hampton** Nebraska U.S.A.
95 R4 **Hampton** New Hampshire U.S.A.
100 E6 **Hampton** Oregon U.S.A.
112 F5 **Hampton** South Carolina U.S.A.
95 L9 **Hampton** Virginia U.S.A.
101 P8 **Hampton** Wyoming U.S.A.
95 P6 **Hampton Bays** Long I, New York U.S.A.
143 F9 **Hampton Tableland** W Australia Australia
27 H10 **Hamra** Sweden
27 J11 **Hamränge** Sweden
79 G4 **Ḩamrāt, Al** Syria
101 P7 **Hams Fork** *R* Wyoming U.S.A.
9 G5 **Hamstreet** England
68 H7 **Ham Tan** Vietnam
135 T3 **Hana** Hawaiian Is
126 D3 **Hanábana** *R* Cuba
135 O1 **Hanalei** Hawaiian Is
135 T3 **Hanamanioa, C** Hawaiian Is
135 O1 **Hanamaulu** Hawaiian Is
135 O1 **Hanapepe** Hawaiian Is
61 N13 **Hanare-iwa** *islds* Japan
36 F3 **Hanau** Germany
102 S12 **Hanauma B** Hawaiian Is
121 L5 **Hanbury** Ontario Canada
117 M10 **Hanceville** British Columbia Canada
111 K7 **Hanceville** Alabama U.S.A.
58 F4 **Hancheng** China
67 D1 **Hanchuan** China
95 T2 **Hancock** Maine U.S.A.
94 J7 **Hancock** Maryland U.S.A.
99 S2 **Hancock** Michigan U.S.A.
99 L4 **Hancock** Minnesota U.S.A.
95 P4 **Hancock** New Hampshire U.S.A.
95 M5 **Hancock** New York U.S.A.
99 R5 **Hancock** Wisconsin U.S.A.
113 F10 **Hancock, L** Florida U.S.A.
61 K11 **Handa** Japan
58 F4 **Handan** China
28 B4 **Handbjerg** Denmark
9 F5 **Handcross** England
118 J6 **Handel** Saskatchewan Canada
27 K12 **Handen** Sweden
88 G4 **Handeni** Tanzania
28 D3 **Handest** Denmark
65 D1 **Handgai** China
109 K3 **Handley** Texas U.S.A.
119 P9 **Handsworth** Saskatchewan Canada
32 K4 **Hanerau** Germany
102 E5 **Hanford** California U.S.A.
76 B3 **Hangal** India
68 C5 **Hangan** Burma
65 G6 **Hangang** *R* S Korea
145 F3 **Hangaroa** New Zealand
27 C11 **Hangastöl** Norway
145 E3 **Hangatiki** New Zealand
58 C2 **Hangayn Nuruu** *mt* Mongolia
Hangchow *see* **Hangzhou**
33 T8 **Hangelsberg** Germany
27 G14 **Hånger** Sweden
58 E3 **Hanggin Houqi** China
94 E8 **Hanging Rock** Ohio U.S.A.
89 A10 **Hangklip, C** S Africa
100 H2 **Hangman Cr** Washington U.S.A.
29 K12 **Hango** Finland
65 D5 **Hangu** China
67 D4 **Hanguang** China
59 H5 **Hangzhou** China
59 H5 **Hangzhou Wan** *B* China
79 F4 **Ḩanīdiyah, Al** Syria
32 M7 **Hänigsen** Germany
86 H3 **Ḩanīsh al Kabīr** *islds* Red Sea
80 D1 **Ḩanita** Israel
Hanjiang *see* **Yangzhou**
67 F4 **Hanjiang** China
29 M9 **Hankasalmi** Finland
85 C4 **Hank, El** Mauritania
98 J3 **Hankinson** North Dakota U.S.A.
58 F5 **Hankou** China
103 O3 **Hanksville** Utah U.S.A.
118 L7 **Hanley** Saskatchewan Canada
8 D1 **Hanley** England
99 L5 **Hanley Falls** Minnesota U.S.A.
144 D5 **Hanmer Springs** New Zealand
118 F7 **Hanna** Alberta Canada
101 P9 **Hanna** Utah U.S.A.
101 T8 **Hanna** Wyoming U.S.A.
98 H2 **Hannaford** North Dakota U.S.A.
119 T10 **Hannah** North Dakota U.S.A.
120 K1 **Hannah B** Ontario Canada
99 P10 **Hannibal** Missouri U.S.A.
99 Q4 **Hannibal** Wisconsin U.S.A.
28 A4 **Hanning Kirke** Denmark
142 F3 **Hann, Mt** W Australia Australia
32 L8 **Hannover** Germany
98 E2 **Hannover** North Dakota U.S.A.
140 C6 **Hann Ra** N Terr Australia
22 J2 **Hannut** Belgium
27 H16 **Hanöbukten** *B* Sweden
68 G2 **Hanoi** Vietnam
48 D4 **Hanót** Hungary
120 J8 **Hanover** Ontario Canada
127 H1 **Hanover** *parish* Jamaica
89 D8 **Hanover** S Africa
107 O2 **Hanover** Kansas U.S.A.
99 N4 **Hanover** Minnesota U.S.A.
101 Q2 **Hanover** Montana U.S.A.
95 P3 **Hanover** New Hampshire U.S.A.
133 C8 **Hanover, I** Chile
48 E6 **Han Pijesak** Bosnia-Herzegovina
48 D3 **Hanság** Hungary
117 N8 **Hansard** British Columbia Canada
98 G1 **Hansboro** North Dakota U.S.A.
120 F3 **Hansen** Ontario Canada
146 J10 **Hansen mts** Antarctica
67 F1 **Hanshan** China
67 D2 **Hanshou** China
58 E5 **Han Shui** *R* China
67 D1 **Han Shui** *R* China
74 F4 **Hansi** India
27 G10 **Hansjö** Sweden
140 C5 **Hanson** *R* N Terr Australia
138 D4 **Hanson, L** South Australia Australia
119 P4 **Hanson L** Saskatchewan Canada
28 D5 **Hansted** Vejle Denmark
28 B2 **Hanstholm** Denmark
28 B2 **Hanstholm Havn** *C* Denmark
65 D2 **Han Sum** China
22 J3 **Han-sur-Lesse** Belgium
25 B6 **Hansweert** Netherlands
Hantan *see* **Handan**
66 C3 **Hantengri Feng** *mt* Kazakhstan
Hanting *see* **Wei Xian**
Hants *co see* **Hampshire**
122 H8 **Hantsport** Nova Scotia Canada
36 C7 **Hantz, Col du** *pass* France
79 H3 **Ḩānūbah, Al** Syria
65 D2 **Han Ul** China
20 B5 **Hanvec** France
67 A1 **Hanwang** China
83 K11 **Hanwella** Sri Lanka
58 F5 **Hanyang** China
57 K4 **Hanyaylak** China
61 N9 **Hanyū** Japan
58 D6 **Hanyuan** China
58 E5 **Hanzhong** China
65 D7 **Hanzhuang** China
135 N10 **Hao** *atoll* Tuamotu Arch Pacific Oc
65 H1 **Haolianghe** China
80 F3 **Ha On** Israel
75 N7 **Hāora** India
26 N6 **Haparanda** Sweden
71 B1 **Hapo** Halmahera Indonesia
9 H2 **Happisburgh** England
100 B8 **Happy Camp** California U.S.A.
140 E5 **Happy Cr** N Terr Australia
144 D5 **Hapuku** New Zealand
83 L11 **Haputale** Sri Lanka
79 E9 **Ḩaql** Saudi Arabia
26 M5 **Harads** Sweden
86 H4 **Hara Fanna** Ethiopia
111 H12 **Harahan** New Orleans, Louisiana U.S.A.
26 B9 **Haram** Norway
59 M4 **Haramachi** Japan
86 H4 **Hārar** Ethiopia
88 C10 **Harare** Zimbabwe
58 E2 **Har-ayrag** Mongolia
86 C3 **Haraz Djombo** Chad
86 D3 **Haraz-Mangueigne** Chad
80 E8 **Har Ben Yai'r** Israel
65 G2 **Harbin** China
27 J11 **Harbo** Sweden
77 K5 **Harboi Hills** Pakistan
28 J7 **Hårbølle** Denmark
22 D4 **Harbonnières** France
28 A3 **Harboør** Denmark
28 A3 **Harboør Tange** *pen* Denmark
100 A7 **Harbor** Oregon U.S.A.
94 E3 **Harbor Beach** Michigan U.S.A.
117 E6 **Harbor Pt** Alaska U.S.A.
94 B1 **Harbor Springs** Michigan U.S.A.
13 F3 **Harbottle** England
123 R6 **Harbour Breton** Newfoundland Canada
123 S6 **Harbour Buffett** Newfoundland Canada
113 K12 **Harbour Cay, Little** *isld* Bahamas
123 Q3 **Harbour Deep** Newfoundland Canada
123 T6 **Harbour Grace** Newfoundland Canada
113 L12 **Harbour I** Bahamas
123 S6 **Harbour Mille** Newfoundland Canada
122 H8 **Harbourville** Nova Scotia Canada
37 K6 **Harburg** Bayern Germany
32 L6 **Harburg** Niedersachsen Germany
28 E6 **Hårby** Denmark
122 G7 **Harcourt** New Brunswick Canada
103 L7 **Harcuvar Mts** Arizona U.S.A.
74 G7 **Harda Khās** India
27 B11 **Hardanger** Norway
27 B11 **Hardanger-fjorden** *inlet* Norway
27 C11 **Hardangervidda** *plateau* Norway
27 B11 **Hardangervidda Nat. Park** Norway
89 A5 **Hardap Dam** Namibia
111 F9 **Hardee** Mississippi U.S.A.
112 F5 **Hardeeville** South Carolina U.S.A.
25 E2 **Hardegarijp** Netherlands
32 L9 **Hardegsen** Germany
22 B2 **Hardelot-Plage** France
25 G3 **Hardenberg** Netherlands
70 D2 **Harden, Bt** *mt* Kalimantan
25 E4 **Harderwijk** Netherlands
107 J5 **Hardesty** Oklahoma U.S.A.
142 B6 **Hardey, R** W Australia Australia
36 H4 **Hardheim** Germany
110 F2 **Hardin** Illinois U.S.A.
110 C2 **Hardin** Missouri U.S.A.
101 S4 **Hardin** Montana U.S.A.
87 E12 **Harding** S Africa
99 M3 **Harding** Minnesota U.S.A.
116 M6 **Harding Icefield** Alaska U.S.A.
119 T2 **Harding L** Manitoba Canada
111 L9 **Harding, L** Georgia U.S.A.
110 K4 **Hardinsburg** Kentucky U.S.A.
118 F6 **Hardisty** Alberta Canada
117 P3 **Hardisty L** Northwest Territories Canada
21 P2 **Hardivillers** France
100 F4 **Hardman** Oregon U.S.A.
142 E4 **Hardman, Mt** W Australia Australia
80 D8 **Hardof** *R* Jordan
98 K6 **Hardwick** Minnesota U.S.A.
95 P2 **Hardwick** Vermont U.S.A.
8 D4 **Hardwicke** England
138 D5 **Hardwicke B** South Australia Australia
119 N9 **Hardy** Saskatchewan Canada
110 E5 **Hardy** Arkansas U.S.A.
101 O2 **Hardy** Montana U.S.A.
Hardy, Mt *see* **Rangipova**
133 D9 **Hardy, Pen** Chile
94 B3 **Hardy Res** Michigan U.S.A.
123 S5 **Hare B** Newfoundland Canada
80 E4 **Hare Gilboa** Israel
26 B9 **Hareid** Norway
22 E2 **Harelbeke** Belgium
32 F7 **Haren** Germany
115 O3 **Hareøen** *isld* Greenland
86 H4 **Hārergē** *prov* Ethiopia
13 G6 **Harewood** England
79 F5 **Harf el Mreffi** *mt* Lebanon
21 L2 **Harfleur** France
27 K11 **Harg** Sweden
36 B5 **Hargarten aux Mines** France
86 H4 **Hargele** Ethiopia
86 H4 **Hargeysa** Somalia
48 K4 **Harghita, Muntii** *mt* Romania
22 E4 **Hargicourt** France
109 J9 **Hargill** Texas U.S.A.
22 J3 **Hargimont** Belgium
22 H3 **Hargnies** France
119 Q9 **Hargrave** Manitoba Canada
119 S4 **Hargrave L** Manitoba Canada
79 E8 **Har Hakippa** *mt* Israel
79 E8 **Har Harif** Israel
80 D8 **Har Ḩezron** Israel
66 F4 **Har Hu** *L* China
61 M9 **Hari** Japan
74 H4 **Haridwār** India
76 B3 **Harihar** India
144 C5 **Harihari** New Zealand
79 G2 **Hārim** Syria
60 H11 **Harima-nada** *sea* Japan
25 B5 **Haringvliet** Netherlands
74 E1 **Haripur** Pakistan
77 J2 **Hari Rud** *R* Afghanistan/Iran
79 G6 **Ḩarīr, Wādī adh** *watercourse* Syria
87 C10 **Haris** Namibia
26 G10 **Härjån** *R* Sweden
29 J10 **Harjavalta** Finland
26 F10 **Härjehågna** *mt* Sweden
80 F2 **Har Kena'an** *pk* Israel
112 L3 **Harkers I** North Carolina U.S.A.
99 L8 **Harlan** Iowa U.S.A.
107 M2 **Harlan** Kansas U.S.A.
94 D10 **Harlan** Kentucky U.S.A.
98 G9 **Harlan County Lake** *res* Nebraska U.S.A.
22 K4 **Harlange** Luxembourg
32 G5 **Harle** Germany
8 B2 **Harlech** Wales
112 E4 **Harlem** Georgia U.S.A.
101 R1 **Harlem** Montana U.S.A.
32 L5 **Harlesiel** Germany
9 H3 **Harleston** England
28 D4 **Harlev** Denmark
28 J6 **Hårlev** Denmark
112 G4 **Harleyville** South Carolina U.S.A.
25 D2 **Harlingen** Netherlands
109 K9 **Harlingen** Texas U.S.A.
32 G5 **Harlinger Land** Germany
33 M9 **Harlingerode** Germany
9 G4 **Harlow** England
98 G1 **Harlow** North Dakota U.S.A.
101 Q3 **Harlowton** Montana U.S.A.
94 H8 **Harman** West Virginia U.S.A.
47 K5 **Harmancık** Turkey
26 J10 **Harmånger** Sweden
25 C4 **Harmelen** Netherlands
80 E2 **Har Meron** *pk* Israel
107 L5 **Harmon** Oklahoma U.S.A.
118 A2 **Harmon R** Alberta Canada
95 S2 **Harmony** Maine U.S.A.
99 O6 **Harmony** Minnesota U.S.A.
79 E8 **Har Natḩa** *mt* Israel
100 F6 **Harney Basin** *reg* Oregon U.S.A.
113 F9 **Harney, L** Florida U.S.A.
100 F6 **Harney L** Oregon U.S.A.
98 C6 **Harney Pk** South Dakota U.S.A.
28 E6 **Harnorup** Denmark
26 J9 **Härnösand** Sweden
65 E2 **Har Nur** China
58 B2 **Har Nuur** *L* Mongolia
80 E3 **Harod** *R* Israel
26 B9 **Haröy** *isld* Norway
9 F4 **Harpenden** England
85 C8 **Harper** Liberia
107 M4 **Harper** Kansas U.S.A.
100 H6 **Harper** Oregon U.S.A.
109 H5 **Harper** Texas U.S.A.
116 L4 **Harper Bend** Alaska U.S.A.
117 Q6 **Harper Cr** Alberta Canada
102 G6 **Harper L** California U.S.A.
116 Q4 **Harper, Mt** Alaska U.S.A.
144 C5 **Harper Pass** New Zealand
94 K7 **Harpers Ferry** West Virginia U.S.A.
110 J5 **Harpeth** *R* Tennessee U.S.A.
8 C6 **Harpford** England
9 G2 **Harpley** England
27 F15 **Harplinge** Sweden
32 J7 **Harpstedt** Germany
119 M9 **Harptree** Saskatchewan Canada
65 D4 **Harqin** China
65 D4 **Harqin Qi** China
103 L8 **Harquahala Mts** Arizona U.S.A.
85 E1 **Harrach, El** Algeria
107 N6 **Harrah** Oklahoma U.S.A.
26 F7 **Harran** Norway
37 K3 **Harras** Germany
28 B3 **Harre** Denmark
111 D8 **Harrell** Arkansas U.S.A.
144 D5 **Harrelville** New Zealand
121 L2 **Harricana** *R* Quebec Canada
28 E3 **Harridslev** Denmark
94 B2 **Harrietta** Michigan U.S.A.
112 C2 **Harriman** Tennessee U.S.A.
95 M8 **Harrington** Delaware U.S.A.
95 U2 **Harrington** Maine U.S.A.
100 G2 **Harrington** Washington U.S.A.
123 N3 **Harrington-Harbour** Quebec Canada
119 P2 **Harriot L** Saskatchewan Canada
118 K7 **Harris** Saskatchewan Canada
15 B3 **Harris** *div* Scotland
100 B9 **Harris** California U.S.A.
99 N9 **Harris** Missouri U.S.A.
110 F6 **Harrisburg** Arkansas U.S.A.
110 H4 **Harrisburg** Illinois U.S.A.
98 C8 **Harrisburg** Nebraska U.S.A.
94 D7 **Harrisburg** Ohio U.S.A.
100 B5 **Harrisburg** Oregon U.S.A.
95 L6 **Harrisburg** Pennsylvania U.S.A.
98 K6 **Harrisburg** South Dakota U.S.A.
118 H2 **Harris Hill** Ontario Canada
138 D4 **Harris, L** South Australia Australia
113 F9 **Harris, L** Florida U.S.A.
143 C10 **Harrismith** W Australia Australia
89 F7 **Harrismith** S Africa
140 A6 **Harris, Mt** N Terr Australia
144 B6 **Harris Mts** New Zealand
110 C5 **Harrison** Arkansas U.S.A.
112 E5 **Harrison** Georgia U.S.A.
100 J2 **Harrison** Idaho U.S.A.
94 C2 **Harrison** Michigan U.S.A.
101 O4 **Harrison** Montana U.S.A.
98 C7 **Harrison** Nebraska U.S.A.
98 H6 **Harrison** South Dakota U.S.A.
116 L1 **Harrison B** Alaska U.S.A.
111 E10 **Harrisonburg** Louisiana U.S.A.
94 J8 **Harrisonburg** Virginia U.S.A.
115 O7 **Harrison, C** Labrador, Nfld Canada
117 M11 **Harrison L** British Columbia Canada
83 K12 **Harrison, Mt** Mahé I Indian Oc
110 B3 **Harrisonville** Missouri U.S.A.
94 D2 **Harrisville** Michigan U.S.A.
95 M2 **Harrisville** New York U.S.A.
94 F7 **Harrisville** West Virginia U.S.A.
110 K2 **Harrodsburg** Indiana U.S.A.
94 C9 **Harrodsburg** Kentucky U.S.A.
13 G6 **Harrogate** England
98 G5 **Harrold** South Dakota U.S.A.
109 H1 **Harrold** Texas U.S.A.
120 H10 **Harrow** Ontario Canada
9 F4 **Harrow** England
119 Q8 **Harrowby** Manitoba Canada
26 H7 **Harrsjön** Sweden
27 F14 **Härryda** Sweden
110 C3 **Harry S. Truman Res** Missouri U.S.A.
98 F9 **Harry Strunk L** Nebraska U.S.A.
79 E8 **Har Saggi** *mt* Israel
32 K6 **Harsefeld** Germany
32 H9 **Harsewinkel** Germany
26 L5 **Harsprånget** Sweden
26 J3 **Harstad** Norway
32 L8 **Harsum** Germany
28 A4 **Harsyssel** *reg* Denmark
119 M9 **Hart** Saskatchewan Canada
13 G4 **Hart** England
99 U6 **Hart** Michigan U.S.A.
65 E3 **Hartao** China
89 B7 **Hartbees** *watercourse* S Africa
89 E5 **Hartbeespoortdam** S Africa
38 N7 **Hartberg** Austria
27 B11 **Hårteigen** *mt* Norway
118 C8 **Hartell** Alberta Canada
22 E5 **Hartennes-et-Taux** France
36 E2 **Hartenrod** Germany
37 O2 **Hartenstein** Germany
37 J5 **Hartershofen** Germany
15 E5 **Hart Fell** Scotland
9 G5 **Hartfield** England
111 L10 **Hartford** Alabama U.S.A.
109 N1 **Hartford** Arkansas U.S.A.
95 P5 **Hartford** Connecticut U.S.A.
107 P3 **Hartford** Kansas U.S.A.
110 K4 **Hartford** Kentucky U.S.A.
94 A4 **Hartford** Michigan U.S.A.
94 E6 **Hartford** Ohio U.S.A.
112 D2 **Hartford** Tennessee U.S.A.
99 S6 **Hartford** Wisconsin U.S.A.
94 B6 **Hartford City** Indiana U.S.A.
95 P5 **Hartford, E** Connecticut U.S.A.
37 O1 **Hartha** Germany
37 O2 **Harthau** Germany
12 E2 **Harthill** Scotland
9 E1 **Hartington** England
98 J7 **Hartington** Nebraska U.S.A.
80 E2 **Har Tir'an** Israel
122 D2 **Hart-jaune, R** Quebec Canada
138 D4 **Hart, L** South Australia Australia
122 E7 **Hartland** New Brunswick Canada
8 B6 **Hartland** England
95 S2 **Hartland** Maine U.S.A.
8 B5 **Hartland Pt** England
8 D3 **Hartlebury** England
13 G4 **Hartlepool** England
13 G3 **Hartley** England
99 L6 **Hartley** Iowa U.S.A.
108 B8 **Hartley** Texas U.S.A.
117 J9 **Hartley Bay** British Columbia Canada
9 F5 **Hartley Wintney** England
100 F2 **Hartline** Washington U.S.A.
106 H3 **Hartman** Colorado U.S.A.
37 P5 **Hartmanice** Czechoslovakia
37 O2 **Hartmannsdorf** Germany
36 G3 **Hartmannshain** Germany
142 E3 **Hart, Mt** W Australia Australia
119 Q6 **Hart Mt** Manitoba Canada
100 F7 **Hart Mt** Oregon U.S.A.
119 R9 **Hartney** Manitoba Canada
29 M10 **Hartola** Finland
13 G4 **Harton** England
106 E2 **Hartsel** Colorado U.S.A.
111 K7 **Hartselle** Alabama U.S.A.
37 J6 **Härtsfeld** *mts* Germany
107 P7 **Hartshorne** Oklahoma U.S.A.
138 C4 **Harts I** South Australia Australia
140 C6 **Harts Range Police Station** N Terr Australia
112 G3 **Hartsville** South Carolina U.S.A.
110 K5 **Hartsville** Tennessee U.S.A.
89 D6 **Hartswater** S Africa
80 C6 **Hartuv** Israel
110 D4 **Hartville** Missouri U.S.A.
98 B7 **Hartville** Wyoming U.S.A.
112 E3 **Hartwell** Georgia U.S.A.
112 E3 **Hartwell L** *res* South Carolina U.S.A.
120 H3 **Harty** Ontario Canada
89 D6 **Hartz** *R* S Africa
84 F4 **Harūj al Aswad, Al** Libya
79 G1 **Haruniye** Turkey
58 B2 **Har Us Nuur** *L* Mongolia
80 C7 **Ḩaruvit** Israel
102 H7 **Harvard** California U.S.A.
100 J3 **Harvard** Idaho U.S.A.
99 S7 **Harvard** Illinois U.S.A.
98 H9 **Harvard** Nebraska U.S.A.
116 O6 **Harvard Gl** Alaska U.S.A.
106 D3 **Harvard, Mt** Colorado U.S.A.
143 F7 **Harvest, Mt** W Australia Australia
143 B10 **Harvey** W Australia Australia
99 T8 **Harvey** Illinois U.S.A.
99 O8 **Harvey** Iowa U.S.A.
111 J13 **Harvey** New Orleans, Louisiana U.S.A.
98 F2 **Harvey** North Dakota U.S.A.
102 C1 **Harvey Mt** California U.S.A.
122 F8 **Harvey Stn** New Brunswick Canada
107 P3 **Harveyville** Kansas U.S.A.
110 F5 **Harviell** Missouri U.S.A.
9 E4 **Harwell** England
9 H4 **Harwich** England
109 K6 **Harwood** Texas U.S.A.
36 E4 **Harxheim** Germany
74 F4 **Haryana** *prov* India
80 E8 **Har Yonatan** Israel
33 N9 **Harz** *mts* Germany
33 O9 **Harzegerode** Germany
79 F8 **Hāsā** Jordan
72 F4 **Hasā, Al** *reg* Saudi Arabia
78 H3 **Hasakah, Al** Syria
78 E2 **Hasan Daği** *mt* Turkey
74 H9 **Hasanparti** India
80 E7 **Hasasa** *R* Jordan
79 F5 **Hâsbaiya** Lebanon
32 G8 **Hasbergen** Germany
36 B5 **Hasborn-Dautweiler** Germany
32 G7 **Hase** *R* Germany
37 K2 **Hasel** *R* Germany
32 L5 **Haseldorf** Germany
32 F7 **Haselünne** Germany
80 D4 **Hashimiye** Jordan
61 J11 **Hashimoto** Japan
26 H8 **Håsjö** Sweden
111 D7 **Haskell** Arkansas U.S.A.
107 P6 **Haskell** Oklahoma U.S.A.
108 H2 **Haskell** Texas U.S.A.
38 K4 **Haslach** Austria
36 E7 **Haslach** Germany
27 G16 **Hasle** Denmark
109 M8 **Haslet** Texas U.S.A.
28 H6 **Haslev** Denmark
13 F6 **Haslingden** England
41 H4 **Hasli Tal** Switzerland
28 E4 **Haslund** Denmark
28 E5 **Hasmark** Denmark
22 E3 **Hasnon** France
80 D3 **Ha Solelim** Israel
18 E9 **Hasparren** France
32 F10 **Haspe** Germany
80 G2 **Haspin** Syria
22 E3 **Haspres** France
76 C4 **Hassan** India
103 M8 **Hassayampa** *R* Arizona U.S.A.
37 K3 **Hassberge** *mts* Germany
36 C5 **Hassel** Germany
26 J9 **Hassela** Sweden
33 N9 **Hasselfelde** Germany
115 K2 **Hassel Sd** Northwest Territories Canada
22 J2 **Hasselt** Belgium
25 F3 **Hasselt** Netherlands
28 F4 **Hassensør** *C* Denmark
33 N9 **Hasserode** Germany
37 K3 **Hassfurt** Germany
17 F10 **Hassi Berkane** Morocco
85 E2 **Hassi-Bou-Zid** Algeria
85 E3 **Hassi Chebaba** Algeria
28 A3 **Hassing** Denmark
37 L3 **Hasslach** Germany
33 T6 **Hassleben** Germany
37 K1 **Hassleben** Thüringen Germany
27 G15 **Hässleholm** Sweden
27 G13 **Hasslerör** Sweden
36 E5 **Hassloch** Germany
22 H3 **Hastière-Lavaux** Belgium
139 L4 **Hastings** *R* New South Wales Australia
139 H9 **Hastings** Tasmania Australia
127 P6 **Hastings** Barbados
121 N8 **Hastings** Ontario Canada
9 G6 **Hastings** England
145 F3 **Hastings** New Zealand
113 F8 **Hastings** Florida U.S.A.
99 L9 **Hastings** Iowa U.S.A.
94 B4 **Hastings** Michigan U.S.A.
99 O5 **Hastings** Minnesota U.S.A.
98 H9 **Hastings** Nebraska U.S.A.
107 M7 **Hastings** Oklahoma U.S.A.
94 J6 **Hastings** Pennsylvania U.S.A.
28 E6 **Håstrup** Denmark
27 G15 **Hästveda** Sweden
106 H3 **Hasty** Colorado U.S.A.
26 M1 **Hasvik** Norway
106 G3 **Haswell** Colorado U.S.A.
79 G2 **Hatay** Turkey
95 M6 **Hatboro** Pennsylvania U.S.A.
106 C9 **Hatch** New Mexico U.S.A.
103 M4 **Hatch** Utah U.S.A.
140 D5 **Hatches Cr** N Terr Australia
126 F2 **Hatchet Bay** Eleuthera Bahamas
110 G6 **Hatchie** *R* Tennessee U.S.A.
98 B7 **Hat Cr** Wyoming U.S.A.
100 D9 **Hat Creek** California U.S.A.
48 H5 **Haţeg** Romania
145 F3 **Hatepe** New Zealand
67 H4 **Haterumashima** Japan
139 G5 **Hatfield** New South Wales Australia
119 M7 **Hatfield** Saskatchewan Canada
9 F4 **Hatfield** England
111 B7 **Hatfield** Arkansas U.S.A.
98 K6 **Hatfield** Minnesota U.S.A.
9 G4 **Hatfield Peverel** England
101 T3 **Hathaway** Montana U.S.A.
138 F6 **Hatherleigh** South Australia Australia
8 B6 **Hatherleigh** England
9 E1 **Hathersage** England
74 H5 **Hathras** India
68 G7 **Ha Tien** Vietnam
80 G3 **Hatim** Jordan
68 G3 **Ha Tinh** Vietnam
71 M9 **Hatohudo** Indonesia
127 K5 **Hato Mayor** Dominican Rep
56 C3 **Hatskiy** Russian Federation
60 F11 **Hatsukaichi** Japan
138 F5 **Hattah** Victoria Australia
70 F2 **Hattan, Mt** Sabah
25 F4 **Hattem** Netherlands
36 D6 **Hatten** France
112 M2 **Hatteras** North Carolina U.S.A.
112 M2 **Hatteras Inlet** North Carolina U.S.A.
36 E3 **Hattersheim** Germany
26 G6 **Hattfjelldal** Norway
111 G10 **Hattiesburg** Mississippi U.S.A.
36 B6 **Hattigny** France
28 D5 **Hatting** Denmark
32 F10 **Hattingen** Germany
118 H8 **Hatton** Saskatchewan Canada
21 P3 **Hatton** France
98 J2 **Hatton** North Dakota U.S.A.
100 G3 **Hatton** Washington U.S.A.
68 C6 **Hattras Passage** Burma
40 F1 **Hattstatt** France
29 L10 **Hattula** Finland
126 F4 **Hatuey** Cuba
145 F4 **Hatuma** New Zealand
48 F3 **Hatvan** Hungary
38 O8 **Hatzendorf** Austria
36 C3 **Hatzenport** Germany
36 F2 **Hatzfeld** Germany
22 D2 **Haubourdin** France
86 A2 **Haud** *reg* Ethiopia
80 G4 **Haufa** Jordan
28 C4 **Hauge** Denmark
27 C10 **Hauge** Norway
99 P4 **Haugen** Wisconsin U.S.A.
27 A12 **Haugesund** Norway
111 C9 **Haughton** Louisiana U.S.A.
31 J7 **Haugsdorf** Austria
29 L10 **Hauho** Finland
145 E3 **Hauhungaroa Ra** New Zealand
27 B12 **Haukeliseter** Norway
29 L6 **Haukipudas** Finland
29 N9 **Haukivesi** *L* Finland
29 N9 **Haukivuori** Finland
145 F3 **Haumoana** New Zealand
36 H2 **Haune** *R* Germany
36 H2 **Hauneck** Germany
36 H2 **Haunetal** Hessen Germany
37 K7 **Haunstetten** Germany
144 C5 **Haupiri, L** New Zealand
37 O5 **Hauptenberg** *mt* Germany
145 E2 **Hauraki Gulf** New Zealand
144 A6 **Hauroko, L** New Zealand
27 A11 **Haus** Norway
36 E7 **Hausach** Germany
32 J8 **Hausberge** Germany
101 O3 **Hauser L. Dam** Montana U.S.A.
38 H5 **Hausruck** *mts* Austria
Haussez Iles d' *see* **Mercury Is**
41 K4 **Hausstock** *mt* Switzerland
29 O5 **Hautajarvi** Finland
22 B3 **Haut Banc, Pte du** France
40 B2 **Haut du Sec** *mt* France
18 L10 **Haute-Corse** *dept* Corsica
19 O12 **Hautecourt** France
18 F7 **Hautefort** France
18 F9 **Haute-Garonne** *dept* France
18 H7 **Haute-Loire** *dept* France
40 E6 **Hauteluce** France
19 J4 **Haute-Marne** *dept* France
121 Q4 **Haute Mauricie, Parc de** Quebec Canada
122 D4 **Hauterive** Quebec Canada
19 Q15 **Hautes Alpes** *dept* France
19 J5 **Haute-Saône** *dept* France
40 D6 **Haute-Savoie** *dept* France
22 L2 **Hautes Fagnes** Belgium
18 E9 **Hautes-Pyrénées** *dept* France
22 H4 **Hautes Rivières** France
18 F7 **Haute-Vienne** *dept* France
20 G4 **Hauteville-sur-Mer** France
36 B5 **Haut-Hombourg** France
95 T2 **Haut, I. au** Maine U.S.A.
22 F3 **Hautmont** France
19 K5 **Haut-Rhin** *dept* France
85 D2 **Hauts Plateaux** Morocco/Algeria
86 E5 **Haut-Zaire** *prov* Zaire
135 Q2 **Hauula** Hawaiian Is
145 E4 **Hauwai** New Zealand
Havana Cuba *see* **Habana**
110 C6 **Havana** Arkansas U.S.A.
111 M11 **Havana** Florida U.S.A.
99 R9 **Havana** Illinois U.S.A.
107 P4 **Havana** Kansas U.S.A.
98 J4 **Havana** North Dakota U.S.A.
9 F6 **Havant** England
103 K7 **Havasu, L** Cal/Ariz U.S.A.
28 C3 **Havbro** Denmark
28 J5 **Havdrup** Denmark
33 R6 **Havel** Germany
22 J3 **Havelange** Belgium
33 Q7 **Havelberg** Germany
33 R7 **Havelland** *reg* Germany
33 R7 **Havelland Grosse Haupt-kanal** Germany
122 G8 **Havelock** New Brunswick Canada
121 N8 **Havelock** Ontario Canada
145 D4 **Havelock** New Zealand
112 L3 **Havelock** North Carolina U.S.A.
98 D3 **Havelock** North Dakota U.S.A.
140 C2 **Havelock Falls** N Terr Australia
68 A7 **Havelock I** Andaman Is
145 F3 **Havelock North** New Zealand
107 N4 **Haven** Kansas U.S.A.
107 O2 **Havensville** Kansas U.S.A.
8 B4 **Haverfordwest** Wales
9 G3 **Haverhill** England
95 Q4 **Haverhill** Massachusetts U.S.A.
95 Q3 **Haverhill** New Hampshire U.S.A.
76 B3 **Haveri** India
26 H9 **Haverö** Sweden
22 J3 **Haversin** Belgium
28 C2 **Haverslev** Denmark
28 D3 **Haverslev** Nordjylland Denmark
95 N5 **Haverstraw** New York U.S.A.
107 L4 **Haviland** Kansas U.S.A.
94 C5 **Haviland** Ohio U.S.A.
120 F6 **Haviland Bay** Ontario Canada
65 B2 **Havirga** Mongolia
48 K2 **Havirna** Romania
31 J6 **Havlíčkův Brod** Czechoslovakia
28 D6 **Havnbjerg** Denmark
28 E3 **Havndal** Denmark
28 B6 **Havneby** Denmark
28 G5 **Havnebyen** Denmark
28 G5 **Havnsø** Denmark
28 B4 **Havnstrup** Denmark
26 O1 **Havoysund** Norway
47 J5 **Havran** Turkey
22 G3 **Havre** Belgium
101 Q1 **Havre** Montana U.S.A.
21 L2 **Havre Antifer, Pont du** France
123 L6 **Havre Aubert** Madeleine Is, Quebec Canada
28 G6 **Havrebjerg** Denmark
123 L8 **Havre Boucher** Nova Scotia Canada
95 L7 **Havre de Grace** Maryland U.S.A.
122 J3 **Havre-St-Pierre** Quebec Canada
137 Q8 **Havre Trench** *sea feature* Pacific Oc
28 A5 **Havrvig** Denmark
26 H7 **Havsnäs** Sweden
78 E1 **Havza** Turkey
135 U5 **Hawaii** *isld* Hawaiian Is
135 **Hawaiian Is** Pacific Oc
86 B3 **Hawal** *R* Nigeria
118 L7 **Hawarden** Saskatchewan Canada
144 D5 **Hawarden** New Zealand
98 K6 **Hawarden** Iowa U.S.A.
8 C1 **Hawarden** Wales
138 F6 **Hawdon, L** South Australia Australia
144 B6 **Hawea** New Zealand
144 B6 **Hawea Flat** New Zealand
145 E3 **Hawera** New Zealand
102 G7 **Hawes** California U.S.A.
110 K4 **Hawesville** Kentucky U.S.A.
13 F5 **Hawes Water** England
135 U4 **Hawi** Hawaiian Is
13 F3 **Hawick** Scotland
144 B6 **Hawkdun Range** New Zealand
145 F3 **Hawke Bay** New Zealand
139 L4 **Hawke, C** New South Wales Australia
138 E4 **Hawker** South Australia Australia
138 F3 **Hawker Gate** New South Wales Australia
145 F3 **Hawke's Bay** *admin region* New Zealand
141 F1 **Hawkesbury I** Queensland Australia
140 C1 **Hawkesbury Pt** N Terr Australia
139 K5 **Hawkesbury R** New South Wales Australia
9 G5 **Hawkhurst** England
103 L4 **Hawkins Pk** Utah U.S.A.
112 D5 **Hawkinsville** Georgia U.S.A.
120 F4 **Hawk Junct** Ontario Canada
118 J1 **Hawk Lake** Ontario Canada
110 E3 **Hawk Point** Missouri U.S.A.
94 D1 **Hawks** Michigan U.S.A.
126 F2 **Hawksbill Cay** *isld* Bahamas
13 E5 **Hawkshead** England
126 G2 **Hawks Nest Pt** Cat I Bahamas
98 B8 **Hawk Springs** Wyoming U.S.A.
141 K7 **Hawkwood** Queensland Australia
106 G4 **Hawley** Colorado U.S.A.
98 K3 **Hawley** Minnesota U.S.A.
95 M5 **Hawley** Pennsylvania U.S.A.
108 H3 **Hawley** Texas U.S.A.
68 D2 **Hawng Luk** Burma
13 G6 **Haworth** England
107 Q8 **Haworth** Oklahoma U.S.A.
112 H2 **Haw R** North Carolina U.S.A.
78 H5 **Hawran, Wadi** Iraq
78 L5 **Hawr as S'adiyah** *L* Iraq
13 H5 **Hawsker** England
113 E8 **Hawthorn** Florida U.S.A.
102 F3 **Hawthorne** Nevada U.S.A.
99 P3 **Hawthorne** Wisconsin U.S.A.
80 D5 **Hawwara** Jordan
85 B3 **Hawza** Western Sahara
65 F2 **Haxat** China
65 B2 **Haxat Hudag** China
101 T2 **Haxby** Montana U.S.A.
98 D9 **Haxtun** Colorado U.S.A.
139 G5 **Hay** New South Wales Australia
117 N6 **Hay** *R* British Columbia Canada
100 H3 **Hay** Washington U.S.A.
99 P4 **Hay** *R* Wisconsin U.S.A.
61 P6 **Hayachine-san** *mt* Japan
60 P3 **Hayakita** Japan
19 K3 **Hayange** France
60 E12 **Hayasui-seto** *str* Japan
101 T9 **Haybro** Colorado U.S.A.
47 N10 **Haydarpaşa** Turkey
103 O8 **Hayden** Arizona U.S.A.
101 S9 **Hayden** Colorado U.S.A.
100 J2 **Hayden L** Idaho U.S.A.
141 F4 **Haydon** Queensland Australia
13 F4 **Haydon Br** England
20 G3 **Haye-du-Puits, la** France
21 N3 **Haye, la** France
20 H4 **Haye-Pesnel, la** France
115 K6 **Hayes** *R* Manitoba Canada
111 D11 **Hayes** Louisiana U.S.A.
98 E5 **Hayes** South Dakota U.S.A.
21 M4 **Haye-St.Sylvestre, la** France
98 E9 **Hayes Center** Nebraska U.S.A.
116 L6 **Hayes Glaciers** Alaska U.S.A.
115 N2 **Hayes Halvø** *pen* Greenland
68 C7 **Hayes I** Burma
116 O5 **Hayes, Mt** Alaska U.S.A.
112 D2 **Hayesville** North Carolina U.S.A.
13 G6 **Hayfield** England
99 O6 **Hayfield** Minnesota U.S.A.
103 J8 **Hayfield Res** Carolina U.S.A.
102 A1 **Hayfork** California U.S.A.
13 F5 **Haygarth** England
36 G7 **Hayingen** Germany
117 O6 **Hay L** Alberta Canada
118 D5 **Hay Lakes** Alberta Canada
8 A7 **Hayle** England
9 F6 **Hayling** England
113 E7 **Haylow** Georgia U.S.A.
141 J5 **Hayman I** Queensland Australia
94 K8 **Haymarket** Virginia U.S.A.
140 C6 **Hay, Mt** N Terr Australia
109 O3 **Haynesville** Louisiana U.S.A.
95 T8 **Haynesville** Maine U.S.A.
111 K9 **Hayneville** Alabama U.S.A.
21 N2 **Hayons, les** France
8 C3 **Hay-on-Wye** England
141 J5 **Hay Point** Queensland Australia
140 D6 **Hay R** N Terr Australia
47 J3 **Hayrabolu** *R* Turkey
47 J3 **Hayrabolu** Turkey
117 Q5 **Hay River** Northwest Territories Canada
118 F8 **Hays** Alberta Canada
107 L3 **Hays** Kansas U.S.A.
101 R1 **Hays** Montana U.S.A.
98 D7 **Hay Springs** Nebraska U.S.A.
100 K8 **Haystack Mt** Nevada U.S.A.
103 L2 **Haystack Pk** Utah U.S.A.
118 G6 **Hayter** Alberta Canada
110 G5 **Hayti** Missouri U.S.A.
98 J5 **Hayti** South Dakota U.S.A.
13 H6 **Hayton** England
102 B4 **Hayward** California U.S.A.
99 N6 **Hayward** Minnesota U.S.A.
107 N5 **Hayward** Oklahoma U.S.A.
99 P4 **Hayward** Wisconsin U.S.A.
140 B2 **Hayward, Mt** N Terr Australia
9 F6 **Haywards Heath** England
119 T9 **Haywood** Manitoba Canada
80 E2 **Hazan** Israel
77 J3 **Hazarajat** *reg* Afghanistan
94 D9 **Hazard** Kentucky U.S.A.
95 P4 **Hazardville** Connecticut U.S.A.
75 L7 **Hazāribag** India
77 F1 **Hazar Masjed, Kūh-e** *mts* Iran
22 D2 **Hazebrouck** France
98 K1 **Hazel** Minnesota U.S.A.
98 J5 **Hazel** South Dakota U.S.A.
119 V9 **Hazelridge** Manitoba Canada
117 K8 **Hazelton** British Columbia Canada
107 M4 **Hazelton** Kansas U.S.A.
98 F3 **Hazelton** North Dakota U.S.A.
110 E7 **Hazen** Arkansas U.S.A.
102 E2 **Hazen** Nevada U.S.A.
98 E2 **Hazen** North Dakota U.S.A.
116 E6 **Hazen B** Alaska U.S.A.
115 N1 **Hazen, L** Northwest Territories Canada
118 K9 **Hazenmore** Saskatchewan Canada
114 H2 **Hazen Str** Northwest Territories Canada
80 B8 **Haẕerim** Israel
25 C4 **Hazerswoude** Netherlands
112 E2 **Hazewood** North Carolina U.S.A.
112 E6 **Hazlehurst** Georgia U.S.A.
111 F10 **Hazlehurst** Mississippi U.S.A.
95 M6 **Hazleton** Pennsylvania U.S.A.
142 G5 **Hazlett, L** W Australia Australia
37 N3 **Hazlov** Czechoslovakia
80 F2 **Ḩaẕor** Israel
80 F3 **HaZore'im** Israel
80 C7 **He** Israel
9 G2 **Heacham** England
9 G5 **Headcorn** England
14 B3 **Headford** Ireland
122 E9 **Head Harbor I** Maine U.S.A.
140 E5 **Headingly** Queensland Australia
111 L10 **Headland** Alabama U.S.A.
144 B6 **Headlong Pk** New Zealand
138 B4 **Head of Bight** *B* South Australia Australia
100 K3 **Headquarters** Idaho U.S.A.
83 M9 **Headridge Hill** Christmas I Indian Oc
100 A7 **Heads, The** *C* Oregon U.S.A.
99 R4 **Heafford Junct** Wisconsin U.S.A.
102 B3 **Healdsburg** California U.S.A.
109 K1 **Healdton** Oklahoma U.S.A.
139 H7 **Healesville** Victoria Australia
116 P4 **Healy** *R* Alaska U.S.A.
116 N5 **Healy** Alaska U.S.A.
107 K3 **Healy** Kansas U.S.A.
116 P5 **Healy L** Alaska U.S.A.
119 Q3 **Heaman** Manitoba Canada
9 E1 **Heanor** England
81 K16 **Heard I** Southern Oc
119 M8 **Hearne** Saskatchewan Canada
109 L5 **Hearne** Texas U.S.A.
117 R4 **Hearne L** Northwest Territories Canada
120 G3 **Hearst** Ontario Canada
102 A2 **Hearst** California U.S.A.
146 D5 **Hearst I** Antarctica
98 D3 **Heart** *R* North Dakota U.S.A.
118 F3 **Heart L** Alberta Canada
101 P5 **Heart L** Wyoming U.S.A.
118 A3 **Heart R** Alberta Canada
123 T6 **Heart's Content** Newfoundland Canada
123 T6 **Heart's Delight** Newfoundland Canada
98 H9 **Heartwell** Nebraska U.S.A.
128 E6 **Heath** *R* Bolivia/Peru
139 G6 **Heathcote** Victoria Australia
6 L2 **Heather** *oil rig* North Sea
123 O5 **Heatherton** Newfoundland Canada
9 G6 **Heathfield** England
123 L4 **Heath Pt** Anticosti I, Quebec
9 F5 **Heathrow Airport** England
112 G3 **Heath Springs** South Carolina U.S.A.
122 F6 **Heath Steel Mines** New Brunswick Canada
95 L9 **Heathsville** Virginia U.S.A.
107 Q7 **Heavener** Oklahoma U.S.A.
109 J8 **Hebbronville** Texas U.S.A.
13 F6 **Hebden Br** England
65 C5 **Hebei** *prov* China
141 J8 **Hebel** Queensland Australia
32 L6 **Heber** Germany
103 O7 **Heber** Arizona U.S.A.
101 O9 **Heber City** Utah U.S.A.
110 D6 **Heber Springs** Arkansas U.S.A.
121 P3 **Hébert, L** Quebec Canada

121 T4 Hébertville Station Quebec Canada
101 O5 Hebgen L Montana U.S.A.
65 C7 Hebi China
100 B4 Hebo Oregon U.S.A.
115 N6 Hebron Labrador, Nfld Canada
122 F10 Hebron Nova Scotia Canada
80 D7 Hebron Jordan
101 T9 Hebron Colorado U.S.A.
99 S7 Hebron Illinois U.S.A.
99 T8 Hebron Indiana U.S.A.
98 J9 Hebron Nebraska U.S.A.
98 E3 Hebron North Dakota U.S.A.
96 E7 Hebron Ohio U.S.A.
27 J12 Heby Sweden
117 H9 Hecate Str British Columbia Canada
100 A5 Heceta Head Oregon U.S.A.
117 G8 Hecate I Alaska U.S.A.
67 C4 Hechi China
36 F7 Hechingen Germany
22 J1 Hechtel Belgium
32 K5 Hechthausen Germany
36 E4 Hechuan China
67 B1 Hechuan China
33 T7 Heckelberg Germany
9 F2 Heckington England
33 P9 Hecklingen Germany
98 H4 Hecla South Dakota U.S.A.
114 H2 Hecla & Griper B Northwest Territories Canada
119 V7 Hecla I Manitoba Canada
119 V7 Hecla Prov. Park Manitoba Canada
122 F9 Hectanooga Nova Scotia Canada
144 C4 Hector New Zealand
99 M5 Hector Minnesota U.S.A.
117 P10 Hector, Mt Alberta Canada
145 E4 Hector, Mt New Zealand
127 M2 Hector Mts New Zealand
27 H12 Hector's River Jamaica
61 M11 Heda Japan
27 D11 Hedal Norway
21 P1 Hédauville France
26 K6 Hedberg Sweden
27 D12 Heddal Norway
36 F4 Heddesheim Germany
13 G3 Heddon-on-the-Wall England
20 G5 Hédé France
26 G9 Hede Sweden
25 D5 Hedel Netherlands
27 H11 Hedemora Sweden
32 L10 Hedemunden Germany
28 E6 Heden Sweden
26 M6 Heden Sweden
26 N5 Hedensted Sweden
28 D5 Hedensted Denmark
33 O9 Hedersleben Germany
27 J11 Hedesunda Sweden
26 G9 Hedeviken Sweden
144 B7 Hedgehope New Zealand
101 Q3 Hedgesville Montana U.S.A.
94 J7 Hedgesville West Virginia U.S.A.
67 C6 Hedi Shuiku res China
117 N11 Hedley British Columbia Canada
27 E10 Hedmark county Norway
27 E11 Hedmark Norway
61 Q12 Hedo Okinawa
61 Q12 Hedo-misaki C Okinawa
13 H6 Hedon England
8 L11 Hedo Oya R I Sri Lanka
99 O8 Hedrick Iowa U.S.A.
28 A4 Hee Denmark
32 F7 Heede Germany
33 T7 Heegermühle Germany
32 F8 Heek Germany
25 C4 Heemstede Netherlands
32 J8 Heepen Germany
22 H3 Heer Belgium
26 P1 Heines Norway
59 J3 Helong China
142 G3 Helong China
32 L5 Helotes Texas U.S.A.
8 D6 Helper Utah U.S.A.
142 B6 Helsby England
32 L5 Helsby England
9 H5 Herne Bay England
103 M9 Hickwan Arizona U.S.A.
13 G6 Hickleton England
110 G5 Hickman Kentucky U.S.A.
98 K9 Hickman Nebraska U.S.A.
106 C7 Hickman Nevada U.S.A.
113 T5 Hickman's Hbr Newfoundland Canada
109 G2 Hillington England
85 F4 Hillion France
145 E2 Hirakimata New Zealand
75 K8 Hirakud Res India
95 R3 Hiram Maine U.S.A.
60 C12 Hirara Japan
61 R9 Hira shima isld Japan
60 F10 Hirata Japan
124 D5 Hiray Mexico

65 B4 Hekou China
67 D5 Hekou Guangdong China
67 A3 Hekou Yunnan China
31 L1 Hel Poland
80 E2 Hela Israel
26 F9 Helagsfjället mt Sweden
58 E4 Helan Shan mt ra China
37 K1 Helbe R Germany
28 E3 Helberskov Denmark
33 O9 Helbra Germany
58 C6 Helchtren Belgium
37 K3 Heldburg Germany
36 F3 Heldenbergen Germany
37 P6 Helden's Pt St Kitts W Indies
67 F2 Helen, Mt Queensland
141 F5 Helen, Mt Queensland
15 D4 Helensburgh Scotland
140 C4 Helen Springs N Terr Australia
145 E2 Helensville New Zealand
33 P10 Helfta Germany
26 F6 Helgeland reg Norway
27 D12 Helgen Norway
32 G4 Helgoland isld Germany
32 H4 Helgoländer Bucht Germany
26 K1 Helgøy Norway
65 H1 Heli China
99 R8 Heliopolis Egypt
79 B8 Heliopolis Egypt
28 E8 Hell Norway
107 N5 Helena Oklahoma U.S.A.
Hell's Canyon see Snake River Canyon
127 L3 Hellshire Hills Jamaica
28 E8 Hellum Denmark
32 M6 Hellwege Germany
101 O7 Helm California U.S.A.
99 R8 Helm Illinois U.S.A.
146 D7 Helmand R Afghanistan
115 N4 Helmand R Afghanistan
100 G7 Helmand R Afghanistan
111 K8 Helmeringhausen Namibia
37 J2 Helmershausen Germany
9 H3 Helmingham England
68 A6 Helmond Netherlands
32 J4 Helmsand sandbank Germany
100 K1 Helmsdale R Scotland
103 O4 Helmsdale Scotland
142 B6 Helmsley England
32 L5 Helmstadt Germany
110 L3 Helmstedt Germany
110 J9 Helmville Montana U.S.A.
110 J4 Helnæs Denmark
110 P4 Helnæs Bugt B Denmark
12 E5 Helong China
59 J6 Helong China
103 Q2 Helper Utah U.S.A.
33 T6 Helpter Berge pk Germany
29 K4 Helsingborg Sweden
28 J4 Helsinge Denmark
Helsingfors see Helsinki
29 K4 Helsingør Denmark
118 L6 Helsinki Finland
67 E4 Helston England
37 L7 Helstorf Germany
103 K3 Heltonville Indiana U.S.A.
112 E4 Helvécia Brazil
14 D4 Helvick Hd Ireland
84 J4 Helwan Egypt
36 B2 Hem Vejle Denmark
36 F4 Hem Viborg Denmark
118 F7 Hemau Germany
50 F4 Hemau Germany
68 J2 Hepu China
9 F4 Hepworth Ontario Canada
65 B5 Hequ China
27 E11 Heradsbygd Norway
141 J3 Herald Cays islds St Barrier Reef Aust
74 H2 Herat Afghanistan
37 F13 Hérault R France
18 H9 Hérault R France
38 E4 Hérault dept France
28 A5 Herbault France
32 F10 Herbede Germany
32 G9 Herberge, K mt Germany
141 H4 Herbert R Queensland
118 K8 Herbert Saskatchewan Canada
145 D5 Herbert New Zealand
68 A7 Herbertabad Andaman Is
140 D5 Herbert Downs Queensland
29 D5 Hersley Denmark
28 D5 Hersom Denmark
22 J2 Herstal Belgium
9 F3 Herstmonceux England
86 B6 Hermandsdorp S Africa
32 F9 Hertford England
9 F4 Hertfordshire co England
12 D3 Hertford North Carolina U.S.A.
95 S6 Hervey Junction Quebec Canada
142 B1 Hervey Ra Queensland

94 H7 Hendricks West Virginia U.S.A.
129 G3 Hendrik Top mt Suriname
89 D8 Hendrik Verwoerd Dam S Africa
8 B4 Hendy Wales
101 O8 Henefer Utah U.S.A.
65 H2 Hengdaohezi China
65 G3 Hengdaozi China
67 D3 Hengdong China
58 C6 Hengduan Shan mts China
37 N3 Hengelo Netherlands
58 F2 Hengelo Netherlands
37 P6 Hengersberg Germany
37 J1 Henriksen Germany
28 H6 Henrlev Denmark
20 F3 Henrichemont France
144 C6 Herriot New Zealand
13 F2 Herriot Scotland
117 L10 Heriot Bay British Columbia Canada
41 K3 Herisau Switzerland
22 J2 Herk-de-Stad Belgium
117 H4 Herkimer New York U.S.A.
107 N3 Herkimer New York U.S.A.
58 F2 Herlaigrän Germany
28 J7 Herlev Denmark
37 J1 Herleshausen Germany
20 P3 Herlufmagle Denmark
20 F3 Herlufsholm Denmark
21 P3 Hermagor Austria
94 C2 Herman Michigan U.S.A.
107 N3 Heston Kansas U.S.A.
99 M3 Herman Minnesota U.S.A.
98 K8 Herman Nebraska U.S.A.
68 J2 Hermann Missouri U.S.A.
124 J4 Hermanas Mexico
106 C10 Hermanas New Mexico
36 E4 Hermann Missouri U.S.A.
98 D3 Hermannsberg Germany
32 M7 Hermannsburg Germany
140 C6 Hermannsburg N Terr Australia
37 P4 Heřmanova Hut' Czechoslovakia
99 T4 Hermansville Michigan U.S.A.
89 A10 Hermanus S Africa
111 F10 Hermanville Mississippi U.S.A.
79 G4 Hermel Lebanon
21 P3 Hermes France
36 B4 Hermeskeil Germany
22 H3 Hermeton-sur-Meuse Belgium
139 H4 Hermidale New South Wales Australia
22 E3 Hermès France
100 F4 Hermiston Oregon U.S.A.
123 R6 Hermitage Newfoundland Canada
119 O9 Heward Saskatchewan Canada
111 D8 Hermitage Arkansas U.S.A.
123 Q5 Hermitage B Newfoundland Canada
20 E5 Hermitage, I' France
142 B5 Hermite I W Australia
67 F1 Hermite, Is Chile
133 D9 Hermite, Is Chile
21 M6 Hermites, les France
140 B2 Hermit Hill N Terr Australia
136 K2 Hermit Is Bismarck Arch
103 M5 Hermits Rest Arizona U.S.A.
108 G3 Hermleigh Texas U.S.A.
140 F5 Hermón, Mt see Sheikh, J. esh
22 F5 Hermonville France
98 C6 Hermosa South Dakota U.S.A.
124 D3 Hermosillo Mexico
130 C9 Hernandarias Paraguay
113 E9 Hernando Florida U.S.A.
110 G7 Hernando Mississippi U.S.A.
111 F7 Hernay Germany
80 F2 Herodshvotn R Iceland
21 Q2 Héricourt France
102 H7 Herington Kansas U.S.A.
22 G2 Herinnes Belgium
144 B6 Heriot New Zealand
110 A3 Heron Montana U.S.A.
101 P3 Heron Bay Ontario Canada
107 J4 Herongen Germany
141 H1 Heron I Gt Barrier Reef Aust
144 C5 Heron L New Zealand
99 L6 Heron L Minnesota U.S.A.
112 F2 Herowābād see Khalkhāl
26 A9 Herøy Norway
130 B10 Herradura Argentina
16 D5 Herrara del Duque Spain
17 G3 Herre el France
16 C5 Herrera de Alcántara Spain
17 G3 Herrera de los Navarros Spain
124 G5 Herreras Mexico
32 F6 Herrested Denmark
139 J8 Herrick Tasmania Australia
98 G6 Herrick South Dakota U.S.A.
109 J4 Herrin Illinois U.S.A.
30 G1 Herring Neck Newfoundland Canada
141 H4 Hidden Valley Queensland Australia
37 K5 Hesselberg mt Germany
28 H4 Hessele isld Denmark
33 N8 Hessen Germany
36 F2 Hessen land Germany
37 M3 Hessenstein Germany
34 H5 Hessenthal Germany
36 H1 Hessisch Lichtenau Germany
117 H4 Hess Mts Yukon Territory Canada
107 N3 Heston Kansas U.S.A.
107 C7 Hestnehoved C Denmark
95 N6 Hestøyri Iceland
28 J7 Hesteyri Iceland
26 F5 Hestmannen isld Norway
27 G14 Hestra, N Sweden
22 G3 Hestrud France
102 C4 Hetch Hetchy California U.S.A.
94 C2 Hetherton Michigan U.S.A.
25 E2 Het Loo Netherlands
68 J2 Hetou China
72 L5 Hettange Gde France
145 E3 Hettihini New Zealand
79 G5 Hitjanah, Al Syria
17 G3 Hijar Spain

107 O3 Herington Kansas U.S.A.
22 G2 Herinnes Belgium
144 B6 Heriot New Zealand
13 F2 Heriot Scotland
117 L10 Heriot Bay British Columbia Canada
112 H2 High Point North Carolina U.S.A.
117 P8 High Prairie Alberta Canada
100 B4 High River Alberta Canada
119 R3 Highrock Manitoba Canada
113 J11 High Rock Grand Bahama I
112 G2 High Rock L North Carolina U.S.A.
139 H9 High Rocky Pt Tasmania Australia
113 E8 Highsprings Florida U.S.A.
95 N6 Hightstown New Jersey U.S.A.
99 S7 Highwood Illinois U.S.A.
101 P2 Highwood Montana U.S.A.
9 E4 Highworth England
9 F4 High Wycombe England
116 O6 Hinchinbrook Entrance str Alaska U.S.A.
141 H4 Hinchinbrook I Queensland Australia
116 O6 Hinchinbrook I Alaska U.S.A.
119 P6 Hinchliffe Saskatchewan Canada
9 E2 Hinckley England
99 O3 Hinckley Minnesota U.S.A.
103 M2 Hinckley Utah U.S.A.
95 N3 Hinckley Res New York U.S.A.
74 G5 Hindaun India
41 M2 Hindelang Germany
25 D3 Hindeloopen Netherlands
Hindenburg see Lindenhagen
28 A7 Hindenburg-damm causeway Germany
26 N6 Hinderön isld Sweden
109 J7 Hindes Texas U.S.A.
9 F5 Hindhead England
13 F6 Hindley England
138 F6 Hindmarsh, L Victoria Australia
9 D5 Hindon England
112 F6 Hindsholm Denmark
123 P5 Hinds L Newfoundland Canada
28 F5 Hindsholm Denmark
123 P5 Hinds L Newfoundland Canada
75 K8 Hindubagh Pakistan
72 K1 Hindu Kush mts Afghanistan
76 C4 Hindupur India
118 G5 Hindville Alberta Canada
68 G4 Hine Laos
95 O2 Hinesburg Vermont U.S.A.
117 O7 Hines Creek Alberta Canada
112 F6 Hinesville Georgia U.S.A.
74 H8 Hinganghat India
28 D4 Hinge Denmark
101 P1 Hingham Montana U.S.A.
77 J7 Hinglaj Pakistan
20 F5 Hinglé, le France
77 J7 Hingol R India
74 G9 Hingoli India
102 G7 Hinkley California U.S.A.
143 G7 Hinkley, Mt W Australia Australia
80 D4 Hinnant Jordan
29 J11 Hinnerjoki Finland
26 F4 Hinnerup Denmark
26 E4 Hinnøya isld Norway
61 K9 Hino R Japan
27 P6 Hinoba-an Philippines
28 E13 Hinokage Japan
60 F10 Hinomi saki C Japan
99 S8 Hinsdale Massachusetts U.S.A.
91 S1 Hinsdale Illinois U.S.A.
94 J4 Hinsdale New York U.S.A.
8 D2 Hinstock England
36 E3 Hinterdilmingen Germany
41 K4 Hinterrhein Switzerland
41 J3 Hinter Riss Austria
28 E4 Hinterstoder Austria
36 D5 Hinter Tux Austria
37 M7 Hinter Weidenthal Germany
117 P9 Hinton Alberta Canada
107 N6 Hinton Oklahoma U.S.A.
61 O9 Hi-numa Japan
78 B2 Hiocolândia Brazil
135 P2 Hīo Pt Hawaiian Is
124 J5 Hipólito Mexico
25 C3 Hippolytushoef Netherlands
80 F2 Hippos Syria
60 C12 Hirado-gawa isld Japan
60 C12 Hirado-shima isld Japan
76 K8 Hirakata Japan

65 B4 Hekou China
37 K5 Hesselberg mt Germany
112 H2 High Point North Carolina U.S.A.
116 O6 Hinchinbrook Entrance str Alaska U.S.A.

27 G13 Hjo Sweden
28 C4 Hjøllund Denmark
28 C6 Hjordkær Denmark
Hjørring co see Nordjylland co
28 D2 Hjørring Denmark
28 E7 Hjortø Denmark
28 E4 Hjortshøj Denmark
28 C5 Hjortsvang Denmark
26 B9 Hjörundfjord Norway
27 D12 Hjuksebö Norway
68 D2 Hka R Burma
68 D2 Hkok R Burma
68 C4 Hlegu Burma
28 S10 Hlidharendi Iceland
37 P3 Hlinec R Czechoslovakia
31 K7 Hlohovec Czechoslovakia
28 A5 Ho Denmark
85 E7 Ho Ghana
67 B6 Hoa Binh Vietnam
89 A4 Hoachanas Namibia
118 C6 Hoadley Alberta Canada
98 F8 Hoagland Nebraska U.S.A.
68 J5 Hoai Nhon Vietnam
68 G1 Hoang Su Phi Vietnam
87 B9 Hoanib R Namibia
60 E12 Hoashi Japan
101 P6 Hoback R Wyoming U.S.A.
101 P6 Hoback Pk Wyoming U.S.A.
138 F8 Hobart Tasmania Australia
99 T8 Hobart Indiana U.S.A.
107 L6 Hobart Oklahoma U.S.A.
108 D3 Hobbs New Mexico U.S.A.
111 K7 Hobbs Island Alabama U.S.A.
113 G10 Hobe Sound Florida U.S.A.
112 K1 Hobgood North Carolina U.S.A.
22 G1 Hoboken Belgium
112 E6 Hoboken Georgia U.S.A.
Hobot Xar see Xianghuang Qi
28 D3 Hobro Denmark
101 Q3 Hobson Montana U.S.A.
112 L2 Hobucken North Carolina U.S.A.
28 A5 Ho Bugt B Denmark
27 K15 Hoburgen lighthouse Sweden
86 A2 Hobyo Somalia
71 D5 Hoc isld Philippines
47 K6 Hocalar Turkey
111 B7 Hochatown Oklahoma U.S.A.
38 N8 Hocheck mt Austria
87 C10 Hochfeld Namibia
36 D6 Hochfelden France
38 G7 Hochfilzen Austria
41 N4 Hochfinstermünz Austria
38 F8 Hochgall mt Italy
36 E3 Hochheim Germany
37 K2 Hochheim Germany
109 K6 Hochheim Texas U.S.A.
Ho Chi Minh see Saigon
38 K8 Hochobir mt Austria
41 N2 Hoch Platte mt Germany
38 M6 Hochschwab mt Austria
36 D5 Hochspeyer Germany
37 K4 Höchstadt Germany
37 K6 Höchstädt Germany
36 D2 Höchstenbach Germany
144 C5 Hochstetter, L New Zealand
38 K9 Hochstuhl mt Slovenia
36 F5 Hockenheim Germany
94 E7 Hocking R Ohio U.S.A.
94 F7 Hockingport Ohio U.S.A.
109 M5 Hockley Texas U.S.A.
9 E3 Hockley Heath England
9 F4 Hockliffe England
6 N6 Hod oil rig North Sea
28 B5 Hodde Denmark
13 F6 Hodder, R England
9 F4 Hoddesdon England
Hodeida see Ḥudaydah, Al
111 D9 Hodge Louisiana U.S.A.
110 L4 Hodgenville Kentucky U.S.A.
98 B3 Hodges Montana U.S.A.
112 E3 Hodges South Carolina U.S.A.
123 Q4 Hodges Hill pk Newfoundland Canada
102 G8 Hodges, L California U.S.A.
118 L8 Hodgeville Saskatchewan Canada
119 U7 Hodgson Manitoba Canada
140 C3 Hodgson Downs N Terr Australia
85 C5 Hodh reg Mauritania
80 B7 Hodiyya Israel
48 F4 Hódmezővásárhely Hungary
85 E1 Hodna, Mts. du Algeria
8 D2 Hodnet England
31 K7 Hodonín Czechoslovakia
48 C4 Hodoš Slovenia
28 B4 Hodsager Denmark
116 N3 Hodzana, R Alaska U.S.A.
28 F4 Hoed Denmark
25 A6 Hoedekenskerke Netherlands
20 E7 Hoëdic isld France
106 F4 Hoehne Colorado U.S.A.
25 B5 Hoeksche Waard Netherlands
25 B5 Hoek van Holland Netherlands
119 M6 Hoey Saskatchewan Canada
37 M3 Hof Germany
36 H2 Hofbieber Germany
Hofei see Hefei
36 F6 Höfen Germany
37 J6 Hofen Germany
98 L4 Hoffman Minnesota U.S.A.
112 H2 Hoffman North Carolina U.S.A.
113 K12 Hoffmans Cay isld Bahamas
32 K10 Hofgeismar Germany
36 E3 Hofheim Germany
37 K3 Hofheim Germany
37 P6 Hofkirchen Germany
29 T9 Hofn Iceland
28 S9 Hofsjökull ice cap Iceland
28 S9 Hofsos Iceland
60 E11 Hōfu Japan
29 K4 Höganäs Sweden
139 H7 Hogan Group islds Tasmania Australia
102 D3 Hogan Res California U.S.A.
111 M8 Hogansville Georgia U.S.A.
141 H7 Hoganthulla R Queensland Australia
119 P1 Hogarth Ontario Canada
140 D5 Hogarth, Mt N Terr Australia
116 K3 Hogatza Alaska U.S.A.
116 K3 Hogatza R R Alaska U.S.A.
101 N5 Hogback Mt Montana U.S.A.
27 F12 Hogboda Sweden
27 J14 Högby Sweden
28 C7 Högel Germany
101 R1 Hogeland Montana U.S.A.
27 H12 Högfors Sweden
85 F4 Hoggar mt reg Algeria
119 V1 Hogg L Manitoba Canada
48 J5 Hoghiz Romania
94 B1 Hog I Michigan U.S.A.
95 M9 Hog I Virginia U.S.A.
28 B4 Høgild Denmark
80 C4 Hogla Israel
27 H14 Högsby Sweden
126 H4 Hogsty Reef Bahamas
26 G5 Högtuvbre mt Norway
100 A2 Hoh R Washington U.S.A.
33 R10 Hohburg Germany
36 C3 Hohe Acht mt Germany
41 N3 Hohe Geige mt Austria
37 K6 Hohen-Altheim Germany
38 N6 Hohenberg Austria
37 M3 Hohenberg Germany
33 S9 Hohenbucke Germany
37 M5 Hohenburg Germany
33 N10 Hohenebra Germany
32 M8 Hoheneggelsen Germany
36 H1 Hoheneiche Germany
41 L3 Hohenems Austria
37 M5 Hohenfels Germany
33 Q7 Hohengöhren Germany
36 G6 Hohenheim Germany
37 M7 Hohenkammer Germany
33 Q10 Hohenleina Germany
37 N2 Hohenleuben Germany
32 G10 Hohenlimburg Germany
32 L5 Hohenlockstedt Germany
33 S5 Hohenmocker Germany
37 N1 Hohenmölsen Germany
33 Q7 Hohennauen Germany
36 H2 Hohenroda Germany
33 Q8 Hohenseeden Germany
33 S9 Hohenseefeld Germany
36 E2 Hohensolms Germany
36 H6 Hohenstaufen Germany
36 G7 Hohenstein Germany
37 O2 Hohenstein-Ernstthal Germany
110 J6 Hohenwald Tennessee U.S.A.
37 L6 Hohenwart Germany
32 K9 Hohenwepel Germany
32 L4 Hohenwestedt Germany
33 N6 Hohenzethen Germany
36 F7 Hohenzollern Germany
41 M3 Hoher Ifen mt Austria
41 M3 Hohes Licht mt Austria
37 J5 Hohe Steig mt Germany
38 F7 Hohe Tauern Austria
58 F3 Hohhot China
36 E6 Hohloh mt Germany
33 M7 Hohne Germany
19 K4 Hohneck mt France
33 N6 Hohnstorf Germany
116 J6 Hoholitna R Alaska U.S.A.
32 K4 Hohrr Germany
66 E4 Hoh Sai Hu L China
33 N4 Hohwacht Germany
36 C7 Hohwald France
66 D4 Hoh Xil Shan ra China
68 J5 Hoi An Vietnam
107 M3 Hoisington Kansas U.S.A.
66 F4 Hoit Taria China
67 B6 Hoi-Xuan Vietnam
75 P6 Hojai India
28 E6 Højby Denmark
28 C5 Højen Denmark
28 B7 Højer Denmark
29 K6 Højerup Denmark
60 F12 Hōjō Japan
28 B6 Højrup Denmark
28 C3 Højslev Denmark
68 D2 Hok R Burma
99 P6 Hokah Minnesota U.S.A.
Hokang see Hegang
27 K11 Hökhuvud Sweden
61 N9 Hōki R Japan
145 D1 Hokianga Harbour New Zealand
144 C5 Hokitika New Zealand
60 Q2 Hokkaidō isld Japan
27 D12 Hokksund Norway
61 O9 Hokota Japan
61 K10 Hokunō Japan
61 K10 Hokuriku Tunnel Japan
27 C11 Hol Norway
27 E12 Höland Norway
Holbæk co see Vestjælland co
28 E3 Holbæk Denmark
28 H5 Holbæk Denmark
9 G2 Holbeach England
117 K10 Holberg British Columbia Canada
28 C7 Holbøl Denmark
141 J4 Holbourne I Queensland Australia
139 H6 Holbrook New South Wales Australia
103 O7 Holbrook Arizona U.S.A.
101 N7 Holbrook Idaho U.S.A.
98 F9 Holbrook Nebraska U.S.A.
13 F6 Holcombe England
99 P4 Holcombe Wisconsin U.S.A.
118 E5 Holden Alberta Canada
95 Q4 Holden Massachusetts U.S.A.
110 C3 Holden Missouri U.S.A.
103 M2 Holden Utah U.S.A.
94 E9 Holden West Virginia U.S.A.
107 O6 Holdenville Oklahoma U.S.A.
13 H6 Holderness pen England
119 M8 Holdfast Saskatchewan Canada
99 M4 Holdingford Minnesota U.S.A.
32 H7 Holdorf Germany
98 G9 Holdrege Nebraska U.S.A.
28 G7 Holeby Denmark
113 K12 Hole in the Wall pt Bahamas
27 E12 Hölen Norway
76 C4 Hole Narsipur India
31 K6 Holešov Czechoslovakia
127 P6 Holetown Barbados
94 C5 Holgate Ohio U.S.A.
126 F4 Holguín Cuba
48 D2 Holič Czechoslovakia
116 H5 Holikachuk Alaska U.S.A.
116 J6 Holitna R Alaska U.S.A.
27 F11 Höljes Sweden
119 T9 Holland Manitoba Canada
9 F2 Holland div England
99 U7 Holland Michigan U.S.A.
98 K5 Holland Minnesota U.S.A.
94 J4 Holland New York U.S.A.
100 B7 Holland Oregon U.S.A.
109 K5 Holland Texas U.S.A.
111 F8 Hollandale Mississippi U.S.A.
127 M3 Holland B Jamaica
120 K8 Holland Centre Ontario Canada
143 C9 Holland,Mt W Australia Australia
141 K2 Holland Park dist Brisbane, Qnsld Australia
25 C5 Hollandsch Diep Netherlands
22 K4 Hollange Belgium
32 M8 Holle Germany
33 N5 Hollenbek Germany
32 L6 Hollenstedt Germany
38 N6 Hollen-Tal V Austria
38 F7 Hollersbach Austria
9 H3 Hollesley B England
94 J3 Holley New York U.S.A.
37 L4 Hollfeld Germany
109 J2 Holliday Texas U.S.A.
94 J6 Hollidaysburg Pennsylvania U.S.A.
107 L7 Hollis Oklahoma U.S.A.
102 C5 Hollister California U.S.A.
101 L7 Hollister Idaho U.S.A.
110 C5 Hollister Missouri U.S.A.
107 M7 Hollister Oklahoma U.S.A.
22 J2 Hollogne-sur-Geer Belgium
111 D10 Holloway Louisiana U.S.A.
29 K6 Höllviken C Sweden
106 H3 Holly Colorado U.S.A.
94 D4 Holly Michigan U.S.A.
111 F9 Holly Bluff Mississippi U.S.A.
144 B6 Hollyford R New Zealand
111 E7 Holly Grove Arkansas U.S.A.
113 F8 Holly Hill Florida U.S.A.
112 G4 Holly Hill South Carolina U.S.A.
112 K3 Holly Ridge North Carolina U.S.A.
110 G7 Holly Springs Mississippi U.S.A.
113 G11 Hollywood Florida U.S.A.
95 L8 Hollywood Maryland U.S.A.
28 D6 Holm Denmark
26 F6 Holm Norway
26 J9 Holm Sweden
106 E5 Holman New Mexico U.S.A.
114 H3 Holman Island Northwest Territories Canada
28 S9 Holmavik Iceland
28 B5 Holme Å R Denmark
99 P6 Holmen Wisconsin U.S.A.
8 D1 Holmes Chapel England
119 V1 Holmes L Manitoba Canada
101 P5 Holmes, Mt Wyoming U.S.A.
141 J3 Holmes Reef Great Barrier Reef Aust
27 D12 Holmestr Norway
119 S9 Holmfield Manitoba Canada
13 G6 Holmfirth England
26 K6 Holmfors Sweden
115 O3 Holm Ø isld Greenland
26 L8 Holmögadd lighthouse Sweden
26 L8 Holmön Sweden
13 J6 Holmpton England
27 D12 Holmsbu Norway
26 J8 Holmsjö Sweden
26 H9 Holmsjön L Sweden
28 A4 Holmsland Klit sand spit Denmark
28 E6 Holmstrup Fyn Denmark
28 G5 Holmstrup Vestjælland Denmark
26 L8 Holmsund Sweden
27 K14 Holmudden lighthouse Gotland Sweden
111 C11 Holmwood Louisiana U.S.A.
37 M5 Holnstein Germany
27 J12 Hölö Sweden
88 C5 Holoholo Tanzania
80 C5 Ḥolon Israel
87 C11 Holoog Namibia
113 F9 Holopaw Florida U.S.A.
80 B6 Ḥolot Ashdod Israel
142 F2 Holothuria Reefs W Australia Australia
80 B6 Ḥolot Yavne Israel
26 E9 Holöydal Norway
141 F2 Holroyd R Queensland Australia
28 B4 Holstebro Denmark
28 B5 Holsted Denmark
120 K8 Holstein Ontario Canada
99 L7 Holstein Iowa U.S.A.
98 H9 Holstein Nebraska U.S.A.
28 G6 Holsteinborg Denmark
115 O4 Holsteinsborg Greenland
112 E1 Holston R Tennessee U.S.A.
94 F10 Holston R Virginia U.S.A.
33 N4 Holst Schweiz Germany
8 B6 Holsworthy England
9 H2 Holt England
111 J8 Holt Alabama U.S.A.
111 K11 Holt Florida U.S.A.
94 C4 Holt Michigan U.S.A.
98 K1 Holt Minnesota U.S.A.
8 D1 Holt Wales
98 G7 Holt Cr Nebraska U.S.A.
29 K5 Holte Denmark
33 O9 Holtemme R Germany
25 F4 Holten Netherlands
101 O3 Holter L. Dam Montana U.S.A.
33 O5 Holthusen Germany
94 B7 Holton Indiana U.S.A.
107 P2 Holton Kansas U.S.A.
94 B3 Holton Michigan U.S.A.
65 D2 Holt Sum China
28 C4 Holtum Å R Denmark
103 J9 Holtville California U.S.A.
120 K4 Holtyre Ontario Canada
135 U5 Holualoa Hawaiian Is
27 C13 Holum Norway
25 E2 Holwerd Netherlands
116 H5 Holy Cross Alaska U.S.A.
8 B1 Holyhead Wales
8 B1 Holyhead B Wales
Holy I see Lindisfarne
12 C3 Holy I Scotland
8 B1 Holy I Wales
118 G4 Holyoke Alberta Canada
106 H1 Holyoke Colorado U.S.A.
95 P4 Holyoke Massachusetts U.S.A.
123 T6 Holyrood Newfoundland Canada
107 M3 Holyrood Kansas U.S.A.
37 P4 Holýšov Czechoslovakia
8 D6 Holywell England
8 C1 Holywell Wales
14 F2 Holywood N Ireland
36 D3 Holzappel Germany
33 S9 Holzdorf Germany
33 P5 Holzendorf Germany
32 H8 Holzhausen Germany
36 D3 Holzhausen Germany
37 K6 Holzheim Germany
32 K9 Holzminden Germany
32 G10 Holzwickede Germany
28 H6 Høm Denmark
86 G6 Homa Bay Kenya
75 Q6 Homalin Burma
36 G1 Homberg Germany
60 R2 Hombetsu Japan
22 E4 Homblières France
85 D5 Hombori Mali
Homburg see Nümbrecht
36 H4 Homburg Bayern Germany
36 C5 Homburg Rheinland-Pfalz Germany
115 N4 Home B Northwest Territories Canada
100 J6 Homedale Idaho U.S.A.
141 H4 Home Hill Queensland Australia
83 M8 Home I Cocos Is Indian Oc
116 M7 Homer Alaska U.S.A.
99 T9 Homer Illinois U.S.A.
111 C9 Homer Louisiana U.S.A.
94 C4 Homer Michigan U.S.A.
94 H6 Homer City Pennsylvania U.S.A.
9 H3 Homersfield England
144 A6 Homer Tun New Zealand
112 E6 Homerville Georgia U.S.A.
80 D4 Homesh Jordan
141 H5 Homestead Queensland Australia
113 G12 Homestead Florida U.S.A.
99 P8 Homestead Iowa U.S.A.
98 B1 Homestead Montana U.S.A.
107 M5 Homestead Oklahoma U.S.A.
100 J4 Homestead Oregon U.S.A.
98 K9 Homestead Nat Mon Nebraska U.S.A.
145 E4 Homewood New Zealand
111 K8 Homewood Alabama U.S.A.
68 A6 Homfray's Str Andaman Is
107 O5 Hominy Oklahoma U.S.A.
26 E9 Hommelfjell mt Norway
26 E8 Hommelvik Norway
25 E3 Hommerts Netherlands
21 L7 Hommes France
74 G10 Homnabad India
89 H5 Homoine Mozambique
48 G6 Homoljske Planina mt Serbia Yugoslavia
71 G5 Homonhon Philippines
48 J4 Homorod Romania
113 E9 Homosassa Florida U.S.A.
Homs see Hims
Homs Libya see Khums, Al
60 F12 Honai Japan
Honan prov see Henan
76 B3 Honavar India
68 G7 Hon Chong Vietnam
102 C2 Honcut California U.S.A.
128 D2 Honda Colombia
71 D6 Honda B Palawan Philippines
125 P8 Hondo R Belize
118 D3 Hondo Alberta Canada
60 D13 Hondo Japan
106 E8 Hondo New Mexico U.S.A.
109 H6 Hondo Texas U.S.A.
22 D2 Hondschoote France
125 L2 Honduras rep Central America
119 Q2 Hone Manitoba Canada
112 E3 Honea Path South Carolina U.S.A.
36 H2 Hönebach Germany
27 D11 Hönefoss Norway
95 M5 Honesdale Pennsylvania U.S.A.
102 A1 Honeydew California U.S.A.
98 J1 Honeyford North Dakota U.S.A.
109 M2 Honey Grove Texas U.S.A.
109 N5 Honey Island Texas U.S.A.
100 E9 Honey L California U.S.A.
120 K8 Honeywood Ontario Canada
21 L3 Honfleur France
28 G5 Høng Denmark
65 G2 Hongai China
68 H2 Hon Gai Vietnam
67 E1 Hong'an China
67 B6 Hon Gay Vietnam
65 B2 Honggor China
67 E5 Honghai Wan B China
58 F5 Hong He R China
67 D2 Honghu China
67 C3 Hongjiang China
67 G6 Hong Kong colony E Asia
67 F4 Honglai China
68 G7 Hong Ngu Vietnam
Hongning see Wulian
58 F2 Hongor Mongolia
65 B2 Hongor Mongolia
67 D7 Hongqizhen China
68 E3 Hongsa Laos
67 B4 Hongshui He R China
65 B6 Hongtong China
61 J12 Hongū Japan
122 H4 Honguedo Passage Canada
66 E3 Hongxing Sichang China
67 A2 Hongya China
58 G5 Hongze Hu L China
137 N3 Honiara Guadalcanal I Solomon Is
9 H2 Honingham England
8 C6 Honiton England
61 O6 Honjō Japan
29 J10 Honkajoki Finland
68 H3 Hon Matt isld Vietnam
68 G3 Hon Me isld Vietnam
76 B3 Honnali India
26 P1 Honningsvåg Norway
102 V13 Honokaa Hawaiian Is
135 S3 Honokahua Hawaiian Is
145 F2 Honokawa New Zealand
135 S3 Honokohau Hawaiian Is
102 S12 Honolulu Hawaiian Is
135 V5 Honomu Hawaiian Is
102 R12 Honouliuli Hawaiian Is
68 H7 Hon Quan Vietnam
17 F5 Honrubia Spain
59 K4 Honshū isld Japan
28 H5 Hønsinge Denmark
135 U6 Honuapo Hawaiian Is
100 D4 Hood, Mt Oregon U.S.A.
143 C10 Hood Pt W Australia Australia
100 D4 Hood River Oregon U.S.A.
100 B2 Hoodsport Washington U.S.A.
32 K10 Hoof Germany
25 C4 Hoofddorp Netherlands
25 A6 Hoofdplaat Netherlands
25 F3 Hooger Smilde Netherlands
25 G3 Hoogeveen Netherlands
25 G2 Hoogezand Netherlands
25 G3 Hooghalen Netherlands
22 D2 Hoogstade Belgium
22 H1 Hoogstraten Belgium
41 K2 Höohster mt Germany
9 F5 Hook England
144 C6 Hook New Zealand
135 U5 Hookena Hawaiian Is
107 J5 Hooker Oklahoma U.S.A.
140 B4 Hooker Creek N Terr Australia
14 E4 Hook Hd Ireland
141 J5 Hook I Queensland Australia
141 L7 Hook Pt Queensland Australia
141 J4 Hook Reef Gt Barrier Reef Aust
109 N2 Hooks Texas U.S.A.
95 Q3 Hooksett New Hampshire U.S.A.
32 H5 Hooksiel Germany
102 V13 Hoolehua Hawaiian Is
117 F6 Hoonah Alaska U.S.A.
100 B8 Hoopa California U.S.A.
106 E4 Hooper Colorado U.S.A.
98 K8 Hooper Nebraska U.S.A.
101 N8 Hooper Utah U.S.A.
100 G3 Hooper Washington U.S.A.
116 D6 Hooper Bay Alaska U.S.A.
95 L8 Hooper I Maryland U.S.A.
99 T9 Hoopeston Illinois U.S.A.
123 Q3 Hooping Hbr Newfoundland Canada
98 J1 Hoople North Dakota U.S.A.
89 D6 Hoopstad S Africa
27 G16 Höör Sweden
25 D3 Hoorn Noord Netherlands
25 C2 Hoorn Texel Netherlands
95 O4 Hoosick Falls New York U.S.A.
118 H7 Hoosier Saskatchewan Canada
98 C4 Hoover South Dakota U.S.A.
103 K5 Hoover Dam Arizona U.S.A.
94 E6 Hoover Res Ohio U.S.A.
94 J6 Hooversville Pennsylvania U.S.A.
78 H1 Hopa Turkey
95 M5 Hop Bottom Pennsylvania U.S.A.
9 E4 Hopcrofts Holt England
117 N11 Hope British Columbia Canada
103 L8 Hope Arizona U.S.A.
111 C8 Hope Arkansas U.S.A.
94 B7 Hope Indiana U.S.A.
107 N3 Hope Kansas U.S.A.
98 J2 Hope North Dakota U.S.A.
127 M2 Hope Bay Jamaica
115 N6 Hopedale Labrador, Nfld Canada
Hopeh prov see Hebei
138 E3 Hope, L South Australia Australia
143 D9 Hope,L W Australia Australia
138 E3 Hopeless, Mt South Australia Australia
112 J3 Hope Mills North Carolina U.S.A.
147 J12 Hopen isld Arctic Oc
144 D5 Hope Pass New Zealand
116 D2 Hope, Pt Alaska U.S.A.
138 F6 Hopetoun Victoria Australia
143 D10 Hopetoun W Australia Australia
113 L11 Hope Town Bahamas
89 D7 Hopetown S Africa
141 H3 Hopevale Queensland Australia
122 K8 Hopewell Nova Scotia Canada
94 J6 Hopewell Pennsylvania U.S.A.
95 K9 Hopewell Virginia U.S.A.
115 M6 Hopewell Is Northwest Territories Canada
103 O6 Hopi Buttes mt Arizona U.S.A.
67 E4 Ho-p'ing China
139 G7 Hopkins R Victoria Australia
94 B4 Hopkins Michigan U.S.A.
99 M9 Hopkins Missouri U.S.A.
143 G6 Hopkins,L W Australia Australia
144 B5 Hopkins, Mt New Zealand
110 J5 Hopkinsville Kentucky U.S.A.
102 A3 Hopland California U.S.A.
68 C2 Hopong Burma
33 T7 Hoppegarten Germany
26 Q1 Hopseidet Norway
32 G8 Hopsten Germany
9 H2 Hopton England
28 C6 Hoptrup Denmark
94 H7 Hopwood Pennsylvania U.S.A.
141 G5 Hopwood,Mt Queensland Australia
100 B2 Hoquiam Washington U.S.A.
107 J3 Horace Kansas U.S.A.
37 P2 Hora Svatého Šebastiána Czechoslovakia
37 P2 Hora Svaté Katering Czechoslovakia
111 B8 Horatio Arkansas U.S.A.
30 H6 Horaždovice Czechoslovakia
36 F7 Horb Germany
28 J7 Horbelev Denmark
37 O7 Horbering Germany
118 B6 Horburg Alberta Canada
13 G6 Horbury England
28 E2 Hørby Nordjylland Denmark
28 D3 Hørby Nordjylland Denmark
27 G16 Hörby Sweden
16 D5 Horcajo de los Montes Spain
16 E5 Horcajo de Santiago Spain
124 G3 Horcasitas Mexico
36 E4 Horchheim Germany
27 A11 Hordaland reg Norway
109 H4 Hords Cr. Res Texas U.S.A.
28 A3 Hørdum Denmark
8 B3 Horeb Wales
88 C6 Hore B Zambia
48 H5 Horezu Romania
48 F4 Horgoš Serbia Yugoslavia
31 J5 Hořice Czechoslovakia
99 S6 Horicon Wisconsin U.S.A.
58 F3 Horinger China
22 J2 Horion Hozémont Belgium
119 M9 Horizon Saskatchewan Canada
137 S6 Horizon Depth Pacific Oc
31 H4 Horka Germany
9 F5 Horley England
146 D9 Horlick Mts Antarctica
28 E2 Hørmested Denmark
Hormo see Nyima
77 E6 Hormoz isld Iran
77 D6 Hormozgān prov Iran
77 E6 Hormoz, Strait of Iran
31 J7 Horn Austria
28 R8 Horn C Iceland
25 E6 Horn Netherlands
27 H14 Horn Sweden
48 F2 Hornad R Czechoslovakia
26 J5 Hornavan L Sweden
36 C5 Hornbach Germany
32 J9 Horn-Bad Meinog Germany
29 K4 Hornbæk Denmark
111 C10 Hornbeck Louisiana U.S.A.
36 E7 Hornberg Germany
27 G13 Hornborgasjön L Sweden
100 C8 Hornbrook California U.S.A.
33 N8 Hornburg Germany
9 F1 Horncastle England
27 H11 Horndal Sweden
33 N6 Horndorf Germany
28 E1 Horne Denmark
28 B5 Horne Ribe Denmark
32 L5 Horneburg Germany
26 L8 Hörnefors Sweden
28 E6 Horneland Denmark
94 K4 Hornell New York U.S.A.
120 F3 Hornepayne Ontario Canada
110 F5 Hornersville Missouri U.S.A.
27 C13 Hornesund Norway
28 G2 Hornfiskrøn isld Denmark
14 C1 Horn Hd Ireland
33 O8 Hornhsleben Germany
141 F1 Horn I Queensland Australia
111 H11 Horn I Mississippi U.S.A.
31 K6 Horni Benešov Czechoslovakia
137 R4 Horn, Îles de Îles Wallis Pacific Oc
124 E4 Hornillos Mexico
26 B10 Hornindal Norway
26 B10 Hornindalsvatn L Norway
36 E6 Hornisgrinde mt Germany
37 O3 Horní Slavkov Czechoslovakia
41 J3 Hörnli mt Switzerland
117 N4 Horn Mts Northwest Territories Canada
116 H6 Horn Mts Alaska U.S.A.
27 C13 Hornnes Norway
133 C6 Hornopiren mt Chile
124 H5 Hornos Mexico
133 D9 Hornos, C. de Chile
21 O2 Hornoy-le Bourg France
117 O4 Horn R Northwest Territories Canada
139 K5 Hornsby New South Wales Australia
110 H6 Hornsby Tennessee U.S.A.
8 B6 Horns Cross England
13 H6 Hornsea England
26 L8 Hörnsjö Sweden
28 E4 Hornslet Denmark
80 E2 Horns of Hittin Israel
37 K1 Hornsömmern Germany
33 P5 Hornstorf Germany
28 D5 Hornstrup Denmark
28 D5 Hornum Vejle Denmark
28 A7 Hørnum Germany
33 S6 Horn Zieritz Germany
60 T1 Horobetsu Japan
60 R3 Horoizumi Japan
60 Q1 Horonai Japan
145 E3 Horopito New Zealand
144 C5 Hororata New Zealand
60 Q3 Horoshiri-dake mt Japan
65 A5 Horo Sum China
30 H6 Hořovice Czechoslovakia
145 E4 Horowhenua admin region New Zealand
83 K9 Horowupotana Sri Lanka
21 K5 Horps,le France
59 H2 Horqin Youyi Qianqi China
65 E2 Horqin Youyi Zhongqi China
65 F2 Horqin Zouyi Zhongqi China
65 E3 Horqin Zuoyi Houqi China
129 G8 Horqueta Paraguay
133 F2 Horqueta Paraguay
28 H7 Horreby Denmark
27 F14 Horred Sweden
36 B2 Horrem Germany
143 A8 Horrocks W Australia Australia
83 M8 Horsburgh I Cocos Is Indian Oc
37 J1 Hörschel Germany
110 K4 Horse Branch Kentucky U.S.A.
9 G6 Horsebridge E Sussex England
94 B9 Horse Cave Kentucky U.S.A.
106 G3 Horse Cr Colorado U.S.A.
110 B4 Horse Cr Missouri U.S.A.
98 A8 Horse Cr Wyoming U.S.A.
117 N9 Horsefly British Columbia Canada
98 F2 Horsehead L North Dakota U.S.A.
95 L4 Horseheads New York U.S.A.
123 R3 Horse Is Newfoundland Canada
37 J2 Hörsel R Germany
102 D1 Horse L California U.S.A.
37 J2 Hörsel Berge mt Germany
28 D5 Horsens Vejle Denmark
28 E5 Horsens Fjord inlet Denmark
118 F2 Horse, R Alberta Canada
113 D8 Horseshoe Florida U.S.A.
111 L9 Horseshoe Band Nat. Mil. Park Alabama U.S.A.
138 C2 Horseshoe Bend N Terr Australia
140 C7 Horseshoe Bend N Terr Australia
100 J6 Horse Shoe Bend Idaho U.S.A.
127 P4 Horse Shoe Pt St Kitts W Indies
103 N7 Horseshoe Res Arizona U.S.A.
106 B8 Horse Springs New Mexico U.S.A.
138 F6 Horsham Victoria Australia
118 H8 Horsham Saskatchewan Canada
9 F5 Horsham England
29 K5 Hørsholm Denmark
13 G4 Horsley England
28 G7 Horslunde Denmark
37 O4 Horšovský Týn Czechoslovakia
32 L5 Horst Germany
33 S4 Horst Germany
25 F6 Horst Netherlands
32 G8 Hörstel Germany
25 F6 Hörstgen Germany
32 F8 Horstmar Germany
48 E2 Hor Stubňa Czechoslovakia
27 D12 Horten Norway
112 F6 Hortense Georgia U.S.A.
26 M6 Hortlax Sweden
114 G4 Horton R Northwest Territories Canada
107 P2 Horton Kansas U.S.A.
27 C10 Horungane Norway
28 C7 Hörup Germany
28 G5 Hørve Denmark
27 G15 Hörvik Sweden
13 F6 Horwich England
120 H5 Horwood L Ontario Canada
37 P5 Hory Matky Boží Czechoslovakia
31 J5 Hory Orlické mts Czechoslovakia
47 K7 Horzom R Turkey
86 G4 Hosa'ina Ethiopia
36 G3 Hösbach Germany
76 C4 Hosdurga India
70 C3 Hose Mts Sarawak
84 G5 Hosenofu Libya
77 A3 Hoseynābad Iran
111 M11 Hosford Florida U.S.A.
74 C10 Hoshab Pakistan
77 H6 Hoshāb Pakistan
74 G7 Hoshangabad India
74 F3 Hoshiarpur India
98 J7 Hoskins Nebraska U.S.A.
98 G4 Hosmer South Dakota U.S.A.
60 E13 Hososhima Japan
106 C6 Hospah New Mexico U.S.A.
76 C3 Hospet India
14 C4 Hospital Ireland
131 G3 Hospital, Cuchilla del mt Uruguay
29 O6 Hossa Finland
106 B6 Hosta Butte mt New Mexico U.S.A.
133 D9 Hoste, I Chile
18 E8 Hostens France
27 G13 Höstholmen Sweden
37 O4 Hostouň Czechoslovakia
28 A5 Hostrup Ribe Denmark
28 B7 Hostrup Sønderjylland Denmark
28 D7 Hostrup Germany
28 C7 Hostrup Sø L Denmark
76 C4 Hosur India
26 G8 Hotagen Sweden
61 L9 Hotaka Japan
66 B4 Hotan China
66 C4 Hotan He R China
87 D11 Hotazel S Africa
117 P7 Hotchkiss Alberta Canada
106 C3 Hotchkiss Colorado U.S.A.
102 H3 Hot Creek Ra Nevada U.S.A.
33 O8 Hötensleben Germany
140 B1 Hotham,C N Terr Australia
116 F3 Hotham Inlet Alaska U.S.A.
139 H6 Hotham, Mt Victoria Australia
26 H7 Hoting Sweden
80 E8 Hot Springs Israel
109 O1 Hot Springs nat park Arkansas U.S.A.
111 C7 Hot Springs Arkansas U.S.A.
101 L2 Hot Springs Montana U.S.A.
112 E2 Hot Springs North Carolina U.S.A.
98 C6 Hot Springs South Dakota U.S.A.
108 D6 Hot Springs Texas U.S.A.
94 H9 Hot Springs Virginia U.S.A.
106 D1 Hot Sulphur Springs Colorado U.S.A.
117 O3 Hottah L Northwest Territories Canada
22 J3 Hotton Belgium
108 B5 Hot Wells Texas U.S.A.
32 L6 Hötzingen Germany
28 E2 Hou Denmark
20 E7 Houat isld France
22 D3 Houdain France
21 O4 Houdan France
22 G3 Houdeng Belgium
18 E8 Houeillès France
22 K3 Houffalize Belgium
107 J5 Hough Oklahoma U.S.A.
141 H4 Houghton R Queensland Australia
99 S2 Houghton Michigan U.S.A.
94 J4 Houghton New York U.S.A.
98 H4 Houghton South Dakota U.S.A.
94 C2 Houghton L Michigan U.S.A.
13 G4 Houghton-le-Spring England
145 D1 Houhora New Zealand
80 F1 Houla Lebanon
21 K3 Houlgate France
111 G7 Houlka Mississippi U.S.A.
21 N2 Houlme,le France
95 T7 Houlton Maine U.S.A.
65 B7 Houma China
111 F12 Houma Louisiana U.S.A.
85 G2 Houmt Souk Tunisia
85 D6 Houndé Burkina
9 F5 Hounslow England
18 E7 Hourtin France
95 O5 Housatonic R Connecticut U.S.A.
108 D1 House New Mexico U.S.A.
123 L6 House Hbr Madeleine Is, Quebec Canada
12 D3 House o'-Hill Scotland
118 E3 House R Alberta Canada
103 L2 House Ra Utah U.S.A.
117 K8 Houston British Columbia Canada
99 P6 Houston Minnesota U.S.A.
111 H8 Houston Mississippi U.S.A.
110 E4 Houston Missouri U.S.A.
109 F9 Houston Texas U.S.A.
110 C3 Houstonia Missouri U.S.A.
109 M5 Houston, L Texas U.S.A.
111 C11 Houston R Louisiana U.S.A.
89 F4 Hout R S Africa
89 A10 Hout B S Africa
25 D4 Houten Netherlands
22 J1 Houthalen Belgium
143 A8 Houtman Abrolhos arch W Australia Australia
94 J6 Houtzdale Pennsylvania U.S.A.
22 J3 Houyet Belgium
28 E5 Hov Denmark
29 K4 Hov Sweden
27 G13 Hova Sweden
28 B5 Hovborg Denmark
58 B2 Hovd Mongolia
27 B12 Hovden Norway
26 H9 Hovdsjö Sweden
28 A3 Hove Denmark
28 G5 Høve Vestjælland Denmark
9 F6 Hove England
28 D5 Hovedgård Denmark
32 J9 Hövelhof Germany
28 B5 Hoven Denmark
98 G4 Hoven South Dakota U.S.A.
103 P4 Hovenweep Nat. Mon Utah U.S.A.
28 A4 Hover Denmark
28 A4 Hover Å R Denmark
77 A4 Hoveyzeh Iran
99 R2 Hovland Minnesota U.S.A.
28 C6 Hovslund Denmark
58 D3 Hövüün Mongolia
141 L7 Howard Queensland Australia
107 O4 Howard Kansas U.S.A.
94 E6 Howard Ohio U.S.A.
94 K5 Howard Pennsylvania U.S.A.
98 J5 Howard South Dakota U.S.A.
99 S5 Howard Wisconsin U.S.A.
94 B3 Howard City Michigan U.S.A.
108 F5 Howard Cr Texas U.S.A.
140 D1 Howard I N Terr Australia
99 M4 Howard L Minnesota U.S.A.
116 J2 Howard Pass Alaska U.S.A.
99 T6 Howards Grove Wisconsin U.S.A.
86 D2 Howar, Wadi watercourse Sudan
13 H6 Howden England
101 M6 Howe Idaho U.S.A.
94 B5 Howe Indiana U.S.A.
109 N1 Howe Oklahoma U.S.A.
109 L2 Howe Texas U.S.A.
139 J6 Howe, C New South Wales Australia
83 L13 Howe, Î Kerguelen Indian Oc
94 D4 Howell Michigan U.S.A.
101 N8 Howell Utah U.S.A.
98 J8 Howells Nebraska U.S.A.
138 C2 Howe, Mt South Australia Australia
15 F4 Howe of Mearns Scotland
98 D5 Howes South Dakota U.S.A.
117 M11 Howe Sound British Columbia Canada
121 R7 Howick Quebec Canada
145 E2 Howick New Zealand
141 H2 Howick Group islds Gt Barrier Reef Aust
138 E2 Howitt, L South Australia Australia
139 H6 Howitt, Mt Victoria Australia
95 T1 Howland Maine U.S.A.
137 R1 Howland I Pacific Oc
123 P4 Howley Newfoundland Canada
117 P10 Howser British Columbia Canada
14 E3 Howth Ireland
68 H4 Ho Xa Vietnam
110 F5 Hoxie Arkansas U.S.A.
107 K2 Hoxie Kansas U.S.A.
32 K9 Höxter Germany
66 D2 Hoxtolgay China
15 E2 Hoy Scotland
32 K7 Hoya Germany
31 H4 Hoyerswerda Germany
8 C1 Hoylake England
26 F7 Höylandet Norway
120 J4 Hoyle Ontario Canada
110 G3 Hoyleton Illinois U.S.A.
33 O9 Hoym Germany
16 C4 Hoyos Spain
15 E2 Hoy Snd Scotland
122 F8 Hoyt New Brunswick Canada
107 P2 Hoyt Kansas U.S.A.
29 O9 Höytiäinen L Finland
101 O9 Hoyt Pk Utah U.S.A.
Hpa-an see Pa-an
68 C2 Hpa Lai Burma
68 C3 Hpasawg Burma
37 P4 Hracholuská Nádrž res Czechoslovakia
31 J5 Hradec Králové Czechoslovakia
37 P3 Hradiště mt Czechoslovakia
31 K6 Hranice Czechoslovakia
Hranice Czechoslovakia see Rossbach
48 F2 Hriňová Czechoslovakia
31 L7 Hron R Czechoslovakia
37 O3 Hroznetín Czechoslovakia
31 O5 Hrubieszów Poland
31 J7 Hrušovany Czechoslovakia
Hrvatska see Croatia
68 C2 Hsa Mong Hkam Burma
66 D5 Hsia-ju Ts'o L China
67 G6 Hsiao-lan Hsü isld Taiwan
58 G5 Hsieh-chia-chi China
68 C2 Hsi Hkip Burma
68 C2 Hsi-hseng Burma
58 G4 Hsin-chi China
58 F4 Hsin-ch'iang China
67 G4 Hsin-chu Taiwan
68 J3 Hsing-ying China
59 H3 Hsin-min China
68 C1 Hsipaw Burma
66 D5 Hsi-tsang Kao-yüan reg China
68 C1 Hsumhsai Burma
68 K2 Hsü-wen China
67 F4 Hua'an China
128 C6 Huacho Peru
65 H1 Huachuan China
128 C5 Huacrachuco Peru
65 C4 Huade China
59 J3 Huadian China
67 G2 Huading Shan mt China
68 D6 Hua Hin Thailand
68 F5 Huai R Thailand
65 C4 Huai'an China
58 G5 Huaibei China
65 F3 Huaide China
65 F3 Huaidezhen China
58 F5 Huai He R China
67 C3 Huaihua China
67 D5 Huaiji China
65 C4 Huailai China
68 F4 Huai Luang R Thailand
58 G5 Huainan China
67 E1 Huaining China
58 F4 Huairen China
65 C4 Huairou China
68 F4 Huai Yang Res Thailand
59 G5 Huaiyin China
67 C4 Huaiyuan China
125 L9 Huajuápan de León Mexico
71 N8 Huaki Indonesia
103 L6 Hualapai Mts Arizona U.S.A.
67 E2 Hualin China
128 C5 Huallaga R Peru
128 C5 Huallanca Peru
65 H1 Huama China
65 H1 Huanan China
128 E7 Huanay Bolivia
128 C6 Huancabamba Pasco Peru
128 C5 Huancabamba Piura Peru
128 E7 Huancane Peru
128 C6 Huancavelica Peru
128 C6 Huancayo Peru
128 E8 Huanchaca Bolivia
128 F6 Huanchaca, Sa. de mts Bolivia
128 C5 Huanchaco Peru
Huang'an see Hong'an
67 G1 Huangang China
Huangcaoba see Qianxinan
58 G5 Huangchuan China
67 E1 Huanggang China
65 D3 Huangganglliang mt China
67 F3 Huanggang Shan mt China
Huang Hai see Yellow Sea
58 D4 Huang He R China
65 D5 Huanghua China
65 C7 Huangkou China
67 E2 Huanglaomen China
65 A7 Huangling China
68 J3 Huangliu China
65 A7 Huanglong China
65 C7 Huanglongsi China
67 E1 Huangmei China
67 C4 Huangmian China
65 G3 Huangnihe China
67 E1 Huangpi China
67 B3 Huangpin China
67 C6 Huangpo China
67 D5 Huangpu China
67 E2 Huangshagang China
67 F1 Huang Shan mts China
67 F2 Huangshan China
65 E6 Huangshanguan China
58 D4 Huang Shui R China
65 G3 Huangsongdian China
65 D4 Huangtuliangzi China
65 E6 Huang Xian China
67 G2 Huangyan China
67 D3 Huangyangsi China
Huangzhou see Huanggang
67 C7 Huangzhu China
67 G1 Huaniao Shan isld China
67 A4 Huaning China
58 E4 Huan Jiang R China
67 C4 Huanjiang China
65 F4 Huanren China
Huanshan see Yuhuan
58 G5 Huanshi China
128 D6 Huanta Peru
65 D6 Huantai China
128 C5 Huánuco Peru
128 D6 Huanzo, Cord. de mts Peru
125 N3 Huaonta Nicaragua
67 G4 Hua-p'ing Hsü isld Taiwan
128 E7 Huara Chile
128 C5 Huaraz Peru
128 C6 Huariaca Peru
128 C6 Huarmey Peru
67 D2 Huarong China
128 C5 Huascarán mt Peru
133 C3 Huasco Chile
131 B2 Huasco, R Chile
67 D3 Huashi China
125 M2 Huaspuc Honduras
124 E4 Huatabampo Mexico
58 E4 Huating China
65 E3 Hua Tugal China
125 L8 Huatusco Mexico
125 K7 Huauchinango Mexico
65 A7 Hua Xian China
65 C7 Hua Xian China

Hua Xian — Indispensable Reefs 185

67 D5 **Hua Xian** China
65 A7 **Huayin** China
67 B1 **Huaying Shan** *mts* China
67 E1 **Huayuan** China
67 C2 **Huayuan** China
67 C6 **Huazhou** China
65 F4 **Huazi** China
119 O7 **Hubbard** Saskatchewan Canada
99 N7 **Hubbard** Iowa U.S.A.
109 L4 **Hubbard** Texas U.S.A.
109 H3 **Hubbard Cr. Res** Texas U.S.A.
117 C5 **Hubbard Glacier** Alaska U.S.A.
94 D2 **Hubbard L** Michigan U.S.A.
117 D5 **Hubbard, Mt** Alaska/Yukon Terr U.S.A./Canada
122 H9 **Hubbards** Nova Scotia Canada
98 J9 **Hubbell** Nebraska U.S.A.
103 P6 **Hubbell Trading Post Nat. Hist. Site** Arizona U.S.A.
58 F5 **Hubei** *prov* China
41 N3 **Huben** Austria
121 Q7 **Huberdeau** Quebec Canada
33 T7 **Hubertusstock** Germany
76 B3 **Hubli** India
32 J6 **Huchting** Germany
25 F6 **Hückelhoven-Ratheim** Germany
36 C1 **Hückeswagen** Germany
140 D6 **Huckitta** N Terr Australia
9 E1 **Hucknall** England
22 B2 **Hucqueliers** France
72 E6 **Ḩudaydah, Al** Yemen
13 G6 **Huddersfield** England
27 J12 **Huddinge** Sweden
32 H6 **Hude** Germany
32 L7 **Hudemühlen** Germany
26 J10 **Hudiksvall** Sweden
20 H4 **Hudimesnil** France
115 K7 **Hudson** Ontario Canada
133 C7 **Hudson** *mt* Chile
106 F1 **Hudson** Colorado U.S.A.
113 E9 **Hudson** Florida U.S.A.
110 G1 **Hudson** Illinois U.S.A.
94 B5 **Hudson** Indiana U.S.A.
99 O7 **Hudson** Iowa U.S.A.
107 M3 **Hudson** Kansas U.S.A.
94 C5 **Hudson** Michigan U.S.A.
95 O3 **Hudson** *R* New York U.S.A.
95 O4 **Hudson** New York U.S.A.
94 F5 **Hudson** Ohio U.S.A.
101 R7 **Hudson** Wyoming U.S.A.
115 L6 **Hudson Bay** Canada
119 P6 **Hudson Bay** Saskatchewan Canada
146 C13 **Hudson, Cape** *C* Antarctica
95 O3 **Hudson Falls** New York U.S.A.
107 P5 **Hudson, L.** Oklahoma U.S.A.
117 N7 **Hudson's Hope** British Columbia Canada
115 M5 **Hudson Str** Canada
94 B4 **Hudsonville** Michigan U.S.A.
119 W5 **Hudwin L** Manitoba Canada
68 H4 **Hue** Vietnam
16 C4 **Huebra** *R* Spain
131 B7 **Huechulafquén, L** Argentina
108 B4 **Hueco Mts** Texas U.S.A.
48 H4 **Huedin** Romania
124 G5 **Huehueto, Cerro** *mt* Mexico
125 K7 **Huejutla** Mexico
20 C5 **Huelgoat** France
16 E7 **Huelma** Spain
16 C7 **Huelva** *R* Spain
16 C7 **Huelva** *prov* Spain
16 C7 **Huelva** Spain
68 G4 **Huen** Laos
131 B3 **Huentelauquén** Chile
124 D3 **Huépac** Mexico
133 C6 **Huequi, Pen** Chile
17 F7 **Huércal Overa** Spain
106 F3 **Huerfano** *R* Colorado U.S.A.
131 C3 **Huerta, Sa. de la** *ra* Argentina
17 G6 **Huertas, C. de las** Spain
124 J5 **Huertecillas** Mexico
17 G3 **Huerva** *R* Spain
17 G2 **Huesca** *prov* Spain
17 G2 **Huesca** Spain
17 F7 **Huéscar** Spain
16 D7 **Huesna** *R* Spain
108 B5 **Hueso, Sierra del** *mts* Mexico
125 J8 **Huétamo** Mexico
17 F4 **Huete** Spain
98 F3 **Huff** North Dakota U.S.A.
36 G5 **Hüffenhardt** Germany
98 H4 **Huffton** South Dakota U.S.A.
77 A7 **Hufuf, Al** Saudi Arabia
116 K4 **Huggins I** Alaska U.S.A.
98 F9 **Hugh Butler L** Nebraska U.S.A.
141 G5 **Hughenden** Queensland Australia
118 F6 **Hughenden** Alberta Canada
121 L4 **Hughes** Ontario Canada
110 F7 **Hughes** Arkansas U.S.A.
119 R2 **Hughes R** Manitoba Canada
109 N3 **Hughes Springs** Texas U.S.A.
110 C3 **Hughesville** Missouri U.S.A.
140 C6 **Hugh R** N Terr Australia
118 K7 **Hughton** Saskatchewan Canada
9 F7 **Hugh Town** Isles of Scilly England
75 M8 **Hugli** *R* India
106 G2 **Hugo** Colorado U.S.A.
99 N4 **Hugo** Minnesota U.S.A.
107 P7 **Hugo** Oklahoma U.S.A.
100 B7 **Hugo** Oregon U.S.A.
107 P7 **Hugo L** Oklahoma U.S.A.
107 J4 **Hugoton** Kansas U.S.A.
36 D7 **Hugsweier** Germany
65 B6 **Huguan** China
Huhehot *see* **Hohhot**
58 F3 **Huhehot** China
67 F4 **Hui'an** China
145 F3 **Huiarau Range** New Zealand
67 E4 **Huichang** China
Huicheng *see* **She Xian**
124 H7 **Huicholes, Sa. de los** *mts* Mexico
59 J3 **Hŭich'ŏn** N Korea
67 E5 **Huidong** China
65 G2 **Huifaheng** China
128 C3 **Huila** *div* Colombia
58 G4 **Huimin** China
65 G3 **Huinan** China
67 B3 **Huishui** China
21 L7 **Huismes** France
21 M5 **Huîsne** *R* France
21 N6 **Huisseau-sur-Cosson** France
65 C7 **Huiting** China
67 C3 **Huitong** China
29 K10 **Huittinen** Finland
125 K8 **Huitzuco** Mexico
65 B7 **Hui Xian** China
125 N10 **Huixtla** Mexico
Huiyang *see* **Huizhou**
25 D4 **Huizen** Netherlands
67 E5 **Huizhou** China
58 D2 **Hujirt** Mongolia
145 F3 **Huka Falls** New Zealand
145 E4 **Hukanui** New Zealand
144 C5 **Hukarere** New Zealand
75 R5 **Hukawng Valley** Burma
145 E1 **Hukerenui** New Zealand
67 E2 **Hukou** China
87 D10 **Hukuntsi** Botswana
107 O5 **Hulah** Oklahoma U.S.A.
107 O5 **Hulah L** Oklahoma U.S.A.
59 J2 **Hulan** China
65 F1 **Hulan Ergi** China
65 G1 **Hulan He** *R* China
80 F1 **Ḩulata** Israel
98 B5 **Hulett** Wyoming U.S.A.
Huliao *see* **Dabu**
65 J2 **Hulin** China
65 E2 **Hulin He** *R* China
121 P7 **Hull** Quebec Canada
99 P10 **Hull** Illinois U.S.A.
98 K6 **Hull** Iowa U.S.A.
98 F3 **Hull** North Dakota U.S.A.
109 N5 **Hull** Texas U.S.A.
140 A6 **Hull Cr** N Terr Australia
22 G2 **Hulpe, la** Belgium
28 E1 **Hulsig** Denmark
25 B6 **Hulst** Netherlands
27 H14 **Hultsfred** Sweden
65 E4 **Huludao** China
69 E11 **HUlu Kali, Gunung** Malaysia
58 G2 **Hulun Nur** *L* China
69 E10 **Hulu Soh, Gunung** *mt* Malaysia
59 J1 **Huma** China
127 M5 **Humacao** Puerto Rico
59 H1 **Huma He** *R* China
128 F5 **Humaitá** Brazil
130 B10 **Humaitá** Paraguay
87 D12 **Humansdorp** S Africa
110 C4 **Humansville** Missouri U.S.A.
128 C6 **Humay** Peru
87 C9 **Humbe** Angola
123 P5 **Humbermouth** Newfoundland Canada
13 H6 **Humber, R** England
13 H6 **Humberside** *co* England
99 Q5 **Humbird** Wisconsin U.S.A.
28 F7 **Humble** Denmark
109 M6 **Humble** Texas U.S.A.
106 G9 **Humble City** New Mexico U.S.A.
119 M6 **Humboldt** Saskatchewan Canada
103 M7 **Humboldt** Arizona U.S.A.
99 S10 **Humboldt** Illinois U.S.A.
99 M7 **Humboldt** Iowa U.S.A.
107 P4 **Humboldt** Kansas U.S.A.
102 F1 **Humboldt** *R* Nevada U.S.A.
102 F1 **Humboldt** Nevada U.S.A.
110 H6 **Humboldt** Tennessee U.S.A.
100 A9 **Humboldt B** California U.S.A.
115 N2 **Humboldt Gletscher** *gla* Greenland
102 F2 **Humboldt L** Nevada U.S.A.
144 B6 **Humboldt Mts** New Zealand
100 G9 **Humboldt Range** Nevada U.S.A.
102 F1 **Humboldt Rge** Nevada U.S.A.
102 G2 **Humboldt Salt Marsh** Nevada U.S.A.
94 J8 **Hume** Virginia U.S.A.
141 H7 **Humeburn** Queensland Australia
77 F7 **Hūmedān** Iran
48 G2 **Humenné** Czechoslovakia
139 H6 **Hume Res** New South Wales Australia
99 N9 **Humeston** Iowa U.S.A.
29 K5 **Humlebæk** Denmark
28 B3 **Humlum** Denmark
32 K9 **Humme** Germany
95 L6 **Hummelstown** Pennsylvania U.S.A.
32 G7 **Hümmling** *hills* Germany
144 C6 **Hummock** *mt* New Zealand
127 K10 **Humocaro Bajo** Venezuela
131 A5 **Humos, C** Chile
87 B9 **Humpata** Angola
111 E7 **Humphrey** Arkansas U.S.A.
101 N5 **Humphrey** Idaho U.S.A.
98 J8 **Humphrey** Nebraska U.S.A.
100 D2 **Humphrey** Washington U.S.A.
102 E5 **Humphreys** California U.S.A.
110 C1 **Humphreys** Missouri U.S.A.
103 N6 **Humphreys Pk** Arizona U.S.A.
140 C7 **Humphries, Mt** N Terr Australia
31 J6 **Humpolec** Czechoslovakia
29 K11 **Humppila** Finland
100 B2 **Humptulips** Washington U.S.A.
140 B2 **Humpty Doo** N Terr Australia
84 F4 **Hūn** Libya
28 S9 **Húna-flói** *B* Iceland
67 C3 **Hunan** *prov* China
65 H3 **Hunchun** China
144 D5 **Hundalee** New Zealand
28 A3 **Hundborg** Denmark
28 B6 **Hunderup** Denmark
28 H5 **Hundested** Denmark
117 N10 **Hundred Mile House** British Columbia Canada
26 M6 **Hundsjö** Sweden
28 E5 **Hundslund** Denmark
38 G7 **Hundstein** *mt* Austria
28 D2 **Hune** Denmark
48 H5 **Hunedoara** *reg* Romania
48 H5 **Hunedoara** Romania
36 H2 **Hünfeld** Germany
36 E3 **Hünfelden** Germany
48 D3 **Hungary** *rep* Europe
26 H9 **Hunge** Sweden
36 F3 **Hungen** Germany
141 G8 **Hungerford** Queensland Australia
9 E5 **Hungerford** England
58 B2 **Hüngiy** Mongolia
65 G5 **Hŭngnam** N Korea
101 L1 **Hungry Horse Dam** Montana U.S.A.
101 M1 **Hungry Horse Res** Montana U.S.A.
68 H2 **Hung Yen** Vietnam
65 B4 **Hun He** *R* China
65 E4 **Hun He** *R* China
65 F4 **Hun Jiang** *R* China
65 G4 **Hunjiang** China
13 H5 **Hunmanby** England
99 P10 **Hunnewell** Missouri U.S.A.
25 F7 **Hünshoven** Germany
9 G2 **Hunstanton** England
28 B2 **Hunstrup** Denmark
76 C4 **Hunsur** India
65 E2 **Hunt** China
109 H5 **Hunt** Texas U.S.A.
120 J3 **Hunta** Ontario Canada
32 H8 **Hunte** *R* Germany
32 H8 **Hunteburg** Germany
139 K4 **Hunter** *R* New South Wales Australia
144 C6 **Hunter** New Zealand
137 P6 **Hunter** *isld* Pacific Oc
110 E6 **Hunter** Arkansas U.S.A.
107 M2 **Hunter** Kansas U.S.A.
98 J2 **Hunter** North Dakota U.S.A.
107 N5 **Hunter** Oklahoma U.S.A.
109 J6 **Hunter** Texas U.S.A.
139 G8 **Hunter I** Tasmania Australia
117 J10 **Hunter I** British Columbia Canada
99 P1 **Hunter I** Ontario Canada
116 M5 **Hunter, Mt** Alaska U.S.A.
144 A6 **Hunter Mts** New Zealand
144 B6 **Hunter R** New Zealand
122 J7 **Hunter River** Prince Edward I Canada
100 G1 **Hunters** Washington U.S.A.
68 A3 **Hunter's B** Burma
144 C6 **Hunter's Hills, The** New Zealand
12 D2 **Hunterston** Scotland
112 G2 **Huntersville** North Carolina U.S.A.
94 G8 **Huntersville** West Virginia U.S.A.
94 B5 **Huntertown** Indiana U.S.A.
145 E3 **Hunterville** New Zealand
110 K3 **Huntingburg** Indiana U.S.A.
121 Q7 **Huntingdon** Quebec Canada
9 F3 **Huntingdon** England
94 J6 **Huntingdon** Pennsylvania U.S.A.
110 H6 **Huntingdon** Tennessee U.S.A.
Huntingdon and Peterborough *co see* **Cambridgeshire**
122 J3 **Hunting I** Quebec Canada
112 G5 **Hunting I** South Carolina U.S.A.
94 B6 **Huntington** Indiana U.S.A.
95 O6 **Huntington** Long I, New York U.S.A.
100 H5 **Huntington** Oregon U.S.A.
111 B10 **Huntington** Texas U.S.A.
103 O2 **Huntington** Utah U.S.A.
94 E8 **Huntington** West Virginia U.S.A.
102 F8 **Huntington Beach** California U.S.A.
102 E4 **Huntington L** California U.S.A.
8 D4 **Huntley** England
101 R4 **Huntley** Montana U.S.A.
98 G9 **Huntley** Nebraska U.S.A.
98 B8 **Huntley** Wyoming U.S.A.
32 H7 **Huntlosen** Germany
145 E2 **Huntly** New Zealand
15 F3 **Huntly** Scotland
117 J5 **Hunt, Mt** Yukon Territory Canada
138 D3 **Hunt Pen** South Australia Australia
101 S5 **Hunts Mt** Wyoming U.S.A.
122 H10 **Hunts Pt** Nova Scotia Canada
121 L7 **Huntsville** Ontario Canada
110 K7 **Huntsville** Alabama U.S.A.
110 C5 **Huntsville** Arkansas U.S.A.
110 D2 **Huntsville** Missouri U.S.A.
109 M5 **Huntsville** Texas U.S.A.
101 O8 **Huntsville** Utah U.S.A.
32 E9 **Hünxe** Germany
88 C10 **Hunyani Rge** *mts* Zimbabwe
65 B5 **Hunyuan** China
66 A4 **Hunza** Kashmir
25 G2 **Hunze** *R* Netherlands
66 C3 **Huocheng** China
65 F1 **Huodifangzi** China
65 B7 **Huojia** China
139 H9 **Huon** *R* Tasmania Australia
68 H4 **Huong Hoa** Vietnam
68 G3 **Huong Khe** Vietnam
68 H8 **Huong My** Vietnam
68 G3 **Huong Son** Vietnam
68 H4 **Huong Thuy** Vietnam
139 H9 **Huonville** Tasmania Australia
65 B6 **Huo Shan** *mt* China
67 E1 **Huoshan** China
67 G5 **Huo-shao Tao** *isld* Taiwan
65 B6 **Huo Xian** China
Hupeh *prov see* **Hubei** *prov*
21 O1 **Huppy** France
33 M10 **Hüpstedt** Germany
48 E3 **Hurbanovo** Czechoslovakia
27 E11 **Hurdals** *L* Norway
120 J7 **Hurd, Cape** Ontario Canada
86 B1 **Hurdiyo** Somalia
110 D1 **Hurdland** Missouri U.S.A.
98 F2 **Hurdsfield** North Dakota U.S.A.
65 E3 **Hure Qi** China
80 E1 **Hurfeish** Israel
84 J4 **Hurghada** Egypt
18 G6 **Huriel** France
119 P2 **Hurkett** Ontario Canada
9 F4 **Hurley** England
111 H11 **Hurley** Mississippi U.S.A.
106 B9 **Hurley** New Mexico U.S.A.
98 J6 **Hurley** South Dakota U.S.A.
99 Q3 **Hurley** Wisconsin U.S.A.
12 D2 **Hurlford** Scotland
15 E2 **Hurliness** Scotland
95 M8 **Hurlock** Maryland U.S.A.
143 C10 **Hurlstone, L** W Australia Australia
102 D5 **Huron** California U.S.A.
94 E5 **Huron** Ohio U.S.A.
98 H5 **Huron** South Dakota U.S.A.
99 S3 **Huron B** Michigan U.S.A.
94 E2 **Huron City** Michigan U.S.A.
94 E2 **Huron, L** U.S.A./Canada
99 T3 **Huron Mts** Michigan U.S.A.
103 L4 **Hurricane** Utah U.S.A.
94 E8 **Hurricane** West Virginia U.S.A.
112 E6 **Hurricane Cr** Georgia U.S.A.
126 E3 **Hurricane Flats** Bahamas
110 J6 **Hurricane Mills** Tennessee U.S.A.
9 E5 **Hursley** England
109 M9 **Hurst** Texas U.S.A.
9 E5 **Hurstbourne Tarrant** England
9 G5 **Hurst Green** England
9 F6 **Hurstpierpoint** England
131 B3 **Hurtado** *R* Chile
36 B2 **Hürtgen** Germany
36 B2 **Hürth** Germany
111 L9 **Hurtsboro** Alabama U.S.A.
70 C4 **Hurung, Gunung** *mt* Kalimantan
88 B10 **Hurungwe** *dist* Zimbabwe
144 D5 **Hurunui R** New Zealand
28 E3 **Hurup** Denmark
28 D7 **Hurup** Germany
28 S9 **Husavik** Iceland
9 E3 **Husbands Bosworth** England
28 A4 **Husby** Denmark
71 L10 **Husdale** Indonesia
Hushan *see* **Cixi**
65 H2 **Hushan** China
48 L4 **Huşi** Romania
80 D3 **Ḩusifa** Israel
139 K6 **Huskisson** New South Wales Australia
27 G14 **Huskvarna** Sweden
116 J4 **Huslia** Alaska U.S.A.
80 G4 **Husn** Jordan
101 L2 **Huson** Montana U.S.A.
27 A10 **Husöy** Norway
118 E7 **Hussar** Alberta Canada
26 B9 **Hustadvika** Norway
28 B6 **Husum** Denmark
30 E1 **Husum** Germany
131 H6 **Husvik** S Georgia
58 D2 **Hutag** Mongolia
69 D12 **Hutanopan** Sumatra
109 O10 **Hutchins** Texas U.S.A.
107 N3 **Hutchinson** Kansas U.S.A.
99 M5 **Hutchinson** Minnesota U.S.A.
113 G10 **Hutchinson I** Florida U.S.A.
103 N7 **Hutch Mt** Arizona U.S.A.
68 D4 **Huthi** Burma
59 K2 **Hutou** China
110 J2 **Hutsonville** Illinois U.S.A.
38 H7 **Hüttau** Austria
21 L5 **Hutte, la** France
37 L4 **Hüttenbach** Germany
38 L8 **Hüttenberg** Austria
36 G3 **Hüttengesäss** Germany
37 P6 **Hutthurm** Germany
111 D8 **Huttig** Arkansas U.S.A.
109 K5 **Hutto** Texas U.S.A.
6 L1 **Hutton** *oil rig* North Sea
141 J7 **Hutton, Mt** Queensland Australia
143 E6 **Hutton Ra** W Australia Australia
94 G8 **Huttonsville** West Virginia U.S.A.
40 G3 **Huttwil** Switzerland
66 D3 **Hutubi** China
58 F4 **Hutuo He** *R* China
73 L8 **Huvadu Atoll** Maldives
79 G3 **Ḩuwayz, Al** Syria
118 D7 **Huxley** Alberta Canada
142 F4 **Huxley, Mt** W Australia Australia
144 B6 **Huxley, Mt** New Zealand
116 R6 **Huxley, Mt** Alaska U.S.A.
22 J3 **Huy** Belgium
67 G1 **Huzhou** China
27 E12 **Hvaler** *isld* Norway
28 C3 **Hvalpsund** Denmark
115 M2 **Hvalsund** *Sd* Greenland
28 C3 **Hvam** Denmark
42 G5 **Hvar** Croatia
42 H5 **Hvar** *isld* Croatia
28 S10 **Hveragerdhi** Iceland
28 S9 **Hveravellir** Iceland
28 B3 **Hvidbjerg** Denmark
28 B6 **Hviding** Denmark
28 E4 **Hvilsager** Denmark
28 D3 **Hvilsom** Denmark
28 E4 **Hvilsted** Denmark
28 S9 **Hvita** *R* Iceland
27 E12 **Hvitsten** Norway
27 D12 **Hvittingfoss** Norway
Hwainan *see* **Huainan**
89 E2 **Hwange** Zimbabwe
87 E9 **Hwange Nat. Park** Zimbabwe
Hwang Hai *see* **Yellow Sea**
61 P14 **Hyakuna** Okinawa
101 P4 **Hyalite Pk** Montana U.S.A.
100 B9 **Hyampom** California U.S.A.
95 R5 **Hyannis** Massachusetts U.S.A.
98 E8 **Hyannis** Nebraska U.S.A.
58 B2 **Hyargas Nuur** *L* Mongolia
100 C7 **Hyatt Res** Oregon U.S.A.
95 L8 **Hyattsville** Maryland U.S.A.
101 S5 **Hyattville** Wyoming U.S.A.
111 J10 **Hybart** Alabama U.S.A.
121 N7 **Hybla** Ontario Canada
27 H14 **Hycklinge** Sweden
117 G8 **Hydaburg** Alaska U.S.A.
13 F6 **Hyde** England
144 C6 **Hyde** New Zealand
143 C9 **Hyden** W Australia Australia
94 D9 **Hyden** Kentucky U.S.A.
117 H8 **Hyder** Br Col/Alaska Canada/U.S.A.
74 H10 **Hyderabad** India
77 L7 **Hyderabad** Pakistan
Hydra *isld see* **Ídhra** *isld*
109 J5 **Hye** Texas U.S.A.
20 H4 **Hyenville** France
19 Q18 **Hyères** France
59 J3 **Hyesan** N Korea
98 A9 **Hygiene** Colorado U.S.A.
117 J5 **Hyland** *R* Yukon Territory Canada
139 L4 **Hyland, Mt** New South Wales Australia
117 J7 **Hyland Post** British Columbia Canada
28 D5 **Hylke** Denmark
28 G7 **Hyllekrog** *C* Denmark
27 A10 **Hyllestad** Norway
28 F4 **Hyllested** Denmark
28 H5 **Hyllinge** Denmark
118 E4 **Hylo** Alberta Canada
27 B12 **Hylsfjorden** *inlet* Norway
110 J2 **Hymera** Indiana U.S.A.
138 F6 **Hynam** South Australia Australia
12 E2 **Hyndford Br** Scotland
94 J7 **Hyndman** Pennsylvania U.S.A.
101 L6 **Hyndman Peak** Idaho U.S.A.
94 K5 **Hyner** Pennsylvania U.S.A.
60 J10 **Hyōgo** *prefect* Japan
86 D4 **Hyrra Banda** Cent Afr Republic
101 O8 **Hyrum** Utah U.S.A.
29 N7 **Hyrynsalmi** Finland
52 C3 **Hyrynsalmi** Finland
101 S3 **Hysham** Montana U.S.A.
117 O8 **Hythe** Alberta Canada
9 H5 **Hythe** England
9 E6 **Hythe** Hampshire England
60 E13 **Hyūga** Japan
29 L11 **Hyvinkää** Finland

I

68 J6 **Ia Ayun** *R* Vietnam
128 E6 **Iaco** *R* Brazil
48 J3 **Iacobeni** Romania
129 K6 **Iaçu** Brazil
94 F9 **Iaeger** West Virginia U.S.A.
36 B7 **Iaintrux** France
48 K6 **Ialomiţa** *reg* Romania
48 K6 **Ialomiţa** *R* Romania
47 R14 **Ialysus** *hist site* Rhodes Greece
113 C7 **Iamonia, L** Florida U.S.A.
48 L5 **Ianca** Romania
88 C7 **Iangano Nat. Park** Zambia
144 C5 **Ianthe, L** New Zealand
48 H4 **Iara** Romania
14 B3 **Iar Connaught** Ireland
129 H3 **Iaripo** Brazil
53 C10 **Iasi** Romania
46 G3 **Íasmos** Greece
111 D10 **Iatt, L** Louisiana U.S.A.
128 E3 **Iauareté** Brazil
52 H4 **Ib** Russian Federation
71 D3 **Iba** Luzon Philippines
85 E7 **Ibadan** Nigeria
128 C3 **Ibagué** Colombia
130 E8 **Ibaiti** Brazil
101 M9 **Ibapah** Utah U.S.A.
46 D1 **Ibar** *R* Serbia Yugoslavia
60 G11 **Ibara** Japan
61 O9 **Ibaraki** *prefect* Japan
128 C3 **Ibarra** Ecuador
32 G8 **Ibbenbüren** Germany
80 G4 **Ibbin** Jordan
86 C5 **Ibenga** *R* Congo
131 F2 **Iberá, Esteros del** *marshes* Argentina
131 F2 **Iberá, L** Argentina
110 D3 **Iberia** Missouri U.S.A.
121 R7 **Iberville** Quebec Canada
26 J3 **Ibestad** Norway
85 F6 **Ibeto** Nigeria
85 F7 **Ibi** Nigeria
129 J7 **Ibiá** Brazil
130 G5 **Ibiaí** Brazil
129 K4 **Ibiapaba, Serra da** *mts* Brazil
131 G3 **Ibicui da Cruz** *R* Brazil
131 G2 **Ibicuí, R** Brazil
133 F4 **Ibicuy** Argentina
61 K10 **Ibigawa** Japan
80 D2 **I'billin** Israel
130 D8 **Ibiporã** Brazil
130 H6 **Ibiraçu** Brazil
130 E10 **Ibirama** Brazil
130 H5 **Ibiranhém** Brazil
131 G3 **Ibirapuita** *R* Brazil
130 E7 **Ibitinga** Brazil
17 H5 **Ibiza** *isld* Balearic Is
80 F8 **Ibn Hammad** Jordan
88 H8 **Ibo** Mozambique
129 K6 **Ibotirama** Brazil
86 D3 **Ibra., Wadi** *watercourse* Sudan
52 G6 **Ibresi** Russian Federation
47 H3 **İbriktepe** Turkey
79 A9 **Ibshawâi** Egypt
9 E6 **Ibsley** England
61 Q12 **Ibu** Okinawa
60 D14 **Ibusuki** Japan
128 E4 **Içá** *R* Brazil
128 C6 **Ica** Peru
128 F3 **Icabaru** *R* Venezuela
127 N3 **Icacos Pt** Trinidad
71 D5 **Icadambanauan** Philippines
131 G2 **Icamaqua** *R* Brazil
128 E3 **Icana** Brazil
103 K5 **Iceberg Canyon** Nev/Ariz U.S.A.
100 G3 **Ice Harbor Dam** Washington U.S.A.
İçel *see* **Mersin**
28 **Iceland** *rep* N Atlantic Oc
90 H2 **Iceland-Faeroe Rise** Atlantic Oc
56 B3 **Icha** *R* Russian Federation
76 B2 **Ichalkaranji** India
37 J7 **Ichenhausen** Germany
60 G11 **Ichi** Japan
60 E13 **Ichifusa-yama** *mt* Japan
61 O10 **Ichihara** Japan
61 P5 **Ichinohe** Japan
59 L4 **Ichinomiya** Japan
54 D6 **Ichnya** Ukraine
22 E1 **Ichtegem** Belgium
37 K2 **Ichtershausen** Germany
130 H7 **Iconha** Brazil
Iconium *see* **Konya**
116 R6 **Icy B** Alaska U.S.A.
116 F1 **Icy Cape** Alaska U.S.A.
117 E6 **Icy Pt** Alaska U.S.A.
109 O3 **Ida** Louisiana U.S.A.
94 D5 **Ida** Michigan U.S.A.
109 N2 **Idabel** Oklahoma U.S.A.
99 L7 **Ida Grove** Iowa U.S.A.
85 F7 **Idah** Nigeria
101 M6 **Idaho** *state* U.S.A.
100 K6 **Idaho City** Idaho U.S.A.
101 N6 **Idaho Falls** Idaho U.S.A.
106 E2 **Idaho Springs** Colorado U.S.A.
106 H2 **Idalia** Colorado U.S.A.
36 C4 **Idar Oberstein** Germany
56 E4 **Idarskoye Belogor'ye** *mts* Russian Federation
36 C4 **Idarwald** *mts* Germany
144 C6 **Ida Valley** New Zealand
27 E12 **Idd** Norway
77 C7 **Idd al Sharqi** *oil well* Persian Gulf
118 F8 **Iddesleigh** Alberta Canada
111 M9 **Ideal** Georgia U.S.A.
52 D3 **Idel'** Russian Federation
85 F4 **Idelès** Algeria
86 B6 **Idemba** Gabon
28 H7 **Idestrup** Denmark
84 J5 **Idfu** Egypt
84 E4 **Idhān Awbārī** Libya
84 E5 **Idhān Murzuq** Libya
46 G9 **Ídhi Óros** *mt* Crete Greece
46 F7 **Ídhra** *isld* Greece
69 C10 **Idi** Sumatra
Idi Amin Dada, L *see* **Edward, L**
45 K3 **Idice** *R* Italy
116 H5 **Iditarod** Alaska U.S.A.
27 H11 **Idkerberget** Sweden
79 G3 **Idlib** Syria
80 C7 **Idna** Jordan
140 C6 **Idracowra** N Terr Australia
26 F10 **Idre** Sweden
102 D5 **Idria** California U.S.A.
52 C6 **Idritsa** Russian Federation
42 C3 **Idro, L. d'** Italy
21 P8 **Ids St. Roch** France
36 E3 **Idstein** Germany
76 C6 **Idukki** India
28 A4 **Idum** Denmark
87 E12 **Idutywa** S Africa
61 P12 **Ie-jima** *isld* Okinawa
45 R6 **Ielsi** Italy
22 H3 **Iemeppe** Belgium
130 D8 **Iepê** Brazil
22 D2 **Ieper** Belgium
47 H9 **Ierápetra** Crete Greece
46 F8 **Iérax, Akr** *C* Greece
59 G2 **I-erh-hsieh** China
46 F4 **Ierissós** Greece
43 C9 **Ierzu** Sardinia
45 O4 **Iesi** Italy
61 P12 **Ie-suidō** *str* Okinawa
48 J5 **Iezeru** *mt* Romania
17 H6 **Ifach, Pta** Spain
87 H12 **Ifanadiana** Madagascar
85 E7 **Ife** Nigeria
85 F5 **Iférouane** Niger
141 F4 **Iffley** Queensland Australia
138 B4 **Ifould L** South Australia Australia
85 C2 **Ifrane** Morocco
85 E5 **Igadiane** *watercourse* Mali
70 B3 **Igan** Sarawak
88 D1 **Iganga** Uganda
16 E10 **Igá, Oued** *R* Morocco
130 J9 **Igaraçu** Brazil
129 J4 **Igarape-Açu** Brazil
147 P14 **Igarka** Russian Federation
130 C9 **Igatimi** Paraguay
74 E9 **Igatpuri** India
71 F5 **Igbon** *isld* Philippines
21 M5 **Igé** France
36 B4 **Igel** Germany
27 J10 **Iggesund** Sweden
133 D4 **Iglesia** Argentina
43 B9 **Iglesias** Sardinia
98 C6 **Igloo** South Dakota U.S.A.
147 E4 **Igloolik** Northwest Territories Canada
41 O3 **Igls** Austria
79 D9 **'Igma, Gebel el** *mts* Egypt
115 K8 **Ignace** Ontario Canada
106 C4 **Ignacio** Colorado U.S.A.
124 H5 **Ignacio Allende** Mexico
52 C6 **Ignalina** Lithuania
47 J3 **İğneada** Turkey
68 A7 **Ignoitijala** Andaman Is
76 G5 **Ignoitijala** Andaman Is
102 B1 **Igo** California U.S.A.
71 C3 **Igom** W Irian
87 F7 **Igoma** Tanzania
70 B3 **Igon** *R* Sarawak
46 D5 **Igoumenitsa** Greece
52 H5 **Igra** Russian Federation
130 E9 **Iguaçu, R** Brazil
130 H4 **Iguaí** Brazil
125 K8 **Iguala** Mexico
17 J3 **Igualda** Spain
129 J8 **Iguapé** Brazil
130 D8 **Iguaraçu** Brazil
130 F7 **Iguatama** Brazil
130 C8 **Iguatemi** Brazil
129 L5 **Iguatu** Brazil
Iguazú Falls *see* **Cataratas del Iguazú** *waterfalls*
86 A6 **Iguéla** Gabon
86 A6 **Iguéla, Lagune** *Lagoon* Gabon
116 K8 **Igvak, C** Alaska U.S.A.
87 H10 **Iharaña** Madagascar
87 H12 **Ihosy** Madagascar
68 F6 **Ihr** Cambodia
22 L3 **Ihren** Germany
32 F6 **Ihrhove** Germany
40 G1 **Ihringen** Germany
58 E2 **Ihsuuj** Mongolia
29 L6 **Ii** Finland
61 L10 **Iida** Japan
61 N8 **Iide-san** *mt* Japan
29 N2 **Iijärvi** *L* Finland
29 N6 **Iijoki** *R* Finland
52 C5 **Iisaku** Estonia
29 N9 **Iisvesi** Finland
61 M9 **Iiyama** Japan
61 O8 **Iizaka** Japan
60 D12 **Iizuka** Japan
71 K9 **Ija** *isld* Indonesia
70 P9 **Ijang** *isld* Indonesia
85 E7 **Ijebu Ode** Nigeria
25 E2 **IJlst** Netherlands
25 D4 **IJmeer** Netherlands
25 C4 **IJmuiden** Netherlands
25 F3 **IJonger** *R* Netherlands
25 C4 **Ijsel** *R* Netherlands
25 F4 **IJssel** *R* Netherlands
25 D3 **IJsselmeer** Netherlands
25 C5 **IJsselmonde** Netherlands
25 E3 **IJsselmuiden** Netherlands
25 D4 **IJsselstein** Netherlands
133 G3 **Ijuí** Brazil
131 G2 **Ijuí, R** Brazil
25 A6 **IJzendijke** Netherlands
22 D2 **Ijzer** *R* Belgium
52 H6 **Ik** *R* Russian Federation
29 K10 **Ikaalinen** Finland
144 C5 **Ikamatua** New Zealand
115 O4 **Ikamiut** Greenland
86 D6 **Ikanda** Zaire
47 H7 **Ikaria** *isld* Greece
28 C4 **Ikast** Denmark
56 H4 **Ikatskiy Khrebet** *mts* Russian Federation
145 F3 **Ikawhenua Range** New Zealand
60 J11 **Ikeda** Japan
60 G12 **Ikegawa** Japan
61 P13 **Ikei-jima** *isld* Okinawa
85 E7 **Ikeja** Nigeria
86 D6 **Ikela** Zaire
115 O3 **Ikerasak** Greenland
46 F2 **Ikhtiman** Bulgaria
60 C12 **Iki** *isld* Japan
88 C2 **Ikimba L** Tanzania
60 C12 **Iki-suidō** *str* Japan
116 K8 **Ikolik, C** Alaska U.S.A.
85 F7 **Ikom** Nigeria
88 D6 **Ikomba** Tanzania
87 H12 **Ikongo** Madagascar
87 H11 **Ikopa** *R* Madagascar
116 K1 **Ikpikpuk** *R* Alaska U.S.A.
56 B3 **Iksa** *R* Russian Federation
54 J1 **Iksha** Russian Federation
88 C1 **Ikulwe** Uganda
60 H10 **Ikuno** Japan
60 R2 **Ikutahara** Japan
71 E2 **Ilagan** Philippines
78 L5 **Īlām** Iran
75 M5 **Ilam** Nepal
56 E3 **Ilanskiy** Russian Federation
41 K4 **Ilanz** Switzerland
85 E7 **Ilaro** Nigeria
31 M2 **Iława** Poland
28 E2 **Ilbro** Denmark
138 D2 **Ilbunga** South Australia Australia
8 D5 **Ilchester** England
120 J9 **Ilderton** Ontario Canada
13 G3 **Ilderton** England
118 J3 **Ile-à-la Crosse** Saskatchewan Canada
118 K3 **Ile-à-la-Crosse L** Saskatchewan Canada
48 H3 **Ileanda** Romania
83 L13 **Ile aux Bénitiers** Mauritius
86 D6 **Ilebo** Zaire
21 P3 **Île de France** *reg* France
20 G8 **Île D'Olonne** France
25 E5 **Ileijen** Netherlands
55 B5 **Ilek** Russian Federation
85 E4 **Ilerh** *watercourse* Algeria
127 N5 **Îles des Saintes** Guadeloupe W Indies
85 F7 **Ilesha** Nigeria
52 G6 **Ilet'** *R* Russian Federation
20 B6 **Ile-Tudy** France
33 N9 **Ilfeld** Germany
119 W2 **Ilford** Manitoba Canada
9 G4 **Ilford** England
141 G6 **Ilfracombe** Queensland Australia
8 B5 **Ilfracombe** England
56 F4 **Ilga** *R* Russian Federation
78 D1 **Ilgaz Dağ** Turkey
130 F8 **Ilhabela** Brazil
128 F4 **Ilha Grande** Brazil
130 G8 **Ilha Grande, B. de** Brazil
130 D7 **Ilha Solteira Dam** Brazil
16 B4 **Ílhavo** Portugal
130 H4 **Ilhéus** Brazil
48 H5 **Ilia** Romania
116 L6 **Iliamna** Alaska U.S.A.
116 K7 **Iliamna L** Alaska U.S.A.
71 L9 **Ili Boleng** *vol* Indonesia
48 N4 **Il'ichevsk** Ukraine
98 C9 **Iliff** Colorado U.S.A.
71 G6 **Iligan** Philippines
71 G6 **Iligan B** Philippines
71 F1 **Iligan Pt** Philippines
86 A2 **Ilig, Raas** *C* Somalia
46 F6 **Ilikí, L** Greece
56 F3 **Ilim** *R* Russian Federation
56 F1 **Ilimpeya** *R* Russian Federation
56 F3 **Ilimskiy, Khrebet** *mts* Russian Federation
71 E4 **Ilin** *isld* Philippines
55 C6 **Il'inka** Kazakhstan
52 F5 **Il'ino-Zaborskoye** Russian Federation
55 C2 **Il'inskiy** Russian Federation
71 E4 **Ilin Str** Philippines
48 M1 **Il'intsy** Ukraine
46 F5 **Iliodhrómia** *isld* Greece
95 M3 **Ilion** New York U.S.A.
42 F3 **Ilirska Bistrica** Slovenia
76 C3 **Ilkal** India
13 G6 **Ilkley** England
36 D7 **Ill** *R* France
128 E7 **Illampu** *mt* Bolivia
17 F4 **Illana** Spain
71 F7 **Illana B** Philippines
131 B3 **Illapel** Chile
131 B3 **Illapel, R** Chile
54 G8 **Illarionovo** Ukraine
41 O7 **Illasi** Italy
41 O6 **Illasi, Val d'** Italy
138 C2 **Illbillee, Mt** South Australia Australia
18 D4 **Ille-et-Vilaine** *dept* France
37 J7 **Iller** *R* Germany
37 J7 **Illertissen** Germany
16 E4 **Illescas** Spain
21 N5 **Illiers-Combray** France
20 F5 **Illifaut** France
128 E7 **Illimani** *mt* Bolivia
36 F6 **Illingen** Germany
99 R9 **Illinois** *state* U.S.A.
110 G1 **Illinois** *R* Illinois U.S.A.
110 B5 **Illinois** *R* Oklahoma U.S.A.
100 B7 **Illinois** *R* Oregon U.S.A.
99 R8 **Illinois & Mississippi Canal** Illinois U.S.A.
110 G2 **Illiopolis** Illinois U.S.A.
128 G3 **Illiwa** *R* Guyana
85 F3 **Illizit** Algeria
36 D6 **Illkirch** France
110 G4 **Illmo** Missouri U.S.A.
140 D6 **Illogwa** *R* N Terr Australia
21 O2 **Illois** France
16 E7 **Illora** Spain
Illorsuit *see* **Ubekendt Ejland**
37 M5 **Illschwang** Germany
28 E6 **Illumø** *isld* Denmark
37 M6 **Ilm** *R* Germany
29 K9 **Ilmajoki** Finland
33 M6 **Ilmenau** *R* Germany
37 K2 **Ilmenau** Germany
52 D5 **Il'men', Ozero** *L* Russian Federation
8 D6 **Ilminster** England
128 D7 **Ilo** Peru
71 F5 **Iloilo** Philippines
29 P9 **Ilomantsi** Finland
85 E7 **Ilorin** Nigeria
54 K9 **Ilovaysk** Ukraine
53 F9 **Ilovlya** Russian Federation
116 L7 **0il Pt** Alaska U.S.A.
33 N8 **Ilse** *R* Germany
33 N9 **Ilsenburg** Germany
36 G5 **Ilsfeld** Germany
36 H5 **Ilshofen** Germany
28 C4 **Ilskov** Denmark
86 F4 **Īlubabor** *prov* Ethiopia
88 D3 **Ilula** Tanzania
Ilulissat *see* **Jakobshavn**
48 J3 **Ilva Mică** Romania
100 A3 **Ilwaco** Washington U.S.A.
52 J4 **Ilych** *R* Russian Federation
52 D6 **Il'yino** Russian Federation
31 N4 **Iłża** Poland
31 N4 **Iłżanka** *R* Poland
59 K5 **Imabari** Japan
60 O4 **Imabetsu** Japan
61 N9 **Imaichi** Japan
61 K10 **Imajō** Japan
124 F5 **Imala** Mexico
78 K6 **Imām al Ḩamzah** Iraq
57 B6 **Imambaba** Turkmenistan
İmamoğlu *see* **Kırmıt**
Iman *see* **Dal'nerechensk**
52 D1 **Imandra** Russian Federation
130 C10 **Iman, Sa. del** *ra* Argentina
55 E4 **Imantau, Oz** *L* Kazakhstan
60 C12 **Imari** Japan
128 F2 **Imataca, Sa de** *mts* Venezuela
29 O10 **Imatra** Finland
61 J10 **Imazu** Japan
79 B8 **Imbâba** Egypt
128 C3 **Imbabura** *prov* Ecuador
127 J5 **Imbert** Dominican Rep
133 H3 **Imbituba** Brazil
130 E9 **Imbituva** Brazil
100 H4 **Imbler** Oregon U.S.A.
110 E5 **Imboden** Arkansas U.S.A.
52 F5 **Imeni-Babushkina** Russian Federation
52 F5 **Imeni Kalinina** Russian Federation
53 F11 **Imeni Lenina, Kanal** *canal* Russian Federation
53 G7 **Imeni VI Lenina** Russian Federation
128 E3 **Imeri, Sa** *mts* Venezuela
113 F7 **Imeson** *airport* Florida U.S.A.
55 F2 **Imgyt** *R* Russian Federation
86 H4 **Īmī** Ethiopia
46 F7 **Imittós** *mt* Greece
65 G5 **Imjin** *R* N Korea
102 F1 **Imlay** Nevada U.S.A.
98 D6 **Imlay** South Dakota U.S.A.
94 D3 **Imlay City** Michigan U.S.A.
85 A4 **Imlili** *well* Western Sahara
32 K10 **Immenhausen** Germany
41 M2 **Immenstadt** Germany
113 F11 **Immokalee** Florida U.S.A.
100 J4 **Imnaha** Oregon U.S.A.
99 L9 **Imogene** Iowa U.S.A.
45 L3 **Imola** Italy
42 H5 **Imotski** Croatia
128 E5 **Imperatriz** Brazil
44 D4 **Imperia** Italy
119 M7 **Imperial** Saskatchewan Canada
103 J9 **Imperial** California U.S.A.
98 E9 **Imperial** Nebraska U.S.A.
102 G9 **Imperial Beach** California U.S.A.
103 K9 **Imperial Dam** Cal/Ariz U.S.A.
103 J9 **Imperial Valley** California U.S.A.
142 C4 **Imperieuse Reef** W Australia Australia
122 J9 **Imperoyal** Nova Scotia Canada
36 E5 **Impflingen** Germany
86 C5 **Impfondo** Congo
75 P6 **Imphal** India
18 H6 **Imphy** France
52 D4 **Impilakhti** Russian Federation
45 K4 **Impruneta** Italy
80 F8 **Imra** Jordan
47 K4 **İmralı** *isld* Turkey
İmroz *isld see* **Gökçeada** *isld*
47 H4 **İmroz** Turkey
41 N3 **Imst** Austria
124 D2 **Imuris** Mexico
71 D5 **Imuruan B** Philippines
116 D4 **Imuruk Basin** Alaska U.S.A.
116 F4 **Imuruk L** Alaska U.S.A.
16 E9 **Imzouren** Morocco
61 L10 **Ina** Japan
31 J2 **Ina** *R* Poland
90 A16 **Inaccessible I** Atlantic Oc
71 D6 **Inagauan** Philippines
61 N8 **Ina-gawa** *R* Japan
127 H4 **Inagua I., Little** Bahamas
61 N12 **Inamba-jima** *isld* Japan
128 D6 **Inambiri** *R* Peru
85 F3 **In Aménas** Algeria
85 E4 **In Amguel** Algeria
70 E1 **Inanam** Sabah
144 C4 **Inangahua Junction** New Zealand
51 K2 **Inarigda** Russian Federation
29 N3 **Inarijärvi** *L* Finland
61 N11 **Inatori** Japan
61 O8 **Inawashiro** Japan
61 O8 **Inawashiro ko** *L* Japan
85 F4 **In Azaoua** Algeria
85 E3 **In Belbel** Algeria
133 D3 **Incahuasi** *mt* Chile/Arg
78 E2 **İncesu** Turkey
14 E4 **Inch** Ireland
100 G1 **Inchelium** Washington U.S.A.
37 L6 **Inchenhofen** Germany
21 O1 **Incheville** France
13 E1 **Inchkeith** *isld* Scotland
15 D2 **Inchnadamph** Scotland
65 G6 **Inch'ŏn** S Korea
116 B3 **Inchoun** Russian Federation
13 E1 **Inchture** Scotland
22 E3 **Inchy** France
45 K4 **Incisa in Valdarno** Italy
89 H5 **Incomati** *R* Mozambique
22 H2 **Incourt** Belgium
18 M11 **Incudine, L'** *mt* Corsica
12 B2 **Indaal, L** Scotland
85 D4 **In Dagouber** Mali
130 D6 **Indaia Grande, R** Brazil
26 J9 **Indal** Sweden
26 H8 **Indalsälven** *R* Sweden
68 C2 **Indaw** Burma
75 R6 **Indawgyi Lake** Burma
124 G5 **Indé** Mexico
7 M9 **Indefatigable** *oil rig* North Sea
102 F5 **Independence** California U.S.A.
99 P7 **Independence** Iowa U.S.A.
107 P4 **Independence** Kansas U.S.A.
111 F11 **Independence** Louisiana U.S.A.
110 B2 **Independence** Missouri U.S.A.
100 B5 **Independence** Oregon U.S.A.
94 F10 **Independence** Virginia U.S.A.
99 P5 **Independence** Wisconsin U.S.A.
147 H9 **Independence Fj** Greenland
100 J8 **Independence Mts** Nevada U.S.A.
69 E13 **Inderapura** Sumatra
69 E13 **Inderapura, Tg** *C* Sumatra
55 B6 **Inderborskiy** Kazakhstan
26 E8 **Inderöy** Norway
55 B6 **Inder, Oz** *L* Kazakhstan
100 D2 **Index** Washington U.S.A.
74 G10 **Indi** India
74 **India** *rep* S Asia
107 M7 **Indiahoma** Oklahoma U.S.A.
117 D4 **Indian** *R* Yukon Territory Canada
95 M2 **Indian** *R* New York U.S.A.
140 D6 **Indiana** N Terr Australia
94 B6 **Indiana** *state* U.S.A.
94 H6 **Indiana** Pennsylvania U.S.A.
81 G11 **Indian-Antarctic Basin** Southern Oc
81 J11 **Indian-Antarctic Ridge** Southern Oc
94 A7 **Indianapolis** Indiana U.S.A.
123 T4 **Indian B** Newfoundland Canada
123 M7 **Indian Brook** Nova Scotia Canada
117 P6 **Indian Cabins** Alberta Canada
115 O7 **Indian Hbr** Labrador, Nfld Canada
122 J9 **Indian Hbr** Nova Scotia Canada
119 O8 **Indian Head** Saskatchewan Canada
95 K8 **Indian Head** Maryland U.S.A.
95 N3 **Indian L** New York U.S.A.
101 P7 **Indian Mt** Wyoming U.S.A.
81 **Indian Ocean**
83 **Indian Ocean Islands**
99 N8 **Indianola** Iowa U.S.A.
111 F8 **Indianola** Mississippi U.S.A.
98 F9 **Indianola** Nebraska U.S.A.
107 P6 **Indianola** Oklahoma U.S.A.
130 F6 **Indianópolis** Brazil
103 L3 **Indian Peak** Utah U.S.A.
101 Q5 **Indian Pk** Wyoming U.S.A.
113 G10 **Indian R** Florida U.S.A.
94 C1 **Indian River** Michigan U.S.A.
113 G9 **Indian River City** Florida U.S.A.
103 J5 **Indian Sp** Nevada U.S.A.
113 G10 **Indian Town** Florida U.S.A.
100 J5 **Indian Valley** Idaho U.S.A.
98 E2 **Indian Villages Nat. Hist. Site** North Dakota U.S.A.
103 O6 **Indian Wells** Arizona U.S.A.
122 A2 **Indicator L** Quebec Canada
52 G1 **Indiga** Russian Federation
147 L15 **Indiga** Russian Federation
51 O2 **Indigirka** *R* Russian Federation
52 G1 **Indigskaya Guba** *B* Russian Federation
48 F5 **Indija** Serbia Yugoslavia
117 Q3 **Indin L** Northwest Territories Canada
103 H8 **Indio** California U.S.A.
109 K9 **Indios** Mexico
137 N4 **Indispensable Reefs** Pacific Oc

70 D7 **Indonesia** *rep* S E Asia
141 K2 **Indooroopilly** *dist* Brisbane, Qnsld Australia
74 F7 **Indore** India
69 F13 **Indragiri** *R* Sumatra
70 M9 **Indramayu** Java
69 E14 **Indrapura** Sumatra
69 E14 **Indrapura, Tanjong** *C* Sumatra
73 N5 **Indravati** *R* India
18 G6 **Indre** *dept* France
20 G7 **Indre** France
21 N7 **Indre** *R* France
18 F5 **Indre-et-Loire** *dept* France
113 G10 **Indrio** Florida U.S.A.
21 N7 **Indrois** *R* France
31 O2 **Indura** Belorussia
118 D8 **Indus** Alberta Canada
73 L2 **Indus** *R* S W Asia
74 B6 **Indus, Mouths of** Pakistan
110 F1 **Industry** Illinois U.S.A.
109 L6 **Industry** Texas U.S.A.
89 E8 **Indwe** S Africa
85 F4 **In Ebeggi** Algeria
78 D1 **İnebolu** Turkey
47 J4 **İnecik** Turkey
85 F4 **In Ecker** Algeria
85 E5 **In Edek** Niger
78 B1 **İnegöl** Turkey
71 K9 **Inerie** *mt* Flores Indonesia
21 P8 **Ineuil** France
109 L7 **Inez** Texas U.S.A.
85 G4 **In Ezzane** Algeria
89 B10 **Infanta, C** S Africa
128 F5 **Infernão, Cach** *rapids* Brazil
124 H8 **Infiernillo, L** Mexico
16 D1 **Infiesto** Spain
130 J9 **Ingá** Brazil
29 L11 **Inga** Finland
68 B4 **Ingabu** Burma
85 F5 **Ingal** Niger
140 C5 **Ingallanna** *R* N Terr Australia
94 B7 **Ingalls** Indiana U.S.A.
107 K4 **Ingalls** Kansas U.S.A.
99 T4 **Ingalls** Michigan U.S.A.
100 E10 **Ingalls, Mt** California U.S.A.
55 F3 **Ingaly** Russian Federation
9 G4 **Ingatestone** England
36 H5 **Ingelfingen** Germany
36 E4 **Ingelheim** Germany
22 E2 **Ingelmunster** Belgium
86 C6 **Ingende** Zaire
133 E5 **Ingeniero Luiggi** Argentina
131 E7 **Ingeniero, Pto** Argentina
117 L7 **Ingenika** *R* British Columbia Canada
116 E7 **Ingeramuit** Alaska U.S.A.
107 M5 **Ingersoll** Oklahoma U.S.A.
71 B2 **Inggelang** *isld* Halmahera Indonesia
141 H4 **Ingham** Queensland Australia
83 K11 **Ingiriya** Sri Lanka
13 F5 **Ingleborough** *mt* England
115 N2 **Inglefield Land** Greenland
109 K8 **Ingleside** Texas U.S.A.
13 F5 **Ingleton** England
141 K8 **Inglewood** Queensland Australia
139 G6 **Inglewood** Victoria Australia
145 E3 **Inglewood** New Zealand
140 D1 **Inglis** *isld* N Terr Australia
119 Q8 **Inglis** Manitoba Canada
116 G4 **Inglutalik** *R* Alaska U.S.A.
58 F1 **Ingoda** *R* Russian Federation
118 F1 **Ingolf** Ontario Canada
29 T10 **Ingolfshöfdhi** *C* Iceland
86 C7 **Ingololo** Zaire
37 L6 **Ingolstadt** Germany
138 C3 **Ingomar** South Australia Australia
101 S3 **Ingomar** Montana U.S.A.
123 M7 **Ingonish** C Breton I, Nova Scotia
102 B1 **Ingot** California U.S.A.
26 N1 **Ingöy** Norway
75 N6 **Ingrāj Bāzār** India
109 H5 **Ingram** Texas U.S.A.
99 Q4 **Ingram** Wisconsin U.S.A.
122 J9 **Ingramport** Nova Scotia Canada
21 M8 **Ingrandes** Indre France
21 J7 **Ingrandes** Maine-et-Loire France
21 M8 **Ingrandes** Vienne France
117 P3 **Ingray L** Northwest Territories Canada
21 O6 **Ingré** France
146 J11 **Ingrid Christensen Coast** Antarctica
28 D2 **Ingstrup** Denmark
85 F5 **In Guezzam** Algeria
20 D6 **Inguiniel** France
54 D9 **Ingul** *R* Ukraine
54 E9 **Ingulets** Ukraine
54 D10 **Ingulets** *R* Ukraine
55 F1 **Inguyagun** *R* Russian Federation
89 G6 **Ingwavuma** S Africa
19 K4 **Ingwiller** France
89 H6 **Inhaca Pen** Mozambique
87 G10 **Inhambane** Mozambique
130 C7 **Inhandui, R** Brazil
130 C7 **Inhanduizinho, R** Brazil
88 E10 **Inhangoma I** Mozambique
130 C10 **Inhanhora** *R* Brazil
130 G6 **Inhapim** Brazil
87 G10 **Inharrime** Mozambique
47 L4 **İnhisar** Turkey
130 H4 **Inhobim** Brazil
129 J7 **Inhumas** Brazil
116 L3 **Iniakuk** *R* Alaska U.S.A.
71 K9 **Inielika** *mt* Flores Indonesia
17 F5 **Iniesta** Spain
85 E3 **Inifel, Hassi** Algeria
27 M11 **Iniö** Finland
128 E3 **Inírida** *R* Colombia
14 A3 **Inishark** *isld* Ireland
14 C1 **Inishbofin** *isld* Ireland
14 A3 **Inishbofin** *isld* Ireland
14 B2 **Inishcrone** Ireland
14 B3 **Inisheer** *isld* Ireland
14 A2 **Inishkea** *isld* Ireland
14 B3 **Inishmaan** *isld* Ireland
14 B3 **Inishmore** *isld* Ireland
14 C2 **Inishmurray** *isld* Ireland
14 D1 **Inishowen** *dist* Ireland
14 E1 **Inishowen Hd** Ireland
14 D1 **Inishtrahull** *isld* Ireland
14 A3 **Inishturk** *isld* Ireland
65 D2 **Injgan Sum** China
141 J7 **Injune** Queensland Australia
141 F3 **Inkerman** Queensland Australia
122 H6 **Inkerman** New Brunswick Canada
86 C7 **Inkis** *R* Zaire
86 C7 **Inkisi-Kisantu** Zaire
117 G6 **Inklin** British Columbia Canada
101 N7 **Inkom** Idaho U.S.A.
52 F5 **Inkovo** Russian Federation
98 J1 **Inkster** North Dakota U.S.A.
68 C2 **Inle, L** Burma
98 H7 **Inman** Nebraska U.S.A.
95 N2 **Inman** New York U.S.A.
112 E2 **Inman** South Carolina U.S.A.
41 O3 **Inn** *R* Austria
38 F6 **Inn** *R* Germany
138 F2 **Innamincka** South Australia Australia
15 E5 **Innerleithen** Scotland
Inner Mongolia *aut reg see* **Nei Mongol Zizhiqu**
41 K3 **Inner-Rhoden** *dist* Switzerland
15 C3 **Inner Sound** Scotland
32 M8 **Innerste** *R* Germany
41 H4 **Innertkirchen** Switzerland
38 F8 **Innervillgraten** Austria
6 M6 **Innes** *oilfield* North Sea
26 E8 **Innherad** *reg* Norway
Innien *see* **Aukrug**
14 C5 **Inniscarra Res** Ireland
141 H3 **Innisfail** Queensland Australia
118 D6 **Innisfail** Alberta Canada
118 F5 **Innisfree** Alberta Canada
116 J5 **Innoko** *R* Alaska U.S.A.
60 G11 **Inno-shima** Japan
41 O3 **Innsbruck** Austria
26 K3 **Innset** Norway
26 B10 **Innvik** Norway
116 A3 **Innymney, Gora** *mt* Russian Federation
130 D6 **Inocência** Brazil
107 P5 **Inola** Oklahoma U.S.A.
47 L5 **İnönü** Turkey
31 L3 **Inowrocław** Poland
128 E7 **Inquisivi** Bolivia
85 E3 **In Rhar** Algeria
40 F3 **Ins** Switzerland
85 E3 **In Salah** Algeria
15 F3 **Insch** Scotland
143 A7 **Inscription,C** W Australia Australia
68 B4 **Insein** Burma
37 J2 **Inselsberg** *mt* Germany
119 O7 **Insinger** Saskatchewan Canada
31 J2 **Insko** Poland
36 B6 **Insming** France
Insterburg *see* **Chernyakhovsk**
146 D7 **Institute Ice Stream** *ice stream* Antarctica
118 J9 **Instow** Saskatchewan Canada
8 B5 **Instow** England
48 L6 **Însurăţei** Romania
52 K2 **Inta** Russian Federation
98 B2 **Intake** Montana U.S.A.
57 F1 **Intaly** Kazakhstan
85 E5 **In Tebezas** Mali
47 H4 **İntepe** Turkey
98 E6 **Interior** South Dakota U.S.A.
113 F8 **Interlachen** Florida U.S.A.
139 H8 **Interlaken** Tasmania Australia
40 G4 **Interlaken** Switzerland
99 N1 **International Falls** Minnesota U.S.A.
119 R10 **International Peace Gdn** Canada/U.S.A.
117 O9 **Intersection Mt** Alberta/Br Col Canada
68 A6 **Interview I** Andaman Is
48 K5 **Intorsura Buzăului** Romania
41 J5 **Intragna** Switzerland
32 G8 **Intrup** Germany
52 F2 **Intsy** Russian Federation
61 O10 **Inubō saki** Japan
115 O3 **Inugsulik Bugt** *B* Greenland
115 M6 **Inukjuak** Quebec Canada
133 C8 **Inútil, B** Chile
114 F4 **Inuvik** Northwest Territories Canada
114 F4 **Inuvik** *dist* Northwest Territories Canada
128 D6 **Inuya** *R* Peru
52 J5 **In'va** *R* Russian Federation
15 C4 **Inveraray** Scotland
15 F4 **Inverbervie** Scotland
144 B7 **Invercargill** New Zealand
12 C2 **Invercloy** Scotland
139 K3 **Inverell** New South Wales Australia
15 D3 **Invergordon** Scotland
15 E4 **Inverkeithing** Scotland
12 D2 **Inverkip** Scotland
140 F4 **Inverleigh** Queensland Australia
12 D1 **Inverlochlarig** Scotland
119 O7 **Invermay** Saskatchewan Canada
117 P10 **Invermere** British Columbia Canada
Inverness *co see* **Highland** *reg*
121 T6 **Inverness** Quebec Canada
123 L7 **Inverness** C Breton I, Nova Scotia
15 D3 **Inverness** Scotland
113 E9 **Inverness** Florida U.S.A.
101 P1 **Inverness** Montana U.S.A.
15 D3 **Invershin** Scotland
15 F3 **Inverurie** Scotland
140 A4 **Inverway** N Terr Australia
68 C6 **Investigator Chan** Burma
138 C5 **Investigator Group** *islds* South Australia Australia
138 D6 **Investigator Str** South Australia Australia
68 A7 **Invisible Bank** Andaman Is
120 J10 **Inwood** Ontario Canada
102 C1 **Inwood** California U.S.A.
56 B3 **Inya** *R* Russian Federation
87 F9 **Inyanga** Zimbabwe
87 F9 **Inyanga Nat. Park** Zimbabwe
98 B5 **Inyan Kara Cr** Wyoming U.S.A.
56 G3 **Inyaptuk, Gora** *mt* Russian Federation
102 G6 **Inyokern** California U.S.A.
55 C4 **Inzer** Russian Federation
86 C7 **Inzia** *R* Zaire
20 D6 **Inzinzac-Lochrist** France
46 D5 **Ioánnina** Greece
38 H9 **Iôf di Montasio** *mt* Italy
47 H9 **Ioinianísia** *isld* Greece
61 N13 **Iō-Jima** *isld* Japan
52 E1 **Iokanga** Russian Federation
106 C3 **Iola** Colorado U.S.A.
107 P4 **Iola** Kansas U.S.A.
109 L5 **Iola** Texas U.S.A.
45 L2 **Iolanda di Savoia** Italy
57 B6 **Iolotan'** Turkmenistan
123 M8 **Iona** C Breton I, Nova Scotia
12 B1 **Iona** *isld* Scotland
101 O6 **Iona** Idaho U.S.A.
99 L6 **Iona** Minnesota U.S.A.
98 G6 **Iona** South Dakota U.S.A.
87 B9 **Iona Nat. Park** Angola
47 J1 **Ion Corvin** Romania
102 G3 **Ione** Nevada U.S.A.
100 F4 **Ione** Oregon U.S.A.
100 H1 **Ione** Washington U.S.A.
48 J6 **Ioneşti** Romania
47 H6 **Ionia** *hist reg* Turkey
99 O6 **Ionia** Iowa U.S.A.
94 B3 **Ionia** Michigan U.S.A.
110 C3 **Ionia** Missouri U.S.A.
Ionian Is *see* **Iónioi Nísoi**
43 H10 **Ionian Sea** S Europe
46 D5 **Iónioi Nísoi** *islds* Greece
116 A4 **Ioniveen** *R* Russian Federation
78 K1 **Iori** *R* Azerbaijan/Georgia
46 G8 **Íos** *isld* Greece
52 H3 **Iosser** Russian Federation
99 N7 **Iowa** *state* U.S.A.
99 N7 **Iowa** *R* Iowa U.S.A.
111 C11 **Iowa** Louisiana U.S.A.
99 P8 **Iowa City** Iowa U.S.A.
99 N7 **Iowa Falls** Iowa U.S.A.
109 J2 **Iowa Park** Texas U.S.A.
124 G7 **Ipala** Mexico
83 K9 **Ipalogama** Sri Lanka
130 E5 **Ipameri** Brazil
130 H6 **Ipanema** Brazil
130 H10 **Ipanema** *R* Brazil
130 H8 **Ipanguacu** Brazil
99 Q9 **Ipava** Illinois U.S.A.
48 E2 **Ipel'** *R* Czechoslovakia
116 E2 **Ipewik** *R* Alaska U.S.A.
37 J4 **Iphofen** Germany
128 C3 **Ipiales** Colombia
129 L6 **Ipiau** Brazil
Ipin *see* **Yibin**
128 E4 **Ipiranga** Amazonas Brazil
130 E9 **Ipiranga** Paraná Brazil
128 D5 **Ipixuna** Amazonas Brazil
128 F5 **Ipixuna** *R* Amazonas Brazil
69 E10 **Ipoh** Malaysia
130 J10 **Ipojuca** *R* Brazil
71 C6 **Ipolote B** Palawan Philippines
129 H7 **Iporá** Brazil
130 E9 **Iporanga** Brazil
120 J9 **Ipperwash Prov. Park** Ontario Canada
37 J4 **Ippesheim** Germany
86 D4 **Ippy** Cent Afr Republic
78 A1 **İpsala** Turkey
141 L8 **Ipswich** Queensland Australia
9 H3 **Ipswich** England
127 J2 **Ipswich** Jamaica
95 R4 **Ipswich** Massachusetts U.S.A.
98 G4 **Ipswich** South Dakota U.S.A.
129 K4 **Ipu** Brazil
54 C4 **Iput'** *R* Belorussia/Rus Fed
78 K2 **Iqdir** Turkey
58 B4 **Iqe** China
66 E4 **Iqe** China
128 D8 **Iquique** Chile
128 D4 **Iquitos** Peru
80 F6 **'Ira** Jordan
108 F5 **Iraan** Texas U.S.A.
61 L11 **Irago-misaki** Japan
130 D10 **Irai** Brazil
46 G8 **Iráklia** *isld* Greece
46 G9 **Iráklion** Crete
130 C9 **Irala** Paraguay
77 C4 **Iran** *rep* S W Asia
130 D10 **Irani** *R* Brazil
77 G6 **Irānshahr** Iran
128 F1 **Irapa** Venezuela
124 J7 **Irapuato** Mexico
78 H5 **Iraq** *rep* S W Asia
95 P2 **Irasburg** Vermont U.S.A.
129 H3 **Iratapuru** *R* Brazil
130 E9 **Irati** Brazil
133 G3 **Irati** Brazil
17 G2 **Irati** *R* Spain
84 E4 **Īrāwan** Libya
52 J3 **Irayel'** Russian Federation
Irbenskiy Proliv *see* **Kura Kurk**
80 G3 **Irbid** Jordan
55 D2 **Irbit** *R* Russian Federation
55 D3 **Irbit** Russian Federation
9 G1 **Irby** England
38 K7 **Irdning** Austria
54 C7 **Irdyn'** Ukraine
109 K4 **Iredell** Texas U.S.A.
109 K4 **Ireland** Texas U.S.A.
90 A2 **Ireland I** Bermuda
14 **Ireland, Rep of**
14 E3 **Ireland's Eye** *isld* Ireland
55 C3 **Iren** *R* Russian Federation
98 J6 **Irene** South Dakota U.S.A.
98 K7 **Ireton** Iowa U.S.A.
57 B1 **Irgiz** *R* Kazakhstan
85 F5 **Irhazer Wan Agadez** *V* Niger
85 C2 **Irhil M'Goun** *mt* Morocco
136 G2 **Irian Jaya** *prov* Indonesia
86 D2 **Iriba** Chad
129 G3 **Iricoumé, Serra** *mts* Brazil
71 F4 **Iriga** Philippines
55 C5 **Iriklinskiy** Russian Federation
87 G7 **Iringa** Tanzania
67 H4 **Iriomote-shima** *isld* Japan
125 M2 **Iriona** Honduras
129 H5 **Iriri** *R* Brazil
139 H8 **Irishtown** Tasmania Australia
56 E2 **Irkineyeva** *R* Russian Federation
56 F5 **Irkutsk** Russian Federation
56 F3 **Irkutskaya Oblast'** Russian Federation
118 F6 **Irma** Alberta Canada
99 R4 **Irma** Wisconsin U.S.A.
36 E2 **Irmgarteichen** Germany
112 F3 **Irmo** South Carolina U.S.A.
20 G5 **Irodouer** France
20 A5 **Iroise** *G* France
86 C3 **Iro, L** Chad
138 D4 **Iron Baron** South Australia Australia
120 G6 **Iron Bridge** Ontario Canada
8 D2 **Ironbridge** England
110 J6 **Iron City** Tennessee U.S.A.
121 M8 **Irondale** Ontario Canada
110 F4 **Irondale** Missouri U.S.A.
94 G6 **Irondale** Ohio U.S.A.
138 D4 **Iron Knob** South Australia Australia
99 S4 **Iron Mountain** Michigan U.S.A.
100 A7 **Iron Mt** Oregon U.S.A.
103 L4 **Iron Mt** Utah U.S.A.
98 G5 **Iron Nation** South Dakota U.S.A.
141 G2 **Iron Range** Queensland Australia
99 S6 **Iron Ridge** Wisconsin U.S.A.
99 S3 **Iron River** Michigan U.S.A.
99 P3 **Iron River** Wisconsin U.S.A.
94 B2 **Irons** Michigan U.S.A.
100 H5 **Ironside** Oregon U.S.A.
103 L4 **Iron Sp** Utah U.S.A.
94 B1 **Ironton** Michigan U.S.A.
110 F4 **Ironton** Missouri U.S.A.
94 E8 **Ironton** Ohio U.S.A.
99 Q3 **Ironwood** Michigan U.S.A.
99 T9 **Iroquois** *R* Illinois U.S.A.
98 J5 **Iroquois** South Dakota U.S.A.
120 K4 **Iroquois Falls** Ontario Canada
71 G4 **Irosin** Philippines
61 M11 **Irō zaki** *C* Japan
45 R8 **Irpinia** Italy
68 B4 **Irrawaddy** *prov* Burma
68 B5 **Irrawaddy** *R* Burma
68 B5 **Irrawaddy, Mouths of** Burma
36 B4 **Irrel** Germany
118 D7 **Irricana** Alberta Canada
85 D5 **Irrigi** *reg* Mali/Mauritania
56 D3 **Irsha** Russian Federation
48 H2 **Irshava** Ukraine
52 G4 **Irta** Russian Federation
13 F3 **Irthing, R** England
55 D3 **Irtyash, Oz** *L* Russian Federation
55 E2 **Irtysh** *R* Russian Federation
55 F4 **Irtysh** Russian Federation
55 G4 **Irtyshsk** Kazakhstan
86 E5 **Irumu** Zaire
17 F1 **Irún** Spain
17 F2 **Irurzun** Spain
18 D10 **Irurzun** Spain
128 E8 **Iruya** Argentina
Irves Šaurums *see* **Kura Kurk**
118 G9 **Irvine** Alberta Canada
15 D5 **Irvine** *R* Scotland
15 D5 **Irvine** Scotland
110 N4 **Irvine** Kentucky U.S.A.
141 H3 **Irvinebank** Queensland Australia
14 D2 **Irvinestown** N Ireland
107 O2 **Irving** Kansas U.S.A.
109 N9 **Irving** Texas U.S.A.
143 F7 **Irving, Mt** W Australia Australia
110 K4 **Irvington** Kentucky U.S.A.
95 L9 **Irvington** Virginia U.S.A.
94 J6 **Irvona** Pennsylvania U.S.A.
13 F6 **Irwell, R** England
143 B8 **Irwin** W Australia Australia
101 O6 **Irwin** Idaho U.S.A.
99 L8 **Irwin** Iowa U.S.A.
98 D7 **Irwin** Nebraska U.S.A.
112 D5 **Irwinton** Georgia U.S.A.
138 F5 **Irymple** Victoria Australia
141 J6 **Isaac** *R* Queensland Australia
117 N9 **Isaac L** British Columbia Canada
123 L8 **Isaacs Hbr** Nova Scotia Canada
17 G2 **Isaba** Spain
107 M4 **Isabel** Kansas U.S.A.
98 E4 **Isabel** South Dakota U.S.A.
71 E7 **Isabela** Philippines
71 F5 **Isabela** Negros Philippines
127 L5 **Isabela** Puerto Rico
126 D3 **Isabela de Sagua** Cuba
128 A8 **Isabela, Isla** Galapagos Is
125 M3 **Isabelia, Cord** *ra* Nicaragua
119 Q8 **Isabella** Manitoba Canada
102 F6 **Isabella** California U.S.A.
99 P2 **Isabella** Minnesota U.S.A.
142 F5 **Isabella, L** W Australia Australia
48 L5 **Isaccea** Romania
147 N11 **Isachenko, Ostrov** *isld* Russian Federation
114 J2 **Isachsen** Northwest Territories Canada
28 R8 **Isafjardhardjup** *inlet* Iceland
28 R8 **Isafjördhur** Iceland
60 D13 **Isahaya** Japan
52 F3 **Isakogorka** Russian Federation
48 H6 **Işalniţat** Romania
87 H12 **Isalo, Parc National de L'** *nat park* Madagascar
86 D5 **Isangi** Zaire
37 N7 **Isar** *R* Germany
42 D2 **Isarco** *R* Italy
46 E7 **Isari** Greece
41 O2 **Isar Tal** Germany
111 J7 **Isbell** Alabama U.S.A.
22 C2 **Isbergues** France
15 G1 **Isbister** Scotland
40 C1 **Isches** France
41 M3 **Ischgl** Austria
45 P8 **Ischia** Italy
142 F3 **Isdell,R** W Australia Australia
21 P6 **Isdes** France
59 L5 **Ise** Japan
28 H5 **Isefjord** *inlet* Denmark
41 O3 **Isel Berg** *mt* Austria
81 H14 **Iselin Seamount** Southern Oc
36 D3 **Isenburg** Germany
33 N8 **Isenbüttel** Germany
33 N7 **Isenhagen** Germany
28 C4 **Isenvad** Denmark
42 C3 **Iseo** Italy
42 C3 **Iseo, L. d'** Italy
19 O14 **Isère** *R* France
19 P14 **Isère** *dept* France
32 G10 **Iserlohn** Germany
32 L8 **Isernhagen** Germany
43 F7 **Isernia** Italy
61 N9 **Isesaki** Japan
61 K11 **Ise shima Nat. Park** Japan
55 E3 **Isetskoye** Russian Federation
61 K11 **Ise-wan** *B* Japan
85 E7 **Iseyin** Nigeria
Isfahan *see* **Eşfahān**
57 E5 **Isfana** Kyrgyzstan
57 F4 **Isfara** Tajikistan
80 D3 **Isfiya** Israel
52 J4 **Isherim, Gora** *mt* Russian Federation
128 G3 **Isherton** Guyana
88 C7 **Ishiba Ngandu** Zambia
67 H4 **Ishigaki** Japan
67 H4 **Ishigaki-shima** *isld* Japan
61 K9 **Ishika** *prefect* Japan
60 P2 **Ishikari** Japan
60 R2 **Ishikari dake** *mt* Japan
59 M3 **Ishikari-wan** *B* Japan
55 E5 **Ishim** *R* Kazakhstan/Rus Fed
55 E3 **Ishim** Russian Federation
55 C4 **Ishimbay** Russian Federation
55 F3 **Ishimskaya Step** *steppe* Russian Federation
55 E5 **Ishimskoye** Kazakhstan
59 M4 **Ishinomaki** Japan
60 G12 **Ishizuchi-san** *mt* Japan
21 H4 **Isigny-le-Buat** France
21 H3 **Isigny sur Mer** Calvados France
47 J4 **Işıklar Dağı** *mts* Turkey
86 G6 **Isiolo** Kenya
87 F11 **Isipingo Bch** S Africa
86 E5 **Isiro** Zaire
141 G6 **Isisford** Queensland Australia
86 G1 **Is, Jebel** *mt* Sudan
55 E3 **Iska** *R* Russian Federation
80 D5 **Iskāka** Jordan
57 E4 **Iskander** Uzbekistan
47 J8 **İskandil Burun** *C* Turkey
78 F3 **İskenderun** Turkey
78 E1 **İskilip** Turkey
57 G4 **Iski-Naukat** Kyrgyzstan
56 B4 **Iskitim** Russian Federation
46 G1 **Iskŭr** *R* Bulgaria
46 F2 **Iskŭr, Yazovir** *res* Bulgaria
117 H7 **Iskut** *R* British Columbia Canada
117 J7 **Iskut** British Columbia Canada
119 O3 **Iskwatam L** Saskatchewan Canada
15 E4 **Isla** *R* Scotland
78 F3 **Islâhiye** Turkey
74 E2 **Islamabad** Pakistan
113 G13 **Islamorada** Florida U.S.A.
117 N5 **Island** *R* Northwest Territories Canada
110 J4 **Island** Kentucky U.S.A.
71 D6 **Island B** Palawan Philippines
100 H4 **Island City** Oregon U.S.A.
120 J3 **Island Falls** Ontario Canada
119 P3 **Island Falls** Saskatchewan Canada
95 S7 **Island Falls** Maine U.S.A.
141 K5 **Island Hd** Queensland Australia
95 N7 **Island Heights** New Jersey U.S.A.
115 K7 **Island L** Manitoba Canada
120 K7 **Island L** Ontario Canada
138 D4 **Island Lagoon** South Australia Australia
99 W3 **Island Lake** Ontario Canada
100 B9 **Island Mountain** California U.S.A.
101 O5 **Island Park** Idaho U.S.A.
123 Q5 **Island Pond** *L* Newfoundland Canada
95 Q2 **Island Pond** Vermont U.S.A.
143 B9 **Island Pt** W Australia Australia
123 O4 **Islands, Bay of** Newfoundland Canada
145 E1 **Islands, Bay of** New Zealand
16 B2 **Islas Cíes** Spain
127 M5 **Isla Verde** *airport* Puerto Rico
118 G5 **Islay** Alberta Canada
15 B5 **Islay** *isld* Scotland
18 F7 **Isle** *R* France
99 N3 **Isle** Minnesota U.S.A.
21 P3 **Isle-Adam,l'** France
123 O6 **Isle aux Morts** Newfoundland Canada
95 T2 **Isleboro** Maine U.S.A.
18 F9 **Isle en Dodon, L'** France
18 F9 **Isle Jourdain, L'** Gers France
18 F6 **Isle Jourdain, L'** Vienne France
118 H4 **Isle, Lac des** Saskatchewan Canada
122 A5 **Isle Maligne** Quebec Canada
112 F6 **Isle of Hope** Georgia U.S.A.
15 G2 **Isle of Noss** Scotland
12 D4 **Isle of Whithorn** Scotland
99 S1 **Isle Royale** Michigan U.S.A.
22 G5 **Isles-sur-Suippes** France
18 H5 **Isle-sur-Serein, L'** France
106 D7 **Isleta** New Mexico U.S.A.
102 C3 **Isleton** California U.S.A.
122 C5 **Isle Verte** Quebec Canada
9 E4 **Islip** England
127 N3 **Islote Pt** Trinidad
128 E7 **Isluga** *vol* Chile
133 D1 **Isluga** *mt* Chile
131 F4 **Ismael Cortinas** Uruguay
84 J3 **Ismâ'ilîya** Egypt
37 M7 **Ismaning** Germany
98 B3 **Ismay** Montana U.S.A.
78 A2 **Ismir Körfezi** Turkey
84 J4 **Isna** Egypt
87 H12 **Isoanala** Madagascar
29 J9 **Isojoki** Finland
87 F8 **Isoka** Zambia
29 J8 **Isokyrö** Finland
41 O7 **Isola** Italy
111 F8 **Isola** Mississippi U.S.A.
45 P6 **Isola d. Liri** Italy
45 M5 **Isola Farnese** Italy
87 H12 **Isola, Massif de L'** *mts* Madagascar
45 K1 **Isola Rizza** Italy
20 C6 **Isole** *R* France
110 L5 **Isoline** Tennessee U.S.A.
45 J1 **Isorella** Italy
29 N6 **Iso-syöte** *mt* Finland
78 C3 **Isparta** Turkey
78 C3 **Isparta** *R* Turkey
47 M10 **Ispartakula** Turkey
47 H1 **Isperikh** Bulgaria
78 H1 **İspir** Turkey
80 **Israel** *state* S W Asia
143 E10 **Israelite B** W Australia Australia
20 H6 **Issé** France
28 F4 **Issehoved** *C* Denmark
143 A8 **Isseka** W Australia Australia
25 F5 **Isselburg** Germany
85 C7 **Issia** Ivory Coast
71 H4 **Issimu** Sulawesi Indonesia
18 H7 **Issoire** France
19 Q18 **Issole** *R* France
21 O8 **Issoudun** France
25 F5 **Issum** Germany
57 H4 **Issyk-Kul'** Kyrgyzstan
57 H4 **Issyk-Kul, Ozero** *L* Kyrgyzstan
57 J4 **Issyk-Kul'skaya Oblast'** Kyrgyzstan
77 L2 **Istalif** Afghanistan
47 M10 **İstanbul** Turkey
120 J7 • **Isthmus Bay** Ontario Canada
46 F6 **Istiaía** Greece
128 C2 **Istmina** Colombia
42 F3 **Istra** *pen* Croatia
54 H1 **Istra** Russian Federation
19 N18 **Istres** France
47 Q14 **Ístrios** Rhodes Greece
61 M11 **Isu hantō** *pen* Japan
55 C5 **Isyangulovo** Russian Federation
130 B9 **Itá** Paraguay
129 L6 **Itabaiana** Brazil
130 H7 **Itabapoana** Brazil
130 E8 **Itaberá** Brazil
130 E5 **Itaberaí** Brazil
129 K7 **Itabira** Brazil
130 G7 **Itabirito** Brazil
128 F4 **Itaboca** Brazil
129 L6 **Itabuna** Brazil
129 J5 **Itacajá** Brazil
129 H5 **Itacajuna** *R* Brazil
130 G4 **Itacarambi** Brazil
129 L6 **Itacaré** Brazil
128 G4 **Itacoatiara** Brazil
128 D5 **Itacuai** *R* Brazil
130 C9 **Itacurubí del Rosario** Paraguay
130 H6 **Itaguaçu** Brazil
130 D8 **Itaguaje** Brazil
129 J6 **Itaguari** *R* Brazil
130 E8 **Itaí** Brazil
130 E10 **Itaiópolis** Brazil
129 G4 **Itaituba** Brazil
130 E10 **Itajai Acú, R** Brazil
129 J8 **Itajuba** Brazil
130 H4 **Itajuipe** Brazil
61 O10 **Itako** Japan
Itala *see* **Cadale**
42 **Italy** *rep* S Europe
109 L3 **Italy** Texas U.S.A.
130 G5 **Itamarandiba** Brazil
129 J4 **Itamatare** Brazil
130 H6 **Itambacuri** Brazil
129 K7 **Itambé** Brazil
130 G6 **Itambe, P. de** *mt* Brazil
60 J11 **Itami** Japan
130 F9 **Itanhaém** Brazil
129 K7 **Itanhém** *R* Brazil
129 H3 **Itany** *R* Suriname
130 H5 **Itaobim** Brazil
129 J6 **Itapaci** Brazil
130 E6 **Itapajipe** Brazil
130 H4 **Itapebi** Brazil
130 F7 **Itapecerica** Brazil
129 K4 **Itapecuru Mirim** Brazil
130 H7 **Itapemirim** Brazil
129 K8 **Itaperuna** Brazil
129 K7 **Itapetinga** Brazil
129 J8 **Itapetininga** Brazil
129 J8 **Itapeva** Brazil
129 G3 **Itapi** *R* Brazil
129 K5 **Itapicura** *R* Brazil
129 J5 **Itapicuru, Serra do** *mts* Brazil
128 F5 **Itapinima** Brazil
129 L4 **Itapipoca** Brazil
128 G4 **Itapira** Brazil
130 E10 **Itapocu, R** Brazil
130 E7 **Itápolis** Brazil
130 H9 **Itaporanga** Brazil
130 C10 **Itapuá** *reg* Paraguay
129 H7 **Itapuranga** Brazil
131 G2 **Itaqui** Brazil
133 F2 **Itaquyry** Paraguay
129 J8 **Itararé** Brazil
74 G7 **Itarsi** India
130 D6 **Itarumã** Brazil
109 K3 **Itasca** Texas U.S.A.
99 L2 **Itasca State Park** Minnesota U.S.A.
131 A6 **Itata, R** Chile
130 F8 **Itatiba** Brazil
131 F2 **Itati, L** Argentina
130 E8 **Itatinga** Brazil
128 F5 **Itatuba** Brazil
130 E5 **Itauçu** Brazil
130 G7 **Itaúna** Brazil
129 L7 **Itaúnas** Brazil
130 H6 **Itaúnas** Brazil
9 E5 **Itchin, R** England
55 F4 **Itemgen, Oz** *L* Kazakhstan
Ithaca *isld* Greece *see* **Itháki** *isld*
94 C3 **Ithaca** Michigan U.S.A.
95 L4 **Ithaca** New York U.S.A.
46 D6 **Itháki** *isld* Greece
8 C3 **Ithon, R** Wales
115 O4 **Itilleq** Greenland
86 D5 **Itimbiri** *R* Zaire
130 H5 **Itinga** Brazil
129 H7 **Itiquira** Brazil
129 K6 **Itiúba, Serra de** *mts* Brazil
116 M2 **Itkillik** *R* Alaska U.S.A.
61 N11 **Itō** Japan
61 L8 **Itoigawa** Japan
86 D6 **Itoko** Zaire
61 P14 **Itoman** Okinawa
21 N4 **Iton** *R* France
45 P7 **Itri** Italy
79 A9 **Itsa** Egypt
111 F8 **Itta Bena** Mississippi U.S.A.
25 E6 **Ittervoort** Netherlands
43 B8 **Ittiri** Sardinia
Ittoqqortoormiit *see* **Scoresbysund**
130 F8 **Itu** Brazil
131 G2 **Itú** *R* Brazil
129 J7 **Ituiutaba** Brazil
88 A3 **Itula** Zaire
88 E5 **Itumba** Tanzania
129 J7 **Itumbiara** Brazil
119 O7 **Ituna** Saskatchewan Canada
128 G2 **Ituni** Guyana
130 E10 **Ituporanga** Brazil
128 E8 **Iturbe** Argentina
130 C10 **Iturbe** Paraguay
59 N3 **Iturup, Ostrov** *isld* Russian Federation
130 F7 **Ituverava** Brazil
130 C10 **Ituzaingo** Argentina
37 K3 **Itz** *R* Germany
32 L5 **Itzehoe** Germany
32 K5 **Itzwärden** Germany
88 D6 **Iufira** *R* Malawi
110 H3 **Iuka** Illinois U.S.A.
107 M4 **Iuka** Kansas U.S.A.
110 H7 **Iuka** Mississippi U.S.A.
130 H7 **Iúna** Brazil
112 E3 **Iva** South Carolina U.S.A.
129 H8 **Ivai** *R* Brazil
29 N3 **Ivalo** Finland
29 N3 **Ivalojoki** *R* Finland
48 E7 **Ivančići** Bosnia-Herzegovina
52 C5 **Ivangorod** Russian Federation
46 D2 **Ivangrad** Montenegro Yugoslavia
139 G5 **Ivanhoe** New South Wales Australia
142 G3 **Ivanhoe** W Australia Australia
120 H4 **Ivanhoe** *R* Ontario Canada
98 K5 **Ivanhoe** Minnesota U.S.A.
94 G10 **Ivanhoe** Virginia U.S.A.
54 M1 **Ivanishchi** Russian Federation
48 F7 **Ivanjica** Serbia Yugoslavia
53 B9 **Ivano-Frankovsk** Ukraine
48 L1 **Ivanopol'** Ukraine
55 B4 **Ivanovka** Russian Federation
55 G3 **Ivanovka** Omskaya obl Russian Federation
52 F6 **Ivanovo** Russian Federation
103 J6 **Ivanpah** California U.S.A.
54 J1 **Ivanteyvka** Russian Federation
53 C7 **Ivatsevichi** Belorussia
47 H3 **Ivaylovgrad** Bulgaria
55 D1 **Ivdel'** Russian Federation
33 R5 **Ivenack** Germany
99 S10 **Ivesdale** Illinois U.S.A.
17 H8 **Ivi, C** Algeria
86 B5 **Ivindo** *R* Gabon
9 F4 **Ivinghoe** England
129 H8 **Ivinheima** *R* Brazil
52 E4 **Ivinskiy Razliv, Vodokhranilishche** *res* Russian Federation
116 N2 **Ivishak** *R* Alaska U.S.A.
115 P5 **Ivittuut** Greenland
Iviza *see* **Ibiza**
95 L10 **Ivor** Virginia U.S.A.
85 C7 **Ivory Coast** *rep* W Africa
27 G15 **Ivösjön** Sweden
54 F3 **Ivot** Russian Federation
42 B3 **Ivrea** Italy
47 J5 **İvrindi** Turkey
21 N4 **Ivry-la-Bataille** France
115 M5 **Ivugivik** Quebec Canada
8 C7 **Ivybridge** England
94 F8 **Ivydale** West Virginia U.S.A.
61 O7 **Iwadeyama** Japan
61 O7 **Iwai-gawa** *R* Japan
61 P6 **Iwaizumi** Japan
61 O5 **Iwaki** *R* Japan
61 O9 **Iwaki** Japan
61 O5 **Iwaki-san** *mt* Japan
59 K5 **Iwakuni** Japan
60 P2 **Iwamizawa** Japan
70 D3 **Iwan** *R* Kalimantan
60 O3 **Iwanai** Japan
61 O7 **Iwanuma** Japan
61 O9 **Iwase** Japan
61 M9 **Iwasuge-yama** *mt* Japan
61 L11 **Iwata** Japan
61 P6 **Iwate** Japan
60 H11 **Iwaya** Japan
85 E7 **Iwo** Nigeria
Iwo Jima *see* **Iō-Jima**
140 C6 **Iwupataka** N Terr Australia
22 E3 **Iwuy** France
128 E6 **Ixiamas** Bolivia
125 K8 **Ixtaccihuatl** *vol* Mexico
125 M9 **Ixtepec, Ciudad** Mexico
124 H8 **Ixtlahuacán** Mexico
124 G7 **Ixtlán del Río** Mexico
9 G3 **Ixworth** England
56 F4 **Iya** *R* Russian Federation
55 E3 **Iyevlevo** Russian Federation
60 G12 **Iyomishima** Japan
60 F12 **Iyo-nada** *sea* Japan
56 C4 **Iyus** Russian Federation
48 J3 **Iza** *R* Romania
125 P10 **Izabal, L. de** Guatemala
17 G2 **Izalzu** Spain
116 F6 **Izaviknek** *R* Alaska U.S.A.
57 K5 **Izbaskan** Uzbekistan
31 O5 **Izbica** Poland
54 E1 **Izdeshkovo** Russian Federation
22 E2 **Izegem** Belgium
19 O14 **Izeron** France
52 H6 **Izhevsk** Russian Federation
52 H2 **Izhma** Russian Federation
53 C10 **Izmail** Ukraine
78 A2 **Izmir** Turkey
Izmit *see* **Kocaeli**
78 C1 **Izmit** Turkey
47 N11 **İzmit Körfezi** *B* Turkey
16 E7 **Iznajar** Spain
16 E7 **Iznalloz** Spain
78 B1 **Iznik** Turkey
78 B1 **Iznik Gölü** Turkey
53 F10 **Izobil'nyy** Russian Federation
128 F7 **Izozog, Bañados de** Bolivia
79 G6 **Izra'** Syria
48 E4 **Izsák** Hungary
60 C11 **Izuhara** Japan
60 D13 **Izumi** Japan
61 O7 **Izumi** Japan
60 J11 **Izumi-ōtsu** Japan
60 F10 **Izumo** Japan
61 M8 **Izumozaki** Japan
55 D3 **Izumrud** Russian Federation
55 F6 **Izumrudnyy** Kazakhstan
57 F1 **Izumrudnyy** Kazakhstan
61 N11 **Izu-shotō** *islds* Japan
50 H1 **Izvestiy Tsentral'nogo Ispolnitel'nogo Komiteta, Ostrova** *isld* Russian Federation
48 K3 **Izvoru Muntelui, Lacul** *L* Romania
57 A2 **Izyndy** Kazakhstan
54 J7 **Izyum** Ukraine

J

29 M10 **Jaala** Finland
29 L5 **Jaatila** Finland
77 E2 **Jaba** *R* Iran
80 G1 **Jabā** Syria
77 C7 **Jabal az Zannah** U.A.E.
16 E6 **Jabalón** *R* Spain
74 H7 **Jabalpur** India
22 E1 **Jabbeke** Belgium
33 R5 **Jabel** Germany
140 C2 **Jabiru** N Terr Australia
79 F3 **Jablah** Syria
46 D3 **Jablanica** Albania
46 E2 **Jablanica** *R* Serbia Yugoslavia
31 J5 **Jablonec nad Nisou** Czechoslovakia
31 K7 **Jablonica** Czechoslovakia
31 L2 **Jabłonowo** Poland
31 L6 **Jablunkov** Czechoslovakia
129 M5 **Jaboatão** Brazil
129 J8 **Jaboticabal** Brazil
69 G13 **Jabung, Tanjung** *C* Sumatra
128 F5 **Jaburu** Brazil
17 G2 **Jaca** Spain
130 B6 **Jacadigo** *L* Brazil
130 G4 **Jacaraci** Brazil
129 K6 **Jacaré** *R* Brazil
129 G5 **Jacareacanga** Brazil
130 F8 **Jacareí** Brazil
128 G5 **Jacaretinga** Brazil
130 E8 **Jacarezinho** Brazil
133 D4 **Jachal** Argentina
37 O3 **Jáchymov** Czechoslovakia
130 H5 **Jacinto** Brazil
109 M5 **Jacinto, S** *R* Texas U.S.A.
128 F5 **Jaciparaná** Brazil
120 D4 **Jackfish** Ontario Canada
118 J5 **Jackfish L** Saskatchewan Canada
117 R6 **Jackfish River** Alberta Canada
119 U7 **Jackhead Harbour** Manitoba Canada
115 N6 **Jack Lane B** Labrador, Nfld Canada
95 R1 **Jackman** Maine U.S.A.
100 E1 **Jack Mt** Washington U.S.A.
120 C3 **Jackpine** Ontario Canada
141 G3 **Jack R** Queensland Australia
112 C1 **Jacksboro** Tennessee U.S.A.
109 J2 **Jacksboro** Texas U.S.A.
94 K6 **Jacks Mt** Pennsylvania U.S.A.
141 J7 **Jackson** Queensland Australia
111 J10 **Jackson** Alabama U.S.A.
102 D3 **Jackson** California U.S.A.
112 D4 **Jackson** Georgia U.S.A.
94 D9 **Jackson** Kentucky U.S.A.
111 E11 **Jackson** Louisiana U.S.A.
111 F9 **Jackson** Mississippi U.S.A.
110 G4 **Jackson** Missouri U.S.A.
101 M4 **Jackson** Montana U.S.A.
112 K1 **Jackson** North Carolina U.S.A.
94 E7 **Jackson** Ohio U.S.A.
112 F4 **Jackson** South Carolina U.S.A.
110 H6 **Jackson** Tennessee U.S.A.
94 H8 **Jackson** *R* Virginia U.S.A.
101 P6 **Jackson** Wyoming U.S.A.
117 L10 **Jackson Bay** British Columbia Canada
144 B5 **Jackson Bay** New Zealand
145 E4 **Jackson, C** New Zealand
110 M1 **Jackson Cen** Ohio U.S.A.
106 B4 **Jackson Gulch Res** Colorado U.S.A.
113 C7 **Jackson, L** Florida U.S.A.
112 D4 **Jackson L** Georgia U.S.A.
101 P6 **Jackson L** Wyoming U.S.A.
143 C9 **Jackson, Mt** W Australia Australia
100 G8 **Jackson Mts** Nevada U.S.A.
141 F8 **Jackson Oil Field** Queensland Australia
144 A6 **Jackson Peaks** New Zealand
99 T5 **Jacksonport** Wisconsin U.S.A.
111 G9 **Jackson Prairie** Mississippi U.S.A.
106 F1 **Jackson Res** Colorado U.S.A.
144 C5 **Jacksons** New Zealand
123 Q4 **Jackson's Arm** Newfoundland Canada
111 L8 **Jacksonville** Alabama U.S.A.
110 D7 **Jacksonville** Arkansas U.S.A.
113 F7 **Jacksonville** Florida U.S.A.
99 Q10 **Jacksonville** Illinois U.S.A.
110 D2 **Jacksonville** Missouri U.S.A.
112 K3 **Jacksonville** North Carolina U.S.A.
100 C7 **Jacksonville** Oregon U.S.A.
109 M4 **Jacksonville** Texas U.S.A.
113 F7 **Jacksonville Beach** Florida U.S.A.
127 H5 **Jacmel** Haiti
124 G4 **Jaco** Mexico
74 C4 **Jacobabad** Pakistan
129 K6 **Jacobina** Brazil
103 M5 **Jacob L** Arizona U.S.A.
80 E5 **Jacob's Well** Jordan
124 H8 **Jacona** Mexico
121 T9 **Jacques Cartier** Quebec Canada
121 T5 **Jacques Cartier, L** Quebec Canada
122 G4 **Jacques Cartier, Mt** Quebec Canada
122 F6 **Jacquet R** New Brunswick Canada
130 J9 **Jacú** *R* Brazil
130 F7 **Jacuí** Minas Gerais Brazil
131 H2 **Jacui** *R* Rio Grande do Sul Brazil
131 H2 **Jacui** Rio Grande do Sul Brazil
129 L6 **Jacuípe** *R* Brazil
103 H9 **Jacumba** California U.S.A.
129 H4 **Jacunda** *R* Brazil
129 J4 **Jacundá** Brazil
130 F9 **Jacupiranga** Brazil
129 E4 **Jaçura** Brazil
80 G8 **Jad'a** Jordan
48 E6 **Jadar** *R* Serbia Yugoslavia
32 H6 **Jade** *R* Germany
32 H6 **Jade** Germany
85 C2 **Jadida, El** Morocco
87 E8 **Jadotville** Zaire
31 N3 **Jadów** Poland
17 F4 **Jadraque** Spain
84 E3 **Jādū** Libya
28 H5 **Jægerspris** Denmark
22 F3 **Jaeibise** Belgium
83 J10 **Ja-Ela** Sri Lanka
143 C8 **Jaellan Hill** W Australia Australia
71 E3 **Jaen** Luzon Philippines
16 E7 **Jaén** *prov* Spain
16 E7 **Jaén** Spain
27 A13 **Jaeren** *R* Norway
26 F7 **Jaevsjo** Norway
77 A2 **Ja'farābād** Iran
80 C5 **Jaffa** Israel
138 E6 **Jaffa, C** South Australia Australia
83 K8 **Jaffna** Sri Lanka
75 K9 **Jagdalpur** India
75 J5 **Jagdishpur** India
87 E11 **Jagersfontein** S Africa
84 G4 **Jaghbūb, Al** Libya
116 Q2 **Jago** *R* Alaska U.S.A.
36 H5 **Jagst** *R* Germany
37 J5 **Jagstzell** Germany
74 H9 **Jagtial** India
129 K6 **Jaguaquara** Brazil
131 H4 **Jaguarão** Brazil
131 G2 **Jaguari** *R* Brazil
129 H8 **Jaguariaiva** Brazil
129 L5 **Jaguaribe** *R* Brazil
131 C2 **Jagüe, R** Argentina
126 D3 **Jagüey Grande** Cuba
140 B1 **Jahleel, Pt** N Terr Australia
78 K7 **Jahmah** Iraq
48 E7 **Jahorina** *mt* Bosnia-Herzegovina
77 C5 **Jahrom** Iran
74 G3 **Jaijon** India
75 P6 **Jaintia Hills** India
74 F5 **Jaipur** India
74 D5 **Jaisalmer** India
42 H4 **Jajce** Bosnia-Herzegovina
75 M8 **Jajpur** India
63 **Jakarta** *conurbation* Indonesia
70 L9 **Jakarta** Java
84 G4 **Jakharrah** Libya
26 J5 **Jäkkvik** Sweden
71 N9 **Jako** *isld* Timor
26 S2 **Jakobselv** *R* Norway/Rus Fed
115 O4 **Jakobshavn** Greenland
29 K8 **Jakobstad** Finland
46 E3 **Jakupica** Macedonia Yugoslavia
106 G9 **Jal** New Mexico U.S.A.
77 H6 **Jāla** Iran
58 G2 **Jalai Nur** China
77 L2 **Jalalabad** Afghanistan
74 F3 **Jalandhar** India
125 L3 **Jalapa** Nicaragua
125 L8 **Jalapa Enriquez** Mexico
29 K9 **Jalasjärvi** Finland
74 H5 **Jalaun** India
140 C2 **Jalboi** *R* N Terr Australia
130 E7 **Jales** Brazil
75 M8 **Jaleshwar** India
74 F8 **Jalgaon** India
22 K2 **Jalhay** Belgium
78 L6 **Jalibah** Iraq
86 B4 **Jalingo** Nigeria
124 G8 **Jalisco** *state* Mexico
21 J7 **Jallais** France
74 F9 **Jalna** India
17 F3 **Jalón** *R* Spain
Jalo Oasis *see* **Jālu**
74 E6 **Jalor** India
124 H7 **Jalostotitlán** Mexico
124 H7 **Jalpa** Mexico
75 N5 **Jalpaiguri** India
124 K7 **Jalpan** Mexico
77 L2 **Jalrez** Afghanistan
84 G4 **Jālu** Libya

84 G4 **Jālu** *oilfield* Libya
78 K4 **Jalūlā** Iraq
84 G4 **Jālu, Waḩat** *oasis* Libya
77 G2 **Jam** *reg* Iran
128 B4 **Jama** Ecuador
86 H5 **Jamaame** Somalia
126 G4 **Jamaica** Cuba
95 P3 **Jamaica** Vermont U.S.A.
127 K2 **Jamaica** W Indies
126 G5 **Jamaica Chan** Caribbean
27 M13 **Jämaja** Estonia
75 N6 **Jamalpur** Bangladesh
75 M6 **Jamalpur** India
126 A2 **Jamanota** *hill* Aruba W Indies
129 G5 **Jamanxim** *R* Brazil
128 F5 **Jamari** Brazil
66 C2 **Jamati** China
139 K5 **Jamberoo** New South Wales Australia
69 F13 **Jambi** Sumatra
141 K6 **Jambin** Queensland Australia
69 C10 **Jamboaye** *R* Sumatra
70 E1 **Jambongan** *isld* Sabah
122 F4 **Jambon, Pte** Quebec Canada
70 E5 **Jambu** Kalimantan
69 C10 **Jambuair, Tanjung** *C* Sumatra
110 C5 **James** *R* Missouri U.S.A.
98 H3 **James** *R* North Dakota U.S.A.
98 J6 **James** *R* South Dakota U.S.A.
115 L7 **James B** Canada
95 N6 **Jamesburg** New Jersey U.S.A.
112 K2 **James City** North Carolina U.S.A.
94 J5 **James City** Pennsylvania U.S.A.
112 F2 **James, L** North Carolina U.S.A.
99 N9 **Jameson** Missouri U.S.A.
115 R3 **Jameson Land** Greenland
143 G7 **Jameson Ra** W Australia Australia
99 N10 **Jamesport** Missouri U.S.A.
113 L12 **James Pt** Bahamas
140 D5 **James R** N Terr Australia
95 L9 **James R** Virginia U.S.A.
140 C6 **James Ranges** N Terr Australia
146 D4 **James Ross I** Antarctica
115 K4 **James Ross Str** Northwest Territories Canada
138 E5 **Jamestown** South Australia Australia
90 A13 **Jamestown** St Helena
110 K2 **Jamestown** Indiana U.S.A.
107 N2 **Jamestown** Kansas U.S.A.
94 B4 **Jamestown** Michigan U.S.A.
94 H4 **Jamestown** New York U.S.A.
98 H3 **Jamestown** North Dakota U.S.A.
94 D7 **Jamestown** Ohio U.S.A.
94 G5 **Jamestown** Pennsylvania U.S.A.
95 Q5 **Jamestown** Rhode I U.S.A.
112 H4 **Jamestown** South Carolina U.S.A.
94 C10 **Jamestown** Tennessee U.S.A.
95 L9 **Jamestown Nat. Hist. Site** Virginia U.S.A.
95 L4 **Jamesville** New York U.S.A.
112 L2 **Jamesville** North Carolina U.S.A.
22 J5 **Jametz** France
139 H6 **Jamieson** Victoria Australia
100 H5 **Jamieson** Oregon U.S.A.
29 K10 **Jämijärvi** Finland
125 L9 **Jamilzepec** Mexico
98 G7 **Jamison** Nebraska U.S.A.
76 B2 **Jamkhandi** India
74 F9 **Jamkhed** India
76 D3 **Jammalamadugu** India
28 C2 **Jammerbugt** *B* Denmark
28 F5 **Jammerland Bugt** *B* Denmark
74 F2 **Jammu** Kashmir
Jammu and Kashmir *see* **Kashmir**
74 G1 **Jammu and Kashmir** *prov* India/Pakistan
74 D7 **Jamnagar** India
31 J1 **Jamno, Jezioro** *L* Poland
22 J4 **Jamoigne** Belgium
71 K8 **Jampea** Indonesia
74 D4 **Jampur** Pakistan
29 L10 **Jämsä** Finland
29 L10 **Jämsänkoski** Finland
75 M7 **Jamshedpur** India
26 F8 **Jämtland** Sweden
26 H8 **Jämtl Sikås** Sweden
71 C3 **Jamtup, Tg** *C* W Irian
70 E3 **Jamuk, G** *mt* Kalimantan
102 H9 **Jamul** California U.S.A.
75 N6 **Jamuna** *R* Bangladesh
128 C3 **Jamundí** Colombia
75 M5 **Janakpur** Nepal
129 K7 **Janaúba** Brazil
129 H3 **Janaucu, I** Brazil
130 E5 **Jandaia** Brazil
142 B3 **Jandakot** *dist* Perth, W Aust Australia
142 B3 **Jandakot, L** W Australia Australia
77 D2 **Jandaq** Iran
28 A5 **Janderup** Denmark
128 E5 **Jandiatuba** *R* Brazil
141 K7 **Jandowae** Queensland Australia
94 G7 **Jane Lew** West Virginia U.S.A.
144 B6 **Jane Pk** New Zealand
100 E9 **Janesville** California U.S.A.
99 O7 **Janesville** Iowa U.S.A.
99 N5 **Janesville** Minnesota U.S.A.
99 R7 **Janesville** Wisconsin U.S.A.
130 D10 **Jangada** Brazil
130 C7 **Jango** Brazil
69 G13 **Jang, Tanjung** *C* Indonesia
33 S8 **Jänickendorf** Germany
46 E2 **Janjevo** Serbia Yugoslavia
89 D6 **Jan Kemp** S Africa
119 P4 **Jan L** Saskatchewan Canada
90 H1 **Jan Mayen** *isld* Arctic Oc
77 G2 **Jannatabad** Iran
124 E2 **Janos** Mexico
48 E4 **Jánoshalma** Hungary
48 D3 **Jánosháza** Hungary
37 P5 **Janovice nad Uhlavou** Czechoslovakia
33 S5 **Janow** Germany
31 K3 **Janowiec** Poland
31 N5 **Janów Lubelski** Poland
31 O3 **Janów Podlaski** Poland
119 N7 **Jansen** Saskatchewan Canada
98 K9 **Jansen** Nebraska U.S.A.
130 G4 **Januária** Brazil
21 O5 **Janville** France
20 H6 **Janzé** France
130 G5 **Jaoquim Felício** Brazil
74 F7 **Jaora** India
61 **Japan** *empire* E Asia
59 K3 **Japan, Sea of** E Asia
29 N9 **Jäppilä** Finland
128 E4 **Japurá** Brazil
127 J5 **Jarabacoa** Dominican Rep
78 F3 **Jarābulus** Syria
129 J7 **Jaraguá** Brazil
130 E10 **Jaraguá do Sul** Brazil
130 C7 **Jaraguari** Brazil
130 E10 **Jaraguá Serra** *mts* Brazil
16 D5 **Jaraicejo** Spain
16 E4 **Jarama** *R* Spain
133 D7 **Jaramillo** Argentina
16 D4 **Jarandilla** Spain
129 H4 **Jarauçu** *R* Brazil
100 K7 **Jarbidge** *R* Idaho U.S.A.
100 K8 **Jarbidge** Nevada U.S.A.
27 J11 **Järbo** Sweden
130 G9 **Jardim** Ceará Brazil
130 C7 **Jardim** Mato Grosso Brazil
130 H9 **Jardim do Seridó** Brazil
141 F1 **Jardine** *R* Queensland Australia
122 E6 **Jardine Brook** New Brunswick Canada
141 G1 **Jardine River Nat. Park** Queensland Australia
126 E4 **Jardines de la Reina, Arch. de las** *islds* Cuba
130 E6 **Jardinésia** Brazil
130 F7 **Jardinópolis** Brazil
27 H14 **Järeda** Sweden
27 E11 **Jaren** Norway
38 N8 **Jarenina** Slovenia
58 G2 **Jargalant** Mongolia
21 P6 **Jargeau** France
129 H3 **Jari** *R* Brazil
128 F4 **Jari, L** Brazil
33 S5 **Jarmen** Germany
27 J12 **Järna** Sweden
18 E7 **Jarnac** France
27 H13 **Järnlunden** *L* Sweden
71 F5 **Jaro** Panay Philippines
31 K4 **Jarocin** Poland
31 J5 **Jaroměř** Czechoslovakia
31 J6 **Jaroměřice** Czechoslovakia
126 F4 **Jaronu** Cuba
31 O5 **Jaroslaw** Poland
106 E4 **Jaroso** Colorado U.S.A.
26 F8 **Järpen** Sweden
80 F8 **Jarra** *R* Jordan
94 K10 **Jarratt** Virginia U.S.A.
26 K5 **Jarre** *mt* Sweden
109 K5 **Jarrell** Texas U.S.A.
68 F3 **Jarres, Plaine des** Laos
118 F6 **Jarrow** Alberta Canada
13 G4 **Jarrow** England
128 F6 **Jaru** Brazil
65 E2 **Jarud Qi** China
52 C5 **Järva-Jaani** Estonia
118 D4 **Jarvie** Alberta Canada
134 B3 **Jarvis I** Pacific Oc
26 H10 **Järvsö** Sweden
21 K6 **Jarzé** France
48 F5 **Jaša Tomic** Serbia Yugoslavia
74 D7 **Jasdan** India
33 T8 **Jasdorf** Germany
85 E7 **Jasikan** Ghana
77 E7 **Jāsk** Iran
31 N6 **Jasło** Poland
119 O7 **Jasmin** Saskatchewan Canada
30 H1 **Jasmund** *pen* Germany
133 E8 **Jason Is** Falkland Is
146 D4 **Jason Pen** Antarctica
110 J2 **Jasonville** Indiana U.S.A.
117 O9 **Jasper** Alberta Canada
121 P8 **Jasper** Ontario Canada
111 J8 **Jasper** Alabama U.S.A.
110 C5 **Jasper** Arkansas U.S.A.
106 D4 **Jasper** Colorado U.S.A.
113 E7 **Jasper** Florida U.S.A.
111 M7 **Jasper** Georgia U.S.A.
110 K3 **Jasper** Indiana U.S.A.
94 C5 **Jasper** Michigan U.S.A.
98 K6 **Jasper** Minnesota U.S.A.
110 B4 **Jasper** Missouri U.S.A.
94 K4 **Jasper** New York U.S.A.
112 B2 **Jasper** Tennessee U.S.A.
111 C11 **Jasper** Texas U.S.A.
117 O9 **Jasper Nat. Park** Alberta Canada
78 K5 **Jassan** Iraq
Jassy *see* **Iasi**
31 L1 **Jastarnia** Poland
46 E1 **Jastrebac** *mt* Serbia Yugoslavia
31 K2 **Jastrowie** Poland
48 F3 **Jászapáti** Hungary
48 F3 **Jászarokszállás** Hungary
48 F3 **Jászberény** Hungary
48 F3 **Jászfényszaru** Hungary
48 F3 **Jászladány** Hungary
129 H7 **Jataí** Brazil
128 G4 **Jatapu** *R* Brazil
76 B2 **Jath** India
70 M9 **Jatibarang** Java
126 E4 **Jatibonico** Cuba
17 G6 **Játiva** Spain
129 H4 **Jatobá** Brazil
80 D4 **Jatt** Israel
128 F5 **Jatuarana** Brazil
33 T5 **Jatzke** Germany
33 T5 **Jatznick** Germany
128 F4 **Jaú** *R* Brazil
129 J8 **Jaú** Brazil
128 F3 **Jauaperi** *R* Brazil
22 H2 **Jauche** Belgium
126 G4 **Jauco** Cuba
20 D4 **Jaudy** *R* France
128 C6 **Jauja** Peru
21 L8 **Jaulnay** France
128 G5 **Jauna** *R* Brazil
21 L8 **Jaunay Clan** France
52 B6 **Jaunjelgava** Latvia
52 C6 **Jaunpiebalga** Latvia
75 K6 **Jaunpur** India
38 L8 **Jauntal** *V* Austria
129 G7 **Jauru** *R* Brazil
130 D6 **Jauru, R** Brazil
22 D5 **Jaux** France
Java *isld* *see* **Jawa**
76 D4 **Javadi Hills** India
129 J6 **Javaés, Serra dos** *mts* Brazil
17 G4 **Javalambre, Sierra de** *mts* Spain
128 D4 **Javari** *R* Brazil/Peru
70 M8 **Java Sea** Indonesia
136 D4 **Java Trench** Indian Oc
17 H6 **Jávea** Spain
Javhlant *see* **Uliastay**
133 C7 **Javier** *B* Chile
48 E6 **Javor** *mts* Bosnia-Herzegovina
48 E2 **Javoria** *mt* Czechoslovakia
38 K9 **Javornik** Slovenia
48 E1 **Javorniky** *mt* Czechoslovakia
26 M6 **Jävre** Sweden
21 K5 **Javron-les-Chapelles** France
70 **Jawa** *isld* Indonesia
80 G6 **Jawa** Jordan
79 H2 **Jawbān Bayk** Syria
86 J5 **Jawhar** Somalia
31 J4 **Jawor** Poland
31 L5 **Jaworzno** Poland
107 Q5 **Jay** Oklahoma U.S.A.
75 N5 **Jayanti** India
136 H2 **Jaya Pk** *mt* W Irian
136 J2 **Jayapura** W Irian
98 B7 **Jay Em** Wyoming U.S.A.
33 P7 **Jayenitz** Germany
75 K9 **Jaypur** India
79 G5 **Jayrūd** Syria
9 H4 **Jaywick Sands** England
78 H4 **Jazirah, Al** Iraq
124 J5 **Jazminal** Mexico
77 F6 **Jaz Murian, Hamun-e** *L* Iran
79 F4 **Jbail** Lebanon
79 F4 **Jdaidet Ghazir** Lebanon
85 B3 **Jdiriya** Western Sahara
103 J6 **Jean** Nevada U.S.A.
109 J2 **Jean** Texas U.S.A.
111 E12 **Jeanerette** Louisiana U.S.A.
122 E1 **Jean L** Quebec Canada
111 G12 **Jean Lafitte Nat. Hist. Park** Louisiana U.S.A.
117 N5 **Jean Marie River** Northwest Territories Canada
6 M6 **Jeanne** *oil rig* North Sea
94 H6 **Jeannette** Pennsylvania U.S.A.
127 H5 **Jean Rabel** Haiti
13 G5 **Jeater Houses** England
77 F5 **Jebāl Bārez, Kūh-e** *mts* Iran
85 E7 **Jebba** Nigeria
80 F1 **Jebel** Lebanon
86 E2 **Jebel Abyad Plateau** Sudan
16 D9 **Jebha** Morocco
28 B3 **Jebjerg** Denmark
88 E8 **Jeci** *mt* Mozambique
119 P7 **Jedburgh** Saskatchewan Canada
13 F2 **Jedburgh** Scotland
Jedda *see* **Jiddah**
94 E3 **Jeddo** Michigan U.S.A.
43 C12 **Jedeida** Tunisia
13 F3 **Jedfoot Br** Scotland
31 M5 **Jędrzejów** Poland
31 N2 **Jedwabne** Poland
117 H9 **Jedway** British Columbia Canada
29 M4 **Jeesiö** Finland
33 O6 **Jeetze** *R* Germany
33 O7 **Jeetze** Germany
99 L5 **Jeffers** Minnesota U.S.A.
106 E2 **Jefferson** Colorado U.S.A.
112 D3 **Jefferson** Georgia U.S.A.
94 K7 **Jefferson** Maryland U.S.A.
94 G5 **Jefferson** Ohio U.S.A.
107 N5 **Jefferson** Oklahoma U.S.A.
100 C5 **Jefferson** Oregon U.S.A.
98 K7 **Jefferson** South Dakota U.S.A.
111 B9 **Jefferson** Texas U.S.A.
99 S6 **Jefferson** Wisconsin U.S.A.
110 D3 **Jefferson City** Missouri U.S.A.
101 N3 **Jefferson City** Montana U.S.A.
112 D1 **Jefferson City** Tennessee U.S.A.
101 O4 **Jefferson Island** Montana U.S.A.
100 D5 **Jefferson, Mt** Oregon U.S.A.
94 B8 **Jeffersontown** Kentucky U.S.A.
110 L3 **Jeffersontown** Kentucky U.S.A.
112 D5 **Jeffersonville** Georgia U.S.A.
94 B8 **Jeffersonville** Indiana U.S.A.
95 N5 **Jeffersonville** New York U.S.A.
94 D7 **Jeffersonville** Ohio U.S.A.
95 P2 **Jeffersonville** Vermont U.S.A.
101 S7 **Jeffrey City** Wyoming U.S.A.
71 C3 **Jef Lio** W Irian
85 E6 **Jega** Nigeria
28 B3 **Jegindø** *isld* Denmark
18 F9 **Jegun** France
77 G4 **Jehīle Pūzak** *L* Iran
28 B7 **Jejsing** Denmark
130 C9 **Jejui Guazú, R** Paraguay
52 C6 **Jēkabpils** Latvia
112 F6 **Jekyll I** Georgia U.S.A.
86 H4 **Jeldēsa** Ethiopia
31 J5 **Jelenia Góra** Poland
52 B6 **Jelgava** Latvia
120 C3 **Jellicoe** Ontario Canada
28 C5 **Jelling** Denmark
102 B1 **Jelly** California U.S.A.
31 L5 **Jełowa** Poland
27 E12 **Jelöy** *isld* Norway
28 C6 **Jels** Denmark
27 B12 **Jelsa** Norway
48 F2 **Jelšava** Czechoslovakia
69 G11 **Jemaja** Indonesia
22 F3 **Jemappes** Belgium
70 O10 **Jember** Java
33 N8 **Jembke** Germany
85 G1 **Jem, El** Tunisia
22 J3 **Jemelle** Belgium
106 D6 **Jemez** *R* New Mexico U.S.A.
106 D6 **Jemez Pueblo** New Mexico U.S.A.
106 D6 **Jemez Springs** New Mexico U.S.A.
32 F6 **Jemgum** Germany
43 D13 **Jemmel** Tunisia
31 J6 **Jemnice** Czechoslovakia
70 E5 **Jempang, Danao** *L* Kalimantan
122 F8 **Jemseg** New Brunswick Canada
37 M2 **Jena** Germany
111 D10 **Jena** Louisiana U.S.A.
38 E7 **Jenbach** Austria
80 E4 **Jenin** Jordan
94 F9 **Jenkinjones** West Virginia U.S.A.
94 E9 **Jenkins** Kentucky U.S.A.
99 M3 **Jenkins** Minnesota U.S.A.
140 A7 **Jenkins,Mt** N Terr Australia
118 F8 **Jenner** Alberta Canada
102 A3 **Jenner** California U.S.A.
117 H6 **Jennings** *R* British Columbia Canada
113 D7 **Jennings** Florida U.S.A.
107 K2 **Jennings** Kansas U.S.A.
111 D11 **Jennings** Louisiana U.S.A.
107 O5 **Jennings** Oklahoma U.S.A.
127 O4 **Jennings** Antigua W Indies
114 J4 **Jenny Lind I** Northwest Territories Canada
139 K5 **Jenolan Caves** New South Wales Australia
101 Q9 **Jensen** Utah U.S.A.
113 G10 **Jensen Beach** Florida U.S.A.
115 P5 **Jensen Nunatakker** *pk* Greenland
115 L4 **Jens Munk I** Northwest Territories Canada
70 N9 **Jepara** Java
138 F6 **Jeparit** Victoria Australia
29 K8 **Jeppo** Finland
129 K6 **Jequie** Brazil
130 G5 **Jequitai** Brazil
129 K7 **Jequitinhonha** Brazil
85 D2 **Jerada** Morocco
69 F11 **Jerantut** Malaysia
85 G2 **Jerba, I de** Tunisia
126 G5 **Jérémie** Haiti
129 L6 **Jeremoabo** Brazil
71 H9 **Jerewan** Indonesia
124 H6 **Jerez de García Salinas** Mexico
16 C8 **Jerez de la Frontera** Spain
16 C6 **Jerez de los Caballeros** Spain
141 H6 **Jericho** Queensland Australia
80 E6 **Jericho** Jordan
33 Q8 **Jerichow** Germany
129 K4 **Jericoaquara, Pta** *C* Brazil
69 G14 **Jerigi** Sumatra
26 N5 **Jerijärvi** Sweden
70 B3 **Jerijih, Tanjong** *C* Sarawak
139 H6 **Jerilderie** New South Wales Australia
29 L4 **Jerisjärvi** *L* Finland
130 E4 **Jeroaquara** Brazil
120 H5 **Jerome** Ontario Canada
103 M7 **Jerome** Arizona U.S.A.
101 L7 **Jerome** Idaho U.S.A.
129 H7 **Jerônimo, Serra do** *mts* Brazil
143 C10 **Jerramungup** W Australia Australia
20 F3 **Jersey** *isld* Channel Is
95 N6 **Jersey City** New Jersey U.S.A.
95 K5 **Jersey Shore** Pennsylvania U.S.A.
110 F2 **Jerseyville** Illinois U.S.A.
28 E2 **Jerslev** Denmark
28 C6 **Jerstal** Denmark
16 D4 **Jerte** *R* Spain
70 D2 **Jerudong** Brunei
129 K5 **Jerumenha** Brazil
28 E1 **Jerup** Denmark
80 D6 **Jerusalem** Israel
145 E3 **Jerusalem** New Zealand
140 D6 **Jervais Ra** N Terr Australia
139 K6 **Jervis Bay** New South Wales Australia
138 E6 **Jervis, C** South Australia Australia
117 M10 **Jervis Inlet** British Columbia Canada
140 D6 **Jervois Ra** N Terr Australia
33 N8 **Jerxheim** Germany
36 G2 **Jesberg** Germany
37 P3 **Jesenice** Czechoslovakia
42 F2 **Jesenice** Slovenia
31 K5 **Jesenik** Czechoslovakia
48 F2 **Jesenské** Czechoslovakia
33 Q8 **Jeserig** Germany
33 R10 **Jesewitz** Germany
Jesselton *see* **Kota Kinabalu**
27 E11 **Jessheim** Norway
98 H2 **Jessie** North Dakota U.S.A.
33 Q9 **Jessnitz** Germany
113 F9 **Jessup, L** Florida U.S.A.
32 L6 **Jesteburg** Germany
112 F6 **Jesup** Georgia U.S.A.
99 O7 **Jesup** Iowa U.S.A.
133 E4 **Jesús María** Argentina
124 H7 **Jesús María** Mexico
126 F4 **Jesús Mendéndez** Cuba
107 M5 **Jet** Oklahoma U.S.A.
119 Q2 **Jetait** Manitoba Canada
94 J9 **Jetersville** Virginia U.S.A.
20 F3 **Jethou** *isld* Channel Is
107 L3 **Jetmore** Kansas U.S.A.
37 J7 **Jettingen** Germany
37 L7 **Jetzendorf** Germany
22 G3 **Jeumont** France
32 L4 **Jevenau** *R* Germany
32 L4 **Jevenstedt** Germany
32 G5 **Jever** Germany
48 D1 **Jevičko** Czechoslovakia
27 D11 **Jevnaker** Norway
98 C6 **Jewel Cave Nat. Mon** South Dakota U.S.A.
99 N7 **Jewell** Iowa U.S.A.
107 M2 **Jewell** Kansas U.S.A.
100 B4 **Jewell** Oregon U.S.A.
110 H2 **Jewett** Illinois U.S.A.
94 G6 **Jewett** Ohio U.S.A.
109 L4 **Jewett** Texas U.S.A.
95 Q5 **Jewett City** Connecticut U.S.A.
46 D2 **Jezerce** *mt* Albania
37 P5 **Jezerni** *mt* Czechoslovakia
42 H4 **Jezero** Bosnia-Herzegovina
31 M2 **Jeziorak, Jezioro** *L* Poland
31 M2 **Jeziorany** Poland
31 L4 **Jeziorsko, Jezioro** *res* Poland
31 P1 **Jeznas** Lithuania
31 M4 **Jeżów** Poland
79 F5 **Jezzine** Lebanon
74 F7 **Jhabua** India
74 G4 **Jhajjar** India
74 G6 **Jhalawar** India
74 E3 **Jhang Maghiana** Pakistan
74 H6 **Jhansi** India
75 M5 **Jhapa** Nepal
74 E2 **Jhelum** India
74 E2 **Jhelum** *R* Pakistan
74 F4 **Jhunjhunūn** India
65 E3 **Jiade He** *R* China
67 G1 **Jiading** China
67 C4 **Jiagui** China
67 D4 **Jiahe** China
Jiaji *see* **Qionghai**
67 A2 **Jiajiang** China
58 E5 **Jialing Jiang** *R* China
59 K2 **Jiamusi** China
65 H1 **Jiamusi** China
65 G4 **Ji'an** China
67 E3 **Ji'an** China
65 D4 **Jianchang** China
65 F4 **Jianchang** China
67 F2 **Jiande** China
67 B2 **Jiang'an** China
67 B2 **Jiangbei** China
68 E1 **Jiangcheng** China
67 C3 **Jiangdong** China
67 F1 **Jiangdu** China
67 C6 **Jianghong** China
67 D4 **Jianghua** China
67 B2 **Jiangjin** China
Jiangkou *see* **Fengkai**
67 D1 **Jiangkou** China
67 C3 **Jiangkou** China
67 F3 **Jiangle** China
67 D1 **Jiangling** China
67 D5 **Jiangmen** China
67 F1 **Jiangpu** China
67 F2 **Jiangshan** China
58 G5 **Jiangsu** *prov* China
67 E3 **Jiangxi** *prov* China
65 B7 **Jiang Xian** China
67 F1 **Jiangxiang** China
67 G1 **Jiangyin** China
67 D4 **Jiangyong** China
67 A1 **Jiangyou** China
67 C3 **Jianhe** China
67 D2 **Jianli** China
67 E3 **Jianning** China
67 F3 **Jian'ou** China
65 D4 **Jianping** China
65 D5 **Jianping** China
67 C1 **Jianshi** China
67 A5 **Jianshui** China
58 D5 **Jianyang** China
67 F3 **Jianyang** China
65 B6 **Jiaocheng** China
59 J3 **Jiaohe** China
65 B6 **Jiaokou** China
67 E4 **Jiaoling** China
65 E7 **Jiaonan** China
65 D6 **Jiao Xian** China
58 F4 **Jiaozuo** China
65 G3 **Jiapigou** China
58 G5 **Jiashan** China
67 G1 **Jiashan** China
57 H5 **Jiashi** China
65 D7 **Jiawang** China
65 A5 **Jia Xian** China
65 B7 **Jia Xian** China
59 H5 **Jiaxing** China
67 C4 **Jiaya** China
59 K2 **Jiayin** China
67 D2 **Jiayu** China
58 C4 **Jiayuguan** China
65 E7 **Jiazohou Wan** *B* China
77 B7 **Jiban, Al** Saudi Arabia
129 J7 **Jibao, Serra do** *mts* Brazil
88 G6 **Jibondo** *isld* Tanzania
48 H3 **Jibou** Romania
67 B3 **Jichang** China
31 J5 **Jičín** Czechoslovakia
86 G1 **Jiddah** Saudi Arabia
65 H2 **Jidong** China
Jiehu *see* **Yinan**
26 L2 **Jiekkevarre** *mt* Norway
67 E5 **Jieshi** China
67 E5 **Jieshi Wan** *B* China
26 O2 **Jiesjavrre** *L* Norway
67 E5 **Jiexi** China
65 B6 **Jiexiu** China
143 D6 **Jiggalong** W Australia Australia
100 K9 **Jiggs** Nevada U.S.A.
67 E1 **Jigong Shan** *mt* China
79 H4 **Jihar, Wādī el** *watercourse* Syria
31 J6 **Jihlava** Czechoslovakia
31 H6 **Jihočesky** *reg* Czechoslovakia
31 J6 **Jihomoravský** *reg* Czechoslovakia
85 F1 **Jijel** Algeria
48 L3 **Jijia** *R* Romania
86 H4 **Jijiga** Ethiopia
80 G3 **Jijjin** Jordan
17 G6 **Jijona** Spain
48 K6 **Jilava** Romania
86 H5 **Jilib** Somalia
59 H2 **Jilin** *prov* China
65 G3 **Jilin** China
65 F3 **Jilin Hada Ling** *mt ra* China
59 H1 **Jiliu He** *R* China
17 G4 **Jiloca** *R* Spain
116 M3 **Jim** *R* Alaska U.S.A.
86 G4 **Jima** Ethiopia
69 G14 **Jimar** Sumatra
142 F5 **Jimberingga** W Australia Australia
48 F5 **Jimbolia** Romania
141 L8 **Jimboomba** Queensland Australia
16 D8 **Jimena de la Frontera** Spain
124 G4 **Jiménez** Mexico
140 C2 **Jim Jim Cr** N Terr Australia
65 E6 **Jimo** China
65 C6 **Jinan** China
65 B7 **Jincheng** China
139 J6 **Jindabyne** New South Wales Australia
37 O3 **Jindřichovice** Czechoslovakia
31 J6 **Jindřichův Hradec** Czechoslovakia
67 E2 **Jing'an** China
67 F1 **Jingde** China
67 F2 **Jingdezhen** China
Jingfeng *see* **Hexigten Qi**
65 D5 **Jinghai** China
65 E6 **Jinghaiwei** China
58 E5 **Jing He** *R* China
66 C3 **Jinghe** China
68 E2 **Jinghong** China
67 G1 **Jingjiang** China
65 B5 **Jingle** China
67 D1 **Jingmen** China
Jingping *see* **Pinglu**
65 G2 **Jingpo** China
65 G3 **Jingpo Hu** *L* China
58 F5 **Jing Shan** *mt ra* China
67 D1 **Jingshan** China
58 D4 **Jingtai** China
65 C6 **Jing Xian** China
67 F1 **Jing Xian** China
59 H2 **Jingxing** China
67 A2 **Jingyan** China
65 A7 **Jingyang** China
65 G3 **Jingyu** China
58 D4 **Jingyuan** China
Jingzhou *see* **Jiangling**
67 F2 **Jinhua** China
65 C7 **Jining** China
65 B4 **Jining** Nei Monggol Zizhiqu China
88 D1 **Jinja-Bugembe** Uganda
67 E2 **Jin Jiang** *R* China
67 C3 **Jin Jiang** *R* China
67 F4 **Jinjiang** China
67 D2 **Jinjing** China
65 E6 **Jinkou** China
67 E1 **Jinkou** China
67 F4 **Jinlong Jiang** *R* China
67 C7 **Jinmu Jiao** China
68 J3 **Jinmu Jiao** *C* China
125 M3 **Jinotega** Nicaragua
125 L4 **Jinotepe** Nicaragua
67 C3 **Jinping** China
68 F1 **Jinping** China
Jinsha *see* **Nantong**
67 B3 **Jinsha** China
58 C6 **Jinsha Jiang** *R* China
Jinshan *see* **Harqin Qi**
67 G1 **Jinshan** China
67 D2 **Jinshi** China
67 F1 **Jintan** China
67 A1 **Jintang** China
67 C5 **Jintian Shuiku** *res* China
71 F5 **Jintotolo** *isld* Philippines
71 F5 **Jintotolo Ch** Philippines
59 H3 **Jinxi** China
67 E3 **Jinxi** China
67 F3 **Jin Xi** China
67 B5 **Jinxi** China
65 E4 **Jin Xian** China
65 C5 **Jin Xian** China
65 E5 **Jin Xian** China
67 E2 **Jinxian** China
65 C7 **Jinxiang** China
67 G3 **Jinxiang** China
67 C4 **Jinxiu** China
67 G2 **Jinyun** China
67 E1 **Jinzhai** China
65 E4 **Jinzhou** China
65 E5 **Jinzhou Wan** *B* China
128 B4 **Jipijapa** Ecuador
126 F4 **Jiquani** Cuba
130 H5 **Jiquitaia** Brazil
77 C7 **Jirāb, Al** *isld* U.A.E.
143 F9 **Jirina Rockholes** *rockhole* W Australia Australia
65 D2 **Jirin Gol** China
37 P3 **Jirkov** Czechoslovakia
48 L5 **Jirlău** Romania
86 A2 **Jirriiban** Somalia
65 A7 **Jishan** China
67 C2 **Jishou** China
67 E3 **Jishui** China
79 G3 **Jisr ash Shughūr** Syria
16 C2 **Jistredo, Sa. de** *mts* Spain
143 C10 **Jitarning** W Australia Australia
Jitian *see* **Lianshan**
69 E9 **Jitra** Malaysia
48 H6 **Jiu** *R* Romania
Jiucheng *see* **Wucheng**
67 A1 **Jiuding Shan** *mt* China
58 G6 **Jiujiang** China
67 E2 **Jiujiang** China
67 D1 **Jiukou** China
67 E4 **Jiulian Shan** *mts* China
67 E2 **Jiuling Shan** *mt ra* China
58 C4 **Jiuquan** China
65 E6 **Jiurongcheng** China
59 J3 **Jiutai** China
67 C4 **Jiuwan Dashan** *mts* China
65 C5 **Jiuwuqing** China
65 C5 **Jiuxincheng** China
67 B4 **Jiuxu** China
67 F1 **Jiuyuhang** China
67 B4 **Jiuzhou** China
77 G7 **Jiwani** Iran
74 B10 **Jiwani** Pakistan
65 H2 **Jixi** China
67 F1 **Jixi** China
59 K2 **Jixian** China
65 D4 **Ji Xian** China
65 A6 **Ji Xian** China
65 C6 **Ji Xian** China
65 C7 **Ji Xian** China
65 D6 **Jiyang** China
65 B7 **Jiyuan** China
79 F7 **Jiza** Jordan
80 G7 **Jiza** Jordan
65 C6 **Jize** China
31 H5 **Jizera** *R* Czechoslovakia
60 G10 **Jizō zaki** *C* Japan
86 E1 **J. Kissu** *mt* Sudan
120 G1 **Joab L** Ontario Canada
130 D10 **Joaçaba** Brazil
33 T7 **Joachimsthal** Germany
130 H5 **Joaíma** Brazil
85 A6 **Joal-Fadiout** Senegal
129 L5 **Joao Camara** Brazil
129 J4 **João Coelho** Brazil
131 H4 **João Maria, Albardão do** Brazil
130 E10 **João Paulo** *R* Brazil
130 J9 **João Pessoa** Brazil
130 F5 **João Pinheiro** Brazil
111 B10 **Joaquin** Texas U.S.A.
126 F4 **Jobabo** Cuba
61 O9 **Jōban** Japan
71 G6 **Jobo Pt** Mindanao Philippines
20 G2 **Jobourg** France
102 F2 **Job Pk** Nevada U.S.A.
120 D2 **Jobrin** Ontario Canada
38 F7 **Jochberg** Austria
16 E7 **Jódar** Spain
74 E5 **Jodhpur** India
74 D7 **Jodiya Bandar** India
22 H2 **Jodoigne** Belgium
123 S4 **Joe Batt's Arm** Newfoundland Canada
29 O9 **Joensuu** Finland
106 H2 **Joes** Colorado U.S.A.
26 G6 **Joeström** Sweden
61 M8 **Jōetsu** Japan
87 F10 **Jofane** Mozambique
106 E7 **Joffre** New Mexico U.S.A.
117 Q10 **Joffre, Mt** British Columbia Canada
61 L9 **Joganji** *R* Japan
75 M5 **Jogbani** India
65 C3 **Jogdor** China
52 C5 **Jõgeva** Estonia
122 H8 **Joggins** Nova Scotia Canada
74 G3 **Jogindarnagar** India
120 E2 **Jog L** Ontario Canada
38 N7 **Joglland** Austria
61 K9 **Jōhana** Japan
32 J9 **Johannaberg** Germany
89 A1 **Johannesburg** S Africa
102 G6 **Johannesburg** California U.S.A.
37 O3 **Johanngeorgenstadt** Germany
115 M2 **Johan Pen** Northwest Territories Canada
60 F13 **Jōhen** Japan
116 L3 **John** *R* Alaska U.S.A.
122 J8 **John, C** Nova Scotia Canada
127 M2 **John Crow Mts** Jamaica
100 E4 **John Day** *R* Oregon U.S.A.
100 G5 **John Day** Oregon U.S.A.
100 E5 **John Day Fossil Beds Nat. Mon.** Oregon U.S.A.
117 Q6 **John d'Or Prairie** Alberta Canada
113 G9 **John F. Kennedy Space Center** Florida U.S.A.
94 J10 **John H. Kerr Res** N Carolina/Virg U.S.A.
106 H3 **John Martin Res** Colorado U.S.A.
142 G3 **John,Mt** W Australia Australia
15 E2 **John O'Groats** Scotland
107 P3 **John Redmond Res** Kansas U.S.A.
107 J4 **Johnson** Kansas U.S.A.
99 K9 **Johnson** Nebraska U.S.A.
94 J5 **Johnsonburg** Pennsylvania U.S.A.
95 M4 **Johnson City** New York U.S.A.
94 E10 **Johnson City** Tennessee U.S.A.
109 J5 **Johnson City** Texas U.S.A.
99 S6 **Johnson Cr** Wisconsin U.S.A.
117 G5 **Johnsons Crossing** Yukon Territory Canada
127 P4 **Johnsons Pt** Antigua W Indies
112 H4 **Johnsonville** South Carolina U.S.A.
112 F4 **Johnston** South Carolina U.S.A.
8 A4 **Johnston** Wales
110 H4 **Johnston City** Illinois U.S.A.
15 D5 **Johnstone** Scotland
117 K10 **Johnstone Str** British Columbia Canada
88 B7 **Johnston Falls** Zambia
143 D9 **Johnston,L** W Australia Australia
143 C8 **Johnston Ra** W Australia Australia
14 E3 **Johnstown** Ireland
98 F7 **Johnstown** Nebraska U.S.A.
95 N4 **Johnstown** New York U.S.A.
94 E6 **Johnstown** Ohio U.S.A.
94 J6 **Johnstown** Pennsylvania U.S.A.
94 E9 **John W Flannagan Res** Virginia U.S.A.
61 P5 **Jōhōji** Japan
69 F12 **Johor** Malaysia
69 F12 **Johor Baharo** Malaysia
37 P2 **Jöhstadt** Germany
52 C5 **Jõhvi** Estonia
18 H5 **Joigny** France
110 F6 **Joiner** Arkansas U.S.A.
130 E10 **Joinville** Brazil
19 J4 **Joinville** France
146 D3 **Joinville I** Antarctica
125 K8 **Jojutla** Mexico
26 N5 **Jokk** Sweden
26 L5 **Jokkmokk** Sweden
27 C10 **Jokuleggi** *mt* Norway
29 T9 **Jökulsá á Fjöllum** *R* Iceland
29 T9 **Jökulsa o Bru** *R* Iceland
78 K2 **Jolfā** Iran
99 S8 **Joliet** Illinois U.S.A.
101 Q4 **Joliet** Montana U.S.A.
121 R6 **Joliette** Quebec Canada
119 U10 **Joliette** North Dakota U.S.A.
142 A1 **Jolimont** *dist* Perth, W Aust Australia
99 M7 **Jolley** Iowa U.S.A.
117 S3 **Jolly L** Northwest Territories Canada
71 E7 **Jolo** Philippines
102 C6 **Jolon** California U.S.A.
26 B10 **Jölstervatn** *L* Norway
26 G7 **Joma** *mt* Norway
29 H11 **Jomala** Finland
71 F3 **Jomalig** *isld* Luzon Philippines
70 O9 **Jombang** Java
66 F5 **Jomda** China
71 A3 **Jome** Indonesia
27 D13 **Jomfruland** *isld* Norway
52 B6 **Jonava** Lithuania
22 F5 **Jonchery-sur-Vesle** France
7 E13 **Jones Bank** Atlantic Oc
110 F6 **Jonesboro** Arkansas U.S.A.
111 M8 **Jonesboro** Georgia U.S.A.
110 G4 **Jonesboro** Illinois U.S.A.
109 P3 **Jonesboro** Louisiana U.S.A.
95 U2 **Jonesboro** Maine U.S.A.
112 H2 **Jonesboro** North Carolina U.S.A.
100 H6 **Jonesboro** Oregon U.S.A.
112 E1 **Jonesboro** Tennessee U.S.A.
109 K4 **Jonesboro** Texas U.S.A.
116 N1 **Jones Is** Alaska U.S.A.
146 B7 **Jones Mts** Antarctica
95 U2 **Jonesport** Maine U.S.A.
83 M9 **Jones Pt** Christmas I Indian Oc
115 L2 **Jones Sound** Northwest Territories Canada
111 F7 **Jonestown** Mississippi U.S.A.
94 B7 **Jonesville** Indiana U.S.A.
111 E10 **Jonesville** Louisiana U.S.A.
94 C5 **Jonesville** Michigan U.S.A.
112 F3 **Jonesville** South Carolina U.S.A.
94 D10 **Jonesville** Virginia U.S.A.
86 F4 **Jonglei** *prov* Sudan
52 B6 **Joniskis** Lithuania
27 G14 **Jönköping** Sweden
27 G14 **Jönköping** *county* Sweden
121 T4 **Jonquière** Quebec Canada
29 K4 **Jönstorp** Sweden
18 E7 **Jonzac** France
110 B4 **Joplin** Missouri U.S.A.
101 P1 **Joplin** Montana U.S.A.
80 B5 **Joppa** Israel
110 H4 **Joppa** Illinois U.S.A.
141 H6 **Jordan** *R* Queensland Australia
80 F1 **Jordan** *R* Israel/Jordan
80 **Jordan** *kingdom* S W Asia
99 N5 **Jordan** Minnesota U.S.A.
101 T2 **Jordan** Montana U.S.A.
95 L3 **Jordan** New York U.S.A.
100 H7 **Jordan** *R* Oregon U.S.A.
129 K7 **Jordânia** Brazil
122 G9 **Jordan L** Nova Scotia Canada
111 K9 **Jordan L** Alabama U.S.A.
48 F1 **Jordanow** Poland
100 H7 **Jordan Valley** Oregon U.S.A.
130 D9 **Jordão, R** Brazil
28 C3 **Jordbro Å** *R* Denmark
33 R5 **Jördenstorf** Germany
27 F10 **Jordet** Norway
28 E6 **Jordløse** Denmark
28 C5 **Jordrup** Denmark
28 B6 **Jordsand** *isld* Denmark
26 P2 **Jorgastak** Norway
133 B8 **Jorge Montt, I** Chile
75 Q5 **Jorhat** India
32 L5 **Jork** Germany
57 F6 **Jorm** Afghanistan
26 G7 **Jormlien** Sweden
26 L6 **Jörn** Sweden
106 C9 **Jornada del Muerto** *reg* New Mexico U.S.A.
27 B12 **Jörpeland** Norway
21 K4 **Jort** France
85 F7 **Jos** Nigeria
71 G8 **Jose Abad Santos** Mindanao Philippines
133 C6 **José de San Martín** Argentina
129 J8 **José dos Campos** Brazil
130 C5 **Joselândia** Brazil
133 E5 **José Maria Blanco** Argentina
27 B12 **Josenfjord** *inlet* Norway
71 F3 **Jose Pañganiban** Philippines
100 J4 **Joseph** Idaho U.S.A.
100 H4 **Joseph** Oregon U.S.A.
142 G2 **Joseph Bonaparte G** Australia
142 G2 **Joseph Bonaparte Gulf** Australia
103 O7 **Joseph City** Arizona U.S.A.
6 M6 **Josephine** *oil rig* North Sea
115 N7 **Joseph L** Labrador, Nfld Canada
123 K4 **Joseph Pt** Anticosti I, Quebec
144 B6 **Josephville** New Zealand
61 M9 **Jō-Shin-Etsu Nat. Park** Japan
109 K3 **Joshua** Texas U.S.A.
102 H7 **Joshua Tree** California U.S.A.
21 O6 **Josnes** France
36 H3 **Jossatal** Germany
20 E6 **Josselin** France
26 E7 **Jössund** Nord-Tröndelag Norway
26 D8 **Jössund** Sör-Tröndelag Norway
26 B10 **Jostedal** Norway
26 B10 **Jostedalsbreen** *gla* Norway
48 F2 **Josvafö** Hungary
26 N2 **Jotkajavrre** Norway
27 C10 **Jotunheimen** *mt* Norway
79 F5 **Jouaiya** Lebanon
21 O4 **Jouars** France
21 K4 **Joué-du-Bois** France
21 M7 **Joué-lès-Tours** France
20 H7 **Joué-sur-Erdre** France
19 K3 **Jœuf** France
29 N6 **Joukokylä** Finland
113 J12 **Joulters Cays** *islds* Bahamas
79 F5 **Jôunié** Lebanon
109 J7 **Jourdanton** Texas U.S.A.
25 E3 **Joure** Netherlands
118 B3 **Joussard** Alberta Canada
121 M3 **Joutel** Quebec Canada
29 M10 **Joutsa** Finland
29 N5 **Joutsijärvi** Finland
40 D4 **Joux, L.de** Switzerland
21 O4 **Jouy** France
21 O6 **Jouy-le-Potier** France
126 D3 **Jovellanos** Cuba
75 P6 **Jowai** India
77 J1 **Jowzjān** *prov* Afghanistan
14 B3 **Joyce's Country** Ireland
117 G4 **Joy, Mt** Yukon Territory Canada
60 O3 **Jōzankei** Japan
31 N4 **Józefów** Poland
110 K5 **J. Percy Priest L** Tennessee U.S.A.
71 B3 **Ju** *isld* Indonesia
124 H5 **Juan Aldama** Mexico
65 C7 **Juancheng** China
141 J7 **Juandah** *R* Queensland Australia
127 K2 **Juan de Bolas** *pk* Jamaica
100 A1 **Juan de Fuca, Str. of** Canada/U.S.A.
87 G11 **Juan de Nova** *isld* Madagascar
133 A9 **Juan Fernández, Is** Pacific Oc
127 N9 **Juangriego** Venezuela
88 G6 **Juani** *isld* Tanzania
128 C5 **Juanjui** Peru
29 N8 **Juankoski** Finland
44 B4 **Juan les Pins** France
124 E2 **Juan M. Ortíz** Mexico
131 B2 **Juan Soldado, C.de** Chile
133 B7 **Juan Stuven, I** Chile
133 F5 **Juárez** Argentina
103 J9 **Juárez, Sa** *ra* Mexico
129 K5 **Juazeiro** Brazil
130 G9 **Juàzeiro do Norte** Brazil
86 F5 **Juba** Sudan
77 A6 **Jubayl, Al** Saudi Arabia
80 G5 **Jubba** Jordan
86 H5 **Jubba** *R* Somalia
80 G1 **Jubbāta el Khashab** Syria
123 R5 **Jubilee L** Newfoundland Canada
143 F8 **Jubilee Lake** W Australia Australia
102 H6 **Jubilee Peak** California U.S.A.
21 K5 **Jublains** France
85 B3 **Juby, Cap** *C* Morocco
17 F5 **Júcar** *R* Spain
36 B1 **Jüchen** Germany
124 H7 **Juchipila** Mexico
125 M9 **Juchitán** Mexico
124 H7 **Juchitlán** Mexico
129 K7 **Jucurucú** *R* Brazil
98 H3 **Jud** North Dakota U.S.A.
99 R7 **Juda** Wisconsin U.S.A.
80 B7 **Judaea** Israel
79 G5 **Judaydat al Wadī** Syria
123 S6 **Jude I** Newfoundland Canada
80 D2 **Judeida** Israel
37 L3 **Judenbach** Germany
38 L7 **Judenburg** Austria
146 B16 **Judge and Clerk Is** *islds* S Pacific Oc
123 L8 **Judique** C Breton I, Nova Scotia
101 Q2 **Judith** *R* Montana U.S.A.
101 Q2 **Judith Basin** *reg* Montana U.S.A.
101 Q3 **Judith Gap** Montana U.S.A.
98 E3 **Judson** North Dakota U.S.A.
Juegang *see* **Rudong**
28 E5 **Juelsminde** Denmark
130 H5 **Juerana** Brazil
128 F4 **Jufari** *R* Brazil
84 F4 **Jufrah Oasis, Al** Libya
20 F5 **Jugon-les-Lacs** France
65 E4 **Juhua Dao** *isld* China
21 H6 **Juigné-des-Moutiers** France
18 F7 **Juillac** France
21 P4 **Juine** *R* France
32 E5 **Juist** *isld* Germany
32 F5 **Juist** Germany
129 K8 **Juiz de Fora** Brazil
65 D3 **Jujinchang** China
69 E13 **Jujuhan** *R* Sumatra
19 O12 **Jujurieux** France
128 E8 **Jujuy** *prov* Argentina
26 L7 **Juken** Sweden
26 L4 **Jukkasjärvi** Sweden
67 D3 **Jukoupu** China
26 H6 **Juktån** *R* Sweden
128 E8 **Julaca** Bolivia
98 D9 **Julesburg** Colorado U.S.A.
128 E7 **Julí** Peru
141 F5 **Julia** *R* Queensland Australia
128 D7 **Juliaca** Peru
141 F5 **Julia Creek** Queensland Australia
100 J3 **Juliaetta** Idaho U.S.A.
102 H8 **Julian** California U.S.A.
115 P5 **Julianehåb** Greenland
14 E3 **Julianstown** Ireland
36 B2 **Jülich** Germany
42 E2 **Julijske A** *mts* Slovenia
124 G3 **Julimes** Mexico
80 D2 **Jūlis** Israel
27 H12 **Julita** Sweden
140 E5 **Julius L.** Queensland Australia
20 G4 **Jullouville** France
Jullundur *see* **Jalandhar**
28 D4 **Julsø** *L* Denmark
65 C6 **Julu** China
80 G8 **Jumaiyil** Jordan
86 H6 **Jumba** Somalia
117 P10 **Jumbo Mt** British Columbia Canada
21 K7 **Jumelles** France
21 J7 **Jumellière,la** France
22 G3 **Jumet** Belgium
21 M3 **Jumièges** France
17 G6 **Jumilla** Spain
75 K4 **Jumla** Nepal
74 D8 **Junagadh** India
65 D7 **Junan** China
65 D2 **Jun Bulen** China
124 D5 **Juncal** Mexico
131 D8 **Juncal, L** Argentina
108 H5 **Junction** Texas U.S.A.
103 M3 **Junction** Utah U.S.A.
140 C1 **Junction B** N Terr Australia

111 D8 **Junction City** Arkansas U.S.A.
111 M9 **Junction City** Georgia U.S.A.
107 O2 **Junction City** Kansas U.S.A.
94 C9 **Junction City** Kentucky U.S.A.
110 M4 **Junction City** Kentucky U.S.A.
100 B5 **Junction City** Oregon U.S.A.
99 R5 **Junction City** Wisconsin U.S.A.
141 G6 **Jundah** Queensland Australia
65 C4 **Jundu Shan** mt ra China
117 F6 **Juneau** Alaska U.S.A.
99 S6 **Juneau** Wisconsin U.S.A.
139 J5 **Junee** New South Wales Australia
113 F10 **June in Winter, L** Florida U.S.A.
102 E4 **June Lake** California U.S.A.
65 A5 **Jungar Qi** China
40 G4 **Jungfrau** mt Switzerland
40 G4 **Jungfraujoch** Switzerland
22 L4 **Junglinster** Luxembourg
100 G9 **Jungo** Nevada U.S.A.
98 H9 **Juniata** Nebraska U.S.A.
95 K6 **Juniata** R Pennsylvania U.S.A.
131 E5 **Junin** Argentina
128 D7 **Junin** Chile
128 C6 **Junin** Peru
133 C5 **Junin de los Andes** Argentina
94 H8 **Junior** West Virginia U.S.A.
95 T1 **Junior L** Maine U.S.A.
122 E7 **Juniper** New Brunswick Canada
103 L6 **Juniper Mts** Arizona U.S.A.
102 C5 **Junipero Sierra Pk** California U.S.A.
61 O5 **Jūni sho** Japan
22 G5 **Juniville** France
116 O2 **Junjik** R Alaska U.S.A.
36 B3 **Jünkerath** Germany
26 H5 **Junkerdal** Norway
67 A2 **Junlian** China
108 F5 **Juno** Texas U.S.A.
118 K5 **Junor** Saskatchewan Canada
26 M4 **Junosuando** Sweden
26 J8 **Junsele** Sweden
67 E2 **Junshan Hu** L China
16 A5 **Junto** mt Portugal
65 A5 **Juntuliang** China
100 G6 **Juntura** Oregon U.S.A.
29 O6 **Juntusranta** Finland
29 O9 **Juojärvi** L Finland
26 N5 **Juoksengi** Sweden
130 H6 **Juparaña, Lagoa** L Brazil
130 D7 **Jupia** Brazil
130 D7 **Jupia Dam** Brazil
22 K2 **Jupille** Belgium
21 L6 **Jupilles** France
113 G11 **Jupiter** Florida U.S.A.
122 J4 **Jupiter R** Quebec Canada
129 J8 **Juquiá** Brazil
86 E4 **Jur** R Sudan
40 C4 **Jura** dept France
15 C4 **Jura** Scotland
40 F3 **Jura** canton Switzerland
128 C2 **Jurado** Colombia
31 L5 **Jura Krakowska** reg Poland
130 G5 **Juramento** Brazil
52 B6 **Jurbarkas** Lithuania
12 D5 **Jurby** I of Man U.K.
79 F8 **Jurf ed Darāwīsh** Jordan
65 E2 **Jurh** China
143 B9 **Jurien** W Australia Australia
143 B9 **Jurien B** W Australia Australia
48 M6 **Jurilovca** Romania
52 B6 **Jurmala** Latvia
67 F1 **Jurong** China
38 N9 **Juršinci** Slovenia
128 E4 **Juruá** Brazil
128 D5 **Juruá** R Brazil
128 G6 **Juruena** Brazil
129 G4 **Juruti** Brazil
29 J9 **Jurva** Finland
61 O5 **Jūsan-ko** L Japan
127 N10 **Jusepín** Venezuela
79 G4 **Jūsīyah** Syria
19 J5 **Jussey** France
119 S8 **Justice** Manitoba Canada
108 F2 **Justiceburg** Texas U.S.A.
109 K2 **Justin** Texas U.S.A.
133 D4 **Justo Daract** Argentina
128 E5 **Jutaí** Brazil
33 S9 **Jüterbog** Germany
130 C8 **Juti** Brazil
125 L2 **Juticalpa** Honduras
26 J5 **Jutis** Sweden
Jutland see **Jylland**
26 E10 **Jutulhugget** pass Norway
146 H6 **Jutulstraumen** ice stream Antarctica
29 O8 **Juuka** Finland
29 N10 **Juva** Finland
126 C4 **Juventud, Isla de la** Cuba
21 H5 **Juvigné** France
21 H4 **Juvigny-le-Tertre** France
21 J4 **Juvigny-sous-Andaine** France
21 P4 **Juvisy** France
28 B6 **Juvre** Denmark
70 N9 **Juwana** Java
79 H5 **Juwayf, Al** Syria
65 D7 **Ju Xian** China
65 C7 **Juye** China
77 F2 **Jūymand** Iran
40 A1 **Juzennecourt** France
Jye Kundo see **Yushu**
28 B4 **Jylland** reg Denmark
29 M9 **Jyväskylä** Finland

K

66 B4 **K2** mt Kashmir/China
85 E6 **Ka** R Nigeria
102 S11 **Kaaawa** Hawaiian Is
89 B7 **Kaaing Veld** plateau S Africa
57 A5 **Kaakhka** Turkmenistan
102 R11 **Kaala** pk Hawaiian Is
26 L4 **Kaalasjarvi** L Sweden
135 U6 **Kaalualu** Hawaiian Is
29 N2 **Kaamanen** Finland
86 H6 **Kaambooni** Somalia
89 C7 **Kaap Plato** S Africa
33 O6 **Kaarssen** Germany
29 N9 **Kaavi** Finland
48 G3 **Kaba** Hungary
70 G7 **Kabaena** isld Sulawesi
85 B7 **Kabala** Sierra Leone
86 F5 **Kabalega Falls** Uganda
86 E7 **Kabalo** Zaire
88 A4 **Kabambare** Zaire
69 D11 **Kabanjahe** Sumatra
85 D5 **Kabara** Mali
53 F11 **Kabardino Balkarskaya Respublika** Russian Federation
88 B3 **Kabare** Zaire
86 F5 **Kabarole** Uganda
71 F7 **Kabasalang** Philippines
60 C13 **Kaba shima** isld Japan
68 C3 **Kabaung** R Burma
85 F7 **Kabba** Nigeria
26 G3 **Kabelvåg** lighthouse Norway
120 E4 **Kabenung L** Ontario Canada
70 G4 **Kabetan. I** Sulawesi
99 O1 **Kabetogama** Minnesota U.S.A.
99 N1 **Kabetogama L** Minnesota U.S.A.
120 F3 **Kabinakagami** R Ontario Canada
86 D7 **Kabinda** Zaire
71 M9 **Kabir** Indonesia
79 F3 **Kabīr** R Syria/Lebanon
57 E5 **Kabla** Tajikistan
47 J2 **Kableshkovo** Bulgaria
86 C4 **Kabo** Cent Afr Republic
87 D8 **Kabompo** R Zambia
70 B4 **Kabong** Sarawak
87 E7 **Kabongo** Zaire
68 C6 **Kabosa I.** Burma
85 G1 **Kaboudia, Rass** C Tunisia
52 E5 **Kabozha** Russian Federation
80 D1 **Kabri** Israel
77 F1 **Kabūd Gonbad** Iran
71 E2 **Kabugao** Philippines
77 L2 **Kābul** Afghanistan
80 D2 **Kābūl** Israel
88 C2 **Kabula** Uganda
87 E8 **Kabunda** Zaire
88 B7 **Kabunda** Zambia
71 H9 **Kabunduk** Indonesia
86 F2 **Kabushiya** Sudan
88 B9 **Kabwe** Zambia
55 F3 **Kabyrdak** Russian Federation
55 D5 **Kabyrga** R Kazakhstan
46 E2 **Kačanik** Serbia Yugoslavia
71 B3 **Kacepi** Indonesia
87 F8 **Kachalola** Zambia
74 C7 **Kachchh, Gulf of** India
74 C6 **Kachchh, Rann of** India
116 M7 **Kachemak B** Alaska U.S.A.
100 D2 **Kachess L** Washington U.S.A.
85 F7 **Kachia** Nigeria
75 R5 **Kachin State** prov Burma
55 G4 **Kachiry** Kazakhstan
55 C2 **Kachkanar** Russian Federation
56 G4 **Kachug** Russian Federation
78 H1 **Kaçkar Dağlar** mt Turkey
60 J11 **Kada** Japan
68 C4 **Kadaingti** Burma
76 A5 **Kadamatt** isld Indian Oc
86 F5 **Kadam Mt** Uganda
37 P3 **Kadaň** Czechoslovakia
68 D6 **Kadan Kyun** isld Burma
70 D7 **Kadapongan** isld Indonesia
48 D4 **Kadarkút** Hungary
71 H7 **Kadatung** isld Indonesia
137 Q5 **Kadavu** isld Fiji
41 H2 **Kadelburg** Germany
61 P13 **Kadena** Okinawa
71 K9 **Kadesa** Indonesia
143 F7 **Kadgo L** W Australia Australia
78 K5 **Kādhimain** Iraq
74 E7 **Kadi** India
85 C6 **Kadiana** Mali
46 F3 **Kadijica** mt Macedonia Yugoslavia
47 N11 **Kadıköy** Turkey
138 E5 **Kadina** South Australia Australia
78 D2 **Kadınhanı** Turkey
74 F9 **Kadirabad** India
47 J8 **Kadirga Burun** C Turkey
76 D3 **Kadiri** India
78 F3 **Kadirli** Turkey
70 G7 **Kadjang** Sulawesi
73 L6 **Kadmat** isld Lakshadweep Indian Oc
52 F5 **Kadnikov** Russian Federation
68 C4 **Kado** Burma
60 E13 **Kadogawa** Japan
98 E6 **Kadoka** South Dakota U.S.A.
89 F2 **Kadoma** Zimbabwe
68 B5 **Kadonkani** Burma
46 E3 **Kadrifakovo** Macedonia Yugoslavia
86 E3 **Kadugli** Sudan
86 A3 **Kaduna** Nigeria
76 C4 **Kadur** India
52 E5 **Kaduy** Russian Federation
56 E5 **Kadyr-Egi-Tayga, Khrebet** mts Russian Federation
52 F5 **Kadyy** Russian Federation
57 H4 **Kadzhi-Say** Kyrgyzstan
85 B5 **Kaedi** Mauritania
123 R5 **Kaegudeck L** Newfoundland Canada
86 B3 **Kaélé** Cameroon
145 D1 **Kaeo** New Zealand
28 D6 **Kærum** Denmark
65 G5 **Kaesŏng** N Korea
87 D7 **Käfakumba** Zaire
85 F7 **Kafanchan** Nigeria
85 A6 **Kaffrine** Senegal
71 C3 **Kafiau** isld W Irian
46 G7 **Kafiréos, Porthmós** str Greece
46 G6 **Kafirévs, Akr** C Greece
26 L2 **Kåfjord** inlet Norway
26 N2 **Kåfjord** Norway
80 E1 **Kafra** Lebanon
80 D5 **Kafr 'Abbush** Jordan
80 D5 **Kafr 'Ain** Jordan
79 G3 **Kafr Buhum** Syria
80 F6 **Kafrein** R Jordan
79 A7 **Kafr el Dauwâr** Egypt
80 D4 **Kafr-el-Labad** Jordan
79 A7 **Kafr el Sheik** Egypt
79 A8 **Kafr el Zaiyât** Egypt
80 D2 **Kafr Mandā** Israel
80 C5 **Kafr Qāsim** Israel
80 D4 **Kafr Qud** Jordan
80 D4 **Kafr Ra'i** Jordan
80 D4 **Kafr Rumman** Jordan
79 G4 **Kafrūn Bashūr** Syria
80 D5 **Kafr Zibad** Jordan
88 B9 **Kafue** Zambia
87 E8 **Kafue Nat. Park** Zambia
87 E7 **Kafulwe** Zambia
55 C4 **Kaga** Russian Federation
86 C4 **Kaga Bandoro** Cent Afr Republic
60 G10 **Kagami** Japan
57 C5 **Kagan** Uzbekistan
116 G7 **Kagati L** Alaska U.S.A.
60 G11 **Kagawa** prefect Japan
120 H7 **Kagawong** Ontario Canada
26 M7 **Kåge** Sweden
88 C2 **Kagera** reg Tanzania
88 C2 **Kagera National Park** Rwanda
28 J5 **Kagerup** Denmark
120 C2 **Kagianagami L** Ontario Canada
120 D3 **Kagiano L** Ontario Canada
47 M10 **Kâğıthane** Turkey
78 J1 **Kağızman** Turkey
69 D13 **Kagologolo** Indonesia
60 D14 **Kagoshima** Japan
48 L5 **Kagul** Moldavia
48 L5 **Kagul, Ozero** L Ukraine
116 L8 **Kaguyak** Alaska U.S.A.
70 D6 **Kahajan** R Kalimantan
70 E5 **Kahala** Kalimantan
135 O1 **Kahala Pt** Hawaiian Is
102 S12 **Kahaluu** Hawaiian Is
88 D3 **Kahama** Tanzania
74 C4 **Kahan** Pakistan
102 S11 **Kahana** Hawaiian Is
145 F3 **Kaharoa** mt New Zealand
71 A2 **Kahatola** isld Halmahera Indonesia
87 C7 **Kahemba** Zaire
102 R12 **Kahe Pt** Hawaiian Is
144 A6 **Kaherekoau Mts** New Zealand
116 M5 **Kahiltna Gl** Alaska U.S.A.
36 G3 **Kahl** R Germany
37 M2 **Kahla** Germany
36 F1 **Kahler-Asten** mt Germany
100 G3 **Kahlotus** Washington U.S.A.
117 N6 **Kahntah** British Columbia Canada
77 E6 **Kahnuj** Iran
110 E1 **Kahoka** Missouri U.S.A.
61 K9 **Kahoku-gata** L Japan
102 V13 **Kahoolawe** isld Hawaiian Is
29 J2 **Kahperusvaara** mt Finland
78 F3 **Kahramanmaraş** Turkey
135 Q1 **Kahuku** Hawaiian Is
102 S11 **Kahuku Pt** Hawaiian Is
135 T3 **Kahului** Hawaiian Is
Kahutara Pt see **Table Cape**
85 E7 **Kaiama** Nigeria
144 D5 **Kaiapoi** New Zealand
119 O1 **Kaiashk** R Ontario Canada
103 M5 **Kaibab Plat** Arizona U.S.A.
60 J10 **Kaibara** Japan
103 N5 **Kaibito Plat** Arizona U.S.A.
66 D3 **Kaidu He** R China
128 G2 **Kaieteur Falls** Guyana
65 C7 **Kaifeng** China
145 D1 **Kaihu** New Zealand
67 F2 **Kaihua** China
145 E3 **Kai-Iwi** New Zealand
67 B1 **Kaijiang** China
136 G3 **Kai, Kep** islds Moluccas Indonesia
145 D1 **Kaikohe** New Zealand
67 B3 **Kaikou** China
144 D5 **Kaikoura** New Zealand
144 D5 **Kaikoura Range** New Zealand
Kailas Range see **Gangdisê Shan**
36 G4 **Kailbach** Germany
67 B3 **Kaili** China
65 E3 **Kailu** China
102 S12 **Kailua** Hawaiian Is
135 T5 **Kailua** Hawaiian Is
145 E2 **Kaimai Ra** New Zealand
46 E4 **Kaïmakchalán** mt Greece
136 G2 **Kaimana** W Irian
145 E3 **Kaimanawa Mts** New Zealand
144 C5 **Kaimata** New Zealand
60 D14 **Kaimon-dake** pk Japan
135 V5 **Kaimu** Hawaiian Is
27 N13 **Käina** Estonia
38 M7 **Kainach** R Austria
135 U5 **Kainaliu** Hawaiian Is
60 J11 **Kainan** Japan
46 G3 **Kainchal** mt Greece
57 G3 **Kainda** Kyrgyzstan
68 B2 **Kaing** Burma
145 F3 **Kaingaroa Forest** New Zealand
145 F3 **Kaingaroa Plat.** New Zealand
38 J6 **Kainisch** Austria
85 E6 **Kainji Res** Nigeria
71 H7 **Kaioba** Indonesia
145 E2 **Kaipara Flats** New Zealand
103 N4 **Kaiparowits Plat** Utah U.S.A.
65 D5 **Kaiping** China
67 D5 **Kaiping** China
29 N4 **Kairala** Finland
43 C13 **Kairouan** Tunisia
38 F6 **Kaiser-Gebirge** mts Austria
102 E4 **Kaiser Pk** California U.S.A.
36 C3 **Kaisersesch** Germany
36 D5 **Kaiserslautern** Germany
40 G1 **Kaiserstuhl** mt Germany
32 E10 **Kaiserswerth** Germany
60 F11 **Kaita** Japan
145 D1 **Kaitaia** New Zealand
144 B7 **Kaitangata** New Zealand
145 F3 **Kaitawa** New Zealand
145 D4 **Kaiteriteri** New Zealand
74 G4 **Kaithal** India
145 E4 **Kaitoki** New Zealand
Kaitong see **Tongyu**
26 L4 **Kaitum** Sweden
26 K4 **Kaitumälven** R Sweden
26 K4 **Kaitumj** Sweden
26 L3 **Kaivare** mt Sweden
145 E2 **Kaiwaka** New Zealand
71 N9 **Kaiwatu** Indonesia
102 V13 **Kaiwi Ch** Hawaiian Is
67 C1 **Kai Xian** China
67 B3 **Kaiyang** China
59 H3 **Kaiyuan** China
67 A5 **Kaiyuan** China
116 H5 **Kaiyuh Mts** Alaska U.S.A.
60 J11 **Kaizuka** Japan
70 E3 **Kaja** Kalimantan
29 N7 **Kajaani** Finland
141 F5 **Kajabbi** Queensland Australia
77 J3 **Kajaki Dam** Afghanistan
71 L9 **Kajan** isld Indonesia
69 E11 **Kajang** Malaysia
88 F2 **Kajiado** Kenya
61 M10 **Kajikazawa** Japan
60 D14 **Kajiki** Japan
71 A2 **Kajoa** isld Halmahera Indonesia
86 F5 **Kajo Kaji** Sudan
71 K8 **Kajuadi** isld Indonesia
85 F6 **Kajuru** Nigeria
86 F3 **Kaka** Sudan
103 M9 **Kaka** Arizona U.S.A.
70 F3 **Kakaban** isld Kalimantan
119 O2 **Kakabeka Falls** Ontario Canada
71 L8 **Kakabia** isld Indonesia
140 C2 **Kakadu Nat Park** N Terr Australia
118 J1 **Kakagi L** Ontario Canada
145 E3 **Kakahi** New Zealand
71 G7 **Kakal** R Mindanao Philippines
70 F5 **Kakali** Sulawesi
87 D11 **Kakamas** S Africa
88 E1 **Kakamega** Kenya
69 A8 **Kakana** Nicobar Is
144 C6 **Kakanui** New Zealand
135 T3 **Kaka Pt** Hawaiian Is
145 E3 **Kakaramea** New Zealand
85 B7 **Kakata** Liberia
145 E3 **Kakatahi** New Zealand
57 D5 **Kakaydy** Uzbekistan
60 F11 **Kake** Japan
117 G7 **Kake** Alaska U.S.A.
61 M11 **Kakegawa** Japan
56 E5 **Ka-Khem** R Russian Federation
116 K7 **Kakhonak** Alaska U.S.A.
54 E10 **Kakhovka** Ukraine
54 E10 **Kakhovskoye Vdkhr** res Ukraine
77 F2 **Kakht** Iran
77 B5 **Kākī** Iran
76 F2 **Kākināda** India
117 P5 **Kakisa L** Northwest Territories Canada
61 M8 **Kakizaki** Japan
60 H11 **Kakogawa** Japan
55 E4 **Kak, Oz** L Kazakhstan
85 D7 **Kakpin** Ivory Coast
66 B3 **Kak Shaal Too, Khrebet** mts Kazakhstan
116 Q1 **Kaktovik** Alaska U.S.A.
61 O8 **Kakuda** Japan
61 O6 **Kakumagawa** Japan
61 O6 **Kakunodate** Japan
70 C3 **Kakus** R Sarawak
86 E7 **Kakuyu** Zaire
117 O8 **Kakwa** R Alberta Canada
48 F3 **Kál** Hungary
43 D13 **Kalaâ Kebira** Tunisia
Kalaallit Nunaat see **Greenland**
43 B13 **Kalaat Es Senam** mt Tunisia
71 M9 **Kalabahi** Indonesia
46 E5 **Kalabáka** Greece
70 E2 **Kalaban** Sabah
138 F4 **Kalabity** South Australia Australia
87 D8 **Kalabo** Zambia
54 N6 **Kalach** Russian Federation
55 F3 **Kalachinsk** Russian Federation
53 F9 **Kalach-na-donu** Russian Federation
54 M6 **Kalachskaya Vozvyshennost'** uplands Russian Federation
68 A2 **Kaladan** Burma
121 N8 **Kaladar** Ontario Canada
102 V14 **Kalae** Hawaiian Is
70 G6 **Kalaena** R Sulawesi
47 R14 **Kaláfou** Rhodes Greece
68 C1 **Kalagwe** Burma
89 B4 **Kalahari Desert** Botswana
89 B6 **Kalahari Game Res** S Africa
89 B5 **Kalahari Gemsbok Nat. Park** S Africa
57 F5 **Kalai-Khumb** Tajikistan
57 B6 **Kala-I-Mor** Turkmenistan
29 K7 **Kalajoki** Finland
29 L8 **Kalajoki** R Finland
58 G1 **Kalakan** Russian Federation
135 O1 **Kalalau Lookout** Hawaiian Is
70 G5 **Kalaliok** Sulawesi
74 E1 **Kalam** Pakistan
100 C3 **Kalama** Washington U.S.A.
46 E7 **Kalámai** Greece
Kalamata Greece see **Kalámai**
94 B4 **Kalamazoo** Michigan U.S.A.
70 D7 **Kalambau** isld Indonesia
87 F7 **Kalambo Falls** Tanzania
46 D6 **Kálamos** isld Greece
46 F6 **Kálamos** Greece
143 B9 **Kalamunda** W Australia Australia
138 E3 **Kalamurra, L** South Australia Australia
143 B9 **Kalannie** W Australia Australia
29 J11 **Kalanti** Finland
71 K8 **Kalao** isld Indonesia
71 G7 **Kalaong** Mindanao Philippines
71 K8 **Kalaotoa** isld Indonesia
83 K9 **Kala Oya** R Sri Lanka
69 G13 **Kalapa** Indonesia
58 G1 **Kalar** R Russian Federation
48 L3 **Kalarash** Moldavia
26 H9 **Kälarne** Sweden
83 L9 **Kal Aru** R Sri Lanka
74 B4 **Kalat** Pakistan
77 G6 **Kalateh-Masjed** Iran
135 S2 **Kalaupapa** Hawaiian Is
53 F10 **Kalaus** R Russian Federation
47 R14 **Kalavardha** Rhodes Greece
46 E6 **Kalávrita** Greece
68 C2 **Kalaw** Burma
83 K9 **Kalawewa** Sri Lanka
36 H3 **Kalbach** Germany
143 A8 **Kalbarri** W Australia Australia
143 A8 **Kalbarri Nat Park** W Australia Australia
33 O7 **Kalbe** Germany
56 B6 **Kalbinskiy Khrebet** mts Kazakhstan
77 F2 **Kalbū** Iran
42 F3 **Kalce** Slovenia
55 B5 **Kaldygayty** R Kazakhstan
47 K7 **Kale** Turkey
78 D1 **Kalecik** Turkey
71 H7 **Kaledupa** isld Indonesia
68 C5 **Kalegauk I** Burma
88 E6 **Kalehe** Zaire
68 B3 **Kaleindaung** inlet Burma
86 D6 **Kalema** Zaire
88 B4 **Kalémié** Zaire
32 K7 **Kalenberg** reg Germany
31 L5 **Kalety** Poland
94 B2 **Kaleva** Michigan U.S.A.
29 P6 **Kalevala** Russian Federation
28 S10 **Kalfafell** Iceland
52 E3 **Kalgachikha** Russian Federation
Kalgan see **Zhangjiakou**
58 G3 **Kalgan** China
143 C10 **Kalgan,R** W Australia Australia
108 F2 **Kalgary** Texas U.S.A.
116 M6 **Kalgin I** Alaska U.S.A.
143 D9 **Kalgoorlie** W Australia Australia
46 E4 **Kalí** Greece
47 L6 **Kalı** R Turkey
46 E6 **Kaliakoúdha** mt Greece
47 J1 **Kaliakra, N** Bulgaria
70 K8 **Kalianda** Sumatra
70 O9 **Kalianget** Indonesia
55 F4 **Kalibek, Oz** L Kazakhstan
71 F5 **Kalibo** Philippines
94 C6 **Kalida** Ohio U.S.A.
69 D14 **Kaliet** Indonesia
86 E6 **Kalima** Zaire
70 **Kalimantan** Borneo
70 B4 **Kalimantan Barat** Borneo
70 D6 **Kalimantan Selatan** Kalimantan
70 C5 **Kalimantan Tengah** Kalimantan
70 E3 **Kalimantan Timur** Kalimantan
47 H8 **Kálimnos** isld Greece
75 N5 **Kālimpang** India
71 H7 **Kalingsusuh Tk** B Indonesia
Kalinin see **Tver'**
57 E5 **Kalininabad** Tajikistan
27 L17 **Kaliningrad** Russian Federation
55 C3 **Kalinino** Russian Federation
53 F8 **Kalininsk** Russian Federation
Kaliniskaya Oblast' see **Tverskaya Oblast'**
48 E7 **Kalinovik** Bosnia-Herzegovina
55 C6 **Kalinovka** Kazakhstan
48 M1 **Kalinovka** Ukraine
55 D3 **Kalinovo** Russian Federation
70 O10 **Kalisat** Java
101 L1 **Kalispell** Montana U.S.A.
31 L4 **Kalisz** Poland
53 F9 **Kalitva** R Russian Federation
88 C4 **Kaliua** Tanzania
26 N6 **Kalix** Sweden
26 N5 **Kalix älv** R Sweden
26 L4 **Kalixfors** Sweden
74 G3 **Kalka** India
55 G5 **Kalkaman** Kazakhstan
47 K8 **Kalkan** Turkey
25 F5 **Kalkar** Germany
94 B2 **Kalkaska** Michigan U.S.A.
33 T8 **Kalkberge** Germany
87 C10 **Kalkfeld** Namibia
Kalkfontein see **Tsootsha**
33 O5 **Kalkhorst** Germany
47 J5 **Kalkım** Turkey
89 A5 **Kalk Plateau** Namibia
87 C10 **Kalkrand** Namibia
83 L10 **Kalkudah** Sri Lanka
138 D2 **Kallakoopah** R South Australia Australia
52 C5 **Kallaste** Estonia
29 N9 **Kallavesi** L Finland
33 O7 **Kallehne** Germany
32 H10 **Kallenhardt** Germany
32 J8 **Kalletal** Germany
37 P2 **Kallich** Czechoslovakia
47 V16 **Kallidhiés** Rhodes Greece
80 F7 **Kallirhoe Hot Sp** Jordan
46 D3 **Kallmet** Albania
37 M5 **Kallmünz** Germany
47 H5 **Kalloní** Greece
47 H5 **Kallonís Kólpos** Greece
26 F8 **Kallsjön** Sweden
29 O5 **Kallunki** Finland
57 D2 **Kalmakkyrgan** R Kazakhstan
27 H14 **Kalmar** county Sweden
27 H15 **Kalmar** Sweden
27 H15 **Kalmarsund** chan Sweden
36 E5 **Kalmit** mt Germany
53 E10 **Kal'mius** R Ukraine
22 H1 **Kalmthout** Belgium
83 L10 **Kalmunai** Sri Lanka
55 B6 **Kalmykovo** Kazakhstan
53 G9 **Kalmytskaya Respublika** Russian Federation
48 E4 **Kalocsa** Hungary
46 G2 **Kalofer** Bulgaria
135 S3 **Kalohi Ch** Hawaiian Is
79 C3 **Kalokhorio** Cyprus
74 E7 **Kalol** India
87 E9 **Kalomo** Zambia
46 F4 **Kalón** Greece
99 P8 **Kalona** Iowa U.S.A.
117 K9 **Kalone Peak** British Columbia Canada
71 F3 **Kalongkooan** isld Luzon Philippines
71 F3 **Kalotkot** isld Luzon Philippines
28 E4 **Kalø Vig** B Denmark
46 G2 **Kaloyanovc** Bulgaria
73 L6 **Kalpeni I** Lakshadweep Indian Oc
74 H5 **Kalpi** India
57 J4 **Kalpin** China
83 J9 **Kalpitiya** Sri Lanka
28 E5 **Kalsenakke** Denmark
77 E1 **Kāl-Shūr, Rūd-e** R Iran
6 F1 **Kalsoy** isld Faeroes
116 H4 **Kaltag** Alaska U.S.A.
56 C4 **Kaltan** Russian Federation
41 M3 **Kalte Berg** mt Austria
37 M4 **Kaltenbrunn** Germany
32 L5 **Kaltenkirchen** Germany
37 J2 **Kaltennordheim** Germany
37 J2 **Kaltensundheim** Germany
54 H2 **Kaluga** Russian Federation
83 K11 **Kalu Ganga** R Sri Lanka
70 E7 **Kalukalukuang** isld Indonesia
70 F6 **Kaluku** Sulawesi
70 D3 **Kalulong, Bt** mt Sarawak
87 E8 **Kalulushi** Zambia
142 F2 **Kalumburu** W Australia Australia
70 F6 **Kalumpang** Sulawesi
28 G5 **Kalundborg** Denmark
28 F5 **Kalundborg Fjord** inlet Denmark
88 D6 **Kalungu** R Zambia
88 B6 **Kalungwishi** R Zambia
70 E1 **Kalupis Falls** Sabah
48 J1 **Kalush** Ukraine
31 N3 **Kałuszyn** Poland
83 J11 **Kalutara** Sri Lanka
53 D7 **Kaluzhskaya Oblast'** prov Russian Federation
31 O1 **Kalvarija** Lithuania
28 J6 **Kalvehave** Denmark
29 K8 **Kälviä** Finland
29 N10 **Kalvitsa** Finland
29 L10 **Kalvola** Finland
28 B6 **Kalvslund** Denmark
38 L7 **Kalwang** Austria
55 C1 **Kal'ya** Russian Federation
74 E9 **Kalyan** India
76 C3 **Kalyāndurg** India
74 G10 **Kalyani** India
52 H5 **Kama** R Russian Federation
55 G3 **Kama** Novosibirskaya obl Russian Federation
55 D1 **Kama** Sverdlovskaya obl Russian Federation
86 B1 **Kamada** Niger
60 E13 **Kamae** Japan
61 P6 **Kamaishi** Japan
61 N13 **Kama iwa** islds Iwo Jima Japan
135 S2 **Kamakou** pk Hawaiian Is
61 N10 **Kamakura** Japan
70 O9 **Kamal** Indonesia
74 E3 **Kamalia** Pakistan
135 S3 **Kamalo** Hawaiian Is
85 B7 **Kamalu** Sierra Leone
68 C4 **Kamamaung** Burma
78 D2 **Kaman** Turkey
87 D8 **Kamapanda** Zambia
72 E5 **Kamarān** isld Yemen
77 K2 **Kamard** reg Afghanistan
74 H9 **Kamareddi** India
75 N7 **Kamarhati** India
74 B9 **Kamarod** Pakistan
101 O9 **Kamas** Utah U.S.A.
87 E9 **Kamativi** Zimbabwe
119 P2 **Kamatsi L** Saskatchewan Canada
60 H11 **Kamatsushima** Japan
143 D9 **Kambalda** W Australia Australia
52 G1 **Kambal'nitskiye Koshki, Ova** islds Russian Federation
76 C6 **Kambam** India
69 E13 **Kambang** Sumatra
70 M9 **Kambangan** isld Java
71 H7 **Kambara** Indonesia
52 H6 **Kambarka** Russian Federation
85 B7 **Kambia** Sierra Leone
83 M8 **Kambling** isld Cocos Is Indian Oc
65 H4 **Kambo Ho** mt N Korea
70 F6 **Kambuno** mt Sulawesi
51 Q3 **Kamchatka** pen Russian Federation
51 Q3 **Kamchatskaya Oblast'** prov Russian Federation
47 J1 **Kamchiya** R Bulgaria
47 H2 **Kamchiya, Yazovir** res Bulgaria
52 F4 **Kamchuga** Russian Federation
61 N8 **Kameda** Japan
100 G4 **Kamela** Oregon U.S.A.
32 G9 **Kamen** Germany
52 D6 **Kamenets** Russian Federation
48 K2 **Kamenets-Podol'skiy** Ukraine
46 D4 **Kamenicë** Albania
42 F4 **Kamenjak. Rt** C Croatia
52 H1 **Kamenka** Russian Federation
52 F2 **Kamenka** Russian Federation
56 E2 **Kamenka** R Russian Federation
53 B8 **Kamenka-Bugskaya** Ukraine
54 F9 **Kamenka-Dneprovskaya** Ukraine
56 B4 **Kamen'na-Obi** Russian Federation
29 O11 **Kamennogorsk** Russian Federation
52 D3 **Kamennoye, Oz** L Russian Federation
47 J2 **Kameno** Bulgaria
54 M9 **Kamenolomni** Russian Federation
59 K3 **Kamen Rybolov** Russian Federation
56 G5 **Kamensk** Russian Federation
55 E3 **Kamenskoye** Russian Federation
53 F9 **Kamensk-Shakhtinskiy** Russian Federation
55 D3 **Kamensk-Ural'skiy** Russian Federation
31 O3 **Kamenyuki** Belorussia
30 H4 **Kamenz** Germany
61 J10 **Kameoka** Japan
12 C2 **Kames** Scotland
54 N1 **Kameshkovo** Russian Federation
74 H3 **Kamet** mt India/Xizang Zizhiqu
61 K11 **Kameyama** Japan
100 J3 **Kamiah** Idaho U.S.A.
31 K2 **Kamien** Poland
31 J5 **Kamienna Góra** Poland
31 H2 **Kamień Pomorski** Poland
31 L4 **Kamieńsk** Poland
87 C12 **Kamieskroon** S Africa
89 A8 **Kamies Sektor Berg** mt S Africa
60 Q2 **Kami-Furano** Japan
60 Q2 **Kamikawa** prefect Japan
60 C14 **Kami-Koshiki-jima** isld Japan
140 F4 **Kamileroi** Queensland Australia
114 J5 **Kamilukuak L** Northwest Territories Canada
87 D7 **Kamina** Zaire
115 K5 **Kaminak L** Northwest Territories Canada
99 R1 **Kaministikwia** Ontario Canada
60 C11 **Kami no-shima** isld Japan
115 K5 **Kaminuriak L** Northwest Territories Canada
61 L9 **Kamioka** Japan
47 Q14 **Kamiros** hist site Rhodes Greece
116 L7 **Kamishak B** Alaska U.S.A.
60 R2 **Kami-Shihoro** Japan
Kamishli see **Qāmishlī, Al**
88 B3 **Kamituga** Zaire
61 O13 **Kamiyama-jima** isld Okinawa
60 R1 **Kami-Yūbetsu** Japan
57 F3 **Kamkaly** Kazakhstan
56 C5 **Kamlak** Russian Federation
117 N10 **Kamloops** British Columbia Canada
68 B3 **Kamma** Burma
29 P7 **Kammenoye, Oz** L Russian Federation
60 E12 **Kammon Kaikyō** str Japan
60 D12 **Kammon Tunnels** Japan
60 J10 **Kammuri shima** isld Japan
60 F11 **Kammuri-yama** mt Japan
42 F2 **Kamnik** Slovenia
56 H3 **Kamniokan** Russian Federation
78 K1 **Kamo** Armenia
61 M8 **Kamo** Japan
145 E1 **Kamo** New Zealand
56 E1 **Kamo** R Russian Federation
128 G3 **Kamoa Mts** Guyana
60 O2 **Kamoenai** Japan
61 O10 **Kamogawa** Japan
60 H11 **Kamojima** Japan
122 C6 **Kamouraska** Quebec Canada
38 N4 **Kamp** R Austria
69 G13 **Kampa** Indonesia
86 F5 **Kampala** Uganda
69 E12 **Kamparkiri** R Sumatra
36 D3 **Kamp-Bornhofen** Germany
28 A7 **Kampen** Germany
25 E3 **Kampen** Netherlands
86 E6 **Kampene** Zaire
22 H2 **Kampenhout** Belgium
38 M5 **Kamp, Gr** R Austria
68 D4 **Kamphaeng Phet** Thailand
88 B6 **Kampinda** Zambia
88 B7 **Kampolombo, L** Zambia
68 G7 **Kampong Cham** Cambodia
68 G6 **Kampong Chhnang** Cambodia
68 G7 **Kampot** Cambodia
85 D6 **Kampti** Burkina
Kampuchea rep see **Cambodia**
99 N7 **Kamrar** Iowa U.S.A.
119 Q7 **Kamsack** Saskatchewan Canada
52 G6 **Kamskoye Ust'ye** Russian Federation
74 H8 **Kāmthi** India
119 P2 **Kamuchawie L** Saskatchewan Canada
60 Q3 **Kamui-dake** mt Japan
46 E4 **Kamvoúnia, Óri** mts Greece
53 G8 **Kamyshin** Russian Federation
55 D3 **Kamyshlov** Russian Federation
57 B2 **Kamyshlybash** Kazakhstan
55 D5 **Kamyshnoye** Kazakhstan
54 F6 **Kamyshnya** Ukraine
54 H9 **Kamysh-Zarya** Ukraine
68 B1 **Kan** Burma
85 G6 **Kan** Nigeria
56 D3 **Kan** R Russian Federation
89 E2 **Kana** R Zimbabwe
103 M4 **Kanab** Utah U.S.A.
103 M5 **Kanab Cr** Arizona U.S.A.
70 C3 **Kana, Bt** mt Sarawak
61 O5 **Kanagi** Japan
42 F2 **Kanal** Slovenia
46 F5 **Kanália** Greece
69 A9 **Kanalla** Nicobar Is
118 C8 **Kananaskis L** Alberta Canada
86 D7 **Kananga** Zaire
55 C4 **Kananikol'skoye** Russian Federation
103 L4 **Kanarraville** Utah U.S.A.
52 G6 **Kanash** Russian Federation
46 F5 **Kanastraion, Ákr** C Greece
116 K8 **Kanatak** Alaska U.S.A.
52 H4 **Kanava** Russian Federation
99 N7 **Kanawha** Iowa U.S.A.
109 M2 **Kanawha** Texas U.S.A.
94 E8 **Kanawha** R West Virginia U.S.A.
94 F7 **Kanawha, Little** R West Virginia U.S.A.
61 M11 **Kanaya** Japan
61 K9 **Kanazawa** Japan
61 K9 **Kanazu** Japan
75 Q7 **Kanbalu** Burma
68 C5 **Kanbauk** Burma
68 D5 **Kanchanaburi** Thailand
Kanchenjunga see **Kanychenjunga**
57 J1 **Kanchingiz, Khrebet** mt Kazakhstan
76 D4 **Kanchipuram** India
60 D12 **Kanda** Japan
74 B4 **Kanda** Pakistan
77 J4 **Kandahār** Afghanistan
119 N7 **Kandahar** Saskatchewan Canada
52 D2 **Kandalaksha** Russian Federation
52 D2 **Kandalalakshskaya Guba** B Russian Federation
69 C11 **Kandang** Sumatra
70 D6 **Kandangan** Kalimantan
46 F9 **Kándanos** Crete Greece
52 B6 **Kandava** Latvia
36 E5 **Kandel** Germany
40 G2 **Kandern** Germany
28 E1 **Kandestederne** Denmark
74 C4 **Kandhkot** Pakistan
85 E6 **Kandi** Benin
76 D2 **Kandi** India
77 K5 **Kandi** Pakistan
116 R4 **Kandik** R Alaska U.S.A.
47 L3 **Kandıra** Turkey
70 G4 **Kandi, Tg** C Sulawesi
74 D7 **Kandla** India
139 J5 **Kandos** New South Wales Australia
87 H11 **Kandreho** Madagascar
55 B4 **Kandry** Russian Federation
76 D3 **Kandukur** India
83 K10 **Kandy** Sri Lanka
110 F2 **Kane** Illinois U.S.A.
94 J5 **Kane** Pennsylvania U.S.A.
101 R5 **Kane** Wyoming U.S.A.
115 M2 **Kane Basin** Canada/Greenland
116 G7 **Kanektok** R Alaska U.S.A.
86 C3 **Kanem** dist Chad
102 S12 **Kaneohe** Hawaiian Is
102 S12 **Kaneohe Bay** Hawaiian Is
54 C7 **Kanev** Ukraine
52 E2 **Kanevka** Russian Federation
54 C7 **Kanevskoye Vodokhranilishche** res Ukraine
61 O7 **Kaneyama** Japan
42 F3 **Kanfanar** Croatia
87 D10 **Kang** Botswana
115 O4 **Kangaamiut** Greenland
Kangaarsussiaq see **Parry, Kap**
115 O4 **Kangaatsiak** Greenland
85 C6 **Kangaba** Mali
78 F2 **Kangal** Turkey
77 C6 **Kangan** Iran
69 E9 **Kangar** Malaysia
138 D6 **Kangaroo I** South Australia Australia
140 E4 **Kangaroo Pt** Queensland Australia
29 L7 **Kangas** Finland
29 N9 **Kangaslampi** Finland
29 M9 **Kangasniemi** Finland
77 A2 **Kangāvar** Iran
48 M4 **Kangaz** Moldavia
65 C4 **Kangbao** China
75 N5 **Kangchenjunga** mt Nepal/India
58 D5 **Kangding** China
70 P9 **Kangean** isld Indonesia
115 N4 **Kangeeak Pt** Northwest Territories Canada
Kangeq C see **Cort Adelaer, Kap**
Kanger lussuaq see **Søndre Strømfjord**
Kangerlua see **Kobberminebugt**
115 Q4 **Kangerlussuaq** inlet Greenland
Kangersuatsiaq see **Prøven**
115 Q4 **Kangertittivatsiaq** inlet Greenland
86 G5 **Kangetet** Kenya
59 J3 **Kanggye** N Korea
Kangikajik C see **Brewster, Kap**
Kangilinnguit see **Grønnedal**
115 M5 **Kangiqsujuaq** Quebec Canada
65 B5 **Kangjiahui** China
65 G1 **Kangjinjing** China
59 J4 **Kangnūng** S Korea
86 B5 **Kango** Gabon
61 N13 **Kangoku-iwa** islds Iwo Jima Japan
26 N4 **Kangosfors** Sweden
65 F3 **Kangping** China
75 J3 **Kangrinboqê Feng** mt Xizang Zizhiqu
71 E8 **Kang Tipayan Dakula** isld Philippines
Kan-hsien see **Ganzhou**
68 B1 **Kani** Burma
87 D7 **Kaniama** Zaire
57 F4 **Kanibadam** Tajikistan
144 C5 **Kaniere** New Zealand
144 C5 **Kaniere, L** New Zealand
76 D3 **Kanigiri** India
57 D4 **Kanimekh** Uzbekistan
52 F1 **Kanin Nos, Mys** C Russian Federation
52 F1 **Kanin, Poluostrov** pen Russian Federation
52 F1 **Kaninskiy Bereg** coast Russian Federation
61 O5 **Kanita** Japan
26 N5 **Kaniulasjärvi** Sweden
138 F6 **Kaniva** Victoria Australia
48 F4 **Kanjiža** Serbia Yugoslavia
29 J10 **Kankaanpää** Finland
99 S8 **Kankakee** R Illinois U.S.A.
85 C6 **Kankan** Guinea
75 J8 **Kanker** India
83 J8 **Kankesanturai** Sri Lanka
29 L4 **Kankonen** Finland
74 E6 **Kankroli** India
68 D7 **Kanmaw Kyun** isld Burma
56 D5 **Kanmegirskiy Khrebet** mts Russian Federation
27 G15 **Kånna** Sweden
112 G2 **Kannapolis** North Carolina U.S.A.
22 K2 **Kanne** Belgium
74 G7 **Kannod** India
29 L9 **Kannonkoski** Finland
Kannur see **Cannanore**
29 K8 **Kannus** Finland
71 J6 **Kano** isld Indonesia
60 E11 **Kano** Japan
85 F6 **Kano** Nigeria
107 K2 **Kanona** Kansas U.S.A.
55 G5 **Kanonerka** Kazakhstan
60 G11 **Kanonji** Japan
126 B2 **Kanon, Pt** Curaçao
107 M3 **Kanopolis** Kansas U.S.A.
103 M3 **Kanosh** Utah U.S.A.
70 C3 **Kanowit** Sarawak
60 D14 **Kanoya** Japan
74 J5 **Kanpur** India
107 K3 **Kansas** state U.S.A.
99 T10 **Kansas** Illinois U.S.A.
107 P2 **Kansas** R Kansas U.S.A.
107 Q5 **Kansas** Oklahoma U.S.A.
107 Q2 **Kansas City** Kansas U.S.A.
110 B2 **Kansas City** Missouri U.S.A.
67 E4 **Kanshi** China
56 E3 **Kansk** Russian Federation
56 E4 **Kanskoye Belogor'ye** mts Russian Federation
88 A5 **Kansonge** Zaire
Kansu prov see **Gansu**
57 G3 **Kant** Kyrgyzstan
29 N9 **Kantala** Finland
85 E6 **Kantchari** Burkina
85 E6 **Kanté** Togo
68 G5 **Kantharalak** Thailand
75 M8 **Kānthi** India
116 M4 **Kantishna** R Alaska U.S.A.
134 A6 **Kanton I** isld Phoenix Is Pacific Oc
61 M10 **Kanto sanchi** mts Japan
68 C2 **Kantulong** Burma
14 C4 **Kanturk** Ireland
77 J5 **Kanuk** Afghanistan
102 S11 **Kanuku** Hawaiian Is
128 G3 **Kanuku Mts** Guyana
61 N9 **Kanuma** Japan
87 C11 **Kanus** Namibia
116 M3 **Kanuti** R Alaska U.S.A.
89 D5 **Kanye** Botswana
68 B3 **Kanyinngu** Burma
68 C3 **Kanyutkwin** Burma
38 J8 **Kanzel** mt Austria
87 E8 **Kanzenze** Zaire
137 R5 **Kao** isld Tonga
87 B9 **Kaoko Veld** reg Namibia
85 A6 **Kaolack** Senegal
47 J1 **Kaolinovo** Bulgaria
87 D8 **Kaoma** Zambia
65 F2 **Kaoshan** China
102 V13 **Kapaa** Hawaiian Is
102 V13 **Kapaau** Hawaiian Is
74 E7 **Kapadvanj** India
57 J2 **Kapal** Kazakhstan
71 O9 **Kapala** isld Indonesia
71 A3 **Kapalabuaya** Indonesia
71 M9 **Kapan** Timor Indonesia
87 D7 **Kapanga** Zaire
87 F7 **Kapatu** Zambia
66 B3 **Kapchagay** Kazakhstan
57 H3 **Kapchagayskoye Vdkhr.** res Kazakhstan
22 G1 **Kapellen** Belgium
25 F5 **Kapellen** Germany
86 G5 **Kapenguria** Kenya
38 M7 **Kapfenberg** Austria
88 E9 **Kapichira Falls** waterfall Malawi
47 J4 **Kapıdağı Yar** pen Turkey
70 G5 **Kapinyu, Tanjong** C Sulawesi
87 E8 **Kapiri Mposhi** Zambia
77 L2 **Kāpīsā** Afghanistan
115 L7 **Kapiskau** Ontario Canada
70 C4 **Kapit** Sarawak
54 C8 **Kapitanovka** Ukraine
145 E4 **Kapiti I** New Zealand
111 D11 **Kaplan** Louisiana U.S.A.
31 H7 **Kaplice** Czechoslovakia
69 D8 **Kapoe** Thailand
86 F5 **Kapoeta** Sudan
135 V5 **Kapoho** Hawaiian Is
71 L9 **Kapondai, Tanjong** Indonesia
145 E3 **Kaponga** New Zealand
70 F7 **Kapoposang** isld Indonesia
48 E4 **Kapos** R Hungary
48 D4 **Kaposvár** Hungary
71 C3 **Kapotjol** W Irian
74 B10 **Kappar** Pakistan
28 G7 **Kappel** Denmark
36 C3 **Kappel** Germany
28 D7 **Kappeln** Germany
36 E6 **Kappelrodeck** Germany
27 K14 **Kappelshamn** isld Gotland Sweden
41 M3 **Kappl** Austria
38 G7 **Kaprun** Austria
Kapsukas see **Marijampolė**
88 C9 **Kapsuku** mt Zimbabwe
70 B4 **Kapuas** R Kalimantan
70 D5 **Kapuas** R Kalimantan
70 C4 **Kapuas Hulu, Peg** Kalimantan
138 E5 **Kapunda** South Australia Australia
145 E3 **Kapuni** New Zealand
74 F3 **Kapurthala** India
120 H3 **Kapuskasing** Ontario Canada
120 H4 **Kapuskasing** R Ontario Canada
139 K4 **Kaputar** mt New South Wales Australia
48 D3 **Kapuvár** Hungary
56 H4 **Kapylyushi, Oz** L Russian Federation
66 B4 **Kaqung** China
85 E7 **Kara** Togo
78 G2 **Kara** R Turkey
79 G6 **Karā', Arḑ al** Syria
57 G5 **Karaart** Tajikistan

57 G3 **Kara Balta** Kyrgyzstan
54 K1 **Karabanovo** Russian Federation
57 H2 **Karabas** Kazakhstan
57 C5 **Karabekaul** Turkmenistan
47 J4 **Karabiğa** Turkey
57 C6 **Karabil', Vozvyshennost'** *uplands* Turkmenistan
78 D1 **Karabük** Turkey
57 J4 **Karabulak** China
46 C4 **Karaburun** Albania
47 H6 **Kara Burun** *C* Turkey
47 H6 **Karaburun** Turkey
47 J8 **Kara Burun** *C* Turkey
55 D6 **Karabutak** Kazakhstan
47 J4 **Karacabey** Turkey
47 J3 **Karacaköy** Turkey
79 C2 **Karaçal Tepe** *mt* Turkey
47 J3 **Karacaoğlan** Turkey
47 K7 **Karacasu** Turkey
53 F11 **Karachayevo-Cherkesskaya Avtonomnyy Oblast'** Russian Federation
54 F3 **Karachev** Russian Federation
74 B6 **Karachi** Pakistan
76 B2 **Karad** India
78 D3 **Kara Dağ** *mt* Turkey
57 G4 **Karadar'ya** *R* Kyrgyzstan
47 M11 **Karadeniz Boğazı** *str* Turkey
55 F2 **Karagach** Russian Federation
55 F6 **Karaganda** Kazakhstan
57 H1 **Karagayly** Kazakhstan
51 Q4 **Karaginskiy, Ostrova** *islds* Russian Federation
47 K8 **Kara Göl** *L* Turkey
56 B5 **Karaguzhikha** Kazakhstan
47 K6 **Karahalh** Turkey
47 J7 **Karahayıt** Turkey
55 C3 **Karaidel'** Russian Federation
76 D5 **Kāraikāl** India
Kara Irtysh *R see* **Ertix He**
79 F1 **Karaisalı** Turkey
70 E4 **Karaitan** Kalimantan
83 J9 **Karaitivu** Sri Lanka
77 B2 **Karaj** Iran
79 F7 **Karak** Jordan
47 H6 **Karaka Burun** *C* Turkey
57 A3 **Karakalpakskaya Respublika** Uzbekistan
57 C2 **Karaketken** Kazakhstan
143 B9 **Karakin Ls** W Australia Australia
57 E2 **Karakoin, Ozero** *L* Kazakhstan
57 H4 **Karakolka** Kyrgyzstan
74 F1 **Karakoram** *ra* Kashmir
74 G1 **Karakoram Pass** Kashmir
85 B5 **Karakoro** *R* Mauritania/Mali
58 D2 **Karakorum** Mongolia
55 G5 **Karakuduk** Kazakhstan
55 F4 **Kara-Kuga** Kazakhstan
57 G4 **Kara Kul'** Kyrgyzstan
57 C5 **Karakul'** Uzbekistan
52 H6 **Karakulino** Russian Federation
57 G5 **Kara-Kul', Ozero** *L* Tajikistan
55 D4 **Karakul'skoye** Russian Federation
57 C5 **Karakumskiy Kanal** Turkmenistan
50 E5 **Karakumy** Turkmenistan
57 A5 **Karakumy, Peski** *desert* Turkmenistan
60 D14 **Karakuni-dake** *mt* Japan
38 M8 **Karalpe** *mts* Austria
143 C7 **Karalundi** W Australia Australia
70 F6 **Karam** *R* Sulawesi
80 F6 **Karama** Jordan
47 K7 **Karaman** Turkey
47 K7 **Karamanlı** Turkey
66 C2 **Karamay** China
145 D4 **Karamea** New Zealand
70 D7 **Karamian** *isld* Indonesia
47 L6 **Karamık Gölü** *L* Turkey
66 C4 **Karamiran He** *R* China
66 D4 **Karamiran Shankou** *pass* China
86 F5 **Karamoja** *dist* Uganda
47 K4 **Karamürsel** Turkey
78 L4 **Karand** Iran
69 G14 **Karangagung** Sumatra
70 K8 **Karangan** Sumatra
144 B5 **Karangarua R** New Zealand
70 P10 **Karangasem** Indonesia
70 M9 **Karangbolong Tanjong** *C* Java
70 F7 **Karang Bril** Indonesia
70 F5 **Karang, Tg** *C* Sulawesi
74 G8 **Karanja** India
47 J7 **Karaova** Turkey
57 G2 **Karaoy** Kazakhstan
57 D3 **Karaozek** Kazakhstan
47 J1 **Karapelit** Bulgaria
78 D3 **Karapınar** Turkey
145 E2 **Karapiro** New Zealand
66 C4 **Karasay** China
57 J4 **Karasay** Kyrgyzstan
89 A7 **Karasburg** Namibia
147 M12 **Kara Sea** Arctic Oc
55 G5 **Karashoky** Kazakhstan
26 O2 **Karasjok** Norway
26 O2 **Karasjokka** *R* Norway
55 G5 **Karasor** Kazakhstan
55 F4 **Karasu** Kokchetavskaya obl Kazakhstan
55 D5 **Karasu** Kustanayskaya Kazakhstan
47 L3 **Karasu** Turkey
78 H1 **Karasu** *R* Turkey
55 G4 **Karasuk** Russian Federation
56 B4 **Karasuk** *R* Russian Federation
61 O9 **Karasuyama** Japan
55 E2 **Karas'ye, Oz** *L* Russian Federation
57 L1 **Karatal** Kazakhstan
57 H2 **Karatal** *R* Kazakhstan
78 E3 **Karataş** Turkey
57 F3 **Kara Tau** Kazakhstan
68 D7 **Karathuri** Burma
83 J9 **Karativu** *isld* Sri Lanka
26 K5 **Karatjaur** *L* Sweden
55 B6 **Karatobe** Kazakhstan
57 B2 **Karatobe, Mys** *C* Kazakhstan
55 D5 **Karatomarskoye Vodokhranilishche** *res* Kazakhstan
60 C12 **Karatsu** Japan
57 A2 **Karatup, Poluostrov** *pen* Kazakhstan
55 E6 **Karaturgay** *R* Kazakhstan
Karaul *see* **Qongkol**
57 J1 **Karaul** Kazakhstan
50 H1 **Karaul** Russian Federation
57 A3 **Kara-uzyak** Uzbekistan
46 E5 **Karáva** *mt* Greece
57 F4 **Karavan** Kyrgyzstan
46 C4 **Karavastasë, Këneta e** Albania
79 C4 **Karavostasi** Cyprus
70 L9 **Karawang** Java
70 L8 **Karawang Tg.** *C* Java
38 K8 **Karawanken** *mt* Austria
57 F1 **Karazhal** Kazakhstan
57 G2 **Karazhingil** Kazakhstan
78 J5 **Karbala** Iraq
78 J5 **Karbalā'** *prov* Iraq
36 F3 **Karben** Germany
26 H10 **Kårböle** Sweden
33 Q6 **Karbow-Vietlübbe** Germany
55 G6 **Karbushevka** Kazakhstan
28 B3 **Karby** Denmark
48 F3 **Karcag** Hungary
46 E8 **Kardhamíla** Greece
47 H6 **Kardhámila** Greece
46 E5 **Kardhítsa** Greece
26 N5 **Kardis** Sweden
52 B5 **Kärdla** Estonia
138 B2 **Karee** N Terr Australia
52 D3 **Karel'skaya Masel'ga** Russian Federation
52 D3 **Karel'skaya Respublika** Russian Federation
87 F7 **Karema** Tanzania
Karen State *see* **Kayin State**
85 C4 **Karet** Mauritania
145 F2 **Karewa I** New Zealand
55 C5 **Kargala** Russian Federation
57 G1 **Kargaly** Kazakhstan
55 D3 **Kargapolye** Russian Federation
56 B3 **Kargat** *R* Russian Federation
Karghalik *see* **Yecheng**
78 E1 **Kargı** Turkey
52 E4 **Kargopol'** Russian Federation
33 R6 **Kargow** Germany
31 J3 **Kargowa** Poland
85 G6 **Kargueri** Niger
117 G8 **Karheen** Alaska U.S.A.
29 M11 **Karhula** Finland
88 B10 **Kariba** Zimbabwe
88 B10 **Kariba Dam** Zimbabwe/Zambia
88 B10 **Kariba,L** Zimbabwe/Zambia
60 N3 **Kariba yama** *mt* Japan
87 C10 **Karibib** Namibia
89 C9 **Kariega** *watercourse* S Africa
29 M2 **Karigasniemi** Finland
29 J9 **Karijoki** Finland
145 D1 **Karikari, C** New Zealand
86 F2 **Karima** Sudan
75 P6 **Karimganj** India
74 H9 **Karimnagar** India
69 F12 **Karimun Besar** *isld* Indonesia
70 N8 **Karimundjawa** *isld* Indonesia
70 N8 **Karimundjawa, Pulau Pulau** *islds* Indonesia
86 A1 **Karin** Somalia
145 E2 **Karioi** *mt* New Zealand
145 E3 **Karioi** New Zealand
29 K11 **Karis** Finland
28 J6 **Karise** Denmark
88 E6 **Karisimbi. Mt** Zaire
46 G6 **Káristos** Greece
144 C6 **Karitane** New Zealand
76 B4 **Karkal** India
Karkamiş *see* **Barak**
136 K2 **Karkar** *isld* Papua New Guinea
57 H1 **Karkaralinsk** Kazakhstan
77 F7 **Kärkīn Dar** Iran
29 L11 **Karkkila** Finland
29 L11 **Kärkölä** Finland
138 D5 **Karkoo** South Australia Australia
Karlá *L see* **Voïvïis** *L*
54 G5 **Karla Libknekhta** Russian Federation
57 G6 **Karla Marksa, Pik** *mt* Tajikistan
28 F4 **Karlby** Denmark
26 R1 **Karlebotn** Norway
28 J7 **Karleby** Denmark
31 J1 **Karlino** Poland
Karl-Marx-Stadt *see* **Chemnitz**
42 G4 **Karlobag** Croatia
54 G7 **Karlovka** Ukraine
46 G2 **Karlovo** Bulgaria
37 O3 **Karlovy Vary** Czechoslovakia
26 K8 **Karlsbäck** Sweden
36 E6 **Karlsbad** Germany
29 K6 **Karlsberg** Sweden
27 G13 **Karlsborg** Sweden
37 L7 **Karlsfeld** Germany
32 K9 **Karlshafen** Germany
27 G15 **Karlshamn** Sweden
27 G12 **Karlskoga** Sweden
27 H15 **Karlskrona** Sweden
26 L1 **Karlsöy** Norway
36 E5 **Karlsruhe** Germany
98 F1 **Karlsruhe** North Dakota U.S.A.
27 F12 **Karlstad** Sweden
98 K1 **Karlstad** Minnesota U.S.A.
36 H4 **Karlstadt** Germany
116 K8 **Karluk L** Alaska U.S.A.
57 D5 **Karlyuk** Turkmenistan
76 B1 **Karmala** India
52 E6 **Karmanovo** Russian Federation
80 D8 **Karmel** Jordan
80 C2 **Karmel, Cape** Israel
80 C6 **Karmé Yoséf** Israel
80 E2 **Karmi'el** Israel
80 B7 **Karmiyya** Israel
27 A12 **Karmöy** *isld* Norway
109 N3 **Karnack** Texas U.S.A.
110 H4 **Karnak** Illinois U.S.A.
74 G4 **Karnal** India
76 B3 **Karnataka** *prov* India
109 K7 **Karnes City** Texas U.S.A.
38 G8 **Karnische Alpen** *mts* Austria
47 H2 **Karnobat** Bulgaria
27 E13 **Kärnsj** *L* Sweden
38 H8 **Kärnten** Austria
87 E9 **Karoi** Zimbabwe
77 H2 **Karokh** Afghanistan
68 C5 **Karokpi** Burma
71 K8 **Karompalompo** *isld* Indonesia
128 G3 **Karona Fall** Guyana
88 D6 **Karonga** Malawi
143 D9 **Karonie** W Australia Australia
57 H4 **Karool-Dëbë** Kyrgyzstan
89 C9 **Karoo National Park** S Africa
138 E6 **Karoonda** South Australia Australia
47 H8 **Káros** *isld* Greece
70 F5 **Karossa** Sulawesi Indonesia
71 J9 **Karossa, Tg** *C* Indonesia
47 O12 **Karousádhes** Greece
33 Q5 **Karow** Germany
47 J9 **Kárpathos** *isld* Greece
47 J9 **Kárpathos** Kárpathos I Greece
47 J9 **Karpathos Str** Greece
46 E6 **Karpenision** Greece
41 K4 **Kärpf** *mt* Switzerland
37 P7 **Karpfham** Germany
55 C2 **Karpinsk** Russian Federation
52 F3 **Karpogory** Russian Federation
55 D2 **Karpuniskiy** Russian Federation
55 C2 **Karpushikha** Russian Federation
79 C2 **Karpuz** *R* Turkey
47 J7 **Karpuzlu** Turkey
142 A1 **Karrakatta** *dist* Perth, W Aust Australia
142 B5 **Karratha** W Australia Australia
115 O3 **Karrats Fjord** Greenland
28 H6 **Karrebæk** Denmark
28 H6 **Karrebæksminde** Denmark
28 G6 **Karrebæksminde Bugt** *B* Denmark
89 B8 **Karreeberge** *mts* S Africa
143 B10 **Karridale** W Australia Australia
78 J1 **Kars** Turkey
57 D1 **Karsakpay** Kazakhstan
119 S2 **Karsakuwigamak L** Manitoba Canada
29 M8 **Kärsämäki** Finland
52 C6 **Kārsava** Latvia
57 D5 **Karshi** Uzbekistan
57 D5 **Karshinskaya Step'** Uzbekistan
75 N5 **Kārsiyāng** India
50 E1 **Karskiye Vorota, Proliv** *str* Russian Federation
33 P6 **Karstädt** Germany
28 B5 **Karstoft** Denmark
29 L9 **Karstula** Finland
26 H10 **Karsvall** Sweden
46 G3 **Kartál** *mt* Greece
47 N11 **Kartal** Turkey
55 D4 **Kartaly** Russian Federation
52 H3 **Kartayël** Russian Federation
36 B4 **Karthaus** Germany
94 J5 **Karthaus** Pennsylvania U.S.A.
29 N9 **Karttula** Finland
31 L1 **Kartuzy** Poland
87 E9 **Karubwe** Zambia
61 M9 **Karuizawa** Japan
143 F9 **Karulbie Rockhole** *rockhole* W Australia Australia
140 F3 **Karumba** Queensland Australia
77 A4 **Karun** *R* Iran
26 N5 **Karungi** Sweden
71 J9 **Karuni** Indonesia
142 G3 **Karunjie** W Australia Australia
106 G3 **Karval** Colorado U.S.A.
29 K9 **Karvia** Finland
26 K2 **Kårvik** Norway
31 L6 **Karviná** Czechoslovakia
48 E1 **Karvina** Czechoslovakia
76 B3 **Karwar** India
41 O3 **Karwendel Geb** *mts* Austria
55 E1 **Karym** Russian Federation
28 D2 **Kås** Denmark
56 C2 **Kas** *R* Russian Federation
47 K8 **Kaş** Turkey
88 C6 **Kasaba B** Zambia
86 D6 **Kasai** *prov* Zaire
87 D7 **Kasai** *R* Zaire
87 D8 **Kasaji** Zaire
61 O9 **Kasama** Japan
88 C7 **Kasama** Zambia
57 D5 **Kasan** Uzbekistan
88 C6 **Kasanga** Tanzania
57 F4 **Kasansay** Uzbekistan
76 B4 **Kasaragod** India
75 O7 **Kasba** Bangladesh
114 J5 **Kasba L** Northwest Territories Canada
27 G16 **Kåseberga** Sweden
60 D14 **Kaseda** Japan
116 F1 **Kasegaluk Lag** Alaska U.S.A.
87 E8 **Kasempa** Zambia
37 L3 **Kasendorf** Germany
88 B7 **Kasenga** Zaire
86 F5 **Kasenyi** Zaire
77 B5 **Kāserūn** Iran
88 C1 **Kasese** Uganda
86 E6 **Kasese** Zaire
68 F5 **Kaset Wisai** Thailand
119 N2 **Kashabowie** Ontario Canada
77 B2 **Kāshān** Iran
Kashgar *see* **Kashi**
66 B4 **Kashi** China
61 J11 **Kashihara** Japan
60 D12 **Kashima** Japan
52 E6 **Kashin** Russian Federation
74 H4 **Kashipur** India
54 K2 **Kashira** Russian Federation
119 O1 **Kashishibog L** Ontario Canada
61 M8 **Kashiwazaki** Japan
57 D5 **Kashkadar'in-skaya Oblast** Uzbekistan
57 G2 **Kashkanteniz** Kazakhstan
52 D4 **Kashkany** Russian Federation
52 E2 **Kashkarantsy** Russian Federation
57 H4 **Kashkasu** Kyrgyzstan
77 F2 **Kāshmar** Iran
66 B5 **Kashmir** *prov* India/Pakistan
74 C4 **Kashmor** Pakistan
88 G3 **Kasigao** *mt* Kenya
70 G5 **Kasimbar** Sulawesi
71 A3 **Kasiruta** *isld* Indonesia
110 G2 **Kaskaskia** *R* Illinois U.S.A.
26 K6 **Kasker** Sweden
29 J9 **Kaskinen** Finland
Kaskö *see* **Kaskinen**
68 F7 **Kas Kong** Cambodia
55 D3 **Kasli** Russian Federation
117 P11 **Kaslo** British Columbia Canada
69 F14 **Kasmaran** Sumatra
70 C5 **Kasongan** Kalimantan
86 E6 **Kasongo** Zaire
87 C7 **Kasongo-Lunda** Zaire
47 H9 **Kásos** *isld* Greece
47 H9 **Kásos Str** Greece
47 J1 **Kaspichan** Bulgaria
54 C1 **Kasplya** *R* Belorussia/Rus Fed
68 H6 **Kas Preas** Cambodia
68 F7 **Kas Prins** *isld* Cambodia
68 F7 **Kas Rong** *isld* Cambodia
68 F7 **Kas Rong Sam Lem** *isld* Cambodia
86 G2 **Kassala** Sudan
46 F4 **Kassándra** Greece
32 L10 **Kassel** Germany
85 F1 **Kasserine** Tunisia
47 O12 **Kassiópi** Greece
68 F7 **Kas Smach** *isld* Cambodia
99 O5 **Kasson** Minnesota U.S.A.
78 D1 **Kastamonu** Turkey
47 H3 **Kastanéai** Greece
28 E3 **Kastbjerg** Denmark
36 E3 **Kastel** Germany
36 C3 **Kastellaun** Germany
46 F9 **Kastélli** Crete Greece
46 G9 **Kastéllion** Crete Greece
47 K8 **Kastellórizon** *isld* Greece
36 B1 **Kaster** Germany
22 H1 **Kasterlee** Belgium
37 M5 **Kastl** Germany
27 H15 **Kastlösa** Sweden
33 N5 **Kastorf** Germany
46 E4 **Kastoría** Greece
46 E4 **Kastorías, L** Greece
46 G5 **Kástron** Límnos I Greece
46 F4 **Kástron Nigrita** Greece
46 D5 **Kastrosikiá** Greece
29 K5 **Kastrup** Denmark
60 F10 **Kasubuchi** Japan
60 D12 **Kasuga** Japan
61 K10 **Kasugai** Japan
61 O9 **Kasumiga-ura** *L* Japan
70 C6 **Kasungan** Kalimantan
87 F8 **Kasungu** Malawi
88 E9 **Kasupe** Malawi
74 F3 **Kasur** Pakistan
85 G6 **Katagum** Nigeria
95 S8 **Katahdin, Mt** Maine U.S.A.
86 D6 **Katako-Kombe** Zaire
46 E7 **Katákolon** Greece
116 P2 **Katakturuk** *R* Alaska U.S.A.
116 P6 **Katalla** Alaska U.S.A.
86 D7 **Katanda** Zaire
56 F2 **Katanga** *R* Russian Federation
74 H8 **Katangi** India
59 M1 **Katangli** Russian Federation
143 C10 **Katanning** W Australia Australia
75 J4 **Katarnian Ghat** India
46 D7 **Katastári** Greece
61 J10 **Katata** Japan
88 C5 **Katavi Nat. Park** Tanzania
77 L3 **Katāwāz-Urgan** Afghanistan
55 D3 **Kataysk** Russian Federation
69 A9 **Katchall** *isld* Nicobar Is
38 J7 **Katchberg** Austria
87 C8 **Katchiungo** Angola
116 H4 **Kateel** *R* Alaska U.S.A.
119 O8 **Katepwa** Saskatchewan Canada
46 F4 **Katerini** Greece
25 F4 **Katerveer** Netherlands
117 G7 **Kates Needle** *mt* British Columbia Canada
75 K7 **Katghora** India
75 R6 **Katha** Burma
84 J4 **Katherina, Gebel** *hill* Egypt
140 B2 **Katherine** N Terr Australia
140 C2 **Katherine R** N Terr Australia
74 H4 **Kathgodam** India
74 D8 **Kathiawar** *reg* India
83 L9 **Kathiraveli** Sri Lanka
113 E9 **Kathleen** Florida U.S.A.
140 B2 **Kathleen Falls** N Terr Australia
143 D7 **Kathleen Valley** W Australia Australia
75 L5 **Kathmandu** Nepal
118 D7 **Kathryn** Alberta Canada
98 H3 **Kathryn** North Dakota U.S.A.
74 F2 **Kathwa** Kashmir
85 C6 **Kati** Mali
70 C4 **Katibas** *R* Sarawak
75 M6 **Katihar** India
145 E2 **Katikati** New Zealand
87 D9 **Katima Mulilo** Namibia
119 S6 **Katimik L** Manitoba Canada
85 C7 **Katiola** Ivory Coast
29 L3 **Kätkätunturi** *mt* Finland
89 A8 **Katkop Hills** S Africa
48 M5 **Katlabuk, Oz** *L* Ukraine
32 M9 **Katlenburg** Germany
116 K8 **Katmai B** Alaska U.S.A.
116 K7 **Katmai Nat Park and Preserve** Alaska U.S.A.
116 K7 **Katmai Vol., Mt** Alaska U.S.A.
74 J7 **Katni** India
46 E6 **Káto Akhaïa** Greece
46 E6 **Katokhi** Greece
88 C9 **Katondwe** Zambia
46 F3 **Káto Nevrokópion** Greece
139 K5 **Katoomba** New South Wales Australia
70 G5 **Katoposa, Gunung** *mt* Sulawesi
46 F4 **Káto Stavrós** Greece
55 C4 **Katov-Ivanovsk** Russian Federation
31 L5 **Katowice** Poland
75 N7 **Kātoya** India
47 L7 **Katrancı Dağ** *mt* Turkey
27 H10 **Katrineberg** Sweden
27 H13 **Katrineholm** Sweden
12 D1 **Katrine, L** Scotland
85 F6 **Katsina** Nigeria
61 P13 **Katsuren-zaki** *C* Okinawa
61 O9 **Katsuta** Japan
61 O10 **Katsuura** Japan
61 N10 **Katsuyama** Japan
61 K9 **Katsuyama** Fukui Japan
60 G10 **Katsuyama** Okayama Japan
57 D5 **Kattakurgan** Uzbekistan
142 F5 **Kattamudda Well** W Australia Australia
29 K4 **Kattarp** Sweden
47 J9 **Kattavia** Rhodes Greece
47 Q15 **Kattaviá** Rhodes Greece
120 K3 **Kattawagami L** Ontario Canada
28 E3 **Kattegat** *str* Denmark
32 G8 **Kattenvenne** Germany
27 K14 **Katthammarsvik** *isld* Gotland Sweden
28 D5 **Kattrup** Denmark
88 A8 **Katue** *R* Zambia
87 E7 **Katumba** Zaire
88 D7 **Katumbi** Malawi
56 C5 **Katun'** *R* Russian Federation
83 J10 **Katunayaka** Sri Lanka
56 C6 **Katunskiy Khr** *mts* Russian Federation
88 B2 **Katwe** Uganda
25 B4 **Katwijk aan Zee** Netherlands
31 K4 **Katy Wrocł** Poland
36 G5 **Katzenbuckel** *mt* Germany
36 D3 **Katzenelnbogen** Germany
37 L2 **Katzhütte** Germany
71 A2 **Kau** Halmahera Indonesia
102 V13 **Kauai** *isld* Hawaiian Is
102 V13 **Kauai Ch** Hawaiian Is
144 B7 **Kauana** New Zealand
36 D3 **Kaub** Germany
89 D2 **Kaucaca Pans** Botswana
135 U6 **Kau Desert** Hawaiian Is
41 N2 **Kaufbeuren** Germany
41 N1 **Kaufering** Germany
109 L3 **Kaufman** Texas U.S.A.
32 L10 **Kaufungen** Germany
29 K8 **Kauhava** Finland
135 T3 **Kauiki Hd** Hawaiian Is
145 E2 **Kaukapakapa** New Zealand
99 S5 **Kaukauna** Wisconsin U.S.A.
102 U13 **Kaula** *isld* Hawaiian Is
102 U13 **Kaulakahi Ch** Hawaiian Is
135 U5 **Kauluoa Pt** Hawaiian Is
135 O1 **Kaumakani** Hawaiian Is
38 N5 **Kaumberg** Austria
135 R2 **Kaunakakai** Hawaiian Is
135 U6 **Kauna Pt** Hawaiian Is
53 B7 **Kaunas** Lithuania
29 L11 **Kauniainen** Finland
145 E3 **Kaupokonui Stream** New Zealand
85 F6 **Kaura Namoda** Nigeria
48 M4 **Kaushany** Moldavia
29 K8 **Kaustinen** Finland
22 L4 **Kautenbach** Luxembourg
71 A2 **Kau, Tk** *B* Halmahera Indonesia
26 N3 **Kautokeino** Norway
68 D7 **Kau-ye Kyun** *isld* Burma
47 K5 **Kavacık** Turkey
46 E3 **Kavadarci** Macedonia Yugoslavia
46 D3 **Kavajë** Albania
47 J7 **Kavaklıdere** Turkey
59 K3 **Kavalerovo** Russian Federation
76 E3 **Kavali** India
46 G4 **Kavála** Greece
87 C9 **Kavango** *R* Namibia
87 C9 **Kavango** *homeland* Namibia
73 L6 **Kavaratti** *isld* Lakshadweep Indian Oc
47 J1 **Kavarna** Bulgaria
33 Q4 **Kavelstorf** Germany
136 L2 **Kavieng** New Ireland
116 O2 **Kavik** *R* Alaska U.S.A.
27 F16 **Kävlinge** Sweden
47 P13 **Kavos** Greece
47 H9 **Kavoúsi** Crete Greece
88 C5 **Kavu** *R* Tanzania
80 D2 **Kavul** Israel
87 D8 **Kavungo** Angola
129 H3 **Kaw** Fr Guiana
121 M7 **Kawagama L** Ontario Canada
61 N10 **Kawagoe** Japan
61 N10 **Kawaguchi** Japan
60 H10 **Kawahara** Japan
61 M7 **Kawaharada** Japan
135 U4 **Kawaihae** Hawaiian Is
135 N1 **Kawaihoa Pt** Hawaiian Is
135 O1 **Kawaikini** *pk* Hawaiian Is
102 R11 **Kawailoa Bch** Hawaiian Is
61 M10 **Kawakami** Japan
145 E1 **Kawakawa** New Zealand
145 E2 **Kawakawa B** New Zealand
60 E13 **Kawakita** Japan
61 O8 **Kawamata** Japan
88 B6 **Kawambwa** Zambia
61 N11 **Kawana** Japan
71 J4 **Kawangkoan** Sulawesi
60 G11 **Kawanoe** Japan
144 B6 **Kawarau R** New Zealand
75 J7 **Kawardha** India
121 M8 **Kawartha Lakes** Ontario Canada
61 N10 **Kawasaki** Japan
60 D11 **Kawashiri-misaki** *C* Japan
71 H5 **Kawato** Sulawesi Indonesia
60 O4 **Kawauchi** Japan
145 E2 **Kawau I** New Zealand
107 O5 **Kaw City** Oklahoma U.S.A.
71 C2 **Kawe** *isld* Indonesia
102 E5 **Kaweah** *R* California U.S.A.
145 F3 **Kaweka** *mt* New Zealand
102 R11 **Kawela B** Hawaiian Is
145 F3 **Kawerau** New Zealand
145 E3 **Kawhia** New Zealand
102 H4 **Kawich Ra** Nevada U.S.A.
88 C6 **Kawimbe** Zambia
119 S6 **Kawinaw L** Manitoba Canada
71 J9 **Kawinda** Sumbawa Indonesia
68 D4 **Kawkareik** Burma
107 O5 **Kaw L** Oklahoma U.S.A.
68 C3 **Kawludo** Burma
68 D6 **Kawmapyin** Burma
68 D7 **Kawthaung** Burma
66 B4 **Kaxgar He** *R* China
52 H4 **Kay** Russian Federation
85 D6 **Kaya** Burkina
68 C3 **Kayah State** Burma
116 P7 **Kayak I** Alaska U.S.A.
47 N11 **Kayalar** Turkey
47 N11 **Kayali Dag** *mt* Turkey
68 C4 **Kayan** Burma
70 E3 **Kayan** *R* Kalimantan
76 C6 **Kayankulam** India
71 J5 **Kayasa** Indonesia
55 E4 **Kaybagar, Oz** *L* Kazakhstan
101 T6 **Kaycee** Wyoming U.S.A.
120 D2 **Kayedon L** Ontario Canada
103 O5 **Kayenta** Arizona U.S.A.
85 B6 **Kayes** Mali
94 F8 **Kayford** West Virginia U.S.A.
55 D5 **Kaygy** Kazakhstan
68 C3 **Kayin State** Burma
47 J6 **Kayışlar** Turkey
55 G4 **Kaymanachikha** Kazakhstan
55 G2 **Kaymysovy** Russian Federation
37 N2 **Kayna** Germany
48 M4 **Kaynary** Moldavia
116 S2 **Kay Pt** Yukon Territory Canada
129 G3 **Kayser Geb** *mts* Suriname
78 E2 **Kayseri** Turkey
101 O8 **Kaysville** Utah U.S.A.
69 G14 **Kayuagung** Sumatra
119 M9 **Kayville** Saskatchewan Canada
121 P7 **Kazabazua** Quebec Canada
56 G3 **Kazachinskoye** Russian Federation
78 K1 **Kazakh** Azerbaijan
57 A3 **Kazakhdar'ya** Uzbekistan
Kazakhskaya S.S.R. *see* **Kazakhstan**
57 D1 **Kazakhskiy Melkosopochnik** *reg* Kazakhstan
57 B2 **Kazakhstan** *rep* C Asia
57 B2 **Kazalinsk** Kazakhstan
115 K5 **Kazan** *R* Northwest Territories Canada
52 G6 **Kazan'** Russian Federation
52 G6 **Kazanka** *R* Russian Federation
46 G2 **Kazanlŭk** Bulgaria
54 K3 **Kazanovka** Russian Federation
55 E3 **Kazanskoye** Russian Federation
57 G4 **Kazarman** Kyrgyzstan
48 M1 **Kazatin** Ukraine
47 H5 **Kaz Dağı** *mt* Turkey
55 E5 **Kazgorodok** Kazakhstan
55 F4 **Kazgorodok** Kokchetavskaya obl Kazakhstan
52 H4 **Kazhym** Russian Federation
31 N4 **Kazimierz** Poland
48 F2 **Kazincbarcika** Hungary
54 L3 **Kazinka** Russian Federation
37 P4 **Kaznějov** Czechoslovakia
61 N9 **Kazo** Japan
86 D7 **Kazumba** Zaire
61 O5 **Kazuno** Japan
50 F2 **Kazym** *R* Russian Federation
56 D4 **Kazyr** *R* Russian Federation
77 G4 **Kbash** Afghanistan
31 K3 **Kcynia** Poland
37 P5 **Kdyně** Czechoslovakia
46 G7 **Kéa** *isld* Greece
135 V5 **Keaau** Hawaiian Is
14 E2 **Keady** N Ireland
135 T5 **Keahole Pt** Hawaiian Is
135 S3 **Kealaikahiki Pt** Hawaiian Is
102 V14 **Kealakekue B** Hawaiian Is
135 U5 **Kealia** Hawaiian Is
102 R11 **Keamapapa Pt** Hawaiian Is
103 O6 **Keams Canyon** Arizona U.S.A.
Kéamu *isld see* **Anatom** *isld*
121 L7 **Kearney** Ontario Canada
98 G9 **Kearney** Nebraska U.S.A.
102 F5 **Kearsarge Pass** California U.S.A.
109 O3 **Keatchie** Louisiana U.S.A.
100 H5 **Keating** Oregon U.S.A.
94 K5 **Keating** Pennsylvania U.S.A.
118 K6 **Keatley** Saskatchewan Canada
113 D8 **Keatons Beach** Florida U.S.A.
135 V5 **Keaukaha** Hawaiian Is
78 G2 **Keban** Turkey
78 G2 **Keban Baraji** *res* Turkey
68 H2 **Ke Bao, I de** Vietnam
17 F10 **Kebdana, Jbel** *mts* Morocco
85 A5 **Kébémer** Senegal
85 F2 **Kebili** Tunisia
86 D3 **Kebkabiya** Sudan
26 K4 **Kebnekaise** Sweden
70 M9 **Kebumen** Java
69 F14 **Kebur** Sumatra
48 E4 **Kecel** Hungary
60 C11 **Kechi** Japan
117 K6 **Kechika** *R* British Columbia Canada
47 L7 **Keçiborlu** Turkey
48 F4 **Kecskemet** Hungary
69 E9 **Kedah** *prov* Malaysia
52 B6 **Kédainiai** Lithuania
100 E9 **Keddie** California U.S.A.
80 F1 **Kedesh Naphtali** Israel
122 E6 **Kedgewick** New Brunswick Canada
70 O9 **Kediri** Java
85 B6 **Kédougou** Senegal
46 E4 **Kedriki Makedhonia** *admin region* Greece
141 K1 **Kedron** *dist* Brisbane, Qnsld Australia
111 D7 **Kedron** Arkansas U.S.A.
141 K1 **Kedron Brook** Brisbane, Qnsld Australia
55 D3 **Kedrovoye** Russian Federation
55 E1 **Kedrovyy** Russian Federation
70 B4 **Kedukul** Kalimantan
70 M9 **Kedungwuni** Java
52 H3 **Kedvavom** Russian Federation
117 N10 **Keefers** British Columbia Canada
117 J4 **Keele Pk** Yukon Territory Canada
119 M8 **Keeler** Saskatchewan Canada
118 J4 **Keeley L** Saskatchewan Canada
Keeling Is *see* **Cocos Is**
123 T5 **Keels** Newfoundland Canada
71 D7 **Keenapusan** Philippines
102 F6 **Keene** California U.S.A.
95 P4 **Keene** New Hampshire U.S.A.
95 O2 **Keene** New York U.S.A.
111 L7 **Keener** Alabama U.S.A.
98 B9 **Keenesburg** Colorado U.S.A.
14 C4 **Keeper Hill** Ireland
141 F2 **Keer-weer,C** Queensland Australia
95 O2 **Keeseville** New York U.S.A.
89 A6 **Keetmanshoop** Namibia
115 K5 **Keewatin** *dist* Northwest Territories Canada
118 H1 **Keewatin** Ontario Canada
99 N2 **Keewatin** Minnesota U.S.A.
86 G4 **Kefa** *prov* Ethiopia
46 D5 **Kefali, Kep** *C* Albania
46 D6 **Kefallinia** *isld* Greece
71 M9 **Kefamenanu** Timor Indonesia
80 C6 **Kefar Bilu** Israel
80 F1 **Kefar Blum** Israel
80 C6 **Kefar Daniyyel** Israel
80 D7 **Kefar 'Ezyon** Jordan
80 C2 **Kefar Gallim** Israel
80 F1 **Kefar Gil'adi** Israel
80 C6 **Kefar Ḥabad** Israel
80 D2 **Kefar Ḥa Maccabi** Israel
80 B6 **Kefar Ha Nagid** Israel
80 F2 **Kefar HaNasi** Israel
80 B7 **Kefar Ha No'ar Nizzanim** Israel
80 C5 **Kefar Hess** Israel
80 C5 **Kefar Mallal** Israel
80 C7 **Kefar Menaḥem** Israel
80 D1 **Kefar Rosh HaNiqra** Israel
80 F4 **Kefar Ruppin** Israel
80 D6 **Kefar Rut** Jordan
80 C5 **Kefar Sava** Israel
80 F1 **Kefar Szold** Israel
80 E5 **Kefar Tappuaḥ** Jordan
80 E3 **Kefar Tavor** Israel
80 C6 **Kefar Uriyya** Israel
80 C4 **Kefar Vitkin** Israel
80 C4 **Kefar Ya'vetz** Israel
80 C4 **Kefar Yona** Israel
80 C7 **Kefar Zekharya** Israel
80 C4 **Kefer Monash** Israel
85 F7 **Keffi** Nigeria
47 L3 **Kefken Adasi** *isld* Turkey
28 R9 **Keflavik** Iceland
83 K10 **Kegalla** Sri Lanka
123 L3 **Kégashka, L** Quebec Canada
123 L3 **Kegaska** Quebec Canada
28 D7 **Kegnæs** Denmark
117 P7 **Keg River** Alberta Canada
84 F5 **Kegueur Terbi** *mt* Chad
52 B6 **Ķegums** Latvia
9 E2 **Kegworth** England
32 K5 **Kehdingen Das Alte Ld** *reg* Germany
84 J6 **Keheili** Sudan
77 C3 **Kehi** Iran
36 D6 **Kehl** Germany
52 C5 **Kehra** Estonia
36 C3 **Kehrig** Germany
13 G6 **Keighley** England
52 B5 **Keila** Estonia
86 E3 **Keilak, L** Sudan
86 C4 **Keita** *R* Chad
85 F6 **Keïta** Niger
29 M8 **Keitele** Finland
138 F6 **Keith** South Australia Australia
117 M3 **Keith Arm** *B* Northwest Territories Canada
117 N9 **Keithley Creek** British Columbia Canada
99 Q8 **Keithsburg** Illinois U.S.A.
109 O3 **Keithville** Louisiana U.S.A.
135 N1 **Kekaha** Hawaiian Is
57 H4 **Këkaygyr** Kyrgyzstan
145 E5 **Kekerenga** New Zealand
115 N4 **Kekertuk** Northwest Territories Canada
48 F3 **Kékes** *mt* Hungary
71 B3 **Kekik** *isld* Indonesia
83 K9 **Kekirawa** Sri Lanka
47 K8 **Kekova Adası** *isld* Turkey
74 F6 **Kekri** India
86 H4 **K'elafo** Ethiopia
73 L7 **Kelai** *isld* Maldives
65 B5 **Kelan** China
69 E11 **Kelang** Malaysia
69 F9 **Kelantan** *R* Malaysia
69 E10 **Kelantan** *prov* Malaysia
70 F7 **Kelara** *R* Sulawesi
69 J13 **Kelawar** *isld* Indonesia
36 B3 **Kelberg** Germany
33 O10 **Kelbra** Germany
38 F7 **Kelchsau** Austria
13 F5 **Keld** England
52 F3 **Kel'da** *R* Russian Federation
29 K6 **Keldby** Denmark
80 C8 **Kelekh** *R* Israel
57 E4 **Keles** Kazakhstan
47 K5 **Keles** Turkey
118 J7 **Kelfield** Saskatchewan Canada
112 K1 **Kelford** North Carolina U.S.A.
37 M6 **Kelheim** Germany
43 D12 **Kelibia** Tunisia
77 K1 **Kelif** Turkmenistan
57 C5 **Kelifskiy Uzboy** Turkmenistan
98 B9 **Kelim** Colorado U.S.A.
71 K9 **Keli Mutu** *mt* Flores Indonesia
36 E3 **Kelkheim** Germany
78 G1 **Kelkit** Turkey
86 B6 **Kéllé** Congo
95 M9 **Keller** Virginia U.S.A.
100 G1 **Keller** Washington U.S.A.
143 C9 **Kellerberrin** W Australia Australia
117 N4 **Keller L** Northwest Territories Canada
118 K2 **Keller L** Saskatchewan Canada
33 N4 **Kellersee** Germany
99 M9 **Kellerton** Iowa U.S.A.
114 G3 **Kellet, C** Northwest Territories Canada
94 H5 **Kellettville** Pennsylvania U.S.A.
94 E5 **Kelleys I** Ohio U.S.A.
119 O7 **Kelliher** Saskatchewan Canada
99 M2 **Kelliher** Minnesota U.S.A.
32 L5 **Kellinghusen** Germany
41 M1 **Kellmünz** Germany
100 J2 **Kellogg** Idaho U.S.A.
99 O8 **Kellogg** Iowa U.S.A.
29 O5 **Kelloselkä** Finland
14 E3 **Kells** Ireland
15 D5 **Kells Range** Scotland
140 E6 **Kelly** *R* Queensland Australia
116 F2 **Kelly** *R* Alaska U.S.A.
110 J5 **Kelly** Kentucky U.S.A.
111 D10 **Kelly** Louisiana U.S.A.
101 P6 **Kelly** Wyoming U.S.A.
140 B7 **Kelly Hills** N Terr Australia
117 K3 **Kelly L** Northwest Territories Canada
9 F3 **Kelmarsh** England
52 B6 **Kelme** Lithuania
48 K2 **Kel'mentsy** Ukraine
142 C3 **Kelmscott** *dist* Perth, W Aust Australia
86 C4 **Kélo** Chad
26 M3 **Kelottijarvi** *L* Sweden
117 O11 **Kelowna** British Columbia Canada
8 D1 **Kelsall** England
36 F3 **Kelsberbach** Germany
119 V2 **Kelsey** Manitoba Canada
117 L10 **Kelsey Bay** British Columbia Canada
119 Q5 **Kelsey L** Manitoba Canada
102 B3 **Kelseyville** California U.S.A.
119 Q9 **Kelso** Saskatchewan Canada
144 B6 **Kelso** New Zealand
13 F2 **Kelso** Scotland
103 J6 **Kelso** California U.S.A.
98 J2 **Kelso** North Dakota U.S.A.
100 C3 **Kelso** Washington U.S.A.
9 E1 **Kelstedge** England
28 H5 **Kelstrup** Denmark
28 D6 **Kelstrupstrand** Denmark
101 M8 **Kelton** Utah U.S.A.
109 N4 **Keltys** Texas U.S.A.
69 F11 **Keluang** Malaysia
70 O9 **Kelud G** *mt* Java
9 G4 **Kelvedon** England
103 O8 **Kelvin** Arizona U.S.A.
119 O6 **Kelvington** Saskatchewan Canada
119 P1 **Kelvin I** Ontario Canada
119 S8 **Kelwood** Manitoba Canada
52 D3 **Kem'** Russian Federation
52 E4 **Kema** *R* Russian Federation
71 J4 **Kema** Sulawesi
70 D2 **Kemabung** Sabah
78 G2 **Kemah** Turkey
78 G2 **Kemaliye** Turkey
47 J6 **Kemalpasa** Turkey
117 K9 **Kemano** British Columbia Canada
69 F10 **Kemasik** Malaysia
70 B4 **Kembayan** Kalimantan
86 D5 **Kembe** Cent Afr Republic
33 R9 **Kemberg** Germany
56 D3 **Kemchug** *R* Russian Federation
47 K8 **Kemer** Turkey
47 L8 **Kemer** Lycia Turkey
47 K7 **Kemer Baraji** *L* Turkey
47 M10 **Kemerburgaz** Turkey
56 C3 **Kemerovo** Russian Federation
56 C4 **Kemerovskaya Oblast'** *prov* Russian Federation
29 L6 **Kemi** Finland
29 N5 **Kemijärvi** Finland
29 M5 **Kemijoki** *R* Finland
101 P8 **Kemmerer** Wyoming U.S.A.
37 M4 **Kemnath** Germany
119 R9 **Kemnay** Manitoba Canada
33 T4 **Kemnitz** Germany
109 L3 **Kemp** Texas U.S.A.
29 L7 **Kempele** Finland
25 F6 **Kempen** Germany
36 C3 **Kempenich** Germany
22 H1 **Kempenland** *reg* Belgium
36 C4 **Kempfeld** Germany
22 J1 **Kempisch Kan** Belgium
109 H2 **Kemp, L** Texas U.S.A.
146 K10 **Kemp Land** Antarctica
109 K4 **Kempner** Texas U.S.A.
146 D5 **Kemp Pen** Antarctica
126 F2 **Kemp's Bay** Andros Bahamas
139 L4 **Kempsey** New South Wales Australia
36 D4 **Kempten** Germany
41 M2 **Kempten** Germany
121 Q5 **Kempt, L** Quebec Canada
139 H8 **Kempton** Tasmania Australia
99 S9 **Kempton** Illinois U.S.A.
98 J2 **Kempton** North Dakota U.S.A.
121 P7 **Kemptville** Ontario Canada
70 N8 **Kemudjan** *isld* Indonesia
85 D2 **Kenadsa** Algeria
116 M6 **Kenai** Alaska U.S.A.
116 N6 **Kenai Fjords Nat Park** Alaska U.S.A.
116 N6 **Kenai L** Alaska U.S.A.
116 N6 **Kenai Pen** Alaska U.S.A.
70 K8 **Kenam, Tg** *C* Sumatra
86 F4 **Kenamuke Swamp** Sudan
118 L7 **Kenaston** Saskatchewan Canada
70 D3 **Kenawang, Bt** *mt* Sarawak
94 J10 **Kenbridge** Virginia U.S.A.
70 O10 **Kencong** Java
139 L4 **Kendal** New South Wales Australia
119 O8 **Kendal** Saskatchewan Canada
13 F5 **Kendal** England
127 K2 **Kendal** Jamaica
70 N9 **Kendal** Java
141 F2 **Kendall** *R* Queensland Australia
113 G12 **Kendall** Florida U.S.A.
107 J4 **Kendall** Kansas U.S.A.
94 J3 **Kendall** New York U.S.A.
115 L5 **Kendall, C** Northwest Territories Canada
145 D4 **Kendall, Mt** New Zealand
94 B5 **Kendallville** Indiana U.S.A.
71 H6 **Kendari** Sulawesi
143 C10 **Kendenup** W Australia Australia
86 C3 **Kendigué** Chad
75 M8 **Kendrāparha** India
100 J3 **Kendrick** Idaho U.S.A.
103 N6 **Kendrick Pk** Arizona U.S.A.
75 L8 **Kendujhargarh** India
57 L1 **Kendyrlik** Kazakhstan
139 J4 **Kenebri** New South Wales Australia
109 K7 **Kenedy** Texas U.S.A.
107 O7 **Kenefick** Oklahoma U.S.A.
98 F4 **Kenel** South Dakota U.S.A.
85 B7 **Kenema** Sierra Leone
70 B4 **Kenepai** *mt* Kalimantan
145 D4 **Kenepuru Sound** New Zealand
98 H9 **Kenesaw** Nebraska U.S.A.
56 B3 **Kenga** *R* Russian Federation
86 C6 **Kenge** Zaire
57 A3 **Kenges** Uzbekistan
26 N4 **Kengis** Sweden
68 G4 **Keng Kaboa** Laos
68 G4 **Keng Kok** Laos
68 E2 **Keng Lap** Burma
68 D1 **Keng Lon** Burma
68 D2 **Keng Tawng** Burma
68 D2 **Kengtung** Burma
87 D11 **Kenhardt** S Africa
116 L6 **Kenibuna L** Alaska U.S.A.
85 B6 **Keniéba** Mali
9 E3 **Kenilworth** England
70 E2 **Keningau** Sabah
85 C2 **Kénitra** Morocco
12 D3 **Ken, L** Scotland
65 D6 **Kenli** China
112 J2 **Kenly** North Carolina U.S.A.
14 B5 **Kenmare** Ireland
98 E1 **Kenmare** North Dakota U.S.A.
14 A5 **Kenmare, R** Ireland
141 K2 **Kenmore** *dist* Brisbane, Qnsld Australia
15 E4 **Kenmore** Scotland
108 D2 **Kenna** New Mexico U.S.A.
94 F8 **Kenna** West Virginia U.S.A.
95 R1 **Kennebago Lake** Maine U.S.A.
95 S2 **Kennebec** *R* Maine U.S.A.
98 G6 **Kennebec** South Dakota U.S.A.
95 R3 **Kennebunk** Maine U.S.A.
109 M10 **Kennedale** Texas U.S.A.
141 H4 **Kennedy** Queensland Australia
119 P8 **Kennedy** Saskatchewan Canada
98 J1 **Kennedy** Minnesota U.S.A.
98 F7 **Kennedy** Nebraska U.S.A.
94 J4 **Kennedy** New York U.S.A.
115 N1 **Kennedy Channel** Canada/Greenland
141 G4 **Kennedy Highway** Queensland Australia
119 P5 **Kennedy L** Saskatchewan Canada
117 D5 **Kennedy, Mt** Yukon Territory Canada
141 G3 **Kennedy R** Queensland Australia
143 B6 **Kennedy Ra** W Australia Australia
145 E2 **Kennedy's B** New Zealand
95 M7 **Kennedyville** Maryland U.S.A.
111 F11 **Kenner** Louisiana U.S.A.
111 H12 **Kenner** New Orleans, Louisiana U.S.A.
122 J8 **Kennetcook** Nova Scotia Canada
143 B6 **Kenneth Ra** W Australia Australia
9 E5 **Kennet, R** England
110 F5 **Kennett** Missouri U.S.A.
100 F3 **Kennewick** Washington U.S.A.
110 G1 **Kenney** Illinois U.S.A.
117 L9 **Kenney Dam** British Columbia Canada
116 Q6 **Kennicott** Alaska U.S.A.
9 H3 **Kenninghall** England
137 M6 **Kenn Reef** Coral Sea
100 D7 **Keno** Oregon U.S.A.
120 E2 **Kenogami** *R* Ontario Canada
121 T4 **Kénogami L** *res* Quebec Canada
120 J4 **Kenogamissi L** Ontario Canada
117 F4 **Keno Hill** Yukon Territory Canada
118 H1 **Kenora** Ontario Canada
99 T7 **Kenosha** Wisconsin U.S.A.
94 E8 **Kenova** West Virginia U.S.A.
52 E4 **Kenozero, Oz** *L* Russian Federation
12 D3 **Ken, R** Scotland
98 H2 **Kensal** North Dakota U.S.A.
127 H5 **Kenscoff** Haiti
110 E6 **Kensett** Arkansas U.S.A.
99 N6 **Kensett** Iowa U.S.A.
122 J7 **Kensington** Prince Edward I Canada
107 M2 **Kensington** Kansas U.S.A.
9 G5 **Kent** *co* England

12 E4 **Kirkbean** Scotland
13 E4 **Kirkbride** England
13 F5 **Kirkby Lonsdale** England
13 H5 **Kirkbymoorside** England
13 F5 **Kirkby Stephen** England
118 D8 **Kirkcaldy** Alberta Canada
13 E1 **Kirkcaldy** Scotland
12 C4 **Kirkcolm** Scotland
12 D4 **Kirkcowan** Scotland
Kirkcudbright *co see* **Dumfries and Galloway** *reg*
12 D4 **Kirkcudbright** Scotland
12 D4 **Kirkcudbright B** Scotland
13 G6 **Kirk Deighton** England
28 F6 **Kirkeby** Fyn Denmark
28 B6 **Kirkeby** Sønderjylland Denmark
28 G5 **Kirke Helsinge** Denmark
28 H5 **Kirke Hvalsø** Denmark
28 H5 **Kirke Hyllinge** Denmark
119 Q8 **Kirkella** Manitoba Canada
36 C5 **Kirkel-Neuhausel** Germany
26 R2 **Kirkenes** Norway
28 H5 **Kirke Såby** Denmark
28 G6 **Kirke Stillinge** Denmark
26 K3 **Kirkestind** *mt* Norway
12 E2 **Kirkfieldbank** Scotland
13 F6 **Kirkham** England
12 D4 **Kirkinner** Scotland
12 D2 **Kirkintilloch** Scotland
29 L11 **Kirkkonummi** Finland
12 E3 **Kirkland** Scotland
103 M7 **Kirkland** Arizona U.S.A.
99 S7 **Kirkland** Illinois U.S.A.
120 K4 **Kirkland Lake** Ontario Canada
47 J3 **Kirklareli** Turkey
94 A6 **Kirklin** Indiana U.S.A.
9 F1 **Kirklington** England
13 G5 **Kirklington** N Yorks England
12 E2 **Kirkliston** Scotland
144 C6 **Kirkliston Range** New Zealand
99 L8 **Kirkman** Iowa U.S.A.
12 D3 **Kirkmichael** Scotland
13 F4 **Kirkoswald** England
12 D3 **Kirkoswald** Scotland
13 E3 **Kirkpatrick-Fleming** Scotland
146 D10 **Kirkpatrick,Mt** Antarctica
13 F5 **Kirkstone Pass** England
110 D1 **Kirksville** Missouri U.S.A.
78 K4 **Kirkūk** Iraq
15 F2 **Kirkwall** Scotland
89 D9 **Kirkwood** S Africa
102 B2 **Kirkwood** California U.S.A.
95 M4 **Kirkwood** New York U.S.A.
98 E5 **Kirley** South Dakota U.S.A.
79 F1 **Kırmıt** Turkey
36 C4 **Kirn** Germany
12 D2 **Kirn** Scotland
54 F2 **Kirov** Kaluga Russian Federation
52 G5 **Kirov** Kirovskaya obl Russian Federation
Kirovabad *see* **Gyandzha**
78 K1 **Kirovakan** Armenia
55 D3 **Kirovo** Russian Federation
54 D8 **Kirovograd** Ukraine
52 D1 **Kirovsk** Russian Federation
52 G5 **Kirovskaya Oblast'** *prov* Russian Federation
57 E5 **Kirovskiy** Tajikistan
118 G7 **Kirriemuir** Alberta Canada
15 E4 **Kirriemuir** Scotland
52 H5 **Kirs** Russian Federation
78 E2 **Kırşehir** Turkey
87 D11 **Kirstonia** S Africa
98 B7 **Kirtley** Wyoming U.S.A.
13 H6 **Kirton** England
9 F2 **Kirton Holme** England
36 G2 **Kirtorf** Germany
26 L4 **Kiruna** Sweden
86 E6 **Kirundu** Zaire
144 D5 **Kirwee** New Zealand
107 M2 **Kirwin** Kansas U.S.A.
61 N9 **Kiryū** Japan
54 K1 **Kirzhach** Russian Federation
27 H14 **Kisa** Sweden
61 N6 **Kisakata** Japan
87 G7 **Kisaki** Tanzania
46 F9 **Kisámou, K** *B* Crete Greece
86 E5 **Kisangani** Zaire
71 N9 **Kisar** *isld* Indonesia
116 G6 **Kisaralik** *R* Alaska U.S.A.
69 D11 **Kisaran** Sumatra
61 N10 **Kisarazu** Japan
48 D3 **Kisbér** Hungary
119 P9 **Kisbey** Saskatchewan Canada
56 C4 **Kiselevsk** Russian Federation
74 F5 **Kishangarh** India
85 E7 **Kishi** Nigeria
55 F4 **Kishikaroy, Oz** *L* Kazakhstan
48 M3 **Kishinev** Moldavia
60 J11 **Kishiwada** Japan
74 F2 **Kishtwar** Kashmir
Kisi *see* **Jixi**
88 G3 **Kisigau Mt** Kenya
88 E5 **Kisigo** *R* Tanzania
88 E2 **Kisii** Kenya
119 T4 **Kiskittogisu L** Manitoba Canada
119 T4 **Kiskitto L** Manitoba Canada
48 D4 **Kiskomárom** Hungary
48 E4 **Kiskörei-viztárole** *L* Hungary
48 F3 **Kisköreiviztároló** *L* Hungary
48 F4 **Kiskundorozsma** Hungary
48 F4 **Kiskunfélegyháza** Hungary
48 E4 **Kiskunhalas** Hungary
48 F4 **Kiskunmajsa** Hungary
53 F11 **Kislovodsk** Russian Federation
86 H6 **Kismaayo** Somalia
61 L10 **Kiso** Japan
61 L10 **Kiso-Fukushima** Nagano Japan
61 L10 **Kiso-sammyaku** *mts* Japan
48 E3 **Kispest** Hungary
117 J8 **Kispiox** *R* British Columbia Canada
28 H5 **Kisserup** Denmark
85 B7 **Kissidougou** Guinea
113 F9 **Kissimmee** Florida U.S.A.
113 F10 **Kissimmee** *R* Florida U.S.A.
119 Q3 **Kississing L** Manitoba Canada
41 L2 **Kisslegg** Germany
84 H5 **Kissu, Jebel** *mt* Sudan
26 L3 **Kistefjell** *mt* Norway
48 F4 **Kistelek** Hungary
48 F2 **Kisterenye** Hungary
26 O1 **Kistrand** Norway
48 F3 **Kisújszállás** Hungary
88 E2 **Kisumu** Kenya
48 G2 **Kisvárda** Hungary
79 G5 **Kiswah, Al** Syria
85 C6 **Kita** Mali
57 D5 **Kitab** Uzbekistan
60 H12 **Kitagawa** Japan
61 O9 **Kita-Ibaraki** Japan
26 L5 **Kitajaur** Sweden
61 P6 **Kitakami** Japan
61 N8 **Kitakata** Japan
60 D12 **Kita-Kyūshū** Japan
86 G5 **Kitale** Kenya
60 R2 **Kitami** Japan
60 Q1 **Kitami-sanchi** *mts* Japan
61 N9 **Kitamoto** Japan
88 G7 **Kitangari** Tanzania
61 N13 **Kitano-hana** *C* Japan
61 O9 **Kita-ura** *L* Japan
61 J12 **Kitayama** *R* Japan
48 M5 **Kitay, Ozero** *L* Ukraine
106 H3 **Kit Carson** Colorado U.S.A.
120 K9 **Kitchener** Ontario Canada
112 E5 **Kite** Georgia U.S.A.
29 P9 **Kitee** Finland
86 F5 **Kitgum** Uganda
46 F6 **Kithairón** *mt* Greece
46 F8 **Kíthira** *isld* Greece
46 G7 **Kíthnos** *isld* Greece
120 H3 **Kitigan** Ontario Canada
114 H3 **Kitikmeot** *dist* Northwest Territories Canada
80 G4 **Kitim** Jordan
117 J8 **Kitimat** British Columbia Canada
117 J9 **Kitimat Mill** Alberta Canada
29 M3 **Kitinen** *R* Finland
29 M4 **Kitinen** *R* Finland
52 C1 **Kitinen** *R* Finland
46 E2 **Kitka** *mt* Serbia Yugoslavia
46 F4 **Kítros** Greece
118 G5 **Kitscoty** Alberta Canada
48 K2 **Kitsman'** Ukraine
60 E12 **Kitsuki** Japan
61 O9 **Kitsuregawa** Japan
138 E3 **Kittakittaooloo, L** South Australia Australia
94 H6 **Kittanning** Pennsylvania U.S.A.
95 N5 **Kittatinny Mts** New Jersey U.S.A.
33 R5 **Kittendorf** Germany
95 R3 **Kittery** Maine U.S.A.
29 L4 **Kittilä** Finland
112 M1 **Kitty Hawk** North Carolina U.S.A.
88 G2 **Kitui** Kenya
88 D5 **Kitunda** Tanzania
117 J8 **Kitwanga** British Columbia Canada
88 B8 **Kitwe-Nkana** Zambia
38 F7 **Kitzbüheler Alpen** *mts* Austria
37 J4 **Kitzingen** Germany
27 M10 **Kiukainen** Finland
116 L7 **Kiukpalik I** Alaska U.S.A.
68 D3 **Kiu Lom Dam** Thailand
86 E7 **Kiumbi** Zaire
29 M8 **Kiuruvesi** Finland
116 A4 **Kivak** Russian Federation
116 E3 **Kivalina** Alaska U.S.A.
53 C8 **Kivertsy** Ukraine
116 E3 **Kividlo** Alaska U.S.A.
29 L8 **Kivijärvi** Finland
27 G17 **Kivik** Sweden
52 C5 **Kiviõli** Estonia
46 E4 **Kivotós** Greece
88 B2 **Kivu, Lac** Zaire/Rwanda
145 D4 **Kiwi** New Zealand
56 C3 **Kiya** *R* Russian Federation
55 E6 **Kiyakty, Oz** *L* Kazakhstan
61 O14 **Kiyan** Okinawa
61 O14 **Kiyan-zaki** *C* Okinawa
54 B6 **Kiyev** Ukraine
55 F5 **Kiyevka** Kazakhstan
54 B5 **Kiyevskoy Vdkr** *res* Ukraine
47 J3 **Kiyiköy** Turkey
47 L5 **Kıyır** *R* Turkey
118 H7 **Kiyiu L** Saskatchewan Canada
55 E5 **Kiyma** Kazakhstan
52 J5 **Kizel** Russian Federation
52 F4 **Kizema** Russian Federation
47 M11 **Kızıl Adalar** *islds* Turkey
79 D2 **Kızıl Burun** *C* Turkey
79 D2 **Kızılca** Turkey
47 K7 **Kızılcabölük** Turkey
47 K7 **Kızılcadağ** Turkey
47 K8 **Kızılca Dağ** *mt* Turkey
78 D1 **Kızılcahamam** Turkey
47 K7 **Kızılhişar** Turkey
78 E1 **Kızılırmak** *R* Turkey
47 L7 **Kızılkaya** Turkey
55 C5 **Kizil'skoye** Russian Federation
47 N11 **Kiziltoprak** Turkey
79 C1 **Kızılyaka** Turkey
56 D4 **Kizir** *R* Russian Federation
53 G11 **Kizlyar** Russian Federation
50 E5 **Kizyl-Arvat** Turkmenistan
26 M2 **Kjaekan** Norway
28 C4 **Kjellerup** Denmark
26 P1 **Kjelvik** Norway
26 G4 **Kjerringöy** Norway
26 Q1 **Kjöllefjord** Norway
71 J4 **Klabat** *mt* Sulawesi
48 E6 **Kladanj** Bosnia-Herzegovina
30 H5 **Kladno** Czechoslovakia
48 H6 **Kladovo** Serbia Yugoslavia
37 O4 **Kladruby** Czechoslovakia
70 E2 **Klagan** Sabah
38 K8 **Klagenfurt** Austria
103 P6 **Klagetoh** Arizona U.S.A.
52 B6 **Klaipėda** Lithuania
28 D5 **Klakring** Denmark
6 F1 **Klaksvik** Faeroes
100 A8 **Klamath** California U.S.A.
100 B8 **Klamath** *R* California U.S.A.
100 D7 **Klamath Falls** Oregon U.S.A.
100 B8 **Klamath Mts** California U.S.A.
100 C8 **Klamath River** California U.S.A.
71 C3 **Klamono** W Irian
70 D4 **Klampo** Kalimantan
117 J7 **Klappan** *R* British Columbia Canada
27 F12 **Klarä** *R* Sweden
27 F11 **Klarabro** Sweden
27 F11 **Klarälven** *R* Sweden
37 P3 **Klášterec** Czechoslovakia
70 N9 **Klaten** Java
37 P5 **Klatovy** Czechoslovakia
38 O5 **Klausen-Leopoldsdorf** Austria
41 J4 **Klausen P** *mt* Switzerland
117 G8 **Klawock** Alaska U.S.A.
31 K3 **Kłecko** Poland
31 L3 **Kleczew** Poland
122 J3 **Kleczkowski L** Quebec Canada
117 L10 **Kleena Kleene** British Columbia Canada
101 S5 **Kleenburn** Wyoming U.S.A.
33 S5 **Kleeth** Germany
25 F5 **Klefe** Germany
28 S9 **Kleifar** Iceland
101 R3 **Klein** Montana U.S.A.
33 P6 **Kleinberge** Germany
22 J1 **Kleine-Brogel** Belgium
33 S9 **Kleine Elster** *R* Germany
32 J9 **Kleinenberg** Germany
22 H1 **Kleine Nete** *R* Belgium
33 R8 **Klein Kreutz** Germany
37 N6 **Klein Laaber** *R* Germany
36 F2 **Klein Linden** Germany
89 B9 **Klein Roggeveld Berge** *mts* S Africa
89 B9 **Klein Swartberge** *mts* S Africa
33 N5 **Klein Thurow** Germany
33 Q8 **Klein Wusterwitz** Germany
38 N6 **Klein Zell** Austria
28 D3 **Klejtrup** Denmark
42 H4 **Klekovača** *mt* Bosnia-Herzegovina
99 N6 **Klemme** Iowa U.S.A.
22 E1 **Klemskerke** Belgium
117 J9 **Klemtu** British Columbia Canada
48 F6 **Klenak** Serbia Yugoslavia
33 N7 **Klenze** Germany
89 E6 **Klerksdorp** S Africa
116 G3 **Klery Creek** Alaska U.S.A.
54 E3 **Kletnya** Russian Federation
53 F9 **Kletskiy** Russian Federation
41 H2 **Klettgau** *R* Germany
33 T9 **Klettwitz** Germany
100 D3 **Klickitat** *R* Washington U.S.A.
79 E3 **Klidhes Is** Cyprus
33 Q7 **Klietz** Germany
28 C2 **Klim** Denmark
31 N5 **Klimontów** Poland
54 C3 **Klimovichi** Belorussia
52 H5 **Klimovka** Russian Federation
54 D4 **Klimovo** Russian Federation
54 J1 **Klimovsk** Russian Federation
26 G6 **Klimpfjäll** Sweden
54 H1 **Klin** Russian Federation
117 L10 **Klinaklini** *R* British Columbia Canada
112 F4 **Kline** South Carolina U.S.A.
71 G8 **Kling** Mindanao Philippines
36 G4 **Klingenberg** Germany
37 Q2 **Klingenberg** Germany
36 D5 **Klingenmünster** Germany
37 N3 **Klingenthal** Germany
70 B4 **Klingkang Ra** Sarawak
41 H2 **Klingnau** Germany
33 R6 **Klink** Germany
37 O3 **Klínovec** *mt* Czechoslovakia
28 E5 **Klinte** Denmark
27 K14 **Klintehamn** Sweden
54 D4 **Klintsy** Russian Federation
47 H5 **Klió** Greece
27 F15 **Klippan** Sweden
89 A8 **Kliprug Berg** *mt* S Africa
46 G2 **Klisura** Bulgaria
28 B2 **Klitmøller** Denmark
28 B7 **Klixbüll** Germany
42 H4 **Ključ** Bosnia-Herzegovina
31 L5 **Kłobuck** Poland
121 M6 **Klock** Ontario Canada
33 U6 **Klockow** Germany
31 L3 **Kłodawa** Poland
31 K5 **Kłodzko** Poland
27 E11 **Klöfta** Norway
117 F6 **Klondike Gold rush National Historic Park** Alaska U.S.A.
25 B6 **Kloosterzande** Netherlands
46 D3 **Klos** Albania
41 L3 **Kloster** *R* Austria
33 S7 **Klosterfelde** Germany
28 A4 **Klosterhede Plantage** Denmark
41 M3 **Klösterle** Austria
33 Q6 **Kloster Malchow** Germany
33 O9 **Kloster Mansfeld** Germany
31 J7 **Klosterneuburg** Austria
36 E6 **Klosterreichenbach** Germany
41 L4 **Klosters** Switzerland
33 S8 **Kloster Zinna** Germany
27 H12 **Kloten** Sweden
36 C3 **Klotten** Germany
33 O7 **Klötze** Germany
28 C5 **Klovborg** Denmark
26 G9 **Klövsjö** Sweden
117 D5 **Kluane** Yukon Territory Canada
117 D5 **Kluane Nat. Park** Yukon Territory Canada
31 L5 **Kluczbork** Poland
117 F6 **Klukwan** Alaska U.S.A.
70 E6 **Klumpang, Teluk** *B* Kalimantan
25 C5 **Klundert** Netherlands
70 P10 **Klungkung** Indonesia
36 C1 **Kluppelberg** Germany
116 P6 **Klutina L** Alaska U.S.A.
26 L7 **Klutmark** Sweden
33 O5 **Klütz** Germany
52 H7 **Klyavlino** Russian Federation
52 F6 **Klyazma** *R* Russian Federation
52 F2 **Klyuchevaya** Russian Federation
51 Q3 **Klyuchevskaya Sopka** *mt* Russian Federation
55 D2 **Klyuchi** Russian Federation
55 G4 **Klyuchi** Russian Federation
56 C2 **Klyuvinka** Russian Federation
27 B13 **Knabengruber** Norway
38 J7 **Knallstein, Gross** *mt* Austria
99 O5 **Knapp** Wisconsin U.S.A.
13 G5 **Knaresborough** England
13 F4 **Knarsdale** England
37 M2 **Knau** Germany
9 F4 **Knebworth** England
32 H5 **Knechtsand** *sandbank* Germany
118 K3 **Knee L** Saskatchewan Canada
33 N7 **Knesebeck** Germany
22 E1 **Knesselare** Belgium
37 K4 **Knetsgau** Germany
117 L9 **Knewstubb L** British Columbia Canada
46 G1 **Knezha** Bulgaria
98 D2 **Knife** *R* North Dakota U.S.A.
116 K7 **Knife Pk** Alaska U.S.A.
99 P3 **Knife River** Minnesota U.S.A.
101 P8 **Knight** Wyoming U.S.A.
116 O6 **Knight I** Alaska U.S.A.
117 K10 **Knight Inlet** British Columbia Canada
8 C3 **Knighton** Wales
94 B7 **Knightstown** Indiana U.S.A.
110 J2 **Knightsville** Indiana U.S.A.
42 G4 **Knin** Croatia
32 H5 **Kniphausen** Germany
109 H6 **Knippa** Texas U.S.A.
38 L7 **Knittelfeld** Austria
27 J12 **Knivsta** Sweden
46 E1 **Knjaževac** Serbia Yugoslavia
110 F5 **Knobel** Arkansas U.S.A.
142 G2 **Knob Pk** W Australia Australia
14 C3 **Knock** Ireland
14 B5 **Knockboy** *mt* Ireland
14 B5 **Knockbrack** *mt* Ireland
14 E1 **Knocklayd** *mt* N Ireland
14 D4 **Knockmealdown Mts** Ireland
14 B5 **Knockowen** *mt* Ireland
22 E1 **Knokke** Belgium
29 O5 **Knolayarvi** Russian Federation
101 M9 **Knolls** Utah U.S.A.
29 L10 **Knorevesi** Finland
28 E2 **Knøsen** *hill* Denmark
46 G9 **Knossos** Crete Greece
108 F3 **Knott** Texas U.S.A.
9 E3 **Knowle** England
107 K5 **Knowles** Oklahoma U.S.A.
146 D5 **Knowles, Cape** *C* Antarctica
121 S7 **Knowlton** Quebec Canada
99 R5 **Knowlton** Wisconsin U.S.A.
99 U8 **Knox** Indiana U.S.A.
98 G1 **Knox** North Dakota U.S.A.
94 H5 **Knox** Pennsylvania U.S.A.
117 G8 **Knox, C** Graham I, Br Col Canada
110 E1 **Knox City** Missouri U.S.A.
108 H2 **Knox City** Texas U.S.A.
146 G13 **Knox Coast** Antarctica
102 B3 **Knoxville** California U.S.A.
99 Q9 **Knoxville** Illinois U.S.A.
99 N8 **Knoxville** Iowa U.S.A.
111 E10 **Knoxville** Mississippi U.S.A.
94 K5 **Knoxville** Pennsylvania U.S.A.
112 C1 **Knoxville** Tennessee U.S.A.
83 K10 **Knuckles** *mt* Sri Lanka
115 N2 **Knud Rasmussen Land** Greenland
28 H6 **Knudshoved** *C* Denmark
36 G2 **Knüllwald** Germany
8 D1 **Knutsford** England
52 D2 **Knyazhaya Guba** Russian Federation
52 F5 **Knyazhevo** Russian Federation
87 D12 **Knysna** S Africa
31 O2 **Knyszyn** Poland
29 M2 **Koarvikods** *mt* Finland
69 H14 **Koba** Indonesia
60 D14 **Koba** Japan
28 H6 **Kobanke** *hill* Denmark
69 D8 **Ko Ban Sa Ket** Thailand
42 F2 **Kobarid** Slovenia
60 D13 **Kobayashi** Japan
115 P5 **Kobberminebugt** *B* Greenland
28 C3 **Kobberup** Denmark
Kobdo Jargalant *see* **Hovd**
71 A2 **Kobe** Halmahera Indonesia
60 J11 **Kōbe** Japan
28 G7 **Købelev** Denmark
54 F7 **Kobelyaki** Ukraine
89 A8 **Kobe Mts** S Africa
29 K5 **København** Denmark
38 H5 **Kobernausser Wald** *reg* Austria
36 C3 **Kobern-Gondorf** Germany
67 H4 **Kōbi-sho** *isld* Japan
36 D3 **Koblenz** Germany
86 F4 **Kobowem Swamp** Sudan
52 E5 **Kobozha** *R* Russian Federation
52 H4 **Kobra** Russian Federation
52 H5 **Kobra** *R* Russian Federation
61 M10 **Kobuchizawa** Japan
116 H3 **Kobuk** *R* Alaska U.S.A.
116 J3 **Kobuk** Alaska U.S.A.
116 H3 **Kobuk Valley Nat Park** Alaska U.S.A.
31 K4 **Kobylin** Poland
47 K8 **Koca** *R* Turkey
Kocaeli *see* **Izmit**
46 E3 **Kočani** Macedonia Yugoslavia
47 J7 **Koçarlı** Turkey
47 L6 **Koca Tepe** *mt* Turkey
48 F6 **Koceljevo** Serbia Yugoslavia
42 F3 **Kočevje** Slovenia
75 N5 **Koch Bihār** India
52 F4 **Kochen'ga** Russian Federation
36 H5 **Kocher** *R* Germany
46 F2 **Kocherinovo** Bulgaria
54 M4 **Kochetovka** Russian Federation
52 H5 **Kochevo** Russian Federation
115 M4 **Koch I** Northwest Territories Canada
60 F11 **Kōchi** Japan
60 G12 **Kōchi** *prefect* Japan
60 G12 **Kōchi** Japan
61 P14 **Kochinada** Okinawa
52 D3 **Kochkoma** Russian Federation
57 H4 **Kochkorka** Kyrgyzstan
52 K2 **Kochmes** Russian Federation
101 O4 **Koch Mt** Montana U.S.A.
53 G11 **Kochubey** Russian Federation
31 K4 **Kocie Góry** *mts* Poland
31 N4 **Kock** Poland
33 O7 **Köckte** Germany
48 E4 **Kocsola** Hungary
52 J3 **Kodachdikost** Russian Federation
76 C5 **Kodaikanal** India
60 O4 **Kodamari misaki** *C* Japan
75 L6 **Kodarma** India
83 L9 **Koddiyar B** Sri Lanka
31 O4 **Kodeń** Poland
116 L8 **Kodiak** Alaska U.S.A.
116 L8 **Kodiak I** Alaska U.S.A.
83 K8 **Kodikamam** Sri Lanka
52 F4 **Kodima** Russian Federation
74 D8 **Kodinar** India
52 E3 **Kodino** Russian Federation
76 D5 **Kodiyakkari** India
86 F4 **Kodok** Sudan
60 O4 **Kodomari** Japan
48 M2 **Kodyma** Ukraine
102 G6 **Koehn L** California U.S.A.
22 D1 **Koekelare** Belgium
22 J1 **Koersel** Belgium
87 C11 **Koës** Namibia
60 P1 **Koetoi** Japan
103 L8 **Kofa Mts** Arizona U.S.A.
37 N6 **Köfering** Germany
87 E11 **Koffiefontein** S Africa
85 D7 **Koforidua** Ghana
61 M10 **Kōfu** Japan
47 K8 **Kofu Tepe** *mt* Turkey
61 N9 **Koga** Japan
141 K7 **Kogan** Queensland Australia
28 J6 **Køge** Denmark
29 K6 **Køge Bugt** *B* Denmark
52 J3 **Kogel'** *R* Russian Federation
48 M4 **Kogil'nik** *R* Moldavia/Ukraine
116 H6 **Kogrukluk** *R* Alaska U.S.A.
60 D11 **Kogushi** Japan
74 D2 **Kohat** Pakistan
52 B5 **Kohila** Estonia
75 Q6 **Kohima** India
68 G6 **Koh Ker** Cambodia
146 B8 **Kohler Ra** Antarctica
74 C4 **Kohlu** Pakistan
37 O1 **Kohren Sahlis** Germany
77 G2 **Kohsun** Afghanistan
68 F7 **Koh Tang** *isld* Cambodia
52 C5 **Kohtla-Järve** Estonia
145 E3 **Kohuratahi** New Zealand
61 M8 **Koide** Japan
116 R6 **Koidern** Yukon Territory Canada
69 A8 **Koihoa** Nicobar Is
52 H3 **Koin** *R* Russian Federation
78 K3 **Koi Sanjaq** Iraq
29 P8 **Koitere** *L* Finland
29 L5 **Koivu** Finland
65 G7 **Köje** *isld* S Korea
31 K6 **Kojetín** Czechoslovakia
60 N4 **Ko jima** *isld* Japan
143 B10 **Kojonup** W Australia Australia
95 S1 **Kokadjo** Maine U.S.A.
83 L10 **Kokagala** *mt* Sri Lanka
86 G4 **K'ok'a Hāyk'** *L* Ethiopia
55 D6 **Kokalaat** Kazakhstan
57 F4 **Kokand** Uzbekistan
117 P11 **Kokanee Glacier Nat. Park** British Columbia Canada
57 B2 **Kokaral** Kazakhstan
48 F2 **Kokava** Czechoslovakia
60 J11 **Kokawa** Japan
56 C5 **Kokbesh** Russian Federation
57 F6 **Kokcha** *R* Afghanistan
55 E4 **Kokchetav** Kazakhstan
29 K10 **Kokemäenjoki** *R* Finland
29 J10 **Kokemäki** Finland
136 H2 **Kokenau** W Irian
54 A2 **Kokhanovo** Belorussia
80 B7 **Kokhav** Israel
80 E6 **Kokhav HaShaḥar** Jordan
80 C5 **Kokhav Ya'ir** Jordan
29 K8 **Kokkola** Finland
85 E6 **Koko** Nigeria
136 K3 **Kokoda** Papua New Guinea
102 S12 **Koko Head** Hawaiian Is
116 F2 **Kokolik** *R* Alaska U.S.A.
94 A6 **Kokomo** Indiana U.S.A.
144 C6 **Kokonga** New Zealand
Koko Nor *L see* **Qinghai Hu** *L*
52 C4 **Kokonselka** *L* Finland
54 F4 **Kokorevka** Russian Federation
69 B11 **Kokos** *isld* Indonesia
116 K4 **Kokrines Hills** Alaska U.S.A.
57 E4 **Koksaray** Kazakhstan
52 G6 **Kokshaga** *R* Russian Federation
52 F4 **Kokshen'ga** *R* Russian Federation
22 D1 **Koksijde** Belgium
115 N6 **Koksoak** *R* Quebec Canada
54 M8 **Koksovyy** Russian Federation
89 F8 **Kokstad** S Africa
60 D14 **Kokubu** Japan
60 D12 **Kokura** Japan
70 G7 **Koku, Tg** *C* Sulawesi
116 H7 **Kokwok** *R* Alaska U.S.A.
57 G4 **Kok-Yangak** Kyrgyzstan
52 D1 **Kola** Russian Federation
70 G7 **Kolaka** Sulawesi
71 F6 **Kolambugan** Mindanao Philippines
76 D4 **Kolar** India
76 D4 **Kolar Gold Fields** India
29 K4 **Kolari** Finland
Kolarovgrad *see* **Shumen**
48 D3 **Kolárovo** Czechoslovakia
26 F8 **Kolåsen** Sweden
46 D2 **Kolašin** Montenegro Yugoslavia
27 H12 **Kolbäck** Sweden
71 M10 **Kolbano** Timor
38 H8 **Kölbnitz** Austria
26 D9 **Kolbotn** Norway
31 N5 **Kolbuszowa** Poland
28 F5 **Kolby** Denmark
52 E6 **Kol'chugino** Russian Federation
85 A6 **Kolda** Senegal
28 B3 **Koldby** Denmark
28 C6 **Kolding** Denmark
86 E5 **Kole** Zaire
135 T3 **Kolekole** *pk* Hawaiian Is
48 M4 **Kolesnoye** Ukraine
37 P5 **Koleveč** Czechoslovakia
52 C5 **Kolga laht** *G* Estonia
50 D2 **Kolguyev Ostrov** *isld* Russian Federation
76 B2 **Kolhapur** India
29 O8 **Koli** Finland
48 L5 **Kolibash** Moldavia
116 J7 **Koliganek** Alaska U.S.A.
47 R14 **Kolimbia** Rhodes Greece
31 J5 **Kolin** Czechoslovakia
101 Q2 **Kolin** Montana U.S.A.
28 F4 **Kolind** Denmark
37 P5 **Kolinec** Czechoslovakia
28 C4 **Kølkær** Denmark
121 N7 **Kol. Kienitz** Ontario Canada
33 T7 **Kol Kienitz** Germany
Kollam *see* **Quilon**
37 L1 **Kölleda** Germany
76 C4 **Kollegal** India
76 D5 **Kollidam** *R* India
46 E7 **Kollinai** Greece
25 F2 **Kollum** Netherlands
28 C4 **Kollund** Ringkøbing Denmark
28 C7 **Kollund** Sønderjylland Denmark
36 B2 **Köln** Germany
31 N2 **Kolno** Poland
31 L3 **Koło** Poland
135 O1 **Koloa** Hawaiian Is
31 J1 **Kołobrzeg** Poland
33 S9 **Kolochau** Germany
54 D2 **Kolodnya** Russian Federation
52 F5 **Kologriv** Russian Federation
71 B3 **Kolok** Indonesia
85 C6 **Kolokani** Mali
137 M3 **Kolombangara** *isld* Solomon Is
56 B2 **Kolominskiye Grivy** Russian Federation
54 K1 **Kolomna** Russian Federation
48 J2 **Kolomyya** Ukraine
70 G6 **Kolonedale** Sulawesi
71 B2 **Kolorai** *isld* Halmahera Indonesia
55 F3 **Kolosovka** Russian Federation
Kolozsvar *see* **Cluj-Napoca**
52 E5 **Kolp'** *R* Russian Federation
56 B2 **Kolpashevo** Russian Federation
33 R6 **Kölpin-See** *L* Germany
33 Q10 **Kölsa** Germany
26 G9 **Kolsätt** Sweden
52 D1 **Kol'skiy Poluostrov** *pen* Russian Federation
52 D1 **Kol'skiy Zaliv** *G* Russian Federation
28 F6 **Kølstrup** Denmark
27 H12 **Kolsva** Sweden
52 A3 **Kol'tsovo** Russian Federation
48 F6 **Kolubara** *R* Serbia Yugoslavia
145 D1 **Koluikohu** New Zealand
73 L8 **Kolumadulu Atoll** Maldives
31 M4 **Koluszki** Poland
55 E5 **Koluton** Kazakhstan
52 J1 **Kolva** *R* Komi Respublika Russian Federation
52 J4 **Kolva** *R* Permskaya obl Russian Federation
26 E7 **Kolvereid** Norway
26 O1 **Kolvik** Norway
52 D2 **Kolvitsa** Russian Federation
87 E8 **Kolwezi** Zaire
54 K1 **Kolyberovo** Russian Federation
51 P2 **Kolyma** *R* Russian Federation
54 H1 **Kolyubakino** Russian Federation
147 P2 **Kolyuchinskaya** Russian Federation
116 A3 **Kolyuchinskaya Guba** *G* Russian Federation
56 B5 **Kolyvan'** Russian Federation
27 G14 **Kölzby** Sweden
46 F1 **Kom** *mt* Bulgaria
68 D5 **Koma** Burma
86 G4 **Koma** Ethiopia
61 P6 **Kōma** Japan
85 G6 **Komadugu Gana** *R* Nigeria
61 L10 **Komagane** Japan
60 O3 **Komaga-take** *mt* Hokkaido Japan
61 N8 **Komaga-take** *mt* Honshu Japan
26 N1 **Komagfjord** Norway
26 S1 **Komagvaer** Norway
55 C2 **Komarikhinskiy** Russian Federation
119 U8 **Komarno** Manitoba Canada
48 E3 **Komárno** Czechoslovakia
48 E3 **Komárom** *co* Hungary
48 E3 **Komárom** Hungary
89 G6 **Komati** *R* Swaziland
89 G5 **Komatipoort** S Africa
103 M8 **Komatke** Arizona U.S.A.
61 K9 **Komatsu** Ishikawa Japan
61 O7 **Komatsu** Yamagata Japan
71 L8 **Komba** *isld* Indonesia
71 J4 **Kombot** Sulawesi
46 E5 **Kombóti** Greece
28 E3 **Komdrup** Denmark
88 D2 **Kome I** Uganda
89 E9 **Komga** S Africa
61 O5 **Kominato** Japan
52 H5 **Komi-Permyatskiy Avtonomnyy Okrug** *dist* Russian Federation
52 H3 **Komi Respublika** Russian Federation
48 E2 **Komjatice** Czechoslovakia
48 E4 **Komló** Hungary
53 E9 **Kommunarsk** Ukraine
57 F5 **Kommunizma, Pik** *mt* Tajikistan
71 J9 **Komodo** *isld* Indonesia
85 D7 **Komoé** *R* Ivory Coast
85 D7 **Komoé Nat. Park** Ivory Coast
84 J5 **Kôm Ombo** Egypt
61 M9 **Komoro** Japan
46 G3 **Komotiní** Greece
46 D2 **Komovi** *mt* Montenegro Yugoslavia
89 D8 **Kompas Berg** *mt* S Africa
68 G6 **Kompong Kleang** Cambodia
68 F7 **Kompong Som** Cambodia
68 G7 **Kompong Speu** Cambodia
68 G6 **Kompong Sralao** Cambodia
68 G6 **Kompong Thom** Cambodia
68 G6 **Kompong Trabek** Cambodia
68 G7 **Kompong Trach** Cambodia
68 G7 **Kompong Tralach** Cambodia
48 M4 **Komrat** Moldavia
89 B9 **Komsbergeskarp** *mts* S Africa
55 D4 **Komsomolets** Kazakhstan
51 J1 **Komsomolets, Ostrov** *isld* Russian Federation
52 F6 **Komsomol'sk** Russian Federation
54 E8 **Komsomol'sk** Ukraine
55 D1 **Komsomol'skiy** Russian Federation
54 K9 **Komsomol'skoye** Ukraine
59 L1 **Komsomol'skoye-na-Amure** Russian Federation
103 M10 **Kom Vo** Arizona U.S.A.
53 G12 **Konagkend** Azerbaijan
52 E6 **Konakovo** Russian Federation
75 M9 **Konārka** India
77 B5 **Konār Takhteh** Iran
109 L1 **Konawa** Oklahoma U.S.A.
42 H3 **Končanica** Croatia
55 E2 **Konda** *R* Russian Federation
71 C3 **Konda** W Irian
76 E1 **Kondagaon** India
121 O6 **Kondiaronk, L** Quebec Canada
143 C10 **Kondinin** W Australia Australia
88 E4 **Kondoa** Tanzania
52 D4 **Kondopoga** Russian Federation
48 F4 **Kondoros** Hungary
54 G2 **Kondrovo** Russian Federation
86 B3 **Konduga** Nigeria
143 B9 **Kondut** W Australia Australia
56 D2 **Konduyak** Russian Federation
77 L1 **Kondūz** Afghanistan
52 J3 **Konetsbor** Russian Federation
52 E4 **Konevo** Russian Federation
28 H6 **Køng** Denmark
85 D7 **Kong** Ivory Coast
116 R2 **Kongakut** *R* Alaska U.S.A.
115 Q4 **Kong Christian IX Land** Greenland
115 R3 **Kong Christian X Land** Greenland
28 B6 **Kongeå** *R* Denmark
29 K5 **Kongens Lyngby** Denmark
115 P5 **Kong Frederik VI Kyst** *coast* Greenland
29 M9 **Konginkangas** Finland
68 F7 **Kong Kaôh Kong** Cambodia
50 B1 **Kong Karls Land** *isld* Spitzbergen
70 E4 **Kong Kat** *mt* Kalimantan
70 E4 **Kongkemul** *mt* Kalimantan
87 D9 **Kongola** Namibia
86 E7 **Kongolo** Zaire
86 F4 **Kongor** Sudan
147 E10 **Kong Oscars Fj** Greenland
26 J3 **Kongsbakktind** *mt* Norway
27 D12 **Kongsberg** Norway
26 R1 **Kongsfjord** *inlet* Norway
26 R1 **Kongsfjord** Norway
28 B6 **Kongsmark** Denmark
26 F7 **Kongsmoen** Norway
28 J6 **Kongsted** Denmark
27 E11 **Kongsvinger** Norway
66 B4 **Kongur Shan** *mt* China
88 F5 **Kongwa** Tanzania
31 M5 **Koniecpol** Poland
36 H4 **Königheim** Germany
36 F6 **Königsbach** Germany
Königsberg *see* **Kaliningrad**
36 D4 **Königsberg** *mt* Germany
37 J6 **Königsbronn** Germany
33 T10 **Königsbrück** Germany
37 K7 **Königsbrunn** Germany
41 O2 **Königsdorf** Germany
37 L2 **Königsee** Germany
37 L4 **Königsfeld** Germany
Königshofen *see* **Lauda-Königshofen**
36 H4 **Königshofen** Germany
33 N8 **Königslutter** Germany
36 F5 **Königsstuhl** *mt* Germany
36 E3 **Königstein** Germany
38 L5 **Königswiesen** Austria
36 C2 **Königswinter** Germany
33 T8 **Königs Wusterhausen** Germany
31 L3 **Konin** Poland
145 E4 **Konini** New Zealand
46 D5 **Konispol** Albania
42 H5 **Konjic** Bosnia-Herzegovina
88 B1 **Konjo** *tribal dist* Zaire
48 E6 **Konjuh** *mt* Bosnia-Herzegovina
26 M3 **Konkämä Älv** *R* Sweden/Finland
88 A8 **Konkola** Zambia
85 B6 **Konkouré** *R* Guinea
33 P9 **Könnern** Germany
37 N3 **Konnersreuth** Germany
29 M9 **Konnevesi** Finland
85 D7 **Konongo** Ghana
88 C5 **Konongo** Tanzania
61 N9 **Kōnosu** Japan
54 E5 **Konotop** Ukraine
66 D3 **Konqi He** *R* China
85 C7 **Konsankoro** Guinea
31 M4 **Końskie** Poland
53 F10 **Konstantinovsk** Russian Federation
41 K2 **Konstanz** Germany
85 F6 **Kontagora** Nigeria
86 B4 **Kontcha** Cameroon
22 G1 **Kontich** Belgium
29 N7 **Kontiomäki** Finland
47 O12 **Kontókali** Greece
116 L6 **Kontrashibuna L** Alaska U.S.A.
68 J6 **Kontum, Plat. du** Vietnam
52 F2 **Konushin, Mys** *C* Russian Federation
78 D3 **Konya** Turkey
36 B4 **Konz** Germany
88 F2 **Konza** Kenya
37 O5 **Konzell** Germany
55 C2 **Konzhakovskiy Kamen', G** *mt* Russian Federation
25 C4 **Koog** Netherlands
116 C5 **Kookooligit Mts** St Lawrence I, Alaska U.S.A.
143 D8 **Kookynie** W Australia Australia
140 D2 **Koolatong** *R* N Terr Australia
102 S11 **Koolauloa** Hawaiian Is
102 S12 **Koolaupoko** Hawaiian Is
142 B6 **Kooline** W Australia
140 E6 **Koolivoo,L** Queensland Australia
143 C9 **Koolyanobbing** W Australia Australia
143 G9 **Koonalda** South Australia Australia
142 B6 **Koorabooka** *R* W Australia Australia
143 B6 **Koorabooka** W Australia Australia
143 B9 **Koorda** W Australia Australia
142 B5 **Koordarrie** W Australia Australia
29 T8 **Kópasker** Iceland
48 L2 **Kopaygorod** Ukraine
144 A7 **Kopeka B** New Zealand
33 T8 **Kopenick** Germany
26 K8 **Köpmanholmen** Sweden
27 F10 **Kopparberg** *county* Sweden
79 C2 **Köprülü** Turkey
145 E2 **Kopu** New Zealand
145 E4 **Kopuaranga** New Zealand
77 C4 **Kor** *R* Iran
86 H4 **K'orahē** Ethiopia
47 O12 **Korakiána** Greece
75 K7 **Korba** India
32 J10 **Korbach** Germany
100 B9 **Korbel** California U.S.A.
69 E10 **Korbu, G.** *mt* Malaysia
46 D4 **Korcë** Albania
42 H6 **Korčula** Croatia
36 B4 **Kordel** Germany
77 A2 **Kordestān** Iran
77 D1 **Kord Kūy** Iran
Kordofan *prov* Sudan *see* **Northern and Southern Kordofan** *provs*
77 G6 **Kords** *reg* Iran
59 H4 **Korea Bay** China/Korea
65 G4 **Korea, North** *rep* E Asia
65 H6 **Korea, South** *rep* E Asia
52 D2 **Korelaksha** Russian Federation
52 J4 **Korelino** Russian Federation
54 F5 **Korenevo** Russian Federation
146 D7 **Korff Ice Rise** *ice rise* Antarctica
26 G5 **Korgen** Norway
85 C7 **Korhogo** Ivory Coast
60 D14 **Kori** Japan
46 F4 **Korinós** Greece
28 E6 **Korinth** Denmark
46 E6 **Korinthiakós Kólpos** *G* Greece
46 F7 **Kórinthos** Greece
46 D2 **Koritnik** *mt* Serbia Yugoslavia
Koritsa *see* **Korcë**
61 O8 **Kōriyama** Japan
55 D4 **Korkino** Russian Federation
47 L7 **Korkuteli** Turkey
66 D3 **Korla** China
54 B3 **Korma** Belorussia
120 G5 **Kormak** Ontario Canada
48 D3 **Körmend** Hungary
55 F3 **Kormilovka** Russian Federation
42 G5 **Kornat** *isld* Croatia
37 L5 **Kornburg** Germany
25 F7 **Kornelimünster** Germany
37 K1 **Körner** Germany
48 L3 **Korneshty** Moldavia
55 E4 **Korneyevka** Kazakhstan
55 F5 **Korneyevka** Kazakhstan
27 E13 **Kornsjö** Norway
28 C3 **Kornum** Denmark
36 G6 **Kornwestheim** Germany
70 G5 **Koro** *R* Sulawesi
54 J6 **Korocha** Russian Federation
78 C1 **Köröglu D** Turkey
88 G4 **Korogwe** Tanzania
138 F7 **Koroit** Victoria Australia
144 D4 **Koromiko** New Zealand
113 F8 **Korona** Florida U.S.A.
85 E7 **Koronga** *mt* Togo
139 G6 **Korong Vale** Victoria Australia
46 E8 **Koróni** Greece
46 F4 **Korónia, L** Greece
31 K2 **Koronowo** Poland
54 D5 **Korop** Ukraine
48 J2 **Koropets** Ukraine
46 F7 **Koropí** Greece
48 F4 **Körös** *R* Hungary
53 C8 **Korosten** Ukraine
53 C8 **Korostyshev** Ukraine
86 C2 **Koro Toro** Chad
54 L6 **Korotoyak** Russian Federation
116 G9 **Korovin I** Alaska U.S.A.
29 M9 **Korpilahti** Finland
26 N5 **Korpilombolo** Sweden
29 J11 **Korpo** Finland
59 M2 **Korsakov** Russian Federation
27 H14 **Korsberga** Sweden
36 B1 **Korschenbroich** Germany
28 H5 **Korshage** *C* Denmark
48 J2 **Korshev** Ukraine
28 E3 **Korsholm** *isld* Denmark
27 H11 **Korsnäs** Sweden
26 H3 **Korsnes** Norway
28 G6 **Korsør** Denmark
54 C7 **Korsun' Shevchenkovskiy** Ukraine
22 E1 **Kortemark** Belgium
29 K8 **Kortesjärvi** Finland
22 J2 **Kortessem** Belgium
27 G12 **Kortfors** Sweden
25 A5 **Kortgene** Netherlands
52 H4 **Kortkeros** Russian Federation
22 E2 **Kortrijk** Belgium
52 F5 **Kortsovo** Russian Federation
47 J5 **Korucu** Turkey
139 H7 **Korumburra** Victoria Australia
29 O3 **Korvatunturi** *mt* Finland
29 O4 **Korya** Russian Federation
52 G4 **Koryazhma** Russian Federation
54 D5 **Koryukovka** Ukraine
47 J8 **Kos** *isld* Greece
52 H5 **Kosa** Russian Federation
53 E10 **Kosa Arabatskaya Strelka** *spit* Ukraine
55 D5 **Kosagal** Kazakhstan
61 L11 **Kosai** Japan
61 O5 **Kosaka** Japan
69 E8 **Ko Samui** *isld* Thailand
57 D1 **Kosay** Kazakhstan
54 J2 **Kosaya Gora** Russian Federation
56 E2 **Kosaya, Shiv** Russian Federation
57 C4 **Kosboget** Uzbekistan
37 M6 **Kösching** Germany
31 K3 **Kościan** Poland
31 K1 **Kościerzyna** Poland
111 G8 **Kosciusko** Mississippi U.S.A.
117 G7 **Kosciusko I** Alaska U.S.A.
139 J6 **Kosciusko, Mt** New South Wales Australia
139 J6 **Kosciusko Nat Park** New South Wales Australia
33 S10 **Koselitz** Germany
33 U4 **Koserow** Germany
56 B1 **Koses** *R* Russian Federation
76 C2 **Kosgi** India
56 C6 **Kosh Agach** Russian Federation
55 D2 **Koshay** Russian Federation
57 G4 **Kosh-Děbě** Kyrgyzstan
60 S2 **Koshikawa** Japan
60 C14 **Koshiki-kaikyō** *str* Japan
60 C14 **Koshiki-rettō** *islds* Japan
110 E5 **Koshkonong** Missouri U.S.A.
57 K2 **Koshkorkol', Ozero** *L* Kazakhstan
57 B4 **Kosh-Kupyr** Uzbekistan
61 M9 **Kōshoku** Japan
57 D4 **Koshrabad** Uzbekistan
48 G2 **Košice** Czechoslovakia
68 E6 **Ko Si Chang** *isld* Thailand
76 C3 **Kosigi** India
89 H6 **Kosi L** S Africa
55 C5 **Kos-Istek** Kazakhstan
48 E5 **Koška** Croatia
123 R6 **Koskaecodde L** Newfoundland Canada
29 K11 **Koski** Finland
26 M5 **Koskivaara** Sweden
57 D1 **Koskol'** Kazakhstan
57 H3 **Koskuduk** Kazakhstan
26 L4 **Koskullskulle** Sweden
52 G3 **Koslan** Russian Federation
52 G2 **Kosma** *R* Russian Federation
48 J2 **Kosmach** Ukraine
100 C3 **Kosmos** Washington U.S.A.
59 J4 **Kosŏng** N Korea
48 J2 **Kosov** Ukraine
46 D2 **Kosovo** *aut rep* Serbia Yugoslavia
46 E2 **Kosovo Polje** Serbia Yugoslavia
33 S10 **Kossdorf** Germany
109 L4 **Kosse** Texas U.S.A.
33 P9 **Kösseln** Germany
37 O1 **Kössern** Germany
37 P7 **Kösslarn** Germany
31 N3 **Kossów** Poland
27 H15 **Kosta** Sweden
33 T9 **Kostebrau** Germany
46 F2 **Kostenets** Bulgaria
28 J7 **Koster** Denmark
54 L1 **Kosterevo** Russian Federation
48 L2 **Kosteshty-Synka, Vodokhranilishche** *res* Moldavia
48 L3 **Kostesty** Moldavia
86 F3 **Kosti** Sudan
46 F2 **Kostinbrod** Bulgaria
50 H2 **Kostino** Russian Federation
52 D3 **Kostomuksha** Russian Federation
52 F5 **Kostroma** Russian Federation
52 F5 **Kostromskaya Oblast'** *prov* Russian Federation
31 H3 **Kostrzyn** Poland
54 D3 **Kostyukovichi** Belorussia
54 B4 **Kostyukovka** Belorussia
61 L9 **Kosugi** Japan
52 J2 **Kos'yu** Russian Federation
52 J2 **Kos'yuvom** Russian Federation
31 J1 **Koszalin** Poland
48 D3 **Köszeg** Hungary
75 K7 **Kota** India
70 K8 **Kotaagung** Sumatra
69 F9 **Kota Baharu** Malaysia
70 B5 **Kotabaru** Kalimantan
70 E6 **Kotabaru** Kalimantan
69 C11 **Kotabaru** Sumatra
69 E13 **Kotabaru** Sumatra
70 E1 **Kota Belud** Sabah
70 C6 **Kotabesi** Kalimantan

Kyaka — Langhe
193

88 C2 **Kyaka** Tanzania
56 G5 **Kyakhta** Russian Federation
139 G5 **Kyalite** New South Wales Australia
138 D5 **Kyancutta** South Australia Australia
52 E3 **Kyanda** Russian Federation
52 D3 **Kyargozero** Russian Federation
68 C3 **Kyaukhnyat** Burma
68 B3 **Kyaukkyi** Burma
68 C1 **Kyaukme** Burma
68 B1 **Kyaukmyaung** Burma
68 A3 **Kyaukpyu** Burma
68 C2 **Kyaukse** Burma
68 A2 **Kyauktaw** Burma
68 B2 **Kyaukyit** Burma
68 B4 **Kyaunggon** Burma
138 F6 **Kybybolite** South Australia Australia
26 G7 **Kycklingvattnet** Sweden
68 C3 **Kyebogyi** Burma
144 C6 **Kyeburn** New Zealand
68 D5 **Kyeikdon** Burma
68 D4 **Kyeikywa** Burma
68 B3 **Kyeintali** Burma
33 O10 **Kyffhäuser** *mt* Germany
143 E7 **Kyffin-Thomas Hill** W Australia Australia
28 F5 **Kyholm** *isld* Denmark
68 C3 **Kyidaunggan** Burma
58 D4 **Kyikug** China
68 A2 **Kyindwe** Burma
31 K6 **Kyjov** Czechoslovakia
118 J8 **Kyle** Saskatchewan Canada
98 D6 **Kyle** South Dakota U.S.A.
109 K6 **Kyle** Texas U.S.A.
101 T8 **Kyle** Wyoming U.S.A.
15 C3 **Kyleakin** Scotland
87 F10 **Kyle Dam** Zimbabwe
15 D2 **Kyle of Durness** Scotland
15 C3 **Kyle of Lochalsh** Scotland
15 D2 **Kyle of Tongue** Scotland
12 C2 **Kyles of Bute** *chan* Scotland
36 B3 **Kyll** *R* Germany
36 B3 **Kyllburg** Germany
29 N10 **Kymi** *prov* Finland
29 M11 **Kymijoki** *R* Finland
55 C2 **Kyn** Russian Federation
139 G6 **Kyneton** Victoria Australia
37 O3 **Kynšperk nad Ohří** Czechoslovakia
141 F5 **Kynuna** Queensland Australia
61 P12 **Kyoda** Okinawa
86 F5 **Kyoga, L** Uganda
60 J10 **Kyōga-misaki** *C* Japan
139 L3 **Kyogle** New South Wales Australia
65 F5 **Kyŏmip'o** N Korea
68 D4 **Kyondo** Burma
141 H5 **Kyong** Queensland Australia
68 C2 **Kyong** Burma
60 J10 **Kyōto** *prefect* Japan
62 **Kyōto** *conurbation* Japan
55 E6 **Kypshak, Oz** *L* Kazakhstan
79 D3 **Kyrenia** Cyprus
57 F4 **Kyrgyzstan** *rep* C Asia
33 Q7 **Kyritz** Germany
Kyrkslätt *see* **Kirkkonummi**
29 J8 **Kyröjoki** *R* Finland
29 K10 **Kyrösjärvi** *L* Finland
52 J3 **Kyrta** Russian Federation
55 D2 **Kyrtym'ya** Russian Federation
55 C2 **Kyr'ya** Russian Federation
55 G3 **Kyshtovka** Russian Federation
55 D3 **Kyshtym** Russian Federation
68 G3 **Ky Son** Vietnam
52 G3 **Kyssa** Russian Federation
79 D3 **Kythrea** Cyprus
55 C2 **Kytlym** Russian Federation
57 H3 **Kyungëy-Ala-Too, Khrebet** *mts* Kazakhstan/Kyrgyzstan
68 D5 **Kyungyaung** Burma
68 C7 **Kyun Pila** *islds* Burma
117 K10 **Kyuquot** British Columbia Canada
60 D13 **Kyūshū** *isld* Japan
60 E13 **Kyūshū-sanchi** *mts* Japan
46 F2 **Kyustendil** Bulgaria
51 M1 **Kyusyur** Russian Federation
139 H6 **Kywong** New South Wales Australia
29 L8 **Kyyjärvi** Finland
56 D5 **Kyzyl** Russian Federation
57 E1 **Kyzyldyykan** Kazakhstan
56 E5 **Kyzyl-Khem** *R* Russian Federation
57 J2 **Kyzylkiya** Kazakhstan
57 F4 **Kyzyl-Kiya** Kyrgyzstan
57 E1 **Kyzyl-Kommuna** Kazakhstan
57 C4 **Kyzylkum, Peski** *desert* Kazakhstan/Uzbekistan
57 G5 **Kyzylrabot** Tajikistan
55 F5 **Kyzyltas** Kazakhstan
57 H1 **Kyzyltu** Kazakhstan
57 D1 **Kyzyluy** Kazakhstan
57 C1 **Kyzylzhar** Kazakhstan
57 E1 **Kyzylzhar** Kazakhstan
57 J3 **Kyzylzhide** Kazakhstan
57 D3 **Kzyl-Orda** Kazakhstan
55 F4 **Kzyltu** Kazakhstan

L

31 J7 **Laa** Austria
37 M5 **Laaber** Germany
36 C3 **Laacher See** *L* Germany
33 Q5 **Laage** Germany
25 F4 **Laag Keppel** Netherlands
124 C4 **La Angostura** Mexico
29 N3 **Laanila** Finland
131 A7 **La Araucanía** *prov* Chile
86 A2 **Laascaanood** Somalia
86 A1 **Laas Dhuura** Somalia
86 A1 **Laasgoray** Somalia
86 A1 **Laaso Dawaco** Somalia
36 E2 **Laasphe** Germany
127 N9 **La Asunción** Venezuela
135 R2 **Laau Pt** Hawaiian Is
85 B3 **Laâyoune** W Sahara
108 E7 **La Babia** Mexico
110 F3 **Labadie** Missouri U.S.A.
7 E12 **Labadie Bank** Atlantic Oc
111 F12 **Labadieville** Louisiana U.S.A.
121 U4 **La Baie** Quebec Canada
71 L9 **Labala** Indonesia
19 P12 **Labalme** France
79 F8 **Labān** Jordan
16 D2 **La Baneza** Spain
124 H7 **La Barca** Mexico
101 P7 **La Barge** Wyoming U.S.A.
137 Q5 **Labasa** Vanua Levu Fiji
19 P17 **La Bastide-des-Jourdans** France
18 G8 **Labastide Murat** France
19 Q13 **La Bathie** France
19 Q15 **La Bâtie-Neuve** France
68 A2 **Labawa** Burma
52 H2 **Labazhskoye** Russian Federation
26 J5 **Labbas** Sweden
80 D1 **Labbouna** Lebanon
26 R3 **Labdshy'aur, Oz** *L* Russian Federation
31 J5 **Labe** *R* Czechoslovakia
85 B6 **Labé** Guinea
19 Q17 **La Bégude Blanche** France
121 Q6 **Labelle** Quebec Canada
99 P9 **La Belle** Missouri U.S.A.
71 H6 **Labengke** *isld* Sulawesi
19 Q15 **La Bérarde** France
117 F5 **Laberge, L** Yukon Territory Canada
131 E7 **Laberinto, Pta** Argentina
37 N6 **Laberweinting** Germany
70 D2 **Labi** Brunei
117 L5 **La Biche** *R* Yukon Terr/Br Col Canada
71 B2 **Labilabi** Halmahera Indonesia
42 F3 **Labin** Croatia
69 F11 **Labis** Malaysia
127 M9 **La Blanquilla, I** Venezuela
71 F3 **Labo** Philippines
71 H5 **Labobo** *isld* Indonesia
103 J10 **La Bomba** Mexico
101 U7 **Labonte Cr** Wyoming U.S.A.
124 G4 **La Boquilla** Mexico
48 G1 **Laborec** *R* Czechoslovakia
143 C7 **Labouchere, Mt** W Australia Australia
79 G4 **Laboué** Lebanon
18 E8 **Labouheyre** France
133 E4 **Laboulaye** Argentina
115 N7 **Labrador** *dist* Newfoundland Canada
115 N7 **Labrador City** Labrador, Nfld Canada
115 O6 **Labrador Sea** Nfld/Greenland
128 F5 **Labrea** Brazil
128 B4 **La Brea, Cer. de** *hill* Peru
124 E5 **La Brecha** Mexico
18 E8 **Labrède** France
122 C4 **Labrieville** Quebec Canada
122 C4 **Labrieville, Parc de** Quebec Canada
18 E8 **Labrit** France
118 E1 **La Broquerie** Manitoba Canada
22 B3 **Labroye** France
18 G9 **Labruguière** France
70 G5 **Labuanbajo** Sulawesi
136 F2 **Labuha** Moluccas Indonesia
70 K9 **Labuhan** Java
71 J9 **Labuhanbadjo** Sumba Indonesia
69 E11 **Labuhanbilik** Sumatra
69 C11 **Labuhanhaji** Sumatra
70 K8 **Labuhanmeringgai** Sumatra
69 D11 **Labuhanruku** Sumatra
71 H9 **Labuhansepakah** Indonesia
19 P14 **La Buisse** France
70 E2 **Labuk** *R* Sabah
70 E1 **Labuk, Telukan** *B* Sabah
68 B4 **Labutta** Burma
138 D4 **Labyrinth, L** South Australia Australia
50 F2 **Labytnangi** Russian Federation
46 D3 **Laç** Albania
118 J8 **Lacadena** Saskatchewan Canada
124 G5 **La Cadena** Mexico
22 L2 **La Calamine** Belgium
122 J3 **Lac Allard** Quebec Canada
111 D10 **Lacamp** Louisiana U.S.A.
18 E8 **Lacanau** France
128 F2 **La Canoa** Venezuela
125 O9 **Lacantum** *R* Mexico
18 G8 **Lacapelle-Marival** France
131 B8 **Lacar, L** Argentina
133 E4 **La Carlota** Argentina
71 F5 **La Carlota** Negros Philippines
16 E6 **La Carolina** Spain
18 G9 **Lacaune** France
Laccadive Is *see* **Lakshadweep**
122 B8 **Lac-Drolet** Quebec Canada
99 R4 **Lac du Flambeau** Wisconsin U.S.A.
13 H6 **Laceby** England
125 L2 **La Ceiba** Honduras
128 D2 **La Ceiba** Venezuela
138 E6 **Lacepede B** South Australia Australia
142 D3 **Lacepede Is** W Australia Australia
100 C2 **Lacey** Washington U.S.A.
19 Q14 **La Chambre** France
52 E4 **Lacha, Oz** *L* Russian Federation
21 O3 **Lachapelle-aux-Pots** France
19 O15 **La Chapelle-en-Vercors** France
128 C6 **Lachay, Pta** *pt* Peru
36 E5 **Lachen** Germany
41 J3 **Lachen** Switzerland
94 D1 **Lachine** Michigan U.S.A.
139 H5 **Lachlan** *R* New South Wales Australia
125 P5 **La Chorrera** Panama
33 M7 **Lachte** *R* Germany
121 Q7 **Lachute** Quebec Canada
19 P18 **La Ciotat** France
94 J4 **Lackawanna** New York U.S.A.
118 E4 **Lac la Biche** Alberta Canada
117 N10 **Lac La Hache** British Columbia Canada
119 M3 **Lac la Ronge** Saskatchewan Canada
100 J1 **Laclede** Idaho U.S.A.
99 N10 **Laclede** Missouri U.S.A.
19 Q13 **La Clusaz** France
133 D3 **La Cocha** Argentina
8 D5 **Lacock** England
121 R7 **Lacolle** Quebec Canada
124 D3 **La Colorada** Mexico
118 D6 **Lacombe** Alberta Canada
111 G11 **Lacombe** Louisiana U.S.A.
99 R8 **Lacon** Illinois U.S.A.
99 N8 **Lacona** Iowa U.S.A.
95 L3 **Lacona** New York U.S.A.
43 C9 **Laconi** Sardinia
95 Q3 **Laconia** New Hampshire U.S.A.
113 E9 **Lacoochee** Florida U.S.A.
130 B9 **La Cordillera** *dept* Paraguay
121 N4 **Lacorne** Quebec Canada
16 B1 **Lá Coruña** Spain
109 J6 **Lacoste** Texas U.S.A.
19 O14 **La Côte St. André** France
127 J2 **Lacovia** Jamaica
98 K4 **Lac Qui Parle** Minnesota U.S.A.
98 E6 **Lacreek L** South Dakota U.S.A.
126 A3 **Lacre Pt** Bonaire W Indies
99 P6 **La Crescent** Minnesota U.S.A.
99 O1 **La Croix,L** Ontario Canada
99 U8 **La Crosse** Indiana U.S.A.
107 L3 **La Crosse** Kansas U.S.A.
94 J10 **La Crosse** Virginia U.S.A.
99 P6 **La Crosse** Wisconsin U.S.A.
133 F3 **La Cruz** Argentina
125 M4 **La Cruz** Costa Rica
124 G4 **La Cruz** Mexico
124 F6 **La Cruz** Mexico
120 G3 **Lac Ste. Thérèse** Ontario Canada
108 E7 **La Cuesta** Mexico
133 C5 **La Cueva** Chile
106 E6 **La Cueva** New Mexico U.S.A.
119 N6 **Lac Vert** Saskatchewan Canada
107 Q3 **La Cygne** Kansas U.S.A.
130 H5 **Ladainha** Brazil
74 G1 **Ladakh Range** Kashmir
54 D6 **Ladan'** Ukraine
69 D9 **Ladang, Ko** *isld* Thailand
129 G7 **Ladário** Brazil
70 K9 **Lada, Teluk** *B* Java
9 E3 **Ladbroke** England
99 R8 **Ladd** Illinois U.S.A.
107 J3 **Ladder Cr** Kansas U.S.A.
110 E2 **Laddonia** Missouri U.S.A.
111 E8 **Ladelle** Arkansas U.S.A.
28 C7 **Ladelund** Germany
126 C4 **La Demajagua** Cuba
36 F5 **Ladenburg** Germany
127 O4 **La Désirade** *isld* Guadeloupe W Indies
79 F3 **Ladhiqīyah, Al** Syria
46 E7 **Ládhon** *R* Greece
83 J12 **La Digue** *isld* Seychelles
28 D4 **Lading** Denmark
89 B9 **Ladismith** S Africa
77 G5 **Ladīz** Iran
98 C4 **Ladner** South Dakota U.S.A.
48 G6 **Ladne Vode** Serbia Yugoslavia
74 F5 **Ladnun** India
8 B7 **Ladock** England
Ladoga *L* *see* **Ladozhskoye Oz**
110 K2 **Ladoga** Indiana U.S.A.
109 M2 **Ladonia** Texas U.S.A.
128 D2 **La Dorada** Colombia
52 D4 **Ladozhskoye Oz** *L* Russian Federation
106 C7 **Ladrones Pk** New Mexico U.S.A.
116 R5 **Ladue** *R* Alaska/Yukon Terr U.S.A./Canada
124 E3 **La Dura** Mexico
52 D4 **Ladva Vetka** Russian Federation
115 L2 **Lady Ann Str** Northwest Territories Canada
15 E4 **Ladybank** Scotland
139 J8 **Lady Barron** Tasmania Australia
89 E7 **Ladybrand** S Africa
142 F5 **Lady Edith L** W Australia Australia
141 L6 **Lady Elliot I** Gt Barrier Reef Aust
120 K5 **Lady Evelyn L** Ontario Canada
100 B1 **Ladysmith** British Columbia Canada
89 F7 **Ladysmith** S Africa
99 P4 **Ladysmith** Wisconsin U.S.A.
55 E5 **Ladyzhenka** Kazakhstan
48 M2 **Ladyzhin** Ukraine
136 K3 **Lae** Papua New Guinea
68 E3 **Lae** Thailand
28 C5 **Læborg** Denmark
22 G2 **Laeken** Belgium
69 D8 **Laem Ao Kham** *C* Thailand
68 F6 **Laem Ngop** Thailand
69 D8 **Laem Sui** *C* Thailand
17 G6 **La Encina** Spain
127 L10 **La Encrucijada** Venezuela
27 B10 **Laerdalsöyri** Norway
128 F8 **La Esmeralda** Paraguay
28 G2 **Læsø** *isld* Denmark
28 F2 **Læsø Rende** *str* Denmark
133 D5 **La Esperanza** Argentina
126 F4 **La Esperanza** Cuba
16 B2 **La Estrada** Spain
26 P2 **Laevajoki** Norway
131 D3 **La Falda** Argentina
95 M2 **La Fargeville** New York U.S.A.
19 Q18 **La Farlède** France
111 L9 **Lafayette** Alabama U.S.A.
106 E2 **Lafayette** Colorado U.S.A.
112 B3 **Lafayette** Georgia U.S.A.
110 K1 **Lafayette** Indiana U.S.A.
111 E11 **Lafayette** Louisiana U.S.A.
99 M5 **Lafayette** Minnesota U.S.A.
94 B10 **Lafayette** Tennessee U.S.A.
95 Q2 **Lafayette, Mt** New Hampshire U.S.A.
126 B3 **La Fé** Cuba
126 C4 **La Fé** Cuba
109 K9 **La Feria** Texas U.S.A.
121 M4 **Laferte** Quebec Canada
85 F7 **Lafia** Nigeria
85 F7 **Lafiagi** Nigeria
121 N3 **Laflamme** *R* Quebec Canada
118 L9 **Lafleche** Saskatchewan Canada
38 O7 **Lafnitz** *R* Austria
94 C10 **La Follette** Tennessee U.S.A.
121 M5 **Laforce** Quebec Canada
120 J5 **Laforest** Ontario Canada
18 F8 **Lafrançaise** France
112 E3 **La France** South Carolina U.S.A.
36 C6 **Lafrimbole** France
16 C4 **La Fuente de San Esteban** Spain
69 A9 **Laful** Nicobar Is
124 G5 **La Gallega** Mexico
14 E2 **Lagan** *R* N Ireland
27 G15 **Lagan** *R* Sweden
16 B2 **La Gañiza** Spain
36 B6 **Lagarde** France
41 N6 **Lagarina, Val** Italy
106 D4 **La Garita Mts** Colorado U.S.A.
129 H8 **Lagarto, Serra do** *mts* Brazil
85 B3 **Lag'Ayda** Western Sahara
32 J8 **Lage** Germany
la Geltrú *see* **Geltrú**
26 D10 **Lågen** *R* Norway
32 L5 **Lägerdorf** Germany
54 H7 **Lagery** Ukraine
12 C2 **Lagg** Scotland
15 D3 **Laggan** Scotland
12 B2 **Laggan B** Scotland
77 L2 **Laghmān** *prov* Afghanistan
85 E2 **Laghouat** Algeria
46 C3 **Lagjit, kepi i** *C* Albania
40 B6 **Lagnieu** France
16 B7 **Lagôa** Portugal
130 G6 **Lagoa Santa** Brazil
130 E4 **Lagolândia** Brazil
43 G8 **Lagonegro** Italy
71 F4 **Lagonoy Gulf** Philippines
133 C7 **Lago Posadas** Argentina
85 E7 **Lagos** Nigeria
16 B7 **Lagos** Portugal
45 M2 **Lagosanto** Italy
100 G4 **La Grande** Oregon U.S.A.
115 M7 **La Grande 2, Réservoir** *res* Quebec Canada
115 M7 **La Grande 3, Réservoir** *res* Quebec Canada
115 M7 **La Grande-Riviére** *R* Quebec Canada
142 D4 **Lagrange** W Australia Australia
111 L8 **La Grange** Georgia U.S.A.
94 B5 **Lagrange** Indiana U.S.A.
94 B8 **La Grange** Kentucky U.S.A.
99 P9 **La Grange** Missouri U.S.A.
112 K2 **La Grange** North Carolina U.S.A.
94 E5 **Lagrange** Ohio U.S.A.
109 L6 **La Grange** Texas U.S.A.
98 B8 **La Grange** Wyoming U.S.A.
128 F2 **La Gran Sabana** *reg* Venezuela
19 Q14 **La Grave** France
83 M13 **Lagrave** *mt* Mauritius
20 G6 **La Grigonnais** France
127 J10 **La Grita** Venezuela
27 L12 **Lågskär** Finland
29 H11 **Lågskär** *lighthouse* Finland
127 L9 **La Guaira** Venezuela
133 D3 **La Guardia** Argentina
16 B3 **La Guardia** Portugal
17 F2 **Laguardia** Spain
16 C2 **La Gudiña** Spain
18 G8 **Laguiole** France
133 H3 **Laguna** Brazil
42 E3 **Laguna** Italy
106 C6 **Laguna** New Mexico U.S.A.
141 L7 **Laguna B** Queensland Australia
102 G8 **Laguna Beach** California U.S.A.
103 O5 **Laguna Cr** Arizona U.S.A.
103 K9 **Laguna Dam** Cal/Ariz U.S.A.
102 H9 **Laguna Mts** California U.S.A.
128 C5 **Lagunas** Peru
71 J9 **Lagunda, Tanjong** *C* Sumbawa Indonesia
133 E1 **Lagunillas** Bolivia
127 J9 **Lagunillas** Venezuela
65 F4 **Lagushao** China
70 F2 **Lahad Datu** Sabah
70 F2 **Lahad Datu, Telukan** *B* Sabah
68 F1 **Lahadi** China
135 S3 **Lahaina** Hawaiian Is
99 Q9 **La Harpe** Illinois U.S.A.
69 F14 **Lahat** Sumatra
70 K7 **Lahat** Sumatra
80 C8 **Lahav** Israel
122 H9 **La Have** Nova Scotia Canada
80 F1 **Lahavot HaBashan** Israel
32 J8 **Lahde** Germany
124 D4 **La Higuera** Mexico
77 B1 **Lāhījān** Iran
102 R12 **Lahilahi Pt** Hawaiian Is
37 K3 **Lahm** Germany
30 D5 **Lahn** Germany
36 E2 **Lahn** *R* Germany
36 F2 **Lahntal** Germany
27 F15 **Laholm** Sweden
27 F15 **Laholmsbukten** Sweden
71 F4 **Lahong** Philippines
102 E2 **Lahontan Res** Nevada U.S.A.
74 F3 **Lahore** Pakistan
36 D7 **Lahr** Germany
32 M8 **Lahstedt** Germany
29 M11 **Lahti** Finland
124 G8 **La Huerta** Mexico
80 G8 **Lahun** Jordan
71 F4 **Lahuy** *isld* Philippines
86 C4 **Lai** Chad
67 F1 **Lai'an** China
133 F3 **La Iberá** *L* Argentina
67 C5 **Laibin** China
68 F2 **Lai Chau** Vietnam
36 H7 **Laichingen** Germany
141 K8 **Laidley** Queensland Australia
102 S11 **Laie** Hawaiian Is
67 C2 **Laifeng** China
22 H4 **Laifour** France
21 H5 **Laignelet** France
18 H5 **Laignes** France
44 D4 **Laigueglia** Italy
29 J9 **Laihia** Finland
68 C2 **Lai-Hka** Burma
68 C2 **Lai-Hsak** Burma
21 O6 **Lailly-en-Val** France
71 E1 **Lai-Lo** Luzon Philippines
71 H7 **Laimea** Sulawesi
47 H3 **Lainá** Greece
38 L6 **Lainbach** Austria
89 B9 **Laingsburg** S Africa
94 C4 **Laingsburg** Michigan U.S.A.
26 K6 **Lainijaur** Sweden
26 M4 **Lainio** Sweden
26 M3 **Lainio älv** *R* Sweden
118 L6 **Laird** Saskatchewan Canada
98 D9 **Laird** Colorado U.S.A.
15 D2 **Lairg** Scotland
71 G7 **Lais** Mindanao Philippines
70 G4 **Lais** Sulawesi
86 G5 **Laisamis** Kenya
52 G6 **Laishevo** Russian Federation
65 C5 **Laishui** China
21 K4 **Laison** *R* France
18 G8 **Laissac** France
26 J5 **Laisvall** Sweden
20 C6 **Laïta** *R* France
26 K4 **Laitaure** *L* Sweden
29 J11 **Laitila** Finland
65 D6 **Laiwu** China
65 E6 **Laixi** China
71 E4 **Laiya** Philippines
59 H4 **Laiyang** China
65 C5 **Laiyuan** China
21 K3 **Laize** *R* France
65 D6 **Laizhou Wan** *B* China
79 G6 **Lajā, Al** *mts* Syria
131 B6 **Laja, L. de** Chile
133 D5 **La Japonesa** Argentina
131 A6 **Laja, R** Chile
106 E4 **La Jara** Colorado U.S.A.
70 E7 **Lajar, Tg** *C* Kalimantan
19 Q16 **La Javie** France
130 F9 **Laje dos Santos** *isld* Brazil
71 O8 **Lajeni** Indonesia
130 E10 **Lajes** Brazil
108 D6 **Lajitas** Texas U.S.A.
133 E2 **Lajitas, Las** Argentina
48 F6 **Lajkovac** Serbia Yugoslavia
102 G9 **La Jolla** California U.S.A.
119 N8 **Lajord** Saskatchewan Canada
48 F3 **Lajosmizse** Hungary
124 F4 **La Joya** Mexico
106 D7 **La Joya** New Mexico U.S.A.
128 F7 **La Junta** Bolivia
124 F3 **La Junta** Mexico
106 G4 **La Junta** Colorado U.S.A.
26 J8 **Lakasjö** Sweden
26 M5 **Lakaträsk** Sweden
101 O5 **Lake** Idaho U.S.A.
94 B3 **Lake** Michigan U.S.A.
100 E6 **Lake** Oregon U.S.A.
113 F9 **Lake Alfred** Florida U.S.A.
119 N9 **Lake Alma** Saskatchewan Canada
109 P5 **Lake Arthur** Louisiana U.S.A.
106 F8 **Lake Arthur** New Mexico U.S.A.
98 K5 **Lake Benton** Minnesota U.S.A.
143 C10 **Lake Biddy** W Australia Australia
139 G6 **Lake Boga** Victoria Australia
98 K1 **Lake Bronson** Minnesota U.S.A.
143 C9 **Lake Brown** W Australia Australia
137 R5 **Lakebu** *isld* Fiji
113 E7 **Lake Butler** Florida U.S.A.
143 C10 **Lake Camm** W Australia Australia
109 O5 **Lake Charles** Louisiana U.S.A.
100 E1 **Lake Chelan Nat. Recreation Area** Washington U.S.A.
110 F6 **Lake City** Arkansas U.S.A.
100 E8 **Lake City** California U.S.A.
106 C3 **Lake City** Colorado U.S.A.
113 E7 **Lake City** Florida U.S.A.
99 M7 **Lake City** Iowa U.S.A.
94 B2 **Lake City** Michigan U.S.A.
99 O5 **Lake City** Minnesota U.S.A.
94 G4 **Lake City** Pennsylvania U.S.A.
112 H4 **Lake City** South Carolina U.S.A.
98 J4 **Lake City** South Dakota U.S.A.
94 C10 **Lake City** Tennessee U.S.A.
116 L6 **Lake Clark Nat Park and Preserve** Alaska U.S.A.
144 C5 **Lake Coleridge** New Zealand
110 F7 **Lake Cormorant** Mississippi U.S.A.
100 J8 **Lake Cr** Nevada U.S.A.
99 M5 **Lake Crystal** Minnesota U.S.A.
99 R6 **Lake Delton** Wisconsin U.S.A.
118 F5 **Lake Eliza** Alberta Canada
102 G8 **Lake Elsinore** California U.S.A.
145 E4 **Lake Ferry** New Zealand
141 G2 **Lakefield** Queensland Australia
121 M8 **Lakefield** Ontario Canada
99 L6 **Lakefield** Minnesota U.S.A.
141 G2 **Lakefield Nat. Park** Queensland Australia
99 T7 **Lake Forest** Illinois U.S.A.
99 S7 **Lake Geneva** Wisconsin U.S.A.
106 E3 **Lake George** Colorado U.S.A.
95 O3 **Lake George** New York U.S.A.
115 N5 **Lake Harbour** Northwest Territories Canada
101 U8 **Lake Hattie Res** Wyoming U.S.A.
103 K7 **Lake Havasu City** Arizona U.S.A.
102 F7 **Lake Hughes** California U.S.A.
95 N6 **Lakehurst** New Jersey U.S.A.
109 M6 **Lake Jackson** Texas U.S.A.
143 C10 **Lake King** W Australia Australia
112 D6 **Lakeland** Georgia U.S.A.
119 N6 **Lake Lenore** Saskatchewan Canada
99 S2 **Lake Linden** Michigan U.S.A.
117 P10 **Lake Louise** Alberta Canada
140 B5 **Lake Mackay Aboriginal Land** N Terr Australia
108 C8 **Lake Meredith Recreation Area** Texas U.S.A.
99 N6 **Lake Mills** Iowa U.S.A.
94 G5 **Lake Milton** Ohio U.S.A.
116 L5 **Lake Minchumina** Alaska U.S.A.
95 S1 **Lake Moxie** Maine U.S.A.
140 E5 **Lake Nash** N Terr Australia
37 P5 **Laken Berg** *mt* Czech/Germany
9 G3 **Lakenheath** England
94 B4 **Lake Odessa** Michigan U.S.A.
99 M1 **Lake of the Woods** *L* Ontario Canada
94 D4 **Lake Orion** Michigan U.S.A.
100 C4 **Lake Oswego** Oregon U.S.A.
107 Q5 **Lake O' The Cherokees** *L* Oklahoma U.S.A.
109 N3 **Lake O'The Pines** *L* Texas U.S.A.
101 P5 **Lake Outlet** Wyoming U.S.A.
144 B5 **Lake Paringa** New Zealand
113 G11 **Lake Park** Florida U.S.A.
113 D7 **Lake Park** Georgia U.S.A.
99 L6 **Lake Park** Iowa U.S.A.
113 F10 **Lake Placid** Florida U.S.A.
95 O2 **Lake Placid** New York U.S.A.
102 B2 **Lakeport** California U.S.A.
113 F11 **Lakeport** Florida U.S.A.
94 E3 **Lakeport** Michigan U.S.A.
98 J5 **Lake Preston** South Dakota U.S.A.
111 E9 **Lake Providence** Louisiana U.S.A.
144 C6 **Lake Pukaki** New Zealand
100 F9 **Lake Range** *mts* Nevada U.S.A.
115 L7 **Lake River** Ontario Canada
139 J7 **Lakes Entrance** Victoria Australia
102 E4 **Lakeshore** California U.S.A.
103 P7 **Lakeside** Arizona U.S.A.
102 H9 **Lakeside** California U.S.A.
98 D7 **Lakeside** Nebraska U.S.A.
101 N8 **Lakeside** Utah U.S.A.
120 F5 **Lake Superior Prov. Park** Ontario Canada
144 C5 **Lake Tekapo** New Zealand
101 O8 **Laketown** Utah U.S.A.
121 M7 **Lake Traverse** Ontario Canada
118 L8 **Lake Valley** Saskatchewan Canada
106 C9 **Lake Valley** New Mexico U.S.A.
109 J5 **Lake Victor** Texas U.S.A.
99 L7 **Lake View** Iowa U.S.A.
94 B3 **Lakeview** Michigan U.S.A.
101 O5 **Lakeview** Montana U.S.A.
100 E7 **Lakeview** Oregon U.S.A.
112 H3 **Lake View** South Carolina U.S.A.
109 N9 **Lakeview** Texas U.S.A.
111 E8 **Lake Village** Arkansas U.S.A.
95 O5 **Lakeville** Connecticut U.S.A.
94 A5 **Lakeville** Indiana U.S.A.
99 N5 **Lakeville** Minnesota U.S.A.
94 K4 **Lakeville** New York U.S.A.
113 F10 **Lake Wales** Florida U.S.A.
98 G2 **Lake Williams** North Dakota U.S.A.
102 F8 **Lakewood** California U.S.A.
106 E2 **Lakewood** Colorado U.S.A.
95 N6 **Lakewood** New Jersey U.S.A.
106 F9 **Lakewood** New Mexico U.S.A.
94 H4 **Lakewood** New York U.S.A.
94 F5 **Lakewood** Ohio U.S.A.
113 G11 **Lake Worth** Florida U.S.A.
47 Q15 **Lakhaniá** Rhodes Greece
52 D4 **Lakhdenpokh'ya** Russian Federation
74 J5 **Lakhimpur** India
80 B6 **Lakhish** Israel
80 C7 **Lakhish** *R* Israel
80 C7 **Lakhish** Israel
74 C7 **Lakhpat** India
107 J4 **Lakin** Kansas U.S.A.
54 L1 **Lakinsk** Russian Federation
47 P13 **Lákka** Greece
74 D2 **Lakki** Pakistan
71 M9 **Laklo** *R* Timor
71 K9 **Lakohembi** Sumba Indonesia
28 A6 **Lakoik** Denmark
47 O12 **Lákones** Greece
46 F8 **Lakonikós Kólpos** *B* Greece
71 O9 **Lakor** *isld* Indonesia
85 C7 **Lakota** Ivory Coast
99 M6 **Lakota** Iowa U.S.A.
98 H1 **Lakota** North Dakota U.S.A.
68 G3 **Lak Sao** Laos
26 P1 **Lakse Fjord** *inlet* Norway
26 O1 **Lakselv** Norway
26 F6 **Laksfors** Norway
76 A5 **Lakshadweep** *islds* Indian Oc
71 F7 **Lala** Mindanao Philippines
88 C8 **Lala** Zambia
87 B7 **Lalama** Angola
47 H3 **Lâlapaşa** Turkey
86 B5 **Lalare** Gabon
87 G8 **Lalaúa** Mozambique
18 G8 **Lalbenque** France
77 E5 **Lāleh Zar, Kūh-e** *mt* Iran
33 Q5 **Lalendorf** Germany
46 C3 **Lalëzit, Gjiri i** *B* Albania
77 A3 **Lāli** Iran
128 B4 **La Libertad** Ecuador
125 O9 **La Libertad** Guatemala
133 C4 **La Ligua** Chile
71 N8 **Laliki** Indonesia
71 H6 **Lalimboee** Sulawesi
65 G2 **Lalin** China
16 B2 **Lalin** Spain
18 F8 **Lalinde** France
65 G2 **Lalin He** *R* China
74 H6 **Lalitpur** India
19 P15 **Lalley** France
70 G7 **Laloa** Sulawesi
118 H2 **La Loche West** Saskatchewan Canada
52 G4 **Lal'sk** Russian Federation
124 H6 **La Luz** Mexico
37 P5 **Lam** Germany
52 E6 **Lama** *R* Russian Federation
128 D3 **La Macarena** Colombia
106 D5 **La Madera** New Mexico U.S.A.
65 D4 **Lamadong** China
124 J4 **Lamadrid** Mexico
70 E2 **Lamag** Sabah
68 C5 **Lamaing** Burma
68 D6 **Lamaingkaw** Burma
71 L9 **Lamakera** Indonesia
122 B6 **La Malbaie** Quebec Canada
123 R7 **Lamaline** Newfoundland Canada
45 J3 **Lama Mocogno** Italy
124 H5 **La Mancha** Mexico
17 F5 **La Mancha** *reg* Spain
125 M4 **La Mansión** Costa Rica
110 C6 **Lamar** Arkansas U.S.A.
106 H3 **Lamar** Colorado U.S.A.
110 G7 **Lamar** Mississippi U.S.A.
110 B4 **Lamar** Missouri U.S.A.
98 E9 **Lamar** Nebraska U.S.A.
107 O6 **Lamar** Oklahoma U.S.A.
112 G3 **Lamar** South Carolina U.S.A.
101 P5 **Lamar** *R* Wyoming U.S.A.
40 C1 **Lamarche** France
40 A2 **Lamargelle** France
133 D5 **Lamarque** Argentina
109 N6 **La Marque** Texas U.S.A.
122 B6 **Lamartine** Quebec Canada
125 L2 **La Masica** Honduras
19 N15 **Lamastre** France
126 G4 **La Maya** Cuba
69 B11 **Lamayang** Indonesia
20 E5 **Lamballe** France
86 B6 **Lambaréné** Gabon
130 F7 **Lambari** Brazil
70 G7 **Lambasina** *isld* Sulawesi
128 B5 **Lambayeque** *dept* Peru
14 E3 **Lambay I** Ireland
70 D5 **Lambeng** Kalimantan
9 G5 **Lamberhurst** England
112 F6 **Lambert** Georgia U.S.A.
111 F7 **Lambert** Mississippi U.S.A.
98 B2 **Lambert** Montana U.S.A.
142 B5 **Lambert, C** W Australia Australia
146 H10 **Lambert Glacier** Antarctica
99 L5 **Lamberton** Minnesota U.S.A.
87 C12 **Lamberts B** S Africa
95 N6 **Lambertville** New Jersey U.S.A.
19 O17 **Lambesc** France
120 J10 **Lambeth** Ontario Canada
46 E7 **Lámbia** Greece
9 E5 **Lambourn** England
36 E5 **Lambrecht** Germany
41 K7 **Lambro** *R* Italy
94 G10 **Lambsburg** Virginia U.S.A.
14 A5 **Lambs Hd** Ireland
36 E4 **Lambsheim** Germany
121 T7 **Lambton** Quebec Canada
114 G3 **Lambton, C** Northwest Territories Canada
70 G7 **Lambuya** Sulawesi
68 F5 **Lam Chi** *R* Thailand
68 G5 **Lam Dom Noi** *R* Thailand
69 C11 **Lame** Sumatra
101 T4 **Lame Deer** Montana U.S.A.
16 B3 **Lamego** Portugal
127 N4 **Lamentin** Guadeloupe W Indies
122 H6 **Lameque** New Brunswick Canada
122 H6 **Lamèque, Ile** New Brunswick Canada
133 D3 **La Merced** Argentina
138 F6 **Lameroo** South Australia Australia
102 G9 **La Mesa** California U.S.A.
106 D9 **La Mesa** New Mexico U.S.A.
108 F3 **Lamesa** Texas U.S.A.
43 F7 **La Meta** *mt* Italy
20 G5 **La Meziére** France
46 E6 **Lamia** Greece
127 K10 **La Miel** Venezuela
71 G7 **Lamigan Pt** Mindanao Philippines
15 E5 **Lamington** Scotland
124 D3 **La Misa** Mexico
71 F7 **Lamitan** Philippines
85 B3 **Lamjaybir** Western Sahara
109 J4 **Lamkin** Texas U.S.A.
71 C3 **Lamlam** Indonesia
15 C5 **Lamlash** Scotland
144 B6 **Lammerlaw Range** New Zealand
141 G5 **Lammermoor** Queensland Australia
15 F5 **Lammermuir Hills** Scotland
25 F7 **Lammersdorf** Germany
27 G14 **Lammhult** Sweden
29 L10 **Lammi** Finland
68 G5 **Lam Nam Mun** *R* Thailand
21 M5 **Lamnay** France
99 R8 **La Moille** Illinois U.S.A.
103 J1 **Lamoille** Nevada U.S.A.
95 P2 **Lamoille** *R* Vermont U.S.A.
110 F1 **La Moine** *R* Illinois U.S.A.
100 G2 **Lamona** Washington U.S.A.
71 E3 **Lamon B** Luzon Philippines
42 D4 **Lamone** *R* Italy
70 O9 **Lamongan** Java
110 C1 **Lamoni** Iowa U.S.A.
118 E5 **Lamont** Alberta Canada
102 F6 **Lamont** California U.S.A.
113 D7 **Lamont** Florida U.S.A.
101 O6 **Lamont** Idaho U.S.A.
99 P7 **Lamont** Iowa U.S.A.
107 N5 **Lamont** Oklahoma U.S.A.
101 S7 **Lamont** Wyoming U.S.A.
124 G3 **La Morita** Mexico
19 P14 **La Morte** France
22 J4 **Lamorteau** Belgium
121 M4 **La Motte** Quebec Canada
21 P6 **Lamotte-Beuvron** France
19 P15 **La Motte d'Aveillans** France
19 P13 **La Motte-Servolex** France
98 H3 **La Moure** North Dakota U.S.A.
68 F4 **Lam Pao Res** Thailand
109 J4 **Lampasas** Texas U.S.A.
109 K5 **Lampasas** *R* Texas U.S.A.
20 A5 **Lampaul-Plouarzel** France
125 K4 **Lampazos** Mexico
43 E13 **Lampedusa, I. di** Italy
36 E4 **Lampertheim** Germany
33 T10 **Lampërtswalde** Germany
8 B3 **Lampeter** Wales
8 B4 **Lamphey** Wales
46 F5 **Lampinoú** Greece
43 E13 **Lampione, I. di** Italy
68 F5 **Lam Plai** *R* Thailand
119 P9 **Lampman** Saskatchewan Canada
45 J4 **Lamporecchio** Italy
9 F3 **Lamport** England
52 F2 **Lampozhnya** Russian Federation
29 O6 **Lämpsä** Finland
70 K8 **Lampung** *prov* Sumatra
70 K8 **Lampung Teluk** *B* Sumatra
68 G5 **Lam Si Bai** *R* Thailand
32 M9 **Lamspringe** Germany
32 K5 **Lamstedt** Germany
68 B3 **Lamu** Burma
86 H6 **Lamu** Kenya
19 P15 **La Mure** France
19 N12 **Lamure-sur-Azergues** France
106 E6 **Lamy** New Mexico U.S.A.
141 G5 **Lana** Queensland Australia
42 D2 **Lana** Italy
135 S3 **Lanai** *isld* Hawaiian Is
135 S3 **Lanai City** Hawaiian Is
135 S3 **Lanaihale** *pk* Hawaiian Is
22 K2 **Lanaken** Belgium
74 H1 **Lanak Pass** Kashmir/Xizang Zizhiqu
71 G7 **Lanao** *L* Mindanao Philippines
Lanark *co* *see* **Strathclyde** *reg*
121 O7 **Lanark** Ontario Canada
12 E2 **Lanark** Scotland
113 C8 **Lanark** Florida U.S.A.
99 R7 **Lanark** Illinois U.S.A.
70 E2 **Lanas** Sabah
68 C7 **Lanbi Kyun** *isld* Burma
71 F6 **Lanboyan Pt** Mindanao Philippines
68 D1 **Lancang** China
Lancang Jiang *R* *see* **Mekong**
13 F6 **Lancashire** *co* England
121 Q7 **Lancaster** Ontario Canada
13 F5 **Lancaster** England
102 F7 **Lancaster** California U.S.A.
110 M4 **Lancaster** Kentucky U.S.A.
98 K1 **Lancaster** Minnesota U.S.A.
110 D1 **Lancaster** Missouri U.S.A.
95 Q2 **Lancaster** New Hampshire U.S.A.
94 J4 **Lancaster** New York U.S.A.
94 E7 **Lancaster** Ohio U.S.A.
95 L6 **Lancaster** Pennsylvania U.S.A.
112 G3 **Lancaster** South Carolina U.S.A.
109 L3 **Lancaster** Texas U.S.A.
95 L9 **Lancaster** Virginia U.S.A.
99 Q7 **Lancaster** Wisconsin U.S.A.
115 L3 **Lancaster Sd** Northwest Territories Canada
98 B6 **Lance Cr** Wyoming U.S.A.
143 B9 **Lancelin** W Australia Australia
143 B9 **Lancelin I** W Australia Australia
143 E7 **Lancelot, Mt** W Australia Australia
19 O16 **Lance, Mt. de la** France
118 J8 **Lancer** Saskatchewan Canada
21 O1 **Lanchères** France
13 G4 **Lanchester** England
66 C5 **Lan-chia Ts'o** *L* China
48 J2 **Lanchin** Ukraine
Lanchow *see* **Lanzhou**
42 F6 **Lanciano** Italy
20 F4 **Lancieux** France
94 C10 **Lancing** Tennessee U.S.A.
19 O17 **Lançon** France
31 N5 **Łańcut** Poland
27 D11 **Land** *reg* Norway
98 F1 **Landa** North Dakota U.S.A.
32 K10 **Landau** Hessen Germany
36 E5 **Landau** Rheinland-Pfalz Germany
21 H5 **Landéan** France
41 N3 **Landeck** Austria
26 G4 **Landegode** *isld* Norway
20 C5 **Landeleau** France
21 H4 **Landelles-et-Coupigny** France
22 J2 **Landen** Belgium
140 C5 **Lander** *R* N Terr Australia
101 R7 **Lander** Wyoming U.S.A.
20 B5 **Landerneau** France
140 B5 **Lander R** N Terr Australia
27 F14 **Landeryd** Sweden
18 E8 **Landes** *reg* France
18 E8 **Landes** *dept* France
21 N6 **Landes** Loir-et-Cher France
94 H8 **Landes** West Virginia U.S.A.
28 G7 **Landet** Denmark
17 G5 **Landete** Spain
20 D6 **Landévant** France
20 B5 **Landevennec** France
20 G8 **Landevieille** France
68 A6 **Landfall I** Andaman Is
133 C8 **Landfall, I** Chile
9 E6 **Landford** England
33 S5 **Landgraben** *R* Germany
32 J5 **Land Hadeln** Germany
69 E13 **Landik, Gunung** *mt* Sumatra
74 D1 **Landi Khana** Pakistan
77 H4 **Landi Md. Amin Khan** Afghanistan
119 U3 **Landing L** Manitoba Canada
118 J6 **Landis** Saskatchewan Canada
112 G2 **Landis** North Carolina U.S.A.
20 B5 **Landivisiau** France
21 H5 **Landivy** France
112 F3 **Lando** South Carolina U.S.A.
99 R3 **Land O Lakes** Wisconsin U.S.A.
143 B7 **Landor** W Australia Australia
26 G8 **Landösjön** *L* Sweden
22 F3 **Landrecies** France
22 J5 **Landres** Ardennes France
22 K5 **Landres** Meurthe-et-Moselle France
121 N4 **Landrienne** Quebec Canada
142 F4 **Landrigan Cliffs** W Australia Australia
38 F8 **Landro** Italy
112 E2 **Landrum** South Carolina U.S.A.
40 E6 **Landry** France
26 M5 **Landså** Sweden
33 Q9 **Landsberg** Germany
41 N1 **Landsberg** Germany
141 G5 **Landsborough** *R* Queensland Australia
144 B5 **Landsborough** *R* New Zealand
114 G2 **Lands End** *C* Northwest Territories Canada
9 F7 **Land's End** England
37 N6 **Landshut** Germany
29 K5 **Landskrona** Sweden
36 D5 **Landstuhl** Germany
20 C5 **Landudal** France
20 B6 **Landudec** France
101 R2 **Landusky** Montana U.S.A.
32 L10 **Landwehrhagen** Germany
37 N3 **Landwüst** Germany
112 H4 **Lane** South Carolina U.S.A.
98 H5 **Lane** South Dakota U.S.A.
109 L6 **Lane City** Texas U.S.A.
22 G3 **Laneffe** Belgium
99 P6 **Lanesboro** Minnesota U.S.A.
111 L9 **Lanett** Alabama U.S.A.
22 D5 **Laneuvilleroy** France
22 J5 **Laneuville-sur-Meuse** France
20 E5 **Lanfains** France
Lanfeng *see* **Lankao**
118 G7 **Lanfine** Alberta Canada
119 N9 **Lang** Saskatchewan Canada
28 F6 **Langå** Denmark
66 C5 **La'nga Co** *L* China
16 E3 **Langa de Duero** Spain
46 F4 **Langadhás** Greece
46 E7 **Langádhia** Greece
29 T8 **Langanes** *pen* Iceland
86 G4 **Langano Hāyk'** *L* Ethiopia
71 H7 **Langara** Sulawesi
117 G8 **Langara I** British Columbia Canada
77 A1 **Langarūd** Iran
119 P8 **Langbank** Saskatchewan Canada
67 B6 **Lang Chanh** Vietnam
Lang-ch'u Ho *see* **Sutlej**
111 L9 **Langdale** Alabama U.S.A.
118 D8 **Langdon** Alberta Canada
107 M4 **Langdon** Kansas U.S.A.
98 H1 **Langdon** North Dakota U.S.A.
13 F4 **Langdon Beck** England
18 H7 **Langeac** France
21 L7 **Langeais** France
89 A9 **Langeberg** *mts* S Africa
89 C7 **Langebergen** *mts* S Africa
19 P18 **L'Ange, Col de** France
28 F7 **Langeland** *isld* Denmark
29 L10 **Längelmäki** Finland
29 L10 **Längelmävesi** *L* Finland
33 M9 **Langelsheim** Germany
22 D2 **Langemark** Belgium
32 J5 **Langen** Germany
36 F4 **Langen** Hessen Germany
37 P2 **Langenau** Germany
37 J7 **Langenau** Germany
32 F10 **Langenberg** Germany
37 N2 **Langenberg** Thüringen Germany
37 M4 **Langenbruck** Germany
119 Q8 **Langenburg** Saskatchewan Canada
36 H5 **Langenburg** Germany
26 H2 **Langenes** *lighthouse* Norway
28 B7 **Langeness** *isld* Germany
32 L8 **Langenhagen** Germany
28 B7 **Langenhorn** Germany
37 O6 **Langenisarhofen** Germany
38 N5 **Langenlois** Austria
36 D4 **Langenlonsheim** Germany
33 S9 **Langennaundorf** Germany
36 G3 **Langenselbold** Germany
37 J5 **Langensteinach** Germany
36 F6 **Langensteinbach** Germany
40 G3 **Langenthal** Switzerland
38 N6 **Langenwang** Austria
37 K5 **Langenzenn** Germany
32 F5 **Langeoog** Germany
28 E2 **Lange-Rak** *inlet* Denmark
28 F6 **Langeskov** Denmark
28 H5 **Langesø** *L* Denmark
27 D12 **Langesund** Norway
27 D13 **Langesundsfjord** *inlet* Norway
26 B9 **Langevag** Norway
37 K2 **Langewiesen** Germany
21 N5 **Langey** France
Langfang *see* **Anci**
26 M1 **Langfjord** Norway
26 Q1 **Langfjord** *inlet* Finnmark Norway
26 C9 **Langfjord** *inlet* Möre og Romsdal Norway
98 J4 **Langford** South Dakota U.S.A.
32 H7 **Langförden** Germany
69 E12 **Langgam** Sumatra
69 D12 **Langgapayung** Sumatra
118 L6 **Langham** Saskatchewan Canada
44 D2 **Langhe** Italy

Lemsid — Lioppa
195

85 B3 Lemsid Western Sahara
43 G7 Le Murge dist Italy
19 Q18 Le Muy France
28 A3 Lemvig Denmark
32 J6 Lemwerder Germany
68 B4 Lemyethna Burma
56 G3 Lena R Russian Federation
99 R7 Lena Illinois U.S.A.
109 P4 Lena Louisiana U.S.A.
111 G9 Lena Mississippi U.S.A.
100 F4 Lena Oregon U.S.A.
99 S5 Lena Wisconsin U.S.A.
101 Q9 Lena, Mt Utah U.S.A.
71 H9 Lenangguar Indonesia
107 P5 Lenapah Oklahoma U.S.A.
21 L8 Lencloître France
38 H7 Lend Austria
12 D3 Lendalfoot Scotland
29 P8 Lendery Russian Federation
45 L1 Lendinara Italy
118 K6 Leney Saskatchewan Canada
33 M8 Lengede Germany
37 P2 Lengefeld Germany
32 G8 Lengerich Germany
66 E4 Lenghu China
58 D4 Lenglong Ling mt ra China
67 D3 Lengshuijiang China
131 B3 Lengua de Vaca,Pta Chile
65 E4 Lengzipu China
9 G5 Lenham England
27 H15 Lenhovda Sweden
70 D5 Lenili Kalimantan
Leninabad Tajikistan see Khodzhent
57 A3 Leninabad Uzbekistan
78 J1 Leninakan Armenia
57 G5 Lenina, Pik mt Tajikistan
36 B6 Léning France
Leningrad see Sankt-Peterburg
146 C13 Leningradskaya former U.S.S.R. Base Antarctica
52 D5 Leningradskaya Oblast' prov Russian Federation
Lenin I.V. Kanal see Volgo-Balt
56 B5 Leninogorsk Kazakhstan
55 C4 Leninsk Chelyabinskaya obl Russian Federation
57 A4 Leninsk Turkmenistan
55 G5 Leninskiy Kazakhstan
52 G6 Leninskiy Mariyskaya Respublika Russian Federation
54 J2 Leninskiy Tul'skaya obl Russian Federation
56 B4 Leninsk-Kuznetskiy Russian Federation
55 E4 Leninskoye Kazakhstan
57 G4 Leninskoye Kyrgyzstan
52 G5 Leninskoye Kirovskaya obl Russian Federation
48 G3 Leninváros Hungary
88 B9 Lenje Zambia
55 H4 Len'ki Russian Federation
142 E3 Lennard,R W Australia Australia
27 E12 Lennartsfors Sweden
36 E1 Lenne R Germany
101 P3 Lennep Montana U.S.A.
36 E1 Lennestadt Germany
143 F7 Lennis Hills W Australia Australia
98 K6 Lennox South Dakota U.S.A.
133 D9 Lennox, I Chile/Arg
12 D2 Lennoxtown Scotland
121 T7 Lennoxville Quebec Canada
56 F4 Leno-Angarskoye Plato plateau Russian Federation
112 F2 Lenoir North Carolina U.S.A.
112 C2 Lenoir City Tennessee U.S.A.
107 K2 Lenora Kansas U.S.A.
119 R9 Lenore Manitoba Canada
119 M6 Lenore L Saskatchewan Canada
100 F2 Lenore, L Washington U.S.A.
112 D6 Lenox Georgia U.S.A.
99 M9 Lenox Iowa U.S.A.
95 O4 Lenox Massachusetts U.S.A.
22 F2 Lens Belgium
22 D3 Lens France
33 N4 Lensahn Germany
26 D8 Lensvik Norway
25 E5 Lent Netherlands
37 L6 Lenting Germany
43 F11 Lentini Sicily
29 O7 Lentüra Finland
26 K2 Lenvik Norway
68 D7 Lenya Burma
33 O6 Lenzen Germany
12 D2 Lenzie Scotland
85 D6 Léo Burkina
38 M7 Leoben Austria
127 H5 Léogane Haiti
38 G7 Leogang Austria
38 G7 Leoganger Austria
70 G4 Leok Sulawesi Indonesia
8 D3 Leominster England
95 Q4 Leominster Massachusetts U.S.A.
18 E9 Léon France
20 A5 Léon reg France
124 J7 Leon Mexico
125 L3 León Nicaragua
16 D2 León prov Spain
16 D2 León Spain
99 N9 Leon Iowa U.S.A.
107 O4 Leon Kansas U.S.A.
94 F8 Leon West Virginia U.S.A.
109 M4 Leona Texas U.S.A.
109 H7 Leona R Texas U.S.A.
94 D4 Leonard Michigan U.S.A.
99 O10 Leonard Missouri U.S.A.
98 J3 Leonard North Dakota U.S.A.
109 L2 Leonard Texas U.S.A.
89 A4 Leonardville Namibia
107 O2 Leonardville Kansas U.S.A.
79 E3 Leonarisso Cyprus
36 G6 Leonberg Germany
36 F5 Leonbronn Germany
19 O15 Léoncel France
131 B2 Leoncito,L Argentina
128 F8 Leon,Co mt Paraguay
108 E4 Leon Cr Texas U.S.A.
46 E5 Leondári Greece
139 H7 Leongatha Victoria Australia
46 F7 Leonídhion Greece
16 C2 León, Montañas de mts Spain
143 D8 Leonora W Australia Australia
109 J6 Leon Springs Texas U.S.A.
116 F9 Leontovitch,C Alaska U.S.A.
142 F4 Leopold Downs W Australia Australia
130 G7 Leopoldina Brazil
129 J7 Leopoldo de Bulhões Brazil
22 J1 Leopoldsburg Belgium
33 T5 Leopoldshagen Germany
40 G1 Leopoldskan canal Germany
Leopoldville see Kinshasa
107 J3 Leoti Kansas U.S.A.
118 K5 Leoville Saskatchewan Canada
48 L4 Leovo Moldavia
125 M5 Lepanto Costa Rica
110 F6 Lepanto Arkansas U.S.A.
69 H14 Lepar isld Indonesia
125 L2 Lepaterique Honduras
87 E10 Lephepe Botswana
67 F2 Leping China
45 O6 Lepini, Mti mts Italy
121 R7 L'Epiphanie Quebec Canada
55 D1 Leplya R Russian Federation
71 H7 Lepolepo Sulawesi
42 B2 Lepontine,Alpi mts Italy
70 G7 Leppangeng Sulawesi
29 N9 Leppävirta Finland
145 E3 Lepperton New Zealand
122 F8 Lepreau New Brunswick Canada
122 F8 Lepreau, Pt New Brunswick Canada
57 J2 Lepsa R Kazakhstan
48 E4 Lepsény Hungary
57 K2 Lepsinsk Kazakhstan
57 J2 Lepsy Kazakhstan
19 O17 Le Puy Ste Réparade France
95 L5 Le Raysville Pennsylvania U.S.A.
33 M9 Lerbach Germany
29 K4 Lerberget Sweden
28 D4 Lerbjerg Denmark
43 F11 Lercara Friddi Sicily
86 B4 Léré Chad
70 F5 Lereh, Tanjong C Sulawesi
121 T5 Le Relais Quebec Canada
29 K4 Lerhamn Sweden
141 G5 Lerida Queensland Australia
128 D3 Lérida Colombia
17 H3 Lérida prov Spain
17 H3 Lérida Spain
28 C3 Lerkenfeld Å R Denmark
16 E2 Lerma Spain
53 F11 Lermontov Russian Federation
41 N3 Lermoos Austria
99 S10 Lerna Illinois U.S.A.
21 L7 Lerné France
127 L4 Le Robert Martinique W Indies
47 H7 Léros isld Greece
119 O7 Leross Saskatchewan Canada
19 J4 Lérouville France
119 N7 Leroy Saskatchewan Canada
99 S9 Le Roy Illinois U.S.A.
99 N9 Le Roy Iowa U.S.A.
107 P3 Le Roy Kansas U.S.A.
94 B2 Le Roy Michigan U.S.A.
99 O6 Le Roy Minnesota U.S.A.
94 J4 Leroy New York U.S.A.
101 P8 Le Roy Wyoming U.S.A.
40 D1 Lerrain France
27 F14 Lerum Sweden
15 G2 Lerwick Scotland
21 N3 Léry France
111 G12 Lery,L Louisiana U.S.A.
48 G4 Leş Romania
41 J6 Lesa Italy
19 P13 Les Abrets France
38 G8 Lesach Tal V Austria
38 G8 Lesachtal Austria
19 N18 Le Salin de Giraud France
19 P13 Les Avenières France
19 N17 Les Baux France
Lesbos isld see Lésvos isld
13 G3 Lesbury England
83 M13 L'Escalier Mauritius
18 E9 Lescar France
126 H5 Les Cayes Haiti
143 B9 Leschenault, C W Australia Australia
122 B6 Les Éboulements Quebec Canada
19 P14 Les Echelles France
122 C5 Les Escoumins Quebec Canada
122 D6 Les Étroits Quebec Canada
67 A2 Leshan China
20 E3 Les Hanois Lt.Ho English Chan
40 G5 Les Haudères Switzerland
52 G3 Leshukonskoye Russian Federation
69 C11 Lesikin Indonesia
44 F2 Lésima mt Italy
42 G7 Lesina,L.di Italy
26 C9 Lesja Norway
26 C9 Lesjaskog Norway
26 C9 Lesjaskogsvatn L Norway
27 G12 Lesjöfors Sweden
31 N6 Lesko Poland
46 E1 Leskovac Serbia Yugoslavia
146 G2 Leskov I S Sandwich Is S Atlantic Oc
46 D4 Leskovik Albania
13 E1 Leslie Scotland
110 D6 Leslie Arkansas U.S.A.
112 C6 Leslie Georgia U.S.A.
101 M6 Leslie Idaho U.S.A.
94 C4 Leslie Michigan U.S.A.
119 O7 Leslie Stn Saskatchewan Canada
118 C6 Leslieville Alberta Canada
12 E2 Lesmahagow Scotland
127 N4 Les Mangles Guadeloupe
19 P16 Les Mées France
19 Q16 Les Monges mt France
31 O3 Lesnaya R Belorussia
20 B4 Lesneven France
48 E6 Lešnica Serbia Yugoslavia
55 E3 Lesnoy Russian Federation
52 D2 Lesnoy Murmanskaya obl Russian Federation
52 E5 Lesnoye Russian Federation
59 M2 Lesogorsk Russian Federation
52 C4 Lesogorskiy Russian Federation
56 D2 Lesosibirsk Russian Federation
89 E7 Lesotho kingdom Africa
65 J2 Lesozavodsk Russian Federation
18 E7 Lesparre-Medoc France
19 O18 Les-Pennes-Mirabeau France
83 K12 L'Espérance Mahé I Indian Oc
22 F4 Lesquielles-St Germain France
38 J7 Lessach Austria
127 N5 Les Saintes islds Guadeloupe W Indies
20 G3 Lessay France
22 J3 Lesse R Belgium
32 M8 Lesse Germany
27 H15 Lessebo Sweden
146 B8 Lesser Antarctica Antarctica
127 N6 Lesser Antilles islds W Indies
Lesser Khingan Range see Xiao Hinggan Ling
117 Q8 Lesser Slave L Alberta Canada
118 C3 Lesser Slave R Alberta Canada
22 F2 Lessines Belgium
41 O6 Lessini mt Italy
40 G7 Lessolo Italy
98 K6 Lester Iowa U.S.A.
98 H9 Lester Nebraska U.S.A.
94 F9 Lester West Virginia U.S.A.
99 M5 Lester Prairie Minnesota U.S.A.
98 J6 Lesterville South Dakota U.S.A.
29 L8 Lestijärvi Finland
119 N7 Lestock Saskatchewan Canada
127 L4 Les Trois Îlets Martinique W Indies
99 N5 Le Sueur Minnesota U.S.A.
142 F2 Lesueur I W Australia Australia
143 B9 Lesueur, Mt W Australia Australia
70 D4 Lesung, Bt mt Kalimantan
47 H5 Lésvos isld Greece
12 C4 Leswalt Scotland
31 K4 Leszno Poland
89 G4 Letaba R S Africa
111 K9 Letchatchee Alabama U.S.A.
98 H6 Letcher South Dakota U.S.A.
9 F4 Letchworth England
119 U9 Letellier Manitoba Canada
100 J6 Letha Idaho U.S.A.
118 E9 Lethbridge Alberta Canada
123 T5 Lethbridge Newfoundland Canada
71 N9 Leti isld Indonesia
48 L1 Letichev Ukraine
128 E4 Leticia Colombia
71 N9 Leti, Kepulauan islds Indonesia
65 D5 Leting China
37 P4 Letiny Czechoslovakia
52 G5 Letka R Russian Federation
32 G10 Letmathe Germany
52 D3 Letnerechenskiy Russian Federation
46 G1 Letnitsa Bulgaria
52 D2 Letnyaya-Reka Russian Federation
52 E3 Letnyaya Zolotitsa Russian Federation
38 F8 Le Tofane mt Italy
19 P14 Le Touvet France
68 B4 Letpadan Burma
139 G5 Lette New South Wales Australia
14 D2 Letterkenny Ireland
8 B4 Letterston Wales
94 B7 Letts Indiana U.S.A.
69 G11 Letung Indonesia
17 F6 Letur Spain
33 O8 Letzlingen Germany
48 J6 Leu Romania
87 D8 Leua Angola
37 N2 Leubnitz Germany
18 H10 Leucate France
15 F4 Leuchars Scotland
37 N4 Leuchtenberg Germany
37 M2 Leuchtenburg Germany
22 G3 Leugnies France
20 C5 Leuhan France
40 G5 Leuk Switzerland
40 G5 Leukerbad Switzerland
36 E2 Leun Germany
33 Q10 Leuna Germany
37 M3 Leupoldsdorf Germany
69 B10 Leupung Sumatra
141 J6 Leura Queensland Australia
69 C11 Leuser,Gunung mt Sumatra
48 L4 Leusheny Moldavia
55 E2 Leushi Russian Federation
55 E2 Leushinskiy Tuman, Oz L Russian Federation
33 O6 Leussow Germany
41 O3 Leutasch Austria
37 L2 Leutenberg Germany
37 J5 Leutershausen Germany
41 M2 Leutkirch Germany
38 M8 Leutschach Austria
22 H2 Leuven Belgium
22 F2 Leuze Belgium
120 J6 Levack Ontario Canada
46 F6 Levádhia Greece
19 Q18 Le Val France
46 C4 Levan Albania
103 N2 Levan Utah U.S.A.
26 E8 Levanger Norway
44 B1 Levanna mt Italy
40 F7 Levanna, M Italy
107 J2 Levant Kansas U.S.A.
19 Q18 Levant,I.du France
44 F3 Levanto Italy
43 E10 Levanzo, I. di Sicily
21 J5 Levare France
127 M4 Le Vauclin Martinique W Indies
55 E1 Levdym Russian Federation
108 E2 Levelland Texas U.S.A.
144 C6 Levels New Zealand
13 H6 Leven England
13 E1 Leven Scotland
41 J5 Leventina, Valle Switzerland
142 E3 Lévêque,C W Australia Australia
98 B6 Leverett Wyoming U.S.A.
36 B1 Leverkusen Germany
117 P3 Lever L Northwest Territories Canada
32 H8 Levern Germany
9 F4 Leverstock Green England
21 N5 Lèves France
48 E2 Levice Czechoslovakia
41 O5 Levico Italy
55 C2 Levikha Russian Federation
145 E4 Levin New Zealand
52 F5 Levinskoye Russian Federation
140 B6 Levi Ra N Terr Australia
121 T6 Lévis Quebec Canada
94 E9 Levisa Fork R Kentucky U.S.A.
47 H7 Levítha isld Greece
95 N6 Levittown Pennsylvania U.S.A.
46 G9 Lévka Óri mt Crete Greece
46 F9 Lévka Óri National Park Crete Greece
46 D6 Levkás isld Greece
47 P13 Levkimmi Greece
31 M6 Levoča Czechoslovakia
85 A4 Lévrier,B.du Mauritania
28 C4 Levring Denmark
21 O8 Levroux France
46 G1 Levski Bulgaria
106 F5 Levy New Mexico U.S.A.
20 H2 Levy,C France
113 E8 Levy,L Florida U.S.A.
71 J9 Lewa Indonesia
98 F7 Lewanna Nebraska U.S.A.
68 C3 Lewe Burma
98 D8 Lewellen Nebraska U.S.A.
9 F6 Lewes England
142 D5 Lewin,Mt W Australia Australia
15 B2 Lewis dist Scotland
99 L8 Lewis Iowa U.S.A.
94 K6 Lewis Pennsylvania U.S.A.
100 D3 Lewis R Washington U.S.A.
98 J7 Lewis and Clark L South Dakota U.S.A.
138 D3 Lewis B South Australia Australia
110 K5 Lewisburg Kentucky U.S.A.
94 C7 Lewisburg Ohio U.S.A.
95 K6 Lewisburg Pennsylvania U.S.A.
110 K6 Lewisburg Tennessee U.S.A.
94 G9 Lewisburg West Virginia U.S.A.
123 O5 Lewis Hills Newfoundland Canada
68 A6 Lewis Inlet Andaman Is
101 P5 Lewis L Wyoming U.S.A.
144 D5 Lewis Pass New Zealand
123 R4 Lewisporte Newfoundland Canada
142 G5 Lewis Ra W Australia Australia
101 M1 Lewis Ra Montana U.S.A.
94 J5 Lewis Run Pennsylvania U.S.A.
103 O10 Lewis Sps Arizona U.S.A.
100 J3 Lewiston Idaho U.S.A.
95 R2 Lewiston Maine U.S.A.
94 C2 Lewiston Michigan U.S.A.
110 E1 Lewiston Missouri U.S.A.
94 J3 Lewiston New York U.S.A.
112 K1 Lewiston North Carolina U.S.A.
101 O8 Lewiston Utah U.S.A.
99 Q9 Lewistown Illinois U.S.A.
101 Q2 Lewistown Montana U.S.A.
111 C8 Lewisville Arkansas U.S.A.
101 N6 Lewisville Idaho U.S.A.
99 M6 Lewisville Minnesota U.S.A.
94 K5 Lewisville Pennsylvania U.S.A.
109 L2 Lewisville Texas U.S.A.
109 L2 Lewisville, L Texas U.S.A.
33 P6 Lewitz Germany
71 L9 Lewoleba Indonesia
71 L9 Lewotobi mt Flores Indonesia
119 N8 Lewvan Saskatchewan Canada
111 F7 Lexa Arkansas U.S.A.
99 S9 Lexington Illinois U.S.A.
94 B8 Lexington Indiana U.S.A.
94 C8 Lexington Kentucky U.S.A.
94 E3 Lexington Michigan U.S.A.
111 F8 Lexington Mississippi U.S.A.
110 C2 Lexington Missouri U.S.A.
98 G9 Lexington Nebraska U.S.A.
112 G2 Lexington North Carolina U.S.A.
109 K1 Lexington Oklahoma U.S.A.
100 F4 Lexington Oregon U.S.A.
112 F4 Lexington South Carolina U.S.A.
110 H6 Lexington Tennessee U.S.A.
109 K5 Lexington Texas U.S.A.
94 H9 Lexington Virginia U.S.A.
95 L8 Lexington Park Maryland U.S.A.
98 J1 Leyden North Dakota U.S.A.
95 M3 Leyden,W New York U.S.A.
67 B4 Leye China
83 L13 Leygues Kerguelen Indian Oc
13 F6 Leyland England
18 E8 Leyre R France
9 G5 Leysdown England
71 G5 Leyte isld Philippines
71 G5 Leyte Gulf Philippines
19 N16 Lez R France
31 N5 Leżajsk Poland
20 D4 Lèzardrieux France
18 E6 Lezay France
52 F5 Lezha Russian Federation
46 D3 Lezhë Albania
67 B1 Lezhi China
52 F6 Lezhnevo Russian Federation
18 G9 Lézignan France
18 H7 Lezoux France
17 F6 Lezuza Spain
99 R3 L. Gogebic Michigan U.S.A.
54 G5 L'gov Russian Federation
54 G5 L'govskiy Russian Federation
66 E5 Lhari China
143 A7 Lharidon Bight W Australia Australia
Lhariguo see Lhari
66 E6 Lhasa China
Lhatse Dzong see Lhazê
66 D6 Lhazê China
Lho Dzong see Lhorong
69 B10 Lhokkreut Sumatra
69 C10 Lhokseumawe Sumatra
69 C10 Lhoksukon Sumatra
66 F5 Lhorong China
Liancheng see Qinglong
67 E4 Liancheng China
21 P3 Liancourt France
Liancourt Rocks see Tok-to
22 B2 Liane R France
71 H5 Liang Indonesia
71 G6 Lianga Mindanao Philippines
65 B4 Liangcheng China
65 D7 Liangcheng China
58 E5 Liangdang China
67 C2 Lianghekou China
Liangjiayoufang see Youyu
71 E8 Liang Liang Philippines
67 B1 Liangping China
70 D4 Liangpran, Bukit mt Kalimantan
Liangshizhen see Shaodong
67 D4 Liangtan China
69 E11 Liang Timur, Gunung mt Malaysia
67 A4 Liangwang Shan mts China
67 E1 Liangzi Hu L China
67 D3 Lianhua China
67 E5 Lianhua Shan mts China
67 F3 Lianjiang China
67 B4 Lian Jiang R China
68 K2 Lianjiang China
65 H1 Lianjiangkou China
67 D4 Liannan China
67 E4 Lianping China
67 D4 Lianshan China
65 F4 Lianshanguan China
67 D3 Lian Shui R Hunan China
68 E6 Liant C Thailand
67 D5 Liantan China
Liantang see Nanchang
67 D1 Liantuo China
67 D4 Lian Xian China
67 D3 Lianyuan China
65 D7 Lianyungang China
Lianzhou see Lian Xian
Lianzhou see Hepu
65 H2 Lianzhushan China
58 G4 Liaocheng China
59 H4 Liaodong pen China
59 H3 Liaodong Wan B China
59 H3 Liao He R China
65 E4 Liaoning prov China
Liaotung pen see Liaodong pen
Liaotung, Gulf of see Liaodong Wan
59 H3 Liaoyang China
65 F3 Liaoyangwopu China
59 J3 Liaoyuan China
65 E4 Liaozhong China
47 O12 Liapádhes Greece
117 M5 Liard R Br Col/N W Terr Canada
117 J5 Liard R Yukon Territory Canada
117 M5 Liard Ra Northwest Territories Canada
117 K6 Liard River British Columbia Canada
77 K7 Liari Pakistan
22 G4 Liart France
69 H14 Liat isld Indonesia
79 F5 Liban, Jebel mts Lebanon
117 Q11 Libby Idaho U.S.A.
100 K1 Libby Montana U.S.A.
86 C5 Libenge Zaire
107 K4 Liberal Kansas U.S.A.
110 B4 Liberal Missouri U.S.A.
116 H2 Liberator L Alaska U.S.A.
129 H6 Liberdade R Brazil
130 G8 Liberdade Brazil
31 J5 Liberec Czechoslovakia
85 C7 Liberia rep W Africa
127 P4 Liberta Antigua W Indies
128 C5 Libertad dept Peru
127 K10 Libertad Venezuela
133 E2 Libertador Gen. San Martín Argentina
124 C3 Libertad,Pto Mexico
13 E2 Liberton Scotland
116 R4 Liberty Alaska U.S.A.
110 E2 Liberty Illinois U.S.A.
94 B7 Liberty Indiana U.S.A.
110 M4 Liberty Kentucky U.S.A.
111 F10 Liberty Mississippi U.S.A.
110 B2 Liberty Missouri U.S.A.
98 K9 Liberty Nebraska U.S.A.
95 N5 Liberty New York U.S.A.
112 H2 Liberty North Carolina U.S.A.
95 K5 Liberty Pennsylvania U.S.A.
109 N5 Liberty Texas U.S.A.
100 E2 Liberty Washington U.S.A.
94 C5 Liberty Center Ohio U.S.A.
112 G3 Liberty Hill South Carolina U.S.A.
109 K5 Liberty Hill Texas U.S.A.
95 K7 Libertytown Maryland U.S.A.
99 T7 Libertyville Illinois U.S.A.
99 O9 Libertyville Iowa U.S.A.
22 J4 Libin Belgium
37 Q4 Liblín Czechoslovakia
71 F4 Libmanan Philippines
67 B4 Libo China
71 B3 Libobo, Tg C Indonesia
46 D4 Libohovë Albania
69 D9 Libong,Ko isld Thailand
86 B5 Liboumba R Gabon
18 E8 Libourne France
22 J4 Libramont Belgium
46 D3 Librazhd Albania
131 F2 Libres,P.de los Argentina
86 A5 Libreville Gabon
71 G7 Libuganon R Mindanao Philippines
84 F4 Libya rep Africa
84 G4 Libyan Desert Libya
84 H3 Libyan Plateau Egypt
47 N11 Libyssa hist site Turkey
43 F11 Licata Sicily
36 F2 Lich Germany
65 B6 Licheng China
65 C6 Licheng China
9 E2 Lichfield England
145 E3 Lichfield New Zealand
88 E8 Lichinga Mozambique
36 E6 Lichtenau Baden-Württemberg Germany
32 J9 Lichtenau Nordrhein-Westfalen Germany
37 P2 Lichtenberg Germany
37 M3 Lichtenberg Germany
89 E6 Lichtenburg S Africa
36 G7 Lichtenstein Germany
37 O2 Lichtenstein Germany
37 N2 Lichtentanne Germany
36 E6 Lichtenthal Germany
25 G5 Lichtenvoorde Netherlands
33 S8 Lichterfelde Germany
22 E1 Lichtervelde Belgium
67 C1 Lichuan China
67 E3 Lichuan China
110 E4 Licking Missouri U.S.A.
94 D8 Licking R Kentucky U.S.A.
42 G4 Ličko Petrovo Selo Bosnia-Herzegovina
43 F8 Licosa,P Italy
22 B2 Licques France
53 C7 Lida Belorussia
102 G4 Lida Nevada U.S.A.
65 E6 Lidao China
99 M7 Lidderdale Iowa U.S.A.
15 F5 Liddesdale Valley Scotland
26 L7 Liden Sweden
26 J9 Liden Sweden
98 J3 Lidgerwood North Dakota U.S.A.
27 F15 Lidhult Sweden
27 K12 Lidingo Sweden
27 F13 Lidköping Sweden
26 M3 Lidnatjärro mt Sweden
45 M1 Lido Italy
42 E7 Lido di Ostia Italy
31 M2 Lidzbark Poland
31 M1 Lidzbark Warmiński Poland
20 E5 Lié R France
32 K9 Liebenau Hessen Germany
32 K7 Liebenau Niedersachsen Germany
37 M2 Liebengrün Germany
118 H8 Liebenthal Saskatchewan Canada
33 S7 Liebenwalde Germany
33 S9 Liebenwerda Germany
140 B6 Liebig, Mt N Terr Australia
144 C5 Liebig Range New Zealand
48 G5 Liebling Romania
41 L3 Liechtenstein princ Europe
26 M3 Liedakka Sweden
22 K2 Liège Belgium
21 N7 Liège, le France
29 P8 Lieksa Finland
32 G8 Lienen Germany
Lienyünkang see Lianyungang
27 M15 Liepāja Latvia
33 S5 Liepen Germany
36 C7 Liepvre France
22 H1 Lier Belgium
27 E11 Lier Norway
22 K3 Lierneux Belgium
22 K2 Liers Belgium
21 O3 Lierville France
36 D3 Liesenfeld Germany
38 J8 Lieser R Austria
36 B3 Lieser R Germany
29 K11 Liesjärvi Nat. Park Finland
22 F4 Liesse France
25 E6 Liessel Netherlands
40 G3 Liestal Switzerland
48 L5 Lieşti Romania
21 M3 Lieurey France
21 L3 Lieuvin France
22 D3 Liévin France
121 P7 Lièvre R Quebec Canada
122 B6 Lievres, I. aux Quebec Canada
38 K6 Liezen Austria
71 M9 Lifan Indonesia
14 E3 Liffey R Ireland
19 J4 Liffol le Grand France
14 D2 Lifford Ireland
20 H5 Liffre France
78 J6 Lifiyah, Al Saudi Arabia
137 O6 Lifu Îles Loyauté Pacific Oc
133 D6 Lifue Mahuida mt Argentina
45 Q8 Li Galli Italy
71 F4 Ligao Philippines
Ligen-i Shkodrës see Skadarsko Jez
65 B7 Ligeta China
65 E6 Ligezhuang China
26 L5 Ligga Sweden
8 A7 Ligger Bay England
109 H7 Light Texas U.S.A.
143 E8 Lightfoot L W Australia Australia
113 C8 Lighthouse Pt Florida U.S.A.
142 F4 Lightjack Hill W Australia Australia
119 N2 Light L Ontario Canada
139 J3 Lightning Rdg New South Wales Australia
20 H7 Ligne France
21 K4 Lignieres France
21 P8 Lignières France
21 K4 Lignières-Orgères France
98 D1 Lignite North Dakota U.S.A.
20 D5 Lignol France
94 K8 Lignum Virginia U.S.A.
22 H3 Ligny Belgium
19 J4 Ligny en Barrois France
21 O6 Ligny-le-Ribault France
45 H3 Ligonchio Italy
88 G9 Ligonha R Mozambique
94 B5 Ligonier Indiana U.S.A.
94 H6 Ligonier Pennsylvania U.S.A.
46 F7 Ligoúrion Greece
65 D7 Ligouyi China
131 B4 Ligua,B de la Chile
21 M7 Ligueil France
124 D5 Ligui Mexico
44 F2 Ligure reg Italy
44 D3 Ligure Italy
44 E4 Ligurian Sea Italy
103 K9 Ligurta Arizona U.S.A.
137 L2 Lihir Group Bismarck Arch
28 B3 Lihme Denmark
22 D4 Lihons France
141 K3 Lihou Reef Coral Sea
141 K3 Lihou Reef & Cays Gt Barrier Reef Aust
102 V13 Lihue Hawaiian Is
52 B5 Lihula Estonia
52 D1 Liinakhamari Russian Federation
65 D6 Lijin China
68 F3 Lik R Laos
86 D5 Likati Zaire
117 N9 Likely British Columbia Canada
100 E8 Likely California U.S.A.
52 E6 Likhoslavl' Russian Federation
54 M8 Likhovskoy Russian Federation
54 K1 Likino-Dulevo Russian Federation
71 M9 Likisia Timor
46 D3 Likmetaj Albania
86 C6 Likouala R Congo
69 J12 Liku Indonesia
70 D2 Liku Sarawak
71 J4 Likupang Sulawesi
110 G5 Lilbourn Missouri U.S.A.
28 B2 Lildstrand Denmark
143 F8 Lilian, Pt W Australia Australia
38 N5 Lilienfeld Austria
32 J6 Lilienthal Germany
67 D3 Liling China
22 H1 Lille Belgium
22 E2 Lille France
28 B4 Lilleå R Denmark
28 D6 Lille Bælt chan Denmark
21 M2 Lillebonne France
27 D10 Lillehammer Norway
22 C2 Lillers France
27 C13 Lillesand Norway
27 E12 Lilleström Norway
28 E3 Lille Vildmose Denmark
26 G10 Lillhärdal Sweden
26 G8 Lillholmsjön Sweden
26 K6 Lillholmträsk Sweden
123 L2 Lillian L Quebec Canada
109 P3 Lillie Louisiana U.S.A.
13 F3 Lilliesleaf Scotland
112 J2 Lillington North Carolina U.S.A.
107 O2 Lillis Kansas U.S.A.
22 G1 Lillo Belgium
16 E5 Lillo Spain
117 M10 Lillooet R British Columbia Canada
117 N10 Lillooet British Columbia Canada
94 J6 Lilly Pennsylvania U.S.A.
88 D8 Lilongwe Malawi
88 E8 Lilongwe R Malawi
71 F6 Liloy Mindanao Philippines
98 J4 Lily South Dakota U.S.A.
138 F5 Lilydale South Australia Australia
139 H8 Lilydale Tasmania Australia
48 F7 Lim R Serbia Yugoslavia
130 C8 Lima Paraguay
128 C6 Lima Peru
16 B3 Lima R Portugal
27 F11 Lima Sweden
99 P9 Lima Illinois U.S.A.
101 N5 Lima Montana U.S.A.
94 K4 Lima New York U.S.A.
94 C6 Lima Ohio U.S.A.
133 C4 Limache Chile
130 G7 Lima Duarte Brazil
80 D1 Liman Israel
70 N9 Liman, G mt Java
48 F1 Limanowa Poland
71 N8 Limar Indonesia
133 C4 Limari R Chile
131 B3 Limari,R Chile
69 G12 Limas Indonesia
79 E2 Limas R Turkey
71 G6 Limasawa isld Philippines
79 D4 Limassol Cyprus
14 E1 Limavady N Ireland
21 O4 Limay France
133 D5 Limay Mahuida Argentina
131 C7 Limay,R Argentina
36 C5 Limbach Germany
37 O2 Limbach Germany
37 O2 Limbach-Oberfrohna Germany
70 D2 Limbang R Sarawak
43 C8 Limbara, Monte mt Sardinia
52 B6 Limbaži Latvia
85 F8 Limbe Cameroon
127 H5 Limbé Haiti
88 E9 Limbe Malawi
71 H4 Limboto Sulawesi
71 H4 Limboto, Danau L Sulawesi
22 K2 Limbourg Belgium
70 F7 Limbung Sulawesi
70 D6 Limbungan Kalimantan
140 A3 Limbunya N Terr Australia
57 J6 Limbur Uzbekistan
22 J2 Limburg prov Belgium
36 E3 Limburg Germany
144 B7 Limchills New Zealand
100 H5 Lime Oregon U.S.A.
27 F11 Limedsforsen Sweden
116 K6 Lime Hills Alaska U.S.A.
130 F8 Limeira Brazil
45 L1 Limena Italy
46 G4 Limenária Greece
47 H7 Limén Vathéos Greece
118 L9 Limerick Saskatchewan Canada
14 C4 Limerick co Ireland
14 C4 Limerick Ireland
95 R3 Limerick Maine U.S.A.
20 F6 Limerzel France
22 J4 Limes Belgium
99 O6 Lime Springs Iowa U.S.A.
113 F10 Limestone Florida U.S.A.
95 T7 Limestone Maine U.S.A.
94 J4 Limestone New York U.S.A.
119 W2 Limestone L Manitoba Canada
119 T5 Limestone Pt Manitoba Canada
21 M2 Limésy France
28 B3 Limfjorden inlet Denmark
29 K5 Limhamn Sweden
16 B2 Limia R Spain
Limin isld see Thásos isld
26 G7 Limingen L Norway
29 L7 Liminka Finland
41 H3 Limmat R Switzerland
25 C3 Limmen Netherlands
140 D2 Limmen Bight N Terr Australia
140 D3 Limmen Bight R N Terr Australia
46 F6 Límni Greece
46 G5 Límnos isld Greece
129 L5 Limoeiro Brazil
129 L5 Limoeiro do Norte Brazil
121 P7 Limoges Ontario Canada
18 F7 Limoges France
125 N5 Limón Costa Rica
125 M2 Limón Honduras
106 G2 Limon Colorado U.S.A.
128 F7 Limoquije Bolivia
18 F7 Limousin reg France
18 G9 Limoux France
108 D5 Limpia Cr Texas U.S.A.
8 D5 Limpley Stoke England
89 E4 Limpopo R Botswana
9 G5 Limpsfield England
45 P1 Limski Zaljev Croatia
67 C4 Limu China
28 D4 Lina Denmark
26 L4 Linaälv Sweden
26 M5 Lina älv R Sweden
67 F1 Lin'an China
71 F7 Linao B Mindanao Philippines
71 D5 Linapacan isld Philippines
71 D5 Linapacan Str Philippines
131 B5 Linares Chile
131 B6 Linares prov Chile
125 K5 Linares Mexico
16 E6 Linares Spain
21 P4 Linas France
43 B9 Linas, M mt Sardinia
70 D3 Linau Balui Plateau Sarawak
67 E3 Linchuan China
133 E4 Lincoln Argentina
9 F1 Lincoln England
144 A4 Lincoln New Zealand
111 K8 Lincoln Alabama U.S.A.
102 C3 Lincoln California U.S.A.
95 M8 Lincoln Delaware U.S.A.
99 R9 Lincoln Illinois U.S.A.
107 M2 Lincoln Kansas U.S.A.
95 T1 Lincoln Maine U.S.A.
94 D2 Lincoln Michigan U.S.A.
99 M3 Lincoln Minnesota U.S.A.
101 N3 Lincoln Montana U.S.A.
98 K9 Lincoln Nebraska U.S.A.
95 Q2 Lincoln New Hampshire U.S.A.
106 E8 Lincoln New Mexico U.S.A.
110 K3 Lincoln City Indiana U.S.A.
100 A5 Lincoln City Oregon U.S.A.
98 J9 Lincoln Cr Nebraska U.S.A.
138 E4 Lincoln Gap South Australia Australia
9 F1 Lincolnshire co England
112 E4 Lincolnton Georgia U.S.A.
112 F2 Lincolnton North Carolina U.S.A.
123 L8 Lincolnville Nova Scotia Canada
95 S2 Lincolnville Maine U.S.A.
100 G3 Lind Washington U.S.A.
140 E6 Linda R Queensland Australia
52 F6 Linda Nizhegorodskaya obl Russian Federation
13 F5 Lindale England
111 L7 Lindale Georgia U.S.A.
109 M3 Lindale Texas U.S.A.
27 A11 Lindas Norway
33 Q8 Lindau Germany
41 L2 Lindau Germany
118 G5 Lindbergh Alberta Canada
98 B8 Lindbergh Wyoming U.S.A.
101 M2 Lindbergh L Montana U.S.A.
28 A4 Linde Denmark
28 F7 Lindelse Denmark
141 J5 Lindeman I Queensland Australia
32 L8 Linden Germany
128 G2 Linden Guyana
111 J9 Linden Alabama U.S.A.
94 J4 Linden New York U.S.A.
112 J2 Linden North Carolina U.S.A.
110 J6 Linden Tennessee U.S.A.
111 B8 Linden Texas U.S.A.
37 K3 Lindenau Friedrichshall Germany
33 Q6 Lindenberg Germany
28 D3 Lindenborg Å R Denmark
36 F4 Lindenfels Germany
33 T6 Lindenhagen Germany
33 Q9 Lindenhayn Germany
115 P5 Lindenow Fjord Greenland
25 F6 Lindern Germany
32 G7 Lindern Germany
143 B10 Lindesay, Mt W Australia Australia
27 H12 Lindesberg Sweden
27 B14 Lindesnes lighthouse Norway
9 F5 Lindfield England
27 G12 Lindfors Sweden
28 F5 Lindholm isld Denmark
88 G6 Lindi Tanzania
88 F6 Lindi reg Tanzania
86 E5 Lindi R Zaire
65 F1 Lindian China
13 G2 Lindisfarne England
144 B6 Lindis Valley New Zealand
28 C5 Lindknud Denmark
106 D1 Lindland Colorado U.S.A.
36 C1 Lindlar Germany
32 K8 Lindnorst Germany
106 G2 Lindon Colorado U.S.A.
13 E1 Lindores Scotland
47 V17 Lindos Rhodes Greece
33 R7 Lindow Germany
36 B6 Lindre,Etg de L France
121 M8 Lindsay Ontario Canada
102 E5 Lindsay California U.S.A.
101 U2 Lindsay Montana U.S.A.
98 J8 Lindsay Nebraska U.S.A.
107 N7 Lindsay Oklahoma U.S.A.
143 D7 Lindsay Gordon, L W Australia Australia
140 A6 Lindsay, Mt N Terr Australia
107 N3 Lindsborg Kansas U.S.A.
94 D5 Lindsey Ohio U.S.A.
33 P7 Lindstedt Germany
83 K11 Lindula Sri Lanka
28 D3 Lindum Denmark
37 P4 Líně Czechoslovakia
94 G5 Linesville Pennsylvania U.S.A.
111 L8 Lineville Alabama U.S.A.
99 N9 Lineville Iowa U.S.A.
56 B4 Linevo Russian Federation
58 F4 Linfen China
68 J3 Lingao China
71 E2 Lingayen Luzon Philippines
71 E2 Lingayen Gulf Luzon Philippines
65 B7 Lingbao China
27 J10 Lingbo Sweden
65 B7 Lingchuan China
67 C4 Lingchuan China
21 N8 Lingé France
25 D5 Linge R Netherlands
32 F7 Lingen Germany
69 G13 Lingga Indonesia
70 B4 Lingga Sarawak
69 G13 Lingga,Kep islds Indonesia
27 H11 Linghed Sweden
70 E3 Lingkas Kalimantan
98 B7 Lingle Wyoming U.S.A.
86 D5 Lingomo Zaire
58 F4 Lingqiu China
68 J1 Lingshan China
65 E7 Lingshan Dao isld China
65 B6 Lingshi China
101 O3 Lingshire Montana U.S.A.
65 C5 Lingshou China
68 K3 Lingshui China
76 C2 Lingsugur India
67 D7 Lingtou China
43 G11 Linguaglossa Sicily
85 B5 Linguère Senegal
67 C4 Lingui China
Lingxi see Yongshun
65 C6 Ling Xian China
67 D3 Ling Xian China
67 B4 Lingyang China
65 D4 Lingyuan China
67 B4 Lingyun China
67 G2 Linhai China
130 H6 Linhares Brazil
68 G3 Linh Cam Vietnam
65 D7 Linhong Kou B China
122 B7 Liniere Quebec Canada
21 O7 Liniez France
65 G4 Linjiang China
67 G2 Lin Jiang R China
65 F4 Linjiatai China
65 A7 Linjin China
36 E5 Linkenheim Germany
27 H13 Linköping Sweden
59 K2 Linkou China
67 A3 Linkou China
52 B6 Linkuva Lithuania
67 D2 Linli China
15 E5 Linlithgow Scotland
32 E10 Linn Germany
107 N2 Linn Kansas U.S.A.
110 E3 Linn Missouri U.S.A.
109 J9 Linn Texas U.S.A.
29 N9 Linnansaari Nat. Park Finland
95 S7 Linneus Maine U.S.A.
99 N10 Linneus Missouri U.S.A.
8 A4 Linney Hd Wales
25 F7 Linnich Germany
100 C9 Linn,Mt California U.S.A.
15 E4 Linn of Dee Scotland
43 E13 Linosa, I. di Italy
33 R6 Linow Germany
Linping see Yuhang
65 B7 Linqi China
65 C6 Linqing China
65 D6 Linqu China
65 B7 Linru China
130 E7 Lins Brazil
32 K7 Linsburg Germany
26 G9 Linsell Sweden
65 A7 Lin Shan hist site China
67 B2 Linshizhen China
65 D7 Linshu China
67 B1 Linshui China
127 L2 Linstead Jamaica
71 J9 Lintah,Selat str Indonesia
58 D5 Lintan China
58 D4 Lintao China
41 K3 Linth R Switzerland
41 J4 Linthal Switzerland
119 O6 Lintlaw Saskatchewan Canada
121 S5 Linton Quebec Canada
145 E4 Linton New Zealand
110 J2 Linton Indiana U.S.A.
98 F3 Linton North Dakota U.S.A.
65 A7 Lintong China
32 E10 Lintorf Germany
33 R7 Linum Germany
112 F1 Linville North Carolina U.S.A.
94 J8 Linville Virginia U.S.A.
107 P2 Linwood Kansas U.S.A.
94 D3 Linwood Michigan U.S.A.
98 K8 Linwood Nebraska U.S.A.
67 D4 Linwu China
58 G3 Linxi China
58 D4 Linxia China
65 A6 Lin Xian China
67 D2 Linxiang China
65 C6 Linyi China
65 A7 Linyi China
65 D7 Linyi China
38 K5 Linz Austria
36 C2 Linz Germany
65 C6 Linzhang China
65 D6 Linzi China
70 D3 Lio Matoh Sarawak
21 J6 Lion-d' Angers, le France
89 G1 Lion's Den Zimbabwe
120 J8 Lions Head Ontario Canada
21 K3 Lion-sur-Mer France
71 N8 Lioppa Indonesia

196 Liouesso — Longwy

86 C5 **Liouesso** Congo
54 B1 **Liozno** Belorussia
42 G4 **Lipa** Bosnia-Herzegovina
71 E4 **Lipa** Philippines
65 J3 **Lipadiya** Russian Federation
109 J3 **Lipan** Texas U.S.A.
43 F10 **Lipari, I** *islds* Italy
43 F10 **Lipari, I** Italy
69 E12 **Lipatkain** Sumatra
29 O9 **Liperi** Finland
54 L4 **Lipetsk** Russian Federation
9 F5 **Liphook** England
31 H2 **Lipiany** Poland
52 E4 **Lipin Bor** Russian Federation
67 C3 **Liping** China
48 K2 **Lipkany** Moldavia
46 E2 **Lipljan** Serbia Yugoslavia
48 D1 **Lipnik** Czechoslovakia
48 L6 **Lipniţa** Romania
31 L3 **Lipno** Poland
89 F3 **Lipokolo Hills** Botswana
48 G4 **Lipova** Romania
48 M1 **Lipovets** Ukraine
32 H9 **Lippe** *R* Germany
32 H9 **Lipperode** Germany
32 H9 **Lippetal** Germany
32 H9 **Lippstadt** Germany
108 D7 **Lipscomb** Texas U.S.A.
31 O2 **Lipsk** Poland
47 H7 **Lipsói** *isld* Greece
119 O8 **Lipton** Saskatchewan Canada
48 F1 **Liptovský Mikuláš** Czechoslovakia
139 H7 **Liptrap,C** Victoria Australia
67 C4 **Lipu** China
86 F5 **Lira** Uganda
71 M8 **Liran** *isld* Indonesia
86 C6 **Liranga** Congo
128 D6 **Lircay** Peru
21 H7 **Liré** France
45 O6 **Liri** *R* Italy
45 P7 **Liri** Italy
69 F13 **Lirik** Sumatra
55 D4 **Lisakovsk** Kazakhstan
86 D5 **Lisala** Zaire
127 O2 **Lisas B** Trinidad
16 A6 **Lisboa** Portugal
Lisbon *see* **Lisboa**
99 S8 **Lisbon** Illinois U.S.A.
95 Q2 **Lisbon** New Hampshire U.S.A.
95 M2 **Lisbon** New York U.S.A.
98 J3 **Lisbon** North Dakota U.S.A.
94 G6 **Lisbon** Ohio U.S.A.
95 R2 **Lisbon Falls** Maine U.S.A.
14 E2 **Lisburn** N Ireland
116 D2 **Lisburne,C** Alaska U.S.A.
14 B4 **Liscannor B** Ireland
98 D8 **Lisco** Nebraska U.S.A.
123 K8 **Liscomb** Nova Scotia Canada
14 B3 **Lisdoonvarna** Ireland
28 H4 **Liseleje** Denmark
67 D1 **Lishan** China
65 B6 **Lishi** China
65 F3 **Lishu** China
67 C2 **Li Shui** *R* China
67 F1 **Lishui** Jiangsu China
67 G2 **Lishui** Zhejiang China
54 K8 **Lisichansk** Ukraine
118 L9 **Lisieux** Saskatchewan Canada
21 L3 **Lisieux** France
56 C2 **Lisitsa** *R* Russian Federation
8 B7 **Liskeard** England
54 L6 **Liski** Russian Federation
95 L4 **Lisle** New York U.S.A.
18 G9 **Lisle sur Tarn** France
111 H9 **Lisman** Alabama U.S.A.
123 K8 **Lismore** Nova Scotia Canada
14 D4 **Lismore** Ireland
15 C4 **Lismore** *isld* Scotland
14 D2 **Lisnaskea** N Ireland
21 H3 **Lison** France
21 N3 **Lisors** France
142 G3 **Lissadell** W Australia Australia
25 C4 **Lisse** Netherlands
28 A6 **List** Germany
27 B13 **Lista** *isld* Norway
27 B13 **Listerfj** *inlet* Norway
140 E7 **Listore** *R* Queensland Australia
14 B4 **Listowel** Ireland
141 H7 **Listowel Downs** Queensland Australia
56 C6 **Listvyaga,Khr** *mts* Kazakhstan/Rus Fed
56 G5 **Listvyanka** Russian Federation
26 G8 **Lit** Sweden
58 D5 **Litang** China
67 C5 **Litang** China
58 D6 **Litang Qu** *R* China
79 F5 **Līṭāni** *R* Lebanon
9 G2 **Litcham** England
100 E9 **Litchfield** California U.S.A.
95 O5 **Litchfield** Connecticut U.S.A.
110 G2 **Litchfield** Illinois U.S.A.
94 C4 **Litchfield** Michigan U.S.A.
99 M4 **Litchfield** Minnesota U.S.A.
98 G8 **Litchfield** Nebraska U.S.A.
103 M8 **Litchfield Pk** Arizona U.S.A.
98 H3 **Litchville** North Dakota U.S.A.
48 K3 **Liteni** Romania
18 E8 **Lit et Mixe** France
46 D7 **Lithakiá** Greece
46 G6 **Lithári,Akr** *C* Greece
139 K5 **Lithgow** New South Wales Australia
46 G10 **Lithinon, Akr** *C* Crete Greece
27 M16 **Lithuania** *rep* E Europe
37 P4 **Litice** Czechoslovakia
42 F2 **Litija** Slovenia
48 L1 **Litin** Ukraine
95 L6 **Lititz** Pennsylvania U.S.A.
6 F1 **Litla Dimun** *isld* Faeroes
86 A6 **Lit. Loango Nat. Park** Gabon
46 F4 **Litókhoron** Greece
31 H5 **Litoměřice** Czechoslovakia
31 J6 **Litomyšl** Czechoslovakia
59 K2 **Litovko** Russian Federation
Litovskaya S.S.R. *see* **Lithuania**
27 J12 **Litslena** Sweden
110 D6 **Little** *R* Arkansas U.S.A.
112 E4 **Little** *R* Georgia U.S.A.
110 J5 **Little** *R* Kentucky U.S.A.
111 D10 **Little** *R* Louisiana U.S.A.
112 J2 **Little** *R* North Carolina U.S.A.
107 O6 **Little** *R* Oklahoma U.S.A.
109 M1 **Little** *R* Oklahoma U.S.A.
109 L5 **Little** *R* Texas U.S.A.
68 A7 **Little Andaman** *isld* Andaman Is
99 T4 **Little Bay de Noc** Michigan U.S.A.
123 R4 **Little Bay Is** Newfoundland Canada
119 N4 **Little Bear L** Saskatchewan Canada
101 P3 **Little Belt Mts** Montana U.S.A.
101 S4 **Little Bighorn River** Montana U.S.A.
116 Q3 **Little Black** *R* Alaska U.S.A.
13 F6 **Littleborough** England
118 E8 **Little Bow Prov. Park** Alberta Canada
118 D8 **Little Bow R** Alberta Canada
123 R2 **Little Brehat** Newfoundland Canada
117 R5 **Little Buffalo R** Northwest Territories Canada
119 V7 **Little Bullhead** Manitoba Canada
123 R4 **Little Burnt Bay** Newfoundland Canada
9 G3 **Littlebury** England
89 A7 **Little Bushman Land** *reg* S Africa
99 S5 **Little Chute** Wisconsin U.S.A.
103 N6 **Little Colorado** *R* Arizona U.S.A.
103 M4 **Little Creek Pk** Utah U.S.A.
120 J7 **Little Current** Ontario Canada
111 B9 **Little Cypress Cr** Texas U.S.A.
138 F6 **Little Desert** Victoria Australia
116 C3 **Little Diomede** *isld* Alaska U.S.A.
101 T2 **Little Dry Cr** Montana U.S.A.
99 M4 **Little Falls** Minnesota U.S.A.
95 N4 **Little Falls** New York U.S.A.
103 L5 **Littlefield** Arizona U.S.A.
108 E2 **Littlefield** Texas U.S.A.
99 N1 **Little Fork** *R* Minnesota U.S.A.
99 N1 **Little Fork** Minnesota U.S.A.
117 N10 **Little Fort** British Columbia Canada
110 G4 **Little Grassy L** Illinois U.S.A.
6 K4 **Little Halibut Bank** North Sea
9 F6 **Littlehampton** England
113 L11 **Little Harbour** Bahamas
89 A6 **Little Karas Berg** *mts* Namibia
89 B9 **Little Karoo** *reg* S Africa
116 H9 **Little Koniuji I** Alaska U.S.A.
102 G6 **Little L** California U.S.A.
111 F12 **Little L** Louisiana U.S.A.
127 H2 **Little London** Jamaica
101 M5 **Little Lost R** Idaho U.S.A.
101 N7 **Little Malad** *R* Idaho U.S.A.
122 E2 **Little Manicouagan,L** Quebec Canada
95 L5 **Little Meadows** Pennsylvania U.S.A.
115 N7 **Little Mecatina** *R* Quebec/Labrador Canada
98 A7 **Little Medicine** Wyoming U.S.A.
110 M2 **Little Miami** *R* Ohio U.S.A.
15 B3 **Little Minch** *chan* Hebrides Scotland
98 B5 **Little Missouri** *R* Wyoming U.S.A.
69 A9 **Little Nicobar** *isld* Nicobar Is
107 Q3 **Little Osage** *R* Kansas/Missouri U.S.A.
112 H3 **Little Pee Dee R** South Carolina U.S.A.
9 G3 **Littleport** England
98 A5 **Little Powder** *R* Wyoming U.S.A.
123 Q5 **Little R** Newfoundland Canada
144 D5 **Little River** New Zealand
111 J10 **Little River** Alabama U.S.A.
107 N3 **Little River** Kansas U.S.A.
112 J4 **Little River Inlet** North Carolina U.S.A.
110 D7 **Little Rock** Arkansas U.S.A.
102 G7 **Littlerock** California U.S.A.
88 E6 **Little Ruaha** *R* Tanzania
99 U6 **Little Sable Pt** Michigan U.S.A.
110 C4 **Little Sac** *R* Missouri U.S.A.
117 F4 **Little Salmon L** Yukon Territory Canada
103 M4 **Little Salt L** Utah U.S.A.
119 T1 **Little Sand L** Manitoba Canada
101 Q7 **Little Sandy Cr** Wyoming U.S.A.
112 E6 **Little Satilla** *R* Georgia U.S.A.
99 L7 **Little Sioux** *R* Iowa U.S.A.
117 P8 **Little Smoky River** Alberta Canada
101 R9 **Little Snake** *R* Colorado U.S.A.
9 G6 **Littlestone-on-Sea** England
95 K7 **Littlestown** Pennsylvania U.S.A.
99 T5 **Little Suamico** Wisconsin U.S.A.
122 F7 **Little S.W. Miramichi R** New Brunswick Canada
112 C2 **Little Tennessee** *R* Tennessee U.S.A.
127 N1 **Little Tobago** *isld* Tobago
106 E2 **Littleton** Colorado U.S.A.
99 Q9 **Littleton** Illinois U.S.A.
95 Q2 **Littleton** New Hampshire U.S.A.
112 K1 **Littleton** North Carolina U.S.A.
94 G7 **Littleton** West Virginia U.S.A.
95 N2 **Little Tupper L** New York U.S.A.
94 J4 **Little Valley** New York U.S.A.
100 K7 **Little Valley Cr** Idaho U.S.A.
111 J7 **Littleville** Alabama U.S.A.
110 H3 **Little Wabash** *R* Illinois U.S.A.
9 G4 **Little Waltham** England
98 E6 **Little White** *R* South Dakota U.S.A.
101 L6 **Little Wood** *R* Idaho U.S.A.
8 D2 **Littleworth** England
78 J4 **Little Zab** *R* Iraq
37 Q2 **Litvínov** Czechoslovakia
67 C4 **Liucheng** China
67 B3 **Liuchong He** *R* China
Liuchuan *see* **Jianhe**
67 B2 **Liudu** China
67 B3 **Liuguang** China
65 E3 **Liu He** *R* China
65 F3 **Liu He** *R* China
65 F3 **Liuhe** China
67 B1 **Liuhechang** China
67 G2 **Liuheng Dao** *isld* China
65 E2 **Liuhu** China
67 D1 **Liujiachang** China
67 C4 **Liu Jiang** *R* China
88 E7 **Liuli** Tanzania
65 C5 **Liulihezhen** China
67 B4 **Liuma** China
Liupai *see* **Tian'e**
67 D1 **Liushuigou** China
67 C4 **Liutang** China
67 D2 **Liuyang** China
67 D2 **Liuyang He** *R* China
67 B4 **Liuzhai** China
Liuzhangzhen *see* **Qinghe**
Liuzhangzhen *see* **Yuanqu**
67 C4 **Liuzhou** China
65 C7 **Liuzhuang** China
48 H3 **Livade** Romania
52 C6 **Līvāni** Latvia
21 L3 **Livarot** France
118 J5 **Livelong** Saskatchewan Canada
116 N4 **Livengood** Alaska U.S.A.
42 E3 **Livenza** *R* Italy
102 C2 **Live Oak** California U.S.A.
113 E7 **Live Oak** Florida U.S.A.
142 E4 **Liveringa** W Australia Australia
102 C4 **Livermore** California U.S.A.
99 M7 **Livermore** Iowa U.S.A.
110 J4 **Livermore** Kentucky U.S.A.
95 R2 **Livermore Falls** Maine U.S.A.
108 C5 **Livermore, Mt** Texas U.S.A.
139 K5 **Liverpool** New South Wales Australia
140 C1 **Liverpool** *R* N Terr Australia
122 H9 **Liverpool** Nova Scotia Canada
11 B2 **Liverpool** *conurbation* England
95 L3 **Liverpool** New York U.S.A.
114 G3 **Liverpool B** Northwest Territories Canada
115 M3 **Liverpool,C** Northwest Territories Canada
139 K4 **Liverpool Plains** New South Wales Australia
139 K4 **Liverpool Ra** *mts* New South Wales Australia
143 F7 **Livesey Ra** W Australia Australia
19 P14 **Livet** France
41 M4 **Livigno** Italy
125 P10 **Livingston** Guatemala
15 E5 **Livingston** Scotland
111 H9 **Livingston** Alabama U.S.A.
110 M4 **Livingston** Kentucky U.S.A.
111 F11 **Livingston** Louisiana U.S.A.
101 P4 **Livingston** Montana U.S.A.
109 N5 **Livingston** Texas U.S.A.
99 Q7 **Livingston** Wisconsin U.S.A.
144 C6 **Livingstone** New Zealand
89 D1 **Livingstone** Zambia
117 F5 **Livingstone Creek** Yukon Territory Canada
88 C8 **Livingstone Memorial** Zambia
144 B6 **Livingstone Mts** New Zealand
88 E6 **Livingstone Mts** Tanzania
118 C8 **Livingstone Ra** Alberta Canada
146 C3 **Livingston I** S Shetland Is Antarctica
87 F8 **Livingstonia** Malawi
95 N5 **Livingston Manor** New York U.S.A.
42 H5 **Livno** Bosnia-Herzegovina
54 J4 **Livny** Russian Federation
28 B3 **Livø** *isld* Denmark
29 M6 **Livojoki** *R* Finland
111 E11 **Livonia** Louisiana U.S.A.
94 D4 **Livonia** Michigan U.S.A.
99 O9 **Livonia** Missouri U.S.A.
44 H4 **Livorno** Italy
18 H7 **Livradois,Mts.du** France
133 F4 **Livramento** Brazil
20 H5 **Livré** France
19 N15 **Livron** France
87 G7 **Liwale** Tanzania
88 G6 **Liwale** Tanzania
31 N3 **Liwiec** *R* Poland
67 E2 **Lixi** China
65 C5 **Li Xian** China
67 D2 **Li Xian** Hunan China
67 A1 **Li Xian** Sichuan China
36 B5 **Lixing les St.Avold** France
46 D6 **Lixoúrion** Greece
67 F1 **Liyang** China
67 C4 **Liyong** China
9 G7 **Lizard** *pen* England
129 J5 **Lizarda** Brazil
101 Q7 **Lizard Head Pk** Wyoming U.S.A.
141 H2 **Lizard I** Gt Barrier Reef Aust
112 D5 **Lizella** Georgia U.S.A.
94 F8 **Lizemores** West Virginia U.S.A.
52 D4 **Lizhma** Russian Federation
18 F7 **Lizonne** *R* France
121 S4 **Lizotte** Quebec Canada
110 K2 **Lizton** Indiana U.S.A.
45 J3 **Lizzano in Belvedere** Italy
27 F10 **Ljöra** *R* Norway
28 S9 **Ljosafoss** Iceland
42 H4 **Ljubija** Bosnia-Herzegovina
42 J6 **Ljubinje** Bosnia-Herzegovina
46 C1 **Ljubišnja** *mt* Bosnia-Herzegovina/Yugoslavia
42 F2 **Ljubljana** Slovenia
46 E2 **Ljuboten** *mt* Serbia Yugoslavia
48 E6 **Ljubovija** Serbia Yugoslavia
42 H5 **Ljubuški** Bosnia-Herzegovina
27 K14 **Ljugarn** Gotland Sweden
26 H9 **Ljunga** Sweden
26 H9 **Ljungan** *R* Sweden
26 H9 **Ljungaverk** Sweden
27 G15 **Ljungby** Sweden
27 G15 **Ljungby, Ö** Sweden
26 F9 **Ljungdalen** Sweden
26 H10 **Ljusdal** Sweden
26 H9 **Ljusnan** *R* Sweden
27 J10 **Ljusne** Sweden
27 K12 **Ljusterö** Sweden
133 C5 **Llaima** *mt* Chile
131 B7 **Llaima,Vol** Chile
8 B2 **Llanaelhaearn** Wales
8 B3 **Llanarth** Wales
8 B2 **Llanbedr** Wales
8 B2 **Llanbedrog** Wales
8 B1 **Llanberis** Wales
8 C3 **Llanbister** Wales
131 B5 **Llancanelo, L** Argentina
131 C5 **Llancanelo,Salina** Argentina
8 C5 **Llandaf** Wales
8 C4 **Llandarcy** Wales
8 B4 **Llanddarog** Wales
8 B4 **Llandefeilog** Wales
8 B1 **Llandegai** Wales
8 D4 **Llandegfedd Resr.** *res* Wales
8 B4 **Llandeilo** Wales
8 B4 **Llandissilio** Wales
8 C4 **Llandovery** Wales
8 B4 **Llandowror** Wales
8 C2 **Llandrillo** Wales
8 C3 **Llandrindod Wells** Wales
8 C1 **Llandudno** Wales
8 B3 **Llandyssul** Wales
8 B4 **Llanelli** Wales
8 C2 **Llanelltyd** Wales
8 B1 **Llanerchymedd** Wales
16 D1 **Llanes** Spain
8 B1 **Llanfaethlu** Wales
8 C1 **Llanfairfechan** Wales
8 C1 **Llanfair Talhaiarn** Wales
8 B3 **Llanfarian** Wales
8 C1 **Llanferres** Wales
8 C2 **Llanfyllin** Wales
8 C2 **Llangadfan** Wales
8 C4 **Llangadog** Wales
8 C3 **Llangammarch Wells** Wales
8 B1 **Llangefni** Wales
8 B3 **Llangeler** Wales
8 B2 **Llangelynin** Wales
8 C1 **Llangernyw** Wales
8 C2 **Llangollen** Wales
8 C3 **Llangurig** Wales
8 C2 **Llangynog** Wales
8 C3 **Llanidloes** Wales
8 B3 **Llanilar** Wales
8 B1 **Llanllyfni** Wales
8 B4 **Llanmadog** Wales
124 D2 **Llano** Mexico
109 H5 **Llano** *R* Texas U.S.A.
109 J5 **Llano** Texas U.S.A.
124 G6 **Llano Grande** Mexico
128 D2 **Llanos** *prairies* Colombia/Venezuela
17 H3 **Llanos de Urgel** *reg* Spain
131 C3 **Llanos,Sa.de los** *mts* Argentina
133 C6 **Llanquihue** *prov* Chile
131 A8 **Llanquihue,L** Chile
141 F5 **Llanrheidol** Queensland Australia
8 B4 **Llanrhidian** Wales
8 B3 **Llanrhystyd** Wales
8 C1 **Llanrwst** Wales
18 H10 **Llansa** Spain
8 C1 **Llansannan** Wales
8 B3 **Llansantffraid** Wales
8 B4 **Llanstephan** Wales
8 C4 **Llanthony** Wales
8 C4 **Llantrisant** Wales
8 C4 **Llanwrda** Wales
8 C3 **Llanwrtyd Wells** Wales
8 B3 **Llanybydder** Wales
8 C2 **Llanymynech** England
77 E5 **Llazārān, Kūh-e** *mt* Iran
8 B3 **Llechryd** Wales
Lleida *see* **Lérida**
17 H3 **Llena,Sierra de la** *mts* Spain
16 C6 **Llerena** Spain
133 C4 **Llico** Chile
17 G5 **Lliria** Spain
17 J3 **Llobregat** *R* Spain
17 J3 **Lloret de Mar** Spain
101 Q1 **Lloyd** Montana U.S.A.
141 G2 **Lloyd B** Queensland Australia
117 L7 **Lloyd George, Mt** British Columbia Canada
118 H5 **Lloydminster** Alberta/Sask Canada
127 K2 **Lluidas Vale** Jamaica
133 D2 **Llullaillaco** *mt* Arg/Chile
128 E7 **Lluta** *R* Chile
8 B2 **Llwyngwril** Wales
8 C3 **Llyswen** Wales
128 E8 **Loa** *R* Chile
103 N3 **Loa** Utah U.S.A.
70 E5 **Loakulu** Kalimantan
99 R10 **Loami** Illinois U.S.A.
130 D8 **Loanda** Brazil
86 D6 **Loanga** *R* Zaire
86 B6 **Loango** Congo
13 E2 **Loanhead** Scotland
110 G2 **Loann** Illinois U.S.A.
44 D3 **Loano** Italy
71 G6 **Loay** Philippines
52 H5 **Loban'** *R* Russian Federation
54 K3 **Lobanovo** Russian Federation
70 G6 **Lobata** Sulawesi
89 D5 **Lobatse** Botswana
31 H4 **Löbau** Germany
86 C5 **Lobaye** *R* Cent Afr Republic
22 G3 **Lobbes** Belgium
37 M2 **Lobeda** Germany
33 P9 **Löbejün** Germany
37 M3 **Lobenstein** Germany
133 F5 **Lobería** Argentina
31 J2 **Łobez** Poland
87 B8 **Lobito** Angola
33 R4 **Löbnitz** Germany
54 J1 **Lobnya** Russian Federation
85 C7 **Lobo** *R* Ivory Coast
16 C6 **Lobón** Spain
27 H10 **Lobonäs** Sweden
131 F5 **Lobos** Argentina
124 D4 **Lobos** *isld* Mexico
128 D7 **Lobos,C** Chile
124 C3 **Lobos,C** Mexico
126 F3 **Lobos Cay** *isld* Cuba
128 B5 **Lobos de Tierra** *isld* Peru
133 D6 **Lobos,Pta** Argentina
131 A5 **Lobos,Pta** Colchagua Chile
37 N1 **Lobstädt** Germany
115 N7 **Lobstick L** Labrador, Nfld Canada
33 Q8 **Loburg** Germany
55 D2 **Lobva** Russian Federation
31 K2 **Łobżenica** Poland
40 G7 **Locana** Italy
41 J5 **Locarno** Switzerland
67 B6 **Loc Binh** Vietnam
32 K8 **Loccum** Germany
15 D4 **Lochaber** Scotland
122 K8 **Lochaber Mines** Nova Scotia Canada
15 C4 **Lochaline** Scotland
120 F4 **Lochalsh** Ontario Canada
15 C2 **Loch Assynt** Scotland
15 C4 **Loch Awe** Scotland
15 A3 **Loch Boisdale** Outer Hebrides Scotland
15 C3 **Loch Broom** Scotland
15 C4 **Lochbuie** Scotland
15 C3 **Loch Clunie** Scotland
15 D4 **Lochearnhead** Scotland
15 C4 **Loch Eil** Scotland
25 F4 **Lochem** Netherlands
15 D2 **Loch Eriboll** Scotland
15 D4 **Loch Ericht** Scotland
15 B2 **Loch Erisort** Scotland
21 M7 **Loches** France
21 N7 **Loché-sur-Indrois** France
15 C4 **Loch Etive** Scotland
15 C3 **Loch Ewe** Scotland
15 E4 **Loch Faskally** Scotland
15 C4 **Loch Fyne** Scotland
12 C1 **Lochgilphead** Scotland
15 C4 **Lochgilphead** Scotland
15 D3 **Loch Glass** Scotland
12 D1 **Lochgoilhead** Scotland
15 C3 **Loch Hourn** Scotland
144 B7 **Lochie** New Zealand
15 C2 **Loch Inchard** Scotland
15 C2 **Lochinver** Scotland
15 D4 **Loch Laggan** Scotland
15 B2 **Loch Langavat** Scotland
15 C2 **Loch Laxford** Scotland
15 E4 **Loch Leven** Scotland
15 D4 **Loch Lochy** Scotland
15 D4 **Loch Long** Scotland
15 C3 **Loch Loyne** Scotland
12 E3 **Lochmaben** Scotland
15 E5 **Lochmaben** Scotland
15 A3 **Lochmaddy** Outer Hebrides Scotland
15 C3 **Loch Maree** Scotland
15 C3 **Loch Monar** Scotland
15 C4 **Loch Morar** Scotland
15 D2 **Loch More** Scotland
144 B6 **Lochnagar** *L* New Zealand
15 E4 **Lochnagar** *mt* Scotland
15 D2 **Loch Naver** Scotland
15 D3 **Loch Ness** Scotland
15 D3 **Loch Oich** Scotland
15 C3 **Loch Quoich** Scotland
15 D4 **Loch Rannoch** Scotland
12 C2 **Lochranza** Scotland
22 F1 **Lochristi** Belgium
15 C4 **Loch Sheil** Scotland
15 D2 **Loch Shin** Scotland
15 C4 **Loch Sunart** Scotland
15 D4 **Loch Tay** Scotland
15 C3 **Loch Torridon** Scotland
68 J2 **Lo Chuc San** *isld* Vietnam
15 D4 **Loch Vennacher** Scotland
12 D2 **Lochwinnoch** Scotland
138 D5 **Lock** South Australia Australia
95 L4 **Locke** New York U.S.A.
100 H1 **Locke** Washington U.S.A.
122 G10 **Lockeport** Nova Scotia Canada
109 J4 **Locker** Texas U.S.A.
15 E5 **Lockerbie** Scotland
142 A5 **Locker Pt** W Australia Australia
103 J3 **Lockes** Nevada U.S.A.
111 B8 **Lockesburg** Arkansas U.S.A.
109 H1 **Lockett** Texas U.S.A.
139 H6 **Lockhart** New South Wales Australia
111 K10 **Lockhart** Alabama U.S.A.
98 K2 **Lockhart** Minnesota U.S.A.
112 F3 **Lockhart** South Carolina U.S.A.
109 K6 **Lockhart** Texas U.S.A.
141 G2 **Lockhart River** Queensland Australia
94 K5 **Lock Haven** Pennsylvania U.S.A.
143 B6 **Lockier Ra** W Australia Australia
108 F1 **Lockney** Texas U.S.A.
33 P6 **Löcknitz** *R* Germany
99 S8 **Lockport** Illinois U.S.A.
111 F12 **Lockport** Louisiana U.S.A.
94 J3 **Lockport** New York U.S.A.
99 P9 **Lockridge** Iowa U.S.A.
119 N7 **Lockwood** Saskatchewan Canada
110 C4 **Lockwood** Missouri U.S.A.
116 J3 **Lockwood Hills** Alaska U.S.A.
19 K5 **Locle, Le** France
20 D7 **Locmaria** Belle Isle, Nfld France
20 E6 **Locmaria** Morbihan France
20 E6 **Locmariaquer** France
20 E6 **Locminé** France
68 H7 **Loc Ninh** Vietnam
107 N7 **Loco** Oklahoma U.S.A.
101 P3 **Loco Mt** Montana U.S.A.
20 C4 **Locquirec** France
43 G10 **Locri** Italy
20 B5 **Locronan** France
20 B6 **Loctudy** France
99 N9 **Locust Cr** *R* Missouri U.S.A.
111 K7 **Locust Fork** *R* Alabama U.S.A.
94 D8 **Locust Grove** Ohio U.S.A.
107 P5 **Locust Grove** Oklahoma U.S.A.
80 C6 **Lod** Israel
99 S9 **Loda** Illinois U.S.A.
26 B10 **Lodalskåpa** *mt* Norway
139 G6 **Loddon** *R* Victoria Australia
9 H2 **Loddon** England
33 P10 **Lodersleben** Germany
18 H9 **Lodève** France
52 D4 **Lodeynoye-Pole** Russian Federation
101 Q1 **Lodge Cr** Mont/Sask U.S.A./Canada
101 S4 **Lodge Grass** Montana U.S.A.
117 E6 **Lodge, Mt** Br Col/Alaska Canada/U.S.A.
98 D8 **Lodgepole** Nebraska U.S.A.
98 C8 **Lodgepole Cr** Nebraska U.S.A.
98 B8 **Lodgepole Cr** Wyoming U.S.A.
74 D4 **Lodhran** Pakistan
41 L7 **Lodi** Italy
102 C3 **Lodi** California U.S.A.
94 E5 **Lodi** Ohio U.S.A.
99 R6 **Lodi** Wisconsin U.S.A.
26 G4 **Løding** Norway
26 H3 **Lödingen** Norway
86 D6 **Lodja** Zaire
71 A3 **Lodji** Indonesia
88 E3 **Lodmalasin** *mt* Tanzania
18 D10 **Lodosa** Spain
40 D3 **Lods** France
86 G5 **Lodwar** Kenya
31 L4 **Łódź** Poland
16 E4 **Loeches** Spain
86 F4 **Loelli** Sudan
25 F4 **Loenen** Netherlands
26 B10 **Loenvatn** *L* Norway
21 P2 **Loeuilly** France
38 G6 **Lofer** Austria
38 G6 **Loferer St Ulrich** Austria
36 E6 **Loffenau** Germany
15 E1 **L. of Harray** Scotland
26 F3 **Lofoten** *islds* Norway
26 F9 **Lofsdalen** Sweden
28 B5 **Loft** Denmark
27 J14 **Loftahammar** Sweden
13 G5 **Lofthouse** England
13 H4 **Loftus** England
143 C6 **Lofty Ra** W Australia Australia
141 H5 **Logan** *R* Queensland Australia
141 L8 **Logan** *R* Queensland Australia
99 L8 **Logan** Iowa U.S.A.
107 L2 **Logan** Kansas U.S.A.
101 O4 **Logan** Montana U.S.A.
98 F8 **Logan** Nebraska U.S.A.
106 G6 **Logan** New Mexico U.S.A.
101 O8 **Logan** Utah U.S.A.
94 F9 **Logan** West Virginia U.S.A.
98 K8 **Logan Cr** Nebraska U.S.A.
103 K5 **Logandale** Nevada U.S.A.
116 R6 **Logan Glacier** Alaska/Yukon Terr U.S.A./Canada
118 F3 **Logan L** Alberta Canada
122 E5 **Logan,Mt** Quebec Canada
117 C5 **Logan,Mt** Yukon Territory Canada
100 E1 **Logan, Mt** Washington U.S.A.
117 K5 **Logan Mts** Yukon Terr/N W Terr Canada
101 M1 **Logan Pass** Montana U.S.A.
94 A6 **Logansport** Indiana U.S.A.
111 B10 **Logansport** Louisiana U.S.A.
95 K5 **Loganton** Pennsylvania U.S.A.
99 Q6 **Loganville** Wisconsin U.S.A.
98 A9 **Logcabin** Colorado U.S.A.
26 K8 **Logde älv** *R* Sweden
100 F5 **Logdell** Oregon U.S.A.
87 B7 **Loge** *R* Angola
21 L2 **Loges, les** France
8 D2 **Loggerheads** England
55 D3 **Loginovo** Russian Federation
86 B3 **Logone** *R* Cameroon
21 N5 **Logron** France
17 F2 **Logroño** Spain
16 D5 **Logrosan** Spain
28 C3 **Løgstør** Denmark
28 C3 **Løgstrup** Denmark
28 E4 **Løgten** Denmark
20 D4 **Loguivy-Plougras** France
28 B6 **Løgumkloster** Denmark
28 F6 **Lohals** Denmark
80 D2 **Lohame HaGeta'ot** Israel
75 L7 **Lohardaga** India
20 G6 **Lohéac** France
32 L10 **Lohfelden** Germany
37 M7 **Lohhof** Germany
29 L5 **Lohijärvi** Finland
29 L11 **Lohja** Finland
101 Q1 **Lohman** Montana U.S.A.
33 Q5 **Lohmen** Germany
109 H4 **Lohn** Texas U.S.A.
36 E3 **Löhnberg** Germany
32 J8 **Löhne** Germany
36 D4 **Lohnsfeld** Germany
70 G6 **Loholoho** Sulawesi
36 H4 **Lohr** Germany
36 F2 **Lohra** Germany
99 M7 **Lohrville** Iowa U.S.A.
29 K7 **Lohtaja** Finland
68 C2 **Loi-ai** Burma
45 K3 **Loiano** Italy
38 K8 **Loibl Pass** Austria/Italy
21 J6 **Loigne** France
68 C3 **Loikaw** Burma
68 C3 **Loi Lan** *mt* Burma
68 C2 **Loi-Lem** Burma
68 D1 **Loi Lun** Burma
29 K11 **Loimaa** Finland
18 G4 **Loing** *R* France
21 L6 **Loir** *R* France
18 H7 **Loire** *R* France
21 K7 **Loire** *R* France
21 J6 **Loiré** Maine-et-Loire France
18 D5 **Loire-Atlantique** *dept* France
18 G5 **Loiret** *dept* France
18 F5 **Loir-et-Cher** *dept* France
21 J5 **Loiron** France
41 O2 **Loisach** *R* Germany
68 C2 **Loi Sang** *mt* Burma
22 J5 **Loison** *R* France
40 B4 **Loisy** France
33 S5 **Loitz** Germany
128 C4 **Loja** *prov* Ecuador
16 E7 **Loja** Spain
28 C6 **Løjt** Denmark
86 F5 **Loka** Sudan
29 J11 **Lokalahti** Finland
70 E2 **Lokan** *R* Sabah
86 E6 **Lokandu** Zaire
29 N4 **Lokantekojärvi** *L* Finland
70 D6 **Lokbatu** Kalimantan
52 H4 **Lokchim** *R* Russian Federation
22 D2 **Loker** Belgium
22 F1 **Lokeren** Belgium
37 O3 **Loket** Czechoslovakia
54 E6 **Lokhvitsa** Ukraine
86 G5 **Lokichar** Kenya
70 G5 **Lokilalaki, G** *mt* Sulawesi
86 G5 **Lokitaung** Kenya
29 N4 **Lokka** Finland
28 D2 **Løkken** Denmark
26 D8 **Lökken** Norway
52 D6 **Loknya** Russian Federation
86 A4 **Loko** Nigeria
86 D6 **Lokolo** *R* Zaire
53 C7 **Lokoml'skoye, Ozero** *L* Belorussia
86 C6 **Lokoro** *R* Zaire
55 F1 **Lokosovo** Russian Federation
54 F4 **Lokot'** Russian Federation
52 C5 **Loksa** Estonia
59 K1 **Lokshak** Russian Federation
115 N5 **Loks Land** Northwest Territories Canada
86 E4 **Lol** *R* Sudan
71 J4 **Lolak** Sulawesi
121 P4 **Lola, L** Quebec Canada
100 A9 **Loleta** California U.S.A.
20 H4 **Lolif** France
88 E3 **Loliondo** Tanzania
28 G7 **Lolland** *isld* Denmark
36 F2 **Lollar** Germany
101 L3 **Lolo** Montana U.S.A.
71 B2 **Lolobata** Halmahera Indonesia
71 A2 **Loloda** Halmahera Indonesia
71 A2 **Loloda,Tk** *B* Halmahera Indonesia
71 A1 **Loloda Utara, Pulau Pulau** *islds* Halmahera Indonesia
86 B5 **Lolodorf** Cameroon
52 H4 **Lolog** *R* Russian Federation
101 L3 **Lolo Hot Springs** Montana U.S.A.
69 C12 **Lolomoyo** Indonesia
101 L3 **Lolo Pass** Idaho/Montana U.S.A.
71 M9 **Lolotoi** Indonesia
69 C12 **Lolowau** Indonesia
46 F1 **Lom** Bulgaria
37 O4 **Lom** Czechoslovakia
37 P4 **Lom** *mt* Czechoslovakia
26 C10 **Lom** Norway
106 B2 **Loma** Colorado U.S.A.
101 P2 **Loma** Montana U.S.A.
98 H1 **Loma** North Dakota U.S.A.
16 E6 **Loma de Chiclana** Spain
16 E6 **Loma de Úbeda** Spain
88 B10 **Lomagundi** *dist* Zimbabwe
86 E6 **Lomami** *R* Zaire
85 B7 **Loma Mts** Sierra Leone/Guinea
99 N1 **Loman** Minnesota U.S.A.
131 D6 **Loma Negra,Planicie de la** *plain* Argentina
133 D6 **Lomas Coloradas** *hills* Argentina
130 B10 **Lomas de Vallejos** Argentina
133 F4 **Lomas de Zamora** Argentina
142 E3 **Lombadina** W Australia Australia
101 O3 **Lombard** Montana U.S.A.
129 H3 **Lombarda, Serra** *mts* Brazil
42 C3 **Lombardia** *prov* Italy
22 D1 **Lombardsijde** Belgium
18 F9 **Lombez** France
71 L9 **Lomblen** *isld* Indonesia
70 Q10 **Lombok** Indonesia
70 P10 **Lombok,Selat** *str* Indonesia
21 L5 **Lombron** France
85 E7 **Lomé** Togo
86 D6 **Lomela** Zaire
109 J4 **Lometa** Texas U.S.A.
86 B5 **Lomié** Cameroon
99 S6 **Lomira** Wisconsin U.S.A.
37 P1 **Lommatzsch** Germany
22 D2 **Lomme** France
22 J1 **Lommel** Belgium
118 E8 **Lomond** Alberta Canada
123 P4 **Lomond** Newfoundland Canada
6 M5 **Lomond** *oil rig* North Sea
15 E4 **Lomond Hills** Scotland
12 D1 **Lomond, Loch** *L* Scotland
52 D6 **Lomonosovo** Russian Federation
55 E4 **Lomonosovskaya** Kazakhstan
52 F3 **Lomovoye** Russian Federation
68 H6 **Lomphat** Cambodia
70 G7 **Lompobattang, G** *mt* Sulawesi
102 D7 **Lompoc** California U.S.A.
68 E4 **Lom Sak** Thailand
26 C10 **Lomseggja** *mt* Norway
26 J7 **Lomsjö** Sweden
31 N2 **Łomza** Poland
106 E7 **Lon** New Mexico U.S.A.
94 J7 **Lonaconing** Maryland U.S.A.
74 E9 **Lonāvale** India
28 A5 **Lønborg** Denmark
133 C5 **Loncoche** Chile
133 C5 **Loncopue** Argentina
22 F2 **Londerzeel** Belgium
120 J9 **Londesborough** Ontario Canada
21 N2 **Londinières** France
120 J10 **London** Ontario Canada
10 **London** *conurbation* England
110 C6 **London** Arkansas U.S.A.
94 C9 **London** Kentucky U.S.A.
94 D7 **London** Ohio U.S.A.
109 H5 **London** Texas U.S.A.
122 J8 **Londonderry** Nova Scotia Canada
14 D1 **Londonderry** N Ireland
14 D2 **Londonderry** *co* N Ireland
95 Q4 **Londonderry** New Hampshire U.S.A.
95 P3 **Londonderry** Vermont U.S.A.
142 F2 **Londonderry, C** W Australia Australia
133 C9 **Londonderry, I** Chile
Londorf *see* **Rabenau**
130 D8 **Londrina** Brazil
107 N7 **Lone Grove** Oklahoma U.S.A.
120 J7 **Lonely I** Ontario Canada
102 G4 **Lone Mt** Nevada U.S.A.
109 M3 **Lone Oak** Texas U.S.A.
102 F5 **Lone Pine** California U.S.A.
101 L2 **Lonepine** Montana U.S.A.
118 H5 **Lone Rock** Saskatchewan Canada
100 F4 **Lonerock** Oregon U.S.A.
99 Q6 **Lone Rock** Wisconsin U.S.A.
101 P8 **Lonetree** Wyoming U.S.A.
98 F2 **Lonetree Res** North Dakota U.S.A.
107 L7 **Lone Wolf** Oklahoma U.S.A.
87 C8 **Longa** Angola
129 K4 **Longa** *R* Brazil
46 E8 **Longá** Greece
70 D3 **Longagung** Kalimantan
70 D3 **Long Akah** Sarawak
67 B5 **Long'an** China
141 F5 **Longara** Queensland Australia
45 L1 **Longara** Italy
45 L1 **Longare** Italy
42 E2 **Longarone** Italy
133 C5 **Longavi** *mt* Chile
127 K3 **Long B** Jamaica
70 D3 **Longbawan** Kalimantan
127 M2 **Long Bay** Jamaica
112 J4 **Long Bay** South Carolina U.S.A.
144 C6 **Longbeach** New Zealand
102 F8 **Long Beach** California U.S.A.
95 O6 **Long Beach** Long I, New York U.S.A.
111 G11 **Long Beach** Mississippi U.S.A.
100 A3 **Long Beach** Washington U.S.A.
9 F2 **Long Bennington** England
70 D3 **Longberini** Kalimantan
70 E3 **Longbia** Kalimantan
113 E10 **Longboat Key** *isld* Florida U.S.A.
70 D4 **Longboh** Kalimantan
95 N6 **Long Branch** New Jersey U.S.A.
8 D5 **Longbridge Deverill** England
145 E4 **Longburn** New Zealand
8 D6 **Long Burton** England
22 K3 **Longchamps** Belgium
67 B2 **Longchang** China
67 E4 **Longchuan** China
9 E3 **Long Compton** England
138 C3 **Long Cr** South Australia Australia
119 O9 **Long Cr** Saskatchewan Canada
98 C1 **Long Cr** North Dakota U.S.A.
100 F5 **Long Creek** Oregon U.S.A.
68 H4 **Long Dai** Vietnam
107 M5 **Longdale** Oklahoma U.S.A.
58 E4 **Longde** China
9 E2 **Longdon** England
9 E2 **Long Eaton** England
40 B3 **Longecourt** France
95 M5 **Long Eddy** New York U.S.A.
36 B1 **Longerich** Germany
95 R1 **Long Falls Dam** Maine U.S.A.
108 E5 **Longfellow** Texas U.S.A.
144 D5 **Longfellow, Mt** New Zealand
65 G2 **Longfengshan Shuiku** *res* China
139 H8 **Longford** Tasmania Australia
14 D3 **Longford** *co* Ireland
14 D3 **Longford** Ireland
145 D4 **Longford** New Zealand
107 N2 **Longford** Kansas U.S.A.
13 F2 **Longformacus** Scotland
6 K5 **Long Forties** *bank* North Sea
13 G3 **Longframlington** England
65 G3 **Longgang Shan** *mt ra* China
70 E4 **Longgi** *R* Kalimantan
65 C4 **Longguan** China
65 C7 **Longguji** China
67 C7 **Longgun** China
67 F4 **Longhai** China
9 E6 **Longham** England
123 T6 **Long Harbour** Newfoundland Canada
13 G3 **Longhorsley** England
13 G3 **Longhoughton** England
65 D4 **Longhua** China
67 D3 **Longhui** China
112 J1 **Longhurst** North Carolina U.S.A.
68 A6 **Long I** Andaman Is
141 J5 **Long I** Queensland Australia
126 G3 **Long I** Bahamas
115 M7 **Long I** Northwest Territories Canada
122 F9 **Long I** Nova Scotia Canada
83 K12 **Long I** Mahé I Indian Oc
144 A6 **Long I** New Zealand
136 K3 **Long I** Papua New Guinea
95 P6 **Long I** New York U.S.A.
100 A3 **Long I** Washington U.S.A.
127 M4 **Long, I** Martinique W Indies
70 E5 **Longikis** Kalimantan
70 D5 **Longiram** Kalimantan
95 P5 **Long I Sd** Conn/New York U.S.A.
107 L2 **Long Island** Kansas U.S.A.
59 H2 **Longjiang** China
67 B4 **Long Jiang** *R* China
65 H3 **Longjing** China
21 P4 **Longjumeau** France
Longjuzhai *see* **Danfeng**
36 C4 **Longkamp** Germany
70 D4 **Longkay** Kalimantan
65 E6 **Longkou** China
122 F6 **Long L** New Brunswick Canada
120 D3 **Long L** Ontario Canada
116 K6 **Long L** Alaska U.S.A.
95 S6 **Long L** Maine U.S.A.
94 B2 **Long L** Michigan U.S.A.
99 M3 **Long L** Minnesota U.S.A.
95 N2 **Long L** New York U.S.A.
98 G3 **Long L** North Dakota U.S.A.
122 J1 **Long, Lac** Labrador, Nfld Canada
120 D3 **Longlac** Ontario Canada
95 N3 **Long Lake** New York U.S.A.
99 S4 **Long Lake** Wisconsin U.S.A.
70 D3 **Long Lama** Sarawak
8 D5 **Longleat House** England
67 B3 **Longli** China
22 J4 **Longlier** Belgium
67 B4 **Longlin** China
12 D1 **Long, Loch** *L* Scotland
118 E4 **Long L. Prov. Park** Alberta Canada
100 F2 **Long L.Res** Washington U.S.A.
70 E3 **Longmalinau** Kalimantan
9 G3 **Long Melford** England
67 C6 **Longmen** China
65 A7 **Longmen Shan** *mts* China
98 A9 **Longmont** Colorado U.S.A.
70 D3 **Long Murum** Sarawak
67 E4 **Longnan** China
70 D4 **Longnawan** Kalimantan
21 O4 **Longnes** France
9 E1 **Longnor** England
21 M4 **Longny** France
43 H9 **Longobucco** Italy
88 F2 **Longonot,Mt** Kenya
70 D4 **Longpahangai** Kalimantan
69 H8 **Long Phu** Vietnam
98 G7 **Long Pine** Nebraska U.S.A.
Longping *see* **Luodian**
99 S8 **Long Point** Illinois U.S.A.
120 K10 **Long Point B** Ontario Canada
123 U6 **Long Pond** Newfoundland Canada
22 E5 **Longpont** France
123 Q5 **Long Pound** *res* Newfoundland Canada
99 M4 **Long Prairie** Minnesota U.S.A.
21 O1 **Longpré-les-Corps-Saints** France
119 T5 **Long Pt** Manitoba Canada
123 O5 **Long Pt** Newfoundland Canada
144 A7 **Long Pt** New Zealand
71 D6 **Long Pt** Philippines
70 D3 **Longpujungan** Kalimantan
67 F2 **Longquan** China
67 F3 **Longquan Xi** *R* China
123 P4 **Long Range Mts** Newfoundland Canada
141 G6 **Longreach** Queensland Australia
142 F2 **Long Reef** W Australia Australia
13 F6 **Longridge** England
112 J4 **Longs** South Carolina U.S.A.
144 A7 **Long Sd** New Zealand
70 E3 **Longsegah** Kalimantan
67 D2 **Longshan** China
67 C4 **Longsheng** China
67 D5 **Longsheng** China
Longshi *see* **Ninggang**
98 A9 **Longs Peak** *mt* Colorado U.S.A.
140 B6 **Longs Ra** N Terr Australia
9 H3 **Long Stratton** England
9 G2 **Long Sutton** England
67 B2 **Longtan** China
70 D3 **Long Teru** Sarawak
67 C3 **Longtian** China
117 P3 **Longtom L** Northwest Territories Canada
100 K6 **Long Tom Res** Idaho U.S.A.
141 H5 **Longton** Queensland Australia
8 D2 **Longton** England
13 F6 **Longton** Lancs England
107 O4 **Longton** Kansas U.S.A.
13 F2 **Longtown** England
110 G4 **Longtown** Missouri U.S.A.
83 M14 **Longue** *isld* Kerguelen Indian Oc
21 P2 **Longueau** France
22 D5 **Longueil-St.Marie** France
21 K7 **Longué-Jumelles** France
22 D3 **Longueval** France
18 H4 **Longueville** Seine-et-Marne France
21 N2 **Longueville** Seine-Inférieure France
19 J3 **Longuyon** France
98 E6 **Longvalley** South Dakota U.S.A.
102 F4 **Long Valley Res** California U.S.A.
40 B3 **Longvic** France
118 C8 **Longview** Alberta Canada
109 N3 **Longview** Texas U.S.A.
100 C3 **Longview** Washington U.S.A.
109 O5 **Longville** Louisiana U.S.A.
22 K3 **Longvilly** Belgium
70 E4 **Longwai** Kalimantan
65 J2 **Longwangmiao** China
65 F5 **Longwangmiao** China
113 F9 **Longwood** Florida U.S.A.
111 E8 **Longwood** Mississippi U.S.A.
108 G3 **Longworth** Texas U.S.A.
22 K4 **Longwy** France

58 D5 **Longxi** China
Longxian *see* **Wengyuan**
58 E5 **Long Xian** China
67 B2 **Longxing** China
Longxu *see* **Cangwu**
68 G7 **Long Xuyen** Vietnam
67 F4 **Longyan** China
65 C6 **Longyao** China
147 H11 **Longyearbyen** Spitzbergen
67 F2 **Longyou** China
67 B5 **Longzhou** China
45 K1 **Lonigo** Italy
32 G7 **Löningen** Germany
21 J4 **Lonlay-L'Abbaye** France
25 G4 **Lonneker** Netherlands
33 S10 **Lonnewitz** Germany
22 H4 **Lonny** France
110 E7 **Lonoke** Arkansas U.S.A.
26 H5 **Lönsdal** Norway
99 N5 **Lonsdale** Minnesota U.S.A.
139 G6 **Lonsdale L** Victoria Australia
36 H6 **Lonsee** Germany
26 D9 **Lønset** Norway
28 D2 **Lønstrup** Denmark
129 H4 **Lontra** Brazil
130 D7 **Lontra, R** Brazil
22 C2 **Looberghe** France
71 F4 **Looc** Philippines
8 B7 **Looe, E** England
110 K3 **Loogootee** Indiana U.S.A.
107 M6 **Lookeba** Oklahoma U.S.A.
94 C4 **Lookingglass** *R* Michigan U.S.A.
100 D8 **Lookout** California U.S.A.
116 H5 **Lookout Mt** Alaska U.S.A.
102 F5 **Lookout Mt** California U.S.A.
112 B3 **Lookout Mt** Georgia U.S.A.
106 B6 **Lookout Mt** New Mexico U.S.A.
100 K2 **Lookout Pass** Mont/Idaho U.S.A.
141 H2 **Lookout Pt** Queensland Australia
141 L7 **Lookout, Pt** Queensland Australia
94 D2 **Lookout, Pt** Michigan U.S.A.
100 C6 **Lookout Pt.Res** Oregon U.S.A.
116 H2 **Lookout Ridge** Alaska U.S.A.
112 F2 **Lookout Shoal** North Carolina U.S.A.
118 D5 **Looma** Alberta Canada
118 J9 **Loomis** Saskatchewan Canada
98 G9 **Loomis** Nebraska U.S.A.
100 F1 **Loomis** Washington U.S.A.
117 Q7 **Loon** *R* Alberta Canada
120 B4 **Loon** Ontario Canada
123 S4 **Loon Bay** Newfoundland Canada
143 F9 **Loongana** W Australia Australia
95 R7 **Loon L** Maine U.S.A.
118 H4 **Loon Lake** Saskatchewan Canada
22 C2 **Loon Plage** France
119 Q2 **Loon R** Manitoba Canada
117 N9 **Loos** British Columbia Canada
110 G6 **Loosahatchie** *R* Tennessee U.S.A.
22 D3 **Loos-en-Gohelle** France
54 F4 **Lopandino** Russian Federation
55 E4 **Lopatki** Russian Federation
68 E5 **Lop Buri** Thailand
59 H1 **Lopcha** Russian Federation
71 F4 **Lopez** Philippines
86 A6 **Lopez, C** Gabon
25 C5 **Lopik** Netherlands
Lop Nor *L see* **Lop Nur** *L*
66 E3 **Lop Nur** *L* China
71 H9 **Lopok** Indonesia
86 D5 **Lopori** *R* Zaire
26 M1 **Loppa** Norway
26 M1 **Lopphavet** *chan* Norway
52 G3 **Loptyuga** Russian Federation
31 M5 **Łopuszno** Poland
52 H4 **Lopydino** Russian Federation
20 C5 **Loqueffret** France
138 C3 **Lora** *R* South Australia Australia
16 D7 **Lora del Rio** Spain
77 J5 **Lora, Hamun-i-** Pakistan
94 E5 **Lorain** Ohio U.S.A.
99 P9 **Loraine** Illinois U.S.A.
98 E1 **Loraine** North Dakota U.S.A.
77 L4 **Loralai** Pakistan
70 G6 **Lorana** Sulawesi
131 A5 **Lora, Pta** Chile
77 K4 **Lora** *R* Afghanistan
17 F7 **Lorca** Spain
36 H6 **Lorch** Baden-Württemberg Germany
36 D3 **Lorch** Hessen Germany
26 C9 **Lord** *R* Norway
137 M8 **Lord Howe I** Pacific Oc
137 M7 **Lord Howe Seamounts** Pacific Oc
68 C7 **Lord Loughborough I** Burma
115 K4 **Lord Mayor B** Northwest Territories Canada
106 B9 **Lordsburg** New Mexico U.S.A.
118 L7 **Loreburn** Saskatchewan Canada
36 D3 **Loreley** *cliffs* Germany
130 F8 **Lorena** Brazil
109 K4 **Lorena** Texas U.S.A.
38 F9 **Lorenzago di Cadore** Italy
33 S10 **Lorenzkirch** Germany
101 O6 **Lorenzo** Idaho U.S.A.
98 C8 **Lorenzo** Nebraska U.S.A.
131 F4 **Lorenzo Geyres** Uruguay
45 M1 **Loreo** Italy
77 A3 **Lorestan** Iran
130 B10 **Loreto** Argentina
124 D4 **Loreto** Mexico
130 B8 **Loreto** Paraguay
128 C5 **Loreto** *dept* Peru
71 G5 **Loreto** Philippines
99 Q4 **Loretta** Wisconsin U.S.A.
119 V9 **Lorette** Manitoba Canada
121 T6 **Loretteville** Quebec Canada
94 B9 **Loretto** Kentucky U.S.A.
110 J6 **Loretto** Tennessee U.S.A.
19 Q18 **Lorgues** France
126 G10 **Lorica** Colombia
20 D6 **Lorient** France
121 Q7 **L'Orignal** Ontario Canada
99 M8 **Lorimor** Iowa U.S.A.
141 F2 **Lorim Point** Queensland Australia
48 F3 **Lőrinci** Hungary
101 S1 **Loring** Montana U.S.A.
112 J3 **Loris** South Carolina U.S.A.
119 O8 **Lorlie** Saskatchewan Canada
111 E10 **Lorman** Mississippi U.S.A.
22 B2 **Lormel, Pte de** France
18 H5 **Lormes** France
15 C4 **Lorn** Scotland
143 D7 **Lorna Glen** W Australia Australia
140 D4 **Lorne** *R* N Terr Australia
141 H6 **Lorne** Queensland Australia
122 F6 **Lorne** New Brunswick Canada
135 L11 **L'Orne Bank** Pacific Oc
12 C1 **Lorn, Firth of** Scotland
45 L4 **Loro Ciuffenna** Italy
20 H7 **Loroux-Bottereau, le** France
36 C6 **Lorquin** France
40 G2 **Lörrach** Germany
140 E4 **Lorraine** Queensland Australia
36 B5 **Lorraine** *hist reg* France
107 M3 **Lorraine** Kansas U.S.A.
121 L5 **Lorrainville** Quebec Canada
36 F4 **Lorsch** Germany
28 B3 **Lørslev** Denmark
13 E4 **Lorton** England
32 G7 **Lorup** Germany
26 H10 **Los** Sweden
124 H3 **Los Alamos** Mexico
102 D7 **Los Alamos** California U.S.A.
106 D6 **Los Alamos** New Mexico U.S.A.
131 B5 **Los Angeles** Chile
124 H3 **Los Angeles** Mexico
104 **Los Angeles** *conurbation* California U.S.A.
109 H7 **Los Angeles** Texas U.S.A.
102 F6 **Los Angeles Aqueduct** California U.S.A.
126 D3 **Los Arabos** Cuba
17 F4 **Losares** *mt* Spain
70 M9 **Losari** Java
124 F4 **Los Baños** Mexico
102 D4 **Los Banos** California U.S.A.
128 F8 **Los Blancos** Argentina
124 D2 **Los Chirriones** Mexico
131 C2 **Los Colorados** Argentina
109 J9 **Los Comales** Mexico
124 D5 **Los Dolores** Mexico
109 J9 **Los Ebanos** Texas U.S.A.
38 K6 **Losenstein** Austria
17 F7 **Los Filabres** *mts* Spain
109 K9 **Los Fresnos** Texas U.S.A.
102 C4 **Los Gatos** California U.S.A.
22 L3 **Losheim** Belgium
36 B5 **Losheim** Germany
128 F1 **Los Hermanos** *islds* Venezuela
109 H10 **Los Herreras** Mexico
124 E2 **Los Hoyos** Mexico
27 G15 **Loshult** Sweden
31 O3 **Łosice** Poland
85 B7 **Los, Iles de** Guinea
42 F4 **Lošinj** *isld* Croatia
56 C2 **Losinoborskoye** Russian Federation
55 D3 **Losinyy** Russian Federation
89 F5 **Loskop Dam** S Africa
131 A8 **Los Lagos** *prov* Chile
108 A4 **Los Médanos** Mexico
124 E5 **Los Mochis** Mexico
100 C9 **Los Molinos** California U.S.A.
131 B3 **Los Molles, R** Chile
27 D10 **Losna** Norway
16 D5 **Los Navalmorales** Spain
28 D5 **Løsning** Denmark
102 D7 **Los Olivos** California U.S.A.
126 C3 **Los Palacios** Cuba
16 D6 **Los Pedroches** *reg* Spain
124 D3 **Los Pocitos** Mexico
133 C3 **Los Pozos** Chile
124 H8 **Los Reyes** Mexico
128 C4 **Los Rios** *R* Ecuador
127 L9 **Los Roques, Is** Venezuela
127 L8 **Los Roques Trench** Caribbean
37 L1 **Lossa** Germany
16 C6 **Los Santos de Maimona** Spain
36 E7 **Lossburg** Germany
15 E3 **Lossie** *R* Scotland
15 E3 **Lossiemouth** Scotland
37 O2 **Lössnitz** Germany
101 S6 **Lost Cabin** Wyoming U.S.A.
94 J8 **Lost City** West Virginia U.S.A.
101 R7 **Lost Cr** Wyoming U.S.A.
127 K9 **Los Teques** Venezuela
127 N9 **Los Testigos** *islds* Venezuela
102 E6 **Lost Hills** California U.S.A.
133 E3 **Los Tigres** Argentina
100 H4 **Lostine** Oregon U.S.A.
111 E12 **Lost L** Louisiana U.S.A.
94 J8 **Lost River** West Virginia U.S.A.
101 M5 **Lost River Ra** Idaho U.S.A.
107 O3 **Lost Springs** Kansas U.S.A.
98 B7 **Lost Springs** Wyoming U.S.A.
101 M4 **Lost Trail Pass** Idaho/Montana U.S.A.
8 B7 **Lostwithiel** England
98 D1 **Lostwood** North Dakota U.S.A.
71 B1 **Losuwo** Halmahera Indonesia
133 C4 **Los Vilos** Chile
16 E5 **Los Yebenes** Spain
18 G8 **Lot** *dept* France
18 G8 **Lot** *R* France
131 A6 **Lota** Chile
86 F5 **Lotagipi Swamp** Sudan
68 A1 **Lotaw** Burma
18 F8 **Lot et Garonne** *dept* France
77 F1 **Lotfābād** Iran
101 O1 **Lothair** Montana U.S.A.
15 E5 **Lothian** *reg* Scotland
20 J3 **Lothiers** France
86 D6 **Loto** Zaire
54 G1 **Lotoshino** Russian Federation
89 E4 **Lotsane** *R* Botswana
40 G5 **Lötschberg Tunnel** Switzerland
40 G5 **Lotschen** *R* Switzerland
54 G8 **Lotsmano-Kamenka** Ukraine
109 K4 **Lott** Texas U.S.A.
52 C1 **Lotta** *R* Russian Federation
37 N3 **Lottengrün** Germany
41 J5 **Lottigna** Switzerland
112 F5 **Lotts Cr** Georgia U.S.A.
88 D2 **Lotui** *isld* Uganda
100 J2 **Lotus** Idaho U.S.A.
99 S9 **Lotus** Illinois U.S.A.
21 K6 **Louailles** France
68 F3 **Louang-Phrabang** Laos
20 D4 **Louannec** France
21 M7 **Louans** France
20 D4 **Louargat** France
86 B6 **Loubomo** Congo
20 E5 **Loudéac** France
46 E4 **Loudhias** *R* Greece
86 B6 **Loudima** Zaire
95 Q3 **Loudon** New Hampshire U.S.A.
112 C2 **Loudon** Tennessee U.S.A.
94 E6 **Loudonville** Ohio U.S.A.
21 L7 **Loudun** France
21 K6 **Loué** France
40 C3 **Loue** *R* France
65 B5 **Loufan** China
9 E2 **Loughborough** England
118 F6 **Lougheed** Alberta Canada
114 J2 **Lougheed I** Northwest Territories Canada
8 B4 **Loughor** Wales
14 C3 **Loughrea** Ireland
19 J6 **Louhans** France
111 G9 **Louin** Mississippi U.S.A.
94 D8 **Louisa** Kentucky U.S.A.
94 J8 **Louisa** Virginia U.S.A.
142 E3 **Louisa, L** W Australia Australia
70 C1 **Louisa Reef** S China Sea
123 N8 **Louisbourg** C Breton I, Nova Scotia
107 Q3 **Louisburg** Kansas U.S.A.
112 J1 **Louisburg** North Carolina U.S.A.
123 L8 **Louisdale** C Breton I, Nova Scotia
109 L6 **Louise** Texas U.S.A.
117 P5 **Louise Falls** Northwest Territories Canada
117 H9 **Louise I** British Columbia Canada
117 P10 **Louise, L** Alberta Canada
116 O6 **Louise, L** Alaska U.S.A.
121 S6 **Louiseville** Quebec Canada
137 L6 **Louisiade Arch** *islds* Papua New Guinea
111 E11 **Louisiana** *state* U.S.A.
110 E2 **Louisiana** Missouri U.S.A.
109 O6 **Louisiana Pt** Louisiana U.S.A.
89 F4 **Louis Trichardt** S Africa
111 L10 **Louisville** Alabama U.S.A.
98 A10 **Louisville** Colorado U.S.A.
112 E4 **Louisville** Georgia U.S.A.
94 B8 **Louisville** Kentucky U.S.A.
111 G8 **Louisville** Mississippi U.S.A.
99 L9 **Louisville** Nebraska U.S.A.
94 F6 **Louisville** Ohio U.S.A.
115 M7 **Louis XIV, Pte** Quebec Canada
52 D2 **Loukhi** Russian Federation
16 B7 **Loule** Portugal
30 H5 **Louny** Czechoslovakia
98 J8 **Loup** *R* Nebraska U.S.A.
98 H8 **Loup City** Nebraska U.S.A.
21 N5 **Loupe, la** France
22 J5 **Louppy-sur-Loison** France
22 E3 **Lourches** France
123 N5 **Lourdes** Newfoundland Canada
18 F9 **Lourdes** France
130 B5 **Lourenço** *R* Brazil
Lourenço Marques *see* **Maputo**
16 A6 **Loures** Portugal
16 A5 **Lourinã** Portugal
46 D5 **Loúros** Greece
21 J6 **Louroux-Beconnais, le** France
21 P5 **Loury** France
16 B4 **Lousã** Portugal
118 D6 **Lousana** Alberta Canada
47 H1 **Lousa, Serra Da** *mts* Portugal
Lousy Bank *see* **Outer Bailey**
6 B2 **Lousy Bank** N Atlantic Oc
139 H4 **Louth** New South Wales Australia
13 H6 **Louth** England
14 E3 **Louth** *co* Ireland
14 E3 **Louth** Ireland
46 F6 **Loutrá** Evvoia Greece
46 E7 **Loutrá** Dhytikí Ellás Greece
47 O12 **Loútsa** Greece
Louvain *see* **Leuven**
22 K2 **Louveigne** Belgium
21 P1 **Louvencourt** France
21 J5 **Louverne** France
22 G3 **Louvière, La** Belgium
21 N3 **Louviers** France
106 E2 **Louviers** Colorado U.S.A.
20 H5 **Louvigné-de-Bais** France
21 H5 **Louvigné-du-Désert** France
28 H6 **Lov** Denmark
26 M7 **Lövånger** Sweden
48 E3 **Lovasberény** Hungary
48 D3 **Lovászpatona** Hungary
54 B1 **Lovat'** *R* Russian Federation
26 K6 **Lövberg** Sweden
26 H8 **Lövberga** Sweden
42 J6 **Lovćen** *mt* Montenegro Yugoslavia
119 N5 **Love** Saskatchewan Canada
28 G5 **Love** Denmark
68 F6 **Lovea** Cambodia
47 G1 **Lovech** Bulgaria
109 O9 **Love Field Airport** Texas U.S.A.
28 C3 **Løvel** Denmark
109 M4 **Lovelady** Texas U.S.A.
106 E2 **Loveland** Colorado U.S.A.
110 M2 **Loveland** Ohio U.S.A.
106 E2 **Loveland Pass** Colorado U.S.A.
101 R5 **Lovell** Wyoming U.S.A.
94 C2 **Lovells** Michigan U.S.A.
100 G9 **Lovelock** Nevada U.S.A.
103 O1 **Lovenia, Mt** Utah U.S.A.
95 L7 **Love Point** Maryland U.S.A.
42 C3 **Lovere** Italy
118 H7 **Loverna** Saskatchewan Canada
113 D7 **Lovett** Florida U.S.A.
26 F10 **Lövhögen** Sweden
26 N4 **Lovikka** Sweden
106 F9 **Loving** New Mexico U.S.A.
109 J2 **Loving** Texas U.S.A.
94 J9 **Lovingston** Virginia U.S.A.
99 S10 **Lovington** Illinois U.S.A.
106 G9 **Lovington** New Mexico U.S.A.
16 B3 **Lovios** Spain
29 M11 **Lovisa** Finland
26 J5 **Lövnäs** Sweden
28 C3 **Lovns Bredning** *B* Denmark
30 H5 **Lovosice** Czechoslovakia
52 E1 **Lovozero** Russian Federation
52 E1 **Lovozero, Ozero** *L* Russian Federation
45 P1 **Lovre čica** Croatia
48 F5 **Lovrin** Romania
26 H7 **Lövsjön** Sweden
26 F5 **Lovunden** *isld* Norway
103 L1 **Low** Utah U.S.A.
86 E6 **Lowa** Zaire
144 B6 **Lowburn** New Zealand
120 K4 **Low Bush River** Ontario Canada
115 L5 **Low, C** Northwest Territories Canada
99 P8 **Lowden** Iowa U.S.A.
100 E6 **Low Desert** Oregon U.S.A.
9 F1 **Lowdham** England
103 P10 **Lowell** Arizona U.S.A.
110 B5 **Lowell** Arkansas U.S.A.
100 K3 **Lowell** Idaho U.S.A.
99 T8 **Lowell** Indiana U.S.A.
95 Q4 **Lowell** Massachusetts U.S.A.
94 B4 **Lowell** Michigan U.S.A.
94 F7 **Lowell** Ohio U.S.A.
100 C6 **Lowell** Oregon U.S.A.
100 J6 **Lowell, L** Idaho U.S.A.
33 S7 **Löwenberg** Germany
28 C7 **Löwenstedt** Germany
36 G5 **Löwenstein** Germany
117 P11 **Lower Arrow L** British Columbia Canada
98 G5 **Lower Brule** South Dakota U.S.A.
101 P5 **Lower Falls** Wyoming U.S.A.
119 V8 **Lower Fort Garry** Manitoba Canada
103 L6 **Lower Granite Gorge** Arizona U.S.A.
145 G4 **Lower Hutt** New Zealand
123 U6 **Lower Island Cove** Newfoundland Canada
100 D8 **Lower Klamath L** California U.S.A.
102 B3 **Lower L** California U.S.A.
117 F5 **Lower Laberge** Yukon Territory Canada
115 K4 **Lower Macdougall L** Northwest Territories Canada
122 G6 **Lower Neguac** New Brunswick Canada
122 G10 **Lower Ohio** Nova Scotia Canada
135 T3 **Lower Paia** Hawaiian Is
117 J6 **Lower Post** British Columbia Canada
99 L2 **Lower Red L** Minnesota U.S.A.
101 O5 **Lower Red Rock L** Montana U.S.A.
115 N5 **Lower Savage Is** Northwest Territories Canada
122 G10 **Lower West Pubnico** Nova Scotia Canada
15 F1 **Lower Whitehall** Scotland
110 H5 **Lowes** Kentucky U.S.A.
9 H2 **Lowestoft** England
77 L2 **Lowgar** *R* Afghanistan
77 L3 **Lowgar** *prov* Afghanistan
139 H8 **Low Head** Tasmania Australia
146 C3 **Low I** *isld* Antarctica
13 G2 **Lowick** England
13 E3 **Lowick Br** England
31 M3 **Łowicz** Poland
141 H3 **Low Is** Queensland Australia
100 K5 **Lowman** Idaho U.S.A.
111 K8 **Lowndesboro** Alabama U.S.A.
83 M9 **Low Pt** Christmas I Indian Oc
139 H9 **Low Rocky Pt** Tasmania Australia
110 C3 **Lowry City** Missouri U.S.A.
87 H10 **Lowry, Iles** Madagascar
112 F3 **Lowrys** South Carolina U.S.A.
13 F4 **Lowther** England
115 K3 **Lowther I** Northwest Territories Canada
121 P8 **Lowville** New York U.S.A.
125 L9 **Loxicha** Mexico
111 J11 **Loxley** Alabama U.S.A.
138 F5 **Loxton** South Australia Australia
99 Q5 **Loyal** Wisconsin U.S.A.
118 F7 **Loyalist** Alberta Canada
94 D10 **Loyall** Kentucky U.S.A.
95 L5 **Loyalsock Cr** Pennsylvania U.S.A.
102 D2 **Loyalton** California U.S.A.
98 G4 **Loyalton** South Dakota U.S.A.
Loyang *see* **Luoyang**
137 O6 **Loyauté, Îs** Pacific Oc
54 B5 **Loyev** Belorussia
52 G4 **Loyma** Russian Federation
52 H5 **Loyno** Russian Federation
47 H2 **Lozarevo** Bulgaria
18 H8 **Lozère** *dept* France
18 H8 **Lozère, Mt** France
42 J4 **Loznica** Serbia Yugoslavia
47 H1 **Loznitsa** Bulgaria
54 K7 **Lozovaya** Ukraine
55 G4 **Lozovoye** Kazakhstan
55 D1 **Loz'va** *R* Russian Federation
86 C5 **Lua** *R* Zaire
87 D8 **Luacano** Angola
87 D7 **Luachimo** Angola
69 D13 **Luahasibuka** Indonesia
88 F10 **Luala** *R* Mozambique
86 E6 **Lualaba** *R* Zaire
88 C6 **Luama** *R* Zaire
87 F8 **Luambe** Zambia
87 D9 **Luampa** Zambia
58 G5 **Lu'an** China
127 J2 **Luana Pt** Jamaica
68 F2 **Luan Chau** Vietnam
65 C6 **Luancheng** China
67 C5 **Luancheng** China
65 B8 **Luanchuan** China
87 B7 **Luanda** Angola
87 C8 **Luando** *R* Angola
71 O9 **Luang** *isld* Indonesia
87 D8 **Luanganga** *R* Angola
69 D8 **Luang, Khao** *mt* Thailand
69 E9 **Luang, Thale** *L* Thailand
87 C7 **Luangue** *R* Angola
88 C8 **Luangwa** *R* Zambia
88 C9 **Luangwa** Zambia
65 D5 **Luan He** *R* China
65 D5 **Luannan** China
88 B9 **Luano** Zambia
65 D4 **Luanping** China
88 B8 **Luanshya** Zambia
65 D5 **Luan Xian** China
88 B8 **Luapula** Zambia
87 F7 **Luapula** *R* Zaire
16 C1 **Luarca** Spain
70 C4 **Luar, D** *L* Kalimantan
87 D8 **Luashi** Zaire
88 F8 **Luatize** *R* Mozambique
87 B8 **Luau** Angola
85 F8 **Luba** Bioko Equat Guinea
125 P9 **Lubaantum** Belize
31 O5 **Lubaczów** Poland
87 C7 **Lubalo** Angola
31 J4 **Lubań** Poland
52 C6 **Lubāna** Latvia
52 C6 **Lubānasezers** *L* Latvia
71 E4 **Lubang** Philippines
87 B8 **Lubango** Angola
88 C7 **Lubansenshi** *R* Zambia
87 E7 **Lubao** Zaire
33 Q8 **Lübars** Germany
31 O4 **Lubartów** Poland
31 M2 **Lubawa** Poland
32 J8 **Lübbecke** Germany
33 T9 **Lübben** Germany
33 T9 **Lübbenau** Germany
108 F2 **Lubbock** Texas U.S.A.
139 G6 **Lubeck** Victoria Australia
33 N5 **Lübeck** Germany
33 O4 **Lübecker Bucht** Germany
86 D6 **Lubefu** Zaire
37 P3 **Lubenec** Czechoslovakia
55 B5 **Lubenka** Kazakhstan
88 B2 **Lubero** Zaire
19 O17 **Lubéron, Montagne du** *mts* France
88 C8 **Lubi** *R* Zambia
71 E5 **Lubic** *isld* Philippines
118 B2 **Lubicon L** Alberta Canada
31 L3 **Lubie, Jezioro** *L* Poland
31 L3 **Lubień** Poland
87 E8 **Lubilash** *R* Zaire
31 J4 **Lubin** Poland
31 O4 **Lublin** Poland
99 Q4 **Lublin** Wisconsin U.S.A.
31 L5 **Lubliniec** Poland
33 T4 **Lubmin** Germany
15 D4 **Lubnaig, L** Scotland
54 E7 **Lubny** Ukraine
70 B4 **Lubok Anto** Sarawak
29 P8 **Lubosalma** Russian Federation
17 F7 **Lubrín** Spain
31 K4 **Lubsko** Poland
33 O6 **Lübtheen** Germany
71 E3 **Lubuagan** Luzon Philippines
87 D7 **Lubudi** *R* Zaire
87 E7 **Lubudi** Zaire
70 K8 **Lubukbatang** Sumatra
69 F14 **Lubuklinggau** Sumatra
69 D11 **Lubukpakam** Sumatra
69 E12 **Lubuksikaping** Sumatra
88 B6 **Lubule** *R* Zaire
87 E8 **Lubumbashi** Zaire
86 E6 **Lubutu** Zaire
37 N3 **Luby** Czechoslovakia
33 Q6 **Lübz** Germany
21 K3 **Luc** Calvados France
87 C7 **Lucala** Angola
120 J9 **Lucan** Ontario Canada
14 E3 **Lucan** Ireland
116 R6 **Lucania, Mt** Yukon Territory Canada
43 G8 **Lucano, Appennino** *mts* Italy
129 G6 **Lucas** Brazil
99 N8 **Lucas** Iowa U.S.A.
107 M2 **Lucas** Kansas U.S.A.
94 E6 **Lucas** Ohio U.S.A.
142 G5 **Lucas, L** W Australia Australia
126 E1 **Lucaya** Grand Bahama I
21 N7 **Luçay-le-Mâle** France
71 E3 **Lucban** Luzon Philippines
45 J4 **Lucca** Italy
98 J3 **Lucca** North Dakota U.S.A.
129 G3 **Luce** *R* Suriname
127 H1 **Lucea** Jamaica
15 D6 **Luce B** Scotland
111 H11 **Lucedale** Mississippi U.S.A.
130 E7 **Lucélia** Brazil
71 E4 **Lucena** Philippines
17 G4 **Lucena del Cid** Spain
16 D7 **Lucena, Sa. de** *mts* Spain
48 E2 **Lučenec** Czechoslovakia
43 G7 **Lucera** Italy
Lucerne *see* **Luzern**
102 B2 **Lucerne** California U.S.A.
99 N9 **Lucerne** Missouri U.S.A.
100 E1 **Lucerne** Washington U.S.A.
101 R6 **Lucerne** Wyoming U.S.A.
102 H7 **Lucerne L** California U.S.A.
102 H7 **Lucerne Valley** California U.S.A.
124 F2 **Lucero** Mexico
122 D5 **Luceville** Quebec Canada
65 B6 **Lucheng** China
67 B4 **Lucheng** China
88 E9 **Luchenza** Malawi
21 L6 **Luché-Pringé** France
111 F11 **Lucher** Louisiana U.S.A.
54 B2 **Luchesa** *R* Belorussia
21 P1 **Lucheux** France
33 O7 **Lüchow** Germany
68 K1 **Luchuan** China
21 P2 **Luchy** France
102 C5 **Lucia** California U.S.A.
121 M2 **Lucie, L** Quebec Canada
100 J4 **Lucile** Idaho U.S.A.
16 C2 **Lucillo** Spain
101 M8 **Lucin** Utah U.S.A.
141 H4 **Lucinda** Queensland Australia
94 H5 **Lucinda** Pennsylvania U.S.A.
138 F6 **Lucindale** South Australia Australia
87 B8 **Lucira** Angola
99 O4 **Luck** Wisconsin U.S.A.
37 N1 **Lucka** Germany
33 T9 **Luckau** Germany
33 S8 **Luckenwalde** Germany
143 E8 **Luck, Mt** W Australia Australia
140 F6 **Lucknow** Queensland Australia
120 J9 **Lucknow** Ontario Canada
74 J5 **Lucknow** India
118 K8 **Lucky Lake** Saskatchewan Canada
100 K6 **Lucky Peak Res** Idaho U.S.A.
118 F9 **Lucky Strike** Alberta Canada
18 E6 **Luçon** France
45 O6 **Luco ne Marsi** Italy
22 G4 **Lucquy** France
126 G4 **Lucrecia, C** Cuba
20 H8 **Lucs-sur-Boulogne, les** France
87 D8 **Lucusse** Angola
106 E7 **Lucy** New Mexico U.S.A.
140 D5 **Lucy Creek** N Terr Australia
68 G1 **Luc Yen** Vietnam
140 C6 **Lucy, Mt** N Terr Australia
Lüda *see* **Dalian**
13 H6 **Ludborough** England
98 H3 **Ludden** North Dakota U.S.A.
21 L6 **Lude, le** France
107 K2 **Ludell** Kansas U.S.A.
32 G10 **Lüdenscheid** Germany
33 P7 **Lüderitz** Germany
87 C11 **Lüderitz** Namibia
120 K7 **Ludgate** Ontario Canada
9 E5 **Ludgershall** England
74 F3 **Ludhiana** India
32 F9 **Lüdinghausen** Germany
99 U6 **Ludington** Michigan U.S.A.
122 F7 **Ludlow** New Brunswick Canada
8 D3 **Ludlow** England
103 H7 **Ludlow** California U.S.A.
106 F4 **Ludlow** Colorado U.S.A.
99 S9 **Ludlow** Illinois U.S.A.
94 J5 **Ludlow** Pennsylvania U.S.A.
98 C4 **Ludlow** South Dakota U.S.A.
95 P3 **Ludlow** Vermont U.S.A.
47 H1 **Ludogorie** Bulgaria
52 C5 **Ludoni** Russian Federation
112 F6 **Ludowici** Georgia U.S.A.
36 E5 **Ludswigshöhe** Germany
48 J4 **Luduş** Romania
27 H11 **Ludvika** Sweden
36 H2 **Ludwigsau** Germany
36 G6 **Ludwigsburg** Germany
37 M3 **Ludwigschorgast** Germany
36 E5 **Ludwigshafen** Germany
37 L5 **Ludwigs Kanal** *canal* Germany
33 O6 **Ludwigslust** Germany
37 L3 **Ludwigsstadt** Germany
52 C6 **Ludza** Latvia
86 D7 **Luebo** Zaire
109 H3 **Lueders** Texas U.S.A.
86 E6 **Lueki** Zaire
87 C8 **Luena** Angola
87 D8 **Luena** *R* Angola
87 D8 **Luena** *R* Zambia
88 D10 **Luenha** *R* Mozambique
128 F2 **Luepa** Venezuela
87 D7 **Lueta** Zaire
87 D9 **Lueti** *R* Zambia
58 E5 **Lüeyang** China
67 E5 **Lufeng** China
88 D6 **Lufira** *R* Malawi
111 B10 **Lufkin** Texas U.S.A.
88 C6 **Lufubu** *R* Zambia
88 B10 **Lufya** *R* Zambia
48 F6 **Lug** *R* Serbia Yugoslavia
52 C5 **Luga** *R* Russian Federation
52 C5 **Luga** Russian Federation
88 B4 **Lugamba** Zaire
41 J5 **Lugano** Switzerland
42 B3 **Lugano, L. di** Italy
54 L8 **Lugansk** Ukraine
126 F4 **Lugareño** Cuba
32 K9 **Lügde** Germany
88 F10 **Lugela** *R* Mozambique
88 F10 **Lugela** Mozambique
88 F8 **Lugenda** *R* Mozambique
144 B6 **Luggate** New Zealand
8 D3 **Lugg, R** England
Lugh Ferrandi *see* **Luuq**
14 E4 **Lugnaquilla** *mt* Ireland
41 K4 **Lugnezer Tal** Switzerland
45 L3 **Lugo** Italy
16 B1 **Lugo** *prov* Spain
16 B1 **Lugo** Spain
48 G5 **Lugoj** Romania
55 E1 **Lugovskoy** Russian Federation
12 D2 **Lugton** Scotland
86 E6 **Lugulu** *R* Zaire
71 E8 **Lugus** *isld* Philippines
70 G6 **Luha** *isld* Celebes
29 M10 **Luhanka** Finland
72 E5 **Luḥayyah, Al** Yemen
67 F1 **Luhe** China
32 M6 **Luhe** *R* Germany
37 N4 **Luhe** Germany
65 D1 **Luhin Sum** China
33 T4 **Lühmannsdorf** Germany
87 C7 **Lui** *R* Angola
88 D10 **Luia** *R* Mozambique
87 D9 **Luiana** Angola
Luichow Pen *see* **Leizhou Bandao**
Luik *see* **Liège**
86 D6 **Luilaka** *R* Zaire
15 C4 **Luing** *isld* Scotland
42 B2 **Luino** Italy
29 N4 **Luira** *R* Finland
124 E4 **Luis** Mexico
130 E10 **Luís Alves** Brazil
130 H9 **Luís Gomes** Brazil
87 E8 **Luishia** Zaire
124 H5 **Luis Moya** Mexico
146 E7 **Luitpold Coast** Antarctica
87 D7 **Luiza** Zaire
88 A5 **Luizi** *R* Zaire
131 F5 **Lujan** *R* Argentina
133 D4 **Lujan** Argentina
67 F1 **Lujiang** China
67 C5 **Lujing** China
70 Q10 **Luk** Indonesia
37 P3 **Luka** Czechoslovakia
87 E8 **Lukafu** Zaire
88 A8 **Lukanga** *R* Zambia
88 A9 **Lukanga Sw** Zambia
143 B7 **Luke, Mt** W Australia
86 C6 **Lukenie** *R* Zaire
52 F6 **Lukh** Russian Federation
54 L2 **Lukhovitsy** Russian Federation
46 G3 **Lŭki** Bulgaria
41 J4 **Lukmanier Pass** Switzerland
86 C6 **Lukolela** Zaire
67 D3 **Lukou** China
46 G1 **Lukovit** Bulgaria
46 D3 **Lukovo** Macedonia Yugoslavia
31 N4 **Łuków** Poland
52 F6 **Lukoyanov** Russian Federation
86 B7 **Lukula** Zaire
88 G7 **Lukuledi** *R* Tanzania
87 D8 **Lukulu** Zambia
88 C8 **Lukulu** *R* Zambia
87 G7 **Lukumburu** Tanzania
88 D8 **Lukuzye** *R* Zambia
112 D3 **Lula** Georgia U.S.A.
111 F7 **Lula** Mississippi U.S.A.
26 M6 **Luleä** Sweden
26 M6 **Lule älv** *R* Sweden
47 J3 **Lüleburgaz** Turkey
87 D7 **Lulembe** *R* Angola
67 A4 **Luliang** China
65 B6 **Lüliang Shan** *ra* China
111 F12 **Luling** Louisiana U.S.A.
109 K6 **Luling** Texas U.S.A.
65 D5 **Lulong** China
86 C5 **Lulonga** *R* Zaire
113 E7 **Lulu** Florida U.S.A.
86 D7 **Lulua** *R* Zaire
Luluabourg *see* **Kananga**
8 D6 **Lulworth Cove** England
143 C7 **Lulworth, Mt** W Australia Australia
70 O10 **Lumajang** Java
70 D2 **Lumaku** *mt* Sabah
87 D8 **Lumbala Kaquenque** Angola
87 D8 **Lumbala N'guimbo** Angola
112 H3 **Lumber** *R* North Carolina U.S.A.
112 E6 **Lumber City** Georgia U.S.A.
94 J6 **Lumber City** Pennsylvania U.S.A.
94 G7 **Lumberport** West Virginia U.S.A.
111 G10 **Lumberton** Mississippi U.S.A.
106 D5 **Lumberton** New Mexico U.S.A.
112 H3 **Lumberton** North Carolina U.S.A.
18 E10 **Lumbier** Spain
70 E2 **Lumbis** Kalimantan
88 H9 **Lumbo** Mozambique
52 F1 **Lumbovka** Russian Federation
16 C4 **Lumbrales** Spain
22 C2 **Lumbres** France
28 E6 **Lumby** Denmark
75 P6 **Lumding** India
29 L7 **Lumijoki** Finland
88 D8 **Lumimba** *R* Zambia
22 J2 **Lummen** Belgium
29 H11 **Lumparland** Finland
111 M9 **Lumpkin** Georgia U.S.A.
28 H5 **Lumsås** Denmark
123 T4 **Lumsden** Newfoundland Canada
119 N8 **Lumsden** Saskatchewan Canada
144 B6 **Lumsden** New Zealand
15 F3 **Lumsden** Scotland
69 E10 **Lumut** Malaysia
70 D5 **Lumut, Bt** *mt* Kalimantan
71 E2 **Luna** Luzon Philippines
106 B8 **Luna** New Mexico U.S.A.
131 G2 **Luna, L** Argentina
67 A4 **Lunan** China
15 F4 **Lunan B** Scotland
74 E7 **Lunavada** India
117 L10 **Lund** British Columbia Canada
28 D5 **Lund** Denmark
27 F16 **Lund** Sweden
103 J3 **Lund** Nevada U.S.A.
103 L3 **Lund** Utah U.S.A.
27 J13 **Lunda** Sweden
88 B7 **Lunda Chishinga** Zambia
29 K5 **Lundåkrabukten** *B* Sweden
119 T8 **Lundar** Manitoba Canada
87 F8 **Lundazi** Zambia
88 D8 **Lundazi** *R* Zambia
118 C9 **Lundbreck** Alberta Canada
28 H6 **Lundby** Denmark
28 A5 **Lunde** Denmark
28 F6 **Lundeborg** Denmark
28 C6 **Lunderskov** Denmark
27 B13 **Lunde-Vatn** *L* Norway
28 C3 **Lundø** Denmark
28 D5 **Lundum** Denmark
8 B5 **Lundy** *isld* England
32 J6 **Lüne** *R* Germany
33 M6 **Lüne** Germany
36 B3 **Lünebach** Germany
33 M6 **Lüneburg** Germany
32 M6 **Lüneburger Heide** *reg* Germany
18 H9 **Lunel** France
32 G9 **Lünen** Germany
122 H9 **Lunenburg** Nova Scotia Canada
95 Q2 **Lunenburg** Vermont U.S.A.
21 M2 **Luneray** France
41 L3 **Lüner See** *L* Austria
21 P8 **Lunery** France
19 K4 **Lunéville** France
87 D8 **Lunga** *R* Zambia
68 H1 **Lung-chou** China
66 C5 **Lungdo** China
66 C5 **Lunggar** China
44 G3 **Lungiana** Italy
26 H8 **Lungsjön** Sweden
27 G12 **Lungsund** Sweden
88 C6 **Lungu** Zambia
87 C8 **Lungue Bungo** *R* Angola
102 F3 **Luning** Nevada U.S.A.
71 H9 **Lunjuk** Sumbawa Indonesia
15 G2 **Lunna** Scotland
32 F8 **Lünne** Germany
85 B7 **Lunsar** Sierra Leone
88 B8 **Lunsemfwa** *R* Zambia
66 C3 **Luntai** China
38 M6 **Lunz am See** Austria
37 O2 **Lunzenau** Germany
88 D7 **Lunzi** *R* Zambia
67 C4 **Luocheng** China
58 E4 **Luochuan** China
67 B4 **Luodian** China
67 D5 **Luoding** China
65 A7 **Luo He** *R* China
65 B7 **Luo He** *R* China
67 A1 **Luojiang** China
67 D5 **Luojing** China
67 B2 **Luolong** China
65 A7 **Luonan** China
26 M4 **Luongastunturi** *mt* Sweden
88 B7 **Luongo** *R* Zambia
65 B7 **Luoning** China
67 A4 **Luoping** China
67 C4 **Luoqing Jiang** *R* China
67 C4 **Luorong** China
67 E1 **Luoshan** China
67 D2 **Luoshan** China
67 E1 **Luotian** China
65 E1 **Luotuobozi** China
67 B1 **Luowenba** China
65 B7 **Luoyang** China
67 F3 **Luoyuan** China
86 B6 **Luozi** Zaire
88 D6 **Lupa** *R* Tanzania
88 D8 **Lupachi** *R* Malawi
89 E2 **Lupane** Zimbabwe
89 F2 **Lupani** *R* Zimbabwe
71 D7 **Lupa pula** Philippines
70 B4 **Lupar** *R* Sarawak
31 K1 **Łupawa** *R* Poland
37 M5 **Lupburg** Germany
48 H5 **Lupeni** Romania
127 J5 **Luperón** Dominican Rep
41 J1 **Lupfen** *mt* Germany
87 G8 **Lupilichi** Mozambique
67 B3 **Luping** China
87 C8 **Lupire** Angola
42 F3 **Lupoglav** Croatia
54 B3 **Lupolovo** Belorussia
71 G7 **Lupon** Mindanao Philippines
33 R10 **Luppa** Germany
110 D3 **Lupus** Missouri U.S.A.
87 D7 **Luputa** Zaire
52 H4 **Lup'ya** *R* Russian Federation
130 B9 **Luque** Paraguay
107 M2 **Luray** Kansas U.S.A.
94 J8 **Luray** Virginia U.S.A.
112 E2 **Lure, L** North Carolina U.S.A.
19 P16 **Lure, Mt de** France
14 E2 **Lurgan** N Ireland
128 E7 **Luribay** Bolivia
128 C6 **Lurín** Peru
87 H8 **Lurio** Mozambique
26 F5 **Luröy** Norway
19 P17 **Lurs** France
110 C6 **Lurton** Arkansas U.S.A.
21 P7 **Lury sur-Arnon** France
88 B9 **Lusaka** Zambia
86 D6 **Lusambo** Zaire
86 C6 **Lusanga** Zaire
88 C8 **Lusangazi** Zambia
20 G6 **Lusanger** France
117 P9 **Luscar** Alberta Canada
118 H6 **Luseland** Saskatchewan Canada
88 C6 **Lusenga Plain Nat. Park** Zambia
75 P7 **Lushai Hills** India
65 D6 **Lu Shan** *mt* China
58 F5 **Lushi** China
142 F3 **Lush, Mt** W Australia Australia
88 G4 **Lushoto** Tanzania
65 E5 **Lüshun** China
67 G1 **Lüsi** China
70 N9 **Lusi** *R* Java
18 F6 **Lusignan** France
98 B7 **Lusk** Wyoming U.S.A.
19 P15 **Lus-la-Croix Haute** France
38 E8 **Luson** Italy
26 L4 **Luspebryggan** Sweden
15 D4 **Luss** Scotland
18 F6 **Lussac les Châteaux** France
12 C3 **Lussa, L** Scotland
129 H8 **Lussanvira** Brazil
78 J6 **Lussuf, Al** Iraq
141 J7 **Lussvale** Queensland Australia
36 E5 **Lustadt** Germany
41 L3 **Lustenau** Austria
37 J5 **Lustenau** Germany
27 B10 **Luster** Norway
22 H3 **Lustin** Belgium
101 U1 **Lustre** Montana U.S.A.
Lutai *see* **Ninghe**
77 E3 **Lut, Dasht-e** *desert* Iran
87 D8 **Lutembo** Angola
110 G4 **Lutesville** Missouri U.S.A.
99 N8 **Luther** Iowa U.S.A.
107 N6 **Luther** Oklahoma U.S.A.
108 G1 **Lutie** Texas U.S.A.
33 N4 **Lütjenburg** Germany
9 F4 **Luton** England
40 E4 **Lutry** Switzerland
87 C7 **Lutshima** *R* Zaire
32 M9 **Lutter am Barenberge** Germany
32 M7 **Lutterloh** Germany
9 E3 **Lutterworth** England
22 G3 **Luttre** Belgium
112 D1 **Luttrell** Tennessee U.S.A.
36 C1 **Lüttringhausen** Germany
54 L8 **Lutugino** Ukraine
113 E9 **Lutz** Florida U.S.A.
36 C6 **Lutzelbourg** France
36 C6 **Lutzelhouse** France
33 Q10 **Lützen** Germany
36 B3 **Lutzerath** Germany
33 O5 **Lützow** Germany
146 J8 **Lützow-Holmbukta** *B* Antarctica
29 N11 **Luumäki** Finland
86 H5 **Luuq** Somalia
29 N5 **Luusua** Finland
111 K10 **Luverne** Alabama U.S.A.
99 M7 **Luverne** Iowa U.S.A.
98 K6 **Luverne** Minnesota U.S.A.
98 J2 **Luverne** North Dakota U.S.A.
29 J10 **Luvia** Finland
26 K5 **Luvos** Sweden
29 P7 **Luvozero** Russian Federation
87 E7 **Luvua** *R* Zaire
87 D8 **Luvuei** Angola
88 F6 **Luwegu** *R* Tanzania
87 F8 **Luwingu** Zambia
71 B2 **Luwo** *isld* Halmahera Indonesia
68 J1 **Luwu** China
70 B5 **Luwuhuyu** Kalimantan
71 H5 **Luwuk** Sulawesi
88 D7 **Luwumbu** *R* Zambia
111 J8 **Luxapallila** *R* Alabama U.S.A.
22 L4 **Luxembourg** *Grand Duchy* Europe
22 L4 **Luxembourg** Luxembourg
99 P7 **Luxemburg** Iowa U.S.A.
40 D2 **Luxeuil-les-Bains** France
67 C2 **Luxi** China
67 A4 **Luxi** China
67 B2 **Lu Xian** China
84 J4 **Luxor** Egypt
18 E9 **Luy** *R* France
21 M7 **Luynes** France
18 E10 **Luz** France
52 G4 **Luza** Russian Federation
52 J2 **Luza** *R* Komi Respublika Russian Federation
21 P3 **Luzarches** France
18 F8 **Luzech** France
21 N8 **Luzeret** France
41 H3 **Luzern** Switzerland
94 C2 **Luzerne** Michigan U.S.A.
95 O3 **Luzerne** New York U.S.A.
67 C4 **Luzhai** China
67 B3 **Luzhi** China
67 B2 **Luzhou** China
130 F5 **Luziânia** Brazil
21 N7 **Luzillé** France
31 H6 **Lužnice** *R* Czechoslovakia
71 E2 **Luzon** Philippines
18 H6 **Luzy** France
45 J2 **Luzzara** Italy
48 J1 **L'vov** Ukraine
88 B7 **Lwela** *R* Zambia
88 C7 **Lwitikila** *R* Zambia
31 J3 **Lwówek** Poland
31 J4 **Lwówek Śląski** Poland
52 E4 **Lyadiny** Russian Federation
48 L2 **Lyadova** *R* Ukraine
147 Q7 **Lyakhovskiye 0s** *isld* Russian Federation
144 A6 **Lyall, Mt** New Zealand
Lyallpur *see* **Faisalabad**
57 E5 **Lyal'-Mikar** Uzbekistan
55 D2 **Lyalya** *R* Russian Federation
55 F1 **Lyamin** *R* Russian Federation
57 D4 **Lyangar** Uzbekistan
52 D4 **Lyaskelya** Russian Federation
47 H1 **Lyaskovets** Bulgaria
106 C5 **Lybrook** New Mexico U.S.A.
15 E2 **Lybster** Scotland
28 C3 **Lyby** Denmark
106 H4 **Lycan** Colorado U.S.A.
33 S6 **Lychen** Germany
52 D5 **Lychkovo** Russian Federation
47 K8 **Lycia** Turkey
Lyck *see* **Ełk**
26 K7 **Lycksele** Sweden
9 G6 **Lydd** England
Lydda *see* **Lod**
119 T3 **Lyddal** Manitoba Canada
146 F6 **Lyddan Ice Rise** *ice rise* Antarctica
89 G5 **Lydenburg** S Africa
8 B6 **Lydford** England
8 D2 **Lydham** England
47 J6 **Lydia** *hist reg* Turkey
112 G3 **Lydia** South Carolina U.S.A.
119 V8 **Lydiatt** Manitoba Canada
8 D4 **Lydney** England
8 B6 **Lyd, R** England
28 A5 **Lydum** Denmark
21 N7 **Lye** France
145 D4 **Lyell** New Zealand
140 B6 **Lyell Brown, Mt** N Terr Australia
117 H9 **Lyell I** British Columbia Canada
139 H8 **Lyell, Mt** Tasmania Australia
111 L7 **Lyerly** Georgia U.S.A.
26 K2 **Lyfjord** Norway
109 K9 **Lyford** Texas U.S.A.
113 K9 **Lyford Cay** *isld* New Providence I Bahamas
27 B13 **Lygna** *R* Norway
95 L6 **Lykens** Pennsylvania U.S.A.
52 D5 **Lykoshino** Russian Federation
99 O6 **Lyle** Minnesota U.S.A.
100 D4 **Lyle** Washington U.S.A.
110 J6 **Lyles** Tennessee U.S.A.
119 Q9 **Lyleton** Manitoba Canada
111 G11 **Lyman** Mississippi U.S.A.
107 O5 **Lyman** Oklahoma U.S.A.
112 E3 **Lyman** South Carolina U.S.A.
101 P8 **Lyman** Wyoming U.S.A.
117 O8 **Lymburn** Alberta Canada
95 P3 **Lyme** New Hampshire U.S.A.
8 D6 **Lyme B** England

8 D6 **Lyme Regis** England
9 H5 **Lyminge** England
9 E6 **Lymington** England
31 M1 **Lyna** R Poland
28 H5 **Lynaes** Denmark
98 H7 **Lynch** Nebraska U.S.A.
94 D7 **Lynchburg** Ohio U.S.A.
110 K6 **Lynchburg** Tennessee U.S.A.
94 H9 **Lynchburg** Virginia U.S.A.
112 G3 **Lynches** R South Carolina U.S.A.
95 R2 **Lynchville** Maine U.S.A.
141 G3 **Lynd** R Queensland Australia
141 G2 **Lynd** Queensland Australia
28 H5 **Lynby** Denmark
100 C1 **Lynden** Washington U.S.A.
141 G4 **Lyndhurst** Queensland Australia
138 E4 **Lyndhurst** South Australia Australia
9 E6 **Lyndhurst** England
144 C5 **Lyndhurst** New Zealand
143 B6 **Lyndon** W Australia Australia
107 P3 **Lyndon** Kansas U.S.A.
95 P2 **Lyndon** Vermont U.S.A.
109 J5 **Lyndon B. Johnson, L** Texas U.S.A.
143 A6 **Lyndon, R** W Australia Australia
94 J3 **Lyndonville** New York U.S.A.
95 P2 **Lyndonville** Vermont U.S.A.
28 A5 **Lyne** Denmark
13 E2 **Lyne** Scotland
28 D4 **Lyngby** Denmark
28 D4 **Lyngbygård Å** R Denmark
28 H6 **Lyngdal** Norway
28 H6 **Lyngdal** Denmark
26 L2 **Lyngen** Norway
27 D13 **Lyngör** Norway
28 A3 **Lyngs** Denmark
28 B2 **Lyngså** Denmark
26 L2 **Lyngseidet** Norway
26 L2 **Lyngsfjord** inlet Norway
142 D3 **Lynher Reef** W Australia Australia
8 C5 **Lynmouth** England
111 J7 **Lynn** Alabama U.S.A.
94 C6 **Lynn** Indiana U.S.A.
95 R4 **Lynn** Massachusetts U.S.A.
101 M8 **Lynn** Utah U.S.A.
117 F6 **Lynn Canal** Alaska U.S.A.
103 M2 **Lynndyl** Utah U.S.A.
111 L11 **Lynn Haven** Florida U.S.A.
119 O2 **Lynn Lake** Manitoba Canada
99 O8 **Lynnville** Iowa U.S.A.
110 J6 **Lynnville** Tennessee U.S.A.
143 A6 **Lynton** W Australia Australia
8 C5 **Lynton** England
28 E6 **Lye** Denmark
18 N13 **Lyon** France
94 B2 **Lyon Manor** Michigan U.S.A.
95 O2 **Lyon Mountain** New York U.S.A.
18 H7 **Lyonnais, Mts.du** France
Lyons see Lyon
138 C4 **Lyons** South Australia Australia
98 A9 **Lyons** Colorado U.S.A.
112 E5 **Lyons** Georgia U.S.A.
110 J3 **Lyons** Indiana U.S.A.
107 M3 **Lyons** Kansas U.S.A.
94 C4 **Lyons** Michigan U.S.A.
98 K8 **Lyons** Nebraska U.S.A.
95 L3 **Lyons** New York U.S.A.
94 C5 **Lyons** Ohio U.S.A.
100 C5 **Lyons** Oregon U.S.A.
98 K6 **Lyons** South Dakota U.S.A.
109 L5 **Lyons** Texas U.S.A.
99 S7 **Lyons** Wisconsin U.S.A.
95 M3 **Lyons Falls** New York U.S.A.
18 H7 **Lyons-la-Forêt** France
143 B6 **Lyons, R** W Australia Australia
137 L2 **Lyra Reef** Bismarck Arch
22 D2 **Lys** R France
42 B3 **Lys** R Italy
31 H5 **Lysá** Czechoslovakia
27 B12 **Lyse** Norway
27 B13 **Lysefjorden** inlet Norway
27 E13 **Lysekil** Sweden
79 D3 **Lysi** Cyprus
101 S6 **Lysite** Wyoming U.S.A.
14 **Lyss** Switzerland
121 T6 **Lyster** Quebec Canada
55 C2 **Lys'va** Russian Federation
27 F11 **Lysvik** Sweden
53 F8 **Lysyye Gory** Russian Federation
8 D6 **Lytchett** England
13 E6 **Lytham St.Anne's** England
68 J5 **Ly Tin** Vietnam
109 J6 **Lytle** Texas U.S.A.
144 B4 **Lyttleton** New Zealand
117 N10 **Lytton** British Columbia Canada
121 O6 **Lytton** Quebec Canada
102 B3 **Lytton** California U.S.A.
52 D5 **Lyuban'** Russian Federation
48 N3 **Lyubashevka** Ukraine
52 E6 **Lyubertsy** Russian Federation
54 J1 **Lyubertsy** Russian Federation
52 F5 **Lyubim** Russian Federation
47 H3 **Lyubimets** Bulgaria
55 C2 **Lyubimovo** Russian Federation
55 F3 **Lyubinskiy** Russian Federation
52 D5 **Lyublino** Russian Federation
52 E6 **Lyubokhna** Russian Federation
54 G7 **Lyubotin** Ukraine
54 F3 **Lyudinovo** Russian Federation
52 H6 **Lyuk** Russian Federation
52 G6 **Lyunda** R Russian Federation
52 J2 **Lyzha** R Russian Federation

M

68 D1 **Ma** R Burma
78 B9 **Ma'ad** Jordan
80 B3 **Ma'ädi** Egypt
80 A3 **Ma'agan** Israel
80 C3 **Ma'agan Mikha'el** Israel
87 H8 **Maaia** Mozambique
135 T3 **Maalaea** Hawaiian Is
80 E6 **Ma'ale Adummim** Jordan
80 D7 **Ma'alé 'Amos** Jordan
73 L7 **Maalosmadulu Atoll** Maldives
79 F8 **Ma'ãn** Jordan
29 N8 **Maaninka** Finland
58 E2 **Maanit** Mongolia
29 O8 **Maanselkä** Finland
75 H5 **Ma'anshan** China
76 A6 **Maos** see Negros Philippines
25 E6 **Maarheeze** Netherlands
79 G2 **Ma'arrat al Ikhwän** Syria
79 G3 **Ma'arrat an Nu'mãn** Syria
25 D5 **Maarssen** Netherlands
25 E5 **Maarssenbroek** Netherlands
25 D5 **Maas** R Netherlands
25 E7 **Maasbracht** Netherlands
22 K1 **Maaseik** Belgium
25 B5 **Maassluis** Netherlands
25 E7 **Maastricht** Netherlands
143 K5 **Maatsuyker Is** Tasmania Australia
Maba see Qujiang China
71 H2 **Maba** Halmahera Indonesia
87 F10 **Mabalane** Mozambique
109 L3 **Mabank** Texas U.S.A.
60 C4 **Mabarot** Israel
71 F4 **Mabatobato** Philippines
6 M4 **Mabel** oil rig North Sea
99 P6 **Mabel** Minnesota U.S.A.

138 C3 **Mabel Creek** South Australia Australia
142 G3 **Mabel Downs** W Australia Australia
119 O2 **Mabella** Ontario Canada
94 F9 **Maben** West Virginia U.S.A.
121 O8 **Maberly** Ontario Canada
122 K2 **Mabille, L** Quebec Canada
28 B4 **Måbjerg** Denmark
9 G1 **Mablethorpe** England
123 L7 **Mabou** C Breton I, Nova Scotia
84 D5 **Mabrouk** Mali
84 E5 **Mabrous** Niger
84 F4 **Mabruk** Libya
100 E3 **Mabton** Washington U.S.A.
89 D5 **Mabule** Botswana
61 P14 **Mabuni** Okinawa
89 C5 **Mabutsane** Botswana
91 C7 **Maca** mt Chile
122 C8 **McAdam** New Brunswick Canada
143 B7 **Macadam Plains** W Australia Australia
140 A2 **Macadam Ra** N Terr Australia
130 H8 **Macaé** Brazil
130 J8 **Macaiba** Brazil
71 G6 **Macajalar B** Philippines
109 M1 **McAlester** Oklahoma U.S.A.
139 J5 **Macalister, Mt** New South Wales Australia
109 J9 **McAllen** Texas U.S.A.
101 O4 **McAllister** Montana U.S.A.
113 E7 **McAlpin** Florida U.S.A.
114 J4 **MacAlpine L** Northwest Territories Canada
121 L4 **Macamic** Quebec Canada
Macan, Kepulauan isld see **Taka' Bonerate, Kepulauan**
67 D5 **Macao** terr E Asia
112 D4 **Macon** Georgia U.S.A.
67 E1 **Macheng** China
128 E5 **Macapá** Amazonas Brazil
130 H4 **Macarani** Brazil
127 O10 **Macareo R** Venezuela
141 F3 **Macaroni** Queensland Australia
141 G4 **Macarthur** Victoria Australia
100 D8 **McArthur** Ohio U.S.A.
94 E7 **McArthur** Ohio U.S.A.
76 E2 **Macchilipatnam** India
88 G6 **Machinga** Tanzania
88 D8 **Machinji** Malawi
127 H9 **Machiques** Venezuela
94 C2 **Macau** see Macao
129 L5 **Macau** Brazil
119 Q8 **McAuley** Manitoba Canada
137 R8 **Macauley I** Kermadec Is Pacific Oc
112 F4 **McBean** Georgia U.S.A.
119 U6 **McBeth Pt** Manitoba Canada
117 N9 **McBride** British Columbia Canada

106 B6 **McGaffey** New Mexico U.S.A.
118 J7 **McGee** Saskatchewan Canada
87 E12 **McGee Creek Res** Oklahoma U.S.A.
111 E8 **McGehee** Arkansas U.S.A.
103 K2 **McGill** Nevada U.S.A.
100 K1 **McGillvray Range** mts British Columbia Canada
116 K5 **McGrath** Alaska U.S.A.
95 L4 **McGraw** New York U.S.A.
119 T9 **McGregor** Manitoba Canada
94 E3 **McGregor** Michigan U.S.A.
109 K4 **McGregor** Minnesota U.S.A.
118 E8 **McGregor** Texas U.S.A.
117 N8 **McGregor R** British Columbia Canada
141 F7 **McGregor Ra** Queensland Australia
83 M9 **McGrew** Nebraska U.S.A.
77 K5 **Mach** Pakistan
89 F7 **Machache Mt** Lesotho
128 C4 **Machachi** Ecuador
130 D6 **Machado** Brazil
80 F7 **Machaerus** Jordan
87 F10 **Machaila** Mozambique
83 H10 **Machakos** Kenya
128 C4 **Machala** Ecuador
70 C4 **Machan** Sarawak
67 B3 **Machanging** China
133 E2 **Machareti** Bolivia
140 E6 **Machattie L** Queensland Australia
22 G5 **Machault** France
20 G8 **Machecoul** France
99 S7 **Machen** China
67 E1 **Macheng** China
76 D4 **Macherla** India
33 H10 **Machern** Germany
95 U2 **Machias** Maine U.S.A.
95 S7 **Machias** R Maine U.S.A.
17 F1 **Machichaco, C** Spain
109 K5 **McNeil** Texas U.S.A.
122 G5 **Machault** France

118 H2 **McLean L** Saskatchewan Canada
110 H3 **McLeansboro** Illinois U.S.A.
139 L4 **Maclear** S Africa
88 E8 **Maclear, C** Malawi
139 N3 **Macleay R** New South Wales Australia
143 A3 **McLennan** Alberta Canada
119 Q7 **McLennan Lake** Saskatchewan Canada
93 J12 **McLeod B** Northwest Territories Canada
74 G7 **McLeod, L** W Australia Australia
65 H3 **McLeod Lake** British Columbia Canada
70 C4 **McLeods I** Burma
118 K8 **McMahon** Kansas U.S.A.
94 G7 **McMechen** West Virginia U.S.A.
72 D4 **Madinah, Al** Saudi Arabia
86 B6 **Madimba** Zaire
81 C5 **Madingley Rise** Indian Oc
86 B6 **Madingo-Kayes** Congo
86 B6 **Madingou** Congo
78 G4 **Ma'din Jadid** Syria
117 F4 **Macmillan** R Yukon Territory Canada
99 V3 **McMillan** Michigan U.S.A.
106 F9 **McMillan, L** New Mexico U.S.A.
100 C6 **McMinns Cr** N Terr Australia
100 C6 **McMinnville** Oregon U.S.A.
110 L6 **McMinnville** Tennessee U.S.A.
118 J7 **McMorran** Saskatchewan Canada
118 F1 **McMunn** Manitoba Canada
146 D11 **McMurdo** U.S.A. Base Antarctica

124 E5 **Madera** Mexico
102 D5 **Madera** California U.S.A.
94 A6 **Madera** Pennsylvania U.S.A.
102 E5 **Madera Canal** California U.S.A.
108 E5 **Madera** Sonora Mexico
106 C7 **Madera** New Mexico U.S.A.
83 J12 **Madge Rocks** Seychelles
75 M5 **Madhubani** India
74 G7 **Madhya Pradesh** prov India
65 H3 **Madida** China
81 E6 **Madidi** R Bolivia
70 C4 **Madi, Dtt** Kalimantan
138 E3 **Madigan Gulf** South Australia Australia
76 B4 **Madikeri** India
111 G10 **Madill** Oklahoma U.S.A.
14 F2 **Madingo** Congo
116 K7 **Madirovalo** Madagascar
70 N9 **Madela** Java
8 D3 **Madelane** England
A0 A8 **Madely** England
86 B6 **Madingou** Congo

37 L2 **Magdala** Germany
128 F6 **Magdalena** Bolivia
128 D2 **Magdalena** div Colombia
128 C2 **Magdalena** R Colombia
126 C3 **Magdalena** Sonora Mexico
106 C7 **Magdalena** New Mexico U.S.A.
133 C6 **Magdalena, I** Chile
124 C5 **Magdalena, I** Mexico
70 E2 **Magdalena, Mt** Sabah
Magdalen Is see Madeleine, Iles de la
33 P8 **Magdeburg** Germany
68 J2 **Magdeburgerforth** Germany
141 K3 **Magdelaine Cays** isld Gt Barrier Reef Aust
33 O9 **Magdesprung** Germany
34 B3 **Magdiel** Israel
112 F2 **Magee** Mississippi U.S.A.
8 D5 **Magee, I N** Ireland
116 K7 **Mageik Vol** Alaska U.S.A.
8 D5 **Magelang** Java
99 O5 **Magellan, Str. of** Chile

117 L3 **Mahony L** Northwest Territories Canada
17 F5 **Mahora** Spain
85 G2 **Mahrès** Tunisia
134 E6 **Mahuhura** New Zealand
74 D8 **Mahua** India
137 P1 **Maiana** atoll Kiribati
71 M9 **Maibang** Indonesia
61 K10 **Maibara** Japan
41 B5 **Măicănesţi** Romania
19 K5 **Maich** France
40 E3 **Maiche** France
68 J2 **Maichen** China
129 H3 **Mai-ch'u** China
129 H3 **Maicuru** R Brazil
142 C1 **Maida Vale** W Australia Australia
112 F2 **Maiden** North Carolina U.S.A.
8 D5 **Maiden Bradley** England
8 D5 **Maidenhead** England
8 D6 **Maiden Newton** England
99 O5 **Maiden Rock** Wisconsin U.S.A.
9 G5 **Maidenhead** England
86 P3 **Magerøya** mt Switzerland
86 B3 **Magerøya** isld Norway
42 F6 **Maiella, M.della** Italy
41 L3 **Maienfeld** Switzerland
21 P2 **Maignelay** France
48 L4 **Magialida, Sierra** mts Venezuela
14 C4 **Maigue** R Ireland
34 J8 **Maikala Range** India
36 E5 **Maikammer** Germany
86 E6 **Maiko, Parc Nacional de** nat park Zaire
69 D14 **Maileppe** Indonesia
102 R12 **Maili** Hawaiian Is
21 N4 **Maillebois** France
21 M3 **Mailleraye-sur-Seine, la** France
22 M3 **Mailly Maillet** France
44 C5 **Mailsi** Pakistan
144 C5 **Maimai** New Zealand
127 J5 **Maimon, B.de** Dominican Rep
14 F3 **Main** R Germany
8 D5 **Main** R Ireland
80 F7 **Ma'in** Jordan
8 D5 **Main** N Ireland
129 N8 **Main-à-Dieu** C Breton I, Nova Scotia
37 J4 **Mainbernheim** Germany
123 Q2 **Main Brook** Newfoundland Canada
37 M6 **Mainburg** Germany
118 K8 **Main Centre** Saskatchewan Canada
120 J7 **Main Channel Cave I** Ontario Canada
86 C6 **Mai Ndombe, L** Zaire
121 O9 **Main Duck I** Ontario Canada
19 K4 **Maine** R France
19 K4 **Maine** R France
21 J7 **Maine** R France
16 F3 **Maine** reg France
103 N6 **Maine** Arizona U.S.A.
110 J5 **Maine** state U.S.A.
123 N8 **Main-à-Dieu** C Breton I, Nova Scotia

37 L2 **Magdala** Germany (see above)

52 J2 **Makarikha** Russian Federation
144 B6 **Makarora** *R* New Zealand
59 M2 **Makarov** Russian Federation
42 H5 **Makarska** Croatia
52 G3 **Makar-Yb** Russian Federation
52 G5 **Makar'ye** Russian Federation
Makassar *see* **Ujung Pandang**
70 F5 **Makassar Str** Indonesia
89 H6 **Makatini Flats** *reg* S Africa
135 T3 **Makawao** Hawaiian Is
71 C3 **Makbon** W Irian
Makedonija *see* **Macedonia**
135 N10 **Makemo** *atoll* Pacific Oc
85 B7 **Makeni** Sierra Leone
145 F2 **Maketu** New Zealand
54 K8 **Makeyevka** Ukraine
89 D3 **Makgadikgadi** *salt pans* Botswana
Makharadze *see* **Ozurgety**
16 D9 **Makhazen, Oued** *R* Morocco
55 D2 **Makhnevo** Russian Federation
55 E4 **Makhorovka** Kazakhstan
80 F3 **Makhraba** Jordan
61 M8 **Maki** Japan
71 A2 **Makian** Halmahera Indonesia
144 C6 **Makikihi** New Zealand
119 S8 **Makinak** Manitoba Canada
55 F4 **Makinsk** Kazakhstan
115 M2 **Makinson Inlet** Northwest Territories Canada
26 S1 **Makkaur** Norway
25 F3 **Makkinga** Netherlands
115 O6 **Makkovik** Labrador, Nfld Canada
25 D2 **Makkum** Netherlands
48 F4 **Makó** Hungary
120 C1 **Makokibatan L** Ontario Canada
87 F7 **Makongolosi** Tanzania
145 F3 **Makorako** *mt* New Zealand
98 E2 **Makoti** North Dakota U.S.A.
145 F4 **Makotuku** New Zealand
86 C5 **Makoua** Congo
31 L6 **Makov** Czechoslovakia
31 M6 **Maków** Poland
31 N3 **Maków Mazowiecki** Poland
80 D2 **Makr** Israel
47 H8 **Makrá** *isld* Greece
74 F5 **Makrana** India
77 J7 **Makran Coast Range** Pakistan
47 H4 **Mákri** Greece
76 E1 **Makri** India
46 G7 **Makronísi** *isld* Greece
52 J3 **Maksim** Russian Federation
56 C2 **Maksimkin Yar** Russian Federation
85 F1 **Makthar** Tunisia
78 K2 **Maku** Iran
70 C4 **Makup, Bt** *mt* Kalimantan
60 D14 **Makurazaki** Japan
86 A4 **Makurdi** Nigeria
55 E3 **Makushino** Russian Federation
116 D10 **Makushin Vol** Aleutian Is
88 D7 **Makutu Mts** Zambia
118 H4 **Makwa L** Saskatchewan Canada
89 G1 **Makwiro** Zimbabwe
128 C6 **Mala** Peru
71 G7 **Malabang** Mindanao Philippines
113 G9 **Malabar** Florida U.S.A.
76 B5 **Malabar Coast** India
70 L9 **Malabar, G** *mt* Java
85 F8 **Malabo** Fernando Póo Equat Guinea
71 C6 **Malabuñgan** Palawan Philippines
69 E11 **Malacca, Str. of** Malaysia
118 H1 **Malachi** Ontario Canada
31 K7 **Malacky** Czechoslovakia
101 N7 **Malad City** Idaho U.S.A.
17 H2 **Maladeta** Spain
31 L6 **Malá Fatra** *mts* Czechoslovakia
16 D8 **Málaga** *prov* Spain
16 E8 **Málaga** Spain
100 E2 **Malaga** Washington U.S.A.
88 C4 **Malagarasi** Tanzania
Malagasy Rep *see* **Madagascar**
16 E5 **Malagón** Spain
71 K9 **Malahar** Indonesia
14 E3 **Malahide** Ireland
87 G12 **Malaimbandy** Madagascar
137 N3 **Malaita** *isld* Solomon Is
71 J9 **Malaka** *mt* Sumbawa Indonesia
86 F4 **Malakal** Sudan
42 G4 **Mala Kapela** *mts* Croatia
109 L3 **Malakoff** Texas U.S.A.
71 B2 **Malaku** *islds* Indonesia
137 O5 **Malakula** *isld* Vanuatu
45 L2 **Malalbergo** Italy
71 A3 **Malamala** *isld* Indonesia
70 G6 **Malamala** Sulawesi
71 E7 **Malamaui** *isld* Philippines
45 M1 **Malamocco** Italy
71 D5 **Malampaya Snd** Philippines
141 H3 **Malanda** Queensland Australia
70 O10 **Malang** Java
88 E6 **Malangali** Tanzania
70 M9 **Malangbong** Java
26 K2 **Malangen** *inlet* Norway
26 K2 **Malangen** Norway
26 J2 **Malangsgrunnen** *shoal* Norway
75 L5 **Malangwa** Nepal
71 F7 **Malanipa** *isld* Philippines
87 C7 **Malanje** Angola
20 F6 **Malansac** France
71 D6 **Malanut B** Philippines
85 E6 **Malanville** Benin
65 D4 **Malanyu** China
131 C3 **Malanzaán, Sa. de** *mts* Argentina
76 C5 **Malappuram** India
27 J12 **Mälaren** *L* Sweden
131 B5 **Malargue** *R* Argentina
133 D5 **Malargue** Argentina
129 H3 **Malaripo** Brazil
121 M4 **Malartic** Quebec Canada
70 F7 **Malasoro, Tk** *B* Sulawesi
117 C6 **Malaspina Gl** Alaska U.S.A.
144 A6 **Malaspina Reach** New Zealand
117 L11 **Malaspina Str** British Columbia Canada
26 K6 **Malåtrask** Sweden
78 G2 **Malatya** Turkey
19 O16 **Malaucène** France
21 N2 **Malaunay** France
70 E1 **Malawali** *isld* Sabah
88 D8 **Malawi** *rep* Africa
Malawi, L *see* **Nyasa, L**
29 J9 **Malax** Finland
55 D1 **Malaya Sos'va** *R* Russian Federation
52 D5 **Malaya Vishera** Russian Federation
77 A2 **Malāyer** Iran
141 J4 **Malay Reef** Gt Barrier Reef Aust
69 **Malaysia** S E Asia
69 E10 **Malaysia, Peninsular** S E Asia
14 B4 **Mal B** Ireland
122 H5 **Mal Baie** Quebec Canada
122 B6 **Malbaie** *R* Quebec Canada
131 B6 **Malbarco, L** Argentina
140 F5 **Malbon** Queensland Australia
38 J9 **Malborghetto** Italy
31 L1 **Malbork** Poland
41 N6 **Malcesine** Italy
33 R5 **Malchin** Germany
33 Q6 **Malchow** Germany
143 D8 **Malcolm** W Australia Australia
116 R2 **Malcolm** *R* Yukon Territory Canada
68 D7 **Malcolm I** Burma
143 E10 **Malcolm,Pt** W Australia Australia
99 O8 **Malcom** Iowa U.S.A.
22 E1 **Maldegem** Belgium
95 Q4 **Malden** Massachusetts U.S.A.
110 G5 **Malden** Missouri U.S.A.
100 H2 **Malden** Washington U.S.A.
94 F8 **Malden** West Virginia U.S.A.
135 M8 **Malden I** Pacific Oc
73 L8 **Maldive Is** *rep* Indian Oc
43 B9 **Mal di Ventre, I. di** Sardinia
73 L9 **Maldive Ridge** Indian Oc
9 G4 **Maldon** England
131 G5 **Maldonado** *dept* Uruguay
131 G5 **Maldonado** Uruguay
41 N5 **Male** Italy
73 L8 **Male** Maldives
46 F8 **Maléa, Akr** *C* Greece
47 H5 **Maléa, Akr** Turkey
74 F8 **Malegaon** India
70 G6 **Malehu** Sulawesi
48 D2 **Malé Karpaty** Czechoslovakia
121 P4 **Mâle, L.du** Quebec Canada
88 F9 **Malema** Mozambique
87 E7 **Malemba Nkulu** Zaire
46 F9 **Máleme** Crete
52 E3 **Malen'ga** Russian Federation
33 N4 **Malente** Germany
74 F3 **Maler Kotla** India
47 H9 **Máles** Crete Greece
21 P5 **Malesherbes** France
20 F6 **Malestroit** France
54 K3 **Malevka** Russian Federation
89 B10 **Malgas** S Africa
37 O6 **Malgersdorf** Germany
86 E2 **Malha** Sudan
13 F5 **Malham** England
100 H5 **Malheur** Oregon U.S.A.
100 H6 **Malheur** *R* Oregon U.S.A.
83 K12 **Malheureu, Cap** Mahé I Indian Oc
100 G6 **Malheur L** Oregon U.S.A.
66 F6 **Mali** *R* Burma
85 D5 **Mali** *rep* W Africa
71 M9 **Maliana** Indonesia
21 K6 **Malicorne-sur-Sarthe** France
71 F7 **Maligoy B** Mindanao Philippines
80 F4 **Malih** *R* Jordan
19 Q16 **Malijai** France
70 D6 **Maliku** Kalimantan
71 H5 **Maliku** Sulawesi
68 D6 **Mali Kyun** *isld* Burma
70 G6 **Malili** Sulawesi
27 H14 **Målilla** Sweden
88 B5 **Malimba** *mts* Zaire
70 K9 **Malimping** Java
100 D7 **Malin** Oregon U.S.A.
71 G5 **Malinao Inlet** Philippines
71 F6 **Malindang, Mt** Mindanao Philippines
88 H3 **Malindi** Kenya
48 F2 **Malinec** Czechoslovakia
Malines *see* **Mechelen**
70 G4 **Maling, G** *mt* Sulawesi
27 H12 **Malingsbo** Sweden
14 D1 **Malin Hd** Ireland
48 K3 **Malini** Romania
14 C2 **Malin More** Ireland
70 F7 **Malino** Sulawesi
54 H7 **Malinovka** Ukraine
55 G5 **Malinovoye Ozero** *L* Russian Federation
68 G1 **Malipo** China
42 F4 **Mali Rajinac** *mt* Croatia
71 G7 **Malita** Mindanao Philippines
71 G5 **Malitbog** Leyte Philippines
68 D7 **Maliwun** Burma
106 G9 **Maljamar** New Mexico U.S.A.
48 F6 **Maljen** *mt* Serbia Yugoslavia
80 F3 **Malka** Jordan
53 F11 **Malka** *R* Russian Federation
47 J2 **Malkapapiye** Bulgaria
74 G8 **Malkapur** India
47 H4 **Malkara** Turkey
56 G5 **Malkhanskiy Khr** *mts* Russian Federation
31 N3 **Małkinia** Poland
80 F1 **Malkiyya** Israel
139 J7 **Mallacoota** Victoria Australia
118 F4 **Mallaig** Alberta Canada
15 C3 **Mallaig** Scotland
99 M7 **Mallard** Iowa U.S.A.
84 J4 **Mallawi** Egypt
131 A7 **Malleco** *prov* Chile
19 O17 **Mallemort** France
37 N6 **Mallersdorf** Germany
41 N4 **Malles Venosta** Italy
130 E9 **Mallét** Brazil
142 C5 **Mallina** W Australia Australia
28 E4 **Malling** Denmark
38 H8 **Mallnitz** Austria
17 J5 **Mallorca** *isld* Balearic Is
94 F9 **Mallory** West Virginia U.S.A.
121 P8 **Mallorytown** Ontario Canada
14 C4 **Mallow** Ireland
142 E5 **Mallowa Well** W Australia Australia
8 B1 **Malltraeth B** Wales
8 C2 **Mallwyd** Wales
22 F5 **Malmaison, la** France
27 G14 **Malmbäck** Sweden
26 L4 **Malmberget** Sweden
22 L3 **Malmédy** Belgium
8 D4 **Malmesbury** England
89 A9 **Malmesbury** S Africa
26 K6 **Malmesjaure** *L* Sweden
27 J12 **Malmköping** Sweden
29 K5 **Malmö** Sweden
27 F16 **Malmöhus** *county* Sweden
126 A2 **Malmok** *pt* Bonaire W Indies
52 H6 **Malmyzh** Russian Federation
26 G3 **Malnes** Norway
137 O5 **Malo** *isld* Vanuatu
54 H4 **Maloarkhangel'sk** Russian Federation
129 G3 **Maloca** Amapá Brazil
129 H5 **Maloca** Pará Brazil
41 L5 **Maloggia** Switzerland
71 E3 **Malolos** Luzon Philippines
55 C2 **Malomal'sk** Russian Federation
88 E9 **Malombe,L** Malawi
47 H2 **Malomir** Bulgaria
47 R14 **Malóna** Rhodes Greece
121 N8 **Malone** Ontario Canada
113 B7 **Malone** Florida U.S.A.
95 N2 **Malone** New York U.S.A.
109 L4 **Malone** Texas U.S.A.
98 F8 **Maloney Res** Nebraska U.S.A.
67 A4 **Malong** China
87 D8 **Malonga** Zaire
26 N6 **Malören** Sweden
31 P4 **Malorita** Belorussia
52 E3 **Maloshuyka** Russian Federation
89 F7 **Maloti Mts** Lesotho
100 F1 **Malott** Washington U.S.A.
26 A10 **Måløy** Norway
54 H1 **Maloyaroslavets** Russian Federation
55 E2 **Maloye Gorodishche** Russian Federation
52 H1 **Malozemel'skaya Tundra** *plain* Russian Federation
106 C10 **Malpais** New Mexico U.S.A.
138 F5 **Malpas** South Australia Australia
8 D1 **Malpas** England
124 H6 **Malpaso** Mexico
90 A8 **Malpelo I** Pacific Oc
122 J7 **Malpeque B** Prince Edward I Canada
16 D5 **Malpica** Spain
16 B1 **Malpica de Bergantiños** Spain
131 B4 **Malpo** *R* Chile
73 L5 **Malprabha** *R* India
74 F5 **Malpura** India
36 E6 **Malsch** Germany
31 H7 **Malše** *R* Czechoslovakia
26 K2 **Målselv** *R* Norway
26 K2 **Målselv** Norway
36 H1 **Malsfeld** Germany
77 A7 **Malsūnīyah, Al** Saudi Arabia
38 J8 **Malta** Austria
43 F13 **Malta** *rep* Mediterranean Sea
106 D2 **Malta** Colorado U.S.A.
101 M7 **Malta** Idaho U.S.A.
101 S1 **Malta** Montana U.S.A.
94 F7 **Malta** Ohio U.S.A.
43 F12 **Malta Ch** Mediterranean Sea
87 C10 **Maltahöhe** Namibia
38 H7 **Maltatel** *V* Austria
9 G1 **Maltby** England
13 G6 **Maltby** S Yorks England
144 C5 **Malte Brun** *mt* New Zealand
47 N11 **Maltepe** Turkey
121 L9 **Malton** *airport* Ontario Canada
13 H5 **Malton** England
48 K6 **Malu** Romania
71 D5 **Malubutglubut** *isld* Philippines
85 F6 **Malumfashi** Nigeria
70 F6 **Malunda** Sulawesi
27 G11 **Malung** Sweden
41 K5 **Malvaglia** Switzerland
76 A2 **Malvan** India
127 J2 **Malvern** Jamaica
127 J3 **Malvern** *pk* Jamaica
109 P1 **Malvern** Arkansas U.S.A.
99 L9 **Malvern** Iowa U.S.A.
94 F6 **Malvern** Ohio U.S.A.
8 D3 **Malvern Wells** England
20 G7 **Malville** France
Malvinas, Is *see* **Falkland Is.**
74 F7 **Malwa Plateau** India
83 K9 **Malwatu Oya** *R* Sri Lanka
78 K1 **Maly Kavkaz** *mts* Armenia/Azerbaijan
55 E1 **Malyy Atlym** Russian Federation
55 F1 **Malyy Balyk** *R* Russian Federation
55 G4 **Malyye Chany, Oz** *L* Russian Federation
52 G6 **Malyy Kundysh** *R* Russian Federation
51 O1 **Malyy Lyakhovski,Ostrov** *isld* Russian Federation
51 K1 **Malyy Taymyr, Ostrov** *isld* Russian Federation
55 G2 **Malyy Yugan** *R* Russian Federation
56 H2 **Mama** *R* Russian Federation
56 H2 **Mama** Russian Federation
52 H6 **Mamadysh** Russian Federation
48 M6 **Mamaia** Romania
120 F5 **Mamainse Point** Ontario Canada
145 F3 **Mamaku** New Zealand
76 E4 **Māmallapuram** India
145 D1 **Mamaranui** New Zealand
70 F6 **Mamasa** Sulawesi
71 D7 **Mambahenauhan** *isld* Philippines
71 G6 **Mambajao** Philippines
89 F3 **Mambala Cave** Zimbabwe
86 E5 **Mambasa** Zaire
136 H2 **Mamberamo** *R* W Irian
86 C4 **Mambéré** *R* Cent Afr Republic
70 F6 **Mambi** Sulawesi
79 H2 **Mambij** Syria
71 E4 **Mamburao** Philippines
118 K1 **Mameigwess L** Ontario Canada
83 J12 **Mamelle** *isld* Seychelles
118 D6 **Ma-Me-O Beach** Alberta Canada
118 D5 **Ma-Me-O Beach Prov. Park** Alberta Canada
22 K4 **Mamer** Luxembourg
21 L5 **Mamers** France
86 A4 **Mamfé** Cameroon
128 F4 **Mamiá, L** Brazil
40 D3 **Mamirolle** France
55 E4 **Mamlyutka** Kazakhstan
120 F2 **Mammamattawa** Ontario Canada
28 D4 **Mammen** Denmark
37 L7 **Mammendorf** Germany
37 O6 **Mamming** Germany
43 G10 **Mammola** Italy
94 F8 **Mammoth** West Virginia U.S.A.
110 K4 **Mammoth Cave** Kentucky U.S.A.
101 P5 **Mammoth Hot Springs** Wyoming U.S.A.
102 F4 **Mammoth lakes** California U.S.A.
110 E5 **Mammoth Spring** Arkansas U.S.A.
126 G9 **Mamonal** Colombia
130 G4 **Mamonas** Brazil
31 M1 **Mamo-novo** Russian Federation
128 E6 **Mamore** *R* Bolivia/Brazil
128 F4 **Mamoré, L** Brazil
85 B6 **Mamou** Guinea
111 D11 **Mamou** Louisiana U.S.A.
87 H11 **Mampikony** Madagascar
16 D1 **Mampodre** *mt* Spain
85 D7 **Mampong** Ghana
83 J9 **Mampuri** Sri Lanka
31 N1 **Mamry,Jezioro** *L* Poland
15 C3 **Mam Soul** *mt* Scotland
Mamuji *see* **Yucheng**
70 F6 **Mamuji** Sulawesi
87 D10 **Mamuno** Botswana
55 C5 **Mamyt** Kazakhstan
85 C7 **Man** Ivory Coast
94 F9 **Man** West Virginia U.S.A.
129 H3 **Mana** *R* Fr Guiana
135 N1 **Mana** Hawaiian Is
56 D3 **Mana** *R* Russian Federation
128 B4 **Manabí** Ecuador
128 F4 **Manacapuru** Brazil
128 F4 **Manacapuru,L.Grande de** Brazil
17 K5 **Manacor** Majorca
71 J4 **Manado** Sulawesi
71 J4 **Manadotua** *isld* Sulawesi
22 G3 **Manage** Belgium
140 D3 **Manageoora** N Terr Australia
125 L3 **Managua** Nicaragua
145 E4 **Mana I** New Zealand
145 E3 **Manaia** New Zealand
87 H12 **Manakara** Madagascar
144 D5 **Manakau** *mt* New Zealand
145 E4 **Manakau** New Zealand
136 K2 **Manam** *isld* Papua New Guinea
76 D6 **Manamadurai** India
77 B6 **Manamah,Al** Bahrain
87 G11 **Manambaho** *R* Madagascar
127 N10 **Mánamo** *R* Venezuela
71 E5 **Manamoc** *isld* Philippines
102 S12 **Manana** Hawaiian Is
87 H11 **Mananara** Madagascar
139 G6 **Manangatang** Victoria Australia
87 H12 **Mananjary** Madagascar
128 F2 **Manano,Caño** *creek* Venezuela
85 B6 **Manantali, Lac de** *res* Mali
76 C5 **Mānantavādi** India
87 H12 **Manantenina** Madagascar
144 A6 **Manapouri** New Zealand
66 D3 **Manas** China
Manasarowar Lake *see* **Mapam Yumco**
74 H3 **Mana Shankou** *pass* India/China
66 D3 **Manas He** *R* China
66 D2 **Manas Hu** *L* China
75 L4 **Manaslu** *mt* Nepal
95 N6 **Manasquan** New Jersey U.S.A.
106 E4 **Manassa** Colorado U.S.A.
94 K8 **Manassas** Virginia U.S.A.
71 M9 **Manatang** Indonesia
127 L5 **Manati** Puerto Rico
128 G4 **Manaus** Brazil
78 C3 **Manavgat** Turkey
99 S5 **Manawa** Wisconsin U.S.A.
119 P3 **Manawan L** Saskatchewan Canada
145 E2 **Manawaru** New Zealand
145 F4 **Manawatu** *admin region* New Zealand
145 E4 **Manawatu R** New Zealand
71 G7 **Manay** Mindanao Philippines
140 B2 **Manbulloo** N Terr Australia
94 C2 **Mancelona** Michigan U.S.A.
16 E7 **Mancha Real** Spain
18 E3 **Manche** *dept* France
21 P5 **Manchecourt** France
Manche,la *see* **English Channel**
74 H9 **Mancheral** India
11 E2 **Manchester** *conurbation* England
127 K3 **Manchester** *parish* Jamaica
102 A3 **Manchester** California U.S.A.
95 P5 **Manchester** Connecticut U.S.A.
112 C5 **Manchester** Georgia U.S.A.
110 F2 **Manchester** Illinois U.S.A.
99 P7 **Manchester** Iowa U.S.A.
107 N2 **Manchester** Kansas U.S.A.
110 N4 **Manchester** Kentucky U.S.A.
94 C4 **Manchester** Michigan U.S.A.
95 Q4 **Manchester** New Hampshire U.S.A.
95 K4 **Manchester** New York U.S.A.
94 D8 **Manchester** Ohio U.S.A.
107 M5 **Manchester** Oklahoma U.S.A.
95 L6 **Manchester** Pennsylvania U.S.A.
110 K6 **Manchester** Tennessee U.S.A.
95 O3 **Manchester** Vermont U.S.A.
37 M6 **Manching** Germany
127 M2 **Manchioneal** Jamaica
65 E1 **Manchuria** *reg* China
42 D6 **Manciano** Italy
128 B4 **Mâncora** Peru
106 B4 **Mancos** Colorado U.S.A.
77 B5 **Mand** *R* Iran
87 F8 **Manda** Tanzania
130 D8 **Mandaguari** Brazil
80 F3 **Mandah** Jordan
69 F13 **Mandah** Sumatra
88 D7 **Manda Hd** Zambia
77 G3 **Mandal** Afghanistan
58 D2 **Mandal** Mongolia
27 B13 **Mandal** Norway
68 C2 **Mandalay** Burma
78 A3 **Mandalaya** *isld* Turkey
58 E2 **Mandalgovĭ** Mongolia
78 K5 **Mandalī** Iraq
27 B13 **Mandalsåni** *R* Norway
Mandalt *see* **Sonid Zuoqi**
98 F3 **Mandan** North Dakota U.S.A.
69 E12 **Mandau** Sumatra
36 C5 **Mandelbachtal** Germany
127 K2 **Mandeville** Jamaica
144 B7 **Mandeville** New Zealand
111 F11 **Mandeville** Louisiana U.S.A.
69 F10 **Mandi Angin, Gunung** *mt* Malaysia
130 B6 **Mandioré, Lagoa** *L* Bolivia/Brazil
74 J7 **Mandla** India
69 J12 **Mandor** Indonesia
46 F6 **Mandoúdhion** Greece
74 F6 **Mandsaur** India
143 B10 **Mandurah** W Australia Australia
48 K5 **Maneciu** Romania
41 N6 **Manerba del Garda** Italy
17 G7 **Manga del Mar Menor** Spain
145 E3 **Mangakino** New Zealand
76 E2 **Mangalagiri** India
76 B4 **Mangalore** India
145 E4 **Mangamahoe** New Zealand
145 E3 **Mangamahu** New Zealand
144 D5 **Mangamaunu** New Zealand
145 D1 **Mangamuka** New Zealand
145 E3 **Mangapehi** New Zealand
145 E4 **Mangatainoka** New Zealand
145 E3 **Mangaweka** New Zealand
145 E2 **Mangawhai** New Zealand
142 A4 **Mangles B** W Australia Australia
66 E4 **Mangnai** China
85 E6 **Mango** Togo
88 E9 **Mangochi** Malawi
87 G12 **Mangoky** *R* Madagascar
145 D1 **Mangonui** New Zealand
87 H12 **Mangoro** Madagascar
74 D8 **Māngral** India
113 J11 **Mangrove Cay** *isld* Bahamas
126 F2 **Mangrove Cay** Andros Bahamas
71 E4 **Mangsoagui Pt** Philippines
130 H10 **Manguaba,L** Brazil
16 B4 **Mangualde** Portugal
86 D3 **Mangueigne** Chad
131 H4 **Mangueira, L** Brazil
130 D9 **Mangueirinha** Brazil
84 E5 **Mangueni,Pl.du** Niger
59 H1 **Mangui** China
87 G7 **Mangula** Tanzania
108 E9 **Mangum** Oklahoma U.S.A.
67 A5 **Manhao** China
99 T8 **Manhattan** Illinois U.S.A.
107 O2 **Manhattan** Kansas U.S.A.
101 O4 **Manhattan** Montana U.S.A.
102 G3 **Manhattan** Nevada U.S.A.
22 K3 **Manhay** Belgium
130 H7 **Manhuaçu** Brazil
130 H6 **Manhuaçu,R** Brazil
113 L12 **Man I** Bahamas
87 E7 **Mani** Zaire
87 H11 **Mania** *R* Madagascar
42 E2 **Maniago** Italy
88 E8 **Maniamba** Mozambique
87 F9 **Manica** Mozambique
71 G5 **Manicani** *isld* Philippines
122 D4 **Manic Deux Dam** Quebec Canada
128 F5 **Manicoré** *R* Brazil
122 D3 **Manicouagan** Quebec Canada
122 D4 **Manicouagan Pen** Quebec Canada
122 D4 **Manicouagan R** Quebec Canada
122 D2 **Manicouagan, Res** Quebec Canada
141 K6 **Manifold, C** Queensland Australia
119 V7 **Manigotagan** Manitoba Canada
Maniitsoq *see* **Sukkertoppen Iskappe**
71 E3 **Manila** Luzon Philippines
110 F6 **Manila** Arkansas U.S.A.
101 Q9 **Manila** Utah U.S.A.
71 E3 **Manila B** Luzon Philippines
139 J5 **Manildra** New South Wales Australia
139 K4 **Manilla** New South Wales Australia
99 L8 **Manilla** Iowa U.S.A.
70 F5 **Manimbaja,Tg** *C* Sulawesi
69 E13 **Manindjan,Danau** *L* Sumatra
87 H11 **Maningory** Madagascar
140 C1 **Maningrida** N Terr Australia
85 C6 **Maninian** Ivory Coast
69 E13 **Maninjau Danau** *L* Sumatra
73 P4 **Manipur** *R* Burma
75 P6 **Manipur** *prov* India
47 J6 **Manisa** Turkey
17 G5 **Manises** Spain
12 D5 **Man,Isle of** U.K.
70 B6 **Manismata** Kalimantan
94 B2 **Manistee** *R* Michigan U.S.A.
99 U5 **Manistee** Michigan U.S.A.
99 U3 **Manistique** *R* Michigan U.S.A.
99 U4 **Manistique** Michigan U.S.A.
99 V3 **Manistique L** Michigan U.S.A.
99 R9 **Manito** Illinois U.S.A.
114 J6 **Manitoba** Canada
119 S7 **Manitoba, L** Manitoba Canada
118 H6 **Manito L** Saskatchewan Canada
119 T9 **Manitou** Manitoba Canada
109 J1 **Manitou** Oklahoma U.S.A.
119 M7 **Manitou Bch** Saskatchewan Canada
99 T2 **Manitou I** Michigan U.S.A.
99 W4 **Manitou Island, North** Michigan U.S.A.
99 W4 **Manitou Island, South** Michigan U.S.A.
120 J7 **Manitou L** Ontario Canada
122 G3 **Manitou,L** Quebec Canada
120 H7 **Manitoulin I** Ontario Canada
122 G2 **Manitou R** Quebec Canada
106 F3 **Manitou Springs** Colorado U.S.A.
120 E3 **Manitouwadge** Ontario Canada
120 J7 **Manitowaning** Ontario Canada
120 F4 **Manitowik L** Ontario Canada
99 T5 **Manitowoc** Wisconsin U.S.A.
121 P6 **Maniwaki** Quebec Canada
128 C2 **Manizales** Colombia
80 G6 **Manja** Jordan
87 G12 **Manja** Madagascar
143 B10 **Manjimup** W Australia Australia
38 M5 **Mank** Austria
107 M2 **Mankato** Kansas U.S.A.
99 N5 **Mankato** Minnesota U.S.A.
89 G6 **Mankayane** Swaziland
86 B5 **Mankim** Cameroon
109 J2 **Mankins** Texas U.S.A.
85 C7 **Mankono** Ivory Coast
118 K9 **Mankota** Saskatchewan Canada
48 N2 **Man'kovka** Ukraine
83 K8 **Mankulam** Sri Lanka
95 M3 **Manlius** New York U.S.A.
17 J2 **Manlleu** Spain
139 K5 **Manly** New South Wales Australia
145 E2 **Manly** New Zealand
99 N6 **Manly** Iowa U.S.A.
74 F8 **Manmad** India
139 K3 **Mann** *R* New South Wales Australia
140 C2 **Mann** *R* N Terr Australia
138 F4 **Mannahill** South Australia Australia
83 J9 **Mannar** Sri Lanka
73 M7 **Mannar,G.of** India/Sri Lanka
76 D5 **Mannargudi** India
83 J8 **Mannar I** Sri Lanka
36 F5 **Mannheim** Germany
14 A3 **Mannin B** Ireland
139 K4 **Manning** *R* New South Wales Australia
117 P7 **Manning** Alberta Canada
109 P1 **Manning** Arkansas U.S.A.
99 L8 **Manning** Iowa U.S.A.
98 D2 **Manning** North Dakota U.S.A.
112 G4 **Manning** South Carolina U.S.A.
109 N4 **Manning** Texas U.S.A.
117 N11 **Manning Prov. Park** British Columbia Canada
94 G7 **Mannington** West Virginia U.S.A.
9 H4 **Manningtree** England
140 A7 **Mann, Mt** N Terr Australia
140 A7 **Mann Ranges** N Terr/S Aust Australia
112 M2 **Manns Harbor** North Carolina U.S.A.
95 L3 **Mannsville** New York U.S.A.
43 C9 **Mannu** *R* Sardinia
43 B8 **Mannu,C** Sardinia
138 E5 **Mannum** South Australia Australia
118 F5 **Mannville** Alberta Canada
85 B7 **Mano** Sierra Leone
128 E5 **Manoa** Bolivia
80 B8 **Manoah** *R* Israel
127 N1 **Man of War B** Tobago
116 H7 **Manokotak** Alaska U.S.A.
136 G2 **Manokwari** W Irian
46 E6 **Manolás** Greece
87 G12 **Manombo** Madagascar
88 A5 **Manono** Zaire
119 Q9 **Manor** Saskatchewan Canada
112 E6 **Manor** Georgia U.S.A.
109 K5 **Manor** Texas U.S.A.
8 B4 **Manorbier** Wales
144 B6 **Manorburn Res** New Zealand
14 C2 **Manorhamilton** Ireland
85 B7 **Mano River** Liberia
68 D7 **Manoron** Burma
19 P17 **Manosque** France
21 M4 **Manou** France
121 Q5 **Manouane** Quebec Canada
122 B3 **Manouane L** Quebec Canada
61 M8 **Mano-wan** *B* Japan
68 C1 **Man Pan** Burma
134 K9 **Manra** *isld* Phoenix Is Pacific Oc
17 J3 **Manresa** Spain
88 B7 **Mansa** Zambia
85 A6 **Mansaba** Guinea-Bissau
85 A6 **Mansa Konko** The Gambia
71 E4 **Mansalay B** Philippines
71 H5 **Mansalean** Indonesia
68 C1 **Man Sam** Burma
142 G4 **Mansbridge, Mt** W Australia Australia
115 L5 **Mansel I** Northwest Territories Canada
33 O9 **Mansfeld** Germany
139 H6 **Mansfield** Victoria Australia
9 E1 **Mansfield** England
110 B6 **Mansfield** Arkansas U.S.A.
112 D4 **Mansfield** Georgia U.S.A.
99 S9 **Mansfield** Illinois U.S.A.
109 O3 **Mansfield** Louisiana U.S.A.
95 Q4 **Mansfield** Massachusetts U.S.A.
110 D4 **Mansfield** Missouri U.S.A.
94 E6 **Mansfield** Ohio U.S.A.
98 H4 **Mansfield** South Dakota U.S.A.
109 K3 **Mansfield** Texas U.S.A.
100 F2 **Mansfield** Washington U.S.A.
95 P2 **Mansfield,Mt** Vermont U.S.A.
21 L6 **Mansigne** France
56 D4 **Manskoye Belogor'ye** *mts* Russian Federation
18 F7 **Mansle** France
99 M7 **Manson** Iowa U.S.A.
100 E2 **Manson** Washington U.S.A.
117 L8 **Manson Creek** British Columbia Canada
130 C4 **Manso,R** Brazil
80 D1 **Mansoura** Israel
8 D6 **Manston** England
111 D10 **Mansura** Louisiana U.S.A.
79 B7 **Mansûra,El** Egypt
128 B4 **Manta** Ecuador
71 C6 **Mantalingajan, Mt** Palawan Philippines
71 C1 **Mantanani Besar** *isld* Sabah
86 D6 **Mantantale** Zaire
65 H4 **Mantap-san** *mt* N Korea
71 J5 **Mantarara** Indonesia
118 H7 **Mantario** Saskatchewan Canada
128 C6 **Mantaro** *R* Peru
102 C4 **Manteca** California U.S.A.
111 G8 **Mantee** Mississippi U.S.A.
71 J4 **Mantehase** *isld* Sulawesi
37 N4 **Mantel** Germany
130 H6 **Mantena** Brazil
99 T8 **Manteno** Illinois U.S.A.
112 M2 **Manteo** North Carolina U.S.A.
107 J4 **Manter** Kansas U.S.A.
21 O4 **Mantes-la-Jolie** France
25 E2 **Mantgum** Netherlands
74 H9 **Manthani** India
21 M7 **Manthelan** France
103 N2 **Manti** Utah U.S.A.
130 F8 **Mantiqueira,Serra da** *mts* Brazil
100 D9 **Manton** California U.S.A.
94 B2 **Manton** Michigan U.S.A.
65 B5 **Mantou Shan** *mt ra* China
45 J1 **Mantova** Italy
29 L11 **Mäntsälä** Finland
29 L10 **Mänttä** Finland
126 B3 **Mantua** Cuba
Mantua Italy *see* **Mantova**
94 F5 **Mantua** Ohio U.S.A.
141 H6 **Mantuan Downs** Queensland Australia
52 F5 **Manturovo** Russian Federation
29 J10 **Mäntyluoto** Finland
128 D6 **Manú** Peru
Manuan *see* **Manouane**
122 B3 **Manuanis,L** Quebec Canada
71 F6 **Manucan** Mindanao Philippines
129 J5 **Manuel Alves** *R* Brazil
106 B6 **Manuelito** New Mexico U.S.A.
130 D9 **Manuel Ribas** Brazil
133 C8 **Manuel Rodriguez, I** Chile
128 E5 **Manuel Urbano** Brazil
129 H5 **Manuelzinho** Brazil
71 H6 **Manui** *isld* Indonesia
77 E6 **Manūjān** Iran
145 G2 **Manukau** New Zealand
145 E2 **Manukau Hbr** New Zealand
70 F2 **Manuk Manka** Philippines
138 E4 **Manunda** *R* South Australia Australia
145 E3 **Manunui** New Zealand
71 C3 **Manuran** *isld* W Irian
128 E6 **Manuripe** *R* Bolivia/Peru
136 K2 **Manus** *isld* Bismarck Arch
145 E3 **Manutahi** New Zealand
138 E3 **Manuwalkaninna** South Australia Australia
98 J1 **Manvel** North Dakota U.S.A.
76 C3 **Manvi** India
98 B7 **Manville** Wyoming U.S.A.
109 O4 **Many** Louisiana U.S.A.
52 K4 **Man'ya** Russian Federation
88 B10 **Manyangau** *mt* Zimbabwe
88 G3 **Manyara,L** Tanzania
47 J4 **Manyas** Turkey
118 G9 **Manyberries** Alberta Canada
54 M9 **Manych** *R* Russian Federation
118 G8 **Many Island I** Alberta Canada
88 E4 **Manyoni** Tanzania
141 K6 **Many Peaks** Queensland Australia
143 C10 **Many Peaks, Mt** W Australia Australia
79 B7 **Manzala,El** Egypt
84 J3 **Manzala, L** Egypt
89 E2 **Manzamnyama** *R* Zimbabwe
16 E5 **Manzanares** Spain
127 P2 **Manzanilla B** Trinidad
126 F4 **Manzanillo** Cuba
124 G8 **Manzanillo** Mexico
106 D7 **Manzano** New Mexico U.S.A.
131 A8 **Manzano,B del** Chile
106 G3 **Manzanola** Colorado U.S.A.
106 D7 **Manzano Mts** New Mexico U.S.A.
58 G2 **Manzhouli** China
79 G7 **Manzil** Jordan
89 G6 **Manzini** Swaziland
Manzovka *see* **Sibirtsevo**
86 C3 **Mao** Chad
65 G2 **Mao'ershan** China
136 H2 **Maoke, Pegunungan** *ra* W Irian
65 F4 **Maokui Shan** *mt* China
65 G3 **Maolin** China
67 C6 **Maoming** China
80 D8 **Ma'on** Jordan
67 C1 **Maoping** China
67 G6 **Mao-pi T'ou** *C* Taiwan
67 B3 **Maotai** China
67 A1 **Maowen** China
65 F2 **Maoxing** China
80 F4 **Ma'oz** Israel
87 F10 **Mapai** Mozambique
66 C5 **Mapam Yumco** *L* China
70 G5 **Mapane** Sulawesi
71 D7 **Mapin** Philippines
67 D1 **Maping** China
128 F2 **Mapire** Venezuela
129 H3 **Mapireme** Brazil
128 E7 **Mapiri** *R* La Paz Bolivia
128 F4 **Mapixari, L** Brazil
99 L7 **Maple** *R* Iowa U.S.A.
94 C3 **Maple** *R* Michigan U.S.A.
118 H9 **Maple Creek** Saskatchewan Canada
99 N6 **Maple Island** Minnesota U.S.A.
111 K9 **Maplesville** Alabama U.S.A.
122 H8 **Mapleton** Nova Scotia Canada
99 L7 **Mapleton** Iowa U.S.A.
95 S7 **Mapleton** Maine U.S.A.
99 N6 **Mapleton** Minnesota U.S.A.
100 B5 **Mapleton** Oregon U.S.A.
100 C2 **Maple Valley** Washington U.S.A.
95 L3 **Maple View** New York U.S.A.
141 F1 **Mapoon** Queensland Australia
69 G12 **Mapor** *isld* Indonesia
144 C5 **Mapourika, L** New Zealand
13 H6 **Mappleton** England
129 G4 **Mapuera** *R* Brazil
87 F11 **Maputo** Mozambique
89 H6 **Maputo** *R* Mozambique
80 F8 **Maqam en Nabi Yusha** Jordan
78 H6 **Maqar an Naam** Iraq
46 D3 **Maqellarë** Albania
58 C5 **Maqên Gangri** *mt* China
65 H2 **Maqiaohe** China
79 E10 **Maqnā** Saudi Arabia
66 C6 **Maquan He** *R* China
71 G4 **Maqueda Chan** Philippines
122 H5 **Maquereau Pte.au** Quebec Canada
133 D6 **Maquinchao** Argentina
131 B8 **Maquinchao, R** Argentina
99 Q7 **Maquoketa** Iowa U.S.A.
99 Q9 **Maquon** Illinois U.S.A.
70 G7 **Mara** Sulawesi
127 J9 **Mara** Venezuela
128 E4 **Maraa** Brazil
129 J5 **Marabá** Brazil
70 D6 **Marabahan** Kalimantan
40 B2 **Marac** France
127 J9 **Maracaibo** Venezuela
127 J9 **Maracaibo, L. de** Venezuela
129 H3 **Maracá, Ilha de** Amapá Brazil
128 F3 **Maracá, Ilha de** Roraima Brazil
133 F2 **Maracaju** Brazil
130 C7 **Maracaju,Serra de** *mts* Brazil
129 J4 **Maracana** Brazil
127 O2 **Maracas B** Trinidad
127 L9 **Maracay** Venezuela
84 F4 **Marādah** Libya
85 F6 **Maradi** Niger
145 E3 **Maraetai** New Zealand
78 L3 **Marāgheh** Iran
130 J10 **Maragogi** Brazil
144 D4 **Marahau** New Zealand
128 E3 **Marahuaca,Co** *mt* Venezuela
65 E2 **Marain Sum** China
110 A3 **Marais des Cygnes** *R* Kansas/Missouri U.S.A.
21 L3 **Marais-Vernier** France
129 J4 **Marajó,I.de** Brazil
86 G5 **Maralal** Kenya
55 G4 **Maraldy** Kazakhstan
86 C4 **Marali** Cent Afr Republic
137 N3 **Maramasike** *isld* Solomon Is
Maramba *see* **Livingstone** Zambia
48 H3 **Maramures** *old prov* Romania
69 F11 **Maran** Malaysia
103 N9 **Marana** Arizona U.S.A.
140 C2 **Maranboy** N Terr Australia
17 F3 **Maranchón** Spain
78 K2 **Marand** Iran
45 J2 **Maranello** Italy
68 D7 **Marang** Burma
69 F10 **Marang** Malaysia
129 L4 **Maranguape** Brazil
129 J4 **Maranhão** *state* Brazil
130 E4 **Maranhão** *R* Brazil
141 J7 **Maranoa** *R* Queensland Australia
45 Q8 **Marano di Napoli** Italy
128 D4 **Marañón** *R* Peru
18 E6 **Marans** France
40 A1 **Maranville** France
16 B3 **Marão, Sa do** *mts* Portugal
129 G3 **Marapi** *R* Brazil
43 B8 **Marargiu, C** Sardinia
128 E5 **Marari** Brazil
144 B6 **Mararoa** *R* New Zealand
70 F7 **Marasende** *isld* Indonesia
48 L5 **Mărășești** Romania
71 C6 **Marasi B** Palawan Philippines
16 B6 **Marateca** Portugal
46 D7 **Marathiás,Akr** *C* Greece
120 D4 **Marathon** Ontario Canada
46 F6 **Marathón** Greece
113 F13 **Marathon** Florida U.S.A.
95 L4 **Marathon** New York U.S.A.
108 D5 **Marathon** Texas U.S.A.
99 R5 **Marathon** Wisconsin U.S.A.
70 F3 **Maratua** *isld* Indonesia
129 L6 **Maraú** Brazil
128 E3 **Marauai** *R* Brazil
127 O2 **Maraval** Trinidad
108 E6 **Maravillas Cr** Texas U.S.A.
71 G7 **Marawi** Mindanao Philippines
38 M5 **Marbach** Austria
36 F2 **Marbach** Germany
22 K4 **Marbehan** Belgium
106 C2 **Marble** Colorado U.S.A.
100 H1 **Marble** Washington U.S.A.
142 C5 **Marble Bar** W Australia Australia
103 N5 **Marble Canyon** Arizona U.S.A.
110 B6 **Marble City** Oklahoma U.S.A.
109 J5 **Marble Falls** Texas U.S.A.
87 E10 **Marble Hall** S Africa
99 P10 **Marblehead** Illinois U.S.A.
95 R4 **Marblehead** Massachusetts U.S.A.
94 E5 **Marblehead** Ohio U.S.A.
99 O7 **Marble Rock** Iowa U.S.A.
121 T7 **Marbleton** Quebec Canada
101 P7 **Marbleton** Wyoming U.S.A.
36 F2 **Marburg** Germany
95 K8 **Marbury** Maryland U.S.A.
26 G8 **Marby** Sweden
48 D3 **Marcal** *R* Hungary
47 J7 **Marçal Dag** *mt* Turkey
48 D4 **Marcali** Hungary
45 J1 **Marcaria** Italy
122 F2 **Marceau,L** Quebec Canada
118 L6 **Marcelin** Saskatchewan Canada
110 D2 **Marceline** Missouri U.S.A.
133 G3 **Marcelino Ramos** Brazil
110 E6 **Marcella** Arkansas U.S.A.
94 B4 **Marcellus** Michigan U.S.A.
100 G2 **Marcellus** Washington U.S.A.
45 O5 **Marcetelli** Italy
9 G2 **March** England
21 M4 **Marchainville** France
118 E2 **Marchand** Manitoba Canada
138 E4 **Marchant Hill** South Australia Australia
40 D3 **Marchaux** France
18 F6 **Marche** *reg* France
45 N4 **Marche** *reg* Italy
22 J3 **Marche-en-Famenne** Belgium
128 A7 **Marchena** *isld* Galapagos Is
16 D7 **Marchena** Spain
21 N6 **Marchenoir** France
20 H3 **Marchésieux** France
127 P6 **Marchfield** Barbados
22 E3 **Marchiennes-Ville** France
22 J3 **Marchin** Belgium
140 D1 **Marchinbar I** N Terr Australia
131 E3 **Mar Chiquita, L** Córdoba Argentina
45 Q7 **Marcianise** Italy
18 H6 **Marcigny** France
18 G8 **Marcillac** France
21 J5 **Marcille-la-Ville** France
20 H4 **Marcilly** Manche France
21 O7 **Marcilly-en-Gault** France
21 P6 **Marcilly-en-Villette** France
21 N4 **Marcilly-sur-Eure** France
40 G1 **Marckolsheim** France
122 J1 **Marc,L** Labrador, Nfld Canada
113 F12 **Marco** Florida U.S.A.
110 J3 **Marco** Indiana U.S.A.
43 G9 **Marco Argentano, S** Italy
22 E3 **Marcoing** France
100 C5 **Marcola** Oregon U.S.A.
21 M6 **Marçon** France
118 C1 **Marconi** Manitoba Canada
22 K3 **Marcourt** Belgium
19 Q16 **Marcoux** France
99 L7 **Marcus** Iowa U.S.A.
100 G1 **Marcus** Washington U.S.A.
116 O6 **Marcus Baker,Mt** Alaska U.S.A.
134 G5 **Marcus I** Pacific Oc
95 M3 **Marcy** New York U.S.A.
95 O2 **Marcy, Mt** New York U.S.A.
80 D5 **Marda** Jordan
74 E1 **Mardan** Pakistan
131 F6 **Mar del Plata** Argentina
9 G5 **Marden** England
142 B5 **Mardie** W Australia Australia
78 H3 **Mardin** Turkey
26 M5 **Mårdsel** Sweden
26 K7 **Mårdsele** Sweden
26 J7 **Mårdsjö** Sweden
26 H8 **Mårdsjön** Sweden
71 A2 **Mare** *isld* Halmahera Indonesia
137 O6 **Maré** *isld* Îles Loyauté Pacific Oc
126 F5 **Marea de Portillo** Cuba
45 M3 **Marecchia** *R* Italy
130 J10 **Marechal Deodoro** Brazil
141 H3 **Mareeba** Queensland Australia
86 A3 **Mareeq** Somalia
86 A2 **Mareer-Gur** Somalia
118 H7 **Marengo** Saskatchewan Canada
41 N7 **Marengo** Italy
110 K3 **Marengo** Indiana U.S.A.
99 P8 **Marengo** Iowa U.S.A.
94 E6 **Marengo** Ohio U.S.A.
100 G2 **Marengo** Washington U.S.A.
99 Q3 **Marengo** Wisconsin U.S.A.
99 R3 **Marenisco** Michigan U.S.A.
18 E7 **Marennes** France
145 E2 **Mareretu** New Zealand
9 G6 **Maresfield** England
43 E11 **Marettimo, I** Sicily
22 E3 **Maretz** France
18 F7 **Mareuil** France
21 P8 **Mareuil-sur-Arnon** France
20 H8 **Mareuil-sur-Lay** France
108 C5 **Marfa** Texas U.S.A.
66 D4 **Margai Caka** *L* China
75 M1 **Margai Caka** *L* China
8 C4 **Margam** Wales
123 L7 **Margaree Harbour** C Breton I, Nova Scotia
123 L7 **Margaree I** Nova Scotia Canada
123 M7 **Margaree Valley** C Breton I, Nova Scotia
138 D3 **Margaret** *R* South Australia Australia
108 H1 **Margaret** Texas U.S.A.
141 G1 **Margaret Bay** Queensland Australia
117 K10 **Margaret Bay** British Columbia Canada
117 Q6 **Margaret L** Alberta Canada
117 P3 **Margaret L** Northwest Territories Canada
142 C5 **Margaret, Mt** W Australia Australia

143 B10 **Margaret R** W Australia Australia
95 N4 **Margaretville** New York U.S.A.
130 C7 **Margarida** Brazil
127 N9 **Margarita I. de** Venezuela
46 D5 **Margarition** Greece
139 H9 **Margate** Tasmania Australia
9 H5 **Margate** England
89 G8 **Margate** S Africa
95 N7 **Margate City** New Jersey U.S.A.
18 H8 **Margeride, Mts de la** France
Margherita *see* **Jamaame** Somalia
48 G3 **Marghita** Romania
118 F3 **Margie** Alberta Canada
99 N1 **Margie** Minnesota U.S.A.
57 F4 **Margilan** Uzbekistan
48 G5 **Margina** Romania
48 G5 **Margita** Serbia Yugoslavia
119 O7 **Margo** Saskatchewan Canada
77 H4 **Margo, Dasht-i-** *desert* Afghanistan
71 F7 **Margosatubig** Mindanao Philippines
94 C2 **Margrethe, L** Michigan U.S.A.
117 M9 **Marguerite** British Columbia Canada
146 C5 **Marguerite B** Antarctica
22 J4 **Margut** France
80 F3 **Marhaba** Jordan
122 F5 **Maria** Quebec Canada
124 F7 **Maria Cleofas, I** Mexico
28 D3 **Mariager** Denmark
32 M7 **Mariaglück** Germany
140 D2 **Maria I** N Terr Australia
139 J8 **Maria I** Tasmania Australia
68 C7 **Maria I** Burma
36 C3 **Maria Laach** Germany
38 G8 **Maria Luggau** Austria
124 F7 **Maria Madre, I** Mexico
124 F7 **Maria Magdalena, I** Mexico
103 K8 **Maria Mts** California U.S.A.
141 J5 **Marian** Queensland Australia
130 G7 **Mariana** Brazil
118 E3 **Mariana Lake** Alberta Canada
126 C3 **Marianao** Cuba
134 E6 **Marianas, Northern** *islds* Pacific Oc
75 Q5 **Mariani** India
117 P4 **Marian L** Northwest Territories Canada
110 F7 **Marianna** Arkansas U.S.A.
113 B7 **Marianna** Florida U.S.A.
27 H14 **Mariannelund** Sweden
37 O4 **Mariánské Lázně** Czechoslovakia
119 T9 **Mariapolis** Manitoba Canada
101 N1 **Marias** *R* Montana U.S.A.
17 F7 **Maria,Sierra de** *mts* Spain
124 F5 **Marías, Islas** *islds* Mexico
101 M1 **Marias Pass** Montana U.S.A.
38 F6 **Mariastein** Austria
135 M12 **Maria Theresa Reef** Pacific Oc
145 D1 **Maria van Diemen, C** New Zealand
38 M6 **Mariazell** Austria
99 T5 **Maribel** Wisconsin U.S.A.
Maribo *co see* **Storstrøm** *co*
28 G7 **Maribo** Denmark
38 N8 **Maribor** Slovenia
71 E4 **Maricaban** *isld* Philippines
89 E5 **Marico** *R* Botswana
103 M8 **Maricopa** Arizona U.S.A.
102 E6 **Maricopa** California U.S.A.
103 M8 **Maricopa Mts** Arizona U.S.A.
Maricourt *see* **Kangiqsujuaq**
86 E5 **Maridi** Sudan
128 E4 **Marié** *R* Brazil
83 K12 **Marie Anne I** Seychelles
146 C8 **Marie Byrd Land** Antarctica
146 A8 **Marie Byrd Seamount** *seamount* Antarctica
27 H13 **Mariedam** Sweden
27 J12 **Mariefred** Sweden
127 N5 **Marie Galante** *isld* Guadeloupe W Indies
27 L11 **Mariehamn** Finland
118 G4 **Marie L** Alberta Canada
126 C3 **Mariel** Cuba
Marienbad *see* **Mariánské Lázně**
32 L8 **Marienberg** Germany
37 P2 **Marienberg** Germany
25 G3 **Marienberg** Netherlands
22 H3 **Marienbourg** Belgium
Marienburg *see* **Malbork**
36 C2 **Marienburg** Nordrhein-Westfalen Germany
37 N3 **Marieney** Germany
32 F5 **Marienhafe** Germany
36 C1 **Marienheide** Germany
28 G7 **Marienleuchte** *C* Germany
89 A5 **Mariental** Namibia
107 J3 **Marienthal** Kansas U.S.A.
94 H5 **Marienville** Pennsylvania U.S.A.
140 B1 **Marie Shoal** N Terr Australia
27 G13 **Mariestad** Sweden
112 C4 **Marietta** Georgia U.S.A.
94 F7 **Marietta** Ohio U.S.A.
109 K2 **Marietta** Oklahoma U.S.A.
112 E2 **Marietta** South Carolina U.S.A.
121 R7 **Marieville** Quebec Canada
19 O18 **Marignane** France
21 J6 **Marigné** Maine-et-Loire France
21 L6 **Marigné** Sarthe France
20 H3 **Marigny** France
127 N5 **Marigot** Saint Martin W Indies
55 A3 **Mariinsk** Russian Federation
56 C3 **Mariinsk** Russian Federation
55 D4 **Mariinskoye** Russian Federation
52 G6 **Mariinsky Posad** Russian Federation
31 O1 **Marijampolė** Lithuania
71 J5 **Marikasu,Tg** *C* Indonesia
130 D8 **Marila** Brazil
133 H2 **Marilia** Brazil
142 C5 **Marillana** W Australia Australia
130 E7 **Marimbondo Cachoeira** *rapids* Brazil
70 D5 **Marimun** Kalimantan
16 B2 **Marin** Spain
127 M4 **Marin** Martinique W Indies
102 B4 **Marina** California U.S.A.
44 H3 **Marina di Carrara** Italy
44 H3 **Marina di Massa** Italy
44 H4 **Marina di Pisa** Italy
45 M3 **Marina di Ravenna** Italy
128 G2 **Marina Fall** Guyana
53 C7 **Mar"ina Gorka** Belorussia
71 E4 **Marinduque** *isld* Philippines
110 G3 **Marine** Illinois U.S.A.
113 F8 **Marineland** Florida U.S.A.
21 P3 **Marines** France
99 T4 **Marinette** Wisconsin U.S.A.
129 H8 **Maringá** Brazil
86 D5 **Maringa** *R* Zaire
111 E11 **Maringouin** Louisiana U.S.A.
87 F9 **Maringue** Mozambique
16 B5 **Marinha Grande** Portugal
54 D9 **Mar'inka** Ukraine
42 E7 **Marino** Italy
128 E3 **Marinuma** Colombia
111 J9 **Marion** Alabama U.S.A.
110 F6 **Marion** Arkansas U.S.A.
117 Q11 **Marion** Idaho U.S.A.
110 H4 **Marion** Illinois U.S.A.
94 B6 **Marion** Indiana U.S.A.
99 P7 **Marion** Iowa U.S.A.
107 O3 **Marion** Kansas U.S.A.
110 H4 **Marion** Kentucky U.S.A.
111 D9 **Marion** Louisiana U.S.A.
95 U2 **Marion** Maine U.S.A.
94 B2 **Marion** Michigan U.S.A.
111 H9 **Marion** Mississippi U.S.A.
101 L1 **Marion** Montana U.S.A.
98 F9 **Marion** Nebraska U.S.A.
112 E2 **Marion** North Carolina U.S.A.
98 H3 **Marion** North Dakota U.S.A.
94 D6 **Marion** Ohio U.S.A.
112 H3 **Marion** South Carolina U.S.A.
98 J6 **Marion** South Dakota U.S.A.
109 J6 **Marion** Texas U.S.A.
94 F10 **Marion** Virginia U.S.A.
99 S5 **Marion** Wisconsin U.S.A.
139 J8 **Marion B** Tasmania Australia
140 E6 **Marion Downs** Queensland Australia
111 J9 **Marion Junction** Alabama U.S.A.
141 K4 **Marion Reef** Gt Barrier Reef Aust
141 L4 **Marion Reef** Coral Sea
110 C4 **Marionville** Missouri U.S.A.
128 E2 **Maripa** Venezuela
71 G5 **Maripipi** *isld* Philippines
102 D4 **Mariposa** *R* California U.S.A.
102 E4 **Mariposa** California U.S.A.
70 G4 **Marisa** Sulawesi
133 E2 **Mariscal Estigarribia** Paraguay
110 G3 **Marissa** Illinois U.S.A.
46 G2 **Maritsa** *R* Bulgaria
47 R14 **Maritsa** Rhodes Greece
44 B3 **Marittime, Alpi** *mts* Italy/France
52 G6 **Mari Turek** Russian Federation
54 J9 **Mariupol'** Ukraine
127 O10 **Mariusa** *R* Venezuela
78 L4 **Marivān** Iran
52 G6 **Mariyskaya Respublika** Russian Federation
77 J4 **Marja** Afghanistan
84 G3 **Marj, Al** Libya
77 A5 **Marjan, Al** *oil well* Persian Gulf
26 N5 **Marjärv** Sweden
79 F5 **Marjayoûn** Lebanon
25 C5 **Mark** *R* Netherlands
80 G6 **Marka** Jordan
86 H5 **Marka** Somalia
26 E8 **Markabygd** Norway
56 C6 **Markakal', Oz** *L* Kazakhstan
52 J4 **Markalasta** Russian Federation
58 C6 **Markam** China
76 D3 **Markapur** India
77 A2 **Markazī** *prov* Iran
120 K8 **Markdale** Ontario Canada
41 K2 **Markdorf** Germany
110 F6 **Marked Tree** Arkansas U.S.A.
25 G4 **Markelo** Netherlands
28 G7 **Markelsdorfer Huk** *C* Germany
25 D4 **Marken** Netherlands
25 D3 **Markerwaard** Netherlands
99 S6 **Markesan** Wisconsin U.S.A.
9 F2 **Market Deeping** England
8 D2 **Market Drayton** England
9 F3 **Market Harborough** England
14 E2 **Markethill** N Ireland
13 H6 **Market Rasen** England
9 E1 **Market Warsop** England
13 H6 **Market Weighton** England
36 G6 **Markgröningen** Germany
121 L9 **Markham** Ontario Canada
109 L7 **Markham** Texas U.S.A.
100 B3 **Markham** Washington U.S.A.
146 K7 **Markham Moor** England
146 D10 **Markham, Mt** Antarctica
31 N3 **Marki** Poland
119 N8 **Markinch** Saskatchewan Canada
15 E4 **Markinch** Scotland
33 T8 **Märkisch Buchholz** Germany
66 B4 **Markit** China
26 M4 **Markitta** Sweden
102 E3 **Markleeville** California U.S.A.
37 O6 **Marklkofen** Germany
37 N3 **Markneukirchen** Germany
26 J4 **Markotjåkko** *mt* Sweden
33 Q10 **Markranstädt** Germany
111 F7 **Marks** Mississippi U.S.A.
8 D5 **Marksbury** England
120 K6 **Markstay** Ontario Canada
9 G4 **Marks Tey** England
37 J2 **Marksuhl** Germany
111 D10 **Marksville** Louisiana U.S.A.
37 J5 **Marktbergel** Germany
37 J4 **Markt Bibart** Germany
37 J4 **Marktbreit** Germany
37 J3 **Marktgraitz** Germany
36 H4 **Marktheidenfeld** Germany
37 L7 **Markt Indersdorf** Germany
37 O7 **Marktl** Germany
37 M3 **Marktleugast** Germany
37 J6 **Marktoffingen** Germany
37 N4 **Marktredwitz** Germany
37 N3 **Marktschorgast** Germany
37 J4 **Marktsteft** Germany
38 M7 **Markt-Übelbach** Austria
110 E2 **Mark Twain L** Missouri U.S.A.
41 N1 **Markt Wald** Germany
37 N4 **Marktzeuln** Germany
99 O3 **Markville** Minnesota U.S.A.
32 F9 **Marl** Germany
107 N5 **Marland** Oklahoma U.S.A.
143 B8 **Marlandy Hill** W Australia Australia
121 N8 **Marlbank** Ontario Canada
95 P4 **Marlboro** New Hampshire U.S.A.
141 J6 **Marlborough** Queensland Australia
9 E5 **Marlborough** England
128 G2 **Marlborough** Guyana
145 D4 **Marlborough** *admin region* New Zealand
95 Q4 **Marlborough** Massachusetts U.S.A.
22 F4 **Marle** France
33 S8 **Marlendorf** Germany
33 S8 **Marlenfelde** Germany
94 D3 **Marlette** Michigan U.S.A.
19 O12 **Marlieux** France
109 L4 **Marlin** Texas U.S.A.
94 G8 **Marlinton** West Virginia U.S.A.
139 J7 **Marlo** Victoria Australia
22 J3 **Marloie** Belgium
9 F4 **Marlow** England
33 R4 **Marlow** Germany
95 P3 **Marlow** New Hampshire U.S.A.
109 K1 **Marlow** Oklahoma U.S.A.
22 F4 **Marly** France
19 P9 **Marma** Sweden
110 F5 **Marmaduke** Arkansas U.S.A.
21 P7 **Marmagne** Cher France
18 F8 **Marmande** France
47 J4 **Marmara Adası** *isld* Turkey
47 J4 **Marmara Denizi** Turkey
47 J10 **Marmaraereglisi** Turkey
47 J6 **Marmara Gölü** *L* Turkey
Marmara, Sea of *see* **Marmara Denizi**
47 J8 **Marmaris** Turkey
98 C3 **Marmarth** North Dakota U.S.A.
26 K3 **Mårmatj** *mt* Sweden
94 E4 **Marme City** Michigan U.S.A.
16 B2 **Marmed,Sa des S** *mts* Spain
128 F5 **Marmelos** *R* Brazil
94 F8 **Marmet** West Virginia U.S.A.
121 P4 **Marmette,L** Quebec Canada
118 L1 **Marmion L** *res* Ontario Canada
143 C8 **Marmion, Mt** W Australia Australia
45 J1 **Marmirolo** Italy
42 D2 **Marmolada** *mt* Italy
16 E6 **Marmolejo** Spain
116 L7 **Marmot B** Alaska U.S.A.
125 M9 **Mar Muerto** *B* Mexico
19 P11 **Marnay** France
18 H3 **Marne** *dept* France
40 B1 **Marne** *R* France
32 K5 **Marne** Germany
36 B6 **Marne, Canal de la** France
36 D4 **Marnheim** Germany
33 P6 **Marnitz** Germany
139 G6 **Marnoo** Victoria Australia
145 F3 **Maroa** New Zealand
99 S9 **Maroa** Illinois U.S.A.
87 H11 **Maroantsetra** Madagascar
74 C2 **Marobi** Pakistan
22 F3 **Marolles** France
37 K3 **Maroldsweisach** Germany
21 L5 **Marolles-les-Braults** France
87 H10 **Maromandia** Madagascar
21 N3 **Maromme** France
21 O8 **Mâron** Indre France
89 G2 **Marondera** Zimbabwe
47 H4 **Marónia** Greece
18 G7 **Maronne** *R* France
141 L7 **Maroochydore** Queensland Australia
143 B6 **Maroonah** W Australia Australia
127 J2 **Maroon Town** Jamaica
70 F7 **Maros** *R* Sulawesi
70 F7 **Maros** Sulawesi
145 E1 **Marotiri Is** New Zealand
86 B3 **Maroua** Cameroon
20 E5 **Maroué** France
121 L4 **Marouf Jct** Quebec Canada
22 D3 **Mareuil** France
129 H3 **Marouini** *R* Fr Guiana
87 H11 **Marovoay** Madagascar
78 H4 **Marqādah** Syria
110 F4 **Marquand** Missouri U.S.A.
135 U13 **Marquesas Is** Pacific Oc
113 E13 **Marquesas Keys** *islds* Florida U.S.A.
130 G8 **Marquês de Valença** Brazil
118 D1 **Marquette** Manitoba Canada
99 P6 **Marquette** Iowa U.S.A.
107 N3 **Marquette** Kansas U.S.A.
99 T3 **Marquette** Michigan U.S.A.
99 U6 **Marquette** *R* Michigan U.S.A.
98 H8 **Marquette** Nebraska U.S.A.
106 C6 **Marquez** New Mexico U.S.A.
109 L4 **Marquez** Texas U.S.A.
17 F4 **Marquina** Spain
22 E3 **Marquion** France
119 M8 **Marquis** Saskatchewan Canada
22 B2 **Marquise** France
139 G4 **Marra** New South Wales Australia
139 H4 **Marra** *R* New South Wales Australia
87 G11 **Marracuene** Mozambique
89 H5 **Marradi** Italy
45 L3 **Marradong** W Australia Australia
143 B10 **Marrah, Jebel** *mts* Sudan
86 D3 **Marrakai** N Terr Australia
140 B2 **Marrakech** Morocco
85 C2 **Marraket, Hassi** Algeria
85 E2 **Marrar** New South Wales Australia
139 H5 **Marrawah** Tasmania Australia
139 G8 **Marrebæk** Denmark
28 H7 **Marree** South Australia Australia
138 E3 **Marrero** New Orleans, Louisiana U.S.A.
111 J13 **Marromeu** Mozambique
87 G9 **Marroquí,Pta** Spain
16 D8 **Marrupa** Mozambique
88 F8 **Mars** Pennsylvania U.S.A.
94 G6 **Marsā Alam** Egypt
84 K4 **Marsa Ben Mehidi** Algeria
17 F9 **Marsabit** Kenya
86 G5 **Marsa Brega** *see* **Al Burayqah**
20 G6 **Marsac-sur-Don** France
130 F8 **Mar,Sa.do** *mts* Brazil
36 B6 **Marsal** France
43 E11 **Marsala** Sicily
17 F9 **Marsanne** France
19 N15 **Marsden** New South Wales Australia
139 J5 **Marsden** Saskatchewan Canada
118 H6 **Marsden** England
13 G4 **Marseille** France
19 O18 **Marseille-en-Beauvaisis** France
21 O2 **Marseille-Rhône, Canal** France
19 N18 **Marseilles** France *see* **Marseille**
99 S8 **Marseilles** Illinois U.S.A.
94 D6 **Marseilles** Ohio U.S.A.
98 B3 **Marsh** Montana U.S.A.
79 E10 **Marsha, J** *mt* Saudi Arabia
118 H5 **Marshall** Saskatchewan Canada
110 D6 **Marshall** Arkansas U.S.A.
99 T10 **Marshall** Illinois U.S.A.
94 C4 **Marshall** Michigan U.S.A.
99 L5 **Marshall** Minnesota U.S.A.
110 C2 **Marshall** Missouri U.S.A.
112 E2 **Marshall** North Carolina U.S.A.
98 D2 **Marshall** North Dakota U.S.A.
107 N5 **Marshall** Oklahoma U.S.A.
109 N3 **Marshall** Texas U.S.A.
94 K8 **Marshall** Virginia U.S.A.
101 U7 **Marshall** Wyoming U.S.A.
139 J7 **Marshall B** Tasmania Australia
134 G7 **Marshall Is** Pacific Oc
120 C2 **Marshall L** Ontario Canada
99 O7 **Marshalltown** Iowa U.S.A.
8 D3 **Marshbrook** England
8 D5 **Marshfield** England
110 D4 **Marshfield** Missouri U.S.A.
99 Q5 **Marshfield** Wisconsin U.S.A.
113 K11 **Marsh Harbour** Great Abaco I Bahamas
145 L5 **Marsh Hill** Pennsylvania U.S.A.
95 T7 **Mars Hill** Maine U.S.A.
111 D12 **Marsh Island** Louisiana U.S.A.
117 F5 **Marsh L** Yukon Territory Canada
98 K4 **Marsh Lake** Minnesota U.S.A.
101 Q9 **Marsh Pk** Utah U.S.A.
112 G3 **Marshville** North Carolina U.S.A.
100 J6 **Marsing** Idaho U.S.A.
13 G4 **Marske-by-the-Sea** England
98 G8 **Marsland** Nebraska U.S.A.
20 K5 **Mars la Tour** France
28 E4 **Mårslet** Denmark
28 F6 **Marslev** Denmark
25 E2 **Marssum** Netherlands
27 J12 **Märsta** Sweden
28 F4 **Marstal** Denmark
28 E7 **Marstal Bugt** *B* Denmark
101 Q8 **Marston** Wyoming U.S.A.
27 E14 **Marstrand** Sweden
28 C6 **Marstrup** Denmark
55 D1 **Marsyaty** Russian Federation
109 L4 **Mart** Texas U.S.A.
42 D6 **Marta** *R* Italy
68 C4 **Martaban** Burma
73 Q5 **Martaban,G.of** Burma
18 E4 **Martaizé** France
70 D6 **Martapura** Kalimantan
70 K8 **Martapura** Sumatra
18 G8 **Martel** France
22 K4 **Martelange** Belgium
45 M1 **Martellago** Italy
44 D2 **Martello, Val** Italy
41 H1 **Marten** Bulgaria
99 N8 **Martensdale** Iowa U.S.A.
32 F9 **Martés,Sierra** *mts* Spain
139 J4 **Marthaguy** *R* New South Wales Australia
110 E3 **Marthasville** Missouri U.S.A.
95 R5 **Marthas Vineyard** Massachusetts U.S.A.
36 B6 **Marthille** France
126 F4 **Marti** Cuba
45 M5 **Martignano,L.di** Italy
21 J5 **Martigné** France
21 K7 **Martigné Briand** France
20 H6 **Martigné-Ferchaud** France
40 F5 **Martigny** Switzerland
40 C1 **Martigny-les-Bains** France
19 O18 **Martigues** France
16 D9 **Martil** Morocco
31 L6 **Martin** Czechoslovakia
17 G4 **Martín** *R* Spain
116 N4 **Martin** Alaska U.S.A.
94 E9 **Martin** Kentucky U.S.A.
94 B4 **Martin** Michigan U.S.A.
98 E6 **Martin** South Dakota U.S.A.
110 H5 **Martin** Tennessee U.S.A.
41 M4 **Martina** Switzerland
43 H8 **Martina Franca** Italy
145 E4 **Martinborough** New Zealand
109 K6 **Martindale** Texas U.S.A.
125 L7 **Martinez** Mexico
102 B3 **Martinez** California U.S.A.
32 M10 **Martinfeld** Germany
130 F6 **Martinho Campos** Brazil
127 L4 **Martinique** *isld* Lesser Antilles
111 L9 **Martin L** Alabama U.S.A.
130 D8 **Martinópolis** Brazil
146 B8 **Martin Pen** Antarctica
116 Q1 **Martin Pt** Alaska U.S.A.
144 A6 **Martins B** New Zealand
38 M5 **Martinsberg** Austria
Martinsbrück *see* **Martina**
110 E2 **Martinsburg** Missouri U.S.A.
95 M3 **Martinsburg** New York U.S.A.
94 E6 **Martinsburg** Ohio U.S.A.
94 J6 **Martinsburg** Pennsylvania U.S.A.
94 K7 **Martinsburg** West Virginia U.S.A.
101 P3 **Martinsdale** Montana U.S.A.
94 G6 **Martins Ferry** Ohio U.S.A.
99 T10 **Martinsville** Illinois U.S.A.
94 A7 **Martinsville** Indiana U.S.A.
94 H10 **Martinsville** Virginia U.S.A.
20 G2 **Martinvast** France
21 N8 **Martizay** France
9 H3 **Martlesham** England
8 D6 **Martock** England
28 F5 **Martofte** Denmark
9 F1 **Marton** England
145 E4 **Marton** New Zealand
17 J3 **Martorell** Spain
16 E7 **Martos** Spain
117 O4 **Martre, Lac La** Northwest Territories Canada
117 P4 **Martre, Lac la** Northwest Territories Canada
29 N4 **Martti** Finland
29 K11 **Marttila** Finland
55 C5 **Martuk** Kazakhstan
52 J2 **Martyn** Russian Federation
80 G3 **Maru** Jordan
70 B6 **Marua** Kalimantan
77 H2 **Maruchak** Afghanistan
70 D2 **Marudi** Sarawak
70 E1 **Marudu Bay** Sabah
77 L2 **Maruf** Afghanistan
60 G11 **Marugame** Japan
144 D5 **Maruia** New Zealand
144 D5 **Maruia Springs** New Zealand
129 L6 **Maruim** Brazil
139 J5 **Marulan** New South Wales Australia
28 J4 **Marum** Denmark
25 F2 **Marum** Netherlands
145 F3 **Marumaru** New Zealand
140 C2 **Marumba Mt** N Terr Australia
86 G4 **Marungu** *mts* Zaire
61 K9 **Maruoka** Japan
77 D4 **Marvast** Iran
27 C11 **Mår-vatn** *L* Norway
18 H8 **Marvejols** France
111 F7 **Marvell** Arkansas U.S.A.
143 C9 **Marvel Loch** W Australia Australia
22 J5 **Marville** France
98 K4 **Marvin** South Dakota U.S.A.
106 C1 **Marvine** Colorado U.S.A.
103 N3 **Marvine,Mt** Utah U.S.A.
77 H2 **Marwa** Afghanistan
74 E6 **Marwar** India
118 G5 **Marwayne** Alberta Canada
15 E1 **Marwick Hd** Orkney Scotland
32 G6 **Marx** Germany
33 S9 **Marxdorf** Germany
37 M3 **Marxgrün** Germany
77 G1 **Mary** Turkmenistan
55 F3 **Mar'yanovka** Russian Federation
139 G6 **Maryborough** New South Wales Australia
141 L7 **Maryborough** Queensland Australia
87 D11 **Marydale** S Africa
55 E4 **Mar'yevka** Kazakhstan
119 Q9 **Maryfield** Saskatchewan Canada
117 L6 **Mary Henry,Mt** British Columbia Canada
12 D2 **Maryhill** Scotland
111 E10 **Mary,L** Mississippi U.S.A.
95 K7 **Maryland** *state* U.S.A.
89 G1 **Maryland** Zimbabwe
108 G3 **Maryneal** Texas U.S.A.
12 E4 **Maryport** England
141 K7 **Mary R** Queensland Australia
123 R1 **Mary's Hbr** Labrador, Nfld Canada
100 K8 **Marys R** Nevada U.S.A.
123 R6 **Marystown** Newfoundland Canada
103 M3 **Marysvale** Utah U.S.A.
122 F8 **Marysville** New Brunswick Canada
101 O5 **Marysville** Idaho U.S.A.
107 O2 **Marysville** Kansas U.S.A.
94 E4 **Marysville** Michigan U.S.A.
94 D6 **Marysville** Ohio U.S.A.
100 C1 **Marysville** Washington U.S.A.
141 H4 **Maryvale** Queensland Australia
141 K8 **Maryvale** Queensland Australia
99 M9 **Maryville** Missouri U.S.A.
112 D2 **Maryville** Tennessee U.S.A.
45 K3 **Marzabotto** Italy
85 D5 **Marzafal** Mali
130 E5 **Marzagão** Brazil
33 R8 **Marzahna** Germany
33 R7 **Marzahne** Germany
20 F6 **Marzan** France
128 C2 **Marzo,C** Colombia
70 O9 **Mas** *R* Java
69 D13 **Masa** *isld* Indonesia
Masada *see* **Mezada**
80 F1 **Mas'ada** Syria
88 F3 **Masai Mara Game Reserve** Kenya
88 E2 **Masai Mara National Reserve** *nat park* Kenya
88 F4 **Masai Steppe** Tanzania
88 C3 **Masaka** Uganda
86 C3 **Masalasef** Chad
70 D7 **Masalembu Besar** *isld* Indonesia
70 D7 **Masalembu Kecil** *isld* Indonesia
70 G6 **Masamba** Sulawesi
65 G7 **Masan** S Korea
71 N8 **Masapun** Indonesia
95 S3 **Masardis** Maine U.S.A.
88 G7 **Masasi** Tanzania
Mas Atierra *isld see* **Robinson Crusoe** *isld*
71 E3 **Masbate** *isld* Philippines
71 F4 **Masbeck** Germany
17 H9 **Mascara** Algeria
81 C7 **Mascarene Basin** Indian Oc
81 C7 **Mascarene Is** Indian Oc
81 C7 **Mascarene Rge** Indian Oc
98 G9 **Mascot** Nebraska U.S.A.
112 D1 **Mascot** Tennessee U.S.A.
110 G3 **Mascoutah** Illinois U.S.A.
19 P12 **Mas d'Azil, le** France
118 K9 **Masefield** Saskatchewan Canada
70 E3 **Ma Sekatok** Kalimantan
71 O9 **Masela** *isld* Indonesia
38 N7 **Masenberg** *mt* Austria
45 L1 **Masera di P** Italy
121 P4 **Masères,L** Quebec Canada
89 E7 **Maseru** Lesotho
40 E2 **Masevaux** France
13 G5 **Masham** England
65 H2 **Mashan** China
67 C5 **Mashan** China
80 G1 **Masharah** Syria
80 E7 **Mashash** *R* Jordan
87 F9 **Mashava** Zimbabwe
80 F2 **Mashfa** Syria
77 F1 **Mashhad** Iran
85 F7 **Mashi** *R* Nigeria
60 P2 **Mashike** Japan
77 E5 **Mashīz** Iran
77 H5 **Mashkel, Hāmūn-i-** *marsh* Pakistan
77 H6 **Mashkel** *R* Pakistan
120 F5 **Mashkode** Ontario Canada
88 C10 **Mashonaland Central** *prov* Zimbabwe
88 D10 **Mashonaland East** *prov* Zimbabwe
88 B10 **Mashonaland West** *prov* Zimbabwe
89 C6 **Mashowing** *watercourse* S Africa
95 R5 **Mashpee** Massachusetts U.S.A.
60 S2 **Mashū-ko** *L* Japan
26 N2 **Masi** Norway
124 E4 **Masiáca** Mexico
86 C6 **Masi-Manimba** Zaire
70 F5 **Masimbu** Sulawesi
86 F5 **Masindi** Uganda
71 D3 **Masinloc** Luzon Philippines
72 H4 **Maşīrah** *isld* Oman
77 B4 **Masiri** Iran
89 G5 **Masitonto** *R* S Africa
77 A4 **Masjed Soleymān** Iran
125 P9 **Maskall** Belize
78 G3 **Maskanah** Syria
121 R6 **Maskinongé** Quebec Canada
14 B3 **Mask,L** Ireland
29 J11 **Masku** Finland
46 F3 **Maslen Nos, N.** Bulgaria
70 Q10 **Maslovo** Russian Federation
56 B4 **Maslyanino** Russian Federation
55 F3 **Maslyanskiy** Russian Federation
28 H7 **Masnedsund** Denmark
22 E3 **Masnieres** France
87 I11 **Masoala, Tanjona** *C* Madagascar
110 H3 **Mason** Illinois U.S.A.
94 C4 **Mason** Michigan U.S.A.
102 E3 **Mason** Nevada U.S.A.
110 M2 **Mason** Ohio U.S.A.
110 G6 **Mason** Tennessee U.S.A.
108 H5 **Mason** Texas U.S.A.
99 P3 **Mason** Wisconsin U.S.A.
101 P7 **Mason** Wyoming U.S.A.
144 A7 **Mason Bay** New Zealand
99 R9 **Mason City** Illinois U.S.A.
99 N6 **Mason City** Iowa U.S.A.
98 G8 **Mason City** Nebraska U.S.A.
117 M7 **Mason Creek** British Columbia Canada
88 F3 **Masongaleni** Kenya
71 J5 **Masoni** *isld* Indonesia
143 C8 **Mason, L** W Australia Australia
94 H7 **Masontown** Pennsylvania U.S.A.
94 H7 **Masontown** West Virginia U.S.A.
26 O1 **Måsöy** *isld* Norway
77 F7 **Masqat** Oman
99 R3 **Mass** Michigan U.S.A.
44 H3 **Massa** Italy
95 P4 **Massachusetts** *state* U.S.A.
95 R4 **Massachusetts B** U.S.A.
45 H4 **Massaciuccoli,L.di** Italy
100 F8 **Massacre L** Nevada U.S.A.
80 F4 **Massada** Israel
106 B1 **Massadona** Colorado U.S.A.
45 M2 **Massa Fiscāglia** Italy
86 C3 **Massaguet** Chad
86 C3 **Massakoti** Chad
45 L3 **Massa Lombarda** Italy
45 Q8 **Massa Lubrense** Italy
45 J4 **Massa Marittima** Italy
42 D5 **Massa Marittima** Italy
87 F10 **Massanga** Mozambique
87 F8 **Massangena** Mozambique
94 J8 **Massanutten Mt** Virginia U.S.A.
129 K4 **Massape** Brazil
94 K8 **Massaponax** Virginia U.S.A.
45 H4 **Massarosa** Italy
18 F10 **Massat** France
55 D1 **Massava** Russian Federation
Massawa *see* **Mits'iwa**
21 O7 **Massay** France
37 J3 **Massbach** Germany
99 M8 **Massena** Iowa U.S.A.
95 N2 **Massena** New York U.S.A.
86 C3 **Massenya** Chad
20 G6 **Masserac** France
117 G9 **Masset** British Columbia Canada
18 F9 **Masseube** France
120 H6 **Massey** Ontario Canada
18 H7 **Massiac** France
45 P7 **Massico, M** *mt* Italy
94 H9 **Massies Mill** Virginia U.S.A.
18 H7 **Massif Central** *plateau* France
18 F10 **Massif de Néouvielle** *mt* France
86 D4 **Massif des Bongos** *mts* Cent Afr Republic
19 Q18 **Massif des Maures** *mts* France
85 F4 **Massif de Tarazit** *mts* Niger
85 G5 **Massif de Termit** *mts* Niger
19 O15 **Massif du Diois** *mts* France
19 Q15 **Massif du Pelvoux** *mts* France
86 D4 **Massif du Tondou** *mts* Cent Afr Republic
94 F5 **Massillon** Ohio U.S.A.
87 G10 **Massinga** Mozambique
89 G4 **Massingir** Mozambique
121 P7 **Masson** Quebec Canada
146 H13 **Masson I** Antarctica
77 B4 **Mastang** Pakistan
27 K14 **Mästerby** Sweden
145 E4 **Masterton** New Zealand
95 P6 **Mastic Beach** Long I, New York U.S.A.
126 E2 **Mastic Point** Andros Bahamas
47 H6 **Mástikho,Akr** *C* Greece
37 P3 **Maštov** Czechoslovakia
74 E1 **Mastuj** Pakistan
72 F4 **Masuda** Japan
60 E11 **Masuda** Japan
Masulipatnam *see* **Machilipatnam**
89 G3 **Masvingo** Zimbabwe
79 G3 **Masyāf** Syria
46 D3 **Mat** *R* Albania
18 H3 **Matabeleland North** *prov* Zimbabwe
133 C7 **Mata Amarilla** Argentina
89 E2 **Matabeleland North** *prov* Zimbabwe
89 F3 **Matabeleland South** *prov* Zimbabwe
71 H4 **Matabulawa** *mt* Sulawesi
118 H2 **Mataban** *R* Burma
120 K5 **Matachewan** Ontario Canada
86 B7 **Matadi** Zaire
118 K8 **Matador** Saskatchewan Canada
108 G1 **Matador** Texas U.S.A.
125 M2 **Matagalpa** Nicaragua
121 N3 **Matagami** Quebec Canada
109 M7 **Matagorda** Texas U.S.A.
109 L7 **Matagorda I** Texas U.S.A.
130 H10 **Mata Grande** Brazil
145 E3 **Matahina** New Zealand
145 F3 **Matahiwi** New Zealand
134 C12 **Mataiea** Tahiti Pacific Oc
145 F4 **Mataikona** New Zealand
69 H11 **Matak** *isld* Indonesia
139 H5 **Matakana** New South Wales Australia
145 E2 **Matakana** New Zealand
145 F2 **Matakana I** New Zealand
145 G2 **Matakaoa Pt** New Zealand
144 D5 **Matakitaki** *R* New Zealand
145 D4 **Matakitaki** New Zealand
145 E2 **Matakohe** New Zealand
87 C8 **Matala** Angola
85 B5 **Matam** Senegal
145 E2 **Matamata** New Zealand
145 F4 **Matamau** New Zealand
85 F6 **Matameye** Niger
95 N5 **Matamoras** Pennsylvania U.S.A.
124 H5 **Matamoros** Coahuila Mexico
125 L5 **Matamoros** Tamaulipas Mexico
70 G6 **Matana, Danao** *L* Sulawesi
71 F7 **Matanal Pt** Philippines
84 G5 **Ma'tan as Sārah** Libya
84 G5 **Ma'ṭan Bishrah** *well* Libya
88 G6 **Matandu** *R* Tanzania
122 E5 **Matane** Quebec Canada
122 F5 **Matane,Parc** Quebec Canada
122 E5 **Matane R** Quebec Canada
145 E2 **Matangi** New Zealand
145 E2 **Matangi I** New Zealand
113 J10 **Matanilla Reef** Bahamas
116 O6 **Matanuska** *mt* Alaska U.S.A.
126 D3 **Matanzas** Cuba
113 F8 **Matanzas Inlet** Florida U.S.A.
131 C6 **Matanzilla, Pampa de la** *plain* Argentina
129 H5 **Matão, Serra do** *mts* Brazil
Matapan, C Greece *see* **Tainaron, Akr**
122 F6 **Matapedia** Quebec Canada
122 E5 **Matapedia L** Quebec Canada
122 E5 **Matapedia R** Quebec Canada
16 D3 **Matapozuelos** Spain
131 B5 **Mataquito** *R* Chile
83 K12 **Matara** Sri Lanka
70 Q10 **Mataram** Indonesia
128 D7 **Matarani** Peru
140 C2 **Mataranka** N Terr Australia
71 H6 **Matarape,Tk** *B* Sulawesi
17 J3 **Mataró** Spain
145 E3 **Mataroa** New Zealand
70 G6 **Matarombeo** *R* Sulawesi
17 F3 **Mata,Sierra de la** *mts* Spain
70 D7 **Matasiri** *isld* Indonesia
145 F2 **Matata** New Zealand
87 E12 **Matatiele** S Africa
144 B7 **Mataura** New Zealand
145 F3 **Matawai** New Zealand
121 R6 **Matawin** *R* Quebec Canada
57 J2 **Matay** Kazakhstan
57 E5 **Matcha** Tajikistan
121 N5 **Matchi-Manitou, L** Quebec Canada
128 F6 **Mategua** Bolivia
125 J6 **Matehuala** Mexico
89 G3 **Mateke Hills** Zimbabwe
127 P1 **Matelot** Trinidad
145 E3 **Matemateaonga Ra** New Zealand
88 H8 **Matemo** *isld* Mozambique
43 H8 **Matera** Italy
45 Q7 **Matese** *L* Italy
45 Q7 **Matese, Monti del** *mts* Italy
48 G3 **Mátészalka** Hungary
43 C11 **Mateur** Tunisia
129 K7 **Mateus** *R* Brazil
129 L7 **Mateus** Brazil
94 E9 **Matewan** West Virginia U.S.A.
107 O3 **Matfield Green** Kansas U.S.A.
26 J9 **Matfors** Sweden
18 E7 **Matha** France
102 E4 **Mather** California U.S.A.
94 H7 **Mather** Pennsylvania U.S.A.
74 E9 **Matheran** India
99 Q8 **Matherville** Illinois U.S.A.
120 K4 **Matheson** Ontario Canada
106 G2 **Matheson** Colorado U.S.A.
119 V7 **Matheson Island** Manitoba Canada
111 K9 **Mathews** Alabama U.S.A.
95 L9 **Mathews** Virginia U.S.A.
109 K7 **Mathis** Texas U.S.A.
111 G8 **Mathiston** Mississippi U.S.A.
80 F8 **Mathluthah** Jordan
21 N2 **Mathonville** France
139 G6 **Mathoura** New South Wales Australia
8 A4 **Mathry** Wales
74 G5 **Mathura** India
71 G7 **Mati** Mindanao Philippines
125 M9 **Matías Romero** Mexico
145 E3 **Matiere** New Zealand
20 F4 **Matignon** France
22 E4 **Matigny** France
16 D4 **Matilla de los Caños del Rio** Spain
120 H6 **Matinenda L** Ontario Canada
134 C13 **Matiti** Tahiti Pacific Oc
89 E5 **Matlabas** *R* S Africa
119 V8 **Matlock** Manitoba Canada
100 B2 **Matlock** Washington U.S.A.
9 E1 **Matlock Bath** England
94 F9 **Matoaka** West Virginia U.S.A.
129 G6 **Mato Grosso** *reg* Brazil
130 D4 **Mato Grosso,Chapada de** *hills* Brazil
130 C7 **Mato Grosso do Sul** *state* Brazil
130 C4 **Mato Grosso,Planalto de** *plateau* Brazil
122 C2 **Matonipi L** Quebec Canada
122 C2 **Matonipis L** Quebec Canada
89 F3 **Matopo Hills Nat. Park** Zimbabwe
87 E10 **Matopos Nat. Park** Zimbabwe
130 D10 **Matos Costa** Brazil
16 B3 **Matosinhos** Portugal
Matou *see* **Qiu Xian**
86 B6 **Matouti, Pto** Gabon
130 G4 **Mato Verde** Minas Gerais Brazil
48 F3 **Mátra** *mts* Hungary
72 H4 **Maṭraḥ** Oman
27 F11 **Matrand** Norway
83 K13 **Mât, R. du** Réunion Indian Oc
27 A11 **Matre** Norway
41 O3 **Matrei am Brenner** Austria
89 A9 **Matroos Berg** *mt* S Africa
59 M2 **Matrosov** Russian Federation
84 J3 **Maṭrūḥ** Egypt
61 N10 **Matsudo** Japan
59 K4 **Matsue** Japan
60 O4 **Matsumae** Japan
61 L9 **Matsumoto** Japan
60 G11 **Matsunaga** Japan
61 K11 **Matsusaka** Japan
61 M9 **Matsushiro** Japan
67 G3 **Matsu Tao** *isld* Taiwan
61 K9 **Matsutō** Japan
60 C12 **Matsuura** Japan
61 P7 **Matsuyama** Honshu Japan
60 F12 **Matsuyama** Shikoku Japan
61 M11 **Matsuzaki** Japan
120 J4 **Mattagami Heights** Ontario Canada
120 J5 **Mattagami L** Ontario Canada
120 H2 **Mattagami R** Ontario Canada
112 L2 **Mattamuskeet L** North Carolina U.S.A.
76 C6 **Mattancheri** India
95 K9 **Mattaponi** *R* Virginia U.S.A.
121 M6 **Mattawa** Ontario Canada
95 T1 **Mattawamkeag** Maine U.S.A.
89 E3 **Mattengwe** *R* Botswana
40 G6 **Matterhorn** *mt* Switzerland
100 H4 **Matterhorn** *mt* Oregon U.S.A.
48 C3 **Mattersburg** Austria
137 P6 **Matthew** *isld* Pacific Oc
126 H4 **Matthew Town** Great Inagua I Bahamas
103 M7 **Matthie** Arizona U.S.A.
120 G3 **Mattice** Ontario Canada
38 H5 **Mattig** *R* Austria
95 P6 **Mattituck** Long I, New York U.S.A.
26 G8 **Mattmar** Sweden
102 A1 **Mattole** *R* California U.S.A.
99 S10 **Mattoon** Illinois U.S.A.
110 H4 **Mattoon** Kentucky U.S.A.
99 R4 **Mattoon** Wisconsin U.S.A.
113 E7 **Mattox** Georgia U.S.A.
115 K4 **Matty I** Northwest Territories Canada
70 B3 **Matu** Sarawak
128 C6 **Matucana** Peru
144 B6 **Matukituki** *R* New Zealand
Matūn *see* **Khowst** *reg*
145 D1 **Matupia I** New Zealand
56 C4 **Matur** Russian Federation
127 P2 **Matura** Trinidad
127 N10 **Maturín** Venezuela
55 B4 **Matveyevka** Russian Federation
54 K9 **Matveyev Kurgan** Russian Federation
75 K6 **Mau** India
87 G8 **Maua** Mozambique
71 M9 **Maubara** Timor
18 F10 **Maubermé, Pic de** *mt* France/Spain
22 G4 **Maubert-Fontaine** France
22 F3 **Maubeuge** France
68 B4 **Maubin** Burma
18 E9 **Maubourguet** France
12 D3 **Mauchline** Scotland
94 A8 **Mauckport** Indiana U.S.A.
107 O6 **Maud** Oklahoma U.S.A.
109 N2 **Maud** Texas U.S.A.
146 G6 **Maudheimvidda** *ra* Antarctica
101 O3 **Maudlow** Montana U.S.A.
90 J15 **Maud Rise** S Atlantic Oc
146 J5 **Maud Rise** *seamount* S Atlantic Oc
87 F10 **Mau-é-ele** Mozambique
129 G4 **Maués** Brazil
134 A1 **Maugaafi** *pk* Western Samoa
94 K7 **Maugansville** Maryland U.S.A.
20 H7 **Mauges, Les** *reg* France
12 D5 **Maughold Hd** I of Man U.K.
135 T3 **Maui** *isld* Hawaiian Is
70 L9 **Mauk** Java
36 F6 **Maulbronn** Germany
22 E3 **Maulde** France
131 A5 **Maule** *prov* Chile
131 B5 **Maule** *R* Chile
21 O4 **Maule** France
21 J8 **Mauléon** France
18 E9 **Mauléon Licharre** France
21 J7 **Maulévrier** France
14 B2 **Maumakeogh** *mt* Ireland
94 D5 **Maumee** Ohio U.S.A.
94 D5 **Maumee Bay** Michigan/Ohio U.S.A.
110 D7 **Maumelle, L** Arkansas U.S.A.
71 L9 **Maumere** Flores Indonesia
87 D9 **Maun** Botswana
135 U5 **Mauna Kea** *pk* Hawaiian Is
135 R2 **Mauna Loa** Hawaiian Is
135 U6 **Mauna Loa** *vol* Hawaiian Is
102 S12 **Maunalua Bay** Hawaiian Is
116 K3 **Mauneluk** *R* Alaska U.S.A.
145 F3 **Maungaharuru Ra** New Zealand
145 F3 **Maungahaumi** *mt* New Zealand
145 F3 **Maungapohatu** New Zealand
145 F3 **Maungataniwha** *mt* New Zealand
145 E1 **Maungatapere** New Zealand
145 E2 **Maungaturoto** New Zealand
68 A2 **Maungdaw** Burma
68 C7 **Maungmagan** *islds* Burma
68 D6 **Maungthama** Burma
114 G4 **Maunoir,L** Northwest Territories Canada
138 D6 **Maupertuis B** South Australia Australia
100 D4 **Maupin** Oregon U.S.A.
38 E7 **Maurach** Austria
19 Q16 **Maure,Col de** *pass* France
20 G6 **Maure-de-Bretagne** France
6 M4 **Maureen** *oil rig* North Sea
111 F11 **Maurepas,L** Louisiana U.S.A.
18 G7 **Mauriac** France
145 E4 **Mauriceville** New Zealand
111 C11 **Mauriceville** Texas U.S.A.
19 Q14 **Maurienne** *dist* France
40 D7 **Maurienne** *V* France
98 D4 **Maurine** South Dakota U.S.A.
85 B4 **Mauritania** *rep* W Africa
83 L12 **Mauritius** *isld* Indian Oc
20 F5 **Mauron** France
18 G8 **Maurs** France
19 N17 **Maussane** France
99 Q6 **Mauston** Wisconsin U.S.A.
38 N5 **Mautern** Austria
38 J7 **Mauterndorf** Austria
38 L5 **Mauthausen** Austria
40 B2 **Maûtz** France
19 N14 **Mauves** France
18 B9 **Mauvezin** France
18 E6 **Mauzé** France
21 K8 **Mauzé Thouarsais** France
128 E3 **Mavaca** *R* Venezuela
21 N6 **Maves-Pontijou** France
87 D9 **Mavinga** Angola
127 L2 **Mavis Bank** Jamaica
144 B6 **Mavora L, N** New Zealand
46 F5 **Mavrovoúni** *mt* Greece
46 D3 **Mavrovsko** *mt* Macedonia Yugoslavia
88 D9 **Mavudzi** *R* Mozambique
88 C10 **Mavuradonha Mts** Zimbabwe
70 C4 **Mawa, Bt** *mt* Kalimantan
71 H7 **Mawasangka** Indonesia
68 C3 **Mawchi** Burma
68 D7 **Mawdaung** *pass* Burma/Thailand
119 R4 **Mawdesley L** Manitoba Canada
118 L8 **Mawer** Saskatchewan Canada
144 C5 **Mawheraiti** New Zealand
68 D4 **Mawkhi** Burma
68 C2 **Mawkmai** Burma
75 Q7 **Mawlaik** Burma
Mawlamyine *see* **Mawkhi**
78 J3 **Mawsil, Al** Iraq
146 K10 **Mawson** *Australia Base* Antarctica
146 J11 **Mawson Coast** Antarctica
146 H10 **Mawson Escarpt** Antarctica
146 C13 **Mawson Pen** Antarctica
98 E2 **Max** Nebraska U.S.A.
98 E3 **Max** North Dakota U.S.A.
86 A3 **Maxaas** Somalia
98 E1 **Maxbass** North Dakota U.S.A.
20 F6 **Maxent** France
112 D4 **Maxeys** Georgia U.S.A.
117 M6 **Maxhamish L** British Columbia Canada
37 N5 **Maxhütte-Haidof** Germany
36 E5 **Maximiliansau** Germany
94 G10 **Max Meadows** Virginia U.S.A.
29 J8 **Maxmo** Finland
18 L9 **Maxstone** Saskatchewan Canada
112 H3 **Maxton** North Carolina U.S.A.
121 Q7 **Maxville** Ontario Canada
113 E7 **Maxville** Florida U.S.A.
101 M3 **Maxville** Montana U.S.A.
102 B2 **Maxwell** California U.S.A.
99 N8 **Maxwell** Iowa U.S.A.
98 F8 **Maxwell** Nebraska U.S.A.
106 F5 **Maxwell** New Mexico U.S.A.
12 E3 **Maxwelltown** Scotland
141 G5 **Maxwelton** Queensland Australia

May — Meteor Depth 201

101 M5 **May** Idaho U.S.A.
108 E7 **May** Oklahoma U.S.A.
109 J4 **May** Texas U.S.A.
59 K1 **Maya** *R* Russian Federation
55 C4 **Mayachnyy** Russian Federation
78 H4 **Mayādīn, Al** Syria
126 H3 **Mayaguana Passage** Bahamas
127 L5 **Mayagüez** Puerto Rico
85 F6 **Mayahi** Niger
55 C5 **Mayakskiy** Russian Federation
17 H3 **Mayals** Spain
77 D1 **Mayamey** Iran
80 D3 **May 'Ami** Israel
125 P9 **Maya Mts** Belize
80 F1 **Ma'yan Barukh** Israel
67 C3 **Mayang** China
126 G4 **Mayari** Cuba
127 P3 **Mayaro** *co* Trinidad
94 D4 **Maybee** Michigan U.S.A.
106 B1 **Maybell** Colorado U.S.A.
12 D3 **Maybole** Scotland
86 G3 **Maych'ew** Ethiopia
86 A1 **Mayd** Somalia
52 F2 **Mayda** Russian Federation
79 G2 **Maydān Ikbis** Syria
77 L2 **Maydān Shahr** Afghanistan
127 K3 **May Day Mts** Jamaica
109 M4 **Maydelle** Texas U.S.A.
139 H9 **Maydena** Tasmania Australia
86 A1 **Mayd, Jasiired** *isld* Somalia
36 C3 **Mayen** Germany
18 E4 **Mayenne** *dept* France
21 J5 **Mayenne** France
21 J5 **Mayenne** *R* France
90 H1 **Mayen Ridge** Arctic Oc
103 M7 **Mayer** Arizona U.S.A.
118 B5 **Mayerthorpe** Alberta Canada
112 G4 **Mayesville** South Carolina U.S.A.
21 L6 **Mayet** France
107 P2 **Mayetta** Kansas U.S.A.
118 K5 **Mayfair** Saskatchewan Canada
9 E1 **Mayfield** England
9 G5 **Mayfield** England
144 C5 **Mayfield** New Zealand
100 K6 **Mayfield** Idaho U.S.A.
110 H5 **Mayfield** Kentucky U.S.A.
107 L6 **Mayfield** Oklahoma U.S.A.
95 M5 **Mayfield** Pennsylvania U.S.A.
103 N2 **Mayfield** Utah U.S.A.
110 D7 **Mayflower** Arkansas U.S.A.
111 H8 **Mayhew** Mississippi U.S.A.
106 E9 **Mayhill** New Mexico U.S.A.
65 G2 **Mayi He** *R* China
13 F1 **May, I. of** Scotland
55 G5 **Maykain** Kazakhstan
57 H2 **Maykamys** Kazakhstan
53 F11 **Maykop** Russian Federation
52 J5 **Maykor** Russian Federation
110 L5 **Mayland** Tennessee U.S.A.
142 B1 **Maylands** *dist* Perth, W Aust Australia
57 C2 **Maylibash** Kazakhstan
57 D2 **Maylykum** Kazakhstan
56 C5 **Mayma** Russian Federation
57 F3 **Maymak** Kazakhstan
118 K6 **Maymont** Saskatchewan Canada
68 C1 **Maymyo** Burma
99 P7 **Maynard** Iowa U.S.A.
143 C8 **Maynard Hills** W Australia Australia
141 F6 **Mayne** *R* Queensland Australia
121 N7 **Maynooth** Ontario Canada
14 E3 **Maynooth** Ireland
51 R2 **Maynopil'gyn** Russian Federation
117 F4 **Mayo** Yukon Territory Canada
14 B3 **Mayo** *co* Ireland
128 C5 **Mayo** *R* Peru
113 D7 **Mayo** Florida U.S.A.
95 L8 **Mayo** Maryland U.S.A.
71 G7 **Mayo B** Mindanao Philippines
86 B4 **Mayo Daga** Nigeria
94 G10 **Mayodan** North Carolina U.S.A.
71 F4 **Mayon** *mt* Philippines
17 F4 **Mayor** *R* Spain
16 D2 **Mayorga** Spain
145 F2 **Mayor I** New Zealand
133 E2 **Mayor Pablo Lagerenza** Paraguay
87 H10 **Mayotte** *isld* Comoros
127 K3 **May Pen** Jamaica
113 F7 **Mayport** Florida U.S.A.
142 E3 **May R** W Australia
71 E1 **Mayraira Pt** Luzon Philippines
38 E7 **Mayrhofen** Austria
78 L5 **Maysān** *prov* Iraq
55 G2 **Maysk** Russian Federation
54 M9 **Mayskiy** Russian Federation
59 J1 **Mayskiy** Amurskaya obl Russian Federation
55 G5 **Mayskoye** Kazakhstan
95 N7 **Mays Landing** New Jersey U.S.A.
21 J7 **May-sur-Evre, le** France
112 D3 **Maysville** Georgia U.S.A.
94 D8 **Maysville** Kentucky U.S.A.
99 M10 **Maysville** Missouri U.S.A.
112 K3 **Maysville** North Carolina U.S.A.
107 N7 **Maysville** Oklahoma U.S.A.
71 D5 **Maytiguid** Philippines
68 A2 **Mayu** *R* Burma
86 B6 **Mayumba** Gabon
94 D3 **Mayville** Michigan U.S.A.
94 H4 **Mayville** New York U.S.A.
98 J2 **Mayville** North Dakota U.S.A.
100 E4 **Mayville** Oregon U.S.A.
99 S6 **Mayville** Wisconsin U.S.A.
98 F9 **Maywood** Nebraska U.S.A.
133 E5 **Maza** Argentina
98 G1 **Maza** North Dakota U.S.A.
88 A9 **Mazabuka** Zambia
129 H4 **Mazagão** Brazil
22 H5 **Mazagram** France
46 G2 **Mazalat** *mt* Bulgaria
100 E1 **Mazama** Washington U.S.A.
18 G9 **Mazamet** France
77 B1 **Māzandarān** *prov* Iran
21 M6 **Mazange** France
124 J5 **Mazapil** Mexico
79 F7 **Mazār** Jordan
43 E11 **Mazara del Vallo** Sicily
77 K1 **Mazār-e-Sharīf** Afghanistan
16 D9 **Mazari,C** Morocco
133 D7 **Mazarredo** Argentina
17 G7 **Mazarrón** Spain
80 F8 **Mazar Saiyidna Suleiman** Jordan
128 F2 **Mazaruni** *R* Guyana
124 D3 **Mazatán** Mexico
125 O10 **Mazatenango** Guatemala
124 F6 **Mazatlán** Mexico
103 N7 **Mazatzal Pk** Arizona U.S.A.
77 B3 **Mazdaj** Iran
52 B6 **Mazeikiai** Lithuania
118 D8 **Mazeppa** Alberta Canada
21 L7 **Mazières** Touraine France
52 B5 **Mazirbe** Latvia
80 C6 **Mazliaḥ** Israel
99 R6 **Mazomanie** Wisconsin U.S.A.
99 S8 **Mazon** Illinois U.S.A.
88 C10 **Mazowe** *R* Zimbabwe
89 G1 **Mazowe** Zimbabwe
80 F8 **Mazra'** Jordan
86 E3 **Mazrub** Sudan
87 E10 **Mazunga** Zimbabwe
22 H4 **Mazures, les** France
31 M2 **Mazury** *reg* Poland
89 G6 **Mbabane** Swaziland
86 C5 **Mbaéré** *R* Cent Afr Republic
85 D7 **Mbahiakro** Ivory Coast
86 C5 **Mbaiki** Cent Afr Republic
88 C6 **Mbala** Zambia
87 E10 **Mbalabala** Zimbabwe
86 F5 **Mbale** Uganda
86 B5 **Mbalmayo** Cameroon
86 B4 **Mbam** *R* Cameroon
87 F8 **Mbamba B** Tanzania
86 C5 **Mbandaka** Zaire
85 F8 **Mbanga** Cameroon
86 B7 **M'banza Congo** Angola
86 B7 **Mbanza-Ngungu** Zaire
88 C2 **Mbarara** Uganda
88 F6 **Mbarika** *mt* Tanzania
89 F9 **Mbashe** S Africa
88 G6 **Mbemkuru** *R* Tanzania
88 D6 **Mbeya** *mt* Tanzania
88 D6 **Mbeya** Tanzania
Mbini *see* **Rio Muni**
87 F10 **Mbizi** Zimbabwe
86 C4 **Mbo** Cent Afr Republic
85 A6 **Mbour** Senegal
85 B5 **Mbout** Mauritania
86 C4 **Mbrés** Cent Afr Republic
87 B7 **M'Bridge** *R* Angola
86 D7 **Mbuji-Mayi** Zaire
86 F5 **Mbulamuti** Uganda
88 E3 **Mbulu** Tanzania
88 F6 **Mbungu** Tanzania
133 F3 **Mburucuyá** Argentina
117 F5 **M'Clintock** Yukon Territory Canada
115 M1 **M'Clintock, C** Northwest Territories Canada
115 L1 **M'Clintock Inlet** Northwest Territories Canada
85 C3 **Mdakane, Hassi** Algeria
43 B12 **M'Daourouch** Algeria
85 C4 **Mdennah** Mali/Mauritania
68 J6 **Mdrak** Vietnam
119 M6 **Meacham** Saskatchewan Canada
100 G4 **Meacham** Oregon U.S.A.
120 G3 **Mead** Ontario Canada
100 H2 **Mead** Washington U.S.A.
116 K1 **Meade** *R* Alaska U.S.A.
107 K4 **Meade** Kansas U.S.A.
101 O7 **Meade Pk** Idaho U.S.A.
103 K5 **Mead,L** Nev/Ariz U.S.A.
103 K6 **Mead, L. National Recreational Area** Arizona U.S.A.
143 A7 **Meadow** W Australia Australia
98 D4 **Meadow** South Dakota U.S.A.
108 E2 **Meadow** Texas U.S.A.
94 G9 **Meadow Bridge** West Virginia U.S.A.
109 M9 **Meadowbrook** Texas U.S.A.
94 G9 **Meadow Creek** West Virginia U.S.A.
98 B7 **Meadowdale** Wyoming U.S.A.
118 J4 **Meadow Lake** Saskatchewan Canada
99 O2 **Meadowlands** Minnesota U.S.A.
118 H4 **Meadow L. Prov. Park** Saskatchewan Canada
119 S7 **Meadow Portage** Manitoba Canada
100 J5 **Meadows** Idaho U.S.A.
103 K4 **Meadow Val.Mts** Nevada U.S.A.
103 K5 **Meadow Val.Wash** *R* Nevada U.S.A.
110 C2 **Meadville** Missouri U.S.A.
98 G7 **Meadville** Nebraska U.S.A.
94 G5 **Meadville** Pennsylvania U.S.A.
120 K8 **Meaford** Ontario Canada
122 J9 **Meaghers Grant** Nova Scotia Canada
60 R2 **Me-akan dake** *mt* Japan
16 B4 **Mealhada** Portugal
13 E4 **Mealsgate** England
115 N7 **Mealy Mts** Labrador, Nfld Canada
141 J7 **Meandarra** Queensland Australia
117 P6 **Meander River** Alberta Canada
100 B4 **Meares,Cape** Oregon U.S.A.
80 C3 **Me 'Arot Karmel** Israel
99 U6 **Mears** Michigan U.S.A.
15 C3 **Measach Falls** Scotland
9 E2 **Measham** England
14 E3 **Meath** *co* Ireland
119 M5 **Meath Park** Saskatchewan Canada
18 G4 **Meaux** France
112 H1 **Mebane** North Carolina U.S.A.
17 G9 **Mebtoub** *R* Algeria
71 H7 **Mebula** Indonesia
70 P10 **Mebulu,Tg** *C* Bali Indonesia
101 S2 **Mecaha** Montana U.S.A.
123 O3 **Mecatina I.,Gt** Quebec Canada
123 N3 **Mecatina I.,Little** Quebec Canada
123 M1 **Mecatina,Riv.du Petite** Quebec Canada
86 G1 **Mecca** Saudi Arabia
103 H8 **Mecca** California U.S.A.
95 R2 **Mechanic Falls** Maine U.S.A.
94 D6 **Mechanicsburg** Ohio U.S.A.
95 K6 **Mechanicsburg** Pennsylvania U.S.A.
95 L8 **Mechanicsville** Maryland U.S.A.
95 O4 **Mechanicville** New York U.S.A.
111 F12 **Mechant,L** Louisiana U.S.A.
22 G1 **Mechelen** Belgium
85 D2 **Mecheria** Algeria
36 B2 **Mechernich** Germany
122 F5 **Méchins,Les** Quebec Canada
37 Q3 **Mecholupy** Czechoslovakia
17 F10 **Mechra Saf Saf** Morocco
33 M6 **Mechtersen** Germany
47 H4 **Mecidiye** Turkey
37 P5 **Měčin** Czechoslovakia
41 L2 **Meckenbeuren** Germany
36 C2 **Meckenheim** Germany
36 E5 **Meckenheim** Germany
36 F5 **Meckesheim** Germany
33 O5 **Mecklenburg** Germany
30 F1 **Mecklenburger Bucht** *B* Germany
33 P5 **Mecklenburg-Vorpommern** *land* Germany
88 G9 **Meconta** Mozambique
94 B3 **Mecosta** Michigan U.S.A.
48 E4 **Mecsek** *mts* Hungary
88 G9 **Mecuburi** *R* Mozambique
88 H8 **Mecufi** Mozambique
87 G8 **Mecula** Mozambique
16 C4 **Meda** Portugal
42 G4 **Medak** Croatia
74 H9 **Medak** India
69 D11 **Medan** Sumatra
71 H9 **Medang** *isld* Indonesia
124 D4 **Médano** Mexico
133 E5 **Médanos** Argentina
133 D7 **Medanosa,Pta** Argentina
99 U8 **Medaryville** Indiana U.S.A.
17 K2 **Medas** *isld* Spain
83 K9 **Medawachchiya** Sri Lanka
144 D5 **Medbury** New Zealand
95 U1 **Meddybemps L** Maine U.S.A.
85 E1 **Médéa** Algeria
36 F1 **Medebach** Germany
41 J4 **Medel** *mt* Switzerland
28 C7 **Medelby** Germany
128 C2 **Medellín** Colombia
32 J5 **Medem** *R* Germany
25 D3 **Medemblik** Netherlands
85 G2 **Medenine** Tunisia
85 A5 **Mederdra** Mauritania
22 L4 **Medernach** Luxembourg
79 E1 **Medetsiz Tepe** *mt* Turkey
95 Q4 **Medford** Massachusetts U.S.A.
107 N5 **Medford** Oklahoma U.S.A.
100 C7 **Medford** Oregon U.S.A.
99 Q4 **Medford** Wisconsin U.S.A.
116 K5 **Medfra** Alaska U.S.A.
48 L6 **Medgidia** Romania
99 P8 **Mediapolis** Iowa U.S.A.
48 J4 **Mediaş** Romania
100 H2 **Medical Lake** Washington U.S.A.
45 L3 **Medicina** Italy
101 T8 **Medicine Bow** *R* Wyoming U.S.A.
101 T8 **Medicine Bow** Wyoming U.S.A.
106 D1 **Medicine Bow Mts** Wyo/Colo U.S.A.
101 T8 **Medicine Bow Pk** Wyoming U.S.A.
118 G8 **Medicine Hat** Alberta Canada
100 D8 **Medicine L** California U.S.A.
98 B1 **Medicine L** Montana U.S.A.
107 M4 **Medicine Lodge** Kansas U.S.A.
109 H1 **Medicine Mound** Texas U.S.A.
118 C6 **Medicine R** Alberta Canada
98 B3 **Medicine Rocks** Montana U.S.A.
Medina *see* **Madīnah, Al**
143 B9 **Medina** W Australia Australia
130 H5 **Medina** Brazil
94 J3 **Medina** New York U.S.A.
98 G3 **Medina** North Dakota U.S.A.
94 F5 **Medina** Ohio U.S.A.
110 H6 **Medina** Tennessee U.S.A.
109 H6 **Medina** Texas U.S.A.
17 F3 **Medinaceli** Spain
16 D3 **Medina del Campo** Spain
16 D3 **Medina de Rioseco** Spain
131 F2 **Medina,L** Argentina
16 D8 **Medina Sidonia** Spain
33 N6 **Medingen** Germany
75 M7 **Medinīpur** India
84 F2 **Mediterranean Sea** Europe/Africa
85 F1 **Medjerda** *R* Tunisia
43 B12 **Medjerda, Monts de la** Algeria/Tunisia
118 G4 **Medley** Alberta Canada
55 C5 **Mednogorsk** Russian Federation
18 E7 **Medoc** *reg* France
45 J1 **Médole** Italy
110 H6 **Medon** Tennessee U.S.A.
119 R9 **Medora** Manitoba Canada
110 F2 **Medora** Illinois U.S.A.
107 N3 **Medora** Kansas U.S.A.
98 C3 **Medora** North Dakota U.S.A.
86 B5 **Médouneu** Gabon
20 F5 **Médréac** France
118 J5 **Medstead** Saskatchewan Canada
122 E8 **Meductic** New Brunswick Canada
Medu Kongkar *see* **Maizhokunggar**
46 E2 **Medveda** Serbia Yugoslavia
55 E2 **Medvedchikovo** Russian Federation
52 E6 **Medveditsa** *R* Russian Federation
52 H6 **Medvedok** Russian Federation
51 J1 **Medvezhiy Yar** Russian Federation
59 L2 **Medvezh'ya, Gora** *mt* Russian Federation
55 F3 **Medvezh'ye** Russian Federation
52 D3 **Medvezh'yegorsk** Russian Federation
95 T1 **Medway** Maine U.S.A.
9 G5 **Medway,R** England
83 M9 **Medwin Pt** Christmas I Indian Oc
54 G2 **Medyn** Russian Federation
48 L1 **Medzhibozh** Ukraine
31 N6 **Medzilaborce** Czechoslovakia
141 L1 **Meeandah** *dist* Brisbane, Qnsld Australia
143 B7 **Meeberrie** W Australia Australia
37 K3 **Meeder** Germany
143 C7 **Meekatharra** W Australia Australia
106 C1 **Meeker** Colorado U.S.A.
107 O6 **Meeker** Oklahoma U.S.A.
123 Q5 **Meelpaeg L** *res* Newfoundland Canada
37 N2 **Meerane** Germany
36 B3 **Meerfeld** Germany
25 F5 **Meerlo** Netherlands
25 E7 **Meerssen** Netherlands
74 G4 **Meerut** India
101 R5 **Meeteetse** Wyoming U.S.A.
118 E6 **Meeting Cr** Alberta Canada
14 E4 **Meeting of the Waters** Ireland
118 K5 **Meetoos** Saskatchewan Canada
33 R5 **Meetschow** Germany
22 K1 **Meeuwen** Belgium
80 B7 **Mefallesim** Israel
86 G5 **Mēga** Ethiopia
69 E14 **Mega** *isld* Indonesia
71 C3 **Mega** W Irian
80 C3 **Megadim** Israel
18 H7 **Megal** *mt* France
86 H4 **Megalo** Ethiopia
47 J8 **Megálo Khorió** Tílos I Greece
46 E7 **Megalópolis** Greece
46 D6 **Meganisi** *mt* Greece
122 B8 **Mégantic** Quebec Canada
122 B8 **Megantic,L** Quebec Canada
46 F6 **Mégara** Greece
109 J2 **Megargel** Texas U.S.A.
46 E5 **Mégdhova** *R* Greece
25 E5 **Megen** Netherlands
40 E6 **Megève** France
36 E1 **Meggen** Germany
13 E3 **Megget Res** Scotland
112 G5 **Meggett** South Carolina U.S.A.
85 F2 **Meghaiër, El** Algeria
75 O6 **Meghalaya** *prov* India
75 O6 **Meghna** *R* Bangladesh
121 P4 **Mégiscane, L** Quebec Canada
100 B3 **Megler** Washington U.S.A.
52 F2 **Megra** Arkhangel'skaya obl Russian Federation
52 E4 **Megra** Vologodskaya obl Russian Federation
48 G6 **Mehadia** Romania
26 Q1 **Mehamn** Norway
77 C2 **Mehdi Shahr** Iran
48 H6 **Mehedinti** *reg* Romania
74 G8 **Mehekar** India
94 J9 **Meherrin** Virginia U.S.A.
94 J10 **Meherrin** *R* Virginia U.S.A.
37 N2 **Mehitheuer** Germany
75 K5 **Mehndawal** India
78 L5 **Mehran** Iran
36 B3 **Mehren** Germany
36 B4 **Mehring** Germany
77 D4 **Mehriz** Iran
77 L2 **Mehtar Lām** Afghanistan
21 P7 **Mehun-sur-Yèvre** France
130 E5 **Meia Ponte,R** Brazil
67 D2 **Meichengzhen** China
67 E1 **Meichuan** China
8 C2 **Meifod** Wales
86 B4 **Meiganga** Cameroon
114 J1 **Meighen I** Northwest Territories Canada
112 C6 **Meigs** Georgia U.S.A.
25 E6 **Meijel** Netherlands
67 E5 **Mei Jiang** *R* China
117 O7 **Meikle** *R* Alberta Canada
68 B2 **Meiktila** Burma
Meilin *see* **Gan Xian**
20 G5 **Meillac** France
20 H6 **Meilleraye-de-Bretagne,la** France
117 L5 **Meilleur Cr** Northwest Territories Canada
33 N8 **Meine** Germany
33 M8 **Meinersen** Germany
36 D1 **Meinerzhagen** Germany
37 J2 **Meiningen** Germany
16 C1 **Meira, Sa. de** *mts* Spain
41 H4 **Meiringen** Switzerland
80 C3 **Me'ir Shefeya** Israel
36 D4 **Meisenheim** Germany
67 A1 **Meisham** China
Meishan *see* **Jinzhai**
67 E1 **Meishan Shuiku** *res* China
80 E1 **Meiss ej Jabal** Lebanon
37 P1 **Meissen** Germany
32 L7 **Meissendorf** Germany
36 H1 **Meissner** *mt* Germany
67 B3 **Meitan** China
37 K6 **Meitingen** Germany
Meixian *see* **Meizhou**
65 E2 **Meiyao** China
67 E4 **Meizhou** China
43 C12 **Mejerda** *R* Tunisia
43 C12 **Mejez El Bab** Tunisia
133 C2 **Mejillones** Chile
28 B4 **Mejrup** Denmark
86 B5 **Mékambo** Gabon
120 F5 **Mekatina** Ontario Canada
86 G3 **Mek'elē** Ethiopia
55 D3 **Mekhonskoye** Russian Federation
74 C3 **Mekhtar** Pakistan
98 J1 **Mekinock** North Dakota U.S.A.
85 C2 **Meknès** Morocco
68 G6 **Mekong** *R* S E Asia
70 G7 **Mekongga, Tk** *B* Sulawesi
69 H8 **Mekong, Mouths of the** Vietnam
116 D6 **Mekoryuk** Alaska U.S.A.
85 E6 **Mekrou** *R* Benin/Niger
69 F11 **Melaka** Malaysia
69 G13 **Melalo, Tanjong** *C* Indonesia
46 G9 **Mélambes** Crete Greece
134 E8 **Melanesia** Pacific Oc
137 P4 **Melanesian Border Plat** Pacific Oc
70 D2 **Melapap** Sabah
70 E2 **Melaut** *mt* Sabah
118 L9 **Melaval** Saskatchewan Canada
70 C5 **Melawi** *R* Kalimantan
21 J7 **Melay** Maine-et-Loire France
100 J6 **Melba** Idaho U.S.A.
33 M6 **Melbeck** Germany
9 G3 **Melbourn** England
138 C7 **Melbourne** Victoria Australia
9 E2 **Melbourne** England
113 G9 **Melbourne** Florida U.S.A.
99 N8 **Melbourne** Iowa U.S.A.
113 G9 **Melbourne Beach** Florida U.S.A.
26 G3 **Melbu** Norway
28 H5 **Melby** Denmark
99 N8 **Melcher** Iowa U.S.A.
120 D2 **Melchett L** Ontario Canada
124 J5 **Melchor Ocampo** Coahuila Mexico
124 H8 **Melchor Ocampo** Michigan U.S.A.
26 D8 **Meldal** Norway
26 M6 **Melderstein** Sweden
45 M3 **Meldola** Italy
32 K4 **Meldorf** Germany
112 F5 **Meldrim** Georgia U.S.A.
120 G7 **Meldrum Bay** Ontario Canada
80 D3 **Melea** Israel
119 U8 **Meleb** Manitoba Canada
44 F1 **Melegnano** Italy
46 G9 **Melékhas, Akr** *C* Crete Greece
52 J5 **Melekhina** Russian Federation
87 G9 **Melela** *R* Mozambique
52 F6 **Melenki** Russian Federation
55 D3 **Melent'yevskoye** Russian Federation
20 G5 **Melesse** France
21 L4 **Mêle-sur-Sarthe,le** France
55 C4 **Meleuz** Russian Federation
45 P6 **Melfa** *R* Italy
95 M9 **Melfa** Virginia U.S.A.
86 C3 **Melfi** Chad
43 G8 **Melfi** Italy
119 N6 **Melfort** Saskatchewan Canada
20 C6 **Melgven** France
28 E2 **Melholt** Denmark
26 D8 **Melhus** Norway
36 F4 **Melibocus** *mt* Germany
21 M4 **Melicourt** France
Melide *see* **Mellid**
130 E9 **Mel, I. do** Brazil
46 E7 **Meligalá** Greece
71 H5 **Melilis** *isld* Indonesia
85 D1 **Melilla** *Spanish exclave* Morocco
133 C6 **Melimoyu** *mt* Chile
144 B6 **Melina, Mt** New Zealand
48 H6 **Melineşti** Romania
70 E5 **Melintang, D** *L* Kalimantan
133 C4 **Melipilla** Chile
119 R9 **Melita** Manitoba Canada
43 G11 **Melito di Porto Salvo** Italy
54 G10 **Melitopol'** Ukraine
38 M5 **Melk** Austria
86 G5 **Melka Guba** Ethiopia
8 D5 **Melksham** England
44 H1 **Mella** *R* Italy
26 K8 **Mellansel** Sweden
26 H9 **Mellansjö** Sweden
22 F2 **Melle** Belgium
32 H8 **Melle** Germany
43 B12 **Mellégue** *R* Tunisia
99 Q3 **Mellen** Wisconsin U.S.A.
32 L7 **Mellendorf** Germany
27 F13 **Mellerud** Sweden
18 E6 **Melle S. Bretonne** France
98 H4 **Mellette** South Dakota U.S.A.
16 B2 **Mellid** Spain
22 K4 **Mellier** Belgium
37 L2 **Mellingen** Germany
137 M5 **Mellish Rise** Coral Sea
86 E3 **Mellit** Sudan
13 F6 **Mellor Brook** England
32 H5 **Mellun** *isld* Germany
111 E7 **Mellwood** Arkansas U.S.A.
13 F4 **Melmerby** England
46 F3 **Melnik** Bulgaria
31 H5 **Mělník** Czechoslovakia
48 K2 **Mel'nitsa-Podol'skaya** Ukraine
131 G4 **Melo** Uruguay
52 G2 **Melogorskoye** Russian Federation
71 A3 **Meloku** Indonesia
71 K9 **Melolo** Sumba Indonesia
54 M7 **Melovoye** Ukraine
26 F5 **Melöy** Norway
116 K4 **Melozitna** *R* Alaska U.S.A.
20 D6 **Melrand** France
22 J3 **Melreux** Belgium
17 G9 **Melrir** *R* Algeria
143 D8 **Melrose** W Australia Australia
123 K8 **Melrose** Nova Scotia Canada
13 F2 **Melrose** Scotland
100 J3 **Melrose** Idaho U.S.A.
99 M4 **Melrose** Minnesota U.S.A.
101 N4 **Melrose** Montana U.S.A.
106 G7 **Melrose** New Mexico U.S.A.
100 B6 **Melrose** Oregon U.S.A.
99 P5 **Melrose** Wisconsin U.S.A.
101 S3 **Melstone** Montana U.S.A.
99 U3 **Melstrand** Michigan U.S.A.
36 H1 **Melsungen** Germany
70 E2 **Melta, Mt** Sabah
29 L5 **Meltaus** Finland
13 G6 **Meltham** England
9 F2 **Melton Mowbray** England
88 G10 **Meluli** *R* Mozambique
68 A2 **Melun** Burma
18 G4 **Melun** France
86 F3 **Melut** Sudan
107 P3 **Melvern** Kansas U.S.A.
15 E2 **Melvich** Scotland
119 P8 **Melville** Saskatchewan Canada
111 E11 **Melville** Louisiana U.S.A.
101 Q3 **Melville** Montana U.S.A.
98 G2 **Melville** North Dakota U.S.A.
140 D1 **Melville B** N Terr Australia
115 N2 **Melville Bugt** *B* Greenland
141 G2 **Melville, C** Queensland Australia
71 C6 **Melville, Cape** Philippines
114 G4 **Melville Hills** Northwest Territories Canada
140 B1 **Melville I** N Terr Australia
114 H2 **Melville I** Northwest Territories Canada
115 O7 **Melville, L** Labrador, Nfld Canada
115 L4 **Melville Pen** Northwest Territories Canada
142 A1 **Melville Water** *B* Perth, W Aust Australia
109 H4 **Melvin** Texas U.S.A.
119 R1 **Melvin L** Manitoba Canada
14 C2 **Melvin, L** Ireland
48 E4 **Mélykút** Hungary
68 H6 **Meman** Cambodia
88 H9 **Memba** Mozambique
71 J9 **Memboro** Sumba Indonesia
22 H4 **Membre** France
21 M7 **Membrolle,la** France
Memel *see* **Klaipėda**
32 E5 **Memmert** *isld* Germany
41 M2 **Memmingen** Germany
70 D2 **Mempakul** Sabah
69 J12 **Mempawah** Indonesia
84 J4 **Memphis** *ruins* Egypt
99 O9 **Memphis** Missouri U.S.A.
110 G6 **Memphis** Tennessee U.S.A.
108 G1 **Memphis** Texas U.S.A.
121 S8 **Memphremagog, L** Vermont U.S.A.
122 H7 **Memramcook** New Brunswick Canada
60 R3 **Memuro** Japan
71 M9 **Ména** Timor Indonesia
54 D5 **Mena** Ukraine
110 B7 **Mena** Arkansas U.S.A.
80 F3 **Menaḥemya** Israel
99 L3 **Menahga** Minnesota U.S.A.
8 B1 **Menai Brigde** Wales
8 B1 **Menai Str** Wales
85 E5 **Menaka** Mali
101 O4 **Menard** Montana U.S.A.
108 H5 **Menard** Texas U.S.A.
99 S5 **Menasha** Wisconsin U.S.A.
123 L2 **Menaskwagama, L** Quebec Canada
45 M2 **Menate** Italy
69 H14 **Mendanau** *isld* Indonesia
130 G6 **Mendanha** Brazil
69 H12 **Mendarik** Indonesia
70 C6 **Mendawai** Kalimantan
18 H8 **Mende** France
86 G4 **Mendebo Mts** Ethiopia
56 D3 **Mendel'** *R* Russian Federation
32 G10 **Menden** Germany
111 G10 **Mendenhall** Mississippi U.S.A.
116 D7 **Mendenhall, C** Alaska U.S.A.
47 K6 **Menderes** *R* Turkey
55 E5 **Mendesh** Kazakhstan
71 E3 **Mendez-Nuñez** Luzon Philippines
118 H8 **Mendham** Saskatchewan Canada
136 J3 **Mendi** Papua New Guinea
8 D5 **Mendip Hills** England
100 A9 **Mendocino, C** California U.S.A.
135 N4 **Mendocino Seascarp** Pacific Oc
94 B4 **Mendon** Michigan U.S.A.
110 M1 **Mendon** Ohio U.S.A.
139 J4 **Mendooran** New South Wales Australia
102 D5 **Mendota** California U.S.A.
99 R8 **Mendota** Illinois U.S.A.
108 D8 **Mendota** Texas U.S.A.
99 R6 **Mendota, L** Wisconsin U.S.A.
131 C4 **Mendoza** Argentina
131 C5 **Mendoza** *prov* Argentina
128 C5 **Mendoza** Peru
16 B6 **Mendro** *mt* Portugal
20 F5 **Ménéac** France
44 G2 **Menegosa** *mt* Italy
127 J10 **Mene Grande** Venezuela
47 J6 **Menemen** Turkey
22 E2 **Menen** Belgium
21 P6 **Ménestreau** France
21 P7 **Ménétréol-sous-Sancerre** France
20 B5 **Ménez Hom** *mt* France
20 F5 **Menez, Landes du** *reg* France
43 E11 **Menfi** Sicily
70 D1 **Mengalum** *isld* S China Sea
58 G5 **Mengcheng** China
65 D5 **Mengcun** China
41 K1 **Mengen** Germany
32 J10 **Mengeringhausen** Germany
36 E2 **Mengerskirchen** Germany
70 K8 **Menggala** Sumatra
68 E2 **Menghai** China
65 H1 **Mengjiagang** China
67 C5 **Mengjiang** China
65 A5 **Mengjiawan** China
65 B7 **Mengjin** China
70 D6 **Mengkatip** Kalimantan
70 B4 **Mengkiang** *R* Kalimantan
37 N6 **Mengkofen** Germany
70 G6 **Mengkoka, Gunung** *mt* Sulawesi
68 E2 **Mengla** China
68 D1 **Menglian** China
68 E1 **Mengman** China
67 C4 **Mengshan** China
68 E1 **Mengwang** China
65 B7 **Meng Xian** China
65 D7 **Mengyin** China
68 E2 **Mengyuan** China
67 A5 **Mengzi** China
115 N7 **Menihek, Lac** Labrador, Nfld Canada
83 L11 **Menik Ganga** *R* Sri Lanka
21 N3 **Menilles** France
36 B7 **Ménil-sur-Bélvitte** France
Menin *see* **Menen**
139 G4 **Menindee** New South Wales Australia
138 E6 **Meningie** South Australia Australia
21 K7 **Ménitre,la** France
70 E4 **Menjapa, Gt** *mt* Kalimantan
51 M2 **Menkere** Russian Federation
112 B3 **Menlo** Georgia U.S.A.
99 M8 **Menlo** Iowa U.S.A.
107 K2 **Menlo** Kansas U.S.A.
102 B4 **Menlo Pk** California U.S.A.
21 P4 **Mennecy** France
21 O7 **Mennetou-sur-Cher** France
98 J6 **Menno** South Dakota U.S.A.
12 E3 **Mennock P** Scotland
99 T4 **Menominee** *R* Michigan U.S.A.
99 S6 **Menomonee Falls** Wisconsin U.S.A.
99 P5 **Menomonie** Wisconsin U.S.A.
17 K4 **Menorca** *isld* Balearic Is
19 P15 **Mens** France
70 E3 **Mensalong** Kalimantan
47 N10 **Menşari** Turkey
55 G3 **Men'shchikovo** Russian Federation
66 C5 **Men-shih** China
32 G7 **Menslage** Germany
12 E1 **Menstrie** Scotland
28 H6 **Menstrup** Denmark
70 C5 **Mentaja** *R* Kalimantan
45 N5 **Mentana** Italy
70 E2 **Mentapok** Sabah
70 E3 **Mentarang** *R* Kalimantan
116 Q5 **Mentasta Mts** Alaska U.S.A.
69 D13 **Mentawai, Kepulauan** *island group* Indonesia
69 F11 **Mentekab** Malaysia
19 Q13 **Menthon** France
69 G14 **Mentok** Sumatra
44 B4 **Menton** France
94 A5 **Mentone** Indiana U.S.A.
108 D4 **Mentone** Texas U.S.A.
98 K2 **Mentor** Minnesota U.S.A.
94 F5 **Mentor** Ohio U.S.A.
65 C5 **Mentougou** China
70 C5 **Mentubar** *R* Kalimantan
89 D9 **Mentz, L** S Africa
70 C5 **Menukung** Kalimantan
58 E2 **Menza** *R* Mongolia
56 G5 **Menza** *R* Russian Federation
56 G6 **Menza** Russian Federation
43 C11 **Menzel Bourguiba** Tunisia
52 H6 **Menzelinsk** Russian Federation
43 D12 **Menzel Temime** Tunisia
143 D8 **Menzies** W Australia Australia
146 H10 **Menzies,Mt** Antarctica
Menzingen *see* **Kraichtal**
21 N8 **Méobecq** France
9 G5 **Meopham** England
124 G3 **Meoqui** Mexico
118 J5 **Meota** Saskatchewan Canada
25 F3 **Meppel** Netherlands
32 F7 **Meppen** Germany
17 H3 **Mequinenza** Spain
99 T6 **Mequon** Wisconsin U.S.A.
21 O6 **Mer** France
52 F5 **Mera** *R* Russian Federation
47 H9 **Merabéllou, Kólpos** *B* Crete Greece
70 E4 **Merah** Kalimantan
70 K8 **Merak** Java
26 E8 **Meråker** Norway
138 B3 **Meramangye, L** South Australia Australia
110 F3 **Meramec Park** Missouri U.S.A.
Meran *see* **Merano**
41 O4 **Merano** Italy
70 P9 **Merapi, G** *mt* Java
69 E13 **Merapi, Gunung** *mt* Sumatra
123 S6 **Merasheen** Newfoundland Canada
70 D6 **Meratus, Peg** *mts* Kalimantan
136 J3 **Merauke** W Irian
69 F12 **Merbau** Sumatra
138 F5 **Merbein** Victoria Australia
22 G3 **Merbes-le-Château** Belgium
70 P10 **Merbuk** *mt* Indonesia
45 M4 **Mercato Saraceno** Italy
102 D4 **Merced** *R* California U.S.A.
102 D4 **Merced** California U.S.A.
131 B3 **Mercedario, Cerro** *mt* Chile/Arg
131 D4 **Mercedes** Argentina
131 F5 **Mercedes** Buenos Aires Argentina
131 F2 **Mercedes** Corrientes Argentina
131 F4 **Mercedes** Uruguay
109 K9 **Mercedes** Texas U.S.A.
133 C3 **Merceditas** Chile
145 E2 **Mercer** New Zealand
99 N9 **Mercer** Missouri U.S.A.
98 F2 **Mercer** North Dakota U.S.A.
94 G5 **Mercer** Pennsylvania U.S.A.
110 H6 **Mercer** Tennessee U.S.A.
99 Q3 **Mercer** Wisconsin U.S.A.
94 J7 **Mercersburg** Pennsylvania U.S.A.
22 G2 **Merchtem** Belgium
121 O6 **Mercier Dam** Quebec Canada
117 P9 **Mercoal** Alberta Canada
45 R8 **Mercogliano** Italy
103 M1 **Mercur** Utah U.S.A.
48 H5 **Mercurea** Romania
19 Q13 **Mercury** France
109 H4 **Mercury** Texas U.S.A.
145 E2 **Mercury Is** New Zealand
114 H3 **Mercy B** Northwest Territories Canada
115 N5 **Mercy, C** Northwest Territories Canada
20 H3 **Merderet** *R* France
20 F5 **Merdrignac** France
8 D5 **Mere** England
21 P7 **Méreau** France
86 G3 **Mereb** *R* Ethiopia
95 Q3 **Meredith** New Hampshire U.S.A.
133 E8 **Meredith, C** Falkland Is
108 C8 **Meredith, L** Texas U.S.A.
99 Q10 **Meredosia** Illinois U.S.A.
85 E3 **Meredoua** Algeria
54 H7 **Merefa** Ukraine
85 C5 **Mereié, El** *reg* Mauritania/Mali
137 O4 **M̃éré Lava** *isld* Vanuatu
36 E3 **Merenberg** Germany
56 B4 **Meret'** Russian Federation
21 P5 **Méréville** France
9 G5 **Mereworth** England
Merga *see* **Nukheila**
68 D6 **Mergui** Burma
68 C7 **Mergui Arch** Burma
138 F5 **Meribah** South Australia Australia
47 H3 **Meriç** *R* Greece
47 H3 **Meriç** Turkey
118 H7 **Merid** Saskatchewan Canada
125 P7 **Mérida** Mexico
16 C6 **Mérida** Spain
128 D2 **Mérida** Venezuela
95 O5 **Meriden** Connecticut U.S.A.
107 P2 **Meriden** Kansas U.S.A.
95 P3 **Meriden** New Hampshire U.S.A.
98 B8 **Meriden** Wyoming U.S.A.
102 C2 **Meridian** California U.S.A.
100 J6 **Meridian** Idaho U.S.A.
111 H9 **Meridian** Mississippi U.S.A.
95 L3 **Meridian** New York U.S.A.
109 K4 **Meridian** Texas U.S.A.
137 O4 **M̃érig** *isld* Vanuatu
21 M8 **Merigny** France
29 J10 **Merikarvia** Finland
139 J6 **Merimbula** New South Wales Australia
141 J4 **Merinda** Queensland Australia
19 O17 **Mérindol** France
37 L7 **Mering** Germany
138 F5 **Meringur** Victoria Australia
138 F6 **Merino** Victoria Australia
106 G1 **Merino** Colorado U.S.A.
Merioneth *co see* **Gwynedd**
70 C3 **Merit** Sarawak
141 J7 **Merivale** *R* Queensland Australia
57 G3 **Merke** Kazakhstan
22 D2 **Merkem** Belgium
37 K5 **Merkendorf** Germany
26 H5 **Merkenes** Sweden
31 P1 **Merkine** Lithuania
37 O3 **Merklín** Czechoslovakia
37 P4 **Merklín** Czechoslovakia
22 G1 **Merksem** Belgium
22 H1 **Merksplas** Belgium
55 E2 **Merkushino** Tyumenskaya obl Russian Federation
36 C3 **Merl** Germany
45 K1 **Merlara** Italy
21 L4 **Merlerault,le** France
22 B3 **Merlimont** France
120 H10 **Merlin** Ontario Canada
100 B7 **Merlin** Oregon U.S.A.
141 F2 **Merluna** Queensland Australia
69 F13 **Merlung** Sumatra
142 C3 **Mermaid Reef** Indian Oc
111 C12 **Mermentau** *R* Louisiana U.S.A.
28 J6 **Mern** Denmark
98 G8 **Merna** Nebraska U.S.A.
101 P7 **Merna** Wyoming U.S.A.
69 A9 **Meroe** *isld* Nicobar Is
143 D8 **Merolia** W Australia Australia
80 E2 **Meron** Israel
86 F2 **Merowe** Sudan
143 C9 **Merredin** W Australia Australia
110 B2 **Merriam** Kansas U.S.A.
15 D5 **Merrick Mt** Scotland
121 P8 **Merrickville** Ontario Canada
98 H3 **Merricourt** North Dakota U.S.A.
98 K7 **Merrill** Iowa U.S.A.
94 C3 **Merrill** Michigan U.S.A.
111 H11 **Merrill** Mississippi U.S.A.
100 D7 **Merrill** Oregon U.S.A.
99 R4 **Merrill** Wisconsin U.S.A.
99 Q5 **Merrillan** Wisconsin U.S.A.
99 R6 **Merrimac** Wisconsin U.S.A.
95 Q3 **Merrimack** *R* New Hamps/Mass U.S.A.
98 E7 **Merriman** Nebraska U.S.A.
117 N10 **Merritt** British Columbia Canada
98 F7 **Merritt Res** Nebraska U.S.A.
139 K4 **Merriwa** New South Wales Australia
111 E9 **Mer Rouge** Louisiana U.S.A.
9 F5 **Merrow** England
139 J4 **Merrygoen** New South Wales Australia
109 O5 **Merryville** Louisiana U.S.A.
86 H3 **Mersa Fatma** Ethiopia
22 L4 **Mersch** Luxembourg
9 G4 **Mersea I** England
33 P10 **Merseburg** Germany
17 G9 **Mers el Kébir** Algeria
8 D1 **Mersey, R** England
13 F6 **Merseyside** *co* England
Mersin *see* **Içel**
79 E2 **Mersin** Turkey
69 F11 **Mersing** Malaysia
21 N1 **Mers-les-Bains** France
52 B6 **Mērsrags** Latvia
21 O8 **Mers-sur-Indre** France
74 F5 **Merta** India
8 C4 **Merthyr Tydfil** Wales
37 K6 **Mertingen** Germany
16 B7 **Mértola** Portugal
8 B6 **Merton** England
143 D8 **Mertondale** W Australia Australia
146 D14 **Mertz Glacier** Antarctica
108 G4 **Mertzon** Texas U.S.A.
21 P3 **Méru** France
88 F1 **Meru** Kenya
88 F3 **Meru** *mt* Tanzania
74 C8 **Merui** Pakistan
70 G4 **Merunu** Sulawesi
70 E2 **Merutai** Sabah
22 D2 **Merville** France
118 J5 **Mervin** Saskatchewan Canada
100 C4 **Merwin, L** Washington U.S.A.
18 H4 **Méry-sur-Seine** France
78 E1 **Merzifon** Turkey
36 B5 **Merzig** Germany
146 D5 **Merz Peninsula** *pen* Antarctica
71 B2 **Mesa** Halmahera Indonesia
17 F3 **Mesa** *R* Spain
103 N8 **Mesa** Arizona U.S.A.
100 J5 **Mesa** Idaho U.S.A.
106 F8 **Mesa** New Mexico U.S.A.
99 N2 **Mesabi Ra** *mts* Minnesota U.S.A.
43 H8 **Mesagne** Italy
117 Q3 **Mesa L** Northwest Territories Canada
116 K6 **Mesa Mt** Alaska U.S.A.
47 Q14 **Mesanagrós** Rhodes Greece
69 G12 **Mesanak** *isld* Indonesia
20 H7 **Mésanger** France
70 D2 **Mesapo** Sabah
46 G10 **Mesarás, Kólpos** *B* Crete Greece
106 B4 **Mesa Verde Nat. Park** Colorado U.S.A.
103 O10 **Mescal** Arizona U.S.A.
106 E8 **Mescalero** New Mexico U.S.A.
32 H10 **Meschede** Germany
26 J7 **Meselefors** Sweden
68 C3 **Mesenan** Burma
48 H3 **Meseşului, Muntii** *mts* Romania
128 F2 **Meseta del Cerro Jaua** *mts* Venezuela
52 G6 **Mesha** *R* Russian Federation
54 L1 **Meshcherskaya Nizina** *lowland* Russian Federation
54 G2 **Meshchovsk** Russian Federation
52 H3 **Meshchura** Russian Federation
Meshed *see* **Mashhad**
57 B4 **Meshekli** Uzbekistan
116 H8 **Meshik** Alaska U.S.A.
86 E4 **Meshra er Req** Sudan
94 B2 **Mesick** Michigan U.S.A.
117 L7 **Mesilinka** *R* British Columbia Canada
106 D9 **Mesilla** New Mexico U.S.A.
80 C6 **Mesillat Ẕiyyon** Israel
28 F5 **Mesinge** Denmark
21 J6 **Meslay-du-Maine** France
27 E10 **Mesna** *L* Norway
21 N2 **Mesnières-en-Béthune** France
21 J4 **Mesnil-Auzouf,le** France
21 P2 **Mesnil-St.Firmin,le** France
20 H3 **Mesnil-Vigot,le** France
21 K4 **Mesnil-Villement,le** France
41 K5 **Mesocco** Switzerland
45 M2 **Mésola** Italy
41 K5 **Mesolcina, Valle** Switzerland
46 E6 **Mesolóngion** Greece
78 J4 **Mesopotamia** Iraq
20 F7 **Mesquer** France
130 G6 **Mesquita** Brazil
103 K5 **Mesquite** Nevada U.S.A.
106 D9 **Mesquite** New Mexico U.S.A.
109 O9 **Mesquite** Texas U.S.A.
103 J6 **Mesquite L** California U.S.A.
20 G6 **Messac** France
Messalo *R see* **Mualo** *R*
87 G8 **Messalo** *R* Mozambique
22 K4 **Messancy** Belgium
85 F2 **Messaoud, Hassi** Algeria
33 P7 **Messdorf** Germany
21 J4 **Messei** France
Messick *see* **Poquoson**
133 C7 **Messie, Can** *str* Chile
89 F4 **Messina** S Africa
43 G10 **Messina** Sicily
22 J4 **Messincourt** France
121 O6 **Messines** Quebec Canada
13 H6 **Messingham** England
46 E7 **Messíni** Greece
46 E8 **Messiniakós Kólpos** *B* Greece
41 K2 **Messkirch** Germany
47 O12 **Messongi** Greece
Mesta *R see* **Néstos** *R*
46 F3 **Mesta** *R* Bulgaria
16 E6 **Mestanza** Spain
33 P5 **Mestlin** Germany
42 G3 **Mesto, N** Slovenia
37 P4 **Město-Touškov** Czechoslovakia
42 E3 **Mestre** Italy
45 L1 **Mestrino** Italy
128 D3 **Meta** *div* Colombia
45 Q8 **Meta** Italy
110 D3 **Meta** Missouri U.S.A.
128 E2 **Meta** *R* Venezuela/Colombia
115 N5 **Meta Incognita Pen** Northwest Territories Canada
111 F11 **Metairie** Louisiana U.S.A.
111 H12 **Metairie** New Orleans, Louisiana U.S.A.
120 C2 **Meta L** Ontario Canada
48 H4 **Metalici, Muntii** *mts* Romania
117 P11 **Metaline Falls** Washington U.S.A.
42 D5 **Metallifere, Colline** *hills* Italy
99 R9 **Metamora** Illinois U.S.A.
133 E3 **Metán** Argentina
70 D6 **Metangai** Kalimantan
87 F8 **Metangula** Mozambique
43 H8 **Metaponto** Italy
80 C8 **Metar** Israel
42 E5 **Metauro** *R* Italy
80 E3 **Metav** Israel
122 F9 **Meteghan** Nova Scotia Canada
32 F8 **Metelen** Germany
86 G3 **Metema** Ethiopia
141 J6 **Meteor** *R* Queensland Australia
90 G14 **Meteor Depth** S Atlantic Oc

202 Meteor Seamount — Misumi

90 K14 Meteor Seamount S Atlantic Oc
22 D2 Méteren France
46 F7 Méthana Greece
119 S7 Methley Manitoba Canada
46 E8 Methóni Greece
100 E1 Methow R Washington U.S.A.
95 Q4 Methuen Massachusetts U.S.A.
142 E3 Methuen,Mt W Australia Australia
144 C5 Methven New Zealand
12 E1 Methven Scotland
143 D7 Methwin,Mt W Australia Australia
9 G2 Methwold England
119 N1 Metionga L Ontario Canada
118 G6 Metiskow Alberta Canada
122 E5 Metis L Quebec Canada
42 H5 Metković Croatia
117 H8 Metlakatla Alaska U.S.A.
85 F2 Metlaoui Tunisia
38 K8 Metnitz Austria
46 D2 Metohija mts Serbia Yugoslavia
46 D2 Metohija Serbia Yugoslavia
100 D5 Metolius Oregon U.S.A.
46 E1 Metovnica Serbia Yugoslavia
70 K8 Metro Sumatra
110 H4 Metropolis Illinois U.S.A.
29 N6 Metsäkylä Finland
25 F2 Metslawier Netherlands
46 E5 Métsovon Greece
37 O6 Metten Germany
36 B4 Mettendorf Germany
112 E5 Metter Georgia U.S.A.
22 H3 Mettet Belgium
32 G8 Mettingen Germany
36 B4 Mettlach Germany
32 E10 Mettmann Germany
36 B4 Mettnich Germany
21 M7 Mettray France
76 C5 Mettuppalaiyam India
76 C5 Mettur India
88 H7 Metudo isld Mozambique
79 F5 Metulla Israel
19 K3 Metz France
40 F1 Metzeral France
22 L5 Metzervisse France
36 G6 Metzingen Germany
20 F5 Meu R France
88 G9 Meucate Mozambique
36 D3 Meudt Germany
69 C10 Meulaboh Sumatra
21 O3 Meulan France
22 E2 Meulebeke Belgium
21 L4 Meulles France
21 O6 Meung-sur-Loire France
69 C10 Meureudu Sumatra
40 A4 Meursault France
19 K4 Meurthe R France
36 B6 Meurthe et Moselle dept France
22 H3 Meuse R Belgium
19 J3 Meuse R France
19 J4 Meuse dept France
37 N1 Meuselwitz Germany
21 O7 Meusnes France
8 B7 Mevagissey England
80 D6 Meva Horon Jordan
80 C6 Meva Modiin Jordan
13 G6 Mexborough England
109 L4 Mexia Texas U.S.A.
129 J3 Mexiana isld Brazil
103 J9 Mexicali Mexico
103 P4 Mexican Hat Utah U.S.A.
124 F3 Mexicanos, Lago de los Mexico
103 P5 Mexican Water Arizona U.S.A.
124 G6 Mexico rep N America
94 A6 Mexico Indiana U.S.A.
95 R2 Mexico Maine U.S.A.
110 E2 Mexico Missouri U.S.A.
95 L3 Mexico New York U.S.A.
125 K8 Mexico City Mexico
125 M6 Mexico, G. of Mexico
40 B6 Meximieux France
71 E3 Meycawayan Luzon Philippines
77 D5 Meydān-e-Gel salt lake Iran
33 Q6 Meyenburg Germany
117 G8 Meyers Chuck Alaska U.S.A.
94 H7 Meyersdale Pennsylvania U.S.A.
18 G7 Meymac France
77 J2 Meymaneh Afghanistan
77 B3 Meymeh Iran
118 L8 Meyronne Saskatchewan Canada
18 H8 Meyrueis France
18 G7 Meyssac France
80 E8 Mezada Israel
80 F2 Mezar Syria
125 N9 Mezcalapa R Mexico
46 F1 Mezdra Bulgaria
18 H9 Mèze France
19 Q17 Mézel France
52 G3 Mezen' R Russian Federation
52 F2 Mezen' Arkhangel'skaya obl Russian Federation
52 F2 Mezenskaya Guba B Russian Federation
80 D4 Mezer Israel
54 C1 Mezha R Russian Federation
52 G3 Mezhdurechensk Russian Federation
56 C4 Mezhdurechensk Russian Federation
55 E2 Mezhdurechenskiy Russian Federation
31 N1 Mezhdurech'ye Russian Federation
50 D1 Mezhdusharskiy Ostrov isld Russian Federation
48 H2 Mezhgor'ye Ukraine
42 F2 Mežica Slovenia
21 K3 Mézidon-Canon France
21 N8 Mézières-en-Brenne France
21 O4 Mézières-sur-Seine France
31 H6 Mezimostí Czechoslovakia
18 F8 Mézin France
54 M1 Mezinovskiy Russian Federation
48 G4 Mezőberény Hungary
48 F3 Mezőcsát Hungary
48 F4 Mezőhegyes Hungary
48 F4 Mezőkovacsháza Hungary
48 F3 Mezőkövesd Hungary
18 E8 Mézos France
48 F3 Mezőtúr Hungary
124 G6 Mezquital R Mexico
124 G6 Mezquital Mexico
124 H6 Mezquitic Mexico
41 N5 Mezzana Italy
45 M3 Mezzano Italy
41 O4 Mezzaselva Italy
45 M2 Mezzogoro Italy
41 K5 Mezzola, Lago di Italy
41 L5 Mezzoldo Italy
42 D2 Mezzolombardo Italy
89 G7 Mfolozi R S Africa
52 D5 Mga Russian Federation
74 F10 Mhasvad India
89 G6 Mhlume Swaziland
125 L9 Miahuatián de Porfirio Diaz Mexico
16 D5 Miajadas Spain
119 T9 Miami Manitoba Canada
103 O8 Miami Arizona U.S.A.
113 G12 Miami Florida U.S.A.
94 C7 Miami R Ohio U.S.A.
107 Q5 Miami Oklahoma U.S.A.
108 D8 Miami Texas U.S.A.
113 G12 Miami Beach Florida U.S.A.
113 G11 Miami Canal Florida U.S.A.
94 C6 Miami, Great R Ohio U.S.A.
94 C7 Miami, Little R Ohio U.S.A.
94 C7 Miamisburg Ohio U.S.A.
113 G12 Miami Shores Florida U.S.A.
113 G12 Miami Springs Florida U.S.A.
65 B7 Mianchi China
78 L3 Miandowab Iran
87 H11 Miandrivazo Madagascar
77 A1 Mīāneh Iran
67 E4 Mian Shui R China
58 E5 Mian Xian China
67 D1 Mianyang China
67 A1 Mianzhu China
65 E6 Miao Dao isld China
65 E5 Miaodao Qundao islds China
65 H3 Miaoling China
67 B3 Miao Ling mt ra China
67 C4 Miaoping China
87 H11 Miarinarivo Madagascar
55 D3 Miass R Russian Federation
31 K1 Miastko Poland
117 O9 Mica Dam British Colombia Canada
103 O9 Mica Mt Arizona U.S.A.
58 E5 Micang Shan mt ra China
113 E8 Micanopy Florida U.S.A.
128 C3 Micay Colombia
113 C7 Miccosukee Florida U.S.A.
52 H3 Michaichmon' Russian Federation
48 G2 Michal'any Czechoslovakia
48 G2 Michalovce Czechoslovakia
118 C9 Michel British Columbia Canada
118 H3 Michel Saskatchewan Canada
38 N5 Michelbach Austria
36 E3 Michelbach Germany
116 Q2 Michelson, Mt Alaska U.S.A.
36 G4 Michelstadt Germany
33 S8 Michendorf Germany
127 K5 Miches Dominican Rep
118 E7 Michichi Alberta Canada
112 J1 Michie, L North Carolina U.S.A.
99 S3 Michigamme Michigan U.S.A.
99 S3 Michigamme L Michigan U.S.A.
99 S3 Michigamme Res Michigan U.S.A.
94 A1 Michigan state U.S.A.
98 H1 Michigan North Dakota U.S.A.
94 C4 Michigan Center Michigan U.S.A.
99 U8 Michigan City Indiana U.S.A.
94 A4 Michigan, L U.S.A.
110 K1 Michigantown Indiana U.S.A.
120 F5 Michipicoten Ontario Canada
31 N4 Michów Poland
47 J2 Michurin Bulgaria
54 M4 Michurinsk Russian Federation
13 F4 Mickle Fell mt England
9 E3 Mickleton England
127 O8 Micoud St Lucia
134 F7 Micronesia Pacific Oc
69 H11 Midai isld Indonesia
119 O9 Midale Saskatchewan Canada
100 J8 Midas Nevada U.S.A.
90 E6 Mid-Atlantic Ridge Atlantic Oc
12 E2 Mid Calder Scotland
25 A6 Middelburg Netherlands
87 D12 Middelburg S Africa
89 D8 Middelburg Cape Prov S Africa
89 F5 Middelburg Transvaal S Africa
25 B5 Middelharnis Netherlands
22 D1 Middelkerke Belgium
89 B9 Middel Roggeveld reg S Africa
87 E10 Middelwit S Africa
25 C3 Middenbeemster Netherlands
90 A7 Middle America Trench Pacific Oc
68 A6 Middle Andaman isld Andaman Is
138 D5 Middleback, Mt South Australia Australia
95 R5 Middleboro Massachusetts U.S.A.
94 G7 Middlebourne West Virginia U.S.A.
118 F1 Middlebro Manitoba Canada
95 K6 Middleburg Pennsylvania U.S.A.
94 K8 Middleburg Virginia U.S.A.
95 N4 Middleburgh New York U.S.A.
94 B5 Middlebury Indiana U.S.A.
95 O2 Middlebury Vermont U.S.A.
108 G4 Middle Concho R Texas U.S.A.
28 D5 Middlefart Denmark
144 A6 Middle Fiord New Zealand
13 G5 Middleham England
143 E10 Middle I W Australia Australia
69 C8 Middle I Thailand
90 B16 Middle I Tristan da Cunha
94 D1 Middle I Michigan U.S.A.
100 F8 Middle L Nevada U.S.A.
119 M6 Middle Lake Saskatchewan Canada
98 G8 Middle Loup R Nebraska U.S.A.
144 C6 Middlemarch New Zealand
8 D6 Middlemarsh England
94 J3 Middleport New York U.S.A.
94 E8 Middleport Ohio U.S.A.
83 M9 Middle Pt Christmas I Indian Oc
94 C6 Middle Pt Ohio U.S.A.
98 K1 Middle R Minnesota U.S.A.
123 R5 Middle Rge Newfoundland Canada
95 L7 Middle River Maryland U.S.A.
118 G8 Middle Sand Hills, The Alberta Canada
94 D10 Middlesboro Kentucky U.S.A.
13 G4 Middlesbrough England
125 P9 Middlesex Belize
95 K4 Middlesex New York U.S.A.
141 F5 Middleton Queensland Australia
122 G9 Middleton Nova Scotia Canada
13 F5 Middleton Cumbria England
13 F6 Middleton Greater Manchester England
13 H6 Middleton Humberside England
100 J6 Middleton Idaho U.S.A.
94 C3 Middleton Michigan U.S.A.
110 H6 Middleton Tennessee U.S.A.
99 R6 Middleton Wisconsin U.S.A.
116 P7 Middleton I Alaska U.S.A.
13 F4 Middleton in Teesdale England
8 C2 Middletown England
95 P5 Middletown Connecticut U.S.A.
95 M7 Middletown Delaware U.S.A.
94 B6 Middletown Indiana U.S.A.
94 K7 Middletown Maryland U.S.A.
95 N5 Middletown New York U.S.A.
110 M2 Middletown Ohio U.S.A.
95 L6 Middletown Pennsylvania U.S.A.
8 D2 Middletown Wales
94 B4 Middleville Michigan U.S.A.
95 N3 Middleville New York U.S.A.
108 B8 Middle Water Texas U.S.A.
8 D1 Middlewich England
122 H9 Middlewood Nova Scotia Canada
85 D2 Midelt Morocco
109 L7 Midfield Texas U.S.A.
8 C4 Mid Glamorgan co Wales
145 E3 Midhirst New Zealand
121 L8 Midhurst Ontario Canada
9 F6 Midhurst England
18 G9 Midi, Canal du France
18 E10 Midi d'Ossau, Pic du mt France
18 F10 Midi du Bigorre, Pic du mt France
143 B9 Midland W Australia Australia
110 B6 Midland Arkansas U.S.A.
103 K8 Midland California U.S.A.
94 J7 Midland Maryland U.S.A.
94 C3 Midland Michigan U.S.A.
98 E5 Midland South Dakota U.S.A.
108 E4 Midland Texas U.S.A.
111 L10 Midland City Alabama U.S.A.
89 F2 Midlands prov Zimbabwe
14 C5 Midleton Ireland
Midlothian co see Lothian and Borders regions
109 K3 Midlothian Texas U.S.A.
94 K9 Midlothian Virginia U.S.A.
32 J5 Midlum Germany
111 F8 Midnight Mississippi U.S.A.
87 H12 Midongy Atsimo Madagascar
60 D13 Midori-kawa R Japan
18 E9 Midouze R France
134 G5 Mid-Pacific Mountains Pacific Oc
71 G7 Midsayap Philippines
100 J5 Midvale Idaho U.S.A.
101 O9 Midvale Utah U.S.A.
112 E5 Midville Georgia U.S.A.
117 O11 Midway British Columbia Canada
111 L9 Midway Alabama U.S.A.
112 F6 Midway Georgia U.S.A.
94 C8 Midway Kentucky U.S.A.
109 M4 Midway Texas U.S.A.
135 U2 Midway Is atoll Hawaiian Is
116 O1 Midway Is Alaska U.S.A.
122 E1 Midway L Quebec Canada
143 E6 Midway Well W Australia Australia
101 T6 Midwest Wyoming U.S.A.
107 N6 Midwest City Oklahoma U.S.A.
25 F2 Midwolde Netherlands
78 H3 Midyat Turkey
15 G1 Mid Yell Scotland
46 F1 Midžor mt Serbia Yugoslavia
61 K11 Mie prefect Japan
31 M5 Miechów Poland
40 F3 Miécourt Switzerland
31 J3 Międzychód Poland
31 K5 Międzylesie Poland
31 O4 Międzyrzec Poland
31 J3 Międzyrzecz Poland
31 K4 Miejska Gorka Poland
29 L5 Miekojärvi L Finland
18 F9 Miélan France
31 N5 Mielec Poland
41 N3 Mieminger Kette mt Austria
27 G15 Mien L Sweden
139 H8 Miena Tasmania Australia
67 G4 Mien-hua Hsü isld Taiwan
109 H9 Mier Mexico
106 D7 Miera New Mexico U.S.A.
48 K4 Miercurea-Ciuc Romania
16 D1 Mieres Spain
26 N2 Mieron Norway
38 E6 Miesbach Germany
86 H4 Mī 'ēso Ethiopia
33 O8 Mieste Germany
31 H3 Mieszkowice Poland
94 K6 Mifflin Pennsylvania U.S.A.
95 K6 Mifflinburg Pennsylvania U.S.A.
95 K6 Mifflintown Pennsylvania U.S.A.
83 L9 Migaswewa Sri Lanka
80 F2 Migdal Israel
80 D3 Migdal Ha'Émeq Israel
80 D7 Migdal Oz Jordan
80 D7 Migdal'Oz Jordan
77 F4 Mighān Iran
45 L2 Migliarino Italy
21 L8 Mignaloux Beauvoir France
45 P7 Mignano Italy
44 G2 Mignano, L. di Italy
21 N8 Migné Indre France
21 L8 Migné-Auxances Vienne France
44 L5 Mignone R Italy
122 F5 Miguasha-Ouest Quebec Canada
124 H5 Miguel Auza Mexico
88 H2 Migwani Kenya
68 B3 Migyaunye Burma
48 K3 Mihăileni Romania
60 G11 Mihara Japan
61 N11 Mihara-yama vol Japan
61 O8 Miharu Japan
37 J1 Mihla Germany
60 G10 Miho wan B Japan
40 D5 Mijoux France
119 P7 Mikado Saskatchewan Canada
94 D2 Mikado Michigan U.S.A.
60 P2 Mikasa Japan
61 K9 Mikawa Japan
61 L11 Mikawa-wan B Japan
Mikha Tskhakaya see Senaki
54 L2 Mikhaylov Russian Federation
46 F1 Mikhaylovgrad Bulgaria
146 J12 Mikhaylov I Antarctica
48 L1 Mikhaylovka Ukraine
47 H2 Mikhaylovo Bulgaria
55 C3 Mikhaylovsk Russian Federation
55 G4 Mikhaylovskiy Altayskiy Kray Russian Federation
80 C4 Mikhmoret Israel
79 E9 Mikhrot Timna Israel
88 H7 Mikindani Tanzania
100 E4 Mikkalo Oregon U.S.A.
29 N10 Mikkeli Finland
117 Q7 Mikkwa R Alberta Canada
31 N2 Mikołajki Poland
31 L5 Mikołow Poland
46 G1 Mikre Bulgaria
46 E4 Mikrí Préspa L Greece
47 H3 Mikrón Dhérion Greece
52 G1 Mikulkin, Mys C Russian Federation
48 D2 Mikulov Czechoslovakia
87 G7 Mikumi Tanzania
88 F5 Mikumi Nat. Park Tanzania
61 N8 Mikuni sammyaku mts Japan
61 N12 Mikura-jima isld Japan
99 N4 Milaca Minnesota U.S.A.
73 L7 Miladunmadulu Atoll Maldives
130 H9 Milagres Brazil
Milan see Milano
122 A8 Milan Quebec Canada
94 B7 Milan Indiana U.S.A.
107 N4 Milan Kansas U.S.A.
94 D4 Milan Michigan U.S.A.
99 L4 Milan Minnesota U.S.A.
99 N9 Milan Missouri U.S.A.
94 E5 Milan Ohio U.S.A.
110 H6 Milan Tennessee U.S.A.
100 H2 Milan Washington U.S.A.
138 E6 Milang South Australia Australia
88 E10 Milange Mozambique
39 Milano conurbation Italy
109 L5 Milano Texas U.S.A.
17 G4 Milares R Spain
47 J7 Milâs Turkey
43 G10 Milazzo Sicily
98 K4 Milbank South Dakota U.S.A.
95 U2 Milbridge Maine U.S.A.
94 A4 Milburg Michigan U.S.A.
144 B7 Milburn New Zealand
9 G3 Mildenhall England
120 J8 Mildmay Ontario Canada
118 K5 Mildred Saskatchewan Canada
98 A3 Mildred Montana U.S.A.
95 L5 Mildred Pennsylvania U.S.A.
117 R7 Mildred Lake Alberta Canada
138 F5 Mildura Victoria Australia
67 A4 Mile China
46 F5 Miléai Greece
127 J2 Mile Gully Jamaica
141 K7 Miles Queensland Australia
100 G2 Miles Washington U.S.A.
101 U3 Miles City Montana U.S.A.
21 L5 Milesse,la France
119 N9 Milestone Saskatchewan Canada
43 G10 Mileto Italy
45 Q7 Miletto, M mt Italy
143 B7 Mileura W Australia Australia
31 H6 Milevsko Czechoslovakia
9 F5 Milford Surrey England
102 D1 Milford California U.S.A.
95 O5 Milford Connecticut U.S.A.
95 M8 Milford Delaware U.S.A.
99 T9 Milford Illinois U.S.A.
94 B5 Milford Indiana U.S.A.
99 L6 Milford Iowa U.S.A.
107 O2 Milford Kansas U.S.A.
95 T2 Milford Maine U.S.A.
95 Q4 Milford Massachusetts U.S.A.
94 D4 Milford Michigan U.S.A.
98 J9 Milford Nebraska U.S.A.
95 Q4 Milford New Hampshire U.S.A.
95 N4 Milford New York U.S.A.
109 L3 Milford Texas U.S.A.
103 L3 Milford Utah U.S.A.
94 K8 Milford Virginia U.S.A.
94 D6 Milford Center Ohio U.S.A.
8 A4 Milford Haven Wales
9 E6 Milford on Sea England
144 A6 Milford Sound New Zealand
140 F4 Milgarra Queensland Australia
143 C8 Milgoo, Mt W Australia Australia
143 C7 Milgun W Australia Australia
85 E1 Miliana Algeria
43 C12 Miliane R Tunisia
31 K4 Milicz Poland
140 B1 Milikapiti N Terr Australia
143 B9 Miling W Australia Australia
140 C1 Milingimbi N Terr Australia
20 A5 Milizac France
51 P3 Milkovo Russian Federation
118 F9 Milk R Alberta/Montana Canada/U.S.A.
127 K3 Milk River Bath Jamaica
86 E2 Milk, Wadi el watercourse Sudan
25 E5 Mill Netherlands
141 H4 Millaa Millaa Queensland Australia
21 O7 Millançay France
99 O9 Millard Missouri U.S.A.
141 H5 Millaroo Queensland Australia
98 H3 Millarton North Dakota U.S.A.
94 H9 Millboro Virginia U.S.A.
121 M8 Millbrook Ontario Canada
95 O5 Millbrook New York U.S.A.
102 F1 Mill City Nevada U.S.A.
100 C5 Mill City Oregon U.S.A.
102 C1 Mill Creek California U.S.A.
109 L1 Mill Creek Oklahoma U.S.A.
94 H8 Mill Creek West Virginia U.S.A.
112 D4 Milledgeville Georgia U.S.A.
99 R8 Milledgeville Illinois U.S.A.
101 O2 Millegan Montana U.S.A.
99 N3 Mille Lacs L Minnesota U.S.A.
119 N2 Mille Lacs, Lac des Ontario Canada
112 F5 Millen Georgia U.S.A.
138 D3 Miller R South Australia Australia
110 C4 Miller Missouri U.S.A.
98 G9 Miller Nebraska U.S.A.
98 H5 Miller South Dakota U.S.A.
124 B3 Miller, Desembarcadero de Mexico
116 Q6 Miller, Mt Alaska U.S.A.
54 M8 Millerovo Russian Federation
103 O10 Miller Pk Arizona U.S.A.
102 G3 Millers Nevada U.S.A.
94 B5 Millersburg Indiana U.S.A.
110 M3 Millersburg Kentucky U.S.A.
94 D1 Millersburg Michigan U.S.A.
94 F6 Millersburg Ohio U.S.A.
95 L6 Millersburg Pennsylvania U.S.A.
138 D4 Millers Creek South Australia Australia
95 P4 Millers Falls Massachusetts U.S.A.
111 J9 Millers Ferry Alabama U.S.A.
144 B6 Miller's Flat New Zealand
12 D2 Millerston Scotland
94 H6 Millerstown Pennsylvania U.S.A.
108 H4 Millersview Texas U.S.A.
122 G7 Millerton New Brunswick Canada
144 C4 Millerton New Zealand
95 O5 Millerton New York U.S.A.
102 E4 Millerton L California U.S.A.
123 Q5 Millertown Newfoundland Canada
123 Q4 Millertown Junct Newfoundland Canada
118 D5 Millet Alberta Canada
94 E9 Millet West Virginia U.S.A.
102 G2 Millett Nevada U.S.A.
109 H7 Millett Texas U.S.A.
18 G7 Millevaches, Plateau de France
14 D1 Millford Ireland
94 K5 Mill Hall Pennsylvania U.S.A.
146 H13 Mill I Antarctica
115 M5 Mill I Northwest Territories Canada
100 E6 Millican Oregon U.S.A.
109 L5 Millican Texas U.S.A.
138 F6 Millicent South Australia Australia
118 F8 Millicent Alberta Canada
143 D8 Millicent,Mt W Australia Australia
111 K11 Milligan Florida U.S.A.
98 J9 Milligan Nebraska U.S.A.
106 F1 Milliken Colorado U.S.A.
95 M7 Millington Maryland U.S.A.
94 D3 Millington Michigan U.S.A.
110 G6 Millington Tennessee U.S.A.
95 S8 Millinocket Maine U.S.A.
141 K8 Millmerran Queensland Australia
13 E5 Millom England
12 D2 Millport Scotland
111 H8 Millport Alabama U.S.A.
95 L4 Millport New York U.S.A.
111 H10 Millry Alabama U.S.A.
141 G5 Mills R Queensland Australia
106 F5 Mills New Mexico U.S.A.
101 T7 Mills Wyoming U.S.A.
109 J3 Millsap Texas U.S.A.
102 B2 Millsaps California U.S.A.
95 M8 Millsboro Delaware U.S.A.
94 G7 Millsboro Pennsylvania U.S.A.
117 O5 Mills L Northwest Territories Canada
99 Q5 Millston Wisconsin U.S.A.
142 B5 Millstream W Australia Australia
14 B4 Millstreet Ireland
8 C2 Milltir Cerig mt Wales
122 E8 Milltown New Brunswick Canada
123 R6 Milltown Newfoundland Canada
14 B4 Milltown Malbay Ireland
141 F4 Millungera Queensland Australia
102 B4 Mill Valley California U.S.A.
122 H9 Mill Village Nova Scotia Canada
122 E7 Millville New Brunswick Canada
94 C7 Millville Ohio U.S.A.
95 L5 Millville Pennsylvania U.S.A.
109 N2 Millwood Res Arkansas U.S.A.
21 P5 Milly-la-Forêt France
143 B7 Milly Milly W Australia Australia
21 P3 Milly-sur Thérain France
33 T6 Milmersdorf Germany
13 E1 Milnathort Scotland
115 R3 Milne Land Greenland
112 C4 Milner Georgia U.S.A.
101 L7 Milner Idaho U.S.A.
118 E1 Milner Ridge Manitoba Canada
120 K6 Milnet Ontario Canada
12 D2 Milngavie Scotland
98 J3 Milnor North Dakota U.S.A.
13 F5 Milnthorpe England
118 E8 Milo Alberta Canada
88 E6 Milo Tanzania
99 N8 Milo Iowa U.S.A.
95 S1 Milo Maine U.S.A.
100 B7 Milo Oregon U.S.A.
135 U6 Milolii Hawaiian Is
31 M2 Miłomłyn Poland
46 G8 Mílos isld Greece
31 K3 Miłosław Poland
33 Q7 Milow Germany
31 L6 Milówka Poland
138 F3 Milparinka New South Wales Australia
102 C4 Milpitas California U.S.A.
110 L2 Milroy Indiana U.S.A.
94 K6 Milroy Pennsylvania U.S.A.
37 O5 Miltach Germany
36 G4 Miltenberg Germany
139 K6 Milton New South Wales Australia
122 H9 Milton Nova Scotia Canada
144 B7 Milton New Zealand
12 D2 Milton Scotland
95 M8 Milton Delaware U.S.A.
111 J11 Milton Florida U.S.A.
99 Q10 Milton Illinois U.S.A.
110 D1 Milton Iowa U.S.A.
107 N4 Milton Kansas U.S.A.
95 R3 Milton Maine U.S.A.
94 H10 Milton North Carolina U.S.A.
98 J1 Milton North Dakota U.S.A.
95 L5 Milton Pennsylvania U.S.A.
95 O2 Milton Vermont U.S.A.
94 E8 Milton West Virginia U.S.A.
99 S7 Milton Wisconsin U.S.A.
8 B6 Milton Abbot England
139 J3 Milton Downs New South Wales Australia
100 G4 Milton Freewater Oregon U.S.A.
12 D3 Miltonish Scotland
9 F3 Milton Keynes England
107 N2 Miltonvale Kansas U.S.A.
86 C3 Miltou Chad
33 S4 Miltzow Germany
67 D2 Miluo China
8 C5 Milverton England
99 T6 Milwaukee Wisconsin U.S.A.
127 K5 Milwaukee Depth Caribbean
60 E13 Mimitsu Japan
18 E8 Mimizan France
60 O4 Mimmaya Japan
31 H5 Mimoň Czechoslovakia
86 B6 Mimongo Gabon
60 H10 Mimuro yama mt Japan
102 A2 Mina California U.S.A.
102 F3 Mina Nevada U.S.A.
77 A5 Mina' al Ahmadi Iran
77 E6 Mīnāb Iran
60 J12 Minabe Japan
124 F3 Miñaca Mexico
119 T4 Minago R Manitoba Canada
71 H4 Minahassa Peninsula Sulawesi Indonesia
77 D7 Mina Jebel Ali U.A.E.
79 H2 Mīnakh Syria
118 H1 Minaki Ontario Canada
100 H4 Minam Oregon U.S.A.
60 D13 Minamata Japan
61 L10 Minami Alps Nat. Park Japan
85 C6 Mina, Mt Mali
126 F4 Minas Cuba
69 E12 Minas Sumatra
131 G5 Minas Uruguay
77 A5 Mina' Sa'ud Kuwait
122 H8 Minas Basin Nova Scotia Canada
126 C3 Minas de Matahambre Cuba
16 C7 Minas de Riotinto Spain
16 C7 Minas de Tharsis Spain
130 F5 Minas Gerais state Brazil
129 K7 Minas Novas Brazil
130 G5 Minas Novas Brazil
125 P10 Minas, Sa. de las mts Guatemala
98 C8 Minatare Nebraska U.S.A.
120 B2 Minataree Ontario Canada
125 M9 Minatitlán Mexico
68 B2 Minbu Burma
118 F5 Minburn Alberta Canada
99 M8 Minburn Iowa U.S.A.
68 A2 Minbya Burma
116 M5 Minchumina, L Alaska U.S.A.
45 J1 Mincio R Italy
107 N6 Minco Oklahoma U.S.A.
31 M6 Minčol mt Czechoslovakia
71 G7 Mindanao Philippines
71 G6 Mindanao Sea Philippines
138 F5 Mindarie South Australia Australia
68 A2 Mindat Sakan Burma
37 J7 Mindel R Germany
41 M1 Mindelheim Germany
121 M8 Minden Ontario Canada
32 J8 Minden Germany
111 C9 Minden Louisiana U.S.A.
98 G9 Minden Nebraska U.S.A.
102 E3 Minden Nevada U.S.A.
94 F9 Minden West Virginia U.S.A.
94 E3 Minden City Michigan U.S.A.
142 B5 Minderoo W Australia Australia
68 B3 Mindon Burma
138 F5 Mindona L New South Wales Australia
71 E4 Mindoro isld Philippines
71 E4 Mindoro Str Philippines
48 H5 Mîndra Romania
48 F4 Mindszent Hungary
55 C4 Mindyak Russian Federation
60 E11 Mine Japan
99 O1 Mine Centre Ontario Canada
14 D5 Mine Hd Ireland
8 C5 Minehead England
130 D5 Mineiros Brazil
21 J3 Mine,la France
99 L8 Mineola Iowa U.S.A.
109 M3 Mineola Texas U.S.A.
101 P4 Miner Montana U.S.A.
102 C1 Mineral California U.S.A.
109 K7 Mineral Texas U.S.A.
94 K8 Mineral Virginia U.S.A.
100 C3 Mineral Washington U.S.A.
125 K7 Mineral del Monte Mexico
103 M3 Mineral Mts Utah U.S.A.
99 Q7 Mineral Pt Wisconsin U.S.A.
109 O2 Mineral Springs Arkansas U.S.A.
109 J3 Mineral Wells Texas U.S.A.
45 K2 Minerbio Italy
103 M3 Minersville Utah U.S.A.
94 F6 Minerva Ohio U.S.A.
137 R6 Minerva Rfs Pacific Oc
43 G7 Minervino Murge Italy
95 L3 Minetto New York U.S.A.
94 E8 Minford Ohio U.S.A.
68 C4 Mingaladon Burma
122 H3 Mingan Quebec Canada
122 J3 Mingan Chan Quebec Canada
122 J3 Mingan Is Quebec Canada
138 F4 Mingary South Australia Australia
67 D5 Mingcheng China
78 L1 Mingechaur Azerbaijan
78 L1 Mingechaurskoye Vdkhr res Azerbaijan
141 H4 Mingela Queensland Australia
143 B8 Mingenew W Australia Australia
140 E5 Mingera R Queensland Australia
68 B1 Mingin Burma
75 Q6 Mingin Range Burma
67 B5 Mingjiang China
58 G5 Ming-kuang China
17 G5 Minglanilla Spain
67 C4 Minglun China
99 N8 Mingo Iowa U.S.A.
107 K2 Mingo Kansas U.S.A.
94 G6 Mingo Junct Ohio U.S.A.
87 G8 Mingoyo Tanzania
67 A1 Mingshan China
Mingshui see Zhangqiu
65 F1 Mingshui China
109 J3 Mingus Texas U.S.A.
67 F3 Mingxi China
68 G8 Minh Hoa, Hon isld Vietnam
68 B4 Minhla Burma
16 B3 Minho prov Portugal
16 B2 Minho R Spain/Portugal
127 K2 Minho, R Jamaica
67 F3 Minhou China
20 G4 Miniac Morvan France
46 E1 Minićevo Serbia Yugoslavia
73 L7 Minicoy I Lakshadweep Indian Oc
101 M7 Minidoka Idaho U.S.A.
99 R9 Minier Illinois U.S.A.
143 E8 Minigwal,L W Australia Australia
143 A6 Minilya W Australia Australia
143 A6 Minilya R W Australia Australia
110 K4 Mining City Res Kentucky U.S.A.
119 Q8 Miniota Manitoba Canada
83 K10 Minipe Sri Lanka
123 L1 Minipi L Labrador, Nfld Canada
118 H4 Ministikwan L Saskatchewan Canada
17 F3 Ministra, Sierra Spain
119 Q6 Minitonas Manitoba Canada
58 D5 Min Jiang R China
67 F3 Min Jiang R China
140 C1 Minjilang N Terr Australia
102 E5 Minkler California U.S.A.
48 L2 Min'kovtsy Ukraine
57 G4 Min-Kush Kyrgyzstan
138 D5 Minlaton South Australia Australia
85 F7 Minna Nigeria
146 D11 Minna Bluff pt Antarctica
61 P12 Minna-jima isld Okinawa
107 N2 Minneapolis Kansas U.S.A.
99 N4 Minneapolis Minnesota U.S.A.
119 S8 Minnedosa Manitoba Canada
107 L4 Minneola Kansas U.S.A.
99 N3 Minnesota state U.S.A.
99 M5 Minnesota R Minnesota U.S.A.
99 P5 Minnesota City Minnesota U.S.A.
99 N6 Minnesota Lake Minnesota U.S.A.
27 E11 Minnesund Norway
99 N5 Minnetonka Minnesota U.S.A.
118 B7 Minnewanka, L Alberta Canada
99 L4 Minnewaska L Minnesota U.S.A.
98 G1 Minnewaukan North Dakota U.S.A.
143 B6 Minnie Creek W Australia Australia
141 H7 Minnie Downs Queensland Australia
142 B5 Minnie,Mt W Australia Australia
138 D5 Minnipa South Australia Australia
120 G4 Minnipuka Ontario Canada
118 K1 Minnitaki L Ontario Canada
61 K10 Mino Japan
16 B2 Miño R Spain
61 M10 Minobu Japan
99 R4 Minocqua Wisconsin U.S.A.
61 K10 Minokamo Japan
61 K11 Minokuchi Japan
99 P3 Minong Wisconsin U.S.A.
99 R9 Minonk Illinois U.S.A.
99 S8 Minooka Illinois U.S.A.
40 A2 Minot France
98 E1 Minot North Dakota U.S.A.
67 F3 Minqing China
65 C7 Minquan China
20 F4 Minquiers,les English Chan
32 G5 Minsen Germany
65 A4 Minsheng Canal China
53 C7 Minsk Belorussia
31 N3 Mińsk Mazowieckie Poland
9 H5 Minster England
94 C6 Minster Ohio U.S.A.
74 F1 Mintaka Pass China/Kashmir
111 J9 Minter Alabama U.S.A.
111 F8 Minter City Mississippi U.S.A.
119 S9 Minto Manitoba Canada
122 F7 Minto New Brunswick Canada
117 E4 Minto Yukon Territory Canada
114 J3 Minto Hd Northwest Territories Canada
114 H3 Minto Inlet Northwest Territories Canada
115 M6 Minto, L Quebec Canada
98 B1 Minton Saskatchewan Canada
106 D2 Minturn Colorado U.S.A.
45 P7 Minturno Italy
79 A8 Minûf Egypt
56 D4 Minusinsk Russian Federation
58 D5 Min Xian China
79 A10 Minya, El Egypt
79 B8 Minya el Qamn Egypt
Minya Konka mt see Gongga Shan mt
55 C3 Min'yar Russian Federation
138 F6 Minyip Victoria Australia
68 B1 Minywa Burma
94 C2 Mio Michigan U.S.A.
83 J10 Mi Oya R Sri Lanka
78 K5 Miqdādiyah Iraq
123 Q6 Miquelon isld Atlantic Oc
123 Q6 Miquelon Miquelon I Atlantic Oc
121 O3 Miquelon Quebec Canada
123 Q6 Miquelon, C Miquelon I Atlantic Oc
118 E5 Miquelon Prov. Park Alberta Canada
123 N7 Mira C Breton I, Nova Scotia
45 M1 Mira Italy
16 B7 Mira R Portugal
17 G5 Mira Spain
19 P17 Mirabeau France
130 G5 Mirabela Brazil
45 R7 Mirabella Eclano Italy
130 G7 Miracema Brazil
128 D2 Miraflores Boyaca Colombia
124 E6 Miraflores Mexico
102 G7 Mirage L California U.S.A.
130 G7 Miraí Brazil
76 B2 Miraj India
130 G5 Miralta Brazil
19 O17 Miràmas France
18 E7 Mirambeau France
122 G6 Miramichi B New Brunswick Canada
18 F8 Miramont de Guyenne France
133 F5 Miranda Argentina
145 E2 Miranda New Zealand
128 E1 Miranda state Venezuela
17 F2 Miranda de E.Haro Spain
16 C3 Miranda do D Portugal
141 F3 Miranda Downs Queensland Australia
130 C6 Miranda, R Brazil
18 F9 Mirande France
16 C3 Mirandela Portugal
109 J8 Mirando City Texas U.S.A.
45 K2 Mirandola Italy
130 D7 Mirandópolis Brazil
45 M1 Mirano Italy
130 E8 Mirante Serra do mts Brazil
60 F11 Mirasaka Japan
17 G5 Mira, Sierra de mts Spain
130 E7 Mirassol Brazil
16 C2 Miravalles mt Spain
46 E3 Miravci Macedonia Yugoslavia
77 L2 Mīr Bacheh Kowt Afghanistan
25 E3 Mirdum Netherlands
21 K6 Miré France
86 G1 Mirear I Egypt
127 H5 Mirebalais Haiti
19 J5 Mirebeau Côte-d'Or France
21 L8 Mirebeau Vienne France
18 G9 Mirepoix France
54 E7 Mirgorod Ukraine
70 D2 Miri Sarawak
141 K6 Miriam Vale Queensland Australia
85 A5 Mirik, C Mauritania
127 K9 Mirimire Venezuela
131 H4 Mirim, L Brazil/Uruguay
131 F2 Miriñay, R Argentina
141 G8 Mirintu R Queensland Australia
128 D4 Miriti-Paraná R Colombia
77 G5 Mīrjāveh Iran
80 D4 Mirka Jordan
45 P1 Mirna R Croatia
146 H13 Mirnyy former U.S.S.R. Base Antarctica
56 H1 Mirnyy Russian Federation
40 E3 Miroir, Mt France
144 D5 Miromiro mt New Zealand
119 P3 Mirond L Saskatchewan Canada
54 B7 Mironovka Ukraine
31 J2 Mirosławiec Poland
33 R6 Mirow Germany
77 L7 Mirpur Khas Pakistan
140 D7 Mirranponga Pongunna L N Terr Australia
85 F6 Mirria Niger
118 D6 Mirror Alberta Canada
48 J6 Mîrşani Romania
56 D5 Mirskoy Khrebet mts Russian Federation
141 H5 Mirtna Queensland Australia
46 F7 Mirtoan Sea Greece
59 J4 Miryang S Korea
56 E1 Miryuginskiy Porog falls Russian Federation
57 B5 Mirzachiria Turkmenistan
75 K6 Mirzapur India
45 O4 Misa R Italy
60 G11 Mi-saki C Japan
60 F12 Misaki Japan
61 L10 Misakubo Japan
45 N4 Misano Monte Italy
61 P13 Misato Okinawa
61 P5 Misawa Japan
32 L8 Misburg Germany
40 G5 Mischabel mt Switzerland
122 J7 Miscouche Prince Edward I Canada
122 H6 Miscou I New Brunswick Canada
122 H5 Miscou, Pt New Brunswick Canada
127 P4 Misery, Mt St Kitts W Indies
80 F1 Misgav 'Am Israel
69 A9 Misha Nicobar Is
77 A5 Mish'ab, Al U.A.E.
128 D6 Mishahua R Peru
65 H2 Mishan China
94 A5 Mishawaka Indiana U.S.A.
116 G2 Misheguk Mt Alaska U.S.A.
56 F4 Mishelevka Russian Federation
120 E4 Mishibishu L Ontario Canada
99 T5 Mishicot Wisconsin U.S.A.
60 E11 Mi shima isld Japan
61 M10 Mishima Japan
55 C3 Mishkino Bashkirskaya Respublika Russian Federation
55 D3 Mishkino Sverdlovskaya obl Russian Federation
80 F7 Mishmaqa Jordan
80 C6 Mishmar 'Ayyalon Israel
80 B8 Mishmar Ha Negev Israel
80 F1 Mishmar Ha Yarden Israel
121 P5 Mishomis Quebec Canada
52 J2 Mishvan' Russian Federation
80 E4 Misilya Jordan
137 L4 Misima isld Louisiade Arch
128 E6 Misión Cavinas Bolivia
130 C10 Misiones prov Argentina
130 B10 Misiones dept Paraguay
130 C10 Misiones, Sa.de ra Argentina
88 B4 Misisi Zaire
125 N2 Miskito, Cayos islds Nicaragua
48 F2 Miskolc Hungary
38 M9 Mislinja Slovenia
79 G5 Mīsmīyah, Al Syria
60 G10 Misogu chi Japan
71 C3 Misoöl isld W Irian
99 Q2 Misquah Hills Minnesota U.S.A.
84 F3 Mişrātah Libya
84 F3 Mişrātah, Ra's C Libya
120 F4 Missanabie Ontario Canada
130 G9 Missão Velhá Brazil
20 F7 Missillac France
120 G4 Missinaibi L Ontario Canada
120 H2 Missinaibi R Ontario Canada
100 C1 Mission British Columbia Canada
98 F6 Mission South Dakota U.S.A.
109 J9 Mission Texas U.S.A.
117 M11 Mission City British Columbia Canada
98 J7 Mission Hill South Dakota U.S.A.
101 M2 Mission Range Montana U.S.A.
121 L1 Missisicabi R Quebec Canada
120 G6 Mississagi R Ontario Canada
121 L9 Mississauga Ontario Canada
94 B6 Mississinewa L Indiana U.S.A.
110 L1 Mississinewa L Indiana U.S.A.
111 F9 Mississippi state U.S.A.
111 E10 Mississippi R U.S.A.
111 G12 Mississippi Delta Louisiana U.S.A.
121 O7 Mississippi, L Ontario Canada
111 H11 Mississippi Sound Mississippi U.S.A.
Missolonghi Greece see Mesolóngion
120 H4 Missonga Ontario Canada
101 L3 Missoula Montana U.S.A.
110 C3 Missouri state U.S.A.
110 C2 Missouri R Missouri U.S.A.
109 O2 Missouri, Lit R Arkansas U.S.A.
98 F3 Missouri Res North Dakota U.S.A.
99 L8 Missouri Valley Iowa U.S.A.
141 H5 Mistake Cr Queensland Australia
140 A3 Mistake Creek N Terr Australia
123 K2 Mistanipisipou R Quebec Canada
121 S4 Mistassini Quebec Canada
115 M7 Mistassini, Lac Quebec Canada
119 O6 Mistatim Saskatchewan Canada
121 M3 Mistawak L Quebec Canada
31 K7 Mistelbach Austria
27 J14 Misterhult Sweden
126 C5 Misteriosa Bank Caribbean
8 D6 Misterton England
128 D7 Misti mt Peru
122 E5 Mistigougèche L Quebec Canada
37 P3 Misto Czechoslovakia
131 D3 Mistolar, L Argentina
26 E10 Mistra R Norway
43 F11 Mistretta Sicily
117 H8 Misty Fjords Nat Mon Alaska U.S.A.
60 E11 Misumi Japan
60 D13 Misumi Japan

Mitai — Moorpark 203

60 E13 **Mitai** Japan
127 P2 **Mitan** Trinidad
124 G7 **Mita, Pta.de** *C* Mexico
8 D4 **Mitcheldean** England
141 J7 **Mitchell** Queensland Australia
120 J9 **Mitchell** Ontario Canada
8 A7 **Mitchell** England
110 K3 **Mitchell** Indiana U.S.A.
98 C8 **Mitchell** Nebraska U.S.A.
100 E5 **Mitchell** Oregon U.S.A.
98 H6 **Mitchell** South Dakota U.S.A.
111 K9 **Mitchell L** Alabama U.S.A.
94 B2 **Mitchell, L** Michigan U.S.A.
112 E2 **Mitchell, Mt** North Carolina U.S.A.
140 A1 **Mitchell Pt** N Terr Australia
141 F3 **Mitchell River** Queensland Australia
14 C4 **Mitchelstown** Ireland
121 Q5 **Mitchinamecus, L** Quebec Canada
74 C6 **Mithi** Pakistan
47 H5 **Míthimna** Greece
71 B2 **Miti** *isld* Halmahera Indonesia
47 H5 **Mitilíni** Greece
52 G2 **Mitina** Russian Federation
119 S4 **Mitishto R** Manitoba Canada
117 G7 **Mitkof I** Alaska U.S.A.
79 C8 **Mitla Pass** Egypt
61 O9 **Mito** Japan
86 A5 **Mitra** *mt* Equat Guinea
137 P4 **Mitre** *isld* Santa Cruz Is
145 E4 **Mitre, Mt** New Zealand
144 A6 **Mitre Pk** New Zealand
52 J3 **Mitrofan-Dikost** Russian Federation
116 H9 **Mitrofania I** Alaska U.S.A.
46 D2 **Mitrovica** Serbia Yugoslavia
46 D5 **Mitsikéli** *R* Greece
86 G2 **Mits'iwa** Ethiopia
86 H2 **Mits'iwa** Ethiopia
60 F11 **Mitsu** Japan
60 F12 **Mitsuhama** Japan
60 Q3 **Mitsuishi** Japan
60 H11 **Mitsuishi** Japan
61 N9 **Mitsukaidō** Japan
61 M8 **Mitsuke** Japan
60 R2 **Mitsumata** Japan
139 K5 **Mittagong** New South Wales Australia
141 F4 **Mittagong** Queensland Australia
41 L3 **Mittagspitze** *mt* Austria
139 J6 **Mitta Mitta** Victoria Australia
41 N4 **Mittelberg** Austria
37 J5 **Mittelfranken** *dist* Bayern Germany
40 F4 **Mittelland** *dist* Switzerland
32 H8 **Mittellandkanal** Germany
33 R8 **Mittelmark** *reg* Germany
36 H3 **Mittelsinn** Germany
41 O3 **Mittenwald** Germany
33 T8 **Mittenwalde** Germany
38 M6 **Mitterbach** Austria
37 O6 **Mitterfels** Germany
38 G7 **Mitter Pinzgau** *V* Austria
36 B6 **Mittersheim** France
37 N4 **Mitterteich** Germany
140 D4 **Mittiebah** *R* N Terr Australia
37 O2 **Mittweida** Germany
128 D3 **Mitú** Colombia
88 B3 **Mitumba** *mts* Zaire
87 E7 **Mitwaba** Zaire
55 D1 **Mityayevo** Russian Federation
86 B5 **Mitzic** Gabon
61 N10 **Miura** Japan
54 K9 **Mius** *R* Rus Fed/Ukraine
54 K9 **Miusskiy Liman** *lagoon* Russian Federation
65 B7 **Mi Xian** China
38 M7 **Mixnitz** Austria
61 K11 **Miya-gawa** *R* Japan
61 O7 **Miyagi** *prefect* Japan
61 Q12 **Miyagi** Okinawa
61 P13 **Miyagusuku-jima** *isld* Okinawa
78 G4 **Miyāh, Wadi Al** Syria
61 N11 **Miyake-jima** *isld* Japan
61 P6 **Miyako** Japan
60 E14 **Miyakonojō** Japan
55 B6 **Miyaly** Kazakhstan
60 E13 **Miyazaki** *prefect* Japan
60 E14 **Miyazaki** Japan
60 J10 **Miyazu** Japan
60 F11 **Miyoshi** Japan
65 C4 **Miyun** China
65 D4 **Miyun Shuiku** *res* China
86 G4 **Mīzan Teferī** Ethiopia
84 E3 **Mizdah** Libya
111 G10 **Mize** Mississippi U.S.A.
14 B5 **Mizen Hd** Cork Ireland
14 E4 **Mizen Hd** Wicklow Ireland
65 A6 **Mizhi** China
48 K6 **Mizil** Romania
46 F1 **Miziya** Bulgaria
75 P7 **Mizoram** *prov* India
99 M2 **Mizpah** Minnesota U.S.A.
79 E7 **Mizpe Ramon** Israel
61 P6 **Mizusawa** Japan
26 K9 **Mjällom** Sweden
88 C1 **Mjanji** Uganda
27 F14 **Mjöbäck** Sweden
27 H13 **Mjölby** Sweden
28 B6 **Mjolden** Denmark
27 D12 **Mjöndalen** Norway
27 F14 **Mjörn** *L* Sweden
27 E11 **Mjösa** *L* Norway
88 C9 **Mkokomo** *mt* Zambia
88 G4 **Mkokotoni** Tanzania
88 B8 **Mkuku** Zambia
87 E8 **Mkushi** Zambia
88 B8 **Mkushi** *R* Zambia
89 H6 **Mkuze** S Africa
31 H5 **Mladá Boleslav** Czechoslovakia
48 F6 **Mladenovac** Serbia Yugoslavia
37 P4 **Mladotice** Czechoslovakia
88 C5 **Mlala Hills** Tanzania
48 G6 **Mlava** *R* Serbia Yugoslavia
31 M2 **Mława** Poland
88 G10 **M'lela** *R* Mozambique
87 G7 **Mlimba** Tanzania
42 H6 **Mljet** *isld* Croatia
88 E7 **Mlowe** Malawi
89 D5 **Mmabatho** S Africa
89 E3 **Mmashoro** Botswana
37 O3 **Mnichov** Czechoslovakia
31 H5 **Mnichovo Hradiště** Czechoslovakia
48 F2 **Mníšek** Czechoslovakia
26 K8 **Mo** Sweden
128 D5 **Moa** *R* Brazil
71 N9 **Moa** *isld* Indonesia
85 B7 **Moa** *R* Sierra Leone/Guinea
103 P3 **Moab** Utah U.S.A.
126 G4 **Moa Grande, Cayo** *isld* Cuba
141 F1 **Moa I** Queensland Australia
119 U3 **Moak L** Manitoba Canada
139 G6 **Moama** New South Wales Australia
89 H5 **Moamba** Mozambique
144 C5 **Moana** New Zealand
138 F3 **Moanba, L** South Australia Australia
86 B6 **Moanda** Gabon
86 B7 **Moanda** Zaire
103 K5 **Moapa** Nevada U.S.A.
71 N8 **Moapora** *isld* Indonesia
14 D3 **Moate** Ireland
88 D10 **Moatize** Mozambique
145 E3 **Moawhango** New Zealand
87 E7 **Moba** Zaire
61 O10 **Mobara** Japan
77 B3 **Mobārakeh** Iran
86 D5 **Mobaye** Cent Afr Republic
86 D5 **Mobayi-Mbongo** Zaire
110 D2 **Moberly** Missouri U.S.A.
117 N8 **Moberly Lake** British Columbia Canada
120 E4 **Mobert** Ontario Canada
111 H11 **Mobile** Alabama U.S.A.
103 M8 **Mobile** Arizona U.S.A.
111 J11 **Mobile Pt** Alabama U.S.A.
141 G7 **Moble** *R* Queensland Australia
71 F4 **Mobo** Philippines
28 A4 **Møborg** Denmark
98 F4 **Mobridge** South Dakota U.S.A.
Mobutu, L *see* **Albert, L**
127 J5 **Moca** Dominican Rep
129 J4 **Mocajuba** Brazil
Moçambique *see* **Mozambique**
88 H9 **Moçambique** *dist* Mozambique
Moçâmedes *see* **Namibe**
95 L5 **Mocanaqua** Pennsylvania U.S.A.
103 M5 **Moccasin** Arizona U.S.A.
101 Q2 **Moccasin** Montana U.S.A.
68 G2 **Moc Chau** Vietnam
125 Q7 **Mocche** Mexico
Mocha *see* **Mukha, Al**
131 A7 **Mocha** *isld* Chile
124 E5 **Mochicahui** Mexico
127 K2 **Mocho Mts** Jamaica
89 E5 **Mochudi** Botswana
88 H7 **Mocímboa da Praia** Mozambique
48 H4 **Mociu** Romania
27 G15 **Möckeln** *L* Sweden
33 P8 **Möckern** Germany
95 M9 **Mockhorn** *isld* Virginia U.S.A.
106 D8 **Mockingbird Gap** *gap* New Mexico U.S.A.
27 J15 **Möckleby, N** Sweden
27 H15 **Möckleby, S** Sweden
36 G5 **Mockmühl** Germany
33 R9 **Mockrehna** Germany
112 G2 **Mocksville** North Carolina U.S.A.
100 A2 **Moclips** Washington U.S.A.
128 C3 **Mocoa** Colombia
130 F7 **Mococa** Brazil
131 F3 **Mocoretá** *R* Argentina
124 F5 **Mocorito** Mexico
124 F2 **Moctezuma** Chihuahua Mexico
124 E3 **Moctezuma** Sonora Mexico
88 F10 **Mocuba** Mozambique
40 E7 **Modane** France
83 K9 **Modaragam Aru** *R* Sri Lanka
74 E7 **Modasa** India
22 J3 **Modave** Belgium
8 C7 **Modbury** England
89 D7 **Modder** *R* S Africa
106 F4 **Model** Colorado U.S.A.
45 J2 **Modena** Italy
45 J3 **Modena** *prov* Italy
103 L4 **Modena** Utah U.S.A.
19 L4 **Moder** *R* France
38 K7 **Moderbrugg** Austria
102 C4 **Modesto** California U.S.A.
43 F12 **Modica** Sicily
45 L3 **Modigliana** Italy
80 C6 **Modi'im** Israel
86 D5 **Modjamboli** Zaire
94 B6 **Modoc** Indiana U.S.A.
107 J3 **Modoc** Kansas U.S.A.
112 E4 **Modoc** South Carolina U.S.A.
100 D7 **Modoc Point** Oregon U.S.A.
58 E2 **Modot** Mongolia
36 B2 **Mödrath** Germany
48 E6 **Modriča** Bosnia-Herzegovina
48 E2 **Modrý Kameň** Czechoslovakia
68 J5 **Mo Đuc** Vietnam
139 H7 **Moe** Victoria Australia
145 E2 **Moehau** *mt* New Zealand
20 C6 **Moelan** France
8 B1 **Moelfre** Wales
8 C2 **Moel Sych** *mt* Wales
27 E11 **Moelv** Norway
129 H2 **Moengo** Suriname
103 N5 **Moenkopi** Arizona U.S.A.
144 B5 **Moeraki, L** New Zealand
22 F1 **Moerbeke** Belgium
25 C5 **Moerdijk** Netherlands
22 D1 **Moere** Belgium
20 G7 **Moëre,la** France
145 E1 **Moerewa** New Zealand
145 E3 **Moeroa** New Zealand
Moero, Lac *see* **Mweru, L**
13 E3 **Moffat** Scotland
106 E3 **Moffat** Colorado U.S.A.
144 B6 **Moffat Pk** New Zealand
98 F3 **Moffit** North Dakota U.S.A.
48 H3 **Moftin** Romania
74 F3 **Moga** India
Mogadiscio *see* **Muqdisho**
Mogadishu *see* **Muqdisho**
94 F5 **Mogadore** Ohio U.S.A.
16 C3 **Mogadouro** Portugal
89 F4 **Mogalakwena** *R* S Africa
61 N7 **Mogami-gawa** *R* Japan
67 F1 **Mogan Shan** *mt* China
75 R6 **Mogaung** Burma
28 B7 **Møgeltønder** Denmark
17 G6 **Mogente** Spain
36 H6 **Mögglingen** Germany
60 C13 **Mogi** Japan
129 J8 **Mogi das Cruzes** Brazil
31 M4 **Mogielnica** Poland
130 F7 **Mogi Guaçu** *R* Brazil
54 H9 **Mogila-Bel'mak Gora** *mt* Ukraine
54 B3 **Mogilëv** Belorussia
48 L2 **Mogilev-Podol'skiy** Ukraine
139 J3 **Mogil-Mogil** New South Wales Australia
31 K3 **Mogilno** Poland
130 F8 **Mogi Mirim** Brazil
88 H9 **Mogincual** Mozambique
45 J2 **Móglia** Italy
42 E3 **Mogliano Veneto** Italy
45 M1 **Mogliano Veneto** Italy
46 D4 **Moglicë** Albania
19 N12 **Mogneneins** France
59 G1 **Mogocha** Russian Federation
68 C1 **Mogok** Burma
89 E4 **Mogol** *R* S Africa
106 B8 **Mogollon** New Mexico U.S.A.
106 B8 **Mogollon Mts** New Mexico U.S.A.
103 O7 **Mogollon Rim** *tableland* Arizona U.S.A.
106 D4 **Mogote** Colorado U.S.A.
56 F5 **Mogoyty** Russian Federation
16 C7 **Moguer** Spain
143 B9 **Mogumber** W Australia Australia
48 E5 **Mohács** Hungary
145 F3 **Mohaka** New Zealand
98 E1 **Mohall** North Dakota U.S.A.
17 H9 **Mohammadia** Algeria
85 C2 **Mohammedia** Morocco
103 K6 **Mohave, L** Nev/Ariz U.S.A.
103 K7 **Mohave Mts** Cal/Ariz U.S.A.
103 L9 **Mohawk** Arizona U.S.A.
99 S2 **Mohawk** Michigan U.S.A.
95 N4 **Mohawk** *R* New York U.S.A.
103 L9 **Mohawk Mts** Arizona U.S.A.
59 H1 **Mohe** China
27 G14 **Moheda** Sweden
87 G10 **Mohéli** *isld* Comoros
87 D9 **Mohembo** Botswana
74 C5 **Mohenjo Daro** *anc site* Pakistan
14 B4 **Moher, Cliffs of** Ireland
116 D6 **Mohican, C** Alaska U.S.A.
14 D3 **Mohill** Ireland
100 J3 **Mohler** Idaho U.S.A.
32 H10 **Möhne** *R* Germany
32 H10 **Möhnesee** Germany
32 H10 **Möhnestausee** *L* Germany
27 G13 **Moholm** Sweden
20 E5 **Mohon** France
103 L7 **Mohon Pk** Arizona U.S.A.
88 G6 **Mohoro** Tanzania
124 H4 **Mohovano Ranch** Mexico
37 J2 **Möhra** Germany
36 G6 **Möhringen** Germany
28 D7 **Mohrkirch** Germany
27 B13 **Moi** Norway
16 B4 **Moimenta da Beira** Portugal
66 C5 **Moincêr** China
21 H7 **Moine** *R* France
95 N2 **Moira** New York U.S.A.
26 G5 **Mo i Rana** Norway
19 P14 **Moirans** France
46 G9 **Moíres** Crete Greece
52 C5 **Mõisaküla** Estonia
20 H6 **Moisdon** France
55 G2 **Moiseyevka** Russian Federation
122 F3 **Moisie** Quebec Canada
19 Q17 **Moissac** France
86 C4 **Moissala** Chad
21 O3 **Moisson** France
21 N6 **Moisy** France
27 K12 **Möja** Sweden
17 F7 **Mojácar** Spain
102 F6 **Mojave** California U.S.A.
102 G7 **Mojave** *R* California U.S.A.
102 G6 **Mojave Desert** California U.S.A.
60 E12 **Moji** Japan
130 F8 **Moji das Cruzes** Brazil
120 B2 **Mojikit L** Ontario Canada
86 G4 **Mojo** Ethiopia
71 H9 **Mojo** *isld* Indonesia
86 F5 **Mojo** Uganda
70 O9 **Mojokerto** Java
128 E7 **Mojos, Llanos de** *plain* Bolivia
129 J4 **Moju** *R* Brazil
61 O9 **Mōka** Japan
145 E3 **Mokai** New Zealand
75 L6 **Mokāma** India
110 E3 **Mokane** Missouri U.S.A.
102 S12 **Mokapu Pen** Hawaiian Is
145 E3 **Mokau** New Zealand
102 D3 **Mokelumne** *R* California U.S.A.
89 F7 **Mokhotlong** *mt* Lesotho
55 F3 **Mokhovoy Prival** Russian Federation
27 J11 **Möklinta** Sweden
85 G1 **Moknine** Tunisia
145 E1 **Mokohinau Is** New Zealand
145 E3 **Mokoia** New Zealand
75 Q5 **Mokokchung** India
86 B3 **Mokolo** Cameroon
144 B7 **Mokoreta** New Zealand
144 B7 **Mokotua** New Zealand
65 G7 **Mokp'o** S Korea
46 D2 **Mokra Gora** *mt* Montenegro/Serbia Yugoslavia
48 F5 **Mokrin** Serbia Yugoslavia
55 E3 **Mokrousovo** Russian Federation
29 L8 **Möksy** Finland
102 S11 **Mokuauia I** Hawaiian Is
135 U5 **Mokuaweoweo Crater** Hawaiian Is
102 R11 **Mokuleia** Hawaiian Is
102 S12 **Mokulua Is** Hawaiian Is
22 J1 **Mol** Belgium
20 F6 **Molac** France
100 C4 **Molalla** Oregon U.S.A.
125 K7 **Molango** Mexico
46 F8 **Moláoi** Greece
42 F4 **Molat** *isld* Croatia
70 G6 **Molawe** Sulawesi
21 J3 **Molay-Littry, le** France
32 G7 **Molbergen** Germany
28 B5 **Mølby** Denmark
8 C1 **Mold** Wales
48 G2 **Moldava nad Bodvon** Czechoslovakia
53 C10 **Moldavia** *rep* E Europe
48 K4 **Moldavia** *reg* Romania
Moldavskaya S.S.R *see* **Moldavia** E Europe
26 B9 **Molde** Norway
Moldova *see* **Moldavia**
48 K3 **Moldova** *R* Romania
48 J5 **Moldoveanu** *mt* Romania
48 K3 **Moldoviţa** Romania
28 D3 **Møldrup** Denmark
40 D5 **Môle** *mt* France
20 A5 **Molène** *isld* France
89 D5 **Molepolole** Botswana
8 C6 **Mole, R** England
9 F5 **Mole, R** England
144 D5 **Molesworth** New Zealand
43 H7 **Molfetta** Italy
133 C5 **Molina** Chile
17 F4 **Molina de Aragón** Spain
17 G6 **Molina de Segura** Spain
99 Q8 **Moline** Illinois U.S.A.
107 O4 **Moline** Kansas U.S.A.
94 B4 **Moline** Michigan U.S.A.
45 L2 **Molinella** Italy
38 E8 **Molini** Italy
124 D3 **Molino** Mexico
111 J11 **Molino** Florida U.S.A.
42 F7 **Molise** *prov* Italy
40 D2 **Mollans** France
29 K4 **Mölle** Sweden
28 C5 **Møllebjerg** *hill* Denmark
33 S6 **Möllenbeck** Germany
128 D7 **Mollendo** Peru
33 R5 **Möllenhagen** Germany
143 C9 **Mollerin L** W Australia Australia
28 D4 **Mollerup** Denmark
17 H3 **Mollerusa** Spain
26 O2 **Mollesjok** Norway
21 P2 **Molliens-Dreuil** France
12 D2 **Mollinsburn** Scotland
26 M2 **Mollius** *mt* Norway
33 N5 **Mölln** Germany
33 S5 **Mölln** Germany
38 G8 **Molltal** *V* Austria
27 F14 **Mölndal** Sweden
54 G9 **Molochansk** Ukraine
53 E10 **Molochnyy, Liman** Ukraine
88 G10 **Molocue** *R* Mozambique
146 K9 **Molodezhnaya** *former U.S.S.R. Base* Antarctica
54 D8 **Molodezhnoye** Ukraine
55 F5 **Molodezhnyy** Kazakhstan
56 B2 **Molodezhnyy** Russian Federation
55 F4 **Molodogvardeyskoye** Kazakhstan
52 D6 **Molodoy-Tud** Russian Federation
52 E5 **Mologa** *R* Russian Federation
102 V13 **Molokai** *isld* Hawaiian Is
135 S3 **Molokini** *isld* Hawaiian Is
52 E5 **Molokovo** Russian Federation
52 G5 **Moloma** *R* Russian Federation
139 J5 **Molong** New South Wales Australia
89 B6 **Molopo** *R* S Africa
46 F6 **Mólos** Greece
86 C5 **Moloundou** Cameroon
28 F4 **Mols B** *hill* Denmark
89 F5 **Molsgat** S Africa
36 D6 **Molsheim** France
118 E1 **Molson** Manitoba Canada
119 V4 **Molson L** Manitoba Canada
101 R4 **Molt** Montana U.S.A.
87 E12 **Molteno** S Africa
Moluccas *see* **Malaku** *islds*
88 G10 **Moma** Mozambique
51 O2 **Moma** *R* Russian Federation
86 D6 **Moma** Zaire
139 G4 **Momba** New South Wales Australia
88 D6 **Momba** *R* Tanzania
45 N4 **Mombaroccio** Italy
88 G4 **Mombasa** Kenya
60 R1 **Mombetsu** Japan
60 Q3 **Mombetsu** Japan
130 D6 **Mombuca, Serra da** *mts* Brazil
46 G3 **Momchilgrad** Bulgaria
99 T8 **Momence** Illinois U.S.A.
22 G3 **Momignies** Belgium
36 D6 **Mommenheim** France
70 G5 **Momo** Sulawesi
71 F4 **Mompog Passage** Philippines
86 D5 **Mompono** Zaire
126 G10 **Mompós** Colombia
Môn *isld* *see* **Anglesey**
68 B2 **Mon** *R* Burma
68 C3 **Mon** Burma
29 K7 **Møn** *isld* Denmark
127 L2 **Mona** Jamaica
103 N2 **Mona** Utah U.S.A.
94 G6 **Monaca** Pennsylvania U.S.A.
15 A3 **Monach I** Outer Hebrides Scotland
44 B4 **Monaco** *princ* W Europe
15 D3 **Monadhliath Mts** Scotland
29 J8 **Monå Fjärd** *inlet* Finland
128 F2 **Monagas** *state* Venezuela
14 E2 **Monaghan** *co* Ireland
14 E2 **Monaghan** Ireland
108 E4 **Monahans** Texas U.S.A.
127 L5 **Mona, I** Puerto Rico
98 H3 **Monango** North Dakota U.S.A.
87 C7 **Mona Quimbundo** Angola
118 D9 **Monarch** Alberta Canada
106 D3 **Monarch** Colorado U.S.A.
101 P2 **Monarch** Montana U.S.A.
117 L10 **Monarch Mt** British Columbia Canada
103 N2 **Mona Res** Utah U.S.A.
117 O10 **Monashee Mts** British Columbia Canada
14 D3 **Monasterevin** Ireland
18 H8 **Monastier, le** France
43 D13 **Monastir** Tunisia
48 J1 **Monastyriska** Ukraine
55 D2 **Monastyrskoye** Russian Federation
44 C2 **Moncalieri** Italy
16 B2 **Monção** Portugal
17 F3 **Moncayo, Sierra del** Spain
22 F4 **Monceau-le-Neuf** France
38 L5 **Mönchdorf** Austria
52 D1 **Monchegorsk** Russian Federation
36 B1 **Mönchengladbach** Germany
30 H1 **Mönchgut** *pen* Germany
16 B7 **Monchique** Portugal
101 R1 **Monchy** Saskatchewan Canada
112 G4 **Moncks Corner** South Carolina U.S.A.
124 J4 **Monclova** Mexico
20 E5 **Moncontour** Côtes d'Armor France
21 K8 **Moncontour** Vienne France
122 A5 **Moncouche, L** Quebec Canada
21 J8 **Moncoutant** France
122 H7 **Moncton** New Brunswick Canada
130 D10 **Mondai** Brazil
99 L8 **Mondamin** Iowa U.S.A.
45 N4 **Mondavio** Italy
130 C9 **Monday, R** Paraguay
16 B4 **Mondego** *R* Portugal
16 B4 **Mondego, C** Portugal
16 E4 **Mondéjar** Spain
21 K3 **Mondeville** France
89 G3 **Mondi** *R* Zimbabwe
89 G6 **Mondlo** S Africa
86 C3 **Mondo** Chad
45 O4 **Mondolfo** Italy
16 C1 **Mondoñedo** Spain
22 L4 **Mondorf-les-Bains** Luxembourg
21 M6 **Mondoubleau** France
44 C3 **Mondovi** Italy
99 P5 **Mondovi** Wisconsin U.S.A.
19 N16 **Mondragon** France
45 P7 **Mondragone** Italy
143 E10 **Mondrain I** W Australia Australia
41 P3 **Mondschein Spitze** *mt* Austria
38 H6 **Mondsee** Austria
127 K2 **Moneague** Jamaica
44 F3 **Moneglia** Italy
18 E9 **Monein** France
46 F8 **Monemvasia** Greece
94 H9 **Moneta** Virginia U.S.A.
101 S6 **Moneta** Wyoming U.S.A.
110 C5 **Monett** Missouri U.S.A.
110 F6 **Monette** Arkansas U.S.A.
42 F3 **Monfalcone** Italy
68 D3 **Mon Fang** Thailand
44 C2 **Monferrato** *dist* Italy
86 D5 **Monga** Zaire
95 N5 **Mongaup Vall** New York U.S.A.
68 H2 **Mong Cai** Vietnam
142 A1 **Monger L** Perth, W Aust Australia
143 B8 **Monger, L** W Australia Australia
68 D2 **Mong Hai** Burma
68 D2 **Mong Hang** Burma
45 K3 **Monghidoro** Italy
68 E2 **Mong Hkan** Burma
68 D2 **Mong Hkok** Burma
68 D2 **Mong Hpayak** Burma
68 D2 **Mong Hsat** Burma
68 C2 **Mong Hsawk** Burma
68 D2 **Mong Hsu** Burma
44 C3 **Mongioie** *mt* Italy
68 F6 **Mongkol Borey** Cambodia
68 D3 **Mong Kyawt** Burma
68 D2 **Mong La** Burma
68 E2 **Mong Lin** Burma
68 E2 **Mong Loi** Burma
68 C1 **Mong Long** Burma
68 C2 **Mong Long** Burma
68 C3 **Mong Mau** Burma
68 C2 **Mong Nai** Burma
68 D2 **Mong Nawng** Burma
17 H6 **Mongo** *mt* Spain
94 B5 **Mongo** Indiana U.S.A.
58 C2 **Mongolia** *rep* Asia
Mongolküre *see* **Zhaosu**
85 G8 **Mongomo** Mbini Equat Guinea
142 F3 **Mongona,Mt** W Australia Australia
86 B3 **Mongonu** Nigeria
68 C3 **Mong Pai** Burma
68 D2 **Mong Pan** Burma
68 D1 **Mong Pat** Burma
68 D1 **Mong Pawk** Burma
68 C2 **Mong Pawn** Burma
68 D2 **Mong Ping** Burma
68 D2 **Mong Pu** Burma
68 D2 **Mong Pu-awn** Burma
124 H9 **Mongrove, Pta** *C* Mexico
68 D2 **Mong Ton** Burma
68 D2 **Mong Tum** Burma
68 C1 **Mong Tung** Burma
87 D9 **Mongu** Zambia
38 F8 **Monguelfo** Italy
68 E2 **Mong Un** Burma
68 D1 **Mong Yai** Burma
68 D2 **Mong Yang** Burma
68 D2 **Mong Yawn** Burma
68 E2 **Mong Yawng** Burma
95 S3 **Monhegan I** Maine U.S.A.
37 K6 **Monheim** Bayern Germany
36 B1 **Monheim** Nordrhein-Westfalen Germany
113 E7 **Moniac** Georgia U.S.A.
12 E3 **Moniaive** Scotland
19 O16 **Monieux** France
13 F1 **Monifieth** Scotland
18 H7 **Monistrol-sur-Loire** France
118 G7 **Monitor** Alberta Canada
102 H3 **Monitor** *pk* Nevada U.S.A.
14 C3 **Monivea** Ireland
28 B7 **Mönkebüll** Germany
140 F6 **Monkira** Queensland Australia
86 D6 **Monkoto** Zaire
120 J9 **Monkton** Ontario Canada
12 D3 **Monkton** Scotland
Monmouth *co see* **Gwent**
99 Q9 **Monmouth** Illinois U.S.A.
95 R2 **Monmouth** Maine U.S.A.
8 D4 **Monmouth** Wales
117 M10 **Monmouth, Mt** British Columbia Canada
21 L4 **Monnai** France
21 M7 **Monnaie** France
25 D3 **Monnickendam** Netherlands
85 E7 **Mono** *R* Togo
102 F3 **Mono L** California U.S.A.
47 U17 **Monólithos** Rhodes Greece
95 S5 **Monomoy Pt** Massachusetts U.S.A.
99 U9 **Monon** Indiana U.S.A.
99 P6 **Monona** Iowa U.S.A.
94 G7 **Monongah** West Virginia U.S.A.
94 H6 **Monongahela** Pennsylvania U.S.A.
43 H8 **Monopoli** Italy
48 E3 **Monor** Hungary
127 N1 **Monos I** Trinidad
86 D2 **Monou** Chad
17 G6 **Monóvar** Spain
144 A6 **Monowai** New Zealand
98 H7 **Monowi** Nebraska U.S.A.
18 F8 **Monpont** France
36 C3 **Monreal** Germany
17 G4 **Monreal del Campo** Spain
43 E10 **Monreale** Sicily
102 A2 **Monroe** California U.S.A.
112 D4 **Monroe** Georgia U.S.A.
94 C6 **Monroe** Indiana U.S.A.
99 N8 **Monroe** Iowa U.S.A.
111 D9 **Monroe** Louisiana U.S.A.
94 D5 **Monroe** Michigan U.S.A.
95 N5 **Monroe** New York U.S.A.
112 G3 **Monroe** North Carolina U.S.A.
100 B5 **Monroe** Oregon U.S.A.
95 L5 **Monroe** Pennsylvania U.S.A.
98 J6 **Monroe** South Dakota U.S.A.
103 M3 **Monroe** Utah U.S.A.
94 H9 **Monroe** Virginia U.S.A.
100 D2 **Monroe** Washington U.S.A.
99 R7 **Monroe** Wisconsin U.S.A.
99 P10 **Monroe City** Missouri U.S.A.
113 F9 **Monroe, L** Florida U.S.A.
110 K2 **Monroe L** Indiana U.S.A.
111 J10 **Monroeville** Alabama U.S.A.
94 C6 **Monroeville** Indiana U.S.A.
94 E5 **Monroeville** Ohio U.S.A.
85 B7 **Monrovia** Liberia
102 G7 **Monrovia** California U.S.A.
17 G4 **Monroyo** Spain
22 F3 **Mons** Belgium
16 C4 **Monsanto** Portugal
130 H6 **Monsarás, Pta. de** Brazil
22 L2 **Monschau** Germany
71 H7 **Monse** Indonesia
42 D3 **Monselice** Italy
36 E4 **Monsheim** Germany
29 K7 **Møns Klint** *cliffs* Denmark
95 P4 **Monson** Massachusetts U.S.A.
68 C3 **Mon State** Burma
28 C4 **Mønsted** Denmark
25 B4 **Monster** Netherlands
27 H14 **Mönsterås** Sweden
45 J4 **Monsummano Terme** Italy
22 K3 **Mont** Belgium
36 D3 **Montabaur** Germany
41 L3 **Montafon** *V* Austria
45 K1 **Montagnana** Italy
89 B9 **Montagu** S Africa
122 K7 **Montague** Prince Edward I Canada
100 C8 **Montague** California U.S.A.
94 A3 **Montague** Michigan U.S.A.
109 K2 **Montague** Texas U.S.A.
139 K6 **Montague I** New South Wales Australia
103 K10 **Montague, I** Mexico
116 O6 **Montague I** Alaska U.S.A.
143 C7 **Montague Ra** W Australia Australia
142 F2 **Montague Sd** W Australia Australia
116 N7 **Montague Str** Alaska U.S.A.
146 G3 **Montagu I** S Sandwich Is S Atlantic Oc
20 H8 **Montaigu** France
18 F8 **Montaigu-de-Quercy** France
40 D7 **Montaimont** France
45 J4 **Montaione** Italy
70 D5 **Montalat** *R* Kalimantan
17 G4 **Montalbán** Spain
127 K9 **Montalbán** Venezuela
45 K4 **Montale** Italy
16 B3 **Montalegre** Portugal
40 B6 **Montalieu** France
19 O13 **Montalieu Vercieu** France
43 G10 **Montalto** *mt* Italy
21 L8 **Montamise** France
101 P3 **Montana** *state* U.S.A.
116 N5 **Montana** Alaska U.S.A.
40 G7 **Montanaro** Italy
16 C5 **Montánchez** Spain
121 T5 **Mont-Apica** Quebec Canada
18 G5 **Montargis** France
21 P3 **Montataire** France
18 F9 **Montauban** France
20 F5 **Montauban-de-Bretagne** France
21 J5 **Montaudin** France
18 H5 **Montbard** France
40 C3 **Montbarrey** France
21 M7 **Montbazon** France
40 E2 **Montbéliard** France
109 N6 **Mont Belvieu** Texas U.S.A.
40 D4 **Montbenoit** France
20 H7 **Montbert** France
40 E6 **Mont Blanc** *mt* France
17 H3 **Montblanch** Spain
Montblanc Vilanovai *see* **Montblanch Vilanuevay**
40 D3 **Montbozon** France
21 H4 **Montbray** France
18 H7 **Montbrison** France
Montcalm, L *see* **Dogai Coring**
18 F10 **Montcalm, Pic** *mt* France
21 J4 **Montchamp** France
22 G4 **Montcornet** France
18 E9 **Mont de Marsan** France
22 D4 **Montdidier** France
43 G9 **Montea** *mt* Italy
110 L6 **Monteagle** Tennessee U.S.A.
129 H4 **Monte Alegre** Brazil
17 G6 **Montealegre del Castillo** Spain
130 E6 **Monte Alegre de Minas** Brazil
130 G4 **Monte Azul** Brazil
121 Q7 **Montebello** Quebec Canada
142 B5 **Monte Bello Is** W Australia Australia
45 K1 **Montebello Vic** Italy
42 E3 **Montebelluna** Italy
20 H3 **Montebourg** France
45 N4 **Montecalvo in Foglia** Italy
45 S7 **Montecalvo Irpino** Italy
133 G3 **Montecarlo** Argentina
44 B4 **Monte-Carlo** Monaco
129 J7 **Monte Carmelo** Brazil
45 O4 **Montecarotto** Italy
131 F3 **Monte Caseros** Argentina
45 J4 **Montecatini Terme** Italy
45 J2 **Montécchio Emilia** Italy
45 K1 **Montecchio Maggiore** Italy
45 H2 **Montecchio nell'Emilia** Italy
45 N5 **Montecélio** Italy
18 F9 **Montech** France
112 H3 **Monte Clare** South Carolina U.S.A.
45 R8 **Montecorvino Rovella** Italy
45 J3 **Montecreto** Italy
127 J5 **Montecristi** Dominican Rep
128 F6 **Monte Cristo** Bolivia
42 C6 **Montecristo, I.di** Italy
41 O4 **Montecroce, Pta di** *mt* Italy
124 H6 **Monte Escobedo** Mexico
45 M4 **Montefeltro** Italy
45 J3 **Montefiorino** Italy
45 R8 **Monteforte Irpina** Italy
16 E7 **Montefrio** Spain
127 J1 **Montego Bay** Jamaica
45 M4 **Monte Grimano** Italy
130 H9 **Monteiro** Brazil
140 B3 **Montejinnie** N Terr Australia
45 O6 **Montelanico** Italy
131 E6 **Monte, L.del** Argentina
19 N15 **Montélimar** France
129 G8 **Monte Lindo** Paraguay
108 G6 **Montell** Texas U.S.A.
45 S8 **Montella** Italy
16 D8 **Montellanto** Spain
101 L8 **Montello** Nevada U.S.A.
99 R6 **Montello** Wisconsin U.S.A.
45 K4 **Montelupo Fiorentino** Italy
45 R8 **Montemárano** Italy
45 O4 **Montemarciano** Italy
133 D6 **Montemayor, Meseta de** *hills* Argentina
45 L4 **Montemignaio** Italy
45 R7 **Montemiletto** Italy
125 K5 **Montemorelos** Mexico
45 K4 **Montemurio** Italy
21 J5 **Montenay** France
18 E7 **Montendre** France
46 C2 **Montenegro** *reg* Yugoslavia
46 C2 **Montenegro** *rep* Yugoslavia
20 F6 **Monteneuf** France
42 D6 **Montepescali** Italy
127 K5 **Monte Plata** Dominican Rep
45 O4 **Monteporzio** Italy
88 G8 **Montepuez** Mozambique
42 D5 **Montepulciano** Italy
18 G4 **Montereau** France
45 K3 **Monterenzio** Italy
102 C5 **Monterey** California U.S.A.
99 U8 **Monterey** Indiana U.S.A.
110 L5 **Monterey** Tennessee U.S.A.
94 H8 **Monterey** Virginia U.S.A.
102 B5 **Monterey B** California U.S.A.
126 G10 **Montería** Colombia
128 F7 **Montero** Bolivia
21 N2 **Montérolier** France
45 M5 **Monterosi** Italy
44 M5 **Monterosi, L** Italy
45 N5 **Monterotondo** Italy
125 J5 **Monterrey** Mexico
42 G7 **Monte S. Angelo** Italy
100 B3 **Montesano** Washington U.S.A.
130 G11 **Monte Santo** Brazil
130 F7 **Monte Santo de Minas** Brazil
45 R7 **Montesarchio** Italy
45 O7 **Monte S. Biágio** Italy
129 K7 **Montes Claros** Brazil
45 J3 **Montese** Italy
45 O4 **Montesicuro** Italy
45 K4 **Montespértoli** Italy
18 F9 **Montesquieu-Volvestre** France
18 H6 **Montet, le** France
19 N16 **Monteux** France
111 K8 **Montevallo** Alabama U.S.A.
42 D5 **Montevarchi** Italy
45 K3 **Monteveglio** Italy
45 O5 **Monte Velino** Italy
131 G5 **Montevideo** Uruguay
99 L5 **Montevideo** Minnesota U.S.A.
101 N6 **Monteview** Idaho U.S.A.
106 D4 **Monte Vista** Colorado U.S.A.
103 L8 **Montezuma** Arizona U.S.A.
112 C5 **Montezuma** Georgia U.S.A.
99 T10 **Montezuma** Indiana U.S.A.
99 O8 **Montezuma** Iowa U.S.A.
107 K4 **Montezuma** Kansas U.S.A.
106 E6 **Montezuma** New Mexico U.S.A.
103 N7 **Montezuma Castle Nat.Mon** Arizona U.S.A.
102 G4 **Montezuma Pk** Nevada U.S.A.
20 H2 **Montfarville** France
21 H7 **Montfaucon** Maine-et-Loire France
22 J5 **Montfaucon** Meuse France
19 P14 **Montferrat** France
21 O4 **Montfort-l'Amaury** France
21 L5 **Montfort-le-Rotrou** France
20 G5 **Montfort-sur-Meu** France
21 M3 **Montfort-sur-Risle** France
19 N17 **Montfrin** France
Montgomery *co see* **Powys**
111 K9 **Montgomery** Alabama U.S.A.
111 D10 **Montgomery** Louisiana U.S.A.
94 C5 **Montgomery** Michigan U.S.A.
99 N5 **Montgomery** Minnesota U.S.A.
109 M5 **Montgomery** Texas U.S.A.
94 F8 **Montgomery** West Virginia U.S.A.
8 C2 **Montgomery** Wales
110 E3 **Montgomery City** Missouri U.S.A.
100 D9 **Montgomery Creek** California U.S.A.
142 E3 **Montgomery I** W Australia Australia
18 E7 **Montguyon** France
22 H4 **Monthermé** France
40 E5 **Monthey** Switzerland
22 H5 **Monthois** France
40 C1 **Monthureux-sur-Saône** France
43 C8 **Monti** Sardinia
111 E8 **Monticello** Arkansas U.S.A.
113 D7 **Monticello** Florida U.S.A.
112 D4 **Monticello** Georgia U.S.A.
110 H1 **Monticello** Illinois U.S.A.
110 K1 **Monticello** Indiana U.S.A.
99 P7 **Monticello** Iowa U.S.A.
110 M5 **Monticello** Kentucky U.S.A.
95 T7 **Monticello** Maine U.S.A.
99 N4 **Monticello** Minnesota U.S.A.
111 F10 **Monticello** Mississippi U.S.A.
110 E1 **Monticello** Missouri U.S.A.
106 C8 **Monticello** New Mexico U.S.A.
95 N5 **Monticello** New York U.S.A.
103 P4 **Monticello** Utah U.S.A.
99 R7 **Monticello** Wisconsin U.S.A.
45 J1 **Montichiari** Italy
43 C8 **Monti del Gennargentu** Sardinia
131 F3 **Montiel, Cuchilla de** *mts* Argentina
21 O8 **Montierchaume** France
19 J4 **Montier en Der** France
22 D5 **Montiers** France
18 F7 **Montignac** France
18 F7 **Montignac-Charente** France
21 H4 **Montigny** Manche France
36 B6 **Montigny** Meurthe-et-Moselle France
40 B2 **Montigny-le-Roi** France
16 B6 **Montijo** Portugal
16 C6 **Montijo** Spain
125 O6 **Montijo, G.de** Panama
16 D7 **Montilla** Spain
21 O8 **Montipouret** France
45 N5 **Monti Sabini** Italy
130 D5 **Montividiu** Brazil
21 L2 **Montivilliers** France
21 J7 **Montjean** Maine-et-Loire France
21 J5 **Montjean** Mayenne France
21 H4 **Montjoie** France
122 D5 **Mont-Joli** Quebec Canada
138 F2 **Montkeleary** *R* South Australia Australia
21 N5 **Montlandon** France
121 P6 **Mont-Laurier** Quebec Canada
40 E3 **Montlebon** France
21 P4 **Montlhéry** France
18 E7 **Montlieu** France
122 G4 **Mont Louis** Quebec Canada
18 G10 **Mont Louis** France
18 G6 **Montluçon** France
19 O13 **Montluel** France
122 B7 **Montmagny** Quebec Canada
20 G4 **Montmartin-sur-Mer** France
119 O8 **Montmartre** Saskatchewan Canada
22 J4 **Montmédy** France
19 Q14 **Montmélian** France
40 A5 **Montmerle** France
19 Q17 **Montmeyan** France
19 N15 **Montmeyran** France
18 H4 **Montmirail** Marne France
21 M5 **Montmirail** Sarthe France
18 F7 **Montmoreau St Cybard** France
21 P4 **Montmorency** France
122 A6 **Montmorency, R** Quebec Canada
18 F6 **Montmorillon** France
19 P16 **Montmorin** France
141 K6 **Monto** Queensland Australia
20 F7 **Montoir-de-Bretagne** France
21 M6 **Montoire-sur-le-Loir** France
45 M3 **Montone** *R* Italy
16 E6 **Montoro** Spain
99 O8 **Montour** Iowa U.S.A.
95 L4 **Montour Falls** New York U.S.A.
21 J8 **Montournais** France
95 L5 **Montoursville** Pennsylvania U.S.A.
106 F6 **Montoya** New Mexico U.S.A.
127 J2 **Montpelier** Jamaica
101 O7 **Montpelier** Idaho U.S.A.
110 L1 **Montpelier** Indiana U.S.A.
98 H3 **Montpelier** North Dakota U.S.A.
94 C5 **Montpelier** Ohio U.S.A.
95 P2 **Montpelier** Vermont U.S.A.
121 P7 **Montpellier** Quebec Canada
18 H9 **Montpellier** France
40 B4 **Montpont** France
120 K5 **Montreal** *R* Ontario Canada
121 R7 **Montréal** Quebec Canada
18 G9 **Montréal** France
99 Q3 **Montreal** Wisconsin U.S.A.
120 F5 **Montreal I** Ontario Canada
119 M4 **Montreal Lake** Saskatchewan Canada
119 M4 **Montreal R** Saskatchewan Canada
120 F5 **Montreal River** Ontario Canada
18 G9 **Montredon Labessonié** France
18 F9 **Montrejeau** France
21 N7 **Montrésor** France
22 B3 **Montreuil** France
21 K7 **Montreuil Bellay** France
21 K5 **Montreuil-le-Chetif** France
20 G5 **Montreuil-sur-Ille** France
40 E5 **Montreux** Switzerland
21 H7 **Montrevault** France
21 N7 **Montrichard** France
19 P18 **Montrieux le Vieux** France
6 L5 **Montrose** *oil rig* North Sea
15 F4 **Montrose** Scotland
111 E8 **Montrose** Arkansas U.S.A.
106 C3 **Montrose** Colorado U.S.A.
110 H2 **Montrose** Illinois U.S.A.
99 P9 **Montrose** Iowa U.S.A.
98 C7 **Montrose** Nebraska U.S.A.
95 L5 **Montrose** Pennsylvania U.S.A.
98 J6 **Montrose** South Dakota U.S.A.
95 L8 **Montross** Virginia U.S.A.
22 G3 **Mont. St.Christophe** Belgium
22 H2 **Mont.St.Guibert** Belgium
22 G2 **Mont-St.Jean** Belgium
22 K4 **Mont St.Martin** France
20 G4 **Mont-St. Michel, B. du** France
20 G4 **Mont-St.Michel, le** France
21 J4 **Montsecret** France
17 H2 **Montseny** *mt* Spain
17 J3 **Montseny, Sierra de** *mts* Spain
127 N6 **Montserrat** *isld* Lesser Antilles
17 J3 **Montserrat** *dist* Spain
129 H3 **Montsinery** Fr Guiana
21 L7 **Montsoreau** France
21 P3 **Montsoult** France
115 N8 **Monts, Pointe des** Quebec Canada
21 L8 **Mont-sur-Guesnes** France
21 J5 **Montsûrs** France
121 Q6 **Mont Tremblant** Quebec Canada
21 L4 **Montviette** France
95 P5 **Montville** Connecticut U.S.A.
106 F2 **Monument** Colorado U.S.A.
107 J2 **Monument** Kansas U.S.A.
108 D3 **Monument** New Mexico U.S.A.
100 F5 **Monument** Oregon U.S.A.
116 F4 **Monument Mt** Alaska U.S.A.
103 O4 **Monument V** Utah/Ariz U.S.A.
86 D5 **Monveda** Zaire
21 N2 **Monville** France
68 B1 **Monywa** Burma
41 K6 **Monza** Italy
87 E9 **Monze** Zambia
17 H3 **Monzón** Spain
45 K3 **Monzuno** Italy
109 K4 **Moody** Texas U.S.A.
95 O2 **Mooers** New York U.S.A.
138 E3 **Moolawatana** South Australia Australia
138 E2 **Moolionburrinna, L** South Australia Australia
138 F3 **Moomba Oil & Gas Field** South Australia Australia
139 J3 **Moomin** *R* New South Wales Australia
138 D4 **Moonaree** South Australia Australia
120 H3 **Moonbeam** Ontario Canada
140 F7 **Moonda L** Queensland Australia
141 J8 **Moonie** *R* Queensland Australia
141 K8 **Moonie** Queensland Australia
103 O1 **Moon L.Res** Utah U.S.A.
139 K4 **Moonoi Ra** *mts* New South Wales Australia
138 D5 **Moonta** South Australia Australia
143 B9 **Moora** W Australia Australia
140 F7 **Mooraberree** Queensland Australia
98 B5 **Moorcroft** Wyoming U.S.A.
101 M6 **Moore** Idaho U.S.A.
101 Q3 **Moore** Montana U.S.A.
107 N6 **Moore** Oklahoma U.S.A.
109 H6 **Moore** Texas U.S.A.
134 A11 **Moorea** *isld* Society Is Pacific Oc
116 J5 **Moore Creek** Alaska U.S.A.
98 F9 **Moorefield** Nebraska U.S.A.
94 J7 **Moorefield** West Virginia U.S.A.
113 F11 **Moore Haven** Florida U.S.A.
143 C8 **Moore, L** W Australia Australia
108 E7 **Mooreland** Oklahoma U.S.A.
140 D2 **Moore, Mt** N Terr Australia
143 E7 **Moore, Mt** W Australia Australia
143 C9 **Moore, Mt** W Australia Australia
143 A8 **Moore, Pt** W Australia Australia
95 Q2 **Moore Res** Vermont U.S.A.
112 J3 **Moores Cr. Nat. Mil. Park** North Carolina U.S.A.
113 K11 **Moore's I** Bahamas
122 E8 **Moore's Mills** New Brunswick Canada
110 K2 **Mooresville** Indiana U.S.A.
112 G2 **Mooresville** North Carolina U.S.A.
98 J3 **Mooreton** North Dakota U.S.A.
127 M2 **Moore Town** Jamaica
13 E2 **Moorfoot Hills** Scotland
98 K3 **Moorhead** Minnesota U.S.A.
111 F8 **Moorhead** Mississippi U.S.A.
101 U4 **Moorhead** Montana U.S.A.
109 O3 **Mooringsport** Louisiana U.S.A.
121 N6 **Moor Lake** Ontario Canada
99 M7 **Moorland** Iowa U.S.A.
110 J4 **Moorman** Kentucky U.S.A.
139 G5 **Moornanyah L** New South Wales Australia
87 F7 **Moorokosa** Zambia
141 K2 **Moorooka** *dist* Brisbane, Qnsld Australia
140 D1 **Mooroongga I** N Terr Australia
139 H6 **Mooroopna** Victoria Australia
102 F7 **Moorpark** California U.S.A.

22 G2 **Moorsel** Belgium
22 E2 **Moorslede** Belgium
89 F5 **Moos** *R* S Africa
37 N4 **Moosbach** Germany
32 L9 **Moosberg** *mt* Germany
37 M7 **Moosburg** Germany
120 J2 **Moose** *R* Ontario Canada
101 P6 **Moose** Wyoming U.S.A.
120 K1 **Moose Factory** Ontario Canada
95 S1 **Moosehead L** Maine U.S.A.
119 O2 **Moose Hill** Ontario Canada
119 T7 **Moosehorn** Manitoba Canada
119 U7 **Moose I** Manitoba Canada
119 M8 **Moose Jaw** Saskatchewan Canada
119 N8 **Moosejaw Cr** Saskatchewan Canada
99 O3 **Moose L** Minnesota U.S.A.
119 R5 **Moose Lake** Manitoba Canada
95 R2 **Mooselookmeguntic L** Maine U.S.A.
119 P9 **Moose Mt. Prov. Park** Saskatchewan Canada
119 W2 **Moose Nose L** Manitoba Canada
116 N6 **Moose Pass** Alaska U.S.A.
120 J2 **Moose River** Ontario Canada
37 N6 **Moosham** Germany
38 M8 **Mooskirchen** Austria
119 Q8 **Moosomin** Saskatchewan Canada
120 K1 **Moosonee** Ontario Canada
95 Q5 **Moosup** Connecticut U.S.A.
89 G7 **Moot** *R* S Africa
138 F4 **Mootwingee** New South Wales Australia
87 G9 **Mopeia** Mozambique
85 D6 **Mopti** Mali
77 K3 **Moqor** Afghanistan
99 P3 **Moquah** Wisconsin U.S.A.
128 D7 **Moquegua** *dept* Peru
128 D7 **Moquegua** Peru
48 E3 **Mór** Hungary
86 B3 **Mora** Cameroon
16 B6 **Mora** Portugal
16 E5 **Mora** Spain
27 G10 **Mora** Sweden
100 J6 **Mora** Idaho U.S.A.
99 N4 **Mora** Minnesota U.S.A.
106 E6 **Mora** New Mexico U.S.A.
46 C2 **Morača** *R* Montenegro Yugoslavia
131 B5 **Mora, Cerro** *pk* Arg/Chile
74 H4 **Moradabad** India
16 B5 **Moradal, Sa. do** *mts* Portugal
130 F6 **Morada Nova de Minas** Brazil
17 H3 **Mora de Ebro** Spain
17 G4 **Mora de Rubielos** Spain
87 G11 **Morafenobe** Madagascar
31 M2 **Morąg** Poland
83 K11 **Moragala** Sri Lanka
133 C6 **Moraleda, Canal** *str* Chile
109 L6 **Morales** Texas U.S.A.
87 H11 **Moramanga** Madagascar
110 A4 **Moran** Kansas U.S.A.
109 H3 **Moran** Texas U.S.A.
101 P6 **Moran** Wyoming U.S.A.
141 J5 **Moranbah** Queensland Australia
21 K6 **Morannes** France
43 G9 **Morano Cal** Italy
126 G6 **Morant Cays** *reefs* W Indies
16 C1 **Morás** *C* Spain
16 E4 **Moras** *R* Spain
16 E4 **Morata de T** Spain
17 F6 **Moratalla** Spain
83 J11 **Moratuwa** Sri Lanka
31 K7 **Morava** *R* Czechoslovakia
48 G6 **Morava** *R* Serbia Yugoslavia
48 D1 **Moravia** Czechoslovakia
99 O9 **Moravia** Iowa U.S.A.
95 L4 **Moravia** New York U.S.A.
46 D1 **Moravica** *R* Serbia Yugoslavia
31 K6 **Moravice** *R* Czechoslovakia
31 K6 **Moravská Třebová** Czechoslovakia
31 J6 **Moravski Budějovice** Czechoslovakia
143 B8 **Morawa** W Australia Australia
128 G2 **Morawhanna** Guyana
Moray *co see* **Grampian** *reg*
141 H5 **Moray Downs** Queensland Australia
15 E3 **Moray Firth** Scotland
140 B3 **Moray Ra** N Terr Australia
36 C4 **Morbach** Germany
22 C2 **Morbecque** France
41 L5 **Morbegno** Italy
74 D7 **Morbi** India
20 E6 **Morbihan, le** *B* France
27 H15 **Mörbylånga** Sweden
18 E8 **Morcenx** France
45 N4 **Morciano di Romagna** Italy
124 G5 **Morcillo** Mexico
45 R7 **Morcone** Italy
9 F2 **Morcott** England
59 H1 **Mordaga** China
20 G5 **Mordelles** France
98 H1 **Morden** Manitoba Canada
122 H8 **Morden** Nova Scotia Canada
139 H7 **Mordialloc** Victoria Australia
52 H4 **Mordino** Russian Federation
53 F7 **Mordovskaya Respublika** Russian Federation
116 E9 **Mordvinof, C** Aleutian Is
31 N3 **Mordy** Poland
20 E6 **Moréac** France
98 E4 **Moreau** *R* South Dakota U.S.A.
111 E10 **Moreauville** Louisiana U.S.A.
13 F3 **Morebattle** Scotland
13 F5 **Morecambe** England
7 H9 **Morecambe** *oil rig* Irish Sea
16 E7 **Moreda** Spain
139 J3 **Moree** New South Wales Australia
21 N6 **Morée** France
141 G2 **Morehead** *R* Queensland Australia
94 D8 **Morehead** Kentucky U.S.A.
112 L3 **Morehead City** North Carolina U.S.A.
110 G5 **Morehouse** Missouri U.S.A.
128 F4 **Moreira** Brazil
101 N6 **Moreland** Idaho U.S.A.
124 J8 **Morelia** Mexico
141 G6 **Morella** Queensland Australia
124 H6 **Morelos** Mexico
74 H5 **Morena** India
102 H9 **Morena Res** California U.S.A.
16 C7 **Morena, Sa** *mts* Spain
103 P8 **Morenci** Arizona U.S.A.
94 C5 **Morenci** Michigan U.S.A.
48 K6 **Moreni** Romania
124 D3 **Moreno** Mexico
26 C9 **More og Romsdal** *reg* Norway
145 F3 **Morere** New Zealand
12 E4 **Moresby** England
22 K2 **Moresnet** Belgium
40 B6 **Morestel** France
18 G4 **Moret** France
141 L7 **Moreton B** Queensland Australia
8 C6 **Moretonhampstead** England
141 L7 **Moreton I** Queensland Australia
9 E4 **Moreton in Marsh** England
95 P2 **Moretown** Vermont U.S.A.
21 P2 **Moreuil** France
40 D4 **Morez** France
36 F4 **Mörfelden** Germany
29 M3 **Morgam Viibus** *mt* Finland
138 E5 **Morgan** South Australia Australia
112 C6 **Morgan** Georgia U.S.A.
109 K3 **Morgan** Texas U.S.A.
101 O8 **Morgan** Utah U.S.A.
110 J4 **Morganfield** Kentucky U.S.A.
102 C4 **Morgan Hill** California U.S.A.
109 J3 **Morgan Mill** Texas U.S.A.
140 D4 **Morgan, Mt** N Terr Australia
102 F4 **Morgan, Mt** California U.S.A.
113 K12 **Morgan's Bluff** Bahamas
112 F2 **Morganton** North Carolina U.S.A.
110 K2 **Morgantown** Indiana U.S.A.
110 K4 **Morgantown** Kentucky U.S.A.
111 F10 **Morgantown** Mississippi U.S.A.
94 H7 **Morgantown** West Virginia U.S.A.
111 E11 **Morganza** Louisiana U.S.A.
20 A5 **Morgat** France
40 E4 **Morges** Switzerland
40 F6 **Morgex** Italy
21 O3 **Morgny** France
36 B6 **Morhange** France
22 K4 **Morhet** Belgium
122 K2 **Morhiban, L.de** Quebec Canada
66 E3 **Mori** China
41 N6 **Mori** Italy
60 O3 **Mori** Japan
127 M2 **Moriah** Tobago
95 O2 **Moriah** New York U.S.A.
103 K2 **Moriah, Mt** Nevada U.S.A.
22 H3 **Morialme** Belgium
108 A1 **Moriarty** New Mexico U.S.A.
141 H8 **Moriarty's Ra** Queensland Australia
117 K8 **Morice L** British Columbia Canada
128 D3 **Morichal** Colombia
45 N5 **Moricone** Italy
118 J4 **Morin Creek** Saskatchewan Canada
59 H2 **Morin Dawa** China
32 L9 **Moringen** Germany
52 D5 **Morino** Russian Federation
118 D5 **Morinville** Alberta Canada
61 P6 **Morioka** Japan
124 E3 **Moris** Mexico
139 K5 **Morisset** New South Wales Australia
122 B7 **Morisset Sta** Quebec Canada
32 L8 **Moritzberg** Germany
37 L5 **Moritzberg** *mt* Germany
61 O6 **Moriyashi-zan** *mt* Japan
138 F5 **Morkalla** Victoria Australia
28 E4 **Mørke** Denmark
52 G6 **Morki** Russian Federation
28 G5 **Mørkøv** Denmark
20 C4 **Morlaix** France
107 K2 **Morland** Kansas U.S.A.
36 F4 **Mörlenbach** Germany
118 C7 **Morley** Alberta Canada
13 G6 **Morley** England
106 F4 **Morley** Colorado U.S.A.
110 G4 **Morley** Missouri U.S.A.
117 G5 **Morley River** Yukon Territory Canada
45 N5 **Morlupe** Italy
43 G9 **Mormanno** Italy
19 O16 **Mormoiron** France
103 N7 **Mormon L** Arizona U.S.A.
101 L4 **Mormon Mt** Idaho U.S.A.
103 K5 **Mormon Mts** Nevada U.S.A.
19 N13 **Mornant** France
19 N16 **Mornas** France
83 M14 **Morne, Pte** Kerguelen Indian Oc
141 F7 **Morney** *R* Queensland Australia
141 F7 **Morney** Queensland Australia
140 F4 **Morning Inlet** *R* Queensland Australia
141 K1 **Morningside** *dist* Brisbane, Qnsld Australia
99 P8 **Morning Sun** Iowa U.S.A.
140 E3 **Mornington** Queensland Australia
140 E3 **Mornington I** Queensland Australia
133 B7 **Mornington, I** Chile
46 E6 **Mórnos** *R* Greece
36 F2 **Mornshausen** Germany
37 L6 **Mörnsheim** Germany
110 F7 **Moro** Arkansas U.S.A.
100 E4 **Moro** Oregon U.S.A.
136 K3 **Morobe** Papua New Guinea
85 C3 **Morocco** *kingdom* N Africa
99 T9 **Morocco** Indiana U.S.A.
88 F5 **Morogoro** Tanzania
71 F7 **Moro Gulf** Philippines
89 C6 **Morokweng** S Africa
124 J7 **Moroleón** Mexico
71 J7 **Moromaho** *isld* Indonesia
87 G12 **Morombe** Madagascar
126 E3 **Morón** Cuba
58 D2 **Mörön** Mongolia
40 F3 **Moron** *mt* Switzerland
127 K9 **Morón** Venezuela
128 C4 **Morona** Ecuador
128 C4 **Morona-Santiago** *prov* Ecuador
87 G12 **Morondava** Madagascar
17 F3 **Morón de Almazán** Spain
16 D7 **Morón de la Frontera** Spain
87 G10 **Moroni** Comoros
103 N2 **Moroni** Utah U.S.A.
66 E5 **Moron Us He** *R* China
61 K11 **Morosaki** Japan
71 B1 **Morotai** *isld* Halmahera Indonesia
48 E5 **Morovič** Serbia Yugoslavia
70 G5 **Morowali** Sulawesi
55 D2 **Morozkovo** Russian Federation
120 J10 **Morpeth** Ontario Canada
13 G3 **Morpeth** England
79 C3 **Morphou B** Cyprus
94 D6 **Morral** Ohio U.S.A.
130 E9 **Morretes** Brazil
99 L10 **Morrill** Kansas U.S.A.
98 C8 **Morrill** Nebraska U.S.A.
110 D6 **Morrilton** Arkansas U.S.A.
118 E7 **Morrin** Alberta Canada
130 E5 **Morrinhos** Brazil
145 E2 **Morrinsville** New Zealand
119 U9 **Morris** Manitoba Canada
99 S8 **Morris** Illinois U.S.A.
99 L4 **Morris** Minnesota U.S.A.
95 M4 **Morris** New York U.S.A.
107 P6 **Morris** Oklahoma U.S.A.
95 K5 **Morris** Pennsylvania U.S.A.
121 P8 **Morrisburg** Ontario Canada
112 H5 **Morris I** South Carolina U.S.A.
138 B2 **Morris, Mt** South Australia Australia
142 D4 **Morris, Mt** W Australia Australia
99 R8 **Morrison** Illinois U.S.A.
107 O5 **Morrison** Oklahoma U.S.A.
110 L6 **Morrison** Tennessee U.S.A.
144 C6 **Morrisons** New Zealand
110 G2 **Morrisonville** Illinois U.S.A.
113 E8 **Morriston** Florida U.S.A.
8 C4 **Morriston** Wales
103 M8 **Morristown** Arizona U.S.A.
99 N5 **Morristown** Minnesota U.S.A.
95 N6 **Morristown** New Jersey U.S.A.
95 M2 **Morristown** New York U.S.A.
98 E4 **Morristown** South Dakota U.S.A.
112 D1 **Morristown** Tennessee U.S.A.
95 M4 **Morrisville** New York U.S.A.
95 N6 **Morrisville** Pennsylvania U.S.A.
95 P2 **Morrisville** Vermont U.S.A.
94 K8 **Morrisville** Virginia U.S.A.
130 G4 **Morro** Brazil
130 E7 **Morro Agudo** Brazil
102 D6 **Morro B** California U.S.A.
131 A7 **Morro Bonifacio** *C* Chile
130 H6 **Morro d'Anta** Brazil
131 A8 **Morro del Compas** *C* Chile
129 G6 **Morro Do Sinal** Brazil
133 C3 **Morro, Pta** Chile
131 D4 **Morro, Sa. del** *pk* Argentina
126 G10 **Morrosquillo, G. de** Colombia
111 D11 **Morrow** Louisiana U.S.A.
110 M2 **Morrow** Ohio U.S.A.
88 E10 **Morrumbala** Mozambique
87 G10 **Morrumbene** Mozambique
28 B3 **Mors** *isld* Denmark
20 H2 **Morsalines** France
36 D2 **Morsbach** Germany
36 E6 **Mörsch** Germany
37 M2 **Mörsdorf** Germany
118 K8 **Morse** Saskatchewan Canada
111 D11 **Morse** Louisiana U.S.A.
108 C7 **Morse** Texas U.S.A.
53 F7 **Morshansk** Russian Federation
52 D3 **Morskaya Maselga** Russian Federation
27 E11 **Morskogen** Norway
33 O8 **Morsleben** Germany
118 H1 **Morson** Ontario Canada
43 B13 **Morsott** Algeria
140 E4 **Morstone** Queensland Australia
28 A7 **Morsum** Germany
26 H4 **Morsvik** Norway
140 F5 **Mort** *R* Queensland Australia
36 B7 **Mortagne** *R* France
21 M4 **Mortagne-au-Perche** France
21 J8 **Mortagne-sur-Sèvre** France
16 B4 **Mortágua** Portugal
21 J4 **Mortain** France
138 C5 **Mortana** South Australia Australia
41 J7 **Mortara** Italy
40 E3 **Morteau** France
21 K4 **Morteaux-Coulibœuf** France
8 B5 **Mortehoe** England
130 G7 **Mortes** *R* Brazil
129 H6 **Mortes, Rio das** *R* Brazil
22 F4 **Mortiers** France
8 D3 **Mortimers Cross** England
118 L8 **Mortlach** Saskatchewan Canada
139 G7 **Mortlake** Victoria Australia
99 R9 **Morton** Illinois U.S.A.
99 M5 **Morton** Minnesota U.S.A.
111 G9 **Morton** Mississippi U.S.A.
108 E2 **Morton** Texas U.S.A.
100 C3 **Morton** Washington U.S.A.
139 J5 **Morton Nat Park** New South Wales Australia
110 J4 **Mortons Gap** Kentucky U.S.A.
21 L4 **Mortrée** France
22 G1 **Mortsel** Belgium
28 E6 **Morud** Denmark
127 O3 **Moruga** Trinidad
139 H5 **Morundah** New South Wales Australia
139 K6 **Moruya** New South Wales Australia
18 H5 **Morvan** *mts* France
141 H7 **Morven** Queensland Australia
144 C6 **Morven** New Zealand
15 E2 **Morven** *mt* Scotland
113 D7 **Morven** Georgia U.S.A.
112 G3 **Morven** North Carolina U.S.A.
15 C4 **Morvern** Scotland
8 D2 **Morville** England
56 B3 **Moryakovskiy Zaton** Russian Federation
52 F2 **Morzhovets, Os** *isld* Russian Federation
116 F9 **Morzhovoi B** Alaska U.S.A.
54 F2 **Mosal'sk** Russian Federation
28 E1 **Mosbjerg** Denmark
101 S2 **Mosby** Montana U.S.A.
Moscow *see* **Moskva**
100 J3 **Moscow** Idaho U.S.A.
107 J4 **Moscow** Kansas U.S.A.
110 F3 **Moscow** Missouri U.S.A.
110 M3 **Moscow** Ohio U.S.A.
95 M5 **Moscow** Pennsylvania U.S.A.
110 G6 **Moscow** Tennessee U.S.A.
146 F14 **Moscow University Ice Shelf** *ice shelf* Antarctica
146 E14 **Mose, C** Antarctica
36 C3 **Mosel** *R* Germany
37 N2 **Mosel** Germany
94 K9 **Moseley** Virginia U.S.A.
36 C3 **Moselkern** Germany
36 B5 **Moselle** *dept* France
40 E1 **Moselle** *R* France
111 G10 **Moselle** Mississippi U.S.A.
40 E2 **Moselotte** *R* France
123 K9 **Moser River** Nova Scotia Canada
106 G5 **Moses** New Mexico U.S.A.
100 F2 **Moses Coulee** *R* Washington U.S.A.
100 H9 **Moses, Mt** Nevada U.S.A.
116 F4 **Moses Point** Alaska U.S.A.
60 P2 **Moseushi** Japan
52 G2 **Moseyevo** Russian Federation
144 C6 **Mosgiel** New Zealand
52 F4 **Mosha** *R* Russian Federation
52 C5 **Moshchnyy, Ostrov** *isld* Russian Federation
112 E1 **Mosheim** Tennessee U.S.A.
120 F4 **Mosher** Ontario Canada
88 F3 **Moshi** Tanzania
52 F6 **Moshok** Russian Federation
52 H3 **Mosh'yuga** Russian Federation
33 Q9 **Mosigkau** Germany
31 K3 **Mosina** Poland
99 R5 **Mosinee** Wisconsin U.S.A.
26 F6 **Mosjöen** Norway
55 F3 **Moskalenki** Russian Federation
59 M1 **Moskalvo** Russian Federation
98 B5 **Moskee** Wyoming U.S.A.
26 F4 **Moskenes** Norway
26 F4 **Moskenesöy** *isld* Norway
26 F4 **Moskenstraumen** *isld* Norway
26 M4 **Moskijärvi** Sweden
26 L6 **Moskosel** Sweden
29 M4 **Moskuvaara** Finland
49 **Moskva** *conurbation* Russian Federation
54 G1 **Moskva** *R* Russian Federation
56 D4 **Moskva, Gora** *mt* Russian Federation
54 J1 **Moskvy, Kanal Imeni** Russian Federation
42 H3 **Moslavacka Gora** *mt* Croatia
21 N7 **Mosnes** France
41 O4 **Moso** Italy
87 E10 **Mosomane** Botswana
48 D3 **Mosonmagyarovar** Hungary
89 D5 **Mosopa** Botswana
54 K9 **Mospino** Ukraine
128 C3 **Mosquera** Colombia
125 M2 **Mosquitia** *reg* Honduras
130 H4 **Mosquito** *R* Brazil
94 G5 **Mosquito Cr.Res** Ohio U.S.A.
113 G9 **Mosquito Lagoon** Florida U.S.A.
125 N3 **Mosquitos, Costa de** Nicaragua
27 E12 **Moss** Norway
130 E5 **Mossâmedes** Brazil
118 L9 **Mossbank** Saskatchewan Canada
15 G2 **Mossbank** Scotland
144 B6 **Mossburn** New Zealand
89 C10 **Mosselbaai** S Africa
86 B6 **Mossendjo** Congo
139 G5 **Mossgiel** New South Wales Australia
36 G7 **Mössingen** Germany
119 T1 **Moss L** Manitoba Canada
13 F6 **Mossley** England
141 H3 **Mossman** Queensland Australia
28 D4 **Mossø** *L* Denmark
129 L5 **Mossoro** Brazil
13 F3 **Mosspaul** Scotland
111 H11 **Moss Point** Mississippi U.S.A.
88 H9 **Mossuril** Mozambique
139 K5 **Moss Vale** New South Wales Australia
113 A7 **Mossy Head** Florida U.S.A.
119 U6 **Mossy Pt** Manitoba Canada
119 O4 **Mossy R** Saskatchewan Canada
100 C3 **Mossyrock** Washington U.S.A.
47 H3 **Most** Bulgaria
30 H5 **Most** Czechoslovakia
17 H9 **Mostaganem** Algeria
42 H5 **Mostar** Bosnia-Herzegovina
31 O6 **Mostiska** Ukraine
55 C3 **Mostovaya** Russian Federation
55 E3 **Mostovskoye** Russian Federation
31 P2 **Mosty** Belorussia
70 F2 **Mostyn** Sabah
8 C1 **Mostyn** Wales
27 C12 **Mös-vatn** *L* Norway
26 E8 **Mosvik** Norway
86 G3 **Mot'a** Ethiopia
86 C5 **Motaba** *R* Congo
17 F5 **Mota del Cuervo** Spain
16 D3 **Mota del Marqués** Spain
125 O10 **Motagua** *R* Guatemala
27 H13 **Motala** Sweden
127 J10 **Motatán** Venezuela
61 O9 **Motegi** Japan
20 G8 **Mothe-Achard, la** France
116 J8 **Mother Goose L** Alaska U.S.A.
12 E2 **Motherwell** Scotland
58 D5 **Motian Ling** *mt ra* China
40 F4 **Môtier** Switzerland
75 L5 **Motihari** India
71 A2 **Moti, I** California U.S.A.
17 F5 **Motilla del Palancar** Spain
145 F2 **Motiti I** New Zealand
27 G12 **Motjärnshyttan** Sweden
99 M3 **Motley** Minnesota U.S.A.
89 F3 **Motloutse** *R* Botswana
89 C5 **Motokwe** Botswana
60 O4 **Motomachi** Japan
71 J4 **Motongkat** Sulawesi
52 D1 **Motovskiy Zaliv** *G* Russian Federation
42 F3 **Motovun** Croatia
60 G12 **Motoyama** Japan
61 N13 **Moto-yama** *pk* Iwo Jima Japan
61 P7 **Motoyoshi** Japan
16 E8 **Motril** Spain
48 H6 **Motru** Romania
60 N3 **Motsuta misaki** *C* Japan
98 D3 **Mott** North Dakota U.S.A.
45 J1 **Motteggiana** Italy
20 E5 **Motte, la** France
36 H3 **Motten** Germany
21 M2 **Motteville** France
145 F3 **Motu** New Zealand
145 G3 **Motu Ahiauru** New Zealand
145 D4 **Motueka** New Zealand
145 F2 **Motuhora I** New Zealand
144 D5 **Motukarara** New Zealand
145 D1 **Motukawanui I** New Zealand
Motukorea I *see* **Browns I**
144 D5 **Motunau Beach** New Zealand
144 D5 **Motunau I** New Zealand
135 L10 **Motu One** *isld* Society Is Pacific Oc
145 G3 **Motuoroi I** New Zealand
145 D4 **Motupiko** New Zealand
145 F2 **Motu R** New Zealand
145 D1 **Moturoa Is** New Zealand
145 E3 **Motutaiko I** New Zealand
145 D1 **Motutang** New Zealand
145 E2 **Motutapu I** New Zealand
28 E3 **Mou** Denmark
122 C2 **Mouchalagane R.** Quebec Canada
21 H8 **Mouchamps** France
127 J4 **Mouchoir Passage** Caribbean
46 G5 **Moúdhros** Greece
85 B5 **Moudjéria** Mauritania
40 E4 **Moudon** Switzerland
86 B6 **Mouila** Gabon
21 J8 **Mouilleron-en-Pareds** France
86 D4 **Mouka** Cent Afr Republic
139 G6 **Moulamein** New South Wales Australia
16 C10 **Moulay-Bouselham** Morocco
114 H2 **Mould Bay** Northwest Territories Canada
127 N4 **Moule** Guadeloupe W Indies
86 H3 **Moulhoute** Djibouti
21 M4 **Moulicent** France
21 L7 **Mouliherne** France
18 H6 **Moulins** Allier France
21 K5 **Moulins** Sarthe France
18 H6 **Moulins-Engilbert** France
21 L4 **Moulins-la-Marche** France
21 O7 **Moulins-sur-Cephons** France
68 C4 **Moulmein** Burma
85 D2 **Moulouya, Oued** *R* Morocco
111 J7 **Moulton** Alabama U.S.A.
101 M7 **Moulton** Idaho U.S.A.
110 D1 **Moulton** Iowa U.S.A.
109 K6 **Moulton** Texas U.S.A.
112 D6 **Moultrie** Georgia U.S.A.
112 G4 **Moultrie, L** South Carolina U.S.A.
86 B6 **Mounana** Gabon
46 D6 **Moúnda, Akr** *C* Greece
111 F8 **Mound Bayou** Mississippi U.S.A.
110 G4 **Mound City** Illinois U.S.A.
110 B3 **Mound City** Kansas U.S.A.
99 L9 **Mound City** Missouri U.S.A.
98 F4 **Mound City** South Dakota U.S.A.
94 D7 **Mound City Nat.Mon** Ohio U.S.A.
86 C4 **Moundou** Chad
107 N3 **Mound Ridge** Kansas U.S.A.
110 G4 **Mounds** Illinois U.S.A.
107 O6 **Mounds** Oklahoma U.S.A.
94 G7 **Moundsville** West Virginia U.S.A.
110 A4 **Mound Valley** Kansas U.S.A.
111 J9 **Moundville** Alabama U.S.A.
68 F6 **Moung** Cambodia
68 F1 **Moung Hat Hin** Laos
98 J1 **Mountain** North Dakota U.S.A.
94 G7 **Mountain** West Virginia U.S.A.
108 A1 **Mountainair** New Mexico U.S.A.
8 C4 **Mountain Ash** Wales
100 K8 **Mountain City** Nevada U.S.A.
109 N10 **Mountain Creek L** Texas U.S.A.
109 N1 **Mountain Fork** *R* Oklahoma U.S.A.
110 D4 **Mountain Grove** Missouri U.S.A.
110 D5 **Mountain Home** Arkansas U.S.A.
100 K6 **Mountain Home** Idaho U.S.A.
109 H5 **Mountain Home** Texas U.S.A.
103 O1 **Mountain Home** Utah U.S.A.
112 G2 **Mountain Island L** North Carolina U.S.A.
117 P9 **Mountain Park** Alberta Canada
109 J1 **Mountain Park** Oklahoma U.S.A.
109 O1 **Mountain Pine** Arkansas U.S.A.
118 D9 **Mountain View** Alberta Canada
135 V5 **Mountain View** Hawaiian Is
110 D6 **Mountain View** Arkansas U.S.A.
110 E5 **Mountain View** Missouri U.S.A.
107 M6 **Mountain View** Oklahoma U.S.A.
101 P8 **Mountainview** Wyoming U.S.A.
116 F5 **Mountain Village** Alaska U.S.A.
95 K7 **Mount Airy** Maryland U.S.A.
112 G1 **Mount Airy** North Carolina U.S.A.
99 S4 **Mountan** Wisconsin U.S.A.
100 C4 **Mount Angel** Oregon U.S.A.
144 B6 **Mount Aspiring Nat. Park** New Zealand
118 B8 **Mount Assiniboine Prov Park** Br Col/Alberta Canada
99 R10 **Mount Auburn** Illinois U.S.A.
143 B6 **Mount Augustus** W Australia Australia
89 F8 **Mount Ayliff** S Africa
99 M9 **Mount Ayr** Iowa U.S.A.
138 E6 **Mount Barker** South Australia Australia
143 C10 **Mount Barker** W Australia Australia
142 F3 **Mount Barnett** W Australia Australia
14 C3 **Mount Bellew Br** Ireland
138 F3 **Mount Browne** New South Wales Australia
145 E4 **Mount Bruce** New Zealand
139 H6 **Mount Buller** Victoria Australia
120 J4 **Mount Byers** Ontario Canada
109 L4 **Mount Calm** Texas U.S.A.
141 H3 **Mount Carbine** Queensland Australia
123 T6 **Mount Carmel** Newfoundland Canada
110 J3 **Mount Carmel** Illinois U.S.A.
95 L6 **Mount Carmel** Pennsylvania U.S.A.
99 R7 **Mount Carroll** Illinois U.S.A.
140 C7 **Mount Cavenagh** N Terr Australia
98 H9 **Mount Clare** Nebraska U.S.A.
94 G7 **Mount Clare** West Virginia U.S.A.
143 C7 **Mount Clere** W Australia Australia
144 C5 **Mount Cook** New Zealand
141 H5 **Mount Coolon** Queensland Australia
88 C10 **Mount Darwin** Zimbabwe
140 B5 **Mount Denison** N Terr Australia
95 T2 **Mount Desert I** Maine U.S.A.
95 T3 **Mount Desert Rock** Maine U.S.A.
108 A7 **Mount Dora** New Mexico U.S.A.
140 B5 **Mount Doreen** N Terr Australia
141 H5 **Mount Douglas** Queensland Australia
138 D2 **Mount Dutton** South Australia Australia
138 D4 **Mount Eba** South Australia Australia
140 C7 **Mount Ebenezer** N Terr Australia
117 F7 **Mount Edgecumbe** Alaska U.S.A.
117 H7 **Mount Edziza Prov. Park** British Columbia Canada
101 P9 **Mount Emmons** Utah U.S.A.
141 G5 **Mount Emu Plains** Queensland Australia
109 N4 **Mount Enterprise** Texas U.S.A.
140 C6 **Mount Ertwa** N Terr Australia
89 F8 **Mount Fletcher** S Africa
89 F8 **Mount Frere** S Africa
138 F6 **Mount Gambier** South Australia Australia
141 H4 **Mount Garnet** Queensland Australia
112 H2 **Mount Gilead** North Carolina U.S.A.
94 E6 **Mount Gilead** Ohio U.S.A.
141 L2 **Mount Gravatt** *dist* Brisbane, Qnsld Australia
136 J3 **Mount Hagen** Papua New Guinea
106 C1 **Mount Harris** Colorado U.S.A.
100 C8 **Mount Hebron** California U.S.A.
95 N6 **Mount Holly** New Jersey U.S.A.
94 K6 **Mount Holly** Pennsylvania U.S.A.
138 D5 **Mount Hope** South Australia Australia
107 N4 **Mount Hope** Kansas U.S.A.
99 R6 **Mount Horeb** Wisconsin U.S.A.
142 F3 **Mount House** W Australia Australia
141 F7 **Mount Howitt** Queensland Australia
144 C5 **Mount Hutt** New Zealand
109 O1 **Mount Ida** Arkansas U.S.A.
100 J4 **Mount Idaho** Idaho U.S.A.
140 E5 **Mount Isa** Queensland Australia
94 J8 **Mount Jackson** Virginia U.S.A.
94 J5 **Mount Jewett** Pennsylvania U.S.A.
120 H6 **Mount L** Ontario Canada
141 K6 **Mount Larcom** Queensland Australia
83 J11 **Mount Lavinia** Sri Lanka
142 B1 **Mount Lawley** *dist* Perth, W Aust Australia
138 E6 **Mount Lofty Ra** S Australia Australia
141 H5 **Mount McConnell** Queensland Australia
143 C8 **Mount Magnet** W Australia Australia
139 G4 **Mount Manara** New South Wales Australia
141 G6 **Mount Marlow** Queensland Australia
145 F2 **Mount Maunganui** New Zealand
100 E9 **Mount Meadows Res** California U.S.A.
14 D3 **Mountmellick** Ireland
141 H3 **Mount Molloy** Queensland Australia
102 F4 **Mount Montgomery** Nevada U.S.A.
141 K6 **Mount Morgan** Queensland Australia
110 C1 **Mount Moriah** Missouri U.S.A.
99 R7 **Mount Morris** Illinois U.S.A.
94 K4 **Mount Morris** New York U.S.A.
139 G4 **Mount Murchison** New South Wales Australia
106 D2 **Mount of the Holy Cross** Colorado U.S.A.
110 G2 **Mount Olive** Illinois U.S.A.
111 G10 **Mount Olive** Mississippi U.S.A.
110 M3 **Mount Olivet** Kentucky U.S.A.
110 N2 **Mount Orab** Ohio U.S.A.
121 S7 **Mount Orford, Parc de** Quebec Canada
141 K7 **Mount Perry** Queensland Australia
99 P9 **Mount Pleasant** Iowa U.S.A.
94 C3 **Mount Pleasant** Michigan U.S.A.
94 H6 **Mount Pleasant** Pennsylvania U.S.A.
110 J6 **Mount Pleasant** Tennessee U.S.A.
109 N2 **Mount Pleasant** Texas U.S.A.
103 N2 **Mount Pleasant** Utah U.S.A.
95 M5 **Mount Pocono** Pennsylvania U.S.A.
99 R9 **Mount Pulaski** Illinois U.S.A.
100 D3 **Mount Rainier Nat.Pk** Washington U.S.A.
14 D3 **Mountrath** Ireland
117 O10 **Mount Revelstoke Nat. Park** British Columbia Canada
106 C10 **Mount Riley** New Mexico U.S.A.
98 C6 **Mount Rushmore Nat.Mem** South Dakota U.S.A.
140 B3 **Mount Sanford** N Terr Australia
94 J7 **Mount Savage** Maryland U.S.A.
9 F7 **Mount's B** England
109 M3 **Mount Selman** Texas U.S.A.
140 C7 **Mount Squires** N Terr Australia
99 Q10 **Mount Sterling** Illinois U.S.A.
110 M3 **Mount Sterling** Kentucky U.S.A.
94 D7 **Mount Sterling** Ohio U.S.A.
122 K7 **Mount Stewart** Prince Edward I Canada
94 H7 **Mount Storm** West Virginia U.S.A.
142 B5 **Mount Stuart** W Australia Australia
141 G5 **Mount Sturgeon** Queensland Australia
141 G4 **Mount Surprise** Queensland Australia
140 D6 **Mount Swan** N Terr Australia
103 L5 **Mount Trumbull** Arizona U.S.A.
122 J9 **Mount Uniacke** Nova Scotia Canada
94 K6 **Mount Union** Pennsylvania U.S.A.
143 C6 **Mount Vernon** W Australia Australia
111 J10 **Mount Vernon** Alabama U.S.A.
110 D6 **Mount Vernon** Arkansas U.S.A.
112 E5 **Mount Vernon** Georgia U.S.A.
110 H3 **Mount Vernon** Illinois U.S.A.
110 J4 **Mount Vernon** Indiana U.S.A.
99 P8 **Mount Vernon** Iowa U.S.A.
110 M4 **Mount Vernon** Kentucky U.S.A.
110 C4 **Mount Vernon** Missouri U.S.A.
95 O6 **Mount Vernon** New York U.S.A.
94 E6 **Mount Vernon** Ohio U.S.A.
100 F5 **Mount Vernon** Oregon U.S.A.
98 H6 **Mount Vernon** South Dakota U.S.A.
109 M2 **Mount Vernon** Texas U.S.A.
95 K8 **Mount Vernon** Virginia U.S.A.
100 C1 **Mount Vernon** Washington U.S.A.
94 D6 **Mount Victory** Ohio U.S.A.
140 B6 **Mount Wedge** N Terr Australia
138 D5 **Mount Wedge** South Australia Australia
111 K9 **Mount Willing** Alabama U.S.A.
138 C3 **Mount Willoughby** South Australia Australia
142 B1 **Mount Yokine** *dist* Perth, W Aust Australia
110 H2 **Mount Zion** Illinois U.S.A.
99 P9 **Mount Zion** Iowa U.S.A.
141 J6 **Moura** Queensland Australia
128 D5 **Moura** *R* Brazil
16 C6 **Moura** Portugal
85 C6 **Mourdiah** Mali
19 N17 **Mouriès** France
141 H4 **Mourilyan Harbour** Queensland Australia
14 D2 **Mourne** *R* N Ireland
14 E2 **Mourne Mts** N Ireland
15 G2 **Mousa** *isld* Shetland Scotland
22 E2 **Mouscron** Belgium
98 E1 **Mouse** *R* North Dakota U.S.A.
18 F7 **Mousin** *reg* France
36 B6 **Moussey** Moselle France
36 C7 **Moussey** Vosges France
86 C3 **Moussoro** Chad
20 D4 **Mousterus** France
19 Q17 **Moustiers** France
12 E3 **Mouswald** Scotland
36 C6 **Mouterhouse** France
40 D4 **Mouthe** France
40 D3 **Mouthier** France
40 F3 **Moutier** Switzerland
40 E7 **Moutiers** France
21 M5 **Moutiers-au-Perche** France
70 G4 **Moutong** Sulawesi
21 P3 **Mouy** France
22 J5 **Mouzay** France
22 J4 **Mouzon** France
124 E3 **Movas** Mexico
14 D1 **Moville** Ireland
99 L7 **Moville** Iowa U.S.A.
142 E3 **Mowanjum** W Australia Australia
141 K7 **Mowbullan, Mt** Queensland Australia
99 S10 **Moweaqua** Illinois U.S.A.
145 E3 **Mowhanau** New Zealand
100 D6 **Mowich** Oregon U.S.A.
100 E3 **Moxee City** Washington U.S.A.
130 H10 **Moxotó,R** Brazil
14 B3 **Moy** *R* Ireland
17 J3 **Moyá** Spain
106 F6 **Moya** *R* New Mexico U.S.A.
124 H7 **Moyahua** Mexico
86 G5 **Moyale** Kenya
85 B7 **Moyamba** Sierra Leone
21 L3 **Moyaux** France
22 E4 **Moy-de-l'Aisne** France
65 E6 **Moye Dao** *isld* China
36 B7 **Moyenmoutier** France
83 K12 **Moyenne** *isld* Mahé I Indian Oc
21 O1 **Moyenneville** France
36 B6 **Moyenvic** France
100 K1 **Moyie** British Columbia Canada
100 J1 **Moyie Springs** Idaho U.S.A.
86 C4 **Moyo** Chad
128 C5 **Moyobamba** Peru
86 C3 **Moyto** Chad
57 E2 **Moyynkum** *desert* Kazakhstan
57 G3 **Moyynkum** Kazakhstan
57 E3 **Moyynkum, Peski** *desert* Kazakhstan
57 G2 **Moyynty** Kazakhstan
87 G9 **Mozambique** *rep* Africa
81 B9 **Mozambique Ridge** Indian Oc
120 H6 **Mozhabong L** Ontario Canada
52 E6 **Mozhaysk** Russian Federation
52 H6 **Mozhga** Russian Federation
77 G2 **Mozhnābād** Iran
68 B1 **Mozo** Burma
45 J1 **Mozzecane** Italy
87 E7 **Mpala** Zaire
89 D2 **Mpandamatenga** Botswana
88 C7 **Mpika** Zambia
88 C6 **Mporokoso** Zambia
86 C6 **M'Pouya** Congo
85 D7 **Mpraeso** Ghana
87 F7 **Mpulungu** Zambia
87 G7 **Mpwapwa** Tanzania
31 N2 **Mragowo** Poland
55 C4 **Mrakovo** Russian Federation
56 C4 **Mras-Su** *R* Russian Federation
85 C4 **Mreiti,El** Mauritania
88 C10 **Mrewa** Zimbabwe
42 H4 **Mrkonjič Grad** Bosnia-Herzegovina
31 J5 **Mrlina** *R* Czechoslovakia
31 J1 **Mrzeżyno** Poland
43 D13 **M'saken** Tunisia
31 H5 **Mšeno** Czechoslovakia
52 D5 **Msta** *R* Russian Federation
54 C2 **Mstislavl'** Belorussia
31 M4 **Mszczonów** Poland
88 C5 **Mtakuja** Tanzania
89 G6 **Mtambama Mt** Swaziland
88 C5 **Mtambo** *R* Tanzania
89 F8 **Mtata** S Africa
120 J10 **Mt. Brydges** Ontario Canada
103 M4 **Mt Carmel** Utah U.S.A.
89 G8 **Mtentu** S Africa
144 C5 **Mt Hutt** New Zealand
89 G3 **Mtilikwe** *R* Zimbabwe
141 G6 **Mt Marlow** Queensland Australia
144 C5 **Mt Somers** New Zealand
87 F11 **Mtubatuba** S Africa
88 H7 **Mtwara** Tanzania
88 G7 **Mtwara** *reg* Tanzania
16 B7 **Mu** *mt* Portugal
88 G7 **Mualo** *R* Mozambique
88 C8 **Muamadzi** *R* Zambia
21 K3 **Muance** *R* France
68 F6 **Muang** Cambodia
68 E4 **Muang Botene** Thailand
68 G5 **Muang Bua** Thailand
68 E5 **Muang Chainat** Thailand
68 E3 **Muang Chaiyaphum** Thailand
68 E4 **Muang Chiang Khan** Thailand
68 D3 **Muang Chiang Rai** Thailand
68 G4 **Muang Hinboun** Laos
68 F4 **Muang Kalasin** Thailand
68 G5 **Muang Khong** Laos
68 G5 **Muang Khong-Xedon** Laos
68 D4 **Muang Kosamphi** Thailand
69 D8 **Muang Krabi** Thailand
68 D3 **Muang Lampang** Thailand
68 D3 **Muang Lamphun** Thailand
68 E4 **Muang Loei** Thailand
68 D3 **Muang Long** Thailand
68 G4 **Muang Nakhon Phanom** Thailand
68 D5 **Muang Nakhon Sawan** Thailand
68 D3 **Muang Ngao** Thailand
68 E3 **Muang Oi** Thailand
68 G4 **Muang Phaluka** Thailand
68 D3 **Muang Phan** Thailand
68 F4 **Muang Phannanikhom** Thailand
68 D3 **Muang Phayao** Thailand
68 E4 **Muang Phetchabun** Thailand
68 E4 **Muang Phichai** Thailand
68 E4 **Muang Phichit** Thailand
68 E3 **Muang Phrae** Thailand
68 G4 **Muang Renu Nakhon** Thailand
68 F5 **Muang Roi Et** Thailand
68 F4 **Muang Sakon Nakhon** Thailand
68 G5 **Muang Sam Sip** Thailand
68 G5 **Muang Si Chalalai** Thailand
68 F4 **Muang Song** Thailand
68 D4 **Muang Thoen** Thailand
69 F11 **Muar** *R* Malaysia
69 F11 **Muar** Malaysia
70 D2 **Muara** Brunei
70 E3 **Muara** Kalimantan
70 E4 **Muaraancalong** Kalimantan
70 E4 **Muaraatap** Kalimantan
70 K9 **Muarabinuangeun** Java
69 F13 **Muarabulian** Sumatra
69 E13 **Muarabungo** Sumatra
70 K8 **Muaradua** Sumatra
69 F14 **Muaraenim** Sumatra
70 D5 **Muarainu** Kalimantan
70 E5 **Muarajawa** Kalimantan
70 E5 **Muarakaman** Kalimantan
70 C5 **Muarakayang** Kalimantan
69 E13 **Muaralabuh** Sumatra
69 F14 **Muaralakitan** Sumatra
70 D5 **Muaralaung** Kalimantan
70 E4 **Muaralesan** Kalimantan
70 E4 **Muaramayang** Kalimantan
70 E4 **Muaranawai** Kalimantan
69 F14 **Muararupit** Sumatra
69 F13 **Muarasabak** Sumatra
69 D13 **Muarasiberut** Indonesia
69 D13 **Muarasigep** Indonesia
69 D12 **Muarasipongi** Sumatra
69 D12 **Muarasoma** Sumatra
70 F4 **Muaras Rf** Indonesia
69 F13 **Muaratebo** Sumatra
69 F13 **Muaratembesi** Sumatra
70 D5 **Muarateweh** Kalimantan
70 E4 **Muarawahau** Kalimantan
71 A3 **Muari** Halmahera Indonesia
57 D5 **Mubarek** Uzbekistan
77 A7 **Mubarraz,Al** Saudi Arabia
88 C1 **Mubende** Uganda
80 G5 **Mubis** Jordan
79 F8 **Mubrak, J** *mt* Jordan
69 H11 **Mubur** *isld* Indonesia
142 C5 **Muccan** W Australia Australia
36 C2 **Much** Germany
117 K11 **Muchalat** British Columbia Canada
15 F3 **Muchalls** Scotland
143 B9 **Muchea** W Australia Australia
33 P10 **Mücheln** Germany
88 C8 **Muchinga Escarpment** Zambia
52 G3 **Muchkas** Russian Federation
67 A2 **Muchuan** China
8 D2 **Much Wenlock** England
15 B4 **Muck** *isld* Inner Hebrides Scotland
141 J7 **Muckadilla** Queensland Australia
14 D1 **Muckish Mt** Ireland
15 G1 **Muckle Flugga** *isld* Shetland Scotland
15 G2 **Muckle Roe** *isld* Shetland Scotland
9 E2 **Muckley Corner** England
14 C2 **Muckros Hd** Ireland
88 H8 **Mucojo** Mozambique
87 D8 **Muconda** Angola
130 H6 **Mucuri** Brazil
130 H5 **Mucuri,R** Brazil
87 D9 **Mucusso** Angola
69 E10 **Muda** *R* Malaysia
80 G7 **Mudaiyina** Jordan
65 H2 **Mudan Jiang** *R* China
65 H2 **Mudanjiang** China
47 K4 **Mudanya** Turkey
47 N10 **Mudarlı** Turkey
36 G4 **Mudau** Germany
98 D4 **Mud Butte** South Dakota U.S.A.
98 G8 **Mud Cr** Nebraska U.S.A.
76 C2 **Muddebihāl** India
26 L5 **Muddus Nat. Park** Sweden
107 O7 **Muddy Boggy Cr** Oklahoma U.S.A.
103 N3 **Muddy Cr** Utah U.S.A.
101 T7 **Muddy Cr** Wyoming U.S.A.
101 P8 **Muddy Cr** Wyoming U.S.A.
101 S8 **Muddy Cr** Wyoming U.S.A.
101 S7 **Muddy Gap** *pass* Wyoming U.S.A.
118 H6 **Muddy L** Saskatchewan Canada
103 K5 **Muddy Pk** Nevada U.S.A.
33 M7 **Müden** Germany
139 J4 **Mudgee** New South Wales Australia
141 H6 **Mudge, Mt** Queensland Australia
76 B2 **Mudhol** India
74 G9 **Mudhol** Andhra Pradesh India
101 N6 **Mud L** Idaho U.S.A.
101 Q1 **Mud L** Montana U.S.A.
102 G4 **Mud L** Nevada U.S.A.
98 H4 **Mud L.Res** South Dakota U.S.A.
68 C4 **Mudon** Burma
47 L4 **Mudurnu** *R* Turkey

52 E3 **Mud'yuga** Russian Federation
88 D10 **Mudzi** *R* Zimbabwe
21 K3 **Mue** *R* France
88 G7 **Mueda** Mozambique
20 F5 **Muel** France
17 G4 **Muela de Ares** *mt* Spain
17 G3 **Muela,Sierra de la** Spain
142 G4 **Mueller, Mt** W Australia Australia
142 F4 **Mueller Ra** W Australia Australia
141 F6 **Muellers Ra** Queensland Australia
119 N6 **Muenster** Saskatchewan Canada
109 K2 **Muenster** Texas U.S.A.
125 N2 **Muerto,Cayo** *isld* Nicaragua
126 D2 **Muertos Cays** *reefs* Bahamas
52 G3 **Muftyuga** Russian Federation
88 B8 **Mufulira** Zambia
67 E2 **Mufu Shan** *mts* Jiangxi/Hubei China
67 B5 **Mugang** China
16 B5 **Muge** Portugal
87 G9 **Mugeba** Mozambique
45 K4 **Mugello** Italy
33 S10 **Mügeln** Germany
37 L4 **Muggendorf** Germany
79 H9 **Mughayrā', Al** Saudi Arabia
59 K5 **Mugi** Japan
16 A1 **Mugia** Spain
88 B5 **Mugila** *mts* Zaire
47 J7 **Muğla** Turkey
47 H2 **Müglizh** Bulgaria
57 A1 **Mugodzhary** *mts* Kazakhstan
18 E9 **Mugron** France
75 K4 **Mugu** Nepal
86 G1 **Muhammad Qol** Sudan
77 B6 **Muharraq,Al** Bahrain
36 F6 **Mühlacker** Germany
36 H2 **Mühlbach** Germany
33 S10 **Mühlberg** Brandenburg Germany
37 K2 **Mühlberg** Thüringen Germany
38 G5 **Mühldorf** Germany
41 K3 **Mühlehorn** Switzerland
33 S7 **Mühlenbeck** Germany
33 O5 **Mühlen Eichsen** Germany
37 J1 **Mühlhausen** Germany
37 K4 **Mühlhausen** Germany
36 C4 **Mühlheim** Germany
146 H6 **Mühlig-Hofmannfjella** *mts* Antarctica
37 M2 **Mühltroff** Germany
29 M7 **Muhos** Finland
38 H7 **Muhr** Austria
80 D3 **Muhraqa** Israel
36 F7 **Mühringen** Germany
52 B5 **Muhu** Estonia
88 C2 **Muhutwe** Tanzania
88 F7 **Muhuwesi** *R* Tanzania
69 G8 **Mui Bai Bung** Vietnam
68 J4 **Mui Chon May Dong** *C* Vietnam
68 J7 **Mui da Vaich** *C* Vietnam
25 D4 **Muiden** Netherlands
21 O6 **Muides-sur-Loire** France
68 J7 **Mui Dinh** *C* Vietnam
21 N3 **Muids** France
61 M8 **Muikamachi** Japan
71 B3 **Muilijk** *isld* Indonesia
14 E4 **Muine Bheag** Ireland
94 C3 **Muir** Michigan U.S.A.
88 D10 **Muira** *R* Mozambique
13 F1 **Muirdrum** Scotland
117 E6 **Muir Gl** Alaska U.S.A.
13 E1 **Muirhead** Scotland
12 D3 **Muirkirk** Scotland
143 B10 **Muir, L** W Australia Australia
143 G7 **Muir, Mt** W Australia Australia
142 A5 **Muiron I., N** W Australia Australia
102 B4 **Muir Woods Nat.Mon** California U.S.A.
87 G8 **Muite** Mozambique
68 J6 **Mui Yen** *C* Vietnam
125 Q7 **Mujeres, I** Mexico
80 F8 **Mujib** *R* Jordan
87 D8 **Mujimbeji** Zambia
70 C3 **Mujong** *R* Sarawak
48 H2 **Mukachevo** Ukraine
70 C3 **Mukah** Sarawak
72 F6 **Mukallā, Al** Yemen
80 E6 **Mukallik** *R* Jordan
60 P3 **Mukawa** Japan
60 Q3 **Mu-kawa** *R* Japan
80 F7 **Mukawir** Jordan
86 G1 **Mukawwar I** Sudan
68 G4 **Mukdahan** Thailand
Mukden *see* **Shenyang**
13 F5 **Muker** England
72 E6 **Mukha, Al** Yemen
84 G3 **Mukhaylī, Al** Libya
74 G9 **Mukher** India
80 E6 **Mukhmas** Jordan
58 F1 **Mukhor-Konduy** Russian Federation
143 C9 **Mukinbudin** W Australia Australia
69 D9 **Muk,Ko** *isld* Thailand
69 E14 **Mukomuko** Sumatra
33 P9 **Mukrena** Germany
57 D5 **Mukry** Turkmenistan
75 K4 **Muktinath** Nepal
86 D7 **Mukumbi** Zaire
86 G5 **Mukutan** Kenya
119 U5 **Mukutawa R** Manitoba Canada
87 D9 **Mukwe** Namibia
99 S7 **Mukwonago** Wisconsin U.S.A.
17 G6 **Mula** Spain
73 L8 **Mulaku Atoll** Maldives
57 J2 **Mulaly** Kazakhstan
65 G2 **Mulan** China
71 F4 **Mulanay** Philippines
88 E9 **Mulanje** *mt* Malawi
88 E10 **Mulanje** Malawi
129 H4 **Mulata** Brazil
124 E3 **Mulatos** Mexico
125 Q5 **Mulatupo Sasardi** Panama
110 B6 **Mulberry** Arkansas U.S.A.
110 C6 **Mulberry** *R* Arkansas U.S.A.
113 F10 **Mulberry** Florida U.S.A.
110 K1 **Mulberry** Indiana U.S.A.
107 Q4 **Mulberry** Kansas U.S.A.
110 B4 **Mulberry** Missouri U.S.A.
111 K8 **Mulberry Fork** *R* Alabama U.S.A.
110 G3 **Mulberry Grove** Illinois U.S.A.
116 K6 **Mulchatna** *R* Alaska U.S.A.
133 C5 **Mulchen** Chile
37 P2 **Mulda** Germany
28 E3 **Muldbjerge** *hill* Denmark
33 Q9 **Mulde** *R* Germany
101 M6 **Muldoon** Idaho U.S.A.
108 E5 **Mule Cr** Texas U.S.A.
98 B6 **Mule Cr** Wyoming U.S.A.
106 B8 **Mule Creek** New Mexico U.S.A.
124 C4 **Mulegé** Mexico
80 G7 **Muleih** Jordan
88 C8 **Mulembo** *R* Zambia
86 D6 **Mulenda** Zaire
71 K9 **Mules** *isld* Flores Indonesia
108 E1 **Muleshoe** Texas U.S.A.
87 G9 **Mulevala** Mozambique
36 H5 **Mulfingen** Germany
142 C5 **Mulga Downs** W Australia Australia
140 B7 **Mulga Park** N Terr Australia
138 C4 **Mulgathing** South Australia Australia
138 C4 **Mulgathing Rocks** *mt* South Australia Australia
123 L8 **Mulgrave** Nova Scotia Canada
116 F3 **Mulgrave Hills** Alaska U.S.A.
143 C6 **Mulgul** W Australia Australia
16 E7 **Mulhacén** *mt* Spain
107 N5 **Mulhall** Oklahoma U.S.A.
32 E10 **Mülheim** Germany
40 F2 **Mulhouse** France
65 H2 **Muling** China
65 D6 **Muling Guan** *pass* China
65 J2 **Muling He** *R* China
138 E3 **Mulka** South Australia Australia
76 B4 **Mulki** India
15 C4 **Mull** *isld* Scotland
14 B4 **Mullaghareirk Mts** Ireland
83 K8 **Mullaittivu** Sri Lanka
139 J4 **Mullaley** New South Wales Australia
100 K2 **Mullan** Idaho U.S.A.
98 E7 **Mullen** Nebraska U.S.A.
109 J4 **Mullen** Texas U.S.A.
139 H4 **Mullengudgery** New South Wales Australia
94 F9 **Mullens** West Virginia U.S.A.
140 C6 **Muller** *R* N Terr Australia
70 C4 **Muller,Peg** *mts* Kalimantan
113 E10 **Mullet Key** *isld* Florida U.S.A.
94 C1 **Mullett L** Michigan U.S.A.
143 B8 **Mullewa** W Australia Australia
15 F1 **Mull Head** Orkney Scotland
40 G2 **Müllheim** Germany
95 N7 **Mullica** *R* New Jersey U.S.A.
140 E6 **Mulligan** *R* Queensland Australia
14 D3 **Mullingar** Ireland
112 H3 **Mullins** South Carolina U.S.A.
107 L4 **Mullinville** Kansas U.S.A.
139 J5 **Mullion Creek** New South Wales Australia
83 K8 **Mulliyavalai** Sri Lanka
15 D6 **Mull of Galloway** Scotland
15 C5 **Mull of Kintyre** Scotland
12 B2 **Mull of Oa** Scotland
27 G14 **Mullsjö** Sweden
15 C4 **Mull, Sound of** Scotland
139 L3 **Mullumbimby** New South Wales Australia
80 F6 **Mul Nevo** Jordan
87 E9 **Mulobezi** Zambia
87 C9 **Mulondo** Angola
87 E7 **Mulongo** Zaire
138 E3 **Muloorina** South Australia Australia
14 D1 **Mulroy B** Ireland
21 L6 **Mulsanne** France
33 P5 **Mulsow** Germany
74 D3 **Multan** Pakistan
55 F1 **Multanovy** Russian Federation
29 L9 **Multia** Finland
26 J8 **Multrå** Sweden
70 D2 **Mulu, G** *mt* Sarawak
130 J9 **Mulungu** Brazil
107 N4 **Mulvane** Kansas U.S.A.
119 T8 **Mulvihill** Manitoba Canada
139 G4 **Mulyah,Mt** New South Wales Australia
55 E1 **Mulym'ya** *R* Russian Federation
138 F4 **Mulyungarie** South Australia Australia
8 C4 **Mumbles** Wales
87 B8 **Mumbondo** Angola
87 C8 **Mumbué** Angola
87 E8 **Mumbwa** Zambia
87 E8 **Mumena** Zaire
109 L5 **Mumford** Texas U.S.A.
69 D9 **Mum Nauk,Laem** *C* Thailand
71 H7 **Muna** *isld* Indonesia
125 P7 **Muna** Mexico
67 B5 **Munankwan Lin** *pass* Vietnam/China
141 G2 **Munburra** Queensland Australia
37 M3 **Münchberg** Germany
30 H3 **Müncheberg** Germany
39 **München** *conurbation* Germany
37 M2 **Münchenbernsdorf** Germany
36 F2 **Münchhausen** Germany
117 L6 **Muncho Lake** British Columbia Canada
37 N5 **Münchshofen** Germany
37 O6 **Münchshofen** Germany
37 M6 **Münchsmünster** Germany
110 L1 **Muncie** Indiana U.S.A.
140 E7 **Muncoonie, L** Queensland Australia
95 L5 **Muncy** Pennsylvania U.S.A.
118 E5 **Mundare** Alberta Canada
109 H2 **Munday** Texas U.S.A.
99 S7 **Mundelein** Illinois U.S.A.
83 J10 **Mundel L** Sri Lanka
32 L10 **Münden** Germany
98 J10 **Munden** Kansas U.S.A.
36 H7 **Munderkingen** Germany
9 H2 **Mundesley** England
9 G2 **Mundford** England
143 D6 **Mundiwindi** W Australia Australia
141 F4 **Mundjuro** *R* Queensland Australia
17 F6 **Mundo** *R* Spain
129 K6 **Mundo Nôvo** Brazil
143 G9 **Mundrabilla** W Australia Australia
141 K7 **Mundubbera** Queensland Australia
56 C4 **Mundybash** Russian Federation
46 D3 **Munella** *mt* Albania
17 F5 **Munera** Spain
110 L4 **Munfordville** Kentucky U.S.A.
141 J7 **Mungallala** Queensland Australia
141 H8 **Mungallala** *R* Queensland Australia
141 G3 **Mungana** Queensland Australia
87 F9 **Mungari** Mozambique
142 C5 **Mungaroona Ra** W Australia Australia
56 D5 **Mungash-Kul', Gora** *mt* Russian Federation
86 E5 **Mungbere** Zaire
75 J7 **Mungeli** India
75 M6 **Munger** India
94 D3 **Munger** Michigan U.S.A.
138 E3 **Mungerannie** South Australia Australia
69 J12 **Mungguresak, Tanjong** *C* Indonesia
141 J8 **Mungindi** Queensland Australia
87 C8 **Munhango** Angola
Munich Germany *see* **München**
98 H1 **Munich** North Dakota U.S.A.
88 B8 **Muniengashi** *R* Zaire
17 G3 **Muniesa** Spain
130 H7 **Muniz Freire** Brazil
28 H5 **Munke Bjergby** Denmark
28 F6 **Munkebo** Denmark
27 E13 **Munkedal** Sweden
26 G8 **Munkflohögen** Sweden
27 G12 **Munkfors** Sweden
28 A7 **Munkmarsch** Germany
26 M6 **Munksund** Sweden
56 F5 **Munku-Sardyk,Gora** *mt* Mongolia/Rus Fed
37 J3 **Münnerstadt** Germany
22 J4 **Muno** Belgium
71 E3 **Muñoz** Luzon Philippines
133 C8 **Muñoz Gamero, Pen** Chile
139 J8 **Munro,Mt** Tasmania Australia
36 H7 **Münsingen** Germany
118 E7 **Munson** Alberta Canada
111 K11 **Munson** Florida U.S.A.
40 F1 **Munster** France
32 M7 **Münster** Niedersachsen Germany
32 G9 **Münster** Nordrhein-Westfalen Germany
14 B4 **Munster** *prov* Ireland
41 H5 **Münster** Switzerland
36 C3 **Münstermaifeld** Germany
143 C9 **Muntadgin** W Australia Australia
70 F4 **Munte** Sulawesi
48 H4 **Muntelui Mare** *mt* Romania
70 P10 **Muntjar** Java
87 E9 **Munyati** *R* Zimbabwe
36 F3 **Münzenberg** Germany
26 N4 **Muodoslompolo** Sweden
29 O6 **Muojärvi** *L* Finland
68 F1 **Muong Boum** Vietnam
68 F2 **Muong Hiem** Laos
68 F2 **Muong Hun Xieng Hung** Laos
68 F3 **Muong Khao** Laos
68 F2 **Muong Khoua** Laos
68 G1 **Muong Khuong** Vietnam
68 E3 **Muong Ki** Laos
68 G3 **Muong Lam** Vietnam
68 E3 **Muong Liep** Laos
68 E2 **Muong Louang Namtha** Laos
68 H7 **Muong Man** Vietnam
68 F3 **Muong May** Laos
68 F3 **Muong Moc** Laos
68 F2 **Muong Ngoi** Laos
68 F1 **Muong Nhie** Vietnam
68 H4 **Muong Nong** Laos
68 E3 **Muong Oua** Laos
68 E1 **Muong ou Neua** Laos
68 E1 **Muong ou Tay** Laos
68 E3 **Muong Pa** Laos
68 G4 **Muong Phalane** Laos
68 E3 **Muong Phiang** Laos
68 E2 **Muong Sai** Laos
68 E3 **Muong Saiapoun** Laos
68 E2 **Muong Sing** Laos
68 F2 **Muong Son** Laos
68 G4 **Muong Song Khone** Laos
68 F3 **Muong Soui** Laos
68 F3 **Muong Soum** Laos
68 F1 **Muong Te** Vietnam
68 E3 **Muong Tha Deua** Laos
68 E3 **Muong Thong** Laos
68 F2 **Muong Va** Laos
Muong Xen *see* **Ky Son**
29 K4 **Muonio** Finland
26 N3 **Muonio älv** *R* Sweden/Finland
29 K4 **Muoniojoki** *R* Finland
26 N4 **Muonionalusta** Sweden
71 B2 **Muor** *isld* Halmahera Indonesia
41 J4 **Muotathal** Switzerland
88 B9 **Mupata Gorge** Zambia
65 E6 **Muping** China
80 G4 **Muqbilla** Jordan
86 J5 **Muqdisho** Somalia
130 H7 **Muqui** Brazil
38 J7 **Mur** *R* Austria
56 E2 **Mura** *R* Russian Federation
48 C4 **Mura** *R* Slovenia
80 G1 **Murāba 'āt** Syria
47 J6 **Muradiye** Turkey
45 L4 **Muraglione,Pso.di** *pass* Italy
61 N7 **Murakami** Japan
48 D4 **Murakeresztúr** Hungary
133 C7 **Murallón** *mt* Chile/Arg
61 N8 **Muramatsu** Japan
88 F2 **Murang'a** Kenya
45 M1 **Murano** Italy
52 G5 **Murashi** Russian Federation
18 G7 **Murat** France
78 H2 **Murat** *R* Turkey
78 J2 **Murat** *R* Turkey
47 K6 **Murat Dağı** Turkey
47 J3 **Muratlı** Turkey
38 K7 **Murau** Austria
77 C7 **Murban** U.A.E.
16 C3 **Murça** Portugal
77 B3 **Murcheh Khvort** Iran
33 T5 **Murchin** Germany
139 H6 **Murchison** Victoria Australia
145 D4 **Murchison** New Zealand
6 M1 **Murchison** *oil rig* North Sea
Murchison Falls Uganda *see* **Kabalega Falls**
143 B7 **Murchison, Mt** W Australia Australia
144 C5 **Murchison, Mt** New Zealand
145 D4 **Murchison, Mt** New Zealand
144 A6 **Murchison Mts** New Zealand
143 A8 **Murchison, R** W Australia Australia
140 C5 **Murchison Ra** N Terr Australia
89 G4 **Murchison Ra** S Africa
88 E9 **Murchison Rapids** Malawi
17 F6 **Murcia** *reg* Spain
17 F7 **Murcia** *prov* Spain
17 G7 **Murcia** Spain
71 F6 **Murcielagos B** Mindanao Philippines
18 G8 **Mur-de-Barrez** France
20 E5 **Mur-de-Bretagne** France
21 O7 **Mur-de-Sologne** France
98 F6 **Murdo** South Dakota U.S.A.
141 G2 **Murdoch Pt** Queensland Australia
122 G5 **Murdochville** Quebec Canada
113 E10 **Murdock** Florida U.S.A.
61 M9 **Mure** Japan
21 O4 **Mureaux, Les** France
38 N8 **Mureck** Austria
47 J4 **Mürefte** Turkey
86 G4 **Murel** Ethiopia
48 J4 **Mureş** *R* Romania
48 J4 **Mureş** *reg* Romania
18 F9 **Muret** France
111 C7 **Murfreesboro** Arkansas U.S.A.
95 K10 **Murfreesboro** North Carolina U.S.A.
110 K6 **Murfreesboro** Tennessee U.S.A.
36 E6 **Murg** *R* Germany
57 G5 **Murgab** *R* Tajikistan
57 G5 **Murgab** Tajikistan
46 D5 **Murgána** *mt* Greece
46 F2 **Murgash** *mt* Bulgaria
140 C1 **Murgenella Cr** N Terr Australia
48 L4 **Murgeni** Romania
77 H2 **Murghab** *R* Afghanistan
74 C3 **Murgha Kibzai** Pakistan
48 K4 **Murgoci** *mt* Romania
141 K7 **Murgon** Queensland Australia
143 B7 **Murgoo** W Australia Australia
58 D4 **Muri** China
75 L7 **Muri** India
130 G7 **Muriaé** Brazil
70 N9 **Muria, Gunung** *mt* Java
16 C2 **Murias de Paredes** Spain
87 D7 **Muriege** Angola
118 G4 **Muriel L** Alberta Canada
60 R2 **Murii-dake** *mt* Japan
119 O2 **Murill** Ontario Canada
17 G2 **Murillo de Gállego** Spain
20 G6 **Murin, L. de** France
33 R6 **Müritz** *L* Germany
145 F3 **Muriwai** New Zealand
26 L5 **Murjek** Sweden
36 B3 **Mürlenbach** Germany
52 D1 **Murmansk** Russian Federation
52 D1 **Murmanskaya Oblast'** *prov* Russian Federation
52 D1 **Murmashi** Russian Federation
54 M2 **Murmino** Russian Federation
41 O2 **Murnau** Germany
18 L11 **Muro, Cap di** *C* Corsica
102 G7 **Muroc L** California U.S.A.
52 F6 **Murom** Russian Federation
55 G3 **Muromtsevo** Russian Federation
60 O3 **Muroran** Japan
16 A2 **Muros** Spain
60 H12 **Muroto** Japan
60 H12 **Muroto-zaki** Japan
60 N3 **Murotsu-shima** *isld* Japan
48 L2 **Murovanyye Kurilovtsy** Ukraine
31 K3 **Murowana Goslina** Poland
60 E12 **Murozumi** Japan
100 J6 **Murphy** Idaho U.S.A.
112 C2 **Murphy** North Carolina U.S.A.
100 B7 **Murphy** Oregon U.S.A.
102 D3 **Murphys** California U.S.A.
110 G4 **Murphysboro** Illinois U.S.A.
141 H8 **Murra Murra** Queensland Australia
139 G6 **Murray** *R* New South Wales Australia
99 N8 **Murray** Iowa U.S.A.
110 H5 **Murray** Kentucky U.S.A.
99 K9 **Murray** Nebraska U.S.A.
103 N1 **Murray** Utah U.S.A.
138 E6 **Murray Bridge** South Australia Australia
94 E7 **Murray City** Ohio U.S.A.
135 L5 **Murray Deep** Pacific Oc
140 C5 **Murray Downs** N Terr Australia
122 K7 **Murray Hbr** Prince Edward I Canada
123 K8 **Murray Hd** Prince Edward I Canada
83 M9 **Murray Hill** *pk* Christmas I Indian Oc
107 N7 **Murray,L** Oklahoma U.S.A.
112 F3 **Murray, L** South Carolina U.S.A.
143 B10 **Murray, R** W Australia Australia
117 N8 **Murray R** British Columbia Canada
143 G7 **Murray Ra** W Australia Australia
122 K7 **Murray River** Prince Edward I Canada
89 C8 **Murraysburg** S Africa
135 M5 **Murray Seascarp** Pacific Oc
138 E5 **Murray Town** South Australia Australia
138 F6 **Murrayville** Victoria Australia
99 Q10 **Murrayville** Illinois U.S.A.
112 H4 **Murrells Inlet** South Carolina U.S.A.
40 G4 **Mürren** Switzerland
36 H6 **Murrhardt** Germany
139 J5 **Murringo** New South Wales Australia
143 D8 **Murrin Murrin** W Australia Australia
14 B3 **Murrisk** *mts* Ireland
139 G5 **Murrumbidgee** *R* New South Wales Australia
139 J5 **Murrumburrah & Harden** New South Wales Australia
139 K4 **Murrurundi** New South Wales Australia
19 O17 **Murs** France
38 O8 **Murska Sobota** Slovenia
74 G8 **Murtajāpur** India
38 K7 **Mur Tal** *V* Austria
41 M4 **Murtarol,Piz** *mt* Italy
101 L7 **Murtaugh** Idaho U.S.A.
139 G4 **Murtee** New South Wales Australia
40 F4 **Murten See** *L* Switzerland
42 G5 **Murter** *isld* Croatia
138 F3 **Murteree,L** South Australia Australia
117 O9 **Murtle L** British Columbia Canada
138 F6 **Murtoa** Victoria Australia
29 O6 **Murtovaara** Finland
74 E9 **Murud** India
70 D3 **Murud** *mt* Kalimantan
65 E3 **Muruin Sum Shuiku** *res* China
70 D5 **Murui, R** Kalimantan
70 D4 **Murung,R** Kalimantan
145 F3 **Murupara** New Zealand
128 F3 **Murupu** Brazil
109 N3 **Murvaul Res** Texas U.S.A.
22 K5 **Murville** France
74 J7 **Murwara** India
139 L3 **Murwillumbah** New South Wales Australia
52 G5 **Murygino** Russian Federation
38 M6 **Mürzsteg** Austria
38 M7 **Murz Tal** *V* Austria
84 E4 **Murzuq** Libya
38 N6 **Mürzzuchlag** Austria
78 H2 **Muş** Turkey
86 D6 **Musadi** Zaire
79 D10 **Mûsa, G** *mt* Egypt
74 C3 **Musa Khel Bazar** Pakistan
47 N10 **Musaköyalçaği Burun** *C* Turkey
46 F2 **Musala** *mt* Bulgaria
69 D12 **Musala** *isld* Sumatra
59 J3 **Musan** N Korea
77 E6 **Musandam** *pen* Oman
77 J3 **Musa Qala** Afghanistan
77 B7 **Musay'īd** Qatar
Muscat *see* **Masqat**
99 P8 **Muscatine** Iowa U.S.A.
Muscat & Oman *sultanate see* **Oman**
110 J7 **Muscle Shoals** Alabama U.S.A.
99 Q6 **Muscoda** Wisconsin U.S.A.
95 S3 **Muscongus B** Maine U.S.A.
88 C9 **Muse** *R* Mozambique
80 G8 **Museitiba** Jordan
141 G2 **Musgrave** Queensland Australia
138 B2 **Musgrave Ranges** South Australia Australia
123 S5 **Musgravetown** Newfoundland Canada
89 G3 **Mushandike Dam** Zimbabwe
80 G8 **Musheirifa** Jordan
14 C5 **Musheramore** *mt* Ireland
86 C6 **Mushie** Zaire
28 G6 **Musholm** *isld* Denmark
103 L6 **Music Mt** Arizona U.S.A.
103 N2 **Musinia Pk** Utah U.S.A.
117 M5 **Muskeg** *R* Northwest Territories Canada
99 L1 **Muskeg B** Minnesota U.S.A.
95 R5 **Muskeget Chan** Massachusetts U.S.A.
119 O1 **Muskeg L** Ontario Canada
94 A3 **Muskegon** *R* Michigan U.S.A.
94 A3 **Muskegon** Michigan U.S.A.
94 A3 **Muskegon Heights** Michigan U.S.A.
26 H4 **Musken** Norway
94 F7 **Muskingum** *R* Ohio U.S.A.
27 K13 **Muskö** Sweden
110 A6 **Muskogee** Oklahoma U.S.A.
121 L7 **Muskoka,L** Ontario Canada
101 S6 **Muskrat Cr** Wyoming U.S.A.
77 F6 **Mūskutān** Iran
118 C2 **Muskwa R** Alberta Canada
79 H2 **Muslimīyah** Syria
52 H6 **Muslyumovo** Russian Federation
86 G2 **Musmar** Sudan
80 D3 **Musmus** Israel
88 D2 **Musoma** Tanzania
45 M1 **Musone** *R* Italy
45 O4 **Musone** Italy
123 L3 **Musquanus L** Quebec Canada
123 L3 **Musquaro** Quebec Canada
122 F8 **Musquash** New Brunswick Canada
122 J8 **Musquodoboit** Nova Scotia Canada
122 J9 **Musquodoboit Hbr** Nova Scotia Canada
28 H7 **Musse** Denmark
25 H3 **Mussel Aa** *R* Netherlands
13 E2 **Musselburgh** Scotland
101 R3 **Musselshell** Montana U.S.A.
101 S3 **Musselshell** *R* Montana U.S.A.
87 C8 **Mussende** Angola
18 F7 **Mussidan** France
43 F11 **Mussomeli** Sicily
47 K4 **Mustafakemalpaşa** Turkey
47 K5 **Mustafakemalpaşa** *R* Turkey
86 H4 **Mustahīl** Ethiopia
75 K4 **Mustang** Nepal
107 N6 **Mustang** Oklahoma U.S.A.
108 E3 **Mustang Cr** Texas U.S.A.
109 K8 **Mustang I** Texas U.S.A.
55 B5 **Mustayevo** Russian Federation
133 D7 **Muster,L** Argentina
98 K4 **Mustinka** *R* Minnesota U.S.A.
127 O8 **Mustique** *isld* Lesser Antilles
27 M13 **Mustjala** Estonia
52 C5 **Mustla** Estonia
29 N3 **Mustola** Finland
13 H5 **Muston** England
52 C5 **Mustvee** Estonia
65 H4 **Musu-dan** *C* N Korea
139 K4 **Muswellbrook** New South Wales Australia
48 F1 **Muszyna** Poland
84 H4 **Mut** Egypt
78 D3 **Mut** Turkey
38 M8 **Muta** Slovenia
88 C1 **Mutai** Uganda
89 G4 **Mutale** *R* S Africa
87 E8 **Mutanda** Zambia
Mutankiang *see* **Mudanjiang**
88 E10 **Mutarara** Mozambique
87 F9 **Mutare** Zimbabwe
37 O4 **Mutěnin** Czechoslovakia
88 C10 **Mutepatepa** Zimbabwe
78 K6 **Muthanna, Al** *prov* Iraq
12 E1 **Muthill** Scotland
71 M9 **Mutis** *mt* Timor Indonesia
52 J2 **Mutnyy-Materik** Russian Federation
88 D10 **Mutoko** Zimbabwe
87 D7 **Mutombo Mukulu** Zaire
138 F4 **Mutooroo** South Australia Australia
88 C10 **Mutorashanga** Zimbabwe
65 D4 **Mutoudeng** China
65 D3 **Mutougou** China
45 R7 **Mutria, M** *mt* Italy
87 G10 **Mutsamudu** Comoros
87 D8 **Mutshatsha** Zaire
60 P4 **Mutsu** Japan
61 O5 **Mutsu-wan** *B* Japan
141 G6 **Muttaburra** Queensland Australia
40 G1 **Muttersholtz** France
36 E5 **Mutterstadt** Germany
41 M4 **Muttler** *mt* Switzerland
123 O3 **Mutton Bay** Quebec Canada
144 B7 **Muttonbird Is.** New Zealand
14 B4 **Mutton I** Ireland
107 L5 **Mutual** Oklahoma U.S.A.
87 G8 **Mutuala** Mozambique
129 H7 **Mutum** Mato Grosso Brazil
130 H6 **Mutum** Minas Gerais Brazil
128 F5 **Mutumparaná** Brazil
83 L9 **Mutur** Sri Lanka
36 C6 **Mutzig** France
33 R10 **Mutzschen** Germany
29 M9 **Muurame** Finland
29 L5 **Muurola** Finland
65 A5 **Mu Us Shamo** *desert* China
Muxia *see* **Mugia**
58 F1 **Muya** *R* Russian Federation
88 C3 **Muyinga** Burundi
125 M3 **Muy Muy** Nicaragua
57 A3 **Muynak** Uzbekistan
87 E7 **Muyumba** Zaire
67 C1 **Muyuping** China
74 E1 **Muzaffarabad** Kashmir
74 D3 **Muzaffargarh** Pakistan
74 G4 **Muzaffarnagar** India
75 L5 **Muzaffarpur** India
130 F7 **Muzambinho** Brazil
57 K4 **Muzat He** *R* China
50 F2 **Muzhi** Russian Federation
20 F6 **Muzillac** France
40 A3 **Muzin** *R* France
117 G8 **Muzon, C** Alaska U.S.A.
108 F8 **Múzquiz** Mexico
66 C4 **Muztag** *mt* China
66 D4 **Muztag** *mt* China
66 B4 **Muztagata** *mt* China
88 E8 **Mvera** Malawi
86 E4 **Mvolo** Sudan
87 G7 **Mvomero** Tanzania
86 B6 **M'Vouti** Congo
89 G2 **Mvuma** Zimbabwe
88 C10 **Mvurwi Ra** *mts* Zimbabwe
88 D7 **Mwambwa** *R* Zambia
88 D3 **Mwanza** Tanzania
88 D6 **Mwaya** Tanzania
14 B3 **Mweelrea** *mts* Ireland
86 D6 **Mweka** Zaire
87 D7 **Mwene Ditu** Zaire
87 F10 **Mwenezi** Zimbabwe
89 G3 **Mwenezi** *R* Zimbabwe
89 G3 **Mwenezi** Zimbabwe
88 B3 **Mwenga** Zaire
88 G6 **Mwera** Tanzania
89 G2 **Mwerihari** *R* Zimbabwe
88 B6 **Mweru, L** Zaire/Zambia
88 B6 **Mweru Wantipa** Zambia
89 F3 **Mwewe** *R* Zimbabwe
87 D7 **Mwimba** Zaire
87 D8 **Mwinilunga** Zambia
68 B2 **Myaing** Burma
113 E10 **Myakka** Florida U.S.A.
113 E10 **Myakka City** Florida U.S.A.
52 E5 **Myaksa** Russian Federation
31 H3 **Myálibórz** Poland
139 K4 **Myall L** New South Wales Australia
68 B3 **Myanaung** Burma
52 D3 **Myanduselga** Russian Federation
Myanmar *see* **Burma**
54 G2 **Myatlevo** Russian Federation
68 A2 **Myaungbwe** Burma
68 B4 **Myaungmya** Burma
68 D4 **Myawadi** Burma
46 F7 **Mycenae** Greece
68 A2 **Myebon** Burma
95 L6 **Myerstown** Pennsylvania U.S.A.
68 B2 **Myingyan** Burma
68 C2 **Myinkyado** Burma
68 D6 **Myinmoletkat** *mt* Burma
68 B2 **Myinmu** Burma
68 B2 **Myitche** Burma
68 D5 **Myitta** Burma
68 C2 **Myittha** Burma
48 D2 **Myjava** Czechoslovakia
26 F5 **Myken** *lighthouse* Norway
6 E1 **Mykines** *isld* Faeroes
52 H2 **Myla** Russian Federation
37 N2 **Mylau** Germany
29 M11 **Myllykoski** Finland
98 G1 **Mylo** North Dakota U.S.A.
75 O6 **Mymensingh** Bangladesh
29 J11 **Mynämäki** Finland
57 G2 **Mynaral** Kazakhstan
57 C4 **Mynbulak** Uzbekistan
8 B3 **Mynydd Bach** *mts* Wales
8 C3 **Mynydd Eppynt** *mts* Wales
68 A2 **Myohaung** Burma
68 B2 **Myohla** Burma
68 B2 **Myotha** Burma
68 B2 **Myothit** Burma
47 K8 **Myra** Turkey
109 K2 **Myra** Texas U.S.A.
141 F3 **Myra Vale** Queensland Australia
27 B11 **Myrdal** Norway
28 S10 **Myrdalsjökull** *ice cap* Iceland
26 H3 **Myre** Norway
27 G14 **Myresjö** Sweden
26 L6 **Myrheden** Sweden
118 F5 **Myrnam** Alberta Canada
119 U9 **Myrtle** Manitoba Canada
121 M8 **Myrtle** Ontario Canada
100 J3 **Myrtle** Idaho U.S.A.
111 G7 **Myrtle** Mississippi U.S.A.
112 J4 **Myrtle Beach** South Carolina U.S.A.
100 B6 **Myrtle Cr** Oregon U.S.A.
139 H6 **Myrtleford** Victoria Australia
100 A6 **Myrtle Point** Oregon U.S.A.
138 E4 **Myrtle Springs** South Australia Australia
141 L1 **Myrtletown** Queensland Australia
65 H3 **Mys Gamova** *lighthouse* Russian Federation
52 E5 **Myshkino** Russian Federation
47 J5 **Mysia** *hist reg* Turkey
56 C4 **Myski** Russian Federation
31 M6 **Myślenice** Poland
76 C4 **Mysore** India
147 P3 **Mys Shmidta** Russian Federation
26 G9 **Myssjo** Sweden
119 U3 **Mystery L** Manitoba Canada
112 D6 **Mystic** Georgia U.S.A.
99 O9 **Mystic** Iowa U.S.A.
52 H4 **Mysy** Permskaya obl Russian Federation
31 L5 **Myszków** Poland
31 N2 **Myszyniec** Poland
52 F6 **Myt** Russian Federation
68 H7 **My Tho** Vietnam
54 J1 **Mytishchi** Russian Federation
101 P9 **Myton** Utah U.S.A.
68 J6 **My Trach** Vietnam
29 T9 **Myvatn** *L* Iceland
57 H1 **Myylybulak** Kazakhstan
37 O4 **Mže** *R* Czechoslovakia
85 C4 **Mzereb,El** Mali
88 D7 **Mzimba** Malawi
89 F8 **Mzimvubu** *R* S Africa
88 E7 **Mzuzu** Malawi

N

37 M5 **Naab** *R* Germany
25 B5 **Naaldwijk** Netherlands
135 U6 **Naalehu** Hawaiian Is
80 C6 **Na'an** Israel
86 E4 **Naandi** Sudan
29 J11 **Naantali** Finland
25 D4 **Naarden** Netherlands
14 E3 **Naas** Ireland
29 N2 **Näätämönjoki** *R* Finland
89 A7 **Nababeep** S Africa
16 B5 **Nabaõ** *R* Portugal
75 K9 **Nabarangapur** India
61 K11 **Nabari** Japan
140 C1 **Nabarlek** N Terr Australia
71 F5 **Nabas** Panay Philippines
80 G1 **Nab'as Şakhr** Syria
79 F5 **Nabatīyet Ett Tahta** Lebanon
143 D7 **Nabberu, L** W Australia Australia
71 E2 **Nabbuan** Luzon Philippines
37 N5 **Nabburg** Germany
52 H6 **Naberezhnyye Chelny** Russian Federation
116 Q5 **Nabesna Gl** Alaska U.S.A.
43 D12 **Nabeul** Tunisia
139 K4 **Nabiac** New South Wales Australia
130 B7 **Nabileque,R** Brazil
136 H2 **Nabire** W Irian
123 K3 **Nabisipi R** Quebec Canada
79 F5 **Nabi Younés, Ras en** *C* Lebanon
80 E5 **Nablus** Jordan
79 E10 **Nabq** Egypt
71 F6 **Nabulao B** Negros Philippines
68 D5 **Nabule** Burma
88 H9 **Nacala** Mozambique
88 H9 **Nacala-a-Velha** Mozambique
125 L3 **Nacaome** Honduras
67 B5 **Nacham** Vietnam
100 E3 **Naches** Washington U.S.A.
100 D2 **Naches Pass** Washington U.S.A.
87 G8 **Nachingwea** Tanzania
74 D5 **Nāchna** India
66 E5 **Na Ch'u** *R* China
68 A7 **Nachuge** Andaman Is
102 C6 **Nacimiento** *R* California U.S.A.
102 C6 **Nacimiento Res** California U.S.A.
33 R7 **Nackel** Germany
103 P10 **Naco** Mexico
111 B10 **Nacogdoches** Texas U.S.A.
68 B6 **Nacondam I** Andaman Is
124 E2 **Nacozari de Garcia** Mexico
Nada *see* **Dan Xian**
103 L3 **Nada** Utah U.S.A.
61 M8 **Nadachi** Japan
124 J4 **Nadadores** Mexico
67 B6 **Nadang** China
99 T4 **Nadeau** Michigan U.S.A.
Nådendal *see* **Naantali**
55 D4 **Nadezhdinka** Kazakhstan
137 Q5 **Nadi** Viti Levu Fiji
74 E7 **Nadiad** India
48 F4 **Nădlac** Romania
85 D1 **Nador** Morocco
48 G3 **Nádudvar** Hungary
77 C3 **Nadūshan** Iran
52 D3 **Nadvoitsy** Russian Federation
48 J2 **Nadvornaya** Ukraine
50 G2 **Nadym** Russian Federation
27 A13 **Naerbö** Norway
26 E7 **Naeröy** Norway
29 K5 **Nærum** Denmark
28 B5 **Næsbjerg** Denmark
28 C3 **Næsborg** Denmark
28 H6 **Næsby** Denmark
28 E6 **Næsbyhoved** Denmark
28 A3 **Næs Sund** *inlet* Denmark
28 H6 **Næstelsø** Denmark
28 H6 **Næstved** Denmark
68 A2 **Naf** *R* Burma
101 M7 **Naf** Idaho U.S.A.
85 G6 **Nafada** Nigeria
77 A4 **Naft-e Safīd** Iran
78 K4 **Naft Shahr** Iran
77 J6 **Nāg** Pakistan
71 F4 **Naga** Philippines
120 F3 **Nagagami** Ontario Canada
120 F3 **Nagagamisis L** Ontario Canada
60 F12 **Nagahama** Japan
75 Q5 **Nagaland** *prov* India
139 H6 **Nagambie** Victoria Australia
61 O13 **Nagannu-jima** *isld* Okinawa
61 L9 **Nagano** *prefect* Japan
61 M9 **Nagano** Japan
61 M9 **Naganohara** Japan
61 M8 **Nagaoka** Japan
75 P5 **Nagaon** India
76 D5 **Nagappattinam** India
76 E1 **Nāgāram** India
76 D2 **Nāgārjuna Sāgar** *res* India
76 D2 **Nagar Karnul** India
74 D6 **Nagar Parkar** Pakistan
60 C12 **Nagasaki** *prefect* Japan
60 C13 **Nagasaki** Japan
60 D14 **Nagasaki-bana** Japan
60 F12 **Naga-shima** *isld* Japan
60 D13 **Naga shima** *isld* Japan
60 E12 **Nagasu** Japan
60 E11 **Nagato** Japan
74 E5 **Nagaur** India
Nagchu Dzong *see* **Nagqu**
76 C6 **Nagercoil** India
26 H9 **Naggen** Sweden
74 H4 **Nagina** India
75 Q5 **Nāginimāra** India
61 P12 **Nago** Okinawa
74 J6 **Nagod** India
36 F6 **Nagold** *R* Germany
36 F6 **Nagold** Germany
78 L2 **Nagornyy Karabakh** *aut reg* Azerbaijan
52 H5 **Nagorsk** Russian Federation
61 P13 **Nago-wan** *B* Okinawa
61 K10 **Nagoya** Japan
74 H8 **Nagpur** India
66 E5 **Nagqu** China
29 J11 **Nagu** Finland
127 K5 **Nagua** Dominican Rep
71 E2 **Naguilian** Luzon Philippines
71 G4 **Nagumbuaya Pt** Philippines
48 D4 **Nagyatád** Hungary
48 D4 **Nagybajom** Hungary
48 G3 **Nagyecsed** Hungary
48 G3 **Nagykálló** Hungary
48 D4 **Nagykanizsa** Hungary
48 F3 **Nagykáta** Hungary
48 F3 **Nagykörös** Hungary
48 G3 **Nagyléta** Hungary
48 E3 **Nagymaros** Hungary
Nagyvárad *see* **Oradea**
66 F4 **Nagza** China
61 P13 **Naha** Okinawa
70 D4 **Nahabuan** Kalimantan
80 D3 **Nahalal** Israel
80 C7 **Naḩalat** Israel
80 C8 **Naḩal Eshkolot** Jordan
80 E4 **Naḩal Ginnat** Jordan
80 E4 **Naḩal 'Irit** Jordan
80 C8 **Naḩal Negohot** Jordan
80 C8 **Naḩal Zohar** Jordan
74 G3 **Nahan** India
117 M5 **Nahanni Butte** Northwest Territories Canada
117 L5 **Nahanni Nat. Park** Northwest Territories Canada
80 D1 **Nahariyya** Israel
77 A2 **Nahāvand** Iran
36 C4 **Nahbollenbach** Germany
36 C4 **Nahe** *R* Germany
80 G4 **Nahla** Jordan
137 O4 **Nahoï, C** Vanuatu
21 O7 **Nahon** *R* France
79 H2 **Nahr Sājūr** *R* Syria
80 C3 **Naḩsholim** Israel
131 B8 **Nahuel Huapi, L** Argentina
133 D6 **Nahuel Niyeu** Argentina
112 E6 **Nahunta** Georgia U.S.A.
71 E3 **Naic** Luzon Philippines
124 G4 **Naica** Mexico
119 N6 **Naicam** Saskatchewan Canada
66 E4 **Naij Tal** China
71 L9 **Naikliu** Timor Indonesia
37 M3 **Naila** Germany
65 D4 **Nailin** China
8 D5 **Nailsea** England
8 D4 **Nailsworth** England
65 E3 **Naiman Qi** China
66 E3 **Naimin Bulak** *spring* China
115 N6 **Nain** Labrador, Nfld Canada
77 C3 **Nā'īn** Iran
74 J7 **Nainpur** India
21 L8 **Naintré** France
Nairn *co see* **Highland** *reg*
120 J6 **Nairn** Ontario Canada
15 E3 **Nairn** Scotland
143 B7 **Nairn, Mt** W Australia Australia
15 D3 **Nairn,R** Scotland
88 F2 **Nairobi** Kenya
52 B5 **Naissaar** *isld* Estonia
88 F2 **Naivasha** Kenya
20 E6 **Naizin** France
77 B3 **Najafābād** Iran
78 K6 **Najaf, An** Iraq
78 J6 **Najaf, An** *prov* Iraq
126 F4 **Najasa** *R* Cuba
17 F2 **Nájera** Spain
17 F2 **Najerilla** *R* Spain
65 H3 **Najin** N Korea
77 B2 **Najmabad** Iran
60 H12 **Naka** *R* Japan
60 C13 **Nakadōri shima** *isld* Japan
60 C12 **Nakagumi** Japan
61 P13 **Nakagusuku-wan** *B* Okinawa
61 N7 **Nakajō** Japan
60 C14 **Naka koshiki jima** *isld* Japan
60 D12 **Nakama** Japan
61 O9 **Nakaminato** Japan
60 F13 **Nakamura** Japan
60 E14 **Nakamura** Japan
61 M9 **Nakano** Japan
61 M9 **Nakanojō** Japan
60 G9 **Nakano-shima** *isld* Japan
67 H4 **Nakanougan-jima** *isld* Japan
61 Q12 **Nakaoshi** Okinawa
77 L3 **Naka Pass** Afghanistan
61 O5 **Nakasato** Japan
60 R3 **Nakasatsunai** Japan
60 T2 **Naka-shibetsu** Japan
55 D2 **Nakatay** Russian Federation
60 Q1 **Naka-Tombetsu** Japan
60 E12 **Nakatsu** Japan
61 L10 **Nakatsugawa** Japan
60 G10 **Naka-umi** Japan
116 J8 **Nakchamik I** Alaska U.S.A.
116 O6 **Naked I** Alaska U.S.A.
86 G2 **Nak'fa** Ethiopia
78 K2 **Nakhichevan** Azerbaijan
78 K2 **Nakhichevanskaya Respublika** Azerbaijan
84 J4 **Nakhl** Egypt
65 J3 **Nakhodka** Russian Federation
68 E5 **Nakhon Nayok** Thailand
68 D6 **Nakhon Pathom** Thailand
68 F5 **Nakhon Ratchasima** Thailand
69 E8 **Nakhon Si Thammarat** Thailand
68 E4 **Nakhon Thai** Thailand
59 L2 **Nakhtakhe** Russian Federation
61 P12 **Nakijin** Okinawa
117 G6 **Nakina** British Columbia Canada
120 D2 **Nakina** Ontario Canada
29 K3 **Näkkälä** Finland
29 J10 **Nakkila** Finland
31 K2 **Nakło** Poland
116 J7 **Naknek** Alaska U.S.A.
61 O9 **Nakoso** Japan
67 F3 **Nakou** China
Naksho Biru *see* **Biru**
28 G7 **Nakskov** Denmark
26 G9 **Näkten** *L* Sweden
65 G7 **Naktong** *R* S Korea
88 F2 **Nakuru** Kenya
88 E2 **Nakuru, L** Kenya
117 P10 **Nakusp** British Columbia Canada
68 C1 **Na-lang** Burma
58 E2 **Nalayh** Mongolia
53 F11 **Nal'chik** Russian Federation
74 G10 **Naldurg** India
76 D2 **Nalgonda** India
22 G3 **Nalinnes** Belgium
76 D3 **Nallamala Hills** India
94 G8 **Nallen** West Virginia U.S.A.
21 M8 **Nalliers** Vienne France
78 C1 **Nallıhan** Turkey
87 D9 **Nalolo** Zambia
6 M2 **N Alwyn** *oil rig* North Sea
68 C1 **Nam** *R* Burma
68 F3 **Nam** *R* Laos
65 G5 **Nam** *R* N Korea
60 C12 **Nama** Japan
87 C9 **Namacunde** Angola
88 F10 **Namacurra** Mozambique
118 D8 **Namaka** Alberta Canada
118 K2 **Namakan L** Minnesota/Ontario U.S.A./Canada
77 F4 **Namakiār-e Shadād** *salt lake* Iran
77 E2 **Namak, Kavīr-e** *salt waste* Iran
69 H14 **Namang** Indonesia
57 F4 **Namangan** Uzbekistan
88 G8 **Namapa** Mozambique
88 G9 **Namaponda** Mozambique
87 C11 **Namaqualand** *tribal area* Namibia
87 C12 **Namaqualand** *dist* S Africa
88 F9 **Namarroi** Mozambique
86 F5 **Namasagali** Uganda
87 E9 **Nambala** Zambia
68 E2 **Nam Beng** *R* Laos
141 L7 **Nambour** Queensland Australia
139 L4 **Nambucca Heads** New South Wales Australia
68 G3 **Nam Ca Dinh** *R* Laos
69 G8 **Nam Can** Vietnam
66 E5 **Nam Co** *L* China
26 F7 **Namdalen** *V* Norway
26 E7 **Namdalseid** Norway
68 G2 **Nam Ðing** Vietnam
88 G8 **Namecala** Mozambique
99 P3 **Namekagon** *R* Wisconsin U.S.A.
61 L9 **Namerikawa** Japan
48 E1 **Námestovo** Czechoslovakia
88 G9 **Nametil** Mozambique

Grid	Name
119 P4	Namew L Saskatchewan Canada
68 F2	Nam Het R Laos
68 D2	Nam Hsin R Burma
87 B10	Namib Des Namibia
87 B9	Namibe Angola
87 B10	Namib Game Res. Namibia
87 C10	Namibia rep Africa
88 F9	Namibia L North Carolina U.S.A.
61 O8	Namie Japan
61 O5	Namioka Japan
56 D6	Namir Mongolia
87 C11	Namisis mt Namibia
66 F6	Namjagbarwa Feng mt China
68 F3	Nam Khan R Laos
68 D2	Nam Kok R Thailand
68 C1	Namlan Burma
68 C2	Namlang R Burma
68 E2	Nam Loi R Burma
68 C3	Nam Ma R Laos
68 C2	Nammekon Burma
68 G3	Nam Muone R Laos
68 F1	Nam Na R Vietnam
68 O4	Nam One R Laos
68 E2	Nam Ngaou R Laos
68 F2	Nam Noud R Vietnam
139 J4	Namoi R New South Wales Australia
68 E1	Nam Ou R Laos
85 D2	Namous watercourse Algeria
118 A2	Nampa Alberta Canada
29 M5	Nampa Finland
100 J6	Nampa Idaho U.S.A.
68 E4	Nampala Mali
68 E4	Nam Pa Sak R Thailand
68 E4	Nam Pat Thailand
68 F4	Nam Phong Thailand
65 F5	Namp'o N Korea
22 B3	Nampont France
68 G4	Nampula Mozambique
68 G4	Nam Pung Res Thailand
26 F7	Namsen R Norway
68 F2	Nam Seng R Laos
26 E7	Namsos Norway
68 F2	Nam Suong R Laos
26 G7	Namsvatn L Norway
68 D2	Nam Teng Burma
68 E2	Nam Tha Laos
68 G4	Nam Theun R Laos
68 D2	Namtok Burma
68 D5	Nam Tok Thailand
68 D1	Namton Burma
51 M2	Namtsy Russian Federation
88 F9	Namuli mt Mozambique
87 G8	Namuno Mozambique
83 L11	Namunukula mt Sri Lanka
22 H3	Namur Belgium
121 O7	Namur Quebec Canada
117 R7	Namur L Alberta Canada
87 C9	Namutoni Namibia
87 E9	Namwala Zambia
68 D4	Nam Wang R Thailand
88 E9	Namwera Malawi
31 L4	Namysłaki Poland
68 E3	Nan Thailand
100 B1	Nanaimo British Columbia Canada
102 R12	Nanakuli Hawaiian Is
65 H4	Nanam N Korea
67 F4	Nan'an China
67 B6	Nanan China
141 N7	Nanango Queensland Australia
67 F5	Nan'ao China
61 K8	Nanao Japan
67 F5	Nan'ao Dao isld China
61 L8	Nanao wan B Japan
61 K8	Nanatsu-jima isld Japan
67 B3	Nanbai China
67 B1	Nanbazhen China
67 B1	Nanbu China
21 P7	Nançay France
59 J2	Nancha China
67 E2	Nanchang China
65 E6	Nanchangshan Dao isld China
67 E3	Nancheng China
67 B1	Nanchong China
69 A9	Nancowry isld Nicobar Is
19 K4	Nancy France
144 A6	Nancy Sd New Zealand
74 H3	Nanda Devi mt India
67 B4	Nandan China
74 G9	Nanded India
139 K4	Nandewar Ra mts New South Wales Australia
37 M6	Nandstadt Germany
22 J3	Nandrin Belgium
67 C7	Nandu Jiang R China
74 F8	Nandurbar India
76 D3	Nandyal India
36 D4	Nane R Germany
65 F4	Nanfen China
98 Q8	Nanfeng China
75 P4	Nang China
70 C4	Nangabadau Kalimantan
70 C4	Nangabulik Kalimantan
86 B5	Nanga Eboko Cameroon
70 C4	Nangahbunut Kalimantan
70 C4	Nangahdangkan Kalimantan
70 B5	Nangah Dedai Kalimantan
70 C4	Nangahembaloh Kalimantan
70 B4	Nangahkantuk Kalimantan
70 B4	Nangahketungau Kalimantan
70 B5	Nangahmau Kalimantan
70 B4	Nangah Merakai Kalimantan
70 B5	Nangahpinoh Kalimantan
70 C4	Nangahserawai Kalimantan
70 C4	Nangahsuruk Kalimantan
70 C4	Nangahtempuai Kalimantan
74 G9	Nangal India
71 E5	Nangalao isld Philippines
74 H2	Nanga Parbat mt Kashmir
71 K9	Nangarendi Indonesia
77 L2	Nangarhar prov Afghanistan
70 B5	Nangatayap Indonesia
68 D7	Nangin Burma
18 G4	Nangis France
65 G5	Nangnim Sanmaek mts N Korea
65 G5	Nangong China
76 C6	Nanguneri India
87 D9	Nangweshi Zambia co Shangyi
65 C6	Nanhe China
67 D1	Nan He R China
67 G1	Nanhui China
66 F4	Nan Hulsan Hu L China
67 E4	Nanhua China
58 E5	Nanjiang China
67 D2	Nanjiangqiao China
	Nanjie see Guangning
67 F1	Nanjing China
67 F4	Nanjing China
67 E4	Nanjing China
67 C4	Nankang China
	Nanking see Nanjing
65 C4	Nankouzhen China
65 C6	Nanle China
67 F1	Nan Ling China
67 E3	Nan Ling mts China
	Nanma see Yiyuan
65 C4	Nanma China
68 G4	Nanmiao Jiangxi China
37 L7	Nannhofen Germany
143 D7	Nannine W Australia Australia
67 C5	Nanning China
143 B10	Nannup W Australia Australia
127 M2	Nanny Town hist site Jamaica
115 P5	Nanortalik Greenland
67 A4	Nanpan Jiang R China
75 J5	Nanpara India
67 F3	Nanpeng Liedao islds China
65 H3	Nanpi China
65 G3	Nan Poul R China
65 D5	Nanpu China
67 F3	Nanpu Xi R China
	Nanqiao see Fengxian
67 F4	Nanri Dao isld China
68 C2	Nansang Burma
65 B6	Nanweiquan China
67 A2	Nanxi China
67 B3	Nan Xian China
67 F7	Nanxiang China
67 F2	Nanxiong China
58 F5	Nanyang China
67 C2	Nanyangzhen China
65 C7	Nanyi China
67 F1	Nanyi Hu China
61 O7	Nan'yō Japan
65 C5	Nanyuan China
88 F1	Nanyuki Kenya
65 F4	Nanzamu China
67 D1	Nanzhang China
65 F4	Nanzhao China
17 H6	Nao,C.de la Spain
115 M7	Naococane,L Quebec Canada
61 M8	Naoetsu Japan
75 N6	Naogaon Bangladesh
74 C6	Naokot Pakistan
59 K2	Naoli He R China
77 G3	Naomid, Dasht-e desert Iran
101 O8	Naomi Pk Utah U.S.A.
46 E4	Náoussa Greece
67 C6	Napa China
102 B3	Napa California U.S.A.
71 H7	Napabalana Indonesia
122 F7	Napadogan New Brunswick Canada
121 O8	Napanee Ontario Canada
116 G6	Napaskiak Alaska U.S.A.
115 C4	Napasoq Greenland
100 C3	Napavine Washington U.S.A.
71 F4	Napayauan Philippines
68 G3	Nape Laos
99 S8	Naperville Illinois U.S.A.
123 O2	Napetipi R Quebec Canada
40 D1	Napf mt Switzerland
145 F3	Napier New Zealand
94 J6	Napier Broome B W Australia
145 F3	Napier Mts Antarctica
140 D1	Napier Pen N Terr Australia
142 J2	Napier Ra W Australia Australia
121 R7	Napierville Quebec Canada
119 P9	Napinka Manitoba Canada
	Naples see Napoli Italy
113 H5	Naples Florida U.S.A.
95 K4	Naples New York U.S.A.
109 N2	Naples Texas U.S.A.
67 B5	Napo China
128 C4	Napo R Peru/Ecuador
94 B7	Napoleon Indiana U.S.A.
98 G3	Napoleon North Dakota
110 D6	Napoleon Ohio U.S.A.
36 D3	Napoleon Germany
111 E12	Napoleonville Louisiana
43 G7	Napoletano, Appennino mts Italy
42 D7	Napoli Italy
94 Q8	Napoli Nebraska U.S.A.
135 U5	Napopoo Hawaiian Is
131 E7	Naposta R Argentina
141 F8	Nappamerry Queensland Australia
94 A5	Nappanee Indiana U.S.A.
33 S7	Nappenheide Germany
84 J5	Nasser, L Egypt
27 G14	Nässjö Sweden
22 J3	Nassogne Belgium
38 N6	Nassy Austria
115 M6	Nastapoka Is Northwest Territories Canada
36 D3	Nastätten Germany
61 N8	Nasu-Yumoto Japan
129 L6	Nasza R Brazil
26 J10	Näsviken Sweden
130 J9	Nata Botswana
89 B3	Nata R Botswana
141 H5	Natabua Queensland Australia
128 B4	Natagaima Colombia
118 D2	Natal British Columbia Canada
95 M6	Natal Brazil
130 E5	Natal prov S Africa
69 D12	Natal I Indonesia
90 M13	Natal R Thailand
141 H5	Natal Downs Queensland Australia
89 F7	Natal prov S Africa
135 R3	Nathorsts Land Greenland
106 D3	Nathrop Colorado U.S.A.
80 A4	Natili Jordan
61 G4	Natimuk Victoria Australia
116 R4	Nation Alaska U.S.A.
101 G1	National Bison Ra Montana U.S.A.
102 G9	National City California U.S.A.
86 C3	National Park Chad
4 L1	N Brae oil rig North Sea
117 L8	Natron R British Columbia Canada
123 A7	Natuashish Anticosti I, Quebec
124 D4	Natividad isld Mexico
129 J6	Natividade Brazil
61 C8	Natkyizin Burma
54 A8	Natkzin Burma
61 O7	Natori Japan
61 N8	Natoye Japan
101 T6	Natrona Wyoming U.S.A.
61 O8	Natron L Tanzania
145 M7	Natsui-gawa R Japan
71 K9	Natuna Flores Indonesia
80 J10	Nattaïm Indonesia
25 N3	Nattavaara Sweden
37 O6	Nattenberg Germany
37 M1	Nattheim Germany
26 L5	Nättraby Sweden
69 H10	Natuna Besar isld Indonesia
69 H11	Natuna, Kepulauan islds Indonesia
69 H10	Natuna Utara isld Indonesia
95 M2	Natural Bridge New York U.S.A.
94 H9	Natural Bridge Virginia U.S.A.
103 O4	Natural Br.Nat.Mon Utah
4 L1	Natural Dam L Texas U.S.A.
143 B10	Naturaliste, C W Australia Australia
143 A7	Naturaliste Chan W Australia Australia
116 J9	Naturaliste Plateau Indian Oc
8 C4	Neath Wales
21 O4	Neauphle-le-Château France
76 D3	Nellore India
59 L2	Nel'ma Russian Federation
138 F7	Nel'sha Russian Federation
138 D1	Nelson Victoria Australia
25	Nelson Victoria Australia
118 F6	Nelson British Columbia Canada
98 H9	Nelson Nebraska U.S.A.
103 L6	Nelson Nevada U.S.A.
112 J2	Nelson North Carolina U.S.A.
99 K5	Nelson Pennsylvania U.S.A.
99 P5	Nelson Wisconsin U.S.A.
8 C4	Nelson Wales
145 E5	Nelson New Zealand
30 C2	Nelson, Victoria Australia
144 C5	Nelson Creek New Zealand
133 C8	Nelson,Estrecho chan Chile
117 M6	Nelson Forks British Columbia Canada
119 T3	Nelson House Manitoba Canada
116 E6	Nelson I Alaska U.S.A.
145 D4	Nelson Lakes Nat. Park New Zealand
119 V3	Nelson R Manitoba Canada
101 S1	Nelson Res Montana U.S.A.
36 H1	Nelsonville Ohio U.S.A.
89 G5	Nelspruit S Africa
52 J4	Néma Mauritania
52 H5	Neman R Russian Federation
21 M3	Nemanan India
45 K3	Neman R Belorussia
52 B6	Neman Russian Federation
52 F5	Nemda R Russian Federation
40 E3	Nemea R Greece
32 M2	Neuckrug Germany
119 P8	Neudorf Saskatchewan Canada
37 M3	Neudrossenfeld Germany
32 L10	Neu-Eichenberg Germany
36 F6	Neuenburg Baden-Württemberg Germany

Neustift — Njoko

207

37 M7 **Neustift** Germany
33 S6 **Neustrelitz** Germany
37 J7 **Neu Ulm** Germany
22 D2 **Neuve Chapelle** France
21 M4 **Neuve-Lyre,la** France
40 F3 **Neuveville** Switzerland
18 G7 **Neuvic** France
109 N4 **Neuville** Texas U.S.A.
21 P5 **Neuville-aux-Bois** France
21 L8 **Neuville-de-Poitou** Vienne France
22 G5 **Neuville-en-Tourne-à-Fuy** France
19 O12 **Neuville-les-Dames** France
21 N2 **Neuville-les-Dieppe** France
21 K8 **Neuvy Bouin** France
21 M6 **Neuvy-le-Roi** France
21 O8 **Neuvy Pailloux** France
21 O8 **Neuvy St. Sépulchre** France
21 P7 **Neuvy-sur-Barangeon** France
33 O8 **Neuwegersleben** Germany
36 E6 **Neuweier** Germany
32 H5 **Neuwerk** *isld* Germany
36 C3 **Neuwied** Germany
36 C6 **Neuwiller** France
32 L6 **Neu-Wulmstorf** Germany
52 D5 **Neva** *R* Russian Federation
27 G11 **Neva** Sweden
99 R4 **Neva** Wisconsin U.S.A.
102 F2 **Nevada** *state* U.S.A.
99 N7 **Nevada** Iowa U.S.A.
110 B4 **Nevada** Missouri U.S.A.
109 L2 **Nevada** Texas U.S.A.
102 C2 **Nevada City** California U.S.A.
128 D2 **Nevada de Cocuy,Sa** *mts* Colombia
124 H8 **Nevada de Colima** Mexico
16 E7 **Nevada, Sierra** *mts* Spain
131 C5 **Nevado, Cerro** *pk* Argentina
131 B6 **Nevados Chillán** *mt* Chile
131 C5 **Nevado, Sierra del** *ra* Argentina
54 A1 **Nevel'** Russian Federation
59 M2 **Nevel'sk** Russian Federation
59 H1 **Never** Russian Federation
8 B3 **Nevern** Wales
26 F6 **Nevernes** Norway
18 H5 **Nevers** France
139 J4 **Nevertire** New South Wales Australia
48 E7 **Nevesinje** Bosnia-Herzegovina
20 C6 **Névez** France
45 H2 **Neviano d'Arduini** Italy
32 F10 **Neviges** Germany
118 K9 **Neville** Saskatchewan Canada
21 M2 **Neville** France
112 F5 **Nevils** Georgia U.S.A.
53 F11 **Nevinnomyssk** Russian Federation
79 E9 **Neviot** Egypt
118 D6 **Nevis** Alberta Canada
127 P4 **Nevis** *isld* Lesser Antilles
99 M3 **Nevis** Minnesota U.S.A.
127 P4 **Nevis Pk** Nevis W Indies
80 E6 **Nevit HaGedud** Jordan
78 E2 **Nevşehir** Turkey
65 J2 **Nevskoye** Russian Federation
55 D2 **Nev'yansk** Russian Federation
103 J9 **New** *R* California U.S.A.
112 F1 **New** *R* North Carolina U.S.A.
94 F9 **New** *R* Virginia/W Virginia U.S.A.
12 E4 **New Abbey** Scotland
95 S3 **Newagen** Maine U.S.A.
87 G8 **Newala** Tanzania
94 B8 **New Albany** Indiana U.S.A.
111 G7 **New Albany** Mississippi U.S.A.
95 L5 **New Albany** Pennsylvania U.S.A.
99 P6 **New Albin** Iowa U.S.A.
99 S4 **Newald** Wisconsin U.S.A.
9 E5 **New Alresford** England
141 J8 **New Angledool** New South Wales Australia
9 F1 **Newark** England
110 E6 **Newark** Arkansas U.S.A.
102 B4 **Newark** California U.S.A.
95 M7 **Newark** Delaware U.S.A.
99 S8 **Newark** Illinois U.S.A.
98 G9 **Newark** Nebraska U.S.A.
95 N6 **Newark** New Jersey U.S.A.
95 K3 **Newark** New York U.S.A.
94 E6 **Newark** Ohio U.S.A.
95 L4 **Newark Valley** New York U.S.A.
110 G3 **New Athens** Illinois U.S.A.
99 P4 **New Auburn** Wisconsin U.S.A.
111 G10 **New Augusta** Mississippi U.S.A.
94 E4 **New Baltimore** Michigan U.S.A.
94 J7 **New Baltimore** Pennsylvania U.S.A.
95 R5 **New Bedford** Massachusetts U.S.A.
100 C4 **Newberg** Oregon U.S.A.
99 Q10 **New Berlin** Illinois U.S.A.
95 M4 **New Berlin** New York U.S.A.
111 J9 **Newbern** Alabama U.S.A.
112 K2 **New Bern** North Carolina U.S.A.
110 G5 **Newbern** Tennessee U.S.A.
102 H7 **Newberry** California U.S.A.
113 E8 **Newberry** Florida U.S.A.
110 J3 **Newberry** Indiana U.S.A.
99 V3 **Newberry** Michigan U.S.A.
112 F3 **Newberry** South Carolina U.S.A.
94 H5 **New Bethlehem** Pennsylvania U.S.A.
13 G3 **Newbiggin by-the-Sea** England
13 E3 **Newbigging** Scotland
110 D3 **New Bloomfield** Missouri U.S.A.
99 R4 **Newbold** Wisconsin U.S.A.
121 O8 **Newboro** Ontario Canada
8 B1 **Newborough** Wales
99 Q8 **New Boston** Illinois U.S.A.
109 N2 **New Boston** Texas U.S.A.
109 J6 **New Braunfels** Texas U.S.A.
94 C6 **New Bremen** Ohio U.S.A.
12 E3 **New Bridge** Scotland
8 C3 **Newbridge** Wales
118 G7 **New Brigden** Alberta Canada
136 K3 **New Britain** *isld* Papua New Guinea
95 P5 **New Britain** Connecticut U.S.A.
111 L10 **New Brockton** Alabama U.S.A.
122 F7 **New Brunswick** *prov* Canada
95 N6 **New Brunswick** New Jersey U.S.A.
9 H3 **New Buckenham** England
99 U8 **New Buffalo** Michigan U.S.A.
99 O8 **Newburg** Iowa U.S.A.
110 E4 **Newburg** Missouri U.S.A.
94 K6 **Newburg** Pennsylvania U.S.A.
94 H7 **Newburg** West Virginia U.S.A.
121 O8 **Newburgh** Ontario Canada
15 F3 **Newburgh** Scotland
15 E4 **Newburgh** Fife Scotland
110 J4 **Newburgh** Indiana U.S.A.
95 N5 **Newburgh** New York U.S.A.
123 T5 **New Burnt Cove** Newfoundland Canada
9 E5 **Newbury** England
95 R4 **Newburyport** Massachusetts U.S.A.
85 E6 **New Bussa** Nigeria
137 N6 **New Caledonia** *isld* Pacific Oc
95 O5 **New Canaan** Connecticut U.S.A.
99 P10 **New Canton** Illinois U.S.A.
122 G5 **New Carlisle** Quebec Canada
94 C7 **New Carlisle** Ohio U.S.A.
139 K5 **Newcastle** New South Wales Australia
122 G6 **Newcastle** New Brunswick Canada
121 M9 **Newcastle** Ontario Canada
14 E3 **Newcastle** Ireland
127 L2 **Newcastle** Jamaica
14 F2 **Newcastle** N Ireland
89 F6 **Newcastle** S Africa
102 C3 **Newcastle** California U.S.A.
106 C2 **New Castle** Colorado U.S.A.
94 B7 **New Castle** Indiana U.S.A.
110 L3 **New Castle** Kentucky U.S.A.
98 K7 **Newcastle** Nebraska U.S.A.
95 M7 **New Castle** New Jersey U.S.A.
107 N6 **Newcastle** Oklahoma U.S.A.
94 G6 **New Castle** Pennsylvania U.S.A.
109 J2 **Newcastle** Texas U.S.A.
103 L4 **Newcastle** Utah U.S.A.
94 G9 **New Castle** Virginia U.S.A.
98 B6 **Newcastle** Wyoming U.S.A.
127 P4 **Newcastle** Nevis W Indies
141 G1 **Newcastle B** Queensland Australia
122 F7 **Newcastle Br** New Brunswick Canada
8 B3 **Newcastle Emlyn** Wales
118 E7 **Newcastle Mine** Alberta Canada
141 G4 **Newcastle Ra** Queensland Australia
15 F5 **Newcastleton** Scotland
8 D1 **Newcastle Under Lyme** England
13 G4 **Newcastle-upon-Tyne** England
140 C3 **Newcastle Waters** N Terr Australia
14 B4 **Newcastle West** Ireland
9 F5 **New Chapel** England
106 B5 **Newcomb** New Mexico U.S.A.
94 F6 **Newcomerstown** Ohio U.S.A.
94 F7 **New Concord** Ohio U.S.A.
12 D3 **New Cumnock** Scotland
12 D3 **New Dailly** Scotland
119 R8 **Newdale** Manitoba Canada
101 O6 **Newdale** Idaho U.S.A.
118 E9 **New Dayton** Alberta Canada
15 F3 **New Deer** Scotland
143 C10 **Newdegate** W Australia Australia
76 **New Delhi** India
117 P11 **New Denver** British Columbia Canada
111 M7 **New Echota Nat.Mon** Georgia U.S.A.
111 D8 **New Edinburg** Arkansas U.S.A.
113 E7 **Newell** Georgia U.S.A.
99 L7 **Newell** Iowa U.S.A.
112 G2 **Newell** North Carolina U.S.A.
98 C5 **Newell** South Dakota U.S.A.
112 F4 **New Ellenton** South Carolina U.S.A.
143 F6 **Newell,L** W Australia Australia
118 E8 **Newell L** Alberta Canada
111 E9 **Newellton** Louisiana U.S.A.
98 D3 **New England** North Dakota U.S.A.
139 K4 **New England Ra** *mts* New South Wales Australia
90 D4 **New England Seamount Chain** Atlantic Oc
116 F7 **Newenham,C** Alaska U.S.A.
8 D4 **Newent** England
94 A3 **New Era** Michigan U.S.A.
80 F3 **Newe Ur** Israel
80 C3 **Newe Yam** Israel
94 J3 **Newfane** New York U.S.A.
95 P3 **Newfane** Vermont U.S.A.
141 K1 **New Farm** *dist* Brisbane, Qnsld Australia
95 R3 **Newfield** Maine U.S.A.
95 M7 **Newfield** New Jersey U.S.A.
117 P8 **New Fish Creek** Alberta Canada
110 E3 **New Florence** Missouri U.S.A.
98 K1 **Newfolden** Minnesota U.S.A.
9 E6 **New Forest** England
95 Q3 **Newfound L** New Hampshire U.S.A.
115 N6 **Newfoundland** *prov* Canada
123 P5 **Newfoundland** *isld* Newfoundland Canada
95 M5 **Newfoundland** Pennsylvania U.S.A.
90 F4 **Newfoundland Basin** Atlantic Oc
90 E4 **Newfoundland Rise** Atlantic Oc
110 D2 **New Franklin** Missouri U.S.A.
95 L7 **New Freedom** Pennsylvania U.S.A.
8 A4 **Newgale** Wales
12 D3 **New Galloway** Scotland
118 B9 **Newgate** British Columbia Canada
137 M3 **New Georgia** *isld* Solomon Is
122 H9 **New Germany** Nova Scotia Canada
99 R7 **New Glarus** Wisconsin U.S.A.
122 K8 **New Glasgow** Nova Scotia Canada
95 R3 **New Gloucester** Maine U.S.A.
127 O3 **New Grant** Trinidad
136 J3 **New Guinea** *isld* S E Asia
109 M6 **Newgulf** Texas U.S.A.
100 D1 **Newhalem** Washington U.S.A.
116 K7 **Newhalen** Alaska U.S.A.
102 F7 **Newhall** California U.S.A.
116 F5 **New Hamilton** Alaska U.S.A.
95 Q4 **New Hampshire** *state* U.S.A.
99 O6 **New Hampton** Iowa U.S.A.
99 M9 **New Hampton** Missouri U.S.A.
95 S3 **New Harbor** Maine U.S.A.
110 J3 **New Harmony** Indiana U.S.A.
95 O5 **New Hartford** Connecticut U.S.A.
9 G6 **Newhaven** England
95 P5 **New Haven** Connecticut U.S.A.
94 B5 **New Haven** Indiana U.S.A.
110 E3 **New Haven** Missouri U.S.A.
94 F8 **New Haven** West Virginia U.S.A.
98 B5 **New Haven** Wyoming U.S.A.
117 K8 **New Hazelton** British Columbia Canada
New Hebrides *see* **Vanuatu**
13 F6 **New Hey** England
13 H6 **New Holland** England
99 R9 **New Holland** Illinois U.S.A.
99 S6 **New Holstein** Wisconsin U.S.A.
109 O1 **Newhope** Arkansas U.S.A.
12 E2 **Newhouse** Scotland
111 E12 **New Iberia** Louisiana U.S.A.
9 H5 **Newington** England
112 F5 **Newington** Georgia U.S.A.
137 L2 **New Ireland** *isld* Bismarck Arch
95 N7 **New Jersey** *state* U.S.A.
94 H6 **New Kensington** Pennsylvania U.S.A.
95 L9 **New Kent** Virginia U.S.A.
106 F6 **Newkirk** New Mexico U.S.A.
107 N5 **Newkirk** Oklahoma U.S.A.
143 E8 **Newland Ra** W Australia Australia
98 E3 **New Leipzig** North Dakota U.S.A.
94 E7 **New Lexington** Ohio U.S.A.
99 Q6 **New Lisbon** Wisconsin U.S.A.
121 L5 **New Liskeard** Ontario Canada
99 P9 **New London** Iowa U.S.A.
99 M4 **New London** Minnesota U.S.A.
99 P10 **New London** Missouri U.S.A.
95 P3 **New London** New Hampshire U.S.A.
94 E5 **New London** Ohio U.S.A.
99 S5 **New London** Wisconsin U.S.A.
12 D4 **New Luce** Scotland
110 G5 **New Madrid** Missouri U.S.A.
12 E2 **Newmains** Scotland
143 C6 **Newman** W Australia Australia
145 E4 **Newman** New Zealand
102 C4 **Newman** California U.S.A.
99 T10 **Newman** Illinois U.S.A.
106 D9 **Newman** New Mexico U.S.A.
98 J8 **Newman Gr** Nebraska U.S.A.
142 C6 **Newman,Mt** W Australia Australia
123 T5 **Newman's Cove** Newfoundland Canada
141 K1 **Newmarket** *dist* Brisbane, Qnsld Australia
121 L8 **Newmarket** Ontario Canada
9 G3 **Newmarket** England
14 B4 **Newmarket** Ireland
127 J2 **Newmarket** Jamaica
110 K7 **New Market** Alabama U.S.A.
99 M9 **New Market** Iowa U.S.A.
95 Q3 **Newmarket** New Hampshire U.S.A.
94 J8 **New Market** Virginia U.S.A.
94 E7 **New Marshfield** Ohio U.S.A.
94 G7 **New Martinsville** West Virginia U.S.A.
94 F7 **New Matamoras** Ohio U.S.A.
100 J5 **New Meadows** Idaho U.S.A.
102 D4 **New Melones Res** California U.S.A.
106 D6 **New Mexico** *state* U.S.A.
94 C7 **New Miami** Ohio U.S.A.
95 O5 **New Milford** Connecticut U.S.A.
95 M5 **New Milford** Pennsylvania U.S.A.
12 D2 **Newmilns** Scotland
108 E2 **New Moore** Texas U.S.A.
111 M8 **Newnan** Georgia U.S.A.
113 E8 **Newnan L** Florida U.S.A.
139 K5 **Newnes** New South Wales Australia
8 D4 **Newnham** England
143 B9 **New Norcia** W Australia Australia
139 H8 **New Norfolk** Tasmania Australia
118 E6 **New Norway** Alberta Canada
111 F11 **New Orleans** Louisiana U.S.A.
119 O6 **New Osgoode** Saskatchewan Canada
95 K7 **New Oxford** Pennsylvania U.S.A.
95 N5 **New Paltz** New York U.S.A.
94 C7 **New Paris** Ohio U.S.A.
94 A8 **New Pekin** Indiana U.S.A.
94 F6 **New Philadelphia** Ohio U.S.A.
100 E7 **New Pine Creek** Oregon U.S.A.
15 F3 **New Pitsligo** Scotland
145 E3 **New Plymouth** New Zealand
100 J6 **New Plymouth** Idaho U.S.A.
122 H5 **Newport** Quebec Canada
126 B2 **New Port** Curaçao
8 D2 **Newport** England
9 G4 **Newport** England
9 E6 **Newport** England
14 B3 **Newport** Ireland
127 K3 **Newport** Jamaica
110 E6 **Newport** Arkansas U.S.A.
99 T10 **Newport** Indiana U.S.A.
110 M2 **Newport** Kentucky U.S.A.
94 D5 **Newport** Michigan U.S.A.
99 O5 **Newport** Minnesota U.S.A.
98 G7 **Newport** Nebraska U.S.A.
95 P3 **Newport** New Hampshire U.S.A.
95 M7 **Newport** New Jersey U.S.A.
112 L3 **Newport** North Carolina U.S.A.
100 A5 **Newport** Oregon U.S.A.
95 K6 **Newport** Pennsylvania U.S.A.
95 Q5 **Newport** Rhode I U.S.A.
112 D2 **Newport** Tennessee U.S.A.
109 J2 **Newport** Texas U.S.A.
95 P2 **Newport** Vermont U.S.A.
100 H1 **Newport** Washington U.S.A.
8 B3 **Newport** Wales
8 D4 **Newport** Wales
8 B3 **Newport B** Wales
102 G8 **Newport Beach** California U.S.A.
95 L10 **Newport News** Virginia U.S.A.
13 F1 **Newport-on-Tay** Scotland
9 F3 **Newport Pagnell** England
113 E9 **New Port Richey** Florida U.S.A.
112 D1 **New Powell** Tennessee U.S.A.
99 N5 **New Prague** Minnesota U.S.A.
113 L9 **New Providence** *isld* Bahamas
8 A7 **Newquay** England
8 B3 **New Quay** Wales
113 E8 **New R** Florida U.S.A.
8 C3 **New Radnor** Wales
106 G1 **New Raymer** Colorado U.S.A.
99 N6 **New Richland** Minnesota U.S.A.
122 G5 **New Richmond** Quebec Canada
94 C8 **New Richmond** Ohio U.S.A.
99 O4 **New Richmond** Wisconsin U.S.A.
110 M5 **New River** Tennessee U.S.A.
112 K3 **New River Inlet** North Carolina U.S.A.
111 E11 **New Roads** Louisiana U.S.A.
98 G2 **New Rockford** North Dakota U.S.A.
9 G6 **New Romney** England
14 E4 **New Ross** Ireland
110 K2 **New Ross** Indiana U.S.A.
140 A3 **Newry** N Terr Australia
14 E2 **Newry** N Ireland
95 R2 **Newry** Maine U.S.A.
94 J6 **Newry** Pennsylvania U.S.A.
14 E2 **Newry Canal** N Ireland
98 E3 **New Salem** North Dakota U.S.A.
94 H7 **New Salem** Pennsylvania U.S.A.
13 E1 **New Scone** Scotland
99 O8 **New Sharon** Iowa U.S.A.
New Siberian Is *see* **Novosibirskiye Ostrova**
113 G8 **New Smyrna Beach** Florida U.S.A.
139 G5 **New South Wales** *state* Australia
94 E7 **New Straitsville** Ohio U.S.A.
85 D7 **New Tamale** Ghana
94 D10 **New Tazewell** Tennessee U.S.A.
116 E6 **Newtok** Alaska U.S.A.
9 G2 **Newton** England
13 E3 **Newton** Scotland
111 L10 **Newton** Alabama U.S.A.
110 H3 **Newton** Illinois U.S.A.
99 N8 **Newton** Iowa U.S.A.
107 N3 **Newton** Kansas U.S.A.
95 Q4 **Newton** Massachusetts U.S.A.
111 G9 **Newton** Mississippi U.S.A.
112 F2 **Newton** North Carolina U.S.A.
109 O5 **Newton** Texas U.S.A.
8 C6 **Newton Abbot** England
13 E4 **Newton Arlosh** England
95 M2 **Newton Falls** New York U.S.A.
94 G5 **Newton Falls** Ohio U.S.A.
8 B7 **Newton Ferrers** England
112 J2 **Newton Grove** North Carolina U.S.A.
94 K6 **Newton Hamilton** Pennsylvania U.S.A.
13 F6 **Newton-le-Willows** England
12 D2 **Newton Mearns** Scotland
15 D3 **Newtonmore** Scotland
101 O8 **Newton Res** Utah U.S.A.
12 D4 **Newton Stewart** Scotland
123 T4 **Newtown** Newfoundland Canada
110 C1 **Newtown** Missouri U.S.A.
95 K9 **Newtown** Virginia U.S.A.
8 C3 **Newtown** Wales
14 E2 **Newtownabbey** N Ireland
14 F2 **Newtownards** N Ireland
14 D2 **Newtownbutler** N Ireland
14 E2 **Newtownhamilton** N Ireland
14 E3 **Newtown Mt.Kennedy** Ireland
98 D2 **New Town Sanish** North Dakota U.S.A.
14 D2 **Newtown Stewart** N Ireland
99 M5 **New Ulm** Minnesota U.S.A.
109 L6 **New Ulm** Texas U.S.A.
98 D5 **New Underwood** South Dakota U.S.A.
111 L10 **Newville** Alabama U.S.A.
102 B2 **Newville** California U.S.A.
94 K6 **Newville** Pennsylvania U.S.A.
99 N8 **New Virginia** Iowa U.S.A.
94 E6 **New Washington** Ohio U.S.A.
123 M7 **New Waterford** C Breton I, Nova Scotia
109 M5 **New Waverly** Texas U.S.A.
117 J11 **New Westminster** British Columbia Canada
95 K7 **New Windsor** Maryland U.S.A.
123 S4 **New World I** Newfoundland Canada
100 F8 **New Year L** Nevada U.S.A.
96 **New York** *conurbation*
95 K4 **New York** *state* U.S.A.
103 J6 **New York Mts** California U.S.A.
144 **New Zealand** *dominion* S W Pacific
94 C5 **Ney** Ohio U.S.A.
52 F5 **Neya** Russian Federation
8 B4 **Neyland** Wales
77 D5 **Neyrīz** Iran
77 F1 **Neyshābūr** Iran
76 D5 **Neyveli** India
55 D2 **Neyvo Shaytanskiy** Russian Federation
31 H6 **Nežárka** *R* Czechoslovakia
54 C5 **Nezhin** Ukraine
100 J3 **Nezperce** Idaho U.S.A.
61 N7 **Nezugaseki** Japan
86 C6 **N'Gabé** Congo
88 E10 **N'gabu** Malawi
68 D5 **Nga Chong,Khao** *mt* Burma/Thailand
68 H5 **Ngac Linh** *mt* Vietnam
71 J9 **Ngadubolu** Sumba Indonesia
68 A2 **Ngahan** Burma
144 C5 **Ngahere** New Zealand
71 K10 **Ngalu** Indonesia
145 E3 **Ngamatapouri** New Zealand
145 F3 **Ngamatea Swamp** New Zealand
66 F5 **Ngamda** China
87 D10 **Ngami, L** Botswana
66 C5 **Ngangla Ringco** *L* China
74 J2 **Nganglong Kangri** *mt ra* China
75 M3 **Ngangzê Co** *L* China
70 N9 **Nganjuk** Java
68 G3 **Ngan Pha** *R* Vietnam
68 G3 **Ngan Sau** *R* Vietnam
68 G1 **Ngan Son** Vietnam
86 C6 **N'Gao** Congo
86 B4 **Ngaoundéré** Cameroon
144 C6 **Ngapara** New Zealand
68 B2 **Ngape** Burma
144 C6 **Ngapuna** New Zealand
70 K8 **Ngaras** Sumatra
145 E3 **Ngaroma** New Zealand
145 E2 **Ngaruawahia** New Zealand
145 F3 **Ngaruroro R** New Zealand
145 D1 **Ngataki** New Zealand
145 F3 **Ngatapo** New Zealand
145 E2 **Ngatea** New Zealand
68 B4 **Ngathainggyaung** Burma
145 E3 **Ngatira** New Zealand
145 E3 **Ngauruhoe** *vol* New Zealand
68 D7 **Ngawan Chaung** *R* Burma
145 F2 **Ngawaro** New Zealand
70 N9 **Ngawi** Java
68 B4 **Ngayok B** Burma
Ngemda *see* **Ngamda**
89 G2 **Ngezi** *R* Zimbabwe
89 G3 **Ngezi** *R* Zimbabwe
89 G3 **Ngezi** Zimbabwe
89 G2 **Ngezi Dam** Zimbabwe
Nghia Hung *see* **Thai Hoa**
68 G2 **Nghia Lô** Vietnam
71 M9 **Ngilmina** Indonesia
70 O9 **Ngimbang** Java
88 F6 **Ngindo** Tanzania
86 C5 **Ngoko** *R* Congo
87 E9 **Ngoma** Zambia
88 F2 **Ngong** Kenya
145 F3 **Ngongotaha** New Zealand
88 D7 **Ngoni** Malawi
66 F5 **Ngoring Hu** *L* China
88 E3 **Ngorongoro Crater** Tanzania
71 A2 **Ngotakiaha** Halmahera Indonesia
86 B6 **Ngounié** *R* Gabon
86 B2 **N'Gourti** Niger
88 B3 **Ngozi** Burundi
86 B3 **N'Guigmi** Niger
140 B1 **Nguiu** N Terr Australia
140 C2 **Ngukurr** N Terr Australia
68 F3 **Ngum** *R* Laos
71 K10 **Ngundju,Tg** *C* Sumba Indonesia
145 E1 **Ngunguru** New Zealand
88 E7 **Nguni** Tanzania
70 O10 **Ngunut** Java
85 G6 **Nguru** Nigeria
67 B5 **Nguyen Binh** Vietnam
89 D5 **Ngwaketse** *dist* Botswana
89 B4 **Ngwatlhe Pan** Botswana
87 G10 **Nhachengue** Mozambique
128 G6 **Nhambiquara** Brazil
129 G4 **Nhamunda** Brazil
67 A6 **Nhan Nghia** Vietnam
68 J6 **Nha Trang** Vietnam
74 E9 **Nhava-Sheva** India
130 C6 **Nhecolândia** Brazil
68 F3 **Nhiep** *R* Laos
138 F6 **Nhill** Victoria Australia
68 G4 **Nhommarath** Laos
140 D1 **Nhulunbuy** N Terr Australia
68 G3 **Nhu Xuan** Vietnam
144 B7 **Niagara** New Zealand
98 H1 **Niagara** North Dakota U.S.A.
99 S4 **Niagara** Wisconsin U.S.A.
121 L9 **Niagara Falls** Ontario Canada
94 J3 **Niagara Falls** New York U.S.A.
121 L9 **Niagara-on-the-Lake** Ontario Canada
70 C3 **Niah** Sarawak
85 C7 **Niakaramandougou** Ivory Coast
85 E6 **Niamey** Niger
86 E5 **Niangara** Zaire
85 D5 **Niangaye,L** Mali
85 C7 **Niangbo,Pic de** *mt* Ivory Coast
85 D6 **Niangoloko** Burkina
110 D4 **Niangua** *R* Missouri U.S.A.
Niangxi *see* **Xinshao**
86 E5 **Nia Nia** Zaire
95 P5 **Niantic** Connecticut U.S.A.
65 E1 **Nianzishan** China
101 L2 **Niarada** Montana U.S.A.
86 B6 **Niari** *R* Congo
69 C12 **Nias** *isld* Indonesia
88 F8 **Niassa** Mozambique
46 F8 **Niata** Greece
101 R4 **Nibbe** Montana U.S.A.
28 D3 **Nibe** Denmark
28 D2 **Nibe Bredning** *B* Denmark
121 R3 **Nicabau** Quebec Canada
125 L3 **Nicaragua** *rep* Central America
125 M4 **Nicaragua, Lac de** Nicaragua
95 T1 **Nicatous L**
44 B4 **Nice** France
102 B2 **Nice** California U.S.A.
111 K11 **Niceville** Florida U.S.A.
115 M7 **Nichicun, L** Quebec Canada
60 E11 **Nichihara** Japan
112 E6 **Nicholls** Georgia U.S.A.
99 P8 **Nichols** Iowa U.S.A.
95 L4 **Nichols** New York U.S.A.
140 E4 **Nicholson** *R* Queensland Australia
142 G4 **Nicholson** W Australia Australia
143 B7 **Nicholson Ra** W Australia Australia
95 N2 **Nicholville** New York U.S.A.
99 O1 **Nickel L** Ontario Canada
129 G2 **Nickerie** *R* Suriname
107 M3 **Nickerson** Kansas U.S.A.
142 B5 **Nickol B** W Australia Australia
122 F3 **Nicman** Quebec Canada
69 A8 **Nicobar Is** Bay of Bengal
117 N10 **Nicola** British Columbia Canada
121 S6 **Nicolet** Quebec Canada
99 M5 **Nicollet** Minnesota U.S.A.
Nicomedia *see* **Kocaeli**
78 D4 **Nicosia** Cyprus
43 F11 **Nicosia** Sicily
43 G10 **Nicotera** Italy
125 M4 **Nicoya** Costa Rica
125 M5 **Nicoya,Pen.de** Costa Rica
122 E6 **Nictau** New Brunswick Canada
31 M5 **Nida** *R* Poland
76 E2 **Nidadavole** India
40 F3 **Nidau** Switzerland
36 F3 **Nidda** *R* Germany
36 G3 **Nidda** Germany
36 F3 **Niddatal** Germany
36 B2 **Nideggen** Germany
27 C13 **Nidelv** *R* Norway
41 H4 **Nidwalden** *canton* Switzerland
31 M2 **Nidzica** Poland
30 D1 **Niebüll** Germany
36 G1 **Niedenstein** Germany
37 N6 **Niederaichbach** Germany
37 L6 **Niederarnbach** Germany
36 H2 **Nieder Aula** Germany
37 N6 **Niederbayern** *dist* Germany
36 C3 **Niederbieber** Germany
19 L4 **Niederbronn** France
33 O6 **Nieder Elde** *R* Germany
36 G2 **Nieder Gemünden** Germany
33 R9 **Niedergörsdorf** Germany
36 C2 **Niederkassel** Germany
25 F6 **Niederkrüchten** Germany
36 D3 **Nieder Lahnstein** Germany
32 J10 **Nieder Marsberg** Germany
33 M6 **Nieder Marschacht** Germany
36 H5 **Niedernhall** Germany
36 E3 **Niedernhausen** Germany
36 E4 **Nieder Olm** Germany
36 E3 **Nieder Ouembach** Germany
32 J7 **Niedersachsen** *land* Germany
36 D2 **Nieder Schelden** Germany
36 E3 **Niederselters** Germany
32 J10 **Niedersfeld** Germany
36 H5 **Niederstetten** Germany
37 J6 **Niederstotzingen** Germany
36 D4 **Niederwald** Germany
36 E2 **Nieder Weidbach** Germany
36 F2 **Nieder Weimar** Germany
37 P2 **Niederwiesa** Germany
36 F3 **Nieder Wöllstadt** Germany
36 C3 **Nieder Zissen** Germany
33 T8 **Nieder Zittau** Germany
32 K9 **Nieheim** Germany
98 K2 **Nielsville** Minnesota U.S.A.
88 B4 **Niemba** Zaire
88 B5 **Niemba** *R* Zaire
33 Q9 **Niemberg** Germany
31 K5 **Niemcza** Poland
33 R8 **Niemegk** Germany
26 N5 **Niemis** Sweden
26 M5 **Niemisel** Sweden
31 K5 **Niemodlin** Poland
33 N7 **Nienbergen** Germany
32 F8 **Nienborg** Germany
32 K7 **Nienburg** Germany
33 P9 **Nienburg** Germany
33 N5 **Niendorf** Germany
31 M5 **Niepołomice** Poland
22 D2 **Nieppe** France
25 F5 **Niers** *R* Germany
36 E4 **Nierstein** Germany
31 H4 **Niesky** Germany
31 L3 **Nieszawa** Poland
85 C7 **Niete, Mt** Liberia
33 P10 **Nietleben** Germany
20 H8 **Nieul le Dolent** France
129 G2 **Nieuw Amsterdam** Suriname
25 D4 **Nieuwegein** Netherlands
25 B5 **Nieuwe Maas** Netherlands
25 C5 **Nieuwendijk** Netherlands
25 D4 **Nieuwersluis** Netherlands
32 F6 **Nieuweschans** Germany
25 H2 **Nieuweschans** Netherlands
22 D2 **Nieuwkerke** Belgium
25 C4 **Nieuwkoop** Netherlands
129 G2 **Nieuw Nickerie** Suriname
25 G2 **Nieuwolda** Netherlands
22 D1 **Nieuwpoort** Belgium
25 C5 **Nieuwpoort** Netherlands
25 E6 **Nieuwstadt** Netherlands
25 C4 **Nieuw-Vennep** Netherlands
18 H5 **Nièvre** *dèpt* France
122 G6 **Nigadoo** New Brunswick Canada
78 E3 **Niğde** Turkey
85 F5 **Niger** *rep* W Africa
85 B6 **Niger** *R* W Africa
85 F7 **Nigeria** *rep* W Africa
85 F8 **Niger,Mouths of the** Nigeria
144 B6 **Nightcaps** New Zealand
100 F1 **Nighthawk** Washington U.S.A.
141 G2 **Night I** Great Barrier Reef Aust
Nightingale I *see* **Bach Long Vi,I.**
90 B16 **Nightingale I** Tristan da Cunha
116 K2 **Nigu** *R* Alaska U.S.A.
21 O8 **Niherne** France
102 U13 **Nihoa** Hawaiian Is
131 C5 **Nihuili, Embalse del** *res* Argentina
61 N8 **Niigata** Japan
60 G12 **Niihama** Japan
135 N1 **Niihau** *isld* Hawaiian Is
61 N11 **Nii-jima** *isld* Japan
60 Q3 **Niikappu** *R* Japan
60 G10 **Niimi** Japan
60 D4 **Niitomi** Japan
61 N8 **Niitsu** Japan
17 F8 **Nijar** Spain
25 F2 **Nijega** Netherlands
60 S2 **Nijibetsu** Japan
79 F8 **Nijil** Jordan
25 D4 **Nijkerk** Netherlands
25 E5 **Nijmegen** Netherlands
25 F4 **Nijverdal** Netherlands
116 K6 **Nikabuna Lakes** Alaska U.S.A.
Nikaria *isld see* **Ikaría** *isld*
26 S2 **Nikel'** Russian Federation
55 C5 **Nikel'tau** Kazakhstan
71 M9 **Nikiniki** Timor Indonesia
46 F4 **Nikitas** Greece
52 D6 **Nikitinka** Russian Federation
54 K8 **Nikitovka** Ukraine
85 E7 **Nikki** Benin
61 N9 **Nikkō** Japan
61 N9 **Nikkō Nat. Park** Japan
40 G5 **Niklaus** Switzerland
116 K5 **Nikolai** Alaska U.S.A.
48 H1 **Nikolayev** Ukraine
54 D10 **Nikolayev** Ukraine
55 E4 **Nikolayevka** Kazakhstan
53 G8 **Nikolayevsk** Russian Federation
55 D4 **Nikolayevskiy** Russian Federation
59 M1 **Nikolayevsk-na-Amure** Russian Federation
52 G5 **Nikol'sk** Russian Federation
52 F5 **Nikolskoye** Russian Federation
55 C5 **Nikol'skoye** Russian Federation
88 C3 **Nikonga** *R* Tanzania
46 G1 **Nikopol** Bulgaria
54 F9 **Nikopol'** Ukraine
78 F1 **Niksar** Turkey
77 G6 **Nīkshahr** Iran
42 J6 **Nikšić** Montenegro Yugoslavia
137 S2 **Nikumaroro** *isld* Phoenix Is Pacific Oc
71 O8 **Nila** *isld* Indonesia
103 J8 **Niland** California U.S.A.
73 L8 **Nilande Atoll** Maldives
83 L9 **Nilaveli** Sri Lanka
84 J4 **Nile** *R* N E Africa
86 F2 **Nile** *prov* Sudan
102 B4 **Niles** California U.S.A.
107 N3 **Niles** Kansas U.S.A.
94 A5 **Niles** Michigan U.S.A.
94 G5 **Niles** Ohio U.S.A.
121 N6 **Nilgaut, L** Quebec Canada
76 C5 **Nilgiri Hills** India
116 E6 **Nilikluguk** Alaska U.S.A.
57 K3 **Nilka** China
29 N8 **Nilsiä** Finland
47 K4 **Nilüfer** *R* Turkey
57 F5 **Nil'van** Tajikistan
83 K11 **Nilwala** *R* Sri Lanka
28 D5 **Nim** Denmark
74 F6 **Nimach** India
85 C7 **Nimba, Mts** Guinea/Liberia/ Ivory Co
142 E6 **Nimberra Well** W Australia Australia
139 L3 **Nimbin** New South Wales Australia
18 H9 **Nîmes** France
47 O12 **Nímfai** Greece
74 F5 **Nimka Thana** India
139 J6 **Nimmitabel** New South Wales Australia
101 M3 **Nimrod** Montana U.S.A.
Nimrod Bay *see* **Xiangshan Gang**
110 C7 **Nimrod L** Arkansas U.S.A.
144 C6 **Nimrod, Mt** New Zealand
109 O1 **Nimrod Res** Arkansas U.S.A.
77 H4 **Nīmrūz** *reg* Afghanistan
28 F4 **Nimtofte** Denmark
42 G4 **Nin** Croatia
78 H4 **Nīnawá** *prov* Iraq
71 F4 **Nin Bay** Philippines
87 D8 **Ninda** Angola
141 J8 **Nindigully** Queensland Australia
73 L7 **Nine Degree Chan** Lakshadweep Indian Oc
13 E2 **Nine Mile Burn** Scotland
139 G4 **Nine Mile L** New South Wales Australia
103 H2 **Ninemile Pk** Nevada U.S.A.
108 D6 **Nine Point Mesa** *mt* Texas U.S.A.
119 S9 **Ninette** Manitoba Canada
139 J7 **Ninety Mile Beach** Victoria Australia
145 D1 **Ninety Mile Beach** New Zealand
112 E3 **Ninety Six** South Carolina U.S.A.
94 G7 **Ninevah** Pennsylvania U.S.A.
133 E6 **Ninfas,Pta** Argentina
9 G6 **Ninfield** England
143 A6 **Ningaloo** W Australia Australia
59 J3 **Ning'an** China
67 G2 **Ningbo** China
65 D4 **Ningcheng** China
67 F3 **Ningde** China
67 E3 **Ningdu** China
67 D3 **Ninggang** China
67 F1 **Ningguo** China
67 G2 **Ninghai** China
65 D5 **Ninghe** China
Ning-hsia *see* **Yinchuan**
67 E3 **Ninghua** China
58 F4 **Ningjin** China
65 C6 **Ningjin** China
66 F5 **Ningjing Shan** *ra* China
65 C7 **Ningling** China
67 B5 **Ningming** China
Ningpo *see* **Ningbo**
Ningsia *aut reg see* **Ningxia**
65 B5 **Ningwu** China
58 E4 **Ningxia** *aut reg* China
67 D2 **Ningxiang** China
65 C7 **Ningyang** China
67 D4 **Ningyuan** China
67 B6 **Ninh Binh** Vietnam
68 J6 **Ninh Hoa** Vietnam
6 L2 **Ninian** *oil rig* North Sea
116 M6 **Ninilchik** Alaska U.S.A.
142 C5 **Niningarra** W Australia Australia
107 N7 **Ninnekah** Oklahoma U.S.A.
107 N4 **Ninnescah** *R* Kansas U.S.A.
146 D14 **Ninnis Glacier** Antarctica
111 C9 **Ninock** Louisiana U.S.A.
61 P5 **Ninohe** Japan
60 E14 **Ninokata** Japan
22 G2 **Ninove** Belgium
130 C7 **Nioaque** Brazil
94 H4 **Niobe** New York U.S.A.
98 E7 **Niobrara** *R* Nebraska U.S.A.
98 J7 **Niobrara** Nebraska U.S.A.
86 C6 **Nioki** Zaire
85 B6 **Niokolo-koba,Parc Nat.du** Senegal
85 A6 **Nioro du Rip** Senegal
85 C5 **Nioro du Sahel** Mali
18 E6 **Niort** France
Nios *isld see* **Íos** *isld*
99 P9 **Niota** Illinois U.S.A.
112 C2 **Niota** Tennessee U.S.A.
85 C5 **Niout** Mauritania
76 B2 **Nipani** India
71 H6 **Nipanipa,Tg** *C* Sulawesi
119 N5 **Nipawin** Saskatchewan Canada
119 N4 **Nipawin Prov.Park** Saskatchewan Canada
120 B3 **Nipigon** Ontario Canada
120 C4 **Nipigon B** Ontario Canada
120 B3 **Nipigon, Lake** Ontario Canada
118 H3 **Nipin R** Saskatchewan Canada
118 C3 **Nipisi R** Alberta Canada
122 G6 **Nipisquit,B** New Brunswick Canada
121 L6 **Nipissing Junc** Ontario Canada
120 K6 **Nipissing,L** Ontario Canada
122 F3 **Nipissis L** Quebec Canada
122 F3 **Nipissis R** Quebec Canada
122 G3 **Nipisso L** Quebec Canada
102 D6 **Nipomo** California U.S.A.
103 J6 **Nipton** California U.S.A.
84 J5 **Niqrûb el Fuqâni, Gebel** *mt* Egypt
126 F4 **Niquero** Cuba
80 E6 **Niran** Jordan
61 M10 **Nirasaki** Japan
80 C3 **Nir 'Ezyon** Israel
80 B6 **Nir Gallim** Israel
80 B7 **Nir H̱en** Israel
74 H9 **Nirmal** India
75 M5 **Nirmali** India
80 B8 **Nir Moshe** Israel
94 B3 **Nirvana** Michigan U.S.A.
80 C6 **Nir Ẕevi** Israel
46 E1 **Niš** Serbia Yugoslavia
16 B5 **Nisa** Portugal
72 F6 **Niṣāb** Yemen
46 F1 **Nisava** *R* Serbia Yugoslavia
95 K5 **Nisbet** Pennsylvania U.S.A.
60 O3 **Niseko** Japan
67 C2 **Nishi** China
61 P5 **Nishi-Hōji** Japan
60 J11 **Nishinomiya** Japan
60 F9 **Nishino-shima** *isld* Japan
61 L11 **Nishio** Japan
60 C13 **Nishi-Sonogi-hantō** *pen* Japan
60 C11 **Nishi-suidō** *str* Japan
60 H10 **Nishiwaki** Japan
116 H6 **Nishlik L** Alaska U.S.A.
99 L8 **Nishnabotna, E** *R* Iowa U.S.A.
99 L8 **Nishnabotna, W** *R* Iowa U.S.A.
130 J9 **Nísia Floresta** Brazil
48 J3 **Nisipitul** Romania
47 J8 **Nísiros** *isld* Greece
31 N5 **Nisko** Poland
98 C5 **Nisland** South Dakota U.S.A.
117 D4 **Nisling** *R* Yukon Territory Canada
48 L3 **Nisporeny** Moldavia
100 C3 **Nisqually** *R* Washington U.S.A.
27 F15 **Nissan** *R* Sweden
27 C12 **Nissedal** Norway
27 C12 **Nisserv** *L* Norway
28 A3 **Nissum Bredning** *B* Denmark
28 A4 **Nissum Fjord** *inlet* Denmark
117 G5 **Nisutlin** *R* Yukon Territory Canada
115 M7 **Nitchequon** Quebec Canada
130 G8 **Niterói** Brazil
15 E5 **Nith,R** Scotland
15 E5 **Nithsdale** Scotland
71 M9 **Nitibe** Timor
80 G7 **Nitil** Jordan
100 A1 **Nitinat L** British Columbia Canada
9 E6 **Niton** England
31 L7 **Nitra** *R* Czechoslovakia
48 E2 **Nitra** Czechoslovakia
94 F8 **Nitro** West Virginia U.S.A.
55 D2 **Nitsa** *R* Russian Federation
29 N2 **Nitsjärvi** *L* Finland
37 N5 **Nittenau** Germany
37 M5 **Nittendorf** Germany
137 R5 **Niuafo'ou** *isld* Pacific Oc
137 S5 **Niuatoputapu** *isld* Pacific Oc
137 T5 **Niue** *isld* Pacific Oc
137 Q4 **Niulakita** *isld* Tuvalu
65 F4 **Niumaowu** China
69 F13 **Niur, Pulau** *isld* Sumatra
Niushan *see* **Donghai**
137 Q3 **Niutao** *isld* Tuvalu
65 E4 **Niuzhuang** China
29 K5 **Nivå** Denmark
29 L8 **Nivala** Finland
141 H7 **Nive** *R* Queensland Australia
18 E9 **Nive** *R* France
141 H7 **Nive Downs** Queensland Australia
22 G2 **Nivelles** Belgium
18 H5 **Nivernais** *prov* France
118 D1 **Niverville** Manitoba Canada
21 P3 **Nivillers** France
102 G4 **Nivloc** Nevada U.S.A.
40 B6 **Nivolas-Vermelle** France
52 D2 **Nivskiy** Russian Federation
74 J7 **Niwas** India
102 E2 **Nixon** Nevada U.S.A.
109 K6 **Nixon** Texas U.S.A.
47 N11 **Niyandros** *isld* Turkey
70 B4 **Niyat, Gunung** *mt* Kalimantan
74 H9 **Nizamabad** India
52 F6 **Nizhegorodskaya Oblast'** *prov* Russian Federation
52 E3 **Nizhmozero** Russian Federation
56 G3 **Nizhneangarsk** Russian Federation
52 H2 **Nizhne Bugayevo** Russian Federation
54 L9 **Nizhne Gnilovskoy** Russian Federation
52 H6 **Nizhnekamsk** Russian Federation
52 H6 **Nizhnekamskoye Vodokhranilishche** *res* Russian Federation
55 B4 **Nizhne-troitskiy** Russian Federation
56 E4 **Nizhneudinsk** Russian Federation
55 G1 **Nizhnevartovsk** Russian Federation
55 B4 **Nizhneye Il'yasovo** Russian Federation
52 D2 **Nizhneye Kuyto, Oz** *L* Russian Federation
52 F6 **Nizhniy Novgorod** Russian Federation
55 C2 **Nizhniy Tagil** Russian Federation
52 H6 **Nizhniy Takanysh** Russian Federation
56 F5 **Nizhniy Torey** Russian Federation
52 E2 **Nizhniy Vyalozerskiy** Russian Federation
52 G4 **Nizhniy Yenangsk** Russian Federation
55 E2 **Nizhnyaya Aremzyan** Russian Federation
55 C3 **Nizhnyaya Irga** Russian Federation
55 F3 **Nizhnyaya Omka** Russian Federation
52 J3 **Nizhnyaya-Omra** Russian Federation
52 G2 **Nizhnyaya Pesha** Russian Federation
56 E3 **Nizhnyaya Pomya** Russian Federation
55 D2 **Nizhnyaya Salda** Russian Federation
55 G4 **Nizhnyaya Suyetka** Russian Federation
55 E2 **Nizhnyaya Tavda** Russian Federation
52 F3 **Nizhnyaya Toyma** *R* Russian Federation
56 G1 **Nizhnyaya Tunguska** *R* Russian Federation
55 C2 **Nizhnyaya Tura** Russian Federation
52 H4 **Nizhnyaya Voch'** Russian Federation
52 F2 **Nizhnyaya Zolotitsa** Russian Federation
29 Q4 **Nizh Pirengskoye Ozero** *L* Russian Federation
56 G2 **Nizh Tunguska** *R* Russian Federation
116 Q6 **Nizina** Alaska U.S.A.
78 F3 **Nizip** Turkey
31 L7 **Nízké Tatry** *mts* Czechoslovakia
48 F2 **Nižm Medzev** Czechoslovakia
22 G4 **Nizy-le-Comte** France
44 D2 **Nizza** Italy
79 E8 **Nizzana** *hist site* Israel
80 C4 **Niẕẕane 'Oz** Israel
80 B7 **Niẕẕanim** Israel
70 D4 **Njaän** *mt* Kalimantan
42 J6 **Njegoš** *mt* Montenegro Yugoslavia
87 G7 **Njinjo** Tanzania
87 D9 **Njoko** *R* Zambia

88 E5 **Njombe** *R* Tanzania
88 E6 **Njombe** Tanzania
88 G10 **Njoro** *isld* Mozambique
26 J9 **Njurundabommen** Sweden
27 J10 **Njutånger** Sweden
89 G7 **Nkandla** S Africa
88 D7 **Nkanka** *R* Zambia
88 E7 **Nkhata B** Malawi
88 E8 **Nkhotakota** Malawi
86 A6 **Nkomi, Lagune** *Lagoon* Gabon
86 A5 **Nkongsamba** Cameroon
88 D5 **Nkululu** *R* Tanzania
28 A4 **No** Denmark
21 P3 **Noailles** France
75 O7 **Noakhali** Bangladesh
45 M1 **Noale** Italy
128 C3 **Noanama** Colombia
95 Q5 **Noank** Connecticut U.S.A.
26 O3 **Noarvas** *mt* Norway
40 F7 **Noasca** Italy
116 F3 **Noatak** Alaska U.S.A.
116 G3 **Noatak Nat Preserve** Alaska U.S.A.
14 E3 **Nobber** Ireland
120 K7 **Nobel** Ontario Canada
60 E13 **Nobeoka** Japan
110 H3 **Noble** Illinois U.S.A.
107 N6 **Noble** Oklahoma U.S.A.
118 D9 **Nobleford** Alberta Canada
111 E7 **Noble Lake** Arkansas U.S.A.
94 A6 **Noblesville** Indiana U.S.A.
60 P3 **Noboribetsu** Japan
130 C4 **Nobres** Brazil
141 G8 **Noccundra** Queensland Australia
21 M5 **Noce** France
41 O5 **Noce** *R* Italy
45 R8 **Nocera Inferiore** Italy
44 H2 **Noceto** Italy
124 H7 **Nochistlán** Mexico
141 G8 **Nockatunga** Queensland Australia
109 K2 **Nocona** Texas U.S.A.
48 J5 **Nocrich** Romania
61 P5 **Noda** Japan
133 D7 **Nodales,B.de los** Argentina
99 M8 **Nodaway** *R* Iowa U.S.A.
99 M9 **Nodaway** Iowa U.S.A.
98 B7 **Node** Wyoming U.S.A.
20 G6 **Noé-Blanche** France
130 D4 **Noedori** *R* Brazil
110 B5 **Noel** Missouri U.S.A.
123 Q5 **Noel Paul's Brook** Newfoundland Canada
120 K6 **Noelville** Ontario Canada
22 D3 **Noeux les Mines** France
124 D2 **Nogales** Sonora Mexico
125 L8 **Nogales** Vera Cruz Mexico
103 O10 **Nogales** Arizona U.S.A.
116 J6 **Nogamut** Alaska U.S.A.
45 K1 **Nogara** Italy
18 E9 **Nogaro** France
31 L1 **Nogat** *R* Poland
60 D12 **Nōgata** Japan
40 B1 **Nogent en Bassigny** France
21 L5 **Nogent-le-Bernard** France
21 O4 **Nogent-le-Roi** France
21 M5 **Nogent-le-Rotrou** France
21 P3 **Nogent-sur-Oise** France
18 H4 **Nogent-sur-Seine** France
54 K1 **Noginsk** Russian Federation
59 M1 **Nogliki** Russian Federation
40 C4 **Nogno** France
141 K7 **Nogo** *R* Queensland Australia
141 J6 **Nogoa** *R* Queensland Australia
61 K10 **Nōgohaku-san** *mt* Japan
131 F4 **Nogoya** *R* Argentina
48 E3 **Nógrád** *co* Hungary
16 C3 **Nogueira** *mt* Portugal
17 H2 **Noguera Pallarésa** *R* Spain
17 H2 **Noguera Ribagorzana** *R* Spain
21 O8 **Nohant Vicq** France
74 F4 **Nohar** India
61 P5 **Noheji** Japan
36 C4 **Nohfelden** Germany
36 B3 **Nohn** Germany
Noia *see* **Noya**
121 N6 **Noire** *R* Quebec Canada
67 A6 **Noire** *R* Vietnam
16 E9 **Noire, Pt** Morocco
20 C5 **Noires,Mtgnes** France
20 F7 **Noirmoutier** France
20 F8 **Noirmoutier,Ile de** France
20 C5 **Noir,Mt** France
21 K8 **Noirterre** France
17 H9 **Noisy les Bains** Algeria
61 N11 **Nojima-zaki** *C* Japan
61 M9 **Nojiri-ko** *L* Japan
87 D9 **Nokaneng** Botswana
29 K10 **Nokia** Finland
74 B8 **Nok Kundi** Pakistan
77 H5 **Nok Kundi** Pakistan
144 B6 **Nokomai** New Zealand
119 N7 **Nokomis** Saskatchewan Canada
110 G2 **Nokomis** Illinois U.S.A.
86 C5 **Nola** Cent Afr Republic
45 R8 **Nola** Italy
119 O2 **Nolalu** Ontario Canada
98 J2 **Nolan** North Dakota U.S.A.
108 G3 **Nolan** Texas U.S.A.
28 E5 **Nølev** Denmark
44 D3 **Noli** Italy
112 E1 **Nolichucky** *R* Tennessee U.S.A.
112 E1 **Nolichucky Dam** Tennessee U.S.A.
52 G5 **Nolinsk** Russian Federation
21 N3 **Nolléval** France
6 F1 **Nólsoy** *isld* Faeroes
69 E9 **Nol,Thale** *L* Thailand
66 E3 **Nom** China
111 L11 **Noma** Florida U.S.A.
60 D14 **Noma-misaki** *C* Japan
95 R5 **No Mans Land** *isld* Massachusetts U.S.A.
116 E4 **Nome** Alaska U.S.A.
98 J3 **Nome** North Dakota U.S.A.
116 E4 **Nome C** Alaska U.S.A.
19 K4 **Nomeny** France
121 P6 **Nominingue** Quebec Canada
60 C13 **Nomo-zaki** *C* Japan
87 C10 **Nomtsas** Namibia
137 S6 **Nomuka** *isld* Tonga
114 J5 **Nonacho L** Northwest Territories Canada
21 N4 **Nonancourt** France
21 J3 **Nonant** France
21 L4 **Nonant-le-Pin** France
45 K2 **Nonantola** Italy
52 H2 **Nonburg** Russian Federation
65 F2 **Nong'an** China
68 F3 **Nong Het** Laos
68 F5 **Nong Hong** Thailand
68 F4 **Nong Khai** Thailand
87 F11 **Nongoma** S Africa
19 N15 **Nonières** France
Nonni *R see* **Nen Jiang** *R*
138 D4 **Nonning** South Australia Australia
138 D4 **Nonning,Mt** South Australia Australia
36 B4 **Nonnweiler** Germany
130 D10 **Nonoaí** Brazil
124 F4 **Nonoava** Mexico
71 G6 **Nonoc** *isld* Philippines
137 P2 **Nonouti** *atoll* Kiribati
119 W2 **Nonsuch** Manitoba Canada
68 E6 **Nonthaburi** Thailand
18 F7 **Nontron** France
116 K7 **Nonvianuk L** Alaska U.S.A.
143 B7 **Nookawarra** W Australia Australia
138 D2 **Noolyeanna,L** South Australia Australia
140 B2 **Noonamah** N Terr Australia
98 C1 **Noonan** North Dakota U.S.A.
143 C9 **Noongaar** W Australia Australia
142 E4 **Noonkanbah** W Australia Australia
141 H8 **Noorama** *R* Queensland Australia
25 A5 **Noord-Beveland** Netherlands
25 D5 **Noord Brabant** Netherlands
25 C5 **Noordeloos** Netherlands
25 C3 **Noord-Holland** Netherlands
25 E3 **Noordoost Polder** Netherlands
126 A1 **Noord Pt** Curaçao
25 B4 **Noordwijk aan zee** Netherlands
7 N9 **Noordwinning** *oil rig* North Sea
25 F3 **Noordwolde** Netherlands
25 C4 **Noordzee-Kanaal** Netherlands
29 J10 **Noormarkku** Finland
116 G3 **Noorvik** Alaska U.S.A.
141 L7 **Noosa Heads** Queensland Australia
117 K11 **Nootka** British Columbia Canada
117 K11 **Nootka I** British Columbia Canada
103 H5 **Nopah Ra** California U.S.A.
99 T4 **Noquebay,L** Wisconsin U.S.A.
119 O6 **Nora** Saskatchewan Canada
59 J1 **Nora** *R* Russian Federation
27 H12 **Nora** Sweden
98 J9 **Nora** Nebraska U.S.A.
28 D3 **Nørager** Denmark
86 G2 **Nora I** Ethiopia
71 G7 **Norala** Mindanao Philippines
121 L4 **Noranda** Quebec Canada
99 O6 **Nora Springs** Iowa U.S.A.
98 G4 **Norbeck** South Dakota U.S.A.
27 H11 **Norberg** Sweden
110 C2 **Norborne** Missouri U.S.A.
107 K2 **Norcatur** Kansas U.S.A.
42 E6 **Norcia** Italy
143 D9 **Norcott,Mt** W Australia Australia
111 M8 **Norcross** Georgia U.S.A.
18 H2 **Nord** *dept* France
27 D12 **Nordaguta** Norway
26 K7 **Nordanås** Sweden
27 D11 **Nord-Aurdal** Norway
50 B1 **Nordaustlandet** *isld* Spitzbergen
28 D6 **Nordborg** Denmark
28 F5 **Nordby** Denmark
28 A6 **Nordby** Denmark
Nord Cap *see* **Horn**
26 B9 **Norddal** Norway
32 F5 **Norddeich** Germany
28 A7 **Norddorf** Germany
32 L7 **Norddrebber** Germany
118 B6 **Nordegg R** Alberta Canada
9 G2 **Nordelph** England
32 F5 **Norden** Germany
37 K6 **Nordendorf** Germany
32 H5 **Nordenham** Germany
51 J1 **Nordenshel'da Arkhipelag** Russian Federation
117 E5 **Nordenskiold** *R* Yukon Territory Canada
28 A7 **Norder Aue** *chan* Germany
32 J5 **Nordergründe** *sandbank* Germany
32 F5 **Norderney** *isld* Germany
32 F5 **Norderney** Germany
26 A10 **Nordfjord** *reg* Norway
26 A10 **Nordfjord** *inlet* Norway
26 B10 **Nordfjordeid** Norway
26 H4 **Nordfold** Norway
30 D1 **Nord-friesische Inseln** *islds* Germany
28 B7 **Nordfriesland** *reg* Germany
37 M3 **Nordhalben** Germany
33 N10 **Nordhausen** Germany
109 K7 **Nordheim** Texas U.S.A.
32 J5 **Nordholz** Germany
27 A11 **Nordhordland** *reg* Norway
32 F8 **Nordhorn** Germany
26 K9 **Nordingrå** Sweden
80 C4 **Nordiyya** Israel
28 C3 **Nordjylland** *co* Denmark
26 P1 **Nordkapp** *C* Norway
26 Q1 **Nordkinn** Norway
26 L2 **Nordkjosbotn** Norway
26 F6 **Nordland Fylker** Norway
26 G7 **Nordli** Norway
37 K6 **Nördlingen** Germany
26 K8 **Nordmaling** Sweden
100 J1 **Nordman** Idaho U.S.A.
27 G12 **Nordmark** Sweden
27 D11 **Nordmarka** *reg* Norway
26 B9 **Nordmöre** *reg* Norway
98 F7 **Nordon** Nebraska U.S.A.
32 K4 **Nord-Ostsee Kanal** Germany
28 F2 **Nordre Rønner** *isld* Denmark
115 O4 **Nordre Strømfjord** *inlet* Greenland
32 E9 **Nordrhein Westfalen** *land* Germany
28 C7 **Nord Schleswig** Germany
28 B6 **Nord Slesvig** *reg* Denmark
32 L8 **Nord-Stemmen** Germany
30 D1 **Nordstrand** *isld* Germany
26 E7 **Nord-Tröndelag Fylker** Norway
51 L1 **Nordvik** Russian Federation
32 F8 **Nordwalde** Germany
14 D4 **Nore** *R* Ireland
27 C11 **Nore** Norway
27 D11 **Norefjell** *mt* Norway
122 E1 **Nore,L** Quebec Canada
120 K4 **Norembego** Ontario Canada
17 K2 **Norfeo,C** Spain
9 H2 **Norfolk** *co* England
110 D5 **Norfolk** Arkansas U.S.A.
95 O5 **Norfolk** Connecticut U.S.A.
98 J7 **Norfolk** Nebraska U.S.A.
95 L10 **Norfolk** Virginia U.S.A.
137 O7 **Norfolk I** Pacific Oc
110 D5 **Norfolk L** Arkansas U.S.A.
25 F2 **Norg** Netherlands
13 F2 **Norham** England
109 K9 **Norias** Texas U.S.A.
61 L9 **Norikura-dake** *mt* Japan
51 H2 **Noril'sk** Russian Federation
141 G8 **Norley** Queensland Australia
112 J1 **Norlina** North Carolina U.S.A.
45 N6 **Norma** Italy
110 K7 **Normal** Alabama U.S.A.
99 S9 **Normal** Illinois U.S.A.
141 F4 **Norman** *R* Queensland Australia
111 C7 **Norman** Arkansas U.S.A.
98 H9 **Norman** Nebraska U.S.A.
107 N6 **Norman** Oklahoma U.S.A.
141 G2 **Normanby** *R* Queensland Australia
13 H5 **Normanby** England
145 E3 **Normanby** New Zealand
141 K5 **Normanby Ra** Queensland Australia
21 H4 **Normandie** *reg* France
20 H4 **Normandie, Collines de** *hills* France
121 S4 **Normandin** Quebec Canada
110 K6 **Normandy** Tennessee U.S.A.
109 L4 **Normangee** Texas U.S.A.
143 E7 **Norman Hurst,Mt** W Australia Australia
112 F2 **Norman, L** North Carolina U.S.A.
109 K7 **Normanna** Texas U.S.A.
141 K2 **Norman Park** *dist* Brisbane, Qnsld Australia
141 F4 **Normanton** Queensland Australia
117 K3 **Norman Wells** Northwest Territories Canada
121 L4 **Normetal** Quebec Canada
143 B10 **Nornalup** W Australia Australia
124 F4 **Norogachic** Mexico
111 D8 **Norphlet** Arkansas U.S.A.
119 Q7 **Norquay** Saskatchewan Canada
133 C5 **Norquin** Argentina
133 C6 **Norquinco** Argentina
29 J8 **Norra Kvarken** *chan* Finland/Sweden
27 J10 **Norrala** Sweden
27 G15 **Norraryd** Sweden
26 J4 **Norrbotten** *reg* Sweden
28 D4 **Nørreå** *R* Denmark
28 C5 **Nørre Bramdrup** Denmark
28 A5 **Nørre Nebel** Denmark
22 C2 **Norrent-Fontès** France
28 D2 **Nørre Saltum** Denmark
28 D2 **Nørresundby** Denmark
26 M6 **Norrfjärden** Sweden
26 K8 **Norrfors** Sweden
26 J9 **Norrhassel** Sweden
95 S2 **Norridgewock** Maine U.S.A.
99 Q9 **Norris** Illinois U.S.A.
101 O4 **Norris** Montana U.S.A.
98 E6 **Norris** South Dakota U.S.A.
112 C1 **Norris** Tennessee U.S.A.
101 P5 **Norris** Wyoming U.S.A.
123 R4 **Norris Arm** Newfoundland Canada
110 H4 **Norris City** Illinois U.S.A.
112 C1 **Norris Dam** Tennessee U.S.A.
112 D1 **Norris Lake** Tennessee U.S.A.
123 P4 **Norris Point** Newfoundland Canada
95 M6 **Norristown** Pennsylvania U.S.A.
27 H13 **Norrköping** Sweden
29 H8 **Norrskär** *lighthouse* Finland
27 J11 **Norrsundet** Sweden
27 K12 **Norrtälje** Sweden
26 H6 **Norrvik** Sweden
27 F12 **Norsä** *R* Sweden
143 D9 **Norseman** W Australia Australia
145 F4 **Norsewood** New Zealand
27 H13 **Norsholm** Sweden
27 D12 **Norsjö** *L* Norway
26 K7 **Norsjö** Sweden
26 Q1 **Norskholmen** Norway
28 B2 **Nors Sø** *L* Denmark
129 H3 **Norte,C** Brazil
128 D2 **Norte de Santander** *div* Colombia
32 L9 **Nörten Hardenburg** Germany
133 E6 **Norte,Pta** Argentina
131 D3 **Norte,Sa de** *ra* Argentina
128 G6 **Norte,Serra do** *mts* Brazil
111 J8 **North** *R* Alabama U.S.A.
112 F4 **North** South Carolina U.S.A.
94 C5 **North Adams** Michigan U.S.A.
13 G5 **Northallerton** England
143 B9 **Northam** W Australia Australia
98 F1 **North America, Center of** North Dakota U.S.A.
90 C6 **North American Basin** Atlantic Oc
143 A8 **Northampton** W Australia Australia
9 F3 **Northampton** England
95 P4 **Northampton** Massachusetts U.S.A.
141 H6 **Northampton Downs** Queensland Australia
9 F3 **Northamptonshire** *co* England
68 A6 **North Andaman** *isld* Andaman Is
94 K8 **North Anna** *R* Virginia U.S.A.
95 S2 **North Anson** Maine U.S.A.
Northants *co see* **Northamptonshire** *co*
117 Q4 **North Arm** *inlet* Northwest Territories Canada
112 E4 **North Augusta** Georgia U.S.A.
115 N6 **North Aulatsivik I** Labrador, Nfld Canada
94 D5 **North Baltimore** Ohio U.S.A.
118 J6 **North Battleford** Saskatchewan Canada
123 O6 **North Bay** Newfoundland Canada
121 L6 **North Bay** Ontario Canada
98 K8 **North Bend** Nebraska U.S.A.
100 A6 **North Bend** Oregon U.S.A.
13 F1 **North Berwick** Scotland
99 L9 **Northboro** Iowa U.S.A.
139 H4 **North Bourke** New South Wales Australia
118 H2 **North Branch** Ontario Canada
94 D3 **North Branch** Michigan U.S.A.
99 O4 **North Branch** Minnesota U.S.A.
121 N8 **North Brook** Ontario Canada
13 H5 **North Burton** England
123 M6 **North,C** C Breton I, Nova Scotia
127 J4 **North Caicos** *isld* Turks & Caicos Is
108 B7 **North Canadian** *R* Oklahoma U.S.A.
145 D1 **North Cape** New Zealand
137 P8 **North Cape Rise** *sea feature* Pacific Oc
115 L7 **North Caribou L** Ontario Canada
112 E2 **North Carolina** *state* U.S.A.
100 D1 **North Cascades Nat. Park** Washington U.S.A.
113 H12 **North Cat Cay** *isld* Bahamas
113 L9 **North Cay** *isld* New Providence I Bahamas
14 F1 **North Chan** N Ireland/ Scotland
120 G6 **North Channel** Ontario Canada
112 H5 **North Charleston** South Carolina U.S.A.
13 G2 **North Charlton** England
99 T7 **North Chicago** Illinois U.S.A.
143 B10 **Northcliffe** W Australia Australia
108 F4 **North Concho** *R* Texas U.S.A.
100 A3 **North Cove** Washington U.S.A.
95 N3 **North Creek** New York U.S.A.
98 F2 **North Dakota** *state* U.S.A.
122 F8 **North Devon** New Brunswick Canada
9 F5 **North Downs** England
94 H4 **North East** Pennsylvania U.S.A.
95 R8 **North East Carry** Maine U.S.A.
141 L5 **North-East Cay** *isld* Gt Barrier Reef Aust
90 G3 **North Eastern Atlantic Basin** Atlantic Oc
122 A3 **Northeast Mistassibi R** Quebec Canada
126 F2 **Northeast Providence Chan** Bahamas
123 R1 **Northeast Pt** Belle Isle, Nfld
83 M9 **North East Pt** *C* Christmas I Indian Oc
32 L9 **Northeim** Germany
99 O8 **North English** Iowa U.S.A.
86 E2 **Northern** *prov* Sudan
123 T5 **Northern Bight** Newfoundland Canada
86 E2 **Northern Darfur** *prov* Sudan
113 L12 **Northern Eleuthera** *dist* Bahamas
122 F9 **Northern Hd** New Brunswick Canada
119 U1 **Northern Indian L** Manitoba Canada
12 A4 **Northern Ireland** U.K.
86 E2 **Northern Kordofan** *prov* Sudan
99 Q1 **Northern Light L** Ontario Canada
83 M9 **Northern Plateau** Christmas I Indian Oc
127 O2 **Northern Range** Trinidad
Northern Sporades *islds see* **Vorίai Sporádhes** *islds*
138 B1 **Northern Territory** Australia
139 H8 **North Esk** *R* Tasmania Australia
9 E3 **Northfield** England
95 P4 **Northfield** Massachusetts U.S.A.
99 N5 **Northfield** Minnesota U.S.A.
95 P2 **Northfield** Vermont U.S.A.
144 A6 **North Fiord** New Zealand
99 S6 **North Fond du Lac** Wisconsin U.S.A.
9 H5 **North Foreland** *hd* England
102 E4 **North Fork** California U.S.A.
101 M4 **North Fork** Idaho U.S.A.
100 K8 **North Fork** Nevada U.S.A.
94 B1 **North Fox I** Michigan U.S.A.
99 R6 **North Freedom** Wisconsin U.S.A.
120 J2 **North French** *R* Ontario Canada
13 H6 **North Frodingham** England
141 K1 **Northgate** *dist* Brisbane, Qnsld Australia
119 P9 **Northgate** Saskatchewan Canada
13 G3 **Northgate** England
95 P5 **North Haven** Connecticut U.S.A.
144 D5 **North Hd.** New Zealand
122 F9 **North Head** New Brunswick Canada
123 O4 **North Head** Newfoundland Canada
141 H2 **North Horn** *C* Gt Barrier Reef Aust
86 G5 **North Horr** Kenya
83 J12 **North I** Seychelles
112 H4 **North I** South Carolina U.S.A.
9 G6 **Northiam** England
145 E3 **North Island** New Zealand
71 E6 **North Islet** Philippines
103 O6 **North Jadito Canyon** *R* Arizona U.S.A.
83 M8 **North Keeling I** Cocos Is Indian Oc
115 L2 **North Kent I** Northwest Territories Canada
94 G5 **North Kingsville** Ohio U.S.A.
119 V1 **North Knife L** Manitoba Canada
59 J3 **North Korea** *rep* E Asia
North Land *see* **Severnaya Zemlya**
145 D1 **Northland** *admin region* New Zealand
99 T3 **Northland** Michigan U.S.A.
103 J5 **North Las Vegas** Nevada U.S.A.
9 E4 **Northleach** England
99 U8 **North Liberty** Indiana U.S.A.
110 D7 **North Little Rock** Arkansas U.S.A.
98 H8 **North Loup** *R* Nebraska U.S.A.
98 H8 **North Loup** Nebraska U.S.A.
88 D7 **North Luangwa Nat. Park** Zambia
70 C2 **North Luconia Shoals** S China Sea
106 C2 **North Mam Pk** Colorado U.S.A.
94 B5 **North Manchester** Indiana U.S.A.
99 U4 **North Manitou I** Michigan U.S.A.
113 G12 **North Miami** Florida U.S.A.
15 B2 **North Minch** Scotland
142 E4 **North, Mt** W Australia Australia
94 A3 **North Muskegon** Michigan U.S.A.
112 J4 **North Myrtle Beach** South Carolina U.S.A.
117 L4 **North Nahanni** *R* Northwest Territories Canada
113 G11 **North New River Can** Florida U.S.A.
94 E5 **North Olmsled** Ohio U.S.A.
99 M2 **Northome** Minnesota U.S.A.
8 C1 **Northop** Wales
North Ossetia *see* **Severo-Osetinskaya Respublika**
102 F4 **North Palisade** *pk* California U.S.A.
98 D8 **North Platte** *R* Nebraska U.S.A.
98 F8 **North Platte** Nebraska U.S.A.
101 T8 **North Platte** *R* Wyoming U.S.A.
116 O4 **North Pole** Alaska U.S.A.
122 J8 **Northport** Nova Scotia Canada
111 J8 **Northport** Alabama U.S.A.
99 V4 **Northport** Michigan U.S.A.
98 C8 **Northport** Nebraska U.S.A.
100 H1 **Northport** Washington U.S.A.
100 H4 **North Powder** Oregon U.S.A.
99 S7 **North Prairie** Wisconsin U.S.A.
139 J7 **North Pt** Flinders I, Tasmania Australia
122 H6 **North Pt** Prince Edward I Canada
83 J12 **North Pt** Mahé I Indian Oc
94 D1 **North Pt** Michigan U.S.A.
100 B3 **North R** Washington U.S.A.
142 A4 **North Rankin Gas Field** W Australia Australia
68 A6 **North Reef I** Andaman Is
109 M9 **North Richland Hills** Texas U.S.A.
123 M7 **North River Bridge** C Breton I, Nova Scotia
15 C1 **North Rona** Scotland
15 F1 **North Ronaldsay** Orkney Scotland
15 F1 **North Ronaldsay Firth** Orkney Scotland
122 J7 **North Rustico** Prince Edward I Canada
102 C2 **North San Juan** California U.S.A.
100 C5 **North Santiam** *R* Oregon U.S.A.
118 B6 **North Sask R** Alberta Canada
90 J3 **North Sea** W Europe
68 A7 **North Sentinel I** Andaman Is
13 G3 **North Shields** England
102 G2 **North Shoshone Pk** Nevada U.S.A.
99 O8 **North Skunk** *R* Iowa U.S.A.
116 M1 **North Slope** Alaska U.S.A.
117 P7 **North Star** Alberta Canada
110 M1 **North Star** Ohio U.S.A.
141 L8 **North Stradbroke I** Queensland Australia
109 M2 **North Sulphur** *R* Texas U.S.A.
123 M7 **North Sydney** C Breton I, Nova Scotia
8 C6 **North Tawton** England
144 A7 **North Trap** *islds* New Zealand
71 E7 **North Ubian** *isld* Philippines
15 A3 **North Uist** *isld* Scotland
141 J5 **Northumberland** *islds* Queensland Australia
13 F3 **Northumberland** *co* England
138 F7 **Northumberland,C** South Australia Australia
122 H7 **Northumberland Str** Nova Scotia Canada
117 G10 **North Vancouver** British Columbia Canada
71 D5 **North Verde** Philippines
117 P6 **North Vermilion** Alberta Canada
94 B7 **North Vernon** Indiana U.S.A.
95 N3 **Northville** New York U.S.A.
98 H4 **Northville** South Dakota U.S.A.
9 H2 **North Walsham** England
116 R5 **Northway Junc** Alaska U.S.A.
116 B5 **Northwest C.** St Lawrence I, Alaska U.S.A.
113 K11 **Northwest Cay** *isld* Bahamas
74 D2 **North West Frontier Prov** Pakistan
142 B5 **North West I** W Australia Australia
126 E1 **Northwest Providence Chan** Bahamas
83 M9 **North-West Pt** *C* Christmas I Indian Oc
115 N7 **North West River** Labrador, Nfld Canada
123 N2 **Northwest St.Augustin R** Quebec Canada
114 H4 **Northwest Territories** *prov* Canada
8 D1 **Northwich** England
112 F1 **North Wilkesboro** North Carolina U.S.A.
99 N6 **Northwood** Iowa U.S.A.
98 J2 **Northwood** North Dakota U.S.A.
120 C9 **North York** Ontario Canada
13 G5 **North Yorkshire** *co* England
109 L5 **North Zulch** Texas U.S.A.
32 G6 **Nortmoor** Germany
122 G8 **Norton** New Brunswick Canada
94 E10 **Norton** Virginia U.S.A.
89 G1 **Norton** Zimbabwe
116 G4 **Norton B** Alaska U.S.A.
116 E5 **Norton Sound** Alaska U.S.A.
107 P2 **Nortonville** Kansas U.S.A.
98 H3 **Nortonville** North Dakota U.S.A.
32 L4 **Nortorf** Germany
32 G7 **Nortrup** Germany
20 H7 **Nort-sur-Erdre** France
28 E5 **Norup** Denmark
116 K3 **Norutak L** Alaska U.S.A.
146 G6 **Norvegia Kapp** *C* Antarctica
36 B2 **Nörvenich** Germany
102 F8 **Norwalk** California U.S.A.
95 O5 **Norwalk** Connecticut U.S.A.
99 N8 **Norwalk** Iowa U.S.A.
99 U5 **Norwalk** Michigan U.S.A.
94 E5 **Norwalk** Ohio U.S.A.
99 Q6 **Norwalk** Wisconsin U.S.A.
99 P8 **Norway** Iowa U.S.A.
95 R2 **Norway** Maine U.S.A.
99 T4 **Norway** Michigan U.S.A.
112 F4 **Norway** South Carolina U.S.A.
68 H2 **Norway** *isld* Vietnam
26 **Norway** *kingdom* W Europe
119 U5 **Norway House** Manitoba Canada
115 K2 **Norwegian B** Northwest Territories Canada
147 E13 **Norwegian Basin** Arctic Oc
147 E12 **Norwegian Sea** Arctic Oc
120 K10 **Norwich** Ontario Canada
9 H2 **Norwich** England
95 P5 **Norwich** Connecticut U.S.A.
107 N4 **Norwich** Kansas U.S.A.
95 M4 **Norwich** New York U.S.A.
141 J6 **Norwich Park** Queensland Australia
15 G1 **Norwick** Scotland
121 N8 **Norwood** Ontario Canada
95 Q4 **Norwood** Massachusetts U.S.A.
95 N2 **Norwood** New York U.S.A.
112 G2 **Norwood** North Carolina U.S.A.
71 E3 **Norzagaray** Luzon Philippines
60 T2 **Nosappu-misaki** *C* Japan
36 G2 **Nösberts** Germany
61 N5 **Noshiro** Japan
52 G4 **Noshul'** Russian Federation
55 E2 **Noska** *R* Russian Federation
89 B5 **Nosop** *R* Botswana
52 E3 **Nosovshchina** Russian Federation
77 F5 **Nosratābād** Iran
130 H11 **Nossa Senhora das Dores** Brazil
130 C4 **Nossa Senhora do Livramento** Brazil
27 F13 **Nossebro** Sweden
22 H2 **Nossegem** Belgium
37 P1 **Nossen** Germany
33 Q5 **Nossentin** Germany
89 A4 **Nossob** Namibia
87 G11 **Nosy Barren** Madagascar
87 H10 **Nosy Be** *isld* Madagascar
87 H10 **Nosy Lava** Madagascar
87 H10 **Nosy Mitsio** *isld* Madagascar
87 H10 **Nosy Radamà** Madagascar
87 H12 **Nosy Varika** Madagascar
111 L9 **Notasulga** Alabama U.S.A.
103 L2 **Notch Pk** Utah U.S.A.
31 K2 **Noteć** *R* Poland
80 F1 **Notera** Israel
100 B5 **Noti** Oregon U.S.A.
46 E3 **Notia** Greece
114 H6 **Notikewin** Alberta Canada
117 O7 **Notikewin** *R* Alberta Canada
46 G8 **Nótion Aiyaíon** *admin region* Greece
43 G12 **Noto** Sicily
27 D12 **Notodden** Norway
43 G12 **Noto, Golfo di** Sicily
61 K8 **Noto-hantō** *pen* Japan
61 L8 **Noto-jima** *isld* Japan
60 S1 **Notoro-ko** *L* Japan
60 S1 **Notoro-misaki** *C* Japan
Notozero, Oz. *see* **Verkhnetulomskoye, Vodokhranilishche**
122 H7 **Notre Dame** New Brunswick Canada
122 A8 **Notre Dame** Quebec Canada
123 R4 **Notre Dame B** Newfoundland Canada
21 L4 **Notre Dame-de-Courson** France
21 M3 **Notre Dame de Gravenchon** France
115 M5 **Notre Dame de Koartáo** Quebec Canada
121 S4 **Notre-Dame-de-la-Doré** Quebec Canada
119 T9 **Notre Dame de Lourdes** Manitoba Canada
20 F8 **Notre Dame-de-Monts** France
121 P6 **Notre Dame du Laus** Quebec Canada
121 L5 **Notre Dame du-Nord** Quebec Canada
122 A5 **Notre Dame du Rosaire** Quebec Canada
85 E7 **Notsé** Togo
60 T2 **Notsuke-saki** *C* Japan
60 T2 **Notsuke-suidō** *str* Japan/ Rus Fed
120 K8 **Nottawasaga Bay** Ontario Canada
121 M2 **Nottaway R** Quebec Canada
27 H14 **Nottebäck** Sweden
112 C3 **Nottely L** Georgia U.S.A.
27 E12 **Nötteröy** *isld* Norway
9 E1 **Nottingham** *co* England
9 E2 **Nottingham** England
115 M5 **Nottingham Island** Northwest Territories Canada
27 G15 **Nöttja** Sweden
37 K2 **Nottleben** Germany
94 K10 **Nottoway** *R* Virginia U.S.A.
100 J6 **Notus** Idaho U.S.A.
85 A4 **Nouadhibou** Mauritania
85 A5 **Nouakchott** Mauritania
21 P6 **Nouan-le-Fuzelier** France
21 N7 **Nouans-les-Fontaines** France
21 O6 **Nouan-sur-Loire** France
22 J5 **Nouart** France
137 O6 **Nouméa** New Caledonia
85 D6 **Nouna** Burkina
89 D8 **Noupoort** S Africa
115 M7 **Nouveau-Comptoir** Quebec Canada
115 M5 **Nouveau Québec, Cratèr du** Quebec Canada
115 M5 **Nouveau Québec, Cratére du** Canada
122 D4 **Nouvel,L** Quebec Canada
Nouvelle Calédonie *isld see* **New Caledonia**
115 M5 **Nouvelle-France,Cap de** Quebec Canada
18 H9 **Nouvelle, la** France
122 F5 **Nouvelle,R** Quebec Canada
21 O1 **Nouvion-en-Pontheiu** France
22 F3 **Nouvion-en-Thiérache,Le** France
21 M6 **Nouzilly** France
22 H4 **Nouzonville** France
71 M9 **Nova Anadia** Timor
48 E2 **Nová Baňa** Czechoslovakia
87 B7 **Nova Caipemba** Angola
48 H5 **Novaci** Romania
45 M4 **Novafeltria** Italy
130 G8 **Nova Friburgo** Brazil
Nova Gaia *see* **Cambundi-Catembo**
42 H3 **Nova Gradiška** Croatia
130 G8 **Nova Iguaçu** Brazil
129 K5 **Nova Iorque** Brazil
130 G6 **Nova Lima** Brazil
87 C8 **Nova Lisboa** Angola
87 F10 **Nova Mambone** Mozambique
128 G4 **Nova Olinda do Norte** Brazil
129 K5 **Nova Pilão Arcado** Brazil
41 J7 **Novara** Italy
129 K5 **Nova Remanso** Brazil
129 K4 **Nova Russas** Brazil
122 G9 **Nova Scotia** *prov* Canada
129 K5 **Nova Sento Sé** Brazil
41 K5 **Novate** Italy
102 B3 **Novato** California U.S.A.
130 E10 **Nova Trento** Brazil
48 F7 **Nova Varš** Serbia Yugoslavia
128 F6 **Nova Vida** Brazil
55 C5 **Novaya Akkermanovka** Russian Federation
55 E3 **Novaya Aptula** Russian Federation
56 F3 **Novaya Igirma** Russian Federation
54 E10 **Novaya Kakhovka** Ukraine
53 F8 **Novaya Kriusha** Russian Federation
55 D2 **Novaya Lyala** Russian Federation
51 O1 **Novaya Sibir', Ostrov** *isld* Russian Federation
56 E3 **Novaya Solyanka** Russian Federation
48 J1 **Novaya Strelishcha** Ukraine
48 L2 **Novaya Ushitsa** Ukraine
55 E3 **Novaya Zaimka** Russian Federation
50 E1 **Novaya Zemlya** *isld* Russian Federation
47 H2 **Nova Zagora** Bulgaria
45 J2 **Novellara** Italy
110 D1 **Novelty** Missouri U.S.A.
45 L1 **Noventa V** Italy
33 N7 **Növenthien** Germany
48 E3 **Nové Zámky** Czechoslovakia
52 D5 **Novgorod** Russian Federation
54 E5 **Novgorod Severskiy** Ukraine
52 D5 **Novgorodskaya Oblast'** *prov* Russian Federation
47 J1 **Novgradets** Bulgaria
44 E2 **Novi** Italy
109 H4 **Novice** Texas U.S.A.
45 J2 **Novi di Modena** Italy
42 F3 **Novigrad** Croatia
42 G4 **Novigrad** Croatia
46 F2 **Novi Iskŭr** Bulgaria
48 F4 **Novi Kneževac** Serbia Yugoslavia
59 M2 **Novikovo** Russian Federation
45 N4 **Novilara** Italy
124 G6 **Novillero** Mexico
99 O9 **Novinger** Missouri U.S.A.
22 G4 **Novion-Porcien** France
47 J1 **Novi Pazar** Bulgaria
46 D1 **Novi Pazar** Serbia Yugoslavia
48 F5 **Novi Sad** Serbia Yugoslavia
42 F3 **Novi Vinodolski** Croatia
54 N1 **Novki** Russian Federation
28 B4 **Nøvling** Denmark
129 H4 **Nôvo Acôrdo** Brazil
53 F10 **Novoaleksandrovsk** Russian Federation
55 C5 **Novoalekseyevka** Kazakhstan
56 B4 **Novoaltaysk** Russian Federation
52 B4 **Novoandreyevka** Russian Federation
128 F5 **Novo Aripuana** Brazil
53 D9 **Novo Arkhangelsk** Ukraine
55 D2 **Novoasbest** Russian Federation
54 K9 **Novoazovsk** Ukraine
54 C4 **Novobelitsa** Belorussia
55 C3 **Novobelokatay** Russian Federation
55 E3 **Novoberezovka** Russian Federation
55 D3 **Novoburino** Russian Federation
54 M9 **Novocherkassk** Russian Federation
55 F5 **Novodolinka** Kazakhstan
52 D6 **Novo Dugino** Russian Federation
52 F3 **Novodvinsk** Arkhangel'skaya obl Russian Federation
53 C8 **Novograd-Volynskiy** Ukraine
53 C7 **Novogrudok** Belorussia
54 J2 **Novogurovskiy** Russian Federation
131 H2 **Novo Hamburgo** Brazil
59 L1 **Novoilinovka** Russian Federation
55 F5 **Novoishimka** Kazakhstan
56 F4 **Novokadinskiy** Russian Federation
53 G7 **Novokashpirskiy** Russian Federation
57 B2 **Novokazalinsk** Kazakhstan
53 F8 **Novokhopersk** Russian Federation
59 J1 **Novokiyevskiy Uval** Russian Federation
56 C4 **Novokuznetsk** Russian Federation
129 H3 **Novo, L** Brazil
146 H7 **Novolazarevskaya** *former U.S.S.R. Base* Antarctica
43 J8 **Novoli** Italy
71 M9 **Novo Luso** Timor
54 L2 **Novomichurinsk** Russian Federation
53 E11 **Novomikhaylovskiy** Russian Federation
48 F5 **Novo Miloševo** Serbia Yugoslavia
54 C8 **Novomirgorod** Ukraine
54 K2 **Novomoskovsk** Russian Federation
54 G8 **Novomoskovsk** Ukraine
55 E3 **Novonikolskoye** Russian Federation
55 C5 **Novoorsk** Russian Federation
52 C6 **Novopolotsk** Belorussia
Novo Redondo *see* **Sumbe**
56 B4 **Novoromanovka** Russian Federation
53 E11 **Novorossiysk** Russian Federation
55 C5 **Novorossiyskoye** Kazakhstan
54 M3 **Novoryazhsk** Russian Federation
55 F5 **Novorybinka** Kazakhstan
51 K1 **Novorybnoye** Russian Federation
52 C6 **Novorzhev** Russian Federation
52 H7 **Novo Sakhcha** Russian Federation
48 K2 **Novoselitsa** Ukraine
55 B5 **Novosergiyevka** Russian Federation
54 L9 **Novoshakhtinsk** Russian Federation
52 H6 **Novo Sheshminsk** Russian Federation
56 B4 **Novosibirsk** Russian Federation
55 G3 **Novosibirskaya Oblast'** *prov* Russian Federation
51 O1 **Novosibirskiye Ostrova** *islds* Russian Federation
54 J4 **Novosil'** Russian Federation
55 D3 **Novosineglazovskiy** Russian Federation
52 D6 **Novosokol'niki** Russian Federation
55 C5 **Novotroitsk** Russian Federation
55 G3 **Novotroitsk** Novosibirskaya obl Russian Federation
57 G3 **Novotroitskoye** Kazakhstan
54 K2 **Novougol'nyy** Russian Federation
54 C8 **Novoukrainka** Ukraine
55 C5 **Novouralets** Russian Federation
53 G8 **Novo Uzensk** Russian Federation
55 F4 **Novovarshavka** Russian Federation
55 G2 **Novovaya Vasyugan** Russian Federation
54 L5 **Novovoronezhskiy** Russian Federation
52 G5 **Novo-Vyatsk** Russian Federation
56 D2 **Novoyeniseysk** Russian Federation
56 F3 **Novoye Prirech'ye** Russian Federation
52 E6 **Novozavidovskiy** Russian Federation
52 H3 **Novozhilovskaya** Russian Federation
42 H3 **Novska** Croatia
31 L6 **Novy Bohumin** Czechoslovakia
31 J5 **Nový Bydžov** Czechoslovakia
22 G4 **Novy-Chevrières** France
54 K8 **Novy Donbass** Ukraine
54 F7 **Novye Sanzhary** Ukraine
48 D1 **Nový Jičin** Czechoslovakia
54 J6 **Novy Oskol** Russian Federation
52 D1 **Novyy** Russian Federation
52 H2 **Novyy Bor** Russian Federation
54 D9 **Novyy Bug** Ukraine
54 B3 **Novyy Bykhov** Belorussia
54 D6 **Novyy Bykov** Ukraine
48 M4 **Novyye Aneny** Moldavia
55 E1 **Novyy Karymkary** Russian Federation
55 E2 **Novyy Katysh** Russian Federation
50 G2 **Novyy Port** Russian Federation
52 G6 **Novyy Tor'yal** Russian Federation
56 H3 **Novyy Uoyan** Russian Federation
50 G2 **Novyy Urengoy** Russian Federation
31 J5 **Nowa Ruda** Poland
31 J4 **Nowa Sól** Poland
107 P5 **Nowata** Oklahoma U.S.A.
77 A2 **Nowbarān** Iran
31 L2 **Nowe** Poland
142 E5 **No.34 Well** W Australia Australia
142 F5 **No.37 Well** W Australia Australia
142 F5 **No.41 Well** W Australia Australia
142 F5 **No.45 Well** W Australia Australia
31 M2 **Nowe Miasto** Poland
Nowgong *see* **Nagaon**
116 K4 **Nowitna** *R* Alaska U.S.A.
31 J2 **Nowógard** Poland
31 N2 **Nowogród** Poland
31 J4 **Nowogrodziec** Poland
101 S5 **Nowood Cr** Wyoming U.S.A.
139 K5 **Nowra** New South Wales Australia
77 A5 **Nowruz** *oil well* Persian Gulf
77 B1 **Now Shahr** Iran
74 E1 **Nowshera** Pakistan
31 O2 **Nowy Dwór** Poland
31 M3 **Nowy Dwor** Poland
31 L1 **Nowy Dwór Gdański** Poland
31 M5 **Nowy Korczyn** Poland
48 F1 **Nowy Sącz** Poland
48 F1 **Nowy Targ** Poland
31 J3 **Nowy Tomysl** Poland
111 G9 **Noxapater** Mississippi U.S.A.
95 L5 **Noxen** Pennsylvania U.S.A.
100 K2 **Noxon** Montana U.S.A.
111 H8 **Noxubee** *R* Mississippi U.S.A.
16 B2 **Noya** Spain
17 J3 **Noya** *R* Spain
20 F6 **Noyal Muzillac** France
20 E6 **Noyalo** France
20 E5 **Noyal-Pontivy** France
20 G5 **Noyal-sur-Vilaine** France
21 J6 **Noyant-la-Gravoyère** France
21 K7 **Noyant-la-Plaine** France
21 L6 **Noyant-sous-le-Lude** France
21 P2 **Noye** *R* France
21 O1 **Noyelles-sur-Mer** France
21 K6 **Noyen** France
21 N7 **Noyers-sur-Cher** Loir-et-Cher France
117 G8 **Noyes I** Alaska U.S.A.
102 A2 **Noyo** California U.S.A.
22 E4 **Noyon** France
123 O2 **Noyrot,L** Quebec Canada
20 G6 **Nozay** France
86 C6 **N'Sah** Congo
88 E10 **Nsanje** Malawi
85 D7 **Nsawam** Ghana
88 C9 **Nsenga** Zambia
87 E9 **Nsiza** Zimbabwe
89 F2 **Nsiza** *R* Zimbabwe
88 E9 **Ntcheu** Malawi
86 B5 **Ntem** *R* Cameroon
83 L13 **Nuageuses** *isld* Kerguelen Indian Oc
21 J7 **Nuaillé** Maine-et-Loire France
52 C3 **Nuasjärvi** *L* Finland
84 J5 **Nuba, L** Sudan
86 F3 **Nuba Mts** Sudan
84 J5 **Nubian Des** Sudan
100 D8 **Nubieber** California U.S.A.
131 B6 **Nuble** *R* Chile
131 B6 **Nuble** *prov* Chile
48 H4 **Nucet** Romania
65 D2 **Nudam** China
65 A3 **Nüden** Mongolia
141 K1 **Nudgee** *dist* Brisbane, Qnsld Australia
109 J7 **Nueces** *R* Texas U.S.A.
21 J8 **Nueil-sur-Argent** France
21 K7 **Nueil-sur-Layon** France
115 K5 **Nueltin L** Northwest Territories Canada
65 E4 **Nü'erhe** China
128 F8 **Nueva Asunción** *dept* Paraguay
124 F2 **Nueva Casas Grandes** Mexico
109 H9 **Nueva Ciudad** Mexico

125 K4 **Nueva Ciudad Guerrero** Mexico
128 F1 **Nueva Esparta** *state* Venezuela
128 F7 **Nueva Esperanza** Bolivia
130 C8 **Nueva Germania** Paraguay
126 C4 **Nueva Gerona** Cuba
133 D9 **Nueva, I** Chile/Arg
133 C5 **Nueva Imperial** Chile
133 C6 **Nueva Lubecka** Argentina
124 J4 **Nueva Rosita** Mexico
133 E5 **Nueve de Julio** Argentina
126 F4 **Nuevitas** Cuba
71 F5 **Nuevo** Cebu Philippines
133 E6 **Nuevo,G** Argentina
124 G5 **Nuevo Ideal** Mexico
125 K4 **Nuevo Laredo** Mexico
109 H8 **Nuevo Laredo** Texas U.S.A.
125 J5 **Nuevo Leon** *state* Mexico
128 C4 **Nuevo Rocafuerte** Ecuador
141 J6 **Nuga Nuga, L** Queensland Australia
84 J5 **Nugrus,Gebel** *mt* Egypt
137 L2 **Nuguria Is** Bismarck Arch
145 F3 **Nuhaka** New Zealand
137 Q3 **Nui** *atoll* Tuvalu
68 H5 **Nui Ti On** *mt* Vietnam
18 H5 **Nuits** France
19 J5 **Nuits St.Georges** France
66 E5 **Nu Jiang** *R* China
116 M7 **Nuka I** Alaska U.S.A.
138 D4 **Nukey Bluff** South Australia Australia
80 G8 **Nukheila** *R* Jordan
86 E2 **Nukheila** Sudan
137 R6 **Nuku'alofa** *isld* Tonga
137 Q3 **Nukufetau** *atoll* Tuvalu
135 N9 **Nuku Hiva** *isld* Marquesas Is Pacific Oc
137 Q3 **Nukulaelae** *atoll* Tuvalu
137 M2 **Nukumanu Is** Solomon Is
137 Q2 **Nukunau** *isld* Kiribati
57 A4 **Nukus** Uzbekistan
17 G5 **Nules** Spain
142 D5 **Nullagine** W Australia Australia
142 D5 **Nullagine R** W Australia Australia
138 B4 **Nullarbor** South Australia Australia
138 B4 **Nullarbor Nat Park** South Australia Australia
143 F9 **Nullarbor Plain** S/W Australia Australia
65 D4 **Nulu'erhu Shan** *mt ra* China
43 B8 **Nulvi** Sardinia
61 L8 **Numaho** Japan
61 P6 **Numakunai** Japan
141 G8 **Numalla, L** Queensland Australia
86 B4 **Numan** Nigeria
45 O4 **Numana** Italy
17 F3 **Numancia** Spain
25 B5 **Numansdorp** Netherlands
60 P2 **Numata** Japan
86 E4 **Numatinna** *R* Sudan
61 M10 **Numazu** Japan
36 D2 **Nümbrecht** Nordrhein-Westfalen Germany
140 D2 **Numbulwar** N Terr Australia
27 D11 **Numedal** *V* Norway
27 D12 **Numedalsågen** *R* Norway
136 G2 **Numfor** *isld* W Irian
29 K11 **Nummi** Finland
139 H6 **Numurkah** Victoria Australia
116 J7 **Nunachuak** Alaska U.S.A.
116 F6 **Nunapitchuk** Alaska U.S.A.
116 E6 **Nunavakanuk L** Alaska U.S.A.
94 K4 **Nunda** New York U.S.A.
141 K1 **Nundah** *dist* Brisbane, Qnsld Australia
139 K4 **Nundle** New South Wales Australia
138 B4 **Nundroo** South Australia Australia
9 E2 **Nuneaton** England
143 C9 **Nungarin** W Australia Australia
65 D2 **Nungnain Sum** China
87 G8 **Nungo** Mozambique
116 E7 **Nunivak I** Alaska U.S.A.
106 F1 **Nunn** Colorado U.S.A.
110 J6 **Nunnelly** Tennessee U.S.A.
8 D5 **Nunney** England
25 E4 **Nunspeet** Netherlands
138 F4 **Nuntherungie** New South Wales Australia
70 E3 **Nunukan** *isld* Kalimantan
59 H2 **Nuomin He** *R* China
43 C8 **Nuoro** Sardinia
26 L5 **Nuortikon** Sweden
137 O4 **Nupani** Santa Cruz Is
128 C2 **Nuquí** Colombia
57 G1 **Nura** *R* Kazakhstan
57 G1 **Nura** Kazakhstan
Nurakita *see* **Niulakita**
57 D4 **Nuratau, Khr** *mts* Uzbekistan
57 D4 **Nuratau, Khrebet** *mts* Uzbekistan
36 B3 **Nürburg** Germany
78 F3 **Nur Dalari** *mts* Turkey
44 G2 **Nure** *R* Italy
57 E5 **Nurek** Tajikistan
57 E5 **Nurek Vodokhranilishche** *res* Tajikistan
Nuremberg *see* **Nürnberg**
95 L6 **Nuremburg** Pennsylvania U.S.A.
21 N8 **Nuret-le-Ferron** France
124 E3 **Nuri** Mexico
138 E5 **Nuriootpa** South Australia Australia
74 D1 **Nuristan** *reg* Afghanistan
52 H7 **Nurlat** Russian Federation
52 G6 **Nurlaty** Russian Federation
29 O8 **Nurmes** Finland
29 K9 **Nurmo** Finland
37 L5 **Nürnberg** Germany
71 G7 **Nuro** Mindanao Philippines
138 A3 **Nurrari Lakes** South Australia Australia
43 C9 **Nurri** Sardinia
36 G6 **Nürtingen** Germany
66 E4 **Nur Turu** China
31 O3 **Nurzec** *R* Poland
71 H9 **Nusa Tenggara Barat** Indonesia
71 K9 **Nusa Tenggara Timur** Indonesia
78 H3 **Nusaybin** Turkey
79 G3 **Nusayrīyah, Jebel al** *mts* Syria
116 J6 **Nushagak** *R* Alaska U.S.A.
116 H7 **Nushagak B** Alaska U.S.A.
116 H7 **Nushagak Pen** Alaska U.S.A.
66 F6 **Nu Shan** *mt ra* China
74 B4 **Nushki** Pakistan
33 N5 **Nusse** Germany
115 N6 **Nutak** Labrador, Nfld Canada
33 S8 **Nuthe** *R* Germany
119 O6 **Nut L** Saskatchewan Canada
9 G5 **Nutley** England
128 E2 **Nutrias** Venezuela
14 E2 **Nutts Corner** N Ireland
140 C3 **Nutwood Downs** N Terr Australia
116 Q5 **Nutzotin Mts** Alaska U.S.A.
115 O3 **Nuugaabsiaq** Greenland
Nuuk *see* **Godthåb**
29 M5 **Nuupas** Finland
Nuussuaq *see* **Kraulshavn**
115 O3 **Nuussuaq** *area* Greenland
115 O3 **Nuussuaq** *pen* Greenland
75 K4 **Nuwakot** Nepal
83 K11 **Nuwara Eliya** Sri Lanka
79 E10 **Nuweiba el Muzeina** Egypt
89 B9 **Nuweveldreeks** *mts* S Africa
116 J7 **Nuyakuk** *R* Alaska U.S.A.
116 H7 **Nuyakuk,L** Alaska U.S.A.
138 C4 **Nuyts Arch** South Australia Australia
138 B4 **Nuyts,C** South Australia Australia
143 B11 **Nuyts, Pt** W Australia Australia
122 F6 **N.W. Miramichi R** New Brunswick Canada
143 C10 **Nyabing** W Australia Australia
88 B3 **Nyabisindu** Rwanda
101 M1 **Nyack** Montana U.S.A.
88 D10 **Nyaderi** *R* Zimbabwe
139 G6 **Nyah** Victoria Australia
88 F1 **Nyahururu** Kenya
66 D6 **Nyainqêntanglha Shan** *ra* China
88 D3 **Nyakabindi** Tanzania
26 K8 **Nyåker** Sweden
55 D1 **Nyaksimvol'** Russian Federation
86 D3 **Nyala** Sudan
66 D6 **Nyalam** China
88 D3 **Nyalikungu** Tanzania
55 E1 **Nyalinskoye** Russian Federation
87 E9 **Nyamandhlovu** Zimbabwe
88 C10 **Nyamanji** *mt* Zimbabwe
88 D10 **Nyamapanda** Zimbabwe
87 D8 **Nyamboma Falls** Zambia
86 E4 **Nyamlell** Sudan
87 G8 **Nyamtumba** Tanzania
Nyanda *see* **Masvingo**
52 F4 **Nyandoma** Russian Federation
88 C10 **Nyangadzi** *R* Zimbabwe
88 D10 **Nyangadzi** *R* Zimbabwe
143 F8 **Nyanga, L** W Australia Australia
88 E10 **Nyanja** Malawi
87 F8 **Nyanji** Zambia
52 H4 **Nyanyayel'** Russian Federation
70 E4 **Nyapa, Gunung** *mt* Kalimantan
117 R5 **Nyarling** *R* Northwest Territories Canada
88 E7 **Nyasa** *tribe* Tanzania
88 E7 **Nyasa,L** Malawi/Moz
Nyasaland *see* **Malawi**
52 H2 **Nyashabozh** Russian Federation
68 B3 **Nyaungbinzeik** Burma
68 C4 **Nyaunglebin** Burma
68 B2 **Nyaungu** Burma
55 C3 **Nyazepetrovsk** Russian Federation
87 F9 **Nyazura** Zimbabwe
89 G2 **Nyazvidzi** *R* Zimbabwe
28 F6 **Nyborg** Denmark
26 R1 **Nyborg** Norway
27 H15 **Nybro** Sweden
50 G2 **Nyda** Russian Federation
27 G14 **Nydala** Sweden
115 O1 **Nyeboe Land** Greenland
Nyenchen Tanglha Range *see* **Nyainqêntanglha Shan**
86 F4 **Nyerol** Sudan
27 G11 **Nyhammar** Sweden
29 K4 **Nyhamn** Sweden
26 H9 **Nyhem** Sweden
88 D6 **Nyiha** Tanzania
66 D5 **Nyima** China
87 F8 **Nyimba** Zambia
66 E6 **Nyingchi** China
48 G3 **Nyiradony** Hungary
48 G3 **Nyírbátor** Hungary
48 G3 **Nyíregyháza** Hungary
88 F3 **Nyiri Desert** Kenya
86 G5 **Nyiru** *mt* Kenya
29 K8 **Nykarleby** Finland
27 H13 **Nykil** Sweden
28 J5 **Nykøbing** Denmark
28 H7 **Nykøbing** Falster Denmark
28 B3 **Nykøbing** Mors Denmark
27 J13 **Nyköping** Sweden
27 G12 **Nykroppa** Sweden
89 F5 **Nyl** *R* S Africa
26 J8 **Nyland** Sweden
89 F5 **Nylstroom** S Africa
26 K6 **Nylund** Sweden
139 H4 **Nymagee** New South Wales Australia
139 L3 **Nymboida** New South Wales Australia
139 L3 **Nymborda** *R* New South Wales Australia
31 J5 **Nymburk** Czechoslovakia
7 F11 **Nymphe Bank** Atlantic Oc
27 J13 **Nynäshamn** Sweden
139 H4 **Nyngan** New South Wales Australia
21 J6 **Nyoiseau** France
86 B5 **Nyong** *R* Cameroon
19 O16 **Nyons** France
37 P4 **Nýřany** Czechoslovakia
52 J4 **Nyrob** Russian Federation
37 P5 **Nýrsko** Czechoslovakia
26 R2 **Nyrud** Norway
31 K5 **Nysa** Poland
27 F11 **Nyskoga** Sweden
100 H6 **Nyssa** Oregon U.S.A.
Nystad *see* **Uusikaupunki**
55 C2 **Nyta** Russian Federation
52 H5 **Nytva** Russian Federation
61 N5 **Nyūdō zaki** *C* Japan
52 G3 **Nyukhcha** Arkhangel'skaya obl Russian Federation
52 E3 **Nyukhcha** Karel'skaya Respublika Russian Federation
52 D3 **Nyuk, Oz** *L* Russian Federation
52 F4 **Nyuksenitsa** Russian Federation
59 H1 **Nyukzha** *R* Russian Federation
51 L2 **Nyurba** Russian Federation
55 E1 **Nyurkoy** Russian Federation
69 H14 **Nyurun** Indonesia
52 H4 **Nyuvchim** Russian Federation
56 H1 **Nyuya** *R* Russian Federation
88 D4 **Nzega** Tanzania
85 C7 **Nzérékoré** Guinea
87 B7 **N'Zeto** Angola

O

98 G6 **Oacoma** South Dakota U.S.A.
98 F5 **Oahe Dam** South Dakota U.S.A.
98 F5 **Oahe, L** South Dakota U.S.A.
102 S11 **Oahu** *isld* Hawaiian Is
103 N7 **Oak** *R* Arizona U.S.A.
60 S2 **O-akan-dake** *mt* Japan
122 E8 **Oak B** New Brunswick Canada
138 F5 **Oakbank** South Australia Australia
95 R5 **Oak Bluffs** Massachusetts U.S.A.
112 G2 **Oakboro** North Carolina U.S.A.
119 R8 **Oakburn** Manitoba Canada
112 K2 **Oak City** North Carolina U.S.A.
103 M2 **Oak City** Utah U.S.A.
109 N9 **Oak Cliff** Texas U.S.A.
101 T9 **Oak Creek** Colorado U.S.A.
102 D4 **Oakdale** California U.S.A.
111 D11 **Oakdale** Louisiana U.S.A.
98 J7 **Oakdale** Nebraska U.S.A.
98 H3 **Oakes** North Dakota U.S.A.
100 H2 **Oakesdale** Washington U.S.A.
140 F7 **Oakes, Mt** Queensland Australia
141 K7 **Oakey** Queensland Australia
99 S6 **Oakfield** Wisconsin U.S.A.
99 R9 **Oakford** Illinois U.S.A.
111 E9 **Oak Grove** Louisiana U.S.A.
9 F2 **Oakham** England
94 D5 **Oak Harbor** Ohio U.S.A.
113 G9 **Oak Hill** Florida U.S.A.
107 N2 **Oak Hill** Kansas U.S.A.
94 E8 **Oak Hill** Ohio U.S.A.
94 F9 **Oak Hill** West Virginia U.S.A.
119 R9 **Oak Lake** Manitoba Canada
102 B4 **Oakland** California U.S.A.
99 S10 **Oakland** Illinois U.S.A.
99 L8 **Oakland** Iowa U.S.A.
95 S2 **Oakland** Maine U.S.A.
94 H7 **Oakland** Maryland U.S.A.
111 G7 **Oakland** Mississippi U.S.A.
98 K8 **Oakland** Nebraska U.S.A.
100 B6 **Oakland** Oregon U.S.A.
95 M5 **Oakland** Pennsylvania U.S.A.
110 G6 **Oakland** Tennessee U.S.A.
109 L6 **Oakland** Texas U.S.A.
110 J3 **Oakland City** Indiana U.S.A.
113 G11 **Oakland Park** Florida U.S.A.
139 H6 **Oaklands** New South Wales Australia
99 T8 **Oak Lawn** Illinois U.S.A.
145 E1 **Oakleigh** New Zealand
102 C4 **Oakley** California U.S.A.
101 M7 **Oakley** Idaho U.S.A.
107 K2 **Oakley** Kansas U.S.A.
94 C3 **Oakley** Michigan U.S.A.
112 C3 **Oakman** Georgia U.S.A.
94 H6 **Oakmont** Pennsylvania U.S.A.
119 R8 **Oakner** Manitoba Canada
142 D5 **Oakover, R** W Australia Australia
141 G4 **Oak Park** Queensland Australia
112 E5 **Oakpark** Georgia U.S.A.
119 T8 **Oak Pt** Manitoba Canada
111 E9 **Oak Ridge** Louisiana U.S.A.
110 G4 **Oak Ridge** Missouri U.S.A.
100 C6 **Oakridge** Oregon U.S.A.
112 C1 **Oak Ridge** Tennessee U.S.A.
119 R8 **Oak River** Manitoba Canada
145 D3 **Oakura** New Zealand
138 F5 **Oakvale** South Australia Australia
119 T9 **Oakville** Manitoba Canada
121 L9 **Oakville** Ontario Canada
109 J7 **Oakville** Texas U.S.A.
141 H7 **Oakwood** Queensland Australia
110 J1 **Oakwood** Illinois U.S.A.
110 E2 **Oakwood** Missouri U.S.A.
94 C5 **Oakwood** Ohio U.S.A.
107 M6 **Oakwood** Oklahoma U.S.A.
144 C6 **Oamaru** New Zealand
61 O10 **Ōami** Japan
144 D5 **Oaro** New Zealand
71 F4 **Oas** Philippines
60 F11 **Ōasa** Japan
102 G4 **Oasis** California U.S.A.
101 L8 **Oasis** Nevada U.S.A.
146 C13 **Oates Land** Antarctica
139 H8 **Oatlands** Tasmania Australia
103 K6 **Oatman** Arizona U.S.A.
125 L9 **Oaxaca de Juárez** Mexico
56 B4 **Ob'** *R* Russian Federation
120 F3 **Oba** Ontario Canada
120 E3 **Obakamiga L** Ontario Canada
120 F4 **Oba L** Ontario Canada
86 B5 **Obala** Cameroon
121 Q3 **Obalski** Quebec Canada
61 J10 **Obama** Japan
118 J6 **Oban** Saskatchewan Canada
15 C4 **Oban** Scotland
61 O7 **Obanazawa** Japan
106 G6 **Obar** New Mexico U.S.A.
O Barco *see* **El Barco de Valdeorras**
120 E4 **Obatanga Prov. Park** Ontario Canada
121 Q3 **Obatogamau L** Quebec Canada
26 L8 **Obbola** Sweden
38 L7 **Obdach** Austria
117 P9 **Obed** Alberta Canada
38 J5 **Ober** *dist* Austria
40 G3 **Ober Aargau** *dist* Switzerland
30 F8 **Oberammergau** Germany
37 Q1 **Oberau** Germany
41 O2 **Oberau** Germany
36 H2 **Oberaula** Germany
36 H3 **Oberbach** Germany
38 E5 **Oberbayern** *dist* Germany
25 F6 **Oberbruch-Dremmen** Germany
39 C2 **Oberbrunn** Germany
36 H7 **Oberdischingen** Germany
38 H8 **Ober-Drau-Tal** *V* Austria
37 J4 **Obereisenheim** Germany
37 J2 **Oberellen** Germany
41 L4 **Oberengadin** *dist* Switzerland
38 K7 **Oberenns Tal** Austria
37 K3 **Oberessfeld** Germany
37 P1 **Ober Eula** Germany
37 L4 **Oberfranken** *dist* Germany
Oberfrohna *see* **Limbach-Oberfrohna**
38 H8 **Obergailtal** *V* Austria
41 O4 **Obergurgl** Austria
41 L4 **Oberhalbstein** *R* Switzerland
36 E7 **Oberharmersbach** Germany
36 C6 **Oberhaslach** France
32 E10 **Oberhausen** Germany
36 F3 **Oberhausen** Hessen Germany
36 E4 **Ober Hilbersheim** Germany
37 K2 **Oberhof** Germany
36 E6 **Oberkirch** Germany
36 F3 **Oberkleen** Germany
37 J6 **Ober-Kochen** Germany
37 M3 **Ober Kotzau** Germany
37 J3 **Ober Lauringen** Germany
36 H6 **Oberlenningen** Germany
107 K2 **Oberlin** Kansas U.S.A.
111 D11 **Oberlin** Louisiana U.S.A.
94 E5 **Oberlin** Ohio U.S.A.
36 H7 **Ober Marchthal** Germany
32 J10 **Ober Marsberg** Germany
37 J2 **Obermassfeld-Grimmenthal** Germany
36 D4 **Ober Moschel** Germany
36 C7 **Obernai** France
36 G4 **Obernburg** Germany
32 K8 **Obernkirchen** Germany
139 J5 **Oberon** New South Wales Australia
98 G2 **Oberon** North Dakota U.S.A.
39 C2 **Oberpfaffenhofen** Germany
37 M5 **Oberpfalz** *dist* Germany
37 N4 **Oberpfalzer Wald** *mts* Germany
36 C2 **Oberpleis** Germany
36 F4 **Ober Ramstadt** Germany
41 K3 **Oberri** Switzerland
37 O3 **Ober Rittersgrün** Germany
33 P10 **Ober Röblingen** Germany
36 F3 **Ober Rosbach** Germany
36 G5 **Ober Schefflenz** Germany
40 F4 **Ober Simmen Tal** Switzerland
36 H5 **Obersontheim** Germany
33 N10 **Oberspier** Germany
41 M3 **Oberstdorf** Germany
36 D5 **Obersteinbach** France
37 J3 **Obertheres** Germany
37 N6 **Obertraubling** Germany
37 O7 **Ober Trennbach** Germany
33 T6 **Oberueckersee** *L* Germany
36 F3 **Oberursel** Germany
37 N5 **Oberviechtach** Germany
41 H4 **Oberwald** Switzerland
38 O7 **Oberwart** Austria
36 D3 **Oberwesel** Germany
37 O3 **Oberwiesenthal** Germany
36 C2 **Oberwinter** Germany
38 K7 **Oberwölz** Austria
71 A3 **Obi** *isld* Indonesia
60 E14 **Obi** Japan
129 G4 **Obidos** Brazil
16 A5 **Obidos** Portugal
60 R3 **Obihiro** Japan
71 A3 **Obi,Kep** *isld* Indonesia
71 A3 **Obilatu** *isld* Indonesia
38 F5 **Obing** Germany
110 G5 **Obion** Tennessee U.S.A.
19 P15 **Obiou, l'** *mt* France
110 J3 **Oblong** Illinois U.S.A.
59 K2 **Obluch'ye** Russian Federation
54 H1 **Obninsk** Russian Federation
86 H3 **Obock** Djibouti
54 A1 **Obol'** *R* Belorussia
120 A3 **Obonga L** Ontario Canada
70 D2 **Obong, G** *mt* Sarawak
31 K3 **Oborniki** Poland
52 F1 **Obornyy, Mys** *C* Russian Federation
86 C6 **Obouya Mossaka** Congo
54 H5 **Oboyan'** Russian Federation
52 F3 **Obozerskiy** Russian Federation
124 E4 **Obregón, Presa** *res* Mexico
120 K5 **O'Brien** Ontario Canada
42 G4 **Obrovac** Croatia
137 M6 **Observatoire, Caye de l'** *islds* Coral Sea
117 H8 **Observatory Inlet** British Columbia Canada
54 D1 **Obsha** *R* Russian Federation
55 B5 **Obshciy Syrt** *reg* Russian Federation
101 L5 **Obsidian** Idaho U.S.A.
50 G2 **Obskaya Guba** *G* Russian Federation
85 D7 **Obuasi** Ghana
52 J5 **Obva** *R* Russian Federation
41 H4 **Obwalden** *canton* Switzerland
52 G4 **Ob'yachevo** Russian Federation
16 E2 **Oca** *R* Spain
113 E8 **Ocala** Florida U.S.A.
124 E3 **Ocampo** Chihuahua Mexico
124 H4 **Ocampo** Coahuila Mexico
16 E2 **Oca,Mt.de** Spain
126 H10 **Ocaña** Colombia
16 E5 **Ocaña** Spain
106 E5 **Ocate** New Mexico U.S.A.
45 L2 **Occhiobello** Italy
95 M8 **Ocean City** Maryland U.S.A.
95 N7 **Ocean City** New Jersey U.S.A.
100 A2 **Ocean City** Washington U.S.A.
117 K9 **Ocean Falls** British Columbia Canada
95 N7 **Ocean Gate** New Jersey U.S.A.
Ocean I *see* **Banaba**
101 R6 **Ocean L** Wyoming U.S.A.
102 D6 **Oceano** California U.S.A.
90 F5 **Oceanographer Fracture** Atlantic Oc
100 A3 **Ocean Park** Washington U.S.A.
102 G8 **Oceanside** California U.S.A.
100 B4 **Oceanside** Oregon U.S.A.
111 H11 **Ocean Springs** Mississippi U.S.A.
95 M8 **Ocean View** Delaware U.S.A.
16 E3 **Ocejón,Pic** *mt* Spain
108 G4 **O. C. Fisher L** Texas U.S.A.
54 C10 **Ochakov** Ukraine
53 F11 **Ochamchira** Georgia
56 H1 **Ochchuguy Botuobuya** *R* Russian Federation
52 H5 **Ocher** Russian Federation
60 C12 **Ōchi** Japan
60 G10 **Ochiai** Japan
60 T2 **Ochiishi-misaki** *C* Japan
15 E4 **Ochil Hills** Scotland
15 D5 **Ochiltree** Scotland
113 C7 **Ochlocknee** Georgia U.S.A.
111 M11 **Ochlockonee** *R* Florida U.S.A.
100 E5 **Ochoco Res** Oregon U.S.A.
32 G6 **Ocholt** Germany
113 F12 **Ochopee** Florida U.S.A.
127 K2 **Ocho Rios** Jamaica
119 S7 **Ochre River** Manitoba Canada
40 F4 **Ochsen** *mt* Switzerland
37 J4 **Ochsenfurt** Germany
41 L1 **Ochsenhausen** Germany
37 M3 **Ochsenkopf** *mt* Germany
32 L5 **Ochsenzoll** Germany
36 C3 **Ochtendung** Germany
33 O8 **Ochtmersleben** Germany
32 F8 **Ochtrup** Germany
112 D6 **Ocilla** Georgia U.S.A.
27 J11 **Ockelbo** Sweden
28 B7 **Ockholm** Germany
9 F5 **Ockley** England
48 J4 **Ocland** Romania
112 D4 **Ocmulgee** *R* Georgia U.S.A.
112 D5 **Ocmulgee Nat Mon** Georgia U.S.A.
48 H4 **Ocna Mureş** Romania
48 J5 **Ocna Sibiului** Romania
48 H3 **Ocna Sugătag** Romania
48 J5 **Ocnele Mari** Romania
113 F9 **Ocoee** Florida U.S.A.
112 C2 **Ocoee** Tennessee U.S.A.
128 D7 **Ocoña** Peru
112 E5 **Oconee** *R* Georgia U.S.A.
110 G2 **Oconee** Illinois U.S.A.
98 J8 **Oconee** Nebraska U.S.A.
141 G5 **O'Connell** *R* Queensland Australia
98 G8 **Oconto** Nebraska U.S.A.
99 T5 **Oconto** Wisconsin U.S.A.
99 S5 **Oconto Falls** Wisconsin U.S.A.
124 E5 **Ocoroni** Mexico
125 M3 **Ocotal** Nicaragua
124 H7 **Ocotlán** Mexico
125 N9 **Ocozocoautla** Mexico
22 J3 **Ocquier** Belgium
112 M2 **Ocracoke** North Carolina U.S.A.
48 E3 **Ocsa** Hungary
48 F4 **Öcsöd** Hungary
20 G2 **Octeville** Manche France
21 L2 **Octeville** Seine-Inférieure France
120 D3 **Octopus** Ontario Canada
127 L9 **Ocumare del Tuy** Venezuela
71 M9 **Ocussi Ambeno** Timor
27 F14 **Od** Sweden
85 D7 **Oda** Ghana
60 F10 **Ōda** Japan
28 S9 **Odádhahraun** *lava field* Iceland
61 K11 **Ōdaigahara-zan** *mt* Japan
61 O8 **Odaka** Japan
27 E11 **Odal,N** Norway
27 E11 **Odal,S** Norway
99 Q3 **Odanah** Wisconsin U.S.A.
61 O5 **Ōdate** Japan
61 N10 **Odawara** Japan
27 B11 **Odda** Norway
86 G1 **Odda,Jebel** *mt* Sudan
28 E3 **Odde** Denmark
28 E5 **Odder** Denmark
27 C13 **Oddernes** Norway
99 L7 **Odebolt** Iowa U.S.A.
16 B7 **Odeleite** Portugal
99 S8 **Odell** Illinois U.S.A.
98 K9 **Odell** Nebraska U.S.A.
109 H1 **Odell** Texas U.S.A.
37 L7 **Odelzhausen** Germany
109 K8 **Odem** Texas U.S.A.
16 B7 **Odemira** Portugal
47 J6 **Ödemiş** Turkey
110 C7 **Oden** Arkansas U.S.A.
36 D4 **Odenbach** Germany
89 E6 **Odendaalsrus** S Africa
36 F5 **Odenheim** Germany
36 B1 **Odenkirchen** Germany
Odense *co see* **Fyn** *co*
28 E6 **Odense** Denmark
28 F5 **Odense Fjord** *inlet* Denmark
36 G4 **Odenwald** *mts* Germany
Oder *R see* **Odra** *R*
33 U7 **Oderberg** Germany
33 T8 **Oderin** Germany
36 E4 **Odernheim** Germany
33 T8 **Oder-Spree-Kanal** Germany
42 E3 **Oderzo** Italy
27 G13 **Ödeshög** Sweden
121 O8 **Odessa** Ontario Canada
119 O8 **Odessa** Saskatchewan Canada
48 N4 **Odessa** Ukraine
110 C3 **Odessa** Missouri U.S.A.
95 L4 **Odessa** New York U.S.A.
108 E4 **Odessa** Texas U.S.A.
100 G2 **Odessa** Washington U.S.A.
55 F4 **Odesskoye** Russian Federation
20 C5 **Odet** *R* France
119 T3 **Odhill** Manitoba Canada
87 E10 **Odiakwe** Botswana
85 C7 **Odienné** Ivory Coast
9 F5 **Odiham** England
6 M2 **Odin** *oil rig* North Sea
110 G3 **Odin** Illinois U.S.A.
32 E9 **Öding** Germany
54 J1 **Odintsovo** Russian Federation
48 L5 **Odobeşti** Romania
31 K4 **Odolanów** Poland
21 J3 **Odon** *R* France
110 K3 **Odon** Indiana U.S.A.
108 F3 **O'Donnell** Texas U.S.A.
25 G3 **Odoorn** Netherlands
48 J4 **Odorheiu Secuiesc** Romania
31 J4 **Odra** *R* Poland
16 E2 **Odra** *R* Spain
25 F6 **Odt** Germany
112 E6 **Odum** Georgia U.S.A.
48 E5 **Odžaci** Serbia Yugoslavia
33 O8 **Oebisfelde** Germany
37 J2 **Oechsen** Germany
22 E1 **Oedelem** Belgium
37 P2 **Oederan** Germany
36 E1 **Oedingen** Germany
129 K5 **Oeiras** Brazil
16 A6 **Oeiras** Portugal
16 B7 **Oeiras** *R* Portugal
32 H9 **Oelde** Germany
98 C6 **Oelrichs** South Dakota U.S.A.
37 N3 **Oelsnitz** Germany
99 P7 **Oelwein** Iowa U.S.A.
37 L2 **Oelze** Germany
135 O11 **Oeno** *atoll* Pacific Oc
140 C1 **Oenpelli** N Terr Australia
32 F9 **Oer-Erkenschwick** Germany
32 J9 **Oerlinghausen** Germany
37 L3 **Oeslau** Germany
71 M9 **Oessilo** Timor
36 E3 **Oestrich-Winkel** Germany
133 E3 **Oetling** Argentina
37 K6 **Oettingen** Germany
32 H10 **Oeventrop** Germany
111 G9 **Ofahoma** Mississippi U.S.A.
43 G7 **Ofanto** *R* Italy
80 B8 **Ofaqim** Israel
41 M5 **Ofenpass** Italy
80 C3 **Ofer** Israel
14 D3 **Offaly** *co* Ireland
36 F3 **Offenbach am Main** Germany
36 D7 **Offenburg** Germany
26 G8 **Offerdal** Sweden
112 E6 **Offerman** Georgia U.S.A.
138 B2 **Officer Cr.,The** South Australia Australia
37 J7 **Offingen** Germany
21 N2 **Offranville** France
36 E4 **Offstein** Germany
47 H8 **Ofidhoúsa** *isld* Greece
79 E11 **Ofira** Egypt
26 J3 **Ofotfjord** *inlet* Norway
80 D6 **Ofra** Jordan
61 N6 **Oga** Japan
70 D4 **Oga** *R* Kalimantan
86 J4 **Ogadēn** *reg* Ethiopia
120 E2 **Ogahalla** Ontario Canada
61 N6 **Oga-hantō** *pen* Japan
61 K10 **Ōgaki** Japan
107 L3 **Ogallah** Kansas U.S.A.
98 E8 **Ogallala** Nebraska U.S.A.
54 J3 **Ogarevka** Russian Federation
59 M6 **Ogasawara-shoto** Japan
121 M5 **Ogascanan, L** Quebec Canada
61 O7 **Ogawara** Japan
61 P5 **Ogawara ko** *L* Japan
85 E7 **Ogbomosho** Nigeria
9 E5 **Ogbourne St.George** England
123 L8 **Ogden** Nova Scotia Canada
110 J1 **Ogden** Illinois U.S.A.
99 M7 **Ogden** Iowa U.S.A.
107 O2 **Ogden** Kansas U.S.A.
101 O8 **Ogden** Utah U.S.A.
117 G6 **Ogden,Mt** Br Col/Alaska Canada/U.S.A.
95 M2 **Ogdensburg** New York U.S.A.
112 F5 **Ogeechee** *R* Georgia U.S.A.
119 N9 **Ogema** Saskatchewan Canada
98 K2 **Ogema** Minnesota U.S.A.
32 G5 **Ogenbargen** Germany
36 B6 **Ogéviller** France
41 K6 **Oggiono** Italy
61 M8 **Ogi** Japan
120 F6 **Ogidaki** Ontario Canada
103 K9 **Ogilby** California U.S.A.
143 A8 **Ogilvie** W Australia Australia
99 N4 **Ogilvie** Minnesota U.S.A.
114 F5 **Ogilvie Mts** Yukon Territory Canada
61 Q12 **Ōgimi** Japan
98 D6 **Oglala** South Dakota U.S.A.
99 R8 **Oglesby** Illinois U.S.A.
109 K4 **Oglesby** Texas U.S.A.
112 C5 **Oglethorpe** Georgia U.S.A.
55 F3 **Oglukhino** Russian Federation
141 J6 **Ogmore** Queensland Australia
55 G2 **Ognev Yar** Russian Federation
19 J5 **Ognon** *R* France
70 G4 **Ogoamas, G** *mt* Celebes
59 K1 **Ogodzha** Russian Federation
85 F7 **Ogoja** Nigeria
120 C2 **Ogoki L** Ontario Canada
120 D2 **Ogoki R** Ontario Canada
120 B2 **Ogoki Res** Ontario Canada
86 A6 **Ogooué** *R* Gabon
46 F1 **Ogosta** *R* Bulgaria
70 G4 **Ogotomubu** Sulawesi
61 K9 **Ogoya** Japan
143 B9 **O'Grady, L** W Australia Australia
47 H3 **Ogražden** *hills* Greece
46 F3 **Ogražden Planina** *mt* Macedonia Yugoslavia
52 B6 **Ogre** Latvia
61 N10 **Oguchi Dam** Japan
85 D4 **Oguilet Khenachich** Mali
124 F4 **Oguivo** Mexico
85 E7 **Ogun** *R* Nigeria
60 E12 **Oguni** Japan
95 R3 **Ogunquit** Maine U.S.A.
85 F7 **Ogwashi-Uku** Nigeria
145 D1 **Ohaeawai** New Zealand
144 A6 **Ohai** New Zealand
145 E3 **Ohakune** New Zealand
86 D2 **O Haouach** *dist* Chad
61 O10 **Ōhara** Japan
61 P6 **Ōhasama** Japan
60 P4 **Ōhata** Japan
118 E6 **Ohaton** Alberta Canada
145 E4 **Ohau** New Zealand
144 B6 **Ohau, L** New Zealand
145 E2 **Ohaupo** New Zealand
32 G7 **Ohe** *R* Germany
22 J3 **Ohey** Belgium
131 B5 **O'Higgins** *prov* Chile
133 C7 **O'Higgins, L** Chile/Arg
133 C7 **O'Higgins Pirámide** *mt* Chile
145 E2 **Ohinewai** New Zealand
145 E3 **Ohingaiti** New Zealand
94 C6 **Ohio** *state* U.S.A.
110 H4 **Ohio** *R* U.S.A.
99 R8 **Ohio** Illinois U.S.A.
94 C8 **Ohio** *R* Indiana U.S.A.
94 C6 **Ohio City** Ohio U.S.A.
32 G10 **Ohle** Germany
36 F2 **Ohm** *R* Germany
33 M8 **Ohof** Germany
116 G6 **Ohogamiut** Alaska U.S.A.
112 E5 **Ohoopee** *R* Georgia U.S.A.
145 F2 **Ohope** New Zealand
33 N7 **Ohrdorf** Germany
37 K2 **Ohrdruf** Germany
37 O3 **Ohře** *R* Czechoslovakia
33 O8 **Ohre** *R* Germany
46 D3 **Ohrid** Macedonia Yugoslavia
46 D3 **Ohridsko ezero** *L* Albania/Yugoslavia
36 H5 **Öhringen** Germany
36 G5 **Ohrnberg** Germany
26 N5 **Ohtanajärvi** Sweden
145 E3 **Ohura** New Zealand
129 H3 **Oiapoque** Fr Guiana
66 E6 **Oiga** China
22 H3 **Oignies** Belgium
29 M6 **Oijärvi** Finland
106 G9 **Oil Center** New Mexico U.S.A.
102 F6 **Oil City** California U.S.A.
111 C9 **Oil City** Louisiana U.S.A.
94 H5 **Oil City** Pennsylvania U.S.A.
120 H10 **Oil Springs** Ontario Canada
107 O5 **Oilton** Oklahoma U.S.A.
109 J8 **Oilton** Texas U.S.A.
94 K9 **Oilville** Virginia U.S.A.
47 H6 **Oinoúsa** *isld* Greece
58 C6 **Oi Qu** *R* China
61 P5 **Oirase-gawa** *R* Japan
21 K8 **Oiron** France
25 D5 **Oirschot** Netherlands
19 Q14 **Oisans** *dist* France
18 G3 **Oise** *dept* France
21 P3 **Oise** *R* France
21 O2 **Oisemont** France
21 J5 **Oisseau** France
21 N3 **Oissel** France
25 D5 **Oisterwijk** Netherlands
127 P6 **Oistins** Barbados
22 E3 **Oisy-le-Verger** France
60 E12 **Ōita** Japan
46 E6 **Oíti** *mt* Greece
48 K4 **Oituz** *pass* Romania
60 P3 **Oiwake** Japan
102 E7 **Ojai** California U.S.A.
27 G11 **Öje** Sweden
61 J11 **Ōji** Japan
60 B12 **Ojika-jima** *isld* Japan
124 G3 **Ojinaga** Mexico
61 M8 **Ojiya** Japan
124 H6 **Ojocaliente** Mexico
106 B7 **Ojo Caliente** New Mexico U.S.A.
133 E3 **Ojo de Agua** Argentina
124 F3 **Ojo de Laguna** Mexico
124 C4 **Ojo de Liebre** Mexico
16 E5 **Ojos del Guadiana** *mt* Spain
133 D3 **Ojos del Salado, Nev** *mt* Chile/Arg
17 F4 **Ojos Negros** Spain
113 G12 **Ojus** Florida U.S.A.
27 F10 **Öjvallberget** Sweden
121 Q7 **Oka** Quebec Canada
54 G4 **Oka** *R* Russian Federation
56 F4 **Oka** *R* Russian Federation
87 C10 **Okahandja** Namibia
145 E1 **Okahu** New Zealand
145 E3 **Okahukura** New Zealand
145 E3 **Okaiawa** *R* New Zealand
145 D1 **Okaihau** New Zealand
115 N6 **Okak Is** Labrador, Nfld Canada
113 F11 **Okaloacoochee Slough** *swamp* Florida U.S.A.
117 O10 **Okanagan Centre** British Columbia Canada
117 O11 **Okanagan Falls** British Columbia Canada
86 B6 **Okanda Nat. Park** Gabon
100 F1 **Okanogan** Washington U.S.A.
100 F1 **Okanogan Range** Wash/Br Col U.S.A./Canada
74 E3 **Okara** Pakistan
107 N6 **Okarche** Oklahoma U.S.A.
144 C5 **Okarito** New Zealand
60 D14 **Okasaki** Japan
145 F3 **Okataina L** New Zealand
145 D3 **Okato** New Zealand
111 G10 **Okatoma** *R* Mississippi U.S.A.
87 C9 **Okaukuejo** Namibia
87 D9 **Okavango Basin** Botswana
60 D12 **Ōkawa** Japan
61 N8 **Ō-kawa** *R* Japan
110 G3 **Okawville** Illinois U.S.A.
107 P6 **Okay** Oklahoma U.S.A.
61 L9 **Okaya** Japan
60 G11 **Okayama** *prefect* Japan
60 G11 **Okayama** Japan
61 L11 **Okazaki** Japan
113 G10 **Okeechobee** Florida U.S.A.
113 G11 **Okeechobee,L** Florida U.S.A.
107 M5 **Okeene** Oklahoma U.S.A.
113 E7 **Okefenokee Swamp** Georgia U.S.A.
8 B6 **Okehampton** England
107 O6 **Okemah** Oklahoma U.S.A.
85 F7 **Okene** Nigeria
33 N8 **Oker** *R* Germany
33 M9 **Oker** Germany
60 R2 **Oketo** Japan
98 K10 **Oketo** Kansas U.S.A.
74 C7 **Okha** India
59 M1 **Okha** Russian Federation
75 M5 **Okhaldhunga** Nepal
46 G6 **Ókhi** *mt* Greece
51 O3 **Okhotsk** Russian Federation
59 N1 **Okhotskoye More** *sea* E Asia
Okhotsk,Sea of *see* **Okhotskoye More**
60 G9 **Oki** *islds* Japan
89 A7 **Okiep** S Africa
85 F7 **Okigwi** Nigeria
61 P13 **Okinawa** *isld* Japan
61 P13 **Okinawa** Okinawa
60 D11 **Okino-shima** *isld* Japan
60 F13 **Okino-shima** Japan
56 E4 **Okinskiy Khrebet** *mts* Russian Federation
85 E7 **Okitipupa** Nigeria
68 B4 **Okkan** Burma
107 N6 **Oklahoma** *state* U.S.A.
107 N6 **Oklahoma City** Oklahoma U.S.A.
109 H1 **Oklaunion** Texas U.S.A.
113 F8 **Oklawaha** *R* Florida U.S.A.
107 P6 **Okmulgee** Oklahoma U.S.A.
48 L2 **Oknitsa** Moldavia
48 K2 **Okno** Ukraine
99 L6 **Okoboji L** Iowa U.S.A.
98 F5 **Okobojo** South Dakota U.S.A.
145 E3 **Okoia** New Zealand
111 H7 **Okolona** Mississippi U.S.A.
86 B6 **Okondja** Gabon
112 D4 **Okonee, L** Georgia U.S.A.
31 K2 **Okonek** Poland
60 R1 **Okoppe** Japan
145 E2 **Okoroire** New Zealand
118 D8 **Okotoks** Alberta Canada
86 B6 **Okoyo** Congo
85 E7 **Okpara** *R* Benin/Nigeria
98 F6 **Okreek** South Dakota U.S.A.
28 A5 **Oksby** Denmark
26 C9 **Oksendal** Norway
26 M1 **Öksfjord** Norway
26 M1 **Öksfjord-jökel** *mt* Norway
52 H1 **Oksino** Russian Federation
54 M3 **Oksko-Donskaya Ravnina** *plain* Russian Federation
26 G3 **Öksnes** Norway
52 E3 **Oksovskiy** Russian Federation
26 G5 **Okstinderne** *mt* Norway
107 P6 **Oktaha** Oklahoma U.S.A.
68 C3 **Oktwin** Burma
55 C6 **Oktyabr'sk** Kazakhstan
56 B6 **Oktyabr'skiy** Kazakhstan
55 D4 **Oktyabr'skiy** Kustanayskaya Kazakhstan
56 E2 **Oktyabr'skiy** Russian Federation
55 C3 **Oktyabr'skiy** Bashkirskaya Respublika Russian Federation
55 D3 **Oktyabr'skiy** Chelyabinskaya obl Russian Federation
52 F5 **Oktyabr'skiy** Kostromskaya obl Russian Federation
55 E2 **Oktyabr'skiy** Tyumenskaya obl Russian Federation
57 E5 **Oktyabr'skiy** Tajikistan
55 E5 **Oktyabr'skoye** Turgayskaya obl Kazakhstan
55 D4 **Oktyabr'skoye** Chelyabinskaya obl Russian Federation
55 E1 **Oktyabr'skoye** Khanty-Mansiyskiy aut ok Russian Federation
55 C4 **Oktyabr'skoye** Orenburgskaya obl Russian Federation
54 D10 **Oktyabr'skoye** Ukraine
51 J1 **Oktyabr'skoy Revolyutsii, Os** *isld* Russian Federation
61 Q12 **Oku** Okinawa
60 D13 **Ōkuchi** Japan
144 D5 **Okuku** *R* New Zealand
52 D5 **Okulovka** Russian Federation
144 B5 **Okuru** New Zealand
60 N3 **Okushiri-kaikyō** *str* Japan
60 N3 **Okushiri-tō** *isld* Japan
60 J10 **Okutango-hantō** *pen* Japan
89 B4 **Okwa** *watercourse* Botswana
110 C6 **Ola** Arkansas U.S.A.
100 J5 **Ola** Idaho U.S.A.
28 S8 **Olafsfjordhur** Iceland
28 R9 **Olafsvik** Iceland
80 D1 **Olailé** Israel
16 C7 **Olalla de Cala, Sta** Spain
95 T1 **Olamon** Maine U.S.A.
28 D2 **Øland** *reg* Denmark
27 J15 **Oland** *isld* Sweden
29 P5 **Olanga** *R* Finland/Rus Fed
52 D2 **Olanga** Russian Federation
112 H4 **Olanta** South Carolina U.S.A.
18 G9 **Olargues** France
138 C2 **Olarinna** *R* South Australia Australia
138 F4 **Olary** South Australia Australia
107 Q3 **Olathe** Kansas U.S.A.
131 E6 **Olavarria** Argentina
31 K5 **Oława** Poland
103 N8 **Olberg** Arizona U.S.A.
37 P2 **Olbernhau** Germany
37 L1 **Olbersleben** Germany
43 C8 **Olbia** Sardinia
37 L7 **Olching** Germany
94 J3 **Olcott** New York U.S.A.
126 E3 **Old Bahama Chan** Caribbean
14 D3 **Oldcastle** Ireland
142 F4 **Old Cherrabun** W Australia Australia
141 F6 **Old Cork** Queensland Australia
116 R3 **Old Crow** Yukon Territory Canada
116 R2 **Old Crow** *R* Alaska/Yukon Terr U.S.A./Canada
88 E3 **Oldeani** Tanzania
109 J3 **Olden** Texas U.S.A.
32 H6 **Oldenbrok** Germany
33 N4 **Oldenburg** Germany
33 N6 **Oldendorf** Germany
33 N7 **Oldenstadt** Germany
25 G4 **Oldenzaal** Netherlands
32 F6 **Oldersum** Germany
26 B10 **Oldevatn** *L* Norway
101 P5 **Old Faithful** Wyoming U.S.A.
95 M3 **Old Forge** New York U.S.A.
95 M5 **Old Forge** Pennsylvania U.S.A.
112 E2 **Old Fort** North Carolina U.S.A.
123 O2 **Old Fort Bay** Quebec Canada
143 C8 **Old Gidgee** W Australia Australia
108 G2 **Old Glory** Texas U.S.A.
13 F6 **Oldham** England
98 J5 **Oldham** South Dakota U.S.A.
116 L8 **Old Harbor** Alaska U.S.A.
127 K3 **Old Harbour** Jamaica
110 K5 **Old Hickory L** Tennessee U.S.A.
117 L8 **Old Hogem** British Columbia Canada
9 F3 **Old Hurst** England
33 O10 **Oldisleben** Germany
116 P2 **Old John L** Alaska U.S.A.
95 P5 **Old Lyme** Connecticut U.S.A.
15 F3 **Oldmeldrum** Scotland
110 F3 **Old Monroe** Missouri U.S.A.
95 R3 **Old Orchard Beach** Maine U.S.A.
123 T5 **Old Perlican** Newfoundland Canada
123 L3 **Old Post Pt** Quebec Canada
116 R3 **Old Rampart** Alaska U.S.A.
113 G12 **Old Rhodes Key** *isld* Florida U.S.A.
127 O5 **Old Road** Antigua W Indies
127 P4 **Old Road Town** St Kitts W Indies
118 C7 **Olds** Alberta Canada
95 R2 **Old Speck Mt** Maine U.S.A.
9 F3 **Old Stratford** England
28 A7 **Oldsum** Germany
113 E10 **Old Tampa B** Florida U.S.A.
138 E4 **Old Telichie** South Australia Australia
113 D8 **Old Town** Florida U.S.A.
95 T2 **Old Town** Maine U.S.A.
88 E3 **Olduvai Gorge** Tanzania
Old Viking Bank *see* **Bergen Bank**
118 L8 **Old Wives L** Saskatchewan Canada
116 H5 **Old Woman** *R* Alaska U.S.A.
103 J7 **Old Woman Mts** California U.S.A.
65 A2 **Öldziyt** Mongolia
94 J4 **Olean** New York U.S.A.
122 H7 **O'Leary** Prince Edward I Canada
31 N1 **Olecko** Poland
16 B5 **Oleiros** Portugal
59 G1 **Olekminski Stanovik** *mt ra* Russian Federation
52 G3 **Olema** Russian Federation
27 A12 **Ölen** Norway
100 D7 **Olene** Oregon U.S.A.
52 D1 **Olenegorsk** Russian Federation
51 L2 **Olenek** *R* Russian Federation
52 D6 **Olenino** Russian Federation
52 E2 **Olenitsa** Russian Federation
55 B5 **Olenty** *R* Kazakhstan
18 E7 **Oléron,Ile d'** France
48 J1 **Olesko** Ukraine
31 K4 **Oleśnica** Poland
31 L5 **Olesno** Poland
45 O6 **Olevano Romano** Italy
100 E4 **Olex** Oregon U.S.A.
32 F9 **Olfen** Germany
59 L3 **Ol'ga** Russian Federation
113 F11 **Olga** Florida U.S.A.
98 H1 **Olga** North Dakota U.S.A.
116 K8 **Olga B** Alaska U.S.A.
121 N3 **Olga,L** Quebec Canada
140 B7 **Olga, Mt** N Terr Australia
54 J9 **Ol'ginka** Ukraine
66 D2 **Ölgiy** Mongolia
28 B5 **Ølgod** Denmark
48 M2 **Ol'gopol'** Ukraine
16 B7 **Olhão** Portugal
29 L6 **Olhava** Finland
85 E7 **Oli** *R* Benin/Nigeria
138 A2 **Olia Chain** *mts* N Terr Australia
140 A7 **Olia Chain** *mts* N Terr Australia
17 H2 **Oliana** Spain
42 F4 **Olib** *isld* Croatia
17 G4 **Oliete** Spain
87 C10 **Olifants** *R* Namibia
89 A5 **Olifants** *watercourse* Namibia
89 G5 **Olifants** *R* S Africa
89 A8 **Olifants** S Africa
87 D11 **Olifantshoek** S Africa

210

Olifants R. Berge — Ottenshlag

89 A9 **Olifants R. Berge** *mts* S Africa
131 G4 **Olimar** *R* Uruguay
46 E7 **Olimbia** Greece
46 E4 **Ólimbos** *mt* Greece
133 F2 **Olimpo** Paraguay
99 P7 **Olin** Iowa U.S.A.
100 C9 **Olinda** California U.S.A.
141 G1 **Olinda Ent** Gt Barrier Reef Aust
129 L6 **Olindina** Brazil
141 G5 **Olio** Queensland Australia
17 F2 **Olite** Spain
17 G6 **Oliva** Spain
131 B2 **Oliva, Cord. de** *mt ra* Arg/Chile
16 C6 **Oliva de Mérida** Spain
131 B3 **Olivares,Cerro del** *pk* Arg/Chile
17 F5 **Olivares de Júcar** Spain
98 A4 **Olive** Montana U.S.A.
110 G7 **Olive Branch** Mississippi U.S.A.
94 D8 **Olive Hill** Kentucky U.S.A.
130 G7 **Oliveira** Brazil
16 B4 **Oliveira de Azemeis** Portugal
16 B4 **Oliveira do Hospital** Portugal
112 J2 **Olive, Mt** North Carolina U.S.A.
Olivenca *see* **Lupilichi**
16 C6 **Olivenza** Spain
117 O11 **Oliver** British Columbia Canada
112 F5 **Oliver** Georgia U.S.A.
21 O6 **Olivet** France
94 C4 **Olivet** Michigan U.S.A.
98 J6 **Olivet** South Dakota U.S.A.
99 M5 **Olivia** Minnesota U.S.A.
109 L7 **Olivia** Texas U.S.A.
144 B6 **Olivine Range** New Zealand
41 J5 **Olivone** Switzerland
31 L1 **Oliwa** Poland
65 D3 **Olji Moron He** *R* China
54 L6 **Ol'khovatka** Russian Federation
55 D3 **Ol'khovka** Russian Federation
31 M5 **Olkusz** Poland
111 D10 **Olla** Louisiana U.S.A.
133 D2 **Ollague** *vol* Bolivia/Chile
9 E1 **Ollerton** England
98 B3 **Ollie** Montana U.S.A.
29 N2 **Ollila** Finland
131 B3 **Ollita, Cord. de** *ra* Arg/Chile
131 B3 **Ollitas** *pk* Argentina
27 G12 **Ölme** Sweden
16 D3 **Olmeda** Spain
131 D4 **Olmos,L** Argentina
9 F3 **Olney** England
110 H3 **Olney** Illinois U.S.A.
101 L1 **Olney** Montana U.S.A.
109 J2 **Olney** Texas U.S.A.
106 G3 **Olney Springs** Colorado U.S.A.
26 K8 **Olofsfors** Sweden
27 G15 **Olofström** Sweden
123 M3 **Olomane R** Quebec Canada
86 C6 **Olombo** Congo
48 D1 **Olomouc** Czechoslovakia
41 K7 **Olona** *R* Italy
48 M4 **Oloneshty** Moldavia
52 D4 **Olonets** Russian Federation
71 E3 **Olongapo** Luzon Philippines
70 D5 **Olongliko** Kalimantan
20 G8 **Olonne-sur-Mer** France
18 G9 **Olonzac** France
18 E9 **Oloron-St.Marie** France
17 J2 **Olot** Spain
37 O3 **Olovi** Czechoslovakia
48 E6 **Olovo** Bosnia-Herzegovina
58 G1 **Olovyannaya** Russian Federation
36 D1 **Olpe** Germany
107 O3 **Olpe** Kansas U.S.A.
41 P3 **Olperer** *mt* Austria
107 O2 **Olsburg** Kansas U.S.A.
31 L6 **Olše** *R* Czechoslovakia
54 G6 **Ol'shany** Ukraine
25 F4 **Olst** Netherlands
31 M2 **Olsztyn** Poland
31 M2 **Olsztynek** Poland
48 K4 **Olt** *R* Romania
40 G3 **Olten** Switzerland
48 K6 **Oltenița** Romania
133 D6 **Olte,Sa.de** *mts* Argentina
48 H6 **Olteț** *R* Romania
108 E1 **Olton** Texas U.S.A.
78 H1 **Oltu** Turkey
67 G6 **O-luan-pi** *C* Taiwan
113 E7 **Olustee** Florida U.S.A.
107 L7 **Olustee** Oklahoma U.S.A.
71 F7 **Olutanga** *isld* Philippines
33 P8 **Olvenstedt** Germany
16 D8 **Olvera** Spain
46 E7 **Olympia** Greece
100 C2 **Olympia** Washington U.S.A.
100 B2 **Olympic Mts** Washington U.S.A.
100 A2 **Olympic Nat. Park** Washington U.S.A.
100 B2 **Olympic Nat. Park** Washington U.S.A.
Olympus *mt* Cyprus *see* **Troödos** *Mt*
Olympus *mt* Greece *see* **Ólimbos** *mt*
100 B2 **Olympus,Mt** Washington U.S.A.
95 M5 **Olyphant** Pennsylvania U.S.A.
51 Q2 **Olyutorskiy** Russian Federation
36 B3 **Olzheim** Germany
56 B3 **Om'** *R* Russian Federation
60 O4 **Ōma** Japan
52 G2 **Oma** Russian Federation
111 F10 **Oma** Mississippi U.S.A.
61 L9 **Ōmachi** Japan
61 M11 **Omae zaki** *C* Japan
14 D2 **Omagh** N Ireland
128 D4 **Omaguas** Peru
110 C5 **Omaha** Arkansas U.S.A.
99 L8 **Omaha** Nebraska U.S.A.
109 N2 **Omaha** Texas U.S.A.
126 F4 **Omaja** Cuba
100 F1 **Omak** Washington U.S.A.
144 B6 **Omakau** New Zealand
145 F4 **Omakere** New Zealand
72 H5 **Oman** *sultanate* Arabian Pen
77 F7 **Oman, Gulf of** Iran/Oman
145 D1 **Omapere, L** New Zealand
94 E9 **Omar** West Virginia U.S.A.
144 B6 **Omarama** New Zealand
87 C10 **Omaruru** Namibia
128 D7 **Omate** Peru
71 J9 **Omatema** Indonesia
60 O4 **Ōma-zaki** *C* Japan
120 C2 **Ombabika** Ontario Canada
120 B2 **Ombabika B** Ontario Canada
71 M9 **Ombai,Selat** *str* Indonesia
61 N11 **Ombase-jima** *isld* Japan
8 D3 **Ombersley** England
69 C12 **Ombolata** Indonesia
86 A6 **Omboue** Gabon
45 J4 **Ombrone** *R* Italy
66 D5 **Ombu** China
86 F2 **Omdurman** Sudan
61 N10 **Ōme** Japan
111 L10 **Omega** Alabama U.S.A.
112 D6 **Omega** Georgia U.S.A.
107 M6 **Omega** Oklahoma U.S.A.
121 M8 **Omemee** Ontario Canada
98 F1 **Omemee** North Dakota U.S.A.
94 B1 **Omena** Michigan U.S.A.
80 C8 **'Omer** Israel
94 D2 **Omer** Michigan U.S.A.
47 J5 **Ömerköy** Turkey
47 N10 **Ömerli Baraji** *dam* Turkey
14 A3 **Omey I** Ireland
86 G3 **Om Hājer** Ethiopia
61 L8 **Ōmi** Japan
22 D4 **Omiecourt** France
144 D5 **Omihi** New Zealand
60 P4 **Ōminato** Japan
117 L8 **Omineca** *R* British Columbia Canada
117 K7 **Omineca Mts** British Columbia Canada
42 H5 **Omis** Croatia
60 E11 **Ōmi-shima** *isld* Japan
60 F11 **Ōmi-shima** *isld* Japan
61 N10 **Ōmiya** Japan
117 F7 **Ommaney,C** Alaska U.S.A.
114 J3 **Ommanney B** Northwest Territories Canada
28 B5 **Omme Å** *R* Denmark
25 F3 **Ommen** Netherlands
28 G6 **Omø** Denmark
86 G4 **Omo** *R* Ethiopia
43 B8 **Omodeo, L** Sardinia
51 P2 **Omolon** *R* Russian Federation
51 N2 **Omoloy** *R* Russian Federation
61 O6 **Omono-gawa** *R* Japan
22 H4 **Omont** France
20 G2 **Omonville-la Rogue** France
61 O6 **Ōmori** Japan
61 P6 **Omoto** Japan
61 P6 **Omoto-gawa** *R* Japan
99 S5 **Omro** Wisconsin U.S.A.
55 F3 **Omsk** Russian Federation
55 G3 **Omskaya Oblast'** *prov* Russian Federation
68 D1 **O-mu** Burma
60 Q1 **Ōmu** Japan
31 N2 **Omulew** *R* Poland
83 L10 **Omuna** Sri Lanka
60 C13 **Ōmura** Japan
60 C13 **Ōmura wan** *B* Japan
47 H1 **Omurtag** Bulgaria
60 D12 **Ōmuta** Japan
55 E3 **Omutinskiy** Russian Federation
52 H5 **Omutninsk** Russian Federation
26 B9 **Ona** Norway
56 C5 **Ona** *R* Russian Federation
16 E2 **Oña** Spain
113 F10 **Ona** Florida U.S.A.
107 O2 **Onaga** Kansas U.S.A.
61 P7 **Onagawahama** Japan
61 P7 **Onagawa-wan** *B* Japan
61 O9 **Onahama** Japan
98 G4 **Onaka** South Dakota U.S.A.
120 J2 **Onakawana** Ontario Canada
120 J1 **Onakwehegan** *R* Ontario Canada
100 C3 **Onalaska** Washington U.S.A.
99 P6 **Onalaska** Wisconsin U.S.A.
120 C2 **Onaman L** Ontario Canada
99 N3 **Onamia** Minnesota U.S.A.
95 M9 **Onancock** Virginia U.S.A.
70 F6 **Onang** Sulawesi
86 B6 **Onangue, L** Gabon
120 J5 **Onaping L** Ontario Canada
110 H1 **Onarga** Illinois U.S.A.
121 U3 **Onatchiway,L** Quebec Canada
124 F2 **Oñate** Mexico
124 E3 **Onavas** Mexico
98 K7 **Onawa** Iowa U.S.A.
94 C1 **Onaway** Michigan U.S.A.
87 B9 **Oncocua** Angola
17 G5 **Onda** Spain
87 C9 **Ondangwa** Namibia
31 N6 **Ondava** *R* Czechoslovakia
25 G2 **Onderdendam** Netherlands
87 C9 **Ondjiva** Angola
85 E7 **Ondo** Nigeria
58 F2 **Öndörhaan** Mongolia
65 E2 **Ondor Had** China
73 L8 **One and Half Degree Chan** Indian Oc
113 E10 **Oneco** Florida U.S.A.
Onega *L* *see* **Onezhskoye, Oz**
52 E3 **Onega** Russian Federation
52 E4 **Onega** *R* Russian Federation
44 D4 **Oneglia** Italy
141 H2 **One & Half Mile Opening** *str* Gt Barrier Reef Aust
99 Q8 **Oneida** Illinois U.S.A.
99 P7 **Oneida** Iowa U.S.A.
94 D9 **Oneida** Kentucky U.S.A.
95 M3 **Oneida** New York U.S.A.
110 M5 **Oneida** Tennessee U.S.A.
95 L3 **Oneida L** New York U.S.A.
98 H7 **O'Neill** Nebraska U.S.A.
145 D4 **Onekaka** New Zealand
94 A2 **Onekama** Michigan U.S.A.
86 D6 **Onema** Zaire
111 K8 **Oneonta** Alabama U.S.A.
95 M4 **Oneonta** New York U.S.A.
145 E1 **Onerahi** New Zealand
145 E2 **Oneroa I** New Zealand
118 J1 **One Sided Lake** Ontario Canada
48 K4 **Onești** Romania
52 E4 **Onezhskoye,Oz** *L* Russian Federation
145 F3 **Ongaonga** New Zealand
9 G4 **Ongar** England
145 E3 **Ongarue** New Zealand
89 C8 **Ongers** *watercourse* S Africa
143 C10 **Ongerup** W Australia Australia
65 B3 **Onggon Ul** China
19 P16 **Ongles** France
65 D3 **Ongniud Qi** China
76 E3 **Ongole** India
56 G4 **Onguren** Russian Federation
15 C4 **Onich** Scotland
98 G5 **Onida** South Dakota U.S.A.
87 G12 **Onilahy** *R* Madagascar
118 H5 **Onion Lake** Saskatchewan Canada
60 P1 **Onishika** Japan
122 A3 **Onistagan L** Quebec Canada
85 F7 **Onitsha** Nigeria
21 N1 **Onival** France
29 N8 **Onkivesi** *L* Finland
95 M9 **Onley** Virginia U.S.A.
61 P13 **Onna** Okinawa
61 P13 **Onna-dake** *mt* Okinawa
22 F3 **Onnaing** France
60 O4 **Ōno** Japan
60 E11 **Onoda** Japan
61 N11 **Ōnohara-jima** *isld* Japan
137 R6 **Ono-i-lau** *isld* Pacific Oc
145 E4 **Onoke, L** New Zealand
60 G11 **Onomichi** Japan
58 G1 **Onon** *R* Russian Federation
69 C12 **Ononamolo** Indonesia
94 C4 **Onondaga** Michigan U.S.A.
58 F2 **Onon Gol** *R* Mongolia
61 O8 **Ono-Niimachi** Japan
59 M1 **Onor** Russian Federation
128 E2 **Onoto** Venezuela
137 Q2 **Onotoa** *atoll* Kiribati
118 C5 **Onoway** Alberta Canada
28 F5 **Onsbjerg** Denmark
16 B2 **Ons., I.de** Spain
28 H7 **Ønslev** Denmark
142 B5 **Onslow** W Australia Australia
112 K3 **Onslow B** North Carolina U.S.A.
144 B6 **Onslow, L** New Zealand
94 C4 **Onsted** Michigan U.S.A.
36 G7 **Onstmettingen** Germany
25 H2 **Onstwedde** Netherlands
61 L10 **Ontake-san** *mt* Japan
115 K7 **Ontario** *prov* Canada
102 G7 **Ontario** California U.S.A.
100 J5 **Ontario** Oregon U.S.A.
99 Q6 **Ontario** Wisconsin U.S.A.
94 J3 **Ontario,L** U.S.A./Canada
17 G6 **Onteniente** Spain
99 R3 **Ontonagon** Michigan U.S.A.
137 M3 **Ontong Java Is** Solomon Is
17 G6 **Ontur** Spain
60 O4 **Onuma** Japan
111 F9 **Onward** Mississippi U.S.A.
102 F6 **Onyx** California U.S.A.
21 N6 **Onzain** France
138 E5 **Oodla Wirra** South Australia Australia
138 D2 **Oodnadatta** South Australia Australia
135 V4 **Ookala** Hawaiian Is
138 B4 **Ooldea** South Australia Australia
138 B4 **Ooldea Ra** South Australia Australia
110 K3 **Oolitic** Indiana U.S.A.
107 P5 **Oologah** Oklahoma U.S.A.
107 P5 **Oologah L** Oklahoma U.S.A.
25 B5 **Ooltgensplaat** Netherlands
140 C6 **Ooraminna Ra** N Terr Australia
140 D5 **Ooratippra** *R* N Terr Australia
140 D5 **Ooratippra** N Terr Australia
141 F5 **Oorindi** Queensland Australia
111 L7 **Oostanaula** *R* Georgia U.S.A.
25 A6 **Oostburg** Netherlands
22 D2 **Oost Cappel** France
22 D1 **Oostduinkerke** Belgium
22 D1 **Oostende** Belgium
25 E5 **Oosterbeër** Netherlands
25 D2 **Oosterend** Netherlands
25 C5 **Oosterhout** Netherlands
25 A5 **Oosterschelde** Netherlands
25 F3 **Oosterwolde** Netherlands
22 F2 **Oosterzele** Belgium
25 D3 **Oosthuizen** Netherlands
25 E4 **Oostlijk-Flevoland** *prov* Netherlands
25 F2 **Oostmahoorn** Netherlands
22 H1 **Oostmalle** Belgium
22 F1 **Oost Vlaanderen** Belgium
25 D2 **Oost Vlieland** Netherlands
25 B5 **Oostvoorne** Netherlands
25 G4 **Ootmarsum** Netherlands
117 L9 **Ootsa Lake** British Columbia Canada
119 S2 **Opachuanau L** Manitoba Canada
102 R11 **Opaeula** *R* Hawaiian Is
47 H1 **Opaka** Bulgaria
145 E4 **Opaki** New Zealand
118 D5 **Opal** Alberta Canada
124 H5 **Opal** Mexico
101 P8 **Opal** Wyoming U.S.A.
51 P3 **Opala** Russian Federation
86 D6 **Opala** Zaire
31 J3 **Opalenica** Poland
113 G12 **Opa-Locka** Florida U.S.A.
83 K11 **Opanake** Sri Lanka
86 F5 **Opari** Sudan
52 G5 **Oparino** Russian Federation
120 H3 **Opasatika** Ontario Canada
120 G3 **Opasatika L** Ontario Canada
42 F3 **Opatija** Croatia
31 N5 **Opatów** Poland
31 L4 **Opatówek** Poland
31 K5 **Opava** *R* Czechoslovakia
31 K6 **Opava** Czechoslovakia
121 P3 **Opawica, L** Quebec Canada
111 L9 **Opelika** Alabama U.S.A.
111 D11 **Opelousas** Louisiana U.S.A.
120 D2 **Opemisha** Ontario Canada
144 B5 **Open Bay Is** New Zealand
121 M7 **Opeongo L** Ontario Canada
22 F2 **Ophasselt** Belgium
101 T1 **Opheim** Montana U.S.A.
100 A7 **Ophir** Oregon U.S.A.
101 N9 **Ophir** Utah U.S.A.
69 E12 **Ophir, Gunung** *mt* Sumatra
22 K1 **Ophoven** Belgium
142 C6 **Ophthalmia Ra** W Australia Australia
45 P6 **Opi** Italy
86 E5 **Opienge** Zaire
144 C6 **Opihi R** New Zealand
36 B1 **Opladen** Germany
85 F8 **Opobo** Nigeria
52 C6 **Opochka** Russian Federation
122 F1 **Opocopa L** Quebec Canada
31 M4 **Opoczno** Poland
124 D3 **Opodepe** Mexico
31 K5 **Opole** Poland
145 F3 **Oponae** New Zealand
145 D1 **Opononi** New Zealand
Oporto *see* **Porto**
54 F7 **Oposhnya** Ukraine
145 F3 **Opotiki** New Zealand
145 E2 **Opoutere** New Zealand
111 K10 **Opp** Alabama U.S.A.
61 P7 **Oppa-gawa** *R* Japan
61 P7 **Oppa-wan** *B* Japan
26 D9 **Oppdal** Norway
45 K1 **Oppeano** Italy
33 T9 **Oppelhaun** Germany
36 E7 **Oppenau** Germany
36 E4 **Oppenheim** Germany
36 G6 **Oppenweiler** Germany
28 J5 **Oppe Sundby** Denmark
27 D10 **Oppland** *county* Norway
119 Q4 **Optic Lake** Manitoba Canada
107 J5 **Optima** Oklahoma U.S.A.
145 E1 **Opua** New Zealand
145 E1 **Opuawhanga** New Zealand
145 D3 **Opunake** New Zealand
124 E2 **Oputo** Mexico
87 B9 **Opuwo** Namibia
22 G2 **Opwijk** Belgium
99 Q9 **Oquawka** Illinois U.S.A.
124 D2 **Oquitoa** Mexico
95 R2 **Oquossoc** Maine U.S.A.
55 C5 **Or'** *R* Kazakhstan/Rus Fed
27 G15 **Ör** Sweden
41 O5 **Ora** Italy
84 F4 **Ora** Libya
143 D9 **Ora Banda** W Australia Australia
127 L2 **Oracabessa** Jamaica
103 O9 **Oracle** Arizona U.S.A.
48 G3 **Oradea** Romania
18 F7 **Oradour-sur-Vayres** France
29 T9 **Oræfajökull** *ice cap* Iceland
74 H6 **Orai** India
103 O6 **Oraibi** Arizona U.S.A.
103 O5 **Oraibi Wash** *creek* Arizona U.S.A.
29 M4 **Orajärvi** *L* Finland
29 L5 **Orajärvi** Finland
98 C6 **Oral** South Dakota U.S.A.
85 D1 **Oran** Algeria
110 G4 **Oran** Missouri U.S.A.
139 J5 **Orange** New South Wales Australia
19 N16 **Orange** France
87 C11 **Orange** *R* S Africa/Namibia
102 G8 **Orange** California U.S.A.
95 P4 **Orange** Massachusetts U.S.A.
109 O5 **Orange** Texas U.S.A.
94 J8 **Orange** Virginia U.S.A.
111 J11 **Orange Beach** Alabama U.S.A.
112 G4 **Orangeburg** South Carolina U.S.A.
129 H3 **Orange,C** Brazil
126 E2 **Orange Cay** *isld* Bahamas
113 F9 **Orange City** Florida U.S.A.
116 Q3 **Orange Cr** Alaska U.S.A.
123 L8 **Orangedale** C Breton I, Nova Scotia
113 F7 **Orangedale** Florida U.S.A.
95 N6 **Orange, E** New Jersey U.S.A.
89 D7 **Orange Free State** *prov* S Africa
129 G3 **Orange Gebergte** *mts* Suriname
109 K8 **Orange Grove** Texas U.S.A.
113 E8 **Orange L** Florida U.S.A.
113 F7 **Orange Park** Florida U.S.A.
99 R7 **Orangeville** Illinois U.S.A.
103 N2 **Orangeville** Utah U.S.A.
145 E3 **Orangimea** New Zealand
71 E3 **Orani** Luzon Philippines
43 C8 **Orani** Sardinia
33 Q9 **Oranienbaum** Germany
33 S7 **Oranienburg** Germany
80 D3 **Oranim** Israel
87 C11 **Oranjemund** Namibia
126 A1 **Oranjestad** Aruba W Indies
127 N6 **Oranjestad** St Eustatius W Indies
14 C3 **Oranmore** Ireland
133 E2 **Orán, N** Argentina
Orantes *R* *see* **'Āsi** *R*
143 G6 **Orantjugurr,L** W Australia Australia
80 C3 **Or'Aqiva** Israel
144 C6 **Orari** New Zealand
71 G4 **Oras** Philippines
71 G4 **Oras B** Philippines
48 E5 **Orašje** Bosnia-Herzegovina
48 H5 **Orăştie** Romania
48 H3 **Oraşu Nou** Romania
124 H5 **Oratario** Mexico
48 M1 **Oratov** Ukraine
31 L6 **Orava** *R* Czechoslovakia
29 J8 **Oravais** Finland
48 G5 **Oravița** Romania
31 L6 **Oravská Magura** *mts* Czechoslovakia
144 A7 **Orawia** New Zealand
18 H9 **Orb** *R* France
44 E2 **Orba** *R* Italy
66 C5 **Orba Co** *L* China
21 L3 **Orbec** France
42 D6 **Orbetello** Italy
21 N7 **Orbigny** France
16 D2 **Orbigo** *R* Spain
94 K6 **Orbisonia** Pennsylvania U.S.A.
139 J7 **Orbost** Victoria Australia
28 F5 **Ørby** Denmark
27 F14 **Örby** Sweden
27 J11 **Örbyhus** Sweden
116 O6 **Orca B** Alaska U.S.A.
146 E3 **Orcadas** *Argentina Base* S Orkney Is S Atlantic Oc
146 G4 **Orcadas Seamounts, Islas** *seamounts* Antarctica
21 L8 **Orches** France
113 G10 **Orchid Island** Florida U.S.A.
128 E1 **Orchila, La** *isld* Venezuela
16 B1 **Órdenes** Spain
103 M4 **Orderville** Utah U.S.A.
Órdes *see* **Órdenes**
28 B3 **Ørding** Denmark
142 F3 **Ord,Mt** W Australia Australia
102 H7 **Ord Mt** California U.S.A.
52 D3 **Ordozero** Russian Federation
142 G3 **Ord River** W Australia Australia
78 F1 **Ordu** Turkey
78 K2 **Ordubail** Azerbaijan
16 E2 **Orduña** Spain
106 G3 **Ordway** Colorado U.S.A.
98 H4 **Ordway** South Dakota U.S.A.
Ordzhonikidze *see* **Vladikavkaz**
55 D4 **Ordzhonikidze** Kazakhstan
56 C4 **Ordzhonikidzevskiy** Russian Federation
28 E5 **Ore** Denmark
26 C9 **Öre** Norway
26 K7 **Oreälv** *R* Sweden
100 J6 **Oreana** Idaho U.S.A.
102 F1 **Oreana** Nevada U.S.A.
27 G12 **Örebro** *county* Sweden
27 H12 **Örebro** Sweden
109 N3 **Ore City** Texas U.S.A.
100 E6 **Oregon** *state* U.S.A.
99 R7 **Oregon** Illinois U.S.A.
110 A2 **Oregon** Missouri U.S.A.
99 R7 **Oregon** Wisconsin U.S.A.
100 B7 **Oregon Caves Nat. Mon** Oregon U.S.A.
100 C4 **Oregon City** Oregon U.S.A.
112 M2 **Oregon Inlet** North Carolina U.S.A.
27 K11 **Öregrund** Sweden
54 G9 **Orekhov** Ukraine
46 G1 **Orekhovitsa** Bulgaria
55 F3 **Orekhovo** Russian Federation
52 E6 **Orekhovo Zuyevo** Russian Federation
54 B2 **Orekhovsk** Belorussia
54 H4 **Orël** Orlovskaya obl Russian Federation
52 J5 **Orël** Permskaya obl Russian Federation
54 F8 **Orel'** *R* Ukraine
98 C7 **Orella** Nebraska U.S.A.
128 C5 **Orellana** Peru
16 D5 **Orellana, Embalse de** *res* Spain
53 E7 **Orel Oblast'** *prov* Russian Federation
59 L1 **Orel', Oz** *L* Russian Federation
103 N1 **Orem** Utah U.S.A.
47 J7 **Ören** Turkey
55 C5 **Orenburg** Russian Federation
50 E3 **Orenburgskaya Oblast'** *prov* Russian Federation
16 B2 **Orense** *prov* Spain
16 B2 **Orense** Spain
46 F6 **Oreoí** Greece
144 A7 **Orepuki** New Zealand
47 H3 **Orestiás** Greece
29 K5 **Öresund** *str* Sweden/Denmark
80 G1 **Oretal** Syria
144 B7 **Oreti R** New Zealand
145 E2 **Orewa** New Zealand
22 J2 **Oreye** Belgium
139 J8 **Orford** Tasmania Australia
9 H3 **Orford** England
95 P3 **Orford** New Hampshire U.S.A.
141 G1 **Orford Ness** Queensland Australia
9 H3 **Orford Ness** England
106 D9 **Organ** New Mexico U.S.A.
106 D9 **Organ** *mt* New Mexico U.S.A.
126 C3 **Organos, Sa. de los** *hills* Cuba
103 M9 **Organ Pipe Cactus Nat. Mon** Arizona U.S.A.
16 E5 **Orgaz** Spain
21 P4 **Orge** *R* France
40 C4 **Orgelet** France
21 O5 **Orgères-en-Beauce** France
21 O4 **Orgeval** France
48 M3 **Orgeyev** Moldavia
45 K1 **Orgiano** Italy
16 E8 **Órgiva** Spain
47 N10 **Örgök Burun** *C* Turkey
65 B3 **Orgon Tal** China
52 F6 **Orgtrud** Russian Federation
77 L3 **Orgūn** Afghanistan
47 K5 **Orhaneli** *R* Turkey
47 K5 **Orhaneli** Turkey
47 K4 **Orhangazi** Turkey
Orhanie *see* **Botevgrad**
47 J5 **Orhanlar** Turkey
58 D2 **Orhon Gol** *R* Mongolia
17 F1 **Oria** *R* Spain
17 F7 **Oria** Spain
52 G5 **Orichi** Russian Federation
100 A8 **Orick** California U.S.A.
141 G8 **Orient** Queensland Australia
106 E3 **Orient** Colorado U.S.A.
99 M8 **Orient** Iowa U.S.A.
98 G5 **Orient** South Dakota U.S.A.
108 G4 **Orient** Texas U.S.A.
100 G1 **Orient** Washington U.S.A.
112 L2 **Oriental** North Carolina U.S.A.
120 B3 **Orient Bay** Ontario Canada
95 P5 **Orient I** New York U.S.A.
138 F3 **Orientos** New South Wales Australia
141 F8 **Orientos** Queensland Australia
22 G4 **Origny-en-Thiérache** France
22 E4 **Origny-St.-Benoîte** France
17 G6 **Orihuela** Spain
121 L8 **Orillia** Ontario Canada
29 M11 **Orimattila** Finland
98 A7 **Orin** Wyoming U.S.A.
48 K2 **Orinin** Ukraine
128 F2 **Orinoco** *R* Venezuela
128 F2 **Orinoco, Mouths of the** Venezuela
43 G8 **Oriolo** Italy
118 G9 **Orion** Alberta Canada
99 Q8 **Orion** Illinois U.S.A.
98 J3 **Oriska** North Dakota U.S.A.
95 M4 **Oriskany Falls** New York U.S.A.
75 K8 **Orissa** *prov* India
43 B9 **Oristano** Sardinia
43 B9 **Oristano, G. di** Sardinia
128 E2 **Orituco** *R* Venezuela
29 O9 **Orivesi** *L* Finland
129 G4 **Oriximiná** Brazil
125 L8 **Orizaba** Mexico
47 J2 **Orizare** Bulgaria
42 J6 **Orjen** *mt* Bosnia-Herzegovina
26 D8 **Orkdalen** *V* Norway
27 F15 **Örkelljunga** Sweden
27 G15 **Örkened** Sweden
26 D9 **Orkla** *R* Norway
118 K9 **Orkney** Saskatchewan Canada
87 E11 **Orkney** S Africa
15 F1 **Orkney** *isld* Scotland
37 M2 **Orla** *R* Germany
31 K4 **Orla** *R* Poland
108 D4 **Orla** Texas U.S.A.
37 M2 **Orlamünde** Germany
102 B2 **Orland** California U.S.A.
94 B5 **Orland** Indiana U.S.A.
95 T2 **Orland** Maine U.S.A.
113 F9 **Orlando** Florida U.S.A.
107 N5 **Orlando** Oklahoma U.S.A.
43 F10 **Orlando, C.d'** Sicily
21 N5 **Orléanais** *reg* France
21 O6 **Orléans** France
100 B8 **Orleans** California U.S.A.
110 K3 **Orleans** Indiana U.S.A.
95 S5 **Orleans** Massachusetts U.S.A.
98 K1 **Orleans** Minnesota U.S.A.
98 G9 **Orleans** Nebraska U.S.A.
95 P2 **Orleans** Vermont U.S.A.
121 U6 **Orleans, Île d'** Quebec Canada
Orléansville *see* **Ech Cheliff**
31 J5 **Orlice** *R* Czechoslovakia
56 E5 **Orlik** Russian Federation
31 L6 **Orlová** Czechoslovakia
56 C2 **Orlovka** Russian Federation
55 F3 **Orlovo** Russian Federation
53 E7 **Orlovskaya Oblast'** *prov* Russian Federation
52 F2 **Orlovskiy, Mys** *C* Russian Federation
21 P4 **Orly** *airport* France
74 C10 **Ormara** Pakistan
13 G4 **Ormesby** England
36 C5 **Ormesheim** Germany
21 M8 **Ormes,les** France
119 M9 **Ormiston** Saskatchewan Canada
71 G5 **Ormoc** Philippines
145 F3 **Ormond** New Zealand
113 F8 **Ormond** Florida U.S.A.
113 F8 **Ormond Beach** Florida U.S.A.
145 F4 **Ormondville** New Zealand
38 O9 **Ormož** Slovenia
99 M6 **Ormsby** Minnesota U.S.A.
99 R4 **Ormsby** Wisconsin U.S.A.
26 H7 **Ormsjö** Sweden
13 F6 **Ormskirk** England
121 R7 **Ormstown** Quebec Canada
19 J4 **Ornain** *R* France
19 K5 **Ornans** France
41 H6 **Ornavasso** Italy
37 K5 **Ornbau** Germany
18 E4 **Orne** *dept* France
21 L5 **Orne** *R* France
31 M1 **Orneta** Poland
27 K12 **Orno** Sweden
26 K8 **Örnsköldsvik** Sweden
28 H5 **Orø** Denmark
41 L5 **Orobie, Alpi** *mt* Italy
42 C2 **Orobie, Alpi** *mts* Italy
51 M3 **Orochen** Russian Federation
128 D3 **Orocué** Colombia
85 D6 **Orodara** Burkina
100 J3 **Orofino** Idaho U.S.A.
102 G7 **Oro Grande** California U.S.A.
100 K4 **Orogrande** Idaho U.S.A.
106 D9 **Orogrande** New Mexico U.S.A.
61 P13 **Oroku** Okinawa
122 F8 **Oromocto** New Brunswick Canada
122 F8 **Oromocto L** New Brunswick Canada
79 F8 **Oron** Israel
134 K9 **Orona** *isld* Phoenix Is Pacific Oc
121 M9 **Orono** Ontario Canada
95 T2 **Orono** Maine U.S.A.
110 B4 **Oronogo** Missouri U.S.A.
12 B1 **Oronsay** *isld* Scotland
16 D5 **Oropesa** Spain
127 P2 **Oropuche** *R* Trinidad
59 H1 **Oroqen Zizhiqi** China
71 F6 **Oroquieta** Mindanao
129 L5 **Orós, Açude** *res* Brazil
43 C8 **Orosei** Sardinia
43 C8 **Orosei, G.di** Sardinia
48 F4 **Orosháza** Hungary
48 E3 **Oroszlany** Hungary
51 P2 **Orotukan** Russian Federation
145 E4 **Oroua R** New Zealand
100 H8 **Orovada** Nevada U.S.A.
102 C2 **Oroville** California U.S.A.
100 F1 **Oroville** Washington U.S.A.
101 U7 **Orpha** Wyoming U.S.A.
141 H4 **Orpheus I** Queensland Australia
21 O4 **Orphin** France
19 P16 **Orpierre** France
98 J1 **Orr** North Dakota U.S.A.
107 N7 **Orr** Oklahoma U.S.A.
28 B4 **Ørre** Denmark
27 H15 **Orrefors** Sweden
15 D3 **Orrin** *R* Scotland
98 F1 **Orrin** North Dakota U.S.A.
119 U2 **Orr L** Manitoba Canada
26 G10 **Orrmosjön** *L* Sweden
138 E4 **Orroroo** South Australia Australia
27 J11 **Orrskog** Sweden
94 K6 **Orrstown** Pennsylvania U.S.A.
94 F6 **Orrville** Ohio U.S.A.
27 G10 **Orsa** Sweden
44 H3 **Orsaro** *mt* Italy
21 P4 **Orsay** France
9 G5 **Orsett** England
54 B2 **Orsha** Belorussia
52 G6 **Orshanka** Russian Federation
27 H15 **Örsjö** Sweden
55 C5 **Orsk** Russian Federation
27 F13 **Örslösa** Sweden
28 E2 **Ørsø** Denmark
48 G6 **Orșova** Romania
32 E9 **Orsoy** Germany
26 B9 **Ørsta** Norway
27 J12 **Örsundsbro** Sweden
47 K8 **Ortaca** Turkey
47 J7 **Ortaklar** Turkey
80 G1 **Or Tal** Syria
41 H6 **Orta, L. d'** Italy
26 K7 **Örtäsk** Sweden
42 E6 **Orte** Italy
16 B1 **Ortegal, C** Spain
36 G3 **Ortenberg** Germany
37 P6 **Ortenburg** Germany
30 F1 **Orth** Germany
18 E9 **Orthez** France
45 L4 **Ortignano Raggiolo** Italy
16 B1 **Ortigueira** Spain
28 E5 **Ørting** Denmark
100 C2 **Orting** Washington U.S.A.
124 D3 **Ortiz** Mexico
106 D4 **Ortiz** Colorado U.S.A.
128 E2 **Ortiz** Venezuela
41 N4 **Ortles** *mt* Italy
37 O2 **Ortmannsdorf** Germany
127 P3 **Ortoire R** Trinidad
128 E6 **Orton** *R* Bolivia
13 F5 **Orton** England
42 F6 **Ortona** Italy
98 K4 **Ortonville** Minnesota U.S.A.
57 H4 **Orto-Tokoy** Kyrgyzstan
33 T10 **Ortrand** Germany
32 M7 **Ortze** *R* Germany
51 M2 **Orulgan, Khrebet** *mt* Russian Federation
28 E2 **Ørum** Denmark
28 D4 **Ørum** Denmark
78 K3 **Orūmīyeh** Iran
78 K3 **Orūmīyeh, Daryācheh-ye** *L* Iran
133 D1 **Oruro** Bolivia
145 D1 **Oruru** New Zealand
27 E13 **Orust** *isld* Sweden
77 J3 **Orūzgān** Afghanistan
20 G7 **Orvault** France
42 E6 **Orvieto** Italy
21 O4 **Orvilliers** France
45 N5 **Orvinio** Italy
94 K5 **Orviston** Pennsylvania U.S.A.
95 L3 **Orwell** New York U.S.A.
94 G5 **Orwell** Ohio U.S.A.
95 O3 **Orwell** Vermont U.S.A.
58 G2 **Orxon Gol** *R* China
46 F1 **Oryakhovo** Bulgaria
41 L7 **Orzinuovi** Italy
31 M2 **Orzyc** *R* Poland
31 N2 **Orzysz** Poland
26 E9 **Os** Norway
27 G14 **Os** Sweden
27 E10 **Osa** *R* Norway
119 O9 **Osage** Saskatchewan Canada
99 O6 **Osage** Iowa U.S.A.
107 O5 **Osage** Oklahoma U.S.A.
98 B6 **Osage** Wyoming U.S.A.
107 P3 **Osage City** Kansas U.S.A.
110 D4 **Osage Fork** *R* Missouri U.S.A.
62 **Ōsaka** *conurbation* Japan
55 F5 **Osakarovka** Kazakhstan
99 L4 **Osakis** Minnesota U.S.A.
99 L4 **Osakis L** Minnesota U.S.A.
107 Q3 **Osawatomie** Kansas U.S.A.
120 E3 **Osawin** *R* Ontario Canada
142 F2 **Osborne Is** W Australia Australia
27 G15 **Osby** Sweden
142 F4 **Oscar Ra** W Australia Australia
110 G6 **Osceola** Arkansas U.S.A.
99 N8 **Osceola** Iowa U.S.A.
110 C3 **Osceola** Missouri U.S.A.
98 J8 **Osceola** Nebraska U.S.A.
94 J6 **Osceola** Pennsylvania U.S.A.
99 O4 **Osceola** Wisconsin U.S.A.
33 S10 **Oschatz** Germany
33 O8 **Oschersleben** Germany
94 D2 **Oscoda** Michigan U.S.A.
106 D8 **Oscura** New Mexico U.S.A.
26 E7 **Osen** Norway
54 K2 **Osetr** *R* Russian Federation
60 B13 **Ōse-zaki** *C* Japan
94 B7 **Osgood** Indiana U.S.A.
110 C1 **Osgood** Missouri U.S.A.
121 P7 **Osgoode Station** Ontario Canada
100 H8 **Osgood Mts** Nevada U.S.A.
57 G4 **Osh** Kyrgyzstan
55 F3 **Osha** *R* Russian Federation
87 C9 **Oshakati** Namibia
60 O3 **Oshamambe** Japan
121 M9 **Oshawa** Ontario Canada
60 P1 **Oshidomari** Japan
61 P7 **Oshika-Hantō** *pen* Japan
59 J6 **O-shima** *isld* Japan
61 N11 **Ō-shima** *isld* Japan
98 D8 **Oshkosh** Nebraska U.S.A.
99 S6 **Oshkosh** Wisconsin U.S.A.
52 J2 **Oshkur'ya** Russian Federation
55 D1 **Oshmar'ye** Russian Federation
78 K3 **Oshnoviyeh** Iran
85 E7 **Oshogbo** Nigeria
98 B5 **Oshoto** Wyoming U.S.A.
77 A3 **Oshtorān Kūh** *mt* Iran
52 K2 **Oshvor** Russian Federation
86 C6 **Oshwe** Zaire
46 G1 **Osica** Romania
48 J6 **Osica de Jos** Romania
48 E5 **Osijek** Croatia
45 O4 **Osimo** Italy
56 C4 **Osinniki** Russian Federation
54 B2 **Osintorf** Belorussia
74 E5 **Osiyān** India
26 N3 **Oskal** Norway
99 O8 **Oskaloosa** Iowa U.S.A.
107 P2 **Oskaloosa** Kansas U.S.A.
27 H14 **Oskarshamn** Sweden
27 F15 **Oskarström** Sweden
121 P4 **Oskelaneo** Quebec Canada
54 J7 **Oskol** *R* Rus Fed/Ukraine
31 J6 **Oslava** *R* Czechoslovakia
118 L6 **Osler** Saskatchewan Canada
27 E12 **Oslo** Norway
98 J1 **Oslo** Minnesota U.S.A.
71 F6 **Oslob** Cebu Philippines
27 E13 **Oslofjord** *inlet* Norway
28 C2 **Øsløs** Denmark
54 E2 **Os'ma** *R* Russian Federation
74 G9 **Osmanabad** India
78 E1 **Osmancık** Turkey
47 K4 **Osmaneli** Turkey
52 C5 **Osmino** Russian Federation
27 J13 **Ösmo** Sweden
98 J7 **Osmond** Nebraska U.S.A.
98 H1 **Osnabrock** North Dakota U.S.A.
32 H8 **Osnabrück** Germany
31 H3 **Ośno** Poland
46 E2 **Osogovske Planina** *mt* Macedonia Yugoslavia
41 N7 **Osone** *R* Italy
60 O4 **Osore yama** *mt* Japan
131 A8 **Osorno** *prov* Chile
131 A8 **Osorno** Chile
16 E2 **Osorno** Spain
131 A8 **Osorno, Vol** *pk* Chile
133 C6 **Osorro** *mt* Chile
100 F1 **Osoyoos** British Columbia Canada
44 C4 **Ospedaletti** Italy
117 M7 **Ospika** *R* British Columbia Canada
113 E10 **Osprey** Florida U.S.A.
141 H2 **Osprey Reef** Gt Barrier Reef Aust
9 G5 **Ospringe** England
25 E5 **Oss** Netherlands
46 F5 **Óssa** *mt* Greece
112 F6 **Ossabaw I** Georgia U.S.A.
139 H8 **Ossa, Mt** Tasmania Australia
16 B6 **Ossa, Sa. d'** *mts* Portugal
85 F7 **Osse** *R* Nigeria
99 P5 **Osseo** Wisconsin U.S.A.
38 J8 **Ossiach** Austria
99 P6 **Ossian** Iowa U.S.A.
94 D2 **Ossineke** Michigan U.S.A.
95 O5 **Ossining** New York U.S.A.
95 Q3 **Ossipee L** New Hampshire U.S.A.
27 E10 **Os-sjöen** *L* Norway
32 J8 **Ossning** *hills* Germany
41 H5 **Ossola, Val d'** Italy
51 Q3 **Ossora** Russian Federation
71 N9 **Ossu** Timor
121 M5 **Ostaboningue, L** Quebec Canada
77 A2 **Ostan-e Markazi** Iran
52 E6 **Ostashevo** Russian Federation
52 D6 **Ostashkov** Russian Federation
26 H9 **Östavell** Sweden
32 G8 **Ostbevern** Germany
32 K5 **Oste** *R* Germany
113 F9 **Osteen** Florida U.S.A.
45 L2 **Ostellato** Italy
32 K5 **Osten** Germany
Ostend *see* **Oostende**
32 L7 **Ostenholz** Germany
41 K6 **Osteno** Italy
54 D3 **Oster** *R* Belorussia/Rus Fed
33 P7 **Osterburg** Germany
94 J6 **Osterburg** Pennsylvania U.S.A.
36 G5 **Osterburken** Germany
27 J11 **Österby** Sweden
27 H14 **Österbymo** Sweden
32 H8 **Ostercappeln** Germany
27 G10 **Osterdalälven** *R* Sweden
32 E5 **Osterems** *est* Germany
27 H13 **Östergotland** *county* Sweden
37 P6 **Osterhofen** Germany
32 J6 **Osterholz-Scharmbeck** Germany
38 H6 **Osterhorn Gruppe** *mts* Austria
28 D3 **Øster Hornum** Nordjylland Denmark
27 J11 **Österlövsta** Sweden
26 J7 **Östernoret** Sweden
32 M9 **Osterode** Germany
27 A11 **Osteröy** *isld* Norway
38 H5 **Osterreich** *dist* Austria
26 G8 **Östersund** Sweden
28 H7 **Øster Ulslev** Denmark
27 J11 **Östervåla** Sweden
33 N9 **Osterwieck** Germany
36 G6 **Ostfildern** Germany
27 E12 **Östfold** *reg* Norway
32 F5 **Ostfriesische Inseln** *islds* Germany
32 F6 **Ostfriesland** *reg* Germany
32 G6 **Ostgrossefehn** Germany
27 K11 **Östhammar** Sweden
36 C7 **Ostheim** France
37 J3 **Ostheim** Germany
45 M6 **Ostia** Italy
45 K1 **Ostiglia** Italy
27 F11 **Östmark** Sweden
33 R5 **Ost Peene** *R* Germany
45 O4 **Ostra** Italy
94 D6 **Ostrander** Ohio U.S.A.
37 P1 **Ostrau** Germany
31 L6 **Ostrava** Czechoslovakia
45 O4 **Ostra Vetere** Italy
31 M2 **Ostróda** Poland
31 N2 **Ostrołęka** Poland
120 J5 **Ostrom** Ontario Canada
37 O3 **Ostrov** Czechoslovakia
48 L6 **Ostrov** Romania
52 C6 **Ostrov** Russian Federation
55 F3 **Ostrovnaya** Russian Federation
51 Q2 **Ostrovnoye** Russian Federation
65 J3 **Ostrov Russkiy** *isld* Russian Federation
31 K4 **Ostrów** Poland
31 N5 **Ostrowiec** Poland
31 O4 **Ostrów Lubelski** Poland
31 N3 **Ostrów Mazowiecka** Poland
28 C3 **Østrup** Denmark
37 P5 **Ostrý** *mt* Czechoslovakia
31 K4 **Ostrzeszów** Poland
33 O5 **Ostseebad Boltenhagen** Germany
33 Q4 **Ostseebad Graal-Müritz** Germany
33 P4 **Ostseebad Kühlungsborn** Germany
33 P4 **Ostseebad Nienhagen** Germany
33 P4 **Ostseebad Rerik** Germany
43 H8 **Ostuni** Italy
52 D6 **Osuga** *R* Russian Federation
100 F3 **O'Sullivan Dam** Washington U.S.A.
120 D2 **O'Sullivan, L** Ontario Canada
121 P5 **O'Sullivan, L** Quebec Canada
46 D4 **Osum** *R* Albania
46 G1 **Osūm** *R* Bulgaria
60 D14 **Ōsumi-hantō** *pen* Japan
16 D7 **Osuna** Spain
52 C6 **Osveya** Belorussia
13 G5 **Oswaldkirk** England
94 J5 **Oswayo** Pennsylvania U.S.A.
95 M2 **Oswegalchie** *R* New York U.S.A.
99 S8 **Oswego** Illinois U.S.A.
107 P4 **Oswego** Kansas U.S.A.
101 U1 **Oswego** Montana U.S.A.
95 L3 **Oswego** New York U.S.A.
8 C2 **Oswestry** England
31 L5 **Oświęcim** Poland
111 F10 **Osyka** Mississippi U.S.A.
60 F11 **Ōta** *R* Japan
61 N9 **Ōta** Japan
144 D7 **Otago Peninsula** New Zealand
144 C6 **Otaio** New Zealand
60 F11 **Ōtake** Japan
145 E3 **Otakeho** New Zealand
61 M10 **Ōtaki** Japan
145 E4 **Otaki** New Zealand
61 O8 **Ōtakine-yama** *mt* Japan
145 F3 **Otane** New Zealand
145 F2 **Otanewainuku** New Zealand
29 N7 **Otanmäki** Finland
83 K9 **Otappuwa** Sri Lanka
57 H3 **Otar** Kazakhstan
60 O2 **Otaru** Japan
144 B7 **Otatara** New Zealand
144 B7 **Otautau** New Zealand
30 H6 **Otava** *R* Czechoslovakia
128 C3 **Otavalo** Ecuador
87 C9 **Otavi** Namibia
87 B9 **Otchinjau** Angola
95 M4 **Otego** New York U.S.A.
144 C6 **Otekaieke** New Zealand
48 F5 **Otelec** Romania
48 G5 **Oțelu Roșu** Romania
144 C6 **Otematata** New Zealand
52 C5 **Otepää** Estonia
22 K5 **Othain** *R* France
22 J2 **Othée** Belgium
18 H4 **Othe, Forêt d'** France
100 F3 **Othello** Washington U.S.A.
27 K14 **Othem** Sweden
8 D5 **Othery** England
46 C5 **Othonoí** *isld* Greece
46 F5 **Óthris** *mt* Greece
70 F5 **Oti** Sulawesi
85 E7 **Oti** *R* W Africa
124 G5 **Otinapa** Mexico
144 C5 **Otira** New Zealand
106 H1 **Otis** Colorado U.S.A.
107 L3 **Otis** Kansas U.S.A.
95 O4 **Otis** Massachusetts U.S.A.
95 L4 **Otisco L** New York U.S.A.
122 B1 **Otish Mts** Quebec Canada
95 N5 **Otisville** New York U.S.A.
87 C10 **Otjiwarongo** Namibia
31 K5 **Otmuchów** Poland
60 O3 **Otobe-dake** *mt* Japan
42 G4 **Otočac** Croatia
99 K9 **Otoe** Nebraska U.S.A.
60 R2 **Otofuke** Japan
60 Q1 **Otoineppu** Japan
145 F3 **Otoko** New Zealand
145 E3 **Otorohanga** New Zealand
119 P5 **Otosquen** Saskatchewan Canada
27 C13 **Otra** *R* Norway
126 B1 **Otrabanda** Curaçao
54 H3 **Otradinskiy** Russian Federation
43 J8 **Otranto** Italy
43 J8 **Otranto, C.d'** Italy
46 C4 **Otranto, Str of** Adriatic Sea
94 C2 **Otsego** Michigan U.S.A.
95 N4 **Otsego I** New York U.S.A.
94 C2 **Otsego Lake** Michigan U.S.A.
95 M4 **Otselic, South** New York U.S.A.
60 R3 **Ōtsu** Hokkaido Japan
61 J10 **Ōtsu** Honshu Japan
61 P6 **Ōtsuchi-wan** *B* Japan
61 M10 **Ōtsuki** Japan
26 C10 **Otta** *R* Norway
26 D10 **Otta** Norway
22 L5 **Ottange** France
27 F16 **Ottarp** Sweden
45 Q8 **Ottaviano** Italy
120 D9 **Ottawa** Ontario Canada
99 S8 **Ottawa** Illinois U.S.A.
107 P3 **Ottawa** Kansas U.S.A.
94 C5 **Ottawa** Ohio U.S.A.
115 L6 **Ottawa Is** Northwest Territories Canada
121 L6 **Ottawa R** Ontario/Quebec
32 K9 **Ottbergen** Germany
27 H15 **Ottenby** Sweden
36 H5 **Ottendorf** Germany
37 M2 **Ottendorf-Okrilla** Germany
36 E6 **Ottenhöfen** Germany
38 M5 **Ottenshlag** Austria

212 Pará de Minas — Pensford

130 G6 **Pará de Minas** Brazil
126 A1 **Paradera** Aruba W Indies
121 O4 **Paradis** Quebec Canada
144 B6 **Paradise** New Zealand
102 C2 **Paradise** California U.S.A.
107 M2 **Paradise** Kansas U.S.A.
101 L2 **Paradise** Montana U.S.A.
109 K2 **Paradise** Texas U.S.A.
101 O8 **Paradise** Utah U.S.A.
118 H5 **Paradise Hill** Saskatchewan Canada
116 H5 **Paradise Hill** Alaska U.S.A.
113 L9 **Paradise I.** New Providence I Bahamas
102 G3 **Paradise Pk** Nevada U.S.A.
118 G5 **Paradise Valley** Alberta Canada
100 H8 **Paradise Valley** Nevada U.S.A.
71 J9 **Parado** Sumbawa Indonesia
75 M8 **Pārādwīp** India
110 K2 **Paragon** Indiana U.S.A.
103 M4 **Paragonah** Utah U.S.A.
110 F5 **Paragould** Arkansas U.S.A.
128 F6 **Paraguá** *R* Bolivia
128 F2 **Paragua** *R* Venezuela
130 E8 **Paraguaca Paulista** Brazil
129 L6 **Paraguaçu** *R* Brazil
133 F2 **Paraguai** *R* Paraguay
127 J9 **Paraguaipoa** Venezuela
127 J9 **Paraguaná, Pen. de** Venezuela
130 B10 **Paraguari** *dept* Paraguay
133 F3 **Paraguay** *R* Paraguay
133 F2 **Paraguay** *rep* S America
130 H9 **Paraíba** *state* Brazil
130 G8 **Paraiba do Sul** Brazil
130 H7 **Paraíba, R** Brazil
Parainen *see* **Pargas**
133 G1 **Paraisa** Brazil
85 E7 **Parakou** Benin
138 D4 **Parakylia** South Australia Australia
75 L9 **Paralākhemundi** India
76 D6 **Paramakkudi** India
129 G2 **Paramaribo** Suriname
20 G4 **Paramé** France
131 B4 **Paramillos, Sa. de los** *mts* Argentina
129 K6 **Paramirim** Brazil
46 D5 **Paramithiá** Greece
128 C6 **Paramonga** Peru
133 E4 **Paraná** Argentina
130 D9 **Paraná** *state* Brazil
130 B10 **Paraná** *R* Brazil
130 E9 **Paranaguá** Brazil
133 G1 **Paranaíba** Brazil
130 E6 **Paranaiba, R** Brazil
131 F4 **Paraná Ibicuy** *R* Argentina
131 F2 **Paraná, L** Argentina
129 G2 **Paranam** Suriname
129 H8 **Paranapanema** *R* Brazil
131 F3 **Paraná, R** Argentina
133 G2 **Paranaval** Brazil
46 G3 **Paranéstion** Greece
70 N8 **Parang** *isld* Indonesia
71 E8 **Parang** Philippines
86 F5 **Paranga** Uganda
83 K8 **Parangi Aru** *R* Sri Lanka
76 D5 **Parangipettai** India
83 K8 **Paranthan** Sri Lanka
130 G6 **Paraopeba** Brazil
145 E4 **Paraparaumu** New Zealand
128 F8 **Parapeti** *R* Bolivia
46 F8 **Parapóla** *isld* Greece
128 E2 **Paraque, Cerro** *mt* Venezuela
71 G5 **Parasan** *isld* Philippines
138 E4 **Paratoo** South Australia Australia
129 H5 **Parauapebas** *R* Brazil
18 H6 **Paray-le-Monial** France
56 B3 **Parbig** *R* Russian Federation
122 J3 **Parc Archipelago Mingan** *nat park* Quebec Canada
21 L7 **Parçay-les-Pins** France
20 H5 **Parcé** Ille-et-Vilaine France
21 K6 **Parcé** Sarthe France
55 E5 **Parchevka** Kazakhstan
33 P6 **Parchim** Germany
45 O7 **Parco Naz. del Circeo** Italy
22 C3 **Parcq, le** France
31 O4 **Parczew** Poland
102 D3 **Pardee Res** California U.S.A.
99 R6 **Pardeeville** Wisconsin U.S.A.
80 C4 **Pardes Ḥanna-Karkur** Israel
129 H8 **Pardo** *R* Brazil
130 F4 **Pardo** *R* Minas Gerais Brazil
131 H2 **Pardo** *R* Rio Grande do Sul Brazil
142 C5 **Pardoo** W Australia Australia
130 D7 **Pardo, R** Mato Grosso Brazil
31 J5 **Pardubice** Czechoslovakia
70 O9 **Pare** Java
129 G6 **Parecis** Brazil
128 F6 **Parecis, Sa. dos** *mts* Brazil
133 D3 **Pareditas** Argentina
145 D1 **Parengarenga Harbour** New Zealand
70 C6 **Parenggean** Kalimantan
21 K5 **Parennes** France
121 Q5 **Parent** Quebec Canada
18 E8 **Parentis en Born** France
121 O4 **Parent L** Quebec Canada
144 C6 **Pareora** New Zealand
70 F7 **Parepare** Sulawesi
33 P8 **Parey** Germany
52 F5 **Parfen'yevo** Russian Federation
46 D5 **Párga** Greece
29 J11 **Pargas** Finland
52 D4 **Pargolovo** Russian Federation
127 P4 **Parham** Antigua W Indies
103 N4 **Paria** *R* Utah U.S.A.
128 F1 **Paria, G. of** Venezuela/Trinidad
128 F2 **Pariaguán** Venezuela
69 E13 **Pariaman** Sumatra
128 F1 **Paria, Pen. de** Venezuela
103 M5 **Paria Plat** Arizona U.S.A.
128 E4 **Paricá, L** Brazil
70 G5 **Parigi** Sulawesi
21 L6 **Parigné-l'Eveque** France
128 G2 **Parika** Guyana
144 D5 **Parikawa** New Zealand
145 E3 **Parikino** New Zealand
29 O10 **Parikkala** Finland
128 F3 **Parima, Sa** *mts* Brazil/Venezuela
128 D7 **Parinacocha, L** Peru
128 D4 **Parinari** Peru
128 B4 **Pariñas, Pta** Peru
48 L4 **Parincea** Romania
138 F5 **Paringa** South Australia Australia
129 G4 **Parintins** Brazil
23 **Paris** *conurbation* France
110 C6 **Paris** Arkansas U.S.A.
101 O7 **Paris** Idaho U.S.A.
99 T10 **Paris** Illinois U.S.A.
110 M3 **Paris** Kentucky U.S.A.
110 E2 **Paris** Missouri U.S.A.
110 H5 **Paris** Tennessee U.S.A.
109 M2 **Paris** Texas U.S.A.
95 L3 **Parish** New York U.S.A.
99 W3 **Parisienne, Ile** Ontario Canada
69 E10 **Parit Buntar** Malaysia
71 L10 **Pariti** Timor Indonesia
55 D4 **Parizh** Russian Federation
26 N4 **Parkajoki** Sweden
29 K9 **Parkano** Finland
118 L8 **Parkbeg** Saskatchewan Canada
110 K4 **Park City** Kentucky U.S.A.
101 R4 **Park City** Montana U.S.A.
103 N1 **Park City** Utah U.S.A.
106 E3 **Parkdale** Colorado U.S.A.
100 D4 **Parkdale** Oregon U.S.A.
103 K7 **Parker** Arizona U.S.A.
106 F2 **Parker** Colorado U.S.A.
101 O6 **Parker** Idaho U.S.A.
107 Q3 **Parker** Kansas U.S.A.
98 J6 **Parker** South Dakota U.S.A.
110 L1 **Parker City** Indiana U.S.A.
94 H5 **Parker City** Pennsylvania U.S.A.
103 K7 **Parker Dam** California U.S.A.
143 D9 **Parker Hill** W Australia Australia
140 E3 **Parker Pt** Queensland Australia
143 C9 **Parker Range** W Australia Australia
99 O7 **Parkersburg** Iowa U.S.A.
94 F7 **Parkersburg** West Virginia U.S.A.
99 L3 **Parkers Prairie** Minnesota U.S.A.
119 O7 **Parkerview** Saskatchewan Canada
139 J5 **Parkes** New South Wales Australia
95 M6 **Parkesburg** Pennsylvania U.S.A.
99 Q4 **Park Falls** Wisconsin U.S.A.
102 D6 **Parkfield** California U.S.A.
12 E3 **Parkgate** Scotland
95 L8 **Park Hall** Maryland U.S.A.
57 E5 **Parkhar** Tajikistan
120 J9 **Parkhill** Ontario Canada
26 K5 **Parkijaur** *L* Sweden
110 F6 **Parkin** Arkansas U.S.A.
118 E9 **Park Lake Prov. Park** Alberta Canada
118 D8 **Parkland** Alberta Canada
119 Q9 **Parkman** Saskatchewan Canada
101 S5 **Parkman** Wyoming U.S.A.
99 L3 **Park Rapids** Minnesota U.S.A.
99 T8 **Park Ridge** Illinois U.S.A.
98 J1 **Park River** North Dakota U.S.A.
103 N6 **Parks** Arizona U.S.A.
98 E9 **Parks** Nebraska U.S.A.
111 L13 **Parks Airport** St Louis
118 L5 **Parkside** Saskatchewan Canada
95 M9 **Parksley** Virginia U.S.A.
140 C6 **Parks, Mt** N Terr Australia
109 K2 **Park Springs** Texas U.S.A.
37 N4 **Parkstein** Germany
98 J6 **Parkston** South Dakota U.S.A.
95 L7 **Parkton** Maryland U.S.A.
112 H3 **Parkton** North Carolina U.S.A.
101 M8 **Park Valley** Utah U.S.A.
106 D1 **Park View Mt** Colorado U.S.A.
100 D3 **Parkway** Washington U.S.A.
26 K5 **Pärlälven** *R* Sweden
127 M1 **Parlatuvier** Tobago
74 G9 **Parli Vaijnāth** India
45 H2 **Parma** *R* Italy
45 H2 **Parma** Italy
100 J6 **Parma** Idaho U.S.A.
94 C4 **Parma** Michigan U.S.A.
110 G5 **Parma** Missouri U.S.A.
94 F5 **Parma** Ohio U.S.A.
129 K6 **Parnaguá** Brazil
129 K4 **Parnaíba** Brazil
129 J5 **Parnaíba** *R* Brazil
46 F6 **Parnassós** *mt* Greece
144 D5 **Parnassus** New Zealand
99 O8 **Parnell** Iowa U.S.A.
99 M9 **Parnell** Missouri U.S.A.
108 G1 **Parnell** Texas U.S.A.
46 F6 **Párnis** *mt* Greece
46 F7 **Párnon Óros** *mts* Greece
52 B5 **Pärnu** Estonia
52 B5 **Pärnu laht** *G* Estonia
144 C5 **Paroa** New Zealand
59 M1 **Paromay** Russian Federation
110 D7 **Paron** Arkansas U.S.A.
141 G8 **Paroo** *R* Queensland Australia
139 G4 **Paroo Chan** New South Wales Australia
77 G2 **Paropamisus** *mts* Afghanistan
70 F6 **Paroreang, Bk** *mt* Sulawesi
46 G7 **Páros** *isld* Greece
127 J3 **Parottee Pt** Jamaica
103 M4 **Parowan** Utah U.S.A.
129 H6 **Parque Indigena do Xingu** *nat park* Brazil
99 T8 **Parr** Indiana U.S.A.
112 F3 **Parr** South Carolina U.S.A.
8 C5 **Parracombe** England
133 C5 **Parral** Chile
139 K5 **Parramatta** New South Wales Australia
95 M9 **Parramore I** Virginia U.S.A.
124 H5 **Parras de la Fuente** Mexico
8 D5 **Parrett, R** England
111 J8 **Parrish** Alabama U.S.A.
113 E10 **Parrish** Florida U.S.A.
112 G5 **Parris I** South Carolina U.S.A.
112 C6 **Parrott** Georgia U.S.A.
94 G9 **Parrott** Virginia U.S.A.
122 H8 **Parrsboro** Nova Scotia Canada
119 N9 **Parry** Saskatchewan Canada
115 L4 **Parry B** Northwest Territories Canada
120 K7 **Parry I** Ontario Canada
114 H2 **Parry Is** Northwest Territories Canada
115 M2 **Parry, Kap** Greenland
127 N3 **Parrylands** Trinidad
142 B5 **Parry Ra** W Australia Australia
77 B6 **Pars** *oil well* Persian Gulf
33 N7 **Parsau** Germany
37 M5 **Parsberg** Germany
41 M3 **Parseier Spitze** *mt* Austria
98 D2 **Parshall** North Dakota U.S.A.
103 K3 **Parsnip Pk** Nevada U.S.A.
107 P4 **Parsons** Kansas U.S.A.
110 H6 **Parsons** Tennessee U.S.A.
94 H7 **Parsons** West Virginia U.S.A.
123 P3 **Parson's Pond** Newfoundland Canada
43 E11 **Partanna** Sicily
26 J4 **Pårtefjället** *mt* Sweden
36 E4 **Partenheim** Germany
21 K8 **Parthenay** France
46 F7 **Parthénion** Greece
124 D5 **Partida** *isld* Mexico
43 E10 **Partinico** Sicily
56 D2 **Partizansk** Russian Federation
59 K3 **Partizansk** Russian Federation
120 K2 **Partridge** *R* Ontario Canada
107 M4 **Partridge** Kansas U.S.A.
123 R5 **Partridgeberry Hills** Newfoundland Canada
119 U1 **Partridge Breast L** Manitoba Canada
123 Q3 **Partridge Pt** Newfoundland Canada
129 H4 **Paru** *R* Brazil
145 E1 **Parua Bay** New Zealand
77 L2 **Parvan** *prov* Afghanistan
66 C6 **Paryang** China
27 H15 **Påryd** Sweden
89 E6 **Parys** S Africa
102 G7 **Pasadena** California U.S.A.
109 G9 **Pasadena** Texas U.S.A.
128 B4 **Pasado, C** Ecuador
133 E3 **Pasaje** *R* Argentina
124 H5 **Pasaje** Mexico
106 G5 **Pasamonte** New Mexico U.S.A.
70 F5 **Pasangkaiu** Sulawesi
69 E14 **Pasarbantal** Sumatra
77 C4 **Pasargadae** Iran
69 E14 **Pasarseblat** Sumatra
71 H7 **Pasarwadjo** Indonesia
111 H11 **Pascagoula** *R* Mississippi U.S.A.
121 N4 **Pascalis** Quebec Canada
48 K3 **Paşcani** Romania
128 C6 **Pasco** *dept* Peru
100 F3 **Pasco** Washington U.S.A.
95 Q5 **Pascoag** Rhode I U.S.A.
130 H5 **Pascoal, Mte** Brazil
142 B5 **Pascoe I** W Australia Australia
140 E3 **Pascoe Inlet** Queensland Australia
141 G2 **Pascoe, R** Queensland Australia
120 A2 **Pascopee** Ontario Canada
133 C7 **Pascua** *R* Chile
18 G2 **Pas-de-Calais** *dept* France
22 C3 **Pas en Artois** France
33 T5 **Pasewalk** Germany
52 D4 **Pasha** Russian Federation
52 J3 **Pashnya** Russian Federation
71 E3 **Pasig** Luzon Philippines
71 J4 **Pasige** *isld* Indonesia
78 H1 **Pasinler** Turkey
70 O10 **Pasirian** Java
69 E12 **Pasirpangarayan** Sumatra
69 F10 **Pasir Putih** Malaysia
71 K8 **Pasitelu, Pulau Pulau** *islds* Indonesia
27 H14 **Påskallavik** Sweden
102 B2 **Paskenta** California U.S.A.
31 M1 **Pasłęk** Poland
143 E10 **Pasley, C** W Australia Australia
29 L4 **Pasmajärvi** Finland
42 G5 **Pašman** *isld* Croatia
138 E4 **Pasmore** *R* South Australia Australia
77 H7 **Pasni** Pakistan
133 D6 **Paso de Indios** Argentina
125 M4 **Paso del Cascal** *mt* Nicaragua
133 F3 **Paso de los Libres** Argentina
133 F4 **Paso de los Toros** Uruguay
130 B10 **Paso de Patria** Paraguay
68 B2 **Pasok** Burma
133 C6 **Paso Limay** Argentina
125 M2 **Paso Reál** Honduras
133 C7 **Paso Rio Mayo** Argentina
102 D6 **Paso Robles** California U.S.A.
122 G5 **Paspébiac** Quebec Canada
119 M8 **Pasqua** Saskatchewan Canada
119 O5 **Pasquia Hills** Saskatchewan Canada
119 Q5 **Pasquia R** Manitoba Canada
112 L1 **Pasquotank R** North Carolina U.S.A.
77 C5 **Pas Rūdak** Iran
95 T1 **Passadumkeag** Maine U.S.A.
20 F8 **Passage du Gois** France
120 B4 **Passage I** Ontario Canada
99 S1 **Passage I** Michigan U.S.A.
113 E10 **Pass-a-Grille Beach** Florida U.S.A.
95 N6 **Passaic** New Jersey U.S.A.
21 J4 **Passais** France
38 H4 **Passau** Germany
40 D2 **Passavant** France
111 G11 **Pass Christian** Mississippi U.S.A.
101 T8 **Pass Cr** Wyoming U.S.A.
22 E2 **Passendale** Belgium
43 G12 **Passero, C** Sicily
123 Q6 **Pass I** Newfoundland Canada
71 F5 **Passi** Philippines
41 O4 **Passiria, Val** Italy
99 S1 **Pass L** Ontario Canada
120 B4 **Pass Lake** Ontario Canada
15 C4 **Pass of Brander** Scotland
133 H2 **Passos** Brazil
128 C4 **Pastaza** *prov* Ecuador
122 F3 **Pasteur, L** Quebec Canada
128 C3 **Pasto** Colombia
116 F5 **Pastol B** Alaska U.S.A.
9 H2 **Paston** England
103 P5 **Pastora Pk** Arizona U.S.A.
129 K5 **Pastos Bons** Brazil
71 E1 **Pasuquin** Luzon Philippines
70 O9 **Pasuruan** Java
52 B6 **Pasvalys** Lithuania
52 C1 **Pasvikelv** *R* Norway
119 O6 **Paswegin** Saskatchewan Canada
31 M2 **Pasym** Poland
48 F3 **Pásztó** Hungary
86 D4 **Pata** Cent Afr Republic
71 E8 **Pata** *isld* Philippines
133 C7 **Patagonia** *terr* Chile/Arg
103 O10 **Patagonia** Arizona U.S.A.
100 H3 **Pataha** *R* Washington U.S.A.
77 K1 **Pata Kesar** Afghanistan
130 G10 **Patamuté** Brazil
75 L5 **Patan** Nepal
71 B2 **Patani** Indonesia
95 L7 **Patapsco** *R* Maryland U.S.A.
21 O5 **Patay** France
138 F6 **Patchewollock** Victoria Australia
95 P6 **Patchogue** Long I, New York U.S.A.
88 H3 **Pate** *isld* Kenya
145 E3 **Patea** New Zealand
144 C6 **Patearoa** New Zealand
85 F7 **Pategi** Nigeria
43 F11 **Paternò** Sicily
45 R8 **Paternopoli** Italy
100 F1 **Pateros** Washington U.S.A.
141 H8 **Paterson** *R* Queensland Australia
95 N6 **Paterson** New Jersey U.S.A.
100 F4 **Paterson** Washington U.S.A.
144 B7 **Paterson Inlet** New Zealand
142 D5 **Paterson Ra** W Australia Australia
25 G2 **Paterswolde** Netherlands
74 F2 **Pathankot** India
74 F9 **Pathardi** India
Pathein *see* **Bassein**
101 T7 **Pathfinder Res** Wyoming U.S.A.
13 F2 **Pathhead** Lothian Scotland
12 D3 **Pathhead** Strathclyde Scotland
68 D7 **Pathiu** Thailand
119 N6 **Pathlow** Saskatchewan Canada
74 G9 **Pathri** India
68 E5 **Pathum Thani** Thailand
70 N9 **Pati** Java
128 C3 **Patia** *R* Colombia
74 G3 **Patiala** India
143 F6 **Patience Well** W Australia Australia
70 G7 **Patiro Tg** *C* Sulawesi
128 C6 **Pativilca** Peru
70 N10 **Patjitan** Java
75 Q5 **Pātkai Bum** *reg* India
109 M2 **Pat Mayse Res** Texas U.S.A.
47 H7 **Pátmos** *isld* Greece
111 C8 **Patmos** Arkansas U.S.A.
75 L6 **Patna** India
12 D3 **Patna** Scotland
75 K8 **Patnagarh** India
71 F3 **Patnanongan** *isld* Luzon Philippines
78 J2 **Patnos** Turkey
145 F3 **Patoka** New Zealand
110 G3 **Patoka** Illinois U.S.A.
110 K3 **Patoka** *R* Indiana U.S.A.
99 M7 **Paton** Iowa U.S.A.
130 H9 **Patos** Brazil
129 J7 **Patos de Minas** Brazil
127 N1 **Patos, I** Trinidad
100 C1 **Patos I** Washington U.S.A.
131 H3 **Patos, Lagoa dos** Brazil
108 A5 **Patos, Laguna de** Mexico
131 E3 **Patos, L. de los** Santa Fé Argentina
131 B3 **Patos, R. de los** Argentina
133 D4 **Patquia** Argentina
46 E6 **Pátrai** Greece
Patras Greece *see* **Pátrai**
28 R9 **Patreksfjördhur** *inlet* Iceland
118 F8 **Patricia** Alberta Canada
98 E6 **Patricia** South Dakota U.S.A.
140 B5 **Patricia, Mt** N Terr Australia
133 B7 **Patricio Lynch, I** Chile
13 G5 **Patrick Brompton** England
121 T7 **Patrie, La** Quebec Canada
110 M3 **Patriot** Indiana U.S.A.
133 H1 **Patrocinio** Brazil
111 K10 **Patsaliga** *R* Alabama U.S.A.
41 O3 **Patscherkofel** *mt* Austria
52 C1 **Patsoyoki** *R* Russian Federation
43 C8 **Pattada** Sardinia
57 D6 **Pattakesar** Uzbekistan
70 F7 **Pattalasa** Sulawesi Indonesia
76 C6 **Pattanapuram** India
69 E9 **Pattani** *R* Thailand
69 E9 **Pattani** Thailand
95 S7 **Patten** Maine U.S.A.
32 L8 **Pattensen** Germany
13 F5 **Patterdale** England
102 C4 **Patterson** California U.S.A.
112 E6 **Patterson** Georgia U.S.A.
101 M5 **Patterson** Idaho U.S.A.
111 E12 **Patterson** Louisiana U.S.A.
94 H7 **Patterson Cr** West Virginia U.S.A.
117 F3 **Patterson, Mt** Yukon Territory Canada
102 E5 **Patterson Mt** California U.S.A.
99 V4 **Patterson, Pt** Michigan U.S.A.
71 N9 **Patti** Indonesia
43 F10 **Patti** Sicily
140 B4 **Pattie Cr** N Terr Australia
43 G10 **Patti, G. di** Sicily
80 B8 **Pattish** *R* Israel
111 F10 **Pattison** Mississippi U.S.A.
94 J6 **Patton** Pennsylvania U.S.A.
99 M9 **Pattonsburg** Missouri U.S.A.
130 H9 **Patu** Brazil
78 H2 **Patu** Turkey
75 O7 **Patuakhali** Bangladesh
118 K3 **Patuanak** Saskatchewan Canada
48 H6 **Pătuele** Romania
70 L9 **Patuha, G** *mt* Java
117 J7 **Patullo, Mt** British Columbia Canada
144 D4 **Paturau River** New Zealand
145 F3 **Patutahi** New Zealand
145 E3 **Patutu** *mt* New Zealand
95 L8 **Patuxent** *R* Maryland U.S.A.
18 E9 **Pau** France
145 D1 **Paua** New Zealand
129 J5 **Pau D'Arco** Brazil
21 O7 **Paudy** France
121 O7 **Paugan Falls** Quebec Canada
18 E7 **Pauillac** France
128 E5 **Pauini** Brazil
68 B2 **Pauk** Burma
68 A2 **Pauktaw** Burma
101 M7 **Paul** Idaho U.S.A.
38 H8 **Paularo** Italy
114 G4 **Paulatuk** Northwest Territories Canada
103 M7 **Paulden** Arizona U.S.A.
94 C5 **Paulding** Ohio U.S.A.
18 H9 **Paulhan** France
115 N6 **Paul I** Labrador, Nfld Canada
116 H9 **Paul I** Alaska U.S.A.
100 F5 **Paulina** Oregon U.S.A.
33 R7 **Paulinenaue** Germany
Paulis *see* **Isiro**
130 J9 **Paulista** Brazil
129 K5 **Paulistana** Brazil
99 L7 **Paullina** Iowa U.S.A.
41 K7 **Paullo** Italy
21 N8 **Paulnay** France
130 H10 **Paulo Alfonso, Cachoeira de** *falls* Brazil
25 C3 **Paulowna** Netherlands
107 N7 **Pauls Valley** Oklahoma U.S.A.
37 M5 **Paulushofen** Germany
20 G8 **Paulx** France
68 C4 **Paung** Burma
68 B3 **Paungde** Burma
74 H8 **Pauni** India
74 H3 **Pauri** India
37 M2 **Pausa** Germany
128 D7 **Pausa** Peru
33 S7 **Pausin** Germany
128 D2 **Pauto** *R* Colombia
26 J7 **Pauträsk** Sweden
22 G5 **Pauvres** France
135 T3 **Pauwela** Hawaiian Is
103 M3 **Pavant Ra** Utah U.S.A.
55 C2 **Pavda** Russian Federation
46 G2 **Pavel Banya** Bulgaria
54 L3 **Pavelets** Russian Federation
44 F1 **Pavia** Italy
117 N10 **Pavilion** British Columbia Canada
94 K4 **Pavilion** New York U.S.A.
101 R6 **Pavillion** Wyoming U.S.A.
21 M2 **Pavilly** France
27 M15 **Pāvilosta** Latvia
52 G5 **Pavino** Russian Federation
46 G1 **Pavlikeni** Bulgaria
55 G4 **Pavlodar** Kazakhstan
116 G9 **Pavlof** Alaska U.S.A.
116 F9 **Pavlof Harbour** Aleutian Is
116 G9 **Pavlof Vol** Alaska U.S.A.
54 G8 **Pavlograd** Ukraine
55 F4 **Pavlogradka** Russian Federation
55 F5 **Pavlovka** Kazakhstan
55 C3 **Pavlovka** Bashkirskaya Respublika Russian Federation
52 F6 **Pavlovo** Russian Federation
56 B4 **Pavlovsk** Altayskiy Kray Russian Federation
52 D5 **Pavlovsk** Leningradskaya obl Russian Federation
55 D4 **Pavlovskiy** Kazakhstan
52 H5 **Pavlovskiy** Permskaya obl Russian Federation
113 D7 **Pavo** Georgia U.S.A.
45 J3 **Pavullo nel Frignano** Italy
107 O5 **Pawhuska** Oklahoma U.S.A.
119 Q3 **Pawistik** Manitoba Canada
95 O3 **Pawlet** Vermont U.S.A.
8 D5 **Pawlett** England
112 H4 **Pawleys Island** South Carolina U.S.A.
68 C3 **Pawn** *R* Burma
99 R10 **Pawnee** Illinois U.S.A.
107 O5 **Pawnee** Oklahoma U.S.A.
109 K7 **Pawnee** Texas U.S.A.
99 L9 **Pawnee City** Nebraska U.S.A.
98 C9 **Pawnee Cr** Colorado U.S.A.
107 L3 **Pawnee Rock** Kansas U.S.A.
94 B4 **Paw Paw** Michigan U.S.A.
94 J7 **Paw Paw** West Virginia U.S.A.
95 Q5 **Pawtucket** Rhode I U.S.A.
46 G9 **Paximádhia** *isld* Crete Greece
Paxoi *see* **Paxos**
47 P13 **Paxos** *isld* Greece
116 P5 **Paxson** Alaska U.S.A.
116 P5 **Paxson L** Alaska U.S.A.
99 S9 **Paxton** Illinois U.S.A.
98 E8 **Paxton** Nebraska U.S.A.
68 C4 **Payagyi** Burma
71 A2 **Payahe** Halmahera Indonesia
79 G2 **Payas** Turkey
58 E3 **Pa-yen-kao-le** China
40 E4 **Payerne** Switzerland
100 J5 **Payette** *R* Idaho U.S.A.
100 J5 **Payette** Idaho U.S.A.
109 L3 **Pay Hubbard, L** Texas U.S.A.
50 F2 **Pay-Khoy, Khrebet** *mt* Russian Federation
112 D5 **Payne** Georgia U.S.A.
94 C5 **Payne** Ohio U.S.A.
115 M6 **Payne, L** Quebec Canada
102 C1 **Paynes Cr** California U.S.A.
143 C8 **Payne's Find** W Australia Australia
99 M4 **Paynesville** Minnesota U.S.A.
118 J5 **Paynton** Saskatchewan Canada
131 F4 **Paysandu** Uruguay
21 K3 **Pays-d'Auge** *reg* France
21 O2 **Pays-de-Bray** *reg* France
19 N13 **Pays de Dombes** *reg* France
40 F5 **Pays d'Enhaut** Switzerland
103 N7 **Payson** Arizona U.S.A.
103 N1 **Payson** Utah U.S.A.
57 K6 **Paytug** Uzbekistan
131 B6 **Payún** *vol* Argentina
70 C3 **Payung Tanjong** *C* Sarawak
131 B6 **Payún Matru, Cerros** *hills* Argentina
77 A4 **Pāzanūn** Iran
46 G2 **Pazardzhik** Bulgaria
47 J5 **Pazarköy** Turkey
47 J6 **Pazaryeri** Turkey
124 D5 **Paz, B. de la** Mexico
128 D2 **Paz de Rio** Colombia
42 F3 **Pazin** Croatia
41 M3 **Paznauntal** Austria
52 D5 **Pchevzha** Russian Federation
31 M6 **Pcim** Poland
46 E2 **Pčinja** *R* Serbia/Macedonia Yugoslavia
68 D6 **Pe** Burma
111 L10 **Pea** *R* Alabama U.S.A.
117 R6 **Peace Point** Alberta Canada
118 A2 **Peace R** Alberta Canada
117 M7 **Peace R** Br Col/Alberta Canada
113 F10 **Peace R** Florida U.S.A.
117 P7 **Peace River** Alberta Canada
117 O11 **Peachland** British Columbia Canada
103 L6 **Peach Sp** Arizona U.S.A.
94 B2 **Peacock** Michigan U.S.A.
141 J5 **Peak Downs** Queensland Australia
138 D3 **Peake** *R* South Australia Australia
71 D5 **Peaked Pt** Philippines
140 B3 **Peake, Mt** N Terr Australia
143 C7 **Peak Hill** W Australia Australia
102 E7 **Peak Mt** California U.S.A.
141 J6 **Peak Ra** Queensland Australia
103 P3 **Peale, Mt** Utah U.S.A.
100 B9 **Peanut** California U.S.A.
118 D9 **Pearce** Alberta Canada
103 P10 **Pearce** Arizona U.S.A.
140 A2 **Pearce Pt** N Terr Australia
111 C7 **Pearcy** Arkansas U.S.A.
116 H1 **Peard B** Alaska U.S.A.
110 C5 **Pea Ridge Nat. Mil. Park** Arkansas U.S.A.
119 P2 **Pearl** Ontario Canada
110 F2 **Pearl** Illinois U.S.A.
111 F9 **Pearl** Mississippi U.S.A.
111 G11 **Pearl** *R* Miss/Louisiana U.S.A.
109 G10 **Pearland** Texas U.S.A.
134 K5 **Pearl and Hermes Atoll** Hawaiian Is U.S.A.
102 S12 **Pearl City** Hawaiian Is
99 R7 **Pearl City** Illinois U.S.A.
102 S12 **Pearl Hbr** Hawaiian Is
144 A7 **Pearl I** New Zealand
109 H7 **Pearsall** Texas U.S.A.
112 E6 **Pearson** Georgia U.S.A.
138 C5 **Pearson Is** South Australia Australia
119 V2 **Pearson L** Manitoba Canada
114 J2 **Peary Ch** Northwest Territories Canada
109 H1 **Pease** *R* Texas U.S.A.
20 F6 **Péaule** France
99 S3 **Peavy Falls Res** Michigan U.S.A.
142 C5 **Peawah, R** W Australia Australia
88 G10 **Pebane** Mozambique
128 D4 **Pebas** Peru
133 F8 **Pebble I** Falkland Is
70 G5 **Pebengko** Sulawesi
46 D2 **Peć** Serbia Yugoslavia
111 D12 **Pecan Island** Louisiana U.S.A.
130 E9 **Peças, I. das** Brazil
99 R7 **Pecatonica** *R* Illinois U.S.A.
99 R7 **Pecatonica** Illinois U.S.A.
45 J4 **Péccioli** Italy
48 L5 **Pechea** Romania
48 J2 **Pechenezhin** Ukraine
54 H6 **Pechenezhskoye Vodokhranilishche** *res* Ukraine
29 P2 **Pechenga** Russian Federation
55 D1 **Pecherakh** Russian Federation
52 J2 **Pechora** Russian Federation
52 J3 **Pechora** *R* Russian Federation
50 E2 **Pechorskaya Guba** *sea* Russian Federation
52 C5 **Pechory** Russian Federation
48 G4 **Pecica** Romania
100 B7 **Peck** Oregon U.S.A.
33 S5 **Peckatel** Germany
32 K9 **Peckelsheim** Germany
43 B9 **Pecora, C** Sardinia
43 G10 **Pecoraro, M** *mt* Italy
106 E6 **Pecos** New Mexico U.S.A.
106 F6 **Pecos** *R* New Mexico U.S.A.
108 D4 **Pecos** Texas U.S.A.
108 F5 **Pecos** *R* Texas/Mexico U.S.A./Mexico
106 E6 **Pecos Nat. Mon** New Mexico U.S.A.
48 E4 **Pécs** Hungary
48 E4 **Pécsvárad** Hungary
110 B3 **Peculiar** Missouri U.S.A.
125 O6 **Pedasí** Panama
139 H9 **Pedder, L** Tasmania Australia
100 B5 **Pedee** Oregon U.S.A.
127 J5 **Pedernales** Dominican Rep
124 F3 **Pedernales** Mexico
127 N10 **Pedernales** Venezuela
28 H6 **Pedersborg** Denmark
70 L9 **Pedes** Java
79 C4 **Pedhoulas** Cyprus
138 D2 **Pedirka** South Australia Australia
71 A2 **Pediwang** Indonesia
129 K7 **Pedra Azul** Brazil
130 J9 **Pedra, Pta. de** *C* Brazil
128 F6 **Pedras Negras** Brazil
124 H5 **Pedriceña** Mexico
129 J5 **Pedro Afonso** Brazil
126 E6 **Pedro Bank** Caribbean
116 K7 **Pedro Bay** Alaska U.S.A.
126 D3 **Pedro Betancourt** Cuba
126 F6 **Pedro Cays** *reefs* Caribbean
Peebles *co see* **Borders** *reg*
140 D7 **Peebles, Mt** N Terr Australia
142 B5 **Peedamulla** W Australia Australia
12 D5 **Peel** I of Man U.K.
144 C5 **Peel, Mt** New Zealand
103 M7 **Peeples Valley** Arizona U.S.A.
117 Q7 **Peerless L** Alberta Canada
118 A5 **Peers** Alberta Canada
139 G4 **Peery, L** New South Wales Australia
106 G1 **Peetz** Colorado U.S.A.
98 K4 **Peever** South Dakota U.S.A.
144 D5 **Pegasus Bay** New Zealand
37 N1 **Pegau** Germany
38 M7 **Peggau** Austria
44 E3 **Pegli** Italy
37 M4 **Pegnitz** Germany
17 G6 **Pego** Spain
45 J2 **Pegognaga** Italy
101 O7 **Pegram** Idaho U.S.A.
13 G3 **Pegswood** England
69 F13 **Peg Tigabuluh** *mt* Sumatra
68 C4 **Pegu** Burma
69 E13 **Pegunungan Barisan** *mt* Sumatra
69 K12 **Pegunungan Bayang** *mt* Indonesia
68 B3 **Pegu Yoma** *ra* Burma
9 H5 **Pegwell B** England
52 H3 **Pegysh** Russian Federation
46 F3 **Pehčevo** Macedonia Yugoslavia
67 B1 **Peijiangchang** China
67 G3 **Pei-Kan-t'ang Tao** *isld* Taiwan
20 F6 **Peillac** France
38 M5 **Peilstein** *mt* Austria
32 M8 **Peine** Germany
133 C8 **Peineta** *mt* Chile
68 B2 **Peinwa** Burma
19 P16 **Peipin** France
Peipsi Järv *see* **Peipus, L**
52 C5 **Peipus, L** Estonia/Rus Fed
41 N2 **Peiting** Germany
133 G2 **Peixe** *R* Brazil
130 C5 **Peixe de Couro, R** Brazil
65 C7 **Pei Xian** China
65 D7 **Pei Xian** China
69 H12 **Pejantan** *isld* Indonesia
48 G6 **Pek** *R* Serbia Yugoslavia
70 F6 **Pekabata** Sulawesi
70 M9 **Pekalongan** Java
69 F11 **Pekan** Malaysia
69 E12 **Pekanbaru** Sumatra
99 R9 **Pekin** Illinois U.S.A.
110 G1 **Pekin** Illinois U.S.A.
98 H2 **Pekin** North Dakota U.S.A.
Peking *see* **Beijing**
117 Q10 **Pekisko** Alberta Canada
29 M5 **Pekkala** Finland
68 C3 **Pekon** Burma
69 E11 **Pelabuhan Kelang** Malaysia
43 E13 **Pelagie, Isole** Italy
45 L4 **Pelago** Italy
46 G5 **Pélagos** *isld* Greece
111 G9 **Pelahatchee** Mississippi U.S.A.
69 F12 **Pelalawan** Sumatra
17 G4 **Pelarda, Sa** *mts* Spain
46 F6 **Pelasyía** Greece
89 F7 **Pelatsoeu** *mt* Lesotho
70 F4 **Pelawanbesar** Kalimantan
31 J2 **Pełczyce** Poland
48 H5 **Peleaga** *mt* Romania
56 H2 **Peleduy** *R* Russian Federation
120 H10 **Pelee Island** Ontario Canada
127 L4 **Pelée, Mt** Martinique W Indies
47 O12 **Pélekas** Greece
71 H5 **Peleng** *isld* Indonesia
71 H5 **Peleng, Selat** *str* Sulawesi
71 H5 **Peleng, Tk** *B* Indonesia
112 C6 **Pelham** Georgia U.S.A.
31 J6 **Pelhřimov** Czechoslovakia
119 R6 **Pelican B** Manitoba Canada
113 L11 **Pelican Harbour** Bahamas
118 D3 **Pelican L** Alberta Canada
119 S9 **Pelican L** Manitoba Canada
119 O3 **Pelican L** Saskatchewan Canada
99 O1 **Pelican L** Minnesota U.S.A.
99 R4 **Pelican L** Wisconsin U.S.A.
118 E3 **Pelican Portage** Alberta Canada
141 G3 **Pelican R** Queensland Australia
119 R6 **Pelican Rapids** Manitoba Canada
98 K3 **Pelican Rapids** Minnesota U.S.A.
48 L3 **Peliniya** Moldavia
59 L1 **Peliny Osipenko, imeni** Russian Federation
112 F4 **Pelion** South Carolina U.S.A.
26 J5 **Peljekaise Nat. Park** Sweden
42 H6 **Pelješac** *pen* Croatia
29 N4 **Pelkosenniemi** Finland
52 D3 **Pelkula** Russian Federation
32 G9 **Pelkum** Germany
43 G8 **Pella** Italy
80 F4 **Pella** Jordan
99 O8 **Pella** Iowa U.S.A.
111 K8 **Pell City** Alabama U.S.A.
133 E5 **Pellegrini** Argentina
133 D5 **Pellegrini, L** Argentina
21 H5 **Pellerine, la** France
20 G7 **Pellerin, le** France
45 M1 **Pellestrina** Italy
119 U2 **Pelletier L** Manitoba Canada
21 N8 **Pellevoisin** France
140 D3 **Pellew C** N Terr Australia
36 B4 **Pellingen** Germany
29 L5 **Pello** Finland
21 K6 **Pellouailles** France
94 C1 **Pellston** Michigan U.S.A.
30 D1 **Pellworm** *isld* Germany
119 Q7 **Pelly** Saskatchewan Canada
117 E4 **Pelly** *R* Yukon Territory Canada
115 L4 **Pelly Bay** Northwest Territories Canada
117 E4 **Pelly Crossing** Yukon Territory Canada
114 J4 **Pelly L** Northwest Territories Canada
117 G5 **Pelly Mts** Yukon Territory Canada
71 J8 **Pelokang** *isld* Indonesia
46 E7 **Pelopónnisos** *admin region* Greece
43 G11 **Peloritani, Mi** *mts* Sicily
145 D4 **Pelorus Sound** New Zealand
131 H3 **Pelotas** Brazil
130 D10 **Pelotas, R.das** Brazil
46 G1 **Pelovo** Bulgaria
31 L2 **Pelplin** Poland
143 A8 **Pelsart Group** *islds* W Australia Australia
33 T5 **Pelsin** Germany
110 C6 **Pelsor** Arkansas U.S.A.
29 L3 **Peltovuoma** Finland
44 B2 **Pelvo d'Elva** *mt* Italy
19 Q15 **Pelvoux, Mt** France
55 D1 **Pelym** *R* Russian Federation
55 D2 **Pelym** Russian Federation
55 D1 **Pelymskiy Tuman, Oz** *L* Russian Federation
8 B7 **Pelynt** England
112 E3 **Pelzer** South Carolina U.S.A.
33 N4 **Pelzerhaken** Germany
120 G5 **Pemache, R** Ontario Canada
95 S1 **Pemadumcook L** Maine U.S.A.
70 M9 **Pemalang** Java
70 M9 **Pemalang, Ujung** *C* Java
71 H5 **Pemali, Tg** *C* Sulawesi
69 J12 **Pemangkat** Indonesia
70 E5 **Pemarung, P** Kalimantan
69 D11 **Pematangsiantar** Sumatra
88 H8 **Pemba** Mozambique
87 E9 **Pemba** Zambia
87 H8 **Pemba, B.de** Mozambique
88 G4 **Pemba I** Tanzania
143 B10 **Pemberton** W Australia Australia
117 M10 **Pemberton** British Columbia Canada
98 H1 **Pembina** *R* Manitoba Canada
119 U10 **Pembina** North Dakota U.S.A.
119 T9 **Pembina Mt** Manitoba Canada
118 B5 **Pembina Oil Fields** Alberta Canada
118 C5 **Pembina Prov. Park** Alberta Canada
118 C4 **Pembina R** Alberta Canada
99 T4 **Pembine** Wisconsin U.S.A.
Pembroke *co see* **Dyfed**
121 N7 **Pembroke** Ontario Canada
112 F5 **Pembroke** Georgia U.S.A.
110 J5 **Pembroke** Kentucky U.S.A.
112 H3 **Pembroke** North Carolina U.S.A.
94 G9 **Pembroke** Virginia U.S.A.
8 B4 **Pembroke** Wales
133 F8 **Pembroke, C** Falkland Is
144 A6 **Pembroke, Mt** New Zealand
9 G5 **Pembury** England
70 B5 **Pemuar** Kalimantan
127 J5 **Peña** Dominican Rep
106 D6 **Penablanca** New Mexico U.S.A.
95 Q3 **Penacook** New Hampshire U.S.A.
17 G2 **Peña de Oroel** *mt ra* Spain
16 B3 **Penafiel** Portugal
16 E3 **Peñafiel** Spain
17 G4 **Peñagolosa** *mt* Spain
127 O3 **Penal** Trinidad
8 B4 **Penally** Wales
70 D3 **Penambo Ra** Kalimantan
16 C3 **Peña Mira** *mt* Spain
70 E2 **Penampang** Sabah
131 B2 **Peña Negra, Pasco de** Arg/Chile
125 K6 **Peña Nevada, Cerro** *mt* Mexico
Penang *see* **Pinang** *isld*
130 E7 **Penápolis** Brazil
16 D1 **Peña Prieta** *mt* Spain
16 D4 **Peñaranda de Bracamonte** Spain
95 M6 **Pen Argyl** Pennsylvania U.S.A.
139 G5 **Penarie** New South Wales Australia
17 G4 **Peñarroya** *mt* Spain
16 D6 **Peñarroya-Pueblonuevo** Spain
8 C5 **Penarth** Wales
16 C1 **Peña Rubia** *mt* Spain
17 G2 **Peña, Sa. de la** *mts* Spain
124 M4 **Peñas Blancas** Nicaragua
16 D1 **Peñas, C. de** Spain
106 E5 **Penasco** New Mexico U.S.A.
108 C3 **Penasco, Rio** *R* New Mexico U.S.A.
16 E3 **Peñas de Cervera** Spain
17 F6 **Peñas de San Pedro** Spain
133 C7 **Penas, G.de** Chile
69 B10 **Penasi, Pulau** *isld* Sumatra
127 N9 **Peñas, Pta** Venezuela
16 C2 **Peña Trevinca** *mt* Spain
16 D1 **Peña Vieja** *mt* Spain
100 H3 **Penawawa** Washington U.S.A.
65 F4 **Pen-ch'i** China
146 J12 **Penck, C** Antarctica
131 C4 **Pencoso, Alto de** *mt* Argentina
70 C5 **Pendadahian** Kalimantan
46 E4 **Pendálofon** Greece
118 F9 **Pendant d'Oreille** Alberta Canada
86 C4 **Pende** *R* Cent Afr Republic
46 F6 **Pendelikón** *mt* Greece
85 B7 **Pendembu** Sierra Leone
130 H8 **Pendencia** Brazil
142 E3 **Pender** W Australia Australia
98 K7 **Pender** Nebraska U.S.A.
142 E3 **Pender Bay** W Australia Australia
144 A6 **Pender, Mt** New Zealand
47 N11 **Pendik** Turkey
8 B4 **Pendine** Wales
13 F6 **Pendlebury** England
13 F6 **Pendle Hill** England
94 B7 **Pendleton** Indiana U.S.A.
100 G4 **Pendleton** Oregon U.S.A.
112 E3 **Pendleton** South Carolina U.S.A.
117 J6 **Pendleton, Mt** British Columbia Canada
69 F14 **Pendopo** Sumatra
100 H1 **Pend Oreille** *R* Washington U.S.A.
117 P11 **Pend Oreille, L** Idaho U.S.A.
101 N1 **Pendroy** Montana U.S.A.
69 J13 **Penebangan** *isld* Indonesia
16 B3 **Peneda** *mt* Portugal
129 L6 **Penedo** Brazil
20 F7 **Penestin** France
94 J5 **Penfield** Pennsylvania U.S.A.
70 L9 **Pengalengan** Java
67 B1 **Peng'an** China
67 G4 **P'eng-chia Hsü** *isld* Taiwan
86 D7 **Penge** Zaire
67 F5 **P'eng-hu Lieh-tao** *isld* Taiwan
67 F5 **P'eng-hu Tao** *isld* Taiwan
69 J12 **Pengiki** *isld* Indonesia
67 E4 **Pengkou** China
65 E6 **Penglai** China
58 G5 **Peng-pu** China
67 A1 **Pengshan** China
67 C2 **Pengshui** China
139 H8 **Penguin** Tasmania Australia
142 F2 **Penguin Deeps** Timor Sea
67 B1 **Pengxi** China
67 A1 **Peng Xian** China
67 E2 **Pengze** China
130 E10 **Penha** Brazil
20 A5 **Penhir, Pte de** France
118 D6 **Penhold** Alberta Canada
8 D4 **Penhow** Wales
120 F3 **Penhurst** Ontario Canada
44 F2 **Penice** *mt* Italy
16 A5 **Peniche** Portugal
13 E2 **Penicuik** Scotland
70 P10 **Penida** *isld* Indonesia
37 O2 **Penig** Germany
71 G5 **Peninsula Pt** Philippines
69 E10 **Peninsular Malaysia** S E Asia
17 H4 **Peñiscola** Spain
13 G6 **Penistone** England
70 M9 **Penju, Teluk** *B* Java
78 K4 **Penjwin** Iran
38 H8 **Penk** Austria
56 B3 **Pen'ki** Russian Federation
8 D2 **Penkridge** England
8 C1 **Penmaenmawr** Wales
20 B6 **Penmarc'h** France
20 B6 **Penmarc'h, Pte de** France
118 K5 **Penn** Saskatchewan Canada
45 M4 **Pennabilli** Italy
45 L4 **Penna, M** *mt* Italy
118 J8 **Pennant** Saskatchewan Canada
122 J9 **Pennant Pt** Nova Scotia Canada
42 F6 **Penna, Pta. della** Italy
42 F6 **Penne** Italy
18 F8 **Penne d'Agenais** France
146 C11 **Pennell Bank** *sea feature* Antarctica
146 C12 **Pennell Coast** *coast* Antarctica
138 E6 **Penneshaw** South Australia Australia
122 F8 **Pennfield** New Brunswick Canada
40 G5 **Pennine, Alpi** *mts* Switzerland
7 J8 **Pennine Chain** *mts* England
26 G7 **Penningkejsen** *mt* Norway/Sweden
95 N6 **Pennington** New Jersey U.S.A.
109 M4 **Pennington** Texas U.S.A.
94 D10 **Pennington Gap** Virginia U.S.A.
42 E5 **Pennino, M** *mt* Italy
95 M6 **Pennsburg** Pennsylvania U.S.A.
95 M7 **Penns Grove** New Jersey U.S.A.
94 H6 **Pennsylvania** *state* U.S.A.
95 K4 **Penn Yan** New York U.S.A.
12 B1 **Pennyghael** Scotland
115 N4 **Penny Ice Cap** Northwest Territories Canada
146 D11 **Penny Point** *pt* Antarctica
115 K2 **Penny Str** Northwest Territories Canada
52 D6 **Peno** Russian Federation
95 T1 **Penobscot** *R* Maine U.S.A.
95 T2 **Penobscot B** Maine U.S.A.
122 G8 **Penobsquis** New Brunswick Canada
138 F6 **Penola** South Australia Australia
124 G5 **Peñón Blanco** Mexico
138 C4 **Penong** South Australia Australia
125 O5 **Penonomé** Panama
100 C8 **Penoyar** California U.S.A.
8 B2 **Penrhyndeudraeth** Wales
139 K5 **Penrith** New South Wales Australia
13 F4 **Penrith** England
8 A7 **Penryn** England
111 J11 **Pensacola** Florida U.S.A.
113 K10 **Pensacola Cay** Bahamas
146 E8 **Pensacola Mts** Antarctica
119 N8 **Pense** Saskatchewan Canada
8 D5 **Pensford** England

Ref	Name
138 F7	Penshurst Victoria Australia
9 G5	Penshurst England
70 E2	Pensiangan Sabah
137 O5	Pentecost I Vanuatu
142 G3	Pentecost, R W Australia Australia
	Pentecôte, I see Pentecost I
122 E4	Pentecôte, L Quebec Canada
48 K5	Penteleu mt Romania
117 O11	Penticton British Columbia Canada
141 H5	Pentland Queensland Australia
15 E2	Pentland Firth Scotland
13 E2	Pentland Hills Scotland
15 F2	Pentland Skerries Orkney Scotland
8 B1	Pentraeth Wales
8 C1	Pentre-Foelas Wales
94 A3	Pentwater Michigan U.S.A.
131 E5	Penuajo Argentina
69 G13	Penuba Indonesia
69 G14	Penuguan Indonesia
69 F10	Penunjuk, Tanjong C Malaysia
20 D4	Penwenan France
68 C3	Penwegon Burma
8 C1	Pen-y-benclog Wales
8 C3	Penybont Wales
8 B1	Pen-y-groes Wales
53 F7	Penza Russian Federation
119 M7	Penzance Saskatchewan Canada
9 F6	Penzance England
21 O4	Penzberg Germany
51 Q2	Penzhinskaya Guba G Russian Federation
33 S6	Penzlin Germany
100 H3	Peola Washington U.S.A.
101 R1	Peoples Cr Montana U.S.A.
103 M8	Peoria Arizona U.S.A.
99 R9	Peoria Illinois U.S.A.
99 C8	Peotillos mt Mexico
89 C6	Pepani watercourse S Africa
85 B7	Pepel Sierra Leone
25 F3	Peperga Netherlands
145 D4	Pepin I New Zealand
99 Q5	Pepin, L Wisconsin U.S.A.
22 K2	Pepinster Belgium
130 D10	Pepiri Guaçu, R Brazil
44 B3	Pêpori, Mt France
46 D3	Peqin Albania
131 H3	Pequena, L Brazil
124 C4	Pequeña, Pta C Mexico
103 K1	Pequop Mts Nevada U.S.A.
103 K1	Pequot Lakes Minnesota U.S.A.
37 O7	Perach Germany
141 F2	Pera Hd Queensland Australia
70 M9	Perahu, Gunung mt Java
69 E10	Perai Malaysia
69 D10	Perak isld Malaysia
69 E10	Perak prov Malaysia
46 F6	Perakhóra Greece
38 G8	Peralta mt Italy
106 D7	Peralta New Mexico U.S.A.
46 G9	Pérama Crete Greece
69 F13	Peranap Sumatra
29 M5	Perä-Posio Finland
29 K9	Peräseinäjoki Finland
82 D4	Perazson Israel
122 H5	Percé Quebec Canada
21 J3	Percée, Pte. de la France
18 G10	Perche, Col de la pass France
21 M4	Perche, Coteaux du hills France
8 B2	Percilan Hd Wales
45 N5	Percile Italy
99 L3	Percival Iowa U.S.A.
142 E5	Percival Ls W Australia Australia
21 H4	Percy France
110 G3	Percy Illinois U.S.A.
99 N8	Percy Iowa U.S.A.
141 K5	Percy Is Queensland Australia
143 D9	Percy, L W Australia Australia
133 D6	Perdido R Argentina
17 H2	Perdido mt Spain
111 J11	Perdido R Alabama/Florida U.S.A.
18 F10	Perdido, M mt Spain
130 B7	Perdido, R Brazil
118 K6	Perdue Saskatchewan Canada
122 B3	Perdu, L Quebec Canada
99 U6	Père R Michigan U.S.A.
48 G2	Perechin Ukraine
48 J2	Pereginskoye Ukraine
50 F2	Peregrebnoye Russian Federation
128 C3	Pereira Colombia
130 D7	Pereira Barreto Brazil
130 E6	Pereira de Eça see Ondjiva
129 G5	Pereirinha Brazil
17 H4	Perello Spain
94 A3	Pere Marquette R Michigan U.S.A.
146 G13	Peremennyy, C Antarctica
48 J1	Peremyshlyany Ukraine
143 B8	Perenjori W Australia Australia
116 L7	Perenosa B Alaska U.S.A.
52 E6	Pereslavl' Zalesskiy Russian Federation
45 O5	Pereto Italy
48 H2	Pereval Veretski mt Ukraine
55 B5	Perevolotskiy Russian Federation
54 C6	Pereyaslav Khmel'nitskiy Ukraine
133 D3	Pérez Chile
100 D8	Perez California U.S.A.
131 E4	Perforated I Thailand
131 E4	Pergamino Argentina
	Pergamum see Bergama
45 N4	Pergola Italy
29 M8	Perham Minnesota U.S.A.
69 F10	Perhentian Besar isld Malaysia
29 L8	Perho Finland
29 L8	Perhojoki R Finland
48 F4	Periam Romania
121 T3	Péribonka R Quebec Canada
121 S4	Péribonca Quebec Canada
122 A3	Péribonca, L Quebec Canada
133 D2	Perico Argentina
124 F5	Pericos Mexico
20 H3	Périers France
18 F7	Périgueux France
127 H9	Perijá, Sa. de mts Colombia/Venezuela
123 P2	Peril Rock Quebec Canada
72 E6	Perim isld Yemen
37 P6	Perimeter Highway Canada
130 H10	Periquito, Sa do mts Brazil
46 E8	Periš Romania
46 K6	Peristéri mt Greece
129 O5	Perito Moreno Argentina
47 P13	Perivóli Greece
76 C5	Periyakulam India
95 M6	Perkasie Pennsylvania U.S.A.
69 G13	Perkak, Tanjong C Indonesia
111 C11	Perkins Georgia U.S.A.
111 C11	Perkins Louisiana U.S.A.
99 T4	Perkins Michigan U.S.A.
111 G11	Perkins Mississippi U.S.A.
103 M7	Perkinsville U.S.A.
57 C5	Per Klukhorskiy pass Georgia
42 G5	Perković Croatia
22 L5	Perl Germany
125 P5	Perlas, Arch. de las islds Panama
33 P6	Perleberg Germany
37 P6	Perlesreut Germany
54 K5	Perlevka Russian Federation
98 K2	Perley Minnesota U.S.A.
48 F5	Perlez Serbia Yugoslavia
69 E9	Perlis prov Malaysia
52 J5	Perm' Russian Federation
101 L2	Perma Montana U.S.A.
53 F11	Per Mamiosnskiy pass Georgia/Rus Fed
53 F11	Per Marukhskiy pass Georgia/Rus Fed
111 G10	Permas Russian Federation
29 J9	Permantoo R North Carolina U.S.A.
55 C2	Permskaya Oblast' prov Russian Federation
	Pernambuco see Recife
130 H9	Pernambuco state Brazil
138 D4	Pernatty Lagoon South Australia Australia
107 N7	Pernell Oklahoma U.S.A.
22 C3	Pernes France
46 F2	Pernik Bulgaria
25 B5	Pernis Netherlands
40 O5	Pernio France
143 A7	Pernon, I R C W Australia Australia
140 B2	Peron Is N Terr Australia
22 D4	Péronne France
22 G3	Péronnes Belgium
143 A7	Peron Pen W Australia Australia
8 A7	Péronville France
18 G10	Perpignan France
112 L1	Perquimans R North Carolina U.S.A.
15 F3	Perranporth England
15 G3	Perranporth England
13 G4	Perrault France
21 N9	Perray-sur-Andelle France
115 O1	Perrine Florida U.S.A.
143 G6	Perron, Laguna del New Mexico U.S.A.
121 N4	Perron Quebec Canada
36 F2	Perros-Guirec France
120 F5	Perry Ontario Canada
110 D5	Perry Arkansas U.S.A.
113 D7	Perry Florida U.S.A.
112 D5	Perry Georgia U.S.A.
110 F2	Perry Illinois U.S.A.
99 H1	Perry Iowa U.S.A.
94 C4	Perry Michigan U.S.A.
94 C4	Perry Missouri U.S.A.
94 C4	Perry New York U.S.A.
107 N5	Perry Oklahoma U.S.A.
116 O6	Perry I Kansas U.S.A.
120 F2	Perry L Ontario Canada
110 A2	Perry L Kansas U.S.A.
94 F7	Perryman Maryland U.S.A.
94 D5	Perrysburg Ohio U.S.A.
108 D7	Perryton Texas U.S.A.
118 D4	Perryvale Alberta Canada
9 F5	Perryville Arkansas U.S.A.
32 J8	Perryville Missouri U.S.A.
21 P3	Perryville Maryland U.S.A.
128 F6	Persepolis see Takht-e Jamshid
121 O4	Perseverancia Bolivia
116 M5	Pershing Quebec Canada
143 E7	Pershore England
123 R4	Pershotravensk Ukraine
123 R4	Pershotravneve Ukraine
43 H9	Persia sea Iran
21 H5	Persia Iowa U.S.A.
29 M10	Persian Gulf S W Asia
52 G5	Persnäs Sweden
127 N5	Perth Tasmania Australia
143 B9	Perth W Australia Australia
121 O8	Perth Ontario Canada
12 E1	Perth Scotland
107 N4	Perth Kansas U.S.A.
112 C4	Perth North Dakota U.S.A.
127 N4	Perth Amboy New Jersey U.S.A.
122 G5	Perth-Andover New Brunswick Canada
38 L4	Pertholz Austria
41 P3	Pertisau Austria
52 E3	Pertominsk Russian Federation
122 D7	Pertre, le France
29 M10	Pertunmaa Finland
52 G5	Pertyugskiy Russian Federation
128 D6	Peru rep S America
99 U6	Pere R Michigan U.S.A.
94 A6	Peru Indiana U.S.A.
99 J9	Peru Nebraska U.S.A.
99 O2	Peru New York U.S.A.
135 S12	Peru-Chile Trench Pacific Oc
42 G4	Perugia Italy
42 G4	Peruíbe Brazil
123 N5	Perushtitsa Bulgaria
42 G2	Perušić Croatia
95 U2	Peruwelz Belgium
73 J3	Pervari Turkey
91 U2	Perwick France
36 B6	Pervomayka Ukraine
54 K8	Pervomaysk Ukraine
56 B5	Pervomayskiy Kazakhstan
58 G1	Pervomayskiy Kazakhstan
145 G4	Pervomayskiy Kazakhstan
133 C4	Pervomaysky Chile
94 C1	Pervomaysk Michigan U.S.A.
55 C4	Pervomayskiy Bashkirskaya Respublika Russian
55 B5	Pervomayskiy Orenburgskaya obl Russian Federation
43 F11	Pervomayskiy Sverdlovskaya obl Russian Federation
65 H3	Pervomayskoye Russian Federation
56 C3	Pervomayskoye Russian Federation
51 Q2	Pervorechenskiy Russian Federation
54 J4	Pervoural'sk Russian Federation
55 C3	Pervouralsk Russian Federation
46 F3	Perwez Belgium
22 H2	Pes' R Russian Federation
52 D5	Pesa R Italy
45 K6	Pesagot Jordan
54 F8	Pesagua Kalimantan
45 P6	Pesaro Italy
129 L5	Pescadero California U.S.A.
8 B6	Pescadores, Pta C Peru
42 F6	Pescaglia Italy
45 P6	Pescara R Italy
45 P6	Pescasseroli Italy
45 P6	Peschici Italy
45 N4	Peschiera del Garda Italy
45 J4	Pescina Italy
45 R7	Pesco Sannita Italy
46 F6	Pescocostanzo Italy
54 D1	Pesha R Russian Federation
77 N4	Peshawar Pakistan
48 C4	Peshkopi Albania
99 R3	Peshtera Bulgaria
99 R3	Peshtigo R Wisconsin U.S.A.
99 T4	Peshtigo Wisconsin U.S.A.
55 E4	Peski Kazakhstan
129 K8	Peski Priaral'skie Karkumy Kazakhstan
57 C5	Peski Sundukli Turkmenistan
48 H5	Peskova Russian Federation
48 H5	Pésnica R Slovenia
16 B3	Peso de Regua Portugal
129 L5	Pesqueira Brazil
18 D3	Pessac France
33 R7	Pessin Germany
48 E3	Pest co Hungary
48 H6	Peşteana Jiu Romania
52 E5	Pestovo Russian Federation
52 E6	Pestyaki Russian Federation
56 G5	Petah Tiqwa Israel
29 L9	Petäjävesi Finland
71 B2	Petak, Tg C Halmahera Indonesia
29 J9	Petäjäskoski Finland
46 G7	Petalíon Kólpos G Greece
14 D2	Petaluma California U.S.A.
22 K4	Petange Luxembourg
70 E6	Petangis Kalimantan
127 L9	Petare Venezuela
88 C9	Petauke Zambia
121 P6	Petawaga, L Quebec Canada
121 N7	Petawawa Ontario Canada
125 P9	Petén Itzá, L Guatemala
99 R5	Petenwell Lake res Wisconsin U.S.A.
138 E5	Peterborough South Australia Australia
121 M8	Peterborough Ontario Canada
9 F2	Peterborough England
95 Q4	Peterborough New Hampshire U.S.A.
15 F3	Petercutter Scotland
15 G3	Peterhead Scotland
146 B7	Peter I Øy isld Antarctica
13 G4	Peterlee England
140 B6	Petermann Aboriginal Land N Terr Australia
115 O1	Petermann Gletscher gla Greenland
143 G6	Petermann Ra N Terr/W Aust Australia
131 B5	Peteroa, Vol pk Arg/Chile
118 H2	Petersberg Germany
18 H9	Pézenas France
31 K7	Pezinok Czechoslovakia
52 H4	Pezmog Russian Federation
37 N6	Pfaffenberg Germany
45 J1	Pfaffenhofen an der Ilm Germany
122 B2	Pfaffenhoffen France
141 L7	Pfäffikon Switzerland
139 J4	Pian R New South Wales Australia
45 P5	Piana del Fucino Italy
41 K5	Pianazzo Italy
42 E2	Piancó R Brazil
45 K3	Pian del Vóglio Italy
45 J3	Pian di Cento Italy
45 M4	Pian di Meleto Italy
37 O7	Pfarrkirchen Germany
139 G6	Piangil Victoria Australia
45 M1	Pianiga Italy
42 G6	Pianosa isld Adriatic Sea
42 C6	Pianosa, I Italy
45 J1	Piaopuk China
122 F7	Piapot Saskatchewan Canada
127 K3	Piapon L Laura Canada
98 B8	Pine Ridge South Dakota
119 R7	Pine River Manitoba Canada
118 K3	Pine River Saskatchewan Canada
99 M3	Pine River Minnesota U.S.A.
44 B2	Pinerolo Italy
120 J9	Pinery Prov. Park Ontario Canada
112 H5	Pines, I of South Carolina
111 B9	Pines, L O'The Texas U.S.A.
108 C4	Pines Springs Texas U.S.A.
89 G7	Pinetown S Africa
110 B7	Pine Valley Oklahoma U.S.A.
103 L4	Pine Valley Utah U.S.A.
103 L4	Pine Valley Mts Utah U.S.A.
94 D10	Pineville Kentucky U.S.A.
110 D5	Pineville Louisiana U.S.A.
110 D5	Pineville Missouri U.S.A.
112 H5	Pineville North Carolina U.S.A.
94 F9	Pineville West Virginia U.S.A.
99 M1	Pinewood Ontario Canada
99 L2	Pinewood Minnesota U.S.A.
112 G4	Pinewood South Carolina U.S.A.
119 T9	Piney Manitoba Canada
101 T2	Piney Buttes hills Montana
110 C6	Piney Cr Arkansas U.S.A.
113 D8	Piney Pt Florida U.S.A.
118 D4	Ping'an China
143 C10	Pingaring W Australia
67 A5	Pingbian China
67 B3	Pingchang China
67 C4	Pingdeng China
67 D7	Pingding China
65 B6	Pingdingbu see Guyan
67 D7	Pingdingshan China
65 G1	Pingding Shan mt China
66 C3	Pingdu China
143 C10	Pingelly W Australia Australia
67 A5	Pingguo China
67 C5	Pinghai China
67 C5	Pingho China
67 C5	Pinghu China
67 B5	Pingjiang China
67 G1	Pingle China
67 D1	Pingli China
67 C1	Pingliang China
65 F6	Pingling China
	Pingluo see Xinyang
67 B3	Pingnan China
101 N6	Pingree Idaho U.S.A.
98 G2	Pingree North Dakota U.S.A.
143 C10	Pingrup W Australia Australia
67 C5	Pingshan China
67 D7	Pingshan China
67 B5	Pingtan China
67 D2	Pingtan Dao isld China
67 C5	Pingtang China
67 E2	P'ing-tung Taiwan
67 C5	Pingxiang China
67 A5	Pingxiang China
67 C5	Pingxiang China
65 B6	Pingyao China
65 G1	Pingyi China
66 C3	Pingyin China
66 C3	Pinhal Brazil
130 N7	Pinhal Brazil
16 A3	Pinhão Portugal
129 J4	Pinheiro Brazil
16 A3	Pinhel Portugal
69 G12	Pini, P isld Indonesia
46 E7	Piniós R Greece
143 B10	Pinjarra W Australia Australia
38 O7	Pinka R Austria
65 C6	Pinkafeld Austria
141 K1	Pinkenba dist Brisbane, Qnsld Australia
140 A3	Pinkerton Ra N Terr Australia

99 S9 Pontiac Illinois U.S.A.
94 D4 Pontiac Michigan U.S.A.
70 A5 Pontianak Kalimantan
43 E7 Pontinia Italy
20 E5 Pontivy France
20 B6 Pont-l'Abbé France
122 H6 Pont Lafrance New Brunswick Canada
40 A1 Pont la Ville France
21 L3 Pont-l'Evêque France
21 N7 Pontlevoy France
20 D5 Pont-Melvez France
119 S4 Ponton Manitoba Canada
143 E9 Ponton Ck W Australia Australia
20 H4 Pontorson France
111 G7 Pontotoc Mississippi U.S.A.
109 J5 Pontotoc Texas U.S.A.
44 G3 Pontremoli Italy
41 L4 Pontresina Switzerland
8 C3 Pontrhydfendigaid Wales
8 B1 Pont Rhythallt Wales
20 D4 Pontrieux France
119 N5 Pontrilas Saskatchewan Canada
8 D4 Pontrilas England
121 T6 Pont Rouge Quebec Canada
19 N16 Pont-St. Esprit France
22 D5 Pont-Ste. Maxence France
20 D6 Pont-Scorff France
21 J7 Ponts-de-Cé, les France
22 F3 Pont-sur-Sambre France
18 H4 Pont-sur-Yonne France
20 B4 Pontusval, Pte.de France
21 L6 Pontvallain France
121 M8 Pontypool Ontario Canada
8 C4 Pontypool Wales
8 C4 Pontypridd Wales
145 E2 Ponui I New Zealand
101 O4 Pony Montana U.S.A.
43 E8 Ponza, I di Italy
43 E8 Ponziane, Isole *islds* Italy
138 C4 Poochera South Australia Australia
13 G6 Pool England
138 D2 Poolawanna L South Australia Australia
144 B6 Poolburn Dam New Zealand
9 E6 Poole England
138 F3 Poole, Mt New South Wales Australia
112 F5 Pooler Georgia U.S.A.
95 K7 Poolesville Maryland U.S.A.
15 C3 Poolewe Scotland
12 E1 Pool of Muckart Scotland
109 K3 Poolville Texas U.S.A.
Poona *see* Pune
139 G5 Pooncarie New South Wales Australia
143 B8 Poondarrie,Mt W Australia Australia
139 G4 Poopelloe, L New South Wales Australia
128 E7 Poopó Bolivia
145 E1 Poor Knights Is New Zealand
116 K4 Poorman Alaska U.S.A.
86 C7 Popakabaka Zaire
129 G3 Popakai Suriname
54 K8 Popasnaya Ukraine
128 C3 Popayan Colombia
27 M14 Pope Latvia
103 J8 Pope California U.S.A.
111 G7 Pope Mississippi U.S.A.
99 N7 Popejoy Iowa U.S.A.
58 F1 Poperechnoye Russian Federation
22 D2 Poperinge Belgium
95 L8 Popes Creek Maryland U.S.A.
95 S3 Popham Beach Maine U.S.A.
51 K1 Popigay *R* Russian Federation
138 F5 Popiltah New South Wales Australia
98 A1 Poplar Montana U.S.A.
99 P3 Poplar Wisconsin U.S.A.
110 F5 Poplar Bluff Missouri U.S.A.
101 U1 Poplar Cr Montana U.S.A.
119 U6 Poplar Pt Manitoba Canada
111 G11 Poplarville Mississippi U.S.A.
125 K8 Popocatepetl *vol* Mexico
116 G9 Popof I Alaska U.S.A.
70 N10 Popoh Java
45 P5 Popoli Italy
136 K3 Popondetta Papua New Guinea
47 H1 Popovo Bulgaria
37 M5 Poppberg *mt* Germany
25 H4 Poppe Netherlands
22 J1 Poppel Belgium
37 J3 Poppenhausen Germany
45 L4 Poppi Italy
31 M6 Poprad Czechoslovakia
48 F1 Poprad *R* Czechoslovakia
128 E8 Poquis *mt* Chile/Arg
95 L9 Poquoson Virginia U.S.A.
145 F4 Porangahau New Zealand
74 C8 Porbander India
117 H9 Porcher I British Columbia Canada
54 B1 Porch'ye Pskovskaya obl Russian Federation
133 D1 Porco Bolivia
16 E7 Porcuna Spain
141 G5 Porcupine *R* Queensland Australia
116 R3 Porcupine *R* Alaska/Yukon Terr U.S.A./Canada
90 H3 Porcupine Bank Atlantic Oc
101 T1 Porcupine Cr Montana U.S.A.
118 C8 Porcupine Hills Alberta Canada
119 Q6 Porcupine Hills Manitoba/Sask Canada
99 R3 Porcupine Mts Michigan U.S.A.
119 O6 Porcupine Plain Saskatchewan Canada
42 E3 Pordenoné Italy
46 G1 Pordim Bulgaria
42 F3 Poreč Croatia
130 D8 Porecatu Brazil
55 D2 Porech'ye Russian Federation
52 G6 Poretskoye Russian Federation
145 E4 Porewa New Zealand
85 E6 Porga Benin
29 J10 Pori Finland
145 F4 Porirua New Zealand
80 F3 Poriyya Israel
26 L5 Porjus Sweden
29 L12 Porkala Finland
52 C5 Porkhov Russian Federation
128 F1 Porlamar Venezuela
41 K5 Porlezza Italy
8 C5 Porlock England
37 L6 Pörnbach Germany
20 F7 Pornic France
20 F7 Pornichet France
71 G5 Poro *isld* Philippines
52 E3 Porog Arkhangel'skaya obl Russian Federation
52 J4 Porog Komi Respublika Russian Federation
59 M2 Poronaysk Russian Federation
68 G6 Porong *R* Cambodia
143 C10 Porongorup W Australia Australia
60 Q1 Poronupuri yama *mt* Japan
145 E3 Porootarao New Zealand
46 F7 Póros *isld* Greece
60 Q1 Poroshiri yama *mt* Japan
52 D3 Porosozero Russian Federation
52 H3 Porozhsk Russian Federation
56 F3 Porozhskiy Russian Federation
146 E14 Porpoise B Antarctica
19 Q18 Porquerolles, I. de France
120 K4 Porquis Junct Ontario Canada
40 F3 Pörrentruy Switzerland
45 J3 Porretta Terme Italy
16 B2 Porriño Spain
26 N1 Porsa Norway
26 O1 Pôrsangen *inlet* Norway
27 D12 Porsgrunn Norway
20 A4 Porspoder France
33 Q9 Porst Germany
47 L5 Porsük *R* Turkey
128 F7 Portachuelo Bolivia
138 E5 Port Adelaide South Australia Australia
14 E2 Portadown N Ireland
144 B7 Port Adventure New Zealand
14 F2 Portaferry N Ireland
122 H7 Portage Prince Edward I Canada
116 N6 Portage Alaska U.S.A.
95 S7 Portage Maine U.S.A.
101 O2 Portage Montana U.S.A.
94 D5 Portage *R* Ohio U.S.A.
94 J6 Portage Pennsylvania U.S.A.
101 N8 Portage Utah U.S.A.
110 F3 Portage des Sioux Missouri U.S.A.
122 G6 Portage I New Brunswick Canada
119 T9 Portage la Prairie Manitoba Canada
110 G5 Portageville Missouri U.S.A.
94 J4 Portageville New York U.S.A.
103 P10 Portal Arizona U.S.A.
112 F5 Portal Georgia U.S.A.
98 D1 Portal North Dakota U.S.A.
14 D3 Portalaoise Ireland
117 L11 Port Alberni British Columbia Canada
139 H7 Port Albert Victoria Australia
120 J9 Port Albert Ontario Canada
145 E2 Port Albert New Zealand
16 C5 Portalegre Portugal
106 G7 Portales New Mexico U.S.A.
117 F7 Port Alexander Alaska U.S.A.
89 E9 Port Alfred S Africa
117 K10 Port Alice British Columbia Canada
94 J5 Port Allegany Pennsylvania U.S.A.
111 E11 Port Allen Louisiana U.S.A.
141 K6 Port Alma Queensland Australia
117 M11 Port Angeles Washington U.S.A.
109 K8 Port Aransas Texas U.S.A.
102 A3 Port Arena California U.S.A.
14 D3 Portarlington Ireland
Port Arthur *see* Lüshun
139 J9 Port Arthur Tasmania Australia
109 N6 Port Arthur Texas U.S.A.
12 B2 Port Askaig Scotland
138 D4 Port Augusta South Australia Australia
123 N5 Port-au-Port *pen* Newfoundland Canada
123 O5 Port-au-Port Newfoundland Canada
127 H5 Port-au-Prince Haiti
94 D2 Port Austin Michigan U.S.A.
32 J8 Porta Westfalica Germany
20 G3 Portbail France
12 C2 Port Bannatyne Scotland
111 E11 Port Barre Louisiana U.S.A.
71 D5 Port Barton Palawan Philippines
123 L8 Port Bickerton Nova Scotia Canada
68 A7 Port Blair Andaman Is
109 N6 Port Bolivar Texas U.S.A.
17 K2 Port Bou Spain/France
85 D8 Port Bouet Ivory Coast
140 D2 Port Bradshaw *inlet* N Terr Australia
21 J5 Port Brillet France
120 J10 Port Bruce Ontario Canada
120 K10 Port Burwell Ontario Canada
99 Q8 Port Byron Illinois U.S.A.
95 L3 Port Byron New York U.S.A.
139 G7 Port Campbell Victoria Australia
75 N7 Port Canning India
121 L7 Port Carling Ontario Canada
13 E4 Port Carlisle England
122 F3 Port Cartier Quebec Canada
144 D7 Port Chalmers New Zealand
145 E2 Port Charles New Zealand
15 B5 Port Charlotte Scotland
95 O6 Port Chester New York U.S.A.
111 G12 Port Chicot I Louisiana U.S.A.
117 F6 Port Chilkoot Alaska U.S.A.
116 D4 Port Clarence *hbr* Alaska U.S.A.
117 G9 Port Clements British Columbia Canada
141 K5 Port Clinton *inlet* Queensland Australia
94 E5 Port Clinton Ohio U.S.A.
95 S3 Port Clyde Maine U.S.A.
121 L10 Port Colborne Ontario Canada
117 M11 Port Coquitlam British Columbia Canada
68 A6 Port Cornwallis Andaman Is
121 L9 Port Credit Ontario Canada
19 Q18 Port Cros, I. de France
141 K6 Port Curtis *inlet* Queensland Australia
121 L9 Port Dalhousie Ontario Canada
122 H5 Port Daniel Quebec Canada
139 H9 Port Davey Tasmania Australia
19 N18 Port de Bouc France
19 N18 Port de Fos *hbr* France
102 A1 Port Delgada California U.S.A.
127 H5 Port-de-Paix Haiti
21 M7 Port-de-Piles France
69 E11 Port Dickson Malaysia
8 B1 Port Dinorwic Wales
141 H3 Port Douglas Queensland Australia
120 K10 Port Dover Ontario Canada
123 K9 Port Dufferin Nova Scotia Canada
111 G12 Porte a la Hache Louisiana U.S.A.
Porte d'Annam *see* Vinh Son
99 U4 Porte des Morts Wisconsin U.S.A.
117 H8 Port Edward British Columbia Canada
89 G8 Port Edward S Africa
130 G4 Porteirinha Brazil
129 H4 Portel Brazil
16 B6 Portel Portugal
130 H7 Portela Brazil
122 H7 Port Elgin New Brunswick Canada
120 J8 Port Elgin Ontario Canada
127 O8 Port Elizabeth Lesser Antilles
89 D9 Port Elizabeth S Africa
22 B2 Portel, le France
12 B2 Port Ellen Scotland
130 B9 Porteña *R* Argentina
21 J3 Port-en-Bessin-Huppain France
98 K5 Porter Minnesota U.S.A.
98 C7 Porter Nebraska U.S.A.
106 D6 Porter New Mexico U.S.A.
107 P6 Porter Oklahoma U.S.A.
112 D4 Porterdale Georgia U.S.A.
99 T4 Porterfield Wisconsin U.S.A.
12 D5 Port Erin I of Man U.K.
117 H6 Porter Landing British Columbia Canada
15 G3 Port Errol Scotland
87 C12 Porterville S Africa
102 E5 Porterville California U.S.A.
127 K3 Port Esquivel Jamaica
8 B4 Port Eynon Wales
138 F7 Port Fairy South Australia Australia
123 L8 Port Felix Nova Scotia Canada
145 E2 Port Fitzroy New Zealand
Port Francqui *see* Ilebo
86 A6 Port Gentil Gabon
122 G9 Port George Nova Scotia Canada
111 E10 Port Gibson Mississippi U.S.A.
12 D2 Port Glasgow Scotland
14 E2 Portglenone N Ireland
15 E3 Portgordon Scotland
145 E4 Port Gore New Zealand
116 M7 Port Graham Alaska U.S.A.
143 A8 Port Gregory *B* W Australia Australia
122 H8 Port Greville Nova Scotia Canada
8 C4 Porth Wales
85 F8 Port Harcourt Nigeria
117 K10 Port Hardy British Columbia Canada
145 D4 Port Hardy New Zealand
Port Harrison *see* Inukjuak
123 L8 Port Hastings C Breton I, Nova Scotia
123 L8 Port Hawkesbury C Breton I, Nova Scotia
8 C5 Porthcawl Wales
8 B2 Porth Dinlleyn *B* Wales
142 C5 Port Hedland W Australia Australia
127 L3 Port Henderson Jamaica
95 O3 Port Henry New York U.S.A.
Port Herald *see* Nsanje
100 J1 Porthill Idaho U.S.A.
8 B2 Porthmadog Wales
8 B2 Porth Neigwl *B* Wales
123 L8 Port Hood C Breton I, Nova Scotia
121 M9 Port Hope Ontario Canada
94 E3 Port Hope Michigan U.S.A.
123 Q1 Port Hope Simpson Labrador, Nfld Canada
102 E7 Port Hueneme California U.S.A.
120 H10 Port Huron Ontario Canada
94 E4 Port Huron Michigan U.S.A.
45 Q8 Portici Italy
16 B7 Portimão Portugal
29 M5 Portimo Finland
12 C1 Portinnisherrich Scotland
107 M2 Portis Kansas U.S.A.
8 B6 Port Isaac England
109 K9 Port Isabel Texas U.S.A.
99 T2 Port Isabelle Michigan U.S.A.
8 D5 Portishead England
139 K5 Port Jackson New South Wales Australia
95 O6 Port Jefferson Long I, New York U.S.A.
95 N5 Port Jervis New York U.S.A.
20 F8 Port Joinville France
127 J3 Port Kaiser Jamaica
140 A2 Port Keats N Terr Australia
139 K5 Port Kembla New South Wales Australia
138 C5 Port Kenney South Australia Australia
139 J5 Portland New South Wales Australia
138 F7 Portland Victoria Australia
127 P6 Portland Barbados
121 O8 Portland Ontario Canada
127 M2 Portland *parish* Jamaica
145 E1 Portland New Zealand
106 E3 Portland Colorado U.S.A.
94 C6 Portland Indiana U.S.A.
95 R3 Portland Maine U.S.A.
94 C4 Portland Michigan U.S.A.
98 J2 Portland North Dakota U.S.A.
100 C4 Portland Oregon U.S.A.
110 K5 Portland Tennessee U.S.A.
109 K8 Portland Texas U.S.A.
127 K3 Portland Bight Jamaica
8 D7 Portland, Bill of *head* England
139 J8 Portland, C Tasmania Australia
117 H8 Portland Canal Br Col/Alaska Canada/U.S.A.
123 P3 Portland Cr. Pond Newfoundland Canada
8 D6 Portland Hbr England
145 F3 Portland I New Zealand
117 H8 Portland Inlet British Columbia Canada
127 K3 Portland Ridge Jamaica
141 G2 Portland Roads Queensland Australia
126 F6 Portland Rock Caribbean
71 E8 Port Languyan Philippines
139 H8 Port Latta Tasmania Australia
109 L7 Port Lavaca Texas U.S.A.
14 D4 Portlaw Ireland
144 B4 Port Levy New Zealand
95 M3 Port Leyden New York U.S.A.
138 D5 Port Lincoln South Australia Australia
12 D4 Port Logan Scotland
120 K7 Port Loring Ontario Canada
20 D6 Port-Louis France
83 L12 Port Louis Mauritius
127 N4 Port Louis Guadeloupe W Indies
140 D3 Port McArthur *B* N Terr Australia
138 F7 Port MacDonnell South Australia Australia
121 L8 Port McNicoll Ontario Canada
139 L4 Port Macquarie New South Wales Australia
122 F10 Port Maitland Nova Scotia Canada
121 L10 Port Maitland Ontario Canada
109 K9 Port Mansfield Texas U.S.A.
115 N6 Port Manvers Labrador, Nfld Canada
127 L2 Port Maria Jamaica
94 J6 Port Matilda Pennsylvania U.S.A.
113 G11 Port Mayaca Florida U.S.A.
122 H9 Port Medway Nova Scotia Canada
117 M11 Port Mellon British Columbia Canada
122 H4 Port Menier Quebec Canada
116 G8 Port Moller Alaska U.S.A.
117 M11 Port Moody British Columbia Canada
127 M3 Port Morant Jamaica
136 K3 Port Moresby Papua New Guinea
123 N7 Port Morien C Breton I, Nova Scotia
21 N3 Port-Mort France
122 H10 Port Mouton Nova Scotia Canada
122 H10 Port Mouton I Nova Scotia Canada
141 F1 Port Musgrave *inlet* Queensland Australia
15 C4 Portnacroish Scotland
12 B2 Portnahaven Scotland
20 E6 Port Navalo France
109 O6 Port Neches Texas U.S.A.
138 D5 Port Neill South Australia Australia
126 G3 Port Nelson Bahamas
101 N7 Portneuf Idaho U.S.A.
121 S5 Portneuf, Parc Quebec Canada
122 C5 Portneuf, R Quebec Canada
122 C5 Portneuf-sur-Mer Quebec Canada
145 G4 Port Nicholson New Zealand
138 E6 Port Noarlunga South Australia Australia
87 C11 Port Nolloth S Africa
95 M7 Port Norris New Jersey U.S.A.
115 N6 Port-Nouveau Québec Quebec Canada
129 K4 Pôrto Brazil
16 B3 Porto Portugal
128 E5 Pôrto Acre Brazil
130 D7 Pôrto Alegre Mato Grosso Brazil
131 H3 Pôrto Alegre Rio Grande do Sul Brazil
Porto Alexandre *see* Tombua
87 B8 Porto Amboim Angola
Porto Amelia *see* Pemba Mozambique
129 G6 Porto Artur Brazil
144 D7 Portobello New Zealand
13 E2 Portobello Scotland
130 E10 Pôrto Belo Brazil
116 L8 Port O'Brian Alaska U.S.A.
43 C7 Porto Cervo Sardinia
109 L7 Port O'Connor Texas U.S.A.
16 B3 Porto de Leixões Portugal
129 H4 Pôrto de Mos Brazil
129 H6 Pôrto dos Meinacos Brazil
43 F11 Porto Empedocle Sicily
128 G7 Pôrto Espiridião Brazil
42 C6 Portoferraio Elba Italy
44 F3 Portofino Italy
12 D1 Port of Menteith Scotland
15 B2 Port of Ness Scotland
127 O2 Port of Spain Trinidad
45 M2 Porto Garibaldi Italy
129 H3 Pôrto Grande Brazil
42 E3 Portogruaro Italy
129 G7 Pôrto Jofre Brazil
102 D2 Portola California U.S.A.
130 C10 Porto Luceno Brazil
29 J9 Pörtom Finland
45 L2 Portomaggiore Italy
45 J1 Porto Mantovano Italy
44 D4 Porto Maurizio Italy
88 H9 Porto Mocambo Mozambique
129 G8 Pôrto Murtinho Brazil
129 J6 Pôrto Nacional Brazil
85 E7 Porto Novo Benin
113 G8 Port Orange Florida U.S.A.
117 M12 Port Orchard Washington U.S.A.
42 F5 Porto Recanati Italy
100 A7 Port Orford Oregon U.S.A.
133 G2 Pôrto San José Brazil
42 D6 Porto San Stefano Italy
85 A2 Pôrto Santo *isld* Madeira
129 H8 Pôrto São José Brazil
130 H5 Pôrto Seguro Brazil
45 M2 Porto Tolle Italy
43 B8 Porto Torres Sardinia
133 G3 Pôrto União Brazil
128 F5 Pôrto Velho Brazil
44 G3 Portovenere Italy
128 B4 Portoviejo Ecuador
12 C4 Portpatrick Scotland
140 B2 Port Patterson *inlet* N Terr Australia
144 A7 Port Pegasus New Zealand
121 M8 Port Perry Ontario Canada
139 G7 Port Phillip B Victoria Australia
138 E5 Port Pirie South Australia Australia
114 H4 Port Radium Northwest Territories Canada
8 A7 Portreath England
15 B3 Portree Scotland
118 J8 Portreeve Saskatchewan Canada
83 M8 Port Refuge Cocos Is Indian Oc
100 A1 Port Renfrew British Columbia Canada
123 T5 Port Rexton Newfoundland Canada
102 A4 Port Reyes California U.S.A.
100 B1 Port Roberts Washington U.S.A.
144 D5 Port Robinson New Zealand
140 D2 Port Roper *inlet* N Terr Australia
120 K10 Port Rowan Ontario Canada
127 L3 Port Royal Jamaica
112 G5 Port Royal South Carolina U.S.A.
95 K8 Port Royal Virginia U.S.A.
122 G9 Port Royal Nat. Hist. Park Ontario Canada
14 E1 Portrush N Ireland
79 C7 Port Said Egypt
113 B8 Port St. Joe Florida U.S.A.
89 F8 Port St Johns S Africa
19 N18 Port St. Louis France
18 F8 Port St. Marie France
20 G7 Port St.Père France
20 A4 Portsall France
14 D1 Portsalon Ireland
94 E3 Port Sanilac Michigan U.S.A.
123 P3 Port Saunders Newfoundland Canada
Port Say *see* Marsa Ben Mehdi
38 K8 Pörtschach Austria
89 G8 Port Shepstone S Africa
117 H8 Port Simpson British Columbia Canada
142 D4 Port Smith *B* W Australia Australia
121 O8 Portsmouth Ontario Canada
127 O7 Portsmouth Dominica
9 E6 Portsmouth England
99 L8 Portsmouth Iowa U.S.A.
95 R3 Portsmouth New Hampshire U.S.A.
112 L2 Portsmouth North Carolina U.S.A.
94 E8 Portsmouth Ohio U.S.A.
95 Q5 Portsmouth Rhode I U.S.A.
95 L10 Portsmouth Virginia U.S.A.
12 C1 Portsonachan Scotland
15 F3 Portsoy Scotland
120 J10 Port Stanley Ontario Canada
139 K5 Port Stephens New South Wales Australia
141 G2 Port Stewart *inlet* Queensland Australia
14 E1 Port Stewart N Ireland
86 G2 Port Sudan Sudan
8 C4 Port Talbot Wales
71 F4 Port Tambang Philippines
79 C9 Port Taufiq Egypt
127 O2 Port Tembladora Trinidad
29 M3 Porttipahdan tekojärvi *L* Finland
117 M11 Port Townsend Washington U.S.A.
16 B7 Portugal *rep* W Europe
83 J9 Portugal B Sri Lanka
123 U6 Portugal Cove Newfoundland Canada
17 F1 Portugalete Spain
128 E2 Portuguesa *state* Venezuela
Portuguese Guinea *see* Guinea-Bissau *rep*
14 C3 Portumna Ireland
123 T5 Port Union Newfoundland Canada
18 H10 Port Vendres France
102 F8 Port Vicente California U.S.A.
88 D1 Port Victoria Kenya
137 O5 Port-Vila Vanuatu
94 J4 Portville New York U.S.A.
138 E5 Port Vincent South Australia Australia
52 D1 Port Vladimir Russian Federation
138 E5 Port Wakefield South Australia Australia
142 F2 Port Warrender *inlet* W Australia Australia
99 T6 Port Washington Wisconsin U.S.A.
142 B5 Port Weld *B* W Australia Australia
116 N6 Port Wells *inlet* Alaska U.S.A.
112 F5 Port Wentworth Georgia U.S.A.
12 D4 Port William Scotland
122 H8 Port Williams Nova Scotia Canada
99 P3 Port Wing Wisconsin U.S.A.
107 P6 Porum Oklahoma U.S.A.
127 K2 Porus Jamaica
133 C8 Porvenir Chile
108 C5 Porvenir Texas U.S.A.
29 M11 Porvoo Finland
36 C2 Porz Germany
16 E5 Porzuna Spain
16 E5 Porzuna, Sa. de *mts* Spain
43 C8 Posada *R* Sardinia
133 F3 Posadas Argentina
16 D7 Posadas Spain
41 M5 Poschiavo Switzerland
94 D1 Posen Michigan U.S.A.
110 J3 Poseyville Indiana U.S.A.
52 E5 Poshekhonye Russian Federation
119 O1 Poshkokagan L Ontario Canada
46 F5 Posidhion, Ákr *C* Greece
41 O6 Posina *R* Italy
37 O5 Pösing Germany
29 N5 Posio Finland
45 Q8 Positano Italy
70 G5 Poso Sulawesi
78 J1 Posof Turkey
129 J6 Posse Brazil
37 N3 Posseck Germany
146 C12 Possession Is Antarctica
37 M2 Pössneck Germany
21 J7 Possonnière, la France
38 M8 Possruck Slovenia
109 J3 Possum Kingdom L Texas U.S.A.
100 E5 Post Oregon U.S.A.
37 N6 Postau Germany
37 L5 Postbauer-Heng Germany
8 C6 Postbridge England
115 M6 Poste-de-la-Baleine Quebec Canada
68 H6 Poste Deshayes Cambodia
Poste Maurice Cortier *see* Bidon 5
83 M12 Poste, R du Mauritius
85 E4 Poste Weygand Algeria
100 J2 Post Falls Idaho U.S.A.
71 J8 Postiljon Pulau *isld* Indonesia
89 C7 Postmasburg S Africa
129 H6 Pôsto Alto Manissaua Brazil
128 C4 Posto Bobonazo Peru
42 F3 Postojna Slovenia
99 P6 Postville Iowa U.S.A.
42 H5 Posušje Bosnia-Herzegovina
71 K9 Pota Indonesia
124 D4 Pótam Mexico
46 G3 Potamoi Greece
46 F8 Potamós Greece
47 O12 Potamós Greece
50 H2 Potapovo Russian Federation
128 G2 Potaro *R* Guyana
89 E6 Potchefstroom S Africa
48 J6 Potcoava Romania
130 H5 Poté Brazil
107 Q7 Poteau *R* Okla/Ark U.S.A.
107 Q6 Poteau Oklahoma U.S.A.
109 J6 Poteet Texas U.S.A.
130 J8 Potengi *R* Brazil
43 G8 Potenza Italy
144 A7 Poteriteri, L New Zealand
16 D1 Potes Spain
89 F5 Potgietersrus S Africa
109 J6 Poth Texas U.S.A.
100 F2 Potholes Res Washington U.S.A.
129 K5 Poti *R* Brazil
21 K4 Potigny France
85 G6 Potiskum Nigeria
71 K9 Potjo Mandasawu *mt* Indonesia
100 J3 Potlatch Idaho U.S.A.
89 B8 Potloer *mt* S Africa
48 K6 Potlogi Romania
101 M3 Potomac Montana U.S.A.
94 J7 Potomac S. Branch *R* West Virginia U.S.A.
133 D1 Potosí Bolivia
133 D2 Potosí *dept* Bolivia
110 F4 Potosi Missouri U.S.A.
103 J6 Potosi Mt Nevada U.S.A.
71 F5 Pototan Panay Philippines
133 D3 Potrerillos Chile
131 B2 Potro, Cerro de *pk* Chile
33 S8 Potsdam Germany
95 N2 Potsdam New York U.S.A.
37 L4 Pottenstein Germany
120 K4 Potter Ontario Canada
98 C8 Potter Nebraska U.S.A.
9 E5 Potterne England
9 F4 Potter's Bar England
102 A2 Potter Valley California U.S.A.
94 C4 Potterville Michigan U.S.A.
37 L6 Pottmes Germany
9 F3 Potton England
109 L2 Pottsboro Texas U.S.A.
111 G7 Potts Camp Mississippi U.S.A.
95 M6 Pottstown Pennsylvania U.S.A.
95 L6 Pottsville Pennsylvania U.S.A.
109 J4 Pottsville Texas U.S.A.
83 L11 Pottuvil Sri Lanka
107 N4 Potwin Kansas U.S.A.
21 H6 Pouancé France
68 F3 Pou Bia *mt* Laos
117 N8 Pouce Coupé British Columbia Canada
123 U6 Pouch Cove Newfoundland Canada
21 J6 Poueze la France
95 O5 Poughkeepsie New York U.S.A.
18 H5 Pougues les Eaux France
21 N7 Pouillé France
18 E9 Pouillon France
18 J5 Pouilly en Auxois France
21 O7 Poulaines France
20 B5 Pouldergat France
20 B6 Pouldreuzic France
20 C6 Pouldu,le France
21 N8 Pouligny St. Pierre France
20 F7 Pouliguen,le France
122 B5 Poulin de Courval, L Quebec Canada
20 C5 Poullaouen France
68 J5 Poulo Canton, Is de Vietnam
69 G8 Poulo Dama, Iles Vietnam
68 J6 Poulo Gambir, Cu Lao *isld* Vietnam
95 O3 Poultney Vermont U.S.A.
13 E6 Poulton-le-Fylde England
68 E4 Pou Miang *mt* Thailand
99 S4 Pound Wisconsin U.S.A.
9 F5 Pound Hill England
19 P18 Pourcieux France
145 F4 Pourerere New Zealand
145 G3 Pourewa I New Zealand
40 E6 Pourri, Mont France
21 N2 Pourville France
68 F3 Pou San *mt* Laos
68 F3 Pou Sao *mt* Laos
68 H5 Pou Set *mt* Laos
129 G6 Pouso Alegre Mato Grosso Brazil
130 F8 Pouso Alegre Minas Gerais Brazil
29 O6 Poussu Finland
144 A7 Poutama I New Zealand
68 F6 Pouthisat Cambodia
145 E2 Pouto New Zealand
121 Q3 Poutrincourt, L Quebec Canada
40 D1 Pouxeux France
21 J8 Pouzauges France
21 M7 Pouzay France
48 E1 Pov Bystrica Czechoslovakia
52 D3 Povenets Russian Federation
145 F3 Poverty Bay New Zealand
9 F5 Povey Cross England
45 J2 Poviglio Italy
48 F6 Povlen *mt* Serbia Yugoslavia
16 B3 Póvoa de Varzim Portugal
65 J3 Povorotnyy, Mys *C* Russian Federation
115 M5 Povungnituk Quebec Canada
121 L6 Powassan Ontario Canada
101 T5 Powder *R* Wyo/Mont U.S.A.
106 C3 Powderhorn Colorado U.S.A.
100 H5 Powder R Oregon U.S.A.
98 A4 Powderville Montana U.S.A.
141 G7 Powell *R* Queensland Australia
103 K7 Powell Arizona U.S.A.
98 E5 Powell South Dakota U.S.A.
94 D10 Powell *R* Tenn/Virg U.S.A.
99 R3 Powell Wisconsin U.S.A.
101 R5 Powell Wyoming U.S.A.
100 D5 Powell Butte Oregon U.S.A.
113 K11 Powell Cay *isld* Bahamas
103 O4 Powell, L Ariz/Utah U.S.A.
106 D2 Powell, Mt Colorado U.S.A.
102 F3 Powell Mt Nevada U.S.A.
126 F2 Powell Pt Eleuthera Bahamas
117 L10 Powell River British Columbia Canada
94 F8 Powellton West Virginia U.S.A.
101 O2 Power Montana U.S.A.
99 T4 Powers Michigan U.S.A.
100 A7 Powers Oregon U.S.A.
98 D1 Powers L North Dakota U.S.A.
111 C10 Powhatan Louisiana U.S.A.
94 K9 Powhatan Virginia U.S.A.
107 P2 Powhattan Kansas U.S.A.
8 D3 Powick England
141 H5 Powlathanga Queensland Australia
95 O4 Pownal Vermont U.S.A.
8 C3 Powys *co* Wales
130 C5 Poxoreu *R* Brazil
67 E2 Poyang Hu *L* China
111 D7 Poyen Arkansas U.S.A.
99 S5 Poygan, L Wisconsin U.S.A.
31 K7 Poysdorf Austria
124 C5 Poza Grande Mexico
78 E3 Pozantı Turkey
48 G6 Požarevac Serbia Yugoslavia
125 L7 Poza Rica Mexico
48 F7 Požega Serbia Yugoslavia
Pozen *see* Poznań
59 K2 Pozharskoye Russian Federation
52 J5 Pozhva Russian Federation
22 D3 Pozières France
140 D5 Pozieres,Mt N Terr Australia
31 K3 Poznań Poland
102 D6 Pozo California U.S.A.
17 F7 Pozo Alcón Spain
133 D2 Pozo Almonte Chile
16 D6 Pozoblanco Spain
103 J9 Pozo Cenizo Mexico
17 F6 Pozohondo Spain
103 J9 Pozo Salado Mexico
103 N10 Pozo Verde Mexico
52 H4 Poztykeros Russian Federation
133 D2 Pozuelos, L. de Argentina
45 J1 Pozzolengo Italy
45 L1 Pozzonova Italy
45 Q8 Pozzuoli Italy
68 F2 P. Phac Mo *mt* Vietnam
85 D7 Pra *R* Ghana
69 G14 Prabumulih Sumatra
31 L2 Prabuty Poland
45 J3 Pracchia Italy
68 D7 Pracham Hiang, Laem Thailand
30 H7 Prachatice Czechoslovakia
68 E5 Prachin Buri Thailand
68 D7 Prachuap Khiri Khan Thailand
16 C1 Pradairo Spain
31 K5 Praděd *mt* Czechoslovakia
18 G10 Prades France
70 P9 Pradjekan Java
28 E2 Præstbro Denmark
Præstø *co see* Storstrøm and Roskilde *counties*
28 J6 Præsto Denmark
38 N9 Pragersk Slovenia
38 F7 Prägraten Austria
Prague *see* Praha
107 O6 Prague Oklahoma U.S.A.
31 H5 Praha Czechoslovakia
48 K5 Prahova Romania
48 K6 Prahova *R* Romania
48 H6 Prahova Serbia Yugoslavia
85 B8 Praia Cape Verde
133 G4 Praia Albardão *beach* Brazil
48 J4 Praid Romania
129 H4 Prainha Brazil
122 B3 Praires, L. des Quebec Canada
109 K6 Prairia Lea Texas U.S.A.
141 G5 Prairie Queensland Australia
100 K6 Prairie Idaho U.S.A.
110 F1 Prairie City Illinois U.S.A.
100 G5 Prairie City Oregon U.S.A.
107 K2 Prairie Dog Cr Kansas U.S.A.
108 F1 Prairie Dog Town Fork *R* Texas U.S.A.
99 P6 Prairie du Chien Wisconsin U.S.A.
99 R6 Prairie du Sac Wisconsin U.S.A.
110 B6 Prairie Grove Arkansas U.S.A.
109 L4 Prairie Hill Texas U.S.A.
119 P6 Prairie River Saskatchewan Canada
119 Q7 Prairies, L of the Manitoba/Sask Canada
110 J2 Prairieton Indiana U.S.A.
107 L2 Prairie View Kansas U.S.A.
111 F11 Prairieville Louisiana U.S.A.
94 E9 Praise Kentucky U.S.A.
68 F5 Prakhon Chai Thailand
40 E7 Pralognan France
42 E2 Pramaggiore, Mont *mt* Italy
70 N9 Prambanan Java
37 O3 Prameny Czechoslovakia
69 D8 Pram, Khao *mt* Thailand
68 D6 Pran *R* Thailand
68 D6 Pran Buri Thailand
38 K7 Prankerhöhe *mt* Austria
69 D11 Prapat Sumatra
40 B2 Praslay France
83 J12 Praslin *isld* Seychelles
47 Q15 Prasonísi *isld* Greece
47 J9 Prasonísí, Akr *C* Rhodes Greece
31 L4 Praszka Poland
129 J7 Prata *R* Brazil
Pratas *isld see* Dongsha Qundao
33 R9 Pratau Germany
17 J3 Prat de Llobregat Spain
41 L4 Prätigau *V* Switzerland
45 K4 Prato Italy
45 R8 Prátola Serra Italy
42 D5 Pratomagno *mt* Italy
45 L4 Pratomagno Italy
45 H3 Prato, Mt Italy
45 L4 Pratovecchio Italy
18 G10 Prats-de-Mollo France
119 T9 Pratt Manitoba Canada
107 M4 Pratt Kansas U.S.A.
95 N4 Prattsville New York U.S.A.
111 K9 Prattville Alabama U.S.A.
40 B2 Prauthoy France
31 N1 Pravdinsk Russian Federation
54 J1 Pravdinskiy Russian Federation
46 F2 Pravets Bulgaria
16 C1 Pravia Spain
8 C7 Prawle Pt England
70 Q10 Praya Indonesia
21 N7 Préaux France
37 O3 Přebuz Czechoslovakia
20 H4 Precey France
52 D6 Prechistoye Russian Federation
21 K6 Précigné France
21 P3 Précy-sur-Oise France
45 L3 Predappio Italy
42 D2 Predazzo Italy
37 O5 Predigtstuhl *mt* Germany
38 M8 Preding Austria
38 J7 Predlitz Austria
38 F7 Predoi Italy
44 E2 Predosa Italy
51 O2 Predporozhnyy Russian Federation
119 P7 Preeceville Saskatchewan Canada
21 K5 Pré-en-Pail France
33 M4 Preetz Germany
20 F7 Préfailles France
31 M1 Pregolya *R* Russian Federation
127 J10 Pregonero Venezuela
18 E8 Preignac France
52 C6 Preiļi Latvia
121 M4 Preissac Quebec Canada
68 G6 Prek Kak Cambodia
68 H6 Prek Preas *R* Cambodia
68 G7 Prek Sandek Cambodia
68 F7 Prek Taley *R* Cambodia
8 B3 Pren-gwyn Wales
46 D4 Prenjas Albania
33 T6 Prenzlau Germany
59 K3 Preobrazheniye Russian Federation
42 A3 Pré-St.-Didier Italy
144 A7 Preservation Inlet New Zealand
130 D8 Presidente Prudente Brazil
108 C6 Presidio Texas U.S.A.
95 T7 Presque Isle Maine U.S.A.
18 F6 Pressac France
8 C1 Prestatyn Wales
8 C3 Presteigne Wales
13 F6 Preston England
101 O7 Preston Idaho U.S.A.
95 M8 Preston Maryland U.S.A.
99 O6 Preston Minnesota U.S.A.
110 C4 Preston Missouri U.S.A.
103 J3 Preston Nevada U.S.A.
107 P6 Preston Oklahoma U.S.A.
9 E5 Preston Candover England
109 O9 Preston Hollow Texas U.S.A.
13 F2 Prestonpans Scotland
94 E9 Prestonsburg Kentucky U.S.A.
13 F6 Prestwich England
12 D3 Prestwick Scotland
129 K6 Preto *R* Bahia Brazil
129 J7 Prêto *R* Minas Gerais Brazil
128 F4 Prêto do Igapó Açu *R* Brazil
89 F5 Pretoria S Africa
20 H3 Prétot France
33 R9 Prettin Germany
95 L7 Prettyboy Res Maryland U.S.A.
107 M4 Pretty Prairie Kansas U.S.A.
33 O7 Pretzier Germany
33 R9 Pretzsch Germany
21 M8 Preuilly-sur-Claise France
38 L8 Prevalje Slovenia
46 D6 Préveza Greece
106 B6 Prewitt New Mexico U.S.A.
106 G1 Prewitt Res Colorado U.S.A.
21 N4 Prey France
68 G7 Prey Lovea Cambodia
68 G7 Prey Veng Cambodia
45 P5 Prezza Italy
69 B10 Priala Sumatra
54 H9 Priazovskaya Vozvyshenost' *uplands* Ukraine
116 D8 Pribilof Is Bering Sea
30 H6 Příbram Czechoslovakia
122 D5 Price Quebec Canada
95 M7 Price Maryland U.S.A.
98 F2 Price North Dakota U.S.A.
103 O2 Price *R* Utah U.S.A.
103 O2 Price Utah U.S.A.
68 A6 Price, C Andaman Is
106 B1 Price Creek Colorado U.S.A.
117 J9 Price I British Columbia Canada
111 H11 Prichard Alabama U.S.A.
100 K2 Prichard Idaho U.S.A.
54 E9 Prichernomorskaya Nizmennost' *lowland* Ukraine
37 J4 Prichsenstadt Germany
127 P5 Prickly Pt Grenada
109 J4 Priddy Texas U.S.A.
54 D7 Pridneprovskaya Nizmennost' *lowland* Ukraine
54 C8 Pridneprovskaya Vozvyshennost' *uplands* Ukraine
17 F4 Priego Spain
16 E7 Priego de C Spain
27 M15 Priekule Latvia
27 M16 Priekulė Lithuania
33 Q5 Priemerburg Germany
89 C7 Prieska S Africa
37 M1 Priessnitz Germany
33 T10 Priestewitz Germany
100 J1 Priest L Idaho U.S.A.
127 M2 Priestman's River Jamaica
100 F3 Priest Rapids Washington U.S.A.
100 E3 Priest Rapids Lake *res* Washington U.S.A.
100 J1 Priest River Idaho U.S.A.
117 P11 Priest River Idaho U.S.A.
31 L7 Prievidza Czechoslovakia
33 Q6 Prignitz *reg* Germany
56 C4 Priiskovyy Russian Federation
42 H4 Prijedor Bosnia-Herzegovina
53 G9 Prikaspiyskaya Nizmennost *lowlands* Kazakhstan/Rus Fed
46 E3 Prilep Macedonia Yugoslavia
54 D6 Priluki Ukraine
40 B7 Primarette France
118 H6 Primate Saskatchewan Canada
37 O4 Přimda Czechoslovakia
20 C4 Primel,Pte.de France
20 C4 Primel-Trégastel France
126 E4 Primero de Enero Cuba
131 D3 Primero, R Argentina
139 J8 Prime Seal I Tasmania Australia
99 L6 Primghar Iowa U.S.A.
52 C4 Primorsk Russian Federation
53 E10 Primorsk Ukraine
59 K3 Primorskiy Russian Federation
56 F5 Primorskiy Khrebet *mts* Russian Federation
59 K2 Primorskiy Kray *reg* Russian Federation
47 J2 Primorsko Bulgaria
48 M5 Primorskoye Ukraine
48 N5 Primorskoye Ukraine
54 J9 Primorskoye Ukraine
122 J7 Prim, Pt Prince Edward I Canada
117 F5 Primrose *R* Br Col/Yukon Terr Canada
118 H4 Primrose L Saskatchewan Canada
36 B5 Prims *R* Germany
36 C4 Primstal Germany
118 J6 Prince Saskatchewan Canada
119 M5 Prince Albert Saskatchewan Canada
89 C9 Prince Albert S Africa
146 D11 Prince Albert Mts Antarctica
118 L5 Prince Albert Nat. Park Saskatchewan Canada
114 H3 Prince Albert Pen Northwest Territories Canada
114 G3 Prince Alfred, C Northwest Territories Canada

216 **Prince Charles I — Quesnoy-sur-Deule, le**

115 M4 **Prince Charles I** Northwest Territories Canada
146 H10 **Prince Charles Mts** Antarctica
121 O9 **Prince Edward B** Ontario Canada
122 J7 **Prince Edward I** *prov* Canada
90 M14 **Prince Edward I** Indian Oc
122 J7 **Prince Edward I. Nat. Park** Canada
95 L8 **Prince Frederick** Maryland U.S.A.
142 F3 **Prince Frederick Harb** W Australia Australia
117 M9 **Prince George** British Columbia Canada
114 J2 **Prince Gustaf Adolf Sea** Northwest Territories Canada
116 C4 **Prince of Wales, C** Alaska U.S.A.
141 F1 **Prince of Wales I** Queensland Australia
114 J3 **Prince of Wales I** Northwest Territories Canada
117 G8 **Prince of Wales I** Alaska U.S.A.
114 H3 **Prince of Wales Str** Northwest Territories Canada
114 H2 **Prince Patrick I** Northwest Territories Canada
115 K3 **Prince Regent Inlet** Northwest Territories Canada
142 F3 **Prince Regent R** W Australia Australia
117 H8 **Prince Rupert** British Columbia Canada
130 H9 **Princesa Isabel** Brazil
Princes Is *see* **Kızıl Adalar**
Princes Lake Ontario *see* **Wallace**
9 F4 **Princes Risborough** England
95 M8 **Princess Anne** Maryland U.S.A.
141 G2 **Princess Charlotte B** Queensland Australia
146 H12 **Princess Elizabeth Land** Antarctica
142 F3 **Princess May Ra** W Australia Australia
144 A6 **Princess Mts** New Zealand
143 D7 **Princess Ra** W Australia Australia
117 J9 **Princess Royal I** British Columbia Canada
127 O3 **Prince's Town** Trinidad
9 E3 **Princethorpe** England
117 N11 **Princeton** British Columbia Canada
102 B2 **Princeton** California U.S.A.
99 R8 **Princeton** Illinois U.S.A.
110 J3 **Princeton** Indiana U.S.A.
110 J4 **Princeton** Kentucky U.S.A.
95 U1 **Princeton** Maine U.S.A.
99 T3 **Princeton** Michigan U.S.A.
99 N4 **Princeton** Minnesota U.S.A.
99 N9 **Princeton** Missouri U.S.A.
95 N6 **Princeton** New Jersey U.S.A.
112 J2 **Princeton** North Carolina U.S.A.
94 F9 **Princeton** West Virginia U.S.A.
99 R6 **Princeton** Wisconsin U.S.A.
8 C6 **Princetown** England
121 T6 **Princeville** Quebec Canada
99 R9 **Princeville** Illinois U.S.A.
116 O6 **Prince William Sound** Alaska U.S.A.
86 A5 **Principe** *isld* G of Guinea
128 F6 **Principe da Beira** Brazil
100 E5 **Prineville** Oregon U.S.A.
98 C6 **Pringle** South Dakota U.S.A.
108 C8 **Pringle** Texas U.S.A.
19 Q13 **Pringy** France
115 P5 **Prins Christian Sund** Greenland
25 C5 **Prinsenhage** Netherlands
68 C6 **Prinsep I** Burma
146 H7 **Prinsesse Astrid Kyst** *coast* Antarctica
146 J7 **Prinsesse Ragnhild Kyst** *coast* Antarctica
146 J8 **Prins Harald Kyst** *coast* Antarctica
50 A1 **Prins Karls Forland** Spitzbergen
123 L4 **Prinsta B** Anticosti I, Quebec
125 N3 **Prinzapolca** Nicaragua
54 L2 **Priokskiy** Russian Federation
16 B1 **Prior, C** Spain
52 D4 **Priozersk** Russian Federation
52 K3 **Pripolyarnyy Ural** *mts* Russian Federation
53 C8 **Pripyat** *R* Belorussia/Ukraine
29 P3 **Prirechnyy** Russian Federation
37 P3 **Přísečnice** Czechoslovakia
48 J3 **Prislop Pass** Romania
46 E4 **Prispansko ezero** *L* Albania/Greece/Yugoslavia
46 E2 **Priština** Serbia Yugoslavia
106 H4 **Pritchett** Colorado U.S.A.
33 Q8 **Pritzerbe** Germany
33 O6 **Pritzier** Germany
33 Q6 **Pritzwalk** Germany
19 N15 **Privas** France
45 O7 **Priverno** Italy
45 O6 **Privernum** Italy
42 F3 **Privka** Slovenia
52 F6 **Privolzhsk** Russian Federation
53 G7 **Privolzhskaya Vozvyshennost** *uplands* Russian Federation
53 G7 **Privolzh'ye** Russian Federation
20 D5 **Priziac** France
46 D2 **Prizren** Serbia Yugoslavia
43 E11 **Prizzi** Sicily
48 K1 **Probezhnaya** Ukraine
70 O9 **Probolinggo** Java
37 L2 **Probstzella** Germany
8 B7 **Probus** England
31 J4 **Prochowice** Poland
43 F8 **Procida** *isld* Italy
45 Q8 **Procida** Italy
106 H1 **Proctor** Colorado U.S.A.
109 J4 **Proctor** Texas U.S.A.
95 O3 **Proctor** Vermont U.S.A.
109 J3 **Proctor Res** Texas U.S.A.
95 P3 **Proctorsville** Vermont U.S.A.
16 B5 **Proènca a Nova** Portugal
37 N1 **Profen** Germany
22 H3 **Profondeville** Belgium
125 L2 **Progreso** Honduras
125 P7 **Progreso** Mexico
59 J2 **Progress** Russian Federation
106 E7 **Progresso** New Mexico U.S.A.
56 B6 **Prokhladnoye** Kazakhstan
55 G2 **Prokhorkino Proryto** Russian Federation
54 H5 **Prokhorovka** Russian Federation
46 D2 **Prokletije** Montenegro Yugoslavia
56 C4 **Prokop'yevsk** Russian Federation
46 E1 **Prokuplje** Serbia Yugoslavia
52 D5 **Proletariy** Russian Federation
53 F10 **Proletarsk** Russian Federation
54 K8 **Proletarsk** Ukraine
54 J1 **Proletarskiy** Russian Federation
54 G6 **Proletarskiy** Russian Federation
59 N2 **Proliv Frizi** *str* Russian Federation
50 E1 **Proliv Matochkin Shar** Russian Federation
37 K4 **Prolsdorf** Germany
Prome *see* **Pyè**
99 N9 **Promise City** Iowa U.S.A.
101 N8 **Promontory** Utah U.S.A.
56 C3 **Promyshlennaya** Russian Federation
53 G10 **Promyslovka** Russian Federation
52 F5 **Pronino** Russian Federation
100 G9 **Pronto** Nevada U.S.A.
54 M2 **Pronya** *R* Russian Federation
117 M6 **Prophet River** British Columbia Canada
99 R8 **Prophetstown** Illinois U.S.A.
130 H11 **Propriá** Brazil
33 S10 **Prösen** Germany
141 J5 **Proserpine** Queensland Australia
33 Q9 **Prosigk** Germany
31 K3 **Prosna** *R* Poland
52 H5 **Prosnitsa** Russian Federation
46 F3 **Prosotsáni** Greece
95 M3 **Prospect** New York U.S.A.
94 D6 **Prospect** Ohio U.S.A.
100 C7 **Prospect** Oregon U.S.A.
94 G6 **Prospect** Pennsylvania U.S.A.
127 M3 **Prospect Pt** Jamaica
100 A6 **Prosper** Oregon U.S.A.
112 F3 **Prosperity** South Carolina U.S.A.
98 H9 **Prosser** Nebraska U.S.A.
100 F3 **Prosser** Washington U.S.A.
48 D1 **Prostějov** Czechoslovakia
141 K7 **Proston** Queensland Australia
52 H2 **Prosunduy** Russian Federation
54 H8 **Prosyanaya** Ukraine
31 M5 **Proszowice** Poland
107 L4 **Protection** Kansas U.S.A.
99 O6 **Protivin** Iowa U.S.A.
54 J2 **Protva** *R* Russian Federation
33 T7 **Prötzel** Germany
47 J1 **Provadiya** Bulgaria
115 O3 **Prøven** Greenland
111 C10 **Provencal** Louisiana U.S.A.
19 O17 **Provence** *prov* France
36 C7 **Provenchères-sur-Fave** France
127 P5 **Providence** Grenada
110 J4 **Providence** Kentucky U.S.A.
112 J1 **Providence** North Carolina U.S.A.
95 Q5 **Providence** Rhode I U.S.A.
101 O8 **Providence** Utah U.S.A.
120 H7 **Providence Bay** Ontario Canada
144 A7 **Providence, C** New Zealand
116 J8 **Providence, C** Alaska U.S.A.
87 J9 **Providence I** Br Indian Oc Terr
103 J7 **Providence Mts** California U.S.A.
127 H4 **Providenciales** *isld* Turks & Caicos Is
128 F6 **Providencia, Sa. da** *mts* Brazil
116 A4 **Provideniya** Russian Federation
141 G2 **Providential Chan** Gt Barrier Reef Aust
95 R4 **Provincetown** Massachusetts U.S.A.
18 H4 **Provins** France
98 C6 **Provo** South Dakota U.S.A.
103 N1 **Provo** Utah U.S.A.
118 G6 **Provost** Alberta Canada
22 D4 **Proyart** France
42 H5 **Prozor** Bosnia-Herzegovina
130 E9 **Prudentópolis** Brazil
94 C2 **Prudenville** Michigan U.S.A.
13 G4 **Prudhoe** England
116 N1 **Prudhoe Bay** Alaska U.S.A.
141 J5 **Prudhoe I** Queensland Australia
115 N2 **Prudhoe Land** Greenland
119 M6 **Prud'homme** Saskatchewan Canada
31 K5 **Prudnik** Poland
54 H6 **Prudyanka** Ukraine
36 B3 **Prüm** Germany
21 M6 **Prunay** France
21 O5 **Prunay-le-Gillon** France
45 J3 **Prunetta** Italy
19 Q15 **Prunières** France
21 P8 **Pruniers** Indre France
21 O7 **Pruniers** Loir-et-Cher France
52 H4 **Prupt** *R* Russian Federation
31 K2 **Pruszcz** Poland
31 M3 **Pruszków** Poland
48 L4 **Prut** *R* Moldavia/Romania
48 L3 **Prutul** *R* Romania
41 N3 **Prutz** Austria
52 D4 **Pryazha** Russian Federation
146 J11 **Prydz B** Antarctica
101 R4 **Pryor** Montana U.S.A.
107 P5 **Pryor** Oklahoma U.S.A.
31 M2 **Przasnysz** Poland
31 K2 **Przechlewo** Poland
31 M4 **Przedbórz** Poland
31 O6 **Przemyśl** Poland
31 N5 **Przeworsk** Poland
31 H4 **Przewóz** Poland
57 J4 **Przheval'sk** Kyrgyzstan
31 M4 **Przysucha** Poland
46 F6 **Psakhná** Greece
47 H6 **Psará** *isld* Greece
46 G5 **Psathoúra** *isld* Greece
31 K4 **Psie Pole** Poland
47 R14 **Psíndhos** Rhodes Greece
47 H9 **Psíra** *isld* Greece
52 C5 **Pskov** Russian Federation
52 C5 **Pskovskaya Oblast'** *prov* Russian Federation
52 C5 **Pskovskoye, Ozero** *L* Russian Federation
31 L1 **Pszczółki** Poland
31 L6 **Pszczyna** Poland
53 C7 **Ptich'** *R* Belorussia
46 E4 **Ptolemaís** Greece
38 N9 **Ptuj** Slovenia
135 U4 **Puako** Hawaiian Is
116 K8 **Puale B** Alaska U.S.A.
133 E5 **Puán** Argentina
67 C5 **Pubei** China
122 G10 **Pubnico** Nova Scotia Canada
128 C5 **Pucacaca** Peru
128 D5 **Pucallpa** Peru
21 O3 **Puchay** France
38 N6 **Puchberg** Austria
65 A7 **Pucheng** China
65 C7 **Pucheng** China
67 F3 **Pucheng** China
52 F6 **Puchezh** Russian Federation
31 L6 **Puchov** Czechoslovakia
71 E5 **Pucio Pt** Panay Philippines
31 L1 **Puck** Poland
99 R6 **Puckaway L** Wisconsin U.S.A.
9 G4 **Puckeridge** England
111 G9 **Puckett** Mississippi U.S.A.
143 B7 **Puckford,Mt** W Australia Australia
29 M6 **Pudasjärvi** Finland
8 D6 **Puddletown** England
52 H5 **Pudem** Russian Federation
70 E6 **Pudi** Kalimantan
67 B3 **Puding** China
123 Q5 **Pudops L** Newfoundland Canada
52 E4 **Pudozh** Russian Federation
52 E4 **Pudozhgora** Russian Federation
13 G6 **Pudsey** England
125 K8 **Puebla** Mexico
16 D5 **Puebla de Alcocer** Spain
17 F7 **Puebla de Don Fadrique** Spain
16 D5 **Puebla de Don Rodrigo** Spain
16 C2 **Puebla de Sanabria** Spain
16 C2 **Puebla de Trives** Spain
106 F3 **Pueblo** Colorado U.S.A.
106 C5 **Pueblo Bonito** New Mexico U.S.A.
133 C3 **Pueblo Hundido** Chile
100 G7 **Pueblo Mts** Oregon U.S.A.
124 G6 **Pueblo Nuevo** Mexico
125 N9 **Pueblo Viejo** Mexico
125 L6 **Pueblo Viejo, L. de** Mexico
133 D5 **Puelches** Argentina
133 D5 **Puelén** Argentina
16 B2 **Puenteareas** Spain
16 B2 **Puente-Caldelas** Spain
16 D7 **Puente Genil** Spain
103 P7 **Puerco** *R* Arizona U.S.A.
106 C6 **Puerco, R** New Mexico U.S.A.
128 C2 **Puerta Mutis** Colombia
133 C7 **Puerto Aisén** Chile
125 N5 **Puerto Armuelles** Panama
128 C3 **Puerto Asis** Colombia
128 E2 **Puerto Ayacucho** Venezuela
125 P10 **Puerto Barrios** Guatemala
128 D6 **Puerto Bermúdez** Peru
128 D2 **Puerto Berrio** Colombia
133 C7 **Puerto Bertrand** Chile
128 C6 **Puerto Caballas** Peru
128 E1 **Puerto Cabello** Venezuela
125 N2 **Puerto Cabezas** Nicaragua
Puerto Capaz Morocco *see* **Jebha**
128 E2 **Puerto Carreño** Colombia
130 B8 **Puerto Casado** Paraguay
128 C5 **Puerto Chicama** Peru
133 C6 **Puerto Cisnes** Chile
133 D8 **Puerto Coig** Argentina
128 D1 **Puerto Colombia** Colombia
125 Q10 **Puerto Cortés** Honduras
128 E1 **Puerto Cumarebo** Venezuela
125 L10 **Puerto Escondido** Mexico
127 J8 **Puerto Estrella** Colombia
128 C5 **Puerto Eten** Peru
133 C5 **Puerto Fuy** Chile
128 F7 **Puerto Grether** Bolivia
133 D8 **Puerto Harberton** Argentina
128 E6 **Puerto Heath** Bolivia
128 D3 **Puerto Huitoto** Colombia
133 E5 **Puerto Ingeniero White** Argentina
125 Q7 **Puerto Juárez** Mexico
127 M9 **Puerto La Cruz** Venezuela
128 D4 **Puerto Leguizamo** Colombia
125 N2 **Puerto Lempira** Honduras
16 E6 **Puertollano** Spain
128 D7 **Puerto Lomas** Peru
127 J9 **Puerto López** Colombia
17 F7 **Puerto Lumbreras** Spain
133 D6 **Puerto Madryn** Argentina
128 E6 **Puerto Maldonado** Peru
126 F4 **Puerto Manatí** Cuba
128 D4 **Puerto Miraña** Colombia
133 C6 **Puerto Montt** Chile
133 C8 **Puerto Natales** Chile
128 E2 **Puerto Nuevo** Colombia
133 F3 **Puerto Ocampo** Argentina
128 F2 **Puerto Ordaz** Venezuela
126 F4 **Puerto Padre** Cuba
133 C2 **Puerto Patillos** Chile
124 C2 **Puerto Penasco** Mexico
133 F2 **Puerto Pinasco** Paraguay
133 E6 **Puerto Pirámides** Argentina
128 F1 **Puerto Piritu** Venezuela
127 J5 **Puerto Plata** Dominican Rep
128 D5 **Puerto Portillo** Peru
130 C9 **Puerto Presidente Stroessner** Paraguay
71 D6 **Puerto Princesa** Palawan Philippines
125 M5 **Puerto Quepos** Costa Rica
128 E6 **Puerto Rico** Bolivia
113 J7 **Puerto Rico** *terr* Caribbean
127 L5 **Puerto Rico Trench** Caribbean
126 G4 **Puerto Samá** Cuba
125 L3 **Puerto Sandino** Nicaragua
130 B8 **Puerto Sastre** Paraguay
128 E6 **Puerto Siles** Bolivia
130 B6 **Puerto Suárez** Bolivia
124 G7 **Puerto Vallarta** Mexico
133 C6 **Puerto Varas** Chile
128 F7 **Puerto Velarde** Bolivia
128 D5 **Puerto Victoria** Peru
128 D2 **Puerto Villamizar** Colombia
133 D7 **Puerto Visser** Argentina
128 D2 **Puerto Wilches** Colombia
133 C7 **Pueyrredón, L** Chile/Arg
25 F7 **Puffendorf** Germany
124 G7 **Puga** Mexico
52 H6 **Pugachevo** Russian Federation
74 E4 **Pugal** India
88 G10 **Puga Puga** *isld* Mozambique
100 C2 **Puget Sound** Washington U.S.A.
19 P13 **Pugieu** France
43 G8 **Puglia** *prov* Italy
71 K9 **Pugubengo** Flores Indonesia
70 K8 **Pugung, G** *mt* Sumatra
122 J8 **Pugwash** Nova Scotia Canada
145 F3 **Puha** New Zealand
135 O1 **Puhi** Hawaiian Is
145 E2 **Puhoi** New Zealand
48 H5 **Pui** Romania
48 L4 **Puieşti** Romania
17 J2 **Puigcerda** Spain
71 G7 **Pujada B** Mindanao Philippines
65 G4 **Pujan Res** N Korea
19 N16 **Pujaut** France
67 A1 **Pujiang** China
67 F2 **Pujiang** China
119 Q3 **Pukatawagan** Manitoba Canada
46 D2 **Pukë** Albania
145 G2 **Pukeamaru** *mt* New Zealand
145 E3 **Pukearuhe** New Zealand
145 F3 **Pukehou** New Zealand
145 E2 **Pukekawa** New Zealand
145 E2 **Pukekohe** New Zealand
144 C5 **Pukekura** New Zealand
145 E2 **Pukemiro** New Zealand
145 D1 **Pukenui** New Zealand
145 F3 **Pukeokahu** New Zealand
144 C6 **Pukerangi** New Zealand
144 B7 **Pukerau** New Zealand
145 E3 **Pukeroa** New Zealand
145 G3 **Puketawai** New Zealand
144 D5 **Puketeraki Range** New Zealand
145 F3 **Puketitiri** New Zealand
145 F2 **Puketoetoe** *mt* New Zealand
145 F4 **Puketoi Range** New Zealand
145 E3 **Puketutu** New Zealand
145 F2 **Puketutu I** New Zealand
144 C6 **Pukeuri Junction** New Zealand
29 M11 **Pukkila** Finland
67 F1 **Pukou** China
52 F3 **Puksa** Russian Federation
52 H5 **Puksib** Russian Federation
52 F3 **Puksoozero** Russian Federation
98 G6 **Pukwana** South Dakota U.S.A.
42 F4 **Pula** Croatia
128 E8 **Pulacayo** Bolivia
43 C9 **Pula, C. di** Sardinia
69 C11 **Pulaksama** Sumatra
Pulandian *see* **Xinjin**
71 G6 **Pulangi** *R* Mindanao Philippines
70 D6 **Pulangpisau** Kalimantan
70 K8 **Pulao Seribu** *isld* Sumatra
70 K9 **Pulasari** *mt* Java
71 K8 **Pulasi** *isld* Indonesia
99 O9 **Pulaski** Iowa U.S.A.
95 L3 **Pulaski** New York U.S.A.
110 J6 **Pulaski** Tennessee U.S.A.
94 G9 **Pulaski** Virginia U.S.A.
99 S5 **Pulaski** Wisconsin U.S.A.
69 F13 **Pulaukidjang** Sumatra
70 B4 **Pulaumadjang** Kalimantan
69 E13 **Pulaupunjung** Sumatra
31 N4 **Puławy** Poland
9 F6 **Pulborough** England
76 D3 **Pulivendla** India
76 C6 **Puliyangudi** India
83 K9 **Puliyankulam** Sri Lanka
29 M7 **Pulkkila** Finland
100 H3 **Pullman** Washington U.S.A.
71 E2 **Pulog, Mt** Luzon Philippines
83 K8 **Puloli** Sri Lanka
52 F2 **Pulonga** Russian Federation
52 D1 **Pulozero** Russian Federation
124 D4 **Púlpito, Pta** *C* Mexico
33 T10 **Pulsnitz** *R* Germany
31 M3 **Pułtusk** Poland
66 C4 **Pulu** China
70 P10 **Pulukan** Bali Indonesia
66 E6 **Puma Yumco** *L* China
Pumiao *see* **Yongning**
98 A4 **Pumpkin Cr** Montana U.S.A.
98 C8 **Pumpkin Cr** Nebraska U.S.A.
108 F6 **Pumpville** Texas U.S.A.
8 C3 **Pumsaint** Wales
128 B4 **Puná** *isld* Ecuador
70 G5 **Puna** *R* Sulawesi
144 C5 **Punakaiki** New Zealand
83 L10 **Punani** Sri Lanka
74 F2 **Punch** Kashmir
117 M9 **Punchaw** British Columbia Canada
52 F4 **Punduga** Russian Federation
76 A1 **Pune** India
55 D1 **Punga** *R* Russian Federation
112 L2 **Pungo** North Carolina U.S.A.
59 J3 **Pungsan** N Korea
86 E6 **Punia** Zaire
70 Q10 **Punikan, G** *mt* Indonesia
131 B2 **Punilla, Sa. de la** *mts* Chile
74 F3 **Punjab** *prov* India
74 D3 **Punjab, The** *prov* Pakistan
140 E4 **Punjaub** Queensland Australia
29 O10 **Punkaharju** Finland
29 K10 **Punkalaidun** Finland
119 N7 **Punnichy** Saskatchewan Canada
128 D6 **Puno** *dept* Peru
128 D7 **Puno** Peru
106 D7 **Punta** New Mexico U.S.A.
131 E7 **Punta Alta** Argentina
133 C8 **Punta Arenas** Chile
43 C7 **Puntaccia, Monte** *mt* Sardinia
133 C3 **Punta Colorada** Chile
108 B8 **Punta de Agua Cr.** *R* Texas/New Mex U.S.A.
17 H4 **Punta de la Baña** Spain
125 P9 **Punta Gorda** Belize
125 N4 **Punta Gorda** Nicaragua
100 A9 **Punta Gorda** California U.S.A.
113 E11 **Punta Gorda** Florida U.S.A.
131 G6 **Punta Norte** Argentina
127 J5 **Punta Palenque** Dominican Rep
124 B3 **Punta Prieta** Mexico
125 M5 **Puntarenas** Costa Rica
128 G8 **Punta Rieles** Paraguay
125 N5 **Punta San Pedrillo** Costa Rica
127 M5 **Punta Tuna** Puerto Rico
128 D1 **Punto Fijo** Venezuela
46 G4 **Punto Lágo** Greece
133 D7 **Puntudo, Cerro** *mt* Argentina
116 C5 **Punuk Is** Bering Sea
94 J6 **Punxsutawney** Pennsylvania U.S.A.
68 F6 **Puok** Cambodia
29 N7 **Puolanka** Finland
26 L5 **Puottaure** Sweden
128 E6 **Puoya** *mt* Bolivia
145 D4 **Puponga** New Zealand
58 F6 **Puqi** China
128 D6 **Puquio** Peru
133 D3 **Puquios** Chile
50 G2 **Pur** *R* Russian Federation
128 C3 **Puracé** *vol* Colombia
70 M9 **Purbalingga** Java
107 N7 **Purcell** Oklahoma U.S.A.
116 J3 **Purcell Mt** Alaska U.S.A.
117 P10 **Purcell Mts** British Columbia Canada
100 K1 **Purcell Range** Montana U.S.A.
94 K7 **Purcellville** Virginia U.S.A.
17 F7 **Purchena** Spain
99 N10 **Purdin** Missouri U.S.A.
98 F7 **Purdum** Nebraska U.S.A.
110 C5 **Purdy** Missouri U.S.A.
145 E3 **Pureora** *mt* New Zealand
124 H8 **Purépero** Mexico
145 E1 **Purerua** New Zealand
9 E6 **Purewell** England
106 G4 **Purgatoire** *R* Colorado U.S.A.
116 N3 **Purgatory** Alaska U.S.A.
38 M5 **Purgstall** Austria
75 L9 **Puri** India
128 D3 **Purificación** Colombia
145 E2 **Puriri** New Zealand
9 F5 **Purley** England
25 C3 **Purmerend** Netherlands
74 G9 **Purna** India
138 B2 **Purndu Saltpan** South Australia Australia
52 E3 **Purnema** Russian Federation
75 M6 **Pūrnia** India
118 F9 **Purple Springs** Alberta Canada
128 E4 **Purué** *R* Brazil
70 D5 **Purukcahu** Kalimantan
128 F4 **Purus** *R* Brazil
29 O10 **Puruvesi** *L* Finland
111 G10 **Purvis** Mississippi U.S.A.
46 G2 **Pŭrvomay** Bulgaria
70 L9 **Purwakarta** Java
70 M9 **Purwarejo** Java
70 N9 **Purwodadi** Java
70 M9 **Purwokerto** Java
110 H5 **Puryear** Tennessee U.S.A.
66 B4 **Pusa** China
52 C6 **Puša** Latvia
70 B4 **Pusa** Sarawak
74 G9 **Pusad** India
52 B6 **Pušalotas** Lithuania
65 H7 **Pusan** S Korea
71 G7 **Pusan Pt** Mindanao Philippines
70 B4 **Pusatdamai** Kalimantan
79 D2 **Pusatlı Dağı** *mt* Turkey
65 D6 **Pushang** China
95 T2 **Pushaw L** Maine U.S.A.
52 D5 **Pushkin** Russian Federation
54 J1 **Pushkino** Russian Federation
52 E3 **Pushlakhta** Russian Federation
123 Q6 **Pushthrough** Newfoundland Canada
77 H4 **Pusht-i-Rud** *reg* Afghanistan
120 E4 **Puskaskwa Nat. Park** Ontario Canada
121 O3 **Puskitamika L** Quebec Canada
48 G3 **Püspökladány** Hungary
21 O5 **Pussay** France
22 H4 **Pussemange** Belgium
38 K7 **Pusterwald** Austria
52 C6 **Pustoshka** Russian Federation
102 B3 **Putah Cr** California U.S.A.
67 G5 **Pu-tai** Taiwan
71 M9 **Putain** Timor Indonesia
21 K4 **Putanges-Pont-Ecrepin** France
75 R5 **Putao** Burma
145 E3 **Putaruru** New Zealand
30 G1 **Putbus** Germany
70 P9 **Puteran** *isld* Indonesia
83 K8 **Puthukkudiyiruppu** Sri Lanka
67 F4 **Putian** China
43 H8 **Putignano** Italy
48 J3 **Putila** Ukraine
52 F5 **Putilovo** Russian Federation
70 B6 **Puting Tg** *C* Kalimantan
54 E5 **Putivl'** Ukraine
33 Q6 **Putlitz** Germany
48 K3 **Putna** Romania
95 Q5 **Putnam** Connecticut U.S.A.
108 E8 **Putnam** Oklahoma U.S.A.
109 H3 **Putnam** Texas U.S.A.
112 C6 **Putney** Georgia U.S.A.
98 H4 **Putney** South Dakota U.S.A.
95 P4 **Putney** Vermont U.S.A.
51 J2 **Putorana, Plato** *mt* Russian Federation
145 F3 **Putorino** New Zealand
83 J9 **Puttalam** Sri Lanka
83 J9 **Puttalam Lag** Sri Lanka
22 G1 **Putte** Belgium
36 B5 **Puttelange** France
33 O5 **Püttelkow** Germany
25 E4 **Putten** Netherlands
28 G7 **Puttgarden** Germany
36 B5 **Püttlingen** Germany
128 C3 **Putumayo** *div* Colombia
128 D4 **Putumayo** *R* Peru/Colombia
67 G2 **Putuo** China
67 G1 **Putuo Shan** *isld* China
70 C4 **Putusibau** Kalimantan
33 T5 **Putzar** Germany
135 U5 **Puuanahulu** Hawaiian Is
135 U5 **Puu Hualalei** *crater* Hawaiian Is
135 S3 **Puukoli** Hawaiian Is
29 M10 **Puulavesi** *L* Finland
29 N10 **Puumala** Finland
22 G1 **Puurs** Belgium
135 N1 **Puuwai** Hawaiian Is
Puxian *see* **Pucheng**
65 A6 **Pu Xian** China
117 M12 **Puyallup** Washington U.S.A.
65 C7 **Puyang** China
18 G7 **Puy de Dôme** *dept* France
18 G7 **Puy-de-Sancy** *mt* France
131 A8 **Puyehue, L de** Chile
131 B8 **Puyehue, P. de** Argentina
131 A8 **Puyehue, V** Chile
21 M8 **Puye, La** France
19 Q14 **Puy Gris** *mt* France
18 G9 **Puylaurens** France
18 H7 **Puy, le** France
18 F8 **Puy l'Evêque** France
18 G7 **Puy Mary** *mt* France
21 K7 **Puy Notre Dame, le** France
21 N2 **Puys** France
52 H4 **Puzla** Russian Federation
88 G5 **Pwani** *prov* Tanzania
88 B6 **Pweto** Zaire
68 B2 **Pwinbyu** Burma
8 B2 **Pwllheli** Wales
52 E2 **Pyalitsa** Russian Federation
52 E4 **Pyal'ma** Russian Federation
68 B3 **Pyalo** Burma
68 B5 **Pyamalaw** *R* Burma
52 F6 **Pyana** *R* Russian Federation
57 E6 **Pyandzh** Tajikistan
57 E6 **Pyandzh** *R* Tajikistan/Afghanistan
52 J4 **Pyanteg** Russian Federation
52 D2 **Pyaozero, Oz** *L* Russian Federation
76 C3 **Pyapalli** India
68 B4 **Pyapon** Burma
51 H1 **Pyasina** *R* Russian Federation
53 F11 **Pyatigorsk** Russian Federation
54 E8 **Pyatikhatki** Ukraine
52 H4 **Pyatiqory** Russian Federation
110 D5 **Pyatt** Arkansas U.S.A.
52 H6 **Pychas** Russian Federation
68 B3 **Pyè** Burma
116 M7 **Pye Is** Alaska U.S.A.
29 M9 **Pyhä-Häki Nat. Park** Finland
27 M11 **Pyhajärvi** *L* Finland
29 M8 **Pyhäjärvi** Finland
29 L7 **Pyhäjoki** Finland
29 M7 **Pyhäntä** Finland
29 J11 **Pyhäranta** Finland
29 O9 **Pyhäselkä** Finland
29 M4 **Pyhätunturi Nat. Park** Finland
38 N5 **Pyhra** Austria
68 C3 **Pyinmana** Burma
8 C4 **Pyle** Wales
29 L9 **Pylkönmäki** Finland
94 G5 **Pymatuning Res** Ohio/Penn U.S.A.
69 A9 **Pymgalion Pt** Nicobar Is
59 J3 **Pyöktong** N Korea
65 F5 **P'yŏngyang** N Korea
100 F9 **Pyramid** Nevada U.S.A.
103 K6 **Pyramid Canyon** Ariz/Nev U.S.A.
139 G6 **Pyramid Hill** Victoria Australia
106 C1 **Pyramid Pk** Colorado U.S.A.
94 A2 **Pyramid Pt** Michigan U.S.A.
102 E2 **Pyramid Rge** Nevada U.S.A.
18 F9 **Pyrénées** *mts* France/Spain
18 E9 **Pyrénées Atlantiques** *dept* France
18 G10 **Pyrénées-Orientales** *dept* France
142 B5 **Pyrton,Mt** W Australia Australia
31 H2 **Pyrzyce** Poland
52 G5 **Pyshchug** Russian Federation
55 D3 **Pyshma** Russian Federation
31 L5 **Pyskowice** Poland
52 C6 **Pytalovo** Russian Federation
121 O6 **Pythonga, L** Quebec Canada
68 C3 **Pyu** *R* Burma
68 C3 **Pyu** Burma
68 C4 **Pyuntaza** Burma
31 K3 **Pyzdry** Poland

Q

Qaanaaq *see* **Thule**
84 E3 **Qaddāhīyah, Al** Libya
74 F3 **Qadian** India
78 K6 **Qādisīyah, Al** *prov* Iraq
77 C1 **Qāem Shahr** Iran
80 G4 **Qafqafa** Jordan
58 G2 **Qagan** China
Qagan Nur *see* **Zhengxiangbai Qi**
65 F2 **Qagan Nur** *L* China
65 B3 **Qagan Nur** China
65 C3 **Qagan Nur** *L* China
65 B4 **Qagan Nur** *L* China
65 D1 **Qagan Qulut** China
65 D3 **Qagan Us** China
65 B4 **Qahar Youyi Houqi** China
65 B4 **Qahar Youyi Qianqi** China
65 B4 **Qahar Youyi Zhongqi** China
Qâhira, El *see* **Cairo**
66 E4 **Qaidam Pendi** *reg* China
66 F4 **Qaidam Shan** *mts* China
77 J4 **Qala Bist** Afghanistan
86 G3 **Qala'en Nahl** Sudan
77 J3 **Qala-i-Ghor** Afghanistan
77 H3 **Qala-i-Kāl** Afghanistan
77 K3 **Qalāt** Afghanistan
79 G4 **Qal 'at al Hisn** Syria
79 F3 **Qal'at al Marqab** Syria
78 H4 **Qal'at as Salihīyah** Syria
80 F4 **Qal'at er Rabad** Jordan
78 L6 **Qal'at Sālih** Iraq
77 J4 **Qal'eh-ye Bost** Afghanistan
77 H2 **Qal'eh-ye Now** Afghanistan
80 C5 **Qalqīlya** Israel
80 E6 **Qalya** Jordan
79 B8 **Qalyûb** Egypt
80 G3 **Qam** Jordan
74 C5 **Qambar** Pakistan
66 F5 **Qamdo** *reg* China
84 F3 **Qaminis** Libya
78 H3 **Qāmishlī, Al** Syria
74 C3 **Qamruddin Karez** Pakistan
80 D5 **Qana** Jordan
86 A1 **Qandala** Somalia
65 C3 **Qangdin Gol** China
65 C3 **Qangdin Sum** China
79 C8 **Qanṭara, El** Egypt
79 G6 **Qanwāt, Al** Syria
Qaqortoq *see* **Julianehåb**
84 H4 **Qara** Egypt
79 F5 **Qaraaoun** Lebanon
77 L2 **Qarah Bāgh** Afghanistan
80 D5 **Qarawat Bani Ḥassan** Jordan
79 G3 **Qardāhah, Al** Syria
86 A2 **Qardho** Somalia
78 L2 **Qareh Su** *R* Iran
79 C10 **Qarn el Kabsh, G** *mt* Egypt
66 D4 **Qarqan He** *R* China
79 F4 **Qartaba** Lebanon
84 E3 **Qaryāt, Al** Libya
79 H4 **Qaryatayn, Al** Syria
80 G7 **Qaryat Falha** Jordan
77 H2 **Qasa Murg** Afghanistan
Qasigiangguit *see* **Christianshåb**
80 F8 **Qasr** Jordan
79 H4 **Qasr al Ḥayr** Syria
79 F8 **Qasr ed Deir, J** *mt* Jordan
84 H4 **Qasr, El** Egypt
78 K4 **Qasr-e-Shirin** Iran
80 G8 **Qasr eth Thuraiya** Jordan
84 H4 **Qasr Farâfra** Egypt
115 P5 **Qassimiut** Greenland
79 G5 **Qatana** Syria
77 B7 **Qatar** *state* Persian Gulf
77 B6 **Qatīf, Al** Saudi Arabia
79 G7 **Qatrāna** Jordan
84 E5 **Qaṭrūn, Al** Libya
84 H4 **Qattara Depression** Egypt
77 F3 **Qāyen** Iran
78 J4 **Qayyarah** Iraq
80 F2 **Qazrin** Syria
77 A1 **Qazvīn** Iran
80 F1 **Qela'** Syria
84 J4 **Qena** Egypt
Qeqertarsuaq *see* **Godhavn**
Qeqertarsuaq *isld see* **Disko** *isld*
Qeqertarsuatsiaat *see* **Fiskenæsset**
Qeqertarsuatsiaq *see* **Hareøen**
77 E6 **Qeshm** Iran
77 A1 **Qeydār** Iran
77 C6 **Qeys** *isld* Iran
77 A1 **Qezel Owzan** *R* Iran
79 E8 **Qeẓi'ot** Israel
65 F2 **Qian'an** China
65 D4 **Qian'an** China
67 C3 **Qiancheng** China
65 F2 **Qian Gorlos** China
67 C3 **Qiangu'ao** China
Qianguozhen *see* **Qian Gorlos**
65 D7 **Qiangwei He** *R* China
67 D1 **Qianjiang** China
67 C2 **Qianjiang** *R* China
67 C5 **Qianjiang** China
59 K2 **Qianjin** China
65 F4 **Qian Shan** *mt ra* China
66 E3 **Qianshan** China
67 E1 **Qianshan** China
65 E4 **Qianwei** China
67 A2 **Qianwei** China
65 D4 **Qianxi** China
67 B3 **Qianxi** China
67 A4 **Qianxinan** China
67 C3 **Qianyang** China
65 D3 **Qiaotou** China
67 E3 **Qiaotou** China
67 E1 **Qichun** China
80 F1 **Qidmat Ẓevi** Syria
67 G1 **Qidong** China
67 D3 **Qidong** China
66 D4 **Qiemo** China
67 C2 **Qifeng Guan** *pass* China
65 C6 **Qihe** China
65 B3 **Qihreg** China
58 E6 **Qijiang** China
66 E3 **Qijiaojing** China
Qike *see* **Xunke**
65 D5 **Qikou** China
77 H6 **Qila Lādgasht** Pakistan
65 D4 **Qilaotu Shan** *mt ra* China
74 A8 **Qila Safed** Pakistan
74 C3 **Qila Saifullah** Pakistan
Qili *see* **Shitai**
66 F4 **Qilian Shan** *mt ra* China
65 E4 **Qilihe** China
67 F2 **Qimen** China
65 G1 **Qing'an** China
65 D6 **Qingcheng** China
65 E6 **Qingdao** China
65 E5 **Qingduizi** China
65 C7 **Qingfeng** China
67 A2 **Qingfu** China
65 G1 **Qinggang** China
Qinggil *see* **Qinghe**
65 C7 **Qingguji** China
66 E4 **Qinghai** *prov* China
58 D4 **Qinghai Hu** *L* China
65 H1 **Qinghe** China
65 C6 **Qinghe** China
66 E2 **Qinghe** China
65 F4 **Qinghecheng** China
65 E4 **Qinghemen** China
65 F3 **Qinghe Shuiku** *res* China
67 F2 **Qinghu** China
65 A6 **Qingjian** China
67 C1 **Qing Jiang** *R* China
67 E2 **Qingjiang** China
65 A6 **Qingjian He** *R* China
Qingkou *see* **Ganyu**
67 C7 **Qinglan** China
67 D7 **Qinglan Gang** *inlet* China
67 D4 **Qinglian** China
67 E3 **Qingliu** China
65 D4 **Qinglong** China
67 B4 **Qinglong** China
65 D4 **Qinglong He** *R* China
65 C6 **Qingping** China
68 J2 **Qingping** China
67 G1 **Qingpu** China
67 A2 **Qingshen** China
58 E4 **Qingshui He** *R* China
65 B5 **Qingshuihe** China
67 C3 **Qingshui Jiang** *R* China
67 G2 **Qingtian** China
65 C5 **Qing Xian** China
65 B6 **Qingxu** China
Qingyang *see* **Jinjiang**
58 E4 **Qingyang** China
67 F1 **Qingyang** China
Qingyuan *see* **Yishan**
59 J3 **Qingyuan** China
67 F3 **Qingyuan** China
67 D5 **Qingyuan** China
65 D6 **Qingyun** China
65 B7 **Qin He** *R* China
65 D5 **Qinhuangdao** China
67 C6 **Qin Jiang** *R* China
58 E5 **Qin Ling** *mt ra* China
65 B7 **Qinshui** China
67 C5 **Qintang** China
58 F4 **Qin Xian** China
58 F4 **Qinyang** China
67 G3 **Qinyu** China
65 B6 **Qinyuan** China
67 C6 **Qinzhou** China
68 J2 **Qinzhou Wan** *B* China
68 K3 **Qionghai** China
58 D5 **Qionglai** China
58 D5 **Qionglai Shan** *mt ra* China
67 C7 **Qiongshan** China
67 C7 **Qiongzhong** China
68 J2 **Qiongzhou Haixia** China
67 B1 **Qiping** China
59 H2 **Qiqihar** China
77 C5 **Qīr** Iran
80 D7 **Qiryat Arba'** Jordan
80 D2 **Qiryat Ata** Israel
80 D8 **Qiryatayim** Jordan
80 D2 **Qiryat Bialik** Israel
80 C7 **Qiryat Gat** Israel
80 D2 **Qiryat Motmkin** Israel
80 D5 **Qiryat Netafim** Jordan
80 F1 **Qiryat Shemona** Israel
80 D3 **Qiryat Tiv'on** Israel
80 D2 **Qiryat Yam** Israel
80 D6 **Qiryat Yearim** Israel
67 C6 **Qisha** China
80 D3 **Qishon 'Eneq Yizre'el** Israel
68 J2 **Qishui** China
66 D3 **Qitai** China
65 H2 **Qitaihe** China
67 A4 **Qiubei** China
65 C6 **Qiu Xian** China
65 E6 **Qixia** China
65 B6 **Qi Xian** China
65 C7 **Qi Xian** China
65 B4 **Qixiaying** China
65 J1 **Qixing He** *R* China
65 H1 **Qixingpao** China
67 D3 **Qiyang** China
67 E1 **Qizhou** China
Qogir Feng *mt pk see* **K2** *mt*
65 C2 **Qog Ul** China
77 B2 **Qom** Iran
77 B3 **Qomisheh** Iran
Qomolangma Feng *mt see* **Everest, Mt**
66 D3 **Qongkol** China
115 O5 **Qoornoq** Greenland
77 A2 **Qorveh** Iran
79 G4 **Qoubaiyat** Lebanon
95 P4 **Quabbin Res** Massachusetts U.S.A.
122 G8 **Quaco Hd** New Brunswick Canada
74 D2 **Quaidabad** Pakistan
102 H6 **Quail Mts** California U.S.A.
143 B9 **Quairading** W Australia Australia
32 G7 **Quakenbrück** Germany
95 M6 **Quakertown** Pennsylvania U.S.A.
45 Q8 **Qualiano** Italy
85 E6 **Quallam** Niger
139 G6 **Quambatook** Victoria Australia
139 J4 **Quambone** New South Wales Australia
140 F5 **Quamby** Queensland Australia
108 H1 **Quanah** Texas U.S.A.
128 F4 **Quanaru, Ilha** Brazil
68 H2 **Quan Dao Co To** *isld* Vietnam
68 J5 **Quang Nam** Vietnam
68 J5 **Quang Ngai** Vietnam
68 H4 **Quang Tri** Vietnam
67 B6 **Quang Yen** Vietnam
67 F1 **Quanjiao** China
69 G8 **Quan Long** Vietnam
67 E4 **Quannan** China
68 F7 **Quan Phu Quoc** *isld* Vietnam
94 K8 **Quantico** Virginia U.S.A.
120 E1 **Quantz L** Ontario Canada
67 C4 **Quanzhou** China
119 O8 **Qu'Appelle** Saskatchewan Canada
119 P8 **Qu'Appelle R** Saskatchewan Canada
118 L7 **Qu'Appelle R. Dam** Saskatchewan Canada
133 F4 **Quaraí** Brazil
131 G3 **Quaraí, R** Brazil
32 L4 **Quarnbek** Germany
122 G7 **Quarryville** New Brunswick Canada
95 L7 **Quarryville** Pennsylvania U.S.A.
40 F6 **Quart** Italy
45 L2 **Quartesana** Italy
45 N6 **Quartière Mt. Sacro** Italy
83 M12 **Quartier Militaire** Mauritius
43 C9 **Quartu Sant'Elena** Sardinia
102 H4 **Quartzite Mt** Nevada U.S.A.
102 G2 **Quartz Mt** Nevada U.S.A.
100 G1 **Quartz Mt** Washington U.S.A.
103 K8 **Quartzsite** Arizona U.S.A.
99 P7 **Quasqueton** Iowa U.S.A.
22 G2 **Quatre Bras** Belgium
22 H5 **Quatre-Champs** France
117 K10 **Quatsino** British Columbia Canada
45 H2 **Quattro Castella** Italy
106 G7 **Quay** New Mexico U.S.A.
77 F1 **Qūchān** Iran
101 P8 **Quealy** Wyoming U.S.A.
139 J6 **Queanbeyan** New South Wales Australia
115 M7 **Quebec** *prov* Canada
121 T6 **Québec** Quebec Canada
130 F6 **Quebra Anzol** *R* Brazil
88 D9 **Quebrabasa Rapids** Mozambique
133 E3 **Quebracho Coto** Argentina
131 A8 **Quedal, C. de** Chile
33 O9 **Quedlinburg** Germany
17 G9 **Qued Tlélat** Algeria
95 L8 **Queen Anne** Maryland U.S.A.
117 L10 **Queen Bess, Mt** British Columbia Canada
9 G5 **Queenborough** England
115 M5 **Queen, C** Northwest Territories Canada
133 E8 **Queen Charlotte B** Falkland Is
117 G9 **Queen Charlotte Is** British Columbia Canada
117 J10 **Queen Charlotte Sd** British Columbia Canada
145 E4 **Queen Charlotte Sound** New Zealand
117 K10 **Queen Charlotte Str** British Columbia Canada
99 O9 **Queen City** Missouri U.S.A.
109 N2 **Queen City** Texas U.S.A.
115 K2 **Queen Elizabeth Is** Northwest Territories Canada
146 H12 **Queen Mary Land** Antarctica
117 D5 **Queen Mary, Mt** Yukon Territory Canada
114 J4 **Queen Maud Gulf** Northwest Territories Canada
146 D9 **Queen Maud Mts** Antarctica
13 G6 **Queensbury** England
140 A2 **Queens Chan** N Terr Australia
115 K2 **Queens Chan** Northwest Territories Canada
139 G7 **Queenscliff** Victoria Australia
13 E2 **Queensferry** Scotland
140 F6 **Queensland** *state* Australia
142 B2 **Queens Park** *dist* Perth, W Aust Australia
123 L8 **Queensport** Nova Scotia Canada
139 H8 **Queenstown** Tasmania Australia
118 E8 **Queenstown** Alberta Canada
144 B6 **Queenstown** New Zealand
89 E8 **Queenstown** S Africa
95 L8 **Queenstown** Maryland U.S.A.
100 A2 **Queets** Washington U.S.A.
131 F4 **Queguay Grande** *R* Uruguay
36 E5 **Queich** *R* Germany
16 C2 **Queija, S. de** *mts* Spain
129 L6 **Queimadas** Brazil
87 C7 **Quela** Angola
21 J6 **Quelaines** France
87 B7 **Quele** Angola
88 F10 **Quelimane** Mozambique
124 F6 **Quelite** Mexico
133 C6 **Quellen** Chile
106 B7 **Quemado** New Mexico U.S.A.
108 G7 **Quemado** Texas U.S.A.
20 B5 **Quéménéven** France
Quemoy *see* **Chin-men**
133 E5 **Quemu Quemu** Argentina
22 B3 **Quend** France
9 G4 **Quendon** England
22 B3 **Quend Plage** France
107 P3 **Quenemo** Kansas U.S.A.
111 F10 **Quentin** Mississippi U.S.A.
Que Que *see* **Kwekwe**
133 F5 **Quequén** Argentina
22 C2 **Quercamps** France
130 D8 **Querência do Norte** Brazil
125 J7 **Querétaro** Mexico
33 P10 **Querfurt** Germany
124 D2 **Querobabi** Mexico
20 G2 **Querqueville** France
20 C6 **Querrien** France
21 P2 **Querrieu** France
117 M9 **Quesnel** British Columbia Canada
117 N9 **Quesnel L** British Columbia Canada
22 D4 **Quesnoy** France
22 F3 **Quesnoy, le** France
22 E2 **Quesnoy-sur-Deule, le** France

20 E5 **Quessoy** France
106 E5 **Questa** New Mexico U.S.A.
20 F6 **Questembert** France
133 D2 **Quetena** Bolivia
99 Q1 **Quetico** Ontario Canada
118 L2 **Quetico L** Ontario Canada
99 P1 **Quetico Provincial Park** Ontario Canada
74 B3 **Quetta** Pakistan
20 H2 **Quettehou** France
21 L3 **Quetteville** France
20 H4 **Quettreville** France
111 D11 **Queue de Tortue** *R* Louisiana U.S.A.
21 O4 **Queue-lèz-Yvelines,la** France
21 P2 **Quevauvillers** France
121 O3 **Quévillon** Quebec Canada
125 O10 **Quezaltenango** Guatemala
71 C6 **Quezon** Palawan Philippines
71 E3 **Quezon City** Luzon Philippines
65 D7 **Qufu** China
87 B8 **Quibala** Angola
87 B7 **Quibate** Angola
128 C2 **Quibdó** Colombia
118 J1 **Quibell** Ontario Canada
20 D7 **Quiberon** France
20 D6 **Quiberon,B.de** France
21 M2 **Quiberville** France
127 K10 **Quíbor** Venezuela
87 B7 **Quicama Nat. Park** Angola
68 G3 **Qui Chau** Vietnam
32 L5 **Quickborn** Germany
36 C5 **Quierschied** Germany
117 G5 **Quiet L** Yukon Territory Canada
22 F3 **Quievrain** Belgium
22 E3 **Quiévy** France
118 G2 **Quigley** Alberta Canada
133 F3 **Quiindy** Paraguay
103 M9 **Quijotoa** Arizona U.S.A.
124 F5 **Quilá** Mexico
133 C6 **Quilán, C** Chile
16 E9 **Quilates, C** Morocco
128 D7 **Quilca** Peru
100 C2 **Quilcene** Washington U.S.A.
87 B8 **Quilengues** Angola
133 E4 **Quilino** Argentina
128 D6 **Quillabamba** Peru
128 E7 **Quillacollo** Bolivia
Quillak *see* **Dannebrog Ø**
18 G10 **Quillan** France
21 M3 **Quillebeuf** France
131 B7 **Quillén, L** Argentina
119 N6 **Quill Lake** Saskatchewan Canada
131 B4 **Quillota** Chile
119 N7 **Quillsks L** Saskatchewan Canada
20 G7 **Quilly** France
76 C6 **Quilon** India
141 G7 **Quilpie** Queensland Australia
87 C8 **Quimbango** Angola
20 B5 **Quimerch** France
20 B6 **Quimper** France
20 C6 **Quimperlé** France
71 F3 **Quinabucasan Pt** Philippines
71 F4 **Quinalasag** *isld* Philippines
100 A2 **Quinault** *R* Washington U.S.A.
100 B2 **Quinault** Washington U.S.A.
21 N2 **Quincampoix** France
21 L8 **Quinçay** France
128 D6 **Quince Mil** Peru
102 D2 **Quincy** California U.S.A.
111 M11 **Quincy** Florida U.S.A.
99 P10 **Quincy** Illinois U.S.A.
95 R4 **Quincy** Massachusetts U.S.A.
110 N1 **Quincy** Ohio U.S.A.
100 B3 **Quincy** Oregon U.S.A.
100 F2 **Quincy** Washington U.S.A.
20 H2 **Quineville** France
68 F2 **Quinh Nhai** Vietnam
128 E3 **Quinigua, Cerro** *mts* Venezuela
71 E5 **Quiniluban** *isld* Philippines
109 L3 **Quinlan** Texas U.S.A.
98 D6 **Quinn** South Dakota U.S.A.
103 J4 **Quinn Canyon Ra** Nevada U.S.A.
100 G8 **Quinn River Crossing** Nevada U.S.A.
19 Q17 **Quinson** France
16 E5 **Quintanar de la Orden** Spain
125 P8 **Quintana Roo** *terr* Mexico
107 K2 **Quinter** Kansas U.S.A.
20 E5 **Quintin** France
131 D5 **Quinto** *R* Argentina
17 G3 **Quinto** Spain
119 N7 **Quinton** Saskatchewan Canada
107 P6 **Quinton** Oklahoma U.S.A.
45 L1 **Quinto Vicentino** Italy
8 A7 **Quintrel Downs** England
94 G8 **Quinwood** West Virginia U.S.A.
88 H7 **Quionga** Mozambique
130 J10 **Quipapá** Brazil
87 B8 **Quipungo** Angola
15 B3 **Quirang** Scotland
87 C8 **Quirima** Angola
139 K4 **Quirindi** New South Wales Australia
131 A6 **Quiriquina** *isld* Chile
127 N10 **Quiriquire** Venezuela
120 H6 **Quirke L** Ontario Canada
36 C5 **Quirnbach** Germany
16 C2 **Quiroga** Spain
123 R2 **Quirpon** Newfoundland Canada
123 R2 **Quirpon I** Newfoundland Canada
88 H8 **Quissanga** Mozambique
87 F10 **Quissico** Mozambique
45 J1 **Quistello** Italy
20 D6 **Quistinic** France
87 C8 **Quitapa** Angola
126 D7 **Quita Sueño Bank** Caribbean
130 D6 **Quitéria** *R* Brazil
110 D6 **Quitman** Arkansas U.S.A.
113 D7 **Quitman** Georgia U.S.A.
109 P3 **Quitman** Louisiana U.S.A.
111 H9 **Quitman** Mississippi U.S.A.
109 M3 **Quitman** Texas U.S.A.
128 C4 **Quito** Ecuador
103 M10 **Quitovac** Mexico
21 N3 **Quittebeuf** France
103 M6 **Quivero** Arizona U.S.A.
128 C5 **Quivilla** Peru
129 L4 **Quixadá** Brazil
67 B1 **Qu Jiang** *R* China
67 D4 **Qujiang** China
67 C6 **Qujie** China
67 A4 **Qujing** China
46 D3 **Qukës-Shkumbin** Albania
80 G6 **Quleib** *R* Jordan
66 E4 **Qumar He** *R* China
58 C5 **Qumarlêb** China
89 F8 **Qumbu** S Africa
80 G1 **Qunayṭirah, El** Syria
84 G4 **Qunayyin, S. al** Libya
72 E5 **Qunfudhah, Al** Saudi Arabia
66 D5 **Qungtag** China
143 A6 **Quobba,Pt** W Australia Australia
83 M12 **Quoin Channel** Mauritius
140 A2 **Quoin I** N Terr Australia
141 K6 **Quoin I** Queensland Australia
89 A10 **Quoin Pt** S Africa
138 E4 **Quorn** South Australia Australia
119 N1 **Quorn** Ontario Canada
80 G6 **Qureiyat Nafi** Jordan
80 G6 **Qureiyat Salim** Jordan
129 J4 **Qurem** Brazil
84 J4 **Qus** Egypt
80 G1 **Quşaybah** Syria
84 J4 **Quseir** Egypt
77 G6 **Quşr-e-Qand** Iran
67 C1 **Qutang Xia Wu Xia** China
87 E12 **Quthing** Lesotho
79 H2 **Quwayq** *R* Syria
79 B8 **Quweisna** Egypt
65 B7 **Quwo** China
58 E4 **Quwu Shan** *mt ra* China
67 A5 **Quxi** China
Qu Xian *see* **Quzhou**
67 B1 **Qu Xian** China
75 O4 **Qüxü** China
65 C5 **Quyang** China
67 E3 **Quyang** China
67 B7 **Quynh Luu** Vietnam
68 J6 **Quy Nhon** Vietnam
121 O7 **Quyon** Quebec Canada
65 C6 **Quzhou** China
67 F2 **Quzhou** China

R

29 K5 **Rå** Sweden
27 F16 **Råå** Sweden
Raab *see* **Györ**
31 J7 **Raabs** Austria
38 N7 **Raab Tal** *V* Austria
29 L7 **Raahe** Finland
138 F5 **Raak Plain** Victoria Australia
29 O9 **Rääl-kylä** Finland
25 F4 **Raalte** Netherlands
115 L2 **Raanes Pen** Northwest Territories Canada
29 L5 **Raanujärvi** Finland
70 P9 **Raas** *isld* Indonesia
77 A5 **Ra'as Al Khafji** Saudi Arabia
15 B3 **Raasay, Sd of** Scotland
42 F4 **Rab** *isld* Croatia
48 D3 **Rába** *R* Hungary
71 J9 **Raba** Sumbawa Indonesia
80 E4 **Raba** Jordan
48 F1 **Raba** *R* Poland
16 C3 **Rabaçal** *R* Portugal
18 F9 **Rabastens de Bigorre** Hautes-Pyrénées France
85 C2 **Rabat** Morocco
137 L2 **Rabaul** New Britain
Rabbah *see* **'Ammān**
117 K6 **Rabbit** *R* British Columbia Canada
98 D4 **Rabbit Cr** South Dakota U.S.A.
106 D1 **Rabbit Ears Pass** Colorado U.S.A.
145 D4 **Rabbit I** New Zealand
118 K5 **Rabbit Lake** Saskatchewan Canada
117 N5 **Rabbitskin** *R* Northwest Territories Canada
28 D7 **Rabel** Germany
36 F2 **Rabenau** Germany
77 E5 **Rābor** Iran
52 F6 **Rabotki** Russian Federation
37 P3 **Rabštejn** Czechoslovakia
112 D3 **Rabun, L** Georgia U.S.A.
84 G5 **Rabyānah** *well* Libya
84 G5 **Rabyānah, Ramlat** *sands* Libya
46 D1 **Rača** Serbia Yugoslavia
44 C2 **Racconigi** Italy
99 M8 **Raccoon** *R* Iowa U.S.A.
126 G3 **Raccoon Cay** Bahamas
94 E8 **Raccoon Cr** Ohio U.S.A.
38 N9 **Rače** Slovenia
123 T7 **Race, C** Newfoundland Canada
94 E8 **Raceland** Kentucky U.S.A.
111 F12 **Raceland** Louisiana U.S.A.
113 E7 **Race Pond** Florida U.S.A.
95 R4 **Race Pt** Massachusetts U.S.A.
100 B1 **Race Rocks** British Columbia Canada
101 N3 **Race Track** Montana U.S.A.
80 E1 **Rachaf** Lebanon
79 F5 **Rachaiya** Lebanon
109 J9 **Rachal** Texas U.S.A.
69 D9 **Racha Noi, Ko** *isld* Thailand
69 D9 **Racha Yai, Ko** *isld* Thailand
68 G8 **Rach Gia** Vietnam
31 L5 **Racibórz** Poland
37 P3 **Račic** Czechoslovakia
94 F8 **Racine** Ohio U.S.A.
99 T7 **Racine** Wisconsin U.S.A.
122 D1 **Racine-de-Bouleau, R** Quebec Canada
120 G4 **Racine L** Ontario Canada
33 Q10 **Rackwitz** Germany
37 O4 **Racovský** *mt* Czechoslovakia
46 E1 **Radan** *mt* Serbia Yugoslavia
48 K3 **Rădăuţi** Romania
37 P4 **Radbuza** *R* Czechoslovakia
110 L4 **Radcliff** Kentucky U.S.A.
13 F6 **Radcliffe** England
99 N7 **Radcliffe** Iowa U.S.A.
27 E12 **Råde** Norway
30 H4 **Radeberg** Germany
37 Q1 **Radebeul** Germany
33 T10 **Radeburg** Germany
19 Q18 **Rade d'Hyères** *B* France
33 Q9 **Radegast** Germany
38 M8 **Radel Pass** Austria
36 C1 **Radevormwald** Germany
94 G9 **Radford** Virginia U.S.A.
140 B1 **Radford Pt** N Terr Australia
74 D7 **Radhanpur** India
118 K6 **Radisson** Saskatchewan Canada
99 P4 **Radisson** Wisconsin U.S.A.
101 T10 **Radium** Colorado U.S.A.
98 K1 **Radium** Minnesota U.S.A.
37 N3 **Radiumbad-Brambach** Germany
138 F4 **Radium Hill** *pk* South Australia Australia
117 P10 **Radium Hot Springs** British Columbia Canada
106 D9 **Radium Springs** New Mexico U.S.A.
70 O9 **Radja, I** Indonesia
77 F1 **Rādkān** Iran
Radldorf *see* **Bergstorf**
38 L6 **Radmer-an-dem-Hasel** Austria
47 H2 **Radnevo** Bulgaria
30 H6 **Radnice** Czechoslovakia
Radnor *co see* **Powys**
41 J2 **Radolfzell** Germany
31 N4 **Radom** Poland
86 D4 **Radom** Sudan
46 F2 **Radomir** Bulgaria
31 L4 **Radomsko** Poland
37 P3 **Radonice** Czechoslovakia
31 K7 **Radošina** Czechoslovakia
31 M4 **Radoszyce** Poland
46 E3 **Radoviš** Macedonia Yugoslavia
54 L1 **Radovitskiy** Russian Federation
42 F2 **Radovljica** Slovenia
38 H7 **Radstadt** Austria
8 D5 **Radstock** England
38 L9 **Raduha** *mt* Slovenia
42 H5 **Raduša** *mt* Bosnia-Herzegovina
52 B6 **Radviliškis** Lithuania
119 N9 **Radville** Saskatchewan Canada
118 E4 **Radway** Alberta Canada
31 O6 **Radymno** Poland
31 M3 **Radzanów** Poland
31 L3 **Radziejów** Poland
31 N3 **Radzymin** Poland
31 O4 **Radzyń Podlaski** Poland
117 P4 **Rae** Northwest Territories Canada
75 J5 **Rae Bareli** India
112 H3 **Raeford** North Carolina U.S.A.
115 L4 **Rae Isthmus** Northwest Territories Canada
114 H5 **Rae L** Northwest Territories Canada
118 B8 **Rae, Mt** British Columbia Canada
28 B2 **Rær** Denmark
22 L2 **Raeren** Belgium
32 E9 **Raesfeld** Germany
143 D8 **Raeside, L** W Australia Australia
115 K4 **Rae Str** Northwest Territories Canada
145 D1 **Raetea** *mt* New Zealand
145 E3 **Raetihi** New Zealand
131 E3 **Rafaela** Argentina
79 E7 **Rafaḥ** Egypt
86 D5 **Rafaï** Cent Afr Republic
53 C8 **Rafalovka** Ukraine
80 D5 **Rafat** Jordan
17 G5 **Rafelbuñol** Spain
78 J7 **Rafḥā'** Saudi Arabia
77 E4 **Rafsanjān** Iran
101 M7 **Raft** *R* Idaho U.S.A.
119 Q3 **Rafter** Manitoba Canada
101 M8 **Raft R. Mts** Utah U.S.A.
26 H3 **Raftsund** Norway
86 E4 **Raga** Sudan
71 G7 **Ragang, Mt** Philippines
71 F4 **Ragay G** Philippines
28 J4 **Rågeleje** Denmark
33 R6 **Rägelin** Germany
126 G3 **Ragged I** Bahamas
143 E10 **Ragged,Mt** W Australia Australia
127 P6 **Ragged Pt** Barbados
145 E2 **Raglan** New Zealand
8 D4 **Raglan** Wales
111 K8 **Ragland** Alabama U.S.A.
108 D1 **Ragland** New Mexico U.S.A.
145 D4 **Raglan Range** New Zealand
107 M4 **Rago** Kansas U.S.A.
44 G2 **Ragola Monte** Italy
33 R8 **Ragösen** Germany
28 G7 **Rågø Sund** *chan* Denmark
33 Q9 **Raguhn** Germany
26 H8 **Ragunda** Sweden
Ragusa *see* **Dubrovnik**
43 F12 **Ragusa** Sicily
71 H7 **Raha** Indonesia
86 G3 **Rahad** *R* Sudan
86 D3 **Rahad el Berdi** Sudan
Rahaeng *see* **Tak**
80 E8 **Raḥaf** Israel
27 J11 **Råhällan** Sweden
32 J8 **Rahden** Germany
86 E2 **Rahib** Sudan
80 D8 **Rahiya** Jordan
145 D3 **Raholu** New Zealand
74 F9 **Rahuri** India
16 B6 **Raia** *R* Portugal
45 P5 **Raiano** Italy
Raibu *see* **Air**
76 C2 **Raichur** India
71 K10 **Raidjua** *isld* Indonesia
75 K8 **Raigarh** India
102 G2 **Railroad Pass** Nevada U.S.A.
103 J3 **Railroad Valley** Nevada U.S.A.
37 K6 **Rain** Germany
37 N6 **Rain** Germany
37 J6 **Rainau** Germany
138 F6 **Rainbow** Victoria Australia
103 O4 **Rainbow Br. Nat. Mon** Utah U.S.A.
124 E9 **Rainbow City** Panama
111 K8 **Rainbow City** Alabama U.S.A.
141 G1 **Raine I** Gt Barrier Reef Aust
9 G4 **Rainham** England
100 C3 **Rainier** Oregon U.S.A.
100 C3 **Rainier** Washington U.S.A.
100 D3 **Rainier, Mt** Washington U.S.A.
100 B5 **Rainrock** Oregon U.S.A.
94 J7 **Rainsburg** Pennsylvania U.S.A.
94 C1 **Rainy** *R* Michigan U.S.A.
99 M1 **Rainy** *R* Minnesota U.S.A.
118 J2 **Rainy L** Minnesota/Ontario U.S.A./Canada
99 N1 **Rainy Lake** Ontario Canada
100 E1 **Rainy Pass** Washington U.S.A.
116 L5 **Rainy Pass Lodge** Alaska U.S.A.
118 H2 **Rainy R** Ontario Canada
99 M1 **Rainy River** Ontario Canada
29 J8 **Raippaluoto** *isld* Finland
75 J8 **Raipur** India
74 G7 **Raisen** India
27 M11 **Raisio** Finland
22 E3 **Raismes** France
29 N5 **Raistakka** Finland
119 O2 **Raith** Ontario Canada
68 A1 **Raithaw** Burma
145 D4 **Rai Valley** New Zealand
70 F4 **Raja** Kalimantan
70 B5 **Raja, Bt** *mt* Kalimantan
70 C5 **Raja, Bt** *mt* Kalimantan
76 E2 **Rajahmundry** India
76 D3 **Rajampet** India
70 B3 **Rajang** Sarawak
74 D4 **Rajanpur** Pakistan
76 C6 **Rajapalaiyam** India
74 D5 **Rajasthan** *prov* India
69 C11 **Raja, Ujung** *C* Sumatra
46 D2 **Rajë** Albania
75 L6 **Rajgir** India
31 O2 **Rajgród** Poland
80 F5 **Rajib** *R* Jordan
80 F5 **Rajib** Jordan
69 G14 **Rajik** Bangka Indonesia
75 J8 **Rajim** India
74 D7 **Rajkot** India
75 J8 **Raj Nandgaon** India
74 E8 **Rajpipla** India
75 N6 **Rajshahi** Bangladesh
76 D1 **Rajura** India
88 C2 **Rakai** Uganda
144 D5 **Rakaia** New Zealand
Rakata *isld see* **Krakatau** *isld*
145 F3 **Rakauroa** New Zealand
99 N6 **Rake** Iowa U.S.A.
144 A7 **Rakeahua** *mt* New Zealand
56 C6 **Rakhmanoviskoye** Kazakhstan
56 C6 **Rakhmanovskiye Klyuchi** Kazakhstan
48 J2 **Rakhov** Ukraine
77 J6 **Rakhshan** *R* Pakistan
145 E2 **Rakino I** New Zealand
26 L3 **Rakisvaara** *mt* Sweden
70 M8 **Rakit** *isld* Indonesia
71 C7 **Rakit** Sabah
46 G3 **Rakitovo** Bulgaria
145 E2 **Rakitu I** New Zealand
55 C5 **Rakityanka** Russian Federation
Raki-ura *isld see* **Stewart I**
27 E12 **Rakkestad** Norway
69 D8 **Ra, Ko** *isld* Thailand
31 J3 **Rakoniewice** Poland
87 D10 **Rakops** Botswana
30 H5 **Rakovník** Czechoslovakia
46 G2 **Rakovski** Bulgaria
33 S4 **Rakow** Germany
52 F3 **Rakula** Russian Federation
52 G4 **Rakulka** Russian Federation
52 C5 **Rakvere** Estonia
111 G9 **Raleigh** Mississippi U.S.A.
112 J2 **Raleigh** North Carolina U.S.A.
98 E3 **Raleigh** North Dakota U.S.A.
112 L3 **Raleigh B** North Carolina U.S.A.
101 M1 **Raley** Alberta Canada
70 F7 **Ralla** Sulawesi
108 F2 **Ralls** Texas U.S.A.
99 T3 **Ralph** Michigan U.S.A.
98 C4 **Ralph** South Dakota U.S.A.
107 O5 **Ralston** Oklahoma U.S.A.
95 L5 **Ralston** Pennsylvania U.S.A.
100 G3 **Ralston** Washington U.S.A.
101 R5 **Ralston** Wyoming U.S.A.
117 M5 **Ram** *R* Northwest Territories Canada
79 F9 **Ram** Jordan
119 P7 **Rama** Saskatchewan Canada
80 D4 **Rāma** Jordan
125 M3 **Rama** Nicaragua
78 J5 **Ramādi, Ar** Iraq
106 F2 **Ramah** Colorado U.S.A.
106 B6 **Ramah** New Mexico U.S.A.
16 E1 **Ramales de la Victoria** Spain
129 K6 **Ramalho, Sa. do** *mts* Brazil
133 E4 **Ramalio** Argentina
80 D6 **Ramallah** Jordan
76 D6 **Ramanathapuram** India
75 K8 **Rāmapur** India
89 E3 **Ramaquabane** *R* Zimbabwe
54 E4 **Ramasukha** Russian Federation
80 C5 **Ramatayim** Israel
80 C5 **Ramat Gan** Israel
80 C5 **Ramat Ha Kovesh** Israel
80 C5 **Ramat Ha Sharon** Israel
80 D3 **Ramat HaShofet** Israel
80 E7 **Ramat Qidron** Jordan
80 D2 **Ramat Yoḥanan** Israel
83 K10 **Rambe** Sri Lanka
36 E5 **Ramberg** Germany
36 B7 **Rambervillers** France
83 K9 **Rambewa** Sri Lanka
127 J2 **Ramble** Jamaica
133 D4 **Ramblon** Argentina
21 O4 **Rambouillet** France
33 P6 **Rambow** Germany
76 B3 **Ramdurg** India
123 P6 **Ramea** Newfoundland Canada
139 J7 **Rame Hd** Victoria Australia
52 E6 **Ramenskoye** Russian Federation
111 K9 **Ramer** Alabama U.S.A.
52 E6 **Rameshki** Russian Federation
83 J8 **Rameswaram** India
75 L7 **Ramgarh** India
77 A4 **Rāmhormoz** Iran
44 B2 **Ramière, Punta** *mt* Italy/France
22 H2 **Ramillies-Offus** Belgium
140 D1 **Ramingining** N Terr Australia
109 K10 **Ramírez** Mexico
109 J8 **Ramirez** Texas U.S.A.
109 J9 **Ramirito** Texas U.S.A.
86 H4 **Ramis** *R* Ethiopia
80 E1 **Râmîye** Lebanon
27 G14 **Ramkvilla** Sweden
80 C6 **Ramla** Israel
80 C6 **Ramle** Israel
28 J4 **Ramløse** Denmark
27 G11 **Rämmen** Sweden
75 K6 **Ramnagar** India
27 H12 **Ramnäs** Sweden
89 E3 **Ramokgwebana** Botswana
80 E3 **Ram On** Israel
54 L5 **Ramon'** Russian Federation
102 H8 **Ramona** California U.S.A.
94 B3 **Ramona** Michigan U.S.A.
107 P5 **Ramona** Oklahoma U.S.A.
98 J5 **Ramona** South Dakota U.S.A.
120 K4 **Ramore** Ontario Canada
124 G5 **Ramos** Mexico
71 C6 **Ramos** *isld* Philippines
80 F1 **Ramot Naftali** Israel
87 E10 **Ramotsua** Botswana
116 M4 **Rampart** Alaska U.S.A.
116 R3 **Rampart House** Yukon Territory Canada
13 E5 **Rampside** England
74 H4 **Rampur** India
74 F6 **Rampura** India
68 A3 **Ramree** Burma
142 F4 **Ramsay Ra** W Australia Australia
32 H10 **Ramsbeck** Germany
27 H12 **Ramsberg** Sweden
13 F6 **Ramsbottom** England
32 E9 **Ramsdorf** Germany
32 F7 **Ramsel** Germany
26 H8 **Ramsele** Sweden
112 H2 **Ramseur** North Carolina U.S.A.
120 H5 **Ramsey** Ontario Canada
9 F3 **Ramsey** England
12 D5 **Ramsey** I of Man U.K.
110 G2 **Ramsey** Illinois U.S.A.
95 N5 **Ramsey** New Jersey U.S.A.
8 A4 **Ramsey I** Wales
9 H5 **Ramsgate** England
13 G5 **Ramsgill** England
28 B3 **Ramsing** Denmark
26 H9 **Ramsjö** Sweden
22 D1 **Ramskapelle** Belgium
74 H8 **Ramtek** India
79 G6 **Ramtha** Jordan
71 J9 **Ramu** *mt* Sumbawa Indonesia
136 K3 **Ramu** *R* Papua New Guinea
26 J9 **Ramvik** Sweden
127 M4 **Ramville, I** Martinique
52 B6 **Ramygala** Lithuania
26 G5 **Rana** *inlet* Norway
16 C1 **Rañadoiro, Sa. de** *mts* Spain
26 F5 **Ranafjord** *inlet* Norway
75 N7 **Ranaghat** India
69 J10 **Ranai** Indonesia
145 E3 **Ranana** New Zealand
27 K12 **Rånäs** Sweden
27 E11 **Rånåsfoss** Norway
70 K8 **Ranau, D** *L* Sumatra
131 B5 **Rancagua** Chile
22 G3 **Rance** Belgium
20 G4 **Rance** *R* Côtes d'Armor France
133 G2 **Rancharia** Brazil
117 F5 **Rancheria** Yukon Territory Canada
101 S5 **Ranchester** Wyoming U.S.A.
75 L7 **Ranchi** India
129 G6 **Rancho de Caça dos Tapiúnas** Brazil
124 H6 **Rancho Grande** Mexico
106 E5 **Ranchos de Taos** New Mexico U.S.A.
126 D3 **Rancho Veloz** Cuba
131 A8 **Ranco, L. de** Chile
106 D1 **Rand** Colorado U.S.A.
109 J8 **Randado** Texas U.S.A.
99 N7 **Randall** Iowa U.S.A.
107 M2 **Randall** Kansas U.S.A.
99 M3 **Randall** Minnesota U.S.A.
14 E2 **Randalstown** N Ireland
43 F11 **Randazzo** Sicily
89 A1 **Randburg** S Africa
Randers *co see* **Århus** *co*
28 E4 **Randers** Denmark
37 J4 **Randersacker** Germany
26 L5 **Randijaur** *L* Sweden
100 D3 **Randle** Washington U.S.A.
112 H2 **Randleman** North Carolina U.S.A.
109 J1 **Randlett** Oklahoma U.S.A.
103 P1 **Randlett** Utah U.S.A.
28 E5 **Randlev** Denmark
99 L9 **Randolph** Iowa U.S.A.
107 O2 **Randolph** Kansas U.S.A.
95 S2 **Randolph** Maine U.S.A.
111 G7 **Randolph** Mississippi U.S.A.
98 J7 **Randolph** Nebraska U.S.A.
94 J4 **Randolph** New York U.S.A.
101 O8 **Randolph** Utah U.S.A.
95 P3 **Randolph** Vermont U.S.A.
99 S6 **Randolph** Wisconsin U.S.A.
123 T5 **Random I** Newfoundland Canada
99 T6 **Random Lake** Wisconsin U.S.A.
21 M4 **Randonnai** France
102 G6 **Randsburg** California U.S.A.
27 D11 **Randsfjord** Norway
32 E5 **Randzel** *sandbank* Germany
26 N6 **Råneå** Norway
21 K4 **Rânes** France
118 F5 **Ranfurly** Alberta Canada
144 C6 **Ranfurly** New Zealand
69 E9 **Rangae** Thailand
70 F6 **Rangasa, Tanjong** *C* Sulawesi
70 F6 **Rangas, Tanjong** *C* Sulawesi
145 E3 **Rangataua** New Zealand
145 D1 **Rangaunu Harbour** New Zealand
111 J10 **Range** Alabama U.S.A.
95 R2 **Rangeley** Maine U.S.A.
101 R9 **Rangely** Colorado U.S.A.
109 J3 **Ranger** Texas U.S.A.
94 E8 **Ranger** West Virginia U.S.A.
120 G6 **Ranger L** Ontario Canada
75 O5 **Rangia** India
144 D5 **Rangiora** New Zealand
145 F2 **Rangipoua** New Zealand
145 F3 **Rangitaiki** New Zealand
145 F3 **Rangitaiki R** New Zealand
144 C6 **Rangitata** New Zealand
145 E4 **Rangitikei R** New Zealand
145 E2 **Rangitoto I** New Zealand
145 E3 **Rangitoto Ra** New Zealand
145 G2 **Rangitukia** New Zealand
69 D10 **Rangkalanberandan** Sumatra
70 L9 **Rangkasbitung** Java
Rangoon *see* **Yangon**
68 C4 **Rangoon** *R* Burma
75 N6 **Rangpur** Bangladesh
69 F12 **Rangsang** *isld* Sumatra
33 S8 **Rangsdorf** Germany
28 C6 **Rangstrup** Denmark
76 B3 **Ranibennur** India
99 N1 **Ranier** Minnesota U.S.A.
75 M7 **Raniganj** India
37 M2 **Ranis** Germany
74 E6 **Raniwara** India
140 D5 **Ranken** *R* N Terr Australia
140 D4 **Ranken Store** N Terr Australia
110 J1 **Rankin** Illinois U.S.A.
108 F4 **Rankin** Texas U.S.A.
115 K5 **Rankin Inlet** Northwest Territories Canada
139 H5 **Rankin's Springs** New South Wales Australia
80 B8 **Rannen** Israel
141 K6 **Rannes** Queensland Australia
55 B5 **Ranneye** Russian Federation
15 D4 **Rannoch Moor** Scotland
87 H12 **Ranohira** Madagascar
120 J2 **Ranoke** Ontario Canada
68 D7 **Ranong** Thailand
69 E9 **Ranot** Thailand
26 G6 **Ransarn** *L* Sweden
36 D3 **Ransel** Germany
99 S8 **Ransom** Illinois U.S.A.
107 L3 **Ransom** Kansas U.S.A.
94 K7 **Ranson** West Virginia U.S.A.
36 G3 **Ranstadt** Germany
29 N9 **Rantasalmi** Finland
70 D6 **Rantau** Kalimantan
69 F12 **Rantau** *isld* Sumatra
69 E12 **Rantaukampar** Sumatra
70 E3 **Rantaupandjang** Kalimantan
70 C5 **Rantaupanjang** Kalimantan
69 D11 **Rantauprapat** Sumatra
70 C6 **Rantaupulut** Kalimantan
70 F6 **Rantemario, Gunung** *mt* Sulawesi
70 F6 **Rantepao** Sulawesi
21 P3 **Rantigny** France
110 H1 **Rantoul** Illinois U.S.A.
102 H1 **Rant Pass** Nevada U.S.A.
29 M7 **Rantsila** Finland
29 M6 **Ranua** Finland
131 A8 **Ranue, R** Chile
28 C3 **Ranum** Denmark
78 K3 **Ranya** Iraq
68 G3 **Rao Go** *mt* Laos
65 J1 **Raohe** China
36 B7 **Raon-l'Etape** France
36 C6 **Raon-sur-Plaine** France
67 E5 **Raoping** China
41 O6 **Raossi** Italy
137 R7 **Raoul** *isld* Kermadec Is Pacific Oc
65 C5 **Raoyang** China
144 C5 **Rapahoe** New Zealand
44 F3 **Rapallo** Italy
131 B4 **Rapel** *R* Chile
101 Q4 **Rapelje** Montana U.S.A.
115 N4 **Raper, C** Northwest Territories Canada
94 H9 **Raphine** Virginia U.S.A.
14 D2 **Raphoe** Ireland
116 R3 **Rapid** *R* Alaska U.S.A.
99 M1 **Rapid** *R* Minnesota U.S.A.
94 J8 **Rapidan** Virginia U.S.A.
94 K8 **Rapidan** *R* Virginia U.S.A.
138 E6 **Rapid B** South Australia Australia
119 R8 **Rapid City** Manitoba Canada
98 C5 **Rapid City** South Dakota U.S.A.
121 R5 **Rapide Blanc** Quebec Canada
121 N6 **Rapides des Joachims** Quebec Canada
141 H2 **Rapid Horn** *C* Gt Barrier Reef Aust
99 U4 **Rapid River** Michigan U.S.A.
118 H4 **Rapid View** Saskatchewan Canada
52 C5 **Räpina** Estonia
52 B5 **Rapla** Estonia
95 K8 **Rappahannock** *R* Virginia U.S.A.
70 F6 **Rappang** Sulawesi
41 J3 **Rapperswil** Switzerland
46 F5 **Rapsáni** Greece
128 E6 **Rapulo** *R* Bolivia
71 G4 **Rapu Rapu** Philippines
80 G1 **Raqqādīyah** Syria
95 N2 **Raquette** *R* New York U.S.A.
95 N3 **Raquette Lake** New York U.S.A.
140 D1 **Raragala I** N Terr Australia
71 K9 **Rarakah** *mt* Flores Indonesia
95 N6 **Raritan B** New Jersey U.S.A.
40 G5 **Raron** Switzerland
134 A10 **Rarotonga** *isld* Pacific Oc
42 F3 **Raša** Croatia
71 D6 **Rasa** *isld* Palawan Philippines
79 F3 **Ra's al Basiţ** *C* Syria
77 D7 **Ras al Khaimah** U.A.E.
Ra's al Khaymah *see* **Ras al Khaimah**
131 E8 **Rasa, Pta** *C* Argentina
133 E6 **Rasa, Pta** Argentina
79 G4 **Ras Baalbek** Lebanon
86 G3 **Ras Dashen** *mt* Ethiopia
52 B6 **Raseiniai** Lithuania
80 G4 **Ras el Aqra** Jordan
80 F8 **Ras el Ghor** Jordan
84 H3 **Râs el Kenâyis** *C* Egypt
85 D5 **Ras el Ma** Mali
72 G5 **Ra's Fartak** *C* Yemen
79 D10 **Râs Ghârib** Egypt
86 F3 **Rashad** Sudan
86 G1 **Râs Hadarba** *C* Egypt
79 F8 **Rashādīya** Jordan
79 A7 **Rashîd** Egypt
77 A1 **Rasht** Iran
76 D5 **Rasipuram** India
77 G6 **Rāsk** Iran
46 D1 **Raška** Serbia Yugoslavia
86 G2 **Râs Kasar** *C* Sudan
28 D5 **Raskmølle** Denmark
77 J5 **Raskoh** *reg* Pakistan
84 F3 **Ra's Lānūf** Libya
31 N6 **Raslavice** Czechoslovakia
72 H5 **Ra's Madrakah** *C* Oman
72 G6 **Ra's Māmī** *C* Socotra
79 C9 **Râs Matarma** Egypt
84 J4 **Ras Muhammad** *C* Egypt
85 A4 **Ras Nouadhibou** Mauritania
133 D6 **Raso, C** Argentina
130 H10 **Raso da Catarina** Brazil
143 E8 **Rason L** W Australia Australia
46 F1 **Rasovo** Bulgaria
116 L7 **Raspberry I** Alaska U.S.A.
79 D10 **Râs Shukheir** Egypt
53 F7 **Rasskazov** Russian Federation
26 P1 **Rásstigáisa** *mt* Norway
77 B6 **Ras Tannurah** Saudi Arabia
Ras Tarf *see* **Quilates,C**
16 D9 **Ras Targa** Morocco
36 E6 **Rastatt** Germany
28 A4 **Råsted** Denmark
32 H6 **Rastede** Germany
38 M4 **Rastenfeld** Austria
38 E7 **Rastkogel** *mt* Austria
26 M3 **Råstoätno** *R* Sweden
43 B8 **Rasu, M** *mt* Sardinia
80 G4 **Rasun** Jordan
145 E3 **Rata** New Zealand
71 J4 **Ratahan** Sulawesi
70 K8 **Ratai, Gunung** *mt* Sumatra Indonesia
31 H6 **Rataje** Czechoslovakia
26 L8 **Ratan** Sweden
26 G9 **Rätan** Sweden
74 F4 **Ratangarh** India
68 D6 **Rat Buri** Thailand
55 B4 **Ratchino** Russian Federation
110 C6 **Ratcliff** Arkansas U.S.A.
109 M4 **Ratcliff** Texas U.S.A.
33 N5 **Ratekau** Germany
74 H6 **Rath** India
99 N9 **Rathburn Lake** *res* Iowa U.S.A.
14 E4 **Rathdrum** Ireland
100 J2 **Rathdrum** Idaho U.S.A.
68 A2 **Rathedaung** Burma
33 Q7 **Rathenow** Germany
14 E2 **Rathfriland** N Ireland
14 C4 **Ráth Luirc** Ireland
14 D1 **Rathmelton** Ireland
14 E4 **Rathnew** Ireland
119 T9 **Rathwell** Manitoba Canada
32 E10 **Ratingen** Germany
116 L10 **Rat Is** Aleutian Is
Ratisbon *see* **Regensburg**
119 S2 **Rat L** Manitoba Canada
74 F7 **Ratlam** India
116 C4 **Ratmanova, Ostrov** *isld* Russian Federation
76 A2 **Ratnagiri** India
83 K11 **Ratnapura** Sri Lanka
119 N5 **Ratner** Saskatchewan Canada
106 F5 **Raton** New Mexico U.S.A.
19 O18 **Ratonneau, I** France
106 F4 **Raton Pass** Colorado U.S.A.
115 K7 **Rat Rapids** Ontario Canada
117 R5 **Rat River** Northwest Territories Canada
109 M1 **Rattan** Oklahoma U.S.A.
37 K3 **Rattelsdorf** Germany
38 N7 **Ratten** Austria
38 E7 **Rattenberg** Austria
106 F4 **Rattlesnake Buttes** *mts* Colorado U.S.A.
107 L4 **Rattlesnake Cr** Kansas U.S.A.
100 H7 **Rattlesnake Cr** Oregon U.S.A.
101 S7 **Rattlesnake Ra** Wyoming U.S.A.
123 Q4 **Rattling Brook** Newfoundland Canada
15 G3 **Rattray Head** Scotland
27 H11 **Rättvik** Sweden
33 N5 **Ratzeburg** Germany
33 N5 **Ratzeburger See** *L* Germany
71 B1 **Rau** Halmahera Indonesia
69 E11 **Raub** Malaysia
133 F5 **Rauch** Argentina
22 H4 **Raucourt** France
29 M5 **Raudanjoki** *R* Finland
29 T8 **Raufarhöfn** Iceland
27 E11 **Raufoss** Norway
36 G7 **Rauhe Alb** *mts* Germany
37 K4 **Rauhe Ebrach** *R* Germany
37 K4 **Rauhenebrach** Germany
145 F2 **Raukokore** New Zealand
145 G2 **Raukumara** New Zealand
145 F3 **Raukumara Range** New Zealand
27 C12 **Rauland** Norway
27 M10 **Rauma** Finland
26 C9 **Rauma** *R* Norway
145 E4 **Raumati** New Zealand
36 E6 **Raumünzach** Germany
52 C6 **Rauna** Latvia
27 B11 **Raundal** *R* Norway
70 P10 **Raung, G** *mt* Java
145 E3 **Raurimu** New Zealand
29 K4 **Raus** Sweden
36 F2 **Rauschenberg** Germany
60 T1 **Rausu** Japan
29 M9 **Rautalampi** Finland
26 K3 **Rautasjaure** *L* Sweden
29 N8 **Rautavaara** Finland
29 O10 **Rautjärvi** Finland
101 L2 **Ravalli** Montana U.S.A.
48 E6 **Ravan** *mt* Bosnia-Herzegovina
31 O5 **Rava Russkaya** Ukraine
45 R8 **Ravello** Italy
94 F9 **Raven** Virginia U.S.A.
95 O4 **Ravena** New York U.S.A.
119 O5 **Ravendal** Saskatchewan Canada
102 D1 **Ravendale** California U.S.A.
22 C4 **Ravenel** France
13 E5 **Ravenglass** England
45 L3 **Ravenna** *reg* Italy
45 M3 **Ravenna** Italy
102 F7 **Ravenna** California U.S.A.
110 N4 **Ravenna** Kentucky U.S.A.
98 H8 **Ravenna** Nebraska U.S.A.
94 F5 **Ravenna** Ohio U.S.A.
20 H3 **Ravenoville** France
141 H6 **Ravensbourne** *R* Queensland Australia
33 S6 **Ravensbrück** Germany
41 L2 **Ravensburg** Germany
13 H5 **Ravenscar** England
118 H9 **Ravenscrag** Saskatchewan Canada
141 H4 **Ravenshoe** Queensland Australia
7 L8 **Ravenspurn** *gas field* North Sea
25 E5 **Ravenstein** Netherlands
143 D10 **Ravensthorpe** W Australia Australia
141 H5 **Ravenswood** Queensland Australia
94 F8 **Ravenswood** West Virginia U.S.A.
121 L7 **Ravensworth** Ontario Canada
74 E3 **Ravi** *R* Pakistan
109 L1 **Ravia** Oklahoma U.S.A.
18 H5 **Ravières** France
46 E1 **Ravna Reka** Serbia Yugoslavia
38 L8 **Ravne Na Koroškem** Slovenia
57 C2 **Ravnina Dar'yalytakyr** Kazakhstan
115 K4 **Ravn, Kap** Greenland
28 D3 **Ravnkilde** Denmark
42 H6 **Ravno** Bosnia-Herzegovina
74 E2 **Rawalpindi** Pakistan
117 Q3 **Rawalpindi L** Northwest Territories Canada
31 M4 **Rawa Mazowiecka** Poland
78 K3 **Rawandiz** Iraq
121 R6 **Rawdon** Quebec Canada
119 R4 **Rawebb** Manitoba Canada
145 D1 **Rawene** New Zealand
98 B7 **Rawhide Cr** Wyoming U.S.A.
31 K4 **Rawicz** Poland
69 D9 **Rawi, Ko** *isld* Thailand
143 F9 **Rawlinna** W Australia Australia
101 S8 **Rawlins** Wyoming U.S.A.
143 F7 **Rawlinson, Mt** W Australia Australia
143 G7 **Rawlinson Mt** W Australia Australia
133 D6 **Rawson** Argentina
94 D6 **Rawson** Ohio U.S.A.
38 N6 **Raxalpe** *mts* Austria
116 M4 **Ray** *R* Alaska U.S.A.
99 N1 **Ray** Minnesota U.S.A.
98 C1 **Ray** North Dakota U.S.A.
76 D3 **Rayachoti** India
76 C3 **Rāyadurg** India
75 K9 **Rāyagarha** India
79 G5 **Rayak** Lebanon
26 R3 **Rayakoski** Russian Federation
86 B4 **Ray-Bouba** Cameroon
123 N6 **Ray, C** Newfoundland Canada
59 J2 **Raychikhinsk** Russian Federation
112 D6 **Ray City** Georgia U.S.A.
77 E5 **Rāyen** Iran
55 B4 **Rayevskiy** Russian Federation
54 J8 **Raygorodok** Ukraine
80 G1 **Rayhānīyah** Syria
9 G4 **Rayleigh** England
118 E9 **Raymond** Alberta Canada
102 E4 **Raymond** California U.S.A.
110 G2 **Raymond** Illinois U.S.A.
111 F9 **Raymond** Mississippi U.S.A.
98 B1 **Raymond** Montana U.S.A.
98 J5 **Raymond** South Dakota U.S.A.
109 N3 **Raymond** Texas U.S.A.
100 B3 **Raymond** Washington U.S.A.
139 K5 **Raymond Terrace** New South Wales Australia
109 K9 **Raymondville** Texas U.S.A.
119 N7 **Raymore** Saskatchewan Canada
116 L4 **Ray Mts** Alaska U.S.A.
111 D11 **Rayne** Louisiana U.S.A.
101 P2 **Raynesford** Montana U.S.A.
108 A1 **Rayo** New Mexico U.S.A.
68 E6 **Rayong** Thailand
110 B3 **Raytown** Missouri U.S.A.
66 E5 **Rayü** China
111 E9 **Rayville** Louisiana U.S.A.
77 A2 **Razan** Iran
48 N4 **Razdel'naya** Ukraine
56 D2 **Razdolinsk** Russian Federation
47 H1 **Razgrad** Bulgaria
48 M6 **Razim, Lacul** *L* Romania
46 F3 **Razlog** Bulgaria
20 A5 **Raz, Pte.du** France
110 B1 **Rea** Missouri U.S.A.
142 A1 **Reabold Hill** W Australia Australia
117 D6 **Reaburn, Mt** Alaska U.S.A.
109 O2 **Reader** Arkansas U.S.A.
119 Q5 **Reader L** Manitoba Canada
9 F5 **Reading** England
127 J2 **Reading** Jamaica
94 C5 **Reading** Michigan U.S.A.
99 L6 **Reading** Minnesota U.S.A.
95 M6 **Reading** Pennsylvania U.S.A.
119 M9 **Readlyn** Saskatchewan Canada
95 P4 **Readsboro** Vermont U.S.A.
99 Q6 **Readstown** Wisconsin U.S.A.
109 L4 **Reagan** Texas U.S.A.
128 E7 **Real, Cord** *mts* Bolivia
128 C4 **Real, Cord** *mts* Ecuador
44 C1 **Reale** Italy
133 E5 **Realico** Argentina
109 J8 **Realitos** Texas U.S.A.
68 F7 **Ream** Cambodia
100 H2 **Reardan** Washington U.S.A.
15 G2 **Reawick** Scotland
112 D6 **Rebecca** Georgia U.S.A.
143 D9 **Rebecca, L** W Australia Australia
100 H8 **Rebel Creek** Nevada U.S.A.
33 T5 **Rebelow** Germany
117 P3 **Rebesca L** Northwest Territories Canada
28 D3 **Rebild** Denmark
128 G5 **Reboja, Cachoeira de** Brazil
29 P8 **Reboly** Russian Federation
46 F2 **Rebrovo** Bulgaria
60 P1 **Rebun-suidō** *str* Japan
60 P1 **Rebun-tō** *isld* Japan
133 E5 **Recalde** Argentina
48 G5 **Recaş** Romania
44 F3 **Recco** Italy
40 A2 **Recey** France
19 J5 **Recey-sur-Ource** France
143 D10 **Recherche, Arch.of the** W Australia Australia
36 B6 **Réchicourt le Château** France
54 B4 **Rechitsa** Belorussia
33 R6 **Rechlin** Germany
22 L3 **Recht** Belgium
130 J10 **Recife** Brazil
89 D10 **Recife, C** S Africa
83 J12 **Recif I** Seychelles
32 G8 **Recke** Germany
32 F9 **Recklinghausen** Germany
101 U5 **Recluse** Wyoming U.S.A.
22 J4 **Recogne** Belgium
131 F2 **Reconquista** Argentina
19 O15 **Recoubeau** France
146 E7 **Recovery Glacier** Antarctica
133 D3 **Recreo** Argentina
31 J2 **Recz** Poland
110 E6 **Red** *R* Arkansas U.S.A.
98 K2 **Red** *R* Minnesota U.S.A.
69 F10 **Redang** *isld* Malaysia
22 K4 **Redange** Luxembourg
122 G7 **Red Bank** New Brunswick Canada
95 N6 **Red Bank** New Jersey U.S.A.
Red Basin *see* **Sichuan Pendi**
123 Q2 **Red Bay** Labrador, Nfld Canada
120 J8 **Red Bay** Ontario Canada
111 H7 **Red Bay** Alabama U.S.A.
113 B7 **Redbay** Florida U.S.A.
118 K6 **Redberry L** Saskatchewan Canada
109 N10 **Redbird Airport** Texas U.S.A.
143 C6 **Red Bluff** *mt* W Australia Australia
102 B1 **Red Bluff** California U.S.A.
108 D4 **Red Bluff L** Texas/New Mex U.S.A.
9 F4 **Redbourn** England
110 G3 **Red Bud** Illinois U.S.A.
103 M6 **Red Butte** *mt* Arizona U.S.A.
98 A8 **Red Buttes** Wyoming U.S.A.
99 M2 **Redby** Minnesota U.S.A.
13 G4 **Redcar** England
106 D2 **Red Cliff** Colorado U.S.A.
141 L7 **Redcliffe** Queensland Australia
89 F2 **Redcliffe** Zimbabwe
143 D8 **Redcliffe, Mt** W Australia Australia
138 F5 **Red Cliffs** Victoria Australia
111 H11 **Red Cr** Mississippi U.S.A.
101 R8 **Red Cr** Wyoming U.S.A.
95 L3 **Red Creek** New York U.S.A.
118 D6 **Red Deer** Alberta Canada
119 Q6 **Red Deer L** Manitoba Canada
119 P6 **Red Deer R** Saskatchewan Canada
111 D11 **Reddell** Louisiana U.S.A.
13 E4 **Red Dial** England
113 E8 **Reddick** Florida U.S.A.
102 B1 **Redding** California U.S.A.
118 H1 **Reddit** Ontario Canada
9 E3 **Redditch** England
33 O6 **Redefin** Germany
98 E4 **Red Elm** South Dakota U.S.A.
129 K5 **Redenção** Brazil
20 D6 **Redené** France
85 F2 **Redeyef** Tunisia
111 D7 **Redfield** Arkansas U.S.A.
99 M8 **Redfield** Iowa U.S.A.
98 H5 **Redfield** South Dakota U.S.A.
101 L5 **Redfish L** Idaho U.S.A.
108 C6 **Redford** Texas U.S.A.
99 R5 **Redgranite** Wisconsin U.S.A.
75 L8 **Redhākhol** India
9 F5 **Redhill** England
145 D4 **Red Hill** *mt* New Zealand
111 K10 **Red Hills** Alabama U.S.A.
95 O5 **Red Hook** New York U.S.A.
100 H8 **Red House** Nevada U.S.A.
123 S6 **Red I** Newfoundland Canada
98 C4 **Redig** South Dakota U.S.A.
123 Q5 **Red Indian L** Newfoundland Canada
103 O9 **Redington** Arizona U.S.A.
98 C8 **Redinqton** Nebraska U.S.A.
85 D2 **Redjem Demouch** Algeria
110 L1 **Red Key** Indiana U.S.A.
52 E6 **Redkino** Russian Federation
117 O5 **Redknife** *R* Northwest Territories Canada
103 K6 **Red L** Arizona U.S.A.

115 K7 Red Lake Ontario Canada
103 M6 Red Lake Arizona U.S.A.
102 G7 Redlands California U.S.A.
98 K2 Red L. Falls Minnesota U.S.A.
95 L7 Red Lion Pennsylvania U.S.A.
101 Q4 Red Lodge Montana U.S.A.
118 C7 Red Lodge Prov. Park Alberta Canada
145 E2 Red Mercury I New Zealand
13 G5 Redmire England
110 J2 Redmon Illinois U.S.A.
100 D5 Redmond Oregon U.S.A.
103 N2 Redmond Utah U.S.A.
102 G6 Red Mt California U.S.A.
112 C1 Red Mt Tennessee U.S.A.
37 L5 Rednitz R Germany
99 L8 Red Oak Iowa U.S.A.
103 A7 Red Oak Oklahoma U.S.A.
109 L3 Red Oak Texas U.S.A.
20 F6 Redon France
127 N6 Redonda isld Antigua & Barbuda W Indies
16 B2 Redondela Spain
18 B6 Redondo Portugal
102 F8 Redondo Beach California U.S.A.
128 F3 Redondo, Pico mt Brazil
116 L6 Redoubt Vol Alaska U.S.A.
117 O9 Red Pass British Columbia Canada
118 J6 Red Pheasant Saskatchewan Canada
141 G2 Red Pt Queensland Australia
117 J6 Red R British Columbia Canada
119 U9 Red R Manitoba Canada
111 D10 Red R Louisiana U.S.A.
109 J1 Red R Texas U.S.A.
Red R Vietnam see Song-koi R
122 E7 Red Rapids New Brunswick Canada
101 K4 Red Rk. Hot Springs Idaho U.S.A.
119 P2 Red Rock Ontario Canada
103 N9 Redrock Arizona U.S.A.
106 B9 Red Rock New Mexico U.S.A.
107 N5 Red Rock Oklahoma U.S.A.
109 K6 Red Rock Texas U.S.A.
117 Q3 Redrock L Northwest Territories Canada
99 N8 Red Rock Res Iowa U.S.A.
143 G9 Red Rocks Pt W Australia Australia
8 A7 Redruth England
86 G1 Red Sea Africa/Arabian Pen
112 H3 Red Springs North Carolina U.S.A.
117 M9 Redstone British Columbia Canada
117 K4 Redstone R Northwest Territories Canada
120 J4 Redstone R Ontario Canada
101 V1 Redstone Montana U.S.A.
124 E9 Red Tank Panama
22 J4 Redu Belgium
119 Q9 Redvers Saskatchewan Canada
118 D5 Redwater Alberta Canada
98 A2 Redwater R Montana U.S.A.
109 N2 Redwater Texas U.S.A.
8 B1 Red Wharf B Wales
118 E6 Red Willow Alberta Canada
98 E9 Red Willow Cr Nebraska U.S.A.
99 O5 Red Wing Minnesota U.S.A.
102 B4 Redwood City California U.S.A.
99 L5 Redwood Falls Minnesota U.S.A.
100 A8 Redwood Nat. Park California U.S.A.
102 A2 Redwood Valley California U.S.A.
71 C5 Reed Bank S China Sea
98 D3 Reed City Michigan U.S.A.
98 D3 Reeder North Dakota U.S.A.
102 E5 Reedley California U.S.A.
101 Q4 Reedpoint Montana U.S.A.
106 C8 Reeds Pk New Mexico U.S.A.
100 A6 Reedsport Oregon U.S.A.
112 E3 Reedy R South Carolina U.S.A.
94 F8 Reedy West Virginia U.S.A.
138 D4 Reedy Lagoon South Australia Australia
141 G4 Reedy Springs Queensland Australia
144 C5 Reefton New Zealand
98 G5 Ree Heights South Dakota U.S.A.
14 C3 Ree, L Ireland
110 G5 Reelfoot L Tennessee U.S.A.
32 G6 Reepsholt Germany
28 C5 Reerse Denmark
25 F5 Rees Germany
26 L2 Reese Michigan U.S.A.
100 H9 Reese R Nevada U.S.A.
120 Q3 Reesor Ontario Canada
33 P6 Reetz Germany
78 G2 Refahiye Turkey
111 J8 Reform Alabama U.S.A.
133 D3 Refresco Chile
28 F6 Refs Denmark
27 G14 Reftele Sweden
109 K7 Refugio Texas U.S.A.
31 J2 Rega R Poland
120 E4 Regan Ontario Canada
80 D3 Regavim Israel
37 N5 Regen R Germany
37 N5 Regensburg Germany
37 N5 Regenstauf Germany
119 R9 Regent Manitoba Canada
121 O7 Regent Ontario Canada
85 E3 Reggane Algeria
45 L4 Reggello Italy
43 G10 Reggio di Calabria Italy
45 K3 Reggiolo Italy
45 J2 Reggio nell Emilia Italy
119 N8 Regina Saskatchewan Canada
37 N1 Regis Germany
43 G4 Registan Afghanistan
22 G4 Regniowez France
37 K4 Regnitz R Germany
16 B6 Reguengos de Monsaraz Portugal
20 E6 Reguiny France
80 D4 Rehan Jordan
37 N3 Rehau Germany
36 D5 Rehberg mt Germany
33 Q7 Rehden Germany
72 J8 Rehli India
33 Q5 Rehna Germany
87 C10 Rehoboth Namibia
95 M8 Rehoboth Beach Delaware U.S.A.
80 C6 Rehovot Israel
36 F5 Reichelshausen Germany
37 N2 Reichenbach Germany
38 L7 Reichenfels Germany
37 J1 Reichensachsen Germany
37 M3 Reichertsheim Germany
37 L6 Reichertshofen Germany
101 N4 Reichle Montana U.S.A.
36 D2 Reichshoffen Germany
36 D6 Reichshoffen France
143 G9 Reid W Australia Australia
140 B4 Reid, Mt N Terr Australia
112 E5 Reid R Queensland Australia
112 H1 Reidsville North Carolina U.S.A.
9 F5 Reigate England
21 M7 Reignac-sur-Indre Indre-et-Loire France

25 C5 Reijen Netherlands
37 J4 Reiley Pk Arizona U.S.A.
36 F5 Reilingen Germany
19 P17 Reillanne France
22 G5 Reims France
18 H3 Reims, Mt de France
133 C8 Reina Adelaida, Arch. de la islds Chile
99 O7 Reinbeck Iowa U.S.A.
32 M5 Reinbek Germany
33 S4 Reinberg Germany
119 U6 Reindeer I Manitoba Canada
119 Q1 Reindeer L Manitoba/Sask Canada
26 F4 Reine Norway
140 D6 Reinecke, Mt N Terr Germany
27 C11 Reineskarvet mt Norway
33 M5 Reinfeld Germany
17 G5 Reinga, C New Zealand
32 L10 Reinhausen Germany
18 G8 Reinheim Germany
21 P7 Reins R France
145 F3 Rerewhakaaitu L New Zealand
15 G2 Rerwick Scotland
78 F1 Reşadiye Turkey
41 G8 Resag, G mt Sumatra
102 F7 Reseda California U.S.A.
26 J8 Resele Sweden
28 C3 Resen Denmark
28 C4 Resen Denmark
46 E3 Resen Macedonia Yugoslavia
119 P6 Reserve Saskatchewan Canada
111 F11 Reserve Louisiana U.S.A.
98 B1 Reserve New Mexico U.S.A.
106 B8 Reserve New Mexico U.S.A.
54 F7 Reshetilovka Ukraine
45 M6 Resia Italy
133 F3 Resistencia Argentina
48 G5 Reşiţa Romania
122 E6 Resitgouche R New Brunswick Canada
115 K3 Reklaw Texas U.S.A.
109 N4 Rekovac Serbia Yugoslavia
144 A6 Relecq-Kerhoun,le France
115 N5 Reliance South Dakota U.S.A.
101 Q8 Reliance Wyoming U.S.A.
85 E1 Reliana Algeria
124 G4 Reliano Mexico
21 M5 Rémalard France
138 E4 Remarkable, Mt South Australia Australia
70 N9 Rembang Java
26 H9 Remchingen Germany
37 L2 Remda Germany
124 F5 Remedios Cuba
124 F5 Remedios Mexico
126 L6 Remedios Panama
72 F6 Remeshk Iran
36 E6 Remich Luxembourg
22 G5 Rémigny Quebec Canada
120 H3 Remi L Ontario Canada
22 J4 Remilly-Allicourt France
99 T9 Remington Indiana U.S.A.
94 K8 Remington Virginia U.S.A.
33 N8 Remlingen Germany
100 B6 Remote Oregon U.S.A.
22 K3 Remouchamps Belgium
19 N17 Remoulins France
83 K14 Remparts, R. des Réunion Indian Oc
9 G4 Rempstone England
33 R5 Remscheid Germany
31 J7 Remse Germany
25 E8 Remseck Germany
99 L7 Remsen Iowa U.S.A.
99 P7 Remsen New York U.S.A.
20 E6 Remungol France
21 M7 Remus Michigan U.S.A.
22 L3 Rémuzat France
33 N9 Renaix, Pulau isld Indonesia
71 D2 Rena Pt Luzon Philippines
128 E4 Renascença Brazil
41 J4 Renaul I isld Antarctica
33 Q10 Renazé France
36 E6 Renchen Germany
26 E10 Rendal Norway
33 R5 Renderne Germany
32 L4 Rendsburg Germany
37 N4 Renens Germany
123 U7 Renews Newfoundland Canada
Renfrew co see Strathclyde reg
121 O7 Renfrew Ontario Canada
12 D2 Renfrew Scotland
70 L9 Rengat Sumatra
69 F13 Rengat Sumatra
70 L9 Renge Java
69 N6 Ren He R China
67 C1 Renhua China
67 B1 Renhuai China
141 N8 Renick West Virginia U.S.A.
48 L5 Reni Ukraine
120 J2 Renison Ontario Canada
139 H8 Renison Bell Tasmania Australia
45 L4 Renk Sudan
29 L11 Renko Finland
25 F5 Renkum Netherlands
115 M7 Renland reg Greenland
138 F5 Renmark South Australia Australia
65 F1 Renmin China
14 A5 Rennedøl Norway
79 E7 Rennebu Norway
137 N4 Rennell isld Solomon Is
26 O1 Rennerod Germany
37 L6 Renner Springs N Terr Australia
88 D9 Rennes France
94 J5 Rennes France
75 J6 Rennick glacier Antarctica
118 H6 Rennie Saskatchewan Canada
74 G4 Rewari India
99 Q7 Rewey Wisconsin U.S.A.
45 J8 Riccione Italy
110 C1 Rexburg Idaho U.S.A.
107 K7 Rexford Kansas U.S.A.
100 K1 Rexford Montana U.S.A.
22 D2 Rexpoede France
122 H7 Rexton New Brunswick Canada
80 D2 Reyba Israel
29 T9 Reydarfjördur inlet Iceland
107 L6 Reydon Oklahoma U.S.A.
144 E6 Reyes Pk New Zealand
118 K5 Reyes, les France
118 N6 Reykir Iceland
119 T7 Reykjavik Manitoba Canada
28 R9 Reykjavik Iceland
119 M6 Reynaud Saskatchewan Canada
140 B2 Reynella R N Terr Australia
112 G7 Reynolds Georgia U.S.A.
100 J8 Reynolds Idaho U.S.A.
109 J3 Reynolds Indiana U.S.A.
109 K1 Reynolds Indiana U.S.A.
138 D4 Reynolds, L South Australia Australia
117 D7 Reynolds I Northwest Territories Canada
140 C5 Reynolds Ra N Terr Australia
143 C8 Reynolds Range W Australia Australia
92 C4 Reynosa Mexico
40 B5 Reyssouze R France
78 K3 Rezaiyeh Iran
119 N8 Rezat R Germany
20 G7 Reze France
52 K6 Rēzekne Latvia
48 M3 Rezh Russian Federation
71 A7 Rezzonico Italy
98 K3 Rhade Germany
94 J2 Rhame North Dakota U.S.A.
38 H7 Rhätikon mt Switzerland
8 C3 Rhayader Wales

32 H9 Rheda-Wiedenbrück Germany
32 F6 Rhede Niedersachsen Germany
32 E9 Rhede Nordrhein-Westfalen Germany
25 F4 Rheden Netherlands
9 F3 Rhee, R England
119 P7 Rhein Saskatchewan Canada
W N Europe Rhein R
110 B3 Rich Hill Missouri U.S.A.
122 H7 Richibucto New Brunswick Canada
118 F4 Rich Lake Alberta Canada
112 G3 Richland Georgia U.S.A.
94 B4 Richland Michigan U.S.A.
110 D4 Richland Missouri U.S.A.
101 T1 Richland Montana U.S.A.
95 N7 Richland New Jersey U.S.A.
100 H5 Richland Oregon U.S.A.
100 F3 Richland Washington U.S.A.
99 Q6 Richland Center Wisconsin U.S.A.
109 L4 Richland Cr Texas U.S.A.
112 K3 Richlands North Carolina U.S.A.
94 J9 Richlands Virginia U.S.A.
109 J4 Richland Springs Texas U.S.A.
118 J7 Richlea Saskatchewan Canada
119 K5 Richmond New South Wales Australia
141 G5 Richmond Queensland Australia
139 H8 Richmond Tasmania Australia
121 P7 Richmond Ontario Canada
45 N3 Richmond Prince Edward I Canada
121 S7 Richmond Quebec Canada
9 F5 Richmond England
13 G5 Richmond North Yorkshire England
127 L2 Richmond Jamaica
145 D4 Richmond New Zealand
87 G4 Richmond S Africa
102 B4 Richmond California U.S.A.
110 M2 Richmond Indiana U.S.A.
110 M4 Richmond Kentucky U.S.A.
96 S2 Richmond Maine U.S.A.
99 M4 Richmond Minnesota U.S.A.
100 F5 Richmond Oregon U.S.A.
109 M6 Richmond Texas U.S.A.
103 O1 Richmond Utah U.S.A.
94 K9 Richmond Virginia U.S.A.
121 L9 Richmond Hill Ontario Canada
112 F6 Richmond Hill Georgia U.S.A.
70 Q10 Richmond, L W Australia Australia
139 L3 Richmond R New South Wales Australia
139 J8 Richmond Ra mts New South Wales Australia
74 F5 Ringas India
42 F3 Risnjak mt Croatia
48 J5 Ringeltu Romania
41 K4 Ringelspitz mt Switzerland
27 D11 Ringerike L Norway
12 D4 Ringford Scotland
37 J3 Ringgau Germany
109 L8 Ringgold Louisiana U.S.A.
108 G6 Ringgold Texas U.S.A.
26 D8 Ringlove Denmark
101 Q3 Ringkøbing Montana U.S.A.
100 K1 Ringling Montana U.S.A.
109 J9 Ringmer Oklahoma U.S.A.
109 M1 Ringold Oklahoma U.S.A.
27 E11 Ringsaker Norway
28 H6 Ringsted Denmark
108 B7 Ringstead England
26 K2 Ringvassøy isld Norway
140 C6 Ringwood N Terr Australia
9 E6 Ringwood England
118 C8 Ringwood Victoria Australia
133 C5 Rinihue Chile
117 H7 Riñihue, L Chile
99 R6 Rinkabyholm Sweden
32 M10 Rinkenæs Denmark
41 O3 Rinn Austria
32 K8 Rinteln Germany
47 N6 Rio Italy
47 N10 Rio Turkey
47 N11 Riva R Italy
47 N11 Riva Italy
47 N10 Riva Turkey
32 K3 Rivadavia Argentina
133 C3 Rivadavia Chile
45 K3 Rio di Tures Italy
22 K3 Rivage Belgium
19 N14 Rival France
12 C6 Rives Junction Michigan U.S.A.

130 J9 Rio Tinto Brazil
100 K8 Rio Tinto Nevada U.S.A.
71 C6 Rio Tuba Philippines
133 C8 Rio Turbio Mines Argentina
128 C3 Rioverde Ecuador
130 C6 Rio Verde Mexico
130 G9 Rio Verde de Mato Grosso Brazil
149 X3 Rio Vista California U.S.A.
130 C6 Riozinho, R Brazil
48 F6 Ripani Serbia Yugoslavia
44 B1 Riparia Italy
9 F5 Ripley N Yorks England
13 G5 Ripley England
13 G5 Ripley England
103 K8 Ripley California U.S.A.
110 H3 Ripley Mississippi U.S.A.
94 H7 Ripley Ohio U.S.A.
110 G6 Ripley Tennessee U.S.A.
94 F8 Ripley West Virginia U.S.A.
17 J2 Ripoll Spain
13 G5 Ripon Canada
102 C4 Ripon Canada
99 S6 Ripon Wisconsin U.S.A.
142 D5 Ripon Hills W Australia Australia
99 M8 Rippey Iowa U.S.A.
100 J4 Riqqins England
103 K8 Riqnano Flaminio Italy
110 G6 Ripley Tennessee U.S.A.

94 G7 **Rivesville** West Virginia U.S.A.
103 K6 **Riviera** Nevada U.S.A.
109 K8 **Riviera** Texas U.S.A.
113 G11 **Riviera Beach** Florida U.S.A.
44 F3 **Riviera di Levante** Italy
44 D4 **Riviera di Ponente** Italy
21 J4 **Rivière** Orne France
22 D3 **Rivière** Pas-de-Calais France
122 G4 **Rivière à Claude** Quebec Canada
122 J4 **Rivière-à-la-Loutre** Quebec Canada
121 S6 **Rivière à Pierre** Quebec Canada
122 H5 **Rivière-au-Renard** Quebec Canada
122 G3 **Rivière aux Graines** Quebec Canada
121 S5 **Rivière-aux-Rats** Quebec Canada
122 D6 **Rivière Bleue** Quebec Canada
122 K4 **Rivière-de-la-Chaloupe** Quebec Canada
83 M13 **Rivière des Anguilles** Mauritius
122 C6 **Rivière du Loup** Quebec Canada
121 S5 **Rivière du Milieu** Quebec Canada
122 B5 **Rivière du Moulin** Quebec Canada
121 M4 **Rivière Héva** Quebec Canada
122 G4 **Rivière La Madeleine** Quebec Canada
122 B6 **Rivière Ouelle** Quebec Canada
122 E4 **Rivière Pentecôte** Quebec Canada
122 G3 **Rivière Pigou** Quebec Canada
127 M4 **Rivière Pilote** Martinique W Indies
122 H3 **Rivière St. Jean** Quebec Canada
21 L3 **Rivière-St. Sauveur, la** France
127 L4 **Rivière Salée** Martinique W Indies
122 D6 **Rivière-Verte** New Brunswick Canada
122 C6 **Rivière Verte** Quebec Canada
44 C1 **Rivoli** Italy
138 E6 **Rivoli B** South Australia Australia
145 D4 **Riwaka** New Zealand
72 F4 **Riyāḑ, Ar** Saudi Arabia
Riyadh *see* **Riyāḑ, Ar**
71 E3 **Rizal** Luzon Philippines
78 H1 **Rize** Turkey
65 D7 **Rizhao** China
Rizhskiy Zaliv *see* **Riga, Gulf of**
79 E3 **Rizokarpaso** Cyprus
46 E5 **Rizoma** Greece
43 H10 **Rizzuto, C** Italy
27 C12 **Rjukan** Norway
27 B12 **Rjuven** Norway
85 A5 **Rkiz, L** Mauritania
80 E1 **Rmaich** Lebanon
68 H5 **Ro** Vietnam
27 E11 **Roa** Norway
16 E3 **Roa** Spain
110 K2 **Roachdale** Indiana U.S.A.
9 F3 **Roade** England
106 B9 **Road Forks** New Mexico U.S.A.
127 M5 **Road Town** Virgin Is
28 B6 **Roager** Denmark
103 P2 **Roan Cliffs** Utah U.S.A.
106 B2 **Roan Cr** Colorado U.S.A.
112 E1 **Roan Mt** North Carolina U.S.A.
18 H6 **Roanne** France
111 L8 **Roanoke** Alabama U.S.A.
99 R9 **Roanoke** Illinois U.S.A.
94 B6 **Roanoke** Indiana U.S.A.
109 K3 **Roanoke** Texas U.S.A.
94 H9 **Roanoke** Virginia U.S.A.
112 M2 **Roanoke I** North Carolina U.S.A.
112 K1 **Roanoke Rapids** North Carolina U.S.A.
106 B2 **Roan Plateau** Colorado U.S.A.
103 P2 **Roan Plateau** Utah U.S.A.
109 M5 **Roans Prairie** Texas U.S.A.
95 L5 **Roaring Branch** Pennsylvania U.S.A.
112 F1 **Roaring Gap** North Carolina U.S.A.
108 G2 **Roaring Springs** Texas U.S.A.
14 B5 **Roaringwater B** Ireland
77 D4 **Robāt** Iran
77 B2 **Robāṭ Karim** Iran
109 J9 **Robberson** Texas U.S.A.
112 H2 **Robbins** North Carolina U.S.A.
139 G8 **Robbins I** Tasmania Australia
112 D2 **Robbinsville** North Carolina U.S.A.
44 E1 **Robbio** Italy
138 E6 **Robe** South Australia Australia
14 B3 **Robe** *R* Ireland
33 R6 **Röbel** Germany
109 O4 **Robeline** Louisiana U.S.A.
138 F4 **Robe, Mt** New South Wales Australia
122 K3 **Robe Noir, L. de la** Quebec Canada
142 B5 **Robe R** W Australia Australia
112 K2 **Robersonville** North Carolina U.S.A.
108 G4 **Robert Lee** Texas U.S.A.
140 B7 **Robert, Mt** N Terr Australia
13 F3 **Roberton** Scotland
101 N6 **Roberts** Idaho U.S.A.
101 Q4 **Roberts** Montana U.S.A.
100 E5 **Roberts** Oregon U.S.A.
123 R4 **Robert's Arm** Newfoundland Canada
9 G6 **Robertsbridge** England
102 H2 **Roberts Cr. Mt** Nevada U.S.A.
111 J11 **Robertsdale** Alabama U.S.A.
26 L7 **Robertsfors** Sweden
110 A6 **Robert S. Kerr Res** Oklahoma U.S.A.
141 K8 **Roberts, Mt** Queensland Australia
101 Q7 **Roberts Mt** Wyoming U.S.A.
141 G4 **Robertson** *R* Queensland Australia
89 A9 **Robertson** S Africa
101 P8 **Robertson** Wyoming U.S.A.
146 C12 **Robertson Bay** Antarctica
146 D4 **Robertson I** Antarctica
142 D6 **Robertson Ra** W Australia Australia
121 T6 **Robertsonville** Quebec Canada
85 B7 **Robertsport** Liberia
138 E5 **Robertstown** South Australia Australia
14 E3 **Robertstown** Ireland
122 G6 **Robertville** New Brunswick Canada
121 S4 **Roberval** Quebec Canada
115 N1 **Robeson Chan** Canada/Greenland
8 B4 **Robeston Wathen** Wales
101 N7 **Robin** Idaho U.S.A.
100 J5 **Robinette** Oregon U.S.A.
13 H5 **Robin Hoods Bay** England
141 J7 **Robinson** *R* Queensland Australia
110 J2 **Robinson** Illinois U.S.A.
98 G2 **Robinson** North Dakota U.S.A.
133 B9 **Robinson Crusoe** *isld* Juan Fernández Is Pacific Oc
138 D2 **Robinson, Mt** South Australia Australia
142 C6 **Robinson, Mt** W Australia Australia
116 Q6 **Robinson Mts** Alaska U.S.A.
143 C7 **Robinson Ras** W Australia Australia
140 D3 **Robinson River** N Terr Australia
122 F6 **Robinsonville** New Brunswick Canada
139 G5 **Robinvale** New South Wales Australia
17 F6 **Robledo** Spain
103 N9 **Robles Pass** Arizona U.S.A.
103 N9 **Robles Ranch** Arizona U.S.A.
118 A1 **Roblin Park** Manitoba Canada
128 G7 **Robore** Bolivia
118 H9 **Robsart** Saskatchewan Canada
117 O9 **Robson, Mt** Alberta/Br Col Canada
117 O9 **Robson, Mt** British Columbia Canada
109 K8 **Robstown** Texas U.S.A.
16 A6 **Roca, C. da** Portugal
119 Q8 **Rocanville** Saskatchewan Canada
129 M4 **Rocas** *isld* Brazil
124 B5 **Rocas Alijos** *isld* Mexico
43 G8 **Roccadaspide** Italy
45 P5 **Rocca di Mezzo** Italy
45 N6 **Rocca di Papa** Italy
45 O6 **Roccagorga** Italy
43 H8 **Rocca Imperiale** Italy
Rocca Littorio *see* **Gaalkacyo**
45 P7 **Roccamonfina** Italy
38 E9 **Rocca Pietore** Italy
45 L3 **Rocca San Casciano** Italy
45 P6 **Roccasecca** Italy
45 N5 **Rocca Sinibalda** Italy
42 D5 **Roccastrada** Italy
44 B1 **Rocciamelone** *mt* Italy
40 E5 **Roc d'Enfer** *mt* France
131 G4 **Rocha** *dept* Uruguay
131 G5 **Rocha** Uruguay
21 K5 **Rochard, Mt** France
13 F6 **Rochdale** England
121 N4 **Rochebaucourt** Quebec Canada
20 F6 **Roche-Bernard, la** France
21 H7 **Roche Blanche, la** France
18 F7 **Rochechouart** France
20 D4 **Roche-Derrien, la** France
22 K3 **Roche-en-Ardenne, La** Belgium
22 J3 **Rochefort** Belgium
18 E7 **Rochefort** France
19 N17 **Rochefort-du-Gard** France
20 F6 **Rochefort-en-Terre** France
18 G7 **Rochefort-Montagne** France
18 F7 **Rochefoucauld, la** France
21 O3 **Roche-Guyon, la** France
22 J4 **Rochehaut** Belgium
113 E8 **Rochelle** Florida U.S.A.
112 D6 **Rochelle** Georgia U.S.A.
99 R8 **Rochelle** Illinois U.S.A.
111 D10 **Rochelle** Louisiana U.S.A.
109 H4 **Rochelle** Texas U.S.A.
18 E6 **Rochelle, la** France
119 P9 **Roche Percee** Saskatchewan Canada
110 D3 **Rocheport** Missouri U.S.A.
21 M8 **Roche-Posay, la** France
127 L4 **Rocher du Diamant** Martinique W Indies
123 O2 **Rocher, L. du** Quebec Canada
117 R5 **Rocher River** Northwest Territories Canada
122 E3 **Rochers, R. aux** Quebec Canada
20 E3 **Roches Douvres** *islds* English Chan
20 H8 **Rocheservière** France
83 M12 **Roches, Plaine des** Mauritius
40 E1 **Rochesson** France
139 G6 **Rochester** Victoria Australia
118 D4 **Rochester** Alberta Canada
9 G5 **Rochester** England
13 F3 **Rochester** Northumberland England
110 G2 **Rochester** Illinois U.S.A.
94 A5 **Rochester** Indiana U.S.A.
94 D4 **Rochester** Michigan U.S.A.
99 O5 **Rochester** Minnesota U.S.A.
95 Q3 **Rochester** New Hampshire U.S.A.
95 K3 **Rochester** New York U.S.A.
121 N9 **Rochester** New York U.S.A.
94 E5 **Rochester** Ohio U.S.A.
94 G6 **Rochester** Pennsylvania U.S.A.
108 H2 **Rochester** Texas U.S.A.
100 B3 **Rochester** Washington U.S.A.
20 H8 **Roche-sur-Yon, La** France
9 G4 **Rochford** England
98 C5 **Rochford** South Dakota U.S.A.
118 B5 **Rochfort Br** Alberta Canada
37 O1 **Rochlitz** Germany
118 E6 **Rochon Sands Prov. Park** Alberta Canada
21 P3 **Rochy-Condé** France
117 K5 **Rock** *R* Yukon Territory Canada
98 K6 **Rock** *R* Iowa/Minnesota U.S.A.
107 O4 **Rock** Kansas U.S.A.
99 T3 **Rock** Michigan U.S.A.
99 S6 **Rock** *R* Wisconsin U.S.A.
6 B5 **Rockall** N Atlantic Oc
90 H3 **Rockall Bank** Atlantic Oc
144 C6 **Rock and Pillar Range** New Zealand
117 L10 **Rock Bay** British Columbia Canada
12 E4 **Rockcliffe** Scotland
101 S1 **Rock Cr** Montana U.S.A.
101 M3 **Rock Cr** Montana U.S.A.
94 G5 **Rock Cr** Ohio U.S.A.
100 E4 **Rock Cr** Oregon U.S.A.
101 T8 **Rock Cr** Wyoming U.S.A.
117 D3 **Rock Creek** Yukon Territory Canada
101 L7 **Rockcreek** Idaho U.S.A.
109 K5 **Rockdale** Texas U.S.A.
146 B10 **Rockefeller Mts** Antarctica
146 C9 **Rockefeller Plat** Antarctica
36 D4 **Rockenhausen** Germany
99 R8 **Rock Falls** Illinois U.S.A.
94 J9 **Rockfish** Virginia U.S.A.
111 K9 **Rockford** Alabama U.S.A.
101 N6 **Rockford** Idaho U.S.A.
99 R7 **Rockford** Illinois U.S.A.
94 B3 **Rockford** Michigan U.S.A.
99 N4 **Rockford** Minnesota U.S.A.
94 C6 **Rockford** Ohio U.S.A.
100 H2 **Rockford** Washington U.S.A.
119 M9 **Rockglen** Saskatchewan Canada
98 H5 **Rockham** South Dakota U.S.A.
141 K6 **Rockhampton** Queensland Australia
140 D4 **Rockhampton Downs** N Terr Australia
99 S1 **Rock Harbor** Michigan U.S.A.
118 J6 **Rockhaven** Saskatchewan Canada
112 F3 **Rock Hill** South Carolina U.S.A.
99 Q8 **Rock I** Illinois U.S.A.
143 B9 **Rockingham** W Australia Australia
112 H3 **Rockingham** North Carolina U.S.A.
141 H4 **Rockingham B** Queensland Australia
121 S7 **Rock Island** Quebec Canada
109 L6 **Rock Island** Texas U.S.A.
98 G1 **Rock L** North Dakota U.S.A.
100 H2 **Rock L** Washington U.S.A.
121 P7 **Rockland** Ontario Canada
101 N7 **Rockland** Idaho U.S.A.
95 S2 **Rockland** Maine U.S.A.
99 R3 **Rockland** Michigan U.S.A.
109 N4 **Rockland** Texas U.S.A.
140 E4 **Rocklands** Queensland Australia
138 F6 **Rocklands Res** Victoria Australia
141 K2 **Rocklea** *dist* Brisbane, Qnsld Australia
142 B6 **Rocklea** W Australia Australia
100 G2 **Rocklyn** Washington U.S.A.
112 B3 **Rockmart** Georgia U.S.A.
117 Q3 **Rocknest L** Northwest Territories Canada
33 R10 **Röcknitz** Germany
95 L8 **Rock Point** Maryland U.S.A.
102 A2 **Rockport** California U.S.A.
110 E2 **Rockport** Illinois U.S.A.
110 J4 **Rockport** Indiana U.S.A.
95 S2 **Rockport** Maine U.S.A.
95 R4 **Rockport** Massachusetts U.S.A.
110 A1 **Rock Port** Missouri U.S.A.
109 K7 **Rockport** Texas U.S.A.
100 D1 **Rockport** Washington U.S.A.
101 U8 **Rock River** Wyoming U.S.A.
113 L13 **Rock Sound** Bahamas
126 F2 **Rock Sound** Eleuthera Bahamas
103 M7 **Rock Springs** Arizona U.S.A.
101 T3 **Rock Springs** Montana U.S.A.
108 G5 **Rocksprings** Texas U.S.A.
101 Q8 **Rock Springs** Wyoming U.S.A.
144 D4 **Rocks Pt.** New Zealand
128 G2 **Rockstone** Guyana
99 R7 **Rockton** Illinois U.S.A.
98 K6 **Rock Valley** Iowa U.S.A.
145 D4 **Rockville** New Zealand
95 P5 **Rockville** Connecticut U.S.A.
110 J2 **Rockville** Indiana U.S.A.
95 K7 **Rockville** Maryland U.S.A.
100 H6 **Rockville** Oregon U.S.A.
112 G5 **Rockville** South Carolina U.S.A.
103 L4 **Rockville** Utah U.S.A.
109 L3 **Rockwall** Texas U.S.A.
99 N7 **Rockwell** Iowa U.S.A.
112 G2 **Rockwell** North Carolina U.S.A.
99 M7 **Rockwell City** Iowa U.S.A.
106 C4 **Rockwood** Colorado U.S.A.
95 S1 **Rockwood** Maine U.S.A.
94 H7 **Rockwood** Pennsylvania U.S.A.
112 C2 **Rockwood** Tennessee U.S.A.
109 H4 **Rockwood** Texas U.S.A.
112 G2 **Rocky** *R* North Carolina U.S.A.
107 L6 **Rocky** Oklahoma U.S.A.
112 E3 **Rocky** *R* South Carolina U.S.A.
100 K6 **Rocky Bar** Idaho U.S.A.
139 H8 **Rocky C** Tasmania Australia
118 D7 **Rockyford** Alberta Canada
106 G3 **Rocky Ford** Colorado U.S.A.
112 F5 **Rocky Ford** Georgia U.S.A.
98 D6 **Rockyford** South Dakota U.S.A.
94 D7 **Rocky Fork Res** Ohio U.S.A.
94 H5 **Rocky Grove** Pennsylvania U.S.A.
143 B10 **Rocky Gully** W Australia Australia
120 H5 **Rocky Island L** Ontario Canada
119 Q4 **Rocky L** Manitoba Canada
112 K2 **Rocky Mount** North Carolina U.S.A.
94 H10 **Rocky Mount** Virginia U.S.A.
118 C6 **Rocky Mountain House** Alberta Canada
101 N2 **Rocky Mt** Montana U.S.A.
98 A9 **Rocky Mt Nat. Park** Colorado U.S.A.
118 B8 **Rocky Mts** British Columbia Canada
106 C1 **Rocky Mts** N America
127 K3 **Rocky Point** Jamaica
95 P6 **Rocky Point** Long I, New York U.S.A.
98 A5 **Rockypoint** Wyoming U.S.A.
113 K11 **Rocky Pt** Bahamas
116 F4 **Rocky Pt** Alaska U.S.A.
94 F5 **Rocky River** Ohio U.S.A.
131 D7 **Ró Colorado** Argentina
20 F3 **Rocque Pt. La** Channel Is
22 H4 **Rocroi** France
37 M2 **Roda** *R* Germany
36 D5 **Rodalben** Germany
27 C11 **Rödberg** Norway
28 G7 **Rødby** Denmark
28 G7 **Rødbyhavn** Denmark
123 Q3 **Roddickton** Newfoundland Canada
28 B3 **Rødding** Denmark
28 C6 **Rødding** Sønderjylland Denmark
27 H15 **Rödeby** Sweden
36 F4 **Rödemark** Germany
25 F2 **Roden** Netherlands
32 K8 **Rodenberg** Germany
27 E12 **Rödenes** Norway
32 H6 **Rodenkirchen** Germany
37 L3 **Rödental** Germany
124 G5 **Rodeo** Mexico
106 B10 **Rodeo** New Mexico U.S.A.
33 S10 **Röderau** Germany
109 O3 **Rodessa** Louisiana U.S.A.
32 K7 **Rodewald** Germany
37 N2 **Rodewisch** Germany
18 G8 **Rodez** France
36 F3 **Rodgau** Germany
36 F2 **Rodheim-Bieber** Germany
46 F4 **Rodholívos** Greece
47 V14 **Ródhos** *isld* Greece
47 V14 **Ródhos** Greece
45 J1 **Rodigo** Italy
37 O5 **Roding** Germany
140 C6 **Rodinga** N Terr Australia
52 J2 **Rodionovo** Russian Federation
28 C4 **Rødkærsbro** Denmark
77 J6 **Rodkhan** Pakistan
48 J3 **Rodnei, Muntii** Romania
120 J10 **Rodney** Ontario Canada
94 B3 **Rodney** Michigan U.S.A.
116 D4 **Rodney, C** Alaska U.S.A.
52 F6 **Rodniki** Russian Federation
55 C5 **Rodnikovka** Kazakhstan
54 D3 **Rodnya** Belorussia
139 H7 **Rodondo** *isld* Victoria Australia
46 C3 **Rodonit, kepi i** *C* Albania
13 E3 **Rodono** Scotland
46 G3 **Rodopi Planina** Bulgaria
Rodosto *see* **Tekirdağ**
26 F5 **Rödöy** Norway
128 D5 **Rodrigues** Brazil
81 D7 **Rodrigues I** Indian Oc
28 H7 **Rødsand** *sandbank* Denmark
28 D3 **Rød Sø** Denmark
29 K6 **Rødvig** Denmark
14 E2 **Roe** *R* N Ireland
111 E7 **Roe** Arkansas U.S.A.
142 B5 **Roebourne** W Australia Australia
142 D4 **Roebuck B** W Australia Australia
142 D4 **Roebuck Plains** W Australia Australia
143 E9 **Roe, L** W Australia Australia
21 H6 **Roë, la** France
143 G9 **Roe Plains** W Australia Australia
25 E6 **Roermond** Netherlands
22 D2 **Roesbrugge-Haringe** Belgium
22 E2 **Roeselare** Belgium
115 L5 **Roes Welcome Sound** Northwest Territories Canada
45 L2 **Ro Ferrarese** Italy
109 L1 **Roff** Oklahoma U.S.A.
54 B3 **Rogachev** Belorussia
128 E7 **Rogaguado, L** Bolivia
128 E6 **Rogagua, L** Bolivia
27 A12 **Rogaland** *county* Norway
54 H7 **Rogan'** Ukraine
109 O5 **Roganville** Texas U.S.A.
48 J1 **Rogatin** Ukraine
33 P8 **Rogatz** Germany
26 F9 **Rogen** *L* Sweden
121 M5 **Roger, Lac** Quebec Canada
110 B5 **Rogers** Arkansas U.S.A.
98 H2 **Rogers** North Dakota U.S.A.
109 K5 **Rogers** Texas U.S.A.
94 D1 **Rogers City** Michigan U.S.A.
102 G7 **Rogers L.** California U.S.A.
117 P10 **Rogers, Mt** British Columbia Canada
101 L7 **Rogerson** Idaho U.S.A.
122 G7 **Rogersville** New Brunswick Canada
110 J7 **Rogersville** Alabama U.S.A.
110 C4 **Rogersville** Missouri U.S.A.
112 D1 **Rogersville** Tennessee U.S.A.
98 B9 **Roggen** Colorado U.S.A.
33 O5 **Roggendorf** Germany
89 A8 **Roggeveld Berge** *mts* S Africa
8 D4 **Rogiet** Wales
43 G9 **Rogliano** Italy
19 O18 **Rognac** France
26 H4 **Rognan** Norway
19 O17 **Rognes** France
33 O6 **Rögnitz** *R* Germany
44 B2 **Rognosa, Punta** *mt* Italy
46 D1 **Rogozna** *mt* Serbia Yugoslavia
31 K3 **Rogoźno** Poland
100 A7 **Rogue** *R* Oregon U.S.A.
20 E5 **Rohan** France
121 Q3 **Rohault, L** Quebec Canada
33 P6 **Rohlsdorf** Germany
28 J6 **Roholte** Denmark
37 M6 **Rohr** Germany
38 J4 **Rohrbach** Austria
36 C5 **Rohrbach** France
37 O7 **Rohrbach** Germany
33 O7 **Rohrberg** Germany
36 G4 **Rohrbrunn** Germany
74 C5 **Rohri** Pakistan
37 L7 **Röhrmoos** Germany
74 G4 **Rohtak** India
111 E8 **Rohwer** Arkansas U.S.A.
21 L7 **Roiffe** France
22 E4 **Roisel** France
22 F3 **Roisin** Belgium
33 R9 **Roitzsch** Sachsen Germany
33 Q9 **Roitzsch** Sachsen-Anhalt Germany
52 B6 **Roja** Latvia
26 G9 **Röjan** Sweden
133 E4 **Rojas** Argentina
127 L5 **Rojo, C** Puerto Rico
141 G2 **Rokeby** Queensland Australia
119 P7 **Rokeby** Saskatchewan Canada
29 O5 **Rokhmoyva, G** *mt* Russian Federation
52 C6 **Rokiškis** Lithuania
53 C8 **Rokitnoye** Ukraine
77 L2 **Rokkah** Afghanistan
61 P5 **Rokkasho** Japan
26 M6 **Roknäs** Sweden
29 M7 **Rokua Nat. Park** Finland
61 O6 **Rokugō** Japan
61 L8 **Rokugō-saki** *C* Japan
30 H6 **Rokycany** Czechoslovakia
44 C4 **Rola** *R* Italy
40 B2 **Rolampont** France
118 D1 **Roland** Manitoba Canada
83 L13 **Roland** *isld* Kerguelen Indian Oc
110 D7 **Roland** Arkansas U.S.A.
99 N7 **Roland** Iowa U.S.A.
130 D8 **Rolândia** Brazil
28 D3 **Rold** Denmark
27 B12 **Röldal** Norway
25 G3 **Rolde** Netherlands
98 G1 **Rolette** North Dakota U.S.A.
99 M7 **Rolfe** Iowa U.S.A.
94 J5 **Rolfe** Pennsylvania U.S.A.
141 H6 **Rolfes** Queensland Australia
103 L9 **Roll** Arizona U.S.A.
117 N8 **Rolla** British Columbia Canada
107 J4 **Rolla** Kansas U.S.A.
110 E4 **Rolla** Missouri U.S.A.
98 G1 **Rolla** North Dakota U.S.A.
27 D11 **Rollag** Norway
141 J6 **Rolleston** Queensland Australia
144 D5 **Rolleston** New Zealand
144 C5 **Rolleston, Mt** New Zealand
144 C5 **Rolleston Range** New Zealand
121 L5 **Rollet** Quebec Canada
21 L2 **Rolleville** France
110 L4 **Rolling Fork** *R* Kentucky U.S.A.
111 F9 **Rolling Fork** Mississippi U.S.A.
101 L2 **Rollins** Montana U.S.A.
45 J2 **Rolo** Italy
33 R4 **Rolofshagen** Germany
68 G6 **Rolous** Cambodia
121 N6 **Rolphton** Ontario Canada
28 F6 **Rolsted** Denmark
26 N1 **Rolvsöy** *isld* Norway
28 A3 **Rom** Denmark
141 J7 **Roma** Queensland Australia
71 N8 **Roma** *isld* Indonesia
44 M6 **Roma** Italy
27 K14 **Roma** Sweden
45 H3 **Romagna** *reg* Italy
42 B3 **Romagnano Sesia** Italy
20 H5 **Romagné** France
22 J5 **Romagne-sous-Montfaucon** France
144 B7 **Romahapa** New Zealand
122 J3 **Romaine, R** Quebec Canada
109 H9 **Roma Los Saenz** Texas U.S.A.
46 F1 **Roman** Bulgaria
48 K4 **Roman** Romania
126 F3 **Romana, Cayo** *isld* Cuba
19 P14 **Romanche** *R* France
90 H8 **Romanche Gap** Atlantic Oc
19 N12 **Romanèche-Thorins** France
48 G5 **Romania** *rep* E Europe
113 F12 **Romano, C** Florida U.S.A.
58 F1 **Romanovka** Russian Federation
55 D2 **Romanovo** Russian Federation
36 C6 **Romanswiller** France
116 D6 **Romanzof, C** Alaska U.S.A.
116 Q2 **Romanzof Mts** Alaska U.S.A.
128 F4 **Romão** Brazil
20 H5 **Romazy** France
71 F4 **Romblon** Philippines
Rome *see* **Roma**
111 L7 **Rome** Georgia U.S.A.
95 M3 **Rome** New York U.S.A.
95 L5 **Rome** Pennsylvania U.S.A.
110 K5 **Rome** Tennessee U.S.A.
106 E4 **Romeo** Colorado U.S.A.
94 D4 **Romeo** Michigan U.S.A.
36 E5 **Römerberg** Germany
22 H3 **Romerée** Belgium
27 E11 **Romerike** *reg* Norway
125 K8 **Romero** Mexico
106 E6 **Romeroville** New Mexico U.S.A.
36 H7 **Römerstein** Germany
40 C6 **Romey, Val** France
9 G4 **Romford** England
37 K3 **Römhild** Germany
20 G5 **Romille** France
18 H4 **Romilly** France
21 M3 **Romilly** Eure France
21 N3 **Romilly-sur-Andelle** France
142 F5 **Romily, Mt** W Australia Australia
57 E5 **Romit** Tajikistan
57 C5 **Romitan** Uzbekistan
36 B1 **Rommerskirchen** Germany
94 J7 **Romney** West Virginia U.S.A.
54 E6 **Romny** Ukraine
28 A6 **Rømo** *isld* Denmark
54 E6 **Romodan** Ukraine
21 O7 **Romorantin** France
69 F11 **Rompin** Malaysia
36 G2 **Romrod** Germany
26 C9 **Romsdal** *V* Norway
26 B9 **Romsdalsfjord** *inlet* Norway
9 E6 **Romsey** England
28 F5 **Romsø** *isld* Denmark
94 D4 **Romulus** Michigan U.S.A.
68 H4 **Ron** Vietnam
15 C3 **Rona** *isld* Scotland
101 L2 **Ronan** Montana U.S.A.
28 B3 **Rønbjerg** Denmark
126 D8 **Roncador Bank** Caribbean
129 H6 **Roncador, Sa. do** *mts* Brazil
94 G9 **Ronceverte** West Virginia U.S.A.
20 H4 **Roncey** France
40 E2 **Ronchamp** France
44 M5 **Ronciglione** Italy
45 M3 **Ronco** *R* Italy
45 J1 **Roncoferraro** Italy
45 M3 **Roncofreddo** Italy
22 E2 **Roncq** France
16 D8 **Ronda** Spain
26 D10 **Rondane** Norway
16 D8 **Ronda, Sa. de** *mts* Spain
128 F7 **Rondas-das-Salinas** Brazil
28 E4 **Rønde** Denmark
120 J10 **Rondeau Prov. Park** Ontario Canada
83 L14 **Ronde I** Kerguelen Indian Oc
26 D10 **Rondeslottet** *mt* Norway
128 D2 **Rondón** Colombia
128 F6 **Rondônia** Brazil
130 C5 **Rondonópolis** Brazil
128 F3 **Rondon, Pico** *mt* Brazil
88 G7 **Rondo Plat** Tanzania
36 B2 **Rondorf** Germany
95 N5 **Rondout Res** New York U.S.A.
27 K14 **Ronehamn** Sweden
67 C4 **Rong'an** China
67 B2 **Rongchang** China
65 C5 **Rongcheng** China
65 E6 **Rongcheng** China
67 C4 **Rong Jiang** *R* China
67 C4 **Rongjiang** China
68 A1 **Rongklang Ra** Burma
70 G6 **Rongko** *R* Sulawesi
145 E4 **Rongotea** New Zealand
67 C4 **Rongshui** China
88 H7 **Rongüi** *isld* Mozambique
67 A2 **Rong Xian** China
67 C5 **Rong Xian** China
28 A3 **Rønland** *C* Denmark
27 G16 **Rønne** Denmark
27 F15 **Rönnea** *R* Sweden
37 N2 **Ronneburg** Germany
27 H15 **Ronneby** Sweden
146 C6 **Ronne Entrance** Antarctica
146 D6 **Ronne Ice Shelf** Antarctica
32 L8 **Ronnenberg** Germany
26 G8 **Rönnöfors** Sweden
142 C5 **Ronsard I** W Australia Australia
22 F2 **Ronse** Belgium
129 H6 **Ronuro** *R* Brazil
25 G2 **Roodeschool** Netherlands
110 F2 **Roodhouse** Illinois U.S.A.
22 L4 **Roodt** Luxembourg
89 F4 **Rooiberg** *mt* S Africa
25 B5 **Roosendaal** Netherlands
103 N8 **Roosevelt** Arizona U.S.A.
99 L1 **Roosevelt** Minnesota U.S.A.
109 H1 **Roosevelt** Oklahoma U.S.A.
108 G5 **Roosevelt** Texas U.S.A.
101 P9 **Roosevelt** Utah U.S.A.
100 E4 **Roosevelt** Washington U.S.A.
103 N8 **Roosevelt Dam** Arizona U.S.A.
117 O12 **Roosevelt, F.D., L** Washington U.S.A.
135 L16 **Roosevelt I** Antarctica
146 C10 **Roosevelt I** Antarctica
117 L6 **Roosevelt, Mt** British Columbia Canada
14 D3 **Roosky** Ireland
89 F5 **Roossenekal** *mt* S Africa
117 L4 **Root** *R* Northwest Territories Canada
99 P6 **Root** *R* Minnesota U.S.A.
116 E9 **Rootok I** Aleutian Is
52 B6 **Ropaži** Latvia
52 H3 **Ropcha** Russian Federation
31 N5 **Ropczyce** Poland
140 D2 **Roper** *R* N Terr Australia
112 L2 **Roper** North Carolina U.S.A.
140 C2 **Roper Bar Police Station** N Terr Australia
29 J3 **Ropi** *mt* Finland
36 D6 **Roppenheim** France
18 E8 **Roquefort** France
121 L4 **Roquemaure** Quebec Canada
19 N16 **Roquemaure** France
19 P18 **Roquevaire** France
15 E2 **Rora Head** Scotland
128 F3 **Roraima** *state* Brazil
128 F2 **Roraima** *mt* Guyana
27 F10 **Rörbäcksnäs** Sweden
28 D3 **Rørbæk** Denmark
28 G5 **Rørby** Denmark
89 G7 **Rorke's Drift** S Africa
119 S7 **Rorketon** Manitoba Canada
26 E9 **Röros** Norway
41 L3 **Rorschach** Switzerland
26 H4 **Rörstad** Norway
28 H5 **Rørvig** Denmark
26 E7 **Rörvik** Norway
48 N1 **Ros'** *R* Ukraine
26 G6 **Röså** *R* Norway
43 B12 **Rosa, C** Algeria
122 B7 **Rosaire** Quebec Canada
107 O4 **Rosalia** Kansas U.S.A.
100 H2 **Rosalia** Washington U.S.A.
118 E6 **Rosalind** Alberta Canada
126 D6 **Rosalind Bank** Caribbean
102 F7 **Rosamond** California U.S.A.
102 F7 **Rosamond L** California U.S.A.
40 G6 **Rosa, Monte** *mt* Italy
124 G6 **Rosamorada** Mexico
109 K6 **Rosanky** Texas U.S.A.
41 M3 **Rosanna** *R* Austria
19 P16 **Rosans** France
124 E4 **Rosa, Pta** *C* Mexico
131 E4 **Rosario** Argentina
129 K4 **Rosário** Brazil
128 E8 **Rosario** Chile
124 E4 **Rosario** Mexico
124 B2 **Rosario** Baja California Mexico
124 H4 **Rosario** Coahuila Mexico
130 B9 **Rosario** Paraguay
71 E4 **Rosario** Philippines
127 H9 **Rosario** Venezuela
126 B5 **Rosario Bank** Caribbean
126 D4 **Rosario, Cayo del** Cuba
133 E3 **Rosario de la Frontera** Argentina
133 D2 **Rosario de Lerma** Argentina
133 F4 **Rosario del Tala** Argentina
126 C3 **Rosario, Sa. del** *hills* Cuba
124 B3 **Rosarito** Mexico
124 D4 **Rosarito** Mexico
16 D4 **Rosarito Embalse de** *res* Spain
17 K2 **Rosas** Spain
20 A5 **Roscanvel** France
33 N7 **Rosche** Germany
99 S7 **Roscoe** Illinois U.S.A.
101 Q4 **Roscoe** Montana U.S.A.
95 N5 **Roscoe** New York U.S.A.
98 G4 **Roscoe** South Dakota U.S.A.
108 G3 **Roscoe** Texas U.S.A.
20 C4 **Roscoff** France
14 C3 **Roscommon** *co* Ireland
14 C3 **Roscommon** Ireland
94 C2 **Roscommon** Michigan U.S.A.
14 D4 **Roscrea** Ireland
98 G7 **Rose** Nebraska U.S.A.
127 O7 **Roseau** Dominica
98 K1 **Roseau** *R* Minnesota U.S.A.
139 H8 **Roseberry** Tasmania Australia
100 J5 **Roseberry** Idaho U.S.A.
140 E7 **Roseberth** Queensland Australia
123 O6 **Rose Blanche** Newfoundland Canada
112 J3 **Roseboro** North Carolina U.S.A.
118 D7 **Rosebud** Alberta Canada
110 E3 **Rosebud** Missouri U.S.A.
101 T3 **Rosebud** Montana U.S.A.
108 A8 **Rosebud** New Mexico U.S.A.
98 F6 **Rosebud** South Dakota U.S.A.
109 L4 **Rosebud** Texas U.S.A.
101 T4 **Rosebud Cr** Montana U.S.A.
101 S4 **Rosebud Mts** Montana U.S.A.
100 B6 **Roseburg** Oregon U.S.A.
94 C3 **Rosebush** Michigan U.S.A.
94 C2 **Rose City** Michigan U.S.A.
102 G1 **Rose Creek** Nevada U.S.A.
141 K6 **Rosedale** Queensland Australia
118 E7 **Rosedale** Alberta Canada
110 J2 **Rosedale** Indiana U.S.A.
111 F8 **Rosedale** Mississippi U.S.A.
13 H5 **Rosedale Abbey** England
22 H3 **Rosée** Belgium
38 K8 **Rosegg** Austria
127 J1 **Rose Hall** Jamaica
83 L12 **Rose Hill** Mauritius
99 O8 **Rose Hill** Iowa U.S.A.
112 J3 **Rose Hill** North Carolina U.S.A.
113 K12 **Rose I** Bahamas
111 F11 **Roseland** Louisiana U.S.A.
118 F7 **Rose Lynn** Alberta Canada
118 E8 **Rosemary** Alberta Canada
6 D3 **Rosemary Bank** N Atlantic Oc
142 B5 **Rosemary I** W Australia Australia
99 N5 **Rosemount** Minnesota U.S.A.
102 E2 **Rose, Mt** Nevada U.S.A.
38 J8 **Rosenbach** *mt* Austria
33 O5 **Rosenberg** Germany
36 G5 **Rosenberg** Germany
109 M6 **Rosenberg** Texas U.S.A.
22 C1 **Rosendaël** France
32 F8 **Rosendahl** Germany
110 B1 **Rosendale** Missouri U.S.A.
121 M8 **Roseneath** Ontario Canada
12 D1 **Roseneath** Scotland
36 F7 **Rosenfeld** Germany
32 L6 **Rosengarten** Germany
38 F6 **Rosenheim** Germany
38 M8 **Rosenkopf** *mt* Austria
38 J8 **Rosennock** *mt* Austria
38 K8 **Rosental** *V* Austria
36 F2 **Rosenthal** Germany
109 O5 **Rosepine** Louisiana U.S.A.
117 H8 **Rose Pt** British Columbia Canada
140 D2 **Rose R** N Terr Australia
118 J8 **Roseray** Saskatchewan Canada
126 G3 **Roses** Long I Bahamas
118 K7 **Rosetown** Saskatchewan Canada
141 H5 **Rosetta** *R* Queensland Australia
Rosetta Egypt *see* **Rashîd**
101 M8 **Rosette** Utah U.S.A.
119 O6 **Rose Valley** Saskatchewan Canada
110 F1 **Roseville** Illinois U.S.A.
94 E7 **Roseville** Ohio U.S.A.
118 A5 **Rosewear** Alberta Canada
140 B3 **Rosewood** N Terr Australia
141 K8 **Rosewood** Queensland Australia
101 L7 **Roseworth** Idaho U.S.A.
52 E6 **Roshal'** Russian Federation
109 M6 **Rosharon** Texas U.S.A.
52 C4 **Roshchino** Russian Federation
55 E4 **Roshchinskoye** Kazakhstan
36 C6 **Rosheim** France
80 C5 **Rosh Ha 'Ayin** Israel
77 F2 **Roshkhvār** Iran
98 K4 **Rosholt** South Dakota U.S.A.
99 R5 **Rosholt** Wisconsin U.S.A.
80 F2 **Rosh Pinna** Israel
57 F6 **Roshtkala** Tajikistan
80 D7 **Rosh Ẕurim** Jordan
31 J6 **Rosice** Czechoslovakia
110 H4 **Rosiclare** Illinois U.S.A.
22 D4 **Rosières-en-Santerre** France
122 H5 **Rosiers, C.des** Quebec Canada
21 K7 **Rosiers, les** France
142 A5 **Rosily I** W Australia Australia
48 J6 **Roşiori de Vede** Romania
46 G1 **Rositsa** *R* Bulgaria
47 J1 **Rositsa** Bulgaria
37 N1 **Rositz** Germany
28 J5 **Roskilde** *co* Denmark
28 J5 **Roskilde** Denmark
33 R8 **Roskow** Germany
103 N9 **Roskruge Mts** Arizona U.S.A.
54 D3 **Roslavl'** Russian Federation
14 D2 **Roslea** N Ireland
28 B3 **Roslev** Denmark
52 F5 **Roslyatino** Russian Federation
98 J4 **Roslyn** South Dakota U.S.A.
100 D2 **Roslyn** Washington U.S.A.
120 C3 **Roslyn L** Ontario Canada
28 F4 **Rosmus** Denmark
28 F5 **Røsnæs** *C* Denmark
21 N8 **Rosnay** France
20 B5 **Rosnoen** France
45 M1 **Rosolina** Italy
20 C6 **Rosporden** France
22 L4 **Rosport** Luxembourg
36 C2 **Rosrath** Germany
139 J8 **Ross** Tasmania Australia
83 L14 **Ross** *mt* Kerguelen Indian Oc
144 C5 **Ross** New Zealand
98 D1 **Ross** North Dakota U.S.A.
101 U6 **Ross** Wyoming U.S.A.
41 K5 **Rossa** Switzerland
37 K3 **Rossach** Germany
Ross and Cromarty *co see* **Highland** *reg*
43 H9 **Rossano** Italy
14 C2 **Rossan Pt** Ireland
37 N3 **Rossbach** Czechoslovakia
33 P10 **Rossbach** Germany
111 G9 **Ross Barnett Res** Mississippi U.S.A.
119 R8 **Rossburn** Manitoba Canada
14 B5 **Ross Carbery** Ireland
108 F3 **Ross City** Texas U.S.A.
146 A10 **Ross Dependency** Antarctica
37 J2 **Rossdorf** Germany
121 L7 **Rosseau** Ontario Canada
137 L4 **Rossel** *isld* Louisiade Arch
119 T9 **Rossendale** Manitoba Canada
109 L3 **Rosser** Texas U.S.A.
8 D1 **Rossett** Wales
26 K2 **Rossfjord** Norway
83 M9 **Ross Hill** *mt* Christmas I Indian Oc
146 C11 **Ross I** Antarctica
119 U4 **Ross I** Manitoba Canada
146 C10 **Ross Ice Shelf** Antarctica
22 J4 **Rossignal** Belgium
122 G9 **Rossignol Res** Nova Scotia Canada
94 J6 **Rossiter** Pennsylvania U.S.A.
143 E10 **Rossiter B** W Australia Australia
Rossiyskaya SFSR *see* **Russian Federation**
100 D1 **Ross L** Washington U.S.A.
33 O10 **Rossla** Germany
100 E1 **Ross Lake Nat. Recreation Area** Washington U.S.A.
100 H1 **Rossland** British Columbia Canada
14 E4 **Rosslare** Ireland
33 Q9 **Rosslau** Germany
33 O10 **Rossleben** Germany
145 E4 **Ross, Mt** New Zealand
85 A5 **Rosso** Mauritania
26 H8 **Rossön** Sweden
8 D4 **Ross-on-Wye** England
54 L6 **Rossosh'** Russian Federation
33 R6 **Rossow** Germany
120 C4 **Rossport** Ontario Canada
140 C6 **Ross River** N Terr Australia
117 G4 **Ross River** Yukon Territory Canada
146 B11 **Ross Sea** Antarctica
37 K5 **Rosstal** Germany
108 E7 **Rosston** Oklahoma U.S.A.
33 O9 **Rosstrappe** Germany
26 G6 **Rössvassbukt** Norway
26 G6 **Røssvatnet** *L* Norway
110 J5 **Rossview Res** Tennessee U.S.A.
112 B3 **Rossville** Georgia U.S.A.
110 J1 **Rossville** Illinois U.S.A.
107 P2 **Rossville** Kansas U.S.A.
37 P1 **Rosswein** Germany
117 J8 **Rosswood** British Columbia Canada
26 F4 **Röst** *isld* Norway
26 L3 **Rosta** Norway
26 L3 **Rostaelv** *R* Norway
26 L2 **Rostafjord** *mt* Norway
77 C7 **Rostam** *oil well* Persian Gulf
27 F16 **Röstånga** Sweden
77 L1 **Rostāq** Afghanistan
118 L6 **Rosthern** Saskatchewan Canada
36 C2 **Rostingen** Germany
33 Q4 **Rostock** Germany
26 M3 **Rostonsölkä** *reg* Sweden
52 E6 **Rostov** Russian Federation
53 E10 **Rostov-na-Donu** Russian Federation
53 F10 **Rostovskaya Oblast'** *prov* Russian Federation
20 D5 **Rostrenen** France
28 D3 **Rostrup** Denmark
46 D3 **Rostuša** Macedonia Yugoslavia
26 D9 **Röstvangen** Norway
52 H2 **Rosvinskoye** Russian Federation
112 C3 **Roswell** Georgia U.S.A.
108 C2 **Roswell** New Mexico U.S.A.
41 M1 **Rot** *R* Germany
27 G10 **Rot** Sweden
26 F5 **Rota** *C* Norway
16 C8 **Rota** Spain
37 J5 **Rot am See** Germany
108 G3 **Rotan** Texas U.S.A.
37 N5 **Rot Buhl** *mt* Germany
71 L10 **Rote** *isld* Timor Indonesia
80 F4 **Rotem** Jordan
36 H2 **Rotenburg** Hessen Germany
32 K6 **Rotenburg/Wümme** Niedersachsen Germany
38 G8 **Roter Kopf** *mt* Austria
37 L3 **Roter Main** *R* Germany
32 H5 **Roter Sand** Germany
41 L3 **Rote Wand** *mt* Austria
25 F7 **Rotgen** Germany
36 D2 **Roth** Germany
37 N1 **Rötha** Germany
36 E1 **Rothaargebirge** *mts* Germany
36 C7 **Rothau** France
13 G3 **Rothbury** England
99 U6 **Rothbury** Michigan U.S.A.
36 D2 **Rothe Mühle** Germany
37 L5 **Röthenbach** Germany
41 L2 **Röthenbach** Germany
33 P9 **Rothenburg** Germany
37 J5 **Rothenburg ober der Tauber** Germany
20 G4 **Rothéneuf** France
36 H4 **Rothenfels** Germany
36 E6 **Rothenfels** Baden-Württemberg Germany
37 L3 **Rothenkirchen** Germany
33 O10 **Rothenschirmbach** Germany
146 C5 **Rothera** *U.K. Base* Antarctica
13 G6 **Rotherham** England
144 D5 **Rotherham** New Zealand
9 G5 **Rother, R** England
15 E3 **Rothes** Scotland
122 G8 **Rothesay** New Brunswick Canada
12 C2 **Rothesay** Scotland
40 H4 **Rothorn** *mt* Switzerland
98 K3 **Rothsay** Minnesota U.S.A.
146 C5 **Rothschild I** Antarctica
Roti *see* **Rote**
71 L10 **Roti** Indonesia
71 L10 **Roti, Selat** Indonesia
139 H5 **Roto** New South Wales Australia
145 E3 **Rotoaira, L** New Zealand
145 F2 **Rotoehu, L** New Zealand
145 F3 **Rotoiti, L** New Zealand
145 D4 **Rotoiti, L** New Zealand
145 F3 **Rotomahana** New Zealand
145 F3 **Rotoma, L** New Zealand
144 C5 **Rotomanu** New Zealand
43 H8 **Rotondella** Italy
45 O5 **Rotondo, M** *mt* Italy
144 D4 **Rotoroa** New Zealand
145 D4 **Rotoroa, L** New Zealand
145 F3 **Rotorua** New Zealand
145 E2 **Rotowaro** New Zealand
21 K3 **Rots** France
37 O7 **Rott** *R* Germany
41 N2 **Rott** Germany
33 R9 **Rotta** Germany
36 F7 **Rottenburg** Germany
37 J4 **Rottendorf** Germany
38 K6 **Rottenmann** Austria
38 K7 **Rottenmanner Tauern** *mts* Austria
25 C5 **Rotterdam** Netherlands
37 P7 **Rotthalmünster** Germany
9 F6 **Rottingdean** England
36 H4 **Rottingen** Germany
33 N9 **Rottleberode** Germany
143 B9 **Rottnest I** W Australia Australia
33 R8 **Rottstock** Germany
25 G1 **Rottumeroog** *isld* Netherlands
25 F2 **Rottumerplaat** Netherlands
41 J1 **Rottweil** Germany
137 Q4 **Rotuma** *isld* Pacific Oc
37 O5 **Rötz** Germany
20 G7 **Rouans** France
22 E2 **Roubaix** France
19 N15 **Roubion** *R* France
31 H5 **Roudnice** Czechoslovakia
20 C5 **Roudouallec** France
21 N3 **Rouen** France
40 F2 **Rouffach** France
20 H6 **Rougé** France
40 D3 **Rougemont** France
7 L9 **Rough** *oil rig* North Sea
8 D2 **Roughclose** England
144 B6 **Rough Ridge** New Zealand
110 K4 **Rough River L** Kentucky U.S.A.
19 P18 **Rougiers** France
18 E7 **Rouillac** France
119 N8 **Rouleau** Saskatchewan Canada
Roulers *see* **Roeselare**
94 J5 **Roulette** Pennsylvania U.S.A.
121 L5 **Roulier** Quebec Canada
22 G3 **Rœulx** Belgium
18 F7 **Roumazières** France
116 J4 **Roundabout Mt** Alaska U.S.A.

101 L2 **Round Butte** Montana U.S.A.
123 R4 **Round Harbour** Newfoundland Canada
118 E5 **Round Hill** Alberta Canada
141 K6 **Round Hill Hd** Queensland Australia
87 G12 **Round I** Mauritius
116 H7 **Round I** Alaska U.S.A.
109 J5 **Round Mountain** Texas U.S.A.
139 K4 **Round Mt** New South Wales Australia
102 G3 **Round Mt** Nevada U.S.A.
123 R5 **Round Pond** Newfoundland Canada
95 S3 **Round Pond** Maine U.S.A.
109 K5 **Round Rock** Texas U.S.A.
117 R3 **Roundrock L** Northwest Territories Canada
110 E4 **Round Spring** Missouri U.S.A.
101 R3 **Roundup** Montana U.S.A.
119 S9 **Rounthwaite** Manitoba Canada
129 H3 **Roura** Fr Guiana
44 B2 **Roure** Italy
75 L7 **Rourkela** India
15 F1 **Rousay** Orkney Scotland
106 F4 **Rouse** Colorado U.S.A.
94 H5 **Rouseville** Pennsylvania U.S.A.
142 A2 **Rous Hd** Perth, W Aust Australia
133 D9 **Rous, Pen** Chile
19 O17 **Roussillon** France
22 L5 **Roussy-le-Village** France
19 P15 **Route Napoléon** France
21 M3 **Routot** France
25 F3 **Rouveen** Netherlands
121 U3 **Rouvray, L** Quebec Canada
40 A2 **Rouvres** France
22 H4 **Rouvroy-sur-Audry** France
22 G3 **Roux** Belgium
89 E8 **Rouxville** S Africa
121 M4 **Rouyn** Quebec Canada
48 L1 **Rov** *R* Ukraine
41 M6 **Rovato** Italy
26 A9 **Rovde** Norway
52 F4 **Rovdino** Russian Federation
54 L8 **Roven'ki** Ukraine
45 J1 **Roverbella** Italy
41 O6 **Rovereto** Italy
68 F6 **Rovieng** Cambodia
45 L1 **Rovigo** Italy
45 P1 **Rovinj** Croatia
45 P1 **Rovinjsko Selo** Croatia
53 C8 **Rovno** Ukraine
87 G8 **Rovuma** *R* Mozambique
99 N7 **Rowan** Iowa U.S.A.
118 J1 **Rowan L** Ontario Canada
106 E6 **Rowe** New Mexico U.S.A.
139 J3 **Rowena** New South Wales Australia
108 G4 **Rowena** Texas U.S.A.
112 G4 **Rowesville** South Carolina U.S.A.
100 K8 **Rowland** Nevada U.S.A.
94 H7 **Rowlesburg** West Virginia U.S.A.
118 E7 **Rowley** Alberta Canada
115 M4 **Rowley I** Northwest Territories Canada
142 C3 **Rowley Shoals** W Australia Australia
103 M9 **Rowood** Arizona U.S.A.
9 E1 **Rowsley** England
103 K5 **Rox** Nevada U.S.A.
71 E2 **Roxas** Luzon Philippines
71 E4 **Roxas** Mindoro Philippines
71 D5 **Roxas** Palawan Philippines
71 F5 **Roxas** Panay Philippines
112 H1 **Roxboro** North Carolina U.S.A.
127 N2 **Roxborough** Tobago
140 E6 **Roxborough Downs** Queensland Australia
Roxburgh *co see* **Borders** *reg*
144 B6 **Roxburgh** New Zealand
144 B6 **Roxburgh,L** New Zealand
95 N4 **Roxbury** New York U.S.A.
95 P2 **Roxbury** Vermont U.S.A.
138 D4 **Roxby Downs** South Australia Australia
27 H13 **Roxen** *L* Sweden
111 E10 **Roxie** Mississippi U.S.A.
109 M2 **Roxton** Texas U.S.A.
121 S7 **Roxton-Sud** Quebec Canada
101 N7 **Roy** Idaho U.S.A.
101 R2 **Roy** Montana U.S.A.
106 F6 **Roy** New Mexico U.S.A.
101 N8 **Roy** Utah U.S.A.
100 C2 **Roy** Washington U.S.A.
98 H7 **Royal** Nebraska U.S.A.
14 E3 **Royal Canal** Ireland
99 U9 **Royal Center** Indiana U.S.A.
70 C1 **Royal Charlotte Reef** S China Sea
113 L12 **Royal I** Bahamas
120 B3 **Royal, Mount** Ontario Canada
119 P1 **Royal, Mt** Ontario Canada
89 F7 **Royal Natal Nat. Park** S Africa
94 D4 **Royal Oak** Michigan U.S.A.
113 F12 **Royal Palm Hammock** Florida U.S.A.
113 G12 **Royal Palm Ranger Sta** Florida U.S.A.
118 C8 **Royalties** Alberta Canada
9 G5 **Royal Tunbridge Wells** England
18 E7 **Royan** France
19 O14 **Roybon** France
22 D4 **Roye** France
95 M6 **Royersford** Pennsylvania U.S.A.
142 C5 **Roy Hill** W Australia Australia
27 D11 **Röykenvik** Norway
122 C4 **Roy, L** Quebec Canada
26 G7 **Röyrvik** Norway
109 L3 **Royse City** Texas U.S.A.
26 C10 **Röysheim** Norway
9 F3 **Royston** England
112 D3 **Royston** Georgia U.S.A.
29 L6 **Röytta** Finland
31 N3 **Różan** Poland
46 E3 **Rožden** Macedonia Yugoslavia
20 F3 **Rozel** Channel Is
107 L3 **Rozel** Kansas U.S.A.
20 G3 **Rozel, Pte du** France
98 A5 **Rozet** Wyoming U.S.A.
31 L1 **Rozewie** *C* Poland
55 F5 **Rozhdestvenka** Kazakhstan
52 G5 **Rozhdestvenskoye** Russian Federation
22 G4 **Rozoy** France
31 M4 **Rozprza** Poland
Rozwadów *see* **Stalowa Wola**
46 D3 **Rrëshen** Albania
R.S.F.S.R. *see* **Russian Federation**
46 E1 **Rtanj** *mt* Serbia Yugoslavia
87 B9 **Ruacana** Namibia
87 G7 **Ruaha, Gt** *R* Tanzania
88 E5 **Ruaha Nat. Park** Tanzania
145 F4 **Ruahine Range** New Zealand
145 E1 **Ruakaka** New Zealand
71 J4 **Ruang** *isld* Indonesia
145 E3 **Ruapehu** *vol* New Zealand
144 B7 **Ruapuke I** New Zealand
145 F3 **Ruatahuna** New Zealand
144 C5 **Ruatapu** New Zealand
71 J9 **Rua, Tg** *C* Sumba Indonesia
145 F3 **Ruatoki** New Zealand
145 G2 **Ruatoria** New Zealand
145 E2 **Ruawai** New Zealand
77 C7 **Ru'ays, Ar** U.A.E.
54 B1 **Ruba** Belorussia
72 F5 **Rub al Khālī** *desert* Saudi Arabia
53 G12 **Rubas** *R* Russian Federation
33 N9 **Rübeland** Germany
60 R2 **Rubeshibe** Japan
54 K7 **Rubezhnoye** Ukraine
15 C2 **Rubha Coigeach** Scotland
15 B3 **Rubha Hunish** Scotland
15 C3 **Rubha Reidh** Scotland
86 E5 **Rubi** *R* Zaire
102 D3 **Rubicon** *R* California U.S.A.
45 J2 **Rubiera** Italy
133 G2 **Rubinéia** Brazil
124 F3 **Rubio** Mexico
16 E3 **Rubio** *mt* Spain
28 D2 **Rubjerg Knude** *hill* Denmark
56 B5 **Rubtsovsk** Russian Federation
116 K4 **Ruby** Alaska U.S.A.
103 N10 **Ruby** Arizona U.S.A.
101 N4 **Ruby** *R* Montana U.S.A.
100 H1 **Ruby** Washington U.S.A.
103 J1 **Ruby Dome** *pk* Nevada U.S.A.
103 J1 **Ruby L** Nevada U.S.A.
103 J1 **Ruby Mts** Nevada U.S.A.
141 J6 **Rubyvale** Queensland Australia
103 J1 **Ruby Valley** Nevada U.S.A.
52 H4 **Ruch'** Russian Federation
100 B7 **Ruch** Oregon U.S.A.
67 D4 **Rucheng** China
52 F2 **Ruch'i** Russian Federation
Ruchugi *see* **Uvinza**
27 H14 **Ruda** Sweden
138 D5 **Rudall** South Australia Australia
143 E6 **Rudall, R** W Australia Australia
142 D5 **Rudall River Nat Park** W Australia Australia
140 B6 **Rudalls** *R* N Terr Australia
77 E6 **Rudan** Iran
75 J5 **Rudauli** India
77 H4 **Rudbar** Afghanistan
77 A1 **Rudbār** Iran
28 B7 **Rudbøl** Denmark
118 K6 **Ruddell** Saskatchewan Canada
22 E1 **Ruddervoorde** Belgium
119 R3 **Ruddock** Manitoba Canada
116 P6 **Rude** *R* Alaska U.S.A.
38 L8 **Ruden** Austria
33 T4 **Ruden** *isld* Germany
36 H6 **Rudersberg** Germany
33 T8 **Rudersdorf** Germany
36 D4 **Rüdesheim** Germany
31 O6 **Rudki** Ukraine
28 F7 **Rudkøbing** Denmark
31 J4 **Rudna** Poland
59 L3 **Rudnaya Pristan'** Russian Federation
52 H5 **Rudnichnyy** Russian Federation
55 D2 **Rudnichnyy** Sverdlovskaya obl Russian Federation
31 N5 **Rudnik** Poland
54 C2 **Rudnya** Russian Federation
55 D4 **Rudnyy** Kazakhstan
Rudok *see* **Rutog**
46 D3 **Rudoka Planina** *mt* Serbia/Macedonia Yugoslavia
50 E1 **Rudol'fa, O** *isld* Russian Federation
Rudolf, L *see* **Turkana, L**
37 L2 **Rudolstadt** Germany
67 G1 **Rudong** China
46 G3 **Rudozem** Bulgaria
77 B1 **Rūdsar** Iran
28 G5 **Ruds Vedby** Denmark
101 P1 **Rudyard** Montana U.S.A.
22 B3 **Rue** France
120 J5 **Ruel** Ontario Canada
21 P3 **Rue St. Pierre, la** France
86 F3 **Rufa'a** Sudan
18 F6 **Ruffec** France
21 N8 **Ruffec** Indre France
20 F6 **Ruffiac** France
20 H6 **Ruffigne** France
112 G4 **Ruffin** South Carolina U.S.A.
88 F6 **Rufiji** *R* Tanzania
45 K4 **Rufina** Italy
131 E5 **Rufino** Argentina
85 A6 **Rufisque** Senegal
88 C9 **Rufunsa** *R* Zambia
100 F1 **Rufus Woods L** Washington U.S.A.
67 G1 **Rugao** China
9 E3 **Rugby** England
98 G1 **Rugby** North Dakota U.S.A.
9 E2 **Rugeley** England
30 H1 **Rügen** *isld* Germany
144 A7 **Rugged Is** New Zealand
37 K5 **Rügland** Germany
21 M4 **Rugles** France
52 D3 **Rug Oz** *L* Russian Federation
52 D3 **Rugozero** Russian Federation
80 B7 **Ruhama** Israel
75 N5 **Ruhea** Bangladesh
33 N7 **Rühen** Germany
29 L11 **Rühimäki** Finland
37 J2 **Ruhla** Germany
33 T10 **Ruhland** Germany
33 S7 **Ruhleben** Germany
37 O6 **Ruhmannsfelden** Germany
33 P5 **Rühn** Germany
33 P6 **Ruhner Bge** *mt* Germany
32 F10 **Ruhr** *R* Germany
35 **Ruhr, The** *reg* Germany
88 E6 **Ruhudji** *R* Tanzania
88 E7 **Ruhuhu** *R* Tanzania
67 G3 **Rui'an** China
67 E2 **Ruichang** China
65 A7 **Ruicheng** China
108 C6 **Ruidosa** Texas U.S.A.
106 E8 **Ruidoso** New Mexico U.S.A.
108 B2 **Ruidoso** New Mexico U.S.A.
67 E4 **Ruijin** China
80 G7 **Ruim el Hiri** Jordan
22 E1 **Ruiselede** Belgium
9 F4 **Ruislip** England
25 H3 **Ruiten Aa** *R* Netherlands
124 G7 **Ruiz** Mexico
128 C3 **Ruiz, Nevada del** *vol* Colombia
80 G7 **Rujeim Salim** Jordan
46 E2 **Rujen** *mt* Macedonia Yugoslavia
52 C5 **Rūjiena** Latvia
70 D5 **Rujon** Kalimantan
29 O5 **Rukatunturi** *mt* Finland
88 C10 **Rukovakuona Mts** Zimbabwe
88 D7 **Rukuru** *R* Malawi
71 H7 **Rukuwa** Indonesia
88 C5 **Rukwa** *reg* Tanzania
88 D5 **Rukwa, L** Tanzania
107 J2 **Ruleton** Kansas U.S.A.
111 F8 **Ruleville** Mississippi U.S.A.
26 G10 **Rullbo** Sweden
99 L9 **Rulo** Nebraska U.S.A.
36 E5 **Rülzheim** Germany
15 B3 **Rum** *isld* Scotland
48 F5 **Ruma** Serbia Yugoslavia
Rumania *see* **Romania**
71 J4 **Rumbai** Sulawesi
140 C7 **Rumbalara** N Terr Australia
86 E4 **Rumbek** Sudan
31 H5 **Rumburk** Czechoslovakia
126 G3 **Rum Cay** *isld* Bahamas
22 E3 **Rumegies** France
22 L5 **Rumelange** Luxembourg
47 N10 **Rumelifeneri** Turkey
95 R2 **Rumford** Maine U.S.A.
22 G4 **Rumigny** France
22 E2 **Rumillies** Belgium
140 B2 **Rum Jungle** N Terr Australia
80 E2 **Rummāna** Israel
Rummelsburg *see* **Miastko**
60 P2 **Rumoi** Japan
88 D7 **Rumphi** Malawi
118 E7 **Rumsey** Alberta Canada
95 N6 **Rumson** New Jersey U.S.A.
144 C5 **Rumu** New Zealand
144 C5 **Runanga** New Zealand
127 K1 **Runaway Bay** Jamaica
8 D1 **Runcorn** England
89 G3 **Runde** *R* Zimbabwe
36 C1 **Ründeroth** Germany
28 D7 **Rundhof** Germany
26 A9 **Rundöy** Norway
87 C9 **Rundu** Namibia
71 J7 **Runduma** *isld* Indonesia
29 G8 **Rundvik** Sweden
71 M8 **Rung** *isld* Indonesia
70 C6 **Rungan** *R* Kalimantan
109 K7 **Runge** Texas U.S.A.
29 K5 **Rungsted** Denmark
88 D5 **Rungwa** *R* Tanzania
88 D6 **Rungwe** *pk* Tanzania
27 J11 **Runhällen** Sweden
36 E3 **Runkel** Germany
27 H11 **Runn** *L* Sweden
99 N8 **Runnells** Iowa U.S.A.
108 E1 **Running Water Cr** Texas/Okla U.S.A.
119 Q7 **Runnymede** Saskatchewan Canada
143 E6 **Runton Ra** W Australia Australia
29 O10 **Ruokolahti** Finland
66 D4 **Ruoqiang** China
58 D3 **Ruo Shui** *R* China
29 L10 **Ruovesi** Finland
131 A8 **Rupanco, L** Chile
139 G6 **Rupanyup** Victoria Australia
88 D8 **Rupashe** *R* Malawi
69 E12 **Rupat** *isld* Sumatra
48 J4 **Rupea** Romania
141 F5 **Rupert** *R* Queensland Australia
101 M7 **Rupert** Idaho U.S.A.
95 O3 **Rupert** Vermont U.S.A.
94 G9 **Rupert** West Virginia U.S.A.
121 L1 **Rupert B** Quebec Canada
121 N1 **Rupert, R** Quebec Canada
37 L6 **Rupertsbuch** Germany
146 B9 **Ruppert Coast** Antarctica
36 G2 **Ruppertenrod** Germany
36 F2 **Ruppertsberg** Germany
36 C2 **Ruppichteroth** Germany
33 S7 **Ruppiner Kanal** Germany
128 G3 **Rupununi** *R* Guyana
80 G2 **Ruqqād** *R* Syria
80 G1 **Ruqqād Sakhr** Syria
25 F6 **Rur** *R* Germany
112 G1 **Rural Hall** North Carolina U.S.A.
94 F10 **Rural Retreat** Virginia U.S.A.
128 E6 **Rurrenabaque** Bolivia
28 C6 **Rurup** Denmark
17 F5 **Rus** *R* Spain
71 L9 **Rusah** *isld* Indonesia
87 F9 **Rusape** Zimbabwe
Ruschuk *see* **Ruse**
47 H1 **Ruse** Bulgaria
38 M8 **Ruše** Slovenia
37 P6 **Rusel** Germany
146 F6 **Rüser-Larsenisen** *ice shelf* Antarctica
14 E3 **Rush** Ireland
106 F3 **Rush** Colorado U.S.A.
9 E5 **Rushall** England
65 E6 **Rushan** China
57 F5 **Rushanskiy Khrebet** *mts* Tajikistan
107 L3 **Rush Center** Kansas U.S.A.
99 O4 **Rush City** Minnesota U.S.A.
106 G3 **Rush Cr** Colorado U.S.A.
9 F3 **Rushden** England
99 P6 **Rushford** Minnesota U.S.A.
94 J4 **Rushford** New York U.S.A.
118 K8 **Rush Lake** Saskatchewan Canada
107 N7 **Rush Springs** Oklahoma U.S.A.
110 F1 **Rushville** Illinois U.S.A.
110 L2 **Rushville** Indiana U.S.A.
98 D7 **Rushville** Nebraska U.S.A.
139 H6 **Rushworth** Victoria Australia
109 M4 **Rusk** Texas U.S.A.
113 E10 **Ruskin** Florida U.S.A.
26 K7 **Rusksele** Sweden
26 K7 **Rusksträsk** Sweden
98 F2 **Ruso** North Dakota U.S.A.
129 L4 **Russas** Brazil
38 H6 **Russbachsaag** Austria
113 L12 **Russel I** Bahamas
119 Q8 **Russell** Manitoba Canada
121 P7 **Russell** Ontario Canada
145 E1 **Russell** New Zealand
99 N9 **Russell** Iowa U.S.A.
107 M3 **Russell** Kansas U.S.A.
94 E8 **Russell** Kentucky U.S.A.
99 L5 **Russell** Minnesota U.S.A.
95 M2 **Russell** New York U.S.A.
94 H5 **Russell** Pennsylvania U.S.A.
112 B3 **Russell Cave National Monument** Alabama U.S.A.
143 E6 **Russell Headland** *mt* W Australia Australia
115 K3 **Russell I** Northwest Territories Canada
137 M3 **Russell Is** Solomon Is
119 Q2 **Russell L** Manitoba Canada
117 Q4 **Russell L** Northwest Territories Canada
143 C7 **Russell,Mt** W Australia Australia
116 M5 **Russell, Mt** Alaska U.S.A.
143 E10 **Russell Ra** W Australia Australia
110 L4 **Russell Springs** Kentucky U.S.A.
110 N1 **Russells Pt** Ohio U.S.A.
111 J7 **Russellville** Alabama U.S.A.
110 D6 **Russellville** Arkansas U.S.A.
110 K5 **Russellville** Kentucky U.S.A.
110 D3 **Russellville** Missouri U.S.A.
94 D8 **Russellville** Ohio U.S.A.
45 M3 **Russi** Italy
50 **Russian Federation** Asia/Europe
116 G6 **Russian Mission** Alaska U.S.A.
116 H6 **Russian Mts** Alaska U.S.A.
50 F1 **Russkaya Gavan'** Russian Federation
55 F4 **Russkaya-Polyana** Russian Federation
55 D3 **Russkaya-Techa** Russian Federation
54 M6 **Russkaya-Zhuravka** Russian Federation
52 H6 **Russkiy Aktash** Russian Federation
51 J1 **Russkiy, Ostrova** *islds* Russian Federation
78 K1 **Rustavi** Georgia
94 H9 **Rustburg** Virginia U.S.A.
26 Q1 **Rustefjelbma** Norway
89 E5 **Rustenburg** S Africa
32 H5 **Rustersiel** Germany
100 C7 **Rustler Peak** *mt* Oregon U.S.A.
109 P3 **Ruston** Louisiana U.S.A.
71 A3 **Ruta** Indonesia
88 C3 **Rutana** Burundi
16 E7 **Rute** Spain
27 K14 **Rute** Sweden
33 S6 **Rutenberg** Germany
32 F7 **Rütenbrock** Germany
71 K9 **Ruteng** Flores Indonesia
146 D7 **Rutford Ice Stream** *ice stream* Antarctica
102 A1 **Ruth** California U.S.A.
103 K2 **Ruth** Nevada U.S.A.
32 H10 **Rüthen** Germany
112 F2 **Rutherfordton** North Carolina U.S.A.
121 L6 **Rutherglen** Ontario Canada
12 D2 **Rutherglen** Scotland
94 K9 **Ruther Glen** Virginia U.S.A.
116 M5 **Ruth Glacier** Alaska U.S.A.
118 J7 **Ruthilda** Saskatchewan Canada
8 C1 **Ruthin** Wales
98 K5 **Ruthton** Minnesota U.S.A.
141 G6 **Ruthven** Queensland Australia
99 M6 **Ruthven** Iowa U.S.A.
88 E7 **Rutikira** *R* Tanzania
52 G6 **Rutka** *R* Russian Federation
Rutland *co see* **Leicestershire**
99 R9 **Rutland** Illinois U.S.A.
98 J3 **Rutland** North Dakota U.S.A.
94 E7 **Rutland** Ohio U.S.A.
95 P3 **Rutland** Vermont U.S.A.
68 A7 **Rutland I** Andaman Is
141 F3 **Rutland Plains** Queensland Australia
118 H6 **Rutland Station** Saskatchewan Canada
9 F2 **Rutland Water** *L* England
99 O3 **Rutledge** Minnesota U.S.A.
110 D1 **Rutledge** Missouri U.S.A.
66 B5 **Rutog** China
25 E3 **Rutten** Netherlands
120 K6 **Rutter** Ontario Canada
25 F4 **Ruurlo** Netherlands
87 G7 **Ruvu** Tanzania
88 G5 **Ruvu** *R* Tanzania
88 E7 **Ruvuma** Tanzania
88 G7 **Ruvuma** *R* Tanzania
89 G1 **Ruwa** Zimbabwe
86 E2 **Ruweiba** Sudan
88 C1 **Ruwenzori Rge** *mts* Uganda
36 B4 **Ruwer** Germany
87 F9 **Ruya** *R* Zimbabwe
65 B7 **Ruyang** China
67 D4 **Ruyuan** China
55 E4 **Ruzayevka** Kazakhstan
48 M1 **Ruzhin** Ukraine
48 E1 **Ružomberok** Czechoslovakia
88 B2 **Rwanda** *rep* Cent Africa
28 D4 **Ry** Denmark
28 D2 **Ryå** Denmark
47 H1 **Ryakhovo** Bulgaria
144 C5 **Ryall,Mt** New Zealand
99 P7 **Ryan** Iowa U.S.A.
109 K1 **Ryan** Oklahoma U.S.A.
12 C4 **Ryan, Loch** Scotland
101 T8 **Ryan Park** Wyoming U.S.A.
101 L6 **Ryan Pk** Idaho U.S.A.
53 E7 **Ryazan'** Russian Federation
54 M3 **Ryazhsk** Russian Federation
Rybach'ye *see* **Issyk-Kul'**
37 O3 **Rybáře** Czechoslovakia
52 E5 **Rybinsk** Russian Federation
52 E5 **Rybinskoye Vdkhr** *res* Russian Federation
31 L5 **Rybnik** Poland
48 M3 **Rybnitsa** Moldavia
54 L2 **Rybnoye** Russian Federation
55 D2 **Rychkovo** Russian Federation
31 J5 **Rychnov** Czechoslovakia
31 L3 **Rychwał** Poland
33 S4 **Ryckgraben** *R* Germany
117 O8 **Rycroft** Alberta Canada
120 G6 **Rydal Bank** Ontario Canada
146 C6 **Rydberg Peninsula** *pen* Antarctica
28 B4 **Ryde** Denmark
28 G7 **Ryde** Denmark
9 E6 **Ryde** England
98 E2 **Ryder** North Dakota U.S.A.
100 B3 **Ryderwood** Washington U.S.A.
27 H14 **Ryd, V** Sweden
28 D4 **Rye** Denmark
28 H5 **Rye** Denmark
9 G6 **Rye** England
106 F4 **Rye** Colorado U.S.A.
95 R3 **Rye** New Hampshire U.S.A.
109 N5 **Rye** Texas U.S.A.
77 B5 **R-ye Dalaki** *R* Iran
101 Q3 **Ryegate** Montana U.S.A.
100 G9 **Rye Patch** Nevada U.S.A.
102 F1 **Rye Patch Res** Nevada U.S.A.
119 Q9 **Ryerson** Saskatchewan Canada
21 J3 **Ryes** France
27 A12 **Ryfylke** Norway
13 G4 **Ryhope** England
31 N4 **Ryki** Poland
120 G3 **Ryland** Ontario Canada
118 E5 **Ryley** Alberta Canada
54 F5 **Ryl'sk** Russian Federation
139 J5 **Rylstone** New South Wales Australia
31 N6 **Rymanow** Poland
31 K6 **Rýmařov** Czechoslovakia
55 F1 **Rymovy** Russian Federation
31 N2 **Ryn** Poland
52 E1 **Rynda** Russian Federation
53 G9 **Ryn Peski** *desert* Kazakhstan
28 F4 **Ryomgard** Denmark
61 P7 **Ryōri-zaki** *C* Japan
61 M7 **Ryōtsu** Japan
31 L2 **Rypin** Poland
48 L3 **Ryshkany** Moldavia
48 F1 **Rysk** *mt* Czech/Poland
28 F6 **Ryslinge** Denmark
32 F6 **Rysum** Germany
31 M6 **Rysy** *mt* Czech/Poland
61 O10 **Ryūgasaki** Japan
31 H3 **Rzepin** Poland
31 N5 **Rzeszów** Poland
54 E3 **Rzhanitsa** Russian Federation
52 D6 **Rzhev** Russian Federation

S

77 C4 **Sa'ādatābād** Iran
33 R4 **Saal** Germany
36 F5 **Saal** *R* Germany
37 J3 **Saal** Germany
38 G7 **Saalach** *R* Austria
36 F3 **Saalburg** Germany
37 M3 **Saalburg** Germany
33 P9 **Saale** *R* Germany
37 M3 **Saale** *R* Germany
36 C7 **Saales** France
37 L2 **Saalfeld** Germany
40 F5 **Saanen** Switzerland
117 M11 **Saanich** British Columbia Canada
36 B5 **Saar** *R* Germany
19 K3 **Saarbrücken** France
36 B5 **Saarbrücken** Germany
36 B4 **Saarburg** Germany
27 M14 **Sääre** Estonia
27 M13 **Saaremaa** Estonia
29 M5 **Saarenkylä** Finland
29 O10 **Saari** Finland
29 L9 **Saarijärvi** Finland
29 N3 **Saariselkä** *mts* Finland
36 B5 **Saarland** *land* Germany
115 P5 **Saarloq** Greenland
36 B5 **Saarlouis** Germany
33 S8 **Saarmund** Germany
36 B5 **Saar-Wellingen** Germany
36 D7 **Saasenheim** France
40 G5 **Saas Tal** Switzerland
133 E5 **Saavedra** Argentina
131 A7 **Saavedra, Pto** Chile
125 L2 **Sabá** Honduras
127 N6 **Saba** *isld* Lesser Antilles
32 L9 **Sababurg** Germany
48 F6 **Sabac** Serbia Yugoslavia
17 J3 **Sabadell** Spain
70 E2 **Sabah** *state* Borneo
69 E11 **Sabak** Malaysia
71 J8 **Sabalana, Kepulauan** *islds* Indonesia
44 M5 **Saba, Mt** Italy
126 D3 **Sabana, Arch. de** *islds* Cuba
127 K5 **Sabana de la Mar** Dominican Rep
127 J10 **Sabana de Mendoza** Venezuela
128 D1 **Sabanalarga** Colombia
127 K9 **Sabaneta** Venezuela
70 F4 **Sabang** Sulawesi
70 G6 **Sabang** Sulawesi
69 B10 **Sabang** Sumatra
83 K11 **Sabaragamuwa** *reg* Sri Lanka
71 J8 **Sabaru** *isld* Indonesia
80 D4 **Sabastiya** Jordan
45 O7 **Sabaudia** Italy
128 E7 **Sabaya** Bolivia
41 M6 **Sabbia, V** Italy
45 H2 **Sabbioneta** Italy
77 G4 **Şāberi, Hāmūn-e** *L* Iran
107 P2 **Sabetha** Kansas U.S.A.
84 E4 **Sabhā** Libya
87 F10 **Sabi** *R* Zimbabwe
89 G5 **Sabie** *R* S Africa
52 B6 **Sabile** Latvia
45 N5 **Sabina** Italy
94 D7 **Sabina** Ohio U.S.A.
124 F2 **Sabinal** Mexico
109 H6 **Sabinal** Texas U.S.A.
126 F4 **Sabinal, Pen. de** Cuba
17 G2 **Sabiñánigo** Spain
108 F8 **Sabinas** Mexico
125 J4 **Sabinas Hidalgo** Mexico
111 C11 **Sabine** *R* Louisiana/Texas U.S.A.
111 C12 **Sabine L** Louisiana U.S.A.
111 C12 **Sabine Pass** Louisiana U.S.A.
42 E6 **Sabini, Monti** Italy
79 H2 **Sabkhat al Jabbūl** Syria
79 H3 **Sabkhat al Marāghah** *salt lake* Syria
79 D7 **Sabkhet el Bardawīl** Egypt
71 E4 **Sablayan** Philippines
137 M5 **Sable** *isld* Coral Sea
123 N10 **Sable I** Nova Scotia Canada
122 G10 **Sable River** Nova Scotia Canada
18 D6 **Sables-d'Olonne, les** France
20 F4 **Sables d'Or** France
120 H6 **Sables, L. aux** Ontario Canada
120 H6 **Sables, River Aux** Ontario Canada
21 K6 **Sable-sur-Sarthe** France
19 O16 **Sablet** France
19 N18 **Sablon, Pte. du** France
19 N14 **Sablons** France
16 C3 **Sabor** *R* Portugal
131 G2 **Sã Borja** Brazil
94 H7 **Sabraton** West Virginia U.S.A.
18 E8 **Sabres** France
146 F14 **Sabrina Coast** Antarctica
28 E4 **Sabro** Denmark
16 C4 **Sabugal** Portugal
99 Q7 **Sabula** Iowa U.S.A.
70 G5 **Sabulu** Sulawesi
47 L5 **Sabuncu** Turkey
70 P9 **Sabunten** *isld* Indonesia
Sabzawar *see* **Shīndand**
77 E1 **Sabzevār** Iran
110 C4 **Sac** *R* Missouri U.S.A.
128 E7 **Sacaca** Bolivia
103 N8 **Sacaton** Arizona U.S.A.
99 L7 **Sac City** Iowa U.S.A.
43 E7 **Sacco** *R* Italy
45 L1 **Saccolongo** Italy
17 F4 **Sacedón** Spain
115 K7 **Sachigo** *R* Ontario Canada
109 O8 **Sachse** Texas U.S.A.
37 O2 **Sachsen** *land* Germany
33 O8 **Sachsen-Anhalt** *land* Germany
36 F1 **Sachsenberg** Germany
38 H8 **Sachsenburg** Austria
33 O10 **Sachsenburg** Germany
32 K8 **Sachsenhagen** Germany
32 K10 **Sachsenhausen** Germany
114 G3 **Sachs Harbour** Northwest Territories Canada
42 E3 **Sacile** Italy
95 L3 **Sackets Harbor** New York U.S.A.
122 H8 **Sackville** New Brunswick Canada
110 B3 **Sac, L** Missouri U.S.A.
21 P5 **Saclas** France
95 R3 **Saco** Maine U.S.A.
101 S1 **Saco** Montana U.S.A.
71 F7 **Sacol** *isld* Philippines
40 B2 **Sacquenay** France
102 B2 **Sacramento** *R* California U.S.A.
102 C3 **Sacramento** California U.S.A.
108 B3 **Sacramento Mts** New Mexico U.S.A.
102 B1 **Sacramento V** California U.S.A.
103 K6 **Sacramento Wash** *R* Arizona U.S.A.
16 E8 **Sacratif, C** Spain
122 D5 **Sacré Coeur** Quebec Canada
122 C5 **Sacré-Coeur Saguenay** Quebec Canada
130 F6 **Sacremento** Brazil
48 G3 **Săcueni** Romania
18 E10 **Sadaba** Spain
77 B5 **Sa'dabad** Iran
72 E5 **Şa'dah** Yemen
60 F12 **Sada-misaki** Japan
69 E9 **Sadao** Thailand
13 G4 **Sadberge** England
74 D2 **Sadda** Pakistan
141 G2 **Saddle Hill** Queensland Australia
142 D4 **Saddle Hill** W Australia Australia
100 A7 **Saddle Mt** Oregon U.S.A.
101 Q5 **Saddle Mt** Wyoming U.S.A.
68 A6 **Saddle Pk** Andaman Is
68 G7 **Sa Dec** Vietnam
48 K2 **Sadgora** Ukraine
127 O3 **Sadhoowa** Trinidad
94 C8 **Sadieville** Kentucky U.S.A.
85 B6 **Sadiola** Mali
74 D4 **Sadiqabad** Pakistan
16 B6 **Sado** *R* Portugal
61 M7 **Sado-shima** *isld* Japan
46 G2 **Sadovo** Bulgaria
74 E6 **Sadri** India
26 H5 **Sadvajaur** *L* Sweden
28 F2 **Sæby** Nordjylland Denmark
28 G5 **Sæby** Vestjælland Denmark
28 J6 **Sædder** Denmark
28 B4 **Sædding** Denmark
60 E13 **Saeki** Japan
60 E13 **Saeki-wan** *B* Japan
17 F5 **Saelices** Spain
32 G8 **Saerbeck** Germany
28 E5 **Særslev** Denmark
28 E2 **Saesing** Denmark
22 K4 **Saeul** Luxembourg
Safad *see* **Zefat**
55 D4 **Safakulevo** Russian Federation
48 F2 **Šáfárikovo** Czechoslovakia
57 F5 **Safed Khirs** *reg* Afghanistan
77 L2 **Safed Koh** *mt* Afghanistan
38 O7 **Safen** *R* Austria
77 J4 **Safer** Afghanistan
142 A4 **Safety Bay** *dist* W Australia Australia
80 D5 **Saffārin** Jordan
79 B9 **Şaff, El** Egypt
27 F12 **Säffle** Sweden
111 J9 **Safford** Alabama U.S.A.
103 P9 **Safford** Arizona U.S.A.
20 G7 **Saffré** France
9 G3 **Saffron Walden** England
85 C2 **Safi** Morocco
77 G4 **Safidabeh** Iran
77 A1 **Safid Rud** *R* Iran
41 K4 **Safier Tal** Switzerland
130 H6 **Safiras, Sa. das** *mts* Brazil
54 K3 **Safonovka** Russian Federation
52 G2 **Safonovo** Russian Federation
78 D1 **Safranbolu** Turkey
27 G11 **Säfsnäs** Sweden
80 G5 **Safut** Jordan
66 D6 **Saga** China
60 D12 **Saga** *prefect* Japan
60 D12 **Saga** Kyūshū Japan
60 G12 **Saga** Shikoku Japan
60 C11 **Saga** Tsushima Japan
57 C1 **Saga** Kazakhstan
61 O7 **Sagae** Japan
68 B2 **Sagaing** Burma
59 L5 **Sagami-nada** *B* Japan
61 N10 **Sagami-wan** *B* Japan
94 H6 **Sagamore** Pennsylvania U.S.A.
119 N2 **Saganaga L** Ontario Canada
120 H3 **Saganash L** Ontario Canada
60 E12 **Saganoseki** Japan
68 D6 **Saganthit Kyun** *isld* Burma
56 E5 **Sagan-Tologoy** Russian Federation
76 C2 **Sagar** India
61 M11 **Sagara** Japan
88 F5 **Sagara** Tanzania
116 N2 **Sagavanirktok** *R* Alaska U.S.A.
32 H7 **Sage** Germany
101 P8 **Sage** Wyoming U.S.A.
101 P1 **Sage Cr** Montana U.S.A.
101 S8 **Sage Cr** Wyoming U.S.A.
27 G11 **Sågen** Sweden
71 C3 **Sageurin** W Irian
26 H4 **Sagfjord** Norway
26 J5 **Saggat** *L* Sweden
95 P6 **Sag Harbor** Long I, New York U.S.A.
94 D3 **Saginaw** Michigan U.S.A.
109 L9 **Saginaw** Texas U.S.A.
94 D3 **Saginaw Bay** Michigan U.S.A.
88 D2 **Sagitu** *isld* Uganda
115 N6 **Saglek B** Labrador, Nfld Canada
71 H6 **Sago** *isld* Indonesia
99 S3 **Sagola** Michigan U.S.A.
17 F7 **Sagra, La** *mt* Spain
85 F8 **Sagre, Pto.de** Bioko Equat Guinea
16 B8 **Sagres** Portugal
71 L9 **Sagu** Indonesia
106 D3 **Saguache** Colorado U.S.A.
126 G4 **Sagua de Tánamo** Cuba
126 D3 **Sagua la Grande** Cuba
103 N8 **Saguaro L** Arizona U.S.A.
103 O9 **Saguaro Nat.Mon** Arizona U.S.A.
115 M8 **Saguenay** *R* Quebec Canada
85 B3 **Saguia al Hamra, As** *R* Western Sahara
17 G5 **Sagunto** Spain
116 N2 **Sagwan** Alaska U.S.A.
80 G3 **Saham** Jordan
85 C4 **Sahara** *desert* N Africa
79 E10 **Sahara, G** *mt* Egypt
74 G4 **Saharanpur** India
142 E5 **Sahara Well** W Australia Australia
75 L5 **Sahibganj** India
28 D4 **Sahl** Denmark
124 E3 **Sahuaripa** Mexico
103 O10 **Sahuarita** Arizona U.S.A.
124 H7 **Sahuayo** Mexico
136 F4 **Sahul Shelf** Timor Sea
19 O16 **Sahune** France
68 J5 **Sa Huynh** Vietnam
61 L9 **Sai** *R* Japan
136 J3 **Saibai I** Papua New Guinea
69 E9 **Sai Buri** *R* Thailand
69 E9 **Sai Buri** Thailand
85 E2 **Saïda** Algeria
79 F5 **Saïda** Lebanon
77 D5 **Sa'īdābād** Iran
68 F6 **Sai Dao Tai, Khao** *mt* Thailand
86 D4 **Said Bundas** Sudan
75 N6 **Saidpur** Bangladesh
74 E1 **Saidu** Pakistan
40 E3 **Saignelégier** Switzerland
60 G9 **Saigō** Japan
68 H7 **Saigon** *R* Vietnam
68 H7 **Saigon** Vietnam
29 O4 **Saija** Finland
60 G12 **Saijō** Japan
60 C13 **Saikai Nat. Park** Japan
71 C3 **Saileen** W Irian
19 O15 **Saillans** France
71 C3 **Sailolo** W Irian
100 K7 **Sailor Cr** Idaho U.S.A.
76 C1 **Sailu** India
65 F4 **Saima** China
29 N10 **Saimaa** *L* Finland
29 N11 **Saimaa Canal** Finland/Rus Fed
124 H6 **Sain Alto** Mexico
77 G5 **Saindak** Pakistan
78 L3 **Sa'īndezh** Iran
22 D2 **Sainghin-en-Weppes** France
22 G3 **Sains-du-Nord** France
22 F4 **Sains-Richaumont** France
15 F5 **St. Abb's Head** Scotland
122 H5 **Ste. Adelaide** Quebec Canada
121 Q7 **Ste.Adèle** Quebec Canada
21 L2 **Ste.Adresse** France
38 N6 **St.Aegyd** Austria
18 G9 **St.Affrique** France
121 T6 **St.Agapit** Quebec Canada
119 U9 **Ste.Agathe** Manitoba Canada
121 Q6 **Ste.Agathe des Monts** Quebec Canada
21 M5 **St.Agil** France
121 L4 **Ste.Agnes** Quebec Canada
8 A7 **St.Agnes** England
9 F7 **St.Agnes** *isld* Isles of Scilly England
21 N7 **St.Aignan** France
21 H6 **St.Aignan-sur-Roë** France
28 D3 **Ste. Ajstrup** Denmark
20 E4 **St.Alban** France
19 P13 **St.-Alban-Leysee** France
40 C6 **St.-Alban-Leysse** France
123 R6 **St.Alban's** Newfoundland Canada
9 F4 **St.Albans** England
95 P2 **St.Albans** Vermont U.S.A.
94 F8 **St.Albans** West Virginia U.S.A.
118 D5 **St.Albert** Alberta Canada
122 C6 **St.Alexandre** Quebec Canada
121 R6 **St.Alexis des Monts** Quebec Canada
22 E3 **St.Amand-les-Eaux** France
21 N6 **St. Amand-Longpré** France
18 G6 **St. Amand Mont Rond** France
21 J8 **St.Amand-sur-Sèvre** France
40 F2 **St.Amarin** France
121 T4 **St.-Ambroise** Quebec Canada
21 P8 **St.Ambroix** Cher France
122 D5 **St.Anaclet** Quebec Canada
19 N17 **St.-Andiol** France
38 L8 **St. Andra-im-Lavanttal** Austria
83 K13 **St.André** Réunion Indian Oc
83 M12 **Saint-André** Mauritius
33 M9 **St. Andreasberg** Germany
19 N13 **St.Andre-de-Corcy** France
18 E8 **St.André-de-Cubzac** France
21 N4 **St.André-de-l'Eure** France
20 F7 **St.-André-des-Eaux** France
21 N4 **St.André,Plaine de** France
127 L2 **St.Andrew** *parish* Jamaica
127 P2 **St.Andrew** *co* Trinidad
111 L11 **St.Andrew** Florida U.S.A.
123 N6 **St.Andrew's** Newfoundland Canada
144 C6 **St. Andrews** New Zealand
13 F1 **St.Andrews** Scotland
123 M7 **St.Andrew's Chan** Nova Scotia Canada
113 F7 **St.Andrew Sd** Georgia U.S.A.
127 K2 **St.Ann** *parish* Jamaica
98 F9 **St.Ann** Nebraska U.S.A.
126 B2 **St. Anna-Baai** *B* Curaçao
119 V9 **Ste.Anne** Manitoba Canada
21 M4 **Ste.Anne** France
99 T8 **St.Anne** Illinois U.S.A.
127 N4 **Ste.Anne** Guadeloupe W Indies
127 L4 **Ste.Anne** Martinique W Indies
20 E6 **Ste.-Anne-d'Auray** France
121 U5 **Ste.-Anne-de-Beaupré** Quebec Canada
121 S6 **Ste. Anne de la Pérade** Quebec Canada
122 B6 **Ste.Anne de la Pocatière** Quebec Canada
122 F4 **Ste.Anne des Monts** Quebec Canada
121 P6 **Ste.Anne du Lac** Quebec Canada
122 E3 **Ste.Anne, L** Quebec Canada
118 C5 **Ste. Anne, Lac** Alberta Canada
122 B6 **Ste.Anne, R** Quebec Canada
20 F2 **St.Annes** Channel Is
117 Q9 **St.Ann, L** Alberta Canada
123 M7 **St. Anns** Nova Scotia Canada
127 K2 **St. Ann's Bay** Jamaica
12 E3 **St Ann's Bridge** Scotland
99 O6 **St.Ansgar** Iowa U.S.A.
25 E5 **St.Anthonis** Netherlands
123 R2 **St.Anthony** Newfoundland Canada
101 O6 **St.Anthony** Idaho U.S.A.
19 O18 **St.Antoine** France
41 M3 **St.Anton** Austria
122 C6 **St.Antonin** Quebec Canada
18 G8 **St.Antonin** France
21 O8 **St.Août** France
21 N3 **St.Aquilin-de-Pacy** France
139 G6 **St.Arnaud** Victoria Australia
145 D4 **St. Arnaud** New Zealand
21 O4 **St. Arnoult-en-Yvelines** France
122 C6 **St.Arsène** Quebec Canada
8 C1 **St. Asaph** Wales
140 B1 **St.Asaph B** N Terr Australia
18 F7 **St.Astier** France
122 C6 **St.Athanase** Quebec Canada
122 B6 **St.Aubert** Quebec Canada
20 F3 **St.Aubin** Channel Is
21 K3 **St.Aubin** Calvados France
20 G5 **St.Aubin-d'Aubigné** France
21 L3 **St.Aubin-de-Scellon** France
20 H4 **St.Aubin-de-Terregatte** France
20 H5 **St.Aubin-du-Cormier** France
21 N2 **St.Aubin-le-Cauf** France
123 O2 **St.Augustin** Quebec Canada
36 C2 **St. Augustin** Germany
123 O2 **St.Augustin B** Quebec Canada
87 G12 **St.Augustin, B.de** Madagascar
21 J7 **St.Augustin-des-Bois** France
127 O2 **St.Augustine** Trinidad
113 F8 **St.Augustine** Florida U.S.A.
123 N2 **St.Augustin R** Quebec Canada
18 F7 **St.Aulaye** France
8 B7 **St. Austell** England
21 M7 **St.Avertin** France
19 K3 **St.Avold** France
123 Q2 **St. Barbe** Newfoundland Canada
121 S6 **St.Barnabé Nord** Quebec Canada
121 R6 **St.Barthélémi** Quebec Canada
18 G10 **St.Barthélemy** France
127 N5 **St. Barthélemy** *isld* Lesser Antilles
144 B6 **St. Bathans** New Zealand
21 P8 **St.Baudel** France
19 P18 **Ste.Baume** France
18 F10 **St. Béat** France
12 E5 **St.Bees** England
119 M6 **St.Benedict** Saskatchewan Canada
99 M6 **St.Benedict** Iowa U.S.A.
21 L8 **St.Benoit** Vienne France
18 F6 **St.-Benoît-du-Sault** France
122 B7 **St.Benoit Labre** Quebec Canada
21 P6 **St.Benoît-sur-Loire** France
122 H5 **Ste.Bernadette** Quebec Canada
121 T6 **St.Bernard** Quebec Canada
144 D5 **St. Bernard** *mt* New Zealand
40 F6 **St. Bernard, Col du Gd.** Switz/Italy
42 A3 **St. Bernard, Petit** *pass* Italy/France
110 J2 **St.Bernice** Indiana U.S.A.
19 P13 **St.Beron** France
21 J5 **St.Berthevin** France
36 C7 **St.Blaise** France
122 D5 **Ste.Blandine** Quebec Canada
8 B7 **St.Blazey** England
118 D1 **St.Boniface** Manitoba Canada
118 L8 **St.Boswells** Saskatchewan Canada
13 F2 **St. Boswells** Scotland
21 M7 **St. Branchs** France
123 T5 **St.Brendan's** Newfoundland Canada
20 F7 **St.Brévin-les-Pins** France
20 F4 **St.Briac** France
20 H5 **St.Brice-en-Cogles** France
118 B7 **St.Bride, Mt** Alberta Canada
123 S7 **St.Bride's** Newfoundland Canada
8 A4 **St. Bride's** Wales
20 E4 **St.Brieuc** France
20 E4 **St.Brieuc,B.de** France
119 N6 **St.Brieux** Saskatchewan Canada
20 G4 **St.Broladre** France
121 L5 **St. Bruno de Guiques** Quebec Canada
21 M6 **St.Calais** France
119 T9 **St.Calude** Manitoba Canada
122 B7 **St.Camille** Quebec Canada
20 E5 **St.Caradec** France
20 E5 **St. Carreuc** France
121 S6 **St.Casimir** Quebec Canada
20 F4 **St.Cast** France
121 L9 **St. Catharines** Ontario Canada
127 K2 **St. Catherine** *parish* Jamaica
127 P5 **St.Catherine, Mt** Grenada
112 F6 **St.Catherines I** Georgia U.S.A.
9 E6 **St.Catherines Pt** England
122 B8 **Ste.Cécile** Quebec Canada
18 G8 **St. Céré** France
18 G7 **St.Cernin** France
121 R7 **St.Césaire** Quebec Canada
18 H7 **St.Chamond** France
118 A1 **St.Charles** Manitoba Canada
101 O7 **St.Charles** Idaho U.S.A.
99 S8 **St.Charles** Illinois U.S.A.
94 C3 **St.Charles** Michigan U.S.A.
99 O6 **St.Charles** Minnesota U.S.A.
110 F3 **St.Charles** Missouri U.S.A.
21 O8 **St.Chartier** France
19 O13 **St. Chef** France
18 H8 **St. Chély l'Apcher** France
21 P4 **St.Chéron** France
18 G9 **St.Chinian** France
126 A1 **St.Christoffel Berg** *mt* Curaçao
19 Q15 **St.Christophe d'Oisans** France
20 G8 **St.Christophe-du-Ligneron** France
21 O7 **St. Christophe-en-Bazelle** France
St. Christopher *isld see* **St Kitts**
121 T4 **St.-Cîour-de-Marie** Quebec Canada
21 H3 **St.Clair** France
94 E4 **St.Clair** Michigan U.S.A.
99 N5 **St.Clair** Minnesota U.S.A.
110 F3 **St.Clair** Missouri U.S.A.
94 E4 **St. Clair, L** U.S.A./Canada
120 H9 **St.Clair R** Ontario/Michigan Canada/U.S.A.
21 O3 **St.Clair-sur-Epte** France
19 J6 **St.Claude** France
127 N4 **St.Claude** Guadeloupe W Indies
8 B4 **St.Clears** Wales
122 C6 **St.Clement** Quebec Canada
21 J6 **St. Clement-de-la-Place** France

Ste.Clothilde — Salado, R 221

121 S7 **Ste.Clothilde** Quebec Canada
113 F9 **St.Cloud** Florida U.S.A.
99 M4 **St.Cloud** Minnesota U.S.A.
8 B7 **St.Columb** England
20 G7 **St. Columban** France
121 R6 **St.Côme** Quebec Canada
20 H3 **St.Côme-du-Mont** France
21 L5 **St.Cosme-de-Vair** France
122 E8 **Ste.Croix** New Brunswick Canada
40 D4 **Ste.Croix** Switzerland
99 O4 **St. Croix** *R* Wisconsin U.S.A.
95 T8 **St. Croix** *R* Maine/New Brunswick U.S.A./Canada
36 C7 **Ste.Croix aux Mines** France
113 L8 **St.Croix I** Virgin Is
122 C6 **St.Cyprien** Quebec Canada
18 F8 **St.Cyprien** France
19 P18 **St.Cyr** France
21 K5 **St.Cyr** Mayenne France
21 J4 **St.Cyr-du-Bailleul** France
21 K7 **St.Cyr-en-Bourg** France
21 O6 **St.Cyr-en-Val** France
121 S7 **St.Cyrille** Quebec Canada
121 P4 **St.Cyr, L** Quebec Canada
118 J4 **St. Cyr Lake** Saskatchewan Canada
21 M7 **St.-Cyr-sur-Loire** France
122 B7 **St.Damien** Quebec Canada
127 P1 **St.David** *co* Trinidad
110 F1 **St.David** Illinois U.S.A.
122 A5 **St.David-de-Falardeau** Quebec Canada
123 O5 **St. David's** Newfoundland Canada
8 A4 **St. David's** Wales
90 D1 **St.Davids I** Bermuda
22 G3 **St.Denis** Belgium
121 R7 **St.Denis** Quebec Canada
21 P4 **St. Denis** France
83 J13 **St.Denis** Réunion Indian Oc
21 K6 **St.Denis-d'Anjou** France
21 J5 **St. Denis-de-Gastines** France
21 O8 **St.Denis-de-Jouhet** France
21 K5 **St.Denis-d'Orques** France
20 H8 **St. Denis la Chevasse** France
21 K5 **St.Denis-sur-Sarthon** France
20 F4 **St.Denoual** France
19 O16 **St.Didier** France
36 B7 **St. Dié** France
19 J4 **St.Dizier** France
20 F6 **St.Dolay** France
20 G5 **St Domineuc** France
19 N14 **St.Donat sur l'Herbasse** France
98 J8 **St.Edward** Nebraska U.S.A.
116 P7 **St.Elias, C** Alaska U.S.A.
117 D5 **St. Elias Mts** Alaska/Yukon Terr U.S.A./Canada
121 S4 **Ste.Elisabeth** Quebec Canada
127 J2 **St.Elizabeth** *parish* Jamaica
110 H2 **St.Elmo** Illinois U.S.A.
122 C5 **St.Eloi** Quebec Canada
18 G6 **St Éloy-les-Mines** France
121 R6 **Ste.Emélie** Quebec Canada
18 H8 **Ste.Enimie** France
20 H3 **Sainteny** France
21 M7 **St.Epain** France
122 B7 **St.Ephrem** Quebec Canada
121 L3 **St.Ephrem de Paradis** Quebec Canada
122 C6 **St.-Epiphane** Quebec Canada
20 G5 **St.Erblon** France
22 F5 **St.Erme-Outre-et-Ramecourt** France
18 E7 **Saintes** France
127 L4 **St. Ésprit, Le** Martinique W Indies
22 B2 **St.Étienne-au-Mont** France
18 E9 **St. Étienne de Baïgorry** France
20 G7 **St.Étienne-de-Montluc** France
19 O14 **St.Étienne de St.Geoirs** France
21 N3 **St.Étienne-du-Rouvray** France
121 M4 **St. Eugène** Quebec Canada
121 S4 **St.-Eugène** Quebec Canada
122 D6 **St.Eusèbe** Quebec Canada
121 R7 **St.Eustache** Quebec Canada
127 N6 **Sint Eustatius** *isld* Lesser Antilles
21 L4 **St.Evroult Notre Dame-du-Bois** France
122 D5 **St.Fabien** Quebec Canada
122 B7 **Ste.Familie** Quebec Canada
121 P6 **Ste.Famille d'Aumond** Quebec Canada
18 H5 **St.Fargeau** France
121 S4 **St.Félicien** Quebec Canada
122 E5 **Ste.Félicité** Quebec Canada
121 R6 **St. Félix de Valois** Quebec Canada
12 D1 **St.Fillans** Scotland
14 A5 **St. Finan's B** Ireland
123 O5 **St.Fintan's** Newfoundland Canada
19 Q15 **St. Firmin** France
20 G8 **Ste. Flaive-des-Loups** France
121 T6 **St.Flavien** Quebec Canada
122 E5 **Ste.Florence** Quebec Canada
20 H8 **St.Florent-des-Bois** France
18 H4 **St.Florentin** France
21 H7 **St.Florent-le-Vieil** France
21 P8 **St.Florent-sur-Cher** France
18 H7 **St.Flour** France
21 N8 **St.Flovier** France
121 T7 **St.Fortunat** Quebec Canada
19 N15 **St.Fortunat** France
121 T6 **Ste. Foy** Quebec Canada
18 F8 **Ste.Foy-la-Grande** France
107 J2 **St.Francis** Kansas U.S.A.
110 F5 **St. Francis** *R* Missouri/Ark U.S.A.
95 R6 **St. Francis** *R* Maine/New Brunswick U.S.A./Canada
89 D10 **St. Francis B** S Africa
123 U6 **St.Francis, C** Newfoundland Canada
89 D10 **St. Francis C** S Africa
138 C4 **St.Francis, I.of** South Australia Australia
110 J3 **St. Francisville** Illinois U.S.A.
111 E11 **St.Francisville** Louisiana U.S.A.
121 S7 **St. François** *R* Quebec Canada
127 N4 **St.François** Guadeloupe W Indies
121 T7 **St. François, L** Quebec Canada
110 F4 **St. Francois Mts** Missouri U.S.A.
121 S7 **St.François Xavier** Quebec Canada
95 S7 **St.Froid L** Maine U.S.A.
21 H8 **St.Fulgent** France
111 E11 **St.Gabriel** Louisiana U.S.A.
121 R6 **St.Gabriel de Brandon** Quebec Canada
122 H5 **St.Gabriel de Gaspé** Quebec Canada
41 K3 **St. Gallen** Switzerland
21 L4 **Ste.Gauburge-Ste.Colombe** France
18 F9 **St.Gaudens** France
21 N8 **St.Gaultier** France
122 B8 **St.Gédéon** Quebec Canada
21 N8 **Ste.Gemme** France
21 P3 **Ste. Geneviève** Oise France
110 F4 **Ste.Genevieve** Missouri U.S.A.
123 P2 **St.Genevieve B** Quebec Canada
18 G8 **St.Geniez** France
21 N8 **St.Genou** France
19 P14 **St Geoire-en-Valdaine** France
141 G3 **St. George** *R* Queensland Australia
141 J8 **St.George** Queensland Australia
127 P6 **St.George** *parish* Barbados
90 C1 **St.George** Bermuda
122 F8 **St.George** New Brunswick Canada
127 O2 **St.George** *co* Trinidad
113 E7 **St.George** Georgia U.S.A.
112 G4 **St.George** South Carolina U.S.A.
103 L4 **St.George** Utah U.S.A.
123 N5 **St.George, C** Newfoundland Canada
139 K6 **St.George Hd** New South Wales Australia
116 D8 **St. George I** Pribilof Is Bering Sea
113 C8 **St.George I** Florida U.S.A.
41 H1 **St.Georgen** Germany
100 A8 **St.George, Pt** California U.S.A.
142 E4 **St.George Ra** W Australia Australia
123 O5 **St.George's** Newfoundland Canada
122 B7 **St.Georges** Quebec Canada
36 B6 **St.Georges** France
129 H3 **St.Georges** Fr Guiana
127 P5 **St.George's** Grenada
123 N5 **St.George's B** Newfoundland Canada
125 P9 **St. Georges Cay** *isld* Belize
7 F11 **St Georges Chan** U.K.
137 L2 **St.George's Channel** Bismarck Arch
14 E5 **St. Georges Channel** Ireland/U.K.
69 A9 **St.George's Channel** Nicobar Is
20 H8 **St.Georges-de-Montaigu** France
20 H4 **St.Georges-de-Reintembault** France
21 M3 **St.Georges-du-Mesnil** France
21 M3 **St. Georges du-Vièvre** France
90 C1 **St.George's I** Bermuda
21 L8 **St.Georges-les-Baillargeaux** France
21 N4 **St.Georges-Motel** Eure France
21 N5 **St.Georges-sur-Eure** France
21 O7 **St.Georges-sur-la Prée** France
21 J7 **St.Georges-sur-Loire** France
22 H3 **St.Gérard** Belgium
121 M4 **St. Gerard-Centre** Quebec Canada
19 N13 **St. Germain au Mt D'Or** France
21 J5 **St.Germain-d'Anxure** France
19 P12 **St. Germain-de-Joux** France
21 M5 **St.Germain-de-la-Coudre** France
18 H6 **St.Germain-des-Fosses** France
19 J6 **St.Germain du Bois** France
122 B7 **Ste.Germaine** Quebec Canada
21 P4 **St. Germain-en-Laye** France
20 G3 **St. Germain, Hâvre de** France
21 L3 **St.Germain-la-Campagne** France
18 G7 **St.Germain-les-Belles** France
20 G3 **St.Germain-sur-Ay** France
8 B7 **St.Germans** England
21 O3 **St. Germer-de-Fly** France
41 N5 **St. Gertrude** Italy
20 G8 **St.Gervais** Vendée France
40 E6 **St. Gervais-les-Bains** France
21 L8 **St. Gervais-les-Trois-Clochers** France
22 F3 **St.Ghislain** Belgium
20 E6 **St.Gildas-de-Rhuis** France
20 F6 **St.Gildas-des-Bois** France
20 F7 **St.Gildas,Pte.de** France
121 T6 **St.-Giles** Quebec Canada
127 N1 **St. Giles Is** Tobago
20 G8 **St. Gilles-Croix-de-Vie** France
20 D5 **St.Gilles-Pligeaux** France
22 G1 **St. Gillis-bij-Dendermonde** Belgium
22 G1 **St.Gillis-Waas** Belgium
18 F10 **St.Girons** France
27 F12 **St.Gla** *L* Sweden
36 D3 **St.Goar** Germany
20 C5 **St.Goazec** France
22 E4 **St.Gobain** France
122 G5 **St.Godefroi** Quebec Canada
41 J4 **St.Gotthard** *pass* Switzerland
8 B4 **St.Govan's Hd** Wales
119 N6 **St.Gregor** Saskatchewan Canada
123 O4 **St.Gregory, Mt** Newfoundland Canada
20 B6 **St.Guénolé** France
121 S7 **St. Guillaume** Quebec Canada
19 Q15 **St. Guillaume, Mt** France
94 C2 **St.Helen** Michigan U.S.A.
90 B14 **St. Helena** *isld* Atlantic Oc
102 B3 **St.Helena** California U.S.A.
89 A9 **St.Helena B** S Africa
90 H10 **St Helena Fracture** Atlantic Oc
94 B1 **St.Helena I** Michigan U.S.A.
112 G5 **St.Helena Sd** South Carolina U.S.A.
122 B6 **Ste.Hélène** Quebec Canada
18 E8 **Ste.Hélène** France
139 J8 **St.Helens** Tasmania Australia
13 F6 **St.Helens** England
100 C4 **St.Helens** Oregon U.S.A.
100 C3 **St.Helens, Mt** Washington U.S.A.
139 J8 **St.Helens Pt** Tasmania Australia
122 H4 **St.Helier** Quebec Canada
20 F3 **St Hélier** Channel Is
121 U6 **Ste.Hénédine** Quebec Canada
121 T6 **St.Henri** Quebec Canada
20 G7 **St.-Herblain** France
121 T7 **St.Herménégilde** Quebec Canada
21 H8 **Ste.Hermine** France
18 G9 **St.Hilaire** France
98 K1 **St.Hilaire** Minnesota U.S.A.
20 G7 **St. Hilaire-de-Chaléons** France
20 H7 **St. Hilaire-de-Loulay** France
20 G8 **St. Hilaire-de-Riez** France
21 H4 **St. Hilaire-du-Harcouet** France
21 K7 **St. Hilaire St. Florent** France
21 O6 **St.Hilaire-St.Mesmin** France
140 D6 **Sainthill,Mt** N Terr Australia
19 K5 **St.Hippolyte** Doubs France
21 N7 **St.Hippolyte** Indre-et-Loire France
18 H9 **St.Hippolyte du Fort** France
122 A5 **St.Honoré** Quebec Canada
122 C6 **St.Honoré** Quebec Canada
21 J3 **Ste.Honorine** France
21 K3 **Ste.Honorine-du-Fay** France
22 J3 **St.Hubert** Belgium
25 F6 **St.Hubert** Germany
29 K5 **St Ibb** Sweden
94 C1 **St.Ignace** Michigan U.S.A.
121 R6 **St.Ignace du Lac** Quebec Canada
120 C4 **St. Ignace, Isle** Ontario Canada
101 L2 **St.Ignatius** Montana U.S.A.
40 E3 **St.Imier** Switzerland
36 C5 **St.Ingbert** Germany
122 B6 **St.Irénée** Quebec Canada
121 L5 **St.Isidore** Quebec Canada
121 T7 **St.Isidore** Quebec Canada
26 K3 **St.Istind** *mt* Norway
8 A7 **St.Ives** England
9 F3 **St.Ives** England
20 C6 **St.Ivy** France
25 E2 **St.Jacobi Parochie** Netherlands
122 D6 **St.Jacques** New Brunswick Canada
20 G5 **St.Jacques-de-la-Lande** France
38 F8 **St.Jakob** Austria
118 A1 **St.James** Manitoba Canada
20 H4 **St.James** France
127 J2 **St.James** *parish* Jamaica
99 V4 **St.James** Michigan U.S.A.
99 M5 **St.James** Minnesota U.S.A.
110 E3 **St.James** Missouri U.S.A.
117 H10 **St.James, C** British Columbia Canada
113 E11 **St.James City** Florida U.S.A.
22 D2 **Sint Jan** Belgium
121 L4 **St.Janvier** Quebec Canada
121 R7 **St.Jean** Quebec Canada
21 K5 **St.Jean** France
119 U9 **St.Jean Baptiste** Manitoba Canada
121 S5 **St.Jean Bosco** Quebec Canada
20 E6 **St.Jean-Brévelay** France
18 E7 **St.-Jean-d'Angély** France
21 L5 **St.Jean-d'Asse** France
19 O13 **St.Jean-de-Bournay** France
21 O6 **St.-Jean-de-Braye** France
21 H3 **St.Jean-de-Daye** France
122 C5 **St.Jean de Dieu** Quebec Canada
21 O6 **St.-Jean-de-la-Ruelle** France
19 J5 **St.Jean de Losne** France
18 D9 **St.Jean-de-Luz** France
121 R6 **St. Jean-de-Matha** Quebec Canada
19 Q14 **St.Jean-de-Maurienne** France
20 F8 **St.Jean-de-Monts** France
21 L8 **St.Jean-de-Sauves** France
18 H8 **St.Jean du Gard** France
19 O14 **St.Jean-en-Royans** France
121 S4 **Saint-Jean, Lac** Quebec Canada
20 G4 **St.Jean-le-Thomas** France
18 E9 **St.Jean Pied de Port** France
122 B6 **St.Jean Port Joli** Quebec Canada
122 H3 **St.Jean, R** Quebec Canada
36 B5 **St.Jean Rohrbach** France
20 H5 **St.Jean-sur-Couesnon** France
121 Q7 **St.Jérôme** Quebec Canada
19 N14 **St. Jeure D'Ay** France
109 K2 **St.Jo** Texas U.S.A.
122 B6 **St.Joachim** Quebec Canada
20 F7 **St.Joachim** France
41 O3 **St.Jodok** Austria
110 D5 **St.Joe** Arkansas U.S.A.
100 J2 **St.Joe** Idaho U.S.A.
94 C5 **St.Joe** Indiana U.S.A.
36 E4 **St.Johann** Germany
38 G8 **St. Johann-im-Walde** Austria
127 P6 **St.John** *parish* Barbados
122 F8 **St.John** New Brunswick Canada
107 M3 **St.John** Kansas U.S.A.
95 R7 **St. John** *R* Maine U.S.A.
119 S10 **St.John** North Dakota U.S.A.
103 M1 **St.John** Utah U.S.A.
100 H2 **St.John** Washington U.S.A.
123 P3 **St John B** Newfoundland Canada
123 R3 **St.John, C** Newfoundland Canada
113 L7 **St.John I** Virgin Is
123 S5 **St.John, L** Newfoundland Canada
122 E7 **St. John R** New Brunswick Canada
122 G5 **St. John R** Quebec Canada
123 T6 **St. John's** Newfoundland Canada
103 P7 **St.Johns** Arizona U.S.A.
94 C3 **St.Johns** Michigan U.S.A.
127 P4 **St.John's** Antigua W Indies
95 P2 **St.Johnsbury** Vermont U.S.A.
13 F4 **St.John's Chapel** England
14 C2 **St.John's Pt** Ireland
113 F7 **St.Johns R** Florida U.S.A.
95 N3 **St.Johnsville** New York U.S.A.
20 H3 **St.Jores** France
22 H2 **St.Joris-Winge** Belgium
127 P6 **St.Joseph** *parish* Barbados
121 U6 **St.Joseph** Quebec Canada
83 K14 **St.Joseph** Réunion Indian Oc
127 P2 **St.Joseph** Mayoro Trinidad
127 O2 **St.Joseph** St George Trinidad
111 E10 **St.Joseph** Louisiana U.S.A.
94 A5 **St. Joseph** *R* Michigan U.S.A.
99 U7 **St.Joseph** Michigan U.S.A.
99 M10 **St.Joseph** Missouri U.S.A.
127 L4 **St.Joseph** Martinique W Indies
113 B8 **St. Joseph Bay** Florida U.S.A.
120 G6 **St. Joseph I** Ontario Canada
109 L8 **St. Joseph I** Texas U.S.A.
115 K7 **St. Joseph, L** Ontario Canada
123 T6 **St.Joseph's** Newfoundland Canada
22 B3 **St.Josse** France
20 F5 **St. Jouan-de-l'Isle** France
20 G4 **St Jouan-des-Guerets** France
21 L2 **St.Jouin** France
21 K8 **St.Jouin-de-Marnes** France
121 Q6 **St. Jovite** Quebec Canada
126 A1 **St. Jozefsdal** Curaçao
19 N14 **St.Julian Molin-Molette** France
40 D5 **St.Julien** France
20 E5 **St.Julien** Côtes d'Armor France
20 H7 **St.Julien-de-Concelles** France
20 G8 **St. Julien-des-Landes** France
20 H6 **St.Julien-de-Vouvantes** France
19 O15 **St.Julien en Quint** France
21 L8 **St.Julien-l'Ars** France
21 L3 **St.Julien-le-Faucon** France
18 F7 **St.Junien** France
9 F7 **St.Just** England
21 P2 **St.Just-en-Chaussée** France
18 H7 **St.Just-en-Chevalet** France
38 M7 **St.Katherein** Austria
15 A1 **St. Kilda** *isld* Scotland
127 P4 **St.Kitts** *isld* Lesser Antilles
127 P4 **St. Kitts-Nevis** *islds* West Indies
126 A1 **St.Kruis** Curaçao
121 T6 **St.Lambert** Quebec Canada
121 R7 **St.Lambert** Quebec Canada
142 G2 **St.Lambert,C** W Australia Australia
21 K7 **St. Lambert des Levées** France
21 J7 **St.Lambert-du-Lattay** France
111 D11 **St.Landry** Louisiana U.S.A.
119 U8 **St.Laurent** Manitoba Canada
121 L4 **Saint-Laurent** Quebec Canada
19 J6 **St. Laurent** France
129 H2 **St.Laurent** Fr Guiana
18 G10 **St.Laurent de la Salanque** France
19 O13 **St.Laurent-de-Mûre** France
21 H7 **St. Laurent-des-Autels** France
21 O6 **St.Laurent-des-Eaux** France
19 P14 **St.Laurent-du-Pont** France
21 M2 **St.Laurent-en-Caux** France
21 M6 **St.Laurent-en-Gâtines** France
18 E7 **St.Laurent-et-Benon** France
121 U5 **St.Laurent, R** Quebec Canada
21 J3 **St.Laurent-sur-Mer** France
22 K5 **St.Laurent-sur-Othain** France
21 J8 **St. Laurent-sur-Sèvre** France
141 J5 **St.Lawrence** Queensland Australia
123 R7 **St.Lawrence** Newfoundland Canada
95 M2 **St. Lawrence** *R* Canada/U.S.A.
122 K5 **St.Lawrence, G.of** Canada
116 B5 **St.Lawrence I** Bering Sea
121 O8 **St. Lawrence I Nat. Park** Ontario Canada
121 P8 **St.Lawrence Seaway** Canada/U.S.A.
119 Q8 **St.Lazare** Manitoba Canada
22 K4 **St.Léger** Belgium
21 O4 **St.Léger-en-Yvelines** France
22 H1 **St.Lenaarts** Belgium
122 E5 **St.Léon** Quebec Canada
122 E6 **St.-Léonard** New Brunswick Canada
121 S6 **St.Léonard** Quebec Canada
36 B7 **St. Léonard** France
18 G7 **St.-Léonard-de-Noblat** France
9 G6 **St.Leonards** England
121 T4 **St.-Léon-de-Chicoutimi** Quebec Canada
122 B7 **St.Léon de Standon** Quebec Canada
38 L8 **St.Leonhard** Kärnten Austria
38 N4 **St.Leonhard** Nieder Österreich Austria
123 Q1 **St.Lewis R** Labrador, Nfld Canada
121 S7 **St.Liboire** Quebec Canada
18 F8 **Ste. Livrade** France
21 P7 **Ste.Lizaigne** France
18 F9 **St.Lizier** France
21 H3 **St.Lô** France
122 H7 **St.Louis** Prince Edward I Canada
119 M6 **St.Louis** Saskatchewan Canada
83 J14 **St.Louis** Réunion Indian Oc
85 A5 **St.Louis** Mauritania
94 C3 **St.Louis** Michigan U.S.A.
99 O2 **St. Louis** *R* Minnesota U.S.A.
105 **St.Louis** *conurbation* Missouri U.S.A.
127 N4 **St.Louis** Marie Galante W Indies
122 H7 **St.Louis de Kent** New Brunswick Canada
122 D6 **St.Louis du Ha Ha** Quebec Canada
126 H5 **St.Louis du Sud** Haiti
122 B6 **Ste.Louise** Quebec Canada
121 R7 **St.Louis, L** Quebec Canada
36 C5 **St. Louis-lès-Bitche** France
94 E6 **St.Louisville** Ohio U.S.A.
21 K8 **St. Loup-Lamaire** France
40 D2 **St. Loup-sur-Semoise** France
21 N4 **St.Lubin-des-Joncherets** France
127 L4 **Ste.Luce** Martinique W Indies
141 K2 **St.Lucia** *dist* Brisbane, Qnsld Australia
127 O8 **St. Lucia** *isld* Lesser Antilles
87 F11 **St. Lucia, C** S Africa
121 Q6 **Ste.Lucie** Quebec Canada
113 G10 **St. Lucie Canal** Florida U.S.A.
127 P6 **St.Lucy** *parish* Barbados
122 B8 **St.Ludger** Quebec Canada
127 H5 **St.Luis du Nord** Haiti
123 R2 **St Lunaire** Newfoundland Canada
20 F4 **St.Lunaire** France
20 F7 **St.Lyphard** France
127 N5 **Sint Maarten** *isld* Lesser Antilles
25 B5 **St.Maartens-dijk** Netherlands
18 E8 **St. Macaire** Gironde France
21 J7 **St. Macaire-en-Mauges** France
15 G2 **St.Magnus B** Scotland
122 B7 **St.Malachie** Quebec Canada
20 F4 **St.Malo** France
20 G3 **St.Malo-de-la-Lande** France
20 F4 **St.Malo,G.de** France
20 F5 **St.Malon-sur-Mel** France
19 P18 **St.Mandrier** France
20 B5 **St.Marc** Finistère France
20 F7 **St.Marc** Loire-Inférieure France
127 H5 **St.Marc** Haiti
121 S6 **St.Marc des Carrières** Quebec Canada
122 B7 **St.Marcel** Quebec Canada
21 O8 **St.Marcel** Indre France
19 O14 **St.Marcellin** France
21 H3 **St.Marcouf,Is** France
20 H5 **St.Marc-sur-Couesnon** France
22 K4 **St.Mard** Belgium
123 P2 **St.Margaret B** Newfoundland Canada
122 J9 **St.Margaret B** Nova Scotia Canada
38 K8 **St.Margarethen** Austria
32 K5 **St.Margarethen** Germany
9 H5 **St. Margaret's at Cliffe** England
15 F2 **St.Margarets Hope** Scotland
20 F7 **Ste.Marguerite** France
122 F3 **Ste.Marguerite, R** Quebec Canada
122 B5 **Ste.Marguerite, R** Quebec Canada
121 T6 **Ste.Marie** Quebec Canada
83 K13 **Ste.Marie** Réunion Indian Oc
110 H3 **Ste.Marie** Illinois U.S.A.
127 L4 **Ste.Marie** Martinique W Indies
19 K4 **Ste.Marie aux Mines** France
36 C7 **Ste. Marie, Col de** *pass* France
20 H3 **Ste.Marie-du-Mont** France
19 Q17 **St Marie Mourre de Chanier** *mt* France
100 J2 **St.Maries** Idaho U.S.A.
113 C7 **St.Marks** Florida U.S.A.
21 L6 **St. Mars-d'Outille** France
20 H7 **St.Mars-du-Désert** France
21 L5 **St.Mars-la-Brière** France
21 H6 **St.Mars-la-Jaille** France
21 H5 **St.Mars-sur-la-Futaie** France
122 F4 **Ste.Marthe de Gaspé** Quebec Canada
18 E6 **St.Martin** France
19 P17 **St.-Martin** France
20 F6 **St.Martin** Morbihan France
127 N5 **St.Martin** *isld* Lesser Antilles
22 B2 **St.Martin-Boulogne** France
89 A9 **St.Martin, C** S Africa
127 L4 **St. Martin, C** Martinique W Indies
21 O4 **St.Martin-de-Bretencourt** France
19 N17 **St.Martin-de-Crau** France
21 H4 **St.Martin-de-Landelle** France
21 J3 **St.Martin-des-Besaces** France
21 H8 **St.Martin-des-Noyers** France
16 E4 **St.Martin de Valdeiglesias** Spain
19 P14 **St.-Martin-d'Heres** France
19 P12 **St.Martin-du-Fresne** France
19 O12 **St.Martin-du-Mont** France
40 B4 **St.Martin en Bresse** France
21 N2 **St.Martin-en-Campagne** France
99 U4 **St.Martin I** Michigan U.S.A.
119 T7 **St. Martin, L** Manitoba Canada
21 M7 **St. Martin-le-Beau** France
122 G8 **St. Martin's** New Brunswick Canada
9 F7 **St. Martin's** *isld* Isles of Scilly England
68 A2 **St.Martin's I** Burma
20 E3 **St.Martin's Pt** Channel Is
119 T7 **St. Martin Station** Manitoba Canada
111 E11 **St.Martinville** Louisiana U.S.A.
20 F3 **St.Mary** Channel Is
127 L2 **St.Mary** *parish* Jamaica
101 M1 **St. Mary** *R* Montana/Alberta U.S.A./Canada
123 N3 **St. Mary Is** Quebec Canada
101 M1 **St.Mary L** Montana U.S.A.
117 P11 **St. Mary, Mt** British Columbia Canada
144 B6 **St. Mary, Mt** New Zealand
123 N3 **St.Mary Reefs** Quebec Canada
118 D9 **St.Mary Res** Alberta Canada
139 J8 **St.Marys** Tasmania Australia
123 T7 **St.Marys** Newfoundland Canada
9 F7 **St.Mary's** *isld* Isles of Scilly England
15 F2 **St. Marys** Scotland
127 O3 **St. Mary's** Trinidad
116 F5 **St. Marys** Alaska U.S.A.
113 F7 **St. Marys** Georgia U.S.A.
94 B6 **St. Marys** *R* Indiana U.S.A.
107 O2 **St Marys** Kansas U.S.A.
110 G4 **St.Marys** Missouri U.S.A.
94 C6 **St.Marys** Ohio U.S.A.
94 J5 **St.Marys** Pennsylvania U.S.A.
94 F7 **St.Marys** West Virginia U.S.A.
123 T7 **St.Mary's B** Newfoundland Canada
122 F9 **St.Mary's B** Nova Scotia Canada
95 L8 **St. Marys City** Maryland U.S.A.
89 H6 **St.Mary's Hill** S Africa
15 E5 **St. Marys Loch** Scotland
123 K8 **St.Mary's, R** Nova Scotia Canada
113 F7 **St.Marys R** Florida/Georgia U.S.A.
112 G4 **St. Mathews** South Carolina U.S.A.
121 M4 **St.Mathieu** Quebec Canada
20 A5 **St.Mathieu,Pte de** France
20 G8 **St.Mathurin** France
116 C6 **St.Matthew I** Bering Sea
136 K2 **St. Matthias Group** *islds* Bismarck Arch
21 M7 **Ste.Maure-de-Touraine** France
40 E2 **St.Maurice** France
21 K7 **St. Maurice la Fougereuse** Deux Sèvres France
21 M4 **St. Maurice-les-Charencey** France
8 A7 **St. Mawes** England
122 B7 **St. Maxime** Quebec Canada
19 P18 **St.Maximin** France
20 D5 **St.Mayeux** France
22 J4 **St. Médard** Belgium
18 E8 **St Medard en Jalles** France
20 F5 **St.Meen** France
110 K3 **St.Meinrad** Indiana U.S.A.
8 C4 **St.Mellons** Wales
20 G4 **St.Méloir-des-Ondes** France
19 J3 **St. Menehould** France
22 H4 **St.Menges** France
20 H3 **Ste.Mère-Église** France
21 J8 **St.Mesmin** Vendée France
127 P6 **St.Michael** *parish* Barbados
98 H8 **St.Michael** Nebraska U.S.A.
32 K5 **St.Michaelisdonn** Germany
103 P6 **St.Michaels** Arizona U.S.A.
95 L8 **St.Michaels** Maryland U.S.A.
22 G4 **St.Michel** Aisne France
21 H6 **St.Michel** Maine-et-Loire France
20 F7 **St.Michel-Chef-Chef** France
127 H5 **St.Michel de L'Atalaye** Haiti
121 R6 **St.Michel des Saints** Quebec Canada
21 J8 **St.Michel-Mont Mercure** France
20 C5 **St.Michel,Mt** Finistère France
20 C5 **St.Michel,Res.de** France
36 B7 **St.Michel-sur-Meurthe** France
126 B1 **St.Michiel** Curaçao
19 J4 **St Mihiel** France
22 C2 **St.Momelin** France
13 F1 **St.Monance** Scotland
41 L5 **St.Moritz** Switzerland
20 F7 **St.Nazaire** Loire-Atlantique France
19 O14 **St.Nazaire-en-Royans** France
9 F3 **St.Neots** England
20 B5 **St.Nic** France
126 A2 **Sint Nicolaas** Aruba W Indies
St.Nicolas *see* **St.Niklaas**
21 N2 **St.Nicolas-d'Aliermont** France
20 F6 **St.Nicolas-de-Redon** France
20 D5 **St.Nicolas-du-Pélem** France
22 G1 **St.Niklaas** Belgium
21 P4 **St.-Nom-la-Bretêche** France
119 U9 **St.Norbert** Manitoba Canada
25 F6 **St.Odilienberg** Netherlands
25 D5 **St.Oedenrode** Netherlands
122 F5 **St.Omer** Quebec Canada
22 C2 **St.Omer** France
145 D4 **St. Omer** New Zealand
21 P2 **St.-Omer-en-Chaussée** France
18 E7 **Saintonge** *prov* France
98 C5 **St.Onge** South Dakota U.S.A.
20 H4 **St.Osvin** France
21 P4 **St.-Ouen** France
21 J5 **St.Ouen-des-Toits** France
21 P3 **St.Ouen-l'Aumône** France
121 R7 **St.Ours** Quebec Canada
122 C6 **St.Pacôme** Quebec Canada
20 G4 **St.Pair** France
18 E9 **St.Palais** France
122 C7 **St.Pamphile** Quebec Canada
18 F7 **St.Pardoux la Rivière** France
94 D6 **St.Paris** Ohio U.S.A.
122 C6 **St.Pascal** Quebec Canada
21 L6 **St. Paterne** Indre-et-Loire France
21 L5 **St. Paterne** Sarthe France
121 N6 **St.Patrice, L-** Quebec Canada
127 O3 **St.Patrick** *co* Trinidad
38 L8 **St.Paul** Austria
118 F4 **St.Paul** Alberta Canada
18 E9 **St.Paul** France
85 C7 **St. Paul** *R* Guinea/Liberia
83 J13 **St.Paul** Réunion Indian Oc
110 C6 **St.Paul** Arkansas U.S.A.
94 B7 **St.Paul** Indiana U.S.A.
107 P4 **St.Paul** Kansas U.S.A.
99 N4 **St.Paul** Minnesota U.S.A.
98 H8 **St.Paul** Nebraska U.S.A.
112 G4 **St.Paul** South Carolina U.S.A.
94 E10 **St.Paul** Virginia U.S.A.
18 G10 **St. Paul de Fenouillet** France
122 C6 **St.-Paul-de-la-Croix** Quebec Canada
122 B7 **St.Paul de Montriny** Quebec Canada
122 C5 **St.Paul du Nord** Quebec Canada
116 D8 **St. Paul I** Pribilof Is Bering Sea
123 M6 **St.Paul I** C Breton I, Nova Scotia
81 E9 **St. Paul, Î** Indian Oc
18 H7 **St.Paulien** France
121 R6 **St.Paulin** Quebec Canada
19 P17 **St.Paul-les-Durance** France
123 P2 **St.Paul R** Quebec Canada
90 G8 **St.Paul Rocks** Atlantic Oc
112 H3 **St.Pauls** North Carolina U.S.A.
127 P4 **St.Pauls** St Kitts W Indies
123 P4 **St.Paul's Inlet** Newfoundland Canada
19 N16 **St Paul-Trois-Châteaux** France
20 G7 **St. Pazanne** France
18 E9 **St.Pé de B** France
21 O5 **St. Peravy-la-Colombe** France
20 F7 **St. Père-en-Retz** France
122 C6 **Ste.Perpétue** Quebec Canada
32 J4 **Sankt Peter** Germany
110 H3 **St.Peter** Illinois U.S.A.
38 K7 **St.Peter-am-Kammersberg** Austria
123 R1 **St.Peter B** Labrador, Nfld Canada
32 J4 **St Peter-Ording** Germany
20 E3 **St. Peter Port** Channel Is
122 H5 **St.Peter, Pt** Quebec Canada
122 K7 **St.Peters** Prince Edward I Canada
123 M8 **St.Peters** C Breton I, Nova Scotia
St.Petersburg *see* **Sankt-Peterburg**
113 E10 **St.Petersburg** Florida U.S.A.
69 J12 **St.Petrus** *isld* Indonesia
20 G8 **St. Philbert-de-Bouaine** France
20 G7 **St. Philbert-de-Grandlieu** France
122 B7 **St.Philémon** Quebec Canada
127 P6 **St. Philip** *parish* Barbados
25 B5 **St.Philipsland** Netherlands
121 S7 **St.Pie** Quebec Canada
123 Q7 **St. Pierre** St. Pierre I Atlantic Oc
119 V9 **St.Pierre** Manitoba Canada
20 D6 **St. Pierre** Morbihan France
83 J14 **St.Pierre** Réunion Indian Oc
127 L4 **St.Pierre** Martinique W Indies
123 Q7 **St. Pierre and Miquelon** *islds* Atlantic Oc
19 Q13 **St Pierre d'Albigny** France
21 N3 **St. Pierre-d'Autils** France
21 M8 **St. Pierre-de-Maillé** France
20 G5 **St. Pierre-de-Plesguen** France
21 M7 **St.-Pierre-des-Corps** France
21 J8 **St. Pierre-des-Echaubrognes** France
21 K5 **St. Pierre-des-Nids** France
21 J8 **St. Pierre-du-Chemin** France
21 N3 **St. Pierre-du-Vauvray** France
20 H2 **St. Pierre-Église** France
21 L2 **St. Pierre-en-Port** France
123 Q7 **St. Pierre, I** Atlantic Oc
81 C6 **St. Pierre I** Indian Oc
121 S6 **St.Pierre, L** Quebec Canada
21 H5 **St. Pierre-la-Cour** France
20 H4 **St. Pierre-Langers** France
18 H6 **St. Pierre le Môutier** France
21 N3 **St. Pierre-lès-Elbeuf** France
20 A5 **St. Pierre-Quilbignon** France
21 K3 **St. Pierre-sur-Dives** France
21 K5 **St. Pierre-sur-Orthe** France
21 H4 **St. Pois** France
21 H6 **St. Poix** France
22 C1 **St.Pol** France
22 C3 **St.Pol** France
20 C4 **St. Pol-de-Leon** France
38 N5 **St.Pölten** Austria
19 K6 **St.Pon, L.de** France
18 G9 **St Pons** France
18 H6 **St.Pourcain-sur-Sioule** France
121 S4 **St.-Prime** Quebec Canada
21 J8 **St. Prouant** France
20 E4 **St. Quay-Portrieux** France
122 E6 **St.Quentin** New Brunswick Canada
22 E4 **St.Quentin** Aisne France
21 J6 **St.-Quentin** Maine-et-Loire France
21 P4 **St. Quentin-en-Yvelines** France
22 B3 **St.Quentin, Pte.de** France
36 C6 **St.Quirin** France
18 H7 **St.Rambert** France
122 B7 **St.Raphaël** Quebec Canada
121 T6 **St.Raymond** Quebec Canada
101 L2 **St.Regis** Montana U.S.A.
95 N2 **St. Regis Falls** New York U.S.A.
121 R7 **St.Rémi** Quebec Canada
19 N17 **St. Rémy** Bouches du Rhône France
21 K4 **St. Rémy** Calvados France
21 L5 **St. Rémy-des-Monts** France
20 G5 **St Remy du Plain** France
21 L5 **St. Rémy-du-Plain** France
21 N4 **St. Rémy-sur-Avre** France
18 H7 **St. Rémy-sur-Durolle** France
20 A5 **St. Renan** France
40 F6 **St.Rhémy** Italy
19 J6 **St. Rigaud, Mt** France
21 O1 **St. Riquier** France
121 R7 **St.Robert** Quebec Canada
122 A8 **St.Romain** Quebec Canada
21 L2 **St. Romain-de-Colbosc** France
21 N7 **St. Romain-sur-Cher** France
121 T6 **St.Romuald** Quebec Canada
141 G4 **St. Ronans** Queensland Australia
121 R7 **Ste.Rose** Quebec Canada
127 N4 **Ste.Rose** Guadeloupe W Indies
119 S7 **Ste.Rose de Lac** Manitoba Canada
122 D6 **Ste.Rose du Dégelé** Quebec Canada
38 N7 **St.Ruprecht-an-der-Raab** Austria
21 N2 **St. Saëns** France
20 E3 **St. Sampson** Channel Is
20 E5 **St. Samson** France
21 P8 **St. Saturnin** France
19 O17 **St.Saturnin d'Apt** France
19 N17 **St Saturnin-lès-Avig-non** France
21 P2 **St. Sauflieu** France
121 Q7 **St.Sauveur** Quebec Canada
19 O16 **St. Sauveur** France
20 B5 **St. Sauveur** Finistère France
21 K4 **St. Sauveur** Orne France
20 H3 **St. Sauveur-Lendelin** France
20 G3 **St. Sauveur-le-Vicomte** France
21 N4 **St. Sauveur-Marville** Eure France
18 E7 **St.Savin** France
21 M8 **St. Savin** Vienne France
21 L4 **Ste. Scolasse** France
20 B5 **St. Segal** France
18 G9 **St.Sernin-sur-Rance** France
20 F4 **St. Servan** France
18 E9 **St.Sever** France
21 H4 **St. Sever-Calvados** France
21 P8 **Ste. Sévère-sur-Indre** Indre France
123 T7 **St.Shott's** Newfoundland Canada
122 C5 **St.Simon** Quebec Canada
22 E4 **St.Simon** France
112 F6 **St. Simons** Georgia U.S.A.
26 J4 **St. Sjöfallets Nat. Park** Sweden
122 E8 **St.Stephen** New Brunswick Canada
112 H4 **St.Stephen** South Carolina U.S.A.
101 R7 **St.Stephens** Wyoming U.S.A.
18 G9 **St.Sulpice** France
21 M4 **St. Sulpice** Orne France
20 G6 **St. Sulpice-des-Landes** France
18 F6 **St. Sulpice Laurière** France
21 K5 **Ste. Suzanne** France
83 K13 **Ste.Suzanne** Réunion Indian Oc
21 K3 **St. Sylvain** France
121 T6 **St.-Sylvestre** Quebec Canada
18 E8 **St.Symphorien** France
117 F6 **St. Terese** Alaska U.S.A.
122 E5 **St.Tharsicius** Quebec Canada
121 S6 **Ste.Thècle** Quebec Canada
20 C4 **St. Thégonnec** France
122 B8 **St. Théophile** Quebec Canada
121 R7 **Ste.Thérèse** Quebec Canada
117 N3 **Ste. Thérèse, Lac** Northwest Territories Canada
40 C1 **St.Thiébault** France
127 P6 **St.Thomas** *parish* Barbados
120 J10 **St.Thomas** Ontario Canada
127 M3 **St.Thomas** *parish* Jamaica
98 J1 **St.Thomas** North Dakota U.S.A.
113 K7 **St.Thomas I** Virgin Is
20 C6 **St Thurien** France
121 S6 **St.Tite** Quebec Canada
122 B6 **St.Tite des Caps** Quebec Canada
40 B5 **St.Trivier de Courtes** France
19 N12 **St. Trivier-Moignans** France
St.Trond *see* **St.Truiden**
22 J2 **St.Truiden** Belgium
8 B2 **St. Tudwal's Is** Wales
27 H11 **St.Tuna** Sweden
122 E5 **St.Ulric** Quebec Canada
122 B6 **St.Urbain** Quebec Canada
21 M2 **St. Vaast** France
20 H2 **St. Vaast-la-Hougue** France
21 M2 **St. Valéry-en-Caux** France
21 O1 **St. Valery-sur-Somme** France
122 B7 **St.Vallier** Quebec Canada
21 K8 **St. Varent** France
38 H7 **St.Veit** Austria
38 K8 **St.Veit-an-der-Glan** Austria
22 D2 **St.Venant** France
20 F5 **St. Véran** Côtes d'Armor France
121 Q6 **Ste.Véronique** Quebec Canada
21 O6 **St. Viâtre** France
20 F7 **St Viaud** France
20 G7 **St. Viaud** France
19 P17 **Ste Victoire, Mt** France
20 F6 **St. Vincent** France
127 O8 **St. Vincent** *isld* Lesser Antilles
21 L6 **St Vincent-de-Larouer** France
18 E9 **St.Vincent-de-Tyrosse** France
138 E5 **St.Vincent, G** South Australia Australia
113 B8 **St. Vincent I** Florida U.S.A.
139 H9 **St.Vincent, Pt** Tasmania Australia
123 T7 **St.Vincent's** Newfoundland Canada
118 A2 **St.Vital** Manitoba Canada
94 C1 **St. Vital Pt** Michigan U.S.A.
22 L3 **St.Vith** Belgium
18 E7 **St.Vivien-de-Médoc** France
106 G7 **St.Vrain** New Mexico U.S.A.
118 H5 **St.Walburg** Saskatchewan Canada
21 M2 **St. Wandrille** France
36 C5 **St.Wendel** Germany
126 A1 **St. Willebrordus** Curaçao
120 K10 **St.Williams** Ontario Canada
101 S4 **St.Xavier** Montana U.S.A.
18 F7 **St. Yrieix** France
122 H4 **St.Yvon** Quebec Canada
19 P18 **St.Zacharie** France
21 O5 **Sainville** France
134 E6 **Saipan** *isld* Mariana Is Pacific Oc
20 H2 **Saire** *R* France
20 H2 **Saire, Pte. de** France
18 E9 **Saison** *R* France
61 M10 **Saitama** *prefect* Japan
68 A1 **Saitlai** Burma
60 E13 **Saito** Japan
26 N3 **Saivomuotka** Sweden
77 L2 **Saiydabad** Afghanistan
77 L1 **Saiyid** Afghanistan
74 E3 **Saiyidwala** Pakistan
71 B2 **Sajafi** *isld* Indonesia
128 E7 **Sajama** *mt* Bolivia
128 E7 **Sajama** Bolivia
71 B2 **Sajang** *isld* Indonesia
48 F2 **Sajó** *R* Hungary
89 B7 **Sak** *watercourse* S Africa
88 G2 **Saka** Kenya
Saka Dzong *see* **Saga** China
59 L5 **Sakai** Japan
60 G11 **Sakaide** Japan
60 G10 **Sakai Minato** Japan
78 H7 **Sākākah** Saudi Arabia
98 E2 **Sakakawea, L** North Dakota U.S.A.
70 Q9 **Sakala** *isld* Indonesia
61 N7 **Sakamachi** Japan
115 M7 **Sakami, L** Quebec Canada
88 B8 **Sakania** Zaire
47 H3 **Sakar** *hills* Bulgaria
57 C5 **Sakar** Turkmenistan
87 G12 **Sakaraha** Madagascar
57 B5 **Sakar-chaga** Turkmenistan
47 J5 **Sakar Dağı** *mt* Turkey
78 C1 **Sakarya** *R* Turkey
78 C2 **Sakarya** *R* Turkey
59 L4 **Sakata** Japan
111 H8 **Sakatonchee** *R* Mississippi U.S.A.
85 E7 **Sakete** Benin
59 M1 **Sakhalin** *isld* Russian Federation
51 O4 **Sakhalinskaya Oblast'** Russian Federation
51 O3 **Sakhalinskiy Zaliv** *B* Russian Federation
85 F2 **Sakhira** Tunisia
54 G7 **Sakhnovshchina** Ukraine
77 B1 **Sakht-Sar** Iran
52 B7 **Šakiai** Lithuania
80 G4 **Sakib** Jordan
60 H12 **Sakihama** Japan
67 H4 **Sakishima-guntō** *islds* Japan
55 C5 **Sakmara** Russian Federation
85 B3 **Sakn, As** Western Sahara
68 C3 **Sa-koi** Burma
95 Q5 **Sakonnet R** Rhode I U.S.A.
87 D12 **Sakrivier** S Africa
28 E5 **Saksild** Denmark
28 H7 **Sakskøbing** Denmark
75 K7 **Sakti** India
51 M1 **Saktyakh** Russian Federation
61 M9 **Saku** Japan
61 L10 **Sakuma** Japan
61 J11 **Sakurai** Japan
60 D14 **Sakura jima** *isld* Japan
27 M10 **Säkylä** Finland
80 G3 **Sal** Jordan
53 F9 **Sal** *R* Russian Federation
48 D2 **Šala** Czechoslovakia
27 J12 **Sala** Sweden
68 F7 **Sala Andong Tuk** Cambodia
71 H6 **Salabangka** *isld* Sulawesi
52 B5 **Salacgriva** Latvia
43 G8 **Sala Consilina** Italy
109 K5 **Salad** Texas U.S.A.
133 C3 **Salada, B** Chile
131 G6 **Salada, L** Buenos Aires Argentina
131 F2 **Salada, L** Corrientes Argentina
124 B1 **Salada, L** Mexico
103 J9 **Salada, Laguna** *L* Mexico
131 E4 **Saladillo** *R* Argentina
131 B2 **Salado** *R* La Rioja Argentina
131 E2 **Salado, R** Santa Fé Argentina

106 C7 **Salado, R** New Mexico U.S.A.
85 D7 **Salaga** Ghana
68 F7 **Sala Hintoun** Cambodia
56 C4 **Salair** Russian Federation
56 C4 **Salairskiy Kryazh** *ridge* Russian Federation
48 H3 **Sălaj** *prov* Romania
70 G7 **Salajar, Selat** *str* Sulawesi
70 L9 **Salak, G** *mt* Java
86 C3 **Salal** Chad
72 G5 **Şalālah** Oman
125 O10 **Salamá** Guatemala
16 C4 **Salamanca** *prov* Spain
16 D4 **Salamanca** Spain
94 J4 **Salamanca** New York U.S.A.
86 C4 **Salamat** *R* Chad
70 D6 **Salamban** Kalimantan
128 C2 **Salamina** Colombia
79 D3 **Salamis** Cyprus
46 F7 **Salamís** Greece
79 H3 **Salamīyah** Syria
94 B6 **Salamonie** *R* Indiana U.S.A.
26 J3 **Salangen** Norway
52 B6 **Salantai** Lithuania
45 K2 **Salara** Italy
48 G3 **Sălard** Romania
133 D2 **Salar de Arizaro** *salt pan* Argentina
133 D2 **Salar de Atacama** *salt pan* Chile
133 D2 **Salar de Cauchari** *salt pan* Argentina
133 D1 **Salar de Coipasa** *salt pan* Bolivia
133 D3 **Salar del Hombre Muerto** *salt pan* Argentina
133 D2 **Salar de Uyuni** *salt pan* Bolivia
16 C1 **Salas** Spain
46 E1 **Salaš** Serbia Yugoslavia
16 E2 **Salas de los Infantes** Spain
18 F9 **Salat** *R* France
70 N9 **Salatiga** Java
18 F10 **Salau, Pont de** *pass* France/Spain
52 H6 **Salaushi** Russian Federation
55 C4 **Salavat** Russian Federation
128 C5 **Salaverry** Peru
133 E3 **Salavina** Argentina
71 C3 **Salawati** *isld* W Irian
71 G6 **Salay** Mindanao Philippines
135 Q11 **Sala y Gómez** *isld* Pacific Oc
Salazar *see* **N'dalatando**
21 P7 **Salbris** France
126 D3 **Sal, Cay** *isld* Bahamas
127 J5 **Salcedo** Dominican Rep
116 P4 **Salcha** *R* Alaska U.S.A.
116 O4 **Salchaket** Alaska U.S.A.
33 P8 **Salchau** Germany
37 O6 **Salching** Germany
46 G1 **Salcia** Romania
8 C7 **Salcombe** England
47 K7 **Salda Gölü** *L* Turkey
16 D2 **Saldaña** Spain
87 C12 **Saldanha** S Africa
41 N4 **Saldura, Pta** *mt* Italy
52 B6 **Saldus** Latvia
139 H7 **Sale** Victoria Australia
68 B2 **Sale** Burma
8 D1 **Sale** England
85 C2 **Salé** Morocco
70 G5 **Salea** Sulawesi
112 C6 **Sale City** Georgia U.S.A.
112 B2 **Sale Creek** Tennessee U.S.A.
77 A2 **Sālehābad** Iran
71 H9 **Saleh, Teluk** *B* Indonesia
147 N15 **Salekhard** Russian Federation
76 D5 **Salem** India
111 L9 **Salem** Alabama U.S.A.
110 E5 **Salem** Arkansas U.S.A.
113 D8 **Salem** Florida U.S.A.
110 H3 **Salem** Illinois U.S.A.
110 K3 **Salem** Indiana U.S.A.
95 R4 **Salem** Massachusetts U.S.A.
110 E4 **Salem** Missouri U.S.A.
95 Q4 **Salem** New Hampshire U.S.A.
95 M7 **Salem** New Jersey U.S.A.
106 C9 **Salem** New Mexico U.S.A.
95 O3 **Salem** New York U.S.A.
94 G6 **Salem** Ohio U.S.A.
100 B5 **Salem** Oregon U.S.A.
112 E3 **Salem** South Carolina U.S.A.
98 J6 **Salem** South Dakota U.S.A.
94 G9 **Salem** Virginia U.S.A.
99 S7 **Salem** Wisconsin U.S.A.
43 E11 **Salemi** Sicily
15 C4 **Salen** Scotland
27 F10 **Sälen** Sweden
142 E3 **Sale, R** W Australia Australia
19 Q17 **Salernes** France
43 F8 **Salerno** Italy
113 G10 **Salerno** Florida U.S.A.
43 F8 **Salerno, Golfo di** Italy
45 L1 **Saletto** Italy
21 P2 **Saleux** France
19 Q12 **Salève, Mt** France
13 F6 **Salford** England
130 H9 **Salgado** *R* Brazil
131 H2 **Salgado Filho** *airport* Brazil
48 F2 **Salgótarján** Hungary
130 G10 **Salgueiro** Brazil
80 E1 **Sâlhâni** Lebanon
79 C8 **Sâlhîya, El** Egypt
127 P2 **Salibea** Trinidad
106 D3 **Salida** Colorado U.S.A.
18 E9 **Salies de Béarn** France
18 F9 **Salies du Salat** France
47 J6 **Salihli** Turkey
87 F8 **Salima** Malawi
70 E3 **Salimbatu** Kalimantan
68 B2 **Salin** *R* Burma
68 B2 **Salin** Burma
107 N3 **Salina** Kansas U.S.A.
110 A5 **Salina** Oklahoma U.S.A.
103 N3 **Salina** Utah U.S.A.
125 M9 **Salina Cruz** Mexico
43 F10 **Salina, I** Italy
133 D4 **Salina La Antigua** *salt pan* Argentina
126 G3 **Salina Pt** Acklins I Bahamas
129 K7 **Salinas** Brazil
128 B4 **Salinas** Ecuador
128 C6 **Salinas** Peru
102 C5 **Salinas** *R* California U.S.A.
102 C5 **Salinas** California U.S.A.
133 D4 **Salinas Grandes** Argentina
106 D7 **Salinas Nat. Mon** New Mexico U.S.A.
108 A1 **Salinas Nat.Mon** New Mexico U.S.A.
131 C3 **Salinas, Pampa de la** Argentina
106 D8 **Salinas Pk** New Mexico U.S.A.
87 B8 **Salinas, Pte. das** Angola
12 E1 **Saline** Scotland
111 D8 **Saline** *R* Arkansas U.S.A.
110 H4 **Saline** *R* Illinois U.S.A.
107 L2 **Saline** *R* Kansas U.S.A.
94 D4 **Saline** Michigan U.S.A.
127 P2 **Saline B** Trinidad
109 P3 **Saline Bayou** *R* Louisiana U.S.A.
109 P4 **Saline L** Louisiana U.S.A.
127 P5 **Salines, Pt** Grenada
102 G5 **Saline V** California U.S.A.
94 G6 **Salineville** Ohio U.S.A.
68 B1 **Salingyi** Burma
133 C3 **Salinitas** Chile
129 J4 **Salinópolis** Brazil
Salisbury *see* **Harare** Zimbabwe
141 K2 **Salisbury** *dist* Brisbane, Qnsld Australia
138 E5 **Salisbury** South Australia Australia
122 G7 **Salisbury** New Brunswick Canada
9 E5 **Salisbury** England
95 O4 **Salisbury** Connecticut U.S.A.
95 M8 **Salisbury** Maryland U.S.A.
110 D2 **Salisbury** Missouri U.S.A.
112 G2 **Salisbury** North Carolina U.S.A.
94 H7 **Salisbury** Pennsylvania U.S.A.
95 O3 **Salisbury** Vermont U.S.A.
115 M5 **Salisbury I** Northwest Territories Canada
86 F5 **Salisbury, L** Uganda
116 O2 **Salisbury, Mt** Alaska U.S.A.
9 E5 **Salisbury Plain** England
48 H5 **Săliste** Romania
129 K6 **Salitre** *R* Brazil
80 G8 **Saliya** Jordan
45 K1 **Salizzole** Italy
112 F4 **Salkehatchie** *R* South Carolina U.S.A.
79 G6 **Şalkhad** Syria
28 D4 **Sall** Denmark
38 L7 **Salla** Austria
29 O5 **Salla** Finland
21 J7 **Salle-de-Vihiers, la** France
17 G2 **Sallent de G** Spain
19 N16 **Salles** France
18 G8 **Salles-Curan** France
112 F4 **Salley** South Carolina U.S.A.
33 T9 **Sallgast** Germany
28 B3 **Salling** *reg* Denmark
107 Q6 **Sallisaw** Oklahoma U.S.A.
86 G2 **Sallom** Sudan
78 K6 **Salman, As** Iraq
78 K2 **Salmās** Iran
17 F4 **Salmerón** Spain
29 N5 **Salmivaara** Finland
100 H1 **Salmo** British Columbia Canada
117 M8 **Salmon** *R* British Columbia Canada
116 Q3 **Salmon** Alaska U.S.A.
101 M4 **Salmon** Idaho U.S.A.
117 O10 **Salmon Arm** British Columbia Canada
123 P2 **Salmon Bay** Quebec Canada
101 L7 **Salmon Cr.Res** Idaho U.S.A.
142 F3 **Salmond R** W Australia Australia
101 L7 **Salmon Falls** Idaho U.S.A.
116 R4 **Salmon Fork** *R* Alaska U.S.A.
143 D10 **Salmon Gums** W Australia Australia
123 T6 **Salmonier** Newfoundland Canada
100 B8 **Salmon Mt** California U.S.A.
122 G7 **Salmon R** New Brunswick Canada
122 K4 **Salmon, R** Quebec Canada
95 M3 **Salmon Res** New York U.S.A.
100 K5 **Salmon River Mts** Idaho U.S.A.
36 G3 **Salmünster** Germany
52 E2 **Sal'nitsa** Russian Federation
42 D3 **Salò** Italy
52 G6 **Salobelyak** Russian Federation
130 C7 **Salobra, R** Brazil
29 L7 **Saloinen** Finland
99 L1 **Salol** Minnesota U.S.A.
103 L8 **Salome** Arizona U.S.A.
127 L4 **Salomon, C** Martinique W Indies
40 C2 **Salon** *R* France
19 O17 **Salon-de-Provence** France
86 D6 **Salonga, Parc Nacional de la** *nat park* Zaire
Salonica *see* **Thessaloníki**
48 G4 **Salonta** Romania
Salop *co see* **Shropshire**
17 H3 **Salou, C** Spain
29 M11 **Salpausselkä** *reg* Finland
53 F10 **Sal'sk** Russian Federation
43 F11 **Salso** *R* Sicily
44 G2 **Salsomaggiore Terme** Italy
80 F5 **Salt** Jordan
103 N8 **Salt** *R* Arizona U.S.A.
110 L3 **Salt** *R* Kentucky U.S.A.
110 E2 **Salt** *R* Missouri U.S.A.
133 D2 **Salta** Argentina
55 F3 **Saltaim, Oz** *L* Russian Federation
8 B7 **Saltash** England
28 G5 **Saltbæk Vig** *lagoon* Denmark
108 B4 **Salt Basin** Texas U.S.A.
13 H4 **Saltburn-by-the-Sea** England
119 P7 **Saltcoats** Saskatchewan Canada
12 D2 **Saltcoats** Scotland
99 R9 **Salt Cr** *R* Illinois U.S.A.
110 G1 **Salt Cr** Illinois U.S.A.
94 E7 **Salt Cr** Ohio U.S.A.
101 T6 **Salt Cr** Wyoming U.S.A.
138 E6 **Salt Creek** South Australia Australia
26 H4 **Saltdal** Norway
108 C4 **Salt Draw** *R* Texas U.S.A.
14 E4 **Saltee Is** Ireland
26 H5 **Saltelv** *R* Norway
26 G4 **Salten** *reg* Norway
28 D4 **Salten Langsø** *L* Denmark
26 G4 **Saltfjord** *inlet* Norway
108 B4 **Salt Flat** Texas U.S.A.
13 J6 **Saltfleet** England
107 M5 **Salt Fork** *R* Oklahoma U.S.A.
108 F2 **Salt Fork** *R* Texas U.S.A.
109 H4 **Salt Gap** Texas U.S.A.
29 K5 **Saltholm** *isld* Denmark
125 J5 **Saltillo** Mexico
94 J6 **Saltillo** Pennsylvania U.S.A.
110 H6 **Saltillo** Tennessee U.S.A.
106 G9 **Salt L** New Mexico U.S.A.
108 C4 **Salt L** Texas U.S.A.
101 O9 **Salt Lake City** Utah U.S.A.
94 D8 **Salt Lick** Kentucky U.S.A.
133 E4 **Salto** Argentina
130 F8 **Salto** Brazil
42 E6 **Salto** *R* Italy
131 F3 **Salto** *dept* Uruguay
131 F3 **Salto** Uruguay
130 D7 **Salto do Urubupungá** *falls* Brazil
131 F3 **Salto Grande, Embalse de** *res* Arg/Uruguay
45 O5 **Salto, L. del** Italy
26 K4 **Saltoluokta** Sweden
103 J8 **Salton Sea** California U.S.A.
Saltos do Iguaçu *see* **Cataratas del Iguazú** *waterfalls*
107 M5 **Salt Plains L** Oklahoma U.S.A.
127 L3 **Salt Ponds, The** Jamaica
74 E2 **Salt Range** Pakistan
127 K3 **Salt River** Jamaica
127 H5 **Saltrou** Haiti
101 P7 **Salt R. Ra** Wyoming U.S.A.
27 K12 **Saltsjöbaden** Sweden
27 L11 **Saltvik** Finland
94 F10 **Saltville** Virginia U.S.A.
102 F2 **Salt Wells** Nevada U.S.A.
112 E3 **Saluda** *R* South Carolina U.S.A.
112 F3 **Saluda** South Carolina U.S.A.
71 H5 **Salue** *isld* Indonesia
71 H5 **Salue Timpaus, Selat** *str* Indonesia
84 H3 **Salûm** Egypt
45 N4 **Saluoecio** Italy
71 F7 **Saluping** *isld* Philippines
76 F1 **Salur** India
110 C6 **Salus** Arkansas U.S.A.
129 H2 **Salut, I.du** Fr Guiana
44 B2 **Saluzzo** Italy
129 L6 **Salvador** Brazil
118 H6 **Salvador** Saskatchewan Canada
84 E5 **Salvador** Niger
111 F12 **Salvador, L** Louisiana U.S.A.
123 T5 **Salvage** Newfoundland Canada
16 B5 **Salvaterra de Magos** Portugal
125 J7 **Salvatierra** Mexico
103 N3 **Salvation Cr** Utah U.S.A.
141 H6 **Salvator, L** Queensland Australia
18 G8 **Salvetat, la** Aveyron France
18 G9 **Salvetat, la** Hérault France
117 J8 **Salvus** British Columbia Canada
68 C4 **Salween** *R* Burma/Thailand
75 K4 **Salyan** Nepal
94 D9 **Salyersville** Kentucky U.S.A.
55 F1 **Salym** Russian Federation
38 L6 **Salza** *R* Austria
32 F8 **Salzbergen** Germany
38 H6 **Salzburg** Austria
38 H7 **Salzburg** *prov* Austria
32 L9 **Salzderhelden** Germany
33 M8 **Salzgitter** Germany
33 M8 **Salzgitter-Bad** Germany
38 J6 **Salzkammer-gut** *res* Austria
32 J9 **Salzkotten** Germany
33 P9 **Salzmünde** Germany
33 O7 **Salzwedel** Germany
101 O6 **Sam** Idaho U.S.A.
80 G3 **Sama** Jordan
80 G4 **Samad** Jordan
71 J5 **Samada** *isld* Indonesia
16 D1 **Sama de Langreo** Spain
56 E5 **Samagaltay** Russian Federation
84 F4 **Samāh** Libya
80 F2 **Samak** Syria
71 G7 **Samal** *isld* Mindanao Philippines
69 C10 **Samalanga** Sumatra
69 J12 **Samalantan** Indonesia
108 A4 **Samalayuca** Mexico
71 E7 **Samales Group** *islds* Philippines
76 F2 **Samalkot** India
84 J4 **Samâlût** Egypt
127 K5 **Samaná** Dominican Rep
126 H3 **Samana Cay** *isld* Bahamas
78 E3 **Samandağı** Turkey
47 N11 **Samandira** Turkey
60 Q3 **Samani** Japan
70 N10 **Samanu** Java
121 S3 **Samaqua** *R* Quebec Canada
80 G3 **Samar** Jordan
71 G5 **Samar** *isld* Philippines
53 H7 **Samara** Russian Federation
53 H7 **Samara** *R* Russian Federation
136 L4 **Samarai** Papua New Guinea
80 D4 **Samaria** Jordan
101 N7 **Samaria** Idaho U.S.A.
46 E4 **Samarina** Greece
70 E5 **Samarinda** Kalimantan
57 D5 **Samarkand** Uzbekistan
78 J4 **Sāmarrā'** Iraq
71 G5 **Samar Sea** Philippines
53 G7 **Samarskaya Oblast'** Russian Federation
71 C3 **Samate** W Irian
78 K6 **Samāwah, Aq** Iraq
70 C5 **Samba** *R* Kalimantan
86 D5 **Samba** Equateur Zaire
86 E6 **Samba** Kasai Oriental Zaire
87 C7 **Samba Caju** Angola
71 A3 **Sambaki, Selat** Indonesia
70 F4 **Sambaliung** *mts* Kalimantan
75 L8 **Sambalpur** India
70 G7 **Sambapolulu, G** *mt* Sulawesi
87 J10 **Sambava** Madagascar
25 E5 **Sambeek** Netherlands
74 H4 **Sambhal** India
71 H5 **Sambiat** Sulawesi
21 N7 **Sambin** France
70 F4 **Sambit** *isld* Kalimantan
129 K5 **Sambito** *R* Brazil
70 F6 **Sambo** Sulawesi
70 E5 **Sambodja** Kalimantan
68 H6 **Sambor** Cambodia
48 H1 **Sambor** Ukraine
131 G6 **Samborombón, B** Argentina
22 H3 **Sambre** *R* Belgium
69 F12 **Sambu** Indonesia
70 D5 **Sambuah** Kalimantan
45 J3 **Sambuca Pistojese** Italy
59 J4 **Samchŏk** S Korea
68 D6 **Same** Burma
88 F4 **Same** Tanzania
22 B2 **Samer** France
68 E6 **Samet, Ko** *isld* Thailand
87 E8 **Samfya** Zambia
68 A2 **Sami** Burma
46 D6 **Sámi** Greece
71 H4 **Samia, Tg** *C* Sulawesi Indonesia
128 D5 **Samiria** *R* Peru
85 E5 **Samit** Mali
68 C2 **Samka** Burma
29 K11 **Sammatti** Finland
80 F3 **Sammu'** Jordan
68 F5 **Samnak Kado** Thailand
41 M3 **Samnaun Gruppe** *mt* Austria
80 E6 **Samniya Auja** *R* Jordan
84 F4 **Samnū** Libya
100 A9 **Samoa** California U.S.A.
Samoa i Sisifo *islds see* **Western Samoa**
42 G3 **Samobor** Croatia
52 F3 **Samoded** Russian Federation
40 E5 **Samoëns** France
46 F2 **Samokov** Bulgaria
68 C2 **Samon** *R* Burma
47 H7 **Sámos** *isld* Greece
Samothrace *see* **Samothráki**
46 D5 **Samothráki** *isld* Ionian Is Greece
47 H4 **Samothráki** *isld* Anatolikí Makedhonía Kaí Thráki Greece
133 E4 **Sampacho** Argentina
70 F6 **Sampaga** Sulawesi
71 E3 **Sampaloc Pt** Luzon Philippines
70 O9 **Sampang** Indonesia
17 G3 **Samper de Calanda** Spain
113 L12 **Samphire Cay** *isld* Bahamas
70 C6 **Sampit** Kalimantan
70 C6 **Sampit, Teluk** *B* Kalimantan
87 E7 **Sampwe** Zaire
80 F8 **Samra** Jordan
109 N4 **Sam Rayburn L** Texas U.S.A.
111 B10 **Sam Rayburn Res** Texas U.S.A.
22 K3 **Samrée** Belgium
68 F6 **Samrong** *R* Cambodia
28 F5 **Samsø** *isld* Denmark
111 K10 **Samson** Alabama U.S.A.
68 G3 **Sam Son** Vietnam
78 F1 **Samsun** Turkey
67 A6 **Sam Teu** Laos
140 C4 **Samuel, Mt** N Terr Australia
47 H1 **Samuil** Bulgaria
56 B3 **Samus'** Russian Federation
68 E6 **Samut Prakan** Thailand
68 E6 **Samut Sakhon** Thailand
68 E6 **Samut Songkhram** Thailand
71 J5 **Samuya** Indonesia
85 D6 **San** Mali
31 N6 **San** *R* Poland
42 H4 **Sana** *R* Bosnia-Herzegovina
72 E5 **Şan'ā'** Yemen
106 D7 **San Acacia** New Mexico U.S.A.
146 H6 **Sanae** *S Africa Base* Antarctica
86 B5 **Sanaga** *R* Cameroon
106 D10 **San Agustin** Mexico
71 G7 **San Agustin, C** Mindanao Philippines
133 D4 **San Agustín de Valle Fértil** Argentina
106 B8 **San Agustin, Plains of** *high plain* New Mexico U.S.A.
116 F9 **Sanak I** Aleutian Is
45 M2 **San Alberto** Italy
79 G5 **Şanamayn, Aş** Syria
135 S12 **San Ambrosio** *isld* Pacific Oc
102 D3 **San Andreas** California U.S.A.
125 P9 **San Andrés** Guatemala
106 D9 **San Andres Mts** New Mexico U.S.A.
125 M8 **San Andrés Tuxtla** Mexico
41 K7 **San Angelo** Italy
108 G4 **San Angelo** Texas U.S.A.
126 C3 **San Anton de los Baños** Cuba
125 P9 **San Antonio** Belize
131 B4 **San Antonio** Chile
125 L2 **San Antonio** Honduras
124 E6 **San Antonio** Mexico
71 E2 **San Antonio** Luzon Philippines
113 E9 **San Antonio** Florida U.S.A.
106 D8 **San Antonio** New Mexico U.S.A.
109 J6 **San Antonio** Texas U.S.A.
109 K7 **San Antonio** *R* Texas U.S.A.
128 E3 **San Antonio** Venezuela
17 H6 **San Antonio Abad** Ibiza
71 C6 **San Antonio B** Palawan Philippines
109 L7 **San Antonio B** Texas U.S.A.
133 F5 **San Antonio, C** Argentina
126 B4 **San Antonio, C** Cuba
17 H6 **San Antonio, C** Spain
133 D2 **San Antonio de los Cobres** Argentina
124 E3 **San Antonio del Rio** Mexico
127 N9 **San Antonio de Maturín** Venezuela
127 L10 **San Antonio de Tamanaco** Venezuela
102 G7 **San Antonio, Mt** California U.S.A.
108 B4 **San Antonio Mt** Texas U.S.A.
133 E6 **San Antonio Oeste** Argentina
130 J9 **San Antonio, Pta. de** *C* Brazil
128 E2 **Sanariapo** Venezuela
19 P18 **Sanary** France
111 B10 **San Augustine** Texas U.S.A.
74 G7 **Sanawad** India
16 B7 **San Bartolómeu de Messines** Portugal
45 R7 **San Bartolomew in Galdo** Italy
42 F6 **San Benedetto del Tronto** Italy
45 J1 **San Benedetto Po** Italy
125 P9 **San Benito** Guatemala
102 C5 **San Benito** *R* California U.S.A.
109 K9 **San Benito** Texas U.S.A.
102 D5 **San Benito Mt** California U.S.A.
71 G4 **San Bernadino Str** Philippines
109 M6 **San Bernard** *R* Texas U.S.A.
130 B9 **San Bernardino** Paraguay
102 G7 **San Bernardino** California U.S.A.
103 J8 **San Bernardino Mts** California U.S.A.
41 K5 **San Bernardino P** Switzerland
131 B4 **San Bernardo** Chile
124 G4 **San Bernardo** Mexico
128 C2 **San Bernardo, I.de** Colombia
60 F10 **Sanbe-san** *mt* Japan
45 L2 **San Biagio** Italy
124 G7 **San Blas** Nayarit Mexico
124 E4 **San Blas** Sonora Mexico
113 B7 **San Blas** Florida U.S.A.
125 P5 **San Blas, Archipélago de** *islds* Panama
113 B8 **San Blas, C** Florida U.S.A.
125 P5 **San Blas, Serrania de** *mts* Panama
41 O7 **San Bonifacio** Italy
128 E6 **San Borja** Bolivia
124 C3 **San Borja** Mexico
99 L6 **Sanborn** Iowa U.S.A.
99 L5 **Sanborn** Minnesota U.S.A.
98 H3 **Sanborn** North Dakota U.S.A.
95 Q3 **Sanbornville** New Hampshire U.S.A.
124 J4 **San Buenaventura** Mexico
68 E5 **San Buri** Thailand
128 F8 **San Camilo** Argentina
133 D4 **San Carlos** Argentina
131 B6 **San Carlos** Chile
124 C4 **San Carlos** Baja Cal Sur Mexico
124 H5 **San Carlos** Coahuila Mexico
71 E3 **San Carlos** Luzon Philippines
71 F5 **San Carlos** Negros Philippines
133 G4 **San Carlos** Uruguay
103 O8 **San Carlos** Arizona U.S.A.
127 K10 **San Carlos** Venezuela
131 B8 **San Carlos de Bariloche** Argentina
17 H4 **San Carlos de la Rápita** Spain
128 D2 **San Carlos del Zulia** Venezuela
128 E3 **San Carlos de Rio Negro** Venezuela
124 B3 **San Carlos, Mesa de** *mt* Mexico
103 O8 **San Carlos Res** Arizona U.S.A.
45 K4 **San Casciano in Valdi Pesa** Italy
17 J3 **San Celoni** Spain
18 G5 **Sancergues** France
18 G5 **Sancerre** France
45 K2 **San Cesario sul Panaro** Italy
21 O5 **Sancheville** France
127 K5 **Sánchez** Dominican Rep
106 E4 **Sanchez Res** Colorado U.S.A.
52 G6 **Sanchursk** Russian Federation
125 K7 **San Ciro de Acosta** Mexico
17 F5 **San Clemente** Spain
102 G8 **San Clemente** California U.S.A.
102 F9 **San Clemente** *isld* California U.S.A.
18 G6 **Sancoins** France
71 G6 **Sanco Pt** Mindanao Philippines
130 B10 **San Cosme** Argentina
133 F3 **San Cosme** Paraguay
45 O4 **San Costanzo** Italy
131 E3 **San Cristóbal** Argentina
127 J5 **San Cristóbal** Dominican Rep
128 B8 **San Cristóbal** *isld* Galapagos Is
137 N4 **San Cristobal** Solomon Is
128 D2 **San Cristóbal** Venezuela
125 N9 **San Cristóbal de las Casas** Mexico
103 L9 **San Cristobal Wash** *R* Arizona U.S.A.
45 J4 **San Croce sulee Arno** Italy
133 C4 **San Cruz** Chile
126 E4 **Sancti Spiritus** Cuba
118 J7 **Sanctuary** Saskatchewan Canada
22 K5 **Sancy** France
27 B12 **Sand** Norway
89 E7 **Sand** *R* Orange Free State S Africa
89 F4 **Sand** *R* Transvaal S Africa
60 J11 **Sanda** Japan
15 C5 **Sanda** *isld* Scotland
28 D6 **Sandager** Denmark
70 F2 **Sandakan** Sabah
70 F2 **Sandakan, Pelabuhan** *hbr* Sabah
68 H6 **Sandan** Cambodia
26 B10 **Sandane** Norway
46 F3 **Sandanski** Bulgaria
65 H2 **Sandaotong** China
65 G1 **Sandaozhen** China
85 B6 **Sandare** Mali
27 J10 **Sandarne** Sweden
106 H4 **Sand Arroyo** *R* Colo/Kansas U.S.A.
33 Q7 **Sandau** Germany
15 F1 **Sanday** Scotland
8 D5 **Sand B** England
8 D1 **Sandbach** England
37 P6 **Sandbach** Germany
27 G15 **Sandbäck** Sweden
12 D2 **Sandbank** Scotland
120 H1 **Sandbank L** Ontario Canada
89 E4 **Sandbult** S Africa
28 G7 **Sandby** Denmark
26 F7 **Sanddöla** *R* Norway
32 H5 **Sande** Germany
26 A9 **Sande** Norway
27 A10 **Sande** Norway
27 D12 **Sandefj** Norway
146 J10 **Sandercock Nunataks** *mt peaks* Antarctica
103 P6 **Sanders** Arizona U.S.A.
100 J2 **Sanders** Idaho U.S.A.
37 M6 **Sandersdorf** Germany
33 P9 **Sandersleben** Germany
113 E7 **Sanderson** Florida U.S.A.
108 E5 **Sanderson** Texas U.S.A.
112 E5 **Sandersville** Georgia U.S.A.
111 H10 **Sandersville** Mississippi U.S.A.
33 M5 **Sandesneben** Germany
28 B5 **Sandet** Denmark
142 D4 **Sandfire Flat Roadhouse** W Australia Australia
118 L3 **Sandfly L** Saskatchewan Canada
94 G8 **Sand Fork** West Virginia U.S.A.
141 L7 **Sandgate** Queensland Australia
9 H5 **Sandgate** England
36 F5 **Sandhausen** Germany
12 D4 **Sandhead** Scotland
26 G4 **Sandhornöy** *isld* Norway
9 F5 **Sandhurst** England
99 Q3 **Sand I** Wisconsin U.S.A.
109 K7 **Sandia** Texas U.S.A.
106 D6 **Sandia Pk** New Mexico U.S.A.
124 G3 **San Diego** Mexico
102 G9 **San Diego** California U.S.A.
109 J8 **San Diego** Texas U.S.A.
102 G8 **San Diego Aqueduct** California U.S.A.
133 D8 **San Diego, C** Argentina
128 F2 **San Diego de Cabrutica** Venezuela
47 L6 **Sandıklı** Turkey
74 J5 **Sandila** India
118 E1 **Sandilands** Manitoba Canada
113 M9 **Sandilands Village** New Providence I Bahamas
21 P6 **Sandillon** France
143 B6 **Sandiman, Mt** W Australia Australia
124 G5 **San Dimas** Mexico
69 E14 **Sanding** *isld* Indonesia
116 D5 **Sand Is** Alaska U.S.A.
52 J2 **Sandivey** *R* Russian Federation
32 H6 **Sandkrug** Germany
38 L4 **Sandl** Austria
120 F5 **Sand Lake** Ontario Canada
110 K7 **Sand Mountain** Alabama U.S.A.
27 C13 **Sandnes** Aust Agder Norway
27 A13 **Sandnes** Rogaland Norway
15 G2 **Sandness** Scotland
26 F5 **Sandnessjöen** Norway
Sandø *see* **Sandoy**
87 D7 **Sandoa** Zaire
31 N5 **Sandomierz** Poland
45 P6 **San Donato Val di Comino** Italy
110 G3 **Sandoval** Illinois U.S.A.
106 D6 **Sandoval** New Mexico U.S.A.
140 D5 **Sandover** *R* N Terr Australia
52 E5 **Sandovo** Russian Federation
68 B3 **Sandoway** Burma
9 E6 **Sandown** England
89 A10 **Sandown B** S Africa
6 F1 **Sandoy** *isld* Faeroes
116 G9 **Sand Point** Alaska U.S.A.
117 P11 **Sandpoint** Idaho U.S.A.
118 F4 **Sand R** Alberta Canada
47 K7 **Sandras Daği** *mt* Turkey
140 E6 **Sandringham** Queensland Australia
9 G2 **Sandringham** England
99 T3 **Sands** Michigan U.S.A.
27 G14 **Sandsjö, N** Sweden
113 G12 **Sands Key** *isld* Florida U.S.A.
117 H9 **Sandspit** British Columbia Canada
38 G8 **Sandspitze** *mt* Austria
101 S2 **Sand Springs** Montana U.S.A.
107 O5 **Sand Springs** Oklahoma U.S.A.
102 F2 **Sand Springs Salt Flat** Nevada U.S.A.
26 D8 **Sandstad** Norway
32 J6 **Sandstedt** Germany
95 K9 **Sandston** Virginia U.S.A.
143 C8 **Sandstone** W Australia Australia
99 O3 **Sandstone** Minnesota U.S.A.
103 M9 **Sand Tanks Mts** Arizona U.S.A.
123 L4 **Sandtop, C** Anticosti I, Quebec
67 B3 **Sandu** China
67 B4 **Sandu** Guizhou China
67 E2 **Sandu** Jiangxi China
94 E3 **Sandusky** Michigan U.S.A.
94 D5 **Sandusky** *R* Ohio U.S.A.
94 E5 **Sandusky** Ohio U.S.A.
28 H6 **Sandved** Denmark
87 C11 **Sandverhaar** Namibia
27 G16 **Sandvig** Denmark
27 D12 **Sandvika** Norway
27 J11 **Sandviken** Sweden
9 H5 **Sandwich** England
99 S8 **Sandwich** Illinois U.S.A.
95 R5 **Sandwich** Massachusetts U.S.A.
115 O7 **Sandwich B** Labrador, Nfld Canada
141 H4 **Sandwich, C** Queensland Australia
15 G2 **Sandwick** Scotland
118 J5 **Sandwith** Saskatchewan Canada
95 R2 **Sandy** *R* Maine U.S.A.
103 J6 **Sandy** Nevada U.S.A.
100 C4 **Sandy** Oregon U.S.A.
103 N1 **Sandy** Utah U.S.A.
119 P3 **Sandy Bay** Saskatchewan Canada
127 H1 **Sandy Bay** Jamaica
118 K1 **Sandybeach L** Ontario Canada
141 L6 **Sandy C** Queensland Australia
139 G8 **Sandy C** Tasmania Australia
101 O9 **Sandy City** Utah U.S.A.
109 L6 **Sandy Cr** Texas U.S.A.
101 Q7 **Sandy Cr** Wyoming U.S.A.
121 O7 **Sandy Creek** Quebec Canada
95 L3 **Sandy Creek** New York U.S.A.
95 O5 **Sandy Hook** Connecticut U.S.A.
94 D8 **Sandy Hook** Kentucky U.S.A.
111 G10 **Sandy Hook** Mississippi U.S.A.
95 N6 **Sandy Hook** *pt* New Jersey U.S.A.
57 C6 **Sandykachi** Turkmenistan
123 Q4 **Sandy L** Newfoundland Canada
115 K7 **Sandy L** Ontario Canada
119 R8 **Sandy Lake** Manitoba Canada
119 O3 **Sandy Narrows** Saskatchewan Canada
112 L2 **Sandy Pt** North Carolina U.S.A.
127 P4 **Sandy Pt** St Kitts W Indies
126 G9 **San Estanislao** Colombia
129 G8 **San Estanislao** Paraguay
71 E2 **San Fabian** Luzon Philippines
45 O7 **San Felice Circeo** Italy
45 K2 **San Felice sul Panaro** Italy
131 B4 **San Felipe** Chile
128 E3 **San Felipe** Colombia
124 B2 **San Felipe** Baja California Mexico
124 F4 **San Felipe** Chihuahua Mexico
127 K9 **San Felipe** Venezuela
126 C4 **San Felipe, Cayos de** *islds* Cuba
17 F4 **San Felipe, Cerro de** *pk* Spain
103 H8 **San Felipe Cr** California U.S.A.
106 D6 **San Felipe Pueblo** New Mexico U.S.A.
17 K3 **San Feliú de Guixols** Spain
17 J3 **San Feliu de Llobregat** Spain
135 S12 **San Félix** *isld* Pacific Oc
131 B5 **San Fernando** Chile
124 B3 **San Fernando** Mexico
71 E2 **San Fernando** Luzon Philippines
16 C8 **San Fernando** Spain
127 O3 **San Fernando** Trinidad
102 F7 **San Fernando** California U.S.A.
128 E2 **San Fernando de Apure** Venezuela
128 E3 **San Fernando de Atabape** Venezuela
26 G9 **Sånfjället** *mt* Sweden
118 D1 **Sanford** Manitoba Canada
106 E4 **Sanford** Colorado U.S.A.
113 F9 **Sanford** Florida U.S.A.
95 R3 **Sanford** Maine U.S.A.
112 H2 **Sanford** North Carolina U.S.A.
108 C8 **Sanford** Texas U.S.A.
94 C3 **Sanford L** Michigan U.S.A.
116 Q5 **Sanford, Mt** Alaska U.S.A.
143 B7 **Sanford, R** W Australia Australia
127 N3 **San Francique** Trinidad
131 E3 **San Francisco** Argentina
106 B8 **San Francisco** *R* Ariz/New Mex U.S.A.
104 **San Francisco** *conurbation* California U.S.A.
127 J9 **San Francisco** Venezuela
102 B4 **San Francisco Bay** California U.S.A.
108 E6 **San Francisco Cr** Texas U.S.A.
124 G4 **San Francisco de Conchos** Mexico
133 E3 **San Francisco del Chanar** Argentina
133 D4 **San Francisco del Monte de Oro** Argentina
124 G4 **San Francisco del Oro** Mexico
124 H7 **San Francisco del Rincón** Mexico
127 J5 **San Francisco de Macoris** Dominican Rep
133 D7 **San Francisco de Paula, C** Argentina
133 G4 **San Gabriel** Brazil
102 G7 **San Gabriel Mts** California U.S.A.
124 C3 **San Gabriel, Pta** *C* Mexico
69 G14 **Sangaigerong** Sumatra
76 B1 **Sangammer** India
74 F9 **Sangamner** India
99 R10 **Sangamon** *R* Illinois U.S.A.
77 J3 **Sangan, Koh-i** *mt* Afghanistan
51 M2 **Sangar** Russian Federation
76 D2 **Sangāreddi** India
70 E5 **Sangasanga** Kalimantan
70 F2 **Sanga Sanga** *isld* Philippines
85 C6 **Sangasso** Mali
22 B2 **Sangatte** France
43 B9 **San Gavino Monreale** Sardinia
128 C4 **Sangay** *vol* Ecuador
71 E7 **Sangboy Island** Philippines
71 J9 **Sangeang** *isld* Indonesia
102 E5 **Sanger** California U.S.A.
98 E2 **Sanger** North Dakota U.S.A.
109 K2 **Sanger** Texas U.S.A.
33 O10 **Sangerhausen** Germany
127 L5 **San Germán** Puerto Rico
65 C4 **Sanggan He** *R* China
71 J9 **Sanggar** Sumbawa Indonesia
71 J9 **Sanggar, Teluk** *B* Indonesia
70 B4 **Sanggau** Kalimantan
69 J12 **Sanggauledo** Indonesia
65 E6 **Sanggou Wan** *B* China
86 C5 **Sangha** *R* Congo
74 C5 **Sānghār** Pakistan
56 B1 **Sangil'ka** *R* Russian Federation
45 R7 **San Giorgio del Sannio** Italy
45 J1 **San Giórgio di Mántova** Italy
42 E3 **San Giorgio di N** Italy
45 K2 **San Giorgio di Piano** Italy
45 R7 **San Giorgio la Molara** Italy
38 E8 **San Giovanni** Italy
45 Q8 **San Giovanni a Teducio** Italy
45 J1 **San Giovanni in Croce** Italy
45 K2 **San Giovanni in Persiceto** Italy
45 K1 **San Giovanni Lupatoto** Italy
43 G10 **San Giovanni, V** Italy
45 L4 **San Giovanni Valdarno** Italy
71 E3 **Sangitan** Luzon Philippines
45 M1 **San Giuliano** Italy
45 H4 **San Giuliano Terme** Italy
45 R8 **San Giuseppe Vesuviano** Italy
45 M4 **San Giustino** Italy
65 G6 **Sangju** S Korea
70 F7 **Sangkarang, Kep** *isld* Sulawesi
68 D5 **Sangkhla Buri** Thailand
70 E4 **Sangkulirang** Kalimantan
70 F4 **Sangkulirang, Teluk** *B* Kalimantan
74 E3 **Sangla** Pakistan
76 B2 **Sangli** India
86 B5 **Sangmélima** Cameroon
89 G4 **Sango** Zimbabwe
45 L4 **San Godenzo** Italy
17 G7 **Sangonera** *R* Spain
102 H7 **San Gorgonio Mt** California U.S.A.
71 B1 **Sangowo** Halmahera Indonesia
106 E5 **Sangre de Cristo Mts** New Mex/Colo U.S.A.
102 B4 **San Gregorio** California U.S.A.
127 P2 **Sangre Grande** Trinidad
42 F6 **Sangro** *R* Italy
74 F3 **Sangrur** India
88 E5 **Sangu** Tanzania
118 C5 **Sangudo** Alberta Canada
129 G6 **Sangue** *R* Brazil
18 E10 **Sangüesa** Spain
41 O7 **Sanguinetto** Italy
Sangyuan *see* **Wuqiao**
67 C2 **Sangzhi** China
Sanhe *see* **Sandu** Guizhou
59 H1 **Sanhe** China
65 D4 **Sanhe** China
67 D1 **Sanhedian** China
59 J1 **Sanhezhan** China
124 D5 **San Hilario** Mexico
59 H1 **San-ho** China
67 D1 **San Hu** *L* China
67 B1 **Sanhuizhen** China
113 E11 **Sanibel I** Florida U.S.A.
130 C10 **San Ignacio** Argentina
128 E6 **San Ignacio** Beni Bolivia
128 F7 **San Ignacio** Santa Cruz Bolivia
124 D2 **San Ignacio** Mexico
124 C4 **San Ignacio, Laguna** Mexico
16 E4 **San Ildefonso** Spain
106 D6 **San Ildefonso** New Mexico U.S.A.
71 F2 **San Ildefonso, C** Luzon Philippines
79 H3 **Saniman, Wādī** *watercourse* Syria
60 H10 **San'in** Japan
106 E4 **San Isabel** Colorado U.S.A.
133 F4 **San Isidro** Argentina
124 H5 **San Isidro** Mexico
71 G5 **San Isidro** Leyte Philippines
33 Q4 **Sanitz** Germany
126 G10 **San Jacinto** Colombia
71 F4 **San Jacinto** Philippines
101 L8 **San Jacinto** Nevada U.S.A.
102 H8 **San Jacinto Mts** California U.S.A.
133 F4 **San Javier** Argentina
124 F4 **San Javier** Mexico
131 F2 **San Javier, R** Argentina
125 J9 **San Jerónimo** Mexico
Sanjiang *see* **Liannan** Guangdong
67 C4 **Sanjiang** China
65 F3 **Sanjiangkou** China
65 F3 **Sanjiazi** China
61 M8 **Sanjō** Japan
128 F6 **San Joaquin** Bolivia
130 C9 **San Joaquin** Paraguay
102 D4 **San Joaquin** *R* California U.S.A.
102 D5 **San Joaquin** California U.S.A.
102 D5 **San Joaquin Valley** California U.S.A.
108 A8 **San Jon** New Mexico U.S.A.
128 C2 **San Jorge** *R* Colombia
133 D7 **San Jorge, G** Argentina
17 H4 **San Jorge, G.de** Spain
131 B4 **San Jose** *vol* Chile
125 M5 **San José** Costa Rica
124 D5 **San José** *isld* Mexico
71 E4 **San Jose** Philippines
131 G5 **San José** *dept* Uruguay
131 G5 **San José** Uruguay
102 C4 **San Jose** California U.S.A.
99 R9 **San Jose** Illinois U.S.A.
106 E6 **San Jose** New Mexico U.S.A.
131 F3 **San José, Cuchilla de** *mts* Uruguay
128 F2 **San José de Amacuro** Venezuela
128 F7 **San José de Chiquitos** Bolivia
124 D3 **San José de Dimas** Mexico
133 F4 **San José de Feliciano** Argentina
124 F4 **San José de Gracia** Sinaloa Mexico
127 M10 **San José de Guaribe** Venezuela
127 J5 **San José de las Matas** Dominican Rep
124 E6 **San José del Cabo** Mexico
128 D3 **San José del Gauviare** Colombia
127 J5 **San José de Ocoa** Dominican Rep
128 D3 **San José de Ocuné** Colombia
106 C6 **San Jose, R** New Mexico U.S.A.
131 B3 **San Juan** *prov* Argentina
131 C3 **San Juan** Argentina
128 F7 **San Juan** Bolivia
128 C3 **San Juan** *R* Colombia
125 M4 **San Juan** *R* Costa Rica
126 D4 **San Juan** *mt* Cuba
127 J5 **San Juan** Dominican Rep
124 F4 **San Juan** Chihuahua Mexico
124 J4 **San Juan** Coahuila Mexico
128 D7 **San Juan** Peru
71 G6 **San Juan** Mindanao Philippines
127 L5 **San Juan** Puerto Rico
102 D6 **San Juan** *R* California U.S.A.
109 J9 **San Juan** Texas U.S.A.
103 P4 **San Juan** *R* Utah U.S.A.
128 E2 **San Juan** Venezuela
102 C5 **San Juan Bautista** California U.S.A.
128 C7 **San Juan, B. de** *B* Peru
133 E8 **San Juan, C** Argentina
102 G8 **San Juan Capistrano** California U.S.A.
124 H5 **San Juan de Guadalupe** Mexico
18 G10 **San Juan de las Abadesas** Spain
124 H8 **San Juan de Lima, Pta** *C* Mexico
125 N4 **San Juan del Norte** Nicaragua
127 K9 **San Juan de los Cayos** Venezuela
124 H7 **San Juan de los Lagos** Mexico
127 L10 **San Juan de los Morros** Venezuela
125 J7 **San Juan del Río** Mexico
100 C1 **San Juan Is** Washington U.S.A.
124 F7 **San Juanito, I** Mexico
106 C4 **San Juan Mts** Colo/New Mex U.S.A.
125 L9 **San Juan Quiotepec** Mexico
131 C3 **San Juan, R** Argentina
126 C3 **San Juan y Martinez** Cuba
133 D7 **San Julián** Argentina
133 E4 **San Justo** Argentina
17 G4 **San Just, Sa. de** *mts* Spain
85 C6 **Sankarani** *R* Guinea/Mali
76 C6 **Sankarankovil** India
76 B2 **Sankeshwar** India
88 E10 **Sankhulani** Malawi
49 **Sankt-Peterburg** *conurbation* Russian Federation
86 D6 **Sankuru** *R* Zaire
45 H2 **San Lazzaro** Italy
102 B4 **San Leandro** California U.S.A.
45 M4 **San Leo** Italy
124 C3 **San Lino, Sa** *mt* Mexico
78 G3 **Şanlıurfa** Turkey
133 E4 **San Lorenzo** Argentina
128 E6 **San Lorenzo** Bolivia
133 C7 **San Lorenzo** *mt* Chile/Arg
128 C3 **San Lorenzo** Ecuador
125 P9 **San Lorenzo** Guatemala
124 C3 **San Lorenzo** *isld* Mexico
124 F3 **San Lorenzo** Mexico
128 E6 **San Lorenzo** Peru
106 C9 **San Lorenzo** New Mexico U.S.A.
127 J10 **San Lorenzo** Venezuela
44 C4 **San Lorenzo al Mare** Italy
128 B4 **San Lorenzo, C** Ecuador
16 E4 **San Lorenzo de El Escorial** Spain
17 F5 **San Lorenzo de la Parrilla** Spain
17 J2 **San Lorenzo de Morunys** Spain
128 C6 **San Lorenzo, I** Peru
45 N4 **San Lorenzo in Campo** Italy
16 C8 **Sanlúcar de Barrameda** Spain
16 C7 **Sanlúcar la Mayor** Spain
128 E8 **San Lucas** Bolivia
124 E6 **San Lucas** Mexico
102 C5 **San Lucas** California U.S.A.
131 C4 **San Luis** *prov* Argentina
131 C4 **San Luis** Argentina
126 G4 **San Luis** Cuba
125 P9 **San Luís** Guatemala
125 J9 **San Luis** Mexico
124 F4 **San Luis** Chihuahua Mexico
124 D3 **San Luis** Sonora Mexico
71 E2 **San Luis** Luzon Philippines
103 K9 **San Luis** Arizona U.S.A.
106 E4 **San Luis** Colorado U.S.A.
127 K9 **San Luis** Venezuela
124 E4 **San Luis Babarocos** Mexico
125 J7 **San Luis de la Paz** Mexico
128 F6 **San Luis, L** Bolivia
103 K9 **San Luis, Mesa de** Mexico

102 D6 **San Luis Obispo** California U.S.A.
109 M6 **San Luis Pass** Texas U.S.A.
106 D3 **San Luis Pk** Colorado U.S.A.
125 J6 **San Luis Potosí** Mexico
102 G8 **San Luis Rey** *R* California U.S.A.
124 B1 **San Luis Río Colorado** Mexico
131 C4 **San Luis, Sa. de** *mts* Argentina
71 E3 **San Marcelino** Luzon Philippines
124 D3 **San Marcial** Mexico
106 C8 **San Marcial** New Mexico U.S.A.
124 D5 **San Marcial, Pta** *C* Mexico
43 B9 **San Marco, C** Sardinia
126 G10 **San Marcos** Colombia
124 C4 **San Marcos** *isld* Mexico
124 G7 **San Marcos** Mexico
109 K6 **San Marcos** Texas U.S.A.
42 E5 **San Marino** *rep* S Europe
128 F6 **San Martín** *R* Bolivia
128 D3 **San Martín** Colombia
128 C5 **San Martín** *dept* Peru
133 C6 **San Martín de los Andes** Argentina
133 C7 **San Martín, L** Chile/Arg
45 L2 **San Martino in Argine** Italy
38 E8 **San Martino in Badia** Italy
45 J2 **San Martino in Rio** Italy
45 K2 **San Martino in Spino** Italy
125 M5 **San Mateo** Costa Rica
17 H4 **San Mateo** Spain
102 B4 **San Mateo** California U.S.A.
106 C6 **San Mateo** New Mexico U.S.A.
127 M10 **San Mateo** Venezuela
106 C8 **San Mateo Pk** New Mexico U.S.A.
128 G7 **San Matías** Bolivia
131 D8 **San Matías, G** Argentina
121 R5 **Sanmaur** Quebec Canada
127 L10 **San Mauricio** Venezuela
44 C1 **San Mauro Torinese** Italy
67 G2 **Sanmen** China
67 G2 **Sanmen Wan** *B* China
65 B7 **Sanmenxia** China
45 K1 **San Michele Extra** Italy
128 F7 **San Miguel** Bolivia
128 C3 **San Miguel** *R* Ecuador
125 O11 **San Miguel** Honduras
124 D3 **San Miguel** *R* Mexico
124 J5 **San Miguel** Mexico
128 D6 **San Miguel** Peru
71 D6 **San Miguel** *islds* Philippines
103 N10 **San Miguel** Arizona U.S.A.
102 D6 **San Miguel** California U.S.A.
106 B3 **San Miguel** *R* Colorado U.S.A.
71 F4 **San Miguel B** Philippines
109 J9 **San Miguel Camargo** Mexico
109 J7 **San Miguel Cr** Texas U.S.A.
125 J7 **San Miguel de Allende** Mexico
128 E7 **San Miguel de Huachi** Bolivia
133 D3 **San Miguel de Tucumán** Argentina
102 D7 **San Miguel I** California U.S.A.
67 F3 **Sanming** China
45 J4 **San Miniato** Italy
71 E3 **San Narciso** Luzon Philippines
44 E1 **Sannazzaro de 'Burgondi** Italy
42 G7 **Sannicandro Garganico** Italy
131 E4 **San Nicolás** Argentina
124 G5 **San Nicolás** Mexico
71 E1 **San Nicolas** Luzon Philippines
71 E2 **San Nicolas** Luzon Philippines
102 E8 **San Nicolas I** California U.S.A.
45 L2 **San Nicolo Ferrarese** Italy
27 D13 **Sannidal** Norway
51 O1 **Sannikoya, Proliv** *str* Russian Federation
45 R7 **Sannio** *mts* Italy
61 N9 **Sano** Japan
31 N6 **Sanok** Poland
133 D8 **San Pablo** Argentina
128 F7 **San Pablo** *R* Bolivia
133 D2 **San Pablo** Bolivia
71 E3 **San Pablo** Luzon Philippines
124 F4 **San Pablo Balleza** Mexico
124 B4 **San Pablo, Pta** *C* Mexico
124 H6 **San Pascual** Mexico
131 F4 **San Pedro** Buenos Aires Argentina
128 F8 **San Pedro** Jujuy Argentina
130 C10 **San Pedro** Misiones Argentina
124 E4 **San Pedro** Mexico
130 B9 **San Pedro** Paraguay
103 O9 **San Pedro** *R* Arizona U.S.A.
102 F8 **San Pedro** California U.S.A.
128 F2 **San Pedro** Venezuela
71 G5 **San Pedro B** Philippines
131 A8 **San Pedro, B.de** Chile
102 F8 **San Pedro Chan** California U.S.A.
128 D3 **San Pedro de Arimena** Colombia
124 E3 **San Pedro de la Cueva** Mexico
124 H5 **San Pedro de las Colonias** Mexico
128 C5 **San Pedro de Lloc** Peru
17 G7 **San Pedro del Pinatar** Spain
127 K5 **San Pedro de Macorís** Dominican Rep
133 C3 **San Pedro, Pta** *C* Chile
16 C5 **San Pedro, Sa. de** *mts* Spain
125 P10 **San Pedro Sula** Honduras
41 L6 **San Pellegrino Terme** Italy
44 E3 **San Pier d'Arena** Italy
45 K4 **San Piero a Sieve** Italy
99 U8 **San Pierre** Indiana U.S.A.
45 K1 **San Pietro di Morubio** Italy
45 K2 **San Pietro di Piano** Italy
43 H8 **San Pietro, I** Italy
43 B9 **San Pietro, I. di** Sardinia
42 C3 **San Pietro, Pte** Italy
100 G1 **Sanpoil** *R* Washington U.S.A.
45 J2 **San Polo d'Enza** Italy
45 H2 **San Polo d'Enza in Caviano** Italy
45 J2 **San Possidónio** Italy
45 K2 **San Prospero** Italy
15 E5 **Sanquhar** Scotland
124 A2 **San Quintín** Mexico
131 C5 **San Rafael** Argentina
128 F7 **San Rafael** Bolivia
102 B4 **San Rafael** California U.S.A.
106 C6 **San Rafael** New Mexico U.S.A.
103 O2 **San Rafael** *R* Utah U.S.A.
127 K10 **San Rafael** Venezuela
127 K5 **San Rafael, C** Dominican Rep
127 K5 **San Rafael del Yuma** Dominican Rep
103 O3 **San Rafael Knob** *mt* Utah U.S.A.
102 E7 **San Rafael Mts** California U.S.A.
125 M3 **San Ramón** Nicaragua
128 C6 **San Ramón** Peru
67 E5 **Sanrao** China
44 C4 **San Remo** Italy
108 F7 **San Rodrigo** *R* Mexico
127 J8 **San Román, C** Venezuela
16 D8 **San Roque** Spain
108 G5 **San Saba** *R* Texas U.S.A.
109 J4 **San Saba** Texas U.S.A.
126 A3 **San Salvador** *isld* Bahamas
125 P11 **San Salvador** El Salvador
128 A8 **San Salvador** *isld* Galapagos Is
131 F4 **San Salvador** *R* Uruguay
133 D2 **San Salvador de Jujuy** Argentina
133 D8 **San Sebastián** Argentina
85 A3 **San Sebastian** Canary Is
124 C3 **San Sebastián** *isld* Mexico
17 F1 **San Sebastian** Spain
127 L10 **San Sebastián** Venezuela
129 J8 **San Sebastião** Brazil
42 E5 **Sansepolcro** Italy
42 G7 **San Severo** Italy
67 G3 **Sansha** China
66 D3 **Sanshichang** China
67 D5 **Sanshui** China
128 E6 **San Silvestre** Bolivia
127 J10 **San Silvestre** Venezuela
102 C6 **San Simeon** California U.S.A.
103 P9 **San Simon** Arizona U.S.A.
103 P9 **San Simon Cr** Arizona U.S.A.
42 H4 **Sanski Most** Bosnia-Herzegovina
145 E4 **Sanson** New Zealand
108 B6 **San Sostenes** Mexico
44 C4 **San Stefano al Mare** Italy
127 N4 **Sans Toucher** *mt* Guadeloupe W Indies
67 C3 **Sansui** China
128 C5 **Santa** Peru
125 O9 **Santa Amelia** Guatemala
128 E6 **Santa Ana** Bolivia
128 B4 **Santa Ana** Ecuador
125 P11 **Santa Ana** El Salvador
124 D2 **Santa Ana** Mexico
102 G8 **Santa Ana** *R* California U.S.A.
102 G8 **Santa Ana** California U.S.A.
127 M10 **Santa Ana** Venezuela
124 F3 **Santa Ana Babicora** Mexico
102 G8 **Santa Ana Mts** California U.S.A.
44 F1 **Santa Angelo** Italy
109 H4 **Santa Anna** Texas U.S.A.
130 G6 **Santa Bárbara** Brazil
124 G4 **Santa Bárbara** Mexico
102 E7 **Santa Barbara** California U.S.A.
127 N10 **Santa Bárbara** Venezuela
102 D7 **Santa Barbara Ch** California U.S.A.
102 E8 **Santa Barbara I** California U.S.A.
102 E7 **Santa Barbara Res** California U.S.A.
130 D7 **Santa Barbara, Sa de** *mts* Brazil
128 E8 **Santa Catalina** Argentina
133 D3 **Santa Catalina** Chile
124 D5 **Santa Catalina** *isld* Mexico
102 G8 **Santa Catalina, G.of** California U.S.A.
102 F8 **Santa Catalina, I** California U.S.A.
133 G3 **Santa Catarina** *state* Brazil
124 B3 **Santa Catarina** Mexico
124 G5 **Santa Catarina de Tepehuanes** Mexico
126 B1 **Santa Catharina** Curaçao
128 E4 **Santa Clara** Colombia
126 E3 **Santa Clara** Cuba
103 K10 **Santa Clara** Mexico
133 B9 **Santa Clara** *isld* Juan Fernández Is Pacific Oc
102 B4 **Santa Clara** California U.S.A.
102 E7 **Santa Clara** *R* California U.S.A.
95 N2 **Santa Clara** New York U.S.A.
103 L4 **Santa Clara** Utah U.S.A.
110 K3 **Santa Claus** Indiana U.S.A.
17 J3 **Santa Coloma de Farnés** Spain
16 B1 **Santa Comba** Spain
133 C7 **Santa Cruz** *prov* Argentina
128 F7 **Santa Cruz** Bolivia
128 D5 **Santa Cruz** Amazonas Brazil
130 J9 **Santa Cruz** Rio Grande do Norte Brazil
128 A8 **Santa Cruz** *isld* Galapagos Is
124 D5 **Santa Cruz** *isld* Mexico
128 C5 **Santa Cruz** Peru
71 E2 **Santa Cruz** Luzon Philippines
71 D3 **Santa Cruz** Luzon Philippines
71 E3 **Santa Cruz** Luzon Philippines
71 F6 **Santa Cruz** Negros Philippines
102 B5 **Santa Cruz** California U.S.A.
106 D6 **Santa Cruz** New Mexico U.S.A.
126 A1 **Santa Cruz** Aruba W Indies
130 H5 **Santa Cruz Cabralia** Brazil
85 A3 **Santa Cruz de la Palma** Canary Is
16 E5 **Santa Cruz de la Zarza** Spain
126 F4 **Santa Cruz del Sur** Cuba
16 E6 **Santa Cruz de Mudela** Spain
85 A3 **Santa Cruz de Tenerife** Canary Is
133 G3 **Santa Cruz do Sul** Brazil
137 O4 **Santa Cruz Is** Solomon Is
127 J2 **Santa Cruz Mts** Jamaica
102 B4 **Santa Cruz Mts** California U.S.A.
17 F3 **Santa Cruz, Sa. de** *mts* Spain
79 B8 **Santa, El** Egypt
128 B4 **Santa Elena** Ecuador
109 J9 **Santa Elena** Texas U.S.A.
128 F3 **Santa Elena** Venezuela
128 B4 **Santa Elena, B. de** Ecuador
125 M4 **Santa Elena, C** Costa Rica
100 J2 **Santa Emida** Idaho U.S.A.
16 A2 **Santa Eugenia de Ribeira** Spain
17 G4 **Santa Eulalia** Spain
17 J6 **Santa Eulalia del Rio** Ibiza
131 E3 **Santa Fe** Argentina
133 E4 **Santa Fe** *prov* Argentina
128 A8 **Santa Fe** *isld* Galapagos Is
71 F4 **Santa Fe** Philippines
16 E7 **Santafé** Spain
113 E8 **Santa Fe** *R* Florida U.S.A.
106 E6 **Santa Fe** New Mexico U.S.A.
129 J5 **Santa Filomena** Brazil
124 E6 **Santa Genovéva** *mt* Mexico
124 G4 **Santa Gertrudis** Mexico
129 J4 **Santa Helena** Brazil
58 E5 **Santai** China
133 C8 **Santa Ines, I** Chile
133 D5 **Santa Isabel** Argentina
128 G5 **Santa Isabel** Brazil
Santa Isabel Fernando Póo *see* **Malabo** Bioko
137 M3 **Santa Isabel** *isld* Solomon Is
124 B2 **Santa Isabel, Sa** *mts* Mexico
129 J5 **Santa Isobel do Araguaia** Brazil
129 G5 **Santa Julia** Brazil
130 F6 **Santa Juliana** Brazil
58 D4 **Santala** China
126 B3 **Santa Lucía** Cuba
124 G5 **Santa Lucía** Mexico
131 F2 **Santa Lucia, R** Argentina
131 G5 **Santa Lucia, R** Uruguay
102 C5 **Santa Lucia Rge** California U.S.A.
130 C6 **Santa Luisa, Sa. de** *mts* Brazil
130 H9 **Santa Luzia** Brazil
124 D5 **Santa Margarita** *isld* Mexico
102 D6 **Santa Margarita** California U.S.A.
102 G8 **Santa Margarita** *R* California U.S.A.
44 F3 **Santa Margherita** Italy
133 D3 **Santa María** Argentina
133 D5 **Santa María** *mt* Argentina
131 G3 **Santa Maria** *R* Brazil
128 G4 **Santa Maria** Amazonas Brazil
131 H2 **Santa Maria** Rio Grande do Sul Brazil
128 A8 **Santa María** *isld* Galapagos Is
124 F2 **Santa María** *R* Mexico
103 L7 **Santa Maria** *R* Arizona U.S.A.
102 D7 **Santa Maria** California U.S.A.
137 O4 **Santa Maria** *isld* Vanuatu
87 E8 **Santa Maria** Zambia
131 G5 **Santa María, C** Uruguay
43 F7 **Santa Maria Capua Vetere** Italy
126 E3 **Santa María, Cayo** *isld* Cuba
16 B7 **Santa Maria, C. de** Portugal
16 B8 **Santa Maria, C. de** Portugal
130 F4 **Santa Maria, Chapadão de** *hills* Brazil
124 F4 **Santa María de Cuevas** Mexico
127 M10 **Santa María de Ipire** Venezuela
124 G5 **Santa María del Oro** Mexico
43 J9 **Santa Maria di Leuca, C** Italy
45 M1 **Santa Maria di Sala** Italy
131 A6 **Santa María, I** Chile
103 M7 **Santa Maria Mts** Arizona U.S.A.
128 C6 **Santa María, Pta** *C* Peru
130 C7 **Santa Maria, R** Brazil
130 F4 **Santa Maria, Sa. de** *mts* Brazil
131 B6 **Santa Mariá, Vol** Argentina
126 G3 **Santa Marie, C** Long I Bahamas
126 G9 **Santa Marta** Colombia
87 B8 **Santa Marta, C** Angola
126 H9 **Santa Marta, Sa. Nevada de** *mts* Colombia
130 D6 **Santa Martha, Sa. de** *mts* Brazil
Santa Maura *isld see* **Levkás**
41 N6 **Sant Ambrogio di Valpolicella** Italy
108 G7 **Santa Mónica** Mexico
102 F7 **Santa Monica** California U.S.A.
109 K9 **Santa Monica** Texas U.S.A.
102 F8 **Santa Monica B** California U.S.A.
102 H8 **Santa Mts** California U.S.A.
70 E5 **Santan** Kalimantan
129 K6 **Santana** Brazil
131 G3 **Santana, Coxilha de** *mt* Brazil/Uruguay
131 G3 **Santana do Livramento** Brazil
128 C3 **Santander** Colombia
16 E1 **Santander** Spain
67 D3 **Santang** China
66 E3 **Santanghu** China
71 G5 **Santa Niño** Samar Philippines
103 N8 **Santan Mt** Arizona U.S.A.
43 B9 **Sant'Antioco** Sardinia
43 B9 **Sant'Antioco, I. di** Sardinia
102 E7 **Santa Paula** California U.S.A.
109 K9 **Santa Perlita** Texas U.S.A.
17 G6 **Santa Pola, C. de** Spain
101 O10 **Santaquin** Utah U.S.A.
16 B5 **Santarem** Portugal
130 J9 **Santa Rita** Brazil
101 N1 **Santa Rita** Montana U.S.A.
127 J9 **Santa Rita** Venezuela
131 D6 **Santa Rosa** Argentina
128 E3 **Santa Rosa** Colombia
130 C10 **Santa Rosa** Paraguay
102 B3 **Santa Rosa** California U.S.A.
108 C1 **Santa Rosa** New Mexico U.S.A.
125 M2 **Santa Rosa de Aguán** Honduras
128 F7 **Santa Rosa de la Roca** Bolivia
125 L3 **Santa Rosa de Lima** El Salvador
111 J11 **Santa Rosa I** Florida U.S.A.
109 H2 **Santa Rosa L** Texas U.S.A.
124 C4 **Santa Rosalía** Mexico
130 C10 **Santa Rosa, R** Brazil
100 H8 **Santa Rosa Range** Nevada U.S.A.
103 N9 **Santa Rosa Wash** *R* Arizona U.S.A.
133 E3 **Santa Sylvina** Argentina
129 J6 **Santa Teresa** *R* Brazil
124 G6 **Santa Teresa** Mexico
43 C7 **Santa Teresa Gallura** Sardinia
129 H6 **Santa Teresinha** Brazil
140 C6 **Santa Theresa** N Terr Australia
133 G4 **Santa Vitória do Palmar** Brazil
43 C9 **Santa Vittoria, Monte** *mt* Sardinia
102 D7 **Santa Ynez** California U.S.A.
102 D7 **Santa Ynez Mts** California U.S.A.
102 H8 **Santa Ysabel** California U.S.A.
112 H4 **Santee** *R* South Carolina U.S.A.
112 H4 **Santee Pt** South Carolina U.S.A.
112 D2 **Santeetlah, L** North Carolina U.S.A.
125 O5 **Santé Fé** Panama
124 A2 **San Telmo** Mexico
124 H8 **San Telmo, Pta** *C* Mexico
45 O5 **Sante Marie** Italy
21 N6 **Santenay** France
42 D4 **Santerno** *R* Italy
21 O5 **Santeuil** France
44 D1 **Santhià** Italy
131 B4 **Santiago** *prov* Chile
131 B4 **Santiago** Chile
127 J5 **Santiago** Dominican Rep
124 D6 **Santiago** Baja California Mexico
124 G8 **Santiago** Colima Mexico
125 O5 **Santiago** Panama
130 C10 **Santiago** Paraguay
128 C4 **Santiago** *R* Peru
16 B2 **Santiago de Compostela** Spain
126 G4 **Santiago de Cuba** Cuba
17 F6 **Santiago de la Espana** Spain
133 E3 **Santiago del Estero** *prov* Argentina
16 B6 **Santiago do Cacem** Portugal
124 G7 **Santiago Ixcuintla** Mexico
108 D6 **Santiago Mts** Texas U.S.A.
124 G5 **Santiago Papasquiaro** Mexico
102 G8 **Santiago Pk** California U.S.A.
124 H7 **Santiago, Rio Grande de** Mexico
128 G7 **Santiago, Serranía de** *mts* Bolivia
124 G5 **Santiaguillo, L. de** Mexico
70 G4 **Santigi** Sulawesi Indonesia
70 G4 **Santiki, Tanjong** *C* Sulawesi
16 E1 **Santillana** Spain
16 E6 **Santisteban del Puerto** Spain
109 J3 **Santo** Texas U.S.A.
130 F8 **Santo Amaro, I. de** Brazil
130 G6 **Santo Antônia** *R* Brazil
128 F5 **Santo Antonio** Brazil
129 K6 **Santo Antônio de Jesus** Brazil
128 E4 **Santo Antônio do Içá** Brazil
86 B7 **Santo Antonio do Zaire** Angola
130 C10 **Santo Cristo** *R* Brazil
87 D9 **Santo Cruz do Cuando** Angola
126 D3 **Santo Domingo** Cuba
127 K5 **Santo Domingo** Dominican Rep
124 B3 **Santo Domingo** Baja California Mexico
124 H3 **Santo Domingo** Coahuila Mexico
126 G4 **Santo Domingo, Cay** *isld* Bahamas
17 F2 **Santo Domingo de la Calza** Spain
124 C5 **Santo Domingo del Pacifico** Mexico
130 G6 **Santo Maria do Suaçuí** Brazil
127 M10 **San Tomé** Venezuela
128 F2 **San Tome de Guayana** Venezuela
16 E1 **Santoña** Spain
65 G3 **Santong He** *R* China
Santorini *isld see* **Thira** *isld*
130 F8 **Santos** Brazil
128 E5 **Santos Dumont** Amazonas Brazil
130 G7 **Santos Dumont** Minas Gerais Brazil
16 D6 **Santos, Sa. de los** *mts* Spain
44 G1 **Santo Stéfano Lodigiano** Italy
16 B3 **Santo Tirso** Portugal
124 F3 **Santo Tomás** Mexico
128 D6 **Santo Tomás** Peru
125 P10 **Santo Tomás de Castilla** Guatemala
133 F3 **Santo Tomé** Argentina
43 C8 **Santu, C. di M** *mt* Sardinia
65 D4 **Santunying** China
103 L6 **Sanup Plat** Arizona U.S.A.
80 D4 **Sa Nur** Jordan
133 C7 **San Valentín** *mt* Chile
21 L2 **Sanvic** France
124 A2 **San Vicente** Mexico
71 F1 **San Vicente** Luzon Philippines
16 A7 **San Vicente, C. de** Portugal
128 C6 **San Vicente de Cañete** Peru
16 E1 **San Vicente de la Barquera** Spain
45 P6 **San Vicenze Falle Roveto** Italy
42 E3 **San Vito al Tag** Italy
43 E10 **San Vito, C** Sicily
38 F9 **San Vito di Cadore-Antelao** Italy
45 N6 **San Vito Romano** Italy
67 C7 **Sanya** China
88 B10 **Sanyati** *R* Zimbabwe
109 H8 **San Ygnacio** Texas U.S.A.
102 G9 **San Ysidro** California U.S.A.
106 D6 **San Ysidro** New Mexico U.S.A.
58 E5 **Sanyuan** China
65 F3 **Sanyuanpu** China
87 C7 **Sanza Pomba** Angola
65 F2 **Sanzhan** China
130 F8 **São Bernardo do Campo** Brazil
87 B7 **São Brás, Cabo de** *C* Angola
130 F8 **São Carlos** Brazil
129 L6 **São Cristóvão** Brazil
129 J6 **São Domingos** Brazil
130 D6 **São Domingos, R** Brazil
129 K7 **São Felippe, Serra de** *mts* Brazil
129 H5 **São Felix do Xingu** Brazil
129 K7 **São Francisco** Brazil
130 F6 **São Francisco** *R* Brazil
130 E10 **São Francisco do Sul** Brazil
130 E10 **São Francisco, I.de** Brazil
129 J7 **São Gabriel de Goias** Brazil
87 G7 **Sao Hill** Tanzania
130 D8 **São João** *R* Brazil
129 J6 **São João da Alianca** Brazil
130 F7 **São João da Boa Vista** Brazil
130 G7 **São João del Rei** Brazil
129 K5 **São João do Piauí** Brazil
129 J5 **São João du Araguaia** Brazil
129 K4 **São João, I. de** Brazil
128 F5 **São João, Sa. de** *mts* Brazil
128 E4 **São Joaquim** Brazil
128 E4 **São José** Brazil
128 F3 **São José do Anauá** Brazil
133 G4 **São José do Norte** Brazil
130 E7 **São José do Rio Prêto** Brazil
130 F8 **São José dos Campos** Brazil
130 E9 **São José dos Pinhais** Brazil
133 G3 **São Leopoldo** Brazil
130 C5 **São Lourenço** Brazil
133 G4 **São Lourenço do Sul** Brazil
130 C5 **São Lourenço, Pantanal de** *swamp* Brazil
129 J4 **São Luís** Brazil
128 F5 **São Luis de Cassianá** Brazil
133 G3 **São Luis Gonzaga** Brazil
128 E3 **São Marcelino** Brazil
129 K4 **São Marco, B. de** Brazil
130 F5 **São Marcos, R** Brazil
130 H6 **São Mateus** Brazil
130 F4 **São Miguel** *R* Brazil
127 K5 **Saona, I** Dominican Rep
19 N12 **Saône** *R* France
18 H6 **Saône-et-Loire** *dept* France
71 C3 **Saonek** W Irian
130 F8 **São Paulo** Brazil
128 E4 **São Paulo de Olivença** Brazil
128 F5 **São Pedro** Brazil
129 L5 **São Rafael** Brazil
129 J5 **São Raimundo das Mangabeiras** Brazil
129 K5 **São Raimundo Nonato** Brazil
128 E5 **São Romáo** Brazil
129 H5 **São Sebastião** Brazil
130 F7 **São Sebastião do Paraiso** Brazil
130 F8 **São Sebastião, I. de** Brazil
128 F6 **São Simão** *R* Brazil
86 A5 **Sao Tome and Principe** *rep* West Africa
130 H7 **São Tomé, C. de** Brazil
19 O15 **Saou** France
68 F7 **Sa Oui** Cambodia
85 D3 **Saoura** *watercourse* Algeria
129 J8 **Sao Vicente** Brazil
68 F1 **Sa Pa** Vietnam
47 H3 **Sápai** Greece
69 D13 **Sapako** Indonesia
47 L4 **Sapanca** Turkey
71 E3 **Sapangbato** Luzon Philippines
46 F2 **Sapareva Banya** Bulgaria
71 J9 **Sape** Sumbawa Indonesia
85 F7 **Sapele** Nigeria
106 E6 **Sapello** New Mexico U.S.A.
112 F6 **Sapelo I** Georgia U.S.A.
16 C4 **Sa. Peña de Francia** *mt* Spain
71 J9 **Sape Selat** Indonesia
71 J9 **Sape Teluk** *B* Indonesia
47 K5 **Şaphane** Turkey
68 G2 **Sa Phin, Pou** *mt* Vietnam
46 E8 **Sapiéntza** *isld* Greece
106 C3 **Sapinero** Colorado U.S.A.
21 L4 **Sap, le** France
71 E2 **Sapocoy, Mt** Luzon Philippines
125 P6 **Sapo, Serranía del** *ra* Panama
128 C5 **Saposoa** Peru
54 M3 **Sapozhok** Russian Federation
98 F10 **Sappa Cr** Kansas U.S.A.
38 G8 **Sappada** Italy
141 J6 **Sapphire** Queensland Australia
101 M3 **Sapphire Mts** Montana U.S.A.
26 M4 **Sappisaasi** Sweden
59 M3 **Sapporo** Japan
43 G8 **Sapri** Italy
129 G4 **Sapucua, L. de** Brazil
70 P9 **Sapudi** *isld* Indonesia
70 E2 **Sapulot** Sabah
107 O5 **Sapulpa** Oklahoma U.S.A.
70 O9 **Sapulu** Java
115 O3 **Saqqaq** Greenland
78 L3 **Saqqez** Iran
78 L3 **Sarab** Iran
68 E5 **Sara Buri** Thailand
106 E6 **Sarafina** New Mexico U.S.A.
108 D4 **Saragosa** Texas U.S.A.
Saragossa *see* **Zaragoza** Spain
128 C4 **Saraguro** Ecuador
29 M7 **Säräisniemi** Finland
48 E7 **Sarajevo** Bosnia-Herzegovina
140 J5 **Saraji** Queensland Australia
77 G1 **Sarakhs** Iran
46 F4 **Saraklí** Greece
55 C5 **Saraktash** Russian Federation
129 G2 **Saramacca R** Suriname
18 F9 **Saramon** France
138 D2 **Sara, Mt** South Australia Australia
57 G1 **Saran'** Kazakhstan
94 B4 **Saranac** Michigan U.S.A.
95 N2 **Saranac Lake** New York U.S.A.
46 D5 **Sarandë** Albania
130 D10 **Sarandi** Brazil
133 F4 **Sarandi del Yi** Uruguay
70 B5 **Saran, G** *mt* Kalimantan
71 G8 **Sarangani** *isld* Mindanao Philippines
75 K8 **Sarangarh** India
53 G7 **Saransk** Russian Federation
59 L2 **Sarapul'skoye** Russian Federation
79 F3 **Sarārā** Syria
113 E10 **Sarasota** Florida U.S.A.
111 B11 **Saratoga** Texas U.S.A.
101 T8 **Saratoga** Wyoming U.S.A.
95 O3 **Saratoga Springs** New York U.S.A.
70 B4 **Saratok** Sarawak
53 G8 **Saratov** Russian Federation
77 H6 **Saravan** Iran
68 H5 **Saravan** Laos
68 D6 **Sarawa** *R* Burma
70 **Sarawak** *state* Malaysia
47 J3 **Saray** Turkey
47 K7 **Sarayköy** Turkey
77 G6 **Sarbāz** Iran
42 D3 **Sarca** *R* Italy
21 P4 **Sarcelles** France
33 T9 **Särchen** Germany
133 C3 **Sarco** Chile
110 B4 **Sarcoxie** Missouri U.S.A.
74 F4 **Sardarshahr** India
43 C8 **Sardegna** *isld* Italy
86 G5 **Sardindida Plain** Kenya
Sardinia *see* **Sardegna**
94 D7 **Sardinia** Ohio U.S.A.
47 J6 **Sardis** Turkey
112 F5 **Sardis** Georgia U.S.A.
111 G7 **Sardis** Mississippi U.S.A.
110 H6 **Sardis** Tennessee U.S.A.
107 P7 **Sardis Lake** Oklahoma U.S.A.
71 J8 **Sarege** *isld* Indonesia
45 K1 **Sarego** Italy
26 J4 **Sarektjåkko** *mt* Sweden
70 D5 **Sarempaka** *mt* Kalimantan
86 G3 **Sarenga** *mt* Ethiopia
41 O4 **Sarentina, V** Italy
42 D2 **Sarentine, Alpi** *mts* Italy
41 O4 **Sarentino** Italy
77 J1 **Sar-e-Pol** Afghanistan
111 C9 **Sarepta** Louisiana U.S.A.
77 D4 **Sar e Yazd** Iran
41 K3 **Sargans** Switzerland
90 C6 **Sargasso Sea** Atlantic Oc
55 F3 **Sargatskoye** Russian Federation
21 L5 **Sarge** France
102 C5 **Sargent** California U.S.A.
98 G8 **Sargent** Nebraska U.S.A.
116 N6 **Sargent Icefield** Alaska U.S.A.
106 D3 **Sargents** Colorado U.S.A.
21 M6 **Sargé-sur-Braye** France
74 E2 **Sargodha** Pakistan
86 C4 **Sarh** Chad
85 C2 **Sarhro, Jbel** *mts* Morocco
77 C1 **Sārī** Iran
47 J9 **Sária** *isld* Greece
57 E5 **Sariasiya** Uzbekistan
124 D2 **Sáric** Mexico
116 E9 **Sarichef, C** Aleutian Is
80 D3 **Sarid** Israel
47 K6 **Sarigöl** Turkey
78 J1 **Sarıkamış** Turkey
78 C2 **Şarıkaraağaç** Turkey
79 D2 **Sarıkavac** Turkey
70 B3 **Sarikei** Sarawak
141 J5 **Sarina** Queensland Australia
17 G3 **Sariñena** Spain
77 K2 **Sar-i-Pul** Afghanistan
84 G4 **Sarīr** Libya
109 K8 **Sarita** Texas U.S.A.
59 J4 **Sariwŏn** N Korea
78 C1 **Sarıyar Barajı** *dam* Turkey
29 L7 **Sarjakylä** Finland
20 F3 **Sark** *isld* Channel Is
57 J2 **Sarkand** Kazakhstan
78 F2 **Sarkisla** Turkey
47 J4 **Şarköy** Turkey
18 F8 **Sarlat** France
77 K4 **Sarlath Range** Afghanistan/Pakistan
98 H1 **Sarles** North Dakota U.S.A.
119 T10 **Sarles** North Dakota U.S.A.
52 H6 **Sarmanovo** Russian Federation
48 J4 **Sărmaşu** Romania
136 H2 **Sarmi** W Irian
133 D7 **Sarmiento** Argentina
133 C8 **Sarmiento** *mt* Chile
27 F10 **Särna** Sweden
27 M14 **Sārnate** Latvia
8 B3 **Sarnau** Wales
41 H4 **Sarnen** Switzerland
120 H10 **Sarnia** Ontario Canada
41 L6 **Sarnico** Italy
43 F8 **Sarno** Italy
53 C8 **Sarny** Ukraine
27 E14 **Särö** Sweden
70 G6 **Saroako** Sulawesi
69 F14 **Sarolangun** Sumatra
60 R1 **Saroma-ko** *L* Japan
46 F7 **Saronikós Kólpos** *B* Greece
42 C3 **Saronno** Italy
47 H4 **Saros Körfezi** *B* Turkey
77 L2 **Sarowbī** Afghanistan
46 D2 **Šar Planina** *mt* Serbia/Macedonia Yugoslavia
27 E12 **Sarpsborg** Norway
101 T4 **Sarpy** Montana U.S.A.
36 C6 **Sarralbe** France
36 C6 **Sarraltroff** France
19 N14 **Sarras** France
36 C6 **Sarrebourg** France
19 K3 **Sarreguemines** France
16 C2 **Sarria** Spain
19 N16 **Sarrians** France
17 G4 **Sarrión** Spain
80 G5 **Sarrut** Jordan
55 C3 **Sars** Russian Federation
52 H6 **Sarsak Omga** Russian Federation
45 M4 **Sarsina** Italy
22 D3 **Sars, le** France
22 G3 **Sars-Poteries** France
32 L8 **Sarstedt** Germany
22 K2 **Sart** Belgium
74 D5 **Sartanahu** Pakistan
51 N2 **Sartang** *R* Russian Federation
18 F5 **Sarthe** *dept* France
21 K5 **Sarthe** *R* France
20 H4 **Sartilly** France
Sartu *see* **Daqing**
60 R3 **Sarubetsu** *R* Japan
60 F10 **Sarumasay** Japan
75 O5 **Sarupeta** India
79 G3 **Sarūt** *R* Syria
78 L4 **Sarvabad** Iran
48 E4 **Sarviz** *R* Hungary
26 F9 **Särvsjö** Sweden
57 G2 **Sarykomey** Kazakhstan
55 D5 **Sarykopa, Oz** *L* Kazakhstan
55 D5 **Sarymoin, Oz** *L* Kazakhstan
57 J3 **Sary-Ozek** Kazakhstan
57 G2 **Sary-Shagan** Kazakhstan
57 E2 **Sarysu** *R* Kazakhstan
57 G5 **Sary-Tash** Kyrgyzstan
52 J3 **Sar'yudin** Russian Federation
57 B6 **Saryyazinskoye Vodokhranilishche** *res* Turkmenistan
57 H2 **Saryyesik-Atyray** *desert* Kazakhstan
57 J3 **Saryzhaz** Kazakhstan
44 G3 **Sarzana** Italy
20 E6 **Sarzeau** France
124 D2 **Sásabe** Mexico
103 N10 **Sasabe** Arizona U.S.A.
86 H4 **Sasabeneh** Ethiopia
69 D12 **Sasak** Sumatra
75 L6 **Sasaram** India
71 J9 **Sasar Tg** *C* Sumba Indonesia
60 J10 **Sasayama** Japan
40 G1 **Sasbach** Germany
60 C12 **Sasebo** Japan
114 J7 **Saskatchewan** *prov* Canada
119 O5 **Saskatchewan** *R* Canada
118 L6 **Saskatoon** Saskatchewan Canada
119 Q5 **Saskeram L** Manitoba Canada
51 L1 **Saskylakh** Russian Federation
125 M3 **Saslaya** *mt* Nicaragua
89 E6 **Sasolburg** S Africa
109 J6 **Saspamco** Texas U.S.A.
112 E2 **Sassafras Mt** South Carolina U.S.A.
77 C7 **Sassan** *oil well* Persian Gulf
85 C7 **Sassandra** *R* Ivory Coast
85 C8 **Sassandra** Ivory Coast
37 K4 **Sassanfahr** Germany
43 B8 **Sassari** Sardinia
33 S4 **Sassen** Germany
19 P14 **Sassenage** France
32 H9 **Sassenberg** Germany
33 N7 **Sassenburg** Germany
25 C4 **Sassenheim** Netherlands
21 M2 **Sassetot** France
30 H1 **Sassnitz** Germany
45 N4 **Sassocorvaro** Italy
45 K3 **Sasso Marconi** Italy
38 E8 **Sass Rigais** *mt* Italy
45 J2 **Sassuolo** Italy
17 G3 **Sástago** Spain
133 E4 **Sastre** Argentina
60 C11 **Sasuna** Japan
25 A6 **Sas-van Gent** Netherlands
57 K2 **Sasykkol', Ozero** *L* Kazakhstan
48 M5 **Sasyk, Oz** *L* Ukraine
53 D10 **Sasyk, Ozero** *L* Ukraine
85 B6 **Satadougou** Mali
60 D14 **Sata-misaki** *C* Japan
106 B6 **Satan Pass** New Mexico U.S.A.
107 K4 **Satanta** Kansas U.S.A.
76 A2 **Satara** India
114 H2 **Satellite B** Northwest Territories Canada
113 G9 **Satellite Beach** Florida U.S.A.
71 H8 **Satengar** *isld* Indonesia
27 H11 **Säter** Sweden
32 G6 **Saterland** *reg* Germany
112 E6 **Satilla** *R* Georgia U.S.A.
19 N14 **Satillieu** France
128 D6 **Satipo** Peru
26 K4 **Satisjaure** *L* Sweden
55 C4 **Satka** Russian Federation
13 G4 **Satley** England
Satluj *R see* **Sutlej** *R*
74 F8 **Satmala Hills** India
71 H9 **Satonda** *isld* Indonesia
86 D6 **Satonga** *R* Zaire
42 H4 **Šator** *mt* Bosnia-Herzegovina
48 G2 **Sátoraljaújhely** Hungary
33 P5 **Satow** Germany
74 F8 **Satpura Range** India
28 D7 **Satrup** Germany
60 D14 **Satsuma-hantō** *pen* Japan
26 N4 **Sattajärvi** Sweden
29 M4 **Sattanen** Finland
41 J3 **Sattel** Switzerland
76 E2 **Sattenapalle** India
68 B3 **Satthwa** Burma
26 J9 **Sättna** Sweden
38 K8 **Sattnitz** *reg* Austria
70 D6 **Satui** Kalimantan
48 H3 **Satu Mare** Romania
69 D9 **Satun** Thailand
100 B1 **Saturna I** British Columbia Canada
100 E3 **Satus** Washington U.S.A.
76 C5 **Satyamangalam** India
55 D2 **Satyga** Russian Federation
38 L8 **Saualpe** *mts* Austria
70 P9 **Saubi** *isld* Indonesia
122 H2 **Saubosq, L** Quebec Canada
124 J5 **Sauceda** Mexico
103 M9 **Sauceda Mts** Arizona U.S.A.
131 E7 **Sauce, R** Argentina
124 G4 **Sauces** Mexico
111 G11 **Saucier** Mississippi U.S.A.
124 G3 **Saucillo** Mexico
27 B12 **Sauda** Norway
128 F5 **Saudade** Brazil
28 S9 **Saudhárkrókur** Iceland
72 E4 **Saudi Arabia** *kingdom*
36 D1 **Sauerland** *reg* Germany
129 G6 **Saueruina** *R* Brazil
71 G7 **Saug** *R* Mindanao Philippines
99 U7 **Saugatuck** Michigan U.S.A.
120 J8 **Saugeen** *R* Ontario Canada
117 K9 **Saugstad, Mt** British Columbia Canada
18 H8 **Saugues** France
129 G4 **Sauiá** Brazil
18 E7 **Saujon** France
99 M4 **Sauk** *R* Minnesota U.S.A.
100 D1 **Sauk** *R* Washington U.S.A.
99 M4 **Sauk Center** Minnesota U.S.A.
99 R6 **Sauk City** Wisconsin U.S.A.
52 B6 **Šaukenai** Lithuania
19 N15 **Saulce** France
22 G4 **Saulces-Monclin** France
21 K5 **Saule, Mt.du** France
41 L1 **Saulgau** Germany
41 O2 **Saulgrub** Germany
18 H5 **Saulieu** France
52 B6 **Saulkrasti** Latvia
122 F9 **Saulnierville** Nova Scotia Canada
19 O16 **Sault** France
122 C5 **Sault au Mouton** Quebec Canada
122 C5 **Sault-aux-Cochons, R** Quebec Canada
120 F6 **Sault Ste. Marie** Ontario Canada
120 F6 **Sault Ste. Marie** Michigan U.S.A.
36 C7 **Saulxures** France
80 G3 **Saum** Jordan
141 L5 **Saumarez Reef** Gt Barrier Reef Aust
127 J5 **Saumâtre, Etang** *L* Haiti
21 N5 **Saumeray** France
136 G3 **Saumlakki** Moluccas Indonesia
21 K7 **Saumur** France
122 K2 **Saumur, L** Quebec Canada
29 N4 **Saunavaara** Finland
118 B6 **Saunders** Alberta Canada
146 C10 **Saunders Coast** *coast* Antarctica
8 B4 **Saundersfoot** Wales
146 G2 **Saunders I** S Sandwich Is S Atlantic Oc
140 B2 **Saunders, Mt** N Terr Australia
8 B5 **Saunton** England
87 D7 **Saurimo** Angola
57 L2 **Saur, Khrebet** *mts* Kazakhstan
41 K4 **Sauronstock** *mt* Switzerland
38 M8 **Sausal** *reg* Austria
102 B4 **Sausalito** California U.S.A.
71 C3 **Sausapor** W Irian
20 H2 **Saussemesnil** France
19 O18 **Sausset-les-Pins** France
40 A3 **Saussy** France
70 G5 **Sausu** Sulawesi
87 C8 **Sautar** Angola
122 H2 **Sauterelles, Lac aux** Quebec Canada
127 P5 **Sauteurs** Grenada
20 G7 **Sautron** France
18 E9 **Sauveterre** France
18 F8 **Sauveterre-de-Guyenne** France
29 K11 **Sauvo** Finland
25 G2 **Sauwerd** Netherlands
20 D7 **Sauzon** France
42 H3 **Sava** *R* Croatia/Slovenia/Yugoslavia
95 L7 **Savage** Maryland U.S.A.
111 F7 **Savage** Mississippi U.S.A.
98 B2 **Savage** Montana U.S.A.
139 H8 **Savage River** Tasmania Australia
101 U6 **Savageton** Wyoming U.S.A.
134 A1 **Savaii** *isld* Western Samoa
85 E7 **Savalou** Benin
122 A2 **Savan'e, R** Quebec Canada
126 A2 **Savaneta** Aruba W Indies
99 Q7 **Savanna** Illinois U.S.A.
107 P7 **Savanna** Oklahoma U.S.A.
112 F5 **Savannah** Georgia U.S.A.
110 B2 **Savannah** Missouri U.S.A.
94 E6 **Savannah** Ohio U.S.A.
112 E3 **Savannah** *R* South Carolina U.S.A.
110 H6 **Savannah** Tennessee U.S.A.
112 F6 **Savannah Beach** Georgia U.S.A.
113 L12 **Savannah Sound** Bahamas
126 F2 **Savannah Sound** Eleuthera Bahamas
68 G4 **Savannakhet** Laos
127 H2 **Savanna la Mar** Jamaica
Sāvantvadi *see* **Vādi**
76 B3 **Savanur** India
26 L8 **Sävar** Sweden
26 L7 **Sävarån** *R* Sweden
40 F6 **Savaranche, V** Italy
26 M6 **Sävast** Sweden
47 J5 **Savaştepe** Turkey
85 E7 **Savé** Benin
18 F9 **Save** *R* France
87 F10 **Save** *R* Mozambique
77 B2 **Sāveh** Iran
85 D7 **Savelugu** Ghana
56 F3 **Savel'yevka** Russian Federation
45 K3 **Savena** *R* Italy
20 G7 **Savenay** France
18 G9 **Saverdun** France
36 C6 **Saverne** France
101 S8 **Savery** Wyoming U.S.A.
44 C2 **Savigliano** Italy
45 M3 **Savignano** Italy
21 L6 **Savigne** France
21 L5 **Savigné-l'Evêque** France
21 L7 **Savigné-sur-Lathan** France
45 K3 **Savigno** Italy
21 L7 **Savigny-en-Véron** Indre-et-Loire France
21 M6 **Savigny-sur-Braye** France
19 Q15 **Savines** France
42 F2 **Savinja** *R* Slovenia
52 H2 **Savino** Russian Federation
52 J3 **Savinobor** Russian Federation
45 M3 **Savio** Italy
45 M4 **Sàvio** *R* Italy
29 N10 **Savitaipale** Finland
42 J6 **Šavnik** Montenegro Yugoslavia
120 F3 **Savoff** Ontario Canada
19 K7 **Savoie** *dept* France
117 N10 **Savona** British Columbia Canada
44 D3 **Savona** Italy
95 K4 **Savona** New York U.S.A.
29 O10 **Savonlinna** Finland
29 O9 **Savonranta** Finland
116 B5 **Savoonga** St Lawrence I, Alaska U.S.A.
111 H9 **Savoy** Mississippi U.S.A.
101 R1 **Savoy** Montana U.S.A.
48 N2 **Savran'** Ukraine
27 G14 **Sävsjö** Sweden
27 H15 **Sävsjöström** Sweden
71 K10 **Savu** *isld* Indonesia
42 E3 **Savudrija Rtič** *pt* Croatia
29 N4 **Savukoski** Finland
78 H3 **Savur** Turkey
71 K9 **Savu Sea** Indonesia
80 C5 **Savyon** Israel
68 B2 **Saw** Burma
69 E13 **Sawahlunto** Sumatra
74 G6 **Sawai Madhopur** India
70 M9 **Sawall, G** *mt* Java
70 D5 **Sawan** Kalimantan
68 F4 **Sawang Daen Din** Thailand
68 D4 **Sawankhalok** Thailand
60 O3 **Sawara** Hokkaido Japan
61 O10 **Sawara** Honshu Japan
61 M8 **Sawasaki-bana** *C* Japan
106 D2 **Sawatch Ra** Colorado U.S.A.
121 L1 **Sawayan Pt** Quebec Canada
119 Q1 **Sawbill** Manitoba Canada
84 E4 **Sawdā', Jabal as** *mts* Libya
118 D4 **Sawdy** Alberta Canada
14 D2 **Sawel** *mt* N Ireland
69 A8 **Sawi B** Nicobar Is
80 E5 **Sāwīya** Jordan
107 L4 **Sawlog Cr** Kansas U.S.A.
117 O3 **Sawmill Bay** Northwest Territories Canada
9 G3 **Sawston** England
116 N4 **Sawtooth Mt** Alaska U.S.A.
99 P2 **Sawtooth Mts** Minnesota U.S.A.
101 L6 **Sawtooth Range** Idaho U.S.A.
100 E1 **Sawtooth Range** Washington U.S.A.
Sawu *see* **Savu**
71 L10 **Sawu** Indonesia
107 M4 **Sawyer** Kansas U.S.A.
98 E1 **Sawyer** North Dakota U.S.A.
99 T5 **Sawyer** Wisconsin U.S.A.
100 B8 **Sawyers Bar** California U.S.A.
121 T7 **Sawyerville** Quebec Canada
141 F4 **Saxby** *R* Queensland Australia
141 G5 **Saxby Downs** Queensland Australia
9 F1 **Saxilby** England
9 H3 **Saxmundham** England
26 H7 **Saxnäs** Sweden
99 Q3 **Saxon** Wisconsin U.S.A.
94 J6 **Saxton** Pennsylvania U.S.A.
144 D5 **Saxton Pass** New Zealand
85 E6 **Say** Niger
79 F3 **Şāyā** Syria
81 C6 **Saya de Malha Bank** Indian Oc
57 H2 **Sayak Pervyy** Kazakhstan
128 C6 **Sayán** Peru
56 D4 **Sayano-Shushenskoye Vodokhranilishche** *res* Russian Federation
56 D3 **Sayanskiy** Russian Federation
56 D5 **Sayanskiy Khrebet** *mt* Russian Federation
57 C5 **Sayat** Turkmenistan
125 O9 **Sayaxché** Guatemala
37 P2 **Sayda** Germany
69 C8 **Sayer I** Thailand
72 G5 **Sayḩūt** Yemen
86 H3 **Saylac** Somalia
56 C6 **Saylyugem, Khrebet** *mts* Russian Federation
29 M9 **Säynätsalo** Finland
58 F3 **Saynshand** Mongolia
108 E8 **Sayre** Oklahoma U.S.A.
95 L5 **Sayre** Pennsylvania U.S.A.
124 H8 **Sayula** Mexico
72 F5 **Say'ūn** Yemen
117 L10 **Sayward** British Columbia Canada
46 C4 **Sazan** *isld* Albania
31 J6 **Sázava** *R* Czechoslovakia
55 C3 **Sazhino** Russian Federation
47 M10 **Sazli** *R* Turkey
47 M10 **Sazlibosna Çitlihan** Turkey

Seriana, Val — Shoshone Cavern Nat. Mon 225

41 L6 **Seriana, Val** Italy
69 D11 **Seribudolok** Sumatra
130 H9 **Seridó** *R* Brazil
21 O3 **Sérifontaine** France
46 G7 **Sérifos** *isld* Greece
20 C5 **Sérignac** France
19 N16 **Sérignan** France
68 D5 **Serim** Burma
142 D2 **Seringapatam Reef** Indian Oc
129 H5 **Seringa, Serra da** *mts* Brazil
45 R8 **Serino** Italy
41 L7 **Serio** *R* Italy
85 F4 **Serkout, Dj** *mt* Algeria
138 E4 **Serle, Mt** South Australia Australia
21 P5 **Sermaises** France
71 O9 **Sermata** *isld* Indonesia
45 K1 **Sermide** Italy
45 N6 **Sermoneta** Italy
38 H9 **Sernio** *mt* Italy
33 U6 **Sernitz** *R* Germany
33 Q8 **Serno** Germany
60 T2 **Sernovodsk** Russian Federation
57 A5 **Sernyy-Zavod** Turkmenistan
31 N3 **Serock** Poland
126 A2 **Seroe Colorado** Aruba W Indies
17 F7 **Serón** Spain
85 F4 **Serouenout** Algeria
55 D2 **Serov** Russian Federation
89 E4 **Serowe** Botswana
16 B7 **Serpa** Portugal
87 C8 **Serpa Pinto** Angola
43 C9 **Serpeddi, Pta** *mt* Sardinia
116 E4 **Serpentine Hot Springs** Alaska U.S.A.
138 A3 **Serpentine Lakes** South Australia Australia
143 B9 **Serpentine, R** W Australia Australia
122 A3 **Serpent, R. au** Quebec Canada
128 F1 **Serpents Mouth** *str* Venezuela
17 G6 **Serpis** *R* Spain
54 J2 **Serpukhov** Russian Federation
21 O2 **Serqueux** Seine-Inférieure France
21 M3 **Serquigny** France
130 H7 **Serra** Brazil
45 L4 **Serra, Alpe di** *mts* Italy
130 E10 **Serra Alta** Brazil
130 F4 **Serra Bonita** Brazil
130 F4 **Serra das Araras** Brazil
129 H3 **Serra do Navio** Brazil
33 Q5 **Serrahn** Germany
46 F3 **Sérrai** Greece
45 J3 **Serramazzoni** Italy
125 O2 **Serrana Bank** Caribbean
125 P2 **Serranilla Bank** Caribbean
43 G10 **Serra San Bruno** Italy
43 C11 **Serrat, Cape** *C* Tunisia
45 J4 **Serravalle Pistojese** Italy
22 F4 **Serre** *R* France
18 G10 **Serrére, Pic de** *mt* France
19 P16 **Serres** France
133 D4 **Serrezuela** Argentina
19 N14 **Serrières** France
129 L6 **Serrinha** Brazil
45 M4 **Serriola, Bocca** *pass* Italy
43 B12 **Sers** Tunisia
16 B5 **Sertã** Portugal
130 F7 **Sertãozinho** Brazil
70 K9 **Sertung** *isld* Sumatra
69 D10 **Seruai** Sumatra
70 C6 **Serujan** *R* Kalimantan
89 E3 **Serule** Botswana
40 E2 **Servance** France
46 E4 **Sérvia** Greece
100 E5 **Service Creek** Oregon U.S.A.
138 F6 **Serviceton** Victoria Australia
106 E5 **Servilleta** New Mexico U.S.A.
71 N9 **Serwaro** Indonesia
66 F5 **Sêrxü** China
22 G4 **Séry** France
22 E4 **Séry-les-Mezières** France
68 G4 **Se Sang Soi** *R* Laos
70 E3 **Sesatap** Kalimantan
88 D2 **Sese Is** Uganda
120 K4 **Sesekinika** Ontario Canada
71 A3 **Sesepe** Indonesia
87 B9 **Sesfontein** Namibia
87 D9 **Sesheka** Zambia
41 H7 **Sesia R** Italy
16 A6 **Sesimbra** Portugal
26 N6 **Seskarön** *isld* Sweden
47 Q14 **Seskli** *isld* Greece
61 P12 **Sesoko-jima** *isld* Okinawa
43 F7 **Sessa Aurunca** Italy
36 D6 **Sessenheim** France
110 G3 **Sesser** Illinois U.S.A.
37 K3 **Sesslach** Germany
71 K9 **Sessok** Flores Indonesia
45 M4 **Sestino** Italy
45 K4 **Sesto Fiorentino** Italy
31 O1 **Seštokai** Lithuania
45 J3 **Sestola** Italy
52 E6 **Sestra** *R* Russian Federation
44 E3 **Sestri** Italy
44 F3 **Sestri Levante** Italy
29 O11 **Sestroretsk** Russian Federation
60 D12 **Setaka** Japan
60 N3 **Setana** Japan
9 G2 **Setchey** England
18 H9 **Sète** France
130 G6 **Sete Lagoas** Brazil
130 D8 **Sete Quedas, Ilha Grande ou** *isld* Brazil
27 B12 **Setesdal** Norway
94 F8 **Seth** West Virginia U.S.A.
85 F1 **Sétif** Algeria
60 C13 **Seto** Japan
60 F12 **Seto Naikai** *sea* Japan
60 G11 **Seto Naikai Nat. Park** Japan
68 B4 **Setsan** Burma
85 C2 **Settat** Morocco
86 A6 **Sette Cama** Gabon
119 U1 **Settee L** Manitoba Canada
119 T3 **Setting L** Manitoba Canada
13 F5 **Settle** England
140 E3 **Settlement Cr** Queensland Australia
90 C15 **Settlement of Edinburgh** Tristan da Cunha
16 B6 **Setúbal** Portugal
37 M5 **Seubersdorf** Germany
Seu d'Urgell, la *see* **Seo de Urgel**
37 K5 **Seukendorf** Germany
55 E1 **Seul'** *R* Russian Federation
99 V4 **Seul Choix Pt** Michigan U.S.A.
69 B10 **Seulimeum** Sumatra
115 K7 **Seul, Lac** Ontario Canada
21 J3 **Seulles** *R* France
69 C11 **Seumayan** Sumatra
40 B3 **Seurre** France
78 K1 **Sevan, Ozero** Armenia
53 D11 **Sevastopol'** Ukraine
54 H6 **Sev Donets** *R* Rus Fed/Ukraine
28 B4 **Sevel** Denmark
100 J4 **Seven Devils Mts** Idaho U.S.A.
140 D3 **Seven Emu** N Terr Australia
14 C5 **Seven Hd** Ireland
122 F3 **Seven Is. Bay** Quebec Canada
106 C6 **Seven Lakes** New Mexico U.S.A.
9 G5 **Sevenoaks** England
118 G9 **Seven Persons** Alberta Canada
109 J7 **Seven Sisters** Texas U.S.A.
112 K2 **Seven Springs** North Carolina U.S.A.
141 K6 **Seventeen Seventy** Queensland Australia
102 F1 **Seven Troughs** Nevada U.S.A.
117 N10 **Seventy Mile House** British Columbia Canada
25 F6 **Sevenum** Netherlands
20 F6 **Sévérac** France
18 H8 **Séverac-le-Château** France
107 P2 **Severance** Kansas U.S.A.
139 K3 **Severn** *R* New South Wales Australia
121 L8 **Severn** *R* Ontario Canada
52 J4 **Severnaya Mylva** *R* Russian Federation
51 K1 **Severnaya Zemlya** *arch* Arctic Oc
55 G3 **Severnoye** Russian Federation
8 D4 **Severn, R** England
55 D3 **Severnyy** Russian Federation
52 J3 **Severnyy Ural** *mts* Russian Federation
56 G3 **Severobaykal'sk** Russian Federation
51 L3 **Severo-Baykal'skoye Nagor'ye** *uplands* Russian Federation
37 P3 **Severocesky Kraj** *reg* Czechoslovakia
52 E3 **Severodvinsk** Russian Federation
55 E4 **Severo-Kazakhstanskaya Oblast'** *prov* Kazakhstan
31 K6 **Severomoravský** *reg* Czechoslovakia
52 D1 **Severomorsk** Russian Federation
53 F11 **Severo-Osetinskaya Respublika** Russian Federation
55 C1 **Severouralsk** Russian Federation
54 K2 **Severo Zadonsk** Russian Federation
107 O4 **Severy** Kansas U.S.A.
20 H3 **Séves** *R* France
29 O2 **Sevettijarvi** Finland
56 D5 **Sevi** Russian Federation
103 M2 **Sevier** *R* Utah U.S.A.
103 M3 **Sevier** Utah U.S.A.
103 M2 **Sevier Bridge Res** Utah U.S.A.
103 M2 **Sevier Des** Utah U.S.A.
112 D2 **Sevierville** Tennessee U.S.A.
20 F5 **Sévignac** France
22 G4 **Sevigny** France
126 F4 **Sevilla** *R* Cuba
16 D7 **Sevilla** *prov* Spain
16 D7 **Sevilla** Spain
Seville *see* **Sevilla**
46 G2 **Sevlievo** Bulgaria
48 J2 **Sevola** *mt* Ukraine
21 J8 **Sèvre** *R* France
18 E6 **Sèvre-Niortaise** *R* France
40 B5 **Sevron** *R* France
54 F4 **Sevsk** Russian Federation
85 B7 **Sewa** *R* Sierra Leone
110 L6 **Sewanee** Tennessee U.S.A.
116 N6 **Seward** Alaska U.S.A.
107 M3 **Seward** Kansas U.S.A.
98 J9 **Seward** Nebraska U.S.A.
107 N6 **Seward** Oklahoma U.S.A.
94 H6 **Seward** Pennsylvania U.S.A.
116 R6 **Seward Glacier** Yukon Terr/Alaska Canada/U.S.A.
146 D6 **Seward Mts** Antarctica
116 E4 **Seward Pen** Alaska U.S.A.
133 C4 **Sewell** Chile
40 E2 **Sewen** France
94 G6 **Sewickley** Pennsylvania U.S.A.
117 O8 **Sexsmith** Alberta Canada
124 G4 **Sextín** Mexico
77 H3 **Seyah Band Koh** *mts* Afghanistan
43 B12 **Seybouse** *R* Algeria
83 J12 **Seychelles** *rep* Indian Oc
33 R9 **Seyda** Germany
52 K2 **Seyda** Russian Federation
29 T9 **Seydhisfjördhur** Iceland
78 C3 **Seydişehir** Turkey
20 G3 **Seye** *R* France
78 E3 **Seyhan** *R* Turkey
79 F1 **Seyhan Barajı** *res* Turkey
47 L5 **Seyit** *R* Turkey
47 L5 **Seyitgazi** Turkey
54 D5 **Seym** *R* Ukraine
139 H6 **Seymour** Victoria Australia
95 O5 **Seymour** Connecticut U.S.A.
94 B8 **Seymour** Indiana U.S.A.
110 C1 **Seymour** Iowa U.S.A.
110 D4 **Seymour** Missouri U.S.A.
109 H2 **Seymour** Texas U.S.A.
99 S5 **Seymour** Wisconsin U.S.A.
140 C6 **Seymour Ra** N Terr Australia
19 Q16 **Seyne-les-Alpes** France
42 F3 **Sežana** Slovenia
18 H4 **Sezanne** France
52 D6 **Sezha** *R* Russian Federation
45 O6 **Sezze** Italy
85 G2 **Sfax** Tunisia
46 F9 **Sfinári** Crete Greece
48 K5 **Sfîntu Gheorghe** Romania
48 M6 **Sfîntu Gheorghe** *R* Romania
's-Gravenhage *see* **Den Haag**
25 B5 **'s-Gravenzande** Netherlands
15 D3 **Sgurr Mor** *mt* Scotland
80 D2 **Sha'ab** Israel
80 F1 **Sha'al** Syria
58 E4 **Shaanxi** *prov* China
80 F3 **Sha'ar** Israel
87 E7 **Shaba** *reg* Zaire
Shabani *see* **Zvishavane**
119 O2 **Shabaqua** Ontario Canada
99 S8 **Shabbona** Illinois U.S.A.
84 H5 **Shab, El** Egypt
53 E10 **Shabel'skoye** Russian Federation
78 K2 **Shabestar** Iran
79 F9 **Shabibī, J. esh** *mt* Jordan
47 J1 **Shabla** Bulgaria
86 E6 **Shabunda** Zaire
55 D2 **Shaburovo** Russian Federation
67 B3 **Shachang** China
66 B4 **Shache** China
118 J8 **Shackleton** Saskatchewan Canada
146 D11 **Shackleton Coast** Antarctica
146 D10 **Shackleton Glacier** Antarctica
146 H13 **Shackleton Ice Shelf** Antarctica
146 D10 **Shackleton Inlet** Antarctica
146 F7 **Shackleton Ra** Antarctica
78 H3 **Shadādah, Ash** Syria
74 B5 **Shadadkot** Pakistan
68 C3 **Shadaw** Burma
98 D4 **Shadehill Res** South Dakota U.S.A.
67 E3 **Shadi** China
55 D3 **Shadrinsk** Russian Federation
84 J4 **Shadwân** Egypt
111 K10 **Shady Grove** Alabama U.S.A.
113 D7 **Shady Grove** Florida U.S.A.
146 C12 **Shafer Peak** *mt* Antarctica
57 C4 **Shafirkan** Uzbekistan
55 C4 **Shafranovo** Russian Federation
102 E6 **Shafter** California U.S.A.
101 L9 **Shafter** Nevada U.S.A.
108 C6 **Shafter** Texas U.S.A.
8 D5 **Shaftesbury** England
55 G5 **Shagan** *R* Kazakhstan
65 E4 **Shagang** China
48 M5 **Shagany, Oz** *L* Ukraine
Shagedu *see* **Jungar Qi**
55 F4 **Shaglyteniz, Oz** *L* Kazakhstan
56 D5 **Shagonar** Russian Federation
144 C6 **Shag R** New Zealand
57 A2 **Shagray, Plato** *plateau* Kazakhstan
146 E1 **Shag Rocks** S Georgia S Atlantic Oc
76 C2 **Shahabad** India
76 B3 **Shahapur** India
80 B7 **Shahar** Israel
74 C6 **Shahbadpur** Pakistan
74 B6 **Shahbandar** Pakistan
75 J7 **Shahdol** India
65 C6 **Shahe** China
65 D6 **Shahe** China
67 E2 **Shahezhen** China
Shahezi *see* **Wan Xian**
77 K2 **Shah Fuladi** *mt* Afghanistan
84 G3 **Shahhāt** Libya
Shāhī *see* **Qāem Shahr**
74 H5 **Shahjahanpur** India
77 E1 **Shāh Jehān, Kuh-e** *mts* Iran
77 K3 **Shāh Jūy** Afghanistan
65 E4 **Shahousuo** China
74 G7 **Shahpur** India
74 F6 **Shahpura** India
77 J2 **Shahrak** Afghanistan
77 G3 **Shāhrakht** Iran
77 D4 **Shahr-e Bābak** Iran
77 B3 **Shahr-e Kord** Iran
77 B2 **Shahr Rey** Iran
77 D2 **Shahrud Bustam** Iran
77 F5 **Shāh Savāran, Kūh-e** *mts* Iran
55 D1 **Shaim** Russian Federation
79 H4 **Shā'īr, Jabal** *mt* Syria
80 G3 **Shajara** Jordan
65 F4 **Shajianzi** China
52 E6 **Shakhovskaya** Russian Federation
57 D5 **Shakhrisabz** Uzbekistan
59 M2 **Shakhtersk** Sakhalin Russian Federation
54 K8 **Shakhtersk** Ukraine
55 F6 **Shakhtinsk** Kazakhstan
54 M9 **Shakhty** Russian Federation
52 G5 **Shakhun'ya** Russian Federation
85 E7 **Shaki** Nigeria
99 N5 **Shakopee** Minnesota U.S.A.
59 L3 **Shakotan misaki** *C* Japan
55 C4 **Shaksha** Russian Federation
116 G4 **Shaktolik** Alaska U.S.A.
86 G4 **Shala Hāyk'** *L* Ethiopia
52 F4 **Shalakusha** Russian Federation
117 M10 **Shalalth** British Columbia Canada
65 G2 **Shalan** China
67 D6 **Shalang** China
55 G4 **Shalday** Kazakhstan
52 F6 **Shaldezh** Russian Federation
9 F5 **Shalford** England
52 E4 **Shalgachëva** Russian Federation
57 F2 **Shalgiya** Kazakhstan
80 C8 **Shalhavi** Israel
66 E4 **Shaliangzi** China
77 E4 **Shalidab** Iran
55 D5 **Shalkar Karashatau** *L* Kazakhstan
55 D5 **Shalkar-Yega-Kara** *L* Russian Federation
57 J3 **Shalkudysu** Kazakhstan
80 G3 **Shallala** Jordan
112 J4 **Shallotte** North Carolina U.S.A.
108 E2 **Shallowater** Texas U.S.A.
120 J8 **Shallow Lake** Ontario Canada
80 C7 **Shalwa** Israel
55 C3 **Shalya** Russian Federation
56 C4 **Shalym** Russian Federation
88 D5 **Shama** *R* Tanzania
56 C5 **Shaman, Khrebet** *mts* Russian Federation
55 C3 **Shamary** Russian Federation
86 F4 **Shambe** Sudan
80 D2 **Shamerat** Israel
75 O5 **Shamgong** Bhutan
77 E6 **Shamīl** Iran
80 F1 **Shamir** Israel
78 K6 **Shamiya Des** Iraq
95 L6 **Shamokin** Pennsylvania U.S.A.
118 L8 **Shamrock** Saskatchewan Canada
113 D8 **Shamrock** Florida U.S.A.
107 O6 **Shamrock** Oklahoma U.S.A.
108 D8 **Shamrock** Texas U.S.A.
88 C10 **Shamva** Zimbabwe
68 C2 **Shan** *prov* Burma
80 G6 **Sha'nab** Jordan
Shanchengzhen *see* **Nanjing**
77 G5 **Shāndak** Iran
58 D4 **Shandan** China
65 C3 **Shandian He** *R* China
12 D1 **Shandon** Scotland
102 D6 **Shandon** California U.S.A.
65 C6 **Shandong** *prov* China
65 E6 **Shandong Bandao** *pen* China
87 E9 **Shangani** *R* Zimbabwe
65 D4 **Shangbancheng** China
67 E1 **Shangcheng** China
65 F3 **Shangchengzhen** China
67 D6 **Shangchuan Dao** *isld* China
65 B4 **Shangdu** China
Shangdundu *see* **Linchuan**
67 E2 **Shangfu** China
67 E2 **Shanggao** China
63 **Shanghai** *conurbation* China
67 G1 **Shanghai** China
67 E4 **Shanghang** China
65 D6 **Shanghe**
65 C4 **Shanghuangqi** China
67 C1 **Shangkan** China
67 C5 **Shanglin** China
87 D9 **Shangombo** Zambia
Shangpaihe *see* **Feixi**
58 G5 **Shangqiu** China
67 F2 **Shangrao** China
67 B5 **Shangsi** China
Shangxian *see* **Shangzhou**
65 B5 **Shangyangwu** China
65 C4 **Shangyi** China
67 E4 **Shangyou** China
66 C3 **Shangyou Shuiku** *res* China
67 G1 **Shangyu** China
59 J2 **Shangzhi** China
58 E5 **Shangzhou** China
65 D5 **Shanhaiguan** China
65 G2 **Shanhetun** China
100 E4 **Shaniko** Oregon U.S.A.
9 E6 **Shanklin** England
67 E2 **Shankou** China
94 J6 **Shanksville** Pennsylvania U.S.A.
145 E4 **Shannon** New Zealand
112 B3 **Shannon** Georgia U.S.A.
99 R7 **Shannon** Illinois U.S.A.
111 H7 **Shannon** Mississippi U.S.A.
14 C4 **Shannon Airport** Ireland
99 M9 **Shannon City** Iowa U.S.A.
14 D2 **Shannon Pot** Ireland
14 C2 **Shannon R** Ireland
Shansi *prov see* **Shanxi** *prov*
65 G3 **Shansonggang** China
80 G4 **Shantana** Jordan
51 N3 **Shantarskiye, Ostrova** *islds* Russian Federation
67 E5 **Shantou** China
Shantung *prov see* **Shandong** *prov*
Shantung Peninsula *see* **Shandong Bandao**
67 E5 **Shanwei** China
58 F4 **Shanxi** *prov* China
65 C7 **Shan Xian** China
67 F4 **Shanyao** China
58 F4 **Shanyin** China
67 F1 **Shaobo** China
67 D3 **Shaodong** China
67 D3 **Shaoshan** China
67 F3 **Shaowu** China
59 H5 **Shaoxing** China
67 D3 **Shaoyang** China
15 F1 **Shapinsay** Scotland
52 H2 **Shapkina** *R* Russian Federation
56 C5 **Shapshal'skiy Khrebet** *mts* Russian Federation
80 D4 **Shaqéd** Jordan
Shara Gol *R see* **Dang He** *R*
52 H7 **Sharan** Russian Federation
52 G6 **Sharanga** Russian Federation
121 O8 **Sharbot Lake** Ontario Canada
56 E6 **Sharga** Mongolia
48 L2 **Shargorod** Ukraine
58 D3 **Sharhulsan** Mongolia
60 S2 **Shari** Japan
79 H4 **Sharīfah** Syria
56 G6 **Sharīngol** Mongolia
Shāriqah, Ash *see* **Sharjah**
77 D7 **Sharjah** U.A.E.
52 H6 **Sharkan** Russian Federation
71 D5 **Shark Fin B** Philippines
52 C6 **Sharkovshchina** Belorussia
141 H2 **Shark Reef** Gt Barrier Reef Aust
55 B4 **Sharlyk** Russian Federation
79 F10 **Sharmah** Saudi Arabia
95 O5 **Sharon** Connecticut U.S.A.
112 E4 **Sharon** Georgia U.S.A.
107 M4 **Sharon** Kansas U.S.A.
94 B2 **Sharon** Michigan U.S.A.
98 J2 **Sharon** North Dakota U.S.A.
108 E7 **Sharon** Oklahoma U.S.A.
110 H5 **Sharon** Tennessee U.S.A.
95 P3 **Sharon** Vermont U.S.A.
99 S7 **Sharon** Wisconsin U.S.A.
80 C5 **Sharon, Plain of** Israel
107 J3 **Sharon Springs** Kansas U.S.A.
54 G6 **Sharovka** Ukraine
98 F5 **Sharpe, L** South Dakota U.S.A.
95 L9 **Sharps** Virginia U.S.A.
99 M9 **Sharpsburg** Iowa U.S.A.
94 K7 **Sharpsburg** Maryland U.S.A.
94 A6 **Sharpsville** Indiana U.S.A.
79 F5 **Sharqi, Jebel esh** *mts* Lebanon
52 G5 **Shar'ya** Russian Federation
56 C3 **Sharypovo** Russian Federation
89 F3 **Shashani** *R* Zimbabwe
89 E3 **Shashe** Botswana
89 G2 **Shashe** *R* Zimbabwe
87 E10 **Shashe** *R* Zimbabwe/Botswana
86 G4 **Shashemenē** Ethiopia
67 D1 **Shashi** China
100 C9 **Shasta L** California U.S.A.
100 C8 **Shasta, Mt** California U.S.A.
67 D4 **Shatian** China
52 F6 **Shatki** Russian Federation
55 D3 **Shatrovo** Russian Federation
108 E7 **Shattuck** Oklahoma U.S.A.
54 L1 **Shatura** Russian Federation
79 F8 **Shaubak** Jordan
57 J2 **Shaukar, Poluostrov** *pen* Kazakhstan
80 G3 **Shaumar** Jordan
118 J9 **Shaunavon** Saskatchewan Canada
52 D3 **Shaverki** Russian Federation
102 E4 **Shaver L** California U.S.A.
94 H8 **Shavers Fork** *R* West Virginia U.S.A.
80 D4 **Shavé Shomeron** Jordan
80 D2 **Shave Ẕiyyon** Israel
111 F8 **Shaw** Mississippi U.S.A.
120 K7 **Shawanaga** Ontario Canada
95 N5 **Shawangunk Mts** New York U.S.A.
99 S5 **Shawano** Wisconsin U.S.A.
99 S5 **Shawano L** Wisconsin U.S.A.
121 R7 **Shawbridge** Quebec Canada
8 D2 **Shawbury** England
141 J5 **Shaw I** Queensland Australia
121 S6 **Shawinigan** Quebec Canada
79 H4 **Shawmarīyah, Jabal ash** *mt* Syria
101 Q3 **Shawmut** Montana U.S.A.
94 E7 **Shawnee** Ohio U.S.A.
107 O6 **Shawnee** Oklahoma U.S.A.
98 A7 **Shawnee** Wyoming U.S.A.
110 H4 **Shawneetown** Illinois U.S.A.
121 O7 **Shawville** Quebec Canada
67 F3 **Sha Xi** *R* China
67 F3 **Sha Xian** China
67 D1 **Shayang** China
142 D5 **Shay Gap** W Australia Australia
84 J4 **Shayib el Banât, Gebel** *mt* Egypt
79 G6 **Shaykh Miskīn** Syria
52 J4 **Shaytanovka** Russian Federation
67 G1 **Shazhou** China
57 F5 **Shazud** Tajikistan
54 J3 **Shchekino** Russian Federation
54 K1 **Shchelkovo** Russian Federation
52 H2 **Shchel'yayur** Russian Federation
55 G4 **Shcherbakty** Kazakhstan
54 J1 **Shcherbinka** Russian Federation
54 H5 **Shchigry** Russian Federation
54 C5 **Shchors** Ukraine
54 F8 **Shchorsk** Ukraine
55 F4 **Shchuchinsk** Kazakhstan
55 D3 **Shchuch'ye** Russian Federation
54 M5 **Shchuch'ye** Voronezhskaya obl Russian Federation
55 C3 **Shchuch'ye Ozero** Russian Federation
54 K1 **Shchurovo** Russian Federation
128 G3 **Shea** Guyana
100 H6 **Sheaville** Oregon U.S.A.
119 O2 **Shebandowan L** Ontario Canada
54 H6 **Shebekino** Russian Federation
86 H4 **Shebelē, Wabē** *R* Ethiopia
77 J1 **Sheberghān** Afghanistan
99 T6 **Sheboygan** Wisconsin U.S.A.
86 B4 **Shebshi Mts** Nigeria
100 B5 **Shedd** Oregon U.S.A.
120 J10 **Shedden** Ontario Canada
122 H7 **Shediac** New Brunswick Canada
14 D3 **Sheelin, L** Ireland
121 N7 **Sheenboro** Quebec Canada
116 Q2 **Sheenjek** *R* Alaska U.S.A.
117 O9 **Sheep Cr** Alberta Canada
101 U7 **Sheep Cr** Wyoming U.S.A.
14 D1 **Sheep Haven** Ireland
101 T10 **Sheephorn** Colorado U.S.A.
106 C2 **Sheep Mt** Colorado U.S.A.
103 J5 **Sheep Pk** Nevada U.S.A.
103 J5 **Sheep Ra** Nevada U.S.A.
14 B5 **Sheep's Hd** Ireland
118 F7 **Sheerness** Alberta Canada
9 G5 **Sheerness** England
122 K9 **Sheet Harbour** Nova Scotia Canada
80 D2 **Shefar'am** Israel
80 C7 **Shefela** Israel
139 H8 **Sheffield** Tasmania Australia
13 G6 **Sheffield** England
144 D5 **Sheffield** New Zealand
110 J7 **Sheffield** Alabama U.S.A.
99 R8 **Sheffield** Illinois U.S.A.
99 N7 **Sheffield** Iowa U.S.A.
95 O4 **Sheffield** Massachusetts U.S.A.
94 H5 **Sheffield** Pennsylvania U.S.A.
108 F5 **Sheffield** Texas U.S.A.
94 E5 **Sheffield Lake** Ohio U.S.A.
56 B3 **Shegarka** *R* Russian Federation
52 G3 **Shegmas** Russian Federation
120 J7 **Sheguiandah** Ontario Canada
119 O7 **Sheho** Saskatchewan Canada
67 B1 **Shehong** China
133 C7 **Shehuén** *R* Argentina
79 F5 **Sheikh, J. esh** *mt* Lebanon/Syria
120 F3 **Shekak** *R* Ontario Canada
Shekar Dzong *see* **Tingri**
Shekhem *see* **Nablus**
54 M4 **Shekhman'** Russian Federation
74 F3 **Shekhupura** Pakistan
53 G12 **Sheki** Azerbaijan
52 E5 **Sheksna** *R* Russian Federation
52 E5 **Sheksna** Russian Federation
94 E9 **Shelbiana** Kentucky U.S.A.
110 D2 **Shelbina** Missouri U.S.A.
110 J2 **Shelburn** Indiana U.S.A.
122 G10 **Shelburne** Nova Scotia Canada
120 K8 **Shelburne** Ontario Canada
95 O2 **Shelburne** Vermont U.S.A.
141 G1 **Shelburne B** Queensland Australia
95 P4 **Shelburne Falls** Massachusetts U.S.A.
99 T8 **Shelby** Indiana U.S.A.
99 L8 **Shelby** Iowa U.S.A.
99 U6 **Shelby** Michigan U.S.A.
111 F8 **Shelby** Mississippi U.S.A.
101 O1 **Shelby** Montana U.S.A.
98 J8 **Shelby** Nebraska U.S.A.
112 F2 **Shelby** North Carolina U.S.A.
94 E6 **Shelby** Ohio U.S.A.
110 H2 **Shelbyville** Illinois U.S.A.
110 L2 **Shelbyville** Indiana U.S.A.
110 L3 **Shelbyville** Kentucky U.S.A.
110 E2 **Shelbyville** Missouri U.S.A.
110 K6 **Shelbyville** Tennessee U.S.A.
109 N4 **Shelbyville** Texas U.S.A.
99 T9 **Sheldon** Illinois U.S.A.
99 L6 **Sheldon** Iowa U.S.A.
110 B4 **Sheldon** Missouri U.S.A.
98 J3 **Sheldon** North Dakota U.S.A.
117 H4 **Sheldon, Mt** Yukon Territory Canada
95 P2 **Sheldon Springs** Vermont U.S.A.
122 H3 **Sheldrake** Quebec Canada
56 F5 **Shelekhov** Russian Federation
51 P3 **Shelikhova, Zaliv** *B* Russian Federation
116 K8 **Shelikof Str** Alaska U.S.A.
99 L3 **Shell** *R* Minnesota U.S.A.
101 S5 **Shell** Wyoming U.S.A.
111 G12 **Shell Beach** Louisiana U.S.A.
118 L5 **Shellbrook** Saskatchewan Canada
101 R8 **Shell Cr** Wyoming U.S.A.
101 N6 **Shelley** Idaho U.S.A.
139 K5 **Shellharbour** New South Wales Australia
99 P4 **Shell L** Wisconsin U.S.A.
118 K5 **Shell Lake** Saskatchewan Canada
143 F8 **Shell Lakes** W Australia Australia
111 M10 **Shellman** Georgia U.S.A.
119 Q8 **Shellmouth** Manitoba Canada
102 A1 **Shell Mt** California U.S.A.
99 O7 **Shell Rock** Iowa U.S.A.
99 O7 **Shellrock** *R* Iowa U.S.A.
99 P7 **Shellsburg** Iowa U.S.A.
80 D1 **Shelomi** Israel
58 G1 **Shelopugino** Russian Federation
102 A1 **Shelter Cove** California U.S.A.
95 P5 **Shelter I** Long I, New York U.S.A.
144 B7 **Shelter Pt** New Zealand
95 O5 **Shelton** Connecticut U.S.A.
98 H9 **Shelton** Nebraska U.S.A.
117 M12 **Shelton** Washington U.S.A.
52 E4 **Sheltozero** Russian Federation
78 M1 **Shemakha** Azerbaijan
56 B5 **Shemonaikha** Kazakhstan
52 H6 **Shemordan** Russian Federation
52 G6 **Shemursha** Russian Federation
99 L9 **Shenandoah** Iowa U.S.A.
95 L6 **Shenandoah** Pennsylvania U.S.A.
94 J8 **Shenandoah** Virginia U.S.A.
94 H8 **Shenandoah Mts** W Virginia/Virginia U.S.A.
94 J8 **Shenandoah Nat. Park** Virginia U.S.A.
94 G5 **Shenango Res** Ohio/Penn U.S.A.
57 D1 **Shenber** Kazakhstan
65 B5 **Shenchi** China
86 A4 **Shendam** Nigeria
86 F2 **Shendi** Sudan
65 J1 **Shending Shan** *mt* China
57 J3 **Shengel'dy** Kazakhstan
46 D3 **Shëngjin** Albania
65 F1 **Shengping** China
67 G1 **Shengsi** China
67 G1 **Shengsi Liedao** *islds* China
67 G2 **Sheng Xian** China
52 F4 **Shenkursk** Russian Federation
65 A5 **Shenmu** China
67 C1 **Shennongjia** China
Shensi *prov see* **Shaanxi**
52 H7 **Shentala** Russian Federation
143 E8 **Shenton, Mt** W Australia Australia
Shentza Dzong *see* **Xainza**
65 C5 **Shen Xian** China
65 C6 **Shen Xian** China
59 H3 **Shenyang** China
65 C5 **Shenze** China
Shenzhen *see* **Bao'an**
74 G6 **Sheopur** India
118 D7 **Shepard** Alberta Canada
94 C3 **Shepherd** Michigan U.S.A.
101 R4 **Shepherd** Montana U.S.A.
109 M5 **Shepherd** Texas U.S.A.
137 O5 **Shepherd Is** Vanuatu
94 K7 **Shepherdstown** West Virginia U.S.A.
94 B9 **Shepherdsville** Kentucky U.S.A.
117 G7 **Sheppard, Mt** British Columbia Canada
139 H6 **Shepparton** Victoria Australia
9 G5 **Sheppey** *isld* England
8 D5 **Shepton Mallet** England
80 C7 **Sheqef** Israel
77 K1 **Sherabad** Uzbekistan
115 M3 **Sherard, C** Northwest Territories Canada
55 F4 **Sherbakul'** Russian Federation
8 D6 **Sherborne** England
85 B7 **Sherbro I** Sierra Leone
121 T7 **Sherbrooke** Quebec Canada
122 H9 **Sherbrooke L** Nova Scotia Canada
13 H5 **Sherburn** England
13 G6 **Sherburn** England
99 M6 **Sherburn** Minnesota U.S.A.
95 M4 **Sherburne** New York U.S.A.
86 C1 **Sherda** Chad
9 F5 **Shere** England
84 J6 **Shereik** Sudan
54 J1 **Sheremet'yevo** *airport* Russian Federation
74 E5 **Shergarh** India
111 D7 **Sheridan** Arkansas U.S.A.
94 A6 **Sheridan** Indiana U.S.A.
94 B3 **Sheridan** Michigan U.S.A.
101 N4 **Sheridan** Montana U.S.A.
100 B4 **Sheridan** Oregon U.S.A.
101 T5 **Sheridan** Wyoming U.S.A.
115 N1 **Sheridan, C** Northwest Territories Canada
106 H3 **Sheridan L** Colorado U.S.A.
101 P5 **Sheridan, Mt** Wyoming U.S.A.
138 D5 **Sheringa** South Australia Australia
9 H2 **Sheringham** England
111 H7 **Sherman** Mississippi U.S.A.
94 H4 **Sherman** New York U.S.A.
109 L2 **Sherman** Texas U.S.A.
95 S8 **Sherman Mills** Maine U.S.A.
103 J1 **Sherman Mt** Nevada U.S.A.
101 O7 **Sherman Pk** Idaho U.S.A.
98 H8 **Sherman Res** Nebraska U.S.A.
77 L2 **Sherpur** Afghanistan
119 Q3 **Sherridon** Manitoba Canada
95 M3 **Sherrill** New York U.S.A.
25 D5 **'s-Hertogenbosch** Netherlands
141 K2 **Sherwood** *dist* Brisbane, Qnsld Australia
122 J7 **Sherwood** Prince Edward I Canada
98 E1 **Sherwood** North Dakota U.S.A.
108 G4 **Sherwood** Texas U.S.A.
144 C5 **Sherwood Downs** New Zealand
9 E1 **Sherwood Forest** England
52 H6 **Sheshma** *R* Russian Federation
77 E1 **Sheshtamad** Iran
67 E1 **She Shui** *R* China
117 H6 **Sheslay** British Columbia Canada
52 H5 **Shestakovo** Russian Federation
99 L5 **Shetek, L** Minnesota U.S.A.
15 G2 **Shetland** *reg* Scotland
50 E4 **Shevchenko** Kazakhstan
48 M5 **Shevchenko, Liman** *B* Ukraine
57 B2 **Shevchenko, Zaliv** *G* Kazakhstan
99 L2 **Shevlin** Minnesota U.S.A.
86 G4 **Shewa** *prov* Ethiopia
86 G4 **Shewa Gīmīra** Ethiopia
65 B6 **She Xian** China
67 F2 **She Xian** China
98 G2 **Sheyenne** North Dakota U.S.A.
98 J3 **Sheyenne** *R* North Dakota U.S.A.
77 C6 **Sheykh Sho'eyb** *isld* Iran
80 E2 **Shezor** Israel
15 B3 **Shiant** *isld* Scotland
94 C3 **Shiawassee** *R* Michigan U.S.A.
61 N8 **Shibata** Japan
65 B4 **Shibatai** China
60 S2 **Shibecha** Japan
60 T2 **Shibetsu** Japan
84 J3 **Shibîn el Kom** Egypt
79 B8 **Shibîn el Qanâtir** Egypt
67 C3 **Shibing** China
61 M9 **Shibukawa** Japan
60 E14 **Shibushi-wan** Japan
65 D6 **Shibuzi** China
67 B3 **Shichang** China
67 E3 **Shicheng** China
61 P5 **Shichinohe** Japan
98 J9 **Shickley** Nebraska U.S.A.
95 L5 **Shickshinny** Pennsylvania U.S.A.
122 F5 **Shickshock Mts** Quebec Canada
Shicun *see* **Xiangfen**
65 E6 **Shidao** China
65 E6 **Shidao Wan** *B* China
55 F5 **Shiderty** Kazakhstan
55 F5 **Shiderty** *R* Kazakhstan
107 O5 **Shidler** Oklahoma U.S.A.
60 H11 **Shido** Japan
15 C3 **Shieldaig** Scotland
140 D2 **Shield, C** N Terr Australia
107 K3 **Shields** Kansas U.S.A.
98 E3 **Shields** North Dakota U.S.A.
67 A1 **Shifang** China
8 D2 **Shifnal** England
61 K10 **Shiga** *prefect* Japan
Shigatse *see* **Xigazê**
122 G5 **Shigawake** Quebec Canada
65 A4 **Shiguaigou** China
67 F1 **Shih-chiu Hu** *L* China
58 G5 **Shi He** *R* China
66 D3 **Shihezi** China
Shihkiachwang *see* **Shijiazhuang**
86 J4 **Shiikh** Somalia
61 M8 **Shiiya** Japan
46 D3 **Shijak** Albania
67 A1 **Shijiaba** China
Shijiao *see* **Fogang**
65 B5 **Shijiazhuang** China
65 C5 **Shijiazhuang** China
67 F1 **Shijiu Hu** China
65 D7 **Shijiusuo** China
60 O3 **Shikabe** Japan
119 N1 **Shikag L** Ontario Canada
60 H11 **Shikama** Japan
68 J2 **Shikang** China
77 L2 **Shikar, Darya-i-** *R* Afghanistan
76 B3 **Shikarpur** India
74 C5 **Shikarpur** Pakistan
61 N11 **Shikine-jima** *isld* Japan
60 G12 **Shikoku** *isld* Japan
60 F12 **Shikoku-sanchi** *mts* Japan
59 N3 **Shikotan** *isld* Japan
60 O3 **Shikotsu Toya Nat. Park** Japan
86 H4 **Shilabo** Ethiopia
52 G4 **Shilador** Russian Federation
80 D6 **Shilat** Jordan
55 D5 **Shil'da** Russian Federation
75 N5 **Shiliguri** India
Shiliu *see* **Changjiang**
59 G1 **Shilka** *R* Russian Federation
14 E4 **Shillelagh** Ireland
9 E4 **Shillingford** England
120 K4 **Shillington** Ontario Canada
95 M6 **Shillington** Pennsylvania U.S.A.
80 E5 **Shillo** Jordan
75 O6 **Shillong** India
110 H6 **Shiloh Nat. Mil. Park** Tennessee U.S.A.
67 C5 **Shilong** China
67 D5 **Shilong** China
65 A6 **Shilou** China
54 M2 **Shilovo** Russian Federation
Shima *see* **Longhai**
67 E3 **Shima** China
60 D13 **Shimabara** Japan
61 M11 **Shimada** Japan
60 F10 **Shimane** *prefect* Japan
59 J1 **Shimanovsk** Russian Federation
60 F13 **Shimanto** Japan
67 D2 **Shimen** China
65 D4 **Shimenzhai** China
61 M11 **Shimizu** Japan
74 G3 **Shimla** India
61 L9 **Shimminato** Japan
61 M11 **Shimoda** Japan
61 O9 **Shimodate** Japan
60 P4 **Shimofuro** Japan
76 B4 **Shimoga** India
60 E11 **Shimogo** Japan
60 Q1 **Shimokawa** Japan
61 O8 **Shimo-kitaba** Japan
60 O4 **Shimokita-hantō** *pen* Japan
60 C14 **Shimo koshiki jima** *isld* Japan
61 M9 **Shimonita** Japan
59 K5 **Shimonoseki** Japan
60 D14 **Shimo-Taniguchi** Japan
60 E13 **Shimo-Tashima** Japan
61 N9 **Shimotsuma** Japan
80 D3 **Shimron** Israel
52 D5 **Shimsk** Russian Federation
67 C5 **Shinan** China
59 L4 **Shinano** *R* Japan
77 H3 **Shīndand** Afghanistan
61 K11 **Shindō** Japan
109 K6 **Shiner** Texas U.S.A.
94 J5 **Shinglehouse** Pennsylvania U.S.A.
145 D4 **Shingle Pk** New Zealand
99 U3 **Shingleton** Michigan U.S.A.
100 D9 **Shingletown** California U.S.A.
61 J12 **Shingū** Japan
120 J5 **Shining Tree** Ontario Canada
61 O7 **Shinjō** Japan
60 E11 **Shin-Nan'yō** Japan
94 G7 **Shinnston** West Virginia U.S.A.
61 M9 **Shinonoi** Japan
79 G4 **Shinshār** Syria
61 L11 **Shinshiro** Japan
60 Q2 **Shintoku** Japan
88 D3 **Shinyanga** Tanzania
61 P7 **Shiogama** Japan
61 L9 **Shiojiri** Japan
61 J12 **Shiono-misaki** *C* Japan
Shipai *see* **Huaining**
126 F2 **Ship Chan. Cay** *isld* Bahamas
123 S6 **Ship Cove** Newfoundland Canada
9 G2 **Shipdham** England
111 H11 **Ship I** Mississippi U.S.A.
52 G4 **Shipitsino** Russian Federation
46 G2 **Shipka P** Bulgaria
74 H3 **Shipki Pass** India/Xizang Zizhiqu
13 G6 **Shipley** England
119 N5 **Shipman** Saskatchewan Canada
94 K6 **Shippensburg** Pennsylvania U.S.A.
106 B5 **Shiprock** New Mexico U.S.A.
121 T4 **Shipshaw Dam** Quebec Canada
111 E13 **Ship Shoal Lt. Hse** Louisiana U.S.A.
13 G5 **Shipton** N Yorks England
9 E4 **Shipton under Wychwood** England
Shipu *see* **Huanglong**
67 G2 **Shipu** China
67 C3 **Shiqian** China
Shiqiao *see* **Panyu**
67 D5 **Shiqiao** China
80 A7 **Shiqma** Israel
80 C8 **Shiqma** *R* Israel
58 E5 **Shiquan** China
66 C5 **Shiquan He** *R* China
74 H2 **Shiquanhe** China
60 J12 **Shirahama** Japan
60 O4 **Shirakami-misaki** *C* Japan
61 O8 **Shirakawa** Fukushima, Honshu Japan
61 K9 **Shirakawa** Toyama, Honshu Japan
78 L1 **Shirakskaya Step'** Azerbaijan/Georgia
61 N9 **Shirane-san** *mt* Tochigi Japan
61 M10 **Shirane san** *mt* Yamanashi Japan
60 S3 **Shiranuka** Japan
60 P3 **Shiraoi** Japan
146 C10 **Shirase Coast** Antarctica
77 C5 **Shīrāz** Iran
79 B7 **Shirbîn** Egypt
88 E9 **Shire** *R* Malawi
65 B2 **Shireet** Mongolia
88 E9 **Shire Highlands** Malawi
65 G4 **Shiren** China
60 T1 **Shiretoko misaki** *C* Japan
60 O3 **Shiribeshi** *prefect* Japan
57 C3 **Shirikrabat** Kazakhstan
60 O4 **Shiriuchi** Japan
60 P4 **Shiriya-zaki** *C* Japan
9 E3 **Shirley** England
9 E6 **Shirley** England
110 D6 **Shirley** Arkansas U.S.A.
101 T7 **Shirley Mts** Wyoming U.S.A.
61 O8 **Shiroishi** Japan
54 E9 **Shirokoye** Ukraine
61 K10 **Shirotori** Japan
61 L9 **Shirouma-dake** *mt* Japan
77 E1 **Shīrvān** Iran
116 E9 **Shishaldin Vol** Aleutian Is
60 H12 **Shishikui** Japan
60 C11 **Shishimi** Japan
116 D3 **Shishmaref** Alaska U.S.A.
116 E3 **Shishmaref Inlet** Alaska U.S.A.
67 D2 **Shishou** China
67 F1 **Shitai** China
61 L10 **Shitara** Japan
74 D5 **Shiv** India
74 G6 **Shivpuri** India
103 L5 **Shivwits Plat** Arizona U.S.A.
67 B6 **Shiwan Dashan** *mts* China
87 F8 **Shiwa Ngandu** Zambia
67 E4 **Shixing** China
67 B2 **Shiyangchang** China
67 C2 **Shiye** China
Shizhaihe *see* **Zhenping**
67 C2 **Shizhu** China
Shizilu *see* **Junan**
67 A4 **Shizong** China
61 P7 **Shizugawa** Japan
58 E4 **Shizuishan** China
65 A6 **Shizuiyi** China
61 O6 **Shizukuishi** Japan
60 Q3 **Shizunai** Japan
59 L5 **Shizuoka** Japan
61 M10 **Shizuoka** *prefect* Japan
54 B2 **Shklov** Belorussia
46 D2 **Shkodër** Albania
46 D3 **Shkumbin** *R* Albania
52 D5 **Shlino** *R* Russian Federation
51 J1 **Shmidta, Ostrova** *islds* Russian Federation
61 L9 **Shō** *R* Japan
113 A7 **Shoal** *R* Florida U.S.A.
140 B1 **Shoal B** N Terr Australia
123 T5 **Shoal Harb** Newfoundland Canada
139 K5 **Shoalhaven R** New South Wales Australia
119 U8 **Shoal L** Manitoba Canada
118 F1 **Shoal L** Ontario Canada
110 K3 **Shoals** Indiana U.S.A.
141 K5 **Shoalwater B** Queensland Australia
60 F11 **Shōbara** Japan
60 H11 **Shōdo-shima** *isld* Japan
9 G4 **Shoeburyness** England
123 R4 **Shoe Cove** Newfoundland Canada
145 E2 **Shoe I** New Zealand
77 F1 **Shoghlābād** Iran
51 K1 **Shokal'skogo, Proliv** *str* Russian Federation
60 P2 **Shokambetsu dake** *mt* Japan
57 E6 **Shokh** Tajikistan
60 R1 **Shokotsu** Japan
52 E4 **Shola** *R* Russian Federation
55 D5 **Sholaksay** Kazakhstan
55 F5 **Sholakshalkar, Oz** *L* Kazakhstan
142 B5 **Sholl I** W Australia Australia
52 D2 **Shomba** Russian Federation
80 E1 **Shomera** Israel
52 H3 **Shomvukva** Russian Federation
57 A2 **Shomyshkol'** Kazakhstan
88 B9 **Shona** Zambia
55 G5 **Shoptykul'** Kazakhstan
52 G6 **Shora** *R* Russian Federation
76 C5 **Shoranur** India
76 C2 **Shorapur** India
77 J5 **Shorawak** *reg* Afghanistan
9 F6 **Shoreham-by-Sea** England
99 T6 **Shorewood** Wisconsin U.S.A.
55 F5 **Shortandy** Kazakhstan
103 M5 **Short Cr** Arizona U.S.A.
119 Q7 **Shortdale** Manitoba Canada
111 L9 **Shorter** Alabama U.S.A.
138 E2 **Short, L** South Australia Australia
143 C10 **Short, Mt** W Australia Australia
95 K4 **Shortsville** New York U.S.A.
57 A2 **Shoshkakol'** Kazakhstan
102 H6 **Shoshone** California U.S.A.
101 L7 **Shoshone** Idaho U.S.A.
101 R5 **Shoshone** *R* Wyoming U.S.A.
101 Q5 **Shoshone Cavern Nat. Mon** Wyoming U.S.A.

101 P5 **Shoshone L** Wyoming U.S.A.
102 G2 **Shoshone Mts** Nevada U.S.A.
102 H5 **Shoshone Pk** Nevada U.S.A.
101 R6 **Shoshoni** Wyoming U.S.A.
54 E5 **Shostka** Ukraine
9 H4 **Shotley** England
144 B6 **Shotover R** New Zealand
67 F2 **Shouchang** China
67 C4 **Shoucheng** China
65 D6 **Shouguang** China
116 Q3 **Shoulder Mt** Alaska U.S.A.
118 E8 **Shouldice** Alberta Canada
67 F3 **Shouning** China
101 L4 **Shoup** Idaho U.S.A.
65 B6 **Shouyang** China
80 B8 **Shoval** Israel
99 N3 **Shovel L** Minnesota U.S.A.
146 J9 **Showa** *Japan Base* Antarctica
86 G3 **Showak** Sudan
60 O3 **Shōwa-Shinzan** *mt* Japan
103 O7 **Show Low** Arizona U.S.A.
52 F1 **Shoyna** Russian Federation
52 F4 **Shozhma** Russian Federation
54 C7 **Shpola** Ukraine
94 F6 **Shreve** Ohio U.S.A.
111 C9 **Shreveport** Louisiana U.S.A.
8 D2 **Shrewsbury** England
111 H12 **Shrewsbury** New Orleans, Louisiana U.S.A.
9 E5 **Shrewton** England
76 B1 **Shrigonda** India
76 B1 **Shrirampur** India
9 E4 **Shrivenham** England
8 D2 **Shropshire** *co* England
54 K8 **Shterovka** Ukraine
65 G2 **Shuang-ch'eng** China
65 F2 **Shuangchengpu** China
67 D3 **Shuangfeng** China
65 E2 **Shuanggang** China
67 D1 **Shuanggou** China
65 G3 **Shuanghezhen** China
Shuanghuyu *see* **Zizhou**
Shuangjiang *see* **Tongdao**
59 H3 **Shuangliao** China
67 A1 **Shuangliu** China
65 F3 **Shuangshan** China
65 F3 **Shuangyang** China
59 K2 **Shuangyashan** China
55 C6 **Shubar-Kuduk** Kazakhstan
79 H3 **Shubayţ, Jebel ash** *mts* Syria
122 J8 **Shubenacadie** Nova Scotia Canada
122 J9 **Shubenacadie L** Nova Scotia Canada
99 L9 **Shubert** Nebraska U.S.A.
116 P2 **Shublik Mts** Alaska U.S.A.
79 A7 **Shubra Khît** Egypt
111 H10 **Shubuta** Mississippi U.S.A.
67 E1 **Shucheng** China
80 F6 **Shu'eib** *R* Jordan
80 F6 **Shu'eib Br** Jordan
80 D4 **Shufa** Jordan
57 H5 **Shufu** China
55 G4 **Shuga** Kazakhstan
57 F5 **Shugnan** Tajikistan
57 F5 **Shugnanskiy Khrebet** *mts* Tajikistan
52 D5 **Shugozero** Russian Federation
55 E1 **Shugur** Russian Federation
52 H6 **Shugurovo** Russian Federation
65 D7 **Shu He** *R* China
67 B2 **Shuibatang** China
67 A3 **Shuicheng** China
Shuiji *see* **Laixi**
67 F3 **Shuiji** China
67 F3 **Shuikou** China
67 C4 **Shuikou** China
67 D5 **Shuikou** China
65 G2 **Shuiquliu** China
65 E5 **Shuishiying** China
74 D4 **Shujaabad** Pakistan
74 G7 **Shujalpur** India
55 D1 **Shukhtungort** Russian Federation
100 D1 **Shuksan, Mt** Washington U.S.A.
59 J3 **Shulan** China
57 H5 **Shule** China
58 C3 **Shule He** *R* China
Shulinzhao *see* **Dalad Qi**
99 Q7 **Shullsburg** Wisconsin U.S.A.
65 C6 **Shulu** China
116 G9 **Shumagin Is** Alaska U.S.A.
116 Q3 **Shuman House** Alaska U.S.A.
60 Q1 **Shumarinai** Japan
55 D5 **Shumekty** Kazakhstan
47 H1 **Shumen** Bulgaria
52 G6 **Shumerlya** Russian Federation
55 D3 **Shumikha** Russian Federation
54 A1 **Shumilino** Belorussia
52 H4 **Shumino** Russian Federation
56 E4 **Shumskiy** Russian Federation
65 E1 **Shumugou** China
103 O7 **Shumway** Arizona U.S.A.
80 F6 **Shunat Nimrin** Jordan
67 F3 **Shunchang** China
67 D5 **Shunde** China
52 D3 **Shunga** Russian Federation
65 C4 **Shunyi** China
67 B5 **Shuolong** China
58 F4 **Shuo Xian** China
80 F8 **Shuqeiq** *R* Jordan
111 H9 **Shuqualak** Mississippi U.S.A.
77 G4 **Shur** *R* Iran
57 F4 **Shurab** Tajikistan
52 G6 **Shuran** Russian Federation
61 P13 **Shuri** Okinawa
58 F1 **Shurinda** Russian Federation
52 H6 **Shurma** Russian Federation
87 E9 **Shurugwi** Zimbabwe
77 A3 **Shūsh** Iran
78 L2 **Shusha** Azerbaijan
46 D4 **Shushicë** *R* Albania
77 A3 **Shūshtar** Iran
117 O10 **Shuswap L** British Columbia Canada
139 H4 **Shuttleton** New South Wales Australia
80 B8 **Shuva** Israel
52 F6 **Shuya** Ivanovskaya obl Russian Federation
52 D4 **Shuya** Karel'skaya Respublika Russian Federation
116 L7 **Shuyak I** Alaska U.S.A.
65 D8 **Shuyang** China
52 D3 **Shuyeretskoye** Russian Federation
55 G4 **Shuyreksor, Oz** *L* Kazakhstan
52 F5 **Shuyskoye** Russian Federation
61 M11 **Shuzenji** Japan
68 B3 **Shwebandaw** Burma
68 B1 **Shwebo** Burma
68 B3 **Shwedaung** Burma
68 C4 **Shwegun** Burma
68 C4 **Shwegyin** Burma
68 C2 **Shwenyaung** Burma
74 H1 **Shyok** Kashmir
69 D12 **Siabu** Sumatra
77 H6 **Siahan Range** Pakistan
69 E12 **Siak Sri Inderapura** Sumatra
74 F2 **Sialkot** Pakistan
Siam *see* **Thailand**
Sian *see* **Xi'an**
Siangtan *see* **Xiangtan**
47 Q14 **Siánna** Rhodes Greece
31 J1 **Sianów** Poland
69 H11 **Siantan** *isld* Indonesia
69 D8 **Si Ao Ban Don, Laem** Thailand
128 E3 **Siapa** *R* Venezuela
71 G6 **Siargao** *isld* Philippines
95 S5 **Siasconset** Massachusetts U.S.A.
71 E8 **Siasi** Philippines
71 F6 **Siaton** Negros Philippines
52 B6 **Siauliai** Lithuania
84 J4 **Sibâi, Gebel** *mt* Egypt
126 F4 **Sibanicú** Cuba
71 E5 **Sibay** *isld* Philippines
55 C4 **Sibay** Russian Federation
89 H6 **Sibayi** S Africa
118 G7 **Sibbald** Alberta Canada
146 C12 **Sibbald, Cape** *C* Antarctica
29 L11 **Sibbo** Finland
42 G5 **Sibenik** Croatia
69 D13 **Siberut** *isld* Indonesia
74 B4 **Sibi** Pakistan
69 B11 **Sibigo** Indonesia
42 E6 **Sibillini, Monti** Italy
59 K3 **Sibirtsevo** Russian Federation
86 B6 **Sibiti** Congo
48 J5 **Sibiu** Romania
9 G4 **Sible Hedingham** England
99 S9 **Sibley** Illinois U.S.A.
99 L6 **Sibley** Iowa U.S.A.
109 O3 **Sibley** Louisiana U.S.A.
120 B4 **Sibley Prov. Park** Ontario Canada
70 G4 **Siboa** Sulawesi
69 D12 **Sibolga, Tel** *B* Sumatra
71 E4 **Sibolon** *isld* Philippines
126 G5 **Siboney** Cuba
69 D11 **Siborongborong** Sumatra
41 M3 **Sibratsgfäll** Austria
75 Q5 **Sibsagar** India
9 G1 **Sibsey** England
70 B3 **Sibu** Sarawak
71 F7 **Sibuco** Mindanao Philippines
71 F7 **Sibuguey Bay** Mindanao Philippines
86 C4 **Sibut** Cent Afr Republic
70 C2 **Sibuti** Sarawak
71 F4 **Sibuyan** *isld* Philippines
48 H4 **Sic** Romania
71 E1 **Sicapoo** *mt* Luzon Philippines
128 E7 **Sicasica** Bolivia
71 F6 **Sicayac** Mindanao Philippines
138 E4 **Siccus** *R* South Australia Australia
68 E6 **Si Chang, Ko** *isld* Thailand
67 A1 **Sichuan** *prov* China
67 B1 **Sichuan Pendi** *basin* China
43 E11 **Sicilia** *isld* Italy
43 D11 **Sicilian Chan** S Europe
Sicily *see* **Sicilia**
111 E10 **Sicily Island** Louisiana U.S.A.
119 R2 **Sickle L** Manitoba Canada
71 F5 **Sicogon** *isld* Philippines
128 D6 **Sicuani** Peru
48 E5 **Šid** Serbia Yugoslavia
71 A2 **Sidangoli** Halmahera Indonesia
47 O12 **Sidari** Greece
85 F5 **Sidawet** Niger
8 D5 **Sidcot** England
9 G5 **Sidcup** England
140 B6 **Siddeley Ra** N Terr Australia
74 E7 **Siddhapur** India
76 D3 **Siddhavattam** India
8 D1 **Siddington** England
76 D1 **Siddipet** India
29 J9 **Sideby** Finland
99 T10 **Sidell** Illinois U.S.A.
70 F6 **Sidenreng, D** *L* Sulawesi
26 K8 **Sidensjö** Sweden
85 D6 **Sidéradougou** Burkina
43 H10 **Siderno Marina** Italy
118 H8 **Sidewood** Saskatchewan Canada
46 G4 **Sidherítis** *isld* Greece
47 H9 **Sídheros, Akra** *C* Crete Greece
75 J6 **Sidhi** India
46 F3 **Sidhirókastron** Greece
17 H8 **Sidi Ali** Algeria
84 H3 **Sidi Barrani** Egypt
85 D1 **Sidi Bel Abbès** Algeria
43 C13 **Sidi Bou Ali** Tunisia
85 B3 **Sidi Ifni** Morocco
85 C2 **Sidi Kacem** Morocco
69 D11 **Sidikalang** Sumatra
85 B4 **Sidi Mhamed** Western Sahara
13 E1 **Sidlaw Hills** Scotland
146 B9 **Sidley, Mt** Antarctica
8 C6 **Sidmouth** England
141 G2 **Sidmouth, C** Queensland Australia
99 S3 **Sidnaw** Michigan U.S.A.
100 B1 **Sidney** British Columbia Canada
117 M11 **Sidney** British Columbia Canada
119 S9 **Sidney** Manitoba Canada
99 S9 **Sidney** Illinois U.S.A.
99 L9 **Sidney** Iowa U.S.A.
98 B2 **Sidney** Montana U.S.A.
98 D8 **Sidney** Nebraska U.S.A.
95 M4 **Sidney** New York U.S.A.
110 M1 **Sidney** Ohio U.S.A.
85 C6 **Sido** Mali
70 G4 **Sidoan** Sulawesi
70 O9 **Sidoardjo** Java
68 B2 **Sidoktaya** Burma
Sidon *see* **Saïda**
84 F3 **Sidrah, As** Libya
130 C7 **Sidrolândia** Brazil
36 C2 **Siebengebirge** *mt* Germany
37 P1 **Siebenlehn** Germany
32 J7 **Siedenburg** Germany
31 N3 **Siedlce** Poland
36 D2 **Sieg** *R* Germany
36 E2 **Siegbach** Germany
36 C2 **Siegburg** Germany
Siegelsdorf *see* **Seukendorf**
37 M6 **Siegenburg** Germany
31 O3 **Siemiatycze** Poland
68 H5 **Siem Pang** Cambodia
68 F6 **Siem Reap** Cambodia
42 D5 **Siena** Italy
31 O5 **Sieniawa** Poland
20 H4 **Sienne** *R* France
29 K4 **Sieppijärvi** Finland
31 L4 **Sieradz** Poland
31 J3 **Sieraków** Poland
22 L5 **Sierck** France
40 F2 **Sierentz** France
31 M3 **Sierpc** Poland
108 B4 **Sierra Blanca** Texas U.S.A.
102 D2 **Sierra Buttes** *pk* California U.S.A.
133 D6 **Sierra Colorada** Argentina
133 D6 **Sierra Grande** Argentina
124 J6 **Sierra Hermosa** Mexico
85 B7 **Sierra Leone** *rep* W Africa
90 H8 **Sierra Leone Basin** Atlantic Oc
90 H8 **Sierra Leone Rise** Atlantic Oc
125 J9 **Sierra Madre del Sur** *mts* Mexico
102 D7 **Sierra Madre Mts** California U.S.A.
125 J5 **Sierra Madre Oriental** *mts* Mexico
124 H4 **Sierra Mojada** Mexico
102 D2 **Sierraville** California U.S.A.
36 D3 **Siershahn** Germany
130 B8 **Siete Puntas, R** Paraguay
33 R6 **Sietow** Germany
48 J4 **Şieu** Romania
45 K4 **Sieve** *R* Italy
33 Q7 **Sieversdorf** Germany
32 M8 **Sievershausen** Germany
29 L8 **Sievi** Finland
67 C5 **Sifang Ling** *mts* China
65 G1 **Sifangtai** China
80 E1 **Sifsufa** Israel
119 R7 **Sifton** Manitoba Canada
117 K7 **Sifton Pass** British Columbia Canada
17 G9 **Sig** Algeria
28 B5 **Sig** Denmark
52 D2 **Sig** Russian Federation
27 D11 **Sigdal** Norway
18 G9 **Sigean** France
110 H2 **Sigel** Illinois U.S.A.
94 H5 **Sigel** Pennsylvania U.S.A.
26 H3 **Sigerfjord** Norway
48 H3 **Sighetu Marmaţiei** Romania
48 J4 **Sighişoara** Romania
47 J4 **Sığırcı** Turkey
69 B10 **Sigli** Sumatra
28 S8 **Siglufjördhur** Iceland
71 F5 **Sigma** Panay Philippines
41 K1 **Sigmaringen** Germany
45 K4 **Signa** Italy
103 L7 **Signal** Arizona U.S.A.
18 G7 **Signal du Luguet** *mt* France
112 B2 **Signal Mt** Tennessee U.S.A.
103 K8 **Signal Pk** Arizona U.S.A.
19 P18 **Signes** France
146 E3 **Signy** *U.K. Base* S Orkney Is S Atlantic Oc
22 G4 **Signy-l'Abbaye** France
22 G4 **Signy-le-petit** France
69 D14 **Sigoisooinan** Indonesia
99 O8 **Sigourney** Iowa U.S.A.
128 C4 **Sigsig** Ecuador
27 J12 **Sigtuna** Sweden
125 L2 **Siguatepeque** Honduras
17 F3 **Sigüenza** Spain
85 C6 **Siguiri** Guinea
103 N3 **Sigurd** Utah U.S.A.
21 N2 **Sigy-en-Bray** France
68 B1 **Sihaung Myauk** Burma
65 D4 **Siheyong** China
41 J3 **Sihl** *R* Switzerland
41 J3 **Sihl See** *L* Switzerland
74 J7 **Sihora** India
67 D5 **Sihui** China
29 J10 **Siikainen** Finland
52 C3 **Siikajoki** *R* Finland
29 N8 **Siilinjärvi** Finland
78 H3 **Siirt** Turkey
69 E13 **Sijunjung** Sumatra
69 E14 **Sikakap** Indonesia
117 M7 **Sikanni Chief** British Columbia Canada
74 F5 **Sikar** India
77 L2 **Sikaram** *mt* Afghanistan
85 C6 **Sikasso** Mali
70 G7 **Sikeli** Sulawesi
110 G5 **Sikeston** Missouri U.S.A.
59 K3 **Sikhote Alin'** *mts* Russian Federation
46 G8 **Sikinos** *isld* Greece
46 F6 **Sikionia** Greece
75 N5 **Sikkim** *prot* India
48 E5 **Siklós** Hungary
116 B5 **Siknik C** Alaska U.S.A.
71 A2 **Siko** *isld* Halmahera Indonesia
70 E1 **Sikuati** Sabah
16 C2 **Sil** *R* Spain
52 B6 **Šilale** Lithuania
41 N4 **Silandro** Italy
70 B4 **Silantek, G** *mt* Sarawak/Kalimantan
71 G4 **Sila Pt** Philippines
111 H10 **Silas** Alabama U.S.A.
69 B10 **Silawaih Agam** *vol* Sumatra
71 F5 **Silay** Negros Philippines
75 P6 **Silchar** India
26 M1 **Silda** *isld* Norway
47 N10 **Şile** Turkey
22 G3 **Silenrieux** Belgium
27 F12 **Silen, V** *L* Sweden
112 H2 **Siler City** North Carolina U.S.A.
31 K4 **Silesia** *reg* Poland/Czech
101 R4 **Silesia** Montana U.S.A.
85 E4 **Silet** Algeria
55 F4 **Siletiteniz, Ozero** *L* Kazakhstan
20 D5 **Silfiac** France
74 J4 **Silgarhi** Nepal
83 J12 **Silhouette I** Seychelles
67 C4 **Silian** China
43 C12 **Siliana** Tunisia
99 N2 **Silica** Minnesota U.S.A.
66 D5 **Siling Co** *L* China
43 B9 **Siliqua** Sardinia
47 J1 **Silistra** Bulgaria
47 J3 **Silivri** Turkey
27 G11 **Siljan** *L* Sweden
28 C4 **Silkeborg** Denmark
13 G6 **Silkstone** England
128 E7 **Sillajhuay** *mt* Chile/Bolivia
52 C5 **Sillamäe** Estonia
45 H3 **Sillano** Italy
45 L3 **Sillaro** *R* Italy
21 K5 **Sillé-le-Guillaume** France
38 F8 **Sillian** Austria
21 L4 **Silli-en-Gouffern** France
20 D4 **Sillon-de-Talbert** France
47 H3 **Silo** *mt* Greece
110 B5 **Siloam Springs** Arkansas U.S.A.
109 N5 **Silsbee** Texas U.S.A.
119 W3 **Silsby L** Manitoba Canada
106 C2 **Silt** Colorado U.S.A.
119 N8 **Silton** Saskatchewan Canada
86 C2 **Siltou** Chad
70 Q10 **Silungblanak** Indonesia
52 B6 **Šilutė** Lithuania
78 H2 **Silvan** Turkey
130 E5 **Silvânia** Brazil
Silva Porto *see* **Kuito**
74 E8 **Silvassa** India
127 K4 **Silver Bank** Caribbean
99 P2 **Silver Bay** Minnesota U.S.A.
103 N9 **Silver Bell** Arizona U.S.A.
101 N3 **Silver Bow** Montana U.S.A.
121 L5 **Silver Centre** Ontario Canada
100 J6 **Silver City** Idaho U.S.A.
111 F8 **Silver City** Mississippi U.S.A.
106 B9 **Silver City** New Mexico U.S.A.
103 M2 **Silver City** Utah U.S.A.
98 J8 **Silver Cr** Nebraska U.S.A.
100 F6 **Silver Cr** Oregon U.S.A.
111 F10 **Silver Creek** Mississippi U.S.A.
94 H4 **Silver Creek** New York U.S.A.
98 A8 **Silver Crown** Wyoming U.S.A.
145 E2 **Silverdale** New Zealand
107 O4 **Silverdale** Kansas U.S.A.
118 F6 **Silver Heights** Alberta Canada
120 B4 **Silver Islet** Ontario Canada
99 T3 **Silver L** Michigan U.S.A.
100 E6 **Silver L** Oregon U.S.A.
100 D6 **Silver Lake** Oregon U.S.A.
123 P4 **Silver Mt** Newfoundland Canada
102 G4 **Silverpeak** Nevada U.S.A.
7 L9 **Silver Pit** North Sea
141 G2 **Silver Plains** Queensland Australia
94 J4 **Silver Springs** New York U.S.A.
141 J8 **Silver Springs Gas Field** Queensland Australia
101 N4 **Silver Star** Montana U.S.A.
117 O10 **Silver Star Prov. Park** British Columbia Canada
117 K10 **Silverthrone Mt** British Columbia Canada
106 C4 **Silverton** Colorado U.S.A.
100 C5 **Silverton** Oregon U.S.A.
108 F1 **Silverton** Texas U.S.A.
100 D1 **Silverton** Washington U.S.A.
128 G4 **Silves** Brazil
16 B7 **Silves** Portugal
131 C4 **Silveyra, L** Argentina
100 F6 **Silvies** *R* Oregon U.S.A.
41 M4 **Silvretta Gruppe** *mt* Switzerland
41 M4 **Silvrettahorn** *mt* Switz/Austria
80 D6 **Silwād** Jordan
36 B5 **Silwingen** Germany
55 C3 **Sim** Russian Federation
70 B4 **Simanggang** Sarawak
68 E1 **Simao** China
71 F4 **Simara** *isld* Philippines
121 M5 **Simàrd, Lac** Quebec Canada
70 G4 **Simatang** *isld* Sulawesi
47 J4 **Simav** *R* Turkey
47 K5 **Simav** Turkey
47 J5 **Simav Dağlari** *mts* Turkey
47 K5 **Simav Gölü** *L* Turkey
37 O6 **Simbach** Germany
71 E7 **Simbahan** Philippines
79 B8 **Simbillâwein, El** Egypt
45 O6 **Simbruini, Monti** *mt* Italy
120 K10 **Simcoe** Ontario Canada
98 F7 **Simeon** Nebraska U.S.A.
116 H9 **Simeonof I** Alaska U.S.A.
47 H2 **Simeonovgrad** Bulgaria
48 H5 **Simeria** Romania
28 D3 **Simested** Denmark
43 F11 **Simeto** *R* Sicily
69 C11 **Simeulue** *isld* Indonesia
53 D11 **Simferopol'** Ukraine
47 Q14 **Simi** Greece
47 U14 **Simi** *isld* Greece
46 F3 **Simitli** Bulgaria
102 F7 **Simi Valley** California U.S.A.
Simla *see* **Shimla**
106 F2 **Simla** Colorado U.S.A.
48 H3 **Şimleu Silvaniei** Romania
37 L4 **Simmelsdorf** Germany
40 G4 **Simmental** *R* Switzerland
36 C4 **Simmer** *R* Germany
22 L2 **Simmerath** Germany
36 D4 **Simmern** Germany
111 E11 **Simmesport** Louisiana U.S.A.
118 J9 **Simmie** Saskatchewan Canada
102 E6 **Simmler** California U.S.A.
109 J7 **Simmons** Texas U.S.A.
126 G3 **Simms** Long I Bahamas
101 O2 **Simms** Montana U.S.A.
111 B8 **Simms** Texas U.S.A.
113 K9 **Simms Pt** New Providence I Bahamas
31 O1 **Simnas** Lithuania
29 L6 **Simo** Finland
27 D12 **Simoa** *R* Norway
29 M6 **Simojoki** *R* Finland
29 N11 **Simola** Finland
143 E9 **Simon** W Australia Australia
102 G3 **Simon** Nevada U.S.A.
117 O8 **Simonette** *R* Alberta Canada
119 Q4 **Simonhouse** Manitoba Canada
121 P7 **Simon, L** Quebec Canada
13 G5 **Simon Seat** *mt* England
27 H13 **Simonstorp** Sweden
89 A10 **Simon's Town** S Africa
117 K10 **Simoom Sd** British Columbia Canada
69 G13 **Simpang** Sumatra
69 C11 **Simpangkiri** Sumatra
29 O10 **Simpele** Finland
25 E7 **Simpelveld** Netherlands
129 K5 **Simplicio Mendes** Brazil
40 H5 **Simplon Tunnel** Italy/Switz
119 M7 **Simpson** Saskatchewan Canada
107 N2 **Simpson** Kansas U.S.A.
99 O6 **Simpson** Minnesota U.S.A.
101 P1 **Simpson** Montana U.S.A.
140 D6 **Simpson Des** N Terr Australia
138 E2 **Simpson Desert Conservation Park** South Australia Australia
140 E7 **Simpson Desert Nat Park** Queensland Australia
143 F7 **Simpson Hill** W Australia Australia
120 C4 **Simpson I** Ontario Canada
133 C7 **Simpson, I** Chile
117 R5 **Simpson Is** Northwest Territories Canada
115 L4 **Simpson Pen** Northwest Territories Canada
102 H2 **Simpson Pk Mts** Nevada U.S.A.
112 E3 **Simpsonville** South Carolina U.S.A.
27 G16 **Simrishamn** Sweden
100 C8 **Sims** California U.S.A.
100 D5 **Simtustus, L** Oregon U.S.A.
69 C13 **Simuk** *isld* Indonesia
69 D13 **Simulubek** Indonesia
70 B4 **Simunjan** Sarawak
70 F2 **Simunul** *isld* Philippines
69 C11 **Sinabang** Indonesia
69 D11 **Sinabung** *mt* Sumatra
42 G4 **Sinac** Croatia
86 J4 **Sina Dhaqa** Somalia
84 J4 **Sinai** *pen* Egypt
98 J5 **Sinai** South Dakota U.S.A.
48 K5 **Sinaia** Romania
124 F5 **Sinaloa** *state* Mexico
42 D5 **Sinalunga** Italy
127 J9 **Sinamaica** Venezuela
67 C3 **Sinan** China
46 D4 **Sinanaj** Albania
55 D3 **Sinara** *R* Russian Federation
47 O12 **Sinarádhes** Greece
68 B3 **Sinbaungwe** Burma
75 R6 **Sinbo** Burma
68 D6 **Sinbyubyin** Burma
68 D6 **Sinbyudaing** Burma
68 B2 **Sinbyugyun** Burma
126 G10 **Sincé** Colombia
126 G10 **Sincelejo** Colombia
22 E4 **Sinceny** France
101 S8 **Sinclair** Wyoming U.S.A.
112 D4 **Sinclair L** Georgia U.S.A.
117 N9 **Sinclair Mills** British Columbia Canada
138 C4 **Sinclair, Pt** South Australia Australia
15 E2 **Sinclairs B** Scotland
94 H4 **Sinclairville** New York U.S.A.
28 E2 **Sindal** Denmark
71 F6 **Sindañgan** Mindanao Philippines
70 L9 **Sindangbarang** Java
71 K9 **Sindeh, Tk** *B* Flores Indonesia
47 J1 **Sindel** Bulgaria
36 G6 **Sindelfingen** Germany
55 D1 **Sindeya** Russian Federation
76 C2 **Sindgi** India
74 B6 **Sindh** *prov* Pakistan
76 C3 **Sindhnur** India
52 B5 **Sindi** Estonia
47 J5 **Sındırği** Turkey
48 K4 **Sîndominic** Romania
52 H3 **Sindor** Russian Federation
75 M7 **Sindri** India
36 G5 **Sindringen** Germany
54 M9 **Sinegorskiy** Russian Federation
52 H5 **Sinegor'ye** Russian Federation
47 J4 **Sinekçi** Turkey
47 J3 **Sinekli** Turkey
54 G8 **Sinel'nikoyo** Ukraine
16 B7 **Sines** Portugal
29 L5 **Sinettä** Finland
Sinfu *see* **Jianping**
68 D2 **Sing** Burma
86 F3 **Singa** Sudan
68 C2 **Singaingmyo** Burma
69 G12 **Singapore** *rep* S E Asia
69 B14 **Singapore** *city* Singapore
69 F12 **Singapore, Str. of** S E Asia
70 P10 **Singaraja** Indonesia
68 E5 **Sing Buri** Thailand
41 J2 **Singen** Germany
48 J4 **Sîngeorgiu de Pădure** Romania
48 J3 **Sîngeorz-Bąi** Romania
111 C11 **Singer** Louisiana U.S.A.
88 E4 **Singida** Tanzania
46 F4 **Singitikós, Kólpos** *G* Greece
75 Q5 **Singkaling Hkamti** Burma
70 G7 **Singkang** Sulawesi
69 E13 **Singkarak** Sumatra
69 G13 **Singkep** Indonesia
69 C11 **Singkil** Sumatra
69 D12 **Singkuang** Sumatra
139 K4 **Singleton** New South Wales Australia
140 C5 **Singleton** N Terr Australia
9 F6 **Singleton** England
109 M5 **Singleton** Texas U.S.A.
140 B5 **Singleton, Mt** N Terr Australia
143 B8 **Singleton, Mt** W Australia Australia
Singora *see* **Songkhla**
68 B1 **Singu** Burma
47 O12 **Siniais** Greece
46 E4 **Siniátsikon** *mt* Greece
71 E3 **Siniloan** Luzon Philippines
Sining *see* **Xining**
Sining Ho *R* *see* **Huang Shui** *R*
70 F5 **Sinio, Gunung** *mt* Sulawesi
43 C8 **Siniscola** Sardinia
55 D5 **Siniy-Shikhan** Russian Federation
70 G7 **Sinjai** Sulawesi
46 C2 **Sinjavina** *mt* Montenegro Yugoslavia
86 G2 **Sinkat** Sudan
Sinkiang *see* **Xinjiang Uygur Zizhiqu**
Sinkiang *aut reg see* **Xinjiang Uygur Zizhiqu**
94 D7 **Sinking Spring** Ohio U.S.A.
65 F5 **Sinmi** *isld* N Korea
36 E2 **Sinn** Germany
36 H3 **Sinn** *R* Germany
129 H2 **Sinnamary** Fr Guiana
76 B1 **Sinnar** India
94 J5 **Sinnemahoning** Pennsylvania U.S.A.
43 H8 **Sinni** *R* Italy
13 H5 **Sinnington** England
36 H3 **Sinntal** Germany
79 A9 **Sinnûris** Egypt
48 M6 **Sinoe, L** Romania
78 E1 **Sinop** Turkey
124 D2 **Sinoquipe** Mexico
131 H2 **Sinos** *R* Brazil
59 J3 **Sinp'o** N Korea
36 F5 **Sinsheim** Germany
36 B4 **Sinspelt** Germany
119 O8 **Sintaluta** Saskatchewan Canada
70 B4 **Sintang** Kalimantan
109 K7 **Sinton** Texas U.S.A.
16 A6 **Sintra** Portugal
59 H3 **Sinŭiju** N Korea
86 A2 **Sinujiif** Somalia
126 G10 **Sinú, R** Colombia
52 C6 **Sinyaya** *R* Russian Federation
36 E6 **Sinzheim** Germany
36 C2 **Sinzig** Germany
28 F7 **Siø** *isld* Denmark
48 E4 **Sió** *R* Hungary
71 F7 **Siocon** Mindanao Philippines
20 G6 **Sion** France
40 F5 **Sion** Switzerland
18 G6 **Sioule** *R* France
98 K6 **Sioux Center** Iowa U.S.A.
98 K7 **Sioux City** Iowa U.S.A.
98 K6 **Sioux Falls** South Dakota U.S.A.
118 L1 **Sioux Lookout** Ontario Canada
99 L7 **Sioux Rapids** Iowa U.S.A.
71 F6 **Sipalay** Negros Philippines
127 O3 **Siparia** Trinidad
Siping *see* **Huangpin**
59 H3 **Siping** China
70 D2 **Sipitang** Sabah
119 U3 **Sipiwesk** Manitoba Canada
146 C10 **Siple Coast** Antarctica
146 A8 **Siple I** *isld* Antarctica
146 A8 **Siple, Mt** Antarctica
29 N11 **Sippola** Finland
111 J7 **Sipsey** Alabama U.S.A.
111 J8 **Sipsey** *R* Alabama U.S.A.
111 J8 **Sipsey Fork** *R* Alabama U.S.A.
69 D14 **Sipura** *isld* Indonesia
71 F6 **Siquijor** Philippines
128 E1 **Siquisique** Venezuela
80 G6 **Sir** *R* Jordan
76 C4 **Sira** India
27 B13 **Sira** *R* Norway
128 D5 **Sira** *mt* Peru
77 D7 **Şir Abū Nu'āyr** *isld* U.A.E.
19 Q15 **Sirac** *mt* France
68 E6 **Si Racha** Thailand
43 G11 **Siracusa** Sicily
117 N9 **Sir Alexander, Mt** British Columbia Canada
85 E6 **Sirba** *watercourse* Niger/Burkina
123 S4 **Sir Charles Hamilton Sd** Newfoundland Canada
141 G1 **Sir Charles Hardy Is** Gt Barrier Reef Aust
27 B13 **Sirdalsvatn** *L* Norway
118 B8 **Sir Douglas, Mt** Alberta Canada
140 D3 **Sir Edward Pellew Group** *islds* N Terr Australia
99 O4 **Siren** Wisconsin U.S.A.
45 P5 **Sirente, M** *mt* Italy
48 K3 **Siret** *R* Romania
80 F8 **Sirfa** Jordan
140 B1 **Sir George Hope Is** N Terr Australia
142 F2 **Sir Graham Moore Is** W Australia Australia
79 H7 **Sirhān, Wādī** *watercourse* Saudi Arabia
68 E4 **Siri Kit Dam** Thailand
70 B3 **Sirik, Tg** *C* Sarawak
138 D5 **Sir Isaac Pt** South Australia Australia
117 J4 **Sir James McBrien, Mt** Northwest Territories Canada
143 D7 **Sir James, Mt** W Australia Australia
138 D5 **Sir Joseph Banks Group** *islds* South Australia Australia
29 L4 **Sirkka** Finland
29 L5 **Sirkkakoski** Finland
74 G5 **Sir Muttra** India
47 H8 **Sirna** *isld* Greece
78 J3 **Sirnak** Turkey
74 E6 **Sirohi** India
42 H5 **Široki Brijeg** Bosnia-Herzegovina
45 O4 **Sirolo** Italy
69 C12 **Sirombu** Indonesia
76 E1 **Sironcha** India
74 G6 **Sironj** India
46 G7 **Siros** Greece
76 D1 **Sirpur** India
102 F6 **Sirretta Pk** California U.S.A.
77 D7 **Sīrrī, Jazīreh-ye** *isld* Iran
74 F4 **Sirsa** India
117 P10 **Sir Sandford** *mt* British Columbia Canada
117 P10 **Sir Sanford, Mt** British Columbia Canada
76 B3 **Sirsi** India
Sirte *see* **Surt**
84 F3 **Sirte Desert** Libya
84 F3 **Sirte, G. of** Libya
138 A2 **Sir Thomas, Mt** South Australia Australia
71 M9 **Sirung** *isld* Indonesia
117 O9 **Sir Wilfrid Laurier, Mt** British Columbia Canada
141 G2 **Sir William Thompson Ra** Queensland Australia
68 G5 **Sisaket** Thailand
16 B1 **Sisargas** *isld* Spain
87 D11 **Sishen** S Africa
65 D7 **Sishui** China
119 S6 **Sisib L** Manitoba Canada
56 D4 **Sisim** *R* Russian Federation
Sisimiut *see* **Holsteinsborg**
119 Q3 **Sisipuk L** Manitoba Canada
99 S2 **Siskiwit B** Michigan U.S.A.
100 B8 **Siskiyou Mts** Cal/Oregon U.S.A.
124 F4 **Sisogúichic** Mexico
68 F4 **Si Song Khram** Thailand
68 F6 **Sisophon** Cambodia
102 D7 **Sisquoc** California U.S.A.
40 G3 **Sissach** Switzerland
98 J4 **Sisseton** South Dakota U.S.A.
122 E6 **Sisson Branch Res** New Brunswick Canada
22 F4 **Sissonne** France
77 G4 **Sistan, Daryacheh ye** *L* Afghanistan
109 J6 **Sisterdale** Texas U.S.A.
19 P16 **Sisteron** France
68 A7 **Sisters** *islds* Andaman Is
100 D5 **Sisters** Oregon U.S.A.
143 F7 **Sisters, The** *mt* W Australia Australia
83 J12 **Sisters, The** *isld* Seychelles
116 G5 **Sisters, The** *mt* Alaska U.S.A.
94 G7 **Sistersville** West Virginia U.S.A.
36 B3 **Sistig** Germany
45 O7 **Sisto** *R* Italy
52 E5 **Sit** *R* Russian Federation
75 L5 **Sitamarhi** India
70 F2 **Sitangkai** Philippines
74 J5 **Sitapur** India
26 J3 **Sitasjaure** *L* Sweden
89 G6 **Siteki** Swaziland
17 J3 **Sitges** Spain
46 F4 **Sithoniá** Greece
47 H9 **Sitía** Crete Greece
66 E3 **Sitian** China
130 F4 **Sítio da Abadia** Brazil
129 K6 **Sítio de Mato** Brazil
117 F7 **Sitka** Alaska U.S.A.
107 L4 **Sitka** Kansas U.S.A.
116 L8 **Sitkalidak I** Alaska U.S.A.
117 F7 **Sitka Nat Historical Park** Alaska U.S.A.
116 L8 **Sitkinak I** Alaska U.S.A.
100 B6 **Sitkum** Oregon U.S.A.
46 D2 **Sitnica** *R* Serbia Yugoslavia
55 E3 **Sitnikovo** Russian Federation
26 K4 **Sitojaure** *L* Sweden
84 H4 **Sitra** *oasis* Egypt
77 B6 **Sitrah** Bahrain
68 C4 **Sittang** *R* Burma
25 E7 **Sittard** Netherlands
Sitten *see* **Sion**
32 K6 **Sittensen** Germany
9 G5 **Sittingbourne** England
68 A2 **Sittwe** Burma
70 P9 **Situbondo** Java
33 R10 **Sitzenroda** Germany
71 H7 **Siumpu** *isld* Indonesia
125 M3 **Siuna** Nicaragua
29 M6 **Siuruanjoki** *R* Finland
59 J1 **Sivaki** Russian Federation
78 F2 **Sivas** Turkey
53 E10 **Sivash, Zaliv** *B* Ukraine
47 K6 **Sivaslı** Turkey
78 G3 **Siverek** Turkey
52 D5 **Siverskiy** Russian Federation
52 K2 **Sivomaskinskiy** Russian Federation
47 M11 **Sivri** *isld* Turkey
78 C2 **Sivrihisar** Turkey
22 G3 **Sivry** Belgium
22 J5 **Sivry-sur-Meuse** France
84 H4 **Siwa** Egypt
70 G6 **Siwa** Sulawesi
100 A7 **Sixes** Oregon U.S.A.
19 P18 **Six Fours-la-Plage** France
14 C4 **Sixmilebridge** Ireland
111 E12 **Six Mile L** Louisiana U.S.A.
20 F6 **Sixt** Ille-et-Vilaine France
40 E5 **Sixt Vallorcine** France
52 F3 **Siya** Russian Federation
86 G1 **Siyâl I** Egypt
52 G6 **Siyava** Russian Federation
101 M1 **Siyeh, Mt** Montana U.S.A.
56 E5 **Sizim** Russian Federation
59 M1 **Siziman** Russian Federation
65 B4 **Siziwang Qi** China
20 B5 **Sizun** France
52 H2 **Sizyabsk** Russian Federation
28 G5 **Sjælland** *isld* Denmark
28 G5 **Sjællands Odde** *C* Denmark
26 K8 **Själevad** Sweden
46 D1 **Sjenica** Serbia Yugoslavia
26 D10 **Sjoa** *R* Norway
27 G16 **Sjöbo** Sweden
127 M10 **S. José de Guanipa** Venezuela
26 G7 **Sjoutnäs** Sweden
27 F14 **Sjövik** Sweden
26 G7 **Sjulsåsen** Sweden
26 M6 **Sjulsmark** Sweden
26 O2 **Sjusjavrre** Norway
26 F8 **Skäckerfjällen** *mt* Sweden
42 J6 **Skadarsko Jez** *L* Albania/Yugoslavia
28 G6 **Skælskør** Denmark
28 S10 **Skaftárós** *est* Iceland
27 J14 **Skaftet** Sweden
27 K11 **Skäfthammar** Sweden
28 S9 **Skagafjördhur** *inlet* Iceland
27 C10 **Skagastölstindane** *mt* Norway
28 S9 **Skagastrand** Iceland
28 F1 **Skagen** Denmark
27 G13 **Skagern** *L* Sweden
27 C14 **Skagerrak** *chan* Denmark/Norway
27 D10 **Skaget** *mt* Norway
100 D1 **Skagit** *R* Washington U.S.A.
117 F6 **Skagway** Alaska U.S.A.
79 D4 **Skala** Cyprus
46 F8 **Skála** Greece
48 K2 **Skala-Podol'skaya** Ukraine
27 F15 **Skälderviken** *B* Sweden
26 K5 **Skalka** *L* Sweden
26 S1 **Skallelv** Norway
28 A5 **Skallingen** *pen* Denmark
27 F14 **Skallsjö** Sweden
27 J13 **Skällvik** Sweden
31 K4 **Skalmierzyce** Poland
37 N3 **Skalná** Czechoslovakia
28 G7 **Skalø** *isld* Denmark
28 C3 **Skals Å** *R* Denmark
100 C4 **Skamania** Washington U.S.A.
28 E5 **Skamby** Denmark
28 D6 **Skamlingsbanken** *hill* Denmark
Skanderborg *co see* **Vejle** *co*
99 T3 **Skandia** Michigan U.S.A.
27 F16 **Skåne** *physical reg* Sweden
95 L4 **Skaneateles** New York U.S.A.
99 S3 **Skanee** Michigan U.S.A.
26 J3 **Skånland** Norway
28 D4 **Skannerup** Denmark
27 F16 **Skanör** Sweden
26 H7 **Skansholm** Sweden
26 J6 **Skansnäs** Sweden
46 G5 **Skantzoúra** *isld* Greece
27 F13 **Skara** Sweden
27 F13 **Skaraborg** *reg* Sweden
26 F9 **Skardörfjell** *mt* Norway
74 F1 **Skardu** Kashmir
27 M12 **Skärgårdshavets Nat. Park** Finland
27 E11 **Skarnes** Norway
28 E6 **Skarø** *isld* Denmark
28 F6 **Skårop** Denmark
28 B5 **Skarrild** Denmark
26 F9 **Skarsfjället** *mt* Sweden
31 L1 **Skarszewy** Poland
26 J7 **Skarvsjö** Sweden
31 N4 **Skaryszew** Poland
31 M4 **Skarżysko-Kamienna** Poland
28 B5 **Skast** Denmark
26 H10 **Skästra** Sweden
27 G15 **Skatelöv** Sweden
13 F2 **Skateraw** Scotland
27 G12 **Skattkärr** Sweden
27 G10 **Skattungen** *L* Sweden
52 B6 **Skaudvilė** Lithuania
28 B4 **Skave** Denmark
31 M6 **Skawina** Poland
120 K6 **Skead** Ontario Canada
117 J8 **Skeena** *R* British Columbia Canada
117 K8 **Skeena Crossing** British Columbia Canada
117 J7 **Skeena Mts** British Columbia Canada
9 G1 **Skegness** England
28 H6 **Skelby** Denmark
28 H7 **Skelby** Storstrøm Denmark
28 D7 **Skelde** Denmark
140 D3 **Skeleton** *R* N Terr Australia
87 B9 **Skeleton Coast Nat. Park** Namibia
28 C4 **Skelhøje** Denmark
26 L7 **Skellefteå** Sweden
26 L6 **Skellefte älv** *R* Sweden
26 M7 **Skelleftehamm** Sweden
13 F6 **Skelmersdale** England
146 D11 **Skelton Glacier** *glacier* Antarctica
28 E3 **Skelund** Denmark
27 F14 **Skene** Sweden
28 J5 **Skensved** Denmark
46 F6 **Skhimatárion** Greece
46 E8 **Skhíza** *isld* Greece
46 G8 **Skhoinoúsa** *isld* Greece
27 E12 **Ski** Norway
46 F5 **Skíathos** *isld* Greece
107 O5 **Skiatook** Oklahoma U.S.A.
14 B5 **Skibbereen** Ireland
28 B4 **Skibbild** Denmark
28 H5 **Skibby** Denmark
28 C5 **Skibet** Denmark
28 J6 **Skibinge** Denmark
26 L2 **Skibotn** Norway
28 A3 **Skibsted Fjord** Denmark
112 F6 **Skidaway I** Georgia U.S.A.
117 H9 **Skidegate** British Columbia Canada
31 P2 **Skidel'** Belorussia
95 L8 **Skidmore** Maryland U.S.A.
109 K7 **Skidmore** Texas U.S.A.
27 D12 **Skien** Norway
31 M4 **Skierniewice** Poland
118 F9 **Skiff** Alberta Canada
29 J11 **Skiftet Kihti** Finland
85 F1 **Skikda** Algeria
116 M6 **Skilak L** Alaska U.S.A.
46 F7 **Skillaion, Akra** *C* Greece
27 G14 **Skillengaryd** Sweden
110 H3 **Skillet** *R* Illinois U.S.A.
46 D7 **Skinári, Akra** *C* Greece
28 B3 **Skinnerup** Denmark
27 H12 **Skinnskatteberg** Sweden
26 Q1 **Skipagurra** Norway
12 C2 **Skipness** Scotland
144 B6 **Skippers** New Zealand
144 B6 **Skippers Range** New Zealand
13 H6 **Skipsea** England
139 G6 **Skipton** Victoria Australia
13 F6 **Skipton** England
46 G6 **Skiros** *isld* Greece
28 C3 **Skive** Denmark
28 C3 **Skive Fj** *inlet* Denmark
26 C10 **Skjåk** Norway
28 S9 **Skjalfandafljot** *R* Iceland
28 S8 **Skjálfandi** *B* Iceland
26 G5 **Skjelåtind** *mt* Norway
28 D3 **Skjellerup** Denmark
28 A5 **Skjern** Ringkøbing Denmark
28 D4 **Skjern** Viborg Denmark
28 C5 **Skjern Å** *R* Denmark
26 H4 **Skjerstad** Norway
26 L1 **Skjervöy** Norway
28 D4 **Skjød** Denmark
27 A12 **Skjold** Norway
28 B3 **Skjoldborg** Denmark
27 C10 **Skjolden** Norway
28 E7 **Skjoldnæs** *C* Denmark
115 P5 **Skjoldungen** Greenland
26 J3 **Skjomen** Norway
26 H4 **Skjönstå** Norway
26 E6 **Sklinna** *lighthouse* Norway
26 D6 **Sklinnabanken** Norway
48 E1 **Skoczow** Poland
28 C6 **Skodborg** Denmark
28 A5 **Skodsbøl** Denmark
29 K5 **Skodsborg** Denmark
28 E4 **Skødstrup** Denmark
42 F2 **Skofja Loka** Slovenia
26 K9 **Skog** Sweden
26 O2 **Skoganvarre** Norway
26 R2 **Skogerøy** Norway
27 F12 **Skoghall** Sweden
8 A4 **Skokholm I** Wales
99 T8 **Skokie** Illinois U.S.A.
55 D6 **Skol'** Kazakhstan
31 O6 **Skole** Ukraine
48 H1 **Skole** Ukraine
27 H12 **Sköllersta** Sweden
8 A4 **Skomer I** Wales
26 F4 **Skomvoer** Norway
117 Q11 **Skookumchuk** British Columbia Canada
46 F5 **Skópelos** *isld* Greece
46 G6 **Skópelos Kaloyeroi** *isld* Greece
54 L3 **Skopin** Russian Federation
46 E2 **Skopje** Macedonia Yugoslavia
31 L2 **Skórcz** Poland
55 F2 **Skorodum** Russian Federation
26 F7 **Skorovatn** Norway
26 J8 **Skorped** Sweden
28 D3 **Skørping** Denmark
28 G7 **Skørringe** Denmark
27 D12 **Skotselv** Norway
28 F7 **Skovballe** Denmark
28 D4 **Skovby** Århus Denmark
28 E5 **Skovby** Fyn Denmark
28 D7 **Skovby** Sønderjylland Denmark
27 G13 **Skövde** Sweden
28 B5 **Skovlund** Denmark
59 H1 **Skovorodino** Russian Federation
95 S2 **Skowhegan** Maine U.S.A.
119 S7 **Skownan** Manitoba Canada
28 C2 **Skræm** Denmark
27 E11 **Skreia** Norway
28 F7 **Skrøbelev** Denmark
26 M5 **Skröven** Sweden
28 C6 **Skrydstrup** Denmark
27 A12 **Skudeneshavn** Norway
27 E12 **Skulerud** Norway
103 H5 **Skull Pk** Nevada U.S.A.
103 M7 **Skull V** Arizona U.S.A.
48 L3 **Skulyany** Moldavia
111 G8 **Skuna** *R* Mississippi U.S.A.
110 E1 **Skunk** *R* Iowa U.S.A.
27 M15 **Skuodas** Lithuania
27 F16 **Skurup** Sweden
31 J6 **Skuteč** Czechoslovakia
27 J11 **Skutskär** Sweden
26 H3 **Skutvik** Norway
6 F1 **Skúvoy** *isld* Faeroes
48 M1 **Skvira** Ukraine
116 M6 **Skwentna** Alaska U.S.A.
31 J3 **Skwierzyna** Poland
15 B3 **Skye, I. of** Scotland
100 D2 **Skykomish** Washington U.S.A.
146 D7 **Skytrain Ice Rise** *ice rise* Antarctica
55 D2 **Sladkovskoye** Russian Federation
28 G6 **Slagelse** Denmark
13 F4 **Slaggyford** England
111 C10 **Slagle** Louisiana U.S.A.
28 H5 **Slaglille** Denmark
26 K6 **Slagnäs** Sweden
70 N9 **Slahung** Java
13 F6 **Slaidburn** England
12 E2 **Slamannan** Scotland
70 M9 **Slamet, G** *mt* Java
48 F2 **Slana** *R* Czechoslovakia
116 P5 **Slana** Alaska U.S.A.
14 E3 **Slane** Ireland
14 E4 **Slaney** *R* Ireland
89 B8 **Slang Berg** *mt* S Africa
28 J5 **Slangerup** Denmark
89 A10 **Slang Kop Pt** S Africa
48 K5 **Slănic** Romania
48 K4 **Slănic-Moldova** Romania
42 H6 **Slano** Croatia
52 C5 **Slantsy** Russian Federation
30 H5 **Slaný** Czechoslovakia
37 N3 **Slapany** Czechoslovakia
15 B3 **Slapin, L** Scotland
141 H4 **Slashers Reefs** Gt Barrier Reef Aust
120 D4 **Slate I** Ontario Canada
101 S9 **Slater** Colorado U.S.A.
110 C2 **Slater** Missouri U.S.A.

98 B8 **Slater** Wyoming U.S.A.
102 G6 **Slate Ra** California U.S.A.
111 G8 **Slate Springs** Mississippi U.S.A.
48 J6 **Slatina** Romania
42 H3 **Slatina, P** Croatia
108 F2 **Slaton** Texas U.S.A.
27 H11 **Slättberg** Sweden
26 O1 **Slåtten** Norway
94 G8 **Slatyfork** West Virginia U.S.A.
111 E11 **Slaughter** Louisiana U.S.A.
51 Q2 **Slautnoye** Russian Federation
118 C3 **Slave Lake** Alberta Canada
117 Q5 **Slave Pt** Northwest Territories Canada
117 R5 **Slave R** Northwest Territories Canada
54 C3 **Slavgorod** Belorussia
54 G8 **Slavgorod** Dnepropetrovskaya obl Ukraine
31 N1 **Slavinek** Russian Federation
48 D1 **Slavkov** Czechoslovakia
52 C5 **Slavkovichi** Russian Federation
42 H3 **Slavonia** *reg* Croatia
46 F2 **Slavovvrŭkh** *mt* Bulgaria
42 H3 **Slav Požega** Croatia
48 H2 **Slavskoye** Ukraine
46 G1 **Slavyanovo** Bulgaria
54 J8 **Slavyansk** Ukraine
31 J4 **Sława** Poland
31 O4 **Sławatycze** Poland
31 K1 **Sławno** Poland
31 J2 **Sławoborze** Poland
99 L6 **Slayton** Minnesota U.S.A.
9 F1 **Sleaford** England
138 D6 **Sleaford B** South Australia Australia
116 D4 **Sledge I** Alaska U.S.A.
118 K4 **Sled L** Saskatchewan Canada
13 H5 **Sledmere** England
115 M6 **Sleeper Is** Northwest Territories Canada
99 W5 **Sleeping Bear Dunes Nat. Lakeshore** *nat park* Michigan U.S.A.
94 A2 **Sleeping Bear Pt** Michigan U.S.A.
99 M5 **Sleepy Eye** Minnesota U.S.A.
116 J6 **Sleetmute** Alaska U.S.A.
22 F1 **Sleidinge** Belgium
6 M4 **Sleipner** *oil rig* North Sea
70 N9 **Sleman** Java
52 C5 **Slepino** Russian Federation
31 L3 **Ślesiń** Poland
146 F7 **Slessor Glacier** Antarctica
28 F4 **Sletterhage** *C* Denmark
28 C2 **Slettestrand** Denmark
26 Q1 **Slettnes** Norway
111 G11 **Slidell** Louisiana U.S.A.
109 K2 **Slidell** Texas U.S.A.
27 D10 **Slidre** Norway
25 C5 **Sliedrecht** Netherlands
14 D2 **Slieve Anierin** *mt* Ireland
14 C3 **Slieve Aughty** *mts* Ireland
14 D2 **Slieve Beagh** *mt* Ireland
14 C4 **Slieve Bernagh** Ireland
14 D3 **Slieve Bloom Mts** Ireland
14 B2 **Slieve Car** *mt* Ireland
14 F2 **Slieve Donard** *mt* N Ireland
14 B3 **Slieve Elva** *mt* Ireland
14 C4 **Slievefelim Cullaun Mts** Ireland
14 B2 **Slieve Gamph** *mt* Ireland
14 E2 **Slieve Gullion** *mt* N Ireland
14 C2 **Slieve League** *mt* Ireland
14 B4 **Slieve Mish** *mts* Ireland
14 B5 **Slieve Miskish** *mt* Ireland
14 A3 **Slievemore** *mt* Ireland
14 D2 **Slievenakilla** *hill* Ireland
14 D4 **Slievenamon** *mt* Ireland
14 D1 **Slieve Snaght** *mt* Ireland
14 C2 **Slieve Tooey** *mt* Ireland
15 B3 **Sligachan** Scotland
14 C2 **Sligo** *co* Ireland
14 C2 **Sligo** Ireland
94 H5 **Sligo** Pennsylvania U.S.A.
28 H6 **Slimminge** Denmark
99 S6 **Slinger** Wisconsin U.S.A.
15 C3 **Slioch Mt** Scotland
145 E2 **Slipper I** New Zealand
94 G5 **Slippery Rock** Pennsylvania U.S.A.
27 K14 **Slite** Sweden
47 H2 **Sliven** Bulgaria
46 F2 **Slivnitsa** Bulgaria
98 K7 **Sloan** Iowa U.S.A.
101 L2 **Sloan** Montana U.S.A.
103 J6 **Sloan** Nevada U.S.A.
102 D2 **Sloat** California U.S.A.
52 H5 **Slobedskoy** Russian Federation
54 M5 **Sloboda** Russian Federation
52 G4 **Slobodchikovo** Russian Federation
48 M3 **Slobodka** Ukraine
48 M4 **Slobodzeya** Moldavia
48 L6 **Slobozia** Ialomita Romania
48 J6 **Slobozia** Teleorman Romania
117 P11 **Slocan** British Columbia Canada
25 G2 **Slochteren** Netherlands
111 L10 **Slocomb** Alabama U.S.A.
117 G6 **Sloko** *R* British Columbia Canada
27 F15 **Slömge** Sweden
31 H3 **Słońsk** Poland
25 E3 **Sloten** Netherlands
25 E3 **Sloter Meer** Netherlands
28 G6 **Slots** Denmark
81 B9 **Slot van Capelle** Indian Oc
9 F4 **Slough** England
48 F2 **Slovakia** Czechoslovakia
42 F3 **Slovenia** *rep* S Europe
Slovenija *see* **Slovenia**
38 N8 **Slovenske Gorice** *mts* Slovenia
48 E2 **Slovenské Pravno** Czechoslovakia
31 L7 **Slovenské Rudohorie** *mts* Czechoslovakia
48 F2 **Slovensko** *aut reg* Czechoslovakia
116 L5 **Slow Fork** *R* Alaska U.S.A.
12 D1 **Sloy, L** Scotland
31 H3 **Słubice** Poland
53 C8 **Sluch'** *R* Ukraine
52 H4 **Sludka** Komi Respublika Russian Federation
25 A6 **Sluis** Netherlands
25 A6 **Sluiskil** Netherlands
31 H4 **Słuknov** Czechoslovakia
31 K3 **Słupca** Poland
31 K1 **Słupsk** Poland
14 A3 **Slyne Hd** Ireland
111 D8 **Smackover** Arkansas U.S.A.
15 E4 **Sma Glen** Scotland
13 F2 **Smailholm** Scotland
27 G15 **Småland** *physical reg* Sweden
28 G6 **Smålandsfarvandet** Denmark
27 F14 **Smål Burseryd** Sweden
101 N5 **Small** Idaho U.S.A.
119 U1 **Small L** Manitoba Canada
95 S3 **Small Pt** Maine U.S.A.
115 N7 **Smallwood Res** Labrador, Nfld Canada
9 G5 **Smarden** England
119 N5 **Smeaton** Saskatchewan Canada
48 F6 **Smederevo** Serbia Yugoslavia
48 F6 **Smederevska Palanka** Serbia Yugoslavia
27 H11 **Smedjebacken** Sweden
54 C7 **Smela** Ukraine
26 S1 **Smelror** Norway
94 J5 **Smethport** Pennsylvania U.S.A.
59 K2 **Smidovich** Russian Federation
28 J4 **Smidstrup** Denmark
31 K3 **Śmigiel** Poland
118 H7 **Smiley** Saskatchewan Canada
109 K6 **Smiley** Texas U.S.A.
52 C6 **Smiltene** Latvia
46 G3 **Smilyan** Bulgaria
46 G1 **Smirdiasa** Romania
31 J5 **Smiřice** Czechoslovakia
55 E4 **Smirnovo** Kazakhstan
59 M2 **Smirnykh** Russian Federation
117 Q8 **Smith** Alberta Canada
102 E3 **Smith** Nevada U.S.A.
94 H10 **Smith** *R* Virginia/N Carolina U.S.A.
114 G4 **Smith Arm** *B* Northwest Territories Canada
115 M2 **Smith B** Northwest Territories Canada
116 K1 **Smith B** Alaska U.S.A.
110 G3 **Smithboro** Illinois U.S.A.
140 F3 **Smithburne R** Queensland Australia
107 M2 **Smith Center** Kansas U.S.A.
117 K8 **Smithers** British Columbia Canada
89 E8 **Smithfield** S Africa
98 G9 **Smithfield** Nebraska U.S.A.
112 J2 **Smithfield** North Carolina U.S.A.
94 H7 **Smithfield** Pennsylvania U.S.A.
109 M9 **Smithfield** Texas U.S.A.
101 O8 **Smithfield** Utah U.S.A.
95 L9 **Smithfield** Virginia U.S.A.
94 G7 **Smithfield** West Virginia U.S.A.
68 A6 **Smith I** Andaman Is
146 C3 **Smith I** S Shetland Is Antarctica
115 M5 **Smith I** Northwest Territories Canada
95 M8 **Smith I** Maryland U.S.A.
112 K4 **Smith I** North Carolina U.S.A.
95 M9 **Smith I** Virginia U.S.A.
100 C1 **Smith I** Washington U.S.A.
94 H9 **Smith Mountain Lake** Virginia U.S.A.
146 D6 **Smith Peninsula** *pen* Antarctica
100 J1 **Smith Pk** *mt* Idaho U.S.A.
140 B1 **Smith Pt** *inlet* N Terr Australia
122 J8 **Smith Pt** Nova Scotia Canada
101 O2 **Smith R** Montana U.S.A.
117 K6 **Smith River** British Columbia Canada
100 A8 **Smith River** California U.S.A.
121 O8 **Smiths Falls** Ontario Canada
100 J5 **Smiths Ferry** Idaho U.S.A.
110 K4 **Smiths Grove** Kentucky U.S.A.
7 M10 **Smiths Knoll** *oil rig* North Sea
115 M2 **Smith Sound** Northwest Territories Canada
139 H8 **Smithton** Australia
110 C3 **Smithton** Missouri U.S.A.
139 L4 **Smithtown-Gladstone** New South Wales Australia
111 M10 **Smithville** Georgia U.S.A.
110 B2 **Smithville** Missouri U.S.A.
107 O7 **Smithville** Oklahoma U.S.A.
110 L6 **Smithville** Tennessee U.S.A.
109 K6 **Smithville** Texas U.S.A.
94 F7 **Smithville** West Virginia U.S.A.
98 C6 **Smithwick** South Dakota U.S.A.
46 D4 **Smilkas** *mt* Greece
102 E1 **Smoke Creek Desert** Nevada U.S.A.
94 H8 **Smoke Hole** West Virginia U.S.A.
117 O8 **Smoky** *R* Alberta Canada
138 C4 **Smoky B** South Australia Australia
139 L4 **Smoky C** New South Wales Australia
123 M7 **Smoky C** Nova Scotia Canada
120 H2 **Smoky Falls** Ontario Canada
106 H2 **Smoky Hill** *R* Colo/Kansas U.S.A.
107 L2 **Smoky Hills** Kansas U.S.A.
118 E4 **Smoky Lake** Alberta Canada
26 C8 **Smøla** *isld* Norway
31 N2 **Smolensk** Russian Federation
53 D7 **Smolenskaya Oblast'** *prov* Russian Federation
54 E2 **Smolensko-Moskovskaya Vozvyshennost'** *upland* Russian Federation
46 G3 **Smolyan** Bulgaria
101 P7 **Smoot** Wyoming U.S.A.
120 J3 **Smooth Rock Falls** Ontario Canada
120 A2 **Smooth Rock L** Ontario Canada
118 L3 **Smoothstone R** Saskatchewan Canada
48 K2 **Smotrich** Ukraine
47 J1 **Smyadovo** Bulgaria
54 G1 **Smychka** Russian Federation
27 F16 **Smygehamn** Sweden
146 C6 **Smyley** *isld* Antarctica
Smyrna *see* **Izmir**
95 M7 **Smyrna** Delaware U.S.A.
112 C4 **Smyrna** Georgia U.S.A.
95 L4 **Smyrna** New York U.S.A.
110 K6 **Smyrna** Tennessee U.S.A.
95 S7 **Smyrna Mills** Maine U.S.A.
28 T9 **Snaefell** *mt* Iceland
12 D5 **Snaefell** *mt* I of Man U.K.
139 H9 **Snag** Tasmania Australia
68 G7 **Snaipol** Cambodia
13 G6 **Snaith** England
101 O6 **Snake** *R* Idaho/Wyoming U.S.A.
98 E7 **Snake** *R* Nebraska U.S.A.
100 G3 **Snake** *R* Washington U.S.A.
103 K2 **Snake Ra** Nevada U.S.A.
100 J4 **Snake R. Canyon** Idaho/Oregon U.S.A.
101 N6 **Snake R. Plain** Idaho U.S.A.
126 F3 **Snap Pt** Andros Bahamas
28 E5 **Snaptun** Denmark
117 Q3 **Snare L** Northwest Territories Canada
117 P4 **Snare River** Northwest Territories Canada
26 F7 **Snåsa** Norway
26 F8 **Snasahögarna** *mt* Sweden
26 E7 **Snåsavatn** *L* Norway
111 M11 **Sneads** Florida U.S.A.
25 E2 **Sneek** Netherlands
25 E2 **Sneeker Meer** Netherlands
14 B5 **Sneem** Ireland
89 D8 **Sneeuberg** *mts* S Africa
89 A9 **Sneeukop** *mt* S Africa
29 K4 **Snekkersten** Denmark
102 D4 **Snelling** California U.S.A.
28 B5 **Snesere** Denmark
54 L8 **Snezhnoye** Ukraine
31 J5 **Sněžka** *mt* Czechoslovakia
42 F3 **Snežnik** *mt* Slovenia
31 N2 **Śniadowo** Poland
31 N2 **Śniardwy, Jezioro** *L* Poland
31 N7 **Snina** Czechoslovakia
118 A3 **Snipe L** Alberta Canada
15 B3 **Snizort, Loch** Scotland
28 F6 **Snøde** Denmark
28 D5 **Snoghøj** Denmark
26 D9 **Snøhetta** *mt* Norway
100 C2 **Snohomish** Washington U.S.A.
28 J5 **Snoldelev** Denmark
127 M3 **Snook Pt** Jamaica
100 D2 **Snoqualmie Pass** Washington U.S.A.
26 G10 **Snössvallen** Sweden
68 H6 **Snoul** Cambodia
54 D4 **Snov** *R* Rus Fed/Ukraine
94 D3 **Snover** Michigan U.S.A.
116 L6 **Snowcap Mt** Alaska U.S.A.
119 N5 **Snowden** Saskatchewan Canada
100 B8 **Snowden** California U.S.A.
8 B1 **Snowdon** *mt* Wales
114 H5 **Snowdrift** Northwest Territories Canada
119 T9 **Snowflake** Manitoba Canada
103 O7 **Snowflake** Arizona U.S.A.
95 M8 **Snow Hill** Maryland U.S.A.
112 K2 **Snow Hill** North Carolina U.S.A.
146 D4 **Snow Hill I** Antarctica
146 C3 **Snow I** S Shetland Is Antarctica
119 R4 **Snow Lake** Manitoba Canada
111 E7 **Snow Lake** Arkansas U.S.A.
106 C2 **Snowmass Mt** Colorado U.S.A.
121 O8 **Snow Road** Ontario Canada
94 K5 **Snow Shoe** Pennsylvania U.S.A.
100 K1 **Snowshoe Pk** *mt* Montana U.S.A.
138 E5 **Snowtown** South Australia Australia
101 N8 **Snowville** Utah U.S.A.
103 K1 **Snow Water L** Nevada U.S.A.
139 J6 **Snowy Mts** Vict/N S W Australia
48 K2 **Snyatyn** Ukraine
98 K8 **Snyder** Nebraska U.S.A.
107 M7 **Snyder** Oklahoma U.S.A.
108 G3 **Snyder** Texas U.S.A.
27 H12 **Snyten** Sweden
143 E6 **Soakage Well** W Australia Australia
144 A6 **Soaker, Mt** New Zealand
87 H11 **Soalala** Madagascar
40 G7 **Soana, Val di** Italy
87 H11 **Soanierana Ivongo** Madagascar
65 G7 **Soan kundo** *isld* S Korea
100 F2 **Soap Lake** Washington U.S.A.
48 J5 **Soarş** Romania
71 A2 **Soa-Siu** Halmahera Indonesia
45 K1 **Soave** Italy
15 B3 **Soay** Scotland
41 K5 **Soazza** Switzerland
85 F6 **Soba** Nigeria
86 F4 **Sobat** *prov* Sudan
86 F4 **Sobat** *R* Sudan
36 D4 **Sobernheim** Germany
31 H6 **Sobeslav** Czechoslovakia
54 M1 **Sobinka** Russian Federation
53 H8 **Sobolevo** Russian Federation
60 E13 **Sobo-san** *mt* Japan
38 M8 **Soboth** Austria
31 K5 **Sobotka** Poland
129 K6 **Sobradinho, Barragem de** *res* Brazil
129 K4 **Sobral** Brazil
48 G2 **Sobrance** Czechoslovakia
18 F10 **Sobrarbe** *dist* Spain
68 H1 **Soc Bang Giang** *R* Vietnam
68 H1 **Soc Giang** Vietnam
31 M3 **Sochaczew** Poland
40 E2 **Sochaux** France
53 E11 **Sochi** Russian Federation
112 D4 **Social Circle** Georgia U.S.A.
112 H3 **Society Hill** South Carolina U.S.A.
135 M10 **Society Is** Pacific Oc
Socna *see* **Sūknah**
128 E8 **Socompa** *vol* Chile/Arg
73 F8 **Socorro** Brazil
108 A1 **Socorro** New Mexico U.S.A.
133 B6 **Socorro, I** Chile
Socotra *see* **Suquţrā**
17 F5 **Socuéllamos** Spain
117 M9 **Soda Creek** British Columbia Canada
103 H6 **Soda L** California U.S.A.
29 M4 **Sodankylä** Finland
101 O7 **Soda Springs** Idaho U.S.A.
102 F3 **Sodaville** Nevada U.S.A.
112 B2 **Soddy-Daisy** Tennessee U.S.A.
36 F3 **Södel** Germany
27 K12 **Söderby-Karl** Sweden
27 J9 **Söderfjärden** Sweden
27 J11 **Söderfors** Sweden
27 D7 **Söderhamn** Sweden
27 H13 **Söderköping** Sweden
27 H12 **Södermanland** *reg* Sweden
27 J12 **Södertälje** Sweden
86 E3 **Sodiri** Sudan
86 G4 **Sodo** Ethiopia
94 K3 **Sodus** New York U.S.A.
89 H6 **Sodwana B** S Africa
71 M9 **Soë** Timor Indonesia
60 D12 **Soeda** Japan
87 E10 **Soekmekaar** S Africa
52 B5 **Soela Väin** *chan* Estonia
32 H9 **Soest** Germany
25 D4 **Soest** Netherlands
32 G7 **Soeste** *R* Germany
46 E5 **Sofádhes** Greece
Sofala *see* **Beira** Mozambique
139 J5 **Sofala** New South Wales Australia
79 F5 **Sofar** Lebanon
Sofia *see* **Sofiya**
87 H11 **Sofia** *R* Madagascar
106 G5 **Sofia** New Mexico U.S.A.
46 F7 **Sofikón** Greece
46 F2 **Sofiya** Bulgaria
36 H7 **Söflingen** Germany
52 D2 **Sofporog** Russian Federation
75 P3 **Sog** China
128 D2 **Sogamoso** Colombia
32 G7 **Sögel** Germany
45 M3 **Sogliano al Rubicone** Italy
27 B10 **Sogn** *reg* Norway
27 B10 **Sogndal** Norway
27 B10 **Sognefjorden** *inlet* Norway
26 B10 **Sogn og Fjordane** Norway
71 G5 **Sogod** Philippines
55 E1 **Sogom** Russian Federation
47 K5 **Söğüt** Turkey
78 C1 **Söğüt** Turkey
47 K7 **Söğüt Gölü** *L* Turkey
84 J4 **Sohâg** Egypt
75 J7 **Sohagpur** India
9 G3 **Soham** England
137 L3 **Sohano** Bougainville I Papua New Guinea
68 D5 **Sohng Gwe, Khao** *mt* Burma/Thailand
36 H1 **Söhrewald** Germany
65 F7 **Sohŭksan** *isld* S Korea
22 G3 **Soignies** Belgium
21 O7 **Soings-en-Sologne** France
29 L9 **Soini** Finland
22 E5 **Soissons** France
60 G11 **Sōja** Japan
74 E6 **Sojat** India
71 F6 **Sojoton Pt** Philippines
53 H7 **Sok** *R* Russian Federation
78 A3 **Soke** Turkey
46 E6 **Sokhós** Greece
48 L6 **Sokiryany** Ukraine
48 E2 **Soko Banja** Serbia Yugoslavia
85 E7 **Sokodé** Togo
52 F5 **Sokol** Russian Federation
31 O2 **Sokółka** Poland
31 L4 **Sokolniki** Poland
85 C6 **Sokolo** Mali
37 O3 **Sokolov** Czechoslovakia
55 E3 **Sokolovka** Kazakhstan
52 J2 **Sokolovo** Russian Federation
31 N5 **Sokołów Małopolski** Poland
31 N3 **Sokołów Podlaski** Poland
52 D2 **Sokolozero** Russian Federation
52 F6 **Sokol'skoye** Russian Federation
31 O3 **Sokoły** Poland
115 R4 **Søkongen Ø** *isld* Greenland
61 Q12 **Sokoniya** Okinawa
85 F6 **Sokoto** *R* Nigeria
85 F6 **Sokoto** Nigeria
56 B3 **Sokur** Russian Federation
56 C3 **Sokur** Russian Federation
126 F4 **Sola** Cuba
27 A13 **Sola** Norway
88 F1 **Solai** Kenya
74 G3 **Solan** India
144 A7 **Solander I** New Zealand
71 E2 **Solano** Luzon Philippines
106 F6 **Solano** New Mexico U.S.A.
76 B2 **Solāpur** India
45 Q8 **Solaro, M** *mt* Italy
41 O3 **Solbad Hall** Austria
26 J8 **Solberg** Sweden
26 J2 **Solbergfjord** *inlet* Norway
27 E12 **Solbergfoss** Norway
28 E3 **Solbjerg** Denmark
28 D4 **Solbjerg Sø** *L* Denmark
48 K3 **Solca** Romania
41 O4 **Sölden** Austria
99 L8 **Soldier** Iowa U.S.A.
107 P2 **Soldier** Kansas U.S.A.
94 D8 **Soldier** Kentucky U.S.A.
31 L2 **Solec Kujawski** Poland
126 G9 **Soledad** Colombia
124 C5 **Soledad** Mexico
102 C5 **Soledad** California U.S.A.
127 N10 **Soledad** Venezuela
128 E5 **Soledade** Brazil
100 A1 **Soleduck** *R* Washington U.S.A.
55 F3 **Solenoye, Ozero** *L* Russian Federation
125 M4 **Solentiname, Is. de** Nicaragua
9 E6 **Solent, The** *chan* England
7 L9 **Sole Pit** North Sea
45 L1 **Solesino** Italy
22 F3 **Solesmes** Nord France
21 K6 **Solesmes** Sarthe France
41 N5 **Sole, Val. di** Italy
29 J8 **Solf** Finland
45 J1 **Solferino** Italy
52 F4 **Solginskiy** Russian Federation
56 D3 **Solgonskiy Kryzah** *ra* Russian Federation
27 A11 **Solheim** Norway
52 F5 **Soligalich** Russian Federation
21 M4 **Soligny-la-Trappe** France
9 E3 **Solihull** England
52 J5 **Solikamsk** Russian Federation
55 B5 **Sol'Iletsk** Russian Federation
43 C12 **Soliman** Tunisia
128 E4 **Solimões** *R* Brazil
36 C1 **Solingen** Germany
127 J10 **Solita** Venezuela
139 L3 **Solitary I, North** New South Wales Australia
139 L4 **Solitary I, South** New South Wales Australia
17 H3 **Solivella** Spain
38 F7 **Söll** Austria
26 J8 **Sollefteå** Sweden
27 J12 **Sollentuna** Sweden
26 D10 **Sollia** Norway
33 R9 **Söllichau** Germany
32 K9 **Solling** *hills* Germany
33 N8 **Söllingen** Germany
36 E3 **Solms** Germany
26 E10 **Søln** *mt* Norway
27 J12 **Solna** Sweden
54 H1 **Solnechnogorsk** Russian Federation
37 K6 **Solnhofen** Germany
26 D10 **Sølnkletten** *mt* Norway
54 H5 **Solntsevo** Russian Federation
70 N9 **Solo** *R* Java
70 G6 **Solo** *R* Sulawesi
45 R8 **Solofra** Italy
21 N7 **Sologne** *reg* France
71 J4 **Solok** Sulawesi
69 E13 **Solok** Sumatra
52 D4 **Solomennoye** Russian Federation
103 P9 **Solomon** Arizona U.S.A.
107 M2 **Solomon** *R* Kansas U.S.A.
107 N3 **Solomon** Kansas U.S.A.
137 M3 **Solomon Is** Pacific Oc
137 L3 **Solomon Sea** Pacific Oc
80 G7 **Solomon's Pools** Jordan
59 H2 **Solon** China
99 P8 **Solon** Iowa U.S.A.
94 F5 **Solon** Ohio U.S.A.
55 F5 **Solonichki** Kazakhstan
54 H6 **Solonitsevka** Ukraine
99 P3 **Solon Springs** Wisconsin U.S.A.
58 G1 **Solontsovo** Russian Federation
45 R7 **Solopaca** Italy
71 L9 **Solor** *isld* Indonesia
17 F3 **Solorio, Sa. del** *mts* Spain
71 L9 **Solor, Kepulauan** *isld* Indonesia
40 F3 **Solothurn** Switzerland
48 J2 **Solotvin** Ukraine
52 E2 **Solovetskiye Ostrova** *islds* Russian Federation
59 H1 **Solov'yevsk** Russian Federation
22 G3 **Solre-le-Château** France
28 J5 **Solrød Strand** Denmark
38 N6 **Solstein** *mt* Austria
42 G5 **Šolta** *isld* Croatia
32 L7 **Soltau** Germany
52 D5 **Sol'tsy** Russian Federation
27 A10 **Solund** Norway
46 E3 **Solunska** *mt* Macedonia Yugoslavia
102 D7 **Solvang** California U.S.A.
95 L3 **Solvay** New York U.S.A.
27 G15 **Sölvesborg** Sweden
52 G4 **Sol'vychegodsk** Russian Federation
15 E6 **Solway Firth** Scotland
87 E8 **Solwezi** Zambia
61 O8 **Sōma** Japan
47 J5 **Soma** Turkey
22 E3 **Somain** France
86 H5 **Somalia** *rep* E Africa
72 G7 **Somali Basin** Indian Oc
70 E3 **Sombang, Gunung** *mt* Kalimantan
87 D7 **Sombo** Angola
48 E5 **Sombor** Serbia Yugoslavia
120 H10 **Sombra** Ontario Canada
22 H2 **Sombreffe** Belgium
124 H6 **Sombrerete** Mexico
127 N5 **Sombrero** *isld* Lesser Antilles
69 A9 **Sombrero Chan** Nicobar Is
113 F13 **Sombrero Key** *isld* Florida U.S.A.
48 H3 **Şomcuţa Mare** Romania
48 H3 **Şomcuta Mare** Romania
25 E6 **Someren** Netherlands
29 K11 **Somero** Finland
99 M7 **Somers** Iowa U.S.A.
101 L1 **Somers** Montana U.S.A.
99 T7 **Somers** Wisconsin U.S.A.
139 H8 **Somerset** Tasmania Australia
119 T9 **Somerset** Manitoba Canada
8 C5 **Somerset** *co* England
106 C3 **Somerset** Colorado U.S.A.
94 C9 **Somerset** Kentucky U.S.A.
95 Q5 **Somerset** Massachusetts U.S.A.
94 E7 **Somerset** Ohio U.S.A.
94 H6 **Somerset** Pennsylvania U.S.A.
109 J6 **Somerset** Texas U.S.A.
87 E12 **Somerset East** S Africa
90 A2 **Somerset I** Bermuda
147 F4 **Somerset I** Northwest Territories Canada
141 L7 **Somerset Res** Queensland Australia
95 P4 **Somerset Res** Vermont U.S.A.
89 A10 **Somerset West** S Africa
95 N7 **Somers Point** New Jersey U.S.A.
95 Q3 **Somersworth** New Hampshire U.S.A.
8 D5 **Somerton** England
103 K9 **Somerton** Arizona U.S.A.
95 Q4 **Somerville** Massachusetts U.S.A.
95 N6 **Somerville** New Jersey U.S.A.
110 G6 **Somerville** Tennessee U.S.A.
109 L5 **Somerville Res** Texas U.S.A.
48 H3 **Someş** *R* Romania
100 B8 **Somesbar** California U.S.A.
48 H4 **Somesul Cald** *R* Romania
48 J3 **Someşul Mare** *R* Romania
77 K7 **Somiani Bay** *B* Pakistan
45 J1 **Sommacampagna** Italy
22 H5 **Sommauthe** France
45 Q8 **Somma Vesuvio** Italy
18 G3 **Somme** *dept* France
21 O1 **Somme** *R* France
22 D4 **Somme** *R* France
22 J3 **Somme-Leuze** Belgium
27 G13 **Sommen** Sweden
27 H13 **Sommen** *L* Sweden
37 L1 **Sömmerda** Germany
18 H4 **Sommesous** France
18 H9 **Sommières** France
68 G2 **Som Mong** Vietnam
48 D4 **Somogy** *co* Hungary
48 D4 **Somogyszob** Hungary
48 D4 **Somogyvár** Hungary
99 S8 **Somonauk** Illinois U.S.A.
16 E3 **Somosierra, Pto. de** Spain
54 L5 **Somovo** Russian Federation
31 L3 **Sompolno** Poland
131 C8 **Somuncurá, Mesa Vol. de** *mt* Argentina
22 G3 **Somzée** Belgium
73 N4 **Son** *R* India
27 E12 **Son** Norway
21 O4 **Sonchamp** France
44 G1 **Soncino** Italy
41 M5 **Sondalo** Italy
52 D3 **Sondaly** Russian Federation
28 C7 **Sønderå** *R* Denmark
28 D7 **Sønderborg** Denmark
28 A6 **Sønderjylland** *co* Denmark
28 D3 **Sønder Onsild** Denmark
33 N10 **Sondershausen** Germany
28 E6 **Sønderse** Denmark
111 E9 **Sondheimer** Louisiana U.S.A.
115 O4 **Søndre Strømfjord** *inlet* Greenland
115 O3 **Søndre Upernavik** Greenland
42 C2 **Sondrio** Italy
25 E5 **Son en Breugel** Netherlands
76 C1 **Sonepat** India
128 E8 **Sonequera** *mt* Bolivia
95 L5 **Sonestown** Pennsylvania U.S.A.
70 C4 **Song** Sarawak
71 A3 **Songa** Indonesia
65 J2 **Song'acha He** *R* China/Rus Fed
88 G6 **Songa Manara** *isld* Tanzania
27 B12 **Songa Totak** *R* Norway
68 J6 **Song Ba** *R* Vietnam
68 H2 **Song Ba Che** *R* Vietnam
67 D3 **Songbai** China
Song Bo *R see* **Noire** *R*
68 G2 **Song Boi** *R* Vietnam
67 E1 **Songbu** China
67 A4 **Song Ca** *R* Vietnam
68 J6 **Song Cai** *R* Vietnam
67 B5 **Song Cau** *R* Vietnam
68 J6 **Song Cau** Vietnam
68 G2 **Song Chay** *R* Vietnam
67 A7 **Song Chu** *R* Vietnam
69 H8 **Song Co Chien** *R* Vietnam
69 G8 **Song Cua Lon** *R* Vietnam
88 E7 **Songea** Tanzania
21 O2 **Songeons** France
68 J5 **Song Ha Giao** *R* Vietnam
65 G3 **Songhua Hu** *res* China
65 F2 **Songhua Jiang** *R* China
Songjiachuan *see* **Wubu**
Songjiang *see* **Antu**
67 G1 **Songjiang** China
59 J3 **Songjin** N Korea
67 B2 **Songkan** China
57 G4 **Song-Kël'-Too, Ozero** *L* Kyrgyzstan
69 E9 **Songkhla** Thailand
68 F4 **Song Khram** *R* Thailand
67 A5 **Song-koi** *R* Vietnam
67 E4 **Songkou** China
67 B5 **Song Ky Cung** *R* Vietnam
65 E4 **Song Ling** *mts* China
68 D1 **Songlong** Burma
67 B5 **Song Luy** *R* Vietnam
68 G2 **Song Ma** *R* Vietnam
67 A4 **Songming** China
68 H7 **Song Nha Be** *R* Vietnam
87 B8 **Songo** Angola
86 B7 **Songololo** Zaire
69 G8 **Song Ong Doc** *R* Vietnam
58 D5 **Songpan** China
88 G6 **Song Songo** *isld* Tanzania
67 C2 **Songtao** China
68 J5 **Song Tra Khuc** *R* Vietnam
68 H7 **Song Vam Co Dong** *R* Vietnam
68 H7 **Song Vam Co Tay** *R* Vietnam
88 D6 **Songwe** Tanzania
67 F3 **Song Xi** *R* China
67 F3 **Songxi** China
65 B7 **Song Xian** China
65 F1 **Song Zhan** China
67 D1 **Songzi** China
68 J5 **Son Ha** Vietnam
68 J5 **Son Hai** Vietnam
68 J6 **Son Hoa** Vietnam
65 B3 **Sonid Youqi** China
65 B3 **Sonid Zuoqi** China
74 G4 **Sonīpat** India
29 N8 **Sonkajärvi** Finland
68 F2 **Son La** Vietnam
74 B6 **Sonmiani** Pakistan
38 H7 **Sonnblick, Gross** *mt* Austria
37 L3 **Sonneberg** Germany
37 L3 **Sonnefeld** Germany
37 P6 **Sonnen Wald** *mts* Germany
33 T9 **Sonnewalde** Germany
118 K6 **Sonningdale** Saskatchewan Canada
45 O7 **Sonnino** Italy
129 J5 **Sono** *R* Brazil
60 J10 **Sonobe** Japan
41 J5 **Sonogno** Switzerland
103 M10 **Sonoita** Mexico
103 O10 **Sonoita** Arizona U.S.A.
103 M1 **Sonoita** *R* Utah U.S.A.
103 L10 **Sonoita R** Mexico
102 B3 **Sonoma** California U.S.A.
100 H9 **Sonoma Range** Nevada U.S.A.
123 L8 **Sonora** Nova Scotia Canada
124 D3 **Sonora** *state* Mexico
124 D3 **Sonora** *R* Mexico
103 O8 **Sonora** Arizona U.S.A.
102 D4 **Sonora** California U.S.A.
108 G5 **Sonora** Texas U.S.A.
92 C4 **Sonoran Desert** Cal/Ariz U.S.A.
102 E3 **Sonora Pk** California U.S.A.
25 F5 **Sonsbeck** Germany
56 D4 **Sonskiy** Russian Federation
128 C2 **Sonsón** Colombia
125 P11 **Sonsonate** El Salvador
68 G1 **Son Tay** Vietnam
37 J6 **Sontheim** Germany
41 M2 **Sonthofen** Germany
36 H1 **Sontra** Germany
94 K4 **Sonyea** New York U.S.A.
21 L6 **Sonzay** France
Soochow *see* **Suzhou**
116 C5 **Sooghmeghat** Alaska U.S.A.
117 M11 **Sooke** British Columbia Canada
36 D4 **Soonwald** *mts* Germany
131 G3 **Sopas** *R* Uruguay
113 C7 **Sopchoppy** Florida U.S.A.
107 P7 **Soper** Oklahoma U.S.A.
112 E5 **Soperton** Georgia U.S.A.
68 F3 **Sop Khao** Laos
9 E6 **Sopley** England
86 E4 **Sopo** *R* Sudan
46 G2 **Sopot** Bulgaria
31 L1 **Sopot** Poland
26 M3 **Soppero** Sweden
48 D3 **Sopron** Hungary
123 Q4 **Sop's Arm** Newfoundland Canada
71 J4 **Soputan, G** Sulawesi
102 C5 **Soquel** California U.S.A.
16 B5 **Sor** *R* Portugal
42 F7 **Sora** Italy
27 G14 **Söraby** Sweden
60 Q2 **Sorachi** *R* Japan
75 L9 **Sorada** India
26 J9 **Söråker** Sweden
45 N5 **Soratte, M** *mt* Italy
17 F7 **Sorbas** Spain
16 E3 **Sorbe** *R* Spain
27 F10 **Sörberget** Sweden
12 D4 **Sorbie** Scotland
45 H2 **Sorbolo** Italy
26 H9 **Sörbygden** Sweden
28 G6 **Sørbymagle** Denmark
28 B3 **Sørdbjerg** Denmark
70 L9 **Soreang** Java
121 R6 **Sorel** Quebec Canada
139 J8 **Sorell** Tasmania Australia
139 H8 **Sorell, C** Tasmania Australia
80 B6 **Soreq** *R* Israel
44 G1 **Soresina** Italy
27 B11 **Sørfjorden** Norway
26 E7 **Sör Flatanger** Norway
26 H4 **Sørfold** Norway
26 H7 **Sörfors** Sweden
45 J1 **Sorgà** Italy
43 C8 **Sorgono** Sardinia
18 G9 **Sorgues** *R* France
19 N17 **Sorgues** France
79 E2 **Sorgun** *R* Turkey
44 F3 **Sori** Italy
17 F3 **Soria** *prov* Spain
17 F3 **Soria** Spain
133 F4 **Soriano** *dept* Uruguay
21 M7 **Sorigny** France
69 D12 **Sorikmarapi** *mt* Sumatra
52 E5 **Sorka** Russian Federation
50 A1 **Sörkapp** *isld* Svalbard
26 G7 **Sørli** Norway
26 L8 **Sörmjöle** Sweden
12 D3 **Sorn** Scotland
41 J5 **Sornico** Switzerland
Sorø *co see* **Vestjælland** *co*
28 H6 **Sorø** Denmark
130 F8 **Sorocaba** Brazil
52 H6 **Soroch'I Gory** Russian Federation
55 B5 **Sorochinsk** Russian Federation
48 L2 **Soroki** Moldavia
48 E3 **Soroksár** Hungary
57 H2 **Sorolen** Kazakhstan
43 F11 **Soro, M** *mt* Sicily
71 C3 **Sorong** W Irian
86 F5 **Soroti** Uganda
26 N1 **Sørøya** *isld* Norway
26 N1 **Sørøysund** *chan* Norway
32 G10 **Sorpetalsperre** *L* Germany
16 B6 **Sorraia** *R* Portugal
26 K2 **Sørreisa** Norway
139 G7 **Sorrento** Victoria Australia
117 O10 **Sorrento** British Columbia Canada
45 Q8 **Sorrento** Italy
111 F11 **Sorrento** Louisiana U.S.A.
95 T2 **Sorrento** Maine U.S.A.
87 B10 **Sorris-Sorris** Namibia
29 O4 **Sorsatunturi** *mt* Finland
26 J6 **Sorsele** Sweden
56 C4 **Sorsk** Russian Federation
43 B8 **Sorso** Sardinia
71 G4 **Sorsogon** Philippines
18 F10 **Sort** Spain
29 P10 **Sortavala** Russian Federation
26 H3 **Sortland** Norway
52 H4 **Sortopolovskaya** Russian Federation
26 E9 **Sør-Trøndelag** *reg* Norway
28 H7 **Sortsø** Denmark
47 N10 **Sortullu** Turkey
98 D4 **Sorum** South Dakota U.S.A.
28 G7 **Sørup** Denmark
32 L4 **Sörup** Germany
28 B4 **Sørvad** Denmark
26 M1 **Sørvær** Norway
26 F9 **Sörvattnan** Sweden
Sörve Väin *see* **Kura Kurk** *str*
52 G5 **Sorvizhi** Russian Federation
17 G2 **Sos del Rey Catolico** Spain
32 M9 **Sose** *R* Germany
131 B5 **Sosneado** *pk* Argentina
54 D5 **Sosnitsa** Ukraine
52 H3 **Sosnogorsk** Russian Federation
52 D3 **Sosnovets** Russian Federation
52 F2 **Sosnovka** Russian Federation
52 G6 **Sosnovka** Chuvashskaya Respublika Russian Federation
29 P11 **Sosnovo** Russian Federation
58 F1 **Sosnovo-Ozerskoye** Russian Federation
52 C5 **Sosnovyy Bor** Russian Federation
55 E1 **Sosnovyy Mys** Russian Federation
31 L5 **Sosnowiec** Poland
29 M7 **Soso** Finland
111 G10 **Soso** Mississippi U.S.A.
42 G2 **Šoštanj** Slovenia
61 Q12 **Sosu** Okinawa
55 D2 **Sos'va** Russian Federation
53 E10 **Sosyka** *R* Russian Federation
78 H2 **Sothan** Turkey
29 N7 **Sotkamo** Finland
125 K6 **Soto la Marina** Mexico
27 A11 **Sotra** *isld* Norway
54 K6 **Sotsgorodok** Russian Federation
20 G2 **Sottevast** France
21 N3 **Sotteville** France
27 L11 **Sottunga** Finland
21 M5 **Souance** France
85 C7 **Souanké** Congo
85 C7 **Soubré** Ivory Coast
22 D3 **Souchez** France
140 D5 **Soudan** N Terr Australia
20 H6 **Soudan** Loire-Inférieure France
95 M6 **Souderton** Pennsylvania U.S.A.
21 P7 **Souesmes** France
86 B5 **Souflay** Congo
36 D5 **Soufflenheim** France
47 H3 **Souflion** Greece
127 O8 **Soufrière** St Lucia
127 O8 **Soufrière** *mt* St Vincent
127 N4 **Soufrière** *pk* Guadeloupe W Indies
21 K5 **Sougé-le Ganelon** France
21 O5 **Sougy** France
18 G8 **Souillac** France
83 L13 **Souillac** Mauritius
85 F1 **Souk Ahras** Algeria
16 D10 **Souk-el-Arba-du-Rharb** Morocco
16 D9 **Souk-Sebt-des-Beni-Zarfeto** Morocco
16 D9 **Souk Tolba** Morocco
65 G6 **Sŏul** S Korea
121 Q7 **Soulanges Canal** Quebec Canada
21 J5 **Soulgé-sur-Quette** France
21 L5 **Souligné** France
21 L6 **Souligné** France
20 G8 **Soullans** France
36 D6 **Soultz** France
68 A6 **Sound I** Andaman Is
118 G6 **Sounding L** Alberta Canada
15 A3 **Sound of Barra** Scotland
15 A3 **Sound of Harris** Outer Hebrides Scotland
15 C3 **Sound of Sleat** Scotland
46 F7 **Soúnion, Akra** Greece
79 F5 **Soûr** Lebanon
89 F7 **Sources, Mt. aux** Lesotho
21 J4 **Sourdeval** France
129 J4 **Soure** Brazil
16 B4 **Souré** Portugal
85 E1 **Sour El Ghozlane** Algeria
119 R9 **Souris** Manitoba Canada
123 K7 **Souris** Prince Edward I Canada
119 R10 **Souris** North Dakota U.S.A.
119 O9 **Souris** *R* Saskatchewan Canada
46 F5 **Soúrpi** Greece
21 O5 **Sours** France
85 C2 **Sous** *R* Morocco
130 H9 **Sousa** Brazil
129 H4 **Sousel** Brazil
43 D13 **Sousse** Tunisia
18 E9 **Soustons** France
18 G6 **Souterraine, la** France
89 **South Africa** *rep*
9 F5 **Southall** England
9 E3 **Southam** England
98 H1 **Southam** North Dakota U.S.A.
122 H8 **Southampton** Nova Scotia Canada
120 J8 **Southampton** Ontario Canada
9 E6 **Southampton** England
95 P6 **Southampton** Long I, New York U.S.A.
115 L5 **Southampton I** Northwest Territories Canada
68 A6 **South Andaman** *isld* Andaman Is
94 K9 **South Anna** *R* Virginia U.S.A.
102 C6 **South Antonio** *R* California U.S.A.
146 F14 **Southard,C** Antarctica
138 **South Australia** *state* Australia
120 J7 **South B** Ontario Canada
106 C8 **South Baldy** *mt* New Mexico U.S.A.
94 E5 **South Bass I** Ohio U.S.A.
113 G11 **South Bay** Florida U.S.A.
120 H7 **South Baymouth** Ontario Canada
142 A2 **South Beach** *dist* Perth, W Aust Australia
142 B2 **South Belmont** *dist* Perth, W Aust Australia
99 S7 **South Beloit** Illinois U.S.A.
99 U8 **South Bend** Indiana U.S.A.
109 J3 **South Bend** Texas U.S.A.
100 B3 **South Bend** Washington U.S.A.
126 F2 **South Bight** Andros Bahamas
141 J6 **South Blackwater** Queensland Australia
126 G3 **South Bluff** Acklins I Bahamas
94 B2 **South Boardman** Michigan U.S.A.
9 G5 **Southborough** England
94 H10 **South Boston** Virginia U.S.A.
123 N6 **South Branch** Newfoundland Canada
94 D2 **South Branch** Michigan U.S.A.
8 C7 **South Brent** England
144 D5 **Southbridge** New Zealand
95 P4 **Southbridge** Massachusetts U.S.A.
141 K1 **South Brisbane** *dist* Brisbane, Qnsld Australia
123 Q4 **South Brook** Newfoundland Canada
144 D5 **Southbrook** New Zealand
122 H9 **South Brookfield** Nova Scotia Canada
144 C6 **Southburn** New Zealand
127 J4 **South Caicos** *isld* Turks & Caicos Is
112 F3 **South Carolina** *state* U.S.A.
13 H6 **South Cave** England
94 C1 **South Chan** Michigan U.S.A.
94 D7 **South Charleston** Ohio U.S.A.
94 F8 **South Charleston** West Virginia U.S.A.
66 E6 **South China Sea**
95 N2 **South Colton** New York U.S.A.
98 F5 **South Dakota** *state* U.S.A.
94 H4 **South Dayton** New York U.S.A.
13 F3 **Southdean** Scotland
95 P4 **South Deerfield** Massachusetts U.S.A.
9 F6 **South Downs** England
139 H9 **South East C** Tasmania Australia
139 H7 **South East C** Victoria Australia
83 K12 **South East I** Mahé I Indian Oc
135 N15 **South East Pacific Basin** Pacific Oc
114 J6 **Southend** Saskatchewan Canada
9 G4 **Southend** England
12 C3 **Southend** Scotland
99 O8 **South English** Iowa U.S.A.
144 C5 **Southern Alps** *mts* New Zealand
143 C9 **Southern Cross** W Australia Australia
101 M3 **Southern Cross** Montana U.S.A.
86 D3 **Southern Darfur** *prov* Sudan
8 C5 **Southerndown** Wales
123 T6 **Southern Harbour** Newfoundland Canada
119 S2 **Southern Indian L** Manitoba Canada
86 E3 **Southern Kordofan** *prov* Sudan
81 B11 **Southern Ocean**
111 G10 **Southern Pine Hills** Miss/Ala U.S.A.
112 H2 **Southern Pines** North Carolina U.S.A.
142 B2 **Southern R** Perth, W Aust Australia
142 F5 **South Esk Tablelands** W Australia Australia
119 N8 **Southey** Saskatchewan Canada
110 E2 **South Fabius** *R* Missouri U.S.A.
13 H6 **South Ferriby** England
144 A6 **South Fiord** New Zealand
9 H5 **South Foreland** England
118 J8 **South Fork** Saskatchewan Canada
100 B9 **South Fork** California U.S.A.
106 D4 **South Fork** Colorado U.S.A.
112 F1 **South Fork** *R* North Carolina U.S.A.
94 J6 **South Fork** Pennsylvania U.S.A.
110 G6 **South Fork** *R* Tennessee U.S.A.
98 D4 **South Fork R** South Dakota U.S.A.
99 V4 **South Fox I** Michigan U.S.A.
110 H5 **South Fulton** Tennessee U.S.A.
146 F11 **South Geomagnetic Pole** Antarctica
131 H5 **South Georgia** S Atlantic Oc
99 O9 **South Gifford** Missouri U.S.A.
8 C4 **South Glamorgan** *co* Wales
110 B3 **South Grand** *R* Missouri U.S.A.
123 M7 **South Harbour** Nova Scotia Canada

228 **South Haven — Stickhausen**

107 N4 **South Haven** Kansas U.S.A.
99 U7 **South Haven** Michigan U.S.A.
115 K5 **South Henik L** Northwest Territories Canada
94 J10 **South Hill** Virginia U.S.A.
94 F10 **South Holston L** Tenn/Virg U.S.A.
140 C1 **South I** N Terr Australia
83 M8 **South I** Cocos Is Indian Oc
119 T2 **South Indian L** Manitoba Canada
95 P5 **Southington** Connecticut U.S.A.
144 B5 **South Island** New Zealand
71 D6 **South Islet** Sulu Sea
118 F1 **South Junc** Manitoba Canada
99 T7 **South Kenosha** Wisconsin U.S.A.
59 J4 **South Korea** *rep* Asia
109 M8 **Southlake** Texas U.S.A.
102 E3 **South Lake Tahoe** California U.S.A.
144 A6 **Southland** *admin region* New Zealand
123 K9 **South Lochaber** Nova Scotia Canada
98 G8 **South Loup** *R* Nebraska U.S.A.
88 C8 **South Luangwa Nat. Park** Zambia
70 C2 **South Luconia Shoals** S China Sea
94 D4 **South Lyon** Michigan U.S.A.
120 K7 **Southmag** Ontario Canada
146 E14 **South Magnetic Pole** Antarctica
99 U4 **South Manitou I** Michigan U.S.A.
95 L10 **South Mills** North Carolina U.S.A.
99 T7 **South Milwaukee** Wisconsin U.S.A.
9 G4 **Southminster** England
141 H4 **South Mission Beach** Queensland Australia
8 C5 **South Molton** England
109 K10 **Southmost** Texas U.S.A.
95 K6 **South Mt** Pennsylvania U.S.A.
116 J7 **South Naknek** Alaska U.S.A.
122 G7 **South Nelson** New Brunswick Canada
112 F6 **South Newport** Georgia U.S.A.
95 P5 **Southold** Long I, New York U.S.A.
90 F15 **South Orkney Is** S Atlantic Oc
146 E3 **South Orkney Is** S Atlantic Oc
53 F12 **South Ossetia** *aut reg* Georgia
102 B3 **South Pablo B** California U.S.A.
95 R2 **South Paris** Maine U.S.A.
94 F7 **South Parkersburg** West Virginia U.S.A.
101 R7 **South Pass** Wyoming U.S.A.
101 R7 **South Pass City** Wyoming U.S.A.
99 R9 **South Pekin** Illinois U.S.A.
110 L6 **South Pittsburg** Tennessee U.S.A.
106 E2 **South Platte** Colorado U.S.A.
146 E9 **South Pole** Antarctica
120 J4 **South Porcupine** Ontario Canada
141 L8 **Southport** Queensland Australia
139 H9 **Southport** Tasmania Australia
123 T5 **Southport** Newfoundland Canada
13 E6 **Southport** England
94 A7 **Southport** Indiana U.S.A.
112 J4 **Southport** North Carolina U.S.A.
123 K4 **South Pt** Anticosti I, Quebec
83 M9 **South Pt** Christmas I Indian Oc
112 J3 **South R** North Carolina U.S.A.
99 S2 **South Range** Michigan U.S.A.
144 A7 **South Red Head Pt.** New Zealand
113 H12 **South Riding Rock** Bahamas
121 L7 **South River** Ontario Canada
95 N6 **South River** New Jersey U.S.A.
15 F2 **South Ronaldsay** Scotland
131 J7 **South Sandwich Is** S Atlantic Oc
102 B4 **South San Francisco** California U.S.A.
118 J8 **South Sask R** Saskatchewan Canada
9 E6 **Southsea** England
119 S1 **South Seal R** Manitoba Canada
146 C3 **South Shetland Is** S Atlantic Oc
13 G3 **South Shields** England
98 K7 **South Sioux City** Nebraska U.S.A.
98 K6 **South Sioux Falls** South Dakota U.S.A.
117 P11 **South Slocan** British Columbia Canada
103 N2 **South Tent** *pk* Utah U.S.A.
15 A3 **South Uist** Scotland
9 F1 **Southwell** England
South West Africa *see* **Namibia** *rep*
113 K9 **South West B** New Providence I Bahamas
139 H9 **South West C** Tasmania Australia
123 K6 **Southwest C** Madeleine Is, Quebec Canada
144 A7 **Southwest Cape** New Zealand
113 L8 **South West Cape** Virgin Is
139 H7 **South West I** Tasmania Australia
81 C9 **South-West Indian Ridge** Indian Oc
139 H8 **Southwest Nat. Park** Tasmania Australia
135 M12 **South-West Pacific Basin** Pacific Oc
122 J4 **Southwest Pt** Quebec Canada
126 E6 **Southwest Rock** Caribbean
139 L4 **South West Rocks** New South Wales Australia
99 S8 **South Wilmington** Illinois U.S.A.
9 H3 **Southwold** England
9 G4 **South Woodham Ferrers** England
9 G2 **South Wootton** England
South Yemen *see* **Yemen**
13 G6 **South Yorkshire** *co* England
89 F4 **Soutpansberg** *mts* S Africa
144 B6 **Soutra Hill** New Zealand
18 H6 **Souvigny** France
16 B6 **Souzel** Portugal
48 J4 **Sovata** Romania
118 K7 **Sovereign** Saskatchewan Canada
57 G4 **Sovetabad** Uzbekistan
52 G5 **Sovetsk** Russian Federation
52 B6 **Sovetsk** Russian Federation
53 F9 **Sovetskaya** Russian Federation
59 M2 **Sovetskaya Gavan** Russian Federation
52 C4 **Sovetskiy** Leningradskaya obl Russian Federation
55 D1 **Sovetskiy** Tyumenskaya obl Russian Federation
Soviet Union *see* **Union of Soviet Socialist Republics**
28 E5 **Søvind** Denmark
52 F2 **Sovpol'ye** Russian Federation
89 D3 **Sowa Pan** Botswana
119 N1 **Sowden L** Ontario Canada
13 G6 **Sowerby Br** England
60 P1 **Sōya** Japan
60 P1 **Sōya-misaki** *C* Japan
52 F2 **Soyana** *R* Russian Federation
18 F7 **Soyaux** France
60 P1 **Sōya wan** *B* Japan
38 F5 **Soyen** Germany
19 N15 **Soyons** France
124 E3 **Soyopa** Mexico
54 B4 **Sozh** *R* Belorussia/Rus Fed
52 H5 **Sozimskiy** Russian Federation
47 J2 **Sozopol** Bulgaria
22 K3 **Spa** Belgium
126 B2 **Spaanse Baai** *B* Curaçao
146 C6 **Spaatz I** *isld* Antarctica
16 **Spain** *kingdom* W Europe
31 M4 **Spała** Poland
Spalato *see* **Split** Croatia
138 E5 **Spalding** South Australia Australia
119 N6 **Spalding** Saskatchewan Canada
9 F2 **Spalding** England
100 J3 **Spalding** Idaho U.S.A.
98 H8 **Spalding** Nebraska U.S.A.
37 K5 **Spalt** Germany
25 C3 **Spanbroek** Netherlands
33 S7 **Spandau** Berlin
28 B6 **Spandet** Denmark
27 H14 **Spångenäs** Sweden
36 H1 **Spangenberg** Germany
100 H2 **Spangle** Washington U.S.A.
94 J6 **Spangler** Pennsylvania U.S.A.
123 T6 **Spaniard's B** Newfoundland Canada
120 H6 **Spanish** Ontario Canada
101 O9 **Spanish Fork** Utah U.S.A.
106 F4 **Spanish Pks** Colorado U.S.A.
127 L3 **Spanish Town** Jamaica
113 L7 **Spanish Town** Virgin Is
113 L12 **Spanish Wells** Eleuthera Bahamas
45 Q7 **Sparanise** Italy
26 E8 **Sparbu** Norway
28 C4 **Sparkær** Denmark
111 D8 **Sparkman** Arkansas U.S.A.
112 D6 **Sparks** Georgia U.S.A.
98 F7 **Sparks** Nebraska U.S.A.
102 E2 **Sparks** Nevada U.S.A.
107 O6 **Sparks** Oklahoma U.S.A.
99 R8 **Sparland** Illinois U.S.A.
37 M3 **Sparnberg** Germany
94 C1 **Sparr** Michigan U.S.A.
112 E4 **Sparta** Georgia U.S.A.
110 G3 **Sparta** Illinois U.S.A.
94 B3 **Sparta** Michigan U.S.A.
110 C4 **Sparta** Missouri U.S.A.
94 F10 **Sparta** North Carolina U.S.A.
100 H5 **Sparta** Oregon U.S.A.
110 L6 **Sparta** Tennessee U.S.A.
99 Q6 **Sparta** Wisconsin U.S.A.
112 F3 **Spartanburg** South Carolina U.S.A.
94 H5 **Spartansburg** Pennsylvania U.S.A.
16 D9 **Spartel, C** Morocco
47 O12 **Spartílla** Greece
43 G11 **Spartivento, C** Italy
43 B10 **Spartivento, C** Sardinia
54 M1 **Spas-Klepiki** Russian Federation
56 C4 **Spassk** Russian Federation
52 D4 **Spasskaya Guba** Russian Federation
59 K3 **Spassk Dal'niy** Russian Federation
55 E5 **Spasskoye** Kazakhstan
54 M2 **Spassk-Ryazanskiy** Russian Federation
46 F9 **Spátha, Akr** *C* Crete Greece
117 J7 **Spatsizi Plat. Wilderness Prov. Pk** British Columbia Canada
110 A5 **Spavinaw, L** Oklahoma U.S.A.
36 D3 **Spay** Germany
109 L6 **Speaks** Texas U.S.A.
15 D4 **Spean Bridge** Scotland
98 C5 **Spearfish** South Dakota U.S.A.
119 T7 **Spearhill** Manitoba Canada
108 C7 **Spearman** Texas U.S.A.
107 L4 **Spearville** Kansas U.S.A.
142 A3 **Spearwood** *dist* Perth, W Aust Australia
33 R6 **Specker-See** *L* Germany
95 N3 **Speculator** New York U.S.A.
118 F4 **Spedden** Alberta Canada
109 M1 **Speer** Oklahoma U.S.A.
98 B8 **Speer** Wyoming U.S.A.
118 K6 **Speers** Saskatchewan Canada
36 B4 **Speicher** Germany
37 M4 **Speichersdorf** Germany
37 M7 **Speichersee** *L* Germany
127 P6 **Speightstown** Barbados
116 M6 **Spenard** Alaska U.S.A.
115 K4 **Spence Bay** Northwest Territories Canada
101 N5 **Spencer** Idaho U.S.A.
110 K2 **Spencer** Indiana U.S.A.
99 L6 **Spencer** Iowa U.S.A.
95 P4 **Spencer** Massachusetts U.S.A.
98 H7 **Spencer** Nebraska U.S.A.
95 L4 **Spencer** New York U.S.A.
98 J6 **Spencer** South Dakota U.S.A.
94 F8 **Spencer** West Virginia U.S.A.
99 Q5 **Spencer** Wisconsin U.S.A.
138 D6 **Spencer, C** South Australia Australia
117 E6 **Spencer, C** Alaska U.S.A.
138 D5 **Spencer Gulf** South Australia Australia
95 R1 **Spencer L** Maine U.S.A.
94 K3 **Spencerport** New York U.S.A.
116 D4 **Spencer, Pt** Alaska U.S.A.
140 C1 **Spencer Ra** N Terr Australia
94 C6 **Spencerville** Ohio U.S.A.
117 N10 **Spences Bridge** British Columbia Canada
32 H8 **Spenge** Germany
13 G4 **Spennymoor** England
144 D5 **Spenser Mts** New Zealand
33 S8 **Sperenberg** Germany
27 D11 **Sperillen** Norway
46 E6 **Sperkhiós** *R* Greece
118 D1 **Sperling** Manitoba Canada
45 O7 **Sperlonga** Italy
43 B10 **Sperone, C** Sardinia
14 D2 **Sperrin Mts** N Ireland
94 J8 **Sperryville** Virginia U.S.A.
36 G3 **Spessart** *mts* Germany
46 F7 **Spétsai** *isld* Greece
15 E3 **Spey** *R* Scotland
36 E5 **Speyer** Germany
127 N1 **Speyside** Tobago
20 C5 **Spézet** France
44 G3 **Spezia, La** Italy
115 M4 **Spicer Is** Northwest Territories Canada
99 N9 **Spickardsville** Missouri U.S.A.
32 G5 **Spiekeroog** Germany
38 N8 **Spielfeld** Austria
36 C5 **Spiesen-Elversberg** Germany
44 D2 **Spigno** *R* Italy
25 G2 **Spijk** Netherlands
110 C1 **Spikard** Missouri U.S.A.
116 R3 **Spike Mt** Alaska U.S.A.
45 K2 **Spilamberto** Italy
46 G9 **Spili** Crete Greece
42 E2 **Spilimbergo** Italy
9 G1 **Spilsby** England
43 G8 **Spinazzola** Italy
77 K4 **Spīn Būldak** Afghanistan
22 K5 **Spincourt** France
112 F2 **Spindale** North Carolina U.S.A.
45 M1 **Spinea** Italy
44 F1 **Spino d'Adda** Italy
89 B8 **Spioenberg I** *mt* S Africa
89 A8 **Spioenberg II** *mt* S Africa
89 F7 **Spioen Kop** *mt* S Africa
99 L6 **Spirit L** Iowa U.S.A.
100 J2 **Spirit Lake** Idaho U.S.A.
100 C3 **Spirit Lake** Washington U.S.A.
117 O8 **Spirit River** Alberta Canada
145 D1 **Spirits B** New Zealand
118 K5 **Spiritwood** Saskatchewan Canada
98 H3 **Spiritwood** North Dakota U.S.A.
107 Q6 **Spiro** Oklahoma U.S.A.
52 D6 **Spirovo** Russian Federation
48 F1 **Spišská Belá** Czechoslovakia
48 F2 **Spišská Nová Ves** Czechoslovakia
31 M6 **Spišské Podhradie** Czechoslovakia
50 A1 **Spitsbergen** *arch* Arctic Oc
38 H8 **Spittal-an-der-Drau** Austria
38 M5 **Spitz** Austria
28 A4 **Spjald** Denmark
109 M5 **Splendora** Texas U.S.A.
42 H5 **Split** Croatia
122 H8 **Split, C** Nova Scotia Canada
119 V2 **Split L** Manitoba Canada
100 G8 **Split Pk** *mt* Nevada U.S.A.
38 N9 **Spodnje Hoče** Slovenia
28 F7 **Spodsbjerg** Denmark
108 G6 **Spofford** Texas U.S.A.
13 G6 **Spofforth** England
100 H2 **Spokane** Washington U.S.A.
42 E6 **Spoleto** Italy
118 F7 **Spondin** Alberta Canada
68 G6 **Spong** Cambodia
33 S5 **Sponholz** Germany
22 J3 **Spontin** Belgium
99 Q9 **Spoon** *R* Illinois U.S.A.
99 P4 **Spooner** Wisconsin U.S.A.
100 E8 **Spooner Res** California U.S.A.
Sporádes *islds see* **Dhodhekánisos** *islds*
33 P6 **Spornitz** Germany
28 E4 **Spørring** Denmark
44 D3 **Spotorno** Italy
101 U5 **Spotted Horse** Wyoming U.S.A.
103 J5 **Spotted Ra** Nevada U.S.A.
118 F1 **Sprague** Manitoba Canada
111 K9 **Sprague** Alabama U.S.A.
100 H2 **Sprague** Washington U.S.A.
99 Q5 **Sprague** Wisconsin U.S.A.
100 D7 **Sprague River** Oregon U.S.A.
36 H6 **Spraitbach** Germany
33 M7 **Sprakensehl** Germany
100 F5 **Spray** Oregon U.S.A.
48 E6 **Spreča** *R* Bosnia-Herzegovina
54 J4 **Spredne Russkaya Vozvyshennost'** *uplands* Russian Federation
31 H4 **Spree** *R* Germany
33 T9 **Spreewald** Germany
31 H4 **Spremberg** Germany
36 F3 **Sprendlingen** Hessen Germany
36 E4 **Sprendlingen** Rheinland-Pfalz Germany
22 K3 **Sprimont** Belgium
110 E5 **Spring** *R* Arkansas U.S.A.
110 B5 **Spring** *R* Oklahoma U.S.A.
109 M5 **Spring** Texas U.S.A.
101 N8 **Spring B** Utah U.S.A.
89 A7 **Springbok** S Africa
94 G5 **Springboro** Pennsylvania U.S.A.
109 J6 **Spring Branch** Texas U.S.A.
98 C1 **Spring Brook** North Dakota U.S.A.
118 A3 **Springburn** Alberta Canada
144 C5 **Springburn** New Zealand
95 M6 **Spring City** Pennsylvania U.S.A.
112 C2 **Spring City** Tennessee U.S.A.
103 N2 **Spring City** Utah U.S.A.
118 D9 **Spring Coulee** Alberta Canada
140 E4 **Spring Cr** N Terr Australia
140 F6 **Spring Cr** Queensland Australia
98 E9 **Spring Cr** Nebraska U.S.A.
101 L8 **Spring Cr** Nevada U.S.A.
145 D4 **Spring Creek** New Zealand
123 Q4 **Springdale** Newfoundland Canada
110 B5 **Springdale** Arkansas U.S.A.
101 P4 **Springdale** Montana U.S.A.
102 H4 **Springdale** Nevada U.S.A.
103 M4 **Springdale** Utah U.S.A.
100 H1 **Springdale** Washington U.S.A.
32 L8 **Springe** Germany
106 F5 **Springer** New Mexico U.S.A.
109 K1 **Springer** Oklahoma U.S.A.
121 Q3 **Springer, Mt** Quebec Canada
103 P7 **Springerville** Arizona U.S.A.
122 G8 **Springfield** New Brunswick Canada
122 H9 **Springfield** Nova Scotia Canada
144 C5 **Springfield** New Zealand
106 H4 **Springfield** Colorado U.S.A.
113 B7 **Springfield** Florida U.S.A.
112 F5 **Springfield** Georgia U.S.A.
101 N6 **Springfield** Idaho U.S.A.
110 G2 **Springfield** Illinois U.S.A.
94 B9 **Springfield** Kentucky U.S.A.
95 P4 **Springfield** Massachusetts U.S.A.
110 C4 **Springfield** Missouri U.S.A.
94 D7 **Springfield** Ohio U.S.A.
100 C5 **Springfield** Oregon U.S.A.
112 F4 **Springfield** South Carolina U.S.A.
98 J7 **Springfield** South Dakota U.S.A.
110 K5 **Springfield** Tennessee U.S.A.
95 P3 **Springfield** Vermont U.S.A.
89 D8 **Springfontein** S Africa
99 Q6 **Spring Green** Wisconsin U.S.A.
99 P6 **Spring Grove** Minnesota U.S.A.
95 L7 **Spring Grove** Pennsylvania U.S.A.
122 H8 **Springhill** Nova Scotia Canada
111 C9 **Springhill** Louisiana U.S.A.
110 K6 **Spring Hill** Tennessee U.S.A.
112 J2 **Spring Hope** North Carolina U.S.A.
99 U6 **Spring Lake** Michigan U.S.A.
95 N6 **Spring Lake** New Jersey U.S.A.
112 H2 **Spring Lake** North Carolina U.S.A.
108 E1 **Springlake** Texas U.S.A.
103 J5 **Spring Mts** Nevada U.S.A.
126 H3 **Spring Point** Acklins I Bahamas
89 F6 **Springs** S Africa
95 K6 **Springs** Pennsylvania U.S.A.
119 P7 **Springside** Saskatchewan Canada
144 D5 **Springs Junction** New Zealand
144 D5 **Springston** New Zealand
141 J6 **Springsure** Queensland Australia
109 K3 **Springtown** Texas U.S.A.
140 F6 **Springvale** Queensland Australia
141 G3 **Springvale** Queensland Australia
142 G4 **Springvale** W Australia Australia
95 R3 **Springvale** Maine U.S.A.
119 M9 **Spring Valley** Saskatchewan Canada
99 O6 **Spring Valley** Minnesota U.S.A.
98 G7 **Springview** Nebraska U.S.A.
111 K8 **Springville** Alabama U.S.A.
94 J4 **Springville** New York U.S.A.
101 O9 **Springville** Utah U.S.A.
118 J7 **Springwater** Saskatchewan Canada
13 H6 **Sproatley** England
28 F6 **Sprogø** *isld* Denmark
32 L6 **Sprötze** Germany
94 D2 **Spruce** Michigan U.S.A.
123 O5 **Spruce Brook** Newfoundland Canada
121 L7 **Sprucedale** Ontario Canada
118 D5 **Spruce Grove** Alberta Canada
94 H8 **Spruce Knob** *mt* West Virginia U.S.A.
118 H5 **Spruce Lake** Saskatchewan Canada
101 L9 **Spruce Mt** Nevada U.S.A.
112 E2 **Spruce Pine** North Carolina U.S.A.
103 M4 **Spry** Utah U.S.A.
25 B5 **Spui** *R* Netherlands
43 H9 **Spulico, C** Italy
108 G2 **Spur** Texas U.S.A.
118 C3 **Spurfield** Alberta Canada
111 B11 **Spurger** Texas U.S.A.
106 B8 **Spur Lake** New Mexico U.S.A.
116 L6 **Spurr, Mt** Alaska U.S.A.
46 C2 **Spuž** Montenegro Yugoslavia
22 H3 **Spy** Belgium
119 Q8 **Spy Hill** Saskatchewan Canada
117 M11 **Squamish** British Columbia Canada
95 Q3 **Squam L** New Hampshire U.S.A.
95 S7 **Squapan L** Maine U.S.A.
101 P2 **Square Butte** Montana U.S.A.
95 S6 **Square L** Maine U.S.A.
122 D6 **Squattack** Quebec Canada
123 L3 **Squaw L** Quebec Canada
99 M2 **Squaw L** Minnesota U.S.A.
119 O5 **Squaw Rapids** Saskatchewan Canada
43 H10 **Squillace, Golfo di** Italy
43 J8 **Squinzano** Italy
138 C2 **Squires, Mt** N Terr Australia
143 G7 **Squires,Mt** W Australia Australia
120 F2 **Squirrel** *R* Ontario Canada
116 G3 **Squirrel** *R* Alaska U.S.A.
70 N9 **Sragen** Java
46 D2 **Srbica** Serbia Yugoslavia
Srbija *see* **Serbia**
48 F5 **Srbobran** Serbia Yugoslavia
68 F7 **Srê Âmbêl** Cambodia
46 C1 **Srebrenica** Bosnia-Herzegovina
47 J2 **Sredetska** *R* Bulgaria
46 G2 **Sredna Gora** Bulgaria
51 K2 **Sredne-Sibirskoye Ploskogor'ye** *tableland* Russian Federation
52 D2 **Sredneye Kuyto, Oz** *L* Russian Federation
58 G1 **Sredniy Kalar** Russian Federation
55 C3 **Sredniy Ural** *ra* Russian Federation
53 F10 **Sredniy Yegorlyk** Russian Federation
46 G2 **Srednogorie** Bulgaria
53 F9 **Srednyaya Akhtuba** Russian Federation
55 G2 **Sred Vasyugan** Russian Federation
68 H6 **Sre Khtum** Cambodia
31 K3 **Śrem** Poland
48 F6 **Srem Mitrovica** Serbia Yugoslavia
48 E6 **Srem Raca** Serbia Yugoslavia
48 F5 **Sremski Karlovci** Serbia Yugoslavia
58 G1 **Sretensk** Russian Federation
74 F4 **Sri Dūngargarh** India
76 F1 **Srikakulam** India
76 D4 **Sri Kālahasti** India
83 **Sri Lanka** *rep* S Asia
74 F1 **Srinagar** Kashmir
68 E5 **Srinagarind Dam** Thailand
76 B4 **Sringeri** India
76 C6 **Srivilliputtur** India
42 H4 **Srnetica** Bosnia-Herzegovina
31 K3 **Środa** Poland
31 K4 **Środa Śląska** Poland
76 F1 **Srungavarapukota** India
141 F3 **Staaten** *R* Queensland Australia
141 F3 **Staaten River Nat. Park** Queensland Australia
26 O1 **Stabbursdalen Nat. Park** Norway
26 O1 **Stabburselv** *R* Norway
33 Q4 **Stäbelow** Germany
100 D4 **Stabler** Washington U.S.A.
28 A4 **Staby** Denmark
120 J5 **Stackpool** Ontario Canada
15 D1 **Stack Skerry** *isld* Scotland
14 B4 **Stack's Mts** Ireland
16 E4 **Sta. Cruz del Retamar** Spain
100 E9 **Stacy** California U.S.A.
112 L3 **Stacy** North Carolina U.S.A.
32 K5 **Stade** Germany
22 E2 **Staden** Belgium
36 F3 **Staden** Germany
9 E4 **Stadhampton** England
28 A4 **Stadil** Denmark
28 A4 **Stadil Fjord** *inlet* Denmark
26 A9 **Stadlandet** Norway
25 G2 **Stadskanaal** Netherlands
36 F2 **Stadt Allendorf** Germany
37 N5 **Stadtamhof** Germany
37 K7 **Stadtbergen** Germany
32 K8 **Stadthagen** Germany
37 L2 **Stadtilm** Germany
36 B3 **Stadtkyll** Germany
32 H6 **Stadtland** Germany
37 J3 **Stadtlauringen** Germany
37 J2 **Stadtlengsfeld** Germany
32 E8 **Stadtlohn** Germany
32 L9 **Stadtoldendorf** Germany
36 G4 **Stadtprozelten** Germany
37 M2 **Stadtroda** Germany
37 J4 **Stadt Schwarzach** Germany
37 M3 **Stadtsteinach** Germany
15 B4 **Staffa** *isld* Scotland
33 R7 **Staffelde** Germany
37 L3 **Staffelstein** Germany
44 F2 **Staffora** *R* Italy
141 K1 **Stafford** *dist* Brisbane, Qnsld Australia
8 D2 **Stafford** England
107 M4 **Stafford** Kansas U.S.A.
98 H7 **Stafford** Nebraska U.S.A.
94 K8 **Stafford** Virginia U.S.A.
8 D2 **Staffordshire** *co* England
95 P5 **Stafford Springs** Connecticut U.S.A.
70 E6 **Stagen** Kalimantan
117 Q4 **Stagg L** Northwest Territories Canada
45 H4 **Stagno** Italy
9 F3 **Stagsden** England
33 S4 **Stahlbrode** Germany
33 S8 **Stahnsdorf** Germany
52 B5 **Staicele** Latvia
38 K6 **Stainach** Austria
9 F5 **Staines** England
12 D3 **Stair** Scotland
13 H4 **Staithes** England
48 G2 **Stakčin** Czechoslovakia
53 E9 **Stakhanov** Ukraine
28 B5 **Stakroge** Denmark
46 E1 **Stalać** Serbia Yugoslavia
27 J12 **Stålboga** Sweden
8 D6 **Stalbridge** England
9 H2 **Stalham** England
27 B11 **Stalheim** Norway
Stalingrad *see* **Volgograd**
117 L6 **Stalin, Mt** British Columbia Canada
Stalino *see* **Donetsk**
38 H8 **Stall** Austria
37 O5 **Stallwang** Germany
31 N5 **Stalowa Wola** Poland
119 M7 **Stalwart** Saskatchewan Canada
13 F6 **Stalybridge** England
46 G2 **Stamboliyski** Bulgaria
46 G1 **Stamboliyski, Yazovir A.** *res* Bulgaria
141 G5 **Stamford** Queensland Australia
9 F2 **Stamford** England
95 O5 **Stamford** Connecticut U.S.A.
95 N4 **Stamford** New York U.S.A.
98 E6 **Stamford** South Dakota U.S.A.
108 H3 **Stamford** Texas U.S.A.
37 L6 **Stammham** Germany
27 A11 **Stamnes** Norway
Stampalia *isld see* **Astipálaia** *isld*
100 D2 **Stampede** Washington U.S.A.
94 C8 **Stamping Ground** Kentucky U.S.A.
87 C10 **Stampriet** Namibia
25 E6 **Stamproij** Netherlands
109 O2 **Stamps** Arkansas U.S.A.
37 O5 **Stamsried** Germany
26 G3 **Stamsund** Norway
94 J8 **Stanadsville** Virginia U.S.A.
99 M9 **Stanberry** Missouri U.S.A.
147 Q6 **Stanchik** Russian Federation
118 E7 **Standard** Alberta Canada
103 O7 **Standard** Arizona U.S.A.
87 E11 **Standerton** S Africa
94 D3 **Standish** Michigan U.S.A.
101 M8 **Standrod** Utah U.S.A.
100 F4 **Stanfield** Oregon U.S.A.
110 K2 **Stanford** Indiana U.S.A.
110 M4 **Stanford** Kentucky U.S.A.
101 P2 **Stanford** Montana U.S.A.
9 G4 **Stanford-le-Hope** England
8 D3 **Stanford on Teme** England
27 K14 **Stånga** Sweden
27 E11 **Stange** Norway
87 F11 **Stanger** S Africa
45 L1 **Stanghella** Italy
26 C9 **Stangvik** Norway
126 F2 **Staniard Cr** Andros Bahamas
102 D3 **Stanislaus** *R* California U.S.A.
Stanislav *see* **Ivano-Frankovsk**
46 F2 **Stanke Dimitrov** Bulgaria
37 P4 **Staňkov** Czechoslovakia
139 H8 **Stanley** Tasmania Australia
122 F7 **Stanley** New Brunswick Canada
131 G8 **Stanley** Falkland Is
15 E4 **Stanley** Scotland
101 L5 **Stanley** Idaho U.S.A.
106 E6 **Stanley** New Mexico U.S.A.
112 F2 **Stanley** North Carolina U.S.A.
98 D1 **Stanley** North Dakota U.S.A.
109 M1 **Stanley** Oklahoma U.S.A.
94 J8 **Stanley** Virginia U.S.A.
99 Q5 **Stanley** Wisconsin U.S.A.
119 M3 **Stanley Mission** Saskatchewan Canada
139 G8 **Stanley, Mt** Tasmania Australia
88 B1 **Stanley, Mt** Uganda/Zaire
86 C6 **Stanley Pool** Zaire
Stanleyville *see* **Kisangani**
118 F7 **Stanmore** Alberta Canada
145 E2 **Stanmore Bay** New Zealand
99 T2 **Stannard Rock** Michigan U.S.A.
13 G3 **Stannington** England
55 F3 **Stanovka** Russian Federation
55 D2 **Stanovoy** Russian Federation
51 M3 **Stanovoy Khrebet** *mts* Russian Federation
41 P3 **Stans** Austria
138 E5 **Stansbury** South Australia Australia
142 G5 **Stansmore Ra** W Australia Australia
9 G4 **Stansted** England
141 K8 **Stanthorpe** Queensland Australia
147 J1 **Stanton** Northwest Territories Canada
99 L9 **Stanton** Iowa U.S.A.
94 D9 **Stanton** Kentucky U.S.A.
94 B3 **Stanton** Michigan U.S.A.
98 J8 **Stanton** Nebraska U.S.A.
98 E2 **Stanton** North Dakota U.S.A.
110 G6 **Stanton** Tennessee U.S.A.
108 F3 **Stanton** Texas U.S.A.
6 E6 **Stanton Banks** Atlantic Oc
56 B3 **Stantsionno-Oyashinskiy** Russian Federation
94 B3 **Stanwood** Michigan U.S.A.
117 M11 **Stanwood** Washington U.S.A.
41 N3 **Stanzach** Austria
33 N9 **Stapelburg** Germany
25 F3 **Staphorst** Netherlands
9 E5 **Stapleford** England
111 J11 **Stapleton** Alabama U.S.A.
112 E4 **Stapleton** Georgia U.S.A.
54 F3 **Star'** Russian Federation
111 F9 **Star** Mississippi U.S.A.
112 H2 **Star** North Carolina U.S.A.
109 J4 **Star** Texas U.S.A.
31 N4 **Starachowice** Poland
48 F1 **Stara L'ubovňa** Czechoslovakia
37 O3 **Stará-Role** Czechoslovakia
53 G7 **Staraya Drozhzhanoye** Russian Federation
53 G8 **Staraya Kulatka** Russian Federation
52 D5 **Staraya Russa** Russian Federation
48 L1 **Staraya Sinyava** Ukraine
48 L2 **Staraya Ushitsa** Ukraine
55 E1 **Staraya Vorpavla** Russian Federation
47 H2 **Stara Zagora** Bulgaria
119 U9 **Starbuck** Manitoba Canada
99 L4 **Starbuck** Minnesota U.S.A.
100 G3 **Starbuck** Washington U.S.A.
135 L9 **Starbuck I** Pacific Oc
119 N6 **Star City** Saskatchewan Canada
111 E8 **Star City** Arkansas U.S.A.
94 A6 **Star City** Indiana U.S.A.
94 H7 **Star City** West Virginia U.S.A.
141 G2 **Starcke** Queensland Australia
8 C6 **Starcross** England
37 O4 **Staré Sedliště** Czechoslovakia
31 J2 **Stargard** Poland
42 H4 **Stari Majdan** Bosnia-Herzegovina
31 N6 **Starina** Czechoslovakia
52 D6 **Staritsa** Russian Federation
103 O10 **Stark** Arizona U.S.A.
101 L2 **Stark** Montana U.S.A.
95 Q2 **Stark** New Hampshire U.S.A.
55 C6 **Star Karabutak** Kazakhstan
113 E8 **Starke** Florida U.S.A.
100 J5 **Starkey** Idaho U.S.A.
100 G4 **Starkey** Oregon U.S.A.
109 O5 **Starks** Louisiana U.S.A.
106 F4 **Starkville** Colorado U.S.A.
111 H8 **Starkville** Mississippi U.S.A.
98 H1 **Starkweather** North Dakota U.S.A.
99 R3 **Starlake** Wisconsin U.S.A.
41 O1 **Starnberg** Germany
56 C4 **Starobachati** Russian Federation
54 K7 **Star'obel'sk** Ukraine
54 D4 **Starodub** Russian Federation
31 L2 **Starogard** Poland
48 M4 **Starokazach'ye** Ukraine
48 L1 **Starokonstantinov** Ukraine
53 C9 **Starokonstantinov** Ukraine
55 F3 **Staromalinovka** Russian Federation
31 O2 **Starosielce** Poland
55 F3 **Starosoldatskoye** Russian Federation
55 C4 **Starosubkhangulovo** Russian Federation
55 C3 **Staroutkinsk** Russian Federation
52 G5 **Starovercheskaya** Russian Federation
52 H6 **Staroye Baysarovo** Russian Federation
102 F1 **Star Pk** Nevada U.S.A.
8 C7 **Start Pt** England
15 F1 **Start Pt** Scotland
48 F1 **Stary Sącz** Poland
52 H6 **Staryye Zyattsy** Russian Federation
52 H6 **Staryy Menzelyabash** Russian Federation
50 G2 **Staryy Nadym** Russian Federation
54 J5 **Staryy Oskol** Russian Federation
52 D5 **Staryy Ryad** Russian Federation
31 O6 **Staryy Sambor** Ukraine
48 H1 **Staryy Sambor** Ukraine
33 P9 **Stassfurt** Germany
31 N5 **Staszów** Poland
99 N7 **State Center** Iowa U.S.A.
94 K6 **State College** Pennsylvania U.S.A.
111 H10 **State Line** Mississippi U.S.A.
Staten I Argentina *see* **Estados, I de los**
95 N6 **Staten I** New York U.S.A.
112 F5 **Statesboro** Georgia U.S.A.
112 G2 **Statesville** North Carolina U.S.A.
6 M1 **Statfjord** *oil rig* North Sea
27 D12 **Stathelle** Norway
33 S10 **Stauchitz** Germany
36 F2 **Staufenberg** Germany
100 E6 **Stauffer** Oregon U.S.A.
8 D4 **Staunton** England
110 G2 **Staunton** Illinois U.S.A.
94 H8 **Staunton** Virginia U.S.A.
27 A13 **Stavanger** Norway
22 H3 **Stave** Belgium
117 M11 **Stave L** British Columbia Canada
9 E1 **Staveley** England
13 F5 **Staveley** Cumbria England
22 K3 **Stavelot** Belgium
118 D8 **Stavely** Alberta Canada
33 S5 **Staven** Germany
25 B5 **Stavenisse** Netherlands
28 A5 **Stavning** Denmark
28 F3 **Stavnshoved** *C* Denmark
25 D3 **Stavoren** Netherlands
28 J6 **Stavreby** Denmark
28 F6 **Stavreshoved** *C* Denmark
53 F10 **Stavropol'** Russian Federation
55 E4 **Stavropolka** Kazakhstan
53 F10 **Stavropol'skaya Vozvyshennost'** *uplands* Russian Federation
53 F11 **Stavropol'skiy Kray** *reg* Russian Federation
46 E5 **Stavrós** Greece
46 G9 **Stavrós, Akra** *C* Crete Greece
46 G3 **Stavroúpolis** Greece
139 G6 **Stawell** Victoria Australia
31 N2 **Stawiski** Poland
31 L4 **Stawiszyn** Poland
120 K8 **Stayner** Ontario Canada
100 C5 **Stayton** Oregon U.S.A.
45 H4 **Stazzema** Italy
102 E2 **Steamboat** Nevada U.S.A.
106 D1 **Steamboat Springs** Colorado U.S.A.
94 C10 **Stearns** Kentucky U.S.A.
31 M2 **Stębark** Poland
116 F5 **Stebbins** Alaska U.S.A.
33 Q7 **Stechow** Germany
41 J2 **Steckborn** Switzerland
28 B7 **Stedesand** Germany
116 R4 **Steel Creek** Alaska U.S.A.
111 K8 **Steele** Alabama U.S.A.
110 G5 **Steele** Missouri U.S.A.
98 G3 **Steele** North Dakota U.S.A.
98 K9 **Steele City** Nebraska U.S.A.
146 D5 **Steele I** Antarctica
117 C5 **Steele,Mt** Yukon Territory Canada
110 G3 **Steeleville** Illinois U.S.A.
120 D4 **Steel R** Ontario Canada
95 L6 **Steelton** Pennsylvania U.S.A.
110 E4 **Steelville** Missouri U.S.A.
25 B5 **Steenbergen** Netherlands
89 G5 **Steenkamps Berg** *mts* S Africa
22 G2 **Steenkerque** Belgium
117 P6 **Steen River** Alberta Canada
25 D6 **Steensel** Netherlands
100 G7 **Steens Mt** Oregon U.S.A.
115 O2 **Steenstrup Gletscher** *gla* Greenland
22 D2 **Steenvoorde** France
22 D2 **Steenwerck** France
25 F3 **Steenwijk** Netherlands
119 M5 **Steep Cr** Saskatchewan Canada
119 O3 **Steephill L** Saskatchewan Canada
131 F7 **Steeple Jason** *isld* Falkland Is
71 D6 **Steep Pt** Philippines
119 T7 **Steep Rock** Manitoba Canada
118 K2 **Steep Rock** Ontario Canada
143 B6 **Steere, Mt** W Australia Australia
13 G6 **Steeton** England
48 L3 **Stefăneşti** Romania
43 F10 **Stefano di Cam., S** Sicily
146 K10 **Stefansson B** Antarctica
147 H3 **Stefansson I** Northwest Territories Canada
133 C6 **Steffen** *mt* Chile/Arg
36 F2 **Steffenberg** Germany
98 C8 **Stegall** Nebraska U.S.A.
28 J7 **Stege** Denmark
28 J6 **Stege Bugt** *B* Denmark
33 P8 **Stegelitz** Germany
29 K7 **Stege Nor** *L* Denmark
99 T8 **Steger** Illinois U.S.A.
87 F11 **Stegi** Swaziland
33 S8 **Steglitz** Berlin
100 E1 **Stehekin** Washington U.S.A.
48 G4 **Ştei** Romania
38 L7 **Steiermark** *prov* Austria
37 J4 **Steigerwald** *hills* Germany
37 L5 **Stein** Germany
37 L3 **Steinach** Germany
37 J5 **Steinach** Germany
36 H3 **Steinau** Germany
99 K9 **Steinauer** Nebraska U.S.A.
118 E1 **Steinbach** Manitoba Canada
36 E6 **Steinbach** Germany
37 J2 **Steinbach** Germany
37 K2 **Steinbach Hallenberg** Germany
28 D7 **Steinberg** Germany
38 G6 **Steinberge** Austria
36 C6 **Steinbourg** France
129 H6 **Steinen** *R* Brazil
38 G7 **Steinernes Meer** *mts* Austria
32 H7 **Steinfeld** Germany
22 K4 **Steinfort** Luxembourg
32 H8 **Steinhagen** Germany
113 D8 **Steinhatchee** Florida U.S.A.
87 C10 **Steinhausen** Namibia
37 L3 **Steinheid** Germany
36 F3 **Steinheim** Germany
33 M5 **Steinhorst** Germany
32 K8 **Steinhuder Meer** *L* Germany
32 L5 **Steinkirchen** Germany
26 E8 **Steinkjer** Norway
87 C11 **Steinkopf** S Africa
38 L7 **Steinplan** *mt* Austria
106 B9 **Steins** New Mexico U.S.A.
36 F5 **Steinsfurt** Germany
37 L3 **Steinwiesen** Germany
22 G1 **Stekene** Belgium
99 L9 **Stella** Nebraska U.S.A.
112 K3 **Stella** North Carolina U.S.A.
122 K8 **Stellarton** Nova Scotia Canada
45 K2 **Stellata** Italy
32 M6 **Stelle** Germany
87 C12 **Stellenbosch** S Africa
116 Q6 **Steller, Mt** Alaska U.S.A.
42 D2 **Stelvio, Passo di** Italy
112 J1 **Stem** North Carolina U.S.A.
32 K7 **Stemmen** Germany
26 C8 **Stemshaug** Norway
32 H8 **Stemwede** Germany
22 J5 **Stenay** France
28 A3 **Stenbjerg** Denmark
33 P7 **Stendal** Germany
52 B6 **Stende** Latvia
28 D5 **Stenderup** Denmark
28 D7 **Stenderup** Germany
119 P7 **Stenen** Saskatchewan Canada
28 E2 **Stenhøj** Denmark
138 D6 **Stenhouse B** South Australia Australia
28 D3 **Stenild** Denmark
28 H5 **Stenlille** Denmark
28 J5 **Stenløse** Denmark
15 G2 **Stenness** Shetland Scotland
15 E1 **Stenness,L.of** Orkney Scotland
47 P13 **Stenón Kerkiras, Vório** *chan* Greece/Albania
26 J6 **Stensele** Sweden
27 G14 **Stensjön** Sweden
27 G13 **Stenstorp** Sweden
28 E6 **Stenstrup** Denmark
26 L5 **Stenträsk** Sweden
27 E13 **Stenungsund** Sweden
28 F4 **Stenvad** Denmark
78 L2 **Stepanakert** Azerbaijan
78 K1 **Stepanavan** Armenia
55 C5 **Stepanovka** Kazakhstan
33 O5 **Stepenitz** *R* Germany
33 P6 **Stepenitz** *R* Germany
37 O6 **Stephansposching** Germany
98 K1 **Stephen** Minnesota U.S.A.
109 O2 **Stephens** Arkansas U.S.A.
94 J7 **Stephens City** Virginia U.S.A.
138 F4 **Stephens Creek** New South Wales Australia
117 H8 **Stephens I** British Columbia Canada
115 K6 **Stephens L** Manitoba Canada
119 W2 **Stephens L** Manitoba Canada
99 T4 **Stephenson** Michigan U.S.A.
145 D1 **Stephenson I** New Zealand
117 G7 **Stephens Pass** Alaska U.S.A.
123 O5 **Stephenville** Newfoundland Canada
109 J3 **Stephenville** Texas U.S.A.
123 O5 **Stephenville Crossing** Newfoundland Canada
57 D5 **Step' Karnabchul'** Uzbekistan
55 F5 **Stepnogorsk** Kazakhstan
57 G3 **Stepnoye** Kyrgyzstan
55 F4 **Stepnyak** Kazakhstan
116 G9 **Stepovak B** Alaska U.S.A.
28 C6 **Stepping** Denmark
103 K2 **Steptoe** Nevada U.S.A.
36 H3 **Sterbfritz** Germany
46 E6 **Stereá Ellás** *admin region* Greece
87 E12 **Sterkstroom** S Africa
108 F1 **Sterley** Texas U.S.A.
55 C4 **Sterlibashevo** Russian Federation
106 G1 **Sterling** Colorado U.S.A.
99 R8 **Sterling** Illinois U.S.A.
107 M3 **Sterling** Kansas U.S.A.
94 C2 **Sterling** Michigan U.S.A.
98 K9 **Sterling** Nebraska U.S.A.
98 F3 **Sterling** North Dakota U.S.A.
109 J1 **Sterling** Oklahoma U.S.A.
103 N2 **Sterling** Utah U.S.A.
108 G4 **Sterling City** Texas U.S.A.
94 D4 **Sterling Heights** Michigan U.S.A.
55 C4 **Sterlitamak** Russian Federation
33 P5 **Sternberg** Germany
31 K6 **Šternberk** Czechoslovakia
22 H2 **Sterrebeek** Belgium
52 E4 **Steshevskaya** Russian Federation
31 K3 **Stęszew** Poland
41 K1 **Stetten** Germany
Stettin *see* **Szczecin**
33 U5 **Stettiner Haff** Germany
118 E6 **Stettler** Alberta Canada
99 U3 **Steuben** Michigan U.S.A.
99 Q6 **Steuben** Wisconsin U.S.A.
94 G6 **Steubenville** Ohio U.S.A.
33 Q9 **Steutz** Germany
9 F4 **Stevenage** England
120 E3 **Stevens** Ontario Canada
145 D4 **Stevens, Mt** New Zealand
138 C2 **Stevenson** *R* South Australia Australia
119 U9 **Stevenson** Manitoba Canada
110 L7 **Stevenson** Alabama U.S.A.
100 D4 **Stevenson** Washington U.S.A.
119 W5 **Stevenson L** Manitoba Canada
99 R5 **Stevens Pt** Wisconsin U.S.A.
12 D2 **Stevenston** Scotland
116 N4 **Stevens Village** Alaska U.S.A.
94 A4 **Stevensville** Michigan U.S.A.
32 F9 **Stever** *R* Germany
118 F8 **Steveville Prov.Pk** Alberta Canada
29 K6 **Stevns** *pen* Denmark
22 J2 **Stevoort** Belgium
99 S8 **Steward** Illinois U.S.A.
110 H2 **Stewardson** Illinois U.S.A.
141 G2 **Stewart** *R* Queensland Australia
117 H8 **Stewart** British Columbia Canada
117 D4 **Stewart** Yukon Territory Canada
99 M5 **Stewart** Minnesota U.S.A.
102 E2 **Stewart** Nevada U.S.A.
140 C1 **Stewart, C** N Terr Australia
144 A7 **Stewart I** New Zealand
137 N3 **Stewart Is** Pacific Oc
143 C10 **Stewart, Mt** W Australia Australia
15 D5 **Stewarton** Scotland
95 L7 **Stewartstown** Pennsylvania U.S.A.
110 B2 **Stewartsville** Missouri U.S.A.
127 K2 **Stewart Town** Jamaica
118 K8 **Stewart Valley** Saskatchewan Canada
99 O6 **Stewartville** Minnesota U.S.A.
122 J8 **Stewiacke** Nova Scotia Canada
32 K7 **Steyerberg** Germany
9 F6 **Steyning** England
8 A4 **Steynton** Wales
38 K5 **Steyr** Austria
121 S7 **St-Hyacinthe** Quebec Canada
45 L4 **Stia** Italy
8 B6 **Stibb Cross** England
100 K5 **Stibnite** Idaho U.S.A.
9 G1 **Stickford** England
32 G6 **Stickhausen** Germany

Stickney — Suomenniemi

229

9 G1 **Stickney** England
98 H6 **Stickney** South Dakota U.S.A.
33 N9 **Stiege** Germany
25 E2 **Stiens** Netherlands
45 L2 **Stienta** Italy
107 P6 **Stigler** Oklahoma U.S.A.
43 G8 **Stigliano** Italy
26 J9 **Stigsjö** Sweden
117 H7 **Stikine** *R* Alaska/Br Col U.S.A./Canada
117 H6 **Stikine Ranges** British Columbia Canada
117 G7 **Stikine Str** Alaska U.S.A.
108 F4 **Stiles** Texas U.S.A.
110 K2 **Stilesville** Indiana U.S.A.
46 F6 **Stilis** Greece
28 D4 **Stilling** Denmark
13 G5 **Stillington** England
99 R7 **Stillman Valley** Illinois U.S.A.
99 O4 **Stillwater** Minnesota U.S.A.
101 L1 **Stillwater** *R* Montana U.S.A.
102 F2 **Stillwater** Nevada U.S.A.
107 N5 **Stillwater** Oklahoma U.S.A.
102 F2 **Stillwater Ra** Nevada U.S.A.
43 H10 **Stilo, Pta** Italy
48 J5 **Stîlpeni** Romania
110 B6 **Stilwell** Oklahoma U.S.A.
46 E7 **Stimfalías, L** Greece
101 M1 **Stimson,Mt** Montana U.S.A.
12 D3 **Stinchar,R** Scotland
98 E9 **Stinking Water Cr** Nebraska U.S.A.
46 E3 **Štip** Macedonia Yugoslavia
46 G6 **Stira** Greece
Stirling *co see* **Strathclyde and Central** *regions*
140 C5 **Stirling** N Terr Australia
138 E5 **Stirling** South Australia Australia
118 E9 **Stirling** Alberta Canada
121 N8 **Stirling** Ontario Canada
144 B7 **Stirling** New Zealand
12 E1 **Stirling** Scotland
100 D10 **Stirling City** California U.S.A.
143 C9 **Stirling, Mt** W Australia Australia
143 C10 **Stirling Ra** W Australia Australia
44 H2 **Stirone** *R* Italy
98 J3 **Stirum** North Dakota U.S.A.
100 K3 **Stites** Idaho U.S.A.
119 V3 **Stitt** Manitoba Canada
99 Q7 **Stitzer** Wisconsin U.S.A.
27 K14 **Stjärnarve** Sweden
26 N1 **Stjernöya** *isld* Norway
26 E8 **Stjördalselv** *R* Norway
26 E8 **Stjördalshalsen** Norway
18 E6 **St-Maixent-l'École** France
121 R5 **St-Maurice, Parc** Quebec Canada
13 E2 **Stobo** Scotland
41 K2 **Stockach** Germany
27 G14 **Stockaryd** Sweden
9 E5 **Stockbridge** England
95 O4 **Stockbridge** Massachusetts U.S.A.
94 C4 **Stockbridge** Michigan U.S.A.
94 E8 **Stockdale** Ohio U.S.A.
109 K6 **Stockdale** Texas U.S.A.
33 N5 **Stockelsdorf** Germany
48 C2 **Stockerau** Austria
36 B6 **Stock,Etang du** *L* France
101 O2 **Stockett** Montana U.S.A.
98 J9 **Stockham** Nebraska U.S.A.
37 L3 **Stockheim** Germany
119 P8 **Stockholm** Saskatchewan Canada
27 J12 **Stockholm** *county* Sweden
27 K12 **Stockholm** Sweden
95 S6 **Stockholm** Maine U.S.A.
40 G4 **Stockhorn** *mt* Switzerland
139 J5 **Stockinbingal** New South Wales Australia
13 F6 **Stockport** England
94 F7 **Stockport** Ohio U.S.A.
139 K5 **Stockton** New South Wales Australia
119 S9 **Stockton** Manitoba Canada
144 C4 **Stockton** New Zealand
111 J10 **Stockton** Alabama U.S.A.
102 C4 **Stockton** California U.S.A.
99 Q7 **Stockton** Illinois U.S.A.
107 L2 **Stockton** Kansas U.S.A.
95 M8 **Stockton** Maryland U.S.A.
110 C4 **Stockton** Missouri U.S.A.
101 N9 **Stockton** Utah U.S.A.
99 Q3 **Stockton I** Wisconsin U.S.A.
116 O1 **Stockton Is** Alaska U.S.A.
110 C4 **Stockton L** Missouri U.S.A.
13 G4 **Stockton-on-Tees** England
95 T2 **Stockton Springs** Maine U.S.A.
98 F9 **Stockville** Nebraska U.S.A.
31 N4 **Stoczek Łukowski** Poland
37 P4 **Stod** Czechoslovakia
26 E7 **Stod** Norway
99 P6 **Stoddard** Wisconsin U.S.A.
26 J9 **Stöde** Sweden
68 H6 **Stoeng Treng** Cambodia
15 C2 **Stoer,Pt of** Scotland
28 C4 **Stoholm** Denmark
145 D4 **Stoke** New Zealand
9 G2 **Stoke Ferry** England
8 C7 **Stoke Fleming** England
9 F4 **Stokenchurch** England
8 D1 **Stoke-on-Trent** England
120 J7 **Stokes Bay** Ontario Canada
112 H1 **Stokesdale** North Carolina U.S.A.
143 D10 **Stokes Inlet** W Australia Australia
145 E4 **Stokes, Mt** New Zealand
139 G8 **Stokes Pt** Tasmania Australia
140 B3 **Stokes Ra** N Terr Australia
53 C8 **Stokhod** *R* Ukraine
28 G7 **Stokkemarke** Denmark
28 S10 **Stokkseyri** Iceland
26 D7 **Stokksund** Norway
26 G3 **Stokmarknes** Norway
42 H5 **Stolac** Bosnia-Herzegovina
25 F7 **Stolberg** Germany
33 N9 **Stolberg** Germany
147 Q8 **Stolbovoy,Ostrov** Russian Federation
48 F2 **Stolica** *mt* Czechoslovakia
37 O2 **Stollberg** Germany
32 H5 **Stollhamm** Germany
Stolp *see* **Słupsk**
90 A16 **Stoltenhoff I** Tristan da Cunha
32 K7 **Stolzenau** Germany
36 D3 **Stolzenfels** Germany
46 F5 **Stómion** Greece
36 B1 **Stommeln** Germany
8 D2 **Stone** England
94 G5 **Stoneboro** Pennsylvania U.S.A.
9 E3 **Stonebridge** England
106 F3 **Stone City** Colorado U.S.A.
121 N6 **Stonecliffe** Ontario Canada
100 F7 **Stone Corral L** Oregon U.S.A.
122 A7 **Stoneham** Quebec Canada
98 C9 **Stoneham** Colorado U.S.A.
95 N7 **Stone Harbor** New Jersey U.S.A.
15 F4 **Stonehaven** Scotland
141 G6 **Stonehenge** Queensland Australia
9 E5 **Stonehenge** *anc mon* England
8 D4 **Stonehouse** England
99 P4 **Stone L** Wisconsin U.S.A.
112 C4 **Stone Mt** Georgia U.S.A.
117 L6 **Stone Mt. Prov. Park** British Columbia Canada
110 K6 **Stones River Nat. Battlefield** Tennessee U.S.A.
118 D1 **Stonewall** Manitoba Canada
111 H9 **Stonewall** Mississippi U.S.A.
109 L1 **Stonewall** Oklahoma U.S.A.
109 J5 **Stonewall** Texas U.S.A.
121 L9 **Stoney Creek** Ontario Canada
12 D4 **Stoneykirk** Scotland
26 J2 **Stonglandet** Norway
106 H4 **Stonington** Colorado U.S.A.
95 Q5 **Stonington** Connecticut U.S.A.
99 R10 **Stonington** Illinois U.S.A.
95 T2 **Stonington** Maine U.S.A.
119 M8 **Stony Beach** Saskatchewan Canada
94 K10 **Stony Creek** Virginia U.S.A.
8 D3 **Stony Cross** England
102 B2 **Stonyford** California U.S.A.
127 L2 **Stony Hill** Jamaica
118 D1 **Stony Mountain** Manitoba Canada
118 D5 **Stony Plain** Alberta Canada
95 N5 **Stony Point** New York U.S.A.
112 F2 **Stony Point** North Carolina U.S.A.
144 C6 **Stony R** New Zealand
114 J6 **Stony Rapids** Saskatchewan Canada
116 J6 **Stony River** Alaska U.S.A.
9 F3 **Stony Stratford** England
120 H1 **Stooping** *R* Ontario Canada
32 L4 **Stör** *R* Germany
28 C4 **Storå** *R* Denmark
27 H12 **Storå** Sweden
26 G8 **Storåbränna** Sweden
6 F1 **Stóra Dimun** *isld* Faeroes
27 E12 **Stora Le** *L* Sweden
26 L5 **Stora Lule älv** *R* Sweden
26 K4 **Stora Lulevatten** *L* Sweden
26 F9 **Storån** *R* Sweden
26 J4 **Stora Sjoffallet** *L* Sweden
26 K6 **Storavan** *L* Sweden
26 K6 **Storberg** Sweden
27 L11 **Storby** Finland
27 A12 **Stord** Norway
26 B9 **Stordal** Möre og Romsdal Norway
26 E8 **Stordal** Sör-Tröndelag Norway
28 D3 **Store Arden** Denmark
28 F5 **Store Bælt** *chan* Denmark
26 G6 **Store Börgefjeld** *mt* Norway
27 H14 **Storebro** Sweden
28 B6 **Store Darum** Denmark
28 G5 **Store Fuglede** Denmark
29 K6 **Store Heddinge** Denmark
28 C7 **Store Jyndevad** Denmark
29 K7 **Storeklint** *cliffs* Denmark
147 F10 **Store Koldewey** *isld* Greenland
26 P1 **Storelv** *R* Norway
27 E10 **Stor-Elvdal** Norway
29 K5 **Store Magleby** Denmark
28 H5 **Store Merløse** Denmark
26 R1 **Store Molvik** Norway
26 D8 **Stören** Norway
28 E7 **Store Rise** Denmark
28 J6 **Store Spjellerup** Denmark
28 J6 **Store Tårnby** Denmark
28 D2 **Store Vildmose** Denmark
26 H6 **Storfjellet,N** *mt* Sweden
26 G6 **Storfjellet,S** *mt* Sweden
26 B9 **Storfjord** *inlet* Norway
26 G5 **Storfosshei** Norway
26 H8 **Storhögen** Sweden
26 A9 **Storholmen** Norway
26 G7 **Storjorm** *L* Sweden
33 P5 **Störkanal** Germany
114 G3 **Storkerson B** Northwest Territories Canada
26 F8 **Storlien** Sweden
26 K7 **Storlögda** Sweden
32 L5 **Stormarn** *reg* Germany
139 J9 **Storm B** Tasmania Australia
89 E8 **Stormberge** *mts* S Africa
99 L7 **Storm L** Iowa U.S.A.
118 K1 **Stormy L** Ontario Canada
119 P7 **Stornoway** Saskatchewan Canada
15 B2 **Stornoway** Scotland
52 H4 **Storozhevsk** Russian Federation
48 K2 **Storozhinets** Ukraine
26 F8 **Storrensjön** *L* Sweden
9 F6 **Storrington** England
15 B3 **Storr,The** *mt* Scotland
27 E11 **Stor-s** *L* Norway
26 L7 **Storsävarträsk** Sweden
26 F9 **Storsjö** Sweden
27 E10 **Stor-sjöen** *L* Norway
27 F10 **Storsjøen** Sweden
27 J11 **Storsjön** *L* Gävleborg Sweden
26 F9 **Storsjön** *L* Jämtland Sweden
28 H6 **Storstrøm** *co* Denmark
28 H7 **Storstrømmen** *chan* Denmark
119 Q9 **Storthoaks** Saskatchewan Canada
26 J6 **Storuman** Sweden
27 G10 **Storvarden** *mt* Sweden
26 F9 **Storvigelen** *mt* Norway
27 J11 **Storvik** Sweden
26 J6 **Stor-vindein** *L* Sweden
28 E2 **Storvorde** Denmark
101 T5 **Story** Wyoming U.S.A.
99 N7 **Story City** Iowa U.S.A.
133 B7 **Stosch, I** Chile
37 M1 **Stössen** Germany
26 F5 **Stött** Norway
41 N2 **Stotten** Germany
37 L1 **Stotternheim** Germany
28 D5 **Stouby** Denmark
121 L9 **Stouffville** Ontario Canada
119 O9 **Stoughton** Saskatchewan Canada
95 Q4 **Stoughton** Massachusetts U.S.A.
99 R7 **Stoughton** Wisconsin U.S.A.
22 K3 **Stoumont** Belgium
46 E4 **Stoupí** Greece
8 D3 **Stourbridge** England
8 D3 **Stourport** England
9 H5 **Stour,R** England
8 D3 **Stourton** England
94 E7 **Stoutsville** Ohio U.S.A.
28 D3 **Støvring** Denmark
28 E3 **Støvring** Denmark
13 F2 **Stow** Scotland
95 P2 **Stowe** Vermont U.S.A.
109 N6 **Stowell** Texas U.S.A.
9 G3 **Stowmarket** England
9 E4 **Stow on the Wold** England
28 E6 **Stoy** Denmark
59 K1 **Stoyba** Russian Federation
46 C2 **Stožac** *mt* Montenegro Yugoslavia
45 M1 **Stra** Italy
33 R9 **Straach** Germany
14 D2 **Strabane** N Ireland
12 C1 **Strachur** Scotland
14 D3 **Stradbally** Ireland
44 F1 **Stradella** Italy
38 N8 **Straden** Austria
9 G2 **Stradsett** England
25 F6 **Straelen** Germany
110 C4 **Strafford** Missouri U.S.A.
139 H8 **Strahan** Tasmania Australia
103 N4 **Straight Cliffs** Utah U.S.A.
22 J4 **Straimont** Belgium
12 D3 **Straiton** Scotland
30 H6 **Strakonice** Czechoslovakia
47 H2 **Straldzha** Bulgaria
33 S4 **Stralsund** Germany
27 E10 **Strand** Hedmark Norway
27 A12 **Strand** Rogaland Norway
89 A10 **Strand** S Africa
26 B9 **Stranda** Norway
28 C3 **Strandby** Nordjylland Denmark
28 F2 **Strandby** Vendsyssel Denmark
98 J9 **Strang** Nebraska U.S.A.
113 J10 **Strangers Cay** *isld* Bahamas
14 F2 **Strangford** N Ireland
14 F2 **Strangford L** N Ireland
27 J12 **Strängnäs** Sweden
27 H13 **Strångsjö** Sweden
140 C3 **Strangways** *R* N Terr Australia
140 C6 **Strangways Ra** N Terr Australia
14 D2 **Stranorlar** Ireland
118 J7 **Stranraer** Saskatchewan Canada
12 C4 **Stranraer** Scotland
119 N7 **Strasbourg** Saskatchewan Canada
36 D6 **Strasbourg** France
33 T5 **Strasburg** Germany
106 F2 **Strasburg** Colorado U.S.A.
110 H2 **Strasburg** Illinois U.S.A.
98 F3 **Strasburg** North Dakota U.S.A.
94 F6 **Strasburg** Ohio U.S.A.
94 J8 **Strasburg** Virginia U.S.A.
48 M3 **Strasheny** Moldavia
38 N8 **Strass** Steiermark Austria
38 E7 **Strass** Tirol Austria
27 H12 **Stråssa** Sweden
38 K8 **Strassburg** Austria
36 C2 **Strassenhaus** Germany
38 M7 **Strassgang** Austria
37 O6 **Strasskirchen** Germany
38 H6 **Strasswalchen** Austria
139 H7 **Stratford** Victoria Australia
122 A8 **Stratford** Quebec Canada
145 E3 **Stratford** New Zealand
95 O5 **Stratford** Connecticut U.S.A.
99 N7 **Stratford** Iowa U.S.A.
95 Q2 **Stratford** New Hampshire U.S.A.
109 L1 **Stratford** Oklahoma U.S.A.
98 H4 **Stratford** South Dakota U.S.A.
108 B7 **Stratford** Texas U.S.A.
99 Q5 **Stratford** Wisconsin U.S.A.
9 E3 **Stratford-on-Avon** England
9 H4 **Stratford St. Mary** England
138 E6 **Strathalbyn** South Australia Australia
15 D5 **Strathaven** Scotland
12 D2 **Strathblane** Scotland
15 D2 **Strath Brora** Scotland
15 D3 **Strath Carron** Scotland
119 R8 **Strathclair** Manitoba Canada
15 D5 **Strathclyde** *reg* Scotland
117 L11 **Strathcona Prov. Park** British Columbia Canada
15 E3 **Strath Dearn** Scotland
15 D3 **Strath Farrar** Scotland
15 E2 **Strath Halladale** Scotland
141 G3 **Strathleven** Queensland Australia
123 L7 **Strathlorne** Nova Scotia Canada
13 E1 **Strathmiglo** Scotland
141 G4 **Strathmore** Queensland Australia
118 D7 **Strathmore** Alberta Canada
15 E4 **Strathmore** *dist* Scotland
117 M9 **Strathnaver** British Columbia Canada
15 D3 **Strathpeffer** Scotland
120 J10 **Strathroy** Ontario Canada
15 D2 **Strathy Pt** Scotland
12 D1 **Strathyre** Scotland
8 B6 **Stratton** England
106 H2 **Stratton** Colorado U.S.A.
95 R1 **Stratton** Maine U.S.A.
98 E9 **Stratton** Nebraska U.S.A.
37 O6 **Straubing** Germany
26 G4 **Straumen** Norway
30 H3 **Strausberg** Germany
108 A3 **Strauss** New Mexico U.S.A.
37 K1 **Straussfurt** Germany
101 Q3 **Straw** Montana U.S.A.
110 E5 **Strawberry** *R* Arkansas U.S.A.
103 J2 **Strawberry** Nevada U.S.A.
100 G5 **Strawberry Mt** Oregon U.S.A.
99 P7 **Strawberry Pt** Iowa U.S.A.
101 P9 **Strawberry Res** Utah U.S.A.
121 R5 **Strawhat Depot** Quebec Canada
99 S9 **Strawn** Illinois U.S.A.
109 J3 **Strawn** Texas U.S.A.
37 O4 **Stráž** Czechoslovakia
47 H1 **Strazhitsa** Bulgaria
31 K7 **Strážnice** Czechoslovakia
31 M6 **Štrba** Czechoslovakia
138 C5 **Streaky B** South Australia Australia
118 G5 **Streamstown** Alberta Canada
9 F5 **Streatham** England
9 E4 **Streatley** England
99 S8 **Streator** Illinois U.S.A.
31 H6 **Středočeský** *reg* Czechoslovakia
31 L7 **Strědoslovenský** *reg* Czechoslovakia
8 D5 **Street** England
98 G3 **Streeter** North Dakota U.S.A.
109 H5 **Streeter** Texas U.S.A.
109 L4 **Streetman** Texas U.S.A.
48 H6 **Strehaia** Romania
33 S10 **Strehla** Germany
48 H5 **Strei** *R* Romania
143 E9 **Streich Mound** W Australia Australia
37 L4 **Streitberg** Germany
48 J6 **Strejeşti** Romania
37 P4 **Střela** *R* Czechoslovakia
46 G2 **Strelcha** Bulgaria
54 K5 **Strelitsa** Russian Federation
33 S6 **Strelitz-Alt** Germany
56 D2 **Strelka** Russian Federation
28 B5 **Strellev Kirke** Denmark
142 C5 **Strelley** W Australia Australia
142 C5 **Strelley R** W Australia
52 E2 **Strel'na** *R* Russian Federation
52 E2 **Strel'na** Russian Federation
52 C5 **Strenči** Latvia
41 M3 **Strengen** Austria
27 C12 **Strengen** Norway
13 G5 **Strensall** England
46 E2 **Strešer** *mt* Serbia Yugoslavia
54 B4 **Streshin** Belorussia
9 G3 **Stretham** England
43 G10 **Stretto di Messina** Sicily
8 D1 **Stretton** England
9 E1 **Stretton** England
9 F2 **Stretton** England
37 J3 **Streu** *R* Germany
37 K3 **Streufdorf** Germany
6 F1 **Streymoy** *isld* Faeroes
55 G1 **Strezhevoy** Russian Federation
28 D5 **Strib** Denmark
37 P4 **Stříbro** Czechoslovakia
15 F3 **Strichen** Scotland
120 J3 **Strickland** Ontario Canada
25 C5 **Strijen** Netherlands
109 N4 **Striker Cr.Res** Texas U.S.A.
26 G5 **Strimasund** Sweden
46 F3 **Strimón** *R* Greece
46 F4 **Strimonikós,Kólpos** *G* Greece
109 L1 **Stringtown** Oklahoma U.S.A.
12 C2 **Striven,L** Scotland
48 E5 **Strizivojna** Croatia
38 H6 **Strobl** Austria
46 D7 **Strofádhes** *isld* Greece
32 J7 **Ströhen** Germany
54 H6 **Stroitel'** Russian Federation
14 C3 **Strokestown** Ireland
33 T6 **Strom** *R* Germany
15 E2 **Stroma** *isld* Orkney Scotland
32 H9 **Stromberg** Nordrhein-Westfalen Germany
36 D4 **Stromberg** Rheinland-Pfalz Germany
43 G10 **Stromboli, I** Italy
118 E6 **Strome** Alberta Canada
15 C3 **Stromeferry** Scotland
26 L7 **Strömfors** Sweden
15 E2 **Stromness** Orkney Scotland
131 H6 **Stromness** S Georgia
131 H6 **Stromness B** S Georgia
26 J10 **Strömsbruck** Sweden
98 J8 **Stromsburg** Nebraska U.S.A.
27 E13 **Stromstad** Sweden
26 H8 **Strömsund** Sweden
26 H8 **Stromsvattudal** *L* Sweden
12 D1 **Stronachlachar** Scotland
98 A5 **Stroner** Wyoming U.S.A.
111 D8 **Strong** Arkansas U.S.A.
95 R2 **Strong** Maine U.S.A.
111 H8 **Strong** Mississippi U.S.A.
107 O3 **Strong City** Kansas U.S.A.
107 L6 **Strong City** Oklahoma U.S.A.
118 L7 **Strongfield** Saskatchewan Canada
99 Q9 **Stronghurst** Illinois U.S.A.
47 O12 **Strongilí** Greece
43 H9 **Strongoli** Italy
94 F5 **Strongsville** Ohio U.S.A.
15 F1 **Stronsay** Scotland
15 F1 **Stronsay Firth** Scotland
9 G5 **Strood** England
31 N6 **Stropkov** Czechoslovakia
112 F3 **Strother** South Carolina U.S.A.
139 K4 **Stroud** New South Wales Australia
8 D4 **Stroud** England
107 O6 **Stroud** Oklahoma U.S.A.
139 K4 **Stroud Road** New South Wales Australia
95 M6 **Stroudsburg** Pennsylvania U.S.A.
138 F6 **Struan** South Australia Australia
15 E4 **Struan** Scotland
32 G6 **Strücklingen** Germany
38 L5 **Strudengau** *V* Austria
28 B3 **Struer** Denmark
46 D3 **Struga** Macedonia Yugoslavia
52 C5 **Strugi-Krasnyye** Russian Federation
89 B10 **Struisbaai** S Africa
14 D2 **Strule** *R* N Ireland
99 P5 **Strum** Wisconsin U.S.A.
46 F3 **Struma** *R* Bulgaria
8 A3 **Strumble Head** Wales
46 F3 **Strumica** Macedonia Yugoslavia
46 F3 **Strumitsa** *R* Macedonia Yugoslavia
54 K1 **Strunino** Russian Federation
120 E4 **Struthers** Ontario Canada
94 G5 **Struthers** Ohio U.S.A.
37 P3 **Stružná** Czechoslovakia
46 G2 **Stryama** *R* Bulgaria
101 L1 **Stryker** Montana U.S.A.
94 C5 **Stryker** Ohio U.S.A.
31 M4 **Stryków** Poland
28 F7 **Strynø** Denmark
26 B10 **Strynvatn** *L* Norway
31 O6 **Stryy** *R* Ukraine
48 H1 **Stryy** Ukraine
31 J5 **Strzegom** Poland
31 J3 **Strzelce** Poland
31 L5 **Strzelce** Poland
138 F3 **Strzelecki Cr** South Australia Australia
140 C5 **Strzelecki, Mt** N Terr Australia
139 J8 **Strzelecki Pk** Tasmania Australia
31 K5 **Strzelin** Poland
31 L3 **Strzelno** Poland
31 N6 **Strzyżów** Poland
141 K7 **Stuart** *R* Queensland Australia
113 G10 **Stuart** Florida U.S.A.
99 M8 **Stuart** Iowa U.S.A.
98 G7 **Stuart** Nebraska U.S.A.
109 L1 **Stuart** Oklahoma U.S.A.
94 G10 **Stuart** Virginia U.S.A.
140 B6 **Stuart Bluff Ra** N Terr Australia
138 D3 **Stuart Creek** South Australia Australia
116 F5 **Stuart I** Alaska U.S.A.
117 L8 **Stuart L** British Columbia Canada
100 E2 **Stuart, Mt** Washington U.S.A.
144 A6 **Stuart Mts** New Zealand
140 B1 **Stuart Pt** N Terr Australia
138 C3 **Stuart Rge** South Australia Australia
139 J5 **Stuart Town** New South Wales Australia
41 O3 **Stubaier Alpen** *mt* Austria
41 O3 **Stubai Tal** Austria
38 L7 **Stub Alpe** *mts* Austria
28 J7 **Stubbekøbing** Denmark
32 J6 **Stubben** Germany
28 B4 **Stubbergd Sø** *L* Denmark
28 F4 **Stubbe Sø** *L* Denmark
83 M9 **Stubbings Pt** Christmas I Indian Oc
41 M3 **Stuben** Austria
38 N7 **Stubenberg** Austria
38 M6 **Stübming** *R* Austria
47 H3 **Studen Kladenets, Yazovir** *res* Bulgaria
38 N7 **Studenzen** Austria
140 B5 **Studholme Hills** N Terr Australia
144 C6 **Studholme Junction** New Zealand
144 C6 **Studholme, Mt** New Zealand
46 G1 **Studina** Romania
9 E6 **Studland** England
28 B4 **Studsgård** Denmark
26 H8 **Stugun** Sweden
32 J6 **Stuhr** Germany
32 J9 **Stukenbrock** Germany
9 G3 **Stump Cross** England
112 M2 **Stumpy Point** North Carolina U.S.A.
33 Q9 **Stumsdorf** Germany
68 G6 **Stung Chinle** *R* Cambodia
68 G6 **Stung Sen** *R* Cambodia
26 N2 **Stuorajavrre** *L* Norway
117 L9 **Stupendous Mt** British Columbia Canada
54 K2 **Stupino** Russian Federation
40 G7 **Stura** *R* Italy
44 B1 **Stura di Ala** *R* Italy
44 B3 **Stura di Demonte** *R* Italy
44 B1 **Stura di V,Grande** *R* Italy
44 B1 **Stura di Viu** *R* Italy
146 C13 **Sturge I** Antarctica
120 K6 **Sturgeon** *R* Ontario Canada
94 C1 **Sturgeon** *R* Michigan U.S.A.
110 D2 **Sturgeon** Missouri U.S.A.
119 U6 **Sturgeon B** Manitoba Canada
94 B1 **Sturgeon B** Michigan U.S.A.
99 T5 **Sturgeon Bay** Wisconsin U.S.A.
99 T5 **Sturgeon Bay Canal** Wisconsin U.S.A.
120 K6 **Sturgeon Falls** Ontario Canada
117 P8 **Sturgeon L** Alberta Canada
121 M8 **Sturgeon L** Ontario Canada
119 Q4 **Sturgeon Landing** Manitoba Canada
118 C5 **Sturgeon R** Alberta Canada
118 L5 **Sturgeon R** Saskatchewan Canada
119 P7 **Sturgis** Saskatchewan Canada
110 J4 **Sturgis** Kentucky U.S.A.
94 B5 **Sturgis** Michigan U.S.A.
111 G8 **Sturgis** Mississippi U.S.A.
106 H5 **Sturgis** Oklahoma U.S.A.
98 C5 **Sturgis** South Dakota U.S.A.
44 E3 **Sturla** Italy
8 D6 **Sturminster Newton** England
48 E3 **Štúrovo** Czechoslovakia
9 H5 **Sturry** England
138 D6 **Sturt B** South Australia Australia
142 G4 **Sturt Cr** *R* W Australia Australia
142 G4 **Sturt Creek** W Australia Australia
141 F8 **Sturt Des** Qnsld/S Aust Australia
99 T7 **Sturtevant** Wisconsin U.S.A.
138 F3 **Sturt, Mt** New South Wales Australia
138 F3 **Sturt Nat Park** New South Wales Australia
140 C3 **Sturt Plain** N Terr Australia
36 D5 **Stürzelbronn** France
36 E5 **Stutensee** Germany
89 E9 **Stutterheim** S Africa
36 G6 **Stuttgart** Germany
111 E7 **Stuttgart** Arkansas U.S.A.
107 L2 **Stuttgart** Kansas U.S.A.
37 K2 **Stützerbach** Germany
26 H9 **Styggberg** Sweden
28 R9 **Stykkishólmur** Iceland
130 G6 **Suaçuí Grande, R** Brazil
71 M9 **Suai** Indonesia
70 C3 **Suai** Sarawak
86 G2 **Suakin** Sudan
99 T5 **Suamico** Wisconsin U.S.A.
124 E3 **Suaqui** Mexico
128 D2 **Suárez** *R* Colombia
70 L9 **Subang** Java
71 F4 **Suban Pt** Philippines
52 C6 **Subate** Latvia
77 A5 **Subayhīyah, As** Kuwait
45 L4 **Subbiano** Italy
80 F5 **Subeihi** Jordan
57 J4 **Subexi** China
69 J11 **Subi** *isld* Indonesia
142 A1 **Subiaco** *dist* Perth, W Aust Australia
42 E7 **Subiaco** Italy
69 J1 **Subi Kecil** *isld* Indonesia
101 M7 **Sublett** Idaho U.S.A.
99 R8 **Sublette** Illinois U.S.A.
107 K4 **Sublette** Kansas U.S.A.
109 L6 **Sublime** Texas U.S.A.
48 F4 **Subotica** Serbia Yugoslavia
65 D2 **Subrag** China
118 J8 **Success** Saskatchewan Canada
110 D4 **Success** Missouri U.S.A.
44 H3 **Succiso,Alpe di** *mt* Italy
20 G7 **Sucé** France
48 F1 **Sucha** Poland
Suchan *see* **Partizansk**
31 J2 **Suchan** Poland
31 H7 **Suchdol** Czechoslovakia
31 M4 **Suchedniów** Poland
Süchow *see* **Xuzhou**
31 O2 **Suchowola** Poland
25 F6 **Süchteln** Germany
100 C1 **Sucia I** Washington U.S.A.
14 C3 **Suck** *R* Ireland
100 H6 **Sucker Cr** Oregon U.S.A.
116 Q7 **Suckling,C** Alaska U.S.A.
33 P6 **Suckow** Germany
128 E7 **Sucre** Bolivia
126 G10 **Sucre** Colombia
128 G5 **Sucunduri** *R* Brazil
130 D7 **Sucuriu** *R* Brazil
52 E5 **Suda** Russian Federation
86 E3 **Sudan** *rep* Africa
108 E1 **Sudan** Texas U.S.A.
52 F5 **Suday** Russian Federation
55 B5 **Sud'bodarovka** Russian Federation
120 J6 **Sudbury** Ontario Canada
9 G3 **Sudbury** England
86 E4 **Sudd** *dist* Sudan
128 G2 **Suddie** Guyana
33 O6 **Sude** *R* Germany
28 D7 **Süderbrarup** Germany
33 M7 **Suderburg** Germany
32 K4 **Süderhastedt** Germany
32 J4 **Süderhöft** Germany
28 B7 **Süder Lügum** Germany
52 E6 **Sudilova** Russian Federation
52 F5 **Sudislavl'** Russian Federation
32 E9 **Südlohn** Germany
52 F6 **Sudogda** Russian Federation
54 E4 **Sudost'** *R* Russian Federation
83 L13 **Sud Ouest, Pte** Mauritius
79 C9 **Sudr** Egypt
6 F1 **Suðuroy** Faeroes
6 F1 **Suðuroyarfjørður** *fj* Faeroes
54 G5 **Sudzha** Russian Federation
59 K3 **Sudzukhe** Russian Federation
17 G5 **Sueca** Spain
46 G2 **Sŭedinenie** Bulgaria
80 G8 **Su'eida** *R* Jordan
80 F8 **Su'eidat** Jordan
117 G8 **Suemez I** Alaska U.S.A.
108 D6 **Sue Pk** Texas U.S.A.
55 E3 **Suer'** *R* Russian Federation
21 N6 **Suèvres** France
79 C5 **Suez** Egypt
79 C8 **Suez Canal** Egypt
84 J4 **Suez,G.of** Egypt
80 G4 **Suf** Jordan
118 F8 **Suffield** Alberta Canada
9 H3 **Suffolk** *co* England
101 Q2 **Suffolk** Montana U.S.A.
95 L10 **Suffolk** Virginia U.S.A.
61 K11 **Suga-jima** *isld* Japan
101 O6 **Sugar** Idaho U.S.A.
99 R7 **Sugar** *R* Wisconsin U.S.A.
106 G3 **Sugar City** Colorado U.S.A.
94 H5 **Sugar Grove** Pennsylvania U.S.A.
94 F10 **Sugar Grove** Virginia U.S.A.
109 M6 **Sugar Land** Texas U.S.A.
132 C2 **Sugarloaf** *mt* Brazil
143 C6 **Sugarloaf Hill** W Australia Australia
113 F13 **Sugarloaf Key** *isld* Florida U.S.A.
139 L4 **Sugarloaf Pt** New South Wales Australia
90 A13 **Sugar Loaf Pt** St Helena
71 G5 **Sugbuhan Pt** Philippines
37 J4 **Sugenheim** Germany
119 P4 **Suggi L** Saskatchewan Canada
69 F12 **Sugi** Indonesia
60 J10 **Sugi** Japan
78 D3 **Suğla Gölü** *L* Turkey
51 P2 **Sugoy** *R* Russian Federation
70 E1 **Sugut** *R* Sabah
70 E1 **Sugut, Tanjung** *C* Sabah
46 G1 **Suhaia, L** Romania
77 E7 **Şuḥār** Oman
37 K2 **Suhl** Germany
42 H3 **Suhopolje** Croatia
40 H3 **Suhr** *R* Switzerland
47 L6 **Suhut** Turkey
74 C4 **Sui** Pakistan
129 H6 **Suiá-Missu** *R* Brazil
100 E1 **Suiattle Pass** Washington U.S.A.
67 F2 **Suichang** China
67 E3 **Suichuan** China
58 F4 **Suide** China
65 H2 **Suifenhe** China
65 H3 **Suifen He** China
74 D6 **Suigam** India
65 G1 **Suihua** China
67 A2 **Suijiang** China
67 D5 **Sui Jiang** *R* China
59 J2 **Suileng** China
58 E5 **Suining** China
67 C3 **Suining** China
128 E8 **Suipacha** Bolivia
22 G5 **Suippe** *R* France
14 D4 **Suir** *R* Ireland
60 T2 **Suishō tō** *isld* Russian Federation
95 L8 **Suitland** Maryland U.S.A.
68 K2 **Suixi** China
65 C7 **Sui Xian** China
67 D1 **Sui Xian** China
67 B2 **Suiyanchang** China
67 B3 **Suiyang** China
40 B2 **Suize** *R* France
59 H3 **Suizhong** China
74 F5 **Sujangarh** India
Suji *see* **Haixing**
70 L9 **Sukabumi** Java
70 K8 **Sukadana** Sumatra
61 O8 **Sukagawa** Japan
70 L9 **Sukanegara** Java
69 K14 **Sukaraja** Indonesia
70 B6 **Sukaramai** Kalimantan
70 F2 **Sukau** Sabah
29 N8 **Sukeva** Finland
51 L2 **Sukhana** Russian Federation
65 J1 **Sukhanovka** Russian Federation
46 G1 **Sukhindol** Bulgaria
54 G2 **Sukhinichi** Russian Federation
54 K3 **Sukhodol'skiy** Russian Federation
52 F5 **Sukhona** *R* Russian Federation
68 D4 **Sukhothai** Thailand
55 D3 **Sukhoy Log** Russian Federation
53 F11 **Sukhumi** Georgia
115 O4 **Sukkertoppen Iskappe** *ice field* Greenland
74 C5 **Sukkur** Pakistan
76 E1 **Sukma** India
84 E4 **Sūknah** Libya
70 O9 **Sukodadi** Java
70 N9 **Sukohardjo** Java
70 N9 **Sukolilo** Java
71 H5 **Sukon** Sulawesi
69 D9 **Sukon,Ko** *isld* Thailand
33 P5 **Sukow** Germany
59 L2 **Sukpay Datani** Russian Federation
87 C10 **Sukses** Namibia
55 C3 **Suksun** Russian Federation
60 F13 **Sukumo** Japan
60 F13 **Sukumo-wan** *B* Japan
117 N8 **Sukunka** *R* British Columbia Canada
26 F8 **Sul** Norway
27 A10 **Sula** *isld* Norway
54 D7 **Sula** *R* Ukraine
101 M4 **Sula** Montana U.S.A.
125 L2 **Sulaco** Honduras
74 C4 **Sulaiman Range** Pakistan
53 G11 **Sulak** Russian Federation
71 J6 **Sula,Kep** *isld* Indonesia
52 F4 **Sulanda** *R* Russian Federation
15 B1 **Sular Sgeir** *isld* Scotland
70 Q10 **Sulat** *isld* Indonesia
71 G5 **Sulat** Samar Philippines
71 A2 **Sulat, Bukit** *mt* Halmahera Indonesia
116 K4 **Sulatna** *R* Alaska U.S.A.
116 K4 **Sulatna** Alaska U.S.A.
70 **Sulawesi** *isld* Indonesia
70 G7 **Sulawesi Selatan** Sulawesi
71 H4 **Sulawesi Utara** Sulawesi
78 K4 **Sulaymānīyah, As** Iraq
77 A7 **Şulb, Aş** *plain* Saudi Arabia
27 B12 **Suldal** Norway
27 B12 **Suldalsvatn** Norway
28 D3 **Suldrup** Denmark
31 J3 **Sulechów** Poland
31 J3 **Sulęcin** Poland
77 C1 **Suledeh** Iran
31 M4 **Sulejów** Poland
31 N3 **Sulejówek** Poland
31 M4 **Sulejowskie, Jezioro** *res* Poland
70 F4 **Suleman Teluk** *B* Kalimantan
27 B12 **Suleskar** Norway
15 D1 **Sule Skerry** *isld* Scotland
32 M5 **Sülfeld** Germany
66 E4 **Suli Hu** *L* China
69 E13 **Suliki** Sumatra
85 B7 **Sulima** Sierra Leone
48 M5 **Sulina** *R* Romania
48 M5 **Sulina** Romania
32 J7 **Sulingen** Germany
48 K3 **Suliţa** Romania
26 H4 **Sulitjelma** Norway
29 N10 **Sulkava** Finland
128 B4 **Sullana** Peru
111 H8 **Sulligent** Alabama U.S.A.
99 S10 **Sullivan** Illinois U.S.A.
110 E3 **Sullivan** Missouri U.S.A.
117 K10 **Sullivan Bay** British Columbia Canada
Sullivan I *see* **Lanbi Kyun**
118 F6 **Sullivan L** Alberta Canada
15 G12 **Sullom Voe** *B* Shetland Scotland
99 O8 **Sully** Iowa U.S.A.
21 P6 **Sully-la Chapelle** France
21 P6 **Sully-sur-Loire** France
38 N8 **Sulm** *R* Austria
42 F6 **Sulmona** Italy
109 O5 **Sulphur** Louisiana U.S.A.
100 G9 **Sulphur** Nevada U.S.A.
109 L1 **Sulphur** Oklahoma U.S.A.
109 N2 **Sulphur** *R* Texas/Louisiana U.S.A.
103 M3 **Sulphurdale** Utah U.S.A.
109 M2 **Sulphur Springs** Texas U.S.A.
108 E3 **Sulphur Springs Cr** Texas U.S.A.
28 D2 **Sulsted** Denmark
120 H5 **Sultan** Ontario Canada
78 C2 **Sultan Dağları** *mts* Turkey
47 J7 **Sultanhisar** Turkey
75 K5 **Sultanpur** India
33 R5 **Sülten** Germany
71 G5 **Suluan** *isld* Philippines
70 G1 **Sulu Arch** *islds* Philippines
116 K5 **Sulukna** *R* Alaska U.S.A.
84 G3 **Suluq** Libya
57 D3 **Sulutobe** Kazakhstan
57 E5 **Sulyukta** Kyrgyzstan
36 F7 **Sulz** Germany
38 H7 **Sulzau** Austria
36 H5 **Sulzbach** Baden-Württemberg Germany
36 C5 **Sulzbach** Saarland Germany
37 M5 **Sulzbach-Rosenberg** Germany
41 L2 **Sulzberg** Austria
41 M2 **Sulzberg** Germany
146 B10 **Sulzberger B** Antarctica
37 L5 **Sulzbürg** Germany
37 K3 **Sulzdorf** Germany
32 M7 **Sülze** Germany
117 C5 **Sulzer, Mt** Alaska U.S.A.
36 F5 **Sulzfeld** Germany
37 J4 **Sulzheim** Germany
37 J3 **Sulzthal** Germany
71 H4 **Sumalata** Sulawesi Indonesia
70 E1 **Sumangat, Tanjung** *C* Sabah
70 E1 **Sumangat, Tanjung** Sabah
100 C1 **Sumas** Washington U.S.A.
69 D11 **Sumatera** *isld* Indonesia
69 E13 **Sumatera Barat** *prov* Sumatra
69 F14 **Sumatera Selatan** *prov* Sumatra
69 D11 **Sumatera Utara** *prov* Sumatra
Sumatra *see* **Sumatera**
113 C7 **Sumatra** Florida U.S.A.
101 S3 **Sumatra** Montana U.S.A.
128 G5 **Sumaúma** Brazil
71 J9 **Sumba** *isld* Indonesia
71 J9 **Sumba,Selat** *str* Indonesia
71 H9 **Sumbawa** *isld* Indonesia
71 H9 **Sumbawabesar** Indonesia
88 C5 **Sumbawanga** Tanzania
87 B8 **Sumbe** Angola
70 N9 **Sumbing, G** *mt* Java
69 E13 **Sumbing Gunung** *mt* Sumatra
15 G2 **Sumburgh Hd** Scotland
117 G7 **Sumdum** Alaska U.S.A.
130 H9 **Sumé** Brazil
70 L9 **Sumedang** Java
48 D4 **Sümeg** Hungary
70 O9 **Sumenep** Indonesia
78 M1 **Sumgait** Azerbaijan
29 M9 **Sumiainen** Finland
40 G3 **Sumiswald** Switzerland
111 J8 **Sumiton** Alabama U.S.A.
55 E3 **Sumki** Russian Federation
55 E2 **Sumkino** Russian Federation
98 K10 **Summerfield** Kansas U.S.A.
94 F7 **Summerfield** Ohio U.S.A.
108 E1 **Summerfield** Texas U.S.A.
123 S4 **Summerford** Newfoundland Canada
15 C2 **Summer I** Scotland
99 U4 **Summer I** Michigan U.S.A.
100 E7 **Summer L** Oregon U.S.A.
117 O11 **Summerland** British Columbia Canada
94 B10 **Summer Shade** Kentucky U.S.A.
123 P4 **Summerside** Newfoundland Canada
122 J7 **Summerside** Prince Edward I Canada
110 E4 **Summersville** Missouri U.S.A.
94 G8 **Summersville** West Virginia U.S.A.
112 G4 **Summerton** South Carolina U.S.A.
112 E5 **Summertown** Georgia U.S.A.
123 T5 **Summerville** Newfoundland Canada
112 B3 **Summerville** Georgia U.S.A.
94 H5 **Summerville** Pennsylvania U.S.A.
112 G4 **Summerville** South Carolina U.S.A.
120 F5 **Summit** Ontario Canada
145 F4 **Summit** *mt* New Zealand
116 N5 **Summit** Alaska U.S.A.
101 M1 **Summit** Montana U.S.A.
106 B9 **Summit** New Mexico U.S.A.
100 B5 **Summit** Oregon U.S.A.
98 J4 **Summit** South Dakota U.S.A.
103 M4 **Summit** Utah U.S.A.
94 B2 **Summit City** Michigan U.S.A.
116 P5 **Summit L** Alaska U.S.A.
100 F8 **Summit L** Nevada U.S.A.
117 L6 **Summit Lake** British Columbia Canada
102 H2 **Summit Mt** Nevada U.S.A.
106 D4 **Summit Pk** Colorado U.S.A.
106 D4 **Summitville** Colorado U.S.A.
94 B6 **Summitville** Indiana U.S.A.
110 L6 **Summitville** Tennessee U.S.A.
144 B4 **Sumner** New Zealand
110 J3 **Sumner** Illinois U.S.A.
99 O7 **Sumner** Iowa U.S.A.
110 C2 **Sumner** Missouri U.S.A.
144 D5 **Sumner, L** New Zealand
117 G7 **Sumner Str** Alaska U.S.A.
61 N8 **Sumon-dake** *mt* Japan
48 D5 **Sumony** Hungary
60 H11 **Sumoto** Japan
70 F7 **Sumpangbinangae** Sulawesi
31 K6 **Šumperk** Czechoslovakia
100 G5 **Sumpter** Oregon U.S.A.
111 G10 **Sumrall** Mississippi U.S.A.
52 E3 **Sumskiy Posad** Russian Federation
112 G4 **Sumter** South Carolina U.S.A.
54 F6 **Sumy** Ukraine
52 H5 **Suna** Russian Federation
88 C4 **Suna** Tanzania
60 P2 **Sunagawa** Japan
101 R9 **Sunbeam** Colorado U.S.A.
101 L5 **Sunbeam** Idaho U.S.A.
94 C10 **Sunbright** Tennessee U.S.A.
101 O1 **Sunburst** Montana U.S.A.
139 G7 **Sunbury** Victoria Australia
95 L10 **Sunbury** North Carolina U.S.A.
94 E6 **Sunbury** Ohio U.S.A.
95 L6 **Sunbury** Pennsylvania U.S.A.
37 N6 **Sünching** Germany
133 E3 **Suncho Corral** Argentina
89 E5 **Sun City** S Africa
107 M4 **Sun City** Kansas U.S.A.
95 Q3 **Suncook** New Hampshire U.S.A.
98 B5 **Sundance** Wyoming U.S.A.
70 D2 **Sundar** Sarawak
75 N8 **Sundarbans** *tidal forest* India/Bangladesh
70 K9 **Sunda,Selat** *str* Sumatra
140 C3 **Sunday Cr** N Terr Australia
89 D9 **Sundays** *R* S Africa
142 E3 **Sunday Str** W Australia Australia
28 B3 **Sundby** Denmark
27 J12 **Sundbyberg** Sweden
121 L8 **Sunderland** Ontario Canada
13 G4 **Sunderland** England
32 H10 **Sundern** Germany
28 D7 **Sundeved** *reg* Denmark
40 F2 **Sundgau** *reg* France
70 N9 **Sundoro, G** *mt* Java
138 C2 **Sundown** South Australia Australia
118 E1 **Sundown** Manitoba Canada
108 E2 **Sundown** Texas U.S.A.
118 C7 **Sundre** Alberta Canada
27 K15 **Sundre** Sweden
121 L7 **Sundridge** Ontario Canada
28 C4 **Sunds** Denmark
26 J9 **Sundsbruk** Sweden
26 H8 **Sundsjö** Sweden
27 C12 **Sundsli** Norway
28 C3 **Sundstrup** Denmark
26 J9 **Sundsvall** Sweden
32 G10 **Sundwig** Germany
94 B4 **Sunfield** Michigan U.S.A.
111 F8 **Sunflower** Mississippi U.S.A.
69 E12 **Sungaiapit** Sumatra
70 B4 **Sungai Ayak** Kalimantan
69 E13 **Sungaidareh** Sumatra
69 F12 **Sungaiguntung** Sumatra
69 F12 **Sungaikabung** Sumatra
69 H13 **Sungailiat** Indonesia
69 E13 **Sungailimau** Sumatra
70 D5 **Sungaipinang** Kalimantan
69 J12 **Sungaipinyuh** Indonesia
69 B10 **Sungairaya** Sumatra
69 F13 **Sungaisalak** Sumatra
69 G14 **Sungaiselan** Indonesia
Sungari *R see* **Songhua Jiang**
69 E10 **Sungei Patani** Malaysia
70 F7 **Sungguminasa** Sulawesi
86 E3 **Sungikai** Sudan
67 D3 **Sung-pai** China
69 G14 **Sungsang** Sumatra
47 H2 **Sungurlare** Bulgaria
78 E1 **Sungurlu** Turkey
120 C2 **Suni** Ontario Canada
70 E2 **Suniatan Besar, G** *mt* Sabah
65 C5 **Suning** China
37 P3 **Suniperk** Czechoslovakia
42 H3 **Sunja** Croatia
94 B7 **Sunman** Indiana U.S.A.
26 C9 **Sunndal** *R* Norway
26 C9 **Sunndalsöra** Norway
27 F12 **Sunne** Sweden
27 J12 **Sunnersta** Sweden
27 A10 **Sunnfjord** Norway
27 A12 **Sunnhordland** *reg* Norway
113 F11 **Sunniland** Florida U.S.A.
26 B9 **Sunnmöre** Norway
141 K2 **Sunnybank** *dist* Brisbane, Qnsld Australia
122 K8 **Sunnybrae** Nova Scotia Canada
118 C5 **Sunnybrook** Alberta Canada
26 B9 **Sunnylven** Norway
118 F7 **Sunnynook** Alberta Canada
123 T6 **Sunnyside** Newfoundland Canada
103 J3 **Sunnyside** Nevada U.S.A.
103 O2 **Sunnyside** Utah U.S.A.
100 E3 **Sunnyside** Washington U.S.A.
102 B4 **Sunnyvale** California U.S.A.
99 R6 **Sun Prairie** Wisconsin U.S.A.
108 C7 **Sunray** Texas U.S.A.
116 N6 **Sunrise** Alaska U.S.A.
103 O6 **Sunrise** Arizona U.S.A.
98 B7 **Sunrise** Wyoming U.S.A.
101 O2 **Sun River** Montana U.S.A.
111 D11 **Sunset** Louisiana U.S.A.
109 K2 **Sunset** Texas U.S.A.
102 R11 **Sunset Beach** Hawaiian Is
103 N6 **Sunset Crater Nat.Mon** Arizona U.S.A.
117 P8 **Sunset House** Alberta Canada
103 N6 **Sunshine** Arizona U.S.A.
101 Q5 **Sunshine** Wyoming U.S.A.
118 K1 **Sunstrum** Ontario Canada
51 L2 **Suntar** Russian Federation
32 K8 **Süntel** *hills* Germany
85 D7 **Sunyani** Ghana
37 M7 **Sünzhausen** Germany
67 B6 **Suoi Rut** Vietnam
29 M9 **Suolahti** Finland
26 N2 **Suolovuobme** Norway
29 N10 **Suomenniemi** Finland

230
Suomi — Tambov

119 O2 **Suomi** Ontario Canada
29 O7 **Suomussalmi** Finland
60 E12 **Suō-nada** *sea* Japan
29 N9 **Suonenjoki** Finland
29 M10 **Suonne** *L* Finland
29 N3 **Suorsapää** *mt* Finland
26 K4 **Suorva** Sweden
52 D4 **Suoyarvi** Russian Federation
Suozhen *see* **Huantai**
103 M5 **Supai** Arizona U.S.A.
75 M5 **Supaul** India
128 C6 **Supe** Peru
118 H7 **Superb** Saskatchewan Canada
57 D5 **Superfosfatnyy** Uzbekistan
103 N8 **Superior** Arizona U.S.A.
106 E2 **Superior** Colorado U.S.A.
101 L2 **Superior** Montana U.S.A.
98 J9 **Superior** Nebraska U.S.A.
99 O3 **Superior** Wisconsin U.S.A.
101 R8 **Superior** Wyoming U.S.A.
45 J1 **Superiore,L** Italy
99 R2 **Superior,L** U.S.A./Canada
68 E5 **Suphan Buri** Thailand
78 J2 **Süphan D** *mt* Turkey
45 O6 **Supino** Italy
100 F5 **Suplee** Oregon U.S.A.
54 C7 **Supoy** *R* Ukraine
33 N8 **Süpplingen** Germany
31 O2 **Supraśl** Poland
48 H3 **Supuru** Romania
72 G6 **Suqutrá** *isld* Indian Oc
52 G3 **Sura** Russian Federation
52 G6 **Sura** *R* Russian Federation
27 H12 **Sura** Sweden
74 B4 **Surab** Pakistan
70 O9 **Surabaja** Java
77 F7 **Sūrak** Iran
70 N9 **Surakarta** Java
84 E3 **Sūr al Jīn** *watercourse* Libya
70 F5 **Suramana** Sulawesi
40 B5 **Suran** *R* France
79 G3 **Sūrān** Syria
48 E2 **Šurany** Czechoslovakia
141 J7 **Surat** Queensland Australia
74 E8 **Surat** India
74 E4 **Suratgarhi** India
69 D8 **Surat Thani** Thailand
31 O3 **Suraż** Poland
54 D4 **Surazh** Russian Federation
141 H6 **Surbiton** Queensland Australia
9 F5 **Surbiton** England
48 F6 **Surčin** Serbia Yugoslavia
78 K4 **Sūrdāsh** Iraq
21 L4 **Surdon** France
48 H3 **Surduc** Romania
46 E2 **Surdulica** Serbia Yugoslavia
22 L4 **Sure** *R* Luxembourg
48 H5 **Şureanu** Romania
74 D7 **Surendranagar** India
41 K4 **Surettahorn** *mt* Switzerland
102 D7 **Surf** California U.S.A.
95 N7 **Surf City** New Jersey U.S.A.
117 J9 **Surf Inlet** British Columbia Canada
112 J4 **Surfside Beach** South Carolina U.S.A.
18 E6 **Surgères** France
126 C3 **Surgidero de Batabanó** Cuba
55 F1 **Surgut** Russian Federation
50 H2 **Surgutikha** Russian Federation
76 D2 **Suriapet** India
61 N13 **Suribachi-yama** *mt* Japan
71 G6 **Surigao** Mindanao Philippines
71 G5 **Surigao Str** Philippines
68 F5 **Surin** Thailand
83 L13 **Surinam** Mauritius
129 G3 **Surīname** *rep* S America
129 G2 **Suriname** Suriname
99 S4 **Suring** Wisconsin U.S.A.
128 D2 **Suripá** *R* Venezuela
57 D5 **Surkhandar'inskaya Oblast** *prov* Uzbekistan
77 C4 **Surmāq** Iran
26 C9 **Surnadalsöra** Norway
117 G6 **Surprise** British Columbia Canada
98 J8 **Surprise** Nebraska U.S.A.
121 Q3 **Surprise,L.de la** Quebec Canada
133 F5 **Sur,Pta** Argentina
112 E6 **Surrency** Georgia U.S.A.
9 F5 **Surrey** *co* England
98 E1 **Surrey** North Dakota U.S.A.
95 L9 **Surry** Virginia U.S.A.
40 H3 **Sursee** Switzerland
84 F3 **Surt** Libya
20 G3 **Surtainville** France
28 S10 **Surtsey** *isld* Iceland
71 N9 **Surubec,Danau** *L* Timor
78 G3 **Sürüç** Turkey
61 M11 **Suruga-wan** *B* Japan
69 F14 **Surulangun** Sumatra
71 G7 **Surup** Mindanao Philippines
20 E6 **Surzur** France
28 H6 **Suså** *R* Denmark
44 B1 **Susa** Italy
60 E11 **Susa** Japan
42 G6 **Sušac** *isld* Croatia
84 G3 **Sūsah** Libya
60 G12 **Susaki** Japan
60 J12 **Susami** Japan
57 G4 **Susamyr** Kyrgyzstan
102 D1 **Susan** *R* California U.S.A.
77 A4 **Sūsangerd** Iran
52 F5 **Susanino** Russian Federation
102 D1 **Susanville** California U.S.A.
100 G5 **Susanville** Oregon U.S.A.
78 F1 **Suşehri** Turkey
33 N4 **Süsel** Germany
37 Q5 **Sušice** Czechoslovakia
80 F2 **Susitha** Syria
116 M6 **Susitna** Alaska U.S.A.
116 O5 **Susitna L** Alaska U.S.A.
69 D9 **Suso** Thailand
58 G5 **Susong** China
67 E1 **Susong** China
61 M10 **Susono** Japan
95 L5 **Susquehanna** *R* Pennsylvania U.S.A.
95 M5 **Susquehanna** Pennsylvania U.S.A.
33 P10 **Süsser See** *L* Germany
Sussex *co see* **West and East Sussex** *counties*
122 G8 **Sussex** New Brunswick Canada
95 N5 **Sussex** New Jersey U.S.A.
101 T6 **Sussex** Wyoming U.S.A.
25 E6 **Susteren** Netherlands
45 K1 **Sustinente** Italy
117 K7 **Sustut Pk** British Columbia Canada
70 E2 **Susul** Sabah
116 K5 **Susulatna** *R* Alaska U.S.A.
51 O2 **Susuman** Russian Federation
71 A1 **Susupu** Halmahera Indonesia
47 J5 **Susurluk** Turkey
100 F10 **Sutcliffe** Nevada U.S.A.
48 L5 **Şuţeşti** Romania
Sutherland *co see* **Highland** *reg*
87 D12 **Sutherland** S Africa
99 L7 **Sutherland** Iowa U.S.A.
98 E8 **Sutherland** Nebraska U.S.A.
143 F7 **Sutherland Ra** W Australia Australia
98 E8 **Sutherland Res** Nebraska U.S.A.
144 A6 **Sutherland Sd** New Zealand
100 B6 **Sutherlin** Oregon U.S.A.
56 D5 **Sut-Khol'** Russian Federation
74 F3 **Sutlej** *R* India
74 E3 **Sutlej** *R* Pakistan
79 D2 **Sütluce** Turkey
102 D3 **Sutter Cr** California U.S.A.
9 F2 **Sutterton** England
121 L8 **Sutton** Ontario Canada
121 S7 **Sutton** Quebec Canada
9 G3 **Sutton** England
9 F5 **Sutton** England
144 C6 **Sutton** New Zealand
98 J9 **Sutton** Nebraska U.S.A.
98 H2 **Sutton** North Dakota U.S.A.
94 G8 **Sutton** West Virginia U.S.A.
121 L5 **Sutton Bay** Ontario Canada
9 E2 **Sutton Coldfield** England
9 E1 **Sutton-in-Ashfield** England
94 G8 **Sutton Res** West Virginia U.S.A.
9 E5 **Sutton Scotney** England
141 H5 **Suttor** *R* Queensland Australia
116 J8 **Sutwik I** Alaska U.S.A.
89 D9 **Suurberge** *mts* S Africa
52 C5 **Suure-Jaani** Estonia
137 Q5 **Suva** Viti Levu Fiji
46 E1 **Suva Pl** *mt* Serbia Yugoslavia
46 D2 **Suva Reka** Serbia Yugoslavia
29 N9 **Suvasvesi** *L* Finland
Suvla, C *see* **Büyük Kemikli Br.**
54 H2 **Suvorov** Russian Federation
47 J1 **Suvorovo** Bulgaria
48 M5 **Suvorovo** Ukraine
61 M9 **Suwa** Japan
61 M9 **Suwa ko** *L* Japan
70 D5 **Suwakong** Kalimantan
31 O1 **Suwałki** Poland
68 F5 **Suwannaphum** Thailand
113 D8 **Suwannee** Florida U.S.A.
119 R2 **Suwannee L** Manitoba Canada
113 E7 **Suwanoochee Cr** Georgia U.S.A.
78 H4 **Suwar** Syria
70 E4 **Suwaran, G** *mt* Kalimantan
79 G6 **Suwaydā', As** Syria
80 G2 **Suwaysah** Syria
80 F6 **Suweima** Jordan
Suweis,El *see* **Suez**
Su Xian *see* **Suzhou**
88 A9 **Suye,L** Zambia
55 D1 **Suyevatpaul** Russian Federation
57 E3 **Suzak** Kazakhstan
83 M14 **Suzanne,Pte** Kerguelen Indian Oc
52 F6 **Suzdal'** Russian Federation
19 N16 **Suze la Rousse** France
21 L6 **Suze-sur-Sarthe, la** France
58 G5 **Suzhou** China
59 H5 **Suzhou** China
40 B3 **Suzon** *R* France
121 T4 **Suzor Côté** Quebec Canada
61 L8 **Suzu** Japan
61 K11 **Suzuka** Japan
61 L8 **Suzu-misaki** *C* Japan
56 B4 **Suzun** Russian Federation
45 J2 **Suzzara** Italy
27 H10 **Svabensverk** Sweden
28 H6 **Sværdborg** Denmark
26 P1 **Svaerholtklubben** *C* Norway
26 H9 **Svågan** *R* Sweden
26 H5 **Svaipa** *mt* Sweden
147 H12 **Svalbard** *arch* Arctic Oc
28 G5 **Svallerup** Denmark
48 H2 **Svalyava** Ukraine
27 H16 **Svaneke** Denmark
28 E6 **Svanninge** Denmark
27 F12 **Svanskog** Sweden
26 N5 **Svanstein** Sweden
26 R2 **Svanvik** Norway
54 F5 **Svapa** *R* Russian Federation
26 M4 **Svappavaara** Sweden
29 K11 **Svartå** Finland
27 G12 **Svartå** Sweden
26 N5 **Svartbyn** Sweden
115 O3 **Svartenhuk Halvö** *pen* Greenland
26 G5 **Svartisen** *mt* Norway
26 M6 **Svartlå** Sweden
27 H11 **Svartnäs** Sweden
26 M6 **Svartöstaden** Sweden
54 K7 **Svatovo** Ukraine
27 D10 **Svatsum** Norway
68 G7 **Svay Rieng** Cambodia
52 G5 **Svecha** Russian Federation
27 F16 **Svedala** Sweden
26 L7 **Svedun** Sweden
26 G9 **Sveg** Sweden
26 A10 **Svelgen** Norway
27 D12 **Svelvik** Norway
52 C6 **Švenčionėliai** Lithuania
Svendborg *co see* **Fyn** *co*
28 F6 **Svendborg** Denmark
27 F14 **Svenljunga** Sweden
27 H12 **Svennevad** Sweden
26 F6 **Svenningdal** Norway
100 B3 **Svensen** Oregon U.S.A.
26 J2 **Svensgrunnen** *shoal* Norway
28 D6 **Svenstrup** Sønderjylland Denmark
Sverdlovsk *see* **Yekaterinburg**
55 D2 **Sverdlovskaya Oblast'** *prov* Russian Federation
115 K1 **Sverdrup Chan** Northwest Territories Canada
50 G1 **Sverdrup, Ostrov** *isld* Russian Federation
42 G5 **Svetac** *isld* Croatia
46 E3 **Sveti Nikola** Macedonia Yugoslavia
59 L2 **Svetlaya** Russian Federation
53 C8 **Svetlogorsk** Belorussia
31 M1 **Svetlogorsk** Russian Federation
51 J2 **Svetlogorsk** Russian Federation
31 M1 **Svetloye** Russian Federation
31 M1 **Svetlyy** Russian Federation
51 L3 **Svetlyy** Russian Federation
52 C4 **Svetogorsk** Russian Federation
46 E1 **Svetozarevo** Serbia Yugoslavia
37 P5 **Švihov** Czechoslovakia
48 G6 **Svilajnac** Serbia Yugoslavia
47 H3 **Svilengrad** Bulgaria
28 F6 **Svindinge** Denmark
28 G5 **Svinninge** Denmark
Svinø *see* **Svínoy**
6 F1 **Svínoy** *isld* Faeroes
52 D4 **Svir'** *R* Russian Federation
52 D4 **Sviritsa** Russian Federation
56 F4 **Svirsk** Russian Federation
52 D4 **Svir'stroy** Russian Federation
46 G1 **Svishtov** Bulgaria
53 C7 **Svisloch'** *R* Belorussia
31 J6 **Svitavy** Czechoslovakia
52 G6 **Sviyaga** *R* Russian Federation
59 J1 **Svobodnyy** Russian Federation
46 F2 **Svoge** Bulgaria
28 J5 **Svogerslev** Denmark
37 O4 **Svojšin** Czechoslovakia
26 G3 **Svolvaer** Norway
31 J6 **Svratka** *R* Czechoslovakia
46 E1 **Svrljig** Serbia Yugoslavia
46 E1 **Svrljiške Pl** *mt* Serbia Yugoslavia
52 F5 **Svyatogor'ye** Russian Federation
52 E1 **Svyatoy Nos, Mys** *C* Russian Federation
52 D4 **Svyatozero** Russian Federation
68 C3 **Swa** *R* Burma
9 G2 **Swaffham** England
141 K5 **Swain Reefs** Gt Barrier Reef Aust
112 E5 **Swainsboro** Georgia U.S.A.
134 B4 **Swains I** Pacific Oc
87 B10 **Swakopmund** S Africa
9 G5 **Swale,R** England
137 O4 **Swallow Is** Santa Cruz Is
70 C1 **Swallow Reef** S China Sea
106 F3 **Swallows** Colorado U.S.A.
118 D7 **Swalwell** Alberta Canada
9 E6 **Swanage** England
142 A2 **Swanbourne Beach** *dist* Perth, W Aust Australia
139 G6 **Swan Hill** Victoria Australia
118 B4 **Swan Hills** Alberta Canada
139 J8 **Swan Is** Tasmania Australia
126 C6 **Swan Is** W Indies
117 J8 **Swan, L** British Columbia Canada
98 G4 **Swan L** South Dakota U.S.A.
119 T9 **Swan Lake** Manitoba Canada
101 M2 **Swan Lake** Montana U.S.A.
112 E2 **Swannanoa** North Carolina U.S.A.
119 Q6 **Swan Plain** Saskatchewan Canada
142 E3 **Swan Pt** W Australia Australia
112 L2 **Swanquarter** North Carolina U.S.A.
143 B9 **Swan R** W Australia Australia
118 B3 **Swan R** Alberta Canada
138 E5 **Swan Reach** South Australia Australia
119 Q6 **Swan River** Manitoba Canada
99 N2 **Swan River** Minnesota U.S.A.
112 K3 **Swansboro** North Carolina U.S.A.
139 K5 **Swansea** New South Wales Australia
139 J8 **Swansea** Tasmania Australia
103 L7 **Swansea** Arizona U.S.A.
112 F4 **Swansea** South Carolina U.S.A.
8 C4 **Swansea** Wales
95 T2 **Swans I** Maine U.S.A.
118 K7 **Swanson** Saskatchewan Canada
117 J9 **Swanson Bay** British Columbia Canada
98 E9 **Swanson Res** Nebraska U.S.A.
98 J9 **Swanton** Nebraska U.S.A.
94 D5 **Swanton** Ohio U.S.A.
121 R8 **Swanton** Vermont U.S.A.
33 S4 **Swantow** Germany
139 K3 **Swan Vale** New South Wales Australia
101 O6 **Swan Valley** Idaho U.S.A.
99 M4 **Swanville** Minnesota U.S.A.
89 A10 **Swartberg** *mt* S Africa
103 L2 **Swasey Pk** Utah U.S.A.
120 K4 **Swastika** Ontario Canada
89 G6 **Swaziland** *kingdom* Africa
99 M6 **Swea City** Iowa U.S.A.
26 **Sweden** *kingdom* W Europe
95 M7 **Swedesboro** New Jersey U.S.A.
85 D7 **Swedru** Ghana
12 C2 **Sween, L** Scotland
109 M6 **Sweeny** Texas U.S.A.
140 E3 **Sweers I** Queensland Australia
100 J6 **Sweet** Idaho U.S.A.
101 O1 **Sweetgrass** Montana U.S.A.
111 D7 **Sweet Home** Arkansas U.S.A.
100 C5 **Sweet Home** Oregon U.S.A.
109 L6 **Sweet Home** Texas U.S.A.
110 C3 **Sweet Springs** Missouri U.S.A.
107 L6 **Sweetwater** Oklahoma U.S.A.
112 C2 **Sweet Water** Tennessee U.S.A.
108 G3 **Sweetwater** Texas U.S.A.
101 R7 **Sweetwater** *R* Wyoming U.S.A.
87 D12 **Swellendam** S Africa
108 G2 **Swenson** Texas U.S.A.
31 J5 **Świdnica** Poland
31 O4 **Świdnik** Poland
31 J2 **Świdwin** Poland
31 J3 **Świebodzin** Poland
31 L2 **Świecie** Poland
116 K6 **Swift** *R* Alaska U.S.A.
95 R2 **Swift** *R* Maine U.S.A.
123 S6 **Swift Current** Newfoundland Canada
118 K8 **Swiftcurrent** Saskatchewan Canada
116 L5 **Swift Fork** *R* Alaska U.S.A.
110 E6 **Swifton** Arkansas U.S.A.
100 C3 **Swift Res** Washington U.S.A.
117 H5 **Swift River** Yukon Territory Canada
100 A1 **Swiftsure Bank Lightship** British Columbia Canada
14 D1 **Swilly,L** Ireland
8 C5 **Swimbridge** England
9 E4 **Swindon** England
9 F2 **Swineshead** England
14 C3 **Swinford** Ireland
106 G3 **Swink** Colorado U.S.A.
31 H2 **Swinoujście** Poland
13 F2 **Swinton** Scotland
40 F4 **Switzerland** *rep* Europe
15 E2 **Swona** *isld* Orkney Scotland
14 E3 **Swords** Ireland
141 F5 **Swords Ra** Queensland Australia
52 D4 **Syamozero, Oz** *L* Russian Federation
52 F4 **Syamzha** Russian Federation
52 D5 **Syas'** *R* Russian Federation
52 D4 **Syas'stroy** Russian Federation
52 G5 **Syava** Russian Federation
98 A8 **Sybille Cr** Wyoming U.S.A.
14 A4 **Sybil Pt** Ireland
111 K8 **Sycamore** Alabama U.S.A.
99 S8 **Sycamore** Illinois U.S.A.
94 D6 **Sycamore** Ohio U.S.A.
112 F4 **Sycamore** South Carolina U.S.A.
52 D6 **Sychevka** Russian Federation
31 K4 **Sycow** Poland
56 D4 **Syda** *R* Russian Federation
121 O8 **Sydenham** Ontario Canada
9 G2 **Syderstone** England
139 K5 **Sydney** New South Wales Australia
123 M7 **Sydney** Nova Scotia Canada
98 B2 **Sydney** Montana U.S.A.
140 E3 **Sydney I** Queensland Australia
123 M7 **Sydney Mines** Nova Scotia Canada
115 P5 **Sydproven** Greenland
32 J7 **Syke** Germany
98 G2 **Sykeston** North Dakota U.S.A.
94 J5 **Sykesville** Pennsylvania U.S.A.
52 H4 **Syktyvkar** Russian Federation
111 K8 **Sylacauga** Alabama U.S.A.
110 D6 **Sylamore** Arkansas U.S.A.
26 F8 **Sylene** *mt* Norway
75 O6 **Sylhet** Bangladesh
28 A7 **Sylt** *isld* Germany
26 B9 **Sylte** Norway
26 S1 **Sylterfjord** *inlet* Norway
55 C3 **Sylva** Russian Federation
112 D2 **Sylva** North Carolina U.S.A.
94 J7 **Sylvan** Pennsylvania U.S.A.
107 M2 **Sylvan Grove** Kansas U.S.A.
143 D6 **Sylvania** W Australia Australia
119 N6 **Sylvania** Saskatchewan Canada
112 F5 **Sylvania** Georgia U.S.A.
94 D5 **Sylvania** Ohio U.S.A.
118 C6 **Sylvan Lake** Alberta Canada
101 P5 **Sylvan Pass** Wyoming U.S.A.
112 D6 **Sylvester** Georgia U.S.A.
140 D4 **Sylvester, L** N Terr Australia
123 R5 **Sylvester,Mt** Newfoundland Canada
107 M4 **Sylvia** Kansas U.S.A.
117 L6 **Sylvia,Mt** British Columbia Canada
56 C1 **Sym** *R* Russian Federation
15 E5 **Symington** Scotland
124 H5 **Symon** Mexico
8 D4 **Symonds Yat** England
71 F4 **Syndicate** Philippines
142 F3 **Synnot,Mt** W Australia Australia
142 F3 **Synnot Ra** W Australia Australia
56 H3 **Synnyr, Khrebet** *mts* Russian Federation
54 N2 **Syntul** Russian Federation
52 J2 **Synya** Russian Federation
55 E1 **Syn'yakha** *R* Russian Federation
Syowa *see* **Showa**
Syracuse Italy *see* **Siracusa**
94 B5 **Syracuse** Indiana U.S.A.
107 J3 **Syracuse** Kansas U.S.A.
98 K9 **Syracuse** Nebraska U.S.A.
121 O9 **Syracuse** New York U.S.A.
101 N8 **Syracuse** Utah U.S.A.
57 E4 **Syrdarinsk. Obl** Uzbekistan
57 D3 **Syrdar'ya** *R* Kazakhstan etc
57 E4 **Syrdar'ya** Uzbekistan
57 D4 **Syr Dar'ya Oblast'** *prov* Uzbekistan
79 G4 **Syria** *rep* S W Asia
68 C4 **Syriam** Burma
Syrian Desert *see* **Badiet esh Sham**
55 E1 **Syrkovoye, Oz** *L* Russian Federation
28 G2 **Syr Odde** *C* Denmark
54 L4 **Syrskiy** Russian Federation
55 D3 **Sysert'** Russian Federation
95 T1 **Sysladobsis L** Maine U.S.A.
52 H4 **Sysola** *R* Russian Federation
9 E2 **Syston** England
56 D4 **Systyg-Khem** Russian Federation
52 D6 **Syt'kovo** Russian Federation
55 F1 **Sytomino** Russian Federation
52 F4 **Syuma** *R* Russian Federation
52 H6 **Syumsi** Russian Federation
52 H6 **Syun'** *R* Russian Federation
46 F3 **Syutkya** *mt* Bulgaria
53 G7 **Syzran'** Russian Federation
48 E4 **Szabadszállás** Hungary
48 G2 **Szabolcsszatmár** *co* Hungary
31 L4 **Szadek** Poland
31 K2 **Szamocin** Poland
48 G2 **Szamosszeg** Hungary
31 K3 **Szamotuły** Poland
48 D3 **Szany** Hungary
48 F4 **Szarvas** Hungary
31 O5 **Szczebrzeszyn** Poland
31 H2 **Szczecin** Poland
31 K2 **Szczecinek** Poland
31 M5 **Szczekociny** Poland
31 L4 **Szczerców** Poland
31 N5 **Szczucin** Poland
31 N2 **Szczuczyn** Poland
31 M2 **Szczytno** Poland
Szechwan *prov see* **Sichuan** *prov*
48 F2 **Szécsény** Hungary
48 F4 **Szeged** Hungary
48 G3 **Szeghalom** Hungary
48 E3 **Székesfehérvár** Hungary
48 F2 **Szendrö** Hungary
48 E3 **Szentendre** Hungary
48 F4 **Szentes** Hungary
48 C4 **Szentgotthárd** Hungary
48 D4 **Szentlörinc** Hungary
48 G2 **Szerencs** Hungary
48 D3 **Szigetköz** *dist* Hungary
48 D4 **Szigetvár** Hungary
48 F2 **Szikszó** Hungary
31 J5 **Szklarska Poreba** Poland
31 N2 **Szkwa** *R* Poland
31 J4 **Szlichtyngowa** Poland
48 E3 **Szob** Hungary
48 F3 **Szolnok** Hungary
48 D3 **Szombathely** Hungary
31 J4 **Szprotawa** Poland
31 M2 **Szreńsk** Poland
31 L2 **Sztum** Poland
31 K2 **Szubin** Poland
31 M4 **Szydłowiec** Poland

T

79 F5 **Taalabaya** Lebanon
71 E3 **Taal,L** Luzon Philippines
48 E4 **Tab** Hungary
71 F4 **Tabaco** Philippines
128 F5 **Tabajara** Brazil
70 P10 **Tabanan** Indonesia
70 P16 **Tabanan** Bali Indonesia
70 D4 **Tabang** *R* Kalimantan
70 E4 **Tabang** Kalimantan
85 E5 **Tabankort** Mali
89 F8 **Tabankulu** S Africa
127 O2 **Tabaquite** Trinidad
137 L2 **Tabar Is** Bismarck Arch
43 B12 **Tabarka** Tunisia
77 E3 **Ţabas** Iran
77 G3 **Ţabas** Iran
124 H7 **Tabasco** Mexico
125 N8 **Tabasco** *state* Mexico
52 G6 **Tabashino** Russian Federation
123 N3 **Tabatière,La** Quebec Canada
128 E4 **Tabatinga** Brazil
68 B1 **Tabayin** Burma
71 E2 **Tabayoa, Mt** Philippines
68 G6 **Tabeng** Cambodia
118 E9 **Taber** Alberta Canada
27 G14 **Taberg** Sweden
17 F7 **Tabernas** Spain
17 G5 **Tabernes de Valldigna** Spain
16 D10 **Taberrant** Morocco
17 G9 **Tabia** Algeria
101 P9 **Tabiona** Utah U.S.A.
69 F13 **Tabir** *R* Sumatra
71 F4 **Tablas** *isld* Philippines
131 B3 **Tablas,C** Chile
71 E4 **Tablas Strait** Philippines
89 A9 **Table B** S Africa
139 H8 **Table C** Tasmania Australia
145 G3 **Table Cape** New Zealand
71 D6 **Table Hd** Philippines
144 A7 **Table Hill** New Zealand
68 A6 **Table I** Andaman Is
68 H2 **Table,I.de la** Vietnam
142 F3 **Tableland** W Australia Australia
87 C12 **Table Mt** S Africa
116 Q2 **Table Mt** Alaska U.S.A.
71 D5 **Table Pt** Philippines
83 K14 **Table Pt.de la** Réunion Indian Oc
101 R8 **Table Rock** Wyoming U.S.A.
110 C5 **Table Rock Res** Missouri U.S.A.
141 G4 **Tabletop, Mt** Queensland Australia
130 C6 **Taboco,R** Brazil
31 H6 **Tábor** Czechoslovakia
51 P1 **Tabor** Russian Federation
99 L9 **Tabor** Iowa U.S.A.
98 J7 **Tabor** South Dakota U.S.A.
88 D4 **Tabora** Tanzania
88 D4 **Tabora** *reg* Tanzania
112 J3 **Tabor City** North Carolina U.S.A.
80 E3 **Tabor, Mt** Israel
118 E9 **Tabor Prov. Park** Alberta Canada
55 D2 **Tabory** Russian Federation
85 C8 **Tabou** Ivory Coast
78 L2 **Tabrīz** Iran
68 G2 **Ta Bu** Vietnam
135 U9 **Tabuaeran** *atoll* Pacific Oc
79 G10 **Tabūk** Saudi Arabia
60 E12 **Tabuka** Japan
139 L3 **Tabulam** New South Wales Australia
71 H5 **Tabulan** Sulawesi
129 G5 **Tabuleiro** Brazil
55 G4 **Tabuny** Russian Federation
45 R7 **Taburno, M** *mt* Italy
122 G6 **Tabusintac R** New Brunswick Canada
69 D12 **Tabuyung** Sumatra
88 B6 **Tabwe** Zambia
27 K12 **Täby** Sweden
130 H10 **Tacaratú** Brazil
66 C2 **Tacheng** China
67 G4 **Ta-chia** Taiwan
60 C13 **Tachibana-wan** *B* Japan
61 N10 **Tachikawa** Japan
128 D2 **Táchira** *state* Venezuela
37 O4 **Tachov** Czechoslovakia
70 G7 **Tacipi** Sulawesi
139 L4 **Tacking Pt** New South Wales Australia
71 G5 **Tacloban** Philippines
133 C1 **Tacna** Peru
103 K9 **Tacna** Arizona U.S.A.
21 O4 **Tacoignières** France
117 M12 **Tacoma** Washington U.S.A.
133 E3 **Tacò Pozo** Argentina
128 E7 **Tacora** *mt* Chile
130 E7 **Tacquaritinga** Brazil
130 B10 **Tacuaras** Paraguay
131 G3 **Tacuarembó** Uruguay
131 H4 **Tacuari,R** Uruguay
130 C8 **Tacuati** Paraguay
124 E3 **Tacupeto** Mexico
61 N8 **Tadami** *R* Japan
13 G6 **Tadcaster** England
85 F4 **Tadeinte** *watercourse* Algeria
85 E3 **Tadémaït,Pl.du** Algeria
85 B5 **Tadjakant** Mauritania
85 E3 **Tadjmout** Algeria
86 H3 **Tadjoura** Djibouti
9 E3 **Tadmarton** England
145 D4 **Tadmor** New Zealand
78 G4 **Tadmur** Syria
60 Q2 **Tadoshi** Japan
60 G11 **Tadotsu** Japan
122 C5 **Tadoussec** Quebec Canada
76 D3 **Tadpatri** India
Tadzhikskaya S.S.R. *see* **Tajikistan**
65 F6 **Taech'ŏngdo** *isld* S Korea
65 G5 **Taedong** *R* N Korea
65 G7 **Taegu** S Korea
65 F7 **Taehŭksan** *isld* S Korea
65 G6 **Taejon** S Korea
28 J7 **Tæro** *isld* Denmark
137 S5 **Tafahi** *isld* Pacific Oc
17 F2 **Tafalla** Spain
85 F4 **Tafasaset** *watercourse* Algeria
126 A1 **Tafelberg** *mt* Curaçao
16 E9 **Tafersite** Morocco
8 C4 **Taff,R** Wales
79 F8 **Tafila** Jordan
85 C7 **Tafiré** Ivory Coast
26 B9 **Tafjord** Norway
17 F9 **Tafna** *R* Algeria
106 F5 **Tafoya** New Mexico U.S.A.
85 C3 **Tafraoute** Morocco
102 E6 **Taft** California U.S.A.
107 P6 **Taft** Oklahoma U.S.A.
109 K8 **Taft** Texas U.S.A.
77 G5 **Taftan, Kūh-e-** *mt* Iran
95 P5 **Taftville** Connecticut U.S.A.
69 A9 **Tafwap** Nicobar Is
75 N5 **Taga** Bhutan
48 J4 **Ţaga** Romania
116 H4 **Tagagawik** *R* Alaska U.S.A.
61 P7 **Tagajō** Japan
53 E10 **Taganrog** Russian Federation
54 K9 **Taganrogskiy Zaliv** *G* Rus Fed/Ukraine
85 A4 **Tagarzimat** Western Sahara
71 E3 **Tagaytay City** Philippines
71 F6 **Tagbilaran** Philippines
85 D2 **Taghit** Algeria
117 F6 **Tagish L** British Columbia Canada
45 O5 **Tagliacozzo** Italy
42 E2 **Tagliamento** *R* Italy
45 M1 **Táglio di Po** Italy
22 G5 **Tagnon** France
71 F6 **Tagolo Pt** Philippines
85 C3 **Tagounite** Morocco
26 J8 **Tågsjöberg** Sweden
129 J6 **Taguatinga** Brazil
71 F5 **Tagubanhan** *isld* Philippines
61 L11 **Taguchi** Japan
71 E2 **Tagudin** Philippines
137 L4 **Tagula** *isld* Louisiade Arch
Tagus *R* Portugal *see* **Tejo** *R*
Tagus *R* Spain *see* **Tajo** *R*
98 E1 **Tagus** North Dakota U.S.A.
144 B7 **Tahakopa** New Zealand
69 G10 **Tahan, Gunung** Malaysia
61 L11 **Tahara** Japan
85 F4 **Tahat** *mt* Algeria
145 D1 **Taheke** New Zealand
77 C6 **Tāheri** Iran
117 G6 **Tahi** *R* British Columbia Canada
135 M10 **Tahiti** *isld* Pacific Oc
110 B6 **Tahlequah** Oklahoma U.S.A.
117 H6 **Tahltan** British Columbia Canada
102 D2 **Tahoe City** California U.S.A.
114 J4 **Tahoe L** Northwest Territories Canada
102 D2 **Tahoe L** California U.S.A.
102 D3 **Tahoe Valley** California U.S.A.
108 F2 **Tahoka** Texas U.S.A.
100 A2 **Taholah** Washington U.S.A.
145 E3 **Tahora** New Zealand
145 F4 **Tahoraiti** New Zealand
85 F6 **Tahoua** Niger
99 V3 **Tahquamenon Falls** Michigan U.S.A.
59 H2 **Ta-hsing-an Ling** China
59 H2 **Ta Hsing-an-Ling Shan-mo** *ra* China
117 K11 **Tahsis** British Columbia Canada
67 F5 **Ta Hsü** *isld* Taiwan
84 J4 **Tahta** Egypt
47 L8 **Tahtali Dağ** *mt* Turkey
78 E2 **Tahtali Dağları** *mts* Turkey
117 K9 **Tahtsa** *R* British Columbia Canada
128 D6 **Tahuamanu** *R* Peru
145 E2 **Tahuna** New Zealand
85 C7 **Tai** Ivory Coast
65 E4 **Tai'an** China
65 C6 **Tai'an** China
134 D12 **Taiarapu, Presqu'ile de** *pen* Tahiti Pacific Oc
67 F2 **Taibai** China
106 F7 **Taiban** New Mexico U.S.A.
17 F6 **Taibilla,Sa de** *mts* Spain
58 G3 **Taibus Qi** China
65 C4 **Taibus Qi** China
67 G1 **Taicang** China
67 G4 **T'ai-chung** Taiwan
144 C6 **Taieri** *airport* New Zealand
Taigong *see* **Taijiang**
65 B6 **Taigu** China
65 B5 **Taihang Shan** *mt ra* China
65 B7 **Taihang Shan** *ra* China
145 E3 **Taihape** New Zealand
67 E3 **Taihe** China
61 Q12 **Taiho** Okinawa
67 E1 **Taihu** China
67 G1 **Tai Hu** *L* China
67 C3 **Taijiang** China
Taikang *see* **Dorbod**
65 C7 **Taikang** China
60 R3 **Taiki** Japan
68 B4 **Taikkyi** Burma
59 H2 **Tailai** China
69 D13 **Taileleo** Indonesia
138 E6 **Tailem Bend** South Australia Australia
36 G7 **Tailfingen** Germany
21 K4 **Taillebois** France
19 P14 **Taillefer** *mt* France
20 H5 **Taillis** France
15 D3 **Tain** Scotland
46 E8 **Tainaron, Akr** *C* Greece
67 F3 **Taining** China
19 N14 **Tain l'Hermitage** France
67 G5 **T'ain-nan** Taiwan
130 G4 **Taiobeiras** Brazil
70 G5 **Taipa** Sulawesi
29 O9 **Taipale** Finland
29 N10 **Taipalsaari** Finland
67 G4 **T'ai-pei** Taiwan
67 F1 **Taiping** China
67 B5 **Taiping** China
67 C5 **Taiping** China
69 E10 **Taiping** Malaysia
59 H3 **Taipingchuan** China
65 G3 **Taipingchuan** China
65 F4 **Taipingshao** China
130 J8 **Taipu** Brazil
61 O8 **Taira** Japan
61 Q12 **Taira** Okinawa
60 O4 **Tairadate kaikyō** Japan
145 E2 **Tairua** New Zealand
60 N3 **Taisei** Japan
60 Q2 **Taisetsuzan Nat.Park** Japan
60 F10 **Taisha** Japan
67 D5 **Taishan** China
67 F3 **Taishun** China
69 E14 **Taitaitanopo** *isld* Indonesia
133 C7 **Taitao, Pen. de** Chile
65 D4 **Taitouying** China
52 C2 **Taivalkoski** Finland
27 M11 **Taivassalo** Finland
67 G5 **Taiwan** *rep* E Asia
Taiwan Haixia *see* **Taiwan Str**
67 F4 **Taiwan Strait** China/Taiwan
67 G1 **Tai Xian** China
67 G1 **Taixing** China
46 E7 **Taïyetos** *mt* Greece
80 E3 **Taiyiba** Israel
80 D4 **Taiyiba** Israel
80 F3 **Taiyiba** *R* Jordan
65 B6 **Taiyuan** China
65 B6 **Taiyue Shan** *mt* China
Taizhou *see* **Linhai**
67 G1 **Taizhou** China
67 G2 **Taizhou Wan** *B* China
65 F4 **Taizi He** *R* China
72 E6 **Ta'izz** Yemen
86 H3 **Ta'izz** Yemen
84 E5 **Tajarhī** Libya
84 G5 **Tāj, At** Libya
69 H14 **Tajem, Gunung** *mt* Indonesia
43 B13 **Tajerouine** Tunisia
57 E5 **Tajikistan** *rep* C Asia
61 N8 **Tajima** Japan
61 L10 **Tajimi** Japan
106 D7 **Tajique** New Mexico U.S.A.
124 C2 **Tajito** Mexico
16 E4 **Tajo** *R* Spain
70 N9 **Taju** Java
17 F4 **Tajuna** *R* Spain
68 D4 **Tak** Thailand
71 K8 **Taka' Bonerate, Kepulauan** *islds* Indonesia
61 M8 **Takada** Japan
61 P7 **Takagi** Japan
61 O9 **Takahagi** Japan
61 J10 **Takahama** Japan
60 G11 **Takahashi** Japan
61 O8 **Takahata** Japan
60 E13 **Takajō** Japan
145 D4 **Takaka** New Zealand
46 E7 **Táka, L** Greece
83 K12 **Takamaka** Mahé I Indian Oc
60 H11 **Takamatsu** Japan
60 E13 **Takamori** Japan
61 O5 **Takanosu** Japan
61 K9 **Takaoka** Japan
145 F4 **Takapau** New Zealand
145 F1 **Takapuna** New Zealand
70 F7 **Taka Rewataya** *reef* Indonesia
60 H11 **Takasago** Japan
59 L4 **Takasaki** Japan
60 C12 **Taka shima** *isld* Saga Japan
60 E11 **Taka shima** *isld* Shimane Japan
89 B4 **Takatshwaane** Botswana
61 J11 **Takatsuki** Japan
145 E2 **Takatu Pt.** New Zealand
88 G3 **Takaungu** Kenya
68 D2 **Ta-Kaw** Burma
60 D12 **Takawa** Japan
61 L9 **Takayama** Japan
60 D14 **Takazaki** Japan
60 E14 **Takazaki** Japan
69 F9 **Tak Bai** Thailand
60 E13 **Takeda** Japan
61 K10 **Takefu** Japan
60 F11 **Takehara** Japan
9 G4 **Takeley** England
69 C10 **Takengon** Sumatra
68 G7 **Takeo** Cambodia
60 D12 **Takeo** Japan
60 C11 **Takeshiki** Japan
Take-shima *see* **Tok-to**
77 A1 **Takestān** Iran
60 E12 **Taketazu** Japan
71 C3 **Takeum** W Irian
78 K7 **Takhadid** Iraq
77 L1 **Takhār** *reg* Afghanistan
57 A4 **Takhiatash** Uzbekistan
117 F5 **Takhini** *R* Yukon Territory Canada
57 A4 **Takhta** Turkmenistan
57 C6 **Takhta-Bazar** Turkmenistan
55 E4 **Takhtabrod** Kazakhstan
57 B3 **Takhtakupyr** Uzbekistan
77 C5 **Takht-e Jamshīd** Iran
114 H4 **Takijug L** Northwest Territories Canada
60 Q2 **Takikawa** Japan
100 B7 **Takilma** Oregon U.S.A.
60 R1 **Takinoue** Japan
119 R3 **Takipy** Manitoba Canada
70 D6 **Takisung** Kalimantan
144 A6 **Takitimu Mts** New Zealand
117 L8 **Takla Landing** British Columbia Canada
66 B4 **Taklimakan Shamo** *reg* China
57 E5 **Takob** Tajikistan
85 D8 **Takoradi** Ghana
116 J5 **Takotna** Alaska U.S.A.
145 D1 **Takou B** New Zealand
116 F6 **Takslesluk L** Alaska U.S.A.
117 G6 **Taku** British Columbia Canada
60 D12 **Taku** Japan
69 D8 **Takua Pa** Thailand
117 F5 **Taku Arm** *L* Br Col/Yukon Terr Canada
69 D8 **Takua Thung** Thailand
117 F6 **Taku Glacier** Br Col/Alaska Canada/U.S.A.
85 F7 **Takum** Nigeria
74 E2 **Talagang** Pakistan
133 D6 **Talagapa** Argentina
68 H7 **Ta Lai** Vietnam
83 J8 **Talaimannar** Sri Lanka
85 F5 **Talak** *reg* Niger
107 P5 **Talala** Oklahoma U.S.A.
16 E10 **Talamagait** Morocco
69 F14 **Talang** Sumatra
70 K8 **Talangbatu** Sumatra
69 G14 **Talangbetutu** Sumatra
69 F14 **Talanglambangantir** Sumatra
69 G14 **Talangpulaukabung** Sumatra
128 B4 **Talara** Peru
77 H7 **Talar-i-Band** *mts* Pakistan
57 F3 **Talas** Kyrgyzstan
136 L3 **Talasea** New Britain
57 F4 **Talasskiy Alatau, Khr** *mts* Kazakhstan/Uzbekistan etc
70 G5 **Talatakoh** *isld* Sulawesi
79 G4 **Ţal at Mūsá** *mt* Lebanon
16 D5 **Talavera de la Reina** Spain
130 C10 **Talavera,I** Paraguay
140 F4 **Talawanta** Queensland Australia
71 G7 **Talayan** Philippines
65 G3 **Talazhan** China
79 G4 **Talbīsah** Syria
142 F2 **Talbot, C** W Australia Australia
113 F7 **Talbot I** Florida U.S.A.
115 M2 **Talbot Inlet** Northwest Territories Canada
119 S4 **Talbot L** Manitoba Canada
143 F7 **Talbot, Mt** W Australia Australia
139 J4 **Talbragar** New South Wales Australia
131 B5 **Talca** *prov* Chile
131 B5 **Talca** Chile
131 A6 **Talcahuano** Chile
131 B4 **Talca,Pta** Chile
109 M2 **Talco** Texas U.S.A.
94 G9 **Talcott** West Virginia U.S.A.
52 E6 **Taldom** Russian Federation
141 F4 **Taldora** Queensland Australia
57 A3 **Taldyk** Uzbekistan
57 J3 **Taldy-Kurgan** Kazakhstan
77 B4 **Tal-e Khosravī** Iran
100 C7 **Talent** Oregon U.S.A.
8 C2 **Talerddig** Wales
8 C4 **Talgarth** Wales
76 B3 **Talguppa** India
138 C5 **Talia** South Australia Australia
71 G5 **Talibon** Bohol Philippines
110 A7 **Talihina** Oklahoma U.S.A.
76 C2 **Talikota** India
71 G7 **Talikua** *isld* Mindanao Philippines
86 F4 **Tali Post** Sudan
71 F5 **Talisay** Cebu Philippines
70 F4 **Talisayan** Kalimantan
71 G6 **Talisayan** Philippines
71 J4 **Talisei** *isld* Indonesia
55 D1 **Talitsa** Sverdlovskaya obl Russian Federation
55 D3 **Talitsa** Sverdlovskaya obl Russian Federation
54 M4 **Talitskiy Chamlyk** Russian Federation
33 N5 **Talkau** Germany
116 N5 **Talkeetna Mts** Alaska U.S.A.
79 B7 **Talkha** Egypt
29 N3 **Talkkunapää** *mt* Finland
77 B3 **Talkuncheh** Iran
45 L4 **Talla** Italy
84 G5 **Ţallāb, Aţ** Libya
111 K8 **Talladega** Alabama U.S.A.
111 G10 **Tallahala** *R* Mississippi U.S.A.
111 M11 **Tallahassee** Florida U.S.A.
111 F7 **Tallahatchie** *R* Mississippi U.S.A.
139 H6 **Tallangatta** Victoria Australia
111 K9 **Tallapoosa** *R* Alabama U.S.A.
111 L8 **Tallapoosa** Georgia U.S.A.
19 Q16 **Tallard** France
26 H10 **Tallåsen** Sweden
80 G1 **Tall ash Sha'ar** *mt* Syria
111 L9 **Tallassee** Alabama U.S.A.
143 B8 **Tallering Pk** W Australia Australia
8 C4 **Talley** Wales
78 H4 **Tall Fadghāmī** Syria
52 B5 **Tallinn** Estonia
26 M5 **Talljäry** Sweden
79 G4 **Tall Kalakh** Syria
40 D6 **Talloires** France
14 C4 **Tallow** Ireland
119 P6 **Tall Pines** Saskatchewan Canada
80 G3 **Tall Shihāb** Syria
110 G2 **Tallula** Illinois U.S.A.
111 E9 **Tallulah** Louisiana U.S.A.
119 O9 **Talmage** Saskatchewan Canada
102 A2 **Talmage** California U.S.A.
107 N2 **Talmage** Kansas U.S.A.
99 L9 **Talmage** Nebraska U.S.A.
40 B3 **Talmay** France
56 B4 **Tal'menka** Russian Federation
80 B7 **Talmey Yafe** Israel
18 D6 **Talmont** France
48 N2 **Tal'noye** Ukraine
74 F8 **Taloda** India
86 F3 **Talodi** Sudan
107 M5 **Taloga** Oklahoma U.S.A.
70 F4 **Talok** Kalimantan
68 D2 **Ta-Long** Burma
77 L1 **Tāloqān** Afghanistan
106 E5 **Talpa** New Mexico U.S.A.
108 H4 **Talpa** Texas U.S.A.
124 G7 **Talpa de Allende** Mexico
127 O2 **Talparo R** Trinidad
111 M11 **Talquin,L** Florida U.S.A.
80 C6 **Tal Shaḩar** Israel
52 B6 **Talsi** Latvia
26 L7 **Tålsmark** Sweden
133 C3 **Taltal** Chile
69 D12 **Talu** Sumatra
71 H4 **Taludaä** Sulawesi
70 G4 **Taluditi** Sulawesi
71 E8 **Talue** *isld* Philippines
68 G3 **Ta Lus,C** Vietnam
41 O4 **Talvera** *R* Italy
26 N1 **Talvik** Norway
141 J8 **Talwood** Queensland Australia
56 F5 **Tal'yany** Russian Federation
139 G4 **Talyawalka** *R* New South Wales Australia
8 C3 **Talybont** Wales
8 C1 **Tal-y-cafn** Wales
52 J3 **Talyy** Russian Federation
61 M9 **Tama** Japan
61 N10 **Tama** *R* Japan
99 O8 **Tama** Iowa U.S.A.
70 D3 **Tamabo Ra** Sarawak
68 B1 **Tamadaw** Burma
143 A7 **Tamala** W Australia Australia
85 D7 **Tamale** Ghana
16 C4 **Tamames** Spain
60 D13 **Tamana** Japan
130 J10 **Tamandare** Brazil
140 B4 **Tamani Desert** N Terr Australia
60 G11 **Tamano** Japan
85 F4 **Tamanrasset** Algeria
70 G5 **Tamanusi** Sulawesi
95 M6 **Tamaqua** Pennsylvania U.S.A.
45 L2 **Tamara** Italy
100 J5 **Tamarack** Idaho U.S.A.
99 N3 **Tamarack** Minnesota U.S.A.
60 E13 **Tamarai** Japan
17 H3 **Tamarite de Litera** Spain
110 G3 **Tamaroa** Illinois U.S.A.
41 J5 **Tamaro,Mt** Switzerland
139 H8 **Tamar R** Tasmania Australia
8 B6 **Tamar,R** England
60 G11 **Tamashima** Japan
48 E4 **Tamási** Hungary
Tamatave *see* **Toamasina**
61 O9 **Tamatsukuri** Japan
128 D5 **Tamaya** *R* Peru
85 A4 **Tamayya** Western Sahara
124 F5 **Tamazula** Mexico
124 H8 **Tamazula de Gordiano** Mexico
125 K7 **Tamazunchale** Mexico
37 K2 **Tambach Dietharz** Germany
85 B6 **Tambacounda** Senegal
71 K8 **Tambalongang** *isld* Indonesia
70 B5 **Tambangmunjul** Kalimantan
69 F14 **Tambangsawah** Sumatra
88 E10 **Tambara** Mozambique
130 J9 **També** Brazil
70 G7 **Tambea** Sulawesi
69 H12 **Tambelan Besar** *isld* Indonesia
69 H12 **Tambelan, Kepulauan** *islds* Indonesia
143 C10 **Tambellup** W Australia Australia
87 E9 **Tambero** Zambia
70 O9 **Tamberu** Java
131 B2 **Tambillos,Nevado de los** *pk* Chile
141 H6 **Tambo** Queensland Australia
128 D7 **Tambo** *R* Peru
128 C6 **Tambo de Mora** Peru
71 G6 **Tambog Pt** Mindanao Philippines
70 G6 **Tamboli** Sulawesi
124 G5 **Tambor** Mexico
139 H6 **Tamboritha,Mt** Victoria Australia
53 F7 **Tambov** Russian Federation

Tambre,R — Tenghilan 231

16 B2 **Tambre,R** Spain
142 C5 **Tambrey** W Australia Australia
70 F5 **Tambulan** Sulawesi
70 E2 **Tambunan** Sabah
86 E4 **Tambura** Sudan
70 F4 **Tambu, Tk** *B* Sulawesi
83 K9 **Tambutta** Sri Lanka
70 E1 **Tambuyukon, G** *mt* Sabah
85 B5 **Tamchakett** Mauritania
55 C6 **Tamdy** Kazakhstan
57 C4 **Tamdybulak** Uzbekistan
57 C4 **Tamdytau, Gory** *mt* Uzbekistan
128 D2 **Tame** Colombia
16 B3 **Tâmega** *R* Portugal
133 C7 **Tamel Aike** Argentina
Tamenghest *see* **Tamanrasset**
85 F5 **Tamgak, Mts** Niger
57 E2 **Tamgaly, Ozero** *L* Kazakhstan
125 L7 **Tamiahua,L.de** Mexico
113 F12 **Tamiami Canal** Florida U.S.A.
69 C10 **Tamiang** *R* Sumatra
76 C5 **Tamil Nadu** *prov* India
78 J4 **Ta'mīm, At** *prov* Iraq
41 K4 **Tamina** *R* Switzerland
70 D6 **Taminglayang** Kalimantan
84 G3 **Tamīnī,At** Libya
41 K4 **Tamins** Switzerland
58 D2 **Tamirin Gol** *R* Mongolia
48 F5 **Tamis** *R* Serbia Yugoslavia
52 E3 **Tamitsa** Russian Federation
57 C1 **Tamkamys** Kazakhstan
68 J5 **Tam Ky** Vietnam
71 F5 **Tamlang** Negros Philippines
45 R7 **Tammaro** *R* Italy
Tammerfors *see* **Tampere**
110 G4 **Tamms** Illinois U.S.A.
113 E10 **Tampa** Florida U.S.A.
107 N3 **Tampa** Kansas U.S.A.
70 K8 **Tampang** Sumatra
29 K10 **Tampere** Finland
125 L6 **Tampico** Mexico
99 R8 **Tampico** Illinois U.S.A.
101 T1 **Tampico** Montana U.S.A.
69 F11 **Tampin** Malaysia
69 C13 **Tampines** *dist* Singapore
69 C10 **Tamporbur** Sumatra
68 J5 **Tam Quan** Vietnam
80 D2 **Tamra** Israel
58 G2 **Tamsagbulag** Mongolia
75 Q6 **Tamu** Burma
71 E7 **Tamuk** *isld* Philippines
139 K4 **Tamworth** New South Wales Australia
121 O8 **Tamworth** Ontario Canada
9 E2 **Tamworth** England
95 Q3 **Tamworth** New Hampshire U.S.A.
68 F6 **Tamyong** *R* Cambodia
57 H1 **Tan** Kazakhstan
116 Q6 **Tana** *R* Alaska U.S.A.
60 J12 **Tanabe** Japan
130 E7 **Tanabi** Brazil
26 Q1 **Tana-Bru** Norway
116 Q5 **Tanacross** Alaska U.S.A.
116 Q5 **Tanada L** Alaska U.S.A.
26 Q1 **Tanafjord** *inlet* Norway
43 G8 **Tanagro** *R* Italy
61 O8 **Tanagura** Japan
86 G3 **Tana Hāyk'** *L* Ethiopia
69 D13 **Tanahbala** *isld* Indonesia
71 K8 **Tanahdjampea** *isld* Indonesia
70 E5 **Tanahgrogot** Kalimantan
71 K10 **Tanahkadukung** Indonesia
68 D13 **Tanahmasa** *isld* Indonesia
70 E3 **Tanahmerah** Kalimantan
69 F9 **Tanah Merah** Malaysia
26 R1 **Tanahorn** *mt* Norway
69 E12 **Tanahputih** Sumatra
70 M9 **Tanah,Tg** *C* Java
70 F7 **Tanakeke** *isld* Sulawesi
70 F6 **Tanambung** Sulawesi
136 J3 **Tanamerah** W Irian
140 A4 **Tanami** N Terr Australia
71 J4 **Tanamon** Sulawesi
68 H7 **Tan An** Vietnam
116 L4 **Tanana** Alaska U.S.A.
116 N4 **Tanana** *R* Alaska U.S.A.
Tananarive *see* **Antananarivo**
18 H8 **Tanargue, Mt** France
44 E2 **Tanaro** *R* Italy
84 E4 **Tanārūt** Libya
71 G5 **Tanauan** Leyte Philippines
141 F7 **Tanbar** Queensland Australia
21 L3 **Tancarville** France
61 P13 **Tancha** Okinawa
65 D7 **Tancheng** China
59 J3 **Tanch'ŏn** N Korea
124 H8 **Tancitario,Cerro de** *mt* Mexico
125 K7 **Tancuayalab** Mexico
75 K5 **Tanda** India
71 G6 **Tandag** Mindanao Philippines
48 L6 **Ţăndărei** Romania
70 E1 **Tandek** Sabah
28 D6 **Tanderup** Denmark
131 F6 **Tandil** Argentina
131 F6 **Tandil, Sa del** *ra* Argentina
70 F3 **Tandjungbatu** Kalimantan
69 J11 **Tandjung Blitung** Indonesia
70 L9 **Tandjungpriok** Java
70 C5 **Tandjungpusu** Kalimantan
74 C6 **Tando Adam** Pakistan
74 C6 **Tando Muhammad Khan** Pakistan
138 F4 **Tandou L** New South Wales Australia
55 G3 **Tandovo, Oz** *L* Russian Federation
14 E2 **Tandragee** N Ireland
27 G10 **Tandsjöbörg** Sweden
28 D7 **Tandslet** Denmark
71 E8 **Tandubatu** *isld* Philippines
76 C2 **Tandur** India
145 F3 **Taneatua** New Zealand
59 K5 **Tanega-shima** *isld* Japan
61 P5 **Taneichi** Japan
Tanen *mt* *see* **Taunggyi** *mt*
71 A3 **Taneti** Halmahera Indonesia
31 O5 **Tanew** *R* Poland
95 K7 **Taneytown** Maryland U.S.A.
85 E4 **Tanezrouft** *reg* Algeria
84 E4 **Tanezzuft** *watercourse* Libya/Algeria
88 G4 **Tanga** Tanzania
75 N6 **Tangail** Bangladesh
137 L2 **Tanga Is** Bismarck Arch
83 K11 **Tangalla** Sri Lanka
Tanganyika *see* **Tanzania**
88 B5 **Tanganyika,L** E Africa
130 D10 **Tangará** Brazil
67 D3 **Tangdukou** China
28 D4 **Tange Å** *R* Denmark
146 K9 **Tange Promontory** *pen* Antarctica
16 D9 **Tanger** Morocco
70 L9 **Tangerang** Java
33 P8 **Tangerhütte** Germany
33 P7 **Tangermünde** Germany
28 D4 **Tange Sø** *L* Denmark
58 G4 **Tanggu** China
66 D5 **Tanggula Shan** *ra* China
66 E5 **Tanggula Shankou** *pass* China
58 F5 **Tang He** China
65 C5 **Tang He** *R* China
Tangier *see* **Tanger** Morocco
122 K9 **Tangier** Nova Scotia Canada
122 K9 **Tangier Grand L** Nova Scotia Canada
95 M9 **Tangier I** Virginia U.S.A.
145 E4 **Tangimoana** New Zealand
111 F11 **Tangipahoa** *R* Louisiana U.S.A.
70 G6 **Tangkeleboke, G** *mt* Sulawesi
70 K8 **Tangkittebak, Gunung** *mt* Sumatra
70 L9 **Tangkuban Perahu** *mt* Java
66 D5 **Tang-ku-la-yu-mu Ts'o** *L* China
109 L5 **Tanglewood** Texas U.S.A.
Tanglha Range *see* **Tanggula Shan**
66 F5 **Tangmai** China
141 G5 **Tangorin** Queensland Australia
145 D1 **Tangowahine** New Zealand
67 C6 **Tangpeng** China
66 D5 **Tangra Yumco** *L* China
69 B10 **Tangse** Sumatra
65 D5 **Tangshan** China
67 A3 **Tangtang** China
67 C3 **Tangtou** China
67 E5 **Tangtouxia** China
71 F5 **Tangub** Negros Philippines
85 E6 **Tanguiéta** Benin
56 F3 **Tanguy** Russian Federation
59 J2 **Tangwanghe** China
67 F2 **Tangxi** China
65 C5 **Tang Xian** China
67 D1 **Tangxianzhen** China
68 D1 **Tang-Yan** Burma
67 C2 **Tangyan He** *R* China
58 F4 **Tangyin** China
65 C7 **Tangyin** China
65 H1 **Tangyuan** China
29 N4 **Tanhua** Finland
68 G7 **Tani** Cambodia
61 K10 **Tanigumi** Japan
136 G3 **Tanimbar, Kep** *islds* Moluccas Indonesia
40 E5 **Taninges** France
Tanintharyi *see* **Tenasserim**
60 D14 **Taniyama** Japan
71 F6 **Tanjay** Philippines
70 D6 **Tanjung** Kalimantan
69 G13 **Tanjung** Sumatra
69 F12 **Tanjungbalai** Kepulauan Riau Indonesia
69 D11 **Tanjungbalai** Sumatra
69 F12 **Tanjungbatu** Indonesia
69 F13 **Tanjungbojo** Sumatra
70 F4 **Tanjungbuaya** *isld* Kalimantan
70 K7 **Tanjungenim** Sumatra
70 E6 **Tanjunggaru** Kalimantan
70 K8 **Tanjungkarang Telukbetung** Sumatra
69 H14 **Tanjung-pandan** Indonesia
69 G12 **Tanjungpinang** Indonesia
69 D11 **Tanjungpura** Sumatra
69 G14 **Tanjungraja** Sumatra
70 E3 **Tanjungredeb** Kalimantan
69 J13 **Tanjungsaleh** *isld* Indonesia
69 J13 **Tanjungsatai** Indonesia
70 E3 **Tanjungselor** Kalimantan
74 D2 **Tank** Pakistan
138 E3 **Tankamarinna,L** South Australia Australia
29 N3 **Tankapirtti** Finland
108 G4 **Tankersly** Texas U.S.A.
56 G5 **Tankhoy** Russian Federation
68 B3 **Tanlwe** *R* Burma
68 J7 **Tan My** Vietnam
37 O7 **Tann** Bayern Germany
37 J2 **Tann** Hessen Germany
37 M3 **Tanna** Germany
137 O5 **Tanna** *isld* Vanuatu
15 F4 **Tannadice** Scotland
22 H4 **Tannay** France
33 N9 **Tanne** Germany
95 N4 **Tannersville** New York U.S.A.
95 M5 **Tannersville** Pennsylvania U.S.A.
37 N4 **Tännesberg** Germany
37 J6 **Tannhausen** Germany
41 M1 **Tannheim** Germany
29 M6 **Tannila** Finland
119 N1 **Tannin** Ontario Canada
80 C3 **Tanninim** Israel
28 E1 **Tannis Bugt** *B* Denmark
28 E1 **Tannisby** Denmark
37 L2 **Tannroda** Germany
85 D7 **Tano** *R* Ghana
71 F5 **Tañon Str** Philippines
85 F6 **Tanout** Niger
68 G1 **Tan Quang** Vietnam
124 H4 **Tanque Alvarez** Mexico
125 K7 **Tanquian** Mexico
79 F2 **Tanrıverdı** Turkey
75 K5 **Tansing** Nepal
79 A8 **Tanta** Egypt
68 B1 **Tantabin** Sagaing Burma
68 C3 **Tantabin** Tenasserim Burma
119 Q8 **Tantallon** Saskatchewan Canada
85 B3 **Tan-Tan** Morocco
138 F6 **Tantanoola** South Australia Australia
Tantung *see* **Dandong**
140 C3 **Tanumbirini** N Terr Australia
116 E6 **Tanunak** Alaska U.S.A.
138 E5 **Tanunda** South Australia Australia
55 C3 **Tanyp** *R* Russian Federation
88 C4 **Tanzania** *rep* Africa
117 H6 **Tanzilla** *R* British Columbia Canada
65 E2 **Tao'an** China
67 G2 **Taohua Dao** *isld* China
Taohuaping *see* **Longhui**
67 D2 **Taojiang** China
68 D7 **Tao,Ko** *isld* Thailand
65 D7 **Taoluo** China
Taonan *see* **Tao'an**
99 O6 **Taopi** Minnesota U.S.A.
43 G11 **Taormina** Sicily
106 E5 **Taos** New Mexico U.S.A.
85 D4 **Taoudenni** Mali
85 D2 **Taounate** Morocco
85 D2 **Taourirt** Morocco
85 D2 **Taouz** Morocco
67 D2 **Taoyuan** China
55 E3 **Tap** *R* Russian Federation
52 C5 **Tapa** Estonia
71 E8 **Tapaan Passage** Philippines
125 N10 **Tapachula** Mexico
69 E10 **Tapah** Malaysia
129 G5 **Tapajós** *R* Brazil
69 C11 **Tapaktuan** Sumatra
133 E5 **Tapalquén** Argentina
69 E14 **Tapan** Sumatra
129 G3 **Tapanahoni** *R* Suriname
125 M9 **Tapanatapec** Mexico
144 B6 **Tapanui** New Zealand
69 D12 **Tapanuli, Teluk** *B* Sumatra
128 F5 **Tapauá** Brazil
145 D4 **Tapawera** New Zealand
130 H9 **Taperoá** Brazil
131 H3 **Tapes, Pta. de** *C* Brazil
37 K6 **Tapfheim** Germany
74 F8 **Tāpi** *R* India
71 F7 **Tapiantana** *isld* Philippines
128 D5 **Tapiche** *R* Peru
70 B5 **Tapinbini** Kalimantan
29 L11 **Tapiola** Finland
128 E3 **Tapirapeó, Sa** *mts* Venezuela/Brazil
130 B4 **Tapirapuã** Brazil
69 F10 **Tapis** *mt* Malaysia
124 E4 **Tapizuelas** Mexico
75 M5 **Taplejung** Nepal
48 D4 **Tapolca** Hungary
68 D2 **Ta-Pom** Burma
95 L9 **Tappahannock** Virginia U.S.A.
70 F6 **Tappalang** Sulawesi
94 F6 **Tappan Res** Ohio U.S.A.
98 G3 **Tappen** North Dakota U.S.A.
28 J6 **Tappernøje** Denmark
60 O4 **Tappi zaki** *C* Japan
60 P1 **Tappu** Japan
28 C6 **Taps** Denmark
55 D1 **Tapsuy** *R* Russian Federation
145 E2 **Tapu** New Zealand
145 D4 **Tapuaenuku** *mt* New Zealand
71 E8 **Tapul** Philippines
69 D12 **Tapulonanjing** *mt* Sumatra
68 B3 **Tapun** Burma
128 F4 **Tapurucuara** Brazil
133 G3 **Taquara** Brazil
130 D7 **Taquaraçu** *R* Brazil
130 D4 **Taquara,Sa.da** *mts* Brazil
131 H2 **Taquari** *R* Brazil
130 C6 **Taquari,Pantanal do** *swamp* Brazil
112 K2 **Tar** *R* North Carolina U.S.A.
141 K7 **Tara** Queensland Australia
120 J8 **Tara** Ontario Canada
71 E4 **Tara** *isld* Philippines
55 F3 **Tara** Russian Federation
55 G3 **Tara** *R* Russian Federation
48 E7 **Tara** *mt* Serbia Yugoslavia
85 G7 **Taraba** *R* Nigeria
84 E3 **Tarābulus** Libya
128 E3 **Taracua** Brazil
145 F3 **Taradale** New Zealand
84 E4 **Tarāghin** Libya
60 D13 **Taragi** Japan
139 J6 **Tarago** New South Wales Australia
14 E3 **Tara Hill** Ireland
26 L5 **Tårajaure** Sweden
70 E3 **Tarakan** Kalimantan
77 K3 **Tarakki** *reg* Afghanistan
47 L4 **Taraklı** Turkey
48 M4 **Tarakliya** Moldavia
145 D4 **Tarakohe** New Zealand
139 J5 **Taralga** New South Wales Australia
144 C5 **Taramakau R** New Zealand
71 M9 **Taramana** Indonesia
139 J5 **Tarana** New South Wales Australia
145 E3 **Taranaki** *admin region* New Zealand
16 E4 **Tarancón** Spain
145 E1 **Taranga I** New Zealand
76 D5 **Tarangambadi** India
55 D4 **Taranovskoye** Kazakhstan
15 A3 **Taransay** *isld* Scotland
43 H8 **Taranto** Italy
43 H8 **Taranto,G.di** Italy
128 E7 **Tarapacá** *prov* Chile
145 F3 **Taraponui** *mt* New Zealand
128 C5 **Tarapoto** Peru
18 H7 **Tarare** France
145 E4 **Tararua Range** New Zealand
69 A8 **Tarāsa Dwīp** Nicobar Is
19 N17 **Tarascon** France
48 N1 **Tarashcha** Ukraine
41 M4 **Tarasp** Switzerland
85 F3 **Tarat** Algeria
128 D5 **Tarauacá** Brazil
17 F4 **Taravilla** Spain
145 F3 **Tarawera L** New Zealand
145 F3 **Tarawera, Mt** New Zealand
17 F3 **Tarazona** Spain
17 F5 **Tarazona de la Mancha** Spain
29 K5 **Tårbæk** Denmark
57 K2 **Tarbagatay, Khrebet** *mts* Kazakhstan
14 B4 **Tarbert** Ireland
15 B3 **Tarbert** Harris Scotland
12 C2 **Tarbert** Strathclyde Scotland
12 B2 **Tarbert,L** Scotland
18 F9 **Tarbes** France
12 D3 **Tarbolton** Scotland
112 K2 **Tarboro** North Carolina U.S.A.
141 F5 **Tarbrax** Queensland Australia
48 K4 **Tarcăului,Munţii** *mts* Romania
138 C4 **Tarcoola** South Australia Australia
139 H4 **Tarcoon** New South Wales Australia
138 C2 **Tarcoonyinna** *R* South Australia Australia
139 J6 **Tarcutta** New South Wales Australia
18 E9 **Tardets-Sorholus** France
17 G3 **Tardienta** Spain
21 J8 **Tardière,la** France
18 F7 **Tardoire** *R* France
59 L2 **Tardoki-Yami, Gora** *mt* Russian Federation
143 B8 **Tardun** W Australia Australia
139 L4 **Taree** New South Wales Australia
139 G4 **Tarella** New South Wales Australia
26 N4 **Tärendö** Sweden
40 E7 **Tarentaise** *dist* France
94 H6 **Tarentum** Pennsylvania U.S.A.
85 B3 **Tarfaya** Morocco
65 F1 **Targan** China
16 E10 **Targuist** Morocco
112 J3 **Tarheel** North Carolina U.S.A.
84 E3 **Tarhūnah** Libya
65 A4 **Tarian Gol** China
16 D8 **Tarifa** Spain
71 F2 **Tarigtig Pt** Philippines
133 E2 **Tarija** *prov* Bolivia
133 E2 **Tarija** Bolivia
76 B4 **Tarikere** India
145 E3 **Tariki** New Zealand
72 F5 **Tarīm** Yemen
Tarim Basin *see* **Tarim Pendi**
88 F6 **Tarime** Tanzania
66 D3 **Tarim He** *R* China
66 C3 **Tarim Pendi** *basin* China
77 J3 **Tarīn Kowt** Afghanistan
Tari Nor *see* **Dalai Nur** *L*
89 D9 **Tarka** *R* S Africa
87 E12 **Tarkastad** S Africa
110 A1 **Tarkio** Missouri U.S.A.
101 L2 **Tarkio** Montana U.S.A.
50 G2 **Tarko-Sale** Russian Federation
85 D7 **Tarkwa** Ghana
133 C7 **Tar,L** Argentina
71 E3 **Tarlac** Philippines
15 F3 **Tarland** Scotland
13 F6 **Tarleton** England
140 D5 **Tarlton Downs** N Terr Australia
28 B5 **Tarm** Denmark
128 C6 **Tarma** Peru
32 K6 **Tarmstedt** Germany
18 F9 **Tarn** *R* France
18 G9 **Tarn** *dept* France
48 F3 **Tarna** *R* Hungary
26 H6 **Tärnaby** Sweden
77 K3 **Tarnak** *R* Afghanistan
18 F8 **Tarn-et-Garonne** *dept* France
18 H8 **Tarn,Gorges du** France
31 N5 **Tarnobrzeg** Poland
52 F4 **Tarnogskiy Gorodok** Russian Federation
119 M6 **Tarnopo** Saskatchewan Canada
33 Q5 **Tarnow** Germany
31 M5 **Tarnow** Poland
31 L5 **Tarnowskie Gory** Poland
27 J11 **Tärnsjö** Sweden
44 H2 **Taro** *R* Italy
54 F8 **Taromskoye** Ukraine
141 J7 **Taroom** Queensland Australia
85 C2 **Taroudannt** Morocco
28 C7 **Tarp** Germany
140 D4 **Tarpaulin Swamp** N Terr Australia
109 H6 **Tarpley** Texas U.S.A.
113 E9 **Tarpon Springs** Florida U.S.A.
8 D1 **Tarporley** England
113 L12 **Tarpum Bay** Eleuthera Bahamas
44 L5 **Tarquinia** Italy
80 D7 **Tarqumiya** Jordan
17 H3 **Tarragona** *prov* Spain
17 H3 **Tarragona** Spain
139 H8 **Tarraleah** Tasmania Australia
139 H4 **Tarran Hills** New South Wales Australia
111 K8 **Tarrant City** Alabama U.S.A.
8 D6 **Tarrant Hinton** England
140 E3 **Tarrant,Pt** Queensland Australia
144 B6 **Tarras** New Zealand
17 J3 **Tarrasa** Spain
26 J4 **Tarrekaise** *mt* Sweden
41 N3 **Tarrenz** Austria
106 E2 **Tarryall** Colorado U.S.A.
112 E5 **Tarrytown** Georgia U.S.A.
95 O5 **Tarrytown** New York U.S.A.
17 F9 **Tarsa,C** Algeria
45 P1 **Tarski Zaljev** *B* Croatia
84 F5 **Tarso Taro** *mt* Chad
86 C1 **Tarso Tieroko** *mt* Chad
78 E3 **Tarsus** Turkey
79 E1 **Tarsus** *R* Turkey
133 E2 **Tartagal** Argentina
6 L4 **Tartan** *oil rig* North Sea
45 J1 **Tártaro** *R* Italy
18 E9 **Tartas** France
56 A3 **Tartas** *R* Russian Federation
52 C5 **Tartu** Estonia
79 F4 **Tarţūs** Syria
80 C6 **Tarum** Israel
60 P3 **Tarumae-san** *mt* Japan
130 H6 **Tarumirim** Brazil
60 D14 **Tarumizu** Japan
54 J2 **Tarusa** Russian Federation
69 D9 **Tarutao,Ko** *isld* Thailand
48 M4 **Tarutino** Ukraine
69 D11 **Tarutung** Sumatra
26 D8 **Tarva** *isld* Norway
38 J9 **Tarvisio** Italy
56 E5 **Tarys-Arzhan** Russian Federation
120 K5 **Tarzwell** Ontario Canada
108 B6 **Tasajera, Sa** *mts* Mexico
57 G2 **Tasaral** Kazakhstan
84 E4 **Tasāwah** Libya
57 D3 **Tas Buget** Kazakhstan
121 M4 **Taschereau** Quebec Canada
107 K2 **Tasco** Kansas U.S.A.
117 M10 **Taseko, Mt** British Columbia Canada
56 D2 **Taseyeva** *R* Russian Federation
76 B2 **Tasgaon** India
58 A2 **Tashanta** Russian Federation
57 A4 **Tashauz** Turkmenistan
75 O5 **Tashigang** Bhutan
57 E4 **Tashkent** Uzbekistan
57 C6 **Tashkepri** Turkmenistan
57 F4 **Tash-Kumyr** Kyrgyzstan
55 B5 **Tashla** Russian Federation
120 C2 **Tashota** Ontario Canada
56 C4 **Tashtagol** Russian Federation
56 C4 **Tashtyp** Russian Federation
69 F11 **Tasik Dampar** Malaysia
70 M9 **Tasikmalaja** Java
70 L9 **Tasikmalaya** Java
80 G2 **Tasil** Syria
28 F7 **Tåsinge** *isld* Denmark
115 O3 **Tasiusaq** Greenland
26 H7 **Tåsjö** Sweden
26 H7 **Tåsjön** *L* Sweden
85 G5 **Tasker** Niger
47 N11 **Taşkopru** Turkey
56 E5 **Taskyl,Khrebet** *mts* Russian Federation
78 J2 **Taşlıçay** Turkey
144 D4 **Tasman** New Zealand
145 D4 **Tasman Bay** New Zealand
139 H9 **Tasman Hd** Tasmania Australia
139 H8 **Tasmania** *state* Australia
145 D4 **Tasman Mountains** New Zealand
144 C5 **Tasman, Mt** New Zealand
139 J9 **Tasman Pen** Tasmania Australia
134 G13 **Tasman Plateau** Pacific Oc
137 M9 **Tasman Sea** Pacific Oc
48 H3 **Tăşnad** Romania
85 F5 **Tassara** Niger
19 J5 **Tasselot, Mt** France
115 M6 **Tassialouc,L** Quebec Canada
85 E5 **Tassili du Hoggar** *plateau* Algeria
85 F3 **Tassili-n'-Ajjer** *plateau* Algeria
28 J5 **Tåstrup** Denmark
51 M2 **Tas Tumus** Russian Federation
57 E3 **Tasty** Kazakhstan
79 D2 **Taşucu** Turkey
85 C3 **Tata** Morocco
71 H5 **Tataba** Sulawesi Indonesia
48 E3 **Tatabánya** Hungary
71 E7 **Tatalan** *isld* Philippines
122 J8 **Tatamagouche** Nova Scotia Canada
85 G2 **Tataouine** Tunisia
48 M5 **Tatarbunary** Ukraine
47 H3 **Tatarlar** Turkey
55 G3 **Tatarsk** Russian Federation
52 H6 **Tatarskaya Respublika** Russian Federation
59 M1 **Tatarskiy Proliv** *str* Russian Federation
Tatarstan *see* **Tatarskaya Respublika**
70 C3 **Tatau** Sarawak
141 G3 **Tate** *R* Queensland Australia
89 E3 **Tate** *R* Botswana
119 N7 **Tate** Saskatchewan Canada
112 C3 **Tate** Georgia U.S.A.
61 O6 **Tateai** Japan
140 C2 **Tate Bluff** *hill* N Terr Australia
60 O4 **Tateura** Japan
61 L9 **Tate yama** *mt* Japan
61 N11 **Tateyama** Japan
117 P5 **Tathlina L** Northwest Territories Canada
139 K6 **Tathra** New South Wales Australia
116 O6 **Tatitlek** Alaska U.S.A.
117 L10 **Tatla Lake** British Columbia Canada
117 K7 **Tatlatui Prov. Park** British Columbia Canada
116 K5 **Tatlawiksuk** *R* Alaska U.S.A.
117 L10 **Tatlayoko Lake** British Columbia Canada
117 M10 **Tatlow, Mt** British Columbia Canada
101 R5 **Tatman Mt** Wyoming U.S.A.
116 K6 **Tatna L** Alaska U.S.A.
115 K6 **Tatnam,C** Manitoba Canada
139 H6 **Tatong** Victoria Australia
66 D4 **Tatrang** China
31 M6 **Tatry** *mts* Czech/Poland
117 E6 **Tatshenshini** *R* British Columbia Canada
77 K7 **Tatta** Pakistan
9 F1 **Tattershall** England
57 G3 **Tatty** Kazakhstan
130 F8 **Tatuí** Brazil
131 B2 **Tatul,Sa de** *mts* Chile
108 D2 **Tatum** New Mexico U.S.A.
109 N3 **Tatum** Texas U.S.A.
107 N7 **Tatums** Oklahoma U.S.A.
Tatung *see* **Datong**
139 H6 **Tatura** Victoria Australia
129 K5 **Tauá** Brazil
128 F4 **Tauapeçaçu** Brazil
37 L2 **Taubach** Germany
130 F8 **Taubaté** Brazil
36 H5 **Tauber** *R* Germany
33 R10 **Taucha** Germany
38 H7 **Tauerin Tunnel** Austria
37 N7 **Taufkirchen** Germany
36 G2 **Taufstein** *mt* Germany
128 G3 **Tauini** *R* Brazil
145 E2 **Taukoa** New Zealand
20 C4 **Taulé** France
19 N16 **Taulignan** France
28 D5 **Taulov** Denmark
145 E3 **Taumarunui** New Zealand
128 D5 **Taumaturgo** Brazil
110 F4 **Taum Sauk Mt** Missouri U.S.A.
130 C7 **Taunay** Brazil
89 D6 **Taung** S Africa
68 C5 **Taungbon** Burma
68 B2 **Taungdwingyi** Burma
68 C2 **Taung-Gyi** Burma
68 D3 **Taunggyi** *mt* Burma/Thailand
68 C2 **Taunglau** Burma
68 C4 **Taungnyo A** *ra* Burma
68 B2 **Taungtha** Burma
68 B3 **Taungup** Burma
74 D3 **Taunsa** Pakistan
8 C5 **Taunton** England
95 Q5 **Taunton** Massachusetts U.S.A.
95 R5 **Taunton,E** Massachusetts U.S.A.
36 E3 **Taunus** *mts* Germany
145 E2 **Taupiri** New Zealand
145 F3 **Taupo** New Zealand
52 B6 **Tauragė** Lithuania
145 E3 **Taurakawa** *mt* New Zealand
145 F2 **Tauranga** New Zealand
121 R6 **Taureau, L** Quebec Canada
145 D1 **Tauroa Pt** New Zealand
55 F2 **Taurovy** Russian Federation
Taurus Mts *see* **Toroslar Dağlari**
17 G3 **Tauste** Spain
144 B7 **Tautuku Peninsula** New Zealand
137 M2 **Tauu Is** Papua New Guinea
115 K5 **Tavani** Northwest Territories Canada
40 F3 **Tavannes** Switzerland
113 F9 **Tavares** Florida U.S.A.
45 K4 **Tavarnelles Val di Pesa** Italy
47 K7 **Tavas** Turkey
22 F4 **Tavaux** France
55 D2 **Tavda** *R* Russian Federation
55 E2 **Tavda** Russian Federation
26 L7 **Tavelsjö** Sweden
41 J5 **Taverne** Switzerland
45 K1 **Tavernelle** Italy
115 M4 **Taverner B** Northwest Territories Canada
19 Q17 **Tavernes** France
113 G12 **Tavernier** Florida U.S.A.
21 P3 **Taverny** Val d'Oise France
88 F3 **Taveta** Kenya
137 R5 **Taveuni** *isld* Fiji
56 G6 **Tavin** Mongolia
16 B7 **Tavira** Portugal
8 B6 **Tavistock** England
43 C8 **Tavolara, I** Sardinia
55 G4 **Tavolzhan** Kazakhstan
16 B4 **Tâvora** *R* Portugal
68 D5 **Tavoy** Burma
Tavoy I *see* **Mali Kyun**
68 D6 **Tavoy Pt** Burma
65 H3 **Tavrichanka** Russian Federation
55 F4 **Tavricheskoye** Russian Federation
47 N11 **Tavşancıl** Turkey
47 K5 **Tavşanlı** Turkey
47 N11 **Tavşanlı** Turkey
26 L3 **Tavvaätno** *R* Sweden
145 G4 **Tawa** New Zealand
109 M3 **Tawakoni, L** Texas U.S.A.
94 D2 **Tawas City** Michigan U.S.A.
118 D4 **Tawatinaw** Alberta Canada
70 E2 **Tawau** Sabah
70 E2 **Tawau, Telukan** *B* Kalimantan
86 E3 **Taweisha** Sudan
8 C4 **Tawe,R** Wales
145 E1 **Tawhiti Rahi I** New Zealand
70 F2 **Tawitawi** Philippines
8 B5 **Taw,R** England
67 G5 **Ta-wu** Taiwan
84 F3 **Tāwurghā, Sabkhat** *salt flat* Libya
38 G7 **Taxenbach** Austria
27 J12 **Taxinge** Sweden
66 B4 **Taxkorgan** China
128 C5 **Tayabamba** Peru
71 E4 **Tayabas B** Philippines
69 K13 **Tayan** Indonesia
52 D1 **Taybola** Russian Federation
86 H5 **Tayeeglow** Somalia
13 E1 **Tay,Firth of** Scotland
56 C3 **Tayga** Russian Federation
12 C2 **Tayinloan** Scotland
143 D10 **Tay,L** W Australia Australia
140 C5 **Taylor** *R* N Terr Australia
117 N7 **Taylor** British Columbia Canada
103 O7 **Taylor** Arizona U.S.A.
109 O2 **Taylor** Arkansas U.S.A.
111 G7 **Taylor** Mississippi U.S.A.
110 E2 **Taylor** Missouri U.S.A.
98 G8 **Taylor** Nebraska U.S.A.
109 K5 **Taylor** Texas U.S.A.
100 D2 **Taylor** Washington U.S.A.
99 P5 **Taylor** Wisconsin U.S.A.
144 C5 **Taylor, Mt** New Zealand
106 C6 **Taylor, Mt** New Mexico U.S.A.
116 J6 **Taylor Mts** Alaska U.S.A.
106 D3 **Taylor Park Res** Colorado U.S.A.
112 B3 **Taylor Ridge** Georgia U.S.A.
112 E3 **Taylors** South Carolina U.S.A.
142 B3 **Taylors Crossing** W Australia Australia
106 F5 **Taylor Springs** New Mexico U.S.A.
94 B8 **Taylorsville** Kentucky U.S.A.
111 G10 **Taylorsville** Mississippi U.S.A.
112 F2 **Taylorsville** North Carolina U.S.A.
94 F7 **Taylorsville** Ohio U.S.A.
110 G2 **Taylorville** Illinois U.S.A.
122 F7 **Taymouth** New Brunswick Canada
51 K2 **Taymura** *R* Russian Federation
51 K1 **Taymyr,Ozero** *L* Russian Federation
51 J1 **Taymyr,Poluostrov** *pen* Russian Federation
55 E4 **Tayncha** Kazakhstan
68 H7 **Tay Ninh** Vietnam
12 C1 **Taynuilt** Scotland
71 G6 **Tayoloan** *R* Mindanao Philippines
13 F1 **Tayport** Scotland
15 E4 **Tay,R** Scotland
56 E3 **Tayshet** Russian Federation
58 C2 **Tayshir** Mongolia
15 E4 **Tayside** *reg* Scotland
71 E3 **Taytay** Luzon Philippines
71 D5 **Taytay** Palawan Philippines
71 G5 **Taytay Pt** Philippines
77 G2 **Tayyebād** Iran
79 E10 **Ţayyib al Ism** Saudi Arabia
50 H2 **Taz** *R* Russian Federation
85 D2 **Taza** Morocco
85 F5 **Tazalc** Niger
61 O6 **Tazawa ko** *L* Japan
112 D1 **Tazewell** Tennessee U.S.A.
94 F9 **Tazewell** Virginia U.S.A.
65 F1 **Tazicheng** China
116 K7 **Tazimina Lakes** Alaska U.S.A.
84 G4 **Tāzirbū** Libya
48 K4 **Tazlău** *R* Romania
116 O6 **Tazlina L** Alaska U.S.A.
50 G2 **Tazovskaya Guba** *G* Russian Federation
50 G2 **Tazovskiy** Russian Federation
66 F6 **Tazungdam** Burma
61 K8 **Tazuruhama** Japan
78 K1 **Tbilisi** Georgia
85 E7 **Tchaourou** Benin
86 B6 **Tchibanga** Gabon
84 E5 **Tchigaï, Plat. du** Chad/Niger
68 J2 **Tching Lan Xan** *isld* Vietnam
85 F5 **Tchin-Tabaradene** Niger
86 B4 **Tcholliré** Cameroon
111 F8 **Tchula** Mississippi U.S.A.
31 L1 **Tczew** Poland
128 E4 **Tea** *R* Brazil
98 K6 **Tea** South Dakota U.S.A.
48 J4 **Teaca** Romania
124 G6 **Teacapán** Mexico
108 D3 **Teague** New Mexico U.S.A.
109 L4 **Teague** Texas U.S.A.
143 D7 **Teague,L** W Australia Australia
13 G4 **Team Valley** England
144 A6 **Te Anau** New Zealand
145 E3 **Te Anga** New Zealand
45 Q7 **Teano** Italy
101 T6 **Teapot Dome** *hill* Wyoming U.S.A.
145 G2 **Te Araroa** New Zealand
145 E2 **Te Aroha** New Zealand
140 C5 **Tea Tree** N Terr Australia
145 E3 **Te Awamutu** New Zealand
16 D8 **Teba** Spain
69 J12 **Tebas** Indonesia
85 F1 **Tebessa** Algeria
130 B10 **Tebicuary** Paraguay
69 D11 **Tebingtinggi** Sumatra
69 E13 **Tebo** *R* Sumatra
43 C12 **Tébourba** Tunisia
43 C12 **Téboursouk** Tunisia
69 F12 **Tebrau** Malaysia
53 G11 **Tebulosmta** *mt* Georgia/Rus Fed
18 G10 **Tech** *R* France
55 D3 **Techa** *R* Russian Federation
85 D7 **Techiman** Ghana
47 J1 **Techirghiol** Romania
144 D5 **Technical, Mt** New Zealand
33 Q6 **Techow** Germany
79 G1 **Tecirli** Turkey
36 G6 **Teck** Germany
133 C6 **Tecka** Argentina
32 G8 **Tecklenburg** Germany
27 F16 **Teckomatorp** Sweden
124 G7 **Tecolotlán** Mexico
124 H8 **Tecomán** Mexico
103 H6 **Tecopa** California U.S.A.
124 F4 **Tecorichic** Mexico
124 E3 **Tecoripa** Mexico
125 J9 **Tecpan** Mexico
124 G6 **Tecuala** Mexico
48 L5 **Tecuci** Romania
120 H10 **Tecumseh** Ontario Canada
94 D4 **Tecumseh** Michigan U.S.A.
110 D5 **Tecumseh** Missouri U.S.A.
98 K9 **Tecumseh** Nebraska U.S.A.
107 O6 **Tecumseh** Oklahoma U.S.A.
8 C6 **Tedburn St Mary** England
70 P16 **Tedjakula** Indonesia
57 B5 **Tedzhen** Turkmenistan
77 G1 **Tedzhen** Turkmenistan
56 D5 **Teeli** Russian Federation
118 D6 **Tees** Alberta Canada
13 G5 **Tees,R** England
120 J9 **Teeswater** Ontario Canada
71 D6 **Teeth,The** *mt* Palawan Philippines
128 F4 **Tefe** Brazil
47 K7 **Tefenni** Turkey
26 L8 **Teg** Sweden
70 M9 **Tegal** Java
33 S7 **Tegel** Germany
25 F6 **Tegelen** Netherlands
41 P2 **Tegernsee** *L* Germany
85 F6 **Tegina** Nigeria
70 K8 **Tegineneng** Sumatra
141 H8 **Tego** Queensland Australia
125 L2 **Tegucigalpa** Honduras
85 F5 **Teguiddan Tessoum** Niger
89 E3 **Tegwani** *R* Zimbabwe
102 F6 **Tehachapi** California U.S.A.
102 F7 **Tehachapi Mts** California U.S.A.
102 B1 **Tehama** California U.S.A.
102 B2 **Tehama-Colusa Canal** California U.S.A.
145 E2 **Te Hana** New Zealand
145 D1 **Te Hapua** New Zealand
145 F3 **Te Haroto** New Zealand
145 F3 **Te Hauke** New Zealand
115 K4 **Tehek L** Northwest Territories Canada
77 B2 **Tehrān** Iran
77 B2 **Tehrān** *prov* Iran
125 L8 **Tehuacán** Mexico
125 M9 **Tehuantepec** Mexico
37 L2 **Teichel** Germany
8 C3 **Teifi** *R* Wales
8 C6 **Teignmouth** England
8 C6 **Teign,R** England
20 G6 **Teillay** France
20 H7 **Teille** France
21 J4 **Teilleul,le** France
61 Q12 **Teima** Okinawa
Teinach *see* **Bad Teinach-Zavelstein**
36 F6 **Teinach** Germany
37 N6 **Teisbach** Germany
29 K10 **Teisko** Finland
88 G3 **Teita Hills** Kenya
12 D1 **Teith,R** Scotland
48 H4 **Teius** Romania
130 H9 **Teixeira** Brazil
Teixeira de Sousa *see* **Luau**
130 G7 **Teixeiras** Brazil
130 E9 **Teixeira Soares** Brazil
16 E8 **Tejeda,Sa** *mts* Spain
16 B5 **Tejo** *R* Portugal
124 F3 **Tejolocachic** Mexico
102 F7 **Tejon Pk** California U.S.A.
130 E6 **Tejuco,R** Brazil
125 J8 **Tejupilco** Mexico
145 F2 **Te Kaha** New Zealand
98 K8 **Tekamah** Nebraska U.S.A.
145 D1 **Te Kao** New Zealand
145 F3 **Te Karaka** New Zealand
145 E2 **Te Kauwhata** New Zealand
145 E3 **Te Kawa** New Zealand
47 N10 **Teke** Turkey
57 J3 **Tekeli** Kazakhstan
55 F4 **Teke, Oz** *L* Kazakhstan
57 K3 **Tekes** China
66 C3 **Tekes** *R* Kazakhstan
57 K3 **Tekes He** *R* China
86 G3 **Tekezē** *R* Ethiopia
144 C5 **Te Kinga** New Zealand
47 J4 **Tekirdağ** Turkey
145 D3 **Te Kiri** New Zealand
68 A2 **Teknaf** Burma
100 H2 **Tekoa** Washington U.S.A.
144 D5 **Tekoa, Mt** New Zealand
94 C4 **Tekonsha** Michigan U.S.A.
145 D2 **Te Kopuru** New Zealand
86 D2 **Tekro** Chad
71 H5 **Teku** Sulawesi
145 E3 **Te Kuiti** New Zealand
125 Q10 **Tela** Honduras
80 E3 **Tel 'Adashim** Israel
69 C10 **Telagatujuh** Sumatra
17 G10 **Télagh** Algeria
80 B7 **Telamim** Israel
69 G12 **Telan** *isld* Indonesia
116 L6 **Telaquana,L** Alaska U.S.A.
80 B6 **Tel Ashdod** Israel
80 B7 **Tel Ashqelon** Israel
53 G12 **Telavi** Georgia
80 C5 **Tel Aviv** Israel
80 C7 **Tel Azeqa** Israel
56 C4 **Tel'bes** Russian Federation
80 F3 **Tel Bet She'an** Israel
80 C7 **Tel Bet Shemesh** Israel
80 F3 **Tel Bet Yerah** Israel
31 J6 **Telč** Czechoslovakia
48 J3 **Telciu** Romania
80 C8 **Tel Devir** Israel
70 C6 **Telegapulang** Kalimantan
117 H7 **Telegraph Creek** British Columbia Canada
80 F6 **Teleilet el Ghassul** Jordan
27 C12 **Telemark** *prov* Norway
70 E4 **Telen** *R* Kalimantan
48 L3 **Teleneshty** Moldavia
48 J6 **Teleorman** *R* Romania
109 L2 **Telephone** Texas U.S.A.
102 G5 **Telescope Pk** California U.S.A.
127 P5 **Telescope Pt** Grenada
129 G5 **Teles Pires** *R* Brazil
56 C5 **Teletskoye, Oz** *L* Russian Federation
80 C8 **Tel Eyton** Israel
142 D5 **Telfer Mining Centre** W Australia Australia
8 D2 **Telford** England
80 D4 **Tel Gat** Israel
20 B5 **Telgruc** France
32 G9 **Telgte** Germany
80 F1 **Tel Ḥazor** Israel
85 B6 **Télimélé** Guinea
80 F2 **Tel Kinnerot** Israel
78 J3 **Tel Kotchek** Syria
117 K8 **Telkwa** British Columbia Canada
108 G1 **Tell** Texas U.S.A.
80 C7 **Tel Lakhish** Israel
22 K5 **Tellancourt Villers** France
110 K4 **Tell City** Indiana U.S.A.
80 F5 **Tell Deir'Alla** Jordan
26 L5 **Tellejåkk** Sweden
116 D4 **Teller** Alaska U.S.A.
76 B5 **Tellicherry** India
112 C2 **Tellico L** Tennessee U.S.A.
112 C2 **Tellico Plains** Tennessee U.S.A.
122 F3 **Tellier** Quebec Canada
22 J3 **Tellin** Belgium
32 K4 **Tellingstedt** Germany
80 C5 **Tel Litwinsky** Israel
80 F6 **Tell Nimrin** Jordan
106 C4 **Telluride** Colorado U.S.A.
57 B4 **Tel'mansk** Turkmenistan
80 C7 **Tel Maresha** Israel
58 C2 **Telmen Nuur** *L* Mongolia
80 B8 **Tel Mifsah** Israel
80 C4 **Tel Mond** Israel
69 D13 **Telo** Indonesia
100 H4 **Telocaset** Oregon U.S.A.
69 B14 **Telok Blangah** *dist* Singapore
125 K8 **Teloloapán** Mexico
52 J3 **Tel'poziz, Gora** *mt* Russian Federation
80 F1 **Tel Qedesh** Israel
80 A8 **Tel Re'im** Israel
133 D6 **Telsen** Argentina
80 C2 **Tel Shiqmona** Israel
80 C8 **Tel Shoqet** Israel
52 B6 **Telšiai** Lithuania
120 E3 **Teltaka** Ontario Canada
33 S8 **Teltow** Germany
70 E3 **Telukbajur** Kalimantan
69 E13 **Telukbayur** Sumatra
70 K8 **Telukbetung** Sumatra
69 J10 **Telukbutun** Indonesia
69 C12 **Telukdalam** Indonesia
69 E10 **Teluk Intan** Malaysia
69 E13 **Telukkuantan** Sumatra
70 B5 **Telukmelan** Kalimantan
70 L9 **Teluknaga** Java
69 J13 **Telukpakedai** Indonesia
69 F12 **Teluksabah** Sumatra
85 F5 **Telwes** Niger
80 C8 **Tel Ẓiqlag** Israel
85 E7 **Tema** Ghana
69 J12 **Temaju** *isld* Indonesia
94 K9 **Teman** Virginia U.S.A.
70 N9 **Temanggung** Java
85 F4 **Temasint** Algeria
69 E14 **Tembesi** *R* Sumatra
69 F13 **Tembilahan** Sumatra
102 D6 **Temblor Rge** California U.S.A.
87 C7 **Tembo Aluma** Angola
89 E8 **Tembuland** *dist* S Africa
102 G8 **Temecula** California U.S.A.
56 E5 **Temenchulu,Gora** *mt* Russian Federation
8 D3 **Teme,R** England
48 F5 **Temerin** Serbia Yugoslavia
69 F11 **Temerluh** Malaysia
69 F10 **Temiang, Bukit** *hill* Malaysia
71 C3 **Teminabuan** W Irian
57 A1 **Temir** Kazakhstan
56 C4 **Temirtau** Russian Federation
122 A2 **Temiscamie L** Quebec Canada
122 A2 **Temiscamie R** Quebec Canada
121 L6 **Témiscaming** Quebec Canada
121 L5 **Témiscamingue, L** Quebec Canada
122 D6 **Temiscouata L** Quebec Canada
121 L6 **Témiskaming** Quebec Canada
69 G12 **Temiyang** *isld* Indonesia
139 G8 **Temma** Tasmania Australia
56 F5 **Temnik** *R* Russian Federation
139 J5 **Temora** New South Wales Australia
124 F3 **Temósachic** Mexico
103 N8 **Tempe** Arizona U.S.A.
70 F7 **Tempe, L** *isld* Sulawesi
33 S8 **Tempelhof** Germany
94 D5 **Temperance** Michigan U.S.A.
69 F13 **Tempino** Sumatra
43 C8 **Tempio Paus** Sardinia
95 R2 **Temple** Maine U.S.A.
94 C2 **Temple** Michigan U.S.A.
109 J1 **Temple** Oklahoma U.S.A.
95 M6 **Temple** Pennsylvania U.S.A.
109 K4 **Temple** Texas U.S.A.
141 G1 **Temple B** Queensland Australia
8 B3 **Temple Bar** Wales
20 G7 **Temple-de-Bretagne, le** France
140 B6 **Temple Downs** N Terr Australia
9 H5 **Temple Ewell** England
14 D4 **Templemore** Ireland
13 F4 **Temple Sowerby** England
140 E5 **Templeton** *R* Queensland Australia
102 D6 **Templeton** California U.S.A.
94 H6 **Templeton** Pennsylvania U.S.A.
8 B4 **Templeton** Wales
22 E2 **Templeuve** Belgium
33 T6 **Templin** Germany
87 C8 **Tempué** Angola
33 P5 **Tempzin** Germany
55 E2 **Temryak, Oz** *L* Russian Federation
22 G1 **Temse** Belgium
131 A7 **Temuco** Chile
144 C6 **Temuka** New Zealand
98 F3 **Temvik** North Dakota U.S.A.
55 C4 **Temyasovo** Russian Federation
128 C4 **Tena** Ecuador
102 H1 **Tenabo** Nevada U.S.A.
124 G8 **Tenacatita** Mexico
109 N4 **Tenaha** Texas U.S.A.
117 F7 **Tenakee Springs** Alaska U.S.A.
29 K11 **Tenala** Finland
76 E2 **Tenali** India
124 G7 **Tenamaxtlán** Mexico
145 D4 **Te Namu** New Zealand
68 D6 **Tenasserim** Burma
73 Q6 **Tenasserim** *R* Burma
68 C6 **Tenasserim I** Burma
68 E5 **Tenasserim State** Burma
19 P13 **Tenay** France
8 D3 **Tenbury Wells** England
8 B4 **Tenby** Wales
120 G6 **Tenby Bay** Ontario Canada
18 H7 **Tence** France
86 H3 **Tendaho** Ethiopia
73 P7 **Ten Degree Ch** Andaman/Nicobar Is
86 F3 **Tendelti** Sudan
61 O7 **Tendō** Japan
101 M5 **Tendoy** Idaho U.S.A.
85 D2 **Tendrara** Morocco
40 D4 **Tendre, Mt** Switzerland
9 H4 **Tendring** England
21 O8 **Tendu** France
Tenedos *see* **Bozcaada**
85 G4 **Ténéré du Tafassasset** *reg* Niger
85 A3 **Tenerife** *isld* Canary Is
85 E1 **Ténès** Algeria
47 H2 **Tenevo** Bulgaria
71 J4 **Tenga** Sulawesi
71 L9 **Tengahdai** Flores Indonesia
70 N9 **Tengah, Jawa** *prov* Java
Tengchow *see* **Penglai**
70 E5 **Tenggarong** Kalimantan
70 O9 **Tengger** Java
69 F10 **Tenggul** *isld* Malaysia
70 E1 **Tenghilan** Sabah

55 E5 **Tengiz, Oz** L Kazakhstan
71 E7 **Tengolan** isld Philippines
67 C7 **Tengqiao** China
65 D7 **Teng Xian** China
67 C5 **Teng Xian** China
27 G14 **Tenhult** Sweden
44 B3 **Tenibres** mt Italy/France
146 D3 **Teniente Jubany** Argentina Base Antarctica
146 D3 **Teniente Rodolfo Marsh** Chile Base Antarctica
100 C3 **Tenino** Washington U.S.A.
55 F3 **Tenis, Oz** L Russian Federation
55 A4 **Teniz, Oz** L Kazakhstan
76 C6 **Tenkasi** India
52 G6 **Ten'ki** Russian Federation
107 Q6 **Tenkiller Ferry L** Oklahoma U.S.A.
85 D6 **Tenkodogo** Burkina
69 A9 **Tenlaa** Nicobar Is
123 Q2 **Ten Mile L** Newfoundland Canada
42 F5 **Tenna** R Italy
100 D8 **Tennant** California U.S.A.
140 C4 **Tennant Creek** N Terr Australia
38 H6 **Tennen-Geb** mts Austria
110 H6 **Tennessee** state U.S.A.
106 D2 **Tennessee Pass** Colorado U.S.A.
110 J6 **Tennessee R** Tennessee U.S.A.
26 F4 **Tennholmen** Norway
112 E5 **Tennille** Georgia U.S.A.
29 O4 **Tenniöjoki** R Finland
144 D5 **Tennyson L** New Zealand
131 B5 **Teno** R Chile
29 M2 **Tenojoki** R Finland
70 D2 **Tenom** Sabah
125 O9 **Tenosique** Mexico
61 J11 **Tenri** Japan
61 L11 **Tenryū** Japan
111 E9 **Tensas** R Louisiana U.S.A.
111 J11 **Tensaw** R Alabama U.S.A.
100 J2 **Tensed** Idaho U.S.A.
22 C5 **Tensift** R Morocco
99 M2 **Tenstrike** Minnesota U.S.A.
70 G5 **Tenteno** Sulawesi
143 B10 **Tenterden** W Australia Australia
9 G5 **Tenterden** England
139 K3 **Tenterfield** New South Wales Australia
113 F12 **Ten Thousand Is** Florida U.S.A.
70 G4 **Tentolomatinan** mt Sulawesi
124 H7 **Teocaltiche** Mexico
45 M3 **Teodorano** Italy
130 H5 **Teófilo Otôni** Brazil
48 K1 **Teofipol'** Ukraine
71 E7 **Teomabal** isld Philippines
125 L8 **Teotitlan** Mexico
71 O8 **Tepa** Indonesia
124 E3 **Tepache** Mexico
29 L3 **Tepasto** Finland
124 H7 **Tepatitlán de Morelos** Mexico
46 E2 **Tepe** mt Serbia Yugoslavia
125 K8 **Tepeji** Mexico
57 B3 **Tepekul'** Uzbekistan
46 D4 **Tepelenë** Albania
37 O4 **Tepelská Plošina** mts Czechoslovakia
47 N11 **Teperoren** Turkey
70 E4 **Tepianlangsat** Kalimantan
124 G7 **Tepic** Mexico
37 O4 **Teplá** Czechoslovakia
30 H5 **Teplice** Czechoslovakia
37 O3 **Teplicka** Czechoslovakia
48 M2 **Teplik** Ukraine
52 K4 **Teplogorka** Russian Federation
54 K8 **Teplogorsk** Ukraine
124 C2 **Tepoca, C** Mexico
145 F3 **Te Pohue** New Zealand
21 H4 **Tessin** France
43 C7 **Testa, C** Sardinia
42 G7 **Testa del Gargano** Italy
18 E8 **Teste-de-Buch, la** France
32 L6 **Tested** Germany
83 C12 **Testour** Tunisia
9 E5 **Test, R** England
18 G10 **Tet** R France
48 D3 **Tét** Hungary
117 L9 **Tetachuck L** British Columbia Canada
122 F6 **Tetagouche R** New Brunswick Canada
125 J9 **Tetela** Mexico
56 F1 **Tetere** R Russian Federation
46 G2 **Teteven** Bulgaria
48 M1 **Tetiyev** Ukraine
70 C5 **Tetlin** Alaska U.S.A.
101 O2 **Teton** R Montana U.S.A.
101 O6 **Tetonia** Idaho U.S.A.
20 H6 **Tétouan** Morocco
68 C4 **Tétrault** R France
37 N1 **Tetschen** Germany
133 E3 **Teuco** R Argentina
38 N7 **Teufelstein** mt Austria
37 L3 **Teuschnitz** Germany
32 J9 **Teutoburger Wald** Germany
29 J9 **Teuva** Finland
26 H9 **Tevansjö** Sweden
128 F6 **Téven-Kerbrat** France
16 F9 **Tevere** R Italy
144 D6 **Teviot** New Zealand
15 F5 **Teviot** R Scotland
15 F3 **Teviot, R** Scotland
16 O9 **Tévola** isld Greece
20 B4 **Tewah** Kalimantan
108 D1 **Tewantin** Queensland Australia
141 L7 **Tewantin** Queensland Australia
9 F3 **Tewkesbury** England
8 D4 **Texa I** Scotland
109 J2 **Texarkana** Texas/Ark U.S.A.
109 L5 **Texas** Queensland Australia
109 N6 **Texas** state U.S.A.
109 N6 **Texas City** Texas U.S.A.
25 C2 **Texel** isld Netherlands
25 C2 **Texelstroom** Netherlands
107 O7 **Texhoma** Texas/Okla U.S.A.
107 O7 **Texico** New Mexico U.S.A.
108 C7 **Texline** Texas U.S.A.
125 N7 **Texmelucan** Mexico
109 L2 **Texoma,L** Oklahoma U.S.A.
114 E4 **Texon** Texas U.S.A.
56 E5 **Teya** Russian Federation
67 A1 **Te-yang** China
77 J3 **Teykovo** Russian Federation
46 F4 **Teyvareh** Afghanistan
67 G3 **Teza** R Russian Federation

145 E3 **Te Roti** New Zealand
16 D10 **Teroual** Morocco
138 E5 **Terowie** South Australia Australia
59 M2 **Terpeniya,Mys** C Russian Federation
55 E3 **Terpugovo** Russian Federation
94 H7 **Terra Alta** West Virginia U.S.A.
102 E6 **Terra Bella** California U.S.A.
117 J8 **Terrace** British Columbia Canada
120 C4 **Terrace Bay** Ontario Canada
143 D8 **Terraces, The** hills W Australia Australia
45 O7 **Terracina** Italy
45 O7 **Terra Firma** S Africa
73 R6 **Terragal** Italy
90 D8 **Terrak** Norway
67 D6 **Terral** Oklahoma U.S.A.
43 B9 **Terralba** Sardinia
123 S5 **Terra Nova** Newfoundland Canada
45 L4 **Terranuova Bracc** Italy
18 F7 **Terrasson** France
37 J2 **Terrazas** Brazil
146 D15 **Terre Adélie** Antarctica
100 D5 **Terrebonne** Oregon U.S.A.
111 F12 **Terrebonne B** Louisiana U.S.A.
127 N5 **Terre de Bas** isld Guadeloupe W Indies
127 N5 **Terre de Haut** isld Guadeloupe W Indies
110 J2 **Terre Haute** Indiana U.S.A.
109 L3 **Terrell** Texas U.S.A.
123 S6 **Terrenceville** Newfoundland Canada
101 N6 **Terreton** Idaho U.S.A.
20 H3 **Terrette** R France
139 K5 **Terrigal** New South Wales Australia
40 F3 **Terri, M** Switzerland
9 F4 **Terril** England
120 H10 **Terrington** England
68 C5 **Terry** Mississippi U.S.A.
101 U5 **Terry** Montana U.S.A.
55 E6 **Tersakkan** R Kazakhstan
25 D2 **Terschelling** isld Netherlands
25 D2 **Terschellinger Wad** Netherlands
120 J10 **Tersef** Chad
57 H4 **Terskey Ala-Too Khrebet** mts Kyrgyzstan
52 E2 **Terskiy Bereg** coast Russian Federation
43 C9 **Tertenia** Sardinia
17 G4 **Teru-Aygyr** Kyrgyzstan
142 D4 **Teruel** prov Spain
141 K6 **Teruel** Spain
141 K6 **Tervel** Bulgaria
29 L5 **Tervola** Finland
22 H2 **Tervuren** Belgium
42 H4 **Tesanj** Bosnia-Herzegovina
107 N2 **Tescott** Kansas U.S.A.
86 G1 **Teseney** Ethiopia
76 D5 **Teshikaga** Japan
60 H11 **Te-shima** isld Japan
60 R7 **Teshio** R Japan
60 Q2 **Teshio-dake** mt Japan
60 P1 **Teshio-sanchi** mts Japan
40 D1 **Tesin** France
46 F6 **Thaon** France
21 N5 **Thaon les Vosages** France
68 E4 **Tha Pla** Thailand
68 D7 **Thapsake** Thailand
73 L3 **Thar** desert India
37 G2 **Tharandt** Germany
74 D5 **Thar Desert** India
141 G8 **Thargomindah** Queensland Australia
25 E4 **Tharrawaddy** Burma
68 B4 **Tharrawaw** Burma
78 J5 **Thásos** isld Greece
9 F4 **Thatcham** England
94 H7 **Thatcher** Arizona U.S.A.
106 F4 **Thatcher** Colorado U.S.A.
101 O7 **Thatcher** Idaho U.S.A.
67 B5 **Thatha** Pakistan
68 C4 **That Khe** Vietnam
68 B5 **Thaton** Burma
68 E4 **Tha Tum** Thailand
18 H8 **Thau, Étang de** France
67 H8 **Thauryin** R Thailand
68 C6 **Thayawthadang-yi Kyun** isld Burma
144 D5 **Thayer** Missouri U.S.A.
110 H8 **Thaye** Burma
110 E5 **Thayetmyaung** Burma
68 B3 **Thayetmyo** Burma
101 P7 **Thayne** Wyoming U.S.A.
68 A3 **Thazi** Arakan Burma
68 B2 **Thazi** Magwe Burma
68 B2 **Thazi** Mandalay Burma
9 E5 **Theale** England
103 M9 **Theba** Arizona U.S.A.

121 T6 **Thetford Mines** Quebec Canada
75 P5 **Tezpur** India
87 E11 **Thaba Ntlenyana** mt Lesotho
89 F7 **Thaba Putsoa** mt Lesotho
84 D1 **Thabazimbi** S Africa
68 C1 **Thabeikkyin** Burma
79 E10 **Thabt, G. el** mt Egypt
68 C2 **Thabyedaung** Burma
109 K2 **Thackerville** Oklahoma
67 B6 **Thai Binh** Vietnam
68 H4 **Thai Duong Thung** Vietnam
68 H3 **Thai Hoa** Vietnam
68 E5 **Thailand** S E Asia
67 D8 **Thailand, G. of** Thailand
68 D8 **Thai Muang** Thailand
69 D8 **Tha Nguyen** Vietnam
69 D8 **Tha Khanon** Thailand
68 G4 **Thakhek** Laos
74 D2 **Thal** Pakistan
85 F1 **Thala** Tunisia
69 D8 **Thalang** Thailand
66 F6 **Thala Pass** China/Burma
33 O9 **Thale** Germany
69 E9 **Thale Luang** Thailand
37 M3 **Thalfang** Germany
85 A6 **Thalgau** Austria
43 B8 **Thalheim** Germany
41 K4 **Thalkirch** Switzerland
141 J8 **Thallon** Queensland Australia
112 F6 **Thalmann** Georgia U.S.A.
73 L7 **Thaladunmathi Atoll** Maldives
21 O3 **Thilliers-en-Vexin, les** France
40 E2 **Thillot, le** France
21 N4 **Thimert-Gâtelles** France
75 N5 **Thimphu** Bhutan
22 D5 **Thingeyri** Iceland
28 R9 **Thingvellir** Iceland
103 N3 **Thousand Lake Mt** Utah U.S.A.
102 F7 **Thousand Oaks** California U.S.A.
121 O8 **Thousand Spring Cr** Nevada U.S.A.
101 L8 **Thousand Springs** Idaho U.S.A.
101 L7 **Thrace** Turkey
47 H3 **Thrall** Washington U.S.A.
100 K5 **Thrapston** England
9 G2 **Thirty Thousand Is** Ontario Canada
120 K7 **Thiruvananthapuram** see Trivandrum
8 C3 **Thisted** co see Viborg co
101 K7 **Three Cocks** Wales
101 O4 **Three Forks** Montana U.S.A.
118 D7 **Three Hills** Alberta Canada
101 O10 **Three Hummock I** Tasmania
117 J9 **Three I.Res** Tennessee U.S.A.
9 F2 **Threekingham** England
137 O8 **Three Kings Is** Bay Pacific Oc
68 B1 **Thitseingyi** Burma
68 F6 **Thivai** Greece
21 N5 **Thivars** France
140 D3 **Three Knobs** mt N Terr Australia
99 R4 **Three Lakes** Wisconsin U.S.A.
141 G2 **Three Mile Opening, First & Second** straits Gt Barrier Reef Aust
99 U8 **Three Oaks** Michigan U.S.A.
68 D5 **Three Pagodas Pass** Burma/Thailand
119 U3 **Threepoint L** Manitoba Canada

102 F3 **Thorne** Nevada U.S.A.
9 F2 **Thorney** England
12 D1 **Thornhill** Central Scotland
12 E3 **Thornhill** Dumfries & Galloway Scotland
13 E6 **Thornton** Scotland
67 B4 **Thornton** England
109 P2 **Thornton** Arkansas U.S.A.
106 F2 **Thornton** Colorado U.S.A.
99 N7 **Thornton** Iowa U.S.A.
109 L4 **Thornton** Texas U.S.A.
100 C4 **Thornton** Washington U.S.A.
141 F4 **Thorntonia** Queensland Australia
65 H3 **Tianqiaoling** China
110 K1 **Thorntown** Indiana U.S.A.
138 D6 **Thorny Passage** South Australia Australia
66 C3 **Tian Shan** ra China/Kazakhstan
58 E5 **Tianshui** China
67 G2 **Tiantai** China
67 B5 **Tianyang** China
120 Q5 **Thorp** Wisconsin U.S.A.
145 D4 **Thorpe Ness** England
28 E4 **Thorsager** Denmark
67 C3 **Thorsby** Alberta Canada
134 C11 **Thorshavnfjella** mts Antarctica
29 T8 **Thôrshôfn** Iceland
94 D2 **Thornsville** Wisconsin U.S.A.
119 U1 **Thorsteinson L** Manitoba Canada
13 E3 **Tibbie Shiels Inn** Scotland
68 G7 **Thorverton** England
21 K8 **Thot Not** Vietnam
21 K8 **Thouarcé** France
21 J7 **Thouaret** R France
21 J8 **Thouars** France
21 J8 **Thouarsais-Bouildroux** France
121 N4 **Thouet, R** W Australia
142 C5 **Thouin, C** W Australia Australia
46 E7 **Thouria** Greece
20 H6 **Thourie** France
22 D5 **Thourotte** France
95 L2 **Thousand Is** Ontario/New York Canada/U.S.A.
9 G5 **Thousand Is** isld Philippines
110 H1 **Ticha, Yazovir** res Bulgaria
121 O8 **Tichborne** Ontario Canada
45 E4 **Tichitt** Mauritania
44 E1 **Tichla** Western Sahara
41 J5 **Ticino** canton Switzerland
9 E2 **Tickhill** England
139 L11 **Ticknall** England
46 H6 **Ticleni** Romania
95 O3 **Ticonderoga** New York U.S.A.
27 G13 **Tidaholm** Sweden
122 F6 **Tide Hd** New Brunswick Canada
118 F8 **Tide L** Alberta Canada
69 A9 **Tiden** Nicobar Is
100 B5 **Tidewater** Oregon U.S.A.
85 E3 **Tidikelt** reg Algeria
94 H5 **Tidioute** Pennsylvania U.S.A.
85 B4 **Tidjikja** Mauritania
123 M3 **Tidnish** Nova Scotia Canada
42 A2 **Tidone** R Italy
74 A2 **Tidore** Halmahera Indonesia
85 A5 **Tidra, I** Mauritania
9 E5 **Tidworth** England
85 C7 **Tiébissou** Ivory Coast
85 D7 **Tiefenbach** Germany
65 G1 **Tieli** China
122 E6 **Tiekel** Alaska U.S.A.
25 D5 **Tiel** Netherlands
67 B4 **Ti China**
73 W8 **Tien Berg** mt S Africa
21 K6 **Tien Yen** Vietnam
27 J11 **Tierp** Sweden
106 D5 **Tierra** New Mexico U.S.A.
125 L8 **Tierra Blanca** Mexico
133 D8 **Tierra del Fuego, I.Grande** de Arg/Chile
101 O9 **Tie Siding** Wyoming U.S.A.
16 D4 **Tiétar** R Spain
130 E7 **Tietê** Brazil
130 E7 **Tietê** Brazil
101 N9 **Tietkens, Mt** South Australia Australia
100 D5 **Tieton** Washington U.S.A.
100 D3 **Tieton Res** Washington U.S.A.
138 C2 **Tieyon** South Australia Australia

139 K4 **Tia** New South Wales Australia
127 J9 **Tia Juana** Venezuela
65 G3 **Tianboashan** China
21 O5 **Tilay le Peneux** France
67 B5 **Tiandong** China
40 B3 **Tille** R France
53 F12 **Tianeti** Georgia
57 C4 **Tianhe** China
118 F8 **Tianjin** China
82 E5 **Tianjin** China
58 C4 **Tianjun** China
67 B4 **Tianlin** China
21 H7 **Tianmen** China
21 N4 **Tianlières-sur-Avre** France
28 G7 **Tia see Ar Horquin Qi**
112 F5 **Tianqiaoling** China
113 L11 **Tilago Cay** isld Bahamas
13 G2 **Till, R** England
120 K10 **Tilbury** Ontario Canada
21 J3 **Tilly-sur-Seulles** France
71 M9 **Tilos** mt Sulawesi
47 J8 **Tilos** isld Greece
19 G4 **Tilpa** New South Wales Australia
85 E2 **Tilrhemt** Algeria
9 E5 **Tilshead** England
119 Q9 **Tilston** Manitoba Canada
123 S4 **Tilting** Newfoundland Canada
110 J1 **Tilton** Illinois U.S.A.
95 Q3 **Tilton** New Hampshire U.S.A.
28 A4 **Tim** Denmark
54 J5 **Tim** Russian Federation
121 L5 **Timagami** Ontario Canada
52 G2 **Timanskiy Kryazh** ra Russian Federation
144 C6 **Timaru** New Zealand
53 E10 **Timashevsk** Russian Federation
46 G9 **Timbalou** Crete Greece
111 F12 **Timbalier I** Louisiana U.S.A.
70 F2 **Timbang** Sabah
130 C3 **Timbaúba** Brazil
130 J5 **Timbedra** Mauritania
100 B4 **Timber** Oregon U.S.A.
140 B3 **Timber Creek Police Station** N Terr Australia
98 K4 **Timber L** South Dakota U.S.A.
112 J1 **Timberlake** North Carolina U.S.A.
139 G7 **Timboon** Victoria Australia
130 C10 **Timbó** Brazil
Timbuktu see Tombouctou
71 B8 **Timbun Mata** Sabah
85 E5 **Timeliouline** Algeria
85 D5 **Timetrine Mts** Mali
47 H1 **Timfi, Oros** mt Greece
46 E6 **Timfristós** mt Greece
138 C4 **Timia** Niger
85 E3 **Timimoun** Algeria
57 E3 **Timirmannya Kazakhstan**
56 B3 **Timiryazevskiy** Russian Federation
48 G7 **Timiş** R Romania
48 C6 **Timişoara** Romania
55 L1 **Timkapaul'** Russian Federation
33 N5 **Timmendorfer Strand** Germany
27 G13 **Timmernabo** Sweden
85 F5 **Timmersoi** watercourse Niger
115 P5 **Timmiarmiut** Greenland
120 J4 **Timmins** Ontario Canada
112 H3 **Timmonsville** South Carolina U.S.A.
109 M9 **Timpie** Utah U.S.A.
141 L5 **Timpson** Texas U.S.A.
28 B4 **Timra** Sweden
28 B4 **Timring** Denmark
110 K6 **Tim's Ford L** Tennessee U.S.A.
112 A2 **Tims Ford L** Tennessee U.S.A.
54 H4 **Timsher** Russian Federation
57 E3 **Timur** Kazakhstan
70 G9 **Timur, Jawa** prov Java
61 M8 **Timur** Russian Federation
139 H7 **Timumu Headland** New South Wales Australia
141 L7 **Tina** R S Africa
89 F8 **Tina Pt** Mindanao Philippines
127 K10 **Tinaca** Venezuela
127 J3 **Tinaga** isld Philippines
71 G5 **Tinah Bay** England
124 H5 **Tinajas** Mexico
137 O4 **Tinakula** isld Santa Cruz Is
85 D1 **Tin Alkoum** Algeria
127 K10 **Tinaquillo** Venezuela
48 G4 **Tinca** Romania
141 L7 **Tin Can Bay** Queensland Australia
21 J4 **Tinchebray** France
100 K7 **Tincques** France
76 D4 **Tindivanam** India
70 A9 **Tindjil** isld Java
85 C3 **Tindouf** Algeria
85 E4 **Tine** Sudan
85 E4 **Tinef** Algeria
102 H2 **Tinemaha Res** California U.S.A.
16 C1 **Tineo** Spain
85 F5 **Tinfouchy** Algeria
85 F5 **Tin Fouye** Algeria
70 B4 **Tingah** New South Wales Australia
45 F5 **Tinggi** isld Malaysia
85 D4 **Tinghsia** Nepal
28 C7 **Tinglev** Denmark
67 G3 **Tingo María** Peru
67 B5 **Tingping** China
86 C6 **Tingréla** Ivory Coast
66 D6 **Tingri** China
59 G15 **Tingsjao** China
144 A7 **Tinguiririca** mt Chile/Arg
133 D8 **Tinian** isld Marianas
85 D7 **Tinstane, Mt** W Australia Australia
121 T7 **Tingwick** Quebec Canada
138 F8 **Tin Tarabine** watercourse Algeria

20 G5 **Tinténiac** France
8 D4 **Tintern** England
22 K4 **Tintigny** Belgium
133 E3 **Tintina** Argentina
138 F6 **Tintinara** South Australia Australia
16 C7 **Tinto** *R* Spain
15 E5 **Tinto, Mt** Scotland
145 F4 **Tinui** New Zealand
144 C5 **Tinwald** New Zealand
85 E4 **Tin Zaouaten** Algeria/Mali
86 H3 **T'i'o** Ethiopia
111 D10 **Tioga** Louisiana U.S.A.
98 D1 **Tioga** North Dakota U.S.A.
95 K5 **Tioga** Pennsylvania U.S.A.
109 L2 **Tioga** Texas U.S.A.
94 G8 **Tioga** West Virginia U.S.A.
69 G11 **Tioman** *isld* Malaysia
120 H4 **Tionaga** Ontario Canada
41 N5 **Tione** Italy
42 D2 **Tione di Trento** Italy
100 D8 **Tionesta** California U.S.A.
94 H5 **Tionesta** Pennsylvania U.S.A.
94 A5 **Tippecanoe** Indiana U.S.A.
99 U9 **Tippecanoe** *R* Indiana U.S.A.
14 C4 **Tipperary** Ireland
14 D4 **Tipperary** *co* Ireland
111 F8 **Tippo** Mississippi U.S.A.
102 E5 **Tipton** California U.S.A.
110 K1 **Tipton** Indiana U.S.A.
107 M2 **Tipton** Kansas U.S.A.
110 D3 **Tipton** Missouri U.S.A.
109 H1 **Tipton** Oklahoma U.S.A.
103 K6 **Tipton, Mt** Arizona U.S.A.
110 G5 **Tiptonville** Tennessee U.S.A.
120 D4 **Tip Top Hill** Ontario Canada
9 G4 **Tiptree** England
76 C4 **Tiptur** India
128 E3 **Tiquié** *R* Brazil
80 C5 **Tira** Israel
129 J4 **Tiracambu, Sa.do** *mts* Brazil
79 E11 **Tirān** *isld* Saudi Arabia
46 D3 **Tiranë** Albania
41 M5 **Tirano** Italy
83 K9 **Tirappane** Sri Lanka
53 C10 **Tiraspol'** Moldavia
80 C2 **Tirat Karmel** Israel
80 F4 **Tirat Zevi** Israel
145 E2 **Tirau** New Zealand
145 F4 **Tiraumea** New Zealand
47 J6 **Tire** Turkey
78 G1 **Tirebolu** Turkey
15 B4 **Tiree** *isld* Scotland
85 B4 **Tires** *reg* Western Sahara
48 J6 **Tîrgovişte** Romania
48 L5 **Tîrgu Bujor** Romania
48 H6 **Tîrgu Cărbuneşti** Romania
48 L3 **Tîrgu Frumos** Romania
48 H5 **Tîrgu Jiu** Romania
48 H3 **Tîrgu Lăpuş** Romania
48 J4 **Tîrgu Mureş** Romania
48 K3 **Tîrgu Neamt** Romania
48 K4 **Tîrgu Ocna** Romania
48 K4 **Tîrgu Secuiesc** Romania
47 K4 **Tirilye** Turkey
145 E2 **Tiritiri** New Zealand
Tirlemont *see* **Tienen**
55 C4 **Tirlyanskiy** Russian Federation
48 J4 **Tîrnava Mare** *R* Romania
48 J4 **Tîrnava Mică** *R* Romania
48 J4 **Tîrnăveni** Romania
46 E5 **Tirnavos** Greece
94 E6 **Tiro** Ohio U.S.A.
38 F8 **Tirol** *prov* Austria
41 O4 **Tirolo** Italy
80 C6 **Tirosh** Israel
86 D4 **Tiroungoulou** Cent Afr Republic
45 H4 **Tirrenia** Italy
37 N4 **Tirschenreuth** Germany
43 B8 **Tirso** *R* Sardinia
43 B8 **Tirso, L. del** Sardinia
28 G7 **Tirsted** Denmark
131 A7 **Tirua, Pta** Chile
76 D6 **Tiruchchendur** India
76 D5 **Tiruchchirāppalli** India
83 L10 **Tirukkovil** Sri Lanka
76 C6 **Tirunelveli** India
128 D5 **Tiruntán** Peru
76 D4 **Tirupati** India
76 D4 **Tiruppattur** India
76 C5 **Tiruppur** India
76 D4 **Tiruvannamalai** India
48 H2 **Tisa** *R* Ukraine
119 N6 **Tisdale** Saskatchewan Canada
111 H7 **Tishomingo** Mississippi U.S.A.
109 L1 **Tishomingo** Oklahoma U.S.A.
79 G6 **Ţisīyah** Syria
99 R8 **Tiskilwa** Illinois U.S.A.
28 C6 **Tislund** Denmark
27 H13 **Tisnaren** *L* Sweden
31 J6 **Tišnov** Czechoslovakia
48 F2 **Tisovec** Czechoslovakia
83 L11 **Tissamaharama** Sri Lanka
9 E1 **Tissington** England
27 E12 **Tistedal** Norway
48 F3 **Tisza** *R* Hungary
48 F4 **Tiszaföldvár** Hungary
31 N8 **Tiszavasvari** Hungary
85 E3 **Tit** Algeria
116 K2 **Titaluk** *R* Alaska U.S.A.
146 E9 **Titan Dome** *ice dome* Antarctica
9 E6 **Titchfield** England
128 E7 **Titicaca, L** Peru/Bolivia
116 L4 **Titna** *R* Alaska U.S.A.
Titograd *see* **Podgorica**
99 M6 **Titonka** Iowa U.S.A.
52 D1 **Titovka** *R* Russian Federation
26 C8 **Titran** Norway
94 C3 **Tittabawassee** *R* Michigan U.S.A.
37 L6 **Titting** Germany
38 G5 **Tittmoning** Germany
48 K6 **Titu** Romania
86 E5 **Titule** Zaire
113 G9 **Titusville** Florida U.S.A.
94 H5 **Titusville** Pennsylvania U.S.A.
85 A6 **Tivaouane** Senegal
27 G13 **Tived** Sweden
122 F9 **Tiverton** Nova Scotia Canada
120 J8 **Tiverton** Ontario Canada
8 C6 **Tiverton** England
95 Q5 **Tiverton** Rhode I U.S.A.
45 N6 **Tivoli** Italy
95 O4 **Tivoli** New York U.S.A.
109 L7 **Tivoli** Texas U.S.A.
70 G5 **Tiwad** Sulawesi
71 H7 **Tiworo, Selat** *str* Indonesia
68 D6 **Ti-ywa** Burma
124 H7 **Tizapán el Alto** Mexico
17 H9 **Tizi** Algeria
16 E10 **Tizi-Ifri** Morocco
125 P7 **Tizimin** Mexico
85 C3 **Tiznit** Morocco
124 J5 **Tizoc** Mexico
16 E10 **Tiztoutine** Morocco
28 B6 **Tjæreborg** Denmark
28 G6 **Tjæreby** Denmark
27 H13 **Tjällmo** Sweden
70 L9 **Tjamara** Java
26 K5 **Tjåmotis** Sweden
71 L10 **Tjamplong** Timor Indonesia
70 K9 **Tjankuang Tg** *C* Java
26 L4 **Tjårro Keble** *mt* Sweden
26 J5 **Tjeggelvas** *L* Sweden
26 H3 **Tjeldöy** *isld* Norway
28 D3 **Tjele** Denmark
70 D4 **Tjemaru, G** *mt* Kalimantan
71 J9 **Tjempi, Teluk** *B* Sumbawa Indonesia
70 F6 **Tjenrana** Sulawesi
70 N9 **Tjepu** Java
70 M9 **Tjereme** *mt* Java
25 E3 **Tjeuke Meer** Netherlands
70 L9 **Tjiandjur** Java
70 L9 **Tjibadak** Java
70 L9 **Tjibatu** Java
70 L9 **Tjibuni** *R* Java
70 M9 **Tjidjulang** Java
70 L9 **Tjidua** Java
70 L9 **Tjihara** Java
70 L9 **Tjikadjang** Java
70 L9 **Tjikampek** Java
70 M9 **Tjilatjap** Java
70 M9 **Tjiledug** Java
70 L9 **Tjimahi** Java
70 G6 **Tjimpu** Sulawesi
70 K8 **Tjina, Tg** *C* Sumatra
70 M9 **Tjipatudjah** Java
70 M9 **Tjirebon** Java
70 L9 **Tjitarum** *R* Java
27 E12 **Tjöme** *isld* Norway
27 E13 **Tjörn** *isld* Sweden
28 B4 **Tjørring** Denmark
26 F6 **Tjötta** Norway
53 F11 **Tkvarcheli** Georgia
125 L9 **Tlacolula de Matamoros** Mexico
125 M8 **Tlacotalpan** Mexico
125 K8 **Tlalnepantla** Mexico
125 K8 **Tlálpam** Mexico
68 A1 **Tlangtlang** Burma
125 L8 **Tlapacoyán** Mexico
124 H7 **Tlaquepaque** Mexico
125 K8 **Tlaxcala** Mexico
85 D2 **Tlemcen** Algeria
85 E5 **Tlemcès** Niger
48 J2 **Tlumach** Ukraine
31 N3 **Tłuszcz** Poland
52 E6 **T'ma** *R* Russian Federation
84 F4 **Tmassah** Libya
85 D4 **Tni Haïa** Algeria
68 C4 **To** *R* Burma
126 G4 **Toa** *R* Cuba
117 L6 **Toad River** British Columbia Canada
87 H11 **Toamasina** Madagascar
101 L9 **Toana** *mt ra* Nevada U.S.A.
45 J3 **Toano** Italy
95 L9 **Toano** Virginia U.S.A.
145 F3 **Toatoa** New Zealand
133 E5 **Toay** Argentina
70 F5 **Toaya** Sulawesi
61 K11 **Toba** Japan
69 D11 **Toba, Danau** *L* Sumatra
127 M1 **Tobago** *isld* W Indies
117 L10 **Toba Inlet** British Columbia Canada
77 K4 **Toba & Kakar Ranges** Pakistan
78 G4 **Tobaqah** Syria
101 L9 **Tobar** Nevada U.S.A.
17 F6 **Tobarra** Spain
60 D12 **Tobata** Japan
14 C2 **Tobbercurry** Ireland
71 H7 **Tobea** *isld* Indonesia
140 E5 **Tobermorey** N Terr Australia
141 G7 **Tobermory** Queensland Australia
120 J7 **Tobermory** Ontario Canada
15 B4 **Tobermory** Scotland
60 P2 **Tōbetsu** Japan
98 J9 **Tobias** Nebraska U.S.A.
61 N14 **Tobiishi-hana** *C* Iwo Jima Japan
115 R3 **Tobin, Kap** *C* Greenland
142 F5 **Tobin,L** W Australia Australia
119 O5 **Tobin L** Saskatchewan Canada
102 G1 **Tobin, Mt** Nevada U.S.A.
122 E6 **Tobique R** New Brunswick Canada
61 N6 **Tobi-shima** *isld* Japan
69 H14 **Toboali** Indonesia
55 D4 **Tobol** Kazakhstan
55 E2 **Tobol'sk** Russian Federation
68 J6 **To Bong** Vietnam
71 F5 **Toboso** Negros Philippines
Tobruk *see* **Tubruq**
95 M5 **Tobyhanna** Pennsylvania U.S.A.
52 H2 **Tobysh** *R* Russian Federation
52 H3 **Tobysh** Russian Federation
129 J5 **Tocantínia** Brazil
129 J5 **Tocantinópolis** Brazil
129 J4 **Tocantins** *R* Brazil
129 J6 **Tocantins** *state* Brazil
112 D3 **Toccoa** Georgia U.S.A.
41 H5 **Toce** *R* Italy
61 N9 **Tochigi** Japan
61 M8 **Tochio** Japan
133 D2 **Toco** Chile
133 C2 **Tocopilla** Chile
133 D2 **Tocorpuri** *mt* Chile/Bolivia
139 H6 **Tocumwal** New South Wales Australia
127 K9 **Tocuyo** *R* Venezuela
127 K9 **Tocuyo de la Costa** Venezuela
74 F5 **Toda** India
26 C9 **Todal** Norway
116 L3 **Todatonten** Alaska U.S.A.
140 B2 **Todd,Mt** N Terr Australia
122 F7 **Todd Mt** New Brunswick Canada
140 C6 **Todd R** N Terr Australia
143 F7 **Todd Ra** W Australia Australia
32 M5 **Todesfelde** Germany
13 F1 **Todhills** Scotland
42 E6 **Todi** Italy
41 J4 **Tödi** *mt* Switzerland
138 C2 **Todmorden** South Australia Australia
13 F6 **Todmorden** England
61 Q6 **Todoga-saki** *C* Japan
60 P4 **Todohokke** Japan
131 A8 **Todos los Santos, L** Chile
129 L6 **Todos os Santos, B. de** Brazil
124 D6 **Todos Santos** Mexico
56 E5 **Todzha, Oz** *L* Russian Federation
14 B5 **Toe Hd** Ireland
68 D5 **Toe Jaga, Khao** *mt* Burma/Thailand
144 B7 **Toetoes B** New Zealand
118 E5 **Tofield** Alberta Canada
117 L11 **Tofino** British Columbia Canada
26 F9 **Töfsingdalens Nat. Park** Sweden
27 F14 **Tofta** Sweden
27 E12 **Tofte** Norway
28 C6 **Toftlund** Denmark
116 M4 **Tofty** Alaska U.S.A.
137 R5 **Tofua** *isld* Tonga
Tōfutsu *see* **Sernovodsk**
61 O10 **Tōgane** Japan
41 H5 **Togano, Monte** Italy
41 K3 **Toggenburg** *mt* Switzerland
61 K8 **Togi** Japan
116 G7 **Togiak** Alaska U.S.A.
70 G5 **Togian Kep** *isld* Sulawesi
37 O7 **Töging** Germany
60 C13 **Togitsu** Japan
86 G2 **Togni** Sudan
119 Q7 **Togo** Saskatchewan Canada
85 E7 **Togo** *rep* W Africa
Togrog Ul *see* **Qahar Youyi Qianqi**
65 B4 **Togtoh** China
61 P12 **Toguchi** Okinawa
56 B3 **Toguchin** Russian Federation
56 E4 **Togul'skiy Khrebet** *mts* Russian Federation
57 B2 **Togyz** Kazakhstan
102 E1 **Tohakum Pk** Nevada U.S.A.
74 F4 **Tohana** India
106 B6 **Tohatchi** New Mexico U.S.A.
70 C4 **Tohenbatu** *mt* Sarawak
134 A11 **Tohiea** *pk* Moorea Pacific Oc
29 P9 **Tohmajärvi** Finland
29 L8 **Toholampi** Finland
113 F9 **Tohopekaliga, L** Florida U.S.A.
61 M11 **Toi** Japan
68 A7 **Toibalewe** Andaman Is
29 K10 **Toijala** Finland
71 H5 **Toili** Sulawesi
99 P2 **Toimi** Minnesota U.S.A.
60 E14 **Toi-misaki** Japan
71 L10 **Toineke** Indonesia
29 K9 **Toisvesi** *L* Finland
29 M9 **Toivakka** Finland
99 S3 **Toivola** Michigan U.S.A.
102 G2 **Toiyabe Ra** Nevada U.S.A.
70 G5 **Toja** Sulawesi
60 G11 **Tōjō** Japan
30 H6 **Tok** *mt* Czechoslovakia
145 E3 **Tokaanu** New Zealand
60 R2 **Tokachi** *prefect* Japan
60 Q2 **Tokachi dake** *mt* Japan
48 G2 **Tokajo** Hungary
70 G5 **Tokala, G** *mt* Sulawesi
61 M8 **Tōkamachi** Japan
144 B7 **Tokanui** New Zealand
86 G2 **Tokar** Sudan
59 J5 **Tokara-retto** *islds* Japan
55 F5 **Tokarevka** Kazakhstan
52 D4 **Tokari** Russian Federation
52 G5 **Tokarikha** Russian Federation
78 F1 **Tokat** Turkey
145 D2 **Tokatoka** New Zealand
65 F6 **Tŏkchŏk-kundo** *B* S Korea
70 G6 **Toke** Sulawesi
134 K9 **Tokelau** *islds* Pacific Oc
101 P9 **Tokewanna Pk** Utah U.S.A.
56 E1 **Tokhoma** *R* Russian Federation
61 L10 **Toki** Japan
98 H2 **Tokio** North Dakota U.S.A.
116 Q5 **Tok Junc** Alaska U.S.A.
27 D12 **Tokke-Vatn** *L* Norway
116 M4 **Toklat** Alaska U.S.A.
Tokmak *see* **Eşme**
57 H3 **Tokmak** Kyrgyzstan
54 G9 **Tokmak** Ukraine
145 E3 **Toko** New Zealand
145 E4 **Tokomaru** New Zealand
145 G3 **Tokomaru Bay** New Zealand
60 S1 **Tokoro** Japan
145 E3 **Tokoroa** New Zealand
84 G3 **Tokrah** Libya
57 H1 **Tokrau** *R* Kazakhstan
52 E3 **Toksha-Kuznetsova** Russian Federation
66 D3 **Toksun** China
59 K4 **Tok-to** *isld* Japan/Korea
57 G4 **Toktogul Vdkhr** Kyrgyzstan
57 G5 **Toktomush** Tajikistan
57 K2 **Tokty** Kazakhstan
59 K1 **Tokur** Russian Federation
60 H11 **Tokushima** Japan
60 E11 **Tokuyama** Japan
89 G3 **Tokwe** *R* Zimbabwe
62 **Tōkyō** *conurbation* Japan
61 N10 **Tōkyō-wan** *B* Japan
77 K2 **Tokzār** Afghanistan
145 G3 **Tolaga Bay** New Zealand
87 H13 **Tôlañaro** Madagascar
106 G7 **Tolar** New Mexico U.S.A.
109 K3 **Tolar** Texas U.S.A.
78 K1 **Tolavi** Georgia
55 C4 **Tolbazy** Russian Federation
Tolbukhin *see* **Dobrich**
130 D9 **Toledo** Brazil
133 C3 **Toledo** Chile
16 E5 **Toledo** *prov* Spain
16 E5 **Toledo** Spain
110 H2 **Toledo** Illinois U.S.A.
99 O7 **Toledo** Iowa U.S.A.
94 D5 **Toledo** Ohio U.S.A.
100 B5 **Toledo** Oregon U.S.A.
100 C3 **Toledo** Washington U.S.A.
109 O4 **Toledo Bend Res** Louisiana U.S.A.
16 D5 **Toledo, Montes de** *mts* Spain
42 E5 **Tolentino** Italy
44 L5 **Tolfa, Mt.della** Italy
27 G14 **Tolg** Sweden
26 E9 **Tolga** Norway
87 G12 **Toliara** Madagascar
128 C3 **Tolima** *vol* Colombia
128 C3 **Tolima** *div* Colombia
70 G4 **Tolitoli** Sulawesi
27 G16 **Tollarp** Sweden
33 S5 **Tollense** *R* Germany
33 S5 **Tollensesee** *L* Germany
103 M8 **Tolleson** Arizona U.S.A.
98 E1 **Tolley** North Dakota U.S.A.
102 E4 **Tollhouse** California U.S.A.
28 H5 **Tølløse** Denmark
52 C5 **Tolmachevo** Russian Federation
42 E2 **Tolmezzo** Italy
42 F2 **Tolmin** Slovenia
48 E4 **Tolna** *co* Hungary
48 E4 **Tolna** Hungary
28 E2 **Tolne** Denmark
86 C6 **Tolo** Zaire
54 A2 **Tolochin** Belorussia
110 H2 **Tolono** Illinois U.S.A.
17 F1 **Tolosa** Spain
116 N4 **Tolovana** *R* Alaska U.S.A.
65 G7 **Tolsan** *isld* S Korea
15 B2 **Tolsta Head** Scotland
48 K2 **Tolstoye** Ukraine
103 N9 **Toltec** Arizona U.S.A.
133 C5 **Toltén** Chile
131 A7 **Toltén, R** Chile
126 G10 **Tolú** Colombia
125 K8 **Toluca** Mexico
99 R8 **Toluca** Illinois U.S.A.
29 P5 **Tolvand, Ozero** *L* Russian Federation
52 D4 **Tolvayarvi** Russian Federation
52 E4 **Tolvuya** Russian Federation
55 A4 **Tol'yatti** Russian Federation
55 D5 **Tolybay** Kazakhstan
56 B3 **Tom'** *R* Russian Federation
99 Q6 **Tomah** Wisconsin U.S.A.
99 R4 **Tomahawk** Wisconsin U.S.A.
60 P3 **Tomakomai** Japan
70 G5 **Tomali** Sulawesi
60 P1 **Tomamae** Japan
128 F4 **Tomar** Brazil
57 H2 **Tomar** Kazakhstan
16 B5 **Tomar** Portugal
Tomari *see* **Golovnino**
60 N3 **Tomari** Japan
59 M2 **Tomari** Russian Federation
46 D1 **Tomaševo** Montenegro Yugoslavia
31 O4 **Tomashevka** Ukraine
48 M2 **Tomashpol'** Ukraine
130 E8 **Tomasina** Brazil
31 O5 **Tomaszów Lubelski** Poland
31 M4 **Tomaszów Mazowiecka** Poland
15 D3 **Tomatin** Scotland
124 G8 **Tomatlán** Mexico
38 O9 **Tomaz** Slovenia
31 O4 **Tomazy** Poland
109 M5 **Tomball** Texas U.S.A.
60 F10 **Tombara** Japan
86 F4 **Tombe** Sudan
111 H8 **Tombigbee** *R* Mississippi U.S.A.
71 H5 **Tombila** *mt* Sulawesi
87 B7 **Tomboco** Angola
130 G7 **Tombos** Brazil
85 D5 **Tombouctou** Mali
103 O10 **Tombstone** Arizona U.S.A.
87 B9 **Tombua** Angola
131 A6 **Tome** Chile
71 J7 **Tomea** *isld* Indonesia
27 G16 **Tomelilla** Sweden
57 D3 **Tomenaryk** Kazakhstan
80 E5 **Tomer** Jordan
121 L6 **Tomiko** Ontario Canada
139 J4 **Tomingley** New South Wales Australia
70 G4 **Tomini** Sulawesi
70 G5 **Tomini, Teluk** *B* Sulawesi
15 E3 **Tomintoul** Scotland
61 O8 **Tomioka** Japan
42 H5 **Tomislavgrad** Yugoslavia
143 G7 **Tomkinson Ras** S/W Australia Australia
26 F5 **Tomma** *isld* Norway
28 C2 **Tømmerby** Denmark
28 E6 **Tommerup** Denmark
51 M3 **Tommot** Russian Federation
128 E2 **Tomo** *R* Colombia
60 G11 **Tomo** Japan
124 F3 **Tomóchic** Mexico
60 H11 **Tomogashima-suidō** *str* Japan
70 G6 **Tompira** Sulawesi
118 J8 **Tompkins** Saskatchewan Canada
94 C4 **Tompkins Center** Michigan U.S.A.
110 L5 **Tompkinsville** Kentucky U.S.A.
70 F5 **Tompo** Sulawesi
143 C6 **Tom Price** W Australia Australia
142 C6 **Tom Price,Mt** W Australia Australia
66 D5 **Tomra** China
86 H4 **Tomsa** Ethiopia
56 C3 **Tomsk** Russian Federation
56 B2 **Tomskaya Oblast** *prov* Russian Federation
83 M9 **Tom's Ridge** Christmas I Indian Oc
95 N6 **Toms River** New Jersey U.S.A.
Tömük *see* **Elvanlı**
60 Q2 **Tomuraushi yama** *mt* Japan
Tomur Feng *see* **Pobedy, Pik**
116 Q6 **Tom White, Mt** Alaska U.S.A.
124 F4 **Tónachic** Mexico
125 N9 **Tonalá** Mexico
103 O5 **Tonalea** Arizona U.S.A.
42 D2 **Tonale, Pso. di** Italy
61 K9 **Tonami** Japan
128 E4 **Tonantins** Brazil
100 F1 **Tonasket** Washington U.S.A.
121 M9 **Tonawanda** New York U.S.A.
9 G5 **Tonbridge** England
60 J12 **Tonda** Japan
71 J4 **Tondano** Sulawesi
16 B4 **Tondela** Portugal
Tønder *co see* **Sønderjylland** *co*
28 B7 **Tønder** Denmark
120 E3 **Tondern** Ontario Canada
85 E4 **Tondjara** *watercourse* Algeria
88 C10 **Tondongwe** *mt* Zimbabwe
36 B3 **Tondorf** Germany
61 N9 **Tone** *R* Japan
61 O10 **Tone-gawa** *R* Japan
8 C5 **Tone, R** England
139 G4 **Tonga** New South Wales Australia
137 S6 **Tonga** *kingdom* Pacific Oc
86 F4 **Tonga** Sudan
88 B10 **Tonga** Zambia
89 G7 **Tongaat** S Africa
145 D4 **Tonga I** New Zealand
139 G4 **Tonga L** New South Wales Australia
139 G6 **Tongala** Victoria Australia
67 F4 **Tong'an** China
110 A2 **Tonganoxie** Kansas U.S.A.
145 E3 **Tongaporutu** New Zealand
145 E3 **Tongariro** *mt* New Zealand
145 E3 **Tongariro** *admin region* New Zealand
137 R6 **Tongatapu Group** Tonga
58 F5 **Tongbai Shan** *mt ra* China
Tongcheng *see* **Dong'e**
67 E1 **Tongcheng** China
67 D2 **Tongcheng** China
58 E4 **Tongchuan** China
67 C3 **Tongdao** China
22 J2 **Tongeren** Belgium
67 E2 **Tonggu** China
65 A7 **Tongguan** China
67 A4 **Tonghai** China
59 J2 **Tonghe** China
59 J3 **Tonghua** China
59 K2 **Tongjiang** China
67 B1 **Tongjiang** China
59 J2 **Tongken He** *R* China
67 B6 **Tong King, G. of** Vietnam
70 G5 **Tongko** Sulawesi
12 D4 **Tongland** Scotland
67 B2 **Tongliang** China
59 H3 **Tongliao** China
67 F1 **Tongling** China
67 F2 **Tonglu** China
67 B1 **Tongnan** China
68 H6 **Tong Noy** Cambodia
87 G12 **Tongobory** Madagascar
131 B3 **Tongoi, Bahia** Chile
133 C4 **Tongoy** Chile
Tongquan *see* **Malong**
71 E7 **Tongquil** *isld* Philippines
67 C3 **Tongren** China
Tongres *see* **Tongeren**
Tongshan *see* **Xuzhou**
67 E2 **Tongshan** China
68 J3 **Tongshi** China
68 D2 **Tongta** Burma
58 C5 **Tongtian He** *R* China
15 D2 **Tongue** Scotland
101 U3 **Tongue** *R* Montana U.S.A.
126 F2 **Tongue of the Ocean** *chan* Bahamas
101 T4 **Tongue R.Res** Montana U.S.A.
65 C5 **Tong Xian** China
67 G1 **Tongxiang** China
65 D3 **Tongxing** China
65 C7 **Tongxu** China
65 F2 **Tongyu** China
65 F4 **Tongyuanpu** China
67 B4 **Tongzhou** China
67 B2 **Tongzi** China
6 L4 **Toni** *oil rig* North Sea
99 R8 **Tonica** Illinois U.S.A.
124 E3 **Tónichi** Mexico
124 H8 **Tonila** Mexico
86 E4 **Tonj** Sudan
74 F5 **Tonk** India
77 B1 **Tonkābon** Iran
107 N5 **Tonkawa** Oklahoma U.S.A.
52 G6 **Tonkino** Russian Federation
68 H6 **Tonle Kong** *R* Laos/Cambodia
68 G7 **Tonle Sap** *R* Cambodia
18 E7 **Tonnay-Charente** France
18 F8 **Tonneins** France
28 D5 **Tønning** Denmark
32 J4 **Tönning** Germany
102 G3 **Tonopah** Nevada U.S.A.
60 H11 **Tonoshō** Japan
20 D4 **Tonquédec** France
27 D12 **Tönsberg** Norway
27 B13 **Tonstad** Norway
131 B3 **Tontal, Sa** *ra* Argentina
103 N8 **Tonto Basin** Arizona U.S.A.
103 O8 **Tonto Nat.Mon** Arizona U.S.A.
116 L5 **Tonzona** *R* Alaska U.S.A.
141 J8 **Toobeah** Queensland Australia
143 B9 **Toodyay** W Australia Australia
101 N9 **Tooele** Utah U.S.A.
141 K7 **Toogoolawah** Queensland Australia
139 G6 **Tooleyone** New South Wales Australia
143 G9 **Toolgana Rockhole** *rockhole* W Australia Australia
138 D5 **Tooligie** South Australia Australia
116 N2 **Toolik** *R* Alaska U.S.A.
138 F6 **Toolondo** Victoria Australia
139 J6 **Tooma** *R* New South Wales Australia
141 G7 **Toompine** Queensland Australia
139 H7 **Toora** Victoria Australia
141 F5 **Toorak** Queensland Australia
56 E5 **Toora-Khem** Russian Federation
141 K2 **Toowong** *dist* Brisbane, Qnsld Australia
141 K8 **Toowoomba** Queensland Australia
116 J1 **Topagoruk** *R* Alaska U.S.A.
48 L6 **Topalu** Romania
17 F7 **Topares, Sa.de** *mts* Spain
103 N10 **Topawa** Arizona U.S.A.
102 E3 **Topaz L** California U.S.A.
33 T8 **Töpchin** Germany
13 G5 **Topcliffe** England
94 B5 **Topeka** Indiana U.S.A.
107 P2 **Topeka** Kansas U.S.A.
124 F5 **Topia** Mexico
56 C3 **Topki** Russian Federation
48 G1 **Topl'a** *R* Czechoslovakia
118 C4 **Topland** Alberta Canada
117 K8 **Topley Lodge** British Columbia Canada
46 E1 **Toplica** *R* Serbia Yugoslavia
48 J4 **Topliţa** Romania
131 A5 **Topocalma, Pta** Chile
103 K7 **Topock** Arizona U.S.A.
48 F6 **Topola** Serbia Yugoslavia
46 E3 **Topolčane** Macedonia Yugoslavia
48 E2 **Topol'čany** Czechoslovakia
29 O10 **Topol'ki** Russian Federation
46 G2 **Topolnitsa** *R* Bulgaria
124 E5 **Topolobampo** Mexico
48 J6 **Topoloveni** Romania
47 H2 **Topolovgrad** Bulgaria
38 L9 **Topolšica** Slovenia
106 D1 **Toponas** Colorado U.S.A.
52 E5 **Topornya** Russian Federation
52 D2 **Topozero, Ozero** *L* Russian Federation
100 E3 **Toppenish** Washington U.S.A.
47 J1 **Topraisar** Romania
57 B4 **Toprak-kala** Uzbekistan
52 F3 **Topsa** Russian Federation
95 U1 **Topsfield** Maine U.S.A.
8 C6 **Topsham** England
95 R3 **Topsham** Maine U.S.A.
140 B3 **Top Springs** N Terr Australia
95 M6 **Topton** Pennsylvania U.S.A.
103 L4 **Toquerville** Utah U.S.A.
102 G3 **Toquima Ra** Nevada U.S.A.
86 F4 **Tor** Ethiopia
6 N6 **Tor** *oil rig* North Sea
17 H3 **Torá** Spain
71 J4 **Torawitan, Tg** *B* Sulawesi
123 L8 **Tor B** Nova Scotia Canada
47 J6 **Torbalı** Turkey
77 F2 **Torbat-e-Ḩeydarīyeh** Iran
77 G2 **Torbat-e Jām** Iran
123 U6 **Torbay** Newfoundland Canada
123 L8 **Tor Bay** Nova Scotia Canada
143 C11 **Torbay B** W Australia Australia
27 F10 **Torberget** Norway
116 L6 **Torbert, Mt** Alaska U.S.A.
52 D5 **Torbino** Russian Federation
94 B1 **Torch L** Michigan U.S.A.
8 C7 **Torcross** England
21 N2 **Torcy-le-Grand** France
16 D3 **Tordesillas** Spain
26 N6 **Töre** Sweden
27 G13 **Töreboda** Sweden
28 H7 **Toreby** Denmark
27 F15 **Torekov** Sweden
29 K4 **Torekov** Sweden
145 F2 **Torere** New Zealand
27 J12 **Toresund** Sweden
17 F3 **Torete** *R* Spain
54 K8 **Torez** Ukraine
21 H7 **Torfou** France
33 S9 **Torgau** Germany
33 U5 **Torgelow** Germany
26 F6 **Torghatten** *isld* Norway
53 G8 **Torgun** *R* Russian Federation
27 H15 **Torhamn** Sweden
22 E1 **Torhout** Belgium
61 O10 **Toride** Japan
21 J3 **Torigny-sur-Vire** France
44 C1 **Torino** Italy
86 F5 **Torit** Sudan
130 D5 **Torixoreu** Brazil
52 D5 **Torkovichi** Russian Federation
29 N3 **Törmänen** Finland
8 D5 **Tormarton** England
55 G1 **Tormemtor, Ozero** *L* Russian Federation
142 E3 **Torment, Pt** W Australia Australia
16 D4 **Tormes** *R* Spain
117 Q11 **Tornado Mt** Alberta/Br Col Canada
28 D1 **Tornby** Denmark
Torneå *see* **Tornio**
26 M4 **Torne älv** *R* Sweden
32 L5 **Tornesch** Germany
26 K3 **Torneträsk** *L* Sweden
26 L3 **Torneträsk** Sweden
115 N6 **Torngat Mts** Quebec/Labrador Canada
48 F7 **Tornik** *mt* Serbia Yugoslavia
108 A4 **Tornillo** Texas U.S.A.
28 C4 **Torning** Denmark
29 L6 **Tornio** Finland
29 L6 **Tornionjoki** *R* Finland
33 S6 **Tornow** Germany
133 E5 **Tornquist** Argentina
28 D6 **Torø** *isld* Denmark
60 S2 **Tōro** Japan
16 D3 **Toro** Spain
131 B2 **Toro, Cerro de** *pk* Arg/Chile
48 J3 **Toroiaga** *mt* Romania
48 F3 **Törökszentmiklós** Hungary
46 F4 **Toronaios Kólpos** *G* Greece
139 K5 **Toronto** New South Wales Australia
121 D9 **Toronto** Ontario Canada
107 P4 **Toronto** Kansas U.S.A.
94 G6 **Toronto** Ohio U.S.A.
52 D6 **Toropets** Russian Federation
124 H5 **Toro, Pico del** *mt* Mexico
102 H8 **Toro Pk** California U.S.A.
131 B4 **Toro, Pta** Chile
88 E1 **Tororo** Uganda
78 D3 **Toros Dağlari** *mts* Turkey
15 F3 **Torphins** Scotland
52 F6 **Torpino** Russian Federation
8 B7 **Torpoint** England
26 H9 **Torpshammar** Sweden
133 G4 **Torquato Severo** Brazil
139 G7 **Torquay** Victoria Australia
98 C1 **Torquay** Saskatchewan Canada
8 C7 **Torquay** England
12 B3 **Torr** N Ireland
121 L8 **Torrance** Ontario Canada
102 F8 **Torrance** California U.S.A.
16 B6 **Torrão** Portugal
45 Q8 **Torre Annunziata** Italy
41 O6 **Torrebelvicino** Italy
17 H4 **Torreblanca** Spain
17 F2 **Torrecilla en Cameros** Spain
45 Q8 **Torre del Greco** Italy
44 F1 **Torre del Mangano** Italy
16 C3 **Torre de Moncorvo** Portugal
44 H4 **Torre di Lago Puccini** Italy
16 E7 **Torredonjimeno** Spain
45 L1 **Torrēglia** Italy
16 C5 **Torrejoncillo** Spain
16 E1 **Torrelavega** Spain
42 G7 **Torremaggiore** Italy
16 E8 **Torremolinos** Spain
141 H5 **Torrens** *R* Queensland Australia
141 H5 **Torrens Cr** Queensland Australia
138 E4 **Torrens, L** South Australia Australia
17 G5 **Torrente** Spain
124 H5 **Torreón** Mexico
17 G7 **Torre Pacheco** Spain
133 H3 **Tôrres** Brazil
124 D3 **Torres** Mexico
16 E9 **Torres de Alealá** Morocco
137 O4 **Torres Is** Vanuatu
16 B5 **Torres Novas** Portugal
141 F1 **Torres Strait** Queensland Australia
16 A5 **Torres Vedras** Portugal
17 G7 **Torrevieja** Spain
103 N3 **Torrey** Utah U.S.A.
45 N5 **Torricella in Sabina** Italy
8 B6 **Torridge, R** England
45 L1 **Torri di Quartesolo** Italy
28 E5 **Torrild** Denmark
28 C5 **Tørring** Denmark
139 K3 **Torrington** New South Wales Australia
118 D7 **Torrington** Alberta Canada
95 O5 **Torrington** Connecticut U.S.A.
98 B7 **Torrington** Wyoming U.S.A.
98 B7 **Torrington, S** Wyoming U.S.A.
140 C1 **Tor Rock** *mt* N Terr Australia
26 F8 **Torröjen** *L* Sweden
16 E8 **Torrox** Spain
27 H11 **Torsåker** Sweden
27 H15 **Torsås** Sweden
27 G15 **Torsås, V** Sweden
26 F9 **Torsborg** Sweden
27 F11 **Torsby** Sweden
27 H12 **Torshälla** Sweden
6 F1 **Tórshavn** Faeroes
26 J2 **Torsken** Norway
26 L1 **Torsvåg** Norway
57 E3 **Tortkol'** Kazakhstan
55 F5 **Tortkuduk** Kazakhstan
43 F11 **Torto** *R* Sicily
113 L7 **Tortola** *isld* Virgin Is
131 B2 **Tortolas, Cerro las** *pk* Arg/Chile
44 E2 **Tortona** Italy
17 H4 **Tortosa** Spain
127 H4 **Tortue, Île de la** Haiti
77 D2 **Ţorūd** Iran
70 G5 **Torue** Sulawesi
31 L2 **Toruń** Poland
27 F15 **Torup** Sweden
52 C5 **Tōrva** Estonia
27 G13 **Torved** Sweden
13 E5 **Torver** England
26 J7 **Torvsjö** Sweden
121 M8 **Tory Hill** Ontario Canada
14 C1 **Tory I** Ireland
48 G2 **Torysa** *R* Czechoslovakia
31 J3 **Torzym** Poland
60 G12 **Tosa** Japan
60 F13 **Tosa-Shimizu** Japan
60 G12 **Tosa-wan** *B* Japan
60 G12 **Tosa-Yamada** Japan
87 D11 **Tosca** S Africa
45 K4 **Toscana** *reg* Italy
42 C5 **Toscano, Arch** *islds* Italy
124 D5 **Tosca, Pta** *C* Mexico
41 N6 **Toscolano-Moderno** Italy
26 F6 **Tosen** Norway
26 F6 **Tosenfjord** *inlet* Norway
41 N3 **Tösens** Austria
61 K11 **Tōshi-jima** *isld* Japan
61 N11 **To-shima** *isld* Japan
61 P5 **Tōshima-yama** *mt* Japan
52 D5 **Tosno** Russian Federation
58 C4 **Toson Hu** *L* China
58 C2 **Tosontsengel** Mongolia
26 F9 **Tossåsen** Sweden
45 L3 **Tossignano** Italy
133 E3 **Tostado** Argentina
101 O3 **Toston** Montana U.S.A.
60 D12 **Tosu** Japan
78 D1 **Tosya** Turkey
31 L5 **Toszek** Poland
17 F7 **Totana** Spain
83 K11 **Totapola** *mt* Sri Lanka
144 C5 **Totara Flat** New Zealand
145 D1 **Totara North** New Zealand
145 D4 **Totaranui** New Zealand
27 E11 **Toten** *reg* Norway
32 L6 **Tötensen** Germany
21 N2 **Tôtes** France
38 J6 **Totes Gebirge** *mts* Austria
48 F4 **Tótkomlós** Hungary
9 E1 **Totley** England
8 C7 **Totnes** England
129 G2 **Totness** Suriname
89 C6 **Toto** *mt* S Africa
144 B6 **Totoko Pk** New Zealand
125 L9 **Totolápam** Mexico
131 B2 **Totoralillo** Chile
85 C7 **Totota** Liberia
146 G14 **Totten Glacier** Antarctica
139 H4 **Tottenham** New South Wales Australia
121 L8 **Tottenham** Ontario Canada
9 E6 **Totton** England
59 K4 **Tottori** Japan
60 G10 **Tottori** *prefect* Japan
119 M6 **Totzke** Saskatchewan Canada
85 C7 **Touba** Ivory Coast
85 C2 **Toubkal, Jbel** *mt* Morocco
20 H7 **Touches,les** France
100 G3 **Touchet** Washington U.S.A.
119 N7 **Touchwood Hills** Saskatchewan Canada
18 H5 **Toucy** France
65 G3 **Toudao Jiang** *R* China
65 D3 **Toufendi** China
85 D6 **Tougan** Burkina
85 B6 **Tougé** Guinea
85 F2 **Touggourt** Algeria
85 C3 **Touila** Mauritania
19 J4 **Toul** France
85 C7 **Toulépleu** Ivory Coast
20 A5 **Toulinguet,Pte,du** France
122 E3 **Toulnustouc R** Quebec Canada
19 P18 **Toulon** France
99 R8 **Toulon** Illinois U.S.A.
102 F1 **Toulon** Nevada U.S.A.
19 O17 **Touloubre** *R* France
18 F9 **Toulouse** France
84 E5 **Toumma** Niger
85 C7 **Toumodi** Ivory Coast
68 C3 **Toungoo** Burma
21 L3 **Touques** France
21 L3 **Touques** *R* France
22 B2 **Touquet-Paris Plage, le** France
68 F3 **Tourakom** Laos
Tourane *see* **Da Nang**
20 C5 **Tourch** France
22 E2 **Tourcoing** France
21 L7 **Touriane** *reg* France
16 A1 **Touriñan, C** Spain
85 B4 **Tourine** Mauritania
20 G2 **Tourlaville** France
18 F10 **Tourmalet, Col du** France
22 E2 **Tournai** Belgium
128 D5 **Tournavista** Peru
18 F9 **Tournay** France
19 N14 **Tournon** France
21 M8 **Tournon-St.Martin** Indre-et-Loire France
40 A4 **Tournus** France
21 O3 **Tourny** France
130 J8 **Touros** Brazil
21 M4 **Tourouvre** France
21 M7 **Tours** France
21 L7 **Tour-St. Gélin, la** France
40 E5 **Tour Sallière** *mt* Switzerland
22 H4 **Tourteron** France
19 P18 **Tourves** France
21 N3 **Tourville-la-Rivière** France
21 L2 **Tourville-les-Ifs** France
21 O5 **Toury** France
86 C1 **Toussidé Pic** *mt* Chad
21 P1 **Toutencourt** France
119 S7 **Toutes Aides** Manitoba Canada
100 C3 **Toutle** Washington U.S.A.
20 G8 **Touvois** France
89 B9 **Touwsrivier** S Africa
37 O3 **Toužim** Czechoslovakia
127 J10 **Tovar** Venezuela
54 K3 **Tovarkovskiy** Russian Federation
27 C13 **Tovdal** Norway
27 C13 **Tovdalselv** *R* Norway
9 F3 **Tove, R** England
61 O5 **Towada-Hachimantai Nat. Park** Japan
61 O5 **Towada ko** *L* Japan
145 E1 **Towai** New Zealand
128 G2 **Towakaima** Guyana
139 J6 **Towamba** New South Wales Australia
110 H1 **Towanda** Illinois U.S.A.
107 O4 **Towanda** Kansas U.S.A.
95 L5 **Towanda** Pennsylvania U.S.A.
70 G7 **Towari** Sulawesi
9 F3 **Towcester** England
99 O2 **Tower** Minnesota U.S.A.
98 J3 **Tower City** North Dakota U.S.A.
95 L6 **Tower City** Pennsylvania U.S.A.
101 P5 **Tower Falls** Wyoming U.S.A.
110 H2 **Tower Hill** Illinois U.S.A.
144 A6 **Towing Head** New Zealand
106 H3 **Towner** Colorado U.S.A.
98 F1 **Towner** North Dakota U.S.A.
102 G5 **Townes Pass** California U.S.A.
111 J8 **Townley** Alabama U.S.A.
95 M7 **Townsend** Delaware U.S.A.
112 F6 **Townsend** Georgia U.S.A.
101 O3 **Townsend** Montana U.S.A.
112 D2 **Townsend** Tennessee U.S.A.
99 S4 **Townsend** Wisconsin U.S.A.
139 J6 **Townsend, Mt** Victoria Australia
141 K5 **Townshend I** Queensland Australia
141 H4 **Townsville** Queensland Australia
94 H5 **Townville** Pennsylvania U.S.A.
70 G6 **Towori, Teluk** *B* Sulawesi
86 F4 **Towot** Sudan
95 L7 **Towson** Maryland U.S.A.
70 G6 **Towuti** *L* Sulawesi
8 C3 **Towy, R** Wales
112 D2 **Toxaway, L** North Carolina U.S.A.
66 B3 **Toxkan He** *R* China
108 D4 **Toyah L** Texas U.S.A.
60 O3 **Tōya-ko** *L* Japan
61 L9 **Toyama** Japan
61 L8 **Toyama wan** *B* Japan
116 A3 **Toygunen** Russian Federation
61 L10 **Toyo** Japan
61 L10 **Toyoake** Japan
60 G11 **Toyohama** Japan
61 L11 **Toyohashi** Japan
61 L11 **Toyokawa** Japan
60 R3 **Toyokoro** Japan
61 J11 **Toyonaka** Japan
60 H10 **Toyooka** Japan
61 N8 **Toyosaka** Japan
61 L10 **Toyota** Japan
29 K9 **Töysä** Finland
57 E4 **Toytepa** Uzbekistan
85 F2 **Tozeur** Tunisia
116 M4 **Tozitna** *R* Alaska U.S.A.
36 C4 **Traben-Trarbach** Germany
79 F4 **Trâblous** Lebanon
78 G1 **Trabzon** Turkey
122 H6 **Tracadie** New Brunswick Canada
123 L8 **Tracadie** Nova Scotia Canada
122 F8 **Tracey** New Brunswick Canada
69 H8 **Tra Cu** Vietnam
102 C4 **Tracy** California U.S.A.
99 O8 **Tracy** Iowa U.S.A.
99 L5 **Tracy** Minnesota U.S.A.
110 L6 **Tracy City** Tennessee U.S.A.
22 E5 **Tracy-le-Mont** France
41 J6 **Tradate** Italy
119 O3 **Trade L** Saskatchewan Canada
110 J4 **Tradewater** *R* Kentucky U.S.A.
Tradom *see* **Zhongba**
99 O7 **Traer** Iowa U.S.A.
98 F10 **Traer** Kansas U.S.A.
16 C8 **Trafalgar, C** Spain
111 K8 **Trafford** Alabama U.S.A.
113 F11 **Trafford, L** Florida U.S.A.
131 B8 **Traful** *R* Argentina
131 B8 **Traful, L** Argentina
38 L5 **Tragwein** Austria
48 L5 **Traian** Romania
130 J9 **Traição, B. de** Brazil
133 C5 **Traiguén** Chile
133 C7 **Traiguén, I** Chile
100 H1 **Trail** British Columbia Canada
100 C7 **Trail** Oregon U.S.A.
98 F4 **Trail City** South Dakota U.S.A.
115 R3 **Traill Ø** *isld* Greenland
143 D6 **Trainor Hills** W Australia Australia
117 N5 **Trainor L** Northwest Territories Canada
21 P6 **Traînou** France
130 H10 **Traipu** Brazil
130 J9 **Trairi** *R* Brazil
38 N5 **Traismauer** Austria
21 M3 **Trait,le** France
52 H3 **Trakt** Russian Federation
111 F8 **Tralake** Mississippi U.S.A.
14 B4 **Tralee** Ireland
68 J6 **Tram Bo** Vietnam
40 F3 **Tramelan** Switzerland
68 G7 **Tram Kak** Cambodia
68 G7 **Tram Khnan** Cambodia
14 D4 **Tramore** Ireland
118 J6 **Tramping** Saskatchewan Canada
27 H13 **Tranås** Sweden
28 E4 **Tranbjerg** Denmark
133 D3 **Trancas** Argentina
124 G3 **Trancas** Mexico
18 E6 **Tranche, la** France
130 H5 **Trancoso** Brazil
16 C4 **Trancoso** Portugal
27 F14 **Tranemo** Sweden
13 F2 **Tranent** Scotland
69 D9 **Trang** Thailand
139 J4 **Trangie** New South Wales Australia
27 G11 **Trängslet** Sweden
69 H8 **Tranh De, Cua** *R* Vietnam
43 G7 **Trani** Italy
26 J2 **Tranöy** Norway
102 D5 **Tranquillity** California U.S.A.
19 Q18 **Trans** France
20 G4 **Trans** France
20 G5 **Trans** Ille-et-Vilaine France
146 C12 **Transantarctic Mts** Antarctica
118 C1 **Transcona** Manitoba Canada
89 F8 **Transkei** *homeland* S Africa
27 F11 **Transtrand** Sweden
89 E5 **Transvaal** *prov* S Africa
48 J4 **Transylvania** *reg* Romania
Transylvanian Alps *see* **Carpaţii Meridionali** *mts*
68 G8 **Tra On** Vietnam
41 L5 **Traona** Italy
43 E10 **Trapani** Sicily
101 L4 **Trapper Pk** Montana U.S.A.
21 P4 **Trappes** France
131 H3 **Trapua** *R* Brazil
13 E2 **Traquair** Scotland
139 H7 **Traralgon** Victoria Australia
17 F9 **Traras, Mt.des** Algeria
27 G15 **Traryd** Sweden
85 A5 **Trarza** *reg* Mauritania
45 P6 **Trasacco** Italy
42 E5 **Trasimeno, L** Italy
26 L6 **Träskholm** Sweden
109 P1 **Traskwood** Arkansas U.S.A.
16 C3 **Tras os Montes e Alto Douro** *prov* Portugal
16 B1 **Trasparga** Spain
36 B4 **Trassem** Germany
45 H3 **Trassilico** Italy
68 F6 **Trat** Thailand
38 K5 **Traun** Austria
99 U3 **Traunik** Michigan U.S.A.
38 J6 **Traunsee** *L* Austria
38 J6 **Traunstein** *mt* Austria
38 G6 **Traunstein** Germany
33 M5 **Trave** *R* Germany
138 F5 **Travellers L** New South Wales Australia
112 E3 **Travellers Rest** South Carolina U.S.A.
33 N5 **Travemünde** Germany

48 K6 **Tutraken** Romania
117 F5 **Tutshi L** Yukon Territory Canada
101 L7 **Tuttle** Idaho U.S.A.
98 F2 **Tuttle** North Dakota U.S.A.
107 N6 **Tuttle** Oklahoma U.S.A.
37 K2 **Tüttleben** Germany
107 O2 **Tuttle Cr. Lake** Kansas U.S.A.
99 M6 **Tuttle L** Minnesota U.S.A.
41 J2 **Tuttlingen** Germany
Tuttut Nunaat *see* **Renland**
71 N9 **Tutuala** Timor
134 D1 **Tutuila** *isld* Amer Samoa
125 L9 **Tututepec** Mexico
71 O8 **Tutuwawang** Indonesia
111 F7 **Tutwiler** Mississippi U.S.A.
41 O2 **Tutzing** Germany
58 D2 **Tuul Gol** *R* Mongolia
29 L10 **Tuulos** Finland
29 P9 **Tuupovarra** Finland
29 O9 **Tuusniemi** Finland
137 Q3 **Tuvalu** *islds state* Pacific Oc
137 R6 **Tuvana-i-Colo** *isld* Pacific Oc
137 R6 **Tuvana-i-ra** *isld* Pacific Oc
56 E5 **Tuvinskaya Respublika** Russian Federation
70 E4 **Tuwau** *R* Kalimantan
103 L5 **Tuweep** Arizona U.S.A.
65 A5 **Tuwei He** *R* China
116 L6 **Tuxedni B** Alaska U.S.A.
118 A1 **Tuxedo** Manitoba Canada
112 E2 **Tuxedo** North Carolina U.S.A.
41 P3 **Tuxer Gebirge** *mt* Austria
119 M8 **Tuxford** Saskatchewan Canada
9 F1 **Tuxford** England
67 C1 **Tuxiang** China
125 L7 **Tuxpan** Mexico
124 H8 **Tuxpan** Jalisco Mexico
124 G7 **Tuxpan** Nayarit Mexico
125 N9 **Tuxtla Gutiérrez** Mexico
55 F2 **Tuy** *R* Russian Federation
16 B2 **Tuy** Spain
117 H6 **Tuya L** British Columbia Canada
68 J6 **Tuy An** Vietnam
67 B6 **Tuyen Quang** Vietnam
68 J6 **Tuy Hoa** Vietnam
52 H6 **Tuymazy** Russian Federation
77 A2 **Tūysarkān** Iran
78 D2 **Tuz Gölü** *L* Turkey
103 N7 **Tuzigoot Nat.Mon** Arizona U.S.A.
78 K4 **Tuz Khurmātū** Iraq
48 E6 **Tuzla** Bosnia-Herzegovina
78 H2 **Tuzla** *R* Turkey
48 N5 **Tuzly** Ukraine
27 F14 **Tvååker** Sweden
26 L7 **Tvärålund** Sweden
26 M6 **Tvärån** Sweden
28 E4 **Tved** Århus Denmark
28 F6 **Tved** Fyn Denmark
28 E3 **Tvede** Denmark
27 C13 **Tvedestrand** Norway
52 E6 **Tver'** Russian Federation
52 D6 **Tverskaya Oblast'** *prov* Russian Federation
28 E1 **Tversted** Denmark
52 E6 **Tvertsa** *R* Russian Federation
27 H15 **Tving** Sweden
28 D5 **Tvingstrup** Denmark
28 B4 **Tvis** Denmark
6 F1 **Tvøroyri** Faeroes
47 H2 **Tvŭrditsa** Bulgaria
68 B4 **Twante** Burma
31 K4 **Twardogóra** Poland
85 F4 **Twaret** Niger
121 N8 **Tweed** Ontario Canada
139 L3 **Tweed Heads** New South Wales Australia
118 F4 **Tweedie** Alberta Canada
13 E3 **Tweed, R** Scotland
13 E3 **Tweedsmuir** Scotland
117 K9 **Tweedsmuir Prov.Park** British Columbia Canada
87 D11 **Twee Rivieren** S Africa
118 L9 **Twelvemile L** Saskatchewan Canada
116 P4 **Twelvemile Summit** Alaska U.S.A.
14 B3 **Twelve Pins** *mt* Ireland
103 H7 **Twentynine Palms** California U.S.A.
143 F9 **Twilight Cove** W Australia Australia
123 S4 **Twillingate** Newfoundland Canada
38 L8 **Twimberg** Austria
100 B1 **Twin** Washington U.S.A.
101 N4 **Twin Bridges** Montana U.S.A.
98 K4 **Twin Brooks** South Dakota U.S.A.
108 G4 **Twin Buttes Res** Texas U.S.A.
119 O2 **Twin City** Ontario Canada
115 N7 **Twin Falls** Labrador, Nfld Canada
101 L7 **Twin Falls** Idaho U.S.A.
142 F5 **Twin Heads** *mt* W Australia Australia
94 C2 **Twin L** Michigan U.S.A.
99 U6 **Twin Lake** Michigan U.S.A.
117 P7 **Twin Lakes** Alberta Canada
116 K6 **Twin Lakes** Alaska U.S.A.
106 D2 **Twin Lakes** Colorado U.S.A.
101 L6 **Twin Lakes Res** Idaho U.S.A.
123 Q4 **Twin L.,N** Newfoundland Canada
123 R4 **Twin L.,S** Newfoundland Canada
95 Q2 **Twin Mountain** New Hampshire U.S.A.
102 D2 **Twin Peaks** California U.S.A.
101 L5 **Twin Peaks** Idaho U.S.A.
143 C10 **Twin Pks** W Australia Australia
143 D10 **Twin Rocks** W Australia Australia
138 E3 **Twins Cr** South Australia Australia
138 D4 **Twins, The** South Australia Australia
145 D4 **Twins, The** *mt* New Zealand
98 K2 **Twin Valley** Minnesota U.S.A.
100 E1 **Twisp** Washington U.S.A.
32 J7 **Twistringen** Germany
108 D8 **Twitty** Texas U.S.A.
117 J4 **Twitya** *R* Northwest Territories Canada
144 C6 **Twizel** New Zealand
106 H4 **Two Buttes** Colorado U.S.A.
106 H4 **Two Buttes Creek** Colorado U.S.A.
119 R8 **Two Creeks** Manitoba Canada
99 T5 **Two Creeks** Wisconsin U.S.A.
101 P3 **Twodot** Montana U.S.A.
139 K6 **Twofold B** New South Wales Australia
99 P2 **Two Harbors** Minnesota U.S.A.
116 L8 **Two Headed I** Alaska U.S.A.
118 F5 **Two Hills** Alberta Canada
101 P5 **Two Ocean Pass** Wyoming U.S.A.
99 T5 **Two Rivers** Wisconsin U.S.A.
9 E2 **Twycross** England
9 E5 **Twyford** England
9 F5 **Twyford** England
12 D4 **Twynholm** Scotland
48 H2 **Tyachev** Ukraine
28 H6 **Tybjerg** Denmark
28 D6 **Tybrind Vig** *B* Denmark
56 E1 **Tychany** *R* Russian Federation
55 G3 **Tychkino** Russian Federation
31 J2 **Tychowo** Poland
31 L5 **Tychy** Poland
26 E8 **Tydal** Norway
117 F7 **Tyee** Alaska U.S.A.
100 A1 **Tyee** Washington U.S.A.
94 J9 **Tye River** Virginia U.S.A.
94 H8 **Tygart V** West Virginia U.S.A.
59 J1 **Tygda** Russian Federation
101 N7 **Tyhee** Idaho U.S.A.
27 C10 **Tyin** *L* Norway
31 O2 **Tykocin** Poland
98 K5 **Tyler** Minnesota U.S.A.
94 J5 **Tyler** Pennsylvania U.S.A.
109 M3 **Tyler** Texas U.S.A.
100 H2 **Tyler** Washington U.S.A.
111 A9 **Tyler, L** Texas U.S.A.
111 F10 **Tylertown** Mississippi U.S.A.
28 D2 **Tylstrup** Denmark
56 C1 **Tym** *R* Russian Federation
48 F1 **Tymbark** Poland
59 M1 **Tymovskoye** Russian Federation
55 F2 **Tynay** Russian Federation
59 H1 **Tynda** Russian Federation
118 E1 **Tyndall** Manitoba Canada
98 J6 **Tyndall** South Dakota U.S.A.
144 C5 **Tyndall, Mt** New Zealand
26 J9 **Tynderö** Sweden
13 G4 **Tyne and Wear** *co* England
13 G3 **Tynemouth** England
118 J7 **Tyner** Saskatchewan Canada
122 J7 **Tyne Valley** Prince Edward I Canada
27 G11 **Tyngsjö** Sweden
31 H6 **Týn nad Vltava** Czechoslovakia
26 E9 **Tynset** Norway
8 C2 **Tyn-y-Groes** Wales
116 O5 **Tyone** *R* Alaska U.S.A.
Tyre *see* **Soûr**
27 D11 **Tyrifjorden** *L* Norway
27 G15 **Tyringe** Sweden
59 K1 **Tyrma** Russian Federation
48 L2 **Tyrnovo** Moldavia
112 E2 **Tyron** North Carolina U.S.A.
14 D2 **Tyrone** *co* N Ireland
106 B9 **Tyrone** New Mexico U.S.A.
94 J6 **Tyrone** Pennsylvania U.S.A.
139 G6 **Tyrrell** *R* Victoria Australia
43 D8 **Tyrrhenian Sea** S Europe
28 D5 **Tyrsted** Denmark
26 H3 **Tysfjord** Norway
27 A12 **Tysnesöy** *isld* Norway
27 B11 **Tyssedal** Norway
27 J13 **Tystberga** Sweden
28 H6 **Tystrup** Denmark
31 O5 **Tyszowce** Poland
55 F3 **Tyukalinsk** Russian Federation
57 H4 **Tyulek** Kyrgyzstan
53 G11 **Tyulen'i, Ostrova** *islds* Russian Federation
55 C4 **Tyul'gan** Russian Federation
55 E1 **Tyuli** Russian Federation
52 J5 **Tyul'kino** Russian Federation
55 E3 **Tyumen'** Russian Federation
50 F2 **Tyumenskaya Oblast'** *prov* Russian Federation
55 E4 **Tyuntyugur** Kazakhstan
57 C2 **Tyuratam** Kazakhstan
52 D1 **Tyuva Guba** Russian Federation
119 O8 **Tyvan** Saskatchewan Canada
48 M1 **Tyvrov** Ukraine
8 B2 **Tywyn** Wales
25 C3 **t'Zand** Netherlands
87 F10 **Tzaneen** S Africa
Tzepo *see* **Zibo**
46 E5 **Tzoumérka** *mt* Greece
67 G4 **Tz'u-kao Shan** *pk* Taiwan
25 E2 **Tzummarum** Netherlands

U

85 B3 **Uad el Jat** *watercourse* Western Sahara
116 H7 **Ualik, L** Alaska U.S.A.
142 B6 **Uaroo** W Australia Australia
128 G4 **Uatumá** *R* Brazil
129 L5 **Uaua** Brazil
130 G10 **Uauá** Brazil
128 E4 **Uaupés** Brazil
145 G3 **Uawa R** New Zealand
125 P9 **Uaxactún** Guatemala
130 G7 **Ubá** Brazil
56 B5 **Uba** *R* Kazakhstan
22 L2 **Ubach o. Worms** Netherlands
55 E4 **Ubagan** *R* Kazakhstan
130 G5 **Ubaí** Brazil
129 L6 **Ubaitaba** Brazil
86 C5 **Ubangi** *R* Cent Afr Republic/Zaire
Ubari *see* **Awbārī**
78 H6 **Ubayyid, Wadi al** Saudi Arabia
28 G5 **Ubby** Denmark
60 E12 **Ube** Japan
16 E6 **Ubeda** Spain
115 O3 **Ubekendt Ejland** *isld* Greenland
133 H1 **Uberaba** Brazil
130 B5 **Uberaba** *L* Brazil/Bolivia
36 B5 **Überherrn** Germany
130 E6 **Uberlândia** Brazil
41 K2 **Überlingen** Switzerland
85 F7 **Ubiaja** Nigeria
33 S9 **Ubigau** Germany
133 D2 **Ubina** *mt* Bolivia
94 E3 **Ubly** Michigan U.S.A.
68 F4 **Ubolratana** *res* Thailand
87 F11 **Ubombo** S Africa
68 G5 **Ubon Ratchathani** Thailand
36 F5 **Ubstadt-Weiher** Germany
79 C2 **Uçarı** Turkey
128 D5 **Ucayali** *R* Peru
128 D6 **Ucayali** *dept* Peru
47 N11 **Uçburun Yarımada** *pen* Turkey
22 G2 **Uccle** Belgium
16 E3 **Ucero** *R* Spain
47 N11 **Uçgaziler** Turkey
55 C4 **Uchaly** Russian Federation
57 K2 **Ucharal** Kazakhstan
61 O8 **Uchigō** Japan
60 F12 **Uchiko** Japan
115 K7 **Uchi Lake** Ontario Canada
60 O3 **Uchiura wan** *B* Japan
40 A4 **Uchizy** France
57 C4 **Uch Kuduk** Uzbekistan
57 C4 **Uchkuduk** Uzbekistan
57 K5 **Uchkurgan** Uzbekistan
32 J7 **Uchte** Germany
33 P7 **Uchte** *R* Germany
51 N3 **Uchur** *R* Russian Federation
22 L5 **Uckange** France
30 H2 **Ücker** *R* Germany
36 C2 **Uckerath** Germany
33 U4 **Uckeritz** Germany
9 G6 **Uckfield** England
33 T9 **Uckro** Germany
117 L11 **Ucluelet** British Columbia Canada
101 O6 **Ucon** Idaho U.S.A.
101 T5 **Ucross** Wyoming U.S.A.
56 G5 **Uda** *R* Russian Federation
76 C5 **Udagamandalam** India
74 E6 **Udaipur** India
75 M5 **Udaipur Garhi** Nepal
54 D6 **Uday** *R* Ukraine
76 D3 **Udayagiri** India
77 B7 **Udayd, Khawr al'** *inlet* Qatar/Saudi Arabia
42 G4 **Udbina** Croatia
28 H5 **Udby** Denmark
28 E3 **Udby** Århus Denmark
28 D6 **Udby** Fyn Denmark
28 E3 **Udbyhø** Denmark
28 E3 **Udbyneder** Denmark
27 E13 **Uddevalla** Sweden
12 D2 **Uddingston** Scotland
26 J6 **Uddjaur** *L* Sweden
25 E5 **Uden** Netherlands
32 M10 **Uder** Germany
76 C1 **Udgir** India
74 F2 **Udhampur** Kashmir
142 E4 **Udialla** W Australia Australia
42 E2 **Udine** Italy
56 E4 **Udinskiy Khrebet** *mts*
76 B4 **Ūdipi** India
37 P3 **Udlice** Czechoslovakia
55 B3 **Udmurtskaya Respublika** Russian Federation
52 E5 **Udomlya** Russian Federation
61 N11 **Udone-jima** *isld* Japan
68 F4 **Udon Thani** Thailand
140 B6 **Udor, Mt** N Terr Australia
59 L1 **Udskaya Guba** *B* Russian Federation
76 C5 **Udumalaippettai** India
47 H2 **Udvoy** *mt* Bulgaria
59 L1 **Udyl, Oz** *L* Russian Federation
51 L1 **Udzha** Russian Federation
70 G5 **Uëbonti** Sulawesi
33 U5 **Uecker** *R* Germany
33 T6 **Ueckermark** *reg* Germany
33 U5 **Ueckermünde** Germany
61 M9 **Ueda** Japan
25 F5 **Uedem** Germany
32 G8 **Ueffeln** Germany
98 K8 **Uehling** Nebraska U.S.A.
60 D13 **Ueki** Japan
70 G5 **Uekuli** Sulawesi
86 E5 **Uele** *R* Zaire
32 E7 **Uelsen** Germany
33 N7 **Uelzen** Germany
61 K11 **Ueno** Japan
61 N10 **Uenohara** Japan
86 E5 **Uere** *R* Zaire
36 B3 **Uess** *R* Germany
32 L5 **Uetersen** Germany
55 C4 **Ufa** Russian Federation
37 J4 **Uffenheim** Germany
55 C3 **Ufimskiy** Russian Federation
87 C10 **Ugab** *R* Namibia
116 J8 **Ugaiushak I** Alaska U.S.A.
116 L8 **Ugak I** Alaska U.S.A.
88 C4 **Ugalla** *R* Tanzania
116 E9 **Ugamak I** Aleutian Is
86 F5 **Uganda** *rep* Africa
116 L8 **Uganik I** Alaska U.S.A.
116 J8 **Ugashik B** Alaska U.S.A.
116 J8 **Ugashik Lakes** Alaska U.S.A.
28 C7 **Uge** Denmark
43 J9 **Ugento** Italy
28 H5 **Ugerløse** Denmark
28 E4 **Uggelhuse** Denmark
28 E1 **Uggerby** Denmark
28 E5 **Uggerslev** Denmark
16 E8 **Ugijar** Spain
28 E2 **Ugilt** Denmark
19 Q13 **Ugine** France
59 M2 **Uglegorsk** Russian Federation
55 C2 **Ugleural'skiy** Russian Federation
52 E6 **Uglich** Russian Federation
42 G4 **Ugljan** *isld* Croatia
42 H5 **Ugljane** Croatia
48 E6 **Ugljevik** Bosnia-Herzegovina
52 D5 **Uglovka** Russian Federation
Ugoi *see* **Ujiji**
54 G2 **Ugra** *R* Russian Federation
46 G1 **Ugŭrchin** Bulgaria
55 F1 **Ugut** Russian Federation
83 L10 **Uhana** Sri Lanka
31 K6 **Uherské Hradiště** Czechoslovakia
36 H6 **Uhingen** Germany
87 C10 **Uhlenhorst** Namibia
37 K4 **Uhlfeld** Germany
119 T2 **Uhlman L** Manitoba Canada
37 L2 **Uhlstädt** Germany
28 C5 **Uhre** Denmark
94 F6 **Uhrichsville** Ohio U.S.A.
29 N3 **Uhro Kekkosen Nat. Park** Finland
31 O4 **Uhrusk** Poland
15 B3 **Uig** Skye Scotland
87 C7 **Uíge** Angola
65 F4 **Ŭiju** N Korea
55 B6 **Uil** Kazakhstan
55 C6 **Uil** *R* Kazakhstan
128 E7 **Uiñamarco, L** Peru/Bolivia
103 L5 **Uinkaret Plat** Arizona U.S.A.
55 C3 **Uinskoye** Russian Federation
101 P9 **Uinta Mts** Utah U.S.A.
89 D9 **Uitenhage** S Africa
25 C3 **Uitgeest** Netherlands
25 C4 **Uithoorn** Netherlands
25 G2 **Uithuizen** Netherlands
25 G2 **Uithuizerwad** Netherlands
79 G10 **Ujayyijāt, Abu** *well* Saudi Arabia
31 L5 **Ujazd** Poland
48 G3 **Újfehértó** Hungary
61 J11 **Uji** Japan
74 F7 **Ujiain** India
61 N9 **Ujiie** Japan
88 B4 **Ujiji** Tanzania
70 D4 **Ujohbilang** Kalimantan
48 E3 **Újpest** Hungary
31 K2 **Ujście** Poland
69 E12 **Ujungbatu** Sumatra
70 F7 **Ujung Pandang** Sulawesi
61 Q12 **Uka** Okinawa
61 L8 **Ukawa** Japan
88 D3 **Ukerewe** *isld* Tanzania
75 Q6 **Ukhrul** India
52 E4 **Ukhtoma** Russian Federation
89 B4 **Ukhwi Pan** Botswana
100 G4 **Ukiah** Oregon U.S.A.
61 P13 **Ukibaru-jima** *isld* Okinawa
116 D4 **Ukivok** Alaska U.S.A.
Ukkel *see* **Uccle**
115 O3 **Ukkusissat** Greenland
52 B6 **Ukmerge** Lithuania
27 H13 **Ukna** Sweden
54 G7 **Ukraine** *rep* E Europe
55 G3 **Ukrainka** Russian Federation
55 F4 **Ukrainka** Omskaya obl Russian Federation
Ukrainskaya S.S.R. *see* **Ukraine**
42 H4 **Ukrina** *R* Bosnia-Herzegovina
55 D3 **Uksyanskoye** Russian Federation
31 N2 **Ukta** Poland
52 G3 **Uktym** Russian Federation
87 B8 **Uku** Angola
87 C8 **Ukuma** Angola
60 B12 **Uku-shima** *isld* Japan
6 M5 **Ula** *oil rig* North Sea
47 J7 **Ula** Turkey
58 E2 **Ulaanbaatar** Mongolia
65 A1 **Ulaan-Ereg** Mongolia
58 B2 **Ulaangom** Mongolia
139 J4 **Ulan** New South Wales Australia
58 C4 **Ulan** China
Ulan Bator *see* **Ulaanbaatar**
65 C2 **Ulan Hobor** China
Ulan Hot *see* **Horqin Youyi Qianqi**
65 E2 **Ulan Hua** China
53 G10 **Ulan-Khol** Russian Federation
48 L1 **Ulanov** Ukraine
65 A4 **Ulansuhai Nur** *L* China
56 G5 **Ulan-Ude** Russian Federation
131 C3 **Ulapes, Sa** *mts* Argentina
141 H7 **Ularunda** Queensland Australia
56 B5 **Ul'ba** Kazakhstan
51 N3 **Ul'banskiy Zaliv** *B* Russian Federation
28 C3 **Ulbjerg** Denmark
9 G1 **Ulceby Cross** England
42 J7 **Ulcinj** Montenegro Yugoslavia
13 E4 **Uldale** England
28 D5 **Uldum** Denmark
58 F2 **Uldz** *R* Mongolia
Uleåborg *see* **Oulu**
69 B10 **Uleelheue** Sumatra
27 D12 **Ulefoss** Norway
98 K2 **Ulen** Minnesota U.S.A.
52 C6 **Ulena** Lithuania
138 F3 **Ulenia, L** New South Wales Australia
58 F1 **Ulety** Russian Federation
28 A4 **Ulfborg** Denmark
28 A4 **Ulfborg Kirke** Denmark
37 J1 **Ulfen** Germany
65 D2 **Ulgai** China
65 D2 **Ulgain Gol** *R* China
13 G3 **Ulgham** England
76 A1 **Ulhasnagar** India
Uliastai *see* **Dong Ujimqin Qi**
58 C2 **Uliastay** Mongolia
86 E6 **Ulindi** *R* Zaire
48 G5 **Uljma** Serbia Yugoslavia
56 G3 **Ul'kan** Russian Federation
57 C1 **Ul'kayak** *R* Kazakhstan
28 D7 **Ulkebøl** Denmark
28 C5 **Ulkind** Denmark
56 G3 **Ul'kon** *R* Russian Federation
139 K6 **Ulladulla** New South Wales Australia
137 L8 **Ulladulla Trough** Pacific Oc
26 K9 **Ullånger** Sweden
27 F14 **Ullared** Sweden
26 M4 **Ullatti** Sweden
29 K8 **Ullava** Finland
17 H4 **Ulldecona** Spain
27 B11 **Ullensvang** Norway
28 F6 **Ullerslev** Denmark
28 D7 **Ullerup** Denmark
110 G4 **Ullin** Illinois U.S.A.
28 C3 **Ullits** Denmark
26 L2 **Ullsfjord** Norway
13 F4 **Ullswater** *L* England
59 K4 **Ullung Do** *isld* S Korea
36 H7 **Ulm** Germany
111 E7 **Ulm** Arkansas U.S.A.
101 T5 **Ulm** Wyoming U.S.A.
139 L3 **Ulmarra** New South Wales Australia
36 B3 **Ulmen** Germany
48 K5 **Ulmeni** Romania
38 L5 **Ulmerfeld** Austria
125 M2 **Ulmukhuas** Nicaragua
70 G7 **Uloe** Sulawesi
48 E7 **Ulog** Bosnia-Herzegovina
88 E9 **Ulongue** Mozambique
138 E2 **Uloowaranie, L** South Australia Australia
13 E5 **Ulpha** England
56 H1 **Ulqkhan Botuobuya** *R* Russian Federation
27 F14 **Ulricehamn** Sweden
143 E7 **Ulrich Ra** W Australia Australia
36 G2 **Ulrichstein** Germany
26 H8 **Ulriksfors** Sweden
25 F2 **Ulrum** Netherlands
59 J4 **Ulsan** S Korea
28 D7 **Ulsby** Germany
15 G1 **Ulsta** Shetland Scotland
28 E2 **Ulsted** Denmark
26 A9 **Ulstein** Norway
14 D2 **Ulster** *prov* N Ireland
95 L5 **Ulster** Pennsylvania U.S.A.
14 D2 **Ulster Canal** N Ireland
28 F5 **Ulstrup** Denmark
26 K4 **Ultevis** *mt* Sweden
139 G6 **Ultima** Victoria Australia
140 D6 **Ultim, Mt** N Terr Australia
41 O4 **Ultimo.V.d'** Italy
51 M2 **Ulu** Russian Federation
47 N10 **Ulu** *R* Turkey
125 P10 **Ulua** *R* Honduras
47 K4 **Ulubat Gölü** *L* Turkey
47 K6 **Ulubey** Turkey
Uluçinar *see* **Arsuz**
47 K4 **Ulu Dağ** *mt* Turkey
71 D5 **Ulugan B** Philippines
88 F5 **Uluguru** *mts* Tanzania
78 E3 **Ulukışla** Turkey
70 C4 **Ululselua, Bt** *mt* Kalimantan
66 D2 **Ulungur He** *R* China
66 D2 **Ulungur Hu** *L* China
Ulun Hua *see* **Siziwang Qi**
58 F1 **Ulunkhan** Russian Federation
Uluru *see* **Ayers Rock**
140 B7 **Uluru Nat Park** N Terr Australia
47 J5 **Ulus Dağı** *mt* Turkey
56 C2 **Uluyuya** *R* Russian Federation
15 B4 **Ulva** *isld* Scotland
13 E5 **Ulverston** England
139 H8 **Ulverstone** Tasmania Australia
27 B11 **Ulvik** Norway
27 M10 **Ulvila** Finland
26 K8 **Ulvön** *isld* Sweden
29 K6 **Ulvshale** *pen* Denmark
28 J7 **Ulv Sund** *chan* Denmark
52 G6 **Ul'yankovo** Russian Federation
53 G7 **Ul'yanovsk** Russian Federation
55 F5 **Ul'yanovskiy** Kazakhstan
101 L4 **Ulysses** Idaho U.S.A.
107 J4 **Ulysses** Kansas U.S.A.
98 J8 **Ulysses** Nebraska U.S.A.
57 D1 **Ulytau** Kazakhstan
57 D2 **Ulytau, Gory** *mts* Kazakhstan
57 C1 **Uly-Zhylanshyk** *R* Kazakhstan
Ulzburg *see* **Henstedt-Ulzburg**
48 N2 **Uman'** Ukraine
131 C2 **Umango, Cerro** *pk* Argentina
71 M9 **Umarese** Timor Indonesia
74 J7 **Umaria** India
74 C6 **Umarkot** Pakistan
138 E2 **Umaroona, L** South Australia Australia
113 F9 **Umatilla** Florida U.S.A.
100 F4 **Umatilla** Oregon U.S.A.
71 G6 **Umayan** *R* Philippines
95 Q2 **Umbagog L** New Hampshire U.S.A.
140 D2 **Umbakumba** Northern Territory Australia
108 E1 **Umbarger** Texas U.S.A.
140 C7 **Umbeara** N Terr Australia
42 E5 **Umbertide** Italy
136 K3 **Umboi** *isld* Papua New Guinea
52 D1 **Umbozero, Oz** *L* Russian Federation
144 B6 **Umbrella Mts** New Zealand
127 J1 **Umbrella Pt** Jamaica
42 E6 **Umbria** *prov* Italy
26 G5 **Umbukta** Norway
130 J9 **Umbuzeiro** Brazil
26 L8 **Umeå** Sweden
26 K7 **Ume älv** *R* Sweden
80 G5 **Um ed Dananir** Jordan
80 G6 **Um el 'Amad** Jordan
80 G7 **Um el Malid** Jordan
80 G4 **Um el Manabi** Jordan
71 B3 **Umera** Indonesia
80 G7 **Um er Risas** Jordan
26 H6 **Umfors** Sweden
118 L1 **Umfreville** Ontario Canada
88 B10 **Umfuli** *R* Zimbabwe
89 G7 **Umgeni** *R* S Africa
26 K7 **Umgransele** Sweden
41 N3 **Umhausen** Austria
88 B10 **Umi** *R* Zimbabwe
116 L2 **Umiat** Alaska U.S.A.
147 G1 **Umingmakkok** U.S.A.
89 G8 **Umkomaas** *R* S Africa
84 F4 **Umm al Aḩrār** Libya
79 H4 **Umm al'Amad** Syria
84 E4 **Umm al Arānib** Libya
77 D7 **Umm al Qaiwain** U.A.E.
Umm al Qaywayn *see* **Umm al Qaiwain**
86 E3 **Umm Bel** Sudan
79 D10 **Umm Bugma** Egypt
37 K3 **Ummerstadt** Germany
86 E3 **Umm Keddada** Sudan
86 E2 **Umm Lahai** Sudan
77 A4 **Umm Qasr** Iran
86 F3 **Umm Ruwaba** Sudan
Umm Sai'd *see* **Musay'īd**
86 F3 **Umm Saiyala** Sudan
77 C7 **Umm Shaif** *oil well* Persian Gulf
79 D10 **Umm Shomar, G** *mt* Egypt
79 C10 **Umm Tināṣṣib,G** *mt* Egypt
26 H6 **Umnäs** Sweden
37 L2 **Umpferstedt** Germany
100 B6 **Umpqua** *R* Oregon U.S.A.
87 C8 **Umpulo** Angola
80 G4 **Um Qantara** Jordan
80 F3 **Um Qeis** Jordan
80 G8 **Um Quleib** Jordan
80 G6 **Um Quseir** Jordan
74 H8 **Umred** India
80 G7 **Um Rummana** Jordan
80 G7 **Um Shujeira el Gharbiya** Jordan
89 G2 **Umsweswe** *R* Zimbabwe
Umtali *see* **Mutare**
89 F8 **Umtata** S Africa
86 A4 **Umuahia** Nigeria
47 H4 **Umurbey** Turkey
89 G8 **Umzimkulu** *R* S Africa
89 F3 **Umzingwane** *R* Zimbabwe
42 G4 **Una** *R* Bosnia-Herzegovina/Croatia
130 H4 **Una** Brazil
130 J10 **Una** *R* Brazil
60 S2 **Unabetsu-dake** *mt* Japan
128 F6 **Unacurizal** Brazil
112 D5 **Unadilla** Georgia U.S.A.
95 M4 **Unadilla** New York U.S.A.
130 F5 **Unaí** Brazil
116 G5 **Unalakleet** Alaska U.S.A.
116 D10 **Unalaska I** Aleutian Is
144 D5 **Una, Mt** New Zealand
29 T9 **Unaós** Iceland
15 C2 **Unapool** Scotland
128 E2 **Unare** *R* Venezuela
29 M4 **Unari** Finland
70 G5 **Unauna** *isld* Sulawesi
17 G2 **Uncastillo** Spain
133 D1 **Uncia** Bolivia
106 C3 **Uncompahgre Pk** Colorado U.S.A.
106 B3 **Uncompahgre Plateau** Colorado U.S.A.
27 G13 **Unden** *L* Sweden
27 G13 **Undenäs** Sweden
138 F6 **Underbool** Victoria Australia
28 E2 **Understed** Denmark
27 K11 **Understen** *lighthouse* Sweden
27 H10 **Undersvik** Sweden
28 D5 **Underup** Denmark
99 L8 **Underwood** Iowa U.S.A.
98 E2 **Underwood** North Dakota U.S.A.
28 H5 **Undløse** Denmark
71 K10 **Undu,Tg** *C* Sumba Indonesia
54 D4 **Unecha** Russian Federation
128 E4 **Uneiuxi** *R* Brazil
79 F8 **Uneiza** Jordan
37 P4 **Uněšov** Czechoslovakia
52 E3 **Unezhma** Russian Federation
116 G9 **Unga I** Alaska U.S.A.
116 G4 **Ungalik** Alaska U.S.A.
139 H5 **Ungarie** New South Wales Australia
138 D5 **Ungarra** South Australia Australia
115 N6 **Ungava B** Quebec Canada
115 M5 **Ungava, Pen. d'** Quebec Canada
48 L3 **Ungeny** Moldavia
41 M1 **Ungerhausen** Germany
59 K3 **Unggi** N Korea
128 D5 **União** Brazil
130 D10 **União da Vitória** Brazil
128 F4 **União do Marmará** Brazil
130 J10 **União dos Palmares** Brazil
112 E1 **Unicoi** Tennessee U.S.A.
48 D1 **Uničov** Czechoslovakia
31 L4 **Uniejów** Poland
42 F4 **Unije** *isld* Croatia
116 E9 **Unimak** Aleutian Is
116 E9 **Unimak I** Aleutian Is
85 C8 **Uni,Mt** Liberia
128 F4 **Unini** *R* Brazil
133 D5 **Unión** Argentina
127 O8 **Union** *isld* Lesser Antilles
130 C9 **Unión** Paraguay
98 C9 **Union** Colorado U.S.A.
99 N7 **Union** Iowa U.S.A.
111 F11 **Union** Louisiana U.S.A.
95 S2 **Union** Maine U.S.A.
111 G9 **Union** Mississippi U.S.A.
110 E3 **Union** Missouri U.S.A.
99 L9 **Union** Nebraska U.S.A.
107 N6 **Union** Oklahoma U.S.A.
100 H4 **Union** Oregon U.S.A.
112 F3 **Union** South Carolina U.S.A.
94 G9 **Union** West Virginia U.S.A.
131 E7 **Unión, B** Argentina
95 K7 **Union Bridge** Maryland U.S.A.
111 F10 **Union Church** Mississippi U.S.A.
110 M1 **Union City** Indiana U.S.A.
94 B4 **Union City** Michigan U.S.A.
94 C6 **Union City** Ohio/Indiana U.S.A.
94 H5 **Union City** Pennsylvania U.S.A.
110 G5 **Union City** Tennessee U.S.A.
100 C7 **Union Creek** Oregon U.S.A.
95 M5 **Uniondale** Pennsylvania U.S.A.
126 D3 **Unión de Reyes** Cuba
100 H3 **Union Flat Cr** Washington U.S.A.
100 E3 **Union Gap** Washington U.S.A.
17 G7 **Unión,La** Spain
112 F2 **Union Mills** North Carolina U.S.A.
103 M7 **Union,Mt** Arizona U.S.A.
Union of Soviet Socialist Republics *see* **Armenia, Azerbaijan, Belorussia, Estonia, Georgia, Kazakhstan, Kyrgyzstan, Latvia, Lithuania, Moldavia, Russian Federation, Tajikistan, Turkemenistan, Ukraine or Uzbekistan**
101 Q6 **Union Pass** Wyoming U.S.A.
112 D4 **Union Point** Georgia U.S.A.
118 D1 **Union Pt** Manitoba Canada
111 L9 **Union Springs** Alabama U.S.A.
95 L4 **Union Springs** New York U.S.A.
99 M10 **Union Star** Missouri U.S.A.
109 M9 **Union Stock Yards** Texas U.S.A.
111 J9 **Uniontown** Alabama U.S.A.
110 J4 **Uniontown** Kentucky U.S.A.
94 H7 **Uniontown** Pennsylvania U.S.A.
99 O9 **Unionville** Iowa U.S.A.
94 D3 **Unionville** Michigan U.S.A.
99 N9 **Unionville** Missouri U.S.A.
102 F1 **Unionville** Nevada U.S.A.
94 K8 **Unionville** Virginia U.S.A.
31 L2 **Unisław** Poland
77 C7 **United Arab Emirates (UAE)** Persian Gulf
6 **United Kingdom of Gt.Britain & N.Ireland (UK)** W Europe
92 **United States of America (USA)** N America
52 D3 **Unitsa** Russian Federation
118 H6 **Unity** Saskatchewan Canada
95 S2 **Unity** Maine U.S.A.
100 G5 **Unity** Oregon U.S.A.
17 G4 **Universales** *mt* Spain
17 F4 **Universales, Mts** Spain
111 G7 **University** Mississippi U.S.A.
111 K13 **University City** St Louis
110 F3 **University City** Missouri U.S.A.
109 O9 **University Park** Texas U.S.A.
36 C2 **Unkel** Germany
38 G6 **Unken** Austria
55 C3 **Unkurda** Russian Federation
32 G9 **Unna** Germany
74 J5 **Unnao** India
27 G14 **Unnaryd** Sweden
60 F12 **Unomachi** Japan
37 L6 **Unsernherrn** Germany
52 E2 **Unskaya Guba** *B* Russian Federation
15 G1 **Unst** Shetland Scotland
33 O10 **Unstrut** *R* Germany
61 P12 **Unten** Okinawa
38 N6 **Unter Berg** *mt* Austria
39 C2 **Unterbrunn** Germany
Unter Deufstetten *see* **Fichtenau**
41 M4 **Unter Engadin** *dist* Switzerland
36 H4 **Unterfranken** *dist* Germany
38 H8 **Untergailtal** *V* Austria
36 F5 **Unter Grombach** Germany
36 H6 **Untergröningen** Germany
37 M7 **Unterhaching** Germany
38 E7 **Unter inn-tal** *V* Austria
33 M7 **Unterlüss** Germany
37 K3 **Untermerzbach** Germany
36 H5 **Untermünkheim** Germany
37 K5 **Untern-Bibert** Germany
36 F5 **Unter Schwarzach** Germany
Untersteinbach *see* **Rauhenebrach**
38 J7 **Untertal** *R* Austria
38 J7 **Unter Tavern** Austria
41 H4 **Unterwalden** *canton* Switzerland
36 E2 **Unterwilden** Germany
37 M7 **Unter Zolling** Germany
55 E1 **Untor, Oz** *L* Russian Federation
27 G10 **Untorp** Sweden
128 E3 **Unturán, Sa. de** *mts* Venezuela
117 H7 **Unuk** *R* Alaska U.S.A.
21 N5 **Unverre** France
118 H6 **Unwin** Saskatchewan Canada
78 F1 **Ünye** Turkey
60 D13 **Unzen-Amakusa Nat. Park** Japan
60 D13 **Unzen dake** *mt* Japan
52 F5 **Unzha** Russian Federation
38 K7 **Unzmarkt** Austria
61 L9 **Uozu** Japan
54 H3 **Upa** *R* Russian Federation
101 P9 **Upalco** Utah U.S.A.
127 N10 **Upata** Venezuela
9 E5 **Upavon** England
87 E7 **Upemba, L** Zaire
115 O3 **Upernavik** Greenland
Upernavik Kujallek *see* **Søndre Upernavik**
12 E2 **Uphall** Scotland
98 F1 **Upham** North Dakota U.S.A.
89 B7 **Upington** S Africa
94 B6 **Upland** Indiana U.S.A.
98 H9 **Upland** Nebraska U.S.A.
9 G4 **Upminster** England
116 H6 **Upnuk L** Alaska U.S.A.
52 D1 **Upolaksha** Russian Federation
134 C2 **Upolu** *isld* Western Samoa
135 U4 **Upolu Pt** Hawaiian Is
117 P10 **Upper Arrow L** British Columbia Canada
122 G7 **Upper Blackville** New Brunswick Canada
9 F2 **Upper Broughton** England
8 C3 **Upper Chapel** Wales
123 P4 **Upper Humber R** Newfoundland Canada
145 E4 **Upper Hutt** New Zealand
99 P6 **Upper Iowa** *R* Iowa U.S.A.
122 E7 **Upper Kent** New Brunswick Canada
100 D7 **Upper Klamath L** Oregon U.S.A.
14 B5 **Upper L** Ireland
102 B2 **Upper L** California U.S.A.
117 F5 **Upper Laberge** Yukon Territory Canada
117 J5 **Upper Liard** Yukon Territory Canada
118 J1 **Upper Manitou L** Ontario Canada
127 P2 **Upper Manzanilla** Trinidad
95 L8 **Upper Marlboro** Maryland U.S.A.
145 D4 **Upper Moutere** New Zealand
122 K8 **Upper Musquodoboit** Nova Scotia Canada
99 M1 **Upper Red L** Minnesota U.S.A.
101 O5 **Upper Red Rock L** Montana U.S.A.
94 D6 **Upper Sandusky** Ohio U.S.A.
95 N2 **Upper Saranac L** New York U.S.A.
122 J8 **Upper Stewiacke** Nova Scotia Canada
94 H8 **Upper Tract** West Virginia U.S.A.
94 K7 **Upperville** Virginia U.S.A.
Upper Volta *see* **Burkina**
139 H7 **Upper Yarra Res** Victoria Australia
9 F2 **Uppingham** England
27 J12 **Upplands Väsby** Sweden
27 J12 **Uppsala** *county* Sweden
27 K12 **Uppsala** Sweden
116 C6 **Upright,C** St Matthew I, Alaska U.S.A.
119 N1 **Upsala** Ontario Canada
99 M4 **Upsala** Minnesota U.S.A.
122 F6 **Upsalquitch** New Brunswick Canada
74 G2 **Upshi** Kashmir
99 Q3 **Upson** Wisconsin U.S.A.
141 J4 **Upstart, C** Queensland Australia
9 H5 **Upstreet** England
8 D3 **Upton** England
94 B9 **Upton** Kentucky U.S.A.
98 B5 **Upton** Wyoming U.S.A.
84 F3 **Uqaylah,Al** Libya
79 H3 **Uquayribāt** Syria
126 F10 **Urabá,G.de** Colombia
36 G7 **Urach** Germany
128 F2 **Uracoa** Venezuela
58 E3 **Urad Zhongqi** China
61 N10 **Uraga** Japan
83 K11 **Uragasmanhandiya** Sri Lanka
60 Q3 **Urakawa** Japan
139 H5 **Ural** *mt* New South Wales Australia
55 C4 **Ural** *R* Kazakhstan/Rus Fed
100 K1 **Ural** Montana U.S.A.
139 K4 **Uralla** New South Wales Australia
5 R3 **Ural Mts** Russian Federation
50 E3 **Uralskiy Khrebet** *mts* Russian Federation
88 D4 **Urambo** Tanzania
139 H6 **Urana** New South Wales Australia
140 E5 **Urandangie** Queensland Australia
130 G4 **Urandi** Brazil
141 L7 **Urangan** Queensland Australia
111 D10 **Urania** Louisiana U.S.A.
114 J6 **Uranium City** Saskatchewan Canada
83 L10 **Uraniya** Sri Lanka
140 C2 **Urapunga** N Terr Australia
128 F3 **Uraricoera** Brazil
143 E9 **Uraryie Rock** *rock* W Australia Australia
61 P13 **Urasoe** Okinawa
57 E5 **Ura-Tyube** Tajikistan
60 P2 **Urausu** Japan
61 N10 **Urawa** Japan
55 D1 **Uray** Russian Federation
55 C4 **Urazmetova** Russian Federation
52 G6 **Urazovka** Russian Federation
54 K6 **Urazovo** Russian Federation
99 S9 **Urbana** Illinois U.S.A.
94 B6 **Urbana** Indiana U.S.A.
99 P7 **Urbana** Iowa U.S.A.
110 C4 **Urbana** Missouri U.S.A.
94 D6 **Urbana** Ohio U.S.A.
45 N4 **Urbania** Italy
95 L9 **Urbanna** Virginia U.S.A.
129 K4 **Urbano Santos** Brazil
16 E2 **Urbel** *R* Spain
45 N4 **Urbino** Italy
17 F2 **Urbión, Sa. de** *mts* Spain
22 F5 **Urcel** France
128 D6 **Urcos** Peru
18 E10 **Urdos** France
52 H2 **Urdyuzhskoye Oz** *L* Russian Federation
57 K2 **Urdzhar** Kazakhstan
52 G5 **Uren** Russian Federation
50 G2 **Urengoy** Russian Federation
145 E3 **Urenui** New Zealand
137 O4 **Uréparapara** *isld* Vanuatu
13 G5 **Ure,R** England
124 D3 **Ures** Mexico
145 F3 **Urewera Country** New Zealand
55 G3 **Urez** Russian Federation
Urfa *see* **Şanlıurfa**
38 K5 **Urfahr** Austria
41 O2 **Urfeld** Germany
52 G6 **Urga** *R* Russian Federation
59 K1 **Urgal** Russian Federation
17 H2 **Urgel, Seo de** Spain
57 B4 **Urgench** Uzbekistan
41 J4 **Uri** *canton* Switzerland
19 P14 **Uriage** France
111 J10 **Uriah** Alabama U.S.A.
144 C5 **Uriah, Mt** New Zealand
128 D3 **Uribe** Colombia
127 H9 **Uribia** Colombia
110 B3 **Urich** Missouri U.S.A.
101 P8 **Urie** Wyoming U.S.A.
128 F2 **Urimán** Venezuela
124 F4 **Urique** Mexico
41 H4 **Uri Rothstock** *mt* Switzerland
139 G3 **Urisino** New South Wales Australia
55 E4 **Uritskiy** Kazakhstan
29 K10 **Urjala** Finland
25 E3 **Urk** Netherlands
47 H6 **Urla** Turkey
48 K6 **Urlaţi** Romania
28 D5 **Urlev** Denmark
55 C4 **Urman** Russian Federation
79 G6 **'Urmān** Syria
55 E1 **Urmannyy** Russian Federation
52 G6 **Urmary** Russian Federation
59 K2 **Urmi** *R* Russian Federation
Urmia,L *see* **Orūmīyeh, Daryācheh-ye** *L*
55 F2 **Urninskoye Boloto** Russian Federation
52 J5 **Urolka** *R* Russian Federation
46 E2 **Uroševac** Serbia Yugoslavia
131 D7 **Urre Lauquen, L** Argentina
12 E3 **Urr,L** Scotland
99 P9 **Ursa** Illinois U.S.A.
37 J7 **Ursberg** Germany
25 C3 **Ursem** Netherlands
37 M5 **Ursensollen** Germany
52 F6 **Urshelskiy** Russian Federation
56 C4 **Ursk** Russian Federation
36 H6 **Urspring** Germany
26 M7 **Ursviken** Sweden
55 C4 **Urtazym** Russian Federation
58 B4 **Urt Moron** China
124 E4 **Uruáchic** Mexico
130 E4 **Uruaçu** Brazil
130 E4 **Uruana** Brazil
124 H8 **Uruapan del Progreso** Mexico
128 D6 **Urubamba** Peru
128 G4 **Urubu** *R* Brazil
129 G4 **Urucará** Brazil
127 N10 **Urucoa** Venezuela
128 F4 **Urucu** *R* Brazil
129 K5 **Uruçuí** Brazil
130 F5 **Urucuia** Brazil
130 B6 **Urucum** Brazil
129 G4 **Urucurituba** Brazil
131 F2 **Uruguaiana** Brazil
130 D10 **Uruguai,R** Brazil
131 G4 **Uruguay** *rep* S America
131 F4 **Uruguay, R** Argentina
79 G2 **Urūmaş Şughrá** Syria
Urumchi *see* **Ürümqi**
66 D3 **Ürümqi** China
69 C11 **Urung** Indonesia
139 L4 **Urunga** New South Wales Australia
128 F6 **Urupa** *R* Brazil
52 H6 **Urussu** Russian Federation
130 F4 **Urutágua** Brazil
130 E5 **Urutaí** Brazil
145 E3 **Uruti** New Zealand
77 J3 **Urūzgān** *reg* Afghanistan
146 D3 **Urville I, d'** Antarctica
20 G2 **Urville-Nacqueville** France
136 H2 **Urville, Tg. D'** *C* W Irian
89 B4 **Urwi** Botswana
60 P2 **Uryū** Japan
60 Q2 **Uryū** *R* Japan
60 Q1 **Uryū-ko** *L* Japan
58 G1 **Uryum** *R* Russian Federation
56 C3 **Uryup** *R* Russian Federation
53 F8 **Uryupinsk** Russian Federation
52 G6 **Urzhum** Russian Federation
48 K6 **Urziceni** Romania
36 B4 **Urzig** Germany
21 O3 **Us** France
60 E12 **Usa** Japan
71 E7 **Usada** *isld* Philippines
47 K6 **Uşak** Turkey
87 C10 **Usakos** Namibia
80 E5 **Ūsarīn** Jordan
146 C13 **Usarp Mts** *mts* Antarctica
133 F8 **Usborne** *hill* Falkland Is
33 T5 **Usedom** Germany
143 A7 **Useless Loop** W Australia Australia
80 D2 **Usha** Israel
116 L7 **Ushagat I** Alaska U.S.A.
50 G1 **Ushakova, Ostrova** *islds* Russian Federation
55 E3 **Ushakovo** Russian Federation
Ushant *see* **Ouessant, I. d'**
56 E5 **Ush-Bel'dir** Russian Federation
60 D13 **Ushibuka** Japan
48 L2 **Ushitsa** *R* Ukraine
61 L8 **Ushitsu** Japan
60 D12 **Ushizu** Japan
57 J2 **Ushtobe** Kazakhstan
133 D8 **Ushuaia** *airport* Argentina
129 H5 **Usina** Brazil
36 F3 **Usingen** Germany
8 D4 **Usk** Wales
27 A12 **Uskedal** Norway
8 C4 **Usk,R** Wales
Üskub *see* **Skopje**
47 N10 **Üsküdar** Turkey
47 J3 **Üsküp** Turkey
32 L9 **Uslar** Germany
54 L4 **Usman** Russian Federation
100 F3 **U.S. Mil. Res. Yakima Firing Range** Washington U.S.A.
56 D3 **Usolka** *R* Russian Federation
52 J5 **Usol'ye** Russian Federation
55 G4 **Uspenka** Kazakhstan
57 G1 **Uspenskiy** Kazakhstan
40 F7 **Usseglio** Italy
18 G7 **Ussel** France
13 H6 **Usselby** England
32 J10 **Usseln** Germany
29 K5 **Usserød** Denmark
18 F6 **Usson du Poitou** France
U.S.S.R. *see* **Union of Soviet Socialist Republics**

236 **Ussuri — Verbania**

59 K2 **Ussuri** *R* Russian Federation
59 K3 **Ussuriysk** Russian Federation
21 K4 **Ussy** France
52 G6 **Usta** *R* Russian Federation
56 D5 **Ust'-Abakan** Russian Federation
52 G4 **Ust' Alekseyevo** Russian Federation
27 C11 **Ustaoset** Norway
53 G7 **Ust'-Aza** Russian Federation
55 D3 **Ust-Bagaryak** Russian Federation
56 B3 **Ust'-Bakchar** Russian Federation
52 H4 **Ust' Chernaya** Russian Federation
48 H2 **Ust-'Chorna** Ukraine
52 J5 **Ust' Dolgaya** Russian Federation
41 J3 **Uster** Switzerland
43 E10 **Ustica, I. di** Italy
56 F2 **Ust'Ilimsk** Russian Federation
56 F3 **Ust'-Ilimskoye Vodokhranilishche** *res* Russian Federation
52 J3 **Ust'-Ilych** Russian Federation
30 H5 **Usti'nad** Czechoslovakia
Ustinov *see* **Izhevsk**
55 F2 **Ust'-Ishim** Russian Federation
55 G3 **Ust'Izes** Russian Federation
31 K1 **Ustka** Poland
56 B6 **Ust'-Kamenogorsk** Kazakhstan
58 G1 **Ust'Karenga** Russian Federation
55 C4 **Ust'Katav** Russian Federation
58 E1 **Ust'-Kiran** Russian Federation
55 C3 **Ust Kishert** Russian Federation
52 H3 **Ust'Koin** Russian Federation
52 H4 **Ust'Kulom** Russian Federation
56 G3 **Ust'-Kut** Russian Federation
55 D2 **Ust' Loz'va** Russian Federation
52 C5 **Ust' Luga** Russian Federation
52 J2 **Ust' Lyzha** Russian Federation
51 N2 **Ust'Maya** Russian Federation
51 L3 **Ust-Muya** Russian Federation
52 H4 **Ust'Nem** Russian Federation
59 K1 **Ust'Niman** Russian Federation
56 F4 **Ust'-Ordynskiy** Russian Federation
56 F4 **Ust'-Ordynskiy Buryatskiy Avtonomnyy Okrug** *dist* Russian Federation
46 G3 **Ustovo** Bulgaria
52 F4 **Ust' Paden'ga** Russian Federation
52 F3 **Ust' Pinega** Russian Federation
50 H2 **Ust'-Port** Russian Federation
52 F4 **Ust' Puya** Russian Federation
52 G4 **Ust' Reka** Russian Federation
31 O6 **Ustrzyki Dolne** Poland
52 D4 **Ust'Sara** Russian Federation
52 J3 **Ust'-Shchugor** Russian Federation
55 D1 **Ust'-Tapsuy** Russian Federation
55 F3 **Ust'Tara** Russian Federation
55 G3 **Ust'Tarka** Russian Federation
55 F3 **Ust' Tava** Russian Federation
52 H2 **Ust' Tsil'ma** Russian Federation
59 K1 **Ust'Tyrma** Russian Federation
56 F4 **Ust'-Uda** Russian Federation
52 J4 **Ust' Un'ya** Russian Federation
52 F3 **Ust'ura** Russian Federation
59 H1 **Ust'urov** Russian Federation
56 D5 **Ust' Us** Russian Federation
52 J2 **Ust' Usa** Russian Federation
55 D4 **Ust'-Uyskoye** Russian Federation
52 J3 **Ust'-Voya** Russian Federation
52 G3 **Ust' Vyyskaya** Russian Federation
52 F4 **Ust'ya** *R* Russian Federation
52 E5 **Ust'ye** Russian Federation
52 E6 **Ust'ye** *R* Russian Federation
50 E4 **Ustyurt,Plato** Kazakhstan/Uzbekistan
52 E5 **Ustyuzhna** Russian Federation
66 C3 **Usu** China
71 L10 **Usu** *isld* Indonesia
60 E12 **Usuki** Japan
125 P11 **Usulután** El Salvador
125 O9 **Usumacinta** *R* Mexico
70 D3 **Usun Apau Plateau** Sarawak
89 G6 **Usutu** *R* Swaziland
52 D6 **Usvyaty** Russian Federation
71 B2 **Uta** *isld* Indonesia
103 M2 **Utah** *state* U.S.A.
103 N1 **Utah L** Utah U.S.A.
29 M7 **Utajärvi** Finland
71 H9 **Utan** Indonesia
60 Q2 **Utashinai** Japan
79 G5 **Utaybah, Buḩayrat al** *L* Syria
99 L7 **Ute** Iowa U.S.A.
17 G3 **Utebo** Spain
106 G6 **Ute Cr** New Mexico U.S.A.
88 G6 **Utenge,L** Tanzania
106 E5 **Ute Park** New Mexico U.S.A.
37 P4 **Uterý** Czechoslovakia
55 G4 **Utes** Kazakhstan
88 G6 **Utete** Tanzania
68 D5 **U Thai Thani** Thailand
77 K7 **Uthal** Pakistan
32 J6 **Uthlede** Germany
79 H4 **'Uthmānīyah** Syria
68 G5 **Uthumphon Phisai** Thailand
129 G6 **Utiariti** Brazil
107 K3 **Utica** Kansas U.S.A.
94 D4 **Utica** Michigan U.S.A.
99 P6 **Utica** Minnesota U.S.A.
111 F9 **Utica** Mississippi U.S.A.
110 C2 **Utica** Missouri U.S.A.
101 P3 **Utica** Montana U.S.A.
98 J9 **Utica** Nebraska U.S.A.
95 M3 **Utica** New York U.S.A.
94 E6 **Utica** Ohio U.S.A.
17 G5 **Utiel** Spain
26 K7 **Utifällan** Sweden
119 W3 **Utik L** Manitoba Canada
145 E3 **Utiku** New Zealand
118 B3 **Utikuma L** Alberta Canada
27 H16 **Utklippan** *isld* Sweden
27 C10 **Utla** *R* Norway
27 H15 **Utlängan** *isld* Sweden
109 K5 **Utley** Texas U.S.A.
106 G4 **Utleyville** Colorado U.S.A.
74 D1 **Utmanzai** Pakistan
27 M12 **Utö** *lighthouse* Finland
27 K13 **Utö** Sweden
140 C5 **Utopia** N Terr Australia
109 H6 **Utopia** Texas U.S.A.
75 K5 **Utraula** India
25 D4 **Utrecht** Netherlands
89 G6 **Utrecht** S Africa
16 D7 **Utrera** Spain
27 A12 **Utsira** *lighthouse* Norway
29 N2 **Utsjoki** Finland
61 N9 **Utsunomiya** Japan
53 G10 **Utta** Russian Federation
68 E4 **Uttaradit** Thailand
74 H4 **Uttar Pradesh** *prov* India
27 H12 **Uttersberg** Sweden
28 G7 **Utterslev** Denmark
36 H4 **Üttingen** Germany
9 E2 **Uttoxeter** England
116 G2 **Utukok** *R* Alaska U.S.A.
137 O4 **Utupua** *isld* Santa Cruz Is
55 B5 **Utva** *R* Kazakhstan
37 O3 **Útvina** Czechoslovakia
52 H6 **Utyashkino** Russian Federation
32 M8 **Utze** Germany
33 S5 **Utzedel** Germany
29 O10 **Uukuniem** Finland
Uummannaq *see* **Dundas**
115 O3 **Uummannaq** Greenland
Uummannarsuaq Greenland *see* **Farvel,Kap**
29 L9 **Uurainen** Finland
56 D5 **Üüreg Nuur** *L* Mongolia
Uusikaarlepyy *see* **Nykarleby**
29 J11 **Uusikaupunki** Finland
29 L11 **Uusimaa** *prov* Finland
52 H6 **Uva** Russian Federation
48 F7 **Uvac** *R* Serbia Yugoslavia
103 K2 **Uvada** Nevada U.S.A.
128 D3 **Uva, L** Colombia
112 E5 **Uvalda** Georgia U.S.A.
108 H6 **Uvalde** Texas U.S.A.
54 B4 **Uvarovichi** Belorussia
52 E6 **Uvarovka** Russian Federation
55 E2 **Uvat** Russian Federation
137 O6 **Uvéa** *isld* Îles Loyauté Pacific Oc
137 R4 **Uvea** *isld* Îles Wallis Pacific Oc
55 D4 **Uvel'skiy** Russian Federation
55 D3 **Uvil'dy, Oz** *L* Russian Federation
88 C4 **Uvinza** Tanzania
88 B3 **Uvira** Zaire
60 E13 **Uwae** Japan
60 F12 **Uwajima** Japan
84 H5 **Uweinat,Jebel** *mt* Sudan
135 V5 **Uwekahuna** Hawaiian Is
69 H12 **Uwi** *isld* Indonesia
121 L8 **Uxbridge** Ontario Canada
9 F4 **Uxbridge** England
65 A5 **Uxin Ju** China
125 P7 **Uxmal** Mexico
55 D4 **Uy** *R* Kazakhstan/Rus Fed
116 K8 **Uyak B** Alaska U.S.A.
51 O2 **Uyandina** *R* Russian Federation
56 D3 **Uyar** Russian Federation
15 G1 **Uyea** *isld* Scotland
15 G1 **Uyeasound** Scotland
50 H1 **Uyedineniya,Ostrov** *isld* Russian Federation
52 H2 **Uyeg** Russian Federation
47 K8 **Uyluk Tepe** *mt* Turkey
85 F7 **Uyo** Nigeria
47 K6 **Uysal Dağı** *mt* Turkey
55 D4 **Uyskoye** Russian Federation
57 F3 **Uyuk** Kazakhstan
133 D2 **Uyuni** Bolivia
48 G2 **Uz** *R* Czechoslovakia
57 B3 **Uzbekistan** *rep* C Asia
Uzbekskaya S.S.R. *see* **Uzbekistan**
48 F5 **Uzdin** Serbia Yugoslavia
20 E5 **Uzel** France
53 G8 **Uzen', Malyy** *R* Kazakhstan/Rus Fed
57 G4 **Uzgen** Kyrgyzstan
48 G2 **Uzh** *R* Ukraine
48 G2 **Uzhgorod** Ukraine
56 C3 **Uzhur** Russian Federation
48 F7 **Užice** Serbia Yugoslavia
41 J3 **Uznach** Switzerland
52 F6 **Uzola** *R* Russian Federation
47 N10 **Uzümce** Turkey
47 K8 **Üzümlü** Turkey
47 H6 **Uzun** *isld* Turkey
88 E6 **Uzungwa** Tanzania
47 H3 **Uzunköprü** Turkey
57 B3 **Uzynkair** Kazakhstan

V

29 M9 **Vaajakoski** Finland
89 E6 **Vaal** *R* S Africa
29 M7 **Vaala** Finland
89 F6 **Vaal Dam** S Africa
29 N11 **Vaalimaa** Finland
87 E10 **Vaalwater** S Africa
29 M8 **Vaaraslahti** Finland
21 L6 **Vaas** France
29 J8 **Vaasa** Finland
25 E4 **Vaassen** Netherlands
29 L4 **Vaattojärvi** Finland
28 H7 **Våbensted** Denmark
57 C5 **Vabkent** Uzbekistan
130 C7 **Vacaria,R** Brazil
130 C7 **Vacaria,Sa** *mts* Brazil
131 B4 **Vacas,Pta De** Argentina
102 B3 **Vacaville** California U.S.A.
19 N17 **Vaccarès, Etang de** *L* France
52 F6 **Vacha** Russian Federation
126 H5 **Vache, Île-à-** Haiti
40 E5 **Vacheresse** France
19 N16 **Vacqueyras** France
52 F6 **Vad** Russian Federation
100 C3 **Vader** Washington U.S.A.
27 A10 **Vadheim** Norway
76 A3 **Vādi** India
42 G5 **Vadice** Croatia
106 E5 **Vadito** New Mexico U.S.A.
27 B12 **Vadla** Norway
44 D3 **Vado** Italy
44 D3 **Vado, C. di** Italy
74 E7 **Vadodara** India
124 F2 **Vado de Santa Maria** Mexico
52 D1 **Vadozero, Oz** *L* Russian Federation
26 R1 **Vadsö** Norway
27 G13 **Vadstenna** Sweden
48 M6 **Vadu** Romania
28 D2 **Vadum** Denmark
41 L3 **Vaduz** Liechtenstein
26 K3 **Vadvetjåkko Nat. Park** Sweden
28 H7 **Væggerløse** Denmark
29 K5 **Værløse** Denmark
26 F4 **Vaeröy** Norway
28 G5 **Værslev** Denmark
52 F4 **Vaga** *R* Russian Federation
26 J9 **Vaga** Sweden
26 D10 **Vågåmo** Norway
26 G3 **Vagan** Norway
42 G4 **Vaganski** *mt* Croatia
6 F1 **Vágar** *isld* Faeroes
55 E2 **Vagay** Russian Federation
Vağda *see* **Erdemh**
29 O2 **Vaggetem** Russian Federation
26 R2 **Vaggetem-javrre** *L* Norway
45 K4 **Vaglia** Italy
27 J13 **Vagnahärad** Sweden
16 B4 **Vagos** Portugal
27 F11 **Vägsjöfors** Sweden
26 A10 **Vågsöy** *isld* Norway
31 L6 **Váh** *R* Czechoslovakia
29 J8 **Vähäkyrö** Finland
79 F8 **Vahal** Israel
111 G8 **Vaiden** Mississippi U.S.A.
21 K5 **Vaiges** France
36 F6 **Vaihingen** Germany
76 B1 **Vaijapur** India
52 C5 **Väike-Maarja** Estonia
26 L5 **Vaikijaur** Sweden
103 O9 **Vail** Arizona U.S.A.
106 D2 **Vail** Colorado U.S.A.
15 G2 **Vaila** *isld* Scotland
22 F5 **Vailly-sur-Aisne** France
134 B1 **Vailoa** Western Samoa
29 N11 **Vainikkala** Finland
45 Q7 **Vairano Patenora** Italy
20 G8 **Vairé** France
137 Q3 **Vaitupu** *isld* Tuvalu
46 F2 **Vakarel** Bulgaria
27 G11 **Vakern** Sweden
56 B1 **Vakh** *R* Russian Federation
57 F6 **Vakhanskiy Khrebet** *mts* Tajikistan
57 E5 **Vakhsh** Tajikistan
57 E5 **Vakhsh** *R* Tajikistan
57 E5 **Vakhshstroy** Tajikistan
52 G5 **Vakhtan** Russian Federation
52 D3 **Vaknavolok** Russian Federation
27 A11 **Vaksdal** Norway
83 L10 **Valachchenai** Sri Lanka
26 F8 **Vålådalen** Sweden
40 F5 **Valais** *canton* Switzerland
52 H5 **Valamaz** Russian Federation
46 F3 **Valandovo** Macedonia Yugoslavia
20 E4 **Val André, le** France
21 J7 **Valanjou** France
27 G12 **Valåsen** Sweden
95 O4 **Valatie** New York U.S.A.
46 G6 **Valáxa** *isld* Greece
38 E8 **Val Badia** Italy
121 P6 **Val Barrette** Quebec Canada
26 G3 **Valberg** Norway
19 P15 **Valbonnais** France
122 E5 **Val Brilliant** Quebec Canada
25 E5 **Valburg** Netherlands
133 D6 **Valcheta** Argentina
121 S7 **Valcourt** Quebec Canada
41 O6 **Valdagno** Italy
16 D2 **Valdavia** *R* Spain
52 D5 **Valday** Russian Federation
52 D6 **Valdayskaya Vozvyshennost'** *uplands* Russian Federation
17 G4 **Valde Algorfa** Spain
16 D5 **Valdecañas, Embalse de** *res* Spain
17 F5 **Valdeganga** Spain
21 P4 **Val-de-Marne** *dept* France
52 B6 **Valdemārpils** Latvia
27 J13 **Valdemarsvik** Sweden
16 E4 **Valdemoro** Spain
17 F4 **Valdemoro-Sierra** Spain
16 C2 **Valdeorras, El Barco de** Spain
16 E6 **Valdepeñas** Spain
16 D3 **Valderaduey** *R* Spain
17 H4 **Valderrobres** Spain
99 T5 **Valders** Wisconsin U.S.A.
121 P7 **Val des Bois** Quebec Canada
112 F2 **Valdese** North Carolina U.S.A.
133 E6 **Valdés, Pen** Argentina
116 O6 **Valdez** Alaska U.S.A.
106 F4 **Valdez** Colorado U.S.A.
41 M5 **Valdidentro** Italy
131 A7 **Valdivia** Chile
131 A8 **Valdivia** *prov* Chile
20 H5 **Val-d'Izé** France
21 O3 **Val-d'Oise** *dept* France
121 N4 **Val-d'Or** Quebec Canada
113 D7 **Valdosta** Georgia U.S.A.
27 D11 **Valdres** *plateau* Norway
19 P16 **Valdrome** France
20 E3 **Vale** Channel Is
100 H6 **Vale** Oregon U.S.A.
98 C5 **Vale** South Dakota U.S.A.
48 G5 **Valea Bistrei** Romania
48 G3 **Valea Lui Mihai** Romania
48 J3 **Valea Vişeului** Romania
37 P3 **Valeč** Czechoslovakia
45 J1 **Valéggio** Italy
129 L6 **Valença** Brazil
21 O7 **Valençay** France
19 N15 **Valence** France
18 F8 **Valence d'Agen** France
18 F9 **Valence-sur-Baïse** France
17 G5 **Valencia** *prov* Spain
17 G5 **Valencia** Spain
127 K9 **Valencia** Venezuela
16 C5 **Valência de Alcantara** Spain
16 D2 **Valencia de Don Juan** Spain
16 B3 **Valençia do Minho** Portugal
17 H5 **Valencia,G de** Spain
14 A5 **Valencia I** Ireland
127 L9 **Valencia,L.de** Venezuela
22 F3 **Valenciennes** France
19 P17 **Valensole** France
59 K3 **Valentin** Russian Federation
103 L6 **Valentine** Arizona U.S.A.
111 F12 **Valentine** Louisiana U.S.A.
101 R2 **Valentine** Montana U.S.A.
98 F7 **Valentine** Nebraska U.S.A.
108 C5 **Valentine** Texas U.S.A.
44 E1 **Valenza** Italy
27 E11 **Våler** Norway
109 H4 **Valera** Texas U.S.A.
127 J10 **Valera** Venezuela
27 A12 **Valestrand** Norway
130 H5 **Vale Verde** Brazil
41 M4 **Valfurva** *R* Italy
52 C5 **Valga** Estonia
120 K4 **Val Gagné** Ontario Canada
43 F11 **Valguarnera Caropepe** Sicily
6 N6 **Valhall** *oil rig* North Sea
7 M9 **Valiant** *gas field* North Sea
101 N1 **Valier** Montana U.S.A.
29 K4 **Välinge** Sweden
48 F6 **Valjevo** Serbia Yugoslavia
26 P2 **Valjok** Norway
19 Q15 **Valjouffrey** France
29 L10 **Valkeakoski** Finland
29 M11 **Valkeala** Finland
29 L5 **Valkeavaara** *mt* Finland
25 E7 **Valkenburg** Netherlands
25 D6 **Valkenswaard** Netherlands
54 G7 **Valki** Ukraine
Valko *see* **Valkom**
29 M11 **Valkom** Finland
146 G8 **Valkyrjedomen** *ice dome* Antarctica
19 N17 **Vallabrègues** France
16 D3 **Valladolid** *prov* Spain
16 D3 **Valladolid** Spain
121 N4 **Val Laflamme** Quebec Canada
41 P4 **Vallarga** Italy
41 O6 **Vallarsa** *R* Italy
27 C12 **Valle** Norway
103 M6 **Valle** Arizona U.S.A.
38 E7 **Valle Aurina** Italy
106 C4 **Vallecito Res** Colorado U.S.A.
106 D5 **Vallecitos** New Mexico U.S.A.
45 O7 **Vallecorsa** Italy
131 B2 **Valle Cura,Rio Del** Argentina
40 G6 **Valle d'Aosta** *aut reg* Italy
42 A3 **Valle d'Aosta** Italy
124 G7 **Valle de Banderas** Mexico
16 E1 **Valle de Cabuérniga** Spain
127 M10 **Valle de la Pascua** Venezuela
128 C3 **Valle del Cauca** *div* Colombia
124 F4 **Valle de Olivos** Mexico
124 F4 **Valle de Rosario** Mexico
124 G4 **Valle de Zaragoza** Mexico
126 H9 **Valledupar** Colombia
85 E5 **Vallée de Zgarat** Mali
122 B7 **Vallée Jonction** Quebec Canada
85 E5 **Vallée L'Azawak** Mali/Niger
131 C3 **Valle Fértil, Sa. de** *mts* Argentina
128 F7 **Valle Grande** Bolivia
40 C5 **Valleiry** France
102 B3 **Vallejo** California U.S.A.
45 P7 **Vallemaio** Italy
40 H6 **Valle Mosso** Italy
26 M7 **Vallen** Västerbotten Sweden
26 J8 **Vallen** Väster Norrland Sweden
131 B2 **Vallenar** Chile
36 D3 **Vallendar** Germany
28 H6 **Vallensved** Denmark
27 K12 **Vallentuna** Sweden
45 O6 **Vallepretra** Italy
133 E2 **Valle,R.del** Argentina
20 H7 **Vallet** France
43 F13 **Valletta** Malta
122 J8 **Valley** Nova Scotia Canada
111 F9 **Valley** Mississippi U.S.A.
98 K8 **Valley** Nebraska U.S.A.
100 H1 **Valley** Washington U.S.A.
101 Q5 **Valley** Wyoming U.S.A.
8 B1 **Valley** Wales
107 N4 **Valley Center** Kansas U.S.A.
118 K7 **Valley Centre** Saskatchewan Canada
98 J3 **Valley City** North Dakota U.S.A.
107 P2 **Valley Falls** Kansas U.S.A.
100 E7 **Valley Falls** Oregon U.S.A.
121 Q7 **Valleyfield** Quebec Canada
111 L7 **Valley Head** Alabama U.S.A.
94 G8 **Valley Head** West Virginia U.S.A.
109 K4 **Valley Mills** Texas U.S.A.
116 K7 **Valley of Ten Thousand Smokes** Alaska U.S.A.
110 F3 **Valley Park** Missouri U.S.A.
101 L8 **Valley Pass** Nevada U.S.A.
94 B8 **Valley Sta** Kentucky U.S.A.
117 P8 **Valleyview** Alberta Canada
109 K2 **Valley View** Texas U.S.A.
Vallgrund, isld *see* **Raippaluoto**
109 M2 **Valliant** Oklahoma U.S.A.
45 M2 **Valli di Comacchio** *reg* Italy
18 F10 **Vallier, Mt** France
121 P6 **Val Limoges** Quebec Canada
21 M2 **Valliquerville** France
28 J6 **Valløby** Denmark
43 G8 **Vallo di Diano** Italy
43 G8 **Vallo di Lucania** Italy
45 L4 **Vallombrosa** Italy
94 A8 **Vallonia** Indiana U.S.A.
21 K6 **Vallon-sur-Gée** France
40 D4 **Vallorbe** Switzerland
27 D12 **Vallöy** Norway
17 H3 **Valls** Spain
27 H10 **Vallsta** Sweden
41 M3 **Valluga** *mt* Austria
27 J10 **Vallvik** Sweden
118 K9 **Val Marie** Saskatchewan Canada
16 E1 **Valmaseda** Spain
31 K6 **Val. Meziříčí** Czechoslovakia
52 C5 **Valmiera** Latvia
21 P3 **Valmondois** France
21 M2 **Valmont** France
106 E9 **Valmont** New Mexico U.S.A.
45 N6 **Valmontone** Italy
100 H9 **Valmy** Nevada U.S.A.
16 E1 **Valnera** *mt* Spain
20 H2 **Valognes** France
Valona *see* **Vlorë**
16 D3 **Valoria la Buena** Spain
16 C3 **Valpaços** Portugal
76 C5 **Valparai** India
119 N6 **Valparaiso** Saskatchewan Canada
131 B4 **Valparaíso** *prov* Chile
131 B4 **Valparaíso** Chile
124 H6 **Valparaíso** Mexico
111 K11 **Valparaiso** Florida U.S.A.
99 T8 **Valparaiso** Indiana U.S.A.
98 K8 **Valparaiso** Nebraska U.S.A.
40 F6 **Valpelline** *V* Italy
48 E5 **Valpovo** Croatia
40 G7 **Valprato Soana** Italy
122 A8 **Val-Racine** Quebec Canada
19 N16 **Valréas** France
89 E6 **Vals** *R* S Africa
74 E8 **Valsād** India
28 H7 **Vålse** Denmark
100 B5 **Valsetz** Oregon U.S.A.
28 D3 **Valsgård** Denmark
26 G7 **Valsjö** Sweden
27 H12 **Valskog** Sweden
29 J8 **Valsörarna** *lighthouse* Finland
41 L5 **Valtellina** *V* Italy
29 T9 **Valthjofsstadhur** Iceland
45 M4 **Val Tiberina** Italy
29 O8 **Valtimo** Finland
83 M12 **Valton** Mauritius
54 K6 **Valuyki** Russian Federation
85 A3 **Valverde** Canary Is
127 J5 **Valverde** Dominican Rep
17 F5 **Valverde de Júcar** Spain
16 C7 **Valverde del Camino** Spain
26 M5 **Valvträsk** Sweden
48 K3 **Vama** Romania
28 C6 **Vamdrup** Denmark
27 G10 **Våmhus** Sweden
88 H7 **Vamizi** *isld* Mozambique
27 E12 **Vamma** Norway
29 K10 **Vammala** Finland
46 G9 **Vámos** Crete Greece
48 G3 **Vámospéros** Hungary
78 J2 **Van** Turkey
109 M3 **Van** Texas U.S.A.
29 L10 **Vanajanselka** *L* Finland
109 L2 **Van Alstyne** Texas U.S.A.
101 S3 **Vananda** Montana U.S.A.
56 F1 **Vanavara** Russian Federation
68 G1 **Van-Ban** Vietnam
121 S5 **Van Bruyssel** Quebec Canada
110 B6 **Van Buren** Arkansas U.S.A.
94 B6 **Van Buren** Indiana U.S.A.
95 T6 **Van Buren** Maine U.S.A.
110 F5 **Van Buren** Missouri U.S.A.
68 J6 **Van Canh** Vietnam
22 K4 **Vance** Belgium
21 M6 **Vancé** France
112 K2 **Vanceboro** North Carolina U.S.A.
94 D8 **Vanceburg** Kentucky U.S.A.
68 G2 **Van Chan** Vietnam
57 F5 **Vanchskiy Khrebet** *mts* Tajikistan/Afghanistan
117 G11 **Vancouver** British Columbia Canada
100 C4 **Vancouver** Washington U.S.A.
143 C10 **Vancouver,C** W Australia Australia
116 E6 **Vancouver, C** Alaska U.S.A.
117 K10 **Vancouver I** British Columbia Canada
117 D5 **Vancouver, Mt** Alaska/Yukon Terr U.S.A./Canada
110 G3 **Vandalia** Illinois U.S.A.
110 E2 **Vandalia** Missouri U.S.A.
41 L3 **Vandans** Austria
28 A3 **Vandborg** Denmark
119 Q1 **Vandekerckhove** Saskatchewan Canada
28 C5 **Vandel** Denmark
112 L2 **Vandemere** North Carolina U.S.A.
89 E6 **Vanderbijl Pk** S Africa
94 C1 **Vanderbilt** Michigan U.S.A.
109 L7 **Vanderbilt** Texas U.S.A.
94 H6 **Vandergrift** Pennsylvania U.S.A.
117 M8 **Vanderhoof** British Columbia Canada
140 D3 **Vanderlin I** N Terr Australia
109 N1 **Vandervoort** Arkansas U.S.A.
106 B6 **Vanderwagen** New Mexico U.S.A.
28 B2 **Vandet Sø** *L* Denmark
140 B1 **Van Dieman, C** N Terr Australia
140 E3 **Van Diemen,C** Queensland Australia
140 B1 **Van Diemen G** N Terr Australia
55 E1 **Vandmtor, Oz** *L* Russian Federation
121 R5 **Vandry** Quebec Canada
110 G5 **Vanduser** Missouri U.S.A.
100 A9 **Van Duzen** *R* California U.S.A.
27 F13 **Vänern** *L* Sweden
27 F13 **Vänersborg** Sweden
95 L4 **Van Etten** New York U.S.A.
27 C10 **Vang** Norway
88 G4 **Vanga** Tanzania
87 H12 **Vangaindrano** Madagascar
27 F13 **Vanga,N** Sweden
78 J2 **Van Gölü** *L* Turkey
27 C10 **Vangsmjösa** Norway
118 K9 **Vanguard** Saskatchewan Canada
70 A1 **Vanguard Bank** S China Sea
137 M3 **Vangunu** *isld* Solomon Is
68 F3 **Vang Vieng** Laos
98 D2 **Van Hook** North Dakota U.S.A.
108 C4 **Van Horn** Texas U.S.A.
106 F5 **Van Houten** New Mexico U.S.A.
137 O4 **Vanikoro Is** Santa Cruz Is
26 K7 **Vänjaurbäck** Sweden
26 K7 **Vänjaurträsk** Sweden
51 S2 **Vankarem** Russian Federation
121 Q7 **Vankleek Hill** Ontario Canada
98 F5 **Van Metre** South Dakota U.S.A.
26 L1 **Vanna** *isld* Norway
26 L8 **Vännäs** Sweden
83 J9 **Vannativillu** Sri Lanka
20 E6 **Vannes** France
21 P6 **Vannes-sur-Cosson** France
68 J6 **Van Ninh** Vietnam
57 F4 **Vannovka** Kazakhstan
107 O7 **Vanoss** Oklahoma U.S.A.
87 C12 **Vanrhynsdorp** S Africa
141 F3 **Vanrook** Queensland Australia
74 E8 **Vānsada** India
94 E9 **Vansant** Virginia U.S.A.
27 G11 **Vansbro** Sweden
118 L6 **Vanscoy** Saskatchewan Canada
142 F2 **Vansittart B** W Australia Australia
115 L4 **Vansittart I** Northwest Territories Canada
18 H8 **Vans, les** France
29 L11 **Vantaa** *R* Finland
29 L11 **Vantaa** Finland
118 L9 **Vantage** Saskatchewan Canada
100 F3 **Vantage** Washington U.S.A.
98 B7 **Van Tassell** Wyoming U.S.A.
137 O3 **Vanua Lava** *isld* Vanuatu
137 Q5 **Vanua Levu** *isld* Fiji
137 O5 **Vanuatu** *islds* Pacific Oc
99 N9 **Van Wert** Iowa U.S.A.
94 C6 **Van Wert** Ohio U.S.A.
87 D12 **Vanwyksvlei** S Africa
67 A6 **Van Yen** Vietnam
26 A9 **Vanylven** Norway
26 A9 **Vanylvsgapet** *B* Norway
110 D5 **Vanzant** Missouri U.S.A.
48 M2 **Vapnyarka** Ukraine
19 Q18 **Var** *dept* France
44 B4 **Var** *R* France
44 G3 **Vara** *R* Italy
27 F13 **Vara** Sweden
126 D3 **Varadero** Cuba
21 H7 **Varades** France
19 P17 **Varages** France
44 B2 **Varaita** *R* Italy
41 H6 **Varallo** Italy
42 B3 **Varallo** Italy
77 B2 **Varamin** Iran
75 K6 **Varanasi** India
26 R1 **Varangerfjorden** *inlet* Norway
26 R1 **Varangerhalvöya** *mt* Norway
42 G7 **Varano, L. di** Italy
131 A8 **Varas,Pto** Chile
16 D6 **Varas,R** Spain
21 K3 **Varaville** France
44 E3 **Varazze** Italy
27 F14 **Varberg** Sweden
77 L2 **Vardak** *prov* Afghanistan
111 G8 **Vardaman** Mississippi U.S.A.
46 E6 **Vardhoúsia Óri** *mt* Greece
27 L11 **Vårdö** Finland
26 S1 **Vardö** Norway
52 E5 **Varegovo** Russian Federation
32 H6 **Varel** Germany
21 M2 **Varengeville** France
20 G3 **Varenguebec** France
21 J4 **Varenne** *R* France
19 J3 **Varennes en Argonne** France
40 B5 **Varennes St.Sauveur** France
21 O7 **Varennes-sur-Fouzon** France
48 E6 **Vareš** Bosnia-Herzegovina
41 J6 **Varese** Italy
40 A7 **Vareze** *R* France
27 F13 **Vårgårda** Sweden
55 E3 **Vargashi** Russian Federation
130 G10 **Vargem** *R* Brazil
130 F7 **Varginha** Brazil
18 G9 **Varilhes** France
112 J2 **Varina** North Carolina U.S.A.
27 G13 **Väring** Sweden
21 O5 **Varize** France
26 K5 **Varjisträsk** Sweden
29 N9 **Varkaus** Finland
143 C10 **Varley,L** W Australia Australia
27 F12 **Varmland** *reg* Sweden
27 F12 **Värmlands-näs** *pen* Sweden
47 J1 **Varna** Bulgaria
55 D4 **Varna** Russian Federation
111 G11 **Varnado** Louisiana U.S.A.
28 D6 **Varnæs** Denmark
27 G14 **Vårnamo** Sweden
27 F11 **Värnäs** Sweden
52 F5 **Varnavino** Russian Federation
108 B1 **Varney** New Mexico U.S.A.
31 H5 **Varnsdorf** Czechoslovakia
27 F14 **Varnum** Sweden
112 F5 **Varnville** South Carolina U.S.A.
79 D3 **Varosha** Cyprus
48 D3 **Városlöd** Hungary
48 E3 **Várpalota** Hungary
52 G2 **Varsh, Oz** *L* Russian Federation
28 E3 **Vårst** Denmark
78 H2 **Varto** Turkey
27 G13 **Vartofta** Sweden
83 K9 **Varuniya** Sri Lanka
46 E7 **Varvára** *mt* Greece
46 E1 **Varvarin** Serbia Yugoslavia
54 C10 **Varvarovka** Ukraine
130 G9 **Várzea Alegre** Brazil
130 G5 **Várzea da Palma** Brazil
129 G7 **Várzea Grande** Brazil
130 E9 **Várzea,R** Brazil
52 E1 **Varzino** Russian Federation
52 E2 **Varzuga** *R* Russian Federation
52 E2 **Varzuga** Russian Federation
18 H5 **Varzy** France
48 D3 **Vas** *co* Hungary
130 H11 **Vasa Barris,R** Brazil
76 A1 **Vasai** India
52 B5 **Vasalemma** Estonia
48 G2 **Vásárosnamény** Hungary
29 K4 **Väsby** Sweden
16 B7 **Vascão** *R* Portugal
48 G4 **Vaşcău** Romania
21 N3 **Vascœuil** France
52 G3 **Vashka** *R* Russian Federation
48 K2 **Vashkovtsy** Ukraine
100 C2 **Vashon I** Washington U.S.A.
98 G2 **Vashti** North Dakota U.S.A.
109 J2 **Vashti** Texas U.S.A.
54 H8 **Vasil'kovka** Ukraine
52 G3 **Vasil'yevo** Russian Federation
52 G6 **Vasil'yevo** Russian Federation
55 F2 **Vasis** Russian Federation
29 P11 **Vaskelovo** Russian Federation
52 C5 **Vasknarva** Estonia
29 M3 **Vaskojoki** *R* Finland
48 E4 **Vaskút** Hungary
21 K8 **Vasles** France
48 L4 **Vaslui** Romania
112 H2 **Vass** North Carolina U.S.A.
118 F1 **Vassar** Manitoba Canada
94 D3 **Vassar** Michigan U.S.A.
27 B12 **Vassdalseggja** *mt* Norway
26 K3 **Vassijuare** Sweden
21 J4 **Vassy** Calvados France
26 J4 **Vastenjaure** *L* Sweden
27 J12 **Västerås** Sweden
26 H7 **Västerbotten** *reg* Sweden
27 F11 **Vasterdalälven** *R* Sweden
26 J5 **Västerfjäll** Sweden
27 K12 **Västerhaninge** Sweden
27 H12 **Västermo** Sweden
26 J7 **Vastermyrriset** Sweden
26 J8 **Väster Norr Land** Sweden
27 J14 **Västervik** Sweden
27 J11 **Västland** Sweden
27 H12 **Västmanland** *reg* Sweden
42 F6 **Vasto** Italy
33 N6 **Vastorf** Germany
26 L8 **Vastra Kvarken** *chan* Sweden
48 D3 **Vasvár** Hungary
55 G2 **Vasyugan** *R* Russian Federation
21 O7 **Vatan** France
Vaté *isld see* **Éfaté** *isld*
33 P8 **Väthen** Germany
47 H7 **Vathí** Greece
46 E8 **Váthia** Greece
45 M6 **Vaticano, Citta del** Italy
28 S9 **Vatnajökull** *ice cap* Iceland
26 B9 **Vatne** Norway
28 R9 **Vatneyri** Iceland
27 K12 **Vätö** Sweden
137 R5 **Vatoa** *isld* Fiji
87 H11 **Vatomandry** Madagascar
48 J3 **Vatra Dornei** Romania
27 G13 **Vättern** *L* Sweden
27 J11 **Vattholma** Sweden
41 K4 **Vättis** Switzerland
26 J10 **Vattrång** Sweden
40 C5 **Vauche Marlioz,Mt.De** France
19 O17 **Vaucluse** *dept* France
112 F4 **Vaucluse** South Carolina U.S.A.
40 C2 **Vauconcourt** France
21 L2 **Vaucottes** France
19 J4 **Vaucouleurs** France
36 B6 **Vaucourt** France
40 D4 **Vaud** *canton* Switzerland
21 N3 **Vaudreuil, le** France
122 H9 **Vaughan** Nova Scotia Canada
140 B5 **Vaughan Springs** N Terr Australia
101 O2 **Vaughn** Montana U.S.A.
108 B1 **Vaughn** New Mexico U.S.A.
128 D3 **Vaupés** *div* Colombia
21 K8 **Vausseroux** France
18 H9 **Vauvert** France
20 G2 **Vauville** France
40 D2 **Vauvillers** France
118 E8 **Vauxhall** Alberta Canada
87 J11 **Vavatenina** Madagascar
137 S5 **Vava'u Group** *islds* Tonga
52 H6 **Vavozh** Russian Federation
83 K9 **Vavuniya** Sri Lanka
118 J5 **Vawn** Saskatchewan Canada
27 K12 **Vaxholm** Sweden
27 G15 **Växjö** Sweden
20 G6 **Vay** France
76 D4 **Vāyalpād** India
50 F1 **Vaygach, Ostrov** *isld* Russian Federation
52 F3 **Vaymuga** *R* Russian Federation
129 L5 **Vaza** *R* Brazil
130 F5 **Vazante** Brazil
52 G3 **Vazhgort** Russian Federation
54 F1 **Vazuzskoye Vodokhranilishche** *res* Russian Federation
129 J6 **Veadeiras** Brazil
68 F7 **Veal Renh** Cambodia
28 D3 **Vebbestrup** Denmark
27 F16 **Veberöd** Sweden
98 J4 **Veblen** South Dakota U.S.A.
26 M7 **Vebomark** Sweden
33 M8 **Vechelde** Germany
25 F3 **Vecht** *R* Netherlands
32 H7 **Vechta** *R* Germany
32 H7 **Vechta** Germany
32 L10 **Veckerhagen** Germany
29 K5 **Vedbæk** Denmark
27 F14 **Veddige** Sweden
28 E3 **Veddum** Denmark
48 J6 **Vedea** Romania
28 A4 **Vedersø** Denmark
27 H12 **Vedevåg** Sweden
133 E4 **Vedia** Argentina
17 H6 **Vedra** *isld* Balearic Is
22 H3 **Vedrin** Belgium
28 E5 **Vedslet** Denmark
28 C6 **Vedsted** Denmark
28 G6 **Ved Stranden** Denmark
27 F13 **Vedum** Sweden
110 J1 **Veedersburg** Indiana U.S.A.
25 G2 **Veendam** Netherlands
25 E4 **Veenendaal** Netherlands
25 F2 **Veenhuizen** Netherlands
25 E2 **Veenwouden** Netherlands
25 A5 **Veere** Netherlands
25 A5 **Veerse Meer** Netherlands
33 N7 **Veerssen** Germany
28 E6 **Veflinge** Denmark
26 E6 **Vega** *isld* Norway
16 C2 **Vega de Tera** Spain
27 D13 **Vegårs Vatn** *L* Norway
29 K4 **Vegeån** *R* Sweden
32 J6 **Vegesack** Germany
28 D3 **Veggerby** Denmark
27 D11 **Veggli** Norway
46 E4 **Vegorrítis, L** Greece
118 F5 **Vegreville** Alberta Canada
108 A1 **Veguita** New Mexico U.S.A.
33 Q6 **Vehlow** Germany
27 M11 **Vehmaa** Finland
26 P1 **Veidnes** Norway
27 F15 **Veinge** Sweden
120 D3 **Vein L** Ontario Canada
133 D5 **Veinticinco de Mayo** Argentina
45 M5 **Veio** Italy
36 H4 **Veitshöchheim** Germany
28 J4 **Vejby** Denmark
28 C6 **Vejen** Denmark
28 A5 **Vejers** Denmark
28 D4 **Vejerslev** Denmark
28 E2 **Vejgård** Denmark
28 E4 **Vejlby** Århus Denmark
28 D5 **Vejlby** Vejle Denmark
28 C5 **Vejle** *co* Denmark
28 D5 **Vejle** Denmark
28 D5 **Vejle Fjord** *inlet* Denmark
28 H6 **Vejlø** Denmark
28 E7 **Vejnæs Nokke** *C* Denmark
37 P3 **Vejprty** Czechoslovakia
28 G5 **Vejrhøj** *hill* Denmark
28 F5 **Vejrø** *isld* Århus Denmark
28 G6 **Vejrø** *isld* Storstrøm Denmark
28 B5 **Vejrup** Denmark
28 F6 **Vejstrup** Denmark
28 J5 **Veksø** Denmark
52 F4 **Vel** *R* Russian Federation
127 H8 **Vela, C. de la** Colombia
22 E2 **Velaines** Belgium
46 E5 **Velaóra** Greece
106 E5 **Velarde** New Mexico U.S.A.
124 H5 **Velardeña** Mexico
18 H7 **Velay, Mts du** France
32 F10 **Velbert** Germany
37 M5 **Velburg** Germany
37 M4 **Velden** Germany
25 D6 **Veldhoven** Netherlands
47 J2 **Veleka** *R* Bulgaria
32 E9 **Velen** Germany
48 E3 **Velencei Tó** *L* Hungary
42 G2 **Velenje** Slovenia
46 E3 **Veles** Macedonia Yugoslavia
46 F5 **Velestínon** Greece
17 F7 **Vélez Bianco** Spain
16 E8 **Vélez Málaga** Spain
17 F7 **Vélez Rubio** Spain
26 F6 **Velfjord** Norway
33 R4 **Velgast** Germany
130 G6 **Velhas,R** Brazil
42 H3 **Velika** Croatia
42 G3 **Velika Gorica** Croatia
48 G6 **Velika Gradište** Serbia Yugoslavia
42 F3 **Velika Kapela** *dist* Croatia
48 G6 **Velika Plana** Serbia Yugoslavia
52 G2 **Velikaya** Russian Federation
52 G5 **Velikaya** *R* Russian Federation
52 C6 **Velikaya** *R* Russian Federation
52 E4 **Velikaya Guba** Russian Federation
48 K1 **Veliki Borki** Ukraine
48 K1 **Veliki Glubochek** Ukraine
48 G2 **Velikiy Bereznyy** Ukraine
52 D6 **Velikiye-Luki** Russian Federation
52 G4 **Velikiy Ustyug** Russian Federation
54 M1 **Velikodvorskiy** Russian Federation
54 J6 **Velikomikhaylovka** Russian Federation
47 H1 **Veliko Turnovo** Bulgaria
52 H2 **Velikovisochnoye** Russian Federation
52 F5 **Velikovo** Russian Federation
54 M1 **Velikoye, Oz** *L* Russian Federation
85 B6 **Velingara** Senegal
46 F2 **Velingrad** Bulgaria
42 E6 **Velino** *R* Italy
42 E6 **Velino, M** *mt* Italy
54 C1 **Velizh** Russian Federation
48 E2 **Velká Fatra** *mt* Czechoslovakia
48 E1 **Vel Karlovice** Czechoslovakia
48 G2 **Vel'ké Kapušány** Czechoslovakia
31 L6 **Velké Karlovice** Czechoslovakia
48 D3 **Velký Žitný Ostrov'** *reg* Czechoslovakia
38 L8 **Vellach** Austria
33 N6 **Vellahn** Germany
137 M3 **Vella Lavella** *isld* Solomon Is
45 J4 **Vellano** Italy
36 H5 **Vellberg** Germany
21 O8 **Velles** France
45 N6 **Velletri** Italy
28 D4 **Vellev** Denmark
28 A4 **Velling** Denmark
27 F16 **Vellinge** Sweden
45 O5 **Vellino, M** *mt* Italy
76 D4 **Vellore** India
56 D1 **Vel'minskiye Porogi** *falls* Russian Federation
56 D1 **Vel'mo** *R* Russian Federation
22 J5 **Velosnes** France
25 E4 **Velp** Netherlands
25 C4 **Velsen** Netherlands
52 F4 **Vel'sk** Russian Federation
52 H1 **Vel't** Russian Federation
33 S7 **Velten** Germany
22 D3 **Vélu** France
25 E4 **Veluwe** Netherlands
25 E4 **Veluwemeer** Netherlands
98 F1 **Velva** North Dakota U.S.A.
52 J3 **Vel'yu** *R* Russian Federation
90 E7 **Vema Fracture** Atlantic Oc
28 A4 **Vemb** Denmark
26 G9 **Vemdalen** Sweden
28 G6 **Vemmelev** Denmark
28 F7 **Vemmenæs** Denmark
29 K5 **Ven** *isld* Sweden
27 H14 **Vena** Sweden
27 D10 **Venabygd** Norway
12 D1 **Venachar,L** Scotland
131 E4 **Venado Tuerto** Argentina
45 Q7 **Venafro** Italy
128 F2 **Venamo,Cerro** *mt* Venezuela/Guyana
98 E9 **Venango** Nebraska U.S.A.
44 C1 **Venaria** Italy
100 G6 **Venator** Oregon U.S.A.
44 B1 **Venáus** Italy
130 E8 **Venceslau Bráz** Brazil
Venda *see* **Vantaa**
45 L1 **Venda** *mt* Italy
89 G4 **Venda** *homeland* S Africa
16 B6 **Vendas Novas** Portugal
18 E6 **Vendée** *dept* France
52 G3 **Vendenga** Russian Federation
36 D6 **Vendenheim** France
22 D3 **Vendin-le-Viel** France
21 N6 **Vendôme** France
21 N8 **Vendœuvres** France
17 H3 **Vendrell** Spain
22 H4 **Vendresse** France
28 D2 **Vendsyssel** *reg* Denmark
45 M1 **Veneta, Laguna** Italy
116 P3 **Venetie Landing** Alaska U.S.A.
45 K1 **Veneto** *reg* Italy
52 F6 **Venets** Russian Federation
54 K2 **Venev** Russian Federation
45 M1 **Venezia** Italy
42 D3 **Venezia-Euganea** *prov* Italy
42 E3 **Venezia,G.di** Italy
128 E2 **Venezuela** *rep* S America
127 J9 **Venezuela,G.de** Venezuela
28 D4 **Veng** Denmark
55 G3 **Vengerovo** Russian Federation
76 A3 **Vengurla** India
16 D3 **Venialbo** Spain
116 H8 **Veniaminof Vol** Alaska U.S.A.
118 E4 **Venice** Alberta Canada
Venice Italy *see* **Venezia**
111 M12 **Venice** St Louis
113 E10 **Venice** Florida U.S.A.
111 G12 **Venice** Louisiana U.S.A.
19 N13 **Vénissieux** France
27 G11 **Venjan** Sweden
76 D4 **Venkataguri** India
76 E1 **Venkatapuram** India
25 F6 **Venlo** Netherlands
98 J3 **Venlo** North Dakota U.S.A.
119 M7 **Venn** Saskatchewan Canada
28 D2 **Vennebjerg** Denmark
32 E7 **Vennebrügge** Germany
27 C13 **Vennesla** Norway
28 B3 **Venø** Denmark
28 B3 **Venø Bugt** *B* Denmark
19 Q15 **Venosc** France
121 O7 **Venosta** Quebec Canada
41 N4 **Venosta, Val** Italy
41 N4 **Venostie, Alpi** Italy
25 E5 **Venray** Netherlands
27 M14 **Venta** *R* Latvia
124 E5 **Ventana,Pta de la** *C* Mexico
133 E5 **Ventana,Sa** *ra* Argentina
16 E8 **Ventas de Zafarraya** Spain
19 P16 **Ventavon** France
28 H5 **Vented** Denmark
44 C4 **Ventimiglia** Italy
9 E6 **Ventnor** England
43 E8 **Ventotene, I** Italy
19 O16 **Ventoux, Mt** France
33 P5 **Ventschow** Germany
27 M14 **Ventspils** Latvia
128 E3 **Ventuari** *R* Venezuela
102 E7 **Ventura** California U.S.A.
98 G3 **Venturia** North Dakota U.S.A.
113 F10 **Venus** Florida U.S.A.
109 K3 **Venus** Texas U.S.A.
138 C5 **Venus B** South Australia Australia
138 C5 **Venus Bay** South Australia Australia
124 H8 **Venustiano Carranza** Mexico
52 D4 **Vepsovskaya Vozvyshennost'** *uplands* Russian Federation
133 E3 **Vera** Argentina
17 F7 **Vera** Spain
109 H2 **Vera** Texas U.S.A.
133 D6 **Vera, B** Argentina
130 E8 **Vera Cruz** Brazil
125 L8 **Veracruz** Mexico
74 D8 **Veraval** India
42 B3 **Verbania** Italy

111 K9 Verbena Alabama U.S.A.
22 D5 Verberie France
52 E6 Verbilki Russian Federation
41 H7 Vercelli Italy
33 R5 Verchen Germany
21 K7 Verchers,les France
19 O15 Vercors reg France
19 Q16 Verdaches France
26 E8 Verdal Norway
26 E8 Verdalsöra Norway
133 D6 Verde R Argentina
130 E4 Verde R Brazil
133 F2 Verde R Paraguay
71 E4 Verde isld Philippines
103 N7 Verde R Arizona U.S.A.
85 A6 Verde, C Senegal
126 G3 Verde, Cay isld Bahamas
130 G4 Verde Grande R Brazil
98 H7 Verdel Nebraska U.S.A.
32 K7 Verden Germany
109 J1 Verden Oklahoma U.S.A.
131 E7 Verde,Pen Argentina
130 G4 Verde Pequeno, R Brazil
130 D7 Verde,R Brazil
21 N6 Verdes France
98 H7 Verdigre Nebraska U.S.A.
107 O3 Verdigris R Okla/Kansas U.S.A.
118 F9 Verdigris L Alberta Canada
130 D5 Verdinho,Sa.do mts Brazil
19 Q17 Verdon R France
99 L9 Verdon Nebraska U.S.A.
18 E7 Verdon-sur-Mer, le France
19 J3 Verdun France
18 F9 Verdun-sur-Garonne France
19 J6 Verdun-sur-le-Doubs France
124 E5 Verdura Mexico
52 D6 Verech'ye Russian Federation
89 E6 Vereeniging S Africa
119 P7 Veregin Saskatchewan Canada
121 N5 Vérendrye, Parc Prov. de la Quebec Canada
52 H5 Vereshchagino Russian Federation
52 E5 Verestovo, Oz L Russian Federation
54 H1 Vereya Russian Federation
85 B6 Verga,C Guinea
17 F1 Vergara Spain
133 G4 Vergara Uruguay
45 K3 Vergato Italy
36 B6 Vergaville France
141 G6 Vergemont R Queensland Australia
141 G6 Vergemont Queensland Australia
95 O2 Vergennes Vermont U.S.A.
45 L4 Verghereto Italy
45 R8 Vérgine, M mt Italy
16 C3 Verín Spain
41 K1 Veringenstadt Germany
56 H3 Verkh Angara R Russian Federation
55 C3 Verkhiye Kigi Russian Federation
52 J5 Verkhnaya Yarva Russian Federation
56 H3 Verkhneangarskiy Khrebet mts Russian Federation
55 C4 Verkhnearshinskiy Russian Federation
55 C4 Verkhne-Avzyan Russian Federation
54 F8 Verkhnedneprovsk Ukraine
54 E2 Verkhnedneprovskiy Russian Federation
50 H2 Verkhneimbatsk Russian Federation
54 M7 Verkhnemakeyevka Russian Federation
29 Q3 Verkhnetulomskiy Russian Federation
52 D1 Verkhnetulomskoye, Vodokhranilishche L Russian Federation
55 C4 Verkhneural'sk Russian Federation
52 H6 Verkhne Yarkeyevo Russian Federation
54 K8 Verkhneye Ukraine
55 G3 Verkhneye Krasnoyarka Russian Federation
52 D2 Verkhneye Kuyto, Oz L Russian Federation
55 C3 Verkhniye Tatyshly Russian Federation
55 D3 Verkhniy Neyvinskiy Russian Federation
52 H1 Verkhniy Shar Russian Federation
55 C3 Verkhniy Tagil Russian Federation
55 C1 Verkhniy Vizhay Russian Federation
55 D1 Verkhniy Vizhay Russian Federation
55 D3 Verkhnyaya Pyshma Russian Federation
55 D2 Verkhnyaya Salda Russian Federation
55 D4 Verkhnyaya Sanarka Russian Federation
55 G3 Verkhnyaya Tarka Russian Federation
52 G4 Verkhnyaya Toyma Russian Federation
52 G4 Verkhnyaya Toz'ma Russian Federation
55 C2 Verkhnyaya Tura Russian Federation
52 G5 Verkhoshizhemye Russian Federation
55 D2 Verkhotur'ye Russian Federation
52 F4 Verkhovazh'ye Russian Federation
48 J2 Verkhovina Ukraine
54 F8 Verkhovtsevo Ukraine
51 M2 Verkhoyanskiy Khrebet mts Russian Federation
55 D2 Verkhyaya Sinyachikha Russian Federation
54 F8 Verkne Dneprovsk Ukraine
55 D3 Verkniy Ufaley Russian Federation
52 G3 Verkola Russian Federation
118 J8 Verlo Saskatchewan Canada
26 C9 Verma Norway
22 E4 Vermand France
130 D4 Vermelho,R Brazil
18 H5 Vermenton France
118 G5 Vermilion Alberta Canada
99 T10 Vermilion Illinois U.S.A.
111 D11 Vermilion R Louisiana U.S.A.
94 E5 Vermilion Ohio U.S.A.
111 D12 Vermilion B Louisiana U.S.A.
118 J1 Vermilion Bay Ontario Canada
117 Q6 Vermilion Chutes Alberta Canada
103 M4 Vermilion Cliffs Utah U.S.A.
118 K1 Vermilion L Ontario Canada
99 O2 Vermilion L Minnesota U.S.A.
118 F5 Vermilion Prov. Park Alberta Canada
99 O2 Vermilion Ra Minnesota U.S.A.
107 O2 Vermillion Kansas U.S.A.
98 K7 Vermillion South Dakota U.S.A.
103 M5 Vermillion Cliffs ra Arizona U.S.A.
121 R5 Vermillon R Quebec Canada
46 E4 Vérmion mt Greece
95 P2 Vermont state U.S.A.
99 Q9 Vermont Illinois U.S.A.
21 J6 Vern France
41 N4 Vernago, Lago di Italy
101 Q9 Vernal Utah U.S.A.
102 C4 Vernalis California U.S.A.
21 L7 Vernantes France
44 G3 Vernazza Italy
101 P8 Verne Wyoming U.S.A.
87 D11 Verneakpan L S Africa
120 K6 Verner Ontario Canada
21 M4 Verneuil Eure France
18 G4 Verneuil l'Etang France
21 N7 Verneuil sur-Indre France
89 B7 Verneuk Pan S Africa
28 E6 Verninge Denmark
45 K3 Vernio Italy
21 L7 Vernoil France
117 O10 Vernon British Columbia Canada
122 K7 Vernon Prince Edward I Canada
21 N3 Vernon Eure France
46 E4 Vernon mt Greece
111 H8 Vernon Alabama U.S.A.
103 P7 Vernon Arizona U.S.A.
98 D10 Vernon Colorado U.S.A.
111 L11 Vernon Florida U.S.A.
94 B8 Vernon Indiana U.S.A.
95 M3 Vernon New York U.S.A.
109 H1 Vernon Texas U.S.A.
101 N9 Vernon Utah U.S.A.
95 P4 Vernon Vermont U.S.A.
100 B4 Vernonia Oregon U.S.A.
140 B1 Vernon Is N Terr Australia
143 C6 Vernon,Mt W Australia Australia
21 M7 Vernou France
127 N4 Vernou Guadeloupe
21 O7 Vernou-en-Sologne France
20 G5 Vern-sur-Seiche France
113 G10 Vero Beach Florida U.S.A.
46 E4 Véroia Greece
44 H1 Verolanuova Italy
45 O6 Veroli Italy
121 O8 Verona Ontario Canada
45 J1 Verona Italy
110 C5 Verona Missouri U.S.A.
98 H3 Verona North Dakota U.S.A.
99 R7 Verona Wisconsin U.S.A.
101 T5 Verona Wyoming U.S.A.
19 O13 Verpillière France
138 D5 Verran South Australia Australia
111 E12 Verret, L Louisiana U.S.A.
127 H5 Verrettes Haiti
21 J8 Verrie,la France
19 N17 Vers France
21 P4 Versailles France
110 L2 Versailles Indiana U.S.A.
110 M3 Versailles Kentucky U.S.A.
110 D3 Versailles Missouri U.S.A.
94 C6 Versailles Ohio U.S.A.
55 D1 Vershina Russian Federation
58 G1 Vershino-Darasunskiy Russian Federation
32 H8 Versmold Germany
21 K3 Verson France
28 C5 Verst Denmark
21 K3 Ver-sur-Mer France
41 N4 Vertana,Cima mt Italy
122 C5 Verte,l Quebec Canada
20 C6 Verte,l France
18 F7 Verteillac France
129 H6 Vertentes R Brazil
130 J9 Vertentes Brazil
48 E3 Vérteshegység mt Hungary
126 E4 Vertientes Cuba
54 C5 Vertiyevka Ukraine
123 N2 Verton,L Quebec Canada
20 H7 Vertou France
22 H2 Vertrijk Belgium
18 H4 Vertus France
45 M4 Verucchio Italy
89 G7 Verulam S Africa
22 K2 Verviers Belgium
22 F4 Vervins France
119 M9 Verwood Saskatchewan Canada
8 B7 Veryan B England
41 J5 Verzasca,Val Switzerland
38 O8 Veržej Slovenia
29 M9 Vesanto Finland
22 L2 Vesdre R Belgium
21 O4 Vesegre R France
48 D2 Veseh Czechoslovakia
31 K7 Veselí Czechoslovakia
55 C2 Vesělovka Russian Federation
55 G4 Veselovskoye Russian Federation
55 E4 Veselyy Podol Kazakhstan
26 F6 Vesfna R Norway
21 K6 Vesgre R France
52 F3 Veshkoma Russian Federation
18 H3 Vesle R France
28 B2 Vesløs Denmark
20 H3 Vesly France
52 H3 Veslyana Russian Federation
52 H4 Veslyana R Russian Federation
40 D2 Vesoul France
107 M2 Vesper Kansas U.S.A.
99 R5 Vesper Wisconsin U.S.A.
27 F15 Vessige Sweden
99 L5 Vesta Minnesota U.S.A.
27 B13 Vest Agder reg Norway
95 L4 Vestal Center New York U.S.A.
26 H3 Vestbygd Norway
28 G7 Vestenskov Denmark
28 E6 Vester Aby Denmark
26 G3 Vesterålen isld Norway
147 G14 Vesterålen Norway
28 B3 Vester Assels Denmark
28 G7 Vesterborg Denmark
28 H6 Vester Egede Denmark
28 H6 Vester Egesborg Denmark
28 E2 Vester Hassing Denmark
28 D2 Vester Hjermitslev Denmark
29 K4 Vester Karup Sweden
28 C5 Vesterlund Denmark
28 C5 Vester Nebel Denmark
28 B5 Vester Nykirke Denmark
28 F2 Vesterøhavn Denmark
28 E6 Vester Skerninge Denmark
28 D7 Vester Sottrup Denmark
28 D3 Vester Tørslev Denmark
28 A3 Vestervig Denmark
27 C12 Vestfj-Dal Norway
146 G6 Vestfjella mts Antarctica
26 F4 Vestfjorden inlet Norway
27 D12 Vestfold reg Norway
146 J12 Vestfold Hills Antarctica
130 D7 Véstia Brazil
6 F1 Vestmanna Faeroes
28 S10 Vestmannaeyjar islds Iceland
26 B9 Vestnes Norway
29 T9 Vestrahorn C Iceland
28 G5 Vestsjælland co Denmark
26 G3 Vestvågöy Norway
45 Q8 Vesuvio mt Italy
52 E5 Ves'yegonsk Russian Federation
48 D3 Veszprém co Hungary
48 D3 Veszprém Hungary
48 D3 Veszprémvarsány Hungary
48 G4 Vésztö Hungary
89 E7 Vet R S Africa
98 E6 Vetal South Dakota U.S.A.
118 F6 Veteran Alberta Canada
98 B8 Veteran Wyoming U.S.A.
21 O3 Vétheuil France
54 C4 Vetka Belorussia
27 H14 Vetlanda Sweden
52 G5 Vetluga Russian Federation
52 G5 Vetluzhskiy Russian Federation
52 G6 Vetluzhskiy Russian Federation
47 H1 Vetovo Bulgaria
52 C6 Vetrino Belorussia
28 H6 Vetterslev Denmark
45 H3 Vetto Italy
26 M4 Vetträsjärvi Sweden
36 B2 Vettweiss Germany
21 L8 Veude R France
21 M2 Veules France
21 M2 Veulettes France
27 C12 Veum Norway
68 H6 Veun Kham Cambodia
22 D1 Veurne Belgium
94 B8 Vevay Indiana U.S.A.
26 F6 Vevelstad Norway
40 E5 Vevey Switzerland
46 E4 Vévi Greece
19 P15 Veynes France
103 L4 Veyo Utah U.S.A.
19 K4 Vézelise France
18 G7 Vezère R France
46 G2 Vezhen mt Bulgaria
52 H3 Vezh'yudor Russian Federation
22 K5 Vezin France
21 J7 Vezins Maine-et-Loire France
78 E1 Vezirköprü Turkey
36 B6 Vezouse R France
44 G3 Vezzano Ligure Italy
21 O5 Viabon France
45 J2 Viadana Italy
44 B1 Via di Ciamarella mt Italy
107 Q6 Vian Oklahoma U.S.A.
130 H7 Viana Espírito Santo Brazil
129 J4 Viana Maranhão Brazil
16 C2 Viana del Bollo Spain
16 B6 Viana do Alentejo Portugal
16 B3 Viana do Castelo Portugal
22 L4 Vianden Luxembourg
25 D5 Vianen Netherlands
68 F3 Viangchan Laos
45 J2 Viano Italy
130 E5 Vianópolis Brazil
29 L6 Viantie Finland
16 D7 Viar R Spain
44 H4 Viareggio Italy
18 G8 Viaur R France
119 O8 Vibank Saskatchewan Canada
28 B3 Viborg co Denmark
28 C4 Viborg Denmark
98 J6 Viborg South Dakota U.S.A.
43 G10 Vibo Valentia Italy
21 M5 Vibraye France
28 E4 Viby Århus Denmark
28 J5 Viby Roskilde Denmark
Vic see Vich
48 D2 Vičany Czechoslovakia
45 K4 Vicchio Italy
146 D4 Vicecomodoro Marambio Argentina Base Antarctica
18 E9 Vic en Bigorre France
130 F8 Vicente S Brazil
16 D4 Vicente,S mt Spain
45 L1 Vicenza Italy
119 M9 Viceroy Saskatchewan Canada
18 F9 Vic-Fezensac France
17 J3 Vich Spain
128 E3 Vichada dept Colombia
131 G3 Vichadero Uruguay
52 F6 Vichuga Russian Federation
133 C4 Vichuquén Chile
18 H6 Vichy France
107 L5 Vici Oklahoma U.S.A.
109 O9 Vickery Texas U.S.A.
103 L8 Vicksburg Arizona U.S.A.
94 B4 Vicksburg Michigan U.S.A.
111 F9 Vicksburg Mississippi U.S.A.
45 Q8 Vico Equense Italy
42 E6 Vico, L. di Italy
45 J4 Vicopisano Italy
17 G3 Vicort, Sierra de mts Spain
130 H10 Viçosa Alagoas Brazil
130 G7 Viçosa Minas Gerais Brazil
41 L5 Vicosoprano Switzerland
45 N5 Vicovaro Italy
48 K3 Vicovu de Sus Romania
21 P8 Vicq Exemplet France
21 M8 Vicq-sur-Gartempe France
22 E5 Vic-sur-Aisne France
18 G8 Vic-sur-Cère France
7 M9 Victor oil rig North Sea
106 E3 Victor Colorado U.S.A.
101 O6 Victor Idaho U.S.A.
99 O8 Victor Iowa U.S.A.
101 L3 Victor Montana U.S.A.
94 K4 Victor New York U.S.A.
138 E6 Victor Harbour South Australia Australia
131 E4 Victoria R Argentina
131 E4 Victoria Argentina
138 F6 Victoria state Australia
140 B3 Victoria R N Terr Australia
139 G6 Victoria Victoria Australia
123 T6 Victoria Newfoundland Canada
100 B1 Victoria Vancouver I, Br Col Canada
131 A7 Victoria Chile
127 P5 Victoria Grenada
83 K12 Victoria Mahé I Indian Oc
43 F12 Victoria Malta
71 E3 Victoria Luzon Philippines
70 D2 Victoria Sabah
127 O3 Victoria co Trinidad
107 L3 Victoria Kansas U.S.A.
109 K7 Victoria Texas U.S.A.
94 J10 Victoria Virginia U.S.A.
89 G3 Victoria prov Zimbabwe
119 V8 Victoria Beach Manitoba Canada
89 D1 Victoria Falls Zambezi R Zimbabwe
121 L8 Victoria Harb Ontario Canada
126 G2 Victoria Hill San Salvador Bahamas
114 H3 Victoria I Northwest Territories Canada
139 G5 Victoria L New South Wales Australia
123 P5 Victoria L res Newfoundland Canada
121 N5 Victoria, L Quebec Canada
88 D2 Victoria, L E Africa
146 C12 Victoria Land Antarctica
73 P4 Victoria Mt Burma
145 D4 Victoria, Mt New Zealand
136 K3 Victoria, Mt Papua New Guinea
86 F5 Victoria Nile R Uganda
142 B2 Victoria Park dist Perth, W Aust Australia
139 K5 Victoria Pass New South Wales Australia
140 B3 Victoria R N Terr Australia
123 P5 Victoria R Newfoundland Canada
144 D5 Victoria Range New Zealand
140 B3 Victoria River Downs N Terr Australia
114 J4 Victoria Str Northwest Territories Canada
145 D1 Victoria Valley New Zealand
121 T6 Victoriaville Quebec Canada
89 C8 Victoria West S Africa
123 L3 Victor L Quebec Canada
146 J8 Victor, Mt mt Antarctica
102 G7 Victorville California U.S.A.
140 C7 Victory Downs N Terr Australia
133 E4 Vicuña Argentina
133 C4 Vicuña Chile
28 B7 Vidå R Denmark
98 A2 Vida Montana U.S.A.
100 C5 Vida Oregon U.S.A.
103 K7 Vidal California U.S.A.
112 E5 Vidalia Georgia U.S.A.
111 E10 Vidalia Louisiana U.S.A.
83 K8 Vidattaltivu Sri Lanka
19 Q18 Vidauban France
109 K7 Vidauri Texas U.S.A.
28 B4 Videbæk Denmark
130 D10 Videira Brazil
48 K6 Videle Romania
Viderø see Viðoy
47 O12 Vidho isld Greece
16 B6 Vidigueira Portugal
56 F3 Vidim Russian Federation
46 F1 Vidin Bulgaria
16 C1 Vidio, C Spain
74 G7 Vidisha India
52 D4 Vidlitsa Russian Federation
46 E1 Vidojevica mt Serbia Yugoslavia
31 O3 Vidomlya Belorussia
109 N5 Vidor Texas U.S.A.
111 B11 Vidor Texas U.S.A.
118 H9 Vidora Saskatchewan Canada
18 H9 Vidourle France
6 F1 Viðoy isld Faeroes
48 K6 Vidra Romania
26 L6 Vidsel Sweden
28 D2 Vidstrup Denmark
42 J6 Viduša mt Bosnia-Herzegovina
52 C6 Vidzy Belorussia
52 H4 Vidz'yuyar Russian Federation
21 L3 Vie R Calvados France
20 G8 Vie R Vendée France
37 O5 Viechtach Germany
131 D8 Viedma Argentina
133 C7 Viedma, L Argentina
20 H8 Vieillevigne France
108 C5 Vieja, Sa mts Texas U.S.A.
128 C6 Viejas, Islas de las Peru
Vielha see Viella
17 H2 Viella Spain
21 M4 Vielle-Lyre, la France
22 K3 Vielsalm Belgium
28 J6 Viemose Denmark
33 N9 Vienenburg Germany
68 E2 Vieng Pou Kha Laos
Vienna Austria see Wien Austria
110 H4 Vienna Illinois U.S.A.
95 M8 Vienna Maryland U.S.A.
98 J5 Vienna South Dakota U.S.A.
94 F7 Vienna West Virginia U.S.A.
18 F6 Vienne dept France
19 N13 Vienne France
21 L7 Vienne R France
131 B3 Vientes, P. del pk Arg/Chile
Vientiane see Viangchan
131 B6 Viento, Cord. del ra Argentina
127 M5 Vieques isld Puerto Rico
29 N8 Vieremä Finland
32 M6 Vierlande reg Germany
25 E5 Vierlingsbeek Netherlands
36 F4 Viernheim Germany
25 F6 Viersen Germany
21 J3 Vierville-sur-Mer France
41 H3 Vierwaldstätter See L Switzerland
21 P7 Vierzon France
124 H5 Viesca Mexico
33 Q6 Viesecke Germany
37 L1 Vieselbach Germany
52 C6 Viesite Nereta Latvia
21 J4 Viessoix France
42 G7 Vieste Italy
68 G3 Vietnam rep S E Asia
33 R7 Vietnitz Germany
68 G2 Vietri Vietnam
45 R8 Vietri S. Mare Italy
127 O8 Vieux Fort St Lucia
127 N5 Vieux Fort,Pte.du Guadeloupe W Indies
108 H3 View Texas U.S.A.
28 H5 Vig Denmark
52 F5 Viga R Russian Federation
71 E2 Vigan Luzon Philippines
18 H8 Vigan, le France
45 L2 Vigarano Mainarda Italy
45 J1 Vigásio Italy
18 F7 Vigeois France
44 E1 Vigevano Italy
43 G8 Viggiano Italy
129 J4 Vigia Brazil
16 B7 Vigia mt Portugal
133 D7 Vigía, C Argentina
71 E3 Vigia Pt Luzon Philippines
21 P6 Viglain France
45 O6 Viglio mt Italy
21 P1 Vignacourt France
44 D1 Vignale Mon Ferrato Italy
18 E10 Vignemale mt France/Spain
22 G4 Vigneux Hocquet France
45 K3 Vignola Italy
16 B2 Vigo Spain
45 L1 Vigonza Italy
142 C5 Vigors,Mt W Australia Australia
26 A9 Vigra isld Norway
27 A13 Vigrestad Norway
28 B2 Vigsø Denmark
29 L7 Vihanti Finland
21 J7 Vihiers France
29 L11 Vihti Finland
29 K10 Viiala Finland
29 O9 Viinijärvi L Finland
29 M5 Viiri Finland
29 M8 Viitasaari Finland
76 A2 Vijayadurg India
76 E2 Vijayawada India
46 D4 Vijosë R Albania
28 S10 Vik Iceland
26 F6 Vik Norway
27 G11 Vika Sweden
29 M5 Vikajärvi Finland
27 H11 Vikarbyn Sweden
27 A12 Vikedal Norway
71 N9 Vikeke Timor
29 K4 Viken Sweden
27 G12 Vikersvik Sweden
27 D12 Vikesund Norway
46 F3 Vikhren mt Bulgaria
118 F5 Viking Alberta Canada
7 M9 Viking oil rig North Sea
6 M2 Viking Bank North Sea
7 M9 Viking N oil rig North Sea
7 M9 Viking S oil rig North Sea
27 H11 Vikmanshyttan Sweden
26 E7 Vikna isld Norway
26 E7 Vikna Norway
26 J9 Viksjö Sweden
55 F3 Vikulovo Russian Federation
71 M9 Vila Armindo Monteiro Timor
Vila Cabral see Lichinga
131 E4 Vila Constitución Argentina
88 G10 Vila da Maganje Mozambique
16 B7 Vila do Bispo Portugal
16 B3 Vila do Conde Portugal
87 F8 Vila Gamito Mozambique
20 H5 Vilaine R Ille-et-Vilaine France
20 F6 Vilaine R Morbihan France
17 H2 Vilaller Spain
87 F9 Vila Machado Mozambique
128 E6 Vila Murtinho Brazil
87 G11 Vilanandro, Tanjona C Madagascar
87 G10 Vilanculos Mozambique
52 C6 Vilāni Latvia
16 B5 Vila Nova da Barquinha Portugal
16 B3 Vila Nova de Famalicão Portugal
16 C3 Vila Nova de Fozcoa Portugal
16 B3 Vila Nova de Gaia Portugal
71 N9 Vila Nova de Malaca Timor
16 B7 Vila Nova de Mil Fontes Portugal
16 B4 Vila Nova de Paiva Portugal
16 B3 Vila Pouca de Aguiar Portugal
16 B3 Vila Real Portugal
16 C7 Vila Real de Santo António Portugal
16 C4 Vilar Formoso Portugal
106 H4 Vilas Colorado U.S.A.
111 M11 Vilas Florida U.S.A.
98 J5 Vilas South Dakota U.S.A.
71 N9 Vila Salazar Timor
87 F8 Vila Vasco da Gama Mozambique
129 H3 Vila Velha Amapá Brazil
130 H7 Vila Velha Espírito Santo Brazil
16 B5 Vila Velha de Ródão Portugal
16 B3 Vila Verde Portugal
128 D6 Vilcabamba, Cord mts Peru
48 H5 Vîlcanului Muntii mt Romania
48 J5 Vîlcea reg Romania
28 B4 Vildbjerg Denmark
28 B3 Vile Denmark
52 G4 Viled' R Russian Federation
37 P3 Vilémov Czechoslovakia
53 C7 Vileyskoye Vodokhranilishche res Belorussia
52 H4 Vil'gort Komi Respublika Russian Federation
52 J4 Vil'gort Permskaya obl Russian Federation
26 J7 Vilhelmina Sweden
128 F6 Vilhena Brazil
53 C7 Viliya R Belorussia
52 C5 Viljandi Estonia
31 O1 Vilkaviškis Lithuania
51 J1 Vil'kitskogo, Proliv str Russian Federation
48 M5 Vilkovo Ukraine
128 E8 Villa Abecia Bolivia
45 N6 Villa Adriana Italy
108 A5 Villa Ahumada Mexico
127 J5 Villa Altagracia Dominican Rep
133 E3 Villa Angela Argentina
131 C5 Villa Atuel Argentina
45 K1 Villa Bartolomea Italy
38 F8 Villabassa Italy
128 E6 Villa Bella Bolivia
128 E4 Villa Bittencourt Brazil
16 C2 Villablino Spain
16 E5 Villacañas Spain
16 E1 Villacarriedo Spain
16 E6 Villa Carrillo Spain
16 E4 Villacastin Spain
38 J8 Villach Austria
16 C2 Villachica, L. de Spain
43 B9 Villacidro Sardinia
Villa Cisneros see Dakhla, Ad
133 D4 Villa Colón Argentina
133 E4 Villa Concepción del Tio Argentina
133 E4 Villa Constitucion Argentina
124 G4 Villa Coronado Mexico
16 D2 Villada Spain
127 L9 Villa de Cura Venezuela
133 E4 Villa del Rosario Argentina
16 E2 Villadiego Spain
131 D3 Villa Dolores Argentina
41 H5 Villadossola Italy
45 L1 Villa Estense Italy
17 G4 Villafamés Spain
130 B10 Villa Franca Paraguay
16 C2 Villafranca del Bierzo Spain
17 G4 Villafranca del Cid Spain
16 C6 Villafranca de los Barros Spain
17 J3 Villafranca del Penedés Spain
45 J1 Villafranca di Verona Italy
45 L1 Villafranca P Italy
45 L1 Villaga Italy
16 B2 Villagarcía de Arosa Spain
109 N5 Village Cr Texas U.S.A.
109 N5 Village Mills Texas U.S.A.
131 G6 Villa Gesell Argentina
99 S10 Villa Grove Illinois U.S.A.
131 F3 Villaguay Argentina
133 F3 Villa Guillermina Argentina
133 F3 Villa Hayes Paraguay
125 N9 Villahermosa Mexico
133 E4 Villa Huidobro Argentina
21 K5 Villaines-la-Jubel France
21 M7 Villaines-les-Rochers France
21 K6 Villaines-sous-Malicorne France
128 F8 Villa Ingavi Bolivia
133 E5 Villa Iris Argentina
127 J5 Villa Isabel Dominican Rep
16 B1 Villalba Lugo Spain
16 E4 Villalba Madrid Spain
45 Q7 Villa Literno Italy
16 D2 Villalón de Campos Spain
133 E5 Villalonga Argentina
16 D3 Villalpando Spain
17 F6 Villamanriqué Spain
43 B9 Villamar Sardinia
131 D4 Villa Maria Argentina
133 D2 Villa Martín Bolivia
16 D8 Villamartín Spain
124 G4 Villa Matamoros Mexico
17 F5 Villamayor de Santiago Spain
21 O5 Villamblain France
133 D4 Villa Mercedes Argentina
133 E3 Villa Minetti Argentina
45 H3 Villaminozzo Italy
133 E2 Villa Montes Bolivia
16 B3 Villa Nova da Cerveira Portugal
45 L2 Villanova March Italy
127 H9 Villanueva Colombia
124 H6 Villanueva Mexico
106 E6 Villanueva New Mexico U.S.A.
16 D6 Villanueva de Córdoba Spain
17 F6 Villanueva del Arzobispo Spain
16 D6 Villanueva de la Serena Spain
16 D3 Villanueva del Campo Spain
16 E6 Villanueva de los Infantes Spain
17 J3 Villanueva y Geltrú Spain
48 E5 Villány Hungary
124 G4 Villa Ocampo Durango Mexico
16 C1 Villaodrid Spain
124 G4 Villa Orestes Pereyra Mexico
124 E3 Villa Pesqueira Mexico
43 C9 Villaputzu Sardinia
16 E2 Villarcayo Spain
19 P14 Villard France
19 P14 Villard de Lans France
17 G5 Villar del Arzobispo Spain
16 C5 Villar del Rey Spain
133 D5 Villa Regina Argentina
142 D4 Villaret, C W Australia Australia
130 B9 Villa Rey Paraguay
111 M8 Villa Rica Georgia U.S.A.
17 G4 Villarluengo Spain
43 F11 Villarosa Sicily
17 G5 Villarreal Spain
131 A7 Villarrica Chile
130 C9 Villarrica Paraguay
131 B7 Villarrica, Vol Chile
17 F5 Villarrobledo Spain
17 F3 Villarroya de la Sierra Spain
16 E5 Villarubia de los Ojos Spain
95 N7 Villas New Jersey U.S.A.
131 D2 Villa Sanagasta Argentina
131 D2 Villa San Martín Argentina
38 G9 Villa Santina Italy
17 F3 Villasayas Spain
133 D3 Villa Unión Argentina
108 G7 Villa Union Mexico
124 G6 Villa Unión Durango Mexico
124 F6 Villa Unión Sinaloa Mexico
128 D3 Villavicencio Colombia
16 D1 Villaviciosa Spain
16 D6 Villaviciosa de Córdoba Spain
128 C3 Villavieja Colombia
133 D2 Villazón Bolivia
36 C7 Villé France
21 N6 Ville-aux-Clèrcs, la France
21 H4 Villebaudon France
40 B6 Villebois France
18 F7 Villebois Lavalette France
19 Q17 Villecroze France
21 H7 Villedieu-la-Blouère Maine-et-Loire France
20 H4 Villedieu-les-Poêtes France
21 O8 Villedieu-sur-Indre France
21 M2 Villedomer France
21 M6 Villedomer France
18 H8 Villefort France
44 B4 Villefranche France
19 N13 Villefranche Rhône France
18 G9 Villefranche de Lauragais France
18 G8 Villefranche-de-Rouergue France
18 F8 Villefranche-du-Perigord France
21 O7 Villefranche-sur-Cher France
17 G4 Villel Spain
121 L5 Ville-Marie Quebec Canada
21 N4 Villemeux-sur-Eure France
121 M4 Villemontel Quebec Canada
18 G9 Villemur sur le Tarn France
17 G6 Villena Spain
19 N12 Villeneuve France
40 F6 Villeneuve Italy
18 G8 Villeneuve d'Allier France
22 E2 Villeneuve d'Ascq France
19 N15 Villeneuve de Berg France
18 E9 Villeneuve de Marc France
18 H4 Villeneuve l'Archevêque France
19 N17 Villeneuve-lès-Avignon France
21 P3 Villeneuve-les-Sablons France
18 G4 Villeneuve-St Georges France
18 F8 Villeneuve-sur-Lot France
18 H4 Villeneuve-sur-Yonne France
21 N7 Villentrois France
111 D11 Ville Platte Louisiana U.S.A.
21 M2 Villequier France
21 N6 Villeromain France
121 T6 Villeroy Quebec Canada
21 J3 Villers-Bocage Calvados France
21 P2 Villers-Bocage Somme France
21 P3 Villers-Bretonneux France
22 D4 Villers-Carbonnel France
22 E5 Villers Cotterets France
22 J4 Villers Devant-Orval Belgium
21 L4 Villers-en-Ouche France
22 J2 Villers-le-Bouillet Belgium
22 H3 Villers-le-Gambon Belgium
22 E3 Villers-Outreaux France
22 K5 Villerupt-la-Montagne mt France
21 L3 Villerville France
19 N13 Villeurbanne France
131 C3 Villicun, Sa ra Argentina
21 N8 Villiers France
21 J6 Villiers-Charlemagne France
41 J1 Villingen-Schwenningen Germany
99 M9 Villisca Iowa U.S.A.
36 E3 Villmar Germany
Vilna see Vilnius
118 F4 Vilna Alberta Canada
53 C7 Vilnius Lithuania
29 L9 Vilppula Finland
41 N2 Vils Austria
28 B3 Vils Denmark
27 M13 Vilsandi Saar isld Estonia
37 N7 Vilsbiburg Germany
37 M4 Vilseck Germany
37 P6 Vilshofen Germany
27 G15 Vilshult Sweden
28 B6 Vilslev Denmark
28 C3 Vilsted Denmark
28 B3 Vilsund Denmark
76 D5 Viluppuram India
42 J6 Vilusi Montenegro Yugoslavia
52 J5 Vil'va Russian Federation
22 G2 Vilvoorde Belgium
51 L2 Vilyuy R Russian Federation
51 M2 Vilyuysk Russian Federation
56 H1 Vilyuyskoye Vodokhranilishche res Russian Federation
16 C3 Vimioso Portugal
27 H14 Vimmerby Sweden
27 G11 Vimo Sweden
21 L4 Vimoutiers France
29 K8 Vimpeli Finland
30 H6 Vimperk Czechoslovakia
22 D3 Vimy France
111 H7 Vina Alabama U.S.A.
102 B2 Vina California U.S.A.
131 B4 Viña de Mar Chile
17 G6 Vinalapó R Spain
95 T2 Vinalhaven Maine U.S.A.
17 H4 Vinaroz Spain
40 B7 Vinay France
110 J3 Vincennes Indiana U.S.A.
146 G14 Vincennes Bay Antarctica
111 K8 Vincent Alabama U.S.A.
94 F7 Vincent Ohio U.S.A.
16 B7 Vincente, C. de S Portugal
128 C4 Vinces Ecuador
45 R7 Vinchiaturo Italy
133 D3 Vinchina Argentina
45 J4 Vinci Italy
28 B4 Vind Denmark
28 C3 Vindblæs Denmark
28 G7 Vindeby Denmark
26 H5 Vindelälven R Sweden
26 K6 Vindelgransele Sweden
26 L7 Vindeln Sweden
143 B7 Vinden, Mt W Australia Australia
28 C4 Vinderslev Denmark
28 B4 Vinderup Denmark
74 F7 Vindhya Range India
28 B4 Vinding Ringkøbing Denmark
28 D4 Vinding Vejle Denmark
28 D5 Vinding Vejle Denmark
28 F6 Vindinge Denmark
21 O8 Vineuil Indre France
21 N6 Vineuil Loir-et-Cher France
95 R5 Vineyard Haven Massachusetts U.S.A.
48 G4 Vinga Romania
27 H12 Vingåker, V Sweden
40 B2 Vingeanne R France
21 L4 Vingt Hanaps France
68 G3 Vinh Vietnam
16 C3 Vinhais Portugal
68 J7 Vinh Cam Ranh B Vietnam
68 J6 Vinh Giat Vietnam
Vinh Linh see Ho Xa
69 G8 Vinh Loi Vietnam
68 G7 Vinh Long Vietnam
68 H3 Vinh Son B Vietnam
67 B6 Vinh Yen Vietnam
46 E3 Vinica Macedonia Yugoslavia
99 L3 Vining Minnesota U.S.A.
107 P5 Vinita Oklahoma U.S.A.
27 C12 Vinje Norway
26 C8 Vinjeora Norway
48 H6 Vînju Mare Romania
28 D4 Vinkel Denmark
48 E5 Vinkovci Croatia
26 M2 Vinnelys Norway
48 M1 Vinnitsa Ukraine
48 H2 Vinogradov Ukraine
19 P17 Vinon France
107 L7 Vinson Oklahoma U.S.A.
146 C7 Vinson Massif mts Antarctica
27 D10 Vinstra R Norway
71 E1 Vintar Luzon Philippines
99 O7 Vinton Iowa U.S.A.
111 C11 Vinton Louisiana U.S.A.
94 E8 Vinton Ohio U.S.A.
94 H9 Vinton Virginia U.S.A.
27 G12 Vintrosa Sweden
133 E6 Vintter Argentina
48 H4 Vinţu de Jos Romania
76 D2 Vinukonda India
33 P7 Vinzelberg Germany
55 E3 Vinzili Russian Federation
102 C1 Viola California U.S.A.
100 H3 Viola Idaho U.S.A.
99 Q8 Viola Illinois U.S.A.
107 N4 Viola Kansas U.S.A.
99 Q6 Viola Wisconsin U.S.A.
101 P7 Viola Wyoming U.S.A.
118 B5 Violet Grove Alberta Canada
87 C11 Vioolsdrif Namibia
20 H6 Vioreau, Grand Res. de France
41 O4 Vipiteno Italy
33 R6 Vipperow Germany
42 F4 Vir isld Croatia
27 H13 Virå Sweden
71 G4 Virac Philippines
47 K5 Virancık Turkey
52 E3 Virandozero Russian Federation
48 G6 Virciorova Romania
119 R9 Virden Manitoba Canada
99 R10 Virden Illinois U.S.A.
29 J3 Virdni mt Finland
20 H3 Vire R France
21 J4 Vire France
27 G14 Vireda Sweden
142 B5 Virehow, Mt W Australia Australia
87 B9 Virei Angola
22 G3 Virelles Belgium
22 H3 Vireux Belgium
48 H4 Vîrfurile Romania
101 P1 Virgelle Montana U.S.A.
130 G5 Virgem da Lapa Brazil
17 F3 Virgen,Sa.de la mts Spain
107 P4 Virgil Kansas U.S.A.
98 H5 Virgil South Dakota U.S.A.
102 C1 Virgilia California U.S.A.
94 J10 Virgilina Virginia U.S.A.
45 J1 Virgilio Italy
103 L5 Virgin R Arizona U.S.A.
113 L7 Virgin Gorda isld Virgin Is
14 D3 Virginia Ireland
89 E7 Virginia S Africa
94 H9 Virginia state U.S.A.
101 N7 Virginia Idaho U.S.A.
99 Q10 Virginia Illinois U.S.A.
99 O2 Virginia Minnesota U.S.A.
98 K9 Virginia Nebraska U.S.A.
95 M10 Virginia Beach Virginia U.S.A.
101 O4 Virginia City Montana U.S.A.
102 E2 Virginia City Nevada U.S.A.
117 L5 Virginia Falls Northwest Territories Canada
121 L4 Virginiatown Ontario Canada
113 L7 Virgin Is W Indies
103 K5 Virgin Mts Nev/Ariz U.S.A.
130 G6 Virginópolis Brazil
19 P13 Virignin France
26 J4 Virihaure Sweden
19 O14 Viriville France
133 D8 Virjenes, C Argentina
28 D4 Virklund Denmark
29 N9 Virmasvesi L Finland
29 N11 Virolahti Finland
99 Q6 Viroqua Wisconsin U.S.A.
42 H3 Virovitica Croatia
42 J6 Virpazar Montenegro Yugoslavia
29 K9 Virrat Finland
27 H12 Virsbo Sweden
27 H14 Virserum Sweden
29 N9 Virtasalmi Finland
48 J6 Vîrtoapele Romania
46 G1 Vîrtoapele de Sus Romania
22 K4 Virton Belgium
128 C5 Virú Peru
76 C6 Virudunagar India
52 C5 Viru-Jaagup Estonia
42 G5 Vis isld Croatia
27 H14 Vi, S Sweden
102 E5 Visalia California U.S.A.
19 N16 Visan France
45 J1 Visano Italy
71 F5 Visayan Sea Philippines
28 E3 Visborg Denmark
28 B6 Visby Sønderjylland Denmark
28 A3 Visby Viborg Denmark
27 K14 Visby Sweden
130 G7 Visconde do Rio Branco Brazil
119 M7 Viscount Saskatchewan Canada
114 J3 Viscount Melville Sd Northwest Territories Canada
22 K2 Visé Belgium
48 E7 Višegard Bosnia-Herzegovina
45 M3 Viserba Italy
16 B4 Viseu Portugal
48 J3 Vişeu R Romania
48 J3 Vişeu de Sus Romania
76 F2 Vishakhapatam India
52 H4 Vishera R Russian Federation
52 G5 Vishkil' Russian Federation
48 K1 Vishnevets Ukraine
55 F5 Vishnevka Kazakhstan
55 D3 Vishnevogorsk Russian Federation
55 D1 Visim R Russian Federation
55 C2 Visim Russian Federation
55 C2 Visimo-Utkinsk Russian Federation
46 G1 Vişina Veche Romania
27 G13 Visingsö Sweden
27 F14 Viskafors Sweden
27 F14 Viskan R Sweden
52 C6 Višķi Latvia
28 G5 Viskinge Denmark
27 G15 Vislanda Sweden
124 D3 Visnaga Mexico
74 E7 Visnagar India
44 B2 Viso mt Italy
16 E6 Viso del Marqués Spain
48 E7 Visoko Bosnia-Herzegovina
46 E3 Visoko mt Macedonia Yugoslavia
146 G2 Visokoi I S Sandwich Is S Atlantic Oc
40 G5 Visp Switzerland
27 H15 Vissefjärda Sweden
32 L7 Visselhövede Germany
28 E6 Vissenbjerg Denmark
40 G5 Vissoie Switzerland
102 G8 Vista California U.S.A.
128 F3 Vista Alegre Brazil
101 K8 Vista Res Nevada U.S.A.
28 F4 Vistoft Denmark
46 G3 Vistonís, L Greece
Vistula R see Wisła R
46 G1 Vit R Bulgaria
119 V9 Vita Manitoba Canada
76 B2 Vita India
54 B1 Vitebsk Belorussia
42 E6 Viterbo Italy
16 C3 Vitigudino Spain
56 H4 Vitim R Russian Federation
58 F1 Vitimskoye Ploskogor'ye Russian Federation
42 H5 Vitina Bosnia-Herzegovina
46 E7 Vitína Greece
130 H7 Vitória Brazil
17 F2 Vitoria Spain
130 H4 Vitória da Conquista Brazil
130 J10 Vitoria de Sta Antão Brazil
42 H4 Vitorog mts Bosnia-Herzegovina
21 N5 Vitray-en-Beauce France
20 H5 Vitré France
123 N2 Vitré,L Quebec Canada
40 C2 Vitrey France
19 O18 Vitrolles France
21 P6 Vitry-aux-Loges France
22 D3 Vitry-en-Artois France
27 F11 Vitsand Sweden
Vitsi mt see Vérnon mt
26 M4 Vittangi R Sweden
28 A5 Vittarp Denmark
40 C1 Vittel France
28 D4 Vitten Denmark
27 J12 Vittinge Sweden
120 K10 Vittoria Ontario Canada
43 F12 Vittoria Sicily
43 F13 Vittoriosa Malta
42 E3 Vittorio Ven Italy
27 G15 Vittsjö Sweden
45 R7 Vitulano Italy
26 N5 Vitvattnet Sweden
40 F7 Viu Italy
28 C5 Viuf Denmark
18 H7 Vivarais, Mts du France
28 E3 Vive Denmark
Viveiro see Vivero
17 G5 Viver Spain
16 B1 Vivero Spain
44 D1 Viverone, L. di Italy
51 J2 Vivi Russian Federation
109 O3 Vivian Louisiana U.S.A.
98 F6 Vivian South Dakota U.S.A.
19 N16 Viviers France
20 G4 Vivier-sur-Mer, Le France
28 E4 Vivild Denmark
21 L5 Vivoin France
138 D6 Vivonne South Australia Australia
18 F6 Vivonne France
133 F5 Vivorata Argentina
26 M4 Vivunki Sweden

238
Vizcaíno,Des.de — Wancoocha, L

124 C4 **Vizcaíno,Des.de** Mexico
124 B4 **Vizcaíno,Sa** *mts* Mexico
17 F1 **Vizcaya** *prov* Spain
47 J3 **Vize** Turkey
50 G1 **Vize,Ostrova** *islds* Russian Federation
52 G2 **Vizhas** Russian Federation
76 F1 **Vizianagaram** India
45 P1 **Vižinada** Croatia
52 H4 **Vizinga** Russian Federation
48 L6 **Viziru** Romania
48 D1 **Vizovice** Czechoslovakia
43 F11 **Vizzini** Sicily
25 B5 **Vlaardingen** Netherlands
48 L3 **Vlădeni** Romania
46 E2 **Vladičin Han** Serbia Yugoslavia
53 F11 **Vladikavkaz** Russian Federation
52 F6 **Vladimir** Russian Federation
48 F6 **Vladimirci** Serbia Yugoslavia
55 D4 **Vladimirovka** Kazakhstan
52 E6 **Vladimirskaya Oblast'** *prov* Russian Federation
54 E1 **Vladimirskiy Tupik** Russian Federation
53 B8 **Vladimir Volynskiy** Ukraine
59 K3 **Vladivostok** Russian Federation
52 E5 **Vladychnoye** Russian Federation
48 K4 **Vlăhiţa** Romania
46 E2 **Vlajna** *mt* Serbia Yugoslavia
142 A5 **Vlaming Hd** W Australia Australia
48 E6 **Vlasenica** Bosnia-Herzegovina
48 F6 **Vlašić** *mt* Serbia Yugoslavia
46 E2 **Vlasotince** Serbia Yugoslavia
31 K7 **Vlčany** Czechoslovakia
25 C2 **Vlieland** *isld* Netherlands
25 D2 **Vliestroom** Netherlands
25 A6 **Vlissingen** Netherlands
25 F6 **Vlodrop** Netherlands
46 C4 **Vlorë** Albania
32 J8 **Vlotho** Germany
31 H7 **Vltava** *R* Czechoslovakia
52 E6 **Vnukovo** *airport* Russian Federation
45 L1 **Vo** Italy
109 H5 **Voca** Texas U.S.A.
38 J6 **Vöcklabruck** Austria
107 K2 **Voda** Kansas U.S.A.
68 H7 **Vo Dat** Vietnam
28 B6 **Vodder** Denmark
47 H1 **Voditsa** Bulgaria
52 E4 **Vodla** *R* Russian Federation
52 E4 **Vodlozero, Oz** *L* Russian Federation
30 H6 **Vodňany** Czechoslovakia
42 F4 **Vodnjan** Croatia
52 H3 **Vodnyy** Russian Federation
28 E2 **Vodskov** Denmark
15 G2 **Voe** Shetland Scotland
28 D4 **Voel** Denmark
28 E3 **Voer** Denmark
32 E9 **Voerde** Germany
32 F10 **Voerde** Germany
28 D4 **Voerladegard** Denmark
28 F2 **Voerså** Denmark
85 C7 **Vofnjama** Liberia
86 B4 **Vogel** *mt* Nigeria
41 O3 **Vogelkar Sp** *mt* Austria
36 G2 **Vogelsberg** *mt* Germany
44 F2 **Voghera** Italy
45 L2 **Voghiera** Italy
28 C3 **Vognsild** Denmark
41 H5 **Vogogna** Italy
Vohemar *see* **Iharaña**
37 N4 **Vohenstrauss** Germany
Vohibinany *see* **Ampasimanolotra**
87 H13 **Vohimena, Tanjona** *C* Madagascar
36 F1 **Vöhl** Germany
52 C5 **Võhma** Estonia
37 J7 **Vöhringen** Germany
32 F10 **Vohwinkel** Germany
88 G3 **Voi** Kenya
33 S4 **Voigdehgn** Germany
12 D1 **Voil,L** Scotland
48 L3 **Voineşti** Romania
40 C7 **Voiron** France
38 M7 **Voitsberg** Austria
46 F5 **Voïvïïs** *L* Greece
28 C6 **Vojens** Denmark
26 H6 **Vojmsjön** *L* Sweden
37 N3 **Vojtanov** Czechoslovakia
48 E5 **Vojvodina** *aut rep* Serbia Yugoslavia
52 G5 **Vokhma** *R* Russian Federation
29 P7 **Voknavolok** Russian Federation
30 H6 **Vokyně** Czechoslovakia
52 H3 **Vol'** *R* Russian Federation
30 H7 **Volary** Czechoslovakia
98 A4 **Volborg** Montana U.S.A.
131 B3 **Volcan,Cerro del** *pk* Chile
106 D2 **Volcano** Colorado U.S.A.
Volcano B *see* **Uchiura wan** *B*
135 U5 **Volcanoes Nat. Park** Hawaiian Is
131 F6 **Volcán, Sa. del** *ra* Argentina
55 D2 **Volchansk** Russian Federation
55 H4 **Volchikha** Russian Federation
52 E5 **Volchina** *R* Russian Federation
54 H8 **Volch'ya** *R* Ukraine
28 D4 **Voldby** Denmark
28 F4 **Voldby** Denmark
28 E4 **Voldum** Denmark
25 D4 **Volendam** Netherlands
45 J1 **Volfa Mantovana** Italy
52 E5 **Volga** Russian Federation
52 E6 **Volga** *R* Russian Federation
99 P7 **Volga** *R* Iowa U.S.A.
98 K5 **Volga** South Dakota U.S.A.
52 E4 **Volgo-Balt** *canal* Russian Federation
53 F9 **Volgograd** Russian Federation
53 F9 **Volgogradskaya Oblast'** *prov* Russian Federation
52 D6 **Volgo, Oz** *L* Russian Federation
26 J7 **Volgsele** Sweden
98 J7 **Volin** South Dakota U.S.A.
47 H6 **Volissós** Greece
37 J4 **Volkach** Germany
25 B5 **Volkerak** Netherlands
38 L8 **Völkermarkt** Austria
37 J3 **Völkershausen** Germany
52 D5 **Volkhov** Russian Federation
36 B5 **Völklingen** Germany
32 K10 **Volkmarsen** Germany
48 L1 **Volkovintsy** Ukraine
31 P2 **Volkovysk** Belorussia
32 L8 **Völksen** Germany
89 F6 **Volksrust** S Africa
25 E3 **Vollenhove** Netherlands
22 G2 **Vollezele** Belgium
32 J9 **Völmerstod** *mt* Germany
36 C5 **Volmunster** France
21 L6 **Volnay** Sarthe France
99 U6 **Volney** Michigan U.S.A.
44 F3 **Vol Noci, L. di** Italy
54 F8 **Vol'nogorsk** Ukraine
55 F4 **Vol'noye** Russian Federation
54 G9 **Vol'nyansk** Ukraine
51 J1 **Volochanka** Russian Federation
48 K1 **Volochisk** Ukraine
52 F6 **Volodarsk** Russian Federation
55 E4 **Volodarskoye** Kazakhstan
52 F4 **Volodskaya** Russian Federation
52 E5 **Vologda** Russian Federation
36 B7 **Vologne** *R* France
52 E4 **Vologodskaya Oblast'** *prov* Russian Federation
52 D6 **Volok** Russian Federation
52 E6 **Volokolamsk** Russian Federation
52 G2 **Volokovaya** Russian Federation
52 G2 **Volonga** Russian Federation
19 Q16 **Volonne** France
46 F5 **Vólos** Greece
52 E4 **Voloshka** Russian Federation
52 C5 **Volosovo** Russian Federation
48 H2 **Volosyanka** Ukraine
52 D5 **Volot** Russian Federation
48 H2 **Volovets** Ukraine
33 O8 **Völpke** Germany
33 S5 **Völschow** Germany
53 G8 **Vol'sk** Russian Federation
28 E2 **Volstrup** Denmark
130 H10 **Volta** Brazil
85 E7 **Volta** *R* Ghana
41 N7 **Volta** Italy
85 D6 **Volta Blanche** *R* Burkina/Ghana
98 F1 **Voltaire** North Dakota U.S.A.
142 F2 **Voltaire, C** W Australia Australia
85 D7 **Volta,L** Ghana
85 D6 **Volta Noire** *R* Burkina
130 G8 **Volta Redonda** Brazil
85 D6 **Volta Rouge** *R* Burkina/Ghana
42 D5 **Volterra** Italy
52 F3 **Volteva** Russian Federation
44 E3 **Voltri** Italy
45 R8 **Volturara Irpina** Italy
45 Q7 **Volturno** *R* Italy
46 F4 **Vólvi, L** Greece
19 P17 **Volx** France
52 G6 **Volzhsk** Russian Federation
53 F9 **Volzhskiy** Russian Federation
42 F6 **Vomano** *R* Italy
106 H2 **Vona** Colorado U.S.A.
118 L6 **Vonda** Saskatchewan Canada
87 H12 **Vondrozo** Madagascar
22 J3 **Vonêche** Belgium
116 K5 **Von Frank Mt** Alaska U.S.A.
52 F3 **Vonga** Russian Federation
28 C5 **Vonge** Denmark
40 B3 **Vonges** France
46 D6 **Vónitsa** Greece
129 H5 **Von Martius,Cachoeira** *rapids* Brazil
28 D6 **Vonsbæk** Denmark
28 C6 **Vonsild** Denmark
143 E7 **Von Truer Tableland** W Australia Australia
25 B4 **Voorburg** Netherlands
25 B5 **Voorne** Netherlands
25 B4 **Voorschoten** Netherlands
25 F4 **Voorst** Netherlands
25 E4 **Voorthuizen** Netherlands
29 T9 **Vopnafjördhur** *inlet* Iceland
29 T9 **Vopnafjördhur** Iceland
25 F6 **Vopst** Germany
29 J8 **Vörå** Finland
41 K4 **Vorab** *mt* Switzerland
41 L3 **Vorarlberg** *prov* Austria
38 N7 **Vorau** Austria
28 C5 **Vorbasse** Denmark
32 H8 **Vörden** Germany
25 F4 **Vorden** Netherlands
38 L7 **Vordernberg** Austria
41 J4 **Vorder Rhein** *R* Switzerland
28 H6 **Vordingborg** Denmark
46 G5 **Vóreion Aiyaíon** *admin region* Greece
19 P14 **Voreppe** France
54 D3 **Vorga** Russian Federation
28 B4 **Vorgod** Denmark
46 G5 **Voríai Sporádhes** *islds* Greece
50 F2 **Vorkuta** Russian Federation
27 E11 **Vorma** *R* Norway
28 D3 **Vorning** Denmark
55 G3 **Vorob'yevo** Russian Federation
53 F8 **Vorona** *R* Russian Federation
54 C3 **Voronevo** Belorussia
54 L4 **Voronezh** *R* Russian Federation
54 L5 **Voronezh** Voronezhskaya obl Russian Federation
54 E5 **Voronezh** Ukraine
53 E8 **Voronezhskaya Oblast'** *prov* Russian Federation
48 M1 **Voronovitsa** Ukraine
52 F2 **Voronov, Mys** *C* Russian Federation
55 D2 **Vorontsovka** Russian Federation
50 H1 **Vorontsovo** Russian Federation
52 C6 **Vorontsovo** Russian Federation
52 E1 **Voron'ya** *R* Russian Federation
52 F5 **Voron'ye** Russian Federation
Voroshilovgrad *see* **Lugansk**
52 G5 **Voroshno** Russian Federation
54 N1 **Vorovskogo, im** Russian Federation
54 F5 **Vorozhba** Ukraine
33 S5 **Vorpommern** *reg* Germany
33 N8 **Vorsfelde** Germany
54 G6 **Vorskala** *R* Rus Fed/Ukraine
52 F6 **Vorsma** Russian Federation
52 C5 **Võrtsjäry** Estonia
52 C5 **Võru** Estonia
28 E4 **Vorup** Denmark
55 D1 **Vor'ya** *R* Russian Federation
55 D1 **Vor'yapaul'** Russian Federation
52 H3 **Vorykva** *R* Russian Federation
36 B7 **Vosges** *dept* France
40 E2 **Vosges** *mt* France
55 C4 **Voskresenskoye** Bashkirskaya Respublika Russian Federation
52 G6 **Voskresenskoye** Nizhegorodskaya obl Russian Federation
52 E5 **Voskresenskoye** Vologodskaya obl Russian Federation
89 C3 **Vosloosrus** S Africa
55 F4 **Vosnesenka** Kazakhstan
27 B11 **Voss** Norway
54 D9 **Vossiyatskoye** Ukraine
56 B6 **Vost Kazakhstanskaya Oblast'** *prov* Kazakhstan
52 E1 **Vostochnaya Litsa** Russian Federation
57 H2 **Vostochno-Kounradskiy** Kazakhstan
56 E4 **Vostochnyy Sayan** *mts* Russian Federation
146 F11 **Vostok** *former U.S.S.R. Base* Antarctica
135 M9 **Vostok I** Pacific Oc
55 E1 **Vostykhoy** Russian Federation
109 N5 **Votaw** Texas U.S.A.
109 N5 **Voth** Texas U.S.A.
31 H6 **Votice** Czechoslovakia
52 H6 **Votkinsk** Russian Federation
137 O4 **Vot Tandé** *isld* Vanuatu
130 E7 **Votuporanga** Brazil
16 B4 **Vouga** *R* Portugal
21 L8 **Vouillé** Vienne France
46 E5 **Voulgára** *mt* Greece
46 E5 **Voulgarélion** Greece
19 N15 **Voulte, la** France
68 H6 **Vœune** Cambodia
21 M8 **Vouneuil-sur-Vienne** France
46 E4 **Voúrinos** *mt* Greece
21 K5 **Voutré** France
21 J8 **Vouvant** France
21 M7 **Vouvray** France
21 P7 **Vouzeron** France
22 G5 **Vouziers** France
21 P6 **Vouzon** France
21 O5 **Voves** France
27 H10 **Voxna** Sweden
27 H10 **Voxnan** Sweden
27 G14 **Voxtorp** Sweden
52 H5 **Voya** *R* Russian Federation
99 O1 **Voyageurs Nat. Park** Minnesota U.S.A.
51 P3 **Voyampolka** Russian Federation
48 J1 **Voynilov** Ukraine
52 D2 **Voynitsa** Russian Federation
Vöyri *see* **Vörå**
52 H3 **Voy Vozh** Russian Federation
52 J3 **Voyvozh** Russian Federation
52 G3 **Vozhayel'** Russian Federation
52 F4 **Vozhega** Russian Federation
52 E4 **Vozhe, Oz** *L* Russian Federation
52 H5 **Vozhgaly** Russian Federation
52 G3 **Vozhgora** Russian Federation
54 C9 **Voznesensk** Ukraine
52 E4 **Voznesenye** Russian Federation
55 F4 **Vozvyshenka** Kazakhstan
28 D2 **Vrå** Denmark
48 E2 **Vráble** Czechoslovakia
27 C12 **Vrådalsv** *L* Norway
53 D10 **Vradiyevka** Ukraine
28 C4 **Vrads** Denmark
46 E6 **Vrakhnéïka** Greece
42 H5 **Vran** *mt* Bosnia-Herzegovina
48 K5 **Vrancea** *reg* Romania
48 K5 **Vrancei, Muntii** *mts* Romania
47 O13 **Vranganiótika** Greece
65 J3 **Vrangel'** Russian Federation
147 P3 **Vrangelya, Os** *isld* Russian Federation
42 H5 **Vranica** *mt* Bosnia-Herzegovina
46 E2 **Vranje** Serbia Yugoslavia
48 G2 **Vranov** Czechoslovakia
22 G1 **Vrasene** Belgium
46 F1 **Vratsa** Bulgaria
55 E1 **Vray** *L* Russian Federation
42 H4 **Vrbas** *R* Bosnia-Herzegovina
31 K5 **Vrbno** Czechoslovakia
31 J5 **Vrchlabi** Czechoslovakia
48 F5 **Vrdnik** Serbia Yugoslavia
89 F6 **Vrede** S Africa
32 E8 **Vreden** Germany
32 G7 **Vrees** Germany
28 D2 **Vrensted** Denmark
28 F6 **Vresen** *isld* Denmark
22 H4 **Vress** France
20 G3 **Vrétot, le** France
27 G12 **Vretstorp** Sweden
42 H5 **Vrgorac** Croatia
76 D5 **Vriddhachalam** India
28 C4 **Vridsted** Denmark
25 G2 **Vries** Netherlands
25 G4 **Vriezenveen** Netherlands
27 G14 **Vrigstad** Sweden
41 K4 **Vrin** Switzerland
22 H4 **Vringe-aux-Bois** France
28 A3 **Vrist** Denmark
22 F3 **Vrith-St.Léger** France
22 H5 **Vrizy** France
28 A5 **Vrøgum** Denmark
22 B3 **Vron** France
47 H6 **Vrondádhes** Greece
46 F8 **Vrondamás** Greece
25 G4 **Vroomshoop** Netherlands
28 C4 **Vroue** Denmark
48 G5 **Vršac** Serbia Yugoslavia
45 P1 **Vrsar** Croatia
48 E1 **Vrútky** Czechoslovakia
89 D6 **Vryburg** S Africa
89 G6 **Vryheid** S Africa
37 P4 **Všeruby** Czechoslovakia
37 O5 **Všeruby** Czechoslovakia
31 K6 **Vsetín** Czechoslovakia
55 C1 **Vsevolodo Blagodatskoye** Russian Federation
48 E2 **Vtáčnik** *mt* Czechoslovakia
19 P12 **Vuache, Mt de** France
68 G2 **Vu Ban** Vietnam
46 G3 **Vŭcha** *R* Bulgaria
46 D2 **Vučitrn** Serbia Yugoslavia
20 G7 **Vue** France
25 D5 **Vught** Netherlands
48 E5 **Vuka** *R* Croatia
48 E5 **Vukovar** Croatia
118 D8 **Vulcan** Alberta Canada
7 M9 **Vulcan** *gas field* North Sea
48 H5 **Vulcan** Romania
43 G10 **Vulcano, I** Italy
46 F1 **Vŭlchedrŭm** Bulgaria
47 J1 **Vŭlchidol** Bulgaria
67 B7 **Vu Liet** Vietnam
48 L5 **Vulkaneshty** Moldavia
43 G8 **Vulture, Monte** Italy
103 M8 **Vulture Mts** Arizona U.S.A.
68 J4 **Vung Da Nang** *B* Vietnam
68 J7 **Vung Phan Thiet** *B* Vietnam
68 H7 **Vung Tau** Vietnam
89 F2 **Vungu** *R* Zimbabwe
26 M5 **Vuodas** Sweden
29 N7 **Vuokatti** Finland
29 O11 **Vuoksa** *L* Russian Federation
29 O10 **Vuoksenniska** Finland
29 N7 **Vuolijoki** Finland
26 L5 **Vuollerim** Sweden
29 N5 **Vuostimo** Finland
29 N3 **Vuotso** Finland
26 N2 **Vuovdasoaivve** *mt* Norway
47 H2 **Vŭrbitsa** Bulgaria
52 G6 **Vurnary** Russian Federation
46 F1 **Vŭrshets** Bulgaria
28 C2 **Vust** Denmark
48 L4 **Vutcani** Romania
55 D4 **Vvedenka** Kazakhstan
100 F8 **Vya** Nevada U.S.A.
52 E2 **Vyalozero, Oz** *L* Russian Federation
52 F5 **Vyaltsevo** Russian Federation
29 P9 **Vyartsilya** Russian Federation
52 G5 **Vyatka** *R* Russian Federation
52 H6 **Vyatskiye Polyany** Russian Federation
59 K2 **Vyazemskiy** Russian Federation
54 E1 **Vyazma** *R* Russian Federation
54 F1 **Vyaz'ma** Russian Federation
52 F6 **Vyazniki** Russian Federation
52 C6 **Vybor** Russian Federation
29 O11 **Vyborg** Russian Federation
29 N11 **Vyborgskiy Zaliv** *G* Russian Federation
52 H4 **Vychegda** *R* Russian Federation
31 J5 **Vychodočeský** *reg* Czechoslovakia
56 F5 **Vydrino** Russian Federation
52 E3 **Vyg** *R* Russian Federation
48 N4 **Vygoda** Ukraine
54 F3 **Vygonichi** Russian Federation
52 D3 **Vygozero, Oz** *L* Russian Federation
48 G2 **Vyhorlát** *mt* Czechoslovakia
52 F6 **Vyksa** Russian Federation
52 H3 **Vym'** *R* Russian Federation
52 G4 **Vymsk** Russian Federation
52 C5 **Vyra** Russian Federation
52 D5 **Vyritsa** Russian Federation
8 C2 **Vyrnwy, L** Wales
8 C2 **Vyrnwy R** Wales
54 B6 **Vyshgorod** Ukraine
31 K6 **Vyškov** Czechoslovakia
31 L6 **Vysoká** *mt* Czechoslovakia
52 G6 **Vysokaya Gora** Russian Federation
52 J4 **Vysokaya Parma** *plateau* Russian Federation
31 J6 **Vysoké Mýto** Czechoslovakia
59 L1 **Vysokogornyy** Russian Federation
52 E6 **Vysokovsk** Russian Federation
31 O3 **Vysokoye** Belorussia
29 O11 **Vysotsk** Russian Federation
38 K4 **Vyšši Brod** Czechoslovakia
52 E4 **Vytegra** Russian Federation
52 G3 **Vyya** *R* Russian Federation
59 M2 **Vzmor'ye** Russian Federation

W

85 D6 **Wa** Ghana
86 H5 **Waajid** Somalia
25 D5 **Waal** *R* Netherlands
25 B5 **Waalhaven** Netherlands
25 D5 **Waalwijk** Netherlands
80 H2 **Waamo Iidow** Kenya
25 D2 **Waardgronden** Netherlands
22 F1 **Waarschoot** Belgium
120 D2 **Wababimiga L** Ontario Canada
118 C5 **Wabamun** Alberta Canada
123 U6 **Wabana** Newfoundland Canada
117 Q7 **Wabasca** *R* Alberta Canada
118 D3 **Wabasca** Alberta Canada
110 J3 **Wabash** *R* U.S.A.
111 F7 **Wabash** Arkansas U.S.A.
94 B6 **Wabash** Indiana U.S.A.
99 O5 **Wabasha** Minnesota U.S.A.
113 G10 **Wabasso** Florida U.S.A.
99 L5 **Wabasso** Minnesota U.S.A.
120 F4 **Wabatongushi L** Ontario Canada
99 S4 **Wabeno** Wisconsin U.S.A.
Wabern *see* **Egling**
118 K1 **Wabigoon** Ontario Canada
121 R4 **Wabino** *R* Quebec Canada
120 A2 **Wabinosh L** Ontario Canada
120 C2 **Waboose Dam** Ontario Canada
120 F6 **Wabos** Ontario Canada
119 T4 **Wabowden** Manitoba Canada
31 L2 **Wąbrzezno** Poland
58 G5 **Wabu Hu** *L* China
115 N7 **Wabush** Labrador, Nfld Canada
102 E2 **Wabuska** Nevada U.S.A.
112 H4 **Waccamaw** *R* South Carolina U.S.A.
112 J3 **Waccamaw, L** North Carolina U.S.A.
113 D8 **Waccasassa B** Florida U.S.A.
95 M9 **Wachapreague** Virginia U.S.A.
36 H5 **Wachbach** Germany
36 E5 **Wachenheim** Germany
37 K4 **Wachenroth** Germany
33 R7 **Wachow** Germany
22 F1 **Wachtbeke** Belgium
25 F6 **Wachtendonk** Germany
36 G3 **Wächtersbach** Germany
32 G7 **Wachtum** Germany
95 Q4 **Wachusett Res** Massachusetts U.S.A.
135 M11 **Wachusett Shoal** Pacific Oc
71 H7 **Waci** Indonesia
32 K4 **Wacken** Germany
122 G2 **Waco** Quebec Canada
98 J9 **Waco** Nebraska U.S.A.
109 K4 **Waco** Texas U.S.A.
99 N5 **Waconia** Minnesota U.S.A.
122 G2 **Wacouno R** Quebec Canada
77 K6 **Wad** Pakistan
142 D6 **Wadara Ra** W Australia Australia
60 H10 **Wadayama** Japan
86 E3 **Wad Banda** Sudan
139 H8 **Waddamana** Tasmania Australia
84 F4 **Waddān** Libya
25 D2 **Waddenzee** Netherlands
9 F4 **Waddesdon** England
9 F1 **Waddington** England
95 M2 **Waddington** New York U.S.A.
117 L10 **Waddington, Mt** British Columbia Canada
94 B8 **Waddy** Kentucky U.S.A.
141 L7 **Waddy Pt** Queensland Australia
112 J2 **Wade** North Carolina U.S.A.
8 B7 **Wadebridge** England
119 O7 **Wadena** Saskatchewan Canada
99 L3 **Wadena** Minnesota U.S.A.
36 B4 **Wadern** Germany
32 H9 **Wadersloh** Germany
112 G3 **Wadesboro** North Carolina U.S.A.
123 T4 **Wadham Is** Newfoundland Canada
117 K10 **Wadhams** British Columbia Canada
9 G5 **Wadhurst** England
80 G6 **Wadi es Sir** Jordan
84 K5 **Wâdi Gimâl I** Egypt
86 F1 **Wadi Halfa** Sudan
79 F8 **Wādi Mūsā** Jordan
111 L8 **Wadley** Alabama U.S.A.
112 E5 **Wadley** Georgia U.S.A.
86 F3 **Wad Medani** Sudan
31 L6 **Wadowice** Poland
102 E2 **Wadsworth** Nevada U.S.A.
94 F5 **Wadsworth** Ohio U.S.A.
13 G6 **Wadworth** England
65 G7 **Waegwan** S Korea
109 K6 **Waelder** Texas U.S.A.
68 F4 **Waeng** Thailand
65 E2 **Wafang** China
Wafangdian *see* **Fu Xian**
77 A5 **Wafra** Iran
61 O6 **Waga-gawa** *R* Japan
120 B2 **Wagaming** Ontario Canada
111 H10 **Wagarville** Alabama U.S.A.
32 J7 **Wagenfeld** Germany
25 E5 **Wageningen** Netherlands
139 H6 **Wagga Wagga** New South Wales Australia
74 E8 **Waghai** India
36 F5 **Waghäusel** Germany
143 B10 **Wagin** W Australia Australia
101 R1 **Wagner** Montana U.S.A.
98 H6 **Wagner** South Dakota U.S.A.
107 P6 **Wagoner** Oklahoma U.S.A.
106 F5 **Wagon Mound** New Mexico U.S.A.
100 F6 **Wagontire** Oregon U.S.A.
106 D4 **Wagon Wheel Gap** Colorado U.S.A.
112 H3 **Wagram** North Carolina U.S.A.
31 K3 **Wągrowiec** Poland
100 J3 **Waha** Idaho U.S.A.
83 K9 **Wahalkada Tank** Sri Lanka
145 E2 **Waharoa** New Zealand
102 R12 **Wahiawa** Hawaiian Is
145 E2 **Wahi,L** New Zealand
36 F4 **Wahlen** Germany
36 C2 **Wahn** Germany
32 K7 **Wahnebergen** Germany
98 K8 **Wahoo** Nebraska U.S.A.
98 K3 **Wahpeton** North Dakota U.S.A.
33 S9 **Wahrenbrück** Germany
33 N7 **Wahrenholz** Germany
103 L3 **Wah Wah Mts** Utah U.S.A.
76 A2 **Wai** India
135 U6 **Waiahukini** Hawaiian Is
135 T3 **Waiakoa** Hawaiian Is
135 O1 **Waialeale** *pk* Hawaiian Is
102 R11 **Waialee** Hawaiian Is
102 R11 **Waialua** Hawaiian Is
102 R12 **Waianae** Hawaiian Is
102 R12 **Waianae Ra** Hawaiian Is
144 C6 **Waianakarua** New Zealand
144 B7 **Waianiwa** New Zealand
145 G2 **Waiapu** *R* New Zealand
144 B6 **Waiatoto R** New Zealand
144 D5 **Waiau** New Zealand
144 A6 **Waiau** *R* New Zealand
145 F3 **Waiau R** New Zealand
36 G6 **Waiblingen** Germany
37 N4 **Waidhaus** Germany
31 J7 **Waidhofen** Austria
38 L6 **Waidhofen an der Ybbs** Austria
71 B3 **Waigama** Indonesia
143 G8 **Waigen Lakes** W Australia Australia
71 C3 **Waigeo** W Irian
71 C3 **Waigeo** *isld* W Irian
37 J4 **Waigolshausen** Germany
144 C6 **Waihao Forks** New Zealand
145 D1 **Waiharara** New Zealand
145 E2 **Waiheke I** New Zealand
145 E2 **Waihi** New Zealand
144 A7 **Waihoaka** New Zealand
144 C7 **Waihola** New Zealand
145 D4 **Waihopai** *R* New Zealand
145 D1 **Waihopo** New Zealand
144 C5 **Waiho R** New Zealand
145 E2 **Waihou** New Zealand
145 E2 **Waihou R** New Zealand
145 F3 **Waihua** New Zealand
71 J9 **Waikabubak** Sumba Indonesia
144 B6 **Waikaia** New Zealand
144 B6 **Waikaka** New Zealand
145 E4 **Waikanae** New Zealand
102 S12 **Waikane** Hawaiian Is
145 F3 **Waikareiti, L** New Zealand
145 E2 **Waikare, L** New Zealand
145 F3 **Waikaremoana, L** New Zealand
145 E2 **Waikaretu** New Zealand
144 D5 **Waikari** New Zealand
145 E3 **Waikato** New Zealand
145 E2 **Waikato** *admin region* New Zealand
144 B7 **Waikawa** New Zealand
145 E4 **Waikawa** New Zealand
71 J9 **Waikelo Teluk** *B* Sumba Indonesia
138 E5 **Waikerie** South Australia Australia
135 U5 **Waikii** Hawaiian Is
142 A4 **Waikiki** W Australia Australia
102 S12 **Waikiki Beach** Hawaiian Is
71 L9 **Waiklibang** Indonesia
145 F3 **Waikohu** New Zealand
145 F3 **Waikokopu** New Zealand
144 B7 **Waikotkoi** New Zealand
144 C6 **Waikouaiti** New Zealand
144 A7 **Waikouro** New Zealand
102 V13 **Wailuku** Hawaiian Is
144 B7 **Waimahaka** New Zealand
144 A4 **Waimakariri R** New Zealand
145 D1 **Waimamaka** New Zealand
145 F3 **Waimana** New Zealand
102 S12 **Waimanalo** Hawaiian Is
144 C4 **Waimangaroa** New Zealand
71 J9 **Waimanguar** Indonesia
145 F3 **Waimarama** New Zealand
144 C4 **Waimarie** New Zealand
144 C6 **Waimate** New Zealand
145 E2 **Waimauku** New Zealand
135 Q2 **Waimea** Hawaiian Is
135 U4 **Waimea** Hawaiian Is
102 R11 **Waimea B** Hawaiian Is
70 G6 **Waimenda** Sulawesi
22 L3 **Waimes** Belgium
145 E3 **Waimiha** New Zealand
9 G1 **Wainfleet** England
71 K9 **Waingapu** Sumba Indonesia
145 E4 **Waingawa** New Zealand
135 O1 **Wainiha** Hawaiian Is
144 C5 **Wainihinihi** New Zealand
99 S3 **Wainola** Michigan U.S.A.
144 C6 **Wainono Lagoon** New Zealand
118 G6 **Wainwright** Alberta Canada
116 G1 **Wainwright** Alaska U.S.A.
145 F3 **Waioeka R** New Zealand
135 U6 **Waiohinu** Hawaiian Is
145 E1 **Waiolira** New Zealand
145 F3 **Waiotapu** New Zealand
145 E3 **Waiouru** New Zealand
144 B7 **Waipahi** New Zealand
102 R12 **Waipahu** Hawaiian Is
145 F3 **Waipaoa** New Zealand
145 D1 **Waipapakauri** New Zealand
145 E2 **Waipa R** New Zealand
144 D5 **Waipara** New Zealand
145 F3 **Waipawa** New Zealand
144 C6 **Waipiata** New Zealand
135 U4 **Waipio** Hawaiian Is
145 G3 **Waipiro** New Zealand
144 C6 **Waipori, L** New Zealand
145 E1 **Waipu** New Zealand
145 F3 **Waipukurau** New Zealand
145 F3 **Wairakei** New Zealand
145 E4 **Wairarapa** *admin region* New Zealand
145 E4 **Wairarapa, L** New Zealand
145 D4 **Wairau Valley** New Zealand
144 B7 **Wairio** New Zealand
145 F3 **Wairoa** New Zealand
145 E2 **Wairoa R** New Zealand
145 E1 **Wairua** *R* New Zealand
144 B7 **Wairuna** New Zealand
71 L9 **Wairunu** Flores Indonesia
37 L4 **Waischenfeld** Germany
145 F3 **Waitahanui** New Zealand
144 C5 **Waitaha R** New Zealand
144 B6 **Waitahuna** New Zealand
145 E2 **Waitakaruru** New Zealand
144 C6 **Waitaki, L** New Zealand
145 E1 **Waitangi** New Zealand
145 E3 **Waitara** New Zealand
145 E4 **Waitarere** New Zealand
144 D6 **Waitati** New Zealand
140 B5 **Waite** *R* N Terr Australia
145 F1 **Waitemata Harb** New Zealand
143 D8 **Waite, Mt** W Australia Australia
145 E2 **Waitoa** New Zealand
145 E3 **Waitomo** New Zealand
145 E3 **Waitotara** *R* New Zealand
145 E3 **Waitotara** New Zealand
100 G3 **Waitsburg** Washington U.S.A.
119 M6 **Waitville** Saskatchewan Canada
145 E2 **Waiuku** New Zealand
144 C5 **Waiuta** New Zealand
145 E2 **Waiwera** New Zealand
144 B7 **Waiwera South** New Zealand
71 B1 **Wajabula** Halmahera Indonesia
71 C2 **Wajag** *isld* Indonesia
71 B2 **Wajamli** Indonesia
61 K8 **Wajima** Japan
86 H5 **Wajir** Kenya
86 D5 **Waka** Zaire
60 D12 **Wakamatsu** Japan
60 B12 **Wakamatsu-jima** *isld* Japan
120 H5 **Wakami L** Ontario Canada
144 C5 **Wakanui** New Zealand
145 F3 **Wakarara Range** New Zealand
94 A5 **Wakarusa** Indiana U.S.A.
61 J10 **Wakasa-wan** *B* Japan
144 B6 **Wakatipu, L** New Zealand
119 M6 **Wakaw** Saskatchewan Canada
60 J11 **Wakayama** Japan
60 J12 **Wakayama** *prefect* Japan
61 P7 **Wakayanagi** Japan
107 L2 **Wa Keeney** Kansas U.S.A.
121 P7 **Wakefield** Quebec Canada
13 G6 **Wakefield** England
127 J2 **Wakefield** Jamaica
145 D4 **Wakefield** New Zealand
107 O2 **Wakefield** Kansas U.S.A.
99 R3 **Wakefield** Michigan U.S.A.
98 K7 **Wakefield** Nebraska U.S.A.
95 Q5 **Wakefield** Rhode I U.S.A.
95 K10 **Wakefield** Virginia U.S.A.
112 J2 **Wake Forest** North Carolina U.S.A.
134 H6 **Wake I** Pacific Oc
68 B4 **Wakema** Burma
122 H5 **Wakenam** Quebec Canada
94 A5 **Wakerton** Indiana U.S.A.
74 E1 **Wakhan** *reg* Afghanistan
60 H11 **Waki** Japan
60 O4 **Wakinosawa** Japan
107 N5 **Wakita** Oklahoma U.S.A.
60 P1 **Wakkanai** Japan
87 F11 **Wakkerstroom** S Africa
Wako *see* **Watcomb**
120 G6 **Wakomata L** Ontario Canada
139 G6 **Wakool** New South Wales Australia
119 S9 **Wakopa** Manitoba Canada
71 H7 **Wakoru** Indonesia
98 F4 **Wakpala** South Dakota U.S.A.
71 C3 **Wakre** W Irian
71 K9 **Waku** Indonesia
87 C8 **Waku Kungo** Angola
113 C7 **Wakulla** Florida U.S.A.
120 K2 **Wakwayowkastic** *R* Ontario Canada
103 L6 **Walapai** Arizona U.S.A.
83 K11 **Walawe Ganga** *R* Sri Lanka
33 O8 **Walbeck** Germany
36 D6 **Walbourg** France
94 D5 **Walbridge** Ohio U.S.A.
31 J5 **Wałbrzych** Poland
36 H1 **Walburg** Germany
139 K4 **Walcha** New South Wales Australia
38 G7 **Walchen** Austria
41 O2 **Walchensee** *L* Germany
25 A5 **Walcheren** Netherlands
38 F6 **Walchsee** Austria
117 K8 **Walcott** British Columbia Canada
98 K3 **Walcott** North Dakota U.S.A.
101 T8 **Walcott** Wyoming U.S.A.
142 E3 **Walcott Inlet** W Australia
101 M7 **Walcott, L., Res** Idaho U.S.A.
22 G3 **Walcourt** Belgium
31 J2 **Wałcz** Poland
38 L5 **Wald Aist** *R* Austria
36 F5 **Waldangeloch** Germany
36 D4 **Waldböckelheim** Germany
36 C2 **Waldbreitbach** Germany
36 D2 **Waldbröl** Germany
36 G5 **Waldbrunn** Baden-Württemberg Germany
36 G5 **Waldbrunn** Hessen Germany
143 B6 **Waldburg Ra** W Australia
33 T9 **Walddrehna** Germany
118 K8 **Waldeck** Saskatchewan Canada
36 G1 **Waldeck** Germany
101 T9 **Walden** Colorado U.S.A.
95 N5 **Walden** New York U.S.A.
37 O2 **Waldenberg** Germany
36 G6 **Waldenbuch** Germany
36 H5 **Waldenburg** Germany
110 F6 **Waldenburg** Arkansas U.S.A.
37 N4 **Waldershof** Germany
36 D5 **Waldfischbach** Germany
118 L6 **Waldheim** Saskatchewan Canada
37 P1 **Waldheim** Germany
36 H1 **Waldkappel** Germany
40 G1 **Waldkirch** Germany
30 H7 **Waldkirchen** Germany
36 F4 **Waldmichelbach** Germany
37 O5 **Waldmünchen** Germany
37 N4 **Wald Naab** *R* Germany
25 F6 **Waldniel** Germany
118 B9 **Waldo** British Columbia Canada
109 O2 **Waldo** Arkansas U.S.A.
113 E8 **Waldo** Florida U.S.A.
107 M2 **Waldo** Kansas U.S.A.
94 D6 **Waldo** Ohio U.S.A.
99 T6 **Waldo** Wisconsin U.S.A.
100 C6 **Waldo L** Oregon U.S.A.
95 L8 **Waldorf** Maryland U.S.A.
99 N6 **Waldorf** Minnesota U.S.A.
100 A5 **Waldport** Oregon U.S.A.
119 P8 **Waldron** Saskatchewan Canada
109 N1 **Waldron** Arkansas U.S.A.
146 G14 **Waldron, C** Antarctica
37 N3 **Waldsassen** Germany
41 H2 **Waldshut** Germany
37 J7 **Waldstetten** Germany
37 N4 **Waldthurn** Germany
36 B5 **Waldwisse** France
71 H5 **Waleabahi** *isld* Sulawesi
71 H5 **Waleakodi** *isld* Sulawesi
71 H5 **Walea,Selat** *str* Sulawesi
70 N9 **Waleri** Java
8 C3 **Wales** *princ* U.K.
116 C4 **Wales** Alaska U.S.A.
99 P2 **Wales** Minnesota U.S.A.
98 H1 **Wales** North Dakota U.S.A.
103 N2 **Wales** Utah U.S.A.
115 L4 **Wales I** Northwest Territories Canada
85 D6 **Walewale** Ghana
33 O5 **Walfisch** Germany
139 J4 **Walgett** New South Wales Australia
146 B7 **Walgreen Coast** Antarctica
37 N5 **Walhalla** *mt* Germany
98 J1 **Walhalla** North Dakota U.S.A.
112 D3 **Walhalla** South Carolina U.S.A.
70 N9 **Walikukun** Java
143 A8 **Walkaway** W Australia Australia
33 R5 **Walkendorf** Germany
33 N9 **Walkenried** Germany
140 B6 **Walker** *R* N Terr Australia
141 F3 **Walker** *R* Queensland Australia
100 C8 **Walker** California U.S.A.
99 P7 **Walker** Iowa U.S.A.
107 L3 **Walker** Kansas U.S.A.
111 F11 **Walker** Louisiana U.S.A.
99 M2 **Walker** Minnesota U.S.A.
110 B4 **Walker** Missouri U.S.A.
102 E2 **Walker** *R* Nevada U.S.A.
98 E4 **Walker** South Dakota U.S.A.
89 A10 **Walker B** S Africa
13 E2 **Walkerburn** Scotland
113 J10 **Walker Cay** *isld* Bahamas
119 V4 **Walker L** Manitoba Canada
122 E3 **Walker L** Quebec Canada
116 K3 **Walker L** Alaska U.S.A.
102 F3 **Walker L** Nevada U.S.A.
146 B7 **Walker Mts** Antarctica
102 G6 **Walker Pk** California U.S.A.
140 D2 **Walker R** N Terr Australia
70 D2 **Walker Ra** Sabah
141 J5 **Walkerston** Queensland Australia
94 G8 **Walkersville** West Virginia U.S.A.
120 J8 **Walkerton** Ontario Canada
112 G1 **Walkertown** North Carolina U.S.A.
99 U6 **Walkerville** Michigan U.S.A.
101 N3 **Walkerville** Montana U.S.A.
98 D5 **Wall** South Dakota U.S.A.
143 A8 **Wallabi Group** *islds* W Australia Australia
140 E3 **Wallaby I** Queensland Australia
141 F3 **Wallaby I** Queensland Australia
138 C4 **Wallaby,Mt** South Australia Australia
122 J8 **Wallace** Nova Scotia Canada
121 M7 **Wallace** Ontario Canada
100 K2 **Wallace** Idaho U.S.A.
107 J3 **Wallace** Kansas U.S.A.
99 T4 **Wallace** Michigan U.S.A.
98 E9 **Wallace** Nebraska U.S.A.
112 J3 **Wallace** North Carolina U.S.A.
98 J4 **Wallace** South Dakota U.S.A.
94 G7 **Wallace** West Virginia U.S.A.
120 H10 **Wallaceburg** Ontario Canada
109 O3 **Wallace L** Louisiana U.S.A.
118 B3 **Wallace Mt** Alberta Canada
120 J10 **Wallacetown** Ontario Canada
144 B7 **Wallacetown** New Zealand
142 D4 **Wallal Downs** W Australia Australia
143 C9 **Wallambin, L** W Australia Australia
141 K8 **Wallangarra** Queensland Australia
142 D5 **Wallani Well** W Australia Australia
141 H8 **Wallan, R** Queensland Australia
140 B6 **Wallara Ranch** N Terr Australia
138 D5 **Wallaroo** South Australia Australia
8 C1 **Wallasey** England
140 B3 **Wallaston, Mt** N Terr Australia
36 E2 **Wallau** Germany
139 H6 **Walla Walla** New South Wales Australia
100 G4 **Walla Walla** *R* Oregon U.S.A.
100 G3 **Walla Walla** Washington U.S.A.
138 C2 **Wall Cr** N Terr Australia
140 C7 **Wall Creek** N Terr Australia
36 F5 **Walldorf** Germany
37 J2 **Walldorf** Germany
37 L2 **Wallendorf** Germany
37 L3 **Wallenfels** Germany
32 H8 **Wallenhorst** Germany
95 M5 **Wallenpaupack, L** Pennsylvania U.S.A.
41 K3 **Wallen See** *L* Switzerland
32 L8 **Wallensen** Germany
139 K5 **Wallerawang** New South Wales Australia
37 O6 **Wallersdorf** Germany
36 F1 **Wallershöhe** *mt* Germany
37 J6 **Wallerstein** Germany
33 O10 **Wallhausen** Germany
142 B3 **Walliabup** W Australia Australia
9 E4 **Wallingford** England
145 F4 **Wallingford** New Zealand
95 P5 **Wallingford** Connecticut U.S.A.
95 P3 **Wallingford** Vermont U.S.A.
109 L6 **Wallis** Texas U.S.A.
137 R4 **Wallis, Îles** Pacific Oc
139 L4 **Wallis L** New South Wales Australia
99 L7 **Wall L** Iowa U.S.A.
36 D3 **Wallmerod** Germany
142 B6 **Wall, Mt** W Australia Australia
141 K6 **Walloon** Queensland Australia
94 C1 **Walloon L** Michigan U.S.A.
95 M9 **Wallops I** Virginia U.S.A.
100 H4 **Wallowa** Oregon U.S.A.
100 H4 **Wallowa Mts** Oregon U.S.A.
15 G2 **Walls** Scotland
28 C7 **Wallsbüll** Germany
139 K5 **Wallsend** New South Wales Australia
33 O7 **Wallstawe** Germany
32 J8 **Wallucke** Germany
100 G3 **Wallula** Washington U.S.A.
141 J7 **Wallumbilla** Queensland Australia
33 Q9 **Wallwitzhafen** Germany
9 H5 **Walmer** England
13 E5 **Walney I** England
99 R8 **Walnut** Illinois U.S.A.
107 K3 **Walnut** *R* Kansas U.S.A.
107 P4 **Walnut** Kansas U.S.A.
110 H7 **Walnut** Mississippi U.S.A.
103 N6 **Walnut Canyon Nat.Mon** Arizona U.S.A.
112 G1 **Walnut Cove** North Carolina U.S.A.
111 G9 **Walnut Grove** Mississippi U.S.A.
110 C4 **Walnut Grove** Missouri U.S.A.
109 O9 **Walnut Hills** Texas U.S.A.
110 F5 **Walnut Ridge** Arkansas U.S.A.
109 K3 **Walnut Springs** Texas U.S.A.
125 M2 **Walpatanta** Honduras
138 F6 **Walpeup** Victoria Australia
143 B10 **Walpole** W Australia Australia
137 O6 **Walpole** *isld* Pacific Oc
95 P3 **Walpole** New Hampshire U.S.A.
116 D8 **Walrus I** Pribilof Is Bering Sea
116 G7 **Walrus Is** Alaska U.S.A.
9 E2 **Walsall** England
37 K1 **Walschleben** Germany
36 E3 **Walsdorf** Germany
106 F4 **Walsenburg** Colorado U.S.A.
141 G3 **Walsh** *R* Queensland Australia
118 G9 **Walsh** Alberta Canada
106 H4 **Walsh** Colorado U.S.A.
117 D5 **Walsh, Mt** Yukon Territory Canada
22 J2 **Walshoutem** Belgium
25 B6 **Walsoorden** Netherlands
32 L7 **Walsrode** Germany
32 E9 **Walsum** Germany
112 G5 **Walterboro** South Carolina U.S.A.
111 L10 **Walter F. George Res** Alabama/Georgia
109 J1 **Walters** Oklahoma U.S.A.
37 K2 **Waltershausen** Germany
141 G8 **Walter's Ra** Queensland Australia
111 G8 **Walthall** Mississippi U.S.A.
121 O7 **Waltham** Quebec Canada
9 F2 **Waltham** England
101 P2 **Waltham** Montana U.S.A.
9 G4 **Waltham Abbey** England
9 F4 **Waltham Cross** England
98 K7 **Walthill** Nebraska U.S.A.
101 S6 **Waltman** Wyoming U.S.A.
122 J8 **Walton** Nova Scotia Canada
120 J9 **Walton** Ontario Canada
9 F5 **Walton** England
145 E2 **Walton** New Zealand
94 A6 **Walton** Indiana U.S.A.
94 C8 **Walton** Kentucky U.S.A.
95 M4 **Walton** New York U.S.A.
94 F8 **Walton** West Virginia U.S.A.
126 E6 **Walton Bank** Caribbean
94 B2 **Walton Junc** Michigan U.S.A.
9 H4 **Walton-on-the-Naze** England
110 G3 **Waltonville** Illinois U.S.A.
32 F9 **Waltrop** Germany
87 B10 **Walvis Bay** S Africa
90 J12 **Walvis Ridge** Atlantic Oc
99 S7 **Walworth** Wisconsin U.S.A.
143 C9 **Walyahmoing** *hill* W Australia
36 F5 **Walzbuchtal** Germany
87 C8 **Wama** Angola
86 A4 **Wamba** Nigeria
86 E5 **Wamba** Zaire
87 C7 **Wamba** *R* Zaire
139 H5 **Wamboyne** New South Wales Australia
107 O2 **Wamego** Kansas U.S.A.
25 D5 **Wamel** Netherlands
100 D4 **Wamic** Oregon U.S.A.
94 G6 **Wampum** Pennsylvania U.S.A.
101 R8 **Wamsutter** Wyoming U.S.A.
77 L3 **Wana** Pakistan
139 G3 **Wanaaring** New South Wales Australia
144 B6 **Wanaka** New Zealand
67 E3 **Wan'an** China
126 A2 **Wanapa** Bonaire W Indies
120 K6 **Wanapitei L** Ontario Canada
95 N5 **Wanaque Res** New Jersey U.S.A.
99 U8 **Wanatah** Indiana U.S.A.
138 F5 **Wanbi** South Australia Australia
98 E6 **Wanblee** South Dakota U.S.A.
112 M2 **Wanchese** North Carolina U.S.A.
138 E3 **Wancoocha, L** South Australia Australia

Wanda — West Auckland
239

130 C10 **Wanda** Argentina
59 K2 **Wanda Shan** *mt ra* China
118 E3 **Wandering River** Alberta Canada
37 K2 **Wandersleben** Germany
28 C7 **Wanderup** Germany
33 S7 **Wandlitz** Germany
141 J7 **Wandoan** Queensland Australia
141 G4 **Wando Vale** Queensland Australia
22 K2 **Wandre** Belgium
109 K1 **Wanette** Oklahoma U.S.A.
65 E4 **Wanfu** China
65 C7 **Wanfu He** *R* China
145 E3 **Wanganui** New Zealand
145 E4 **Wanganui** *admin region* New Zealand
144 C5 **Wanganui R** New Zealand
139 G6 **Wangaratta** Victoria Australia
138 D5 **Wangary** South Australia Australia
67 B2 **Wangcaoba** China
65 B5 **Wangcun** China
67 C2 **Wangcun** China
67 B4 **Wangdian** China
65 C5 **Wangdu** China
33 N4 **Wangels** Germany
41 L2 **Wangen** Germany
32 G5 **Wangerland** *reg* Germany
32 G5 **Wangerooge** Germany
9 H3 **Wangford** England
71 K10 **Wanggamet, Gunung** *mt* Sumba Indonesia
67 D4 **Wanggao** China
Wanggezhuang *see* **Jiaonan**
71 H7 **Wangiwangi** *isld* Indonesia
67 D2 **Wangjiachang** China
67 E1 **Wangjiadian** China
67 E1 **Wangjiang** China
68 D5 **Wangka** Thailand
65 G1 **Wangkui** China
Wang Mai Khon *see* **Sawankhalok**
67 C5 **Wangmao** China
67 B4 **Wangmo** China
65 H3 **Wangqing** China
68 D2 **Wan hsa-la** Burma
74 H8 **Wani** India
71 H7 **Wani** *mt* Indonesia
86 E5 **Wanie-Rukula** Zaire
111 F10 **Wanilla** Mississippi U.S.A.
65 E5 **Wanjialing** China
74 D7 **Wankaner** India
32 M4 **Wankendorf** Germany
Wankie *see* **Hwange**
86 H5 **Wanlaweyn** Somalia
119 Q4 **Wanless** Manitoba Canada
12 E3 **Wanlockhead** Scotland
143 G8 **Wanna Lakes** W Australia Australia
32 F9 **Wanne-Eickel** Germany
143 B9 **Wanneroo** W Australia Australia
67 F2 **Wannian** China
68 K3 **Wanning** China
33 S8 **Wannsee** Germany
76 D2 **Wanparti** India
65 C4 **Wanquan** China
125 M2 **Wanquibila** Honduras
65 A7 **Wanrong** China
13 G3 **Wansbeck, R** England
9 F2 **Wansford** England
67 C3 **Wanshan** China
67 D6 **Wanshan Qundao** *islds* China
145 F4 **Wanstead** New Zealand
9 E4 **Wantage** England
36 D6 **Wantzenau** France
120 K6 **Wanup** Ontario Canada
67 C1 **Wan Xian** China
67 C1 **Wanxian** China
65 C7 **Wanyang Hu** *L* China
58 E5 **Wanyuan** China
67 E2 **Wanzai** China
Wanzhi *see* **Wuhu**
33 O8 **Wanzleben** Germany
145 E3 **Waotu** New Zealand
94 C6 **Wapakoneta** Ohio U.S.A.
109 L1 **Wapanucka** Oklahoma U.S.A.
100 E3 **Wapato** Washington U.S.A.
119 N4 **Wapawekka Hills** Saskatchewan Canada
119 Q8 **Wapella** Saskatchewan Canada
101 N6 **Wapello** Idaho U.S.A.
99 P8 **Wapello** Iowa U.S.A.
119 S3 **Wapisu L** Manitoba Canada
117 O8 **Wapiti** *R* Alberta Canada
101 Q5 **Wapiti Ra** Wyoming U.S.A.
110 F4 **Wappapello Res** Missouri U.S.A.
95 O5 **Wappingers Falls** New York U.S.A.
99 O7 **Wapsipinicon** *R* Iowa U.S.A.
119 P2 **Wapus L** Saskatchewan Canada
123 N2 **Wapustagamau L** Quebec Canada
94 F9 **War** West Virginia U.S.A.
140 D1 **Waraga** N Terr Australia
86 H4 **Warandab** Ethiopia
76 D1 **Warangal** India
139 H6 **Waranga Res** Victoria Australia
139 H8 **Waratah** Tasmania Australia
139 H7 **Waratah B** Victoria Australia
99 N2 **Warba** Minnesota U.S.A.
9 F3 **Warboys** England
141 G6 **Warbreccan** Queensland Australia
118 C5 **Warburg** Alberta Canada
32 K10 **Warburg** Germany
138 E2 **Warburton** *R* South Australia Australia
139 H7 **Warburton** Victoria Australia
143 F7 **Warburton Mission** W Australia Australia
143 F7 **Warburton Ra** W Australia Australia
141 H7 **Ward** *R* Queensland Australia
145 E4 **Ward** New Zealand
111 H9 **Ward** Alabama U.S.A.
138 D5 **Wardang I** South Australia Australia
87 E11 **Warden** S Africa
100 F3 **Warden** Washington U.S.A.
32 H6 **Wardenburg** Germany
118 E6 **Warden Junc** Alberta Canada
94 J7 **Wardensville** West Virginia U.S.A.
74 H8 **Wardha** India
115 M1 **Ward Hunt I** Northwest Territories Canada
118 F8 **Wardlow** Alberta Canada
144 B5 **Ward, Mt** New Zealand
144 A6 **Ward, Mt** New Zealand
118 B9 **Wardner** British Columbia Canada
13 F5 **Wards Stone** *mt* England
117 L7 **Ware** British Columbia Canada
9 F4 **Ware** England
95 P4 **Ware** Massachusetts U.S.A.
145 D3 **Warea** New Zealand
22 E2 **Waregem** Belgium
8 D6 **Wareham** England
22 J2 **Waremme** Belgium
33 R5 **Waren** Germany
140 F6 **Warenda** Queensland Australia
32 G9 **Warendorf** Germany
144 B7 **Warepa** New Zealand
140 B4 **Ware Ra** N Terr Australia
112 E6 **Waresboro** Georgia U.S.A.
112 E3 **Ware Shoals** South Carolina U.S.A.
95 N7 **Waretown** New Jersey U.S.A.
25 G2 **Warfum** Netherlands
86 A2 **War Galoh** Somalia
9 F5 **Wargrave** England
139 K3 **Warialda** New South Wales Australia
33 P5 **Warin** Germany
68 G5 **Warin Chamrap** Thailand
109 J6 **Waring** Texas U.S.A.
116 H3 **Waring Mts** Alaska U.S.A.
13 F2 **Wark** England
31 N4 **Warka** Poland
121 N8 **Warkworth** Ontario Canada
13 G3 **Warkworth** England
145 E2 **Warkworth** New Zealand
8 D3 **Warley** England
9 F5 **Warlingham** England
21 P1 **Warloy-Baillon** France
89 A7 **Warmbad** Namibia
117 G6 **Warm Bay Hotsprings** British Columbia Canada
37 M4 **Warmensteinach** Germany
22 G5 **Warmeriville** France
9 E3 **Warmington** England
8 D5 **Warminster** England
25 C4 **Warmond** Netherlands
32 J8 **Warmsen** Germany
112 C5 **Warm Springs** Georgia U.S.A.
101 N3 **Warmsprings** Montana U.S.A.
102 H3 **Warm Springs** Nevada U.S.A.
100 D5 **Warm Springs** Oregon U.S.A.
94 H8 **Warm Springs** Virginia U.S.A.
100 G6 **Warm Springs Res** Oregon U.S.A.
89 B9 **Warmwaters Berg** *mt* S Africa
8 D6 **Warmwell** England
22 J2 **Warnant-Dreye** Belgium
120 B3 **Warneford** Ontario Canada
33 Q4 **Warnemünde** Germany
101 N1 **Warner** Alberta Canada
95 Q3 **Warner** New Hampshire U.S.A.
107 P6 **Warner** Oklahoma U.S.A.
98 H4 **Warner** South Dakota U.S.A.
100 F7 **Warner Lakes** Oregon U.S.A.
100 E8 **Warner Mts** California U.S.A.
112 D5 **Warner Robins** Georgia U.S.A.
102 H8 **Warner Springs** California U.S.A.
22 D2 **Warneton** Belgium
139 L3 **Warning,Mt** New South Wales Australia
33 Q5 **Warnow** *R* Germany
143 B10 **Waroona** W Australia Australia
74 H8 **Warora** India
141 K7 **Warra** Queensland Australia
138 F6 **Warracknabeal** Victoria Australia
139 H7 **Warragul** Victoria Australia
138 E3 **Warrakalanna,L** South Australia Australia
138 D5 **Warramboo** South Australia Australia
143 C8 **Warramboo** *mt* W Australia Australia
139 J3 **Warrambool** *R* New South Wales Australia
80 G4 **Warran** *R* Jordan
138 E2 **Warrandininna,L** South Australia Australia
142 D5 **Warrawagine** W Australia Australia
141 H7 **Warrego** *R* Queensland Australia
141 H6 **Warrego Ra** Queensland Australia
139 J4 **Warren** New South Wales Australia
120 K6 **Warren** Ontario Canada
111 D8 **Warren** Arkansas U.S.A.
100 K4 **Warren** Idaho U.S.A.
99 R7 **Warren** Illinois U.S.A.
94 B6 **Warren** Indiana U.S.A.
94 D4 **Warren** Michigan U.S.A.
98 K1 **Warren** Minnesota U.S.A.
101 R4 **Warren** Montana U.S.A.
95 Q3 **Warren** New Hampshire U.S.A.
94 G5 **Warren** Ohio U.S.A.
94 H5 **Warren** Pennsylvania U.S.A.
95 Q5 **Warren** Rhode I U.S.A.
109 N5 **Warren** Texas U.S.A.
94 J9 **Warren** Virginia U.S.A.
115 L3 **Warrender,C** Northwest Territories Canada
119 U5 **Warren Landing** Manitoba Canada
143 E8 **Warren, Mt** W Australia Australia
14 E2 **Warrenpoint** N Ireland
99 Q5 **Warrens** Wisconsin U.S.A.
99 R10 **Warrensburg** Illinois U.S.A.
110 C3 **Warrensburg** Missouri U.S.A.
95 O3 **Warrensburg** New York U.S.A.
89 D7 **Warrenton** S Africa
112 E4 **Warrenton** Georgia U.S.A.
110 E3 **Warrenton** Missouri U.S.A.
112 J1 **Warrenton** North Carolina U.S.A.
100 B3 **Warrenton** Oregon U.S.A.
94 K8 **Warrenton** Virginia U.S.A.
101 Q1 **Warrick** Montana U.S.A.
143 B8 **Warriedar Hill** W Australia Australia
138 D3 **Warrina** South Australia Australia
138 D3 **Warriners Cr** South Australia Australia
13 F6 **Warrington** England
144 D6 **Warrington** New Zealand
111 J11 **Warrington** Florida U.S.A.
111 K8 **Warrior** Alabama U.S.A.
138 E4 **Warriota Creek** South Australia Australia
138 F3 **Warri Warri** New South Wales Australia
138 F7 **Warrnambool** Victoria Australia
99 L1 **Warroad** Minnesota U.S.A.
141 J7 **Warrong** Queensland Australia
138 D5 **Warrow** South Australia Australia
139 J4 **Warrumbungle Ra** New South Wales Australia
141 F8 **Warry Warry** *R* Queensland Australia
Warsaw *see* **Warszawa**
99 P9 **Warsaw** Illinois U.S.A.
94 B5 **Warsaw** Indiana U.S.A.
94 C8 **Warsaw** Kentucky U.S.A.
110 C3 **Warsaw** Missouri U.S.A.
94 J4 **Warsaw** New York U.S.A.
112 J2 **Warsaw** North Carolina U.S.A.
95 L9 **Warsaw** Virginia U.S.A.
38 K6 **Warscheneck** *mt* Austria
86 A3 **Warshiikh** Somalia
118 E4 **Warspite** Alberta Canada
32 H10 **Warstein** Germany
31 M3 **Warszawa** Poland
31 H2 **Warszów** Poland
31 J3 **Warta** *R* Poland
31 L4 **Warta** Poland
38 N6 **Wartberg** Austria
37 J2 **Wartburg** Germany
37 M7 **Wartenberg** Germany
13 H6 **Warter** England
41 M3 **Warth** Austria
118 J7 **Wartime** Saskatchewan Canada
13 F6 **Warton** England
142 F3 **Warton Ra** W Australia Australia
110 K6 **Wartrace** Tennessee U.S.A.
70 E5 **Waru** Kalimantan
141 K8 **Warwick** Queensland Australia
121 T7 **Warwick** Quebec Canada
9 E3 **Warwick** England
13 F4 **Warwick** Cumbria England
112 D6 **Warwick** Georgia U.S.A.
95 N5 **Warwick** New York U.S.A.
98 H2 **Warwick** North Dakota U.S.A.
95 Q5 **Warwick** Rhode I U.S.A.
140 D2 **Warwick Chan** N Terr Australia
9 E3 **Warwickshire** *co* England
117 Q11 **Wasa** British Columbia Canada
120 K8 **Wasaga Beach** Ontario Canada
85 F6 **Wasagu** Nigeria
103 N2 **Wasatch Ra** Utah U.S.A.
102 E6 **Wasco** California U.S.A.
100 E4 **Wasco** Oregon U.S.A.
99 P3 **Wascott** Wisconsin U.S.A.
118 H5 **Waseca** Saskatchewan Canada
99 N5 **Waseca** Minnesota U.S.A.
121 L8 **Washago** Ontario Canada
101 Q6 **Washakie Needles** *mts* Wyoming U.S.A.
9 H3 **Washbrook** England
99 R9 **Washburn** Illinois U.S.A.
95 S7 **Washburn** Maine U.S.A.
98 E2 **Washburn** North Dakota U.S.A.
108 C8 **Washburn** Texas U.S.A.
114 J3 **Washburn L** Northwest Territories Canada
101 P5 **Washburn,Mt** Wyoming U.S.A.
144 C6 **Washdyke** New Zealand
8 C5 **Washford** England
60 H12 **Washiki** Japan
123 M3 **Washikuti** Quebec Canada
74 G8 **Wāshīm** India
121 S3 **Washimeska** *R* Quebec Canada
97 **Washington** *conurbation* District of Columbia
13 G4 **Washington** England
100 F2 **Washington** *state* U.S.A.
109 O2 **Washington** Arkansas U.S.A.
112 E4 **Washington** Georgia U.S.A.
99 R9 **Washington** Illinois U.S.A.
110 J3 **Washington** Indiana U.S.A.
99 P8 **Washington** Iowa U.S.A.
107 N2 **Washington** Kansas U.S.A.
111 D11 **Washington** Louisiana U.S.A.
110 E3 **Washington** Missouri U.S.A.
95 P3 **Washington** New Hampshire U.S.A.
95 N6 **Washington** New Jersey U.S.A.
112 K2 **Washington** North Carolina U.S.A.
94 G6 **Washington** Pennsylvania U.S.A.
109 L5 **Washington** Texas U.S.A.
103 L4 **Washington** Utah U.S.A.
94 J8 **Washington** Virginia U.S.A.
146 C12 **Washington, Cape** Antarctica
94 D7 **Washington Court Ho** Ohio U.S.A.
99 U4 **Washington I** Wisconsin U.S.A.
113 G9 **Washington,L** Florida U.S.A.
115 N1 **Washington Land** Greenland
95 Q2 **Washington, Mt** New Hampshire U.S.A.
109 J1 **Washita** *R* Oklahoma U.S.A.
101 Q4 **Washoe** Montana U.S.A.
100 C4 **Washougal** Washington U.S.A.
119 V7 **Washow B** Manitoba Canada
9 G2 **Wash, The** *G* England
100 G3 **Washtucna** Washington U.S.A.
22 G4 **Wasigny** France
31 O2 **Wasilków** Poland
71 N8 **Wasiri** Indonesia
79 E9 **Wasit** Egypt
78 K5 **Wāsit** *prov* Iraq
98 F1 **Waskada** Manitoba Canada
119 V2 **Waskaiowaka L** Manitoba Canada
118 L5 **Waskesiu L** Saskatchewan Canada
118 L5 **Waskesiu Lake** Saskatchewan Canada
118 E4 **Wasketenau** Alberta Canada
99 M1 **Waskish** Minnesota U.S.A.
109 N3 **Waskom** Texas U.S.A.
22 F3 **Wasmes** Belgium
31 K4 **Wąsosz** Poland
60 Q1 **Wassamu** Japan
112 F6 **Wassaw Sd** Georgia U.S.A.
36 C6 **Wasselonne** France
25 F6 **Wassenberg** Germany
37 J6 **Wasseralfingen** Germany
22 L4 **Wasserbillig** Luxembourg
37 K5 **Wassermungenau** Germany
37 K5 **Wassertrüdingen** Germany
22 F3 **Wassigny** France
102 F3 **Wassuk Ra** Nevada U.S.A.
19 J4 **Wassy** France
98 D5 **Wasta** South Dakota U.S.A.
79 B9 **Wasta,El** Egypt
13 E5 **Wast Water** *L* England
37 J2 **Wasungen** Germany
121 O3 **Waswanipi** Quebec Canada
120 K4 **Watabeag L** Ontario Canada
99 Q8 **Wataga** Illinois U.S.A.
83 L11 **Watagoda** *mt* Sri Lanka
70 G7 **Watampone** Sulawesi
71 L9 **Watanga, Teluk** *B* Flores Indonesia
70 F7 **Watansoppeng** Sulawesi
98 E4 **Watauga** South Dakota U.S.A.
109 M9 **Watauga** Texas U.S.A.
8 C5 **Watchet** England
118 L1 **Watcomb** Ontario Canada
9 G3 **Waterbeach** England
87 C10 **Waterberg Plateau Park** *nat park* Namibia
95 R3 **Waterboro** Maine U.S.A.
95 O5 **Waterbury** Connecticut U.S.A.
95 P2 **Waterbury** Vermont U.S.A.
126 F3 **Water Cays** *islds* Bahamas
112 G3 **Wateree L** South Carolina U.S.A.
120 K10 **Waterford** Ontario Canada
14 D4 **Waterford** *co* Ireland
14 D4 **Waterford** Ireland
102 D4 **Waterford** California U.S.A.
94 H5 **Waterford** Pennsylvania U.S.A.
14 E4 **Waterford Hbr** Ireland
8 A7 **Watergate B** England
119 S6 **Waterhan L** Manitoba Canada
118 J4 **Waterhen L** Saskatchewan Canada
140 C2 **Waterhouse** *R* N Terr Australia
140 C6 **Waterhouse Ra** N Terr Australia
140 A3 **Waterloo** N Terr Australia
22 G2 **Waterloo** Belgium
121 S7 **Waterloo** Quebec Canada
127 O2 **Waterloo** Trinidad
110 H7 **Waterloo** Alabama U.S.A.
109 O2 **Waterloo** Arkansas U.S.A.
110 F3 **Waterloo** Illinois U.S.A.
94 B5 **Waterloo** Indiana U.S.A.
99 O7 **Waterloo** Iowa U.S.A.
101 N4 **Waterloo** Montana U.S.A.
95 L4 **Waterloo** New York U.S.A.
8 C6 **Waterloo Cross** England
99 S8 **Waterman** Illinois U.S.A.
111 E10 **Waterproof** Louisiana U.S.A.
94 C2 **Waters** Michigan U.S.A.
99 R3 **Watersmeet** Michigan U.S.A.
118 D9 **Waterton Pk** Alberta Canada
99 N5 **Watertown** Minnesota U.S.A.
95 M3 **Watertown** New York U.S.A.
98 J5 **Watertown** South Dakota U.S.A.
110 K5 **Watertown** Tennessee U.S.A.
99 S6 **Watertown** Wisconsin U.S.A.
138 E5 **Watervale** South Australia Australia
111 G7 **Water Valley** Mississippi U.S.A.
108 G4 **Water Valley** Texas U.S.A.
95 O4 **Watervhet** New York U.S.A.
122 H8 **Waterville** Nova Scotia Canada
121 T7 **Waterville** Quebec Canada
95 S2 **Waterville** Maine U.S.A.
99 N5 **Waterville** Minnesota U.S.A.
95 M4 **Waterville** New York U.S.A.
100 E2 **Waterville** Washington U.S.A.
118 F2 **Waterways** Alberta Canada
70 N9 **Wates** Java
120 J10 **Watford** Ontario Canada
9 F4 **Watford** England
98 C2 **Watford City** North Dakota U.S.A.
107 P2 **Wathena** Kansas U.S.A.
143 B9 **Watheroo** W Australia Australia
117 P8 **Watino** Alberta Canada
106 F2 **Watkins** Colorado U.S.A.
99 M4 **Watkins** Minnesota U.S.A.
115 R4 **Watkins Bjerge** *mts* Greenland
95 L4 **Watkins Glen** New York U.S.A.
112 D4 **Watkinsville** Georgia U.S.A.
107 M6 **Watonga** Oklahoma U.S.A.
70 K9 **Waton,Tg** *C* Java
22 D2 **Watou** Belgium
71 B2 **Watowato,Bk** *mt* Halmahera Indonesia
119 M7 **Watrous** Saskatchewan Canada
106 F6 **Watrous** New Mexico U.S.A.
86 E5 **Watsa** Zaire
99 T9 **Watseka** Illinois U.S.A.
86 D6 **Watsi-Kengo** Zaire
141 F2 **Watson** *R* Queensland Australia
119 N6 **Watson** Saskatchewan Canada
111 E8 **Watson** Arkansas U.S.A.
99 L4 **Watson** Minnesota U.S.A.
99 L9 **Watson** Missouri U.S.A.
101 Q10 **Watson** Utah U.S.A.
117 J5 **Watson Lake** Yukon Territory Canada
95 L5 **Watsontown** Pennsylvania U.S.A.
83 J10 **Wattala** Sri Lanka
22 C2 **Watten** France
15 E2 **Watten** Scotland
32 F10 **Wattenscheid** Germany
138 D3 **Wattiwarriganna** *R* South Australia Australia
139 G3 **Wattle Vale** New South Wales Australia
143 F7 **Watt, Mt** W Australia Australia
117 P6 **Watt,Mt** Alberta Canada
9 G2 **Watton** England
9 F4 **Watton** England
107 Q5 **Watts** Oklahoma U.S.A.
112 C2 **Watts Bar Lake** Tennessee U.S.A.
94 H4 **Wattsburg** Pennsylvania U.S.A.
71 L9 **Watumanuk, Tanjong** *C* Indonesia
70 G6 **Watuwila,Bk** *mt* Sulawesi
38 G6 **Watzmann** *mt* Germany
136 K3 **Wau** Papua New Guinea
86 E4 **Wau** Sudan
120 K7 **Waubamick** Ontario Canada
121 L8 **Waubaushene** Ontario Canada
98 J4 **Waubay** South Dakota U.S.A.
98 J4 **Waubay L** South Dakota U.S.A.
139 L4 **Wauchope** New South Wales Australia
140 C5 **Wauchope** N Terr Australia
119 Q9 **Wauchope** Saskatchewan Canada
113 F10 **Wauchula** Florida U.S.A.
99 O6 **Waucoma** Iowa U.S.A.
100 G1 **Wauconda** Washington U.S.A.
118 F1 **Waugh** Manitoba Canada
142 D5 **Waukarlycarly, L** W Australia Australia
70 F5 **Waukata, G** *mt* Sulawesi
99 N8 **Waukee** Iowa U.S.A.
99 T7 **Waukegan** Illinois U.S.A.
99 S6 **Waukesha** Wisconsin U.S.A.
107 N5 **Waukomis** Oklahoma U.S.A.
99 P6 **Waukon** Iowa U.S.A.
98 E9 **Wauneta** Nebraska U.S.A.
99 R5 **Waupaca** Wisconsin U.S.A.
99 S6 **Waupun** Wisconsin U.S.A.
109 K1 **Waurika** Oklahoma U.S.A.
98 J7 **Wausa** Nebraska U.S.A.
99 R5 **Wausau** Wisconsin U.S.A.
99 T4 **Wausaukee** Wisconsin U.S.A.
94 C5 **Wauseon** Ohio U.S.A.
81 G8 **W Australian Ridge** Indian Oc
99 R5 **Wautoma** Wisconsin U.S.A.
99 S6 **Wauwatosa** Wisconsin U.S.A.
140 B3 **Wave Hill Police Station** N Terr Australia
110 J2 **Waveland** Indiana U.S.A.
141 K1 **Wavell Heights** *dist* Brisbane, Qnsld Australia
9 H3 **Waveney,R** England
122 J9 **Waverley** Nova Scotia Canada
145 E3 **Waverley** New Zealand
100 H2 **Waverley** Washington U.S.A.
112 F6 **Waverly** Georgia U.S.A.
110 G2 **Waverly** Illinois U.S.A.
99 O7 **Waverly** Iowa U.S.A.
107 P3 **Waverly** Kansas U.S.A.
110 C2 **Waverly** Missouri U.S.A.
98 K9 **Waverly** Nebraska U.S.A.
95 L4 **Waverly** New York U.S.A.
98 K4 **Waverly** South Dakota U.S.A.
110 J5 **Waverly** Tennessee U.S.A.
95 K9 **Waverly** Virginia U.S.A.
111 M9 **Waverly Hall** Georgia U.S.A.
141 F7 **Waverney** Queensland Australia
22 C2 **Wavrans-sur-l'Aa** France
22 H2 **Wavre** Belgium
22 D2 **Wavrin** France
118 E6 **Wavy L** Alberta Canada
68 C4 **Waw** Burma
120 F4 **Wawa** Ontario Canada
121 M3 **Wawagosic** *R* Quebec Canada
120 J4 **Wawaitin Falls** Ontario Canada
70 G6 **Wawalalindu** Sulawesi
119 S9 **Wawanesa** Manitoba Canada
84 F5 **Waw an Nāmūs** Libya
94 B5 **Wawasee,L** Indiana U.S.A.
70 G6 **Wawo** Sulawesi
102 E4 **Wawona** California U.S.A.
119 Q9 **Wawota** Saskatchewan Canada
70 G6 **Wawotebi** Sulawesi
109 L3 **Waxahachie** Texas U.S.A.
112 G3 **Waxhaw** North Carolina U.S.A.
111 F9 **Way** Mississippi U.S.A.
71 A3 **Wayakuba** Indonesia
101 O7 **Wayan** Idaho U.S.A.
Wayaobu *see* **Zichang**
112 E6 **Waycross** Georgia U.S.A.
68 F8 **Way,Ko** *isld* G of Thailand
143 D7 **Way, L** W Australia Australia
99 P8 **Wayland** Iowa U.S.A.
94 E9 **Wayland** Kentucky U.S.A.
94 B4 **Wayland** Michigan U.S.A.
99 P9 **Wayland** Missouri U.S.A.
94 K4 **Wayland** New York U.S.A.
118 E7 **Wayne** Alberta Canada
95 R2 **Wayne** Maine U.S.A.
94 D4 **Wayne** Michigan U.S.A.
110 C5 **Wayne** Missouri U.S.A.
98 J7 **Wayne** Nebraska U.S.A.
107 N7 **Wayne** Oklahoma U.S.A.
94 E8 **Wayne** West Virginia U.S.A.
110 H3 **Wayne City** Illinois U.S.A.
112 F4 **Waynesboro** Georgia U.S.A.
111 H10 **Waynesboro** Mississippi U.S.A.
94 K7 **Waynesboro** Pennsylvania U.S.A.
110 J6 **Waynesboro** Tennessee U.S.A.
94 J8 **Waynesboro** Virginia U.S.A.
94 F6 **Waynesburg** Ohio U.S.A.
94 G7 **Waynesburg** Pennsylvania U.S.A.
99 R9 **Waynesville** Illinois U.S.A.
110 D4 **Waynesville** Missouri U.S.A.
112 E2 **Waynesville** North Carolina U.S.A.
94 C7 **Waynesville** Ohio U.S.A.
107 M5 **Waynoka** Oklahoma U.S.A.
98 C7 **Wayside** Nebraska U.S.A.
108 F1 **Wayside** Texas U.S.A.
77 L3 **Wazi Khwa** Afghanistan
77 K1 **Wazirabad** Afghanistan
74 F2 **Wazirabad** Pakistan
31 L2 **Wda** *R* Poland
7 L11 **Weald, The** *reg* England
13 F4 **Wearhead** England
140 D3 **Wearyan** *R* N Terr Australia
141 H3 **Weary B** Queensland Australia
99 M10 **Weatherby** Missouri U.S.A.
107 M6 **Weatherford** Oklahoma U.S.A.
109 K3 **Weatherford** Texas U.S.A.
95 M6 **Weatherly** Pennsylvania U.S.A.
110 C4 **Weaubleau** Missouri U.S.A.
111 L8 **Weaver** Alabama U.S.A.
8 D1 **Weaverham** England
119 V6 **Weaver L** Manitoba Canada
100 C9 **Weaverville** California U.S.A.
118 J8 **Webb** Saskatchewan Canada
111 L10 **Webb** Alabama U.S.A.
111 F8 **Webb** Mississippi U.S.A.
109 H8 **Webb** Texas U.S.A.
110 B4 **Webb City** Missouri U.S.A.
107 P6 **Webbers Falls Res.** Oklahoma U.S.A.
142 G6 **Webb, Mt** W Australia Australia
145 F4 **Weber** New Zealand
106 G7 **Weber City** New Mexico U.S.A.
106 E2 **Webster** Colorado U.S.A.
113 E9 **Webster** Florida U.S.A.
99 O8 **Webster** Iowa U.S.A.
107 L2 **Webster** Kansas U.S.A.
95 Q4 **Webster** Massachusetts U.S.A.
95 K3 **Webster** New York U.S.A.
98 H1 **Webster** North Dakota U.S.A.
98 J4 **Webster** South Dakota U.S.A.
99 O4 **Webster** Wisconsin U.S.A.
99 N7 **Webster City** Iowa U.S.A.
110 F3 **Webster Groves** Missouri U.S.A.
22 H1 **Wechelderzande** Belgium
109 M4 **Weches** Texas U.S.A.
37 O2 **Wechselburg** Germany
71 A2 **Weda** Halmahera Indonesia
83 L11 **Wedagama** Sri Lanka
71 B2 **Weda,Teluk** *B* Halmahera Indonesia
133 E8 **Weddell I** Falkland Is
146 E4 **Weddell Sea** Antarctica
32 L7 **Weddemark** Germany
144 C6 **Wedderburn** New Zealand
100 A7 **Wedderburn** Oregon U.S.A.
32 K4 **Weddinghusen** Germany
32 K4 **Weddingstedt** Germany
32 L5 **Wedel** Germany
140 B6 **Wedge, Central Mt** N Terr Australia
112 G4 **Wedgefield** South Carolina U.S.A.
117 M10 **Wedge Mt** British Columbia Canada
122 G10 **Wedgeport** Nova Scotia Canada
8 D5 **Wedmore** England
9 D3 **Wednesbury** England
111 L8 **Wedowee** Alabama U.S.A.
100 C8 **Weed** California U.S.A.
121 T7 **Weedon** Quebec Canada
9 E3 **Weedon** England
95 L3 **Weedsport** New York U.S.A.
94 J5 **Weedville** Pennsylvania U.S.A.
71 C3 **Weeim** *isld* W Irian
119 P6 **Weekes** Saskatchewan Canada
111 E12 **Weeks** Louisiana U.S.A.
94 E9 **Weeksbury** Kentucky U.S.A.
Weeks I *see* **Puketutu I**
112 L1 **Weeksville** North Carolina U.S.A.
9 H4 **Weeley** England
142 B6 **Weeli Wolli Ck** W Australia Australia
139 J3 **Weemelah** New South Wales Australia
32 F6 **Weener** Germany
98 K9 **Weeping Water** Nebraska U.S.A.
25 E6 **Weert** Netherlands
109 K7 **Weesatche** Texas U.S.A.
28 C7 **Weesby** Germany
41 K3 **Weesen** Switzerland
25 D4 **Weesp** Netherlands
25 G1 **Weestereems** Netherlands
139 H5 **Weethalle** New South Wales Australia
9 G3 **Weeting** England
32 L8 **Weetzen** Germany
139 J4 **Wee Waa** New South Wales Australia
25 F5 **Weeze** Germany
33 O8 **Wefensleben** Germany
33 O8 **Weferlingen** Germany
33 O9 **Wegeleben** Germany
33 O8 **Wegenstedt** Germany
41 H3 **Weggis** Switzerland
32 J8 **Wegholm** Germany
31 J4 **Węgliniec** Poland
31 N1 **Wegorapa** *R* Poland
31 N1 **Węgorzewo** Poland
31 J2 **Węgorzyno** Poland
31 N3 **Węgrów** Poland
38 M6 **Wegscheid** Austria
38 J4 **Wegscheid** Germany
25 F2 **Wehe** Netherlands
40 G2 **Wehr** Germany
32 K9 **Wehrden** Germany
36 F3 **Wehrheim** Germany
65 D4 **Weichang** China
37 L6 **Weichering** Germany
38 M6 **Weichselboden** Austria
65 C7 **Weichuan** China
37 N2 **Weida** Germany
37 N4 **Weiden** Germany
36 E2 **Weidenau** Germany
37 M4 **Weidenberg** Germany
36 H6 **Weidenstetten** Germany
37 L3 **Weidhausen** Germany
94 C3 **Weidman** Michigan U.S.A.
65 D6 **Weifang** China
65 E6 **Weihai** China
58 E5 **Wei He** *R* China
65 G2 **Weihe** China
37 N6 **Weihmichl** Germany
36 E3 **Weilburg** Germany
36 F6 **Weil-der-Stadt** Germany
36 B2 **Weilerswist** Germany
36 H6 **Weilheim** Germany
36 E3 **Weilmünster** Germany
36 E3 **Weilnau** Germany
37 J5 **Weiltingen** Germany
65 B4 **Weilu** China
37 L2 **Weimar** Germany
109 L6 **Weimar** Texas U.S.A.
58 E5 **Weinan** China
110 F6 **Weiner** Arkansas U.S.A.
41 K2 **Weinfelden** Switzerland
36 E5 **Weingarten** Germany
36 F5 **Weingarten** Germany
36 F4 **Weinheim** Germany
67 A3 **Weining** China
36 G5 **Weinsberg** Germany
36 G6 **Weinstadt** Germany
141 F2 **Weipa** Queensland Australia
100 K3 **Weippe** Idaho U.S.A.
141 J8 **Weir** *R* Queensland Australia
121 Q7 **Weir** Quebec Canada
110 B4 **Weir** Kansas U.S.A.
111 G8 **Weir** Mississippi U.S.A.
109 K5 **Weir** Texas U.S.A.
143 B7 **Weiragoo Ra** W Australia Australia
107 Q4 **Weir City** Kansas U.S.A.
119 M5 **Weirdale** Saskatchewan Canada
95 Q3 **Weirs Beach** New Hampshire U.S.A.
113 F9 **Weirsdale** Florida U.S.A.
94 G6 **Weirton** West Virginia U.S.A.
37 N3 **Weischlitz** Germany
100 J5 **Weiser** Idaho U.S.A.
65 D7 **Weishan** China
65 C7 **Weishan Hu** *L* China
65 C7 **Weishi** China
Weishui *see* **Jingxing**
36 B4 **Weiskirchen** Germany
37 L3 **Weismain** Germany
36 F6 **Weissach** Germany
37 K5 **Weissenburg** Germany
37 M1 **Weissenfels** Germany
37 J7 **Weissenhorn** Germany
33 T7 **Weissensee** Berlin Germany
37 L1 **Weissensee** Thüringen Germany
37 M3 **Weissenstadt** Germany
36 H6 **Weissenstein** Germany
37 M3 **Weisser Main** *R* Germany
37 O5 **Weisser Regen** *R* Germany
40 G5 **Weisshorn** *mt* Switzerland
38 L7 **Weisskirchen** Austria
41 N4 **Weisskugel** *mt* Austria
112 B3 **Weiss Lake** Alabama U.S.A.
89 A5 **Weissrand Mts** Namibia
41 K3 **Weisstannen** Switzerland
33 S4 **Weitenhagen** Germany
41 M2 **Weitnau** Germany
67 F4 **Weitou** China
31 H7 **Weitra** Austria
38 N8 **Weixelbaum** Austria
38 K8 **Weixelsdorf** Austria
65 C6 **Wei Xian** China
65 D6 **Wei Xian** China
67 A3 **Weixin** China
67 A2 **Weiyuan** China
38 N7 **Weiz** Austria
41 H2 **Weizen** Germany
Weizhou *see* **Wenchuan**
68 J2 **Weizhou Dao** *isld* China
31 L1 **Wejherowo** Poland
119 S4 **Wekusko** Manitoba Canada
113 F8 **Welaka** Florida U.S.A.
138 C2 **Welbourn Hill** South Australia Australia
94 F9 **Welch** West Virginia U.S.A.
99 M6 **Welcome** Minnesota U.S.A.
89 A8 **Welcome Kop** *mt* S Africa
37 K7 **Welden** Germany
86 G3 **Weldiya** Ethiopia
143 D8 **Weld, Mt** W Australia Australia
119 M6 **Weldon** Saskatchewan Canada
102 F6 **Weldon** California U.S.A.
99 S9 **Weldon** Illinois U.S.A.
99 N9 **Weldon** Iowa U.S.A.
99 N9 **Weldon** *R* Missouri U.S.A.
112 L1 **Weldon** North Carolina U.S.A.
109 M4 **Weldon** Texas U.S.A.
106 G1 **Weldona** Colorado U.S.A.
13 G3 **Weldon Br** England
143 B7 **Weld Ra** W Australia Australia
107 O6 **Weleetka** Oklahoma U.S.A.
86 G4 **Welega** *prov* Ethiopia
141 G7 **Welford** Queensland Australia
141 G7 **Welford Downs** Queensland Australia
83 K12 **Weligama** Sri Lanka
83 L11 **Weliwewa** Sri Lanka
22 K2 **Welkenraedt** Belgium
89 E6 **Welkom** S Africa
121 L10 **Welland Canal** Ontario Canada
9 F2 **Welland, R** England
142 A4 **Wellard** *dist* Perth, W Aust Australia
83 L11 **Wellawaya** Sri Lanka
113 E7 **Wellborn** Florida U.S.A.
36 H1 **Wellerode Wald** Germany
9 E3 **Wellesbourne** England
140 E3 **Wellesley Is** Queensland Australia
117 D4 **Wellesley L** Yukon Territory Canada
98 F9 **Wellfleet** Nebraska U.S.A.
37 L6 **Wellheim** Germany
22 J3 **Wellin** Belgium
9 F3 **Wellingborough** England
139 J4 **Wellington** New South Wales Australia
138 E6 **Wellington** South Australia Australia
123 S5 **Wellington** Newfoundland Canada
122 J9 **Wellington** Nova Scotia Canada
121 N9 **Wellington** Ontario Canada
122 H7 **Wellington** Prince Edward I Canada
8 D2 **Wellington** England
8 C6 **Wellington** England
145 E4 **Wellington** *admin region* New Zealand
145 F4 **Wellington** New Zealand
89 A9 **Wellington** S Africa
111 L8 **Wellington** Alabama U.S.A.
106 E1 **Wellington** Colorado U.S.A.
99 T9 **Wellington** Illinois U.S.A.
107 N4 **Wellington** Kansas U.S.A.
102 E3 **Wellington** Nevada U.S.A.
94 E5 **Wellington** Ohio U.S.A.
108 G1 **Wellington** Texas U.S.A.
103 O2 **Wellington** Utah U.S.A.
115 K2 **Wellington Chan** Northwest Territories Canada
133 C7 **Wellington, I** Chile
139 H7 **Wellington, L** Victoria Australia
143 D7 **Wellington Ra** W Australia Australia
108 E2 **Wellman** Texas U.S.A.
9 F1 **Wellow** England
8 D5 **Wells** England
107 N2 **Wells** Kansas U.S.A.
99 N6 **Wells** Minnesota U.S.A.
101 L8 **Wells** Nevada U.S.A.
95 N3 **Wells** New York U.S.A.
109 N4 **Wells** Texas U.S.A.
95 K5 **Wellsboro** Pennsylvania U.S.A.
99 O7 **Wellsburg** Iowa U.S.A.
95 L4 **Wellsburg** New York U.S.A.
94 G6 **Wellsburg** West Virginia U.S.A.
145 E2 **Wellsford** New Zealand
117 N9 **Wells Gray Prov. Park** British Columbia Canada
143 E7 **Wells, L** W Australia Australia
119 R1 **Wells L** Manitoba Canada
142 F3 **Wells, Mt** W Australia Australia
9 G2 **Wells-next-the-sea** England
95 P2 **Wells River** Vermont U.S.A.
94 E7 **Wellston** Ohio U.S.A.
110 E2 **Wellsville** Missouri U.S.A.
94 K4 **Wellsville** New York U.S.A.
101 O8 **Wellsville** Utah U.S.A.
103 K9 **Wellton** Arizona U.S.A.
119 S8 **Wellwood** Manitoba Canada
86 G3 **Welo** *prov* Ethiopia
38 K5 **Wels** Austria
25 D6 **Welschap** Netherlands
36 B4 **Welschbillig** Germany
36 E1 **Welschenennest** Germany
122 F8 **Welsford** New Brunswick Canada
109 P5 **Welsh** Louisiana U.S.A.
8 D2 **Welshampton** England
142 B2 **Welshpool** *dist* Perth, W Aust Australia
122 F9 **Welshpool** New Brunswick Canada
8 C2 **Welshpool** Wales
13 H6 **Welton** England
32 G9 **Welver** Germany
119 Q8 **Welwyn** Saskatchewan Canada
9 F4 **Welwyn Garden City** England
36 H6 **Welzheim** Germany
8 D2 **Wem** England
86 D6 **Wema** Zaire
142 A1 **Wembley** *dist* Perth, W Aust Australia
117 O8 **Wembley** Alberta Canada
142 A1 **Wembley Downs** *dist* Perth, W Aust Australia
8 B7 **Wembury** England
37 K6 **Wemding** Germany
25 A5 **Wemeldinge** Netherlands
12 D2 **Wemyss B** Scotland
126 F2 **Wemyss Bight** Eleuthera Bahamas
65 C5 **Wen'an** China
100 E2 **Wenatchee** Washington U.S.A.
67 C7 **Wenchang** China
67 G3 **Wencheng** China
85 D7 **Wenchi** Ghana
67 A1 **Wenchuan** China
102 D1 **Wendel** California U.S.A.
101 L7 **Wendell** Idaho U.S.A.
98 K3 **Wendell** Minnesota U.S.A.
112 J2 **Wendell** North Carolina U.S.A.
36 D4 **Wendelsheim** Germany
37 L5 **Wendelstein** Germany
9 G3 **Wenden** England
36 D2 **Wenden** Germany
103 L8 **Wenden** Arizona U.S.A.
65 E6 **Wendeng** China
33 Q6 **Wendisch Priborn** Germany
33 O7 **Wendland** *reg* Germany
9 G2 **Wendling** England
100 C5 **Wendling** Oregon U.S.A.
86 G4 **Wendo** Ethiopia
33 O5 **Wendorf** Germany
9 F4 **Wendover** England
101 M9 **Wendover** Utah U.S.A.
98 B7 **Wendover** Wyoming U.S.A.
98 F5 **Wendte** South Dakota U.S.A.
22 E1 **Wenduine** Belgium
120 G5 **Wenebegon L** Ontario Canada
67 B3 **Weng'an** China
36 B4 **Wengerohr** Germany
67 D2 **Wengjiang** China
67 E4 **Wengyuan** China
65 D7 **Wen He** *R* China
36 G3 **Wenings** Germany
67 A1 **Wenjiang** China
68 K1 **Wenli** China
67 G2 **Wenling** China
141 F1 **Wenlock** *R* Queensland Australia
141 G2 **Wenlock** Queensland Australia
128 A7 **Wenman** *isld* Galapagos Is
32 L8 **Wennigsen** Germany
41 N3 **Wenns** Austria
99 R8 **Wenona** Illinois U.S.A.
67 C1 **Wenquan** China
67 A5 **Wenshan** China
65 C7 **Wenshang** China
65 B6 **Wenshui** China
67 B2 **Wenshui** China
57 K4 **Wensu** China
13 G6 **Wentbridge** England
138 F5 **Wentworth** New South Wales Australia
13 G6 **Wentworth** England
95 Q3 **Wentworth** New Hampshire U.S.A.
98 K6 **Wentworth** South Dakota U.S.A.
122 J8 **Wentworth Centre** Nova Scotia Canada
110 F3 **Wentzville** Missouri U.S.A.
65 B7 **Wenxi** China
65 B7 **Wen Xian** China
37 N5 **Wenzenbach** Germany
67 G3 **Wenzhou** China
113 F10 **Weohyakapka L** Florida U.S.A.
100 B9 **Weott** California U.S.A.
89 E7 **Wepener** S Africa
22 H3 **Wepion** Belgium
69 B10 **We, Pulau** *isld* Sumatra
33 T7 **Werbellin** Germany
33 T7 **Werbellinsee** *L* Germany
33 P7 **Werben** Germany
33 S9 **Werbig** Germany
22 K3 **Werbomont** Belgium
87 D11 **Werda** Botswana
37 N2 **Werdau** Germany
86 J4 **Werdër** Ethiopia
33 R8 **Werder** Germany
32 G10 **Werdohl** Germany
80 E6 **Wered Yeriḥo** Jordan
32 G9 **Werl** Germany
32 G7 **Werlte** Germany
36 C1 **Wermelskirchen** Germany
33 R10 **Wermsdorf** Germany
36 H4 **Wern** *R* Germany
37 N4 **Wernberg** Germany
32 G9 **Werne** Germany
37 J4 **Werneck** Germany
117 F3 **Wernecke Mts** Yukon Territory Canada
98 D2 **Werner** North Dakota U.S.A.
33 T7 **Werneuchen** Germany
36 H3 **Wernfeld** Germany
119 U2 **Wernham L** Manitoba Canada
25 C6 **Wernhout** Netherlands
33 N9 **Wernigerode** Germany
37 J1 **Werra** *R* Germany
139 G7 **Werribee** Victoria Australia
138 F5 **Werrimull** Victoria Australia
139 K4 **Werris Cr** New South Wales Australia
32 G9 **Werse** *R* Germany
37 K7 **Wertach** *R* Germany
36 H4 **Wertheim** Germany
37 K6 **Wertingen** Germany
71 M9 **Werula** Indonesia
25 D3 **Wervershoof** Netherlands
32 E9 **Wesel** Germany
36 D5 **Weselberg** Germany
33 R6 **Wesenberg** Germany
32 H5 **Weser** *est* Germany
32 L9 **Weser** *R* Germany
107 J3 **Weskan** Kansas U.S.A.
86 G4 **Weska Weka** Ethiopia
109 K9 **Weslaco** Texas U.S.A.
121 N8 **Weslemkoon L** Ontario Canada
95 U2 **Wesley** Maine U.S.A.
123 T4 **Wesleyville** Newfoundland Canada
94 G4 **Wesleyville** Pennsylvania U.S.A.
32 F5 **Wesse** Germany
32 J4 **Wesselburen** Germany
36 B2 **Wesseling** Germany
140 D1 **Wessel Is** N Terr Australia
98 H5 **Wessington** South Dakota U.S.A.
98 H5 **Wessington Springs** South Dakota U.S.A.
111 D8 **Wesson** Arkansas U.S.A.
111 F10 **Wesson** Mississippi U.S.A.
139 G6 **West** Victoria Australia
32 G8 **West** Germany
111 G8 **West** Mississippi U.S.A.
109 K4 **West** Texas U.S.A.
94 C7 **West Alexandria** Ohio U.S.A.
140 B1 **West Alligator** *R* N Terr Australia
99 S7 **West Allis** Wisconsin U.S.A.
138 C5 **Westall,Pt** South Australia Australia
13 G4 **West Auckland** England

240 **West B — Wilton**

113 B7 **West B** Florida U.S.A.
111 G12 **West B** Louisiana U.S.A.
109 N6 **West B** Texas U.S.A.
140 A3 **West Baines** *R* N Terr Australia
8 D6 **West Bay** England
111 L11 **Westbay** Florida U.S.A.
119 O7 **West Bend** Saskatchewan Canada
99 M7 **West Bend** Iowa U.S.A.
99 S6 **West Bend** Wisconsin U.S.A.
75 M7 **West Bengal** *prov* India
111 J8 **West Blockton** Alabama U.S.A.
99 L9 **Westboro** Missouri U.S.A.
99 Q4 **Westboro** Wisconsin U.S.A.
119 T8 **Westbourne** Manitoba Canada
99 P8 **West Branch** Iowa U.S.A.
94 C2 **West Branch** Michigan U.S.A.
13 G6 **West Bretton** England
117 O11 **Westbridge** British Columbia Canada
9 E2 **West Bridgford** England
9 E2 **West Bromwich** England
95 R3 **Westbrook** Maine U.S.A.
99 L5 **Westbrook** Minnesota U.S.A.
108 F3 **Westbrook** Texas U.S.A.
95 Q2 **West Burke** Vermont U.S.A.
15 G2 **West Burra** Shetland Scotland
139 H8 **Westbury** Tasmania Australia
9 E5 **Westbury** England
101 O1 **West Butte** *mt* Montana U.S.A.
139 H6 **Westby** New South Wales Australia
98 C1 **Westby** North Dakota U.S.A.
99 Q6 **Westby** Wisconsin U.S.A.
144 A6 **West C** New Zealand
127 H4 **West Caicos** *isld* Turks & Caicos Is
12 E2 **West Calder** Scotland
143 C11 **West Cape Howe** W Australia Australia
99 S8 **West Chicago** Illinois U.S.A.
106 E3 **Westcliffe** Colorado U.S.A.
144 B5 **West Coast** *admin region* New Zealand
109 M6 **West Columbia** Texas U.S.A.
99 O5 **West Concord** Minnesota U.S.A.
102 G7 **West Covina** California U.S.A.
9 G6 **Westdean** England
99 N8 **West Des Moines** Iowa U.S.A.
122 J9 **West Dover** Nova Scotia Canada
141 K2 **West End** *dist* Brisbane, Qnsld Australia
126 E1 **West End** Grand Bahama I
102 G6 **Westend** California U.S.A.
112 H2 **West End** North Carolina U.S.A.
22 D1 **Westende** Belgium
113 H11 **West End Pt** Bahamas
113 J11 **West End Settlement** Grand Bahama I
32 L4 **Westensee** *L* Germany
25 G3 **Westerbork** Netherlands
144 C5 **Westerfield** New Zealand
9 G5 **Westerham** England
22 H1 **Westerlo** Belgium
98 J9 **Western** Nebraska U.S.A.
86 E4 **Western Equatoria** *prov* Sudan
76 A1 **Western Ghats** *mts* India
122 H10 **Western Hd** Nova Scotia Canada
120 K7 **Western Is** Ontario Canada
15 A3 **Western Isles** *reg* Scotland
139 H7 **Western Port** Victoria Australia
94 H7 **Westernport** Maryland U.S.A.
141 G5 **Western R** Queensland Australia
85 B4 **Western Sahara** *reg* Africa
134 A2 **Western Samoa** *islds* Pacific Oc
32 M9 **Westerode** Germany
32 G6 **Westerstede** Germany
36 D2 **Westerwald** *reg* Germany
107 M3 **Westfall** Kansas U.S.A.
100 H6 **Westfall** Oregon U.S.A.
8 D2 **West Felton** England
142 B3 **Westfield** *dist* Perth, W Aust Australia
99 T10 **Westfield** Illinois U.S.A.
95 P4 **Westfield** Massachusetts U.S.A.
94 H4 **Westfield** New York U.S.A.
94 K5 **Westfield** Pennsylvania U.S.A.
99 R6 **Westfield** Wisconsin U.S.A.
122 F8 **Westfield Beach** New Brunswick Canada
110 B6 **West Fork** Arkansas U.S.A.
99 M6 **West Fork** *R* Minnesota U.S.A.
98 A1 **West Fork** *R* Montana U.S.A.
110 H4 **West Frankfort** Illinois U.S.A.
141 H7 **Westgate** Queensland Australia
9 H5 **Westgate** England
West Germany *see* **Germany**
8 C4 **West Glamorgan** *co* Wales
95 U1 **West Grand L** Maine U.S.A.
112 E6 **West Green** Georgia U.S.A.
9 F6 **West Grinstead** England
141 J7 **Westgrove** Queensland Australia
9 E3 **West Haddon** England
9 G5 **West Ham** England
94 E8 **West Hamlin** West Virginia U.S.A.
95 P6 **Westhampton Beach** Long I, New York U.S.A.
37 K7 **Westheim** Germany
36 E4 **West Hofen** Germany
109 K6 **Westhoff** Texas U.S.A.
36 C6 **Westhoffen** France
100 B1 **Westholme** British Columbia Canada
98 E1 **Westhope** North Dakota U.S.A.
68 A6 **West I** Andaman Is
83 M8 **West I** Cocos Is Indian Oc
146 J12 **West Ice Shelf** Antarctica
32 G10 **Westig** Germany
127 **West Indies** *arch* Caribbean
94 F10 **West Jefferson** North Carolina U.S.A.
94 D7 **West Jefferson** Ohio U.S.A.
22 E1 **Westkapelle** Belgium
25 A6 **Westkapelle** Netherlands
15 D5 **West Kilbride** Scotland
100 F8 **West L** Nevada U.S.A.
110 J1 **West Lafayette** Indiana U.S.A.
94 F6 **West Lafayette** Ohio U.S.A.
100 A6 **Westlake** Oregon U.S.A.
141 G6 **Westland** Queensland Australia
9 H3 **Westleton** England
99 P8 **West Liberty** Iowa U.S.A.
94 D9 **West Liberty** Kentucky U.S.A.
94 D6 **West Liberty** Ohio U.S.A.
13 E2 **West Linton** Scotland
118 D4 **Westlock** Alberta Canada
120 J10 **West Lorne** Ontario Canada
West Lothian *co see* **Lothian and Central** *regions*
122 H2 **West Magpie R** Quebec Canada
9 G5 **West Malling** England
94 C7 **West Manchester** Ohio U.S.A.
141 J8 **Westmar** Queensland Australia
121 O7 **Westmeath** Ontario Canada
14 D3 **Westmeath** *co* Ireland
110 F6 **West Memphis** Arkansas U.S.A.
9 G4 **West Mersea** England
94 G5 **West Middlesex** Pennsylvania U.S.A.
9 E2 **West Midlands** *co* England
94 C7 **West Milton** Ohio U.S.A.
106 E2 **Westminster** Colorado U.S.A.
95 L7 **Westminster** Maryland U.S.A.
112 D3 **Westminster** South Carolina U.S.A.
95 P3 **Westminster** Vermont U.S.A.
140 E3 **Westmoreland** Queensland Australia
107 O2 **Westmoreland** Kansas U.S.A.
95 P4 **Westmoreland** New Hampshire U.S.A.
110 K5 **Westmoreland** Tennessee U.S.A.
Westmorland *co see* **Cumbria**
127 H2 **Westmorland** *parish* Jamaica
103 J8 **Westmorland** California U.S.A.
87 E10 **West Nicholson** Zimbabwe
108 G6 **West Nueces** *R* Texas U.S.A.
8 D2 **Weston** England
144 C6 **Weston** New Zealand
70 D2 **Weston** Sabah
101 O7 **Weston** Idaho U.S.A.
94 C5 **Weston** Michigan U.S.A.
110 B2 **Weston** Missouri U.S.A.
98 K8 **Weston** Nebraska U.S.A.
94 D5 **Weston** Ohio U.S.A.
100 G4 **Weston** Oregon U.S.A.
94 G7 **Weston** West Virginia U.S.A.
98 A5 **Weston** Wyoming U.S.A.
89 E6 **Westonaria** S Africa
8 D5 **Weston-super-Mare** England
109 H2 **Westover** Texas U.S.A.
32 F6 **Westoverledingen** Germany
113 G11 **West Palm Beach** Florida U.S.A.
95 R2 **West Paris** Maine U.S.A.
110 J3 **Westphalia** Indiana U.S.A.
107 P3 **Westphalia** Kansas U.S.A.
94 K5 **West Pike** Pennsylvania U.S.A.
110 E5 **West Plains** Missouri U.S.A.
139 G8 **West Point** Tasmania Australia
122 H4 **West Point** Quebec Canada
116 P4 **West Point** *mt* Alaska U.S.A.
102 D3 **West Point** California U.S.A.
112 B5 **West Point** Georgia U.S.A.
110 J1 **Westpoint** Indiana U.S.A.
99 P9 **West Point** Iowa U.S.A.
94 B9 **West Point** Kentucky U.S.A.
111 H8 **West Point** Mississippi U.S.A.
95 N5 **West Point** New York U.S.A.
95 L9 **West Point** Virginia U.S.A.
111 L8 **West Point L** Alabama/Georgia
West Polder *see* **Markerwaard**
123 Q4 **Westport** Newfoundland Canada
14 B3 **Westport** Ireland
144 C4 **Westport** New Zealand
102 A2 **Westport** California U.S.A.
94 B7 **Westport** Indiana U.S.A.
95 O2 **Westport** New York U.S.A.
100 B3 **Westport** Oregon U.S.A.
98 H4 **Westport** South Dakota U.S.A.
110 H6 **Westport** Tennessee U.S.A.
100 A3 **Westport** Washington U.S.A.
118 A3 **West Prairie R** Alberta Canada
123 M10 **West Pt** Nova Scotia Canada
122 H7 **West Pt** Prince Edward I Canada
98 K8 **West Pt** Nebraska U.S.A.
122 G10 **West Pubnico** Nova Scotia Canada
126 A1 **Westpunt** Curaçao
13 G4 **West Rainton** England
119 Q5 **Westray** Manitoba Canada
15 F1 **Westray Firth** Orkney Scotland
120 J5 **Westree** Ontario Canada
36 C5 **Westrich** *reg* Germany
117 L9 **West Road R** British Columbia Canada
13 F2 **Westruther** Scotland
123 P2 **West St. Modiste** Quebec Canada
110 H3 **West Salem** Illinois U.S.A.
94 E6 **West Salem** Ohio U.S.A.
99 P6 **West Salem** Wisconsin U.S.A.
145 F3 **Westshore** New Zealand
99 L7 **Westside** Iowa U.S.A.
100 E7 **West Side** Oregon U.S.A.
139 J7 **West Sister I** Tasmania Australia
7 L9 **West Sole** *oil rig* North Sea
95 Q2 **West Stewartstown** New Hampshire U.S.A.
9 F6 **West Sussex** *co* England
13 G5 **West Tanfield** England
25 D2 **West Terschelling** Netherlands
110 J2 **West Union** Illinois U.S.A.
99 P7 **West Union** Iowa U.S.A.
94 D8 **West Union** Ohio U.S.A.
94 G7 **West Union** West Virginia U.S.A.
94 C5 **West Unity** Ohio U.S.A.
117 L11 **Westview** British Columbia Canada
122 K8 **Westville** Nova Scotia Canada
111 L11 **Westville** Florida U.S.A.
99 T9 **Westville** Illinois U.S.A.
99 U8 **Westville** Indiana U.S.A.
107 Q6 **Westville** Oklahoma U.S.A.
94 G8 **West Virginia** *state* U.S.A.
22 D1 **West Vlaanderen** Belgium
8 B5 **Westward Ho** England
103 P2 **Westwater** Utah U.S.A.
111 F12 **Westwego** Louisiana U.S.A.
95 M4 **West Winfield** New York U.S.A.
141 K6 **Westwood** Queensland Australia
102 D1 **Westwood** California U.S.A.
109 L9 **Westworth** Texas U.S.A.
139 H5 **West Wyalong** New South Wales Australia
101 O5 **West Yellowstone** Montana U.S.A.
13 G6 **West Yorkshire** *co* England
71 O8 **Wetan** *isld* Indonesia
71 N8 **Wetar** *isld* Indonesia
71 N9 **Wetar, Selat** *str* Indonesia
118 D6 **Wetaskiwin** Alberta Canada
88 G4 **Wete** Tanzania
121 O3 **Wetetnagami** *R* Quebec Canada
37 M1 **Wethau** Germany
13 G6 **Wetherby** England
68 B1 **Wetlet** Burma
106 E3 **Wetmore** Colorado U.S.A.
109 J6 **Wetmore** Texas U.S.A.
106 E3 **Wet Mts** Colorado U.S.A.
98 H4 **Wetonka** South Dakota U.S.A.
32 F10 **Wetter** Germany
36 F2 **Wetter** Germany
36 F3 **Wetter** *R* Germany
36 F3 **Wetterau** *reg* Germany
22 F1 **Wetteren** Belgium
41 M3 **Wetter Spitze** *mt* Austria
41 O3 **Wetterstein Geb** *mt* Austria
33 P9 **Wettin** Germany
32 F8 **Wettringen** Germany
107 O6 **Wetumka** Oklahoma U.S.A.
111 K9 **Wetumpka** Alabama U.S.A.
68 C1 **Wetwun** Burma
36 F2 **Wetzlar** Germany
37 L3 **Wetzstein** *mt* Germany
36 B1 **Wevelinghoven** Germany
110 E1 **Wever** Iowa U.S.A.
113 B7 **Wewahitchka** Florida U.S.A.
136 J2 **Wewak** Papua New Guinea
107 O6 **Wewoka** Oklahoma U.S.A.
14 E4 **Wexford** *co* Ireland
14 E4 **Wexford** Ireland
14 E4 **Wexford B** Ireland
14 E4 **Wexford Harb** Ireland
118 L4 **Weyakwin L** Saskatchewan Canada
99 S5 **Weyauwega** Wisconsin U.S.A.
9 H2 **Weybourne** England
9 F5 **Weybridge** England
119 O9 **Weyburn** Saskatchewan Canada
38 L6 **Weyer** Austria
36 D2 **Weyerbusch** Germany
99 P4 **Weyerhauser** Wisconsin U.S.A.
36 D6 **Weyersheim** France
33 M7 **Weyhausen** Germany
9 E5 **Weyhill** England
122 G9 **Weymouth** Nova Scotia Canada
8 D6 **Weymouth** England
95 R4 **Weymouth** Massachusetts U.S.A.
141 G1 **Weymouth B** Queensland Australia
141 G2 **Weymouth,C** Queensland Australia
9 F5 **Wey, R** England
25 F4 **Wezep** Netherlands
145 E3 **Whakahora** New Zealand
145 E3 **Whakamaru** New Zealand
145 E3 **Whakapapa** New Zealand
145 E1 **Whakapara** New Zealand
145 F3 **Whakapunake** New Zealand
145 F4 **Whakataki** New Zealand
145 F2 **Whakatane** New Zealand
145 F3 **Whakatane** *R* New Zealand
68 D7 **Whale B** Burma
116 D10 **Whalebone C** Aleutian Is
113 K12 **Whale Cay** *isld* Bahamas
Whale I *see* **Motuhora I**
123 P2 **Whale I** Quebec Canada
9 E1 **Whaley Bridge** England
95 L10 **Whaleyville** Virginia U.S.A.
139 J3 **Whallan** *R* New South Wales Australia
13 F6 **Whalley** England
15 G2 **Whalsay** *isld* Shetland Scotland
13 G3 **Whalton** England
145 E4 **Whangaehu** New Zealand
145 E2 **Whangamata** New Zealand
145 E3 **Whangamomona** New Zealand
145 D4 **Whanganui Inlet** New Zealand
145 G2 **Whangaparaoa** New Zealand
145 E2 **Whangaparaoa Pen** New Zealand
145 D1 **Whangape** New Zealand
145 E2 **Whangape, L** New Zealand
145 E1 **Whangarei** New Zealand
145 D1 **Whangaroa** New Zealand
145 E1 **Whangaruru Harbour** New Zealand
145 E4 **Wharanui** New Zealand
145 F4 **Whareama** New Zealand
13 G6 **Wharfe, R** England
95 N6 **Wharton** New Jersey U.S.A.
94 J5 **Wharton** Pennsylvania U.S.A.
109 L6 **Wharton** Texas U.S.A.
144 C5 **Whataroa** New Zealand
145 F3 **Whatatutu** New Zealand
145 E2 **Whatawhata** New Zealand
99 O8 **What Cheer** Iowa U.S.A.
100 C1 **Whatcom, L** Washington U.S.A.
111 J10 **Whatley** Alabama U.S.A.
68 F6 **Whatthana Nakhon** Thailand
102 C2 **Wheatland** California U.S.A.
98 B7 **Wheatland** Wyoming U.S.A.
98 A8 **Wheatland Res** Wyoming U.S.A.
120 H10 **Wheatley** Ontario Canada
9 E4 **Wheatley** England
110 E7 **Wheatley** Arkansas U.S.A.
99 S8 **Wheaton** Illinois U.S.A.
107 O2 **Wheaton** Kansas U.S.A.
98 K4 **Wheaton** Minnesota U.S.A.
110 B5 **Wheaton** Missouri U.S.A.
8 C5 **Wheddon Cross** England
107 J2 **Wheeler** Kansas U.S.A.
100 B4 **Wheeler** Oregon U.S.A.
108 D8 **Wheeler** Texas U.S.A.
117 Q4 **Wheeler L** Northwest Territories Canada
110 J7 **Wheeler L** Alabama U.S.A.
103 K3 **Wheeler Pk** Nevada U.S.A.
106 E5 **Wheeler Pk** New Mexico U.S.A.
102 F6 **Wheeler Ridge** California U.S.A.
94 E8 **Wheelersburg** Ohio U.S.A.
102 E7 **Wheeler Springs** California U.S.A.
94 G6 **Wheeling** West Virginia U.S.A.
98 C1 **Wheelock** North Dakota U.S.A.
94 E9 **Wheelwright** Kentucky U.S.A.
140 E6 **Whelan,Mt** Queensland Australia
13 F5 **Whernside** *mt* England
9 E5 **Wherwell** England
138 C5 **Whidbey I** South Australia Australia
100 C1 **Whidbey I** Washington U.S.A.
111 M11 **Whigham** Georgia U.S.A.
142 C5 **Whim Creek** W Australia Australia
138 B2 **Whinham, Mt** South Australia Australia
99 M2 **Whipholt** Minnesota U.S.A.
122 F9 **Whipple Pt** Nova Scotia Canada
9 F4 **Whipsnade** England
101 N1 **Whiskey Gap** Alberta Canada
119 T4 **Whiskey Jack Landing** Manitoba Canada
100 C9 **Whiskeytown** California U.S.A.
100 C9 **Whiskeytown-Shasta-Trinity Nat. Rec. Area** California U.S.A.
140 D5 **Whistleduck Creek** N Terr Australia
111 H11 **Whistler** Alabama U.S.A.
9 E2 **Whitacre** England
112 K1 **Whitakers** North Carolina U.S.A.
13 E5 **Whitbeck** England
123 T6 **Whitbourne** Newfoundland Canada
13 G4 **Whitburn** England
12 E2 **Whitburn** Scotland
121 M9 **Whitby** Ontario Canada
13 H5 **Whitby** England
8 D2 **Whitchurch** England
9 F4 **Whitchurch** England
9 E5 **Whitchurch** England
8 C4 **Whitchurch** Wales
111 E7 **White** *R* Arkansas U.S.A.
101 S10 **White** *R* Colorado U.S.A.
99 U6 **White** *R* Michigan U.S.A.
103 J3 **White** *R* Nevada U.S.A.
98 K5 **White** South Dakota U.S.A.
98 F6 **White** *R* South Dakota U.S.A.
108 F2 **White** *R* Texas U.S.A.
103 P2 **White** *R* Utah U.S.A.
100 D2 **White** *R* Washington U.S.A.
99 Q3 **White** *R* Wisconsin U.S.A.
123 Q3 **White B** Newfoundland Canada
118 J8 **White Bear** Saskatchewan Canada
123 P5 **White Bear L** *res* Newfoundland Canada
99 O4 **White Bear L** Minnesota U.S.A.
123 P6 **White Bear R** Newfoundland Canada
100 J4 **White Bird** Idaho U.S.A.
110 J5 **White Bluff** Tennessee U.S.A.
100 F3 **White Bluffs** Washington U.S.A.
122 E6 **White Brook** New Brunswick Canada
98 D4 **White Butte** South Dakota U.S.A.
119 W2 **Whitecap L** Manitoba Canada
111 E11 **White Castle** Louisiana U.S.A.
113 G10 **White City** Florida U.S.A.
107 O3 **White City** Kansas U.S.A.
106 F9 **White City** New Mexico U.S.A.
139 G4 **White Cliffs** New South Wales Australia
99 L10 **White Cloud** Kansas U.S.A.
94 B3 **White Cloud** Michigan U.S.A.
118 B4 **White Court** Alberta Canada
98 D1 **White Earth** North Dakota U.S.A.
108 E2 **Whiteface** Texas U.S.A.
95 O2 **Whiteface Mt** New York U.S.A.
120 J6 **Whitefish** Ontario Canada
117 Q11 **Whitefish** Idaho U.S.A.
99 U4 **Whitefish** *R* Michigan U.S.A.
101 L1 **Whitefish** Montana U.S.A.
99 T6 **Whitefish Bay** Wisconsin U.S.A.
118 E4 **Whitefish L** Alberta Canada
119 O2 **Whitefish L** Ontario Canada
116 K6 **Whitefish L** Alaska U.S.A.
99 V3 **Whitefish L** Michigan U.S.A.
99 M3 **Whitefish L** Minnesota U.S.A.
101 L1 **Whitefish L** Montana U.S.A.
119 N5 **White Fox** Saskatchewan Canada
115 N6 **Whitegull L** Quebec Canada
110 F2 **White Hall** Illinois U.S.A.
99 U6 **Whitehall** Michigan U.S.A.
101 N4 **Whitehall** Montana U.S.A.
99 P5 **Whitehall** Wisconsin U.S.A.
12 E5 **Whitehaven** England
95 M5 **White Haven** Pennsylvania U.S.A.
14 F2 **Whitehead** N Ireland
12 D4 **Whitehill** Scotland
116 N2 **White Hills** Alaska U.S.A.
103 K6 **White Hills** Arizona U.S.A.
117 F5 **Whitehorse** Yukon Territory Canada
100 D8 **White Horse** California U.S.A.
101 L9 **White Horse Pass** Nevada U.S.A.
127 M3 **White Horses** Jamaica
White I *see* **Kvitøya**
146 K9 **White I** Antarctica
115 L4 **White I** Northwest Territories Canada
145 F2 **White I** New Zealand
13 F1 **Whitekirk** Scotland
140 A5 **White L** N Terr/W Aust Australia
142 G5 **White, L** W Australia Australia
111 D12 **White L** Louisiana U.S.A.
99 U6 **White L** Michigan U.S.A.
98 H6 **White L** South Dakota U.S.A.
99 S4 **White Lake** Wisconsin U.S.A.
94 A7 **Whiteland** Indiana U.S.A.
139 J8 **Whitemark** Tasmania Australia
116 F4 **White Mountain** Alaska U.S.A.
14 E4 **White Mt** Ireland
116 O4 **White Mts** Alaska U.S.A.
102 F4 **White Mts** California U.S.A.
95 Q2 **White Mts** New Hampshire U.S.A.
117 P7 **Whitemud** *R* Alberta Canada
86 F3 **White Nile** *R* Sudan
86 F3 **White Nile** *prov* Sudan
86 F2 **White Nile Dam** Sudan
89 A4 **White Nossob** *R* Namibia
112 K3 **White Oak** North Carolina U.S.A.
109 M2 **White Oak Cr** Texas U.S.A.
109 O2 **White Oak L** Arkansas U.S.A.
118 K1 **White Otter L** Ontario Canada
98 D5 **White Owl** South Dakota U.S.A.
9 E5 **Whiteparish** England
100 D3 **White Pass** Washington U.S.A.
94 B5 **White Pigeon** Michigan U.S.A.
99 R3 **White Pine** Michigan U.S.A.
100 K2 **Whitepine** Montana U.S.A.
112 D1 **White Pine** Tennessee U.S.A.
103 J2 **White Pine Ra** Nevada U.S.A.
95 N5 **White Plains** New York U.S.A.
112 G1 **White Plains** North Carolina U.S.A.
123 R2 **White Pt** Belle Isle, Nfld
118 B8 **White R** British Columbia Canada
127 L2 **White R** Jamaica
94 B8 **White R** Indiana U.S.A.
98 F6 **White R** South Dakota U.S.A.
120 E4 **White River** Ontario Canada
95 P3 **White River Junc** Vermont U.S.A.
103 J3 **White River Valley** Nevada U.S.A.
100 J8 **White Rock** Nevada U.S.A.
109 O9 **White Rock** Texas U.S.A.
107 M2 **White Rock Cr** Kansas U.S.A.
103 K3 **White Rock Peak** Nevada U.S.A.
White Russia *see* **Belorussia**
117 K9 **Whitesail L** British Columbia Canada
100 D4 **White Salmon** Washington U.S.A.
117 P6 **Whitesand** *R* Alberta Canada
8 B7 **Whitesand B** England
119 P7 **Whitesand R** Saskatchewan Canada
108 A3 **White Sands Missile Ra** New Mexico U.S.A.
108 A3 **White Sands Nat. Mon** New Mexico U.S.A.
95 M3 **Whitesboro** New York U.S.A.
109 L2 **Whitesboro** Texas U.S.A.
112 C4 **Whitesburg** Georgia U.S.A.
94 E9 **Whitesburg** Kentucky U.S.A.
White Sea *see* **Beloye More**
109 L9 **White Settlement** Texas U.S.A.
118 F1 **Whiteshell** Manitoba Canada
100 B4 **Whiteson** Oregon U.S.A.
119 U2 **Whitestone L** Manitoba Canada
101 P3 **White Sulphur Springs** Montana U.S.A.
110 K4 **Whitesville** Kentucky U.S.A.
94 K4 **Whitesville** New York U.S.A.
94 F9 **Whitesville** West Virginia U.S.A.
100 E3 **White Swan** Washington U.S.A.
119 M4 **Whiteswan L** Saskatchewan Canada
98 A1 **Whitetail** Montana U.S.A.
112 J3 **Whiteville** North Carolina U.S.A.
110 G6 **Whiteville** Tennessee U.S.A.
85 D7 **White Volta** *R* Ghana
94 B7 **Whitewater** *R* Indiana U.S.A.
101 S1 **Whitewater** Montana U.S.A.
106 B9 **Whitewater** New Mexico U.S.A.
99 S7 **Whitewater** Wisconsin U.S.A.
113 F12 **Whitewater B** Florida U.S.A.
120 A2 **Whitewater L** Ontario Canada
138 B4 **White Well** South Australia Australia
141 G5 **Whitewood** Queensland Australia
119 P8 **Whitewood** Saskatchewan Canada
98 C5 **Whitewood** South Dakota U.S.A.
98 J5 **Whitewood, L** South Dakota U.S.A.
109 L2 **Whitewright** Texas U.S.A.
139 H6 **Whitfield** Victoria Australia
13 F4 **Whitfield Hall** England
127 H2 **Whithorn** Jamaica
12 D4 **Whithorn** Scotland
145 E2 **Whitianga** New Zealand
117 G6 **Whiting** *R* Br Col/Alaska Canada/U.S.A.
107 P2 **Whiting** Kansas U.S.A.
95 N7 **Whiting** New Jersey U.S.A.
12 C3 **Whiting B** Scotland
95 P4 **Whitingham Res** Vermont U.S.A.
118 K6 **Whitkow** Saskatchewan Canada
118 F9 **Whitla** Alberta Canada
8 B4 **Whitland** Wales
101 O1 **Whitlash** Montana U.S.A.
13 G3 **Whitley Bay** England
94 C10 **Whitley City** Kentucky U.S.A.
98 F4 **Whitlocks Crossing** South Dakota U.S.A.
95 R4 **Whitman** Massachusetts U.S.A.
98 E7 **Whitman** Nebraska U.S.A.
98 H1 **Whitman** North Dakota U.S.A.
100 G3 **Whitman Mission Nat. Hist. Site** Washington U.S.A.
112 F3 **Whitmire** South Carolina U.S.A.
146 C8 **Whitmore Mts** *mts* Antarctica
121 M7 **Whitney** Ontario Canada
8 C3 **Whitney** England
98 C7 **Whitney** Nebraska U.S.A.
103 J5 **Whitney** Nevada U.S.A.
100 G5 **Whitney** Oregon U.S.A.
109 K4 **Whitney, L** Texas U.S.A.
102 F5 **Whitney, Mt** California U.S.A.
109 J7 **Whitsett** Texas U.S.A.
9 H5 **Whitstable** England
141 J5 **Whitsunday I** Queensland Australia
109 J3 **Whitt** Texas U.S.A.
94 G7 **Whittaker** West Virginia U.S.A.
99 M6 **Whittemore** Iowa U.S.A.
94 D2 **Whittemore** Michigan U.S.A.
116 N6 **Whittier** Alaska U.S.A.
102 F8 **Whittier** California U.S.A.
13 G3 **Whittingham** England
139 H7 **Whittlesea** Victoria Australia
9 F2 **Whittlesey** England
139 H5 **Whitton** New South Wales Australia
8 C3 **Whitton** Wales
13 G4 **Whittonstall** England
141 F7 **Whitula** *R* Queensland Australia
9 E1 **Whitwell** England
112 B2 **Whitwell** Tennessee U.S.A.
114 J5 **Wholdaia L** Northwest Territories Canada
138 D5 **Whyalla** South Australia Australia
123 L8 **Whycocomagh** Nova Scotia Canada
139 G3 **Whyjonta** New South Wales Australia
68 D3 **Wiang Pa Pao** Thailand
68 D2 **Wiang Phrao** Thailand
120 J8 **Wiarton** Ontario Canada
31 K5 **Wiązów** Poland
98 B2 **Wibaux** Montana U.S.A.
13 G6 **Wibsey** England
107 N4 **Wichita** Kansas U.S.A.
109 J1 **Wichita** *R* Texas U.S.A.
109 J2 **Wichita Falls** Texas U.S.A.
109 J1 **Wichita Mts** Oklahoma U.S.A.
15 E2 **Wick** Scotland
32 G10 **Wickede** Germany
103 M8 **Wickenburg** Arizona U.S.A.
122 J4 **Wickenden L** Quebec Canada
143 C10 **Wickepin** W Australia Australia
100 C1 **Wickersham** Washington U.S.A.
108 D4 **Wickett** Texas U.S.A.
9 G4 **Wickford** England
95 Q5 **Wickford** Rhode I U.S.A.
142 B5 **Wickham** W Australia Australia
9 E6 **Wickham** England
139 G7 **Wickham, C** Tasmania Australia
140 A3 **Wickham Mt** N Terr Australia
121 S7 **Wickham West** Quebec Canada
100 D6 **Wickiup Res** Oregon U.S.A.
110 G5 **Wickliffe** Kentucky U.S.A.
14 E4 **Wicklow** *co* Ireland
14 E4 **Wicklow** Ireland
8 D4 **Wickwar** England
31 L4 **Widawka** *R* Poland
36 G5 **Widdern** Germany
121 L6 **Widdifield** Ontario Canada
90 A11 **Wideawake** Ascension I
141 L7 **Wide B** Queensland Australia
116 J8 **Wide B** Alaska U.S.A.
8 C6 **Widecombe-in-the-Moor** England
138 B2 **Wide Gum** *R* South Australia Australia
94 G8 **Widen** West Virginia U.S.A.
141 H8 **Widgeegoara** *R* Queensland Australia
143 D9 **Widgiemooltha** W Australia Australia
71 B3 **Widi, Pulau Pulau** *islds* Indonesia
36 F4 **Wiebelsbach** Germany
36 C5 **Wiebelskirchen** Germany
31 K2 **Więcbork** Poland
36 C2 **Wied** Germany
Wiedenbrück *see* **Rheda-Wiedenbrück**
32 H6 **Wiefelstede** Germany
33 O10 **Wiehe** Germany
32 J8 **Wiehengebirge** *hills* Germany
36 D2 **Wiehl** Germany
31 M2 **Wielbark** Poland
31 J3 **Wieleń** Poland
31 M6 **Wieliczka** Poland
31 L4 **Wieluń** Poland
38 O5 **Wien** Austria
38 O6 **Wiener Neustadt** Austria
32 M7 **Wienhausen** Germany
116 M4 **Wien L** Alaska U.S.A.
33 O7 **Wiepke** Germany
31 O5 **Wieprz** *R* Poland
33 N7 **Wieren** Germany
109 O4 **Wiergate** Texas U.S.A.
25 D3 **Wieringen** Netherlands
25 C3 **Wieringermeer** Netherlands
31 L4 **Wieruszów** Poland
Wierzbnik *see* **Starachowice**
31 L2 **Wierzchucin** Poland
31 L2 **Wierzyca** *R* Poland
38 M8 **Wies** Austria
37 N4 **Wiesau** Germany
36 E3 **Wiesbaden** Germany
40 G2 **Wiese** *R* Germany
33 Q8 **Wiesenburg** Germany
36 H6 **Wiesensteig** Germany
37 L4 **Wiesent** *R* Germany
37 J4 **Wiesentherd** Germany
37 L4 **Wiesenttal** Germany
36 F5 **Wiesloch** Germany
32 G6 **Wiesmoor** Germany
32 F7 **Wietmarschen** Germany
32 L7 **Wietz** Germany
32 K7 **Wietzen** Germany
32 L7 **Wietzendorf** Germany
13 F6 **Wigan** England
98 B9 **Wiggins** Colorado U.S.A.
111 G11 **Wiggins** Mississippi U.S.A.
9 E6 **Wight, I. of** England
8 D3 **Wigmore** England
31 O2 **Wigry, Jezioro** *L* Poland
9 E2 **Wigston** England
13 E4 **Wigton** England
Wigtown *co see* **Dumfries and Galloway** *reg*
12 D4 **Wigtown** Scotland
25 F4 **Wijhe** Netherlands
25 E7 **Wijk** Netherlands
25 C4 **Wijk aan Zee** Netherlands
103 L7 **Wikieup** Arizona U.S.A.
120 J7 **Wikwemikong** Ontario Canada
41 K3 **Wil** Switzerland
83 L11 **Wila Oya** *R* Sri Lanka
98 K9 **Wilber** Nebraska U.S.A.
121 M7 **Wilberforce** Ontario Canada
140 D1 **Wilberforce,C** N Terr Australia
144 C5 **Wilberforce R** New Zealand
101 N3 **Wilborn** Montana U.S.A.
100 B6 **Wilbur** Oregon U.S.A.
100 G2 **Wilbur** Washington U.S.A.
94 E10 **Wilbur Dam** Tennessee U.S.A.
110 A7 **Wilburton** Oklahoma U.S.A.
9 F3 **Wilby** England
139 G4 **Wilcannia** New South Wales Australia
119 N8 **Wilcox** Saskatchewan Canada
99 M9 **Wilcox** Missouri U.S.A.
98 G9 **Wilcox** Nebraska U.S.A.
94 J5 **Wilcox** Pennsylvania U.S.A.
33 T8 **Wildau** Germany
36 F6 **Wildbad** Germany
33 R7 **Wildberg** Germany
36 F6 **Wildberg** Germany
123 Q4 **Wild Bight** Newfoundland Canada
102 H2 **Wildcat Pk** Nevada U.S.A.
119 V3 **Wilde** Manitoba Canada
37 J2 **Wildeck** Germany
37 O2 **Wildenfels** Germany
94 B10 **Wilder** Tennessee U.S.A.
41 O4 **Wilder Freiger** *mt* Austria
117 O9 **Wilderness Prov. Park** Alberta Canada
110 H6 **Wildersville** Tennessee U.S.A.
25 G2 **Wildervank** Netherlands
32 H7 **Wildeshausen** Germany
36 H3 **Wildflecken** Germany
120 A4 **Wild Goose** Ontario Canada
40 F5 **Wildhorn** *mt* Switzerland
101 P1 **Wild Horse** Alberta Canada
100 K8 **Wildhorse Res** Nevada U.S.A.
119 P4 **Wildnest L** Saskatchewan Canada
108 B8 **Wildorado** Texas U.S.A.
33 R8 **Wildpark** Germany
98 K2 **Wild Rice** *R* Minnesota U.S.A.
98 K3 **Wild Rice** *R* North Dakota U.S.A.
98 C1 **Wildrose** North Dakota U.S.A.
99 R5 **Wild Rose** Wisconsin U.S.A.
40 G5 **Wildstrubel** *mt* Switzerland
118 B5 **Wildwood** Alberta Canada
113 E9 **Wildwood** Florida U.S.A.
95 N8 **Wildwood** New Jersey U.S.A.
118 B1 **Wildwood Pk** Manitoba Canada
106 H3 **Wiley** Colorado U.S.A.
36 F6 **Wilferdingen** Germany
120 E2 **Wilgar** Ontario Canada
89 F6 **Wilge** *R* S Africa
138 C4 **Wilgena** South Australia Australia
146 H12 **Wilhelm II Land** Antarctica
129 G3 **Wilhelmina Geb** *mts* Suriname
25 D5 **Wilhelmina Kanal** Netherlands
136 J3 **Wilhelm, Mt** Papua New Guinea
Wilhelm Pieck Stadt *see* **Guben**
32 H5 **Wilhelmshaven** Germany
36 F2 **Wilhelmshütte** Germany
33 O5 **Wiligrad** Germany
70 N9 **Wilis** *mt* Java
95 M5 **Wilkes-Barre** Pennsylvania U.S.A.
112 F1 **Wilkesboro** North Carolina U.S.A.
146 E14 **Wilkes Coast** Antarctica
146 E13 **Wilkes Land** Antarctica
37 N2 **Wilkhau Hasslau** Germany
118 J6 **Wilkie** Saskatchewan Canada
146 D5 **Wilkins Coast** Antarctica
146 C5 **Wilkins Ice Shelf** Antarctica
138 C3 **Wilkinson L** South Australia Australia
112 D6 **Willacoochee** Georgia U.S.A.
103 M6 **Willaha** Arizona U.S.A.
100 B4 **Willamette** *R* Oregon U.S.A.
139 G5 **Willandra Billabong** *R* New South Wales Australia
100 B3 **Willapa** *R* Washington U.S.A.
139 G3 **Willara** New South Wales Australia
138 E2 **Willara, L** South Australia Australia
124 D3 **Willard** Mexico
98 C9 **Willard** Colorado U.S.A.
98 B3 **Willard** Montana U.S.A.
106 D7 **Willard** New Mexico U.S.A.
94 E5 **Willard** Ohio U.S.A.
101 N8 **Willard** Utah U.S.A.
95 M8 **Willards** Maryland U.S.A.
142 E4 **Willare Bridge Roadhouse** W Australia Australia
103 P9 **Willcox** Arizona U.S.A.
32 K9 **Willebadessen** Germany
22 G1 **Willebroek** Belgium
22 E2 **Willems** France
25 C5 **Willemsdorp** Netherlands
126 B1 **Willemstad** Curaçao
25 B5 **Willemstad** Netherlands
140 B3 **Willeroo** N Terr Australia
8 D3 **Willersley** England
22 H4 **Willerzie** Belgium
9 F4 **Willesden** England
118 C6 **Willesden Green** Alberta Canada
120 B2 **Willet** Ontario Canada
143 B6 **Williambury** W Australia Australia
138 D3 **William Creek** South Australia Australia
119 S5 **William L** Manitoba Canada
138 F6 **William, Mt** Victoria Australia
143 B10 **William,Mt** W Australia Australia
140 F5 **Williams** *R* Queensland Australia
143 B10 **Williams** W Australia Australia
103 M6 **Williams** Arizona U.S.A.
102 B2 **Williams** California U.S.A.
110 K3 **Williams** Indiana U.S.A.
99 N7 **Williams** Iowa U.S.A.
99 L1 **Williams** Minnesota U.S.A.
99 S7 **Williams Bay** Wisconsin U.S.A.
99 O8 **Williamsburg** Iowa U.S.A.
94 C10 **Williamsburg** Kentucky U.S.A.
95 P4 **Williamsburg** Massachusetts U.S.A.
94 C7 **Williamsburg** Ohio U.S.A.
94 J6 **Williamsburg** Pennsylvania U.S.A.
95 L9 **Williamsburg** Virginia U.S.A.
127 K2 **Williamsfield** Jamaica
120 K8 **Williamsford** Ontario Canada
126 E2 **Williams I** Bahamas
117 M9 **Williams Lake** British Columbia Canada
99 N8 **Williamson** Iowa U.S.A.
95 K3 **Williamson** New York U.S.A.
94 E9 **Williamson** West Virginia U.S.A.
123 Q3 **Williamsport** Newfoundland Canada
99 T9 **Williamsport** Indiana U.S.A.
94 K7 **Williamsport** Maryland U.S.A.
95 K5 **Williamsport** Pennsylvania U.S.A.
94 C4 **Williamston** Michigan U.S.A.
112 K2 **Williamston** North Carolina U.S.A.
112 E3 **Williamston** South Carolina U.S.A.
94 C8 **Williamstown** Kentucky U.S.A.
95 O4 **Williamstown** Massachusetts U.S.A.
95 P2 **Williamstown** Vermont U.S.A.
94 F7 **Williamstown** West Virginia U.S.A.
110 F5 **Williamsville** Missouri U.S.A.
141 G8 **Willie's Ra** Queensland Australia
127 P4 **Willikie's** Antigua W Indies
95 P5 **Willimantic** Connecticut U.S.A.
118 E5 **Willingdon** Alberta Canada
117 P10 **Willingdon, Mt** Alberta Canada
32 J10 **Willingen** Germany
9 G3 **Willingham** England
13 G4 **Willington** England
109 M5 **Willis** Texas U.S.A.
94 G10 **Willis** Virginia U.S.A.
40 G3 **Willisau** Switzerland
141 K3 **Willis Grp** *islds* Gt Barrier Reef Aust
87 D12 **Williston** S Africa
113 E8 **Williston** Florida U.S.A.
98 C1 **Williston** North Dakota U.S.A.
112 F4 **Williston** South Carolina U.S.A.
117 M8 **Williston L** British Columbia Canada
110 G4 **Willisville** Illinois U.S.A.
8 C5 **Williton** England
102 A2 **Willits** California U.S.A.
119 P9 **Willmar** Saskatchewan Canada
99 L4 **Willmar** Minnesota U.S.A.
94 F5 **Willoughby** Ohio U.S.A.
138 E6 **Willoughby, C** South Australia Australia
117 M9 **Willow** *R* British Columbia Canada
116 M6 **Willow** Alaska U.S.A.
108 E8 **Willow** Oklahoma U.S.A.
119 P7 **Willowbrook** Saskatchewan Canada
119 M9 **Willow Bunch L** Saskatchewan Canada
98 F1 **Willow City** North Dakota U.S.A.
100 E9 **Willow Cr** California U.S.A.
100 H5 **Willow Cr** Oregon U.S.A.
118 D8 **Willow Cr. Prov. Park** Alberta Canada
117 O4 **Willow L** Northwest Territories Canada
98 J5 **Willow L** South Dakota U.S.A.
117 N4 **Willowlake** *R* Northwest Territories Canada
89 C9 **Willowmore** S Africa
140 C5 **Willowra** N Terr Australia
100 E8 **Willow Ranch** California U.S.A.
99 R4 **Willow Res** Wisconsin U.S.A.
99 O3 **Willow River** Minnesota U.S.A.
94 D4 **Willow Run** Michigan U.S.A.
119 M9 **Willows** Saskatchewan Canada
102 B2 **Willows** California U.S.A.
110 E5 **Willow Springs** Missouri U.S.A.
139 K4 **Willow Tree** New South Wales Australia
95 O2 **Willsboro** New York U.S.A.
142 G5 **Wills,L** W Australia Australia
109 L3 **Wills Point** Texas U.S.A.
138 E6 **Willunga** South Australia Australia
111 H11 **Wilmer** Alabama U.S.A.
33 T6 **Wilmersdorf** Germany
99 T7 **Wilmette** Illinois U.S.A.
138 E4 **Wilmington** South Australia Australia
95 M7 **Wilmington** Delaware U.S.A.
99 S8 **Wilmington** Illinois U.S.A.
112 K3 **Wilmington** North Carolina U.S.A.
94 D7 **Wilmington** Ohio U.S.A.
95 O4 **Wilmington** Vermont U.S.A.
99 L6 **Wilmont** Minnesota U.S.A.
107 L4 **Wilmore** Kansas U.S.A.
94 C9 **Wilmore** Kentucky U.S.A.
111 E8 **Wilmot** Arkansas U.S.A.
94 F6 **Wilmot** Ohio U.S.A.
144 B6 **Wilmot, L** New Zealand
144 A6 **Wilmot Pass** New Zealand
25 C4 **Wilnis** Netherlands
121 N7 **Wilno** Ontario Canada
36 E2 **Wilnsdorf** Germany
83 J9 **Wilpattu Nat.Park** Sri Lanka
138 E4 **Wilpena** *R* South Australia Australia
138 E4 **Wilpena** South Australia Australia
22 G1 **Wilrijk** Belgium
101 P3 **Wilsall** Montana U.S.A.
37 Q1 **Wilsdruff** Germany
32 L6 **Wilseder Berg** *hill* Germany
141 G7 **Wilson** *R* Queensland Australia
110 F6 **Wilson** Arkansas U.S.A.
107 M3 **Wilson** Kansas U.S.A.
111 E11 **Wilson** Louisiana U.S.A.
94 J3 **Wilson** New York U.S.A.
112 K2 **Wilson** North Carolina U.S.A.
109 K1 **Wilson** Oklahoma U.S.A.
108 F2 **Wilson** Texas U.S.A.
101 P6 **Wilson** Wyoming U.S.A.
138 A4 **Wilson Bluff** South Australia Australia
115 L4 **Wilson, C** Northwest Territories Canada
142 F5 **Wilson Cliffs** *hill* W Australia Australia
100 F2 **Wilson Creek** Washington U.S.A.
103 K3 **Wilson Cr. Ra** Nevada U.S.A.
146 C13 **Wilson Hills** Antarctica
106 H3 **Wilson Junc** Colorado U.S.A.
138 A2 **Wilson, L** South Australia Australia
110 J7 **Wilson L** Alabama U.S.A.
142 G5 **Wilson,Mt** W Australia Australia
102 G7 **Wilson, Mt** California U.S.A.
106 C4 **Wilson, Mt** Colorado U.S.A.
103 K3 **Wilson, Mt** Nevada U.S.A.
107 M3 **Wilson Res** Kansas U.S.A.
110 C4 **Wilson's Creek Battlefield Nat. Park** Missouri U.S.A.
139 H7 **Wilson's Promontory** Victoria Australia
12 E2 **Wilsontown** Scotland
98 F9 **Wilsonville** Nebraska U.S.A.
32 K6 **Wilstedt** Germany
32 K5 **Wilster** Germany
140 C2 **Wilton** *R* N Terr Australia
9 E5 **Wilton** England

Wilton — Xi'an
241

109 N2 **Wilton** Arkansas U.S.A.
99 P8 **Wilton** Iowa U.S.A.
95 Q4 **Wilton** New Hampshire U.S.A.
98 F2 **Wilton** North Dakota U.S.A.
99 Q6 **Wilton** Wisconsin U.S.A.
9 E5 **Wiltshire** *co* England
22 K4 **Wiltz** Luxembourg
143 D7 **Wiluna** W Australia Australia
22 L4 **Wilwerwiltz** Luxembourg
119 S3 **Wimapedi L** Manitoba Canada
113 E10 **Wimauma** Florida U.S.A.
9 F5 **Wimbledon** England
145 F4 **Wimbledon** New Zealand
98 H2 **Wimbledon** North Dakota U.S.A.
118 D7 **Wimborne** Alberta Canada
9 E6 **Wimborne** England
22 B2 **Wimereux** France
113 B8 **Wimico, L** Florida U.S.A.
22 B2 **Wimille** France
38 K8 **Wimitz** *R* Austria
36 C6 **Wimmenau** France
138 F6 **Wimmera** *R* Victoria Australia
118 A3 **Winagami L** Alberta Canada
94 A5 **Winamac** Indiana U.S.A.
88 E2 **Winam Gulf** Kenya
139 G4 **Winbar** New South Wales Australia
87 E11 **Winburg** S Africa
8 D5 **Wincanton** England
12 E2 **Winchburgh** Scotland
9 E4 **Winchcomb** England
109 H4 **Winchell** Texas U.S.A.
9 G6 **Winchelsea** England
95 P4 **Winchendon** Massachusetts U.S.A.
121 P7 **Winchester** Ontario Canada
9 E5 **Winchester** England
144 C6 **Winchester** New Zealand
100 J3 **Winchester** Idaho U.S.A.
99 Q10 **Winchester** Illinois U.S.A.
94 C6 **Winchester** Indiana U.S.A.
94 C9 **Winchester** Kentucky U.S.A.
95 P4 **Winchester** New Hampshire U.S.A.
94 D8 **Winchester** Ohio U.S.A.
110 K6 **Winchester** Tennessee U.S.A.
109 K5 **Winchester** Texas U.S.A.
101 R6 **Winchester** Wyoming U.S.A.
100 A6 **Winchester Bay** Oregon U.S.A.
101 R6 **Wind** *R* Wyoming U.S.A.
138 D4 **Windabout, L** South Australia Australia
101 P2 **Windam** Montana U.S.A.
143 C9 **Windarling Pk** W Australia Australia
Windau *see* **Ventspils**
94 J6 **Windber** Pennsylvania U.S.A.
98 C6 **Wind Cave Nat. Park** South Dakota U.S.A.
36 F3 **Windecken** Germany
36 E5 **Winden** Germany
112 D4 **Winder** Georgia U.S.A.
141 K7 **Windera** Queensland Australia
13 F5 **Windermere** England
120 G5 **Windermere L** Ontario Canada
94 B6 **Windfall** Indiana U.S.A.
95 M6 **Wind Gap** Pennsylvania U.S.A.
95 R3 **Windham, S** Maine U.S.A.
32 K8 **Windheim** Germany
87 C10 **Windhoek** Namibia
143 D7 **Windich Springs** W Australia Australia
121 R5 **Windigo** Quebec Canada
107 P7 **Winding Stair Mts** Oklahoma U.S.A.
37 N4 **Windischeschenbach** Germany
38 K6 **Windischgarsten** Austria
95 M9 **Windmill Pt** Virginia U.S.A.
107 N3 **Windom** Kansas U.S.A.
99 L6 **Windom** Minnesota U.S.A.
106 C4 **Windom Pk** Colorado U.S.A.
141 G7 **Windorah** Queensland Australia
37 P6 **Windorf** Germany
99 T7 **Wind Point** Wisconsin U.S.A.
101 Q7 **Wind R. Ra** Wyoming U.S.A.
37 K5 **Windsbach** Germany
141 K1 **Windsor** *dist* Brisbane, Qnsld Australia
139 K5 **Windsor** New South Wales Australia
123 R5 **Windsor** Newfoundland Canada
122 H9 **Windsor** Nova Scotia Canada
120 H10 **Windsor** Ontario Canada
121 T7 **Windsor** Quebec Canada
9 F5 **Windsor** England
144 C6 **Windsor** New Zealand
106 F1 **Windsor** Colorado U.S.A.
95 P5 **Windsor** Connecticut U.S.A.
99 S10 **Windsor** Illinois U.S.A.
95 P4 **Windsor** Massachusetts U.S.A.
110 C3 **Windsor** Missouri U.S.A.
95 M4 **Windsor** New York U.S.A.
112 L2 **Windsor** North Carolina U.S.A.
112 F4 **Windsor** South Carolina U.S.A.
95 L10 **Windsor** Virginia U.S.A.
94 G6 **Windsor Heights** West Virginia U.S.A.
126 H4 **Windsor L.** Great Inagua I Bahamas
95 P5 **Windsor Locks** Connecticut U.S.A.
109 J2 **Windthorst** Texas U.S.A.
141 F7 **Windula** *R* Queensland Australia
127 O7 **Windward Is** W Indies
126 H5 **Windward Passage** Cuba/Haiti
116 N5 **Windy** Alaska U.S.A.
116 K5 **Windy Fork** *R* Alaska U.S.A.
119 P4 **Windy L** Saskatchewan Canada
117 Q5 **Windy Pt** Northwest Territories Canada
118 G3 **Winefred L** Alberta Canada
99 R3 **Winegar** Wisconsin U.S.A.
94 C3 **Winegars** Michigan U.S.A.
100 E2 **Winesap** Washington U.S.A.
118 C6 **Winfield** Alberta Canada
111 J8 **Winfield** Alabama U.S.A.
107 O4 **Winfield** Kansas U.S.A.
109 M2 **Winfield** Texas U.S.A.
8 D6 **Winfrith** England
98 F2 **Wing** North Dakota U.S.A.
110 J1 **Wingate** Indiana U.S.A.
106 B6 **Wingate** New Mexico U.S.A.
140 B2 **Wingate Mts** N Terr Australia
139 K4 **Wingen** New South Wales Australia
22 E1 **Wingene** Belgium
36 C6 **Wingen-sur-Moder** France
139 L4 **Wingham** New South Wales Australia
120 J9 **Wingham** Ontario Canada
9 H5 **Wingham** England
110 H5 **Wingo** Kentucky U.S.A.
32 K5 **Wingst** Germany
71 M9 **Wini** Timor Indonesia
101 Q2 **Winifred** Montana U.S.A.
98 J6 **Winifred** South Dakota U.S.A.
142 E5 **Winifred,L** W Australia Australia
115 L6 **Winisk** Ontario Canada
68 D5 **Winkana** Burma
25 C3 **Winkel** Netherlands
103 O9 **Winkelman** Arizona U.S.A.
9 F5 **Winkfield** England
37 O5 **Winklarn** Germany
8 C6 **Winkleigh** England
119 U9 **Winkler** Manitoba Canada
38 G8 **Winklern** Austria
100 C3 **Winlock** Washington U.S.A.
95 T1 **Winn** Maine U.S.A.
94 C3 **Winn** Michigan U.S.A.
140 B6 **Winnalls Ridge** N Terr Australia
85 D7 **Winneba** Ghana
99 M6 **Winnebago** Minnesota U.S.A.
98 K7 **Winnebago** Nebraska U.S.A.
99 S5 **Winnebago, L** Wisconsin U.S.A.
142 G6 **Winnecke Hills** N Terr/W Aust Australia
140 B4 **Winnecke,Mt** N Terr Australia
142 E6 **Winnecke Rock** *hill* W Australia Australia
99 S5 **Winneconne** Wisconsin U.S.A.
100 H9 **Winnemucca** Nevada U.S.A.
102 E1 **Winnemucca L** Nevada U.S.A.
36 G6 **Winnenden** Germany
98 G6 **Winner** South Dakota U.S.A.
99 T7 **Winnetka** Illinois U.S.A.
98 H7 **Winnetoon** Nebraska U.S.A.
101 R2 **Winnett** Montana U.S.A.
109 P4 **Winnfield** Louisiana U.S.A.
99 M2 **Winnibigoshish L** Minnesota U.S.A.
109 N6 **Winnie** Texas U.S.A.
118 F9 **Winnifred** Alberta Canada
33 O9 **Winnigen** Germany
142 A6 **Winning** W Australia Australia
36 D3 **Winningen** Germany
118 A1 **Winnipeg** Manitoba Canada
119 V8 **Winnipeg Beach** Manitoba Canada
119 T5 **Winnipeg, L** Manitoba Canada
119 S7 **Winnipegosis** Manitoba Canada
119 R6 **Winnipegosis, L** Manitoba Canada
95 Q3 **Winnipesaukee, L** New Hampshire U.S.A.
111 E9 **Winnsboro** Louisiana U.S.A.
112 F3 **Winnsboro** South Carolina U.S.A.
109 M3 **Winnsboro** Texas U.S.A.
112 E6 **Winokur** Georgia U.S.A.
103 N6 **Winona** Arizona U.S.A.
107 J2 **Winona** Kansas U.S.A.
99 S3 **Winona** Michigan U.S.A.
99 P5 **Winona** Minnesota U.S.A.
110 E4 **Winona** Missouri U.S.A.
109 M3 **Winona** Texas U.S.A.
100 H3 **Winona** Washington U.S.A.
109 P1 **Winona, L** Arkansas U.S.A.
95 O2 **Winooski** Vermont U.S.A.
95 P2 **Winooski** *R* Vermont U.S.A.
25 H2 **Winschoten** Netherlands
32 M6 **Winsen** Germany
32 L7 **Winsen** Germany
8 D1 **Winsford** England
98 J7 **Winside** Nebraska U.S.A.
9 F4 **Winslow** England
103 O6 **Winslow** Arizona U.S.A.
110 B6 **Winslow** Arkansas U.S.A.
110 J3 **Winslow** Indiana U.S.A.
95 S2 **Winslow** Maine U.S.A.
100 C2 **Winslow** Washington U.S.A.
137 R2 **Winslow Reef** Phoenix Is Pacific Oc
101 N5 **Winsper** Idaho U.S.A.
95 O5 **Winsted** Connecticut U.S.A.
9 E1 **Winster** England
13 G4 **Winston** England
101 O3 **Winston** Montana U.S.A.
106 C8 **Winston** New Mexico U.S.A.
112 G1 **Winston Salem** North Carolina U.S.A.
25 G2 **Winsum** Netherlands
118 H6 **Winter** Saskatchewan Canada
38 M6 **Winterbach** Austria
36 F1 **Winterberg** Germany
36 D4 **Winterberg** Germany
8 D6 **Winterbourne Abbas** England
9 E5 **Winterbourne Stoke** England
33 O7 **Winterfeld** Germany
113 F9 **Winter Garden** Florida U.S.A.
114 J3 **Winter Harb** Northwest Territories Canada
103 K9 **Winterhaven** California U.S.A.
113 F9 **Winter Haven** Florida U.S.A.
119 U3 **Wintering L** Manitoba Canada
36 G7 **Winterlingen** Germany
106 E2 **Winter Park** Colorado U.S.A.
113 F9 **Winter Park** Florida U.S.A.
95 T2 **Winterport** Maine U.S.A.
102 C3 **Winters** California U.S.A.
108 H4 **Winters** Texas U.S.A.
103 M8 **Wintersburg** Arizona U.S.A.
99 M8 **Winterset** Iowa U.S.A.
22 K2 **Winterslag** Belgium
25 G5 **Winterswijk** Netherlands
41 J3 **Winterthur** Switzerland
123 T6 **Winterton** Newfoundland Canada
13 H6 **Winterton** England
95 S7 **Winterville** Maine U.S.A.
95 R4 **Winthrop** Massachusetts U.S.A.
99 M5 **Winthrop** Minnesota U.S.A.
95 N2 **Winthrop** New York U.S.A.
100 E1 **Winthrop** Washington U.S.A.
99 T7 **Winthrop Harbor** Illinois U.S.A.
138 C2 **Wintinna** South Australia Australia
141 G5 **Winton** Queensland Australia
113 M9 **Winton** New Providence I Bahamas
144 B7 **Winton** New Zealand
99 P2 **Winton** Minnesota U.S.A.
112 K1 **Winton** North Carolina U.S.A.
95 M5 **Winton** Pennsylvania U.S.A.
100 E2 **Winton** Washington U.S.A.
101 Q8 **Winton** Wyoming U.S.A.
40 F1 **Wintzenheim** France
112 H4 **Winyah B** South Carolina U.S.A.
37 P6 **Winzer** Germany
99 M8 **Wiota** Iowa U.S.A.
33 N10 **Wipper** *R* Germany
36 C1 **Wipperfürth** Germany
33 O9 **Wippra** Germany
41 O3 **Wipp Tal** Austria
83 K11 **Wiraketiya** Sri Lanka
69 G14 **Wiralaga** Sumatra
32 F6 **Wirdum** Germany
25 E2 **Wirdum** Netherlands
9 E1 **Wirksworth** England
145 F2 **Wiroa I** New Zealand
138 E5 **Wirrabara** South Australia Australia
138 D4 **Wirraminna** South Australia Australia
138 F6 **Wirrega** South Australia Australia
138 C3 **Wirrida, L** South Australia Australia
138 C4 **Wirrulla** South Australia Australia
99 N2 **Wirt** Minnesota U.S.A.
22 B2 **Wirwignes** France
9 G2 **Wisbech** England
9 F5 **Wisborough Green** England
95 S2 **Wiscasset** Maine U.S.A.
32 K5 **Wischhafen** Germany
99 R5 **Wisconsin** *state* U.S.A.
99 R4 **Wisconsin** *R* Wisconsin U.S.A.
99 R6 **Wisconsin Dells** Wisconsin U.S.A.
99 R6 **Wisconsin, L** Wisconsin U.S.A.
99 R5 **Wisconsin Rapids** Wisconsin U.S.A.
101 M4 **Wisdom** Montana U.S.A.
94 E9 **Wise** Virginia U.S.A.
116 M3 **Wiseman** Alaska U.S.A.
101 N4 **Wise River** Montana U.S.A.
118 K7 **Wiseton** Saskatchewan Canada
119 O7 **Wishart** Saskatchewan Canada
12 E2 **Wishaw** Scotland
98 G3 **Wishek** North Dakota U.S.A.
100 E4 **Wishram** Washington U.S.A.
86 A2 **Wisil Dabarow** Somalia
31 L2 **Wisła** *R* Poland
48 E1 **Wisla** Poland
31 N6 **Wisłok** *R* Poland
33 O5 **Wismar** Germany
33 O5 **Wismarbucht** Germany
111 E10 **Wisner** Louisiana U.S.A.
98 K8 **Wisner** Nebraska U.S.A.
22 B2 **Wissant** France
36 D5 **Wissembourg** France
36 D2 **Wissen** Germany
9 G2 **Wissey, R** England
32 H8 **Wissingen** Germany
99 P5 **Wissota L** Wisconsin U.S.A.
31 N4 **Wista** *R* Poland
117 K9 **Wistaria** British Columbia Canada
109 N1 **Wister** Oklahoma U.S.A.
107 Q7 **Wister L** Oklahoma U.S.A.
89 F5 **Witbank** S Africa
89 E8 **Witberge** *mts* S Africa
89 A5 **Witbooisvlei** Namibia
119 U3 **Witchai L** Manitoba Canada
143 B10 **Witchcliffe** W Australia Australia
118 K5 **Witchekan L** Saskatchewan Canada
87 D11 **Witdrail** S Africa
9 G4 **Witham** England
9 F1 **Witham, R** England
8 C6 **Witheridge** England
9 G1 **Withern** England
13 J6 **Withernsea** England
106 C8 **Withington, Mt** New Mexico U.S.A.
113 E9 **Withlacoochee** *R* Florida U.S.A.
100 F2 **Withrow** Washington U.S.A.
31 K3 **Witkowo** Poland
123 U6 **Witless B** Newfoundland Canada
9 E4 **Witney** England
89 G5 **Witrivier** S Africa
22 K4 **Witry** Belgium
22 G5 **Witry-les-Reims** France
22 D2 **Witschate** Belgium
110 G2 **Witt** Illinois U.S.A.
28 A7 **Wittdün** Germany
37 L7 **Wittelsbach** Germany
32 F10 **Witten** Germany
98 F6 **Witten** South Dakota U.S.A.
33 S7 **Wittenau** Germany
33 R9 **Wittenberg** Germany
99 R5 **Wittenberg** Wisconsin U.S.A.
33 P7 **Wittenberge** Germany
33 O5 **Wittenburg** Germany
40 F2 **Wittenheim** France
142 C5 **Wittenoom** W Australia Australia
142 G4 **Wittenoom,Mt** W Australia Australia
37 O2 **Wittgensdorf** Germany
125 N2 **Witties, The** *islds* Nicaragua
36 H4 **Wittighausen** Germany
33 N7 **Wittingen** Germany
70 E2 **Witti Ra** Sabah
32 H8 **Wittlage** Germany
36 B4 **Wittlich** Germany
32 K7 **Wittlohe** Germany
103 M8 **Wittmann** Arizona U.S.A.
32 G5 **Wittmund** Germany
13 G4 **Witton Gilbert** England
13 G4 **Witton-le-Wear** England
30 G1 **Wittow** *pen* Germany
33 Q6 **Wittstock** Germany
87 C10 **Witvlei** Namibia
89 E5 **Witwatersberg** *ridge* S Africa
89 C2 **Witwatersrand** S Africa
32 L10 **Witzenhausen** Germany
8 C5 **Wiveliscombe** England
119 W2 **Wivenhoe** Manitoba Canada
139 L2 **Wivenhoe, Lake** *res* Australia
118 L8 **Wives** Saskatchewan Canada
9 H4 **Wix** England
31 O1 **Wizajny** Poland
22 C2 **Wizernes** France
31 M3 **Wkra** *R* Poland
31 L1 **Władysławowo** Poland
31 J4 **Wleń** Poland
31 L3 **Włocławek** Poland
31 O4 **Włodawa** Poland
31 M5 **Włoszczowa** Poland
33 O6 **Wöbbelin** Germany
9 F4 **Woburn** England
142 C5 **Wodgina** W Australia Australia
139 H6 **Wodonga** Victoria Australia
31 L5 **Wodzisław** Poland
25 B6 **Woensdrecht** Netherlands
25 C4 **Woerden** Netherlands
94 C10 **Wofford** Kentucky U.S.A.
25 D3 **Wognum** Netherlands
41 H3 **Wohlen** Switzerland
33 O5 **Wohlenberg** Germany
40 F4 **Wohlen See** *L* Switzerland
146 H7 **Wohlthat Massivet** *mts* Antarctica
36 F2 **Wohratal** Germany
32 J4 **Wöhrden** Germany
121 N7 **Woito** Ontario Canada
143 A8 **Wokarina** W Australia Australia
65 H1 **Woken** China
65 H1 **Woken He** *R* China
117 O8 **Woking** Alberta Canada
9 F5 **Woking** England
141 G5 **Wokingham** *R* Queensland Australia
9 F5 **Wokingham** England
33 S6 **Wokuhl** Germany
31 L4 **Wola** Poland
98 H8 **Wolbach** Nebraska U.S.A.
32 G9 **Wolbeck** Germany
101 T10 **Wolcott** Colorado U.S.A.
95 L3 **Wolcott** New York U.S.A.
32 E2 **Woldbrunn** Germany
33 T6 **Woldegk** Germany
141 J7 **Woleebee** Queensland Australia
117 G5 **Wolf** *R* Yukon Territory Canada
111 G11 **Wolf** *R* Mississippi U.S.A.
110 G6 **Wolf** *R* Tennessee U.S.A.
99 S4 **Wolf** *R* Wisconsin U.S.A.
36 E7 **Wolfach** Germany
37 P6 **Wolfachau** Germany
123 M3 **Wolf Bay** Quebec Canada
108 D7 **Wolf Cr** Texas/Okla U.S.A.
94 B10 **Wolf Cr. Dam** Kentucky U.S.A.
101 N2 **Wolf Creek** Montana U.S.A.
100 B7 **Wolf Creek** Oregon U.S.A.
106 D4 **Wolf Cr. Pass** Colorado U.S.A.
118 J6 **Wolfe** Saskatchewan Canada
95 Q3 **Wolfeboro** New Hampshire U.S.A.
109 L2 **Wolfe City** Texas U.S.A.
121 O8 **Wolfe Island** Ontario Canada
118 G4 **Wolfe L** Alberta Canada
33 Q9 **Wolfen** Germany
33 N8 **Wolfenbüttel** Germany
9 G2 **Wolferton** England
32 K10 **Wolfhagen** Germany
103 L5 **Wolf Hole** Arizona U.S.A.
123 L6 **Wolf I** Madeleine Is, Quebec Canada
117 H5 **Wolf L** Yukon Territory Canada
101 S4 **Wolf Mts** Wyo/Mont U.S.A.
98 G1 **Wolford** North Dakota U.S.A.
98 A1 **Wolf Pt** Montana U.S.A.
37 K5 **Wolframs-Eschenbach** Germany
41 O2 **Wolfratshausen** Germany
7 G13 **Wolf Rock** English Chan
38 L8 **Wolfsberg** Austria
33 N8 **Wolfsburg** Germany
37 N2 **Wolfsgefärth** Germany
36 E4 **Wolfskehlen** Germany
36 D4 **Wolfstein** Germany
122 H8 **Wolfville** Nova Scotia Canada
33 T4 **Wolgast** Germany
33 T4 **Wolgaster Fähre** Germany
31 H2 **Wolin** Poland
37 L3 **Wölkendorf** Germany
37 P2 **Wolkenstein** Germany
33 N10 **Wolkramsh** Germany
114 H3 **Wollaston, C** Northwest Territories Canada
133 D9 **Wollaston, Is** Chile
114 J6 **Wollaston L** Saskatchewan Canada
114 J6 **Wollaston Lake** Saskatchewan Canada
114 H4 **Wollaston Pen** Northwest Territories Canada
36 B2 **Wollersheim** Germany
140 E3 **Wollogorang** N Terr Australia
139 K5 **Wollongong** New South Wales Australia
36 D4 **Wöllstein** Germany
87 E11 **Wolmaransstad** S Africa
33 O9 **Wolmirsleben** Germany
33 P8 **Wolmirstedt** Germany
37 M6 **Wolnzach** Germany
31 N3 **Wołomin** Poland
31 K4 **Wołow** Poland
71 K9 **Wolowaru** Flores Indonesia
138 F6 **Wolseley** South Australia Australia
119 O8 **Wolseley** Saskatchewan Canada
98 H5 **Wolsey** South Dakota U.S.A.
36 B4 **Wolsfeld** Germany
13 G4 **Wolsingham** England
115 M5 **Wolstenholme, C** Quebec Canada
31 J3 **Wolsztyn** Poland
32 L7 **Wolthausen** Germany
33 M8 **Woltorf** Germany
25 F3 **Wolvega** Netherlands
8 D2 **Wolverhampton** England
94 C1 **Wolverine** Michigan U.S.A.
22 G2 **Wolvertem** Belgium
9 E5 **Wolverton** England
98 K3 **Wolverton** Minnesota U.S.A.
9 E3 **Wolvey** England
69 C10 **Wolya** *R* Sumatra
120 H5 **Woman River** Ontario Canada
13 G6 **Wombwell** England
95 L6 **Womelsdorf** Pennsylvania U.S.A.
138 F3 **Wompah** New South Wales Australia
140 D4 **Wonarah** N Terr Australia
143 E10 **Wonberna Rock** *rock* W Australia Australia
141 K7 **Wondai** Queensland Australia
22 F1 **Wondelgem** Belgium
100 B7 **Wonder** Oregon U.S.A.
116 M5 **Wonder L** Alaska U.S.A.
140 E6 **Wonditti,L** Queensland Australia
140 F4 **Wondoola** Queensland Australia
139 G4 **Wongalarroo L** New South Wales Australia
141 G5 **Wongalee** Queensland Australia
143 B9 **Wongan Hills** W Australia Australia
70 G4 **Wonggarasi** Sulawesi
59 J4 **Wŏnju** S Korea
70 N9 **Wonogiri** Java
70 N10 **Wonojoyo** Java
70 O9 **Wonokromo** Java
138 F4 **Wonominta** *R* New South Wales Australia
70 N9 **Wonosari** Java
70 M9 **Wonosobo** Java
71 N9 **Wonreli** Indonesia
59 J4 **Wŏnsan** N Korea
139 H7 **Wonthaggi** Victoria Australia
143 C6 **Wonyulgunna,Mt** W Australia Australia
138 D4 **Woocalla** South Australia Australia
116 O4 **Wood** *R* Alaska U.S.A.
94 J6 **Wood** Pennsylvania U.S.A.
98 F6 **Wood** South Dakota U.S.A.
140 D2 **Woodah I** N Terr Australia
113 F7 **Woodbine** Georgia U.S.A.
99 L8 **Woodbine** Iowa U.S.A.
107 N3 **Woodbine** Kansas U.S.A.
94 C10 **Woodbine** Kentucky U.S.A.
95 N7 **Woodbine** New Jersey U.S.A.
121 L9 **Woodbridge** Ontario Canada
9 H3 **Woodbridge** England
95 K8 **Woodbridge** Virginia U.S.A.
117 R6 **Wood Buffalo Nat. Park** Alberta Canada
139 L3 **Woodburn** New South Wales Australia
99 N8 **Woodburn** Iowa U.S.A.
110 K5 **Woodburn** Kentucky U.S.A.
100 C4 **Woodburn** Oregon U.S.A.
112 C5 **Woodbury** Georgia U.S.A.
95 M7 **Woodbury** New Jersey U.S.A.
110 K6 **Woodbury** Tennessee U.S.A.
112 F5 **Woodcliff** Georgia U.S.A.
140 C4 **Woodcock,Mt** N Terr Australia
139 L3 **Woodenbong** New South Wales Australia
144 B7 **Woodend** New Zealand
117 M11 **Woodfibre** British Columbia Canada
9 G4 **Woodford** England
127 P5 **Woodford** Grenada
14 C3 **Woodford** Ireland
140 C5 **Woodforde** *R* N Terr Australia
102 E3 **Woodfords** California U.S.A.
140 C5 **Woodgreen** N Terr Australia
9 F4 **Wood Green** England
9 F1 **Woodhall Spa** England
13 G6 **Woodhead** England
99 Q8 **Woodhull** Illinois U.S.A.
95 K4 **Woodhull** New York U.S.A.
142 D5 **Woodie Woodie** W Australia Australia
100 C2 **Woodinville** Washington U.S.A.
122 K8 **Wood Is** Prince Edward I Canada
119 U1 **Wood L** Manitoba Canada
119 O3 **Wood L** Saskatchewan Canada
98 F7 **Wood L** Nebraska U.S.A.
102 E5 **Woodlake** California U.S.A.
102 C3 **Woodland** California U.S.A.
110 J1 **Woodland** Illinois U.S.A.
94 J6 **Woodland** Pennsylvania U.S.A.
100 C4 **Woodland** Washington U.S.A.
109 N10 **Woodland Hills** Texas U.S.A.
106 E3 **Woodland Park** Colorado U.S.A.
119 U8 **Woodlands** Manitoba Canada
137 L3 **Woodlark** *isld* Papua New Guinea
110 G3 **Woodlawn** Illinois U.S.A.
142 A3 **Woodman Pt** W Australia Australia
118 L9 **Wood Mt** Saskatchewan Canada
117 C5 **Wood, Mt** Yukon Territory Canada
101 Q4 **Wood, Mt** Montana U.S.A.
138 D2 **Woodmurra Creek** South Australia Australia
117 M9 **Woodpecker** British Columbia Canada
118 E1 **Woodridge** Manitoba Canada
110 F3 **Wood River** Illinois U.S.A.
98 H9 **Wood River** Nebraska U.S.A.
140 E5 **Woodroffe** *R* N Terr/ Queensland Australia
138 B2 **Woodroffe, Mt** South Australia Australia
118 L9 **Woodrow** Saskatchewan Canada
106 G2 **Woodrow** Colorado U.S.A.
103 O7 **Woodruff** Arizona U.S.A.
107 L2 **Woodruff** Kansas U.S.A.
101 O8 **Woodruff** Utah U.S.A.
101 Q4 **Woods** *mt* Montana U.S.A.
109 K7 **Woodsboro** Texas U.S.A.
94 F7 **Woodsfield** Ohio U.S.A.
122 G10 **Woods Harbour** Nova Scotia Canada
139 H7 **Woodside** Victoria Australia
145 E4 **Woodside** New Zealand
103 O2 **Woodside** Utah U.S.A.
140 C4 **Woods,L** N Terr Australia
118 H1 **Woods, Lake of the** Minnesota/Ontario U.S.A./ Canada
111 D7 **Woodson** Arkansas U.S.A.
99 Q10 **Woodson** Illinois U.S.A.
109 H2 **Woodson** Texas U.S.A.
139 H7 **Woods Pt** Victoria Australia
141 H4 **Woodstock** Queensland Australia
122 E7 **Woodstock** New Brunswick Canada
9 E4 **Woodstock** England
99 S7 **Woodstock** Illinois U.S.A.
95 P3 **Woodstock** Vermont U.S.A.
95 Q2 **Woodstock, N** New Hampshire U.S.A.
107 M2 **Woodston** Kansas U.S.A.
95 M7 **Woodstown** New Jersey U.S.A.
95 Q2 **Woodsville** New Hampshire U.S.A.
138 E6 **Woodswell** South Australia Australia
121 M8 **Woodville** Ontario Canada
145 E4 **Woodville** New Zealand
110 K7 **Woodville** Alabama U.S.A.
111 M11 **Woodville** Florida U.S.A.
111 E10 **Woodville** Mississippi U.S.A.
94 D5 **Woodville** Ohio U.S.A.
109 N5 **Woodville** Texas U.S.A.
107 L5 **Woodward** Oklahoma U.S.A.
102 D4 **Woodward Res** California U.S.A.
122 F9 **Woodwards Cove** New Brunswick Canada
109 P4 **Woodworth** Louisiana U.S.A.
98 G2 **Woodworth** North Dakota U.S.A.
8 C5 **Woody B** England
139 L3 **Woody Head** New South Wales Australia
116 L8 **Woody Island** Alaska U.S.A.
123 P4 **Woody Point** Newfoundland Canada
119 Q6 **Woody R** Manitoba Canada
8 D3 **Woofferton** England
71 A3 **Wooi** Indonesia
8 D6 **Wool** England
8 B5 **Woolacombe** England
110 D3 **Wooldridge** Missouri U.S.A.
139 K5 **Woolemi Nat Park** New South Wales Australia
13 F3 **Wooler** England
118 D9 **Woolford Prov. Park** Alberta Canada
143 D9 **Woolgangie** W Australia Australia
141 G4 **Woolgar** Queensland Australia
143 C6 **Woolgathara** W Australia Australia
139 L4 **Woolgoolga** New South Wales Australia
143 D9 **Woolibar** W Australia Australia
140 C5 **Woolla Downs** N Terr Australia
9 G3 **Woolpit** England
102 F1 **Woolsey** Nevada U.S.A.
138 E4 **Wooltana** South Australia Australia
8 D5 **Woolverton** England
9 G5 **Woolwich** England
138 D4 **Woomera** South Australia Australia
138 B3 **Woomera Prohibited Area** South Australia Australia
95 Q5 **Woonsocket** Rhode I U.S.A.
98 H5 **Woonsocket** South Dakota U.S.A.
13 G3 **Wooperton** England
141 J6 **Woorabinda** Queensland Australia
143 A7 **Wooramel R** W Australia Australia
8 D2 **Woore** England
138 C3 **Woorong, L** South Australia Australia
94 F6 **Wooster** Ohio U.S.A.
9 E4 **Wootton Bassett** England
38 O6 **Wopfing** Austria
117 O7 **Wor** Alberta Canada
71 B2 **Wor** *isld* Halmahera Indonesia
33 M10 **Worbis** Germany
141 F2 **Worbody Pt** Queensland Australia
Worcester *co see* **Hereford and Worcester** *co*
8 D3 **Worcester** England
89 A9 **Worcester** S Africa
95 Q4 **Worcester** Massachusetts U.S.A.
95 N4 **Worcester** New York U.S.A.
110 G3 **Worden** Illinois U.S.A.
101 R4 **Worden** Montana U.S.A.
100 D7 **Worden** Oregon U.S.A.
119 P9 **Wordsworth** Saskatchewan Canada
38 F7 **Wörgl** Austria
12 E4 **Workington** England
9 E1 **Worksop** England
25 D3 **Workum** Netherlands
101 S5 **Worland** Wyoming U.S.A.
8 D5 **Worle** England
33 Q9 **Wörlitz** Germany
8 D4 **Wormbridge** England
25 C4 **Wormerveer** Netherlands
22 C2 **Wormhoudt** France
13 F1 **Wormit** Scotland
33 P10 **Wormlitz** Germany
36 E4 **Worms** Germany
8 B4 **Worms Head** Wales
37 K6 **Wörnitz** *R* Germany
32 J6 **Worpswede** Germany
36 B1 **Worringen** Germany
36 E4 **Wörrstadt** Germany
143 E7 **Worsnop,Mt** W Australia Australia
38 G7 **Wörth** Austria
38 O7 **Wörth** Austria
36 D6 **Wœrth** France
37 N6 **Wörth** Bayern Germany
36 E5 **Wörth** Rheinland-Pfalz Germany
99 M9 **Worth** Missouri U.S.A.
109 L4 **Wortham** Texas U.S.A.
8 C2 **Worthen** England
38 K8 **Wörther See** *L* Austria
127 P6 **Worthing** Barbados
9 F6 **Worthing** England
110 K2 **Worthington** Indiana U.S.A.
99 L6 **Worthington** Minnesota U.S.A.
99 O9 **Worthington** Missouri U.S.A.
94 D6 **Worthington** Ohio U.S.A.
109 L9 **Worth, L** Texas U.S.A.
94 B8 **Worthville** Kentucky U.S.A.
13 G6 **Wortley** England
71 A3 **Wosi** Halmahera Indonesia
118 E5 **Wostok** Alberta Canada
70 G6 **Wosu** Sulawesi
31 L4 **Wotczyn** Poland
121 T7 **Wotton** Quebec Canada
8 D4 **Wotton under Edge** England
70 G6 **Wotu** Sulawesi
25 D4 **Woudenberg** Netherlands
25 C5 **Woudrichem** Netherlands
98 D6 **Wounded Knee** South Dakota U.S.A.
25 B5 **Wouw** Netherlands
22 J5 **Wœvre, Forêt de** France
141 K6 **Wowan** Queensland Australia
71 H7 **Wowoni** *isld* Indonesia
31 L5 **Woźniki** Poland
9 F1 **Wragby** England
Wrangel I *see* **Vrangelya, Os**
117 G7 **Wrangell** Alaska U.S.A.
116 Q6 **Wrangell Mts** Alaska/Yukon Terr U.S.A./Canada
116 P5 **Wrangell-St. Elias Nat Park and Preserve** Alaska U.S.A.
9 G1 **Wrangle** England
106 H1 **Wray** Colorado U.S.A.
9 F2 **Wreak, R** England
141 G1 **Wreck B** Gt Barrier Reef Aust
32 H5 **Wremen** Germany
100 B5 **Wren** Oregon U.S.A.
112 E4 **Wrens** Georgia U.S.A.
118 E9 **Wrentham** Alberta Canada
9 H3 **Wrentham** England
95 Q4 **Wrentham** Massachusetts U.S.A.
8 D1 **Wrexham** Wales
30 H3 **Wriezen** Germany
121 O6 **Wright** Quebec Canada
71 G5 **Wright** Samar Philippines
107 L4 **Wright** Kansas U.S.A.
112 M1 **Wright Bros. Nat. Mem** North Carolina U.S.A.
107 P7 **Wright City** Oklahoma U.S.A.
138 A3 **Wright, L** South Australia Australia
138 F4 **Wright, Mt** New South Wales Australia
68 A7 **Wrightmyo** Andaman Is
109 N2 **Wright Patman L** Texas U.S.A.
103 O10 **Wrightson, Mt** Arizona U.S.A.
112 E5 **Wrightsville** Georgia U.S.A.
95 L6 **Wrightsville** Pennsylvania U.S.A.
112 K3 **Wrightsville Beach** North Carolina U.S.A.
102 G7 **Wrightwood** California U.S.A.
117 M4 **Wrigley** Northwest Territories Canada
32 L5 **Wrist** Germany
118 F9 **Writing-on-Stone Prov. Park** Alberta Canada
31 K4 **Wrocław** Poland
119 V6 **Wrong L** Manitoba Canada
31 J3 **Wronki** Poland
9 G5 **Wrotham** England
8 D2 **Wroxeter** England
9 H2 **Wroxham** England
119 Q7 **Wroxton** Saskatchewan Canada
9 E3 **Wroxton** England
31 J4 **Wschowa** Poland
31 L3 **Wtoctawskie, Jezioro** *res* Poland
65 C6 **Wu'an** China
143 B9 **Wubin** W Australia Australia
65 A6 **Wubu** China
65 E1 **Wuchagou** China
65 G2 **Wuchang** China
67 E1 **Wuchang** China
65 B6 **Wucheng** China
65 C6 **Wucheng** China
Wuchow *see* **Wuzhou**
65 B4 **Wuchuan** China
67 C2 **Wuchuan** China
67 B5 **Wucun** China
58 E4 **Wuda** China
65 E5 **Wudao** China
65 F3 **Wudaogou** China
66 E4 **Wudaoliang** China
67 C2 **Wudaoshui** China
65 D6 **Wudi** China
65 A6 **Wuding He** *R* China
138 D5 **Wudinna** South Australia Australia
58 D5 **Wudu** China
67 A1 **Wudu** China
67 C1 **Wufeng** China
67 C3 **Wugang** China
58 E4 **Wuhai** China
67 E1 **Wuhan** China
58 G5 **Wuhe** China
32 J6 **Wuhrden** *reg* Germany
67 F1 **Wuhu** China
65 C5 **Wuji** China
65 G2 **Wujia** China
67 C6 **Wujia** China
67 G1 **Wujiang** China
67 C2 **Wu Jiang** *R* China
65 F2 **Wujiazhan** China
67 F1 **Wukang** China
85 F7 **Wukari** Nigeria
65 G2 **Wulajie** China
32 F9 **Wulfen** Germany
33 P9 **Wulfen** Germany
33 Q6 **Wulfersdorf** Germany
32 F10 **Wülfrath** Germany
32 M6 **Wulfsen** Germany
32 M9 **Wulften** Germany
68 J1 **Wuli** China
65 D7 **Wulian** China
67 B1 **Wulian** China
67 A3 **Wulian Feng** *mts* China
65 B8 **Wulichuan** China
67 C5 **Wuli Jiang** *R* China
116 F3 **Wulik** *R* Alaska U.S.A.
65 H2 **Wulin** China
67 C2 **Wuling Shan** *mts* China
67 C1 **Wulingzhen** China
67 B2 **Wulong** China
71 O8 **Wulur** Indonesia
37 K5 **Wülzburg** Germany
85 G7 **Wum** Cameroon
139 H5 **Wumbulgel** New South Wales Australia
67 A3 **Wumeng Shan** *mts* China
67 C5 **Wuming** China
32 K6 **Wümme** *R* Germany
142 C3 **Wungang R** W Australia Australia
88 D6 **Wungu** Tanzania
67 E2 **Wuning** China
138 F5 **Wunkar** South Australia Australia
32 J9 **Wünnenberg** Germany
33 S8 **Wünsdorf** Germany
37 N3 **Wunsiedel** Germany
32 K8 **Wunstorf** Germany
75 Q7 **Wuntho** Burma
103 N6 **Wupatki Nat. Mon** Arizona U.S.A.
67 E4 **Wuping** China
32 F10 **Wuppertal** Germany
66 B4 **Wuqia** China
65 C5 **Wuqiang** China
65 C6 **Wuqiao** China
65 D5 **Wuqing** China
143 B8 **Wurarga** W Australia Australia
37 O7 **Wurmannsquick** Germany
85 F6 **Wurno** Nigeria
25 F7 **Würselen** Germany
95 N5 **Wurtsboro** New York U.S.A.
37 M3 **Wurzbach** Germany
36 H4 **Würzburg** Germany
33 R10 **Wurzen** Germany
67 C1 **Wu Shan** *mts* China
67 C1 **Wushan** China
67 D1 **Wushan** China
67 B1 **Wusheng** China
67 F2 **Wusheng** China
67 D1 **Wusheng Guan** *pass* China
57 J4 **Wushi** China
68 J2 **Wushi** China
67 C3 **Wu Shui** *R* China
67 G1 **Wusong** China
36 H3 **Wüstensachsen** Germany
33 Q7 **Wusterhausen** Germany
33 R7 **Wustermark** Germany
32 H6 **Wüsting** Germany
33 R7 **Wustrau** Germany
33 P4 **Wustrow** Germany
33 O7 **Wustrow** Germany
59 K2 **Wusuli Jiang** *R* China
41 H2 **Wutach** *R* Germany
65 B5 **Wutai** China
58 F4 **Wutai Shan** *mt ra* China
65 D3 **Wu-tan** China
67 C4 **Wutong** China
67 A2 **Wutongqiao** China
22 H1 **Wuustwezel** Belgium
58 D4 **Wuwei** China
67 F1 **Wuwei** China
67 C1 **Wuxi** China
67 G1 **Wuxi** China
65 B6 **Wuxiang** China
Wuxing *see* **Huzhou**
67 C5 **Wuxuan** China
Wuxue *see* **Guangji**
Wuyang *see* **Zhenyuan**
65 B6 **Wuyang** China
65 C6 **Wuyi** China
67 F1 **Wuyi** China
67 F2 **Wuyi** China
59 J2 **Wuyiling** China
67 E4 **Wuyi Shan** *mts* China
58 E3 **Wuyuan** China
67 F2 **Wuyuan** China
65 B5 **Wuzhai** China
65 G2 **Wuzhan** China
65 A6 **Wuzhen** China
67 D1 **Wuzhen** China
65 B7 **Wuzhi** China
67 C7 **Wuzhi Shan** *pk* China
58 E4 **Wuzhong** China
67 D5 **Wuzhou** China
141 F3 **Wyaaba Cr** Queensland Australia
99 P9 **Wyaconda** *R* Missouri U.S.A.
143 B9 **Wyalkatchem** W Australia Australia
139 H5 **Wyalong** New South Wales Australia
94 D4 **Wyandotte** Michigan U.S.A.
141 H7 **Wyandra** Queensland Australia
139 J5 **Wyangala Res** New South Wales Australia
141 G8 **Wyara** *L* Queensland Australia
101 T5 **Wyarno** Wyoming U.S.A.
110 G5 **Wyatt** Missouri U.S.A.
9 G5 **Wych Cross** England
139 G6 **Wycheproof** Victoria Australia
9 G5 **Wye** England
143 C8 **Wyemandoo** *mt* W Australia
8 D4 **Wye, R** Wales/England
99 Q5 **Wyeville** Wisconsin U.S.A.
109 L2 **Wylie** Texas U.S.A.
142 B6 **Wyloo** W Australia Australia
8 D5 **Wylye, R** England
95 S1 **Wyman Dam** Maine U.S.A.
118 K8 **Wymark** Saskatchewan Canada
100 E3 **Wymer** Washington U.S.A.
9 H2 **Wymondham** England
98 K9 **Wymore** Nebraska U.S.A.
142 G3 **Wyndham** W Australia Australia
144 B7 **Wyndham** New Zealand
142 E3 **Wyndham Ra** W Australia Australia
98 J3 **Wyndmere** North Dakota U.S.A.
110 F6 **Wynne** Arkansas U.S.A.
142 E4 **Wynne,Mt** W Australia Australia
107 N7 **Wynnewood** Oklahoma U.S.A.
114 H3 **Wynniatt B** Northwest Territories Canada
141 L7 **Wynnum** Queensland Australia
107 O5 **Wynona** Oklahoma U.S.A.
98 J7 **Wynot** Nebraska U.S.A.
139 H8 **Wynyard** Tasmania Australia
119 N7 **Wynyard** Saskatchewan Canada
99 R6 **Wyocena** Wisconsin U.S.A.
98 A5 **Wyodak** Wyoming U.S.A.
101 S4 **Wyola** Montana U.S.A.
138 B3 **Wyola, L** South Australia Australia
120 H10 **Wyoming** Ontario Canada
101 R6 **Wyoming** *state* U.S.A.
95 M7 **Wyoming** Delaware U.S.A.
99 R8 **Wyoming** Illinois U.S.A.
94 B4 **Wyoming** Michigan U.S.A.
99 N4 **Wyoming** Minnesota U.S.A.
94 J4 **Wyoming** New York U.S.A.
95 Q5 **Wyoming** Rhode I U.S.A.
101 P7 **Wyoming Pk** Wyoming U.S.A.
101 P7 **Wyoming Ra** Wyoming U.S.A.
139 K5 **Wyong** New South Wales Australia
138 F6 **Wyperfeld Nat Park** Victoria Australia
13 F6 **Wyre, R** England
31 K2 **Wyrzysk** Poland
31 O5 **Wysokie** Poland
31 N3 **Wysokie Mazowieckie** Poland
31 N3 **Wyszków** Poland
31 M3 **Wyszogrod** Poland
13 E5 **Wythburn** England
94 F10 **Wytheville** Virginia U.S.A.
83 M14 **Wyville-Thomson** *mt* Kerguelen Indian Oc

X

86 B1 **Xaafuun** Somalia
86 B1 **Xaafuun, Raas** *C* Somalia
86 A1 **Xadeed, Bannaanka** *plain* Somalia
66 B4 **Xaidulla** China
68 E3 **Xaignabouri** Laos
66 D5 **Xainza** China
87 F11 **Xai-Xai** Mozambique
125 P7 **Xal, Cerro de** *mt* Mexico
86 A2 **Xalin** Somalia
Xamba *see* **Hanggin Houqi**
129 J5 **Xambioa** Brazil
68 F2 **Xam Nua** Laos
65 A3 **Xangdin Hural** China
Xangdoring *see* **Xungba**
87 B9 **Xangongo** Angola
25 F5 **Xanten** Germany
46 G3 **Xánthi** Greece
130 D10 **Xanxerê** Brazil
128 E6 **Xapuri** Brazil
86 A3 **Xarardheere** Somalia
65 C2 **Xar Hudag** China
65 B3 **Xar Moron** China
59 G3 **Xar Moron He** *R* China
65 B3 **Xar Moron Sum** China
87 D10 **Xau, L** Botswana
129 J6 **Xavantes, Sa. dos** *mts* Brazil
57 L4 **Xayar** China
Xêgar *see* **Tingri**
110 H3 **Xenia** Illinois U.S.A.
94 D7 **Xenia** Ohio U.S.A.
128 F4 **Xeriuini** *R* Brazil
46 D5 **Xerovoúni** *R* Greece
67 F3 **Xiabaishi** China
Xiabancheng *see* **Chengde**
65 D4 **Xiabancheng** China
65 H2 **Xiachengzi** China
65 B7 **Xiachuan** China
67 D6 **Xiachuan Dao** *isld* China
Xiacun *see* **Rushan**
65 C4 **Xiahuayuan** China
67 E3 **Xiajiang** China
67 C4 **Xiajiang** China
65 C6 **Xiajin** China
66 F3 **Xiamaya** China
67 F4 **Xiamen** China
58 E5 **Xi'an** China

67 C2 **Xianfeng** China
58 C6 **Xiangcheng** China
65 B8 **Xiangcheng** China
67 D3 **Xiangdong** China
67 B5 **Xiangdu** China
58 F5 **Xiangfan** China
65 B7 **Xiangfen** China
65 D5 **Xianghe** China
65 B3 **Xianghuang Qi** China
67 D3 **Xiang Jiang** *R* China
65 H1 **Xianglan** China
65 A7 **Xiangning** China
66 B5 **Xiangquan He** *R* China
67 G2 **Xiangshan** China
67 G2 **Xiangshan Gang** *B* China
65 D7 **Xiangshui** China
67 D3 **Xiangtan** China
67 D3 **Xiangxiang** China
65 G2 **Xiangyang** China
67 D2 **Xiangyin** China
65 B6 **Xiangyuan** China
67 C5 **Xiangzhou** China
67 G2 **Xianju** China
58 F6 **Xianning** China
Xiannumiao *see* **Jiangdu**
Xiantaozhen *see* **Mianyang**
67 F3 **Xianxia Ling** *mt ra* China
58 E5 **Xianyang** China
67 F4 **Xianyou** China
65 G1 **Xiaobai** China
65 G2 **Xiaocheng** China
65 D3 **Xiaochengzi** China
65 D4 **Xiaochengzi** China
68 J1 **Xiaodong** China
Xiaofan *see* **Wuqiang**
67 D1 **Xiaogan** China
66 C2 **Xiaoguai** China
67 E1 **Xiaohexi** China
59 J1 **Xiao Hinggan Ling** *mt ra* China
Xiaojiang *see* **Pubei**
65 E3 **Xiaojieji** China
66 F4 **Xiao Qaidam** China
65 A7 **Xiao Shan** *ra* China
67 G1 **Xiaoshan** China
65 F4 **Xiaoshi** China
67 D4 **Xiao Shui** *R* China
65 A6 **Xiaosuan** China
65 C5 **Xiaowutai Shan** *mt* China
67 F2 **Xiao Xi** *R* China
65 D7 **Xiao Xian** China
Xiaoxita *see* **Yichang**
Xiaoyi *see* **Gong Xian**
65 B6 **Xiaoyi** China
67 F3 **Xiapu** China
Xiashi *see* **Haining**
65 B7 **Xia Xian** China
65 C7 **Xiayi** China
Xiayingpan *see* **Luzhi**
58 D6 **Xichang** China
67 C6 **Xichang** China
67 C2 **Xiche** China
Xicheng *see* **Yangyuan**
67 B1 **Xichong** China
67 A5 **Xichou** China
65 E2 **Xi Dorolj** China
67 D3 **Xidu** China
Xiedian *see* **Wanrong**
Xiejiaji *see* **Qingyun**
67 D1 **Xiemahe** China
68 F3 **Xieng Khoang** Laos
65 A7 **Xiexian** China
67 C6 **Xieyang Dao** *isld* China
65 F3 **Xifeng** China
67 B3 **Xifeng** China
65 D4 **Xifenqkou** China
66 D6 **Xigazê** China
65 E4 **Xi He** *R* China
65 G1 **Xiji** China
67 D5 **Xi Jiang** *R* China
65 E1 **Xikou** China
67 C2 **Xikou** China
65 B3 **Xil** China
66 E4 **Xiliangzi** China
67 B4 **Xilin** China
65 C2 **Xilin Gol** *R* China
65 H2 **Xilinhe** China
65 C3 **Xilin Hot** China
65 B2 **Xilin Qagan Obo** China
46 F6 **Xilókastron** Greece
65 D3 **Xiluga He** *R* China
67 B3 **Ximahe** China
65 E5 **Ximayi** *isld* China
58 C3 **Ximiao** China
65 E4 **Ximucheng** China
65 B7 **Xin'an** China
67 F2 **Xin'anjiang Shuiku** *res* China
Xin'anzhen *see* **Xinyi**
65 F2 **Xin'anzhen** China
59 H3 **Xinbin** China
Xin Bulag *see* **Xianghuang Qi**
58 G5 **Xincai** China
67 D2 **Xinchang** China
59 H6 **Xinchang** Zhejiang China
65 H1 **Xincheng** China
65 C5 **Xincheng** China
67 C4 **Xincheng** China
65 F3 **Xinchengzi** China
67 C7 **Xincun** China
Xindeng *see* **Chengyang**
65 G2 **Xindian** China
67 C1 **Xindianzi** China
67 A1 **Xindu** China
67 D4 **Xindu** China
67 E3 **Xinfeng** China
67 E4 **Xinfeng** China
67 E3 **Xingan** China
67 C4 **Xing'an** China
65 E4 **Xingcheng** China
65 C5 **Xingchi** China
67 E3 **Xingguo** China
65 B4 **Xinghe** China
65 G1 **Xinghua** China
67 F4 **Xinghua Wan** *B* China
65 J2 **Xingkai Hu** *L* China
65 D4 **Xinglong** China
65 G1 **Xinglongzhen** China
67 E4 **Xingning** China
67 B3 **Xingren** China
67 B4 **Xingren** China
65 F1 **Xingshan** China
67 C1 **Xingshan** China
58 F4 **Xingtai** China
65 C5 **Xingtang** China
67 F3 **Xingtian** China
129 H4 **Xingú** *R* Brazil
67 A2 **Xingwen** China
65 B5 **Xing Xian** China
66 E3 **Xingxingxia** China
65 B7 **Xingyang** China
67 E2 **Xingzi** China
57 L4 **Xinhe** China
65 C6 **Xinhe** China
Xin Hot *see* **Abag Qi**
67 D3 **Xinhua** China
67 C3 **Xinhuang** China
Xinhui *see* **Aohan Qi**
67 D5 **Xinhui** China
46 E5 **Xiniás, L** Greece
58 D4 **Xining** China
Xinji *see* **Shulu**
67 E2 **Xinjian** China
67 E2 **Xin Jiang** *R* China
65 B7 **Xinjiang** Shanxi China
Xinjiangkou *see* **Songzi**
66 C3 **Xinjiang Uygur Zizhiqu** China
65 E5 **Xinjin** China
67 A1 **Xinjin** China
65 E3 **Xinkai He** *R* China
65 C5 **Xinle** China
65 G2 **Xinli** China
65 D3 **Xinlin** China
65 E3 **Xinlitun** China
65 A5 **Xinminzhen** China
67 C3 **Xinning** China
Xinpu *see* **Lianyungang**
67 D2 **Xinqiang** China
67 D3 **Xinshao** China
65 D7 **Xintai** China
67 D1 **Xintankou** China
67 D4 **Xintian** China
65 D7 **Xinwen** China
67 E1 **Xin Xian** China
65 B7 **Xinxiang** China
67 D5 **Xinxing** China
68 J3 **Xinxing** China
67 E1 **Xinyang** China
65 D7 **Xinyi** China
67 C5 **Xinyi** China
65 D7 **Xinyi He** *R* China
67 C7 **Xinying** China
67 E3 **Xinyu** China
66 C3 **Xinyuan** China
65 D6 **Xinzhai** China
65 F2 **Xinzhan** China
65 G3 **Xinzhan** China
65 B7 **Xinzheng** China
65 B5 **Xinzhou** China
67 E1 **Xinzhou** China
Xinzo de Limia *see* **Ginzo de Limia**
58 F5 **Xiong'er Shan** *mt ra* China
65 C5 **Xiong Xian** China
65 E4 **Xiongyuecheng** China
65 B4 **Xiping** China
58 D4 **Xiqing Shan** *mt ra* China
129 K6 **Xique-Xique** Brazil
Xishuanghe *see* **Kenli**
67 B2 **Xishui** Guizhou China
67 E1 **Xishui** Hubei China
65 D2 **Xi Ujimqin Qi** China
67 F2 **Xiuning** China
67 C2 **Xiushan** China
67 E2 **Xiu Shui** *R* China
67 E2 **Xiushui** China
65 B7 **Xiuwu** China
65 F4 **Xiuyan** China
Xiwanzi *see* **Chongli**
66 D6 **Xixabangma Feng** *mt* China
65 A6 **Xi Xian** China
65 B6 **Xiyang** China
67 F3 **Xiyang** China
67 G3 **Xiyang Dao** *isld* China
67 B5 **Xiyang Jiang** *R* China
67 B5 **Xiyangjie** China
75 K1 **Xizang Gaoyuan** *plateau* China
66 C5 **Xizang Zizhiqu** *aut reg* China
65 E5 **Xizhong Dao** *isld* China
125 K8 **Xochimilco** Mexico
58 G5 **Xuancheng** China
67 C1 **Xuan'en** China
67 B1 **Xuanhan** China
58 F3 **Xuanhua** China
68 H7 **Xuan Loc** Vietnam
67 A3 **Xuanwei** China
58 F5 **Xuchang** China
86 H5 **Xuddur** Somalia
67 G2 **Xuedou Shan** *mt* China
67 C3 **Xuefeng Shan** *mts* China
65 A7 **Xuejiaying** China
Xugezhuang *see* **Fengnan**
Xuguit Qi *see* **Yakeshi**
67 E3 **Xu Jiang** *R* China
65 E4 **Xujiatun** China
Xulun Hobot Qagan *see* **Zhengxiangbai Qi**
Xulun Hoh *see* **Zhenglan Qi**
58 C5 **Xümatang** China
67 A4 **Xundian** China
66 C5 **Xungba** China
58 E5 **Xun He** *R* China
59 J2 **Xunke** China
67 E4 **Xunwu** China
65 C7 **Xun Xian** China
67 C3 **Xupu** China
66 D5 **Xuro Co** *L* China
65 C5 **Xushui** China
67 E3 **Xuwan** China
67 C6 **Xuwen** China
68 H7 **Xuyen Moc** Vietnam
58 E6 **Xuyong** China
58 G5 **Xuzhou** China

Y

100 K1 **Yaak** Montana U.S.A.
141 K6 **Yaamba** Queensland Australia
67 A2 **Ya'an** China
138 F6 **Yaapeet** Victoria Australia
71 A3 **Yaba** Indonesia
86 B5 **Yabassi** Cameroon
86 G5 **Yabēlo** Ethiopia
80 F4 **Yabis** *R* Jordan
46 G1 **Yablanitsa** Bulgaria
125 N2 **Yablis** Nicaragua
48 J2 **Yablonitse, Pereval** *pass* Ukraine
48 J2 **Yablonov** Ukraine
54 D6 **Yablonovka** Ukraine
58 E1 **Yablonovyy Khrebet** *mts* Russian Federation
79 G5 **Yabrūd** Syria
Yacacik *see* **Payas**
141 H5 **Yacamunda** Queensland Australia
Yacha *see* **Baisha**
100 A5 **Yachats** Oregon U.S.A.
67 C7 **Yacheng** China
60 D14 **Yachi** Japan
67 B3 **Yachi He** *R* China
130 C10 **Yaciretá** *isld* Paraguay
139 H6 **Yackandandah** Victoria Australia
100 C4 **Yacolt** Washington U.S.A.
133 E2 **Yacuiba** Bolivia
128 E6 **Yacuma** *R* Bolivia
128 E3 **Yacurai** Venezuela
80 D4 **Yad Hanna** Israel
112 F1 **Yadkin** *R* North Carolina U.S.A.
112 G1 **Yadkinville** North Carolina U.S.A.
80 B7 **Yad Mordekhay** Israel
80 C6 **Yad Rambam** Israel
68 H6 **Ya Drang** *R* Cambodia
52 G6 **Yadrin** Russian Federation
80 C5 **Yafo** Israel
84 E3 **Yafran** Libya
61 Q12 **Yagaji-jima** *isld* Okinawa
60 C13 **Yagami** Japan
47 J5 **Yağcılar** Turkey
60 P1 **Yagishiri-tō** *isld* Japan
124 G7 **Yago** Mexico
55 E2 **Yagodnyy** Russian Federation
52 G4 **Yagrysh** Russian Federation
126 E3 **Yaguajay** Cuba
131 G3 **Yaguari** *R* Uruguay
128 D4 **Yaguas** *R* Peru
124 E4 **Yagui** Mexico
80 D3 **Yagur** Israel
69 E9 **Yaha** Thailand
61 L10 **Yahagi-gawa** *R* Japan
100 J1 **Yahk** British Columbia Canada
124 H7 **Yahualica** Mexico
86 D5 **Yahuma** Zaire
78 E2 **Yahyali** Turkey
68 D6 **Yai, Khao** *mt* Burma/Thailand
61 N9 **Yaita** Japan
61 M11 **Yaizu** Japan
80 G5 **Yajuz** Jordan
116 Q6 **Yakataga** Alaska U.S.A.
59 H2 **Yakeshi** China
80 B8 **Yakhini** Israel
54 J1 **Yakhroma** Russian Federation
55 E2 **Yakhtur, Oz** *L* Russian Federation
100 E3 **Yakima** Washington U.S.A.
74 C8 **Yakmach** Pakistan
85 D6 **Yako** Burkina
117 E6 **Yakobi I** Alaska U.S.A.
86 D5 **Yakoma** Zaire
46 F2 **Yakoruda** Bulgaria
86 D4 **Yakossi** Cent Afr Republic
57 K4 **Yakrik** China
52 J4 **Yaksha** Russian Federation
52 G5 **Yakshanga** Russian Federation
52 H6 **Yakshur-Bod'ya** Russian Federation
101 L1 **Yakt** Montana U.S.A.
60 O3 **Yakumo** Japan
59 J5 **Yaku-shima** *isld* Japan
117 D6 **Yakutat** Alaska U.S.A.
117 C6 **Yakutat B** Alaska U.S.A.
51 M2 **Yakutsk** Russian Federation
56 H1 **Yakutskaya Respublika** Russian Federation
69 E9 **Yala** Thailand
47 K4 **Yalakdere** Turkey
83 L11 **Yala Nat. Park** Sri Lanka
138 B4 **Yalatta** South Australia Australia
144 D5 **Yaldhurst** New Zealand
117 N11 **Yale** British Columbia Canada
110 H2 **Yale** Illinois U.S.A.
99 M8 **Yale** Iowa U.S.A.
94 E3 **Yale** Michigan U.S.A.
107 O5 **Yale** Oklahoma U.S.A.
98 H5 **Yale** South Dakota U.S.A.
86 D5 **Yaleko** Zaire
100 C4 **Yale L** Washington U.S.A.
143 B8 **Yalgoo** W Australia Australia
86 D4 **Yalinga** Cent Afr Republic
127 L2 **Yallahs** *R* Jamaica
127 L3 **Yallahs** Jamaica
141 H6 **Yalleroi** Queensland Australia
143 B10 **Yallingup** W Australia Australia
139 H7 **Yallourn** Victoria Australia
111 F8 **Yalobusha** *R* Mississippi U.S.A.
86 C4 **Yaloké** Cent Afr Republic
66 F5 **Yalong Jiang** *R* China
47 K4 **Yalova** Turkey
48 M4 **Yalpug** *R* Moldavia/Ukraine
48 M5 **Yalpug, Ozero** *L* Ukraine
138 F3 **Yalpunga** New South Wales Australia
48 L1 **Yaltushkov** Ukraine
65 E1 **Yalu He** *R* China
65 G4 **Yalu River** China/Korea
55 E4 **Yalym** Russian Federation
60 Q2 **Yamabe Karikachi Pass** Japan
61 Q6 **Yamada wan** *B* Japan
60 D12 **Yamaga** Japan
61 N7 **Yamagata** *prefect* Japan
61 O7 **Yamagata** Japan
60 D14 **Yamagawa** Japan
60 E11 **Yamaguchi** Japan
59 K1 **Yam-Alin', Khrebet** *mt* Russian Federation
50 F1 **Yamal, Poluostrov** *pen* Russian Federation
61 M10 **Yamanaka ko** *L* Japan
61 M10 **Yamanashi** *prefect* Japan
47 J6 **Yamanlar Dağı** *mt* Turkey
58 F1 **Yamarovka** Russian Federation
60 H10 **Yamasaki** Japan
121 S6 **Yamaska** Quebec Canada
113 G11 **Yamato** Florida U.S.A.
139 L3 **Yamba** New South Wales Australia
138 F5 **Yamba** South Australia Australia
139 G7 **Yambacoona** Tasmania Australia
85 B6 **Yambéring** Guinea
128 D3 **Yambi, Mesa de** Colombia
86 E5 **Yambio** Sudan
47 H2 **Yambol** Bulgaria
136 G3 **Yamdena** *isld* Moluccas Indonesia
Yamdrok Tso *L see* **Yamzho Yumco** *L*
68 C2 **Yamethin** Burma
80 E8 **Yam Hamelah** Israel
52 D6 **Yami** Russian Federation
61 O9 **Yamizo-san** *mt* Japan
80 F2 **Yam Kinneret** Israel
52 C5 **Yamm** Russian Federation
141 F7 **Yamma Yamma,L** Queensland Australia
79 E7 **Yammit** Israel
85 D7 **Yamoussoukro** Ivory Coast
101 R9 **Yampa** *R* Colorado U.S.A.
101 T9 **Yampa** Colorado U.S.A.
142 E3 **Yampi Sound** W Australia Australia
48 K1 **Yampol'** Ukraine
48 L2 **Yampol'** Ukraine
100 D7 **Yamsay Mt** Oregon U.S.A.
52 G4 **Yamskoye** Russian Federation
74 G5 **Yamuna** *R* India
74 G3 **Yamunanagar** India
55 G4 **Yamyshevo** Kazakhstan
66 E6 **Yamzho Yumco** *L* China
51 N2 **Yana** *R* Russian Federation
138 F6 **Yanac** Victoria Australia
60 D12 **Yanagawa** Japan
61 O8 **Yanagawa** Japan
61 P12 **Yanaha-jima** *isld* Okinawa
76 F2 **Yanam** India
65 A6 **Yan'an** China
128 D6 **Yanaoca** Peru
56 D2 **Yanashimskiy Polkan** *pk* Russian Federation
139 G4 **Yancannia** New South Wales Australia
109 H6 **Yancey** Texas U.S.A.
112 H1 **Yanceyville** North Carolina U.S.A.
65 A6 **Yanchang** China
77 B3 **Yanchashmeh** Iran
Yancheng *see* **Qihe**
59 H5 **Yancheng** China
67 F1 **Yancheng** China
143 B9 **Yanchep** W Australia Australia
65 A6 **Yanchuan** China
139 H5 **Yanco** New South Wales Australia
139 H6 **Yanco** *R* New South Wales Australia
143 D8 **Yandal** W Australia Australia
138 F3 **Yandama** *R* South Australia Australia
65 A4 **Yandian** China
143 C7 **Yandil** W Australia Australia
141 L7 **Yandina** Queensland Australia
68 B4 **Yandoon** Burma
85 C6 **Yanfolila** Mali
86 D5 **Yangambi** Zaire
66 E5 **Yangbajain** China
65 B7 **Yangcheng** China
Yangchuan *see* **Suiyang**
67 D5 **Yangchun** China
Yangcun *see* **Wuqing**
67 E5 **Yangcun** China
65 F3 **Yangdachengzi** China
142 A3 **Yangebup L** W Australia Australia
65 J2 **Yanggang** China
58 F3 **Yanggao** China
65 C6 **Yanggu** China
57 F4 **Yangibazar** Kyrgyzstan
77 B2 **Yangi Emām** Iran
57 D5 **Yangi-Nishan** Uzbekistan
67 D6 **Yangjiang** China
65 E4 **Yangjiazhangzi** China
67 F3 **Yangkou** China
67 A4 **Yanglin** China
67 D2 **Yangloudong** China
65 C7 **Yangmiao** China
67 D3 **Yangming Shan** *mt* China
68 C4 **Yangon** Burma
52 E3 **Yangory** Russian Federation
67 D7 **Yangpu Gang** *inlet* China
65 B6 **Yangquan** China
67 D3 **Yangquan** China
65 C7 **Yangshan** China
67 D4 **Yangshan** China
Yangshe *see* **Shazhou**
67 C4 **Yangshuo** China
67 F1 **Yangtan** China
Yangtze Gorges *see* **Qutang Xia Wu Xia**
Yangtze Kiang *R see* **Chang Jiang** *R*
55 E2 **Yangutumskiye** Russian Federation
68 D6 **Yangwa** Burma
Yangwu *see* **Yuanyang**
67 E2 **Yangxin** China
65 B4 **Yangyuan** China
67 F1 **Yangzhong** China
67 F1 **Yangzhou** China
65 A6 **Yan He** *R* China
67 C2 **Yanhe** China
138 D5 **Yaninee, L** South Australia Australia
52 D4 **Yanis'yarvi, Oz** *L* Russian Federation
65 H3 **Yanji** China
65 C7 **Yanjin** China
67 A2 **Yanjin** China
67 B2 **Yanjing** China
138 F4 **Yanko Glen** New South Wales Australia
98 J7 **Yankton** South Dakota U.S.A.
65 C7 **Yanling** China
142 B6 **Yannarie** *R* W Australia Australia
Yannina *see* **Ioánnina**
54 B1 **Yanovichi** Belorussia
52 G6 **Yanovo** Russian Federation
83 K9 **Yan Oya** *R* Sri Lanka
66 D3 **Yanqi** China
65 C4 **Yanqing** China
142 A5 **Yanrey** W Australia Australia
65 D4 **Yan Shan** *mts* China
65 D5 **Yanshan** China
67 F2 **Yanshan** China
67 A5 **Yanshan** China
65 B7 **Yanshi** China
67 F4 **Yanshi** China
59 J2 **Yanshou** China
51 N1 **Yanskiy Zaliv** *B* Russian Federation
139 H3 **Yantabulla** New South Wales Australia
59 H4 **Yantai** China
138 F3 **Yantara, L** New South Wales Australia
67 B1 **Yanting** China
65 G3 **Yantongshan** China
67 G2 **Yantou** China
47 H1 **Yantra** *R* Bulgaria
80 D2 **Yanūh** Israel
57 D3 **Yany Kurgan** Kazakhstan
65 C7 **Yanzhou** China
67 B3 **Yanzikou** China
86 C3 **Yao** Chad
61 J11 **Yao** Japan
Yaodu *see* **Dongzhi**
65 A6 **Yaotou** China
86 B5 **Yaoundé** Cameroon
65 D7 **Yaowan** China
65 A7 **Yao Xian** China
69 D9 **Yao Yai, Ko** *isld* Thailand
136 H2 **Yapen** *isld* W Irian
141 F4 **Yappar** *R* Queensland Australia
Yaqian *see* **Yuexi**
80 D8 **Yaqin** Jordan
127 J5 **Yaque del Sur** *R* Dominican Rep
124 E3 **Yaqui** *R* Mexico
100 A5 **Yaquina Head** Oregon U.S.A.
80 C5 **Yaqum** Israel
52 H5 **Yar** Russian Federation
126 F4 **Yara** Cuba
128 E1 **Yaracuy** *state* Venezuela
141 G6 **Yaraka** Queensland Australia
52 G6 **Yaransk** Russian Federation
47 K7 **Yaraşlı Gölü** *L* Turkey
47 K6 **Yarbasan** Turkey
8 C6 **Yarcombe** England
138 D4 **Yardea** South Australia Australia
80 F3 **Yardena** Israel
47 L8 **Yardımcı Burun** *C* Turkey
52 H3 **Yarega** Russian Federation
48 J2 **Yaremcha** Ukraine
52 G3 **Yarenga** Russian Federation
52 G4 **Yarensk** Russian Federation
9 H2 **Yare, R** England
128 D3 **Yari** *R* Colombia
61 L9 **Yariga-take** *mt* Japan
47 L5 **Yarimca** Turkey
47 N11 **Yarimca** Turkey
80 D1 **Yarîne** Lebanon
140 E5 **Yaringa** *R* Queensland Australia
128 E1 **Yaritagua** Venezuela
Yarkand *R see* **Yarkant He**
Yarkant *see* **Shache**
66 B4 **Yarkant He** *R* China
55 E3 **Yarkovo** Russian Federation
138 B4 **Yarle Lakes** South Australia Australia
66 D6 **Yarlung Zangbo Jiang** *R* China
13 G5 **Yarm** England
48 K1 **Yarmolintsy** Ukraine
122 F10 **Yarmouth** Nova Scotia Canada
9 E6 **Yarmouth** England
95 R3 **Yarmouth** Maine U.S.A.
95 R5 **Yarmouth** Massachusetts U.S.A.
80 F3 **Yarmuk** *R* Syria
103 M7 **Yarnell** Arizona U.S.A.
52 E5 **Yaroslavl'** Russian Federation
52 E5 **Yaroslavskaya Oblast'** *prov* Russian Federation
80 E1 **Yârôun** Lebanon
54 J7 **Yarovaya** Ukraine
80 C5 **Yarqon** Israel
139 H7 **Yarra** *R* Victoria Australia
141 G2 **Yarraden** Queensland Australia
142 B5 **Yarraloola** W Australia Australia
139 H7 **Yarram** Victoria Australia
141 K7 **Yarraman** Queensland Australia
140 D4 **Yarran Ra** N Terr Australia
139 H6 **Yarrawonga** Victoria Australia
141 J5 **Yarrawonga Pt** Queensland Australia
143 B8 **Yarra Yarra Ls** W Australia Australia
142 D5 **Yarrie** W Australia Australia
141 H7 **Yarronvale** Queensland Australia
15 E5 **Yarrow** *R* Scotland
141 H5 **Yarrowmere** Queensland Australia
55 F1 **Yarsomovy** Russian Federation
54 D1 **Yartsevo** Russian Federation
128 C2 **Yarumal** Colombia
48 L2 **Yaryshev** Ukraine
86 D5 **Yasanyama** Zaire
137 Q5 **Yasawa Grp** *islds* Fiji
85 F6 **Yashi** Nigeria
85 E7 **Yashikera** Nigeria
60 F12 **Ya-shima** Japan
61 O6 **Yashima** Japan
60 F12 **Yashiro-jima** Japan
55 B4 **Yashkino** Russian Federation
54 J8 **Yasinovataya** Ukraine
48 J2 **Yasinya** Ukraine
54 J2 **Yasnogorsk** Russian Federation
68 G5 **Yasothon** Thailand
139 J5 **Yass** New South Wales Australia
47 M11 **Yassi** *isld* Turkey
60 G12 **Yasuda** Japan
60 G10 **Yasugi** Japan
77 B4 **Yāsūj** Iran
128 E6 **Yata** Bolivia
47 J7 **Yatağan** Turkey
85 E6 **Yatakala** Niger
106 G5 **Yates** New Mexico U.S.A.
94 H6 **Yatesboro** Pennsylvania U.S.A.
107 P4 **Yates Center** Kansas U.S.A.
115 K5 **Yathkyed L** Northwest Territories Canada
80 D5 **Yatma** Jordan
86 D5 **Yatolema** Zaire
Yatou *see* **Rongcheng**
61 M10 **Yatsuga take** *mt* Japan
61 L9 **Yatsuo** Japan
60 D13 **Yatsushiro** Japan
80 D8 **Yatta** Jordan
8 D5 **Yatton** England
128 E3 **Yatua** *R* Venezuela
128 D7 **Yauca** Peru
127 L5 **Yauco** Puerto Rico
112 H4 **Yauhannah** South Carolina U.S.A.
128 C6 **Yauyos** Peru
103 M7 **Yava** Arizona U.S.A.
57 E5 **Yavan** Tajikistan
124 E4 **Yavaros** Mexico
74 H8 **Yavatmāl** India
128 D6 **Yavero** *R* Peru
128 E8 **Yavi** Argentina
128 E2 **Yavi, Co** *mt* Venezuela
128 E3 **Yavita** Venezuela
55 E4 **Yavlenka** Kazakhstan
80 B6 **Yavne** Israel
80 F3 **Yavnee** Israel
31 O6 **Yavorov** Ukraine
29 O3 **Yavr** *R* Finland/Rus Fed
79 H1 **Yavuzeli** Turkey
68 B2 **Yaw** *R* Burma
60 F12 **Yawatahama** Japan
68 C2 **Yawng-hwe** Burma
67 B3 **Yaxi** China
Yaxian *see* **Sanya**
56 C3 **Yaya** Russian Federation
52 J5 **Yayva** *R* Russian Federation
77 C3 **Yazd** Iran
77 C4 **Yazd-e Khvāst** Iran
57 F5 **Yazgulemskiy Khrebet** *mts* Tajikistan
55 C4 **Yazikovo** Russian Federation
111 F9 **Yazoo City** Mississippi U.S.A.
52 J4 **Yaz'va** *R* Russian Federation
38 M5 **Ybbs** Austria
38 L6 **Ybbsitz** Austria
130 C9 **Ybycúi** Paraguay
28 A3 **Ydby** Denmark
28 D5 **Yding Skovhøj** *hill* Denmark
52 J3 **Ydzhid Parma** Russian Federation
52 J3 **Ydzhyd Patok** *R* Russian Federation
68 C5 **Ye** Burma
139 H6 **Yea** Victoria Australia
8 B7 **Yealmpton** England
Yebaishou *see* **Jianping**
86 C1 **Yebbi bou** Chad
21 M2 **Yébleron** France
68 D5 **Yebyu** Burma
66 B4 **Yecheng** China
17 G6 **Yecla** Spain
124 E3 **Yécora** Mexico
68 C3 **Yedashe** Burma
47 K8 **Yedi Burun** *C* Turkey
48 L2 **Yedintsy** Moldavia
52 F3 **Yedoma** Arkhangel'skaya obl Russian Federation
52 H2 **Yedoma** Komi Respublika Russian Federation
84 F5 **Yédri** Chad
142 E4 **Yeeda River** W Australia Australia
138 D5 **Yeelanna** South Australia Australia
143 D7 **Yeelirrie** W Australia Australia
52 D5 **Yefimovskiy** Russian Federation
54 K3 **Yefremov** Russian Federation
55 G6 **Yegindybulak** Kazakhstan
55 E5 **Yegindykol'** Kazakhstan
56 F3 **Yegirma** *R* Russian Federation
53 F10 **Yegorlyk** *R* Russian Federation
54 L1 **Yegor'yevsk** Russian Federation
130 C10 **Yegros** Paraguay
109 K5 **Yegua Cr** Texas U.S.A.
16 D7 **Yeguas, Sa. de** *mts* Spain
131 B5 **Yeguas, Vol** Chile
86 F5 **Yei** Sudan
67 E1 **Yeji** China
85 D7 **Yeji** Ghana
55 D3 **Yekaterinburg** Russian Federation
55 D1 **Yekaterininka** Russian Federation
55 F3 **Yekaterininskoye** Russian Federation
59 J1 **Yekaterinoslavka** Russian Federation
54 K4 **Yekaterinovka** Russian Federation
68 A3 **Ye Kyun** *isld* Burma
52 H6 **Yelabuga** Russian Federation
53 F8 **Yelan'** *R* Russian Federation
55 D2 **Yelan'** Russian Federation
54 N5 **Yelan'-Koleno** Russian Federation
141 K8 **Yelarbon** Queensland Australia
58 F1 **Yeleninskiy** Russian Federation
54 J9 **Yelenovka** Ukraine
54 G3 **Yelenskiy** Russian Federation
54 K4 **Yelets** Russian Federation
55 E1 **Yelizarovo** Russian Federation
55 C5 **Yelizavetinka** Russian Federation
59 M1 **Yelizavety, Mys** *C* Russian Federation
15 G1 **Yell** *isld* Scotland
76 E2 **Yellandu** India
111 K10 **Yellow** *R* Alabama U.S.A.
99 Q5 **Yellow** *R* Wisconsin U.S.A.
119 M6 **Yellow Creek** Saskatchewan Canada
143 C9 **Yellowdine** W Australia Australia
119 N9 **Yellow Grass** Saskatchewan Canada
117 O9 **Yellowhead Pass** Alberta Canada
114 H5 **Yellowknife** Northwest Territories Canada
117 Q4 **Yellowknife** Northwest Territories Canada
99 L5 **Yellow Medicine** *R* Minnesota U.S.A.
139 H4 **Yellow Mt** New South Wales Australia
100 K5 **Yellow Pine** Idaho U.S.A.
Yellow R *see* **Huang He** *R*
59 H4 **Yellow Sea** China/Korea
110 N2 **Yellow Springs** Ohio U.S.A.
98 B2 **Yellowstone** *R* Montana U.S.A.
101 P5 **Yellowstone L** Wyoming U.S.A.
101 P5 **Yellowstone Nat. Park** Wyoming U.S.A.
15 G1 **Yell Sound** Scotland
110 D5 **Yellville** Arkansas U.S.A.
54 E2 **Yel'nya** Russian Federation
56 C1 **Yeloguy** *R* Russian Federation
55 E3 **Yeloshnoye** Russian Federation
55 C3 **Yelovo Barda** Russian Federation
16 C4 **Yeltes** *R* Spain
52 D6 **Yel'tsy** Russian Federation
125 M2 **Yelucá** *mt* Nicaragua
52 H3 **Yelva** *R* Russian Federation
8 B7 **Yelverton** England
115 L1 **Yelverton B** Northwest Territories Canada
85 E6 **Yelwa** Nigeria
55 D4 **Yemanzhelinsk** Russian Federation
112 G5 **Yemassee** South Carolina U.S.A.
72 E6 **Yemen** *rep* S W Asia
55 E3 **Yemets** *R* Russian Federation
52 F3 **Yemetsk** Russian Federation
52 F3 **Yemtsa** Russian Federation
52 D1 **Yena** Russian Federation
54 K8 **Yenakiyevo** Ukraine
68 B2 **Yenangyat** Burma
68 B2 **Yenangyaung** Burma
68 B3 **Yenanma** Burma
67 A6 **Yen Bai** Vietnam
67 A6 **Yen Chau** Vietnam
139 H5 **Yenda** New South Wales Australia
85 E7 **Yendi** Ghana
58 F1 **Yendondin** Russian Federation
55 E1 **Yendra** Russian Federation
55 E1 **Yendyr'** Russian Federation
68 C2 **Yengan** Burma
66 B4 **Yengisar** China
47 J5 **Yenice** Turkey
47 K5 **Yenice** Turkey
47 H6 **Yenifoça** Turkey
78 A3 **Yenihisar** Turkey
47 J5 **Yeniköy** Turkey
47 N10 **Yeniköy** Turkey
31 M1 **Yenino** Russian Federation
47 J7 **Yenipazar** Aydin Turkey
47 L4 **Yenipazar** Bilecik Turkey
47 K4 **Yenişehir** Turkey
56 D2 **Yenisey** *R* Russian Federation
56 D2 **Yeniseysk** Russian Federation
50 H1 **Yeniseyskiy Zaliv** *G* Russian Federation
56 D5 **Yenisey, Verkhn-e** *R* Russian Federation
68 G2 **Yen Lap** Vietnam
68 G1 **Yen Minh** Vietnam
47 Q14 **Yennádhi** Rhodes Greece
19 P13 **Yenne** France
52 E1 **Yenozero, Oz** *L* Russian Federation
68 G3 **Yen Thanh** Vietnam
116 M5 **Yentna** *R* Alaska U.S.A.
143 E8 **Yeo L** W Australia Australia
74 F8 **Yeola** India
Yeóryios *isld see* **Áyios** *isld*
139 J5 **Yeoval** New South Wales Australia
8 D6 **Yeovil** England
124 E3 **Yepachic** Mexico
54 K3 **Yepifan** Russian Federation
141 K6 **Yeppoon** Queensland Australia
46 F7 **Yeráki** Greece
124 J6 **Yerbabuena** Mexico
56 G1 **Yerbogachen** Russian Federation
21 N2 **Yère** *R* Seine-Inférieure France
55 F5 **Yerementau** *mt* Kazakhstan
47 J7 **Yeresik** Turkey
78 K1 **Yerevan** Armenia
53 F9 **Yergeni** *hills* Russian Federation
143 D8 **Yerilla** W Australia Australia
57 C3 **Yerimbet** Kazakhstan
102 E3 **Yerington** Nevada U.S.A.
78 E2 **Yerköy** Turkey
55 G5 **Yermak** Kazakhstan
55 F1 **Yermakovo** Russian Federation
56 D4 **Yermakovskoye** Russian Federation
55 F5 **Yermentau** Kazakhstan
52 H2 **Yermitsa** Russian Federation
124 G4 **Yermo** Mexico
102 H7 **Yermo** California U.S.A.
55 C4 **Yermolayevo** Russian Federation
54 H1 **Yermolino** Russian Federation
59 H1 **Yerofey Pavlovich** Russian Federation
79 E8 **Yeroham** Israel
141 K2 **Yeronga** *dist* Brisbane, Qnsld Australia
52 H2 **Yersa** *R* Russian Federation
25 B6 **Yerseke** Netherlands
52 G3 **Yertom** Russian Federation
52 F4 **Yertsevo** Russian Federation
128 C6 **Yerupaja** *mt* Peru
80 D6 **Yerushalayim** Israel
21 M2 **Yerville** France
68 B2 **Yesagyo** Burma
67 C1 **Yesanguan** China
52 D6 **Yesenovichi** Russian Federation
79 D1 **Yeşidere** Turkey
55 E5 **Yesil'** Kazakhstan
47 K5 **Yesil Dağı** *mt* Turkey
78 F1 **Yeşilırmak** *R* Turkey
Yeşilkent *see* **Erzin**
47 M11 **Yeşilköy** Turkey
47 K7 **Yeşilova** Turkey
79 D1 **Yeşiltepe** Turkey
108 C1 **Yeso** New Mexico U.S.A.
80 C6 **Yesodot** Israel
51 K2 **Yessey** Russian Federation
17 F6 **Yeste** Spain
80 F1 **Yesud Ha Ma'ala** Israel
13 F3 **Yetholm** Scotland
139 K3 **Yetman** New South Wales Australia
85 C3 **Yetti** *tribe* Mauritania
68 B1 **Yeu** Burma
20 F8 **Yeu, I.d'** France
55 F3 **Yevgashchino** Russian Federation
78 L1 **Yevlakh** Azerbaijan
21 P7 **Yèvre** *R* France
59 K2 **Yevreyskaya Avtonomnyy Oblast** *reg* Russian Federation
65 D6 **Ye Xian** China
53 E10 **Yeysk** Russian Federation
52 D6 **Yezerishche** Russian Federation
52 G5 **Yezhikha** Russian Federation
52 G3 **Yezhuga** *R* Russian Federation
20 E5 **Yffiniac** France
130 C9 **Yguazu, R** Paraguay
130 C9 **Yhú** Paraguay
47 J8 **Yiali** *isld* Greece
84 J3 **Yi' Allaq, Gebel** Egypt
79 E3 **Yialousa** Cyprus
47 H9 **Yianisádhes** *isld* Crete Greece
47 O12 **Yiannádhes** Greece
46 E4 **Yiannitsá** Greece
68 E1 **Yibang** China
Yibei *see* **Minglun**
67 A2 **Yibin** China
80 B6 **Yibna** Israel
67 D1 **Yichang** China
65 B7 **Yicheng** China
65 D7 **Yicheng** China
67 D1 **Yicheng** China
65 A6 **Yichuan** China
65 B7 **Yichuan** China
59 J2 **Yichun** China
67 E3 **Yichun** China
58 F5 **Yidu** China
65 D6 **Yidu** China
67 E2 **Yifeng** China
80 F1 **Yiftah** Israel
65 B7 **Yi He** *R* China
65 D7 **Yi He** *R* China
67 E3 **Yihuang** China
65 A7 **Yijun** China
65 H1 **Yilan** China
47 J3 **Yıldız Dağları** *mts* Turkey
78 F2 **Yildizeli** Turkey
67 A3 **Yiliang** China
67 A4 **Yiliang** China
66 E4 **Yiliping** China
143 B10 **Yilliminning** W Australia Australia
67 B1 **Yilong** China
65 G2 **Yimianpo** China
68 B2 **Yin** *R* Burma
65 D7 **Yinan** China
68 C4 **Yinbaing** Burma
65 B7 **Yincheng** China
58 E4 **Yinchuan** China
143 D9 **Yindarlgooda, L** W Australia Australia
67 D1 **Yindian** China
67 D1 **Yingcheng** China
67 F3 **Yingchuan** China
65 J1 **Yingchun** China
67 D4 **Yingde** China
65 F4 **Ying'ebu** China
Yinggen *see* **Qiongzhong**
65 B7 **Ying He** *R* China
65 E4 **Yingkou** China
67 B1 **Yingshan** China
67 D1 **Yingshan** China
67 E2 **Yingtan** China
65 B5 **Ying Xian** China
65 D3 **Yin He** *R* China
66 C3 **Yining** China
67 C2 **Yinjiang** China
138 F5 **Yinkame** South Australia Australia
68 B1 **Yinmabin** Burma
65 F2 **Yinma He** *R* China
68 C4 **Yinnyein** Burma
65 A4 **Yin Shan** *mts* China
Yinxian *see* **Ningbo**
46 G5 **Yioúra** *isld* Greece
Yiquan *see* **Meitan**
131 G4 **Yi, R** Uruguay
86 G4 **Yirga Alem** Ethiopia
80 D2 **Yirka** Israel
86 F4 **Yirol** Sudan
80 E1 **Yir'on** Israel
140 D1 **Yirrkala** N Terr Australia
59 G2 **Yirshi** China
52 G3 **Yirva** *R* Russian Federation
65 D6 **Yi Shan** *mts* China
67 C4 **Yishan** China
65 D7 **Yishui** China
80 E6 **Yitav** Jordan
46 F8 **Yithion** Greece
65 F3 **Yitong** China
65 F2 **Yitong He** *R* China
66 E3 **Yiwu** China
67 G2 **Yiwu** China
68 E2 **Yiwu** China
Yixian *see* **Yicheng**
65 E4 **Yi Xian** China
65 C5 **Yi Xian** China
67 F2 **Yi Xian** China
67 F1 **Yixing** China
65 D4 **Yixun He** *R* China
65 B7 **Yiyang** China
67 D2 **Yiyang** Hunan China
67 F2 **Yiyang** Jiangxi China
65 D6 **Yiyuan** China
67 D4 **Yizhang** China
67 F1 **Yizheng** China
31 K6 **Yizovice** Czechoslovakia
29 N11 **Ylämaa** Finland
29 J11 **Yläne** Finland
29 K8 **Ylihärmä** Finland
29 M6 **Ylikiiminki** Finland
52 C2 **Ylikitka** *L* Finland
29 M6 **Yli-li** Finland
29 K9 **Ylistaro** Finland
29 K5 **Ylitornio** Finland
29 L7 **Ylivieska** Finland
29 L4 **Ylläsuntturi** *mt* Finland
29 K10 **Ylöjärvi** Finland
115 R3 **Ymers Ø** *isld* Greenland
21 O5 **Ymonville** France
52 J4 **Yndin** Russian Federation
27 J13 **Yngaren** *L* Sweden
86 B3 **Yo** Nigeria
109 K6 **Yoakum** Texas U.S.A.
60 O2 **Yobetsu** Japan
60 O2 **Yobetsu-dake** *mt* Japan
60 C12 **Yobuko** Japan
128 E7 **Yocalla** Bolivia
107 L3 **Yocemento** Kansas U.S.A.
111 G7 **Yocono** *R* Mississippi U.S.A.
106 F3 **Yoder** Colorado U.S.A.
98 B8 **Yoder** Wyoming U.S.A.
60 J11 **Yodo** Japan
60 G10 **Yodoe** Japan
80 D5 **Yo'ezer** Jordan
133 D8 **Yogan** *mt* Chile
47 J3 **Yoğuntaş** Turkey
70 N9 **Yogyakarta** Java
117 P10 **Yoho Nat. Park** British Columbia Canada
60 O2 **Yoichi** Japan
60 O2 **Yoichi dake** *mt* Japan
125 L2 **Yojoa, L. de** Honduras
60 H10 **Yōka** Japan
86 C5 **Yokadouma** Cameroon
61 K10 **Yōkaichi** Japan
61 O10 **Yōkaichiba** Japan
111 F9 **Yokena** Mississippi U.S.A.
61 K11 **Yokkaichi** Japan
86 B4 **Yoko** Cameroon
60 F12 **Yokogawara** Japan
62 **Yokohama** *conurbation* Japan
61 N10 **Yokosuka** Japan
61 O6 **Yokote** Japan
60 O4 **Yokotsu-dake** *mt* Japan
86 B4 **Yola** Nigeria
125 M4 **Yolaina, Cord. de** Nicaragua
57 B5 **Yolbarsli** Turkmenistan
65 E2 **Yolin Mod** China
86 D6 **Yolombo** Zaire
61 P13 **Yomitan Airport** Okinawa
61 Q12 **Yona** Okinawa
61 P13 **Yonabaru** Okinawa
60 G10 **Yonago** Japan
67 G4 **Yonagunijima** Japan
61 Q12 **Yonaha-dake** *mt* Okinawa
100 B6 **Yoncalla** Oregon U.S.A.
61 O5 **Yoneshiro-gawa** *R* Japan
61 O8 **Yonezawa** Japan
67 F4 **Yong'an** China
67 D2 **Yong'anshi** China
67 B2 **Yongchuan** China
67 F4 **Yongchun** China
67 C3 **Yongcong** China
67 E4 **Yongding** China
65 C5 **Yongding He** *R* China
59 J4 **Yongdŭngpo** S Korea
67 E3 **Yongfeng** China
67 C4 **Yongfu** China
65 A6 **Yonghe** China
59 J4 **Yonghŭng** N Korea
65 G5 **Yŏnghŭng-man** *B* N Korea
58 F5 **Yongji** China
65 G3 **Yongji** China
67 G2 **Yongjia** China
Yongjing *see* **Xifeng**
67 G2 **Yongkang** China
65 C6 **Yongnian** China
Yongning *see* **Xuyong**
58 D6 **Yongning** China
67 C5 **Yongning** China
65 C5 **Yongqing** China
67 A2 **Yongshan** China
67 C2 **Yongshun** China
67 E3 **Yongtai** China
67 F4 **Yongtai** China
67 E3 **Yongxin** China
67 D3 **Yongxing** China
67 E2 **Yongxiu** China
Yongyang *see* **Weng'an**
118 H6 **Yonker** Saskatchewan Canada
95 O6 **Yonkers** New York U.S.A.
107 P5 **Yonkers** Oklahoma U.S.A.
18 H5 **Yonne** *dept* France
18 H5 **Yonne** *R* France
68 B2 **Yonzingyi** Burma
57 H5 **Yopurga** China
143 B9 **York** W Australia Australia
13 G6 **York** England
111 H9 **York** Alabama U.S.A.
101 O3 **York** Montana U.S.A.
98 J9 **York** Nebraska U.S.A.
98 G1 **York** North Dakota U.S.A.
95 L7 **York** Pennsylvania U.S.A.
112 F3 **York** South Carolina U.S.A.
141 G1 **York, C** Queensland Australia
141 F2 **York Downs** Queensland Australia
138 D5 **Yorke Pen** South Australia Australia
138 D6 **Yorketown** South Australia Australia
115 K6 **York Factory** Manitoba Canada

ACKNOWLEDGEMENTS

PICTURE CREDITS

The sources for the photographs and illustrations appearing on pages 10–41 are listed below. Credits read from top to bottom and left to right on each page.

PAGES
10–23 **Physical Earth maps** by Duncan Mackay, copyright © Times Books, London.

24–25 **Star Charts** Copyright © Bartholomew, Edinburgh.

26–27 **Universe** *Virgo cluster* Hale Observatories; *Fornax cluster* copyright © 1979 Royal Observatory, Edinburgh; *Large Magellanic Cloud* copyright © Royal Observatory, Edinburgh; *Pleiades* Science Photo Library; *Lagoon Nebula, Veil Nebula* and *Trifid Nebula* Hale Observations; *Space Telescope* NASA/Science Photo Library.

28–29 **Solar System** *The Sun* NASA; *1 Deimos, 2 Ganymede, 3 Callisto* NSSDC/NASA; *4 Io* U.S. Geological Survey, Flagstaff, Arizona, *5 Titan, 6 Enceladus, 7 Mimas, 8 Miranda, 9 Ariel, 10 Titania* Jet Propulsion Laboratory/NASA; *Jupiter* NSSDC/NASA; *Saturn* NASA; *Uranus* Jet Propulsion Laboratory/NASA; *Neptune* NASA/Science Photo Library; *Mercury* NSSDC/NASA; *Mars (Mariner 9 images), Mars (Viking orbiter photo), Venus* NASA/Science Photo Library; *Moon* NASA/Science Photo Library.

30–31 **Space flight** *Space Telescope* NASA/Science Photo Library; *launch vehicle* Roger Ressmeyer, Starlight/Science Photo Library; *Mir space-station* Novosti Press Agency/Science Photo Library; *Meteosat image* ESA/PLI/Science Photo Library; *Java* NASA; *Milton Keynes, Faro, Craters of the Moon* Dr D.A. Rothery, Dept. of Earth Sciences, The Open University; *Galileo* NASA/Science Photo Library.

32–33 **Earth Structure** *Magnetosphere* Encyclopaedia Universalis.

34–35 **Dynamic Earth** *Rock and hydrological cycles* Encyclopaedia Universalis.

36–37 **Climate** *Waterspout* Science Photo Library.

38–39 **Vegetation and Minerals** *Manganese nodules* Robert Hessler/Seaphot Planet Earth Pictures.

40–41 **Energy** Data from BP Statistical review of world energy June 1991.

The publishers would like to extend their grateful thanks to the following:

Academy of Sciences and the National Atlas Committee, Moscow, Russian Federation

American Geographical Society, New York, U.S.A.

Professor D.H.K. Amiran, The Hebrew University, Jerusalem, Israel

Antarctic Place-Names Committee, London and G.Hattersley-Smith

Automobile Association of South Africa, Johannesburg, Republic of South Africa

Mr John C. Bartholomew, Edinburgh

The British Petroleum Company Ltd., London

Professor H.A. Brück, lately Astronomer Royal for Scotland, Edinburgh

Bureau of Coast and Geodetic Survey, Manila, Republic of the Philippines

Mrs J.E. Candy, Geographical Research Associates, Maidenhead

Centro de Geografia do Ultramar, Lisbon, Portugal

Ceskoslovenské Akademie Ved, Prague, Czechoslovakia

Columbia University Press, New York, U.S.A.

Defense Mapping Agency, Aerospace Center, St Louis, Missouri, U.S.A.

Defense Mapping Agency Hydrographic Topographic Center, Washington, D.C., U.S.A.

Department of Lands and Survey, Wellington, New Zealand

Department of National Development, Director of National Mapping, Canberra, Australia

Mr John C. Dewdney, University of Durham

Embassy of the Republic of Indonesia, London

Esselte Map Service, Stockholm, Sweden

Dr M.W. Feast, Director, South African Astronomical Observatory, Cape Town, Republic of South Africa

Professor C.A. Fisher, School of Oriental & African Studies, University of London

Food & Agriculture Organisation of the United Nations, Rome, Italy

Foreign and Commonwealth Office, London

French Railways, London

Freytag-Berndt und Artaria, Vienna, Austria

General Directorate of Highways, Ankara, Turkey

General Drafting Company Inc., Convent Station, New Jersey, U.S.A.

Global Seismology Unit, Institute of Geological Sciences, Edinburgh

Office of the Geographer, Department of State, Washington, D.C., U.S.A.

Dr R. Habel, VEB Hermann Haack, Geographisch-Kartographische Anstalt, Gotha, Germany

Mr E. Hausman, Carta, The Israel Map and Publishing Company Ltd., Jerusalem, Israel

Mr Michael Hendrie, Astronomy Correspondent, *The Times*, London

H.M. Stationery Office, London

The High Commission of India, London

Office of the High Commission for Pakistan, London

Hunting Surveys Limited, Borehamwood, Hertfordshire

Hydrographic Office, Ministry of Defence, Taunton

Institute of Geological Sciences, Herstmonceux, Sussex

Institut Géographique Militaire, Brussels, Belgium

Institut Géographique National, Paris, France

Instituto Brasileiro de Geografia, Rio de Janeiro, Brazil

Instituto Geografico e Cadastral, Lisbon, Portugal

Instituto Geografico Militar, Lima, Peru

Instituto Geografico y Cadastral, Madrid, Spain

International Atomic Energy Agency, Vienna, Austria

International Hydrographic Bureau, Monaco

International Road Federation, London

Kongelig Dansk Geodætisk Institut, Copenhagen, Denmark

Mr P. Laffitte, École des Mines, Paris, France

Dr R.I. Lawless, Centre for Middle Eastern & Islamic Studies, University of Durham

Dr S. Lippard, Department of Earth Sciences, The Open University, Milton Keynes

Professor P.McL.D. Duff, University of Strathclyde

Dr D.N. McMaster, University of Edinburgh

Professor R.E.H. Mellor, University of Aberdeen

Dr W.H. Menard, Jr., Scripps Institution of Oceanography, La Jolla, California, U.S.A.

The Meteorological Office, Bracknell, Berkshire

National Aeronautical and Space Administration, Washington, D.C., U.S.A.

National Geographic Society, Washington, D.C., U.S.A.

National Library of Scotland, Edinburgh

Nigerian Land and Survey Department, Lagos, Nigeria

Norges Geografiske Oppmåling, Oslo, Norway

Nuclear Engineering International, London

Ordnance Survey, Director General, Southampton

Permanent Committee of Geographical Names, London: Mr P. Woodman and Miss E. Shipley

Petroleum Information Bureau, London

Petroleum Press Service, London

Petroleum Publishing Co., Tulsa, Oklahoma, U.S.A

Rand McNally & Co., Chicago, U.S.A.

Dr D.A. Rothery, Department of Earth Sciences, The Open University, Milton Keynes

Mr P. Rouveyrol, Bureau de Recherches Géologiques et Minières, Paris, France

Royal Geographical Society, London

Royal Observatory, Schmidt Unit, Edinburgh

Royal Scottish Geographical Society, Edinburgh

Mr John Sallnow, School of Environmental Sciences, Plymouth

Scientific American, New York, U.S.A.

Scottish Development Department, Edinburgh

Soviet Geography: Mr Theodore Shabad, Editor

State of Israel Department of Surveys, Tel-Aviv, Israel

The Statesman's Year Book, London: Editors Dr John Paxton and Dr Brian Hunter

Dr H.J. Störig, Lexikon-Redaktion, Munich, Germany

Survey Department, Singapore

Survey, Lands and Mines Department, Entebbe, Uganda

Survey of India, Dehra Dun, Uttar Pradesh, India

Survey of Kenya, Nairobi, Kenya

Surveyor General, Harare, Zimbabwe

Surveyor General, Ministry of Lands and Natural Resources, Lusaka, Zambia

Surveys and Mapping Branch, Department of Energy, Mines and Resources, Ottawa, Canada

Surveys & Mapping Division, Dar-es-Salaam, Tanzania

Touring Club Italiano and Dr S. Toniolo, Milan, Italy

The Trigonometrical Survey Office, Pretoria, Republic of South Africa

United States Board on Geographic Nam Washington, D.C., U.S.A.

The United States Geological Survey, Washington, D.C., U.S.A.

Mr P.E. Victor, Expéditions Polaires Françaises, Paris, France

Dr D. Whitehouse, Mullard Space Scienc Laboratory, Dorking, Surrey

North America
Key to map plates

116 1:6 000 000

100 1:3 000 000